FOR REFERENCE

Do Not Take
From This Room

COLLINS

Roget's

INTERNATIONAL
Thesaurus®

Edited by

Robert L. Chapman

HarperCollins*Publishers*

British Edition 1996

1 2 3 4 5 6 7 8 9

© HarperCollins Publishers 1996
PO Box, Glasgow G4 0NB.

Standard Edition   ISBN 0 00 470455-X
Thumb-indexed Edition   ISBN 0 00 470718-4

A catalogue record for this book is available
from the British Library

Typeset by Morton Word Processing Ltd.
Scarborough, England

Printed and bound in Great Britain by
Caledonian International Book Manufacturing Ltd, Glasgow, G64

CONTENTS

The author of the "Treasury of Words" could hardly have thought that his name would become forever associated with a particular book, even though he hoped that he was suggesting a unique way of utilizing the richness and flexibility of the English language. But for almost 150 years Roget's work has been the constant companion of all those who aspire to use the language most effectively.

The career of Peter Mark Roget prior to the publication of his *Thesaurus* in 1852 when he was 73 years old, while largely devoted to science and to medicine, required of him a facility with words in the delivery of ideas and concepts. A lifetime of secretaryships for several learned societies had thoroughly familiarized him with the need for clarity and forcefulness of expression. That he was justified in his concept is made obvious by the universal acceptance of his thesaurus as an indispensable tool for all those who wish to write and speak with eloquence.

Born in London the son of a Protestant pastor who died at an early age, Roget was raised by his mother. He studied at Edinburgh University from 1793 to 1798 and received an M.D. after his successful defence of his Latin thesis dealing with the laws of chemical affinity. He was, however, too late to share in that institution's happy days as a stunning example of the Scottish Enlightenment. He was not to know William Cullen, the great nosologist, nor Alexander Monro Primus who brought Hermann Boerhaave's ethos of a medical school from Leyden; but he did learn anatomy from Monro Secundus and medicine from John Gregory. The bright stars of David Hume, denied professorship at the University for his radical thinking, and that of Adam Smith had long since blazed across the Scottish intellectual world. Moreover, Roget was too early for Sir James Young Simpson and chloroform, or for the dexterous Syme who was mentor and father-in-law to the great Lord Lister. While Roget was in Edinburgh, the soil was being prepared for the phenomenon of Paris Medicine, the next wave of medical advance, which would build on the ruin of the French Revolution.

After his graduation, the young physician looked about for the connections he would need to launch a medical career. In this he was fortunate in having the concerned attention of his uncle, Sir Samuel Romilly, whose own promising political potential, shortened by his suicide, provided an entrée to certain segments of English scientific and intellectual life. Through his uncle, Roget was introduced to Lord Lansdowne, for whom he served briefly as personal physician, and to Jeremy Bentham. On his own initiative, Roget spent some time in Bristol in Thomas Beddoes's Pneumatic Institute, devoted to the treatment of human illness using various gases. There he may have met illustrious figures Humphry Davy, James Watt, Samuel Taylor Coleridge, William Wordsworth and Robert Southey.

In the midst of his desultory round of attendance at lectures and dispensary duties, Roget learned that his uncle had manoeuvred for him an opportunity to tutor two scions of a wealthy Manchester manufacturer on a grand tour of Europe. The Peace of Amiens had been signed in 1802 and continental travel was once again open to English families anxious to provide their children with the advantages of foreign scenes.

Roget was twenty-three when he shepherded his charges across the English Channel and on to Paris, where they entered into the round of parties and dinners opened to them through letters from Sir Samuel and from the boys' family. But there was more than that. Roget hired a French tutor and supervised his charges' studies in mathematics, chemistry and geology. He also saw to it that there were the obligatory trips to museums as well as to the theatre and that the boys wrote their impressions and comments after each visit.

The little party pushed on to Geneva, not without encountering obstructions, delays and disappointments injected by the French bureaucracy. In Geneva, although the city had recently been annexed by Napoleon, the group felt secure enough to settle down to a life of studies, parties and local sightseeing. The respite was short-lived, however. The Peace of Amiens was abrogated by Napoleon in 1803 and the position of any Englishman in French territory was in doubt. Warned by Mme. de Stael that he faced internment, Roget undertook to establish for himself Genevan citizenship on the basis of his father's birth in that city. Through prodigious effort and resourcefulness remarkable in so young a man, Roget sneaked the party, dressed as peasants, into Germany. He was successful in making his way to Denmark and thence to England, delivering his charges back to their family.

Manchester now offered the best opportunity to establish a medical practice, since Roget could count on the support of the wealthy Philips family, whose sons had shared his French experience. He quickly became associated with the local infirmary and with the Manchester Literary and Philosophical Society, before which body he gave a series of lectures on physiology that historians credit as forming the basis of what became the School of Medicine in that city. As D. L. Emblen points out in his biography of Roget, "...[he] showed that his chief interest in the new science of physiology lay in the organization and order of several aspects of that subject and in the relationship of the subject to such kindred fields as anatomy." (*Peter Mark Roget: The Word and the Man*, D. L. Emblen, Thomas Crowell: New York, 1970, p. 96). It was Roget's meticulous, precise way of looking at order, at plan and at interdependence in animal economy that would eventually find expression in his unique and practical lexicographic experiment.

But the great metropolis beckoned and the young physician finally decided on a London career. Roget was never outstandingly successful as a medical practitioner. He had, however, become associated with the establishment of the Northern Dispensary, the quintessential Victorian expression of medical charity, to which he devoted a lifetime of practice. Roget's métier was teaching and institutional activities. He lectured in the Theory and Practice of Physic at the Great Windmill Street School, which served as the school of anatomy of Middlesex Hospital before that institution was eclipsed by the new University College on Gower Street. The Medical and Chirurgical Society, founded to bridge the gap between medicine and surgery, commanded much of Roget's attention during his London days. He served as the Society's secretary for twelve years and contributed to its journal *Transactions*. In 1814 he became a Fellow in the Royal Society on the basis of a paper he wrote describing a forerunner of the slide rule. He contributed many articles to the *Encyclopedia Britannica*, which were carried through several editions. In those pages he crossed swords with George Combe, the ardent promoter of phrenology, a discipline which Roget could not support. While serving as secretary of the Royal Society he wrote the Bridgewater Treatise on Physiology, which demonstrated anew Roget's ability to organize and classify the essentials of a rapidly developing science.

Although extremely occupied during these years, as a list of his extensive memberships in scientific and cultural organizations shows, Roget seems never to have captured the attention of his peers to the extent that many of his contemporaries enjoyed. There is a hint that he was always just below the top rank, never in the front. It was, after all, an age of giants, and to be even in the midst of all the ferment was remarkable enough. His active public life came to an end when he was eased out of the secretaryship of the Royal Society after a conflict over the operation of the library, and was literally forced into retirement.

An inactive retirement was not compatible with Roget's lifestyle. Since childhood, putting ideas and concepts in writing had been second nature to him. He dwelt in a world of language and his orderly, systematic mind lent itself to classification. More than a list of synonyms, more than a dictionary, the thesaurus Roget devised and constantly improved upon during this time was a unique ordering of the English language to be used by those desiring to impart an exacting and felicitous tone to written or spoken material. Grouped by ideas rather than by a mere alphabetic listing, the thesaurus enabled the user to find the exact word or phrase needed for a specific purpose. Roget had been keeping such a word list for many years. He now proposed to enlarge it and present it to the world of users of the English language.

The success of this venture was never in doubt. Roget supervised some twenty-five editions and printings of the thesaurus and was actively at work on his masterpiece when he died in 1869 at the age of ninety. *Roget's International Thesaurus* ® continues to be issued. For all those who deal with words and with ideas as expressed in words it has become indispensable. It remains a monument of scholarship and a tribute to the industry and breadth of knowledge of one of the lesser-known Victorian greats.

DONALD F. KENT, M.D.

PREFACE TO THE FIRST EDITION
(1852)

It is now nearly fifty years since I first projected a system of verbal classification similar to that on which the present work is founded. Conceiving that such a compilation might help to supply my own deficiencies, I had, in the year 1805, completed a classed catalogue of words on a small scale, but on the same principle, and nearly in the same form, as the Thesaurus now published. I had often during that long interval found this little collection, scanty and imperfect as it was, of much use to me in my literary composition, and often contemplated its extension and improvement; but a sense of the magnitude of the task, amidst a multitude of other avocations, deterred me from the attempt. Since my retirement from the duties of Secretary of the Royal Society, however, finding myself possessed of more leisure, and believing that a repertory of which I had myself experienced the advantage might, when amplified, prove useful to others, I resolved to embark in an undertaking which, for the last three or four years, has given me incessant occupation, and has, indeed, imposed upon me an amount of labour very much greater than I had anticipated. Notwithstanding all the pains I have bestowed on its execution, I am fully aware of its numerous deficiencies and imperfections, and of its falling far short of the degree of excellence that might be attained. But, in a work of this nature, where perfection is placed at so great a distance, I have thought it best to limit my ambition to that moderate share of merit which it may claim in its present form; trusting to the indulgence of those for whose benefit it is intended, and to the candour of critics who, while they find it easy to detect faults, can at the same time duly appreciate difficulties.

P. M. ROGET

April 29, 1852

FOREWORD TO THE FIFTH EDITION
(1992)

Apart from rigorous updating and the addition of thirty new categories, the chief innovation of this fifth edition is a rearrangement of the classes and categories into which Dr. Roget organized our verbal universe. This was undertaken gingerly, since Roget's scheme had held its own for nearly a century and a half, and one hesitates to tamper with the work of a master.

Nevertheless, my own reflection and the comments of some users have convinced me that the recasting is justified. Dr. Roget wished, as he said in his original Introduction, "to obtain the greatest amount of practical utility." That should be the aim of all lexicography. Hence he adopted principles of order which seemed "the simplest and most natural, and which would not require, either for their comprehension or application, any disciplined acumen, or depth of metaphysical or antiquarian lore."

At this distance from his intellectual milieu, Roget's scheme no longer seems simple and natural. It reflects a Platonic view of the cosmos, combined with an Artistotelian marshalling of concepts. By "Platonic" I mean that he orders things as though abstract ideas exist in some supraterrestrial realm, and are made temporal and physical as they descend to Earth. By "Aristotelian" I mean that he proceeds by strict logic.

However respectable this cosmos and its deployment may be philosophically, it does not coincide with the way most people now apprehend the universe. Casting about for a more fitting arrangement, I chose what I call a "developmental-existential" scheme, which can be examined in the "Synopsis of Categories". The notion has been to make the arrangement analogous with the development of the human individual and the human race. It is more associational and durational than logical. This seems to me "the simplest and most natural" array in the mind of our own time.

Thesaurus means "treasury or storehouse", and that is exactly what *Roget's International Thesaurus* ® is - a rich treasury of words. There are some 325,000 words and phrases stored here, ready to be used. But it is the organization of this storehouse by themes, making it easy to find words, and the arrangement of related and contrasting themes, leading to happy discoveries, that make *Roget's International Thesaurus* ® uniquely helpful and such a delight to use.

Peter Mark Roget, as related in Dr Kent's essay, had a passion for organizing knowledge and understanding how subjects related to one another. This he applied to language itself in creating the system that underlay his Thesaurus. His purpose in creating this all-embracing schema was to enable users to explore a world of ideas encompassed in a few paragraphs of the typical vocabulary of each subject or theme.

Like language, and life itself, *Roget's International Thesaurus* ® has evolved and changed over the century and a half since it was first published. The present text is based on that acquired by Thomas Crowell from Roget's son and first published in 1886. It remained within the Crowell publishing family for almost a century. Each subsequent edition introduced more efficient and useful features, all of which have contributed to the quality of the present edition. Over the years, tens of thousands of new words and phrases were added, the coverage of foreign expressions increased, and the scope of the book expanded to include slang and useful quotations; a recent innovation was the numbering of paragraphs for the user's convenience. Since the mid seventies it has twice been fully revised and updated by Dr Chapman. It is largely upon his work that our text is based.

In creating this edition we have been able to draw on the enormous resource of the Bank of English — a computerized collection of over 200 million words of current English. This has enabled us to verify and update the coverage. We have also drawn on our extensive language monitoring programme for new words and senses and have added these where appropriate. The skills of our computing colleagues have smoothed the path for all users by creating a comprehensive and simple index. In the history and setting up of this project we have benefited from the knowledge and advice of Carol Cohen and the guidance, support, and scholarship of Dr Robert Chapman, for which we are most grateful.

DIANA TREFFRY

Roget's International Thesaurus ® is a true thesaurus, following the principles of Dr. Peter Mark Roget's great original. It has a text of about 325,000 words and phrases, arranged in categories by their meanings, and a comprehensive index.

The search for a word that you need is a simple process that begins in the index. Suppose that you want a word to describe something that first occurred in the past:

1. In the index, look up the word first and pick the subentry closest to the meaning you want.

2. Follow its number into the text and you will find a whole paragraph of adjectives for things "previous" or "prior".

firm up 854.7
first
　noun degree 648.6
　first ever 817.3
　adj leading 165.3
　front 216.10
　chief 249.14
　preceding 813.4
　beginning 817.15
　foremost 817.17
　previous 833.4
　novel 840.11
　adv before 216.12
　preferably 371.28
　firstly 817.18
first aid 91.14
first and foremost
　817.18
first and last 871.9
first appearance 817.5
first attempt 403.2
first-born
　noun senior 304.5
　adj older 841.19
first choice 371.1
first-class superlative
　249.13
　epistolary 553.14
　first-rate 998.17

833 PREVIOUSNESS

nouns

1 **previousness, earliness** *see* 844, **antecedence** *or* antecedency, priority, anteriority, **precedence** *or* precedency *see* 813, precession; *status quo ante* (*Latin*), previous *or* prior state, earlier state; preexistence; **anticipation,** predating, antedating; antedate; **past time** *see* 836
2 **antecedent,** precedent, premise; forerunner, **precursor** *see* 815, ancestor

verbs

3 **to be prior,** be before *or* early *or* earlier, come on the scene *or* appear earlier, **precede, antecede, forerun,** come *or* go before, set a precedent; **herald,** usher in, proclaim, announce; **anticipate,** antedate, predate; **preexist**

adjectives

4 **previous, prior, early** *see* 844.7, **earlier,** *ci-devant* *or* *ci-dessus* (*French*), **former,** fore, prime, first, **preceding** *see* 165.3, foregoing, above, anterior, **anticipatory,** antecedent; **preexistent;** older, elder, senior

Tracking down words in this way is the most obvious and direct use of the thesaurus. The notes that follow explain some of the other ways in which the unique features of *Roget's International Thesaurus* ® will help you to solve a word problem.

The thesaurus is a device for finding specific words or phrases for general ideas. A dictionary will tell you many things about a word - spelling, pronunciation, meaning and origins. You use a thesaurus when you have an idea but do not know, or cannot remember, the word or phrase that expresses it best or when you want a more accurate or effective way of saying what you mean. A thesaurus gives you possibilities and you choose the one that you think is best. The range of possibilities includes not only meaning as we usually think of it, but the special sense and force given by informal and slang words and phrases, of which many are included and labelled.

Roget's International Thesaurus ® is a more efficient word-finder because it has a structure especially designed to stimulate thought and help you organize your ideas. The backbone of this structure is the ingenious overall arrangement of the large categories. The plan is outlined in the "Synopsis of Categories", which begins on page xvi. To make good use of the thesaurus's structure all you need to remember is that it contains many sequences of closely related categories. Beginning at 48, for example, you will see HEARING, DEAFNESS, SOUND, SILENCE, FAINTNESS OF SOUND, LOUDNESS, etc., a procession of similar, contrasting and opposing concepts, all dealing with the perception and quality of sounds. So, when you are not quite satisfied with what you find in one place, glance at the nearby categories too; it may be that your original intention was not the best. If you are having trouble framing a thought in a positive way, you may find that it can be more effectively expressed negatively. Seeing related terms, and antonyms, often opens up lines of thought and chains of association that had not occurred to you.

You will have already noticed that the large categories of ideas are numbered in sequence; there are 1073 of them in this edition of *Roget's International Thesaurus* ®. Within each category the terms are presented in short paragraphs, and these are also numbered. References from the index to the text are made with two-part numbers such as 247.4, the first part being the number of the category, the second the number of the paragraph within that category. This system, unique to this book, makes for quick and easy pinpointing of the place where you will find the words you need.

The terms within a category are organized also by part of speech, in this order: nouns, verbs, adjectives, adverbs, prepositions, conjunctions, and interjections. This grouping by parts of speech is another aspect of the usefulness of *Roget's International Thesaurus* ®. When you are casting about for a way of saying something, rather than looking for a specific word, do not limit your search to the narrow area of the category suggested by the index reference, but examine the offerings in all parts of speech.

There is a further refinement of word arrangement. The sequence of terms within a paragraph, far from being random, is determined by close, semantic relationships. The words closest in meaning are offered in clusters or "domains" that are set off with semicolons; the semicolon signals a slight change in sense or application. A close examination of the groupings will make you aware of the fine distinctions between synonyms, and you will soon recognize that few words are exactly interchangeable. As a help in focusing on the *right* word, terms with special uses - foreign terms and technical terms - are identified by labels in round brackets.

Cross references are an important feature of the text. They suggest additional meanings of the words you are examining. Notice also that the paragraphs of text are highlighted with terms in boldface type. The bold words are those most commonly used for the idea at hand.

"Word elements" such as prefixes, suffixes, and combining forms, are listed when helpful after the final text paragraph of the category, and before any word lists.

The use of an appropriate quotation often enlivens one's prose. Here again, *Roget's International Thesaurus* ® can help you, for it contains thousands of such quotes on scores of subjects. Another bonus of the thesaurus is its dozens of word lists. These contain the names of specific things - animals, poisonous plants, measurements, architectural ornaments - few of which have synonyms. The lists can save you many excursions to specialist reference books.

Thus, *Roget's International Thesaurus* ® can help you in countless ways to improve your writing and speech and to enrich your active vocabulary. But you should remember the caution that very few words are true synonyms and use the thesaurus in conjunction with a good dictionary whenever a selected word or phrase is new to you.

SYNOPSIS OF CATEGORIES

1 BIRTH

nouns

1 **birth**, genesis, **nativity**, nascency, **childbirth, childbearing, having a baby, giving birth, birthing**, parturition, the stork (*informal*); **confinement**, lying-in, being brought to bed, **childbed**, *accouchement* (*French*); **labour**, travail, birth throes *or* pangs; **delivery**, happy event (*informal*); the Nativity; multiparity; **hatching**; littering, whelping, farrowing

verbs

2 **to be born**, have birth, come forth, issue forth, see the light of day, come into the world; **hatch**; be illegitimate *or* born out of wedlock, have the bar sinister; be born on the wrong side of the blanket, come in through a side door (*informal*)

3 **to give birth, bear**, bear *or* have young, **have; have a baby**, bear a child; drop, cast, throw, pup, whelp, kitten, foal, calve, fawn, lamb, yean, farrow, litter; lie in, be confined, labour, travail

adjectives

4 **born**, given birth; **hatched**; cast, dropped, whelped, foaled, calved, etc;
"cast naked upon the naked earth"—PLINY THE ELDER; née; newborn; stillborn; **bearing**, giving birth

2 THE BODY

nouns

1 **body**, the person, carcass *or* carcase, anatomy, frame, bodily *or* corporal *or* corporeal entity, physical self, physical *or* bodily structure, physique, soma; organism, organic complex; the material *or* physical part

2 **the skeleton, the bones**, one's bones, framework, bony framework, endoskeleton; axial skeleton, appendicular skeleton, visceral skeleton; rib cage; skeletology; **bone** (*see list*); cartilage

3 **the muscles**, myon, voluntary muscle, involuntary muscle; **musculature**, physique; **connective tissue**, connectivum; cartilage

4 **the skin, skin**, dermis, **epidermis**, scarfskin, ecderon; hypodermis, hypoderma; dermis, derma, corium, true skin, cutis, *cutis vera* (*Latin*); epithelium, pavement epithelium; endothelium; mesoderm; endoderm, entoderm; blastoderm; ectoderm, epiblast, ectoblast; enderon; connective tissue

5 (*castoff skin*) slough, cast, desquamation, exuviae

6 **membrane**, membrana, pellicle, chorion; basement membrane, membrana propria; allantoic membrane; amnion, amniotic sac, arachnoid membrane; serous membrane, serosa, membrana serosa; **eardrum**, tympanic membrane, tympanum, membrana tympana; **mucous membrane; velum; peritoneum**; periosteum; pleura; pericardium; meninx, **meninges**; perineurium, neurilemma; conjunctiva; **hymen** *or* maidenhead

7 **member, appendage, external organ; head**, bonce *and* napper *and* noddle *and* noggin *and* noodle (*all informal*); **arm**; forearm; wrist; elbow; upper arm, biceps; **leg**, limb, shank, gam *and* pin (*both informal*), legs, wheels (*informal*); shin, cnemis; ankle, tarsus; calf; knee; thigh, ham; popliteal space; **hand**, mauler *and* paw (*informal*); **foot**

8 **teeth**, dentition, ivories *or* Pearly Gates (*both informal*); periodontal tissue, alveolar ridge; **tooth**, fang, tusk, tush (*informal*); snag, snaggletooth, peg; bucktooth, gagtooth *or* gang tooth (*both informal*); pivot tooth; cuspid, bicuspid; canine tooth, canine, dogtooth, eyetooth; molar, grinder; premolar; incisor, cutter, fore-tooth; wisdom tooth; milk tooth, baby tooth, deciduous tooth; permanent tooth

9 **eye**, visual organ, organ of vision, oculus, optic, **orb**, blinker *and* peeper (*both informal*); clear eyes, bright eyes, starry orbs; saucer eyes, popeyes, goggle eyes; naked eye, unassisted *or* unaided eye; corner of the eye; eyeball; retina; lens; cornea; sclera; optic nerve; iris; pupil; eyelid, lid, nictitating membrane

10 **ear**, auditory apparatus, lug (*Scottish*), shell-like (*informal*); external ear, **outer ear**; auricle, pinna; cauliflower ear; concha, conch, shell; ear lobe, lobe, lobule; auditory canal, acoustic *or* auditory meatus; **middle ear**, tympanic cavity, tympanum; eardrum, drumhead, tympanic membrane; auditory ossicles; malleus, hammer, incus, anvil; stapes, stirrup; mastoid process; eustachian *or* auditory tube; **inner ear**; round window, secondary eardrum; oval window; bony labyrinth, membraneous labyrinth; perilymph, endolymph; vestibule; semicircular canals; cochlea; basilar membrane, organ of Corti; auditory *or* acoustic nerve

11 **genitals**, genitalia, sex organs, reproductive organs, pudenda, private parts, privy parts, privates, meat (*informal*); **crotch**, crutch, pubic region, perineum, pelvis; **male organs; penis, phallus**, lingam (*Sanskrit*), chopper *and* knob *and* cock *and* willie *and* John Thomas (*all informal*); gonads; **testes, testicles**, balls *and* nuts *and* goolies *and* cobblers *and* knackers *and* rocks *and* bollocks *and* family jewels (*all informal*), cullions (*old*); spermary; scrotum, bag *and* basket (*both informal*), cod (*old*); **female organs; vulva**, *yoni* (*Sanskrit*), cunt *and* fanny *and* minge *and* quim *and* pussy (*all informal*), box (*Australian informal*); **vagina**; clitoris; labia, labia majora, labia minora, lips, nymphae; cervix; ovary; uterus, womb; secondary sex characteristic, pubic hair, beard, breasts

12 **nervous system, nerves**, central nervous system *or* CNS, peripheral nervous system; autonomic nervous system; sympathetic *or* thoracolumbar nervous system, parasympathetic *or* craniosacral nervous system; **nerve; neuron**; nerve cell, sensory *or* afferent neuron, sensory cell; motor *or* efferent neuron; association *or* internuncial neuron; axon, dendrite, myelin *or* medullary sheath; **synapse**; effector organ; nerve trunk; **ganglion**; plexus, solar plexus; **spinal cord**

13 **brain**, encephalon

14 **viscera, vitals, internal organs, insides, innards** (*informal*), inwards, internals, thoracic viscera, abdominal viscera; inner mechanism, works (*informal*); peritoneum, peritoneal cavity; **guts** *and* kishkes *and* giblets (*all informal*); **heart**, ticker *and*

pump (*both informal*), endocardium; **lung, lungs; liver**; gallbladder; spleen; pancreas; **kidney, kidneys**

15 digestion, ingestion, assimilation, absorption; primary digestion, secondary digestion; predigestion; salivary digestion, gastric *or* peptic digestion, pancreatic digestion, intestinal digestion; digestive system, alimentary canal, gastrointestinal tract; salivary glands, gastric glands, liver, pancreas; digestive secretions, saliva, gastric juice, pancreatic juice, intestinal juice, bile

16 (*digestive system*) mouth, maw, salivary glands; gullet, crop, craw, **throat**, pharynx; oesophagus, gorge, weasand (*old*), wizen (*informal*); fauces, isthmus of the fauces; **abdomen; stomach, belly** (*informal*), **midriff**, diaphragm; swollen *or* distended *or* protruding *or* prominent belly, *embonpoint* (*French*), **paunch**, ventripotence; underbelly; pylorus; **intestine, intestines**, entrails, **bowels**; small intestine, odenum, jejunum, ileum; blind gut, caecum; foregut, hindgut; midgut, mesogaster; **appendix**, vermiform appendix *or* process; large intestine, colon, sigmoid flexure, rectum; anus

17 (*informal terms*) tum, tummy, tum-tum, breadbasket, **gut**, bulge, fallen chest (*informal*), corporation, spare tyre, bay window, **pot**, potbelly, potgut, beerbelly, pusgut, swagbelly; **guts**, tripes, stuffings

18 metabolism, metabolic process, tissue change; basal metabolism, acid-base metabolism, energy metabolism; **anabolism**, substance metabolism, constructive metabolism, assimilation; **catabolism**, energy metabolism, destructive metabolism, disassimilation; endogenous metabolism, exogenous metabolism; pharmacokinetic metabolism; uricotelic metabolism

19 breathing, respiration, aspiration, **inspiration, inhalation; expiration, exhalation**; insufflation, exsufflation; deep breathing, circular breathing; **breath**, wind, breath of air; pant, puff; wheeze, asthmatic wheeze; hyperventilation; broken wind; gasp, gulp; snoring, snore, stertor; sniff, sniffle, snuff, snuffle; sigh, suspiration; sneeze, sternutation; cough, hack; hiccup; **artificial respiration**, kiss of life, mouth-to-mouth resuscitation; Heimlich manoeuvre

20 (*respiratory system*) **lungs**, bellows (*informal*), lights (*old*); **windpipe, trachea**, weasand (*old*), wizen (*informal*); bronchus, bronchi (*plural*), bronchial tube; epiglottis

21 duct, vessel, canal, passage; vasculature, vascularity, vascularization; vas, meatus; thoracic duct, lymphatic; emunctory (*old*); pore; urethra, urete; vagina; oviduct, fallopian tube; salpinx; eustachian tube; ostium; fistula; **blood vessel; artery**, aorta, pulmonary artery, carotid; **vein**, jugular vein, vena cava, pulmonary vein; portal vein, varicose vein; venation; **capillary**; arteriole, veinlet, veinule, venule

22 (*body fluids*) humour, **lymph**, chyle; rheum; serous fluid, serum; **pus, matter**, purulence, peccant humour (*old*); suppuration; ichor, sanies; discharge; gleet, leucorrhoea, the whites; **phlegm**, snot (*informal*); **saliva, spit** (*informal*); **urine, piss** (*informal*); **perspiration, sweat** (*informal*); **tear**,

teardrop, lachryma; **milk**, mother's milk, colostrum, lactation

23 blood, whole blood, lifeblood, venous blood, arterial blood, **gore**; ichor, humour; grume; **serum**, blood serum; blood substitute; **plasma**, synthetic plasma, plasma substitute, dextran, clinical dextran; **blood cell** *or* **corpuscle**, haemocyte; **red corpuscle** *or* **blood cell**, erythrocyte; **white corpuscle** *or* **blood cell**, leucocyte, blood platelet; **haemoglobin**; blood pressure; circulation; **blood group** *or* **type**, type O *or* A *or* B *or* AB; Rh-type, Rh-positive, Rh-negative; **Rh factor** *or* Rhesus factor; antigen, antibody, isoantibody, globulin; opsonin; blood grouping; blood count, blood picture; haematoscope, haematoscopy, haemometer; bloodstream

adjectives

24 skeleton, skeletal; bone, osteal; **bony**, osseous, ossiferous; ossicular; ossified; **spinal**, myelic; **muscle, muscular**, myoid; cartilage, cartilaginous

25 cutaneous, cuticular; skinlike, skinny; skin-deep; **epidermal**, epidermic, ecderonic; hypodermic, hypodermal, subcutaneous; dermal, dermic; ectodermal, ectodermic; endermic, endermatic; cortical; epicarpal; testaceous; membranous

26 eye, optic, ophthalmic; visual; **ear**, otic; aural

27 genital; phallic, penile, penial; testicular; scrotal; spermatic, seminal; vulvar, vulval; vaginal; clitoral; cervical; ovarian; uterine

28 nerve, neural; brain, cerebral, cerebellar

29 digestive; stomachal, stomachic, abdominal; ventral, coeliac, **gastric**, ventricular; big-bellied *see* 257.18; **metabolic**, basal metabolic, anabolic, catabolic; assimilative, dissimilative

30 respiratory, breathing; inspiratory, expiratory; nasal, rhinal; bronchial, tracheal; **lung**, pulmonary, pulmonic, pneumonic; puffing, huffing, snorting, wheezing, wheezy, asthmatic, stertorous, snoring, panting, heaving; sniffy, sniffly, sniffling, snuffy, snuffly, snuffling; sneezy, sternutative, sternutatory, errhine

31 circulatory, vascular, vascularized; vasiform; venous, veinal, venose; capillary; arterial, aortic; **blood**, haemal, haematic; bloody, gory, sanguinary; lymphatic, rheumy, humoral, phlegmy, ichorous, serous, sanious; chylific, chylifactive, chylifactory; **pussy**, purulent, suppurated *or* suppurating, suppurative; teary, tearing, tearlike, **lachrymal**, lacrimatory

32 bones

aitchbone	cheekbone
alveolar bone	chin
anklebone	clavicle
anvil	coccyx
astragalus *or* anklebone	collarbone
backbone *or* spine *or* spinal	costa
column *or* myel	cranial bones
basilar *or* basioccipital	cranium
bone	cuboid
breastbone *or* sternum	edgebone
calcaneus	ethmoid bone
calf bone *or* fibula	floating rib
cannon bone	frontal bone
carpal *or* carpus	funny bone

hallux	palate bone
hammer	parietal bone
haunch bone	pelvis
heel bone	periotic bone *or* otocrane
hipbone	petrosal *or* petrous bone
humerus	phalanx *or* phalanges
hyoid *or* lingual bone	(plural)
ilium	pterygoid bone
incus	pubis
inferior maxillary	pyramidal bone *or* os
innominate bone	triquetrum
intermaxillary *or*	rachidial
premaxillary *or* incisive	rachis *or* vertebral column
bone	radius
interparietal *or* incarial	rib
bone	sacrum *or* resurrection
ischium	bone
kneecap *or* patella *or* whirl	scaphoid bone
bone	scapula
lacrimal bone	semilunar bone
lenticular bone *or* os	sesamoid bones
orbiculare	shinbone
lentiform *or* pisiform *or*	shoulder blade
postular bone	skull
malar *or* zygomatic bone	sphenoid bone
malleus	stapes
mandible *and* maxilla *or*	stirrup
jawbones	sutural *or* wormian bone
mastoid	talus
maxillary	tarsal *or* tarsus
metacarpal *or* metacarpus	temporal bone
metatarsal *or* metatarsus	thighbone *or* femur
multangular bone large *or*	tibia
trapezium	ulna
multangular bone small *or*	vertebra
trapezoid	vomer
nasal bone	wishbone
occipital bone	wristbone

3 HAIR

nouns

1 **hairiness, shagginess,** hirsuteness, pilosity, fuzziness, frizziness, **furriness,** downiness, fluffiness, woolliness, fleeciness, bristliness, stubbliness, burrheadedness, mopheadedness, shockheadedness; crinosity, hispidity, villosity; hypertrichosis, pilosis, pilosism

2 **hair,** pile, **fur** see 4.2, coat, pelt, **fleece,** wool, camel's hair, horsehair; **mane;** shag, tousled *or* matted hair, **mat of hair;** pubescence, pubes, pubic hair; hairlet, villus, capillament, cilium, ciliolum *see* 271.1; seta, setula; bristle *see* 288.3

3 grey hair, grizzle, silver *or* silvery hair, white hair, salt-and-pepper hair *or* beard, greying temples, "hoary hair"—THOMAS GRAY, "the silver livery of advised age"—SHAKESPEARE, "a crown of glory"—BIBLE, "silver threads among the gold"—EBEN E REXFORD, "snow on the mountain"—ANON

4 **head of hair,** head, crine; **crop,** crop of hair, mat, elflock, **thatch,** mop, **shock,** shag, fleece, **mane; locks, tresses,** crowning glory, helmet of hair;

"her native ornament of hair"—OVID, "amber-dropping hair"—MILTON

5 **lock, tress;** flowing locks, flowing tresses; **curl, ringlet,** "wanton ringlets wav'd"—MILTON; earlock, *payess* (*Yiddish*); lovelock; frizz, frizzle; crimp; ponytail

6 **tuft, flock,** fleck; forelock, widow's peak, quiff, fetlock, cowlick, kiss curl; fringe, bang, bangs

7 **braid,** plait, twist; **pigtail,** rat's-tail *or* rat-tail, tail; **queue,** cue; bunches; coil, knot, French pleat; topknot, scalplock, pigtail; bun, chignon; widow's peak; mohican

8 **beard, whiskers;** beaver (*informal*); full beard, chin whiskers, side whiskers; **sideboards,** sideburns, burnsides (*US*), **muttonchops; goatee,** tuft; imperial, **Vandyke,** spade beard; adolescent beard, pappus, down, peach fuzz, "the soft down of manhood"—CALLIMACHUS, "his phoenix down"—SHAKESPEARE; **stubble,** bristles, five o'clock shadow, designer stubble

9 (*plant beard*) awn, brush, arista, pile, pappus

10 (*animal and insect whiskers*) tactile process, tactile hair, **feeler, antenna,** vibrissa; barb, barbel, barbule; cat whisker

11 **moustache,** mustachio, soup-strainer (*informal*), toothbrush, handle bars *or* handlebar moustache, Fu Manchu moustache, Zapata moustache, walrus moustache, tash (*informal*)

12 **eyelashes, lashes,** cilia; **eyebrows,** brows

13 false hair, switch, fall, chignon, hair extensions

14 **wig, peruke, toupee,** hairpiece, rug *and* divot *and* doormat (*all informal*); **periwig**

15 **hairdo, hairstyle, haircut, coiffure,** coif, headdress; wave; marcel, marcel wave; **permanent,** permanent wave, perm; home permanent; cold wave

16 **dye,** tint, rinse, colour; highlights, lowlights; streaks, tips

17 **feather, plume,** pinion; **quill;** pinfeather; contour feather, penna, down feather, plume feather, plumule; filoplume; hackle; scapular; **crest,** tuft, topknot; panache

18 (*parts of feathers*) quill, calamus, barrel; barb, shaft, barbule, barbicel, cilium, filament, filamentule

19 **plumage, feathers,** feather, feathering; contour feathers; breast feathers, mail (*of a hawk*); hackle; flight feathers; remiges, primaries, secondaries, tertiaries; covert, tectrices; speculum, wing bay

20 **down, fluff,** flue, floss, **fuzz, fur,** pile; eiderdown, eider; swansdown; thistledown; lint

verbs

21 to grow *or* sprout hair; whisker, **bewhisker**

22 **to feather, fledge,** feather out; sprout wings

23 to cut *or* dress the hair, trim, **barber, coiffure,** coif, style *or* shape the hair; pompadour, wave, perm, marcel; process; **bob, shingle,** crop; backcomb, tease

adjectives

24 **hairlike,** trichoid, capillary; filamentous, filamentary, filiform; bristlelike *see* 288.10

25 **hairy, hirsute,** barbigerous, crinose, crinite, pubescent; pilose, pilous, pileous, **furry,** furred; villous; villose; ciliate, cirrose; hispid, hispidulous; **woolly, fleecy,** lanate, lanated, flocky, flocculent,

floccose; woolly-headed, woolly-haired, ulotrichous;
bushy, tufty, **shaggy**, shagged; matted, tomentose;
mopheaded, burrheaded, shockheaded, unshorn;
bristly *see* 288.9; fuzzy

26 **bearded**, whiskered, whiskery, **bewhiskered,**
barbate, barbigerous; moustached *or* mustachioed;
awned, awny, pappose; goateed; unshaved,
unshaven; stubbled, stubbly

27 **wigged**, periwigged, peruked, toupeed

28 **feathery, plumy**; hirsute; featherlike, plumelike,
pinnate, pennate; **downy,** fluffy, nappy, velvety,
peachy, fuzzy, flossy, furry

29 **feathered, plumaged**, flighted, **pinioned, plumed,**
pennate, plumate, plumose

30 **tufted, crested**, topknotted

4 CLOTHING MATERIALS

nouns

1 **material, fabric** (*see list*), **cloth, textile**, textile
fabric, texture, tissue, stuff, weave, weft, woof, web,
material, goods, drapery, *étoffe, tissu* (*both French*);
napery, table linen, felt; rag, rags

2 **fur, pelt, hide,** fell, fleece, vair (*heraldry*); imitation
fur, fake fur, synthetic fur; furring; peltry, skins;
leather, rawhide; imitation leather, leather paper,
Leatherette (*trademark*), bonded leather

3 **fabric**

Acrilan (trademark)	chiffon	fearnought *or* fearnaught
alpaca	chintz	felt
armure	cilice	fishnet
baize	ciré	flannel
balbriggan	cloqué	fleece
barathea	cord	folk weave
barège	corduroy	foulard
batik *or* battik	cotton	frieze
batiste	cottonade	frisé
bayadere	cotton flannel	fur
beige	covert cloth	fustian
bengaline	crepe *or* crape	gaberdine
bird's-eye	cretonne	galatea
bobbinet	Crimplene (trademark)	georgette
bombazine *or* bombasine	crinoline	gingham
bouclé	cypress *or* cyprus	gloria
brilliantine	Dacron (trademark)	Gore-Tex (trademark)
broadcloth	damask	gossamer
brocade	delaine	grogram
buckskin	denim	gros de Londres
bunting	diamanté	grosgrain
burlap	dimity	gunny (chiefly US)
calamanco	Donegal tweed	Harris Tweed (trademark)
calico	drab	hessian
calfskin *or* calf	drabbet	honan
cambric	Dralon (trademark)	hopsack
camlet	drugget	huckaback *or* huck
cavalry twill	duck	India print
challis *or* challie	dungaree	jaconet
chambray	duvetyn, duvetine *or*	Jacquard *or* Jacquard
chamois *or* chammy	duvetyne	weave
Charmeuse (trademark)	elastane	jean
cheesecloth	etamine *or* etamin	jersey
chenille	façonné *or* faconne	khaki
cheviot	faille	kid

nainsook	
nankeen *or* nankin	
needlecord	
net	
ninon	
nun's cloth *or* veiling	
oilskin	
organdie	
organza	
organzine	
Orlon (trademark)	
ottoman	
Oxford	
paduasoy	
paisley pattern	
panne	
paramatta *or* parramatta	
peau de soie	
percale	
percaline	
petersham	
pigskin	
piña cloth	
piqué	
plush	
pongee	
poplin	
poult *or* poult-de-soie	
prunella, prunelle *or*	
prunello	
rayon	
russet	
sailcloth	
samite	
sarcenet *or* sarsenet	
sateen	
satin	
kincob	satinet *or* satinette
knit	saxony
lace	say (archaic)
lambskin	schappe
lamé	scrim
lawn	seersucker
leather	sendal
Leatherette (trademark)	serge
linen	shag
linsey-woolsey	shalloon
lisle	shantung
Lurex (trademark)	sharkskin
Lycra (trademark)	sheepskin
madras	sheeting
marabou	shirting
marocain	shoddy
marquisette	silesia
marseille *or* marseilles	silk
melton	silkaline
messaline	slipper satin
mohair	snakeskin
moire *or* moiré	spandex
moleskin	spun silk
monk's cloth	stockinet
moquette	stroud
moreen	stuff
mousseline	suede
mull	
muslin	

suiting
surah
surat
swan's-down
swanskin
swiss muslin
tabaret
tabby
taffeta
tammy
tarlatan
tarpaulin
tartan
tattersall
terry
Terylene (trademark)
tick
ticking
tiffany
toile
towelling

tricot
tricotine
tulle
tussore, tusser *or* (*US*)
 tussah
tweed
twill
velours
velure
velvet
velveteen
Viyella (trademark)
voile
wadmal
webbing
whipcord
wild silk
winceyette
wool
worsted

5 CLOTHING

nouns

1 **clothing, clothes, apparel, wear, wearing apparel, daywear, dress,** dressing, **raiment,** garmenture, **garb, attire, array,** habit, habiliment, fashion, style *see* 578.1, guise, **costume,** costumery, gear, fig *or* full fig, toilette, trim, bedizenment; **vestment,** vesture, investment, investiture; **garments,** robes, robing, rags (*informal*), drapery, finery, feathers; clobber *or* toggery *or* **togs** *or* threads (*all informal*), sportswear; work clothes, boilersuit, fatigues, overall, overalls; linen; menswear, men's clothing, womenswear, women's clothing; unisex clothing, uniwear, gender-crossing clothing; gender bender

2 **wardrobe,** furnishings, things, accoutrements, trappings; **outfit,** livery, harness, caparison; turnout *and* getup *and* rig *and* rig-out (*all informal*); wedding clothes, bridal outfit, trousseau

3 **garment,** vestment, vesture, robe, frock, gown, rag (*informal*), togs *and* duds (*both informal*)

4 **ready-mades,** ready-to-wear, off the peg clothes (*informal*), store *or* store-bought clothes (*US informal*)

5 **rags,** tatters, secondhand clothes, old clothes; worn clothes, **hand-me-downs** *and* reach-me-downs (*both informal*); slops

6 **suit** (*see list*), suit of clothes, **frock,** dress, rig (*informal*), **costume, habit,** bib and tucker (*informal*)

7 **uniform** (*see list*), **livery,** monkey suit (*informal*)

8 **mufti,** civilian dress *or* clothes, **civvies** *and* cits (*both informal*), plain clothes

9 **costume,** costumery, character dress; outfit *and* getup *and* rig (*all informal*); masquerade, disguise; tights, leotard; ballet skirt, tutu; motley, cap and bells; buskin, sock

10 **finery, frippery, fancy dress,** fine *or* full feather (*informal*), full fig (*informal*); **best clothes,** best bib and tucker (*informal*); **Sunday best** *and* Sunday clothes (*both informal*), Sunday-go-to-meeting clothes *and* Sunday-go-to-meetings (*both US informal*), **glad rags** (*informal*), party dress

11 **formal dress,** formals, **evening dress, full dress,** dress clothes, evening wear, white tie and tails; dinner clothes; dress suit, full-dress suit, tails (*informal*); tuxedo, tux (*informal*); **regalia,** court dress; dress uniform, full-dress uniform, special full-dress uniform, social full-dress uniform; whites (*informal*), dress whites; evening gown, dinner dress *or* gown

12 **cloak,** overgarment (*see list*)

13 **outerwear; coat, jacket** (*see list*); **overcoat** (*see list*), great-coat, **topcoat,** surcoat; **rainwear;** rain gear, raincoat, waterproof, slicker (*US & Canadian*), rainsuit, foul weather gear

14 **waistcoat,** weskit (*informal*), vest (*US, Canadian & Australian*)

15 **shirt** (*see list*), linen, sark (*Scottish*); **blouse,** bodice, corsage; dickey; sweater (*see list*)

16 **dress** (*see list*), **gown,** frock; **skirt**

17 **apron,** *tablier* (*French*); pinafore, bib, tucker; smock

18 **trousers,** pair of trousers, pants (*US*), bags (*informal*), trews (*Scottish*), trouse (*Irish*), **breeches,** britches (*informal*), breeks (*Scottish*), **pantaloons,** jeans, **slacks,** hipsters, leggings, ski pants *or* trousers

19 **waistband,** belt *see* 280.3; **sash,** cummerbund; **loincloth,** breechcloth *or* breechclout, waistcloth, **G-string,** loinguard, dhoti, moocha; **nappy,** napkin, diaper (*US*), dydee (*US informal*)

20 **dishabille,** *déshabillé* (*French*), **undress,** something more comfortable; **negligee,** *négligé* (*French*); **wrap,** wrapper; sport clothes, playwear, leisure-wear, **casual clothes** *or* **dress,** fling-on clothes

21 **nightwear,** nightclothes; **nightdress, nightgown, nightie** *and* shortie nightie (*both informal*), bedgown; nightshirt; **pyjamas,** pj's (*US informal*), baby doll pyjamas

22 **underclothes,** underclothing, undergarments (*see list*), bodywear, **underwear, undies** (*informal*), skivvies (*US informal*), body clothes, smallclothes, unmentionables (*informal*), **lingerie, linen,** underlinen; flannels, woollens

23 **corset,** stays, foundation garment, corselet; **girdle,** undergirdle, panty girdle; suspender belt, garter belt (*US*)

24 **brassiere, bra,** bandeau, underbodice, *soutien-gorge* (*French*), uplift brassiere; falsies (*informal*)

25 **headdress,** headgear, headwear, headclothes, headtire; **millinery;** headpiece, **chapeau, cap, hat;** tile *and* titfer *and* lid (*all informal*); headcloth, **kerchief,** coverchief; **handkerchief**

26 **veil,** veiling, veiler; *yashmak* (*Turkish*), chador (*Iranian*); mantilla

27 **footwear,** footgear, *chaussure* (*French*); **shoes, boots;** wooden shoes, sabots, pattens

28 **hosiery** (*see list*), **hose,** stockings; **socks**

29 **swimwear; bathing suit,** swim suit, swimming suit, swimming costume, tank suit, tank top, *maillot* *or* *maillot de bain* (*French*), two-piece suit; **trunks;** bikini, string bikini *or* string, thong, monokini; wet suit

30 **children's wear;** rompers, Babygro (*trademark*);

layette, baby clothes, infantwear, infants' wear, baby linen; swaddling clothes, swaddle

31 garment making, **tailoring; dressmaking, the rag trade** (*informal*), **the garment industry; millinery,** hatmaking, hatting; **shoemaking,** bootmaking, **cobbling;** habilimentation

32 clothier, haberdasher, draper, outfitter; costumier, costumer; glover; hosier; furrier; dry goods dealer, mercer

33 garmentmaker, garmentworker, needleworker; cutter, stitcher, finisher

34 tailor, tailoress, *tailleur* (*French*), sartor; fitter; busheler, bushelman; furrier, cloakmaker

35 dressmaker, modiste, *couturière* or *couturier* (*both French*); seamstress *see* 741.2

36 hatter, hatmaker, **milliner**

37 shoemaker, bootmaker, booter, **cobbler,** souter (*Scottish*)

verbs

38 to clothe, enclothe, **dress, garb, attire,** tire, array, **apparel,** raiment, garment, habilitate, **tog** *and* tog out (*both informal*), robe, enrobe, invest, endue, **deck,** bedeck, dight, rag out *or* up (*informal*); drape, bedrape; wrap, enwrap, lap, envelop, sheathe, shroud, enshroud; wrap *or* bundle *or* muffle up; swathe, swaddle

39 to cloak, mantle; coat, jacket; gown, frock; breech; shirt; **hat,** coif, bonnet, cap, hood; boot, shoe; stocking, sock

40 to outfit; equip, **accoutre,** uniform, caparison, kit out, rig, rig out *or* up, fit, **fit out,** turn out, **costume,** habit, suit; **tailor,** tailor-make, make to order; order, bespeak

41 to dress up, get up, doll *or* **spruce up** (*informal*), **primp** *and* prink *and* prank (*all informal*), gussy up (*informal*), spiff *or* fancy *or* slick up (*informal*), pretty up (*informal*), tart up (*informal*), deck out *or* up, trick out *or* up, tog out *or* up (*informal*), rag out *or* up (*informal*), fig out *or* up (*informal*); titivate, dizen, bedizen; overdress; put on the style, put on the dog (*US & Canadian informal*); **dress down,** underdress

42 to don, put on, slip on *or* into, get on *or* into, try on, assume, dress in; change; suit up

43 to wear, have on, be dressed in, affect, sport (*informal*)

adjectives

44 clothing; dress, vestiary, sartorial; **clothed, clad, dressed, attired, togged** (*informal*), tired, arrayed, **garbed,** garmented, habited, habilimented, decked, bedecked, decked out, turned-out, tricked-out, rigged-out, dight (*old*), vested, vestmented, robed, gowned, raimented, **apparelled,** invested, endued, liveried, uniformed; **costumed,** in costume, cloaked, mantled, disguised; breeched, trousered, pantalooned; coifed, capped, bonneted, hatted, hooded; **shod,** shoed, booted, *chaussé* (*French*)

45 dressed up, dolled *or* **spruced up** (*informal*); spiffed *or* fancied *or* slicked up (*informal*), gussied up (*informal*); spruce, dressed to advantage, dressed to the nines, dressed *or* fit to kill (*informal*); in Sunday best, *endimanché* (*French*), in one's best bib and tucker (*informal*), in fine *or* high feather; *en grande tenue* (*French*), *en grande toilette* (*French*), in full dress, in full feather, in white tie and tails, in tails; **well-dressed, chic,** *soigné* (*French*), stylish, modish, well-turned, well turned-out; **dressy,** preppy; **overdressed; underdressed,** casual, casually dressed

46 in dishabille, *en déshabillé* (*French*), **in negligee; casual,** nonformal, sporty

47 tailored, custom-made, bespoke; ready-made, off the peg *and* off-the-rail (*both informal*), store-bought (*US informal*), ready-to-wear; vestmental; sartorial

48 suits

bodysuit	separates
boiler suit	shell suit
business suit	shirt suit
camouflage suit *or* camo	shirtwaister suit
casual suit	single-breasted suit
cat suit	ski suit
combination	snowsuit
double-breasted suit	sports suit
dress suit	summer suit
ensemble	sun suit
foul-weather suit	sweat suit
jump suit	swimsuit
leisure suit *or* shirt-suit	tailored suit
lounge suit	tank suit *or* top
mod suit	three-piece suit
one-piece suit	town-and-country suit
playsuit	track suit
rain suit	tropical suit
riding habit	trouser suit
romper-suit	two-piece suit
sack suit	zoot suit
safari suit	

49 uniforms

blues	olive-drab *or* OD
continentals	regimentals
dress blues	sailor suit
dress whites	soldier suit
fatigues	stripes (prison uniform)
full dress	undress
khaki	whites
nauticals	

50 cloaks, overgarments

academic gown	frock
academic hood	gabardine
academic robe	gymslip
afghan	haik
bachelor's gown	houppelande
bleaunt	Inverness cape
blouse	judge's robe *or* gown
burnous	kaftan
caftan	kanga *or* khanga
cape	kimono
capote	kirtle
cardinal	manta
cashmere *or* cashmere shawl	manteau
	mantelet
cassock	mantelletta
chlamys	mantellone
doctor's gown	mantilla
domino	mantle
djellaba	mantua
duster	master's gown

military cloak
monk's robe
opera cloak *or* cape
pallium
pelerine
pelisse
peplos
peplum
plaid
poncho
robe
roquelaure
sagum
sarong
serape
shawl

shoulderette
slop
smock
soutane
stole
tabard
talma
tippet
toga
toga virilis
tunic
wrap-around
wrapover
wrapper
wrap-up

51 coats, jackets

blazer
blouse
body coat
body warmer
bolero
bomber jacket
capuchin
car coat
chaqueta (Spanish)
chesterfield
claw-hammer coat *or* claw
  hammer
coach coat
coatee
coolie jacket *or* coat
cutaway coat *or* cutaway
denim jacket
dinner coat *or* jacket
dolman
donkey jacket
double-breasted jacket
doublet
down jacket
dress coat
dressing jacket
duffel *or* duffel coat
Eisenhower jacket
Eton jacket
fingertip coat
fitted coat
flack jacket
frock coat *or* frock
hacking jacket
happi coat
jerkin
jumper
loden coat
lounging jacket
mackinaw *or* mackinaw

coat
Mao jacket
matinee jacket
maxicoat
mess jacket
midicoat
monkey jacket
morning coat
Nehru jacket
Norfolk jacket
oilskins
parka
peacoat *or* pea jacket
pilot jacket
Prince Albert *or* Prince
  Albert coat
redingote
reefer *or* reefer jacket
sack *or* sack coat
san benito
shell jacket
shirt jacket (US)
shooting jacket
single-breasted jacket
ski jacket
sleeve waistcoat
smoking jacket
spencer
spiketail coat *or* spiketail
sport coat *or* jacket
sports jacket
swagger coat
swallow-tailed coat *or*
  swallowtail
tabard
tail coat *or* tails
tuxedo coat *or* jacket
watch coat
woolly

52 sweaters

Aran
bolero
bulky
cardigan *or* cardigan jacket
  or cardie
cashmere sweater

chunky sweater
crewneck sweater
fisherman's sweater
Guernsey *or* gansey
hand-knit
jersey

jumper
pull-on sweater
pullover
shell
shoulderette
ski sweater
slip-on
slipover

sloppy Joe
sweat shirt
turtleneck sweater
twinset
V-neck sweater
windcheater
woolly

53 overcoats

anorak
Barbour (trademark)
benjamin
Burberry (trademark)
cagoule
camelhair coat
capote
chesterfield
cloth coat
dreadnought
duster
fearnought
fur coat
fur-lined coat
fur-trimmed coat
Gannex (trademark)
greatcoat
Inverness
long coat

mackintosh *or* mac *or*
  mack
Newmarket *or* Newmarket
  coat
oilskins
paletot
raglan
raincoat
slicker (US & Canadian)
slip-on
sou'wester
surtout
tarpaulin
trench coat
ulster
waterproof
wet weathers
wrap-around
wraprascal

54 shirts

basque
blouse
body shirt
body suit
button down
coat shirt
dashiki
dickey
doublet
dress shirt
evening shirt
gipon
habit shirt
hair shirt
halter
middy blouse

overblouse
polo shirt
pourpoint
pullover
sark
shirt-jacket (US)
shirtwaister
short-sleeved shirt
sport shirt
sweatshirt
tank top
tee-shirt *or* T-shirt
top
tube top
workshirt

55 dresses, skirts

ballet skirt
backwrap
ball-gown
body dress
cage
cheongsam
chiton
cocktail dress
crinoline
culottes
dinner dress *or* gown
dirndl
divided skirt
evening dress
evening gown
farthingale
fillebeg

full skirt
granny dress
grass skirt
hobble skirt
hoop skirt
kilt *or* filibeg
kirtle
mantua
maxiskirt
microskirt
midiskirt
miniskirt
Mother Hubbard
muu-muu
overdress
overskirt
palazzo pants

pannier
peplum
petticoat
pinafore
sack
sari
sarong
sheath
shift

shirtdress
shirtwaister
slit skirt
T-dress
tea gown
tunic dress
tutu
wrap dress

56 undergarments

all-in-one
Balmoral
bloomers
bodysuit *or* body
body stocking
boxer shorts
brassiere
breechclout *or* loin-cloth
briefs
bustier
bustle
cami-knickers
camisole
chemise
combinations
corset
crinoline
directoire knickers
drawers
foundation garment
French knickers
halter-top briefs
Jockey shorts (trademark)
knickers
leotard
long underwear *or* long
  johns
napkins *or* nappies
pannier

panties
pants
pantyhose
petticoat
scanties
shift
shorts
singlet
slip
smock
step-ins
string vest
teddy
tee-shirt *or* T-shirt
thermal underwear *or*
  thermals
tournure (French)
trunks
underdrawers
underpants
undershirt
undershorts
underskirt
undervest
union suit
unitard
vest
Y-fronts (trademark)

57 hosiery

anklets *or* ankle socks
argyles
athletic socks
bobbysocks
boothose (US)
boot socks
clock hose
crew socks
dress sheers
fleshings
fully-fashioned stockings
half hose
knee-highs
knee-socks
legwarmers
lisle hose

nylons
panty-hose
rayon stockings
seamless stockings
sheer stockings *or* sheers
shin socks
silk stockings
stocking hose
stretch stockings
sweat socks
tights
trunk hose
tube socks
varsity socks
wigglers *or* toe socks
work socks

6 UNCLOTHING

nouns

1 **unclothing**, divestment, divestiture, divesture; **removal**; **stripping**, denudement, denudation; baring, stripping *or* laying bare, uncovering, **exposure**, exposing; indecent exposure, exhibitionism, flashing (*informal*), mooning (*informal*); decortication, excoriation; desquamation, exfoliation; exuviation, ecdysis

2 **disrobing, undressing,** disrobement, unclothing; uncasing, discasing; shedding, moulting, peeling; striptease

3 **nudity, nakedness,** bareness; **the nude, the altogether** *and* **the buff** (*both informal*), **the raw** (*informal*); state of nature, **birthday suit** (*informal*); not a stitch, not a stitch to one's name *or* back; full-frontal nudity; décolleté, décolletage, toplessness; nudism, naturism, gymnosophy; nudist, naturist, gymnosophist; stripper, stripteaser, ecdysiast

4 **hairlessness, baldness,** acomia, alopecia; beardlessness, bald-headedness *or* patedness; baldhead, baldpate, baldy (*informal*), slaphead (*informal*); shaving, tonsure, depilation; hair remover, depilatory

verbs

5 to divest, **strip, strip away, remove; uncover,** uncloak, unveil, **expose,** lay open, bare, lay *or* strip bare, **denude,** denudate; fleece, shear; pluck

6 to **take off, remove, doff,** douse (*informal*), off with, put off, slip *or* step out of, slip off, slough off, cast off, throw off, drop; unwrap, undo

7 to **undress, unclothe,** undrape, ungarment, unapparel, unarray, disarray; **disrobe**; debag (*informal*); unsheathe, discase, uncase; flash (*informal*), moon (*informal*); **strip,** strip to the buff (*informal*), do a strip-tease

8 to **peel, pare, skin, strip,** flay, excoriate, decorticate, bark; scalp

9 to **husk, hull,** pod, **shell,** shuck

10 to **shed, cast,** throw off, **slough, moult,** slough off, exuviate

11 to **scale, flake,** scale *or* flake off, desquamate, exfoliate

adjectives

12 **divested, stripped, bared,** denuded, denudated, **exposed, uncovered,** stripped *or* laid bare, unveiled, showing; unsheathed, discased, uncased

13 **unclad, undressed, unclothed, unattired, disrobed,** ungarmented, undraped, ungarbed, unrobed, unapparelled, uncased; **clothesless,** garbless, garmentless, raimentless; half-clothed, underclothed, *en déshabillé* (*French*), in dishabille, nudish; low-necked, low-cut, décolleté, strapless, topless; **seminude,** scantily clad

14 **naked, nude,** nuddy (*informal*); **bare,** peeled, raw (*informal*), **in the raw** (*informal*), *in puris naturalibus* (*Latin*), in a state of nature, in nature's garb; in one's birthday suit, **in the buff** *and* in native buff *and* stripped to the buff *and* **in the altogether** (*all informal*), with nothing on, without a stitch, without a stitch to one's name *or* on one's back; **stark-naked,** bare as the back of one's hand, naked as the day one was born, naked as a jaybird (*US informal*), starkers (*informal*),

"naked as a worm"—CHAUCER, "naked as a needle"—WILLIAM LANGLAND, "naked as my nail"—JOHN HEYWOOD, "in naked beauty more adorned"—MILTON; nudist, naturistic, gymnosophical

15 barefoot, barefooted, unshod; discalced, discalceate

16 bare-ankled, bare-armed, bare-backed, bare-breasted, topless, bare-chested, bare-faced, bare-handed, bare-headed, bare-kneed, bare-legged, bare-necked, bare-throated

17 hairless, depilous; **bald**, acomous; bald as a coot, bald as an egg; **bald-headed**, bald-pated, tonsured; **beardless**, whiskerless, shaven, clean-shaven, smooth-shaven, smooth-faced; smooth, glabrous

18 exuvial, sloughy; desquamative, exfoliatory; denudant *or* denudatory

adverbs

19 nakedly, barely, baldly

word elements

20 de–, dis–, un–

7 NUTRITION

nouns

1 nutrition, nourishment, nourishing, feeding, nurture; alimentation; **food** *or* **nutritive value, food intake**; food chain *or* cycle

2 nutritiousness, nutritiveness, **digestibility**, assimilability; healthfulness

3 nutrient, nutritive, **nutriment** *see* 10.3, food; nutrilite, growth factor, growth regulator; **natural food**, health food (*see list*); roughage, fibre

4 vitamin (*see list*), vitamin complex; provitamin, provitamin A *or* carotene

5 carbohydrate, carbo *or* carbs (*informal*), simple carbohydrate, complex carbohydrate; hydroxy aldehyde, hydroxy ketone, saccharide, monosaccharide, disaccharide, trisaccharide, polysaccharide *or* polysaccharose; **sugar; starch**

6 protein *or* proteid, simple protein, conjugated protein; **amino acid**, essential amino acid; peptide, dipeptide, polypeptide, etc

7 fat, glyceride, **lipid**, lipoid; fatty acid; steroid, sterol; **cholesterol**, glycerol-cholesterol, cephalin-cholesterol; triglyceride; **lipoprotein**, high-density lipoprotein *or* HDL, low-density lipoprotein *or* LDL; polyunsaturated fat

8 digestion, ingestion, assimilation, absorption; primary digestion, secondary digestion; predigestion; salivary digestion, gastric *or* peptic digestion, pancreatic digestion, intestinal digestion; digestive system, alimentary canal, gastrointestinal tract; salivary glands, gastric glands, liver, pancreas; digestive secretions, saliva, gastric juice, pancreatic juice, intestinal juice, bile

9 digestant, digester, digestive; pepsin; **enzyme**, proteolytic enzyme

10 metabolism, basal metabolism, acid-base metabolism, energy metabolism; **anabolism**, assimilation; **catabolism**, disassimilation

11 diet, dieting, dietary; dietetics; **regimen**, regime; bland diet, soft diet, pap, spoon food *or* meat, spoon victuals (*informal*); balanced diet; diabetic diet, allergy diet, reducing diet, obesity diet; high-calorie diet, low-calorie diet, watching one's weight *or* calories, calorie-counting; liquid diet; protein-sparing diet; high-protein diet, low-carbohydrate diet; high-vitamin diet, vitamin-deficiency diet; acid-ash diet, alkaline-ash diet; low-salt diet, low-sodium diet, salt-free diet; ulcer diet; vegetarianism, veganism, macrobiotic diet; diet book, vitamin chart, calorie chart, calorie counter; fad diet

12 vitaminization, fortification, enrichment, restoration

13 nutritionist, dietitian, vitaminologist, enzymologist

14 (*science of nutrition*) **dietetics**, dietotherapeutics, dietotherapy; vitaminology; enzymology

verbs

15 to nourish, feed, sustain, nutrify (*old*), nurture; **sustain**, strengthen

16 to digest, assimilate, absorb; metabolize; predigest

17 to diet, go on a diet; watch one's weight *or* calories, count calories

18 to vitaminize, fortify, enrich, restore

adjectives

19 nutritious, nutritive, nutrient, **nourishing**; alimentary, alimental; digestible, assimilable

20 digestive, assimilative; peptic

21 dietary, dietetic, dietic (*old*); regiminal

22 health foods

acidophilus milk	peanut flour
blackstrap molasses	powdered milk
brewer's yeast	raw vegetables
brown rice	royal jelly
buckwheat flour	soybeans
caudle	soy flour
fibre	stoneground flour
fortified flour	unrefined flour
fortified milk	vegetables
fruits	wheat germ
liver	wheat grass
nonfat milk	whole wheat
nuts	whole wheat flour
oat bran	yogurt
organic vegetables	

23 vitamins

vitamin A	biotin *or* vitamin H
vitamin A₁ *or*	choline
antiophthalmic factor *or*	folic acid *or*
axerophthol	pteroylglutamic acid *or*
vitamin A₂	para-aminobenzoic acid
carotene	*or* PABA
cryptoxanthin	inositol
vitamin B	niacin *or* nicotinic acid
vitamin B complex	**vitamin C** *or* ascorbic
vitamin B₁ *or* thiamine *or*	acid
aneurin *or* anti-beriberi	**vitamin D** *or* calciferol
factor	ergocalciferol
vitamin B₂ *or* vitamin G	cholecalciferol
or riboflavin *or* lactoflavin	**vitamin E** *or* tocopherol
or ovoflavin *or*	**vitamin K** *or*
hepatoflavin	naphthoquinone
vitamin M *or* vitamin B꜀	menadione
vitamin B₆ *or* pyridoxine	**vitamin P** *or* bioflavinoid
or adermin	

8 EATING

nouns

1 **eating, feeding, dining,** messing; the nosebag (*informal*); ingestion, consumption, deglutition; **tasting,** relishing, savouring; **gourmet eating** *or* **dining,** fine dining, gourmandise; nibbling, pecking, licking, **munching;** snacking; **devouring,** gobbling, wolfing; **gorging, overeating,** gluttony, overconsumption; **chewing,** mastication, manducation, rumination; **feasting, regaling,** regalement; **appetite, hunger** *see* 100.7; nutrition *see* 7; **dieting** *see* 7.11; gluttony *see* 672; carnivorism, carnivorousness, carnivority; herbivorism, herbivority, herbivorousness, grazing, browsing, cropping, pasturing, pasture, vegetarianism, phytophagy; omnivorism, omnivorousness, pantophagy; cannibalism, anthropophagy; omophagia *or* omophagy

2 **bite, morsel, taste,** swallow; mouthful, gob (*informal*); a nibble, a bite, munchies; cud, quid; bolus; **chew,** chaw (*informal*); nip, nibble; munch; gnash; champ, chomp (*informal*); snap

3 **drinking,** imbibing, imbibition, potation; lapping, sipping, tasting, nipping; quaffing, gulping, swigging (*informal*), swilling *and* guzzling (*both informal*), pulling (*informal*); compotation, symposium; drunkenness *see* 88.1, 3

4 **drink,** potation, potion, libation; draught, dram, drench, **swig** (*informal*), swill *and* guzzle (*both informal*), quaff, **sip,** sup, suck, tot, bumper, snort *and* snorter *and* slug (*all informal*), pull (*informal*), lap, gulp, slurp (*informal*); nip, peg; cuppa (*informal*), beverage

5 **meal, repast,** feed *and* sit-down (*both informal*), mess, spread (*informal*), table, board, meat, *repas* (*French*); **refreshment,** refection, regalement, entertainment, treat; frozen meal, meal pack

6 (*meals*) **breakfast,** *petit déjeuner* (*French*), continental breakfast, English breakfast; meat, breakfast, *déjeuner à la fourchette* (*French*); **brunch** (*informal*), elevenses (*informal*); **lunch, luncheon,** tiffin, hot luncheon; **tea,** teatime, high tea, cream tea; **dinner,** *diner* (*French*); **supper,** *souper* (*French*); buffet supper *or* lunch; box lunch, packed lunch; takeaway, takeout (*US & Canadian*); precooked frozen meal, TV dinner, cook-chill meal; **picnic,** cookout, alfresco meal, fête champêtre, **barbecue;** coffee break, tea break

7 **light meal, refreshments,** light repast, light lunch, spot of lunch (*informal*), collation, **snack** *and* nosh (*both informal*), **bite** (*informal*), *casse-croûte* (*French*)

8 **hearty meal, full meal,** healthy meal, large *or* substantial meal, heavy meal, **square meal,** man-sized meal, large order, nosh-up (*informal*), tuck-in (*informal*), fry-up

9 **feast, banquet,** festal board; lavish *or* Lucullan feast; bean-feast *or* beano (*both informal*), blow *or* blowout (*informal*), groaning board

10 **serving, service; portion, helping,** help; second helping; **course;** dish, plate; dish of the day, *plat du jour* (*French*); antepast (*old*); entree, *entrée* (*French*), entremets; dessert, afters; cover, place

11 (*manner of service*) service, table service, counter service, self-service, takeaway service, take-out service, silver service; table d'hôte, ordinary; à la carte; cover, *couvert* (*French*); cover charge

12 **tableware,** dining utensils; **silverware,** silver, silver plate, stainless-steel ware; flatware, flat silver; hollow ware; **cutlery,** knives, forks, spoons; tablespoon, teaspoon; chopsticks; **china, dishes,** plates, cups, glasses, saucers, bowls, fingerbowls; **dish,** salad dish, fruit dish, dessert dish; **bowl,** cereal bowl, fruit bowl, punchbowl; **tea service, tea set,** tea things, tea strainer, tea-caddy, tea-cosy

13 **table linen, napery,** tablecloth, table cover, table-mat, table pad; **napkin, table napkin,** serviette

14 **menu, bill of fare,** carte, tariff, tourist menu

15 **gastronomy,** gastronomics, gastrology, **epicurism,** epicureanism

16 **eater,** feeder, consumer, devourer; **diner,** luncher; picnicker; mouth, hungry mouth; diner-out, eater-out; boarder, board-and-roomer; **gourmet,** gastronome, epicure, gourmand, connoisseur of food *or* wine, bon vivant, high liver, Lucullus, Brillat-Savarin, foodie (*informal*); **glutton,** overeater, pig (*informal*), gourmand; omnivore, pantophagist; **flesh-eater, meat-eater, carnivore,** omophagist, predacean; **man-eater, cannibal; vegetarian, vegan,** lactovegetarian, fruitarian, plant-eater, **herbivore,** phytophagan, phytophage; grass-eater, graminivore; grain-eater, granivore; gourmand, trencherman, **glutton** *see* 672.3

17 **restaurant,** eating place, eating house, dining room; eatery *and* greasy spoon (*both informal*), beanery *and* hashery *and* hash house (*all US informal*); **fast-food restaurant,** hamburger joint (*informal*); *trattoria* (*Italian*); taverna (*Greek*); **lunchroom** (*US & Canadian*), luncheonette (*US & Canadian*); **café,** *caffè* (*Italian*); **tearoom,** bistro (*French*); **coffeehouse,** coffeeroom, **coffee shop,** coffee bar, coffee-pot (*informal*); **tea shop,** tea-room, tea-garden, teahouse; pub, tavern; carvery, chophouse, steakhouse; **grill,** grillroom; buffet, smorgasbord; lunch counter, quick-lunch counter; hot-dog stand, hamburger stand, drive-in restaurant, drive-in, drive-thru; **snack bar,** *buvette* (*French*), cantina (*Spanish*); milk bar; sushi bar; juice bar; raw bar; pizzeria; creperie; **cafeteria,** automat; transport café, pull-in *or* pull-up, roadhouse; mess hall, dining hall, refectory, buttery; canteen; cookhouse, cookshack (*US*), lunch trolley, chuck wagon (*US*); **diner;** takeaway, carry-out, fish-and-chip shop, chippy (*informal*); **kitchen** *see* 11.3

verbs

18 **to feed, dine,** wine and dine, mess; nibble, snack, graze (*informal*); satisfy, gratify; regale; board, sustain; pasture, put out to pasture, graze, grass; forage, fodder; provision *see* 385.9

19 **to nourish, nurture,** nutrify, aliment, foster; **nurse, suckle,** lactate, breast-feed, wet-nurse, dry-nurse; fatten, fatten up, stuff, force-feed

20 **to eat, feed,** fare, take, partake, partake of, break bread, break one's fast; refresh *or* entertain the inner man, feed one's face *and* put on the nosebag (*both informal*), fall to, pitch in (*informal*); **taste,** relish, savour; hunger *see* 100.19; **diet,** go on a diet, watch one's weight, count calories

21 to dine; **sup,** breakfast; lunch; picnic, barbecue; **eat out, dine out;** board; mess with, break bread with

22 to devour, **swallow,** ingest, **consume,** take in, tuck in *or* away *and* tuck into (*all informal*), down, take down, get down, put away (*informal*); **eat up;** dispatch *or* dispose of *and* get away with (*all informal*); surround *and* put oneself outside of (*both informal*)

23 to gobble, gulp, bolt, scoff, wolf, gobble *or* gulp *or* bolt *or* wolf down

24 to feast, banquet, regale; eat heartily, have a good appetite, eat up, lick the platter *or* plate, do oneself proud (*informal*), do one's duty, do justice to, polish the platter, put it away (*informal*)

25 to stuff, gorge *see* 672.4, pig out (*informal*), engorge, glut, cram, eat one's fill, stuff *or* gorge oneself, gluttonize

26 to pick, peck (*informal*), nibble; snack (*informal*), nosh (*informal*); pick at, peck at (*informal*), eat like a bird, show no appetite, play with one's food

27 to chew, chew up, chaw (*informal*), bite into; masticate, manducate; ruminate, chew the cud; bite, grind, champ, chomp (*informal*); munch; gnash; nibble, gnaw; mouth, mumble; gum

28 to feed on *or* upon, feast on *or* upon, batten upon, fatten on *or* upon; prey on *or* upon, live on *or* upon, pasture on, browse, graze, crop

29 to drink, drink in, imbibe, wet one's whistle (*informal*); quaff, sip, sup, bib, swig *and* swill *and* guzzle *and* pull (*all informal*); suck, suckle, suck in *or* up; drink off *or* up, toss off *or* down, drain the cup; wash down; toast, drink to, pledge; tipple, booze *see* 88.23

30 to lap up, sponge *or* soak up, lick, lap, slurp (*informal*)

adjectives

31 eating, feeding, gastronomical, dining, mensal, commensal, prandial, postprandial, preprandial; nourishing, nutritious *see* 7.19; dietetic; omnivorous, pantophagous, gluttonous *see* 672.6; flesh-eating, meat-eating, carnivorous, omophagous, predacious; man-eating, cannibal, cannibalistic; insect-eating, insectivorous; vegetable-eating, vegetarian, demi-vegetarian, lactovegetarian, fruitarian; plant-eating, herbivorous, phytivorous, phytophagous; grass-eating, graminivorous; grain-eating, granivorous

32 chewing, masticatory, manducatory; ruminant, ruminating, cud-chewing

33 edible, eatable, comestible, gustable, esculent; kosher; palatable, succulent, delicious, dainty, savoury; fine, fancy, gourmet

34 drinkable, potable

exclamations

35 chow down!, soup's on!, grub's on!, come and get it!; *bon appétit!* (*French*), eat hearty!, eat up!

word elements

36 phag–, phago–, –phagia, –phagy; –phage, –vore, –vora

9 REFRESHMENT

nouns

1 refreshment, refection, refreshing, bracing, exhilaration, stimulation, enlivenment, vivification, invigoration, reinvigoration, reanimation, revival, revivification, revivescence *or* revivescency, renewal, recreation; regalement, regale; tonic, bracer, breath of fresh air, pick-me-up *and* a shot in the arm *and* an upper (*all informal*); cordial

verbs

2 to refresh, freshen, refreshen, freshen up, fresh up (*informal*); revive, revivify, reinvigorate, reanimate; exhilarate, stimulate, invigorate, fortify, enliven, liven up, animate, vivify, quicken, brisk, brisken; brace, brace up, buck up *and* pick up (*both informal*), perk up (*informal*), set up, set on one's legs *or* feet (*informal*); renew one's strength, put *or* breathe new life into, give a breath of fresh air, give a shot in the arm (*informal*); renew, recreate, charge *or* recharge one's batteries (*informal*); regale, cheer, refresh the inner man

adjectives

3 refreshing, refreshful, fresh, brisk, crisp, crispy, zesty, zestful, bracing, tonic, cordial; analeptic; exhilarating, stimulating, stimulative, stimulatory, invigorating, rousing, energizing; regaling, cheering

4 refreshed, restored, invigorated, exhilarated, stimulated, energized, recharged, animated, reanimated, revived, renewed, recreated

5 unwearied, untired, unfatigued, unexhausted

10 FOOD

nouns

1 food, foodstuff, food and drink, sustenance, kitchen stuff, victualage, comestibles, edibles, eatables, viands, cuisine, tucker (*Australian*), ingesta (*plural*); soul food; fast food, junk food; fare, cheer, creature comfort; provision, provender; meat (*old*), bread, daily bread, bread and butter; health food; board, table, feast *see* 8.9, spread (*informal*)

2 (*informal terms*) grub, eats, chow, chuck (*US*), groceries, nosh, nosh-up, the nosebag, scarf *or* scoff, snap, tack, tuck, victuals *or* vittles

3 nutriment, nourishment, nurture; pabulum, pap; aliment, alimentation; refreshment, refection, commons; sustenance, support, keep

4 feed, fodder, provender, stover; forage, pasture, eatage, pasturage; grain; corn, oats, barley, wheat; meal, bran, chop; hay, timothy, clover, straw; ensilage, silage; chicken feed, scratch, scratch feed, mash; slops, swill; pet food, dog food, cat food; bird seed

5 provisions, groceries, provender, supplies, stores, larder, food supply; fresh foods, tinned *or* canned foods, frozen foods, dehydrated foods, precooked foods; commissariat, commissary, grocery

6 rations, board, meals, commons, mess, allowance, allotment, food allotment, tucker (*Australian*); short commons; emergency rations; K ration, C ration, garrison or field rations

7 dish see 11.1, culinary preparation or concoction; cover, **course** see 8.10; casserole; grill, broil (US & Canadian), roast, fry; **main dish, entree**, pièce de résistance (French), culinary masterpiece, dish fit for a king; side dish

8 delicacy, dainty, goody (informal), treat, kickshaw, **titbit; morsel**, choice morsel, bonne bouche (French); savoury; dessert, sweet; ambrosia, nectar, cate, manna

9 appetizer, whet, apéritif (French); foretaste, antepast (old), antipasto (Italian), **starter**, Vorspeise (German); **hors d'oeuvre**, savoury; crostato (Italian); smorgasbord; canapé, **dip**, guacamole, salsa, taramasalata, cheese dip, hummus, tzatziki; falafel; zakuski (Russia); **pickle**, sour pickle, dill pickle, piccalilli

10 soup, potage (French), zuppa or minestra (both Italian)

11 stew, hotpot, olla, olio, olla podrida (Spanish); meat stew, étuvée (French); Irish stew, mulligan stew or mulligan (informal); goulash, Hungarian goulash; ragout; salmi; bouillabaisse (French), paella (Catalan), oyster stew, chowder; fricassee; curry

12 meat, flesh, red meat, viande (French); butcher's meat, viande de boucherie (French); **cut of meat**; game, menue viande (French); venison, **roast**, joint, rôti (French); pot roast; barbecue, boiled meat, bouilli (French); forcemeat; minced meat, mince; hash, hachis (French); jugged hare, civet (French); pemmican, jerky; sausage meat, Lorne sausage (Scottish), meat loaf; aspic

13 beef, bœuf (French); roast beef, rosbif (French); Kobe beef; hamburger, ground beef, **mince**, minced beef; corned beef, bully or bully beef; dried beef; chipped beef; salt beef; jerky, charqui; pastrami; beef extract, beef tea, bouillon; suet

14 veal, vitello (Italian), veau (French); veal cutlet, côtelette de veau (French); breast of veal, poitrine de veau (French); fricandeau; calf's head, tête de veau (French); calf's liver, foie de veau (French); sweetbread, ris de veau (French); calf's brains

15 mutton, mouton (French); hog or hogget; muttonchop; **lamb**, agneau (French); breast of lamb, poitrine d'agneau (French); leg of lamb, leg of mutton, gigot, jambe de mouton (French); saddle of mutton; baked sheep's head

16 pork, porc (French), pig, pigmeat (informal)

17 steak, popeseye (Scottish), tranche (French), **beefsteak**, bifteck (French), tranche de bœuf (French), bistecca (Italian)

18 chop, cutlet, côtelette (French); pork chop, côtelette de porc frais (French); mutton chop, Saratoga chop; veal cutlet, veal chop, côtelette de veau (French), Wiener Schnitzel (German)

19 (offal) kidneys; heart; brains; liver; gizzard, gralloch; tongue; sweetbread (thymus); beef bread (pancreas); tripe (stomach); marrow; cockscomb; chitterlings or chitlins (intestines); lamb's fry, prairie or mountain oyster (testis); haslet, giblets, abattis (French)

20 sausage, banger (informal), chipolata, saucisse (French), saucisson (French), salsiccia (Italian), Wurst (German); black pudding, white pudding; toad-in-the-hole; **pâté**

21 fowl, bird, edible bird, volaille (French)

22 (parts of fowl) leg, drumstick, thigh, chicken foot, turkey foot, etc, wing, wishbone, breast; white meat, dark meat, giblets, pope's or parson's nose (informal); oyster; neck

23 fish, poisson (French); seafood; coley; white fish; finnan haddie; kipper, kippered salmon or herring, gravlax; smoked salmon, lox; smoked herring, red herring, bloater; eel, anguille (French); fish eggs, roe, caviar; ceviche, sushi; squid, calamari; flatfish, sole, lemon sole, Dover sole, flounder, fluke, dab, sanddab

24 shellfish, coquillage (French); **mollusc**, snail, escargot (French)

25 eggs, œufs (French); fried eggs, œufs sur le plat (French); boiled eggs, œufs à la coque (French), coddled eggs; poached eggs, œufs pochés (French); scrambled eggs, buttered eggs, œufs brouillés (French); baked eggs, shirred eggs, stuffed eggs, devilled eggs; omelette; soufflé; Scotch egg

26 stuffing, dressing, forcemeat or farce

27 bread, pain (French), pane (Italian), the staff of life; loaf of bread, batch, bloomer, cob loaf, cottage loaf, pan loaf, plait, bread stick, baguette; crust, breadcrust, crust of bread; **leaven**, leavening, ferment

28 corn bread; tortilla (Spanish)

29 biscuit, sinker (informal); hardtack, sea biscuit, ship's biscuit, pilot biscuit or bread; **cracker**, soda cracker or saltine, graham cracker, biscotto (Italian), cream cracker, nacho, crisp or potato crisp, potato chip (US & Canadian), water biscuit, butter cracker, oyster cracker, Bath Oliver, oatcake; wheatmeal biscuit, digestive biscuit; wafer; rusk, zwieback, melba toast, Brussels biscuit; pretzel

30 roll, bun; bagel; brioche, croissant; muffin; popover; scone; bap, bridge roll; hard roll

31 sandwich, sarnie (informal), canapé (French), smörgåsbord (Swedish); **toast**, French toast, toastie; club sandwich; hamburger, burger

32 noodles, pasta (Italian), Italian paste, paste; **spaghetti**, spaghettini, ziti, fedellini, fettuccine, radiattore, vermicelli, **macaroni**, lasagne; ravioli, kreplach (Yiddish plural), won ton; **dumpling**; spaetzle, dim sum, gnocchi, linguine; matzo balls, knaydlach (Yiddish)

33 cereal, breakfast food, dry cereal, hot cereal; **flour**, meal

34 vegetables, produce, légumes (French), veg and veggies (both informal); **greens**; potherbs; **beans**, frijoles (Spanish), haricots (French); **potato**, spud (informal), tater (informal), pomme de terre (French), Irish potato, pratie (informal), white potato; **tomato**, love apple; aubergine, eggplant, mad apple; rhubarb; cabbage, Kraut (German)

35 salad, salade (French); **greens**, crudités (French)

36 fruit; produce; stone fruit, drupe; citrus fruit; soft fruit; fruit compote, fruit salad, fruit cocktail

37 nut, noix (French), noisette (French); kernel, meat

38 sweets, sweet stuff, **confectionery**, tuck (informal); **sweet, sweetmeat**, sweetie (informal); **confection**; candy; boiled sweet; truffle; comfit, confiture;

candyfloss; **jelly, jam;** preserve, conserve; marmalade; apple butter; prune butter, lekvar; lemon curd; gelatin, Jell-O (*US trademark*); trifle; fool; compote; mousse; blancmange; roly-poly, tutti-frutti; maraschino cherries; honey; icing, royal icing, frosting, glaze; meringue; whipped cream

39 pastry, *patisserie* (*French*); French pastry, Danish pastry; **tart;** turnover; timbale; **pie,** *tarte* (*French*), fruit pie, tart, tartlet, Bakewell tart; *quiche* or *quiche Lorraine* (*French*); patty, patty cake; patty shell, *vol-au-vent* (*French*); dowdy (*US*), pandowdy (*US*); filo, strudel, baklava; puff pastry; puff, cream puff, *croquembouche* (*French*), profiterole; cream horn, *cannoli* (*Italian*); éclair, chocolate éclair

40 cake, *gâteau* (*French*), *torte* (*German*); petit-four (*French*)

41 biscuit, cookie (*US & Canadian*)

42 bath bun, Banbury cake, Eccles cake; parkin; **doughnut,** jam doughnut; fritter, *beignet* (*French*); apple fritter, *beignet aux pommes* (*French*)

43 pancake, crumpet, teacake, griddlecake, **hot cake,** battercake, flapcake, **flapjack;** buckwheat cake; chapatti *and* nan (*both India*); **waffle;** blintz, cheese blintz, *crêpe, crêpe suzette* (*both French*), *palacsinta* (*Hungarian*), *Pfannkuchen* (*German*), Swedish pancake; Yorkshire pudding

44 pudding, pud (*informal*), custard, mousse, flan

45 ice, *glace* (*French*), frozen dessert; **ice cream,** ice milk, French ice-cream; **sorbet,** sherbet, water ice, Italian ice; gelato; tortoni; parfait; sundae, ice-cream sundae, banana split, knickerbocker glory; ice-cream soda; frappé; ice-cream cone *or* cornet; frozen pudding; frozen custard, soft ice cream; frozen yogurt, **ice lolly** *or* lollipop *or* lolly

46 dairy products, milk products; **cheese; tofu,** bean curd

47 beverage, drink, thirst quencher, potation, potable, drinkable (*informal*), **liquor,** liquid; **soft drink,** nonalcoholic beverage; cold drink; carbonated water, mineral water *or* mineral, soda water, sparkling water, **soda,** pop, soda pop (*US*), ginger (*Scottish*), tonic; squash; milk shake, frosted shake, thick shake, shake *and* frosted (*both informal*); malted milk; hard drink, alcoholic drink

11 COOKING

nouns

1 cooking, cookery, cuisine, culinary art; food preparation; home economics, domestic science, culinary science; catering; nutrition *see* 7; baking, toasting, roasting, frying, searing, blackening, sautéing, boiling, simmering, stewing, basting, braising, poaching, shirring, barbecuing, steeping, brewing, grilling, broiling (*US & Canadian*), pan-frying; grill; **dish,** manner of preparation, style of recipe; **condiment,** spice, herb; **sauce**

2 cook, chef, *cuisinier* or *cuisinière* (*French*), kitchener, culinarian, culinary artist; **chief cook, head chef,** *chef de cuisine* (*French*); sous chef, commis chef; fry cook *or* grease-burner (*informal*), short-order cook; **baker,** *boulanger* (*French*), pastry cook, pastry chef, *patissier* (*French*)

3 kitchen, cookroom, cookery, **scullery,** cuisine; kitchenette; **galley,** caboose *or* camboose (*US & Canadian*); cookhouse; **bakery,** bakehouse; **cookware, kitchen ware,** cooker (*see list*), pots and pans, *batterie de cuisine* (*French*)

verbs

4 to cook, prepare food, prepare, do, cook up, fry up, boil up, rustle up (*informal*); precook; boil, heat, stew, simmer, parboil, blanch; brew; poach, coddle; bake, fire, ovenbake, **microwave,** micro-cook, nuke (*informal*); scallop; shirr; roast; toast; fry, deep-fry *or* deep-fat fry, griddle, pan, pan-fry; sauté, stir-fry; frizz, frizzle; sear, blacken, braise, brown; grill, broil (*US & Canadian*); barbecue; fricassee; steam; devil; curry; baste; **do to a turn,** do to perfection

adjectives

5 cooking, culinary, kitchen

6 cooked, heated, stewed, fried, barbecued, curried, fricasseed, devilled, sautéed, shirred, toasted; roasted, roast; fired, pan-fried, deep-fried *or* deep-fat fried, stir-fried; grilled, broiled (*US & Canadian*); seared, blackened, braised, browned; boiled, simmered, parboiled; steamed; poached, coddled; baked, fired, oven-baked; scalloped

7 done, well-done, well-cooked; *bien cuit* (*French*), done to a turn *or* to perfection; overcooked, **overdone;** medium, medium-rare; doneness

8 underdone, undercooked, not done, **rare,** *saignant* (*French*); sodden, heavy

9 cookers

Aga (trademark)	fireless cooker
alcohol stove	food processor
baker	galley stove
barbecue	griddle *or* girdle
boiler	grill
broiler	hibachi
camp stove	infrared cooker
chafer	microwave oven
chafing dish *or* pan	percolator
coffee maker	pots, pans
cook stove	pressure cooker
corn popper	roaster
deep-fat fryer	rotisserie
double boiler	samovar
Dutch oven	slow cooker
electric cooker	stove
electric frying pan	toaster
electric roaster	waffle iron
electric toaster	waterless cooker
fan-assisted oven	wok
field range	

12 EXCRETION
bodily discharge

nouns

1 excretion, egestion, extrusion, **elimination, discharge; emission;** eccrisis; **exudation,** transudation; extravasation, effusion, flux, flow; ejaculation, ejection *see* 908; **secretion** *see* 13

2 defecation, dejection, **evacuation,** voidance; movement, **bowel movement,** number two (*informal*), **stool, shit** *and* crap (*both informal*); **diarrhoea**, loose bowels, flux; trots *and* runs *and* shits (*all informal*); gippy tummy *and* Montezuma's revenge (*both informal*); lientery; **dysentery**, bloody flux; catharsis, purgation, purge

3 **excrement**, dejection, dejecta, **discharge**, ejection; matter, **waste**, waste matter; **excreta**, egesta, ejecta, ejectamenta; exudation, exudate; transudation, transudate; extravasation, extravasate; effluent

4 **faeces**, feculence; defecation, movement, bowel movement, motion; **stool, shit** (*informal*), **ordure**, night soil, jakes (*informal*), crap *and* doo-doo (*both informal*); turd (*informal*); **manure, dung, droppings**; cowpats; guano; coprolite, coprolith; sewage, sewerage

5 **urine**, water, **piss** (*informal*), number one, pish (*Scottish informal*), pee *and* pee-pee *and* wee *and* wee-wee (*all informal*), piddle, stale; **urination**, micturition, emiction, a piss *and* a pee *and* a slash *and* a wee (*all informal*); urea

6 **pus; matter**, purulence, peccant humour (*old*), ichor, sanies; pussiness; **suppuration, festering**, rankling, mattering, running; gleet, leucorrhoea

7 **sweat, perspiration**, water; exudation, exudate; diaphoresis, sudor; honest sweat, the sweat of one's brow; beads of sweat, beaded brow; cold sweat; **lather**, mucksweat, swelter, streams of sweat; sudoresis; body odour *or* **BO**, perspiration odour

8 **haemorrhage**, haemorrhoea, **bleeding**; nosebleed; ecchymosis, petechia

9 **menstruation**, menstrual discharge *or* flow *or* flux, catamenia, catamenial discharge, flowers (*old*), **the curse** (*informal*), the curse of Eve; **menses, monthlies**, courses, period, that time, time of the month

10 **latrine**, convenience, **toilet**, toilet room, water closet *or* **WC** (*informal*); loo (*informal*), lav (*informal*), cludgie (*Scottish*); **lavatory**, washroom, cloakroom, public convenience, office *and* usual offices (*both informal*); **bathroom; rest room**, comfort station *or* room; ladies, ladies' *or* women's *or* girls' *or* little girls' *or* powder room (*informal*); gents, men's *or* boys' *or* little boys' room (*informal*); head; privy, outhouse, backhouse, shithouse (*informal*), earth closet, closet *and* necessary (*both informal*); urinal

11 **toilet**, stool, **water closet; pan** (*informal*); latrine; commode, closetstool, potty-chair (*informal*); **chamber pot**, chamber, pisspot (*informal*), potty (*informal*), jerry (*informal*), thunder mug (*informal*); throne (*informal*); chemical toilet, chemical closet; urinal; bedpan

verbs

12 **to excrete**, egest, **eliminate, discharge**, emit, give off, pass; ease *or* relieve oneself, go to the bathroom (*informal*); **exude**, exudate, transude; weep; effuse, extravasate; **secrete** *see* 13.5

13 **to defecate, shit** *and* crap (*both informal*), **evacuate**, void, **stool**, dung, have a bowel movement, take a shit *or* crap (*informal*), number two (*informal*)

14 **to urinate, pass** *or* **make water**, wet, stale, **piss** (*informal*), piddle, pee, tinkle; pee-pee *and* wee-wee

and number one (*all informal*), spend a penny, have a slash *and* take a leak (*both informal*)

15 **to fester**, suppurate, matter, rankle, run, weep; ripen, come *or* draw to a head

16 **to sweat, perspire**, exude; break out in a sweat, **get all in a lather** (*informal*); sweat like a pig *or* horse, swelter, wilt

17 **to bleed, haemorrhage**, lose blood, **shed blood**, spill blood; bloody; ecchymose

18 **to menstruate**, come sick, come around, have one's period

adjectives

19 **excretory**, excretive, excretionary; eliminative, egestive; exudative, transudative; **secretory** *see* 13.7

20 **excremental**, excrementary; **faecal**, feculent, shitty *and* crappy (*both informal*), scatologic *or* scatological, stercoral, stercorous, stercoraceous, dungy; **urinary**, urinative

21 **festering**, suppurative, rankling, mattering; pussy, purulent

22 **sweaty**, perspiry (*informal*); sweating, perspiring; wet with sweat, beaded with sweat, **sticky** (*informal*), **clammy**; bathed in sweat, drenched with sweat, wilted; in a sweat; sudatory, sudoric, sudorific, diaphoretic

23 **bleeding, bloody**, haemorrhaging; ecchymosed

24 **menstrual**, catamenial

13 SECRETION

nouns

1 **secretion**, secreta, secernment; **excretion** *see* 12; external secretion, internal secretion; lactation; weeping, lacrimation

2 **digestive secretion** *or* juice, salivary secretion, gastric juice, pancreatic juice, intestinal juice; bile, gall; endocrine; prostatic fluid, semen, sperm; thyroxin; autacoid, **hormone**, chalone; mucus; tears; rheum; gland

3 **saliva, spittle, sputum, spit**, expectoration; salivation, ptyalism, sialorrhea, sialagogue, **slobber**, slabber, slaver, **drivel**, dribble, **drool**; froth, foam; mouth-watering

4 endocrinology, eccrinology, hormonology

verbs

5 **to secrete**, produce, give out; **excrete** *see* 12.12; water; lactate; weep, tear

6 **to salivate**, ptyalize; **slobber**, slabber, slaver, **drool**, **drivel**, dribble; **expectorate, spit**, spit up, gob (*informal*); spew; hawk, clear the throat

adjectives

7 **secretory**, secretive, secretional, secretionary; **excretory** *see* 12.19; lymphatic, serous; seminal, spermatic, watery, watering; lactational; lacteal, lacteous; lachrymal, lacrimatory, lachrymose; rheumy; salivary, salivant, salivous, sialoid, sialagogic

8 **glandular**, glandulous; **endocrine**, humoral (*old*), exocrine, eccrine, apocrine, holocrine, merocrine; **hormonal** *or* hormonic; adrenal, pancreatic, gonadal; ovarian; luteal; prostatic; splenetic; thymic; thyroidal

14 BODILY DEVELOPMENT

nouns

1 **bodily** *or* **physical development,** growth,
development *see* 860.1, maturation, maturing,
maturescence, coming of age, growing up, reaching
one's full growth, upgrowth; growing like a weed
(*informal*); plant growth, vegetation *see* 310.30,
germination, pullulation; sexual maturity, pubescence,
puberty; nubility, marriageability, marriageableness;
adulthood, manhood, womanhood; reproduction,
procreation *see* 78, burgeoning, sprouting; budding,
gemmation; outgrowth, excrescence; overgrowth *see*
257.5

verbs

2 **to grow, develop,** wax, **increase** *see* 251; gather,
brew; **grow up,** mature, maturate, spring up, ripen,
come of age, **shoot up,** sprout up, upshoot,
upspring, upsprout, upspear, overtop, tower; grow
like a weed (*informal*); burgeon, **sprout** *see* 310.31,
blossom *see* 310.32, reproduce *see* 78.7, procreate *see*
78.8, grow out of, germinate, pullulate; vegetate *see*
310.31; **flourish, thrive;** mushroom, balloon;
outgrow; overgrow, hypertrophy, overdevelop, grow
uncontrollably

adjectives

3 **grown, full-grown, grown-up,** developed, well-
developed, fully developed, **mature, adult, full-
fledged; growing,** adolescent, maturescent,
pubescent; nubile, marriageable; **sprouting,** crescent,
budding, flowering *see* 310.35, florescent,
flourishing, blossoming, blooming, burgeoning,
fast-growing, thriving; overgrown, hypertrophied,
overdeveloped

15 STRENGTH
inherent power

nouns

1 **strength, might,** mightiness, powerfulness, stamina;
force, potency, power *see* 18; **energy** *see* 17;
vigour, vitality, vigorousness, heartiness, lustiness,
lustihood; **stoutness, sturdiness,** stalwartness,
robustness, hardiness, ruggedness; **guts** *and* gutsiness
(*both informal*), fortitude, intestinal fortitude
(*informal*), **toughness** *see* 1047, **endurance,**
stamina, staying *or* sticking power, stick-to-itiveness (*informal*); **strength of will,** decisiveness,
obstinacy *see* 361

2 **muscularity,** brawniness; beefiness *and* huskiness
and heftiness *and* hunkiness (*all informal*), thewiness,
sinewiness; **brawn,** beef (*informal*); **muscle,** brawn,
sinew, sinews, thew, thews; musculature, build,
physique; tone, elasticity *see* 1046

3 **firmness, soundness,** staunchness, stoutness,
sturdiness, stability, solidity, **hardness** *see* 1044,
temper

4 **impregnability,** impenetrability, **invulnerability,**
inexpugnability, inviolability; **unassailability,**
unattackableness; resistlessness, **irresistibility;**
invincibility, indomitability, insuperability,
unconquerableness, unbeatableness

5 **strengthening, invigoration,** fortification;
hardening, toughening, firming; case hardening,
tempering; **restrengthening,** reinforcement;
reinvigoration, refreshment, revivification

6 **strong man, stalwart, tower of strength,** muscle
man, piledriver, bulldozer, hunk (*informal*); **giant,**
Samson, Goliath; Charles Atlas, Mr Universe;
Hercules, Atlas, Antaeus, Cyclops, Briareus, colossus,
Polyphemus, Titan, Brobdingnagian, Tarzan,
Superman; the strong, the mighty

7 (*informal terms*) **hunk, powerhouse, muscle man,**
man mountain, big bruiser, strong-arm man, bully,
bullyboy, ape, tough, toughie, tough guy, bozo (*US*),
bimbo, goon (*US*) *see* 671.10, gorilla, meat-eater

8 (*comparisons*) horse, ox, lion; oak, heart of oak; rock,
Gibraltar; iron, steel, nails

verbs

9 **to be strong,** overpower, overwhelm; have what it
takes, pack a punch

10 **to not weaken,** not flag; **bear up, hold up,** keep
up, stand up; **hold out,** stay *or* see it out, not give
up, **never say die,** not let it get one down

11 (*informal terms*) **to tough it out, hang tough, hang
in,** stick *or* take it, take it on the chin, sweat it out,
stay the distance

12 **to exert strength,** put beef *or* one's back into it
(*informal*); use force, get tough (*informal*), muscle *and*
manhandle *and* strong-arm (*all informal*)

13 **to strengthen, invigorate, fortify,** beef up
(*informal*), brace, buttress, prop, shore up, support,
undergird, brace up; gird, gird up one's loins; steel,
harden, case harden, anneal, stiffen, **toughen,**
temper, nerve; confirm, sustain; **restrengthen,**
reinforce; reinvigorate, refresh, revive, recruit
one's strength

14 **to proof,** insulate, weatherproof, soundproof, muffle,
quietize, fireproof, waterproof, idiotproof (*informal*),
etc

adjectives

15 **strong, forceful,** forcible, **mighty, powerful,**
puissant (*informal*), **potent** *see* 18.12; **stout, sturdy,**
stalwart, rugged, hale; hunky *and* husky *and* hefty
and beefy (*all informal*), strapping, doughty
(*informal*), **hardy,** hard, hard as nails, cast-iron,
iron-hard, steely; **robust,** robustious, gutty *and* gutsy
(*both informal*); strong-willed, obstinate *see* 361.8;
vigorous, hearty, nervy, **lusty,** bouncing, full- *or*
red-blooded; bionic, sturdy as an ox, strong as a lion
or an ox *or* a horse, strong as brandy, strong as
strong; full-strength, double-strength, industrial-
strength (*informal*)

16 **able-bodied, well-built,** well-set, well-set-up
(*informal*), well-knit, of good *or* powerful physique,
broad-shouldered, barrel-chested, **athletic;**
muscular, well-muscled, heavily muscled, thickset,
burly, **brawny;** thewy, sinewy, **wiry;** muscle-bound,
all muscle

17 **Herculean,** Briarean, Antaean, Cyclopean, Atlantean,
gigantic, gigantesque, Brobdingnagian, huge *see*
257.20

18 **firm, sound, stout,** sturdy, tough, hard-boiled
(*informal*), **staunch, stable,** solid; sound as a pound,

solid as a rock, firm as Gibraltar, made of iron;
rigid, unbreakable, infrangible

19 impregnable, impenetrable, **invulnerable**,
inviolable, inexpugnable; **unassailable**, unattackable,
insuperable, unsurmountable; resistless, **irresistible**;
invincible, indomitable, **unconquerable**,
unsubduable, unyielding *see* 361.9, incontestable,
unbeatable, more than a match for; overpowering,
overwhelming, avalanchine

20 resistant, proof, tight; impervious; foolproof;
shatterproof; weatherproof, dampproof, watertight,
leakproof; hermetic, airtight; soundproof, noiseproof;
puncture proof, holeproof; bulletproof, ballproof,
shellproof, bombproof; rustproof, corrosionproof;
fireproof, flameproof, fire-resisting; burglarproof

21 unweakened, undiminished, unallayed, unbated,
unabated, unfaded, unwithered, unshaken, unworn,
unexhausted; **unweakening, unflagging, unbowed;**
in full force *or* swing, **going strong** (*informal*); in
the plenitude of power

22 (*of sounds and odours*) **intense, penetrating,**
piercing; **loud,** deafening, thundering *see* 56.12;
pungent, reeking *see* 69.10

adverbs

23 strongly, stoutly, sturdily, stalwartly, robustly,
ruggedly; **mightily, powerfully, forcefully,**
forcibly; **vigorously, heartily,** lustily; **soundly,**
firmly, staunchly; impregnably, invulnerably,
invincibly, irresistibly, unyieldingly; resistantly,
imperviously; **intensely; loudly,** at the top of one's
lungs, clamorously, deafeningly; **pungently**

word elements

24 muscul–, musculo–, my–, myo–; –eus

16 WEAKNESS

nouns

1 weakness, weakliness, **feebleness,** strengthlessness;
flabbiness, flaccidity, softness; **impotence** *or*
impotency *see* 19; **debility,** debilitation, prostration,
invalidism, collapse; **faintness,** faintishness,
dizziness, lightheadedness, shakiness, gone *or* blah
feeling (*informal*); **fatigue** *see* 21, exhaustion,
weariness, dullness, sluggishness, languor, lassitude,
listlessness, tiredness, languishment, atony; anaemia,
bloodlessness, etiolation, asthenia, adynamia, cachexia
or cachexy

2 frailty, slightness, **delicacy, daintiness,** lightness;
flimsiness, unsubstantiality, wispiness, sleaziness,
shoddiness; **fragility,** frangibility *or* frangibleness,
brittleness, breakableness, destructibility;
disintegration *see* 805; **human frailty,**
"amiable weakness"—HENRY FIELDING; gutlessness
(*informal*), cowardice *see* 491; **moral weakness,**
irresolution, **indecisiveness,** infirmity of will,
velleity, changeableness *see* 853; inherent vice

3 infirmity, unsoundness, incapacity, unfirmness,
unsturdiness, **instability, unsubstantiality;**
decrepitude; **unsteadiness, shakiness,** ricketiness,
wobbliness, wonkiness (*informal*), caducity, senility,
invalidism; wishy-washiness, insipidity, vapidity,
wateriness

4 weak point, weakness, weak place, **weak side,**
vulnerable point, chink in one's armour, Achilles'
heel *or* heel of Achilles; feet of clay

5 weakening, enfeeblement, debilitation,
exhaustion, inanition, attrition; languishment;
devitalization, enervation, evisceration; fatigue;
attenuation, extenuation; softening, mitigation,
damping, abatement, slackening, relaxing, relaxation,
blunting, deadening, dulling; **dilution,** watering,
watering-down, attenuation, thinning, reduction

6 weakling, weak *or* meek soul, weak sister (*informal*),
drip (*informal*), hothouse plant, softy (*informal*),
softling, **jellyfish,** invertebrate, chinless wonder
(*informal*), gutless wonder (*informal*), **baby,** big baby,
crybaby, chicken (*informal*), Milquetoast (*US &
Canadian*), sop, **milksop, namby-pamby,**
mollycoddle, mama's boy, mother's boy, mother's
darling, teacher's pet; sissy *and* pansy (*both informal*),
pushover (*informal*), lightweight, pantywaist (*US
informal*); **wimp,** wet (*informal*), poor *or* weak *or* dull
tool (*informal*); **nonentity,** hollow man, doormat *and*
empty suit *and* sad sack (*all informal*)

7 (*comparisons*) a kitten, a reed, thread, matchwood, a
rope of sand; a house of cards, a house built on
sand, a sand castle; water, milk and water, gruel,
dishwater

verbs

8 (*be weak*) **to shake,** tremble, quiver, quaver, cringe,
cower *see* 491.9, totter, teeter, dodder; halt, limp; be
on one's last leg, have one foot in the grave

9 (*become weak*) **to weaken,** grow weak *or* weaker, go
soft (*informal*); **languish, wilt,** faint, **droop,** drop,
sink, decline, flag, pine, fade, tail away *or* **off,**
fail, fall *or* **drop by the wayside;** crumble, go to
pieces, disintegrate *see* 805.3; go downhill, hit the
skids (*informal*), give way, break, collapse, cave in
(*informal*), surrender; give out, have no staying
power, run out of steam (*informal*), conk *or* peter *or*
poop *or* peg *or* fizzle out (*informal*); come apart,
come apart at the seams, come unstuck *or* unglued
(*both informal*); yield; die on the vine (*informal*); wear
thin *or* away

10 (*make weak*) **to weaken, enfeeble, debilitate,**
unstrengthen, unsinew, undermine, soften up
(*informal*), unbrace, unman, unnerve, rattle, shake up
(*informal*), **devitalize, enervate,** eviscerate; **sap,** sap
the strength of, exhaust, gruel, take it out of
(*informal*); shake, unstring; reduce, lay low; attenuate,
extenuate, mitigate, abate; blunt, deaden, dull, damp
or dampen, take the edge off; draw the teeth, defang;
cramp, cripple

11 to dilute, cut (*informal*), **reduce, thin,** thin out,
attenuate, rarefy; **water,** water down, adulterate,
irrigate *and* baptize (*both informal*)

adjectives

12 weak, weakly, **feeble,** debilitated, imbecile;
strengthless, sapless, marrowless, pithless, sinewless,
listless, out of steam (*informal*), nerveless, lustless;
impotent, powerless *see* 19.13; spineless, lily-
livered, whitelivered, wimpy *and* wimpish *and*
chicken *and* gutless (*all informal*), cowardly *see*
491.10; unnerved, shookup (*informal*), unstrung,

faint, faintish, lightheaded, dizzy, gone; dull, slack; **soft, flabby**, flaccid, unhardened; **limp,** limp as a dishcloth, floppy, rubbery; **languorous,** languid, **drooping**, droopy, pooped (*informal*); asthenic, anaemic, bloodless, effete, etiolated; not what one used to be

13 weak as milk and water, weak as a drink of water, weak as a child *or* baby, weak as a chicken, weak as a kitten, weak as a mouse,
"weak as a rained-on bee"—F R TORRENCE, "weak as water"—BIBLE

14 **frail, slight, delicate, dainty,**
"delicately weak"—POPE; puny; light, lightweight; effeminate; namby-pamby, sissified, pansyish, wet; **fragile**, frangible, **breakable**, destructible, shattery, crumbly, brittle, fragmentable, fracturable; **unsubstantial, flimsy**, wispy, cobwebby, gossamery, papery, pasteboardy; gimcrack *and* gimcracky *and* cheap-jack *and* tacky *and* ticky-tacky (*all informal*); jerry-built, jerry

15 **unsound, infirm,** unfirm, **unstable, unsubstantial,** unsturdy, unsolid, decrepit, crumbling, fragmented, fragmentary, disintegrating see 805.5; poor, poorish; rotten, rotten at *or* rotten to the core

16 **unsteady, shaky, rickety,** ricketish, wonky (*informal*), spindly, spidery, teetering, teetery, tottery, tottering, doddering, tumbledown, ramshackle, dilapidated, rocky (*informal*), dicky (*informal*); groggy, wobbly, staggery

17 **wishy-washy,** tasteless, bland, **insipid,** vapid, neutral, watery, milky, milk-and-water, mushy; halfhearted, infirm of will *or* purpose, **indecisive,** irresolute, changeable see 853.7

18 **weakened, enfeebled, disabled,** incapacitated; **devitalized,** drained, exhausted, sapped, burned-out, used up, played out, spent, *ausgespielt* (*German*), effete, etiolated; **fatigued, enervated,** eviscerated; **wasted, run-down,** worn, worn-out, worn to a frazzle (*informal*), worn to a shadow, reduced to a skeleton,
"weakened and wasted to skin and bone"—DU BARTAS

19 **diluted,** cut (*informal*), **reduced, thinned,** rarefied, attenuated; adulterated; watered, watered-down

20 **weakening, debilitating, enfeebling; devitalizing,** enervating, sapping, exhausting, fatiguing, gruelling, trying, draining, unnerving

21 **languishing, drooping,** sinking, declining, flagging, pining, fading, failing

adverbs

22 **weakly, feebly,** strengthlessly, languorously, listlessly; faintly; delicately, effeminately, daintily; infirmly, unsoundly, unstably, unsubstantially, unsturdily, flimsily; shakily, unsteadily, teeteringly, totteringly

17 ENERGY

nouns

1 **energy, vigour, force, power, vitality,** strenuousness, **intensity, dynamism,** demonic energy; **potency** see 18; **strength** see 15; actual *or* kinetic energy; dynamic energy; potential energy;

energy source see 1020.1, electrical energy, hydroelectric energy, hydro power, water power, nuclear energy, solar energy, wind energy; alternative energy

2 **vim, verve,** fire, adrenalin, **dash, drive; aggressiveness, enterprise,** initiative, proactiveness, thrust, spunk; **eagerness** see 101, zeal, heartiness, keenness, gusto

3 (*informal terms*) **pep,** bang, biff, get-up-and-go, ginger, jazz, sizzle, kick, moxie (*US & Canadian*), oomph, **pizzazz**, punch, push, snap, steam, zing, zip, zizz

4 **animation, vivacity,** liveliness, **ardour,** glow, warmth, enthusiasm, lustiness, robustness, mettle, **zest,** zestfulness, **gusto, élan,** impetus, impetuosity, *joie de vivre* (*French*), *brio* (*Italian*), spiritedness, **briskness,** perkiness, pertness, **life, spirit,** life force, vital force *or* principle, *élan vital* (*French*); activity see 330

5 (*energetic disapproval or criticism*) **acrimony,** acridity, acerbity, acidity, **bitterness,** tartness, **causticity,** mordancy *or* mordacity, **virulence; harshness,** fierceness, **rigour,** roughness, **severity, vehemence,** violence see 671, stringency, astringency, stridency see 58.1, **sharpness, keenness, poignancy,** trenchancy; edge, point; bite, teeth, grip, sting

6 **energizer, stimulus,** stimulator, vitalizer, arouser, needle (*informal*), restorative; **stimulant, tonic** see 86.8; **activator,** motivator, motivating force, motive power; **animator,** spark plug *and* human dynamo *and* ball of fire (*all informal*); life, life and soul of the party

7 (*units of energy*) atomerg, dinamode, dyne, erg, energid, foot-pound, horsepower-hour, horsepower-year, joule, calorie see 1018.19, kilogram-metre, kilowatt-hour, photon, quantum

8 **energizing, invigoration, animation, enlivenment,** quickening, **vitalization,** revival, revitalization; **exhilaration, stimulation**

9 **activation,** reactivation; viability

verbs

10 **to energize,** dynamize; **invigorate, animate, enliven, liven, liven up,** vitalize, quicken, jazz up (*informal*); **exhilarate, stimulate,** hearten, galvanize, electrify, fire, build a fire under, inflame, warm, kindle, charge, charge up, psych *or* pump up (*informal*), rouse, arouse, act like a tonic, be a shot in the arm (*informal*), **pep** *or* snap *or* jazz *or* zip *or* perk *or* ginger up (*informal*), put pep *or* zip into it (*informal*)

11 **to have energy,** be energetic, be vigorous, **thrive,** burst *or* overflow with energy, flourish, tingle, feel one's oats (*US & Canadian*), be up and doing, be full of beans *or* pep *or* ginger *or* zip (*informal*), champ at the bit (*informal*)

12 **to activate,** reactivate, recharge

adjectives

13 **energetic, vigorous, strenuous, forceful, forcible, strong, dynamic,** kinetic, intense, acute, keen, incisive, trenchant, vivid, vibrant; **enterprising, aggressive,** proactive, activist, can-do *and* gung ho *and* take-over *and* take-charge (*all informal*); **active,**

lively, living, **animated, spirited,** go-go (*informal*), **vivacious,** brisk, bright-eyed and bushy-tailed (*informal*), lusty, **robust,** hearty, enthusiastic, mettlesome, zesty, zestful, impetuous, spanking, smacking; pumped *and* pumped up *and* jazzed-up *and* charged up *and* switched on (*all informal*), snappy *and* zingy *and* zippy *and* peppy (*all informal*), full of pep *or* pizzazz (*both informal*)

14 **acrimonious, acrid,** acidulous, acid, **bitter,** tart, **caustic,** escharotic (*medicine*), mordant *or* mordacious, **virulent, violent, vehement,** vitriolic; **harsh,** fierce, **rigorous,** severe, rough, stringent, astringent, strident *see* 58.12, **sharp, keen,** sharpish, incisive, trenchant, **cutting,** biting, stinging, **scathing,** stabbing, **piercing, poignant,** penetrating, edged, double-edged

15 **energizing, vitalizing, enlivening,** quickening; tonic, bracing, rousing; **invigorating,** invigorative; **animating,** animative; **exhilarating,** exhilarative; **stimulating,** stimulative, stimulatory; activating; viable

adverbs

16 **energetically, vigorously, strenuously, forcefully,** forcibly, intensely, like a house on fire (*informal*), zestfully, lustily, heartily, keenly; **actively,** briskly; **animatedly, spiritedly,** vivaciously, with pep (*informal*), *con brio* (*Italian*)

18 POWER, POTENCY
effective force

nouns

1 **power, potency** *or* **potence, prepotency, force, might,** mightiness, **vigour,** vitality, vim, push, drive, charge, puissance (*old*); dint, virtue; oomph *and* pizzazz *and* punch *and* bang *and* clout *and* steam (*all informal*); powerfulness, forcefulness; virulence, vehemence; **strength** *see* 15; **energy** *see* 17; **virility** *see* 76.2; cogence *or* cogency, validity, effect, impact, **effectiveness,** effectivity, effectuality, competence *or* competency; productivity, productiveness; power structure; **influence** *see* 893, pull; **authority** *see* 417, weight; **superiority** *see* 249; power pack, amperage, wattage; main force, *force majeure* (*French*), main strength, brute force *or* strength, compulsion, duress; muscle power, sinew, might and main, beef (*informal*), strong arm; full force, full blast; power struggle; Black Power; flower power; mana; charisma

2 **ability, capability, capacity,** potentiality, faculty, facility, fitness, qualification, talent, flair, genius, calibre, **competence,** competency, adequacy, sufficiency, **efficiency,** efficacy; **proficiency** *see* 413.1; the stuff *and* the goods *and* what it takes (*all informal*); susceptibility

3 **omnipotence, almightiness, all-powerfulness;** omnicompetence

4 manpower; horsepower, brake horsepower *or* bhp, electric power, electropower, hydroelectric power; hydraulic power, water power; steam power; geothermal power; solar power; atomic power, nuclear power, thermonuclear power; rocket power, jet power; **propulsion, thrust,** impulse

5 force of inertia, *vis inertiae* (*Latin*); dead force, *vis mortua* (*Latin*); living force, *vis viva* (*Latin*); force of life, *vis vitae* (*Latin*)

6 centrifugal force *or* action, centripetal force *or* action, force of gravity

7 (*science of forces*) dynamics, statics

8 **empowerment, enablement;** investment, endowment, enfranchisement

9 **work force,** hands, men; **fighting force,** troops, units, the big battalions, firepower; **personnel** *see* 577.11, human resources; **forces**

verbs

10 to **empower, enable;** invest, clothe, invest *or* clothe with power, deputize; enfranchise; endue, endow, **authorize;** arm

11 to **be able,** be up to, up to, **lie in one's power; can,** may, can do; make it *or* make the grade (*informal*); hack it *and* cut it *and* cut the mustard (*all informal*); charismatize; **wield power,** possess authority *see* 417.13; **take charge** *see* 417.14, get something under one's control *or* under one's thumb, hold all the aces *and* have the say-so (*both informal*), call the shots

adjectives

12 **powerful, potent,** prepotent, powerpacked, **mighty,** irresistible, avalanchine, **forceful,** forcible, dynamic; **vigorous,** vital, **energetic,** puissant, ruling, in power; **cogent,** striking, telling, effective, impactful, valid, operative, in force; **strong;** high-powered, high-tension, high-pressure, high-performance, high-potency, bionic; **authoritative;** armipotent, mighty in battle

13 **omnipotent, almighty, all-powerful;** plenipotentiary, absolute, unlimited, **sovereign** *see* 417.17; **supreme** *see* 249.13; omnicompetent

14 **able, capable, equal to,** up to, **competent,** adequate, effective, effectual, efficient, efficacious; productive; **proficient** *see* 413.22

adverbs

15 **powerfully, potently, forcefully,** forcibly, mightily, with might and main, **vigorously, energetically,** dynamically; **cogently,** strikingly, tellingly, impactfully; **effectively,** effectually; productively; with telling effect, to good account, to good purpose, with a vengeance

16 **ably, capably, competently,** adequately, effectively, effectually, **efficiently, well; to the best of one's ability,** as lies in one's power, so far as one can, as best one can; with all one's might, with everything that is in one

17 **by force,** by main *or* brute force, by *force majeure,* with the strong arm, with a high hand, high-handedly; **forcibly,** amain, with might and main; by force of arms, at the point of the sword, by storm

prepositions

18 by dint of, by virtue of

word elements

19 dynam–, dynamo–; –dynamia

19 IMPOTENCE

nouns

1 **impotence** *or* impotency, **powerlessness,** impuissance (*old*), forcelessness, feebleness, softness, flabbiness, wimpiness *or* wimpishness (*informal*), **weakness** see 16; power vacuum

2 **inability, incapability, incapacity,** incapacitation, **incompetence** *or* incompetency, inadequacy, insufficiency, ineptitude, **inferiority** see 250, inefficiency, unfitness, imbecility; disability, disablement, disqualification; legal incapacity, wardship, minority, infancy

3 **ineffectiveness, ineffectualness,** ineffectuality, inefficaciousness, **inefficacy,** counterproductiveness *or* counterproductivity, invalidity, **futility, uselessness,** bootlessness, failure see 410; fatuity, inanity

4 **helplessness, defencelessness,** unprotectedness, vulnerability; **debilitation,** invalidism, effeteness, etiolation, enervation

5 **emasculation,** demasculinization, effeminization, neutering, maiming, castration see 255.4

6 **impotent,** weakling see 16.6, invalid, incompetent; flash in the pan, blank cartridge, wimp *and* dud (*both informal*); eunuch, *castrato* (*Italian*), gelding

verbs

7 to be impotent, lack force; be ineffective, avail nothing, not work *or* do not take (*informal*); **waste one's effort,** bang one's head against a brick wall, have one's hands tied, spin one's wheels, tilt at windmills, run round in circles

8 **cannot, not be able,** not have it *and* not hack it *and* not cut it *and* not cut the mustard (*all informal*), not make it *and* not make the grade *and* not make the cut (*all informal*)

9 **to disable,** disenable, unfit, **incapacitate,** drain, de-energize; enfeeble, debilitate, **weaken** see 16.9, 10; cripple, maim, lame, hamstring, knee-cap, defang, pull the teeth of (*informal*); wing, clip the wings of; **inactivate,** disarm, unarm, put out of action, put *hors de combat*; **put out of order,** put out of commission (*informal*), throw out of gear; bugger *and* bugger up *and* queer *and* queer the works *and* gum up *or* screw up (*all informal*), throw a spanner in the works (*informal*), sabotage, scupper, wreck; kibosh *and* put the kibosh on (*both informal*); spike, spike one's guns, put a spoke in one's wheels

10 (*put out of action*) **to paralyse,** prostrate, shoot down in flames (*informal*), put *hors de combat*, knock out (*informal*), break the neck *or* back of; hamstring; nobble; handcuff, tie the hands of, hobble, enchain, manacle, hog-tie (*informal*), **tie hand and foot,** truss up; throttle, strangle, get a stranglehold on; muzzle, gag, silence; **take the wind out of one's sails,** deflate, knock the props out from under, cut the ground from under, not leave a leg to stand on

11 **to disqualify; invalidate,** knock the bottom out of (*informal*)

12 **to unman, unnerve, enervate,** exhaust, etiolate, **devitalize; emasculate,** cut the balls off (*informal*), demasculinize, effeminize; desex, desexualize; sterilize; castrate see 255.11

adjectives

13 **impotent, powerless, forceless, out of steam** (*informal*); feeble, soft, flabby, **weak** see 16.12, weak as a kitten, wimpy *or* wimpish (*informal*), limp-wristed (*informal*)

14 **unable, incapable, incompetent,** inefficient, ineffective; **unqualified,** inept, unendowed, ungifted, untalented, **unfit,** unfitted; **outmatched,** out of one's depth, in over one's head, outgunned; **inferior** see 250.6

15 **ineffective, ineffectual, inefficacious,** counterproductive, feckless, not up to scratch *or* up to snuff (*informal*), **inadequate** see 250.7; **invalid, inoperative,** of no force; nugatory, nugacious; fatuous, fatuitous; **vain, futile, inutile, useless,** unavailing, bootless, fruitless; all talk and no action, all mouth (*informal*); **empty,** inane; **debilitated,** effete, enervated, etiolated, barren, sterile, washed-out (*informal*)

16 **disabled, incapacitated; crippled,** hamstrung; disqualified, invalidated; disarmed; paralysed; hog-tied (*informal*); prostrate, **on one's back,** on one's beam-ends

17 **out of action, out of commission** *and* out of it (*both informal*), out of gear; *hors de combat* (*French, out of action, literally, out of the fight*), out of the battle, off the field, out of the running; laid on the shelf, obsolete, life-expired, past the sell-by date

18 **helpless, defenceless, unprotected;** vulnerable, like a sitting duck (*informal*), aidless, friendless, unfriended; fatherless, motherless; leaderless, guideless; **untenable,** pregnable, vulnerable

19 **unmanned, unnerved, enervated,** debilitated, **devitalized;** nerveless, sinewless, marrowless, pithless, lustless; **castrated,** emasculate, emasculated, gelded, eunuchized, unsexed, deballed (*informal*), demasculinized, effeminized

adverbs

20 **beyond one,** beyond one's power *or* capacity *or* ability, beyond one's depth, out of one's league (*informal*), above one's head, too much for

exclamations

21 no can do!

20 REST, REPOSE

nouns

1 **rest, repose, ease, relaxation,** slippered *or* unbuttoned ease; **comfort** see 121; restfulness, quiet, tranquillity; inactivity see 331; sleep see 22

2 **respite, recess, rest, pause,** halt, stay, lull, **break,** surcease, suspension, interlude, **intermission,** interval, spell (*Australian*), letup (*informal*), pit stop (*informal*), **time out** (*informal*), time to catch one's breath; **breathing spell,** breathing time, breathing place, breathing space, breath; **breather;** coffee break, tea break, cigarette break, smoko *or* smokeho (*Australian & NZ informal*); lunch hour, lunch break; cocktail hour, happy hour (*informal*); enforced respite, downtime

3 **holiday,** vacation; **time off;** day off, week off, month off, etc; **vacation,** long vacation, hols

(*informal*), vac (*informal*), half term; paid holiday, paid vacation (*US & Canadian*); weekend; long weekend; **leave, leave of absence**, furlough; liberty, shore leave; **sabbatical**, sabbatical leave *or* year; **weekend; busman's holiday**; package tour *or* holiday

4 **holiday, day off**; **red-letter day**, gala day, fete day, festival day, day of festivities; bank holiday, national holiday, legal holiday; High Holiday, High Holy Day; holy day; feast, feast day, high day, church feast, fixed feast, movable feast; half-holiday

5 **day of rest**, *dies non* (*Latin*); **Sabbath**, Sunday, Lord's day, First day

verbs

6 **to rest**, repose, take rest, take one's ease, **take it easy** (*informal*), lay down one's tools, rest from one's labours, rest on one's oars, take life easy; go to rest, settle to rest; lie down, have a lie-down, go to bed, snug down, curl up, tuck up, bed, bed down, couch, recline, lounge, drape oneself, sprawl, loll; take off one's shoes, unbuckle one's belt, get *or* take a load off one's feet, put one's feet up

7 **to relax**, unbend, unwind, slack, slacken, **ease**, chill out (*informal*); **ease up, let up**, slack up, slack off, **ease off**, let down, **slow down**, take it slow, let up, take time to catch one's breath; lie back (*informal*)

8 **to take a rest, take a break, break, take time out** (*informal*), pause, lay off, **knock off** (*informal*), recess (*US & Canadian*), **take a recess** (*US & Canadian*), take ten *and* take five (*both informal*); stop for breath, catch one's breath, breathe; stop work, suspend operations, call it a day; sleep in; take a nap, catch some Zs (*informal*)

9 **to get away from it all, holiday**, take a holiday, go on holiday; **take a leave of absence**, take leave, go on leave, go on furlough, take one's sabbatical; weekend; Sunday, Christmas, etc

adjectives

10 **vacational, holiday**, ferial (*old*), festal; sabbatical; **comfortable** *see* 121.11; **restful**, quiet *see* 173.12

adverbs

11 **at rest, at ease**, at one's ease; abed, in bed
12 **on holiday**, on vacation, on leave, on furlough; off duty, on one's own time

21 FATIGUE

nouns

1 **fatigue, tiredness, weariness**, wearifulness; **burnout**, end of one's tether, overtiredness, overstrain; faintness, goneness, weakness, enfeeblement, lack of staying power, enervation, debility, debilitation *see* 16.1; jadedness; lassitude, languor; tension fatigue, stance fatigue, stimulation fatigue; fatigue disease, fatigue syndrome *or* post-viral fatigue syndrome; combat fatigue; mental fatigue; strain, mental strain, heart strain, eyestrain; sleepiness *see* 22.1

2 **exhaustion**, exhaustedness, draining; **collapse, prostration**, breakdown, crack-up (*informal*), nervous exhaustion *or* prostration

3 **breathlessness, shortness of breath**, windedness, short-windedness; panting, gasping; dyspnoea, laboured breathing

verbs

4 **to fatigue, tire, weary, exhaust**, wilt, flag, jade, harass; **wear**, wear on *or* upon, **wear down; tire out, wear out, burn out; use up; do in; wind**, put out of breath; overtire, overweary, overfatigue, overstrain; weaken, enervate, debilitate *see* 16.10; weary *or* tire to death; prostrate

5 **to burn out, get tired, grow weary, tire, weary**, fatigue, jade; **flag, droop**, faint, sink, feel down, wilt; **play out**, run out, run down, burn out; gasp, wheeze, pant, puff, blow, puff and blow, puff like a grampus; collapse, break down, crack up (*informal*), give out, drop, fall *or* drop by the wayside, drop in one's tracks, succumb

6 (*informal terms*) **to beat**, poop (*US*), frazzle, fag, tucker; fag out, tucker out, knock out, knock up, do in, do up; poop out (*US*), peter out

adjectives

7 **tired, weary, fatigued**, wearied, weariful, jaded, run-down, good and tired; unrefreshed, unrestored, in need of rest, ready to drop; **faint**, fainting, feeling faint, **weak**, rocky (*informal*), enfeebled, enervated, debilitated, seedy (*informal*), weakened *see* 16.13, 18; drooping, droopy, wilting, flagging, sagging; languid; worn, worn-down, **worn to a frazzle** *or* shadow, toilworn, weary-worn; wayworn, way-weary; foot-weary, weary-footed, footsore; tired-armed; tired-winged, weary-winged; weary-laden, "tired and weary-laden"—BIBLE

8 (*informal terms*) **beat, bushed**, pooped (*US*), whacked, knackered, shattered, stonkered, paled, frazzled, fagged, done, done in, all in, dead, dead beat, dead on one's feet, gone, half-dead; pooped out (*US*), knocked out, wiped out, tuckered out, played out, fagged out; run ragged; used up, done up, beat-up, washed up

9 **tired-looking**, weary-looking, tired-eyed, tired-faced, haggard, hollow-eyed, ravaged, drawn, cadaverous, worn, wan, zombiish

10 **burnt-out, exhausted**, drained, **spent**, unable to go on, gone; **tired out, worn-out**, beaten; bone-tired, bone-weary; **dog-tired**, dog-weary; **dead-tired**, tired to death, weary unto death, dead-alive *or* dead-and-alive, more dead than alive, ready to drop, on one's last legs; prostrate

11 **burnt-out, overtired, overweary**, overwearied, overstrained, overdriven, overfatigued, overspent

12 **breathless, winded**; wheezing, puffing, panting, **out of breath**, short of breath *or* wind; short-winded, short-breathed, broken-winded, touched in the wind, dyspnoeic

13 **fatiguing, wearying**, wearing, **tiring**, straining, stressful, trying, **exhausting**, draining, **gruelling**, punishing, killing; **tiresome**, fatiguesome, **wearisome**, weariful; toilsome *see* 725.18

adverbs

14 **out**, to the point of exhaustion

22 SLEEP

nouns

1 **sleepiness, drowsiness**, doziness, heaviness, lethargy, oscitation, somnolence *or* somnolency, yawning, stretching, oscitancy, pandiculation; languor *see* 331.6; sand in the eyes, heavy eyelids; REM sleep *or* rapid-eye-movement sleep *or* dreaming sleep

2 **sleep, slumber; repose**, silken repose, *somnus* (*Latin*), the arms of Morpheus; bye-bye *or* beddy-bye (*both informal*); doss *or* kip (*informal*), blanket drill *and* shut eye (*both informal*); light sleep, fitful sleep, **doze, drowse**, snoozle (*informal*); beauty sleep (*informal*); sleepwalking, somnambulism; somniloquy; **land of Nod**, slumberland, sleepland, dreamland; hibernation, winter sleep, aestivation; bedtime, sack time (*informal*); unconsciousness *see* 25.2

3 **nap**, snooze (*informal*), **catnap**, wink, **forty winks** *and* some Zs (*both informal*), kip *and* zizz (*both informal*), wink of sleep, spot of sleep; **siesta**, blanket drill *and* sack time (*both informal*)

4 sweet sleep, balmy sleep, downy sleep, soft sleep, gentle sleep, smiling sleep, golden slumbers;

"folded sleep"—TENNYSON, "dewy-feathered sleep"—MILTON, "care-charmer Sleep, son of the sable night"—SAMUEL DANIEL, "the honey-heavy dew of slumber"—SHAKESPEARE; peaceful sleep, sleep of the just; restful sleep, good night's sleep,

"sleep that knits up the ravell'd sleave of care"—SHAKESPEARE, "Brother of Death"—SIR THOMAS BROWNE

5 **deep sleep**, profound sleep, heavy sleep, **sound sleep**, unbroken sleep, wakeless sleep, drugged sleep, dreamless sleep, the sleep of the dead,

"sleep such as makes the darkness brief"—MARTIAL; paradoxical *or* orthodox *or* dreaming *or* REM sleep, synchronized *or* S *or* NREM sleep

6 **stupor**, sopor, **coma, swoon**, lethargy (*old*); **trance**; narcosis, narcohypnosis, narcoma, narcotization, narcotic stupor *or* trance; sedation; high (*informal*); nod (*informal*); narcolepsy; catalepsy; thanatosis, shock; sleeping sickness, encephalitis lethargica

7 **hypnosis**, mesmeric *or* **hypnotic sleep**, trance, somnipathy, hypnotic somnolence; lethargic hypnosis, somnambulistic hypnosis, cataleptic hypnosis, animal hypnosis; narcohypnosis; autohypnosis, self-hypnosis; hypnotherapy

8 **hypnotism, mesmerism**; hypnology; hypnotization, mesmerization; **animal magnetism**, od, odyl, odylic force; hypnotic suggestion, posthypnotic suggestion, autosuggestion

9 **hypnotist, mesmerist**, hypnotizer, mesmerizer; Svengali, Mesmer

10 **sleep-inducer**, sleep-producer, sleep-provoker, sleep-bringer, hypnotic, soporific, somnifacient; poppy, mandrake, mandragora, opium, opiate, morphine, morphia; nightcap; sedative *see* 86.12; anaesthetic; lullaby

11 **Morpheus**, Somnus, Hypnos;

"sweet father of soft rest"—WM DRUMMOND; sandman

12 **sleeper, slumberer**; sleeping beauty; **sleepyhead**, lie-abed, slugabed, sleepwalker, somnambulist; somniloquist

verbs

13 **to sleep, slumber**, rest in the arms of Morpheus; **doze, drowse; nap, catnap**, take a nap, catch a wink, sleep soundly, **sleep like a top** *or* **log**, sleep like the dead; *dormir sur les deux oreilles* (*French*); snore; have an early night, go to bed betimes; sleep in; oversleep

14 (*informal terms*) **to snooze**, get some shut-eye, get some sack time, flake *or* sack out, crash, catch forty winks *or* some Zs, zizz, have a zizz; pound the ear, kip *or* doss

15 **to hibernate**, aestivate, lie dormant

16 **to go to sleep**, settle to sleep, go off to sleep, **fall asleep**, drop asleep, **drop off**, drift off, drift off to sleep,

"drift gently down the tides of sleep"—LONGFELLOW; **doze off, drowse off**, nod off, dope off (*informal*), noddle (*informal*); close one's eyes,

"let fall the shadow of mine eyes"—SHAKESPEARE

17 **to go to bed, retire**; lay me down to sleep; bed, bed down,

"and so to bed"—PEPYS; go night-night *and* go bye-bye *and* go beddy-bye (*all informal*)

18 (*informal terms*) **to hit the hay, hit the sack**, crash, turn in, crawl in, flop, sack out, sack up, kip down *or* doss down

19 **to put to bed**, bed; nestle, cradle; **tuck in**

20 **to put to sleep; lull to sleep**, rock to sleep; **hypnotize, mesmerize**, magnetize; **entrance**, trance, put in a trance; narcotize, drug, dope (*informal*); anaesthetize, put under; sedate

adjectives

21 **sleepy, drowsy**, dozy, snoozy (*informal*), **slumberous**, slumbery, dreamy; **half asleep**, asleep on one's feet; sleepful, sleep-filled; yawny, stretchy (*informal*), oscitant, yawning, napping, **nodding**, ready for bed; heavy, **heavy-eyed, heavy with sleep**, sleep-swollen, sleep-drowned, sleep-drunk, drugged with sleep; **somnolent**, soporific; **lethargic**, comatose, narcose *or* narcous, stuporose *or* **stuporous, in a stupor**, out of it (*informal*); narcoleptic; cataleptic; narcotized, drugged, doped (*informal*); sedated; anaesthetized; **languid**

22 **asleep, sleeping, slumbering**, in the arms *or* lap of Morpheus, in the land of Nod; **sound asleep, fast asleep**, dead asleep, deep asleep, in a sound sleep, flaked-out (*informal*); **unconscious, oblivious, out**, out like a light, out cold; comatose; dormant; dead, **dead to the world**; unwakened, unawakened

23 **sleep-inducing**, sleep-producing, sleep-bringing, sleep-causing, sleep-compelling, sleep-inviting, sleep-provoking, sleep-tempting; **narcotic**, hypnotic, **soporific, somniferous**, somnifacient; sedative *see* 86.45

24 **hypnotic**, hypnoid, hypnoidal, **mesmeric**; odylic; narcohypnotic

23 WAKEFULNESS

nouns

1 **wakefulness, wake; sleeplessness**, restlessness,

tossing and turning; **insomnia**, insomnolence *or* insomnolency, white night, "the wakey nights"—Sir Thomas Wyatt; vigil, all-night vigil, lidless vigil, *per vigilium* (*Latin*); insomniac; consciousness, sentience; alertness *see* 339.5

2 **awakening, wakening**, rousing, **arousal**; wakey-wakey (*informal*); rude awakening, rousting out (*informal*); reveille

verbs

3 **to keep awake**, keep one's eyes open; keep alert, be vigilant *see* 339.8; stay awake, **toss and turn, not sleep a wink**, not shut one's eyes, count sheep; have a white night

4 **to awake, awaken, wake, wake up, get up**, rouse, come alive (*informal*); open one's eyes, stir (*informal*)

5 (*wake someone up*) **to awaken, waken, rouse, arouse**, awake, wake, **wake up**, shake up, knock up, roust out (*informal*)

6 **to get up, get out of bed, arise**, rise, **rise and shine** (*informal*), greet the day, **turn out** (*informal*); roll out *and* pile out *and* show a leg *and* hit the deck (*all informal*)

adjectives

7 **wakeful, sleepless**, slumberless, **unsleeping**, insomniac, insomnious; restless; watchful, vigilant, lidless

8 **awake**, conscious, **up; wide-awake**, broad awake; alert *see* 339.14

adverbs

9 **sleeplessly, unsleepingly; wakefully**, with one's eyes open; alertly *see* 339.17

24 SENSATION
physical sensibility

nouns

1 **sensation, sense, feeling**; sense impression, sense-datum *or* data, percept, perception, sense perception; experience, sensory experience; **sensuousness**, sensuosity; **consciousness**, awareness, apperception; response, response to stimuli

2 **sensibility**, sensibleness, physical sensibility, sentience *or* sentiency; openness to sensation, readiness of feeling, receptiveness, receptivity; sensation level, threshold of sensation, limen; impressionability, impressibility, affectibility; **susceptibility**, susceptivity, perceptibility

3 **sensitivity, sensitiveness**; perceptivity, perceptiveness; responsiveness; **tact, tactfulness, considerateness**, courtesy, politeness; **compassion, sympathy**; empathy, identification; **concern**, solicitousness, solicitude; capability of feeling, passibility; **delicacy, exquisiteness**, tenderness, fineness; **oversensitiveness**, oversensibility, hypersensitivity, **thin skin**, hyperaesthesia, hyperpathia, supersensitivity, overtenderness; **irritability**, prickliness, soreness, **touchiness**, tetchiness; ticklishness, nervousness *see* 128; allergy, anaphylaxis; sensitization; photophobia

4 **sore spot**, sore point, soft spot, raw, exposed nerve, raw nerve, nerve ending, tender spot, the quick,

where the shoe pinches, where one lives *and* in the gut (*informal*)

5 **senses, five senses**, sensorium; touch *see* 74, taste *see* 62, smell *see* 69, sight *see* 27, hearing *see* 48; sixth sense; sense *or* sensory organ, sensillum, receptor; synaesthesia, chromaesthesia, colour hearing; phonism, photism; kinaesthesia, muscle sense, sense of motion

verbs

6 **to sense, feel**, experience, **perceive**, apprehend, be sensible of, be conscious *or* aware of, apperceive; taste *see* 62.7, smell *see* 69.8, see *see* 27.12, hear *see* 48.11, 12, touch *see* 73.6; respond, respond to stimuli; be sensitive to, have a thing about (*informal*)

7 **to sensitize**, make sensitive; sensibilize, sensify; **sharpen, whet, quicken**, stimulate, excite, stir, cultivate, refine

8 **to touch a sore spot**, touch a soft spot, touch on the raw, touch a raw spot, touch to the quick, hit *or* touch a nerve *or* nerve ending, touch where it hurts, hit one where he lives (*informal*), strike home, tread on someone's toes *or* corns

adjectives

9 **sensory**, sensorial; **sensitive**, receptive; **sensuous**; sensorimotor, sensimotor; kinaesthetic, somatosensory

10 **neural, nervous**, nerval; neurologic, neurological

11 sensible, sentient, sensile; **susceptible**, susceptive; **receptive**, impressionable, impressive (*old*), impressible; **perceptive; conscious**, cognizant, **aware**, sensitive to, alive to

12 **sensitive**, responsive, sympathetic, compassionate; empathic, empathetic; passible; delicate, tactful, considerate, courteous, solicitous, tender, refined; **oversensitive, thin-skinned**; oversensible, hyperaesthetic, hyperpathic, hypersensitive, supersensitive, overtender, overrefined; **irritable, touchy**, tetchy (*informal*), quick on the draw *or* trigger *or* uptake, itchy, ticklish, prickly; goosy (*informal*), skittish; nervous; allergic, anaphylactic

13 (*keenly sensitive*) **exquisite**, poignant, **acute**, sharp, **keen**, vivid, intense, extreme, excruciating

25 INSENSIBILITY
physical unfeeling

nouns

1 **insensibility**, insensibleness, **insensitivity**, insensitiveness, insentience, impassibility; **unperceptiveness**, imperceptiveness, imperception, imperceptivity, impercipience, blindness, lack of concern, obtuseness; inconsiderateness; unsolicitousness; tactlessness; discourtesy, boorishness; **unfeeling**, unfeelingness, **apathy**, affectlessness, lack of affect; thick skin *or* hide, callousness *see* 94.3; **numbness**, dullness, hypothymia, **deadness**; pins and needles; hypaesthesia; anaesthesia, analgesia; narcosis, electronarcosis; narcotization

2 **unconsciousness, senselessness**; nothingness, oblivion, obliviousness, nirvana; nirvana principle; **faint, swoon, blackout**, syncope, athymia, lipothymy *or* lipothymia; **coma; stupor**; catalepsy,

catatony *or* catatonia, sleep *see* 22; knockout *or* KO *or* kayo (*both informal*); semiconsciousness, greyout

3 **anaesthetic**, general anaesthetic, local anaesthetic, analgesic, anodyne, balm, ointment, **pain killer**, pain-reliever, antiodontalgic, soothing syrup; tranquillizer, **sedative**, sleeping pill *or* tablet, knockout drop *and* Mickey Finn (*both informal*); drug, dope (*informal*), narcotic, opiate

verbs

4 to **deaden, numb**, benumb, blunt, dull, obtund, **desensitize**; paralyse, palsy; **anaesthetize, put to sleep**, slip one a Mickey *or* Mickey Finn (*informal*), chloroform, etherize; narcotize, drug, dope (*informal*); freeze, **stupefy, stun**, bedaze, besot; knock unconscious, knock senseless, **knock out, KO** *and* kayo *and* lay out *and* knock stiff (*all informal*)

5 to **faint, swoon**, drop, succumb, keel over (*informal*), fall in a faint, fall senseless, **pass** *or* zonk out (*informal*), **black out**, go out like a light; grey out

adjectives

6 **insensible, unfeeling, insensitive**, insentient, insensate, impassible; unsympathetic, uncompassionate; unconcerned, unsolicitous, non-caring; tactless, boorish, heavy-handed; **unperceptive**, imperceptive, impercipient, blind; thick-skinned, thick-witted, **dull**, obtuse, obdurate; **numb**, numbed, benumbed, dead, **deadened**, asleep, unfelt; **unfeeling, apathetic**, affectless; callous *see* 94.12; anaesthetized, narcotized

7 **stupefied, stunned**, dazed, bedazed

8 **unconscious, senseless, oblivious**, comatose, asleep, dead, **dead to the world**, cold, out, **out cold**; nirvanic; half-conscious, semiconscious; drugged, narcotized; doped *and* stoned *and* spaced out *and* strung out *and* zonked *and* zonked out *and* out of it (*all informal*); catatonic, cataleptic

9 **deadening**, numbing, dulling; **anaesthetic**, analgesic, narcotic; stupefying, stunning, numbing, mind-boggling *or* numbing; anaesthetizing, narcotizing

26 PAIN
physical suffering

nouns

1 pain; **suffering, hurt, hurting**, misery (*informal*), **distress**, *Schmerz* (*German*), dolour (*old*); **discomfort**, malaise; gyp (*informal*); aches and pains

2 **pang**, throe, throes; seizure, spasm, paroxysm; ouch (*informal*); **twinge**, twitch, wrench, jumping pain; crick, kink, hitch, cramp *or* cramps; **nip**, thrill, pinch, tweak, bite, prick, **stab**, stitch, sharp *or* piercing *or* stabbing pain, acute pain, **shooting pain**, darting pain, fulgurant pain, lancinating pain, shooting, shoot; boring *or* terebrant *or* terebrating pain; gnawing, gnawing *or* grinding pain; griping *and* tormen (*both old*); girdle pain; stitch in the side; charley horse (*US & Canadian informal*); phantom limb pain; hunger pang *or* pain; wandering pain; psychalgia, psychosomatic pain, soul pain, mind pain

3 **smart**, smarting, **sting**, stinging, urtication, **tingle**, tingling; **burn**, burning, burning pain, fire

4 **soreness, irritation**, inflammation, tenderness, sensitiveness; algesia; rankling (*old*), festering; sore; sore spot *see* 24.4

5 **ache**, aching, throbbing, throbbing ache *or* pain; **headache**, cephalalgia, misery in the head (*informal*); splitting headache, **sick headache, migraine**, megrim, hemicrania; **backache; earache**, otalgia; **toothache**, odontalgia; **stomachache**, tummyache (*informal*), bellyache *or* gut-ache (*informal*); **colic**, collywobbles, gripes, gripe, gnawing, gnawing of the bowels, fret (*informal*); **heartburn**, pyrosis; **angina**

6 **agony, anguish, torment, torture**, exquisite torment *or* torture, the rack, excruciation, crucifixion, martyrdom, martyrization, excruciating *or* agonizing *or* atrocious pain

verbs

7 to **pain**, give *or* inflict pain, **hurt, wound, afflict, distress; burn**; sting; nip, bite, tweak, pinch; pierce, prick, stab, cut, lacerate; **irritate, inflame**, harshen, exacerbate, intensify; chafe, gall, fret, rasp, rub, grate; gnaw, grind; gripe; fester, rankle (*old*); **torture, torment**, rack, put to torture, put *or* lay on the rack, **agonize, harrow**, crucify, martyr, martyrize, excruciate, wring, twist, contorse, convulse; wrench, tear, rend; prolong the agony, kill by inches

8 to **suffer, feel pain**, feel the pangs, anguish *see* 96.19; **hurt, ache**, have a misery (*informal*), ail; **smart**, tingle; throb, pound; shoot; twinge, thrill, twitch; **wince**, blanch, shrink, make a wry face, grimace; **agonize**, writhe

adjectives

9 **pained**, in pain, **hurt**, hurting, **suffering**, afflicted, wounded, distressed, in distress; **tortured, tormented, racked, agonized, harrowed**, lacerated, crucified, martyred, martyrized, wrung, twisted, convulsed; on the rack, under the harrow

10 **painful**; hurtful, **hurting**, distressing, afflictive; **acute, sharp**, piercing, stabbing, shooting, stinging, biting, gnawing; **poignant**, pungent, **severe**, cruel, harsh, grave, hard; griping, cramping, spasmic, spasmatic, spasmodic, paroxysmal; **agonizing, excruciating**, exquisite, atrocious, torturous, tormenting, martyrizing, racking, **harrowing**

11 **sore**, raw; smarting, tingling, **burning; irritated, inflamed**, tender, sensitive, fiery, angry, red; algetic; chafed, galled; **festering**, rankling (*old*)

12 **aching**, achy, **throbbing**; headachy, migrainous, backachy, toothachy, stomachachy, colicky, griping

13 **irritating**, irritative, irritant; **chafing, galling**, fretting, rasping, boring, grating, grinding, stinging, scratchy

27 VISION
nouns

1 **vision, sight, eyesight**, seeing; **sightedness**; eye, power of sight, sense of sight, visual sense; **perception**, discernment; perspicacity, perspicuity, sharp *or* acute *or* keen sight, visual acuity, quick

sight; farsight, farsightedness; clear sight, unobstructed vision; rod vision, scotopia; cone vision, photopia; colour vision, twilight vision, daylight vision, day vision, night vision; eye-mindedness; **field of vision**, visual field, scope, ken, purview, horizon, sweep, range; line of vision, line of sight, sight-line; peripheral vision, peripheral field; field of view *see* 31.3; sensitivity to light, phototonus

2 **observation**, observance; **looking, watching, viewing, seeing**, witnessing, espial; **notice**, note, respect, **regard**; watch, lookout, cave; spying, espionage

3 **look, sight**, the eye *and* a look-see *and* a gander (*all informal*), dekko *and* shufti *and* butcher's (*all informal*), bo-peep (*Australian*), eye, view, regard; sidelong look; leer, leering look, lustful leer; sly look; look-in; preview; scene, prospect *see* 33.6

4 **glance**, glance *or* flick of the eye, squiz (*Australian*), slant (*informal*), rapid glance, cast, side-glance; **glimpse**, flash, quick sight; **peek, peep**; wink, blink, flicker *or* twinkle of an eye; casual glance, **half an eye**; *coup d'œil* (*French*)

5 **gaze, stare**, gape, goggle; eye contact; sharp *or* piercing *or* penetrating look; **ogle**, glad eye, come-hither look (*informal*), bedroom eyes (*informal*), sheep's eyes (*informal*); **glare, glower**, glaring *or* glowering look; evil eye, *malocchio* (*Italian*); withering look, hostile look, chilly look, the fisheye (*informal*)

6 **scrutiny**, overview, **survey**, contemplation; **examination, inspection** *see* 937.3, scrutiny, the once-over (*informal*), visual examination, a vetting (*informal*), ocular inspection, eyeball inspection (*informal*)

7 **viewpoint, standpoint, point of view**, vantage, vantage point, point *or* coign of vantage, where one stands; bird's-eye view, worm's-eye view, fly on the wall; **outlook**, angle, angle of vision, *optique* (*French*); mental outlook *see* 977.2

8 observation post *or* point; **observatory**; **lookout**, outlook, overlook, scenic overlook; **watchtower**, tower; beacon, lighthouse, pharos; gazebo, belvedere; bridge, conning tower, crow's nest; peephole, sighthole, loophole; **ringside**, ringside seat; **grandstand**, bleachers; **gallery**, top gallery; the gods (*informal*); terraces

9 **eye**, visual organ, organ of vision, oculus, optic, **orb, peeper** (*informal*), baby blues (*informal*); clear eyes, bright eyes, starry orbs; saucer eyes, popeyes *and* goggle eyes *and* googly eyes (*all informal*); naked eye, unassisted *or* unaided eye; corner of the eye; eyeball; iris; pupil; eyelid, lid, nictitating membrane

10 **sharp eye**, keen eye, piercing *or* penetrating eye, gimlet eye, X-ray eye; **eagle eye**, hawkeye, peeled eye (*informal*), watchful eye; **weather eye**

11 (*comparisons*) eagle, hawk, cat, lynx, ferret, weasel; Argus

verbs

12 **to see, behold, observe, view, witness, perceive, discern, spy, espy, sight**, have in sight, make out, pick out, descry, spot (*informal*), twig (*informal*), clock (*informal*), discover, notice, take notice of, have one's eye on, distinguish, recognize, ken (*informal*),

catch sight of, get a load of (*informal*), take in, get an eyeful of (*informal*), look on *or* upon, cast the eyes on *or* upon, **set *or* lay eyes on, clap eyes on** (*informal*); **glimpse**, get *or* catch a glimpse of; see at a glance, see with half an eye; see with one's own eyes

13 **to look, peer**, have a look, take a gander *and* take a look (*both informal*), direct the eyes, turn *or* bend the eyes, cast one's eye, lift up the eyes; **look at**, take a look at, eye, eyeball (*informal*), have a look-see (*informal*), have a dekko (*informal*), have a bo-peep (*Australian*), look on *or* upon, gaze at *or* upon; **watch, observe, view, regard**; keep one's eyes peeled *or* skinned, be watchful *or* observant *or* vigilant, keep one's eyes open, keep cave; keep in sight *or* view, hold in view; look after; **check *and* check out** (*both informal*); keep under observation, spy on, have an eye out, keep an eye out, keep an eye on, keep a weather eye on, follow, tail *and* shadow (*both informal*), stake out; **reconnoitre**, scout, get the lay of the land; **peek, peep**, pry, take a peep *or* peek; play peekaboo

14 **to scrutinize, survey, eye**, contemplate, look over, give the eye *or* the once-over (*informal*); **ogle**, ogle at, **leer**, leer at, give one the glad eye; examine, vet (*informal*), **inspect** *see* 937.23; **pore**, pore over, peruse; take a close *or* careful look; take a long, hard look; size up (*informal*); take stock of

15 **to gaze**, gloat (*old*), fix one's gaze, fix *or* fasten *or* rivet one's eyes upon, keep one's eyes upon, feast one's eyes on; **eye, ogle; stare**, stare at, stare hard, look, goggle, **gape, gawk** *or* gawp (*informal*), gaze open-mouthed; crane, crane the neck, stand on tiptoe; strain one's eyes; look straight in the eye, look full in the face, hold one's eye *or* gaze, stare down

16 **to glare, glower**, look daggers, look black; give one the evil eye, give one a whammy (*informal*); give one the fish eye (*informal*)

17 **to glance, glimpse**, glint, cast a glance, glance at *or* upon, give a *coup d'œil* (*French*), take a glance at, take a squint at (*informal*)

18 **to look askance** *or* askant, give a sidelong look; squint, look asquint; cock the eye; **look down one's nose** (*informal*)

19 **to look away**, look aside, **avert the eyes**, look the other way, break one's eyes away, stop looking, turn away from, turn the back upon; drop one's eyes *or* gaze, cast one's eyes down; avoid one's gaze

adjectives

20 **visual, ocular, eye, eyeball** (*informal*); **sighted**, seeing, having sight *or* vision; **optic, optical**; ophthalmic; retinal; visible *see* 31.6

21 **clear-sighted**, clear-eyed; twenty-twenty; **farsighted**, farseeing, telescopic; **sharp-sighted**, keen-sighted, sharp-eyed, **eagle-eyed**, hawk-eyed, ferret-eyed, lynx-eyed, cat-eyed, Argus-eyed; eye-minded

adverbs

22 **at sight**, as seen, visibly, at a glance; by sight, by eyeball (*informal*), visually; at first sight, **at the first blush**, *prima facie* (*Latin*); out of the corner of one's

eye; from where one stands, from one's viewpoint *or* standpoint

word elements

23 opto–, –opsia, –opsy, –opsis; –opy, –opia; –scopy; ocul–, oculo–, ophthalm–, ophthalmo–

28 DEFECTIVE VISION

nouns

1 faulty eyesight, bad eyesight, defect of vision *or* sight, poor sight, impaired vision, imperfect vision, blurred vision, reduced sight, partial sightedness, partial blindness; legal blindness; **astigmatism,** astigmia; nystagmus; albinism; double vision, double sight; tunnel vision; photophobia; **blindness** *see* 30

2 **dim-sightedness,** dull-sightedness, near-blindness, amblyopia, gravel-blindness, sand-blindness, **purblindness,** dim eyes; blurredness, blearedness, bleariness, redness, lippitude (*old*)

3 **nearsightedness, myopia,** shortsightedness, short sight

4 **farsightedness,** hyperopia, longsightedness, long sight; presbyopia

5 strabismus, heterotropia; cast, cast in the eye; **squint; cross-eye, cross-eyedness;** convergent strabismus, esotropia; upward strabismus, anoöpsia; walleye, exotropia

6 (*defective eyes*) cross-eyes, cockeyes, squint eyes, lazy eye, swivel eyes (*informal*), goggle eyes, walleyes, bug-eyes *and* popeyes (*both informal*), saucer eyes (*informal*)

7 **winking, blinking,** fluttering the eyelids, nictitation; winker, blinkard (*old*)

verbs

8 to see badly *or* poorly, barely see, be half-blind; have a mote in the eye; see double

9 **to squint,** squint the eye, look asquint, screw up the eyes, skew, goggle (*old*)

10 to wink, **blink,** nictitate, bat the eyes (*informal*)

adjectives

11 poor-sighted; visually impaired, sight-impaired; legally blind; **blind** *see* 30.9; **astigmatic,** astigmatical; nystagmic; **nearsighted, shortsighted, myopic,** mope-eyed (*old*); **farsighted,** longsighted, presbyopic; **squinting,** squinty, asquint, squint-eyed, strabismal, strabismic; winking, **blinking,** blinky, blink-eyed; blinkered; photophobic

12 **cross-eyed, cockeyed,** swivel-eyed (*informal*), goggle-eyed, popeyed (*informal*), bug-eyed (*US informal*), **walleyed,** saucer-eyed, glare-eyed; one-eyed, monocular, cyclopean; moon-eyed

13 **dim-sighted,** dim, dull-sighted, dim-eyed, weak-eyed, feeble-eyed, mole-eyed; **purblind,** half-blind, gravel-blind, sand-blind; bleary-eyed, blear-eyed; filmy-eyed, film-eyed; snow-blind

29 OPTICAL INSTRUMENTS

nouns

1 **optical instrument** (*see list*), optical device, viewer;

microscope (*see list*); **spectroscope,** spectrometer (*see list*)

2 **lens,** glass; prism, objective prism; **camera** *see* 714.11

3 **spectacles, specs** (*informal*), **glasses, eyeglasses,** pair of glasses *or* spectacles, barnacles (*informal*), cheaters *and* peepers (*both informal*); reading glasses, readers; bifocals, divided spectacles, halg glasses, trifocals, varifocals, pince-nez, nippers (*informal*); lorgnette, *lorgnon* (*French*); horn-rimmed glasses; harlequin glasses; granny glasses; mini-specs (*informal*); coloured glasses, sunglasses, sun-specs (*informal*), dark glasses, Polaroid (*trademark*), Raybans (*trademark*), glasses, shades (*informal*); goggles, blinkers; eyeglass, monocle, quizzing glass; thick glasses, thick-lensed glasses, thick lenses, pebble glasses (*informal*); **contacts,** contact lenses, hard lenses, soft lenses, disposable lenses

4 **telescope** (*see list*), scope, **spy glass,** terrestrial telescope, glass, **field glass; binoculars,** zoom binoculars, opera glasses

5 **sight;** sighthole; finder, viewfinder; panoramic sight; bombsight; peep sight, open sight, leaf sight

6 **mirror,** glass, **looking glass,** seeing glass (*informal*), reflector, speculum; two-way mirror; hand mirror, handbag mirror, window mirror, rear-view mirror, cheval glass, pier glass, shaving mirror; steel mirror; convex mirror, concave mirror, distorting mirror

7 **optics,** optical physics; **optometry;** microscopy, microscopics; telescopy; stereoscopy; spectroscopy, spectrometry; infrared spectroscopy; spectrophotometry; electron optics; fibre optics; **photography** *see* 714

8 **oculist,** ophthalmologist, **optometrist;** microscopist; telescopist; optician

adjectives

9 **optic, optical,** ophthalmic, ophthalmologic, ophthalmological, optometrical; acousto-optic, acousto-optical; ocular, binocular, monocular

10 microscopic, telescopic, etc; stereoscopic, three-dimensional, 3-D

11 **spectacled, bespectacled,** four-eyed (*informal*); goggled; monocled

12 **optical instruments and viewers**

abdominoscope	oscilloscope
amblyoscope	periscope
bronchoscope	pharyngoscope
chromatoscope	photometer
chromoscope	photomultiplier
cystoscope	photoscope
diaphanoscope	polariscope
diffractometer	polemoscope
epidiascope	prism
eriometer	pseudoscope
gastroscope	radarscope
goniometer	radioscope
image orthicon	rangefinder
kaleidoscope	retinoscope
laser	sniperscope
microfilm viewer *or* reader	snooperscope
ophthalmoscope	spectroscope
optometer	stereopticon

stereoscope	thaumatrope
stroboscope	

13 microscopes

acoustic microscope	pinion focusing microscope
binocular microscope	polarizing microscope
blink microscope	power microscope
compound microscope	projecting microscope
dark-field microscope	scanning electron
dissecting microscope	microscope
electron microscope	scanning microscope
field ion microscope	simple *or* single
fluorescence microscope	microscope
gravure microscope	stereomicroscope *or*
laboratory microscope	stereoscopic microscope
light microscope	surface microscope
metallurgical microscope	transmission electron
optical microscope	microscope
oxyhydrogen microscope	ultramicroscope
phase contrast microscope	ultraviolet microscope
or phase microscope	X-ray microscope

14 spectroscopes, spectrometers

analytical spectrometer	ocular spectroscope
diffraction spectroscope	prism spectroscope
direct-reading spectrometer	reversion spectroscope
direct-reading spectroscope	spectrograph
microspectrophotometer	spectrophotometer
microspectroscope	spectroradiometer
monochromator	star spectroscope

15 telescopes

astronomical telescope	radio telescope
Cassegrainian telescope	reflecting telescope
double-image telescope	refracting telescope
elbow telescope	Schmidt telescope
finder telescope	spotting scope
guiding telescope	telescopic sight
inverting telescope	terrestrial telescope
mercurial telescope	tower telescope
Newtonian telescope	twin telescope
optical telescope	vernier telescope
panoramic telescope	water telescope
prism telescope	zenith telescope *or* tube

30 BLINDNESS

nouns

1 **blindness, sightlessness,** cecity, ablepsia, unseeingness, sightless eyes, lack of vision, eyelessness; stone-blindness, total blindness; darkness, "ever-during dark", "total eclipse without all hope of day"—BOTH MILTON, "the precious treasure of his eyesight lost"—SHAKESPEARE; legal blindness; partial blindness, reduced sight, **blind side; blind spot;** dimsightedness; snow blindness, niphablepsia; amaurosis, *gutta serena (Latin)*, drop serene; cataract; glaucoma; trachoma; mental *or* psychic blindness, mind-blindness, soul-blindness, benightedness, unenlightenment, spiritual blindness; **blinding,** making blind, depriving of sight, putting out the eyes, excecation (*old*); blurring the eyes, blindfolding, hoodwinking, blinkering

2 **day blindness,** hemeralopia; **night blindness,** nyctalopia; moon blindness, moon-blind

3 **colour blindness;** dichromatism; monochromatism, achromatopsia; red blindness, protanopia, green blindness, deuteranopia, red-green blindness, Daltonism; yellow blindness, xanthocyanopia; blue-yellow blindness, tritanopia; violet-blindness

4 **the blind,** the sightless, the unseeing; blind man; bat, mole; "blind leaders of the blind"—BIBLE

5 blindfold; eye patch; blinkers, blinds, blinders, rogue's badge

6 (*aids for the blind*) sensory aid, **braille,** New York point, Gall's serrated type, Boston type, Howe's American type, Moon *or* Moon's type, Alston's Glasgow type, Lucas's type, sight-saver type, Frere's type; line letter, string alphabet, writing stamps; noctograph, writing frame, embosser, high-speed embosser; visagraph; talking book; optophone, Visotoner, Optacon; personal sonar, Pathsounder; ultrasonic spectacles; cane; Seeing Eye dog, guide dog

verbs

7 **to blind,** blind the eyes, deprive of sight, **strike blind,** render *or* make blind, excecate (*old*); darken, dim, obscure, eclipse, **put one's eyes out,** gouge; **blindfold,** hoodwink, bandage; throw dust in one's eyes, benight; **dazzle,** bedazzle, daze; glare; snow-blind

8 **to be blind,** not see, walk in darkness, grope in the dark, feel one's way; go blind, lose one's sight *or* vision; be blind to, close *or* shut one's eyes to, wink *or* blink at, look the other way, blind oneself to, wear blinkers; have a blind spot *or* side

adjectives

9 **blind, sightless, unsighted,** ableptical, eyeless, visionless, **unseeing,** undiscerning, unobserving, unperceiving; in darkness, rayless, bereft of light, dark (*informal*), "dark, dark, dark, amid the blaze of noon"—MILTON; **stone-blind,** stark blind, **blind as a bat,** blind as a mole *or* an owl; amaurotic; dim-sighted *see* 28.13; hemeralopic; nyctalopic; colour-blind; mind-blind, soul-blind, mentally *or* psychically *or* spiritually blind, benighted, unenlightened

10 **blinded,** excecate (*old*), darkened, obscured; **blindfolded,** blindfold, hoodwinked, blinkered; **dazzled,** bedazzled, dazed; snow-blind, snow-blinded

11 **blinding,** obscuring; **dazzling,** bedazzling

31 VISIBILITY

nouns

1 **visibility,** visibleness, perceptibility, discernibleness, observability, detectability, visuality, seeableness; exposure; manifestation; outcrop, outcropping; the visible, the seen, what is revealed, what can be seen; revelation, epiphany

2 **distinctness, plainness,** evidence (*old*), evidentness, obviousness, patentness, manifestness; **clearness, clarity,** crystal-clearness, lucidity, limpidity; **definiteness,** definition, sharpness, microscopical distinctness; resolution, high resolution, low resolution; **prominence, conspicuousness,**

conspicuity; **exposure,** public exposure, high profile, low profile; high or low visibility; atmospheric visibility, seeing, ceiling, ceiling unlimited, visibility unlimited, visibility zero

3 **field of view,** field of vision, range or scope of vision, **sight,** limit of vision, eyereach, **eyesight,** eyeshot, ken; **vista, view, horizon, prospect, perspective, outlook,** survey; range, scan, scope; line of sight, sightline, line of vision; naked eye; command, domination, outlook over; **viewpoint, observation point** see 27.8

verbs

4 **to show,** show up, show through, shine out or through, **surface, appear** see 33.8, **be visible,** be seen, be revealed, be evident, be noticeable, meet the gaze, impinge on the eye, present to the eye, meet or catch or hit or strike the eye; **stand out,** stand forth, loom large, glare, **stare one in the face,** hit one in the eye, **stick out like a sore thumb;** dominate; emerge, come into view, materialize

5 **to be exposed,** be conspicuous, have high visibility, stick out, hang out (*informal*), crop out; live in a glass house; have or keep a high profile

adjectives

6 **visible,** visual, **perceptible,** perceivable, **discernible, seeable,** viewable, witnessable, beholdable, observable, detectable, noticeable, recognizable, to be seen; **in sight,** in view, in plain sight, in full view, present to the eyes, before one's eyes, under one's eyes, open, naked, outcropping, hanging out (*informal*), exposed, showing, open or exposed to view; **evident,** in evidence, **manifest, apparent;** revealed, disclosed, unhidden, unconcealed, unclouded, undisguised

7 **distinct, plain, clear, obvious, evident, patent,** unmistakable, not to be mistaken, much in evidence, plain to be seen, for all to see, showing for all to see, plain as a pikestaff, plain as the nose on one's face, plain as day, clear as day, plain as plain can be, large as life and twice as ugly; **definite, defined, well-defined,** well-marked, well-resolved, in focus; **clear-cut,** clean-cut; crystal-clear, clear as crystal; **conspicuous,** glaring, staring, **prominent,** pronounced, well-pronounced, in bold or strong or high relief, high-profile

adverbs

8 **visibly, perceptibly,** perceivably, discernibly, seeably, recognizably, observably, markedly, noticeably; **manifestly, apparently,** evidently; **distinctly, clearly,** with clarity or crystal clarity, **plainly,** obviously, patently, definitely, unmistakably; conspicuously, undisguisedly, unconcealedly, prominently, pronouncedly, glaringly, starkly, staringly

32 INVISIBILITY

nouns

1 **invisibility,** imperceptibility, unperceivability, undetectability, indiscernibility, unseeableness, viewlessness; nonappearance; disappearance see 34;

the invisible, the unseen; more than meets the eye; unsubstantiality see 763, immateriality see 1051, secrecy see 345, concealment see 346

2 **inconspicuousness,** half-visibility, semivisibility, low profile; **indistinctness, unclearness,** unplainness, **faintness,** paleness, feebleness, weakness, **dimness,** bedimming, bleariness, darkness, shadowiness, **vagueness,** vague appearance, indefiniteness, obscurity, uncertainty, indistinguishability; **blurriness,** blur, soft focus, defocus, **fuzziness, haziness,** mistiness, filminess, fogginess

verbs

3 to be invisible or unseen, escape notice; lie hid see 346.8, **blush unseen;** disappear see 34.3

4 **to blur, dim, pale,** soften, film, mist, fog; defocus, lose resolution or sharpness or distinctness, go soft at the edges

adjectives

5 **invisible; imperceptible,** unperceivable, **indiscernible,** undiscernible, undetectable, **unseeable,** viewless, unbeholdable, unapparent, insensible; **out of sight,** à perte de vue (*French*); **secret** see 345.11, 15; **unseen,** sightless, unbeheld, unviewed, unwitnessed, unobserved, unnoticed, unperceived; behind the curtain or scenes; disguised, camouflaged, hidden, **concealed** see 346.11, 14; undisclosed, unrevealed, in petto (*Latin*); latent, unrealized, submerged

6 **inconspicuous,** half-visible, semivisible, low-profile; **indistinct, unclear,** unplain, **indefinite,** undefined, ill-defined, ill-marked, **faint,** pale, feeble, weak, **dim,** dark, **shadowy, vague, obscure,** indistinguishable, unrecognizable; half-seen, merely glimpsed; uncertain, confused, out of focus, **blurred, blurry,** bleared, bleary, blear, **fuzzy, hazy,** misty, filmy, foggy

33 APPEARANCE

nouns

1 **appearance, appearing,** apparition, coming, forthcoming, showing up, coming forth, coming on the scene, making the scene (*informal*), putting in an appearance; **emergence,** issuing, issuance; **arising,** rise, rising, occurrence; **materialization, materializing,** coming into being; **manifestation,** realization, incarnation, revelation, showing-forth; epiphany, theophany, avatar, ostent (*old*); **presentation, disclosure, exposure,** opening, unfolding, unfoldment, showing; rising of the curtain

2 **appearance,** exterior, externals, **mere externals, facade,** outside, **show, outward show, image,** display, front (*informal*), outward or external appearance, surface appearance, surface show, vain show, apparent character, public image, window dressing, cosmetics; whitewash; whited sepulchre; **glitz** and tinsel (*both informal*), gaudiness, speciousness, meretriciousness, **superficiality;** PR, flack (*US & Canadian informal*)

3 aspect, look, view; feature, lineaments; **seeming, semblance, image,** imago, icon, eidolon, likeness, simulacrum; effect, impression, total effect or

impression; **form, shape,** figure, configuration, gestalt; **manner,** fashion, wise, guise, style; **respect, regard,** reference, light; **phase; facet, side,** angle, viewpoint *see* 27.7, slant *and* twist *and* spin (*all informal*)

4 **looks, features, lineaments,** traits, lines; **countenance,** face, visage, feature, favour, brow, physiognomy; cast of countenance, **cut of one's jib** (*informal*), facial appearance *or* expression, cast, turn; (*informal terms*) clock, dial, mush, phiz *or* phizog, **look, air, mien,** demeanour, carriage, bearing, port, posture, stance, poise, presence; guise, garb, complexion, colour

5 (*thing appearing*) **apparition, appearance,** phenomenon; **vision, image, shape, form,** figure, presence; false image, mirage, phasm (*old*), spectre, **phantom** *see* 987.1

6 **view, scene, sight; prospect, outlook, lookout, vista, perspective; scenery,** scenic view; panorama, sweep; scape, **landscape,** seascape, riverscape, waterscape, airscape, skyscape, cloudscape, cityscape, townscape; bird's-eye view, worm's-eye view

7 **spectacle, sight;** exhibit, **exhibition,** exposition, **show, stage show** *see* 704.4, **display, presentation,** representation; tableau, tableau vivant; panorama, diorama, cosmorama, myriorama, cyclorama, georama; *son et lumière* (*French*), sound-and-light show; phantasmagoria, shifting scene, light show; psychedelic show; **pageant,** pageantry; parade, pomp

verbs

8 **to appear,** become visible; **arrive, make one's appearance,** make *or* put in an appearance, appear on the scene, make the scene *and* weigh in (*both informal*), appear to one's eyes, meet *or* catch *or* strike the eye, **come in sight** *or* **view, show,** show oneself, show one's face, **show up** (*informal*), **turn up,** come, **materialize,** present oneself, present oneself to view, **manifest oneself,** become manifest, **reveal oneself,** discover oneself, uncover oneself, declare oneself, expose *or* betray oneself; **come to light,** see the light, see the light of day; **emerge,** issue, issue forth, stream forth, come forth, come to the fore, come out, come forward, come one's way, come to hand; enter *see* 189.7, come upon the stage; **rise, arise,** rear its head; look forth, peer *or* peep out; crop out, outcrop; loom, heave in sight, appear on the horizon; fade in

9 **to burst forth,** break forth, debouch, erupt, irrupt, explode; **pop up, bob up** (*informal*), start up, spring up, burst upon the view; flare up, flash, gleam

10 **to appear to be,** seem to be, **appear, seem, look,** feel, sound, look to be, appear to one's eyes, have *or* present the appearance of, give the feeling of, strike one as, come on as (*informal*); **appear like, seem like, look like,** have *or* wear the look of, **sound like; have every appearance of,** have all the hallmarks of, have all the features of, show signs of, have every sign *or* indication of; assume the guise of, take the shape of, exhibit the form of

adjectives

11 **apparent,** appearing, **seeming, ostensible;** outward, surface, superficial; **visible** *see* 31.6

adverbs

12 **apparently, seemingly, ostensibly, to** *or* **by all appearances,** to *or* by all accounts, to all seeming, as it seems, to the eye; on the face of it, *prima facie* (*Latin*); on the surface, outwardly, superficially; at first sight *or* view, at the first blush

34 DISAPPEARANCE

nouns

1 **disappearance,** disappearing, **vanishing,** vanishment; **going, passing, departure, loss;** dissipation, dispersion; dissolution, dissolving, melting, evaporation, evanescence, dematerialization *see* 1051.5; fadeout, fading, fadeaway, blackout; wipe, wipeout, wipeoff, erasure; eclipse, occultation, blocking; vanishing point; elimination *see* 772.2; extinction *see* 395.6

2 **the disappeared**

verbs

3 **to disappear, vanish,** vanish from sight, do a vanishing act (*informal*), depart, fly, **flee** *see* 368.10, go, be gone, **go away,** pass, pass out *or* away, pass out of sight, exit, pull up stakes (*informal*), leave the scene *or* stage, clear out, pass out of the picture, pass *or* retire from sight, become lost to sight, be seen no more, walk (*informal*); **perish, die,** die off; die out *or* away, dwindle, wane, fade, **fade out** *or* **away,** do a fade-out (*informal*); sink, sink away, dissolve, melt, melt away, "melt, thaw, and dissolve itself"—SHAKESPEARE, dematerialize *see* 1051.6, evaporate, evanesce, **vanish into thin air,** go up in smoke; disperse, dispel, dissipate; cease, cease to exist, **cease to be;** leave no trace, "leave not a rack behind"—SHAKESPEARE; waste, waste away, erode, be consumed, wear away; undergo *or* suffer an eclipse; **hide** *see* 346.8

adjectives

4 **vanishing, disappearing,** passing, fleeting, fugitive, transient, flying, fading, dissolving, melting, evaporating, evanescent

5 **gone,** away, gone away, past and gone, extinct, missing, disappeared, no more, lost, lost to sight *or* view, long-lost, **out of sight; unaccounted for;** lost in action; missing presumed dead; nonexistent

35 COLOUR

nouns

1 **colour, hue; tint,** tinct, tincture, **tinge, shade, tone,** cast; key; **colouring, coloration;** colour harmony, colour balance, colour scheme; decorator colour; **complexion,** skin colour *or* colouring *or* tone; chromatism, chromism; achromatism *see* 36.1; natural colour; undercolour; pallor *see* 36.2

2 **warmth,** warmth of colour, warm colour; **blush, flush, glow,** healthy glow *or* hue

3 **softness,** soft colour, subtle colour, pale colour, pastel, pastel colour, pastel shade

4 **colourfulness,** colour, bright colour, pure colour, **brightness, brilliance, vividness,** intensity, saturation; **richness,** gorgeousness, gaiety; riot of colour; Technicolor (*trademark*); Day-Glo (*trademark*)

5 **garishness,** loudness, luridness, glitz (*informal*), gaudiness *see* 501.3; loud *or* screaming colour (*informal*); shocking pink, jaundiced yellow, arsenic green; clashing colours, colour clash

6 **colour quality;** chroma, Munsell chroma, brightness, purity, saturation; **hue,** value, lightness; colorimetric quality, chromaticity, chromaticness; tint, **tone;** chromatic colour, achromatic *or* neutral colour; warm colour; cool colour

7 **colour system,** chromaticity diagram, colour triangle, Maxwell triangle; hue cycle, colour circle, chromatic circle, colour wheel, colour cycle *or* gamut; Munsell scale; colour solid; fundamental colours; **primary colour,** primary pigment, primary; secondary colour, secondary; tertiary colour, tertiary; complementary colour; chromaticity coordinate; colour mixture curve *or* function; spectral colour, spectrum colour, pure *or* full colour; metamer; **spectrum,** solar spectrum, colour spectrum, chromatic spectrum, colour index; monochrome; demitint, half tint, halftone

8 (*colouring matter*) **colour, colouring, colorant,** tinction, tincture, **pigment, stain;** chromogen; **dye,** dyestuff, colour filter, colour gelatin; paint, distemper, tempera; coat, coating, **coat of paint; undercoat,** undercoating, **primer,** priming, prime coat, **ground, flat coat,** dead-colour; interior paint, exterior paint, floor enamel; wash, wash coat, flat wash; opaque colour, transparent colour; medium, vehicle; drier; thinner; turpentine, turps (*informal*)

9 (*persons according to hair colour*) **brunette; blonde,** blond (*masculine*), Goldilocks; bleached blonde, peroxide blonde; ash blonde, platinum blonde, strawberry blonde, honey blonde; **towhead; redhead,** carrottop (*informal*)

10 (*science of colours*) chromatology; chromatics, chromatography, chromatoscopy, colorimetry; spectrum analysis, spectroscopy, spectrometry

11 (*applying colour*) **colouring,** coloration; **staining, dyeing; tie-dyeing,** ikat; **tinting,** tinging, tinction; pigmentation; illumination, emblazonry; colour printing; lithography

12 **painting,** paint-work, coating, covering; **enamelling,** glossing, glazing; **varnishing,** japanning, lacquering, shellacking; staining; **calcimining, whitewashing;** gilding; stippling; frescoing, fresco; distempering, undercoating, priming

verbs

13 **to colour,** hue, lay on colour; **tinge, tint,** tinct, **tincture,** tone, complexion; pigment; bedizen; **stain, dye,** dip, tie-dye; imbue; deep-dye, fast-dye, double-dye, dye in the wool, yarn-dye; ingrain, grain; shade, shadow; illuminate, emblazon; **paint,** apply paint, paint up, **coat,** cover, face; dab, **daub,** dedaub, smear, besmear, brush on paint, slap *or* slop on paint; **enamel,** gloss, glaze; **varnish,** japan, **lacquer, shellac; white out; calcimine, whitewash,** parget; wash; **gild,** begild, engild; stipple; fresco; distemper; undercoat, prime

14 (*be inharmonious*) **to clash,** conflict, collide, fight

adjectives

15 **chromatic,** colorational; **colouring,** colorific, colorative, tinctorial, tingent; pigmental, pigmentary; monochrome, monochromic, monochromatic; dichromatic; many-coloured, parti-coloured, medley *or* motley (*both old*), rainbow, **variegated** *see* 47.9, polychromatic, kaleidoscopic; prismatic, spectral; matching, toning, harmonious; warm, glowing; cool, cold

16 **coloured,** hued, in colour, in Technicolor (*trademark*); **tinged, tinted,** tinctured, tinct, toned; **painted, enamelled; stained, dyed;** tie-dyed; imbued; complexioned; full-coloured, full; deep, deep-coloured; wash-coloured; washed

17 **deep-dyed, fast-dyed,** double-dyed, **dyed-in-the-wool;** ingrained, ingrain; colourfast, fast, fadeless, unfading, indelible, constant

18 **colourful,** coloury *or* colory; **bright, vivid,** intense, **rich,** exotic, **brilliant,** burning, **gorgeous, gay,** bright-hued, bright-coloured, rich-coloured, gay-coloured, high-coloured, deep-coloured

19 garish, lurid, loud, screaming, shrieking, glaring, flaring, flashy, glitzy (*informal*), flaunting, crude, blinding, overbright, raw, gaudy *see* 501.20; Day-Glo (*trademark*)

20 **off-colour,** off-tone; **inharmonious, discordant,** incongruous, **harsh,** clashing, conflicting, colliding

21 soft-coloured, soft-hued, **soft,** softened, **subdued,** light, creamy, peaches-and-cream, fondant, **pastel, pale,** palish, subtle, mellow, delicate, quiet, tender, sweet; pearly, nacreous, mother-of-pearl, iridescent, opalescent; patinaed; sombre, simple, sober, sad; flat, eggshell, semigloss, gloss

word elements

22 –chroia, –chromasia, chrom–, chromo–, chromat–, chromato–; –phyll; pigmento–; –chrome, –chromia, –chromy; pallidi–; –chroic, –chroous

36 COLOURLESSNESS

nouns

1 **colourlessness,** lack *or* absence of colour, huelessness, tonelessness, achromatism, achromaticity; dullness, lacklustre *see* 1026.5

2 **paleness, dimness,** weakness, **faintness,** fadedness; lightness, fairness; **pallor,** pallidity, pallidness, prison pallor, **wanness, sallowness,** pastiness, ashiness; wheyface; muddiness, dullness; greyness, griseousness; **anaemia,** hypochromic anaemia, hypochromia, chloranaemia; bloodlessness, exsanguination; **ghastliness, haggardness,** lividness, sickly hue, sickliness, deadly *or* deathly pallor, deathly hue, cadaverousness

3 **decoloration,** decolorizing, decolorization, discolouration, achromatization, lightening; **fading, paling; dimming, bedimming; whitening,** blanching, etiolation; bleeding, bleeding white; **bleaching,** bleach

4 **bleach,** bleacher, bleaching agent *or* substance; decolorant, decolorizer, achromatizer

verbs

5 to decolour, decolorize, discolour, achromatize, etiolate; **fade, wash out; dim, dull, tarnish,** tone down; **pale, whiten,** blanch, drain, drain of colour; **bleach,** peroxide, fume

6 to lose colour, **fade,** fade out; **bleach,** bleach out; **pale, turn pale,** grow pale, **change colour,** turn white, **whiten, blanch,** wan

adjectives

7 **colourless, hueless,** toneless, uncoloured, achromic, achromatic, achromatous; neutral; dull, flat, matt, dead, dingy, muddy, leaden, lustreless, lacklustre *see* 1026.17; **faded, washed-out,** dimmed, discoloured, etiolated; **pale, dim,** weak, **faint; pallid, wan, sallow,** fallow; pale *or* blue *or* green around the gills; **white,** white as a sheet; **pasty,** mealy, waxen; **ashen,** ashy, ashen-hued, cinereous, cineritious, grey, griseous; **anaemic,** hypochromic, chloranaemic; bloodless, exsanguine, exsanguinated, exsanguineous, bled white; **ghastly,** livid, lurid, **haggard,** cadaverous, sickly, deadly *or* deathly pale; pale as death *or* a ghost *or* a corpse,
"pale as a forpined ghost"—CHAUCER, "pale as his shirt"—SHAKESPEARE; pale-faced, tallow-faced, wheyfaced

8 **bleached,** decoloured, decolorized, achromatized, whitened, blanched, lightened, bleached out, bleached white; drained, drained of colour

9 **light, fair,** light-coloured, light-hued; pastel; whitish *see* 37.8

word elements

10 achromat–, achromato–, achro–, achroö–

37 WHITENESS

nouns

1 **whiteness, white, whitishness;** albescence; **lightness, fairness;** paleness *see* 36.2; silveriness; snowiness, frostiness; chalkiness; pearliness; **creaminess;** blondness; hoariness, grizzliness, canescence; milkiness, lactescence; glaucousness; glaucescence; silver; albinism, achroma, achromasia, achromatosis; albino; leucoderma, vitiligo; wheyface; white race *see* 312.2, 3

2 (*comparisons*) alabaster, bone, chalk, lily, lime, milk, cream, pearl, wool, sheet, swan, sheep, fleece, foam, silver, snow, driven snow, paper, phantom, flour, ivory, maggot, tallow, wax

3 **whitening,** albification, blanching; etiolation; **whitewashing; bleaching** *see* 36.3; silvering, frosting, grizzling

4 whitening agent, whiting, whitening, **whitewash,** calcimine; pipe clay, Blanco (*trademark*); correction fluid

verbs

5 to **whiten,** white (*old*), etiolate, **blanch; bleach** *see* 36.5; silver, grizzle, frost, besnow; chalk; whitewash

6 to **whitewash,** white (*old*), calcimine; pipe-clay, Blanco

adjectives

7 **white,** pure white, white as alabaster *or* bone *or* chalk *or* snow, etc *see* 37.2, **snow-white,** snowy, niveous,
"whiter than new snow on a raven's back"— SHAKESPEARE, frosty, frosted; **hoary,** hoar, **grizzled,** grizzly, griseous, canescent; silver, **silvery,** silvered, argent (*heraldry*), argentine; platinum; chalky, cretaceous; fleece- *or* fleecy-white; swan-white; foam-white; **milk-white,** milky, lactescent; marble, marmoreal; lily-white, white as a lily,
"white as the whitest lily on a stream"—LONGFELLOW; white as a sheet, wheyfaced

8 **whitish,** whity, albescent; **light, fair;** pale *see* 36.7; off-white; eggshell; glaucous, glaucescent; pearl, pearly, pearly-white, pearl-white; alabaster, alabastrine; cream, **creamy;** ivory, ivory-white; grey-white; dun-white; lint-white

9 **blond;** flaxen-haired, fair-haired; artificial blonde, bleached-blonde, peroxide-blonde; ash-blonde, platinum-blonde, strawberry-blonde, honey-blonde, blonde-headed, blonde-haired; **towheaded,** tow-haired; golden-haired *see* 43.5

10 **albino,** albinic, albinistic, albinal

word elements

11 alb–, albo–, leuc–, leuco–, leuk–, leuko–

38 BLACKNESS

nouns

1 **blackness,** nigritude, nigrescence; inkiness; **black, sable, ebony;** melanism; black race *see* 312.2, 3; darkness *see* 1026

2 **darkness, darkishness,** darksomeness, blackishness; **swarthiness,** swartness, swarth; **duskiness,** duskness; soberness, sobriety, **sombreness,** graveness, sadness, funereality; hostility, sullenness, anger, black mood, black looks, black words

3 **dinginess, griminess, smokiness,** sootiness, fuliginousness, fuliginosity, smudginess, smuttiness, blotchiness, dirtiness, **muddiness,** murkiness

4 (*comparisons*) ebony *or* ebon (*old*), jet, ink, sloe, pitch, tar, coal, charcoal, smoke, soot, smut, raven, crow, night, hell, sin, one's hat

5 **blackening, darkening,** nigrification, melanization, denigration; shading; **smudging,** smutching, **smirching;** smudge, smutch, smirch, smut

6 **blacking,** blackening, blackening agent, blackwash; charcoal, burnt cork, black ink; lampblack, carbon black, stove black, gas black, soot

verbs

7 to **blacken,** black, nigrify, melanize, denigrate; **darken,** bedarken, shade, shadow; blackwash, ink, charcoal, cork; **smudge,** smutch, **smirch,** besmirch, murk, blotch, blot, dinge; smut, soot; smoke, oversmoke; ebonize; **smear** *see* 661.9, 512.10, **blacken one's name** *or* **reputation,** give one a black eye, tear down

adjectives

8 **black,** black as ink *or* pitch *or* tar etc *see* 38.4; **sable** (*heraldry*), nigrous; **ebony,**

"black as ebony"—Shakespeare; deep black, of the deepest dye; **pitch-black, pitch-dark,** pitchy, black *or* dark as pitch, tar-black, tarry; night-black, night-dark, black *or* dark as night; midnight, black as midnight; **inky,** inky-black, atramentous, ink-black, black as ink; **jet-black,** jetty; **coal-black,** coaly, black as coal, coal-black; sloe, sloe-black, sloe-coloured,
"sloe-black, slow, black, crowblack"—Dylan Thomas; raven, **raven-black,** black as a crow,
"cyprus black as e'er was crow"—Shakespeare; "bible-black"—Dylan Thomas; **dark** *see* 1026.13-16
9 **dark,** dark-coloured, **darkish,** darksome, blackish; nigrescent; **swarthy,** swart; **dusky,** dusk; **sombre,** sombrous, **sober, grave,** sad, funereal; hostile, sullen, angry
10 **dark-skinned,** black-skinned, **dark-complexioned; black, coloured;** melanian, melanic, melanotic, melanistic, melanous
11 **dingy, grimy, smoky,** sooty, fuliginous, **smudgy,** smutty, blotchy, dirty, grotty, **muddy,** murky, smirched, besmirched
12 **livid,** black and blue
13 **black-haired, raven-haired,** raven-tressed, black-locked; brunette

word elements

14 atro–, mel–, mela–, melo–, melano–, melam–

39 GREYNESS

nouns

1 **greyness, grey,** greyishness, canescence; glaucousness, glaucescence; silveriness; ashiness; neutral tint; smokiness; mousiness; slatiness; leadenness; lividness, lividity; dullness, drabness, soberness, sombreness; grisaille
2 **grey-haired** *or* **grey-headed person,** grey-hair, greybeard, grisard

verbs

3 **to grey, grizzle,** silver

adjectives

4 **grey, greyish,** grey-coloured, grey-hued, grey-toned, greyed, griseous; canescent; iron-grey, steely, steel-grey; Quaker-grey, Quaker-coloured, acier, grey-drab; pearl-grey, pearl, pearly; silver-grey, silver, silvery, silvered; **grizzly,** grizzled, grizzle; ash-grey, ashen, ashy, cinerous, cinereous, cineritious, cinereal; dusty, dust-grey; smoky, smoke-grey; charcoal-grey; slaty, slate-coloured; leaden, livid, lead-grey; glaucous, glaucescent; wolf-grey; mousy, mouse-grey, mouse-coloured; taupe; dapple-grey, dappled-grey; grey-spotted, grey-speckled, salt-and-pepper; grey-white, grey-black, grey-blue, grey-brown, grey-green, etc; **dull, dingy,** dismal, **sombre, sober, sad, dreary;** winter-grey, hoar, hoary, frost-grey, rime-grey
5 **grey-haired,** grey-headed, silver-headed; hoar, hoary, hoary-haired, hoary-headed; grey-bearded, silver-bearded

40 BROWNNESS

nouns

1 **brownness, brownishness, brown,** browning, infuscation; brown race *see* 312.2

verbs

2 **to brown,** embrown, infuscate; rust; **tan, bronze,** suntan; sunburn, burn; fry, sauté, scorch, braise

adjectives

3 **brown, brownish;** cinnamon, hazel; fuscous; **brunette,** brune; tawny, fulvous; tan, tan-coloured; tan-faced, tan-skinned, tanned, sun-tanned; khaki, khaki-coloured; drab, olive-drab; **dun,** dun-brown, dun-drab, dun-olive; beige, ecru; **chocolate,** chocolate-coloured, chocolate-brown; cocoa, cocoa-coloured, cocoa-brown; coffee, coffee-coloured, coffee-brown; toast, toast-brown; nut-brown; walnut, walnut-brown; seal, seal-brown; fawn, fawn-coloured; donkey brown; greyish-brown; brownish-grey, fuscous, taupe, mouse-dun, mouse-brown; snuff-coloured, snuff-brown, mummy-brown; umber, umber-coloured, umber-brown; olive-brown; **sepia;** sorrel; yellowish-brown, brownish-yellow; lurid (*old*); brown as a berry, berry-brown
4 **reddish-brown,** rufous-brown, brownish-red; roan; henna; terra-cotta; rufous, foxy; livid-brown; **mahogany,** mahogany-brown; auburn, Titian; **russet,** russety; rust, rust-coloured, rusty, ferruginous, rubiginous; liver-coloured, liver-brown; **bronze,** bronze-brown, bronze-coloured, bronzed, brazen; copper, coppery, copperish, cupreous, copper-coloured; **chestnut,** chestnut-brown, castaneous; bay, bay-coloured; bayard (*old*); sunburned, adust (*old*)
5 **brunette;** brown-haired; auburn-haired; xanthous

41 REDNESS

nouns

1 **redness, reddishness,** rufosity, rubricity; **red,** *rouge* (*French*), gules (*heraldry*); rubicundity, **ruddiness,** colour, high colour, floridness, floridity; rubor, erythema, erythroderma,
"a fire-red cherubim's face"—Chaucer; erythrism; reddish brown; red race *see* 312.3;
"any colour, so long as it's red"—Eugene Field
2 **pinkness, pinkishness; rosiness; pink,** rose
3 **reddening,** rubefaction, rubification, rubescence, erubescence, rufescence; **colouring,** mantling, crimsoning, **blushing, flushing; blush,** flush, glow, bloom; hectic, hectic flush; rubefacient

verbs

4 (*make red*) **to redden, rouge,** ruddle, rubify, rubric; warm, inflame; crimson, encrimson; vermilion, madder, miniate, henna, rust, carmine; incarnadine, pinkify; raddle; red-ink, lipstick
5 **to redden,** turn *or* grow red, **colour,** colour up, **mantle, blush, flush, crimson;** flame, glow

adjectives

6 **red, reddish,** gules (*heraldry*), red-coloured, red-hued, red-dyed, red-looking; **ruddy,** ruddied,

rubicund; rubrical, rubricate, rubricose; rufescent, rufous, rufulous; warm, hot, glowing; fiery, flaming, flame-coloured, flame-red, fire-red, red as fire, lurid, red as a hot *or* live coal; reddened, inflamed; **scarlet, vermilion, vermeil; crimson**; rubiate; maroon; damask; puce; stammel; cerise; iron-red; cardinal, cardinal-red; cherry, cherry-coloured, cherry-red; carmine, incarmined; **ruby**, ruby-coloured, ruby-red; wine, port-wine, wine-coloured, wine-red, vinaceous; carnation, carnation-red; brick-red, brick-coloured, bricky, tile-red, lateritious; rust, rust-red, rusty, ferruginous, rubiginous; lake-coloured, laky; beetroot-red, red as a beetroot; lobster-red, red as a lobster; red as a turkey-cock; copper-red, carnelian; Titian, Titian-red; infrared; reddish-amber, reddish-grey, etc; reddish-brown *see* 40.4

7 **sanguine**, sanguineous, **blood-red**, blood-coloured, bloody-red, bloody, gory, red as blood

8 **pink, pinkish**, pinky; **rose, rosy**, rose-coloured, rose-hued, rose-red, roseate; flesh-colour, flesh-coloured, flesh-pink, incarnadine; coral, coral-coloured, coral-red, coralline; salmon, salmon-coloured, salmon-pink

9 **red-complexioned**, ruddy-complexioned, warm-complexioned, red-fleshed, red-faced, ruddy-faced, apple-cheeked, **ruddy**, rubicund, **florid**, sanguine, full-blooded; blowzy, blowzed; rosy, **rosy-cheeked**; glowing, blooming; hectic, flushed, flush; burnt, sunburned; erythematous

10 **redheaded**, red-haired, red-polled, red-bearded; erythristic; red-crested, red-crowned, red-tufted; carroty, chestnut, auburn, Titian, xanthous

11 reddening, blushing, flushing, colouring; rubescent, erubescent; rubificative, rubrific; rubefacient

42 ORANGENESS

nouns

1 **orangeness**, oranginess; **orange**

adjectives

2 **orange, orangeish**, orangey, orange-hued, reddish-yellow; ochreous *or* ochry, ochreous, ochroid, ochreish; old gold; pumpkin, pumpkin-coloured; tangerine, tangerine-coloured; apricot, peach; carroty, carrot-coloured; orange-red, orange-yellow, red-orange, reddish-orange, yellow-orange, yellowish-orange

43 YELLOWNESS

nouns

1 **yellowness, yellowishness**; goldenness, aureateness; **yellow**, gold, or (*heraldry*); gildedness; fallowness

2 yellow skin, yellow complexion, sallowness; xanthochroism; **jaundice**, yellow jaundice, icterus, xanthoderma, xanthism; yellow race *see* 312.2, 3

verbs

3 to **yellow**, turn yellow; **gild**, begild, engild; aurify; sallow; **jaundice**

adjectives

4 **yellow, yellowish**, yellowy; lutescent, luteous, luteolous; xanthic, xanthous; **gold, golden**, or (*heraldry*), gold-coloured, golden-yellow, gilt, gilded, auric, aureate; **canary**, canary-yellow; citron, citron-yellow, citreous; **lemon**, lemon-coloured, lemon-yellow; sulphur-coloured, sulphur-yellow; pale-yellow, **sallow**, fallow; cream, creamy, cream-coloured; straw, straw-coloured, tow-coloured; flaxen, flaxen-coloured, flax-coloured; sandy, sand-coloured; ochreous *or* ochry, ochreous, ochroid, ochreish; buff, buff-coloured, buff-yellow; beige, ecru; saffron, saffron-coloured, saffron-yellow; primrose, primrose-coloured, primrose-yellow; topaz-yellow

5 **yellow-haired, golden-haired**, tow-headed, tow-haired, auricomous, xanthous; blond *see* 37.9

6 yellow-faced, yellow-complexioned, sallow, yellow-cheeked; **jaundiced**, xanthodermatous, icteric, icterical

44 GREENNESS

nouns

1 **greenness**, viridity; greenishness, virescence, viridescence; verdantness, verdancy, **verdure**, glaucousness, glaucescence; **green**, greensickness, chlorosis, chloremia, chloranaemia; chlorophyll

2 **verdigris, patina**, aerugo; patination

verbs

3 to **green**; verdigris, patinate, patinize

adjectives

4 **green**, virid; **verdant**, verdurous, vert (*heraldry*); grassy, leafy, leaved, foliaged; springlike, summerlike, summery, vernal, vernant, aestival; **greenish**, viridescent, virescent; **grass-green**, green as grass; citrine, citrinous; **olive**, olive-green, olivaceous; beryl-green, berylline; leek-green, porraceous (*old*); holly, holly-green; ivy, ivy-green; emerald, emerald-green, smaragdine; rifle green; chartreuse, yellow-green, yellowish-green, greenish-yellow; glaucous, glaucescent, glaucous-green; blue-green, bluish-green, green-blue, greenish-blue; greensick, chlorotic, chloremic, chloranaemic

5 verdigrisy, verdigrised, patinous, patinaed, patinated *or* patinized, aeruginous

45 BLUENESS

nouns

1 **blueness, bluishness**; azureness; **blue, azure**; lividness, lividity; cyanosis

verbs

2 to **blue**, azure

adjectives

3 **blue, bluish**, cerulescent; cyanic, cyaneous, cyanean; cerulean, ceruleous; **azure** (*heraldry*), azurine, azurean, azureous, azured, azure-blue, azure-coloured, azure-tinted; sky-blue, sky-coloured, sky-dyed; light-blue, lightish-blue, light-bluish, pale-blue; dark-blue, deep-blue; navy, navy blue; indigo; royal

blue; peacock-blue, pavonine, pavonian; beryl-blue, berylline; cobalt, cobalt blue; turquoise, turquoise-blue; ultramarine; sapphire, sapphire-blue, sapphirine; livid; cyanotic

46 PURPLENESS

nouns

1 **purpleness, purplishness,** purpliness; **purple; violet;** lividness, lividity

verbs

2 **to purple,** empurple, purpurate (*old*)

adjectives

3 **purple,** purpure (*heraldry*), purpureal, purpureous, purpurean, purpurate (*old*); **purplish,** purply, purplescent; **violet,** violaceous; plum-coloured, plum-purple; amethystine; **lavender,** lavender-blue; lilac; magenta; mauve; mulberry, murrey; orchid; pansy-purple, pansy-violet; raisin-coloured; livid

47 VARIEGATION
diversity of colours

nouns

1 **variegation, multicolour;** parti-colour; medley *or* mixture of colours, rainbow of colours, riot of colour; polychrome, polychromatism; dichromatism, trichromatism, etc; dichroism, trichroism, etc

2 **iridescence,** iridization, irisation, **opalescence,** nacreousness, pearliness, **play of colours *or* light;** light show; moiré pattern, tabby; burelé *or* burelage

3 **spottiness,** maculation, freckliness, speckliness, mottledness, dappleness, dappledness, stippledness, spottedness, dottedness; **fleck, speck, speckle;** freckle; **spot,** dot, polka dot, macula, macule, blotch, splotch, splodge, patch, splash; **mottle, dapple; stipple,** stippling, pointillism, pointillage

4 **check, chequer,** checks, checking, chequerboard, chessboard; **plaid,** tartan; chequer-work, variegated pattern, harlequin, colours in patches, crazy-work, patchwork; parquet, parquetry, marquetry, mosaic, tesserae, tessellation; crazy-paving

5 **stripe,** striping, candy-stripe, pinstripe; barber pole; **streak, streaking;** striation, striature, stria; striola, striga; crack, craze; bar, band, belt, list

6 (*comparisons*) spectrum, rainbow, iris, chameleon, leopard, jaguar, cheetah, ocelot, zebra, barber pole, candy stick, Dalmatian, peacock, butterfly, mother-of-pearl, nacre, tortoise shell, opal, serpentine, chrysotile, antigorite, serpentine marble, marble, ophite, mackerel, mackerel sky, confetti, crazy quilt, patchwork quilt, shot silk, moiré, watered silk, marbled paper, Joseph's coat, harlequin

verbs

7 **to variegate,** motley; parti-colour; polychrome, polychromize; harlequin; **mottle, dapple,** stipple, **fleck,** flake, **speck, speckle,** bespeckle, freckle, **spot,** bespot, dot, sprinkle, spangle, bespangle, pepper, stud, maculate; blotch, splotch; tattoo, stigmatize (*old*); **check, chequer;** tessellate; **stripe, streak,** striate, band, bar, vein; marble, marbleize; tabby

8 **to opalesce,** opalize; iridesce

adjectives

9 **variegated, many-coloured,** many-hued, diverse-coloured, **multicoloured,** multicolour, multicolorous, **varicoloured,** varicolorous, polychrome, polychromic, polychromatic; parti-coloured, parti-colour; of all manner of colours, of all the colours of the rainbow; versicolour, versicoloured, versicolorate, versicolorous; motley, medley (*old*), harlequin; colourful, coloury; daedal; crazy; thunder and lightning; kaleidoscopic, kaleidoscopical; prismatic, prismatical, prismal, spectral; shot, shot through; bicoloured, bicolour, dichromic, dichromatic; tricoloured, tricolour, trichromic, trichromatic; two-colour *or* coloured, three-colour *or* coloured, two-tone *or* toned, etc

10 **iridescent,** iridal, iridial, iridine, iridian; irised, irisated, **rainbowy,** rainbowlike; **opalescent,** opaline, opaloid; nacreous, nacry, *nacré* (*French*), nacred, **pearly,** pearlish, mother-of-pearl; tortoise-shell; peacock-like, pavonine, pavonian; chatoyant; moiré, burelé

11 **chameleonlike,** chameleonic

12 **mottled, motley; pied, piebald,** skewbald, pinto; **dappled,** dapple,
   "Glory be to God for dappled things"—GM HOPKINS; calico (*US*); marbled; clouded; pepper-and-salt

13 **spotted, dotted,** polka-dot, sprinkled, peppered, studded, pocked, pockmarked; **spotty,** dotty, patchy, pocky; **speckled, specked,** speckledy, speckly, specky; **stippled,** pointillé, pointillistic; **flecked,** fleckered; spangled, bespangled; maculate, maculated, macular; punctate, punctated; freckled, frecked, freckly; blotched, blotchy, splotched, splotchy, splodgy; flea-bitten

14 **checked, chequered,** checkedy, check, **plaid,** plaided; tessellated, tessellate, mosaic

15 **striped,** stripy, candy-stripe, pinstripe; **streaked,** streaky; **striated,** striate, striatal, striolate, strigate *or* strigose; barred, banded, listed; veined; **brindle,** brindled, brinded; marbled, marbleized; watered, tabby

48 HEARING

nouns

1 **hearing,** audition; sense of hearing, auditory *or* aural sense, ear; listening, heeding, attention, hushed attention, rapt attention, eager attention; auscultation, aural examination, examination by ear; audibility

2 **audition,** hearing, tryout, call (*informal*), **audience, interview,** conference; attention, favourable attention, ear; **listening,** listening in; eavesdropping, phone-tapping, wiretapping, electronic surveillance, bugging (*informal*)

3 good hearing, refined *or* acute sense of hearing, sensitive ear, nice *or* quick *or* sharp *or* correct ear; **an ear for;** musical ear, ear for music; ear-mindedness; bad ear, no ear, tin ear (*US informal*)

4 **earshot,** earreach, **hearing,** range, auditory range, reach, carrying distance, **sound of one's voice**

5 **listener**, hearer, auditor, audient, hearkener; **eavesdropper**, overhearer, little pitcher with big ears, snoop, snooper, listener-in (*informal*); fly on the wall

6 **audience**, auditory (*old*), **house, congregation**; studio audience, live audience, captive audience, theatregoers, gallery, crowd, house; orchestra, pit; groundling, spectator *see* 917

7 **ear** *see* 2.10, lug *and* lughole (*both Scottish*), auditory apparatus; external ear, **outer ear**; cauliflower ear

8 listening device; **hearing aid**, hard-of-hearing aid; electronic hearing aid, transistor hearing aid; vacuum-tube hearing aid; ear trumpet; amplifier, speaking trumpet, megaphone; stethoscope

9 (*science of hearing*) otology; otoscopy, auriscopy; otoneurology, otopathy, otography, otoplasty, otolaryngology, otorhinolaryngology; acoustic phonetics, phonetics *see* 524.14; auriscope, otoscope; audiometer

verbs

10 **to listen**, hark, **hearken, heed, hear, attend**, give attention, **give ear**, give *or* lend an ear, bend an ear; **listen to**, listen at (*informal*), attend to, give a hearing to, give audience to, sit in on; **listen in**; **eavesdrop**, phone-tap, wiretap, tap, intercept, bug (*informal*); **keep one's ears open**, be all ears (*informal*), listen with both ears, strain one's ears; prick up the ears, cock the ears; hang on the lips of, hang on every word; hear out; auscultate, examine by ear

11 **to hear**, catch, get (*informal*), take in; **overhear**; **hear of**, hear tell of (*informal*); get an earful (*informal*), get wind of; have an ear for

12 to be heard, **fall on the ear**, sound in the ear, catch *or* reach the ear, come to one's ear, register, make an impression, get across (*informal*); **have one's ear**, reach, contact, get to; make oneself heard, get through to, gain a hearing, reach the ear of; ring in the ear; caress the ear; assault *or* split *or* assail the ear

adjectives

13 **auditory**, audio, audile, **hearing, aural**, auricular, otic; audio-visual; audible; otological, otoscopic, otopathic, etc; acoustic, acoustical, phonic

14 **listening, attentive**, open-eared, **all ears** (*informal*)

15 **eared**, auriculate; big-eared, cauliflower-eared, crop-eared, dog-eared, droop-eared, flap-eared, flop-eared, lop-eared, long-eared, mouse-eared, prick-eared; **sharp-eared**; ear-minded

exclamations

16 **hark!**, hark ye!, hear ye!, hearken!, hear!, oyez!, hear ye, hear ye!, now hear this!, list!, **listen!**, listen up! (*US & Canadian*), attend!, attention!, hist!, whisht!, psst!, yo!

49 DEAFNESS

nouns

1 **deafness, hardness of hearing**, dull hearing, deaf ears,

"ears more deaf than adders"—S<small>HAKESPEARE</small>; **stone-deafness**; nerve-deafness; mind deafness, word deafness; **tone deafness**; impaired hearing, hearing *or* auditory impairment; loss of hearing, **hearing loss**; **deaf-muteness**, deaf-mutism, surdimutism (*old*)

2 **the deaf**, the hard-of-hearing; **deaf-mute**, surdo-mute (*old*), deaf-and-dumb person; lip reader

3 deaf-and-dumb alphabet, manual alphabet, finger alphabet; dactylology, sign language; lip reading, oral method

verbs

4 **to be deaf**; have no ears, be earless; lose one's hearing, suffer hearing loss *or* impairment, go deaf; shut *or* stop *or* close one's ears, **turn a deaf ear**; fall on deaf ears

5 **to deafen, stun**, split the ears *or* eardrums

adjectives

6 **deaf, hard-of-hearing**, dull *or* thick of hearing, deaf-eared, dull-eared; surd (*old*); deafened, stunned; **stone-deaf**, deaf as a stone, deaf as a door *or* a doorknob *or* doornail, **deaf as a post**, deaf as an adder,

"like the deaf adder that stoppeth her ear"—B<small>IBLE</small>; **unhearing**; earless; word-deaf; tone-deaf; half-deaf, quasi-deaf; **deaf and dumb**, deaf-mute

50 SOUND

nouns

1 **sound**, sonance, acoustic, acoustical *or* acoustic phenomenon; auditory phenomenon *or* stimulus, auditory effect; noise; ultrasound; sound wave, sound propagation; sound intensity, sound intensity level, amplitude, loudness *see* 53; phone, speech sound *see* 524.13

2 **tone, pitch, frequency**, audio frequency *or* AF; monotone, monotony, tonelessness; overtone, harmonic, partial, partial tone; fundamental tone, fundamental; intonation *see* 524.7

3 **timbre**, tonality, **tone quality**, tone colour, colour, colouring, clang colour *or* tint, *Klangfarbe* (*German*)

4 **sounding**, sonation, sonification

5 **acoustics**, phonics, radioacoustics; acoustical engineer, acoustician

6 **sonics**; subsonics; **supersonics**, ultrasonics; speed of sound *see* 174.2; sound barrier, transonic barrier, sonic barrier *or* wall; sonic boom

7 (*sound unit*) **decibel**, bel, phon

8 **loudspeaker, speaker**, dynamic speaker; speaker unit, speaker system; crossover network; voice coil; cone, diaphragm; acoustical network; horn (*informal*); **headphone, earphone**, stereo headset, headset

9 **microphone**, mike (*informal*); radiomicrophone; concealed microphone, **bug** (*informal*)

10 **audio amplifier, amplifier, amp** (*informal*); **preamplifier**, preamp (*informal*), graphic equalizer

11 sound reproduction system, audio sound system; **high-fidelity** system *or* hi-fi (*informal*); **record player**, gramophone, phonograph; **jukebox**, nickelodeon; radiogram, radio-phonograph combination, stereogram; midi system, music centre;

personal stereo, Walkman (*trademark*); ghetto blaster; monophonic *or* monaural system, **mono** (*informal*), stereophonic *or* binaural system, stereo (*informal*); four-channel stereo system, discrete four-channel system, derived four-channel system, quadraphonic sound system; multitrack player *or* recorder *or* sound system; **pickup** *or* cartridge, magnetic pickup *or* cartridge, ceramic pickup *or* cartridge, crystal pickup, photoelectric pickup; stylus, needle; tone arm; turntable, transcription turntable, record changer, changer; **public-address system** *or* PA *or* PA system, Tannoy (*trademark*); sound truck; loudhailer, bullhorn (*US & Canadian*); intercommunication system, **intercom** (*informal*), squawk box *and* bitch box (*both US informal*); **tape recorder**, tape deck, cassette *or* audio-cassette player, cassette *or* audio-cassette recorder; compact disc *or* CD player; CD-video; hi-fi fan *or* freak (*informal*), audiophile

12 **record, phonograph record,** disc, wax, long-playing record *or* LP; transcription, electrical transcription, digital transcription, digital recording; **recording**, wire recording, tape recording; digital disc; tape, tape cassette, cassette, musicassette; tape cartridge, cartridge; digital audio tape *or* DAT; compact disk *or* CD; video-cassette recorder *or* VCR

13 **audio distortion, distortion;** scratching, shredding, hum, 60-cycle hum, rumble, hissing, howling, blurping, blooping, woomping, fluttering, flutter, wow, wow-wows, squeals, whistles, birdies, motorboating; feedback; static *see* 1033.21

verbs

14 **to sound,** make a sound *or* noise, give forth *or* emit a sound; noise; speak *see* 524.20; resound; **record,** tape, tape-record; prerecord; play back

adjectives

15 **sounding,** sonorous, soniferous; **sounded;** tonal; monotone, monotonic, toneless, droning

16 **audible,** hearable; **distinct, clear,** plain, definite, articulate; distinctive, contrastive; high-fidelity, hi-fi (*informal*)

17 **acoustic, acoustical,** phonic, **sonic;** subsonic, supersonic, ultrasonic, hypersonic; transonic *or* transsonic, faster than sound

adverbs

18 **audibly, aloud,** out, **out loud;** distinctly, clearly, plainly

51 SILENCE

nouns

1 **silence,** silentness, **soundlessness,** noiselessness, **stillness,**
"lucid stillness"—T S Eliot, **quietness,** quietude, quiescence *see* 173, **quiet, still,** peace, whisht (*Scottish & Irish*), **hush,** mum; lull, rest; golden silence; deathlike *or* tomblike silence, solemn *or* awful silence, the quiet *or* silence of the grave *or* the tomb; hush *or* dead of night, dead; tacitness, taciturnity; inaudibility; tranquillity

2 **muteness, mutism, dumbness,** voicelessness, tonguelessness; speechlessness, wordlessness; inarticulateness; anaudia, aphasia, aphonia; hysterical mutism; deaf-muteness *see* 49.1; standing mute, refusal to speak, stonewalling (*informal*), the code of silence *or* omertà (*Italian*), keeping one's lip buttoned (*informal*)

3 **mute,** dummy; deaf-mute *see* 49.2

4 **silencer, muffler,** muffle, **mute,** baffle *or* baffler, quietener, cushion; **damper,** damp; dampener; **soft pedal,** sordine, sourdine, *sordino* (*Italian*); hushcloth, silence cloth; **gag, muzzle;** antiknock; **soundproofing,** acoustic tile, sound-absorbing material, sound-proofing insulation

verbs

5 **to be silent,** keep silent *or* silence, **keep still *or* quiet; keep one's mouth shut, hold one's tongue,** keep one's tongue between one's teeth, bite one's tongue, put a bridle on one's tongue, seal one's lips, shut *or* close one's mouth, muzzle oneself, **not breathe a word,** forswear speech *or* speaking, **keep mum, hold one's peace,** not let a word escape one, not utter a word, not open one's mouth; make no sign, keep to oneself; not have a word to say, be mute, stand mute; choke up, have one's words stick in one's throat

6 (*informal terms*) **to shut up,** keep one's trap shut, button up, button one's lip, save one's breath, shut one's face, put a sock in it, dummy up, clam up, close up like a clam, not let out a peep, say nothing, not say 'boo', play dumb, stonewall

7 **to fall silent, hush,** quiet, quieten, quiesce, **quiet down,** pipe down (*informal*), check one's speech

8 **to silence, put to silence, hush,** hush one up, hush-hush, **shush,** quiet, quieten, **still; soft-pedal,** put on the soft pedal; squash, squelch (*informal*), stifle, choke, choke off, throttle, put the kibosh on (*informal*), put the lid on *and* shut down on (*both informal*), put the damper on (*informal*), **gag, muzzle,** muffle, stop one's mouth, cut one short; strike dumb *or* mute, dumbfound; tonguetie

9 **to muffle, mute, dull, soften, deaden,** quietize, cushion, baffle, damp, **dampen,** deafen; subdue, stop, tone down, **soft-pedal,** put on the soft pedal

adjectives

10 **silent, still,** stilly, **quiet,** quiescent *see* 173.12, **hushed, soundless,** noiseless; echoless; **inaudible,** subaudible, below the limen *or* threshold of hearing, unhearable; quiet as a mouse, mousy; silent as a post *or* stone,
"noiseless as fear in a wide wilderness"—Keats, "silent as the shadows"—Coleridge, so quiet that one might hear a feather *or* pin drop; silent as the grave *or* tomb, still as death,
"hush as death"—Shakespeare; **unsounded, unvoiced,** unvocalized, unpronounced, unuttered, unarticulated

11 **tacit, wordless, unspoken,** unuttered, unexpressed, unsaid; **implicit** *see* 519.8

12 **mute, mum, dumb,** voiceless, tongueless, **speechless,** wordless, breathless, at a loss for words, choked up; inarticulate; **tongue-tied,** dumbstruck, dumbstricken, stricken dumb, **dumbfounded**; anaudic, aphasic, aphonic

adverbs

13 silently, in silence, **quietly, soundlessly,** noiselessly; inaudibly

exclamations

14 **silence!, hush!, shush!, sh!,** sh-sh!, whist! *or* whish! (*both informal*), whisht! (*Scottish & Irish*), peace!, pax!, *tais toi!* (*French*), **be quiet!,** be silent!, be still!, **keep still!,** keep quiet!, quiet!, quiet please!, soft!, belay that! *or* there!, stow it!; **hold your tongue!,** hold your jaw! *or* lip!, **shut up!** (*informal*), **shut your mouth!** (*informal*), save your breath!, not another word!, not another peep out of you!, mum!, mum's the word!; hush your mouth!, shut your trap!, shut your face!, button your lip!, pipe down!, clam up!, dry up!, can it! (*US*)

52 FAINTNESS OF SOUND

nouns

1 **faintness, lowness, softness,** gentleness, subduedness, dimness, feebleness, weakness; indistinctness, unclearness, flatness; subaudibility; decrescendo

2 muffled tone, veiled voice, *voce velata* (*Italian*), covered tone; **mutedness; dullness, deadness,** flatness

3 **thud,** dull thud; **thump,** flump, crump, clop, clump, clunk, plunk, tunk, plump, bump; pad, pat; **patter,** pitter-patter, pit-a-pat; **tap,** rap, **click,** tick, flick, pop; tinkle, clink, chink, tingaling

4 **murmur,** murmuring, murmuration; **mutter,** muttering; **mumble,** mumbling; soft voice, low voice, small *or* little voice, "still small voice"—BIBLE; **undertone,** underbreath, bated breath; susurration, susurrus; **whisper,** whispering, stage whisper, breathy voice; breath, sigh, exhalation, aspiration

5 **ripple, splash,** ripple of laughter, ripple of applause; titter, chuckle

6 **rustle,** rustling, froufrou, "a little noiseless noise among the leaves"—KEATS

7 **hum, humming,** thrumming, low rumbling, booming, bombilation, bombination, **droning, buzzing,** whizzing, whirring, purring

8 **sigh, sighing, moaning,** sobbing, whining, soughing

verbs

9 **to steal** *or* **waft on the ear,** melt in the air, float in the air

10 **to murmur, mutter, mumble,** mussitate (*old*); coo; susurrate; **lower one's voice, speak under one's breath; whisper,** whisper in the ear; breathe, sigh, aspirate

11 **to ripple, babble, burble,** bubble, **gurgle,** guggle, **purl, trill;** lap, plash, **splash,** swish, swash, slosh, wash

12 **to rustle,** crinkle; **swish,** whish

13 **to hum,** thrum, boom, bombilate, bombinate, **drone, buzz,** whiz, whir, burr, birr (*Scottish*), purr

14 **to sigh, moan, sob, whine,** sough; **whimper**

15 **to thud, thump, patter,** clop, clump, clunk, plunk, flump, crump; pad, pat; **tap,** rap, **click,** tick, tick away; pop; tinkle, clink, chink

adjectives

16 **faint, low, soft, gentle, subdued, dim, feeble, weak,** faint-sounding, low-sounding, soft-sounding; soft-voiced, low-voiced, faint-voiced, weak-voiced; murmured, whispered; half-heard, scarcely heard; distant; indistinct, unclear; barely audible, subaudible, near the limit *or* threshold of hearing; piano, pianissimo; decrescendo

17 **muffled, muted, softened, dampened,** damped, **smothered,** stifled, bated, dulled, deadened, subdued; **dull, dead, flat,** *sordo* (*Italian*)

18 **murmuring,** murmurous, murmurish, **muttering, mumbling;** susurrous, susurrant; **whispering,** whisper, whispery; **rustling**

19 **rippling, babbling, burbling,** bubbling, **gurgling,** guggling, **purling, trilling;** lapping, splashing, plashing, sloshing, swishing

20 **humming,** thrumming, **droning,** booming, bombinating, **buzzing,** whizzing, whirring, purring, burring, birring (*Scottish*)

adverbs

21 **faintly, softly,** gently, subduedly, hushedly, dimly, feebly, weakly, low; piano, pianissimo; *sordo* and *sordamente* (*both Italian*), *à la sourdine* (*French*)

22 **in an undertone,** *sotto voce* (*Italian*), **under one's breath,** with bated breath, in a whisper, in a stage whisper, between the teeth; aside, in an aside; out of earshot

53 LOUDNESS

nouns

1 **loudness,** intensity, volume, amplitude, fullness; sonorousness, sonority; surge of sound, surge, crescendo, swell, swelling; loudishness

2 **noisiness,** noisefulness, **uproariousness,** racketiness, tumultuousness, thunderousness, clamorousness, clangorousness, boisterousness, obstreperousness; vociferousness see 59.5

3 **noise,** loud noise, **blast** see 56.3, tintamarre, **racket, din, clamour;** outcry, **uproar,** hue and cry, noise and shouting; howl; clangour, clatter, clap, jangle, rattle; roar, thunder, thunderclap see 56.5; **crash, boom,** sonic boom; **bang,** percussion; brouhaha, **tumult, hubbub,** bobbery (*India*); fracas, **brawl,** commotion, drunken brawl, kerfuffle (*informal*); **pandemonium,** bedlam, hell *or* bedlam let loose; charivari, shivaree (*informal*); discord see 61

4 (*informal terms for noisy occasions*) row, flap, hullabaloo, shindy, donnybrook, free-for-all, shemozzle, rumble, rhubarb (*US & Canadian*), dustup, rumpus, ruckus, ruction, hell broke loose, hoo-ha

5 **blare, blast,** shriek see 58.4, peal; **toot,** tootle, hoot, **honk,** beep, blat, trumpet; bay, bray; **whistle,** tweedle (*US*), squeal; trumpet call, trumpet blast *or* blare, sound *or* flourish of trumpets, Gabriel's

trumpet *or* horn, **fanfare**, tarantara, tantara, tantarara; tattoo; taps

6 **noisemaker**; bullroarer, whizzer, snapper, cricket, clapper, clack, clacker, cracker; firecracker; rattle, rattlebox; horn, hooter, Klaxon (*trademark*); whistle, steam whistle, siren; boiler room, boiler factory; loud-hailer, bullhorn (*US informal*)

verbs

7 **to din; boom,** thunder *see* 56.9; **resound,** ring, peal, ring *or* resound in the ears, din in the ear, **blast the ear,** pierce *or* split *or* rend the ears, burst *or* rend *or* split the eardrums, split one's head; **deafen,** stun; blast *see* 56.8, **bang, crash** *see* 56.6; **rend the air** *or* skies *or* firmament, rock the sky, fill the air, make the welkin ring; shake *or* rattle the windows; awake *or* startle the echoes, set the echoes ringing, awake the dead; surge, swell, rise, crescendo; **shout** *see* 59.6

8 **to drown out,** outshout, outroar, shout down, overpower, overwhelm; jam

9 **to be noisy, make a noise** *or* **racket,** raise a clamour *or* din *or* hue and cry, noise, racket, **clamour,** roar, clangour; brawl, row, rumpus; **cause an uproar,** kick up a dust *or* racket, kick up *or* raise a hullabaloo, raise the roof, raise Cain, howl like all the devils of hell, raise the devil, raise hell, whoop it up, maffick; not be able to hear oneself think

10 **to blare,** blast; shriek *see* 58.8; **toot,** tootle, hoot, sound, peal, wind, blow, blat; pipe, trumpet, bugle, clarion; bay, bell, bray; **whistle,** tweedle (*US*), squeal; **honk,** honk *or* sound *or* blow the horn, beep; sound taps, sound a tattoo

adjectives

11 **loud,** loud-sounding, forte, fortissimo; loudish; **resounding,** ringing, plangent, pealing; full, sonorous; **deafening,** ear-deafening, **ear-splitting,** head-splitting, ear-rending, ear-piercing, piercing; **thunderous,** thundering, tonitruous, tonitruant; **crashing, booming** *see* 56.12; window-rattling, earthshaking, enough to wake the dead *or* the seven sleepers

12 **loud-voiced, loudmouthed,** fullmouthed, full-throated, big-voiced, clarion-voiced, trumpet-voiced, trumpet-tongued, brazen-mouthed, **stentorian,** stentorious, stentorophonic, like Stentor, Boanergean

13 **noisy,** noiseful, rackety, clattery, clangorous, clanging, **clamorous,** clamant, blatant, blaring, brassy, brazen, blatting; uproarious, **tumultuous,** turbulent, blustering, brawling, **boisterous,** rip-roaring, rowdy, mafficking, strepitous, strepitant, obstreperous; vociferous *see* 59.10

adverbs

14 **loudly, aloud,** loud, lustily; **boomingly, thunderously, thunderingly; noisily,** uproariously; ringingly, resoundingly; with a loud voice, at the top of one's voice, at the pitch of one's breath, in full cry, with one wild yell, with a whoop and a hurrah; forte, *fortemente* (*Italian*), fortissimo

54 RESONANCE

nouns

1 **resonance, resoundingness, sonorousness,** sonority, plangency, **vibrancy;** mellowness, richness, fullness; deepness, lowness, bassness; hollowness; **snore,** snoring

2 **reverberation, resounding; rumble,** rumbling, thunder, thundering, boom, booming, growl, growling, grumble, grumbling, reboation; rebound, resound, **echo,** reecho

3 **ringing,** tintinnabulation, **pealing, chiming, tinkling,** tingling, **jingling,** dinging, donging; **tolling,** knelling; clangour, clanking, clanging; **ring, peal, chime; toll,** knell; **tinkle,** tingle, **jingle,** dingle, ding, dingdong, ding-a-ling, ting-a-ling; clink, tink, ting, ping, chink; clank, clang; jangle, jingle-jangle; campanology, bell ringing, change ringing, peal ringing; tinnitus, ringing of *or* in the ear

4 **bell** (*see list*), tintinnabulum; **gong,** triangle, **chimes,** door chimes, clock chimes, Westminster chimes; clapper, tongue; carillon, set of bells

5 **resonator,** resounder, reverberator; **sounding board,** sound box; resonant chamber *or* cavity; echo chamber; loud pedal, damper pedal, sustaining pedal

verbs

6 **to resonate,** reverb, **vibrate,** pulse, throb; snore

7 **to reverberate, resound,** sound, **rumble,** roll, boom, echo, reecho, rebound, bounce back, be reflected, be sent back, echo back, send back, return

8 **to ring,** tintinnabulate, **peal,** sound; **toll,** knell, sound a knell; **chime;** gong; **tinkle,** tingle, **jingle,** ding, dingdong, dong; clink, tink, ting, chink; clank, clang, clangour; jangle, jinglejangle; ring on the air; ring changes *or* peals; ring in the ear

adjectives

9 **resonant, reverberant, vibrant, sonorous,** plangent, rolling; mellow, rich, full; resonating, reverberating, echoing, reechoing, vibrating, pulsing, throbbing

10 **deep,** deep-toned, deep-pitched, deep-sounding, deepmouthed, deep-echoing; **hollow, sepulchral;** low, low-pitched, low-toned, grave, heavy; **bass;** baritone; contralto

11 **reverberating,** reverberant, reverberatory, reboant, **resounding,** rebounding, repercussive, sounding; **rumbling,** thundering, booming, growling; echoing, reechoing, echoic; undamped; persistent, lingering

12 **ringing, pealing, tolling,** belling, sounding, chiming; **tinkling,** tinkly, tingling, **jingling,** dinging; tintinnabular *or* tintinnabulary *or* tintinnabulous; campanological

13 **bells**

alarm bell	doorbell
Angelus bell	fire bell
breakfast bell	fog bell
call bell	gong bell
chiming bell	hand bell
church bell	harness bell
cowbell	hour bell
dinner bell *or* gong *or* chimes	jingle bell
	minute bell

news bell	sheepbell
night bell	shop bell
passing bell *or* death bell *or* end bell *or* mortbell	shriving bell
	signal bell
Sanctus bell *or* sacring bell *or* saunce *or* saucing bell	sleigh bell
	telephone bell
	watch bell
school bell	

55 REPEATED SOUNDS

nouns

1 staccato; **drum, thrum, beat, pound, roll;** drumming, tom-tom, beating, pounding, thumping; **throb,** throbbing, pulsation *see* 915.3; **palpitation,** flutter; sputter, spatter, splutter; **patter, pitterpatter,** pit-a-pat; rub-a-dub, rattattoo, rataplan, rata-tat, rat-tat, rat-tat-tat, tat-tat, tat-tat-tat; **tattoo,** devil's tattoo, ruff, ruffle; **drumbeat,** drum music; drumfire, barrage

2 **clicking, ticking, tick, ticktock,** ticktack, ticktick

3 **rattle,** rattling, ruckle (*informal*); **clatter,** clitter, **clitterclatter, chatter,** clack, clacket (*informal*); racket *see* 53.3

verbs

4 **to drum, thrum, beat, pound, thump, thump out,** roll; **palpitate,** flutter; sputter, splatter, splutter; patter, pitter-patter, go pit-a-pat *or* pitter-patter; **throb,** pulsate *see* 915.12; beat *or* sound a tattoo, beat a devil's tattoo, ruffle, beat a ruffle

5 **to tick, ticktock,** ticktack, tick away

6 **to rattle,** ruckle (*informal*); **clatter,** clitter, **chatter,** clack; rattle around, clatter about

adjectives

7 staccato; **drumming, thrumming, beating, pounding, thumping; throbbing;** palpitant, fluttering; sputtering, spattering, spluttering; clicking, ticking

8 **rattly,** rattling, chattering, **clattery,** clattering

56 EXPLOSIVE NOISE

nouns

1 **report, crash, crack, clap, bang,** wham, slam, clash, burst; **knock, rap, tap,** smack, whack, thwack, whop, whap, whomp (*US*), splat, crump (*informal*), bump, slap, flap, flop

2 **snap, crack;** click, clack; **crackle,** snapping, cracking, crackling, crepitation, decrepitation, sizzling, spitting; rale

3 **detonation, blast, explosion,** fulmination, **discharge, burst, bang, pop, crack,** bark; **shot,** gunshot; volley, salvo, fusillade

4 **boom,** booming, cannonade, **peal, rumble,** grumble, growl, **roll, roar**

5 **thunder,** thundering, clap *or* crash *or* peal of thunder, **thunderclap,** thunderpeal, thundercrack, thunderstroke;

"heaven's artillery", "the thunder, that deep and dreadful organ-pipe", "dread rattling thunder", "deep, dread-bolted thunder"—ALL SHAKESPEARE, "the crashing of the chariot of God"—WILLIAM CULLEN BRYANT,

"dry sterile thunder without rain"—T S ELIOT; thunderstorm *see* 316.3; Thor *or* Donar, Jupiter Tonans, Indra

verbs

6 **to crack, clap, crash,** wham, slam, **bang,** clash; **knock, rap, tap,** smack, whack, thwack, whop, whap, whomp (*US*), splat, crump (*informal*), bump, slap, flap

7 **to snap, crack;** click, clack; **crackle,** crepitate, decrepitate; spit

8 **to blast, detonate, explode, discharge, burst,** go off, **bang, pop, crack,** bark, fulminate; burst on the ear

9 **to boom, thunder, peal, rumble,** grumble, growl, roll, roar

adjectives

10 **snapping, cracking, crackling,** crackly, crepitant

11 **banging,** crashing, bursting, exploding, explosive, blasting, cracking, popping; knocking, rapping, tapping; slapping, flapping

12 **thundering, thunderous,** thundery, fulminating, tonitruous, tonitruant, thunderlike; **booming,** pealing, rumbling, rolling, roaring; cannonading, volleying

exclamations

13 bang!, boom!, wham!, whammo!, blam!, kerboom!, kerblam!, kapow!, zap!

57 SIBILATION
hissing sounds

nouns

1 sibilation, sibilance *or* sibilancy; **hiss, hissing,** siss, sissing, white noise; hush, hushing, shush, shushing; sizz, sizzle, sizzling; fizz, fizzle, fizzling, effervescing, effervescence; swish, whish, whoosh; whiz, buzz, zip; siffle; wheeze, *râle* (*French*), rhonchus; whistle, whistling; sneeze, sneezing, sternutation; snort; snore, stertor; **sniff,** sniffle, snuff, snuffle; spit, sputter, splutter; squash, squish, squelch; sigmatism, lisp; assibilation; frication, frictional rustling

verbs

2 to sibilate; **hiss,** siss; hush, shush; sizzle, sizz; fizzle, fizz, effervesce; whiz, buzz, zip; swish, whish, whoosh; whistle; wheeze; sneeze; snort; snore; sniff, sniffle, snuff, snuffle; spit, sputter, splutter; squash, squish, squelch; lisp; assibilate

adjectives

3 **sibilant; hissing,** hushing, sissing; sizzling, fizzling, effervescent; **sniffing,** sniffling, snuffling; snoring; wheezing, wheezy

58 STRIDENCY
harsh and shrill sounds

nouns

1 **stridency,** stridence, stridor, stridulousness, stridulation; **shrillness,** highness, sharpness, acuteness, arguteness; **screechiness, squeakiness,** creakiness, reediness, pipingness

2 **raucousness, harshness,** raucity; discord, cacophony *see* 61.1; coarseness, rudeness, ugliness, roughness, gruffness; **raspiness,** scratchiness, scrapiness, **hoarseness,** huskiness, dryness; stertorousness; gutturalness, gutturalism, gutturality, thickness, throatiness; cracked voice

3 **rasp, scratch, scrape,** grind; crunch, craunch, scranch (*old*), scrunch, crump; burr, chirr, buzz; snore; **jangle, clash, jar;** clank, clang, clangour, twang, twanging; blare, blat, bray; croak, caw, cackle; belch; growl, snarl; grumble, groan

4 **screech, shriek, scream, squeal,** shrill, keen, squeak, squawk, skirl, screak, skreak (*informal*), creak; **whistle,** wolf-whistle; pipe; **whine, wail, howl,** ululation, yammer; vibrato; waul, caterwaul

5 (*insect sounds*) **stridulation,** cricking, creaking; crick, creak, chirp, chirping, chirrup

6 (*high voices*) soprano, mezzo-soprano, treble; tenor, alto; male alto, countertenor; head register, head voice, head tone, falsetto

verbs

7 **to stridulate,** crick, creak, chirp, chirrup

8 **to screech, shriek,** screak, skreak (*informal*), creak, squeak, squawk, **scream, squeal,** shrill, keen; **whistle,** wolf-whistle; pipe, skirl; **whine,** wail, howl, yammer, ululate; waul, caterwaul

9 (*sound harshly*) **to jangle, clash, jar;** blare, blat, bray; croak, caw, cackle; belch; burr, chirr, buzz; snore; growl, snarl; grumble, groan; clank, clang, clangour; twang

10 **to grate, rasp, scratch, scrape,** grind; crunch, craunch, scranch (*old*), scrunch, crump

11 **to grate on,** jar on, grate upon the ear, jar upon the ear, offend the ear, pierce *or* split *or* rend the ears, harrow *or* lacerate the ear, **set the teeth on edge, get on one's nerves,** jangle *or* wrack the nerves, make one's skin crawl

adjectives

12 **strident,** stridulant, stridulous; strident-voiced

13 **high,** high-pitched, high-toned, high-sounding; treble, soprano, mezzo-soprano, tenor, alto, falsetto, countertenor

14 **shrill, thin, sharp,** acute, argute, keen, keening, **piercing,** penetrating, ear-piercing; **screechy,** screeching, shrieky, shrieking, **squeaky,** squeaking, screaky, creaky, creaking; whistling, piping, skirling, reedy; whining, wailing, howling, ululating, ululant; vibrato

15 **raucous,** raucid, **harsh,** harsh-sounding; coarse, rude, rough, gruff, ragged; **hoarse, husky,** cracked, dry; **guttural,** thick, throaty, croaky, croaking; choked, strangled; squawky, **squawking;** brassy, brazen, tinny, metallic; stertorous

16 **grating, jarring,** grinding; **jangling,** jangly; **rasping,** raspy; scratching, scratchy; scraping, scrapy

59 CRY, CALL

nouns

1 **cry, call, shout, yell,** hoot; halloo, hollo, yoo-hoo; **whoop, holler** (*informal*); **cheer, hurrah; howl,** yowl, yawl (*informal*); bawl, bellow, roar; **scream,**

shriek, screech, squeal, squall, caterwaul; yelp, yap, yammer, yawp, bark; war cry, battle cry, war whoop, rallying cry

2 **exclamation,** ejaculation, outburst, blurt, ecphonesis; expletive

3 hunting cry; tallyho, yoicks (*old*), view halloo

4 **outcry, vociferation, clamour;** hullabaloo, hubbub, brouhaha, **uproar** *see* 53.3; **hue and cry**

5 vociferousness, vociferance, clamorousness, blatancy; noisiness *see* 53.2

verbs

6 **to cry, call, shout, yell, holler** (*informal*), hoot; hail, halloo, hollo; **whoop; cheer** *see* 116.6; **howl,** yowl, yammer, yawl (*informal*); squawk, yawp; **bawl, bellow, roar,** roar *or* bellow like a bull; cry *or* yell *or* scream bloody murder *or* blue murder; **scream, shriek,** screech, squeal, squall, waul, caterwaul; yelp, yap, bark

7 **to exclaim,** give an exclamation, ejaculate, burst out, blurt, blurt out, jerk out, spout out; stammer out

8 **to vociferate,** outcry, **cry out,** call out, bellow out, yell out, holler out (*informal*), shout out, sing out; sound off (*informal*), pipe up, **clamour,** make *or* raise a clamour; make an outcry, **raise a hue and cry,** make an uproar

9 to cry aloud, raise *or* lift up the voice, give voice *or* tongue, shout *or* cry *or* thunder at the top of one's voice, split the throat *or* lungs, strain the voice *or* throat, rend the air

adjectives

10 **vociferous,** vociferant, vociferating; **clamorous; blatant;** obstreperous, brawling; **noisy;** crying, shouting, **yelling, hollering** (*informal*), **bawling,** screaming; yelping, yapping, yappy, yammering; loud-voiced, loudmouthed, openmouthed, stentorian, Boanergean

11 **exclamatory,** ejaculatory, blurting

60 ANIMAL SOUNDS

nouns

1 animal noise; **call, cry;** mating call *or* cry; grunt, howl, bark, howling, waul, caterwaul, ululation, barking; birdcall, note, woodnote, clang; stridulation *see* 58.5; dawn chorus

verbs

2 to cry, call; **howl,** yowl, yawp, yawl (*informal*), ululate; wail, whine, pule; **squeal,** squall, scream, screech, screak, squeak; troat; **roar; bellow,** blare, **bawl; moo,** low; **bleat,** blate, blat; **bray; whinny, neigh,** whicker, nicker; **bay,** bay at the moon, bell; **bark,** latrate (*old*), give voice *or* tongue; **yelp, yap,** yip; **mew,** mewl, **meow,** miaow, waul, caterwaul

3 **to grunt,** oink; **snort**

4 **to growl, snarl,** grumble, gnarl, snap; hiss, spit

5 (*birds*) **to warble, sing,** carol, call; pipe, whistle; **trill,** chirr, roll; **twitter,** tweet, twit, chatter, chitter; **chirp,** chirrup, chirk, **cheep,** peep, pip; **quack,** honk, cronk; **croak, caw; squawk,** scold; **crow,** cock-a-doodle-doo; **cackle,** gaggle, gabble, guggle, cluck, clack, chuck; **gobble**; **hoot**, hoo; **coo**; cuckoo; drum

adjectives

6 **howling**, yowling, crying, wailing, whining, puling, bawling, ululant, blatant; lowing, mugient

61 DISCORD
dissonant sounds

nouns

1 **discord**, discordance *or* discordancy, **dissonance** *or* dissonancy, diaphony, **cacophony**; stridor; **inharmoniousness**, unharmoniousness, disharmony, inharmony; **unmelodiousness**, unmusicalness, unmusicality, untunefulness, tunelessness; atonality, atonalism; flatness, sharpness, sourness (*informal*); dissonant chord, wolf; false note, sour note (*informal*), clinker (*informal*), off note; cipher; wolf-tone

2 **clash, jangle, jar**; **noise**, mere noise, confusion *or* conflict *or* jarring *or* jostling of sounds; Babel, witches' *or* devils' chorus; harshness *see* 58.2; clamour *see* 53.3

verbs

3 to sound *or* strike *or* hit a sour note (*informal*), hit a clinker (*US informal*); not carry a tune; **clash, jar, jangle**, conflict, jostle; grate *see* 58.10, 11; untune, unstring

adjectives

4 **dissonant, discordant, cacophonous**, absonant (*old*), disconsonant, diaphonic; strident, shrill, harsh, raucous, grating *see* 58.16; **inharmonious**, unharmonious, disharmonious, disharmonic, inharmonic; **unmelodious**, immelodious, nonmelodious; **unmusical**, musicless, untuneful, tuneless; untunable, untuned, atonal; cracked, **out of tune**, out of tone, out of pitch; **off-key, off-tone, off-pitch**, off; flat, sharp, **sour** (*informal*); "above the pitch, out of tune, and off the hinges"— RABELAIS, "like sweet bells jangled, out of tune and harsh"—SHAKESPEARE

5 **clashing, jarring, jangling**, jangly, confused, conflicting, jostling, warring, ajar; **harsh, grating** *see* 58.16

62 TASTE
sense of taste

nouns

1 **taste**, gust (*old*), goût (*French*); **flavour**, sapor; **smack, tang**; **savour, relish**, sapidity; palate, tongue, tooth, stomach; taste in the mouth; sweetness, sourness, bitterness, bittersweetness, saltiness; aftertaste; savouriness *see* 63

2 **sip, sup, lick, bite**

3 tinge, soupçon, hint *see* 248.4

4 **sample, specimen, taste**, taster, little bite, little smack; example *see* 785.2

5 taste bud *or* bulb *or* goblet, taste *or* gustatory cell, taste hair; **tongue**, lingua; **palate**

6 **tasting, savouring**, gustation

verbs

7 **to taste**, taste of, sample; **savour**, savour of; sip, sup (*informal*), roll on the tongue; lick; smack

adjectives

8 **gustatory**, gustative; tastable, gustable (*old*)

9 **flavoured**, flavorous, flavoury, sapid, saporous, saporific; savoury, flavourful *see* 63.9; sweet, sour, bitter, bittersweet, salt

10 **lingual**, glossal; **tonguelike**, linguiform, lingulate

63 SAVOURINESS

nouns

1 **savouriness, palatableness**, palatability, **tastiness**, toothsomeness, goodness, good taste, right taste, **deliciousness**, gustatory delightfulness, scrumptiousness *and* yumminess (*both informal*), lusciousness, delectability, **flavourfulness**, flavoursomeness, flavorousness, flavouriness, good flavour, fine flavour, sapidity; full flavour, full-bodied flavour; gourmet quality; succulence, juiciness

2 **savour, relish, zest, gusto**, goût (*French*)

3 **flavouring, flavour**, flavourer; **seasoning**, seasoner, **relish, condiment, spice**, condiments

verbs

4 **to taste good**, tickle *or* flatter *or* delight the palate, tempt *or* whet the appetite, make one's mouth water, melt in one's mouth

5 **to savour, relish**, like, love, be fond of, be partial to, enjoy, delight in, have a soft spot for, appreciate; smack the lips; do justice to; taste *see* 62.7

6 **to savour of, taste of, smack of**, have a relish of, have the flavour of, taste like

7 **to flavour**, savour; **season**, salt, pepper, **spice**, sauce

adjectives

8 **tasty**, good, fit to eat *and* finger-lickin' good (*both informal*), good-tasting, **savoury**, savorous, **palatable, toothsome**, gustable (*old*), sapid, **good**, good to eat, nice, agreeable, moreish, likable, pleasing, to one's taste, **delicious**, delightful, delectable, exquisite; delicate, dainty; juicy, succulent, **luscious**, lush; for the gods, ambrosial, nectarous, nectareous; fit for a king, gourmet, fit for a gourmet, of gourmet quality; scrumptious *and* yummy (*both informal*)

9 **flavourful, flavoursome**, flavorous, flavoury, well-flavoured; full-flavoured, full-bodied; nutty, fruity; **rich**, rich-flavoured

10 **appetizing, mouth-watering, tempting**, tantalizing, provocative, piquant

64 UNSAVOURINESS

nouns

1 **unsavouriness, unpalatableness**, unpalatability, **distastefulness**, untastefulness; bad taste, bad taste in the mouth

2 **acridness**, acridity, tartness, sharpness, causticity, astringence *or* astringency, acerbity, **sourness** *see* 67;

pungency *see* 68; **bitterness**, bitter taste; gall, gall and wormwood, wormwood, bitter pill

3 **nastiness, foulness, vileness, loathsomeness, repulsiveness, obnoxiousness,** odiousness, offensiveness, disgustingness, nauseousness; **rankness,** rancidity, rancidness, overripeness, rottenness, malodorousness, fetor, fetidness; yuckiness (*informal*); repugnance *see* 99.2; nauseant, emetic, sickener

verbs

4 **to disgust, repel,** turn one's stomach, nauseate; make one's gorge rise

adjectives

5 **unsavoury, unpalatable, unappetizing,** untasteful, untasty, ill-flavoured, foul-tasting, **distasteful,** dislikable, unlikable, uninviting, unpleasant, unpleasing, displeasing, disagreeable

6 **bitter,** bitter as gall *or* wormwood, amaroidal; **acrid,** sharp, caustic, tart, astringent; hard, harsh, rough, coarse; acerb, acerbic, sour; pungent

7 **nasty, offensive** *see* 98.18, fulsome, noisome, noxious, rebarbative, mawkish, cloying, brackish, **foul, vile,** bad; gross *and* icky *and* yucky (*all informal*), **sickening, nauseating,** nauseous, nauseant, vomity *and* barfy (*both informal*); poisonous, rank, rancid, maggoty, weevily, spoiled, overripe, high, rotten, stinking, putrid, malodorous, fetid

8 **inedible, uneatable,** not fit to eat *or* drink, undrinkable, impotable; unfit for human consumption

65 INSIPIDNESS

nouns

1 **insipidness,** insipidity, **tastelessness, flavourlessness,** blandness, savourlessness, saplessness, unsavouriness; **weakness, thinness,** mildness, **wishy-washiness; flatness, staleness,** lifelessness, deadness; vapidity, inanity, jejunity, jejuneness

adjectives

2 **insipid, tasteless, flavourless,** bland, spiceless, **savourless,** sapless, unsavoury, unflavoured; pulpy, pappy, gruelly; **weak, thin,** mild, **wishy-washy,** milktoast, washy, watery, watered, watered-down, diluted, dilute, milk-and-water; **flat, stale,** dead, *fade* (*French*); vapid, inane, jejune; "weary, flat, stale, and unprofitable"—Shakespeare; indifferent, neither one thing nor the other

66 SWEETNESS

nouns

1 **sweetness,** sweet, sweetishness, saccharinity, dulcitude (*old*); **sugariness,** syrupiness; oversweetness, mawkishness, cloyingness, sickly-sweetness

2 **sweetening,** edulcoration (*old*); sweetener; sugar; sweetening agent, sugar-substitute, artificial sweetener, saccharin, aspartame, NutraSweet (*trademark*), cyclamates, sodium cyclamate, calcium cyclamate; molasses, blackstrap, treacle; syrup, golden syrup *or* treacle, black treacle, maple syrup, cane syrup, corn syrup, sorghum; **honey,** honeycomb, honeypot, comb honey, clover honey; honeydew; **nectar, ambrosia; icing sugar,** sugarcoating; sweets; sugar-making; sugaring off; saccharification

verbs

3 **to sweeten,** dulcify, edulcorate *or* dulcorate (*both old*); **sugar,** honey; sugarcoat, glaze, candy; mull; saccharify; sugar off

adjectives

4 **sweet,** sweetish, sweetened; sacchariferous; **sugary,** sugared, candied, **honeyed,** syrupy; mellifluous, mellifluent (*old*); melliferous, nectarous, nectareous, ambrosial; sugarsweet, honeysweet, sweet as sugar *or* honey, sweet as a nut; sugar-coated; bittersweet; sour-sweet, sweet-sour, sweet and sour, sweet and pungent

5 **oversweet,** saccharine, rich, **cloying,** mawkish, luscious (*old*), sickly-sweet

67 SOURNESS

nouns

1 **sourness,** sour, sourishness, **tartness,** tartishness, acerbity, verjuice; acescency; acidity, acidulousness; hyperacidity, subacidity; vinegariness; unsweetness, **dryness; pungency** *see* 68; greenness, unripeness

2 **sour; vinegar,** acidulant; **pickle,** sour pickle, dill pickle, bread-and-butter pickle; verjuice; lemon, lime, crab apple, green apple, sour cherry, chokecherry (*US*); sourdough; sour cream, sour milk, yogurt; **acid**

3 **souring,** acidification, acidulation, acetification, acescence; fermentation

verbs

4 **to sour,** turn sour *or* acid, **acidify,** acidulate, acetify; ferment; set one's teeth on edge

adjectives

5 **sour,** soured, sourish; **tart,** tartish; crab, **crabbed;** acerb, acerbic, acerbate; acescent; **vinegarish,** vinegary, sour as vinegar; pickled; lemony; **pungent** *see* 68.6; unsweet, unsweetened, **dry,** sec; green, unripe

6 **acid,** acidulous, acidulent, acidulated; acetic, acetous, acetose; hyperacid; subacid, subacidulous

68 PUNGENCY

nouns

1 **pungency,** piquancy, poignancy; **sharpness, keenness,** edge, **causticity,** astringency, mordancy, severity, asperity, trenchancy, cuttingness, bitingness, penetratingness, harshness, roughness, **acridity; bitterness** *see* 64.2; acerbity, acidulousness, acidity, **sourness** *see* 67

2 **zest,** zestfulness, zestiness, **briskness,** liveliness, raciness; **nippiness, tanginess,** snappiness; **spiciness,** pepperiness, hotness, fieriness; **tang,**

spice, relish; **nip, bite;** punch, snap, zip, ginger; **kick,** guts (*informal*)

3 **strength,** strongness; high flavour, highness, rankness, gaminess

4 **saltiness, salinity,** brininess; brackishness; **salt; brine**

verbs

5 **to bite, nip,** cut, penetrate, bite the tongue, sting, make the eyes water, go up the nose

adjectives

6 **pungent, piquant, poignant; sharp, keen,** piercing, penetrating, nose-tickling, stinging, **biting, acrid,** astringent, irritating, harsh, rough, severe, asperous, cutting, trenchant; **caustic,** vitriolic, mordant, escharotic; **bitter** *see* 64.6; acerbic, acid, **sour**

7 **zestful,** zesty, **brisk,** lively, racy, zippy, **nippy,** snappy, **tangy,** with a kick; spiced, seasoned, high-seasoned; **spicy,** curried, **peppery,** hot, burning, hot as pepper; mustardy; like horseradish, like Chinese mustard

8 **strong,** strong-flavoured, strong-tasting; **high,** high-flavoured, high-tasted; **rank, gamy**

9 **salty,** salt, salted, saltish, **saline,** briny; brackish; pickled

69 ODOUR

nouns

1 **odour, smell, scent,** aroma, flavour (*old*), savour, niff (*informal*); **essence,** definite odour, redolence, effluvium, emanation, exhalation, fume, breath, subtle odour, whiff, trace, detectable odour; trail, spoor; **fragrance** *see* 70; **stink, stench** *see* 71

2 **odorousness, smelliness,** headiness, pungency *see* 68

3 smelling, olfaction, nosing, scenting; sniffing, snuffing, snuffling, whiffing, odorizing, odorization

4 **sense of smell,** smell, smelling, scent, olfaction, olfactory sense

5 olfactory organ; olfactory pit, olfactory cell, olfactory area, **nose,** beezer *and* conk (*both informal*), neb (*Scottish*); **nostrils,** noseholes (*informal*), nares; olfactory nerves; **olfactories**

verbs

6 (*have an odour*) **to smell,** be aromatic, smell of, be redolent of; emit *or* emanate *or* give out a smell, reach one's nostrils, yield an odour *or* aroma, breathe, exhale; reek, **stink** *see* 71.4

7 to odorize; scent, perfume *see* 70.8

8 **to smell, scent,** nose; **sniff,** snuff, snuffle, inhale, breathe, breathe in; get a noseful of, smell of, catch a smell of, get *or* take a whiff of, whiff

adjectives

9 **odorous,** odoriferous, odored, odorant, **smelling, smelly,** smellful (*Australian*), smellsome, **redolent, aromatic;** effluvious; **fragrant** *see* 70.9; **stinking, malodorous** *see* 71.5

10 **strong,** strong-smelling, strong-scented; **pungent,** penetrating, nose-piercing, sharp; reeking, reeky; suffocating, stifling

11 **smellable,** sniffable, whiffable

12 **olfactory,** olfactive

13 keen-scented, quick-scented, sharp- *or* keen-nosed, **with a nose for**

70 FRAGRANCE

nouns

1 **fragrance,** fragrancy (*old*), **perfume, aroma,** scent, redolence, balminess, **incense, bouquet,** nosegay (*old*), sweet smell, sweet savour; **odour** *see* 69; spice, spiciness; muskiness; fruitiness

2 perfumery, *parfumerie* (*French*); **perfume,** *parfum* (*French*), **scent, essence,** extract; aromatic, ambrosia; attar, essential *or* volatile oil; aromatic water; balsam, **balm,** aromatic gum; balm of Gilead, balsam of Mecca; myrrh; bay oil, myrcia oil; champaca oil; rose oil, attar of roses,
"the perfumed tincture of the roses"—SHAKESPEARE; lavender oil, heliotrope, jasmine oil, bergamot oil; fixative, musk, civet, ambergris

3 **toilet water,** Florida water; rose water, *eau de rose* (*French*); lavender water, *eau de lavande* (*French*); *eau de jasmin* (*French*); cologne, cologne water, eau de Cologne; bay rum; **lotion,** after-shave lotion

4 **incense;** joss stick; pastille; frankincense *or* olibanum; agalloch *or* aloeswood, calambac, lignaloes *or* linaloa, sandalwood

5 **perfumer,** *parfumeur* (*French*); thurifer, censer bearer; **perfuming,** censing, thurification, odorizing

6 (*articles*) perfumer, *parfumoir* (*French*), fumigator, scenter, odorator, odorizer; atomizer, purse atomizer, spray; censer, thurible, incensory, incense burner; vinaigrette, scent bottle, smelling bottle, scent box, scent ball; scent strip; scent bag, sachet; pomander, pouncet-box (*old*); potpourri

verbs

7 **to be fragrant,** smell sweet, **smell good,** please the nostrils

8 **to perfume, scent,** cense, incense, thurify, aromatize, odorize, fumigate, embalm

adjectives

9 **fragrant, aromatic,** odoriferous, redolent, perfumy, **perfumed, scented,** odorate *or* essenced (*both old*), **sweet, sweet-smelling,** sweet-scented, savoury, balmy, ambrosial, incense-breathing; thuriferous; **odorous** *see* 69.9; niffy *and* pongy *and* whiffy (*all informal*), sweet as a rose, fragrant as new-mown hay; flowery; fruity; musky; spicy

71 STENCH

nouns

1 **stench, stink,** funk, malodour, fetidness, fetidity, fetor, foul odour, offensive odour, offence to the nostrils, bad smell, hum *and* niff *and* pong *and* whiff (*all informal*), rotten smell, noxious stench,
"the rankest compound of villainous smell that ever offended nostril"—SHAKESPEARE, smell *or* stench of

decay, **reek**, reeking, nidor; fug *and* frowst
(*informal*); mephitis, miasma, graveolence (*old*); body
odour *or* BO; halitosis, **bad breath**, foul breath

2 **fetidness**, fetidity, malodorousness, **smelliness**,
stinkingness, **odorousness**, noisomeness, **rankness**,
foulness, putridness, offensiveness; repulsiveness;
mustiness, funkiness, must, frowst *or* frowstiness
(*informal*), mouldiness, mildew, fustiness, frowiness
(*informal*), frowziness, frowstiness (*informal*), fug,
stuffiness; **rancidness**, rancidity; rottenness *see* 393.7

3 **stinker**, stinkard; skunk *or* rotten egg; stink ball,
stinkpot, stink bomb; fart

verbs

4 **to stink**, smell, **smell bad**, hum *and* niff *and* pong
and whiff (*all informal*), assail *or* offend the nostrils,
stink in the nostrils, smell to heaven *or* high heaven,
reek; smell up, stink up; stink out

adjectives

5 **malodorous, fetid**, olid, **odorous, stinking,
reeking**, reeky, nidorous, smelling, bad-smelling,
evil-smelling, ill-smelling, heavy-smelling, **smelly**,
smellful (*Australian*), niffy *and* pongy (*both informal*),
stenchy; **foul**, vile, putrid, bad, fulsome, noisome,
faecal, feculent, excremental, offensive, repulsive,
noxious, sulphurous, graveolent (*old*); rotten; **rank**,
strong, high, gamy; **rancid**, reechy (*old*); **musty**,
funky, fusty, frowy (*informal*), frowzy, frowsty,
fuggy, stuffy, mouldy, mildewed, mildewy; mephitic,
miasmic, miasmal

72 ODOURLESSNESS

nouns

1 **odourlessness, inodorousness**, scentlessness,
smell-lessness; inoffensiveness

2 **deodorizing**, deodorization, fumigation, ventilation

3 **deodorant**, deodorizer; antiperspirant; fumigant,
fumigator

verbs

4 **to deodorize**, fumigate; ventilate, freshen the air

adjectives

5 **odourless**, inodorous, nonodorous, smell-less,
scentless, unscented; neutral-smelling; inoffensive

6 **deodorant**, deodorizing

73 TOUCH

nouns

1 **touch**; sense of touch, tactile sense, cutaneous sense;
taction, **contact** *see* 223.5; **feel**, feeling; hand-
mindedness; light touch, lambency, whisper, breath,
kiss, caress, fondling; loving touch; lick, lap; **brush**,
graze, grazing, glance, glancing; stroke, rub; tap,
flick; fingertip caress; tentative poke

2 **touching, feeling, fingering**, palpation; **handling**,
manipulation; petting, caressing, stroking, rubbing,
frottage, frication, friction *see* 1042; fondling;
pressure *see* 901.2; feeling up (*informal*)

3 touchableness, **tangibility, palpability**, tactility

4 **feeler**, tactile organ, tactor; tactile cell; tactile
process, tactile corpuscle, **antenna**; tactile hair,
vibrissa; cat whisker; barbel, barbule; palp, palpus

5 **finger, digit**; forefinger, index finger, index; ring
finger, annulary; middle finger, medius, dactylion;
little finger, pinkie (*Scottish, US, & Canadian*),
minimus; thumb, pollex

verbs

6 **to touch, feel**, feel of, palpate; **finger**, pass *or* run
the fingers over, feel with the fingertips, thumb;
handle, palm, paw; **manipulate**, wield, ply;
twiddle; poke at, prod; tap, flick; come in contact *see*
223.10

7 **to touch lightly**, touch upon; kiss, **brush**, sweep,
graze, brush by, glance, scrape, skim

8 **to stroke, pet, caress**, fondle; **nuzzle**, nose, rub
noses; feel up *or* touch up (*both informal*); rub, rub
against, massage, knead *see* 1042.6

9 **to lick, lap**, tongue, mouth

adjectives

10 **tactile**, tactual; hand-minded

11 touchable, **palpable, tangible**, tactile

12 lightly touching, lambent, playing lightly over, barely
touching

74 SENSATIONS OF TOUCH

nouns

1 **tingle**, tingling, thrill, buzz; **prickle**, prickles,
prickling, pins and needles; **sting**, stinging,
urtication; paraesthesia

2 **tickle**, tickling, **titillation**, pleasant stimulation,
ticklishness, tickliness

3 **itch, itching**, itchiness, yeuk (*Scottish*); pruritus;
prurigo

4 **creeps** *and* **cold creeps** *and* shivers *and* **cold
shivers** (*all informal*), creeping of the flesh;
gooseflesh, goose bumps, goose pimples; formication

verbs

5 **to tingle**, thrill; **itch**; scratch; **prickle**, prick, sting

6 **to tickle, titillate**

7 **to feel creepy**, feel funny, creep, crawl, **have the
creeps** *or* cold creeps *or* the heebie-jeebies (*informal*);
have gooseflesh *or* goose bumps; give one the creeps,
give one the willies *or* the heebie-jeebies (*informal*)

adjectives

8 **tingly**, tingling, atingle; **prickly**, prickling

9 **ticklish**, tickling, tickly, **titillative**

10 **itchy**, itching; pruriginous

11 **creepy, crawly**, creepy-crawly, formicative

75 SEX

nouns

1 **sex**, gender; maleness, masculinity *see* 76, femaleness,
femininity *see* 77; **genitals, genitalia**

2 **sexuality**, sexual nature, sexualism, love-life; **love**
see 104, sexual activity, lovemaking *see* 562, marriage
see 563; heterosexuality; homosexuality; bisexuality,
ambisexuality; **carnality, sensuality** *see* 663;

sexiness, voluptuousness, flesh, fleshiness; **libido**, sex drive, sexual instinct *or* urge; **potency** *see* 76.2; impotence; frigidity, coldness

3 sex appeal, sexual attraction *or* attractiveness *or* magnetism, sexiness

4 sex object; bit *and* bit of all right *and* bit of crumpet *and* bit of skirt *and* bit of stuff *and* bit of tail, piece *and* meat *and* piece of meat (*all informal*); sex queen, sex goddess; stud (*informal*)

5 sexual desire, sensuous *or* carnal desire, bodily appetite, **biological urge**, venereal appetite *or* desire, sexual longing, **lust**, desire, lusts *or* desires of the flesh, itch, lech (*informal*); **erection**, penile erection, hard-on *and* horn (*both informal*); **passion**, carnal *or* sexual passion, fleshly lust, prurience *or* pruriency, concupiscence, hot blood, aphrodisia, the hots *and* hot pants (*all informal*); lustfulness, goatishness, horniness, libidinousness; lasciviousness *see* 665.5; **eroticism**, erotism; indecency *see* 666; erotomania, eromania, *hysteria libidinosa* (*Latin*); nymphomania, andromania, *furore uterinus* (*Latin*); satyrism, satyriasis, gynecomania; infantile sexuality, polymorphous perversity; **heat**, rut; frenzy *or* fury of lust; oestrus, estrum, estral cycle

6 aphrodisiac, love potion, philtre, love philtre; cantharis, blister beetle, Spanish fly

7 copulation, sex act, having sex, having intercourse, *le sport* (*French*), "making the beast with two backs"—SHAKESPEARE, coupling, mating, coition, **coitus**, pareunia, venery, copula (*law*), **sex, intercourse, sexual intercourse**, cohabitation, commerce, sexual commerce, congress, sexual congress, sexual union, sexual relations, relations, marital relations, marriage act, act of love, sleeping together *or* with; screwing *and* shagging *and* bonking *and* nookie *and* grind *and* making it with (*all informal*); intimacy, connection, carnal knowledge, aphrodisia; foreplay, slap and tickle (*informal*); **oral sex**, oral-genital stimulation, fellatio, fellation, blow job (*informal*), cunnilingus; **anal sex**, anal intercourse, sodomy, buggery (*informal*); **orgasm**, climax, sexual climax; unlawful sexual intercourse, adultery, fornication *see* 665.7; coitus interruptus, onanism; group sex, group grope (*informal*); serial sex, gang bang (*informal*); spouse swapping, wife swapping, husband swapping; casual sex, one-night stand, quickie; phone sex; safe sex; sex shop; **lovemaking** *see* 562; **procreation** *see* 78; germ cell, sperm, ovum *see* 305.12

8 masturbation, autoeroticism, self-abuse, onanism, manipulation, playing with oneself, jacking off *and* pulling off *and* tossing off *and* hand job (*all informal*), wanking (*informal*); sexual fantasy; wet dream

9 sexlessness, asexuality, neuterness; **impotence** *see* 19; eunuch, *castrato* (*Italian*), spado, gelding; steer

10 sexual preference; sexual orientation; sexual normality; **heterosexuality; homosexuality**, homosexualism, homosex, homoeroticism, homophilia, *l'amour bleu* (*French*), the love that dare not speak its name, sexual inversion, uranism; autoeroticism; **bisexuality**, bisexualism, ambisexuality, ambisextrousness, amphierotism,

swinging both ways (*informal*); **lesbianism**, sapphism, tribadism *or* tribady; **sexual prejudice**, sexism, genderism, phallicism, heterosexism, homosexism

11 perversion, sexual deviation, sexual deviance, sexual perversion, sexual abnormality, kink (*informal*); sexual pathology; psychosexual disorder; sexual psychopathy, *psychopathia sexualis* (*Latin*); paraphilia; zoophilia, zooerastia, bestiality; paedophilia; algolagnia, algolagny, **sadomasochism**; active algolagnia, **sadism**; passive algolagnia, **masochism**; fetishism; narcissism; pederasty, paedophilia; exhibitionism; necrophilia; coprophilia; scotophilia, voyeurism; transvestitism, cross-dressing; **incest**, incestuousness, **sex crime; sexual abuse**, carnal abuse, molestation

12 intersexuality, intersexualism, epicenism, epicenity; hermaphroditism, pseudohermaphroditism; androgynism, androgyny, gynandry, gynandrism; transsexuality, transsexualism

13 heterosexual, straight (*informal*), breeder (*informal*)

14 homosexual, gay person, homosexualist, homophile, invert; catamite, *mignon* (*French*), Ganymede, punk, gunsel; **bisexual**, bi-guy (*informal*); **lesbian**, sapphist, tribade, fricatrice (*old*)

15 (*informal terms for male homosexuals*) homo, queer, faggot, fag, fruit, flit, fairy, pansy, nance, auntie, queen, drag queen, closet queen, poof *and* poofter *and* poove; (*informal terms for female homosexuals*) dyke, lesbo, lez

16 sexual pervert; pervert, deviant, deviate, sex *or* sexual pervert, sex fiend, sex criminal, sexual psychopath; sodomist, sodomite, bugger; pederast; paraphiliac; zoophiliac; paedophiliac; sadist; masochist; sadomasochist, algolagniac; fetishist; transvestite *or* TV, cross-dresser, gender-bender (*informal*); narcissist; exhibitionist, flasher; necrophiliac; coprophiliac; scotophiliac, voyeur; erotomaniac, nymphomaniac, satyr; rapist *see* 665.12

17 intersex, sex-intergrade, epicene; hermaphrodite, pseudohermaphrodite; androgyne, gynandroid; transsexual, gender-bender (*informal*)

18 sexology, sexologist; sexual counsellor; sexual surrogate; sexual customs *or* mores *or* practices; sexual morality; new morality, sexual revolution; sexual freedom, free love; trial marriage

verbs

19 to sex, sexualize; genderize

20 to lust, lust after, fancy, itch for, have the hots *and* have hot pants for (*all informal*), lech after (*informal*), **desire; be in heat** *or* **rut**, rut, come in; get physical (*informal*); get an erection, get a hard-on (*informal*), tumesce

21 to copulate, couple, **mate**, unite in sexual intercourse, **have sexual relations, have sex**, make out (*informal*), perform the act of love *or* marriage act, come together, cohabit, shack up (*informal*), be intimate; sleep with, lie with, go to bed with; fuck *and* screw *and* lay *and* shag *and* have *and* frig *and* jump *and* knock *and* **make it with** (*all informal*), go all the way, go to bed with, lie together; cover, mount, serve *or* service (*of animals*); commit adultery, fornicate *see* 665.19; **make love**

22 to masturbate, play with *or* abuse oneself, jack off *and* whack off *and* toss off (*all informal*), wank (*informal*); fellate, suck *and* suck off (*informal*); sodomize, bugger *and* ream (*both informal*)

23 to climax, come, achieve satisfaction, achieve *or* reach orgasm; **ejaculate,** get off (*informal*)

adjectives

24 sexual, sex, sexlike, gamic, coital, libidinal; **erotic,** sexy, amorous; nuptial; venereal; **carnal, sensual** *see* 663.5, voluptuous, fleshly; desirable, beddable; **sexy;** erogenous, erogenic, erotogenic; sexed, oversexed, hypersexual, undersexed; procreative *see* 78.15; potent *see* 76.12

25 aphrodisiac, aphroditous, **arousing,** stimulating, eroticizing, venereal; fruity (*informal*)

26 lustful, prurient, hot, steamy, sexy, concupiscent, lickerish, libidinous, **salacious** *see* 666.9, **passionate,** hot-blooded, itching, **horny** *and* hot to trot *and* sexed-up (*all informal*), randy, goatish; sex-starved, unsatisfied; lascivious *see* 665.29; **orgasmic,** orgastic, **ejaculatory**

27 in heat, burning, hot; in rut, rutting, rutty, ruttish; in must, must, musty; oestrous, estral, estrual

28 unsexual, unsexed; **sexless,** asexual, **neuter,** neutral; castrated, emasculated, eunuchized; **cold, frigid; impotent;** frustrated

29 homosexual, homoerotic, gay, queer *and* limp-wristed *and* faggoty (*all informal*); **bisexual,** bisexed, ambisexual, ambisextrous, amphierotic, AC-DC (*informal*), autoerotic; lesbian, sapphic, tribadistic; mannish *see* 76.13, butch *and* dykey (*both informal*); effeminate *see* 77.14; transvestite; **perverted,** deviant

30 hermaphrodite, hermaphroditic, pseudohermaphrodite, pseudohermaphroditic, epicene, monoclinous; androgynous, androgynal, gynandrous, gynandrian

76 MASCULINITY

nouns

1 masculinity, masculineness, maleness; **manliness,** manlihood, **manhood,** manfulness, manlikeness; mannishness; gentlemanliness, gentlemanlikeness

2 male sex, male sexuality, virility, virileness, potence *or* **potency,** sexual power, manly vigour, **machismo;** ultramasculinity; phallicism; male superiority, patriarchy

3 mankind, man, men, manhood, menfolk (*informal*), the sword side

4 male, male being, masculine; he, him, his; **man,** male person, *homme* (*French*), *hombre* (*Spanish*); **gentleman,** gent (*informal*)

5 (*informal terms*) **guy,** fellow, feller, beggar, blighter, lad, chap, beezer, geezer, old boy, old man, cat, bird, duck, fruit, stud, joker, josser, bugger, bastard, bloke *and* cove *and* johnny *and* bod (*all informal*), customer, party, character, warm, body, bean, cookie, dude (*US & Canadian*), gent, Joe (*US & Canadian*)

6 real man, he-man *or* **two-fisted man** (*both informal*), hunk (*informal*), man with hair on his chest; caveman (*informal*)

7 (*forms of address*) **Mister, Mr,** Messrs (*plural*), Master; **sir;** monsieur, M (*both French*), messieurs, MM (*both French plural*); signor, signore (*both Italian*), signorino (*Italian*), señor, Sr (*both Spanish*), don (*Spanish*), senhor (*Portuguese*); Herr (*German*); mein Herr (*German*); mijnheer (*Dutch*), sahib (*Hindustani*), bwana (*Swahili*)

8 (*male animals*) cock, rooster, chanticleer; cockerel; drake; gander; peacock; tom turkey, tom, turkey-cock, bubbly-jock (*Scottish*), gobbler, turkey gobbler; dog; boar; stag, hart, buck; stallion, studhorse, stud, top horse (*informal*), entire horse, entire; tomcat, tom; he-goat, billy goat, billy; ram, tup; wether; bull, bullock, top cow (*informal*); steer, stot (*informal*)

9 (*mannish female*) **amazon,** virago, androgyne; lesbian, butch *and* dyke (*both informal*); **tomboy,** hoyden, romp

verbs

10 to masculinize, virilize

adjectives

11 masculine, male, bull, he–; **manly, manlike, mannish,** manful, andric; uneffeminate; **gentlemanly,** gentlemanlike

12 virile, potent, viripotent; ultramasculine, **macho, he-mannish** *and* hunky (*both informal*), two-fisted (*informal*), broad-shouldered, hairy-chested

13 mannish, mannified; unwomanly, **unfeminine,** uneffeminate, viraginous; **tomboyish,** hoyden, rompish

77 FEMININITY

nouns

1 femininity, feminality, feminacy, feminineness, femaleness; **womanliness,** womanlikeness, womanishness, **womanhood,** womanity, muliebrity; girlishness, little-girlishness; maidenhood, maidenliness; **ladylikeness,** gentlewomanliness; **matronliness,** matronage, matronhood, matronship; the eternal feminine,
"*das Ewig-Weibliche*" (*German*), Goethe

2 effeminacy, unmanliness, effeminateness, epicenity, epicenism, **womanishness,** muliebrity, **sissiness** (*informal*), prissiness (*informal*); androgyny; feminism

3 womankind, woman, women, femininity, **womanhood,** womenfolk (*informal*), the distaff side; **the female sex;** the second sex, **the fair sex,** the gentle sex, the softer sex, **the weaker sex,** the weaker vessel

4 female, female being; she, her

5 woman, Eve, daughter of Eve, Adam's rib, *femme* (*French*), distaff (*old*), weaker vessel; frow, *Frau* (*German*), *vrouw* (*Dutch*), *donna* (*Italian*), wahine (*Hawaii*); **lady,** milady, gentlewoman, *domina* (*Latin*); feme sole *and* feme covert (*both law*); married woman, wife; **matron,** dame, **dowager;** squaw; unmarried woman, bachelor girl (*informal*), single woman, spinster; lass, girl *see* 302.6; career woman, businesswoman; superwoman

6 (*informal terms*) **gal, dame,** bird, hen, biddy, Judy, old girl, skirt, stuff, crumpet, jane, broad, doll, dolly, babe, chick, wench, tomato (*US & Canadian*), bitch, minx, sister, squaw, toots, chapess

7 "the female of the human species, and not a different kind of animal"—G B Shaw, "O fairest of creation! last and best of all God's works"—Milton, "a temple sacred by birth, and built by hands divine"—Dryden, "one of Nature's agreeable blunders"—Hannah Cowley

8 (*forms of address*) **Ms;** Mistress (*old*), **Mrs; madam** *or* ma'am; *madame, Mme* (*both French*); *mesdames, Mmes* (*both French plural*); *Frau* (*German*), *vrouw* (*Dutch*), *signora* (*Italian*), *señora* (*Spanish*), *senhora* (*Portuguese*), *mem-sahib* (*Hindustani*); *dame* (*old*), *donna* (*Italian*), *doña* (*Spanish*), *dona* (*Portuguese*), lady; **Miss;** *mademoiselle, Mlle* (*both French*); *Fraülein* (*German*); *signorina* (*Italian*), *señorita* (*Spanish*), *senhorita* (*Portuguese*)

9 (*female animals*) hen, Partlet, biddy; guinea hen; peahen; bitch, slut, gyp; sow; ewe, ewe lamb; she-goat, nanny goat *or* nanny; doe, hind, roe; jenny; mare, brood mare; filly; cow, bossy; heifer; vixen; tigress; lioness; she-bear, she-lion, etc

10 (*effeminate male*) **mollycoddle,** effeminate, ponce (*informal*); **mother's darling, mother's boy, mummy's boy, mama's boy,** Lord Fauntleroy, sissy, Percy, goody-goody; nancy *or* nance, chicken, lily, pantywaist (*US*); cream puff, weak sister, milksop; old woman

11 feminization, womanization, effemination, effeminization, sissification (*informal*)

verbs

12 to feminize; womanize, demasculinize, effeminize, effeminatize, effeminate, soften, sissify (*informal*); emasculate, castrate, geld

adjectives

13 **feminine, female;** gynic, gynecic, gynaecoid; muliebral, distaff, **womanly, womanish, womanlike,** petticoat; **ladylike,** gentlewomanlike, gentlewomanly; **matronly,** matronal, matronlike; **girlish,** little-girlish, kittenish; maidenly *see* 301.11

14 **effeminate,** womanish, fem (*informal*), old-womanish, **unmanly,** muliebrous, soft, chicken, prissy, **sissified,** sissy, **sissyish**

78 REPRODUCTION, PROCREATION

nouns

1 **reproduction, making, re-creation,** remaking, refashioning, reshaping, redoing, re-formation, reworking, rejiggering (*informal*); **reconstruction,** rebuilding, redesign, restructuring, *perestroika* (*Russian*); **revision;** reedition, reissue, reprinting; reestablishment, **reorganization,** reinstitution, reconstitution; redevelopment; **rebirth,** renascence, resurrection, revival; regeneration, regenesis, palingenesis; **duplication** *see* 873, **imitation** *see* 336, **copy** *see* 784, **repetition** *see* 848; **restoration** *see* 396, renovation; producing *or* making *or* creating anew *or* over *or* again *or* once more; **birth rate,** fertility rate; baby boom *or* boomlet (*informal*); baby bust (*informal*)

2 **procreation, reproduction, generation, begetting, breeding,** engenderment; **propagation, multiplication,** proliferation; linebreeding; inbreeding, endogamy; outbreeding, xenogamy; dissogeny; crossbreeding *see* 796.4

3 **fertilization,** fecundation; **impregnation,** insemination, begetting, getting with child, knocking up (*informal*), mating, servicing; **pollination,** pollinization; cross-fertilization, cross-pollination; self-fertilization, heterogamy, orthogamy; donor insemination; isogamy, artificial insemination; in-vitro fertilization *or* IVF; conjugation, zygosis

4 **conception,** conceiving, inception of pregnancy; superfetation, superimpregnation

5 **pregnancy, gestation, incubation,** parturiency, gravidness *or* gravidity, heaviness, greatness, bigness, the family way (*informal*); brooding, sitting, covering

6 **birth, generation, genesis; development;** procreation; abiogenesis, archigenesis, biogenesis, blastogenesis, digenesis, dysmerogenesis, epigenesis, eumerogenesis, heterogenesis, histogenesis, homogenesis, isogenesis, merogenesis, metagenesis, monogenesis, oögenesis, orthogenesis, pangenesis, parthenogenesis, phytogenesis, sporogenesis, xenogenesis; spontaneous generation

verbs

7 **to reproduce, remake,** make *or* do over, **re-create,** regenerate, resurrect, revive, re-form, refashion, **reshape,** remould, recast, rework, remaster, rejigger (*informal*), redo, **reconstruct,** rebuild, redesign, restructure, **revise;** reprint, reissue; reestablish, reinstitute, reconstitute, refound, **reorganize; redevelop; duplicate** *see* 873.3, **copy** *see* 336.5, **repeat** *see* 848.7, **restore** *see* 396.11, **renovate**

8 **to procreate, generate, breed, beget,** get, **engender;** propagate, multiply; proliferate; mother; father, sire; reproduce in kind, reproduce after one's kind, "multiply and replenish the earth"—Bible; breed true; inbreed, breed in and in; outbreed; cross-pollinate, crossbreed; linebreed; copulate, make love

9 **to lay** (*eggs*), deposit, drop, spawn

10 **to fertilize,** fructify, fecundate, fecundify; **impregnate, inseminate,** spermatize, knock up (*informal*), **get with child** *or* **young; pollinate** *or* pollinize, pollen; cross-fertilize, cross-pollinate *or* cross-pollinize

11 **to conceive,** get in the family way (*informal*); superfetate

12 **to be pregnant,** be gravid, be great with child, **be with child** *or* **young;** be in the family way *and* be in the club *and* have a bun in the oven *and* be expecting *and* anticipate a blessed event (*all informal*); gestate, breed, carry, carry young; **incubate, hatch; brood,** sit, set, cover

13 **to give birth** *see* 1.3

adjectives

14 **reproductive, re-creative, reconstructive,** re-formative; renascent, regenerative, resurgent, reappearing; reorganizational; revisional; **restorative** *see* 396.22; Hydraheaded, phoenixlike

15 reproductive, **procreative**, procreant, **propagative**, life-giving; spermatic, spermatozoic, seminal, germinal, fertilizing, fecundative; multiparous

16 **genetic, generative**, genial, gametic; genital, genitive; abiogenetic, biogenetic, blastogenetic, digenetic, dysmerogenetic, epigenetic, eumerogenetic, heterogenetic, histogenetic, homogenetic, isogenetic, merogenetic, metagenetic, monogenetic, oögenetic, orthogenetic, pangenetic, parthenogenetic, phytogenetic, sporogenous, xenogenetic

17 **bred, impregnated**, inseminated; inbred, endogamic, endogamous; outbred, exogamic, exogamous; crossbred; linebred

18 **pregnant**, *enceinte* (*French*), preggers *and* knocked-up (*both informal*), **with child** *or* **young, in the family way** *and* **in the club** (*both informal*), up the pole *or* stick (*informal*), gestating, breeding, teeming, parturient; heavy with child *or* young, great *or* big with child *or* young, wearing her apron high, in a delicate condition, gravid, heavy, great, big-laden; carrying, carrying a fetus *or* an embryo; **expecting** (*informal*), anticipating *and* anticipating a blessed event (*both informal*); superfetate, superimpregnated

79 CLEANNESS

nouns

1 **cleanness, cleanliness; purity**, squeaky-cleanness (*informal*), pureness; **immaculateness**, immaculacy; **spotlessness**, unspottedness, stainlessness, whiteness; freshness; fastidiousness, daintiness, cleanly habits; asepsis, sterility, hospital cleanliness; tidiness *see* 806.3

2 **cleansing, cleaning**, cleaning up, depuration, detersion (*old*); **purge**, cleanout, cleaning out, purging, purgation, catharsis, abstersion (*old*); **purification**, purifying, lustration; expurgation, bowdlerization

3 **sanitation, hygiene**, hygenics; **disinfection, decontamination, sterilization**, antisepsis; pasteurization, flash pasteurization; fumigation, disinfestation, delousing

4 **refinement, clarification, purification**, depuration; **straining**, colature; elution, elutriation; extraction *see* 192.8; **filtering**, filtration; **percolation**, leaching, edulcoration (*old*), lixiviation; **sifting**, separation, **screening**, sieving, bolting, riddling, winnowing; essentialization; sublimation; **distillation**, destructive distillation, spiritualization (*old*)

5 **washing, ablution**; wash and brush up (*informal*); lavation, laving, lavage; lavabo; **wash, washup**; soaping, lathering; rinse, rinsing; sponge, sponging; shampoo; washout, elution, elutriation; irrigation, flush, flushing, flushing out; douche, douching; enema; **scrub**, scrubbing, swabbing, mopping, scouring; **cleaning up** *or* **out**, washing up, scrubbing up *or* out, mopping up *or* down, wiping up *or* down

6 **laundering, laundry**, tubbing; **wash, washing**; washday

7 **bathing**, balneation

8 **bathe, bath, tub** (*informal*); **shower**, shower bath, needle bath, hot *or* cold shower; douche; sponge

bath, sponge; bed bath, blanket bath; hip bath, sitz bath; sweat bath, Turkish bath, hummum, Russian bath, Swedish bath, Finnish bath, sauna *or* sauna bath, Japanese bath, hot tub, whirlpool bath, Jacuzzi (*trademark*), plunge bath

9 **dip, bath**; acid bath, mercury bath, fixing bath; sheepdip

10 **bathing place, bath, baths**, public baths, **bathhouse**, bagnio (*old*), sauna; *balneum and balneae and thermae* (*all Latin*); mikvah (*Judaism*); watering place, spa; lavatory, washroom, bathroom; steam room, sweat room, sudatorium, sudarium, caldarium, tepidarium; rest room

11 **washery, laundry**; washhouse, washshed; **coin laundry, Launderette** *or* **laundrette** (*trademark*), coin-operated laundry, Laundromat (*US & Canadian trademark*), washateria; automatic laundry; hand laundry; car wash

12 **washbasin, washbowl**, washdish, basin; **lavatory, washstand; bathtub**, tub, bath; bidet; **shower**, showers, shower room, shower bath, shower stall, shower head, shower curtain; **sink**, kitchen sink; dishwasher, automatic dishwasher; washing machine; washer; piscina, lavabo, ewer, aquamanile; washtub, washpot, washing pot, wash boiler, dishpan; finger bowl; wash barrel

13 **refinery; refiner**, purifier, clarifier; **filter; strainer**, colander; **percolator**, lixiviator; **sifter, sieve, screen**, riddle, cribble; winnow, winnower, winnowing machine, winnowing basket *or* fan; cradle, rocker

14 **cleaner**, cleaner-up, cleaner-off, cleaner-out; **janitor**, janitress, custodian; cleaning woman *or* lady *or* man, daily *or* daily woman *and* charwoman *or* char, Mrs Mop (*informal*)

15 **washer**, launderer; **laundress**, laundrywoman, **washerwoman**, washwoman; **laundryman**, washerman, washman; dry cleaner; **dishwasher**, scullion, scullery maid; dishwiper

16 **sweeper; street sweeper**, crossing sweeper, cleanser *or* scavenger; **chimney sweep** *or* sweeper, sweep, flue cleaner

17 **cleanser, cleaner**; cleaning agent; lotion, cream; cold cream, cleansing cream, **soap, detergent**, synthetic detergent, abstergent; shampoo; rinse; **solvent**; cleaning solvent; water softener; purifier, depurant; mouthwash, wash; dentifrice, **toothpaste, tooth powder**; pumice stone, holystone, scouring powder; purge, purgative, cathartic, enema, diuretic, emetic, nauseant; **cleaning device**

verbs

18 **to clean, cleanse, purge**, deterge, depurate; **purify**, lustrate; sweeten, **freshen**; whiten, bleach; clean up *or* out, clear out, sweep out, clean up after; houseclean, clean house, spring-clean, char; spruce, tidy *see* 807.12; scavenge; **wipe**, wipe up *or* out, wipe off; dust, dust off; steam-clean, **dry-clean**; expurgate, bowdlerize

19 **to wash, bathe**, bath, shower, lave; wash and brush up (*informal*); **launder**, tub; wash up *or* out *or* away; **rinse**, rinse out, flush, flush out, irrigate, sluice, sluice out; ritually immerse, baptize, *toivel* (*Yiddish*); sponge, sponge down *or* off; **scrub**, scrub up *or* out, swab, mop, mop up; scour, holystone; muck out; hose out *or* down; rinse off *or* out; soak out *or* away; soap, lather; shampoo; syringe, douche; gargle

20 to groom, dress, fettle, brush up; preen, plume, titivate; manicure

21 to comb, curry, card, hackle *or* hatchel, heckle (*informal*), rake

22 to refine, clarify, clear, purify, rectify, depurate; try; strain; elute, elutriate; extract *see* 192.10; filter, filtrate; percolate, leach, lixiviate, edulcorate (*old*); sift, separate, sieve, screen, bolt, winnow; sublimate, sublime, distil, spiritualize (*old*), essentialize

23 to sweep, sweep up *or* out, brush, brush off, whisk, broom; vacuum (*informal*), vacuum-clean, hoover

24 to sanitize, sanitate, hygienize; disinfect, decontaminate, sterilize, antisepticize, radiosterilize; autoclave, boil; pasteurize, flash-pasteurize; disinfest, fumigate, delouse; chlorinate

adjectives

25 clean, pure; immaculate, spotless, stainless, white, fair, dirt-free, soil-free; unsoiled, unsullied, unmuddied, unsmirched, unbesmirched, unblotted, unsmudged, unstained, untarnished, unspotted, unblemished; smutless, smut-free; bleached, whitened; bright, shiny *see* 1024.33; unpolluted, nonpolluted, untainted, unadulterated, undefiled; kosher, *tahar* (*Hebrew*), ritually pure *or* clean; squeaky-clean *and* clean as a whistle *or* a new penny *or* a hound's tooth (*all informal*); sweet, fresh; cleanly, fastidious, dainty, of cleanly habits; well-washed, well-scrubbed, tubbed (*informal*)

26 cleaned, cleansed, cleaned up; purged, purified; expurgated, bowdlerized; refined; spruce, spick and span, tidy *see* 806.8

27 sanitary, hygienic, prophylactic; sterile, aseptic, antiseptic, uninfected; disinfected, decontaminated, sterilized; autoclaved, boiled; pasteurized

28 cleansing, cleaning; detergent, detersive, abstergent, abstersive, depurative; purifying, purificatory, lustral; expurgatory; purgative, purging, cathartic, diuretic, emetic

adverbs

29 cleanly, clean; purely, immaculately, spotlessly

80 UNCLEANNESS

nouns

1 uncleanness, immundity; impurity, unpureness; dirtiness, grubbiness, dinginess, griminess, messiness, grunginess *and* scuzziness (*both US informal*), scruffiness, slovenliness, sluttishness, untidiness *see* 809.6; miriness, muddiness *see* 1060.4; uncleanliness

2 filthiness, foulness, vileness, scumminess (*informal*), feculence, shittiness (*informal*), muckiness, ordurousness, nastiness, grossness *and* yuckiness *and* ickiness (*all informal*); scurfiness, scabbiness; rottenness, putridness *see* 393.7; rankness, fetidness *see* 71.2; odiousness, repulsiveness *see* 98.2; nauseousness, disgustingness *see* 64.3; hoggishness, piggishness, swinishness, beastliness

3 squalor, squalidness, squalidity, sordidness; slumminess (*informal*)

4 defilement, befoulment, dirtying, soiling, besmirchment; pollution, contamination, infection; abomination; ritual uncleanness *or* impurity *or* contamination

5 soil, soilure, soilage, smut; smirch, smudge, smutch, smear, spot, blot, blotch, splodge, stain *see* 1003.3

6 dirt, grime; dust; soot, smut; mud *see* 1060.8

7 filth, muck, slime, mess, sordes, foul matter; ordure, excrement *see* 12.3; mucus, snot (*informal*); scurf, furfur, dandruff; putrid matter, pus, corruption, gangrene, decay, carrion, rot *see* 393.7; obscenity, smut (*informal*) *see* 666.4

8 slime, slop, scum, sludge, slush; glop *and* gunk (*both informal*), muck, mire, ooze

9 offal, slough, offscourings, scurf, scum, riffraff, scum of the earth; carrion; garbage, swill, slop, slops; dishwater, ditchwater, bilgewater, bilge; sewage, sewerage; waste, refuse *see* 391.4

10 dunghill, manure pile, midden; compost heap; kitchen midden, refuse heap

11 sty, pigsty, pigpen; stable, Augean stables; dump *and* hole (*both informal*); tenement; warren, slum, rookery; the inner city, the ghetto, the slums; plague spot, pesthole; hovel

12 (*receptacle of filth*) sink; sump, cesspool, cesspit, septic tank; catch pit; bilge *or* bilges; sewer, drain, *cloaca* and *cloaca maxima* (*both Latin*); sewage farm, purification plant; dump, rubbish dump, tip, sanitary landfill, landfill; swamp, bog, mire, quagmire, marsh

13 pig, swine, hog, slut, sloven, slattern *see* 809.7; *Struwwelpeter* (*German*)

verbs

14 to wallow in the mire, live like a pig

15 to dirty, dirty up, dirt (*old*), grime, begrime; muck, muck up (*informal*); muddy, bemud (*old*); mire, bemire; slime; dust; soot, smoke, besmoke

16 to soil, besoil; black, blacken; smirch, besmirch, sully, smutch *or* smouch, besmutch, smut, smudge, smear, besmear, daub, bedaub; spot, stain *see* 1003.6; get one's hands dirty, dirty *or* soil one's hands

17 to defile, foul, befoul; sully; foul one's own nest, mess *and* mess up (*both informal*); pollute, corrupt, contaminate, infect; taint, tarnish

18 to spatter, splatter, splash, bespatter, dabble, bedabble, spot, splotch

19 to draggle, bedraggle, drabble, bedrabble, daggle (*old*), drabble in the mud

adjectives

20 unclean, unwashed, unbathed, unscrubbed, unscoured, unswept, unwiped; impure, unpure; polluted, contaminated, infected, corrupted; ritually unclean *or* impure *or* contaminated, *tref* (*Yiddish*), *terefah* (*Hebrew*), nonkosher; not to be handled without gloves; uncleanly

21 soiled, sullied, dirtied, smirched, besmirched, smudged, spotted, tarnished, tainted, stained;

defiled, fouled, **befouled**; draggled, drabbled, bedraggled

22 dirty, grimy, grubby, grotty (*informal*), grungy (*informal*), smirchy, dingy, messy (*informal*), scrubby (*informal*); scruffy, slovenly, untidy *see* 809.15; miry, **muddy** *see* 1060.14; **dusty**; smutty, smutchy, smudgy; sooty, smoky; snuffy

23 filthy, foul, vile, mucky, **nasty,** icky *and* yecchy *and* yucky *and* gross (*all informal*), grungy *and* scuzzy (*both US informal*); malodorous, mephitic, rank, fetid *see* 71.5; **putrid, rotten;** pollutive; nauseating, disgusting; **odious, repulsive** *see* 98.18; **slimy,** scummy (*informal*); barfy *and* vomity *and* puky (*all informal*); sloppy, sludgy; gloppy *and* gunky (*both informal*), scurfy, scabby; wormy, maggoty, flyblown; feculent, ordurous, crappy *and* shitty (*both informal*), excremental, excrementitious, faecal *see* 12.20

24 hoggish, piggish, swinish, beastly

25 squalid, sordid, wretched, shabby; slumlike, slummy

adverbs

26 uncleanly, impurely, unpurely; **dirtily,** grimily; filthily, foully, nastily, vilely

81 HEALTHFULNESS

nouns

1 healthfulness, healthiness, salubrity, salubriousness, salutariness, **wholesomeness,** beneficialness, goodness

2 hygiene, hygienics; sanitation *see* 79.3; public health, epidemiology; health physics; **preventive medicine,** prophylaxis, preventive dentistry, prophylactodontia; prophylactic psychology, mental hygiene; **fitness and exercise** *see* 84

3 hygienist, hygeist, sanitarian; public health doctor *or* physician, epidemiologist; health physicist; preventive dentist, prophylactodontist; dental hygienist

verbs

4 to make for health, conduce to health, **be good for,** agree with

adjectives

5 healthful, healthy, salubrious, salutary, wholesome, health-preserving, health-enhancing, life-promoting, **beneficial,** benign, good, **good for;** hygienic, hygienica!, hygeian, sanitary; constitutional, for one's health; conditioning; bracing, refreshing, invigorating, tonic

82 UNHEALTHFULNESS

nouns

1 unhealthfulness, unhealthiness, insalubrity, insalubriousness, unsalutariness, **unwholesomeness,** badness; noxiousness, noisomeness, injuriousness, harmfulness *see* 999.5; pathenogenicity; health hazard, threat *or* danger *or* menace to health; contamination, pollution, environmental pollution, air *or* water *or* noise pollution

2 innutritiousness, indigestibility

3 poisonousness, toxicity, venomousness; virulence *or* virulency, malignancy, noxiousness, destructiveness, deadliness; **infectiousness,** infectivity, contagiousness, communicability; poison, venom *see* 1000.3

verbs

4 to disagree with, not be good for, sicken

adjectives

5 unhealthful, unhealthy, insalubrious, unsalutary, unwholesome, peccant, bad, **bad for;** noxious, noisome, injurious, baneful, harmful *see* 999.12; **polluted,** contaminated, tainted, foul, septic; unhygienic, unsanitary, insanitary; morbific, pathogenic, pestiferous

6 innutritious, indigestible, unassimilable

7 poisonous, toxic, toxicant; **venomous,** envenomed, venenate, venenous; veneniferous, toxiferous; pollutive; **virulent, noxious, malignant,** malign, destructive, deadly; pestiferous, pestilential; mephitic, miasmal, miasmic, miasmatic; **infectious,** infective, contagious, communicable, catching

83 HEALTH

nouns

1 health, well-being; fitness, health and fitness, physical fitness *see* 84; bloom, flush, glow, rosiness; mental health, emotional health; physical condition; Hygeia

2 healthiness, healthfulness, soundness, wholesomeness; healthy body, good *or* healthy constitution; **good health,** good state of health, "good estate of body"—BIBLE, "*mens sana in corpore sano*"—JUVENAL (*Latin,* a sound mind in a sound body); **robust health,** rugged health, rude health, glowing health, picture of health, "health that snuffs the morning air"—GRAINGER; **fine fettle,** fine whack (*informal*), fine *or* high feather (*informal*), **good shape,** good trim, fine shape, top shape (*informal*), good condition, mint condition; eupepsia, good digestion; clean bill of health

3 haleness, heartiness, robustness, vigorousness, ruggedness, **vitality,** lustiness, hardiness, strength, vigour; longevity

4 immunity, resistance, nonproneness *or* nonsusceptibility to disease; **immunization;** antibody, antigen *see* 86.27

5 health *or* **medical care,** health *or* **medical management, health maintenance, medical care** *see* 91.1; disease prevention, preventive medicine; health education programme; health-care policy, health policy; National Health Service *or* NHS *or* National Health; **health plan, health** *or* **medical insurance,** health service; Department of Health, Ministry of Health, Secretary of State for Health, Minister for Health, Health Service Commissioner; health club

verbs

6 to enjoy good health, have a clean bill of health, be in the pink; be in the best of health; **feel good,** feel fine, feel fit, feel like a million dollars *or* like a million (*informal*), never feel better; be full of pep, feel one's oats (*US & Canadian*); burst with health, bloom, glow, flourish; keep fit, stay in shape; wear well, stay young

7 **to get well, recover** *see* 396.20, mend, be oneself again, feel like a new person, get back on one's feet, get over it; recuperate *see* 396.19

adjectives

8 **healthy, healthful,** enjoying health, **fine,** in health, in shape, in condition, **fit, fit and fine; in good health,** in the pink of condition, in mint condition, in good case, **in good** *or* **fine shape, in fine fettle,** bursting with health, full of life and vigour, feeling one's oats (*US & Canadian*); eupeptic

9 (*informal terms*) **in the pink,** in fine fettle, chipper, right as rain, **fit as a fiddle;** alive and kicking, bright-eyed and bushy-tailed; full of beans

10 **well, unailing, unsick, unsickly,** unfrail; all right, doing nicely, up and about, sitting up and taking nourishment, alive and well

11 **sound,** whole, wholesome; unimpaired *see* 1001.8; sound of mind and body, sound in wind and limb, sound as a pound (*informal*)

12 **hale, hearty,** hale and hearty, **robust,** robustious, robustuous, vital, **vigorous, strong,** strong as a horse *or* an ox, bionic (*informal*), stalwart, stout, sturdy, **rugged,** rude, hardy, lusty, bouncing, well-knit, flush (*old*); **fit,** in condition *or* shape

13 **fresh,** green, youthful, **blooming;** flush, flushed, **rosy,** rosy-cheeked, apple-cheeked, ruddy, pink, pink-cheeked; fresh-faced, fresh as a daisy *or* rose, fresh as April

14 **immune, resistant,** nonprone *or* nonsusceptible to disease; health-conscious, health-protecting; immune response

84 FITNESS, EXERCISE

nouns

1 **fitness, physical fitness, physical conditioning, condition, shape,** trim, tone, fettle, aerobic fitness, anaerobic fitness, cardiovascular fitness, cardiorespiratory fitness; **gymnasium, gym** (*informal*), **fitness centre, health club,** health spa, workout room, weight room, exercise track *or* trail, *parcourse* or *parcours* (*both French*); **weight, barbell,** dumbbell, exercise machine, bench, exercise bike, rowing machine, stair-climbing machine, Indian club, wand; whirlpool bath, Jacuzzi (*trademark*), hot tub, spa

2 **exercise,** motion, movement, manoeuvre; **programme,** routine, drill, workout; **exercise systems; warm-up, stretching,** warm-down; **callisthenics** (*see list*), Callanetics (*trademark*), free exercise, setting-up exercise *or* set-ups, physical jerks, daily dozen (*informal*), constitutional; **parcourse exercise** (*see list*); **gymnastic exercise, gymnastics; isometrics,** isometric *or* no-movement exercise; **violent exercise,** breather, wind sprint; **aerobic exercise, aerobics,** aerobic dancing *or* dance, dancercize *or* dancercizing, jazz ballet *or* jazzercise *and* popmobility; **bodybuilding,** weightlifting, weight training, pumping iron

(*informal*), bench press, arm raise, curl, wrist curl; **running, jogging,** roadwork, distance running; obligate running; cross-training, interval training, *fartlek* (*Swedish*); **walking,** fitness walking, healthwalking, aerobic walking, powerwalking, powerstriding; **swimming,** swimnastics, water exercise, aquarobics *or* aquaerob *or* hydro-robics, aqua-dynamics; tub toner

3 **physical fitness test;** stress test, treadmill test; cardiovascular test

verbs

4 **to exercise, work out,** warm up, aerobicize, stretch, lift weights, pump iron (*informal*), jog, run, bicycle, walk, fitness-walk, power-walk

5 **callisthenic exercises**

arm raise	rebounding
bench stepping	rope skipping
high jump	shuffle
hop and balance	side bend
jump and stretch	sit-up *or* trunk curl
jumping jack	sit-up and leg stretch
leg lift	squat thrust
place running	trunk twist
push-up	

6 **parcourse exercises**

Achilles stretch	knee lift
balance beam	leg-stretch
bench leg-raise	log hop
body-curl	push-up
chin-up	sit and reach
circle body	step-up
hand-walk	toe touch
hop-kick	vault-bar
jumping jack	

85 DISEASE

nouns

1 **disease** (*see list*), **illness, sickness, malady, ailment, indisposition, disorder,** lurgy (*informal*), complaint, morbidity, *morbus* (*Latin*), **affliction,** affection, distemper (*old*), **infirmity; disability,** defect, handicap; deformity *see* 265.3; **birth defect,** congenital defect; abnormality, condition, pathological condition; **signs, symptoms, pathology,** symptomatology, symptomology, syndrome; **sickishness,** malaise; complication, secondary disease *or* condition; plant disease, blight *see* 1000.2

2 **fatal disease,** deadly disease, terminal disease *or* illness, hopeless condition; **death** *see* 307, clinical death, loss of vital signs; apparent death; **brain death,** local death, somatic death; sudden death, unexplained death; liver death; serum death; thymic death *or* mors thymica; cell death, molecular death; cot death *or* crib death (*US & Canadian*) *or* sudden infant death syndrome *or* SIDS

3 **unhealthiness,** healthlessness; **ill health,** poor health, delicate *or* shaky *or* frail *or* fragile health; **sickliness,** peakedness (*informal*), **feebleness,** delicacy, weakliness, fragility, **frailty** *see* 16.2; **infirmity, unsoundness,** debility, debilitation, enervation, exhaustion, decrepitude; wasting, languishing, languishment (*old*), cachexia *or* cachexy;

chronic ill health, invalidity, **invalidism;** unwholesomeness, morbidity, morbidness; hypochondria, hypochondriasis, valetudinarianism

4 **infection, contagion,** contamination, taint, virus; **contagiousness, infectiousness, communicability;** pestiferousness, epidemicity, inoculability; carrier, vector; **epidemiology**

5 **epidemic, plague, pestilence,** pest, pandemic, pandemia, scourge; white plague, tuberculosis; pesthole, plague spot

6 **seizure, attack,** access, visitation; arrest; blockage, stoppage, occlusion, thrombosis, thromboembolism; **stroke,** ictus, apoplexy; **spasm, throes, fit, paroxysm, convulsion,** eclampsia, frenzy; **epilepsy,** falling sickness; tonic spasm, tetany, lockjaw, trismus, tetanus; laryngospasm, laryngismus; clonic spasm, clonus; cramp; vaginismus

7 **fever, feverishness,** febrility, febricity, pyrexia; hyperpyrexia, hyperthermia; **heat, fire, fever heat;** flush, hectic flush; calenture; delirium *see* 925.8

8 **collapse, breakdown, crackup** (*informal*), **prostration,** exhaustion; myalgic encephalomylitis *or* ME, postviral syndrome *or* PVS, postviral fatigue syndrome, Yuppie disease *or* flu (*informal*), nervous breakdown *or* exhaustion *or* prostration, neurasthenia; circulatory collapse

9 (*disease symptoms*) anaemia; ankylosis; asphyxiation, anoxia, cyanosis; ataxia; bleeding, haemorrhage; colic; dizziness, vertigo; ague, chill, chills; hot flush, hot flash (*US & Canadian*); dropsy, hydrops, edema; morning sickness; fainting; fatigue *see* 21; fever; constipation; diarrhoea, flux, dysentery; indigestion, upset stomach, dyspepsia; inflammation *see* 85.9; necrosis; insomnia; itching, pruritus; jaundice, icterus; backache, lumbago; vomiting, nausea; paralysis; skin eruption, rash; sore, abscess; hypertension, high blood pressure; hypotension, low blood pressure; tumour, growth, blastoma; shock; convulsion, seizure, spasm; pain *see* 26; fibrillation, tachycardia; shortness of breath, laboured breathing, apnoea, dyspnoea, asthma; blennorhea; nasal discharge, rheum, coughing, sneezing; wasting, cachexia *or* cachexy, tabes, marasmus, emaciation, atrophy; sclerosis

10 **inflammation,** inflammatory disease, itis; muscle *or* muscular disease *or* disorder, myopathy; collagen disease, connective-tissue disease

11 **deficiency diseases** (*see list*), nutritional disease, vitamin-deficiency disease

12 **genetic disease** (*see list*), gene disease, gene-transmitted disease, hereditary *or* congenital disease

13 **infectious disease** (*see list*), infection

14 **eye disease** (*see list*), ophthalmic disease, disease of the eye *or* of vision; cataract; conjunctivitis *or* pink eye; glaucoma; sty; eye *or* visual defect, defective vision *see* 28

15 **ear disease,** otic disease *or* disorder; **deafness; earache,** otalgia; tympanitis; otosclerosis; **vertigo,** dizziness, loss of balance; Ménière's syndrome *or* disease *or* apoplectical deafness

16 **respiratory disease, upper respiratory disease;** lung disease

17 **tuberculosis** *or* **TB,** white plague, phthisis, consumption

18 **venereal disease** *or* **VD,** sexually-transmitted disease *or* STD, social disease, Cupid's itch *or* Venus's curse, dose (*informal*); chancre, chancroid; gonorrhoea *or* clap *or* the clap *or* claps (*informal*); syphilis *or* syph *or* the syph *or* the pox (*informal*)

19 **cardiovascular disease;** heart disease, heart condition; vascular disease; hypertension *or* high blood pressure; angina *or* angina pectoris; cardiac *or* myocardial infarction; cardiac arrest; congenital heart disease; congestive heart failure; coronary *or* ischemic heart disease; coronary thrombosis; heart attack, coronary, heart failure; tachycardia

20 **blood disease,** haemic *or* haematic disease, haematopathology

21 **endocrine disease,** gland *or* glandular disease, endocrinism, endocrinopathy; diabetes; goitre; hyper- *or* hypoglycaemia; hyper- *or* hypothyroidism

22 **metabolic disease;** acidosis, alkalosis, ketosis; gout, podagra; galactosemia, lactose intolerance, fructose intolerance; phenylketonuria *or* PKU, maple syrup urine disease, congenital hypophosphatasia

23 **liver disease,** hepatic disease; gallbladder disease; jaundice *or* icterus

24 **kidney disease,** renal disease; nephritis

25 **neural** *or* **nerve disease,** neuropathy; brain disease; amyotrophic lateral sclerosis *or* Lou Gehrig's disease; palsy, cerebral palsy, Bell's palsy; chorea *or* St Vitus's dance *or* the jerks (*informal*); Huntington's chorea; headache, migraine; multiple sclerosis *or* MS; Parkinson's disease *or* Parkinsonism; Alzheimer's disease *or* Alzheimer's, sciatica *or* sciatic neuritis; shingles *or* herpes zoster; spina fibida; emotional trauma *see* 92.17

26 **shock, trauma;** traumatism

27 **paralysis,** paralysation, palsy, impairment of motor function; **stroke,** apoplexy; paresis; motor paralysis, sensory paralysis; hemiplegia, paraplegia, diplegia, quadriplegia; cataplexy, catalepsy; infantile paralysis, poliomyelitis, polio (*informal*)

28 **heatstroke;** heat prostration *or* exhaustion; sunstroke, *coup de soleil* (*French*), siriasis, insolation; calenture, thermic fever

29 **gastrointestinal disease,** disease of the digestive tract; stomach condition; colic; colitis; constipation *or* irregularity; diarrhoea *or* dysentery *or* looseness of the bowels *or* flux, the trots *or* the shits *or* the runs (*all informal*); gastritis; indigestion *or* dyspepsia; ulcer, gastric ulcer, peptic ulcer, rodent ulcer

30 **nausea,** nauseation, queasiness, squeamishness, qualmishness; qualm, pukes (*informal*); motion sickness, travel sickness, **seasickness,** *mal de mer* (*French*), airsickness, car sickness; vomiting *see* 908.8

31 **poisoning,** intoxication, venenation; septic poisoning, blood poisoning, sepsis, septicaemia, toxaemia, pyemia, septicopyemia; autointoxication; food poisoning, ptomaine poisoning, milk sickness, gastroenteritis, listeriosis, salmonellosis; ergotism, St Anthony's fire

32 **environmental disease, occupational disease** (*see list*), disease of the workplace, environmental *or* occupational hazard, biohazard

33 allergy, allergic disorder; allergic rhinitis, **hay fever,** pollinosis; **asthma,** bronchial asthma; **hives,** urticaria; eczema; conjunctivitis; cold sore; allergic gastritis; cosmetic dermatitis; Chinese restaurant syndrome *or* Kwok's disease; allergen

34 skin diseases; acne, sebaceous gland disorder; dermatitis; eczema; herpes; hives; itch; psoriasis

35 skin eruption, eruption, **rash,** efflorescence, breaking out; nappy rash; drug rash, vaccine rash; prickly heat, heat rash; hives, urticaria, nettle rash; papular rash; rupia

36 sore, lesion; pustule, papule, papula, fester, **pimple,** zit (*informal*); pock; ulcer, ulceration; bedsore; tubercle; blister, bleb, bulla, blain; whelk, wheal, welt, wale; **boil,** furuncle, furunculus; carbuncle; canker; canker sore; cold sore, fever blister; sty; abscess, gathering, aposteme (*old*); gumboil, parulis; whitlow, felon, paronychia; bubo; chancre; soft chancre, chancroid; haemorrhoids, piles; bunion; chilblain, kibe; polyp; stigma, petechia; scab, eschar; fistula; suppuration, festering; swelling, rising *see* 283.4

37 trauma, wound, injury hurt, lesion; **cut,** incision, scratch, gash; puncture, stab, stab wound; flesh wound; **laceration,** mutilation; abrasion, scuff, scrape, chafe, gall; frazzle, fray; run, **rip,** rent, slash, **tear; burn,** scald, scorch, first- *or* second- *or* third-degree burn; flash burn; **break, fracture,** bone-fracture, comminuted fracture, compound *or* open fracture, greenstick fracture, spiral *or* torsion fracture; rupture; crack, chip, craze, check, crackle; wrench; whiplash injury *or* whiplash; concussion; **bruise, contusion,** ecchymosis, **black-and-blue mark; black eye,** shiner (*informal*); **battering;** battered child syndrome

38 growth, neoplasm; **tumour,** intumescence; benign tumour, nonmalignant tumour, innocent tumour; malignant tumour, malignant growth, metastatic tumour, **cancer,** sarcoma, carcinoma; morbid growth; excrescence, outgrowth; proud flesh; exostosis; cyst, wen; fungus, fungosity; callus, callosity, **corn,** clavus; **wart,** verruca; **mole,** naevus

39 gangrene, mortification, necrosis, sphacelus, sphacelation; noma; moist gangrene, dry gangrene, gas gangrene, hospital gangrene; caries, cariosity, tooth decay; slough; necrotic tissue

40 (*animal diseases*) anthrax, splenic fever, charbon, milzbrand, malignant pustule; malignant catarrh *or* malignant catarrhal fever; bighead; blackleg, black quarter, quarter evil *or* ill; cattle plague, rinderpest; glanders; foot-and-mouth disease, hoof-and-mouth disease, aphthous fever; distemper; gapes; heaves, broken wind; hog cholera; bovine spongiform encephalopathy *or* BSE, mad cow disease (*informal*); loco, loco disease, locoism; mange, scabies; pip; rot, liver rot, sheep rot; staggers, megrims, blind staggers, mad staggers; swine dysentery, bloody flux; stringhalt; Texas fever, blackwater; John's disease, paratuberculosis, pseudotuberculosis; rabies, hydrophobia; myxomatosis

41 germ, pathogen, contagium, bug (*informal*), disease-causing agent, disease-producing microorganism; **microbe,** microorganism; **virus,** filterable virus, nonfilterable virus, adenovirus, echovirus, lentivirus *or* slow virus, parvovirus, reovirus, rhinovirus, enterovirus, picornavirus, retrovirus; HIV *or* human immunodeficiency virus; rickettsia; bacterium, **bacteria,** coccus, meningococcus, streptococcus, staphylococcus, bacillus, spirillum, vibrio, spirochaete, gram-positive bacteria, gram-negative bacteria, aerobe, aerobic bacteria, anaerobe, anaerobic bacteria; protozoon, amoeba, trypanosome; fungus, mould, spore; **carcinogen,** cancer-causing agent

42 sick person, ill person, sufferer, victim; valetudinarian, **invalid,** shut-in (*US & Canadian*); incurable, terminal case; **patient, case;** inpatient, outpatient; apoplectic, consumptive, dyspeptic, epileptic, rheumatic, arthritic, spastic; **the sick, the infirm**

43 carrier, vector, biological vector, mechanical vector; Typhoid Mary

44 cripple, defective, **handicapped person,** incapable; amputee; paraplegic, quadriplegic, paralytic; deformity *see* 265.3; the crippled, the handicapped, "the halt, the lame, and the blind"—BIBLE; idiot, imbecile *see* 923.8

verbs

45 to ail, suffer, labour under, be affected with, complain of; **feel ill,** feel under the weather, feel awful (*informal*), feel something terrible, not feel like anything (*informal*), feel like the walking dead; look green about the gills (*informal*)

46 to take sick *or* **ill, sicken; catch, contract, get,** take, sicken for, **come down with** (*informal*), be stricken *or* seized by, fall a victim to; catch cold; catch one's death (*informal*); **break out,** break out with, break out in a rash, erupt; run a temperature, fever; be laid by the heels, be struck down, be brought down, be felled; drop in one's tracks, **collapse;** overdose *or* **OD** (*informal*); go into shock, be traumatized

47 to fail, weaken, sink, decline, run down, lose strength, lose one's grip, dwindle, droop, flag, wilt, wither, wither away, fade, **languish,** waste, waste away, pine, peak,
"dwindle, peak, and pine"—SHAKESPEARE

48 to go lame, founder

49 to afflict, disorder, derange; sicken, indispose; weaken, enfeeble, enervate, reduce, debilitate, devitalize; **invalid,** incapacitate, **disable;** lay up, hospitalize

50 to infect, disease, contaminate, taint

51 to poison, empoison (*old*), envenom

adjectives

52 disease-causing, disease-producing, pathogenic; threatening, life-threatening; unhealthful *see* 82.5

53 unhealthy, healthless, in poor health; **infirm, unsound,** invalid, valetudinary, valetudinarian, debilitated, cachectic, enervated, exhausted, drained; shut-in, housebound, homebound, wheelchair-bound; **sickly,** peaky *or* peaked (*informal*); **weakly, feeble, frail** *see* 16.12-21; weakened, with low resistance, **run-down,** reduced, reduced in health; **dying** *see* 307.33, **terminal,** moribund, languishing, failing *see* 16.21; pale *see* 36.7

54 unwholesome, unhealthy, unsound, morbid, diseased, pathological

55 ill, ailing, sick, unwell, indisposed, taken ill, down, bad, on the sick list; **sickish, seedy** *and* rocky *and* ropy (*all informal*), **under the weather, out of sorts** (*informal*), below par (*informal*), off-colour, off one's food (*informal*); not quite right, not oneself; faint, faintish, feeling faint; feeling awful *and* feeling something terrible (*both informal*); sick as a dog *or* a pig (*informal*), laid low; in a bad way, critically ill, in danger, on the critical list, on the guarded list (*US & Canadian*), in intensive care; mortally ill, sick unto death

56 nauseated, nauseous, **queasy, squeamish, qualmish,** qualmy; **sick to one's stomach;** pukish *and* puky *and* barfy (*all informal*); travel-sick, seasick, carsick, airsick

57 feverish, fevered, feverous, in a fever, febrile, pyretic; **flushed,** inflamed, **hot, burning,** fiery, hectic; hyperpyretic, hyperthermic; delirious *see* 925.31

58 laid up, invalided, hospitalized, in hospital; **bedridden, bedfast, sick abed; down,** prostrate, flat on one's back; in childbed, confined

59 diseased, morbid, pathological, bad, **infected, contaminated,** tainted, peccant, **poisoned,** septic; cankerous, cankered, ulcerous, ulcerated, ulcerative, gangrenous, gangrened, mortified, sphacelated; **inflamed;** congested; **swollen,** edematous

60 anaemic, chlorotic; bilious; dyspeptic, liverish, colicky; dropsical, edematous, hydropic; gouty, podagric; neuritic, neuralgic; palsied, paralytic; pneumonic, pleuritic, tubercular, tuberculous, phthisic, consumptive; chesty (*informal*); rheumatic, arthritic; osteoporotic; rickety, rachitic; syphilitic, pocky, luetic; tabetic, tabid (*old*); allergic; allergenic; apoplectic; hypertensive; diabetic; encephalitic; epileptic; laryngitic; leprous; malarial; measly; nephritic; scabietic, scorbutic, scrofulous; variolous, variolar; tumorous; cancerous, malignant; **carcinogenic,** tumorigenic

61 contagious, infectious, infective, **catching,** taking, spreading, **communicable,** zymotic, inoculable; pestiferous, pestilential, **epidemic,** epidemial, pandemic; epizootic, epiphytotic; endemic; sporadic; opportunistic

62 kinds of disease

acute disease *or* condition
allergy *or* allergic disease
atrophy
autoimmune disease
bacterial disease
blood disease
bone disease
cardiovascular disease
childhood *or* paediatric disease
chronic disease *or* condition
chronic fatigue syndrome
circulatory disease
collagen disease
congenital disease
connective-tissue disease
contagious *or* infectious disease
deficiency disease
degenerative disease
digestive disease
endemic disease
endocrine disease
endocrine gland disease
epidemic disease
functional disease
fungus *or* fungal disease
gastric *or* stomach disease
gastrointestinal disease
genetic disease
geriatric disease
glandular disease
hepatic *or* liver disease
hereditary disease
hypertrophy
iatrogenic disease
intestinal disease
joint disease
malignant disease
muscular disease
neurological disease
nutritional disease
occupational disease
ophthalmic disease
organic disease
pandemic disease
parasitic disease
protozoan disease
psychogenic *or* psychosomatic disease
pulmonary disease
radiation disease
renal *or* kidney disease
respiratory disease
skin disease
urinogenital *or* urogenital disease
venereal *or* sexually-transmitted disease *or* STD
virus *or* viral disease
wasting disease
worm disease

63 deficiency diseases and disorders

anaemia
ariboflavinosis
beriberi
cachexia
chlorosis
deficiency anaemia
dermatitis
goitre
greensickness
Italian *or* Lombardy leprosy
keratomalacia
kwashiorkor
maidism
malnutrition
night blindness
osteomalacia
osteoporosis
pellagra
pernicious anaemia
protein deficiency
rickets *or* rachitis
scurvy
struma
vitamin deficiency
xerophthalmia

64 genetic diseases and disorders

achromatic vision
albinism
Christmas disease
colour blindness
cystic fibrosis
dichromatic vision
Down's syndrome
dysautonomia
Hartnup's disease
haemophilia
Huntington's chorea
ichthyosis
lipid histiocytosis
maple syrup urine disease
Milroy's disease
mongolism *or* mongolianism (old)
mucoviscidosis
muscular dystrophy
neurofibromatosis
Niemann-Pick disease
pancreatic fibrosis
sickle-cell anaemia *or* disease
Tay-Sachs disease
thalassaemia
Turner's syndrome
Werdnig-Hoffmann disease

65 infectious diseases

acquired immune deficiency syndrome *or* AIDS
acute articular rheumatism
African lethargy *or* encephalitis lethargica
ague
AIDS-related complex *or* ARC *or* pre-AIDS
alkali disease
amebiasis
amoebic dysentery
anthrax *or* pulmonary anthrax *or* woolsorter's disease
bacillary dysentery
bastard measles
black death
black fever
blackwater fever
breakbone fever
brucellosis
bubonic plague
cachectic fever
candidiasis
cerebral rheumatism
Chagres fever
chicken pox *or* varicella
cholera *or* Asiatic cholera
cowpox
Creutzfeldt-Jakob disease
dandy fever
dengue *or* dengue fever
diphtheria

dumdum fever
dysentery
elephantiasis
enteric fever
erysipelas
famine fever
five-day fever
framboesia
German measles
glandular fever
grippe
Hansen's disease *or* leprosy
Haverhill fever
hepatitis
herpes
histoplasmosis
hookworm
inflammatory rheumatism
influenza *or* flu (informal)
jail fever
jungle rot
kala azar
Kew Gardens spotted
  fever
legionnaires' disease
lepra
leprosy
leptospirosis
loaiasis *or* loa loa
Lyme disease
lyssa
malaria *or* malarial fever
marsh fever
measles *or* rubeola
meningitis
milzbrand
mononucleosis *or* infectious
  mononucleosis *or* kissing
  disease (informal)
mumps
ornithosis
osteomyelitis
paratyphoid fever
parotitis
pneumonia
poliomyelitis *or* infantile
  paralysis *or* polio
  (informal)
polyarthritis rheumatism
ponos
psittacosis *or* parrot fever
rabies *or* hydrophobia

rat-bite fever
relapsing fever
rheumatic fever
rickettsial pox
ringworm *or* tinea
Rocky Mountain spotted
  fever
rubella
scarlatina
scarlet fever
schistosomiasis
scrub typhus *or*
  tsutsugamushi disease
septic sore throat
shigellosis
sleeping sickness *or* sleepy
  sickness
smallpox *or* variola
snail fever
splenic fever
spotted fever
St Anthony's fire
strep throat
streptococcus tonsilitis
swamp fever
tetanus *or* lockjaw
thrush
tick-borne typhus
tick fever
toxic shock syndrome
toxocariasis
tracheitis
trench fever
trench mouth *or* Vincent's
  infection *or* Vincent's
  angina
trypanosomiasis
tuberculosis
tularaemia *or* deer fly fever
  or rabbit fever
typhoid fever *or* typhoid
typhus *or* typhus fever
undulant fever
vaccinia
venereal disease *or* VD
viral dysentery
viral pneumonia
whooping cough *or*
  pertussis
yaws
yellow fever *or* yellow jack
zoster *or* shingles *or* zona

**66 environmental and occupational diseases and
  disorders**

aeroembolism *or* caisson
  disease *or* decompression
  sickness *or* tunnel disease
  or diver's palsy *or* the
  bends (informal)
altitude sickness
anoxaemia
anoxia
anoxic anoxia

anthrax *or* pulmonary
  anthrax *or* woolsorter's
  disease
cadmium poisoning
chilblain
frostbite
frozen shoulder
housemaid's knee
immersion foot

jet lag
lead poisoning
mercury poisoning
Minamata disease
motion sickness
pneumoconiosis *or* black
  lung (informal)
radiation sickness
radionecrosis
red-out

repetitive strain injury *or*
  RSI
sick building syndrome
sunstroke
tennis elbow
tenosynovitis
trench foot
writer's cramp *or* palsy *or*
  spasm

86 REMEDY

nouns

1 **remedy, cure, corrective,** alterative, remedial
measure, sovereign remedy; **relief, help, aid,
assistance,** succour; balm, balsam; healing agent;
restorative, analeptic; healing quality *or* virtue;
specific, specific remedy; **prescription,** recipe,
receipt

2 **nostrum,** patent medicine, quack remedy; snake oil

3 **panacea, cure-all,** universal remedy, theriac,
catholicon; polychrest, broad-spectrum drug *or*
antibiotic; elixir, elixir of life, *elixir vitae* (*Latin*)

4 **medicine, medicament, medication,** medicinal,
theraputant, **drug, physic,** preparation, mixture;
herbs, medicinal herbs, simples, vegetable remedies,
"the physic of the field"—Pope; balsam, balm; tisane,
ptisan; drops; powder; inhalant; electuary, elixir,
syrup, lincture, linctus; officinal; specialized drug,
orphan drug; **prescription drug,** ethical drug;
over-the-counter *or* OTC drug, counter drug,
nonprescription drug; proprietary medicine *or*
drug, proprietary, patent medicine; proprietary name,
generic name; materia medica; **placebo,** placebo
effect

5 **drug, narcotic drug, controlled substance**

6 **dose, draught, potion,** portion, **shot,** injection;
broken dose; booster, booster dose, recall dose,
booster shot

7 **pill, bolus, tablet, capsule,** lozenge, troche

8 **tonic, bracer,** cordial, restorative, analeptic,
roborant, **pick-me-up** (*informal*); **shot in the arm**
(*informal*); vitamin shot

9 **stimulant;** Adrenalin (*trademark*), adrenaline,
epinephrine (*US*), aloes; amphetamine sulphate,
aromatic spirits of ammonia, caffeine,
dextroamphetamine sulphate *or* Dexedrine
(*trademark*), digitalin *or* digitalis, methamphetamine
hydrochloride *or* Methedrine (*trademark*), smelling
salts *or* salts

10 **palliative, alleviative, alleviatory, lenitive,
assuasive,** assuager; soothing, abirritant

11 **balm, lotion, salve, ointment, unguent,**
unguentum (*Latin*), cerate, unction, balsam, oil,
emollient, demulcent; **liniment,** embrocation;
vulnerary; collyrium, eyesalve, eyebath, eyewater
(*old*), eyewash; ear-drops

12 **sedative, sedative hypnotic, depressant,**
amobarbital and secobarbital *or* Tuinal (*trademark*),
amobarbital sodium *or* Amytal (*trademark*), atropine,
barbitone, barbituric acid, belladonna, chloral hydrate
or chloral, laudanum, meperidine *or* Demerol

(*trademark*), Mogadon (*trademark*), morphine, pentobarbitone *or* Nembutal (*trademark*), phenobarbitone *or* Luminal (*trademark*), Quaalude (*trademark*), reserpine, scopolamine, secobarbitone *or* Seconal (*trademark*); **sleeping pill** *or* **tablet** *or* potion; **calmative, tranquillizer,** chlorpromazine, diazepam, Equanil (*trademark*), Librium (*trademark*), meprobamate, rauwolfia, reserpine, Thorazine (*trademark*), Triavil (*trademark*), Valium (*trademark*); abirritant, soother, soothing syrup, quietener, pacifier; **analgesic,** acetaminophen *or* Datril (*trademark*), *or* Tylenol (*trademark*), acetanilide, acetophenetidin, aspirin *or* acetylsalicylic acid *or* Bayer (*trademark*), *or* Empirin (*trademark*), buffered aspirin *or* Bufferin (*trademark*), headache *or* aspirin powder, ibuprofen *or* Advil (*trademark*), *or* Motrin (*trademark*), *or* Nuprin (*trademark*), *or* Nurofen (*trademark*), phenacetin, propoxyphene *or* Darvon (*trademark*), sodium salicylate; **anodyne,** paregoric (*old*); **painkiller** *and* **pain pill** (*both informal*); alcohol, liquor *see* 88.13, 14, Brompton *or* Brompton's mixture *or* cocktail

13 psychoactive drug, hallucinogen, psychedelic, psychedelic drug

14 antipyretic, febrifuge, fever-reducer, fever pill (*informal*)

15 anaesthetic; local *or* topical *or* general anaesthetic; differential anaesthetic; chloroform, ether, ethyl chloride, gas, laughing gas, nitrous oxide, novocaine *or* Novocain (*trademark*), thiopental sodium *or* Pentothal (*trademark*), *or* truth serum

16 cough medicine, cough syrup, cough drops; horehound

17 laxative, cathartic, physic, purge, purgative, aperient, carminative, diuretic; stool softener

18 emetic, vomitive *or* vomit (*both archaic*), nauseant

19 enema, clyster, clysma, lavage, lavement (*old*)

20 prophylactic, preventive, preventative, protective

21 antiseptic, disinfectant (*see list*), fumigant, fumigator, **germicide,** bactericide, microbicide; alcohol, carbolic acid, hydrogen peroxide, merbromin *or* Mercurochrome (*trademark*), tincture of iodine

22 dentifrice, toothpaste, tooth powder; mouthwash, gargle

23 contraceptive, birth control device, prophylactic; condom; **rubber** *and* rubber johnny *and* skin *and* bag *and* French letter (*all informal*); female condom, Femidom (*trademark*); oral contraceptive, **birth control pill, the pill** (*informal*), minipill, morning-after pill, abortion pill; diaphragm, pessary, Dutch cap; spermicide, spermicidal jelly, contraceptive foam; intrauterine device *or* IUD, Dalkon shield (*trademark*), Lippes loop

24 vermifuge, vermicide, worm medicine, anthelminthic

25 antacid, gastric antacid, alkalizer

26 antidote, counterpoison, alexipharmic, theriaca *or* theriac

27 antitoxin, antitoxic serum; **antivenin; serum,** antiserum; interferon; **antibody,** antigen-antibody product, anaphylactic antibody, incomplete antibody, inhibiting antibody, sensitizing antibody, monoclonal antibody; gamma globulin, serum gamma globulin,

immune globulin, antitoxic globulin; lysin, precipitin, agglutinin, anaphylactin, bactericidin; antiantibody; antigen, Rh antigen, Rh factor; allergen; **immunosuppressive drug,** immunosuppressant

28 vaccination, inoculation; vaccine

29 antibiotic, ampicillin, bacitracin, erythromycin, gramicidin, neomycin, nystatin, penicillin, polymyxin, streptomycin, tetracycline *or* Terramycin (*trademark*); **miracle drug, wonder drug,** magic bullets; bacteriostat; **sulpha drug** (*see list*), sulpha, sulphanilamide, sulphonamide, sulphathiazole

30 diaphoretic, sudorific

31 vesicant, vesicatory, epispastic

32 miscellaneous drugs, anabolic steroid *or* muscle pill, antihistamine, antispasmodic, beta blocker, counterirritant, decongestant, expectorant, fertility drug *or* pill, hormone, vasoconstrictor, vasodilator

33 dressing, application, epithem (*old*); plaster, court plaster, mustard plaster, sinapism; **poultice,** cataplasm; formentation; **compress,** pledget; stupe; tent; tampon; **bandage, bandaging,** band (*old*), binder, cravat, triangular bandage, roller *or* roller bandage, four-tailed bandage; bandage compress, adhesive compress, sticking plaster, Elastoplast (*trademark*), Band-Aid (*trademark*); butterfly dressing; elastic bandage; rubber bandage; plastic bandage *or* strip; **tourniquet;** sling; splint, brace; cast, plaster cast; tape, **adhesive tape;** lint, cotton wool, cotton, gauze, sponge

34 pharmacology, pharmacy, pharmaceutics; posology; materia medica

35 pharmacist, chemist, pharmaceutist, pharmacopoeist, druggist (*US & Canadian*), **apothecary,** dispenser, gallipot; pharmacologist, pharmaceutical chemist, posologist

36 pharmacy, chemist *and* **chemist's shop,** drugstore (*US & Canadian*), apothecary's shop, dispensary, dispensatory

37 pharmacopoeia, pharmacopedia, dispensatory

verbs

38 to remedy, cure *see* 396.15; prescribe; treat

adjectives

39 remedial, curative, therapeutic, healing, corrective, disease-fighting, alterative, restorative, analeptic, sanative, sanatory; all-healing, panacean; adjuvant; **medicinal,** medicative, theriac, theriacal, iatric; anticancer

40 palliative, lenitive, alleviative, assuasive, soothing, balmy, balsamic, demulcent, emollient

41 antidotal, alexipharmic; **antitoxic; antibiotic,** synthetic antibiotic, semisynthetic antibiotic, bacteriostatic, antimicrobial; antiluetic, antisyphilitic; antiscorbutic; antiperiodic; antipyretic, febrifugal; vermifugal, anthelmintic; **antacid**

42 prophylactic, preventive, protective

43 antiseptic, disinfectant, germicidal, bactericidal

44 tonic, stimulating, bracing, invigorating, reviving, refreshing, restorative, analeptic, strengthening, roborant, corroborant

45 sedative, calmative, calmant, depressant, **soothing, tranquillizing, quietening; narcotic,** opiatic; **analgesic,** anodyne, paregoric (*old*); anti-inflammatory; muscle relaxant; hypnotic, soporific, somniferous, somnifacient, sleep-inducing

46 psychochemical, psychoactive; ataractic; antidepressant, mood drug; hallucinogenic, **psychedelic,** mind-expanding, psychotomimetic

47 anaesthetic, deadening, numbing

48 cathartic, laxative, purgative, aperient; carminative; diuretic

49 emetic, vomitive, vomitory (*old*)

87 SUBSTANCE ABUSE

nouns

1 substance abuse, drug abuse, narcotics abuse, drug use, glue-sniffing, solvent abuse; **addiction, addictedness, drug addiction,** narcotic addiction, opium addiction *or* habit, opiumism, morphine addiction *or* habit, morphinism, heroin addiction *or* habit, cocaine addiction, cocainism, coke habit (*informal*), crack habit, barbiturate addiction, amphetamine addiction; **habit,** drug habit, drug habituation, drug dependence, physical addiction *or* dependence, psychological addiction *or* dependence, monkey on one's back (*informal*); **drug experience, drug intoxication,** high *and* buzz *and* rush (*all informal*); frightening drug experience, bad trip *and* bum trip *and* bummer *and* drag (*all informal*); **alcoholism** see 88.3, alcohol abuse, drinking habit, acute alcoholism, chronic alcoholism, dipsomania; **smoking,** smoking habit, one- *or* two- *or* three-pack-a-day habit, nicotine addiction see 89.10, chain smoking; **tolerance,** acquired tolerance; **withdrawal, withdrawal sickness,** withdrawal syndrome, withdrawal symptoms, coming down *and* crash (*both informal*), abrupt withdrawal *and* cold turkey (*both informal*); **detoxification** *or* detox (*informal*), drying out, taking the cure

2 drug, narcotic, dope (*informal*), gear (*informal*), dangerous drug, controlled substance, abused substance, illegal drug, addictive drug, **hard drug; designer drug;** soft drug, gateway drug; **opiate; sedative, depressant,** sedative hypnotic, **antipsychotic tranquillizer; hallucinogen,** psychedelic, psychedelic drug, psychoactive drug, psychoactive chemical *or* psychochemical, psychotropic drug, psychotomimetic drug, mind-altering drug, mind-expanding drug, mind-blowing drug; **stimulant; antidepressant; inhalant,** volatile inhalant

3 (*informal terms for amphetamines*) bennies, benz, black mollies, brain ticklers, crank, crystal, dexies, diet pills, dolls, ecstasy, footballs, hearts, ice, jelly beans, lid poppers, meth, pep pills, purple hearts, speed, uppers, ups, white crosses

4 (*informal terms for amyl nitrate*) amies, blue angels, blue devils, blue dolls, blue heavens, poppers, snappers; **barbiturates,** barbs, black beauties, candy, dolls, downers, downs, goofballs (*US & Canadian*), gorilla pills, nebbies, nimbies, phennies, phenos, pink ladies, purple hearts, yellow jackets (*US & Canadian*)

5 (*informal terms for chloral hydrate*) joy juice, knockout drops, mickey, Mickey Finn, peter

6 (*informal terms for cocaine*) basuco, bernice, big C, blow, C, charlie, coke, crack, crack cocaine, jumps, dust, flake, girl, gold dust, her, jay, joy powder, lady, lady snow, nose candy, snow, star dust, toot, white, white girl, white lady

7 (*informal terms for hashish*) black hash, black Russian, hash

8 (*informal terms for heroin*) big H, boy, brown, caballo, crap, doojee, flea powder, garbage, H, hard stuff, henry, him, his, horse, hombre, jones, junk, mojo, P-funk, scag, schmeck, smack, white stuff

9 (*informal terms for LSD*) acid, big D, blotter, blue acid, blue cheer, blue heaven, California sunshine, cap, cubes, D, deeda, dots, electric Kool-Aid, haze, L, mellow yellows, orange cubes, pearly gates, pink owsley, strawberry fields, sugar, sunshine, tabs, yellow

10 (*informal terms for marijuana*) Acapulco gold, aunt mary, blow, bomb, boo, bush, doobie, gage, ganja, grass, grefa, hay, hemp, herb, Indian hay, J, jane, kif, mary, maryjane, mary warner, meserole, mighty mezz, moota, muggles, pod, pot, smoke, snop, tea, Texas tea, weed, yerba

11 (*informal terms for marijuana cigarette*) joint, joy stick, kick stick, reefer, roach, spliff, stick, twist

12 (*informal terms for mescaline*) beans, big chief, buttons, cactus, mesc

13 (*informal terms for morphine*) big M, emm, hocus, M, miss emma, miss morph, morph, moocah, white stuff

14 (*informal terms for pentobarbitone*) nebbies, nemmies, nimby, yellow dolls, yellows

15 (*informal terms for opium*) black pills, brown stuff, hop, O, tar

16 (*informal terms for peyote*) bad seed, big chief, buttons, cactus, P, topi

17 (*informal terms for phencyclidine*) angel dust, animal trank, DOA, dust, elephant, hog, PCP, peace, rocket fuel, supergrass, superweed

18 (*informal terms for psilocybin*) magic mushroom, mushroom, shroom

19 dose, hit *and* fix *and* toke *and* rock (*all informal*); **shot, injection,** bang (*informal*); **portion, packet,** bag *and* deck (*both informal*); drug house, shooting gallery *and* needle park (*both informal*), crack house, opium den, balloon room *and* pot party *and* dope den (*all informal*)

20 addict, drug addict, narcotics addict, user, drug user, drug abuser, junkie *and* head *and* druggy *and* doper *and* toker *and* fiend *and* freak *and* space cadet (*all informal*); cocaine user, cokie *and* coke head *and* crackhead *and* sniffer *and* snow drifter *and* flaky (*all informal*); opium user, opium addict, hophead *and* hopdog *and* tar distiller (*all informal*); heroin user *or* addict, smackhead *and* smack-sack *and* schmecker (*all informal*); methedrine user *or* methhead (*informal*); amphetamine user, pillhead *and* pill popper *and* speed freak (*all informal*); LSD user, acidhead *and* acid freak *and* tripper *and* cubehead (*all informal*); marijuana smoker *and* pothead (*both informal*); **drug seller** *or* **dealer,** pusher, contact, connection; **alcoholic, alcohol abuser** see 88; **smoker,** heavy smoker, chain smoker, nicotine addict

verbs

21 **to use, be on,** get on; use occasionally *or* irregularly, have a cotton habit *and* chip *and* chippy *and* joy pop (*all informal*); **get a rush** *or* **flush,** go over the hump (*informal*); **sniff,** snort, blow, toot, one and one (*informal*); **smoke marijuana,** take on a number *and* blow a stick *and* toke *and* blast *and* weed out (*all informal*); **smoke opium,** blow a fill, chase the dragon; freebase; **inject,** mainline, shoot *and* shoot up *and* crank up *and* jab *and* get down *and* get off (*all informal*), pop *and* skin pop (*both informal*), **take pills,** pop pills (*informal*); **withdraw,** crash *and* come down (*both informal*), kick *or* go cold turkey *and* go a la canona *and* hang tough *and* water out (*all informal*), detoxify, disintoxicate, detoxicate, dry out, kick *and* kick the habit (*both informal*); **trip,** blow one's mind (*informal*), wig out (*US informal*); **sell drugs,** deal *and* push (*both informal*); **buy drugs,** score *and* make *and* connect (*all informal*); **have drugs,** be heeled *and* carry *and* hold *and* sizzle (*all informal*); **drink** *or* **booze** *see* 88.24-25; **smoke, smoke tobacco,** puff, puff away, drag, chain-smoke, smoke like a chimney

adjectives

22 **intoxicated,** under the influence, nodding, narcotized, poppied

23 (*informal terms*) **high,** bent, blasted, blind, bombed out, bonged out, buzzed, coked, coked out, flying, fried, geared, geared up, geezed, gonged, gorked, hopped-up, in a zone, junked, luded out, maxed, noddy, ripped, smashed, snowed, spaced, space out, spacey, stoned, strung out, switched on, tanked, totalled, tranqued, tripping, trippy, wired, zoned, zoned out, zonked, zonked out

24 **addicted,** hooked *and* zunked *and* on the needle (*all informal*); dependency-prone; **supplied with drugs,** holding *and* heeled *and* carrying *and* anywhere (*all informal*); using, on, behind acid (*informal*)

88 INTOXICATION, ALCOHOLIC DRINK

nouns

1 intoxication, inebriation, inebriety, insobriety, besottedness, sottedness, **drunkenness, tipsiness,** befuddlement, fuddle, fuddlement, fuddledness, tipsification *and* tiddliness (*both informal*); a high; Dutch courage, pot-valiance *or* pot-valiancy, pot-valour; hangover, katzenjammer, morning after (*informal*)

2 **bibulousness,** bibacity, bibaciousness, bibulosity, sottishness; serious drinking; crapulence, crapulousness; **intemperance** *see* 669; bacchanalianism; Bacchus, Dionysus

3 **alcoholism, dipsomania,** oenomania, alcoholic psychosis *or* addiction, pathological drunkenness, problem drinking, heavy drinking, habitual drunkenness, ebriosity; delirium tremens *see* 925.9,10; grog blossom *and* bottle nose (*both informal*); gin drinker's liver, cirrhosis of the liver

4 **drinking, imbibing; social drinking; tippling,** guzzling, gargling, bibing; winebibbing, winebibbery; toping; hard drinking, serious drinking (*informal*);

boozing *and* swilling (*both informal*), **hitting the booze** *or* **bottle** (*both informal*)

5 **spree, drinking bout,** bout, **celebration,** potation, compotation, symposium, wassail, **carouse, carousal,** drunken carousal *or* revelry; bacchanal, bacchanalia, bacchanalian; **debauch, orgy**

6 (*informal terms*) **binge, drunk,** bust, tear, **bender, pub-crawl,** jag, **booze-up,** piss-up, guzzle, randan, rip

7 **drink,** dram, potation, potion, libation, jar, jug, **nip,** draught, drop, spot, finger or two, sip, sup, suck, drench, guzzle, gargle, jigger; **pint;** peg, swig, swill, pull; **snort,** jolt, **shot,** snifter, wet; quickie; round, round of drinks, shout

8 **bracer, refresher,** reviver, pickup *and* **pick-me-up** (*both informal*), tonic, hair of the dog *or* hair of the dog that bit one (*informal*)

9 **drink, cocktail,** highball (*US*), long drink, mixed drink; **punch; eye-opener** (*informal*), **nightcap** (*informal*), sundowner (*informal*); **chaser** (*informal*), *pousse-café* (*French*), *apéritif* (*French*); parting cup, stirrup cup, doch-an-dorrach *or* wee doch-an-dorrach (*both Scottish*), one for the road; Mickey Finn *or* Mickey *and* knockout drops (*all informal*)

10 **toast, pledge**

11 **drinker,** imbiber, **social drinker,** tippler, bibber; winebibber, oenophilist; **drunkard, drunk, inebriate, sot,** toper, guzzler, swiller, soaker, tosspot, barfly, thirsty soul, **serious drinker,** devotee of Bacchus; swigger; hard drinker, heavy drinker, **alcoholic, dipsomaniac, problem drinker,** chronic alcoholic, chronic drunk, pathological drinker; carouser, reveler, wassailer; bacchanal, bacchanalian; pot companion

12 (*informal terms*) **drunk, lush,** alky *or* alkie, lusher, **soak,** sponge, **boozer,** boozehound, booze fighter, booze freak, dipso, juicehead, loadie, ginhound, elbow bender *or* crooker, bottle sucker, swillbelly, swillpot, swillbowl; **souse, stew,** rummy, rumhound; wino

13 **spirits, liquor,** intoxicating liquor, "the luscious liquor"—Milton, adult beverage, **hard liquor, whisky** *or* **whiskey** (*Irish, US, & Canadian*), firewater, spiritus frumenti, usquebaugh (*Scottish*), schnapps, ardent spirits, strong waters, **intoxicant,** toxicant, inebriant, **potable,** potation, **beverage, drink, strong drink,** strong liquor, alcoholic drink *or* beverage, **alcohol,** aqua vitae, water of life, brew, **grog,** social lubricant, nectar of the gods; **booze** (*informal*); **rum,** the Demon Rum, John Barleycorn; the bottle, the cup, the cup that cheers, "the ruddy cup"—Sir Walter Scott, little brown jug; punch bowl, the flowing bowl

14 (*informal terms*) **juice,** tiger milk, pig *or* tiger sweat, sheepdip, moonshine, white lightning, hooch (*US & Canadian*), sauce (*US & Canadian*); **medicine,** snake medicine, corpse reviver; **rotgut, poison,** rat poison, formaldehyde, embalming fluid; mother's ruin

15 **liqueur, cordial;** brandy, flavoured brandy

16 **beer, ale,** brew *and* brewskie *and* suds *and* swipes *and* wallop (*all informal*), amber fluid (*Australian informal*), "barmy beer"—DRYDEN; bitter, heavy (*Scottish*), mild, light (*Scottish*); barley wine; small beer

17 wine, *vin* (*French*), *vino* (*Spanish & Italian*); vintage wine, nonvintage wine; red wine, white wine, rosé wine, pink wine; dry *or* sweet wine, heavy *or* light wine, full *or* thin wine, rough *or* smooth wine, still wine, sparkling wine; extra sec *or* demi-sec *or* sec *or* brut champagne; new wine, must; imported wine, domestic wine; *vin de pays* (*French*); wine of the country, *vin du campagne* (*French*); table wine, jug wine, plonk, *vin ordinaire* (*French*), *Tafelwein* (*German*)

18 bootleg alcohol, moonshine (*informal*); hooch *and* shine *and* mountain dew (*all informal*), white lightning *or* mule (*informal*); bathtub gin; home brew

19 off-licence owner, victualler, liquor dealer, liquor store owner (*both US*); **vintner,** wine merchant; winegrower, winemaker, wine expert, oenologist; **publican,** innkeeper, bartender, **barperson, barman,** mixologist, barkeeper, barkeep, tapster, potboy *or* potman; barmaid, tapstress; **brewer,** brewmaster; **distiller; bootlegger, moonshiner** (*informal*)

20 bar, barroom, *bistro* (*French*), cocktail lounge; taproom *or* tap; **tavern, pub,** boozer (*informal*), pothouse, alehouse, rumshop, grogshop, dramshop, groggery, gin mill (*informal*), **saloon,** drinking saloon, saloon bar; bierkeller; lounge bar, private bar, piano bar, singles bar, gay bar; waterhole *or* watering hole (*informal*); wine bar; public house, free house, tied house; local (*informal*); beer parlour, beer garden, rathskeller; **nightclub, cabaret;** café, wine shop; dive (*informal*), barrel house *and* honky-tonk (*both US informal*); **speakeasy** *and* blind tiger *and* blind pig *and* after-hours joint (*all US informal*)

21 distillery, still, distiller; **brewery,** brewhouse; **winery,** wine press; bottling works

verbs

22 to intoxicate, inebriate, addle, befuddle, bemuse, besot, go to one's head, make one see double, make one tiddly

23 (*informal terms*) **to plaster,** pickle, swack, crock, stew, souse, stone, pollute, tipsify, booze up, boozify, fuddle, overtake

24 to tipple, drink, dram, nip; grog, **guzzle,** gargle; **imbibe,** have a drink *or* nip *or* dram *or* guzzle *or* gargle, soak, bib, quaff, sip, sup, lap, lap up, take a drop, slake one's thirst, cheer *or* refresh the inner man, drown one's troubles *or* sorrows, commune with the spirits; **down,** sink, toss off *or* down, toss one's drink, knock back, throw one back, drink off *or* up, drain the cup, drink bottoms-up, drink deep; **drink hard,** drink like a fish, drink seriously, **tope;** take to drink *or* drinking, "follow strong drink"—BIBLE

25 (*informal terms*) **to booze,** swig, swill, moisten *or* wet one's whistle; liquor *and* liquor up (*both US & Canadian informal*), lush, souse, tank up, **hit the booze** *or* **bottle,** exercise *or* bend *or* crook *or* raise the elbow, dip the beak, splice the main brace

26 to get drunk, be stricken drunk, get high, put on a high, take a drop too much; **get plastered** *or* **pickled,** etc (*informal*)

27 to be drunk, be intoxicated, have a drop too much, have more than one can hold, be tired and emotional, see double, be feeling no pain; **stagger, reel; pass out** (*informal*)

28 to go on a spree; go on a binge *or* **bender** *or* bat *or* toot (*US & Canadian informal*), **carouse, spree, revel,** wassail, debauch, "eat, drink, and be merry"—BIBLE, paint the town red (*informal*), pub-crawl (*informal*)

29 to drink to, toast, pledge, drink a toast to, drink *or* pledge the health of, give you

30 to distil; brew; bootleg, moonshine (*informal*), moonlight (*informal*)

adjectives

31 intoxicated, inebriated, inebriate, inebrious, **drunk, drunken,** *shikker* (*Yiddish*), **tipsy,** in liquor, **in one's cups, under the influence,** the worse for alcohol, tired and emotional; nappy, beery; **tiddly, giddy, dizzy,** muddled, addled, flustered, bemused, reeling, seeing double; **mellow, merry,** jolly, happy, gay, glorious; **full,** fou (*Scottish*); **besotted,** sotted, sodden, drenched, far-gone; drunk as a lord, drunk as a fiddler *or* piper, drunk as a skunk; staggering drunk; crapulent, crapulous; **maudlin**

32 dead-drunk, blind drunk, overcome, out *and* out cold *and* passed out (*all informal*), helpless, under the table

33 (*informal terms*) **fuddled,** muzzy, **boozy,** overtaken, tired and emotional; **swacked, plastered,** shnockered, stewed, **pickled,** pissed **soused,** soaked, boiled, fried, canned, tanked, potted, corned, corked, bombed, ripped, smashed, screwed, slewed; bent, **crocked,** crocko, shellacked, sloshed, sozzled, zonked, tight, lushy, squiffy, afflicted, jug-bitten, half-cut, oiled, lubricated, feeling no pain, polluted, raddled, organized, **high,** elevated, high as a kite, lit, **lit up,** lit to the gills, illuminated, **loaded, stinko,** tanked, tanked-up, stinking drunk, pie-eyed, pissy-eyed, shitfaced, cockeyed, cockeyed drunk, roaring *or* rip-roaring drunk, skunk-drunk; pissed as a newt, pissed as a fart; half-seas over, three sheets to the wind, **blotto,** stiff, blind, paralysed, paralytic, legless, **stoned**

34 full of Dutch courage, pot-valiant, pot-valorous

35 bibulous, bibacious, drunken, sottish, given *or* addicted to drink, **liquor-loving,** liquor-drinking, drinking, hard-drinking, swilling (*informal*), toping, tippling, winebibbing

36 intoxicating, intoxicative, **inebriating,** inebriative, inebriant, heady

37 alcoholic, spirituous, ardent, strong, hard, with a kick (*informal*); winy, vinous

exclamations

38 (*toasts*) skoal!, skl! (*Norwegian*), prosit! *or* prost!, *à votre santé!* (*French*), ¡salud! (*Spanish*), *l'chaim!* (*Hebrew*), *sláinte!* (*Irish and Scottish*), salute! (*Italian*), *na zdorovye!* (*Russian*), *nazdrowie!* (*Polish*), to your health!, long life!, to life!, cheerio!, cheers!, down the hatch!, bottoms up!, here's how!, here's to you!, here's looking at you!, here's mud in your eye!, here's good luck!, here's to absent friends!, confusion to our enemies!

89 TOBACCO

nouns

1 **tobacco**, *tabac* (*French*), nicotia *or* nicotian (*both old*); **baccy** *and* snout (*both informal*), **the weed** (*informal*), fragrant weed, Indian weed *or* drug, filthy weed, sot-weed (*old*),
   "pernicious weed"—COWPER, "thou weed, who art so lovely fair and smell'st so sweet"—SHAKESPEARE, "sublime tobacco"—BYRON, "divine tobacco"—SPENSER; carcinogenic substance; smoke, tobacco smoke, cigarette smoke, cigar smoke, pipe smoke; secondary smoke, secondhand smoke

2 (*tobaccos*) flue-cured *or* bright, fire-cured, air-cured; Broadleaf, Burley, Cuban, Havana, Havana seed, Latakia, Turkish, Russian, Maryland, Virginia; plug tobacco, bird's-eye, canaster, leaf, lugs, seconds, shag

3 **smoking tobacco**, smokings (*informal*), smoke *and* smokes (*both informal*)

4 **cigar**, seegar (*informal*); rope *and* stinker (*both informal*); **cheroot**, corona, belvedere, Havana, panatella, colorado, trichinopoly, stogie (*US & Canadian*); cigarillo; box of cigars, cigar box, cigar case, humidor; cigar cutter

5 **cigarette**; **fag** *and* butt *and* cig *and* gasper *and* snout *and* coffin nail *and* cancer stick (*all informal*), durry (*Australian*); roll-up; cigarette butt, **butt**, stub, cigarette end, **fag end** (*informal*), bumper (*Australian informal*); snipe (*informal*); roach (*informal*); pack *or* deck of cigarettes, box *or* carton of cigarettes, cigarette case

6 **pipe**, tobacco pipe; corncob, corncob pipe; briar pipe, briar; clay pipe, clay, churchwarden; meerschaum; water pipe, hookah, nargileh, kalian, hubble-bubble; peace pipe, calumet; pipe rack, pipe cleaner, tobacco pouch

7 **chewing tobacco**, eating tobacco (*informal*); navy *or* navy plug, cavendish, twist, pigtail, cut plug; **quid**, cud, fid (*informal*), **chew**, chaw (*informal*); tobacco juice

8 **snuff**; rappee; pinch of snuff; snuff bottle, snuffbox

9 **nicotine**, nicotia (*old*)

10 **smoking**, smoking habit, habitual smoking; chain-smoke; smoke, puff, drag (*informal*); **chewing**; tobacco *or* nicotine addiction, tobaccoism, tabacosis, tabacism, tabagism, nicotinism; passive smoking

11 **tobacco user, smoker**, cigarette *or* pipe *or* cigar smoker, chewer, snuffer, snuff dipper

12 **tobacconist**; snuffman; tobacco store *or* shop, cigar store

13 **smoking room**, smoking car, **smoker**

verbs

14 (*use tobacco*) **to smoke**; inhale, puff, draw, drag (*informal*), pull; smoke like a chimney *or* furnace; chain-smoke; **chew**, chaw (*informal*); **take snuff**, dip *or* inhale snuff

adjectives

15 **tobacco**, tobaccoy *or* tobaccoey, tobaccolike; **nicotinic**; smoking, chewing; snuffy

90 HEALTH CARE

nouns

1 **medicine, medical practice, health care**, health-care industry, health-care delivery, leechcraft *and* leechdom *and* physic (*all old*); **medical specialty** *or* **branch** (*see list*); **treatment, therapy** *see* 91; **health care, health insurance** *see* 83.5; **care**, nursing care, home care, outpatient care, life care

2 **surgery**; operation; surgeoncy

3 **dentistry** (*see list*), dental medicine, dental care

4 **doctor**, doc (*informal*), **physician**, Doctor of Medicine *or* **MD**, **medical practitioner, medical man**, medico (*informal*), leech (*old*), quack *and* sawbones (*both informal*); **general practitioner** *or* **GP**; family doctor; country doctor; **houseman**, intern (*US & Canadian*); **consultant**; registrar, medical registrar; **resident**, house physician, resident physician; fellow; physician in ordinary; medical attendant, attending physician; **specialist**, board-certified physician *or* specialist; **coroner; osteopath, chiropractor**, podiatrist, oculist, **optometrist**

5 **surgeon**, sawbones (*informal*); operator, operative surgeon

6 **dentist**, tooth doctor, toothdrawer; **dental surgeon**, operative dentist; Bachelor of Dental Surgery *or* BDS; Doctor of Dental Surgery *or* DDS; Doctor of Dental Science *or* DDSc; Master of Dental Surgery *or* MDS; **specialist**, dental specialist

7 **veterinary surgeon, vet** (*informal*), veterinary, veterinarian (*US & Canadian*), horse doctor, animal doctor

8 **health-care professional, health-care provider, physician, nurse, midwife, therapist**, therapeutist, practitioner

9 **healer, nonmedical therapist**; theotherapist; Christian *or* spiritual *or* divine healer; Christian Science practitioner, healer; **faith healer**, witch doctor (*informal*)

10 **nurse**, charge nurse, sister *or* nursing sister; **matron** *or* nursing officer, Registered General Nurse *or* RGN; State Enrolled Nurse *or* SEN; State Registered Nurse *or* SRN; district nurse, health visitor

11 (*hospital staff*) paramedic; orderly, attendant, nurse's aide; almoner; dresser; audiologist; anaesthetist; dietitian; radiographer, X-ray technician; laboratory technician; radiotherapist; physiotherapist, physical therapist; dietitian; hospital administrator; ambulance driver; caretaker

12 **Hippocrates**, Galen; Aesculapius, Asclepius

13 **practice of medicine**, medical practice; general practice, restricted *or* limited practice; group practice; British Medical Association *or* BMA, Royal College of Surgeons *or* RCS; family practice, community medicine

verbs

14 **to practice medicine**, doctor (*informal*); treat

adjectives

15 **medical**, iatric, health; surgical; chiropodic, paediatric, orthopaedic, obstetric, obstetrical,

neurological; dental; orthodontic, periodontic, prosthodontic, exodontic; osteopathic, chiropractic, naturopathic, hydropathic, allopathic, homeopathic; clinical

16 branches of medicine

anatomy	neurosurgery
anaesthetics	nosology
audiology	nutrition
bacteriology	obstetrics
cardiography	ophthalmology
cardiology	optometry
chiropody	orthopaedics
dental surgery	orthotics
dentistry	otolaryngology
dermatology	otology
diagnostics	parasitology
dolorology	pathology
embryology	paediatrics
endocrinology	physical medicine
epidemiology	physiopathology
etiology	podiatry
family practice	psychiatry
fetology	psychology
fluoroscopy	psychoneuroimmunology
general medicine	radiology
geriatrics *or* gerontology	rheumatology
gynaecology	serology
haematology	sports medicine
hygiene	surgery
immunochemistry	surgical anatomy
immunology	symptomatology *or*
internal medicine	semeiology
materia medica	teratology
mental hygiene	therapeutics
midwifery	tocology
mycology	toxicology
neonatology	virology
neurology	

17 kinds and specialities of dentistry

endodontics *or* endodontia	orthodontics *or* orthodontia
exodontics *or* exodontia	periodontics *or* periodontia
family dentistry	prosthetic dentistry *or*
general dentistry	prosthodontics *or*
operative dentistry	prosthodontia
oral surgery *or* surgical	radiodontics *or* radiodontia
dentistry	

91 THERAPY, MEDICAL TREATMENT

nouns

1 **therapy, therapeutics,** therapeusis, **treatment, medical care** *or* **treatment,** medication; noninvasive *or* nonsurgical therapy *or* treatment; disease-fighting, healing; healing arts; alternative *or* complementary medicine, holism; psychotherapy *see* 92; medicines *see* 86

2 **nonmedical therapy;** theotherapy; **healing;** Christian *or* spiritual *or* divine healing; **faith healing**

3 **hydrotherapy,** hydrotherapeutics; hydropathy, water cure; cold-water cure; contrast bath, whirlpool bath

4 **heat therapy,** thermotherapy; heliotherapy, solar therapy; fangotherapy; hot bath, sweat bath, sunbath

5 **diathermy,** medical diathermy; electrotherapy, electrotherapeutics; **radiothermy,** high-frequency treatment; shortwave diathermy, ultrashortwave diathermy, microwave diathermy; ultrasonic diathermy; surgical diathermy, radiosurgery, electrosurgery, electrosection, electrocautery, electrocoagulation

6 **radiotherapy,** radiation therapy, radiotherapeutics; adjuvant therapy

7 **radiology,** radiography, radioscopy, fluoroscopy, etc *see* 1036.7

8 (*radiotherapeutic substances*) radium; cobalt; radioisotope, tracer, labelled *or* tagged element, radioelement; radiocarbon, carbon *see* 14, radiocalcium, radiopotassium, radiosodium, radioiodine; atomic cocktail

9 (*diagnostic pictures and graphs*) X-ray, radiograph, radiogram, roentgenogram *or* roentgenograph; photofluorograph; X-ray movie; chest X-ray; pyelogram; orthodiagram; encephalograph, encephalogram; electroencephalograph, electroencephalogram *or* EEG; electrocorticogram; electrocardiogram *or* ECG *or* EKG; electromyogram; computer-assisted tomography *or* CAT, computerized axial tomography *or* computed tomography *or* computer-assisted tomography *or* computerized tomography *or* CAT *or* CT; CAT *or* CT scan; magnetic resonance imaging *or* MRI; MR scan; positron emission tomography *or* PET; PET scan; ultrasound, ultrasonography; sonogram

10 case history, medical history, anamnesis; associative anamnesis; catamnesis, follow-up

11 **diagnostics,** prognostics; symptomatology, semeiology, semeiotics

12 **diagnosis; examination, physical examination;** study, test, work-up (*informal*); blood test, blood work (*informal*), blood count, urinalysis, uroscopy; biopsy; Pap test *or* smear, cervical smear; electrocardiography, electroencephalography, electromyography; mammography

13 **prognosis,** prognostication; prognostic, **symptom, sign**

14 **treatment,** medical treatment *or* attention *or* care; **cure,** curative measures; **medication,** medicamentation; **regimen,** regime, protocol; first aid; hospitalization

15 **immunization;** immunization therapy, immunotherapy; vaccine therapy, vaccinotherapy; toxin-antitoxin immunization; serum therapy, serotherapy, serotherapeutics; tuberculin test, scratch test, patch test; **immunology,** immunochemistry; immunity theory, side-chain theory; immunity; immunodeficiency

16 **inoculation, vaccination; injection,** hypodermic, hypodermic injection, shot (*informal*), hypospray *or* jet injection; booster, booster shot (*informal*); antitoxin, vaccine *see* 86.28

17 (*methods of injection*) cutaneous, percutaneous, subcutaneous, intradermal, intramuscular, intravenous, intramedullary, intracardiac, intrathecal, intraspinal

18 **transfusion,** blood transfusion; serum; blood bank, blood donor centre, bloodmobile; blood donor

19 surgery, surgical treatment, **operation,** surgical operation, surgical intervention, surgical technique *or* measure, the knife (*informal*); **instrument,** device; respirator; unnecessary surgery, *cacoëthes operandi* (*Latin*), tomomania

20 bloodletting, bleeding, venesection, phlebotomy; leeching; cupping

21 hospital, clinic, infirmary, *hôpital* (*French*), treatment centre; sanatorium; general hospital; private hospital; cottage hospital; hospice; nursing home, old peoples' home, rest-home, eventide home (*informal*); sick bay *or* berth, sanatorium; trauma centre; health centre; well-woman clinic; well-man clinic; private practice

22 pesthouse, lazar house, lazaretto *or* lazaret (*all old*)

23 health resort, spa, watering place, hydro, baths; mineral spring, warm *or* hot spring; pump room, pump house

verbs

24 to treat, doctor, minister to, care for, give care to, physic; **diagnose;** nurse; **cure, remedy, heal;** dress the wounds, bandage, poultice, plaster, strap, splint; bathe; massage, rub; operate on; physic, purge, flux (*old*); **operate,** perform a procedure; transplant, replant

25 to medicate, medicine, drug, dope (*informal*), dose; salve, oil, anoint, embrocate

26 to irradiate, radiumize, **X-ray,** roentgenize

27 to bleed, let blood, leech, phlebotomize; cup; **transfuse,** give a transfusion; perfuse

28 to immunize, inoculate, vaccinate, shoot (*informal*)

29 to undergo treatment, take the cure, doctor (*informal*), take medicine; go under the knife (*informal*)

92 PSYCHOLOGY, PSYCHOTHERAPY

nouns

1 psychology (*see list*), science of the mind, science of human behaviour, mental philosophy; psychologism, pop psychology *and* psychobabble (*both informal*)

2 psychological school (*see list*), school *or* system of psychology, psychological theory; Adlerian psychology; behaviourism *or* behaviour *or* behaviouristic psychology *or* stimulus-response psychology; Freudian psychology *or* Freudianism; Gestalt psychology *or* configurationism; Horneyan psychology; Jungian *or* analytical psychology; Pavlovian psychology; Reichian psychology *or* orgone theory; Skinnerian psychology; Sullivanian psychology

3 psychiatry, psychological medicine; neuropsychiatry; social psychiatry; prophylactic psychiatry

4 psychosomatic medicine, psychological medicine, medicopsychology; psychosocial medicine

5 psychotherapy, psychotherapeutics, mind cure

6 psychoanalysis, analysis, the couch (*informal*); psychoanalytic therapy, psychoanalytic method; **depth psychology,** psychology of depths; group analysis; psychognosis, psychognosy; dream analysis, interpretation of dreams, dream symbolism; depth interview

7 psychodiagnostics, psychodiagnosis, psychological *or* psychiatric evaluation

8 psychometrics, psychometry, psychological measurement; **intelligence testing;** psychological screening; psychography; psychogram, psychograph, psychological profile; psychometer, IQ meter (*informal*); lie detector, polygraph, psychogalvanometer

9 psychological test (*see list*), mental test; standardized test; developmental test, achievement test

10 psychologist; psychotherapist, therapist, psychotherapeutist; clinical psychologist; licensed psychologist, psychological practitioner; **psychiatrist,** alienist, somatist; neuropsychiatrist; psychopathist; psychopathologist; psychotechnologist, industrial psychologist; psychobiologist, psychochemist, psychophysiologist, psychophysicist; psychographer; **psychoanalyst, analyst; shrink** *and* headshrinker *and* shrinker (*all informal*); psychiatric social worker; **counsellor,** psychological counsellor; counselling service

11 personality tendency, complexion (*old*), humour; somatotype; **introversion,** introvertedness, ingoingness; inner-directedness; **extroversion,** extrovertedness, outgoingness; other-directedness; syntony, ambiversion; schizothymia, schizothymic *or* schizoid personality; cyclothymia, cyclothymic *or* cycloid personality; mesomorphism, mesomorphy; endomorphism, endomorphy; ectomorphism, ectomorphy

12 (*personality type*) **introvert, extrovert,** syntone, ambivert; schizothyme, schizoid; cyclothymic, cyclothyme, cycloid; choleric, melancholic, sanguine, phlegmatic; endomorph, mesomorph, ectomorph

13 pathological personality, psychopathological personality, sick personality

14 mental disorder, emotional disorder, psychonosema, psychopathyfunctional nervous disorder; reaction; emotional instability; **maladjustment,** social maladjustment; nervous breakdown, crack-up (*informal*); problems in living; **insanity, mental illness** see 925.1; **psychosis** see 925.3; **schizophrenia; paranoia** see 925.4; **manic-depressive psychosis, depression,** melancholia see 925.5; seasonal affective disorder *or* SAD, post-partum depression; pre-menstrual syndrome *or* PMS; **neurosis, psychoneurosis,** neuroticism, neurotic *or* psychoneurotic disorder; brain disease, nervous disorder

15 personality disorder, character disorder, moral insanity, sociopathy, **psychopathy; psychopathic personality;** sexual pathology, sexual psychopathy see 75.18

16 neurotic reaction, overreaction, disproportionate reaction

17 psychological stress, stress; frustration, external frustration, internal frustration; conflict, ambivalence, ambivalence of impulse; **trauma,** psychological *or* emotional trauma, traumatism, mental *or* emotional shock, decompensation; post-traumatic stress disorder; rape trauma syndrome

18 psychosomatic symptom; symptom of emotional disorder, emotional symptom, psychological symptom; **thought disturbance,** thought disorder *or* disturbances, dissociative disorder, delirium, delusion, disorientation, hallucination; **speech abnormality** (*see list*)

19 trance, daze, stupor; catatonic stupor, catalepsy; cataplexy; dream state, reverie, daydreaming *see* 984.2; somnambulism, sleepwalking; hypnotic trance; fugue, fugue state; **amnesia** *see* 989.2

20 dissociation, mental *or* emotional dissociation, disconnection; dissociation of personality, personality disorganization *or* disintegration; **schizoid personality;** double *or* dual personality; multiple personality, split personality, alternating personality; schizoidism, schizothymia, **schizophrenia** *see* 925.4; depersonalization; **paranoid personality; paranoia** *see* 925.4

21 fixation, libido fixation *or* arrest, **arrested development;** infantile fixation, pregenital fixation, father fixation, Freudian fixation, mother fixation, parent fixation; **regression,** retreat to immaturity

22 complex, inferiority complex, superiority complex, parent complex, Oedipus complex, mother complex, Electra complex, father complex, Diana complex, persecution complex; castration complex

23 defence mechanism, defence reaction; ego defence, psychotaxis; biological *or* psychological *or* sociological adjustive reactions; resistance; dissociation; **negativism, alienation; escapism,** escape mechanism, avoidance mechanism; escape, flight, **withdrawal; isolation,** emotional insulation; fantasy, fantasizing, escape into fantasy, dreamlike thinking, autistic *or* dereistic thinking, wishful thinking, autism, dereism; wish-fulfilment, wish-fulfilment fantasy; sexual fantasy; **compensation,** overcompensation, decompensation; substitution; **sublimation; projection,** blame-shifting; displacement; **rationalization**

24 suppression, repression, inhibition, resistance, restraint, censorship; block, psychological block, blockage, blocking; reaction formation; rigid control; **suppressed desire**

25 catharsis, purgation, abreaction, motor abreaction, psychocatharsis, **emotional release,** relief of tension, outlet; release therapy, acting-out, psychodrama; imaging

26 conditioning, classical *or* Pavlovian conditioning; instrumental conditioning; operant conditioning; psychagogy, reeducation, reorientation; conditioned reflex, conditioned stimulus, conditioned response; reinforcement, positive reinforcement, negative reinforcement; simple reflex, unconditioned reflex, **reflex** *see* 902.1; **behaviour** *see* 321

27 adjustment, adjustive reaction; **readjustment, rehabilitation;** psychosynthesis, integration of personality; fulfilment, self-fulfilment; self-actualization, peak experience; integrated personality, syntonic personality

28 psyche, psychic apparatus, **personality, self,** personhood; **mind** *see* 918.1, 3, 4; preconscious, foreconscious, coconscious; **subconscious, unconscious,** subconscious *or* unconscious mind, submerged mind, subliminal, subliminal self; **libido,** psychic *or* libidinal energy, motive force, vital impulse, ego-libido, object libido; **id,** primitive self, pleasure principle, life instinct, death instinct; **ego,** conscious self; **superego,** ethical self, conscience; ego ideal; ego-id conflict; anima, persona; collective unconscious, racial unconscious

29 engram, memory trace, traumatic trace *or* memory; unconscious memory; archetype, archetypal pattern *or* image *or* symbol; imago, image, father image, etc; race *or* racial memory; cultural memory; **memory** *see* 988

30 symbol, universal symbol, father symbol, mother symbol, phallic symbol, fertility symbol, etc; symbolism, symbolization

31 surrogate, substitute; father surrogate, father figure, father image; mother surrogate, mother figure

32 gestalt, pattern, figure, configuration, sensory pattern; figure-ground

33 association, association of ideas, chain of ideas, concatenation, mental linking; controlled association, free association, association by contiguity, association by similarity; association by sound, clang association; stream of consciousness; transference, identification, positive transference, negative transference; synaesthesia *see* 24.5

34 cathexis, cathection, desire concentration; charge, energy charge, cathectic energy; anticathexis, countercathexis, counterinvestment; hypercathexis, overcharge

verbs

35 to psychologize, psychoanalyse; abreact; fixate, obsess on (*informal*)

adjectives

36 psychological; psychiatric, neuropsychiatric; psychometric; **psychopathic,** psychopathological; **psychosomatic,** somatopsychic, psychophysical, psychophysiological, psychobiological; psychogenic, psychogenetic, functional; psychodynamic, psychoneurological, psychosexual, psychosocial, psychotechnical; **psychotic**

37 psychotherapeutic; psychiatric, psychoanalytic, psychoanalytical

38 neurotic, psychoneurotic, disturbed, disordered; neurasthenic, psychasthenic; hysteric(al), hypochondriac, phobic; stressed

39 introverted, introvert, introversive, **subjective, ingoing,** inner-directed

40 extroverted, extrovert, extroversive, **outgoing,** extrospective; other-directed

41 subconscious, unconscious; subliminal, extramarginal; preconscious, foreconscious, coconscious

42 kinds and branches of psychology

abnormal psychology	animal psychology
academic psychology	applied psychology
act psychology	association psychology
analytic *or* introspective psychology	child psychology
	clinical psychology

cognitive psychology
comparative psychology
constitutional psychology
criminal psychology
depth psychology
developmental psychology
differential psychology
dynamic *or* functional
  psychology
ecological psychology
educational psychology
empirical psychology
existential psychology
experimental psychology
faculty psychology
folk *or* ethnic psychology
genetic psychology
group psychology
hormic psychology
individual psychology
industrial psychology
medical psychology
morbid psychology
neuropharmacology
neuropsychology
objective psychology
ontogenetic psychology
parapsychology
phenomenological
  psychology
phylogenetic psychology
physiologic *or* physiological
  psychology
polygenetic psychology
popular psychology
psychoacoustics
psychoasthenics

psychobiochemistry
psychobiology
psychochemistry
psychodiagnostics
psychodynamics
psychoendocrinology
psychogenetics
psychogeriatrics
psychographics
psychohistory
psycholinguistics
psychological medicine
psychological warfare
psychomathematics
psychometrics *or*
  psychometry
psychonomy *or*
  psychonomics
psychopathology
psychopharmacology
psychophysics
psychophysiology
psychosociology
psychosomatics
psychotechnics *or*
  psychotechnology
psychotherapy *or*
  psychotherapeutics
race *or* racial psychology
rational psychology
reactology
reflexology
self psychology
social psychology
structural psychology
voluntaristic psychology

43 psychological and mental tests

alpha test
apperception test
aptitude test
association test
Babcock-Levy test
Bernreuter personality
  inventory
beta test
Binet *or* Binet-Simon test
Brown personality
  inventory
Cattell's infant intelligence
  scale
CAVD test
controlled association test
free association test
Gesell's development
  schedule
Goldstein-Sheerer test
inkblot test
intelligence quotient *or* IQ

intelligence test
interest inventory
IQ test
Kent mental test
Minnesota multiphasic
  personality inventory
Minnesota preschool scale
Oseretsky test
personality test
Rorschach test
Stanford revision
Stanford scientific aptitude
  test
Stanford-Binet test
Szondi test
thematic apperception test
  or TAT
Wechsler-Bellevue
  intelligence scale
word association test

93 FEELING

nouns

1 **feeling, emotion, affect, sentiment,** affection, affections; affective faculty, affectivity; emotional charge, cathexis; **feelings, sensitiveness, sensibility,** susceptibility, thin skin; emotional life; the logic of the heart; **sense,** deep *or* profound sense, gut sense *or* sensation (*informal*); **sensation** *see* 24; **impression,** undercurrent; hunch, feeling in one's bones, presentiment *see* 933.3; foreboding; **reaction, response,** gut reaction (*informal*); **instinct** *see* 365.1; emotional colouring *or* shade *or* nuance, **tone,** feeling tone

2 **passion,** passionateness, strong feeling, powerful emotion; **fervour, fervency,** fervidness, impassionedness, **ardour, ardency,** *empressement* (*French*), warmth of feeling, **warmth, heat, fire,** verve, furore, **fury,** vehemence; heartiness, gusto, relish, savour; spirit, heart, soul; **liveliness** *see* 330.2; **zeal** *see* 101.2; **excitement** *see* 105; **ecstasy**

3 **heart, soul, spirit,** *esprit* (*French*), **breast, bosom,** inmost heart *or* soul, heart of hearts, secret *or* inner recesses of the heart, secret places, heart's core, heartstrings, cockles of the heart, bottom of the heart, being, innermost being, core of one's being; viscera, pit of one's stomach, **gut** *or* guts (*informal*); bones

4 **sensibility, sensitivity, sensitiveness,** delicacy, fineness of feeling, tenderness, affectivity, susceptibility, impressionability *see* 24.2

5 **sympathy, fellow feeling, sympathetic response,** responsiveness, relating, warmth, **caring,** concern; response, echo, chord, sympathetic chord, vibrations, vibes (*informal*); **empathy,** identification; involvement, sharing; pathos

6 **tenderness,** tender feeling, softness, gentleness, delicacy; **tenderheartedness,** softheartedness, warmheartedness, tender *or* sensitive *or* warm heart, soft place *or* spot in one's heart; warmth, **fondness, weakness** *see* 100.2

7 **bad feeling, hard feelings;** immediate dislike, disaffinity, personality conflict, bad vibes *or* chemistry (*informal*), bad blood, **hostility,** scunner, animosity *see* 589.4; **hard-heartedness** *see* 94.3

8 **sentimentality, sentiment, sentimentalism,** oversentimentality, oversentimentalism, bathos; nostalgia, nostomania; romanticism; sweetness and light, hearts-and-flowers; bleeding heart; mawkishness, cloyingness, maudlinness, namby-pamby, namby-pambyness, namby-pambyism; mushiness *or* sloppiness (*both informal*); **mush** and slush *and* slop *and* goo *and* schmaltz (*all informal*); sob story *and* tearjerker (*both informal*), soap opera

9 **emotionalism,** emotionality, lump in one's throat; emotionalizing, emotionalization; emotiveness, emotivity; visceralness; nonrationalness, unreasoningness; demonstrativeness, making scenes; **theatrics, theatricality, histrionics, dramatics,** hamminess *and* chewing up the scenery (*US & Canadian* (*both informal*)); **sensationalism, melodrama,** melodramatics, blood and thunder; yellow journalism; emotional appeal, human interest,

love interest; **overemotionalism**, hyperthymia, excess of feeling

verbs

10 to feel, entertain *or* harbour *or* cherish *or* nurture a feeling; feel deeply, feel in one's viscera *or* bones, feel in one's gut *or* guts (*informal*); experience *see* 830.8; have a sensation, get *or* receive an impression, **sense, perceive**

11 to respond, react, be moved, be affected *or* touched, be inspired, echo, catch the flame *or* infection, be in tune; **respond to,** warm up to, take *or* lay to heart, open one's heart to, be turned on to (*informal*), nourish in one's bosom, feel in one's breast, cherish at the heart's core, treasure up in the heart; enter into the spirit of, be imbued with the spirit of; care about, sympathize with, empathize with, identify with, relate to emotionally, dig *and* be turned on by (*both informal*), be involved, share; colour with emotion

12 to have deep feelings, be all heart, have a tender heart, be a person of heart *or* sentiment; have a soft spot *or* place in one's heart; love *see* 104.18-20; hate *see* 103.5

13 to emotionalize, emote (*informal*), give free play to the emotions, make a scene; be theatrical, theatricalize, ham it up *and* chew up the scenery (*both US & Canadian informal*); **sentimentalize,** gush *and* slobber over (*both informal*)

14 to affect, touch, move, stir; melt, soften, melt the heart, choke one up, give one a lump in the throat; **penetrate,** pierce, go through one, go deep; touch a chord, **touch a sympathetic chord, touch one's heart,** tug at the heart *or* heartstrings, go to one's heart, get under one's skin; come home to; **touch to the quick,** touch on the raw, flick one on the raw, smart, sting

15 to impress, affect, strike, hit, smite, rock; **make an impression, get to one** (*informal*); make a dent in, make an impact upon, sink in (*informal*), strike home, come home to, hit the mark (*informal*); tell, have a strong effect, traumatize, strike hard, impress forcibly

16 to impress upon, bring home to, make it felt; stamp, stamp on, etch, engrave, engrave on

adjectives

17 emotional, affective, emotive, affectional, **feeling;** soulful, of soul, of heart, of feeling, of sentiment; visceral, gut (*informal*); glandular; emotiometabolic, emotiomotor, emotiomuscular, emotiovascular; demonstrative, overdemonstrative

18 fervent, fervid, passionate, impassioned, intense, **ardent; hearty, cordial,** enthusiastic, exuberant, unrestrained, vigorous; keen, breathless, **excited** *see* 105.18, 20, 22; **lively** *see* 330.17; zealous; **warm, burning, heated, hot,** volcanic, red-hot, fiery, flaming, glowing, ablaze, afire, on fire, boiling over, steaming, steamy; delirious, fevered, feverish, febrile, flushed; intoxicated, drunk

19 emotionalistic, emotive, overemotional, hysteric, hysterical, sensational, sensationalistic, melodramatic, theatric, theatrical, histrionic, dramatic, overdramatic,

hammy (*informal*), nonrational, unreasoning; overemotional, hyperthymic

20 sensitive, sensible, emotional, passible (*old*), delicate; responsive, sympathetic, receptive; susceptible, impressionable; **tender, soft, tenderhearted, softhearted,** warmhearted

21 sentimental, sentimentalized, soft, **mawkish, maudlin,** cloying; sticky *and* gooey *and* schmaltzy *and* sappy *and* soppy *and* twee (*all informal*), oversentimental, oversentimentalized, bathetic; **mushy** *or* sloppy *or* gushing *or* teary *or* beery *or* wet *or* treacly (*all informal*); tearjerking (*informal*); namby-pamby, romantic; nostalgic, nostomanic

22 affecting, touching, moving, emotive, pathetic

23 affected, moved, touched, impressed; impressed with *or* by, penetrated with, seized with, imbued with, devoured by, obsessed, obsessed with *or* by; wrought up by; stricken, wracked, racked, torn, agonized, tortured; worked up, all worked up, **excited** *see* 105.18

24 deep-felt, deepgoing, from the heart, heartfelt, homefelt (*old*); **deep, profound;** indelible; pervasive, pervading, absorbing; penetrating, penetrant, piercing; **poignant,** keen, sharp, acute

adverbs

25 feelingly, emotionally, affectively; affectingly, touchingly, movingly, **with feeling,** poignantly

26 fervently, fervidly, passionately, impassionedly, intensely, **ardently,** zealously; keenly, breathlessly, excitedly; warmly, heatedly, glowingly; heartily, cordially; enthusiastically, exuberantly, vigorously; kindly, heart and soul, with all one's heart, from the heart, from the bottom of one's heart

27 sentimentally, mawkishly, maudlinly, cloyingly; mushily *and* sloppily *and* gushingly (*all informal*)

94 LACK OF FEELING

nouns

1 unfeeling, unfeelingness, affectlessness, lack of affect, lack of feeling *or* feeling tone, emotional deadness *or* numbness *or* paralysis, **anaesthesia, emotionlessness,** unemotionalism, unexcitability; **dispassion,** dispassionateness, unpassionateness, objectivity; passionlessness, **spiritlessness, heartlessness,** soullessness; **coldness, coolness, frigidity,** chill, chilliness, frostiness, iciness; coldheartedness, cold-bloodedness; cold heart, cold blood; cold fish; **unresponsiveness,** unsympatheticness; lack of touch *or* contact, autism, self-absorption, withdrawal, catatonia; unimpressionableness, unimpressibility; insusceptibility, unsusceptibility; **impassiveness,** impassibility, impassivity; straight face *and* poker face (*both informal*), dead pan (*informal*); immovability, untouchability; **dullness, obtuseness; inexcitability** *see* 106

2 insensibility, insensibleness, **unconsciousness,** unawareness, **obliviousness,** oblivion; anaesthesia, narcosis

3 callousness, insensitivity, insensitiveness, philistinism; **coarseness, brutalization, hardness,** hardenedness, **hard-heartedness, hardness of**

heart, hard heart, stony-heartedness, heart of stone, stoniness, marbleheartedness, flintheartedness, flintiness; **obduracy**, obdurateness, induration, inuredness; imperviousness, **thick skin**, rhinoceros hide, thick or hard-shell, armour, formidable defences

4 **apathy, indifference, unconcern**, lack of caring, disinterest; withdrawnness, **aloofness, detachment**, ataraxy or ataraxia, **dispassion; passiveness**, passivity, supineness, insouciance, nonchalance; inappetence, lack of appetite; **listlessness, spiritlessness**, burnout, blah or blahs (informal), heartlessness, plucklessness, spunklessness; **lethargy, phlegm**, lethargicalness, phlegmaticalness, phlegmaticness, hebetude, **dullness**, sluggishness, languor, languidness; soporifousness, sopor, coma, comatoseness, torpidness, torpor, torpidity, **stupor**, stupefaction, narcosis; acedia, sloth; **resignation**, resignedness, stoicism; **numbness**, benumbedness; hopelessness see 125

verbs

5 to not be affected by, remain unmoved, not turn a hair, not care less (informal); have a thick skin, have a heart of stone; be cold as ice, be a cold fish, be an icicle; not affect, leave one cold or unmoved, unimpress, underwhelm (informal)

6 to callous, harden, case harden, **harden one's heart**, ossify, steel, indurate, inure; brutalize

7 to dull, blunt, desensitize, obtund, hebetate

8 to numb, benumb, paralyse, **deaden**, anaesthetize, freeze, **stun, stupefy**, drug, narcotize, anaesthetize

adjectives

9 **unfeeling, unemotional**, nonemotional, emotionless, affectless, emotionally dead or numb or paralysed, anaesthetized, drugged, narcotized; **unpassionate, dispassionate**, unimpassioned, **objective**; passionless, **spiritless, heartless**, soulless, lukewarm, Laodicean; **cold, cool, frigid**, frozen, chill, chilly, arctic, frosty, frosted, icy, **coldhearted, cold-blooded**, cold as charity; **unaffectionate**, unloving; **unresponsive**, unresponding, **unsympathetic**; out of touch or contact; in one's shell or armour, behind one's defences; autistic, self-absorbed, self-centred, egocentric, catatonic; unimpressionable, unimpressible, insusceptible, unsusceptible; **impassive**, impassible; **immovable, untouchable**; dull, obtuse, blunt; **inexcitable** see 106.10

10 **insensible, unconscious**, unaware, **oblivious**, blind to, deaf to, dead to, lost to

11 **unaffected, unmoved, untouched**, dry-eyed, unimpressed, unstruck, **unstirred**, unruffled, unanimated, uninspired

12 **callous, calloused, insensitive**, Philistine; **thick-skinned**, pachydermatous; **hard, hard-hearted, hardened**, case-hardened, coarsened, brutalized, indurated, stony, stony-hearted, marblehearted, flinthearted, flinty, steely, impervious, inured, armoured or steeled against, proof against, as hard as nails

13 **apathetic, indifferent, unconcerned**, uncaring, **disinterested, uninterested; withdrawn, aloof, detached**, Olympian, above it all; **passive**, supine;

stoic, stoical; insouciant, nonchalant, blasé, **listless, spiritless**, burned-out, blah (informal), heartless, pluckless, spunkless; **lethargic, phlegmatic**, hebetudinous, **dull**, desensitized, sluggish, torpid, languid, slack, soporific, comatose, **stupefied**, in a stupor, **numb**, numbed, benumbed; resigned; hopeless see 125.12

adverbs

14 **unfeelingly, unemotionally**, emotionlessly; with a straight or poker face (informal), deadpan (informal); **dispassionately**, unpassionately; **spiritlessly, heartlessly**, coldly, coldheartedly, cold-bloodedly, **in cold blood**; with dry eyes

15 **apathetically, indifferently, unconcernedly**, disinterestedly, uninterestedly, impassively; **listlessly, spiritlessly**, heartlessly, plucklessly, spunklessly; **lethargically, phlegmatically**, dully, numbly

95 PLEASURE

nouns

1 **pleasure, enjoyment**; quiet pleasure, euphoria, well-being, good feeling, **contentment**, content, **ease, comfort** see 121; cosiness, warmth; **gratification, satisfaction**, great satisfaction, hearty enjoyment, keen pleasure or satisfaction; **self-gratification**, self-indulgence; instant gratification; luxury; **relish, zest, gusto**, joie de vivre (French); sweetness of life, douceur de vivre (French); kicks (informal), **fun**, entertainment, amusement see 743; intellectual pleasure, pleasures of the mind; **strokes** and stroking and ego massage (all informal); physical pleasure, creature comforts, bodily pleasure, sense or sensuous pleasure; sexual pleasure, voluptuousness, sensual pleasure, volupté (French), animal pleasure, animal comfort, bodily comfort, fleshly or carnal delight; forepleasure, titillation, endpleasure, fruition

2 **happiness, felicity, gladness, delight**, delectation; **joy, joyfulness**, joyance (old); **cheer**, cheerfulness, exhilaration, **exuberance, high spirits, glee**, sunshine; gaiety see 109.4, overjoyfulness, overhappiness; intoxication; **rapture**, ravishment, bewitchment, **enchantment**, unalloyed happiness; elation, exaltation; **ecstasy**, ecstasies, transport; **bliss**, blissfulness; beatitude, beatification, blessedness; paradise, heaven, seventh heaven, cloud nine

3 **treat, regalement**, regale; **feast, banquet** revelment, regale, Lucullan feast; feast or banquet of the soul; round of pleasures, mad round; **festivity**, fete, fiesta, festive occasion, beano, beanfeast, celebration, merrymaking, revel, revelry, jubilation, joyance; carnival, Mardi Gras

4 pleasure-loving, pleasure principle, hedonism, hedonics; epicureanism, Cyrenaicism, eudaemonism

verbs

5 to please, pleasure, give pleasure, afford one pleasure, be to one's liking, sit well with one, meet one's wishes, take or strike one's fancy, feel good or right, strike one right; do one's heart good, warm the cockles of one's heart; **suit**, suit one down to the ground

6 (*informal terms*) **to hit the spot,** be just the ticket, be just what the doctor ordered, **make a hit,** go over big, go over with a bang

7 **to gratify, satisfy,** sate, satiate; slake, appease, allay, assuage, quench; regale, feed, feast; do one's heart good, warm the cockles of the heart

8 **to gladden,** make happy, happify; bless, beatify; cheer *see* 109.7

9 **to delight,** delectate, **tickle, titillate, thrill, enrapture, enthral, enchant,** entrance, fascinate, captivate, bewitch, **charm,** becharm; enravish, ravish, imparadise; ecstasiate, transport, carry away

10 (*informal terms*) to give one a kick *or* charge *or* rush *or* bang, knock out, knock off one's feet *or* dead *or* for a loop, knock one's socks off, thrill to death *or* to pieces, tickle to death, tickle pink, chuff, **wow,** slay, send, freak out; **stroke,** massage one's ego

11 **to be pleased, feel happy,** feel good, sing, purr, smile, laugh, be wreathed in smiles, beam; **delight,** joy, take great satisfaction; look like the cat that got the cream *or* swallowed the canary; brim *or* burst with joy, walk *or* tread on air, have stars in one's eyes, be in heaven *or* seventh heaven *or* paradise, be on cloud nine; fall *or* go into raptures; die with delight *or* pleasure

12 **to enjoy,** pleasure in, be pleased with, receive *or* derive pleasure from, take delight *or* pleasure in, get a kick *or* boot *or* bang *or* charge *or* lift *or* rush out of (*informal*); **like, love,** adore (*informal*); **delight in, rejoice in,** indulge in, luxuriate in, revel in, riot in, bask in, wallow in, swim in; groove on *and* get high on *and* freak out on (*all informal*); feast on, gloat over *or* on; **relish, appreciate,** roll under the tongue, do justice to, savour, smack the lips; devour, eat up

13 **to enjoy oneself,** have a good time, party, rave, live it up (*informal*), have the time of one's life

adjectives

14 **pleased, delighted; glad,** gladsome; **charmed,** intrigued (*informal*); **thrilled; tickled,** tickled to death *and* tickled pink (*both informal*), exhilarated, chuffed; **gratified, satisfied;** pleased with, taken with, favourably impressed with, sold on (*informal*); pleased as Punch, pleased as a child with a new toy; euphoric, eupeptic; **content, contented,** easy, **comfortable** *see* 121.11, cosy, in clover

15 **happy, glad, joyful, joyous,** flushed with joy, radiant, beaming, glowing, starry-eyed, sparkling, laughing, smiling, smirking, smirky, chirping, purring, singing, dancing, leaping, capering, **cheerful, gay** *see* 109.14; **blissful,** "throned on highest bliss"—MILTON; blessed; beatified, beatific; thrice happy, "thrice and four times blessed"—VIRGIL; happy as Larry, happy as a lark, happy as a king, happy as the day is long, happy as a sand boy, happy as a baby boy, happy as a clam at high water, happy as a pig in shit (*informal*)

16 **overjoyed,** overjoyful, overhappy, brimming *or* bursting with happiness, on top of the world; **rapturous,** raptured **enraptured, enchanted,** entranced, enravished, ravished, rapt, possessed; sent *and* high *and* freaked-out (*all informal*), **in raptures,** transported, in a transport of delight, **carried away,** rapt *or* ravished away, beside oneself, beside oneself with joy, all over oneself (*informal*); **ecstatic,** in ecstasies, ecstasiating; rhapsodic, rhapsodical; imparadised, **in paradise,** in heaven, in seventh heaven, on cloud nine (*informal*); **elated,** elate, exalted, jubilant, exultant, flushed, glowing

17 **pleasure-loving,** pleasure-seeking, fun-loving, hedonic, hedonistic; Lucullan; epicurean, Cyrenaic, eudaemonic

adverbs

18 **happily, gladly, joyfully, joyously, delightedly,** with pleasure, to one's delight; blissfully, blessedly; **ecstatically,** rhapsodically, **rapturously; elatedly,** jubilantly, exultantly

19 **for fun,** for the hell *or* heck *or* devil of it (*informal*)

exclamations

20 goody!, goody, goody!, goody gumdrops!, good-oh!; whee!, **wow!,** u-mm!, mmmm!, oooo!, oo-la-la!; oh boy!, boy oh boy!, boy!, man!, whoopee!, yippee!, groovy!, super!, brill!

96 UNPLEASURE

nouns

1 **unpleasure, unpleasantness** *see* 98, **lack of pleasure,** joylessness, cheerlessness; unsatisfaction, nonsatisfaction, ungratification, nongratification; grimness; discontent *see* 108; displeasure, dissatisfaction, **discomfort,** uncomfortableness, misease (*old*), malaise, **painfulness; disquiet,** inquietude, **uneasiness,** unease, discomposure, vexation of spirit, **anxiety;** angst, anguish, dread, nausea, existential woe, existential vacuum; the blahs (*informal*); **dullness,** flatness, staleness, tastelessness, savourlessness; ashes in the mouth; **boredom,** ennui, tedium, tediousness, spleen; emptiness, spiritual void, death of the heart *or* soul; unhappiness *see* 112.2; dislike *see* 99

2 **annoyance, vexation,** bothersomeness, exasperation, *tracasserie* (*French*), **aggravation; nuisance, pest, bother,** botheration (*informal*), public nuisance, aggro, **trouble, problem,** pain (*informal*), difficulty, hot potato (*informal*); **trial; bore,** crashing bore (*informal*); **drag** *and* downer (*both informal*); **worry,** worriment (*informal*); downside *and* the bad news (*both informal*); headache (*informal*); **pain in the neck** *or* in the arse (*informal*); **harassment,** molestation, persecution, dogging, hounding, harrying; devilment, bedevilment; vexatiousness *see* 98.7

3 **irritation, aggravation,** exacerbation, worsening, salt in the wound, twisting the knife in the wound, embitterment, **provocation;** fret, gall, chafe; irritant; pea in the shoe

4 **chagrin, distress; embarrassment, abashment, discomfiture,** egg on one's face (*informal*), disconcertion, disconcertment, discountenance, discomposure, disturbance, confusion; **humiliation, shame,** shamefacedness, mortification, red face

5 **pain, distress, grief,** stress, stress of life, suffering, passion, dolour; ache, aching; pang, wrench, throes, cramp, spasm; wound, injury, hurt; **sore**, sore spot, tender spot, lesion; cut, stroke; shock, blow, hard *or* nasty blow

6 **wretchedness, despair,** bitterness, infelicity, **misery, anguish, agony, woe,** woefulness, woesomeness (*old*), bale, balefulness; **melancholy,** melancholia, **depression, sadness, grief** *see* 112.10; funk *or* blue funk (*informal*); **heartache,** aching heart, heavy heart, bleeding heart, broken heart, agony of mind *or* spirit; suicidal despair, black night of the soul, **despondency,** despond,

"Slough of Despond"—BUNYAN; **desolation,** prostration, crushing; extremity, depth of misery; sloth, acedia

7 **torment, torture,** cruciation (*old*), excruciation, crucifixion, passion, laceration, clawing, lancination, flaying, excoriation; the rack, the iron maiden, thumbscrews; **persecution; martyrdom; purgatory,**

"frigid purgatorial fires"—T S ELIOT, living death, hell, hell upon earth; holocaust; nightmare, horror

8 **affliction,** infliction; **curse, woe,** distress, grievance, **sorrow,** *tsures* (*Yiddish*); **trouble,** peck *or* pack of troubles,

"sea of troubles"—SHAKESPEARE; **care,** burden of care, cankerworm of care; **burden, oppression, cross, cross to bear** *or* **be borne, load,** fardel (*old*), encumbrance, weight, albatross around one's neck, millstone around one's neck; thorn, thorn in the side, crown of thorns; bitter pill, bitter draught, bitter cup, cup *or* waters of bitterness; gall, gall and wormwood;

"the thousand natural shocks that flesh is heir to"—SHAKESPEARE, "all the ills that men endure"—ABRAHAM COWLEY; Pandora's box

9 **trial, tribulation,** trials and tribulations; **ordeal,** fiery ordeal, the iron entering the soul

10 **tormentor,** torment; torturer; **nuisance, pest,** pesterer, pain *and* pain in the neck *or* arse (*informal*), nag, *nudnik* (*Yiddish*), public nuisance; **tease,** teaser; annoyer, harasser, harrier, badgerer, **heckler,** plaguer, persecutor, sadist; molester, **bully**

11 **sufferer,** victim, prey; **wretch,** poor devil (*informal*), object of compassion; martyr

verbs

12 **to give no pleasure** *or* joy *or* cheer *or* comfort, **disquiet,** discompose, leave unsatisfied; discontent; taste like ashes in the mouth; **bore,** be tedious, cheese off (*informal*)

13 **to annoy, irk, vex, nettle, provoke, pique,** miff *and* peeve (*both informal*), distemper, **ruffle, disturb,** discompose, **roil, rile, aggravate,** make a nuisance of oneself, **exasperate,** exercise, try one's patience, try the patience of a saint; **put one's back up,** make one bristle; **gripe;** give one a pain (*informal*); get, get one down, **get one's goat,** get under one's skin, get in one's hair, tread on one's toes, get on one's wick (*informal*); burn up *and* brown off (*both informal*); **torment, molest, bother,** pother; **harass,** harry, drive up the wall (*informal*), **hound,** dog, nag, **persecute; heckle,** pick *or* prod at, rub it in *and* rub one's nose in it (*both informal*), badger, hector,

bait, bullyrag, worry, worry at, nip at the heels of, chivy, hardly give one time to breathe, make one's life miserable, keep on at, fash (*Scottish*); **bug** (*informal*), be on the back of *and* be at *and* ride (*all informal*), **pester, tease, needle,** devil, get after *or* get on (*informal*), **bedevil, pick on** (*informal*), wind up, tweak the nose, pluck the beard, give a bad time to (*informal*); **plague,** beset, beleaguer; catch in the crossfire *or* in the middle; catch one off balance, trip one up

14 **to irritate, aggravate,** exacerbate, worsen, rub salt in the wound, twist the knife in the wound, step on one's corns, barb the dart; touch a soft spot *or* tender spot, touch a raw nerve, touch where it hurts; provoke, **gall, chafe, fret,** grate, grit *and* gravel (*both informal*), rasp; **get on one's nerves, grate on,** set on edge; **set one's teeth on edge,** go against the grain; **rub one** *or* **one's fur the wrong way**

15 **to chagrin, embarrass, abash, discomfit, disconcert,** discompose, confuse, throw into confusion *or* a tizzy *or* a hissy-fit, **upset,** confound, cast down, mortify, put out, put out of face *or* countenance, put to the blush

16 **to distress, afflict, trouble,** burden, give one a hard row to hoe, load with care, **bother, disturb, perturb, disquiet, discomfort, agitate, upset,** put to it; **worry,** give one grey hair

17 **to pain, grieve,** aggrieve, anguish; **hurt, wound,** bruise, **hurt one's feelings;** pierce, prick, stab, cut, sting; **cut up** (*informal*), **cut to the heart,** wound *or* sting *or* cut to the quick, hit one where it hurts (*informal*); be a thorn in one's side

18 **to torture, torment, agonize, harrow,** savage, **rack,** scarify, crucify, impale, excruciate, lacerate, claw, rip, bloody, lancinate, macerate, convulse, wring; prolong the agony, pile *or* put *or* turn on the agony, kill by inches, make life miserable *or* not worth living; martyr, martyrize; **tyrannize,** push around (*informal*); punish *see* 604.10

19 **to suffer, hurt, ache, bleed;** anguish, **suffer anguish; agonize,** writhe; go hard with, have a bad time of it, go through hell; quaff the bitter cup, drain the cup of misery to the dregs, be nailed to the cross

adjectives

20 **pleasureless,** joyless, cheerless, depressed *see* 112.22, grim; **sad, unhappy** *see* 112.21; unsatisfied, unfulfilled, ungratified; **bored,** cheesed off (*informal*); anguished, anxious, suffering angst *or* dread *or* nausea, uneasy, unquiet, prey to malaise; **repelled,** revolted, **disgusted,** sickened, nauseated, nauseous

21 **annoyed, irritated,** bugged (*informal*), chocker, nonformal; galled, chafed; **bothered, troubled, disturbed, ruffled, roiled, riled; irked, vexed, piqued, nettled, provoked, peeved** *and* **miffed** (*both informal*), griped, **aggravated, exasperated,** pindling (*Western English*); burnt-up *and* browned-off *and* cheesed off (*both informal*), resentful, angry *see* 152.28

22 **distressed, afflicted, put-upon,** beset, beleaguered; caught in the middle *or* in the crossfire; **troubled, bothered, disturbed, perturbed, disquieted,**

discomforted, discomposed, agitated, in a funk
(*informal*); hung up (*informal*); **uncomfortable,**
uneasy, ill at ease; **chagrined, embarrassed,**
abashed, discomfited, **disconcerted, upset,**
confused, mortified, **put-out,** out of countenance,
cast down, chapfallen

23 **pained, grieved,** aggrieved; **wounded, hurt,**
injured, **bruised,** mauled; **cut,** cut to the quick;
stung; anguished, aching, bleeding

24 **tormented, plagued, harassed, harried,** dogged,
hounded, persecuted, beset; nipped at, worried,
chivied, **heckled,** badgered, hectored, baited,
bullyragged, ragged, **pestered, teased, needled,**
devilled, **bedevilled, picked on** (*informal*), **bugged**
(*informal*)

25 **tortured, harrowed,** savaged, **agonized,** convulsed,
wrung, racked, crucified, impaled, lacerated,
excoriated, clawed, ripped, bloodied, lancinated; on
the rack, under the harrow

26 **wretched, miserable; woeful,** woebegone, woesome
(*old*); crushed, stricken, **cut up** (*informal*), choked,
heartsick, heart-stricken, heart-struck; deep-troubled;
desolate, disconsolate, suicidal

adverbs

27 to one's displeasure, to one's disgust

97 PLEASANTNESS

nouns

1 **pleasantness,** pleasingness, pleasance, **pleasure** *see*
95, pleasurefulness, **pleasurableness,** pleasurability,
pleasantry (*old*), felicitousness, **enjoyableness; bliss,**
blissfulness; sweetness, mellifluousness, *douceur*
(*French*); mellowness; **agreeableness,** agreeability,
complaisance, rapport, harmoniousness; compatibility;
welcomeness; geniality, congeniality, cordiality,
Gemütlichkeit (*German*), affability, amicability,
amiability; amenity, graciousness; goodness,
goodliness, niceness; **fun** *see* 743.2, 95.1

2 **delightfulness,** exquisiteness, loveliness; **charm,**
winsomeness, grace, **attractiveness, appeal,**
appealingness, winningness; sexiness (*informal*);
glamour; captivation, enchantment, entrancement,
bewitchment, witchery, enravishment, **fascination**
see 377.1; invitingness, temptingness, tantalizingness;
voluptuousness, sensuousness; luxury

3 **delectability,** delectableness, deliciousness,
lusciousness; tastiness, flavorsomeness, savouriness;
juiciness; succulence

4 **cheerfulness;** brightness, sunniness; sunny side;
bright side; fair weather

verbs

5 to make pleasant, brighten, sweeten, gild, gild the
lily *or* pill; sentimentalize, saccharinize

adjectives

6 **pleasant, pleasing, pleasureful, pleasurable;** fair,
fair and pleasant, **enjoyable,** pleasure-giving;
felicitous, felicific; **likable, desirable,** to one's
liking, to one's taste, to *or* after one's fancy, after
one's own heart; **agreeable,** complaisant,
harmonious, *en rapport* (*French*), compatible; **blissful;**

sweet, mellifluous, honeyed, dulcet; mellow;
gratifying, satisfying, rewarding, heartwarming,
grateful; **welcome,** welcome as the roses in May;
genial, congenial, cordial, *gemütlich* (*German*), affable,
amiable, amicable, gracious; good, goodly, nice, fine;
cheerful *see* 109.11

7 **delightful, exquisite, lovely; thrilling,** titillative;
charming, attractive, endearing, engaging,
appealing, prepossessing, heartwarming, sexy
(*informal*), **enchanting,** bewitching, witching,
entrancing, enthralling, intriguing, fascinating;
captivating, irresistible, ravishing, enravishing;
winning, winsome, taking, fetching, heart-robbing;
inviting, tempting, tantalizing; voluptuous, sensuous;
luxurious, delicious

8 (*informal terms*) **fun,** dishy, drooly, sexy, jammy,
plummy, yummy

9 **blissful,** beatific, saintly, divine; sublime; **heavenly,**
paradisal, paradisiac, paradisiacal, paradisic,
paradisical, empyreal *or* empyrean, Elysian; out of
sight *or* of this world (*informal*)

10 **delectable, delicious,** luscious; tasty, flavoursome,
savoury; juicy, succulent

11 **bright, sunny,** fair, mild, balmy; halcyon, Saturnian

adverbs

12 **pleasantly, pleasingly, pleasurably,** fair,
enjoyably; **blissfully; gratifyingly,** satisfyingly;
agreeably, genially, affably, cordially, amiably,
amicably, graciously, kindly; cheerfully *see* 109.17

13 **delightfully, exquisitely; charmingly,**
engagingly, appealingly, enchantingly,
bewitchingly, entrancingly, intriguingly, fascinatingly;
ravishingly, enravishingly; **winningly,** winsomely;
invitingly, temptingly, tantalizingly, voluptuously,
sensuously; luxuriously

14 **delectably,** deliciously, lusciously, tastily,
succulently, savorously

98 UNPLEASANTNESS

nouns

1 **unpleasantness,** unpleasingness, displeasingness,
displeasure; **disagreeableness,** disagreeability,
désagrément (*French*); **abrasiveness,** woundingess,
hostility, unfriendliness; **undesirability,**
unappealingness, unattractiveness, unengagingness,
uninvitingness, unprepossessingness; **distastefulness,**
unsavouriness, unpalatability, **undelectability;**
ugliness *see* 1014

2 **offensiveness,** objectionability, objectionableness;
repugnance, contrariety, **odiousness, repulsiveness,**
repellence *or* repellency, rebarbativeness,
disgustingness, nauseousness, grossness *and* yuckiness
and grottiness (*all informal*), grunginess *and*
scuzziness (*both US informal*); **loathsomeness,**
hatefulness, beastliness (*informal*); **vileness,**
foulness, putridness, putridity, rottenness,
noxiousness; **nastiness,** fulsomeness, noisomeness,
obnoxiousness, abominableness, heinousness;
contemptibleness, contemptibility, despicability,
despicableness, baseness, ignobleness, ignobility;
unspeakableness; coarseness, grossness, crudeness,
obscenity

3 dreadfulness, **horribleness**, horridness, atrociousness, atrocity, hideousness, terribleness, awfulness (*informal*); grimness, direness, banefulness

4 harshness, agony, agonizingness, excruciation, excruciatingness, **torture**, torturesomeness, torturousness, **torment**, tormentingness; desolation, desolateness; heartbreak, heartsickness

5 distressfulness, distress, grievousness, grief; **painfulness**, pain see 26; **harshness**, bitterness, sharpness; lamentability, lamentableness, deplorability, deplorableness, pitiableness, pitifulness, pitiability, regrettableness; **woe, sadness, sorrowfulness, mournfulness**, lamentation, woefulness, woesomeness (*old*), woebegoneness, pathos, poignancy; comfortlessness, discomfort, misease (*old*); dreariness, cheerlessness, joylessness, dismalness, **depression**, bleakness

6 mortification, humiliation, embarrassment, egg on one's face (*informal*); disconcertedness, awkwardness

7 vexatiousness, irksomeness, annoyance, annoyingness, aggravation, exasperation, provocation, provokingness, tiresomeness, wearisomeness; **troublesomeness, bothersomeness**, harassment; worrisomeness, plaguesomeness, peskiness *and* pestiferousness (*both informal*)

8 harshness, oppressiveness, burdensomeness, onerousness, weightiness, heaviness

9 intolerability, intolerableness, unbearableness, insupportableness, insufferableness, **unendurability**

verbs

10 to be unpleasant; displease; be disagreeable *or* undesirable *or* distasteful *or* abrasive

11 to offend, give offence, **repel**, put off, turn off (*informal*), **revolt, disgust**, nauseate, sicken, make one sick, make one sick to *or* in the stomach, make one vomit *or* puke *or* retch, turn the stomach, gross out (*US informal*); stink in the nostrils; stick in one's throat, stick in one's crop *or* craw *or* gizzard (*informal*); **horrify, appal**, shock; make the flesh creep *or* crawl, make one shudder

12 to agonize, excruciate, **torture, torment**, desolate

13 to mortify, humiliate, embarrass, disconcert, disturb

14 to distress, dismay, grieve, mourn, lament, sorrow; pain, discomfort, misease (*old*); get in one's hair, try one's patience, give one a hard time *or* a pain *or* a pain in the neck *or* arse (*informal*)

15 to vex, irk, annoy, **aggravate**, exasperate, provoke; **trouble, worry**, give one grey hair, plague, harass, bother, hassle

16 to oppress, **burden**, weigh upon, weight down, wear one down, be heavy on one, crush one; **tire, exhaust**, weary, wear out, wear upon one; prey on the mind, prey on *or* upon; **haunt**, haunt the memory, obsess

adjectives

17 unpleasant, unpleasing, unenjoyable; **displeasing, disagreeable; unlikable**, dislikable; **abrasive**, wounding, hostile, unfriendly; **undesirable**, unattractive, unappealing, unengaging, uninviting, unalluring; tacky (*informal*), low rent *and* low ride (*both US informal*); unwelcome, thankless; **distasteful**, untasteful, **unpalatable**, unsavoury,

unappetizing, undelicious, **undelectable; ugly** see 1014.6; sour, **bitter**

18 offensive, objectionable, odious, repulsive, repellent, rebarbative, **repugnant, revolting**, forbidding; **disgusting, sickening, loathsome**, gross *and* yucky *and* grotty (*informal*), grungy *and* scuzzy (*both US informal*), beastly (*informal*), **vile, foul, nasty, nauseating** see 64.7; fulsome, mephitic, miasmal, miasmic, malodorous, stinking, fetid, noisome, noxious; coarse, gross, crude, obscene; **obnoxious, abhorrent, hateful, abominable**, heinous, **contemptible, despicable**, detestable, execrable, beneath *or* below contempt, **base**, ignoble

19 horrid, horrible, horrific, **horrifying**, horrendous, unspeakable, beyond words; **dreadful, atrocious, terrible, rotten**, awful *and* beastly (*both informal*), **hideous; tragic**; dire, grim, baneful; appalling, shocking, disgusting

20 distressing, distressful, dismaying; afflicting, afflictive; **painful**, sore, **harsh**, bitter, sharp; **grievous**, dolorous, dolorific, dolorogenic; **lamentable, deplorable**, regrettable, pitiable, piteous, rueful, woeful, woesome (*old*), woebegone, **sad**, sorrowful, wretched, mournful, **depressing**, depressive; **pathetic**, affecting, touching, moving, saddening, poignant; comfortless, discomforting, uncomfortable; **desolate**, dreary, cheerless, joyless, dismal, bleak

21 mortifying, humiliating, **embarrassing**, cringe-making *and* cringeworthy (*both informal*), crushing, disconcerting, awkward, disturbing

22 annoying, irritating, galling, **provoking, aggravating** (*informal*), **exasperating; vexatious**, vexing, irking, **irksome**, tiresome, wearisome; **troublesome, bothersome, worrisome**, bothering, troubling, disturbing, plaguing, plaguesome, plaguey (*informal*), pestilent, pestilential, pesky *and* pesty (*both US & Canadian informal*); tormenting, harassing, worrying; pestering, teasing; importunate, importune

23 agonizing, excruciating, harrowing, racking, rending, **desolating**, consuming; **tormenting**, torturous; **heartbreaking**, heartrending, **heartsickening**, heartwounding

24 oppressive, burdensome, **crushing**, trying, onerous, heavy, weighty; **harsh**, wearing, wearying, exhausting; overburdensome, tyrannous, grinding

25 insufferable, intolerable, insupportable, unendurable, unbearable, past bearing, not to be borne *or* endured, for the birds (*informal*), **too much** *or* a bit much (*informal*), more than flesh and blood can bear, enough to drive one mad, enough to provoke a saint, enough to try the patience of Job

adverbs

26 unpleasantly, distastefully unpleasingly; **displeasingly, offensively, objectionably**, odiously, **repulsively**, repellently, rebarbatively, repugnantly, **revoltingly, disgustingly, sickeningly, loathsomely**, vilely, foully, nastily, fulsomely, mephitically, malodorously, fetidly, noisomely, noxiously, obnoxiously, **abhorrently, hatefully, abominably**, contemptibly, **despicably, detestably**, execrably, nauseatingly

27 **horridly, horribly, dreadfully, terribly,** hideously; **tragically**; grimly, direly, banefully; appallingly, shockingly

28 **distressingly,** distressfully; **painfully,** sorely, **grievously,** lamentably, deplorably, pitiably, ruefully, woefully, woesomely (*old*), sadly, pathetically; **agonizingly, excruciatingly,** harrowingly, heartbreakingly

29 **annoyingly, irritatingly, aggravatingly, provokingly, exasperatingly; vexatiously,** irksomely, tiresomely, wearisomely; **troublesomely, bothersomely,** worrisomely, regrettably

30 **insufferably, intolerably, unbearably, unendurably, insupportably**

exclamations

31 eeyuck! *or* yeeuck! *or* yeeuch!, phew! *or* pugh!, ugh!; *feh!* (*Yiddish*); alas, alack

99 DISLIKE

nouns

1 **dislike, distaste,** disrelish, scunner; **disaffection, disfavour,** disinclination; disaffinity; **displeasure, disapproval,** disapprobation

2 **hostility,** antagonism, **enmity** *see* 589; **hatred, hate** *see* 103; **aversion, repugnance,** repulsion, **antipathy,** allergy (*informal*), grudge, abomination, **abhorrence, horror,** mortal horror; **disgust, loathing;** nausea; shuddering, cold sweat, creeping flesh

verbs

3 **to dislike,** mislike, disfavour, not like, have no liking for, be no love lost between, **have no use for** (*informal*), have *or* get the needle to (*informal*), **not care for,** have no time for, have a disaffinity for, want nothing to do with, not think much of, not go much on, entertain *or* conceive *or* take a dislike to, go off, take a scunner to, not be able to bear *or* endure *or* abide, not give the time of day to (*informal*), **disapprove of;** disrelish, have no taste for, not stomach, not have the stomach for, not be one's cup of tea; be hostile to, have it in for (*informal*); **hate, abhor, detest, loathe** *see* 103.5

4 **to feel disgust,** be nauseated, **sicken at,** choke on, have a bellyful of (*informal*); **gag, retch,** keck (*US*), heave, vomit, puke, spew *and* hurl *and* upchuck *and* barf (*all informal*)

5 **to shudder at,** have one's flesh creep *or* crawl at the thought of; shrink from, **recoil, revolt at; grimace,** make a face, make a wry face *or* mouth, turn up one's nose, look down one's nose, look askance, raise one's eyebrows, take a dim view of, show distaste for, disapprove of

6 **to repel, disgust** *see* 98.11, gross out (*US informal*), sicken; leave a bad taste in one's mouth

adjectives

7 **unlikable, distasteful,** mislikable, dislikable, **uncongenial, displeasing,** unpleasant *see* 98.17; **not to one's taste,** not one's sort, not one's cup of tea, counter to one's preferences, offering no delight,

against the grain, uninviting; unlovable; **abhorrent, odious** *see* 98.18; **intolerable** *see* 98.25

8 **averse, allergic** (*informal*), undelighted, out of sympathy, disaffected, disenchanted, **disinclined, displeased,** put off (*informal*), not charmed, less than pleased; **disapproving, censorious, judgmental,** po-faced (*informal*); unamiable, **unfriendly, hostile** *see* 589.10; death on, down on

9 **disliked, uncared-for, unvalued,** unprized, misprized, undervalued; **despised,** lowly, spat-upon, untouchable; **unpopular, out of favour,** gone begging; **unappreciated,** misunderstood; unsung, thankless; unwept, unlamented, unmourned, undeplored, unmissed, unregretted

10 **unloved,** unbeloved, uncherished, loveless; **lovelorn,** forsaken, **rejected,** jilted, thrown over (*informal*), spurned, crossed in love

11 **unwanted,** unwished, undesired; **unwelcome,** unasked, unbidden, uninvited, uncalled-for, unasked-for

100 DESIRE

nouns

1 **desire, wish,** wanting, **want, need,** desideration; **hope; fancy; will, mind, pleasure,** will and pleasure; heart's desire; **urge,** drive, libido, pleasure principle; concupiscence; horme; wish fulfilment, fantasy; passion, ardour, sexual desire *see* 75.5; **curiosity,** intellectual curiosity, thirst for knowledge, lust for learning; **eagerness** *see* 101

2 **liking, love, fondness;** infatuation, crush; **affection; relish, taste, gusto; passion,** weakness (*informal*)

3 **inclination, penchant, partiality, fancy, favour, predilection, preference,** propensity, proclivity, **leaning, bent,** turn, tilt, bias, **affinity;** mutual affinity *or* attraction; **sympathy,** fascination

4 **wistfulness,** wishfulness, yearnfulness, **nostalgia;** wishful thinking; sheep's eyes, longing *or* wistful eye; daydream, daydreaming

5 **yearning, yen** (*informal*); **longing,** desiderium, **hankering** (*informal*), **pining,** honing (*informal*), aching; languishment, languishing; **nostalgia, homesickness,** *Heimweh* (*German*), *mal du pays* and *maladie du pays* (*both French*); nostomania

6 **craving, coveting, lust; hunger, thirst, appetite,** "appetite, an universal wolf"—SHAKESPEARE, appetition, appetency *or* appetence; aching void; **itch, itching,** prurience *or* pruriency; lech (*informal*), **sexual desire** *see* 75.5; *cacoëthes* (*Latin*), **mania** *see* 925.12

7 **appetite,** stomach, relish, taste; **hunger,** hungriness; the munchies (*informal*), peckishness (*informal*); tapeworm (*informal*), eyes bigger than one's stomach, wolf in one's stomach, canine appetite; empty stomach, emptiness (*informal*), hollow hunger; **thirst,** thirstiness, drought (*informal*), dryness; polydipsia; torment of Tantalus; sweet tooth (*informal*)

8 **greed,** greediness, graspingness, **avarice, cupidity, avidity, voracity, rapacity, lust,** avariciousness, *avaritia* and *cupiditas* (*both Latin*); money-grubbing; avidness, esurience, wolfishness; voraciousness, ravenousness, rapaciousness, sordidness,

covetousness, acquisitiveness; itching palm; grasping; **piggishness, hoggishness,** swinishness; **gluttony** see 672, *gula* (*Latin*); inordinate desire, furore, craze, fury *or* frenzy of desire, overgreediness; insatiable desire, insatiability; incontinence, intemperateness see 669.1

9 **aspiration,** reaching high, upward looking;

"the desire of the moth for the star"—SHELLEY; high goal *or* aim *or* purpose, dream, ideals; **idealism** see 985.7

10 **ambition,** ambitiousness, vaulting ambition; climbing, status-seeking, social climbing, careerism; opportunism; power-hunger;

"the mind's immodesty"—D'AVENANT, "the way in which a vulgar man aspires"—HENRY WARD BEECHER, "the evil shadow of aspiration"—GEORGE MACDONALD, "the avarice of power"—G G COULTON, "avarice on stilts and masked"—W S LANDOR; noble *or* lofty ambition, magnanimity (*old*);

"the spur that makes man struggle with destiny"—DONALD G MITCHELL

11 (*object of desire*) **desire,** heart's desire, desideration, *desideratum* (*Latin*); wish; **hope;** catch, quarry, prey, game, plum, prize, trophy; forbidden fruit, temptation; lodestone, magnet; golden vision, mecca, glimmering goal; the American dream; land of heart's desire see 985.11; something to be desired,

"a consummation devoutly to be wish'd"—SHAKESPEARE; dearest wish, ambition, the height of one's ambition; a sight for sore eyes, a welcome sight; the light at the end of the tunnel

12 **desirer,** wisher, wanter, hankerer (*informal*), yearner, coveter; fancier, collector; addict, freak (*informal*), devotee, votary; **aspirant,** aspirer, solicitant, wannabee *and* hopeful (*both informal*), candidate; **lover,** swain, suitor

13 **desirability; agreeability,** acceptability, unobjectionableness; **attractiveness,** attraction, magnetism, **appeal,** seductiveness, provocativeness, pleasingness; likability, lovability see 104.7

verbs

14 **to desire,** desiderate, be desirous of, **wish,** lust after, bay after, kill for *and* give one's right arm for (*both informal*), die for (*informal*), **want,** have a mind to, choose (*informal*); would fain do *or* have (*old*), would be glad of; **like,** have *or* acquire a taste for, fancy, take to, **take a fancy** *or* a shine to, have a fancy for; have an eye to, have one's eye on; lean toward, tilt toward, have a penchant for, have a weakness *or* soft spot in one's heart for; aim at, set one's cap for, have designs on; wish very much, wish to goodness; **love** see 104.18; lust; prefer, favour see 371.17

15 **to want to, wish to, like to,** love to, dearly love to, choose to; **itch to,** burn to; ache to, long to

16 **to wish for, hope for, yearn for,** yen for *and* have a yen for (*both informal*), **itch for,** lust for, pant for, **long for, pine for,** hone for (*informal*), ache for, be hurting for (*informal*), weary for, languish for, **be dying for,** thirst for, sigh for, gape for (*old*); cry for, clamour for; spoil for (*informal*)

17 **to want with all one's heart, want in the worst way; set one's heart on, have one's heart set on,** give one's kingdom in hell for *or* one's eyeteeth for (*informal*)

18 **to crave, covet, hunger after,** thirst after, crave after, **lust after,** have a lech for (*informal*), pant after, run mad after, **hanker for** *or* **after** (*informal*); crawl after; aspire after, be consumed with desire; have an itchy *or* itching palm *and* have sticky fingers (*all informal*)

19 **to hunger,** hunger for, feel hungry, be peckish (*informal*); starve (*informal*), be ravenous, raven; **have a good appetite,** be a good trencherman, have a tapeworm (*informal*), have a wolf in one's stomach; eye hungrily, lick one's lips *or* chops (*informal*); **thirst,** thirst for

20 **to aspire, be ambitious;** aspire to, try to reach; aim high, keep one's eyes on the stars, raise one's sights, set one's sights, reach for the sky,

"hitch one's wagon to a star"—EMERSON

adjectives

21 **desirous,** desiring, desireful (*old*), lickerish, **wanting, wishing,** needing, hoping; dying to (*informal*); tempted; appetitive, desiderative, optative, libidinous, libidinal; orectic; hormic; **eager;** lascivious, **lustful**

22 **desirous of** *or* **to,** keen on, set on (*informal*), bent on; fond of, with a liking for, partial to (*informal*); fain of *or* to (*old*); inclined toward, leaning toward; **itching for** *or* **to,** aching for *or* to, **dying for** *or* **to;** spoiling for (*informal*); mad on *or* for, wild to *or* for (*informal*), crazy to *or* for (*informal*)

23 **wistful,** wishful; **longing, yearning,** yearnful, **hankering** (*informal*), **languishing, pining,** honing (*informal*); **nostalgic, homesick**

24 **craving,** coveting; **hungering,** hungry, thirsting, thirsty, athirst; **itching,** prurient; fervid; **devoured by desire,** in a frenzy *or* fury of desire, mad with lust, consumed with desire

25 **hungry,** hungering, peckish (*informal*); empty (*informal*), unfilled; ravening, **ravenous,** voracious, sharp-set, **wolfish,** dog-hungry (*informal*), hungry as a bear; **starved, famished,** starving, famishing, perishing *or* pinched with hunger; fasting; half-starved, half-famished

26 **thirsty,** thirsting, athirst; **dry,** parched, droughty (*informal*)

27 **greedy, avaricious, avid, voracious, rapacious,** cupidinous, esurient, **ravening, grasping,** graspy, acquisitive, mercenary, sordid, overgreedy; ravenous, gobbling, devouring; miserly, money-hungry, money-grubbing, money-mad, venal· **covetous,** coveting; **piggish, hoggish,** swinish, a hog for, greedy as a hog; **gluttonous** see 672.6; omnivorous, all-devouring; insatiable, insatiate, unsatisfied, unsated, unappeased, unappeasable, limitless, bottomless, unquenchable, quenchless, unslaked, unslakeable, slakeless

28 **aspiring, ambitious,** aspirational, sky-aspiring, upward-looking, high-reaching; high-flying, social-climbing, upwardly mobile, careerist, careeristic, on the make (*informal*); power-hungry

29 **desired, wanted,** coveted; **wished-for,** hoped-for, longed-for; in demand, popular
30 **desirable,** sought-after, much sought-after, to be desired, **much to be desired; enviable,** worth having; **likable, pleasing,** after one's own heart; **agreeable,** acceptable, unobjectionable; palatable; **attractive,** taking, winning, sexy (*informal*), dishy (*informal*), tasty (*informal*), **seductive, provocative,** tantalizing, exciting; appetizing, tempting, toothsome, mouth-watering; **lovable,** adorable

adverbs

31 **desirously, wistfully,** wishfully, **longingly, yearningly,** piningly, languishingly; cravingly, itchingly; hungrily, thirstily; aspiringly, ambitiously
32 **greedily, avariciously,** avidly, ravenously, raveningly, voraciously, rapaciously, **covetously,** graspingly, devouringly; wolfishly, **piggishly, hoggishly,** swinishly

101 EAGERNESS

nouns

1 **eagerness, enthusiasm, avidity,** avidness, keenness, forwardness, prothymia, **readiness,** promptness, quickness, **alacrity,** cheerful readiness, *empressement* (*French*); keen desire, **appetite** *see* 100.7; anxiousness, anxiety; **zest,** zestfulness, gusto, verve, **liveliness,** life, **vitality,** vivacity, élan, spirit, animation; **impatience,** breathless impatience *see* 135.1; keen interest, fascination; **craze** *see* 925.12
2 **zeal, ardour, ardency, fervour, fervency, fervidness, spirit, warmth, fire, heat,** heatedness, **passion,** passionateness, impassionedness, heartiness, intensity, **abandon,** vehemence; intentness, resolution *see* 359; **devotion,** devoutness, devotedness, dedication, commitment, committedness; **earnestness, seriousness,** sincerity; loyalty, faithfulness, faith, fidelity *see* 644.7; discipleship, followership
3 **overzealousness, overeagerness,** overanxiousness, overanxiety; unchecked enthusiasm, **overenthusiasm, infatuation; overambitiousness; frenzy, fury;** zealotry, zealotism; mania, **fanaticism** *see* 925.11
4 **enthusiast, zealot,** infatuate, energumen, rhapsodist; addict; faddist; pursuer; hobbyist, collector; **fanatic;** visionary *see* 985.13; **devotee,** votary, aficionada, aficionado, **fancier,** admirer, **follower; disciple,** worshipper, idolizer, idolater; amateur, dilettante; collector
5 (*informal terms*) **fan, buff, freak,** hound, fiend, demon, nut, bug, head, junkie, groupie, rooter, booster, great one for, sucker for; fan club, fanzine; eager beaver, aholic

verbs

6 **to jump at,** catch, grab, grab at, snatch, snatch at, fall all over oneself, get excited about, go at hammer and tongs *or* tooth and nail, go wild (*informal*); go to great lengths, lean *or* bend *or* fall over backwards; **desire** *see* 100.14, 18
7 **to be enthusiastic, rave, enthuse** *and* be big on (*both informal*); get stars in one's eyes, **rhapsodize,**

carry on over *and* rave on (*both informal*), make much of, **make a fuss over,** make an ado *or* much ado about, make a to-do over *and* take on over (*both informal*), be *or* go on over *or* about (*informal*), rave about *and* whoop it up about (*both informal*); go nuts *or* gaga *or* ape over (*informal*); gush, gush over; effervesce, bubble over

adjectives

8 **eager, anxious,** agog, all agog; **avid, keen,** forward, prompt, quick, ready, ready and willing, alacritous, bursting to, dying to, raring to; **zestful, lively,** full of life, vital, vivacious, vivid, spirited, sparky, **animated; impatient** *see* 135.6; breathless, panting, champing at the bit; **desirous** *see* 100.21
9 **zealous, ardent, fervent, fervid,** perfervid, **spirited, intense,** hearty, vehement, abandoned, **passionate,** impassioned, **warm,** heated, hot, hot-blooded, red-hot, fiery, white-hot, flaming, burning, afire, aflame, on fire, like a house afire (*informal*); **devout, devoted;** dedicated, committed; **earnest, sincere, serious,** in earnest; loyal, faithful *see* 644.20; intent, intent on, resolute *see* 359.11
10 **enthusiastic,** enthused *and* big (*both informal*), **gung ho** (*informal*), glowing, full of enthusiasm; enthusiastic about, infatuated with
11 (*informal terms*) **wild about, crazy about, mad about,** potty about, ape about *or* over, gone on, all in a dither over, gaga over, starry-eyed over, all hopped up about, hepped up over, hot about *or* for *or* on, steamed up about, **turned-on, switched on;** hipped on, cracked on, bugs on, freaked-out, **nuts on** *or* **over** *or* **about, keen on** *or* **about,** crazy *or* mad *or* nuts about
12 **overzealous,** ultrazealous, **overeager,** over-anxious; **overambitious;** overdesirous; **overenthusiastic,** infatuated; feverish, perfervid, febrile, at fever *or* fevered pitch; hectic, frenetic, furious, **frenzied,** frantic, **wild,** hysteric, hysterical, delirious; **insane** *see* 925.26; **fanatical** *see* 925.32

adverbs

13 **eagerly, anxiously; impatiently,** breathlessly; **avidly,** promptly, quickly, keenly, readily; zestfully, vivaciously, animatedly; **enthusiastically,** with enthusiasm; **with alacrity,** with zest, with gusto, with relish, with open arms
14 **zealously, ardently, fervently, fervidly,** perfervidly, heatedly, heartily, vehemently, **passionately,** impassionedly; intently, intensely; **devoutly, devotedly;** earnestly, sincerely, seriously

102 INDIFFERENCE

nouns

1 **indifference,** indifferentness; indifferentism; halfheartedness, zeallessness, perfunctoriness, fervourlessness; **coolness,** coldness, chilliness, chill, iciness, frostiness; tepidness, **lukewarmness,** Laodiceanism; **neutrality,** neutralness, neuterness; insipidity, vapidity
2 **unconcern, disinterest, detachment; disregard, dispassion,** insouciance, **carelessness,** regardlessness; easygoingness; **heedlessness,**

mindlessness, inattention *see* 983; **unmindfulness, incuriosity** *see* 981; **insensitivity**; disregardfulness, recklessness, negligence *see* 340.1; *je-m'en-foutisme* or *je-m'en-fichisme* (*French*); unsolicitousness, unanxiousness; pococurantism; **nonchalance, inexcitability** *see* 106, ataraxy *or* ataraxia, samadhi; indiscrimination, casualness *see* 944.1; **listlessness**, lackadaisicalness, lack of feeling *or* affect, **apathy** *see* 94.4; sloth, acedia

3 **undesirousness**, desirelessness; nirvana; lovelessness, passionlessness; uneagerness, **unambitiousness**; lack of appetite, inappetence

verbs

4 **to not care, not mind, not give** *or* **care a damn,** not give a hoot *or* shit (*informal*), not care less *or* two hoots (*informal*), care nothing for *or* about, not care a straw about; shrug off; **take no interest in,** have no desire for, have no taste *or* relish for; hold no brief for; be half-hearted, temper one's zeal

5 **to not matter to,** be all one to, take it or leave it; make no difference

adjectives

6 **indifferent, halfhearted,** zealless, perfunctory, fervourless; **cool, cold** *see* 589.9; tepid, **lukewarm,** Laodicean; neither hot nor cold, neither one thing nor the other, "neither fish, nor flesh, nor good red herring"—JOHN HEYWOOD; **neuter, neutral**

7 **unconcerned, uninterested, disinterested,** turned-off, **dispassionate,** insouciant, **careless,** regardless; easygoing; incurious *see* 981.3; mindless, **unmindful, heedless,** inattentive *see* 983.6, disregardful; **devil-may-care,** reckless, negligent *see* 340.10; unsolicitous, unanxious; pococurante, **nonchalant,** inexcitable *see* 106.10; ataractic; **blasé,** undiscriminating, casual *see* 944.5; **listless,** lackadaisical, sluggish; bovine; numb, **apathetic** *see* 94.13

8 **undesirous,** unattracted, desireless; loveless, passionless; inappetent; nirvanic; **unenthusiastic,** uneager; **unambitious,** unaspiring

adverbs

9 **indifferently, with indifference,** with utter indifference; coolly, coldly; lukewarmly, halfheartedly; perfunctorily; for all *or* aught one cares

10 **unconcernedly, uninterestedly, disinterestedly,** dispassionately, insouciantly, **carelessly,** regardlessly; mindlessly; **unmindfully, heedlessly,** recklessly, negligently *see* 340.17; **nonchalantly**; listlessly, lackadaisically; numbly, **apathetically** *see* 94.15

phrases

11 **who cares?,** I don't care, I couldn't care less (*informal*); it's a matter of sublime indifference; never mind!, **what does it matter?,** what's the difference?, what's the diff? (*informal*), what are the odds?, what of it?, what boots it? (*old*), **so what?,** what the hell (*informal*), it's all one to me, it's all the same to me, it's no skin off one's nose (*informal*); like it or lump it

12 **I should worry?,** I should fret?, that's your lookout, that's your problem, I feel for you but I can't reach

you; that's your pigeon (*informal*), that's your tough luck, tough titty *and* shit (*both informal*)

103 HATE

nouns

1 **hate, hatred; dislike** *see* 99; **detestation, abhorrence, aversion, antipathy,** repugnance, **loathing,** execration, **abomination,** odium; **spite,** spitefulness, despite, despitefulness, **malice, malevolence,** malignity; vials of hate *or* wrath; misanthropy, misanthropism; misandry, misogyny; misogamy; misopedia; anti-Semitism; race hatred, racism, racialism; bigotry; Anglophobia, Russophobia, xenophobia, etc; scorn, despising, **contempt** *see* 157

2 **enmity** *see* 589; bitterness, **animosity** *see* 589.4

3 (*hated thing*) **anathema, abomination,** detestation, aversion, abhorrence, antipathy, execration, hate; peeve, pet peeve; phobia

4 hater, man-hater, woman-hater, misanthropist, misanthrope, misogynist, anti-Semite, racist, racialist, white supremacist, bigot, redneck (*informal*); Anglophobe, Russophobe, xenophobe, etc

verbs

5 **to hate, detest, loathe, abhor,** execrate, **abominate,** hold in abomination, take an aversion to, shudder at, utterly detest, be death on, not stand, not stand the sight of, not stomach; scorn, **despise** *see* 157.3

6 **to dislike,** have it in for (*informal*), disrelish *see* 99.3

adjectives

7 **hating, abhorrent,** loathing, despising, venomous, death on; averse to *see* 99.8; disgusted *see* 96.20; scornful, **contemptuous** *see* 157.8

8 **hateful, loathesome,** detestable *see* 98.18; despiteful; unlikable *see* 99.7; **contemptible** *see* 661.12, 98.18

word elements

9 mis–, miso–; –phobia, –phobiac, –phobe

104 LOVE

nouns

1 **love, affection, attachment, devotion, fondness,** sentiment, warm feeling, soft spot in one's heart, weakness (*informal*), like, **liking,** fancy, shine (*informal*); **partiality, predilection; passion,** tender feeling *or* passion, **ardour,** ardency, fervour, heart, flame; physical love, Amor, Eros, bodily love, libido, sexual love, sex *see* 75; desire, yearning *see* 100.5; lasciviousness *see* 665.5; charity, *caritas* (*Latin*), brotherly love, Christian love, Agape, loving concern, **caring;** spiritual love, platonic love; **adoration,** worship, hero worship; **regard,** admiration; idolization, idolism, idolatry; popular regard, popularity; faithful love, truelove; married love, conjugal love, uxoriousness; free love, free-lovism; **lovemaking** *see* 562

2 "an insatiate thirst of enjoying a greedily desired object"—MONTAIGNE, "the heart's immortal thirst to be

completely known and all forgiven"—HENRY VAN DYKE, "Nature's second sun"—GEORGE CHAPMAN, "tyrant sparing none"—CORNEILLE, "the blood of life, the power of reunion of the separated"—TILLICH, "the reflection of a man's own worthiness from other men"—EMERSON, "a spiritual coupling of two souls"—BEN JONSON

3 **amorousness**, amativeness, lovingness, meltingness, **affection, affectionateness**, demonstrativeness; mating instinct, reproductive *or* procreative drive, libido; carnality, sexiness, goatishness, hot pants *and* horniness (*both informal*); romantic love, romanticism, **sentimentality**, susceptibility; lovesickness, lovelornness; ecstasy, rapture; enchantment *see* 95.2

4 **infatuation**, infatuatedness, passing fancy; **crush** *and* mash *and* pash *and* case (*all informal*); **puppy love** *and* calf love (*both informal*); love at first sight

5 **parental love, natural affection**, mother *or* maternal love, father *or* paternal love; filial love; parental instinct

6 **love affair, affair**, affair of the heart, **amour, romance**, romantic tie *or* bond, something between, thing (*informal*), liaison, entanglement, intrigue; **dalliance**, amorous play, the love game, flirtation, hanky-panky, lollygagging (*US informal*); triangle, eternal triangle; illicit *or* unlawful love, forbidden *or* unsanctified love, adulterous affair, adultery, unfaithfulness, infidelity, cuckoldry

7 **loveableness, likeableness**, lovability, likability, adoreableness, adorability, sweetness, loveliness, lovesomeness; cuddliness, cuddlesomeness; amiability, attractiveness *see* 97.2, desirability, agreeability; **charm, appeal**, allurement *see* 377; winsomeness, winning ways

8 Love, Cupid, Amor, Eros, Kama; Venus, Aphrodite, Astarte, Freya

9 (*symbols*) **cupid**, cupidon, amor, amourette, amoretto, *amorino* (*Italian*); love-knot

10 **sweetheart**, loved one, love, beloved, **darling, dear, dear one**, dearly beloved, well-beloved, truelove, beloved object, **object of one's affections**, light of one's eye *or* life, light of love; sex object, prey, quarry, game

11 (*informal terms*) , **sweetie, honey**, honeybunch, honey-bunny, honeypie, hon, main squeeze, sweetie-pie, tootsie, tootsie-pie, dearie, baby, dreamboat, heart-throb, sugar, sugar-bun, sweets

12 **lover, admirer**, adorer, amorist; infatuate, paramour, **suitor, wooer**, pursuer, follower; **flirt**, coquette, vampire, vamp; conquest, catch; devotee; escort, companion, date *and* steady (*both informal*); significant other

13 **beau, inamorato, swain**, man, gallant, cavalier, squire, esquire, *caballero* (*Spanish*); *amoroso, cavaliere servente* (*both Italian*); sugar daddy (*informal*); gigolo; **boyfriend** *and* **fellow** *and* young man *and* flame (*all informal*); toyboy; old man (*informal*); love-maker, lover-boy (*informal*); **seducer, lady-killer**, ladies' man, sheik, philanderer, cocksman (*informal*); Prince Charming, Lothario, Romeo; Casanova, Don Juan

14 **ladylove, inamorata**, *amorosa* (*Italian*), lady, mistress, ladyfriend; lass, lassie, gill, jill, Dulcinea

15 (*informal terms*) **doll, angel**, baby, baby-doll, ducks, ducky, pet, snookums, snooky, **girl, girlfriend**, best girl, dream girl; old lady

16 **favourite**, preference; **darling**, idol, jewel, apple of one's eye, blue-eyed boy, fair-haired boy, man after one's own heart; **pet**, fondling, cosset, minion; spoiled child *or* darling, *enfant gâté* (*French*), lap dog; teacher's pet; matinee idol; tin god, little tin god

17 **fiancé, fiancée**, bride-to-be, affianced, betrothed, future, intended (*informal*)

18 **loving couple**, soul mates, lovebirds, turtledoves, bill-and-cooers; Romeo and Juliet, Anthony and Cleopatra, Tristan and Isolde, Pelléas and Mélisande, Abélard and Héloïse, Daphnis and Chloë, Aucassin and Nicolette

verbs

19 **to love, be fond of**, be in love with, **care for, like, fancy**, have a fancy for, take an interest in, **dote on** *or* **upon**, be desperately in love, burn with love; be partial to, have a soft spot in one's heart for, have a weakness *or* fondness for

20 (*informal terms*) **to go for**, have an eye *or* eyes for, only have eyes for, be sweet on, have a crush *or* mash *or* case on; have it bad, carry a torch *or* the torch for

21 **to cherish, hold dear**, hold in one's heart *or* affections, think much *or* the world of, prize, treasure; **admire, regard**, esteem, revere; **adore, idolize**, worship, dearly love, think worlds *or* the world of, love to distraction

22 **to fall in love, lose one's heart, become enamoured**, be smitten; take to, **take a liking** *or* **fancy to**, take a shine to *and* fall for (*both informal*), become attached to, bestow one's affections on; fall head and ears *or* head over heels in love, be swept off one's feet

23 **to enamour, endear**; win one's heart, win the love *or* affections of, take the fancy of, make a hit with (*informal*); **charm**, becharm, **infatuate**, hold in thrall, command one's affection, **fascinate**, attract, allure, grow on one, strike *or* tickle one's fancy, **captivate**, bewitch, enrapture, carry away, sweep off one's feet, turn one's head, inflame with love; **seduce**, vamp (*informal*), draw on, tempt, tantalize

adjectives

24 **beloved, loved, dear, darling, precious**; pet, favourite; **adored, admired**, esteemed, revered; **cherished**, prized, treasured, held dear; **well-liked**, popular; **well-beloved**, dearly beloved, dear to one's heart, after one's heart *or* own heart, dear as the apple of one's eye

25 **endearing, lovable, likable, adorable**, admirable, lovely, lovesome, sweet, winning, winsome; **charming**; angelic, seraphic; caressable, kissable; cuddlesome, cuddly

26 **amorous**, amatory, amative, erotic; **sexual** *see* 75.28, 29; loverly, loverlike; **passionate, ardent**, impassioned; desirous *see* 100.21, 22; lascivious *see* 665.29

27 **loving**, lovesome, **fond, adoring, devoted, affectionate**, demonstrative, **romantic, sentimental, tender**, soft (*informal*), melting;

lovelorn, lovesick, languishing; wifely, husbandly, conjugal, uxorious, faithful; parental, paternal, maternal, filial; charitable, caritative

28 enamoured, charmed, becharmed, **fascinated, captivated,** bewitched, enraptured, enchanted; **infatuated,** infatuate; **smitten,** heartsmitten, heartstruck, lovestruck

29 in love, head over heels in love, over head and ears in love

30 fond of, enamoured of, partial to, **in love with,** attached to, wedded to, devoted to, wrapped up in; **taken with,** smitten with, struck with

31 (*informal terms*) **crazy about,** mad *or* nuts *or* nutty *or* wild about, swacked on, sweet on, stuck on, gone on, soppy on

adverbs

32 lovingly, fondly, affectionately, tenderly, dearly, **adoringly,** devotedly; amorously, ardently, passionately; with love, with affection, with all one's love

word elements

33 phil–, philo–, –phily; –phile; –philic, –philous

105 EXCITEMENT

nouns

1 excitement, emotion, excitedness, **arousal, stimulation, exhilaration;** a high (*informal*), manic state *or* condition

2 thrill, sensation, titillation; **tingle,** tingling; quiver, shiver, shudder, tremor, **tremor of excitement,** rush (*informal*); flush, rush of emotion, surge of emotion

3 (*informal terms*) **kick, charge,** boot, bang, belt, blast, flash, hit, jolt, large charge, buzz, rush, upper, lift; jollies

4 agitation, perturbation, ferment, **turbulence, turmoil,** tumult, embroilment, uproar, **commotion,** disturbance, ado, kerfuffle, *brouhaha* (*French*), feery-fary (*Scottish*), to-do (*informal*), carry-on (*informal*), song and dance (*informal*); pell-mell, **flurry,** ruffle, bustle, stir, swirl, swirling, whirl, vortex, eddy, hurry, hurry-scurry, hurly-burly; fermentation, yeastiness, effervescence, ebullience, ebullition; fume

5 trepidation, trepidity; **disquiet,** disquietude, inquietude, **unrest, restlessness,** fidgetiness; **fidgets** *or* **shakes** *and* shivers *and* dithers *and* antsyness (*all informal*); **quivering, quavering, quaking, shaking,** trembling; **quiver,** quaver, shiver, shudder, twitter, **tremor,** tremble, flutter; palpitation, pitapatation (*informal*), pit-a-pat, pitter-patter; **throb,** throbbing; panting, heaving

6 dither, tizzy *and* **tiz** *and* **tiz-woz** (*all informal*), **twitter, flutter, fluster,** fret, **fuss,** pother, bother, lather *and* stew (*both informal*), snit (*US & Australian informal*), flap; emotional crisis, *crise* (*French*)

7 fever of excitement, fever pitch, fever, heat, fever heat, fire; sexual excitement, rut

8 fury, furore, fire and fury; **ecstasy,** transport, **rapture,** ravishment; intoxication, abandon; **passion, rage,** raging *or* tearing passion, towering rage *or* passion; **frenzy,** orgy, orgasm; madness, craze, **delirium,** hysteria

9 outburst, outbreak, **burst, flare-up,** blaze, **explosion,** eruption, irruption, upheaval, convulsion, spasm, seizure, fit, paroxysm; storm, tornado, whirlwind, cyclone, hurricane, gale, tempest, gust; steroid rage, roid rage (*informal*)

10 excitability, excitableness, perturbability, agitability; emotional instability, explosiveness, eruptiveness, inflammability, combustibility, tempestuousness, violence, latent violence; **irascibility** *see* 110.2; irritability, edginess, touchiness, prickliness, **sensitivity** *see* 24.3; skittishness, **nervousness** *see* 128; excessive emotion, hyperthymia, **emotionalism** *see* 93.9

11 excitation, excitement, arousal, arousing, **stirring,** stirring up, working up, working into a lather (*informal*), lathering up, whipping up, steaming up, **agitation, perturbation; stimulation, stimulus, exhilaration,** animation; electrification, galvanization; **provocation, irritation,** aggravation, exasperation, exacerbation, fomentation, inflammation, infuriation, **incitement** *see* 375.4

verbs

12 to excite, impassion, arouse, rouse, blow up (*old*), **stir, stir up,** set astir, stir the feelings, stir the blood, cause a stir *or* commotion, play on the feelings; **work up,** work into, work up into a lather (*informal*), lather up, whip up, **key up,** wind up, steam up, ginger up; **move** *see* 375.12; **foment, incite** *see* 375.17; turn on (*informal*); **awaken,** awake, wake, waken, wake up; call up, summon up, call forth; **kindle,** enkindle, light up, light the fuse, **fire, inflame,** heat, warm, set fire to, set on fire, fire *or* warm the blood; fan, fan the fire *or* flame, blow the coals, stir the embers, feed the fire, add fuel to the fire *or* flame, pour oil on the fire; raise to a fever heat *or* pitch, bring to the boiling point; overexcite; **annoy, incense; enrage, infuriate;** frenzy, madden

13 to stimulate, whet, sharpen, pique, provoke, quicken, enliven, liven up, pick up, jazz up (*informal*), animate, **exhilarate,** invigorate, galvanize, fillip, give a fillip to; infuse life into, give new life to, revive, renew, resuscitate

14 to agitate, perturb, disturb, trouble, disquiet, discompose, discombobulate (*informal*), unsettle, **stir, ruffle, shake, shake up, shock, upset,** make waves, jolt, jar, rock, stagger, electrify, bring *or* pull one up short, give one a turn (*informal*); fuss (*informal*), flutter, flurry, rattle, disconcert, **fluster**

15 to thrill, tickle, thrill to death *or* to bits *or* to pieces, give a thrill, **give one a kick** *or* boot *or* charge *or* bang *or* lift *or* buzz (*informal*); intoxicate, fascinate, titillate, take one's breath away

16 to be excitable, excite easily; **get excited, have a fit;** catch the infection; **explode, flare up,** flash up, flame up, fire up, catch fire, take fire; **fly into a passion,** go into hysterics, have a tantrum *or* temper tantrum, come apart; ride off in all directions at once, run around like a headless chicken; **rage, rave, rant,** rant and rave, rave on, bellow, **storm,** ramp; be angry, smoulder, **seethe** *see* 152.15

17 (*informal terms*) **to work oneself up**, work oneself into a sweat, lather, have a short fuse, get hot under the collar, run a temperature, race one's motor, get into a dither *or* tizzy *or* stew; blow up, **blow one's top** *or* stack *or* cool, **flip**, flip out, flip one's lid *or* wig, pop one's cork, wig out, blow a gasket, fly off the handle, **hit the ceiling**, do one's nut, go ape, go hog wild (*US*), go bananas, lose one's cool, go off the deep end

18 (*be excited*) **to thrill**, tingle, **tingle with excitement**, glow; swell, swell with emotion, be full of emotion; thrill to; turn on to *and* get high on *and* freak out on (*all informal*); heave, pant; **throb**, palpitate, go pit-a-pat; **tremble, shiver, quiver, quaver, quake**, flutter, twitter, **shake**, shake like a leaf, have the shakes (*informal*); **fidget**, have the fidgets *and* have ants in one's pants (*both informal*); toss and turn, toss, tumble, twist and turn, wriggle, wiggle, writhe, squirm; twitch, jerk

19 **to change colour**, turn colour, go all colours; **pale**, whiten, blanch, turn pale; darken, look black; turn blue in the face; **flush, blush**, crimson, glow, mantle, colour, redden, turn *or* get red

adjectives

20 **excited**, impassioned; **thrilled**, agog, tingling, tingly, atingle, aquiver, atwitter; **stimulated, exhilarated, high** (*informal*); manic; **moved, stirred**, stirred up, **aroused, roused**, switched *or* turned on (*informal*), on one's mettle, fired, inflamed, wrought up, **worked up**, all worked up, worked up into a lather (*informal*), lathered up, whipped up, steamed up, keyed up, revved up; turned-on (*informal*); carried away; bursting, ready to burst; effervescent, yeasty, ebullient

21 **in a dither, in a tizzy** *or* tizz *or* tiz-woz (*all informal*), in a quiver, **in a twitter**, in a flutter, all of a twitter *or* flutter, in a fluster, in a flurry, in a pother, in a bother, in a ferment, in a turmoil, in an uproar, in a stew *and* in a sweat (*both informal*), in a lather (*informal*)

22 **heated, passionate, warm, hot**, red-hot, flaming, **burning, fiery, glowing, fervent, fervid; feverish**, febrile, hectic, flushed; sexually excited, in rut *see* 75.20; burning with excitement, het up (*informal*), hot under the collar (*informal*); seething, boiling, boiling over, steamy, steaming

23 **agitated, perturbed, disturbed, troubled, disquieted, upset**, antsy (*informal*), unsettled, **discomposed, flustered**, ruffled, **shaken**

24 **turbulent**, tumultuous, tempestuous, boisterous, clamorous, uproarious

25 **frenzied, frantic; ecstatic**, transported, enraptured, ravished, in a transport *or* ecstasy; intoxicated, abandoned; orgiastic, orgasmic; raging, raving, roaring, bellowing, ramping, storming, howling, ranting, fulminating, frothing *or* foaming at the mouth; **wild**, hog-wild (*US informal*); **violent**, fierce, ferocious, feral, **furious; mad**, madding, **rabid**, maniac, maniacal, demonic, demoniacal, possessed; carried away, **distracted, delirious, beside oneself**, out of one's wits; uncontrollable, running mad, amok, berserk; in hysterics; wild-eyed, wild-looking, haggard; blue in the face

26 **overwrought, overexcited, overstimulated, hyper** (*informal*); **overcome**, overwhelmed, overpowered, overmastered; **upset**, *bouleversé* (*French*)

27 **restless**, restive, **uneasy**, unquiet, unsettled, unrestful, tense; **fidgety**, antsy (*informal*), fussy, fluttery

28 **excitable, emotional**, highly emotional, overemotional, hyperthymic, perturbable, flappable (*informal*), agitable; emotionally unstable; explosive, volcanic, eruptive, inflammable; irascible *see* 110.19; irritable, edgy, touchy, prickly, **sensitive** *see* 24.13; **skittish**, startlish; **high-strung**, highly strung, high-spirited, mettlesome, high-mettled; **nervous**

29 **passionate, fiery, vehement**, hotheaded, **impetuous**, violent, volcanic, furious, fierce, **wild**; tempestuous, stormy, tornadic; simmering, volcanic, ready to burst forth *or* explode

30 **exciting, thrilling**, thrilly (*informal*), **stirring, moving, breathtaking**, eye-popping (*informal*); agitating, agitative, perturbing, disturbing, upsetting, troubling, disquieting, unsettling, off-putting, distracting, jolting, jarring; heart-stirring, heart-thrilling, heart-swelling, heart-expanding, soul-stirring, spirit-stirring, deep-thrilling, mind-blowing (*informal*); impressive, striking, telling; **provocative** *see* 375.27, provoking, piquant, tantalizing, sexy (*informal*); **inflammatory** *see* 375.28; **stimulating**, stimulative, stimulatory; exhilarating, heady, intoxicating, maddening, ravishing; **electric**, galvanic, charged, overcharged; **overwhelming**, overpowering, overcoming, overmastering, more than flesh and blood can bear; suspensive, **suspenseful**, cliff-hanging (*informal*)

31 **penetrating, piercing**, stabbing, cutting, stinging, biting, keen, brisk, sharp, caustic, astringent

32 **sensational, lurid**, yellow, **melodramatic**, Barnumesque; spine-chilling, eye-popping (*informal*); blood-and-thunder, cloak-and-dagger

adverbs

33 **excitedly, agitatedly**, perturbedly; with beating *or* leaping heart, with heart beating high, with heart going pitapat *or* pitter-patter (*informal*), thrilling all over, with heart in mouth; with glistening eyes, all agog, all aquiver *or* atwitter *or* atingle; in a sweat *or* stew *or* dither *or* tizzy (*all informal*)

34 **heatedly, passionately**, warmly, hotly, glowingly, fervently, fervidly, **feverishly**

35 **frenziedly, frantically**, wildly, furiously, violently, fiercely, madly, rabidly, distractedly, deliriously, till one is blue in the face (*informal*)

36 **excitingly, thrillingly**, stirringly, movingly; **provocatively**, provokingly; stimulatingly, exhilaratingly

106 INEXCITABILITY

nouns

1 inexcitability, inexcitableness, unexcitableness, **imperturbability**, imperturbableness, unflappability (*informal*); steadiness, evenness; inirritability, unirritableness; **dispassion**, dispassionateness, unpassionateness, ataraxy *or* ataraxia; quietism; stoicism; **even temper,** steady *or* smooth temper, good *or* easy temper; unnervousness *see* 129; **patience** *see* 134; **impassiveness,** impassivity, stolidity; bovinity, dullness

2 **composure,** countenance; **calm, calmness,** calm disposition, **placidity, serenity,** tranquillity, soothingness, peacefulness; mental composure, peace *or* calm of mind; calm *or* quiet mind, easy mind; resignation, resignedness, acceptance, fatalism, stoic calm; philosophicalness, philosophy, philosophic composure; **quiet,** quietness of mind *or* soul, quietude; decompression, imperturbation, indisturbance, unruffledness; **coolness,** coolheadedness, cool (*informal*), sangfroid; icy calm; Oriental calm, Buddha-like composure; shantih, "the peace that passeth all understanding"—BIBLE

3 **equanimity,** equilibrium, equability, balance; **levelheadedness,** level head, well-balanced *or* well-regulated mind; **poise,** aplomb, **self-possession, self-control,** self-command, self-restraint, restraint, possession, **presence of mind;** confidence, assurance, **self-confidence, self-assurance,** centredness

4 **sedateness, staidness,** soberness, sobriety, sober-mindedness, **seriousness,** gravity, solemnity, sobersidedness, gravitas; temperance, moderation; sobersides

5 **nonchalance,** casualness, offhandedness; easygoingness, lackadaisicalness; **indifference,** unconcern *see* 102.2

verbs

6 **to be cool** *or* **composed,** not turn a hair, not have a hair out of place, keep one's cool (*informal*), look as if butter wouldn't melt in one's mouth; **tranquillize, calm** *see* 670.7; **set one's mind at ease** *or* **rest,** make one easy

7 **to compose oneself, control oneself,** restrain oneself, collect oneself, **get hold of oneself,** get a grip on oneself (*informal*), get organized, master one's feelings, regain one's composure, pull oneself together (*informal*), get one's head *or* act together (*informal*); **calm down, cool off,** cool down, sober down, hold *or* keep one's temper, simmer down *and* cool it (*both informal*); **relax,** decompress, unwind, take it easy, lay *or* kick back (*informal*); **forget it,** get it out of one's mind *or* head, drop it, let it go

8 (*control one's feelings*) **to suppress, repress,** keep under, smother, stifle, choke *or* hold back, fight down *or* back, inhibit; sublimate

9 **to keep cool,** keep one's cool (*informal*), **keep calm,** keep one's head, keep one's wool, keep one's hair on *and* keep one's shirt on *and* hang loose *and* chill out (*all informal*), not turn a hair; take things as they come, cross a bridge when one comes to it, roll with the punches (*informal*); keep a stiff upper lip

adjectives

10 **inexcitable, imperturbable,** undisturbable, **unflappable** (*informal*); **unirritable,** inirritable; **dispassionate,** unpassionate; **steady;** stoic, stoical; **even-tempered; impassive,** stolid; bovine, dull; unnervous *see* 129.2; **patient**

11 **unexcited, unperturbed,** undisturbed, untroubled, unagitated, **unruffled,** unflustered, unfazed (*informal*), unstirred, unimpassioned

12 **calm, placid,** quiet, **tranquil, serene,** peaceful; **cool, coolheaded,** cool as a cucumber (*informal*); philosophical

13 **composed, collected,** recollected, **levelheaded; poised,** together (*informal*), in equipoise, equanimous, equilibrious, **balanced,** well-balanced; **self-possessed,** self-controlled, self-restrained; confident, assured, **self-confident, self-assured**

14 **sedate, staid,** sober, sober-minded, **serious,** grave, solemn, sobersided; temperate, moderate

15 **nonchalant, blasé, indifferent,** unconcerned *see* 102.7; **casual, offhand, relaxed, laid-back** *and* throwaway (*both informal*); **easygoing,** easy, free and easy, devil-may-care, lackadaisical, *dégagé* (*French*)

adverbs

16 inexcitably, **imperturbably,** inirritably, **dispassionately;** steadily; stoically; **calmly, placidly,** quietly, **tranquilly, serenely; coolly, composedly,** levelheadedly; impassively, stolidly, stodgily, stuffily

17 **sedately, staidly, soberly, seriously,** sobersidedly

18 **nonchalantly, casually, relaxedly,** offhandedly, easygoingly, lackadaisically

107 CONTENTMENT

nouns

1 **contentment, content,** contentedness, satisfiedness; **satisfaction,** entire satisfaction, fulfilment; ease, peace of mind, composure *see* 106.2; comfort *see* 121; **quality of life;** well-being, euphoria; **happiness** *see* 95.2; **acceptance,** resignation, reconcilement, reconciliation; clear *or* clean conscience, dreamless sleep

2 **complacency,** complacence; **smugness, self-complacence** *or* self-complacency, self-approval, self-approbation, **self-satisfaction, self-content,** self-contentedness *or* self-contentness; bovinity

3 **satisfactoriness,** adequacy, **sufficiency** *see* 990; **acceptability,** admissibility, **tolerability,** agreeability, unobjectionability, unexceptionability, tenability, viability

verbs

4 **to content, satisfy;** gratify; put *or* set at ease, set one's mind at ease *or* rest, achieve inner harmony

5 **to be content, rest satisfied, rest easy,** rest and be thankful, be of good cheer, be reconciled to, take the good the gods provide, accept one's lot, rest on one's laurels, let well enough alone, let sleeping dogs lie, take the rough with the smooth, take the bitter with the sweet; come to terms with oneself, learn to live in one's own skin; not complain, not worry, not sweat it *and* cool it *and* go with the flow (*all informal*); content oneself with, settle for; settle for less, take half a loaf, lower one's sights, cut one's losses; **be pleased** *see* 95.11

6 **to be satisfactory, do, suffice** *see* 990.4; **suit,** suit one down to the ground

adjectives

7 **content, contented, satisfied; pleased** *see* 95.12;
happy; easy, at ease, at one's ease, easygoing;
composed *see* 106.13; **comfortable** *see* 121.11, of
good comfort; euphoric, eupeptic; carefree, without
care, *sans souci* (*French*); accepting, resigned,
reconciled; uncomplaining, unrepining

8 **untroubled, unbothered, undisturbed,**
unperturbed *see* 106.11, unworried, unvexed,
unplagued, untormented

9 **well-content, well-pleased,** well-contented, **well-
satisfied,** highly satisfied

10 **complacent,** bovine; **smug, self-complacent,
self-satisfied,** self-content, **self-contented**

11 **satisfactory, satisfying; sufficient** *see* 990.6,
sufficing, **adequate, enough,** commensurate,
proportionate, proportionable, ample, equal to

12 **acceptable,** admissible, **agreeable,** unobjectionable,
unexceptionable, tenable, viable; **OK** *and* okay *and* all
right *and* alright (*all informal*); **passable,** good
enough

13 **tolerable, bearable, endurable, supportable,**
sufferable

adverbs

14 **contentedly,** to one's heart's content; **satisfiedly,**
with satisfaction; **complacently, smugly,** self-
complacently, self-satisfiedly, self-contentedly

15 **satisfactorily,** satisfyingly; **acceptably, agreeably,**
admissibly; sufficiently, adequately, commensurately,
amply, enough; **tolerably, passably**

16 **to one's satisfaction,** to one's delight, to one's
great glee; to one's taste, to the king's *or* queen's
taste

108 DISCONTENT

nouns

1 discontent, discontentment, discontentedness;
dissatisfaction, unsatisfaction, dissatisfiedness,
unfulfillment; **resentment, envy** *see* 154;
restlessness, restiveness, uneasiness, unease;
dysphoria, malaise; rebelliousness *see* 327.3;
disappointment *see* 132; unpleasure *see* 96;
unhappiness *see* 112.2; ill humour *see* 110;
disgruntlement, sulkiness, sourness, petulance,
peevishness, querulousness; vexation of spirit; cold
comfort; divine discontent; Faustianism

2 **unsatisfactoriness,** dissatisfactoriness; **inadequacy,
insufficiency** *see* 991; **unacceptability,**
inadmissibility, unsuitability, undesirability,
objectionability, untenability, indefensibility;
intolerability *see* 98.9

3 **malcontent,** *frondeur* (*French*); **complainer,**
complainant, **faultfinder, grumbler,** growler,
murmurer, mutterer, griper, croaker, peevish *or*
petulant *or* querulous person, whiner; reactionary,
reactionist; rebel *see* 327.5

4 (*informal terms*) **grouch,** kvetch, kicker, griper,
moaner, moaning Minnie, crank, crab, grouser,
grump, beefer, bellyacher, sorehead (*US &
Canadian*), sourpuss

verbs

5 **to dissatisfy, discontent, disgruntle, displease,**
fail to satisfy, be inadequate, not fill the bill,
disappoint, leave much *or* a lot to be desired,
dishearten, put out (*informal*); **be discontented,
complain**

6 (*informal terms*) **to beef, bitch,** kvetch, bellyache,
crab, gripe, grouch, grouse, grump, have an attitude,
kick, moan, make a stink, squawk

adjectives

7 **discontented, dissatisfied, disgruntled,**
unaccepting, unaccommodating, **displeased,** less
than pleased, let down, disappointed; **unsatisfied,
ungratified,** unfulfilled; resentful, dog-in-the-
manger; envious *see* 154.4; restless, restive, uneasy;
rebellious *see* 327.11; malcontent, malcontented,
complaining, complaintful, sour, **faultfinding,**
grumbling, growling, murmuring, muttering, griping,
croaking, **peevish, petulant,** sulky, grumpy,
querulous, querulant, whiny; unhappy *see* 112.21;
out of humour *see* 110.17

8 (*informal terms*) **grouchy,** cranky, beefing, crabby,
crabbing, grousing, griping, bellyaching, bitching

9 **unsatisfactory,** dissatisfactory; **unsatisfying,
ungratifying,** unfulfilling; **displeasing** *see* 98.17;
disappointing, disheartening, not up to expectation,
not good enough; **inadequate,** incommensurate,
insufficient *see* 991.9

10 **unacceptable,** inadmissible, unsuitable, undesirable,
objectionable, exceptionable, impossible, untenable,
indefensible; **intolerable** *see* 98.25

adverbs

11 **discontentedly, dissatisfiedly**

12 **unsatisfactorily,** dissatisfactorily; **unsatisfyingly,
ungratifyingly; inadequately, insufficiently;
unacceptably,** inadmissibly, unsuitably, undesirably,
objectionably; intolerably *see* 98.30

109 CHEERFULNESS

nouns

1 **cheerfulness,** cheeriness, **good cheer, cheer,** cheery
vein *or* mood; blitheness, blithesomeness; **gladness,**
gladsomeness; **happiness** *see* 95.2; **pleasantness,**
winsomeness, geniality; brightness, radiance,
sunniness; sanguineness, sanguinity, sanguine
humour, euphoric *or* eupeptic mien; optimism, rosy
expectation, hopefulness; **irrepressibility,**
irrepressibleness

2 **good humour,** good spirits; **high spirits,
exhilaration,** rare good humour

3 **lightheartedness,** lightsomeness, lightness, levity;
buoyancy, buoyance, resilience, resiliency, bounce
(*informal*), springiness; spring in one's step;
jauntiness, perkiness, debonairness, carefreeness;
breeziness, airiness, pertness, chirpiness, light heart

4 **gaiety,** gayness, *allégresse* (*French*); **liveliness,
vivacity, vitality, life, animation, spiritedness,
spirit,** esprit, élan, **sprightliness,** high spirits,
zestfulness, zest, vim, zip (*informal*), vigour, verve,
gusto, **exuberance,** heartiness; **spirits,** animal
spirits; **friskiness,** skittishness, coltishness,

rompishness, rollicksomeness, capersomeness; **sportiveness, playfulness, frolicsomeness,** gamesomeness, kittenishness

5 **merriment,** merriness; **hilarity,** hilariousness; **joy,** joyfulness, joyousness; **glee,** gleefulness, high glee; **jollity,** jolliness, **joviality,** jocularity, jocundity; frivolity, **levity; mirth,** mirthfulness, **amusement** *see* 743; **fun; laughter** *see* 116.4

verbs

6 to exude cheerfulness, radiate cheer, not have a care in the world, **beam,** burst *or* brim with cheer, glow, radiate, sparkle, sing, lilt, whistle, **chirp,** chirrup, chirp like a cricket; walk on air, dance, skip, caper, frolic, gambol, romp, caracole; **smile, laugh** *see* 116.8

7 to **cheer, gladden, brighten,** cheer one up, put in good humour; **encourage, hearten,** pick up (*informal*); **inspire,** inspirit, warm the spirits, **raise the spirits,** elevate one's mood, buoy up, boost, give a lift (*informal*), put one on top of the world *and* on cloud nine (*both informal*); **exhilarate,** animate, invigorate, liven, enliven, vitalize; **rejoice,** rejoice the heart, do the heart good

8 to **elate, exalt,** elevate, lift, uplift, flush

9 to **cheer up,** take heart, drive dull care away; **brighten up,** light up, **perk up; buck up** (*informal*); come out of it, snap out of it (*informal*), revive

10 to **be of good cheer,** bear up, **keep one's spirits up,** keep one's chin up (*informal*), keep one's pecker up (*informal*), keep a stiff upper lip (*informal*), grin and bear it

adjectives

11 **cheerful, cheery,** of good cheer, in good spirits; in high spirits, exalted, elated, exhilarated, high (*informal*); irrepressible; **blithe,** blithesome; **glad, gladsome; happy,** happy as Larry, happy as a clam *or* a sand boy *or* a lark, on top of the world, sitting on top of the world, sitting pretty; **pleasant, genial,** winsome; **bright, sunny,** bright and sunny, **radiant,** riant, sparkling, beaming, glowing, flushed, rosy, smiling, laughing; sanguine, sanguineous, euphoric, eupeptic; optimistic, hopeful; **irrepressible**

12 **lighthearted,** light, lightsome; **buoyant,** resilient; **jaunty,** perky, **debonair, carefree,** free and easy; **breezy,** airy

13 **pert,** chirrupy, **chirpy, chipper** (*informal*)

14 **gay,** gay as a lark; **spirited,** sprightly, **lively, animated, vivacious,** vital, zestful, zippy (*informal*), **exuberant,** hearty; **frisky,** antic, skittish, coltish, rompish, capersome; **full of beans** (*informal*), feeling one's oats (*US & Canadian informal*); **sportive, playful,** playful as a kitten, kittenish, **frolicsome,** gamesome; rollicking, rollicky, rollicksome

15 **merry, mirthful, hilarious; joyful, joyous,** rejoicing; **gleeful,** gleesome; **jolly,** buxom; **jovial,** jocund, jocular; **frivolous;** laughter-loving, mirthloving, risible; merry as a cricket *or* grig,

"as merry as the day is long"—Shakespeare

16 **cheering, gladdening; encouraging, heartening,** heartwarming; **inspiring,** inspiriting; **exhilarating,**

animating, enlivening, invigorating; cheerful, cheery, glad, joyful

adverbs

17 **cheerfully,** cheerily, with good cheer, with a cheerful heart; irrepressibly; **lightheartedly,** lightly; jauntily, perkily, airily; **pleasantly,** genially, blithely; **gladly, happily, joyfully,** smilingly; optimistically, hopefully

18 **gaily, exuberantly, heartily, spiritedly, animatedly, vivaciously,** zestfully, with zest, with vim, with élan, with zip (*informal*), with verve, with gusto

19 **merrily, gleefully, hilariously; jovially,** jocundly, jocularly; **frivolously; mirthfully,** laughingly

phrases

20 cheer up!, every cloud has a silver lining; don't let it get you down, illegitimati non carborundum (*Latin,* don't let the bastards grind you down); nil desperandum (*Latin,* never despair), chin up!, keep your pecker up!; it's always darkest before the dawn

110 ILL HUMOUR

nouns

1 **ill humour,** bad humour, **bad temper,** rotten *or* ill *or* evil temper, **ill nature,** filthy *or* rotten *or* evil humour; **sourness,** biliousness, liverishness; choler, bile, gall, spleen; **abrasiveness,** causticity, corrosiveness, asperity *see* 144.8; **anger** *see* 152.5; discontent *see* 108

2 **irascibility, irritability,** excitability, short *or* quick temper, short fuse (*informal*); **crossness,** disagreeableness, disagreeability, gruffness, shortness, peevishness, querulousness, fretfulness, crabbedness, **crankiness, testiness,** crustiness, huffiness, huffishness, churlishness, bearishness, snappishness, waspishness; **perversity,** cross-grainedness, fractiousness

3 (*informal terms*) **crabbiness, grouchiness,** cantankerousness, crustiness, grumpiness *or* grumpishness, cussedness, huffiness *or* huffishness, **meanness, orneriness,** bitchiness, cussedness, feistiness, ugliness, miffiness, saltiness, scrappiness, shirtiness, soreheadedness

4 **hot temper, temper,** quick *or* short temper, irritable temper, warm temper, fiery temper, fierce temper, short fuse (*informal*), pepperiness, feistiness *and* spunkiness (*both informal*), **hotheadedness,** hot blood

5 **touchiness, tetchiness,** ticklishness, prickliness, quickness to take offence, miffiness (*informal*), **sensitiveness,** oversensitiveness, hypersensitiveness, sensitivity, oversensitivity, hypersensitivity, thin skin; temperamentalness

6 **petulance** *or* petulancy, **peevishness,** pettishness, **querulousness, fretfulness,** resentfulness; shrewishness, vixenishness

7 **contentiousness, quarrelsomeness** *see* 456.3; **disputatiousness, argumentativeness,** litigiousness; **belligerence**

8 **sullenness, sulkiness, surliness, moroseness, glumness,** grumness, grimness, mumpishness,

dumpishness, *bouderie* (*French*); **moodiness,**
moodishness; mopishness, mopiness (*informal*);
dejection, melancholy *see* 112.5

9 **scowl, frown,** lower, **glower, pout,** moue, mow,
grimace, wry face; sullen looks, black looks, **long
face**

10 **sulks,** sullens, **mopes,** mumps, dumps, grumps
(*informal*), **blues,** blue devils, **pouts**

11 (*ill-humoured person*) **sorehead, grouch,
curmudgeon, grump, crank, crosspatch,** wasp,
bear, bear with a sore head, grizzly bear, pit bull;
fury, Tartar, dragon, ugly customer (*informal*);
hothead, hotspur; fire-eater

12 **bitch** (*informal*), **shrew, vixen,** virago, termagant,
brimstone, fury, witch, beldam, cat, tigress, she-wolf,
she-devil, spitfire; fishwife; **scold,** common scold;
battle-axe (*informal*)

verbs

13 to have a temper, have a short fuse (*informal*), have a
devil in one, be possessed of the devil; be cross, get
out on the wrong side of the bed

14 to sulk, mope, mope around; grizzle (*informal*),
grump *and* grouch *and* bitch (*all informal*), fret; get
oneself in a sulk

15 to look sullen, look black, look black as thunder,
gloom, pull *or* make a long face; frown, scowl, knit
the brow, lower, glower, pout, make a moue *or*
mow, grimace, make a wry face, make a lip, hang
one's lip, thrust out one's lower lip

16 to sour, acerbate, exacerbate; embitter, bitter,
envenom

adjectives

17 **out of humour,** out of temper, out of sorts, **in a
bad humour,** in a shocking humour, feeling evil
(*informal*); **abrasive,** caustic, corrosive, acid; angry;
discontented *see* 108.5

18 **ill-humoured, bad-tempered,** ill-tempered, evil-
humoured, evil-tempered, **ill-natured,** ill-affected,
ill-disposed

19 **irascible, irritable,** excitable, flappable (*informal*);
cross, cranky, testy; cankered, crabbed, spiteful,
spleeny, splenetic, churlish, bearish, snappish,
waspish; **gruff,** grumbly, grumbling, growling;
disagreeable; perverse, fractious, cross-grained

20 (*informal terms*) **crabby, grouchy,** cantankerous,
crusty, grumpy *or* grumpish, cussed, huffy *or*
huffish, humpy, mean, ornery, bitchy, feisty, ugly,
miffy, narky, ratty, salty, scrappy, shirty, soreheaded,
spiky, stroppy

21 **touchy, tetchy,** miffy (*informal*), ticklish, prickly,
quick to take offence, **thin-skinned, sensitive,**
oversensitive, hypersensitive, high-strung, highly
strung, temperamental, prima-donnaish

22 **peevish, petulant,** pettish, **querulous, fretful,**
resentful; bitchy, catty; shrewish, vixenish, vixenly;
nagging, naggy

23 **sour,** soured, **sour-tempered,** vinegarish; prune-
faced (*informal*); **choleric, dyspeptic, bilious,**
liverish, jaundiced; **bitter,** embittered

24 **sullen, sulky, surly, morose,** dour, mumpish,
dumpish, **glum,** grum, grim; **moody,** moodish;
mopish, mopey (*informal*), moping; **glowering,**

lowering, **scowling, frowning;** dark, black; black-
browed, beetle-browed; dejected, melancholy *see*
112.23

25 **hot-tempered, hotheaded, passionate,** hot, fiery,
peppery, feisty, spunky (*informal*), **quick-tempered,
short-tempered;** hasty, quick,

"sudden and quick in quarrel"—SHAKESPEARE, explosive,
volcanic, combustible

26 **contentious, quarrelsome** *see* 456.17;
disputatious, controversial, litigious, polemic,
polemical; **argumentative,** argumental; on the
warpath, looking for trouble; scrappy (*informal*); cat-
and-doggish, cat-and-dog; **bellicose, belligerent**

adverbs

27 **ill-humouredly, ill-naturedly; irascibly,
irritably, crossly, crankily, testily,** huffily,
cantankerously (*informal*), crabbedly, sourly,
churlishly, crustily, bearishly, snappily; perversely,
fractiously, cross-grainedly

28 **peevishly, petulantly,** pettishly, **querulously,**
fretfully

29 **grouchily** *and* **crabbily** *and* **grumpily** (*all
informal*), grumblingly

30 **sullenly, sulkily, surlily, morosely,** mumpishly,
glumly, grumly, grimly; moodily, mopingly;
gloweringly, loweringly, scowlingly, frowningly

111 SOLEMNITY

nouns

1 **solemnity, solemness, dignity, soberness,
sobriety, gravity,** *gravitas* (*Latin*), weightiness,
sombreness, grimness; sedateness, staidness;
demureness, decorousness; **seriousness,
earnestness, thoughtfulness, sober-mindedness,**
sobersidedness; sobersides; long face, straight face;
formality *see* 580

verbs

2 to honour the occasion, keep a straight face, look
serious, compose one's features, wear an earnest
frown; repress a smile, not crack a smile (*informal*),
wipe the smile off one's face, keep from laughing

adjectives

3 **solemn, dignified, sober, grave,** unsmiling,
weighty, **sombre,** frowning, **grim; sedate, staid;**
demure, decorous; **serious, earnest, thoughtful;
sober-minded,** sober-sided; straight-faced, long-
faced, grim-faced, grim-visaged, stone-faced; sober as
a judge, grave as an undertaker; **formal** *see* 580.7

adverbs

4 **solemnly, soberly, gravely, sombrely, grimly;
sedately, staidly,** demurely, decorously; with
dignity, **seriously, earnestly,** thoughtfully, sober-
mindedly, sobersidedly; with a straight face; formally
see 580.11

112 SADNESS

nouns

1 **sadness,** sadheartedness, weight *or* burden of sorrow; heaviness, **heavyheartedness,** heavy heart, **heaviness of heart;** pathos, bathos

2 **unhappiness,** infelicity; displeasure *see* 96.1; discontent *see* 108; **uncheerfulness,** cheerlessness; **joylessness,** unjoyfulness; mirthlessness, unmirthfulness, humourlessness, infestivity; **grimness; wretchedness, misery**

3 **dejection, depression, oppression,** dejectedness, **downheartedness,** downcastness; **discouragement, disheartenment,** dispiritedness; *Schmerz* and *Weltschmerz* (*both German*); malaise *see* 96.1; lowness, lowness *or* depression *or* oppression of spirit, downer *and* down trip (*both informal*); chill, chilling effect; **low spirits,** drooping spirits, sinking heart; despondence *or* **despondency,** spiritlessness, heartlessness; black *or* blank despondency, "Slough of Despond"—BUNYAN; demotivation, hopelessness *see* 125, **despair** *see* 125.2, pessimism *see* 125.6, suicidal despair, death wish, self-destructive urge; weariness of life, *taedium vitae* (*Latin*); sloth, acedia, noonday demon

4 **hypochondria,** hypochondriasis, morbid anxiety

5 **melancholy, melancholia,** melancholiness, spleen (*old*); gentle melancholy, romantic melancholy; **pensiveness, wistfulness,** tristfulness; **nostalgia,** homesickness, nostalgy (*old*), *mal du pays* (*French*)

6 **blues** *and* blue devils (*both informal*), mumps, **dumps** (*informal*), the hump (*informal*), **doldrums,** dismals, dolefuls (*informal*), mopes *and* megrims *and* sulks (*all informal*)

7 **gloom, gloominess,** darkness, murk, murkiness, **dismalness, bleakness, grimness, sombreness, gravity, solemnity; dreariness,** drearisomeness; wearifulness, wearisomeness

8 **glumness,** grumness, **moroseness, sullenness,** sulkiness, **moodiness,** mumpishness, dumpishness; mopishness, mopiness (*informal*)

9 **heartache, aching heart,** bleeding heart, grieving heart; heartsickness, heartsoreness; **heartbreak, broken heart,** brokenheartedness, heartbrokenness

10 **sorrow,** sorrowing, **grief, care,** carking care, **woe;** heartgrief, heartfelt grief; languishment, pining; **anguish, misery, agony;** prostrating grief, prostration; **lamentation** *see* 115

11 **sorrowfulness, mournfulness,** ruefulness, **woefulness, dolefulness,** woesomeness (*old*), dolorousness, **plaintiveness,** plangency, grievousness, aggrievedness, lugubriousness, funerealness; *lacrimae rerum* (*Latin*), **tearfulness** *see* 115.2

12 **disconsolateness,** disconsolation, **inconsolability,** inconsolableness, unconsolability, comfortlessness; **desolation,** desolateness; forlornness

13 **sourpuss** *and* misery *and* moaning Minnie (*all informal*); mope, brooder; **melancholic, melancholiac;** depressive

14 **killjoy, spoilsport,** crapehanger *and* drag (*both informal*); damp, damper, **wet blanket,** party pooper; gloomster *and* doomster (*both informal*), doomsdayer, apocalypticist, apocalyptician, awfulizer (*informal*), crapehanger, misery *and* Moaning Minnie (*both informal*); skeleton at the feast; pessimist *see* 125.7

verbs

15 to hang one's head, pull *or* make a long face, look blue, sing *or* get *or* have the blues (*informal*); drag one down; carry the weight *or* woe of the world on one's shoulders; apocalypticize, catastrophize, awfulize (*informal*)

16 **to lose heart,** despond, give way, give oneself up *or* over to; despondency; **despair** *see* 125.10, sink into despair, throw up one's hands in despair, be *or* become suicidal, lose the will to live; **droop,** sink, languish; reach *or* plumb the depths, touch bottom, hit rock bottom

17 **to grieve, sorrow; weep, mourn** *see* 115.8, 10; be dumb with grief; **pine,** pine away; **brood over, mope, fret,** take on (*informal*); **eat one's heart out,** break one's heart over; **agonize,** ache, bleed

18 **to sadden,** darken, cast a pall *or* gloom upon, weigh *or* weigh heavy upon; **deject, depress, oppress, crush,** press down, hit one like a ton of bricks (*informal*), **cast down,** lower, lower the spirits, get one down (*informal*), take the wind out of one's sails, rain on one's parade, burst one's bubble, **discourage, dishearten,** take the heart out of, **dispirit;** damp, dampen, damp *or* dampen the spirits; dash, knock down, beat down; sink, sink one's soul, plunge one into despair

19 to aggrieve, oppress, **grieve, sorrow,** plunge one into sorrow, embitter; draw tears, bring to tears; **anguish, tear up** *and* **cut up** (*both informal*), wring *or* pierce *or* lacerate *or* rend the heart, pull at the heartstrings; afflict *see* 96.16, torment *see* 96.18; **break one's heart, make one's heart bleed;** desolate, leave an aching void; prostrate, break down, crush, bear down, inundate, overwhelm

adjectives

20 **sad,** saddened; sadhearted, **sad of heart; heavyhearted,** heavy; oppressed, weighed upon, weighed *or* weighted down, bearing the woe of the world, burdened *or* laden with sorrow; sad-faced, long-faced; sad-eyed; sad-voiced

21 **unhappy, uncheerful,** uncheery, **cheerless, joyless, unjoyful,** unsmiling; mirthless, unmirthful, humourless, infestive; **grim; out of humour,** out of sorts, in bad humour *or* spirits; **sorry,** sorryish; discontented *see* 108.5; **wretched, miserable;** pleasureless *see* 96.20

22 **dejected, depressed, downhearted, down, downcast, cast down,** bowed down, subdued; **discouraged, disheartened, dispirited,** dashed; **low,** feeling low, low-spirited, **in low spirits; down in the mouth** (*informal*), in the doldrums, **down in the dumps** *and* **in the dumps** *and* in the doleful dumps (*all informal*), in the depths, in the slough of despond; **despondent,** desponding; **despairing** *see* 125.12, weary of life, suicidal, world-weary; pessimistic *see* 125.16; spiritless, heartless, **woebegone; drooping,** droopy, languishing, pining, haggard; hypochondriac *or* hypochondriacal

23 melancholy, melancholic, splenetic (*old*), **blue** (*informal*), funky (*informal*); atrabilious, atrabiliar; **pensive**, **wistful**, tristful; **nostalgic**, homesick

24 **gloomy**, **dismal**, **murky**, **bleak**, **grim**, **sombre**, sombrous, **solemn**, **grave**; sad, *triste* (*French*), **funereal**, funebrial, saturnine; **dark**, black, grey; **dreary**, drear, drearisome, dreich (*Scottish*); weary, weariful, wearisome

25 glum, grum, **morose**, **sullen**, sulky, mumpish, dumpish, long-faced, crestfallen, chapfallen; **moody**, moodish, **brooding**, broody; mopish, mopey (*informal*), **moping**

26 **sorrowful**, **sorrowing**, sorrowed, **mournful**, **rueful**, **woeful**, **woesome** (*old*), **doleful**, **plaintive**, plangent; anguished; dolorous, **grievous**, **lamentable**, lugubrious; **tearful**; **care-worn**; grieved, **grief-stricken**, griefful, aggrieved, in grief, plunged in grief, dumb with grief, prostrated by grief, cut-up *and* torn-up (*both informal*), **inconsolable**

27 **sorrow-stricken**, sorrow-wounded, sorrow-struck, sorrow-torn, sorrow-worn, sorrow-wasted, sorrow-beaten, sorrow-blinded, sorrow-clouded, sorrow-shot, sorrow-burdened, sorrow-laden, sorrow-sighing, sorrow-sobbing, sorrow-sick

28 **disconsolate**, **inconsolable**, unconsolable, comfortless, prostrate *or* prostrated, **forlorn**; desolate, *désolé* (*French*); sick, **sick at heart**, **heartsick**, soul-sick, heartsore

29 **overcome**, crushed, borne-down, overwhelmed, inundated, **stricken**, **cut up** (*informal*), desolated, prostrate *or* prostrated, broken-down, undone; **heart-stricken**, heart-struck; **brokenhearted**, heartbroken

30 depressing, depressive, depressant, **oppressive**; discouraging, disheartening, dispiriting; morale-sapping, worst-case, downbeat (*informal*)

adverbs

31 sadly, gloomily, dismally, drearily, heavily, bleakly, grimly, sombrely, sombrously, solemnly, funereally, gravely, with a long face; **depressingly**

32 unhappily, uncheerfully, cheerlessly, joylessly, unjoyfully

33 dejectedly, downheartedly; discouragedly, disheartenedly, dispiritedly; despondently, despairingly, spiritlessly, heartlessly; disconsolately, inconsolably, unconsolably, forlornly

34 melancholily, pensively, wistfully, tristfully; nostalgically

35 glumly, grumly, morosely, sullenly; moodily, moodishly, broodingly, broodily; mopishly, mopily (*informal*), mopingly

36 sorrowfully, mournfully, ruefully, woefully, woesomely (*old*), dolefully, dolorously, plaintively, grievously, grieffully, lugubriously; with a broken voice; **heartbrokenly**, brokenheartedly; **tearfully**, with tears in one's eyes

113 REGRET

nouns

1 **regret**, regrets, regretting, regretfulness; **remorse**, remorsefulness, remorse of conscience; **shame**, shamefulness, shamefacedness, shamefastness; **sorrow**, **grief**, sorriness, repining; **contrition**, contriteness, attrition; bitterness; apologies; wistfulness *see* 100.4

2 **compunction**, **qualm**, **qualms**, qualmishness, scruples, scrupulosity, scrupulousness, pang, pangs, **pangs of conscience**, throes, sting *or* pricking *or* twinge *or* twitch of conscience, touch of conscience, voice of conscience, pricking of heart, better self

3 **self-reproach**, self-reproachfulness, **self-accusation**, **self-condemnation**, self-conviction, self-punishment, self-humiliation, self-debasement, **self-hatred**, self-flagellation; hair shirt; self-analysis, soul-searching, examination of conscience

4 **penitence**, **repentance**, **change of heart**; **apology**, humble *or* heartfelt apology, abject apology; better nature, good angel, guardian angel; reformation *see* 857.2; deathbed repentance; mea culpa; **penance** *see* 658.3; wearing a hairshirt *or* sackcloth *or* sackcloth and ashes, mortification of the flesh

5 **penitent**, confessor,

"a sadder and a wiser man"—COLERIDGE; **prodigal son**, prodigal returned; Magdalen

verbs

6 to **regret**, deplore, repine, be sorry for; **rue**, rue the day; **bemoan**, **bewail**; curse one's folly, **reproach oneself**, kick oneself (*informal*), bite one's tongue, accuse *or* condemn *or* blame *or* convict *or* punish oneself, flagellate oneself, wear a hair shirt, make oneself miserable, humiliate *or* debase oneself, hate oneself for one's actions, hide one's face in shame; examine one's conscience, search one's soul, consult *or* heed one's better self, analyse *or* search one's motives; cry over spilled milk, waste time in regret

7 to **repent**, **think better of**, change one's mind, have second thoughts; laugh on the other side of one's face; **plead guilty**, own oneself in the wrong, humble oneself, **apologize** *see* 658.5, beg pardon *or* forgiveness, throw oneself on the mercy of the court; **do penance** *see* 658.6; reform

adjectives

8 **regretful**, **remorseful**, full of remorse, **ashamed**, shameful, shamefaced, shamefast, **sorry**, **rueful**, **repining**, unhappy about; **conscience-stricken**, conscience-smitten; **self-reproachful**, self-reproaching, self-accusing, self-condemning, self-convicting, self-punishing, self-flagellating, self-humiliating, self-debasing, self-hating; wistful *see* 100.23

9 **penitent**, **repentant**; **penitential**, penitentiary; **contrite**, abject, humble, humbled, **sheepish**, **apologetic**, touched, softened, melted

10 **regrettable**, much to be regretted; **deplorable** *see* 999.9

adverbs

11 **regretfully, remorsefully,** sorrily, ruefully, unhappily

12 **penitently,** repentantly, penitentially; **contritely,** abjectly, **humbly, sheepishly, apologetically**

114 UNREGRETFULNESS

nouns

1 **unregretfulness, unremorsefulness, unsorriness,** unruefulness; **remorselessness,** regretlessness, sorrowlessness; **shamelessness,** unashamedness

2 **impenitence,** impenitentness; nonrepentance, irrepentance; **uncontriteness,** unabjectness; seared conscience, heart of stone, callousness *see* 94.3; **hardness of heart,** hardness, induration, obduracy; **defiance** *see* 454, 327.2; **insolence** *see* 142

verbs

3 **to harden one's heart,** steel oneself; **have no regrets,** not look backward, not cry over spilled milk; have no shame

adjectives

4 **unregretful,** unregretting, **unremorseful, unsorry, unsorrowful,** unrueful; **remorseless,** regretless, sorrowless, griefless; unsorrowing, ungrieving, unrepining; **shameless,** unashamed

5 **impenitent, unrepentant,** unrepenting, unreconstructed; **uncontrite,** unabject; untouched, unsoftened, unmelted, callous *see* 94.12; hard, hardened, obdurate; **defiant** *see* 453.8, 454.7; **insolent** *see* 142.9

6 **unregretted,** unrepented

adverbs

7 **unregretfully, unremorsefully,** unruefully; **remorselessly,** sorrowlessly, impenitently, shamelessly, unashamedly; **without regret,** without looking back, **without remorse,** without compunction, without any qualms *or* scruples

115 LAMENTATION

nouns

1 **lamentation,** lamenting, **mourning, moaning, grieving, sorrowing, wailing, bewailing, bemoaning,** keening, howling, ululation, "weeping and gnashing of teeth"—BIBLE; **sorrow** *see* 112.10

2 **weeping, sobbing, crying,** bawling, greeting (*Scottish*); blubbering, whimpering, snivelling; **tears,** flood of tears, fit of crying; cry *and* good cry (*both informal*); **tearfulness, weepiness** (*informal*), lachrymosity, melting mood; tearful eyes, swimming *or* brimming *or* overflowing eyes; **tear,** teardrop, lachryma; lacrimatory, tear bottle

3 **lament, plaint,** *planctus* (*Latin*); **murmur,** mutter; **moan, groan; whine, whimper; wail,** wail of woe; **sob,** *cri du coeur* (*French*), **cry,** outcry, scream, **howl,** yawl, yowl, bawl, yawp, keen, ululation; jeremiad, tirade, dolorous tirade

4 **complaint, grievance, peeve,** pet peeve, **groan; dissent, protest** *see* 333.2; hard luck story

(*informal*), tale of woe; **complaining,** scolding, groaning, **faultfinding** *see* 510.4, sniping, destructive criticism, **grumbling, murmuring;** whining, petulance, peevishness, querulousness

5 (*informal terms*) **beef, kick, gripe,** kvetch, grouse, bellyache, howl, holler, **squawk,** bitch; **beefing, grousing, kicking, griping,** kvetching, **bellyaching,** squawking, **bitching,** yapping

6 **dirge, funeral** *or* **death song,** coronach, keen, elegy, epicedium, requiem, monody, threnody, threnode, knell, death knell, passing bell, funeral *or* dead march, muffled drums; eulogy, funeral *or* graveside oration

7 (*mourning garments*) **mourning, weeds,** widow's weeds, crape, black; deep mourning; sackcloth, sackcloth and ashes; cypress, cypress lawn, yew; mourning band; mourning ring

8 **lamenter, griever, mourner** *see* 309.7; moaner, weeper; **complainer,** faultfinder, malcontent *see* 108.3

9 (*informal terms*) **grouch,** kvetch, kicker, griper, moaner, moaning Minnie, nark, crank, crab, grouser, beefer, bellyacher, sorehead (*US & Canadian*), sourpuss, misery

verbs

10 **to lament, mourn, moan, grieve, sorrow,** keen, weep over, **bewail, bemoan, deplore, repine, sigh,** give sorrow words; sing the blues (*informal*), elegize, dirge, knell

11 **to wring one's hands,** tear one's hair, gnash one's teeth, beat one's breast, roll on the ground

12 **to weep, sob, cry,** greet (*Scottish*), **bawl,** howl, boo-hoo; **blubber, whimper, snivel,** blub (*informal*), bubble (*Scottish*); **shed tears,** drop a tear; **burst into tears,** burst out crying, give way to tears, melt *or* dissolve in tears, break down, break down and cry, turn on the waterworks (*informal*); cry one's eyes out, cry oneself blind; cry before one is hurt

13 **to wail,** ululate; **moan, groan; howl,** yowl, yawl; **cry, squall,** bawl, yawp, **yell, scream,** shriek; cry out, make an outcry; bay at the moon; tirade

14 **to whine, whimper,** yammer (*informal*), pule, grizzle (*informal*)

15 **to complain, groan; grumble, murmur, mutter,** growl, clamour, croak, grunt, yelp, chunter (*informal*); **fret,** fuss, make a fuss about, fret and fume, create (*informal*); air a grievance, lodge *or* register a complaint; fault, find fault

16 (*informal terms*) **to beef, bitch, kick,** kvetch, bellyache, crab, gripe, grouch, grouse, grump, have an attitude, kick, holler, howl, moan, nark, make a stink, squawk, squeal, yap; raise a howl, put up a squawk *or* howl, take on, cry *or* yell *or* scream blue murder, give one a hard time, piss *or* kick up a storm *or* row *or* fuss, make *or* raise a stink

17 **to go into mourning;** put on mourning, wear mourning

adjectives

18 **lamenting, grieving, mourning, moaning, sorrowing;** wailing, bewailing, bemoaning; **in mourning,** in sackcloth and ashes

19 plaintive, plangent, **mournful**, moanful, wailful, lamentive, ululant; **sorrowful** see 112.26; **howling**, Jeremianic; whining, whiny, whimpering, puling; **querulous, fretful**, petulant, peevish; **complaining, faultfinding** see 510.24

20 (*informal terms*) grouchy, cranky, beefing, crabby, crabbing, grousing, griping, bellyaching, bitching

21 **tearful**, teary, **weepy** (*informal*); lachrymal, lachrymose, lacrimatory; in the melting mood, on the edge of tears, ready to cry; **weeping, sobbing, crying**; blubbering, whimpering, snivelling; **in tears**, with tears in one's eyes, with tearful *or* watery eyes, with swimming *or* brimming *or* overflowing eyes, with eyes suffused *or* bathed *or* dissolved in tears, "like Niobe, all tears"—SHAKESPEARE

22 dirgelike, knell-like, elegiac, elegiacal, epicedial, threnodic

adverbs

23 **lamentingly, plaintively, mournfully**, moanfully, wailfully; **sorrowfully** see 112.36; complainingly, groaningly, querulously, fretfully, petulantly, peevishly

116 REJOICING

nouns

1 **rejoicing, jubilation**, jubilance, jubilant display, jubilee, show of joy, raucous happiness; **exultation**, elation, triumph; the time of one's life; whoopee *and* hoopla (*both informal*), festivity see 743.3, 4, merriment see 109.5; celebration see 487

2 **cheer, hurrah, huzzah**, hurray, hooray, yippee, rah; **cry, shout, yell**; hosanna, hallelujah, alleluia, paean, paean *or* chorus of cheers; **applause** see 509.2

3 **smile**, smiling; bright smile, gleaming *or* glowing smile, beam; silly smile *or* grin; **grin**, grinning; broad grin, ear-to-ear grin, toothful grin; stupid grin, idiotic grin; cheesy *or* big cheesy grin (*informal*), sardonic grin, **smirk, simper**

4 **laughter, laughing, hilarity** see 109.5, risibility; **laugh; titter; giggle; chuckle, chortle**; cackle, crow; **snicker**, snigger, snort; ha-ha, hee-haw, hee-hee, ho-ho, tee-hee, yuk-yuk; guffaw, **horselaugh; hearty laugh, belly laugh** (*informal*), Homeric laughter, cachinnation; **shout, shriek**, shout of laughter, burst *or* outburst of laughter, peal *or* roar of laughter, gales of laughter; fit of laughter, convulsion,
"laughter holding both his sides"—MILTON

verbs

5 **to rejoice, jubilate, exult, glory, joy, delight**, bless *or* thank one's stars *or* lucky stars, congratulate oneself, hug oneself, rub one's hands, clap hands; dance *or* skip *or* jump for joy, dance, skip, frisk, rollick, revel, frolic, caper, gambol, caracole, romp; sing, carol, chirp, chirrup, chirp like a cricket, whistle, lilt

6 **to cheer, give a cheer, give three cheers, cry, shout, yell**, cry for joy, yell oneself hoarse; huzzah, hurrah, hurray, hooray; shout hosanna *or* hallelujah, "make a joyful noise unto the Lord"—BIBLE; **applaud** see 509.10

7 **to smile**, crack a smile (*informal*), break into a smile; **beam**, smile brightly; **grin**, grin like a Cheshire cat (*informal*); **smirk, simper**

8 **to laugh**, burst out laughing, burst into laughter, burst out, laugh outright; laugh it up (*informal*); **titter; giggle; chuckle, chortle**; cackle, crow; **snicker**, snigger, snort; ha-ha, hee-haw, hee-hee, ho-ho, tee-hee, yuk-yuk; **guffaw**, belly laugh, horselaugh; **shout, shriek**, give a shout *or* shriek of laughter; **roar**, cachinnate, roar with laughter; shake with laughter, shake like jelly; be convulsed with laughter, go into convulsions, fall about (*informal*); burst *or* split with laughter, break up *and* crack up (*both informal*), kill oneself laughing, split (*informal*), **split one's sides**, laugh one's head off, laugh fit to burst *or* bust (*informal*), burst a gut *and* pee in *or* wet one's pants laughing (*both informal*), **be in stitches** *or* **knots** (*both informal*), hold one's sides, roll in the aisles (*informal*); laugh oneself sick *or* silly *or* limp, die *or* nearly die laughing; laugh in one's sleeve, laugh up one's sleeve, laugh in one's beard

9 **to make laugh, kill** *and* **slay** (*both informal*), "set the table on a roar"—SHAKESPEARE, break *or* crack one up (*informal*), get a laugh

adjectives

10 **rejoicing**, delighting, exulting; **jubilant, exultant, elated**, elate, flushed

adverbs

11 **rejoicingly**, delightingly, exultingly; **jubilantly, exultantly, elatedly**

117 DULLNESS
being uninteresting

nouns

1 **dullness, dryness**, dustiness, uninterestingness; **stuffiness, stodginess**, woodenness, stiffness; barrenness, sterility, aridity, jejunity; **insipidness**, insipidity, vapidness, vapidity, inanity, hollowness, emptiness, superficiality, **staleness, flatness**, tastelessness; characterlessness, colourlessness, pointlessness; **deadness**, lifelessness, spiritlessness, bloodlessness, paleness, pallor, etiolation, effeteness; **slowness**, pokiness, dragginess (*informal*), unliveliness; **tediousness** see 118.2; **dreariness**, drearisomeness, dismalness; **heaviness**, leadenness, ponderousness; inexcitability see 106; solemnity see 111; lowness of spirit see 112.3

2 **prosaicness**, prosiness; prosaism, prosaicism, prose, plainness; **matter-of-factness**, unimaginativeness; matter of fact; **simplicity** see 797, **plainness** see 499

3 **triteness**, corniness *and* squareness (*both informal*), **banality**, banalness, unoriginality, sameness, **hackneyedness, commonplaceness**, commonness, familiarness, platitudinousness; a familiar ring; redundancy, repetition, **staleness**, mustiness, fustiness; **cliché** see 973.3

verbs

4 **to fall flat**, fall flat as a pancake; leave one cold *or* unmoved, go down like a lead balloon (*informal*), lay an egg *and* bomb (*both informal*), **wear thin**

5 to prose, platitudinize, sing a familiar tune; pedestrianize; warm over; banalize

adjectives

6 dull, dry, dusty, dry as dust; stuffy, stodgy, wooden, stiff; arid, barren, blank, sterile, jejune; insipid, vapid, inane, hollow, empty, superficial; ho-hum and blah (both informal), flat, tasteless, dead-and-alive (informal); characterless, colourless, pointless; dead, lifeless, spiritless, bloodless, pale, pallid, etiolated, effete; cold; slow, poky, draggy (informal), pedestrian, plodding, unlively; boring; tedious; dreary, drearisome, dismal; heavy, leaden, ponderous, elephantine; dull as dish water, "weary, stale, flat and unprofitable"—SHAKESPEARE; inexcitable see 106.10; solemn see 111.3; low-spirited see 112.22

7 uninteresting, uneventful, unexciting; uninspiring; unentertaining, unenjoyable, unamusing, unfunny, unwitty

8 prosaic, prose, prosy, prosing, plain; matter-of-fact, unimaginative, unimpassioned

9 trite; corny and square (both informal), banal, unoriginal, platitudinous, stereotyped, stock, set, commonplace, common, truistic, twice-told, familiar, bromidic (informal), old hat (informal), back-number, bewhiskered, warmed-over, cut-and-dried; hackneyed, hackney; well-known see 927.27; stale, musty, fusty, worn, timeworn, well-worn, moth-eaten, threadbare, worn thin

adverbs

10 dully, dryly, dustily, uninterestingly; stuffily, stodgily; aridly, barrenly, jejunely, insipidly, vapidly, inanely, hollowly, emptily, superficially, tastelessly, colourlessly, pointlessly; lifelessly, spiritlessly, bloodlessly, pallidly, effetely; slowly, draggily (informal), ploddingly; tediously; drearily, drearisomely, dismally; heavily, ponderously

11 tritely, cornily (informal), banally, commonplacely, commonly, familiarly, hackneyedly, unoriginally, truistically, stalely

118 TEDIUM

nouns

1 tedium, monotony, humdrum, irksomeness, irk; sameness, sameliness, wearisome sameness, more of the same, the same old thing, the same damn thing (informal); broken record, parrot; undeviation, unvariation, invariability; the round, the daily round or grind, the weary round, the treadmill, the rat race (informal), the beaten track or path; time on one's hands, time hanging heavily on one's hands; protraction, prolongation see 826.2

2 tediousness, monotonousness, unrelievedness; humdrumness, humdrumminess, dullness see 117; wearisomeness, wearifulness; tiresomeness, irksomeness, drearisomeness, boresomeness, boringness; prolixity, long-windedness see 538.2; redundancy, repetition, tick-tock

3 weariness, tiredness, wearifulness; jadedness, fed-upness, satiation, satiety; boredom, boredness; ennui, spleen (old), melancholy, life-weariness,

taedium vitae (Latin), world-weariness; listlessness see 94.4, dispiritedness see 112.3

4 bore, crashing bore (informal), frightful bore; pest, nuisance; proser, twaddler, wet blanket

5 (informal terms) drag, drip, pill, yawn; headache, pain in the neck or arse

verbs

6 to be tedious, drag on, go on forever; have a certain sameness, be infinitely repetitive; weary, tire, irk, wear, wear on or upon, make one tired, fatigue, weary or tire to death, jade; give one a swift pain in the arse and give one a bellyful and make one fed-up (all informal), pall, satiate, glut

7 to bore, leave one cold, set or send to sleep; bore stiff or to tears or to death or to extinction (informal), bore to distraction, bore out of one's life, bore out of all patience; buttonhole

8 to harp on or upon, dwell on or upon, harp upon one or the same string, play or sing the same old song or tune, play the same broken record, flog or beat a dead horse

adjectives

9 tedious, monotonous, humdrum, singsong, jog-trot, treadmill, unvarying, invariable, uneventful, broken-record, parrotlike, harping, everlasting, too much with us (informal); blah (informal), dreary, drearisome, dry, dusty, dull see 117.6; protracted, prolonged see 826.11; prolix, long-winded see 538.12

10 wearying, wearing, tiring; wearisome, weariful, fatiguing, tiresome, irksome; boring, stupefyingly boring, stuporific, yawny (informal)

11 weary, weariful; tired, wearied, irked; good and tired, tired to death, weary unto death; sick, sick of, tired of, sick and tired of; jaded, satiated, palled, fed up (informal), brassed or browned or cheesed or pissed off (informal); blasé; splenetic (old), melancholy, melancholic, life-weary, world-weary, tired of living; listless see 94.13, dispirited see 112.22

12 bored, uninterested; bored stiff or to death or to extinction or to tears (informal), stupefied or stuporous with boredom

adverbs

13 tediously, monotonously, harpingly, everlastingly, unvaryingly, endlessly; long-windedly; boringly, boresomely; wearisomely, fatiguingly, wearyingly, tiresomely, irksomely, drearisomely; dully see 117.10

14 on a treadmill, on the beaten track, on the same old round; without a change of menu or scenery or pace

phrases

15 ho hum!, heigh ho!, what a life!, que sera sera; plus ça change, plus c'est la même chose (French, the more things change, the more they stay the same); so what else is new?; MEGO or mine eyes glaze over

119 AGGRAVATION

nouns

1 **aggravation, worsening; exacerbation,** embittering, embitterment, souring; deterioration; **intensification, heightening,** stepping-up, sharpening, deepening, **increase,** enhancement, amplification, enlargement, magnification, augmentation; **exasperation, annoyance, irritation** *see* 96.3; deliberate aggravation, provocation; contentiousness

verbs

2 **to aggravate, worsen,** make worse; **exacerbate,** embitter, sour; deteriorate; **intensify, heighten,** step up, sharpen, make acute *or* more acute, bring to a head, deepen, **increase,** enhance, amplify, enlarge, magnify, build up; augment; rub salt in the wound, twist the knife, add insult to injury, pour oil on the fire, add fuel to the fire *or* flame, heat up *and* hot up (*both informal*); increase pressure *or* tension, tighten, tighten up, tighten the screws, put the squeeze on (*informal*); **exasperate, annoy, irritate** *see* 96.14; provoke, be an *agent provocateur*

3 **to worsen,** get *or* grow worse, take a turn for the worse; go from push to shove, **go from bad to worse; jump out of the frying pan and into the fire,** avoid Scylla and fall into Charybdis, "sow the wind and reap the whirlwind"—BIBLE

adjectives

4 **aggravated, worsened, worse,** worse and worse, exacerbated, embittered, soured, deteriorated; **intensified, heightened,** stepped-up, **increased,** enhanced, amplified, magnified, enlarged, augmented, heated *or* hotted up (*informal*); **exasperated, irritated, annoyed** *see* 96.21; provoked, deliberately provoked; worse off, out of the frying pan and into the fire

5 **aggravating,** aggravative; **exasperating,** exasperative; **annoying, irritating** *see* 98.22; provocative; contentious

adverbs

6 from bad to worse; aggravatingly, exasperatingly; annoyingly *see* 98.29

120 RELIEF

nouns

1 **relief, easement, easing,** ease; **relaxation,** relaxing, relaxation *or* easing of tension, decompression, slackening; **reduction,** diminishment, diminution, lessening, abatement, remission; **remedy** *see* 86; **alleviation, mitigation, palliation,** softening, assuagement, allayment, defusing, appeasement, mollification, subduement; soothing, salving, anodyne; lulling; dulling, deadening, numbing, narcotizing, anaesthesia, anaesthetizing, analgesia; sedating, sedation; doping *or* doping up (*informal*)

2 **release, deliverance, freeing,** removal; suspension, intermission, respite, surcease, reprieve; discharge; catharsis, purging, purgation, purge, cleansing, cleansing away, emotional release

3 **lightening, disburdening,** unburdening, unweighting, unloading, disencumbrance, disembarrassment, easing of the load, a load off one's mind, something out of one's system, something off one's chest

4 **sense** *or* **feeling of relief,** sigh of relief

verbs

5 **to relieve,** give relief; **ease,** ease matters; **relax,** slacken; **reduce,** diminish, lessen, abate, remit; **alleviate, mitigate, palliate,** soften, pad, cushion, assuage, allay, defuse, lay, appease, mollify, subdue, soothe; salve, pour balm into, pour oil on; poultice, foment, stupe; slake; lull; **dull, deaden,** dull *or* deaden the pain, numb, benumb, anaesthetize; sedate, narcotize, dope *or* dope up (*informal*); temper the wind to the shorn lamb, lay the flattering unction to one's soul

6 **to release, free, deliver,** reprieve, remove, free from; suspend, intermit, give respite *or* surcease; **relax,** decompress, ease, destress; act as a cathartic, **purge, purge away, cleanse,** cleanse away; give release, cut loose

7 **to lighten, disburden,** unburden, unweight, unload, unfreight, disencumber, disembarrass, ease one's load; **set one's mind at ease** *or* **rest,** set at ease, **take a load off one's mind,** smooth the ruffled brow of care; relieve oneself, let one's hair down, pour one's heart out, talk it out, let it all hang out *and* go public (*both informal*), get it off one's chest, get it out in the open

8 **to be relieved,** feel relief, feel better about, get something out of one's system, feel *or* be oneself again; get out from under (*informal*); **breathe easy** *or* **easier,** breathe more freely, breathe again, rest easier; **heave a sigh of relief,** draw a long *or* deep breath

adjectives

9 **relieving, easing, alleviative,** alleviating, alleviatory, **mitigative,** mitigating, **palliative,** lenitive, assuasive, softening, subduing, soothing, demulcent, emollient, balmy, balsamic; **remedial** *see* 86.39; dulling, deadening, numbing, benumbing, anaesthetic, analgesic, anodyne, pain killing; cathartic, purgative, cleansing; **relaxing**

10 **relieved,** breathing easy *or* easier *or* freely, able to breathe again, out from under *and* out of the woods (*both informal*); **relaxed**

121 COMFORT

nouns

1 **comfort, ease, well-being;** contentment *see* 107; clover, velvet (*informal*), bed of roses; life of ease *see* 1009.1; solid comfort

2 **comfortableness, easiness; restfulness,** reposefulness, peace, peacefulness; softness, cushiness (*informal*), cushioniness; **cosiness, snugness;** friendliness, warmness; **homeliness,** homelikeness, hominess (*informal*); **commodiousness,** roominess,

convenience; luxuriousness *see* 501.5; hospitality *see* 585

3 **creature comforts, comforts, conveniences,** excellent accommodations, amenities, good things of life, beer and skittles, cakes and ale, egg in one's beer (*informal*), all the comforts of home; all the heart can desire, luxuries, the best

4 **consolation, solace,** solacement, easement, heart's ease,
"surcease of sorrow"—Poe; **encouragement,** aid and comfort, **assurance, reassurance,** support, **comfort,** crumb *or* shred of comfort,
"kind words and comfortable"—William Cowper; condolence *see* 147, sympathy; **relief** *see* 120

5 **comforter,** consoler, solacer, encourager; the Holy Spirit *or* Ghost, the Comforter, the Paraclete

verbs

6 **to comfort, console, solace,** give *or* bring comfort, bear up; condole with, sympathize with, extend sympathy; ease, **put** *or* **set at ease;** bolster, support; relieve *see* 120.5; **assure, reassure; encourage, hearten,** pat on the back; **cheer** *see* 109.7; wipe away the tears,
"rejoice with them that do rejoice, and weep with them that weep"—Bible

7 **to be comforted, take comfort, take heart;** take hope, lift up one's heart, pull oneself together, pluck up one's spirits; *sursum corda* (*Latin*)

8 **to be at ease,** be *or* feel easy, stand easy; **make oneself comfortable,** make oneself at home, feel at home, put one's feet up, take a load off (*informal*); **relax,** be relaxed; live a life of ease *see* 1009.10

9 **to snug,** snug down *or* up; tuck in

10 **to snuggle, nestle, cuddle,** cuddle up, curl up; nest; bundle; snuggle up to, snug up *or* together (*old*)

adjectives

11 **comfortable,** comfy (*informal*); contented *see* 107.7, 9, 10; **easy,** easeful; **restful,** reposeful, peaceful, **relaxing;** soft, cushioned, cushy (*informal*), cushiony; comfortable as an old shoe; **cosy, snug,** snug as a bug in a rug; friendly, warm; **homelike,** homy *and* down-home (*both informal*), homely, lived-in; **commodious,** roomy, convenient; luxurious *see* 501.21

12 **at ease,** at one's ease, easy, relaxed, laid-back (*informal*); at rest, resting easy; **at home,** in one's element

13 **comforting, consoling,** consolatory, of good comfort; condoling, condolent, condolatory, sympathetic; **assuring, reassuring,** supportive; **encouraging, heartening; cheering** *see* 109.16; relieving *see* 120.9; hospitable *see* 585.11

adverbs

14 **comfortably, easily,** with ease; **restfully,** reposefully, peacefully; **cosily, snugly; commodiously,** roomily, conveniently; luxuriously, voluptuously

15 **in comfort,** in ease, **in clover, on** *or* **in velvet** (*informal*), on *or* in a bed of roses

16 **comfortingly, consolingly,** assuringly, reassuringly, supportively, encouragingly, hearteningly; hospitably

122 WONDER

nouns

1 **wonder,** wonderment, sense of wonder, marvelling, marvel, **astonishment, amazement,** amaze, **astoundment;** dumbfoundment, stupefaction; **surprise; awe,** breathless wonder *or* awe, sense of mystery, admiration; beguilement, fascination *see* 377.1; bewilderment, puzzlement *see* 970.3

2 **marvel, wonder, prodigy, miracle, phenomenon,** phenom (*informal*); astonishment, amazement, marvelment, wonderment, wonderful thing, nine days' wonder, amazing *or* astonishing thing, quite a thing, really something, **sensation,** rocker *and* stunner (*both informal*); one for the book *and* something to brag about *and* something to shout about *and* something to write home about *and* something else (*all informal*); **rarity,** nonesuch, nonpareil, exception, one in a thousand, one in a way, oner; **curiosity,** gazingstock (*old*), **sight, spectacle;** wonders of the world

3 **wonderfulness,** wondrousness, **marvellousness,** miraculousness, phenomenalness, **prodigiousness, stupendousness, remarkableness,** extraordinariness; beguilingness, fascination, enchantingness, enticingness, seductiveness, **glamorousness; awesomeness, mysteriousness,** mystery, numinousness; **transcendence,** transcendentness, surpassingness

4 **inexpressibility, ineffability,** ineffableness, inenarrability, noncommunicability, noncommunicableness, incommunicability, incommunicableness, indescribability, indefinableness, **unutterability, unspeakability,** unnameableness, innominability, unmentionability

verbs

5 **to wonder, marvel,** be astonished *or* amazed *or* astounded, be seized with wonder; **gaze, gape,** drop one's jaw, look *or* stand aghast *or* agog, gawk, **stare,** stare openmouthed, open one's eyes, rub one's eyes, hold one's breath; not be able to account for, not know what to make of, not believe one's eyes *or* ears *or* senses

6 **to astonish, amaze, astound, surprise,** startle, stagger, **bewilder, perplex** *see* 970.13, flabbergast (*informal*), confound, overwhelm, **boggle, boggle the mind; awe,** strike with wonder *or* awe; **dumbfound** *or* dumbfounder, strike dumb, strike dead; strike all of a heap *and* throw on one's beam ends *and* knock one's socks off *and* bowl down *or* over (*all informal*), dazzle, bedazzle, daze, bedaze; **stun, stupefy,** petrify, paralyse

7 to take one's breath away, turn one's head, make one's head swim, make one's hair stand on end, make one's tongue cleave to the roof of one's mouth, make one stare, make one sit up and take notice, sweep *or* carry off one's feet

8 to beggar *or* baffle description, stagger belief

adjectives

9 **wondering,** wrapped *or* rapt in wonder, marvelling, **astonished, amazed, surprised, astounded,** flabbergasted (*informal*), gobsmacked (*informal*), **bewildered,** puzzled, confounded, **dumbfounded,** dumbstruck, staggered, overwhelmed, unable to believe one's senses *or* eyes; **aghast,** agape, agog, all agog, gazing, gaping, at gaze staring, gawping, wide-eyed, popeyed, open-eyed, openmouthed, **breathless; thunderstruck,** wonder-struck, wonder-stricken, awestricken, awestruck, struck all of a heap (*informal*); **awed, in awe,** in awe of; spellbound, fascinated, captivated, under a charm, beguiled, enthralled, enraptured, enravished, enchanted, entranced, bewitched, hypnotized, mesmerized, stupefied, lost in wonder *or* amazement

10 **wonderful, wondrous, marvellous, miraculous,** fantastic, fabulous, phenomenal, **prodigious, stupendous,** unheard-of, unprecedented, extraordinary, exceptional, rare, unique, singular, **remarkable,** striking, **sensational; strange,** passing strange,

"wondrous strange"—SHAKESPEARE; **beguiling, fascinating;** incredible, inconceivable, outlandish, unimaginable, incomprehensible; **bewildering, puzzling,** enigmatic

11 **awesome,** awful, awing, awe-inspiring; **transcendent,** transcending, surpassing; **mysterious,** numinous; weird, eerie, uncanny, bizarre

12 **astonishing, amazing, surprising,** startling, **astounding,** confounding, staggering, stunning (*informal*), eye-opening, breathtaking, overwhelming, mind-boggling *or* numbing; **spectacular**

13 **indescribable, ineffable,** inenarrable, inexpressible, unutterable, unspeakable, noncommunicable, incommunicable, indefinable, undefinable, unnameable, innominable, unwhisperable, unmentionable

adverbs

14 **wonderfully,** wondrously, **marvellously, miraculously,** fantastically, fabulously, phenomenally, prodigiously, stupendously, extraordinarily, exceptionally, remarkably, strikingly, **sensationally;** strangely, outlandishly, incredibly, inconceivably, unimaginably, incomprehensibly, **bewilderingly, puzzlingly,** enigmatically; **beguilingly,** fascinatingly

15 **awesomely,** awfully, awingly, awe-inspiringly; **mysteriously,** numinously, weirdly, eerily, uncannily, bizarrely; **transcendently,** surpassingly, surpassing, passing (*old*)

16 **astonishingly, amazingly, astoundingly,** staggeringly, confoundingly; **surprisingly,** startlingly, to one's surprise *or* great surprise, to one's astonishment *or* amazement; for a wonder, strange to say, mirabile dictu (*Latin,* wondrous to relate)

17 **indescribably, ineffably,** inexpressibly, unutterably, **unspeakably,** inenarrably, indefinably, unnameably, unmentionably

18 in wonder, in astonishment, in amazement, in bewilderment, in awe, in admiration, with gaping mouth

exclamations

19 (*astonishment or surprise*) my word!, my hat!, I declare!, well I never!, of all things!, as I live and breathe!, what!, indeed!, really!, surely!, how now!, what on earth!, what in the world!, I'll be jiggered!, holy Christ!, holy Christmas!, holy cow!, holy mackerel!, holy Moses!, holy smoke!, holy shit! (*informal*), blow me down!, strike me dead!, shiver my timbers!, stone the crows!, strike a light!

20 oh!, O!, ah!, la!, lo!, lo and behold!, hello!, halloo!, hey!, whew!, phew!, wow!, coo!, yipes!, yike!

21 my!, oh, my!, dear!, dear me!, goodness!, gracious!, goodness gracious!, cor!, cor blimey!, gee! (*US & Canadian*), my goodness!, my stars!, good gracious!, good heavens!, good lack!, lackadaisy!, welladay!, hoity-toity!, zounds!, 'sdeath!, gadzooks!, gad so!, bless my heart!, God bless me!, lumme!, heavens and earth!, for crying out loud! (*informal*)

22 imagine!, fancy!, fancy that!, just imagine!, imagine that!, just think!, to think of it!, well I never!, can you beat that!, it beats the Dutch!, do tell!, you don't say!, the devil *or* deuce you say!, get along!, I'll be!, what do you know!, what do you know about that!, how about that!, who would have thought it!, did you ever!, can it be!, can such things be?, will wonders never cease!

123 UNASTONISHMENT

nouns

1 **unastonishment, unamazement,** unamazedness, nonastonishment, nonamazement, nonamazedness, nonwonder, nonwondering, nonmarvelling, unsurprise, unsurprisedness, awelessness, wonderlessness; **calm,** calmness, coolness, **cool** (*informal*), cool *or* calm *or* nodding acceptance, composure, composedness, sangfroid, inexcitability *see* 106, expectation *see* 130, unimpressibleness, refusal to be impressed *or* awed *or* amazed; poker face, straight face

verbs

2 **to accept, take for granted** *or* as a matter of course *or* in stride *or* as it comes, treat as routine, show no amazement, refuse to be impressed, not blink an eye, not turn a hair, keep one's cool (*informal*)

adjectives

3 **unastonished, unsurprised, unamazed,** unmarvelling, unwondering, unastounded, undumbfounded, unbewildered; undazzled, undazed; unawed, aweless, wonderless; **unimpressed,** unmoved; calm, **cool,** cool as a cucumber, composed, inexcitable *see* 106.10; expecting, expected *see* 130.13, 14

124 HOPE

nouns

1 **hope, hopefulness,** hoping, **hopes,** fond or fervent hope, good hope, good cheer; aspiration, **desire** see 100; prospect, **expectation** see 130; sanguine expectation, happy or cheerful expectation; **trust, confidence, faith,** assured faith, **reliance,** dependence; conviction, assurance, security; well-grounded hope; assumption, presumption; **promise, prospect,** good or bright or fair prospect, good or hopeful prognosis, best case; great expectations, good prospects, high hopes; hoping against hope, prayerful hope; doomed hope or hopes

2 "the second soul of the unhappy"—GOETHE, "the dream of those that wake"—MATTHEW PRIOR, "the thing with feathers that perches in the soul"—EMILY DICKINSON, "the worst of all evils, because it prolongs the torments of man"—NIETZSCHE

3 **optimism,** optimisticalness, cheerful or bright or rosy outlook, rose-coloured glasses; **cheerfulness** see 109; bright side, silver lining;
"the noble temptation to see too much in everything"—CHESTERTON, "the mania of maintaining that everything is well when we are wretched"—VOLTAIRE; philosophical optimism, Leibnizian or Rousseauistic optimism, utopianism, perfectionism, perfectibilism; millenarianism, chiliasm, millennialism

4 **ray of hope,** gleam or glimmer of hope; faint hope

5 **airy hope,** unreal hope, dream, golden dream, pipe dream (informal), bubble, chimera, fool's paradise, quixotic ideal, utopia see 985.11

6 **optimist,** hoper, ray of sunshine (informal), irrepressible optimist, Dr Pangloss (Voltaire);
"a proponent of the doctrine that black is white"—AMBROSE BIERCE, "one who makes the best of it when he gets the worst of it"—ANON, "one who makes the most of all that comes and the least of all that goes"—SARA TEASDALE, Leibnizian optimist, philosophical optimist, utopian, perfectionist, perfectibilist, perfectibilitarian; millenarian, chiliast, millennialist, millennian; aspirer, aspirant, hopeful (informal)

verbs

7 **to hope,** be or live in hopes, have reason to hope, entertain or harbour the hope, cling to the hope, cherish or foster or nurture the hope; look for, prognosticate, **expect** see 130.5; **trust,** confide, presume, feel confident, rest assured; pin one's hope upon, put one's trust in, hope in, rely on, count on, lean upon, bank on, set great store on; hope for, **aspire to, desire** see 100.14; **hope against hope,** hope and pray, hope to God (informal)

8 **to be hopeful, get one's hopes up,** keep one's spirits up, keep one's pecker up, never say die, take heart, be of good hope, be of good cheer, keep hoping, keep hope alive, keep the faith (informal); **hope for the best,** knock on wood, touch wood, cross one's fingers, keep one's fingers crossed, allow oneself to hope; clutch or catch at straws

9 **to be optimistic, look on the bright side; look through** or **wear rose-coloured glasses,** voir en couleur de rose (French); call the glass half full, think positively or affirmatively, be upbeat (informal), think the best of, **make the best of it,** say that all is for the best, put a good or bold face upon, put the best face upon; see the light at the end of the tunnel; count one's chickens before they are hatched, count one's bridges before they are crossed

10 **to give hope, raise hope,** yield or afford hope, hold out hope, justify hope, inspire hope, **raise one's hopes,** raise expectations, **lead one to expect; cheer** see 109.7; inspire, inspirit; **assure, reassure,** support; **promise,** hold out promise, augur well, bid fair or well, make fair promise, have good prospects

adjectives

11 **hopeful,** hoping, **in hopes,** full of hope, in good heart, of good hope, of good cheer; **aspiring** see 100.28; **expectant** see 130.11; **sanguine,** fond; **confident,** assured; undespairing

12 **optimistic,** upbeat (informal), bright, sunny; **cheerful** see 109.11; **rosy,** roseate, rose-coloured, couleur de rose (French); Leibnizian, Rousseauistic, Panglossian; utopian see 985.23, perfectionist, perfectibilitarian, millenarian, chiliastic, millennialistic

13 **promising,** of promise, full of promise, bright with promise, pregnant of good, best-case, **favourable,** looking up; **auspicious, propitious** see 133.18; inspiring, inspiriting, **encouraging,** cheering, reassuring, supportive

adverbs

14 **hopefully,** hopingly; **expectantly** see 130.15; **optimistically; cheerfully** see 109.17; sanguinely, fondly; confidently

125 HOPELESSNESS

nouns

1 **hopelessness,** unhopefulness, no hope, not a prayer and not a hope in hell (both informal), not the ghost of a chance; small hope, bleak outlook or prospect or prognosis, worst case, blank future, no future; inexpectation see 131; futility see 391.2; impossibility see 966

2 **despair, desperation,** desperateness; no way (informal), no way out, no exit, despondency see 112.3; disconsolateness see 112.12; forlornness; cave of despair, cave of Trophonius; acedia, sloth; apathy see 94.4

3 **irreclaimability, irretrievability,** irredeemability, irrecoverableness, unsalvageability, unsalvability; incorrigibility, irreformability; irrevocability, **irreversibility; irreparability, incurability,** irremediableness, curelessness, remedilessness, immedicableness; unrelievability, unmitigability

4 **forlorn hope,** vain expectation, doomed or foredoomed hope, fond or foolish hope; counsel of perfection

5 **dashed hopes,** blighted hope, hope deferred; disappointment see 132

6 **pessimism, cynicism,** malism, nihilism; uncheerfulness see 112.2; **gloominess,** dismalness, gloomy outlook; negativism; defeatism; retreatism;

"the name that men of weak nerve give to wisdom"—BERNARD DE VOTO

7 **pessimist, cynic,** malist, nihilist; killjoy *see* 112.14, worrywart (*informal*), Job's comforter, prophet of doom, Cassandra, Eeyore; negativist; defeatist; retreatist;

"one who is not happy except when he is miserable"—ANON, "a man who feels bad when he feels good for fear he'll feel worse when he feels better"—GEORGE BURNS, "one who is always building dungeons in the air"—JOHN GALSWORTHY, "a man who thinks everybody as nasty as himself, and hates them for it"—G B SHAW

8 **lost cause,** fool's errand, wild-goose chase; **hopeless case;** goner *and* dead duck (*both informal*); terminal case

verbs

9 **to be hopeless,** have not a hope *or* prayer, look bleak *or* dark; **be pessimistic, look on the dark side,** be downbeat (*informal*), think negatively, think *or* make the worst of, put the worst face upon, call the glass half empty;

"fancy clouds where no clouds be"—THOMAS HOOD; not hold one's breath

10 **to despair,** despair of, despond *see* 112.16, falter, lose hope, **lose heart, abandon hope,** give up hope, **give up,** give up all hope *or* expectation, give way *or* over, fall *or* sink into despair, give oneself up *or* yield to despair, throw up one's hands in despair, turn one's face to the wall; curse God and die

11 **to shatter one's hopes,** dash *or* crush *or* blight one's hopes, burst one's bubble (*informal*), bring crashing down around one's head, dash the cup from one's lips, disappoint *see* 132.2, drive to despair *or* desperation

adjectives

12 **hopeless,** unhopeful, without hope, affording no hope, worst-case, bleak, grim, dismal, cheerless, comfortless; **desperate, despairing, in despair;** despondent *see* 112.22; disconsolate *see* 112.28; forlorn; apathetic *see* 94.13

13 **futile, vain** *see* 391.13; doomed, foredoomed

14 **impossible,** out of the question, not to be thought of, no-go *and* no-win *and* lose-lose (*all informal*)

15 **past hope, beyond recall,** past praying for; **irretrievable, irrecoverable, irreclaimable,** irredeemable, unsalvageable, unsalvable; incorrigible, irreformable; irrevocable, **irreversible; irremediable, irreparable,** inoperable, **incurable,** cureless, remediless, immedicable, beyond remedy, terminal; unrelievable, unmitigable; **ruined,** undone, kaput (*informal*); lost, gone, gone to hell *and* gone to hell in a handbasket (*both informal*)

16 **pessimistic,** pessimist, downbeat (*informal*), **cynical,** nihilistic; uncheerful *see* 112.21; **gloomy,** dismal, crepehanging, funereal, lugubrious; negative, negativistic; defeatist; Cassandran *or* Cassandrian, Cassandra-like

adverbs

17 **hopelessly, desperately,** forlornly; impossibly

18 irreclaimably, irretrievably, irrecoverably, irredeemably, unsalvageably, unsalvably; irrevocably, irreversibly; irremediably, incurably, irreparably

126 ANXIETY
troubled thought

nouns

1 **anxiety, anxiousness; apprehension, apprehensiveness,** antsyness (*informal*), misgiving, foreboding, forebodingness, suspense, strain, tension, stress, nervous strain *or* tension; **dread, fear** *see* 127; **concern,** concernment, anxious concern, **solicitude,** zeal *see* 101.2; **care,** cankerworm of care; **distress,** trouble, vexation, unease; **uneasiness, perturbation, disturbance,** upset, **agitation, disquiet,** disquietude, inquietude, unquietness; **nervousness** *see* 128; malaise, angst *see* 96.1; yips *and* stew (*both informal*), pins and needles, tenterhooks; overanxiety; anxious seat *or* bench; anxiety neurosis, anxiety neurosis *or* hysteria

2 **worry,** worriment (*informal*), worriedness; **worries,** worries and cares, troubles, concerns; worrying, fretting; harassment, torment

3 **worrier, worrywart** *and* nervous Nellie (*both informal*)

verbs

4 **to concern,** give concern, **trouble, bother, distress, disturb, upset,** frazzle, **disquiet, agitate;** rob one of ease *or* sleep *or* rest, keep one on edge *or* on tenterhooks *or* on pins and needles (*informal*), lead one a merry dance

5 (*make anxious*) **to worry, upset, vex,** fret, agitate, get to (*informal*), **harass,** harry, **torment,** dog, hound, plague, persecute, haunt, beset

6 (*feel anxious*) **to worry,** worry oneself, worry one's head about, worry oneself sick, trouble one's head *or* oneself, be a prey to anxiety, lose sleep; have one's heart in one's mouth, have one's heart miss *or* skip a beat, have one's heart stand still, get butterflies in one's stomach; **fret, fuss, chafe,** stew *and* take on (*both informal*), fret and fume; tense up, bite one's nails, walk the floor, go up the wall (*informal*), go spare (*informal*), be on tenterhooks *or* pins and needles (*informal*)

adjectives

7 **anxious, concerned, apprehensive,** foreboding, misgiving, suspenseful, strained, tense, tensed up (*informal*), nail-biting, white-knuckle (*informal*); **fearful** *see* 127.32; **solicitous,** zealous *see* 101.9; **troubled, bothered; uneasy, perturbed, disturbed, disquieted, agitated; nervous** *see* 128.11; **on pins and needles,** on tenterhooks, on the anxious seat *or* bench; all hot and bothered *and* in a stew (*both informal*); over-anxious, overapprehensive

8 **worried, vexed,** fretted; **harassed,** harried, tormented, dogged, hounded, persecuted, haunted, beset, plagued; worried sick, worried to a frazzle, worried stiff (*informal*)

9 **careworn,** heavy-laden, overburdened

10 troublesome, bothersome, **distressing**, distressful, **disturbing**, **upsetting**, **disquieting**; **worrisome**, worrying; fretting, chafing; **harassing**, tormenting, plaguing; **annoying** *see* 98.22

adverbs

11 anxiously, concernedly, apprehensively, misgivingly, **uneasily**; worriedly; solicitously, zealously *see* 101.14

127 FEAR, FRIGHTENINGNESS

nouns

1 fear, fright, affright; scare, alarm, consternation, dismay; dread, unholy dread, awe; terror, horror, horrification, mortal *or* abject fear; phobia (*see* list), funk *or* blue funk (*both informal*); panic, panic fear *or* terror; stampede; cowardice *see* 491

2 frighteningness, frightfulness, awfulness, scariness, fearfulness, fearsomeness, alarmingness, dismayingness, disquietingness, startlingness, disconcertingness, terribleness, dreadfulness, horror, horribleness, hideousness, appallingness, direness, ghastliness, grimness, grisliness, gruesomeness, ghoulishness; creepiness, spookiness, eeriness, weirdness, uncanniness

3 fearfulness, afraidness; timidity, timorousness, shyness; shrinkingness, bashfulness, diffidence, stage fright; skittishness, startlishness, jumpiness, gooiness (*informal*)

4 apprehension, apprehensiveness, misgiving, qualm, qualmishness, funny feeling; anxiety *see* 126; doubt *see* 954.2; foreboding

5 trepidation, trepidity, perturbation, fear and trembling; quaking, agitation *see* 105.4; uneasiness, disquiet, disquietude, inquietude; nervousness *see* 128; palpitation, heartquake; shivers *or* cold shivers (*informal*), creeps *or* cold creeps (*informal*), heebie-jeebies (*informal*), chills of fear *or* terror, icy fingers *or* icy clutch of dread, jimjams (*informal*); horripilation, gooseflesh, goose bumps (*informal*); sweat, cold sweat; thrill of fear, spasm *or* quiver of terror; sinking stomach

6 frightening, intimidation, bullying, browbeating, cowing, bulldozing (*informal*), hectoring; demoralization, psychological warfare, war of nerves

7 terrorization, terrorizing, horrification, scaremongering, panic-mongering, scare tactics; terrorism, terror *or* terroristic tactics, *Schrecklichkeit* (*German*), rule by terror, reign of terror

8 alarmist, scaremonger, panic-monger; terrorist, bomber, assassin

9 frightener, scarer, hair-raiser; scarebabe, bogey, bogeyman, bugaboo, bugbear, hobgoblin; scarecrow; horror, terror, holy terror; ogre, ogress, monster, vampire, werewolf, zombie, ghoul, bête noire, fee-faw-fum; incubus, succubus, nightmare; witch, goblin; ghost, spectre, phantom, revenant; Frankenstein, Dracula, Wolf-man; mythical monsters

verbs

10 to fear, be afraid; apprehend, have qualms, misgive, eye askance; dread, stand in dread *or* awe of, be in mortal dread *or* terror of, stand in awe of, stand aghast; be on pins and needles, sit upon thorns; have one's heart in one's mouth, have one's heart stand still, have one's heart skip *or* miss a beat; sweat, break out in a cold sweat, sweat bullets (*informal*)

11 to take fright, take alarm, push *or* press *o:* hit the panic button (*informal*); funk *and* go into a funk (*both informal*), get the wind up (*informal*), have kittens (*informal*); lose courage *see* 491.8; pale, grow *or* turn pale, change *or* turn colour; look as if one had seen a ghost; freeze, be paralysed with fear, throw up one's hands in horror; shit in one's pants *and* shit green (*both informal*)

12 to start, startle, jump, jump out of one's skin, jump a mile, leap like a startled gazelle; shy, fight shy, start aside, boggle, jib; panic, stampede, skedaddle (*informal*)

13 to flinch, shrink, shy, shy away from, draw back, recoil, funk (*informal*), quail, cringe, wince, blench, blink; put one's tail between one's legs

14 to tremble, shake, quake, shiver, quiver, quaver; tremble *or* quake *or* shake in one's boots *or* shoes, tremble like a leaf, quiver like a rabbit, shake all over

15 to frighten, fright, affright, funk (*informal*), frighten *or* scare out of one's wits; scare, spook (*informal*), scare one stiff *or* shitless *or* spitless (*informal*), scare the life out of, scare the pants off of *and* scare hell out of *and* scare the shit out of (*all informal*); scare one to death, scare the daylights *or* the living daylights *or* the wits *or* the shit out of (*informal*); give one a fright *or* scare *or* turn; alarm, disquiet, raise apprehensions; shake, stagger; startle *see* 131.8; unnerve, unman, unstring; give one goose-flesh, horripilate, give one the creeps *or* the willies (*informal*), make one's flesh creep, chill one's spine, make one's nerves tingle, curl one's hair (*informal*), make one's hair stand on end, make one's blood run cold, freeze *or* curdle the blood, make one's teeth chatter, make one tremble, take one's breath away, make one shit one's pants *or* shit green (*informal*)

16 to put in fear, put the fear of God into, throw a scare into (*informal*); panic, stampede, send scuttling, throw blind fear into

17 to terrify, awe, strike terror into; horrify, appal, shock, make one's flesh creep; frighten out of one's wits *or* senses; strike dumb, stun, stupefy, paralyse, petrify, freeze

18 to daunt, deter, shake, stop, stop in one's tracks, set back; discourage, dishearten; faze (*informal*); awe, overawe

19 to dismay, disconcert, appal, astound, confound, abash, discomfit, put out, take aback

20 to intimidate, cow, browbeat, bulldoze (*informal*), bludgeon, dragoon; bully, hector, harass, huff; bluster, bluster out of *or* into; terrorize, put in bodily fear, use terror *or* terrorist tactics, pursue a policy of *Schrecklichkeit*, systematically terrorize; threaten *see* 514.2; demoralize

21 to frighten off, **scare away**, bluff off, put to flight

adjectives

22 afraid, scared, scared to death (*informal*), spooked (*informal*); feared *or* afeared (*both informal*); fear-stricken, fear-struck; haunted with fear, phobic

23 fearful, fearing, fearsome, **in fear; cowardly** *see* 491.10; **timorous, timid, shy**, rabbity *and* mousy (*both informal*), afraid of one's own shadow; **shrinking**, bashful, diffident; scary; **skittish**, skittery (*informal*), startlish, gun-shy, jumpy, goosy (*informal*); **tremulous**, trembling, trepidant, shaky, shivery; **nervous**

24 apprehensive, misgiving, antsy (*informal*), qualmish, qualmy; anxious *see* 126.6

25 frightened, frightened to death, affrighted, in a fright, in a funk *or* blue funk (*informal*); **alarmed**, disquieted; consternated, **dismayed**, daunted; startled *see* 131.13; more frightened than hurt

26 terrified, terror-stricken, terror-struck, terror-smitten, terror-shaken, terror-troubled, terror-riven, terror-ridden, terror-driven, terror-crazed, terror-haunted; awestricken, awestruck; **horrified**, horror-stricken, horror-struck; **appalled, astounded, aghast**; frightened out of one's wits *or* mind, **scared to death, scared stiff** *or* **shitless** *or* spitless (*informal*); unnerved, unstrung, unmanned, undone, **cowed**, awed, **intimidated; stunned, petrified, stupefied**, paralysed, frozen; white as a sheet, pale as death *or* a ghost, deadly pale, ashen, blanched, pallid, grey with fear

27 panicky, panic-prone, panicked, in a panic, panic-stricken, panic-struck, terror-stricken, out of one's mind with fear, prey to blind fear

28 frightening, frightful; fearful, fearsome, fear-inspiring, nightmarish, hellish; **scary**, scaring, chilling; **alarming, startling**, disquieting, dismaying, disconcerting; **unnerving, daunting**, deterring, **deterrent**, discouraging, disheartening, fazing, awing, overawing; stunning, stupefying, mind-boggling *or* numbing

29 terrifying, terrorful, terror-striking, terror-inspiring, terror-bringing, terror-giving, terror-breeding, terror-breathing, terror-bearing, terror-fraught; **bloodcurdling, hair-raising** (*informal*); petrifying, paralysing, stunning, stupefying; **terrorizing, terror, terroristic;** *schrecklich* (*German*)

30 terrible, terrific, tremendous; **horrid, horrible, horrifying**, horrific, horrendous; **dreadful, dread**, dreaded; **awful**; awesome, awe-inspiring; **shocking, appalling**, astounding; **dire**, direful, fell; formidable, redoubtable; **hideous, ghastly**, morbid, grim, grisly, gruesome, ghoulish, macabre

31 creepy, spooky, eerie, weird, uncanny, unco *or* uncolike (*both Scottish*)

adverbs

32 fearfully, apprehensively, **diffidently**, for fear of; **timorously, timidly, shyly**, mousily (*informal*), bashfully, shrinkingly; tremulously, tremblingly, quakingly, **with** *or* **in fear and trembling**; with heart in mouth, with bated breath

33 in fear, in terror, in awe, in alarm, in consternation; in mortal fear, in fear of one's life

34 frightfully, fearfully; alarmingly, startlingly, disquietingly, dismayingly, disconcertingly; **shockingly, appallingly**, astoundingly; **terribly**, terrifically, tremendously; **dreadfully, awfully; horridly, horribly**, horrifyingly, horrifically, horrendously

35 phobias by subject

(albumin in the urine) albuminurophobia	(dirt) mysophobia
(anaemia) anemophobia	(disease) pathophobia
(animals) zoophobia	(dogs) cynophobia
(bacteria) bacteriophobia	(double vision) diplopiaphobia
(beards) pogonophobia	(draught) aerophobia
(bears) ursaphobia	(drink) potophobia
(bees) apiphobia	(drugs) pharmacophobia
(being alone) autophobia *or* monophobia *or* ermitophobia	(duration) chronophobia
	(dust) koniophobia *or* amathophobia
(being idle) thaasophobia	(electricity) electrophobia
(being whipped) mastigophobia	(enclosed places) claustrophobia
(birds) ornithophobia	(English) Anglophobia
(blood) hemaphobia *or* hematophobia *or* hemophobia	(everything) panphobia *or* pantophobia
	(eyes) ommetaphobia
(blushing) erythrophobia	(failure) kakorraphiaphobia
(body odour) bromidrosiphobia	(fatigue) kopophobia
	(fear) phobophobia
(bullets) ballistophobia	(feathers) pteronophobia
(bulls) taurophobia	(faeces) coprophobia
(cancer) cancerphobia *or* cancerophobia *or* carcinophobia	(fever) febriphobia
	(fire) pyrophobia
	(fish) ichthyophobia
(cats) ailurophobia	(floods) antlophobia
(certain places) topophobia	(flowers) anthophobia
(childbirth) tocophobia	(flutes) aulophobia
(children) pedophobia	(fog) homichlophobia
(Chinese) Sinophobia	(food) cibophobia *or* sitophobia *or* sitiophobia
(cholera) cholerophobia	
(church) ecclesiophobia	(foreigners) xenophobia
(clouds) nephelophobia	(freedom) eleutherophobia
(coitus) coitophobia	(French) Francophobia *or* Gallophobia
(cold) cheimaphobia *or* cheimatophobia	
	(fur) doraphobia
(colour) chromophobia	(Germans) Germanophobia *or* Teutonophobia
(comets) cometophobia	
(constipation) coprostasophobia	(germs) spermophobia *or* spermatophobia
(corpses) necrophobia	(ghosts) phasmophobia
(crossing a bridge) gephyrophobia	(God) theophobia
	(going to bed) clinophobia
(crossing a street) agyrophobia	(gold) aurophobia
	(gravity) barophobia
(crowds) demophobia	(gringos) gringophobia
(crystals) crystallophobia	(hair) chaetophobia *or* trichophobia
(dampness) hygrophobia	
(darkness) scotophobia *or* achluophobia	(hair disease) trichopathophobia
(dawn) eosophobia	(heart disease) cardiophobia
(death) thanatophobia	
(demons) demonophobia	(heat) thermophobia
(depth) bathophobia	(heaven) uranophobia *or* ouranophobia
(diabetes) diabetophobia	

(hell) hadephobia *or* stygiophobia
(heredity) patroiophobia
(high places) acrophobia *or* altophobia *or* batophobia *or* hypsophobia
(home) ecophobia *or* oecophobia *or* oikophobia
(homosexuals) homophobia
(horses) hippophobia
(ice, frost) cryophobia
(ideas) ideophobia
(imperfection) atelophobia
(infinity) apeirophobia
(inoculation) trypanophobia *or* vaccinophobia
(insanity) lyssophobia *or* maniaphobia
(insects) entomophobia
(insect stings) cnidophobia
(itching) acarophobia
(Japanese) Japanophobia
(jealousy) zelophobia
(Jews) Judeophobia
(justice) dikephobia
(lakes) limnophobia
(lice) pediculophobia
(light) photophobia
(light flashes) selaphobia
(lightning) astraphobia *or* astrapophobia
(machinery) mechanophobia
(magic) rhabdophobia
(marriage) gametophobia
(men) androphobia
(meningitis) meningitophobia
(metal) metallophobia
(mice) musophobia
(microbes) bacillophobia *or* microbiophobia
(mirrors) eisoptrophobia
(mites) acarophobia
(mobs) ochlophobia
(money) chrometophobia
(monsters) teratophobia
(motion) dromophobia *or* kinetophobia
(music) musicophobia
(names) onomatophobia
(narrowness) anginophobia
(needles) belonephobia
(Negroes) Negrophobia
(new things) neophobia
(night) nyctophobia
(nudity) gymnophobia *or* nudophobia
(old people) gerontophobia
(one thing) monophobia
(open places) agoraphobia
(pain) algophobia
(parasites) parasitophobia
(passing high buildings) batophobia
(pellagra) pellagraphobia
(people) anthropophobia
(philosophy) philosophobia
(pins) enetophobia
(pleasure) hedonophobia
(poison) toxiphobia *or* toxophobia *or* toxicophobia
(politics) politicophobia
(the Pope) papaphobia
(poverty) peniaphobia
(precipices) cremnophobia
(priests) hierophobia
(protein) proteinphobia
(punishment) poinephobia
(rabies) hydrophobophobia
(rectum) rectophobia
(reptiles) batrachophobia *or* herpetophobia
(responsibility) hypegiaphobia
(ridicule) katagelophobia
(rivers) potamophobia
(robbers) harpaxophobia
(ruin) atephobia
(Russians) Russophobia
(saints) hagiophobia
(Satan) Satanophobia
(scabies) scabiophobia
(sea) thalassophobia
(sex) erotophobia *or* genophobia
(shadows) sciophobia
(sharpness) acrophobia
(shock) hormephobia
(sin) hamartophobia *or* peccatiphobia
(skin) dermatosiophobia
(skin disease) dermatopathophobia
(sleep) hypnophobia
(slime) blennophobia *or* myxophobia
(small things) microphobia
(smell) olfactophobia *or* osmophobia *or* ophresiophobia
(smothering) pnigophobia *or* pnigerophobia
(snakes) ophiciophobia *or* ophiophobia *or* snakephobia
(snow) chionophobia
(soiling) rypophobia
(sound) acousticophobia
(sourness) acerophobia *or* acerbophobia
(speech) lalophobia *or* laliophobia *or* glossophobia *or* phonophobia
(speed) tachophobia
(spiders) arachnophobia
(spirits) pneumatophobia
(standing) stasophobia
(stars) siderophobia
(stealing) kleptophobia
(string) linonophobia
(sun) heliophobia
(swallowing) phagophobia
(symmetry) symmetrophobia
(syphilis) syphilophobia
(taste) geumatophobia
(technology) technophobia
(teeth) odontophobia
(telephone) telephonophobia
(thinking) phronemophobia
(thirteen, the number) tredecaphobia *or* triskaidekaphobia
(thunder) brontophobia *or* tonitrophobia *or* keraunophobia
(touch) haptophobia *or* haphophobia *or* thixophobia
(travel) hodophobia

36 phobias by name

acrophobia *or* altophobia *or* batophobia *or* hypsophobia (high places)
acrophobia (sharpness)
aerophobia (draught)
agoraphobia (open places)
agyrophobia (crossing a street)
ailurophobia (cats)
albuminurophobia (albumin in the urine)
algophobia (pain)
ancraophobia (wind)
androphobia (men)
anemophobia (anaemia)
anginophobia (narrowness)
Anglophobia (English)
anthophobia (flowers)
anthropophobia (people)
antlophobia (floods)
apeirophobia (infinity)
apiphobia (bees)
arachnophobia (spiders)
asthenophobia (weakness)
astraphobia *or* astrapophobia (lightning)
atelophobia (imperfection)
atephobia (ruin)
aulophobia (flutes)
aurophobia (gold)
autophobia *or* monophobia *or* ermitophobia (being alone)
bacillophobia *or* microbiophobia (microbes)

(trembling) tremophobia
(trichinosis) trichinophobia
(tuberculosis) tuberculophobia *or* phthisiophobia
(tyrants) tyrannophobia
(urine) urophobia
(vehicles) ochophobia
(venereal disease) venereophobia
(void) kenophobia
(vomiting) emetophobia
(water) hydrophobia
(waves) cymophobia
(weakness) asthenophobia
(wind) ancraophobia
(women) gynephobia
(words) logophobia
(work) ergophobia
(worms) vermiphobia *or* helminthophobia
(wound, injury) traumatophobia
(writing) graphophobia
(young girls) parthenophobia

bacteriophobia (bacteria)
ballistophobia (bullets)
barophobia (gravity)
bathophobia (depth)
batophobia (passing high buildings)
batrachophobia *or* herpetophobia (reptiles)
belonephobia (needles)
blennophobia *or* myxophobia (slime)
bromidrosiphobia (body odour)
brontophobia *or* tonitrophobia *or* keraunophobia (thunder)
cancerphobia *or* cancerophobia *or* carcinophobia (cancer)
cardiophobia (heart disease)
chaetophobia *or* trichophobia (hair)
cheimaphobia *or* cheimatophobia (cold)
chionophobia (snow)
cholerophobia (cholera)
chrometophobia (money)
chromophobia (colour)
chronophobia (duration)
cibophobia *or* sitophobia *or* sitiophobia (food)
claustrophobia (enclosed places)
clinophobia (going to bed)
cnidophobia (insect stings)

coitophobia (coitus)
cometophobia (comets)
coprophobia (faeces)
coprostasophobia (constipation)
cremnophobia (precipices)
cryophobia (ice)
crystallophobia (crystals)
cymophobia (waves)
cynophobia (dogs)
demonophobia (demons)
demophobia (crowds)
dermatopathophobia (skin disease)
dermatosiophobia (skin)
diabetophobia (diabetes)
dikephobia (justice)
diplopiaphobia (double vision)
doraphobia (fur)
dromophobia *or* kinetophobia (motion)
ecclesiophobia (church)
ecophobia *or* oecophobia *or* oikophobia (home)
eisoptrophobia (mirrors)
electrophobia (electricity)
eleutherophobia (freedom)
emetophobia (vomiting)
enetophobia (pins)
entomophobia (insects)
eosophobia (dawn)
ergophobia (work)
erotophobia *or* genophobia (sex)
erythrophobia (blushing)
febriphobia (fever)
Francophobia *or* Gallophobia (French)
gametophobia (marriage)
gephyrophobia (crossing a bridge)
gerontophobia (old people)
Germanophobia *or* Teutonophobia (Germans)
geumatophobia (taste)
graphophobia (writing)
gringophobia (gringos)
gymnophobia *or* nudophobia (nudity)
gynephobia (women)
hadephobia *or* stygiophobia (hell)
hagiophobia (saints)
hamartophobia *or* peccatiphobia (sin)
haptophobia *or* haphophobia *or* thixophobia (touch)
harpaxophobia (robbers)
hedonophobia (pleasure)
heliophobia (sun)
helminthophobia (worms)

hemaphobia *or* hematophobia *or* hemophobia (blood)
hierophobia (priests)
hippophobia (horses)
hodophobia (travel)
homichlophobia (fog)
homophobia (homosexuals)
hormephobia (shock)
hydrophobia (water)
hydrophobophobia (rabies)
hygrophobia (dampness)
hypegiaphobia (responsibility)
hypnophobia (sleep)
ichthyophobia (fish)
ideophobia (ideas)
Japanophobia (Japanese)
Judeophobia (Jews)
kakorraphiaphobia (failure)
katagelophobia (ridicule)
kenophobia (void)
kleptophobia (stealing)
koniophobia *or* amathophobia (dust)
kopophobia (fatigue)
lalophobia *or* laliophobia *or* glossophobia *or* phonophobia (speech)
limnophobia (lakes)
linonophobia (string)
logophobia (words)
lyssophobia *or* maniaphobia (insanity)
mastigophobia (beating)
mechanophobia (machinery)
meningitophobia (meningitis)
metallophobia (metal)
microphobia (small things)
monophobia (one thing)
musicophobia (music)
musophobia (mice)
mysophobia (dirt)
necrophobia (corpses)
Negrophobia (Negroes)
neophobia (new things)
nephophobia (clouds)
nephophobia *or* pathophobia (disease)
nyctophobia (night)
ochlophobia (mobs)
ochophobia (vehicles)
odontophobia (teeth)
olfactophobia *or* osmophobia *or* ophresiophobia (smell)
ommetaphobia (eyes)
onomatophobia (names)
ophiciophobia *or* ophiophobia *or* snakephobia (snakes)
ornithophobia (birds)

panphobia *or* pantophobia (everything)
papaphobia (the Pope)
parasitophobia (parasites)
parthenophobia (young girls)
pathophobia (disease)
patroiophobia (heredity)
pediculophobia (lice)
pedophobia (children)
pellagraphobia (pellagra)
peniaphobia (poverty)
phagophobia (swallowing)
pharmacophobia (drugs)
phasmophobia (ghosts)
philosophobia (philosophy)
phobophobia (fear)
photophobia (light)
phronemophobia (thinking)
pneumatophobia (spirits)
pnigophobia *or* pnigerophobia (smothering)
pogonophobia (beards)
poinephobia (punishment)
politicophobia (politics)
potamophobia (rivers)
potophobia (drink)
proteinphobia (protein)
pteronophobia (feathers)
pyrophobia (fire)
rectophobia (rectum)
rhabdophobia (magic)
Russophobia (Russians)
rypophobia (soiling)
Satanophobia (Satan)
scabiophobia (scabies)
sciophobia (shadows)
selaphobia (light flashes)
siderophobia (stars)
Sinophobia (Chinese)
spermophobia *or* spermatophobia (germs)
stasophobia (standing)
symmetrophobia

(symmetry)
syphilophobia (syphilis)
tachophobia (speed)
taurophobia (bulls)
technophobia (technology)
telephonophobia (telephone)
teratophobia (monsters)
thaasophobia (being idle)
thalassophobia (sea)
thanatophobia (death)
theophobia (God)
thermophobia (heat)
tocophobia (childbirth)
topophobia (certain places)
toxiphobia *or* toxophobia *or* toxicophobia (poison)
traumatophobia (wound, injury)
tredecaphobia *or* triskaidekaphobia (the number thirteen)
tremophobia (trembling)
trichinophobia (trichinosis)
trichopathophobia (hair disease)
trypanophobia *or* vaccinophobia (inoculation)
tuberculophobia *or* phthisiophobia (tuberculosis)
tyrannophobia (tyrants)
uranophobia *or* ouranophobia (heaven)
urophobia (urine)
ursaphobia (bears)
venereophobia (venereal disease)
vermiphobia *or* helminthophobia (worms)
xenophobia (foreigners)
zelophobia (jealousy)
zoophobia (animals)

128 NERVOUSNESS

nouns

1 **nervousness, nerves, disquiet, uneasiness, apprehensiveness,** disquietude, qualmishness, malaise, funny *or* creepy feeling, **qualm, qualms, misgiving;** undue *or* morbid excitability, excessive irritability, state of nerves, case of nerves, spell of nerves, attack of nerves; **agitation, trepidation; fear** *see* 127; panic; **fidgets,** fidgetiness, jitteriness, jumpiness; nail-biting; twitching, tic, vellication; stage fright, buck fever (*informal*); nervous stomach, butterflies in one's stomach (*informal*)

2 (*informal terms*) **jitters,** willies, **heebie-jeebies,** jimjams, **jumps, shakes,** quivers, trembles, dithers, collywobbles, butterflies, shivers, cold shivers, creeps, sweat, cold sweat; antsyness, ants in one's pants, yips

3 tension, tenseness, tautness, **strain, stress,** stress and strain, mental strain, nervous tension *or* strain, pressure

4 frayed nerves, frazzled nerves, jangled nerves, shattered nerves, raw nerves *or* nerve endings, twanging *or* tingling nerves; neurosis; neurasthenia, nervous prostration, crackup, **nervous breakdown**

5 nervous wreck, wreck, a bundle *or* bag of nerves

verbs

6 to fidget, have the fidgets; jitter, have the jitters, etc; **tense up; tremble**

7 to lose self-control, go into hysterics; lose courage *see* 491.8; **go to pieces,** have a nervous breakdown, fall apart *or* to pieces, come apart, fall *or* come apart at the seams

8 (*informal terms*) **to crack, crack up,** go haywire, **blow one's cork** *or* mind *or* stack, **flip,** flip one's lid *or* wig, wig out, freak, freak out, go off one's head, go out of one's skull; lose it, lose the place; come unglued *or* unstuck, go up the wall

9 to get on one's nerves, jangle the nerves, **grate on,** jar on, put on edge, **set one's teeth on edge, go against the grain, send one up the wall** (*informal*), drive one crazy; **irritate** *see* 96.14

10 to unnerve, unman, undo, unstring, unbrace, reduce to jelly, **demoralize, shake, upset,** psych out (*informal*), dash, knock down *or* flat, **crush,** overcome, prostrate

adjectives

11 nervous, nervy (*informal*); **high-strung,** overstrung, highly strung, all nerves; **uneasy, apprehensive,** qualmish, nail-biting, white-knuckle (*informal*); nervous as a cat; **excitable; irritable,** edgy, **on edge,** nerves on edge, on the ragged edge (*informal*), in a funk (*informal*), panicky, **fearful, frightened**

12 jittery (*informal*), **jumpy,** twittery, skittish, skittery, trigger-happy (*informal*), gun-shy; **shaky,** shivery, quivery, in a quiver; tremulous, tremulant, trembly; jumpy as a cat on a hot tin roof; **fidgety,** fidgeting, fluttery, all of a flutter *or* twitter; twitchy; **agitated;** shaking, trembling, quivering, shivering; shook up *and* all shook up (*both informal*)

13 tense, tensed-up, uptight (*informal*), **strained,** stretched tight, taut, unrelaxed, **under a strain**

14 unnerved, unmanned, unstrung, undone, reduced to jelly, unglued (*informal*), **demoralized, shaken, upset,** dashed, stricken, **crushed; shot,** shot to pieces; neurasthenic, prostrate, prostrated, overcome

15 unnerving, nerve-racking, nerve-rending, nerve-shaking, nerve-jangling, nerve-trying, nerve-stretching; jarring, grating

adverbs

16 nervously, shakily, shakingly, tremulously, tremblingly, quiveringly

129 UNNERVOUSNESS

nouns

1 unnervousness, nervelessness; sangfroid, **calmness, inexcitability** *see* 106; unshakiness, untremulousness; **steadiness,** steady-handedness, steady nerves; no nerves, strong nerves, iron nerves, nerves of steel, icy nerves; cool head

adjectives

2 unnervous, nerveless, without a nerve in one's body; strong-nerved, iron-nerved, steel-nerved; coolheaded, **calm, inexcitable** *see* 106.10; calm, cool and collected; cool as a cucumber (*informal*); **steady,** steady as a rock, rock-steady, steady-nerved, steady-handed; unshaky, unshaken, unquivering, untremulous, without a tremor; **unflinching,** unfaltering, unwavering, unshrinking, unblenching, unblinking; **relaxed,** unstrained

130 EXPECTATION

nouns

1 expectation, expectance *or* **expectancy,** state of expectancy; **predictability,** predictableness; **anticipation, prospect,** thought; contemplation; probability *see* 967; confidence, reliance *see* 952.1, overreliance; certainty *see* 969; imminence *see* 839; unastonishment *see* 123

2 sanguine *or* cheerful expectation, optimism, eager expectation, **hope** *see* 124; the light at the end of the tunnel

3 suspense, state of suspense, cliff-hanging *and* nail-biting (*both informal*); **waiting,** expectant waiting, hushed expectancy; uncertainty *see* 970, nervous expectation; **anxiety, dread, pessimism,** apprehension *see* 126.1

4 expectations, prospects, outlook, lookout, hopes, apparent destiny *or* fate, future prospects; likelihoods, probabilities

verbs

5 to expect, be expectant, **anticipate, have in prospect,** face, think, **contemplate,** have in contemplation *or* mind, envision, envisage; **hope** *see* 124.7; presume *see* 950.10; dread; **take for granted;** not be surprised *or* a bit surprised; foresee *see* 960.5

6 to look forward to, reckon *or* calculate *or* count on, predict, foresee; look to, **look for, watch for,** look out for, watch out for, be on the watch *or* lookout for, keep a good *or* sharp lookout for; be ready for; forestall

7 to be expected, be one's probable fate *or* destiny, be one's outlook *or* prospect, be in store

8 to await, wait, wait for, wait on *or* upon, stay *or* tarry for; have *or* keep an eye out for, lie in wait for; wait around *or* about, watch, watch and wait; **bide one's time,** bide, abide, **mark time;** cool one's heels (*informal*); be in suspense, be on tenterhooks, be on pins and needles, hold one's breath, bite one's nails, sweat *or* sweat out *or* sweat it *or* sweat it out (*all informal*); **wait up for,** stay up for, sit up for; cross one's fingers

9 to expect to, plan on *see* 380.4, 6, 7

10 to be as expected, be as one thought *or* looked for, turn out that way, come as no surprise; **be just like one,** be one all over (*informal*); **expect it of,** think that way about, **not put it past** (*informal*); **impend,** be imminent *see* 839.2; lead one to expect *see* 133.13

adjectives

11 **expectant,** expecting, in expectation *or* anticipation; **anticipative,** anticipant, anticipating, anticipatory; **holding one's breath; waiting,** awaiting, waiting for; forewarned, forearmed, forestalling, ready, prepared; **looking forward to,** looking for, watching for, on the watch *or* lookout for; gaping, agape, agog, all agog, atiptoe, atingle, **eager;** sanguine, optimistic, hopeful *see* 124.11; sure, confident *see* 952.21, 969.21; certain *see* 969.13; unsurprised, not surprised

12 **in suspense, on tenterhooks,** on pins and needles, on tiptoe, **on edge, with bated breath,** tense, taut, with muscles tense, quivering, keyed-up, biting one's nails; anxious, **apprehensive; suspenseful,** cliffhanging (*informal*)

13 **expected, anticipated, awaited, predicted, foreseen;** presumed *see* 950.14; probable *see* 967.6; **looked-for,** hoped-for; **due, promised;** long-expected, long-awaited, overdue; **in prospect, prospective; in view,** in one's eye, on the horizon; imminent *see* 839.3

14 **to be expected,** as expected, up to *or* according to expectation, just as one thought, just as predicted, on schedule, **as one may have suspected,** as one might think *or* suppose; **expected of,** counted on, **taken for granted;** just like one, one all over (*informal*), in character

adverbs

15 **expectantly,** expectingly; anticipatively, **anticipatingly,** anticipatorily; hopefully *see* 124.14; **with bated breath,** in hushed expectancy, with breathless expectation; with ears pricked up, with eyes *or* ears strained

131 INEXPECTATION

nouns

1 **inexpectation,** nonexpectation, inexpectance *or* inexpectancy, no expectation, **unanticipation; unexpectedness;** unforeseeableness, unpredictableness, unpredictability; unreadiness, unpreparedness; the unforeseen, the unlooked-for, the last thing one expects; **improbability** *see* 968

2 **surprise,** surprisal; **astonishment** *see* 122.1,2; surpriser, startler, shocker, **blow,** staggerer (*informal*), **eye-opener,** revelation; **bolt out of** *or* **from the blue,** thunderbolt, thunderclap; **bombshell,** bomb; blockbuster, earthshaker; sudden turn *or* development, *peripeteia* (*Greek*), switch; surprise ending, twist, catch (*informal*), joker (*US*), kicker (*US & Canadian informal*); surprise package; surprise party

3 **start,** shock, jar, jolt, turn

verbs

4 **to not expect,** hardly expect, **not anticipate, not look for,** not bargain for, **not foresee,** not think of, have no thought of, have no expectation, think unlikely *or* improbable

5 **to be startled, be taken by surprise,** be taken aback, be given a start, be given a turn *or* jar *or* jolt; **start, startle, jump,** jump a mile (*informal*), jump out of one's skin; **shy,** start aside, flinch

6 **to be unexpected, come unawares,** come as a surprise *or* shock, come out of nowhere, appear unexpectedly, turn up, pop up *and* bob up (*both informal*), drop from the clouds, appear like a bolt out of the blue, come *or* burst like a thunderclap *or* thunderbolt, burst *or* flash upon one, come *or* fall *or* pounce upon, steal *or* creep up on

7 **to surprise, take by surprise,** do the unexpected, spring a surprise (*informal*), **open one's eyes,** give one a revelation; **catch** *or* **take unawares,** catch *or* take short, take aback, pull up short, raise some eyebrows, wrong-foot, **catch off-guard** *see* 940.7; throw a curve (*informal*), come from behind, come from an unexpected quarter, come upon unexpectedly *or* without warning, spring *or* pounce upon; drop a bombshell, drop a brick (*informal*); **blindside** (*informal*), spring a mine under, ambush, bushwhack; drop in on (*informal*); give a surprise party; **astonish** *see* 122.6

8 **to startle, shock, electrify, jar, jolt, shake,** stun, **stagger, give one a turn** (*informal*), give the shock of one's life, make one jump out of his skin, take aback, take one's breath away, throw on one's beam ends, bowl down *or* over (*informal*), strike all of a heap (*informal*); frighten

adjectives

9 **inexpectant,** nonexpectant, unexpecting; **unanticipative,** unanticipating; **unsuspecting, unaware,** unguessing; uninformed, unwarned, unforewarned, unadvised, unadmonished; unready, unprepared; off one's guard *see* 983.8

10 **unexpected, unanticipated, unlooked for,** unhoped for, unprepared for, undivined, unguessed, unpredicted, **unforeseen;** unforeseeable, unpredictable, off-the-wall (*informal*); **improbable** *see* 968.3; contrary to expectation, beyond *or* past expectation, out of one's reckoning, more than expected, more than one bargained for; out of the blue, dropped from the clouds; without warning, unheralded, unannounced; sudden *see* 829.5; out-of-the-way, **extraordinary**

11 **surprising, astonishing** *see* 122.12; eye-opening, eye-popping (*informal*); **startling, shocking,** electrifying, staggering, stunning, jarring, jolting, mind-boggling (*informal*)

12 **surprised,** struck with surprise, openmouthed; **astonished** *see* 122.9; **taken by surprise,** taken unawares, caught short, caught on the hop

13 **startled, shocked, electrified,** jarred, jolted, shaken, shook (*informal*), staggered, **given a turn** *or* **jar** *or* **jolt,** taken aback, bowled down *or* over (*informal*), struck all of a heap (*informal*), able to be knocked down with a feather

adverbs

14 **unexpectedly,** unanticipatedly, improbably, implausibly, unpredictably, **unforseeably,** *à l'improviste* (*French*), **by surprise, unawares,** against *or* contrary to all expectation, when least expected, as no one would have predicted, without notice *or* warning, in an unguarded moment, like a thief in the night; **out of a clear sky, out of the blue, like a bolt from the blue;** suddenly *see* 829.9

15 surprisingly, startlingly, **to one's surprise,** to one's great surprise; shockingly, staggeringly, stunningly, **astonishingly** *see* 122.16

132 DISAPPOINTMENT

nouns

1 **disappointment,** sad *or* sore disappointment, bitter *or* cruel disappointment, failed *or* blasted expectation; **dashed hope, blighted hope,** betrayed hope, hope deferred, forlorn hope; **dash** (*old*), dash to one's hopes; blow, buffet; **frustration,** discomfiture, bafflement, defeat, balk, foiling; **comedown,** setback, **letdown** (*informal*), bummer (*informal*), smack in the eye (*informal*); failure, fizzle (*informal*), fiasco; **disillusionment** *see* 976; tantalization, mirage, tease; dissatisfaction *see* 108.1; fallen countenance

verbs

2 **to disappoint,** defeat expectation *or* hope; **dash,** dash *or* blight *or* blast *or* crush one's hope; **balk,** bilk, **thwart, frustrate, baffle, defeat,** foil, cross; put one's nose out of joint; **let down,** cast down; **disillusion** *see* 976.2; tantalize, tease; dissatisfy; underwhelm

3 **to be disappointing, let one down** (*informal*), not come up to expectation, come to nothing, not live *or* measure up to expectation, go wrong, turn sour, disappoint one's expectations, come *or* fall short; peter out *or* fizzle *or* fizzle out (*all informal*), not make it *and* not hack it (*both informal*), not cut the mustard (*informal*)

4 **to be disappointed,** not realize one's expectations, fail of one's hopes *or* ambitions, run into a stone wall, be let down; look blue, laugh on the other side of one's face (*informal*); be crestfallen *or* chapfallen

adjectives

5 **disappointed,** bitterly *or* sorely disappointed; choked (*informal*), gutted (*informal*); **let down,** betrayed, ill-served, ill done-by; **dashed,** blighted, blasted, crushed; **balked,** bilked, **thwarted, frustrated,** baffled, crossed, dished, defeated, foiled; "hoist with his own petard"—SHAKESPEARE, caught in one's own trap; disillusioned *see* 976.5; crestfallen, chapfallen, out of countenance; soured; dissatisfied; underwhelmed; regretful *see* 113.8

6 **disappointing,** not up to expectation, falling short, out of the running, not up to one's hopes, second- *or* third-best; tantalizing, teasing; **unsatisfactory**

133 PREMONITION

nouns

1 **premonition, presentiment, preapprehension,** forefeeling, presage, presagement; **hunch** *see* 933.3, **feeling in one's bones;** prediction *see* 961

2 foreboding, boding; **apprehension, misgiving,** chill *or* quiver along the spine, creeping *or* shudder of the flesh; wind of change

3 omen, portent; **augury,** auspice, soothsay, prognostic, prognostication; **premonitory sign** *or* **symptom,** premonitory shiver *or* chill, **foretoken,** foretokening, tokening, betokening, betokenment,

foreshowing, prefiguration, presigning (*old*), presignifying, presignification, **preindication,** indicant, indication, **sign, token,** type, **promise,** sign of the times; **foreshadowing, adumbration,** foreshadow, shadow

4 **warning, forewarning,** "warnings, and portents and evils imminent", "the baby figure of the giant mass of things to come"— SHAKESPEARE, handwriting on the wall, "*mene, mene, tekel, upharsin*"—BIBLE (*Aramaic*)

5 **harbinger, forerunner, precursor,** messenger (*old*), **herald,** announcer, *buccinator novi temporis* (*Latin*); presager, premonitor, foreshadower

6 (*omens*) bird of ill omen, owl, raven, magpie, stormy petrel, Mother Carey's chicken; gathering clouds, clouds on the horizon, dark *or* black clouds, angry clouds, storm clouds, thundercloud, thunderhead; black cat; broken mirror; rainbow; ring around the moon; shooting star; halcyon bird

7 **ominousness, portentousness, portent,** bodefulness, presagefulness, suggestiveness, significance, **meaning** *see* 518, meaningfulness; fatefulness, fatality, doomfulness, sinisterness, banefulness, balefulness, direness

8 **inauspiciousness, unpropitiousness, unfavourableness, unfortunateness, unluckiness,** ill-fatedness, ill-omenedness; fatality

9 **auspiciousness, propitiousness, favourableness; luckiness, fortunateness,** prosperousness, beneficence, benignity, benignancy, benevolence; brightness, cheerfulness, cheeriness; good omen, good auspices, *auspicium melioris aevi* (*Latin*)

verbs

10 **to foreshow, presage;** omen, be the omen of, auspicate (*old*); **foreshadow, adumbrate,** shadow, shadow forth, cast their shadows before; **predict** *see* 961.9; have an intimation, have a hunch (*informal*), feel *or* know in one's bones, feel the wind of change

11 **to forebode, bode,** portend, croak; **threaten, menace, lower,** look black, spell trouble; **warn, forewarn,** raise a warning flag, give pause; have a premonition *or* presentiment, apprehend, preapprehend, fear for

12 **to augur,** hint, divine (*old*); **foretoken, preindicate,** presignify, presign, presignal, pretypify, **prefigure,** betoken, token, typify, **signify, mean** *see* 518.8, spell, **indicate,** point to, look like, **be a sign of,** show signs of

13 **to promise, suggest, hint, imply,** give prospect of, make likely, give ground for expecting, raise expectation, **lead one to expect,** hold out hope, make fair promise, have a lot going for, have *or* show promise, **bid fair, stand fair to**

14 **to herald, harbinger, forerun,** run before; speak of, announce, proclaim, preannounce; give notice, notify, talk about

adjectives

15 augured, **foreshadowed, adumbrated, foreshown; indicated, signified; preindicated,** prognosticated, **foretokened,** prefigured, pretypified, presignified, presigned (*old*); presignalled; **presaged; threatened;** predicted *see* 961.14

16 premonitory, forewarning, augural, monitory, warning, presageful, presaging, **foretokening**, **preindicative**, indicative, prognostic, prognosticative, presignificant, prefigurative; **significant, meaningful** see 518.10, speaking; **foreshowing, foreshadowing**; big or pregnant or heavy with meaning; forerunning, precursory, precursive; intuitive see 933.5; predictive see 961.11

17 ominous, portentous, portending; **foreboding**, boding, **bodeful; inauspicious, ill-omened**, ill-boding, of ill or fatal omen, of evil portent, loaded or laden or freighted or fraught with doom, looming, looming over; fateful, doomful; apocalyptic; **unpropitious, unpromising, unfavourable, unfortunate, unlucky; sinister**, dark, black, gloomy, sombre, dreary; **threatening, menacing, lowering**; bad, evil, ill, untoward; dire, baleful, baneful, **ill-fated**, ill-starred, evil-starred, star-crossed

18 auspicious, of good omen, of happy portent; **propitious, favourable**, favouring, fair, good; **promising**, of promise, full of promise; **fortunate, lucky**, prosperous; benign, benignant, bright, happy, golden

adverbs

19 ominously, portentously, bodefully, forebodingly; significantly, meaningly, meaningfully, speakingly, sinisterly; **threateningly, menacingly**, loweringly

20 inauspiciously, unpropitiously, unpromisingly, unfavourably, unfortunately, unluckily

21 auspiciously, propitiously, promisingly, favourably; fortunately, luckily, happily; brightly

134 PATIENCE

nouns

1 patience, patientness; **tolerance, toleration, acceptance; indulgence**, lenience, leniency see 427; sweet reasonableness; **forbearance**, forbearing, forbearingness; **sufferance, endurance; long-suffering**, long-sufferance, longanimity; **stoicism**, fortitude, self-control; patience of Job; "the art of hoping"—Vauvenargues, "a minor form of despair, disguised as a virtue"—Ambrose Bierce; waiting game, waiting it out; **perseverance** see 360

2 resignation, meekness, humility, humbleness; obedience; amenability; submission, **submissiveness** see 433.3; acquiescence, compliance, uncomplainingness; **fatalism**, submission to fate or the inevitable or necessity; quietude, quietism, passivity, **passiveness** see 329.1; *zitzflaysh* (*Yiddish*); passive resistance, nonviolent resistance, nonresistance; Quakerism

3 stoic, Spartan, man of iron; Job, Griselda

verbs

4 to be patient, forbear, bear with composure, **wait**, wait it out, play a waiting game, wait around, wait one's turn, watch for one's moment, not hold one's breath (*informal*); contain oneself, possess oneself, possess one's soul in patience; carry on, carry through;

"have patience and endure"—Ovid

5 to endure, bear, stand, support, sustain, suffer, tolerate, abide, bide, live with; persevere; bear up under, bear the brunt, bear with, put up with, stand for, tolerate, carry or bear one's cross, take what comes, take the rough with the smooth, take the bitter with the sweet, abide with, brook, brave, brave out, hang in there, keep it up, rub along

6 (*informal terms*) to take it, take it on the chin, take it like a man, not let it get one down, stand the gaff; bite the bullet; hold still or stand still for, swallow, stick, hang in, hang in there, hang tough, tough or stick it out; lump it

7 to accept, condone, countenance; overlook, not make an issue of, let go by, let pass; reconcile oneself to, resign oneself to, yield or submit to, obey; accustom or accommodate or adjust oneself to, sit through; accept one's fate, lay in the lap of the gods, take things as they come, roll with the punches (*informal*); make the best of it, make the most of it, make the best of a bad bargain, make a virtue of necessity; submit with a good grace, grin and bear it, grin and abide, shrug, shrug it off, slough off, not let it bother one; take in good part, take in one's stride; rise above

8 to take, pocket, swallow, down, stomach, eat, digest, disregard, turn a blind eye, ignore; swallow an insult, pocket the affront, turn the other cheek, take it lying down, turn aside provocation

adjectives

9 patient, armed with patience, with a soul possessed in patience, patient as Job, Job-like, Griselda-like, "like patience on a monument smiling at grief"—Shakespeare; **tolerant**, tolerative, tolerating, accepting; understanding, **indulgent**, lenient; **forbearing**; philosophical; **long-suffering**, longanimous; **enduring**, endurant; stoic, stoical, Spartan; disciplined, self-controlled; **persevering**

10 resigned, reconciled; wait-and-see; **meek**, humble; obedient, amenable, **submissive** see 433.12; acquiescent, compliant; accommodating, adjusting, adapting, adaptive; unresisting, **passive** see 329.6; **uncomplaining**

adverbs

11 patiently, enduringly, stoically; **tolerantly, indulgently**, longanimously, leniently, forbearantly, forbearingly, philosophically, more in sorrow than in anger; **perseveringly**

12 resignedly, meekly, submissively, passively, acquiescently, compliantly, uncomplainingly

phrases

13 Rome wasn't built in a day; all in good time; all things come to him who waits; don't hold your breath; time will tell

135 IMPATIENCE

nouns

1 impatience, impatientness, unpatientness, breathless impatience; **anxiety, eagerness** see 101; tense readiness, **restlessness**, restiveness, ants in one's pants (*informal*), prothymia; **disquiet**, disquietude, unquietness, uneasiness, **nervousness** *see* 128; sweat *and* lather *and* stew (*all informal*), **fretfulness,** fretting, chafing; **impetuousness** *see* 365.2; **haste** *see* 401; excitement *see* 105

2 **intolerance,** intoleration, unforbearance, nonendurance

3 **the last straw,** the straw that breaks the camel's back, the limit, the limit of one's patience, all one can bear *or* stand

verbs

4 **to be impatient,** hardly wait; hasten *see* 401.4, 5; itch to, burn to; **champ at the bit, pull at the leash,** not be able to sit down *or* stand still, have ants in one's pants; **chafe, fret, fuss,** squirm; **stew,** sweat, sweat and stew, get into a dither, get into a stew (*informal*), work oneself into a lather *or* sweat (*informal*), get excited; wait impatiently, sweat it out (*informal*), pace the floor; beat the gun, jump the gun (*informal*), go off half-cocked, shoot from the hip

5 **to have no patience with,** be out of all patience; **lose patience,** run out of patience, call a halt, have had it (*informal*), blow the whistle (*informal*)

adjectives

6 **impatient,** unpatient; breathless; champing at the bit, rarin' to go (*informal*); dying, **anxious, eager;** in a lather *and* in a sweat *or* stew (*all informal*), excited *see* 105.18; edgy, **on edge; restless,** restive, unquiet, uneasy; **fretful,** fretting, chafing, squirming, squirmy, about to pee *or* piss one's pants (*informal*); **impetuous** *see* 365.9; **hasty** *see* 401.9

7 **intolerant, unforbearing, unindulgent**

adverbs

8 **impatiently,** breathlessly; **anxiously;** fretfully; restlessly, restively, uneasily; intolerantly

136 PRIDE

nouns

1 **pride,** proudness, pridefulness; **self-esteem, self-respect,** self-confidence, self-reliance, self-consequence, face, independence, self-sufficiency; pardonable pride; obstinate *or* stiff-necked pride, stiff-neckedness; **vanity, conceit** *see* 140.4; haughtiness, **arrogance** *see* 141; boastfulness *see* 502.1

2 **proud bearing,** pride of bearing, military *or* erect bearing, stiff *or* straight backbone, **dignity,** dignifiedness, **stateliness,** courtliness, grandeur, **loftiness;** pride of place; **nobility,** lordliness, princeliness; **majesty,** regality, kingliness, queenliness; worthiness, augustness, venerability; **sedateness, solemnity** *see* 111, gravity, *gravitas* (*Latin*), sobriety

3 proudling; stiff neck; egoist *see* 140.5; boaster *see* 502.5; the proud

verbs

4 **to be proud,** hold up one's head, hold one's head high, stand up straight, hold oneself erect, never stoop; look one in the face *or* eye; stand on one's own two feet, pay one's own way

5 **to take pride, pride oneself, preen oneself,** plume oneself on, pique oneself on, **congratulate oneself,** hug oneself; **be proud of,** glory in, exult in, **burst with pride**

6 **to make proud,** do one's heart good, do one proud (*informal*), **gratify, elate,** flush, turn one's head

7 to save face, save one's face, preserve one's dignity, guard *or* preserve one's honour, be jealous of one's repute *or* good name

adjectives

8 **proud, prideful; self-esteeming, self-respecting;** self-confident, self-reliant, **independent, self-sufficient;** proudhearted, proud-minded, proud-spirited, proud-blooded; proud-looking; proud as Punch, proud as Lucifer, proud as a peacock; erect, stiff-backed, **stiff-necked;** purse-proud, house-proud

9 **vain, conceited** *see* 140.11; haughty, **arrogant** *see* 141.9; boastful *see* 502.10

10 **puffed up,** swollen, bloated, swollen *or* bloated *or* puffed-up with pride; elated, flushed, flushed with pride

11 **lofty, elevated,** triumphal, high, high-flown, highfalutin *and* highfaluting (*both informal*), high-toned (*informal*); high-minded, lofty-minded; high-headed, high-nosed (*informal*), toffee-nosed (*informal*)

12 **dignified, stately, imposing, grand, courtly,** magisterial, aristocratic; **noble,** lordly, princely; **majestic,** regal, royal, kingly, queenly; worthy, **august, venerable;** statuesque; **sedate, solemn** *see* 111.3, sober, grave

adverbs

13 **proudly, pridefully, with pride;** self-esteemingly, self-respectingly, self-confidently, self-reliantly, independently, self-sufficiently; erectly, with head erect, with head held high, with nose in air; stiff-neckedly; like a lord, *en grand seigneur* (*French*)

14 **dignifiedly, with dignity;** nobly, stately, imposingly, loftily, grandly, magisterially; majestically, regally, royally; worthily, augustly, venerably; sedately, solemnly, soberly, gravely

137 HUMILITY

nouns

1 **humility, humbleness, meekness; lowliness,** lowlihood, poorness, meanness, smallness, ingloriousness, undistinguishedness; unimportance *see* 997; innocuousness *see* 998.9; teachableness *see* 570.5; submissiveness *see* 433.3; **modesty,** unpretentiousness *see* 139.1; plainness, simpleness, homeliness

2 **humiliation,** mortification (*old*), egg on one's face (*informal*), **chagrin, embarrassment** *see* 96.4, egg on one's face (*informal*); **abasement,** debasement, letdown, setdown, put-down *and* dump (*both informal*); **comedown,** descent, deflation, wounded *or* humbled pride; self-diminishment, **self-abasement, self-abnegation** *see* 652.1; **shame, disgrace;** shamefacedness, shamefastness, hangdog look

3 condescension, condescendence, deigning, lowering oneself, stooping from one's high place

verbs

4 to humiliate, humble; mortify (*old*), **embarrass** *see* 96.15; put out, put out of face *or* countenance; **shame, disgrace,** put to shame, put to the blush, give one a red face; **deflate,** prick one's balloon; take it out of

5 to abase, debase, crush, abash, **degrade, reduce,** diminish, **demean,** lower, **bring low,** bring down, trip up, take down, set down, put in one's place, put down, dump *and* dump on (*both informal*), knock one off his perch; take down a peg *or* notch or two (*informal*), make a fool *or* an arse *or* a monkey of one

6 (*informal terms*) to beat *or* knock *or* cut one **down to size,** take the wind out of one's sails; put one's nose out of joint, put a tuck in one's tail

7 to humble oneself, demean oneself, abase oneself, climb down *and* get down from one's high horse (*both informal*); put one's pride in one's pocket; **eat humble pie,** eat one's words, swallow one's pride, lick the dust, take *or* eat shit *or* dirt (*informal*), eat crow (*US & Canadian informal*); come on bended knee, come cap in hand; go down on one's knees; pull *or* draw in one's horns (*informal*); come down a peg *or* a peg or two; **deprecate** *or* **depreciate oneself,** diminish oneself, discount oneself, belittle oneself; kiss one's arse (*informal*) *see* 138.7

8 to condescend, deign, vouchsafe; stoop, descend, lower *or* demean oneself, trouble oneself, set one's dignity aside *or* to one side; **patronize;** be so good as to, so forget oneself, dirty *or* soil one's hands; talk down to, talk *de haut en bas* (*French*, from high to low)

9 to be humiliated, be put out of countenance; **be crushed, feel small, feel cheap,** look foolish *or* silly, be ready to sink through the floor; **take shame, be ashamed, feel ashamed of oneself,** be put to the blush, have a very red face; bite one's tongue; hang one's head, hide one's face, not dare to show one's face, not have a word to say for oneself; drink the cup of humiliation to the dregs

adjectives

10 humble, lowly, low, poor, mean, small, inglorious, undistinguished; unimportant *see* 997.16; innocuous; biddable, teachable *see* 570.18; **modest, unpretentious** *see* 139.9; **plain, simple,** homely; humble-looking, humble-visaged; humblest, lowliest, lowest, least

11 humble-hearted, humble-minded, humble-spirited, poor in spirit; **meek,** meek-hearted, meek-minded, meek-spirited, lamblike, Christlike; **abject,** submissive *see* 433.12

12 self-abasing, self-abnegating, self-deprecating, self-depreciating *see* 139.10, self-doubting

13 humbled, reduced, diminished, lowered, brought down *or* low, set down, bowed down, in the dust; on one's knees, on one's marrowbones (*informal*)

14 humiliated, humbled, mortified (*old*), **embarrassed, chagrined, abashed, crushed,** out of countenance; blushing, ablush, **red-faced,**

ashamed, shamed, ashamed of oneself, shamefaced, shamefast; crestfallen, chapfallen, hangdog

15 humiliating, humiliative, humbling, chastening, mortifying, **embarrassing,** crushing, cringe-making (*informal*)

adverbs

16 humbly, meekly; modestly *see* 139.14; with due deference, with bated breath, "with bated breath and whispering humbleness"— SHAKESPEARE; submissively *see* 433.17; **abjectly,** on bended knee, **on one's knees,** on one's marrowbones (*informal*), on all fours, with one's tail between one's legs, cap in hand

138 SERVILITY

nouns

1 servility, slavishness, subservience *or* subserviency, menialness, abjectness, **baseness,** meanness; **submissiveness** *see* 433.3; slavery, helotry, helotism, serfdom, peonage

2 obsequiousness, sycophancy, fawningness, fawnery, **toadyism,** flunkyism; parasitism, sponging; **ingratiation,** insinuation; **truckling, fawning, toadying,** toadeating, grovelling, crawling, cringing, **bootlicking** (*informal*), back scratching, tufthunting (*old*); **apple-polishing** *and* **handshaking** (*both US & Canadian informal*); arse-licking *and* arse-kissing *and* brown-nosing *and* sucking up (*all informal*); timeserving; obeisance, prostration; mealymouthedness

3 sycophant, flatterer, toady, toad, toadeater, lickspit, lickspittle, **truckler, fawner,** courtier, led captain *and* tufthunter (*both old*), kowtower, groveller, crawler, cringer, spaniel; flunky, lackey; timeserver; creature, **puppet,** minion, lap dog, **tool,** cat's-paw, dupe, instrument, faithful servant, slave, helot, serf, peon; mealymouth

4 (*informal terms*) **apple-polisher, arse-kisser, brown-nose,** brown-noser, brownie, arse-licker, arse-wiper, bumsucker, suck-arse; **backslapper,** backscratcher, clawback, back-patter; **bootlicker,** bootlick; **yes-man, stooge**

5 parasite, barnacle, leech; **sponger,** sponge (*informal*), freeloader (*informal*); beat *and* deadbeat (*both informal*)

6 hanger-on, adherent, dangler, appendage, **dependent, satellite, follower,** cohort, retainer, servant, man, shadow, tagtail, **henchman,** heeler (*informal*)

verbs

7 to fawn, truckle; flatter; toady, toadeat; **bootlick** (*informal*), lickspittle, lick one's shoes, lick the feet of; **grovel,** crawl, creep, cower, cringe, crouch, stoop, kneel, bend the knee, fall on one's knees, prostrate oneself, throw oneself at the feet of, fall at one's feet, kiss *or* lick *or* suck one's arse *and* brown-nose (*all informal*), kiss one's feet, kiss the hem of one's garment, lick the dust, make a doormat of oneself; kowtow, bow, **bow and scrape**

8 to toady to, truckle to, pander to, cater to, cater for; **wait on** *or* **upon,** wait on hand and foot, dance attendance, do service, fetch and carry, do the dirty work of, do *or* jump at the bidding of

9 to **curry favour, court, pay court to**, make court to, run after (*informal*), dance attendance on; **shine up to**, make up to (*informal*); **suck up to** *and* **play up to** *and* act up to (*all informal*); be a yes-man (*informal*), agree to anything; fawn upon, fall over *or* all over (*informal*); **handshake** *and* back-scratch *and* **polish the apple** (*all informal*)

10 **to ingratiate oneself**, insinuate oneself, worm oneself in, creep into the good graces of, get in with *or* next to (*informal*), **get on the good** *or* **right side of**, rub the right way (*informal*)

11 **to attach oneself to**, pin *or* fasten oneself upon, hang about *or* around, dangle, hang on the skirts of, hang on the sleeve of, become an appendage of, **follow**, follow at heel; follow the crowd, get on the bandwagon, go with the stream, run with the hare and hunt with the hounds

12 **to sponge** *and* **sponge on** *and* **sponge off of** (*all informal*); feed on, fatten on, batten on, live off of, use as a meal ticket

adjectives

13 **servile, slavish**, subservient, **menial, base**, mean; **submissive** *see* 433.12

14 **obsequious, flattering**, sycophantic, sycophantical, toadyish, fawning, flattering, truckling, ingratiating, smarmy (*informal*), slimy (*informal*), toadying, toadeating, **bootlicking** *and* back scratching *and* backslapping *and* arse-licking *and* brown-nosing (*all informal*); **grovelling**, snivelling, cringing, cowering, crouching, crawling; **parasitic**, leechlike, sponging (*informal*); timeserving; **abject**, beggarly, hangdog; obeisant, prostrate, on one's knees, on one's marrowbones (*informal*), on bended knee; mealymouthed

adverbs

15 **servilely, slavishly**, subserviently, menially, "in a bondman's key"—SHAKESPEARE; **submissively** *see* 433.17

16 **obsequiously, sycophantically, ingratiatingly, fawningly, trucklingly**; hat-in-hand, cap-in-hand; **abjectly**, obeisantly, grovellingly, on one's knees; parasitically

139 MODESTY

nouns

1 **modesty, meekness**; humility *see* 137; **unpretentiousness**, unassumingness, unpresumptuousness, **unostentatiousness**, unambitiousness, unobtrusiveness, unboastfulness

2 **self-effacement, self-depreciation**, self-deprecation, self-detraction, undervaluing of self, self-doubt, **diffidence**; hiding one's light under a bushel; low self-esteem, weak ego, lack of self-confidence *or* self-reliance, self-distrust; inferiority complex

3 **reserve, restraint, constraint**, backwardness, retiring disposition; low key, low visibility, low profile

4 **shyness, timidity**, timidness, timorousness, **bashfulness**, shamefacedness, shamefastness, pudicity, pudency, pudibundity *and* pudibundness *and* verecundity (*all old*); **coyness, demureness**, demurity, skittishness, mousiness; self-consciousness, embarrassment; stammering, confusion; stage fright

5 **blushing, flushing**, colouring, mantling, reddening, crimsoning; **blush, flush**, suffusion, red face

6 shrinking violet, modest violet, mouse

verbs

7 **to efface oneself**, depreciate *or* deprecate *or* doubt *or* distrust oneself; have low self-esteem; reserve oneself, retire, shrink, **retire into one's shell, keep in the background**, not thrust oneself forward, **keep a low profile**, keep oneself to oneself, keep one's distance, remain in the shade, take a back seat *and* play second fiddle (*both informal*), hide one's face, hide one's light under a bushel, avoid the limelight, eschew self-advertisement; pursue the noiseless tenor of one's way,
"blush unseen"—THOMAS GRAY, "do good by stealth and blush to find it fame"—POPE

8 **to blush, flush**, mantle, **colour**, change colour, colour up, redden, crimson, turn red, have a red face, get red in the face, blush up to the eyes; stammer; squirm with self-consciousness *or* embarrassment

adjectives

9 **modest, meek**; humble; **unpretentious**, unpretending, **unassuming**, unpresuming, unpresumptuous, **unostentatious**, unobtrusive, unimposing, unboastful; unambitious, unaspiring

10 **self-effacing, self-depreciative, self-depreciating**, self-deprecating; **diffident**, deprecatory, deprecative, self-doubting, unself-confident, unsure of oneself, unself-reliant, self-distrustful, self-mistrustful; low in self-esteem

11 **reserved, restrained, constrained**; quiet; low-keyed, keeping low visibility *or* a low profile; **backward, retiring, shrinking**

12 **shy, timid**, timorous, **bashful**, shamefaced, shamefast, pudibund *and* verecund *and* verecundious (*all old*); **coy, demure**, skittish, mousy; self-conscious, conscious, confused; stammering, inarticulate

13 **blushing**, blushful; **flushed**, red, ruddy, red-faced, red in the face; **sheepish; embarrassed**

adverbs

14 **modestly, meekly**; humbly; **unpretentiously**, unpretendingly, **unassumingly**, unpresumptuously, **unostentatiously**, unobtrusively; quietly, without ceremony, *sans façon* (*French*)

15 **shyly, timidly**, timorously, **bashfully, coyly, demurely**, diffidently; **shamefacedly**, shamefastly, **sheepishly**, blushingly, with downcast eyes

140 VANITY

nouns

1 **vanity, vainness**; overproudness, overweening pride; **self-importance**, consequentiality,

consequentialness, **self-esteem,** high self-esteem *or* self-valuation, positive self-image, self-respect, self-assumption; **self-admiration,** self-delight, self-worship, self-endearment, **self-love,** *amour-propre* (*French*), self-infatuation, narcissism, narcism; autoeroticism, autoerotism, masturbation; **self-satisfaction, self-content,** ego trip (*informal*), self-approbation, self-congratulation, self-gratulation, self-complacency, **smugness,** complacency, self-sufficiency; vainglory, vaingloriousness;

"an itch for the praise of fools"—ROBERT BROWNING

2 pride *see* 136; arrogance *see* 141; boastfulness *see* 502.1

3 egotism, egoism, egoisticalness, egotisticalness, **ego** (*informal*), self-interest, individualism,

"the tongue of vanity"—CHAMFORT; **egocentricity,** egocentrism, self-centredness, self-obsession; selfishness *see* 651

4 conceit, conceitedness, **self-conceit, self-conceitedness, immodesty,** side, self-assertiveness; **stuck-upness** (*informal*), chestiness (*informal*), swollen-headedness, swollen head, big head, large hat size; **cockiness** (*informal*), pertness, perkiness; aggressive self-confidence, obtrusiveness, bumptiousness

5 egotist, egoist, egocentric, individualist; narcissist, narcist, Narcissus; **swellhead** (*informal*), **braggart** *see* 502.5, know-it-all *or* know-all, smart-arse *and* wise-arse (*both informal*), smarty-pants *or* smarty-boots (*informal*), smart aleck, clever dick, clever clogs, no modest violet,

"a person of low taste, more interested in himself than in me"—AMBROSE BIERCE

verbs

6 to be stuck on oneself (*informal*), be impressed *or* overly impressed with oneself; ego-trip *and* be *or* go on an ego trip (*all informal*); think well of oneself, think one is it *or* one's shit doesn't stink (*informal*), get too big for one's breeches, have a swollen head, know it all, have no false modesty, have no self-doubt, love the sound of one's own voice, be blinded by one's own glory, lay the flattering unction to one's soul; fish for compliments; blow one's own trumpet, **boast** *see* 502.6, 7; be vain as a peacock, give oneself airs *see* 501.14

7 to puff up, inflate, swell; go to one's head, turn one's head

adjectives

8 vain, vainglorious, overproud, overweening; **self-important, self-esteeming,** having high self-esteem *or* self-valuation, self-respecting, self-assuming, consequential; **self-admiring,** self-delighting, self-worshipping, self-loving, self-endeared, self-infatuated, narcissistic, narcistic; autoerotic, masturbatory; **self-satisfied, self-content,** self-contented, self-approving, self-gratulating, self-gratulatory, self-congratulating, self-congratulatory, self-complacent, **smug,** complacent, self-sufficient

9 proud *see* 136.8; arrogant *see* 141.9; boastful *see* 502.10

10 egotistic, egotistical, egoistic, egoistical, self-interested; **egocentric,** egocentristic, self-centred, self-obsessed, narcissistic, narcistic; selfish *see* 651.5

11 conceited, self-conceited, immodest, self-opinionated; **stuck-up** (*informal*), toffee-nosed (*informal*), **puffed up,** chesty (*informal*); swollen-headed, **swelled-headed, big-headed** *and* too big for one's boots *or* britches *and* **cocky** (*all informal*), jumped-up (*informal*); pert, perk, perky; peacockish, peacocky; know-all *or* know-it-all, smart-arse *and* wise-arse (*both informal*), smarty, smart-alecky, overwise, wise in one's own conceit; aggressively self-confident, obtrusive, bumptious

12 stuck on oneself (*informal*), impressed with oneself, pleased with oneself, full of oneself, all wrapped up in oneself

adverbs

13 vainly, self-importantly; **egotistically,** egoistically; **conceitedly,** self-conceitedly, immodestly; cockily (*informal*), pertly, perkily

141 ARROGANCE

nouns

1 arrogance, arrogantness; overbearingness, overbearing pride, overweening pride, stiff-necked pride, assumption of superiority, domineering, domineeringness; **pride,** proudness; superbia, sin of pride, chief of the deadly sins; **haughtiness, hauteur; loftiness,** Olympian loftiness *or* detachment; **toploftiness** *and* stuckupness *and* uppishness *and* uppityness (*all informal*), hoity-toitiness, hoity-toity; side (*informal*), haughty airs, airs of *de haut en bas*; high horse (*informal*); **condescension,** condescendence, patronizing, patronization, patronizing attitude

2 presumptuousness, presumption, overweening, overweeningness, assumption, total self-assurance; hubris; insolence *see* 142

3 lordliness, imperiousness, masterfulness, magisterialness, **high-and-mightiness,** aristocratic presumption; elitism

4 aloofness, standoffishness, offishness (*informal*), chilliness, coolness, distantness, remoteness

5 disdainfulness, disdain, aristocratic disdain, **contemptuousness, superciliousness,** contumeliousness, cavalierness

6 snobbery, snobbishness, snobbiness, snobbism; **priggishness, priggery,** priggism; snootiness *and* snottiness *and* sniffiness *and* high-hattedness *and* high-hattiness (*all informal*); tufthunting

7 snob, prig; elitist; **highbrow** *and* egghead (*both informal*), Brahmin, mandarin; name-dropper, tufthunter (*old*);

"he who meanly admires a mean thing"—THACKERAY

verbs

8 to give oneself airs *see* 501.14; **hold one's nose in the air, look down one's nose,** toss the head, bridle; mount *or* get on one's high horse *and* ride the high horse (*all informal*); **condescend, patronize, deign,** vouchsafe, stoop, descend, lower *or* demean oneself, trouble oneself, set one's dignity aside *or* to one side, be so good as to, so forget oneself, dirty *or* soil one's hands; deal with *or* treat *de haut en bas* (*French,* from high to low) or *en grand seigneur* (*French,* like a great lord), talk down to, talk *de haut en bas*

adjectives

9 **arrogant, overbearing, superior,** domineering, **proud, haughty; lofty, top-lofty** (*informal*); high-flown, high-falutin *and* high-faluting (*both informal*); high-headed; high-nosed *and* **stuck-up** *and* **uppish** *and* uppity *and* **upstage** (*all informal*), **toffee-nosed** (*informal*); **hoity-toity,** big, big as you please, six feet above contradiction; on one's high horse; **condescending, patronizing,** *de haut en bas* (*French*)

10 **presumptuous,** presuming, assuming, overweening, would-be, self-elect, self-elected, self-appointed, self-proclaimed, *soi-disant* (*French*); **insolent**

11 **lordly, imperious,** aristocratic, totally self-assured; hubristic; masterful, magisterial, **high-and-mighty;** elitist; U (*informal*); dictatorial *see* 417.16

12 **aloof, standoffish,** standoff, offish (*informal*), chilly, cool, distant, remote, above all that; Olympian

13 **disdainful,** dismissive, **contemptuous, supercilious,** contumelious, cavalier

14 **snobbish,** snobby, toffee-nosed (*informal*), **priggish,** snippy (*informal*); **snooty** *and* **snotty** *and* sniffy (*all informal*); **high-hat** *and* high-hatted *and* high-hatty (*all informal*)

adverbs

15 **arrogantly, haughtily, proudly,** aloofly; **condescendingly, patronizingly,** *de haut en bas* *and* *en grand seigneur* (*both French*); loftily, toploftily (*informal*); imperiously, magisterially; Olympianly; **disdainfully, contemptuously,** superciliously, contumeliously; with nose in air, with nose turned up, with head held high, with arms akimbo

16 **presumptuously,** overweeningly, aristocratically; hubristically; **insolently**

17 snobbishly, snobbily, **priggishly;** snootily *and* snottily (*both informal*)

142 INSOLENCE

nouns

1 **insolence; presumption,** presumptuousness; **audacity, effrontery,** boldness, assurance, hardihood, bumptiousness; **hubris;** overweening, overweeningness; **contempt** *see* 157, **contemptuousness,** contumely; **disdain** *see* 141.5, *sprezzatura* (*Italian*); **arrogance** *see* 141, uppishness *and* uppityness (*both informal*); obtrusiveness, pushiness (*informal*)

2 **impudence, impertinence,** flippancy, procacity *and* malapertness (*both old*), pertness, **sauciness,** sassiness (*informal*), **cockiness,** *and* cheekiness (*both informal*), freshness (*informal*), bounce, **brazenness,** brazenfacedness, brassiness (*informal*), face of brass, **rudeness** *see* 505.1, **brashness,** disrespect, disrespectfulness, derision, ridicule *see* 508

3 (*informal terms*) **cheek,** face, front, brass, brass neck, **nerve, gall, chutzpah,** crust

4 **sauce** *and* sass *and* lip (*informal*), **back talk,** backchat (*informal*)

5 (*impudent person*) malapert (*old*); minx, hussy; whippersnapper, puppy, pup, young pup, upstart; boldface, brazenface; *chutzpadik* (*Yiddish*); swaggerer *see* 503.2

6 (*informal terms*) **smart aleck,** smarty, smart guy, smartmouth, smart-arse, wise-arse, smarty-pants, clever clogs, wisenheimer, wise guy, saucebox

verbs

7 **to have the audacity, have the cheek; have the gall** *or* a nerve *or* one's nerve (*informal*); **get fresh** (*informal*), get smart (*informal*), forget one's place, **dare, presume,** take liberties, make bold *or* free; hold in contempt *see* 157.3, ridicule, taunt, deride *see* 508.8

8 **to sauce** *and* sass (*both informal*), **talk back,** answer back, lip *and* give one lip (*both informal*), provoke

adjectives

9 **insolent,** insulting; **presumptuous,** presuming, overpresumptuous, overweening; **audacious, bold,** assured, hardy, bumptious; **contemptuous** *see* 157.8, contumelious; **disdainful** *see* 141.13, **arrogant** *see* 141.9, uppish *and* uppity (*both informal*); hubristic; forward, pushy (*informal*), obtrusive, familiar; cool, cold

10 **impudent, impertinent, pert,** malapert *and* procacious (*both old*), flip (*informal*), flippant, **cocky** *and* cheeky *and* **fresh** *and* facy *and* crusty *and* nervy (*all informal*), chutzpadik (*Yiddish*); uncalled-for, gratuitous, biggety (*informal*); **rude** *see* 505.4, 6, **disrespectful,** derisive *see* 508.12, brash, bluff; **saucy,** sassy (*informal*); smart *or* smart-alecky (*informal*), smart-arse (*informal*)

11 **brazen,** brazenfaced, boldfaced, barefaced, brassy (*informal*), **bold,** bold as brass (*informal*), unblushing, unabashed, aweless, **shameless,** dead *or* lost to shame; swaggering *see* 503.4

adverbs

12 **insolently, audaciously,** bumptiously, contumeliously; **arrogantly** *see* 141.15; **presumptuously,** obtrusively, pushily (*informal*); **disdainfully** *see* 141.15

13 **impudently, impertinently,** pertly, procaciously *and* malapertly (*both old*), flippantly, **cockily** *and* cheekily (*both informal*), saucily; **rudely** *see* 505.8, brashly, disrespectfully, contemptuously *see* 157.9, derisively *see* 508.15, in a smart-alecky way (*informal*), in a smart-arse fashion (*informal*)

14 **brazenly,** brazenfacedly, **boldly,** boldfacedly, **shamelessly,** unblushingly

143 KINDNESS, BENEVOLENCE

nouns

1 **kindness, kindliness,** kindly disposition; **benignity,** benignancy; **goodness, decency,** niceness; **graciousness; kindheartedness,** goodheartedness, warmheartedness, softheartedness, tenderheartedness, kindness *or* goodness *or* warmth *or* softness *or*

tenderness of heart, affectionateness, warmth, **loving kindness,**
"milk of human kindness"—SHAKESPEARE; soul of kindness, kind heart, heart of gold; **brotherhood,** fellow feeling, **sympathy,** fraternal feeling, feeling of kinship; **pity** *see* 145, **mercy, compassion; humaneness,** humanity; charitableness

2 **good nature, good humour,** good disposition, good temper, sweetness, sweet temper *or* nature, good-naturedness, good-humouredness, good-temperedness, bonhomie; **amiability,** affability, geniality, cordiality; **gentleness,** mildness, lenity

3 **considerateness, consideration, thoughtfulness,** mindfulness, heedfulness, regardfulness, attentiveness, **solicitousness,** solicitude, thought, regard, concern, delicacy, **sensitivity,** tact, tactfulness; indulgence, toleration, leniency *see* 427; complaisance, accommodatingness, **helpfulness,** obligingness, agreeableness

4 **benevolence,** benevolentness, benevolent disposition, well-disposedness, **beneficence, charity,** charitableness, **philanthropy; altruism,** philanthropism, **humanitarianism,** welfarism, do-goodism; utilitarianism, Benthamism, greatest good of the greatest number; **goodwill,** grace, brotherly love, charity, Christian charity *or* love, *caritas* (*Latin*), love of mankind, good will to *or* toward man, love, *agape* (*Greek*), flower power; **bigheartedness,** largeheartedness, greatheartedness; **generosity** *see* 485; giving *see* 478

5 **welfare; welfare work, social service,** social welfare, social work; child welfare, etc; commonweal, public welfare; welfare state, welfare statism, welfarism; social security, the dole, relief

6 **benevolences,** philanthropies, charities; works, **good works,** public service

7 **act of kindness, kindness, favour,** mercy, **benefit,** benefaction, benevolence, benignity, blessing, **service,** turn, break (*informal*), **good turn, good** *or* **kind deed,** *mitzvah* (*Hebrew*), office, good *or* kind offices, obligation, grace, act of grace, courtesy, kindly act, labour of love

8 **philanthropist, altruist,** benevolist, **humanitarian,** man of good will, **do-gooder,** bleeding heart (*informal*), well-doer, power for good; welfare worker, social worker, caseworker; welfare statist; almsgiver, almoner; Robin Hood, Lady Bountiful

verbs

9 **to be kind,** be good *or* nice, show kindness; treat well, do right by; favour, oblige, accommodate

10 **to be considerate,** consider, respect, regard, think of, **be thoughtful of,** have consideration *or* regard for; be at one's service, fuss over one, spoil one (*informal*)

11 **to be benevolent, bear good will,** wish well, have one's heart in the right place; practice *or* follow the golden rule, do as you would be done by, do unto others as you would have others do unto you; make love not war

12 **to do a favour, do good,** do a kindness, do a good turn, do a good *or* kind deed, do a *mitzvah* (*Hebrew*), use one's good offices, render a service, confer a benefit; benefit, help *see* 449.11

adjectives

13 **kind, kindly,** kindly-disposed; **benign,** benignant; good as gold, **good, nice, decent; gracious; kindhearted, warm, warmhearted,** softhearted, tenderhearted, tender, loving, affectionate; **sympathetic,** sympathizing, **compassionate** *see* 145.7, merciful; brotherly, fraternal; humane, human; charitable, caritative; Christian, Christly, Christlike

14 **good-natured,** well-natured, **good-humoured, good-tempered,** bonhomous, **sweet, sweet-tempered; amiable, affable, genial, cordial; gentle,** mild, mild-mannered; easy, easy-natured, easy to get along with, able to take a joke, **agreeable**

15 **benevolent, charitable, beneficent, philanthropic, altruistic,** humanitarian; **bighearted,** largehearted, greathearted, freehearted; **generous** *see* 485.4; almsgiving, eleemosynary; **welfare,** welfarist, welfaristic, welfare statist

16 **considerate, thoughtful,** mindful, heedful, regardful, solicitous, attentive, delicate, tactful, mindful of others; complaisant, **accommodating,** accommodative, at one's service, **helpful,** agreeable, **obliging,** indulgent, tolerant, lenient *see* 427.7

17 **well-meaning, well-meant,** well-affected, well-disposed, **well-intentioned**

adverbs

18 **kindly,** benignly, benignantly; **good,** nicely, well, favourably; **kindheartedly, warmly,** warmheartedly, softheartedly, tenderheartedly; humanely, humanly

19 **good-naturedly, good-humouredly,** bonhomously; **sweetly; amiably,** affably, genially, cordially; graciously, in good part

20 **benevolently, beneficently, charitably, philanthropically, altruistically,** bigheartedly, with good will

21 **considerately, thoughtfully,** mindfully, heedfully, regardfully, tactfully, **sensitively,** solicitously, attentively; well-meaningly, well-disposedly; out of consideration *or* courtesy

144 UNKINDNESS, MALEVOLENCE

nouns

1 **unkindness, unkindliness;** unbenignity, unbenignness; **unamiability,** uncordiality, ungraciousness, inhospitality, inhospitableness, ungeniality, unaffectionateness; unsympatheticness, uncompassionateness; disagreeableness

2 **unbenevolentness, uncharitableness,** ungenerousness

3 **inconsiderateness, inconsideration, unthoughtfulness,** unmindfulness, unheedfulness, **thoughtlessness,** heedlessness, respectlessness, disregardfulness, forgetfulness; **unhelpfulness,** unobligingness, unaccommodatingness

4 **malevolence, ill will,** bad will, bad blood, bad temper, ill nature, ill-disposedness, ill *or* evil disposition; evil eye, *malocchio* (*Italian*), whammy (*informal*), blighting glance

5 **malice, maliciousness,** maleficence; **malignance** *or* **malignancy,** malignity; **meanness** *and* orneriness

and cussedness *and* bitchiness (*all informal*), hatefulness, nastiness, invidiousness; **wickedness,** iniquitousness *see* 654.4; deviltry, devilry, devilment; malice prepense *or* aforethought, evil intent; **harmfulness, noxiousness** *see* 999.5

6 **spite,** despite; **spitefulness,** cattiness; gloating pleasure, unwholesome *or* unholy joy, *Schadenfreude* (*German*)

7 **rancour, virulence,** venomousness, **venom,** vitriol, gall

8 **causticity,** causticness, corrosiveness, mordancy, mordacity, bitingness; **acrimony, asperity,** acidity, acidness, acidulousness, acridity, acerbity, **bitterness,** tartness; sharpness, keenness, incisiveness, piercingness, stabbingness, trenchancy; "sharp-toothed unkindness"—SHAKESPEARE

9 **harshness, roughness,** ungentleness; **severity,** austerity, hardness, sternness, grimness, inclemency; stringency, astringency

10 **heartlessness, unfeeling,** unnaturalness, unresponsiveness, insensitivity, coldness, **cold-heartedness,** cold-bloodedness; **hard-heartedness,** hardness, hardness of heart, heart of stone; **callousness,** callosity; obduracy, induration; **pitilessness, unmercifulness** *see* 146.1

11 **cruelty,** cruelness, sadistic *or* insensate cruelty, sadism, wanton cruelty; **ruthlessness** *see* 146.1; inhumanness, **inhumanity,** atrociousness; **brutality,** mindless *or* senseless brutality, brutalness, **brutishness, bestiality, animality,** beastliness; **barbarity,** barbarousness, vandalism; **savagery, viciousness, violence,** fiendishness; **child abuse** *see* 389.2; truculence, fierceness, ferociousness, **ferocity;** excessive force, piling on (*informal*); bloodthirst, bloodthirstiness, bloodlust, bloodiness, bloody-mindedness, sanguineousness; cannibalism

12 **act of cruelty, atrocity,** cruelty, brutality, bestiality, barbarity, inhumanity

13 **bad deed, disservice,** ill service, **ill turn,** bad turn

14 **beast, animal, brute, monster,** monster of cruelty, **devil,** devil incarnate; **sadist,** torturer, tormenter; Attila, Torquemada, the Marquis de Sade

verbs

15 to bear malice *or* ill will; **harshen, dehumanize,** brutalize, bestialize; torture, torment; **have a cruel streak,** go for the jugular, have the killer instinct

adjectives

16 **unkind, unkindly,** ill; **unbenign,** unbenignant; **unamiable,** disagreeable, **uncordial, ungracious,** inhospitable, **ungenial,** unaffectionate, unloving; **unsympathetic,** unsympathizing, **uncompassionate,** uncompassioned, uncaring

17 **unbenevolent,** unbeneficent, **uncharitable,** unphilanthropic, unaltruistic, ungenerous

18 **inconsiderate, unthoughtful,** unmindful, unheedful, disregardful, **thoughtless,** heedless, respectless, mindless, unthinking, forgetful; **tactless, insensitive;** uncomplaisant; **unhelpful, unaccommodating, unobliging,** disobliging, uncooperative

19 **malevolent, ill-disposed,** evil-disposed, ill-natured, ill-affected, ill-conditioned, ill-intentioned, bloody-minded

20 **malicious,** maleficent, malefic; **malignant,** malign; **mean** *and* **ornery** *and* cussed *and* bitchy (*all informal*), hateful, nasty, baleful, invidious; **wicked,** iniquitous *see* 654.16; **harmful, noxious** *see* 999.12

21 **spiteful,** despiteful; **catty,** cattish, bitchy (*informal*); **snide,** snidey (*informal*)

22 **rancorous, virulent,** vitriolic; **venomous,** venenate, envenomed

23 **caustic,** mordant, mordacious, corrosive, corroding; **acrimonious,** acrid, acid, acidic, acidulous, acidulent, acerb, acerbate, acerbic, **bitter,** tart; **sharp,** sharpish, keen, incisive, trenchant, **cutting,** penetrating, piercing, biting, **stinging,** stabbing, **scathing, scorching,** withering, scurrilous, abusive, thersitical, foulmouthed, harsh-tongued, sarcastic, sarky (*informal*)

24 **harsh, rough,** rugged, ungentle; **severe,** austere, **stringent,** astringent, hard, stern, dour, grim, inclement, unsparing, swingeing

25 **heartless, unfeeling,** unnatural, unresponsive, insensitive, **cold,** cold of heart, coldhearted, **cold-blooded; hard, hardened,** hard of heart, **hard-hearted,** stony-hearted, marble-hearted, flint-hearted; **callous,** calloused; obdurate, indurated; **unmerciful** *see* 146.3

26 **cruel,** cruel-hearted, sadistic; **ruthless** *see* 146.3; **brutal,** brutish, brute, bestial, beastly, animal, animalistic; **mindless, soulless,** insensate, senseless, subhuman, dehumanized, brutalized; sharkish, wolfish, slavering; **barbarous,** barbaric, uncivilized, unchristian; **savage, ferocious,** feral, mean (*informal*), **vicious,** fierce, **atrocious,** truculent, fell; **inhuman,** inhumane, unhuman; fiendish, fiendlike; demoniac *or* demoniacal, diabolic, diabolical, devilish, satanic, hellish, infernal; **bloodthirsty,** bloody-minded, bloody, sanguineous, sanguinary; cannibalistic, anthropophagous; murderous; Draconian, Tartarean

adverbs

27 **unkindly,** ill; **unbenignly,** unbenignantly; **unamiably,** disagreeably, uncordially, ungraciously, inhospitably, ungenially, unaffectionately, unlovingly; unsympathetically, uncompassionately

28 **unbenevolently,** unbeneficently, **uncharitably,** unphilanthropically, unaltruistically, ungenerously

29 **inconsiderately, unthoughtfully,** thoughtlessly, heedlessly, unthinkingly; unhelpfully, uncooperatively

30 **malevolently, maliciously,** maleficently, **malignantly; meanly** *and* **ornerily** *and* cussedly *and* bitchily *and* cattily (*all informal*), hatefully, nastily, invidiously, balefully; **wickedly,** iniquitously *see* 654.19; **harmfully, noxiously** *see* 999.15, spitefully, in spite; with bad intent, with malice prepense *or* aforethought

31 **rancorously, virulently,** vitriolically; venomously, venenately

32 **caustically,** mordantly, mordaciously, corrosively, corrodingly; **acrimoniously,** acridly, acidly, acerbly, acerbically, **bitterly,** tartly; **sharply,** keenly, incisively, trenchantly, **cuttingly,** penetratingly, piercingly, bitingly, **stingingly,** stabbingly,

scathingly, scorchingly, witheringly, thersitically, scurrilously, abusively

33 **harshly, roughly; severely,** austerely, stringently, sternly, grimly, inclemently, unsparingly

34 **heartlessly, soullessly, unfeelingly, callously,** cold-heartedly; cold-bloodedly, **in cold blood**

35 **cruelly, brutally,** brutishly, bestially, animalistically, subhumanly, sharkishly, wolfishly, slaveringly; **barbarously, savagely, ferociously,** ferally, **viciously,** fiercely, **atrociously,** truculently; **ruthlessly** *see* 146.4; **inhumanely,** inhumanly, unhumanly; fiendishly, diabolically, devilishly

145 PITY

nouns

1 **pity, sympathy,** feeling, fellow feeling in suffering, **commiseration,** condolence, condolences; **compassion, mercy,** ruth, rue, humanity; **sensitivity; clemency,** quarter, reprieve, mitigation, relief *see* 120, favour, grace; **leniency,** lenity, gentleness; forbearance; **kindness, benevolence** *see* 143; pardon, **forgiveness** *see* 601.1; self-pity; **pathos**

2 **compassionateness, mercifulness,** ruthfulness, ruefulness, softheartedness, tenderness, lenity, gentleness; bowels of compassion *or* mercy; bleeding heart

verbs

3 **to pity, be** *or* **feel sorry for,** feel sorrow for; **commiserate,** compassionate; open one's heart; **sympathize, sympathize with,** feel for, weep for, lament for, bleed, bleed for, have one's heart bleed for · or go out to, condole with *see* 147.2

4 **to have pity, have mercy upon,** take pity on *or* upon; melt, thaw; relent, forbear, relax, give quarter, spare, temper the wind to the shorn lamb, go easy on *and* let up *or* ease up on (*all informal*), soften, unsteel; **reprieve,** pardon, remit, forgive *see* 601.4; put out of one's misery; be cruel to be kind

5 (*excite pity*) **to move, touch,** affect, reach, **soften,** unsteel, melt, melt the heart, appeal to one's better feelings; sadden, grieve *see* 112.17

6 **to beg for mercy,** ask for pity, cry for quarter, beg for one's life; fall on one's knees, throw oneself at the feet of

adjectives

7 **pitying, sympathetic,** sympathizing, commiserative, condolent, understanding; **compassionate, merciful,** ruthful, rueful, **clement,** gentle, soft, melting, bleeding, tender, **tenderhearted,** softhearted, warmhearted; **humane,** human; lenient, forbearant *see* 427.7; charitable *see* 143.15

8 **pitiful, pitiable, pathetic, piteous, touching, moving, affecting,** heartrending, grievous, doleful *see* 112.26

9 self-pitying, self-pitiful, sorry for oneself

adverbs

10 **pitifully,** sympathetically; **compassionately, mercifully,** ruthfully, ruefully, clemently, humanely

146 PITILESSNESS

nouns

1 **pitilessness, unmercifulness, uncompassionateness,** unsympatheticness, mercilessness, **ruthlessness,** unfeelingness, inclemency, relentlessness, inexorableness, unyieldingness *see* 361.2, unforgivingness; **heartlessness,** heart of stone, hardness, steeliness, flintiness, harshness, induration, **cruelty** *see* 144.11; remorselessness, unremorsefulness; short shrift, tender mercies

verbs

2 **to show no mercy,** give no quarter, turn a deaf ear, claim one's pound of flesh, harden *or* steel one's heart

adjectives

3 **pitiless, unpitying, unpitiful;** blind *or* deaf to pity; **unsympathetic,** unsympathizing; **uncompassionate,** uncompassioned; **merciless, unmerciful,** without mercy, unruing, **ruthless,** dog-eat-dog; unfeeling, bowelless, inclement, relentless, inexorable, unyielding *see* 361.9, unforgiving; **heartless,** hard, hard as nails, steely, flinty, harsh, savage, **cruel;** remorseless, unremorseful

adverbs

4 **pitilessly,** unsympathetically; mercilessly, **unmercifully, ruthlessly,** uncompassionately, inclemently, relentlessly, inexorably, unyieldingly, unforgivingly; heartlessly, harshly, savagely, cruelly; remorselessly, unremorsefully

147 CONDOLENCE

nouns

1 **condolence, condolences,** condolement, **consolation,** comfort, balm, soothing words, **commiseration, sympathy,** sharing of grief *or* sorrow

verbs

2 **to condole with, commiserate, sympathize with,** feel with, empathize with, express sympathy for, send one's condolences; pity *see* 145.3; **console,** wipe away one's tears, comfort, speak soothing words, bring balm to one's sorrow; sorrow with, share *or* help bear one's grief, grieve *or* weep with, grieve *or* weep for, share one's sorrow, "weep with them that weep"—BIBLE

adjectives

3 condoling, condolent, consolatory, comforting, commiserating, commiserative, **sympathetic,** empathic, empathetic; pitying *see* 145.7

148 FORGIVENESS

nouns

1 **forgiveness,** forgivingness; unresentfulness, unrevengefulness; **condoning,** condonation, condonance, overlooking, disregard; **patience** *see*

134; **indulgence, forbearance,** longanimity, long-suffering; **kindness, benevolence** *see* 143; **magnanimity** *see* 652.2; brooking, **tolerance** *see* 978.4

2 **pardon,** excuse, sparing, **amnesty,** indemnity, exemption, immunity, reprieve, grace; **absolution,** shrift, remission, remission of sin; redemption; **exoneration, exculpation** *see* 601.1

verbs

3 **to forgive, pardon, excuse,** give *or* grant forgiveness, spare; amnesty, grant amnesty to, grant immunity *or* exemption; hear confession, **absolve,** remit, give absolution, shrive, grant remission; **exonerate, exculpate** *see* 601.4; blot out one's sins, wipe the slate clean

4 **to condone** *see* 134.7, **overlook, disregard, ignore,** accept, take *and* swallow *and* let go (*all informal*), pass over, give one another chance, let one off this time *and* let one off easy (*both informal*), close *or* shut one's eyes to, **blink** *or* **wink at,** connive at; allow for, make allowances for; bear with, endure, regard with indulgence; pocket the affront, leave unavenged, turn the other cheek, bury *or* hide one's head in the sand, turn a blind eye to

5 **to forget, forgive and forget,** dismiss from one's thoughts, think no more of, not give it another *or* a second thought, let it go (*informal*), let it pass, **let bygones be bygones;** write off, charge off, charge to experience; bury the hatchet

adjectives

6 **forgiving,** sparing, placable, conciliatory; **kind, benevolent** *see* 143.15; **magnanimous, generous** *see* 652.6; **patient** *see* 134.9; **forbearing,** longanimous, long-suffering; unresentful, unrevengeful; **tolerant** *see* 978.11, more in sorrow than in anger

7 **forgiven, pardoned, excused,** spared, amnestied, reprieved, remitted; overlooked, disregarded, forgotten, not held against one, wiped away, removed from the record, blotted, cancelled, **condoned,** indulged; **absolved,** shriven; redeemed; exonerated, exculpated, acquitted; unresented; unavenged, unrevenged; uncondemned

149 CONGRATULATION

nouns

1 **congratulation, congratulations,** congrats (*informal*), gratulation, **felicitation,** blessing, **compliment,** pat on the back; good wishes, best wishes; **applause** *see* 509.2, **praise** *see* 509.5, flattery *see* 511

verbs

2 **to congratulate,** gratulate, **felicitate,** bless, **compliment,** tender *or* offer one's congratulations *or* felicitations *or* compliments; shake one's hand, pat one on the back; **rejoice with one,** wish one joy; **applaud** *see* 509.10, **praise** *see* 509.12, flatter *see* 511.5

adjectives

3 **congratulatory,** congratulant, congratulational; gratulatory, gratulant; **complimentary** *see* 509.16, flattering *see* 511.8

exclamations

4 **congratulations!,** take a bow!, nice going!, **bravo!, well done!,** good show!

5 (*informal terms*) **congrats!,** all right!, **right on!,** way to go!, attaboy!, attagirl!, good deal!, good for you!, looking good!, nice going!, nice one!, that's my boy!, that's my girl!

150 GRATITUDE

nouns

1 **gratitude, gratefulness, thankfulness, appreciation, appreciativeness;** obligation, sense of obligation *or* indebtedness

2 **thanks, thanksgiving,** praise, laud, hymn, paean, benediction; grace, prayer of thanks; **thank-you; acknowledgment,** cognizance, **credit,** crediting, recognition; thank offering, votary offering

verbs

3 **to be grateful, be obliged,** feel *or* be *or* lie under an obligation, be obligated *or* indebted, be in the debt of, give credit *or* due credit; **be thankful,** thank God, thank one's lucky stars, thank *or* bless one's stars; **appreciate,** be appreciative of; never forget; overflow with gratitude; not look a gift horse in the mouth

4 **to thank, extend gratitude** *or* **thanks,** bless; give one's thanks, **express one's appreciation; offer** *or* **give thanks,** tender *or* render thanks, return thanks; acknowledge, make acknowledgments of, credit, recognize, give *or* render credit *or* recognition; fall all over one with gratitude; fall on one's knees

adjectives

5 **grateful, thankful; appreciative,** appreciatory, sensible; **obliged, much obliged,** beholden, indebted to, crediting, under obligation, acknowledging, cognizant of

exclamations

6 **thanks!, thank you!,** I thank you!, *merci!* (*French*), *¡gracias!* (*Spanish*), *grazie!* (*Italian*), *danke! and danke schön!* (*both German*), gramercy!, *domo and domo arrigato* (*both Japanese*), **much obliged!,** many thanks!, thank you kindly!; I thank you very much!, *merci beaucoup!* and *je vous remercie beaucoup!* (*both French*); thanks a lot! *or* a bunch! *or* a heap! *or* a million! (*informal*), ta! (*informal*), cheers! (*informal*)

151 INGRATITUDE

nouns

1 **ingratitude, ungratefulness, unthankfulness,** thanklessness, unappreciation, **unappreciativeness;** nonacknowledgment, nonrecognition, denial of due *or* proper credit;

"benefits forgot"—Shakespeare; grudging *or* halfhearted thanks

2 **ingrate**, ungrateful wretch

verbs

3 **to be ungrateful**, feel no obligation, **not appreciate**, owe one no thanks; look a gift horse in the mouth; bite the hand that feeds one

adjectives

4 **ungrateful, unthankful**, unthanking, thankless, unappreciative, unappreciatory, unmindful, nonrecognitive, unrecognizing

5 unthanked, unacknowledged, unrecognized, nonrecognized, uncredited, denied due *or* proper credit, unrequited, unrewarded, forgotten, neglected, unduly *or* unfairly neglected, ignored; ill-requited, ill-rewarded

152 RESENTMENT, ANGER

nouns

1 **resentment**, resentfulness; **displeasure**, disapproval, disapprobation, dissatisfaction, **discontent; vexation**, irritation, **annoyance**, aggravation (*informal*), exasperation

2 **offence, umbrage, pique**; glower, scowl, angry look, dirty look (*informal*), glare, frown

3 **bitterness, bitter resentment**, bitterness of spirit, heartburning; **rancour**, virulence, **acrimony**, acerbity, asperity; causticity *see* 144.8; **choler**, gall, bile, spleen, acid, acidity, acidulousness; hard feelings, **animosity** *see* 589.4; soreness, rankling, slow burn (*informal*); gnashing of teeth

4 **indignation**, indignant displeasure, righteous indignation

5 **anger, wrath, ire**, *saeva indignatio* (*Latin*), mad (*informal*); angriness, irateness, wrathfulness, soreness (*informal*),
   "a transient madness"—Horace; infuriation, enragement; vials of wrath, grapes of wrath; **heat**, more heat than light (*informal*)

6 **temper**, dander (*informal*), monkey (*informal*); bad temper *see* 110.1

7 **dudgeon**, high dudgeon; **huff**, pique, pet, tiff, miff *and* stew (*both informal*), fret, **fume**, ferment

8 **fit**, fit of anger, fit of temper, rage, wax *and* bate *and* paddy *and* paddywhack (*informal*), **tantrum**, temper tantrum; duck *or* cat fit *and* **conniption** *or* conniption fit (*all US & Canadian informal*), snit (*US & Australian informal*), paroxysm, convulsion; agriothymia

9 **outburst**, outburst of anger, burst, **explosion**, eruption, blowup *and* **flare-up** (*both informal*), access, blaze of temper; **storm, scene**, high words

10 **rage, passion; fury**, furore; livid *or* towering rage *or* passion, blind *or* burning rage, raging *or* tearing passion, furious rage; vehemence, violence; the Furies, the Eumenides, the Erinyes; Nemesis; Alecto, Tisiphone, Megaera; road rage; steroid rage, roid rage (*informal*)

11 **provocation, affront, offence**,
   "head and front of one's offending"—Shakespeare; *casus belli* (*Latin*), red rag, red rag to a bull, sore point, sore spot, tender spot, raw nerve, the quick, where one lives; slap in the face, kick in the teeth

verbs

12 **to resent**, be resentful, feel *or* harbour *or* nurse resentment, feel hurt, smart, feel sore *and* have one's nose out of joint (*both informal*); bear *or* hold *or* have a grudge

13 **to take amiss**, take ill, **take in bad part**, take to heart, take the wrong way, not take it as a joke, **mind; take offence, take umbrage**, get miffed *or* huffy (*informal*); be cut *or* cut to the quick

14 (*show resentment*) to redden, colour, flush, mantle; **growl, snarl**, gnarl, **snap**, show one's teeth, spit; gnash *or* grind one's teeth; **glower**, lower, scowl, **glare, frown**, give a dirty look (*informal*), look daggers; **stew**, stew in one's own juice

15 (*be angry*) to **burn, seethe, simmer**, sizzle, smoke, smoulder, steam; be pissed *or* pissed off *or* browned off *or* hacked off (*all informal*), be livid, be beside oneself, **fume**, stew (*informal*), boil, fret, chafe; foam at the mouth; breathe fire and fury; **rage, storm, rave**, rant, bluster; take on *and* go on *and* carry on (*all informal*), rant and rave, kick up a row *or* dust *or* a shindy (*informal*); raise Cain *or* raise hell *or* raise the devil *or* raise the roof (*all informal*), tear up the earth; throw a fit, have a conniption *or* conniption fit *or* duck fit *or* cat fit (*all US & Canadian informal*), go into a tantrum; stamp one's foot

16 **to vent one's anger**, vent one's rancour *or* choler *or* spleen, pour out the vials of one's wrath; **snap at, bite** *or* **snap one's nose off, bite** *or* **take one's head off, jump down one's throat**; expend one's anger on, take it out on (*informal*)

17 (*become angry*) to **anger, lose one's temper**, become irate, forget oneself, let one's angry passions rise; **get one's gorge up**, get one's blood up, **bridle**, bridle up, **bristle**, bristle up, raise one's hackles, get one's back up; reach boiling point, boil over, climb the wall, go through the roof

18 (*informal terms*) to **see red**, get one's dander *or* hackles up, get one's monkey up, go spare, go into orbit, do one's nut, cut up rough; get mad *or* sore, **get hot under the collar**, flip out, work oneself into a lather *or* sweat *or* stew, get oneself in a tizzy, do a slow burn

19 **to flare up, blaze up**, fire up, flame up, ignite, kindle, take fire

20 **to fly into a rage** *or* **passion** *or* **temper**, fly out, fly off at a tangent; **fly off the handle** *and* **hit the ceiling** *and* go into a tailspin *and* have a haemorrhage (*all informal*); **explode, blow up** (*informal*), go ballistic (*informal*); blow one's top *or* stack (*informal*), blow a fuse *or* gasket (*informal*), flip one's lid *or* wig (*informal*), wig out (*informal*); kick up a fuss *or* a row *or* a storm (*all informal*)

21 **to offend, give offence, give umbrage**, affront, outrage; grieve, aggrieve; wound, hurt, cut, cut to the quick, hit one where one lives (*informal*), **sting**, hurt one's feelings; step *or* tread on one's corns *or* toes

22 **to anger, make angry, make mad**, raise one's gorge *or* choler; make one's blood boil

23 (*informal terms*) **to piss off**, tick off, get one's goat, **get one's back** *or* **dander** *or* **hackles up**, make

sore, make one hot under the collar, put one's nose out of joint, burn one up, steam

24 **to provoke**, **incense**, arouse, inflame, embitter; **vex, irritate**, **annoy**, **aggravate** (*informal*), **exasperate, nettle**, fret, chafe; **pique, peeve** *and* miff (*both informal*), huff; **ruffle, roil, rile** (*informal*), ruffle one's feathers, **rankle**; bristle, put *or* get one's back up, set up, put one's hair *or* fur *or* bristles up, wind up; stick in one's craw (*informal*); **stir up, work up,** stir one's bile, stir the blood, get one going; wave the bloody shirt

25 **to enrage, infuriate, madden**, drive one mad, frenzy, lash into fury, work up into a passion, **make one's blood boil**

adjectives

26 **resentful**, resenting; **bitter**, embittered, rancorous, virulent, **acrimonious**, acerb, acerbic, acerbate; caustic; **choleric**, splenetic, acid, acidic, acidulous, acidulent; **sore** (*informal*), rankled, choked (*informal*), burning *and* stewing (*both informal*)

27 **provoked, vexed, piqued**; **peeved** *and* miffed *and* huffy *and* stroppy *and* narky (*all informal*), **nettled, irritated, annoyed**, aggravated (*informal*), exasperated, put-out

28 **angry**, angered, **incensed**, **indignant, irate**, ireful; **livid**, livid with rage, beside oneself, **wroth, wrathful**, wrathy, **cross**, wrought-up, worked up, riled up (*informal*)

29 **burning, seething**, simmering, smouldering, sizzling, boiling, **steaming**; flushed with anger

30 (*informal terms*) mad, sore, mad as hell, sore as a boil; **pissed-off** *or* PO'd; ticked off, browned-off, waxy *and* stroppy, **hot**, het up, **hot under the collar**, burned up, hot and bothered, boiling, boiling *or* hopping *or* fighting *or* roaring mad, fit to be tied, good and mad, steamed, hacked, bent out of shape, in a lather, hairless

31 in a temper, in a huff, in a pet, in a stew (*informal*), in a snit (*US & Australian informal*); in a wax (*informal*), **in high dudgeon**

32 **infuriated**, infuriate, in a rage *or* passion *or* fury; **furious**, fierce, wild, savage; raving mad (*informal*), **rabid**, foaming *or* frothing at the mouth; **fuming**, in a fume; **enraged, raging, raving, ranting, storming**

adverbs

33 **angrily, indignantly, irately**, wrathfully, infuriatedly, infuriately, furiously, heatedly; **in anger**, in hot blood, in the heat of passion

153 JEALOUSY

nouns

1 **jealousy**, *jalousie* (*French*), jealousness, heartburning, heartburn, **jaundice**, jaundiced eye, green in the eye (*informal*),
"the jaundice of the soul"—DRYDEN;
"green-eyed jealousy", "green-eyed monster", "a monster begot upon itself, born on itself"—ALL SHAKESPEARE; Othello's flaw, horn-madness; **envy** *see* 154

2 **suspiciousness**, suspicion, sus (*informal*), doubt, misdoubt, mistrust, distrust, distrustfulness

verbs

3 to suffer pangs of jealousy, have green in the eye (*informal*), be possessive *or* overpossessive, view with a jaundiced eye; **suspect**, distrust, mistrust, doubt, misdoubt

4 to make one jealous, put someone's nose out of joint

adjectives

5 **jealous, jaundiced**, jaundice-eyed, yellow-eyed, green-eyed, yellow, green, green with jealousy; horn-mad; invidious, **envious** *see* 154.4; **suspicious**, distrustful

154 ENVY

nouns

1 **envy**, enviousness, **covetousness**; invidia, deadly sin of envy, **invidiousness**; grudging, grudgingness; resentment, resentfulness; **jealousy** *see* 153; rivalry; meanness, meanspiritedness, ungenerousness

2 "the tax which all distinction must pay"—EMERSON, "emulation adapted to the meanest capacity"—AMBROSE BIERCE, "a kind of praise"—JOHN GAY

verbs

3 **to envy**, be envious *or* covetous of, **covet**, cast envious eyes, desire for oneself; resent; **grudge, begrudge**

adjectives

4 **envious**, envying, **invidious**, green with envy; **jealous** *see* 153.4; **covetous**, desirous of; resentful; **grudging, begrudging**; mean, mean-spirited, ungenerous

155 RESPECT

nouns

1 **respect, regard**, consideration, appreciation, favour; approbation, approval; **esteem**, estimation, prestige; **reverence, veneration**, awe; **deference**, deferential *or* reverential regard; **honour, homage**, duty; great respect, high regard, **admiration**; adoration, breathless adoration, exaggerated respect, worship, hero worship, **idolization**; idolatry, deification, apotheosis; courtesy *see* 504

2 **obeisance**, reverence, homage; **bow, nod, bob**, bend, inclination, inclination of the head, **curtsy, salaam, kowtow**, scrape, bowing and scraping, making a leg; **genuflection**, kneeling, bending the knee; prostration; salute, salutation, namaste; presenting arms, dipping the colours *or* ensign, standing to attention; **submissiveness, submission** *see* 433; **obsequiousness, servility** *see* 138

3 **respects, regards**, *égards* (*French*); duties, *devoirs* (*French*); attentions

verbs

4 **to respect**, entertain respect for, accord respect to, **regard, esteem**, hold in esteem *or* consideration,

favour, **admire**, think much of, think well of, think
highly of, have *or* hold a high opinion of, think the
sun rises and sets on (*informal*), think the sun shines
out of one's arse (*informal*); **appreciate, value,**
prize; **revere, reverence,** hold in reverence,
venerate, honour, look up to, defer to, bow to,
exalt, put on a pedestal, **worship,** hero-worship,
deify, apotheosize, **idolize, adore,** worship the
ground one walks on, stand in awe of

5 **to do** *or* **pay homage to,** show *or* demonstrate
respect for, pay respect to, pay tribute to, **do** *or*
render honour to, do the honours for; **doff one's
cap to, take off one's hat to;** salute, present arms,
dip the colours *or* ensign, stand at *or* to attention;
give the red-carpet treatment, roll out the red carpet

6 **to bow, make obeisance, salaam, kowtow,** make
one's bow, bow down, **nod,** incline *or* bend *or* bow
the head, bend the neck, **bob,** bob down, **curtsy,**
bob a curtsy, bend, make a leg, scrape, **bow and
scrape;** touch one's cap, touch *or* tug one's forelock,
genuflect, kneel, bend the knee, get down on one's
knees, throw oneself on one's knees, fall on one's
knees, fall down before, fall at the feet of, prostrate
oneself, kiss the hem of one's garment

7 **to command respect,** inspire respect, stand high,
have prestige, rank high, be widely reputed, be up
there *or* way up there (*informal*); awe *see* 122.6

adjectives

8 **respectful, regardful,** attentive; **deferential,**
conscious of one's place, dutiful, honorific,
ceremonious, cap in hand; **courteous** *see* 504.14

9 **reverent,** reverential; admiring, **adoring,
worshipping,** worshipful, hero-worshipping,
idolizing, idolatrous, deifying, apotheosizing;
venerative, venerational; awestruck, awestricken,
awed, in awe; solemn *see* 111.3

10 **obeisant,** prostrate, on one's knees, on bended knee;
submissive *see* 433.12; **obsequious**

11 **respected, esteemed, revered,** reverenced, adored,
worshipped, **venerated, honoured,** well-thought-of,
admired, much-admired, appreciated, valued, prized,
in high esteem *or* estimation, highly considered,
well-considered, held in respect *or* regard *or* favour
or consideration, prestigious

12 **venerable, reverend, estimable, honourable,**
worshipful, august, awe-inspiring, awesome, awful,
dreadful; time-honoured

adverbs

13 **respectfully,** regardfully, deferentially, reverentially;
dutifully

adverbs, prepositions

14 **in deference to,** with due respect, with all respect,
with all due respect to *or* **for,** saving, excusing the
liberty, saving your reverence, sir-reverence; out of
respect *or* consideration for, out of courtesy to

156 DISRESPECT

nouns

1 **disrespect, disrespectfulness,** lack of respect, low
estimate *or* esteem, **disesteem,** dishonour,

irreverence; **ridicule** *see* 508; **disparagement** *see*
512; **discourtesy** *see* 505; **impudence,** insolence *see*
142

2 **indignity, affront, offence, injury,** humiliation;
scurrility, contempt *see* 157, contumely, despite,
flout, flouting, mockery, jeering, jeer, mock, scoff,
gibe, taunt, brickbat (*informal*); **insult, aspersion,**
uncomplimentary remark, slap *or* kick in the face,
left-handed *or* backhanded compliment, damning
with faint praise; cut,
"most unkindest cut of all"—SHAKESPEARE; **outrage,
atrocity,** enormity

3 (*informal terms*) **put-down,** dump, brickbat, **dig,**
dirty dig, rip, shot, slam

verbs

4 **to disrespect,** not respect, disesteem, hold a low
opinion of, not rate, rate *or* rank low, hold in low
esteem, not care much for, pay a lefthanded *or*
backhanded compliment, damn with faint praise;
show disrespect for, show a lack of respect for, **be
disrespectful,** treat with disrespect, be overfamiliar
with; trifle with, make bold *or* free with, take a
liberty, take liberties with, play fast and loose with;
ridicule *see* 508.8; **disparage** *see* 512.8

5 **to offend, affront,** give offence to, disoblige,
outrage, step *or* tread on one's toes; dishonour,
humiliate, treat with indignity; flout, mock, jeer at,
scoff at, fleer at, gibe at, taunt; **insult,** call names,
kick *or* slap in the face, take *or* pluck by the beard;
add insult to injury

6 (*informal terms*) **to bad-mouth, put down, rubbish,**
trash, dump on, dig at, dis, rip *or* rip on, roast,
slam, hurl a brickbat

adjectives

7 **disrespectful, irreverent,** aweless; **discourteous** *see*
505.4; **insolent, impudent;** ridiculing, **derisive** *see*
508.12; **disparaging** *see* 512.13

8 **insulting, insolent, abusive, offensive,**
humiliating, degrading, contemptuous *see* 157.8,
contumelious, calumnious; scurrilous, scurrile;
backhand, backhanded, left-handed; outrageous,
atrocious, unspeakable

9 **unrespected, unregarded, unrevered,** unvenerated,
unhonoured, unenvied

157 CONTEMPT

nouns

1 **contempt, disdain, scorn,** contemptuousness,
disdainfulness, superciliousness, snootiness,
snottiness, sniffiness, toploftiness, scornfulness,
despite, contumely, sovereign contempt;
snobbishness; clannishness, cliquishness,
exclusiveness, exclusivity; hauteur, airs, arrogance *see*
141; **ridicule** *see* 508; **insult** *see* 156.2;
disparagement *see* 512

2 **snub, rebuff,** repulse; **slight,** humiliation, spurning,
spurn, disregard, the go-by (*informal*); kick in the
teeth (*informal*), slap in the face (*informal*), smack in
the eye (*informal*); cut, cut direct, **the cold
shoulder** (*informal*); sneer, snort, sniff;

contemptuous dismissal, **dismissal** *see* 907.2, kiss-off (*informal*); **rejection** *see* 372

verbs

3 to **disdain, scorn, despise,** hold in contempt, contemn, vilipend, disprize, misprize, rate *or* rank low, be contemptuous of, feel contempt for, **hold in contempt,** hold cheap, look down upon, think little *or* nothing of, feel superior to, be above, hold beneath one *or* beneath contempt, look with scorn upon, view with a scornful eye; **put down** *or* dump on (*both informal*); deride, **ridicule** *see* 508.8; insult; **disparage** *see* 512.8; thumb one's nose at, sniff at, sneeze at, snap one's fingers at, sneer at, snort at, curl one's lip at, shrug one's shoulders at; care nothing for, couldn't care less about, think nothing of, set at naught

4 to **spurn,** scout (*old*), **turn up one's nose at,** scorn to receive *or* accept, not want any part of; spit upon

5 to **snub, rebuff,** cut *or* cut dead (*informal*), drop, repulse; **high-hat** *and* upstage (*both informal*); **look down one's nose at,** look cool *or* coldly upon; cold-shoulder *or* turn a cold shoulder upon *or* **give the cold shoulder** (*informal*), give *or* turn the shoulder (*informal*), give the go-by *or* the kiss-off (*informal*); turn one's back upon, turn away from, turn on one's heel, set one's face against, slam the door in one's face, show one his place, put one in his place, wave one aside; not be at home to, not receive

6 to **slight, ignore,** pooh-pooh (*informal*), make little of, dismiss, pretend not to see, disregard, overlook, neglect, pass by, pass up *and* give the go-by (*both informal*), leave out in the cold (*informal*), take no note *or* notice of, look right through (*informal*), pay no attention *or* regard to, refuse to acknowledge *or* recognize

7 to **avoid** *see* 368.6, avoid like the plague, go out of one's way to avoid, shun, dodge, steer clear of *and* have no truck with (*both informal*); **keep one's distance,** keep at a respectful distance, **keep** *or* **stand** *or* **hold aloof;** keep at a distance, hold *or* keep at arm's length; be **stuck-up** (*informal*), act holier than thou, give oneself airs

adjectives

8 **contemptuous, disdainful,** supercilious, snooty, snotty, sniffy, toplofty, toploftical, **scornful,** sneering, withering, contumelious; snobbish, snobby, toffee-nosed (*informal*); clannish, cliquish, exclusive; stuck-up (*informal*), **conceited** *see* 140.11; haughty, **arrogant** *see* 141.9

adverbs

9 **contemptuously, scornfully, disdainfully;** in *or* with contempt, in disdain, in scorn; sneeringly, with a sneer, with curling lip

exclamations

10 **bah!,** pah!, phooey!, boo!, phoo!, pish!, ecch!, yeech!, eeyuck!, eeyuch!, yeeuck!, *feh!* (*Yiddish*)

158 SPACE
indefinite space

nouns

1 **space, extent,** extension, spatial extension, uninterrupted extension, space continuum, continuum; **expanse,** expansion; spread, breadth; depth, deeps; height, vertical space, airspace; **measure,** volume; **dimension,** proportion; **area, expanse,** tract, surface, surface *or* superficial extension; **field,** arena, sphere; acreage; **void,** empty space, emptiness, nothingness; infinite space, outer space, wastes of outer space, deep space, depths of outer space, interstellar *or* intergalactic space

2 **range, scope, compass, reach, stretch, expanse,** radius, sweep, carry, fetch; **gamut, scale,** register, diapason; **spectrum**

3 **room, latitude,** swing, play, way; spare room, room to spare, room to swing a cat (*informal*), **elbowroom, margin, leeway;** breathing space; sea room; headroom, clearance

4 **open space,** clear space; **clearing,** clearance, glade; open country, wide-open spaces, **terrain,** prairie, steppe, plain *see* 236; wilderness, back country, boonies *and* boondocks (*both US & Canadian informal*), outback (*Australian*), desert; distant prospect *or* perspective, empty view, far horizon; **territory;** living space, *Lebensraum* (*German*); national territory, airspace

5 **spaciousness, roominess, size,** commodiousness, capacity, capaciousness, amplitude, extensiveness, extent, expanse

6 **fourth dimension, space-time,** time-space, space-time continuum, four-dimensional space; four-dimensional geometry, Minkowski world *or* universe; spaceworld; other continuums; **relativity,** theory of relativity, Einstein theory, principle of relativity, principle of equivalence, general theory of relativity, special *or* restricted theory of relativity, continuum theory; time warp; cosmic constant

7 **inner space,** psychological space, the realm of the mind; personal space, room to be, room to breathe, individual *or* private space; semantic space

verbs

8 to **extend, reach, stretch,** sweep, spread, run, **go** *or* **go out,** cover, carry, **range,** lie; **reach** *or* stretch *or* thrust out; span, straddle, take in, hold, encompass, surround, environ

adjectives

9 **spatial,** space; **dimensional,** proportional; two-dimensional, flat, surface *or* superficial, three-dimensional *or* 3-D, spherical, cubic, volumetric; galactic, intergalactic, interstellar; stereoscopic; fourth-dimensional; space-time, spatiotemporal

10 **spacious, sizeable, roomy, commodious, capacious,** ample; **extensive,** expansive, extended, wide-ranging; far-reaching, extending, spreading, **vast,** vasty, broad, **wide,** deep, high, voluminous; **widespread** *see* 863.13; **infinite** *see* 822.3

adverbs

11 **extensively, widely,** broadly, vastly, abroad; **far**

and wide, far and near; **right and left,** on all sides, on every side; infinitely

12 everywhere, everywheres (*US informal*), **here, there and everywhere;** in every place, in every clime *or* region, in all places, in every quarter, in all quarters; **all over,** all round, all over hell *and* all over the map *and* all over the place *and* all over town (*all informal*), all over the shop (*informal*), all over the world, the world over, on the face of the earth, under the sun, throughout the world, throughout the length and breadth of the land; from end to end, from pole to pole, from here to the back of beyond (*informal*),

"from Dan to Beersheba"—BIBLE; **high and low,** upstairs and downstairs, inside and out, in every nook and cranny *or* hole and corner; **universally,** in all creation

13 from everywhere, everywhence,

"from the four corners of the earth"—SHAKESPEARE, "at the round earth's imagined corners"—DONNE, from all points of the compass, from every quarter *or* all quarters; everywhere, everywhither, to the four winds, to the uttermost parts of the earth,

"unto the ends of the earth"—BIBLE, to hell and back (*informal*)

159 LOCATION

nouns

1 location, situation, place, position, spot, *lieu* (*French*), **placement, emplacement,** stead; **whereabouts,** whereabout, ubicity, ubiety; **area, district, region** *see* 231; **locality, locale,** locus; **abode** *see* 228; **site,** situs; **spot, point,** pinpoint, exact spot *or* point, very spot *or* point; bench mark (*surveying*); *locus classicus* (*Latin*); bearings, latitude and longitude

2 station, status, **stand, standing,** standpoint, pou sto; **viewpoint,** *optique* (*French*), point of reference, reference-point, angle, perspective, distance; coign of vantage; **seat, post,** base, footing, ground, venue

3 navigation, guidance; dead reckoning, pilotage; coastal navigation; celestial guidance *or* astro-inertial guidance, celestial navigation *or* celo-navigation *or* astronavigation; consolan; loran; radar navigation; radio navigation; **position, orientation,** lay, lie, set, **attitude,** aspect, exposure, frontage, **bearing** *or* **bearings,** radio bearing, azimuth; position line *or* line of position; **fix**

4 place, stead, lieu

5 map, chart; hachure, contour line, isoline, layer tint; **scale,** graphic scale, representative fraction; **legend;** grid line, meridian, parallel, latitude, longitude; inset; index; **projection,** map projection, azimuthal equidistant projection *or* azimuthal projection, conic projection, Mercator projection; **cartography, mapmaking;** chorography, topography, photogrammetry, phototopography; **cartographer, mapmaker, mapper;** chorographer, topographer, photogrammetrist

6 (*act of placing*) **placement, positioning, emplacement, situation, location,** siting, localization, **locating, placing,** putting; **allocation,** collocation, **disposition,** assignment, **deployment,** posting, **stationing,** spotting; deposition, reposition, **deposit,** disposal, dumping; **stowage,** storage, warehousing; loading, lading, packing

7 establishment, foundation, settlement, settling, colonization, population, peopling, plantation; lodgment, fixation; anchorage, mooring; **installation,** instalment, inauguration, investiture, placing in office, initiation

8 topography, geography; **cartography,** chorography; surveying, navigation, geodesy; geodetic satellite, orbiting geophysical observatory *or* OGO

verbs

9 to have place, be there; have its place *or* slot, **belong, go, fit,** fit in

10 to be located *or* **situated, lie,** be found, stand, rest, repose; lie in, have its seat in

11 to locate, situate, site, place, position; emplace, spot (*informal*), **install,** put in place; **allocate,** collocate, **dispose, deploy,** assign; **localize,** narrow *or* pin down; **map, chart,** put on the map *or* chart; put one's finger on, **fix,** assign *or* consign *or* relegate to a place; **pinpoint,** zero in on, home in on; find *or* fix *or* calculate one's position, triangulate, find a line of position; **get a fix on** *or* navigational fix, navigate

12 to place, put, set, lay, pose, posit, site, seat, stick (*informal*), bung (*informal*), **station, post; park,** plump down (*informal*); **dump**

13 (*put violently*) **to clap,** slap, **thrust, fling, hurl,** throw, cast, chuck, toss, bung (*informal*); **plump;** plunk *and* plank *and* plop (*all informal*)

14 to deposit, repose, reposit, rest, **lay,** lodge; **put down,** set down, lay down

15 to load, lade, freight, burden; fill *see* 793.7; **stow,** store, put in storage, warehouse; **pack,** pack away; pile, dump, heap, heap up, stack, mass; bag, sack, pocket

16 to establish, fix, plant, site, pitch, seat, **set; found, base,** ground, lay the foundation; **build,** put up, set up; build in, lay on; **install, invest,** vest, place in office, put in

17 to settle, settle down, sit down, locate, park (*informal*), ensconce, ensconce oneself; take up one's abode *or* quarters, make one's home, **reside, inhabit** *see* 225.7; **move,** locate, relocate, establish residence, make one's home, **take up residence,** take residence at, put up *or* live *or* stay at, lodge at, quarter *or* billet at, move in, hang up one's hat (*informal*); take *or* strike root, put down roots, place oneself, plant oneself, get a footing, stand, take one's stand *or* position; **anchor,** drop anchor, come to anchor, moor; **squat;** camp, bivouac; perch, roost, nest, hive, burrow; domesticate, **set up housekeeping,** keep house; **colonize,** populate, people; **set up in business,** go in business for oneself, set up shop

adjectives

18 located, placed, sited, situated, situate, **positioned,** installed, emplaced, spotted (*informal*), set, seated; **stationed, posted,** deployed, assigned, positioned, prepositioned; **established,** fixed, in place, **settled,** planted, ensconced, embosomed

19 locational, positional, situational, situal; **cartographic**; topographic, geographic, chorographic, geodetic; navigational; **regional** *see* 231.8

adverbs

20 **in place**, in position, in situ, in loco
21 **where**, whereabouts, in what place, in which place; **whither**, to what *or* which place
22 **wherever**, where'er, **wheresoever**, wheresoe'er, whithersoever, wherever it may be; **anywhere**, anyplace (*informal*)
23 **here**, hereat, in this place, just here, on the spot; **hereabouts**, hereabout, in this vicinity, near here; somewhere about *or* near; aboard, on board, with *or* among us; **hither**, hitherward, hitherwards, hereto, hereunto, hereinto, to this place
24 **there**, thereat, in that place, in those parts; **thereabouts**, in that vicinity *or* neighbourhood; **thither**, thitherward, thitherwards, to that place
25 **here and there**, **in places**, in various places, in spots, *passim* (*Latin*)
26 **somewhere**, **someplace**, in some place, someplace or other

prepositions

27 **at**, **in**, **on**, **by**; **near**, **next to**; **with**, **among**, in the midst of; to, toward; from
28 over, all over, here and there on *or* in, at about, round about; through, **all through**, **throughout** *see* 793.17

phrases

29 X marks the spot

160 DISPLACEMENT

nouns

1 **dislocation**, **displacement**; disjointing *see* 801.1, disarticulation, unjointing, unhinging, luxation; heterotopia; **shift**, **removal**, forcible shift *or* removal; eviction; **uprooting**, ripping out, deracination; rootlessness; **disarrangement** *see* 810; incoherence *see* 803.1; discontinuity *see* 812; Doppler effect, red shift, violet shift (*all physics*)
2 **dislodgment**; unplacement, **unseating**, upset, unsaddling, unhorsing; **deposal** *see* 447
3 **misplacement**, **mislaying**, misputting
4 displaced person *or* DP, stateless person, homeless person, Wandering Jew, man without a country, exile, drifter, vagabond, deportee; displaced *or* deported population; *déraciné* (*French*)

verbs

5 **to dislocate**, **displace**, **disjoint**, disarticulate, unjoint, luxate, unhinge, put *or* force *or* push out of place, **put** *or* **throw out of joint**, throw out of gear, **disarrange** *see* 810.2
6 **to dislodge**, unplace; evict; **uproot**, root up *or* out, deracinate; depose *see* 447.4, **unseat**, unsaddle; **unhorse**, dismount; throw off, buck off
7 **to misplace**, **mislay**, misput

adjectives

8 dislocatory, dislocating, heterotopic

9 **dislocated**, **displaced**; **disjointed**, unjointed, unhinged; out, **out of joint**, out of gear; **disarranged** *see* 809.13
10 **unplaced**, unestablished, unsettled; **uprooted**, deracinated; unhoused, evicted, unharboured, houseless, made homeless, homeless, stateless, exiled, outcast
11 **misplaced**, **mislaid**, misput; **out of place**, out of one's element, like a fish out of water, in the wrong place, in the wrong box *or* pew *and* in the right church but the wrong pew (*all informal*)
12 **eccentric**, **off-centre**, off-balance, unbalanced, uncentred

161 DIRECTION
compass direction or course

nouns

1 **direction**, directionality; **line**, direction line, line of direction, point, quarter, **aim**, **way**, track, range, **bearing**, azimuth, compass reading, **heading**, **course**; current, set; tendency, trend, inclination, bent, tenor, run, drift; **orientation**, lay, lie; steering, helmsmanship, piloting; navigation *see* 182.1, 2; line of march
2 (*nautical & aviation terms*) vector, tack; compass direction, azimuth, compass bearing *or* heading, magnetic bearing *or* heading, relative bearing *or* heading, true bearing *or* heading *or* course; lee side, weather side *see* 218.3
3 **points of the compass**, cardinal points, half points, quarter points, degrees, compass rose; compass card, lubber line; rhumb, loxodrome; magnetic north, true north *or* geographic north, magnetic *or* compass directions, true directions; **north**, northward, nor'; **south**, southward; **east**, eastward, orient, sunrise; **west**, westward, occident, sunset; southeast, southwest, northeast, northwest
4 **orientation**, bearings; adaptation, adjustment, accommodation, alignment, collimation; disorientation; deviation

verbs

5 **to direct**, **point**, **aim**, **turn**, **bend**, **train**, fix, set, determine; point to *or* at, hold on, fix on, sight on; take aim, aim at, turn *or* train upon; directionize, give a push in the right direction
6 **to direct to**, give directions to, lead *or* conduct to, point out to, show, **show** *or* **point the way**, steer, put on the track, put on the right track, set straight, set *or* put right
7 (*have or take a direction*) **to bear**, **head**, **turn**, **point**, **aim**, take *or* hold a heading, lead, go, steer, direct oneself, align oneself, hang (*informal*); **incline**, **tend**, **trend**, set, dispose, verge, tend to go
8 to go west, wester, go east, easter, go north, go south
9 **to head for**, **bear for**, **go for**, **make for**, hit *or* hit out for (*informal*), **steer for**, hold for, put for, **set out** *or* **off for**, strike out for, take off for (*informal*), bend one's steps for, lay for, bear up for, bear up to, make up to, set in towards; set *or* direct *or* shape one's course for, set one's compass for, sail for *see*

182.35; align one's march; **break for,** make a break for (*informal*), run *or* dash for, make a run *or* dash for

10 to go directly, go straight, follow one's nose, go straight on, **head straight for,** vector for, go straight to the point, steer a straight course, follow a course, keep *or* hold one's course, hold steady for, arrow for, cleave to the line, keep pointed; **make a beeline,** go as the crow flies; take the air line, stay on the beam

11 to orient, orientate, orient *or* orientate oneself, orient the map *or* chart, **take *or* get one's bearings,** get the lay *or* lie of the land, see which way the land lies, see which way the wind blows; adapt, adjust, accommodate

adjectives

12 directional, azimuthal; **direct, straight,** arrow-straight, ruler-straight, straight-ahead, straightforward, straightaway, straightway; **undeviating,** unswerving, unveering; uninterrupted, unbroken; one-way, unidirectional, irreversible

13 directable, aimable, pointable, trainable; **steerable,** dirigible, guidable, leadable; **directed,** guided, aimed; well-aimed *or* directed *or* placed, on the mark, on the nose *or* money (*informal*); **directional,** directive

14 northern, north, northernmost, northerly, northbound, **arctic,** boreal, hyperborean; **southern,** south, southernmost, southerly, southbound, meridional, **antarctic,** austral; **eastern,** east, easternmost *or* eastermost, easterly, eastbound, **oriental; western,** west, westernmost, westerly, westbound, **occidental; northeastern,** northeast, northeasterly; **southeastern,** southeast, southeasterly; **southwestern,** southwest, southwesterly; **northwestern,** northwest, northwesterly

adverbs

15 north, N, nor', northerly, northward, north'ard, norward, northwards, northwardly; north about

16 south, S, southerly, southward, south'ard, southwards, southwardly; south about

17 east, E, easterly, eastward, eastwards, eastwardly, where the sun rises; eastabout

18 west, W, westerly, westernly, westward, westwards, westwardly, where the sun sets; westabout

19 northeast *or* NE, nor'east, northeasterly, northeastward, northeastwards, northeastwardly; north-northeast *or* NNE; northeast by east *or* NE by E; northeast by north *or* NE by N

20 northwest *or* NW, nor'west, northwesterly, northwestward, northwestwards, northwestwardly; north-northwest *or* NNW; northwest by west *or* NW by W; northwest by north *or* NW by N

21 southeast *or* SE, southeasterly, southeastward, southeastwards, southeastwardly; south-southeast *or* SSE; southeast by east *or* SE by E; southeast by south *or* SE by S

22 southwest *or* SW, southwesterly, southwestward, southwestwards, southwestwardly; south-southwest *or* SSW; southwest by south *or* SW by S

23 directly, direct, straight, straightly, **straightforward,** straightforwards, **undeviatingly,** unswervingly, unveeringly; **straight ahead,** dead

ahead; due, dead, due north, etc; right, forthright; in a direct *or* straight line, in line with, in a line for, **in a beeline, as the crow flies,** straight across; straight as an arrow

24 clockwise, rightward *see* 219.7; **counterclockwise,** anticlockwise, widdershins, leftward *see* 220.6; homeward; landward; seaward; earthward; heavenward; leeward, windward *see* 218.9

25 in every direction, in all directions, in all manner of ways, every which way (*informal*), everywhither, **everyway, everywhere,** at every turn, in all directions at once, in every quarter, on every side, all over the place *or* the map (*informal*), all over the shop (*informal*); around, all round, round about; forty ways *or* six ways from Sunday (*informal*); from every quarter, everywhence; from *or* to the four corners of the earth, from *or* to the four winds

prepositions

26 toward, towards, **in the direction of,** to, up, on, upon; against, over against, versus; headed for, bound for, on the way to, on the road *or* high road to, in transit to, en route to, on route to, in passage to

27 through, by, passing by *or* through, **by way of,** by the way of, **via;** over, around, round about, here and there in, all through

162 PROGRESSION
motion forwards

nouns

1 progression, progress, going, going forward; **ongoing,** on-go, go-ahead (*informal*), onward course, rolling, rolling on; **advance,** advancing, **advancement, promotion, furtherance,** furthering; forward motion, forwarding, forwardal; **headway,** way; **leap, jump,** forward leap *or* jump, quantum jump *or* leap, spring, forward spring; progressiveness, progressivity; **passage,** course, march, career, full career; midpassage, midcourse, midcareer; travel *see* 177; improvement *see* 392

verbs

2 to progress, advance, proceed, go, go *or* move forward, step forward, go on, **go ahead,** go along, push ahead, pass on *or* along; move, travel; go fast *see* 174.8; **make progress,** come on, **get along,** come along (*informal*), **get ahead;** further oneself; **make headway, roll,** gather head, gather way; make strides *or* rapid strides, cover ground, get over the ground, make good time, make the best of one's way, leap *or* jump *or* spring forward, catapult oneself forward, fast-forward; make up for lost time, gain ground, make up leeway, make progress against, make head against, stem

3 to march on, run on, rub on, **jog on, roll on,** flow on; drift along, go with the stream, go with the flow

4 to make *or* wend one's way, work *or* weave one's way, worm *or* thread one's way, inch forward, feel one's way, muddle along *or* through; go slow *see* 175.6; carve one's way; push *or* force one's way, fight one's way, go *or* swim against the current, swim upstream; come a long way, move up in the world; **forge ahead**, drive on *or* ahead, **push** *or* **press on** *or* **onward**, push *or* press forward, push, crowd

5 to **advance**, **further**, **promote**, forward, hasten, contribute to, foster, aid, facilitate, expedite, abet

adjectives

6 **progressive**, progressing, advancing, proceeding, **ongoing**, oncoming, onward, forward, **forward-looking**, go-ahead (*informal*); moving

adverbs

7 **in progress**, in mid-progress, in midcourse, in midcareer, in full career; **going on**; by leaps and bounds

8 **forward**, forwards, onward, onwards, forth, on, along, **ahead**; on the way to, on the road *or* high road to, en route to *or* for

163 REGRESSION
motion backwards

nouns

1 **regression**, regress; recession *see* 168; **retrogression**, retrocession, retroflexion, reflux, refluence, retrogradation, retroaction, retrusion, reaction; return, reentry; **setback, throwback,** rollback; back-pedalling, backward motion, backward step; sternway; **backsliding**, lapse, relapse, recidivism, recidivation

2 **retreat**, *reculade* (*French*), **withdrawal**, withdrawment, strategic withdrawal, exfiltration; **retirement, fallback,** pullout, pullback; advance to the rear; rout; disengagement; **backing down** *or* **off** *or* **out** (*all informal*); reneging, copping *or* weaselling out (*informal*)

3 **reverse, reversal,** reversing, reversion; **backing,** backing up, backup; **about-face,** *volte-face* (*French*), about-turn, right-about, right-about-face, turn to the right-about, U-turn, turnaround, turnabout, swingaround; back track, back trail

4 **countermotion**, countermovement; countermarching, countermarch

verbs

5 to **regress**, go backwards, **recede**, return, revert; **retrogress**, retrograde, retroflex, retrocede; pull back, jerk back, reach back, cock (the arm, fist, etc); *reculer pour mieux sauter* (*French*); fall *or* get *or* go behind, fall astern, lose ground, slip back; **backslide**, lapse, relapse, recidivate

6 to **retreat**, sound *or* beat a retreat, beat a hasty retreat, **withdraw, retire,** pull out *or* back, exfiltrate, advance to the rear, disengage; **fall back,** move back, go back, stand back; run back; **draw back,** draw off; **back out** *or* **out of** *and* **back off** *and* **back down** (*all informal*); defer, give ground, give place, take a back seat, play second fiddle

7 to **reverse**, go into reverse; **back, back up,** backpedal, back off *or* away; **backwater,** make sternway; **backtrack,** backtrail, take the back track; countermarch; reverse one's field; take the reciprocal course; have second thoughts, think better of it, cut one's losses

8 to **turn back**, put back; double, double back, retrace one's steps; turn one's back upon; **return,** go *or* come back, go *or* come home

9 to **turn round** *or* **around** *or* **about**, turn, make a U-turn, turn tail, **come** *or* **go about**, put about, fetch about; veer, veer around; **swivel**, pivot, pivot about, swing, round, swing round; wheel, wheel about, whirl, spin; heel, turn upon one's heel

10 to **about-face**, *volte-face* (*French*), right-about-face, **do an about-face** *or* a right-about-face *or* an about-turn, perform a *volte-face*, **face about,** turn *or* face to the right-about, do a turn to the right-about

adjectives

11 **regressive**, recessive; **retrogressive**, retrocessive, retrograde, retral; retroactive; reactionary

12 **backward**, reversed, reflex, **turned around**, back, **backward**; wrong-way, wrong-way around, counter

adverbs

13 **backwards**, backward, retrally, **hindwards**, hindward, **rearwards**, rearward, arear, astern; **back**, away, fro, *à reculons* (*French*); **in reverse**; against the grain, *à rebours* (*French*); counterclockwise, anticlockwise, widdershins

word elements

14 an–, ana–, re–, retro–

164 DEVIATION
indirect course

nouns

1 **deviation**, deviance *or* deviancy, deviousness, **departure, digression,** diversion, **divergence,** divarication, branching off, divagation, declination, aberration, aberrancy, **variation,** indirection, exorbitation; detour, excursion, excursus, discursion; obliquity, bias, skew, slant; **circuitousness** *see* 913; **wandering**, rambling, **straying**, errantry, perrerration; drift, drifting; turning, shifting, swerving, swinging; **turn, corner, bend, curve,** dogleg, crook, hairpin, zigzag, twist, warp, swerve, **veer**, sheer, sweep; shift, double; tack, yaw; wandering *or* twisting *or* zigzag *or* shifting course *or* path

2 **deflection, bending,** deflexure, flection, flexure; torsion, distortion, contortion, torture *or* torturing, twisting, warping; skewness; **refraction, diffraction, scatter,** diffusion, dispersion

verbs

3 to **deviate**, **depart from**, **vary**, **diverge**, divaricate, branch off, angle, angle off; **digress**, divagate, turn aside, go out of the way, detour, take a side road; **swerve, veer,** sheer, curve, **shift, turn,** trend, bend, heel, bear off; turn right, turn left, hang a right *or* left (*informal*); alter one's course, make a course correction, change the bearing; tack *see* 182.30

4 to **stray**, go astray, lose one's way, err; take a wrong turn *or* turning; drift, go adrift; **wander**, wander off, ramble, rove, straggle, divagate, excurse, pererrate; meander, wind, twist, snake, twist and turn

5 to **deflect**, deviate, **divert**, diverge, **bend**, curve,
pull, crook, dogleg, hairpin, zigzag, corkscrew; **warp**,
bias, twist, distort, contort, torture, skew; refract,
diffract, **scatter**, **diffuse**, **disperse**

6 to **avoid**, **evade**, **dodge**, duck (*informal*), turn aside
or to the side, draw aside, **turn away**, jib, shy, shy
off; gee, haw; **sidetrack**, shove aside, shunt, switch;
avert; **head off**, turn back *see* 907.3; **step aside**,
sidestep, move aside *or* to the side, sidle; **steer clear
of**, make way for, get out of the way of; go off, bear
off, sheer off, veer off, ease off, edge off; fly off, go
or fly off at a tangent; glance, glance off

adjectives

7 **deviative**, deviatory, deviating, **deviant**, departing,
aberrant, aberrational, aberrative, shifting, turning,
swerving, veering; **digressive**, discursive, excursive,
circuitous; **devious**, indirect, out-of-the-way; errant,
erratic, zigzag, doglegged, **wandering**, rambling,
roving, winding, twisting, meandering, snaky,
serpentine, mazy, labyrinthine, vagrant, stray,
desultory, planetary, undirected

8 **deflective**, inflective, flectional, diffractive, refractive;
refractile, refrangible; deflected, flexed, refracted,
diffracted, scattered, diffuse, diffused, dispersed;
distorted, skewed, skew

9 **avertive**, **evasive**, dodging, dodgy

165 LEADING
going ahead

nouns

1 **leading**, **heading**, foregoing; anteposition, the lead,
le pas (*French*); **preceding**, precedence *see* 813;
priority *see* 833.1; front, point, leading edge, cutting
edge, forefront, vanguard, van *see* 216.2; vaunt-
courier (*old*), herald, precursor *see* 815

verbs

2 to **lead**, **head**, spearhead, stand at the head, stand
first, be way ahead (*informal*), head the line; take the
lead, go in the lead, **lead the way**, break the trail,
be the bellwether, lead the pack; be the point *or*
point man; lead the dance; **light the way**, show the
way, beacon, guide; get before, get ahead *or* in front
of, come to the front, come to the fore, lap, outstrip,
pace, set the pace; not look back; get *or* have the
start, get a head start, steal a march upon; **precede**
see 813.2, **go before** *see* 815.3

adjectives

3 **leading**, **heading**, precessional, precedent,
precursory, foregoing; **first**, **foremost**, headmost;
preceding, antecedent *see* 813.4; **prior** *see* 833.4;
chief *see* 249.14

adverbs

4 **before** *see* 813.6, in front, out in front, outfront,
foremost, headmost, in the van, in the forefront, in
advance *see* 216.12

166 FOLLOWING
going behind

nouns

1 **following**, heeling, **trailing**, tailing (*informal*),
shadowing; **hounding**, **dogging**, chasing, **pursuit**,
pursual, pursuance; sequence *see* 814; sequel *see* 816;
series *see* 811.2

2 **follower**, successor; shadow *and* tail (*both informal*);
pursuer, pursuivant; **attendant** *see* 768.4, **satellite**,
hanger-on, dangler, adherent, appendage,
dependent, parasite, stooge (*informal*), flunky;
henchman, ward heeler, partisan, supporter, votary,
sectary; camp follower, groupie (*informal*); fan *and*
buff (*both informal*); courtier, *homme de cour* (*French*),
cavaliere servente (*Italian*); trainbearer; **public**;
entourage, **following** *see* 768.6; disciple *see* 572.2,
discipleship

verbs

3 to **follow**, go after *or* behind, come after *or* behind,
move behind; **pursue**, **shadow** *and* **tail** (*both
informal*), **trail**, trail after, follow in the trail of,
camp on the trail of, **heel**, follow *or* tread *or* step on
the heels of, follow in the steps *or* footsteps *or*
footprints of, tread close upon, breathe down the
neck of, follow in the wake of, hang on the skirts of,
stick like the shadow of, sit on the tail of, tailgate
(*informal*), go in the rear of, bring up the rear, eat
the dust of, take *or* swallow one's dust; tag *and* **tag
after** *and* tag along (*all informal*); string along
(*informal*); **dog**, bedog, **hound**, chase, get after, take
out *or* take off after, **pursue**

4 to **lag**, **lag behind**, **straggle**, lag back, drag, trail,
trail behind, hang back *or* behind, loiter, linger,
loiter *or* **linger behind**, dawdle, get behind, fall
behind *or* behindhand, let grass grow under one's
feet

adjectives

5 **following**, trailing, on the track *or* trail; succeeding
see 814.4; back-to-back (*informal*), consecutive *see*
811.9

adverbs

6 **behind**, **after**, in the rear, in the train *or* wake of;
at *or* to the back of *see* 217.13

167 APPROACH
motion towards

nouns

1 **approach**, approaching, coming *or* going toward,
coming *or* going near, proximation, appropinquation
(*old*), **access**, accession, nearing; advance, oncoming;
advent, **coming**, forthcoming; flowing toward,
afflux, affluxion; appulse; nearness *see* 223;
imminence *see* 839; approximation *see* 223.1

2 **approachability**, **accessibility**, **access**,
getatableness *and* come-at-ableness (*both informal*),
attainability, openness

verbs

3 to **approach**, **near**, **draw near** *or* nigh, go *or* come
near, go *or* come toward, come closer *or* nearer,

come to close quarters; **close**, close in, close in on, close with; zoom in on; **accost**, encounter, confront; proximate, appropinquate (*old*); **advance**, **come**, **come forward**, come on, come up, bear up, step up; ease *or* edge *or* sidle up to; bear down on *or* upon, be on a collision course with; gain upon, narrow the gap; approximate *see* 783.7, 223.8

adjectives

4 **approaching**, **nearing**, advancing; attracted to, drawn to; **coming**, **oncoming**, **forthcoming**, upcoming, to come; approximate, proximate, approximative; near *see* 223.14; imminent *see* 839.3

5 **approachable**, **accessible**, getatable *and* come-at-able (*both informal*), attainable, open, easy to find, meet, etc

168 RECESSION
motion from

nouns

1 **recession**, recedence, receding, retrocedence; **retreat**, **retirement**, **withdrawing**, **withdrawal**; retraction, retractation, retractility; fleetingness, fugitiveness, fugitivity, evanescence

verbs

2 **to recede**, retrocede; **retreat**, **retire**, **withdraw**; move off *or* away, stand off *or* away, stand out from the shore; go, **go away**; **die away**, fade away, drift away; erode, wash away; **diminish**, decline, sink, shrink, dwindle, **fade**, **ebb**, wane; shy away, tail away, tail off; go out with the tide, fade into the distance; pull away, widen the distance

3 **to retract**, withdraw, **draw** *or* **pull back**, pull out, draw *or* pull in; draw in one's claws *or* horns; defer, take a back seat, play second fiddle; **shrink**, wince, cringe, flinch, shy, fight shy, duck

adjectives

4 **recessive**, recessional, recessionary; recedent, retrocedent

5 **receding**, **retreating**, retiring, withdrawing; shy; **diminishing**, **declining**, sinking, shrinking, eroding, dwindling, **ebbing**, waning; **fading**, dying; fleeting, fugitive, evanescent

6 **retractile**, retractable, retrahent

169 CONVERGENCE
coming together

nouns

1 **convergence**, converging, confluence, concourse, conflux; mutual approach, approach *see* 167; **meeting**, congress, concurrence; **concentration**, concentralization, focalization *see* 208.8, focus *see* 208.4; meeting point, point of convergence, vanishing point; union, merger; crossing point, crossroads, crossing *see* 170; collision course, narrowing gap; funnel, bottleneck; hub, spokes; asymptote; radius; tangent

verbs

2 **to converge, come together**, approach *see* 167.3, run together, **meet**, unite, connect, merge; **cross**, **intersect** *see* 170.6; fall in with, link up with; be on a collision course; go toward, narrow the gap, close with, close, close up, close in; funnel; taper, pinch, nip; centralize, centre, **come to a centre**; centre on *or* around, concentralize, concentre, **concentrate**, come *or* tend to a point; **come to a focus** *see* 208.10

adjectives

3 **converging**, convergent; **meeting**, uniting, merging; concurrent, confluent, mutually approaching, approaching; **crossing**, **intersecting** *see* 170.8; connivent; **focal**, confocal, focusing, focused; centrolineal, centripetal; asymptotic, asymptotical; tangent, tangential

170 CROSSING

nouns

1 **crossing**, intercrossing, intersecting, **intersection**; decussation, chiasma; traversal, transversion; cross section, transection; cruciation; **transit**, transiting

2 **crossing**, crosswalk (*US & Canadian*), pedestrian crossing, pelican crossing, puffin crossing, zebra *or* zebra crossing; *carrefour* (*French*); **intersection**, intercrossing; level crossing, grade crossing; flyover, overpass, crossover, viaduct, underpass, undercrossing; subway, tunnel; roundabout, traffic circle *or* rotary (*both US & Canadian*); **interchange**, spaghetti junction, cloverleaf, highway interchange (*US & Canadian*)

3 **network**, **webwork**, **weaving** *see* 740, **meshwork**, tissue, crossing over and under, interlacement, intertwinement, intertexture, texture, reticulum, reticulation;
"Any thing reticulated or decussated, at equal distances, with interstices between the intersections"—SAMUEL JOHNSON; crossing-out, cancellation, scrubbing (*informal*); **net**, netting; **mesh**, meshes; **web**, webbing; weave, weft; lace, lacery, lacing, lacework; screen, screening; sieve, riddle, raddle; wicker, wickerwork; basketwork, basketry; lattice, latticework; hachure *or* hatchure, hatching, cross-hatching; trellis, trelliswork, treillage; grate, grating; grille, grillwork; **grid**, gridiron; tracery, fretwork, fret, arabesque, filigree; plexus, plexure; reticle, reticule; wattle, wattle and daub

4 **cross**, crux, cruciform; **crucifix**, rood, tree *or* rood tree (*old*); Maltese cross, Greek cross, cross of Lorraine, Celtic cross, Saltire *or* Saint Andrew's cross, tau cross *or* Saint Anthony's cross, Saint Bridget's cross, Saint George's cross, Calvary cross, Jerusalem criss *or* cross potent, papal cross; X *or* ex, exing, T, Y; **swastika**, gammadion, fylfot, *Hakenkreuz* (*German*); crossbones; dagger

5 **crosspiece**, traverse, transverse, transversal, transept, transom, cross bitt; diagonal; **crossbar**, crossarm; swingletree, singletree, whiffletree, whippletree; doubletree

verbs

6 **to cross, crisscross,** cruciate; **intersect,** intercross, decussate; **cut across,** crosscut; **traverse,** transverse, lie across; bar, crossbar

7 to net, web, mesh; lattice, trellis; grate, grid

adjectives

8 **cross, crossing, crossed; crisscross, crisscrossed; intersecting, intersected,** intersectional; crosscut, cut across; decussate, decussated; chiasmal *or* chiasmic *or* chiastic; secant

9 **transverse,** transversal, traverse; **across,** cross, crossway, **crosswise** *or* crossways, thwart, athwart, overthwart; oblique *see* 204.13

10 **cruciform, crosslike,** cross-shaped, cruciate, X-shaped, cross, crossed; cruciferous

11 **netlike,** retiform, plexiform; **reticulated,** reticular, reticulate; cancellate, cancelled; **netted,** netty; **meshed,** meshy; laced, lacy, lacelike; filigreed; latticed, latticelike; grated, gridded; barred, crossbarred, mullioned; streaked, striped

12 **webbed,** webby, weblike, woven, interwoven, interlaced, intertwined; web-footed, palmiped

adverbs

13 **crosswise** *or* crossways *or* crossway, decussatively; **cross, crisscross, across,** thwart, thwartly, thwartways, **athwart,** athwartwise, overthwart; **traverse,** traversely; **transverse,** transversely, transversally; obliquely *see* 204.21; **sideways** *or* sidewise; contrariwise, contrawise; crossgrained, across the grain, against the grain; athwartship, athwartships

171 DIVERGENCE
recession from one another

nouns

1 **divergence** *or* divergency, divarication; aberration, deviation *see* 164; **separation,** division, decentralization; centrifugence; **radial, radiating,** radiating out, raying out, beaming out; **spread,** spreading, spreading out, splaying, fanning, fanning out, deployment; ripple effect

2 **radiation,** ray, sunray, radius, spoke; radiance, diffusion, scattering, dispersion, emanation; halo, aureole, glory, corona

3 **forking,** furcation, bifurcation, biforking, trifurcation, divarication; **branching,** branching off *or* out, **ramification;** arborescence, arborization, treelikeness

4 **fork, prong,** trident; Y, V; **branch, ramification,** stem, offshoot; **crotch,** crutch; **fan,** delta, Δ; **groin,** inguen; furcula, furculum, **wishbone**

verbs

5 **to diverge,** divaricate; aberrate; **separate,** divide, separate off, split off; spread, **spread out,** outspread, splay, fan out, deploy; go off *or* away, **fly** *or* **go off at a tangent**

6 **to radiate,** radiate out, ray, ray out, beam out; diffuse, emanate, spread, disperse, scatter

7 **to fork,** furcate, bifurcate, trifurcate, divaricate; **branch,** stem, ramify, branch off *or* out

adjectives

8 **diverging,** divergent; divaricate, divaricating; palmate, palmated; fanlike, fan-shaped; deltoid, deltoidal, deltalike, delta-shaped; splayed; centrifugal

9 **radiating,** radial, radiate, radiated; rayed, spoked; radiative

10 **forked, forking,** furcate, biforked, bifurcate, bifurcated, forklike, trifurcate, trifurcated, tridentlike, pronged; **crotched,** Y-shaped, V-shaped; **branched, branching;** arborescent, arboreal, arboriform, treelike, tree-shaped, dendriform, dendritic; branchlike, ramous

172 MOTION
motion in general

nouns

1 **motion; movement,** moving, **momentum; stir,** unrest, restlessness; **going,** running, stirring; **operation,** operating, **working,** ticking; **activity** *see* 330; kinesis, kinetics, kinematics; dynamics; kinesiatrics, kinesipathy, kinesitherapy; **actuation,** motivation; mobilization

2 **course,** career, set, midcareer, **passage, progress,** trend, **advance,** forward motion, going *or* moving on, momentum; **travel** *see* 177; **flow,** flux, flight, **trajectory; stream, current,** run, rush, onrush, ongoing; drift, driftage; backward motion, **regression,** retrogression, sternway, backing, going *or* moving backwards; backflowing, reflowing, refluence, reflux, ebbing, subsiding, withdrawing; downward motion, **descent,** descending, sinking, plunging; upward motion, mounting, climbing, rising, **ascent,** ascending, **soaring;** oblique *or* crosswise motion; sideward *or* sidewise *or* sideways motion; radial motion, angular motion, axial motion; random motion, Brownian movement; perpetual motion

3 **mobility, motivity,** motility, movableness; **locomotion;** motive power

4 **velocity** *see* 174.1,2, rate, gait, pace, tread, step, stride, clip *and* lick (*both informal*)

verbs

5 **to move, budge, stir;** go, run, flow, stream; **progress,** advance; wend, wend one's way; **back,** back up, regress, retrogress; ebb, subside, wane; **descend,** sink, plunge; **ascend,** mount, rise, climb, soar; go sideways, go crabwise; go round *or* around, circle, rotate, gyrate, spin, whirl; travel; move over, get over; shift, change, shift *or* change place; **speed** *see* 174.8; **hurry** *see* 401.5, do on the fly *or* run

6 **to set in motion, move, actuate,** motivate, push, shove, nudge, **drive,** impel, propel; mobilize

adjectives

7 **moving, stirring, in motion;** transitional; **mobile,** motive, motile, motor, motorial, motoric; motivational, impelling, propelling, propellant, driving; travelling; **active** *see* 330.17

8 **flowing,** fluent, passing, streaming, flying, **running, going, progressive,** rushing, onrushing; drifting; **regressive,** retrogressive, back, **backward;** backflowing, refluent, reflowing; descending, sinking,

plunging, **downward**, down-trending; ascending, mounting, rising, soaring, **upward**, up-trending; sideward, sidewise, sideways; **rotary**, rotatory, rotational, round-and-round; axial, gyrational, gyratory

adverbs

9 **under way**, under sail, on one's way, on the go *or* move *or* fly *or* run *or* march, **in motion, astir**; from pillar to post

word elements

10 moto–; kinesia–, kin–, kine–, kino–, kinesi–, kinesio–, kinet–, kineto–

173 QUIESCENCE
being at rest; absence of motion

nouns

1 **quiescence** *or* quiescency, **stillness**, silence *see* 51, quietness, **quiet**, quietude, "lucid stillness" — T S ELIOT; **calmness**, restfulness, **peacefulness**, imperturbability, passiveness, passivity, "wise passiveness" — WORDSWORTH, placidness, **placidity, tranquillity, serenity, peace, composure**; quietism, contemplation, satori, nirvana, samadhi, ataraxy *or* ataraxia; **rest, repose**, silken repose, statuelike *or* marmoreal repose; sleep, slumber *see* 22.2

2 **motionlessness, immobility**; inactivity, inaction; fixity, fixation *see* 854.2

3 **standstill, stand**, stillstand; **stop, halt, cessation** *see* 856; dead stop, dead stand, full stop; deadlock, lock, dead set; running *or* dying down, subsidence, waning, ebbing, wane, ebb

4 **inertness, dormancy; inertia**, vis inertiae; passiveness, passivity; suspense, abeyance, latency; torpor, apathy, indifference, indolence, lotus-eating, languor; **stagnation**, stagnancy, **vegetation**; stasis; deathliness, deadliness; catalepsy, catatonia; entropy

5 **calm, lull**, lull *or* calm before the storm; dead calm, flat calm, oily calm, windlessness, deathlike calm; doldrums, horse latitudes; anticyclone

6 **stuffiness, airlessness, closeness, oppressiveness,** stirlessness, oppression

verbs

7 **to be still, keep quiet**, lie still; **stop moving**, cease motion, freeze *or* seize up, come to a standstill; **rest, repose; remain, stay**, tarry; remain motionless, freeze (*informal*); stand, **stand still**, be at a standstill; stand *or* stick fast, stick, stand firm, stay put (*informal*); stand like a post; **not stir**, not stir a step, not move a muscle; not breathe, hold one's breath; bide, bide one's time, mark time, tread water, coast; rest on one's oars, put one's feet up, rest and be thankful

8 **to quiet**, quieten, lull, **soothe**, quiesce, **calm**, calm down, tranquillize *see* 670.7, pacify, passivize, pour oil on troubled waters; **stop** *see* 856.7, halt, bring to a standstill; **cease** *see* 856.6, wane, subside, ebb, run *or* die down, die off, dwindle, moulder

9 **to stagnate, vegetate**, fust (*old*); sleep, slumber; smoulder, hang fire; **idle**

10 **to sit, set** (*informal*), **sit down, be seated**, remain seated; perch, roost

11 **to becalm**, take the wind out of one's sails

adjectives

12 **quiescent, quiet, still**, stilly (*old*), stillish, hushed; quiet as a mouse; waning, subsiding, ebbing, dwindling, mouldering; **at rest**, resting, reposing; restful, reposeful, relaxed; cloistered, sequestered, sequestrated, isolated, secluded, sheltered; **calm, tranquil, peaceful**, peaceable, pacific, halcyon; **placid, smooth; unruffled, untroubled**, cool, undisturbed, unperturbed, unagitated, unmoved, unstirring, laid-back (*informal*); stolid, stoic, stoical, impassive; even-tenored; calm as a mill pond; still as death, "quiet as a street at night" — RUPERT BROOKE

13 **motionless, unmoving**, unmoved, moveless, **immobile**, immotive; **still, fixed, stationary, static**, at a standstill; **stock-still**, dead-still; still as a statue, statuelike; still as a mouse; at anchor, riding at anchor; **idle**, unemployed; out of commission, down

14 **inert, inactive, static, dormant**, passive, sedentary; **latent**, unaroused, suspended, abeyant, in suspense *or* abeyance; sleeping, slumbering, smouldering; **stagnant**, standing, foul; **torpid, languorous, languid**, apathetic, phlegmatic, **sluggish**, logy (*US*), dopey (*informal*), groggy, heavy, leaden, **dull**, flat, slack, tame, **dead**, lifeless; catatonic, cataleptic

15 **untravelled, stay-at-home**, stick-in-the-mud (*informal*), home-keeping

16 **stuffy, airless**, breathless, breezeless, windless; **close, oppressive, stifling, suffocating**, fuggy; stirless, unstirring, not a breath of air, not a leaf stirring, "not wind enough to twirl the one red leaf" — COLERIDGE; ill-ventilated, unventilated, unvented

17 **becalmed**, in a dead calm

adverbs

18 quiescently, **quietly**, stilly, still; **calmly, tranquilly, peacefully; placidly**, smoothly, unperturbedly, **coolly**

19 **motionlessly**, movelessly, stationarily, fixedly

20 **inertly, inactively**, statically, dormantly, passively, latently; stagnantly; **torpidly, languorously, languidly**; like a bump on a log; **sluggishly**, heavily, dully, coldly, lifelessly, apathetically, phlegmatically; stoically, stolidly, impassively

174 SWIFTNESS

nouns

1 **velocity, speed; rapidity**, celerity, **swiftness, fastness, quickness**, snappiness (*informal*), nippiness (*informal*), **speediness**; haste *see* 401.1, hurry, flurry, rush, precipitation; **dispatch, expedition, promptness**, promptitude, instantaneousness; flight, flit; lightning speed; fast *or* swift rate, smart *or* rattling *or* spanking *or* lively *or* snappy pace, round

pace; air speed, ground speed, speed over the bottom; miles per hour, knots; rpm *see* 914.3

2 **speed of sound, sonic speed,** Mach, Mach number, Mach one, Mach two, etc; subsonic speed; supersonic *or* ultrasonic *or* hypersonic *or* transsonic speed; transsonic barrier, sound barrier; escape velocity; speed of light, terminal velocity; warp speed

3 **run, sprint; dash, rush,** plunge, headlong rush *or* plunge, **race, scurry, scamper,** scud, scuttle, **spurt,** burst, **burst of speed;** canter, **gallop,** lope; high lope, hand gallop, full gallop; dead run; **trot,** extended trot, dogtrot, jog trot; **full speed,** open throttle, flat-out speed, heavy right foot, maximum speed; **fast-forward;** fast track *or* lane; forced draught *and* flank speed (*both nautical*)

4 **acceleration, quickening; pickup,** getaway; step-up, speedup; thrust, drive, impetus

5 **speeder, sprinter;** flier, goer, stepper; **speed demon** *or* maniac *or* merchant (*informal*), boy racer (*informal*); **racer, runner;** horse racer, turfman, jockey; Jehu

6 (*comparisons*) lightning, greased lightning (*informal*), thunderbolt, flash, streak of lightning, streak, blue streak (*informal*), bat out of hell (*informal*), light, electricity, thought, wind, shot, bullet, cannonball, rocket, bomb, arrow, dart, quicksilver, mercury, express train, jet plane, torrent, eagle, swallow, antelope, courser, gazelle, greyhound, hare, scared rabbit

7 **speedometer,** accelerometer; cyclometer; tachometer, rev counter (*informal*); Mach meter; knotmeter, log, log line, patent log, taffrail log, harpoon log, ground log; windsock; wind gauge, anemometer

verbs

8 **to speed,** go fast, skim, fly, flit, fleet, wing one's way, outstrip the wind; **zoom;** make knots, foot; break the sound barrier, go at warp speed; go like the wind, go like a shot *or* flash, go like lightning *or* a streak of lightning, go like greased lightning; **rush, tear,** dash, dart, shoot, hurtle, bolt, fling, **scamper, scurry,** scour, scud, scuttle, scramble, **race,** careen, pelt; **hasten,** haste, make haste, **hurry** *see* 401.4, hie, post; march in quick *or* double-quick time; **run, sprint, trip,** spring, **bound,** leap; gallop, lollop, lope, canter; trot; **make time,** make good time, **cover ground,** get over the ground, **make strides** *or* **rapid strides,** make the best of one's way

9 (*informal terms*) **to barrel,** clip, spank *or* cut along, tear *or* tear along, bowl along, bucket along, bomb along, thunder along, storm along, breeze *or* breeze along, tear up the track *or* road, eat up the track *or* road, scorch, sizzle, rip, zip, whiz, whisk, sweep, brush, hare, nip, zing, fly low, give it the gun, skedaddle, scoot, step on it, step on the gas, stir one's stumps, hotfoot, hightail, make tracks, step lively, step, step along, hop, hop along, hop it, get, git, go like a bat out of hell, run like a scared rabbit, run like mad, go like a bomb, go at full blast, go all out, go flat out, go at full tilt *or* steam *or* pelt, step on it, go hell for leather, get a move on, go like blazes *or* blue blazes

10 **to accelerate, speed up, step up** (*informal*), **hurry up, quicken; hasten** *see* 401.4; get upsteam, pour

on the coal, put on more speed, open the throttle; quicken one's pace; pick up speed, gain ground; race (*a motor*), rev (*informal*), blind (*informal*)

11 (*nautical terms*) to put on sail, crack *or* pack on sail, crowd sail, press her

12 **to spurt,** make a spurt *or* dash, **dash** *or* dart *or* shoot ahead, rush ahead, put on *or* make a burst of speed; make one's move

13 **to overtake, outstrip, overhaul,** catch up, **catch up with,** come up with *or* to, gain on *or* upon, pass, lap; outpace, outrun, outsail; leave behind, leave standing *or* looking *or* flatfooted

14 **to keep up with,** keep pace with, run neck and neck

adjectives

15 **fast, swift, speedy, rapid; quick,** double-quick, express, **fleet, hasty, expeditious,** hustling, snappy (*informal*), nippy (*informal*), rushing, onrushing, dashing, flying, galloping, running, **agile, nimble,** lively, nimble-footed, light-footed, light-legged, light of heel; winged, eagle-winged; mercurial; quick as lightning, quick as thought, swift as an arrow, "swifter than arrow from the Tartar's bow"— Shakespeare; **breakneck,** reckless, headlong, precipitate; quick as a wink, quick on the trigger (*informal*), hair-trigger (*informal*); **prompt** *see* 844.9

16 **supersonic,** transsonic, ultrasonic, hypersonic, faster than sound; warp; **high-speed,** high-velocity, high-geared; ton-up (*informal*)

adverbs

17 **swiftly, rapidly, quickly,** snappily (*informal*), **speedily,** with speed, **fast, quick,** apace, amain, on eagle's wings, *ventre à terre* (*French*); at a great rate, at a good clip (*informal*), with rapid strides, with giant strides, *à pas de géant* (*French*), **by leaps and bounds,** trippingly; **lickety-split** *and* lickety-cut (*both informal*); hell for leather (*informal*); **posthaste,** post, **hastily,** expeditiously, promptly, with great *or* all haste, whip and spur, **hand over fist;** double-quick, in double time, in double-quick time, on the double *or* the double-quick (*both informal*); in high gear, in high; under press of sail, all sails set, under crowded sails, under press of sail and steam, under forced draught, at flank speed (*all nautical*)

18 (*informal terms*) **like a shot, as if shot out of a cannon, like a flash,** like a rat up a drainpipe, like a streak, like a blue streak, like a streak of lightning, like lightning, like greased lightning, like the clappers, **like a bat out of hell, like a scared rabbit,** like a house afire, like mad *and* crazy *and* fury, like sin, like the devil, to beat the band

19 **in no time,** instantaneously, immediately if not sooner, in less than no time; in a jiff *or* jiffy (*informal*), before you can say Jack Robinson, **in a flash,** in a twink, **in a twinkling,** "in the twinkling of an eye"—Bible, *tout de suite* (*French*), pronto (*informal*), PDQ *or* pretty damn quick (*informal*)

20 **at full speed,** with all speed, at full throttle, **at the top of one's bent, for all one is worth** (*informal*), hit the ground running (*informal*), as fast as one's legs will carry one, as fast as one can lay feet to the ground; **at full blast,** at full drive *or* pelt; under full steam, in full sail; **flat out** (*informal*); full speed ahead

175 SLOWNESS

nouns

1 **slowness, leisureliness,** pokiness, slackness, creeping; **sluggishness,** sloth, laziness, idleness, indolence, sluggardy, languor, inertia, inertness, lentitude *or* lentor (*both old*); deliberateness, deliberation, circumspection, tentativeness, cautiousness, reluctance, foot-dragging (*informal*); drawl

2 **slow motion,** slow-mo *or* slo-mo (*informal*), **leisurely gait,** snail's *or* tortoise's pace; **creep, crawl; walk,** walking pace, footpace, dragging *or* lumbering pace, trudge, waddle, saunter, stroll; slouch, shuffle, plod, shamble; limp, claudication, hobble; dogtrot, jog trot; jog, rack; mincing steps; slow march, dead *or* funeral march, largo, andante

3 **dawdling, lingering, loitering, tarrying,** dalliance, **dallying,** dillydallying, shillyshallying, lollygagging (*US*), dilatoriness, delaying tactic, delayed action, procrastination *see* 845.5, lag, **lagging,** goofing off (*US informal*)

4 **slowing, retardation,** retardment, **slackening,** flagging, slowing down; **slowdown,** slowup, **letup, letdown, slack-up, slack-off,** ease-off, ease-up; **deceleration,** negative *or* minus acceleration; **delay** *see* 845.2, **detention, setback, holdup** (*informal*), check, arrest, obstruction; lag, drag

5 **slowcoach** (*informal*), slowpoke (*informal*), plodder, slow goer, slow-foot, **lingerer, loiterer, dawdler,** dawdle, **laggard,** procrastinator, foot-dragger, drone, slug, sluggard, lie-abed, sleepy-head, goldbrick (*US informal*); tortoise, snail

verbs

6 **to go slow** *or* **slowly,** go at a snail's pace, take it slow; **drag,** drag out; **creep, crawl;** laze, idle; go dead slow, get nowhere fast; inch, inch along; worm, worm along; poke, **poke along;** shuffle *or* stagger *or* totter *or* toddle along; drag along, drag one's feet, walk, traipse *and* **mosey** *and* trog (*all informal*); **saunter, stroll, amble,** waddle, toddle (*informal*); jogtrot, dogtrot; limp, hobble, claudicate

7 **to plod,** plug (*informal*), peg, shamble, **trudge,** tramp, stump, lumber; plod along, plug along (*informal*), schlep (*informal*); rub on, jog on, chug on

8 **to dawdle, linger, loiter, tarry, delay, dally, dillydally,** shilly-shally, lollygag (*US*), waste time, **take one's time,** take one's own sweet time; goof off *or* around (*US informal*); lag, drag, trail; flag, falter, halt

9 **to slow, slow down** *or* **up, let down** *or* **up, ease off** *or* **up, slack off** *or* **up, slacken,** relax, moderate, taper off, lose speed *or* momentum; **decelerate, retard, delay** *see* 845.8, **detain,** impede, obstruct, arrest, stay, **check,** curb, **hold up, hold back,** keep back, set back, hold in check; draw rein, rein in; throttle down, take one's foot off the gas; idle, barely tick over; brake, **put on the**

brakes, put on the drag; reef, take in sail; backwater, backpedal; lose ground; clip the wings

adjectives

10 **slow, leisurely,** slack, moderate, gentle, **easy,** deliberate, go-slow, unhurried, relaxed, gradual, circumspect, tentative, cautious, reluctant, foot-dragging (*informal*); **creeping, crawling;** poking, poky, slow-poky (*informal*); tottering, staggering, toddling, trudging, **lumbering,** ambling, waddling, shuffling, **sauntering,** strolling; **sluggish,** languid, languorous, lazy, slothful, indolent, idle, slouchy; **slow-going, slow-moving,** slow-creeping, slow-crawling, slow-running, slow-sailing; **slow-footed,** slow-foot, slow-legged, slow-gaited, slow-paced, slow-stepped, easy-paced, slow-winged; snail-paced, snail-like, tortoiselike, turtlelike,

"creeping like snail"—SHAKESPEARE; limping, hobbling, hobbled; halting, claudicant; faltering, flagging; slow as slow, slow as treacle, slow as molasses, slow as death, slower than the seven-year itch (*informal*)

11 **dawdling, lingering, loitering, tarrying, dallying, dillydallying,** shilly-shallying, lollygagging (*US*), procrastinatory *or* procrastinative, dilatory, delaying *see* 845.17, **lagging,** dragging

12 **retarded,** slowed-down, eased, slackened; **delayed, detained,** checked, **arrested,** impeded, set back, backward, behind; late, **tardy** *see* 845.16

adverbs

13 **slowly, slow, leisurely,** unhurriedly, relaxedly, easily, moderately, gently; creepingly, crawlingly; pokingly, pokily; **sluggishly,** languidly, languorously, lazily, indolently, idly, deliberately, with deliberation, circumspectly, tentatively, cautiously, reluctantly; **lingeringly,** loiteringly, tarryingly, dilatorily; limpingly, haltingly, falteringly; **in slow motion,** at a funeral pace, with faltering *or* halting steps; at a snail's *or* turtle's pace,

"in haste like a snail"—JOHN HEYWOOD; in slow tempo, in march time; with agonizing slowness; in low gear; under easy sail

14 **gradually,** little by little *see* 245.6

phrases

15 **easy does it,** take it easy, go easy, slack off, slow down

176 TRANSFERRAL, TRANSPORTATION

1 **transference, transferral, transfer; transmission,** transference, transmittal, transmittance; transposition, transposal, transplacement; mutual transfer, interchange, metathesis; translocation, **transplantation,** translation; migration, transmigration; **import, importation; export, exportation;** deportation, extradition, expulsion, **transit,** transition, **passage; communication,** spread, spreading, dissemination, diffusion, contagion, ripple effect; metastasis; transmigration of souls, metempsychosis; passing over; osmosis, diapedesis; transduction, conduction, convection; transfusion, perfusion; transfer of property *or* right *see* 629

2 transferability, conveyability; transmissibility, transmittability; movability, removability; **portability**, transportability; communicability, impartability; deliverability

3 **transportation, conveyance, transport, carrying,** bearing, packing, toting *and* lugging (*both informal*); **carriage,** carry, **hauling,** haulage, portage, porterage, waft, waftage; **cartage, truckage,** drayage, wagonage; ferriage, lighterage, waterage; telpherage; **freightage,** freight, expressage, railway express; **airfreight, air express,** airlift; **package freight,** package service; **shipment, shipping,** transshipment; containerization, cargo-handling; delivery *see* 478.1; travel *see* 177

4 **moving, removal, movement,** relocation, shift, removement; **displacement,** delocalization

5 people mover, moving pavement, automated monorail; conveyor belt; lift, elevator, hoist, escalator *see* 911.4

6 **freight,** freightage; **shipment, consignment,** goods; **cargo,** payload; lading, load, pack; **baggage, luggage,** impedimenta

7 **carrier, conveyor** *or* **conveyer;** transporter, haulier *or* haulage contractor, carter, wagoner, drayman, shipper, trucker, common carrier, lorry driver; freighter; containerizer; stevedore, cargo handler; expressman, express; **bearer, porter,** redcap (*US & Canadian*); coolie; litter-bearer, stretcher-bearer; caddie; shield-bearer, gun bearer; water carrier *or* bearer, water boy, bheesty (*India*); the Water Bearer, Aquarius; letter carrier *see* 353.5; cupbearer, Ganymede, Hebe

8 **beast of burden; pack** *or* **draught animal,** pack horse *or* mule, sumpter, sumpter horse *or* mule; **horse** *see* 311.10-15, ass, mule; ox; camel, ship of the desert, dromedary, llama; reindeer; elephant; sledge dog, husky, malamute, Siberian husky

9 (*geological terms*) **deposit,** sediment; drift, silt, loess, moraine, scree, sinter; alluvium, alluvion, diluvium; detritus, debris

verbs

10 **to transfer, transmit, transpose,** translocate, transplace, metathesize, switch; **transplant,** translate; **pass,** pass over, **hand over,** turn over, carry over, make over, consign, assign; **deliver** *see* 478.13; pass on, pass the buck (*informal*), hand forward, hand on, relay; **import, export;** deport, extradite, expel; communicate, diffuse, disseminate, spread, impart; transfuse, perfuse, transfer property *or* right *see* 629.3

11 **to remove, move, relocate, shift,** send, shunt; second; displace, delocalize, dislodge; **take away,** cart off *or* away, carry off *or* away; manhandle; set *or* lay *or* put aside, put *or* set to one side, side

12 **to transport, convey,** freight, conduct, **take; carry, bear,** pack, tote *and* lug *and* hump (*all informal*), manhandle; lift, waft, whisk, wing, fly

13 **to haul, cart,** truck, bus; **ship,** barge, lighter, ferry; raft, float

14 (*convey through a channel*) **to channel,** put through channels; **pipe,** tube, pipeline, flume, **siphon, funnel,** tap

15 **to send,** send off *or* away, send forth; **dispatch,** transmit, remit, consign, forward; expedite; **ship,** ship off, freight, airfreight, embark, containerize, **transship,** pass along, send on; **express,** air-express; express-mail; package-express; **post, mail,** airmail, drop a letter; messenger; export

16 **to fetch, bring, go get,** go and get, go to get, **go after,** go fetch, **go for,** call for, pick up; **get,** obtain, procure, secure; **bring back, retrieve;** chase after, run after, fetch and carry

17 **to ladle, dip, scoop; bail,** bucket; **dish,** dish out *or* up; **cup; shovel,** spade, fork; spoon; **pour,** decant

adjectives

18 **transferable, conveyable; transmittable,** transmissible, transmissive, consignable, deliverable; **movable,** removable; **portable,** portative; transportable, transportative, transportive; conductive, conductional; transposable, interchangeable; **communicable,** contagious, impartable; transfusable; metastatic *or* metastatical, metathetic *or* metathetical; mailable, expressable; assignable *see* 629.5

adverbs

19 by transfer, from hand to hand, from door to door; by freight, by express, by rail, by trolley, by bus, by steamer, by aeroplane, by mail, by special delivery, by package express, by messenger, by hand

20 **on the way,** along the way, on the road *or* high road, **en route, in transit,** *in transitu* (*Latin*), on the wing, as one goes; in passing, *en passant* (*French*); in mid-progress

177 TRAVEL

nouns

1 **travel,** travelling, going, journeying, touring, moving, **movement, motion, locomotion, transit, progress, passage,** course, crossing; commutation, straphanging; world travel, globe-trotting (*informal*); junketing; **tourism,** touristry

2 **travels,** journeys, **journeyings, wanderings,** voyagings, transits, peregrinations, peripatetics, migrations, transmigrations; odyssey

3 **wandering, roving, roaming, rambling, gadding,** traipsing (*informal*), wayfaring, flitting, straying, drifting, gallivanting, peregrination, peregrinity, pilgrimage, errantry, divagation; roam, rove, ramble; **itinerancy,** itineracy; **nomadism,** nomadization, gypsydom; vagabonding, vagabondism, vagabondage; **vagrancy,** hoboism, waltzing Matilda (*Australian*); bumming (*informal*); the open road; wanderyear, *Wanderjahr* (*German*); **wanderlust;** "afoot and lighthearted"—WHITMAN

4 **migration, transmigration,** passage, trek; run (*of fish*), flight (*of birds and insects*); swarm, swarming (*of bees*); **immigration,** in-migration; **emigration,** out-migration, expatriation; remigration; intermigration

5 **journey, trip,** *jornada* (*Spanish*), peregrination, sally, **trek; progress,** course, run; **tour,** grand tour; tourist season, low season, high season; tourist class; travel agency *or* bureau, holiday company, tour operator; **conducted tour,** package tour *or* holiday; **excursion, jaunt, junket, outing,** pleasure trip, jolly; sight-seeing trip *or* tour, rubberneck tour (*informal*); day trip, awayday; round trip, circuit, turn; **cruise**, package cruise, cruise to nowhere; **expedition**, campaign; safari, hunting expedition, hunting trip, stalk, shoot, photography safari; **pilgrimage**, hajj; **voyage** *see* 182.6

6 riding, driving; motoring, automobiling (*US*); busing *or* bussing, coaching; motorcycling, bicycling, cycling, pedalling, biking (*informal*); **horseback riding**, horse-riding, equitation; horsemanship, manège; pony-trekking

7 ride, drive; spin *and* whirl *and* run (*all informal*), hurl (*Scottish*), burl (*Australian & NZ*); joyride (*informal*); Sunday drive; airing; lift (*informal*), pickup (*informal*)

8 walking, ambulation, perambulation, pedestrianism, shank's mare *or* pony (*informal*), going on foot *or* afoot, footing *or* hoofing, footing it *or* hoofing it; strolling, sauntering, ambling, *flânerie* (*French*); **tramping, marching, hiking**, backpacking, trailhiking, footslogging, trudging, treading; lumbering, waddling; toddling, staggering, tottering; **hitchhiking** *and* hitching (*both informal*), thumbing *and* thumbing a lift (*both informal*); jaywalking

9 nightwalking, noctambulation, noctambulism; night-wandering, noctivagation; **sleepwalking**, somnambulation, somnambulism; sleepwalk

10 walk, ramble, amble, **hike, tramp**, traipse (*informal*); slog, trudge, schlep (*informal*); **stroll**, saunter; **promenade**; *passeggiata* (*Italian*); jaunt, airing; **constitutional** (*informal*), stretch; turn; peripatetic journey *or* exercise, peripateticism; walking tour *or* excursion; **march**, forced march, route march; parade

11 step, pace, stride; footstep, footfall, tread; hoofbeat, clop; hop, jump; skip, hippety-hop (*informal*)

12 gait, pace, walk, step, stride, tread; saunter, stroll, strolling gait; shuffle, shamble, hobble, limp, hitch, waddle; totter, stagger, lurch; toddle, paddle; slouch, droop, drag; mince, mincing steps, scuttle, prance, flounce, stalk, strut, swagger; slink, slither, sidle; jog; swing, roll; amble, single-foot, rack, piaffer; trot, gallop *see* 174.3; lock step; velocity *see* 174.1, 2; slowness *see* 175

13 march; quick *or* quickstep march, quickstep, quick time; lockstep; double march, double-quick, double time; slow march, slow time; half step; goose step

14 leg, limb, shank; hind leg, foreleg; gamb, jamb (*heraldry*); shin, cnemis; ankle, tarsus; hock, gambrel; calf; knee; thigh; popliteal space, ham, drumstick; gigot

15 (*informal terms*) gams, stems, trotters, hind legs, underpinnings, wheels, shanks, sticks, pins, stumps

16 gliding, sliding, slipping, slithering, skiting (*Scottish*), coasting, sweeping, flowing, sailing; **skating, skiing, tobogganing, sledging**; glide, slide, slither, sweep, skim, flow

17 creeping, crawling, going on all fours; sneaking, stealing, slinking, sidling, pussyfooting (*informal*), gumshoeing (*US & Canadian informal*), walking on eggs, padding, prowling, nightwalking; worming, snaking; tiptoeing, tiptoe, tippytoe; creep, crawl, scramble, scrabble; all fours

verbs

18 to travel, go, move, pass, fare, fare forth, fetch, flit, hie, sashay (*informal*), cover ground; **progress** *see* 162.2; move on *or* along, go along; wend, **wend one's way**; betake oneself, direct one's course, bend one's steps *or* course; course, run, flow, stream; roll, roll on; commute, straphang

19 (*go at a given speed*) **to go, go at**, reach, **make, do, hit** (*informal*)

20 to traverse, cross, travel over *or* through, pass through, **go** *or* **pass over, cover**, measure, transit, track, range, range over *or* through, course, do, perambulate, peregrinate, overpass, go over the ground; patrol, reconnoitre, scout; sweep, go *or* make one's rounds, scour, scour the country; ply, voyage *see* 182.13

21 to journey, travel, make *or* take *or* go *or* go on a journey, **take** *or* **make a trip**, fare, **gad around** *or* **about**, get around *or* about, navigate, trek, **jaunt**, peregrinate; junket, go on a junket; **tour**; hit the trail (*informal*), take to the road, go on the road; **cruise, go on a cruise**, voyage *see* 182.13; go abroad, go to foreign places *or* shores, range the world, globe-trot (*informal*); travel light, live out of a suitcase; pilgrimage, pilgrim, go on *or* make a pilgrimage; campaign, go overseas, go on an expedition, go on safari; go on a sight-seeing trip, sight-see, rubberneck (*informal*)

22 to migrate, transmigrate, trek; flit, take wing; run (*of fish*), swarm (*of bees*); **emigrate**, out-migrate, expatriate; **immigrate**, in-migrate; remigrate; intermigrate

23 to wander, roam, rove, range, nomadize, **gad**, gad around *or* about, follow the seasons, flit, traipse (*informal*), gallivant, knock around *or* about *and* bat around *or* about (*all informal*), prowl, **drift, stray**, float around, straggle, **meander, ramble**, stroll, troll (*informal*), trog (*informal*), saunter, jaunt, peregrinate, pererrate, divagate, go *or* run about, go the rounds; **tramp**, bum *or* go on the bum (*informal*), vagabond, vagabondize, take to the road,

"travel the open road"—WHITMAN, beat one's way; **hit the road** *or* **trail** (*informal*), pound the pavement

24 to go for an outing *or* **airing**, take the air, get some air; go for a walk; go for a ride

25 to go to, repair to, resort to, hie to, hie oneself to, arise and go to, direct one's course to, turn one's tracks to, make one's way to, set foot in, bend one's steps to, betake oneself to, **visit**, drop in *or* around *or* by

26 to creep, crawl, scramble, scrabble, grovel, **go on hands and knees**, go on all fours; worm, worm along, worm one's way, snake; inch, inch along; **sneak, steal**, steal along; pussyfoot (*informal*), gumshoe (*US & Canadian informal*), slink, sidle, pad, prowl, nightwalk; **tiptoe**, tippytoe, go on tiptoe

27 to walk, ambulate, peripateticate, pedestrianize, traipse (*informal*); **step, tread, pace, stride**, pad; foot, foot it; leg, leg it; hoof it, go on the heel and toe, ride shank's mare *or* pony (*informal*), stump it (*informal*); peg *or* jog *or* shuffle on *or* along; perambulate; circumambulate; jaywalk; **power walk**, exercise walk, speed walk, race walk

28 (*ways of walking*) **to stroll,** saunter, *flâner* (*French*); shuffle, scuff, scuffle, straggle, shamble, slouch; stride, straddle; **trudge, plod,** peg, traipse (*informal*), clump, stump, slog, footslog, drag, **lumber, barge;** stamp, stomp (*informal*); swing, roll, lunge; hobble, halt, limp, hitch, lurch; totter, stagger; toddle, paddle; waddle, wobble, wamble, wiggle; link, slither, sidle; stalk; **strut, swagger;** mince, sashay (*informal*), scuttle, prance, tittup, flounce, trip, skip, foot; hop, jump, hippety-hop (*informal*); jog, jolt; bundle, bowl along; **amble,** pace; singlefoot, rack; piaffe, piaffer

29 **to go for a walk, perambulate, take a walk, take one's constitutional** (*informal*), take a stretch, stretch the legs; **promenade,** *passeggiare* (*Italian*), parade

30 **to march,** mush, footslog, yomp, **tramp, hike,** backpack, trail-hike; route-march; file, defile, file off; **parade,** go on parade; goose-step, do the goose step; do the lock step

31 **to hitchhike** *or* **hitch** (*informal*), **thumb** *or* **thumb one's way** (*informal*), catch a ride; hitch *or* hook *or* bum *or* cadge *or* thumb a lift (*informal*)

32 **to nightwalk,** noctambulate; **sleepwalk,** somnambulate, walk in one's sleep

33 **to ride, go for a ride** *or* **drive;** go for a spin (*informal*), take *or* go for a Sunday drive; **drive, chauffeur; motor,** taxi; bus; bike *and* cycle *and* wheel *and* pedal (*all informal*); **motorcycle, bicycle;** go by rail, entrain; joyride *or* take a joyride (*informal*); catch *or* make a train (*informal*)

34 **to go on horseback, ride, horse-ride** pony-trek; ride bareback; mount, take horse; hack; ride hard, clap spurs to one's horse; trot, amble, pace, canter, gallop, tittup, lope; prance, frisk, curvet, piaffe, caracole

35 **to glide, coast, skim,** sweep, flow; **sail, fly,** flit; **slide,** slip, skid, skite (*Scottish*), skitter, sideslip, slither, glissade; skate, ice-skate, roller-skate, rollerblade, skateboard; ski; monoski; snowboard; toboggan, sledge, sleigh

adjectives

36 **travelling, going, moving,** trekking, passing; **progressing; itinerant,** itinerary, circuit-riding; **journeying, wayfaring,** strolling; **peripatetic;** ambulant, ambulatory; ambulative; perambulating, perambulatory; peregrine, peregrinative, pilgrimlike; locomotive; **walking, pedestrian, touring,** on tour, globe-trotting (*informal*), mundivagant (*old*); touristic, touristical, touristy (*informal*); expeditionary

37 **wandering, roving, roaming,** ranging, **rambling, meandering,** strolling, **straying,** straggling, shifting, flitting, landloping, errant, divagatory, discursive, circumforaneous; **gadding,** traipsing (*informal*), gallivanting; **nomad,** nomadic, floating, drifting, gypsyish *or* gypsylike; **transient,** transitory, fugitive; **vagrant,** vagabond, vagabondish; **footloose,** footloose and fancy-free; **migratory,** migrational, transmigrant, transmigratory

38 **nightwalking,** noctambulant, noctambulous; night-wandering, noctivagant; **sleepwalking,** somnambulant, somnambular

39 **creeping, crawling,** on hands and knees, on all

fours; reptant, repent, reptile, reptatorial; **on tiptoe,** on tippytoe, atiptoe, tiptoeing, tiptoe, tippytoe

40 **travelled,** well-travelled, cosmopolitan

41 **wayworn,** way-weary, road-weary, leg-weary, **travel-worn,** travel-weary, travel-tired; travel-sated, travel-jaded; travel-soiled, travel-stained, dusty; jet-lagged

adverbs

42 **on the move** *or* **go,** en route, in transit, on the wing *or* fly; on the run, on the jump (*informal*), on the road, on the tramp *or* march; on the gad (*informal*), on the bum (*informal*)

43 **on foot, afoot,** by foot, footback *or* on footback (*informal*); on the heel and toe, on *or* by shank's mare *or* pony (*informal*)

44 **on horseback,** horseback, by horse, mounted

178 TRAVELLER

nouns

1 **traveller,** goer, viator, comer and goer; **wayfarer,** journeyer, trekker; **tourist,** tourer; holiday-maker; **tripper,** day-tripper; cicerone, travel *or* tourist guide; **visitor,** visiting fireman (*informal*); **excursionist, sightseer,** rubberneck *or* rubbernecker (*informal*); **voyager,** cruise-goer, cruiser, sailor, mariner see 183; **globe-trotter** (*informal*), world-traveller, cosmopolite; jet set, jet-setter; **pilgrim,** palmer, hajji; **passenger,** fare; **commuter,** straphanger (*informal*); transient; passerby; adventurer, alpinist, climber, mountaineer; explorer, forty-niner (*US*), pioneer, pathfinder, voortrekker, trailblazer, trailbreaker; camper; astronaut see 1073.8

2 **wanderer, rover, roamer,** rambler, stroller, straggler, mover; **gad, gadabout** (*informal*), runabout, go-about (*informal*); **itinerant,** peripatetic, rolling stone, peregrine, peregrinator, bird of passage, visitant; **drifter** *and* **floater** (*both informal*); Wandering Jew, Ahasuerus, Ancient Mariner (*Samuel Taylor Coleridge*), Argonaut, Flying Dutchman, Oisin, Ossian, Gulliver (*Jonathan Swift*), Ulysses, Odysseus (*Homer*); wandering scholar, Goliard, *vaganti* (*Latin*); strolling player, wandering minstrel, troubadour

3 **vagabond, vagrant,** vag (*US & Australian informal*); **bum** *or* bummer (*informal*), loafer, wastrel, losel (*old*), *lazzarone* (*Italian*); **tramp,** dosser, knight of the road, **hobo** *or* bo (*US & Canadian informal*); landloper, sundowner *or* swagman *or* swagsman *or* bagman (*all Australian informal*); beggar see 440.8; **waif,** homeless waif, dogie (*US & Canadian*), stray, waifs and strays; ragamuffin, tatterdemalion; **gamin,** gamine, urchin, street urchin, dead-end kid (*informal*), grub (*informal*), mudlark, guttersnipe (*informal*); beachcomber, loafer, idler; ski bum, beach bum, surf bum, tennis bum; ragman, ragpicker

4 **nomad,** Bedouin, Arab; gypsy, Bohemian, Romany, *zingaro* (*Italian*), *Zigeuner* (*German*), *tzigane* (*French*), itinerant, travelling person, tinker (*Scottish & Irish*)

5 **migrant,** migrator, trekker; **immigrant,** in-migrant; migrant *or* migratory worker, *Gastarbeiter* (*German*), wetback (*US informal*); **emigrant,** out-migrant, *émigré* (*French*); expatriate, expat; evacuee, *évacué*

(*French*); displaced person *or* DP, stateless person, exile; tax exile

6 pedestrian, walker, walkist; foot traveller, foot passenger, hoofer (*informal*), footbacker (*informal*), ambulator, peripatetic; **hiker,** backpacker, trailsman, tramper, rambler; marcher, footslogger, foot soldier, infantryman, paddlefoot (*informal*); **hitchhiker** *or* hitcher (*informal*); jaywalker; power walker, exercise walker, speed walker, race walker

7 nightwalker, noctambulist, noctambule, **sleepwalker,** somnambulist, somnambulator, somnambule

8 rider, equestrian, horseman, horserider, horseback rider, horsebacker, *caballero* (*Spanish*), cavalier, knight, chevalier; horse soldier, cavalryman, mounted policeman; horsewoman, equestrienne; cowboy, cowgirl, puncher *or* cowpuncher *or* cowpoke (*all informal*), vaquero, gaucho (*both Spanish*); broncobuster (*informal*), buckaroo; postilion, postboy; roughrider; **jockey;** steeplechaser, jump jockey; circus rider, trick rider

9 driver, reinsman, whip, Jehu, skinner (*informal*); **coachman,** coachy (*informal*), *cocher* (*French*), *cochero* (*Spanish*), *voiturier* (*French*), *vetturino* (*Italian*), gharry-wallah (*India*); stage coachman; charioteer; harness racer; **cabdriver,** cabman, cabby *or* cabbie (*informal*), hackman (*US*), hack *or* hacky (*US informal*), jarvey (*informal*); wagoner, wagonman, drayman, truckman; **carter,** cartman, carman; **teamster;** muleteer, mule skinner (*US & Canadian informal*); bullwhacker (*US*); elephant driver, mahout; cameleer

10 driver, motorist, automobilist; **chauffeur; taxidriver,** cabdriver, cabby *or* cabbie (*informal*), hackman (*US*), **hack** *or* hacky (*US informal*), hackdriver (*US*); jitney driver; **lorry driver,** truck driver, teamster, truckman, **trucker; bus driver,** busman; speeder *see* 174.5, road hog (*informal*), amber gambler (*informal*), Sunday driver, joyrider (*informal*); hotter (*informal*); hit-and-run driver; ram raider (*informal*); drunk driver; backseat driver

11 cyclist, cycler (*US*); **bicyclist,** bicycler (*US*); **motorcyclist,** motorcycler (*US*), biker (*informal*), bikie (*Australian & NZ*), Hell's Angel

12 train driver, engine driver, engineer (*US & Canadian*), engineman (*US & Canadian*); **motorman**

13 railwayman, trainman, locoman, railroad man (*US*), railroader (*US*); guard, conductor (*US & Canadian*); brakeman (*US & Canadian*), brakie (*US & Canadian informal*); fireman, footplate man, stoker; pointsman, switchman (*US & Canadian*); yardman; yardmaster; stationmaster, station manager; lineman, platelayer; lengthman; porter, redcap (*US & Canadian informal*)

179 VEHICLE
means of conveyance

nouns

1 vehicle, conveyance, carrier, means of carrying *or* transporting, means of transport, medium of transportation, carriage; watercraft *see* 180.1, aircraft *see* 181

2 wagon, waggon, wain; haywagon, haywain, milkwagon; dray, van, caravan; covered wagon, prairie schooner, Conestoga wagon (*US & Canadian*)

3 cart, two-wheeler; oxcart, horsecart, ponycart, dogcart; hansom *or* hansom cab; dumpcart, coup-cart (*Scottish*); **handcart,** barrow, wheelbarrow; trolley; jinrikisha, ricksha

4 carriage, four-wheeler, growler (*informal*), *voiture* (*French*), gharry (*India*); **chaise,** shay (*informal*),

"one hoss shay"—OLIVER WENDELL HOLMES

5 rig, equipage, turnout (*informal*), coach-and-four; team, pair, span; tandem, random; three-in-hand, four-in-hand, etc; three-up, four-up, etc; fly

6 pram, perambulator (*US & Canadian*); **pushchair,** baby buggy *or* buggy (*informal*), stroller (*US & Canadian*); baby-walker *or* walker, go-cart (*US & Canadian*)

7 wheel chair, Bath chair

8 cycle, wheel (*US & Canadian informal*); **bicycle,** bike (*informal*), push-bike (*informal*), velocipede; BMX *or* bicycle motocross; mountain bike; **tricycle,** three-wheeler, trike (*informal*); **motorcycle,** bike (*informal*), pig (*informal*), hog (*informal*), chopper (*informal*); moped; combination; pedicab

9 automobile (*see list*), **car, auto,** motorcar, motocar, autocar, **machine,** motor, motor vehicle, motorized vehicle, *voiture* (*French*)

10 (*informal terms*) jalopy, banger, bomb (*Australian & NZ*), bus, buggy, wheels, heap, crate, wreck, clunker (*US*), junker (*US*), junkheap, junkpile, old crock, rustbucket

11 police car, patrol car, panda car; **police van,** patrol wagon (*US, Australian & NZ*); Black Maria (*informal*), wagon (*US & Canadian informal*), paddy wagon (*US, Australian & NZ informal*)

12 lorry (*see list*), *camion* (*French*); articulated lorry, trailer truck, truck trailer, tractor trailer, semitrailer, semi (*US, Canad, Australian & NZ informal*), rig (*US & Canadian*); juggernaut, eighteen-wheeler (*informal*)

13 (*public vehicles*) commercial vehicle; bus, omnibus, chartered bus, autobus, motorbus, motor coach, charabanc, articulated bus, jitney (*informal*), double-decker, single-decker; express bus, local bus; schoolbus; **cab, taxicab, taxi,** hackney, hack (*informal*), gypsy cab (*US informal*); minicab; rental car; hired car, limousine, limo *and* stretch limo (*both informal*)

14 train, railway train; choo-choo *and* choo-choo train *and* puff-puff (*all informal*); passenger train; high-speed train, InterCity (*trademark*), *train à grande vitesse or TGV* (*French*); local, commuter train, milk train; shuttle train, shuttle; express train, express; local express; special, limited stop; freight train, goods train, freight, freighter; luggage train, baggage train; electric train; cable railway; funicular; narrow-gauge railway; cog railway, rack-and-pinion railway; underground, subway, tube, *métro* (*French*); elevated (*US*), el (*US informal*); monorail; rolling stock

15 railway carriage, carriage, coach, car; wagon *or* waggon, truck, bogie *or* bogy; luggage van, baggage car (*US & Canadian*), guard's van *or* brake van, caboose (*US & Canadian*), van, boxcar (*US &*

Canadian); restaurant car *or* dining car, buffet car, diner; Pullman *or* Pullman car; sleeper *or* sleeping car, wagon-lit (*French*), roomette (*US & Canadian*); smoker *or* smoking compartment

16 trolley, truck car

17 tram *or* **tramcar, streetcar** *or* **trolley** *or* trolley car (*all US & Canadian*); electric car, electric (*informal*); milk float; trolley bus, trackless trolley; horse box, horsecar; cable car, grip car

18 tractor, traction engine; Caterpillar tractor (*trademark*), Caterpillar (*trademark*), Cat (*informal*), tracked vehicle; **bulldozer,** dozer (*informal*), calfdozer

19 trailer; caravan, mobile home, house trailer (*US & Canadian*); truck trailer, **semitrailer; caravan,** caravanette, camp *or* camping trailer (*US & Canadian*); motor caravan, Dormobile (*trademark*), camper (*US & Canadian*)

20 sledge, sleigh, sled, *traîneau* (*French*); snowmobile, Sno-Cat (*trademark*), weasel; runner; blade; toboggan

21 skates, ice skates, hockey skates, figure skates; roller skates, rollerblades, skateboard, bob skates; **skis, snowshoes;** snowboard

22 Hovercraft (*trademark*)

adjectives

23 vehicular, transportational; automotive, locomotive

24 cars

brougham	roadster
bubble car	rocket car
cabriolet	runabout
compact car	saloon
convertible	sedan
coupé	sedan limousine
drophead coupé	soft top
estate car	sports car
fixed-head coupé	station wagon (Australian,
hardtop	NZ, US & Canadian)
hatchback	stock car
jeep	stretch limousine *or* limo
limousine *or* limo	tourer
mini-bus	touring car
minicar	two-door
people carrier	two-seater
phaeton	veteran car
racing car *or* racer	vintage car

25 lorries

articulated lorry	minivan
delivery van	panel truck (US &
duck *or* DUKW	Canadian)
dumptruck	pantechnicon
dustcart	pick-up truck *or* pickup
flat-bed lorry	six-by-six
fork *or* forklift truck	tractor *or* tractor truck *or*
four-by-four *or* 4x4	truck tractor
gritter	van
juggernaut	

180 SHIP, BOAT

nouns

1 ship, argosy, cargo ship, coaster, collier, container ship, cruise ship, dredge *or* dredger, freighter, liner, merchant ship *or* merchantman, motorship,

oceanographic research ship, paddle boat *or* steamer, refrigeration ship, roll-on/roll-off ship *or* ro-ro, side-wheeler, supertanker, tanker, trawler, ULCC *or* ultra-large crude carrier, VLCC *or* very large crude carrier, whaler; **boat,** ark, canoe, gondola, junk, kayak, lifeboat, motorboat, rowing boat, shell, skiff, whaleboat, workboat; vessel, craft, bottom, bark, hull, hulk, keel, watercraft; tub *and* bucket *and* rustbucket *and* hooker (*all informal*), packet; leviathan; "that packet of assorted miseries which we call a ship"—KIPLING, "the ship, a fragment detached from the earth"—JOSEPH CONRAD

2 steamer, steamboat, steamship; motor ship

3 sailboat, sailing vessel, sailing boat, wind boat, sailing yacht, sailing cruiser, sailing ship, tall *or* taunt ship, sail, sailer, **windjammer** (*informal*), windship, windboat; **galley; yacht,** pleasure boat

4 motorboat, powerboat, speedboat; **launch,** motor launch, steam launch, naphtha launch; **cruiser,** power cruiser, **cabin cruiser,** sedan cruiser, outboard cruiser

5 liner, ocean liner, ocean greyhound (*informal*), passenger steamer, floating hotel *or* palace, luxury liner; **cruise ship**

6 warship, war vessel, naval vessel; warship; **man-of-war,** man-o'-war, ship of war, armoured vessel; HMS *or* His *or* Her Majesty's Ship; USS *or* United States Ship; line-of-battle ship, ship of the line; aircraft carrier, assault transport, battle cruiser, battleship, coast guard cutter, communications ship, corvette, cruiser, destroyer, destroyer escort, frigate, guided missile cruiser, gunboat, heavy cruiser, hospital ship, mine layer, mine ship, mine sweeper, trooper, troopship

7 battleship, capital ship; **cruiser,** battle-cruiser; **destroyer,** can *or* tin can (*US informal*)

8 carrier, aircraft carrier, seaplane carrier

9 submarine, sub, submersible, underwater craft; **U-boat,** *U-boot or Unterseeboot* (*both German*), pigboat (*US informal*); nuclear *or* nuclear-powered submarine; Polaris submarine; Trident submarine; hunter-killer submarine

10 ships, shipping, merchant *or* mercantile marine, merchant navy *or* fleet, bottoms, tonnage; **fleet,** flotilla, argosy; line; fishing fleet, whaling fleet, etc; navy *see* 461.26

11 float, raft; balsa, balsa raft, Kon Tiki; life raft, Carling float; boom; pontoon; buoy, life buoy; **life preserver** *see* 397.5; surfboard; cork; bob

12 rigging, rig, tackle, tackling, **gear; ropework,** roping; service, serving, whipping; standing rigging, running rigging; boatswain's stores; ship chandlery

13 spar, timber; **mast,** pole, stick *and* tree (*both informal*); bare pole

14 sail, canvas, muslin, cloth, rag (*informal*); **full** *or* **plain sail,** press *or* crowd of sail; reduced sail, reefed sail; square sail; fore-and-aft sail; luff, leech, foot, earing, reef point, boltrope, clew, cringle, head

15 oar, remi–; **paddle,** scull, sweep, pole; steering oar

16 anchor, mooring, hook *and* mudhook (*both informal*); **anchorage,** moorings; **berth,** slip; mooring buoy

adjectives

17 rigged, decked, trimmed; square-rigged, fore-and-aft rigged, Marconi-rigged, gaff-rigged, lateen-rigged

18 seaworthy, sea-kindly, fit for sea, **snug, bold; watertight,** waterproof; A1, A1 at Lloyd's; stiff, tender; weatherly; yare

19 trim, in trim; apoise, on an even keel

20 shipshape, Bristol fashion, shipshape and Bristol fashion, trim, trig, neat, tight, taut, ataunt, all ataunto, bungup and bilge-free

181 AIRCRAFT

nouns

1 aircraft, aeroplane, airplane (*US*), **plane, ship,** fixed-wing aircraft, flying machine (*old*), *avion* (*French*); aerodyne, heavier-than-air craft; kite (*informal*); **shuttle, space shuttle,** lifting body; **aeroplane part; flight instrument,** aircraft instrument; **aircraft engine; piston engine,** radial engine, rotary engine, pancake engine; **jet engine,** fan-jet engine, rocket motor, turbofan, turbojet, turboprop, pulse jet, ramjet, reaction engine *or* motor

2 propeller plane, single-prop, double-prop *or* twin-prop, multi-prop; tractor, tractor plane; pusher, pusher plane; piston plane; turbo-propeller plane, turbo-prop, prop-jet; microlight *or* microlite

3 jet plane, jet; turbojet, ramjet, pulse-jet, blowtorch (*informal*); single-jet, twin-jet, multi-jet; Jet Liner, business jet; deltaplanform jet, tailless jet, twin-tailboom jet; jumbo jet; subsonic jet; supersonic jet, supersonic transport *or* SST, Concorde

4 rocket plane, repulsor; rocket ship, spaceship *see* 1073.2; rocket *see* 1072.2

5 rotor plane, rotary-wing aircraft, rotocraft, rotodyne; gyroplane, gyro, **autogiro,** windmill (*informal*); **helicopter,** copter *and* whirlybird *and* chopper *and* eggbeater (*all informal*)

6 ornithopter, orthopter, wind flapper, mechanical bird

7 flying platform, flying ring, Hiller-CNR machine, flying bedstead *or* bedspring; **Hovercraft** (*trademark*), air car, air-cushion vehicle; flying crow's nest, flying motorcycle, flying bathtub

8 seaplane, waterplane, hydroplane, aerohydroplane, aeroboat, **floatplane,** float seaplane, *Canadier* (*French*); **flying boat,** clipper, boat seaplane; **amphibian,** triphibian

9 military aircraft, warplane, battleplane, combat plane; carrier fighter, carrier-based plane, dive bomber, fighter, helicopter gunship, jet bomber, jet fighter, jet tanker, night fighter, photo-reconnaissance plane, Stealth Bomber, Stealth Fighter, tactical support bomber, torpedo bomber, troop carrier *or* transport; suicide plane, kamikaze; bogey, bandit, enemy aircraft; air fleet, air armada; air force *see* 461.28

10 trainer; Link trainer; **flight simulator;** dual-control trainer; basic *or* primary trainer, intermediate trainer, advanced trainer; crew trainer, flying classroom; navigator-bombardier trainer, radio-navigational trainer, etc

11 aerostat, lighter-than-air craft; **airship,** ship, dirigible balloon, **blimp** (*informal*); rigid airship, semirigid airship; **dirigible,** zeppelin, Graf Zeppelin; gasbag, ballonet; **balloon,** *ballon* (*French*)

12 glider, gliding machine; **sailplane,** soaring plane; rocket glider; student glider; air train, glider train

13 parachute, chute (*informal*), umbrella (*informal*), brolly (*informal*); pilot chute, drogue chute; rip cord, safety loop, shroud lines, harness, pack, vent; parachute jump, brolly-hop (*informal*); sky dive; brake *or* braking *or* deceleration parachute; parawing *or* paraglider *or* parafoil

14 kite, box kite, Eddy kite, Hargrave *or* cellular kite, tetrahedral kite

182 WATER TRAVEL

nouns

1 water travel, travel by water, marine *or* ocean *or* sea travel, **navigation,** navigating, **seafaring, sailing,** steaming, passage-making, voyaging, **cruising,** coasting; **boating, yachting,** motorboating, canoeing, rowing, sculling; circumnavigation, periplus; navigability

2 (*methods*) celestial navigation, astronavigation; radio navigation, radio beacon; loran; consolan, shoran; coastal *or* coastwise navigation; dead reckoning; point-to-point navigation; pilotage; sonar, radar, sofar; plane *or* traverse *or* spherical *or* parallel *or* middle *or* latitude *or* Mercator *or* great-circle *or* rhumbline *or* composite sailing; fix, line of position; sextant, chronometer, tables

3 seamanship, shipmanship; seamanliness, seamanlikeness; weather eye; sea legs

4 pilotship, pilotry, pilotage, **helmsmanship;** steerage; proper piloting

5 embarkation *see* 188.3; disembarkation *see* 186.2

6 voyage, ocean *or* sea trip, **cruise,** sail; course, **run, passage; crossing;** shakedown cruise; leg

7 wake, track; wash, backwash

8 (*submarines*) **surfacing,** breaking water; **submergence, dive;** stationary dive, running dive, crash dive

9 way, progress; headway, steerageway, sternway, leeway, driftway

10 seaway, waterway, fairway, road, channel, ocean *or* sea lane, ship route, steamer track *or* lane; approaches

11 aquatics, swimming, bathing, natation, balneation, **swim, bathe;** crawl *or* Australian crawl *or* front crawl, freestyle, trudgen, breaststroke, butterfly, sidestroke, dog *or* doggie paddle, backstroke; treading water; floating; diving *see* 367.3; wading; fin; flipper, flapper; fishtail; jet skiing; waterskiing, aquaplaning, surfboarding, monoskiing; surfing; windsurfing, boardsailing

12 swimmer, bather, natator, merman; bathing girl, mermaid; bathing beauty; frogman; diver *see* 367.4

verbs

13 to navigate, sail, cruise, steam, run, **seafare, voyage,** ply, go on shipboard, go by ship, go on *or* take a voyage, "go down to the sea in ships"—BIBLE; go to sea, sail the sea, sail the ocean blue; **boat, yacht,** motorboat, canoe, row, scull; surf, windsurf, boardsail; steamboat; bear *or* carry sail; cross, traverse, make a passage *or* run; sail round, circumnavigate; coast

14 to pilot, helm, coxswain, **steer,** guide, be at the helm *or* tiller, direct, manage, handle, run, operate, **con** *or* **conn,** be at *or* have the con; **navigate,** shape *or* chart a course

15 to anchor, come to anchor, lay anchor, **cast anchor,** let go the anchor, drop the hook; carry out the anchor; kedge, kedge off; **dock, tie up; moor,** pick up the mooring; run out a warp *or* rope; lash, lash and tie; foul the anchor; disembark *see* 186.8

16 to ride at anchor, ride, lie, rest; ride easy; ride hawse full; lie athwart; set an anchor watch

17 to lay *or* lie to, lay *or* lie by; lie near *or* close to the wind, head to wind *or* windward, be under the sea; lie ahull; lie off, lie off the land; lay *or* lie up

18 to weigh anchor, up-anchor, bring the anchor home, break out the anchor, cat the anchor, break ground, loose for sea; **unmoor,** drop the mooring, cast off *or* loose *or* away

19 to get under way, put *or* have way upon, **put** *or* **push** *or* **shove off;** hoist the blue Peter; **put to sea,** put out to sea, go to sea, head for blue water, go off soundings; **sail,** sail away; embark

20 to set sail, hoist sail, unfurl *or* spread sail, heave out a sail, **make sail,** trim sail; square away, square the yards; **crowd** *or* **clap** *or* **crack** *or* **pack on sail,** put on (*more*), sail; clap on, crack on, pack on; give her beans (*informal*)

21 to make way, gather way, **make headway,** make sternway; make knots, foot; **go full speed ahead,** go full speed astern; go *or* run *or* steam at flank speed

22 to run, **run** *or* **sail before the wind,** run *or* sail with the wind, run *or* sail down the wind, make a spinnaker run, sail off the wind, sail free, sail with the wind aft, sail with the wind abaft the beam; tack down wind; run *or* sail with the wind quartering

23 to bring off the wind, **pay off,** bear off *or* away, put the helm to leeward, bear *or* head to leeward, pay off the head

24 to sail against the wind, sail on *or* by the wind, sail to windward, bear *or* head to windward; **bring in** *or* **into the wind,** bring by *or* on the wind, haul the wind *or* one's wind; uphelm, put the helm up; haul, haul off, haul up; **haul to, bring to, heave to;** sail in *or* into the wind's eye *or* the teeth of the wind; sail to the windward of, weather

25 to sail near the wind, sail close to the wind, lie near *or* close to the wind, sail full and by, hold a close wind, **sail close-hauled,** close-haul; work *or* go *or* beat *or* eat to windward, **beat, ply; luff,** luff up, sail closer to the wind; sail too close to the wind, sail fine, touch the wind, pinch

26 to gain to windward of, eat *or* claw to windward of, eat the wind out of, have the wind of, be to windward of

27 to chart *or* plot *or* lay out a course; shape a course, lay *or* lie a course

28 to take *or* follow a course, **keep** *or* **hold the course** *or* **a course,** hold on the course *or* a course, stand on *or* upon a course, stand on a straight course, maintain *or* keep the heading, keep her steady, keep pointed

29 to drift off course, yaw, yaw off, pay off, bear off, drift, sag; sag *or* bear *or* ride *or* drive to leeward, make leeway, drive, fetch away; be set by the current, drift with the current, fall down

30 to change course, change the heading, bear off *or* away, bear to starboard *or* port; sheer, swerve; **tack,** cast, break, yaw, slew, shift, turn; **cant,** cant round *or* across; **beat, ply; veer, wear, wear ship; jibe** *or* **gybe,** jibe all standing, make a North River jibe; **put about,** come *or* go *or* bring *or* fetch about, beat about, cast *or* throw about; bring *or* swing *or* heave *or* haul round; **about ship,** turn *or* put back, turn on her heel, wind; swing the stern; box off; back and fill; stand off and on; double *or* round a point; miss stays

31 to put the rudder hard left *or* right, put the rudder *or* helm hard over, put the rudder amidships, ease the rudder *or* helm, give her more *or* less rudder

32 to veer *or* wear short, bring by the lee, **broach to,** lie beam on to the seas

33 (*come to a stop*) to fetch up, heave to, haul up, fetch up all standing

34 to backwater, back, reverse, go astern; **go full speed astern;** make sternway

35 to sail for, put away for, make for *or* toward, make at, **run for,** stand for, head *or* steer toward, lay for, **lay a** *or* **one's course for,** bear up for; bear up to, **bear down on** *or* **upon,** run *or* bear in with, **close with;** make, reach, fetch; heave *or* go alongside; lay *or* go aboard; lay *or* lie in; **put in** *or* **into,** put into port, approach anchorage

36 to sail away from, head *or* steer away from, run from, **stand from,** lay away *or* off from; **stand off,** bear off, put off, shove off, haul off; stand off and on

37 to clear the land, bear off the land, lay *or* settle the land, make *or* get sea room

38 to make land, reach land; close with the land, stand in for the land; sight land; smell land; make a landfall

39 to coast, sail coast-wise, stay in soundings, range the coast, skirt the shore, lie along the shore, **hug the shore** *or* **land** *or* **coast**

40 to weather the storm, weather, ride, **ride out,** outride, ride *or* ride out a storm; make heavy *or* bad weather

41 to sail into, run down, run in *or* into, **ram; come** *or* **run foul** *or* **afoul of,** collide, fall aboard; nose *or* head into, run prow *or* end *or* head on, run head and head; run broadside on

42 to shipwreck, wreck, pile up (*informal*), cast away; **go** *or* **run aground,** ground, take the ground, beach, strand, run on the rocks; ground hard and fast

43 to careen, list, heel, tip, cant, heave *or* lay down, lie along; be on beam ends

44 to capsize, upset, overset, **overturn,** turn over, turn turtle, upset the boat, keel, keel over *or* up; pitchpole, somersault; **sink, founder,** be lost, go down, go to the bottom, go to Davy Jones's locker; scuttle

45 to go overboard, go by the board, go over the board *or* side

46 to manoeuvre, execute a manoeuvre; heave in together, keep in formation, maintain position, **keep station,** keep pointed, steam in line, steam in line of bearing; convoy

47 (*submarines*) **to surface,** break water; **submerge, dive,** crash-dive, go below; rig for diving; flood the tanks, flood negative

48 (*activities aboard ship*) **to lay,** lay aloft, lay forward, etc; traverse a yard, brace a yard fore and aft; heave, haul; kedge; warp; boom; heave round, heave short, heave apeak; log, heave *or* stream the log; haul down, board; spar down; ratline down, clap on ratlines; batten down the hatches; unlash, cut *or* cast loose; clear hawse

49 to trim ship, trim, trim up; trim by the head *or* stern, put in proper fore-and-aft trim, give greater draught fore and aft, **put on an even keel; ballast,** shift ballast, wing out ballast; break out ballast, break bulk, shoot ballast; **clear the decks,** clear for action, take action stations

50 to reduce sail, shorten *or* take in sail, hand a sail, **reef,** reef one's sails; double-reef; lower sail, dowse sail; run under bare poles; snug down; **furl,** put on a harbour furl

51 to take bearings, cast a traverse; correct distance and maintain the bearings; run down the latitude, **take a sight,** shoot the sun, bring down the sun; **box the compass; take soundings** *see* 275.9

52 to signal, make a signal, speak, hail and speak; dress ship; unfurl *or* hoist a banner, unfurl an ensign, **break out a flag;** hoist the blue Peter; show one's colours, **exchange colours;** salute, dip the ensign

53 to row, paddle, ply the oar, **pull, scull, punt;** give way, row away; catch *or* cut a crab *or* lobster (*informal*); feather, feather an oar; sky an oar (*informal*); row dry (*informal*); pace, shoot; ship oars

54 to float, ride, drift; **sail, scud, run,** shoot; skim, foot; ghost, glide, slip; ride the sea, plough the deep, walk the waters

55 to pitch, toss, tumble, toss and tumble, pitch and toss, bucket about, **plunge,** hobbyhorse, pound, **rear, rock, roll, reel, swing, sway, lurch, yaw, heave,** scend, flounder, welter, wallow; make heavy weather

56 to swim, bathe, go in swimming *or* bathing, bogey *or* bogie (*Australian*); tread water; **float,** float on one's back, do the deadman's float; **wade,** go in wading; skinny-dip; dive *see* 367.6

adjectives

57 nautical, marine, maritime, naval, navigational; seafaring, seagoing, oceangoing, seaborne, waterborne; seamanly, seamanlike, **salty** (*informal*); pelagic, oceanic *see* 240.8

58 aquatic, water-dwelling, water-living, watergrowing, water-loving; **swimming,** balneal, natant, natatory, natatorial; shore, seashore; tidal, estuarine, littoral, grallatorial; riverine; deep-sea *see* 275.14

59 navigable, boatable

60 floating, afloat, awash; water-borne

61 adrift, afloat, unmoored, untied, loose, unanchored, aweigh; cast-off, started

adverbs

62 on board, on shipboard, on board ship, **aboard,** all aboard, afloat; **on deck,** topside; aloft; in sail; before the mast; athwart the hawse, athwarthawse

63 under way, making way, with steerageway, with way on; **at sea,** on the high seas, off soundings, in blue water; **under sail** *or* **canvas,** with sails spread; under press of sail *or* canvas *or* steam; under steam *or* power; under bare poles; on *or* off the heading *or* course; in soundings, homeward bound

64 before the wind, with the wind, down the wind, running free; off the wind, with the wind aft, with the wind abaft the beam, wing and wing, under the wind, under the lee; on a reach, on a beam *or* broad reach, with wind abeam

65 against the wind, on the wind, in *or* into the wind, up the wind, by the wind, head to wind; in *or* into the wind's eye, in the teeth of the wind

66 near the wind, close to the wind, **close-hauled,** on a beat, full and by

67 coastward, landward, to landward; **coastwise,** coastways

68 leeward, to leeward, alee, downwind; **windward,** to windward, weatherward, aweather, upwind

69 aft, abaft, baft, **astern;** fore and aft

60 alongside, board and board, yardarm to yardarm

61 at anchor, riding at anchor; lying to, hove to; lying ahull

62 afoul, foul, in collision; head and head, head *or* end *or* prow on; broadside on

63 aground, on the rocks; hard and fast

64 overboard, over the board *or* side, by the board; aft the fantail

183 MARINER

nouns

1 mariner, seaman, sailor, sailorman, **navigator, seafarer,** seafaring man, bluejacket, sea *or* water dog (*informal*), boatie (*Australian & NZ informal*), crewman, shipman, jack, jacky, jack afloat, jack-tar, **tar, salt** (*informal*), hearty, lobscouser (*informal*), *matelot* (*French*), windsailor, windjammer; limey *or* limejuicer (*informal*), lascar (*India*); common *or* ordinary seaman, OD, rating; able rating; able *or* able-bodied seaman, AB; deep-sea man, saltwater *or* bluewater *or* deepwater sailor; fresh-water sailor; fair-weather sailor; whaler, fisherman, lobsterman; viking, sea rover, buccaneer, privateer, pirate; Jason, Argonaut, Ancient Mariner, Flying Dutchman; Neptune, Poseidon, Varuna, Dylan; **yachtsman, yachtswoman,** sailor, cruising sailor, racing sailor; sea ranger

2 (*novice*) **lubber, landlubber;** polliwog

3 (*veteran*) **old salt** *and* old sea dog *and* shell-back *and* barnacle-back (*all informal*); **master mariner**

4 navy man, man-of-war's man, **bluejacket; marine,** Royal Marine, **jolly** *and* bootie (*both informal*), leatherneck *and* gyrene *and* devil dog (*all US*

informal); gob *and* swabbie *and* swabber (*all US informal*); Wren; horse marine (*US*); boot (*US informal*); **midshipman**, midshipmate, middy (*informal*), oldster; cadet, naval cadet; coastguard *or* coastguardsman, Naval Reservist, Seabee (*US*), frogman

5 **boatman**, boatsman, boat-handler, **boater**, waterman; **oarsman**, oar, rower, sculler, punter; galley slave; **ferryman**, ferrier; **bargee**, barger, bargemaster; lighterman, wherryman; **gondolier**, *gondoliere* (*Italian*)

6 hand, **deck hand**, deckie, roustabout (*US & Canadian informal*); stoker, fireman, wiper, oiler, boilerman; cabin boy; yeoman, ship's writer; purser; ship's carpenter, chips (*informal*); ship's cooper; ship's tailor, snip *or* snips (*informal*); steward, stewardess, commissary steward, mess steward, hospital steward, loblolly boy; commissary clerk; mail orderly; navigator; radio operator, sparks (*informal*); landing signalman; gunner, gun loader, torpedoman; afterguard; complement; watch

7 (*ship's officers*) **captain**, shipmaster *or* shipman; **master**, **skipper** *or* skip (*informal*), **commander**, the Old Man (*informal*), *patron* (*French*); navigator, navigating officer, sailing master; deck officer, officer of the deck *or* OD; watch officer, officer of the watch; **mate**, first *or* chief mate, second mate, third mate, boatswain's mate; **boatswain**, bos'n, bosun, pipes (*informal*); quartermaster; sergeant-at-arms; chief engineer, engine-room officer; naval officer *see* 575.20

8 **steersman**, **helmsman**, wheelman *or* wheelsman (*both US*), boatsteerer; quartermaster; **coxswain**, cox (*informal*); **pilot**, conner, sailing master; harbour pilot, docking pilot

9 **docker**, dockworker, dockhand, wharf hand, longshoreman (*US & Canadian*), dock-walloper (*US informal*); **stevedore**, loader; **roustabout** (*US informal*), lumper

184 AVIATION

nouns

1 **aviation**, **aeronautics**; planing, skyriding, **flying**, **flight**, winging; volation, volitation; aeronautism, aerodromics; powered flight, jet flight, subsonic *or* supersonic flight; cruising, cross-country flying; bush flying; **gliding**, sail-planing, soaring, sailing; volplaning; ballooning, balloonery, lighter-than-air aviation; barnstorming (*informal*); high-altitude flying; blind *or* instrument flight *or* flying, instrument flight rules *or* IFR; contact flying, visual flight *or* flying, visual flight rules *or* VFR, pilotage; skywriting; in-flight training, ground school; **air traffic**, airline traffic, air-traffic control, air-traffic controller; commercial aviation, general aviation, private aviation, private flying; astronautics *see* 1073.1; air show, flying circus

2 **air sciences** (*see list*), aeronautical sciences

3 **airmanship**, pilotship; **flight plan**; briefing, brief, rundown (*informal*), debriefing; flight *or* pilot training, flying lessons; washout (*informal*)

4 **air-mindedness**, aerophilia; air legs

5 airsickness; aerophobia, aeropathy

6 **navigation**, avigation, aerial *or* air navigation; celestial navigation, astronavigation; electronic navigation, automatic electronic navigation, radio navigation, navar, radar, consolan, tacan, teleran, loran, shoran; omnidirectional range, omni-range, visual-aural range *or* VAR

7 (*aeronautical organizations*) Civil Aviation Authority *or* CAA; Royal Aeronautical Society; British Airline Pilots Association; Air Force *see* 461.28

8 **takeoff**; taxiing, takeoff run, takeoff power, rotation; daisy-clipping *and* grass-cutting (*both informal*); ground loop; level-off; jet-assisted takeoff *or* JATO, booster rocket, takeoff rocket; catapult, electropult

9 **flight**, **trip**, **run**; hop *and* jump (*both informal*); powered flight; solo flight, **solo**; inverted flight; supersonic flight; test flight, **test hop** (*informal*); **airlift**; airdrop

10 **air travel**, air transport, air transportation; **airfreight**, **air cargo**; **airline travel**, **airline**, airline service, air service, feeder airline, commuter airline, scheduled airline, charter airline, nonscheduled airline, short-hop airline; **shuttle**, air shuttle, shuttle service, shuttle trip; air taxi

11 (*Air Force*) **mission**, flight operation; training mission; gunnery mission; combat rehearsal, **dry run** (*informal*); transition mission; reconnaissance mission, reconnaissance, observation flight, search mission; **milk run** (*informal*); box-top mission (*informal*); combat flight; **sortie**, scramble (*informal*); **air raid**; shuttle raid; bombing mission; bombing, strafing *see* 459.7; **air support** (*for ground troops*), **air cover**, cover, umbrella, air umbrella

12 flight formation, formation flying, formation; close formation, loose formation, wing formation; V formation, echelon

13 (*manoeuvres*) acrobatic *or* tactical evolutions *or* manoeuvres, acrobatics, **aerobatics**; stunting *and* **stunt flying** (*both informal*), rolling, crabbing, banking, porpoising, fishtailing, diving; **dive**, nose dive, **power dive**; **zoom**, chandelle; stall, whip stall; **glide**, volplane; spiral, split 'S', lazy eight, sideslip, pushdown, pull-up, pull-out

14 **roll**, **barrel roll**, aileron roll, outside roll, **snap roll**

15 **spin**, autorotation, **tailspin**, flat spin, inverted spin, normal spin, power spin, uncontrolled spin, falling leaf; whipstall

16 **loop**, spiral loop, ground loop, normal loop, outside loop, inverted normal *or* outside loop, dead-stick loop, wingover, looping the loop; Immelmann turn, reverse turn, reversement; flipper turns

17 **buzzing**, flathatting *and* **hedgehopping** (*both informal*)

18 **landing**, coming in (*informal*), touching down, touchdown; arrival; landing run, landing pattern; approach, downwind leg, approach leg; holding pattern, stack up (*informal*); ballooning in, parachute approach; blind *or* instrument landing, dead-stick landing, glide landing, stall landing, fishtail landing, sideslip landing, level *or* two-point landing, normal *or* three-point landing, Chinese landing (*informal*), tail-high landing, tail-low landing, thumped-in landing (*informal*), pancake landing, belly landing,

crash landing, noseover, nose-up; practice landing, bounce drill

19 flying and landing guides marker, pylon; beacon; radio beacon, radio range station, radio marker; fan marker; radar beacon, racon; beam, radio beam; beacon lights; runway lights, high-intensity runway approach lights, sequence flashers, flare path; wind indicator, windsock *or* wind cone *or* wind sleeve, air sleeve *or* sock, drogue; instrument landing system *or* ILS; touchdown rate of descent indicator *or* TRODI; ground-controlled approach *or* GCA; talking-down system, talking down

20 **crash**, prang (*informal*); crash landing; collision, mid-air collision; near miss, near collision, airmiss

21 blackout; greyout; anoxia; useful consciousness; pressure suit, antiblackout suit

22 **airport, airfield, aerodrome** (*US*), drome, port, air harbour (*Canadian*), aviation field, **landing field**, landing, field, airship station, hub airport *or* hub; **air terminal, jetport**; **air base**, air station, naval air station; airpark; **heliport**, helidrome; control tower, island; baggage pickup, baggage carousel

23 **runway, taxiway**, strip, landing strip, **airstrip, flight strip**, take-off strip; fairway, launching way; stopway; clearway; transition strip; apron; **flight deck**, landing deck; helipad

24 **hangar**, housing, dock, airdock, shed, airship shed; mooring mast

25 (*propulsion*) rocket propulsion, rocket power; **jet propulsion**, jet power; turbojet propulsion, pulse-jet propulsion, ram-jet propulsion, resojet propulsion; constant *or* ram pressure, air ram; reaction propulsion, reaction, action and reaction; aeromotor, aircraft engine, power plant

26 **lift**, lift ratio, lift force *or* component, lift direction; aerostatic lift, dynamic lift, gross lift, useful lift, margin of lift

27 **drag**, resistance; drag ratio, drag force *or* component, induced drag, wing drag, parasite *or* parasitic *or* structural drag, profile drag, head resistance, drag direction, cross-wind force

28 **drift**, drift angle; lateral drift, leeway

29 flow, air flow, laminar flow; **turbulence**, turbulent flow, burble, burble point, eddies

30 wash, wake, stream; downwash; backwash, **slipstream**, propeller race, propwash; **exhaust**, jet exhaust, blow wash; **vapour trail**, condensation trail, contrail, vortex

31 (*speed*) **air speed**, true air speed, operating *or* flying speed, cruising speed, knots, minimum flying speed, hump speed, peripheral speed, pitch speed, terminal speed, sinking speed, get-away *or* take-off speed, landing speed, ground speed, speed over the ground; **speed of sound** *see* 174.2; zone of no signal, Mach cone; **sound barrier**, sonic barrier *or* wall; sonic boom, shock wave, Mach wave

32 (*air, atmosphere*) **airspace**, navigable airspace; aerosphere; **aerospace**; space, empty space; **weather, weather conditions**; **ceiling**, ballonet ceiling, service ceiling, static ceiling, absolute ceiling; ceiling and visibility unlimited *or* CAVU; severe clear (*informal*); cloud layer *or* cover, ceiling zero; visibility, visibility zero; **overcast**, undercast; fog, soup (*informal*); high-pressure area, low-pressure area; trough, trough line; front; **air pocket** *or* **hole**, air bump, pocket, hole, bump; **turbulence**; clear-air turbulence *or* CAT; roughness; head wind, unfavourable wind; tail wind, favourable *or* favouring wind; cross wind; atmospheric tides; jetstream

33 **airway, air lane, air line**, air route, skyway, corridor, flight path, lane, path

34 **course, heading**, vector; compass heading *or* course, compass direction, magnetic heading, true heading *or* course

35 (*altitude*) altitude of flight, absolute altitude, critical altitude, density altitude, pressure altitude, sextant altitude; clearance; ground elevation

verbs

36 **to fly**, be airborne, wing, take wing, wing one's way, take *or* make a flight, take to the air, take the air, volitate, be wafted; **jet**; aviate, aeroplane, plane; travel by air, go *or* travel by airline, go by plane *or* air, take to the airways, ride the skies; hop (*informal*); **soar**, drift, hover; **cruise**; **glide**, sailplane, sail, volplane; hydroplane, seaplane; balloon; ferry; airlift; break the sound barrier; navigate, avigate

37 **to pilot**, control, be at the controls, fly, manipulate, drive (*informal*), fly left seat; **copilot**, fly right seat; solo; **barnstorm** (*informal*); fly blind; follow the beam, ride the beam, fly on instruments; fly in formation, take position; peel off

38 **to take off**, hop *or* jump off (*informal*), become airborne, get off *or* leave the ground, take to the air, go *or* fly aloft, clear; rotate, power off; **taxi**

39 **to ascend**, climb, gain altitude, mount; **zoom**, hoick (*informal*), chandelle

40 (*manoeuvre*) **to stunt** (*informal*), perform aerobatics; crab, fishtail; **spin**, go into a tailspin; **loop**, loop the loop; **roll**, wingover, spiral, undulate, porpoise, feather, yaw, sideslip, skid, bank, dip, nose down, nose up, pull up, push down, pull out, plough, mush through

41 **to dive**, nose-dive, power-dive, go for the deck; lose altitude, settle, dump altitude (*informal*)

42 **to buzz**, flathat *and* **hedgehop** (*both informal*)

43 **to land**, set her down (*informal*), **alight**, light, touch down; **descend**, come down, dump altitude (*informal*), fly down; come in, come in for a landing; **level off**, flatten out; upwind, downwind; overshoot, undershoot; make a dead-stick landing; pancake, thump in (*informal*); bellyland, settle down, balloon in; fishtail down; **crash-land**; ditch (*informal*); nose up, nose over; talk down

44 **to crash**, prang (*informal*), spin in, fail to pull out

45 **to stall**, lose power, conk out (*informal*); flame out

46 **to black out**, grey out

47 **to parachute, bail out, jump**, make a parachute jump, hit the silk, make a brollyhop (*informal*), sky-dive

48 **to brief**, give a briefing; debrief

adjectives

49 **aviation, aeronautic, aeronautical**, aerial; **aviatorial**, aviational; aerodontic, **aerospace**, aerotechnical, aerostatic, aerostatical, aeromechanic, aeromechanical, aerodynamic, aerodynamical, avionic, aeronomic, aerophysical; aeromarine; aerobatic; airworthy, air-minded, air-conscious, aeromedical; air-wise; airsick

50 **flying, airborne,** winging, soaring; volant, volitant, volitational, hovering, fluttering; gliding; jet-propelled, rocket-propelled

adverbs

51 **in flight, on the wing** *or* fly, while airborne
52 **air sciences**

aeroballistics	aerotechnics
acronomy	aircraft hydraulics
aerial photography	aviation medicine *or*
aerocartography	aeromedicine
aerodontia	aviation technology
aerodynamics	avionics
aerogeography	climatology
aerogeology	hydrostatics
aerography	jet engineering
aerology	kinematics
aeromechanics	kinetics
aerometry	meteorology
aeronautical engineering	micrometry
aeronautical meteorology	photometry
aerophotography	pneumatics
aerophysics	rocket engineering
aeroscopy	rocketry
aerospace research	supersonic aerodynamics
aerostatics	supersonics
aerostation	

185 AVIATOR

nouns

1 **aviator, airman, flier, pilot,** air pilot, licensed pilot, private pilot, airline pilot, commercial pilot, aeronaut, birdman (*informal*), flyboy (*US informal*); aircrew member; captain, chief pilot; copilot, second officer; flight engineer, third officer; jet pilot; instructor; test pilot; bush pilot; astronaut *see* 1073.8; cloud seeder, rainmaker; cropduster; barnstormer (*informal*); stunt man, stunt flier

2 **aviatrix,** aviatress, **airwoman,** birdwoman (*informal*); stuntwoman

3 **military pilot,** naval pilot, combat pilot; fighter pilot; bomber pilot; observer; **aviation cadet,** air *or* flying cadet, pilot trainee; flyboy (*informal*); ace; air force *see* 461.28

4 **crew, aircrew,** flight crew; leading aircraftman; crewman, crewmate, crewmember, aircraftman; **navigator,** avigator; **bombardier;** gunner, machine gunner, belly gunner, tail gunner; crew chief; aerial photographer; meteorologist; **flight attendant, steward, stewardess,** hostess

5 **ground crew,** landing crew, plane handlers; crew chief

6 aircraftsman, aeromechanic, aircraft mechanic, mechanic, grease monkey (*informal*); rigger; aeronautical engineer, jet engineer, rocket engineer *see* 1072.11; ground tester, flight tester

7 **balloonist,** ballooner, aeronaut

8 **parachutist,** chutist *or* chuter (*informal*), parachute jumper, sports parachutist; sky diver; smoke jumper; **paratrooper;** jumpmaster

9 (*mythological fliers*) Daedalus, Icarus

186 ARRIVAL

nouns

1 **arrival, coming, advent,** approach, appearance, **reaching; attainment, accomplishment,** achievement

2 **landing,** landfall; docking, mooring, tying up, dropping anchor; **getting off, disembarkation,** disembarkment, debarkation, coming *or* going ashore; **deplaning**

3 **return, homecoming,** recursion; reentrance, reentry; remigration

4 **welcome, greetings** *see* 585.3

5 **destination, goal,** bourn (*old*); port, haven, harbour, anchorage, **journey's end;** end of the line, terminus, **terminal,** terminal point; stop, stopping place, last stop; **airport, air terminal** *see* 184.22

verbs

6 **to arrive,** arrive at, arrive in, come, **come** *or* **get to,** approach, access, **reach, hit** (*informal*); find, **gain,** attain, attain to, accomplish, achieve, make, **make it** (*informal*), fetch, fetch up at, get there, reach one's destination, come to one's journey's end, end up; **come to rest,** settle, settle in; **make** *or* **put in an appearance, show up** (*informal*), turn up, **surface,** pop *or* bob up *and* make the scene (*all informal*); **get in, come in,** blow in (*informal*), pull in, roll in; **check in,** book in; clock *or* punch *or* ring *or* time in (*all informal*), sign in; hit town (*informal*); come to hand, be received

7 **to arrive at,** come at, get at, **reach,** arrive upon, **come upon, hit upon,** strike upon, fall upon, light upon, pitch upon, stumble on *or* upon

8 **to land,** come to land, make a landfall, set foot on dry land; reach *or* make land, make port; put in *or* into, put into port; dock, moor, tie up, anchor, drop anchor; go ashore, **disembark,** debark, unboat; **detrain,** debus, **deplane, disemplane;** alight

adjectives

9 **arriving,** approaching, entering, **coming,** incoming; inbound, inwardbound; homeward, homeward-bound

adverbs

10 **arriving,** on arrival *or* arriving

187 RECEPTION

nouns

1 **reception, taking in,** receipt, receiving; **welcome,** welcoming, cordial welcome, open *or* welcoming arms; refuge *see* 1008

2 **admission,** admittance, acceptance; immission (*old*), intromission *see* 191.1; **installation,** instalment, instatement, inauguration, initiation; baptism, investiture, ordination; enlistment, enrolment, induction

3 entree, entrée, in (*informal*), entry, **entrance** *see* 189, **access,** opening, **open door,** open arms; a foot in the door, opening wedge

4 ingestion; **eating** see 8; **drinking** see 8.3, imbibing, imbibition; engorgement, ingurgitation, engulfment; **swallowing**, gulping; swallow, gulp, slurp

5 (*drawing in*) **suction**, suck, sucking; **inhalation**, inhalement, inspiration, aspiration; snuff, snuffle, sniff, sniffle

6 sorption, **absorption**, adsorption, chemisorption *or* chemosorption, engrossment, digestion, **assimilation**, infiltration; **sponging, blotting;** seepage, percolation; **osmosis**, endosmosis, exosmosis, electroosmosis; absorbency; **absorbent**, adsorbent, **sponge, blotter**, blotting paper

7 (*bringing in*) **introduction; importing**, import, **importation**

8 readmission; reabsorption, resorbence

9 receptivity, **receptiveness**, welcoming, welcome, invitingness, openness, hospitality, cordiality, recipience *or* recipiency; receptibility, admissibility

verbs

10 to receive, take in; **admit, let in**, immit (*old*), intromit, give entrance *or* admittance to; **welcome**, bid welcome, give a royal welcome, roll out the red carpet; give an entree, open the door to, give refuge *or* shelter *or* sanctuary to, throw open to

11 to ingest, eat see 8.18, tuck away, put away; imbibe, **drink; swallow, devour**, ingurgitate; **engulf**, engorge; **gulp**, gulp down, swill, swill down, wolf down, gobble, scoff

12 to draw in, **suck**, suckle, suck in *or* up, aspirate; **inhale**, inspire, breathe in; snuff, snuffle, sniff, sniffle, snuff in *or* up, slurp

13 to absorb, adsorb, chemisorb *or* chemosorb, **assimilate**, engross, digest, **drink**, imbibe, take up *or* in, drink up *or* in, slurp up, swill up; blot, **blot up, soak up**, sponge; osmose; infiltrate, filter in; **soak in, seep in**, percolate in

14 to bring in, introduce, import

15 to readmit; reabsorb, resorb

adjectives

16 receptive, recipient; welcoming, open, hospitable, cordial, inviting, invitatory; introceptive; **admissive**, admissory; receivable, receptible, admissible; intromissive, intromittent; ingestive, imbibitory

17 sorbent, **absorbent**, adsorbent, chemisorptive *or* chemosorptive, **assimilative**, digestive; bibulous, imbibitory, thirsty, soaking, blotting; spongy, spongeous; osmotic, endosmotic, exosmotic; resorbent

18 introductory, introductive; **initiatory**, initiative, baptismal

188 DEPARTURE

nouns

1 departure, leaving, going, passing, **parting; exit**, walkout (*informal*); egress see 190.2; **withdrawal**, removal, retreat see 163.2, retirement; evacuation, abandonment, desertion; decampment; escape, flight, flit (*informal*), getaway (*informal*); exodus, hegira; migration, mass migration; defection, voting with one's feet

2 start, starting, start-off, setoff, setout, takeoff *and*

getaway (*both informal*); the starting gun *or* pistol; break; the green light

3 embarkation, embarkment, boarding; entrainment; enplanement *or* emplanement, **takeoff**, hopoff (*informal*)

4 leave-taking, leave, parting, departure, congé; send-off, Godspeed; adieu, one's adieus, farewell, aloha, good-bye; valedictory address, valedictory, valediction, parting words; parting *or* Parthian shot; swan song; viaticum; stirrup cup, one for the road, *doch-an-dorrach or doch-an-dorris* (*Gaelic*)

5 point of departure, starting place *or* point, takeoff, start, base, baseline, basis; line of departure; starting line *or* post *or* gate, starting blocks; stakeboat; port of embarkation

verbs

6 to depart, make off, begone, be off, take oneself off *or* away, take one's departure, take leave *or* take one's leave, **leave, go, go away, go off, get off** *or* away, get under way, come away, go one's way, go *or* get along, be getting along, gang along (*Scottish*), go on, get on; move off *or* away, move out, march off *or* away; **pull out**; decamp; exit; take *or* break *or* tear oneself away, take oneself off, take wing *or* flight

7 (*informal terms*) **to beat it**, split, scram, up and go, trot, toddle, stagger along, mosey *or* sashay along, buzz off, buzz along, bug out, bugger off, fuck off *or* f off, sod off, get rolling, hightail it, pull up stakes, sling one's hook, do a bunk, check out, clear out, cut out, cut along, hit the road *or* trail, piss off, get lost, flake off, get going, shove off, push along, push off, get out, get *or* git, clear out, get the hell out, make oneself scarce, vamoose, take off, skip, skip out, lam, take it on the lam, powder, take a powder, take a runout powder, skedaddle, absquatulate (*old*)

8 to set out, set forth, put forth, go forth, sally forth, sally, issue, issue forth, launch forth, set forward, set off, be off, be on one's way, outset, start, start out *or* off, strike out, get off, get away; get the green light, break; set sail

9 to quit, vacate, evacuate, abandon, desert, turn one's back on, walk away from, leave to one's fate, leave high and dry; leave *or* desert a sinking ship; **withdraw**, retreat, **beat a retreat**, retire, remove; flit, do a bunk (*informal*); walk away, abscond, disappear, vanish; **bow out** (*informal*), make one's exit; jump ship

10 to hasten off, **hurry away; scamper off, dash off**, whiz off, whip off *or* away, nip *and* nip off (*both informal*), tear off *or* out, **light out** (*informal*)

11 to fling out *or* off, flounce out *or* off

12 to run off *or* away, run along, flee, take to flight, fly, take to one's heels, cut and run *and* hightail *and* scarper *and* make tracks *and* absquatulate (*all old informal*); run for one's life; beat a retreat *or* a hasty retreat; run away from see 368.10

13 to check out; clock *and* ring *and* punch out (*all informal*), sign out

14 to decamp, break camp, strike camp *or* tent, **pull up stakes**, mizzle

15 to embark, go aboard, board, go on board; go on shipboard, take ship; hoist the blue Peter; **entrain**, enplane *or* emplane, embus; weigh anchor, up-anchor, put to sea *see* 182.19

16 to say *or* bid good-bye *or* farewell, take leave, make one's adieus; bid Godspeed, give one a send-off *or* a big send-off, see off *or* out,

"speed the parting guest"—Pope; drink a stirrup cup, have one for the road

17 to **leave home**, go from home; leave the country, emigrate, out-migrate, expatriate, defect; vote with one's feet; burn one's bridges

adjectives

18 departing, leaving; parting, last, final, farewell; valedictory; outward-bound

19 departed, left, gone, gone off *or* away

adverbs

20 hence, thence, whence; off, **away**, forth, out; therefrom, thereof

prepositions

21 from, away from; out, out of

exclamations

22 farewell!, good-bye!, adieu!, so long! (*informal*), ta-ta! (*informal*), I'm outa here (*US informal*), cheerio!, cheers! (*informal*), cheery-bye! (*informal*), bye-bye! (*informal*), au revoir! (*French*), ¡adios! (*Spanish*), ¡hasta la vista! (*Spanish*), ¡hasta luego! (*Spanish*), ¡vaya con Dios! (*Spanish*), auf Wiedersehen! (*German*), addio! (*Italian*), arrivederci!, arrivederla! (*both Italian*), ciao! (*Italian informal*), do svidanye! (*Russian*), shalom! (*Hebrew*), sayonara! (*Japanese*), vale!, vive valeque! (*both Latin*), aloha!, **until we meet again!**, until tomorrow!, à demain! (*French*), **see you later!**, see you!, tata, toodleoo, I'll be seeing you!, see you around!, we'll see you!, à bientôt! (*French*), à toute a l'heure! (*French*), a domani (*Italian*); be good!, keep in touch!, come again!; *bon voyage!* (*French*), pleasant journey!, have a nice trip!, *tsetchem leshalom!* (*Hebrew*), glückliche Reise! (*German*), happy landing!; Godspeed!, peace be with you!, *pax vobiscum!* (*Latin*); all good go with you!, God bless you!

23 good night!, nighty-night! (*informal*), bonne nuit! (*French*), gute Nacht! (*German*), ¡buenas noches! (*Spanish*), buona notte! (*Italian*)

189 ENTRANCE

nouns

1 entrance, entry, access, entree, entrée; **ingress**, ingression; **admission, reception** *see* 187; **ingoing, incoming**, income; **importation**, import, importing; **input, intake; penetration**, interpenetration, injection; infiltration, percolation, seepage, leakage; insinuation; intrusion *see* 214; introduction, **insertion** *see* 191

2 influx, inflow, inflooding, incursion, indraught, indrawing, inpour, inrun, inrush; afflux

3 immigration, in-migration, incoming population, foreign influx; border-crossing

4 incomer, entrant, comer, arrival; visitor, visitant;

immigrant, in-migrant; newcomer *see* 773.4; settler *see* 227.9; **trespasser, intruder** *see* 214.3

5 entrance, entry, gate, door, portal, **entranceway**, entryway; **inlet**, ingress, intake, adit, approach, **access**, means of access, in (*informal*), way in; a foot in the door, an opening wedge; **opening** *see* 292; **passageway**, corridor, companionway, hall, hallway, passage, way; jetway, jet bridge; gangway, gangplank; **vestibule** *see* 197.19; air lock

6 porch, propylaeum; **portal, threshold**, doorjamb, gatepost, doorpost, lintel; **door, doorway**, French window, French door (*US*); **gate, gateway; hatch**, hatchway, scuttle; cat flap *or* door

verbs

7 to **enter**, go in *or* into, access, cross the threshold, **come in**, find one's way into, put in *or* into; be admitted, gain admission *or* admittance, have an entree, have an in (*informal*); **set foot in**, step in, walk in; **get in**, jump in, leap in, hop in; **drop in**, look in, visit, drop by *or* in, nip *or* pop in (*both informal*); **breeze in**, come breezing in; break *or* burst in, bust *or* come busting in (*informal*); **barge in** *or* come barging in *and* wade in (*all informal*); thrust in, push *or* press in, crowd in, jam in, wedge in, pack in, squeeze in; slip *or* creep in, wriggle *or* worm oneself into, get one's foot in the door, edge in, work in, insinuate oneself, weigh in (*informal*); irrupt, intrude *see* 214.5; take in, admit *see* 187.10; insert *see* 191.3

8 to **penetrate**, interpenetrate, **pierce**, pass *or* go through, get through, get into, make way into, make an entrance, gain entree; crash (*informal*)

9 to **flow in**, inpour, **pour in**

10 to **filter in**, infiltrate, **seep in**, percolate into, leak in, soak in, perfuse

11 to **immigrate**, in-migrate; cross the border

adjectives

12 entering, ingressive, **incoming, ingoing**; in, inward; **inbound**, inward-bound; inflowing, influent, inflooding, inpouring, inrushing; invasive, intrusive, irruptive; ingrowing

adverbs

13 in, inward, inwards, inwardly; thereinto

prepositions

14 into, in, to

190 EMERGENCE

nouns

1 emergence, coming out, coming forth, coming into view, rising to the surface, surfacing; **issuing**, issuance, issue; extrusion; **emission**, emitting, giving forth, giving out; emanation; **vent**, venting, discharge

2 egress, egression; **exit**, exodus; outgoing, outgo, going out; emersion *or* egress (*astronomy*); **departure** *see* 188; extraction *see* 192

3 outburst *see* 671.6, ejection *see* 908

4 outflow, outflowing; discharge; **outpouring**, outpour; effluence, effusion, exhalation; **efflux**, effluxion, defluxion; **exhaust; runoff, flowoff;** outfall; drainage, drain; gush *see* 238.4

5 **leakage,** leaking, weeping (*informal*); **leak; dripping,** drippings, **drip,** dribble, drop, trickle; distillation

6 **exuding,** exudation, transudation; **filtration,** exfiltration, filtering; straining; **percolation,** percolating; leaching, lixiviation; effusion, extravasation; **seepage,** seep; perfusion; **oozing,** ooze; weeping, weep; **excretion** *see* 12

7 **emigration,** out-migration, remigration; exile, expatriation, defection, deportation

8 **export,** exporting, exportation

9 **outlet,** egress, **exit,** outgo, outcome, out (*informal*), way out; loophole, escape; **opening** *see* 292; outfall, estuary; chute, flume, sluice, weir, floodgate; **vent,** ventage, venthole, port; safety valve; avenue, channel; spout, tap; debouch; **exhaust;** door *see* 189.6; outgate, sally port; vomitory; emunctory; pore; blowhole, spiracle

10 **goer,** outgoer, leaver, departer; **emigrant, émigré,** out-migrant; defector, refugee

verbs

11 to **emerge, come out, issue,** issue forth, come into view, extrude, **come forth; surface,** rise to the surface; sally, sally forth, come to the fore; emanate, effuse, arise, come; debouch, disembogue; jump out, leap out, hop out; bail out; **burst forth, break forth, erupt;** break cover, **come out in the open;** protrude

12 to **exit,** make an exit, **make one's exit;** egress, **go out,** get out, walk out, march out, run out, pass out, bow out *and* include oneself out (*both informal*); walk out on, leave cold (*informal*); **depart** *see* 188.6

13 to **run out,** empty, find vent; **exhaust, drain,** drain out; **flow out,** outflow, outpour, **pour out,** sluice out, well out, gush *or* spout out, spew, flow, pour, well, surge, gush, jet, spout, spurt, vomit forth, blow out, spew out

14 to **leak, leak out, drip,** dribble, drop, trickle, trill, distil

15 to **exude,** exudate, transude, transpire, reek; **emit, discharge,** give off; **filter,** filtrate, exfiltrate; strain; percolate; leach, lixiviate; effuse, extravasate; **seep, ooze;** bleed; weep; excrete *see* 12.12

16 to **emigrate,** out-migrate, remigrate; exile, expatriate, defect; deport

17 to **export,** send abroad

adjectives

18 **emerging,** emergent; **issuing,** arising, surfacing, coming, forthcoming; emanating, emanent, emanative, transeunt, transient

19 **outgoing, outbound,** outward-bound; **outflowing,** outpouring, effusive, effluent; effused, extravasated

20 exudative, exuding, transudative; percolative; porous, permeable, pervious, oozy, runny, weepy, leaky; excretory *see* 12.19

adverbs

21 **forth; out,** outward, outwards, outwardly

prepositions

22 **out of, ex; from; out, forth**

191 INSERTION
putting in

nouns

1 **insertion, introduction,** insinuation, injection, infusion, perfusion, inoculation, intromission; **entrance** *see* 189; **penetration** *see* 292.3; interjection, interpolation *see* 213.2; graft, grafting, engrafting, transplant, transplantation; infixing, implantation, embedment, tessellation, intarsia *or* tarsia, impactment, impaction

2 **insert,** insertion; **inset, inlay;** gore, godet, gusset; **graft,** scion *or* cion; tessera

verbs

3 to **insert, introduce,** insinuate, inject, infuse, perfuse, inoculate, intromit; **enter** *see* 189.7; **penetrate; put in, stick in,** set in, throw in, pop in, tuck in, whip in; slip in, ease in; interject

4 to **install,** instate, inaugurate, initiate, invest, ordain; enlist, enrol, induct, sign up, sign on

5 to **inset, inlay; embed** *or* bed, bed in

6 to **graft,** engraft, **implant,** imp (*old*); bud; inarch

7 to **thrust in, drive in, run in, plunge in,** force in, push in, **ram in,** press in, stuff in, crowd in, squeeze in, cram in, jam in, tamp in, pound in, pack in, poke in, knock in, wedge in, impact

8 to **implant,** transplant; infix *see* 854.9; fit in, **inlay;** tessellate

192 EXTRACTION
taking or drawing out

nouns

1 **extraction, withdrawal,** removal; **drawing, pulling,** drawing out; ripping *or* tearing *or* wresting out; eradication, **uprooting,** unrooting, deracination; squeezing out, pressing out, expressing, expression; avulsion, evulsion, cutting out, exsection, extirpation, excision, enucleation; extrication, evolvement, disentanglement, unravelment; excavation, mining, quarrying, drilling; dredging

2 **disinterment, exhumation,** disentombment, **unearthing,** uncovering, digging out

3 **drawing,** drafting, sucking, **suction,** aspiration, pipetting; pumping, siphoning, tapping, broaching; milking; drainage, draining, emptying; depuration; cupping; bloodletting, bleeding, phlebotomy, venesection

4 **evisceration,** gutting, **disembowelment**

5 **elicitation,** eduction, drawing out *or* forth, bringing out *or* forth; **evocation,** calling forth; arousal

6 **extortion,** exaction, claim, demand; **wresting, wrenching, wringing, rending,** tearing, ripping; wrest, wrench, wring

7 (*obtaining an extract*) squeezing, pressing, expression; **distillation;** decoction; **rendering,** rendition; **steeping,** soaking, infusion; concentration

8 **extract,** extraction; **essence, quintessence, spirit, elixir;** decoction; **distillate,** distillation; **concentrate,** concentration; infusion; refinement, purification

9 **extractor,** separator; siphon; aspirator, pipette; pump, vacuum pump; press, wringer; corkscrew;

forceps, pliers, pincers, tweezers; crowbar, jemmy; smelter

verbs

10 to **extract**, **take out**, get out, **withdraw, remove;** pull, draw; **pull out, draw out,** tear out, rip out, wrest out, pluck out, pick out, weed out, rake out; **pry out,** prize out, winkle out; **pull up,** pluck up; **root up** *or* **out**, **uproot**, unroot, eradicate, deracinate, pull *or* pluck out by the roots, pull *or* pluck up by the roots; cut out, excise, exsect; enucleate; gouge out, avulse, evulse; extricate, evolve, disentangle, unravel; **dig up** *or* **out**, grub up *or* out, excavate, **unearth**, mine, quarry; dredge, dredge up *or* out; smelt

11 to **disinter, exhume**, disentomb, unbury, unsepulchre, dig up, uncover

12 to **draw off, draught off**, draught, draw, draw from; **suck**, suck out *or* up, **siphon off**; pipette; pump, pump out; tap, broach; let, let out; bleed; let blood, venesect, phlebotomize; milk; **drain**, decant; exhaust, empty

13 to **eviscerate, disembowel, gut**

14 to **elicit**, educe, deduce, induce, derive, obtain, procure, secure; **get from**, get out of; **evoke, call up, summon up**, call *or* summon forth, call out; rouse, arouse, stimulate; **draw out** *or* **forth**, bring out *or* forth, pry *or* prize out, winkle out, drag out, worm out, bring to light; wangle, wangle out of, worm out of

15 to **extort, exact**, squeeze, claim, demand; **wrest, wring from, wrench from, rend from**, wrest *or* tear from

16 (*obtain an extract*) to **squeeze** *or* **press out**, express, wring, wring out; **distil**, distil out, elixirate (*old*); **filter**, filter out; decoct; **render**, melt down; refine; **steep**, soak, infuse; **concentrate, essentialize**

adjectives

17 extractive, eductive; educible; eradicative, uprooting; elicitory, **evocative**, arousing; **exacting**, exactive; **extortionate**, extortionary, extortive

18 essential, quintessential, pure see 797.6

193 ASCENT

motion upwards

nouns

1 **ascent**, ascension, levitation, **rise, rising**, uprising, **uprise**, uprisal; **upgoing**, upgo, uphill, upslope, upping, upgang (*Scottish*); upcoming; **taking off**, leaving the ground, takeoff; **soaring**, zooming, gaining altitude, leaving the earth behind; spiralling *or* gyring up; shooting *or* rocketing up; **jump**, vault, spring, saltation, **leap** see 366; mount, **mounting; climb, climbing**, upclimb, anabasis, clamber, escalade; surge, upsurge, upsurgence, upleap, upshoot, uprush; **gush, jet**, spurt, spout, fountain; updraught; upswing, upsweep; upgrowth; upgrade see 204.6; **uplift**, elevation see 911; **uptick** (*informal*), **increase** see 251

2 upturn, uptrend, upcast, upsweep, upbend, upcurve

3 **stairs, stairway, staircase**, *escalier* (*French*), flight of stairs, pair of stairs; **steps**, treads and risers;

stepping-stones; spiral staircase, winding staircase, cockle stairs (*informal*); companionway, companion; stile; back stairs; perron; fire escape; landing, landing stage; ramp, incline

4 **ladder**, scale; stepladder, folding ladder, rope ladder, fire ladder, turntable ladder; hook ladder, extension ladder; Jacob's ladder, companion ladder, accommodation ladder, boarding ladder, side ladder, gangway ladder, quarter ladder, stern ladder

5 **step, stair, footstep**, rest, footrest, stepping-stone; **rung, round**, rundle, spoke, stave, scale; doorstep; tread; riser; bridgeboard, string; step stool

6 **climber**, ascender, upclimber; mountain climber, **mountaineer**, alpinist, rock climber, cragsman

7 (*comparisons*) rocket, skyrocket; lark, skylark, eagle

verbs

8 to **ascend, rise, mount**, arise, up, uprise, levitate, upgo, **go up**, rise up, come up; go onwards and upwards, go up and up; upsurge, **surge**, upstream, upheave; swarm up, upswarm, sweep up; upwind, upspin, spiral, spire, curl upwards; stand up, **rear**, rear up, **tower**, loom; upgrow, grow up

9 to **shoot up, spring up**, jump up, **leap up**, vault up, start up, fly up, pop up, bob up; float up, surface, break water; **gush, jet**, spurt, fountain; upshoot, upstart, upspring, upleap, upspear, rocket, **skyrocket**

10 to **take off**, leave the ground, leave the earth behind, gain altitude, claw skyward; become airborne; **soar**, zoom, fly, plane, kite, fly aloft; aspire; spire, spiral *or* gyre upward; **hover**, hang, poise, float, float in the air

11 to **climb**, climb up, upclimb, **mount**, clamber, **clamber up**, scramble *or* scrabble up, claw one's way up, struggle up, inch up, shin, shin up (*informal*), ramp (*informal*), work *or* inch one's way up, climb the ladder; **scale**, escalade, scale the heights; climb over, surmount

12 to **mount, get on**, climb on, back; **bestride**, bestraddle; **board**, go aboard, go on board; **get in**, jump in, hop in, pile in (*informal*)

13 to **upturn, turn up**, cock up; trend upwards, slope up; upcast, upsweep, upbend, upcurve

adjectives

14 **ascending**, in the ascendant, **mounting, rising**, uprising, upgoing, upcoming; ascendant, ascensional, ascensive, anabatic; **leaping**, springing, saltatory; spiralling, skyrocketing; **upward**; uphill, uphillward, upgrade, upsloping; uparching, rearing, rampant; climbing, scandent, scansorial

15 **upturned, upcast**, uplifted, **turned-up**, retroussé

adverbs

16 **up, upward, upwards**; skyward, heavenward; uplong, upalong; upstream, upstreamward; uphill; uphillward; upstairs; up attic *and* up steps (*both informal*); uptown; up north

exclamations

17 **alley-oop!, upsy-daisy!, upsadaisy!**; excelsior!, onward and upward!

194 DESCENT
motion downward

nouns

1 **descent, descending,** descension *or* downcome (*both old*), **comedown,** down; **dropping, falling,** plummeting, **drop, fall, free-fall,** *chute* (*French*), **downfall,** debacle, **collapse,** crash; **swoop,** stoop, pounce, downrush, downflow, cascade, waterfall, cataract, **downpour,** defluxion; downturn, downcurve, downbend, downward trend, downtrend; declension, declination, inclination; gravitation; downgrade *see* 204.5; **down tick; decrease** *see* 252

2 **sinkage,** lowering, **decline, slump,** subsidence, submergence, lapse, decurrence; cadence; **droop, sag,** swag; catenary

3 **tumble, fall,** *culbute* (*French*), cropper *and* **spill** (*both informal*), **flop** (*informal*); **header** (*informal*); **sprawl; pratfall** (*informal*); **stumble,** trip; **dive, plunge** *see* 367; forced landing

4 **slide; slip,** slippage; **glide,** coast, glissade; glissando; slither; **skid,** sideslip; **landslide,** rockfall, mudslide, landslip, subsidence; **snowslide,** snowslip; **avalanche**

verbs

5 **to descend, go** *or* **come down,** down, dip down, lose altitude, dump altitude (*informal*); gravitate; **fall, drop,** precipitate, rain, rain *or* pour down, fall *or* drop down; **collapse,** crash; **swoop,** stoop, pounce; **pitch, plunge** *see* 367.6, **plummet;** cascade, cataract; parachute; come down a peg (*informal*); **fall off,** drop off; trend downward, down-tick, go downhill

6 **to sink, go down,** sink down, submerge; **set, settle,** settle down; **decline,** lower, **subside,** give way, lapse, cave, cave in; **droop,** slouch, **sag,** swag; **slump,** slump down; flump, flump down; flop *and* flop down (*both informal*); plump, plop *or* plop down, plunk *or* plunk down (*informal*); founder *see* 367.8

7 **to get down, alight,** touch down, **light; land,** settle, perch, come to rest; **dismount, get off,** uphorse; climb down

8 **to tumble, fall, fall down,** come *or* fall *or* get a cropper (*informal*), take a fall *or* tumble, take a flop *or* spill (*informal*), precipitate oneself; **fall over,** tumble over, trip over; **sprawl,** sprawl out, take a pratfall (*informal*), spread-eagle (*informal*), measure one's length; fall headlong, **take a header** (*informal*); fall prostrate, fall flat, fall on one's face, fall flat on one's backside (*informal*); **fall over,** topple down *or* over; capsize, turn turtle; **topple,** lurch, pitch, **stumble,** stagger, totter, careen, list, tilt, trip, flounder

9 **to slide, slip,** slip *or* slide down; **glide,** skim, coast, glissade; **slither; skid,** sideslip; avalanche

10 **to light upon,** alight upon, settle on; **descend upon, come down on, fall on,** drop on, hit *or* strike upon

adjectives

11 **descending,** descendant, on the descendant; **down,** downward, declivitous; decurrent, deciduous; **downgoing,** downcoming; down-reaching; dropping, falling, plunging, plummeting, downfalling; **sinking,** downsinking, foundering, submerging, setting; declining, **subsiding;** collapsing, tumbledown, tottering; drooping, sagging; on the downgrade, downhill *see* 204.16

12 **downcast, downturned;** hanging, down-hanging

adverbs

13 **down, downward, downwards,** from the top down, *de haut en bas* (*French*); adown, below; downright; downhill, downgrade; downstreet; downline; downstream; downstairs; downtown; south, down south

195 CONTAINER

nouns

1 **container, receptacle;** receiver *see* 479.3, holder, vessel, utensil; basin, pot, pan, cup, glass, ladle, bottle, caddy, pannikin; cask; box, case; basket, scuttle, trug; luggage, baggage; cabinet, cupboard

2 **bag, sack,** sac, poke (*informal*); **pocket,** fob; **balloon, bladder**

196 CONTENTS

nouns

1 **contents, content,** what is contained *or* included *or* comprised; **insides** *see* 207.4, innards (*informal*), guts; **components, constituents, ingredients,** elements, **items, parts, divisions,** subdivisions; **inventory,** index, census, list *see* 870; part *see* 792; whole *see* 791; composition *see* 795

2 **load, lading, cargo, freight, charge, burden; payload;** boatload, busload, carload, cartload, container-load, shipload, trailerload, trainload, lorryload, truckload, vanload, wagonload

3 **lining,** liner; **interlining,** interlineation; inlayer, inside layer, **inlay,** inlaying; **filling,** filler; **packing,** padding, wadding, **stuffing;** facing; doubling, doublure; bushing, bush; wainscot; insole

4 (*contents of a container*) cup, cupful, etc

5 (*essential content*) **substance, sum and substance, stuff, material, matter,** medium, building blocks, fabric; **gist, heart, soul, meat, nub;** the nitty-gritty *and* the bottom line *and* the name of the game (*all informal*), **core,** kernel, marrow, pith, sap, spirit, **essence,** quintessence, elixir, distillate, distillation, distilled essence; sine qua non, irreducible *or* indispensable content

6 **enclosure,** the enclosed

verbs

7 **to fill, pack** *see* 793.7, **load; line,** interline, interlineate; inlay; face; wainscot, ceil; **pad, wad, stuff;** feather, fur

197 ROOM
compartment

nouns

1 **room, chamber,** *chambre* (*French*), *salle* (*French*), four walls

2 **compartment,** chamber, space, enclosed space; **cavity,** hollow, hole, concavity; **cell,** cellule; booth, stall, crib, manger; box, pew; **crypt, vault**

3 **nook, corner, cranny, niche, recess,** inglenook, cove, bay, oriel, alcove; cubicle, roomlet, carrel, hole-in-the-wall (*informal*), cubby, **cubbyhole,** snug, snuggery, hidey-hole (*informal*)

4 **hall;** assembly hall, exhibition hall, convention hall; gallery; meetinghouse, meeting room; **auditorium; concert hall; theatre,** music hall; stadium, dome, sports dome, **arena** *see* 463; lecture hall, lyceum, amphitheatre; operating theatre; dance hall; ballroom, grand ballroom; **chapel** *see* 703.3

5 **parlour, living room, sitting room, morning room, lounge, drawing** *or* **withdrawing room, front room,** best room (*informal*), foreroom (*informal*), **salon,** saloon (*old*); stateroom; sun parlour *or* sunroom, sun lounge, sunporch, solarium

6 **library,** stacks; **study,** studio, *atelier (French),* workroom; **office,** workplace; **loft,** sail loft

7 **bedroom, boudoir,** chamber, sleeping chamber, **bedchamber,** master bedroom, guest room, sleeping room, cubicle, cubiculum; nursery; dormitory

8 (*private chamber*) **sanctum,** sanctum sanctorum, holy of holies, adytum; **den,** retreat, closet, cabinet

9 (*ships*) cabin, stateroom; saloon; house, deckhouse, trunk cabin, cuddy, shelter cabin

10 (*trains*) drawing room, stateroom, parlor car (*US & Canadian*), Pullman car, sleeping car, roomette (*US & Canadian*)

11 **dining room,** *salle à manger (French),* dinette, dining hall, refectory, buttery, mess *or* messroom *or* mess hall, commons; dining car *or* diner; **restaurant, cafeteria, canteen**

12 **playroom,** recreation room (*US & Canadian*), rec room (*US & Canadian informal*), family room, game room, games room, **rumpus room** (*US, Canadian & NZ informal*); **gymnasium**

13 **utility room,** boxroom, laundry room, sewing room

14 **kitchen** *see* 11.3, **storeroom** *see* 386.6, smoking room *see* 89.13

15 wardrobe, cupboard, closet, clothes closet, cloakroom; left-luggage office, checkroom (*US & Canadian*); airing cupboard, linen cupboard; dressing room, fitting room; pantry

16 **attic,** attic room, **garret, loft,** sky parlour; cockloft, hayloft; storeroom, junk room, lumber room

17 **cellar,** cellarage, **basement;** subbasement; wine cellar, potato cellar, storm cellar, cyclone cellar; coal bin *or* hole, hold, hole, bunker

18 **corridor, hall,** hallway; passage, **passageway; gallery,** loggia; arcade, colonnade, pergola, cloister, peristyle; areaway; breezeway

19 **vestibule,** portal, **portico,** entry, entryway, entrance, **entrance hall,** entranceway, **threshold; lobby, foyer;** propylaeum, stoa; narthex, galilee

20 **anteroom,** antechamber; side room, byroom; **waiting room,** *salle d'attente (French);* **reception room,** presence chamber *or* room, audience chamber; throne room; lounge, greenroom, wardroom

21 **porch,** stoop, **veranda,** piazza (*informal*), patio, lanai, gallery; sleeping porch

22 **balcony,** gallery, terrace

23 **floor, storey,** level, flat; first floor *or* storey; ground *or* street floor, *rez-de-chaussée (French);* mezzanine, mezzanine floor, *entresol (French);* clerestory *or* clearstory

24 **showroom,** display room, exhibition room, gallery

25 **hospital room; ward,** maternity ward, fever ward, charity ward, prison ward, etc; private room, semi-private room; examining *or* examination room, consulting *or* consultation room, treatment room; **operating theatre,** operating room *or* OR, surgery; labour room, delivery room; recovery room; emergency, emergency room; intensive care unit *or* ICU; pharmacy, dispensary; clinic, nursery; laboratory; blood bank; nurses' station

26 **bathroom, lavatory, washroom** *see* 79.10, **water closet** *or* **WC,** closet, **rest room,** cloakroom, comfort station (*US*), **toilet** *see* 12.10

27 (*for vehicles*) **garage,** carport, lock up; bicycle shed; coach *or* carriage house; carbarn; roundhouse; hangar; boathouse

198 TOP

nouns

1 **top,** top side, upper side, upside; surface *see* 206.2; topside *or* topsides; upper storey, top floor; clerestory *or* clearstory; **roof,** ridgepole *or* roofpole; rooftop

2 **summit,** top; **tip-top, peak** *see* 3.6, pinnacle; **crest, brow;** ridge, edge; **crown, cap, tip,** point, spire, pitch; highest pitch, no place higher, **apex,** vertex, **acme,** *ne plus ultra (French),* **zenith, climax,** apogee, pole; **culmination; extremity, maximum, limit,** upper extremity, highest point, very top, top of the world, extreme limit, utmost *or* upmost *or* uppermost height,

"the very acme and pitch" —POPE; sky, heaven *or* heavens, seventh heaven, cloud nine (*informal*); meridian, noon, high noon; mountaintop

3 **topping,** icing, frosting

4 (*top part*) **head,** heading, **headpiece,** cap, *caput (Latin),* capsheaf, **crown, crest;** topknot; pinhead, nailhead

5 **architectural topping, capital** (*see list*), head, crown, cap; bracket capital; cornice

6 **head,** headpiece, **pate,** poll (*informal*), crown, **bonce** *and* **napper** *and* **noddle** *and* **noggin** *and* **nut** *and* loaf *and* dome *and* chump (*all informal*), noodle *and* bean (*both US & Canadian informal*), sconce (*old*); brow, ridge;

"the dome of Thought, the palace of the Soul"— BYRON

7 **skull,** cranium, pericranium, epicranium; brainpan, brain box *or* case

8 **phrenology,** craniology, metoposcopy, physiognomy; phrenologist, craniologist, metoposcopist, physiognomist

verbs

9 **to top,** top off, **crown, cap,** crest, **head,** tip, peak, surmount; overtop *or* outtop, have the top place *or* spot, over-arch; **culminate,** consummate, climax; ice, frost (*a cake*); fill, top up

adjectives

10 top, topmost, **uppermost**, upmost, overmost, **highest**; tip-top, tip-crowning, **maximum**, maximal, ultimate; summital, apical, vertical, zenithal, climactic, climactical, **consummate**; acmic, acmatic; meridian, meridional; **head**, headmost, capital, chief, paramount, supreme, preeminent; **top-level**, highest level, top-echelon, top-flight, top-ranking, top-drawer (*informal*)
11 topping, **crowning**, **capping**, heading, surmounting, overtopping *or* outtopping, overarching; **culminating**, consummating, perfecting, climaxing
12 topped, headed, **crowned, capped**, crested, plumed, tipped, peaked
13 topless, headless, crownless
14 cranial; cephalic, encephalic

adverbs

15 atop, on top, at *or* on the top, topside (*informal*); at the top of the tree *or* ladder, on top of the roost *or* heap; on the crest *or* crest of the wave; at the head, at the peak *or* pinnacle *or* summit

prepositions

16 atop, on, upon, on top of, surmounting, topping
17 capital styles

Byzantine	Ionic
Corinthian	Moorish
Doric	Roman Corinthian
Gothic	Roman Doric
Greek	Romanesque
Greek Corinthian	Roman Ionic
Greek Ionic	Tuscan

199 BOTTOM

nouns

1 bottom, bottom side, **underside**, nether side, lower side, downside, **underneath**, fundament; belly, underbelly; buttocks see 217.4, breech; **rock bottom, bedrock**, bed, hardpan; **grass roots**; substratum, underlayer, lowest level *or* layer *or* stratum, nethermost level *or* layer *or* stratum; **nadir**, the pits (*informal*)
2 base, basement, **foot**, footing, sole, toe; **foundation** see 900.6; skirting board; wainscot, dado; skeleton, bare bones, chassis, frame; keel, keelson
3 ground covering, **ground**, earth, *terra firma* (*Latin*); **floor**, flooring; parquet; **deck; pavement**, *pavé* (*French*), paving, surfacing, asphalt, blacktop, Tarmacadam *or* Tarmac (*trademark*), macadam, concrete; **cover**, carpet, floor covering, linoleum; artificial turf, Astroturf (*trademark*)
4 bed, bottom, floor, ground, **basin, channel**, coulee; seabed, ocean bottom see 275.4
5 foot, extremity, pes, pedes, *pied* (*French*), trotter, pedal extremity, dog, tootsy (*informal*); **hoof**, ungula; **paw**, pad, pug, *patte* (*French*); forefoot, forepaw; harefoot, splay-foot, clubfoot; **toe**, digit; **heel; sole**, pedi *or* pedio; instep, arch; pastern; fetlock

verbs

6 to base on, found on, ground on, build on,

bottom on, bed on, set on; root in; **underlie**, undergird; bottom, bottom out; hit bottom

adjectives

7 bottom, bottommost, **undermost**, nethermost, lowermost, deepest, **lowest; rock-bottom**, bedrock; ground
8 basic; basal, basilar; **underlying, fundamental**, essential, elementary, elemental, primary, primal, primitive, rudimentary, original, grass-roots; radical; nadiral
9 pedal; plantar; footed, hoofed, ungulate, clawed, taloned; toed

200 VERTICALNESS

nouns

1 verticalness, verticality, verticalism; **erectness, uprightness**; stiffness *or* erectness of posture, position of attention, brace; straight up-and-downness, up-and-downness; steepness, sheerness, precipitousness, plungingness, **perpendicularity**, plumbness, aplomb; right-angledness *or* angularity, squareness, orthogonality
2 vertical, upright, perpendicular, plumb, normal; right angle, orthodiagonal; vertical circle, azimuth circle
3 precipice, cliff, sheer *or* yawning cliff *or* precipice *or* drop, steep, bluff, wall, face, scar; crag, craig (*Scottish*); scarp, **escarpment; palisade**, palisades
4 erection, erecting, **elevation; rearing**, raising; **uprearing**, upraising, lofting, uplifting, heaving up *or* aloft; standing on end *or* upright *or* on its feet *or* on its base *or* on its legs *or* on its bottom
5 rising, uprising, ascension, ascending, ascent; vertical height *or* dimension; **gradient**, rise, uprise
6 (*instruments*) square, T square, try square, set square, carpenter's square; plumb, plumb line, plumb rule, plummet, bob, plumb bob, lead

verbs

7 to stand, stand erect, stand up, stand upright, stand up straight, be erect, be on one's feet; hold oneself straight *or* stiff, stand ramrod-straight, have an upright carriage; stand at attention, brace, stand at parade rest (*all military*)
8 to rise, arise, ascend, mount, uprise, **rise up, get up**, get to one's feet; **stand up, stand on end; stick up**, cock up; bristle; **rear**, ramp, uprear, rear up, rise on the hind legs; upheave; sit up, sit bolt upright; jump up, spring to one's feet
9 to erect, elevate, rear, raise, pitch, **set up**, raise *or* lift *or* cast up; raise *or* heave *or* rear aloft; uprear, upraise, uplift, upheave; **upright; upend**, stand upright *or* on end; set on its feet *or* legs *or* base *or* bottom
10 to plumb, plumb-line, set *à plomb*; **square**, square up

adjectives

11 vertical, upright, bolt upright, ramrod straight, **erect**, upstanding, standing up, stand-up; rearing, rampant; **upended**, upraised, upreared; downright

12 perpendicular, **plumb**, straight-up-and-down, straight-up, **up-and-down**; sheer, steep, precipitous, plunging; **right-angled**, right-angle, right-angular, orthogonal, orthodiagonal

adverbs

13 vertically, erectly, upstandingly, uprightly, **upright**, up, bolt *or* stark upright; **on end**, up on end, right on end, endways; on one's feet *or* legs, on one's hind legs (*informal*); at attention, braced, at parade rest (*all military*)

14 perpendicularly, sheer, sheerly; up and down, **straight up and down**; plumb, *à plomb* (*French*); at right angles, square

201 HORIZONTALNESS

nouns

1 horizontalness, horizontality; **levelness, flatness**, planeness, evenness, smoothness, flushness; unbrokenness, unrelievedness

2 recumbency, recumbence, decumbency *or* decumbence, accumbency; accubation; **prostration**, proneness; supineness, reclining, reclination; lying, lounging, **repose** *see* 20; sprawl, loll

3 horizontal, **plane, level, flat**, dead level *or* flat, homaloid; **horizontal** *or* level plane; horizontal *or* level line; horizontal projection; horizontal surface, fascia; horizontal parallax; horizontal axis; horizontal fault; water level, sea level, mean sea level; ground, earth, steppe, **plain, flatland**, prairie, savanna, sea of grass, bowling green, table, billiard table; floor, platform, ledge, terrace

4 horizon, skyline, rim of the horizon; sea line; apparent *or* local *or* visible horizon, sensible horizon, celestial *or* rational *or* geometrical *or* true horizon, artificial *or* false horizon; azimuth

verbs

5 to lie, lie down, lay (*informal*), **recline, repose**, lounge, sprawl, loll, drape *or* spread oneself, splay, lie limply; **lie flat** *or* prostrate *or* prone *or* supine, lie on one's face *or* back, lie on a level, hug the ground *or* deck; **grovel, crawl**, kowtow

6 to **level, flatten, even, equalize**, align, smooth *or* smoothen, level out, smooth out, flush; grade, roll, roll flat, steamroller; **lay**, lay down *or* out; **raze**, rase, lay level, lay level with the ground; lay low *or* flat; **fell** *see* 912.5

adjectives

7 horizontal, **level, flat**, flattened; **even, smooth**, smoothened, smoothed out; table-like, tabular; **flush**; homaloidal; **plane, plain**; rolled, trodden, squashed, rolled *or* trodden *or* squashed flat; flat as a pancake, "flat as a cake"—ERASMUS, flat as a table *or* billiard table *or* bowling green *or* tennis court, flat as a board, "flat as a flounder"—JOHN FLETCHER, level as a plain

8 recumbent, accumbent, procumbent, decumbent; **prostrate, prone**, flat; **supine**, resupine; couchant, *couché* (*French*); **lying, reclining, reposing**, flat on one's back; sprawling, lolling, lounging; sprawled,

spread, splay, splayed, draped; grovelling, crawling, flat on one's belly *or* nose

adverbs

9 horizontally, **flat**, flatly, flatways, flatwise; **evenly**, flush; **level, on a level**; lengthwise, lengthways, at full length, on one's back *or* belly *or* nose

202 PENDENCY

nouns

1 pendency, pendulousness *or* pendulosity, pensileness *or* pensility; **hanging, suspension**, dangling *or* danglement, suspense, dependence *or* dependency

2 hang, droop, dangle, swing, fall; **sag, swag, bag**

3 overhang, overhanging, impendence *or* impendency, **projection**, beetling, jutting; cantilever

4 pendant, hanger; **hanging**, drape; **lobe**, ear lobe, lobule, lobus, lobation, lappet, wattle; **uvula**

5 suspender, hanger, supporter; **braces**, galluses (*informal*), suspenders (*US & Canadian*)

verbs

6 to hang, hang down, fall; **depend, pend; dangle**, swing, flap, flop (*informal*); flow, drape, cascade; **droop**, lop; nod, weep; **sag, swag, bag**; **trail, drag**, draggle, drabble, daggle

7 to overhang, hang over, hang out, **impend**, impend over, **project**, project over, beetle, **jut**, beetle *or* jut *or* thrust over, stick out over

8 to suspend, **hang, hang up**, put up, fasten up; sling

adjectives

9 pendent, pendulous, pendulant, pendular, penduline, pensile; **suspended**, hung; **hanging, pending**, depending, dependent; **falling; dangling**, swinging, falling loosely; weeping; flowing, cascading

10 drooping, droopy, limp, loose, nodding, floppy (*informal*), loppy, lop; **sagging**, saggy, swag, sagging in folds; **bagging**, baggy, ballooning; lop-eared

11 overhanging, overhung, lowering, **impending**, impendent, **pending**; incumbent, superincumbent; **projecting, jutting; beetling**, beetle; beetle-browed

12 lobular, lobar, lobed, lobate, lobated

203 PARALLELISM
physically parallel direction or state

nouns

1 parallelism, coextension, nonconvergence, nondivergence, collaterality, concurrence, equidistance; collineation, collimation; alignment; parallelization; parallelotropism; **analogy** *see* 942.1

2 parallel, paralleler; parallel line, parallel dash, parallel bar, parallel file, parallel series, parallel column, parallel trench, parallel vector; parallelogram, parallelepiped *or* parallelepipedon

3 (*instruments*) parallel rule *or* rules *or* ruler, parallelograph, parallelometer

verbs

4 to parallel, be parallel, coextend; run parallel, go alongside, go beside, run abreast; match, equal

5 to **parallelize**, place parallel to, equidistance; line up, align, realign; collineate, collimate; match; correspond, follow, equate

adjectives

6 **parallel**, paralleling; coextending, coextensive, nonconvergent, nondivergent, **equidistant**, equispaced, collateral, concurrent; lined up, aligned; equal, even; parallelogrammical, parallelogrammatical; parallelepipedal; parallelotropic; parallelodrome, parallelinervate; analogous *see* 942.8

adverbs

7 in **parallel**, parallelwise, parallelly; side by side, alongside, abreast; equidistantly, nonconvergently, nondivergently; collaterally, coextensively

204 OBLIQUITY

nouns

1 **obliquity**, obliqueness; **deviation** *see* 164, deviance, divergence, digression, divagation, vagary, excursion, skewness, aberration, squint, declination; deflection, deflexure; nonconformity *see* 867; diagonality, crosswiseness, transverseness; indirection, indirectness, deviousness, circuitousness *see* 913

2 **inclination**, **leaning**, lean, angularity; **slant**, slaunch (*informal*), rake, **slope**; **tilt**, **tip**, pitch, **list**, **cant**, swag, sway; leaning tower, tower of Pisa

3 **bias**, **bend**, bent, **crook**, **warp**, **twist**, **turn**, **skew**, slew, veer, sheer, **swerve**, lurch

4 **incline**, inclination, **slope**, **grade**, gradient, pitch, **ramp**, launching ramp, bank, talus, gentle *or* easy slope, glacis; rapid *or* steep slope, stiff climb, scarp, chute; helicline, inclined plane (*physics*); **bevel**, bezel, fleam; hillside, side; hanging gardens; shelving beach

5 **declivity**, **descent**, dip, drop, fall, falling-off *or* away, **decline**; hang, hanging; **downhill**, downgrade

6 **acclivity**, **ascent**, climb, **rise**, rising, uprise, uprising, rising ground; **uphill**, upgrade, upgo, upclimb, uplift, steepness, precipitousness, abruptness, verticalness *see* 200

7 **diagonal**, oblique, transverse, bias, bend (*heraldry*), oblique line, slash, **slant**, virgule, scratch comma, separatrix, solidus; oblique angle *or* figure, rhomboid

8 **zigzag**, zig, zag; zigzaggery, flexuosity, **crookedness**, crankiness; switchback, hairpin, dogleg; chevron

verbs

9 to **oblique**, **deviate**, **diverge**, deflect, divagate, **bear off**; angle, **angle off**, **swerve**, shoot off at an angle, **veer**, sheer, sway, slew, **skew**, **twist**, **turn**, bend, bias; crook

10 to **incline**, **lean**; slope, slant, slaunch (*informal*), rake, pitch, grade, bank, shelve; **tilt**, **tip**, **list**, **cant**, careen, keel, sidle, swag, sway; **ascend**, **rise**, uprise, climb, **go uphill**; **descend**, **decline**, dip, drop, fall, fall off *or* away, **go downhill**; retreat

11 to **cut**, cut *or* slant across, cut crosswise *or* transversely *or* diagonally, catercorner (*US & Canadian informal*), diagonalize, slash, slash across

12 to **zigzag**, zig, zag, **stagger**, crank *or* crankle (*old*), wind in and out

adjectives

13 **oblique**; **devious**, deviant, deviative, divergent, digressive, divagational, deflectional, excursive; **indirect**, side, sidelong; left-handed, sinister, sinistral; backhand, backhanded; circuitous *see* 913.7

14 **askew**, **skew**, skewed; skew-jawed *and* skewgee *and* skewwhiff *and* askewgee *and* agee *and* agee-jawed (*all informal*); **awry**, wry; askance, askant, asquint, squinting, **cockeyed** (*informal*); **crooked** *see* 265.10; wonky (*informal*)

15 **inclining**, inclined, inclinatory, inclinational; **leaning**, recumbent; **sloping**, sloped, aslope; raking, pitched; **slanting**, slanted, slant, aslant, slantways, slantwise; bias, biased; shelving, shelvy; **tilting**, tilted, atilt, tipped, **tipping**, tipsy, listing, **canting**, careening; sideling, sidelong; out of the perpendicular *or* square *or* plumb, bevel, bevelled

16 (*sloping downward*) **downhill**, downgrade; **descending**, falling, dropping, dipping; **declining**, declined; declivous, declivitous, declivate

17 (*sloping upward*) **uphill**, upgrade; **rising**, uprising, **ascending**, climbing; acclivous, acclivitous, acclinate

18 **steep**, **precipitous**, **bluff**, plunging, abrupt, bold, **sheer**, sharp, rapid; headlong, breakneck; vertical *see* 200.11

19 **transverse**, crosswise *or* crossways, thwart, athwart, across *see* 170.9; **diagonal**, bendwise; catercorner *or* catercornered *or* cattycorner *or* cattycornered (*all US & Canadian informal*); slant, bias, biased, biaswise *or* biasways

20 **crooked**, **zigzag**, zigzagged, zigzaggy, zigzagwise *or* zigzagways, dogleg *or* doglegged; flexuous, twisty, hairpin, bendy, curvy; staggered, crankled (*old*); chevrony, chevronwise *or* chevronways (*all architecture*)

adverbs

21 **obliquely**, **deviously**, deviately, **indirectly**, circuitously *see* 913.9; divergently, digressively, excursively, divagationally; **sideways** *or* sidewise, sidelong, sideling, on *or* to one side; at an angle

22 **askew**, **awry**; askance, askant, asquint

23 **slantingly**, **slopingly**, aslant, aslope, atilt, rakingly, tipsily, slopeways, slopeways, slantwise, slantways, aslantwise, on *or* at a slant; off plumb *or* the vertical; **downhill**, downgrade; **uphill**, upgrade

24 transversely, crosswise *or* crossways, athwart, across *see* 170.13

25 **diagonally**, diagonalwise; **on the bias**, bias, biaswise; **cornerwise**, cornerways; catercornerways *or* catercorner *or* cattycorner (*all US & Canadian informal*)

205 INVERSION

nouns

1 **inversion**, turning over *or* around *or* upside down, the other way round; eversion, turning inside out, invagination, intussusception; introversion, turning inward; **reversing**, reversal *see* 858.1, turning back to front *or* side to side; **reversion**, turning back *or* backwards, retroversion, retroflexion, revulsion; devolution, atavism; recidivism; **transposition,**

transposal; topsy-turvydom *or* topsy-turviness; the world turned upside-down, the tail wagging the dog; pronation, supination, resupination

2 **overturn, upset,** overset, **overthrow,** upturn, **turnover,** spill (*informal*); subversion; **revolution** *see* 859; **capsizing,** capsize, capsizal, turning turtle; **somersault,** *culbute* (*French*); turning head over heels

3 (*grammatical and rhetorical terms*) metastasis, metathesis; anastrophe, chiasmus, hypallage, hyperbaton, hysteron proteron, palindrome, parenthesis, synchysis, tmesis

4 **inverse, reverse, converse, opposite** *see* 215.5, other side of the coin *or* picture, the flip side *and* B side (*both informal*)

verbs

5 **to invert,** inverse, turn over *or* around *or* upside down; introvert, turn in *or* inward; **turn down; turn inside out,** turn out, evert, invaginate, intussuscept; **revert,** recidivate, relapse, lapse, back-slide; **reverse** *see* 858.4, **transpose,** convert; put the cart before the horse; turn into the opposite, turn about, turn the tables, turn the tide; rotate, revolve, pronate, supinate, resupinate

6 **to overturn, turn over, turn upside down,** turn bottom side up, upturn, **upset,** overset, **overthrow,** subvert, *culbuter* (*French*); go *or* turn arse over tit (*informal*), turn somersault, go *or* turn head over heels; **turn turtle, turn topsy-turvy; tip over,** keel over, topple over; **capsize;** careen, set on its beam ends, set on its ears

adjectives

7 **inverted,** inversed, back-to-front, **backwards,** retroverted, **reversed, transposed, backside foremost, tail first; inside out,** outside in, everted, invaginated, wrong side out; reverted, lapsed, recidivist *or* recidivistic; atavistic; devolutional; **upside-down, topsy-turvy,** arse over tit *and* arsy-versy (*both informal*); **capsized,** head-over-heels; hyperbatic, chiastic, palindromic; resupinate; introverted

adverbs

8 inversely, **conversely,** contrarily, contrariwise, **vice versa,** the other way around, **backwards,** turned around; **upside down,** over, **topsy-turvy; bottom up,** bottom side up; head over heels, heels over head

206 EXTERIORITY

nouns

1 **exteriority,** externalness, externality, **outwardness,** outerness; appearance, outward appearance, seeming, mien, **front,** manner; window dressing, cosmetics; openness; extrinsicality *see* 767; **superficiality, shallowness** *see* 276; extraterritoriality, foreignness

2 **exterior,** external, **outside; surface,** superficies, covering *see* 295, skin *see* 2.4, outer skin *or* layer, epidermis, integument, envelope, crust, cortex, rind, shell *see* 295.16; cladding, plating; top, superstratum; **periphery, fringe,** circumference, outline, lineaments, border; **face,** outer face *or* side, facade,

front; facet; extrados, back; store-front, shop-front, shop-window, street-front

3 **outdoors,** outside, **the out-of-doors,** the great outdoors, the open, **the open air;** outland

4 **externalization,** exteriorization, bringing into the open, show, showing, display, displaying; **objectification,** actualization, realization

verbs

5 **to externalize,** exteriorize, bring into the open, bring out, show, display, exhibit; **objectify,** actualize, project, realize

6 **to scratch the surface;** give a lick and a promise, do a cosmetic job, give a once-over-lightly, whitewash, give a nod

adjectives

7 **exterior, external;** extrinsic *see* 767; **outer, outside, out, outward,** outward-facing, outlying, outstanding; **outermost,** outmost; surface, superficial *see* 276.5, epidermic, cortical; cosmetic, merely cosmetic; peripheral, **fringe,** roundabout; apparent, seeming; open *see* 348.10, public *see* 352.17; exomorphic

8 **outdoor, outside,** out of doors, out-of-door, withoutdoors; **open-air,** alfresco; out and about

9 extraterritorial, exterritorial; extraterrestrial, exterrestrial, extramundane; extragalactic, extralateral, extraliminal, extramural, extrapolar, extrasolar, extraprovincial, extratribal; foreign, outlandish, **alien**

adverbs

10 **externally, outwardly,** on the outside, exteriorly; **without, outside, outwards, out;** apparently, to all appearances; openly, publicly, to judge by appearances; superficially, on the surface

11 **outdoors,** out of doors, **outside,** abroad; in the open, **in the open air,** alfresco, *en plein air* (*French*)

word elements

12 e–, ec–, ect–, ecto–, ex–, ef–, epi–, eph–, extra–, hyper–, peripher–, periphero–

207 INTERIORITY

nouns

1 interiority, internalness, internality, **inwardness, innerness,** inness; introversion, internalization; **intrinsicality** *see* 766; depth *see* 275

2 **interior, inside,** inner, inward, internal, intern; inner recess, recesses, **innermost** *or* **deepest recesses,** penetralia, intimate places, secret place *or* places; bosom, secret heart, heart, heart of hearts, soul, vitals, vital centre; inner self, inner life, inner landscape, inner *or* interior man, inner nature; intrados; core, centre *see* 208.2

3 **inland,** inlands, **interior,** up-country; **midlands,** midland; heartland; hinterland *see* 233.2

4 **insides, innards** (*informal*), inwards, internals; inner mechanism, what makes it tick *and* works (*both informal*); **guts** (*informal*), **vitals, viscera,** *kishkes* (*Yiddish*), giblets; entrails, bowels, guts; tripes *and* stuffings (*both informal*)

verbs

5 to internalize, put in, keep within; enclose, embed, surround, contain, comprise, include, enfold, take to heart, assimilate

adjectives

6 interior, internal, inner, inside, inward; intestine; innermost, inmost, intimate, private; visceral, gut (*informal*); intrinsic *see* 766.7; deep *see* 275.10; central *see* 208.11; indoor; live-in
7 inland, interior, up-country, up-river; hinterland; midland, mediterranean
8 intramarginal, intramural, intramundane, intramontane, intraterritorial, intracoastal, intragroupal

adverbs

9 internally, inwardly, interiorly, inly, intimately, deeply, profoundly, under the surface; intrinsically *see* 766; centrally
10 in, inside, within; herein, therein, wherein
11 inward, inwards, inwardly; inland, inshore
12 indoors, indoor, withindoors

prepositions

13 in, into; within, at, inside, inside of, in the limits of; to the heart *or* core of

word elements

14 en–, em–, end–, endo–, ent–, ento–, eso–, infra–, in–, im–, il–, ir–, inter–, intra–, ob–

208 CENTRALITY

nouns

1 centrality, centralness, middleness, central *or* middle *or* mid position; equidistance; centricity, centricality; concentricity; centripetalism
2 centre, centrum; middle *see* 818, heart, core, nucleus; core of one's being, where one lives; kernel; pith, marrow, medulla; nub, hub, nave, axis, pivot; navel, umbilicus, omphalos, belly button (*informal*); bull's-eye, bull; dead centre;
"the still point of the turning world"—T S ELIOT; storm centre, eye of the storm
3 (*biological terms*) central body, centriole, centrosome, centrosphere
4 focus, focal point, prime focus, point of convergence; centre of interest *or* attention, focus of attention; centre of consciousness; centre of attraction, centrepiece, clou, mecca, cynosure, cynosure of all eyes; polestar, lodestar; magnet
5 nerve centre, ganglion, centre of activity, vital centre; control centre, guidance centre
6 headquarters *or* HQ, central station, central office, main office, central administration, seat, base, base of operations, centre of authority; general headquarters *or* GHQ, command post *or* CP, company headquarters
7 metropolis, capital; city centre, town centre, community centre, art centre, cultural centre, health centre, shopping centre, shipping centre, manufacturing centre, tourist centre, trade centre, etc

8 centralization, centring; nucleation; focalization, focus, focusing; convergence *see* 169; concentration, concentralization, pooling; centralism

verbs

9 to centralize, centre, middle; centre round, centre on *or* in
10 to focus, focalize, come to a point *or* focus, bring to *or* into focus; bring *or* come to a head, get to the heart of the matter, home in on; zero in on; draw a bead on *and* get a handle on (*informal*); concentrate, concentre, get it together (*informal*); channel, direct, canalize, channelize; converge *see* 169.2

adjectives

11 central, centric, middle *see* 818; centremost, middlemost, midmost; equidistant; centralized, concentrated; umbilical, omphalic; axial, pivotal, key; centroidal; centrosymmetric; geocentric
12 nuclear, nucleate
13 focal, confocal; converging; centrolineal, centripetal
14 concentric; homocentric; coaxial, coaxal

adverbs

15 centrally, in the centre *or* middle of, at the heart of

209 ENVIRONMENT

nouns

1 environment, surroundings, environs, surround, ambience, entourage, circle, circumjacencies, circumambiencies, circumstances, environing circumstances, *alentours* (*French*); precincts, ambit, purlieus, milieu; neighbourhood, vicinity, vicinage; suburbs; outskirts, outposts, borderlands; borders, boundaries, limits, periphery, perimeter, compass, circuit; context, situation; habitat *see* 228; total environment, configuration, gestalt
2 setting, background, backdrop, ground, surround, field, scene, arena, theatre, locale; back, rear, hinterland, distance; stage, stage setting, stage set, *mise-en-scène* (*French*)
3 (*surrounding influence or condition*) milieu, ambience, atmosphere, climate, air, aura, spirit, feeling, feel, quality, colour, local colour, sense, sense of place, note, tone, overtone, undertone
4 (*natural or suitable environment*) element, medium; the environment
5 surrounding, encompassment, environment, circumambience *or* circumambiency, circumjacence *or* circumjacency; containment, enclosure *see* 212; encirclement, cincture, encincture, circumcincture, circling, girdling, girding; envelopment, enfoldment, encompassment, encompassing, compassing, embracement; circumposition; circumflexion; inclusion *see* 771, involvement *see* 897

verbs

6 to surround, environ, compass, encompass, enclose, close; go round *or* around, compass about; envelop, enfold, lap, wrap, enwrap, embrace, enclasp, embosom, embay, involve, invest
7 to encircle, circle, ensphere, belt, belt in, zone,

cincture, encincture; **girdle, gird**, begird, engird; ring, band; loop; wreathe, wreathe *or* twine around

adjectives

8 **environing, surrounding**, encompassing, enclosing; **enveloping**, wrapping, enwrapping, enfolding, embracing; **encircling**, circling; bordering, peripheral; circumjacent, circumferential, circumambient, ambient; circumfluent, circumfluous; circumflex; **roundabout**, suburban, neighbouring

9 **environmental**, environal; **ecological**

10 **surrounded**, environed, compassed, **encompassed**, enclosed; **enveloped**, wrapped, enfolded, lapped, wreathed

11 **encircled, circled**, ringed, cinctured, encinctured, belted, girdled, girt, begirt, zoned

adverbs

12 **around**, round, **about**, round about, in the neighbourhood *or* vicinity *or* vicinage; close, close about

13 **all round, all about**, on every side, on all sides, on all hands, right and left

word elements

14 amph–, amphi–, circum–, peri–

210 CIRCUMSCRIPTION

nouns

1 **circumscription, limiting**, circumscribing, **bounding, demarcation, delimitation, definition,** determination, specification; limit-setting, inclusion-exclusion, circling-in *or* out, encincture, boundary-marking

2 **limitation, limiting, restriction**, restricting, confinement *see* 212.1, prescription, proscription, restraint, discipline, moderation, continence; qualification, **hedging**; bounds *see* 211, boundary, limit *see* 211.3; time limit, time constraint; small space *see* 258.3

3 **patent, copyright**, certificate of invention, *brevet d'invention* (*French*); **trademark, logo** *or* logotype, registered trademark, trade name, service mark (*US*)

verbs

4 **to circumscribe, bound; mark off** *or* mark out, stake out, lay off, rope off, cordon off; **demarcate,** delimit, delimitate, draw *or* mark *or* set *or* lay out boundaries, circle in *or* out, hedge in, set the limit, mark the periphery, beat the bounds; **define,** determine, fix, specify; surround *see* 209.6; enclose *see* 212.5

5 **to limit, restrict, restrain, bound, confine,** ground (*US informal*); straiten, narrow, tighten; specialize; stint, scant; **condition**, qualify, hedge, hedge about; draw the line, set an end point *or* a stopping place; discipline, moderate, contain; restrain oneself, pull one's punches (*informal*); **patent, copyright**, register

adjectives

6 **circumscribed**, circumscript; ringed *or* circled *or* hedged about; **demarcated, delimited, defined,**

definite, determined, determinate, specific, stated, set, fixed; surrounded *see* 209.10, encircled *see* 209.11

7 **limited, restricted**, bound, **bounded, finite; confined** *see* 212.10, prescribed, proscribed, cramped, strait, straitened, narrow; conditioned, qualified, hedged; disciplined, moderated; **deprived,** in straitened circumstances, pinched, on short commons, on short rations, strapped; patented, registered, protected, copyrighted

8 **restricted**, out of bounds, off limits

9 **limiting, restricting**, defining, determining, determinative, confining; limitative, limitary, restrictive, definitive, exclusive

10 **terminal**, limital; limitable, terminable

211 BOUNDS

nouns

1 **bounds, limits**, boundaries, limitations, **confines, pale**, marches, bourns, verges, edges, outlines, outer markings, skirts, outskirts, **fringes**, metes, metes and bounds; periphery, **perimeter**; coordinates, parameters; **compass, circumference,** circumscription *see* 210

2 **outline, contour**, delineation, lines, lineaments, shape, figure, figuration, **configuration**, gestalt; **features**, main features; **profile, silhouette**; relief; skeleton, framework, armature

3 **boundary, bound, limit**, limitation, extremity *see* 793.5; **barrier**, block, claustrum; delimitation, hedge, breaking *or* breakoff point, cutoff, cutoff point, terminus; time limit, time frame, term, deadline, target date, terminal date, time allotment; finish, **end** *see* 819, tail end; **start**, starting line *or* point, mark; **limiting factor**, determinant, limit *or* boundary condition; bracket, brackets, **bookends** (*informal*); threshold, limen; upper limit, ceiling, apogee, high-water mark; lower limit, floor, low-water mark, nadir; **confine**, march, mark, bourn, mete, compass, circumscription; **boundary line, line, border line,** frontier, dividing line, interface, break, boundary, line of demarcation *or* circumvallation

4 **border**, limbus, bordure (*heraldry*), **edge**, limb, **verge, brink**, brow, brim, rim, **margin**, marge, **skirt, fringe, hem**, list, selvage *or* selvedge, side; **forefront, cutting edge**, front line, vanguard *see* 216.2; sideline; shore, bank, coast; **lip**, labium, labrum, labellum; flange; ledge; frame, enframement, mat; featheredge; ragged edge

5 **frontier, border, borderland**, border ground, marchland, march, marches; outskirts, outpost; frontier post; iron curtain, bamboo curtain, Berlin wall; Pillars of Hercules; three-mile *or* twelve-mile limit

6 **kerb**, kerbing, curb (*US & Canadian*); kerbstone, curbstone (*US & Canadian*), border stone, edgestone

7 **edging, bordering**, bordure (*heraldry*), **trimming**, binding, skirting; fringe, fimbriation, fimbria; **hem**, selvage, list, welt; frill, frilling; beading, flounce, furbelow, galloon, motif, ruffle, valance

verbs

8 **to bound**, circumscribe *see* 210.4, surround *see*

209.6, limit *see* 210.5, enclose *see* 212.5, divide, separate

9 **to outline,** contour; **delineate;** silhouette, profile, limn

10 **to border, edge, bound, rim, skirt, hem, hem in, ringe,** befringe, lap, list, margin, marge, marginate, march, verge, line, side; **adjoin** *see* 223.9; frame, enframe, set off; trim, bind; purl; purfle

adjectives

11 **bordering, fringing,** rimming, skirting; **bounding,** boundary, **limiting,** limit, determining *or* determinant *or* determinative; threshold, liminal, limbic; extreme, terminal; **marginal, borderline,** frontier; coastal, littoral

12 **bordered,** edged; margined, marged, marginate, marginated; **fringed,** befringed, trimmed, skirted, fimbriate, fimbriated

13 lipped, labial, labiate

14 outlining, delineatory; peripheral, perimetric, perimetrical, circumferential; outlined, **in outline**

adverbs

15 **on the verge, on the brink,** on the borderline, on the point, on the bounds, on the edge, on the ragged edge, at the threshold, at the limit; **peripherally,** marginally, at the periphery

16 **thus far,** so far, thus far and no farther

212 ENCLOSURE

nouns

1 **enclosure; confinement,** containing, containment, circumscription *see* 210, immurement, walling- *or* hedging- *or* hemming- *or* boxing- *or* fencing-in; **imprisonment,** incarceration, jailing, locking-up, lockdown; **siege,** besieging, beleaguerment, blockade, blockading, cordoning, quarantine, besetment; inclusion *see* 771; **envelopment** *see* 209.5

2 **packaging, packing,** package; boxing, crating, encasement; canning, tinning; bottling; **wrapping,** enwrapment, bundling; shrink-wrapping

3 *(enclosed place)* **enclosure,** close, **confine,** precinct, enclave, pale, paling, list, cincture; **cloister; cage, pen, sty, coop,** fold, cote; **yard,** park, court, courtyard, curtilage, toft; square, quadrangle, quad *(informal);* **field,** delimited field, **arena,** theatre, ground; **container** *see* 195

4 **fence, wall,** boundary *see* 211.3, **barrier;** brick wall, stone wall; paling, palisade; rail, railing; balustrade, balustrading; arcade

verbs

5 **to enclose,** close in, bound, include, **contain;** compass, encompass; **surround,** encircle *see* 209.7; **shut** *or* **pen in,** coop in; **fence in,** wall in, wall up, rail in, rail off, screen off, curtain off; **hem** *or* **hedge in,** box in, pocket; shut *or* coop *or* mew up; pen, coop, corral, cage, impound, mew; **imprison,** incarcerate, jail, lock up, lock in; **besiege,** beset, beleaguer, leaguer *(old),* cordon, cordon off, quarantine, blockade; yard, yard up; house in; chamber; stable, kennel, shrine, enshrine; **wrap** *see* 295.20

6 **to confine, immure;** cramp, straiten, encase; cloister, closet, cabin, crib; entomb, coffin, casket *(US);* bottle up *or* in, box up *or* in

7 **to fence, wall,** fence in, fence up; pale, rail, bar; hem, hem in, hedge, hedge in, hedge out; picket, palisade; bulkhead in

8 **to parenthesize,** bracket, precede and follow, bookend

9 **to package, pack, parcel;** box, box up, case, encase, crate, carton; can, tin; bottle, jar, pot; barrel, cask, tank; sack, bag; basket, hamper; capsule, encyst; **wrap,** enwrap, bundle; shrink-wrap

adjectives

10 **enclosed,** closed-in; **confined,** bound, immured, cloistered,

"cabined, cribbed, confined"—S<small>HAKESPEARE</small>;

imprisoned, incarcerated, jailed; caged, cramped, restrained, corralled; besieged, beleaguered, leaguered *(old),* beset, cordoned, cordoned off, quarantined, blockaded; **shut-in,** pent-up, penned, cooped, mewed, walled- *or* hedged- *or* hemmed- *or* boxed- *or* fenced-in, fenced, walled, paled, railed, barred; hemmed, hedged

11 **enclosing,** confining, **cloistered,** cloisterlike, claustral, parietal, surrounding *see* 209.8; limiting *see* 210.9

12 **packed, packaged,** boxed, crated, canned, tinned, parcelled, cased, encased; bottled; capsuled, encapsuled; **wrapped,** enwrapped, bundled; shrink-wrapped; prepacked; vacuum-packed

213 INTERPOSITION
a putting or lying between

nouns

1 **interposition, interposing,** interposal, interlocation, intermediacy, interjacence; **intervention,** intervenience, intercurrence, slipping-in, sandwiching; leafing-in, interleaving, interfoliation, tipping-in; **intrusion** *see* 214

2 **interjection, interpolation,** introduction, throwing- *or* tossing-in, **injection,** insinuation; intercalation, interlineation; **insertion** *see* 191; interlocution, remark, passing comment, parenthetical *or* side *or* incidental *or* casual remark, *obiter dictum (Latin),* aside, parenthesis; episode; infix, insert

3 **interspersion, interfusion,** interlardment, interpenetration

4 **intermediary,** intermedium, mediary, medium; link, **connecting link,** tie, connection, **go-between,** liaison; middleman, broker, agent, wholesaler, jobber, distributor; **mediator** *see* 466.3

5 **partition,** dividing wall, division, separation, *cloison (French);* **wall, barrier;** panel; paries, parietes; brattice *(mining);* bulkhead; diaphragm, midriff, midsection; septum, interseptum, septulum, dissepiment; **border** *see* 211.4, **dividing line,** property line, party wall; **buffer, bumper,** mat, fender, cushion, pad, shock pad, collision mat; buffer state; Chinese wall

verbs

6 **to interpose, interject, interpolate,** intercalate, interjaculate; **mediate, liaise, go between;**

intervene; put between, sandwich; **insert in**, stick in, introduce in, insinuate in, sandwich in, slip in, inject in, implant in; leaf in, interleaf, tip in, interfoliate; squeeze in, smuggle in, work in, drag in, foist in, fudge in, lug in, drag *or* lug in by the heels, worm in, throw in, run in, thrust in, edge in, wedge in; **intrude** *see* 214.5

7 **to intersperse, interfuse**, interlard, interpenetrate; intersow, intersprinkle

8 **to partition,** set apart, separate, divide; **wall off**, fence off, screen off, curtain off

adjectives

9 interjectional, interpolative, intercalary; parenthetical, episodic

10 **intervening,** intervenient, **interjacent**, intercurrent; **intermediate**, intermediary, medial, mean, medium, mesne, median, **middle**

11 partitioned, walled; mural; septal, parietal

prepositions

12 **between, betwixt,** 'twixt, betwixt and between (*informal*); **among, amongst,** 'mongst; **amid, amidst,** mid, 'mid, midst, 'midst; in the midst of, in the thick of

word elements

13 medi–, medio–, mes–, meso–; inter–, intra–

214 INTRUSION

nouns

1 **intrusion, obtrusion, interloping;** interposition *see* 213, interposal, imposition, insinuation, **interference**, intervention, interventionism, interruption, injection, interjection *see* 213.2; **encroachment**, entrenchment, trespass, trespassing, unlawful entry; impingement, **infringement**, invasion, incursion, inroad, influx, irruption, infiltration; entrance *see* 189

2 meddling, intermeddling; **butting-in** *and* sticking one's nose in (*both informal*), kibitzing (*US & Canadian informal*); **meddlesomeness, intrusiveness, forwardness,** obtrusiveness; **officiousness**, impertinence, presumption, presumptuousness; inquisitiveness *see* 980.1

3 **intruder, interloper, trespasser;** crasher *and* gate-crasher (*both informal*), unwelcome *or* uninvited guest; invader, encroacher, infiltrator

4 interventionist, intervener *or* intervenor, **meddler**, intermeddler; **busybody**, pry, Paul Pry, prier, Nosey Parker *or* nosey Parker *or* Nosy Parker (*all informal*), snoop *or* snooper, backseat driver (*informal*), kibitzer (*US & Canadian informal*), *yenta* (*Yiddish*)

verbs

5 **to intrude, obtrude, interlope;** come between, **interpose** *see* 213.6, insert oneself, **intervene, interfere**, insinuate, impose; **encroach, infringe**, impinge, **trespass**, trespass on *or* upon, trench, entrench, invade, infiltrate; **break in upon**, break in, burst in, charge in, crash in, smash in, storm in; **barge in** (*informal*), irrupt, **cut in**, thrust in *see*

191.7, push in, press in, rush in, throng in, crowd in, squeeze in, elbow in, muscle in (*informal*); jump the queue, queue-jump; **butt in** *and* **horn in** *and* chisel in (*all informal*); appoint oneself; crash *and* gatecrash (*both informal*); **get in,** get in on, creep in, steal in, sneak in, slink in, slip in; worm *or* work in, edge in, put *or* shove one's oar in, foist in; **foist oneself upon**, thrust oneself upon; put on *or* upon, impose on *or* upon, add *or* give one's tuppence-worth (*informal*), put one's two cents in (*informal*)

6 **to interrupt, put in, cut in, break in;** jump in, chime in *and* chip in *and* give one's tuppence-worth *and* put in one's two-cents worth (*all informal*)

7 **to meddle, intermeddle,** busybody, not mind one's own business; **meddle with, tamper with,** mix oneself up with, inject oneself into, monkey with, fool with *or* around with (*informal*), mess with *or* around with (*informal*); **pry**, Paul-Pry, snoop, nose *or* nose around, **stick** *or* **poke one's nose in**, stick one's big nose into (*informal*), butt in; have a finger in, have a finger in the pie; kibitz (*US & Canadian informal*)

adjectives

8 **intrusive**, obtrusive, **interfering**, interventionist, intervenient, invasive, interruptive

9 **meddlesome**, meddling; **officious**, overofficious, self-appointed, impertinent, presumptuous; **busybody**, busy; pushing, pushy, forward; **prying**, nosy *or* nosey *and* snoopy (*both informal*); inquisitive *see* 980.5

phrases

10 (*informal terms*) **none of your business;** what's it to you?, **mind your own business,** keep your nose out of this, **who asked you?**, who rattled your cage?, **butt out** (*US*), go fly a kite (*US & Canadian*), go jump in the lake; too many cooks spoil the broth

215 CONTRAPOSITION
a placing over against

nouns

1 contraposition, anteposition, posing against *or* over against; **opposition**, opposing, opposure; **antithesis**, contrast, ironic *or* contrastive juxtaposition; confrontment, **confrontation**; polarity, polar opposition, **polarization**; **contrariety** *see* 778; contention *see* 457; hostility *see* 451.2

2 **opposites**, antipodes, polar opposites, contraries; **poles**, opposite poles, antipoles, counterpoles, North Pole, South Pole; antipodal points, antipoints; contrapositives (*logic*); night and day, black and white, chalk and cheese

3 opposite side, other side, the other side of the picture *or* coin, other face; **reverse, inverse, obverse,** converse; heads, tails (*of a coin*); flip side *and* B-side (*both informal*)

verbs

4 to contrapose, **oppose**, contrast, match, **set over against**, pose against *or* over against, put in opposition, set *or* pit against one another; **confront,**

face, front, stand *or* lie opposite, stand opposed *or* vis-à-vis; be at loggerheads, be eyeball to eyeball, meet head-on, meet face-to-face, bump heads, **clash;** counteract *see* 451.3; contend; subtend; **polarize;** contraposit (*logic*)

adjectives

5 contrapositive, **opposite,** opposing, **facing,** confronting, confrontational, confrontive, eyeball-to-eyeball, one-on-one; **opposed,** on opposite sides, adversarial, at loggerheads, at daggers drawn, antithetic, antithetical; **reverse, inverse, obverse, converse; antipodal; polar,** polarized one-on-one, up against

adverbs

6 **opposite, poles apart,** at opposite extremes; contrary, contrariwise, counter; just opposite, **face-to-face,** vis-à-vis, *front à front* (*French*), nose to nose, one on one, eyeball-to-eyeball, back-to-back

prepositions

7 **opposite to,** in opposition to, against, over against; versus, v *or* vs; **facing, across, fronting,** confronting, **in front of;** toward

word elements

8 ant–, anti–, anth–, cat–, cata–, cath–, kat–, kata–, co–, contra–, counter–, enantio–, ob–

216 FRONT

nouns

1 **front, fore,** forepart, forequarter, foreside, forefront, forehand; **priority,** anteriority; **frontier** *see* 211.5; foreland; **foreground;** proscenium; frontage; front page; frontispiece; **preface,** front matter, foreword; prefix; front view, front elevation; **head,** heading; **face,** facade, frontal; fascia; **false front,** window dressing, display; front man; bold *or* brave front, brave face; facet; obverse (*of a coin or medal*), head (*of a coin*); lap

2 **vanguard,** van, point *and* point man (*US*); **spearhead,** advance guard, **forefront, cutting edge,** avant-garde, outguard; scout; **pioneer,** trailblazer; outrider; **precursor** *see* 815; **front-runner,** leader, first in line; **front,** battlefront, line, front line, battle line, line of departure; front rank, first line, first line of battle; **outpost,** farthest outpost; **bridgehead,** beachhead, airhead, railhead; advanced base

3 **prow, bow, stem,** rostrum, figurehead, nose, beak; bowsprit, jib boom; forecastle, forepeak; foredeck

4 **face,** facies, **visage;** physiognomy, phiz *or* phizog *and* dial *and* clock (*all informal*); **countenance,** features, lineaments, favour (*old*); mug *and* mush *and* pan *and* kisser *and* map *and* puss (*all informal*), coupon (*Scottish informal*)

5 **forehead, brow,** lofty brow

6 **chin,** point of the chin, button (*informal*)

verbs

7 to be *or* stand in front, **lead, head,** head up; **get ahead of,** steal a march on, take the lead, come to the front *or* fore, hit the front, forge ahead; be the front-runner, lead, lead the pack *or* field, be first, make the running; **pioneer;** front, front for, represent, speak for

8 **to confront, front,** affront (*old*), **face, meet, encounter,** breast, stem, brave, meet squarely, square up to, come to grips with, head *or* wade into, meet face to face *or* eyeball to eyeball *or* one-on-one, go head-to-head with, come face to face with, look in the face *or* eye, stare in the face, stand up to, stand firm *or* fast, stand *or* hold one's ground, hang tough *and* tough it out *and* gut it out (*all US informal*); call someone's bluff, call *or* bring someone to account; **confront with, face with,** bring face to face with, tell one to one's face, cast *or* throw in one's teeth, present to, **put** *or* **bring before,** set *or* place before, lay before, put *or* lay it on the line; bring up, bring forward; put it to; **challenge,** dare, defy, fly in the face *or* teeth of, throw down the gauntlet, ask for trouble, start something, do something about it, make something of it

9 **to front on, face upon, give upon,** face *or* look toward, look out upon, look over, **overlook**

adjectives

10 **front, frontal, anterior; full-face, full-frontal; fore, forward,** forehand; foremost, headmost; first, earliest, **pioneering, trail-blazing, advanced,** cutting-edge; **leading,** up-front (*informal*), first, chief, head, prime, primary; **confronting,** confrontational, head-on, head-to-head, one-on-one *and* eyeball-to-eyeball (*both informal*); **ahead, in front,** one-up, one step *or* jump *or* move ahead

11 **fronting, facing,** looking on *or* out on, opposite

adverbs

12 **before, ahead,** out *or* up ahead, **in front,** in the front, in the lead, in the van, in advance, **in the forefront,** in the foreground; **to the fore,** to the front; foremost, headmost, first; before one's face *or* eyes, under one's nose

13 **frontward,** frontwards, **forward,** forwards, vanward, **headward,** headwards, **onward,** onwards; **facing** *see* 215.7

217 REAR

nouns

1 **rear, rear end, hind end,** hind part, hinder part, afterpart, rearward, **posterior, behind,** breech, stern, tail, tail end; **afterpiece,** tailpiece, heelpiece, heel; **back,** back side, reverse (*of a coin or medal*), tail (*of a coin*); back door, postern, postern door; back seat, rumble seat (*US & Canadian*); hindhead, occiput

2 rear guard, rear, rear area

3 **back,** dorsum, ridge; dorsal region, lumbar region; hindquarter; loin

4 **buttocks, rump,** bottom, posterior, derrière; croup, crupper; podex; haunches; gluteal region; nates

5 (*informal terms*) arse, **behind, backside,** bum, cheeks, rear, rear end, jacksie *or* jacksy, hind end, nether cheeks, stern, tail, ass *and* butt *and* can *and* fanny *and* keister (*all US & Canadian*)

6 tail, cauda, caudation, caudal appendage; tailpiece, scut (*of a hare, rabbit, or deer*), brush (*of a fox*), fantail (*of fowls*); rattail, rat's-tail; dock, stub; caudal fin; **queue, pigtail**

7 stern, heel; poop, transom, counter, fantail; sternpost, rudderpost

verbs

8 (*be behind*) **to bring up the rear,** come last, follow, come after; trail, trail behind, lag behind, draggle, **straggle;** fall behind, fall back, fall astern; **back up, back,** go back, go backwards, regress *see* 163.5, retrogress, get behind; revert *see* 858.4

adjectives

9 rear, rearward, **back,** backward, retrograde, **posterior,** postern, tail; after *or* aft; **hind, hinder; hindmost,** hindermost, hindhand, posteriormost, **aftermost,** aftmost, rearmost

10 (*anatomy*) posterial, dorsal, retral, tergal, lumbar, gluteal, sciatic, occipital

11 tail, caudal, caudate, caudated, tailed; taillike, caudiform

12 backswept, swept-back

adverbs

13 behind, in the rear, in back of; in the background; behind the scenes; behind one's back; back to back; tandem

14 after; aft, abaft, baft, astern; aback

15 rearward, rearwards, to the rear, **hindward,** hindwards, **backward,** backwards, posteriorly, retrad, tailward, tailwards

218 SIDE

nouns

1 side, flank, hand; laterality, sidedness, handedness; unilaterality, unilateralism, bilaterality, bilateralism, etc, multilaterality, many-sidedness; border *see* 211.4; parallelism *see* 203; bank, shore, coast; siding, planking; beam; broadside; quarter; hip, haunch; cheek, jowl, chop; temple; **profile,** side-view, half-face view

2 lee side, lee, leeward; lee shore; lee tide; lee wheel, lee helm, lee anchor, lee sheet, lee tack

3 windward side, windward, windwards, weather side, weather, weatherboard; weather wheel, weather helm, weather anchor, weather sheet, weather tack, weather rail, weather bow, weather deck; weather roll; windward tide, weather-going tide, windward ebb, windward flood

verbs

4 to side, flank; edge, skirt, border *see* 211.10

5 to go sideways, sidle, edge, veer, angle, slant, skew, sidestep; go crabwise; **sideslip, skid;** make leeway

adjectives

6 side, lateral; flanking, skirting; **beside,** to the side, off to one side; **alongside, parallel** *see* 203.6; next-beside; **sidelong,** sidling, **sidewise,** sideway, **sideways,** sideward, **sidewards,** glancing; leeward, lee; windward, weather

7 sided, flanked, handed; lateral; **one-sided,** unilateral, unilateralist, **two-sided, bilateral,** bilateralist, etc; dihedral, bifacial; **three-sided, trilateral,** trihedral, triquetrous; **four-sided, quadrilateral,** tetrahedral, etc; **many-sided, multilateral,** multifaceted, polyhedral

adverbs

8 laterally, laterad; **sideways,** sideway, **sidewise, sidewards,** sideward, sideling, sidling, sidelong, aside, crabwise; side-to-side; **edgeways,** edgeway, **edgewise; widthwise, widthways, thwartwise; askance,** askant, asquint, glancingly; broadside, **broadside on,** on the beam; on its side, on its beam ends; on the other hand; right and left

9 leeward, to leeward, alee, downwind; **windward,** to windward, weatherward, aweather, upwind

10 aside, on one side, **to one side,** to the side, sidelong, on the side, on the one hand, on one hand, on the other hand; **alongside,** in parallel *see* 203.7, side by side; nearby, in juxtaposition *see* 223.21; away

prepositions

11 beside, alongside, abreast, abeam, by, on the flank of, along by, **by the side of,** along the side of

phrases

12 side by side, cheek to cheek, cheek by cheek, cheek by jowl, shoulder to shoulder, yardarm to yardarm

219 RIGHT SIDE

nouns

1 right side, right, offside (*of a horse or vehicle*), starboard; Epistle side, decanal side; recto (*of a book*); right wing; starboard tack; right field (*US & Canadian*); right-winger, conservative, reactionary, blimp, Colonel Blimp

2 rightness, dextrality; dexterity, **right-handedness;** dextroversion, dextrocularity, dextroduction; dextrorotation, dextrogyration

3 right-hander

adjectives

4 right, right-hand, dextral, dexter; off, off-side, **starboard;** rightmost; dextrorse; dextropedal; dextrocardial; dextrocerebral; dextrocular; **clockwise,** dextrorotary, dextrogyrate, dextrogyratory, deasil (*Scottish*); right-wing, right-wingish, right-of-centre, conservative, reactionary, hawkish, dry (*informal*)

5 right-handed, dextromanual, dexterous

6 ambidextrous, ambidextral, ambidexter; dextrosinistral, sinistrodextral

adverbs

7 rightward, rightwards, rightwardly, **right,** to the **right,** dextrally, dextrad; on the right, dexter; starboard, astarboard

220 LEFT SIDE

nouns

1 left side, left, left hand, left-hand side, wrong side (*informal*), near *or* nigh side (*of a horse or vehicle*), portside, port, larboard; Gospel side, cantorial side; verso (*of a book*); left wing; port tack; left field (*US & Canadian*); left-winger, socialist, communist, red *and* pinko (*both informal*), radical, liberal, progressive, dove, wet (*informal*)

2 **leftness**, sinistrality, **left-handedness**, cack-handedness (*informal*), corrie-fistedness (*Scottish*); sinistration; levoversion, levoduction; levorotation, sinistrogyration

3 **left-hander**, southpaw, corrie-fister (*Scottish*), lefty (*informal*)

adjectives

4 **left, left-hand**, sinister, sinistral; near, nearside, nigh; **larboard, port**; sinistrorse; sinistrocerebral; sinistrocular; anticlockwise, counterclockwise, levorotatory, sinistrogyrate, withershins *or* widdershins (*Scottish*); left-wing, left-wingish, left-of-centre, socialist, communist, radical, liberal, progressive, wet (*informal*)

5 **left-handed**, southpaw, sinistromanual, sinistral, cack-handed (*informal*), corrie-fisted (*Scottish*)

adverbs

6 **leftward**, leftwards, leftwardly, **left, to the left**, sinistrally, sinister, sinistrad; on the left; larboard, port, aport

221 PRESENCE

nouns

1 **presence**, being here *or* there, hereness, thereness, physical *or* actual presence, spiritual presence; **immanence**, indwellingness, **inherence**; whereness, **immediacy**; ubiety; availability, accessibility; nearness *see* 223; **occurrence** *see* 830.2, existence *see* 760

2 **omnipresence**, all-presence, **ubiquity**; continuum, plenum; infinity

3 **permeation, pervasion**, penetration; **suffusion**, transfusion, perfusion, diffusion, imbuement; absorption; **overrunning**, overspreading, ripple effect, overswarming, whelming, overwhelming

4 **attendance**, frequenting, frequence; number present; turnout *and* box office *and* draw (*all informal*)

5 **attender, visitor**, churchgoer, filmgoer, etc; **patron**; fan *and* buff (*both informal*), aficionado, supporter; **frequenter**, habitué, haunter; spectator *see* 917; theatregoer; audience *see* 48.6

verbs

6 **to be present**, be located *or* situated *see* 159.10, be there, be found, be met with; **occur** *see* 830.5, exist *see* 760.8; lie, stand, remain; fall in the way of; dwell in, indwell, inhere

7 **to pervade, permeate**, penetrate; **suffuse**, inform, transfuse, perfuse, diffuse, leaven, imbue; **fill**, extend throughout, leave no void, occupy; **overrun**, overswarm, overspread, bespread, run through, meet one at every turn, whelm, overwhelm; creep *or* crawl *or* swarm with, be lousy with (*informal*), teem with; honeycomb

8 **to attend, be at**, be present at, find oneself at, **go** *or* **come to**; **appear** *see* 33.8, turn up, set foot in,

show up (*informal*), show one's face, make *or* put in an appearance, give the pleasure of one's company, make a personal appearance, **visit, take in** *and* do *and* catch (*all informal*); sit in *or* at; be on hand, be on deck (*informal*); watch, see; witness, look on, *assister* (*French*)

9 **to revisit**, return to, go back to, come again

10 **to frequent, haunt**, resort to, hang *and* hang around *and* hang about *and* hang out (*all informal*)

11 **to present oneself, report**; report for duty

adjectives

12 **present**, attendant; **on hand**, on deck (*informal*), on board; **immediate**, immanent, indwelling, inherent, **available, accessible, at hand**, in view, within reach *or* sight *or* call, in place

13 **omnipresent, all-present**, ubiquitous, everywhere; continuous, uninterrupted, infinite

14 **pervasive**, pervading, suffusive, perfusive, suffusing

15 **permeated**, saturated, shot through, filled with, perfused, suffused; honeycombed; crawling, creeping, swarming, teeming, lousy with (*informal*)

adverbs

16 **here, there**

17 **in person**, personally, bodily, **in the flesh** (*informal*), in one's own person, *in propria persona* (*Latin*)

prepositions

18 **in the presence of**, in the face of, under the eyes *or* nose of, **before**

phrases

19 all present and correct; standing room only *or* SRO

222 ABSENCE

nouns

1 **absence**, nonpresence, awayness; nowhereness, **nonexistence** *see* 761; want, **lack**, total lack, blank, deprivation; nonoccurrence, neverness; **subtraction** *see* 255

2 **vacancy**, vacuity, voidness, **emptiness**, blankness, hollowness, inanition; **bareness**, barrenness, desolateness, bleakness, desertedness; **nonoccupancy**, nonoccupation, vacancy, noninhabitance, nonresidence; vacancy, job vacancy, opening, open place *or* post, vacant post

3 **void, vacuum**, blank, emptiness, empty space, inanity; **nothingness**; *tabula rasa* (*Latin*), clean slate; **nothing** *see* 761.2

4 **absence**, nonattendance, **absenting, leaving**, taking leave, **departure** *see* 188;
"to leave is to die a little"—FRENCH SAYING, "Say, is not absence death to those who love?"—POPE; running away, fleeing, decamping, bolting, skedaddling *and* absquatulating (*old informal*), absconding, scarpering (*informal*); **disappearance** *see* 34, escape *see* 369; **absentation**, nonappearance, default, unauthorized *or* unexcused absence; **truancy**, hooky (*informal*), French leave, cut (*informal*); **absence without leave** *or* AWOL; **absenteeism**, truantism; **leave, leave of absence**, furlough, exeat; **holiday**, vacation, paid

holiday, paid vacation, day off, day in lieu; authorized *or* excused absence, sick leave; sabbatical leave *or* sabbatical

5 absentee, truant, no-show

6 nobody, no one, no man, not one, not a single one *or* person, **not a soul** *or* blessed soul *or* **living soul,** never a one, ne'er a one, nary one (*informal*), nobody on earth *or* under the sun, nobody present; nonperson, unperson

verbs

7 to be absent, stay away, keep away, keep out of the way, not come, not show up (*informal*), turn up missing (*informal*), stay away in droves (*informal*), fail to appear, default, sit out, count oneself out (*informal*)

8 to absent oneself, take leave *or* **leave of absence,** go on leave *or* furlough; **holiday,** go on holiday *or* vacation, take time off, take off from work; slip off *or* away, duck *or* sneak out (*informal*), slip out, make oneself scarce (*informal*), leave the scene, bow out, exit, **depart** *see* 188.6, **disappear** *see* 34.3, escape *see* 369.6

9 to play truant, go AWOL, take French leave; play hooky, cut classes, skip off, bunk off *or* wag it (*both informal*), dog it (*Scottish informal*); jump ship

10 (*informal terms*) **to split, beat it,** bugger off, fuck off, eff off, make tracks, pull up stakes, push along, scarper, push off, skedaddle *or* absquatulate (*old*), cut and run, make tracks, vamoose, piss off, scram, shove off

adjectives

11 absent, not present, nonattendant, **away, gone,** departed, disappeared, vanished, absconded, out of sight; **missing,** among the missing, wanting, **lacking,** not found, nowhere to be found, omitted, taken away, subtracted, deleted; no longer present *or* with us *or* among us; long-lost; **nonexistent;** conspicuous by its absence

12 nonresident, not in residence, far from home, **away from home,** on leave *or* vacation *or* holiday, on sabbatical leave *or* on sabbatical; on tour, on the road; abroad, overseas

13 truant, absent without leave *or* **AWOL**

14 vacant, empty, hollow, inane, **bare, vacuous, void,** without content, with nothing inside, devoid, null, null and void; **blank,** clear, white, bleached; featureless, unrelieved, characterless, bland, insipid; **barren** *see* 890.4

15 available, open, free, **unoccupied,** unfilled, **uninhabited,** unpopulated, unpeopled, untaken, untenanted, tenantless, untended, unmanned, unstaffed; **deserted,** abandoned, forsaken, godforsaken (*informal*)

adverbs

16 absently; vacantly, emptily, hollowly, vacuously, blankly

17 nowhere, in no place, neither here nor there; nowhither

18 away *see* 188.21, **elsewhere,** somewhere else, not here; elsewhither

prepositions

19 absent, lacking, sans; void of, empty of, free of, **without** *see* 991.17

223 NEARNESS

nouns

1 nearness, closeness, nighness, **proximity,** propinquity, intimacy, immediacy; approximation, approach, convergence; a rough idea (*informal*); **vicinity,** vicinage, **neighbourhood,** environs, surroundings, surround, setting, grounds, purlieus, confines, precinct; **foreground,** immediate foreground

2 short distance, short way, little ways (*US*), **step,** short step, span, brief span, short piece (*informal*), a little, intimate distance; short range; close quarters *or* range *or* grips; middle distance; **stone's throw,** spitting distance (*informal*), bowshot, gunshot, pistol shot; earshot, earreach, a whoop *and* a whoop and a holler *and* two whoops and a holler (*all informal*), ace, bit (*informal*), **hair, hairbreadth** *or* **hairsbreadth,** cunt-hair (*informal*), finger's breadth *or* width, an inch; hair space

3 juxtaposition, apposition, adjacency; **contiguity,** contiguousness, conterminousness *or* coterminousness; butting, abuttal, abutment; adjunction, junction *see* 799.1, connection, union; **conjunction,** conjugation; appulse, syzygy; perigee, perihelion

4 meeting, meeting up, joining, joining up, **encounter;** confrontation; rencontre; near miss, collision course, near thing, narrow squeak *or* brush, close shave *or* call

5 contact, touch, touching, *attouchement* (*French*), taction, tangency, contingence; gentle *or* tentative contact, caress, brush, glance, nudge, kiss, rub, graze; impingement, impingence; osculation

6 neighbour, next-door *or* immediate neighbour; borderer; abutter, adjoiner; bystander, onlooker, looker-on; tangent

verbs

7 to near, come near, nigh, draw near *or* nigh, **approach** *see* 167.3, come within shouting *or* spitting distance; **converge,** shake hands (*informal*); come within an ace *or* an inch

8 to be near *or* **around,** be in the vicinity *or* neighbourhood, **approximate, approach,** get warm (*informal*), come near, have something at hand *or* at one's fingertips; give *or* get a rough idea (*informal*)

9 to adjoin, join, conjoin, **connect,** butt, **abut,** abut on *or* upon, be contiguous, be in contact; **neighbour,** border, **border on** *or* **upon,** verge on *or* upon; lie by, stand by

10 to contact, come in contact, touch, feel, **impinge,** bump up against, hit; osculate; **graze,** caress, kiss, nudge, rub, brush, glance, scrape, sideswipe, skim, skirt, shave; grope *and* feel up *and* touch up (*all informal*); have a near miss, have a close shave, brush *or* graze *or* squeak by

11 to meet, encounter; come across, run across, meet up, fall across, cross the path of; **come upon,** run upon, fall upon, light *or* alight upon; come among, fall among; **meet with,** meet up with (*informal*), come face to face with, **confront,** meet head-on *or* eyeball to eyeball; **run into, bump into** *and* run smack into (*both informal*), join up with, come *or* run up against (*informal*), run *and* fall foul of; be on a collision course

12 **to stay near, keep close to;** stand by, lie by; go with, march with, follow close upon, breathe down one's neck, tread *or* stay on one's heels, stay on one's tail, shadow, tailgate (*informal*); hang about *or* around, hang upon the skirts of, hover over; **cling to,** clasp, hug, huddle; hug the shore *or* land, keep hold of the land, stay inshore

13 **to juxtapose,** appose, join *see* 799, **adjoin, abut,** butt against, neighbour; bring near, put with, place *or* set side by side

adjectives

14 **near, close, nigh,** close-in, nearish, nighish, intimate, cheek-by-jowl, side by side, hand-in-hand, arm in arm, *bras-dessus-bras-dessous* (*French*); **approaching,** nearing, approximate *or* approximating, proximate, proximal, propinque (*old*); **short-range;** near the mark; warm *or* hot *or* burning (*all informal*)

15 **nearby, handy, convenient,** neighbouring, vicinal, propinquant *or* propinquous, ready at hand, easily reached *or* attained

16 **adjacent, next,** immediate, contiguous, **adjoining, abutting; neighbouring,** neighbour; **juxtaposed,** juxtapositional; **bordering,** conterminous *or* coterminous, connecting; **face-to-face** *see* 215.6; end-to-end, endways, endwise; **joined**

17 **in contact,** contacting, **touching, meeting,** contingent; impinging, impingent; tangent, tangential; osculatory; grazing, kissing, glancing, brushing, rubbing, nudging

18 **nearer,** nigher, **closer**

19 **nearest,** nighest, **closest,** nearmost, next, immediate

adverbs

20 **near, nigh, close;** hard, at close quarters; **nearby, close by,** hard by, fast by, not far *or* far off, in the vicinity *or* **neighbourhood of,** at hand, at close range, **near** *or* **close at hand;** thereabouts *or* thereabouts, hereabout *or* hereabouts; nearabout *or* nearabouts *or* nigh about (*all dialect*); **about, around** (*informal*), close about, along toward (*informal*); at no great distance, only a step; as near as no matter *or* makes no difference (*informal*); **within reach** *or* **range,** within call *or* hearing, within earshot *or* earreach, within a whoop *or* two whoops and a holler (*informal*), within a stone's throw, a stone's throw away, in spitting distance (*informal*), at one's elbow, at one's feet, at one's fingertips, under one's nose, at one's side, within one's grasp; just around the corner, just across the street, next-door, right next door, just next door

21 **in juxtaposition, in conjunction,** in apposition; beside *see* 218.11

22 **nearly, near,** pretty near (*informal*), close, **closely; almost,** all but, not quite, as good as, as near as makes no difference, as near as damn it; **well-nigh, just about;** nigh

23 **approximately,** approximatively, practically (*informal*), for practical purposes *or* all practical purposes, at a first approximation, give or take a little, **more or less; roughly,** roundly, in round numbers; **generally,** generally speaking, roughly speaking, say; in the ballpark (*US & Canadian informal*)

prepositions

24 **near, nigh,** near to, **close to,** near upon, close upon, hard on *or* upon, bordering on *or* upon, **verging on** *or* upon, on the confines of, at the threshold of, **on the brink** *or* **verge of,** on the edge of, at next hand, at *or* on the point of, on the skirts of; **not far from;** next door to, at one's door; nigh about *or* nearabout *or* nigh on *or* nigh onto (*all dial*)

25 **against,** up against, on, upon, over against, opposite, nose to nose with, vis-à vis, in contact with

26 **about, around,** just about, circa, c, somewhere about *or* near, near *or* close upon, give or take, near enough to, pushing, upwards of (*informal*), ish, something; **in the region** *or* **neighbourhood** *or* **vicinity of**

224 INTERVAL
space between

nouns

1 **interval, gap, space** *see* 158, intervening *or* intermediate space, **interspace,** distance *or* space between, interstice; **clearance,** margin, leeway, **room** *see* 158.3; discontinuity *see* 812, jump, leap, interruption; hiatus, caesura, lacuna; half space, single space, double space, em space, en space, hair space, thick space, thin space; time interval, interim *see* 825

2 **crack, cleft,** cranny, chink, check, craze, chap, **crevice,** fissure, scissure, incision, notch, score, cut, gash, slit, split, **rift,** rent; **opening,** excavation, cavity, concavity, hole; **gap,** gape, **abyss,** abysm, **gulf, chasm,** void *see* 222.3; **breach, break,** fracture, rupture; fault, flaw; slot, groove, furrow, moat, ditch, trench, dike; joint, seam; **valley**

verbs

3 **to interspace, space,** make a space, set at intervals, dot, scatter *see* 770.4, **space out, separate,** split off, part, dispart, set *or* keep apart

4 **to cleave, crack,** check, incise, craze, **cut, cut apart,** gash, slit, **split,** rive, rent, rip open; **open; gap,** breach, break, fracture, rupture; slot, groove, furrow, ditch, trench

adjectives

5 **intervallic,** intervallary, interspatial, interstitial

6 **interspaced, spaced,** intervaled, **spaced out,** set at intervals, with intervals *or* an interval, dotted, scattered *see* 770.9, **separated, parted,** disparted, split-off

7 **cleft, cut,** cloven, **cracked,** sundered, rift, rent, chinky, chapped, crazed; **slit, split;** gaping, gappy; hiatal, caesural, lacunar; fissured, fissural

225 HABITATION
an inhabiting

nouns

1 **habitation,** inhabiting, inhabitation, habitancy, inhabitancy, **tenancy, occupancy,** occupation, **residence** *or* **residency,** residing, abiding, **living,** nesting, **dwelling,** commoracy (*law*), lodging, staying, stopping, sojourning, staying over; squatting; cohabitation, living together, sharing quarters; living in sin; **abode, habitat** *see* 228

2 **peopling,** peoplement, empeoplement, **population,** inhabiting; **colonization, settlement,** plantation

3 **housing,** domiciliation; lodgment, **lodging,** transient lodging, doss, **quartering,** billeting, hospitality; living quarters; housing development, **housing estate,** housing scheme (*Scottish*), tract; housing association

4 **camping,** tenting, **encampment,** bivouacking; camp *see* 228.29

5 **sojourn,** sojourning, sojournment, temporary stay; **stay, stop; stopover,** stopoff, stayover, layover

6 **habitability,** inhabitability, **livability**

verbs

7 **to inhabit, occupy,** tenant, move in *or* into, take up one's abode, make one's home; rent, lease; **reside, live, live in, dwell, lodge, stay,** remain, abide, hang out (*informal*), hang (*US informal*), domicile, domiciliate; **room,** bunk, crash (*informal*), berth, doss down; perch *and* roost *and* squat (*all informal*); nest; room together; cohabit, live together, shack up (*informal*); live in sin

8 **to sojourn,** stop, stay, **stop over,** stay over, lay over

9 **to people,** empeople, **populate, inhabit,** denizen; colonize, **settle,** settle in, plant

10 **to house,** domicile, domiciliate; provide with a roof, have as a guest *or* lodger, shelter, harbour; **lodge, quarter, put up,** billet, room, bed, berth, bunk; stable

11 **to camp, encamp,** tent; pitch, **pitch camp,** pitch one's tent, drive stakes (*informal*); bivouac; go camping, camp out, sleep out, rough it

adjectives

12 **inhabited, occupied,** tenanted; **peopled,** empeopled, populated, colonized, settled; populous

13 **resident,** residentiary, **in residence; residing, living, dwelling,** commorant, lodging, **staying,** remaining, abiding, living in; cohabiting, live-in

14 **housed,** domiciled, domiciliated, **lodged,** quartered, billeted; stabled

15 **habitable,** inhabitable, occupiable, lodgeable, tenantable, **livable, fit to live in, fit for occupation;** homelike *see* 228.33

adverbs

16 **at home,** in the bosom of one's family, *chez soi* (*French*); in one's element; back home (*informal*), down home (*US informal*)

226 NATIVENESS

nouns

1 **nativeness,** nativity, native-bornness, indigenousness *or* indigenity, aboriginality, autochthonousness, **nationality;** nativism

2 **citizenship,** native-born citizenship, citizenship by birth, citizenhood, subjecthood; civism

3 **naturalization,** naturalized citizenship, citizenship by naturalization *or* adoption, nationalization, adoption, admission, affiliation, **assimilation;** indigenization; Briticization, Anglicization, etc; acculturation, enculturation; papers, citizenship papers; culture shock

verbs

4 **to naturalize,** grant *or* confer citizenship, adopt, admit, affiliate, **assimilate;** Briticize, Anglicize, etc; acculturate, acculturize; indigenize, go native (*informal*)

adjectives

5 **native,** natal, **indigenous,** endemic, autochthonous; mother, maternal, original, aboriginal, primitive; native-born, home-grown, homebred, native to the soil *or* place *or* heath

6 **naturalized,** adopted, **assimilated;** indoctrinated, Briticized, Anglicized, etc; acculturated, acculturized; indigenized

227 INHABITANT, NATIVE

nouns

1 **population, inhabitants,** habitancy, dwellers, **populace, people,** whole people, people at large, citizenry, folk, souls, living souls, body, whole body, warm bodies (*US informal*); **public,** general public; community, society, **nation,** commonwealth, constituency, body politic, electorate; speech *or* linguistic community, ethnic *or* cultural community; **census,** head count; population statistics, demography, demographics

2 **inhabitant,** inhabiter, habitant; **occupant,** occupier, **dweller, tenant, denizen,** inmate; **resident,** residencer, residentiary, resider; inpatient; resident *or* live-in maid; writer- *or* poet- *or* artist- *or* composer-in-residence; incumbent, *locum tenens* (*Latin*); sojourner; addressee

3 **native,** indigene, autochthon, earliest inhabitant, first comer, primitive settler; primitive; **aborigine,** aboriginal; local *and* local yokel (*both informal*)

4 **citizen, national,** subject; **naturalized citizen,** nonnative citizen, citizen by adoption, immigrant, metic; **cosmopolitan,** cosmopolite, citizen of the world

5 **fellow citizen,** fellow countryman, **compatriot,** congener, **countryman,** countrywoman, *landsman* (*Yiddish*), *paesano* (*Italian*), *paisano* (*Spanish*); fellow townsman, home boy *and* home girl *and* hometowner (*all US informal*)

6 **townsman, townswoman,** townee *and* towner (*both informal*), **villager,** oppidan, city dweller, city person; big-city person, **city slicker** (*informal*);

urbanite; suburbanite; exurbanite; burgher, burgess, *bourgeois* (*French*); townspeople, townfolks, townfolk

7 householder, homeowner, house-owner, owner-occupier, proprietor, freeholder; cottager, cotter, cottier, crofter; head of household

8 lodger, roomer, paying guest; **boarder,** board-and-roomer, **transient,** transient guest *or* boarder; **renter, tenant,** leaser *or* lessee, subleaser *or* sublessee

9 settler, *habitant* (*Canadian & Louisiana French*); **colonist,** colonizer, colonial, immigrant, planter; **homesteader; squatter,** nester; **pioneer;** sooner; precursor *see* 815

10 wilderness settler *or* hinterlander; **frontiersman,** mountain man; **backwoodsman,** bushwhacker, woodlander, woodsman, woodman, woodhick (*informal*); **mountaineer, hillbilly** *and* ridge runner (*both informal*), brush ape *and* briar-hopper (*both informal*); cracker *and* redneck (*both informal*), desert rat (*informal*), clam digger (*informal*), piny (*informal*)

11 (*regional inhabitants*) Southerner; Northerner; Midlander; West Countryman *or* Countrywoman; Highlander; Lowlander; Borderer; Ulsterman *or* Ulsterwoman

228 ABODE, HABITAT
place of habitation or resort

nouns

1 abode, habitation, place, dwelling, dwelling place, abiding place, place to live, where one lives *or* resides, where one is at home, roof, roof over one's head, **residence,** place of residence, **domicile,** *domus* (*Latin*); **lodging,** lodgment, lodging place; seat, nest, living space, houseroom, sleeping place, place to rest one's head; native heath, turf, home territory, home patch; **address,** permanent residence; **housing; affordable housing,** low-cost housing, low-and-middle-income housing, public housing, public-sector housing; council housing; private housing, private-sector housing; sheltered housing, sheltered accommodation

2 home, home sweet home, "the place where, when you go there, They have to take you in"—ROBERT FROST, "the place to do things you want to do"—ZELDA FITZGERALD; **fireside, hearth,** hearth and home, hearthstone, fireplace, *foyer* (*French*), chimney corner, ingle, ingleside *or* inglenook; **household,** ménage; **homestead,** home place, home roof, roof, rooftree, toft; paternal roof *or* domicile, family home, ancestral halls; **hominess** *or* homeyness

3 domesticity; housewifery, **housekeeping, homemaking;** householding, householdry

4 quarters, living quarters; **lodgings,** lodging, lodgment; digs *and* diggings *and* pad *and* crib *and* gaff (*all informal*), room; **rooms,** berth, roost, accommodations; **housing** *see* 225.3, shelter, *gîte* (*French*)

5 house, dwelling, dwelling house, *casa* (*Spanish & Italian*); house and grounds, plot; **building, structure, edifice,** fabric, erection, **hall** *see* 197.4; roof; lodge; manor house, hall; town house, *rus in urbe* (*Latin*); country house, *dacha* (*Russian*), country seat, shooting box, shooting lodge; farmhouse, farm, ranch house (*US*); **detached house, semidetached house,** semi, **terraced house,** terrace, end terrace, back-to-back; prefabricated house, prefab; sod house, adobe house; lake dwelling *see* 241.3; houseboat; cave *or* cliff dwelling; penthouse; split-level; parsonage *see* 703.7, **rectory,** vicarage, deanery, manse; official residence, Buckingham Palace, 10 Downing Street, Number Ten, White House; embassy, consulate

6 farmstead; croft; ranch, *rancho, hacienda* (*both Spanish*), toft, steading (*old*), grange

7 estate; mansion, palatial residence, stately home; **villa, château,** *hôtel* (*French*), **castle,** tower; **palace,** *palais* (*French*), *palazzo* (*Italian*), court

8 cottage, cot *or* cote (*dialect*), **bungalow,** box; tied cottage, tied house; **cabin,** log cabin; **second home, holiday home;** chalet, lodge, snuggery; home from home, *pied-à-terre* (*French*)

9 hut, hutch, **shack, shanty,** crib, hole-in-the-wall (*informal*), **shed; lean-to; booth,** bothy *or* boothy (*both Scottish*), stall; tollbooth *or* tollhouse, sentry box, gatehouse, porter's lodge; **outhouse,** outbuilding; Portakabin; privy; **pavilion,** kiosk; Nissen hut, Quonset hut (*US*); hutment

10 (*American Indian houses*) wigwam, tepee, hogan, wickiup, jacal, longhouse; tupik, igloo (*both Eskimo*); ajouba

11 slum, hovel, dump (*informal*), rathole, hole, sty, pigsty, pigpen (*US & Canadian*), tumbledown shack

12 summerhouse, arbour, bower, **gazebo,** pergola, kiosk, alcove, retreat; **conservatory, greenhouse,** glasshouse, lathhouse

13 flat, apartment, tenement, chambers, rooms; studio flat *or* apartment; bed-sitter, bedsit, bedsitting room, granny flat, flatlet; **suite,** suite *or* set of rooms; walkup (*US & Canadian*), cold-water flat (*US*); **penthouse;** service flat; cottage flat, maisonette; garden flat; duplex apartment (*US*); railroad *or* shotgun flat (*US*)

14 flats, tenement, mansion; duplex (*US*); **block of flats,** apartment complex; condominium *or* condo (*US informal*); high-rise block *or* high rise, tower block

15 inn, hotel, hostel, hostelry, **tavern,** *posada* (*Spanish*), *taverna* (*Greek*); tourist hotel, *parador* (*Spanish*); guest house, bed and breakfast, B & B, roadhouse, caravansary *or* caravanserai; youth hostel, hospice; **lodging house,** rooming house; **boardinghouse,** *pension* (*French*), *pensione* (*Italian*); hall of residence, hall, dormitory (*US*), dorm (*US informal*), fraternity *or* sorority house (*US*); bunkhouse; **dosshouse** (*informal*), spike (*informal*), flophouse *and* fleabag (*both US informal*)

16 motel, motor inn, motor hotel; boatel

17 caravan, mobile home, camper, camper van, **trailer** (*US*), house *or* camp trailer (*US*); caravan site, trailer court *or* camp *or* park (*US*), campground, campsite

18 habitat, home, **range,** stamping ground, locality, native environment

19 zoo, menagerie, *Tiergarten* (*German*), zoological garden *or* park

20 barn, stable, stall; **cowbarn,** cowhouse, cowshed, cowbyre, byre; mews

21 kennel, doghouse; pound, dog pound; cattery

22 coop, chicken house *or* **coop,** henhouse, hencote, hennery; battery, perchery; brooder

23 birdhouse, aviary, bird cage; dovecote, pigeon loft *or* house, columbary; roost, perch, roosting place; rookery, heronry; eyrie

24 vivarium, terrarium, aquarium; fishpond, fishtank, goldfish bowl, stew

25 nest, nidus; **beehive, apiary,** hive, bee tree, hornet's nest, wasp's nest, vespiary

26 lair, den, cave, **hole,** covert, mew, form; **burrow,** tunnel, earth, run, couch, lodge

27 resort, haunt, purlieu, **hangout** (*informal*), **stamping ground** (*informal*); gathering place, rallying point, meeting place, clubhouse, club, howff (*Scottish*); casino, gambling house; health resort; **spa,** baths, springs, watering place

28 (*disapproved place*) **dive** (*informal*), **den, lair,** den of thieves; **hole** *and* dump *and* **joint** (*all informal*); gyp *or* clip joint (*informal*); **whorehouse,** brothel, knocking shop (*informal*), bordello, stews, fleshpots, cathouse (*US & Canadian informal*), sporting house (*US*)

29 camp, encampment, *Lager* (*German*); bivouac; barrack *or* **barracks,** casern, *caserne* (*French*), cantonment, lines; detention camp, concentration camp, *Konzentrationslager* (*German*); campground *or* campsite; holiday camp

30 (*deities of the household*) lares and penates, Vesta, Hestia, household gods

verbs

31 to keep house, housekeep (*informal*), practise domesticity, maintain *or* run a household

adjectives

32 residential, residentiary; domestic, domiciliary, domal; **home, household;** mansional, manorial, palatial

33 homelike, homish, homy (*informal*), homely; comfortable, friendly, cheerful, peaceful, cosy, snug, intimate; simple, plain, unpretentious

34 domesticated, tame, tamed, broken; house-trained, house-broken

229 FURNITURE

nouns

1 furniture, furnishings, fixtures and fittings, fitments, movables, home furnishings, house furnishings, household effects, household goods, soft furnishings, office furniture, school furniture, church furniture, library furniture, furnishments (*old*); **cabinetmaking,** cabinetwork, cabinetry; **furniture design, furniture style** (*see list*); period furniture; **piece of furniture, furniture piece,** chair, sofa, bed, table, desk, cabinet, mirror, clock, screen; **suite, set of furniture,** ensemble, decor

2 furniture styles and periods

Adam	Anglo-Dutch
Adapted Colonial	Art Deco
Adirondack	Art Nouveau
Arts and Crafts	Louis XV
Baroque	Louis XVI
Bauhaus	Mannerist
Biedermeier	Mission
Block-front	Modern
Byzantine	Moderne
Cape Dutch	National Romanticism
Chinese Chippendale	Naturalistic
Chinoiserie	Neoclassical *or le style*
Chippendale	*antique* (French)
Colonial *or* Campaign	Neo-Gothic *or* Cathédrale
Contemporary	Neo-Grec
Cotswold School	Palladian
Country Chippendale	Pop Art
Cromwellian *or*	Queen Anne
Commonwealth	Regency
De Stijl	Renaissance Revival
Desornamentado	Restoration *or* Carolean
Directoire	Rococo
Duncan Phyfe	Rococo Revival *or* Louis
Early Georgian	Philippe *or* Louis XV
Eastlake	Revival
Edwardian	Romano-Byzantine *or*
Egyptian	Italo-Byzantine *or*
Empire	Romanesque
French Provincial	Scandinavian Modern
French Renaissance	Second Empire
Georgian	Shaker
Gothic	Sheraton
Gothic-Renaissance	Spanish Renaissance
Hepplewhite	Stuart
International	Tudor
Italian Renaissance	Turkish
Jacobean	Venetian
Japonisme	Victorian
Late Regency	Viking Revival *or*
Later Victorian	Dragonesque
Louis XIII	William and Mary
Louis XIV	

230 TOWN, CITY

nouns

1 town, township; **city, metropolis,** metropolitan area, greater city, megalopolis, supercity, conurbation, urban complex, spread city, urban sprawl, urban corridor, **municipality,** *urbs* (*Latin*), *polis* (*Greek*), city *or* municipal government; *ville* (*French*), *Stadt* (*German*); **borough, burg** (*informal*), bourg, burgh (*Scottish*); **suburb,** suburbia, outskirts, subtopia, burbs (*US informal*), slurb (*US informal*), *faubourg* (*French*), *banlieue* (*French*); exurb, exurbia; new town, garden city; market town; small town; twin town; boom town, ghost town

2 village, hamlet; ham *and* thorp *and* wick (*all old*); country town, crossroads, wide place in the road; "a little one-eyed, blinking sort o' place"—THOMAS HARDY, "a hive of glass, where nothing unobserved can pass"—C H SPURGEON

3 (*informal terms*) **one-horse town,** whistle-stop, jumping-off place; hick town (*US*); wide place in the road

4 capital, capital city, **seat,** seat of government; **county town** *or* shire town, county seat *or* county site (*US*)

5 town hall, city hall, county hall, civic centre, city chambers (*Scottish*), municipal building; courthouse; police station, nick (*informal*), police house, station house, precinct house (*US*); fire station, station house, firehouse (*US*); community centre

6 (*city districts*) East End, West End; downtown, uptown, midtown (*all US*); city centre, urban centre, inner city, central *or* centre city, core *or* core city (*US*), suburbs, suburbia, commuter belt, stockbroker belt (*informal*), burbs (*US informal*), outskirts, greenbelt, residential district, business district *or* section, shopping centre; Chinatown, Little Italy, Little Hungary, etc; asphalt *or* **concrete jungle,** mean streets; **slum** *or* **slums,** the other side *or* the wrong side of the tracks, back streets, blighted area *or* neighbourhood *or* section, run-down area, tenement district, shanty-town, hell's kitchen *or* half-acre; red-light district, Bowery (*US*), tenderloin (*US informal*), **skid row** *or* skid road (*both informal*); **ghetto, inner city,** urban ghetto, barrio

7 block

8 square, plaza, *place* (*French*), *piazza* (*Italian*), *campo* (*Italian*), **marketplace,** market, mart, rialto, forum, agora

9 circus, circle (*US*); crescent

10 town planning, urban planning; urban studies, urbanology

adjectives

11 urban, metropolitan, municipal, metro, burghal, **civic,** oppidan; citywide; city, town, village; citified; suburban; interurban; downtown, uptown, midtown (*all US*); **inner-city,** core *and* core-city (*both US*), ghetto; small-town; boom-town

231 REGION

nouns

1 region, area, zone, belt, **territory,** terrain; **place** *see* 159.1; **space** *see* 158; **country** *see* 232, **land** *see* 234, ground, soil; territoriality; territorial waters, twelve- *or* three-mile limit, continental shelf, offshore rights; airspace; heartland; hinterland; **district, quarter, section,** department, division; salient, corridor; part, parts; **neighbourhood,** vicinity, vicinage, neck of the woods (*informal*), purlieus; premises, confines, precincts, environs, milieu

2 sphere, hemisphere, orb, **orbit,** ambit, circle; **circuit,** judicial circuit, **beat, round,** walk; **realm,** demesne, **domain,** dominion, jurisdiction, bailiwick, manor (*informal*); border, borderland, march; **province,** department, precinct (*US*); **field,** pale, arena

3 zone; climate *or* clime (*both old*); **longitude,** longitude in arc, longitude in time; meridian, prime meridian; **latitude,** parallel; equator, the line; tropic, Tropic of Cancer, Tropic of Capricorn; tropics, subtropics, Torrid Zone; Temperate *or* Variable Zones; Frigid Zones, Arctic Zone *or* Circle, Antarctic Zone *or* Circle; horse latitudes, roaring forties

4 plot, plot of ground *or* land, parcel of land, plat, **patch, tract, field;** lot (*US & Canadian*); airspace; block, square; close, quadrangle, quad, enclave, croft, pale, *clos* (*French*), kraal (*Africa*); real estate (*US*)

5 (*territorial divisions*) **state, territory, province,** region, duchy, electorate, government, principality; **county,** shire, canton, *oblast, okrug* (*both Russian*), *département* (*French*), *Kreis* (*German*); **borough, ward,** riding, *arrondissement* (*French*); **township,** hundred, commune, wapentake; urban district, metropolis, metropolitan area, **city, town** *see* 230; **village,** hamlet, **parish; district,** congressional district, electoral district, precinct (*all US*); magistracy, soke, bailiwick; shrievalty, sheriffalty, sheriffwick, constablewick; archdiocese, archbishopric, stake; **diocese,** bishopric, parish

6 (*regions of the world*) continent, landmass; **Old World,** the old country (*US*); **New World,** America; **Western Hemisphere, Occident,** West; **Eastern Hemisphere, Orient,** Levant, East, eastland; Far East, Mideast *or* Middle East, Near East; **Northern Hemisphere; Southern Hemisphere;** Asia, Europe, Eurasia, Asia Major, Asia Minor, Africa, North America, Central America, South America, Latin America, Antipodes, down under, Australasia, Oceania

7 (*regions of the UK*) the South, the South coast; the Southeast, Greater London, the Home Counties; the West Country, the Southwest, Wessex; the Cotswolds; the Midlands, Central England, Middle England, Mercia; the West Midlands, the Black Country, the Potteries; the East Midlands; the Peak District; East Anglia, the Fens; the East coast; the North, the North Country; the Northeast, Northumbria; the Northwest, the Lake District; North Wales; South Wales, the valleys; mid Wales; the Scottish Highlands, the Highlands, Highlands and Islands; the Scottish lowlands, the lowlands, central Scotland, the central belt; the kingdom of Fife; the borders; the Western Isles, the Hebrides, the Inner Hebrides, the Outer Hebrides; Ulster, the Six Counties

adjectives

8 regional, territorial, geographical, areal, sectional, zonal, topographic *or* topographical

9 local, localized, of a place, geographically limited, topical, vernacular, parochial, parish pump, provincial, insular, limited, confined

10 English counties

Avon	Essex
Bedfordshire	Gloucestershire
Berkshire	Greater London
Buckinghamshire	Greater Manchester
Cambridgeshire	Hampshire
Cheshire	Hereford and Worcester
Cleveland	Hertfordshire
Cornwall	Humberside
Cumbria	Isle of Wight
Derbyshire	Kent
Devon	Lancashire
Dorset	Leicestershire
Durham	Lincolnshire
East Sussex	Merseyside

Norfolk
Northamptonshire
Northumberland
North Yorkshire
Nottinghamshire
Oxfordshire
Shropshire
Somerset
South Yorkshire

Staffordshire
Suffolk
Surrey
Tyne and Wear
Warwickshire
West Midlands
West Sussex
West Yorkshire
Wiltshire

11 Welsh counties

Clwyd
Dyfed
Gwent
Gwynedd

Mid Glamorgan
Powys
South Glamorgan
West Glamorgan

12 Scottish local authority areas

Aberdeenshire
Angus
Argyll and Bute
Borders
City of Aberdeen
City of Dundee
City of Edinburgh
City of Glasgow
Clackmannan
Dumbarton and Clydebank
Dumfries and Galloway
East Ayrshire
East Dumbartonshire
East Lothian
East Renfrewshire
Falkirk

Fife
Highland
Inverclyde
Midlothian
Moray
North Ayrshire
North Lanarkshire
Orkney Islands
Perthshire and Kinross
Renfrewshire
Shetland Islands
South Ayrshire
South Lanarkshire
Stirling
West Lothian
Western Isles

13 Northern Irish counties

Antrim
Armagh
Down

Fermanagh
Londonderry
Tyrone

14 US state mottoes and nicknames

Alabama "We dare defend our rights"; Heart of Dixie *or* Camellia State
Alaska "North to the future"; The Last Frontier
Arizona "Diat Deus"; Grand Canyon State
Arkansas "Regnat populus"; Land of Opportunity
California "Eureka"; Golden State
Colorado "Nil sine numine"; Centennial State
Connecticut "Qui transtulit sustinet"; Constitution State; Nutmeg State
Delaware "Liberty and independence"; First State *or* Diamond State
District of Columbia "Justitia Omnibus"; Capital City
Florida "In God we trust"; Sunshine State

Georgia "Wisdom, justice, and moderation"; Empire State of the South; Peach State
Hawaii "The life of the land is perpetuated in righteousness"; Aloha State
Idaho "Esto perpetua"; Gem State
Illinois "State sovereignty–national union"; Prairie State
Indiana "Crossroads of America"; Hoosier State
Iowa "Our liberties we prize and our rights we will maintain"; Hawkeye State
Kansas "Ad astra per aspera"; Sunflower State
Kentucky "United we stand, divided we fall"; Bluegrass State
Louisiana "Union, justice and confidence"; Pelican State

Maine "Dirigo"; Pine Tree State
Maryland "Fatti maschii, parole femine"; Old Line State *or* Free State
Massachusetts "Ense petit placidam sub libertate"; Bay State; Colony State
Michigan "Si quaeris peninsulam amoenam"; Great Lake State *or* Wolverine State
Minnesota "L'Etoile du nord"; North Star State *or* Gopher State
Mississippi "Virtute et armis"; Magnolia State
Missouri "Salus populi suprema lex esto"; Show-Me State
Montana "Oro y plato"; Treasure State
Nebraska "Equality before the law"; Cornhusker State
Nevada "All for our country"; Sagebrush State *or* Battle-Born State
New Hampshire "Live free or die"; Granite State
New Jersey "Liberty and prosperity"; Garden State
New Mexico "Crescit eundo"; Land of Enchantment
New York "Excelsior"; Empire State
North Carolina "Esse quam videri"; Tar Heel State *or* Old North State
North Dakota "Liberty and union, now and forever, one and

inseparable"; Peace Garden State
Ohio "With God, all things are possible"; Buckeye State
Oklahoma "Labor omnia vincit"; Sooner State
Oregon "The union"; Beaver State
Pennsylvania "Virtue, liberty and independence"; Keystone State
Rhode Island "Hope"; Little Rhody; Ocean State
South Carolina "Dum spiro spero"; Palmetto State
South Dakota "Under God, the people rule"; Coyote State *or* Sunshine State
Tennessee "Agriculture and commerce"; Volunteer State
Texas "Friendship"; Lone Star State
Utah "Industry"; Beehive State
Vermont "Freedom and unity"; Green Mountain State
Virginia "Sic semper tyrannis"; Old Dominion
Washington "Alki"; Evergreen State
West Virginia "Montani semper liberi"; Mountain State
Wisconsin "Forward"; Badger State
Wyoming "Equal rights"; Equality State

232 COUNTRY

nouns

1 **country,** land; **nation,** nationality, **state,** nation-state, sovereign nation *or* state, polity, **body politic; power,** superpower, world power; microstate; **republic,** people's republic, **commonwealth,** commonweal; **kingdom,** sultanate; **empire,** empery; **realm,** dominion, domain; **principality,** principate; duchy, dukedom; grand duchy, archduchy, archdukedom, earldom, county, palatinate, seneschalty; chieftaincy, chieftainry; toparchy, *toparchia (Greek)*; city-state, *polis (Greek)*, free city; **province,** territory, possession; colony, settlement; protectorate, mandate, mandated territory, mandant, mandatee, mandatory; buffer state; **ally,** military ally, cobelligerent, treaty partner; satellite, puppet regime *or* government; free nation, captive nation;

nonaligned *or* unaligned *or* neutralist state; developed country, industrial *or* industrialized nation; underdeveloped country, third-world country

2 **fatherland,** *Vaterland* (*German*), *patriá* (*Latin*), *la patrie* (*French*), **motherland,** mother country, **native land,** native soil, one's native heath *or* ground *or* soil *or* place, the old country, country of origin, **birthplace,** cradle; **home, homeland,** homeground, "home is where one starts"—T S ELIOT, God's country; the home front

3 **Britain, Great Britain, United Kingdom, the UK,** Britannia, Albion, Blighty (*informal*), Limeyland (*US informal*), Tight Little Island, Land of the Rose, "This royal throne of kings, this sceptred isle, This earth of majesty, this seat of Mars, This other Eden, demi-paradise"—SHAKESPEARE, Sovereign of the Seas; British Empire, Commonwealth of Nations, British Commonwealth of Nations, the Commonwealth; perfidious Albion

4 **United States,** United States of America, US, USA, US of A (*informal*), **America,** Columbia, the States, Uncle Sugar *and* Yankeeland (*both informal*), Land of Liberty, the melting pot; stateside

5 (*national personifications*) John Bull (*England*); Uncle Sam *or* Brother Jonathan (*US*)

6 nationhood, peoplehood, **nationality; statehood, nation-statehood, sovereignty,** sovereign nationhood *or* statehood, independence, self-government, self-determination; internationality, internationalism; **nationalism**

7 (*derogatory terms*) dago, greaseball, wop (*Italian*); frog (*Frenchman*); Kraut, Jerry, Hun, Boche (*German*); Jock (*Scotsman*); Taffy (*Welshman*); Mick, Mickey, Paddy (*Irishman*); Paki (*Pakistani*); polack (*Pole*); Canuck (*Canadian French*); greaser, wetback (*Mexican*); spic (*Latin American*); Chink (*Chinese*); Jap (*Japanese*); limey, pommy *or* pom (*Briton*); Aussie (*Australian*)

233 THE COUNTRY

nouns

1 **the country,** agricultural region, farm country, farmland, arable land, grazing region *or* country, rural district, rustic region, province *or* **provinces,** the shires, countryside, woodland *see* 310.11, grassland *see* 310.8, woods and fields, meadows and pastures, the soil, grass roots; **the sticks** (*informal*); highlands, moors, uplands, foothills; lowlands, veld *or* veldt, savanna *or* savannah, plains, prairies, steppes, wide-open spaces

2 **hinterland,** back country, outback (*Australian*), up-country, boonies *and* boondocks (*both informal*); **the bush,** bush country, bushveld, **woods,** woodlands, **backwoods,** forests, timbers, the big sticks (*US informal*), brush; wilderness, wilds, uninhabited region, virgin land *or* territory; **wasteland** *see* 890.2; **frontier,** borderland, outpost; wild West

3 **rusticity, ruralism,** inurbanity, agrarianism, bucolicism, **provincialism,** provinciality, simplicity, pastoral simplicity, unspoiledness; yokelism, hickishness, backwoodsiness; **boorishness,** churlishness, unrefinement, uncultivation

4 ruralization, countrification, rustication, pastoralization

verbs

5 **to ruralize, countrify, rusticate,** pastoralize; farm *see* 1067.16; return to the soil

adjectives

6 **rustic, rural, country, provincial, farm, pastoral, bucolic,** Arcadian, **agrarian,** agrestic; **agricultural** *see* 1067.20; lowland, low-lying, upland, highland, prairie, plains

7 **countrified,** inurbane; country-born, country-bred, up-country; farmerish, hobnailed, clodhopping, clodhopperish; **boorish,** clownish, loutish, lumpish, lumpen, cloddish, churlish; **uncouth,** unpolished, uncultivated, uncultured, unrefined; country-style, country-fashion

8 (*informal terms*) **hick,** hicky, hickified, from the sticks, rube (*US*), hayseed, yokel, yokelish, down-home (*US*), shit-kicking (*US*), hillbilly, redneck

9 **hinterland,** back, **back-country,** up-country, backroad, outback (*Australian*), wild, wilderness, virgin; wild-West; **waste** *see* 890.4; backwood *or* **backwoods,** back of beyond, backwoodsy; woodland, sylvan

234 LAND

nouns

1 **land, ground,** landmass, earth, glebe (*old*), **sod,** clod, **soil, dirt,** dust, clay, marl, mould (*informal*); *terra* (*Latin*), **terra firma;** terrain; **dry land;** arable land; marginal land; grassland *see* 310.8, woodland *see* 310.11; crust, earth's crust, lithosphere; regolith; topsoil, subsoil; alluvium, alluvion; eolian *or* subaerial deposit; landholdings, acres, territory, freehold, real estate (*US*), real property (*US*); region *see* 231; the country *see* 233; earth science *see* 1069

2 **shore, coast,** *côte* (*French*); **strand,** *playa* (*Spanish*), **beach,** beachfront, beachside shingle, plage, lido, riviera, sands, berm; waterside, **waterfront;** shoreline, coastline; foreshore; bank, embankment; riverside; lakefront, lakeshore; **dockland; seashore, coast, seacoast, seaside, seaboard,** seabeach, seacliff, seabank, sea margin, oceanfront, oceanside, seafront, seaside, shorefront, tidewater, tideland, coastland, littoral; wetland, wetlands; **bay,** bayfront, bayside; drowned *or* submerged coast; rockbound coast, ironbound coast; loom of the land

3 **landsman,** landman, **landlubber**

adjectives

4 **terrestrial,** terrene (*old*), **earth, earthly,** telluric, tellurian; earthbound; sublunar, subastral; geophilous; terraqueous; fluvioterrestrial

5 **earthy,** earthen, soily, loamy, marly, gumbo (*US*); clayey, clayish; adobe

6 **alluvial,** estuarine, fluviomarine

7 **coastal, littoral, seaside, shore,** shoreside; shoreward; riparian *or* riparial *or* riparious; riverain, riverine; riverside; lakefront, lakeshore; oceanfront, oceanside; seaside, seafront, shorefront, shoreline;

beachfront, beachside; bayfront, bayside; tideland, tidal, wetland

adverbs

8 **on land,** on dry land, on terra firma; onshore, ashore; alongshore; shoreward; by land, overland

9 **on earth,** on the face of the earth *or* globe, in the world, in the wide world, in the whole wide world; **under the sun,** under the stars, beneath the sky, under heaven, below, **here below**

235 BODY OF LAND

nouns

1 **continent, mainland,** main (*old*), landform, continental landform, landmass; North America, South America, Africa, Europe, Asia, Eurasia, Eurasian landmass, Australia, Antarctica; subcontinent, India, Greenland; peninsula; **plate,** tectonic plate, crustal plate, crustal segment, Pacific plate, American plate, African plate, Eurasian plate, Antarctic plate, Indian plate; continental divide, continental drift

2 **island, isle; islet,** holm, ait *or* eyot (*British informal*); continental island; oceanic island; **key,** cay; sandbank, sandbar, bar; **reef,** coral reef, coral head; coral island, atoll; archipelago, island group *or* chain; insularity; islandology

3 **continental,** mainlander; continentalist

4 **islander,** islandman, island-dweller, islesman, insular; islandologist

verbs

5 to insulate, isolate, island, enisle; island-hop

adjectives

6 **continental,** mainland

7 **insular,** insulated, isolated; island, islandy *or* islandish, islandlike; islanded, isleted, island-dotted; seagirt; archipelagic *or* archipelagian

236 PLAIN

open country

nouns

1 **plain, plains,** flat country, flatland, **flats,** flat, level; champaign, champaign country, open country, **wide-open spaces; prairie,** grassland *see* 310.8, sea of grass, **steppe, pampas,** *pampa* (*Spanish*), savanna, tundra, vega, campo, llano, sebkha; **veld,** grass veld, bushveld, tree veld; wold, weald; **moor,** moorland, down, **downs,** lande, **heath,** fell; lowland, lowlands, bottomland; basin, playa; sand plain, sand flat, strand flat; tidal flat, salt marsh; salt pan; salt flat, alkali flat; **desert** *see* 890.2; **plateau,** upland, tableland, table, **mesa,** mesilla; peneplain; coastal plain, tidal plain, alluvial plain, delta, delta plain; mare, lunar mare

adjectives

2 champaign, **plain, flat,** open; campestral *or* campestrian

237 HIGHLANDS

nouns

1 **highlands, uplands,** highland, upland, high country, elevated land, dome, **plateau, tableland,** upland area, piedmont, moor, moorland, **hills, heights,** hill *or* hilly country, downs, wold, foothills, rolling country, **mountains,** mountain *or* mountainous country, high terrain, peaks, range, *massif* (*French*)

2 **slope, declivity,** steep, versant, incline, rise, talus, brae (*Scottish*), mountainside, hillside, bank, gentle *or* easy slope, glacis, angle of repose, steep *or* rapid slope, fall line, bluff, cliff, precipice, steep, wall, palisade, scar, escarpment, scarp, fault scarp, rim, face; upper slopes, upper reaches, timberline *or* tree line

3 **plateau, tableland,** high plateau, table, mesa, table mountain, butte, moor, fell, hammada

4 **hill,** down (*chiefly British*),

"the earth's gesture of despair for the unreachable"—RABINDRANATH TAGORE; brae *and* fell (*both Scottish*); **hillock,** knob, butte, kopje, kame, monticle, monticule, monadnock, **knoll,** hummock, hammock, eminence, rise, knap *and* tump (*both dialect*), mound, swell, barrow, tumulus, kop, tel, jebel; **dune,** sand dune; moraine, drumlin; anthill, molehill; **dune,** sand dune, sandhill

5 **ridge,** ridgeline, *arête* (*French*), chine, spine, horst, kame, comb, esker, cuesta, serpent kame, Indian ridge, moraine, terminal moraine; **saddle, hogback,** hog's-back, saddleback, horseback, col; **pass,** gap, notch, wind gap, water gap

6 **mountain** (*see list*), mount, alp, hump, tor, height, dizzying height, nunatak,

"the beginning and the end of all natural scenery"— RUSKIN, dome; **peak, pinnacle, summit** *see* 198.2, mountaintop, point, topmost point *or* pinnacle, **crest,** tor, *pic* (*French*), *pico* (*Spanish*); crag, spur, cloud-capped *or* cloud-topped *or* snow-clad peak, the roof of the world; needle, aiguille, pyramidal peak, horn; **volcano,** volcanic mountain, volcanic spine, volcanic neck; seamount, submarine mountain, guyot; **mountain range,** range, massif; **mountain system, chain,** mountain chain, cordillera, sierra, cordilleran belt, fold belt;

"alps on alps"—POPE, hill heaped upon hill; mountain-building, orogeny, folding, faulting, block-faulting, volcanism

7 **valley,** vale, glen, dale, dell, dene, hollow, holler (*informal*), flume, cleuch (*Scottish*), cwm (*Welsh*); **ravine, gorge, canyon,** box canyon, *arroyo* (*Spanish*), barranca, boison, coulee, gully, gulch, combe, dingle, rift, rift valley, kloof, donga, graben, gully, draw, wadi, basin, cirque, corrie, hanging valley; **crevasse;** chimney, **defile,** pass, passage, col; **crater,** volcanic crater, caldera, meteorite *or* meteoritic crater

adjectives

8 **hilly, rolling,** undulating; **mountainous,** montane, alpine

9 famous and high mountains

Aconcagua (Argentina 22,835 feet)	Lhotse (Nepal and China 27,923 feet)
Annapurna (Nepal 26,504 feet)	Logan (Canada 19,850 feet)
Ararat (Turkey 17,011 feet)	Makalu (China and Nepal 27,824 feet)
Ben Nevis (Scotland 4,406 feet)	Manaslu (Nepal 26,760 feet)
Carstensz (New Guinea 16,503 feet)	Matterhorn (Switzerland 14,690 feet)
Cho Oyo (Nepal and China 26,750 feet)	McKinley (United States 20,320 feet)
Cook (New Zealand 12,349 feet)	Mont Blanc (France 15,771 feet)
Cotopaxi (Ecuador 19,700 feet)	Mount Saint Helens (United States 8,364 feet)
Dhaulagiri (Nepal 26,810 feet)	Mulhacen (Spain 11,420 feet)
Elbert (United States 14,331 feet)	Olympus (Greece 9,570 feet)
Elbrus (Russia 18,481 feet)	Orizaba (Mexico 18,700 feet)
Erebus (Antarctica 13,202 feet)	Pikes Peak (United States 14,110 feet)
Etna (Sicily 10,900 feet)	Popocatépetl (Mexico 17,887 feet)
Everest (Nepal and China 29,028 feet)	Rainier (United States 14,410 feet)
Fuji (Japan 12,388 feet)	Rushmore (United States 6,050 feet)
Grand Teton (United States 13,766 feet)	Snowdon (Wales 3,560 feet)
Jungfrau (Switzerland 13,668 feet)	Teide (Canary Islands 12,198 feet)
K2 (India 28,741 feet)	Toubaki (Morocco 13,881 feet)
Kanchenjunga (Nepal and Sikkim 28,208 feet)	Vesuvius (Italy 3,891 feet)
Kilimanjaro (Tanzania 19,340 feet)	Vinson Massif (Antarctica 16,864 feet)
Kommunizma Peak (Tadzhikistan 24,590 feet)	Whitney (United States 14,494 feet)
Kosciusko (Australia 7,314 feet)	

238 STREAM
running water

nouns

1 **stream, waterway, watercourse** see 239.2, **channel** see 239; meandering stream, flowing stream, lazy stream, racing stream, braided stream; spillway, wasteweir; adolescent stream; **river**; navigable river, underground *or* subterranean river, "moving road"—PASCAL, "a strong brown god"—T S ELIOT; dry stream, stream bed, winterbourne, wadi, *arroyo* (*Spanish*), *donga* (*Africa*), nullah (*India*); **brook,** branch; kill, bourn, run (*informal*), **creek,** crick (*informal*); **rivulet,** rill, **streamlet,** brooklet, runlet, runnel, rundle (*informal*), rindle (*informal*), beck, gill, burn (*Scottish*), sike (*informal*); **freshet,** fresh; millstream, race; midstream, midchannel; stream action, fluviation

2 **headwaters, headstream,** headwater, head, riverhead; **source,** fountainhead see 885.6

3 **tributary,** feeder, **branch, fork,** prong (*informal*), confluent, confluent stream, affluent; effluent, anabranch; broad; bayou; billabong (*Australian*); dendritic drainage pattern

4 **flow,** flowing, **flux,** fluency, profluence, fluid motion *or* movement; hydrodynamics; **stream, current,** set, trend, tide, water flow; drift, driftage; **course,** onward course, **surge, gush, rush,** onrush, spate, run, race; millrace, mill run; undercurrent, undertow; crosscurrent, crossflow; affluence, afflux, affluxion, confluence, concourse, conflux; **downflow,** downpour; defluxion; inflow *see* 189.2; outflow *see* 190.4

5 **torrent, river, flood,** flash flood, wall of water, waterflood, **deluge;** spate, **pour,** freshet, fresh

6 **overflow,** spillage, spill, spillover, overflowing, overrunning, alluvion, alluvium, **inundation, flood, deluge,** whelming, overwhelming, engulfment, submersion *see* 367.2, cataclysm; the Flood, the Deluge; washout

7 **trickle,** tricklet, **dribble, drip,** dripping, stillicide (*old*), drop, spurtle; percolation, leaching, lixiviation; distillation, condensation, sweating; seeping, seepage

8 **lap, swash, wash, slosh, plash, splash;** lapping, washing, etc

9 **jet, spout, spurt,** spurtle, squirt, spit, spew, spray, spritz (*US informal*); rush, **gush,** flush; **fountain,** fount, font, *jet d'eau* (*French*); geyser, spouter (*informal*)

10 **rapids, rapid,** white water, wild water; ripple, **riffle,** riff (*informal*); chute, shoot, sault

11 **waterfall, cataract, fall, falls, Niagara, cascade,** force, linn (*Scottish*), sault; nappe; watershoot

12 **eddy,** back stream, gurge, **swirl,** twirl, whirl; **whirlpool,** vortex, gulf, **maelstrom;** Maelstrom, Charybdis; countercurrent, counterflow, counterflux, backflow, reflux, refluence, regurgitation, backwash, backwater, snye (*Canadian*)

13 **tide,** tidal current *or* stream, tidal flow *or* flood, **tide race; tidewater;** tideway, tide gate; **riptide,** rip, tiderip, overfalls; direct tide, opposite tide; **spring tide; high tide,** high water, full tide; **low tide,** low water; **neap tide,** neap; lunar tide, solar tide; **flood tide, ebb tide;** rise of the tide, flux, flow, flood; ebb, reflux, refluence; ebb and flow, flux and reflux; tidal amplitude, tidal range; tide chart *or* table, tidal current chart; tide gauge, thalassometer

14 **wave, billow,** surge, **swell,** heave, undulation, lift, rise, send, scend; trough, peak; **sea,** heavy swell, ocean swell, ground swell; **roller,** roll; **comber,** comb; **surf, breakers;** wavelet, **ripple,** riffle; **tidal wave,** tsunami; gravity wave, water wave; tide wave; bore, tidal bore, eagre, travelling wave; **whitecap,** white horse; rough *or* heavy sea, rough water, dirty water *or* sea, choppy *or* chopping sea, popple, lop, chop, choppiness; standing wave

15 water gauge, fluviograph, fluviometer; marigraph; Nilometer

verbs

16 to flow, stream, issue, pour, surge, run, course, rush, gush, flush, flood; empty into, flow into, join, join with, mingle waters; set, make, trend; flow in *see* 189.9; flow out *see* 190.13; flow back, surge back, ebb, regurgitate

17 **to overflow,** flow over, wash over, **run over, well over, brim over,** lap, lap at, lap over, overbrim, overrun, pour out *or* over, **spill, slop, slosh,** spill out *or* over; **cataract, cascade; inundate,** engulf, swamp, sweep, whelm, overwhelm, **flood,** deluge, submerge *see* 367.7

18 **to trickle, dribble,** dripple, **drip,** drop, spurtle; **filter,** percolate, leach, lixiviate; distil, condense, sweat; seep, weep; **gurgle** *see* 52.11

19 **to lap, plash, splash, wash, swash, slosh**

20 **to jet, spout, spurt,** spurtle, **squirt,** spit, spew, spray, spritz (*US informal*), play, **gush,** well, surge; vomit, vomit out *or* forth

21 **to eddy,** gurge, **swirl,** whirl, purl, reel, spin

22 **to billow, surge, swell,** heave, lift, rise, send, scend, toss, popple, **roll,** wave, **undulate; peak,** draw to a peak, be poised; comb, **break,** dash, crash, smash; rise and fall, ebb and flow

adjectives

23 **streamy,** rivery, brooky, creeky; streamlike, riverine; fluvial, fluviatile *or* fluviatic

24 **flowing, streaming, running, pouring,** fluxive, fluxional, coursing, racing, gushing, rushing, onrushing, surging, surgy, torrential, rough, whitewater; **fluent,** profluent, affluent, defluent, decurrent, confluent, diffluent; tidal; gulfy, vortical; meandering, mazy, sluggish, serpentine

25 **flooded,** deluged, inundated, engulfed, swamped, swept, whelmed, drowned, overwhelmed, afloat, awash; washed, water-washed; in flood, at flood, in spate

239 CHANNEL

nouns

1 **channel, conduit, duct,** canal, course; **way, passage, passageway;** trough, troughway, troughing; tunnel; ditch, trench *see* 290.2; adit; ingress, entrance *see* 189; egress, exit; **stream** *see* 238

2 **watercourse, waterway, aqueduct,** water channel, water gate, water carrier, culvert, **canal;** side-channel, intrariverine channel, snye (*Canadian*); streamway, riverway; **bed,** stream bed, river bed, creek bed, runnel; water gap; dry bed, *arroyo* (*Spanish*), wadi, winterbourne, *donga* (*Africa*), *nullah* (*India*), **gully,** gullyhole, gulch; swash, swash channel; race, headrace, tailrace; leat; flume; sluice; spillway; spillbox; irrigation ditch, water furrow; waterworks

3 **gutter, trough,** eave *or* eaves trough; downpipe, rainwater pipe; **flume,** chute, shoot; guide

4 (*metal founding*) gate, ingate, runner, sprue, tedge

5 **drain,** sough (*informal*), sluice, scupper; **sink,** sump; piscina; **gutter,** kennel; **sewer,** cloaca, headchute; cloaca maxima

6 **tube; pipe; tubing, piping,** tubulation; tubulure; nipple, pipette, tubulet, tubule; reed, stem, straw; **hose, hosepipe,** garden hose, fire hose; pipeline;

catheter; **siphon;** tap; efflux tube, adjutage; funnel; snorkel; siamese, siamese connection *or* joint

7 **main,** water main, gas main, fire main

8 **spout,** beak, waterspout, downspout; gargoyle

9 **nozzle,** bib nozzle, pressure nozzle, spray nozzle, nose, snout; rose, rosehead; shower head, sprinkler head

10 **valve, gate; tap,** faucet (*US*), spigot (*US*); cock, petcock, draw cock, **stopcock,** sea cock, drain cock, ball cock; bunghole; needle valve; valvule, valvula

11 **floodgate,** flood-hatch, gate, **head gate,** penstock, water gate, **sluice,** sluice gate; tide gate, aboiteau (*Canadian*); weir; **lock,** lock gate, dock gate; air lock

12 **hydrant,** fire hydrant, plug, water plug, fireplug

13 **air passage,** air duct, airway, air shaft, shaft, **air hole,** air tube; speaking tube *or* pipe; **blowhole,** breathing hole, spiracle; nostril; touchhole; spilehole, **vent, venthole,** ventage, ventiduct; **ventilator,** ventilating shaft; transom, louvre, louvrework; wind tunnel

14 **chimney, flue,** flue pipe, funnel, **stovepipe, stack, smokestack,** smoke pipe, smokeshaft; fumarole

verbs

15 **to channel,** channelize, canalize, **conduct, convey,** put through; pipe, funnel, siphon; trench *see* 290.3; direct *see* 573.8

adjectives

16 **tubular,** tubate, tubiform, tubelike, pipelike; cylindrical; tubed, piped; cannular; tubal

17 **valvular,** valval, valvelike; valved

240 SEA, OCEAN

nouns

1 **ocean, sea,** ocean sea, great *or* main sea, *thalassa* (*Greek*), **main** *or* ocean main, the bounding main, tide, salt sea, salt water, blue water, deep water, open sea, **the brine,** the briny *and* the big pond (*both informal*), the briny deep, "the vasty deep"—Shakespeare, **the deep,** the deep sea, the deep blue sea, drink *and* big drink (*both informal*), **high sea, high seas;** the seven seas; hydrosphere; **ocean depths,** ocean deeps and trenches *see* 275.4, 17

2 "great Neptune's ocean", "unpath'd waters", "the always wind-obeying deep"—all Shakespeare, "thou deep and dark blue ocean"—Byron, "Uterine Sea of our dreams and Sea haunted by the true dream", "Sea of a thousand creases, like the infinitely pleated tunic of the god in the hands of women of the sanctuary"—both S-J Perse, "the great naked sea shouldering a load of salt"—Sandburg, "the wine-dark sea"—Homer, "the wavy waste"—Thomas Hood, "old ocean's grey and melancholy waste"—William Cullen Bryant, "the world of waters wild"—James Thomson, "the rising world of waters dark and deep"—Milton, "the glad, indomitable sea"—Bliss Carman, "the clear hyaline, the glassy sea"—Milton

3 **ocean** (*see list*); **sea,** tributary sea (*see list*), gulf, bay

4 **spirit of the sea,**

"the old man of the sea"—Homer, sea devil, Davy, **Davy Jones;** sea god, **Neptune,** Poseidon, Oceanus, Triton, Nereus, Oceanid, Nereid, Thetis; Varuna, Dylan; **mermaid,** siren; merman, seaman

5 (*ocean zones*) pelagic zone, benthic zone, estuarine area, sublittoral, littoral, intertidal zone, splash zone, supralittoral

6 oceanography, thalassography, hydrography, bathymetry; marine biology; aquaculture

7 oceanographer, thalassographer, hydrographer

adjectives

8 **oceanic, marine, maritime,** pelagic, thalassic; nautical *see* 182.57; oceanographic, oceanographical, hydrographic, hydrographical, bathymetric, bathymetrical, bathyorographical, thalassographic, thalassographical; terriginous; deep-sea *see* 275.14

adverbs

9 **at sea,** on the high seas; afloat *see* 182.62; by water, by sea

10 **oversea, overseas,** beyond seas, over the water, transmarine, across the sea

11 **oceanward,** oceanwards, **seaward,** seawards, off; offshore, off soundings, out of soundings, in blue water

word elements

12 mari–, thalass–, thalasso–; oceano–; bathy–

13 oceans

Antarctic	South Atlantic
Arctic	North Pacific
Indian	Pacific
North Atlantic	South Pacific
Atlantic	

14 seas

Adriatic Sea	Gulf of Mexico
Aegean Sea	Gulf of Saint Lawrence
Andaman Sea	Hudson Bay
Arabian Sea	Ionian Sea
Arafura Sea	Irish Sea
Baffin Bay	Java Sea
Bali Sea	Kara Sea
Baltic Sea	Laptev Sea
Banda Sea	Macassar Strait
Barents Sea	Mediterranean Sea
Bay of Bengal	Molukka Sea
Beaufort Sea	North Sea
Bering Sea	Norwegian Sea
Black Sea	Persian Gulf
Caribbean Sea	Red Sea
Celebes Sea	Savu Sea
Ceram Sea	Sea of Azov
Chukchi Sea	Sea of Japan
Coral Sea	Sea of Marmara
East China Sea	Sea of Okhotsk
East Siberian Sea	South China Sea
English Channel	Sulu Sea
Flores Sea	Tasman Sea
Great Australian Bight	Timor Sea
Greenland Sea	Weddell Sea
Gulf of Alaska	White Sea
Gulf of California	Yellow Sea
Gulf of Guinea	

241 LAKE, POOL

nouns

1 **lake,** landlocked water, loch (*Scottish*), lough (*Irish*), nyanza (*Africa*), mere, freshwater lake; oxbow lake, bayou lake, glacial lake; volcanic lake; tarn; inland sea; **pool,** lakelet, **pond,** pondlet, dew pond, linn (*Scottish*), dike, *étang* (*French*); standing water, still water, stagnant water, dead water; water *or* **watering hole,** water pocket; **oasis;** farm pond; fishpond; millpond, millpool; salt pond, salina, tidal pond *or* pool; **puddle,** plash, sump (*informal*); **lagoon,** *laguna* (*Spanish*); **reservoir,** artificial lake, tank; dam; **well, cistern,** tank, artesian well, flowing well, **spring**

2 **lake dweller,** lacustrian, lacustrine dweller *or* inhabitant, pile dweller *or* builder; laker

3 **lake dwelling,** lacustrine dwelling, pile house *or* dwelling, palafitte; crannog

4 limnology, limnologist; limnimeter, limnograph

adjectives

5 **lakish,** laky, lakelike; lacustrine, lacustral, lacustrian; pondy, pondlike, lacuscular; limnologic, limnological

word elements

6 limn–, limno–, limni–, –limnion

242 INLET, GULF

nouns

1 **inlet, cove,** creek, fleet, arm of the sea, arm, armlet, canal, reach, loch (*Scottish*), **bay, fjord,** bight; cove; **gulf; estuary,** firth *or* frith, bayou, mouth, *boca* (*Spanish*); **harbour,** natural harbour; road *or* roads, roadstead; **strait** *or* straits, kyle (*Scottish*), **narrow** *or* **narrows,** euripus, belt, gut, narrow seas; **sound**

adjectives

2 gulfy, gulflike; gulfed, bayed, embayed; estuarine, fluviomarine, tidewater; drowned

243 MARSH

nouns

1 **marsh,** marshland, **swamp,** swampland, fen, fenland, **morass,** mere *or* marish (*both old*), *marais* (*French*), *maremma* (*Italian*), **bog, mire, quagmire,** carr, sump (*informal*), wash, baygall; wetland; glade *and* everglade (*both US*); slough, swale, wallow, sough; bottom, **bottoms,** bottomland, slob land, holm, water meadow, meadow; **moor,** moorland, moss (*Scottish*), peat bog; salt marsh; quicksand; taiga; mud flat, **mud** *see* 1060.8, 9

verbs

2 **to mire,** bemire, sink in, **bog,** mire *or* bog down, stick in the mud; stodge

adjectives

3 **marshy, swampy,** swampish, **moory,** moorish, fenny, marish (*old*), paludal *or* paludous; **boggy,** boggish, **miry,** mirish, quaggy, quagmiry, spouty, poachy; **muddy** *see* 1060.14; swamp-growing, uliginous

244 QUANTITY

nouns

1 **quantity**, quantum, amount, **whole** *see* 791; mass, **bulk**, substance, matter, magnitude, amplitude, **extent, sum; measure**, measurement; strength, force, numbers

2 **amount**, quantity, large amount, small amount, **sum, number**, count, group, total, reckoning, **measure**, parcel, passel (*informal*), **part** *see* 792, **portion**, clutch, ration, share, issue, allotment, lot, deal; **batch**, bunch, heap (*informal*), pack, mess (*informal*), gob *and* chunk *and* hunk *and* wodge (*all informal*), budget (*old*), dose

3 **some**, somewhat, something, summat (*informal*); **aught; any**, anything

verbs

4 **to quantify**, quantize, **count, number off, enumerate, number** *see* 1016.10, rate, fix; parcel, apportion, mete out, issue, allot, divide *see* 801.18; **increase** *see* 251.4, 6, **decrease** *see* 252.7; quantitate, **measure** *see* 300.11

adjectives

5 **quantitative**, quantitive, quantified, quantized, measured; **some**, certain, one; a, an; **any**

adverbs

6 **approximately**, nearly, some, about, circa; more or less, *plus ou moins* (*French*), by and large, upwards of

prepositions

7 **to the amount of**, to the tune of (*informal*); as much as, all of (*informal*), no less than, upwards of

8 **indefinite quantities**

armful *or* armload	lapful
bag *or* bagful	mouthful
bargeload	mug *or* mugful
barrel *or* barrelful	pail *or* pailful
basin *or* basinful	pitcher *or* pitcherful
basket *or* basketful	planeful *or* planeload
bin *or* binful	plate *or* plateful
bottle *or* bottleful	pocketful
bowl *or* bowlful	pot *or* potful
box *or* boxful	roomful
bucket *or* bucketful	sack *or* sackful *or* sackload
can *or* canful	scoop *or* scoopful
cap *or* capful	shovel *or* shovelful
carton *or* cartonful	skepful
case *or* caseful	spoon *or* spoonful
crate *or* crateful	tablespoon *or* tablespoonful
cup *or* cupful	tank *or* tankful
flask *or* flaskful	tankerload
glass *or* glassful	teacup *or* teacupful
handful	teaspoon *or* teaspoonful
jar *or* jarful	thimble *or* thimbleful
keg *or* kegful	tub *or* tubful
kettle *or* kettleful	

245 DEGREE

nouns

1 **degree**, grade, step, *pas* (*French*), leap; round, rung, tread, stair; **point**, mark, peg, tick; **notch**, cut;

plane, level, plateau; **period**, space, interval; **extent, measure**, amount, ratio, proportion, stint, standard, height, pitch, reach, remove, compass, range, scale, scope, calibre; **shade**, shadow, nuance

2 **rank, standing, level**, footing, **status**, station; **position**, place, sphere, orbit, echelon; **order**, estate, precedence, condition; rate, rating; **class**, caste; **hierarchy**, power structure

3 **gradation, graduation**, grading, staging, phasing, tapering, shading

verbs

4 **to graduate, grade**, calibrate; phase in, phase out, taper off, shade off; **increase** *see* 251, **decrease** *see* 252.6, 7

adjectives

5 **gradual**, gradational, calibrated, graduated, phased, staged, tapered, scalar; regular, progressive; hierarchic, hierarchical

adverbs

6 **by degrees**, degreewise; **gradually**, gradatim; **step by step**, grade by grade, *di grado in grado* (*Italian*), **bit by bit, little by little**, inch by inch, inchmeal, step by step, drop by drop; a little, fractionally; a little at a time, by slow degrees, by inches, a little at a time; slowly *see* 175.13

7 **to a degree**, to some extent, in a way, in a measure, in some measure; somewhat, kind of (*informal*), sort of (*informal*), rather, pretty, quite, fairly; a little, a bit; slightly, scarcely, to a small degree *see* 248.9, 10; very, extremely, to a great degree *see* 247.19-22

246 MEAN

nouns

1 **mean, median, middle** *see* 818; **golden mean**, *juste milieu* (*French*); **medium**, happy medium; middle of the road, middle course, *via media* (*Latin*); middle state *or* ground *or* position *or* echelon *or* level *or* point, midpoint; **average**, balance, par, normal, norm, rule, run, generality; **mediocrity**, averageness, passableness, adequacy; averaging, mediocritization; **centre** *see* 208.2

verbs

2 **to average**, average out, **split the difference**, take the average, strike a balance, pair off; strike *or* hit a happy medium; keep to the middle, avoid extremes; **do**, just do, pass, barely pass; mediocritize

adjectives

3 **medium**, mean, **intermediate**, intermediary, median, medial, mid-level, middle-echelon; **average**, normal, standard, par for the course; middle-of-the-road, moderate; **middling, ordinary**, usual, routine, common, mediocre, merely adequate, passing, banal, so-so; **central** *see* 208.11

adverbs

4 **mediumly**, medianly; medially, midway *see* 818.5, intermediately, in the mean; centrally *see* 208.15

5 **on the average**, in the long run, over the long haul; taking one thing with another, taking all

things together, **all in all, on the whole,** all things considered, on balance; **generally** *see* 863.17

word elements

6 medi–, mes–, mezzo–, semi–

247 GREATNESS

nouns

1 **greatness, magnitude,** muchness; **amplitude,** ampleness, fullness, plenitude, great scope *or* compass *or* reach; **grandeur,** grandness; **immensity,** enormousness *or* enormity, **vastness,** vastitude, tremendousness, expanse, boundlessness, infinity *see* 822; stupendousness, formidableness, prodigiousness, humongousness (*informal*); **might,** mightiness, strength, power, intensity; **largeness** *see* 257.6, **hugeness,** gigantism, bulk; **superiority** *see* 249

2 **glory, eminence, preeminence, majesty, loftiness, prominence,** distinction, outstandingness, consequence, notability; **magnanimity,** nobility, sublimity; **fame,** renown, celebrity; heroism

3 **quantity** *see* 244, numerousness *see* 883; **quantities, much, abundance,** copiousness, superabundance, superfluity, profusion, plenty, plenitude; **volume, mass,** mountain, load; peck, bushel; bag, barrel, ton; world, acre, ocean, sea; flood, spate; **multitude** *see* 883.3, countlessness *see* 822.1

4 **lot, lots,** deal, no end of, **good** *or* **great deal, considerable amount,** sight, **heap, pile, stack,** loads, **raft, slew,** whole slew, spate, wad, **batch,** mess, mint, peck, pack, pot, **tidy sum,** bomb (*informal*), quite a little; **oodles, gobs, scads,** bags *and* masses *and* lashings

verbs

5 **to loom, bulk,** loom large, bulk large, stand out; **tower,** rear, soar, outsoar; **tower above,** rise above, overtop; **exceed, transcend,** outstrip

adjectives

6 **great, grand, considerable,** consequential; **mighty,** powerful, strong, irresistible, intense; main, maximum, **total, full,** plenary, comprehensive, exhaustive; grave, **serious,** heavy, deep

7 **large** *see* 257.16, **immense, enormous, huge** *see* 257.20; **gigantic,** mountainous, titanic, colossal, mammoth, Gargantuan, gigantesque, monster, monstrous, outsize, sizable, larger than life, overgrown, king-size, monumental, ginormous (*informal*); **massive,** massy, weighty, bulky, voluminous; **vast,** vasty, boundless, **infinite** *see* 822.3, immeasurable, cosmic, astronomical, galactic; **spacious,** amplitudinous, extensive; **tremendous,** stupendous, awesome, prodigious

8 **much, many,** beaucoup (*informal*), ample, **abundant,** copious, generous, overflowing, superabundant, multitudinous, plentiful, **numerous** *see* 883.6, countless *see* 822.3

9 **eminent, prominent,** outstanding, standout, high, elevated, towering, soaring, overtopping, exalted, **lofty,** sublime; august, majestic, noble, distinguished;

magnificent, magnanimous, heroic, godlike, superb; famous, renowned, lauded, glorious

10 **remarkable, outstanding,** extraordinary, **superior** *see* 249.12, **marked,** of mark, signal, conspicuous, **striking; notable,** much in evidence, noticeable, noteworthy; **marvellous,** wonderful, formidable, exceptional, uncommon, astonishing, appalling, humongous (*informal*), fabulous, fantastic, incredible, egregious

11 (*informal terms*) **terrific,** terrible, horrible, **dreadful, awful,** fearful, frightful, deadly; **whacking, thumping, rousing,** howling

12 **downright, outright, out-and-out; absolute, utter, perfect, consummate,** superlative, surpassing, positive, definitive, classical, pronounced, decided, regular (*informal*), proper (*informal*), precious, profound, stark; **thorough,** thoroughgoing, **complete,** total; **unmitigated,** unqualified, unrelieved, unspoiled, undeniable, unquestionable, unequivocal; **flagrant,** arrant, shocking, shattering, egregious, intolerable, unbearable, unconscionable, glaring, stark-staring, **rank,** crass, gross

13 **extreme, radical,** out of this world, way *or* far out (*informal*), too much (*informal*); **greatest,** furthest, **most, utmost,** uttermost, the max (*informal*); **ultra,** ultra-ultra; at the height *or* peak *or* limit *or* summit *or* zenith

14 **undiminished,** unabated, unreduced, unrestricted, unretarded, unmitigated

adverbs

15 **greatly, largely,** to a large *or* great extent, in great measure, on a large scale; **much,** muchly (*US informal*), pretty much, very much, so, so very much, ever so much, ever so, never so; **considerably,** considerable (*informal*); abundantly, plenty (*informal*), no end of, no end, not a little, galore (*informal*), **a lot,** a deal (*informal*), **a great deal,** *beaucoup* (*French*); **highly,** to the skies; in spades *and* with bells on *and* with brass knobs on (*all informal*), like *or* as all creation (*informal*), like *or* as all get-out (*US informal*); **undiminishedly,** unabatedly, unreducedly, unrestrictedly, unretardedly, unmitigatedly

16 **vastly, immensely, enormously, hugely, tremendously,** gigantically, colossally, titanically, prodigiously, stupendously, humongously (*informal*)

17 **by far, far and away,** far, far and wide, by a long way, by a great deal, by a long shot *or* long chalk (*informal*), out and away, by all odds

18 **very, exceedingly,** awfully *and* terribly *and* terrifically (*all informal*), **quite,** just, so, **really,** jolly, not half (*informal*), real *and* right (*both informal*), **pretty,** only too, mightily, **mighty** *and* almighty *and* powerfully *and* powerful *and* hellish *and* dead (*all informal*)

19 (*in a positive degree*) **positively, decidedly, clearly,** manifestly, unambiguously, patently, **obviously,** visibly, unmistakably, unquestionably, observably, **noticeably,** demonstrably, sensibly, quite; **certainly,** actually, **really, truly,** verily, **undeniably,** indubitably, without doubt, assuredly, **indeed,** for a certainty, for real (*informal*), seriously, in all conscience

20 (*in a marked degree*) **intensely, acutely,** exquisitely, **exceptionally,** surpassingly, superlatively, eminently, preeminently; **remarkably, markedly, notably, strikingly,** signally, emphatically, pointedly, prominently, conspicuously, pronouncedly, impressively, famously, glaringly; **particularly, singularly,** peculiarly; uncommonly, extraordinarily, **unusually; wonderfully,** wondrously, amazingly, magically, surprisingly, astonishingly, marvellously, exuberantly, incredibly, awesomely; **abundantly,** richly, profusely, amply, **generously,** copiously; **magnificently,** splendidly, nobly, worthily, magnanimously

21 (*in a distressing degree*) **distressingly, sadly, sorely, bitterly,** piteously, grievously, miserably, **cruelly,** woefully, lamentably, balefully, dolorously, shockingly; **terribly, awfully, dreadfully, frightfully, horribly,** abominably, **painfully,** excruciatingly, torturously, **agonizingly,** deathly, deadly, something rotten (*informal*), within an inch of one's life; shatteringly, staggeringly; **excessively,** exorbitantly, extravagantly, **inordinately,** preposterously; **unduly, improperly,** intolerably, unbearably; **inexcusably,** unpardonably, unconscionably; **flagrantly,** blatantly, egregiously; **unashamedly,** unabashedly, baldly, nakedly, brashly, openly; **cursedly,** confoundedly, **damnably,** deucedly (*informal*), infernally, hellishly

22 (*in an extreme degree*) **extremely, utterly, totally,** in the extreme, **most,** *à outrance* (*French,* to the utmost); **immeasurably,** incalculably, indefinitely, **infinitely;** beyond compare *or* comparison, **beyond measure,** beyond all bounds, all out *and* flat out (*both informal*); **perfectly, absolutely,** essentially, fundamentally, radically; **purely, totally,** completely; unconditionally, with no strings attached, unequivocally, downright, dead; with a vengeance

23 (*in a violent degree*) **violently,** furiously, hotly, fiercely, severely, **desperately,** madly, **like mad** (*informal*); **wildly,** demonically, like one possessed, **frantically,** frenetically, fanatically, uncontrollably

word elements

24 meg–, mega–, multi–, super–

248 INSIGNIFICANCE

nouns

1 **insignificance,** inconsiderableness, unimportance *see* 997, inconsequentialness, inconsequentiality, lowness, pettiness, meanness, triviality, nugacity, nugaciousness; **smallness,** tininess, diminutiveness, minuteness, exiguity *or* exiguousness; **slightness,** moderateness, scantiness, puniness, picayunishness, meanness, meagreness; daintiness, delicacy; **littleness** *see* 258; **fewness** *see* 884; insufficiency *see* 991

2 **modicum,** minim; **minimum; little, bit,** little *or* wee *or* tiny bit (*informal*), bite, **particle,** fragment, spot, **speck,** flyspeck, fleck, point, dot, jot, tot, tittle, **iota,** ounce, **dab** (*informal*), mote, **mite** (*informal*) *see* 258.7; whit, ace, **hair,** scruple, groat, farthing, pittance, dole, trifling amount, **smidgen** (*informal*), pinch, gobbet, dribble, driblet, dram, drop, skosh *and* smitch (*both US informal*), drop in a bucket *or*

in the ocean, tip of the iceberg; grain, granule, pebble; molecule, **atom;** thimbleful, spoonful, handful, nutshell; trivia, minutiae; dwarf

3 **scrap,** tatter, smithereen (*informal*), patch, **stitch, shred,** tag; snip, **snippet,** snick, chip, nip; splinter, sliver, shiver, tait (*Scottish*); **morsel,** *morceau* (*French*), **crumb**

4 **hint,** *soupçon* (*French*), **suspicion, suggestion,** intimation; tip of the iceberg; **trace, touch, dash,** cast, **smattering,** sprinkling; tinge, tincture; **taste, lick, smack,** sip, sup, **smell;** look, **thought,** idea; **shade,** shadow; gleam, spark, scintilla

5 **hardly anything, mere nothing,** next to nothing, less than nothing, **trifle,** bagatelle, **a drop in the bucket** *or* **in the ocean;** the shadow of a shade, the suspicion of a suspicion

adjectives

6 **insignificant, small, inconsiderable, inconsequential, negligible,** no great shakes, footling, one-horse *and* pint-size (*both informal*), vest-pocket (*US informal*); unimportant, no skin off one's nose, **trivial,** trifling, nugacious, nugatory, petty, mean, niggling, picayune *or* picayunish, Mickey Mouse (*informal*), nickel-and-dime *and* chickenshit (*both US informal*); shallow, depthless, cursory, superficial, skin-deep; **little** *see* 258.10, **tiny** *see* 258.11, **weeny,** tiddly, **miniature** *see* 258.12, **meagre** *see* 991.10, **few** *see* 884.4; **short** *see* 268.8; **low** *see* 274.7

7 **dainty, delicate, gossamer, diaphanous; subtle,** subtile, tenuous, thin *see* 270.16, rarefied *see* 299.4

8 **mere, sheer,** stark, bare, bare-bones, plain, simple, unadorned, unenhanced

adverbs

9 (*in a small degree*) **scarcely, hardly, barely,** only just, by a hair, by an ace *or* a jot *or* a whit *or* an iota, **slightly,** lightly, exiguously, fractionally, scantily, inconsequentially, **insignificantly, negligibly,** imperfectly, minimally, inappreciably, **little; minutely,** meagrely, triflingly, faintly, weakly, feebly; **a little, a bit,** just a bit, to a small extent, on a small scale; ever so little, *tant soit peu* (*French*), as little as may be

10 (*in a certain or limited degree*) **to a degree, to a certain extent, to some degree,** in some measure, to such an extent, *pro tanto* (*Latin*); **moderately,** mildly, **somewhat,** detectably, just visibly, modestly, appreciably, visibly, **fairly,** tolerably, **partially,** partly, part, in part, incompletely, not exhaustively, not comprehensively; **comparatively, relatively; merely,** simply, purely, only; **at least,** at the least, leastwise, at worst, at any rate; **at most,** at the most, at best, at the outside (*informal*); in a manner, in a manner of speaking, **in a way,** after a fashion; so far, thus far

11 (*in no degree*) **noway,** noways (*US informal*), **nowise,** in no wise, in no case, in no respect, **by no means,** by no manner of means, **on no account,** not on any account, not for anything in the world, **under no circumstances,** at no hand, nohow (*informal*), **not in the least,** not much, **not at all,** never, not by a damn sight (*informal*), not by a long chalk (*informal*), not by a long shot (*informal*); not nearly, **nowhere near; not a bit,** not a bit of it, not a whit, not a speck, not a jot, not an iota

249 SUPERIORITY

nouns

1 **superiority, preeminence, greatness** see 247, **lead,** transcendence *or* transcendency, ascendancy *or* ascendance, prestige, favour, prepotence *or* prepotency, preponderance; predominance *or* predominancy, hegemony; precedence see 813, **priority,** prerogative, privilege, right-of-way; **excellence** see 998.1, virtuosity, inimitability, incomparability; **seniority,** precedence, deanship; **success** see 409, accomplishment see 407, **skill** see 413

2 **advantage,** vantage, odds, leg up *and* inside track *and* pole position (*all informal*); **upper hand,** whip hand; start, head *or* flying *or* running start; **edge,** jump *and* drop (*both informal*), bulge (*US informal*); **card up one's sleeve** (*informal*), ace in the hole (*informal*), something extra *or* in reserve; vantage ground *or* point, coign of vantage, bridgehead

3 **supremacy, primacy,** paramountcy, **first place,** height, acme, zenith, be-all and end-all, summit, top spot (*informal*); **sovereignty, rule, hegemony, control** see 417.5; kingship, **dominion** see 417.6, lordship, imperium, world power; **command,** sway; **mastery,** mastership see 417.7; **leadership,** headship, presidency; **authority** see 417, directorship, management, jurisdiction, power, say *and* last word (*both informal*); influence see 893; effectiveness; **maximum,** highest, most, *ne plus ultra* (*Latin,* no more beyond), the max (*informal*); **championship,** crown, laurels, palms, first prize, blue ribbon, new high, record, personal best

4 **superior, chief, head, boss** see 575.1, honcho (*informal*), commander, **ruler, leader,** dean, *primus inter pares* (*Latin,* first among equals), **master** see 575; higher-up (*informal*), senior, principal, gaffer, guv'nor *or* governor (*informal*), big shot (*informal*); superman, **genius** see 413.12; prodigy, nonpareil, paragon, virtuoso, ace, **star, superstar,** champion, winner, top dog (*informal*), top banana (*US informal*), the bee's knees (*informal*), one in a thousand, one in a million, etc, laureate, fugleman, Rolls-Royce (*trademark*), A 1, A number 1, standout, record-breaker, the greatest *and* whizbang *and* world-beater *and* a tough act to follow (*all informal*)

5 **the best** see 998.8, the top of the line (*informal*); the best people, **nobility** see 608; **aristocracy,** barons, top people *and* toffs (*informal*), **elite,** cream, cream of the crop, top of the milk, glitterati (*informal*), upper crust, upper class, one's betters; **top brass** (*informal*), the VIP's (*informal*), higher-ups, movers and shakers, lords of creation, ruling circles, **establishment,** power elite, power structure, **ruling class,** bigwigs (*informal*), heid bummers *and* high heid yins (*both Scottish*)

verbs

6 **to excel, surpass, exceed, transcend,** get *or* have the ascendancy, get *or* have the edge, have it all over (*informal*), overcome, overpass, best, **better,** improve on, perfect, go one better (*informal*); **cap,** trump; top, tower above *or* over, overtop; **predominate,** prevail, preponderate; **outweigh,** overbalance, overbear

7 **to best, beat, beat out, defeat** see 412.6; beat hollow (*informal*), trounce, thrash, clobber *and* take to the cleaners (*informal*), smoke *and* skin *and* skin alive (*all US informal*), worst, whip *and* lick *and* have it all over *and* cut down to size (*all informal*); bear the palm, take the cake (*informal*), bring home the bacon (*informal*); **triumph; win** see 411.4

8 **to overshadow, eclipse, throw into the shade, top,** extinguish, take the shine out of (*informal*); put to shame, show up (*informal*), put one's nose out of joint, put down (*informal*), fake out (*US informal*)

9 **to outdo, outrival,** outvie, outachieve, edge out, inch out, **outclass, outshine,** overmatch, outgun (*informal*); **outstrip,** outgo, outrange, outreach, outpoint, **outperform;** outplay, overplay, outmanoeuvre, outwit, outrun, outstep, outpace, outsprint, outmarch, run rings *or* circles around (*informal*); outride, override; outjump, overjump; outleap, overleap

10 **to outdistance, distance; pass, surpass,** overpass; **get ahead,** pull ahead, shoot ahead, walk away *or* off (*informal*); **leave behind, leave standing,** leave at the post, leave in the dust, leave in the lurch; **come to the front,** have a healthy lead (*informal*), hold the field; steal a march

11 **to rule, command, lead,** possess authority see 417.13, have the authority, have the say *or* the last word, have the whip hand *and* hold all the aces (*both informal*); **take precedence, precede** see 813.2; **come** *or* **rank first, outrank,** rank, rank out (*informal*); **come to the fore,** come to the front, **lead** see 165.2; play first fiddle, **star**

adjectives

12 **superior, greater,** better, finer; **higher,** upper, over, super, above; ascendant, in the ascendant, in ascendancy, coming (*informal*); **eminent,** outstanding, rare, distinguished, marked, of choice, chosen; **surpassing, exceeding, excellent** see 998.12, **excelling, rivalling, eclipsing,** capping, topping, **transcending,** transcendent *or* transcendental; **ahead,** a cut *or* stroke above, one up on (*informal*); more than a match for

13 **superlative, supreme, greatest, best, highest,** maximal, maximum, most, utmost, outstanding; top, topmost, **uppermost,** tip-top, top-level, top-echelon, top-notch *and* top-of-the-line (*both informal*), **first-rate,** first-class, of the first water, top of the line, highest-quality, best-quality, far and away the best, the best by a long shot *or* long chalk, head and shoulders above, of the highest type, A1, A number 1, drop-dead (*informal*)

14 **chief, main, principal,** paramount, **foremost,** headmost, **leading, dominant,** crowning, capital, **cardinal;** great, arch, banner, master, magisterial; central, focal, prime, **primary,** primal, first; **preeminent,** supereminent; **predominant,** preponderant, prevailing, hegemonic *or* hegemonical; ruling, overruling; **sovereign** see 417.17; topflight,

highest-ranking, ranking; **star**, superstar, stellar, world-class

15 **peerless, matchless, champion; unmatched**, unmatchable, makeless (*old*), unrivalled, unparagoned, unparallelled, immortal, **unequalled**, never-to-be-equalled, unpeered, unexampled, unapproached, unapproachable, **unsurpassed, unexcelled**; unsurpassable; inimitable, **incomparable**, beyond compare *or* comparison, **unique**; without equal *or* parallel, *sans pareil* (*French*); in a class by itself, *sui generis* (*Latin*), easily first, *facile princeps* (*Latin*); second to none, *nulli secundus* (*Latin*); **unbeatable**, invincible

adverbs

16 **superlatively, exceedingly, surpassingly**; eminently, egregiously, prominently; supremely, paramountly, preeminently, **the most**, transcendently, to crown all, *par excellence* (*French*); inimitably, incomparably; to *or* in the highest degree, far and away

17 **chiefly, mainly, in the main**, in chief; dominantly, **predominantly; mostly, for the most part; principally, especially, particularly**, peculiarly; **primarily, in the first place**, first of all, **above all**; indeed, even, yea, still more, more than ever, all the more, *a fortiori* (*Latin*); ever so, never so, no end

18 **peerlessly, matchlessly**, unmatchably; unsurpassedly, unsurpassably; inimitably, **incomparably; uniquely**, second to none, *nulli secundus* (*Latin*); **unbeatably**, invincibly

19 **advantageously**, to *or* with advantage, favourably; melioratively, amelioratively, improvingly

word elements

20 preter–, super–, supra–, sur–, trans–, ultra–, arch–, prot–

250 INFERIORITY

nouns

1 inferiority, **subordinacy**, subordination, secondariness; **juniority**, minority; **subservience**, **subjection**, servility, lowliness, humbleness, humility; back seat *and* second fiddle (*both informal*), second *or* third string (*informal*)

2 **inferior, underling**, understrapper, **subordinate**, subaltern, **junior**; secondary, second fiddle *and* second stringer *and* third stringer *and* benchwarmer (*all informal*), low man on the totem pole (*US informal*), loser *and* nonstarter (*both informal*); lightweight, follower, pawn, cog, flunky, yes-man, creature; lower class *or* orders *or* ranks, commonalty; infrastructure *or* commonality, *hoi polloi* (*Greek*), masses

3 inadequacy, mediocrity *see* 1004, deficiency, imperfection, insufficiency *see* 991; **incompetence** *or* incompetency, maladroitness, unskilfulness *see* 414; **failure** *see* 410; smallness *see* 248.1; littleness *see* 258; meanness, lowness, baseness, pettiness, triviality, shabbiness, vulgarity *see* 497; **fewness** *see* 884; subnormality

verbs

4 **to be inferior, not come up to, not measure up, fall** *or* **come short, fail** *see* 410.8, not make *or* hack it *and* not cut the mustard *and* not make the cut (*all informal*); want, leave much to be desired, be found wanting; **not compare**, have nothing on (*informal*), **not hold a candle to** (*informal*), not approach, not come near; serve, subserve, rank under *or* beneath, follow, play second fiddle *and* take a back seat *and* sit on the bench (*all informal*)

5 **to bow to, hand it to** (*informal*), tip the hat to (*informal*), yield the palm; retire into the shade; give in (*informal*), lose face

adjectives

6 **inferior, subordinate**, subaltern, sub, small-scale, **secondary; junior, minor**; second *or* third string *and* one-horse *and* penny-ante *and* dinky (*all informal*), second *or* third rank, low in the pecking order, low-rent *and* downscale (*both informal*); **subservient**, subject, servile, low, **lowly**, humble, modest; **lesser**, less, lower; in the shade, thrown into the shade; **common**, vulgar, **ordinary**; underprivileged, disadvantaged; **beneath one's dignity** *or* station, infra dig, demeaning

7 **inadequate, mediocre**, deficient, imperfect, **insufficient; incompetent**, unskilful, maladroit; small, little, mean, base, petty, trivial, tinpot, shabby, ropy *or* ropey (*informal*); **not to be compared, not comparable, not a patch on** (*informal*); **outclassed**, not in it *and* not in the same street *or* league (*all informal*), out of it *and* out of the picture *and* **out of the running** *and* miles behind (*all informal*)

8 **least, smallest**, littlest, slightest, **lowest**, shortest; minimum, minimal, minim; few *see* 884.4

adverbs

9 **poorly, incompetently, inadequately**, badly, maladroitly; least of all, at the bottom of the scale, at the nadir, at the bottom of the heap *and* in the gutter (*both informal*); at a disadvantage

word elements

10 sub–, hyp–, hypo–

251 INCREASE

nouns

1 **increase, gain**, augmentation, greatening, **enlargement, amplification, growth**, development, widening, spread, broadening, elevation, **extension**, aggrandizement, access, accession, **increment**, accretion; **addition** *see* 253; **expansion** *see* 259; **inflation**, swelling, ballooning, edema, fattening, tumescence, bloating; **multiduplication, proliferation**, productiveness *see* 889; accruement, accrual, accumulation; **advance**, appreciation, ascent, mounting, crescendo, waxing, snowballing, **rise** *or* raise, fattening *and* boost *and* hike (*all informal*), **up** *and* upping (*both informal*), build-up; **upturn**, uptrend, upsurge, upswing, uptick (*US informal*); **leap**, jump; **flood**, surge, gush

2 intensification, **heightening, deepening,** tightening, turn of the screw; **strengthening,** beefing-up (*informal*), enhancement, **magnification,** blowup, blowing up, exaggeration; aggravation, exacerbation, heating-up; **concentration,** condensation, consolidation; **reinforcement,** redoubling; pickup *and* step-up (*both informal*), **acceleration,** speedup, accelerando; **boom, explosion,** baby boom, the bulge, population explosion, information explosion

3 **gains,** winnings, cut *and* take (*both informal*), increase (*old*), **profits** see 472.3

verbs

4 **to increase, enlarge,** aggrandize, **amplify, augment, extend,** maximize, **add to; expand** see 259.4, **inflate;** lengthen, broaden, fatten, fill out, thicken; **raise,** exalt, boost (*informal*), hike *and* hike up *and* jack up *and* jump up (*all informal*), mark up, top up, put up, up (*informal*); **build, build up;** pyramid, parlay

5 **to intensify, heighten, deepen,** enhance, **strengthen,** beef up (*informal*), aggravate, exacerbate; **exaggerate,** blow up *and* puff up (*both informal*), **magnify;** whet, sharpen; **reinforce,** double, redouble, triple; **concentrate,** condense, consolidate; **complicate,** ramify, make complex; give a boost to, **step up** (*informal*), accelerate; key up, soup up *and* jazz up (*both informal*); add fuel to the flame *or* the fire, heat *or* hot up (*informal*)

6 **to grow, increase, advance,** appreciate; **spread, widen,** broaden; **gain,** get ahead; wax, swell, balloon, bloat, mount, **rise,** go up, crescendo, snowball; **intensify, develop,** gain strength, strengthen; accrue, accumulate; **multiply, proliferate,** breed, teem; run *or* shoot up, **boom, explode**

adjectives

7 **increased, heightened,** raised, elevated, stepped-up (*informal*); **intensified,** deepened, reinforced, strengthened, fortified, beefed-up (*informal*), tightened, stiffened; **enlarged, extended,** augmented, aggrandized, amplified, **enhanced,** boosted, hiked (*informal*); broadened, widened, spread; **magnified, inflated, expanded,** swollen, bloated; **multiplied,** proliferated; **accelerated,** souped-up *and* jazzed-up (*both informal*)

8 **increasing, rising,** fast-rising, skyrocketing, meteoric; on the upswing, on the increase, on the rise; crescent, **growing,** fast-growing, flourishing, burgeoning, blossoming, waxing, swelling, lengthening, **multiplying,** proliferating; spreading, spreading like a cancer *or* like wildfire, expanding; tightening, intensifying; incremental; exponential (*informal*); **on the increase,** crescendoing, snowballing, mushrooming, growing like a mushroom

adverbs

9 **increasingly,** growingly, more, **more and more,** on and on, greater and greater, ever more; in a crescendo

252 DECREASE

nouns

1 **decrease,** decrescence, decrement, **diminishment,** diminution, **reduction, lessening, lowering,** waning, shrinking *or* shrinkage, withering, withering away, scaling down, scaledown, downsizing, build-down (*US informal*); miniaturization; depression, damping, dampening; **letup** (*informal*), abatement, easing, easing off; de-escalation; **alleviation,** relaxation, mitigation; attenuation, extenuation, weakening, sagging, dying, dying off *or* away, trailing off, tailing off, tapering off, fade-out, languishment; depreciation, **deflation; deduction** see 255.1; subtraction, **abridgment** see 268.3; **contraction** see 260; simplicity see 797

2 **decline,** declension, **subsidence,** slump (*informal*), lapse, **drop,** downtick (*US informal*); **collapse,** crash; dwindling, wane, ebb; downturn, downtrend, retreat, remission; **fall, plunge,** dive, decline and fall; decrescendo, diminuendo; catabasis, deceleration, slowdown

3 **decrement, waste, loss,** dissipation, wear and tear, erosion, ablation, wearing away, depletion, corrosion, attrition, consumption, shrinkage, exhaustion; deliquescence, dissolution

4 **curtailment, retrenchment,** cut, cutback, drawdown, rollback, scaleback, pullback, downsizing, the axe *and* the chop (*both informal*)

5 **minimization,** minification, making light of, devaluing, undervaluing, **belittling,** belittlement, detraction; qualification see 958

verbs

6 **to decrease, diminish, lessen;** let up, bate, abate; **decline, subside,** shrink, wane, wither, ebb, ebb away, dwindle, languish, sink, sag, die down *or* away, wind down, taper off *and* trail off *or* away *and* tail off *or* away (*all informal*); **drop,** drop off, dive, take a nose dive, plummet, plunge, fall, fall off, fall away, fall to a low ebb, run low; **waste,** wear, waste *or* wear away, crumble, erode, ablate, corrode, consume, consume away, be eaten away; melt away, deliquesce

7 **to reduce, decrease, diminish, lessen,** take from; **lower, depress,** de-escalate, damp, dampen, **step down** *and* tune down *and* phase down *or* out *and* scale back *or* down *and* roll back *or* down (*all informal*); **downgrade;** depreciate, **deflate; curtail,** retrench; **cut,** cut down *or* back, trim away, chip away at, whittle away *or* down, pare, axe, chop, roll back (*informal*); deduct see 255.9; **shorten** see 268.6, abridge; **compress** see 260.7, shrink, downsize; **simplify** see 797.4

8 **to abate,** bate, ease; **weaken,** dilute, water, water down, attenuate, extenuate; alleviate, mitigate, slacken, remit

9 **to minimize,** minify, **belittle,** detract from; dwarf, bedwarf; play down, underplay, downplay, de-emphasize

adjectives

10 **reduced, decreased, diminished, lowered,** dropped, fallen; bated, **abated; deflated,** contracted, shrunk, shrunken; **simplified** see 797.9; back-to-basics, no-frills; dissipated, **eroded,** consumed, ablated, **worn;** curtailed, shorn, retrenched, cutback; weakened, attenuated, watered-down; scaled-down, miniaturized; minimized, belittled; **lower,** less, lesser, smaller, shorter; off-peak

11 **decreasing, diminishing, lessening, subsiding, declining,** languishing, dwindling, waning, on the wane, wasting; decrescent, reductive, deliquescent, **contractive;** diminuendo, decrescendo

adverbs

12 **decreasingly, diminishingly,** less, **less and less,** ever less; decrescendo, diminuendo; on a declining scale, at a declining rate

253 ADDITION

nouns

1 **addition,** accession, annexation, affixation, suffixation, prefixation, agglutination, attachment, junction, **joining** see 799, adjunction, uniting; **increase** see 251; **augmentation, supplementation, complementation,** reinforcement; superaddition, superposition, superjunction, superfetation, suppletion; juxtaposition see 223.3; adjunct see 254, add-on

2 (*maths terms*) plus sign, plus; addend; sum, summation, total; subtotal

3 **adding,** totalizing *or* totalization, computation; **adding machine,** calculator

verbs

4 **to add,** plus (*informal*), put with, **join** *or* **unite with, bring together, affix, attach,** annex, adjoin, append, conjoin, subjoin, prefix, suffix, infix, postfix, tag, tag on, **tack on** (*informal*), slap on (*informal*), hitch on (*informal*); glue on, paste on, agglutinate; superpose, superadd; burden, encumber, saddle with; **complicate,** ornament, decorate

5 **to add to,** augment, **supplement; increase** see 251.4; **reinforce,** strengthen, fortify, beef up (*informal*); recruit, swell the ranks of

6 **to compute,** add up; sum, total, totalize, total up, tot *and* tot up *and* tote *and* tote up (*all informal*), tally

7 **to be added,** advene, supervene

adjectives

8 **additive,** additional, additory; **cumulative,** accumulative; summative *or* summational

9 **added,** affixed, add-on, **attached,** annexed, appended, appendant; adjoined, adjunct, conjoined, subjoined; superadded, superposed, superjoined

10 **additional, supplementary, supplemental; extra,** plus, further, farther, fresh, **more,** new, **other,** another, ulterior; **auxiliary,** ancillary, supernumerary, contributory, **accessory,** collateral; **surplus,** spare

adverbs

11 **additionally, in addition,** also, and then some, even more, more so, and also, and all (*informal*), and so, **as well, too,** else, beside, **besides, to boot,** not to mention, let alone, into the bargain; on top

of, over, above; **beyond, plus; extra,** on the side (*informal*); **more, moreover,** *au reste* (*French*), *en plus* (*French*), thereto, farther, further, **furthermore,** at the same time, then, again, yet; similarly, likewise, by the same token, by the same sign; item; therewith, withal (*old*); all included, altogether; among other things, *inter alia* (*Latin*)

prepositions

12 **with, plus, including,** inclusive of, **along** *or* **together with,** coupled with, **in conjunction with; as well as,** to say nothing of, not to mention, let alone; over and above, **in addition to,** added to, linked to; with the addition of, attended by

conjunctions

13 **and, also,** and also

phrases

14 **et cetera, etc, and so forth, and so on,** *und so weiter* (*German*); **et al,** *et alii* (*Latin*), and all (*informal*), and others, and other things, *cum multis aliis* (*Latin,* with many others); and everything else, **and more of the same, and the rest, and the like;** blah blah blah blah *and* dah-dah dah-dah dah-dah *and* and suchlike *or* and all that sort of thing *and* and all that *and* and stuff like that *and* and all that jazz (*all informal*); and what not *and* **and what have you** *and* and I don't know what *and* and God knows what *and* and then some *and* you name it (*all informal*); and the following, *et sequens* (*Latin*), et seq

word elements

15 super–, pleo–, pleio–

254 ADJUNCT
thing added

nouns

1 **adjunct, addition,** increase, **increment,** augmentation, supplementation, complementation, *additum* (*Latin*), additament, additory, addendum, addenda (*plural*), accession, fixture; **annexe,** annexation; **appendage,** appendant, pendant, appanage, tailpiece, coda; undergirding, reinforcement; appurtenance, appurtenant; **accessory,** attachment, add-on; **supplement,** complement, continuation, extrapolation, extension; offshoot, side issue, corollary, sidebar (*informal*), side effect, spin-off (*informal*), **concomitant, accompaniment** see 768, **additive,** adjuvant

2 (*written text*) postscript, **appendix;** rider, allonge, codicil; **epilogue,** envoi, coda, tail; back matter, front matter, prelims; note, marginalia, scholia, commentary; **interpolation,** interlineation; affix, prefix, suffix, infix; enclitic, proclitic

3 (*building*) wing, **addition, annexe,** extension, ell *or* L

4 **extra, bonus, premium,** something extra, extra dash, extra added attraction, something into the bargain, something for good measure, baker's dozen, lagniappe (*US*); **padding,** stuffing, filling; trimming, **frill,** flourish, filigree, decoration, ornament; bells

and whistles (*informal*); superaddition; fillip, wrinkle, twist

255 SUBTRACTION

nouns

1 **subtraction, deduction,** subduction, **removal,** taking away; abstraction, ablation, sublation; erosion, abrasion, wearing, wearing away; refinement, purification

2 **reduction, diminution,** decrease *see* 252, build-down, phasedown, decrement, impairment, **cut** *or* **cutting,** curtailment, shortening, truncation; **shrinkage,** depletion, **attrition,** remission; **depreciation,** detraction, disparagement, derogation; retraction, retrenchment; **extraction**

3 **excision,** abscission, rescission, extirpation; **elimination,** exclusion, extinction, eradication, destruction *see* 395, annihilation; cancellation, write-off, erasure; **amputation,** mutilation

4 **castration,** gelding, emasculation, altering *and* fixing (*both informal*), spaying

5 (*written text*) **deletion,** erasure, cancellation, omission; editing, blue-pencilling, striking *or* striking out; expurgation, bowdlerization, censoring *or* censorship; abridgment, abbreviation

6 (*maths terms*) subtrahend, minuend; negative; minus sign, minus

7 (*thing subtracted*) **deduction,** decrement, minus

8 (*result*) **difference, remainder** *see* 256, epact (*astronomy*), discrepancy, net, balance, surplus *see* 992.5, deficit, credit

verbs

9 **to subtract, deduct,** subduct, take away, take from, **remove,** withdraw, abstract; **reduce,** shorten, curtail, retrench, lessen, **diminish, decrease,** phase down, impair, bate, abate; **depreciate,** disparage, detract, derogate; **erode,** abrade, eat *or* wear *or* rub *or* shave *or* file away; **extract,** leach, drain, wash away; thin, thin out, weed; **refine,** purify

10 **to excise,** cut out, cut, extirpate, enucleate; **cancel,** write off; **eradicate,** root out, wipe *or* stamp out, **eliminate,** kill, kill off, liquidate, annihilate, destroy *see* 395.10, extinguish; **exclude,** except, take out, cancel, cancel out, censor out, bleep out (*informal*), rule out, bar, ban; set aside *or* apart, isolate, pick out, cull; **cut off** *or* **away,** shear *or* take *or* strike *or* knock *or* lop off, truncate; **amputate,** mutilate, abscind; **prune,** pare, peel, clip, crop, bob, dock, lop, nip, shear, shave, strip, strip off *or* away

11 **to castrate,** geld, emasculate, eunuchize, neuter, spay, fix *or* alter (*both informal*), unsex

12 (*written text*) **to delete,** erase, expunge, **cancel,** omit; **edit,** edit out, blue-pencil; strike, strike out *or* off, rub *or* blot out, cross out *or* off, kill, cut; void, rescind; **censor,** bowdlerize, expurgate; abridge, abbreviate

adjectives

13 **subtractive, reductive,** deductive; ablative, erosive; censorial

prepositions

14 **off, from; minus,** less, without, excluding, except *or* excepting, with the exception of, save, leaving out *or* aside, barring, exclusive of, not counting, exception taken of, discounting

256 REMAINDER

nouns

1 **remainder, remains, remnant, residue,** residuum, **rest, balance;** holdover (*US informal*); **leavings, leftovers, oddments; refuse,** odds and ends, scraps, rags, **rubbish, waste,** orts, candle ends; scourings, offscourings; parings, sweepings, filings, shavings, sawdust; chaff, straw, stubble, husks; **debris,** detritus, ruins; end, fag end; stump, butt *or* butt end, roach (*informal*), rump; survival, vestige, trace, hint, shadow, afterimage, afterglow; **fossil,** relics

2 **dregs, grounds, lees,** dross, slag, draff, scoria, faeces; **sediment, settlings, deposits,** deposition; precipitate, precipitation, sublimate (*chemistry*); alluvium, alluvion, diluvium; silt, loess, moraine; scum, off-scum, froth; ash, ember, cinder, sinter, clinker; scale, fur; soot, smut

3 **survivor,** heir, successor; **widow,** widower, relict, war widow, **orphan**

4 **excess** *see* 992, **surplus,** surplusage, overplus, overage; superfluity, redundancy

verbs

5 **to remain,** be left *or* left over, **survive,** subsist, rest

6 **to leave,** leave over, leave behind

adjectives

7 **remaining, surviving, extant,** vestigial, over, left, **leftover, still around, remnant,** remanent, odd; **spare,** to spare; unused, unconsumed; **surplus,** superfluous; **outstanding,** unmet, unresolved; net

8 **residual,** residuary; sedimental, sedimentary

257 SIZE, LARGENESS

nouns

1 **size, largeness, bigness, greatness** *see* 247, vastness, vastitude, **magnitude,** order of magnitude, amplitude; mass, bulk, **volume,** body; **dimensions, proportions,** dimension, calibre, scantling, proportion; **measure,** measurement *see* 300, gauge, **scale; extent,** extension, expansion, expanse, square footage *or* yardage etc, **scope,** reach, range, ballpark (*informal*), spread, coverage, area, cirumference, ambit, girth, diameter, radius, boundary, border, periphery; linear measure *or* dimension, length, height, procerity (*depth*); depth, breadth, width; wheelbase, wingspan

2 **capacity, volume, content,** holding capacity, cubic capacity, accommodation, room, space, measure, limit, burden; gallonage, tankage; poundage, tonnage, cordage; stowage; **quantity** *see* 244

3 **full size,** full growth; life size

4 large size, economy size, family size, **king size**, queen size, giant size

5 **oversize**, outsize; overlargeness, overbigness; **overgrowth**, wild *or* uncontrolled growth, overdevelopment, sprawl; **overweight**, overheaviness; overstoutness, overfatness, overplumpness, bloat, bloatedness, obesity; gigantism, giantism, titanism; hypertrophy, acromegalic gigantism, pituitary gigantism, normal gigantism

6 (*large size*) **sizableness, largeness, bigness,** greatness, grandness, grandeur, grandiosity; largishness, biggishness; voluminousness, capaciousness, generousness, copiousness, ampleness; tallness, toweringness; broadness, wideness; profundity; extensiveness, expansiveness, comprehensiveness; spaciousness *see* 158.5

7 (*very large size*) hugeness, **vastness,** vastitude; humongousness (*informal*); **enormousness, immenseness, enormity, immensity,** tremendousness, **prodigiousness,** stupendousness, mountainousness; **gigantism,** giganticness, giantism, giantlikeness; monumentalism; **monstrousness, monstrosity**

8 **corpulence, obesity, stoutness,** largeness, bigness, *embonpoint* (*French*); **fatness,** fattishness, adiposis *or* adiposity, fleshiness, beefiness, meatiness, heftiness, grossness; **plumpness,** buxomness, rotundity, fubsiness, tubbiness (*informal*), roly-poliness; pudginess, podginess; chubbiness, chunkiness (*informal*), stockiness, squatness, dumpiness, portliness; paunchiness, bloatedness, puffiness, pursiness, blowziness; middle-age spread; hippiness (*informal*); steatopygia *or* steatopygy; bosominess, bustiness (*informal*)

9 **bulkiness, bulk,** hulkingness *or* hulkiness, **massiveness,** lumpishness, clumpishness; **ponderousness,** cumbrousness, cumbersomeness; clumsiness, awkwardness, unwieldiness, clunkiness (*informal*)

10 lump, clump, **hunk** *and* chunk (*both informal*), wodge (*informal*); **mass, piece, gob** *and* glob (*both informal*), gobbet; batch, **wad,** block, loaf; pat (*of butter*); clod; nugget; **quantity** *see* 244

11 (*something large*) **whopper** *and* thumper *and* lunker *and* whale *and* jumbo *and* boomer *and* stonker (*all informal*); monster, hulk

12 (*corpulent person*) **heavyweight, pig,** porker, heavy (*informal*), human *or* man mountain (*informal*); big *or* large person; **fat person, fatty** *and* **fatso** (*both informal*), roly-poly, **tub,** tub of lard, tun, tun of flesh, whale, blimp (*informal*), hippo (*informal*), sumo (*informal*), humpty dumpty (*informal*), **potbelly,** gorbelly (*old or dialect*), swagbelly

13 giant (*see list*), giantess, **amazon, colossus, titan,** nephilim (*Hebrew plural*)

14 behemoth, leviathan, monster; mammoth, mastodon; elephant, jumbo (*informal*); whale; hippopotamus, hippo (*informal*); **dinosaur**

verbs

15 to size, adjust, grade, group, range, rank, graduate, sort, match; gauge, **measure** *see* 300.11, proportion; **bulk** *see* 247.5; **enlarge** *see* 259.4, 5; fatten

adjectives

16 **large, sizable, big, great** *see* 247.6, **grand,** tall (*informal*), **considerable, goodly,** healthy, tidy (*informal*), **substantial,** bumper; numerous *see* 883.6; largish, biggish; large-scale, larger than life; man-sized (*informal*); large-size *or* sized, man-sized, king-size, queen-size; good-sized, life-size *or* sized

17 **voluminous, capacious, generous, ample,** copious, broad, wide, extensive, expansive, comprehensive; **spacious**

18 **corpulent, stout, fat, overweight,** fattish, **obese,** adipose, gross, fleshy, beefy, meaty, hefty, porky, porcine; paunchy, paunched, bloated, puffy, blowzy, distended, swollen, pursy; abdominous, big-bellied, full-bellied, potbellied, gorbellied (*old or dialect*), swag-bellied, pot-gutted *and* pussle-gutted (*both informal*), **plump, buxom,** zaftig (*Yiddish*), pleasantly plump, full, huggy (*informal*), rotund, fubsy, **tubby** (*informal*), roly-poly; **pudgy,** podgy; thickbodied, thick-girthed, **heavyset, thickset, chubby,** chunky (*informal*), fubsy, **stocky,** squat, squatty, dumpy, square; pyknic, endomorphic; **stalwart, brawny, burly;** lusty, strapping (*informal*); **portly,** imposing; well-fed, corn-fed, grain-fed; chubby-faced, round-faced, moonfaced; hippy (*informal*), full-buttocked, steatopygic *or* steatopygous, fat-bottomed (*informal*), broad in the beam (*informal*); bosomy, full-bosomed, chesty, busty (*informal*), top-heavy; plump as a dumpling *or* partridge, fat as a quail, fat as a pig *or* hog,

"fat as a pork hog"—Malory, "fat as a porpoise"—Swift, "fat as a fool"—John Lyly, "fat as butter"—Shakespeare, fat as brawn *or* bacon

19 **bulky, hulky,** hulking, lumpish, lumpy, lumping (*informal*), clumpish, lumbering, lubberly; **massive,** massy; elephantine, hippopotamic; **ponderous,** cumbrous, cumbersome; **clumsy,** awkward, **unwieldy;** clunky (*informal*)

20 **huge, immense, vast, enormous,** ginormous (*informal*), astronomic, astronomical, humongous *and* jumbo (*both informal*), king-size, queen-size, tremendous, prodigious, stupendous, macro, mega, giga; great big, larger than life, Homeric, mighty, **titanic, colossal, monumental,** heroic, heroical, epic, epical, towering, mountainous; profound, abysmal, deep as the ocean; **monster,** monstrous; **mammoth,** mastodonic; **gigantic, giant,** giantlike, gigantesque, gigantean; Cyclopean, Brobdingnagian, Gargantuan, Herculean, Atlantean; elephantine, jumbo (*informal*); dinosaurian, dinotherian; **infinite** *see* 822.3

21 (*informal terms*) **whopping, walloping, whaling, whacking,** spanking, slapping, lolloping, thumping, thundering, bumping, banging

22 **full-sized,** full-size, full-scale; **full-grown, full-fledged,** full-blown; full-formed, **life-sized,** large as life, larger than life

23 **oversize,** oversized; **outsize,** outsized, giant-size, **king-size, queen-size,** record-size, **overlarge,** overbig, too big; **overgrown,** overdeveloped; **overweight,** overheavy; overfleshed, overstout, overfat, overplump, overfed, obese

24 this big, so big, yay big (*US informal*), this size, about this size

adverbs

25 largely, on a large scale, in a big way; in the large; as can be

word elements

26 hyper–, macr–, macro–, maxi–, meg–, mega–, megal–, megalo–, super–

27 giants

Abominable Snowman *or* yeti	Galligantus
	Gargantua
Aegaeon	Geryoneo
Aegir	Godzilla
Alifanfaron	Gog
Amarant	Goliath
Antaeus	Grantorto
Ascapart	Gyes
Atlas	Hercules *or* Heracles
Balan	Hlér
Bellerus	Hymir
Big Foot *or* Sasquatch *or* Omah	Jötunn
	King Kong
Blunderbore	Magog
Briareüs	Mimir
Brobdingnagian	Morgante
Cormoran	Og
Cottus	Orgoglio
Cyclops	Orion
Enceladus	Pantagruel
Ephialtes	Paul Bunyan
Fafner	Polyphemus
Fenrir	Titan
Ferragus	Tityus
Fierebras	Typhon
Firbauti	Urdar
Galapas	Ymir

258 LITTLENESS

nouns

1 littleness, smallness, smallishness, **diminutiveness,** miniatureness, slightness, exiguity; puniness, pokiness, dinkiness (*informal*); tininess, **minuteness;** undersize; petiteness; dwarfishness, stuntedness, runtiness, shrimpiness; **shortness** *see* 268; **scantiness** *see* 884.1

2 infinitesimalness; undetectability, inappreciability, evanescence; intangibility, impalpability, tenuousness, imponderability; imperceptibility, invisibility

3 (*small space*) **tight spot** *and* corner *and* squeeze *and* **pinch** (*all informal*), not enough room to swing a cat (*informal*); hole, pigeonhole; hole-in-the-wall; cubby, cubbyhole; wendy house, doll's house, playhouse, doghouse; cuddy, cuddy cabin

4 (*small person or creature*) **runt, shrimp** (*informal*), wart (*informal*), diminutive, wisp, chit, slip, snip, snippet, tiddler, pip-squeak, shorty, fingerling, small fry (*informal*), minikin (*old*), peanut *and* peewee (*both US informal*), dandiprat (*old*); lightweight, featherweight; bantam, banty (*US informal*); pony; minnow, mini *and* minny (*both informal*); mouse, tit, titmouse, tomtit (*informal*); nubbin, button

5 (*creature small by species or birth*) **dwarf,** dwarfling, **midget,** midge, **pygmy,** manikin, homunculus, atomy, micromorph, hop-o'-my-thumb; elf, gnome, brownie; Lilliputian, Pigwiggen, Tom Thumb, Thumbelina, Alberich, Alviss, Andvari, Nibelung, Regin

6 miniature, mini; scaled-down *or* miniaturized version; microcosm, microcosmos; baby; doll, puppet; microvolume; Elzevir, Elzevir edition; duodecimo, twelvemo

7 (*minute thing*) minutia, **minutiae** (*plural*), minim, **drop,** droplet, **mite** (*informal*), **point,** vanishing point, decimal point, point of a pin, pinpoint, pinhead, **dot;** mote, fleck, **speck,** flyspeck, jot, tittle, jot nor tittle, iota, **trace,** trace amount, suspicion, *soupçon* (*French*); **particle,** crumb, scrap, bite, snip, snippet; grain, grain of, sand; barleycorn, millet seed, mustard seed; midge, gnat; microbe, **microorganism,** amoeba, bacillus, bacteria, diatom, germ, microbe, paramecium, protozoon, virus

8 atom, atomy, monad; **molecule,** ion; **electron,** proton, meson, neutrino, quark, parton, subatomic *or* nuclear particle

verbs

9 to make small, contract *see* 260.7; **shorten** *see* 268.6; **miniaturize,** minify, scale down; **reduce** *see* 252.7, scale back

adjectives

10 little, small *see* 248.6, smallish; **slight,** exiguous; **puny, trifling,** poky, piffling *and* pindling *and* piddling *and* piddly (*all informal*), **dinky** (*informal*); cramped, limited; one-horse; pintsized (*informal*), half-pint; knee-high, knee-high to a grasshopper; petite; short *see* 268.8

11 tiny; teeny *and* teeny-weeny *and* eentsy-weentsy (*all informal*), tichy *or* titchy (*informal*), tiddly (*informal*), wee (*Scottish*), bitty *and* bitsy *and* little-bitty *and* little-bitsy *and* itsy-bitsy *and* itsy-witsy *and* itty-bitty (*all informal*); **minute,** fine

12 miniature, diminutive, minuscule, minuscular, mini, micro, miniaturized, subminiature, minikin (*old*), **small-scale,** minimal; pony, bantam, banty (*US informal*); **baby,** baby-sized; pocket, pocketsized, vest-pocket (*US*); **toy;** handy, compact; duodecimo, twelvemo

13 dwarf, dwarfed, dwarfish, **pygmy, midget,** nanoid, elfin; Lilliputian, Tom Thumb; **undersized,** undersize, squat, dumpy; **stunted,** undergrown, runty, pint-size *or* sized *and* sawn-off (*all informal*); shrunk, shrunken, wizened, shrivelled; meagre, scrubby, scraggy; rudimentary, rudimental

14 infinitesimal, microscopic, ultramicroscopic; evanescent, thin, tenuous; inappreciable; impalpable, imponderable, intangible; imperceptible, indiscernible, invisible, unseeable; atomic, subatomic; molecular; granular, corpuscular, microcosmic, microcosmical; embryonic, germinal

15 microbic, microbial, **microorganic;** animalcular, bacterial; microzoic; protozoan, microzoan, amoebic *or* amoeboid

adverbs

16 small, little, **slightly** *see* 248.9, fractionally; **on a small scale**, in a small compass, in a small way, on a minuscule *or* infinitesimal scale; **in miniature**, in the small; in a nutshell

word elements

17 micr–, micro–, ultramicr–, ultramicro–; granul–, granulo–, granuli–, chondr–, chondro–; –cle, –ee, –een, –el, –ella, –illa, –et, –ette, –idium, –idion, –ie, –y, –ey, –ium, –kin, –let, –ling, –ock, –sy, –ula, –ule, –ulum, –ulus

259 EXPANSION, GROWTH
increase in size

nouns

1 expansion, extension, enlargement, increase *see* 251, uptick (*US*), crescendo, upping, raising, hiking, magnification, aggrandizement, amplification, ampliation (*old*), broadening, widening; **spread**, spreading, creeping, fanning out, dispersion, ripple effect; **flare**, splay; deployment; augmentation, **addition** *see* 253; adjunct *see* 254

2 distension, stretching; **inflation**, sufflation, blowing up; **dilation**, dilatation, dilating; diastole; **swelling**, swell *see* 283.4; puffing, puff, puffiness, **bloating**, bloat, **flatulence** *or* flatulency, flatus, gassiness, windiness; **turgidity**, turgidness, turgescence; tumidness *or* tumidity, tumefaction; tumescence, intumescence; **swollenness**, bloatedness; dropsy, oedema; tympanites, tympany, tympanism, meteorism

3 growth, development *see* 860.1; bodily development *see* 14, **maturation**, maturing, coming of age, growing up, upgrowth; vegetation *see* 310.30; reproduction, procreation *see* 78, germination, pullulation; burgeoning, sprouting; budding, gemmation; outgrowth, excrescence; overgrowth *see* 257.5

verbs

4 (*make larger*) **to enlarge, expand, extend, widen, broaden**, build, build up, aggrandize, **amplify**, crescendo, **magnify, increase** *see* 251.4, augment, add to *see* 253.5, raise, up, scale up, hike *or* hike up; develop, bulk *or* bulk up; **stretch, distend, dilate, swell, inflate**, sufflate, **blow up**, puff up, huff, puff, bloat; pump, pump up; rarefy

5 (*become larger*) **to enlarge, expand, extend, increase**, greaten, crescendo, **develop, widen, broaden**, bulk; **stretch, distend, dilate, swell, swell up, swell out, puff up, puff out, pump up, bloat**, tumefy, balloon, fill out; snowball

6 to spread, spread out, outspread, outstretch; **expand, extend**, widen; open, **open up**, unfold; flare, flare out, broaden out, splay; sprawl; branch, branch out, ramify; fan, fan out, disperse, deploy; spread like wildfire; overrun, overgrow

7 to grow, develop, wax, **increase** *see* 251; gather, brew; **grow up**, mature, spring up, ripen, come of age, **shoot up**, sprout up, upshoot, upspring, upsprout, upspear, overtop, tower; burgeon, **sprout** *see* 310.31, blossom *see* 310.32, reproduce *see* 78.7, procreate *see* 78.8, grow out of, germinate, pullulate;

vegetate *see* 310.31; **flourish, thrive**, grow like a weed; mushroom; outgrow; overgrow, hypertrophy, overdevelop, grow uncontrollably

8 to fatten, fat, plump, pinguefy *and* engross (*both old*); **gain weight**, gather flesh, take *or* put on weight, become overweight

adjectives

9 expansive, extensive; expansional, extensional; expansile, extensile, elastic; expansible, inflatable; distensive, dilatant; inflationary

10 expanded, extended, enlarged, increased *see* 251.7, upped, raised, hiked, **amplified**, ampliate (*old*), crescendoed, widened, broadened, built-up, beefed-up (*informal*)

11 spread, spreading; sprawling, sprawly; **outspread, outstretched**, spread-out, stretched-out; open, unfolded, gaping, patulous; widespread, wide-open; flared, splayed; flaring, flared, flared-out, splaying; splay; fanned, fanning; fanlike, fan-shaped, fan-shape, flabelliform, deltoid

12 grown, full-grown, grown-up, mature, developed, well-developed, fully developed, full-fledged; growing, sprouting, crescent, budding, flowering *see* 310.35, florescent, **flourishing**, blossoming, blooming, burgeoning, fast-growing, thriving; overgrown, hypertrophied, overdeveloped

13 distended, dilated, inflated, sufflated, **blown up, puffed up, swollen**, swelled, **bloated**, turgid, tumid, plethoric, incrassate; **puffy**, pursy; flatulent, gassy, windy, ventose; tumefacient; dropsical, oedematous; enchymatous; fat; puffed out, bouffant, bouffed up *and* bouffy (*both informal*)

260 CONTRACTION
decrease in size

nouns

1 contraction, contracture; systole; **compression**, compressure, pressurizing, pressurization; **compacting**, compaction, compactedness; **condensation, concentration**, consolidation, solidification; **circumscription, narrowing**; reduction, diminuendo, **decrease** *see* 252; abbreviation, curtailment, shortening *see* 268.3; **constriction**, stricture *or* striction, astriction, strangulation, **choking**, choking off, coarctation; bottleneck, hourglass, hourglass figure, nipped *or* wasp waist; neck, cervix, isthmus, narrow place; astringency, constringency; puckering, pursing; knitting, wrinkling

2 squeezing, compression, clamping *or* clamping down, tightening; **pressure**, press, crush; **pinch**, squeeze, tweak, nip

3 shrinking, shrinkage, atrophy; **shrivelling, withering**; searing, parching, drying *or* drying up; attenuation, thinning; wasting, consumption, emaciation, emaceration (*old*); skin and bones; preshrinking, preshrinkage, Sanforizing (*trademark*)

4 collapse, prostration, cave-in; implosion; **deflation**

5 contractibility, contractility, compactability, **compressibility**, condensability, reducibility; collapsibility

6 contractor, constrictor, clamp, compressor, vice, pincer, squeezer; thumbscrew; **astringent**, styptic; alum, astringent bitters, styptic pencil

verbs

7 to **contract, compress**, cramp, compact, condense, concentrate, consolidate, solidify; **reduce, decrease** *see* 252; abbreviate, curtail, **shorten** *see* 268.6; **constrict**, constringe, circumscribe, coarct, **narrow**, draw, draw in *or* together; strangle, strangulate, choke, choke off; **pucker**, pucker up, **purse; knit, wrinkle**

8 to **squeeze**, compress, clamp, cramp, cramp up, tighten; roll *or* wad up, roll up into a ball, ensphere; **press**, pressurize, crush; **pinch, tweak, nip**

9 to **shrink, shrivel, wither**, sear, parch, dry up; **wizen**, weazen; consume, waste, waste away, attenuate, thin, emaciate, macerate *or* emacerate (*old*); preshrink, Sanforize (*trademark*)

10 to **collapse, cave, cave in**, fall in; fold, fold up; implode; **deflate**, let the air out of, take the wind out of; puncture

adjectives

11 **contractive**, contractional, contractible, contractile, compactable; **astringent**, constringent, styptic; **compressible**, condensable, reducible; **collapsible**, foldable; deflationary; consumptive

12 **contracted, compressed**, cramped, compact *or* compacted, concentrated, condensed, consolidated, solidified; **constricted**, strangled, strangulated, choked, choked off, coarcted, **squeezed**, clamped, nipped, pinched *or* pinched-in, wasp-waisted; puckered, pursed; knitted, wrinkled

13 **shrunk**, shrunken; **shrivelled**, shrivelled up; **withered**, sear, parched, corky, dried-up; **wasted**, wasted away, consumed, emaciated, emacerated, thin, attenuated; **wizened**, wizen, weazened; wizen-faced; preshrunk, Sanforized (*trademark*)

14 **deflated, punctured, flat**, holed

261 DISTANCE, REMOTENESS

nouns

1 **distance, remoteness**, farness, far-offness, longinquity; **separation**, separatedness, divergence, clearance, margin, leeway; **extent, length**, space *see* 158, **reach**, stretch, range, compass, span, stride, haul, a way; perspective, aesthetic distance, distancing; astronomical *or* interstellar *or* galactic *or* intergalactic distance, deep space, depths of space, **infinity** *see* 822; **mileage**, light-years, parsecs

2 **long way**, good way (*informal*), **great distance, far cry**; long step, tidy step, giant step *or* stride; long run *or* haul, long road *or* trail; black stump (*New Zealand*); long range; apogee, aphelion

3 **the distance, remote distance, offing; horizon**, the far horizon, where the earth meets the sky, vanishing point, background

4 (*remote region*) jumping-off place *and* godforsaken place *and* God knows where *and* the middle of nowhere (*all informal*), the back of beyond, the end of the rainbow, Timbuktu, Thule *or* Ultima Thule, Siberia, Darkest Africa, the South Seas, Pago Pago,

the Great Divide, China, Outer Mongolia, pole, antipodes, end of the earth, North Pole, South Pole, Tierra del Fuego, Greenland, Yukon, Pillars of Hercules, remotest corner of the world; outpost, outskirts; backblocks (*Australian & NZ*); the sticks (*informal*), the boondocks *and* the boonies (*both US & Canadian informal*), bundu (*South African informal*); **nowhere**; frontier, outback (*Australian*); the moon; outer space

verbs

5 to **reach out, stretch out**, extend, extend out, go *or* go out, range out, carry out; outstretch, outlie, outdistance, outrange

6 to **extend to**, stretch to, stretch away to, **reach to**, lead to, go to, get to, come to, run to, carry to

7 to **keep one's distance, distance oneself**, remain at a distance, maintain distance *or* clearance, keep at a respectful distance, separate oneself, **keep away**, stand off *or* away; keep away from, keep *or* stand clear of, **steer clear of** (*informal*), hold away from, give a wide berth to, keep a good leeway *or* margin *or* offing, keep out of the way of, keep at arm's length, not touch with a ten-foot pole (*informal*), keep *or* stay *or* stand aloof; maintain one's perspective, keep one's aesthetic distance

adjectives

8 **distant**, distal, **remote, removed, far, far-off**, away, **faraway**, way-off, at a distance, exotic, separated, apart, asunder; long-distance, long-range

9 **out-of-the-way**, godforsaken, back of beyond, upcountry; **out of reach, inaccessible**, unget-at-able, unapproachable, untouchable, hyperborean, antipodean

10 **thither**, ulterior; **yonder**, yon; **farther, further**, remoter, more distant

11 transoceanic, transmarine, ultramarine, oversea, overseas; transatlantic, transpacific; tramontane, transmontane, ultramontane, transalpine; transarctic, transcontinental, transequatorial, transpolar, transpontine, ultramundane

12 **farthest, furthest**, farthermost, farthest off, furthermost, ultimate, extreme, remotest, most distant

adverbs

13 **yonder**, yon; **in the distance**, in the remote distance; **in the offing**, on the horizon, in the background

14 **at a distance, away, off**, aloof, at arm's length; distantly, remotely

15 **far, far off**, far away, **afar**, afar off, a long way off, a good way off (*informal*), a far cry to, "over the hills and far away"—JOHN GAY, as far as the eye can see, out of sight

16 **far and wide**, far and near, distantly and broadly, wide, widely, broadly, abroad

17 **apart, away, aside**, wide apart, wide away, "as wide asunder as pole and pole"—J A FROUDE, "as far as the east is from the west"—BIBLE

18 **out of reach**, beyond reach, **out of range**, beyond the bounds, out-of-the-way, out of the sphere of; out of sight, *à perte de vue* (*French*); out of hearing, out of earshot

19 wide, clear; wide of the mark, abroad, all abroad, astray, afield, far afield

prepositions

20 as far as, to, all the way to, the whole way to
21 beyond, past, over, across, the other *or* far side of

262 FORM

nouns

1 form, shape, figure; figuration, **configuration;** formation, **conformation; structure** *see 266;* **build,** make, frame; **arrangement** *see 807;* makeup, format, layout; **composition** *see 795;* cut, set, stamp, type, turn, cast, mould, impression, pattern, matrix, model, mode, modality; archetype, prototype *see 785.1,* Platonic form *or* idea; style, fashion; aesthetic form, inner form, significant form; art form, genre
2 contour, *tournure* (*French*), *galbe* (*French*); broad lines, silhouette, profile, **outline** *see 211.2;* organization *see 806.1*
3 appearance *see 33,* lineaments, features, physiognomy, phiz *or* phizog (*informal*)
4 (*human form*) **figure, form,** shape, frame, anatomy, **physique,** build, body-build, person; body *see 1050.3*
5 forming, shaping, moulding, modelling, fashioning, making, making up; **formation,** conformation, figuration, configuration; sculpture; morphogeny, morphogenesis; creation
6 (*grammatical terms*) form, morph, allomorph, morpheme; morphology, morphemics

verbs

7 to form, formalize, **shape, fashion,** tailor, frame, figure, **lick into shape;** (*informal*) work, knead; set, fix; **forge,** drop-forge; **mould,** model, sculpt *or* sculpture; cast, found; thermoform; stamp, mint; carve, whittle, cut, chisel, hew, hew out; roughhew, roughcast, rough out, block out, lay out, sketch out; hammer *or* knock out; cobble up; create; organize *see 806.4*
8 (*be formed*) **to form,** take form, shape, **shape up, take shape;** materialize

adjectives

9 formative, formal, formational, plastic, morphotic; **formed, shaped,** patterned, fashioned, tailored, framed; **forged,** moulded, modelled, sculpted; cast, founded; stamped, minted; carved, cut, whittled, chiselled, hewn; roughhewn, roughcast, roughed-out, blocked-out, laid-out, sketched-out; hammered-out, knocked out, cobbled-up; **made, produced**
10 (*biological terms*) plasmatic, plasmic, protoplasmic, plastic, metabolic
11 (*grammatical terms*) morphologic, morphological, morphemic

word elements

12 morph–, morpho–, –morph, –morphism, –morphy, –form, –iform, –morphic, –morphous

263 FORMLESSNESS

nouns

1 formlessness, shapelessness; unformedness, amorphousness, amorphism; misshapenness; **chaos** *see 809.2,* confusion, messiness, mess, muddle *see 809.2,* orderlessness, untidiness; **disorder** *see 809;* entropy; anarchy *see 418.2;* **indeterminateness, indefiniteness,** indecisiveness, vagueness, mistiness, haziness, fuzziness, blurriness, unclearness, obscurity; lumpiness, lumpishness
2 diamond in the rough, raw material

verbs

3 to deform, distort *see 265.5;* misshape; unform, unshape; disorder, jumble, mess up, muddle, confuse; obfuscate, obscure, fog up, blur

adjectives

4 formless, shapeless, featureless, characterless, nondescript, inchoate, lumpy, lumpish, blobby *and* baggy (*both informal*), inform; amorphous, **chaotic, orderless,** disorderly *see 809.13,* unordered, unorganized, confused, anarchic *see 418.6;* kaleidoscopic; **indeterminate, indefinite,** undefined, indecisive, vague, misty, hazy, fuzzy, blurred *or* blurry, unclear, obscure; obfuscatory
5 unformed, unshaped, unshapen, unfashioned, unlicked; unstructured; uncut, unhewn

264 SYMMETRY

nouns

1 symmetry, symmetricalness, **proportion,** proportionality, **balance** *see 789.1,* equilibrium; **regularity,** uniformity *see 780,* evenness; equality *see 789;* finish; harmony, congruity, consistency, conformity *see 866,* **correspondence,** keeping; eurhythmy, eurhythmics; dynamic symmetry; bilateral symmetry, trilateral symmetry, etc, multilateral symmetry; parallelism *see 203,* polarity; shapeliness
2 symmetrization, regularization, balancing, harmonization; evening, equalization; coordination, integration; **compensation,** playing off, playing off against, posing against *or* over against

verbs

3 to symmetrize, regularize, **balance,** balance off, compensate; harmonize; **proportion,** proportionate; even, even up, equalize; coordinate, integrate; play off, play off against

adjectives

4 symmetric, symmetrical, balanced, balanced off, proportioned, eurhythmic, harmonious; **regular,** uniform *see 780.5,* even, equal *see 789.7,* equal on both sides, fifty-fifty (*informal*), square, squared-off; coequal, coordinate, equilateral; **well-balanced, well-set,** well-set-up (*informal*); finished
5 shapely, well-shaped, well-proportioned, well-made, **well-formed,** well-favoured; comely; trim, trig (*old*), neat, spruce, clean, clean-cut, clean-limbed

265 DISTORTION

nouns

1 **distortion,** torsion, twist, twistedness, **contortion, crookedness,** tortuosity; **asymmetry,** unsymmetry, disproportion, lopsidedness, imbalance, irregularity, **deviation; twist,** quirk, turn, screw, wring, wrench, wrest; **warp,** buckle; knot, gnarl; anamorphosis; anamorphism

2 **perversion, corruption,** misdirection, misrepresentation *see 350,* misinterpretation, misconstruction; **falsification** *see 354.9;* **twisting,** false colouring, bending the truth, **spin,** spin control, slanting, straining, torturing; misuse *see 389*

3 **deformity,** deformation, **malformation,** malconformation, monstrosity *see 869.6,* teratology, freakishness, misproportion, **misshapenness,** misshape; **disfigurement, defacement;** mutilation, truncation; humpback, hunchback, crookback, camelback, kyphosis; swayback, lordosis; wryneck, torticollis; clubfoot, talipes, flatfoot, splayfoot; pigeon toes; knock-knee; bow legs, bandy legs; valgus; harelip; cleft palate

4 **grimace, wry face,** wry mouth, mow, rictus, snarl; moue, pout

verbs

5 **to distort, contort,** turn awry; **twist,** turn, screw, wring, wrench, wrest; writhe; **warp,** buckle, crumple; knot, gnarl; **crook,** bend, spring

6 **to pervert, falsify, twist, garble, put a false construction upon, give a spin, give a false colouring,** colour, varnish, slant; put words in someone's mouth; **bias;** misrepresent *see 350.3,* misconstrue, misinterpret, misrender, misdirect; misuse *see 389.4;* send *or* deliver *or* give out the wrong signal *or* message

7 **to deform,** misshape, twist, torture, strain, disproportion; **disfigure, deface;** mutilate, truncate; blemish, mar

8 **to grimace, make a face,** make a wry face *or* mouth, pull a face, **screw up one's face,** make a mug *(informal),* mouth, make a mouth, mop, mow, mop and mow; pout

adjectives

9 distortive, contortive, contortional, torsional
10 **distorted, contorted, warped, twisted, crooked;** tortuous, labyrinthine, buckled, sprung, bent, bowed; cockeyed *(informal),* crazy; crunched, crumpled; unsymmetric, unsymmetrical, asymmetric, asymmetrical, nonsymmetric, nonsymmetrical; irregular, deviative, anamorphous; one-sided, lopsided; askew *see 204.14,* off-centre, left *or* right of centre
11 **falsified, perverted, twisted, garbled,** slanted, doctored, biased, crooked; strained, tortured; misrepresented, misquoted
12 **deformed, malformed, misshapen,** misbegotten, misproportioned, ill-proportioned, ill-made, ill-shaped, **out of shape;** dwarfed, stumpy; bloated; **disfigured,** defaced, blemished, marred; mutilated, truncated; grotesque, **monstrous** *see 869.13;* swaybacked, round-shouldered; bowlegged, bandy-legged,

bandy; knock-kneed; rickety, rachitic; club-footed, talipedic; flatfooted, splayfooted, pigeon-toed, hentoed; pug-nosed, snub-nosed, simous
13 **humpbacked, hunchbacked,** bunchbacked, crookbacked, crookedbacked, camelback, humped, gibbous, kyphotic

266 STRUCTURE

nouns

1 **structure, construction,** architecture, tectonics, architectonics, **frame,** make, **build,** fabric, tissue, warp and woof *or* weft, web, weave, texture, contexture, mould, **shape, pattern, plan,** fashion, arrangement, **organization** *see 806.1;* organism, organic structure, **constitution, composition; makeup,** getup *(informal),* setup; **formation,** conformation, **format; arrangement** *see 807,* configuration; **composition** *see 795;* making, building, creation, production, forging, fashioning, moulding, fabrication, manufacture, shaping, structuring, patterning; anatomy, physique; form *see 262;* **morphology,** science of structure

2 **structure, building, edifice, construction,** construct, erection, establishment, fabric; house; tower, pile, pyramid, skyscraper, ziggurat; prefabrication, prefab, packaged house; air structure, bubble *(informal),* air hall; superstructure; flat-slab construction, post-and-beam construction, steel-cage construction, steel construction

3 **understructure,** understruction, underbuilding, undercroft, crypt; **substructure,** substruction; infrastructure

4 **frame,** framing; braced framing; **framework, skeleton,** fabric, cadre, chassis, shell, armature; lattice, latticework; sash, casement, case, casing; window case *or* frame, doorframe; picture frame

verbs

5 **to construct, build; structure; organize** *see 806.4;* **form** *see 262.7*

adjectives

6 **structural,** formal, morphological, edificial, tectonic, textural; **anatomic,** anatomical, **organic,** organismal, organismic; **structured, patterned,** shaped, formed; **architectural,** architectonic; constructional; superstructural, substructural

267 LENGTH

nouns

1 **length,** longness, lengthiness, overall length; wheelbase; **extent,** extension, **measure, span, reach, stretch; distance** *see 261;* footage, yardage, mileage; infinity *see 822;* perpetuity *see 828;* long time *see 826.4;* linear measures; oblongness; longitude

2 a length, **piece, portion,** part; coil, **strip,** bolt, roll; run

3 **line, strip,** bar; stripe *see 517.6;* string

4 **lengthening, prolongation, elongation,** production, protraction; prolixity, prolixness; **extension,** stretching, stretching *or* spinning *or* stringing out

verbs

5 **to be long, be lengthy, extend,** be prolonged, **stretch; stretch out,** extend out, reach out; stretch oneself, crane, crane one's neck, rubberneck; stand on tiptoes; outstretch, outreach; sprawl, straggle

6 **to lengthen, prolong,** prolongate, **elongate, extend,** produce, **protract,** continue; make prolix; lengthen out, let out, **draw** or drag or stretch or string or spin out; **stretch,** draw, pull

adjectives

7 **long, lengthy;** longish, longsome (*US*); tall; **extensive, far-reaching,** fargoing, far-flung; sesquipedalian, sesquipedal; as long as one's arm, a mile long; **time-consuming,** interminable, without end, no end of or to

8 **lengthened, prolonged,** prolongated, **elongated, extended, protracted; prolix; long-winded; drawn-out,** dragged-out, long-drawn-out, stretched or spun or strung out, straggling; **stretched,** drawn, pulled

9 **oblong,** oblongated, oblongitudinal, **elongated;** rectangular; elliptical

adverbs

10 lengthily, extensively, at length, *in extenso* (*Latin*), *ad infinitum* (*Latin*), ad nauseam

11 **lengthwise** or lengthways, longwise or longways, longitudinally, along, in length, at length; **endwise** or endways, endlong

268 SHORTNESS

nouns

1 **shortness, briefness, brevity; succinctness,** curtness, terseness, summariness, compendiousness, compactness; **conciseness** see 537; **littleness** see 258; transience see 827, short time see 827.3, instantaneousness see 829

2 **stubbiness, stumpiness** (*informal*), **stockiness, fatness** see 257.8, chubbiness, chunkiness (*informal*), blockiness, squatness, squattiness, dumpiness; pudginess, podginess; snubbiness; **lowness** see 274

3 **shortening, abbreviation; reduction; abridgment, condensation,** compression, conspectus, epitome, epitomization, summary, summation, précis, abstract, recapitulation, recap (*informal*), synopsis, encapsulation; **curtailment,** truncation, retrenchment; telescoping; elision, ellipsis, syncope, apocope; foreshortening

4 shortener, cutter, abridger; abstracter, epitomizer or epitomist

5 **shortcut,** cut, cutoff; shortest way; **beeline,** air line (*US*)

verbs

6 **to shorten, abbreviate, cut; reduce** see 260.7; **abridge, condense,** compress, contract, **boil down,** abstract, sum up, summarize, recapitulate, recap (*informal*), wrap up (*informal*), synopsize, epitomize, encapsulate, capsulize; **curtail,** truncate, retrench; bowdlerize; elide, **cut short,** cut down, cut off short, cut back, take in; **dock,** bob, shear, shave, trim, clip,

snub, nip; mow, reap, **crop; prune,** poll, pollard; stunt, check the growth of; telescope; foreshorten

7 **to take a short cut,** short-cut; **cut across,** cut through; **cut a corner,** cut corners; **make a beeline,** take the air line (*US*), go as the crow flies

adjectives

8 **short, brief, abbreviated,** abbreviatory, "short and sweet"—Thomas Lodge; **concise** see 537.6; **curt,** curtal (*old*), curtate, decurtate; **succinct, summary,** synoptic, synoptical, compendious, compact; **little** see 258.10; **low** see 274.7; transient see 827.7, instantaneous see 829.4

9 **shortened, abbreviated; abridged,** compressed, condensed, epitomized, digested, abstracted, capsule, capsulized, encapsulated; bowdlerized; nutshell, pocket; **curtailed,** cut short, **docked,** bobbed, sheared, shaved, trimmed, clipped, snub, snubbed, nipped; mowed, mown, reaped, **cropped; pruned,** polled, pollarded; elided, elliptic, elliptical

10 **stubby,** stubbed, stumpy (*informal*), undergrown, **thickset, stocky,** blocky, **chunky** (*informal*), **fat** see 257.18, **chubby,** tubby (*informal*), dumpy; **squat,** squatty, squattish; **pudgy,** podgy; pug, **pugged;** snub-nosed; turned-up, *retroussé* (*French*)

11 **short-legged,** breviped; **short-winged,** brevipennate

adverbs

12 **shortly, briefly,** summarily, *tout court* (*French*), in brief compass, economically, sparely, curtly, succinctly, in a nutshell, in two or a few words; abbreviatedly, for short; **concisely** see 537.7, compendiously, synoptically

13 **short, abruptly,** suddenly see 829.9, all of a sudden

269 BREADTH, THICKNESS

nouns

1 **breadth, width,** broadness, wideness, fullness, amplitude, latitude, distance across or crosswise or crossways, extent, **span, expanse, spread;** beam

2 **thickness,** the third dimension, distance through, depth; **mass, bulk, body;** corpulence, fatness see 257.8, bodily size; **coarseness,** grossness see 294.2

3 **diameter, bore, calibre; radius,** semidiameter

verbs

4 **to broaden, widen,** deepen; **expand,** extend, extend to the side or sides; **spread** see 259.6, spread out or sidewise or sideways, outspread, outstretch

5 **to thicken,** grow thick, thick; incrassate, inspissate; **fatten** see 259.8

adjectives

6 **broad, wide,** deep; broad-scale, wide-scale, wide-ranging, exhaustive, comprehensive, in-depth, extensive; spread-out, **expansive;** spacious, **roomy;** ample, full; widespread see 863.13; "broad as the world"—James Russell Lowell, "wide as a church door"—Shakespeare

7 broad of beam, broad-beamed, broad-sterned, beamy; broad-ribbed, wide-ribbed, laticostate; broad-toothed, wide-toothed, latidentate

8 thick, three-dimensional; **thickset, heavyset,** thick-bodied, broad-bodied, thick-girthed; **massive, bulky** *see* 257.19, corpulent *see* 257.18; coarse, heavy, gross, crass, fat; full-bodied, full, viscous; **dense** *see* 1043.12; thicknecked, bullnecked

adverbs

9 breadthways *or* breadthwise, in breadth; widthways *or* widthwise; broadways *or* broadwise; broadside, broad side foremost; sideways *or* wise; through, depth-wise *or* ways, in depth

270 NARROWNESS, THINNESS

nouns

1 narrowness, slenderness; closeness, nearness; straitness (*old*), restriction, restrictedness, limitation, strictness, confinement; crowdedness, incapaciousness, incommodiousness; **tightness,** tight squeeze; hair, hair's-breadth *or* hairbreadth; finger's breadth *or* width; narrow gauge

2 narrowing, tapering, taper; **contraction** *see* 260; stricture, constriction, strangulation, coarctation

3 (*narrow place*) narrow, **narrows, strait; bottleneck,** chokepoint; isthmus; channel *see* 239, canal; pass, defile; neck, throat, craw

4 thinness, slenderness, slimness, frailty, slightness, gracility, lightness, airiness, delicacy, flimsiness, wispiness, laciness, paperiness, gauziness, gossameriness, diaphanousness, insubstantiality, ethereality, mistiness, vagueness; light *or* airy texture; **fineness** *see* 294.3; **tenuity, rarity,** subtility, exility, exiguity; **attenuation;** dilution, dilutedness, wateriness *see* 1059.1, weakness

5 leanness, skinniness, fleshlessness, slightness, frailness, twigginess, spareness, meagreness, **scrawniness, gauntness,** lankness, **lankiness,** gawkiness, **boniness,** skin and bones; haggardness, poorness, paperiness, peakedness (*informal*), puniness, "lean and hungry look"—SHAKESPEARE; undernourishment, undernutrition; hatchet face, lantern jaws

6 emaciation, emaceration (*old*), attenuation, atrophy, tabes, marasmus

7 (*comparisons*) paper, wafer, lath, slat, rail, **rake,** splinter, slip, shaving, streak, vein; gruel, soup; shadow, mere shadow; **skeleton**

8 (*thin person*) **slim, lanky;** twiggy, shadow, **skeleton,** stick, walking skeleton, corpse, barebones, bag *or* stack of bones; rattlebones *or* **spindleshanks** *or* spindlelegs (*all informal*), lathlegs *and* sticklegs (*both informal*), **beanpole,** beanstalk, broomstick, clothes pole, stilt

9 reducing, slenderizing, slimming down; weight-watching, calorie-counting

10 thinner, solvent *see* 1062.4

verbs

11 to narrow, constrict, diminish, draw in, go in; restrict, limit, straiten, confine; **taper; contract** *see* 260.7

12 to thin, thin down, thin away *or* off *or* out, down; **rarefy,** subtilize, **attenuate;** dilute, water, water

down, weaken; undernourish; **emaciate,** emacerate (*old*)

13 to slenderize, reduce, reduce *or* lose *or* take off weight, watch one's weight, lose flesh, weight-watch, count calories, diet; slim, **slim down,** thin down

adjectives

14 narrow, slender; narrowish, narrowy; **close,** near; **tight,** strait (*old*), isthmic, isthmian; close-fitting; **restricted,** limited, circumscribed, **confined,** constricted; **cramped;** incapacious, incommodious, crowded; **meagre,** scant, scanty; narrow-gauge *or* narrow-gauged; angustifoliate, angustirostrate, angustiseptal, angustisellate

15 tapered, taper, tapering, cone- *or* wedge-shaped

16 thin, slender, slim, gracile,

"imperially slim"—E A ROBINSON; thin-bodied, thin-set, narrow- *or* wasp-waisted; **svelte,** slinky, sylphlike, willowy; girlish, boyish, gamine; thinnish, slenderish, slimmish; **slight,** slight-made; **frail,** delicate, light, airy, wispy, lacy, gauzy, papery, gossamer, diaphanous, insubstantial, ethereal, misty, vague, flimsy, wafer-thin, **fine; finespun,** thin-spun, fine-drawn, wiredrawn; threadlike, slender as a thread; **tenuous,** subtle, rare, **rarefied;** attenuated, attenuate, **watery, weak,** diluted, watered *or* watered-down, small

17 lean, lean-looking, **skinny** (*informal*), fleshless, lean-fleshed, thin-fleshed, **spare,** meagre, **scrawny,** scraggy, thin-bellied, **gaunt, lank, lanky; gangling** *and* gangly (*both informal*), gawky, **spindling,** spindly; flat-chested, flat (*informal*); **bony, rawboned,** bare-boned, rattleboned (*informal*), skeletal, **mere skin and bones, all skin and bones, nothing but skin and bones;** twiggy, **underweight,** undersized, undernourished, spidery, thin *or* skinny as a rake,

"lean as a rake"—CHAUCER

18 lean-limbed, thin-legged, lath- *or* stick-legged (*informal*), spindle-legged *or* shanked (*informal*), stilt-legged

19 lean- *or* horse- *or* thin-faced, thin-featured, **hatchet-faced;** wizen- *or* weazen-faced; lean- *or* thin-cheeked; lean- *or* lantern-jawed

20 haggard, poor, puny, **peaked** *and* peaky (*both informal*), **pinched;** shrivelled, withered; **wizened,** weazeny; **emaciated,** emaciate, emacerated, **wasted,** attenuated, corpselike, skeletal, hollow-eyed, wraithlike, cadaverous; tabetic, tabid, marantic, marasmic; **starved,** starveling, starved-looking; **undernourished,** underfed, jejune; worn to a shadow,

"worn to the bones"—SHAKESPEARE, "weakened and wasted to skin and bone"—DU BARTAS

21 slenderizing, reducing, slimming

adverbs

22 narrowly, closely, nearly, **barely,** hardly, only just, **by the skin of one's teeth**

23 thinly, thin; meagrely, sparsely, sparingly, scantily

271 FILAMENT

nouns

1 **filament**; **fibre**; **thread**; **strand**, suture; filature; **hair** see 3; artificial fibre, natural fibre, animal fibre; fibril, fibrilla; cilium, ciliolum; **tendril**, cirrus; flagellum; **web**, **cobweb**, gossamer, spider *or* spider's web; denier

2 **cord**, **line**, **rope**, **wire**, braided rope, twisted rope, flattened-strand rope, wire rope, locked-wire rope, **cable**, wire cable; **wool**, **yarn**, spun yarn, skein, hank; **string**, **twine**; braid; **ligament**, ligature, ligation; **tendon**

3 **cordage**, cording, **ropework**, roping; tackle, tack, gear, rigging; ship's ropes

4 **strip**, **strap**, strop; **lace**, thong; **band**, bandage, fillet, fascia, taenia; **belt**, girdle; **ribbon**, ribband; **tape**, tapeline, tape measure; slat, lath, batten, spline, strake, plank; ligule, ligula

5 **spinner**, spinster; silkworm; spider; spinning wheel, spinning jenny, jenny, mule, mule-jenny; spinning frame, bobbin and fly frame; spinneret; rope walk

verbs

6 (*make threads*) **to spin**; **braid**, twist

adjectives

7 **threadlike**, **thready**; **stringy**, ropy, wiry; **hairlike** see 3.24, hairy see 3.25; filamentary, filamentous, filiform, **fibrous**, fibred, fibroid, fibrilliform; ligamental; capillary, capilliform; cirrose, cirrous; funicular, funiculate; flagelliform; taeniate, taeniform; ligulate, ligular; gossamer, gossamery, flossy, silky

272 HEIGHT

nouns

1 **height**, heighth (*informal*), vertical *or* perpendicular distance; **highness**, **tallness**, procerity; **altitude**, **elevation**, ceiling; **loftiness**, sublimity, exaltation; hauteur, toploftiness see 141.1; eminence, prominence; **stature**

2 **height**, **elevation**, eminence, **rise**, raise, **uprise**, lift, rising ground, vantage point *or* ground; **heights**, soaring *or* towering *or* Olympian heights, aerial heights, dizzy *or* dizzying heights; upmost *or* uppermost *or* utmost *or* extreme height; sky, stratosphere, ether *or* aether, heaven *or* heavens; **zenith**, **apex**, **acme**

3 **highlands** see 237.1, highland, upland, uplands, moorland, moors, downs, wold, rolling country

4 **plateau**, tableland, table, mesa, table mountain, bench; **hill**; **ridge**; **mountain**, ben (*Scottish & Irish*), berg (*South African*); **peak**; **mountain range**

5 **watershed**, water parting, **divide**; Great Divide, Continental Divide

6 **tower**; **turret**, *tour* (*French*); campanile, bell tower, belfry,
"topless towers"—Marlowe; **spire**, church spire; **lighthouse**, light tower; cupola, lantern; dome; martello, martello tower; barbican; **derrick**, pole; windmill tower, observation tower, fire tower; **mast**, radio *or* television mast, antenna tower; water tower; standpipe; **spire**, pinnacle; **steeple**, *flèche* (*French*);
minaret; stupa, tope, pagoda; pyramid; pylon; **shaft**, **pillar**, column; pilaster; obelisk; monument; colossus; skyscraper, tower block, high-rise

7 (*tall person*) **longlegs** *and* longshanks (*both informal*); beanpole see 270.8; **giant** see 257.13; six-footer, seven-footer

8 **high tide**, high water, mean high water, flood tide, spring tide, flood; storm surge

9 (*measurement of height*) altimetry, hypsometry, hypsography; altimeter, hypsometer

verbs

10 **to tower**, **soar**, spire,
"buss the clouds"—Shakespeare; **rise**, **uprise**, **ascend**, **mount**, **rear**; stand on tiptoe

11 **to rise above**, **tower above** *or* **over**, clear, overtop, o'ertop, outtop, **top**, **surmount**; **overlook**, look down upon *or* over; **command**, dominate, overarch, overshadow, command a view of; bestride, bestraddle

12 (*become higher*) **to grow**, grow up; uprise, **rise** *or* **shoot up**, mount

13 **to heighten**, elevate see 911.5

adjectives

14 **high**, high-reaching, high-up, **lofty**, **elevated**, altitudinous, uplifted *or* upreared, uprearing, **eminent**, **exalted**, **prominent**, supernal, **superlative**, sublime; **towering**, towery, **soaring**, spiring, aspiring, mounting, ascending; towered, turreted, steepled; **topping**, outtopping *or* overtopping; overarching, **overlooking**, **dominating**; airy, aerial, ethereal; Olympian; monumental, colossal; high as a steeple; topless; high-set, high-pitched; high-rise, multistorey; **haughty** see 141.9, 157.8, toplofty

15 **skyscraping**, **sky-high**, heaven-reaching *or* aspiring, heaven-high, heaven-kissing,
"as high as Heaven and as deep as Hell"—Beaumont and Fletcher; cloud-touching *or* topped *or* capped; **mid-air**

16 **giant** see 257.20, gigantic, colossal, statuesque; **tall**, **lengthy**, long see 267.8; **rangy**, **lanky**, lank, tall as a maypole; **gangling** *and* gangly (*both informal*); **long-legged**, long-limbed, leggy

17 **highland**, upland; hill-dwelling, mountain-dwelling

18 **hilly**, knobby, rolling; **mountainous**, mountained, **alpine**, alpen, alpestrine, alpigene; subalpine; monticuline, monticulous

19 **higher**, superior, greater; **over**, **above**; upper, upmost *or* uppermost, outtopping, overtopping; highest see 198.10

20 altimetric, altimetrical, hypsometrical, hypsographic

adverbs

21 **on high**, high up, high; **aloft**, aloof; **up**, upward, upwards, straight up, to the zenith; **above**, **over**, o'er, **overhead**; above one's head, over head and ears; skyward, airward, in the air, in the clouds; on the peak *or* summit *or* crest *or* pinnacle; upstairs, abovestairs; tiptoe, on tiptoe; on stilts; on the shoulders of; supra, *ubi supra* (*Latin*), hereinabove, hereinbefore

273 SHAFT

nouns

1 **shaft, pole, bar, rod, stick,** scape, scapi–; **stalk, stem;** thill; tongue, wagon tongue; flagstaff; totem pole; Maypole; utility *or* telephone *or* telegraph pole; tent pole

2 **staff,** stave; **cane, stick, walking stick,** handstaff, shillelagh; Malacca cane; baton, marshal's baton, drum-major's baton, conductor's baton; swagger stick, swanking stick; pilgrim's staff, pastoral staff, shepherd's staff, crook; crosier, cross-staff, cross, paterissa; pikestaff, alpenstock; quarterstaff; lituus, thyrsus; **crutch,** crutch-stick

3 **beam, timber,** pole, spar

4 **post, standard, upright,** batten *or* dropper (*NZ*); king post *or* joggle post, queen post, crown post; newel; banister, baluster; balustrade, balustrading; gatepost, swinging *or* hinging post, shutting post; doorpost, jamb, doorjamb; signpost, milepost; stile, mullion; stanchion; hitching post, snubbing post, samson *or* Samson's post; mooring post, bollard

5 **pillar, column,** post, pier, pilaster, stoop; colonnette, columella; caryatid; atlas, atlantes (*plural*); telamon, telamones; **colonnade, arcade,** pilastrade, portico, peristyle

6 **leg,** shank; **stake,** peg; pile, spile, stud; picket, pale, palisade

274 LOWNESS

nouns

1 **lowness, shortness,** squatness, squattiness, stumpiness; **prostration,** supineness, proneness, recumbency, **lying, lying down, reclining;** depression, debasement; subjacency

2 **low tide,** low water, mean low water, dead low water *or* tide, ebb tide, neap tide, neap

3 **lowland, lowlands,** swale (*US*); water meadow

4 **base, bottom** *see* 199, lowest point, nadir; the lowest of the low; lowest *or* underlying level, lower strata, bedrock

verbs

5 **to lie low, squat, crouch,** lay low (*informal*), couch; crawl, grovel, lie prone *or* supine *or* prostrate, hug the earth; lie under, underlie

6 **to lower,** debase, depress *see* 912.4

adjectives

7 **low, unelevated, flat,** low-lying; **short, squat,** squatty, stumpy, runty *see* 258.13; **lowered,** debased, depressed *see* 912.12; demoted; **reduced** *see* 252.10; prone, supine, prostrate *or* prostrated, couchant, crouched, stooped, recumbent; laid low, knocked flat, decked (*informal*); low-set, low-hung; **low-built,** low-sized, low-statured, low-bodied; low-level, low-levelled; neap; knee-high, knee-high to a grasshopper (*informal*)

8 **lower, inferior, under, nether,** subjacent; down; less advanced; earlier; lowest *see* 199.7

adverbs

9 **low,** near the ground; at a low ebb

10 **below,** down below, **under;** infra, hereunder, hereinafter, hereinbelow; thereunder; belowstairs, downstairs, below deck; underfoot; below par, below the mark

prepositions

11 **below, under, underneath, beneath,** neath, at the foot of, at the base of

275 DEPTH

nouns

1 **depth, deepness,** profoundness, profundity; deepdownness, extreme innerness, deep-seatedness, deeprootedness; bottomlessness, plumblessness, fathomlessness; subterraneity, undergroundness; interiority *see* 207

2 **pit, deep, depth, hole,** hollow, **cavity,** shaft, well, **gulf, chasm, abyss,** abysm, yawning abyss; crater; crevasse; valley

3 **depths,** deeps, bowels, bowels of the earth; bottomless pit; infernal pit, hell, nether world, underworld; dark *or* unknown *or* yawning *or* gaping depths, unfathomed deeps; outer *or* deep space

4 **ocean depths, the deep sea, the deep,** trench, deep-sea trench (*see list*), hadal zone, **the deeps, the depths,** bottomless depths, inner space, abyss; bottom waters; abyssal zone, Bassalia *or* Bassalian realm, bathyal zone, pelagic zone; **seabed, bottom of the sea,** ocean bottom *or* floor *or* bed, ground, benthos, benthonic division, benthonic zone; Davy Jones *or* Davy Jones's locker (*informal*)

5 **sounding** *or* **soundings,** fathoming, depth sounding; **echo sounding,** echolocation; **depth indicator;** oceanography, bathometry, bathymetry; fathomage, water (*depth of water*)

6 **draught,** submergence, submersion, sinkage, **displacement**

7 **deepening, lowering, depression;** sinking, sinkage; excavation, digging, mining, tunnelling; drilling, probing

verbs

8 **to deepen, lower, depress, sink;** countersink; **dig,** excavate, tunnel, mine, **drill;** pierce to the depths; **dive** *see* 367.6

9 **to sound, take soundings,** make a sounding, heave *or* cast *or* sling the lead, **fathom, plumb,** plumbline, plumb the depths

adjectives

10 **deep, profound,** deep-down; deepish; **deep-going,** deep-lying, deep-reaching; **deep-set,** deep-laid; deep-sunk, deep-sunken, deep-sinking; **deep-seated, deep-rooted,** deep-fixed, deep-settled; deep-cut, deep-engraven; knee-deep, ankle-deep

11 **abysmal,** abyssal, yawning, cavernous, gaping, plunging; **bottomless,** without bottom, soundless, unsounded, plumbless, **fathomless,** unfathomed, unfathomable; deep as a well, deep as the sea *or* ocean, deep as hell

12 **underground, subterranean,** subterraneous, buried, deep-buried

13 underwater, subaqueous; **submarine, undersea;** submerged, submersed, immersed, buried, engulfed, inundated, flooded, drowned, sunken

14 deep-sea, deep-water, blue-water; oceanographic, bathyal; benthic, benthal, benthonic; abyssal, Bassalian; bathyorographic, bathyorographical, bathymetric, bathymetrical; benthopelagic, bathypelagic

15 deepest, deepmost, profoundest; bedrock, rock-bottom

adverbs

16 deep; beyond one's depth, out of one's depth; over one's head, over head and ears; at bottom, at the core, at rock bottom

17 deep-sea trenches and deeps

Aleutian Trench 29,194 feet	Trench, Bartholomew Deep 26,160 feet
Cayman Trench 24,576 feet	Philippine Trench, Galathea Deep 34,578 feet
Diamantina Fracture, Ob Trench 22,553 feet	Puerto Rico Trench, Milwaukee Deep 27,498 feet
Guatemala Trench 21,228 feet	
Japan Trench, Ramapo Deep 34,038 feet	Romanche Trench 25,050 feet
Java *or* Sunda Trench, Planet Deep 25,344 feet	Solomon Trench 29,988 feet
Kuril-Kamchatka Trench 34,062 feet	South Sandwich Trench, Meteor Deep 27,112 feet
Mariana Trench, Challenger Deep 35,760 feet	Tonga-Kermadec Trench, Vityaz II *or* Tonga Deep 35,589 feet
Nansei Shoto *or* Ryukyu Trench 24,630 feet	Vityaz Trench 20,142 feet
Peru-Chile *or* Atacama	Yap Trench 26,280 feet

276 SHALLOWNESS

nouns

1 shallowness, depthlessness; shoalness, shoaliness, no water, no depth; **superficiality,** exteriority, triviality, **cursoriness,** slightness; insufficiency *see* 991; a lick and a promise *and* once-over-lightly (*both informal*); **surface,** superficies, skin, rind, epidermis; veneer, gloss; pinprick, scratch, mere scratch

2 shoal, shallow, shallows, shallow *or* shoal water, flat, shelf; **bank, bar,** sandbank, sandbar, tombolo; **reef,** coral reef; ford; wetlands, tidal flats

verbs

3 to shoal, shallow; fill in *or* up, silt up

4 to scratch the surface, touch upon, hardly touch, skim, skim over, skim *or* graze the surface, give a lick and a promise *and* give it once over lightly (*both informal*), apply a band-aid

adjectives

5 shallow, shoal, **depthless,** not deep, unprofound; **surface,** on *or* near the surface, merely surface; **superficial, cursory,** slight, light, cosmetic, merely cosmetic, thin, jejune, trivial; **skin-deep,** epidermal; ankle-deep, knee-deep; shallow-rooted, shallow-

rooting; shallow-draught *or* bottomed *or* hulled; shallow-sea

6 shoaly, shelfy; reefy; unnavigable

277 STRAIGHTNESS

nouns

1 straightness, directness, unswervingness, lineality, **linearity,** rectilinearity; verticalness *see* 200; flatness, horizontalness *see* 201

2 straight line, straight, right line, direct line; straight course *or* stretch, straightaway; **beeline,** air line (*US*); **shortcut** *see* 268.5; great-circle course; streamline; edge, side, diagonal, secant, transversal, chord, tangent, perpendicular, normal, segment, directrix, diameter, axis, radius, vector, radius vector (*all mathematics*)

3 straightedge, rule, ruler; square, T square, triangle

verbs

4 to be straight, have no turning *or* turns; arrow; go straight, make a beeline

5 to straighten, set *or* put straight, rectify, make right *or* good, square away; **unbend,** unkink, uncurl, unsnarl, disentangle *see* 797.5; straighten up, square up; straighten out, extend; flatten, smooth *see* 201.6

adjectives

6 straight; straight-lined, dead straight, straight as an edge *or* a ruler, ruler-straight, even, right, true, straight as an arrow, arrowlike; **rectilinear,** rectilineal; **linear,** lineal, in a line; **direct, undeviating, unswerving,** unbending, undeflected; **unbent, unbowed,** unturned, uncurved, undistorted; **uninterrupted, unbroken;** straight-side, straight-front, straight-cut; upright, vertical *see* 200.11; flat, level, smooth, horizontal *see* 201.7

adverbs

7 straight, straightly, on the straight, unswervingly, undeviatingly, **directly;** straight to the mark; on the button *and* on the nose *and* on the beam *and* on the money *and* in the groove (*all informal*)

278 ANGULARITY

nouns

1 angularity, angularness, crookedness, hookedness; squareness, orthogonality, right-angledness, rectangularity; flection, flexure

2 angle, point, bight; vertex, apex *see* 198.2; **corner,** quoin, coin, nook; **crook, hook,** crotchet; **bend,** curve, swerve, veer, inflection, deflection; ell, L; cant; furcation, bifurcation, fork *see* 171.4; zigzag, zig, zag; chevron; elbow, knee, dogleg (*informal*); crank

3 (*angular measurement*) goniometry; trigonometry

4 (*instruments*) goniometer, radiogoniometer; pantometer, clinometer, graphometer, astrolabe; azimuth compass, azimuth circle; theodolite, transit theodolite, transit, transit instrument, transit circle; sextant, quadrant; bevel, bevel square; protractor, bevel protractor

verbs

5 to **angle, crook, hook, bend,** elbow; crank; angle
off *or* away, curve, swerve, veer, veer off, slant off,
go off on a tangent; furcate, bifurcate, branch, fork
see 171.7; zigzag, zig, zag

adjectives

6 **angular;** cornered, **crooked, hooked, bent,** flexed,
flexural; akimbo; knee-shaped, geniculate,
geniculated, doglegged (*informal*); crotched, Y-
shaped, V-shaped; furcate, furcal, forked *see* 171.10;
sharp-cornered, **sharp, pointed;** zigzag, jagged,
serrate, sawtooth *or* saw-toothed

7 **right-angled, rectangular,** right-angular, right-
angle; **orthogonal,** orthodiagonal, orthometric;
perpendicular, normal

8 **triangular, trilateral,** trigonal, oxygonal, deltoid;
wedgeshaped, cuneiform, cuneate, cuneated

9 **quadrangular, quadrilateral,** quadrate,
quadriform; **rectangular, square;** foursquare,
orthogonal; tetragonal, tetrahedral; **oblong;** trapezoid
or trapezoidal, rhombic *or* rhombal, rhomboid *or*
rhomboidal; **cubic** *or* **cubical,** cubiform, cuboid,
cube-shaped, cubed, diced; rhombohedral,
trapezohedral

10 pentagonal, hexagonal, heptagonal, octagonal,
decagonal, dodecagonal, etc; pentahedral, hexahedral,
octahedral, dodecahedral, icosahedral, etc

11 multilateral, multiangular, polygonal; polyhedral,
pyramidal, pyramidic *or* pyramidal; prismatic,
prismoid

279 CURVATURE

nouns

1 **curvature,** curving, curvation, arcing; incurvature,
incurvation; excurvature, excurvation; decurvature,
decurvation; recurvature, recurvity, recurvation;
rondure; **arching, vaulting,** arcuation,
concameration; aduncity, aquilinity, crookedness,
hookedness; sinuosity, sinuousness, tortuosity,
tortuousness; circularity *see* 280; convolution *see* 281;
rotundity *see* 282; convexity *see* 283; concavity *see*
284; curvaceousness

2 **curve,** sinus; **bow, arc; crook, hook;** parabola,
hyperbola, witch of Agnesi; ellipse; caustic,
catacaustic, diacaustic; catenary, festoon, swag;
conchoid; lituus; tracery; circle *see* 280.2; curl *see*
281.2

3 **bend,** bending; **bow,** bowing, oxbow; Cupid's bow;
turn, turning, sweep, meander, hairpin turn *or* bend,
S-bend, U-turn; **flexure,** flex, **flection,** conflexure,
inflection, deflection; reflection *or* reflexion;
geanticline, geosyncline

4 **arch, span, vault,** vaulting, concameration, camber;
ogive; apse; **dome,** cupola, geodesic dome, igloo,
concha; cove; arched roof, ceilinged roof; **arcade,**
archway, arcature; voussoir, keystone, skewback

5 **crescent, semicircle,** scythe, sickle, meniscus;
crescent moon, half-moon; lunula, lunule; horseshoe

verbs

6 to **curve, turn,** arc, sweep; **crook, hook,** loop;
incurve, incurvate; recurve, decurve, bend back,

retroflex; sag, swag (*informal*); **bend,** flex; deflect,
inflect; reflect, reflex; **bow,** embow; **arch,** vault;
dome; **hump,** hunch; wind, curl *see* 281.5; round *see*
282.6

adjectives

7 **curved,** curve, curvate, curvated, **curving,** curvy,
curvaceous (*informal*), curvesome, curviform;
curvilinear, curvilineal; wavy, undulant, billowy,
billowing; sinuous, tortuous, serpentine, mazy,
labyrinthine, meandering; **bent,** flexed, flexural;
incurved, incurving, incurvate, incurvated; recurved,
recurving, recurvate, recurvated; geosynclinal,
geanticlinal

8 **hooked, crooked, aquiline,** aduncous; **hook-**
shaped, hooklike, uncinate, unciform; hamulate,
hamate, hamiform; claw-like, unguiform, down-
curving; **hook-nosed,** beak-nosed, parrot-nosed,
aquiline-nosed, Roman-nosed, crooknosed,
crookbilled; **beaked,** billed; **beak-shaped,** beak-like;
bill-shaped, bill-like; rostrate, rostriform, rhamphoid

9 turned-up, upcurving, upsweeping, *retroussé* (*French*)

10 **bowed,** embowed, bandy; bowlike, bow-shaped,
oxbow, Cupid's-bow; **convex, concave** *see* 284.16,
convexo-concave, concavo-convex; arcuate, arcuated,
arcual, arciform, arclike; **arched,** vaulted; **humped,**
hunched, humpy, hunchy; gibbous, gibbose;
humpbacked *see* 265.13

11 **crescent-shaped,** crescentlike, crescent, crescentic,
crescentiform; meniscoid(al), menisciform; S-shaped,
ess, S, sigmoid; **semicircular,** semilunar; horn-
shaped, hornlike, horned, corniform; bicorn, two-
horned; sickle-shaped, sickle-like, falcate, falciform;
moon-shaped, moonlike, lunar, lunate, lunular,
luniform

12 lens-shaped, lenticular, lentiform

13 parabolic, parabolical, paraboloid, saucer-shaped;
elliptic, elliptical, ellipsoid; bell-shaped, bell-like,
campanular, campanulate, campaniform

14 pear-shaped, pearlike, pyriform

15 heart-shaped, heartlike; cordate, cardioid, cordiform

16 kidney-shaped, kidneylike, reniform

17 turnip-shaped, turniplike, napiform

18 shell-shaped, shell-like; conchate, conchiform

19 shield-shaped, shieldlike, peltate; scutate, scutiform;
clypeate, clypeiform

20 helmet-shaped, helmetlike, galeiform, cassideous

280 CIRCULARITY

nouns

1 **circularity, roundness,** ring-shape, ringliness,
annularity; annulation

2 **circle,** circus, rondure, **ring,** annulus, O;
circumference, radius, **round,** roundel, rondelle;
cycle, circuit; orbit *see* 1070.16; closed circle *or* arc;
vicious circle, eternal return; magic circle, charmed
circle, fairy ring; logical circle, circular reasoning,
petitio principii; **wheel** *see* 914.4; **disc,** discus,
saucer; **loop,** looplet; noose, lasso; crown, diadem,
coronet, corona; garland, chaplet, wreath; halo, glory,
areola, aureole; annular muscle, sphincter

3 (*thing encircling*) **band, belt, cincture,** cingulum, **girdle, girth,** girt, zone, fascia, fillet; collar, collarband, neckband; necktie; necklace, bracelet, bangle, armlet, torque, wristlet, wristband, anklet; ring, earring, sleeper, nose ring, finger ring; hoop; quoit; zodiac, ecliptic, equator, great circle

4 rim, felly; **tyre**

5 circlet, **ringlet,** roundlet, annulet, eye, **eyelet,** grommet

6 oval, ovule, ovoid; ellipse

7 cycloid; epicycloid, epicycle; hypocycloid; lemniscate; cardioid; Lissajous figure

8 **semicircle,** half circle, hemicycle; crescent *see* 279.5; quadrant, sextant, sector

9 (*music and poetry*) **round,** canon; rondo, rondino, rondeau, rondelet

verbs

10 to circle, round; orbit; **encircle** *see* 209.7, surround, encompass, girdle

adjectives

11 **circular, round,** rounded, circinate, annular, annulate, ring-shaped, ringlike; annulose; disclike, discoid; cyclic, cyclical, cycloid, cycloidal; epicyclic; planetary; coronal, crownlike

12 oval, ovate, ovoid, oviform, egg-shaped, obovate

281 CONVOLUTION
complex curvature

nouns

1 **convolution,** involution, circumvolution, **winding, twisting, turning; meander, meandering;** crinkle, crinkling; circuitousness, circumlocution, circumbendibus, circumambages, ambagiousness, ambages; Byzantinism; tortuousness, tortuosity; torsion, intorsion; sinuousness, **sinuosity,** sinuation, slinkiness; anfractuosity; snakiness; flexuousness, flexuosity; undulation, wave, waving; rivulation; **complexity** *see* 798

2 coil, whorl, roll, **curl,** curlicue, ringlet, pigtail, **spiral,** helix, volute, volution, involute, evolute, gyre, scroll; **kink, twist, twirl;** screw, corkscrew; tendril, cirrus; whirl, swirl, vortex

3 curler, roller, curling tongs, curling iron; curlpaper, papillote

verbs

4 to convolve, **wind,** twine, **twirl, twist, turn, twist and turn, meander,** crinkle; serpentine, snake, slink, worm; screw, corkscrew; whirl, swirl; whorl; scallop; wring; intort; contort

5 **to curl, coil;** crisp, kink, crimp

adjectives

6 **convolutional, winding, twisting,** twisty, **turning; meandering,** meandrous, mazy, labyrinthine; **serpentine,** snaky, anfractuous; roundabout, circuitous, ambagious, circumlocutory; labyrinthine; Byzantine; **sinuous,** sinuose, sinuate; **tortuous,** torsional; tortile; flexular, flexuous, flexuose; involutional, involute, involuted; rivose, rivulose; sigmoidal; wreathy, wreathlike; ruffled, whorled

7 **coiled,** tortile, **snakelike, snaky,** snake-shaped, **serpentine,** serpentlike, serpentiform; anguine (*old*), anguiform; eellike, eelshaped, anguilliform; wormlike, vermiform, lumbricoid, lumbricine, lumbriciform

8 **spiral,** spiroid, volute, voluted; **helical,** helicoid, helicoidal; anfractuous; screw-shaped, corkscrew, corkscrewy; verticillate, whorled, scrolled; cochlear, cochleate; turbinal, turbinate

9 **curly, curled; kinky,** kinked; **frizzly,** frizzy, frizzled, frizzed; crisp, crispy, crisped

10 **wavy, undulant,** undulatory, undulative, undulating, undulate, undulated; **billowy,** billowing, surgy, rolling

adverbs

11 **windingly, twistingly,** sinuously, tortuously, serpentinely, meanderingly, meandrously; in waves; wavily; **in and out,** round and round

282 SPHERICITY, ROTUNDITY

nouns

1 **sphericity, rotundity, roundness,** ball-likeness, rotundness, orbicularness, orbicularity, orbiculation, orblikeness, **sphericalness,** sphericality, globularity, globularness, globosity, globoseness; spheroidity, spheroidicity; belly; cylindricality; convexity *see* 283

2 **sphere; ball,** orb, orbit, **globe,** rondure; geoid; spheroid, globoid, ellipsoid, oblate spheroid, prolate spheroid; spherule, globule, globelet, orblet; glomerulus; **pellet;** boll; **bulb,** bulbil *or* bulbel, bulblet; knob, knot; **gob,** glob (*informal*), blob, gobbet; pill, bolus; **balloon,** bladder, bubble

3 **drop,** droplet; dewdrop, raindrop, teardrop; bead, pearl

4 **cylinder,** cylindroid, pillar, column; barrel, drum, cask, pin; pipe, tube; roll, rouleau, roller, rolling pin; bole, trunk

5 **cone,** conoid, conelet; complex cone, cone of a complex; funnel; ice-cream cone, cornet; pine cone; cop

verbs

6 **to round; round out, fill out;** cone

7 **to ball, snowball;** sphere, spherify, globe, conglobulate; roll; bead; balloon, mushroom

adjectives

8 **rotund, round,** rounded, rounded out, round as a ball; bellied, bellylike; convex, bulging

9 **spherical,** sphereic, spheriform, spherelike, sphere-shaped; **globular, global,** globed, globose, globate, globelike, globe-shaped; orbicular, orbiculate, orbiculated, orbed, orb, orby (*old*), orblike; spheroid, spheroidal, globoid, ellipsoid, ellipsoidal; hemispheric, hemispherical; **bulbous,** bulblike, bulging; ovoid, obovoid

10 **beady,** beaded, bead-shaped, bead-like

11 **cylindric, cylindrical,** cylindroid, cylindroidal; **columnar,** columnal, columned, columelliform; **tubular,** tube-shaped, tube-like; barrel-shaped, drum-shaped

12 **conical,** conic, coned, cone-shaped, conelike; conoid, conoidal; spheroconic; funnel–shaped, funnellike, funnelled, funnelform, infundibuliform, infundibular

283 CONVEXITY, PROTUBERANCE

nouns

1 **convexity**, convexness, convexedness; excurvature, excurvation; camber; gibbousness, gibbosity; tuberousness, tuberosity; **bulging**, bellying, puffing, puffing out

2 **protuberance** *or* protuberancy, **projection**, **protrusion**, **extrusion**; prominence, eminence, salience, boldness, **bulging**, bellying; gibbousness, gibbosity; excrescence *or* excrescency; tuberousness, tuberosity, puffiness; salient; relief, high relief, *alto-rilievo* (*Italian*), low relief, bas-relief, *basso-rilievo* (*Italian*), embossment

3 **bulge**, bilge, bow, convex; **bump**; cahot (*Canadian*); sleeping policeman, speed bump; hill, mountain; **hump**, hunch; **lump**, clump, bunch, blob; nubble, nub, nubbin (*US & Canadian*); **mole**, naevus; **wart**, papilloma, verruca; **knob**, boss, bulla, button, bulb; stud, jog, joggle, peg, dowel; flange, lip; tab, ear, flap, loop, ring, handle; **knot**, knur, knurl, gnarl, burl, burr, gall; **ridge**, rib, costi–, chine, spine, shoulder; welt, wale; blister, bleb, vesicle (*anatomy*), blain; bubble; condyle; bubo; tubercle *or* tubercule

4 **swelling**, swollenness, oedema; **rising, lump, bump**, pimple; pock, furuncle, boil, carbuncle; corn; pustule; dilation, dilatation; turgidity, turgescence *or* turgescency, tumescence, intumescence; tumour, tumidity, tumefaction; wen, cyst, sebaceous cyst; bunion; distension *see* 259.2

5 **node**, nodule, nodulus, nodulation, nodosity

6 **breast, bosom, bust, chest**, crop, brisket; thorax; pigeon chest; **breasts**, dugs, teats; **nipple**, papilla, pap, mamilla, *mamelon* and *téton* (*both French*); mammillation, mamelonation; mammary gland, udder, bag

7 (*informal terms*) **tits**, titties, **boobs**, boobies, bubbies, diddies (*Scottish & Irish*), jugs, **knockers**, bristols, *nénés* (*French*), hooters

8 **nose**, olfactory organ; **snout**, snoot (*informal*), snitch (*informal*), nozzle (*informal*), **muzzle**; **proboscis**, antlia, **trunk**; **beak**, rostrum; nib, neb; beezer *and* conk *and* hooter (*all informal*); muffle, rhinarium; nostrils, nares

9 (*point of land*) **point**, hook, spur, **cape**, tongue, bill; **promontory**, foreland, **headland**, head, mull (*Scottish*); naze, ness; **peninsula**, chersonese; **delta**; **spit**, sandspit; **reef**, coral reef; breakwater *see* 900.4

verbs

10 **to protrude**, protuberate, project, extrude; **stick out**, jut out, poke out, stand out, shoot out; **stick up**, bristle up, start up, cock up, shoot up

11 **to bulge**, bilge, **belly**, bag, balloon, **pouch**; pout; **goggle**, bug (*informal*), pop; **swell, swell up, dilate, distend**, billow; swell out, **belly out**, round out

12 **to emboss, boss**, chase, raise; ridge

adjectives

13 **convex**, convexed; excurved, excurvate, excurvated; **bowed**, bowed-out, out-bowed, arched *see* 279.10; gibbous, gibbose; humped *see* 279.10; rotund *see* 282.8

14 **protruding, protrusive**, protrudent; protrusile, protrusible; **protuberant**, protuberating; **projecting, extruding**, jutting, outstanding; goofy (*informal*); prominent, eminent, salient, bold; prognathous; excrescent, excrescential; protrusile, emissile

15 **bulging, swelling**, distended, bloated, potbellied, bellying, pouching; bagging, baggy; rounded, hillocky, hummocky, moutonnée; billowing, billowy, bosomy, ballooning, pneumatic; **bumpy**, bumped; bunchy, bunched; **bulbous**, bulbose; warty, verrucose, verrucated

16 **bulged, bulgy**; swollen *see* 259.13, turgid, tumid, turgescent, tumescent, tumorous; bellied, ventricose; pouched; goggled, goggle; exophthalmic, bug-eyed (*informal*), popeyed (*informal*)

17 **studded, knobbed, knobby**, knoblike, nubbled, nubby, nubbly, torose; **knotty, knotted; gnarled**, knurled, knurly, burled, gnarly; noded, nodal, nodiform; noduled, nodular, nodulated; bubonic; tuberculous, tubercular; tuberous, tuberose

18 **in relief**, in bold *or* high relief, bold, raised, *repoussé* (*French*); chased, bossed, embossed, bossy

19 **pectoral**, chest, thoracic; pigeon-chested; mammary, mamillary, mammiform; mammalian, mammate; papillary, papillose, papulous; breasted, bosomed, chested; teated, titted (*informal*), nippled; busty, bosomy, chesty

20 **peninsular**; deltaic, deltal

284 CONCAVITY

nouns

1 **concavity**, hollowness; incurvature, incurvation; depression, impression; emptiness *see* 222.2

2 **cavity**, concavity, concave; **hollow**, hollow shell, shell; **hole, pit, depression, dip**, sink, fold; scoop, pocket; **basin**, trough, **bowl**, punch bowl, cup, container *see* 195; **crater**; antrum; lacuna; alveola, alveolus, alveolation; vug *or* vugg *or* vugh; crypt; armpit; socket

3 **pothole**, sinkhole *or* swallow hole, pitchhole, chuckhole, **mudhole**, rut *see* 290.1

4 **pit, well, shaft**, sump; **chasm, gulf, abyss**, abysm; **excavation**, dig, diggings, workings; mine, quarry

5 **cave, cavern**, cove (*Scottish*), **hole**, grotto, grot, antre, subterrane; lair *see* 228.26; **tunnel, burrow**, warren; subway; bunker, foxhole, dugout, *abri* (*French*); sewer

6 **indentation**, indent, indention, indenture, **dent**, dint; gouge, **furrow** *see* 290; sunken part *or* place, **dimple**; **pit**, pock, pockmark; impression, impress; imprint, print; alveolus, alveolation; honeycomb, Swiss cheese; notch *see* 289

7 **recess**, recession, **niche, nook**, inglenook, corner; cove, alcove; bay; pitchhole

8 (*hollow in the side of a mountain*) combe, cwm, cirque, corrie, bench (*NZ*)

9 valley, vale, dale, dell, dingle; **glen,** bottom, bottom glade, intervale, strath (*Scottish*), gill, wadi, grove; trench, trough, lunar rill; gap, pass, ravine

10 excavator, **digger;** sapper; **miner;** tunneller, sandhog *and* groundhog (*both US & Canadian informal*), navvy; driller; JCB, steam shovel; dredge, dredger

11 excavation, digging; mining; indentation, engraving

verbs

12 (*be concave*) **to sink, dish,** cup, bowl, hollow; retreat, retire; incurve

13 to hollow, hollow out, concave, **dish,** cup, bowl; cave, cave in

14 to indent, dent, dint, **depress,** press in, stamp, tamp, punch, punch in, impress, imprint; **pit;** pock, pockmark; dimple; **recess,** set back; set in; notch *see* 289.4; engrave

15 to excavate, **dig,** dig out, **scoop,** scoop out, **gouge,** gouge out, grub, shovel, spade, delve, scrape, scratch, scrabble; dredge; **trench,** trough, furrow, groove; **tunnel, burrow;** drive, sink, lower; **mine,** sap; quarry; drill, bore

adjectives

16 concave, concaved, **incurved,** incurving, incurvate; **sunk,** sunken; retreating, recessed, retiring; **hollow,** hollowed, empty; palm-shaped; dish-shaped, dished, dishing, dishlike, bowl-shaped; bowllike, crater-shaped, craterlike, saucer-shaped; spoon-like; **cupped,** cup-shaped, scyphate; funnel-shaped, infundibular, infundibuliform; funnel-chested, funnel-breasted; boat-shaped, boatlike, navicular, naviform, cymbiform, scaphoid; **cavernous,** cavelike

17 indented, dented, depressed; **dimpled; pitted;** cratered; pocked, pockmarked; honeycombed, alveolar, alveolate, faveolate; **notched** *see* 289.5; engraved

285 SHARPNESS

nouns

1 sharpness, keenness, edge; acuteness, acuity; pointedness, acumination; thorniness, prickliness, spinosity; mucronation; cornification; acridity *see* 68.1

2 (*sharp edge*) edge, cutting edge, honed edge, **knife-edge, razor-edge;** featheredge, fine edge; edge tool; weapon *see* 462.21-26

3 point, tip, cusp; acumination, mucro; **nib,** neb; needle; hypodermic needle, hypodermic syringe; **drill,** borer, auger, bit; **prick, prickle;** sting, acus *or* aculeus; **tooth** *see* 2.8

4 (*pointed projection*) **projection,** spur, jag, **snag,** snaggle; **horn,** antler; cornicle; crag, peak, arête; spire, steeple, flèche; **cog, sprocket,** ratchet; sawtooth; harrow, rake; comb, pecten

5 thorn, bramble, brier, nettle, burr, prickle, sticker (*informal*), bindi-eye (*Australian*); **spike,** spikelet, spicule, spiculum; **spine;** bristle; quill; **needle,** pine needle; **thistle,** catchweed, cleavers, goose grass, sticky willie, cactus; yucca, Adam's-needle, Spanish bayonet

verbs

6 to come *or* taper to a point, acuminate; prick, sting, stick, bite; be keen, have an edge, cut; bristle with

7 to sharpen, edge, acuminate, aculeate, spiculate, taper; **whet, hone,** oilstone, file, grind; strop, strap; set, reset; **point;** barb, spur, file to a point

adjectives

8 **sharp, keen, edged, acute,** fine, **cutting,** knifelike; sharp-edged, keen-edged, razor-edged, razor-sharp, knife-edged, sharp as broken glass; featheredged, fine-edged; acrid *see* 68.6; two-edged, double-edged; sharp as a razor *or* needle *or* tack, "sharp as a two-edged sword"—BIBLE, "sharper than a serpent's tooth"—SHAKESPEARE; sharpened, set

9 **pointed,** pointy, acuminate, acuate, aculeate, aculeated, acute, unbated; tapered, tapering; cusped, cuspate, cuspated, cuspidal, cuspidate, cuspidated; **sharp-pointed; needlelike,** needle-sharp, needle-pointed, needly, acicular, aculeiform; mucronate, mucronated; toothed; **spiked,** spiky, spiculate; **barbed, tined, pronged; horned,** horny, cornuted, corniculate, cornified, ceratoid; **spined, spiny,** spinous, hispid, acanthoid, acanthous; "like quills upon the fretful porpentine"—SHAKESPEARE

10 **prickly,** pricky (*informal*), muricate, echinate, acanaceous, aculeolate; pricking, stinging; **thorny,** brambly, briery, thistly, nettly, burry; bristly

11 **arrowlike,** arrowy, arrowheaded; sagittal, sagittate, sagittiform

12 **spearlike,** hastate; lancelike, lanciform, lanceolate, lanceolar; **spindle-shaped,** fusiform

13 **swordlike,** gladiate, ensate, ensiform

14 **toothlike,** dentiform, dentoid, odontoid; **toothed,** toothy, **fanged, tusked;** snaggle-toothed, snaggled

15 **star-shaped, starlike,** star-pointed

286 BLUNTNESS

nouns

1 **bluntness, dullness,** unsharpness, obtuseness, obtundity; bluffness; abruptness; flatness; toothlessness, lack of bite *or* incisiveness

verbs

2 to blunt, dull, disedge, retund, obtund, **take the edge off;** turn, turn the edge *or* point of; weaken, repress; draw the teeth *or* fangs; bate

adjectives

3 **blunt, dull,** obtuse, obtundent; bluntish, dullish; **unsharp,** unsharpened; **unedged,** edgeless; rounded, faired, smoothed, streamlined; **unpointed,** pointless; blunted, dulled; blunt-edged, dull-edged; blunt-pointed, dull-pointed, blunt-ended; bluff, abrupt

4 **toothless,** teethless, edentate, edental, biteless

287 SMOOTHNESS

nouns

1 **smoothness, flatness, levelness,** evenness, uniformity, regularity; **sleekness,** glossiness; **slickness,** slipperiness, lubricity, oiliness, greasiness, frictionlessness; silkiness, satininess, velvetiness; glabrousness, glabriety; downiness; suavity *see* 504.5

2 **polish, gloss, glaze,** burnish, **shine, lustre,** finish; **patina**

3 (*smooth surface*) smooth, **plane, level, flat;** tennis court, bowling green *or* alley, billiard table *or* ball; slide; glass, ice; marble, alabaster, ivory; silk, satin, velvet, a peach, a baby's bottom (*informal*); mahogany

4 **smoother;** roller, lawn-roller; sleeker, slicker; **polish,** burnish; **abrasive,** abrader, abradant; lubricant

verbs

5 **to smooth, flatten, plane,** planish, **level,** even, equalize; **dress,** dub, dab; smooth down *or* out, lay; plaster, plaster down; roll, roll smooth; harrow, drag; grade; mow, shave; lubricate, oil, grease

6 **to press,** hot-press, **iron, mangle,** calender; roll

7 **to polish, shine, burnish, furbish,** sleek, slick, slick down, gloss, glaze, glance, lustre; **rub,** scour, **buff;** wax, varnish; finish

8 **to grind, file, sand, scrape,** sandpaper, emery, pumice; abrade; sandblast

adjectives

9 **smooth;** smooth-textured *or* surfaced, **even, level, plane, flat,** regular, uniform, **unbroken;** unrough, unroughened, unruffled, unwrinkled; glabrous, glabrate, glabrescent; downy; silky, satiny, velvety, smooth as silk *or* satin *or* velvet, smooth as a baby's bottom *or* billiard ball (*informal*); leiotrichous, lissotrichous; smooth-shaven *see* 6.17; suave *see* 504.18

10 **sleek, slick, glossy,** shiny, gleaming; silky, silken, satiny, velvety; **polished,** burnished, furbished; buffed, rubbed, finished; varnished, lacquered, shellacked, glazed, *glacé* (*French*); **glassy,** smooth as glass

11 **slippery,** slippy, **slick,** slithery *and* sliddery (*both informal*), slippery as an eel; lubricious, lubric, oily, oleaginous, greasy, buttery, soaped; lubricated, oiled, greased

adverbs

12 **smoothly, evenly, regularly, uniformly; like clockwork,** on wheels

288 ROUGHNESS

nouns

1 **roughness, unsmoothness, unevenness,** irregularity, ununiformity, nonuniformity *see* 781, inequality; **bumpiness,** pockedness, pockiness, holeyness; **abrasiveness, abrasion,** harshness, asperity; **ruggedness,** rugosity; **jaggedness,** raggedness, cragginess, scraggliness; joltiness, bumpiness; rough air, turbulence; choppiness; tooth; granulation; hispidity, bristliness, spininess, thorniness; nubbiness, nubbliness

2 (*rough surface*) **rough,** broken ground; broken water, chop, lop; **corrugation,** ripple, washboard; washboard *or* corduroy road, corduroy; pebble dash;

gooseflesh, goose bumps, goose pimples, horripilation; sandpaper

3 **bristle,** barb, barbel, striga, setule, setula, seta; **stubble;** whisker

verbs

4 **to roughen,** rough, rough up, harshen; coarsen; granulate; gnarl, knob, stud, boss; pimple, horripilate

5 **to ruffle,** wrinkle, corrugate, crinkle, crumple, **rumple; bristle; rub the wrong way, go against the grain,** set on edge

adjectives

6 **rough, unsmooth; uneven,** ununiform, unlevel, inequal, **broken,** irregular, textured; jolty, **bumpy,** rutty, rutted, pitted, pocky, potholed; horripilant, pimply; **corrugated,** ripply, wimpled; **choppy;** ruffled, unkempt; **shaggy,** shagged; **coarse,** rank, unrefined; unpolished; rough-grained, coarse-grained, cross-grained; grainy, granulated; rough-hewn, rough-cast; homespun, linsey-woolsey

7 **rugged,** ragged, harsh; rugose, rugous, wrinkled, crinkled, crumpled, corrugated; **scratchy, abrasive,** rough as a cob (*informal*); **jagged,** jaggy, **snaggy,** snagged, snaggled; scraggy, scragged, scraggly; sawtooth, sawtoothed, serrate, serrated; **craggy,** cragged; **rocky,** gravelly, stony; rockbound, ironbound

8 **gnarled,** gnarly; **knurled,** knurly; **knotted,** knotty, knobbly, nodose, nodular, studded, lumpy

9 **bristly, bristling,** bristled, hispid, hirsute, whiskery; barbellate, whiskered, glochidiate, setaceous, setous, setose; strigal, strigose, strigate, studded; **stubbled,** stubbly; hairy *see* 3.25

10 bristlelike, setiform, aristate, setarious

adverbs

11 **roughly,** rough, in the rough; **unsmoothly,** brokenly, **unevenly,** irregularly, raggedly, choppily, jaggedly; **abrasively**

12 cross-grained, **against the grain,** the wrong way

289 NOTCH

nouns

1 **notch, nick, nock, cut,** cleft, incision, **gash,** hack, blaze, scotch, score, kerf, crena, depression, jag; jog, joggle; **indentation** *see* 284.6

2 **notching, serration,** serrulation, saw, saw tooth *or* teeth; denticulation, dentil, dentil band, dogtooth; crenation, crenellation, crenature, crenulation; **scallop;** rickrack; picot edge, Vandyke edge; deckle edge; cockscomb, crest

3 battlement, crenel, merlon, embrasure, castellation, machicolation

verbs

4 **to notch, nick, cut,** incise, **gash,** slash, chop, crimp, scotch, **score,** blaze, jag, scarify; **indent** *see* 284.14; **scallop,** crenellate, crenulate, machicolate; serrate, pink, mill, knurl, tooth, picot, Vandyke

adjectives

5 **notched, nicked,** incised, gashed, scotched, scored, chopped, blazed; **indented** *see* 284.17; serrate,

serrated, serrulated, **saw-toothed**, saw-edged, sawlike; crenate, crenated, crenulate, crenellated, battlemented, embrasured; scalloped; dentate, dentated, **toothed**, toothlike, tooth-shaped; lacerate, lacerated; **jagged**, jaggy; erose

290 FURROW

nouns

1 **furrow, groove**, scratch, crack, cranny, chase, chink, score, **cut**, gash, striation, streak, stria, **gouge**, slit, incision; sulcus, sulcation; **rut**, wheeltrack, well-worn groove; wrinkle see 291.3; **corrugation**; flute, fluting; rifling; chamfer, bezel, rabbet, dado; microgroove; engraving see 713.2

2 **trench, trough, channel, ditch**, dike (old), fosse, **canal**, cut, gutter, kennel, leat; moat; sunk fence, ha-ha or haw-haw; aqueduct see 239.2; entrenchment see 460.5; canalization; pleat, crimp, goffer

verbs

3 **to furrow, groove**, score, scratch, incise, cut, carve, chisel, gash, striate, streak, gouge, slit, crack; plough; rifle; **channel, trough, flute**, chamfer, rabbet, dado; **trench**, canal, canalize, **ditch**, dyke or dike, gully, **rut; corrugate**; wrinkle see 291.6; pleat, crimp, goffer; **engrave** see 713.10

adjectives

4 **furrowed, grooved**, scratched, scored, incised, cut, gashed, gouged, slit, striated; **channelled, troughed**, trenched, ditched; fluted, chamfered, rabbeted, dadoed; rifled; sulcate, sulcated; canaliculate, canaliculated; **corrugated**, corrugate; corduroy, corded, **rutted**, rutty; wrinkled see 291.8, pleated, crimped, goffered; **engraved**; ribbed, costate

291 FOLD

nouns

1 **fold, double**, fold on itself, doubling, duplicature; ply; plication, plica, plicature; flection, flexure; **crease**, creasing; crimp; **tuck, gather**; ruffle, frill, ruche, ruching; flounce; lappet; lapel; dog-ear

2 **pleat**, pleating, plait or plat; accordion pleat, box pleat, knife pleat, sunray pleat

3 **wrinkle, corrugation**, ridge, **furrow** see 290, **crease**, crimp, ruck, **pucker**, cockle; **crinkle**, crankle, rimple, ripple, wimple; crumple, rumple; crow's-feet

4 **folding, creasing**, infolding, infoldment or enfoldment; plication, plicature; paper-folding, origami

verbs

5 **to fold**, fold on itself, fold up; **double**, ply, plicate; fold over, double over, lap over, turn over or under; **crease, crimp**; crisp; **pleat**, plait, plat (informal); **tuck, gather**, tuck up, ruck, ruck up; ruffle, ruff, frill; flounce; twill, quill, flute; dog-ear; **fold in**, enfold or infold, wrap, lap; interfold

6 **to wrinkle, corrugate**, shirr, ridge, **furrow, crease**, crimp, crimple, cockle, cocker, **pucker, purse**; knit; ruck, ruckle; **crumple**, rumple; **crinkle**, rimple, ripple, wimple

adjectives

7 **folded, doubled**; plicate, plicated; **pleated**, plaited; **creased**, crimped; tucked, gathered; flounced, ruffled; twilled, quilled, fluted; dog-eared; foldable, folding, flexural, flexible, pliable, pliant, willowy

8 **wrinkled, wrinkly**; **corrugated**, corrugate; **creased**, rucked, **furrowed** see 290.4, ridged; cockled, cockly; puckered, puckery; pursed, pursy; knitted, knotted; rugged, rugose, rugous; **crinkled**, crinkly, rippled; crimped, crimpy; **crumpled**, rumpled

292 OPENING

nouns

1 **opening, aperture, hole**, hollow, **cavity** see 284.2, **orifice; slot**, split, crack, check, leak; opening up, unstopping, uncorking, clearing, throwing open, laying open, broaching, cutting through; passageway; inlet see 189.5; outlet see 190.9; **gap**, gape, yawn, hiatus, lacuna, gat, space, interval; **chasm, gulf**; cleft see 224.2; fontanelle; foramen, fenestra; stoma; pore, porosity; fistula; **disclosure** see 351

2 **gaping, yawning**, oscitation, oscitancy, dehiscence, pandiculation; **gape, yawn**; the gapes

3 **hole, perforation, penetration, piercing**, empiercement, **puncture**, goring, boring, puncturing, punching, pricking, lancing, broach, transforation, terebration; acupuncture, acupunctuation; trephining, trepanning; **impalement**, skewering, fixing, transfixion, transfixation; bore, borehole, drill hole

4 **mouth**; maw, oral cavity, gob (informal), gab (Scottish); **muzzle**, jaw, lips, embouchure; kisser or mug or mush or trap or yap or phiz or phizog (all informal), bazoo (US); **jaws**, mandibles, chops, chaps, jowls; premaxilla

5 **anus**; arsehole and bum (both informal), jacksie or jacksy or jaxie or jaxy (all informal)

6 **door**, doorway see 189.6; **entrance, entry** see 189.5

7 **window**, casement; **windowpane**, window glass, pane, light; window frame, window ledge, window sill, window bay

8 **porousness**, porosity; sievelikeness, cribriformity, cribrosity; screen, sieve, strainer, colander, riddle, cribble, net; honeycomb; sponge

9 **permeability, perviousness**

10 **opener**; tin opener, can opener; corkscrew, bottle screw, bottle opener, church key (US informal); latchstring; **key**, clavis; latchkey; passkey, passe-partout (French); master key, skeleton key; plastic key

verbs

11 **to open**, ope (old), **open up**; lay open, throw open; fly open, spring open, swing open; **tap, broach**; cut open, cut, cleave, split, slit, crack, chink, fissure, crevasse, incise, gap; rift, rive; tear open, rent, tear, rip, rip open, part, dispart, separate, divide, divaricate; spread, spread out, open out, splay, splay out

12 **to unclose**, unshut; **unfold**, unwrap, unroll; **unstop, unclog, unblock**, clear, unfoul, free, deobstruct; **unplug**, uncork, uncap; crack; **unlock,**

unlatch, undo; unseal, unclench, unclutch; **uncover,** uncase, unsheathe, unveil, undrape, uncurtain; **disclose** *see* 351.4, expose, reveal, bare, take the lid off, manifest

13 to make an opening, find an opening, make place *or* space, **make way, make room**

14 to breach, rupture; **break open,** force *or* pry *or* prize open, crack *or* split open, rip *or* tear open; break into, break through; break in, burst in, stave in, cave in

15 to perforate, pierce, empierce, **penetrate, puncture, punch,** clip, **hole,** prick; **tap, broach; stab, stick,** pink, run through; **transfix,** transpierce, fix, **impale,** spit, skewer; gore, spear, lance, spike, needle; **bore, drill,** auger; **ream,** ream out, countersink, gouge, gouge out; trepan, trephine; punch full of holes, make look like Swiss cheese *or* a sieve, **riddle, honeycomb**

16 to gape, yawn, oscitate, dehisce, hang open

adjectives

17 open, unclosed, uncovered; **unobstructed, unstopped, unclogged;** clear, cleared, free; wide-open, unrestricted; **disclosed** *see* 348.10; bare, exposed, unhidden *see* 348.11, naked, bald

18 gaping, yawning, agape, oscitant, slack-jawed, openmouthed; dehiscent, ringent; ajar, half-open, cracked

19 apertured, slotted, **holey;** pierced, **perforated,** perforate, holed; honeycombed, like Swiss cheese, riddled, *criblé* (*French*), shot through, peppered; windowed, fenestrated; leaky

20 porous, porose; poriferous; like a sieve, sievelike, cribose, cribriform; spongy, spongelike; percolating, leachy

21 permeable, pervious, penetrable, openable, accessible

22 mouthlike, oral, orificial; mandibular, maxillary

exclamations

23 open up!, open sesame!, **gangway!,** passageway!, **make way!**

293 CLOSURE

nouns

1 closure, closing, shutting, shutting up, occlusion; **shutdown,** shutting down; **exclusion** *see* 772, shutting out, **ruling out;** blockade, embargo

2 imperviousness, impermeability, impenetrability, impassability; imperforation

3 obstruction, clog, block, blockade, sealing off, **blockage,** strangulation, choking, choking off, **stoppage,** stop, **bar, barrier, obstacle,** impediment; **bottleneck; congestion,** jam, traffic jam, gridlock, snarl-up, rush hour; gorge; constipation, obstipation, costiveness; infarct, infarction; embolism, embolus; bottleneck; **blind alley,** blank wall, **dead end,** cul-de-sac, dead-end street, impasse; caecum, blind gut

4 stopper, stop, **stopple,** stopgap; **plug, cork,** bung, spike, spill, spile, tap, faucet, spigot, valve, check valve, cock, sea cock, peg, pin; lid *see* 295.5

5 stopping, wadding, stuffing, padding, **packing,** pack, tampon; gland; gasket

verbs

6 to close, shut, occlude; close up, shut up, contract, constrict, strangle, strangulate, choke, choke off, squeeze, squeeze shut; **exclude** *see* 772.4, shut out, squeeze out; **rule out** *see* 444.3; **fasten,** secure; **lock,** lock up, lock out, key, padlock, latch, bolt, bar, barricade; **seal,** seal up, seal in, seal off; button, button up; snap; zip up; batten, batten down; put *or* slap the lid on, **cover;** contain; **shut the door,** slam, bang

7 to stop, stop up; obstruct, bar, stay; **block,** block up; **clog,** clog up, foul; gunge, gunge up; **choke,** choke up *or* off; **fill,** fill up; **stuff,** pack, jam; **congest,** stuff up; **plug,** plug up; stopper, stopple, **cork,** bung, spile; cover; **dam,** dam up; stanch, stench (*Scottish*); chink; caulk; blockade, embargo; constipate, obstipate, bind

8 to close shop, close up *or* **down,** shut up, **shut up shop, shut down,** go out of business, fold *or* fold up (*both informal*), shutter, put up the shutters; cease *see* 856.6

adjectives

9 closed, shut, unopen, unopened; unvented, unventilated; **excluded** *see* 772.7, shut out; **ruled out, barred** *see* 444.7; contracted, constricted, choked, choked off, choked up, squeezed shut, strangulated; blank; blind, caecal, dead; dead-end, blind-alley, closed-end, closed-ended; **exclusive,** exclusionary, closed-door, in-camera, private, closed to the public

10 unpierced, pierceless, **unperforated,** imperforate, intact; **untrodden,** pathless, wayless, trackless

11 stopped, stopped up; obstructed, infarcted, **blocked; plugged,** plugged up; **clogged,** clogged up; foul, fouled; **choked,** choked up, strangulated, strangled; **full, stuffed,** packed, jammed, bumper-to-bumper (*informal*), jam-packed, like sardines; **congested,** stuffed up; constipated, obstipated, costive, bound

12 close, tight, compact, fast, shut fast, **snug,** staunch, firm; **sealed;** hermetic, hermetical, hermetically sealed; airtight, dustproof *or* dusttight, gasproof *or* gastight, lightproof *or* lighttight, oil-proof *or* oil-tight, rainproof *or* raintight, smokeproof *or* smoketight, stormproof *or* stormtight, waterproof *or* watertight, windproof *or* windtight; water-repellent *or* resistant

13 impervious, impenetrable, impermeable; impassable, unpassable; unpierceable, unperforable; **punctureproof,** nonpuncturable, holeproof

294 TEXTURE
surface quality

nouns

1 texture, surface texture; **surface; finish,** feel; **grain,** granular texture, fineness *or* coarseness of grain; **weave,** woof *see* 740.3, wale; **nap,** pile, shag, nub, knub, protuberance *see* 283; **pit,** pock, indentation *see* 284.6; structure *see* 266

2 roughness *see* 288; irregularity; bumpiness, lumpiness; **coarseness, grossness, unrefinement,** coarse-grainedness; cross-grainedness; **graininess,** granularity, granulation, grittiness; pockiness; hardness *see* 1044

3 smoothness *see* 287, **fineness, refinement,** fine-grainedness; **delicacy, daintiness;** filminess, gossameriness *see* 1028.1; down, **downiness,** fluff, fluffiness, velvet, velvetiness, fuzz, fuzziness, peach fuzz, pubescence; satin, satininess, silk, silkiness; softness *see* 1045

verbs

4 to coarsen; grain, granulate; tooth, **roughen** *see* 288.4; smooth *see* 287.5

adjectives

5 textural, textured, surfaced

6 rough *see* 288.6, **coarse, gross, unrefined, coarse-grained;** cross-grained; grained, **grainy,** granular, granulated, gritty, gravelly, gravelish

7 nappy, pily, **shaggy,** hairy, hirsute; nubby *or* nubbly; bumpy, lumpy; studded, knobbed; pocked, pitted *see* 284.17

8 smooth *see* 287.9; **fine, refined,** attenuate, attenuated, **fine-grained; delicate, dainty; finespun,** thin-spun, fine-drawn, wire-drawn; gauzy, filmy, gossamer, gossamery *see* 1028.4, **downy,** fluffy, velvety, velutinous, fuzzy, pubescent; satin, satiny, silky

295 COVERING

nouns

1 (*act of covering*) **covering,** coverage, obduction; **coating,** cloaking; **screening,** shielding, hiding, curtaining, **veiling,** clouding, obscuring, befogging, fogging, fuzzing, masking, mantling, shrouding, blanketing; blocking, blotting out, eclipse, eclipsing, occultation; **wrapping,** enwrapping, enwrapment, sheathing, envelopment; **overlaying,** overspreading, laying on *or* over, superimposition, superposition; superincumbence; upholstering, upholstery; plasterwork, stuccowork, brickwork, cementwork, pargeting; incrustation

2 cover, covering, coverage, covert, coverture, housing, hood, cowl, cowling, pelmet, **shelter; screen,** shroud, shield, veil, pall, mantle, curtain, hanging, drape, drapery; **coat,** cloak, mask, guise; vestment *see* 5.1

3 skin, dermis; **cuticle; rind; flesh;** bare skin *or* flesh, the buff; integument, tegument *see* 206.2, tegmen, tegmentum; **pelt, hide coat, jacket, fell, fleece, fur, hair,** vair (*heraldry*); **peel, peeling, rind; skin,** epicarp; **bark;** cork, phellum; cortex, cortical tissue; periderm, phelloderm; peridium; dermatogen

4 overlayer, overlay; appliqué, **lap, overlap,** overlapping, imbrication; **flap,** fly, tentfly

5 cover, lid, top, cap, screw-top, crown cap; operculum; stopper *see* 293.4

6 roof, roofing, roofage, top, **housetop,** rooftop; roof-deck, roof garden, penthouse; roofpole, ridgepole, rooftree; shingles, slates, tiles; eaves; **ceiling,** *plafond* (*French*), overhead; skylight, lantern, cupola

7 umbrella, brolly *or* gamp (*both informal*), bumbershoot (*US informal*); **sunshade, parasol,** beach umbrella

8 tent, canvas; top, big top; tentage

9 rug, carpet, floor cover *or* covering; carpeting, wall-to-wall carpet *or* carpeting; **mat;** drop cloth, ground cloth, groundsheet; **flooring,** floorboards, duckboards; linoleum *or* lino; parquet, **tiling; pavement,** pavé, crazy paving

10 blanket, coverlet, coverlid (*informal*), bluey (*Australian informal*), space blanket, cover, covers, **spread,** robe, **afghan,** rug, throw; **bedspread; bedcover;** counterpane; **duvet, continental quilt, quilt,** feather bed, eiderdown, doona (*Australian*), comforter (*US*); patchwork quilt; candlewick; **bedding, bedclothes,** clothes; **linen,** bed linen; **sheet,** sheeting, bedsheet, fitted sheet, contour sheet; **pillowcase,** pillowslip, case, slip; duvet cover

11 horsecloth, horse blanket; caparison, housing; **saddle blanket,** saddlecloth

12 blanket, coating, coat; **veneer, facing,** veneering, revetment; pellicle, **film, scum,** skin, scale; slick, oil slick; varnish, enamel, lacquer, paint *see* 35.8

13 plating, plate, cladding; nickel plate, silver plate, gold plate, copperplate, chromium plate, anodized aluminium; electroplating, electrocoating

14 crust, incrustation, shell; piecrust, pastry shell; stalactite, stalagmite; scale, scab, eschar

15 shell, seashell, lorication, lorica, conch; test, testa, episperm, pericarp, elytron, scute, scutum; **armour,** mail, **shield; carapace,** plate, chitin; **protective covering,** cortex, thick skin *or* hide, elephant skin

16 hull, shell, pod, capsule, case, **husk, shuck;** cornhusk, corn shuck; bark, jacket; chaff, bran, palea

17 case, casing, encasement; **sheath,** sheathing

18 wrapper, wrapping, gift wrapping, wrap; wrapping paper, waxed paper, aluminium foil, tin foil, clingfilm, plastic wrap; **binder,** binding; **bandage,** bandaging; **envelope,** envelopment; **jacket,** jacketing; dust jacket

verbs

19 to cover, cover up; apply to, **put on,** lay on; **superimpose,** superpose; **lay over,** overlay; **spread over,** overspread; **clothe, cloak,** mantle, muffle, blanket, canopy, cope, cowl, hood, veil, curtain, **screen, shield,** screen off, mask, cloud, obscure, fog, befog, fuzz; block, eclipse, occult; film, film over, scum

20 to wrap, enwrap, wrap up, wrap about *or* around; **envelop, sheathe;** surround, encompass, lap, smother, enfold, embrace, invest; shroud, enshroud; swathe, swaddle; **box, case,** encase, **crate,** pack, embox; containerize; **package,** encapsulate

21 to top, cap, tip, crown; put the lid on, cork, stopper, plug; hood, hat, coif, bonnet; roof, roof in *or* over; ceil; dome, endome

22 to floor; carpet; pave, causeway, cobblestone, flag, pebble; cement, concrete; **pave, surface,** pave over, repave, resurface; tar, asphalt, metal (*old*), macadamize, blacktop (*US & Canadian*)

23 to face, veneer, revet; **sheathe;** board, plank, weatherboard, clapboard, lath; shingle, shake; tile, stone, brick, slate; thatch; glass, glaze, fibreglass; paper, wallpaper; wall in *or* up

24 to coat, spread on, **spread with;** smear, **smear on,** besmear, slap on, dab, daub, bedaub, plaster, beplaster; flow on, pour on; lay on, lay it on thick, slather (*US & Canadian informal*); undercoat, prime; enamel, gild, gloss, lacquer; butter; tar

25 to plaster, parget, stucco, cement, concrete, mastic, grout, mortar; face, line; roughcast, pebble-dash, spatterdash (*US*)

26 to plate, chromium-plate, copperplate, gold-plate, nickel-plate, silver-plate, silver-gilt; **electroplate, galvanize,** anodize

27 to crust, incrust, encrust; loricate; effloresce; scab, scab over

28 to upholster, overstuff

29 to re-cover, reupholster

30 to overlie, lie over; **overlap,** lap, **lap over,** override, imbricate, jut, shingle; **extend over,** span, bridge, bestride, bestraddle, arch over, overarch, hang over, overhang

adjectives

31 covered, covert, under cover; **cloaked,** mantled, blanketed, muffled, canopied, coped, cowled, hooded, **shrouded, veiled,** clouded, obscured, fogged; eclipsed, occulted, curtained, **screened,** screened-in, screened-off; shielded, masked; **housed;** tented, under canvas; roofed, roofed-in *or* over, domed; walled, walled-in; **wrapped,** enwrapped, jacketed, **enveloped,** sheathed, swathed; **boxed, cased,** encased, encapsuled *or* encapsulated, **packaged; coated,** filmed, filmed-over, scummed; shelled, loricate, loricated; armoured; ceiled; **floored; paved, surfaced;** plastered, stuccoed

32 cutaneous, cuticular; skinlike, skinny; skin-deep; **epidermal,** epidermic, dermal, dermic; ectodermal, ectodermic; endermic, endermatic; cortical; epicarpal; testaceous; hairy, furry *see* 3.25; integumental, integumentary, tegumentary, tegumental, tegmental; vaginal; thecal

33 plated, chromium-plated, copperplated, gold-plated, nickel-plated, silver-plated; electroplated, galvanized, anodized

34 upholstered, overstuffed

35 covering, coating; cloaking, blanketing, shrouding, obscuring, **veiling, screening,** shielding, sheltering; wrapping, **enveloping,** sheathing

36 overlying, incumbent, superincumbent, superimposed; **overlapping,** lapping, shingled, equitant; imbricate, imbricated; spanning, bridging; overarched, overarching

prepositions

37 on, upon, over, o'er, above, on top of

296 LAYER

nouns

1 layer, thickness; **level, tier,** stage, storey, floor, gallery, step, ledge, deck; **stratum,** seam, *couche* (*French*), belt, band, **bed, course,** measures; zone; shelf; **overlayer, superstratum,** topsoil;

underlayer, substratum, understratum; floor, bedding

2 lamina, lamella; **sheet,** leaf, *feuille* (*French*), foil; wafer, disc; **plate,** plating, cladding; covering *see* 295, **coat,** coating, veneer, film, patina, scum, membrane, pellicle, peel, skin, rind, hide; slick, oil slick; **slice,** cut, rasher, collop; **slab,** plank, deal, slat, tablet, table; panel, pane; **fold,** lap, flap, **ply,** plait; laminated glass, safety glass; laminated wood, plywood, layered fibreglass

3 flake, flock, floccule, flocculus; **scale, scurf,** dandruff; chip; shaving, paring, swarf

4 stratification, lamination, lamellation; foliation; delamination, exfoliation; desquamation, furfuration; flakiness, scaliness

verbs

5 to layer, lay down, lay up, **stratify,** arrange in layers *or* levels *or* strata *or* tiers, **laminate;** flake, scale; delaminate, desquamate, exfoliate

adjectives

6 layered, in layers; **laminated,** laminate, laminous; lamellated, lamellate, lamellar, lamelliform; plated, coated; veneered, faced; two-ply, three-ply, etc; two-level, bilevel, three-level, trilevel, etc; one-storey, single storey, two-storey, double-storey, etc; **stratified,** stratiform; foliated, foliaceous, leaflike

7 flaky, flocculent; **scaly,** scurfy, squamous, lentiginous, furfuraceous, lepidote; scabby, scabious, scabrous

word elements

8 strati–, lamin–, lamino–, lamini–, lamell–, lamelli–

297 WEIGHT

nouns

1 weight, heaviness, weightiness, ponderousness, ponderosity, ponderability, leadenness, heftiness *and* heft (*both informal*); body weight, avoirdupois (*informal*), fatness *see* 257.8, beef *and* beefiness (*both informal*); poundage, tonnage; deadweight, live weight; gross weight, gr wt; **net weight,** neat weight, nt wt, net, nett; short-weight; underweight; overweight; overbalance, overweightage; **solemnity, gravity** *see* 111.1, 580.1

2 onerousness, **burdensomeness, oppressiveness, deadweight, overburden, cumbersomeness,** cumbrousness; massiveness, massiness (*old*), bulkiness *see* 257.9, lumpishness, unwieldiness

3 (*sports*) bantamweight, cruiserweight, featherweight, flyweight, heavyweight, junior lightweight, light flyweight, light heavyweight, light middleweight, lightweight, light welterweight, middleweight, superheavyweight, welterweight; catchweight; fighting weight; jockey weight

4 counterbalance *see* 899.4; makeweight; **ballast,** ballasting

5 (*physics terms*) **gravity,** gravitation, G, supergravity; specific gravity; gravitational field, gravisphere; graviton; geotropism, positive geotropism, apogeotropism, negative geotropism; G suit, anti-G suit; **mass**; atomic weight, molecular weight, molar weight

6 **weight**, paperweight, letterweight; sinker, lead, plumb, plummet, bob; sash weight; sandbag

7 **burden**, burthen (*old*), pressure, **oppression**, **deadweight**; burdening, saddling, charging, taxing, overburden, overburdening, overtaxing, overweighting, weighing *or* weighting down; charge, **load**, loading, lading, freight, cargo, bale; cumber, cumbrance, **encumbrance**; incubus; incumbency *or* superincumbency (*old*); handicap, drag, millstone; surcharge, overload

8 (*systems of weight*) avoirdupois weight, troy weight, apothecaries' weight, imperial weight; atomic weight, molecular weight; **pound, ounce, gram** etc, **unit of weight** (*see list*)

9 **weighing**, hefting (*informal*), balancing; weighing-in, weigh-in, weighing-out, weigh-out; **scale**, weighing instrument

verbs

10 **to weigh**, weight; heft (*informal*), **balance**, weigh in the balance, strike a balance, hold the scales, put on the scales, lay in the scales; **counterbalance; weigh in**, weigh out; be heavy, weigh heavy, lie heavy, have weight, carry weight; **tip the scales**, turn *or* depress *or* tilt the scales

11 **to weigh on** *or* **upon**, rest on *or* upon, bear on *or* upon, lie on, press, press down, press to the ground

12 **to weight, weigh** *or* **weight down**; hang like a millstone; **ballast**; lead, sandbag

13 **to burden**, burthen (*old*), **load**, load down *or* up, lade, cumber, **encumber, charge, freight**, tax, handicap, hamper, saddle, lumber; **oppress, weigh one down**, weigh on *or* upon, weigh heavy on, bear *or* rest hard upon, lie hard *or* heavy upon, press hard upon, be an incubus to; **overburden**, overweight, overtax, overload *see* 992.15

14 **to outweigh**, overweigh, overweight, overbalance, outbalance, outpoise, overpoise

15 **to gravitate**, descend *see* 194.5, drop, plunge *see* 367.6, precipitate, sink, settle, subside; tend, tend to go, **incline**, point, head, lead, lean

adjectives

16 **heavy, ponderous, massive**, massy, weighty, hefty (*informal*), fat *see* 257.18; **leaden**, heavy as lead; deadweight; heavyweight; overweight; **solemn, grave** *see* 111.3, 580.8

17 **onerous, oppressive, burdensome**, incumbent *or* superincumbent, **cumbersome**, cumbrous; massive; lumpish, **unwieldy**

18 **weighted, weighed** *or* **weighted down; burdened, oppressed, laden**, cumbered, **encumbered**, charged, loaded, fraught, freighted, taxed, saddled, hampered; **overburdened**, overloaded, overladen, overcharged, overfreighted, overfraught, overweighted, overtaxed; borne-down, sinking, foundering

19 **weighable**, ponderable; **appreciable**, palpable, sensible

20 **gravitational**, mass

adverbs

21 **heavily**, heavy, weightily, leadenly; burdensomely, onerously, oppressively; **ponderously**, cumbersomely, cumbrously

22 **units of weight** *or* **force** *or* **mass**

assay ton	metric ton *or* MT *or* t
carat *or* c	microgram *or* mcg
carat grain	milligram *or* mg
centigram *or* cg	mole *or* mol
dead-weight ton	myriagram *or* myg
decagram *or* dkg *or*	net ton
decigram *or* dg	newton
displacement ton	ounce *or* ounce avoirdupois
drachm	*or* oz *or* oz av
dram *or* dram avoirdupois	ounce apothecaries' *or* oz
or dr	ap
dram apothecaries' *or* dr	ounce troy *or* oz t
ap	pearl grain
dyne	pennyweight *or* dwt *or* pwt
grain *or* gr	pound *or* pound
gram *or* g	avoirdupois *or* lb *or* lb av
gram equivalent *or* gram	poundal
equivalent weight	pound apothecaries' *or* lb
gram molecule *or* gram-	ap
molecular weight	pound troy *or* lb t
gross ton	quintal *or* q
hectogram *or* hg	scruple *or* s ap
hundredweight *or* cwt	shipping ton
international carat	short hundredweight
kilogram *or* kilo *or* kg	short ton *or* st
kiloton	slug
long hundredweight	sthene
long ton *or* lt	stone *or* st
measurement ton	tod
megaton	ton *or* tn
metric carat	

298 LIGHTNESS

nouns

1 **lightness, levity**, unheaviness, lack of weight; **weightlessness; buoyancy**, buoyance, floatability; levitation, ascent *see* 193; **volatility; airiness**, ethereality; foaminess, frothiness, bubbliness, yeastiness; downiness, fluffiness, gossameriness *see* 1028.1; softness, gentleness, delicacy, daintiness, tenderness; light touch, gentle touch; frivolity *see* 922.1, 109.5

2 (*comparisons*) air, aether, feather, down, thistledown, flue, fluff, fuzz, sponge, gossamer, cobweb, fairy, straw, chaff, dust, mote, cork, chip, bubble, froth, foam, spume

3 **lightening**, easing, **easement, alleviation, relief;** disburdening, **disencumberment**, unburdening, **unloading**, unlading, unsaddling, untaxing, unfreighting; unballasting

4 **leavening, fermentation; leaven, ferment**

5 (*indeterminacy of weight*) imponderableness *or* imponderability, unweighableness *or* unweighability; imponderables, imponderabilia

verbs

6 to lighten, make light *or* lighter, reduce weight; unballast; **ease, alleviate, relieve; disburden, disencumber,** unburden, unload, unlade, off-load; **be light,** weigh lightly, have little weight

7 to leaven, raise, ferment

8 to buoy, buoy up; float, float high, ride high, waft; **sustain, hold up,** bear up, uphold, upbear, uplift, upraise; refloat

9 to levitate, rise, ascend *see* 193.8; hover, **float**

adjectives

10 light, unheavy, imponderous; **weightless; airy, ethereal; volatile;** frothy, foamy, spumy, spumous, spumescent, bubbly, yeasty; downy, feathery, fluffy, gossamery *see* 1028.4; *soufflé, moussé, léger* (*all French*);
"lighter than vanity"—BIBLE, "light as any wind that blows"—TENNYSON; light as air *or* a feather *or* gossamer, etc *see* 298.2; **frivolous** *see* 921.20,109.15

11 lightened, eased, unburdened, disburdened, disencumbered, unencumbered, relieved, alleviated, out from under, breathing easier; mitigated

12 light, gentle, soft, delicate, dainty, tender, **easy**

13 lightweight, bantamweight, featherweight, junior lightweight, light flyweight; underweight

14 buoyant, floaty, floatable; floating, supernatant

15 levitative, levitational

16 lightening, easing, alleviating, alleviative, alleviatory, relieving, disburdening, unburdening, disencumbering

17 leavening, raising, fermenting, fermentative, working; yeasty, barmy; enzymic, diastatic

18 imponderable, unweighable

299 RARITY
lack of density

nouns

1 rarity, rareness; thinness, tenuousness, tenuity; **subtlety,** subtility; **fineness,** slightness, flimsiness, **unsubstantiality** *or* **insubstantiality** *see* 763; **ethereality,** airiness, immateriality, incorporeality, bodilessness, insolidity; **diffuseness,** dispersedness, scatter, scatteredness;
"airy nothing", — *and* "such stuff as dreams are made on"—BOTH SHAKESPEARE

2 rarefaction, attenuation, subtilization, etherealization; **diffusion,** dispersion, scattering; **thinning,** thinning-out, dilution, adulteration, watering, watering-down; decompression

verbs

3 to rarefy, attenuate, thin, thin out; dilute, adulterate, water, water down, cut; subtilize, etherealize; **diffuse,** disperse, scatter; expand *see* 259.4; decompress

adjectives

4 rare, rarefied; **subtle; thin,** thinned, dilute, attenuated, attenuate; thinned-out, diluted, adulterated, watered, watered-down, cut; **tenuous, fine,** flimsy, slight, **unsubstantial** *or* **insubstantial** *see* 763; **airy, ethereal,** vaporous, gaseous, windy;

diffused, diffuse, dispersed, scattered; uncompact, uncompressed, decompressed

5 rarefactive, rarefactional

300 MEASUREMENT

nouns

1 measurement, measure; mensuration, measuring, **gauging;** admeasurement; metage; **estimation,** estimate, rough measure, approximation; **quantification,** quantitation, quantization; **appraisal,** appraisement, **stocktaking, assay,** assaying; **assessment,** determination, rating, valuation, evaluation; assizement, assize, sizing up (*informal*); **survey,** surveying; triangulation; **instrumentation;** telemetry, telemetering; metric system; metrication; imperial system; calibration, correction, computation, calculation

2 measure, measuring instrument, **meter, instrument, gauge,** barometer, **rule, yardstick,** measuring rod *or* stick, **standard,** norm, canon, **criterion,** test, touchstone, check; **pattern,** model, type; **scale,** graduated *or* calibrated scale; meter-reading, reading, readout, value, degree, quantity; parameter

3 extent, quantity *see* 244, degree *see* 245, size *see* 257, distance *see* 261, length *see* 267, breadth *see* 269; **weight** *see* 297

4 (*measures*) imperial liquid measure, imperial dry measure, apothecaries' measure, linear measure (*see list*), square measure, circular measure, cubic measure, volume measure (*see list*), area measure (*see list*), surface measure, surveyor's measure, land measure, board measure

5 coordinates, Cartesian coordinates, rectangular coordinates, polar coordinates, cylindrical coordinates, spherical coordinates, equator coordinates; latitude, longitude; altitude, azimuth; declination, right ascension; ordinate, abscissa

6 waterline; watermark, tidemark, floodmark, **high-water mark;** load waterline, load line mark, Plimsoll mark *or* line

7 measurability, mensurability, computability, determinability, quantifiability

8 science of measurement, mensuration, metrology

9 measurer, meter, gauger; **geodesist,** geodetic engineer; **surveyor,** land surveyor, quantity surveyor; topographer, cartographer, mapmaker, oceanographer, chorographer; **appraiser, assessor;** assayer; valuer, valuator, evaluator; estimator

verbs

10 to measure, gauge, quantify, quantitate, quantize, mete (*old*), take the measure of, mensurate, triangulate, apply the yardstick to; **estimate,** make an approximation; **assess, rate, appraise, valuate, value,** evaluate, appreciate, prize; **assay;** size *or* size up (*informal*), take the dimensions of; **weigh,** weigh up *see* 297.10; survey; plumb, probe, sound, fathom; span, pace, step; calibrate, graduate; divide; calliper; meter; read the meter, take a reading, check a parameter; compute, calculate

11 to measure off, mark off, lay off, set off, rule

off; **step off,** pace off or out; **measure out,** mark out, lay out; put at

adjectives

12 measuring, metric, metrical, mensural, mensurative, mensurational; valuative, valuational; **quantitative,** numerative; approximative, estimative; geodetic, geodetical, geodesic, geodesical, hypsographic, hypsographical, hypsometric, hypsometrical; topographic, topographical, chorographic, chorographical, cartographic, cartographical, oceanographic, oceanographical

13 measured, gauged, metered, **quantified;** quantitated, quantized; **appraised, assessed, valuated,** valued, rated, ranked; **assayed; surveyed,** plotted, mapped, admeasured, triangulated; known by measurement

14 measurable, mensurable, **quantifiable,** numerable, meterable, gaugeable, fathomable, **determinable,** computable, calculable; quantifiable, quantitatable, quantizable; estimable; assessable, appraisable, ratable; appreciable, perceptible, noticeable

adverbs

15 measurably, appreciably, perceptibly, noticeably

16 linear measures

absolute angstrom	kilometre or km
Admiralty mile	land mile
angstrom or angstrom unit	league
or a or å or A or A	light-year
arpent	line
astronomical unit	link or li
block	metre or m
board foot or bd ft	micron or μ
cable length	mil
centimetre or cm	mile or mi
chain or Gunter's chain or	millimetre or mm
chn	millimicron or
cubit	micromillimetre
decametre or dkm	myriametre or mym
decimetre or dm	nail
ell	nautical mile or naut mi
em	pace
en	palm
fathom or fthm	parsec
fingerbreadth or finger	perch
foot or ft	pica
footstep	point or pt
furlong or fur	pole or p
hand	rod or r
handbreadth or	statute mile or stat mi
handsbreadth	step
hectometre or hm	stride
inch or in	wavelength
international angstrom	yard or yd

17 volume measures

barrel	decalitre or dkl
bushel or bu	decastere or dks
centilitre or cl	decilitre or dl
cord or cd	drop
cubic foot or yard or etc	dry pint or quart or etc
cubic metre	fifth
cup	finger

firkin	magnum
fluidounce or fl oz	millilitre or ml
fluidram or fl dr	minim or min
gallon or gal	nip
gill or gi	peck or pk
hectolitre or hl	pint or pt
hogshead or hhd	pony
jeroboam	quart or qt
jigger	stere or s
kilolitre or kl	tablespoon or tbs
liquid pint or quart or etc	teaspoon or tsp
litre or l	

18 area measures

acre or a or ac	rood
are or a	section or sec
arpent	square inch or foot or mile
centare or ca	or etc
hectare or ha	square metre or kilometre
perch	or etc
pole or p	

301 YOUTH

nouns

1 youth, youthfulness, juvenility, juvenescence, tenderness, tender age, early years, school age, *jeunesse* (*French*), prime of life, flower of life, salad days, springtime or springtide of life, seedtime of life, flowering time, bloom, florescence, budtime, "the very May-morn of his youth"—SHAKESPEARE, "the summer of your youth"—EDWARD MOORE, "the red sweet wine of youth"—RUPERT BROOKE, golden season of life, "the glad season of life"—CARLYLE, heyday of youth or of the blood, young blood, "my burning youth"—YEATS, "my green age"—DYLAN THOMAS

2 childhood, "childhood's careless days"—WILLIAM CULLEN BRYANT; **boyhood; girlhood,** maidenhood or maidenhead; puppyhood, calfhood; pre-teens, subteens (*US & Canadian*)

3 immaturity, undevelopment, inexperience, **callowness, unripeness,** greenness, rawness, sappiness, freshness, juiciness, dewiness; **minority,** juniority, infancy, nonage

4 childishness, childlikeness, **puerility; boyishness,** boylikeness; **girlishness,** girl-likeness, maidenliness

5 infancy, babyhood, the cradle, the crib, the nursery, "my Angel-infancy"—HENRY VAUGHAN

6 adolescence, maturation, maturement, pubescence, **puberty;** nubility

7 teens, teen or teenage years, **awkward age,** age of growing pains (*informal*)

verbs

8 to make young, youthen, **rejuvenate,** reinvigorate; turn back the clock

adjectives

9 young, youngling, youngish, **juvenile,** juvenal, juvenescent, **youthful,** youthlike, in the flower or bloom of youth, blooming, florescent, flowering, dewy, fresh-faced;

"towering in confidence of twenty-one"—SAMUEL JOHNSON; young-looking, well-preserved

10 **immature**, unadult; **inexperienced**, unseasoned, unfledged, new-fledged, **callow**, **unripe**, ripening, unmellowed, **raw**, **green**, vernal, primaveral, dewy, juicy, sappy, budding, tender, virginal, intact, innocent, naive, ingenuous, **undeveloped**, growing, unformed, unlicked, wet *or* not dry behind the ears; **minor**, underage

11 **childish**, childlike, kiddish (*informal*), **puerile**; **boyish**, boylike, beardless; **girlish**, girl-like, maiden, maidenly; puppyish, puppylike, puplike, calflike, coltish, coltlike

12 **infant**, **infantile**, infantine, **babyish**, baby; dollish, doll-like; kittenish, kittenlike; **newborn**, neonatal; in the cradle *or* crib *or* nursery, in swaddling clothes, in nappies, in diapers (*US & Canadian*), in arms, at the breast, tied to mother's apron strings

13 **adolescent**, pubescent, nubile, marriageable

14 **teen-age**, teen-aged, teenish, **in one's teens**; sweet sixteen (*informal*)

15 **junior**, Jr; minor, minimus; **younger**, puisne

phrases

16 "Young men are fitter to invent than to judge"— FRANCIS BACON;

"To be young is to be one of the Immortals"—W C HAZLITT, "To be young was very Heaven!"—WORDSWORTH

302 YOUNGSTER

nouns

1 **youngster**, young person, **youth**, **juvenile**, youngling, young'un (*informal*), juvenal (*old*); **stripling**, slip, sprig, sapling; fledgling; hopeful, young hopeful; **minor**, infant; **adolescent**, pubescent; **teenager**, teener, teenybopper (*informal*); junior, younger, youngest, baby

2 **young people**, **youth**, young, **younger generation**, rising *or* new generation, young blood, young fry (*informal*), *ragazze* (*Italian*); **children**, tots, childkind; small fry *and* **kids** *and* little kids *and* little ones (*all informal*); childhood; boyhood, girlhood; babyhood

3 **child**; nipper, **kid** *and* kiddy (*both informal*), **little one**, little fellow *or* guy, little bugger (*informal*), shaver *and* little shaver (*both informal*), little squirt (*informal*), **tot**, **little tot**, wee tot, trot, tiddler (*informal*), wean (*Scottish*), tad *or* little tad (*US & Canadian*), tyke, mite, chit (*informal*), innocent, little innocent, moppet, poppet; darling, cherub, lamb, lambkin, kitten, **offspring** see 561.3

4 **brat**, urchin; minx, imp, puck, elf, gamin, little monkey, pickle, tinker, **whippersnapper**, young whippersnapper, *enfant terrible* (*French*), little terror, holy terror, limb; spoiled brat; snotnose kid (*informal*); juvenile delinquent, JD (*informal*), yob, yobbo, teddy boy, ted (*informal*), ned (*Scottish*), bodgie (*Australian & NZ*)

5 **boy**, **lad**, laddie, boyo, **youth**, manchild, manling, young man, *garçon* (*French*), *muchacho* (*Spanish*), schoolboy, schoolkid (*informal*), fledgling, hobbledehoy; fellow see 76.5; pup, puppy, whelp, cub, colt; master; sonny, sonny boy; bud *and* buddy (*both US & Canadian informal*); bub (*US, Australian & NZ informal*); buck, young buck; schoolboy

6 **girl**, girlie (*informal*), **maid**, **maiden**, **lass**, girlchild, **lassie**, young thing, young creature, young lady, damsel in distress, **damsel**, damoiselle, demoiselle, *jeune fille* (*French*), mademoiselle (*French*), muchacha (*Spanish*), miss, missy, little missy, slip, wench (*dialect or informal*), colleen (*Irish*)

7 (*informal terms*) gal, dame, chick, bird, tomato (*US & Canadian*), **babe** *or* baby, broad, frail, **doll**, dolly bird, skirt, jill, chit, cutie, filly, heifer; teenybopper (*informal*)

8 **schoolgirl**, schoolmaid, schoolmiss, junior miss, subteen (*US & Canadian*); **tomboy**, bobbysoxer (*US informal*), hoyden, romp; piece (*informal*), nymphet; virgin, *virgo intacta* (*Latin*)

9 **infant**, **baby**, **babe**, bairn (*Scottish*), babe in arms, little darling *or* angel *or* doll *or* cherub, bouncing baby, puling infant, mewling infant, babykins (*informal*), baby bunting; papoose, *bimbo or bambino* (*Italian*); **toddler**; **suckling**, nursling, fosterling, weanling; neonate; yearling, yearold; premature baby, incubator baby; preschooler; sprog *and* ankle-biter *and* rug rat (*all informal*)

10 (*animals*) **fledgling**, birdling, nestling; **chick**, chicky, chickling; **pullet**, fryer; **duckling**; gosling; **kitten**, kit, catling; **pup**, puppy, whelp; **cub**; **calf**, dogie, weaner; **colt**, foal; piglet, pigling, shoat; **lamb**, lambkin; kid, yeanling; fawn; **tadpole**, polliwog; litter, nest

11 (*plants*) **sprout**, **seedling**, set; sucker, shoot, slip; twig, sprig, scion, sapling

12 (*insects*) **larva**, **chrysalis**, aurelia, cocoon, pupa; nymph, nympha; wriggler, wiggler; caterpillar, maggot, grub

303 AGE
time of life

nouns

1 **age**, years, "the days of our years", "the measure of my days"— BOTH BIBLE; time *or* stage of life; lifespan, life expectancy

2 **maturity**, **adulthood**, **majority**, grown-upness, full growth, mature age, legal age, voting age, driving age, drinking age, *legalis homo* (*Latin*); age of consent; ripe age, riper years, full age *or* growth *or* bloom, flower of age, **prime**, **prime of life**, age of responsibility, age *or* years of discretion, age of matured powers; **manhood**, man's estate, virility, *toga virilis* (*Latin*), masculinity, maleness, manliness; **womanhood**, womanness, femininity, femaleness, womanliness

3 **seniority**, **eldership**, deanship, primogeniture

4 **middle age**, middle life, meridian of life, the middle years, the wrong side of forty, the dangerous age,

"in the middle of the road of our life"—Dante

5 old age, oldness, eld (*old*), **elderliness,** senectude, advanced age *or* years; superannuation, pensionable age, age of retirement; **ripe old age,** the golden years, the Third Age, senior citizenship, hoary age, grey *or* white hairs; **decline of life,** declining years, youth deficiency, the vale of years,

"an incurable disease", "the downward slope"—both Seneca, "slow-consuming age"—Thomas Gray, "a tyrant, which forbids the pleasures of youth on pain of death"—La Rochefoucauld, "old age is fifteen years older than I"—Bernard Baruch, "crabbed age"—The Passionate Pilgrim, "the arctic regions of our lives"—Longfellow, the shady side (*informal*);

"the sere, the yellow leaf", "the silver livery of advised age"—both Shakespeare, "a crown of glory"—Bible; sunset *or* twilight *or* evening *or* autumn *or* winter of one's days; **decrepitude,** ricketiness, infirm old age, infirmity of age, infirmity, debility, caducity, feebleness; **dotage,** second childhood; senility *see* 921.10, anility; **longevity,** long life, length of years, green *or* hale old age

6 maturation, development, growth, ripening, blooming, blossoming, flourishing; **mellowing,** seasoning, tempering; **aging,** senescence

7 change of life, menopause, climacteric, grand climacteric; male menopause; midlife crisis

8 geriatrics, gerontology

verbs

9 to mature, grow up, grow, **develop, ripen,** flower, flourish, bloom, blossom; fledge, leave the nest, put up one's hair, not be in pigtails, put on long trousers; **come of age,** come to maturity, attain majority, **reach one's majority,** reach twenty-one, reach voting age, reach the age of consent, reach manhood *or* womanhood, write oneself a man, come to *or* into man's estate, assume the toga virilis, come into years of discretion, be in the prime of life, cut one's wisdom teeth *or* eyeteeth (*informal*), have sown one's wild oats, settle down; **mellow,** season, temper

10 to age, grow old, senesce, get on, get on in years, grow *or* have whiskers, be over the hill (*informal*), turn grey *or* white; **decline,** wane, fade, fail, sink, waste away; **dodder,** totter, shake; wither, wrinkle, shrivel, wizen; **live to a ripe old age,** cheat the undertaker (*informal*); be in one's dotage *or* second childhood

11 to have had one's day, have seen one's day *or* best days, **have seen better days; show one's age,** show marks of age, have one foot in the grave

adjectives

12 adult, mature, of age, out of one's teens, big, grown, **grown-up;** old enough to know better; **marriageable,** of marriageable age, marriable, nubile

13 mature, ripe, ripened, of full *or* ripe age, **developed,** fully developed, well-developed, **full-grown,** full-fledged, fully fledged, full-blown, in full bloom, in one's prime; **mellow** *or* mellowed, seasoned, tempered, aged

14 middle-aged, mid-life, *entre deux âges* (*French*), fortyish, matronly

15 past one's prime, senescent, on the shady side (*informal*), overblown, overripe, of a certain age, over the hill (*informal*);

"fall'n into the sere, the yellow leaf"—Shakespeare

16 aged, elderly, old, grown old in years, along *or* up *or* advanced *or* on in years, years old, advanced, advanced in life, **at an advanced age, ancient,** geriatric, gerontic; **venerable,** old as Methuselah *or* as God *or* as the hills; patriarchal; hoary, hoar, **grey,** white, grey- *or* white-headed, grey- *or* white-haired, grey- *or* white-crowned, grey- *or* white-bearded, grey *or* white with age; wrinkled, prune-faced (*informal*); wrinkly, with crow's feet, marked with the crow's foot

17 ageing *or* **aging,** growing old, senescent, **getting on** *or* **along,** getting on *or* along *or* up in years, not as young as one used to be, long in the tooth; **declining,** sinking, waning, fading, wasting, doting

18 stricken in years, decrepit, infirm, weak, debilitated, feeble, geriatric, timeworn, the worse for wear, rusty, moth-eaten *or* mossbacked (*informal*), fossilized, wracked *or* ravaged with age, run to seed; **doddering,** doddery, doddered, tottering, tottery, rickety, shaky, palsied; on one's last legs, with one foot in the grave; **wizened,** crabbed, **withered,** shrivelled, like a prune, mummylike, papery-skinned; **senile** *see* 921.23, anile

304 ADULT OR OLD PERSON

nouns

1 adult, grownup, mature man *or* woman, grown man *or* woman, big boy *and* big girl (*both informal*); **man, woman;** major, *legalis homo* (*Latin*); no chicken *and* no spring chicken (*both informal*)

2 old man, elder, oldster (*informal*); senior citizen, old age pensioner *or* OAP, pensioner, geriatric, golden-ager, wrinkly (*informal*); old chap, old party, **old gentleman,** old gent (*informal*), old codger (*informal*), geezer *and* old geezer (*both informal*), old boy (*informal*), gramps (*informal*), gaffer, old duffer (*informal*), old dog *and* old-timer (*both informal*), old crock (*informal*), dotard, veteran, pantaloon; **patriarch,** greybeard *or* greybeard, reverend *or* venerable sir; grandfather, grandsire; Father Time, Methuselah, Nestor, Old Paar; sexagenarian, septuagenarian, octogenarian, nonagenarian, centenarian;

"the quiet-voiced elders"—T S Eliot, "a paltry thing, a tattered coat upon a stick"—Yeats

3 old woman, old lady, dowager, granny, old granny, dame, **grandam;** old dame *and* hen *and* bag *and* girl (*all informal*); old bag *and* old bat *and* old battleaxe (*all informal*); **crone,** hag, witch, beldam, frump (*informal*), gammer (*informal*), old wife, babushka; grandmother

4 (*elderly couples*) Darby and Joan, Baucis and Philemon

5 senior, Sr, *senex* (*Latin*), **elder,** older, major; dean, *doyen* (*French*), *doyenne* (*French*); father, sire; first-born, firstling, **eldest,** oldest

verbs

6 to mature *see* 303.9; grow old *see* 303.10

adjectives

7 mature *see* 303.12; middle-aged *see* 303.14; aged *see* 303.16, older *see* 841.19

305 ORGANIC MATTER

nouns

1 organic matter, animate *or* living matter, all that lives, living nature, organic nature, organized matter; **biology** *see* 1066; **flesh, tissue**, fibre, brawn, plasm; **flora and fauna**, plant and animal life, animal and vegetable kingdom, biosphere, biota, ecosphere, noosphere

2 organism, organization, organic being, life-form, form of life, **living being** *or* **thing**, being, creature, created being, **individual**, genetic individual, physiological individual, morphological individual; zoon, zooid; virus; aerobic organism, anaerobic organism; heterotrophic organism, autotrophic organism; microbe, microorganism

3 biological classification, taxonomy, kingdom, phylum, etc

4 cell, bioplast, cellule; procaryotic cell, eucaryotic cell; plant cell, animal cell; germ cell, somatic cell; corpuscle; lymphocyte; unicellularity, multicellularity; germ layer, ectoderm, endoderm, mesoderm; **protoplasm**, energid, trophoplasm; chromatoplasm; germ plasm; cytoplasm; ectoplasm, endoplasm; cellular tissue, reticulum; plasmodium, coenocyte, syncytium

5 organelle; plastid; chromoplast, plastosome, chloroplast; mitochondrion; Golgi apparatus; ribosome; spherosome, microbody; vacuole; central apparatus, cytocentrum; centroplasm; centra body, microcentrum; centrosome; centrosphere; centriole, basal body; pili, cilia, flagella, spindle fibres; aster; kinoplasm; plasmodesmata; cell membrane

6 metaplasm; cell wall, cell plate; structural polysaccharide; bast, phloem, xylem, xyl– *or* xylo–, cellulose, chitin

7 nucleus, cell nucleus; macronucleus, meganucleus; micronucleus; nucleolus; plasmosome; karyosome, chromatin strands; nuclear envelope; chromatin, karyotin; basichromatin, heterochromatin, oxychromatin

8 chromosome; allosome; heterochromosome, sex chromosome, idiochromosome; W chromosome; X chromosome, accessory chromosome, monosome; Y chromosome; Z chromosome; euchromosome, autosome; homologous chromosomes; univalent chromosome, chromatid; centromere; gene-string, chromonema; genome; chromosome complement; chromosome number, diploid number, haploid number; polyploidy

9 genetic material, gene; allele; operon; cistron, structural gene, regulator gene, operator gene; altered gene; deoxyribonucleic acid *or* DNA; DNA double helix, superhelix *or* supercoil; nucleotide, codon; ribonucleic acid *or* RNA; messenger RNA, mRNA; transfer RNA, tRNA; ribosomal RNA; anticodon;

gene pool, gene complex, gene flow, genetic drift; genotype, biotype; **hereditary character**, heredity *see* 560.6; genetic counselling; genetic screening; **recombinant DNA technology**, gene mapping, gene splicing; gene transplantation, gene transfer, germline insertion; intronizing, intron *or* intervening sequence; exonizing, exon; **genetic engineering**; designer gene

10 gamete, germ cell, reproductive cell; macrogamete, megagamete; microgamete; planogamete; genetoid; gamone; gametangium, gametophore; gametophyte; germ plasm, idioplasm

11 sperm, spermatozoa, seed, semen, jism *or* gism *and* come *or* cum *and* scum *and* spunk (*all informal*); seminal *or* spermatic fluid, milt; **sperm cell**, male gamete; spermatozoon, spermatozoid, antherozoid; antheridium; spermatium, spermatiophore *or* spermatophore, spermagonium; pollen; spermatogonium; androcyte, spermatid, spermatocyte

12 ovum, egg, egg cell, female gamete, oösphere; oöcyte; oögonium; ovicell, oöecium; ovule; stirp; ovulation; donor egg

13 spore; microspore; macrospore, megaspore; swarm spore, zoospore, planospore; spore mother cell, sporocyte; zygospore; sporocarp, cystocarp; basidium; sporangium, megasporangium, microsporangium; sporocyst; gonidangium; sporogonium, sporophyte; sporophore; sorus

14 embryo, zygote, oösperm, oöspore, blastula; *Anlage* (*German*); **fetus** *or* **foetus**, germ, germen (*old*), rudiment; **larva**, nymph

15 egg; ovule; bird's egg; **roe**, fish eggs, caviar, spawn, frogspawn; **yolk**, yellow, vitellus; white, **egg white**, albumen, glair; eggshell

16 cell division; mitosis; amitosis; metamitosis, eumitosis; endomitosis, promitosis; haplomitosis, mesomitosis; karyomitosis; karyokinesis; interphase, prophase, metaphase, anaphase, telophase, diaster, cytokinesis; **meiosis**

adjectives

17 organic, organismic; organized; **animate, living**, vital, zoetic; **biological**, biotic; physiological

18 protoplasmic, plasmic, plasmatic; **genetic**, genic, hereditary

19 cellular, cellulous; unicellular, multicellular; corpuscular

20 gametic, gamic, sexual; **spermatic**, spermic, **seminal**, spermatozoal, spermatozoan, spermatozoic; sporal, sporous, sporoid; sporogenous

21 nuclear, nucleal, nucleary, nucleate; multinucleate; nucleolar, nucleolate, nucleolated; **chromosomal**; chromatinic; haploid, diploid, polyploid

22 embryonic, germinal, germinant, germinative, germinational; larval; fetal; in the bud; germiparous

23 egglike, ovicular, eggy; ovular; albuminous, albuminoid; yolked, yolky; oviparous

306 LIFE

nouns

1 life, living, vitality, being alive, having life, animation, animate existence; breath; liveliness, animal spirits, vivacity, spriteliness; long life, longevity; life expectancy, lifespan; viability; lifetime *see* 826.5; immortality *see* 828.3; birth *see* 1; existence *see* 760

2 "one dem'd horrid grind"—Dickens, "a beauty chased by tragic laughter"—John Masefield, "a little gleam of Time between two eternities"—Carlyle, "a tale told by an idiot, full of sound and fury, signifying nothing"—Shakespeare, "a perpetual instruction in cause and effect"—Emerson, "a flame that is always burning itself out"—G B Shaw, "a dome of many-coloured glass"—Shelley, "a long lesson in humility" —J M Barrie, "a fiction made up of contradiction"— William Blake, "a fatal complaint, and an eminently contagious one" —O W Holmes Sr., "a play of passion" —Sir W Raleigh, "a comedy to those who think, a tragedy to those who feel"—H Walpole

3 **life force, soul,** spirit, indwelling spirit, force of life, living force, *vis vitae* or *vis vitalis* (*both Latin*), **vital force** or energy, animating force or power or principle, inspiriting force or power or principle, archeus, élan vital, impulse of life, vital principle, **vital spark** or **flame,** spark of life, divine spark, life principle, vital spirit, vital fluid, anima; **breath,** life breath, **breath of life,** breath of one's nostrils, divine breath, life essence, essence of life, pneuma; prana, atman, jivatma, jiva; blood, **lifeblood,** heartblood, heart's blood; **heart,** heartbeat, beating heart; seat of life; growth force, bathmism; **life process;** biorhythm, biological clock, life cycle

4 **the living,** the living and breathing, all animate nature, the quick; the quick and the dead

5 vivification, vitalization, animation, quickening

6 biosphere, ecosphere, noosphere; biochore, biotype, biocycle

verbs

7 **to live,** be alive or animate or vital, have life, exist *see* 760.8, breathe, respire, live and breathe, fetch or draw breath, draw the breath of life, walk the earth, subsist

8 **to come to life,** come into existence or being, come into the world, see the light, be incarnated, **be born** or begotten or conceived; quicken; **revive, come to,** come alive, show signs of life; **awake, awaken;** rise again, live again, rise from the grave, resurge, resuscitate, reanimate, return to life

9 **to vivify, vitalize, energize, animate, quicken,** inspirit, imbue or endow with life, give life to, put life or new life into, breathe life into, bring to life, bring or call into existence or being; conceive; give birth

10 **to keep alive,** keep body and soul together, endure, survive, persist, last, last out, hang on, hang in (*informal*), be spared, have nine lives like a cat; support life; cheat death

adjectives

11 **living, alive,** having life, live, very much alive, alive and well, alive and kicking (*informal*), conscious, breathing, quick (*old*), **animate,** animated, **vital,** zoetic, instinct with life, imbued or endowed with life, vivified, enlivened, inspirited; in the flesh,

among the living, in the land of the living, on this side of the grave, above-ground; existent *see* 760.13; long-lived, tenacious of life; capable of life or survival, viable

12 **life-giving,** animating, animative, quickening, vivifying, energizing

307 DEATH

nouns

1 **death, dying,** somatic death, clinical death, biological death, abiosis, **decease, demise;** brain death; perishing, release, **passing away,** passing, passing over,

"crossing the bar"—Tennyson, leaving life, making an end, departure, parting, going, going off or away, exit, ending, **end** *see* 819, end of life, cessation of life, end of the road or line (*informal*); **loss of life,** ebb of life, expiration, **dissolution, extinction,** bane, annihilation, extinguishment, quietus; doom, summons of death, final summons, sentence of death, death knell, knell; **sleep, rest,** eternal rest or sleep, last sleep, last rest; **grave** *see* 309.16; reward, debt of nature, last debt; last muster, last roundup, curtains (*informal*); jaws of death, hand or finger of death, shadow or shades of death; rigor mortis; near-death experience or NDE

2 "the journey's end", "the undiscovered country from whose bourn no traveller returns", "dusty death"—all Shakespeare, "that dreamless sleep"—Byron, "a debt we all must pay"—Euripides, "the tribute due unto nature"—Laurence Sterne, "the sleeping partner of life"—Horace Smith, "a knell that summons thee to heaven or to hell", "that fell arrest without all bail"—both Shakespeare, "kind Nature's signal of retreat"—Samuel Johnson, "the latter end", "a little sleep, a little slumber, a little folding of the hands to sleep"—both Bible, "the seamouth of mortality"— Robinson Jeffers, "that good night"—Dylan Thomas, "the downward path"—Horace, "the gate of life"—St Bernard, "the crown of life"—Edward Young, "an awfully big adventure"—J M Barrie;

"the big sleep"—Raymond Chandler

3 (*personifications and symbols*) **Death,** "Black Death"—Ovid, "Pale Death"—Horace, "the pale priest of the mute people"—R Browning, "that grim ferryman", "that fell sergeant"—both Shakespeare, "Hell's grim Tyrant"—Pope, "the king of terrors"— Bible, **Grim Reaper,** Reaper; pale horse, pale rider; angel of death, death's bright angel, Azrael; scythe or sickle of Death; **skull,** death's-head, grinning skull, crossbones, skull and crossbones; *memento mori* (*Latin*); white cross

4 river of death, Styx, Stygian shore, Acheron; Jordan, Jordan's bank;

"valley of the shadow of death"—Bible; Heaven *see* 681; Hell *see* 682

5 early death, early grave, **untimely end,** premature death; sudden death; stroke of death, death stroke; deathblow

6 **violent death;** killing *see* 308; suffocation, smothering, smotheration (*informal*); asphyxiation;

choking, choke, strangulation, strangling; drowning, watery grave; starvation; liver death, serum death; megadeath

7 natural death; easy *or* quiet *or* peaceful death *or* end, euthanasia, blessed *or* welcome release

8 dying day, deathday,

"the supreme day and the inevitable hour"—Vergil; final *or* fatal hour, dying hour, running-out of the sands, deathtime

9 moribundity, extremity, last *or* final extremity; **deathbed;** deathwatch; death struggle, agony, last agony, death agony, death throes, throes of death; last breath *or* gasp, dying breath; **death rattle,** death groan

10 swan song, *chant du cygne* (*French*), death song
11 bereavement see 473.1
12 deathliness, deathlikeness, deadliness; **weirdness, eeriness, uncanniness,** unearthliness; ghostliness, ghostlikeness; **ghastliness, grisliness, gruesomeness,** macabreness; paleness, haggardness, wanness, luridness, pallor; cadaverousness, corpselikeness; *facies Hippocratica* (*Latin*), Hippocratic face *or* countenance, mask of death

13 death rate, death toll; **mortality,** mortalness; transience see 827; mutability see 853.1
14 obituary, obit (*informal*), necrology, necrologue; register of deaths, roll of the dead, death roll, mortuary roll, bill of mortality; casualty list; martyrology; death toll, body count

15 terminal case; dying
16 corpse, dead body, dead man *or* woman, dead person, **cadaver, carcass** *or* **carcase, body;** *corpus delicti* (*Latin*); **stiff** (*informal*); **the dead,** the defunct, **the deceased,** the departed, the loved one; **decedent,** late lamented; **remains,** mortal *or* organic remains, bones, skeleton, dry bones, relics, reliquiae; dust, ashes, earth, clay, tenement of clay; **carrion,** crowbait, food for worms; **mummy,** mummification; embalmed corpse

17 dead, the majority, the great majority; one's fathers, one's ancestors; the choir invisible
18 autopsy, postmortem, inquest, postmortem examination, ex post facto examination, necropsy, necroscopy, coroner, medical examiner

verbs

19 to die, decease, succumb, expire, perish, be taken by death, up and die (*informal*), cease to be *or* live, finish, part, depart, depart this earth, make one's exit, go, go the way of all flesh, go out, pass, pass on *or* over, **pass away, meet one's death** *or* **end** *or* **fate,** end one's life *or* days, depart this life,

"shuffle off this mortal coil"—Shakespeare, put off mortality, **lose one's life,** fall, be lost, relinquish *or* surrender one's life, resign one's life *or* being, **give up the ghost,** yield the ghost *or* spirit, yield one's breath, take one's last breath, breathe one's last, stop breathing, fall asleep, close one's eyes, take one's last sleep, pay the debt of *or* to nature, go out with the ebb,

"go the way of all earth"—Bible, return to dust *or* the earth

20 (*informal terms*) **to croak,** go west, kick the bucket, kick it, pop off, conk out, cop it, snuff it, drop off, go to the wall, go home feet first, shove off, bow out, pass out, peg out, peg it, pop one's clogs, push up daisies, go for a burton, belly up, go belly-up, go bung (*Australian & NZ*), bite the dust, take the last count, hop the twig; check out (*US*), check in (*US*), cash in, hand *or* pass *or* cash in one's checks *or* chips; turn up one's toes; slip one's cable; have one's time *and* have it *and* buy it

21 to meet one's Maker, go to glory, go to kingdom come (*informal*), go to the happy hunting grounds, go to *or* reach a better place *or* land *or* life *or* world, go to one's rest *or* reward, go home, go home feet first (*informal*), go to one's last home, go to one's long account, go over to *or* join the majority *or* great majority, **be gathered to one's fathers,** join one's ancestors, join the angels, join the choir invisible, die in the Lord, go to Abraham's bosom, pass over Jordan,

"walk through the valley of the shadow of death"—Bible, cross the Stygian ferry, give an obolus to Charon; awake to life immortal,

"put on immortality"—Bible

22 to drop dead, fall dead, fall down dead; come to an untimely end; predecease
23 to die in harness, die with one's boots on, make a good end, die fighting, die in the last ditch, die like a man
24 to die a natural death; die a violent death, be killed; **starve,** famish; smother, **suffocate;** asphyxiate; choke, strangle; **drown,** go to a watery grave, go to Davy Jones's locker (*informal*), sleep with the fishes (*informal*); catch one's death, catch one's death of cold

25 to lay down *or* **give one's life for one's country, die for one's country,**

"*pro patria mori*"—Horace, make the supreme sacrifice, do one's bit

26 to be dying, be moribund, be terminal; die out, become extinct
27 to be dead, be no more, sleep *or* be asleep with the Lord, sleep with one's fathers *or* ancestors; lie in the grave, lie in Abraham's bosom (*informal*)
28 to bereave; leave, leave behind; orphan, widow

adjectives

29 deathly, deathlike, deadly; **weird, eerie, uncanny,** unearthly; ghostly, ghostlike; **ghastly, grisly, gruesome, macabre;** pale, deathly pale, wan, lurid, blue, livid, haggard; **cadaverous,** corpselike; mortuary

30 dead, lifeless, breathless, without life, inanimate see 1053.5, exanimate, without vital functions; **deceased, demised, defunct,** croaked (*informal*), departed, departed this life, destitute of life, **gone, passed on,** gone the way of all flesh, gone west (*informal*), dead and gone, done for (*informal*), dead and done for (*informal*), no more, finished (*informal*), taken off *or* away, released, fallen, bereft of life, gone for a burton (*informal*), had one's chips (*informal*), bung (*Australian & NZ informal*); **at rest,** still, out of one's misery; **asleep,** sleeping, reposing; asleep in

Jesus, with the Lord, asleep *or* dead in the Lord; **called home**, out of the world, gone to a better world *or* place *or* land, launched into eternity, gone to glory, joined the choir invisible, gone to kingdom come (*informal*),

"gathered to his fathers"—BIBLE, with the saints, sainted, numbered with the dead; in the grave, six feet under *and* pushing up daisies (*both informal*); carrion, food for worms; martyred; death-struck, death-stricken, smitten with death; stillborn; late, late lamented

31 **stone-dead**; dead as a doornail *and* dead as a dodo *and* dead as a herring *and* dead as mutton (*all informal*); cold, stone-cold,

"as cold as any stone"—SHAKESPEARE, stiff (*informal*)

32 **drowned**, in a watery grave *or* bier, in Davy Jones's locker, sleeping with the fishes

33 **dying, terminal**, expiring, going, slipping, slipping away, sinking, sinking fast, low, despaired of, given up, given up for dead, not long for this world, hopeless, bad, **moribund**, near death, near one's end, at the end of one's rope (*informal*), done for (*informal*), at the point of death, **at death's door**, at the portals of death, *in articulo mortis* (*Latin*), *in extremis* (*Latin*), in the jaws of death, facing *or* in the face of death; **on one's last legs** (*informal*), with one foot in the grave, tottering on the brink of the grave; on one's deathbed; at the last gasp; terminal; nonviable, unviable, incapable of life

34 **mortal, perishable**, subject to death, ephemeral, transient *see* 827.7, mutable *see* 853.6

35 **bereaved**, bereft, deprived; widowed; orphan, **orphaned**, parentless, fatherless, motherless

36 **postmortem**, postmortal, postmortuary, postmundane, post-obit, postobituary, **posthumous**

adverbs

37 **deathly, deadly**; to the death, *à la mort* (*French*)

phrases

38 one's hour is come, one's days are numbered, one's race is run, one's doom is sealed, life hangs by a thread, one's number is up, Death knocks at the door, Death stares one in the face, the sands of life are running out

308 KILLING

nouns

1 **killing** (*see list*), **slaying, slaughter, dispatch, extermination, destruction**, destruction of life, taking of life, death-dealing, dealing of death, bane; kill; **bloodshed**, bloodletting, blood, gore, flow of blood; mercy killing, euthanasia, negative *or* passive euthanasia; ritual murder *or* killing, immolation, sacrifice; *auto-da-fé* (*Sp, literally, act of faith*), martyrdom, martyrization; lynching; stoning, lapidation; defenestration; braining; shooting; poisoning; execution *see* 604.7; mass killing, biocide, ecocide, genocide; Holocaust; mass murder

2 **homicide, manslaughter**; culpable homicide (*Scottish*); **murder**, bloody murder (*informal*); serial killing; hit *and* bump-off *and* bumping-off (*all informal*), gangland-style execution; kiss of death;

foul play; **assassination**; removal, elimination; liquidation, purge, purging; thuggery, thuggism, thuggee; justifiable homicide

3 **butchery**, butchering, **slaughter**, shambles, occision, slaughtering, hecatomb, holocaust

4 **carnage, massacre, bloodbath, decimation,** saturnalia of blood; **mass murder, mass destruction**, mass extermination, wholesale murder, pogrom, race-murder, genocide, race extermination, **the Holocaust**, the final solution

5 **suicide**, autocide, self-murder, self-homicide, self-destruction, death by one's own hand, *felo-de-se* (*Latin*), self-immolation, self-sacrifice; **disembowelment**, ritual suicide, *hara-kiri, seppuku* (*both Japanese*), suttee, sutteeism; car of Jagannath *or* Juggernaut; mass suicide, race suicide

6 **suffocation**, smothering, smotheration (*informal*), **asphyxiation**, asphyxia; **strangulation**, strangling, burking, throttling, stifling, garrotte, garrotting; **choking**, choke; **drowning**

7 **fatality**, fatal accident, violent death, **casualty**, disaster, calamity; DOA *or* dead-on-arrival

8 **deadliness, lethality**, mortality, fatality; **malignance** *or* malignancy, malignity, **virulence, perniciousness**, banefulness

9 **deathblow**, death stroke, final stroke, fatal *or* mortal *or* lethal blow, *coup de grâce* (*French*)

10 **killer, slayer, slaughterer, butcher**, bloodshedder; massacrer; **manslayer, homicide, murderer**, man-killer, bloodletter, Cain; **assassin**, assassinator; **cutthroat**, thug, desperado, bravo, gorilla (*informal*), apache, gunman; professional killer, hired killer, hit man (*informal*), gun *or* gunsel (*both US informal*); **hatchet man**; poisoner; strangler, garrotter, burker; cannibal, maneater, anthropophagus; headhunter; mercy killer; thrill killer, homicidal maniac; serial killer; executioner *see* 604.8; matador; exterminator, eradicator; death squad; poison, pesticide *see* 1000.3

11 (*place of slaughter*) aceldama, field of blood *or* bloodshed; **slaughterhouse**, butchery, shambles, abattoir, knacker's yard; stockyard; gas chamber, concentration camp, death camp, killing fields; Auschwitz, Belsen, etc

verbs

12 **to kill, slay, put to death**, deprive of life, bereave of life, **take life**, take the life of, take one's life away, **do away with**, make away with, **put out of the way**, put to sleep, end, **put an end to**, end the life of, **dispatch, do to death**, do for, finish, finish off, kill off, take off, **dispose of, exterminate, destroy**, annihilate; **liquidate**, purge; carry off *or* away, remove from life; put down, put away, put one out of one's misery; launch into eternity, send to glory, send to kingdom come (*informal*), send to one's last account; **martyr**, martyrize; immolate, sacrifice; lynch; cut down, cut off, nip in the bud; poison; chloroform; starve; euthanatize; **execute**

13 (*informal terms*) **to waste, zap**, nuke, rub out, croak, snuff, bump off, knock off, bushwhack, lay out, polish off, blow away, blot out, erase, wipe out, blast, whack (*US*), do in, hit, ice (*US*), gun down, pick off, put to bed with a shovel, scrag, take care

of, take out, take for a ride, give the business *or* works, get, fix, settle

14 to shed blood, spill blood, let blood, bloody one's hands with, dye one's hands in blood, have blood on one's hands, pour out blood like water, wade knee-deep in blood

15 to murder, commit murder; **assassinate;** remove, **purge, liquidate,** eliminate, get rid of

16 to slaughter, butcher, massacre, decimate, commit carnage, depopulate, murder *or* kill *or* slay en masse; commit mass murder *or* destruction, murder wholesale, commit genocide

17 to strike dead, fell, bring down, lay low; drop, drop *or* stop in one's tracks; **shoot,** shoot down, pistol, shotgun, machinegun, gun down, riddle, shoot to death; cut down, cut to pieces *or* ribbons, **put to the sword,** stab to death, jugulate, cut *or* slash the throat; **deal a deathblow,** give the quietus *or coup de grâce* (*French*), silence; knock in *or* on the head; **brain,** blow *or* knock *or* dash one's brains out, poleaxe; **stone,** lapidate, stone to death; defenestrate; blow up, blow to bits *or* pieces *or* kingdom come; disintegrate, vaporize; burn to death, incinerate, burn at the stake; necklace

18 to strangle, garrote, **throttle, choke,** burke; **suffocate, stifle, smother, asphyxiate,** stop the breath; **drown**

19 to condemn to death, sign one's death warrant, strike the death knell of, finger (*informal*), give the kiss of death to

20 to be killed, get killed, die a violent death, **come to a violent end,** meet with foul play; welter in one's own blood

21 to commit suicide, take one's own life, kill oneself, die by one's own hand, do away with oneself, put an end to oneself; blow one's brains out, take an overdose (*of a drug*), overdose *or* OD (*informal*); commit hara-kiri *or* seppuku; sign one's own death warrant, doom oneself

adjectives

22 deadly, deathly, deathful, **killing, destructive,** death-dealing, death-bringing, feral (*old*); savage, brutal; internecine; **fatal, mortal, lethal, malignant,** malign, **virulent, pernicious,** baneful; **life-threatening, terminal**

23 murderous, slaughterous; cutthroat; redhanded; **homicidal,** man-killing, death-dealing; biocidal, genocidal; suicidal, self-destructive; soul-destroying; cruel; **bloodthirsty,** bloody-minded; **bloody, gory,** sanguinary

24 types of killing and killers

aborticide *or* feticide (fetus)	(woman)
amicicide (friend)	herbicide (plants)
ceticide (whales)	homicide (person)
deicide (god)	infanticide (infant)
elephanticide (elephants)	insecticide (insects)
formicicide (ants)	mariticide (spouse, especially husband)
fratricide (brother)	matricide (mother)
fungicide (fungi)	microbicide *or* germicide (germs)
genocide (race)	
giganticide (giant)	ovicide (sheep)
gynecide *or* femicide	parenticide (parent)
parricide (kinsman)	tauricide (bulls)
patricide (father)	tickicide (ticks)
pesticide (pest)	tyrannicide (tyrant)
regicide (king)	uxoricide (wife)
rodenticide (rodent)	vaticide (prophet)
sororicide (sister)	vermicide *or* filaricide (worms)
spermicide *or* spermatozoicide (spermatozoa)	vespacide (wasps) viricide (viruses)
suicide *or* autocide (self)	

309 INTERMENT

nouns

1 interment, burial, burying, inhumation, sepulture, **entombment;** encoffinment, inurning, inurnment, urn burial; primary burial; secondary burial, reburial; disposal of the dead; burial *or* funeral *or* funerary customs

2 cremation, incineration, burning, reduction to ashes

3 embalmment, embalming; mummification

4 last offices, last honours, **last rites,** funeral rites, last duty *or* service, funeral service, burial service, exequies, **obsequies;** Office of the Dead, Memento of the Dead, requiem, requiem mass, dirge (*old*); **extreme unction;** viaticum; funeral oration *or* sermon, eulogy; **wake,** deathwatch

5 funeral, burial, burying; funeral procession, cortege; dead march, last post, muffled drum, taps; dirge; burial at sea, deep six (*US informal*)

6 knell, passing bell, death bell, funeral ring, tolling, tolling of the knell

7 mourner, griever, lamenter, keener; mute, professional mourner; **pallbearer,** bearer

8 undertaker, mortician, funeral director; cremator; embalmer; gravedigger; sexton

9 mortuary, morgue, deadhouse (*old*), charnel house, lichhouse (*informal*); ossuary *or* ossuarium; **funeral home** *or* **parlour,** undertaker's establishment; **crematorium,** crematory, cinerarium; pyre, funeral pile; burning ghat

10 hearse, funeral car *or* coach; catafalque

11 coffin, casket (*US*), burial case, box, kist (*Scottish*); **sarcophagus;** mummy case

12 urn, cinerary urn, funerary *or* funeral urn *or* vessel, bone pot, ossuary *or* ossuarium

13 bier, litter

14 grave clothes, shroud, winding sheet, cerecloth, cerements; pall

15 graveyard, cemetery, burial ground *or* **place,** burying place *or* ground, *campo santo* (*Italian*), boneyard *and* bone orchard (*both informal*), burial yard, necropolis, polyandrium, **memorial park,** city *or* village of the dead; **churchyard,** God's acre; **potter's field;** Golgotha, Calvary; urnfield; lych-gate

16 tomb, sepulchre; grave, gravesite, burial, pit, deep six (*US informal*); resting place, "the lone couch of his everlasting sleep"—SHELLEY; last home, long home, narrow house, house of death; **crypt, vault,** burial chamber; ossuary *or* ossuarium; charnel house, bone house; **mausoleum; catacombs;** mastaba; cist grave, box grave, passage grave, shaft grave, beehive tomb; **shrine**, reliquary, monstrance, tope, stupa; cenotaph; dokhma, tower of silence; pyramid, mummy chamber; burial mound, tumulus, barrow, cist, cromlech, dolmen

17 monument, gravestone *see* 549.12

18 epitaph, inscription, *hic jacet* (*Latin*), tombstone marking

verbs

19 to inter, inhume, **bury**, sepulture, inearth (*old*), **lay to rest**, **consign to the grave**, commit to the earth, lay in the grave *or* earth, lay under the sod, put six feet under (*informal*); tomb, **entomb**, ensepulchre, hearse; enshrine; inurn; encoffin, coffin; hold *or* conduct a funeral

20 to cremate, incinerate, burn, reduce to ashes

21 to lay out; **embalm**; mummify; lie in state

adjectives

22 funereal, funeral, funerary, funebrial, funebrous *or* funebrious, *funèbre* (*French*), feral (*old*); mortuary, exequial, obsequial; graveside; sepulchral, tomblike; cinerary; necrological, obituary, epitaphic; **dismal** *see* 112.24; **mournful** *see* 112.26; dirgelike

adverbs

23 beneath the sod, underground, six feet under (*informal*),
"in the dark union of insensate dust"—BYRON; at rest, resting in peace

phrases

24 **RIP**, *requiescat in pace* (*Latin singular*), *requiescant in pace* (*Latin plural*), rest in peace; *hic jacet* (*Latin*), *ci-gît* (*French*), here lies;
"ashes to ashes and dust to dust"—BOOK OF COMMON PRAYER

310 PLANTS

nouns

1 plants, vegetation; **flora**, **plant life**, vegetable life; **vegetable kingdom**, plant kingdom; herbage, flowerage, verdure, greenery, greens; botany *see* 1, 5, 6, 7; vegetation spirit *see* 1067.4

2 **growth**, stand, crop; plantation, planting; **clump**, tuft, tussock, hassock

3 **plant**; **vegetable**; **weed**; seedling; cutting; vascular plant; seed plant, spermatophyte; gymnosperm; angiosperm, flowering plant; monocotyledon *or* monocot *or* monocotyl; dicotyledon *or* dicot *or* dicotyl; polycotyledon *or* polycot *or* polycotyl; thallophyte, fungus; gametophyte, sporophyte; exotic, hothouse plant; ephemeral, annual, biennial, triennial, perennial; evergreen, deciduous plant; cosmopolite; aquatic plant, hydrophyte, amphibian

4 (*varieties*) **legume**, pulse, vetch, bean, pea, lentil; **herb** (*see list*), pot-herb; succulent; **vine** (*see list*), grapevine, creeper, ivy, climber, liana; **fern** (*see list*), bracken; **moss**; **wort**, liverwort; **algae**; **seaweed**, kelp, sea moss, rockweed, gulfweed, sargasso *or* sargassum, sea lentil, bladderwrack, wrack, sea wrack; **fungus**, mould, rust, smut, puffball, mushroom, toadstool; lichen; parasitic plant, parasite, saprophyte,

perthophyte, heterophyte, autophyte; plant families *see* 1066.3; fruits and vegetables

5 **grass**, gramineous *or* graminaceous plant, pasture *or* forage grass, lawn grass, ornamental grass; aftergrass, fog (*informal*); **cereal**, cereal plant, farinaceous plant, **grain**, corn; sedge; rush, reed, cane, bamboo

6 **turf**, **sod**, **sward**, greensward; divot

7 **green**, lawn; artificial turf, Astroturf (*trademark*); grassplot, greenyard; grounds; **common**, **park**, **village green**; golf course *or* links, fairway; bowling green, putting green; grass court

8 **grassland**, grass; parkland; **meadow**, meadow land, mead (*old*), swale, lea, haugh *or* haughland (*Scottish*), vega; bottomland, water meadow; **pasture**, pastureland, pasturage, pasture land; **grazing**, grazing land, range, sheepwalk, machair (*Scottish*); prairie, savanna, steppe, steppeland, pampas, pampa, campo, llano, veld, grass veld

9 **shrubbery**; **shrub**, **bush**; scrub, bramble, brier, brier bush; topiary

10 **tree** (*see list*), timber; shade tree, fruit tree, timber tree; softwood tree, hardwood tree; sapling, seedling; conifer, evergreen; pollard, pollarded tree

11 **woodland**, **wood**, **woods**, **timberland**; **timber**, stand of timber, **forest**, forest land, forest cover, forest preserve, state *or* national forest; forestry, dendrology, silviculture; afforestation, reforestation; boondocks (*US & Canadian informal*); wildwood, **bush**, scrub; bushveld, tree veld; shrubland, scrubland; barrens (*US*); hanger; **park**, parkland, chase; park forest; arboretum

12 **grove**, **woodlet**; holt (*informal*), hurst, spinney, tope (*India*), shaw (*informal*), bosk (*old*); **orchard**; wood lot; coppice, copse; *bocage* (*French*)

13 **thicket**, thickset, **copse**, **coppice**, copsewood, frith (*informal*); bosket (*old*), boscage; covert; motte; **brake**; chaparral (*US*)

14 **brush**, scrub, bush, **brushwood**, shrubwood, scrubwood

15 **undergrowth**, **underwood**, **underbrush**, copsewood, undershrubs, boscage, frith (*informal*); ground cover

16 **foliage**, **leafage**, leafiness, umbrage, foliation; frondage, frondescence; vernation

17 **leaf**, **frond**; leaflet, foliole; ligule; lamina, **blade**, spear, spire, pile, flag; **needle**, pine needle; floral leaf, **petal**, sepal; bract, bractlet, bracteole, spathe, involucre, involucrum, glume, lemma; cotyledon, seed leaf; stipule, stipula

18 **branch**, fork, **limb**, **bough**; deadwood; **twig**, **sprig**, switch; spray; **shoot**, offshoot, spear, frond; scion; **sprout**, sprit, slip, burgeon, thallus; sucker; **runner**, stolon, flagellum, sarmentum, sarment; bine; **tendril**; ramage; branchiness, branchedness, ramification

19 **stem**, **stalk**, **stock**, axis, *caulis* (*Latin*); **trunk**, bole; spear, spire; straw; reed; cane; culm, haulm; caudex; footstalk, pedicel, peduncle; leafstalk, petiole, petiolus, petiolule; seedstalk; caulicle; tigella; funicule, funiculus; stipe, anthrophore, carpophore, gynophore

20 **root**, radix, radicle; rootlet; **taproot**, tap; **rhizome**, rootstock; **tuber**, tubercle; **bulb**, bulbil, corm, earthnut

21 bud, burgeon, gemma; gemmule, gemmula; plumule, acrospire; leaf bud, flower bud

22 flower (*see list*), **posy, blossom, bloom,** blow (*old*); floweret, floret, floscule; **wildflower; gardening,** horticulture, floriculture; hortorium

23 bouquet, nosegay, posy, boughpot, flower arrangement; **buttonhole; corsage; spray; wreath;** festoon; **garland,** chaplet, lei

24 flowering, florescence, efflorescence, flowerage, **blossoming, blooming;** inflorescence; **blossom, bloom,** blowing, blow; unfolding, unfoldment; anthesis, full bloom

25 (*types of inflorescence*) raceme, corymb, umbel, panicle, cyme, thyrse, spadix, verticillaster; head, capitulum; spike, spikelet; ament, catkin; strobile, cone, pine cone

26 (*flower parts*) petal, perianth; calyx, epicalyx; corolla, corolla tube, corona; androecium, anther, stamen, microsporophyll; pistil, gynoecium; style; stigma, carpel, megasporophyll; receptacle, torus

27 ear, spike; auricle; ear of corn, mealie (*South African*); **cob,** corncob

28 seed vessel, seedcase, seedbox, pericarp; hull, husk; **capsule, pod,** cod (*dialect*), seed pod; pease cod, legume, legumen, boll, burr, follicle, silique

29 seed; stone, pit, nut; pip; fruit; **grain, kernel, berry;** flaxseed, linseed; hayseed; bird seed

30 vegetation, growth; germination, pullulation; burgeoning, sprouting; budding, luxuriation

verbs

31 to vegetate, grow; germinate, pullulate; root, take root, strike root; sprout up, shoot up, upsprout, upspear; **burgeon,** put forth, burst forth; **sprout,** shoot; **bud,** gemmate, put forth *or* put out buds; **leaf,** leave, leaf out, put out *or* put forth leaves; flourish, luxuriate, riot, grow rank *or* lush; overgrow, overrun

32 to flower, be in flower, **blossom, bloom,** be in bloom, blow, effloresce, floreate, burst into bloom

adjectives

33 vegetable, vegetal, vegetative, vegetational, vegetarian; **plantlike; herbaceous,** herbal, herbous, herbose, herby; leguminous, leguminose, leguminiform; cereal, farinaceous; weedy; fruity, fruitlike; tuberous, bulbous; rootlike, rhizoid, radicular, radicated, radiciform; botanic, botanical

34 algal, fucoid, confervoid; phytoplanktonic, diatomaceous; fungous, fungoid, fungiform

35 floral; flowery, florid (*old*); **flowered,** floreate, floriate, floriated; **flowering, blossoming, blooming,** abloom, bloomy, florescent, inflorescent, efflorescent, in flower, in bloom, in blossom; uniflorous, multiflorous, floriferous; radiciflorous, rhizanthous; **garden,** horticultural, hortulan, floricultural

36 arboreal, arborical, arboresque, arboreous, arborary; **treelike,** arboriform, arborescent, dendroid, dendriform, dendritic; deciduous, nondeciduous; evergreen; softwood, hardwood, piny; coniferous; citrus; bosky, bushy, shrubby, scrubby, scrubbly; bushlike, shrublike, scrublike

37 sylvan, woodland, forest, forestal; dendrologic, dendrological, silvicultural, afforestational, reforestational; **wooded,** timbered, forested, arboreous; **woody,** woodsy, bosky, bushy, shrubby, scrubby; copsy, braky

38 leafy, leavy (*old*), bowery; foliated, foliate, foliose, foliaged, leaved; **branched,** branchy, branching, ramified, ramate, ramous *or* ramose; twiggy

39 verdant, verdurous, verdured; **mossy,** moss-covered, moss-grown; **grassy,** grasslike, gramineous, graminaceous; turfy, swardy, turflike, caespitose, tufted; meadowy

40 luxuriant, flourishing, **rank, lush,** riotous, exuberant; dense, impenetrable, thick, heavy, gross; jungly, jungled; overgrown, overrun; **weedy,** unweeded, weed-choked, weed-ridden; gone to seed

41 perennial, ephemeral; hardy, half-hardy; **deciduous,** evergreen

42 herbs

angelica	horehound
anise	hyssop
balm	liquorice
basil	liverwort
belladonna	mandrake
boneset	marijuana
borage	marjoram
burning bush	mayapple
calendula	mint
camomile	monkshood
caraway	mullein
cardamom	mustard
castor-oil plant	oregano *or* origanum
catnip *or* catmint	parsley
chervil	peppermint
chicory	rosemary
clover	rue
coriander	sage
Cretan dittany	savory
deadly nightshade	sorrel
death camas	spearmint
dill	sweet cicely
dittany	sweet woodruff
fennel	tansy
feverroot	tarragon
figwort	thyme
fraxinella *or* gas plant	tobacco
ginseng	wall rue
hemp	wild marjoram
henbane	wintergreen

43 vines

bittersweet	morning glory
clematis	poison ivy
dewberry	travellers joy
English ivy	trumpet creeper
grape	trumpet flower
greenbrier	trumpet honeysuckle
honeysuckle	Virginia creeper
hop	virgins-bower
ivy	wisteria
jasmine	woodbine
liana	

44 ferns

adder's fern	marsh fern
basket fern	moonwort
beech fern	oak fern
bladder fern	osmunda
boulder fern	ostrich fern
bracken	parsley fern
buckler fern	pillwort
chain fern	rattlesnake fern
cliff brake	rock brake
climbing fern	royal fern
curly grass	shield fern
grape fern	snuffbox fern
hard fern	sword fern
hart's tongue	tree fern
holly fern	Venus's fern
jojoba	walking fern
lady fern	wall fern
lip fern	wood fern
maidenhair	woodsia
male fern	

45 trees

abele	cacao	hazel *or* hazelnut	rain tree
acacia	camphor tree	hemlock	redwood
ailanthus *or* tree of heaven	candleberry	henna	rosewood
akee	carob	hickory	rowan
alder	cashew	holly	rubber plant
allspice	cassia	hop tree	sandalwood
almond	casuarina	hornbeam	sassafras
aloe	catalpa	horse chestnut	satinwood
apple	cedar	ilex	Scots fir
apricot	cherry	ironwood	Scots pine
assegai *or* assagai	chestnut	jacaranda	senna
ash	chinaberry tree *or* China	Judas tree	sequoia
aspen	tree	juniper	serviceberry
avocado *or* alligator pear	chinquapin	kumquat	silk oak
bald cypress	cinnamon	laburnum	silver birch
balsa	citron	lancewood	spruce
balsam	clove	larch	sycamore
banksia	coconut *or* coco	laurel	tamarack
banyan	coolabah	lemon	tamarind
baobob	cork oak	lignum vitae	tamarugo
basswood	cottonwood	lilac	tangerine
bay	cypress	lime	teak
bayberry	date palm	linden	thorn tree
beech	deal	litchi *or* litchi nut	thuja
betel palm	dogwood	locust	torchwood
birch	Douglas fir	logwood	trembling poplar
black bean	ebony	lotus	tulip oak
blackbutt	elder	madroña	tulip tree
blackwood	elm	magnolia	turpentine tree
bonsai	eucalyptus	mahogany	umbrella tree
boobialla	ficus	mango	upas
bottlebrush	fig	mangrove	varnish tree
bottle tree	fir	maple	walnut
boxwood	frankincense	medlar	wandoo
Brazil-nut	ginkgo	mimosa	wax palm
breadfruit	grapefruit	monkey puzzle	wax tree
brigalow	ground ash	mountain ash	wayfaring tree
buckeye	ground oak	mulberry	weeping willow
bunya	guava	myall *or* boree	western hemlock
butternut	gum	nutmeg	white ash
buttonwood	hawthorn	nux vomica	white birch
		oak	white cedar
		olive	white gum
		orange	white oak
		osier	white pine
		palm	white poplar
		papaw	white spruce
		papaya	whitebeam
		peach	whitethorn
		pear	wicopy
		pecan	willow
		persimmon	witch hazel
		pine	woollybutt
		pistachio	wych-elm
		pitch pine	yellow poplar
		plane	yellowwood *or* gopher
		plum	wood
		pomegranate	yew
		poplar	ylang-ylang
		pussy willow	yucca
		quince	zebrawood
		raffia palm	

46 flowers

acacia
acanthus
African violet
agapanthus
alyssum
amaranth
amaryllis
anemone *or* windflower
arbutus
arrowhead
asphodel
aspidistra
aster
azalea
baby's breath
baby-blue-eyes
bachelor button
begonia
betony
bignonia
bitterroot
black-eyed Susan
bleeding heart
bloodroot
bluebell
bluet
bog asphodel
bougainvillaea
bridal wreath
broom
buttercup
cactus
calendula
camas
camellia
camomile
campanula
candytuft
cardinal flower
carnation
cat's-paw
cattail
celandine
century plant
Chinese lantern
Christmas rose
chrysanthemum
cineraria
clematis
clethra
cockscomb
columbine
cornel
cornflower
cosmos
cotoneaster
cowslip
crocus
cyclamen
daffodil
dahlia
daisy

damask rose
dandelion
deadly nightshade
delphinium
deutzia
digitalis
dog rose
dogwood
duckweed
Dutchman's-breeches
edelweiss
eglantine
elderflower
fireweed
flax
fleur-de-lis (French)
forget-me-not
forsythia
foxglove
foxtail
freesia
fuchsia
gardenia
gentian
geranium
gilliflower *or* gillyflower
gladiolus
godetia
goldenrod
groundsel
guelder rose
harebell
hawthorn
heartsease *or* heart's-ease
heather
heliotrope
hellebore
hemlock
hepatica
hibiscus
hollyhock
honeysuckle
horehound
hyacinth
hydrangea
impatience
Indian paintbrush
indigo
iris
jack-in-the-pulpit
japonica
jasmine
jonquil
kingcup
knotweed
lady's-slipper
larkspur
lavender
lilac
lily
lily of the valley
lobelia

London pride
lotus
love-in-idleness
love-lies-bleeding
lupin
magnolia
mallow
marguerite
marigold
marsh marigold
marshmallow
mayflower
meadowsweet
monkshood
Michaelmas daisy
mignonette
mimosa
moccasin flower
mock orange
monkshood
morning-glory
moss rose
motherwort
myrtle
narcissus
nasturtium
old man's beard
oleander
opium poppy
orchid
oxalis
oxeye daisy
oxlip
oxtongue
pansy
passion flower
peony
periwinkle
petunia
phlox
pink
poinsettia
polyanthus
poppy
portulaca
primrose
primula
Queen Anne's lace
ragged robin
ragweed
ragwort
rambler rose
ranunculus
resurrection plant
rhododendron
rose

samphire
scarlet pimpernel *or*
  shepherd's weatherglass
shooting star
smilax
snapdragon
snowball
snowberry
snowdrop
speedwell
spiraea
stock
strawflower
sunflower
sweet alyssum
sweetbrier
sweet pea
sweet william
tick trefoil
tiger lily
trailing arbutus
trillium
trumpet vine
tulip
twayblade
twinflower
umbrella plant
valerian
Venus's flytrap
verbena
vetch
viburnum
viola
violet
wake-robin
wallflower
water hyacinth
water lily
water milfoil
water pimpernel
wax flower
waxplant
white clover
willowherb
wintergreen
wisteria
wolfbane
wood anemone
woodbine
wood hyacinth
woody nightshade
yarrow
yellow water lily
yucca
zinnia

311 ANIMALS, INSECTS

nouns

1 **animal life, animal kingdom,** brute creation,
fauna, Animalia (*zoology*), animality; animal
behaviour, biology; birds, beasts and fish; the beasts

of the field, the fowl of the air, and the fish of the sea; domestic animals, livestock, stock (*informal*), cattle; wild animals *or* beasts, beasts of field, wildlife, denizens of the forest *or* jungle *or* wild, furry creatures; predators, beasts of prey; game, big game, small game

2 **animal**, **creature**, critter (*informal*), living, being *or* thing, creeping thing; **brute**, **beast**, varmint (*informal*), dumb animal *or* creature, dumb friend

3 (*varieties*) **vertebrate**; **invertebrate**; **biped**, **quadruped**; **mammal**, mammalian **primate** (*see list*); **marsupial**, marsupialian; canine; **feline**; **rodent**, gnawer; **ungulate**; **ruminant**; insectivore, herbivore, carnivore, omnivore; cannibal; scavenger; reptile; amphibian; aquatic; cosmopolite; vermin, varmint (*informal*)

4 **pachyderm**; **elephant**, Jumbo, hathi (*India*), "heffalump"—A A MILNE; mammoth, woolly mammoth; mastodon; **rhinoceros**, rhino; **hippopotamus**, hippo, river horse

5 (*hoofed animals*) **deer**, **buck**, **doe**, **fawn**; red deer, **stag**, hart, hind; roe deer, roe, roebuck; musk deer; fallow deer; hogdeer; white-tailed *or* Virginia deer; mule deer; **elk**, wapiti; **moose**; **reindeer**, caribou; deerlet; **antelope**; gazelle, kaama, wildebeest *or* gnu, hartebeest, springbok, reebok, dik-dik, eland *or* Cape elk, koodoo; **camel**, dromedary, ship of the desert; **giraffe**, camelopard, okapi

6 **cattle** (*see list*), kine (*old plural*), neat; beef cattle, beef, beeves (*plural*); dairy cattle *or* cows; bovine animal, **bovine**, critter (*US & Canadian informal*); **cow**, moo-cow (*informal*); milk *or* milch cow, milker, milcher, dairy cow; **bull**, bullock; **steer**, stot (*informal*), **ox**, oxen (*plural*); **calf**, **heifer**, yearling, fatling, stirk, bobby calf (*NZ*); **dogie**; hornless cow, muley cow; zebu, Brahman; yak; musk ox; **buffalo**, water buffalo, Indian buffalo, carabao; bison, aurochs, wisent

7 **sheep** (*see list*), jumbuck (*Australian*); **lamb**, lambkin, yeanling; hog *or* hogget, teg; **ewe**, yow (*informal*); ewe lamb; **ram**, tup, wether; bellwether; mutton

8 **goat**; he-goat, buck, **billy goat** *and* billy (*both informal*); she-goat, doe, **nanny goat** *and* nanny (*both informal*); **kid**; mountain goat

9 **swine** (*see list*), **pig**, **hog**, porker; **shoat**, piggy, piglet, pigling; sucking *or* suckling pig; gilt; **boar**, **sow**; barrow; wild boar, tusker, razorback; warthog, babirusa

10 **horse** (*see list*); **pony**; horseflesh, critter (*US & Canadian informal*); **equine**, mount, **nag** (*informal*); **steed**, prancer, dobbin; charger, courser, war-horse, destrier (*old*); Houyhnhnm (*Jonathan Swift*); **colt**, foal, filly; **mare**, brood mare; **stallion**, **studhorse**, **stud**, entire horse, entire; gelding, thoroughbred horse, purebred horse, blood horse; wild horse, Przewalsky's horse, tarpan, brumby (*Australian*); **bronco**, range horse, Indian pony, cayuse, mustang; stockhorse, roping horse, cow pony

11 (*coloured horses*) appaloosa, bay, bayard, chestnut, grey, dapple-grey, grizzle, roan, sorrel, dun, buckskin (*Western US*), pinto, paint, piebald, skewbald, calico pony, painted pony

12 (*inferior horse*) **nag**, hack, jade, crock, garron (*Scottish & Irish*), scalawag, Rosinante, plug (*US*); stiff (*informal*); roarer, whistler; balky horse, balker; rogue; scrag, stack of bones

13 **hunter**; stalking-horse, **saddle horse**, saddler, rouncy (*old*), **riding horse**, rider, palfrey, **mount**; remount; polo pony; post-horse; cavalry horse; **driving horse**, road horse, roadster, carriage horse, coach horse, gigster; hack, hackney; **draught horse**, dray horse, cart horse, **workhorse**, plough horse; shaft horse, pole horse, thill horse, thiller, fill horse *or* filler; wheelhorse, wheeler, lead, leader; pack horse, jument (*old*), sumpter, sumpter horse, bidet; pit-pony

14 **race horse**; **show-horse**, **gaited horse**, galloper, trotter, pacer; stepper, high-stepper, cob, prancer; ambler, padnag, pad; racker (*US*); single-footer

15 (*distinguished horses*) Al Borak (*Mohammed's winged horse of ascension*), Baiardo (*Rinaldo's bay horse*), Black Beauty, Black Bess (*Dick Turpin's horse*), Black Saladin (*Warwick's horse*), Boxer, Bucephalus (*Alexander the Great's horse*), Buttermilk (*Dale Evans' horse*), Champion (*Gene Autry's horse*), Copenhagen (*Wellington's horse at Waterloo*), Flicka, Grani (*Sigurd's magic horse*), Hercules, Incitatus (*Caligula's horse*), Marengo (*Napoleon's white horse*), Pegasus (*winged horse of the Muses*), Roan Barbary (*favourite horse of Richard II*), Rosinante (*Don Quixote's bony horse*), Silver (*the Lone Ranger's horse*), Sleipnir (*Odin's eight-legged horse*), Topper (*Hopalong Cassidy's horse*), Traveller (*Robert E Lee's horse*), Trigger (*Roy Rogers' horse*), Vegliantino *or* Veillantif (*Orlando's horse*), White Surrey (*favourite horse of Richard III*)

16 **ass**, **donkey**, **burro**, neddy *or* cuddy (*both informal*), moke (*informal*); **jackass**, jack, dickey (*informal*); jenny, jenny ass, jennet; **mule**, sumpter mule, sumpter; hinny, jennet

17 **dog** (*see list*), **canine**, **pooch** *and* bow-wow (*both informal*); **pup**, **puppy**, puppy-dog (*informal*), **whelp**; bitch, slut; toy dog, lap dog; working dog; ratter; guard dog, watchdog, bandog; police dog; sniffer dog; tracker dog; sheep dog, shepherd *or* shepherd's dog, backing dog (*NZ*); cattle dog, blue heeler *or* heeler (*Australian & NZ*), bluey (*Australian informal*); guide dog, hearing dog, support dog; sledge dog; gazehound, sighthound; show dog, fancy dog; kennel, pack of dogs

18 sporting dog, **hunting dog**, hunter, field dog, bird dog, gundog, water dog

19 **cur**, **mongrel**, lurcher, **mutt** (*informal*), bitser (*informal*), brak (*South African*); pye-dog *or* pariah dog

20 **fox**, reynard, tod (*dialect*); **wolf**, timber wolf, **coyote**, brush wolf, prairie wolf; dingo, jackal, **hyena**; Cape hunting dog, African hunting dog

21 **cat** (*see list*), **feline**, pussy *and* puss *and* pussycat (*all informal*), moggy *or* mog (*informal*), tabby, grimalkin; house cat; **kitten**, **kitty** *and* kitty-cat (*both informal*); kit, kitling (*Scottish*); **tomcat**, tom; gib *or* gib-cat (*both informal*); mouser; ratter; Cheshire cat; silver cat, Chinchilla cat; blue cat, Maltese cat; tiger cat, tabby cat; tortoise-shell cat, calico cat; alley cat

22 (*wild cats*) **big cat, jungle cat; lion,** Leo (*informal*), *simba* (*Swahili*); **tiger,** Siberian tiger; **leopard,** panther, jaguar, cheetah; cougar, puma, mountain lion, catamount *or* cat-a-mountain; lynx, ocelot; wildcat, bobcat

23 (*wild animals*) **bear;** guinea pig, cavy; hedgehog, **porcupine; badger,** brock; **woodchuck,** groundhog; **raccoon,** coon; **opossum,** possum, burramys; weasel; **polecat,** foumart; **wolverine,** glutton; ferret; skunk; zorilla *or* zorille, stink cat (*South Africa*), Cape polecat; **primate, simian; ape; monkey,** chimpanzee, chimp

24 hare, leveret, jackrabbit; **rabbit, bunny** *and* bunny rabbit (*both informal*), lapin; cottontail; Belgian hare, leporide; buck, doe

25 reptile, reptilian; **lizard;** dinosaur, saurian; crocodile, crocodilian, alligator, gator (*informal*); tortoise, turtle, terrapin

26 serpent, snake, ophidian; **viper,** pit viper, horned viper; **adder,** death adder, puff adder; anaconda; asp; boa, boa constrictor; **cobra,** king cobra; **python;** sidewinder; grass snake; tree snake; sea snake, water snake

27 amphibian, batrachian, croaker, puddock (*informal*); **frog,** rani–, tree toad *or* frog, bullfrog, Goliath frog, hairy frog, hyla; toad, midwife toad, natterjack, pipa *or* Surinam toad, Queensland cane toad; newt, salamander, axolotl, congo eel *or* snake, hellbender, mud puppy, olm, siren; caecilian; **tadpole, polliwog**

28 bird, fowl; dicky-bird *and* birdy *and* birdie (*all informal*); fowls of the air, birdlife, avifauna, feathered friends; baby bird, chick, nestling, fledgling; wildfowl, game bird; waterfowl, water bird, wading bird, diving bird; sea bird; shore bird; migratory bird, migrant, bird of passage; **songbird,** oscine bird, warbler, passerine bird, perching bird; cage bird; flightless bird, ratite; seed-eating bird, insect-eating bird, fruit-eating bird, fish-eating bird; **raptor,** bird of prey; **eagle,** bird of Jove, eaglet; **hawk, falcon; owl,** bird of Minerva, bird of night, screech owl; crow, raven; peafowl, peahen, **peacock,** bird of Juno; petrel; **swan,** cygnet; **pigeon,** dived, squab

29 poultry, fowl, domestic fowl, barnyard fowl; **chicken** (*see list*), chick, chicky *and* chickabiddy (*both informal*); **cock, rooster,** chanticleer; **hen,** biddy (*informal*), partlet; cockerel, pullet; setting hen, brooder, broody hen; capon, poulard; broiler, fryer, spring chicken, roaster, stewing chicken; Bantam, banty (*informal*); game fowl; guinea fowl, guinea cock, guinea hen; **goose,** gander, gosling; **duck,** drake, duckling; **turkey,** gobbler, turkey gobbler; turkey-cock, tom, tom turkey; hen turkey; poult

30 marine animal (*see list*), denizen of the deep; **whale,** cetacean; **porpoise, dolphin,** sea pig; **sea serpent,** sea snake, Loch Ness monster, sea monster, Leviathan (*Bible*); **fish,** game fish, tropical fish, panfish; **shark,** man-eating shark, man-eater; **salmon,** kipper, grilse, smolt, parr, alevin; **minnow** *or* minny (*informal*), tiddler (*informal*), fry, fingerling; **sponge; plankton,** zooplankton, nekton, benthon, benthos, zoobenthos; **crustacean,** lobster, spiny lobster, **crab,** blueclaw, Dungeness crab, king crab,

spider crab, land crab, stone crab, soft-shell crab; crayfish; **mollusc,** wentletrap, whelk, snail, cockle, mussel, **clam, oyster,** razor clam, quahog, steamer, toheroa, tridachna *or* giant clam

31 insect, bug, creepy-crawly (*informal*); **beetle;** arthropod; hexapod, myriapod; centipede, chilopod; millipede, diplopod; **mite; arachnid, spider,** tarantula, black widow spider, harvestman; **scorpion; tick;** larva, maggot, nymph, **caterpillar; insect; fly,** housefly, blowfly, crane fly, daddy-longlegs (*informal*)

32 ant, emmet (*informal*), pismire (*dialect*); red ant, black ant, fire ant, house ant, agricultural ant, carpenter ant, army ant, bulldog *or* bull ant; slave ant, slave-making ant; **termite,** white ant; queen, worker, soldier

33 bee, honeybee, bumblebee, carpenter bee; queen, queen bee, worker, drone, African bee; **wasp; hornet,** yellow jacket

34 locust, acridian; **grasshopper,** hopper; **cricket;** cicada, cicala, dog-day cicada, seventeen-year locust

35 vermin; parasite; louse, head louse, body louse, greyback, cootie (*US & NZ informal*); crab, crab louse; weevil; nit; **flea,** sand flea, dog flea, cat flea, chigoe, chigger, jigger, red bug, mite, harvest mite; **roach, cockroach,** *cucaracha* (*Spanish*)

36 bloodsucker, parasite; leech; tick, wood tick, deer tick; **mosquito,** mossie (*Australian & NZ informal*), skeeter (*US informal*), culex; bedbug, carpet beetle

37 worm; earthworm, angleworm, fishworm, night crawler; measuring worm, inchworm; tapeworm, helminth

adjectives

38 animal, animalian, animalic, animalistic, animal-like, theriomorphic, zoic, zooidal; zoologic, zoological; **brutish, brutal,** brute, brutelike; **bestial, beastly,** beastlike; **wild,** feral; subhuman, soulless; dumb, "that wants discourse of reason"—SHAKESPEARE; instinctual *or* instinctive, mindless, nonrational; half-animal, half-human, anthropomorphic, therianthropic

39 vertebrate, chordate, mammalian; viviparous; marsupial, cetacean

40 canine, doggish, doggy, doglike; vulpine, foxy, foxlike; lupine, wolfish, wolflike

41 feline, felid, cattish, catty, catlike; kittenish; leonine, lionlike; tigerish, tigerlike

42 ursine, bearish, bearlike

43 rodent, rodential; verminous; mousy, mouselike; ratty, ratlike

44 ungulate, hoofed, hooved; **equine,** hippic, horsy, horselike; **equestrian;** asinine, mulish; bovid, ruminant, "that chew the cud"—BIBLE; **bovine,** cowlike, cowish; bull-like, bullish, taurine; cervine, deerlike; caprine, caprid, hircine, goatish, goatlike; ovine, sheepish, sheeplike; porcine, swinish, piggish, hoggish

45 elephantlike, elephantine, pachydermous

46 reptile, reptilian, **reptilelike,** reptiloid, reptiliform; reptant, repent, creeping, crawling, slithering; **lizardlike,** saurian; crocodilian; **serpentine,** serpentile, serpentoid, serpentiform, **serpentlike;** snakish, **snaky, snakelike,** colubrine, ophidian, anguine (*old*); viperish, viperous, vipery, viperine, viperoid, viperiform, viperlike; amphibian, batrachian, froggy, toadish, salamandrian

47 birdlike, birdy; avian, avicular; gallinaceous, rasorial; oscine, passerine, perching; columbine, columbaceous, dovelike; psittacine; aquiline, hawklike; anserine, anserous, goosy; nidificant, nesting, nest-building; nidicolous, altricial; nidifugous, precocial

48 fishlike, fishy; piscine, pisciform; piscatorial, piscatory; eellike; selachian, sharklike, sharkish

49 invertebrate, invertebral; protozoan, protozoal, protozoic; crustaceous, crustacean; molluscan, molluscoid

50 insectile, insectlike, buggy; verminous; lepidopterous, lepidopteran; weevily

51 wormlike, vermicular, vermiform; wormy

52 planktonic, nektonic, benthonic, zooplanktonic, zoobenthoic

53 primates

angwantibo	howling monkey
anthropoid ape	king monkey
ape	langur
aye-aye	lemur
baboon	lion-tailed monkey *or*
Barbary ape	macaque
Bengal monkey	macaque
bonnet monkey *or*	man
macaque	mandrill
capuchin	marmoset
chacma	mountain gorilla
chimpanzee	orangutan *or* orang
colobus	owl monkey
drill	proboscis monkey
entellus	rhesus
gibbon	saki
gorilla	siamang
grivet	sloth monkey
guenon	spider monkey
guereza	squirrel monkey
hanuman	vervet

54 breeds of cattle

Aberdeen Angus *or* Angus *or* black Angus	Holstein *or* Holstein-Friesian
Afrikander *or* Africandeer	Illawarra
Alderney	Jersey
Ayrshire	Kerry
Belted Galloway	kyloe
Blonde d'Aquitaine	Kobe cattle
Brahman *or* Brahmany	Limousin
Brown Swiss	Lincoln Red *or* Lincoln
cattalo *or* catalo	Red Shorthorn
Charbray	Longhorn
Charolais	Meuse-Rhine-Ijssel
Devon	Normandy
Dexter	Norwegian Red
Durham	Polled Durham *or*
Dutch Belted	Shorthorn
French Canadian	Polled Hereford
Friesian	Red Poll *or* Red Polled
Galloway	Red Sindhi
Guernsey	Santa Gertrudis
Hereford	Shorthorn
Highland	Simmental

Sussex	Welsh *or* Welsh Black
Texas Longhorn	West Highland

55 breeds of sheep

Afrikander *or* Africander	Leicester
bighorn *or* mountain sheep	Lincoln
black face Highland	Merino
blackhead Persian	Oxford *or* Oxfordshire
blue-faced *or* Hexham	Down
Leicester	Panama
Border Leicester	Rambouillet
broadtail	Romanov
Cheviot	Romeldale
Clun Forest	Romney *or* Romney Marsh
Columbia	Ryeland
Corriedale	Scottish blackface
Cotswold	Shropshire
Devon longwool	Soay
Dorset Down	Southdown
Dorset Horn	Suffolk
Hampshire *or* Hampshire	Swaledale
Down	Targhee
Herdwick	Texel
Karaku	Welsh Mountain
Kerry Hill	Wensleydale

56 breeds of swine

Berkshire	Mangalitza
Cheshire	middle white
Chester White	miniature pig
Duroc *or* Duroc-Jersey	Poland China
fastback	Spotted Poland China
Gloucester Old Spot	Tamworth
Hampshire	Vietnamese potbellied pig
Hereford	Welsh
Landrace	Wessex saddleback
large black	Yorkshire
large white	

57 breeds of horse

Akhal-Teke	Dales pony
American Quarter horse	Danish
American Saddle horse	Dartmoor pony
Andalusian	Don
Anglo-Arab	Dutch Draught
Anglo-Norman	Esthonian, Smudish *or*
Appaloosa	Zmudzin
Arab	Exmoor
Ardennes	Fell pony
Balearic	Finnish horse
Barb	Fjord pony
Basuto	Flemish
Batak *or* Deli	Friesian
boerperd	Gelderland
Beetewk	Gidran
Bhutia	Groningen
Bilgoraj	Gudbrandsdal
Bokhara pony	Hackney
Boulonnais	Hafflinger
Brabançon	Hambletonian
Breton	Hanoverian
Burmese *or* Shan	Highland pony
Cleveland Bay	Holstein
Clydesdale	Huçul
Connemara	Iceland pony
Criollo	Iomud

Jutland
Kabarda
Karabair
Karabakh
Karadagh
Kathiawari
Kladruber
Klepper
Knabstrup
Konik
Kurdistan pony
Limousin
Lipizzaner *or* Lippizaner
Lokai
Manipur
Marwari
Mecklenburg
Mongolian
Morgan
Mustang *or* bronco
New Forest pony
Nonius
North Swedish horse
Oldenburg
Orlov Trotter
Palomino
Percheron
Persian Arab
Pinto
Pinzgauer
Polish Arab
Polish Half-bred
Polish Thoroughbred

Quarter horse
racehorse
Rhenish
Russian saddle horse *or*
 Orlov Rostopchin
Schleswig
Shagya
Shetland pony
Shirazi *or* Gulf Arab
Shire horse
Spanish Jennet *or* Genet
Spiti
Standard Bred
Strelet
Suffolk *or* Suffolk Punch
Swedish Ardennes
Tarbenian
Tarpan
Tennessee Walking Horse
 or Walking Horse
Thoroughbred
Timor pony
Trakehner
Turk *or* Turkoman
Viatka
Waler
Welsh Cob
Welsh Mountain pony
Welsh pony
Yamoote
Yorkshire Coach horse
Zeeland horse
Zemaitukas

58 breeds of dogs

affenpinscher
Afghan hound
Airedale *or* Airedale terrier
Akita
Alaskan malamute
Alpine spaniel
Alsatian *or* German
 shepherd
American foxhound
American water spaniel
Australian terrier
badger dog
barbet
Basenji
basset *or* basset hound
beagle
bearded collie
Bedlington terrier
Belgian sheep dog *or*
 shepherd
Belvoir hound
Bernese mountain dog
Bichon Frise
Blenheim spaniel
bloodhound *or* sleuth *or*
 sleuthhound
blue Gascon hound
boarhound
Border collie

Border terrier
borzoi
Boston bull *or* terrier
Bouvier des Flandres
boxer
Briard
Brittany spaniel
Bruxellois
bulldog *or* bull
bull mastiff
bull terrier
Cairn terrier
Chesapeake Bay retriever
Chihuahua
chow *or* chow chow
clumber spaniel
Clydesdale terrier
cocker spaniel
collie
corgi *or* Welsh corgi
Cuban bloodhound
dachshund *or* sausage dog
 or sausage hound
Dalmatian *or* coach dog
Dandie Dinmont terrier
deerhound
Doberman pinscher
Egyptian basset
elkhound

English setter
Eskimo dog
field spaniel
flat-coated retriever
foxhound
fox terrier
French bulldog
gazelle hound
German shepherd
German short-haired
 pointer
German wire-haired
 pointer
giant schnauzer
golden retriever
Gordon setter
Great Dane
Great Pyrenees
greyhound
griffon
Groenendael
harrier
Highland terrier
husky
Irish setter
Irish terrier
Irish water spaniel
Irish wolfhound
Italian greyhound
Jack Russell terrier
Japanese spaniel
Japanese tosa
keeshond
kelpie
Kerry blue terrier
King Charles spaniel
komondor
kuvasz
Labrador retriever
lakeland terrier
Lhasa apso
malamute
Malinois
Maltese
Manchester terrier
mastiff
Mexican hairless
miniature pinscher
miniature poodle
miniature schnauzer
Newfoundland
Nizinny
Norfolk spaniel
Norfolk terrier
Norwegian elkhound
Norwich terrier
Old English sheep dog
otterhound

papillon
Pekingese
pit bull terrier
pointer
Pomeranian
poodle
pug *or* pug dog *or* mops
puli
Pyrenean mountain dog
raccoon dog *or* coonhound
rat terrier
retriever
Rhodesian ridgeback
Rottweiler
rough collie
Russian owtchar
Russian wolfhound
St Bernard
Saluki
Samoyed
schipperke
schnauzer
Scottish deerhound
Scottish terrier
Sealyham terrier
setter
shepherd dog
Shetland sheep dog
Shih-tzu
Siberian husky
silky terrier
Skye terrier
southern hound
spaniel
spitz
springer spaniel
Staffordshire bull terrier
staghound
Sussex spaniel
talbot
terrier
toy poodle
toy spaniel
toy terrier
turnspit
Vizsla
water spaniel
Weimaraner
Welsh collie
Welsh springer spaniel
Welsh terrier
West Highland white
 terrier
whippet
wire-haired terrier
wolfhound
Yorkshire terrier

59 breeds and varieties of domestic cats

Abyssinian cat
Angora cat
Archangel cat
blue-point Siamese cat

Burmese cat
chartreuse cat
Chinese cat
chocolate-point Siamese cat

colourpoint cat
domestic shorthair cat
Egyptian cat
Havana brown cat
Madagascar cat
Maine coon cat
Malayan cat
Maltese *or* blue cat
Manx cat
marmalade cat
Oriental Shorthair

Persian cat
Rex cat
Russian blue cat
seal-point Siamese cat
Siamese cat
Spanish cat
tabby *or* tabby-cat
Tobolsk cat
tortoiseshell cat
Turkish cat

60 breeds of chickens

Ancona
Andalusian
Araucanian
Australorp
Bantam
Barred Plymouth Rock
black Minorca
black Orpington
black Spanish
black Sumatra
blue Andalusian
blue Orpington
Brahma
buff Orpington
Campine
Cochin
Cornish
dark Cornish
Dorking
Faverolle
Hamburg

Houdan
Jersey white giant
Langshan
Leghorn
Minorca
New Hampshire *or* New
   Hampshire red
Orpington
Plymouth Rock
Rhode Island red
Rhode Island white
Rock Cornish
speckled Sussex
Sumatra
Sussex
white Leghorn
white Orpington
white Plymouth Rock
white Wyandotte
Wyandotte

61 marine animals

crustacean
dugong
elephant seal
fur seal
harbour seal
manatee
octopus *or* octopod
sea calf
sea cow

sea dog
sea elephant
seal
sea lion
sea urchin
shellfish
squid
walrus

312 HUMANKIND

nouns

1 **humankind, mankind, man,** human species, **human race,** race of man, human family, the family of man, **humanity,** human beings, mortals, mortality, flesh, mortal flesh, clay; generation of man (*old*), *le genre humain* (*French*),

"the plumeless genus of bipeds"—Plato, homo, genus Homo, **Homo sapiens,** Hominidae, hominids; archaic Homo; **race,** strain, stock, subrace, infrarace, subspecies; **culture** *see* 373.3; ethnic group; ethnicity, ethnicism; **society,** speech community, **ethnic group;** community, **the people, the populace; nationality, nation**

2 (*races of humankind*) **Caucasoid** *or* **Caucasian** *or* **white race;** Nordic subrace, Alpine subrace, Mediterranean subrace; dolichocephalic people, brachycephalic people; xanthochroi, melanochroi;

Archaic Caucasoid *or* archaic white *or* Australoid race; Polynesian race; **Negroid** *or* **black race;** Nilotic race, Melanesian race, Papuan race; Pygmoid race; Bushman race; **Mongoloid** *or* **Mongolian** *or* **yellow race;** Malayan *or* Malaysian *or* brown race; prehistoric races; majority, racial *or* ethnic majority; minority, racial *or* ethnic minority; persons of colour

3 **Caucasian, white man** *or* **woman, white person,** paleface *and* whitey *and* honky (*all informal*), ofay (*US informal*); Australian aborigine, blackfellow (*Australian*); **Negro, black man** *or* **woman, black,** coloured person, person of colour, darky *and* spade *and* nigger (*all informal*); African-American; negritude, Afroism, blackness; pygmy, Negrito, Negrillo; Bushman; **Indian,** American Indian, Amerind, Red Indian, red man *or* woman; injun *and* redskin (*both informal*); Mongolian, yellow man *or* woman, **Oriental;** gook *and* slant-eye (*both informal*); Malayan, brown man

4 **the people** *see* 606, the populace, the population, the public

5 **person, human, human being, man, woman, child,** member of the human race *or* family, Adamite, daughter of Eve; ethnic; **mortal,** life, **soul,** living soul; **being,** creature, clay, ordinary clay; **individual,**

"single, separate person"—Whitman; personage, **personality, personhood,** individuality; **body;** somebody, one, someone; earthling, groundling, terran, worldling, tellurian; **ordinary person;** head, hand, nose; fellow (*informal*) *see* 76.5; gal (*informal*) *see* 77.6

6 **human nature, humanity;** frail *or* fallen humanity, Adam, the generation of Adam, Adam's seed *or* offspring

7 **God's image, lord of creation;** homo faber, symbol-using animal;

"a god in ruins"—Emerson, "the aristocrat amongst the animals"—Heine, "the measure of all things"—Protagoras, "a reasoning animal"—Seneca, "the most intelligent of animals—and the most silly"—Diogenes, "a thinking reed"—Pascal, "a tool-using animal"—Carlyle, "a tool-making animal"—Benjamin Franklin, "the only animal that blushes Or needs to"—Mark Twain, "an intelligence served by organs"—Emerson, rational animal, animal capable of reason,

"an ingenious assembly of portable plumbing"—Christopher Morley, "Nature's sole mistake"—W S Gilbert, "that unfeather'd two-legged thing"—Dryden, "but breath and shadow, nothing more"—Sophocles, "this quintessence of dust"—Shakespeare, "political animal"—Aristotle, "the naked ape"—Desmond Morris

8 **humanness, humanity,** mortality; **human nature,** the way you are; **frailty,** human frailty, weakness, **human weakness,** weakness of the flesh,

"thy nature's weakness"—Whittier, "one touch of nature"—Shakespeare, the weaknesses human flesh is heir to; human equation

9 **humanization, humanizing; anthropomorphism,** pathetic fallacy, anthropopathism, anthropomorphology

10 **anthropology,** science of man; anthropogeny, anthropography, anthropogeography, human geography, demography, human ecology, anthropometry, craniometry, craniology, ethnology, ethnography; behavioural science, sociology, social anthropology, social psychology, psychology *see* 92; anatomy; **anthropologist**, ethnologist, ethnographer; sociologist; demographics, population study, population statistics; demographer

11 **humanism**; naturalistic humanism, scientific humanism, secular humanism; religious humanism; Christian humanism, integral humanism; new humanism; anthroposophy

verbs

12 to **humanize**, anthropomorphize, make human, civilize

adjectives

13 **human**; hominal; creaturely, creatural; Adamite *or* Adamitic; **frail, weak**, fleshly, finite, **mortal; only human**; earthborn, of the earth, earthy, tellurian, unangelic; humanistic; man-centred, homocentric, anthropocentric; anthropological, ethnographic, ethnological; demographic

14 **manlike, anthropoid**, humanoid, hominid; anthropomorphic, anthropopathic, therioanthropic

15 **personal, individual**, private, peculiar, idiosyncratic; person-to-person, one-to-one, one-on-one (*US*)

16 **public, general, common; communal, societal, social**; civic, civil; **national**, state; international, cosmopolitan, supernational, supranational

adverbs

17 **humanly**, mortally, after the manner of men

word elements

18 anthrop–, anthropo–, homin–, homini–

313 SEASON
time of year

nouns

1 **season**, time of year, season of the year, "the measure of the year"—KEATS, **period**, annual period; dry *or* rainy *or* cold season, monsoon; theatrical *or* opera *or* concert season; **social season**, the season; close season; dead *or* off-season; high season, low season; football season, cricket season, etc; seasonality, periodicity *see* 849.2; **seasonableness** *see* 842.1

2 **spring**, springtide, **springtime**, seedtime *or* budtime, Maytime, Eastertide; *primavera* (*Italian*), prime, prime of the year, "the boyhood of the year"—TENNYSON, "Sweet Spring, full of sweet days and roses"—GEORGE HERBERT, "Daughter of heaven and earth, coy Spring"—EMERSON, "the time of the singing of birds"—BIBLE, "when the hounds of spring are on winter's traces"—SWINBURNE

3 **summer**, summertide, **summertime**; growing season; midsummer; **dog days**, canicular days; the silly season

4 **autumn**, fall (*US & Canadian*), harvest, harvest time, harvest home;

"Season of mists and mellow fruitfulness!"—KEATS

5 **Indian summer**, St Martin's summer, St Luke's summer, little summer of St Luke, St Austin's *or* St Augustine's summer, "the dead Summer's soul"—MARY CLEMMER

6 **winter**, wintertide, **wintertime**, "ruler of th'inverted year"—WILLIAM COWPER; midwinter; Christmastime *or* Christmastide, Yule *or* Yuletide

7 **equinox**, vernal equinox, autumnal equinox; **solstice**, summer solstice, winter solstice

verbs

8 to **summer**, winter, overwinter, spend *or* pass the spring, summer, etc

adjectives

9 **seasonal**, in *or* out of season, in season and out of season, off-season; early-season, mid-season, late-season; **spring**, springlike, vernal; **summer**, summery, summerly, summerlike, canicular, aestival; midsummer; **autumn**, autumnal; **winter**, wintry, wintery, hibernal, hiemal, brumal, boreal, arctic *see* 1022.14, winterlike, snowy, icy; midwinter; equinoctial, solstitial

314 MORNING, NOON

nouns

1 **morning**, morn, morningtide, morning time, morntime, matins, morrow (*old*), waking time, reveille, forenoon; *ante meridiem* (*Latin*) *or* **AM**, ack-emma (*old*); "dewy morn"—BYRON, "incense-breathing morn"—THOMAS GRAY, "grey-eyed morn", "the morn, in russet mantle clad"—BOTH SHAKESPEARE, "rosy-finger'd morn"—HOMER; this morning, this AM (*informal*)

2 Morning, Aurora, Eos; "daughter of the dawn"—HOMER, "meek-eyed Morn, mother of dews"—JAMES THOMSON, "mild blushing goddess"—L P SMITH

3 **dawn**, the dawn of day, dawning, **daybreak**, dayspring, day-peep, **sunrise**, sunup (*US informal*), cockcrowing *or* cocklight (*informal*), light *see* 1024, first light, daylight, aurora; **break of day**, peep of day, **crack of dawn**, prime, prime of the morning, first blush *or* flush of the morning, brightening *or* first brightening; "the opening eyelids of the morn"—MILTON, "vestibule of Day"—BAYARD TAYLOR, "golden exhalations of the dawn"—SCHILLER; chanticleer *or* chantecler

4 **foredawn**, twilight, morning twilight, half-light, glow, dawnlight, first light, "the dawn's early light"—FRANCIS SCOTT KEY, crepuscule, aurora; **the small hours**; alpenglow

5 **noon**, noonday, noontide, nooning (*US informal*), noontime, **high noon, midday**, meridian, *meridiem* (*Latin*), twelve o'clock, 1200 hours; noonlight, "the blaze of noon"—MILTON; meridian devil *or* *daemonium meridianum* (*Latin*), "the destruction that wasteth at noonday"—BIBLE

adjectives

6 **morning**, matin, matinal, matutinal, **antemeridian**; auroral, dawn, dawning

7 **noon**, noonday, noonish, **midday**, meridian, twelve-o'clock; noonlit

adverbs

8 **in the morning**, before noon, mornings (*informal*); at sunrise, at dawn, at dawn of day, at cockcrow, at first light, **at the crack** *or* **break of dawn**; with the sun, with the lark

9 at noon, at midday, at twelve-o'clock sharp

315 EVENING, NIGHT

nouns

1 **afternoon**, *post meridiem* (*Latin*) *or* **PM**; arvo (*Australian informal*), this afternoon, this PM (*informal*)

2 **evening**, eve, even, evensong time *or* hour, **eventide**, vesper; **close of day**, decline *or* fall of day, shut of day, grey of the evening, greyness *see* 39, evening's close, when day is done; **nightfall**, **sunset**, **sundown**, setting sun, going down of the sun, cockshut *and* cockshut time *and* cockshut light (*all informal*), retreat; shank of the afternoon *or* evening (*dialect*), the cool of the evening; "the expiring day"—DANTE, "evening's calm and holy hour"—S G BULFINCH, "the grey-hooded Ev'n"—MILTON, "the pale child, Eve, leading her mother, Night"—ALEXANDER SMITH, "the evening is spread out against the sky, Like a patient etherized upon a table"—T S ELIOT

3 **dusk**, dusking time *or* tide, dusk-dark *and* dust-dark *and* dusty-dark (*all informal*), **twilight**, evening twilight, crepuscule, crepuscular light, gloam, **gloaming**, glooming; duskiness, duskishness, brown of dusk, brownness *see* 40, candlelight, candlelighting, owllight *or* owl's light, cocklight (*informal*), "the pale dusk of the impending night"—LONGFELLOW

4 **night**, **nighttime**, nighttide, lights-out, taps, bedtime, sleepy time (*informal*), **darkness** *see* 1026, blackness *see* 38; "sable-vested Night, eldest of things"—MILTON, "sable night", "darkeyed night"—BOTH SHAKESPEARE, "cowlèd night"—FRANCIS THOMPSON, "empress of silence, and the queen of sleep"—CHRISTOPHER MARLOWE; dark of night, "the suit of night"—SHAKESPEARE, "the mystic wine of Night"—LOUIS UNTERMEYER

5 eleventh hour, curfew

6 **midnight**, **dead of night**, hush of night, the witching hour; "the very witching time of night"—SHAKESPEARE, "noonday night", "outpost of advancing day"—BOTH LONGFELLOW

adjectives

7 **afternoon**, postmeridian

8 **evening**, evensong, vesper, vespertine *or* vespertinal; **twilight**, twilighty, crepuscular; **dusk**, dusky, duskish

9 **nocturnal**, night, **nightly**, nighttime; nightlong, all-night; night-fallen; midnight

10 benighted, night-overtaken

adverbs

11 **nightly**, nights (*informal*), at *or* by night; **overnight**, through the night, all through the night, nightlong, the whole night, all night

word elements

12 noc–, nocto–, nocti–, nyct–, nycto–, nycti–

316 RAIN

nouns

1 **rain**, rainfall, fall, **precipitation**, moisture, wet, rainwater; **shower**, **sprinkle**, flurry, patter, pitter-patter, splatter; streams of rain, sheet of rain, splash *or* spurt of rain; **drizzle**, mizzle; **mist**, misty rain, Scotch mist; evening mist; fog drip; blood rain; raindrop, unfrozen hydrometeor

2 **rainstorm**, scud; **cloudburst**, rainburst, burst of rain, torrent of rain, torrential rain *or* downpour; **downpour**, downflow, downfall, pour, pouring *or* pelting *or* teeming *or* drowning rain, spate (*Scottish*), plash (*informal*), **deluge**, **flood**, heavy rain, driving *or* gushing rain, drenching *or* soaking rain, drencher, soak, soaker, waterspout, spout, rainspout, "smoky rain"—CHAUCER, lovely weather for ducks

3 **thunderstorm**, thundershower, thundersquall

4 **wet weather**, **raininess**, rainy weather, stormy *or* dirty weather, spell of rain, wet; rainy day; **rains**, rainy *or* wet season, spring rains, **monsoon**; predominance of Aquarius, reign of St Swithin

5 **rainmaking**, seeding, cloud seeding, nucleation, artificial nucleation; **rainmaker**, rain doctor, cloud seeder; dry ice, silver iodide

6 Jupiter Pluvius, Zeus; Thor

7 **rain gauge**, pluviometer, pluvioscope, pluviograph; ombrometer, ombrograph; udometer, udomograph; hyetometer, hyetometrograph, hyetograph

8 (*science of precipitation*) hydrometeorology, hyetology, hyetography; pluviography, pluviometry, ombrology

verbs

9 **to rain**, **precipitate**, rain down, fall; weep; **shower**, shower down; **sprinkle**, spit (*informal*), spatter, patter, pitter-patter; **drizzle**, mizzle; **pour**, stream, stream down, pour with rain, **pelt**, pelt down, tip down, drum, tattoo, come down in torrents *or* sheets *or* buckets *or* curtains, **rain cats and dogs** (*informal*), "rain dogs and pole-cats"—RICHARD BROME, "rain daggers with their points downward"—ROBERT BURTON; rainmake, seed clouds

adjectives

10 **rainy**, **showery**; pluvious *or* pluviose *or* pluvial; **drizzly**, drizzling, mizzly, drippy; **misty**; torrential, pouring, streaming, pelting, drumming, driving, blinding

11 pluviometric *or* pluvioscopic *or* pluviographic, ombrometric *or* ombrographic, udometric *or* udographic, hyetometric, hyetographic, hyetometrographic; hydrometeorological, hyetological

317 AIR, WEATHER

nouns

1 **air**; ether; ozone (*informal*); thin air

2 **atmosphere**; aerosphere, gaseous envelope *or* environment *or* medium *or* blanket, welkin; biosphere, ecosphere, noosphere; air mass; atmospheric component, atmospheric gas; atmospheric layer *or* stratum *or* belt (*see list*)

3 **weather, climate,** clime; **the elements,** forces of nature; microclimate, macroclimate; fair weather, calm weather, halcyon days, good weather; stormy weather *see* 671.4; rainy weather *see* 316.4; windiness *see* 318.15; heat wave, hot weather *see* 1018.7; cold wave, cold weather *see* 1022.3

4 weather map; isobar, isobaric *or* isopiestic line; isotherm, isothermal line; isometric, isometric line; high, high-pressure area; low, low-pressure area; front, wind-shift line, squall line; cold front, polar front, cold sector; warm front; occluded front, stationary front; air mass; cyclone, anticyclone

5 **meteorology,** weather science, aerology, aerography, air-mass analysis, weatherology, climatology, climatography, microclimatology, forecasting, long-range forecasting; barometry; pneumatics *see* 1038.5; anemology *see* 318.16; nephology *see* 319.4

6 **meteorologist,** weather scientist, aerologist, aerographer, weatherologist; climatologist, microclimatologist; **weatherman, weather forecaster,** weather prophet; **weather report,** weather forecast; weather bureau, Meteorological *or* Met Office; weather ship; weather station; weather-reporting network

7 weather instrument, meteorological *or* aerological instrument; **barometer,** aneroid barometer, glass, weatherglass; barograph, barometrograph, recording barometer; aneroidograph; vacuometer; hygrometer; weather balloon, radiosonde; weather satellite; hurricane-hunter aircraft; weather vane *see* 318.17

8 **ventilation,** cross-ventilation, **airing,** aerage, perflation, refreshment; **aeration; air conditioning,** air cooling; oxygenation, oxygenization

9 **ventilator; aerator; air conditioner,** air filter, air cooler, ventilating *or* cooling system; blower; heat pump; air passage; fan

verbs

10 **to air,** air out, **ventilate,** cross-ventilate, wind, refresh, freshen; **air-condition,** air-cool; **fan,** winnow; **aerate,** airify; oxygenate, oxygenize

adjectives

11 **airy,** aery, **aerial,** aeriform, airlike, **pneumatic,** ethereal; exposed, roomy, light; airish, breezy; open-air, alfresco; **atmospheric,** tropospheric, stratospheric

12 **climatal,** climatic, climatical, climatographical, **elemental;** meteorological, aerologic, aerological, aerographic, aerographical, climatologic, climatological; macroclimatic, microclimatic, microclimatologic; barometric, barometrical, baric, barographic; isobaric, isopiestic, isometric; high-pressure, low-pressure; cyclonic, anti-cyclonic

13 atmospheric layers

boundary layer	mesosphere
chemosphere	outer atmosphere
exosphere	ozone layer *or* ozonosphere
F_1 layer	stratosphere
F_2 *or* Appleton layer	substratosphere
Heaviside *or* Heaviside-Kennelly layer *or* region	thermosphere
	tropopause
ionosphere	troposphere
isothermal region	upper atmosphere
lower atmosphere	Van Allen belt *or* radiation
magnetosphere	belt

318 WIND
air flow

nouns

1 **wind,** current, **air current,** current of air, **draught,** movement of air, stream, stream of air, flow of air; updraught, uprush; downdraught, downrush, microburst; indraught, inflow, inrush; crosscurrent, undercurrent; fall wind, gravity wind, katabatic wind, head wind, tail wind, following wind; wind aloft; jet stream, upper-atmosphere *or* upper-atmospheric wind

2 "scolding winds"—SHAKESPEARE, "the felon winds"—MILTON, "the wings of the wind"—BIBLE, "O wild West Wind, thou breath of Autumn's being"—SHELLEY, "the wind that sang of trees uptorn and vessels tost"—WORDSWORTH

3 (*wind god; the wind personified*) Aeolus, Vayu; Boreas (*north wind*); Eurus (*east wind*); Zephyr *or* Zephyrus, Favonius (*west wind*); Notus (*south wind*); Caurus (*northwest wind*); After (*southwest wind*)

4 **puff,** puff of air *or* wind, breath, breath of air, flatus, waft, capful of wind, whiff, whiffet, stir of air

5 **breeze,** light *or* gentle wind *or* breeze, softblowing wind, **zephyr,** gale (*old*), air, light air, moderate breeze; fresh *or* stiff breeze; cool *or* cooling breeze; sea breeze, onshore breeze, ocean breeze, cat's-paw

6 **gust,** wind gust, **blast,** blow, flaw, **flurry,** scud

7 **hot wind;** snow eater, thawer; chinook, **chinook wind;** simoom, samiel; foehn *or* föhn; khamsin; harmattan; sirocco *or* yugo; solano; Santa Ana; volcanic wind

8 **wintry wind,** winter wind, raw wind, chilling *or* freezing wind, bone-chilling wind, sharp *or* piercing wind, cold *or* icy wind, biting wind, nipping *or* nippy wind,
"a nipping and an eager air"—SHAKESPEARE, icy blasts; Arctic *or* boreal *or* hyperboreal *or* hyperborean blast; wind chill *or* wind chill factor

9 **north wind, norther,** mistral, bise, tramontane, Etesian winds, meltemi, vardarac, Papagayo wind; northeaster, **nor'easter,** Euroclydon *or* gregale *or* gregal *or* gregau, bura, Tehuantepec wind, Tehuantepecer; northwester, **nor'wester;** southeaster, **sou'easter;** southwester, **sou'wester,** kite-wind, libeccio; berg wind (*South African*); **east wind,** easter, easterly, levanter, sharav; **west wind,** wester, westerly; **south wind,** souther, southerly buster *or* buster (*Australian*)

10 prevailing wind; polar easterlies; prevailing westerlies, antitrades; trade wind, trades; doldrums, wind-equator; horse latitudes; roaring forties

11 (*nautical terms*) **head wind, beam wind, tail wind,** following wind, fair *or* favourable wind, apparent *or* relative wind, backing wind, veering wind, slant of wind; onshore wind, offshore wind

12 **windstorm,** big *or* great *or* fresh *or* strong *or* stiff *or* high *or* howling *or* spanking wind, ill *or* dirty *or* ugly wind; storm, storm wind, stormy winds, **tempest,** tempestuous wind; williwaw; **blow,** violent *or* heavy blow; **squall,** thick squall, black squall, white squall; squall line, wind-shift line, line squall; line storm (*US*); equinoctial; **gale,** half a gale, whole gale; tropical cyclone, **hurricane,** typhoon, tropical storm, **blizzard** *see* 1022.8; thundersquall, thundergust; wind shear

13 **dust storm, sandstorm,** shaitan, peesash, devil, khamsin, sirocco, simoom, samiel, harmattan

14 **whirlwind,** whirlblast, tourbillion, wind eddy; **cyclone, tornado, twister,** rotary storm, typhoon, *baguio* (*Spanish*); sandspout, sand column, dust devil; waterspout, rainspout

15 **windiness,** gustiness; airiness, **breeziness;** draughtiness

16 **anemology,** anemometry; **wind direction; wind force, Beaufort scale,** half-Beaufort scale, International scale; wind-chill factor; wind rose, barometric wind rose, humidity wind rose, hyetal *or* rain wind rose, temperature wind rose, dynamic wind rose; wind arrow, wind marker

17 **weather vane, weathercock,** vane, cock, wind vane, wind indicator, wind cone *or* sleeve *or* sock, anemoscope; anemometer, wind-speed indicator, anemograph, anemometrograph

18 **blower,** bellows; blowpipe, blowtube, blowgun

19 **fan,** flabellum; punkah, thermantidote, electric fan, blower, window fan, attic fan, exhaust fan; ventilator; windsail, windscoop, windcatcher

verbs

20 **to blow, waft;** puff, huff, whiff; whiffle; **breeze;** breeze up, freshen; **gather, brew,** set in, blow up, pipe up, come up, **blow up a storm;** bluster, squall; **storm,** rage,
"blow, winds, and crack your cheeks, rage, blow"—
Sʜᴀᴋᴇsᴘᴇᴀʀᴇ, blast, blow great guns, blow a hurricane; blow over

21 **to sigh,** sough, whisper, mutter, murmur, **sob, moan,** groan, growl, snarl, **wail, howl,** scream, screech, shriek, **roar,** whistle, pipe, sing, sing in the shrouds

adjectives

22 **windy, blowy; breezy, draughty,** airy, airish; brisk, fresh; **gusty,** blasty, puffy, flawy; **squally;** blustery, blustering, blusterous; aeolian, favonian, boreal; ventose

23 **stormy, tempestuous,** raging, storming, angry; turbulent; dirty, foul; cyclonic, tornadic, typhonic, typhoonish; rainy *see* 316.10; cloudy *see* 319.7

24 **windblown,** blown; **windswept,** bleak, raw, exposed

25 anemological, anemographic, anemometric, anemometrical

---

319 CLOUD

nouns

1 **cloud,** high fog;
"the clouds—the only birds that never sleep"—Vɪᴄᴛᴏʀ Hᴜɢᴏ, "the argosies of cloudland"—J T Tʀᴏᴡʙʀɪᴅɢᴇ, "islands on a dark-blue sea"—Sʜᴇʟʟᴇʏ, "fair, frail, palaces"—T B Aʟᴅʀɪᴄʜ, "the low'ring element"—Mɪʟᴛᴏɴ; fleecy cloud, cottony cloud, billowy cloud; **cloud bank,** cloud mass, cloud cover, cloud drift; cloudling, cloudlet; cloudscape, cloud band; cloudland, Cloudcuckooland *or* Nephelococcygia (*Aristophanes*)

2 **fog,** pea soup *and* peasouper *and* pea-soup fog (*all informal*); London fog, London special (*informal*); fog-bank; **smog** (*smoke-fog*), smaze (*US*), smoke-haze; frost smoke; mist, drizzling mist, drisk (*informal*), haar; haze, gauze, film; vapour *see* 1065

3 **cloudiness, haziness, mistiness, fogginess,** nebulosity, nubilation, nimbosity, **overcast,** heavy sky, dirty sky, lowering *or* louring sky

4 nephology, nephelognosy; nephologist

5 nephelometer, nepheloscope

verbs

6 **to cloud,** becloud, encloud, cloud over, overcloud, cloud up, clabber up (*informal*), muzz (*informal*), **overcast,** overshadow, shadow, shade, **darken** *see* 1026.9, darken over, nubilate, obnubilate, obscure; **smoke,** oversmoke; **fog,** befog, fog in; smog; **mist,** mist over, mist up, bemist, enmist; **haze**

adjectives

7 **cloudy,** nebulous, nubilous, nimbose, nebulosus; **clouded,** overclouded, **overcast;** dirty, heavy, lowering *or* louring; dark *see* 1026.13; **gloomy** *see* 1026.14; cloud-flecked; cirrous, cirrose; cumulous, cumuliform, stratous, stratiform; lenticularis, mammatus, castellatus; thunderheaded, stormy, squally

8 **cloud-covered,** cloud-laden, cloud-curtained, cloud-crammed, cloud-crossed, cloud-decked, cloud-hidden, cloud-wrapped, cloud-enveloped, cloud-surrounded, cloud-girt, cloud-flecked, cloud-eclipsed, **cloud-capped,** cloud-topped

9 **foggy,** soupy *or* pea-soupy (*informal*), nubilous; fog-bound, fogged-in; smoggy; hazy, misty; so thick you can cut it with a knife

10 nephological

---

320 BUBBLE

nouns

1 **bubble,** bleb, **globule;** vesicle, bulla, **blister,** blood blister, fever blister; balloon, bladder *see* 195.2; air bubble, soap bubble

2 **foam, froth; spume,** sea foam, scud; **spray, surf,** breakers, white water, spoondrift *or* **spindrift,** "stinging, ringing spindrift"—Kɪᴘʟɪɴɢ; **suds, lather,** soap-suds; head, beer-suds; **scum,** off-scum; head, collar; puff, mousse, soufflé, meringue

3 **bubbling,** bubbliness, **effervescence** *or* effervescency, **sparkle,** spumescence, frothiness, frothing, foaming; **fizz,** fizzle, carbonation; ebullience *or* ebulliency; **ebullition**, boiling; **fermentation,** ferment

verbs

4 to bubble, bubble up, burble; **effervesce, fizz, fizzle;** hiss, **sparkle; ferment,** work; **foam, froth,** froth up; have a head, foam over; **boil,** seethe, simmer; plop, blubber; guggle, gurgle; bubble over, **boil over**

5 to foam, froth, spume, cream; **lather,** suds, sud; scum, mantle; **aerate,** whip, beat, whisk

adjectives

6 bubbly, burbly, **bubbling,** burbling; **effervescent,** spumescent, **fizzy, sparkling,** *mousseux* (*French*), *spumante* (*Italian*); carbonated; ebullient; puffed, soufflé *or* souffléed, beaten, whipped, chiffon; **blistered,** blistery, blebby, vesicated, vesicular; blistering, vesicant, vesicatory

7 foamy, foam-flecked, **frothy,** spumy, spumous *or* spumose; yeasty, barmy; **sudsy,** suddy, **lathery,** soapy, soapsudsy, soapsuddy; heady, with a head *or* collar on

321 BEHAVIOUR

nouns

1 behaviour, conduct, deportment, comportment, manner, manners, demeanour, mien, *maintien* (*French*), **carriage, bearing,** port, poise, posture, guise, air, address, presence; tone, style, lifestyle; way of life, habit of life, modus vivendi; **way, way of acting, ways; trait behaviour,** behaviour trait; methods, **method, methodology; practice,** praxis; procedure, proceeding; **actions,** acts, goings-on, doings, what one is up to, movements, moves, tactics; action, doing *see* 328.1; activity *see* 330; objective *or* observable behaviour; motions, gestures; pose, affectation *see* 500; pattern, behaviour pattern; Type A behaviour, Type B behaviour; culture pattern, behavioural norm, folkway, **custom** *see* 373; behavioural science, social science

2 good behaviour, sanctioned behaviour; good citizenship; good manners, correct deportment, etiquette *see* 580.3; **courtesy** *see* 504; social behaviour, sociability *see* 582; bad *or* poor behaviour, **misbehaviour** *see* 322; **discourtesy** *see* 505

3 behaviourism, behavioural science, behaviour *or* behaviouristic psychology, Watsonian psychology, Skinnerian psychology; behaviour modification, behaviour therapy ethology, animal behaviour, human behaviour, social behaviour

verbs

4 to behave, act, do, go on; **behave oneself, conduct oneself,** manage oneself, **handle oneself,** guide oneself, **comport oneself, deport oneself,** demean oneself, **bear oneself, carry oneself;** acquit oneself, quit oneself (*old*); proceed, move, swing into action; **misbehave** *see* 322.4

5 to behave oneself, behave, act well, clean up one's act (*informal*), act one's age, **be good,** be nice, **do right,** do what is right, do the right *or* proper thing, keep out of mischief, play the game *and* mind one's

P's and Q's (*both informal*), be on one's good *or* best behaviour, play one's cards right

6 to treat, use, do by, deal by, act *or* **behave toward,** conduct oneself toward, act with regard to, conduct oneself vis-à-vis *or* in the face of; **deal with,** cope with, **handle;** respond to

adjectives

7 behavioural; behaviourist, behaviouristic; ethological; **behaved, mannered**

322 MISBEHAVIOUR

nouns

1 misbehaviour, misconduct, misdemeanour (*old*); unsanctioned *or* nonsanctioned behaviour; frowned-upon behaviour; **naughtiness,** badness; impropriety; venial sin; **disorderly conduct,** disorder, disorderliness, disruptiveness, disruption, **rowdiness,** rowdyism, riotousness, ruffianism, hooliganism, hoodlumism, aggro (*informal*); vandalism, trashing; roughhouse, horseplay; discourtesy *see* 505; vice *see* 654; misfeasance, malfeasance, misdoing, delinquency, **wrongdoing** *see* 655

2 mischief, mischievousness; devilment, deviltry, devilry; **roguishness,** roguery, scampishness; **waggery,** waggishness; **impishness,** devilishness, puckishness, elfishness; **prankishness,** pranksomeness; sportiveness, playfulness, *espièglerie* (*French*); high spirits, youthful spirits; foolishness *see* 922

3 mischief-maker, mischief, **rogue, devil, knave, rascal,** rapscallion, scapegrace, **scamp; wag** *see* 489.12; buffoon *see* 707.10; funmaker, joker, jokester, practical joker, prankster, life of the party, cutup (*US informal*); **rowdy,** ruffian, hoodlum, hood (*informal*), hooligan, lout, yob *or* yobbo, tearaway; **imp, elf, puck,** pixie, **minx,** pickle, bad boy, little bugger (*informal*), little devil, little rascal, little monkey, *enfant terrible* (*French*)

verbs

4 to misbehave, misdemean (*old*), **misbehave oneself, misconduct oneself,** misdemean oneself (*old*), behave ill; get into mischief; **act up** *and* **play up** *and* make waves *and* **carry on** *and* carry on something scandalous (*all informal*), sow one's wild oats; **muck about** (*informal*), horse around (*informal*), roughhouse (*informal*); play the fool *see* 922.6

adjectives

5 misbehaving, unbehaving; **naughty, bad;** improper, not respectable; out-of-order *and* out-of-line (*both informal*); **disorderly,** disruptive, **rowdy,** rowdyish, **ruffianly**

6 mischievous, mischief-loving, full of mischief, full of the devil *or* old nick; **roguish,** scampish, scapegrace, arch, knavish; **devilish; impish, puckish, elfish,** elvish; **waggish, prankish,** pranky, pranksome, trickish, tricksy; **playful,** sportive, high-spirited, *espiègle* (*French*); foolish *see* 922.8, 9

adverbs

7 mischievously, roguishly, knavishly, scampishly, devilishly; impishly, puckishly, elfishly; waggishly; prankishly, playfully, sportively, in fun

323 WILL

nouns

1 will, volition; **choice**, determination, **decision** *see* 371.1; **wish, mind, fancy**, discretion, pleasure, **inclination, disposition**, liking, appetence, appetency, **desire** *see* 100; half a mind *or* notion, idle wish, velleity; **appetite, passion, lust, sexual desire** *see* 75.5; animus, **objective, intention** *see* 380; **command** *see* 420; **free choice**, one's own will *or* choice *or* discretion *or* initiative, **free will** *see* 430.6; conation, conatus; will power, **resolution** *see* 359

verbs

2 to will, **wish** see *or* think fit, think good, think proper, **choose to, have a mind to**; have half a mind *or* notion to; **choose**, determine, **decide** *see* 371.14, 16; **resolve** *see* 359.7; command, decree; **desire** *see* 100.14, 18

3 to have one's will, **have** *or* **get one's way**, get one's wish, have it all one's way, do *or* go as one pleases, please oneself; take the bit in one's teeth, take charge of one's destiny; stand on one's rights; take the law into one's own hands; have the last word, impose one's will

adjectives

4 volitional, volitive; **willing, voluntary**; conative; *ex gratia* (*Latin*)

adverbs

5 **at will**, at choice, at pleasure, *al piacere* (*Italian*), **at one's pleasure**, *a beneplacito* (*Italian*), at one's will and pleasure, at one's own sweet will, **at one's discretion**, *à discrétion* (*French*), *ad arbitrium* (*Latin*); *ad libitum* (*Latin*), ad lib; as one wishes, as it pleases *or* suits oneself, **in one's own way**, in one's own sweet way *or* time (*informal*), **as one thinks best**, as it seems good *or* best, as far as one desires; of one's own free will, of one's own accord, on one's own; without coercion, unforced

324 WILLINGNESS

nouns

1 **willingness, gameness** (*informal*), readiness; **unreluctance**, unloathness, ungrudgingness; agreeableness, **agreeability**, favourableness; **acquiescence, consent** *see* 441; **compliance**, cooperativeness; receptivity, receptiveness, responsiveness; amenability, tractableness, tractability, docility, biddability, biddableness, pliancy, pliability, malleability; **eagerness**, keenness, promptness, forwardness, alacrity, zeal, zealousness, ardour, enthusiasm; goodwill, cheerful consent; **willing heart** *or* **mind, favourable disposition**, positive *or* right *or* receptive mood, willing ear

2 **voluntariness**, volunteering; **gratuitousness; spontaneity**, spontaneousness, unforcedness; **self-determination**, self-activity, self-action, autonomy, autonomousness, independence, free will *see* 430.5-7; **volunteerism**, voluntaryism, voluntarism; volunteer

verbs

3 **to be willing, be game** (*informal*), be ready, be up for (*informal*); be of favourable disposition, take the trouble, find it in one's heart, find one's heart (*old*), have a willing heart; **incline, lean**; look kindly upon; be open to, bring oneself, **agree**, be agreeable to; **acquiesce, consent** *see* 441.2; not hesitate to, would as lief, would as leave (*informal*), would as lief as not, not care *or* mind if one does (*informal*); **play** *or* **go along** (*informal*), do one's part *or* bit; be eager, be keen, be dying to, fall all over oneself, be spoiling for, be champing at the bit; step into the breach; **enter with a will**, lean *or* bend over backward, go into heart and soul, go the extra mile, plunge into; **cooperate, collaborate** *see* 450.3; lend *or* give *or* turn a willing ear

4 **to volunteer**, do voluntarily, do ex gratia, **do of one's own accord**, do of one's own volition, **do of one's own free will** *or* **choice**, do off one's own bat; do independently

adjectives

5 **willing, willinghearted, ready, game** (*informal*); **disposed, inclined, minded, willed**, fain *and* prone (*both old*); **well-disposed**, well-inclined, favourably inclined *or* disposed; predisposed; **favourable, agreeable, cooperative; compliant**, content (*old*), **acquiescent** *see* 332.13, **consenting** *see* 441.4; **eager**; keen, prompt, quick, alacritous, forward, ready and willing, zealous, ardent, enthusiastic; in the mood *or* vein *or* humour *or* mind, in a good mood; receptive, responsive; amenable, tractable, docile, pliant

6 **ungrudging**, ungrumbling, **unreluctant**, unloath, **nothing loath**, unaverse, unshrinking

7 **voluntary, volunteer; ex gratia** (*Latin*), **gratuitous; spontaneous, free, freewill**; offered, proffered; **discretionary**, discretional, nonmandatory, **optional**, elective; arbitrary; **self-determined**, self-determining, autonomous, independent, self-active, self-acting; **unsought**, unbesought, **unasked**, unrequested, **unsolicited**, **uninvited**, unbidden, uncalled-for; **unforced**, uncoerced, unpressured, unrequired, uncompelled; **unprompted**, uninfluenced

adverbs

8 **willingly, with a will**, with good will, with right good will, *de bonne volonté* (*French*); **eagerly**, with zest, with relish, with open arms, without question, zealously, ardently, enthusiastically; **readily**, promptly, at the drop of a hat (*informal*)

9 **agreeably, favourably, compliantly**; lief, lieve (*informal*), fain, as lief, as lief as not; **ungrudgingly**, ungrumblingly, **unreluctantly, nothing loath**, without reluctance *or* demur *or* hesitation, unstintingly, unreservedly

10 **voluntarily, freely, gratuitously, spontaneously;** optionally, electively, by choice; **of one's own accord,** of one's own free will, of one's own volition, without reservation, of one's own choice, at one's own discretion; without coercion *or* pressure *or* compulsion *or* intimidation; independently

325 UNWILLINGNESS

nouns

1 **refusal** *see* 442, **unwillingness, disinclination,** nolition, **indisposition,** indisposedness, **reluctance,** renitency, renitence, grudgingness, grudging consent; unenthusiasm, lack of enthusiasm *or* zeal *or* eagerness, slowness, backwardness, dragging of the feet *and* foot-dragging (*both informal*); sullenness, sulk, sulks, sulkiness; cursoriness, perfunctoriness; recalcitrance *or* recalcitrancy, disobedience, refractoriness, fractiousness, intractableness, indocility, mutinousness; averseness, aversion, repugnance, antipathy, distaste, disrelish; **obstinacy, stubbornness** *see* 361.1; opposition *see* 451; **resistance** *see* 453; **disagreement,** dissent *see* 456.3

2 **demur,** demurral, **scruple, qualm,** qualm of conscience, reservation, compunction; **hesitation,** hesitancy *or* hesitance, pause, boggle, **falter;** qualmishness, scrupulousness, scrupulosity; **stickling,** boggling; **faltering;** shrinking; shyness, **diffidence,** modesty, bashfulness; recoil; **protest, objection** *see* 333.2

verbs

3 **to refuse** *see* 442.3, **be unwilling, would** *or* **had rather not, not care to,** not feel like (*informal*), not find it in one's heart to, not have the heart *or* stomach to; **mind,** object to, draw the line at, be dead set against, **balk at,** jib; grudge, begrudge

4 **to demur, scruple,** have qualms *or* scruples; **stickle, stick at,** boggle, strain; falter, waver; **hesitate,** pause, be half-hearted, **hang back,** hang off, hold off; **fight shy of,** shy at, shy, crane, shrink, recoil, blench, flinch, wince, quail, pull back; make bones about *or* of

adjectives

5 **unwilling, disinclined, indisposed,** not in the mood, averse; **unconsenting** *see* 442.6; **dead set against, opposed** *see* 451.8; **resistant** *see* 453.5; **disagreeing,** differing, at odds *see* 456.16; disobedient, recalcitrant, refractory, fractious, sullen, sulky, indocile, mutinous; cursory, perfunctory; **involuntary, forced**

6 **reluctant,** renitent, **grudging, loath;** backward, laggard, dilatory, slow, slow to; unenthusiastic, unzealous, indifferent, apathetic, perfunctory; balky, balking, restive

7 **demurring, qualmish,** boggling, stickling, hedging, squeamish, **scrupulous; diffident,** shy, modest, bashful; **hesitant,** hesitating, faltering; shrinking

adverbs

8 **unwillingly, involuntarily, against one's will,** *à contre coeur* (*French*); under compulsion *or* coercion *or* pressure; in spite of oneself, *malgré soi* (*French*)

9 **reluctantly, grudgingly,** sullenly, sulkily; unenthusiastically, perfunctorily; with dragging feet, with a bad *or* an ill grace, **under protest;** with a heavy heart, with no heart *or* stomach; over one's dead body, not on one's life

326 OBEDIENCE

nouns

1 **obedience** *or* **obediency,** compliance; acquiescence, consent *see* 441; **deference** *see* 155.1, self-abnegation, submission, submissiveness *see* 433.3; servility *see* 138; eagerness *or* readiness *or* willingness to serve, **dutifulness,** duteousness; **service,** servitium, homage, fealty, **allegiance, loyalty,** faithfulness, faith, observance (*old*); doglike devotion *or* obedience; **conformity** *see* 866, lockstep; law-abidingness

verbs

2 **to obey, mind, heed, keep, observe,** listen *or* hearken to; **comply, conform** *see* 866.3, walk in lockstep; stay in line *and* not get out of line (*all informal*), **toe the line** *or* mark, follow the party line, fall in, fall in line, obey the rules, go by *or* follow the book, **do what one is told;** do as one says, do the will of, defer to *see* 155.4, do one's bidding, come at one's call, lie down and roll over for (*informal*); take orders, attend to orders, do suit and service, follow the lead of; **submit** *see* 433.6, 9

adjectives

3 **obedient, compliant,** complying, allegiant; **acquiescent,** consenting *see* 441.4, **submissive** *see* 433.12, deferential *see* 155.8, self-abnegating; willing, **dutiful,** duteous; loyal, faithful, devoted; uncritical, unshakeable, doglike; conforming, in conformity; law-abiding

4 **at one's command,** at one's whim *or* pleasure, at one's disposal, at one's nod, at one's call, **at one's beck and call**

5 **henpecked, tied to one's apron strings,** on a string, on a leash, in leading strings; wimpish (*informal*); milk-toast *or* milquetoast, Caspar Milquetoast

adverbs

6 **obediently, compliantly; acquiescently, submissively** *see* 433.17; willingly, **dutifully,** duteously; loyally, faithfully, devotedly; in obedience to, in compliance *or* conformity with

7 **at your service** *or* command *or* orders, as you please, as you will, as thou wilt (*old*)

327 DISOBEDIENCE

nouns

1 **disobedience,** nonobedience, **noncompliance; undutifulness,** unduteousness; wilful disobedience; **insubordination,** indiscipline; **unsubmissiveness, intractability,** indocility *see* 361.4, recusancy; **nonconformity** *see* 867; **disrespect** *see* 156; **lawlessness,** waywardness, frowardness, naughtiness; violation, transgression, infraction, infringement, lawbreaking; civil disobedience, passive resistance;

uncooperativeness, noncooperation; **dereliction,** deliberate negligence, default, delinquency, nonfeasance

2 **defiance, refractoriness, recalcitrance** *or* recalcitrancy, recalcitration, defiance of authority, contumacy, **contumaciousness, obstreperousness, unruliness,** restiveness, fractiousness, orneriness *and* feistiness (*both informal*); wildness *see* 430.3; **obstinacy, stubbornness** *see* 361.1

3 **rebelliousness, mutinousness;** riotousness; insurrectionism, insurgentism; factiousness, **sedition,** seditiousness; treasonableness, traitorousness, subversiveness; extremism *see* 611.5

4 **revolt, rebellion, revolution, mutiny, insurrection, insurgence** *or* insurgency, *émeute* (*French*), **uprising,** rising, outbreak, general uprising, *levée en masse* (*French*), *intifada* (*Arabic*), riot, civil disorder; peasant revolt, *jacquerie* (*French*); putsch, coup d'état; **strike, general strike;** intifada

5 **rebel,** revolter, **insurgent,** insurrectionary, insurrecto, **insurrectionist;** malcontent, *frondeur* (*French*); **insubordinate; mutineer,** rioter, brawler; maverick (*informal*), noncooperator, troublemaker, refusenik (*informal*); nonconformist *see* 867.3; agitator *see* 375.11; extremist *see* 611.17; revolutionary, revolutionist *see* 859.3; traitor, subversive *see* 357.11; freedom fighter

verbs

6 **to disobey,** not mind, not heed, not keep *or* observe, not listen *or* hearken, pay no attention to, **ignore, disregard, defy,** set at defiance, fly in the face of, snap one's fingers at, scoff at, flout, go counter to, set at naught, set naught by, care naught for; be a law unto oneself, step out of line, refuse to cooperate; not conform *see* 867.4, hear a different drummer; **violate,** transgress *see* 435.4; break the law *see* 674.5

7 **to revolt, rebel,** kick over the traces, reluct, reluctate; **rise up,** rise, arise, rise up in arms, mount the barricades; mount *or* make a coup d'état; **mutiny,** mutineer (*old*); insurge *and* insurrect (*both old*), **riot,** run riot; revolutionize, revolution, revolute, subvert, overthrow *see* 859.4; call a general strike, strike *see* 727.8; secede, break away

adjectives

8 **disobedient, transgressive,** uncomplying, violative, lawless, wayward, froward, naughty; recusant, nonconforming *see* 867.5; **undutiful,** unduteous; self-willed, wilful, obstinate *see* 361.8; **defiant** *see* 454.7; bolshie (*informal*); **undisciplined,** ill-disciplined, indisciplined

9 **insubordinate, unsubmissive,** indocile, **uncompliant, uncooperative,** noncooperative, noncooperating, stroppy (*informal*), **intractable** *see* 361.12

10 **defiant, refractory, recalcitrant, contumacious, obstreperous, unruly,** restive, impatient of control *or* discipline; fractious, ornery *and* feisty (*both informal*); wild, untamed *see* 430.29

11 **rebellious,** rebel, breakaway; **mutinous,** mutineering; **insurgent,** insurrectionary, riotous, turbulent; factious, **seditious,** seditionary;

revolutionary; traitorous, treasonable, subversive; extreme, extremistic *see* 611.29

adverbs

12 **disobediently,** uncompliantly, against *or* contrary to order and discipline; **insubordinately, unsubmissively,** indocilely, **uncooperatively;** unresignedly; disregardfully, floutingly, **defiantly;** intractably *see* 361.17; obstreperously, contumaciously, restively, fractiously; **rebelliously,** mutinously; riotously

328 ACTION
voluntary action

nouns

1 **action, activity** *see* 330, act, willed action *or* activity; **acting, doing,** activism, direct action, not words but action; **practice,** actual practice, praxis; **exercise,** drill; **operation,** working, function, functioning; play; **operations,** affairs, workings; **business,** employment, work, occupation; **behaviour** *see* 321

2 **performance, execution,** carrying out, enactment; **transaction; discharge, dispatch;** conduct, **handling,** management, administration; **achievement, accomplishment, effectuation, implementation; commission, perpetration;** completion *see* 407.2

3 **act, action, deed, doing,** thing, thing done; **turn;** feat, stunt *and* trick (*both informal*); **master stroke,** *tour de force* (*French*), **exploit,** adventure, gest, **enterprise, initiative,** achievement, accomplishment, **performance,** production, track record (*informal*); effort, endeavour, job, undertaking; **transaction;** dealing, deal (*informal*); passage; **operation, proceeding, step, measure, manoeuvre, move, movement;** *démarche* (*French*), coup, stroke; blow, go (*informal*); accomplished fact, *fait accompli* (*French*), done deal (*informal*); overt act (*law*); acta, *res gestae* (*Latin*), **doings, dealings; works;** work, handiwork, hand

verbs

4 **to act, serve, function; operate, work, move,** practice, do one's stuff *or* one's thing (*all informal*); **move, proceed;** make, play, behave *see* 321.4

5 **to take action,** take steps *or* measures; **proceed,** proceed with, go ahead with, go with, go through with; do something, go *or* swing into action, **do something about,** act on *or* upon, take it on, run with it (*informal*), get off one's arse (*informal*), get one's finger out (*informal*), get with it *or* the picture (*informal*); put up or shut up *and* put one's money where one's mouth is (*both informal*); **go,** have a go (*informal*), have a whack (*informal*), lift a finger, **take** *or* **bear a hand;** play a role *or* part in; stretch forth one's hand, strike a blow; **manoeuvre,** make moves (*informal*)

6 **to do, effect,** effectuate, **make; bring about,** bring to pass, **bring off,** produce, deliver (*informal*), **do the trick,** put across *or* through; hack it *and* cut it *and* cut the mustard (*all informal*); **do one's part,** carry one's weight, hold up one's end *or* one's end

of the bargain; **achieve, accomplish**, realize *see* 407.4; **render, pay**; **inflict, wreak**, do to; **commit, perpetrate**; pull off (*informal*); go and do, up and do (*informal*)

7 **to carry out**, carry through, go through, fulfil, work out; **bring off**, carry off; **put through**, get through; **implement**; **put into effect, put in** *or* **into practice**, carry into effect, carry into execution, **translate into action**; suit the action to the word, walk the talk; rise to the occasion, come through (*informal*)

8 **to practice, put into practice, exercise, employ, use**; carry on, **conduct, prosecute, wage**; **follow, pursue**; **engage in**, work at, devote oneself to, **do**, turn to, apply oneself to, employ oneself in; play at; **take up**, take to, **undertake, tackle**, take on, address oneself to, have a go at, turn one's hand to, go in for (*informal*), make it one's business, follow as an occupation, set up shop; specialize in *see* 865.4

9 **to perform, execute, enact**; **transact**; **discharge, dispatch**; conduct, **manage, handle**; dispose of, take care of, **deal with**, cope with; **make, accomplish**, complete *see* 407.6

adjectives

10 **acting**, performing, practising, serving, functioning, functional, operating, operative, operational, working; in action *see* 888.11; behavioural *see* 321.7

329 INACTION
voluntary inaction

nouns

1 inaction, passiveness, "a wise passiveness"—WORDSWORTH, **passivity**, passivism; passive resistance, nonviolent resistance; nonresistance, nonviolence; pacifism; neutrality, neutralness, neutralism, **nonparticipation**, noninvolvement; standpattism (*informal*); **do-nothingism**, do-nothingness, do-nothing policy, **laissez-faireism**; *laissez-faire, laissez-aller (both French)*; watching and waiting, watchful waiting, waiting game, a wait-and-see attitude; **inertia**, inertness, **immobility**, dormancy, stagnation, stagnancy, vegetation, stasis, paralysis; **procrastination**; **idleness**, indolence, torpor, torpidness, torpidity, sloth; **immobility** *see* 852.1; equilibrium, dead centre; **inactivity** *see* 331; **quietude**, serenity, quiescence *see* 173; **quietism**, contemplation, meditation, passive self-annihilation; contemplative life, *vita contemplativa (Latin)*

verbs

2 **to do nothing**, not stir, not budge, **not lift a finger** *or* **hand**, not move a foot, **sit back**, sit on one's hands (*informal*), sit on one's arse (*informal*), sit on the sidelines, be a sideliner, sit it out, take a raincheck (*informal*), fold one's arms, twiddle one's thumbs; **cool** *or* **kick one's heels** (*informal*); **bide one's time, delay**, watch and wait, wait and see, play a waiting game, lie low; hang fire, not go off half-cocked; lie *or* sit back, lie *or* rest upon one's oars, rest, put one's feet up (*informal*), be still *see* 173.7; rest on one's laurels; drift, coast; **stagnate**,

vegetate, veg out (*informal*), lie dormant, hibernate; lie down on the job (*informal*), idle *see* 331.11

3 **to refrain, abstain**, hold, **spare, forbear, forgo**, keep from; hold *or* stay one's hand, sit by *or* idly by, sit on one's hands

4 **to let alone**, leave alone, **leave** *or* **let well enough alone**; look the other way, not make waves, not look for trouble, not rock the boat; **let be**, leave be (*informal*), let things take their course, let it have its way; leave things as they are; *laisser faire, laisser passer, laisser aller (all French)*, live and let live; **take no part in**, not get involved in, **have nothing to do with**, have no hand in, stay out of, stand *or* hold *or* remain aloof

5 **to let go**, let pass, **let slip**; procrastinate

adjectives

6 **passive**; **neutral**, neuter; standpat (*informal*), **do-nothing**; *laissez-faire, laissez-aller (both French)*; **inert, immobile**, dormant, stagnant, stagnating, vegetative, vegetable, static, stationary, motionless, immobile, unmoving, paralysed, paralytic; procrastinating; **inactive, idle** *see* 331.16; quiescent *see* 173.12; quietist, quietistic, contemplative, meditative

adverbs

7 **at a stand** *or* **standstill**, at a halt; as a last resort

phrases

8 leave well enough alone, let sleeping dogs lie; *dolce far niente (Italian)*

330 ACTIVITY

nouns

1 **activity, action**, activeness; **movement**, motion, **stir**; **proceedings, doings, goings-on**; **activism**, political activism, judicial activism, etc; **militancy**; business *see* 724

2 **liveliness, animation, vivacity**, vivaciousness, **sprightliness, spiritedness**, bubbliness, **ebullience**, effervescence, **briskness, brightness, breeziness**, peppiness (*informal*); **life, spirit, verve**, energy, adrenalin; pep *and* oomph *and* pizzazz (*all informal*), vim, moxie (*US & Canadian informal*) *see* 17.2

3 **quickness, swiftness, speediness, alacrity**, celerity, readiness, smartness, sharpness, briskness; **promptness**, promptitude; dispatch, expeditiousness, expedition; **agility, nimbleness, spryness**, springiness, nippiness

4 **bustle, fuss, flurry, flutter**, fluster, scramble, ferment, stew, sweat, whirl, swirl, vortex, maelstrom, **stir**, hubbub, hullabaloo, hoo-ha *and* flap (*both informal*), feery-fary (*Scottish*), kerfuffle (*informal*), carry-on (*informal*), ado, to-do (*informal*), song and dance (*informal*), bother, botheration (*informal*), pother; fussiness, flutteriness; tumult, commotion, **agitation**; **restlessness**, unquiet, fidgetiness; **spurt, burst**, fit, spasm

5 **busyness, press of business**; plenty to do, many irons in the fire, much on one's plate; the battle of life, the rat race (*informal*)

6 industry, industriousness, assiduousness, **assiduity**, **diligence**, **application**, concentration, laboriousness, sedulity, **sedulousness**, unsparingness, relentlessness, zealousness, ardour, fervour, vehemence; **energy**, energeticalness, strenuousness, strenuosity, tirelessness, indefatigability

7 **enterprise**, enterprisingness, dynamism, **initiative**, aggression, **aggressiveness**, killer instinct, force, forcefulness, pushfulness, pushingness, **pushiness**, **push, drive, hustle, go, get-up-and-go** (*informal*), go-ahead, go-getting; **adventurousness**, venturousness, venturesomeness, adventuresomeness; spirit, gumption *and* spunk (*both informal*); **ambitiousness** *see* 100.10;

"the strenuous life"—THEODORE ROOSEVELT

8 **man** *or* **woman of action, doer,** man of deeds; **hustler** *and* **self-starter** (*both informal*), bustler; go-getter *and* ball of fire *and* live wire *and* powerhouse *and* human dynamo *and* spitfire (*all informal*); **workaholic**, overachiever; beaver; busy bee, **eager beaver** (*informal*); operator *and* big-time operator *and* wheeler-dealer (*all informal*); winner (*informal*); **activist**, political activist, **militant**; enthusiast *see* 101.4; new broom

9 **overactivity**, hyperactivity; hyperkinesia *or* hyperkinesis; franticness, frenziedness; overexertion, overextension; officiousness *see* 214.2

verbs

10 **to be busy, have one's hands full,** have many irons in the fire, have a lot on one's plate; not have a moment to spare, not have a moment to call one's own, not be able to call one's time one's own; do it on the run; have other things to do, have other fish to fry; **work, labour, drudge** *see* 725.14; **busy oneself** *see* 724.10, 11

11 **to stir,** stir about, **bestir oneself,** stir one's stumps (*informal*), get down to business, sink one's teeth into it, take hold, be up and doing

12 **to bustle, fuss,** make a fuss, stir, stir about, rush around *or* about, tear around, hurry about, buzz *or* whiz about, dart to and fro, run *or* go around like a headless chicken

13 **to hustle** (*informal*), **drive,** drive oneself, **push, scramble,** go all out (*informal*), **make things hum,** step lively (*informal*), make the sparks fly (*informal*); make up for lost time; press on, drive on; go ahead, forge ahead, shoot ahead, go full steam ahead

14 (*informal terms*) **to hump,** break one's neck, bear down on it, put one's back into it, get off one's arse, **set the ball rolling,** shake a leg, go to town, get one's finger out

15 **to keep going, keep on,** keep on the go, **carry on,** peg *or* plug away (*informal*), **keep at it,** keep moving, keep driving, **keep the ball rolling;** keep busy, **keep one's nose to the grindstone,** stay on the treadmill

16 **to make the most of one's time,** make hay while the sun shines, not let the grass grow under one's feet; get up early

adjectives

17 **active, lively, animated, spirited,** bubbly, ebullient, effervescent, **vivacious, sprightly,** chipper

and perky (*both informal*), pert; **spry, breezy, brisk, energetic,** eager, keen, can-do (*informal*); smacking, spanking; alive, live, full of life, full of pep *or* go *and* pizzazz (*informal*); **peppy** *and* snappy *and* zingy *and* zappy *and* zippy (*all informal*); frisky, bouncing, bouncy; mercurial, quicksilver; **activist,** activistic, **militant**

18 **quick, swift, speedy, expeditious, snappy** (*informal*), celeritous, alacritous, dispatchful (*old*), **prompt,** ready, smart, sharp, quick on the draw *or* trigger (*informal*); **agile, nimble, spry,** springy, nippy

19 **astir, stirring,** afoot, on foot; in full swing

20 **bustling,** fussing, fussy; **fidgety,** restless, fretful, jumpy, unquiet, unsettled *see* 105.23; **agitated, turbulent**

21 **busy,** full of business; **occupied, engaged, employed, working;** at it; **at work,** on duty, on the job, in harness; hard at work, **hard at it; on the move, on the go,** on the run, on the hop (*informal*); busy as a bee *or* beaver; up to one's ears *or* elbows *or* arse *or* neck *or* eyeballs in (*informal*); tied up

22 **industrious, assiduous, diligent, sedulous,** laborious, **hardworking;** hard, unremitting, unsparing, relentless, zealous, ardent, fervent, vehement; **energetic,** strenuous; never idle; sleepless, unsleeping; tireless, unwearied, unflagging, indefatigable

23 **enterprising, aggressive, dynamic,** activist, proactive, driving, forceful, **pushing,** pushful, **pushy, up-and-coming, go-ahead** *and* **hustling** (*both informal*); adventurous, venturous, venturesome, adventuresome; **ambitious** *see* 100.28

24 **overactive,** hyperactive, hyper (*informal*); hectic, frenzied, frantic, frenetic; hyperkinetic; intrusive, officious *see* 214.9

adverbs

25 **actively, busily; lively,** sprightly, **briskly,** breezily, **energetically, animatedly, vivaciously, spiritedly,** with life and spirit, with gusto; allegro, allegretto; full tilt, in full swing, all out (*informal*); like a house on fire

26 **quickly, swiftly, expeditiously,** with dispatch, readily, **promptly; agilely, nimbly, spryly**

27 **industriously, assiduously, diligently, sedulously,** laboriously; unsparingly, relentlessly, zealously, ardently, fervently, vehemently; **energetically,** strenuously, tirelessly, indefatigably

331 INACTIVITY

nouns

1 **inactivity, inaction** *see* 329, inactiveness; lull, suspension; suspended animation; dormancy, hibernation; immobility, motionlessness, quiescence *see* 173; **inertia** *see* 329.1; underactivity

2 **idleness,** unemployment, nothing to do, otiosity, inoccupation; **leisure,** leisureliness, unhurried ease; idle hands, idle hours, time on one's hands;

"a life of dignified otiosity"—THACKERAY; **relaxation,** letting down, unwinding, putting one's feet up

3 unemployment, lack of work, joblessness, inoccupation; layoff, furlough; normal unemployment, seasonal unemployment, technological unemployment, cyclical unemployment; unemployment insurance

4 idling, loafing, lazing, *flânerie* (*French*), goofing off (*US informal*), skiving (*informal*); *dolce far niente* (*Italian*); trifling; dallying, dillydallying, mopery, dawdling; loitering, tarrying, lingering; lounging, **lolling**

5 indolence, laziness, sloth, slothfulness, bone-laziness; laggardness, slowness, dilatoriness, remissness, do-nothingness, faineancy, *fainéantise* (*French*); inexertion, inertia; **shiftlessness;** vagrancy, hoboism (*chiefly US*); spring fever; ergophobia

6 languor, languidness, languorousness, languishment (*old*), lackadaisicalness, lotus-eating; **listlessness,** lifelessness, inanimation, enervation, slowness, lenitude *or* lentor (*both old*), **dullness, sluggishness,** heaviness, dopiness (*informal*), hebetude, supineness, **lassitude, lethargy,** loginess (*US*); phlegm, **apathy, indifference, passivity;** torpidness, **torpor,** torpidity; stupor, stuporousness, stupefaction; **sloth,** slothfulness, acedia; **sleepiness, somnolence,** oscitancy, yawning, drowsiness *see* 22.1; **weariness, fatigue** *see* 21; jadedness, satedness *see* 993.2; world-weariness, ennui, boredom *see* 118.3

7 lazybones, lazyboots, lazylegs, indolent, lie-abed, slugabed

8 idler, loafer, lounger, loller, layabout (*informal*), couch potato (*informal*), lotus-eater, *flâneur, flâneuse* (*both French*), *fainéant* (*French*), scrimshanker, shirker, **skiver,** clock watcher; **sluggard,** slug (*US & Canadian informal*), slouch, sloucher, gentleman of leisure; **time waster,** time killer; **dallier, dillydallier,** mope, moper, doodler, diddler (*old*), **dawdler,** dawdle, laggard, **loiterer,** lingerer; waiter on Providence; trifler, **potterer**

9 bum, stiff (*informal*), derelict, *lazzarone* (*Italian*); beachcomber; **good-for-nothing,** good-for-naught, **ne'er-do-well,** wastrel; drifter, vagrant, hobo (*chiefly US*), dosser, tramp *see* 178.3; beggar *see* 440.8

10 homeless person; street person; bag lady *or* woman

11 nonworker, drone; cadger, moocher (*informal*), bummer (*US informal*), **sponger,** freeloader, lounge lizard (*informal*), social parasite, parasite; beggar, mendicant; **the unemployed;** the unemployable; the chronically unemployed, discouraged workers, lumpen proletariat; leisure class, rentiers, idle rich

verbs

12 to idle, do nothing, **laze,** lazy (*informal*), take one's ease *or* leisure, take one's time, **loaf, lounge;** "I loafe and invite my soul, I lean and loafe at my ease"—WALT WHITMAN; **lie around,** lounge around, loll around, lollop about (*informal*), mike, moon, moon around, sit around, sit on one's arse (*informal*), stand *or* hang around, **loiter about** *or* **around,** slouch, slouch around, **bum around** *and* mooch around (*both informal*), muck about, bugger about *or* around (*informal*), fester; **shirk,** avoid work, scrimshank, skive, bob off; sleep at one's post; let the grass grow under one's feet; twiddle one's thumbs, fold one's arms

13 to waste time, consume time, **kill time,** idle *or* trifle *or* fritter *or* fool away time, loiter away *or* loiter out the time, beguile the time, **while away the time,** pass the time, lose time, waste the precious hours, burn daylight (*old*); **trifle,** dabble, fribble, footle, potter, potter, piddle, diddle (*US informal*), doodle

14 to dally, dillydally, piddle, diddle (*US informal*), doodle, **dawdle, loiter,** lollygag (*US informal*), linger, lag, poke, take one's time

15 to take it easy, take things as they come, **drift,** drift with the current, go with the flow, swim with the stream, coast, lead an easy life, **live a life of ease,** lie *or* rest on one's oars; rest *or* repose on one's laurels, lie back on one's record

16 to lie idle, lie fallow; aestivate, hibernate, lie dormant; lie *or* lay off, charge *or* recharge one's batteries (*informal*); lie up, lie on the shelf; ride at anchor, lay *or* lie by, lay *or* lie to; have nothing to do, have nothing on (*informal*)

adjectives

17 inactive, unactive; stationary, static, at a standstill; sedentary; **quiescent,** motionless *see* 173.13

18 idle, fallow, otiose; **unemployed, unoccupied,** disengaged, *désœuvré* (*French*), **jobless, out of work,** out of a job, out of harness; free, available, at liberty, at leisure; at a loose end; unemployable, lumpen; leisure, leisured; off duty, off work, off

19 indolent, lazy, bone-lazy, **slothful,** workshy, ergophobic; *fainéant* (*French*), **laggard,** slow, **dilatory,** procrastinative, remiss, slack, lax; easy; **shiftless; unenterprising,** nonaggressive; good-for-nothing, ne'er-do-well; drony, dronish, parasitic, cadging, sponging, scrounging

20 languid, languorous, listless, lifeless, inanimate, enervated, debilitated, **pepless** (*informal*), lackadaisical, slow, wan, **lethargic,** logy (*US*), hebetudinous, supine, lymphatic, apathetic, **sluggish,** dopey (*informal*), drugged, nodding, droopy, **dull,** heavy, leaden, lumpish, **torpid,** stultified, stuporous, **inert,** stagnant, stagnating, vegetative, vegetable, dormant; phlegmatic, numb, benumbed; moribund, dead, exanimate; sleepy, somnolent *see* 22.21; **pooped** (*informal*), weary; jaded, sated *see* 993.6; **blasé,** world-weary, bored

332 ASSENT

nouns

1 assent, acquiescence, concurrence, concurring, **concurrency, compliance, agreement, acceptance,** accession; eager *or* hearty *or* warm assent, welcome; assentation; agreement in principle, general agreement; support; **consent** *see* 441

2 affirmative; yes, yea, aye, amen; nod, nod of assent; thumbs-up; **affirmativeness,** affirmative attitude, yea-saying; **me-tooism;** toadying, automatic agreement, knee-jerk assent, subservience, arse-licking (*informal*)

3 acknowledgment, recognition, acceptance; appreciation; **admission,** confession, concession, allowance; avowal, profession, declaration

4 ratification, endorsement, acceptance, approval, approbation *see* 509.1, subscription, subscribership, imprimatur, **sanction, permission, the OK** *and* the okay *and* **the green light** *and* **the go-ahead** *and* the nod (*all informal*), **certification, confirmation, validation, authentication,** authorization, warrant; **affirmation,** affirmance; stamp, rubber stamp; **seal of approval;** seal, signet, sigil; **subscription, signature,** John Hancock (*US & Canadian informal*); countersignature; visa, *visé* (*French*); notarization

5 **unanimity,** unanimousness, universal *or* univocal *or* unambiguous assent; **like-mindedness, meeting of minds,** one *or* same mind; total agreement; **understanding,** mutual understanding; **concurrence, consent,** general consent, common assent *or* consent, consentaneity, **accord,** accordance, **concord,** concordance, **agreement,** general agreement; **consensus,** consensus of opinion (*informal*); *consensus omnium* (*Latin*), universal agreement *or* accord, *consensus gentium* (*Latin*), agreement of all, shared sense, sense of the meeting; **acclamation,** general acclamation; unison, harmony, **chorus, concert,** one *or* single voice, one accord; general voice, vox pop, *vox populi* (*Latin*)

6 **assenter, consenter, accepter,** covenanter, covenantor; assentator, yea-sayer; **yes-man,** toady, creature, arse-licker *and* arse-kisser *and* brown-nose *and* boot-licker (*all informal*)

7 **endorser, subscriber, ratifier,** approver, upholder, certifier, confirmer; **signer,** signatory, the undersigned; cosigner, cosignatory, party; underwriter, guarantor, insurer; notary, notary public

verbs

8 **to assent,** give *or* yield assent, **acquiesce, consent** *see* 441.2, **comply, accede, agree,** agree to *or* with, have no problem with; find it in one's heart; take kindly to *and* hold with (*both informal*); **accept,** receive, buy (*informal*), take one up on (*informal*); **subscribe to,** acquiesce in, abide by; yes, **say 'yes' to; nod,** nod assent, vote for, cast one's vote for, give one's voice for; welcome, hail, cheer, acclaim, applaud, accept in toto

9 **to concur, accord,** coincide, **agree, agree with,** agree in opinion; enter into one's view, enter into the ideas *or* feelings of, **see eye to eye,** be at one with, be of one mind with, go with, **go along with,** fall *or* chime *or* strike in with, close with, meet, conform to, side with, join *or* identify oneself with; cast in one's lot, fall in *or* into line, lend oneself to, play *or* go along, take kindly to; **echo,** ditto (*informal*), say 'ditto' to, say 'amen' to; join in the chorus, go along with the crowd (*informal*), run with the pack, go *or* swim with the stream *or* current; get on the bandwagon (*informal*)

10 **to come to an agreement, agree,** concur on, settle on, agree with, **agree on** *or* **upon, arrive at an agreement, come to an understanding, come to terms,** reach an understanding *or* agreement *or* accord, strike *or* hammer out a bargain, covenant, get together (*informal*); **shake hands on,** shake on it (*informal*); come around to

11 **to acknowledge, admit, own, confess, allow,** avow, **grant,** warrant, **concede,** yield (*old*); **accept,**

recognize; agree in principle, express general agreement, go along with, not oppose *or* deny, agree provisionally *or* for the sake of argument; bring oneself to agree, assent grudgingly *or* under protest

12 **to ratify, endorse,** second, support, **certify, confirm, validate, authenticate, accept,** give the nod *or* the green light *or* the go-ahead *or* the OK (*all informal*), give a nod of assent, give one's imprimatur, permit, give permission, **approve** *see* 509.9; sanction, **authorize,** warrant, accredit; **pass,** give thumbs up (*informal*); amen, say amen to; visa, *visé* (*French*); underwrite, subscribe to; **sign,** undersign, sign on the dotted line, put one's John Hancock on (*US & Canadian informal*), initial, put one's mark *or* X *or* cross on; autograph; cosign, countersign; seal, sign and seal, set one's seal, **set one's hand and seal;** affirm, swear and affirm, take one's oath, swear to; rubber stamp (*informal*); notarize

adjectives

13 **assenting, agreeing,** acquiescing, **acquiescent, compliant,** consenting, consentient, consensual, submissive, unmurmuring, conceding, concessive, assentatious, **agreed, content**

14 **accepted, approved,** received; acknowledged, admitted, allowed, granted, conceded, recognized, professed, confessed, avowed, warranted; self-confessed; **ratified, endorsed, certified,** confirmed, validated, authenticated; certificatory, confirmatory, validating, warranting; **signed,** sealed, signed and sealed, countersigned, underwritten; stamped, rubber-stamped (*informal*); sworn to, notarized, affirmed, sworn and affirmed

15 **unanimous, solid,** consentaneous, **with one consent** *or* **voice;** uncontradicted, unchallenged, uncontroverted, uncontested, unopposed; **concurrent,** concordant, **of one accord; agreeing, in agreement, like-minded, of one mind,** of the same mind; of a piece, **at one,** at one with, agreed on all hands, carried by acclamation

adverbs

16 **affirmatively,** assentingly, in the affirmative

17 **unanimously,** concurrently, consentaneously, **by common** *or* **general consent,** with one consent, **with one accord,** with one voice, without contradiction, *nemine contradicente* (*Latin*), nem con, without a dissenting voice, *nemine dissentiente* (*Latin*), in chorus, in concert, in unison, in one voice, univocally, unambiguously, to a man, **together,** all together, all agreeing, **as one,** as one man, one and all, on all hands; by acclamation

exclamations

18 **yes, yea,** aye, *oui* (*French*), *sí* (*Spanish*), *da* (*Russian*), *ja* (*German*); why yes, *mais oui* (*French*); **indeed,** yes indeed; **surely, certainly,** assuredly, most assuredly, **right, right you are, exactly, precisely,** just so, absolutely, positively, really, truly, rather, quite, to be sure; **all right, right, good,** well and good, good enough, **very well,** *très bien* (*French*); naturally, *naturellement* (*French*); **of course,** as you say, **by all means,** by all manner of means; amen; hear hear

19 (*informal terms*) yeah, yep, yup, uh-huh; same here, likewise, indeedy, yes indeedy, sure, sure thing, sure enough; righto!; OK, okay, Roger, Roger-dodger; fine; you bet!, you can bet on it!, you can say that again!, you said it!, you'd better believe it

phrases

20 **so be it**, be it so, so mote it be (*old*), so shall it be, amen (*Hebrew*); so it is, so is it; agreed, done, that's about the size of it; *c'est bien* (*French*); that takes care of that, that's that, that's right; that makes two of us

333 DISSENT

nouns

1 **dissent, dissidence,** dissentience; **nonassent, nonconsent,** nonconcurrence, nonagreement, agreement to disagree; minority opinion *or* report *or* position; **disagreement, difference, variance,** diversity, disparity; **dissatisfaction, disapproval,** disapprobation; repudiation, **rejection; refusal, opposition** see 451; dissension, disaccord see 456; **alienation,** withdrawal, dropping out, secession; recusance *or* recusancy, **nonconformity** see 867; apostasy see 363.2; counterculture, underground

2 **objection, protest; kick** *and* **beef** *and* **bitch** *and* squawk *and* howl (*all informal*), protestation; **remonstrance, remonstration,** expostulation; **challenge; demur,** demurrer; **reservation, scruple,** compunction, qualm, twinge *or* qualm of conscience; **complaint, grievance; exception;** peaceful *or* nonviolent protest; **demonstration, demo** (*informal*), protest demonstration, counterdemonstration, **rally,** march, sit-in, teach-in, boycott, strike, picketing, indignation meeting; grievance committee; **rebellion** see 327.4

3 **dissenter, dissident,** dissentient, recusant; **objector,** demurrer; minority *or* opposition voice; **protester,** protestant; **separatist,** schismatic; sectary, sectarian, opinionist; nonconformist see 867.3; apostate see 363.5

verbs

4 **to dissent,** dissent from, be in dissent, say nay, **disagree,** discord with, **differ,** not agree, disagree with, agree to disagree *or* differ; divide on, be at variance; **take exception,** withhold assent, **take issue, beg to differ,** raise an objection, rise to a point of order; be in opposition to, oppose; refuse to conform, kick against the pricks, march to *or* hear a different drummer, swim against the tide *or* against the current *or* upstream; **split off, withdraw,** drop out, secede, separate *or* disjoin oneself

5 **to object, protest, kick** *and* **beef** (*both informal*), put up a struggle *or* fight; **bitch** *and* **squeal** *and* squawk *and* howl (*all informal*); exclaim *or* cry out against, make *or* create *or* raise a stink about (*all informal*); cry blue *or* bloody murder (*informal*); **remonstrate,** expostulate; raise *or* press objections, raise one's voice against, enter a protest; **complain,** exclaim at, state a grievance, air one's grievances; **dispute, challenge,** call in question; **demur, scruple,** boggle, dig in one's heels; be bolshie (*informal*), be stroppy, be bloody-minded; **demonstrate, demonstrate against,** rally, march,

sit in, teach-in, boycott, black, strike, picket; **rebel** see 327.7

adjectives

6 **dissenting, dissident,** dissentient, recusant; **disagreeing, differing; opposing** see 451.8, in opposition; alienated; counterculture, antiestablishment, underground; breakaway; at variance with, at odds with; schismatic, schismatical, sectarian, sectary; nonconforming see 867.5; rebellious see 327.11; resistant see 453.5

7 **protesting,** protestant; **objecting,** expostulative, expostulatory, remonstrative, remonstrant; under protest

334 AFFIRMATION

nouns

1 **affirmation,** affirmance, **assertion, asseveration,** averment, **declaration,** vouch (*old*), allegation; **avouchment, avowal; position, stand,** stance; profession, **statement, word,** say, saying, say-so (*informal*), positive declaration *or* statement; manifesto, position paper; statement of principles, **creed** see 952.3; **pronouncement, proclamation,** announcement, annunciation, enunciation; proposition, conclusion; predication, predicate; protest, protestation; utterance, dictum, *ipse dixit* (*Latin*)

2 **affirmativeness; assertiveness,** positiveness, absoluteness, speaking out, table-thumping (*informal*)

3 **deposition, sworn statement, affidavit,** statement under oath, notarized statement, sworn testimony, affirmation; **vouching, swearing; attestation;** certification; **testimony**

4 **oath, vow,** avow (*old*), **word, assurance, guarantee, warrant,** solemn oath *or* affirmation *or* word *or* declaration; **pledge** see 436.1; Bible oath, ironclad oath; judicial oath, extrajudicial oath; oath of office, official oath; oath of allegiance, loyalty oath, test oath

verbs

5 **to affirm, assert,** assever (*old*), **asseverate, aver,** protest, lay down, avouch, avow, **declare,** say, say loud and clear, say out loud, sound off (*informal*), have one's say, speak, speak one's piece *or* one's mind, speak up *or* out, **state,** set down, express, put, put it, put in one's twopenny worth (*informal*); **allege,** profess; stand on *or* for; predicate; issue a manifesto *or* position paper, manifesto; announce, **pronounce,** annunciate, enunciate, **proclaim; maintain,** have, **contend,** argue, **insist, hold,** submit, maintain with one's last breath

6 **to depose,** depone; **testify,** take the stand, witness; **warrant, attest,** certify, **guarantee, assure; vouch, vouch for, swear,** swear to, swear the truth, **swear under oath;** make *or* take one's oath, **vow;** swear by bell, book, and candle; call heaven to witness, declare *or* swear to God, swear on the Bible, kiss the book, swear to goodness, hope to die, cross one's heart *or* cross one's heart and hope to die; swear till one is blue in the face (*informal*)

7 to administer an oath, **place** *or* **put under oath**, put to one's oath, put upon oath; **swear, swear in,** adjure (*old*)

adjectives

8 **affirmative,** affirming, affirmatory, certifying, certificatory; **assertive,** assertative, assertional; **declarative,** declaratory; predicative, predicational; **positive,** absolute, emphatic, decided, table-thumping (*informal*), unambiguously, unmistakably, loud and clear, resounding

9 **affirmed, asserted,** asseverated, avouched, avowed, averred, **declared; alleged,** professed; **stated,** pronounced, announced, enunciated; predicated; manifestoed; **deposed,** warranted, **attested, certified,** vouched, **vouched for,** vowed, pledged, **sworn, sworn to**

adverbs

10 **affirmatively,** assertively, declaratively, predicatively; **positively,** absolutely, decidedly, loudly, loud and clear, at the top of one's voice *or* one's lungs; emphatically, with emphasis; without fear of contradiction; under oath, on one's honour *or* one's word

335 NEGATION, DENIAL

nouns

1 **negation,** negating, abnegation; negativeness, negativity, **negativism,** negative attitude, naysaying; **obtuseness,** perversity, orneriness (*informal*), cross-grainedness; **negative, no,** nay, nix (*informal*)

2 **denial, disavowal, disaffirmation, disownment,** disallowance; disclamation, disclaimer; **renunciation, retraction,** retractation, **repudiation,** recantation; revocation, nullification, annulment, abrogation; abjuration, abjurement, forswearing; **contradiction,** flat *or* absolute contradiction, contravention, contrary assertion, controversion, countering, crossing, gainsaying, impugnment; **refutation, disproof** *see* 957; **apostasy, defection** *see* 363.2; **about-face, reversal** *see* 363.1

verbs

3 **to negate,** abnegate, negative; **say 'no';** shake the head

4 **to deny, not admit, not accept,** refuse to admit *or* accept; **disclaim, disown, disaffirm, disavow, disallow,** abjure, forswear, **renounce, retract,** take back, recant; revoke, nullify, **repudiate; contradict,** fly in the face of, cross, assert the contrary, contravene, controvert, impugn, **dispute,** gainsay, **oppose, counter,** go counter to, go contra, contest, take issue with, join issue upon, run counter to; belie, give the lie to; **refute** *see* 957.5, **disprove** *see* 957.4; **reverse oneself** *see* 363.6; **defect, apostatize** *see* 363.7

adjectives

5 **negative,** negatory, abnegative; **denying, disclaiming,** disowning, disaffirming, disallowing, disavowing, renunciative, renunciatory, repudiative, recanting, abjuratory, revocative *or* revocatory;

contradictory, contradicting, **opposing, contrary,** contra, nay-saying, adversative, repugnant; **obtuse,** perverse, ornery (*informal*), crossgrained, contrarious (*informal*)

adverbs

6 **negatively, in the negative;** in denial, in contradiction

conjunctions

7 **neither,** not either, **nor,** nor yet, or not, and not, also not

exclamations

8 **no, nay,** negative, *non* (*French*), *nein* (*German*), *nyet* (*Russian*); certainly not, absolutely no; **not,** not a bit *or* whit *or* jot, I think not, not really; to the contrary, *au contraire* (*French*), quite the contrary, far from it; no such thing, nothing of the kind *or* sort, not so

9 **by no means, by no manner of means;** on no account, in no respect, **in no case, under no circumstances,** on no condition, no matter what; **not at all,** not in the least, **never;** in no wise, noway, nohow (*informal*); out of the question; **not for the world,** not for anything in the world, not if one can help it, not if I know it, not at any price, not for love or money, not for the life of me, over one's dead body; to the contrary, *au contraire* (*French*), quite the contrary, far from it; God forbid *see* 510.27

10 (*informal or informal terms*) nope, nix; no way, no way José, not on your life, not by a long chalk, not by a long shot *or* sight, not by a darn *or* damn sight, not a bit of it, not much, not a chance, fat chance, nothing doing, forget it, that'll be the day

336 IMITATION

nouns

1 **imitation, copying, counterfeiting, repetition; me-tooism** (*informal*), emulation, the sincerest form of flattery, following, mirroring; copycat crime (*informal*); **simulation** *see* 354.3, modelling; fakery, forgery, plagiarism, plagiarizing, plagiary; **imposture, impersonation, takeoff** (*informal*), **send-up** (*informal*), **impression,** burlesque, pastiche, *pasticcio* (*Italian*); mimesis; parody, onomatopoeia

2 **mimicry,** mockery, apery, parrotry, mimetism; protective coloration *or* mimicry, aggressive mimicry, aposematic *or* synaposematic mimicry *and* cryptic mimicry (*both biology*), playing possum

3 **reproduction, duplication, imitation** *see* 784.1, **copy** *see* 784.1, dummy, mock-up, **replica,** facsimile, representation, paraphrase, approximation, model, version, knockoff (*informal*); computer model *or* simulation; parody, burlesque, pastiche, *pasticcio* (*Italian*), travesty *see* 508.6

4 **imitator,** simulator, me-tooer (*informal*), wannabe (*informal*), **impersonator, impostor** *see* 357.6, **mimic,** mimicker, mimer, mime, **mocker;** mockingbird, cuckoo; **parrot, ape,** aper, monkey; **echo,** echoer, echoist; **copier,** copyist, **copycat** (*informal*); **faker, imposter,** counterfeiter, forger, plagiarist; dissimulator, dissembler, deceiver, gay deceiver, hypocrite, phoney (*informal*), poseur; conformist, sheep

verbs

5 **to imitate, copy, repeat,** ditto (*informal*); do like (*informal*), do (*informal*), act *or* go *or* make like (*informal*); **mirror, reflect; echo,** reecho, chorus; **borrow,** steal one's stuff (*informal*), take a leaf out of one's book; assume, **affect; simulate;** counterfeit, fake (*informal*), forge, plagiarize, crib, lift (*informal*); **parody,** pastiche; **paraphrase,** approximate

6 **to mimic, impersonate,** mime, **ape, parrot,** copycat (*informal*); do an impression; take off, send up

7 **to emulate, follow,** follow in the steps *or* footsteps of, walk in the shoes of, put oneself in another's shoes, follow in the wake of, follow the example of, follow suit, follow like sheep, jump on the bandwagon; **copy after,** model after, model on, pattern after, pattern on, shape after, take after, take a leaf out of one's book, take as a model

adjectives

8 **imitation, mock, sham,** cod (*informal*), copied, fake *and* phoney (*both informal*), counterfeit, forged, plagiarized, unoriginal, ungenuine; **pseudo,** synthetic, synthetical, ersatz, hokey *and* hoked-up (*both US & Canadian informal*), quasi

9 **imitative,** simulative, me-too (*informal*); **mimic,** mimetic, **apish,** parrotlike; **emulative;** echoic, onomatopoetic, onomatopoeic

10 **imitable,** copiable, duplicable, replicable

adverbs

11 **imitatively,** apishly, apewise, parrotwise; onomatopoetically; synthetically; quasi

prepositions

12 **like, in imitation of,** after, in the semblance of, on the model of, *à la* (*French*)

word elements

13 quasi–, mim–, ne–, near–, semi–; –ish, –like

337 NONIMITATION

nouns

1 **nonimitation, originality, novelty,** newness, innovation, freshness, uniqueness; **authenticity;** inventiveness, creativity, creativeness *see* 985.3

2 **original, model** *see* 785, archetype, prototype *see* 785.1, **pattern, mould,** pilot model; **innovation,** new departure

3 **autograph,** holograph, first edition

verbs

4 **to originate, invent; innovate; create;** revolutionize

adjectives

5 **original, novel, unprecedented; unique,** *sui generis* (*Latin*); new, fresh *see* 840.7; underived, **firsthand; authentic, imaginative, creative** *see* 985.18;

avant-garde, revolutionary; **pioneer,** bellwether, trail-blazing

6 **unimitated,** uncopied, **unduplicated,** unreproduced, one-off, unprecedented, unexampled; **archetypal,** archetypical, archetypic, prototypal *see* 785.9; **prime,** primary, primal, primitive, pristine

338 COMPENSATION

nouns

1 **compensation, recompense,** repayment, payback, indemnity, indemnification, measure for measure, rectification, restitution, **reparation; amends,** expiation, atonement; **redress,** satisfaction; commutation, substitution; **offsetting,** balancing, **counterbalancing,** counteraction; **retaliation** *see* 506, revenge, *lex talionis* (*Latin*)

2 **offset,** setoff; **counterbalance,** counterpoise, equipoise, counterweight, makeweight; **balance,** ballast; **trade-off,** equivalent, consideration, something of value, *quid pro quo* (*Latin*, something for something), tit for tat, give-and-take *see* 862.1

3 **counterclaim,** counterdemand

verbs

4 **to compensate,** make compensation, make good, set right, restitute, pay back, rectify, **make up for; make amends,** expiate, do penance, atone; **recompense,** pay back, repay, indemnify, cover; **trade off,** give and take; **retaliate** *see* 506

5 **to offset** *see* 778.4, set off, **counteract,** countervail, **counterbalance,** counterweigh, counterpoise, **balance,** play off against, set against, set over against, equiponderate; **square,** square up

adjectives

6 **compensating, compensatory;** recompensive, amendatory, indemnificatory, reparative, rectifying; **offsetting,** counteracting *or* counteractive, countervailing, balancing, **counterbalancing,** zero-sum; **expiatory,** penitential; **retaliatory** *see* 506

adverbs

7 **in compensation,** in return, back; in consideration, for a consideration

advs, conjs

8 **notwithstanding,** but, all the same (*informal*), still, yet, even; **however, nevertheless,** nonetheless; **although,** when, though; albeit, howbeit; **at all events,** in any event, **in any case,** at any rate; **be that as it may,** for all that, even so, **on the other hand,** rather, again, at the same time, all the same, just the same, **however, that may be;** after all, after all is said and done

adverbs, prepositions

9 **in spite of,** spite of (*informal*), **despite,** in despite of, with, even with; **regardless of,** regardless, irregardless (*informal*), irrespective of, without respect *or* regard to; cost what it may, regardless of cost, at any cost, at all costs, whatever the cost

339 CAREFULNESS
close or watchful attention

nouns

1 **carefulness, care, heed, concern, regard; attention** see 982; **heedfulness,** regardfulness, mindfulness, **thoughtfulness; consideration,** solicitude, caring, loving care, tender loving care, TLC (*informal*), caregiving; circumspectness, circumspection; forethought, anticipation, preparedness; **caution** see 494

2 **painstakingness,** painstaking, **pains;** diligence, assiduousness, assiduity, sedulousness, industriousness, industry; **thoroughness,** thoroughgoingness

3 **meticulousness,** exactingness, **scrupulousness,** scrupulosity, **conscientiousness,** punctiliousness, attention to detail, fine-tuning; **particularness,** particularity, circumstantiality; **fussiness, criticalness,** criticality; **finicalness,** finickingness, finickiness, finicality; **exactness, exactitude, accuracy, preciseness, precision,** precisionism, precisianism, punctuality, correctness, prissiness; **strictness, rigour,** rigorousness, spit and polish; nicety, niceness, delicacy, detail, subtlety, refinement, minuteness, exquisiteness

4 **vigilance, wariness,** prudence, **watchfulness,** watching, observance, **surveillance; watch, vigil, lookout;** *qui vive* (*French*); invigilation, proctoring, monitoring; watch and ward; custody, custodianship, guardianship, stewardship; **guard,** guardedness; **sharp eye, weather eye,** peeled eye, watchful eye, eagle eye, lidless *or* sleepless *or* unblinking *or* unwinking eye

5 **alertness, attentiveness; attention** see 982; **wakefulness,** sleeplessness; **readiness,** promptness, promptitude, punctuality; **quickness,** agility, nimbleness; **smartness,** brightness, keenness, sharpness, acuteness, acuity

verbs

6 to **care, mind, heed,** reck, think, consider, regard, pay heed to, take heed *or* thought of; **take an interest,** be concerned; **pay attention** see 982.8

7 to **be careful, take care** *or* good care, take heed, have a care, exercise care, mind out; **be cautious** see 494.5; **take pains,** take trouble, **be painstaking,** go to great pains, go to great lengths, go out of one's way, go the extra mile (*informal*), bend over backwards (*informal*), use every trick in the book, not miss a trick; mind what one is doing *or* about, mind one's business, **mind one's P's and Q's** (*informal*); **watch one's step** (*informal*), pick one's steps, tread on eggs, place one's feet carefully, feel one's way; treat gently, **handle with gloves** *or* **kid gloves**

8 to **be vigilant,** be watchful, never nod *or* sleep, **be on the watch** *or* **lookout,** be on the *qui vive* (*French*), keep a good *or* sharp lookout, keep in sight *or* view; **keep watch,** keep watch and ward, keep vigil; **watch, look sharp,** look about one, look with one's own eyes, **be on one's guard,** keep an eye out, sleep with one eye open, have all one's eyes *or* wits about one, keep one's eye on the ball (*informal*), keep one's eyes open, keep a weather eye open *and* keep one's eyes peeled (*both informal*), keep an ear to the ground, keep a nose to the wind; keep alert, **be on the alert; look out, watch out;** look lively *or* alive; stop, look, and listen

9 to look after, nurture, foster, **tend, take care of** see 1007.19

adjectives

10 **careful, heedful, regardful, mindful, thoughtful, considerate, caring,** solicitous, loving, tender, curious (*old*); circumspect; **attentive** see 982.15; **cautious** see 494.8

11 **painstaking, diligent, assiduous,** sedulous, **thorough, thoroughgoing,** operose, industrious, elaborate

12 **meticulous, exacting, scrupulous, conscientious,** religious, punctilious, punctual, **particular, fussy, critical, attentive,** scrutinizing; **thorough,** thoroughgoing, thoroughpaced; **finical,** finicking, finicky; **exact, precise,** precisionistic, prissy, **accurate, correct;** close, narrow; **strict,** rigid, **rigorous,** spit-and-polish, exigent, demanding; nice, delicate, subtle, fine, refined, minute, detailed, exquisite

13 **vigilant, wary,** prudent, **watchful,** lidless, sleepless, observant; **on the watch, on the lookout,** *aux aguets* (*French*); **on guard,** on one's guard, guarded; with open eyes, with one's eyes open, with one's eyes peeled *or* with a weather eye open (*both informal*); open-eyed, sharp-eyed, keen-eyed, Argus-eyed, eagle-eyed, hawk-eyed; all eyes, all ears, **all eyes and ears;** custodial

14 **alert, on the alert,** on the *qui vive* (*French*), **on one's toes, on top** *and* **on the ball** (*all informal*), **attentive; awake,** wakeful, **wide-awake,** sleepless, unsleeping, unblinking, unwinking, unnodding, alive, ready, prompt, quick, agile, nimble, quick on the trigger *or* draw (*all informal*); **smart, bright, keen, sharp**

adverbs

15 **carefully, heedfully,** regardfully, **mindfully,** thoughtfully, **considerately,** solicitously, tenderly, lovingly; circumspectly; **cautiously** see 494.12; **with care,** with great care; **painstakingly, diligently,** assiduously, industriously, sedulously, thoroughly, thoroughgoingly, to a t *or* a turn (*informal*)

16 **meticulously, exactingly, scrupulously, conscientiously,** religiously, punctiliously, punctually, fussily; strictly, rigorously; exactly, **accurately, precisely, with exactitude, with precision;** nicely, with great nicety, refinedly, minutely, in detail, exquisitely

17 **vigilantly, warily,** prudently, **watchfully,** observantly; **alertly,** attentively; sleeplessly, unsleepingly, unwinkingly, unblinkingly, lidlessly, unnoddingly

340 NEGLECT

nouns

1 **neglect,** neglectfulness, **negligence,** inadvertence *or* inadvertency, malperformance, dereliction, *culpa* (*Latin*), culpable negligence, criminal negligence;

remissness, laxity, laxness, slackness, looseness, laches; unrigorousness, permissiveness; noninterference, *laissez-faire* (*French*), nonrestriction; **disregard**, airy disregard, slighting; **inattention** *see* 983; **oversight**, overlooking; **omission**, nonfeasance, nonperformance, lapse, failure, **default**; poor stewardship *or* guardianship *or* custody; procrastination *see* 845.5

2 **carelessness, heedlessness, unheedfulness,** disregardfulness, regardlessness; unperceptiveness, impercipience, blindness, deliberate blindess; uncaring, unsolicitude, unsolicitousness, **thoughtlessness**, tactlessness, inconsiderateness, **inconsideration**; unthinkingness, unmindfulness, oblivion, forgetfulness; **unpreparedness,** unreadiness, lack of foresight *or* forethought; **recklessness** *see* 493.2; **indifference** *see* 102, *je-m'en-fichisme* and *je-m'en-foutisme* (*both French*); **laziness** *see* 331.5; perfunctoriness; cursoriness, hastiness, offhandedness, casualness; easiness; nonconcern, insouciance; abandon, careless abandon, *sprezzatura* (*Italian*)

3 **slipshodness**, slipshoddiness, **slovenliness,** slovenry, sluttishness, untidiness, **sloppiness** *and* **messiness** (*both informal*); haphazardness; slapdash, slapdashness, a lick and a promise (*all informal*), loose ends; bad job, sad work, botch, slovenly performance; bungling *see* 414.4

4 **unmeticulousness**, unexactingness, **unscrupulousness**, unrigorousness, **unconscientiousness**, unpunctiliousness, unpunctuality, unparticularness, unfussiness, unfinicalness, **uncriticalness**; inexactness, **inexactitude**, inaccuracy, imprecision, unpreciseness

5 **neglecter**, negligent (*old*), ignorer, disregarder; *je-m'en-fichiste* and *je-m'en-foutiste* (*both French*); **procrastinator**, waiter on Providence, Micawber (*Dickens*); slacker, shirker, skiver, malingerer, dodger, idler; skimper (*informal*); trifler; sloven, slut, mawkin; bungler *see* 414.8

verbs

6 to **neglect**, overlook, **disregard**, not heed, not attend to, take for granted, **ignore**; not care for, not take care of; **pass over**, gloss over; **let slip, let slide** (*informal*), let the chance slip by, **let go,** let take its course; let the grass grow under one's feet; not think *or* consider, not give a thought to, take no thought *or* account of, blind oneself to, turn a blind eye to, leave out of one's calculation; lose sight of, lose track of; **be neglectful** *or* **negligent**, fail in one's duty, **fail**, lapse, **default**, let go by default; not get involved; nod, nod *or* sleep through, sleep (*old*), be caught napping, be asleep at the wheel (*informal*)

7 to **leave undone**, leave, **let go**, leave half-done, pretermit, **skip**, jump, **miss, omit**, let be *or* alone, pass over, pass up (*informal*), abandon; leave a loose thread, leave loose ends, let dangle; **slack, shirk,** skive, malinger; trifle; **procrastinate** *see* 845.11

8 to **slight**; turn one's back on, turn a cold shoulder to, get *or* give the cold shoulder *and* get *or* give the go-by *and* cold-shoulder (*all informal*), leave out in the cold; not lift a finger, leave undone; scamp,

skimp (*informal*); slur, **slur over**, pass over, skate over, slubber over, slip *or* **skip over**, dodge, fudge, blink, carefully ignore; skim, **skim over**, skim the surface, **touch upon**, touch upon lightly *or* in passing, pass over lightly, go once over lightly, give a lick and a promise (*informal*); **cut corners**, cut a corner

9 **to do carelessly**, do by halves, do in a half-arsed way (*informal*), do in a slip-shod fashion, do anyhow, do any old how (*informal*), do in any old way (*informal*); botch, **bungle** *see* 414.11; **trifle with,** play *or* play at fast and loose with, mess around *or* about with *and* muck around *or* about with *and* piss around *or* about with (*all informal*); **do offhand,** dash off, knock off *and* throw off (*both informal*), **toss off** *or* **out** (*informal*); **roughhew**, roughcast, rough out; **knock out** (*informal*), hammer *or* pound out; toss *or* **throw together**, knock together, throw *or* slap together, cobble together, cobble up, patch together, patch, patch up, fudge up, fake up; jury-rig

adjectives

10 **negligent, neglectful,** neglecting, derelict, culpably negligent; inadvertent, uncircumspect; **inattentive** *see* 983.6; unwary, unwatchful, asleep at the wheel, off-guard, unguarded; **remiss**, slack, lax, relaxed, laid-back (*informal*), loose, unrigorous, permissive, overly permissive; noninterfering, *laissez-faire* (*French*), nonrestrictive; slighting; slurring, scamping, skimping (*informal*); procrastinating *see* 845.17

11 **careless, heedless, unheeding, unheedful, disregardful,** disregardant, regardless, **unsolicitous, uncaring**; tactless, respectless, **thoughtless, unthinking, inconsiderate,** untactful, undiplomatic, mindless of, **unmindful,** forgetful, oblivious; **unprepared**, unready; **reckless** *see* 493.8; **indifferent** *see* 102.6; lazy; perfunctory, cursory, casual, offhand; easygoing, *dégagé* (*French*), airy, flippant, insouciant, free and easy, free as a bird

12 **slipshod**, slipshoddy, **slovenly**, sloppy *and* **messy** *and* half-arsed (*all informal*), sluttish, untidy; **clumsy, bungling** *see* 414.20; **haphazard**, hit-or-miss, hit-and-miss, promiscuous; deficient, half-arsed (*informal*), botched

13 **unmeticulous**, unexacting, **unpainstaking, unscrupulous**, unrigorous, **unconscientious**, unpunctilious, unpunctual, **unparticular, unfussy, unfinical, uncritical**; inexact, inaccurate, unprecise

14 **neglected**, unattended to, untended, unwatched, unchaperoned, uncared-for; **disregarded**, unconsidered, unregarded, **overlooked, missed,** omitted, passed by, passed over, passed up (*informal*), gathering dust, **ignored**, slighted; unasked, unsolicited; half-done, undone, left undone; deserted, abandoned; in the cold *and* out in the cold (*both informal*); on the shelf, shelved, pigeonholed, on hold *and* on the back burner (*both informal*), **put** *or* **laid aside**, sidetracked *and* sidelined (*both informal*), shunted

15 **unheeded, unobserved, unnoticed, unnoted, unperceived, unseen,** undiscerned, undescried, unmarked, unremarked, unregarded, unminded, unconsidered, unthought-of, unmissed

16 unexamined, unstudied, unconsidered, unsearched, unscanned, unweighed, unsifted, unexplored, uninvestigated, unindagated, unconned

adverbs

17 negligently, neglectfully, inadvertently; **remissly,** laxly, slackly, loosely; **unrigorously,** permissively; nonrestrictively; **slightingly,** lightly, slurringly; scampingly, skimpingly (*informal*)

18 carelessly, heedlessly, unheedingly, unheedfully, disregardfully, regardlessly, **thoughtlessly, unthinkingly, unsolicitously,** tactlessly, **inconsiderately,** unmindfully, forgetfully; **inattentively, unwarily,** unvigilantly, unguardedly, unwatchfully; **recklessly** see 493.11; perfunctorily; once over lightly, cursorily; casually, offhand, offhandedly, airily; clumsily, bunglingly see 414.24; **sloppily** and **messily** (*both informal*), sluttishly, shoddily, shabbily; haphazardly, promiscuously, hit or miss and hit and miss and helter-skelter and slapdash and anyhow and any old how and any old way and any which way (*all informal*)

19 unmeticulously, unscrupulously, unconscientiously, unfussily, **uncritically;** inexactly, inaccurately, unprecisely, imprecisely, unrigorously, unpunctually

341 INTERPRETATION

nouns

1 interpretation, construction, reading, way of seeing or understanding or putting; constructionism, strict constructionism, loose constructionism; **diagnosis; definition,** description; **meaning** see 518; overinterpretation, labouring

2 rendering, rendition; text, edited text, diplomatic text, normalized text; **version;** reading, lection, variant, variant reading; **edition,** critical or scholarly edition; variorum edition or variorum; conflation, composite reading or text

3 translation, transcription, transliteration; **paraphrase,** loose or free translation; decipherment, decoding; amplification, restatement, rewording; metaphrase, literal or verbal or faithful or word-for-word translation; **crib** (*informal*), pony and trot (*both US informal*); interlinear, interlinear translation, bilingual text or edition; **gloss, glossary;** key, *clavis* (*Latin*)

4 explanation, explication, unfolding, **elucidation,** illumination, enlightenment, light, **clarification,** *éclaircissement* (*French*), simplification; take (*informal*); **exposition,** expounding, exegesis; **illustration, demonstration,** exemplification; **reason,** rationale; euhemerism, demythologization, allegorization; decipherment, decoding, cracking, unlocking, **solution** see 939; editing, emendation; critical revision, rescension, diaskeuasis

5 (*explanatory remark*) **comment,** word of **explanation; annotation,** notation, **note,** note of explanation, footnote, gloss, scholium; exegesis; *apparatus criticus* (*Latin*); commentary, commentation (*old*)

6 interpretability, interpretableness, construability;

definability, describability; translatability; **explicability,** explainableness, accountableness

7 interpreter, exegete, exegetist, exegesist, hermeneut; constructionist, strict constructionist, loose constructionist; **commentator,** annotator, scholiast; critic, textual critic, **editor,** diaskeuast, emender, emendator; cryptographer, cryptologist, decoder, decipherer, cryptanalyst; **explainer,** lexicographer, definer, **explicator,** exponent, expositor, expounder, clarifier; demonstrator, euhemerist, demythologizer, allegorist; go-between see 576.4; **translator,** metaphrast, paraphrast; oneirocritic; guide, *cicerone* (*Italian*), dragoman

8 (*science of interpretation*) exegetics, hermeneutics; tropology; criticism, literary criticism, textual criticism; paleography, epigraphy; cryptology, cryptography, cryptanalysis; lexicography; diagnostics, symptomatology, semeiology, semeiotics; pathognomy; physiognomics, physiognomy; metoposcopy; oneirology, oneirocriticism

verbs

9 to interpret, diagnose; **construe,** put a construction on, **take;** understand, **understand by, take to mean,** take it that; **read; read into,** read between the lines; see in a special light, read in view of, take an approach to, **define, describe**

10 to explain, explicate, expound, make of, exposit; **give the meaning,** tell the meaning of; **spell out,** unfold; **account for,** give reason for; **clarify, elucidate,** clear up, clear the air, **cover** and cover the territory (*all informal*), **make clear,** make plain; **simplify,** popularize; **illuminate,** enlighten, **shed** or **throw light upon;** rationalize, euhemerize, demythologize, allegorize; tell or show how, show the way; **demonstrate, show, illustrate,** exemplify; get to the bottom of or to the heart of, make sense of, make head or tails of; decipher, crack, unlock, find the key to, unravel, read between the lines, read into, **solve** see 939.2; explain oneself; explain away; overinterpret

11 to comment upon, commentate, remark upon; **annotate,** gloss; **edit,** make an edition

12 to translate, render, transcribe, transliterate, put or turn into, transfuse the sense of; construe

13 to paraphrase, rephrase, reword, restate, rehash; give a free or loose translation

adjectives

14 interpretative, interpretive, interpretational, exegetic, exegetical, hermeneutic, hermeneutical; constructive, constructional; **diagnostic;** symptomatological, semeiological; tropological; **definitional, descriptive**

15 explanatory, explaining, exegetic, exegetical, **explicative,** explicatory; **expository,** expositive; **clarifying, elucidative, elucidatory; illuminating,** illuminative, enlightening; **demonstrative, illustrative,** exemplificative; glossarial, annotative, critical, editorial, scholiastic; rationalizing, rationalistic, euhemeristic, demythologizing, allegorizing

16 translational, translative; paraphrastic, metaphrastic

17 **interpretable, construable; definable,** describable; translatable, renderable; explainable, explicable, accountable; diagnosable

adverbs

18 **by interpretation,** as here interpreted, as here defined, according to this reading; **in explanation, to explain; that is,** that is to say, as it were, *id est* (*Latin*), i.e.; **to wit, namely,** *videlicet* (*Latin*), viz, *scilicet* (*Latin*), sc; **in other words,** in words to that effect

342 MISINTERPRETATION

nouns

1 **misinterpretation, misunderstanding,** *malentente* (*French*), misintelligence, **misapprehension, misreading, misconstruction,** mistaking, malobservation, **misconception; misrendering,** mistranslation, eisegesis; misexplanation, misexplication, misexposition; misapplication; gloss; **perversion, distortion,** wrenching, twisting, contorting, torturing, squeezing, garbling; reversal; abuse of terms, misuse of words, catachresis; misquotation, miscitation;
"blunders round about a meaning"—POPE; misjudgment *see* 947; **error** *see* 974

verbs

2 **to misinterpret, misunderstand,** misconceive, **mistake, misapprehend; misread, misconstrue,** put a false construction on, miss the point, **take wrong, get wrong,** get one wrong, take amiss, take the wrong way; **get backwards,** reverse, have the wrong way round, put the cart before the horse; misapply; misexplain, misexplicate, misexpound; **misrender,** mistranslate; quote out of context; misquote, miscite, give a false colouring, give a false impression *or* idea, gloss; **garble, pervert, distort,** wrench, contort, torture, squeeze, twist the words *or* meaning, stretch *or* strain the sense *or* meaning, misdeem, **misjudge** *see* 947.2; bark up the wrong tree

adjectives

3 **misinterpreted, misunderstood, mistaken, misapprehended, misread,** eisegetical, misconceived, **misconstrued; garbled, perverted, distorted,** catachrestic, catachrestical; backwards, reversed, arsy-versy (*informal*), backside-foremost (*informal*)

4 **misinterpretable, misunderstandable,** mistakable

343 COMMUNICATION

nouns

1 **communication,** communion, congress, **commerce, intercourse; speaking, speech** *see* 524, utterance, speech act, talking, linguistic intercourse, speech situation, speech circuit, converse, **conversation** *see* 541; **contact, touch, connection; interpersonal communication, intercommunication,** intercommunion, **interplay,** interaction; **exchange,** interchange; answer, response, reply; one-way

communication, two-way communication; **dealings,** dealing, **traffic, truck** (*informal*); information *see* 551; **message** *see* 552.4; ESP, telepathy *see* 689.9; correspondence *see* 553; social intercourse *see* 582.4; miscommunication

2 **informing, telling,** imparting, impartation, impartment, **conveyance, telling, transmission,** transmittal, transfer, transference, sharing, giving, sending, signalling; notification, alerting, **announcement** *see* 352.2, publication *see* 352, **disclosure** *see* 351

3 **communicativeness, talkativeness** *see* 540, **sociability** *see* 582; **unreserve,** unreservedness, **unreticence, unrestraint, unconstraint,** unrestriction; **unrepression,** unsuppression; **unsecretiveness,** untaciturnity; candour, **frankness** *see* 644.4; **openness,** plainness, freeness, outspokenness, plainspokenness; glasnost (*Russian*); **accessibility,** approachability, conversableness; **extroversion,** outgoingness; **uncommunicativeness** *see* 344, reserve, taciturnity

4 **communicability, impartability, conveyability, transmittability,** transmissibility, transferability; contagiousness

5 **communications,** electronic communications, communications industry, media, communications medium *or* media, communications network; telecommunication *see* 347.1; radio communication, wire communication; fibre optics; communication *or* information theory *see* 551.7

verbs

6 **to communicate, be in touch** *or* **contact,** be in connection *or* intercourse, have intercourse, hold communication; **intercommunicate,** interchange, commune with; commerce with, **deal with, traffic with, have dealings with, have truck with** (*informal*); **speak, talk,** be in a speech situation, **converse** *see* 541.9, pass the time of day

7 **to communicate, impart, tell,** lay on one (*informal*), **convey, transmit,** transfer, send, send word, deliver *or* send a signal *or* message, **disseminate,** broadcast, pass, **pass on** *or* **along, hand on;** download; **report, render, make known,** get across *or* over; give *or* send *or* leave word; **signal;** share, share with; **leak,** let slip out, **give** *see* 478.12; tell *see* 551.8

8 **to communicate with, get in touch** *or* **contact with, contact** (*informal*), **make contact with,** raise, reach, get to, get through to, get hold of, make *or* establish connection, get in connection with; **make advances,** make overtures, **approach,** make up to (*informal*); relate to; keep in touch *or* contact with, maintain connection; **answer,** respond *or* reply to, get back to; **question,** interrogate; **correspond,** drop a line

adjectives

9 **communicational, communicating,** communional; transmissional; speech, **verbal,** linguistic, oral; **conversational** *see* 541.13; **intercommunicational,** intercommunicative, intercommunional, interactional, interactive, interacting, interresponsive, responsive, answering; questioning, interrogative, interrogatory; telepathic

10 **communicative, talkative** *see* 540.9, gossipy, newsy; **sociable; unreserved, unreticent,** unshrinking, **unrestrained, unconstrained,** unhampered, unrestricted; demonstrative, expansive, effusive; **unrepressed, unsuppressed; unsecretive,** unsilent, untaciturn; candid, **frank** *see* 644.17; self-revealing, self-revelatory; **open,** free, outspoken, free-speaking, free-spoken, free-tongued; **accessible, approachable,** conversable, easy to speak to; **extroverted,** outgoing; **uncommunicative** *see* 344.8

11 **communicable, impartable, conveyable, transmittable,** transmissible, transferable; contagious

12 communicatively; verbally, talkatively, by word of mouth, orally, viva voce

344 UNCOMMUNICATIVENESS

nouns

1 **uncommunicativeness,** closeness, indisposition to speak, disinclination to communicate; unconversableness, **unsociability** *see* 583; nondisclosure, **secretiveness** *see* 345.1; lack of message *or* meaning, meaninglessness *see* 520

2 **taciturnity, untalkativeness,** unloquaciousness; **silence** *see* 51; **speechlessness,** wordlessness, dumbness, **muteness** *see* 51.2; quietness, quietude; laconicalness, laconism, curtness, shortness, terseness; brusqueness, briefness, brevity, conciseness, economy *or* sparingness of words, pauciloquy (*old*)

3 **reticence** *or* reticency; **reserve,** reservedness, restraint, low key, **constraint;** guardedness, discreetness, discretion; suppression, repression; subduedness; backwardness, retirement, low profile; **aloofness, standoffishness,** distance, remoteness, **detachment,** withdrawal, withdrawnness, reclusiveness, solitariness; impersonality; **coolness,** coldness, frigidity, iciness, frostiness, chilliness; **inaccessibility, unapproachability; undemonstrativeness,** unexpansiveness, unaffability, uncongeniality; **introversion;** modesty, bashfulness *see* 139.4, pudency; expressionlessness, blankness, impassiveness, impassivity; straight *or* poker face, mask

4 **prevarication, equivocation,** tergiversation, **evasion,** shuffle, fencing, dodging, parrying, waffling (*informal*); *suppressio veri* (*Latin*); weasel words

5 **man of few words,** clam (*informal*), strong silent type, laconic (*old*); Spartan, Laconian; evader, weasel

verbs

6 **to keep to oneself,** keep one's own counsel; not open one's mouth, not say a word, not breathe a word, stand mute, **hold one's tongue** *see* 51.5, clam up (*informal*), keep mum, keep shtoom (*informal*); bite one's tongue; have little to say, refuse comment, say neither yes nor no, waste no words, save one's breath; retire; **keep one's distance,** keep at a distance, keep oneself to oneself, **stand aloof,** hold oneself aloof; keep secret *see* 345.7

7 **to prevaricate, equivocate,** waffle (*informal*), flannel (*informal*), tergiversate, evade, dodge, sidestep, say in a roundabout way, parry, duck, weasel *and*

weasel out (*both informal*), palter; hum and haw, **hem and haw,** back and fill; **mince words,** euphemize

adjectives

8 **uncommunicative,** indisposed *or* disinclined to communicate; unconversational, unconversable (*old*); **unsociable** *see* 583.5; **secretive** *see* 345.15; meaningless *see* 520.6

9 **taciturn, untalkative,** unloquacious, indisposed to talk; **silent, speechless,** wordless, **mum,** shtoom (*informal*); **mute** *see* 51.12, dumb, quiet; close, **closemouthed,** close-tongued, **tight-lipped;** close-lipped, tongue-tied; **laconic,** curt, brief, terse, brusque, short, concise, **sparing of words,** economical of words, of few words

10 **reticent, reserved,** restrained, nonassertive, low-key, low-keyed, constrained; **suppressed,** repressed; subdued; guarded, discreet; backward, **retiring,** shrinking; **aloof, standoffish,** standoff, **distant,** remote, removed, **detached,** Olympian, withdrawn; impersonal; **cool,** cold, frigid, icy, frosty, chilled, chilly; **inaccessible, unapproachable,** forbidding; **undemonstrative,** unexpansive, unaffable, uncongenial, ungenial; **introverted;** modest, verecund, verecundious, *pudique* (*French*), bashful *see* 139.12; expressionless, blank, impassive

11 **prevaricating, equivocal,** tergiversating, tergiversant, waffling (*informal*), **evasive,** weaselly, weasel-worded

345 SECRECY

nouns

1 **secrecy,** secretness, airtight secrecy, close secrecy; crypticness; the dark; hiddenness, **concealment** *see* 346; **secretiveness,** closeness; discreetness, discretion, **uncommunicativeness** *see* 344; **evasiveness,** evasion, subterfuge; hugger-mugger, hugger-muggery

2 **privacy,** retirement, isolation, sequestration, seclusion; incognito, anonymity; **confidentialness,** confidentiality; closed meeting, executive session, private conference

3 **veil of secrecy, veil,** curtain, pall, wraps; iron curtain, "curtains of fog and iron"—CHURCHILL, bamboo curtain; wall *or* barrier of secrecy, security blanket; **suppression,** repression, stifling, smothering; **censorship,** blackout (*informal*), **hush-up, cover-up; seal of secrecy,** official secrecy, classification, official classification; security, ironbound security; pledge *or* oath of secrecy; Official Secrets Act

4 **stealth,** stealthiness, **furtiveness, clandestineness,** clandestinity, clandestine behaviour, **surreptitiousness, covertness,** slyness, shiftiness, sneakiness, slinkiness, underhand dealing, undercover *or* underground activity, **covert activity** *or* **operation;** prowl, prowling; stalking

5 **secret, confidence;** private *or* personal matter, privity (*old*); trade secret; confidential *or* **privileged information** *or* **communication;** doctor-patient *or* lawyer-client confidentiality; secret of the

confessional; more than meets the eye; deep, dark secret; solemn secret; guarded secret, hush-hush matter, classified information, eyes-only *or* top-secret information, restricted information; inside information; **mystery, enigma** *see* 522.8; the arcane, arcanum, *arcanum arcanorum* (*Latin*); esoterica, cabala, the occult, hermetism, hermeticism, hermetics; deep *or* profound secret, sealed book, mystery of mysteries; skeleton in the cupboard

6 **cryptography,** cryptoanalysis, cryptoanalytics; **code, cipher;** secret language; code book, code word, code name; **secret writing,** coded message, cryptogram, cryptograph; secret *or* invisible *or* sympathetic ink; cryptographer

verbs

7 **to keep secret, keep mum, veil,** keep dark; keep it a deep, dark secret; secrete, **conceal;** keep to oneself *see* 344.6, keep *in petto* (*Italian*), bosom, keep close, keep snug (*informal*), keep back, keep from, **withhold,** hold out on (*informal*); not let it go further, keep within these walls, keep between us; **not tell,** hold one's tongue *see* 51.5, never let on (*informal*), make no sign, not breathe *or* whisper a word, clam up (*informal*), be the soul of discretion; **not give away** (*informal*),

"tell it not in Gath"—BIBLE, **keep it under one's hat** (*informal*), keep under wraps (*informal*), keep buttoned up (*informal*), keep one's own counsel; keep *or* play one's cards close to one's chest; play dumb; not let the right hand know what the left is doing; keep in ignorance, keep *or* leave in the dark; classify; file and forget; **have secret *or* confidential information,** be in on the secret (*informal*)

8 **to cover up,** muffle up; **hush up, hush,** hush-hush, shush, hugger-mugger; **suppress,** repress, **stifle,** muffle, **smother,** squash, quash, squelch, kill, sit on *or* upon, put the lid on (*informal*); **censor,** black out (*informal*)

9 **to tell confidentially,** tell for one's ears only, mention privately, **whisper, breathe, whisper in the ear;** tell one a secret; take aside, see one alone, talk to in private, speak in privacy; say under one's breath

10 to code, encode, encipher, cipher

adjectives

11 **secret,** close, closed, closet; cryptic, dark; unuttered, unrevealed, undivulged, undisclosed, unspoken, untold; **hush-hush, top secret,** supersecret, eyes-only, classified, restricted, under wraps (*informal*), under security *or* security restrictions; **censored,** suppressed, stifled, smothered, hushed-up, under the seal *or* ban of secrecy; **unrevealable, undivulgable, undisclosable, untellable,** unwhisperable, unbreatheable, unutterable; latent, ulterior, concealed, hidden *see* 346.11; arcane, esoteric, occult, cabalistic, hermetic; enigmatic, mysterious *see* 522.18

12 **covert,** clandestine, quiet, unobtrusive, huggermugger, hidlings (*Scottish*), **surreptitious, undercover,** underground, under-the-counter, under-the-table, **cloak-and-dagger,** backdoor, holeand-corner (*informal*), underhand, **underhanded;**

furtive, **stealthy,** privy, backstairs, **sly, shifty, sneaky,** sneaking, skulking, slinking, slinky, feline

13 **private, privy, closed-door; intimate, inmost,** innermost, interior, inward, **personal; privileged,** protected; **secluded, sequestered,** isolated, withdrawn, retired; incognito, anonymous

14 **confidential,** auricular, **inside** (*informal*), esoteric; *in petto* (*Italian*), close to one's chest (*informal*), under one's hat (*informal*); **off the record,** not for the record, not to be minuted, within these four walls, for no other ears, eyes-only, between us; not to be quoted, not for publication *or* release; not for attribution; unquotable, unpublishable, sealed; sensitive, privileged, under privilege

15 **secretive,** close-lipped, secret, close, dark; discreet; evasive, shifty; **uncommunicative, close-mouthed**

16 coded, encoded; ciphered, enciphered; cryptographic, cryptographical

adverbs

17 **secretly, in secret,** in *or* up one's sleeve; in the closet; nobody the wiser; **covertly,** stownlins *and* in hidlings (*both Scottish*), **undercover,** *à couvert* (*French*), under the cloak of; **behind the scenes,** in the background, in a corner, in the dark, in darkness, behind the veil *or* curtain, behind the veil of secrecy; *sub rosa* (*Latin*), under the rose; underground; *sotto voce* (*Italian*), under the breath, with bated breath, in a whisper

18 **surreptitiously, clandestinely, secretively, furtively, stealthily, slyly,** shiftily, sneakily, sneakingly, skulkingly, slinkingly, slinkily; by stealth, **on the sly** *and* on the fly *and* on the quiet *and* on the qt (*all informal*), *à la dérobée* (*French*), *en tapinois* (*French*), behind one's back, by a side door, **like a thief in the night,** underhand, underhandedly, under the table, in holes and corners *and* in a holeand-corner way (*both informal*)

19 **privately,** privily, **in private,** in privacy, in privy; apart, aside; **behind closed doors,** *januis clausis* (*Latin*), *à huis clos* (*French*), *in camera* (*Latin*), in chambers, in secret *or* closed meeting, in executive session, in private conference

20 **confidentially, in confidence,** in strict confidence, under the seal of secrecy, off the record; **between ourselves,** strictly between us, *entre nous* (*French*), *inter nos* (*Latin*), for your ears *or* eyes only, between you and me, from me to you, between you and me and the gatepost (*informal*)

346 CONCEALMENT

nouns

1 **concealment, hiding, secretion;** burial, burying, interment, putting away; **cover, covering,** covering up, masking, screening *see* 295.1; mystification, obscuration; darkening, obscurement, clouding *see* 1026.6; hiddenness, concealedness, **covertness,** occultation; **secrecy** *see* 345; uncommunicativeness *see* 344; invisibility *see* 32; **subterfuge, deception** *see* 356

2 **veil,** curtain, **cover, screen** *see* 295.2; fig leaf; **wraps** (*informal*); **cover, disguise**

3 **ambush**, ambushment, **ambuscade**, *guet-apens* (*French*); surveillance, shadowing *see* 937.9; lurking hole *or* place; hide, stalking-horse; booby trap, trap

4 **hiding place**, **hideaway**, **hideout**, hidey-hole (*informal*), hiding, concealment, **cover**, secret place; safe house; accommodation address; **recess, corner**, dark corner, nook, cranny, niche; **hole**, bolt-hole, foxhole, funk hole, dugout, lair, den; **asylum, sanctuary, retreat, refuge** *see* 1008; covert, coverture, undercovert; **cache**, stash (*informal*); cubbyhole, cubby, pigeonhole

5 **secret passage**, covert way, secret exit; **back way, back door, side door**; bolt-hole, escape route, escape hatch, escapeway; secret staircase, *escalier dérobé* (*French*), **back stairs**; **underground**, underground route, underground railway

verbs

6 **to conceal, hide**, ensconce; **cover, cover up**, blind, **screen, cloak, veil**, screen off, curtain, blanket, shroud, enshroud, envelop; **disguise, camouflage, mask**, dissemble; plain-wrap, wrap in plain brown paper; whitewash (*informal*); **paper over**, gloss over, varnish, slur over; distract attention from; **obscure**, obfuscate, cloud, becloud, befog, throw out a smoke screen, shade, throw into the shade; **eclipse**, occult; put out of sight, sweep under the carpet, keep under cover; cover up one's tracks, lay a false scent, hide one's trail; hide one's light under a bushel

7 **to secrete, hide away**, keep hidden, put away, store away, stow away, file and forget, bottle up, lock up, seal up, put out of sight; **keep secret** *see* 345.7; **cache**, stash (*informal*), deposit, plant (*informal*); **bury**; bosom, embosom (*old*)

8 (*hide oneself*) **to hide, conceal oneself, take cover**, hide out (*informal*), hide away, **go into hiding**, go to ground; stay in hiding, **lie hidden**, lie *or* lay low (*informal*), lie *perdue*, lie snug *or* close (*informal*), lie doggo *and* sit tight (*both informal*), burrow (*old*), **hole up** (*informal*), **go underground**; play peekaboo *or* bopeep *or* hide and seek; keep out of sight, retire from sight, drop from sight, disappear *see* 34.3, crawl *or* retreat into one's shell, keep in the background, keep a low profile, stay in the shade; **disguise oneself**, masquerade, take an assumed name, assume a cover, change one's identity, go under an alias, remain anonymous, be incognito, go *or* sail under false colours, wear a mask

9 **to lurk**, couch; lie in wait; **sneak, skulk, slink, prowl**, nightwalk, **steal, creep**, pussyfoot (*informal*), gumshoe (*informal*), tiptoe; stalk, shadow *see* 937.34

10 **to ambush**, ambuscade, waylay; **lie in ambush**, lay wait for, **lie in wait for**; stalk; set a trap for

adjectives

11 **concealed, hidden, hid**, occult, recondite (*old*), blind; **covered** *see* 295.31; **covert, under cover**, under wraps (*informal*); code-named; **obscured**, obfuscated, clouded, clouded over, wrapped in clouds, in a cloud *or* fog *or* mist *or* haze, beclouded, befogged; eclipsed, in eclipse, under an eclipse; in the wings; buried; underground; close, secluded, secluse, sequestered; in purdah, under house arrest, incommunicado; **obscure**, abstruse, mysterious *see*

522.18; **secret** *see* 345.11; unknown *see* 929.17, latent *see* 519.5

12 **unrevealed, undisclosed**, undivulged, **unexposed**; unapparent, **invisible, unseen**, unperceived, unspied, undetected; undiscovered, unexplored, untraced, untracked; unaccounted for, unexplained, unsolved

13 **disguised, camouflaged, in disguise**; masked, masquerading; **incognito**, incog (*informal*); in plain wrapping *or* plain brown paper (*informal*)

14 **in hiding**, hidden out, **under cover**, in a dark corner, doggo (*informal*); in ambush *or* ambuscade; waiting concealed, lying in wait; in the wings; lurking, skulking, prowling, sneaking, stealing; pussyfooted, pussyfoot, on tiptoe; stealthy, furtive, surreptitious *see* 345.12

15 **concealing, hiding**, obscuring, obfuscatory; covering; unrevealing, nonrevealing, undisclosing

347 COMMUNICATIONS

nouns

1 **communications**, signalling, telecommunication, comms (*informal*); electronic communication, electrical communication; satellite communication; wire communication, wireless communication; communication engineering, communication technology; communications engineer; media, communications medium *or* media; communication *or* information theory *see* 551.7; communication *or* information explosion

2 **telegraph, telegraph recorder**, ticker; **telegraphy**, telegraphics; **teleprinter**, Telex (*trademark*), teleprinter; teleprinter exchange *or* telex; wire service; code *see* 345.6; electricity *see* 1031; **key**, interrupter, transmitter, sender; receiver, **sounder**

3 **radio** *see* 1033, **radiotelephony, radiotelegraphy**, wireless, wireless telephony, wireless telegraphy; line radio, wire *or* wired radio, wired wireless, wire wave communication; radiophotography; **television** *see* 1034; electronics *see* 1032

4 **telephone, phone** *and* horn (*both informal*), dog *or* dog and bone (*informal*), telephone set; telephony, telephonics, telephone mechanics, telephone engineering; high-frequency telephony; receiver, telephone receiver; mouthpiece, transmitter; telephone extension, extension; wall telephone, desk telephone; dial telephone, touch-tone telephone, push-button telephone; beeper; scrambler; telephone booth, telephone box, call box, kiosk, public telephone, payphone, coin telephone, cardphone; mobile telephone *or* phone (*informal*), mobile (*informal*), car phone, cellular telephone *or* phone (*informal*), cellphone, Cellnet (*trademark*), Vodafone (*trademark*)

5 **radiophone, radiotelephone**, wireless telephone, wireless; headset, headphone *see* 50.8

6 **intercom** (*informal*), Interphone, intercommunication system

7 **telephone exchange**, telephone office; automatic exchange, tandem exchange; step-by-step switching, panel switching, crossbar switching, electronic switching

8 switchboard; **PBX** *or* private branch *or* business exchange; in *or* A board, out *or* B board

9 **telephone operator, operator,** switchboard operator, telephonist; long distance; PBX operator

10 **telephone man;** telephone engineer; telephone mechanic; linesman

11 **telephoner,** phoner (*informal*), caller, **party,** calling party

12 telephone number, **phone number** (*informal*), ex-directory number, unlisted number; telephone directory, phone book (*informal*); telephone exchange, exchange; STD *or* subscriber trunk dialling code, area code, dialling code

13 telephone call, **phone call** (*informal*), **call, ring** *and* buzz *and* tinkle *and* bell (*all informal*); local call, long-distance call; long distance, subscriber trunk dialling, STD; trunk call; business call, personal call; reverse-charge call; Freefone call (*trademark*); mobile call; dial tone, engaged tone, ringing tone; conference call, video teleconference, teleconference; hotline; chat *or* talk line; helpline; telemarketing

14 **telegram, telegraph, wire** (*informal*), telex; **cablegram, cable,** overseas *or* international telegram; **radiogram,** radiotelegram; fast telegram

15 **facsimile, fax** (*informal*); telephotograph, radiophotograph

16 **telegrapher,** telegraphist, telegraph operator; radiotelegrapher; wireman (*US*)

17 **line,** wire line, telegraph line, telephone line; private line, direct line; party line; hotline; trunk, trunk line; cable, telegraph cable; concentric cable, coaxial cable, coax (*informal*)

verbs

18 **to telephone, phone** (*informal*), **call,** call on the phone (*informal*), make a call, **call up, ring,** ring up, give a ring *or* buzz (*informal*), buzz (*informal*), give a bell (*informal*); call in, ring in, phone in; listen in; hold the phone *or* line; hang up, ring off

19 **to telegraph, telegram, flash, wire** *and* send a wire (*both informal*), telex; **cable;** Teletype (*trademark*); radio; sign on, sign off

adjectives

20 **communicational,** telecommunicational, **communications,** communication, signal; **telephonic,** magnetotelephonic, microtelephonic, monotelephonic, thermotelephonic; **telegraphic;** Teletype (*trademark*); facsimile, fax (*informal*); phototelegraphic, telephotographic; **radio,** wireless; radiotelegraphic

348 MANIFESTATION

nouns

1 **manifestation, appearance; expression,** evincement; **indication, evidence,** proof *see* 956; embodiment, incarnation, bodying forth; materialization; epiphany, theophany, angelophany, Satanophany, Christophany, pneumatophany, avatar; **revelation, disclosure** *see* 351, showing forth; dissemination, **publication** *see* 352

2 **display, demonstration, show, showing; presentation,** showing forth, presentment,

ostentation (*old*), **exhibition, exhibit, exposition,** retrospective; production, performance, representation, enactment, projection; opening, unfolding, unfoldment; **showcase,** showcasing, unveiling, exposure, varnishing day, *vernissage* (*French*)

3 **manifestness, apparentness, obviousness, plainness, clearness,** crystal-clearness, perspicuity, distinctness, microscopical distinctness, patency, patentness, palpability, tangibility; evidentness, evidence (*old*), **self-evidence; openness,** openness to sight, overtness; visibility *see* 31; unmistakableness, unquestionability *see* 969.3

4 **conspicuousness, prominence, salience** *or* saliency, bold *or* high *or* strong relief, boldness, **noticeability,** pronouncedness, strikingness, outstandingness; highlighting, spotlighting, featuring; obtrusiveness; **flagrance** *or* flagrancy, arrantness, blatancy, notoriousness, notoriety; ostentation *see* 501

verbs

5 **to manifest, show, exhibit, demonstrate, display,** breathe, unfold, develop; **present,** represent (*old*), **evince, evidence; indicate,** give sign *or* token, token, betoken, mean *see* 518.8; **express,** show forth, set forth; show off, showcase; **make plain, make clear;** produce, bring out, roll out, trot out (*informal*), bring forth, bring forward *or* to the front, bring to notice, expose to view, bring to *or* into view; **reveal, divulge, disclose** *see* 351.4; **illuminate, highlight, spotlight, feature,** bring to the fore, place in the foreground, bring out in bold *or* strong *or* high relief; **flaunt,** dangle, wave, flourish, brandish, parade; affect, make a show *or* a great show of; perform, enact, dramatize; **embody,** incarnate, body forth, **materialize**

6 (*manifest oneself*) **to come out, come into the open,** come out of the closet (*informal*), come forth, surface; **show one's colours** *or* true colours, pin one's colours to the mast, wear one's heart upon one's sleeve; **speak up, speak out,** raise one's voice, **assert oneself,** let one's voice be heard, speak one's piece *or* one's mind, **stand up and be counted,** take a stand; open up, show one's mind, have no secrets; **appear, materialize**

7 **to be manifest,** be there for all to see, make an appearance, be no secret *or* revelation, **surface,** lie on the surface, be seen with half an eye; need no explanation, **speak for itself,** tell its own story *or* tale; **go without saying,** *aller sans dire* (*French*); **leap to the eye,** *sauter aux yeux* (*French*), **stare one in the face,** hit one in the eye, strike the eye, glare, shout; come across, project; stand out, stick out, stick out a mile, stick out like a sore thumb

adjectives

8 **manifest, apparent, evident, self-evident,** axiomatic, indisputable, **obvious, plain, clear,** perspicuous, distinct, palpable, patent, tangible; **visible, perceptible, perceivable, discernible,** seeable, observable, **noticeable, much in evidence; to be seen,** easy to be seen, plain to be seen; plain as day, plain as the nose on one's face, plain as a pikestaff, large as life, large as life and twice as ugly;

crystal-clear, clear as crystal; **express, explicit, unmistakable,** not to be mistaken, open-and-shut (*informal*); self-explanatory, self-explaining; indubitable *see* 969.15

9 **manifesting, manifestative,** showing, displaying, showcasing, demonstrating, **demonstrative,** presentational, expository, expositional, exhibitive, exhibitional, **expressive;** evincive, evidential; **indicative,** indicatory; appearing, incarnating, incarnational, materializing; epiphanic, theophanic, angelophanic, Satanophanic, Christophanic, pneumatophanic; **revelational,** revelatory, **disclosive** *see* 351.10; promulgatory *see* 352.18

10 **open,** overt, open to all, open as day, out of the closet (*informal*); unclassified; **revealed, disclosed, exposed;** bare, bald, naked

11 **unhidden, unconcealed,** unscreened, uncurtained, unshaded, veilless; **unobscure,** unobscured, undarkened, unclouded; **undisguised,** uncamouflaged

12 **conspicuous, noticeable, notable,** ostensible, **prominent, bold, pronounced, salient,** in relief, in bold *or* high *or* strong relief, in bas-relief, **striking, outstanding,** in the foreground, sticking *or* hanging out (*informal*); highlighted, spotlighted, featured; obtrusive; **flagrant,** arrant, blatant, notorious; **glaring,** staring, stark-staring

13 **manifested,** demonstrated, exhibited, shown, displayed, showcased; **manifestable,** demonstrable, exhibitable, displayable

adverbs

14 **manifestly, apparently, evidently, obviously, patently, plainly, clearly,** distinctly, **unmistakably,** expressly, explicitly, palpably, tangibly; **visibly, perceptibly,** perceivably, discernibly, observably, **noticeably**

15 **openly, overtly,** before one, **before one's eyes** *or* very eyes, under one's nose (*informal*); to one's face, face-to-face; **publicly,** in public; **in the open,** out in the open, in open court, **in plain sight,** in broad daylight, in the face of day *or* heaven, for all to see, in public view, in plain view; aboveboard, on the table

16 **conspicuously, prominently, noticeably,** ostensibly, **notably, markedly, pronouncedly, saliently, strikingly, boldly, outstandingly;** obtrusively; **arrantly, flagrantly, blatantly,** notoriously; glaringly, staringly

349 REPRESENTATION, DESCRIPTION

nouns

1 **representation, delineation,** presentment, drawing, **portrayal, portraiture, depiction,** depictment, rendering, rendition, characterization, charactering (*old*), picturization, figuration, limning, imaging; prefigurement; **illustration,** exemplification, demonstration; projection; **realization;** imagery, iconography; **art** *see* 712; **drama** *see* 704.1, 4–6; conventional representation, plan, diagram, schema, schematization, **blueprint, chart, map;** notation, mathematical notation, musical notation, score, tablature; dance notation, Laban dance notation system *or* labanotation, Benesh dance notation

system, choreography; **writing,** script, written word, text; **writing system; alphabet,** syllabary; alphabetic symbol, syllabic symbol, letter, ideogram, pictogram, logogram, logograph, hieroglyphic; printing *see* 548; **symbol**

2 **description, portrayal,** portraiture, **depiction,** rendering, rendition, **delineation,** limning, **representation** *see* 349; imagery; **word painting** *or* **picture, picture, portrait, image,** photograph; evocation, impression; **sketch,** vignette, cameo; **characterization,** character, character sketch, profile; vivid description, exact description, realistic *or* naturalistic description, slice of life, *tranche de vie* (*French*), graphic account; specification, particularization, details, itemization, catalogue, cataloguing; **narration**

3 **account, recounting,** statement, report, word; play-by-play description, blow-by-blow account *or* description; case study

4 **impersonation,** personation; **mimicry,** mimicking, mime, miming, pantomime, pantomiming, aping, dumb show; mimesis, **imitation** *see* 336; personification, embodiment, incarnation; **characterization,** portrayal; **acting,** playing, dramatization, enacting, enactment, performing, performance; **posing,** masquerade

5 **image, likeness; resemblance,** semblance, similitude, simulacrum; **effigy,** icon, idol; **copy** *see* 784, fair copy; **picture; portrait,** likeness; **photograph** *see* 714.3, 6; **perfect** *or* **exact likeness, duplicate, double;** match, fellow, mate, companion, twin; living image, very image, very picture, living picture, dead ringer (*informal*), spitting image *or* spit and image (*informal*); miniature, model; **reflection,** reflexion, shadow, mirroring; trace, tracing; rubbing

6 **figure, figurine; doll,** dolly (*informal*); teddy bear; **puppet, marionette,** *fantoche* (*French*), *fantoccino* and *fantoccio* (*both Italian*), hand puppet, glove puppet, finger puppet; **mannequin** *or* manikin, model, dummy, lay figure; wax figure, waxwork; scarecrow, corn dolly, woman *or* man of straw, snowman, snowwoman, gingerbread woman *or* man; **sculpture, bust, statue, statuette,** statuary, monument (*old*); portrait bust *or* statue; death mask, life mask; carving, wood carving; figurehead

7 **representative, representation, type, specimen,** typification, embodiment, type specimen; **cross section;** exponent; **example** *see* 785.2, exemplar; exemplification, typicality, typicalness, representativeness

verbs

8 **to represent, delineate, depict,** render, characterize, hit off, character (*old*), **portray, picture,** picturize, limn, draw, paint *see* 712.20; **register,** convey an impression of; take *or* catch a likeness; **notate,** write, print, map, chart, diagram, schematize; trace, trace out, trace over; rub, take a rubbing; symbolize *see* 517.18

9 **to describe, portray, picture, render, depict, represent, delineate,** limn, **paint,** draw; evoke, bring to life, make one see; outline, sketch; **characterize,** character; **express,** set forth, give words to; **write** *see* 547.21

10 to go for *or* as, pass for *or* as, count for *or* as, answer for *or* as, stand in the place of, be taken as, be regarded as, be the equivalent of; **serve as,** be accepted for

11 to **image, mirror,** hold the mirror up to nature, reflect, figure; **embody,** body forth, incarnate, **personify,** personate, impersonate; **illustrate,** demonstrate, exemplify; project, realize; shadow, shadow forth; **prefigure, pretypify,** foreshadow, adumbrate

12 to **impersonate,** personate; **mimic,** mime, pantomime, take off, send up, do *or* give an impression of, mock; ape, copy; **pose as, masquerade as,** affect the manner *or* guise of, pass for, pretend to be, represent oneself to be; **act,** enact, perform, do; **play, act as,** act *or* play a part, act the part of, act out

adjectives

13 **representational, representative, depictive, delineatory, resemblant; illustrative,** illustrational; pictorial, graphic, vivid; ideographic, pictographic, figurative; **representing, portraying,** limning, illustrating; **typifying, symbolizing,** personifying, incarnating, embodying; imitative, mimetic, simulative, apish, mimish; echoic, onomatopoeic

14 **descriptive, depictive,** expositive, **representative, delineative; expressive, vivid, graphic,** well-drawn; realistic, naturalistic, true to life, lifelike, faithful

15 **typical,** typic, typal; exemplary, sample; **characteristic,** distinctive, distinguishing, quintessential; **realistic, naturalistic; natural, normal,** usual, regular, par for the course (*informal*); **true to type, true to form,** the nature of the beast (*informal*)

adverbs

16 **descriptively,** representatively; **expressively, vividly, graphically;** faithfully, realistically, naturalistically

350 MISREPRESENTATION

nouns

1 **misrepresentation, perversion, distortion,** deformation, garbling, twisting, slanting; inaccuracy; **colouring,** miscolouring, **false colouring; falsification** see 354.9, **spin,** spin control, disinformation; misteaching see 569; injustice, unjust representation; misdrawing, mispainting; misstatement, misreport, misquotation; nonrepresentationalism, nonrealism, abstractionism, expressionism, calculated distortion; overstatement, exaggeration, hyperbole, overdrawing; understatement, litotes

2 bad likeness, **daub,** botch; scribble, scratch, hen tracks *or* scratches (*informal*); distortion, distorted image, anamorphosis, astigmatism; **travesty,** parody, **caricature, burlesque,** gross exaggeration

verbs

3 to **misrepresent, belie,** give a wrong idea, pass *or* pawn *or* foist *or* fob off as, send *or* deliver the wrong signal *or* message; put in a false light, **pervert, distort, garble, twist,** warp, wrench, slant, put a spin on, twist the meaning of; **colour,** miscolour, **give a false colouring,** put a false construction *or* appearance upon, falsify see 354.18; misteach see 569.3; **disguise,** camouflage; misstate, misreport, misquote, put words into one's mouth, quote out of context; overstate, exaggerate, overdraw, blow up, blow out of all proportion; understate; **travesty,** parody, **caricature, burlesque**

4 to **misdraw, mispaint;** daub, botch, butcher, scribble, scratch

351 DISCLOSURE

nouns

1 **disclosure,** disclosing; **revelation,** revealment, revealing, making public, publicizing, broadcasting; apocalypse; discovery, discovering; manifestation see 348; unfolding, unfoldment, **uncovering,** unwrapping, uncloaking, taking the wraps off, taking from under wraps, removing the veil, **unveiling, unmasking; exposure,** exposition, **exposé; baring,** stripping, stripping *or* laying bare; outing (*informal*); **showing up,** showup

2 **divulgence, divulging,** divulgement, divulgation, evulgation (*old*), letting out; **betrayal,** unwitting disclosure, indiscretion; leak, communication leak; **giveaway** *and* dead giveaway (*both informal*); telltale, telltale sign, obvious clue; **blabbing** *and* blabbering (*both informal*), babbling; **tattling**

3 **confession,** confessing, shrift, **acknowledgment, admission,** concession, avowal, self-admission, self-concession, self-avowal, owning, owning up *and* coming clean (*both informal*), unbosoming, unburdening oneself, getting a load off one's mind (*informal*), fessing up (*US informal*), making a clean breast, baring one's soul; rite of confession

verbs

4 to **disclose, reveal, let out, show,** impart, discover, develop (*old*), **leak,** let slip out, let the cat out of the bag *and* spill the beans *and* blow the gaff (*all informal*); manifest see 348.5; unfold, unroll; **open,** open up, lay open, break the seal, bring into the open, get out in the open, bring out of the closet; **expose, show up; bare,** strip *or* lay bare, blow the lid off *and* blow wide open *and* rip open *and* crack wide open (*all informal*); take the lid off, **bring to light,** bring into the open, hold up to view; hold up the mirror to; **unmask,** tear off the mask, **uncover,** unveil, take the lid off (*informal*), ventilate, take out from under wraps, take the wraps off, lift *or* draw the veil, raise the curtain, unscreen, uncloak, undrape, unshroud, unfurl, unsheathe, unwrap, unpack, unkennel; put one wise *and* fill one in *and* clue one in (*all informal*), bring one up to speed *and* put one in the picture (*both informal*), open one's eyes

5 **to divulge,** divulgate, evulgate (*old*); **reveal, make known, tell,** breathe, utter, vent, ventilate, air, give vent to, **give out, let out,** let get around, come out with; break it to, **break the news;** let in on *or* to, **confide,** confide to, unbosom oneself, let into the secret; **publish** *see* 352.10

6 **to betray,** inform, **inform on** *see* 551.12, talk *and* peach (*both informal*); rat *and* stool *and* sing *and* squeal (*all informal*), turn queen's *or* king's evidence; leak (*informal*), spill (*informal*), **spill the beans** (*informal*), blow the gaff (*informal*); **let the cat out of the bag** (*informal*), speak before one thinks, be unguarded *or* indiscreet, kiss and tell, **give away** *and* give the game away (*both informal*), betray a confidence, tell secrets, reveal a secret; have a big mouth (*informal*), **blab** *or* blabber (*informal*); babble, **tattle,** tell *or* tattle on, tell tales, **tell tales out of school;** talk out of turn, let slip; **blurt, blurt out**

7 **to confess,** break down and confess, **admit, acknowledge,** tell all, avow, concede, grant, **own, own up** (*informal*), let on, implicate *or* incriminate oneself, come clean (*informal*); **tell the truth,** tell all, admit everything, let it all hang out (*informal*), throw off all disguise; **plead guilty,** own oneself in the wrong, cop a plea (*informal*); **unbosom oneself, make a clean breast, get it off one's chest** (*informal*), get it out of one's system (*informal*), disburden *or* unburden one's mind *or* conscience *or* heart, **get a load off one's mind** (*informal*), fess up (*US informal*); out with it *and* spit it out *and* open up (*all informal*); throw oneself on the mercy of the court; **reveal oneself,** show one's true colours, come out of the closet (*informal*), show one's hand *or* cards, put *or* lay one's cards on the table

8 **to be revealed, become known, surface, come to light,** appear, manifest itself, come to one's ears, transpire, **leak out, get out, come out,** out, come home to roost, come out in the wash, break forth, show its face; show its colours, be seen in its true colours, stand revealed; blow one's cover (*informal*)

adjectives

9 **revealed, disclosed** *see* 348.10

10 **disclosive, revealing,** revelatory, revelational; **disclosing,** showing, exposing, betraying; kiss-and-tell; eye-opening; **talkative** *see* 343.10, 540.9; admitted, confessed, self-confessed

11 confessional, admissive

352 PUBLICATION

nouns

1 **publication, publishing, promulgation,** evulgation, **propagation, dissemination, diffusion, broadcast, broadcasting, spread, spreading,** spreading abroad, **circulation,** ventilation, airing, noising, bandying, bruiting, bruiting about; **display;** issue, issuance; telecasting, videocasting; printing *see* 548; book, periodical *see* 555

2 **announcement,** annunciation; enunciation; **proclamation,** pronouncement, pronunciamento; **report,** communiqué, **declaration, statement;** public declaration *or* statement, programme, **notice, notification,** public notice; circular, encyclical,

encyclical letter; manifesto, position paper; broadside; rationale; white paper, white book; ukase, edict *see* 420.4; bulletin board, notice board

3 **press release,** release, handout, bulletin, official bulletin, notice

4 **publicity, publicness, notoriety, fame,** famousness, notoriousness, notice, public notice, **celebrity,** *réclame, éclat* (*both French*); **limelight** *and* **spotlight** (*both informal*), daylight, bright light, glare, public eye *or* consciousness, **exposure, currency,** common *or* public knowledge, widest *or* maximum dissemination; **ballyhoo** (*informal*), hoopla (*US informal*); report, public report; cry, hue and cry; **public relations** *or* PR, flackery (*US informal*); media event, press conference, photo call, photo opportunity; press notice, publicity story; **writeup, puff** (*informal*), **plug** (*informal*), **blurb** (*informal*)

5 **promotion, buildup** *and* promo (*both informal*), flack (*US & Canadian informal*), publicization, publicizing, promoting, advocating, advocacy, bruiting, drumbeating, tub-thumping, boosterism; **advertising,** salesmanship *see* 734.2, huckstery (*informal*); advertising campaign; advertising agency; advertising medium *or* media; advocacy, advocacy group

6 **advertisement, ad** (*informal*), **advert** (*informal*), notice; trailer; **commercial,** message, important message, message *or* words from the sponsor; television *or* TV commercial, spot commercial *or* spot, network commercial; advertising feature, reader advertisement, advertorial; display ad; classified ad, want *or* wanted ad (*informal*), small ad; spread, two-page spread, testimonial

7 **poster, bill, placard, sign,** show card, banner, *affiche* (*French*); **hoarding,** signboard, billboard; sandwich board; marquee

8 **advertising matter,** promotional material, press release, public relations handout *or* release, **literature** (*informal*); **leaflet,** leaf, **folder, pamphlet, handbill, bill, flier,** throwaway (*US*), **handout, circular,** broadside, broadsheet

9 **publicist,** publicizer, public relations man *or* woman, public relations officer, PR man *or* woman, public relations specialist, **publicity man** *or* agent, **press agent,** flack *and* pitchman *or* pitchperson (*all US informal*); **advertiser; adman** *and* huckster (*both informal*), pitchman (*US*); ad writer (*informal*), copywriter; **promoter, booster** (*informal*), plugger (*informal*); **barker,** spieler (*informal*), skywriter; billposter; sign-painter; sandwich boy *or* man

verbs

10 **to publish, promulgate, propagate, circulate,** circularize, **diffuse, disseminate,** distribute, **broadcast,** televise, telecast, videocast, air, **spread,** spread around *or* about, spread far and wide, publish abroad, **pass the word around,** bruit, **bruit about, advertise,** repeat, retail, put about, **bandy about, noise about,** cry about *or* abroad, noise *or* sound abroad, bruit abroad, set news afloat, **spread a report; rumour,** start a rumour, voice (*old*), whisper, buzz, **rumour about,** whisper *or* buzz about

11 to make public, go public with (*informal*); bring *or* lay *or* drag before the public, **display,** take one's case to the public, **give** *or* **put out, make known; divulge** *see 351.5;* **ventilate,** air, give air to, bring into the open, get out in the open, open up, broach, give vent to, ventilate

12 to announce, annunciate, enunciate; **declare, state,** declare roundly, affirm, pronounce, give notice; **say,** make a statement, send a message *or* signal; **report,** make an announcement *or* a report, issue a statement, publish *or* issue a manifesto, present a position paper, present a white paper, hold a press conference

13 to proclaim, cry, cry out, **promulgate,** give voice to; **herald,** herald abroad; **blazon,** blaze, blaze *or* blazon about *or* abroad, blare, blare forth *or* abroad, thunder, declaim, shout, trumpet, trumpet forth, announce with flourish of trumpets *or* beat of drum; shout from the rooftops

14 to issue, bring out, put out, get out, launch, emit, put *or* give *or* send forth, offer to the public

15 to publicize, give publicity; go public with (*informal*); bring *or* drag into the limelight, throw the spotlight on (*informal*); **advertise, promote,** build up, cry up, sell, puff (*informal*), **boost** (*informal*), **plug** (*informal*), ballyhoo (*informal*); put on the map, make a household name of, establish; bark *and* spiel (*both informal*); make a pitch for *and* beat the drum for *and* thump the tub for (*all informal*); **write up,** give a write-up; circularize; bulletin; bill; **post bills,** post, post up, placard; skywrite

16 (*be published*) **to come out, appear,** break, hit the streets (*informal*), **issue,** go *or* come forth, find vent, see the light of day, become public; **circulate, spread,** spread about, have currency, **get around** *or* about, get abroad, get afloat, get exposure, go *or* fly *or* buzz *or* blow about, **do** *or* **go the rounds,** pass from mouth to mouth, be on everyone's lips, go through the length and breadth of the land; spread like wildfire

adjectives

17 published, public, made public, **circulated,** in circulation, promulgated, propagated, **disseminated,** issued, spread, diffused, distributed; in print; **broadcast,** telecast, televised; **announced,** proclaimed, declared, **stated,** affirmed; **reported,** brought to notice; common knowledge, common property, current; **open,** accessible, open to the public

18 publicational, promulgatory, propagatory; proclamatory, annunciatory, enunciative; declarative, declaratory; heraldic; promotional, promo (*informal*)

adverbs

19 publicly, in public; **openly** *see 348.15;* in the public eye, in the glare of publicity, in the limelight *or* spotlight (*informal*), reportedly

353 MESSENGER

nouns

1 messenger, message-bearer, **dispatch-bearer,** commissionaire (*British*), nuncio (*old*), **courier,** diplomatic courier, carrier, **runner,** express, dispatch-rider, pony-express rider (*US*), post (*old*), postboy, postrider, *estafette* (*French*); bicycle *or* motorcycle messenger; **go-between** *see 576.4;* **emissary** *see 576.6;* Mercury, Hermes, Iris, Pheidippides, Paul Revere; post office, courier service, package service, parcel service, message service; answering service

2 herald, harbinger, forerunner, vaunt-courier; evangel, evangelist, bearer of glad tidings; herald angel, Gabriel, *buccinator* (*Latin*)

3 announcer, annunciator, enunciator; nunciate (*old*); **proclaimer; crier, town crier,** bellman

4 errand boy, office boy, messenger-boy; bellhop (*informal*), bellboy, bellman, callboy, caller

5 postman, mailman, mail carrier, letter carrier; postmaster, postmistress; postal clerk

6 (*mail carriers*) carrier pigeon, carrier, homing pigeon, homer (*informal*); pigeon post; post-horse, poster; mailvan; postbus; post boat, packet boat *or* ship, mail boat, mail packet, mailer (*old*); mail train, mail coach, post coach; mailplane

354 FALSENESS

nouns

1 falseness, falsehood, falsity, inveracity, untruth, **truthlessness, untrueness; fallaciousness,** fallacy, **erroneousness** *see 974.1*

2 spuriousness, phoneyness (*informal*), bogusness, **ungenuineness, unauthenticity,** unrealness, artificiality, factitiousness, syntheticness

3 sham, fakery, faking, falsity, feigning, pretending; feint, pretext, **pretence,** hollow pretence, **pretension, false pretence** *or* **pretension;** humbug, humbuggery; **bluff,** bluffing, speciousness, meretriciousness; cheating, fraud; imposture; deception, delusion *see 356.1;* acting, playacting; representation, **simulation,** simulacrum; dissembling, **dissemblance, dissimulation;** seeming, semblance, appearance, face, ostentation, **show, false show,** outward show, false air; window dressing, front, **false front, façade,** gloss, varnish; gilt; colour, colouring, false colour; masquerade, facade, disguise; charade; posture, pose, posing, attitudinizing; mannerism, affectation *see 500*

4 falseheartedness, falseness, doubleheartedness, doubleness of heart, doubleness, **duplicity, two-facedness,** double-facedness, **double-dealing,** ambidexterity; double standard; **dishonesty,** improbity, lack of integrity, Machiavellianism, bad faith; low cunning, **cunning,** artifice, wile *see 415.1, 3;* **deceitfulness** *see 356.3;* faithlessness, treachery *see 645.6*

5 insincerity, uncandidness, uncandour, **unfrankness,** disingenuousness; emptiness, hollowness; mockery, hollow mockery; crossed fingers, tongue in cheek, unseriousness; halfheartedness; sophistry, jesuitry, casuistry *see 935.1*

6 hypocrisy, hypocriticalness; Tartuffery, Tartuffism, Pecksniffery, pharisaism, **sanctimony** *see 693,* sanctimoniousness, religiosity, false piety, ostentatious devotion, pietism, Bible-thumping (*informal*);

mealymouthedness, **unctuousness**, oiliness, smarminess *or* smarm (*informal*); **cant**, mummery, snuffling (*old*), **mouthing; lip service;** tokenism; token gesture, empty gesture; smooth tongue, smooth talk, sweet talk *and* soft soap (*both informal*); crocodile tears

7 **quackery, chicanery,** quackishness, quackism, **mountebankery, charlatanry,** charlatanism; **imposture; humbug,** humbuggery

8 **untruthfulness, dishonesty, falsehood, unveracity,** unveraciousness, truthlessness, **mendaciousness, mendacity;** credibility gap; **lying, fibbing,** fibbery, pseudology; pathological lying, mythomania, *pseudologia phantastica* (*Latin*)

9 **deliberate falsehood, misinformation, disinformation, falsification,** disinforming, falsifying; confabulation; **perversion, distortion,** straining, **bending; misrepresentation,** misconstruction, misstatement, colouring, false colouring, miscolouring, slanting, imparting a spin (*informal*); tampering, cooking *and* fiddling (*both informal*); stretching, fictionalization, **exaggeration** *see* 355; prevarication, equivocation *see* 344.4; perjury, false swearing, oath breaking

10 **fabrication, invention, concoction, disinformation;** canard, base canard; **forgery; fiction,** figment, **myth,** fable, romance, extravaganza

11 **lie, falsehood, falsity, untruth,** untruism, mendacity, **prevarication, fib,** porky *or* pork pie (*informal*), taradiddle (*informal*), flimflam *or* flam, *blague* (*French*); **fiction,** legal fiction, pious opinion; **story** (*informal*), **trumped-up story,** farrago; **yarn** (*informal*), **tale,** fairy tale (*informal*), ghost story; farfetched story, tall tale *and* **tall story** (*both informal*), **cock-and-bull story;** exaggeration *see* 355; half-truth, stretching of the truth, slight stretching, white lie, little white lie; factoid; *suggestio falsi* (*Latin*); a pack of lies

12 **monstrous lie, consummate lie, deep-dyed falsehood,** out-and-out lie, **whopper** (*informal*), gross *or* flagrant *or* shameless falsehood, barefaced lie, dirty lie (*informal*); **slander, libel** *see* 512.3; the big lie

13 **fake, put-up job** (*informal*), **phoney** (*informal*), **rip-off** (*informal*), **sham, mock, imitation,** simulacrum, dummy; paste, tinsel, *clinquant* (*French*), pinchbeck, shoddy, junk; **counterfeit, forgery;** put-up job *and* frame-up (*both informal*), put-on (*informal*); **hoax, cheat, fraud, swindle** *see* 356.8; whited sepulchre, whitewash job (*informal*); impostor *see* 357.6

14 **humbug,** humbuggery; **bunk** (*informal*), **bunkum; hooey** (*informal*), hoke *and* **hokum** (*both US informal*), **bosh** (*informal*), **crap** *and* bull *and* **bullshit** (*all informal*), baloney (*informal*), flimflam, flam, flannel (*informal*), smoke and mirrors (*informal*), claptrap, moonshine, eyewash, hogwash, gammon (*informal*), *blague* (*French*), jiggery-pokery (*British*)

verbs

15 to **ring false, not ring true**

16 to **falsify, belie, misrepresent,** miscolour; misstate, misquote, misreport, miscite; overstate, understate; **pervert, distort,** strain, warp, **slant, twist,** impart spin (*informal*); garble; put a false appearance upon, give a false colouring, give a colour to, **colour, gild,**

gloss, gloss over, whitewash, varnish, paper over (*informal*); fudge (*informal*), dress up, titivate, embellish, embroider, trick *or* prink out; deodorize, make smell like roses; **disguise, camouflage, mask**

17 to **tamper with, manipulate, fake, juggle,** sophisticate, **doctor** *and* **cook** (*both informal*), pochle *or* pauchle (*Scottish*), rig, cook *or* juggle the books *or* the accounts (*informal*); pack, stack; **adulterate;** retouch; **load; salt,** plant (*informal*), salt a mine

18 to **fabricate, invent, manufacture, trump up, make up, hatch, concoct, cook up** (*informal*), fudge (*informal*), fake, hoke up (*US informal*); **counterfeit, forge;** fantasize, fantasize about

19 to **lie, tell a lie, falsify,** speak falsely, speak with forked tongue (*informal*), be untruthful, trifle with the truth, deviate from the truth, **fib; stretch the truth,** strain *or* bend the truth, be economical with the truth; **exaggerate** *see* 355.3; lie flatly, lie in one's throat, lie through one's teeth, lie like a trooper, **prevaricate,** equivocate *see* 344.7; **deceive, mislead**

20 to **swear falsely, forswear** oneself (*old*), **perjure oneself, bear false witness**

21 to **sham, fake** (*informal*), **feign, counterfeit, simulate,** put up (*informal*), gammon (*informal*); **pretend, make a pretence, make believe, make a show of,** make like (*informal*), make as if *or* as though; go through the motions (*informal*); let on, let on like (*informal*); **affect, profess, assume,** put on; **dissimulate, dissemble,** cover up; **act, play,** play-act, **put on an act** *or* a charade (*informal*), act *or* play a part; **put up a front** (*informal*), put on a front *or* false front (*informal*); **bluff,** pull *or* put up a bluff (*informal*); **play possum** (*informal*), roll over and play dead

22 to **pose as, masquerade as,** impersonate, pass for, assume the guise *or* identity of, set up for, act the part of, represent oneself to be, claim *or* pretend to be, **make false pretences,** go under false pretences, **sail under false colours**

23 to **be hypocritical,** act *or* play the hypocrite; cant, be holier than thou, reek of piety; shed crocodile tears, snuffle (*old*), snivel, mouth; render *or* give lip service; sweet-talk, soft-soap, blandish *see* 511.5

24 to **play a double game** *or* **role,** have it both ways at once, have one's cake and eat it too, run with the hare and hunt with the hounds; two-time (*informal*)

adjectives

25 **false, untrue, truthless, not true,** void *or* devoid of truth, contrary to fact, in error, **fallacious, erroneous** *see* 974.16; unfounded *see* 935.13; disinformative

26 **spurious, ungenuine, unauthentic,** supposititious, bastard, **pseudo, quasi,** apocryphal, **fake** (*informal*), **phoney** (*informal*), **sham, mock, cod** (*informal*), **counterfeit,** colourable, snide, **bogus,** queer (*informal*), dummy, **make-believe,** so-called, **imitation** *see* 336.8; not what it's cracked up to be (*informal*); **falsified;** dressed up, titivated, embellished, embroidered; garbled; twisted, distorted, warped, perverted, slanted; **simulated, faked, feigned,** coloured, fictitious, fictive, **counterfeited,**

pretended, affected, assumed, put-on; artificial, synthetic, ersatz; unreal; factitious, unnatural, man-made; illegitimate; *soi-disant* (*French*), self-styled; pinchbeck, brummagem, tinsel, shoddy, tin, junky

27 specious, meretricious, gilded, tinsel, seeming, apparent, coloured, colourable, plausible, ostensible

28 quack, quackish; charlatan, charlatanish, charlatanic

29 fabricated, invented, manufactured, concocted, hatched, trumped-up, made-up, put-up, cooked-up (*informal*); forged; fictitious, fictional, figmental, mythical, fabulous, legendary, fairy-tale; fantastic, fantasied, fancied

30 tampered with, manipulated, cooked *and* doctored (*both informal*), juggled, rigged, engineered, pochled *or* pauchled (*Scottish*); packed

31 falsehearted, false, false-principled, false-dealing; double, duplicitious, ambidextrous, double-dealing, doublehearted, double-minded, double-tongued, double-faced, two-faced, Janus-faced; Machiavellian, dishonest; crooked, deceitful; creative, artful, cunning, crafty *see* 415.12; faithless, perfidious, treacherous *see* 645.21

32 insincere, uncandid, unfrank, mealymouthed, unctuous, oily, disingenuous, smarmy (*informal*); dishonest; empty, hollow, tokenist; tongue-in-cheek, unserious; sophistic *or* sophistical, jesuitic *or* jesuitical, casuistic *see* 935.10

33 hypocritic *or* hypocritical, canting, Pecksniffian, pharisaic, pharisaical, pharisean, sanctimonious, goody-goody (*informal*), holier-than-thou, simon-pure

34 untruthful, dishonest, unveracious, unveridical, truthless, lying, mendacious; perjured, forsworn; prevaricating, equivocal *see* 344.11

adverbs

35 falsely, untruly, truthlessly; erroneously *see* 974.20; untruthfully, unveraciously; spuriously, ungenuinely; artificially, synthetically; unnaturally, factitiously; speciously, seemingly, apparently, plausibly, ostensibly; nominally, in name only

36 insincerely, uncandidly; emptily, hollowly; unseriously; hypocritically, mealy-mouthedly, unctuously

355 EXAGGERATION

nouns

1 exaggeration, exaggerating; overstatement, big talk (*informal*), hyperbole, hyperbolism; superlative; extravagance, profuseness, prodigality *see* 486; magnification, enlargement, amplification (*old*), dilation, dilatation, inflation, expansion, blowing up, puffing up, aggrandizement; stretching, heightening, enhancement; overemphasis, overstressing; overestimation *see* 948; exaggerated lengths, extreme, exorbitance, inordinacy, overkill, excess *see* 992; burlesque, travesty, caricature; sensationalism, puffery *and* ballyhoo (*both informal*), touting, huckstering; grandiloquence *see* 545

2 overreaction, much ado about nothing, storm in a teacup, making a mountain out of a molehill

verbs

3 to exaggerate, hyperbolize; overstate, overspeak (*old*), overreach, overdraw, overcharge; overstress; overdo, carry too far, go to extremes; push to the extreme, indulge in overkill, overestimate *see* 948.2; overpraise, oversell, tout, puff (*informal*); stretch, stretch the truth, stretch the point; magnify, inflate, amplify (*old*); aggrandize, build up; pile *or* lay it on *and* pour *or* spread *or* lay it on thick *and* lay it on with a trowel (*all informal*); talk big (*informal*), talk in superlatives, make much of; overreact, make a Federal case out of it (*informal*), something out of nothing, make a mountain out of a molehill, cry over spilt milk; pile *or* put *or* turn on the agony; caricature, travesty, burlesque

adjectives

4 exaggerated, hyperbolical, magnified, amplified (*old*), inflated, aggrandized; stretched, disproportionate, blown up out of all proportion; sensationalist; overpraised, oversold, touted, puffed (*informal*); overemphasized, overemphatic, overstressed; overstated, overdrawn; overdone, overwrought; overestimated *see* 948.3; overlarge, overgreat; extreme, pushed to the extreme, exorbitant, inordinate, excessive *see* 992.16; superlative, extravagant, profuse, prodigal *see* 486.8; high-flown, grandiloquent *see* 545.8

5 exaggerating, exaggerative, hyperbolical

356 DECEPTION

nouns

1 deception, calculated deception, deceptiveness, subterfuge, gimmickry *or* gimmickery, trickiness; falseness *see* 354; fallaciousness, fallacy; self-deception, fond illusion, wishful thinking, wilful misconception; vision, hallucination, phantasm, mirage, will-o'-the-wisp, delusion, delusiveness, illusion *see* 975; deceiving, victimization, dupery; bamboozlement (*informal*), hoodwinking; swindling, defrauding, conning, flimflam *or* flimflammery (*informal*); fooling, befooling, tricking, kidding on (*informal*), kidology (*informal*); spoofing *and* spoofery (*both informal*); bluffing; circumvention, overreaching, outwitting; ensnarement, entrapment, enmeshment, entanglement

2 misleading, misguidance, misdirection; bum steer (*informal*); misinformation *see* 569.1

3 deceit, deceitfulness, guile, falseness, insidiousness, underhandedness; shiftiness, furtiveness, surreptitiousness, indirection; hypocrisy *see* 354.6; falseheartedness, duplicity *see* 354.4; treacherousness *see* 645.6; artfulness, craft, cunning *see* 415; sneakiness *see* 345.4

4 chicanery, chicane, skulduggery (*informal*), trickery, dodgery, pettifogging, pettifoggery, *supercherie* (*French*), artifice, sleight, machination; sharp practice, underhand dealing, foul play; connivery, connivance, collusion, conspiracy, covin (*law*)

5 juggling, jugglery, trickery, *escamotage* (*French*), prestidigitation, conjuration, legerdemain, sleight

of hand, smoke and mirrors (*informal*); mumbo jumbo, **hocus-pocus**, hanky-panky *and* monkey business *and* hokey-pokey (*all informal*), nobbling *and* jiggery-pokery (*both informal*)

6 **trick, artifice, device,** ploy, gambit, stratagem, **scheme,** design, *ficelle* (*French*), **subterfuge,** blind, **ruse, wile,** chouse, shift, **dodge,** artful dodge, sleight, pass, feint, fetch, chicanery, cod (*informal*); **bluff;** gimmick, joker, catch; googly *or* bosey *or* wrong'un (*all informal*), curve, curve-ball; **dirty trick,** dirty deal, fast deal, scurvy trick; sleight of hand, sleight-of-hand trick, hocus-pocus (*old*); juggle, juggler's trick; **bag of tricks,** tricks of the trade

7 **hoax, deception,** spoof (*informal*), **humbug,** flam, **fake** *and* fakement, **rip-off** (*informal*), **sham;** mare's nest

8 **fraud, fraudulence** *or* fraudulency, **dishonesty; imposture; imposition, cheat, cheating,** cozenage, **swindle,** swizzle *or* swiz (*informal*), dodge, fishy transaction, piece of sharp practice; customer-gouging, insider-trading, short weight, chiselling; gyp joint (*US informal*); **racket** (*informal*), illicit business *see* 732; **graft** (*informal*), grift (*US informal*); bunco (*US*); cardsharping; ballot-box stuffing (*US & Canadian*), gerrymandering

9 (*informal terms*) gyp, diddle, diddling, scam, flimflam *or* flam, ramp, scam, snow job (*US & Canadian*), double cross, fiddle, suckering (*US*), sting

10 **confidence game, con game** (*informal*), **skin game** (*informal*), bunco game (*US informal*); **thimblerig,** thimblerigging, shell game (*US*); bucket shop; switch selling, bait-and-switch

11 **cover, disguise, camouflage,** protective coloration; **false colours, false front** *see* 354.3; **incognito;** smoke screen; **masquerade,** masque, mummery; **mask,** visor, vizard, vizard mask (*old*), false face, domino, domino mask

12 **trap, gin; pitfall,** trapfall, deadfall; flytrap, mousetrap, mole trap, rattrap, bear trap; deathtrap, firetrap; Venus's flytrap, Dionaea; spring gun, set gun; baited trap; **booby trap, mine;** decoy *see* 357.5

13 **snare,** springe; noose, lasso, lariat; bola; **net,** trawl, dragnet, seine, purse seine, pound net, gill net; cobweb; **meshes, toils; fishhook, hook,** sniggle; **bait,** ground bait; **lure,** fly, jig, squid, plug, wobbler, spinner; lime, birdlime

verbs

14 **to deceive, beguile, trick, hoax, dupe,** cod, gammon, **gull,** pigeon, play one for a fool *or* sucker, **bamboozle** *and* diddle (*both informal*), nobble (*informal*), **humbug, take in,** do down, put on *and* hocus-pocus (*both informal*), string along, **put something over** *or* **across,** slip one over on (*informal*), pull a fast one on; **play games** (*informal*); **delude,** mock; **betray,** let down, leave in the lurch, leave holding the baby, play one false, **double-cross** (*informal*), cheat on; two-time (*informal*); juggle, conjure; **bluff;** cajole, **circumvent,** get around, forestall; **overreach,** outreach, outwit, outmanoeuvre, outsmart

15 **to fool,** befool, make a fool of, **pull one's leg,** make an arse of; **trick;** spoof *and* kid *and* put one on (*all*

informal); **play a trick on,** play a practical joke upon, send on a fool's errand

16 **to mislead, misguide, misdirect,** lead astray, lead up the garden path, **give a bum steer** (*informal*); throw off the scent, throw off the track *or* trail, put on a false scent; bowl a googly *or* bosey *or* wrong 'un (*informal*), throw one a curve *or* curve ball (*informal*); misinform *see* 569.3

17 **to hoodwink, blindfold, blind,** blind one's eyes, blear the eyes of (*old*), throw dust in one's eyes, **pull the wool over one's eyes**

18 **to cheat, victimize, gull,** pigeon, fudge, **swindle, defraud,** practise fraud upon, **con,** swiz, swizzle, twist, finagle, **fleece,** mulct, fob (*old*), **bilk,** cozen, cog (*old*), chouse, **cheat out of, do out of,** chouse out of, beguile of *or* out of; obtain under false pretences; live by one's wits; bunco (*US*); shortchange, skim off the top; stack the cards *or* deck, deal off the bottom of the deck, play with marked cards; cog the dice, load the dice; thimblerig; crib (*informal*); throw a fight *or* game (*informal*), take a dive (*informal*)

19 (*informal terms*) to gyp, clip, scam, rope in (*US & Canadian*), shave, beat, rook, flam, flimflam, diddle, do the dirty on, hustle, fuck, screw, have, pull a trick *or* stunt, ramp, sting, burn, chisel, hocus, hocus-pocus, play *or* take for a sucker, do, take for a ride

20 **to trap, entrap, gin, catch,** catch out, catch in a trap; **ensnare, snare,** hook, **hook in,** sniggle, noose; inveigle; net, mesh, enmesh, snarl (*old*), ensnarl, wind, tangle, entangle, entoil, enweb; trip, trip up; **set** *or* **lay a trap for,** bait the hook, spread the toils; lime, birdlime; **lure,** allure, **decoy** *see* 377.3

adjectives

21 **deceptive, deceiving, misleading,** beguiling, **false, fallacious,** delusive, delusory; hallucinatory, illusive, illusory; tricky, trickish, tricksy (*old*), catchy; **fishy** (*informal*), questionable, dubious

22 **deceitful, false; fraudulent, sharp, guileful, insidious,** slippery, slippery as an eel, **shifty, tricky,** trickish, cute, finagling, chiselling (*informal*); underhand, **underhanded, furtive, surreptitious,** indirect; collusive, covinous; **falsehearted, two-faced; treacherous** *see* 645.21; sneaky *see* 345.12; **cunning,** artful, gimmicky (*informal*), **wily, crafty** *see* 415.12; calculating, scheming

adverbs

23 **deceptively,** beguilingly, **falsely,** fallaciously, delusively, **trickily, misleadingly,** with intent to deceive; under false colours, under cover of, under the garb of, in disguise

24 **deceitfully, fraudulently, guilefully,** insidiously, **shiftily, trickily; underhandedly,** furtively, surreptitiously, indirectly, like a thief in the night; **treacherously** *see* 645.25

357 DECEIVER

nouns

1 **deceiver, deluder,** duper, misleader, **beguiler, bamboozler** (*informal*); actor, playactor (*informal*),

role-player; **dissembler**, dissimulator; confidence man; **double-dealer**, Machiavelli, Machiavel, Machiavellian; dodger, Artful Dodger (*Charles Dickens*), **counterfeiter, forger, faker**; plagiarizer, plagiarist; entrancer, **enchanter**, charmer, befuddler, hypnotizer, mesmerizer; **seducer**, Don Juan, Casanova; tease, teaser; jilt, jilter; gay deceiver; **fooler, joker**, jokester, **hoaxer**, practical joker; **kidder** *and* ragger *and* leg-puller (*all informal*)

2 **trickster**, tricker; **juggler**, sleight-of-hand performer, magician, illusionist, conjurer, **prestidigitator**, *escamoteur* (*French*)

3 **cheat, cheater**; two-timer (*informal*); **swindler, defrauder**, fraudster, cozener, juggler; **sharper, sharp**, spieler, pitchman (*US & Canadian*); **confidence man, confidence trickster, horse trader**, horse coper; **cardsharp**, cardsharper; thimblerigger; shortchanger; pettifogger *and* shyster (*both informal*); landshark, mortgage shark; carpetbagger; crimp

4 (*informal terms*) **gyp**, gypper, gyp artist, flimflammer, flimflam man, blackleg, chiseller, bilk, bilker, fleecer, diddler, twister, crook, shark, spiv, file, slicker, con man, con artist, bunco steerer (*US*), scammer, clip artist, smoothie, hustler

5 **shill**, decoy, plant, capper, stool pigeon (*US*); *agent provocateur* (*French*)

6 **impostor, ringer**; **impersonator; pretender**; sham, shammer, **humbug**, *blagueur* (*French*), **fraud** (*informal*), **fake** *and* **faker** *and* **phoney** (*all informal*), fourflusher (*informal*), bluff, bluffer; **charlatan, quack**, quacksalver, quackster, **mountebank**, saltimbanco; **wolf in sheep's clothing**; poser, poseur; malingerer

7 **masquerader**, masker; **impersonator**, personator; mummer, guiser (*Scottish*), guisard; incognito, incognita

8 **hypocrite, phoney** (*informal*), sanctimonious fraud, pharisee, whited sepulchre, **canter**, snuffler, mealy-mouth,

"a saint abroad and a devil at home"—BUNYAN; Tartuffe (*Molière*), Pecksniff *and* Uriah Heep (*both Charles Dickens*), Joseph Surface (*Richard B Sheridan*), Holy Willie (*Robert Burns*); false friend, fair-weather friend

9 **liar, fibber**, fibster, fabricator, fabulist, pseudologist; falsifier; **prevaricator**, equivocator, mudger (*informal*), waffler (*informal*), palterer; **storyteller**; yarner *and* yarn spinner *and* spinner of yarns (*all informal*); Ananias; Satan, Father of Lies; Baron Münchausen; Sir John Mandeville; consummate liar,

"liar of the first magnitude"—CONGREVE; *menteur à triple étage* (*French*), dirty liar; pathological liar, mythomaniac, pseudologue, confirmed *or* habitual liar; **perjurer**, false witness

10 **traitor**, treasonist, **betrayer, quisling, rat** (*informal*), serpent, snake, cockatrice, **snake in the grass, double-crosser** (*informal*), double-dealer; double agent; trimmer; timeserver; turncoat *see* 363.5; informer *see* 551.6; archtraitor; Judas, Judas Iscariot, Benedict Arnold, Quisling, Brutus; **schemer, plotter**, intriguer, *intrigant* (*French*), conspirer, **conspirator**, conniver, machinator

11 **subversive**; **saboteur, fifth columnist**, crypto; security risk; **collaborationist**, collaborator, fraternizer; fifth column, underground; Trojan horse

358 DUPE

nouns

1 **dupe, gull**, gudgeon, *gobe-mouches* (*French*); **victim**; gullible *or* dupable *or* credulous person, trusting *or* simple soul, innocent, *naif* (*French*), babe, babe in the woods; greenhorn; toy, plaything; monkey; **fool** *see* 923; stooge, **cat's-paw**

2 (*informal terms*) **sucker**, pigeon, fall guy, doormat, mug, muggins, jay (*US*), easy mark, sitting duck, Joe Soap, juggin, pushover, cinch, mark, easy meat, easy pickings, charlie, chump, boob, schlemiel, sap, saphead, prize sap, wet, easy touch, soft touch, patsy (*US*)

359 RESOLUTION

nouns

1 **resolution**, resolve, resolvedness, **determination, decision**, fixed *or* firm resolve, **will**, purpose; **resoluteness, determinedness**, determinateness, decisiveness, decidedness, **purposefulness**; definiteness; **earnestness, seriousness**, sincerity, devotion, dedication, commitment, total commitment; "the dauntless spirit of resolution", "the native hue of resolution"—BOTH SHAKESPEARE; single-mindedness, relentlessness, persistence, tenacity, perseverance *see* 360; self-will, obstinacy *see* 361

2 **firmness**, firmness of mind *or* spirit, **staunchness**, settledness, steadiness, constancy, steadfastness, fixedness, unshakableness; **stability** *see* 854; concentration; flintiness, steeliness; inflexibility, rigidity, unyieldingness *see* 361.2; trueness, loyalty *see* 644.7

3 **pluck, spunk** (*informal*), **mettle, backbone** (*informal*), balls (*informal*), bottle (*informal*), **grit**, true grit, spirit, **stamina, guts** (*informal*), moxie (*US & Canadian informal*), pith (*old*), bottom, **toughness** (*informal*); pluckiness, spunkiness (*informal*), **gameness**, feistiness (*informal*), mettlesomeness; courage *see* 492

4 **will power, will**, power, **strong-mindedness**, strength of mind, strength *or* fixity of purpose, strength, fortitude, **moral fibre; iron will**, will of iron *or* steel; a will *or* mind of one's own, law unto oneself; the courage of one's convictions, moral courage

5 **self-control, self-command, self-possession**, self-mastery, self-government, self-domination, **self-restraint**, self-conquest, self-discipline, **self-denial**; control, restraint, constraint, discipline; composure, possession, aplomb; **independence** *see* 430.5

6 **self-assertion**, self-assertiveness, forwardness, **nerve** *and* pushiness (*both informal*), importunateness, importunacy; self-expression, self-expressiveness

verbs

7 **to resolve, determine, decide, will, purpose, make up one's mind**, make *or* take a resolution,

make a point of; **settle**, settle on, fix, seal; **conclude**, come to a determination *or* conclusion *or* decision, determine once for all

8 **to be determined**, be resolved; **have a mind** *or* **will of one's own**, know one's own mind; **be in earnest, mean business** (*informal*), mean what one says; be out for blood (*informal*), **set one's mind** *or* **heart upon**; put one's heart into, devote *or* commit *or* dedicate oneself to, give oneself up to; buckle oneself, buckle down, buckle to; steel oneself, brace oneself, grit one's teeth, set one's teeth *or* jaw; put *or* lay *or* set one's shoulder to the wheel; take the bull by the horns, take the plunge, cross the Rubicon; nail one's colours to the mast, burn one's bridges *or* boats, go for broke (*informal*), kick down the ladder, throw away the scabbard; never say die, die hard, die fighting, die with one's boots on

9 **to remain firm, stand fast** *or* **firm, hold out,** hold fast, get tough (*informal*), **take one's stand**, set one's back against the wall, **stand** *or* **hold one's ground,** keep one's footing, hold one's own, hang in *and* hang in there *and* hang tough (*all informal*), dig in, dig one's heels in; **stick to one's guns**, stick, stick with it, stick fast, stick to one's colours, adhere to one's principles; not listen to the voice of the siren; take what comes; **put one's foot down** (*informal*), stand no nonsense

10 **to not hesitate**, think nothing of, think little of, **make no bones about** (*informal*), have *or* make no scruple of (*old*), **stick at nothing**, stop at nothing; not look back; go the whole hog (*informal*), carry through, face out

adjectives

11 **resolute, resolved, determined,** bound *and* bound and determined (*both informal*), **decided,** decisive, **purposeful;** definite; **earnest, serious,** sincere; devoted, dedicated, committed, wholehearted; single-minded, relentless, persistent, tenacious, persevering; **obstinate see** 361.8

12 **firm, staunch,** fixed, settled, steady, steadfast, constant, set (*informal*), flinty, steely; unshaken, not to be shaken, unflappable (*informal*); undeflectable, **unswerving,** not to be deflected; immovable, unbending, inflexible, **unyielding see** 361.9; true, loyal *see* 644.20

13 **unhesitating,** unhesitant, **unfaltering,** unflinching, unshrinking; stick-at-nothing (*informal*)

14 **plucky, spunky** *and* feisty *and* gutty *or* gutsy (*all informal*), gritty, **mettlesome,** dauntless, **game,** game to the last *or* end; **courageous see** 492.17

15 **strong-willed, strong-minded,** firm-minded; **self-controlled,** controlled, self-disciplined, self-restrained; **self-possessed; self-assertive,** self-asserting, forward, pushy (*informal*), importunate; self-expressive; **independent**

16 **determined upon,** resolved upon, decided upon, intent upon, fixed upon, settled upon, **set on,** dead set on (*informal*), **bent on,** hell-bent on (*informal*)

adverbs

17 **resolutely, determinedly, decidedly,** decisively, resolvedly, **purposefully, with a will;** firmly, steadfastly, steadily, fixedly, with constancy, staunchly; **seriously,** in all seriousness, **earnestly,** in earnest, in good earnest, sincerely; devotedly, with total dedication, committedly; hammer and tongs, tooth and nail, *bec et ongles* (*French*); heart and soul, with all one's heart *or* might, wholeheartedly; **unswervingly;** singlemindedly, relentlessly, persistently, tenaciously, like a bulldog, like a leech, perseveringly; **obstinately, unyieldingly, inflexibly** *see* 361.15

18 **pluckily, spunkily** *and* feistily *and* gutsily (*all informal*), mettlesomely, **gamely,** dauntlessly, manfully, like a man; on one's mettle; **courageously, heroically** *see* 492.23

19 **unhesitatingly,** unhesitantly, **unfalteringly,** unflinchingly, unshrinkingly

phrases

20 **come what may,** *venga lo que venga* (*Spanish*), *vogue la galère* (*French*), *coûte que coûte* (*French*), whatever the cost, at any price *or* cost *or* sacrifice, at all risks *or* hazards, *ruat caelum* (*Latin*), at all events, live or die, survive or perish, sink or swim, rain or shine, come hell or high water; in some way or other

360 PERSEVERANCE

nouns

1 **perseverance, persistence** *or* persistency, insistence *or* insistency, singleness of purpose; **resolution** *see* 359; **steadfastness, steadiness,** stability *see* 854; **constancy, permanence** *see* 852.1; loyalty, fidelity *see* 644.7; **single-mindedness,** concentration, undivided *or* unswerving attention, engrossment, preoccupation *see* 982.3; **endurance,** staying power, bitterendism, **pertinacity,** pertinaciousness, **tenacity,** tenaciousness, **doggedness,** unremittingness, relentlessness, dogged perseverance, bulldog tenacity, unfailing *or* leechlike grip; plodding, plugging, slogging; **obstinacy, stubbornness** *see* 361.1; **diligence,** application, sedulousness, sedulity, industry, industriousness, assiduousness, assiduity; **tirelessness, indefatigability, stamina; patience,** patience of Job *see* 134.1

verbs

2 **to persevere, persist, carry on,** go on, **keep on,** keep up, keep at, **keep at it,** keep going, keep driving, keep trying, try and try again, **keep the ball rolling,** keep the pot boiling, keep up the good work; not take 'no' for an answer; not accept compromise *or* defeat; **endure,** last, **continue** *see* 826.6

3 to keep doggedly at, **plod,** drudge, slog *or* slog away, soldier on, put one foot in front of the other, peg away *or* at *or* on; **plug,** plug at, plug away *or* along; pound *or* hammer away; **keep one's nose to the grindstone**

4 **to stay with it,** hold on, hold fast, **hang on,** hang on like a bulldog *or* leech, **stick to one's guns;** not give up, **never say die;** come up fighting, come up for more; **stay it out, stick out, hold out;** hold up, last out, **bear up,** stand up; **live with it,** live

through it; stay the distance *or* the course; sit tight, be unmoved *or* unmoveable;

"wear this world out to the ending doom", "bears it out even to the edge of doom"—BOTH SHAKESPEARE; brazen it out

5 to prosecute to a conclusion, **go through with it, carry through, follow through, see it through,** see it out, follow out *or* up; go through with it, go to the bitter end, go the distance, go all the way, go to any length, go the whole length; **leave no stone unturned,** leave no avenue unexplored, overlook nothing, exhaust every move; move heaven and earth, go through fire and water

6 to **die trying,** die in the last ditch, die in harness, **die with one's boots on** *or* die in one's boots, die at one's post, die in the attempt, die game, die hard, go down with flying colours, **go out in a blaze of glory**

7 (*informal terms*) **to stick,** stick to it, stick with it, stick it, stick it out, hang on for dear life, hang on in there, hang tough, tough it out, keep on trucking, keep on keeping on; **go the limit,** go the whole hog, go all out, go for broke, go through hell and high water

adjectives

8 **persevering,** perseverant, **persistent,** persisting, insistent; **enduring,** permanent, **constant, lasting;** continuing *see* 852.7; **stable, steady, steadfast** *see* 854.12; immutable, inalterable; **resolute** *see* 359.11; **diligent, assiduous, sedulous,** industrious; dogged, plodding, slogging, plugging; **pertinacious, tenacious;** loyal, faithful *see* 644.20; **unswerving,** unremitting, unabating, unintermitting, uninterrupted; single-minded, utterly attentive; rapt, preoccupied *see* 982.17; **unfaltering, unwavering,** unflinching; relentless, **unrelenting; obstinate, stubborn** *see* 361.8; **unrelaxing,** unfailing, **untiring,** unwearying, unflagging, never-tiring, **tireless,** weariless, **indefatigable,** unwearied, unsleeping, undrooping, unnodding, unwinking, sleepless; undiscouraged, undaunted, indomitable, unconquerable, invincible, game to the last *or* to the end; **patient,** patient as Job *see* 134.9

adverbs

9 **perseveringly, persistently,** persistingly, insistently; resolutely *see* 359.17; loyally, faithfully, devotedly *see* 644.25; **diligently,** industriously, assiduously, sedulously; **doggedly,** sloggingly, ploddingly; pertinaciously, tenaciously; unremittingly, unabatingly, unintermittingly, uninterruptedly; unswervingly, unwaveringly, unfalteringly, unflinchingly; relentlessly, unrelentingly; **indefatigably, tirelessly,** wearilessly, untiringly, unwearyingly, unflaggingly, unrestingly, unsleepingly; **patiently**

10 **through thick and thin,** through fire and water, come hell or high water, rain or shine, fair or foul, in sickness and in health; **come what may** *see* 359.20, **all the way,** down to the wire, to the bitter end

361 OBSTINACY

nouns

1 **obstinacy,** obstinateness, pertinacity, restiveness, **stubbornness, wilfulness,** self-will, hardheadedness, **headstrongness,** strongheadedness; mind *or* will of one's own, set *or* fixed mind, inflexible will; **perseverance** *see* 360, **doggedness, determination,** tenaciousness, tenacity,

"tough tenacity of purpose"—J A SYMONDS; **bullheadedness, pigheadedness, mulishness; obduracy,** unregenerateness; stiff neck, stiff-neckedness; sullenness, sulkiness; balkiness; uncooperativeness; dogmatism, opinionatedness *see* 969.6; overzealousness, fanaticism *see* 925.11; intolerance, bigotry *see* 979.1

2 **unyieldingness,** unbendingness, stiff temper, **inflexibility,** inelasticity, impliability, ungivingness, **obduracy,** toughness, **firmness,** stiffness, adamantness, rigorism, **rigidity,** strait-lacedness *or* straight-lacedness, stuffiness; **hard line,** hard-bitterness, hard-nosedness (*informal*); unalterability, unchangeability, immutability, immovability; irreconcilability, uncompromisingness, **intransigence** *or* intransigency, *intransigeance* (*French*), intransigentism; **implacability,** inexorability, **relentlessness,** unrelentingness; sternness, grimness, dourness, flintiness, **steeliness**

3 **perversity,** perverseness, **contrariness, wrongheadedness, waywardness,** forwardness, difficultness, crossgrainedness, cantankerousness, feistiness *and* orneriness *and* cussedness (*all informal*); sullenness, sulkiness, dourness, stuffiness; irascibility *see* 110.2

4 **ungovernability, unmanageability,** uncontrollability; indomitability, untamableness, **intractability,** refractoriness, shrewishness; incorrigibility; **unsubmissiveness,** unbiddability (*British*), **indocility;** irrepressibility, insuppressibility; unmalleability, unmouldableness; recidivism; **recalcitrance** *or* recalcitrancy, contumacy, contumaciousness; **unruliness,** obstreperousness, restiveness, fractiousness, wildness; defiance *see* 454; resistance *see* 453

5 **unpersuadableness,** deafness, blindness; closed-mindedness; positiveness, dogmatism *see* 969.6

6 (*obstinate person*) **mule** *and* donkey (*both informal*), ass, perverse fool; bullhead, pighead; hardhead (*US & Canadian*), hammerhead (*informal*), hard-liner; standpat *and* **standpatter, stickler; intransigent,** maverick; dogmatist, positivist, bigot, fanatic, purist; **die-hard**

verbs

7 **to balk, stickle;** hold one's ground, not budge, **stand pat** (*informal*), **not yield an inch,** stick to one's guns; hold out, stand out; stick out for; take no denial, not take 'no' for an answer; take the bit in one's teeth; die hard; cut off one's nose to spite one's face; **persevere** *see* 360.2, 7

adjectives

8 **obstinate, stubborn, pertinacious, restive; wilful, self-willed,** strong-willed, hardheaded (*US &*

Canadian), **headstrong**, strongheaded, *entêté* (*French*); **dogged**, bulldogged, **tenacious, perserving; bullheaded, pigheaded, mulish** (*informal*), stubborn as a mule; **set, set in one's ways**, case-hardened, stiff-necked; sullen, sulky; balky, balking; unregenerate, uncooperative; bigoted, intolerant *see* 979.11, overzealous, fanatic, fanatical *see* 925.32; dogmatic, opinionated *see* 969.22

9 **unyielding, unbending, inflexible, hard, hardline**, inelastic, impliable, ungiving, **firm, stiff, rigid**, rigorous, stuffy; rock-hard, rock-like; **adamant**, adamantine; unmoved, unaffected; **immovable**, not to be moved; **unalterable**, unchangeable, immutable; **uncompromising**, intransigent, irreconcilable, hard-core (*informal*); implacable, inexorable, **relentless**, unrelenting; stern, grim, dour; iron, cast-iron, flinty, steely

10 **obdurate**, tough, **hard**, hard-set, hard-mouthed, hard-bitten, hard-nosed *and* hard-boiled (*both informal*)

11 **perverse, contrary, wrongheaded, wayward, froward, difficult**, bloody-minded, cross-grained, cantankerous, feisty, ornery (*informal*); sullen, sulky, stuffy, stroppy; irascible *see* 110.19

12 **ungovernable, unmanageable, uncontrollable, indomitable, untamable, intractable, refractory**; shrewish; **incorrigible, unreconstructed; unsubmissive**, unbiddable, **indocile**; irrepressible, insuppressible; unmalleable, unmouldable; recidivist, recidivistic; **recalcitrant**, contumacious; obstreperous, **unruly, restive**, wild, fractious, bolshie (*informal*); beyond control, out of hand; **resistant, resisting** *see* 453.5; **defiant** *see* 454.7

13 **unpersuadable**, deaf, blind; closed-minded; positive; dogmatic *see* 969.22

adverbs

14 **obstinately, stubbornly**, pertinaciously; wilfully, headstrongly; **doggedly**, tenaciously; **bullheadedly**, pigheadedly, mulishly; unregenerately; uncooperatively; with set jaw, with sullen mouth, with a stiff neck

15 **unyieldingly, unbendingly, inflexibly, adamantly**, obdurately, **firmly**, stiffly, rigidly, rigorously; unalterably, unchangeably, immutably, immovably, unregenerately; uncompromisingly, intransigently, irreconcilably; implacably, inexorably, relentlessly, unrelentingly; sternly, grimly, dourly

16 **perversely, contrarily**, contrariwise, waywardly, wrongheadedly, frowardly, crossgrainedly, cantankerously, feistily, sullenly, sulkily

17 **ungovernably, unmanageably, uncontrollably**, indomitably, untamably, intractably; shrewishly; incorrigibly; unsubmissively; irrepressibly, insuppressibly; contumaciously; unrulily, obstreperously, restively, fractiously

362 IRRESOLUTION

nouns

1 **irresolution, indecision**, unsettlement, unsettledness, irresoluteness, undeterminedness, **indecisiveness**, undecidedness, infirmity of purpose; mugwumpery, mugwumpism, fence-sitting, fence-

straddling; double-mindedness, **ambivalence**, ambitendency; dubiety, dubiousness, **uncertainty** *see* 970; **instability, inconstancy**, changeableness *see* 853; capriciousness, mercuriality, fickleness *see* 364.3; change of mind, second thoughts, tergiversation *see* 363.1

2 **vacillation, fluctuation**, oscillation, pendulation, mood swing, **wavering**, wobbling, dithering, shilly-shally, **shilly-shallying**, blowing hot and cold; equivocation *see* 344.4

3 **hesitation**, hesitance, **hesitancy**, hesitating, holding back, dragging one's feet; falter, faltering, shilly-shally, shilly-shallying; diffidence, tentativeness, caution, cautiousness

4 **weak will, weak-mindedness**; feeblemindedness (*old*), **weakness**, feebleness, faintness, faintheartedness, **frailty, infirmity; wimpiness** *or* wimpishness (*informal*), spinelessness, invertebracy; abulia; fear *see* 127; cowardice *see* 491; **pliability** *see* 1045.2

5 **vacillator, shillyshallyer**, shilly-shally, **waverer**, wobbler; mugwump, fence-sitter, fence-straddler; **wimp** (*informal*), wuss (*informal*), weakling, jellyfish, Milquetoast; quitter

verbs

6 **to not know one's own mind**, not know where one stands, **be of two minds**, have two minds, have mixed feelings, be in conflict, be conflicted (*informal*); stagger, stumble, boggle

7 **to hesitate, pause, falter, hang back**, hover; shilly-shally, hum and haw, **hem and haw**; wait to see how the cat jumps *or* the wind blows, scruple, jib, demur, stick at, stickle, strain at; think twice about, stop to consider, ponder, wrinkle one's brow; debate, deliberate, see both sides of the question, balance, weigh one thing against another, consider both sides of the question; be divided, come down squarely in the middle, sit on *or* straddle the fence, fall between two stools; yield, back down *see* 433.7; retreat, withdraw *see* 163.6, wimp *or* chicken *or* cop out (*all informal*); pull back, drag one's feet; **flinch, shy away from, shy** *see* 902.7, back off (*informal*); fear; not face up to, bury one's head in the sand

8 **to vacillate, waver, waffle** (*informal*), **fluctuate**, pendulate, oscillate, wobble, wobble about, teeter, totter (*old*), dither, swither (*Scottish*), haver, swing from one thing to another, **shilly-shally**, back and fill, keep off and on, will and will not, keep *or* leave hanging in midair; blow hot and cold *see* 364.4; **equivocate** *see* 344.7, fudge and mudge (*informal*), faff about (*informal*); change one's mind, tergiversate; vary, **alternate** *see* 853.5; shift, change horses in midstream, **change** *see* 851.5

adjectives

9 **irresolute**, irresolved, **unresolved; undecided, indecisive, undetermined**, unsettled, infirm of purpose; dubious, uncertain *see* 970.15; at loose ends, at a loose end; **of two minds**, in conflict, double-minded, **ambivalent**, ambitendent; changeable, mutable *see* 853.6; capricious, mercurial, fickle *see* 364.6; mugwumpian, mugwumpish, fence-sitting, fence-straddling

10 **vacillating**, vacillatory, waffling (*informal*), oscillatory, wobbly, **wavering, fluctuating,** pendulating, oscillating, **shilly-shallying,** shilly-shally,

"at war 'twixt will and will not"—SHAKESPEARE

11 **hesitant**, hesitating, pikerish; faltering; shilly-shallying; diffident, tentative, timid, cautious; scrupling, jibbing, demurring (*old*), sticking, straining, stickling

12 **weak-willed, weak-minded,** feebleminded (*old*), weak-kneed, **weak,** wimpy *or* wimpish (*informal*), feeble, fainthearted, **frail, faint, infirm; spineless,** invertebrate; without a will of one's own, unable to say 'no'; abulic; afraid, **chicken** *and* chicken-hearted *and* chicken-livered (*all informal*), cowardly *see* 491.10; like putty, **pliable** *see* 1045.9

adverbs

13 **irresolutely,** irresolvedly, **undecidedly, indecisively, undeterminedly; uncertainly;** hesitantly, hesitatingly, falteringly; waveringly, vacillatingly, shilly-shally, shilly-shallyingly

363 CHANGING OF MIND

nouns

1 **reverse, reversal,** flip *and* flip-flop *and* U-turn (*all informal*), turnabout, turnaround, **about-face,** about-turn, *volte-face* (*French*), right-about-face, right-about turn, right-about, a turn to the right-about; tergiversation, tergiversating; **change of mind;** second thoughts, better thoughts, afterthoughts, mature judgment

2 **apostasy,** recreancy; **treason,** misprision of treason, betrayal, turning traitor, turning one's coat, ratting (*informal*), going over, joining *or* going over to the opposition, siding with the enemy; **defection;** bolt, bolting, secession, breakaway; **desertion** *see* 370.2; **recidivism,** recidivation, relapse, backsliding *see* 394.2; faithlessness, **disloyalty** *see* 645.5

3 **recantation, withdrawal, disavowal, denial,** reneging, **unsaying, repudiation,** palinode, palinody, **retraction,** retractation; **disclaimer,** disclamation, **disownment,** disowning, abjurement, abjuration, **renunciation,** renouncement, forswearing; expatriation, self-exile

4 **timeserver,** timepleaser (*old*), temporizer, opportunist, trimmer, weathercock; mugwump; chameleon, Vicar of Bray

5 **apostate, turncoat,** turnabout, **recreant, renegade,** renegado, renegate *or* runagate (*old*), **defector,** tergiversator, tergiversant; **deserter,** turntail, quisling, fifth columnist, collaborationist, collaborator, **traitor** *see* 357.10; strikebreaker; **bolter, seceder,** secessionist, **separatist,** schismatic; **backslider,** recidivist; reversionist; convert, proselyte

verbs

6 **to change one's mind** *or* **song** *or* **tune** *or* **note,** sing a different tune, dance to another tune; come round, wheel, do an about-face, reverse oneself, do a flip-flop *or* U-turn (*informal*); swing from one thing to another; think better of it, have second thoughts, be of another mind; bite one's tongue

7 **to apostatize** *or* apostacize, go over, change sides, switch, switch over, change one's allegiance, **defect; turn one's coat,** turn cloak; desert *or* leave a sinking ship; secede, break away, bolt, fall off *or* away; desert

8 **to recant, retract, repudiate, withdraw, take back,** unswear, renege, welsh (*informal*), **abjure, disavow, disown; deny,** disclaim, unsay, unspeak; **renounce, forswear, eat one's words,** eat one's hat, swallow, eat crow, eat humble pie; **back down** *or* **out,** climb down, weasel

9 **to be a timeserver,** trim, temporize, change with the times; sit on *or* straddle the fence

adjectives

10 **timeserving, trimming, temporizing;** supple, neither fish, flesh, nor fowl

11 **apostate, recreant,** renegade, tergiversating, tergiversant; **treasonous, treasonable, traitorous,** forsworn; collaborating; faithless, **disloyal** *see* 645.20

12 **repudiative,** repudiatory; abjuratory, renunciative, renunciatory; schismatic; **separatist,** secessionist, breakaway (*informal*); **opportunistic,** mugwumpian, mugwumpish, fence-straddling, fence-sitting

364 CAPRICE

nouns

1 **caprice, whim,** *capriccio* (*Italian*), *boutade* (*French*), humour, **whimsy,** freak, whim-wham; **fancy,** fantasy, **conceit, notion,** flimflam, toy, freakish inspiration, crazy idea, fantastic notion, foolish notion, harebrained idea, brainstorm, **vagary,** megrim; **fad, craze, passing fancy; quirk, crotchet,** crank, kink; maggot, bee in one's bonnet (*informal*)

2 **capriciousness,** caprice, **whimsicalness,** whimsy, whimsicality; humoursomeness, **fancifulness,** fantasticality, **freakishness;** crankiness, crotchetiness, quirkiness, **moodiness,** temperamentalness, prima-donnaism; petulance *see* 110.6; **arbitrariness,** motivelessness

3 **fickleness, flightiness,** skittishness, inconstancy, **lightness, levity,** *légèreté* (*French*); volatility, mercurialness, mercuriality; **mood swing;** faddishness, faddism; **changeableness** *see* 853; unpredictability *see* 970.1; unreliability, undependability *see* 645.4; coquettishness; frivolousness *see* 921.7

verbs

4 **to blow hot and cold,** keep off and on, have as many phases as the moon, chop and change, **fluctuate** *see* 853.5, vacillate *see* 362.8; act on impulse

adjectives

5 **capricious, whimsical,** freakish, humoursome, vagarious; **fanciful, notional,** fantasied (*old*), fantastic *or* fantastical, maggoty, **crotchety,** kinky, harebrained, cranky, quirky; wanton, wayward, vagrant; **arbitrary, unreasonable,** motiveless; **moody, temperamental,** prima-donnaish; petulant *see* 110.22; unrestrained

6 fickle, flighty, skittish, **light**; coquettish, flirtatious, toying; versatile, **inconstant, changeable** *see* 853.7; vacillating *see* 362.10; volatile, mercurial, quicksilver; faddish; **scatterbrained** *see* 984.16, unpredictable; **impulsive**; unreliable, undependable *see* 645.19

adverbs

7 capriciously, whimsically, fancifully, at one's own sweet will (*informal*); **flightily, lightly**; arbitrarily, unreasonably, without rhyme or reason

365 IMPULSE

nouns

1 **impulse**; natural impulse, blind impulse, **instinct**, urge, drive; vagrant *or* fleeting impulse; involuntary impulse, reflex, knee jerk, automatic response; gut response *or* reaction (*informal*); **notion, fancy**; **sudden thought**, flash, inspiration, brainstorm, brain wave

2 **impulsiveness, impetuousness**, impulsivity, impetuosity; **hastiness**, overhastiness, haste, quickness, suddenness; **precipitateness**, precipitance, precipitancy, precipitation; hair-trigger; **recklessness, rashness** *see* 493; impatience *see* 135

3 **thoughtlessness**, unthoughtfulness, **heedlessness** *see* 983.1, **carelessness**, inconsideration, inconsiderateness; **negligence** *see* 102.2, caprice *see* 364

4 **unpremeditation**, indeliberation, **undeliberateness**, uncalculatedness, undesignedness, **spontaneity**, **spontaneousness**, unstudiedness; involuntariness *see* 962.5; snap judgment *or* decision; snap shot, offhand shot

5 **improvisation**, extemporization, improvision, improvising, extempore (*old*), **impromptu, ad-lib**, ad-libbing *and* playing by ear (*both informal*), **ad hoc measure** *or* solution, adhocracy (*informal*), ad hockery *or* hocery *or* hocism (*informal*); extemporaneousness, extemporariness; temporary measure *or* arrangement, *pro tempore* measure *or* arrangement, **stopgap, makeshift**, jury-rig (*nautical*); cannibalization; bricolage

6 **improviser**, improvisator, *improvvisatore* and *improvvisatrice* (*both Italian*), **extemporizer**, ad-libber (*informal*); cannibalizer; bricoleur

verbs

7 **to act on the spur of the moment**, obey one's impulse, let oneself go; shoot from the hip (*informal*), be too quick on the trigger *or* the uptake *or* the draw; **blurt out**, come out with, let slip out, say what comes uppermost, say the first thing that comes into one's head *or* to one's mind; be unable to help oneself

8 **to improvise, extemporize**, improvisate, improv *and* talk off the top of one's head (*both informal*), speak off the cuff, tapdance (*US informal*), think on one's feet, make it up as one goes along, play it by ear (*informal*), throw away *or* depart from the prepared text, throw away the speech, scrap the plan, **ad-lib** (*informal*), **do offhand**, wing it (*informal*), vamp, fake (*informal*), play by ear (*informal*); **dash off, strike off**, knock off, throw off, toss off *or* out; make up, whip up, **cook up**, run up, rustle up (*informal*), slap up *or* together *and* throw *or* slap together (*all informal*), lash up, cobble up; jury-rig; cannibalize

adjectives

9 **impulsive, impetuous, hasty**, overhasty, quick, sudden; quick on the draw *or* trigger *or* uptake, hair-trigger; **precipitate**, headlong; **reckless, rash** *see* 493.7; impatient *see* 135.6

10 **unthinking, unreasoning, unreflecting**, uncalculating, unthoughtful, **thoughtless, inadvertent**, reasonless, **heedless, careless**, inconsiderate; unguarded; arbitrary, capricious *see* 364.5

11 **unpremeditated**, unmeditated, **uncalculated**, undeliberated, **spontaneous, undesigned, unstudied**; unintentional, unintended, inadvertent, unwilled, **indeliberate**, undeliberate; **involuntary**, reflex, reflexive, knee-jerk (*informal*), automatic, goose-step, lockstep; gut (*informal*), unconscious; **unconsidered**, unadvised, snap, casual, offhand, throwaway (*informal*); **ill-considered**, ill-advised, ill-devised; act-first-and-think-later

12 **extemporaneous, extemporary**, extempore, **impromptu**, unrehearsed, **improvised**, improvisatory, improvisatorial, improviso, *improvisé* (*French*); **ad-lib**, *ad libitum* (*Latin*); **ad hoc**, stopgap, makeshift, jury-rigged; **offhand**, off the top of one's head *and* off-the-cuff (*both informal*), **spur-of-the-moment, quick and dirty** (*informal*)

adverbs

13 **impulsively, impetuously, hastily**, suddenly, quickly, **precipitately**, headlong; **recklessly, rashly** *see* 493.10

14 **on impulse**, on a sudden impulse, **on the spur of the moment; without premeditation**, unpremeditatedly, uncalculatedly, undesignedly; unthinkingly, unreflectingly, unreasoningly, unthoughtfully, thoughtlessly, heedlessly, carelessly, inconsiderately, unadvisedly; unintentionally, inadvertently, without willing, indeliberately, involuntarily

15 **extemporaneously, extemporarily**, extempore, *à l'improviste* (*French*), **impromptu, ad lib, offhand**, out of hand; at *or* on sight; by ear, from the hip *and* off the top of one's head *and* off the cuff (*all informal*); at short notice

366 LEAP

nouns

1 **leap, jump, hop, spring, skip, bound**, bounce; **pounce**; upleap, upspring, jump-off; **hurdle; vault**, pole vault; demivolt, curvet, capriole; jeté, grand jeté, tour jeté, saut de basque; jig, galliard, lavolta, Highland fling, morris; standing *or* running *or* flying jump; long jump, broad jump, standing *or* running broad jump; high jump, standing *or* running high jump; leapfrog; jump shot; handspring; buck, buckjump (*US*); ski jump, jump turn, geländesprung, gelände jump; steeplechase; jump-hop; hop, skip and jump

2 caper, dido (*US informal*), **gambol, frisk,** curvet, cavort, caper, **caprice; prance,** caracole; *gambade* (*French*), gambado; falcade

3 **leaping, jumping,** bouncing, bounding, hopping, capering, cavorting, prancing, skipping, **springing,** saltation; **vaulting,** pole vaulting; **hurdling,** the hurdles, high hurdles, hurdle race, steeplechase; leapfrogging

4 **jumper,** leaper, hopper; broad jumper, high jumper; **vaulter,** pole vaulter; **hurdler,** hurdle racer; jumping jack; bucking bronco, buckjumper (*US*), sunfisher (*US informal*); jumping bean; kangaroo, gazelle, stag, jackrabbit, goat, frog, grasshopper, flea; salmon

verbs

5 to **leap, jump, vault, spring, skip, hop, bound,** bounce; upleap, upspring, updive; leap over, jump over, etc; overleap, overjump, overskip, leapfrog; **hurdle,** clear, negotiate; curvet, capriole; buck, buckjump (*US*); ski jump; steeplechase; start, start up, start aside; **pounce,** pounce on *or* upon

6 to **caper, cut capers,** cut a dido (*US informal*), curvet, cavort, capriole, **gambol,** gambado, **frisk,** flounce, **trip, skip,** bob, bounce, jump about; **romp; prance;** caracole

adjectives

7 **leaping, jumping,** springing, hopping, skipping, prancing, bouncing, bounding; saltant, saltatory, saltatorial

367 PLUNGE

nouns

1 **plunge, dive, pitch, drop, fall;** free-fall; header (*informal*); **swoop, pounce,** stoop; swan dive, gainer, jackknife, cannonball; belly flop (*informal*), belly buster *and* belly whopper (*both US informal*); nose dive, power dive; parachute jump, sky dive; bungee jump; crash dive, stationary dive, running dive

2 **submergence, submersion, immersion,** immergence, engulfment, **inundation,** burial; **dipping, ducking,** dousing, sousing, dunking (*informal*), sinking; **dip, duck, souse;** baptism

3 **diving,** plunging; skydiving; bungee jumping; high diving; scuba diving, snorkelling, skin diving, pearl diving, deep-sea diving

4 **diver,** plunger; high diver; bungee jumper; parachute jumper, jumper, sky diver, sport jumper, paratrooper, smoke jumper (*US*); skin diver, snorkel diver, scuba diver, free diver, pearl diver, deep-sea diver, frogman

5 (*diving equipment*) diving bell, diving chamber, bathysphere, bathyscaphe, benthoscope, aquascope; submarine *see* 180.9; diving boat; scuba *or* self-contained underwater breathing apparatus, Aqua-Lung (*trademark*); diving goggles, diving mask, swim fins (*US*); wet suit; air cylinder; diving suit; diving helmet, diving hood; snorkel, periscope

verbs

6 to **plunge, dive, pitch, plummet, drop, fall;** skydive; bungee jump; free-fall; plump, plunk, plop;

swoop, swoop down, stoop, **pounce,** pounce on *or* upon; nose-dive, make *or* take a nose dive; parachute, sky-dive; skin-dive; sound; take a header (*informal*)

7 to **submerge,** submerse, **immerse,** immerge, merge, **sink,** bury, engulf, **inundate,** deluge, drown, overwhelm, whelm; **dip, duck, dunk** (*informal*), douse, souse, plunge in water; baptize

8 to **sink, scuttle,** scupper, send to the bottom, send to Davy Jones's locker; **founder, go down,** go to the bottom, sink like lead, go down like a stone; get out of one's depth

adjectives

9 **submersible,** submergible, immersible, sinkable

368 AVOIDANCE

nouns

1 **avoidance, shunning;** forbearance, refraining; hands-off policy, **nonintervention,** noninvolvement, neutrality; **evasion,** elusion; side-stepping, getting around (*informal*), **circumvention;** prevention, forestalling, forestalment; **escape** *see* 369; evasive action, the runaround (*informal*); zigzag, jink, jouk (*Scottish*), body swerve, slip, dodge, duck, side step, shy; shunting off, sidetracking; evasiveness, elusiveness; **equivocation** *see* 344.4, fudging; avoiding reaction, defence mechanism

2 **shirking, slacking,** skiving, goldbricking (*US informal*), soldiering, goofing *and* goofing off (*both US informal*); clock-watching; **malingering,** skulking; **dodging,** ducking; welshing (*informal*); truancy; tax evasion, tax dodging

3 **shirker,** shirk, **slacker,** skiver, bludger (*Australian*), passenger, old soldier, goldbricker *and* goldbrick (*both US informal*); clock watcher; **welsher** (*informal*); **malingerer,** skulker *or* skulk; truant; tax dodger

4 **flight,** fugitation, exit, quick exit, moonlight flit, making oneself scarce *and* getting the hell out (*both informal*), bolt, scarpering, disappearing act (*informal*), hasty retreat; **running away, decampment;** skedaddle *and* skedaddling (*both informal*), absquatulation (*old*); **elopement;** disappearance *see* 34; French leave, absence without leave *or* AWOL; **desertion** *see* 370.2; hegira

5 **fugitive,** fleer, person on the run, **runaway,** runagate, levanter, **bolter,** skedaddler (*informal*); **absconder, eloper; refugee, evacuee,** boat person, *émigré* (*French*); **displaced person** *or* DP, stateless person; **escapee** *see* 369.5; illegal immigrant, wetback (*US informal*), day-crosser (*US*)

verbs

6 to **avoid, shun, fight shy of, shy away from,** keep from, **keep away from, circumvent,** keep clear of, avoid like the plague, **steer clear of** (*informal*), give a miss to (*informal*), skate around, keep *or* get out of the way of, **give a wide berth,** keep remote from, stay detached from; make way for, give place to; **keep one's distance,** keep at a respectful distance, keep *or* stand *or* hold aloof; give the cold shoulder to (*informal*), have nothing to do with, have no association with, **have no truck with** (*informal*); not meddle with, let alone, leave well alone, keep hands off, not touch, not touch with a bargepole; turn away from, turn one's back upon, slam the door in one's face

7 **to evade, elude, get out of,** shuffle out of, skirt, **get around** (*informal*), circumvent; give one the run-around; ditch *and* shake *and* shake off (*all informal*), get away from, give the runaround *or* the slip (*informal*); throw off the scent; play at hide and seek; lead one a chase *or* merry chase, lead one a dance *or* pretty dance; escape *see 369.6-8*

8 **to dodge, duck; take evasive action,** duck and weave (*informal*), zigzag, jink, jouk (*Scottish*); throw off the track *or* trail; shy, shy off *or* away; swerve, bodyswerve, sheer off; pull away *or* clear; pull back, shrink, recoil *see 902.6, 7;* **sidestep,** step aside; parry, fence, ward off; have an out *or* escape hatch; shift, shift *or* put off; **hedge,** pussyfoot (*informal*), be *or* sit on the fence, beat about the bush, hem and haw, beg the question, tapdance (*US informal*), dance around, equivocate *see 344.7*

9 **to shirk, slack, lie** *or* **rest upon one's oars,** not pull fair, not pull one's weight; **lie down on the job** (*informal*); soldier, duck duty, skive, bludge (*Australian*), scrimshank, goof off *and* dog it (*both US informal*), goldbrick (*US informal*); **malinger,** skulk; **get out of,** sneak *or* slip out of, slide out of, dodge, duck; welsh (*informal*)

10 **to flee, fly, take flight,** take to flight, take wing, fugitate, **run, cut and run** (*informal*), make a precipitate departure, **run off** *or* **away,** run away from, bug out (*US informal*), **decamp,** pull up stakes, **take to one's heels,** make off, **depart** *see* 188.6, do a disappearing act, make a quick exit, **beat a retreat** *or* **a hasty retreat, turn tail,** show a clean pair of heels; **run for it,**

"show it a fair pair of heels and run for it"— SHAKESPEARE, **bolt,** run for one's life; make a run for it; advance to the rear, make a strategic withdrawal; **take French leave,** go AWOL, slip the cable; **desert; abscond,** levant, **elope,** run away with; skip *or* jump bail

11 (*informal terms*) **to beat it, blow, scram,** bugger off, do a bunk, **take it on the lam** (*US*), take a powder *or* runout powder (*US*), make tracks, cut and run, **split, skip,** skip out, duck out, duck and run, vamoose, absquatulate (*old*), skedaddle, **clear out,** make oneself scarce, get the hell out, make a break for it

12 **to slip away, steal away, sneak off,** shuffle off, slink off, slide off, slither off, skulk away, mooch off *and* duck out (*both informal*), slip out of

13 **to not face up to,** hide one's head in the sand, not come to grips with, put off, procrastinate, temporize

adjectives

14 **avoidable, escapable,** eludible; evadable; preventable

15 **evasive, elusive,** elusory; **shifty, slippery, slippery as an eel;** cagey (*informal*); shirking, malingering

16 **fugitive, runaway,** in flight, on the lam (*US informal*), hot (*informal*); disappearing *see 34.4*

369 ESCAPE

nouns

1 **escape; getaway** *and* **break** *and* **breakout** (*all informal*); **deliverance; delivery,** riddance, **release,** setting-free, freeing, **liberation, extrication, rescue;** emergence, issuance, issue, outlet, vent; **leakage,** leak; jailbreak, prisonbreak, break, breakout; evasion *see 368.1;* **flight** *see 368.4;* escapology; escapism

2 **narrow escape,** hairbreadth escape, **close call** *or* **shave** (*informal*), **near miss,** near thing, narrow squeak, close *or* tight squeeze (*informal*), squeaker (*US informal*)

3 **bolt-hole,** escape hatch, fire escape, life net, lifeboat, life raft, life buoy, lifeline, sallyport, slide, inflatable slide, ejection *or* ejector seat, emergency exit, escapeway

4 **loophole, way out,** way of escape, hole to creep out of, escape hatch, escape clause, saving clause; pretext *see 376;* **alternative,** choice *see 371*

5 **escapee,** escaper, evader; escape artist, Houdini; escapologist; **fugitive** *see 368.5;* escapist

verbs

6 **to escape,** make *or* effect one's escape, make good one's escape; **get away, make a getaway** (*informal*); **free oneself,** deliver oneself, save one's bacon (*informal*), gain one's liberty, **get free, get clear of,** bail out, **get out, get out of,** get well out of; **break loose,** cut loose, break away, break one's bonds *or* chains, slip the collar, shake off the yoke; **jump** *and* **skip** (*both informal*); **break jail** *or* **prison,** escape prison, fly the coop (*informal*); leap over the wall; evade *see 368.7;* flee *see 368.10*

7 **to get off, go free,** win freedom, go at liberty, **go scot free,** escape with a whole skin, escape without penalty, walk (*informal*), beat the rap (*US & Canadian informal*); **get away with** (*informal*), get by, get by with, get off easy *or* lightly, get away with murder (*informal*), **get off cheap;** cop a plea (*US informal*)

8 **to scrape** *or* **squeak through,** squeak by, escape with *or* by the skin of one's teeth, have a close call *or* close shave (*informal*)

9 **to slip away, give one the slip,** slip through one's hands *or* fingers; slip *or* sneak through; **slip out of,** slide out of, crawl *or* creep out of, sneak out of, squirm *or* wriggle *or* worm out of, find a loophole

10 **to find vent,** issue forth, come forth, exit, **emerge, issue,** debouch, erupt, break out, break through, come out, run out, **leak out,** ooze out

adjectives

11 **escaped, loose,** on the loose, disengaged, out of, well out of; **fled, flown; fugitive, runaway; free as a bird, scot-free, at large, free**

370 ABANDONMENT

nouns

1 **abandonment, forsaking, leaving;** jettison, jettisoning, throwing overboard *or* away *or* aside, casting away *or* aside; **withdrawal,** evacuation,

pulling out, absentation; cessation *see* 856; disuse, desuetude

2 **desertion, defection,** ratting (*informal*); dereliction; **secession,** bolt, breakaway, walkout; betrayal *see* 645.8; schism, apostasy *see* 363.2; deserter *see* 363.5

3 (*giving up*) **relinquishment, surrender, resignation, renouncement,** renunciation, abdication, waiver, abjurement, abjuration, ceding, cession, handing over, standing *or* stepping down, **yielding, forswearing; withdrawing, dropping out** (*informal*)

4 **derelict,** castoff; jetsam, flotsam, lagan, **flotsam and jetsam;** waifs and strays; **rubbish, junk,** trash, refuse, waste, waste product, solid waste; liquid waste, wastewater; **dump,** dumpsite, rubbish dump, landfill, sanitary landfill, junkheap, junkpile, scrap heap, midden; abandonee, waif, throwaway, orphan, dogie (*informal*); **castaway;** foundling; wastrel, reject, **discard** *see* 390.3

verbs

5 **to abandon, desert, forsake; quit, leave,** leave behind, take leave of, depart from, absent oneself from, turn one's back upon, turn one's tail upon, say goodbye to, bid a long farewell to, walk away, **walk** *or* **run out on** (*informal*), **leave flat** *and* leave high and dry *or* holding the baby *or* in the lurch (*all informal*), leave one to one's fate, throw to the wolves (*informal*); **withdraw, back out, drop out** (*informal*), pull out, stand down (*informal*); **go back on, go back on one's word;** cry off, beg off, renege; **vacate,** evacuate; quit cold *and* leave flat (*both informal*), toss aside; jilt, throw over, dump (*all informal*); maroon; **jettison; junk,** deep-six (*US informal*), discard *see* 390.7; let fall into disuse *or* desuetude

6 **to defect, secede, bolt,** break away; pull out (*informal*), withdraw one's support; sell out *and* sell down the river (*both informal*), betray *see* 645.14; turn one's back on; apostatize

7 **to give up, relinquish, surrender, yield,** yield up, waive, **forgo, resign, renounce,** throw up, abdicate, **abjure, forswear, give up on, have done with,** give up as a bad job, cede, hand over, lay down, wash one's hands of, **write off,** drop, drop all idea of, drop like a hot potato; **desist from,** leave off, give over, **cease** *see* 856.6; hold *or* stay one's hand, cry quits, acknowledge defeat, chuck it in (*informal*), **throw in the towel** *or* **sponge** *see* 433.8

adjectives

8 **abandoned, forsaken, deserted,** left; disused; **derelict,** castaway, jettisoned; marooned; **junk,** junked, discarded *see* 390.11

371 CHOICE

nouns

1 **choice, selection, election,** preference, decision, **pick, choosing,** free choice; alternativity; co-option, co-optation; **will,** volition, free will *see* 430.6, 7; preoption, first choice; the pick *see* 998.7

2 **option,** discretion, **pleasure,** will and pleasure; optionality; possible choice, alternative, alternate choice

3 **dilemma,** Scylla and Charybdis, the devil and the deep blue sea; *embarras de choix* (*French*); choice of Hercules; Hobson's choice, **no choice,** only choice, zero option; limited choice, positive discrimination, affirmative action (*US*)

4 **adoption, embracement,** acceptance, espousal; affiliation

5 **preference, predilection,** proclivity, bent, affinity, prepossession, predisposition, partiality, inclination, leaning, tilt, penchant, bias, tendency, taste; favour, fancy; prejudice; personal choice, particular choice (*old*), druthers (*US informal*); chosen kind *or* sort, style, one's cup of tea (*informal*), type, bag *and* thing (*both informal*); way of life, lifestyle

6 **vote,** voting, **suffrage,** franchise, enfranchisement, voting right, right to vote; **voice, say;** representation; **poll,** polling, canvass, canvassing, division, counting heads, exit poll; **ballot,** balloting, secret ballot, Australian ballot; ballot box, voting machine (*US*); **plebiscite,** plebiscitum, **referendum;** yeas and nays, yea, aye, yes, nay, no; voice vote, *viva voce* vote; hand vote, show of hands; absentee vote, proxy; card vote, block vote; casting vote, deciding vote; postal vote, write-in vote, write-in (*both US*); faggot vote (*old*); single vote, plural vote; transferable vote, nontransferable vote, single transferable vote *or* STV; first-past-the-post system, Hare system, list system, cumulative voting, preferential voting, proportional representation; **straw vote** *or* **poll;** record vote, snap vote

7 **selector,** chooser, optant, elector, **voter; electorate**

8 **nomination, designation,** naming, proposal

9 **election, appointment;** political election

10 **selectivity,** selectiveness, picking and choosing; **choosiness** *see* 495.1; eclecticism; **discrimination** *see* 943

11 **eligibility, qualification, fitness,** fittedness, **suitability,** acceptability, worthiness, desirability; eligible

12 **elect,** elite, the chosen

verbs

13 **to choose, elect,** pick, go with (*informal*), opt, opt for, co-opt, make *or* take one's choice, make choice of, have one's druthers (*US informal*), use *or* take up *or* exercise one's option; **shop around** (*informal*), pick and choose

14 **to select,** make a selection; **pick, handpick, pick out, single out,** choose out, smile on, give the nod (*informal*), jump at, seize on; extract, excerpt; **decide between, choose sides** (*informal*), cull, glean, winnow, sift; separate the wheat from the chaff, separate the sheep from the goats

15 **to adopt;** approve, ratify, pass, carry, endorse; **take up, go in for** (*informal*); accept, take up on (*informal*), **embrace,** espouse; affiliate

16 **to decide upon, determine upon,** settle upon, fix on, resolve upon; make *or* take a decision, **make up one's mind**

17 **to prefer,** have preference, **favour, like better** *or* **best,** prefer to, set before *or* above; **had** *or* **have rather,** choose rather, had rather *or* sooner, had *or*

would as soon; think proper, see *or* think fit, think best, please; tilt *or* incline *or* lean *or* tend toward, have a bias *or* partiality *or* penchant

18 to vote, cast one's vote, ballot, cast a ballot; have a say *or* a voice; hold up one's hand, exercise one's suffrage *or* franchise, stand up and be counted; plump *or* plump for; divide; **poll**, canvass

19 to nominate, name, designate; put up, propose, submit, name for office; run, run *or* stand for office

20 to elect, vote in, place in office; appoint

21 to put to choice, offer, present, set before; put to vote, have a show of hands, have a straw poll

adjectives

22 elective; volitional, voluntary, volitive; optional, discretional; alternative, disjunctive

23 selective, selecting, choosing; eclectic *or* eclectical; elective, electoral; appointing, appointive, constituent; adoptive; exclusive, discriminating see 943.7; choosy (*informal*), particular see 495.9

24 eligible, qualified, fit, fitted, suitable, acceptable, admissible, worthy, desirable, electable; with voice, with vote, with voice and vote, enfranchised

25 preferable, of choice *or* preference, better, preferred, to be preferred, more desirable, favoured; preferential, preferring, favouring

26 chosen, selected, picked; select, elect; handpicked, singled-out; adopted, accepted, embraced, espoused, approved, ratified, passed, carried; elected, unanimously elected, elected by acclamation; appointed; nominated, designated, named

adverbs

27 at choice, at will, at one's will and pleasure, at one's pleasure, electively, at one's discretion, at the option of, if one wishes; on approval; optionally; alternatively

28 preferably, by choice *or* preference, in preference; by vote, by election *or* suffrage; rather than, sooner than, first, sooner, rather, before

conjunctions

29 or, either . . . or; and/or

phrases

30 one man's meat is another man's poison, there's no accounting for taste

372 REJECTION

nouns

1 rejection, repudiation; abjurement, abjuration, renouncement see 370.3; disownment, disavowal, disclamation, recantation see 363.3; exclusion, exception see 772.1; disapproval, nonacceptance, nonapproval, declining, declination, refusal see 442; contradiction, denial see 335.2; passing by *or* up (*informal*), ignoring, nonconsideration, discounting, deselection, dismissal, disregard see 983.1; throwing out *or* away, putting out *or* away, chucking *and* chucking out (*both informal*); discard see 390.3; turning out *or* away, repulse, a flea in one's ear, rebuff see 907.2; spurning, brush-off (*informal*),

kiss-off (*US informal*), scouting (*old*), despising, despisal, contempt see 157; scorn, disdain

verbs

2 to reject, repudiate, abjure, forswear, renounce see 370.7, disown, disclaim, recant; vote out; except, exclude see 772.4, include out (*informal*), close out, close the door on, leave out in the cold, cut out, deselect, blackball, blacklist; disapprove, decline, refuse see 442.3; contradict, deny see 335.4; pass by *or* up (*informal*), waive, ignore, not hear of, wave aside, brush away *or* aside, refuse to consider, discount, dismiss; disregard see 983.2; throw out *or* away, chuck *and* chuck out (*both informal*), discard see 390.7; turn out *or* away, shove away, push aside, repulse, repel, slap *or* smack down (*informal*), rebuff see 907.2; send away with a flea in one's ear, send about one's business, send packing; turn one's back on; spurn, scout (*old*), disdain, scorn, contemn, make a face at, turn up one's nose at, look down one's nose at, raise one's eyebrows at, despise see 157.3

adjectives

3 rejected, repudiated; renounced, forsworn, disowned; denied, refused; excluded, excepted; disapproved, declined; ignored, discounted, not considered, dismissed, dismissed out of hand; discarded; repulsed, rebuffed; spurned, scouted (*old*), disdained, scorned, contemned, despised; out of the question, not to be thought of, declined with thanks

4 rejective; renunciative, abjuratory; declinatory; dismissive; contemptuous, despising, scornful, disdainful

373 CUSTOM, HABIT

nouns

1 custom, convention, use, usage, standard usage, standard behaviour, wont, way, established way, time-honoured practice, tradition, standing custom, folkway, manner, practice, praxis, prescription, observance, ritual, consuetude, mores; proper thing, what is done, social convention see 579; bon ton, fashion see 578; manners, etiquette see 580.3; way of life, lifestyle; conformity see 866; generalization see 863.1, labelling, stereotyping

2 "a second nature, and no less powerful"—Montaigne, "the universal sovereign"—Pindar, "that unwritten law, by which the people keep even kings in awe"—D'Avenant, "often only the antiquity of error"—Cyprian

3 culture, society, civilization; trait, culture trait; key trait; complex, culture complex, trait-complex; culture area; culture centre; shame culture, memory culture; folkways, mores, system of values, ethos, culture pattern; cultural change; cultural lag; culture conflict; acculturation, enculturation; culture contact, cultural drift

4 habit, habitude, custom, second nature; use, usage, trick, wont, way, practice, praxis; bad habit; stereotype;

"the petrifaction of feelings" —L E LANDON; pattern, **habit pattern**; stereotyped behaviour; force of habit; creature of habit; **knee jerk** (*informal*), automatism *see* 962.5; peculiarity, characteristic *see* 864.4

5 **rule, norm,** procedure, **common practice,** the way things are done, form, prescribed *or* set form; common *or* ordinary run of things, matter of course, par for the course (*informal*); standard operating procedure *or* SOP, drill; standing orders

6 **routine,** run, **round,** beat, track, beaten path *or* track; jog trot, **rut, groove,** well-worn groove; **treadmill,** squirrel cage (*US*); the working day, nine-to-five, the grind *or* the daily grind (*informal*); **red tape,** redtapeism, **bureaucracy,** bureaucratism

7 **customariness,** accustomedness, wontedness, **habitualness; inveteracy,** inveterateness, confirmedness, settledness, fixedness; commonness, prevalence *see* 863.2

8 **habituation, accustoming; conditioning,** seasoning, training; **familiarization,** naturalization (*old*), breaking-in (*informal*), orientation; **domestication, taming,** breaking, house-training; acclimation, acclimatization; **inurement,** hardening, case hardening; adaption, adjustment, accommodation *see* 866.1

9 **addiction** *see* 87.1; **addict** *see* 87.2

verbs

10 **to accustom, habituate,** wont; **condition,** season, **train;** familiarize, naturalize (*old*), break in (*informal*), orient, orientate; **domesticate,** domesticize, **tame,** break, gentle, house-train; put through the mill; acclimatize, acclimate; inure, harden, case harden; adapt, adjust, accommodate *see* 787.7; confirm, fix, establish *see* 854.9; acculturate, enculturate

11 **to become a habit,** take root, become fixed, **grow on one,** take hold of one, take one over

12 **to be used to,** be wont, wont, **make a practice of;** get used to, get into the way of, **take to,** accustom oneself to, make a practice of; fall into a habit, addict oneself to

13 **to get in a rut,** be in a rut, move *or* travel in a groove *or* rut, run on in a groove, follow the beaten path *or* track, go round like a horse in a mill

adjectives

14 **customary, wonted,** consuetudinary; traditional, time-honored; familiar, everyday, ordinary, **usual; established,** received, accepted; set, prescribed, prescriptive; **normative, normal; standard,** regular, stock, regulation; prevalent, prevailing, widespread, obtaining, generally accepted, popular, **current** *see* 863.12; **conventional** *see* 579.5; conformist, conformable *see* 866.5

15 **habitual, regular,** frequent, constant, persistent; **repetitive, recurring, recurrent;** stereotyped; knee-jerk (*informal*), lockstep (*US*), automatic *see* 962.14; **routine,** nine-to-five, workaday, well-trodden, well-worn, beaten; trite, hackneyed *see* 117.9

16 **accustomed,** wont, **used to; conditioned,** trained, seasoned; experienced, **familiarized,** naturalized (*old*), broken-in, run-in (*informal*), oriented, orientated; acclimated, acclimatized; inured,

hardened, case-hardened; adapted, adjusted, accommodated; house-trained, potty-trained

17 **used to, familiar with,** conversant with, **at home in** *or* **with,** no stranger to, an old hand at

18 **habituated,** habitué (*French*); **in the habit of,** used to; never free from; **in a rut**

19 **confirmed, inveterate, chronic, established,** long-established, **fixed, settled, rooted,** thorough; incorrigible, irreversible; **deep-rooted,** deep-set, deep-settled, **deep-seated,** deep-fixed, deep-dyed; **infixed, ingrained,** fast, dyed-in-the-wool; implanted, inculcated, instilled; set, **set in one's ways,** settled in habit

adverbs

20 **customarily,** conventionally, accustomedly, wontedly; normatively, normally, **usually; as is the custom;** as is usual, *comme d'habitude* (*French*); as things go, as the world goes

21 **habitually, regularly,** routinely, frequently, persistently, repetitively, recurringly; **inveterately, chronically;** from habit, **by** *or* **from force of habit,** as is one's wont

374 UNACCUSTOMEDNESS

nouns

1 **unaccustomedness, newness,** unwontedness, disaccustomedness, unusedness, unhabituatedness; shakiness (*informal*); **unfamiliarity,** unacquaintance, unconversance, unpractisedness, newness to; inexperience *see* 414.2; ignorance *see* 929

verbs

2 **to disaccustom, cure, break off,** stop, **wean**

3 **to break the habit, cure oneself of,** disaccustom oneself, wean oneself from, break the pattern, break one's chains *or* fetters; **give up,** leave off, **abandon,** drop, stop, discontinue, chuck in (*informal*), kick *and* shake (*both informal*), throw off, rid oneself of; get on the wagon, swear off *see* 668.8

adjectives

4 **unaccustomed,** new, disaccustomed, **unused, unwonted;** uninured, unseasoned, untrained, unhardened; shaky (*informal*), tyronic; unhabituated, **not in the habit of;** out of the habit of, rusty; unweaned; **unused to, unfamiliar with,** unacquainted with, unconversant with, unpractised, new to, a stranger to; cub, greenhorn; inexperienced *see* 414.17; ignorant *see* 929.12

375 MOTIVATION, INDUCEMENT

nouns

1 **motive, reason, cause,** source, spring, mainspring; matter, score, consideration; **ground, basis** *see* 885.1; **sake; aim, goal** *see* 380.2, end, end in view, telos, final cause; **ideal,** principle, **ambition,** aspiration, inspiration, guiding light *or* star, lodestar; calling, vocation; intention *see* 380; ulterior motive

2 **motivation,** moving, **actuation, prompting, stimulation,** animation, triggering, setting-off,

setting in motion, getting under way; direction, inner-direction, other-direction; **influence** *see* 893

3 **inducement**, enlistment, engagement, solicitation, **persuasion**, suasion; exhortation, hortation, preaching, preachment; **selling**, sales talk, salesmanship, hard sell, high pressure, hawking, huckstering, flogging (*informal*); jawboning, arm-twisting (*both informal*); **lobbying**; **coaxing**, wheedling, working on (*informal*), cajolery, cajolement, conning, snow job *and* smoke and mirrors (*both US informal*), blandishment, sweet talk *and* soft soap (*both informal*), soft sell (*informal*); **allurement** *see* 377

4 **incitement**, incitation, **instigation**, **stimulation**, **arousal**, **excitement**, **agitation**, **inflammation**, excitation, fomentation, firing, stirring, stirring-up, impassioning, whipping up, rabble-rousing; **provocation**, irritation, exasperation; pep talk, pep rally (*US*)

5 **urging**, **pressure**, pressing, pushing; **encouragement**, abetment; **insistence**, instance; **goading**, **prodding**, goosing (*informal*), spurring, pricking, needling

6 **urge**, urgency; impulse, impulsion, compulsion; press, **pressure**, **drive**, push; sudden *or* rash impulse; constraint, exigency, stress, pinch

7 **incentive**, **inducement**, **encouragement**, persuasive, **invitation**, **provocation**, **incitement**; **stimulus**, **stimulation**, stimulative, fillip, whet; carrot; reward, payment *see* 624; golden hello, **golden handshake**, golden handcuffs, golden parachute; **profit** *see* 472.3; bait, **lure** *see* 377.2; palm oil (*informal*), bribe *see* 378.2; sweetening *and* sweetener (*both informal*), interest, percentage, what's in it for one (*informal*)

8 **goad**, **spur**, **prod**, prick (*old*), sting, **gadfly**; rowel; whip, lash, whiplash, gad (*US informal*)

9 **inspiration**, **infusion**, infection; fire, firing, spark, sparking; **animation**, **exhilaration**, enlivenment; afflatus, divine afflatus; genius, animus, moving *or* animating spirit; muse; the Muses

10 **prompter**, **mover**, **prime mover**, motivator, impeller, energizer, galvanizer, inducer, **actuator**, **animator**, moving spirit; **encourager**, abettor, **inspirer**, firer, spark, sparker, spark plug (*informal*); persuader; **stimulator**, gadfly; **tempter** *see* 377.3; coaxer, coax (*informal*), wheedler, cajoler, pleader

11 **instigator**, **inciter**, exciter, urger; **provoker**, *provocateur* (*French*), *agent provocateur* (*French*), catalyst; **agitator**, **fomenter**, inflamer; agitprop; **rabble-rouser**, rouser, **demagogue**; **firebrand**, **incendiary**; **seditionist**, seditionary; **troublemaker**, makebate (*old*), mischief-maker, ringleader

verbs

12 **to motivate**, **move**, set in motion, **actuate**, move to action, **impel**, propel; **stimulate**, energize, galvanize, **animate**, **spark**; promote, foster; force, compel *see* 424.4

13 **to prompt**, **provoke**, **evoke**, **elicit**, **call up**, summon up, muster up, call forth, **inspire**; bring about, **cause**

14 **to urge**, **press**, **push**, work on (*informal*), twist one's arm (*informal*); **sell**, flog (*informal*); **insist**,

push for, not take no for an answer, **importune**, **nag**, **pressure**, **high-pressure**, bring pressure to bear upon, throw one's weight around, jawbone *and* build a fire under (*both US informal*), talk round; grind in; **lobby**; **coax**, wheedle, cajole, blandish, plead with, sweet-talk *and* soft-soap (*both informal*), **exhort**, call on *or* upon, advocate, recommend, put in a good word, hype, buck for (*US informal*); insist, insist upon

15 **to goad**, **prod**, poke, nudge, prod at, goose (*informal*), **spur**, prick, sting, needle; whip, lash; pick at *or* on, nibble at, nibble away at

16 **to urge on** *or* **along**, egg on (*informal*), hound on, hie on (*old*), hasten on, hurry on, speed on; **goad on**, **spur on**, drive on, whip on *or* along; cheer on, root on (*US informal*), cheer from the sidelines

17 **to incite**, **instigate**, **put up to** (*informal*); set on, sic on; **foment**, ferment, **agitate**, **arouse**, **excite**, **stir up**, work up, whip up; rally; **inflame**, incense, **fire**, heat, heat up, impassion; **provoke**, pique, whet, tickle; nettle; lash into a fury *or* frenzy; pour oil on the fire, feed the fire, add fuel to the flame, fan, fan the flame, blow the coals, stir the embers

18 **to kindle**, enkindle, **fire**, **spark**, **spark off**, **trigger**, **trigger off**, **touch off**, set off, light the fuse, **enflame**, set afire *or* on fire

19 **to rouse**, **arouse**, raise, raise up, **waken**, **awaken**, wake up, turn on (*informal*), charge *or* psych *or* pump up (*informal*), stir, **stir up**, set astir, **pique**

20 **to inspire**, inspirit, spirit, spirit up; fire, **fire one's imagination**; **animate**, **exhilarate**, enliven; **infuse**, **infect**, inject, inoculate, imbue, inform

21 **to encourage**, **hearten**, **embolden**, give encouragement, pat *or* clap on the back, stroke (*US informal*); **invite**, ask for; **abet**, aid and abet, countenance, keep in countenance; **foster**, **nurture**, nourish, feed

22 **to induce**, **prompt**, move one to, **influence**, sway, incline, **dispose**, carry, bring, lead, **lead one to**; **lure**; **tempt**; determine, decide; enlist, procure, engage (*old*), interest in, get to do, rope in

23 **to persuade**, **prevail on** *or* **upon**, prevail with, sway, convince, lead to believe, **bring round**, bring to reason, bring to one's senses; **win**, **win over**, win around, bring over, draw over, gain, gain over; **talk over**, **talk into**, argue into, out-talk (*informal*); wangle, wangle into; hook *and* hook in (*both US informal*), do a snow job on (*US informal*), sell *and* sell one on (*both informal*), con (*informal*), **charm**, **captivate**; wear down, overcome one's resistance, arm-twist *and* twist one's arm (*both informal*); **bribe** *see* 378.3, grease *or* oil *or* cross one's palm (*informal*)

24 **to persuade oneself**, **make oneself easy about**, make sure of, make up one's mind; be persuaded, rest easy

adjectives

25 **motivating**, **motivational**, **motive**, **moving**, **animating**, **actuating**, **impelling**, **driving**, impulsive, inducive, directive; **urgent**, **pressing**, **driving**; compelling; causal, causative

26 **inspiring**, **inspirational**, inspiriting; infusive; animating, exhilarating, enlivening

27 provocative, provoking, piquant, **exciting,** sexy, challenging, prompting, **rousing, stirring, stimulating,** stimulant, stimulative, stimulatory, energizing, electric, galvanizing, galvanic; **encouraging,** inviting, **alluring**

28 incitive, inciting, incentive; **instigative,** instigating; **agitative,** agitational; **inflammatory, incendiary,** fomenting, rabble-rousing

29 persuasive, suasive, persuading; wheedling, cajoling; hortative, hortatory; exhortative, exhortatory

30 moved, motivated, prompted, impelled, actuated; stimulated, animated; minded, inclined, of a mind to, with half a mind to; inner-directed, other-directed

31 inspired, fired, afire, on fire

376 PRETEXT

nouns

1 pretext, pretence, pretension, lying pretension, **show,** ostensible *or* announced *or* public *or* professed motive; **front,** facade, **sham** see 354.3; **excuse,** apology, protestation, poor excuse, lame excuse; **occasion,** mere occasion; put-off (*informal*); handle, peg to hang on, leg to stand on, *locus standi* (*Latin*); **subterfuge,** refuge, device, stratagem, feint, dipsy-doodle (*US informal*), **trick** see 356.6; dust thrown in the eye, smoke screen, **screen, cover,** stalking-horse, **blind;** guise, semblance; mask, cloak, veil; **cosmetics,** mere cosmetics, gloss, varnish, colour, coat of paint, whitewash (*informal*); spit and polish; **cover,** cover-up, cover story, alibi; band-aid

2 claim, profession, allegation

verbs

3 to pretext, make a pretext of, take as an excuse *or* reason *or* occasion, urge as a motive, **pretend,** make a pretence of; put up a front *or* false front; **allege, claim,** profess, purport, avow; protest too much

4 to hide under, cover oneself with, shelter under, take cover under, wrap oneself in, cloak *or* mantle oneself with, take refuge in; conceal one's motive with; **cover,** cover up, gloss *or* varnish over, apply a coat of paint *or* whitewash

adjectives

5 pretexted, pretended, alleged, claimed, professed, purported, avowed; **ostensible,** hypocritical, **specious;** so-called, in name only

adverbs

6 ostensibly, allegedly, purportedly, professedly, avowedly; for the record, for public consumption; under the pretext of, **as a pretext,** as an excuse, as a cover *or* a cover-up *or* an alibi

377 ALLUREMENT

nouns

1 allurement, allure, enticement, inveiglement, invitation, come-hither (*informal*), blandishment, cajolery; **inducement** see 375.7; **temptation,** tantalization; **seduction,** seducement; **beguilement,** beguiling; **fascination, captivation,** enthralment,

entrapment, snaring; **enchantment,** witchery, bewitchery, bewitchment; **attraction, interest, charm, glamour, appeal,** magnetism, charisma, star quality; wooing; flirtation

2 attractiveness, allure, charmingness, bewitchingness, impressiveness, **seductiveness,** winsomeness, winning ways, winningness; **sexiness,** sex appeal (*informal*)

3 lure, charm, **come-on** (*informal*), attention-getter *or* grabber, **attraction,** draw, crowd-pleaser, headliner; gimmick, hook *and* clou (*both US informal*), drawing card *and* drawcard (*both US & Canadian informal*); **decoy,** decoy duck; **bait,** ground bait, baited trap, baited hook; **snare,** trap; **endearment** see 562; the song of the Sirens, the voice of the tempter, honeyed words; forbidden fruit

4 tempter, seducer, enticer, inveigler, **charmer,** enchanter, fascinator, tantalizer, teaser; coquette, flirt; Don Juan; Pied Piper of Hamelin; **temptress,** enchantress, seductress, **siren;** Siren, Circe, Lorelei, Parthenope; **vampire,** vamp (*informal*), *femme fatale* (*French*)

verbs

5 to lure, allure, **entice, seduce, inveigle, decoy,** draw, **draw on, lead on;** come on to *and* give the come-on *and* give a come-hither look *and* bat the eyes at (*all informal*), flirt with, flirt, chat up; **woo;** coax, cajole, blandish; **ensnare;** draw in, suck in (*informal*); bait, offer bait to, bait the hook, angle with a silver hook

6 to attract, interest, appeal, engage, impress, fetch (*informal*), catch *or* get one's eye, command one's attention, rivet one, attract one's interest, be attractive, take *or* tickle one's fancy; **invite,** summon, beckon; **tempt, tantalize, titillate,** tickle, **tease,** whet the appetite, make one's mouth water, dangle before one

7 to fascinate, captivate, charm, becharm, spell, spellbind, cast a spell, put under a spell, **beguile, intrigue, enthral,** infatuate, **enrapture, transport, enravish, entrance, enchant,** witch, **bewitch;** carry away, sweep off one's feet, turn one's head, knock one's socks off (*informal*); hypnotize, mesmerize; vamp (*informal*); charismatize

adjectives

8 alluring, fascinating, captivating, riveting, charming, glamorous, exotic, **enchanting,** spellful, spellbinding, **entrancing,** ravishing, **enravishing, intriguing, enthralling,** witching, **bewitching; attractive, interesting, appealing,** tasty (*informal*), dishy (*informal*), sexy (*informal*), engaging, taking, eye-catching, catching, fetching, winning, winsome, prepossessing; exciting; charismatic; **seductive,** seducing, **beguiling, enticing, inviting,** come-hither (*informal*); flirtatious, coquettish; coaxing, cajoling, blandishing; **tempting, tantalizing,** teasing, titillating, titillative, tickling; **provocative,** *provoquant* (*French*); appetizing, mouth-watering, piquant; **irresistible;** siren, sirenic; hypnotic, mesmeric

adverbs

9 **alluringly, fascinatingly,** captivatingly, charmingly, enchantingly, entrancingly, enravishingly, intriguingly, beguilingly, glamorously, bewitchingly; attractively, appealingly, engagingly, winsomely; **enticingly, seductively,** with bedroom eyes (*informal*); **temptingly,** provocatively; **tantalizingly,** teasingly; piquantly, appetizingly; irresistibly; hypnotically, mesmerically

378 BRIBERY

nouns

1 **bribery,** bribing, subornation, **corruption, graft,** bribery and corruption

2 **bribe,** bribe money, sop, sop to Cerberus, gratuity, gratification (*old*), payoff (*informal*), bung (*informal*), kickback, sweetener (*informal*), boodle (*informal*), backhander (*informal*); hush money (*informal*); payola (*informal*); slush fund; protection

verbs

3 **to bribe,** throw a sop to; grease *and* **grease the palm** *or* **hand** *and* oil the palm *and* tickle the palm (*all informal*); kick back; **purchase;** buy *and* **buy off** *and* pay off (*all informal*); suborn, **corrupt,** tamper with; reach *and* get at *and* get to (*all informal*); approach, try to bribe; **fix, take care of,** square

adjectives

4 **bribable,** corruptible, purchasable, buyable; approachable; fixable; on the take (*informal*); **venal, corrupt,** bought and paid for, in one's pocket

379 DISSUASION

nouns

1 **dissuasion,** talking out of (*informal*), remonstrance, expostulation, admonition, monition, **warning,** caveat, **caution,** cautioning; intimidation, **determent,** deterrence, scaring *or* frightening off, turning around

2 **deterrent,** determent; **discouragement,** disincentive, chilling effect, demotivation; damp, damper, **wet blanket,** cold water, chill

verbs

3 **to dissuade,** convince to the contrary, convince otherwise, **talk out of** (*informal*), kid out of (*US informal*); unconvince, unpersuade; remonstrate, expostulate, admonish, cry out against; **warn, warn off** *or* **away, caution;** enter a caveat; **intimidate,** scare *or* frighten off, daunt; turn around

4 **to disincline,** indispose, disaffect, disinterest; **deter,** repel, turn from, turn away *or* aside; divert, deflect; distract, put off *and* turn off (*both informal*); wean from; **discourage; pour** *or* **throw cold water on,** throw *or* lay a wet blanket on, damp, dampen, demotivate, **cool, chill,** quench, blunt; take the wind out of one's sails

adjectives

5 **dissuasive,** dissuading, disinclining, **discouraging;**

deterrent, off-putting; expostulatory, admonitory, monitory, cautionary; intimidating

380 INTENTION

nouns

1 **intention, intent,** intendment, mindset, **aim,** effect, meaning, view, study, animus, **point, purpose,** function, set *or* settled *or* fixed purpose; sake; **design, plan, project,** idea, notion; **quest,** pursuit; **proposal,** prospectus; **resolve,** resolution, mind, will; **motive** *see* 375.1; determination *see* 359.1; desideratum, desideration, **ambition,** aspiration, **desire** *see* 100; striving, nisus

2 **objective, object, aim, end, goal,** destination, mark, object in mind, **end in view,** telos, final cause, ultimate aim; end in itself; **target,** butt, bull's-eye, quintain; quarry, prey, game; reason for being, *raison d'être* (*French*); by-purpose, by-end; "the be-all and the end-all"—SHAKESPEARE; teleology

3 **intentionality, deliberation, deliberateness,** directedness; express intention, expressness, **premeditation, predeliberation,** preconsideration, **calculation, calculatedness, predetermination,** preresolution, forethought, aforethought

verbs

4 **to intend, purpose, plan,** purport, **mean,** think, **propose; resolve,** determine *see* 359.7; project, **design,** destine; **aim,** aim at, take aim at, draw a bead on, set one's sights on, have designs on, go for, drive at, aspire to *or* after, be after, set before oneself, purpose to oneself; harbour a design; **desire** *see* 100.14, 18

5 **to contemplate, meditate; envisage,** envision, **have in mind, have in view;** have an eye to, have every intention, have a mind *or* notion, have half a mind *or* notion, have a good *or* great mind *or* notion

6 **to plan, plan on, figure on,** plan for *or* out, count on, figure out, calculate, calculate on, reckon, reckon *or* bargain on, bargain for, bank on *or* upon, make book on (*US informal*)

7 **to premeditate, calculate, preresolve, predetermine,** predeliberate, preconsider, direct oneself, forethink, work out beforehand; plan; plot, scheme

adjectives

8 **intentional, intended,** proposed, purposed, telic, **projected, designed,** of design, aimed, aimed at, **meant, purposeful,** purposive, **wilful, voluntary, deliberate;** deliberated; considered, studied, advised, **calculated, contemplated, envisaged,** envisioned, meditated, **conscious,** knowing, witting; planned; teleological

9 **premeditated, predeliberated,** preconsidered, predetermined, preresolved, prepense, **aforethought**

adverbs

10 **intentionally, purposely,** purposefully, purposively, pointedly, **on purpose,** with purpose, with a view *or* an eye to, **deliberately, designedly,** wilfully, **voluntarily,** of one's own accord *or* one's own free will; **wittingly, consciously, knowingly;**

advisedly, calculatedly, contemplatedly, meditatedly, premeditatedly, **with premeditation, with intent,** with full intent, **by design,** with one's eyes open; with malice aforethought, in cold blood

prepositions, conjunctions

11 for, to; **in order to** *or* **that,** so, **so that, so as to; for the purpose of,** to the end that, with the intent that, with the view of, with a view to, with an eye to; in contemplation of, in consideration of; **for the sake of**

381 PLAN

nouns

1 **plan, scheme, design,** method, **programme,** device, contrivance, game, envisagement, conception, enterprise, **idea, notion;** organization, rationalization, systematization, schematization; charting, mapping, graphing, blueprinting; **planning,** calculation, figuring; planning function; long-range planning, long-range plan; **master plan,** the picture *and* the big picture (*both informal*); approach, attack, plan of attack; way, procedure; **arrangement,** prearrangement, system, disposition, layout, setup, lineup; **schedule,** timetable, time-scheme, time frame; deadline; plan of work; **schema,** schematism, scheme of arrangement; blueprint, **guideline, guidelines,** programme of action; methodology; working plan, ground plan, tactical plan, strategic plan; tactics, **strategy,** game plan (*informal*); contingency plan; operations research; **intention** *see* 380; forethought, foresight *see* 960

2 **project, projection, scheme; proposal,** prospectus, proposition; **scenario, game plan** (*informal*)

3 **diagram, plot, chart, blueprint,** graph, bar graph, pie chart, area graph; flow diagram, flow chart; **table; design, pattern,** copy (*old*), cartoon; **sketch, draft, drawing,** working drawing, rough; *brouillon, ébauche, esquisse (all French);* **outline, delineation,** skeleton, figure, profile; house plan, ground plan, ichnography; elevation, projection; **map, chart** *see* 159.5

4 **policy,** polity, principles, guiding principles; **procedure,** course, line, plan of action; creed *see* 952.3; **platform;** position paper

5 **intrigue,** web of intrigue, **plot, scheme,** deep-laid plot *or* scheme, underplot, game *or* little game (*both informal*), trick, stratagem, finesse; counterplot; **conspiracy,** confederacy, covin, complot (*old*), cabal, omertà (*Spanish*); **complicity, collusion, connivance;** artifice *see* 415.3; **contrivance,** contriving; **scheming,** schemery, plotting; finagling (*informal*), **machination,** manipulation, **manoeuvring,** engineering, rigging; frame-up (*informal*); string-pulling (*informal*)

6 **planner, designer,** deviser, contriver, framer, projector; enterpriser, entrepreneur; organizer, promoter, developer, engineer; expediter, facilitator, animator; **policymaker, decision-maker; architect, tactician, strategist, strategian**

7 **schemer, plotter,** counterplotter, finagler (*informal*), Machiavellian; **intriguer,** *intrigant, intrigante (both French)*, cabalist; **conspirer, conspirator,**

coconspirator, **conniver;** manoeuvrer, machinator, operator (*informal*), opportunist, chancer (*informal*), pot-hunter (*US*), exploiter; string-puller (*informal*)

verbs

8 **to plan, devise, contrive, design,** frame, shape, cast, concert, lay plans; organize, rationalize, systematize, schematize, methodize, configure, pull together, sort out; **arrange,** prearrange, make arrangements, set up, work up, work out; **schedule;** lay down a plan, shape *or* mark out a course; programme; **calculate,** figure; **project,** cut out, make a projection, forecast (*old*), plan ahead; intend *see* 380.4

9 **to plot, scheme, intrigue,** be up to something; **conspire, connive,** collude, complot (*old*), cabal; **hatch, hatch up,** cook up (*informal*), brew, concoct, hatch *or* lay a plot; **manoeuvre,** machinate, finesse, operate (*informal*), engineer, rig, wangle (*informal*), angle, finagle (*informal*); frame *or* frame up (*both informal*); counterplot, countermine

10 **to plot; map, chart** *see* 159.11, **blueprint; diagram,** graph; **sketch,** sketch in *or* out, draw up a plan; map out, plot out, **lay out,** set out, mark out; lay off, mark off

11 **to outline,** line, **delineate,** chalk out, brief; **sketch, draft,** trace; block in *or* out; rough in, rough out

adjectives

12 **planned, devised, designed,** shaped, set, **blueprinted,** charted, **contrived; plotted;** arranged; organized, rationalized, systematized, schematized, methodized; worked out, calculated, figured; **projected; scheduled,** on the agenda, in the works, in the pipeline (*informal*), on the calendar, on the docket (*US*), on the tapis (*old*), *sur le tapis (French)*; tactical, **strategic**

13 **scheming, calculating, designing, contriving, plotting, intriguing;** manipulatory, **manipulative;** opportunist, **opportunistic;** Machiavellian, Byzantine; **conniving,** connivent (*old*), conspiring, collusive; stratagemical

14 schematic, diagrammatic

382 PURSUIT

nouns

1 **pursuit,** pursuing, pursuance, prosecution (*old*); **quest,** seeking, hunting, searching; **following,** follow, follow-up; tracking, trailing, tracking down, dogging, shadowing, stalking; **chase,** hot pursuit; hue and cry

2 **hunting,** gunning, shooting, venery, cynegetics, sport, sporting; **hunt, chase,** shoot, chivy *or* chevy, shikar (*India*), coursing; blood-sport; fox hunt, fox hunting,
"the unspeakable in full pursuit of the inedible"—Oscar Wilde; hawking, falconry; stalking, still hunt

3 **fishing,** fishery; **angling,** piscatology (*old*), halieutics

4 **pursuer,** pursuant, **chaser,** follower, hunter, quester, **seeker**

5 **hunter, huntsman,** sportsman, Nimrod; huntress, sportswoman, **Diana;** stalker; courser; trapper; big game hunter, shikari (*India*), white hunter;

jacklighter (*US*), jacker; gamekeeper; beater, ghillie, whipper-in; falconer; gundog

6 fisher, fisherman, angler, *piscator* (*Latin*), piscatorian, piscatorialist; Waltonian, "The Compleat Angler"—IZAAK WALTON; trawler, trawlerman, dragger, jacker, jigger, bobber, fly fisherman, coarse fisherman, guddler (*Scottish*), tickler, drifter, drift netter, whaler, clam digger, lobsterman, etc

7 quarry, game, prey, venery, beasts of venery, victim, the hunted; kill; big game

verbs

8 to pursue, prosecute (*old*), **follow,** follow up, **go after,** take out *or* off after (*informal*), bay after, run after, run in pursuit of, make after, go in pursuit of; raise the hunt, raise the hue and cry, hollo after; **chase, give chase,** chivy; hound, dog; **quest,** quest after, **seek,** seek out, hunt, **search** *see* 937.29, 30

9 to hunt, go hunting, hunt down, chase, run, shikar (*India*), sport; engage in a blood sport; shoot, gun; course; ride to hounds, follow the hounds; **track, trail, stalk,** prowl after, still-hunt; hound, dog; hawk, falcon; fowl; flush, start; drive, beat; jack, jacklight (*both US*)

10 to fish, go fishing, **angle;** cast one's hook *or* net; bait the hook; shrimp, whale, clam, grig, coarse-fish, fly-fish, tickle, guddle (*Scottish*), troll, bob, dap, dib *or* dibble, gig, jig, etc; reel in

adjectives

11 pursuing, pursuant, following; **questing, seeking, searching** *see* 937.37; **in pursuit,** in hot pursuit, in full cry; hunting, cynegetic, fishing, piscatory, piscatorial, halieutic, halieutical

prepositions

12 after, in pursuit *or* **pursuance of,** in search of, on the lookout for, in the market for, out for; on the track *or* trail of, on the scent of

exclamations

13 (*hunting cries*) view halloo!, yoicks!; so-ho!, tallyho!, tallyho over!, tallyho back!

383 ROUTE, PATH

nouns

1 route, path, way, itinerary, **course,** track, run, line, road; trajectory, traject, *trajet* (*French*); circuit, tour, orbit; walk, beat, round; trade route, **sea lane, air lane,** air bridge, flight path; line *or* path of least resistance, primrose path, garden path; shortcut

2 path, track, trail, pathway, footpath, footway, ridgeway, *piste* (*French*); walkway, catwalk, skybridge *or* skywalk *or* flying bridge *or* walkway; **pavement, sidewalk** (*US*), **walk,** *trottoir* (*French*); boardwalk (*US*); hiking trail; public walk, promenade, esplanade, parade, *prado* (*Spanish*), mall; towpath *or* towing path; bridle path *or* road *or* trail *or* way; cycle path; berm; run, runway; beaten track *or* path, rut, groove; garden path

3 passageway, pass, passage, defile; avenue, artery; corridor, aisle, alley, lane; channel,

conduit *see* 239.1; ford, ferry, traject, *trajet* (*French*); opening, aperture; access, inlet *see* 189.5; exit, outlet *see* 190.9; connection, communication; covered way, gallery, arcade, portico, colonnade, cloister, ambulatory; underpass, subway, overpass, flyover; tunnel, railway tunnel, vehicular tunnel; Channel Tunnel *or* Chunnel *or* Eurotunnel; junction, interchange, **intersection** *see* 170.2

4 byway, bypath, byroad, by-lane, bystreet, side road, side street; **bypass, diversion, detour,** contraflow, roundabout way; bypaths and crooked ways; back way, back stairs, back door, side door; back road, back street

5 road (*see list*), highway, king's highway, queen's highway, roadway, carriageway, right-of-way; **street** (*see list*)

6 pavement, paving; macadam, blacktop, bitumen, asphalt, tarmacadam, tarmac, tarvia, bituminous macadam; cement, concrete; tile, brick, paving brick; stone, paving stone, pavestone, flag, flagstone, flagging; cobblestone, cobble; road metal; gravel; kerbstone, edgestone; kerb, kerbing; gutter, kennel (*old*)

7 railway (*see list*), railroad (*US*), rail, line, track, permanent way; junction; terminus, terminal, the end of the line, bay; point, sleeper, roadbed, embankment; bridge, trestle

8 ropeway, cable *or* rope railway, funicular *or* funicular railway; *téléphérique* (*French*), telpher, telpher line, telpherage; ski lift

9 bridge, span, viaduct, humpback; cantilever bridge, clapper bridge, drawbridge, footbridge, pontoon bridge, rope bridge, skywalk *or* flying bridge *or* walkway, suspension bridge, toll bridge; **flyover,** overpass *or* overcrossing *or* overbridge (*all US*); stepping-stone, stepstone (*US*); Bifrost

10 roads, highways

A-road	motorway
access road	orbital road
arterial road	parkway (US)
artery	pavé (French)
Autobahn (German)	pike
autoroute (French)	post road
autostrada (Italian)	private road
beltway (US)	ring road
B-road	service road
bypass	single-track road
causeway	slip road
clearway	speedway
dual carriageway	superhighway
expressway	throughway
freeway	toll road
highroad	trunk road
main road	turnpike

11 streets, alleys

alley *or* alleyway	cul-de-sac
avenue	dead-end street
blind alley	drive
boulevard	High street
close	lane
court	mews
crescent	one-way street

place
row

vennel (Scottish)
wynd (Scottish)

12 railways

cable railway
cog railway (US)
electric railway
elevated railway
gravity-operated railway
magnetic railway
mainline
métro (French)
monorail

rack *or* rack-and-pinion
  railway
streetcar line (US)
subway
tram *or* tramline *or*
  tramway
trolley car line (US)
trunk *or* trunk line
underground *or* tube

384 MANNER, MEANS

nouns

1 manner, way, wise, **means, mode,** modality, form, **fashion, style,** tone, guise (*old*); **method,** methodology, **system;** algorithm (*maths*); **approach,** attack, tack; **technique, procedure, process,** proceeding, course, practice; order; lines, line, line of action; *modus operandi* (*Latin*), mode of operation, manner of working, mode of procedure; **routine;** the way of, the how, the how-to, the drill

2 means, ways, **ways and means,** means to an end; **wherewithal,** wherewith; funds *see* 728.14; **resources,** disposable resources, capital *see* 728.15; bankroll (*informal*); stock-in-trade, stock, supply *see* 386; power, capacity, ability *see* 18.2; power base, constituency, backing, support; recourses, resorts, devices; method

3 instrumentality, agency; machinery, **mechanism,** modality; gadgetry (*informal*); mediation, going between, intermediation, service; **expedient,** recourse, resort, device *see* 994.2

4 instrument, tool, implement, appliance, device; contrivance, lever, mechanism; **vehicle, organ; agent** *see* 576; medium, mediator, intermedium, intermediary, intermediate, interagent, liaison, go-between *see* 576.4; expediter, facilitator, animator; midwife, servant, slave, handmaid, handmaiden, *ancilla* (*Latin*); **cat's-paw, puppet, dummy, pawn,** creature, minion, stooge (*informal*); stalking horse; toy, plaything; dupe *see* 358

verbs

5 to use, utilize, adopt, effect; **approach, attack;** proceed, practise, go about; routinize

6 to find means, find a way, provide *or* have the wherewithal; get by hook or by crook, obtain by fair means or foul; beg, borrow, or steal

7 to be instrumental, serve, subserve, serve one's purpose, come in handy, stand in good stead, fill the bill; minister to, act for, act in the interests of, **promote, advance, forward, assist,** facilitate; mediate, go between; liaise

adjectives

8 modal; **instrumental, implemental;** agential, agentive, agentival; **useful,** utile, handy, employable, **serviceable; helpful,** conducive, forwarding, favouring, promoting, assisting, facilitating; subservient, ministering, ministerial; mediating, mediatorial, intermediary

adverbs

9 how, in what way *or* **manner,** by what mode *or* means; to what extent; in what condition; by what name; at what price; after this fashion, in this way, in such wise, along these lines; **thus, so,** just so, thus and so; as, like, on the lines of

10 anyhow, anyway, anywise, anyroad (*informal*), in any way, **by any means, by any manner of means;** in any event, at any rate, leastways (*informal*), in any case; **nevertheless, nonetheless, however, regardless,** irregardless (*informal*); at all, nohow (*US informal*)

11 somehow, in some way, in some way or other, someway (*informal*), by some means, **somehow or other,** somehow or another, in one way or another, in some such way, after a fashion; no matter how, **by hook or by crook,** by fair means or foul

12 herewith, therewith, wherewith, wherewithal; whereby, thereby, hereby

prepositions

13 by means of, by *or* **through the agency of,** by *or* through the good offices of, through the instrumentality of, by the aid of, thanks to, by use of, **by way of,** by dint of, by the act of, through the medium of, by *or* in virtue of, at the hand of, at the hands of; **with, through, by,** per

phrases

14 it isn't what you do, it's how you do it; there's more than one way to skin a cat

385 PROVISION, EQUIPMENT

nouns

1 provision, providing; **equipment, accoutrement,** fitting out, outfitting; **supply,** supplying, finding; **furnishing,** furnishment; chandlery, **retailing, selling** *see* 734.2; **logistics;** procurement *see* 472.1; investment, endowment, subvention, subsidy, subsidization; provisioning, victualling, purveyance, catering; armament; resupply, replenishment, reinforcement; supply line, line of supply; **preparation** *see* 405

2 provisions, supplies *see* 386.1; provender *see* 10.5; merchandise *see* 735

3 accommodations, accommodation, facilities; **lodgings;** bed, board, half board, *demi-pension* (*French*), full board; **room and board,** bed and board; **subsistence,** keep, fostering

4 equipment, matériel, equipage, munitions; **furniture, furnishings,** furnishments (*old*); **fixtures, fittings,** fitments, appointments, accoutrements, appurtenances, installations, plumbing; **appliances,** utensils, **conveniences; outfit, apparatus, rig,** machinery; stock-in-trade; **plant,** facility, facilities; paraphernalia, things, **gear, stuff** (*informal*), impedimenta (*plural*), **tackle;** rigging; armament, munition; **kit,** duffel, effects, personal effects

5 harness, caparison, trappings, **tack,** tackle

6 provider, supplier, furnisher; donor *see* 478.11; patron; **purveyor,** provisioner, **caterer,** victualer, sutler (*old*); *vivandier* *or* *vivandière* (*both French*); chandler, retailer, merchant *see* 730.2; commissary, commissariat, quartermaster, storekeeper, stock clerk, steward, manciple

verbs

7 **to provide, supply,** find, **dish up** *and* **rustle up** (*both informal*), **furnish;** accommodate; invest, endow, fund, subsidize; donate, give, afford, contribute, **kick in** (*US & Australian informal*), yield, present *see* 478.12; make available; stock, store, keep; provide for, make provision *or* due provision for; prepare *see* 405.6; support, maintain, keep; fill, fill up; replenish, restock, recruit

8 **to equip, furnish, outfit,** gear, **prepare, fit,** fit up *or* out, **fix up** (*informal*), **rig,** rig up *or* out, **turn out,** appoint, accoutre, clothe, dress; arm, **heel** (*informal*), munition; man, staff

9 **to provision,** provender, cater, victual, **plenish** (*old*); provide a **grubstake** (*US informal*); **board,** feed; forage; fuel, gas, fill up, coal, oil, bunker; **purvey,** sell *see* 734.8

10 **to accommodate,** furnish accommodations; house, lodge *see* 225.10; **put up,** board

11 **to make a living,** earn a living *or* livelihood, **make** *or* **earn one's keep,** earn a crust (*informal*)

12 **to support oneself,** make one's way; **make ends meet, keep body and soul together, keep the wolf from the door,** keep *or* hold one's head above water, keep afloat; **survive, subsist, cope, eke out,** make out, scrape along, manage, get by

adjectives

13 **provided, supplied, furnished,** provisioned, purveyed, catered; invested, endowed; **equipped, fitted,** fitted out, outfitted, rigged, accoutred; armed, **heeled** (*informal*); staffed, manned; readied, in place, **prepared** *see* 405.16

14 **well-provided, well-supplied, well-furnished,** well-stocked, well-found; **well-equipped, well-fitted,** well-appointed; well-armed

386 STORE, SUPPLY

nouns

1 **store, hoard, treasure,** treasury; plenty, plenitude, abundance, cornucopia; heap, mass, stack, pile, dump, rick; **collection, accumulation,** cumulation, **amassment,** budget, **stockpile; backlog;** repertory, repertoire; stock-in-trade; **inventory, stock,** supply on hand; lock, stock and barrel; **stores, supplies, provisions,** provisionment, rations; larder, commissariat, commissary; munitions; matériel; material, materials *see* 1052

2 **supply, fund, resource, resources; means, assets,** liquid assets, balance, **pluses** (*informal*), black-ink items (*US*), **capital,** capital goods, capitalization, available means *or* resources *or* funds, cash flow, stock-in-trade; venture capital; grist, grist to the mill; holdings, property *see* 471

3 **reserve, reserves,** reservoir, resource; proved *or* proven reserve; **stockpile, cache,** backup, reserve supply, something in reserve *or* in hand, something to fall back on, reserve fund, **nest egg, savings,** sinking fund; proved reserves; backlog, unexpended

balance; **ace in the hole** (*informal*), a card up one's sleeve; spare *or* replacement part

4 **source of supply,** source, staple, resource; well, fountain, fount, font (*old*), spring, wellspring; mine, **gold mine, bonanza,** luau (*US informal*); quarry, lode, vein; oilfield, oil well, oil rig; cornucopia

5 **storage, stowage;** preservation, conservation, safekeeping, warehousing; cold storage, cold store, dry storage, dead storage; storage space, shelf-room; custody, guardianship *see* 1007.2; sequestration, escrow

6 **storehouse, storeroom,** stock room, lumber room, store, storage, **depository, repository,** conservatory (*old*), reservoir, repertory, depot, supply depot, supply base, magazine, *magasin* (*French*), warehouse, godown; bonded warehouse, entrepôt; dock; hold, cargo dock; attic, loft, cellar, basement; coal cellar, coal hole (*informal*), bunker; cupboard, closet; wine cellar, buttery, bin; **treasury,** treasure house, treasure room, exchequer; bank, vault *see* 729.12, strongroom, strongbox; **archives, library,** stack room; armoury, arsenal, dump; timberyard, lumberyard; drawer, shelf; bin, bunker, bay, crib; rack, rick; vat, tank; crate, box; chest, locker, kist (*Scottish*); bookcase, stack; sail locker, chain locker, lazaret, lazaretto, glory hole

7 **garner, granary,** grain bin, elevator, grain elevator, **silo;** mow, haymow, hayloft, hayrick, hayrack; crib, corncrib (*US*)

8 **larder, pantry,** buttery; spence, still room; root cellar; dairy, dairy house *or* room

9 **museum; gallery,** art gallery, picture gallery, pinacotheca; salon; Tate Gallery, British Museum, Louvre, National Gallery, Metropolitan Museum, Museum of Modern Art, Guggenheim Museum, Hermitage, Prado, Uffizi, Rijksmuseum; museology, curatorship

verbs

10 **to store, stow,** lay in store; **lay in,** lay in a supply *or* stock *or* store, store away, stow away, **put away, lay away,** put *or* lay by, pack away, bundle away, lay down, stow down, salt down *or* away *and* squirrel away (*all informal*); **deposit,** reposit, lodge; **cache,** stash (*informal*), bury away; **bank,** coffer, hutch (*old*); warehouse, reservoir; file, file away

11 **to store up, stock up, lay up,** put up, **save up,** hoard up, treasure up, garner up, **heap up,** pile up, build up a stock *or* an inventory; **accumulate,** cumulate, **collect, amass, stockpile;** backlog; garner, gather into barns; **hoard,** treasure, save, keep, hold, squirrel, squirrel away; hide, secrete *see* 346.7

12 **to reserve, save, conserve, keep,** retain, husband, husband one's resources, keep *or* hold back, withhold; **keep in reserve,** keep in store, keep on hand, keep by one; sequester, put in escrow; **preserve** *see* 397.7; **set** *or* **put aside,** set *or* put apart, put *or* lay *or* set by; save up, save to fall back upon, keep as a nest egg, **save for a rainy day,** provide for *or* against a rainy day

13 **to have in store** *or* **reserve,** have to fall back upon, have something to draw on, have something put by,

have something saved for a rainy day, have something up one's sleeve

adjectives

14 stored, accumulated, amassed, laid up; gathered, garnered, collected; **stockpiled; backlogged; hoarded,** treasured

15 reserved, preserved, saved, conserved, put by, kept, retained, held, withheld, held back, kept *or* held in reserve; spare

adverbs

16 in store, in stock, in supply, **on hand**

17 in reserve, back, aside, by

387 USE

nouns

1 use, employment, utilization, employ (*old*), **usage; exercise, exertion,** active use; good use; ill use, wrong use, misuse *see* 389; hard use, hard *or* rough usage; hard wear, heavy duty; **application,** appliance; expenditure, expending, using up, exhausting, dissipation, dissipating, **consumption** *see* 388

2 usage, treatment, handling, management; way *or* means of dealing; stewardship, custodianship, guardianship, care

3 utility, usefulness, usability, use, utilizability, avail, good, **serviceability, helpfulness,** functionality, profitability, applicability, availability, **practicability,** practicality, practical utility, operability, **effectiveness,** efficacy, efficiency

4 benefit, use, service, avail, profit, advantage, point, percentage (*informal*), what's in it for one (*informal*), convenience; interest, behalf, behoof; **value, worth**

5 function, use, purpose, role, part, end use, immediate purpose, ultimate purpose, operational purpose, operation; work, duty, office

6 functionalism, utilitarianism; pragmatism, pragmaticism; functional design, functional furniture *or* housing, etc

7 (*law terms*) usufruct, imperfect usufruct, perfect usufruct, right of use, user, enjoyment of property; *jus primae noctis* (*Latin*), *droit du seigneur* (*French*)

8 utilization, using, making use of, making instrumental, using as a means *or* tool; **employment,** employing; **management,** manipulation, handling, working, operation, **exploitation,** recruiting, recruitment, calling upon, calling into service; mobilization, mobilizing

9 user, employer; **consumer,** enjoyer

verbs

10 to use, utilize, make use of, do with; **employ,** practise, ply, work, manage, handle, manipulate, operate, **wield,** play; **have** *or* **enjoy the use of;** exercise, **exert**

11 to apply, put to use *or* **good use,** carry out, put into execution, **put into practice** *or* **operation,** put in force, enforce; bring to bear upon

12 to treat, handle, manage, use, **deal with,** cope

with, come to grips with, take on, tackle (*informal*), contend with, do with; steward, care for

13 to spend, consume, expend, **pass,** employ, **put in;** devote, bestow, give to *or* give over to, devote *or* consecrate *or* dedicate to; while, while away, wile; dissipate, **exhaust, use up**

14 to avail oneself of, make use of, resort to, put to use *or* **good use,** have recourse to, **turn to,** look to, recur to, refer to, take to (*informal*), betake oneself to; revert to, fall back on *or* upon; convert *or* turn to use, put in *or* into requisition, press *or* enlist into service, lay under contribution, impress, **call upon,** call *or* bring into play, draw on *or* upon, recruit, muster

15 to take advantage of, avail oneself of, **make the most of,** use to the full, make good use of, improve, **turn to use** *or* **profit** *or* **account** *or* **good account,** turn to advantage *or* good advantage, use to advantage, put to advantage, find one's account *or* advantage in; improve the occasion *see* 842.8; profit by, **benefit from,** reap the benefit of; **exploit, capitalize on, make capital of,** make a good thing of (*informal*), make hay (*informal*), **trade on,** cash in on (*informal*); make the best of, make a virtue of necessity,

"make necessity a virtue"—QUINTILIAN

16 (*take unfair advantage of*) to exploit, take advantage of, use, make use of, **use for one's own ends; manipulate,** work on, work upon, stroke (*US*), play on *or* upon; play both ends against the middle; **impose upon,** presume upon; use ill, ill-use, abuse, misuse *see* 389.4; batten on; milk, bleed, bleed white (*informal*); drain, suck the blood of *or* from, suck dry; exploit one's position, feather one's nest (*informal*), **profiteer**

17 to avail, be of use, be of service, serve, **suffice, do,** answer, **answer** *or* **serve one's purpose,** serve one's need, fill the bill *and* do the trick (*both informal*); bestead (*old*), **stand one in stead** *or* **good stead,** be handy; advantage, be of advantage *or* service to; **profit, benefit,** pay *and* pay off (*both informal*), give good returns, yield a profit

adjectives

18 useful, employable, of use, of service, **serviceable,** commodious (*old*); good for; **helpful,** of help *see* 449.21; **advantageous, to one's advantage** *or* **profit, profitable,** remunerative, beneficial *see* 998.12; **practical,** banausic, pragmatical, **functional, utilitarian,** of general utility *or* application; fitting, proper, appropriate, expedient *see* 994.5; well-used, well-thumbed

19 using, exploitive, exploitative, manipulative, manipulatory

20 handy, convenient; available, accessible, **ready, at hand,** to hand, **on hand,** on tap, on call, at one's call *or* beck and call, at one's elbow, at one's fingertips, just around the corner, at one's disposal; versatile, adaptable, all-round, general-purpose, all-purpose; crude but effective, quick and dirty (*informal*)

21 effectual, effective, active, efficient, efficacious, operative

22 valuable, of value, all for the best, all to the good, **profitable,** yielding a return, well-spent, **worthwhile,** rewarding; gainful, remunerative

23 usable, utilizable; applicable, appliable; practical, operable; **reusable; exploitable;** manipulable, pliable, compliant *see* 433.12

24 used, employed, exercised, exerted, **applied;** previously owned, secondhand *see* 841.18

25 in use, in practice, in force, in effect, in service, in operation, in commission

adverbs

26 usefully, to good use; **profitably, advantageously, to advantage,** to profit, to good effect; effectually, effectively, efficiently; serviceably, functionally, **practically;** handily, conveniently; by use of, by dint of

388 CONSUMPTION

nouns

1 consumption, consuming, using *or* **eating up;** burning up; absorption, assimilation, digestion, ingestion, **expenditure,** expending, spending; squandering, wastefulness *see* 486.1; finishing; **depletion,** drain, exhausting, **exhaustion,** impoverishment; **waste,** wastage, wasting away, erosion, ablation, wearing down, wearing away, attrition; throwing away

2 consumable, consumable item *or* **goods;** nonrenewable *or* nonreusable *or* nonrecyclable item *or* resource; **throwaway,** throwaway item, disposable goods *or* item; throwaway society *or* culture, instant obsolescence

verbs

3 to consume, spend, expend, use up; absorb, assimilate, digest, ingest, eat, **eat up,** swallow, swallow up, gobble, gobble up; burn up; **finish,** finish off; **exhaust, deplete,** impoverish, drain, drain of resources; suck dry, bleed white (*informal*), suck one's blood; wear away, erode, erode away, ablate; waste away; **throw away, squander** *see* 486.3

4 to be consumed, be used up, waste; **run out, give out,** peter out (*informal*); run dry, dry up

adjectives

5 used up, consumed, eaten up, burnt up; finished, gone; unreclaimable, irreplaceable; nonrenewable, nonrecyclable, nonreusable; **spent,** exhausted, effete, dissipated, depleted, impoverished, drained, worn-out; worn away, eroded, ablated; **wasted** *see* 486.9

6 consumable, expendable, spendable; exhaustible; replaceable; disposable, throwaway, no-deposit, no-deposit-no-return

389 MISUSE

nouns

1 misuse, misusage, abuse; misemployment, misapplication; mishandling, mismanagement, poor stewardship; corrupt administration, malversation, breach of public trust, maladministration; diversion, defalcation,

misappropriation, conversion, **embezzlement,** peculation, pilfering; perversion, prostitution; profanation, violation, pollution, fouling, befoulment, desecration, defilement, debasement; malpractice, abuse of office, misconduct, malfeasance, misfeasance

2 mistreatment, ill-treatment, maltreatment, ill-use, ill-usage, **abuse; molesting, molestation,** child abuse *or* molestation; **violation,** outrage, violence, injury, atrocity; cruel and unusual punishment

3 persecution, oppression, harrying, hounding, tormenting, bashing (*informal*), harassment, sexual harassment, victimization; **witch-hunting,** witch-hunt, McCarthyism; open season, piling on (*US informal*)

verbs

4 to misuse, misemploy, abuse, misapply; mishandle, mismanage, maladminister; divert, misappropriate, convert, defalcate, embezzle, pilfer, peculate, feather one's nest (*informal*); pervert, prostitute; profane, violate, pollute, foul, foul one's own nest, befoul, desecrate, defile, debase

5 to mistreat, maltreat, ill-treat, ill-use, abuse, injure, **molest;** do wrong to, do wrong by; outrage, do violence to, do one's worst to; mishandle, manhandle; buffet, batter, bruise, **savage,** manhandle, maul, knock about, rough, rough up

6 (*informal terms*) **to screw,** shaft, stiff, give the short *or* the shitty end of the stick, fuck, fuck over

7 to persecute, oppress, **torment,** victimize, play cat and mouse with, **harass,** keep after, get at, harry, hound, beset; pursue, hunt

adverbs

8 on one's back *and* on one's case *and* in one's face (*all informal*)

390 DISUSE

nouns

1 disuse, disusage, desuetude; **nonuse, nonemployment; abstinence, abstention;** nonprevalence, unprevalence; **obsolescence,** obsoleteness, obsoletism, obsoletion, planned obsolescence; superannuation, retirement, pensioning off

2 discontinuance, cessation, desisting, desistance; **abdication,** relinquishment, forbearance, resignation, renunciation, renouncement, abjurement, abjuration; waiver, nonexercise; abeyance, suspension, back burner *and* cold storage (*all informal*); **phaseout, abandonment** *see* 370

3 discard, discarding, jettison, deep six (*US informal*), disposal, dumping, **waste disposal,** solid waste disposal, burning, incineration, ocean burning *or* incineration; compacting; **scrapping, junking** (*informal*); removal, elimination *see* 772.2; **rejection** *see* 372; **reject,** throwaway, castaway, castoff, rejectamenta (*plural*); **refuse** *see* 391.4

verbs

4 to cease to use; abdicate, relinquish; **discontinue, disuse,** quit, stop, drop (*informal*), give up, give over, lay off (*informal*), **phase out,** phase down, put behind one, let go, leave off, come off (*informal*), cut out, desist, desist from, have done with; waive, resign, renounce, abjure; not pursue *or* proceed with

5 **to not use, do without,** dispense with, **let alone,** not touch, hold off; **abstain, refrain,** forgo, forbear, spare, waive; keep *or* hold back, reserve, save, save up, put by, squirrel away, tuck away, put under the mattress, hoard; keep in hand, have up one's sleeve; see the last of

6 **to put away,** lay away, **put aside,** lay *or* set *or* wave *or* cast *or* push aside, sideline (*informal*); stow, store *see* 386.10; **pigeonhole, shelve,** put on the shelf, put in mothballs; **table,** lay on the table; put on hold *or* on the back burner (*informal*), postpone, delay *see* 845.8

7 **to discard, reject, throw away, throw out,** chuck *or* chuck away (*both informal*), cast, cast off *or* away *or* aside; **get rid of,** get quit of, get shut of (*informal*), rid oneself of, shrug off, **dispose of,** slough, tip, **dump, ditch** (*informal*), tip, **jettison, throw** *or* **heave** *or* **toss overboard,** deep-six (*US informal*), throw out the window, throw *or* cast to the dogs, cast to the winds; sell off *or* out; throw over, jilt; part with, give away; throw to the wolves, write off, walk away from, **abandon** *see* 370.5; remove, **eliminate** *see* 772.5

8 **to scrap, junk** (*informal*), consign to the scrap heap, throw on the junk heap (*informal*); superannuate, retire, pension off, put out to pasture *or* grass

9 **to obsolesce,** fall into disuse, go out, pass away; be superseded; superannuate

adjectives

10 **disused, abandoned,** deserted, **discontinued,** done with; out, **out of use;** old; relinquished, resigned, renounced, abjured; **outworn,** worn-out, past use, not worth saving; **obsolete,** obsolescent, life-expired, superannuated, superannuate; superseded, outdated, out-of-date, outmoded, desuete; retired, pensioned off; on the shelf; antique, antiquated, old-fashioned, old

11 **discarded,** rejected, **castoff,** castaway

12 **unused,** unutilized, **unemployed,** unapplied, unexercised; in abeyance, suspended; waived; **unspent,** unexpended, unconsumed; held back, held out, put by, put aside, saved, held in reserve, in hand, spare, to spare, extra, reserve; stored *see* 386.14; untouched, unhandled; untapped; untrodden, unbeaten; **new,** brand-new, original, pristine, fresh, fresh off the assembly line, mint, in mint condition, factory-fresh, split-new (*Scottish*)

391 USELESSNESS

nouns

1 **uselessness,** inutility; **needlessness,** unnecessity; unserviceability, **unusability,** unemployability, inoperativeness, inoperability, disrepair; unhelpfulness; inapplicability, unsuitability, unfitness; functionlessness; otioseness, otiosity; **superfluousness** *see* 992.4

2 **futility,** vanity, emptiness, hollowness; **fruitlessness,** bootlessness, unprofitableness, profitlessness, unprofitability, otiosity, worthlessness, valuelessness; triviality, nugacity, nugaciousness; unproductiveness *see* 890; **ineffectuality,** ineffectiveness, inefficacy *see* 19.3; **impotence** *see* 19.1; **pointlessness,** meaninglessness, purposelessness, aimlessness, fecklessness; the absurd, absurdity; inanity, fatuity; vicious circle *or* cycle; **rat race** (*informal*)

3 **labour in vain,** labour lost, labour for naught; labour of Sisyphus, work of Penelope, Penelope's web; **wild-goose chase,** fool's errand; waste of labour, waste of breath, waste of time, wasted effort, wasted breath, wasted labour

4 **refuse, waste,** wastage, waste matter, waste product, solid waste, liquid waste, wastewater, effluent, muck, sewage, sludge; incinerator ash; industrial waste, hazardous waste, toxic waste, atomic waste; medical waste; **offal; leavings,** sweepings, dust, **scraps,** orts (*old*); **garbage,** swill, pig-swill, slop, slops, hogwash (*informal*); bilgewater; draff, lees, **dregs** *see* 256.2; scourings, rinsings, dishwater; parings, raspings, filings, shavings; **scum;** chaff, stubble, husks; weeds, tares; deadwood; rags, bones, wastepaper, shard, potsherd; scrap iron; dross; slag, culm, slack

5 **rubbish, rubble, trash, junk,** riffraff, **scrap,** dust, **debris, litter,** truck (*informal*)

6 **rubbish heap,** junkheap (*informal*), scrap heap, dustheap, midden, kitchen midden; **dump, rubbish dump,** rubbish tip, scrapyard, coup (*Scottish*), junkyard, dumpsite, landfill, sanitary landfill, toxic waste dump

7 wastepaper basket, wastebasket; litter basket, litter bin; **dustbin,** wheelie bin, wastebin, trash can, garbage can; skip, dumpster (*US*); **waste disposal unit,** trash compactor (*US*)

verbs

8 **to be useless, be futile, make no difference, cut no ice; labour in vain,** go on a wild-goose chase *or* fool's errand, run in circles, go around in circles, bang one's head against a brick wall (*informal*), tilt at windmills, bay at the moon, waste one's breath, flog a dead horse, roll the stone of Sisyphus, carry coals to Newcastle, pour water into a sieve, hold a farthing candle to the sun, look for a needle in a haystack, lock the stable door after the horse has bolted

adjectives

9 **useless,** of no use, no go (*informal*); **aimless, meaningless, purposeless,** of no purpose, **pointless,** feckless; **unavailing,** of no avail, failed; ineffective, **ineffectual** *see* 19.15; impotent *see* 19.13; **superfluous** *see* 992.17

10 **needless, unnecessary, unessential,** nonessential, **unneeded, uncalled-for,** unrequired; unrecognized, neglected,
"born to blush unseen"—THOMAS GRAY

11 **worthless, valueless, good-for-nothing,** good-for-naught, no-good (*informal*), no-account (*informal*), dear at any price, not worth a damn *or* a tinker's cuss (*informal*), not worthwhile, not worth having,

not worth mentioning *or* speaking of, not worth a thought, not worth the powder and shot, not worth the pains *or* the trouble, of no earthly use; trivial, tuppeny-ha'penny (*informal*), nugatory, nugacious; **cheap**, shoddy, trashy, **shabby**, low-rent

12 **fruitless**, gainless, profitless, bootless, otiose, **unprofitable**, unremunerative, nonremunerative; uncommercial; **unrewarding**, rewardless; abortive; barren, sterile, unproductive *see* 890.4

13 **vain**, **futile**, hollow, empty,

"weary, stale, flat, and unprofitable"—Shakespeare, idle; absurd; inane, fatuous, fatuitous

14 **unserviceable**, **unusable**, unemployable, inoperative, inoperable, unworkable; out of order, on the blink (*informal*), in disrepair; **unhelpful**, unconducive; inapplicable; unsuitable, unfit; functionless, nonfunctional, otiose, nonutilitarian

adverbs

15 **uselessly**; **needlessly**, unnecessarily; bootlessly, fruitlessly, **futilely**, **vainly**; purposelessly, to little purpose, to no purpose, **aimlessly**, **pointlessly**, fecklessly

392 IMPROVEMENT

nouns

1 **improvement**, **betterment**, bettering, change for the better; melioration, **amelioration**; **mend**, mending, **amendment**; **progress**, progression, headway; breakthrough, quantum leap; **advance**, advancement; upward mobility; **promotion**, **furtherance**, preferment; **rise**, ascent, **lift**, **uplift**, uptick (*informal*), upswing, uptrend, upbeat; **increase** *see* 251, upgrade; gentrification; **enhancement**, **enrichment**; euthenics, eugenics; **restoration**, revival, retro, recovery

2 **development**, **refinement**, elaboration, **perfection**; beautification, embellishment; maturation, coming of age, ripening, evolution, seasoning

3 **cultivation**, **culture**, **refinement**, **polish**, civility; cultivation of the mind; **civilization**; acculturation; enculturation, socialization; enlightenment, education *see* 927.4

4 **revision**, revise, revisal; revised edition; **emendation**, **amendment**, **correction**, **corrigenda**, **rectification**; editing, redaction, recension, revampment; **rewrite**, rewriting, rescript, rescription (*old*); **polishing**, touching up, putting the finishing touches to, putting the gloss on, finishing, perfecting, tuning, fine-tuning; retrofitting

5 **reform**, **reformation**; regeneration *see* 857.2; **transformation**; **conversion** *see* 857; reformism, meliorism; gradualism, Fabianism, revisionism; utopianism; progressiveness, progressivism, progressism; radical reform, extremism, radicalism *see* 611.5; revolution *see* 859

6 **reformer**, reformist, meliorist; gradualist, Fabian, revisionist; utopian, utopist; progressive, progressivist, progressionist, progressist; radical, extremist *see* 611.17; revolutionary *see* 859.3

verbs

7 (*get better*) **to improve**, **grow better**, look better, show improvement, pull one's socks up (*informal*), **mend**, amend (*old*), meliorate, ameliorate; **look up** *or* **pick up** *or* **perk up** (*all informal*); **develop**, shape up; **advance**, **progress**, **make progress**, **make headway**, **gain**, gain ground, go forward, get *or* go ahead, come on, come along *and* come along nicely (*both informal*), get along; make strides *or* rapid strides, take off (*informal*), make up for lost time; graduate

8 **to rally**, come about *or* round, get over (*informal*), take a turn for the better, gain strength; come a long way (*informal*); **recuperate**, **recover** *see* 396.20

9 **to improve**, **better**, change for the better, make an improvement; transform, transfigure; improve upon, refine upon, **mend**, **amend**, emend; meliorate, **ameliorate**; **advance**, **promote**, foster, favour, nurture, forward, bring forward; **lift**, elevate, **uplift**, raise, boost (*informal*); upgrade; gentrify; **enhance**, **enrich**, fatten, lard (*old*); make one's way, better oneself; be the making of; **reform**, put *or* set straight; reform oneself, turn over a new leaf, mend one's ways, straighten out, straighten oneself out, go straight (*informal*); get it together (*informal*); **civilize**, acculturate, socialize; enlighten, edify; **educate**

10 **to develop**, elaborate; beautify, embellish; **cultivate**; come of age, come into its own, mature, ripen, evolve, season

11 **to perfect**, **touch up**, finish, put on the finishing touches, polish, fine-tune (*informal*), tone up, **brush up**, **refurbish**, furbish, furbish up, spruce, **spruce up**, freshen, vamp, vamp up, rub up, brighten up, polish, polish up, shine (*informal*); retouch; **revive**, **renovate** *see* 396.17, 17; **repair**, fix *see* 396.14; retrofit

12 **to revise**, redact, recense, **revamp**, **rewrite**, redraft, **rework**, work over; **emend**, **amend**, emendate, **rectify**, correct; edit, blue-pencil

adjectives

13 **improved**, **bettered**; changed for the better, advanced, ameliorated, enhanced, enriched; developed, perfected; beautified, embellished; upgraded; gentrified; **reformed**; **transformed**, transfigured, converted; **cultivated**, cultured, **refined**, polished, civilized; **educated** *see* 927.18

14 **better**, better off, better for, all the better for; before-and-after

15 **improving**, **bettering**; meliorative, ameliorative, amelioratory; **progressive**, progressing, advancing, ongoing; mending, **on the mend**; on the up (*informal*), looking up (*informal*)

16 **emendatory**, **corrective**; revisory, revisional; reformatory, reformative, reformational; **reformist**, reformistic, progressive, progressivist, melioristic; gradualistic, Fabian, revisionist; utopian; radical *see* 611.29; revolutionary *see* 859.5

17 **improvable**, ameliorable, corrigible, revisable, perfectible; **emendable** *see* 396.25

393 IMPAIRMENT

nouns

1 **impairment, damage, injury, harm,** mischief, scathe (*old*), **hurt, detriment,** loss, weakening, sickening; **worsening,** disimprovement; disablement, incapacitation; encroachment, inroad, infringement *see* 214.1; **disrepair, dilapidation,** ruinousness; breakage; **breakdown, collapse,** crack-up (*informal*); **malfunction, glitch** (*informal*); bankruptcy; hurting, spoiling, ruination; sabotage, monkey-wrenching (*US informal*); mayhem, mutilation, crippling, hobbling, hamstringing, laming, maiming; destruction *see* 395

2 **corruption, pollution, contamination,** vitiation, **defilement,** fouling, befouling; **poisoning,** envenoming; infection, festering, suppuration; **perversion,** prostitution, misuse *see* 389; denaturing, adulteration

3 **deterioration, decadence, degradation, debasement,** derogation, deformation; **degeneration,** degeneracy, degenerateness, effeteness; etiolation, loss of tone, failure of nerve; depravation, depravedness; **retrogression,** retrogradation, retrocession, **regression;** devolution, involution; demotion *see* 447; downward mobility; **decline,** declination, declension, comedown, **descent,** downtrend, downward trend, downturn, depreciation, **decrease** *see* 252, **drop, fall, plunge,** free-fall, falling-off, lessening, slippage, slump, lapse, fading, dying, failing, failure, wane, ebb

4 **waste, wastage, consumption;** withering, wasting, wasting away, atrophy, wilting, marcescence; emaciation *see* 270.6

5 **wear,** use, hard wear; **wear and tear; erosion, weathering,** ablation, ravages of time

6 **decay, decomposition, disintegration, dissolution,** resolution, degradation, biodegradation, breakup, disorganization, **corruption, spoilage, dilapidation;** corrosion, oxidation, oxidization, rust; mildew, mould *see* 1000.2; degradability, biodegradability

7 **rot, rottenness, foulness, putridness,** putridity, rancidness, rancidity, rankness, **putrefaction,** putrescence, spoilage, decay, decomposition; carrion; dry rot, wet rot

8 **wreck, ruins, ruin, total loss;** hulk, carcass, skeleton; mere wreck, wreck of one's former self; nervous wreck; rattletrap

verbs

9 **to impair, damage,** endamage, **injure, harm, hurt,** irritate; **worsen,** make worse, disimprove, deteriorate, put *or* set back, aggravate, exacerbate, embitter; **weaken; dilapidate;** add insult to injury, rub salt in the wound

10 **to spoil, mar,** botch, **ruin, wreck,** blight, **play havoc with;** destroy *see* 395.10

11 (*informal terms*) **to screw up, foul up,** fuck up, cock up, snafu, snarl up, balls up, bugger, bugger up, gum up, bollocks up, **mess up,** hash up, muck up; play hell with, play merry hell with, play the devil with; upset the apple cart, shoot down in flames

12 **to corrupt, debase, degrade, degenerate, deprave, debauch, defile,** violate, desecrate, deflower, ravish, ravage, despoil; **contaminate,** confound, **pollute, vitiate, poison,** infect, **taint;** canker, ulcerate; **pervert,** warp, twist, distort; prostitute, misuse *see* 389.4; denature; **cheapen,** devalue; coarsen, vulgarize, drag in the mud; adulterate, alloy, water, water down

13 (*inflict an injury*) **to injure, hurt;** draw blood, wound; **traumatize;** stab, stick, pierce, puncture; cut, incise, slit, slash, gash, scratch; abrade, eat away at, scuff, scrape, chafe, fret, gall, bark, skin; break, fracture, rupture; crack, chip, craze, check; lacerate, claw, tear, rip, rend; run; frazzle, fray; burn, scorch, scald; mutilate, maim, rough up (*informal*), make mincemeat of, maul, beat up, batter, savage, sort out (*informal*), fill in (*informal*); sprain, strain, wrench; bloody; **blemish** *see* 1003.4; **bruise, contuse;** batter, bash (*informal*), maul, pound, beat, beat black and blue; give a black eye

14 **to cripple, lame, maim; hamstring,** hobble; wing; emasculate, castrate; incapacitate, **disable** *see* 19.9

15 **to undermine,** sap, mine, honeycomb; sabotage, throw a spanner in the works (*informal*), subvert

16 **to deteriorate, sicken, worsen, get worse,** get no better fast (*informal*), disimprove, **degenerate;** slip back, **retrogress,** retrograde, regress, relapse, fall back; jump the track; go to the bad *see* 395.24; let oneself go, let down, slacken; be the worse for, be the worse for wear *and* have seen better days (*both informal*)

17 **to decline, sink, fail, fall,** slip, fade, die, wane, ebb, subside, lapse, **run down,** go down, **go downhill, fall away, fall off,** go off (*informal*), slide, slump, hit a slump, take a nose dive (*informal*), go into a tailspin, take a turn for the worse; hit the skids (*informal*); reach the depths, hit *or* touch bottom, hit rock bottom, have no lower to go

18 **to languish, pine, droop, flag, wilt; fade,** fade away; **wither, shrivel,** shrink, diminish, wither *or* die on the vine, **dry up,** desiccate, wizen, wrinkle, sear; "fall'n into the sere, the yellow leaf"—SHAKESPEARE

19 **to waste, waste away, wither away,** atrophy, consume, consume away, erode away, emaciate, pine away; trickle *or* dribble away; run to waste, run to seed

20 **to wear, wear away, wear down, wear off;** abrade, fret, whittle away, rub off; fray, frazzle, tatter, wear ragged; **wear out;** weather, erode, ablate

21 **to corrode, erode,** eat, gnaw, eat into, eat away, nibble away, gnaw at the root of; canker, **oxidize, rust**

22 **to decay, decompose, disintegrate;** go *or* fall into decay, go *or* fall to pieces, break up, crumble, crumble into dust; **spoil, corrupt,** canker, **go bad; rot, putrefy,** go off (*informal*), putresce; fester, suppurate, rankle (*informal*); **mortify,** necrose, gangrene, sphacelate; mould, moulder, moulder away, rot away, rust away, mildew

23 **to break, break up,** fracture, **come apart,** come unstuck, **come** *or* **fall to pieces, fall apart, disintegrate;** burst, rupture; crack, split, fissure; snap; break open, give way *or* away, start, spring a

leak, come apart at the seams, come unstuck (*informal*)

24 to break down, founder, collapse; crash (*informal*), cave *or* fall in, come crashing *or* tumbling down, topple, topple down *or* over; totter, sway

25 to get out of order, malfunction, get out of gear; get out of joint; go wrong

26 (*informal terms*) **to get out of kilter, go kaput, go on the blink, go haywire,** give out, **break down,** pack up, play up, conk out

adjectives

27 impaired, damaged, hurt, injured, harmed, crocked (*informal*); **deteriorated, worsened,** cut to the quick, aggravated, exacerbated, irritated, embittered; weakened; **worse,** worse off, the worse for, all the worse for; imperfect; lacerated, mangled, cut, split, rent, torn, slit, slashed, mutilated, chewed-up; **broken** *see* 801.24, **shattered, smashed,** in bits, in pieces, in shards, burst, busted (*informal*), ruptured, sprung; cracked, chipped, crazed, checked; burned, scorched, scalded; **damaging, injurious,** traumatic, degenerative

28 spoiled *or* spoilt, **marred,** botched, blighted, **ruined,** wrecked; **destroyed** *see* 395.28

29 (*informal terms*) **screwed up, fouled up,** loused up, snafued, buggered, buggered up, gummed up, snarled up, ballsed up, bollocksed up, **messed up,** hashed up, mucked up, botched up; beat-up, clapped-out; kaput, finished, packed-up, done for, sunk

30 crippled, game (*informal*), bad, handicapped, maimed; **lame, halt,** halting, hobbling, limping; knee-sprung; hamstrung; spavined; **disabled, incapacitated;** emasculated, castrated

31 worn, well-worn, deep-worn, worn-down, the worse for wear, dog-eared; timeworn; shopworn, shopsoiled, shelfworn; worn to the stump, worn to the bone; **worn ragged,** worn to rags, worn to threads; **threadbare,** bare

32 shabby, shoddy, seedy, scruffy, **tacky** (*informal*), dowdy, tatty, ratty; holey, full of holes; ragged, **tattered, torn;** patchy; **frayed, frazzled;** in rags, in tatters, in shreds; **out at the elbows,** out at the heels, down-at-heel

33 dilapidated, ramshackle, decrepit, shacky, tottery, slummy (*informal*), **tumbledown, broken-down, run-down,** clapped-out, in ruins, ruinous, ruined, derelict, gone to wrack and ruin, the worse for wear; **battered,** beaten up, **beat-up** (*informal*)

34 weatherworn, weather-beaten, weathered, weather-battered, weather-wasted, weather-eaten, weather-bitten, weather-scarred; eroded; **faded,** washed-out, bleached, blanched, etiolated

35 wasted, atrophied, shrunken; **withered,** sere, shrivelled, wilted, wizened, dried-up, desiccated; wrinkled, wrinkled like a prune; brittle, papery, parchmenty; **emaciated** *see* 270.20; starved, worn to a shadow, reduced to a skeleton, skin and bones, "worn to the bones"—Shakespeare

36 worn-out, used up (*informal*), worn to a frazzle, frazzled, fit for the dust hole *or* wastepaper basket; **exhausted, tired,** fatigued, knackered (*informal*), pooped (*informal*), **spent,** effete, etiolated, played

out, *ausgespielt* (*German*), jaded, emptied, done *and* done up (*both informal*); **run-down,** dragged-out (*informal*), laid low, at a low ebb, in a bad way, far-gone, on one's last legs

37 in disrepair, out of order, malfunctioning, out of working order, out of condition, out of repair, inoperative; out of gear; out of joint; **broken** *see* 801.24

38 (*informal terms*) **out of kilter** *or* **sync,** out of commission, on the fritz, on the blink, haywire, wonky

39 putrefactive, putrefacient, rotting; **septic;** saprogenic, saprogenous; saprophilous, saprophytic, saprobic

40 decayed, decomposed; spoiled, corrupt, peccant, bad, **gone bad; rotten,** rotting, putrid, **putrefied, foul;** putrescent, **mortified,** necrosed, necrotic, sphacelated, gangrened, gangrenous, carious; cankered, ulcerated, festering, suppurating, suppurative; rotten at *or* to the core

41 tainted, off, blown; **stale; sour,** soured, turned; **rank, rancid,** strong (*informal*), **high,** gamy

42 blighted, blasted, ravaged, despoiled; blown, flyblown, wormy, weevily, maggoty; **moth-eaten, worm-eaten; mouldy,** mouldering, mildewed, smutty, smutted; **musty, fusty,** frowsty

43 corroded, eroded, eaten; **rusty,** rust-eaten, rust-worn, rust-cankered

44 corrupting, corruptive; corrosive, corroding; erosive, eroding, **damaging, injurious** *see* 999.12; pollutive

45 deteriorating, worsening, disintegrating, coming apart *or* unstuck, crumbling, cracking, fragmenting, going to pieces; **decadent, degenerate,** effete; **retrogressive,** retrograde, regressive, from better to worse; **declining, sinking, failing,** falling, waning, subsiding, **slipping,** sliding, slumping; **languishing, pining,** drooping, flagging, wilting; ebbing, draining, dwindling; **wasting,** fading, fading fast, **withering,** shrivelling; tabetic, marcescent

46 on the wane, on the decline, on the downgrade, on the downward track, on the skids (*informal*); tottering, nodding to its fall, on the way out

47 degradable, biodegradable, decomposable, putrefiable, putrescible

adverbs

48 out of the frying pan into the fire, from better to worse; for the worse

394 RELAPSE

nouns

1 relapse, lapse, falling back; **reversion, regression** *see* 858.1; **reverse, reversal,** backward deviation, devolution, **setback,** backset; **return,** recurrence, renewal, recrudescence; throwback, atavism

2 backsliding, backslide; **fall,** fall from grace; recidivism, recidivation; apostasy *see* 363.2

3 backslider, recidivist, reversionist; apostate *see* 363.5

verbs

4 to relapse, lapse, backslide, slide back, lapse back, **slip back, sink back, fall back,** have a relapse, devolve, **return to, revert to,** recur to, yield again to, fall again into, recidivate; revert, **regress** *see* 858.4; **fall, fall from grace**

adjectives

5 **relapsing, lapsing, lapsarian, backsliding,** recidivous; **recrudescent; regressive** *see* 858.7; apostate *see* 363.11

395 DESTRUCTION

nouns

1 **destruction, ruin, ruination,** rack, **rack and ruin,** blue ruin (*informal*); perdition, damnation, eternal damnation; universal ruin; **wreck;** devastation, ravage, havoc, holocaust, firestorm, hecatomb, carnage, shambles, slaughter, bloodbath, **desolation; waste, consumption;** decimation; **dissolution, disintegration,** breakup, disruption, disorganization, undoing, lysis; vandalism, depredation, spoliation, despoliation, despoilment; the road to ruin *or* wrack and ruin

2 **end, fate, doom,** death, death knell, bane, deathblow, death warrant, *coup de grâce* (*French*), final blow, quietus, cutoff

3 **fall, downfall,** prostration; **overthrow, overturn, upset, upheaval,** *bouleversement* (*French*); convulsion, **subversion,** sabotage, throwing a spanner in the works, monkey-wrenching (*US informal*)

4 **debacle, disaster, cataclysm, catastrophe; breakup,** breaking up; **breakdown, collapse; crash,** smash, **smashup,** crack-up (*informal*); **wreck,** wrack, shipwreck; cave-in, cave; washout; total loss

5 **demolition,** demolishment; **wrecking,** wreckage, levelling, razing, flattening, smashing, tearing down, bringing to the ground; **dismantlement,** disassembly, unmaking

6 **extinction, extermination, elimination, eradication,** extirpation; rooting out, deracination, uprooting, tearing up root and branch; **annihilation,** extinguishment, **snuffing out; abolition,** abolishment; annulment, **nullification,** voiding, **negation; liquidation, purge; suppression;** choking, choking off, suffocation, stifling, strangulation; silencing

7 **obliteration, erasure, effacement,** expunction, blot (*old*), blotting, **blotting out, wiping out;** washing out *and* scrubbing (*both informal*), cancellation, cancel; deletion

8 **destroyer, ruiner, wrecker, bane,** wiper-out, demolisher; **vandal,** hun; exterminator, annihilator; **iconoclast,** idoloclast, idol breaker; biblioclast; nihilist; terrorist, syndicalist; **bomber,** dynamiter, dynamitard; burner, arsonist

9 **eradicator,** expunger; eraser, **rubber,** India rubber, sponge

verbs

10 **to destroy,** deal *or* unleash destruction, unleash the hurricane, nuke (*informal*); **ruin,** ruinate (*informal*), bring to ruin, lay in ruins; throw into disorder, upheave; **wreck,** wrack, shipwreck; damn, seal the doom of, **condemn,** confound; **devastate, desolate,** waste, **lay waste, ravage,** havoc, wreak havoc, despoil, depredate; vandalize; **decimate;** devour, consume, engorge, gobble, gobble up, swallow up; gut, gut with fire, incinerate, vaporize, ravage with fire and sword; dissolve, lyse

11 **to do for, fix** (*informal*), settle, sink, cook one's goose *and* cut one down to size *and* cut one off at the knees *and* pull the plug on *and* pull the rug out from under (*all informal*), scuttle, scupper, put the kibosh on *and* put the skids under (*both informal*), do in, **undo,** knock on the head, poleaxe, torpedo, knock out, KO *and* banjax (*both informal*), deal a knockout blow to, zap *and* shoot down *and* shoot down in flames (*all informal*); break the back of; make short work of; **defeat** *see* 412.6

12 **to put an end to,** make an end of, **end, finish,** finish off (*informal*), put paid to, give the *coup de grâce* (*French*), to, give the quietus to, deal a deathblow to, dispose of, get rid of, do in, do away with; cut off, take off, be the death of, sound the death knell of; put out of the way, put out of existence, **slaughter,** put to the sword, make away with, waste *and* blow away (*both informal*), kill off, strike down, **kill** *see* 308.13; nip, nip in the bud *or* head; cut short

13 **to abolish, nullify,** void, abrogate, annihilate, annul, tear up, repeal, revoke, negate, negative, invalidate, **undo, cancel,** cancel out, bring to naught, put *or* lay to rest

14 **to exterminate, eliminate, eradicate,** deracinate, **extirpate, annihilate; wipe out** (*informal*); cut out, root up *or* out, uproot, pull *or* pluck up by the roots, cut up root and branch, strike at the root of, lay the axe to the root of; **liquidate, purge;** remove, sweep away, wash away

15 **to extinguish, quench, snuff out,** put out, stamp *or* trample out, trample underfoot; **smother,** choke, stifle, strangle, suffocate; silence; **suppress, quash,** squash *and* squelch (*both informal*), **quell,** put down

16 **to obliterate, expunge, efface, erase,** raze (*old*), blot, sponge, **wipe out,** wipe off the map, rub out, **blot out,** sponge out, wash away; cancel, strike out, cross out, scratch, scratch out, rule out; blue-pencil; delete, kill

17 **to demolish, wreck,** undo, unbuild, unmake, **dismantle, disassemble; take apart, tear apart, tear asunder, rend,** take *or* pull *or* pick *or* tear **to pieces,** pull in pieces, tear to shreds *or* rags *or* tatters; sunder, cleave, **split; disintegrate, fragment,** break to pieces, make mincemeat of, reduce to rubble, atomize, pulverize, **smash,** shatter *see* 801.13

18 **to blow up,** blast, spring, explode, blow to pieces *or* bits *or* smithereens *or* kingdom come, bomb, bombard, blitz; mine; self-destruct

19 **to raze, fell, level,** flatten, smash, prostrate, raze to the ground *or* dust; steamroller, bulldoze; **pull down, tear down, take down,** bring down, bring down about one's ears, bring tumbling *or* crashing down, break down, throw down, cast down, beat down, knock down *or* over; cut down, chop down, mow down; blow down; burn down

20 to overthrow, overturn; **upset**, overset, upend, **subvert**, throw down *or* over; undermine, honeycomb, **sap**, **weaken**

21 to overwhelm, whelm, swamp, engulf; inundate

22 (*be destroyed*) to fall, fall to the ground, tumble, come tumbling *or* crashing down, topple, tremble *or* nod to its fall, bite the dust (*informal*); **break up**, crumble, crumble to dust, disintegrate, go *or* fall to pieces; go by the board, go out the window *or* up the spout (*informal*), go down the tube *or* tubes (*informal*); self-destruct

23 to perish, expire, succumb, die, cease, end, come to an end, go, pass, **pass away**, vanish, disappear, fade away, run out, peg *or* conk out (*informal*), come to nothing *or* naught, be no more, be done for; be all over with, be all up with (*informal*)

24 to go to ruin, go to rack and ruin, go to rack and manger (*old*), **go to the bad**, go wrong, **go to the dogs** *or* **pot** (*informal*), go *or* run to seed, go to hell in a handcart (*informal*), go to the deuce *or* devil (*informal*), go to hell (*informal*), go to the wall, go to perdition *or* glory (*informal*); go up (*informal*), go under

25 to drive to ruin, drive to the bad, **force to the wall**, drive to the dogs (*informal*), hound *or* harry to destruction

adjectives

26 destructive, destroying; **ruinous**, ruining; demolishing, demolitionary; **disastrous, calamitous, cataclysmic**, cataclysmal, **catastrophic**; fatal, fateful, doomful, baneful; bad news (*informal*); **deadly**; consumptive, consuming, withering; **devastating, desolating**, ravaging, wasting, wasteful, spoliative, depredatory; vandalic, vandalish, vandalistic; subversive, subversionary; nihilist, nihilistic; suicidal, self-destructive; fratricidal, internecine, internecive

27 exterminative, exterminatory, **annihilative, eradicative**, extirpative, extirpatory; all-destroying, all-devouring, all-consuming

28 ruined, destroyed, wrecked, blasted, undone, down and out, broken, bankrupt; spoiled; irremediable *see* 125.15; fallen, overthrown; **devastated, desolated, ravaged**, blighted, wasted; ruinous, in ruins; gone to wrack and ruin

29 (*informal terms*) shot, done for, done in, finished, *ausgespielt* (*German*), kaput; gone to pot, gone to the dogs, gone to hell in a handcart, phut, belly up, dead in the water, washed up, all washed up, history, **dead meat, down the tube** *or* **tubes**, zapped, nuked, wiped out

396 RESTORATION

nouns

1 **restoration, restitution, reestablishment, redintegration, reinstatement,** reinstation, reformation (*old*), reinvestment, reinvestiture, instauration, reversion, reinstitution, reconstitution, recomposition; replacement; **rehabilitation**, redevelopment, reconversion, reactivation, reenactment; improvement *see* 392

2 **reclamation, recovery, retrieval**, salvage, salving; redemption, salvation

3 **revival**, revivification, revivescence *or* reviviscency, **renewal**, resurrection, resuscitation, restimulation, reanimation, resurgence, recrudescence; retro; **refreshment** *see* 9; second wind; renaissance, renascence, **rebirth**, new birth; **rejuvenation**, rejuvenescence, second youth, new lease of life; **regeneration**, regeneracy, regenerateness; regenesis, palingenesis

4 **renovation, renewal**; refreshment; **redecorating; reconditioning**, furbishment, refurbishment, refurbishing; retread *and* retreading (*both informal*); face-lifting *or* face-lift; slum clearance, urban renewal

5 **reconstruction, re-creation, remaking**, recomposition, remodeling, **rebuilding**, refabrication, refashioning; reassembling, reassembly; reformation; restructuring, perestroika

6 **reparation, repair**, repairing, **fixing, mending**, making *or* setting right, repairwork; servicing, maintenance; **overhaul**, overhauling; troubleshooting (*informal*); **rectification, correction, remedy; redress**, making *or* setting right, amends, satisfaction, compensation, **recompense**

7 **cure, curing, healing, remedy** *see* 86; **therapy** *see* 91

8 **recovery, rally, comeback** (*informal*), return; **recuperation, convalescence**

9 **restorability, reparability**, curability, recoverability, reversibility, remediability, retrievability, redeemability, salvageability, corrigibility

10 **mender, fixer**, restorer, renovator, repairer, **repairman, repairwoman**, maintenance man *or* woman, **serviceman, servicewoman**; troubleshooter; Mr Fixit (*informal*); **mechanic**; tinker, tinkerer; cobbler; salvager, salvor *or* salver

verbs

11 to **restore, put back, replace, return**, place in *status quo ante*; **reestablish**, reform (*old*), reenact, **reinstate**, restitute; **reinstall**, reinvest, revest, reinstitute, reconstitute, recompose, recruit, **rehabilitate**, redevelop; reintegrate, reconvert, reactivate; refill, replenish; give back *see* 481.4

12 to **redeem, reclaim, recover, retrieve**; ransom; rescue; **salvage, salve**; recycle; win back, **recoup**

13 to **remedy, rectify, correct, right**, patch up, emend, amend, **redress**, make good *or* right, **put right**, set right, put *or* set to rights, put *or* set straight, set up, heal up, make all square; pay reparations, give satisfaction, requite, restitute, recompense, compensate, remunerate

14 to **repair, mend, fix, fix up** (*informal*), do up, put in repair, put in shape, set to rights, put in order *or* condition; **condition, recondition**, commission, put in commission, ready; **service, overhaul**; patch, **patch up**; tinker, tinker up, fiddle, fiddle around; cobble; sew up, darn; recap, retread

15 to **cure**, work a cure, recure (*old*), **remedy, heal, restore to health**, heal up, knit up, bring round *or* around, pull round *or* around, give a new *or* fresh lease on life, make better, make well, fix up, pull through, set on one's feet *or* legs; snatch from the jaws of death

16 to **revive**, revivify, **renew**, recruit; **reanimate**, reinspire, **regenerate**, **rejuvenate**, **revitalize**, put *or* breathe new life into, restimulate; **refresh** *see* 9.2; **resuscitate**, bring to, bring round *or* around; recharge; **resurrect**, bring back, call back, recall to life, raise from the dead; rewarm, warm up *or* over; **rekindle**, relight, reheat the ashes, stir the embers

17 to **renovate**, **renew**; **recondition**, refit, revamp, furbish, refurbish; refresh, face-lift

18 to **remake**, reconstruct, remodel, recompose, reconstitute, re-create, **rebuild**, refabricate, re-form, refashion, reassemble

19 to **recuperate**, recruit, **gain strength**, renew one's strength, catch one's breath, **get better**; **improve** *see* 392.7; **rally**, **pick up**, perk up (*both informal*), take a new lease on life; turn the corner, be on the mend, be out of the woods, take a turn for the better; **convalesce**; sleep it off

20 to **recover**, **rally**, **revive**, **get well**, **get over**, **pull through**, pull round *or* around, come round *or* around (*informal*), come back (*informal*), make a comeback (*informal*); get back in shape (*informal*), be oneself again, feel like a new person; **survive**, weather the storm; **come to**, come to oneself, show signs of life; come up smiling *and* bounce back (*both informal*), get one's second wind; come *or* pull *or* snap out of it (*informal*)

21 to **heal**, **heal over**, close up, scab over, cicatrize, granulate; heal *or* right itself; **knit**, **set**

adjectives

22 **tonic**, **restorative**, **restitutive**, restitutory, restimulative; analeptic; reparative, reparatory; remedial, **curative** *see* 86.39

23 **recuperative**, recuperatory; reviviscent; **convalescent**; buoyant, resilient, elastic

24 **renascent**, redivivus, redux, resurrected, renewed, revived, reborn, resurgent, recrudescent, reappearing, phoenix-like

25 **remediable**, **curable**; treatable, medicable; emendable, amendable, **correctable**, rectifiable, corrigible; **improvable**, ameliorable; **reparable**, repairable, **mendable**, **fixable**; restorable, recoverable, salvageable, retrievable, reversible, reclaimable, recyclable, redeemable; renewable

397 PRESERVATION

nouns

1 **preservation**, **conservation**, **saving**, **salvation**, salvage, **keeping**, **safekeeping**, maintenance, upkeep, support; custody, custodianship, guardianship, curatorship; protectiveness, protection *see* 1007; conservationism, environmental conservation; nature conservation *or* conservancy, soil conservation, forest conservation, forest management, wildlife conservation, stream conservation, water conservation, wetlands conservation

2 **food preservation**; **curing**, seasoning, salting, brining, pickling, marinating, corning; **drying**, dry-curing, jerking; dehydration, anhydration, evaporation, desiccation; **smoking**, fuming, smoke-

curing, kippering; **refrigeration**, freezing, quick-freezing, blast-freezing; freeze-drying, lyophilization; irradiation; **canning**, tinning; bottling, potting

3 **embalming**, mummification; taxidermy, stuffing; tanning

4 **preservative**, preservative medium; salt, brine, vinegar, formaldehyde, formalin *or* formol, embalming fluid

5 **preserver**, saver, conservator, keeper, safekeeper; taxidermist; lifesaver, rescuer, deliverer, saviour; **conservationist**, preservationist; National Trust, Council for the Protection of Rural England, English Heritage; **park keeper**, **ranger**, **forest ranger**, fire warden, game warden

6 **life jacket**, life belt, life preserver, life belt, float, cork jacket, Mae West (*informal*); life buoy, life ring, buoy, floating cushion; man-overboard buoy; water wings; breeches buoy; lifeboat, life raft, rubber dinghy; life net; lifeline; safety belt; **parachute**; ejector seat *or* ejection seat, ejection capsule

7 **preserve**, reserve, reservation; park, paradise; national park, country park, conservation area, nature reserve; green belt; **refuge**, **sanctuary** *see* 1008.1, game preserve *or* reserve, bird sanctuary, wildlife sanctuary *or* preserve; museum, library *see* 558, archives *see* 549.2, bank, store *see* 386

verbs

8 to **preserve**, **conserve**, **save**, spare, list; **keep**, keep safe, keep inviolate *or* intact; patent, copyright, register; not endanger, not destroy; not use up, not waste, not expend; **guard**, **protect** *see* 1007.18; **maintain**, **sustain**, uphold, support, **keep up**, keep alive

9 to **preserve**, **cure**, season, salt, brine, marinate *or* marinade, pickle, corn, **dry**, **dry-cure**, jerk, dry-salt; dehydrate, anhydrate, evaporate, desiccate; vacuum-pack; **smoke**, fume, **smoke-cure**, smoke-dry, kipper; **refrigerate**, freeze, quick-freeze, blast-freeze; freeze-dry, lyophilize; irradiate

10 to **put up**, do up; **can**, tin; bottle, jar, pot

adjectives

11 **preservative**, preservatory, conservative, conservatory; custodial, curatorial; **green**, **conservational**, conservationist; preserving, conserving, saving, keeping; **protective** *see* 1007.23

12 **preserved**, conserved, scheduled, **kept**, saved, spared; protected *see* 1007.21; **untainted**, **unspoiled**; intact, all in one piece, undamaged *see* 1001.8; **well-preserved**, well-conserved, **well-kept**, in a good state of preservation, none the worse for wear

398 RESCUE

nouns

1 **rescue**, **deliverance**, delivery, **saving**; lifesaving; **extrication**, **release**, **freeing**, **liberation** *see* 431; **bailout**; **salvation**, salvage, **redemption**, ransom; recovery, retrieval

2 **rescuer**, lifesaver, lifeguard; coast guard, lifesaving service, air-sea rescue; saviour *see* 592.2; lifeboat; salvager, salver *or* salvor

verbs

3 **to rescue,** come to the rescue, **deliver, save,** be the saving of, **redeem,** ransom, **salvage; recover, retrieve** *see* 481.6; **free,** set free, **release, extricate,** extract, **liberate** *see* 431.4; snatch from the jaws of death; save one's bacon *and* save one's neck *and* bail one out (*all informal*)

adjectives

4 **rescuable, savable;** redeemable; deliverable, extricable; salvageable

399 WARNING

nouns

1 **warning, caution,** caveat, **admonition,** monition, admonishment; **notice,** notification; **word to the wise,** *verbum sapienti* (*Latin*), verb sap, enough said; **hint,** broad hint, measured words, flea in one's ear (*informal*), little bird (*informal*); tip-off (*informal*); **lesson,** object lesson, **example,** deterrent example, warning piece; moral, moral of the story; **alarm** *see* 400; final warning *or* notice, ultimatum; **threat** *see* 514

2 **forewarning,** prewarning, **premonition,** precautioning; advance warning *or* notice, plenty of notice, prenotification; presentiment, hunch *and* funny feeling (*both informal*), **foreboding; portent,** "warnings, and portents and evils imminent"—
SHAKESPEARE

3 **warning sign,** premonitory sign, danger sign; preliminary sign *or* signal *or* token; **symptom,** early symptom, premonitory symptom, prodrome, prodroma, prodromata (*plural*); **precursor** *see* 815; **omen** *see* 133.3, 6; writing on the wall, "*mene, mene, tekel, upharsin*"—BIBLE (*Aramaic*); straw in the wind; gathering clouds, clouds on the horizon; thundercloud; falling barometer; storm *or* stormy petrel, **red light,** red flag; quarantine flag, yellow flag, yellow jack; death's-head, skull and crossbones; **warning signal, alert,** red alert; siren, klaxon, tocsin, alarm bell

4 **warner,** cautioner, admonisher, monitor; prophet *or* messenger of doom, Cassandra, Jeremiah; **lookout, lookout man; sentinel, sentry; signalman,** signaller, flagman; lighthouse keeper

verbs

5 **to warn, caution,** advise, **admonish; give warning,** give fair warning, utter a caveat, address a warning to, put a flea in one's ear (*informal*), have a word with one, say a word to the wise; **tip** *and* tip off (*both informal*); notify, put on notice, give notice *or* advance notice *or* advance word; tell once and for all; issue an ultimatum; **threaten** *see* 514.2; **alert,** warn against, put on one's guard, warn off; **put on alert,** cry havoc, sound the alarm *see* 400.3

6 **to forewarn,** prewarn, precaution, premonish; prenotify, tell in advance, give advance notice; portend, forebode

adjectives

7 **warning,** cautioning, **cautionary; monitory,**

monitorial, admonitory, admonishing; notifying, notificational; exemplary, deterrent

8 **forewarning, premonitory; portentous,** foreboding *see* 133.17; **precautionary,** precautional; precursive, precursory, forerunning, prodromal, prodromic

400 ALARM

nouns

1 **alarm,** alarum, alarm signal *or* bell, **alert;** hue and cry; **red light,** danger signal, amber light, caution signal; **alarm button,** panic button (*informal*), nurse's signal; **beeper,** buzzer; note of alarm; air-raid alarm; all clear; tocsin, alarm bell; signal of distress, SOS, Mayday, upside-down flag, flare; *sécurité* (*French*), notice to mariners; storm warning, storm flag *or* pennant *or* cone, gale warning; foghorn, fog bell; burglar alarm; fire alarm, fire bell, smoke alarm; siren, whistle, horn, klaxon, hooter; police whistle, watchman's rattle; alarm clock; five-minute gun, two-minute gun; lighthouse, beacon; blinking light, flashing light, occulting light

2 **false alarm,** cry of wolf; bugbear, bugaboo; flash in the pan (*informal*)

verbs

3 **to alarm, alert, arouse,** put on the alert; **warn** *see* 399.5; **sound the alarm,** give *or* raise the alarm, ring *or* sound the tocsin, cry havoc, raise a hue and cry; give a false alarm, cry before one is hurt, **cry wolf;** frighten *or* scare out of one's wits *or* to death, **frighten,** startle *see* 131.8

adjectives

4 **alarmed, aroused;** alerted; frightened to death *or* out of one's wits, **frightened; startled** *see* 131.13

401 HASTE
rapidity of action

nouns

1 **haste, hurry, scurry, rush, race,** dash, drive, scuttle, scamper, **scramble,** hustle (*informal*), **bustle,** flutter, **flurry,** hurry-scurry, helter-skelter; no time to be lost

2 **hastiness, hurriedness,** quickness, swiftness, expeditiousness, alacrity, promptness *see* 330.3; **speed** *see* 174.1, 2; furiousness, feverishness; **precipitousness,** precipitance *or* precipitancy, precipitation; suddenness, abruptness; **impetuousness** *see* 365.2, impetuosity, **impulsiveness, rashness** *see* 493, impulsivity; eagerness, zealousness, **overeagerness, overzealousness**

3 **hastening, hurrying,** festination, speeding, forwarding, quickening, **acceleration;** forced march, double time, double-quick time, double-quick; fast-forward

verbs

4 **to hasten, haste, hurry, accelerate, speed,** speed up, **hurry up,** cut along (*informal*), **rush,** quicken, hustle (*informal*), bustle, bundle, precipitate, forward; **dispatch, expedite; whip,** whip along, spur, **urge**

see 375.14, 16; push, press; crowd, stampede; **hurry on**, hasten on, drive on, hie on, push on, press on; **hurry along**, lollop, rush along, speed along, **speed on its way**; **push through**, bulldoze, steamroll, railroad through (*US informal*)

5 **to make haste**, **hasten**, festinate, **hurry**, **hurry up**, **race**, **run**, post, **rush**, **chase**, **tear**, **dash**, spurt, leap, plunge, **scurry**, hurry-scurry, **scamper**, **scramble**, **scuttle**, hustle (*informal*), bundle, **bustle**; bestir oneself, move quickly *see* 174.9; hurry on, dash on, press *or* push on, crowd; double-time, go at the double; break one's neck *or* fall all over oneself (*both informal*); lose no time, not lose a moment; rush through, romp through, hurry through; dash off; make short *or* fast work of, make the best of one's time *or* way, make up for lost time; do on the run

6 (*informal terms*) **to step on it, snap to it**, hop to it, hotfoot, bear down on it, shake it up, **get moving** *or* **going**, get a move on, get cracking, pull one's finger out, get one's arse in gear, give it the gun, not spare the horses

7 **to rush into**, **plunge into**, dive into, plunge, plunge ahead *or* headlong; **not stop to think**, go off half-cocked *or* at half cock (*informal*), leap before one looks, cross a bridge before one comes to it

8 **to be in a hurry**, be under the gun (*informal*), have no time to lose *or* spare, not have a moment to spare, hardly have time to breathe, work against time *or* the clock, work under pressure, have a deadline

adjectives

9 **hasty**, **hurried**, festinate, **quick**, flying, **expeditious**, prompt *see* 330.18; quick-and-dirty (*informal*), **immediate**, instant, on the spot; onrushing, **swift**, **speedy**; **urgent**; furious, feverish; slap-bang, slapdash, **cursory**, passing, cosmetic, snap (*informal*), superficial; spur-of-the-moment, last-minute

10 **precipitate**, precipitant, precipitous; **sudden**, abrupt; **impetuous, impulsive, rash**; headlong, breakneck; breathless, panting

11 **hurried**, **rushed**, pushed, pressed, crowded, **pressed for time**, hard-pushed *or* pressed, hard-run; double-time, double-quick, on *or* at the double

adverbs

12 **hastily**, **hurriedly**, **quickly**; **expeditiously**, promptly, with dispatch; all in one breath, in one word, in two words; apace, amain (*old*), hand over fist, **immediately**, instantly, in a second *or* split second *or* jiffy, at once, as soon as possible *or* ASAP, before you can say Jack Robinson; **swiftly, speedily**, on *or* at fast-forward; with haste, with great *or* all haste, in *or* with a rush, in a mad rush, at fever pitch; furiously, feverishly, in a sweat *or* lather of haste, hotfoot; by forced marches; **helter-skelter, hurry-scurry**, pellmell; slapdash, cursorily, superficially, in passing, on the spur of the moment

13 **posthaste**, in posthaste; post, express; by express, by airmail, by return mail; by cable, by telegraph, by fax

14 **in a hurry**, **in haste**, in hot haste, in all haste; in short order; against time, against the clock

15 **precipitately**, precipitantly, precipitously, slap-bang; **suddenly**, abruptly; **impetuously, impulsively, rashly**; **headlong**, headfirst, headforemost, head over heels, heels over head (*old*), *à corps perdu* (*French*)

exclamations

16 **make haste!**, make it quick!, **hurry up!**; **now!**; at once!, rush!, immediate!, urgent!; step lively!, look alive!, on the double!

17 (*informal terms*) **step on it!**, snap to it!, **make it snappy!**, get a move on!, chop-chop!, shake a leg!, get moving!, get going!, get cracking!, get with it!, hop to it!, get on the ball!, don't spare the horses!

402 LEISURE

nouns

1 **leisure, ease, convenience**, freedom; retirement, semiretirement; rest, repose *see* 20; **free time, spare time**, odd moments, idle hours; time to spare *or* kill, time on one's hands, time at one's disposal *or* command

2 **leisureliness, unhurriedness**, unhastiness, hastelessness, relaxedness; *dolce far niente* (*Italian*); **inactivity** *see* 331; **slowness** *see* 175; deliberateness, deliberation

verbs

3 **to have time**, have time enough, have time to spare, have plenty of time, have nothing but time, be in no hurry

4 **to take one's leisure**, take it easy, **take one's time**, do at one's leisure *or* convenience *or* pleasure; go slow *see* 175.6; ride the gravy train *and* lead the life of Riley (*both informal*)

adjectives

5 **leisure, leisured**; idle, unoccupied, free, open, spare; retired, semiretired

6 **leisurely, unhurried**, laid-back (*informal*), unhasty, hasteless, easy, relaxed; deliberate; inactive *see* 331.17; **slow** *see* 175.10

adverbs

7 **at leisure**, at one's leisure, at one's convenience, when one gets around to it, when it is handy, when one has the time, when one has a minute to spare, when one has a moment to call one's own

exclamations

8 easy does it!, take it easy!, chill out! (*informal*)

403 ENDEAVOUR

nouns

1 **endeavour, effort**, striving, struggle, strain; **all-out effort, best effort; exertion** *see* 725; determination, resolution *see* 359; **enterprise** *see* 330.7

2 **attempt, trial, effort, essay**, assay (*old*), first attempt, *coup d'essai* (*French*); **endeavour, undertaking**; approach, move; coup, stroke *see* 328.3, step; gambit, offer, **bid**, strong bid; experiment, tentative; tentation, trial and error

3 (*informal terms*) **try, whack, fling, shot, crack,** bash, belt, go, stab, smack

4 **one's best, one's level best, one's utmost,** one's damndest (*informal*), one's best effort *or* endeavour, the best one can, the best one knows how, all one can do, all one's got, all one's got in one, one's all (*informal*), the top of one's bent, as much as in one lies

verbs

5 **to endeavour, strive, struggle,** strain, sweat, sweat blood, labour, get one's teeth into, get to grips with, take it on, make an all-out effort, move heaven and earth, **exert oneself,** apply oneself, use some elbow grease (*informal*); spend oneself; seek, study, aim; resolve, be determined *see* 359.8

6 **to attempt, try, essay,** assay, offer; try one's hand, try it on; **undertake** *see* 404.3, **approach,** get to grips with, engage, take the bull by the horns; venture, venture on *or* upon, chance; **make an attempt** *or* **effort,** lift a finger *or* hand

7 (*informal terms*) **to tackle, take on, make a try, give a try,** have a go, take a shot *or* stab *or* crack *or* try at; try on for size, go for it, **have a fling** *or* **go at,** give it a whirl *or* go, **make a stab at,** have a shot *or* stab *or* crack *or* try at

8 **to try to,** try and (*informal*), **attempt to, endeavour to,** strive to, seek to, study to, aim to, venture to, dare to, pretend to

9 **to try for, strive for,** strain for, struggle for, contend for, pull for (*informal*), bid for, make a bid *or* strong bid for, make a play for (*informal*)

10 **to see what one can do,** see what can be done, see if one can do, do what one can, use one's endeavour; try anything once; **try one's hand,** try one's luck; make a cautious *or* tentative move, experiment, feel one's way, test the waters

11 **to make a special effort, go out of the way,** go out of one's way, take special pains, **put oneself out,** put oneself out of the way, lay oneself out *and* fall *or* bend *or* lean over backward (*all informal*), fall all over oneself, trouble oneself, **go to the trouble,** take trouble, **take pains,** redouble one's efforts

12 **to try hard, push** (*informal*), make a bold push, **put one's back into,** put one's heart into, try until one is blue in the face, die trying, **try and try;** try, try again; exert oneself *see* 725.9

13 **to do one's best** *or* **level best,** do one's utmost, try one's best *or* utmost, **do all** *or* **everything one can,** do the best one can, **do the best one knows how,** do all in one's power, do as much as in one lies, do what lies in one's power; make sterling efforts; put all one's strength into, put one's whole soul in, **strain every nerve;** give it one's all; be on one's mettle, **die trying**

14 (*informal terms*) **to knock oneself out, break one's neck,** break one's balls, bust a gut, knock one's pan in (*Scottish*), bust one's ass *or* hump (*US*), rupture oneself, do *or* try one's damndest, go all out, go the limit, go for broke, give it all one's got, give it one's best shot, go for it

15 **to make every effort, spare no effort** *or* **pains, go all lengths, go to great lengths,** go the whole length, go through fire and water, not rest, not relax, not slacken, move heaven and earth, leave no stone unturned, leave no avenue unexplored

adjectives

16 trial, tentative, experimental; venturesome, willing; determined, resolute *see* 359.11; utmost, damndest

adverbs

17 **out for,** out to, trying for, **on the make** (*informal*)

18 **at the top of one's bent,** at a stretch, to one's utmost, as far as possible

404 UNDERTAKING

nouns

1 **undertaking, enterprise, operation,** work, **venture, project,** proposition *and* deal (*both informal*); **programme, plan** *see* 381; **affair, business, matter, task** *see* 724.2, concern, interest; **initiative,** effort, attempt *see* 403.2; **action** *see* 328.3; **engagement, contract, obligation, commitment** *see* 436.2; *démarche* (*French*)

2 **adventure, emprise, mission;** quest, pilgrimage; expedition, exploration

verbs

3 **to undertake, assume,** accept, **take on, take upon oneself,** take in hand, take upon one's shoulders, take up, go with, **tackle,** attack; engage *or* contract *or* obligate *or* commit oneself; **put** *or* **set** *or* **turn one's hand to, engage in,** devote oneself to, **apply oneself to,** betake oneself to (*old*), address oneself to, give oneself up to; join oneself to, associate oneself with, **come aboard** (*informal*); busy oneself with *see* 724.11; **take up,** move into, go into, **go in for** (*informal*), **enter on** *or* **upon,** proceed to, embark in *or* upon, venture upon, go upon, launch forth, set forward, get going, get under way; set about, go about, lay about, go to do; **go** *or* **swing into action,** set to, turn to, buckle to, **fall to; pitch into** (*informal*), plunge into, fall into, **launch into** *or* **upon;** go at, set at, get stuck into (*informal*), knuckle *or* buckle down to; put one's nose to the grindstone, put one's shoulder to the wheel; roll up one's sleeves; take the bull by the horns; **endeavour, attempt**

4 **to have in hand, have one's hands in,** have on one's hands *or* shoulders

5 **to be in progress** *or* **process,** be on the anvil, be in the fire, be in the works *or* pipeline (*informal*), **be under way**

6 **to bite off more than one can chew** (*informal*), overextend *or* overreach oneself, have too many irons in the fire, have too much on one's plate

adjectives

7 **undertaken, assumed,** accepted, **taken on** (*informal*); **ventured,** attempted, chanced; **in hand,** on the anvil, in the fire, **in progress** *or* **process,** on one's plate, in the works *or* pipeline (*informal*), on the agenda, **under way**

8 **enterprising,** venturesome, adventurous, plucky, keen, eager

405 PREPARATION

nouns

1 **preparation**, preparing, **readying**, getting *or* making ready, makeready; warm-up, getting in shape *or* condition; mobilization; walk-up, **run-up**; **prearrangement** *see* 964, lead time, advance notice, warning, advance warning, alerting; **planning** *see* 381.1; trial, dry run, **tryout** *see* 941.3; **provision, arrangement**; preparatory *or* preliminary act *or* measure *or* step; **preliminary, preliminaries**; clearing the decks (*informal*); **grounding**, propaedeutic, preparatory study *or* instruction; basic training, familiarization, briefing; prerequisite; processing, treatment, pretreatment; equipment *see* 385; training *see* 568.3; manufacture; **spadework**, groundwork, foundation *see* 900.6

2 **fitting**, checking the fit, fit; **conditioning**; **adaptation, adjustment**, tuning; **qualification**, capacitation, enablement; **equipment, furnishing** *see* 385.1

3 (*a preparation*) concoction, decoction, *decoctum* (*Latin*), brew, **confection**; composition, mixture *see* 796.5, combination *see* 804

4 **preparedness, readiness**; fitness, fittedness, suitedness, suitableness, **suitability**; condition, trim; **qualification**, qualifiedness, credentials, record, track record (*informal*); **competence** *or* competency, **ability, capability, proficiency**, mastery; ripeness, maturity, seasoning, tempering

5 **preparer**, preparator, preparationist; trainer, coach, instructor, mentor, teacher; **trailblazer, pathfinder**; forerunner *see* 815.1; **paver of the way**

verbs

6 **to prepare, make** *or* **get ready**, trim (*old*), **ready**, fix (*informal*); provide (*old*), **arrange; make preparations** *or* **arrangements**, sound the note of preparation, clear the decks (*informal*), clear for action, settle preliminaries, tee up (*informal*); mobilize, marshal, deploy, marshal *or* deploy one's forces *or* resources; **prearrange; plan**; try out *see* 941.8; fix up (*informal*), put in *or* into shape; dress; treat, pretreat, process; cure, tan, taw

7 **to make up, get up, fix up** *and* rustle up (*both informal*); concoct, decoct, brew; **compound, compose, put together, mix**; make

8 **to fit, condition, adapt, adjust,** suit, tune, attune, put in tune *or* working order; **qualify, enable,** capacitate; **equip, furnish** *see* 385.7, 8

9 **to prime, load,** charge, cock, set; wind, wind up; steam up, get up steam, warm up

10 **to prepare to, get ready to,** get set for (*informal*), fix to (*informal*); be about to, be on the point of; ready oneself to, hold oneself in readiness

11 **to prepare for, provide for,** arrange for, make arrangements *or* dispositions for, look to, look out for, see to, **make provision** *or* **due provision for**; provide against, make sure against, forearm, **provide for** *or* **against a rainy day**, prepare for the evil day; lay in provisions, lay up a store, keep as a nest egg, save to fall back upon, lay by, husband one's resources, salt *or* squirrel something away; set one's house in order

12 **to prepare the way, pave the way,** smooth the path *or* road, **clear the way,** open the way, open the door to; **break the ice**; go in advance, be the point, **blaze the trail; prepare the ground**, cultivate the soil, sow the seed; do the spadework, lay the groundwork *or* foundation, lay the first stone; lead up to

13 **to prepare oneself**, brace oneself, **get ready, get set** (*informal*), put one's house in order, strip for action, get into shape *or* condition, roll up one's sleeves, spit on one's hands, limber up, warm up, flex one's muscles, gird up one's loins, buckle on one's armour, get into harness, shoulder arms; sharpen one's tools, whet the knife *or* sword; **run up to**, build up to, gear up, tool up

14 **to be prepared, be ready**, stand by, stand ready, hold oneself in readiness, keep one's powder dry, "put your trust in God, my boys, and keep your powder dry"—CROMWELL

15 (*be fitted*) **to qualify, measure up**, meet the requirements, check out (*informal*), have the credentials *or* qualifications *or* prerequisites; be up to *and* be just the ticket *and* fill the bill (*all informal*)

adjectives

16 **prepared, ready, well-prepared,** in readiness *or* ready state, all ready, good and ready, prepared and ready; psyched *or* pumped up (*informal*), eager, keen, champing at the bit; alert, vigilant *see* 339.13; **ripe, mature; set** *and* **all set** (*both informal*), on the mark *and* teed up (*informal*); about to, fixing to (*informal*); **prearranged; planned; primed**, loaded, cocked; familiarized, briefed, informed, put into the picture; groomed, coached; ready for anything, "prepared for either course"—VIRGIL; in the saddle, booted and spurred; armed and ready, in arms, up in arms, **armed** *see* 460.14; in battle array, mobilized; **provided, equipped** *see* 385.13; dressed; treated, pretreated, processed; cured, tanned, tawed; **readied**, available *see* 221.12

17 **fitted, adapted, adjusted, suited; qualified, fit, competent, able, capable,** proficient; well-qualified, well-fitted, well-suited

18 **prepared for, ready for,** alert for, set *or* all set for (*informal*); loaded for, primed for; up for (*informal*); equal to, up to

19 **ready-made,** ready-mixed, ready-cooked, ready-to-eat, pre-cooked, instant; ready-built, prefabricated, prefab (*informal*), preformed; ready-to-wear, ready-for-wear, off-the-peg, off-the-rack, prêt-à-porter (*US*); ready-cut, cut-and-dried *or* cut-and-dry

20 **preparatory**, preparative; propaedeutic; prerequisite; provident, provisional

adjectives, adverbs

21 **in readiness**, in store, in reserve; in anticipation

22 **in preparation**, in course of preparation, **in progress** *or* **process**, under way, **going on**, in embryo, **in production**, on stream, under construction, **in the works** *or* pipeline (*informal*), on the way, **in the making, in hand**, on the anvil, on the fire, in the oven; under revision; brewing, forthcoming

23 **afoot, on foot, afloat, astir**

24 in preparation for, against, for; in order to; ready for, set for (*informal*)

406 UNPREPAREDNESS

nouns

1 **unpreparedness, unreadiness,** unprovidedness, nonpreparedness, nonpreparation, lack of preparation; vulnerability *see* 1005.4; extemporaneousness, improvisation, ad-lib (*informal*), planlessness; **unfitness,** unfittedness, unsuitedness, unsuitableness, **unsuitability, unqualifiedness,** unqualification, lack of credentials, poor track record (*informal*), **disqualification,** incompetence *or* incompetency, incapability

2 **improvidence, thriftlessness, unthriftiness,** poor husbandry, lax stewardship; **shiftlessness,** fecklessness, thoughtlessness, heedlessness; happy-go-luckiness; hastiness *see* 401.2; negligence *see* 340.1

3 (*raw or original condition*) **naturalness,** inartificiality; **natural state,** nature, **state of nature,** nature in the raw; pristineness, intactness, virginity; natural man,
"unaccommodated man" — SHAKESPEARE; artlessness *see* 416

4 **undevelopment,** nondevelopment; **immaturity,** immatureness, callowness, unfledgedness, cubbishness, **rawness, unripeness, greenness; unfinish,** unfinishedness, unpolishedness, **unrefinement, uncultivation; crudity,** crudeness, **rudeness, coarseness,** roughness, the rough; **oversimplification,** oversimplicity, simplism, reductionism

5 **raw material;** crude, crude stuff (*informal*); ore, rich ore, rich vein; unsorted mass; rough diamond, **diamond in the rough;** unlicked cub; **virgin soil**

verbs

6 to **be unprepared** *or* **unready,** not be ready; go off half-cocked *or* at half cock (*informal*); be taken unawares *or* aback, be blindsided (*informal*), be caught napping, be caught with one's trousers down (*informal*), be surprised; **extemporize,** improvise, ad-lib *and* play by ear (*both informal*), wing it (*informal*); have no plan, be innocent of forethought

7 to **make no provision,** take no thought of tomorrow *or* the morrow, seize the day, *carpe diem* (*Latin,* Horace), let tomorrow take care of itself, live for the day, live like the grasshopper, live from hand to mouth;
"eat, drink, and be merry" — BIBLE

adjectives

8 **unprepared, unready,** unprimed; surprised, caught short, caught napping, caught on the hop, caught with one's pants down (*informal*), taken by surprise, taken aback, taken unawares, caught off balance, tripped up; **unarranged,** unorganized, haphazard; makeshift, rough-and-ready, **extemporaneous,** extemporized, improvised, ad-lib *and* off the top of one's head (*both informal*); impromptu, snap (*informal*); **unmade,** unmanufactured, unconcocted,

unhatched, uncontrived, undevised, unplanned, unpremeditated, undeliberated, unstudied; hasty, precipitate *see* 401.10; unbegun

9 **unfitted, unfit,** ill-fitted, **unsuited, unadapted, unqualified,** disqualified, incompetent, incapable; **unequipped, unfurnished,** unarmed, ill-equipped, ill-furnished, **unprovided,** ill-provided *see* 991.12

10 **raw, crude; uncooked,** unbaked, unboiled; underdone, undercooked, rare, red

11 **immature, unripe,** underripe, unripened, impubic, **raw, green,** callow, wet behind the ears, cub, cubbish, unfledged, fledgling, unseasoned, unmellowed; ungrown, half-grown, adolescent, juvenile, puerile, boyish, girlish; undigested, ill-digested; half-baked (*informal*); half-cocked *and* at half cock (*both informal*)

12 **undeveloped, unfinished,** unlicked, unformed; unfashioned, unwrought, unlaboured, unworked, unprocessed, untreated; unblown; uncut, unhewn; **underdeveloped;** backward, arrested, stunted; **crude, rude, coarse,** unpolished, **unrefined; uncultivated, uncultured; rough,** roughcast, roughhewn; **rudimentary,** rudimental; embryonic, in embryo, fetal, *in ovo* (*Latin*); **oversimple, simplistic,** reductive, reductionistic

13 (*in the raw or original state*) **natural, native,** in a **state of nature,** in the raw; inartificial, artless *see* 416.5; virgin, virginal, pristine, untouched, unsullied

14 **fallow,** untilled, uncultivated, unsown

15 **improvident,** prodigal, unproviding; **thriftless, unthrifty,** uneconomical; grasshopper; hand-to-mouth; **shiftless, feckless, thoughtless, heedless;** happy-go-lucky; negligent *see* 340.10

407 ACCOMPLISHMENT

1 **accomplishment, achievement, fulfilment, performance, execution, effectuation,** implementation, carrying out *or* through, **discharge, dispatch, consummation, realization, attainment,** production, fruition; **success** *see* 409; track record (*informal*); *fait accompli* (*French*), accomplished fact, done deal (*informal*); mission accomplished

2 **completion,** completing, **finish,** finishing, **conclusion, end,** ending, **termination,** terminus, **close, windup** (*informal*), rounding off, topping off, wrapping up, wrap-up, finalization; **perfection,** culmination *see* 1001.3; ripeness, maturity, maturation, full development

3 **finishing touch,** final touch (*informal*), icing the cake, the icing on the cake; copestone, capstone, crown, crowning of the edifice; capper (*US informal*), climax *see* 198.2

verbs

4 to **accomplish, achieve, effect, effectuate, compass, consummate, do, execute, produce, deliver, make,** enact, **perform, discharge, realize,** attain, run with (*informal*); **work,** work out; **dispatch, dispose of,** knock off (*informal*), polish off (*informal*), take care of (*informal*), **deal with,** put away, make short work of; succeed, manage *see*

409.12; come through *and* do the job (*both informal*), do the trick (*informal*)

5 to bring about, bring to pass, bring to effect; **implement, carry out, carry through,** carry into execution; **bring off, carry off, pull off** (*informal*); **put through,** get through, **put over** *or* **across** (*informal*); come through with (*informal*)

6 to complete, perfect, finish, finish off, conclude, terminate, end, bring to a close, carry to completion, prosecute to a conclusion; **get through, get done;** come off of, get through with, get it over, get it over with, **finish up;** clean up *and* wind up *and* sew up *and* wrap up *and* mop up (*all informal*); put the lid on *and* call it a day (*both informal*); **round off, wind up** (*informal*), **top off;** top out, crown, cap *see* 198.9; climax, culminate; add the finishing touch, whip into shape, finalize, put the icing on the cake

7 to do to perfection, do to a turn, do to a T (*informal*), not do by halves, do oneself proud (*informal*), use every trick in the book, leave no loose ends, leave nothing hanging; go all lengths, go to all lengths, go the whole length *or* way, go the limit *and* go whole hog *and* go all out *and* go for broke (*all informal*)

8 to ripen, mature, maturate; bloom, blow, blossom, flourish; come to fruition, bear fruit; **mellow;** grow up, reach maturity, reach its season; come to a head; bring to maturity, bring to a head

adjectives

9 completing, completive, completory, **finishing,** consummative, culminating, terminative, conclusive, **concluding,** fulfilling, finalizing, crowning; ultimate, **last, final,** terminal

10 accomplished, achieved, effected, effectuated, implemented, **consummated, executed, discharged, fulfilled, realized,** compassed, **attained; dispatched, disposed of,** set at rest; wrought, wrought out

11 completed, done, finished, concluded, terminated, ended, finished up; signed, sealed and delivered; cleaned up *and* wound up *and* sewn up *and* wrapped up *and* mopped up (*all informal*); washed up (*informal*), **through,** done with; all over with, all said and done, all over bar the shouting; perfective

12 complete, perfect, consummate, polished; exhaustive, thorough *see* 793.10; fully realized

13 ripe, mature, matured, maturated, seasoned; blooming, abloom; **mellow,** full-grown, fully developed

adverbs

14 to completion, to the end, to the full, to the limit; to a turn, to a T (*informal*), to a finish

exclamations

15 so much for that!, that's that!, that's your lot!, that's all, folks!, *voilà!* (*French*)

408 NONACCOMPLISHMENT

nouns

1 nonaccomplishment, nonachievement, nonperformance, inexecution, nonexecution, nondischarging, **noncompletion,** nonconsummation, nonfulfilment, unfulfilment; nonfeasance, omission; **neglect** *see* 340; loose ends, rough edges; endless task, work of Penelope, Sisyphean labour *or* toil *or* task; **disappointment** *see* 132; **failure** *see* 410

verbs

2 to neglect, leave undone *see* 340.7, fail *see* 410.8-10, 13; be disappointed *see* 132.4

adjectives

3 unaccomplished, unachieved, unperformed, unexecuted, undischarged, unfulfilled, unconsummated, unrealized, unattained; **unfinished, uncompleted, undone;** open-ended; **neglected** *see* 340.14; **disappointed** *see* 132.5

409 SUCCESS

nouns

1 success, successfulness, fortunate outcome, prosperous issue, favourable termination; **prosperity** *see* 1009; accomplishment *see* 407; victory *see* 411

2 sure success, foregone conclusion, sure-fire proposition (*informal*); **winner** (*informal*); **sure thing** *and* sure bet *and* **cinch** (*all informal*)

3 great success, triumph, resounding triumph, brilliant success, striking success, meteoric success; **stardom; success story;** brief *or* momentary success, nine days' wonder, flash in the pan, fad; best seller

4 (*informal terms*) **smash, hit,** smash hit, chart-topper, blast, boffo, showstopper, roaring success, one for the book, wow, sensation, overnight success, winner

5 score, hit, bull's-eye; goal; slam, grand slam; hole-in-one; home run, homer (*informal*); touchdown

6 (*successful person*) **winner,** star, star in the firmament, success, superstar *and* megastar (*both informal*); phenom (*US informal*); victor *see* 411.2

verbs

7 to succeed, prevail, be successful, be crowned with success, meet with success, do very well, do famously, deliver, come through *and* make a go of it (*both informal*); **go, come off,** go off; **prosper** *see* 1009.7; fare well, work well, do *or* work wonders, go to town *or* go great guns (*both informal*); **make a hit** (*informal*), go like a bomb (*informal*), catch fire; pass, graduate, qualify, win one's spurs *or* wings, get one's credentials, be blooded; pass with flying colours

8 to achieve one's purpose, gain one's end *or* **ends,** secure one's object, attain one's objective, do what one set out to do, reach one's goal, bring it off, pull it off (*informal*); make one's point; play it *or* handle it just right (*informal*), not put a foot wrong, play it like a master

9 to score a success, score, notch one up (*informal*), hit it, hit the mark, ring the bell (*informal*), turn up trumps, break the bank *or* make a killing (*both informal*), hit the jackpot (*informal*)

10 **to make good, come through, achieve success,** make a success, have a good thing going (*informal*), **make it** (*informal*), hit one's stride, **make one's mark,** give a good account of oneself, bear oneself with credit, do all right by oneself *and* **do oneself proud; advance, progress,** make one's way, make headway, **get on,** come on (*informal*), **get ahead** (*informal*); go places, go far; rise, **rise in the world,** work one's way up, step up, come *or* move up in the world, claw *or* scrabble one's way up, climb the ladder of success, pull oneself up by one's bootstraps; **arrive,** get there (*informal*), make the scene (*informal*); come out on top, come out on top of the heap (*informal*); **be a success,** have it made (*informal*), have the world at one's feet; **make a noise in the world** (*informal*), cut a swath, set the world on fire, set the heather alight; break through, score *or* make a breakthrough

11 **to succeed with,** crown with success; **make a go of it; accomplish,** compass, **achieve** *see* 407.4; **bring off, carry off, pull off** (*informal*), do the trick (*informal*), **put through,** bring through; **put over** *or* **across** (*informal*); get away with it *and* get by (*both informal*)

12 **to manage, contrive, succeed in; make out, get on** *or* **along** (*informal*), come on *or* along (*informal*), go on; **scrape along,** worry along, **muddle through,** get by, **manage somehow; make it** (*informal*), **make the grade,** cut the mustard *and* hack it (*both informal*); **clear,** clear the hurdle; **negotiate** (*informal*), **engineer;** put over (*informal*), put through

13 **to win through, win out** (*informal*), come through (*informal*), rise to the occasion, beat the system (*informal*); **triumph** *see* 411.3; **weather the storm,** live through, keep one's head above water; come out fighting, not know when one is beaten, **persevere** *see* 360.2

adjectives

14 **successful,** succeeding, crowned with success; **prosperous, fortunate** *see* 1009.14; **triumphant;** ahead of the game, out in front, on top, home and dry, sitting on top of the world *and* sitting pretty (*both informal*), on top of the heap (*informal*); assured of success, surefire, made; coming *and* on the up-and-up (*both informal*)

adverbs

15 **successfully,** swimmingly (*informal*), well, to some purpose, to good purpose; beyond all expectation, beyond one's wildest dreams, from rags to riches, with flying colours

410 FAILURE

nouns

1 **failure, unsuccessfulness,** unsuccess, successlessness, nonsuccess; no go (*informal*); ill success; futility, **uselessness** *see* 391; **defeat** *see* 412; losing game, **no-win situation;**

"lame and impotent conclusion"—SHAKESPEARE; nonaccomplishment *see* 408; **bankruptcy** *see* 625.3

2 (*informal terms*) flop, clinker, dud, non-starter, **loser,** washout, turkey, bomb, flat failure, total loss

3 **collapse, crash,** smash, comedown, breakdown, derailment, **fall,** pratfall (*informal*), stumble, tumble, **downfall,** cropper (*informal*); nose dive *and* tailspin (*both informal*); deflation, bursting of the bubble, letdown, **disappointment** *see* 132

4 **miss,** near miss; **slip, slipup; error, mistake** *see* 974.3

5 **abortion, miscarriage,** miscarrying, abortive attempt, vain attempt; wild-goose chase, merry dance; **misfire, flash in the pan,** damp squib, malfunction, glitch (*informal*); **dud** (*informal*); **flunk** (*informal*), **washout** (*informal*)

6 **fiasco, botch,** botch-up, cock-up *and* balls-up (*both informal*), bungle, hash, mess, muddle, bollocks *and* screw-up *and* fuck-up (*all informal*)

7 (*unsuccessful person*) **failure,** flash in the pan; bankrupt *see* 625.4

8 (*informal terms*) **loser, non-starter,** born loser, **flop,** washout, false alarm, **dud,** also-ran, schlemiel (*US*), turkey

verbs

9 **to fail,** be unsuccessful, not work *and* not come off (*both informal*), come to grief, **lose,** not make the grade, be found wanting, not come up to the mark; not pass, plough, flunk (*informal*); go to the wall, **go on the rocks;** labour in vain *see* 391.8; come away empty-handed; go bankrupt *see* 625.7, end up in Queer street

10 (*informal terms*) **to lose out,** get left, **not make it,** not hack it, go for a Burton *and* come a cropper, **flop,** flummox, fall flat, lay an egg, go over like a lead balloon, draw a blank, bomb, drop a bomb; fold, fold up; take it on the chin

11 **to sink, founder,** go down, go under (*informal*); **slip,** go downhill, be on the skids (*informal*)

12 **to fall, fall down** (*informal*), fall *or* drop by the wayside, fall flat, fall flat on one's face; fall down on the job (*informal*); **fall short, fall through,** fall to the ground; fall between two stools; **fall dead; collapse,** fall in; **crash**

13 **to come to nothing,** get nowhere (*informal*); fail miserably *or* ignominiously; fizzle out *and* peter out (*both informal*); **misfire,** flash in the pan, hang fire; **blow up, blow up in one's face, explode, end** *or* **go up in smoke,** go up like a rocket and come down like a stick

14 **to miss, miss the mark,** miss one's aim; slip, slip up (*informal*); **blunder, err** *see* 974.9, goof (*informal*); **botch, bungle** *see* 414.11, 12; waste one's effort, run around in circles, spin one's wheels

15 **to miscarry,** abort, be stillborn, die aborning; **go amiss,** go astray, **go wrong,** go on a wrong tack, take a wrong turn, derail, go off the rails

16 **to stall,** stick, die, go dead, **conk out** (*informal*), run out of gas *or* steam, come to a shuddering halt, come to a dead stop

17 **to flunk** *or* **flunk out** (*both informal*)

adjectives

18 unsuccessful, successless, failing; failed, *manqué* (*French*); **unfortunate** see 1010.14; **abortive**, miscarrying, miscarried, stillborn, died aborning; fruitless, no-win (*informal*), futile, useless see 391.9; lame, **ineffectual**, ineffective, inefficacious, of no effect; malfunctioning, glitchy (*informal*)

adverbs

19 unsuccessfully, successlessly, **without success**; fruitlessly, ineffectually, ineffectively, inefficaciously, lamely; to little *or* no purpose, **in vain**

411 VICTORY

nouns

1 **victory, triumph, conquest**, subduing, subdual; a feather in one's cap (*informal*); total victory, grand slam; **championship**, crown, laurels, cup, trophy, belt, blue ribbon, first prize; V-for-victory sign *or* V-sign, raised arms; victory lap, lap of honour; **winning**, win (*informal*); knockout *or* KO (*informal*); easy victory, walkover (*informal*), pushover (*informal*); runaway win; landslide victory, landslide; Pyrrhic victory, Cadmean victory; moral victory; winning streak (*informal*); winning ways, triumphalism; **success** see 409; ascendancy see 417.6; mastery see 612.2

2 **victor, winner**, victress, victrix, triumpher; **conqueror**, defeater, **vanquisher**, subduer, subjugator, *conquistador* (*Spanish*); top dog (*informal*); master, master of the situation; hero, conquering hero; champion, champ *and* number one (*both informal*); easy winner, sure winner; pancratiast; runner-up

verbs

3 **to triumph, prevail, be victorious**, come out ahead, come out on top (*informal*); **win, gain, capture, carry**; win out (*informal*), **win through**, carry it, carry off *or* away; **win** *or* **carry** *or* **gain the day**, win the battle, come out first, finish in front, make a killing (*informal*), remain in possession of the field; get *or* have the last laugh; **win the prize**, win the palm *or* bays *or* laurels, bear the palm, win one's spurs *or* wings; fluke *and* win by a fluke (*both informal*); **win by a nose** *and* nose out *and* edge out (*all informal*); **succeed**; break the record, set a new mark (*informal*)

4 **to win hands down** *and* win going away (*both informal*), win at a canter (*informal*), romp *or* breeze *or* waltz home (*all informal*), **walk off** *or* **away with**, waltz off with (*informal*), walk off with the game, **walk over** (*informal*); have the game in one's own hands, have it all one's way; **take** *or* **carry by storm**, sweep aside all obstacles, carry all before one, make short work of

5 **to defeat** see 412.6, **triumph over, prevail over**, best, get the best of (*informal*), **beat** (*informal*), **get the better** *or* **best of**; surmount, overcome, outmatch, rise above

6 **to gain the ascendancy**, come out on top (*informal*), **get the advantage, gain the upper** *or*

whip hand, dominate the field, get the edge on (*informal*), get a stranglehold on

adjectives

7 **victorious, triumphant**, triumphal, **winning, prevailing**; conquering, vanquishing, defeating, overcoming; ahead of the game, ascendant, in the ascendant, in ascendancy, sitting on top of the world *and* sitting pretty (*both informal*), dominant see 612.18; successful; flushed with success *or* victory

8 **undefeated, unbeaten, unvanquished, unconquered**, unsubdued, unquelled, unbowed

adverbs

9 **triumphantly**, victoriously, **in triumph**; by a mile

412 DEFEAT

nouns

1 **defeat**; **beating**, drubbing, thrashing; clobbering *and* hiding *and* lathering *and* whipping *and* lambasting *and* licking (*all informal*), trouncing; **vanquishment, conquest, conquering**, mastery, subjugation, subduing, subdual; **overthrow**, overturn, overcoming; **fall, downfall**, collapse, smash, crash, **undoing, ruin**, debacle, derailing, derailment; **destruction** see 395; deathblow, quietus; Waterloo; failure see 410

2 **discomfiture, rout, repulse**, rebuff; **frustration**, bafflement, confusion; **checkmate**, check, balk, foil (*old*); **reverse**, reversal, setback

3 **utter defeat**, total defeat, overwhelming defeat, crushing defeat, smashing defeat, decisive defeat; no contest; pasting *and* hammering (*informal*), gubbing (*Scottish informal*); whitewash *or* **whitewashing** (*informal*), **shutout**, blank sheet

4 **ignominious defeat**, abject defeat, inglorious defeat, disastrous defeat, utter rout, bitter defeat, stinging defeat, embarrassing defeat

5 **loser**, defeatee (*informal*); the vanquished; good loser, game loser, sport *or* **good sport** (*informal*); poor sport, poor loser; **underdog, also-ran**; stooge *and* fall guy (*both informal*); victim see 96.11

verbs

6 **to defeat, worst, best, get the better** *or* **best of**, be too good for, be too much for, be more than a match for; **outdo**, outgeneral, outmanoeuvre, outclass, outshine, outpoint, outsail, outrun, outfight, etc; **triumph over**; knock on the head, deal a deathblow to, put *hors de combat*; **undo, ruin, destroy** see 395.10; beat by a nose *and* nose out *and* edge out (*all informal*)

7 **to overcome, surmount; overpower, overmaster**, overmatch; **overthrow, overturn**, overset; put the skids under (*informal*); **upset**, trip, trip up, lay by the heels, send flying *or* sprawling; silence, floor, deck, make bite the dust; overcome oneself, master oneself; kick the habit (*informal*)

8 **to overwhelm**, whelm, snow under (*informal*), overbear, defeat utterly, deal a crushing *or* smashing defeat; **discomfit, rout, put to rout**, put to flight, scatter, stampede, panic; confound; put out of court

9 (*informal terms*) **to clobber, trim, skin alive, beat,** drub, massacre, marmelize (*informal*), lick, whip, thrash, knock off, hide, cut to pieces, run rings *or* circles around, lather, trounce, **lambaste,** skin alive; fix, settle, beat one's brains out, cook one's goose, make mincemeat out of, wipe the floor with, banjax, bulldoze, steamroller, **smear,** paste, whop

10 to conquer, vanquish, quell, **suppress, put down, subdue, subjugate,** put under the yoke, master; **reduce,** prostrate, fell, **flatten, break, smash, crush, humble,** bend, **bring one to his knees;** roll *or* trample in the dust, tread *or* trample underfoot, trample down, ride down, ride *or* run roughshod over, override; have one's way with

11 to thwart, frustrate, dash, check, checkmate *see* 1011.15

12 to lose, lose out (*informal*), lose the day, come off second best, **get** *or* **have the worst of it, meet one's Waterloo; fall,** succumb, tumble, bow, go down, go under, bite the dust, take the count (*informal*); snatch defeat from the jaws of victory; throw in the towel; have enough

adjectives

13 lost, unwon

14 defeated, worsted, bested, outdone; beaten, discomfited, put to rout, **routed,** scattered, stampeded, panicked; confounded; **overcome, overthrown,** upset, overturned, overmatched, **overpowered, overwhelmed,** whelmed, **overmastered,** overborne, overridden; **fallen,** down; floored, silenced; **undone, done for** (*informal*), **ruined,** kaput *and* on the skids (*both informal*), *hors de combat* (*French*); all up with (*informal*)

15 (*informal terms*) **beat, clobbered,** banjaxed, done in, lathered, creamed, trounced, lambasted, settled, fixed, **licked, whipped;** skinned alive; thrown for a loss

16 shut out, whitewashed (*informal*), scoreless, not on the scoreboard

17 conquered, vanquished, quelled, suppressed, put down, **subdued, subjugated,** mastered; **reduced,** prostrate *or* prostrated, felled, **flattened,** smashed, **crushed,** broken; **humbled,** brought to one's knees

18 irresistible, overpowering, overcoming, overwhelming, overmastering, overmatching, avalanchine

413 SKILL

nouns

1 skill, skilfulness, **expertness, expertise, proficiency,** callidity (*old*), craft, moxie (*US informal*), **cleverness; dexterity,** dexterousness *or* dextrousness; **adroitness,** address, **adeptness, deftness,** handiness, hand, practical ability; coordination, timing; quickness, readiness; **competence,** capability, capacity, ability; efficiency; **facility, prowess,** grace, style, finesse; **tact, tactfulness, diplomacy;** *savoir-faire* (*French*); **artistry;** artfulness; **craftsmanship,** workmanship, artisanship; **know-how** *and* savvy *and* bag of tricks *and* nous (*all informal*); technical skill, **technique, touch,** technical brilliance, technical mastery, **virtuosity,** bravura, wizardry; brilliance *see* 919.2;

cunning *see* 415; **ingenuity,** ingeniousness, resource, resourcefulness, wit; **mastery,** mastership, **command,** control, grip; steady hand; marksmanship, seamanship, airmanship, horsemanship, etc

2 agility, nimbleness, spryness, lightness, nippiness, featliness

3 versatility, ambidexterity, many-sidedness, all-roundedness (*informal*), Renaissance versatility; **adaptability,** adjustability, flexibility; broad-gauge, many hats; Renaissance man *or* woman

4 talent, flair, strong flair, **gift, endowment,** dowry, dower, natural gift *or* endowment, **genius,** instinct, **faculty; power, ability, capability, capacity,** potential; calibre; **forte,** speciality, métier, strong point, long suit; **equipment, qualification;** talents, powers, naturals (*old*), parts; the goods *and* the right stuff *and* what it takes *and* the makings (*all informal*)

5 aptitude, inborn *or* innate aptitude, aptness, felicity, flair; **bent, turn,** propensity, **leaning,** inclination, tendency; turn for, capacity for, gift for, genius for; an eye for, an ear for, a hand for, a way with

6 knack, art, hang, trick, way; **touch,** feel

7 art, science, craft; skill; technique, technic, **technics,** technology, technical knowledge *or* skill, technical know-how (*informal*); **mechanics,** mechanism; method

8 accomplishment, acquirement, attainment; finish

9 experience, practice, practical knowledge *or* skill, hands-on experience (*informal*), field-work; **background,** past experience, seasoning, tempering; **worldly wisdom,** knowledge of the world, blaséness, **sophistication;** sagacity *see* 919.4

10 masterpiece, masterwork, *chef d'œuvre* (*French*); **master stroke,** *coup de maître* (*French*); **feat,** *tour de force* (*French*)

11 expert, adept, proficient; **artist, craftsman,** artisan, skilled workman, journeyman; technician; seasoned *or* experienced hand; hard act to follow (*informal*); graduate; **professional, pro** (*informal*); **jack-of-all-trades,** handy man, Admirable Crichton (*J M Barrie*); **authority,** maven (*informal*); professor; **consultant,** expert consultant, attaché, technical adviser; boffin (*informal*), pundit, savant *see* 928.3; diplomatist, diplomat; politician, statesman, elder statesman; connoisseur, *connaisseur* (*French*); *cordon bleu* (*French*); marksman, crack shot, dead shot

12 talented person, talent, man *or* woman of parts, gifted person, prodigy, natural (*informal*), **genius,** mental genius, intellectual genius, lad o' pairts (*Scottish*); rocket scientist *and* brain surgeon (*both informal*); phenom (*informal*); gifted child, **child prodigy,** wunderkind, whiz kid *and* boy wonder (*both informal*)

13 master, past master; master hand, world-class performer, **good hand,** dab hand (*informal*), skilled *or* practised hand; **prodigy; wizard,** magician; **virtuoso; genius,** man *or* woman of genius; **mastermind;** master spirit, mahatma, sage *see* 920.1

14 (*informal terms*) **ace, star, superstar,** great, all-time great, topnotcher, first-rater, whiz, flash, hot stuff, no slouch, world-beater

15 champion, champ (*informal*), title-holder, world champion, grandmaster; **record holder,** world-record holder; laureate; medal winner, Olympic medal winner, medallist, award winner, prizeman, prizetaker, **prizewinner;** hall of famer (*US*)

16 veteran, seasoned *or* grizzled veteran, **old pro** *and* **old sweat** (*both informal*); **old hand,** one of the old guard, old stager, **old-timer** (*informal*); old campaigner, war-horse *or* old war-horse (*informal*); salt *and* old salt *and* old sea dog (*all informal*)

17 sophisticate, man of experience, **man of the world;** slicker *and* city slicker (*both informal*); man-about-town; **cosmopolitan,** cosmopolite, citizen of the world

verbs

18 to excel in *or* **at, shine in** *or* **at** (*informal*), be master of; write the book (*informal*), have a good command of, feel comfortable with, be at home in; **have a gift** *or* **flair** *or* **talent** *or* **bent** *or* **faculty** *or* **turn for,** be a natural *and* be cut out *or* born to be (*both informal*), **have a good head for,** have an ear for, have an eye for, be born for, show aptitude *or* talent for, have something to spare; have the knack *or* touch, have a way with, have the hang of it, have a lot going for one (*informal*), be able to do it blindfolded *or* standing on one's head (*informal*)

19 to know backwards and forwards, know one's stuff *or* **know one's onions** (*both informal*), **know the ropes** *and* **know all the ins and outs** (*both informal*), know from A to Z, know like the back of one's hand, know from the ground up, know all the tricks *or* moves, know all the tricks of the trade, know all the moves of the game; **know what's what, know a thing or two, know what it's all about, know the score** *and* know all the answers (*both informal*),
"know a hawk from a handsaw"—SHAKESPEARE; have savvy (*informal*); **know one's way about,** know the ways of the world, have been around (*informal*), have been around the block (*informal*), have been through the mill (*informal*), have cut one's wisdom teeth *or* eyeteeth (*informal*), be long in the tooth, **not be born yesterday;** get around (*informal*)

20 to exercise skill, handle oneself well, demonstrate one's ability, **strut one's stuff** *and* grandstand *and* showboat (*all informal*), show expertise; cut one's coat according to one's cloth, play one's cards well

21 to be versatile

adjectives

22 skilful, good, goodish, excellent, **expert, proficient; dexterous,** callid (*old*), **adroit, deft, adept, coordinated,** well-coordinated, **apt,** no mean, **handy;** quick, ready; **clever,** cute *and* slick *and* slick as a whistle (*all informal*), neat, clean; fancy, graceful, stylish; some *or* quite some *or* quite a *or* every bit a (*all informal*); **masterly, masterful;** magisterial; authoritative, professional; the complete; whiz-kid (*informal*); **virtuoso,** bravura, technically superb; **brilliant** see 919.14; cunning see 415.12; tactful, diplomatic, politic, statesmanlike; **ingenious,** resourceful, daedal, Daedalian; **artistic; workmanlike, well-done**

23 agile, nimble, spry, sprightly, fleet, featly, peart (*informal*), light, graceful, nimble-footed, light-footed, sure-footed; nimble-fingered, neat-fingered, neat-handed

24 competent, capable, able, efficient, qualified, fit, fitted, suited, worthy; journeyman; fit *or* fitted for; **equal to, up to;** up to snuff (*informal*), up to the mark (*informal*), *au fait* (*French*); well-qualified, well-fitted, well-suited

25 versatile, ambidextrous, two-handed, **all-round** (*informal*), **well-rounded, many-sided,** generally capable; **adaptable,** adjustable, flexible, resourceful, supple; amphibious

26 skilled, accomplished; practised; professional, career; trained, coached, prepared, primed, finished; at one's best, at concert pitch, on song; initiated, initiate; technical; conversant

27 skilled in, proficient in, adept in, versed in, **good at,** expert at, **handy at, a hand** *or* **good hand at,** master of, strong in, at home in; **up on,** well up on, well-versed see 927.20

28 experienced, practised, mature, matured, ripe, ripened, **seasoned,** tried, well-tried, tried and true, **veteran,** old, an old hand at (*informal*); sagacious see 919.16; **worldly, worldly-wise,** world-wise, wise in the ways of the world, knowing, time-served, **sophisticated,** cosmopolitan, cosmopolite, blasé, not wet behind the ears, not born yesterday, long in the tooth

29 talented, gifted, endowed, with a flair; born for, made for, cut out for (*informal*), with an eye for, with an ear for

30 well-laid, well-devised, well-contrived, well-designed, well-planned, well-worked-out; well-invented, *ben trovato* (*Italian*); **well-weighed, well-reasoned,** well-considered, well-thought-out; **cunning, clever**

adverbs

31 skilfully, expertly, proficiently, excellently, well; **cleverly,** neatly, ingeniously, resourcefully; cunningly see 415.13; **dexterously, adroitly, deftly, adeptly,** aptly, handily; agilely, nimbly, featly, spryly; **competently, capably, ably,** efficiently; **masterfully;** brilliantly, superbly, with genius, with a touch of genius; **artistically,** artfully; with skill, with consummate skill, with finesse

414 UNSKILFULNESS

nouns

1 unskilfulness, skill-lessness, **inexpertness, unproficiency, uncleverness;** unintelligence see 921; inadeptness, **undexterousness,** indexterity, **undeftness;** inefficiency; **incompetence** *or* incompetency, **inability, incapability, incapacity,** inadequacy; ineffectiveness, **ineffectuality; mediocrity,** pedestrianism; **inaptitude,** inaptness, unaptness, ineptness, maladroitness; unfitness, unfittedness; untrainedness, unschooledness; thoughtlessness, inattentiveness; maladjustment; rustiness (*informal*)

2 inexperience, unexperience, unexperiencedness, unpracticedness; **rawness, greenness,** unripeness, callowness, unfledgedness, unreadiness, immaturity; ignorance *see* 929; **unfamiliarity**, unacquaintance, unacquaintedness, unaccustomedness; **amateurishness**, amateurism, unprofessionalness, unprofessionalism

3 **clumsiness, awkwardness**, bumblingness, **maladroitness, unhandiness**, left-handedness, heavy-handedness, ham-fistedness (*informal*); handful of thumbs; **ungainliness**, uncouthness, **ungracefulness**, gracelessness, inelegance; **gawkiness**, gawkishness; **lubberliness, oafishness**, loutishness, boorishness, clownishness, lumpishness; **cumbersomeness**, hulkiness, **ponderousness; unwieldiness, unmanageability**

4 **bungling, blundering**, boggling, **fumbling**, malperformance, muffing, **botching**, botchery, blunderheadedness; **sloppiness, carelessness** *see* 340.2; too many cooks

5 **bungle, blunder, botch**, cockup, screw-up *and* fuck-up (*both informal*), bevue; **fumble, muff**, fluff, miscue; **slip**, trip, stumble; *gaucherie, étourderie, balourdise* (*all French*); **hash** *and* **mess** (*both informal*); bad job, sad work, clumsy performance; off day; **error, mistake** *see* 974.3

6 **mismanagement, mishandling**, misdirection, misguidance, misconduct, **misgovernment**, misrule; misadministration, maladministration; malfeasance, malpractice, misfeasance, wrongdoing *see* 655; nonfeasance, omission, **negligence**, neglect *see* 340.6; bad policy, impolicy, inexpedience *or* inexpediency *see* 995

7 **incompetent**, incapable; mediocrity, duffer *and* hacker (*both informal*), no great shakes, no prize package, no brain surgeon, no rocket scientist, piss artist (*informal*); no conjuror; one who will not set the Thames on fire *or* the heather alight; greenhorn *see* 929.8

8 **bungler, blunderer**, blunderhead, bumbler, **fumbler, botcher**; bull in a china shop, ox; **lout, oaf**, gawk, boor, **clown**, slouch; clodhopper, yokel; **clod**, clot, **dolt**, clown, blockhead *see* 923.4; awkward squad; blind leading the blind

9 (*informal terms*) bonehead, clodhopper, klutz (*US*), **butterfingers**, stumblebum, duffer, **slob**, lump

verbs

10 to not know how, not have the knack, not have it in one (*informal*); not be up to (*informal*); not be versed; muddle along, pedestrianize

11 to **bungle, blunder, muff**, muff one's cue *or* lines, **fumble**, be all thumbs, have a handful of thumbs; **flounder**, muddle, lumber; stumble, **slip**, trip, trip over one's own feet, get in one's own way, miss one's footing, miscue; commit a *faux pas*, commit a gaffe; blunder on *or* upon *or* into; blunder away, be not one's day; **botch**, mar, **spoil, butcher, murder**, make sad work of; play havoc with, play mischief with

12 (*informal terms*) to **cock up**, muck up, lay an egg, put *or* stick one's foot in it, stub one's toe, drop a brick, goof (*US*); **blow**, blow it, **mess up, make a mess** *or* **hash of**, foul up, fuck up, bollocks up, **screw up, gum up**, gum up the works, bugger, bugger up, louse up, goof up (*US*), play the devil *or*

hell *or* merry hell with; put one's foot in one's mouth

13 to **mismanage, mishandle, misconduct**, misdirect, misguide, **misgovern, misrule**; misadminister, maladminister; be negligent *see* 340.6

14 to not know what one is about, not know one's interest, lose one's touch, make an arse of oneself, **make a fool of oneself**, stultify oneself, put oneself out of court, stand in one's own light, not know on which side one's bread is buttered, not know one's arse from one's elbow, kill the goose that lays the golden egg, cut one's own throat, dig one's own grave, behave self-destructively, **play with fire**, burn one's fingers, jump out of the frying pan into the fire,

"sow the wind and reap the whirlwind"—BIBLE, lock the stable door after the horse has bolted, **count one's chickens before they are hatched**, buy a pig in a poke, aim at a pigeon and kill a crow, **put the cart before the horse**, put a square peg into a round hole, run before one can walk

adjectives

15 **unskilful**, skill-less, artless, **inexpert, unproficient, unclever**; inefficient; **undexterous, undeft, inadept, unfacile; unapt**, inapt, **inept**, hopeless, half-arsed (*informal*), **poor**; mediocre, pedestrian; thoughtless, inattentive; unintelligent *see* 921.13

16 **unskilled, unaccomplished, untrained**, untaught, unschooled, untutored, uncoached, unimproved, uninitiated, **unprepared**, unprimed, unfinished, unpolished; **untalented, ungifted, unendowed; amateurish**, unprofessional, unbusinesslike, semiskilled

17 **inexperienced**, unexperienced, unversed, unconversant, **unpractised**; undeveloped, unseasoned; **raw, green**, unripe, callow, unfledged, immature, unmatured, fresh, wet behind the ears, **untried**; unskilled in, unpractised in, unversed in, unconversant with, unaccustomed to, unused to, unfamiliar *or* unacquainted with, new to, uninitiated in, a stranger to, a novice *or* tyro at; ignorant *see* 929.12

18 **out of practice**, out of training *or* form, soft (*informal*), flabby, out of shape *or* condition, stiff, **rusty**; gone *or* run to seed *and* over the hill *and* not what one used to be (*all informal*), losing one's touch, slipping, on the downgrade

19 **incompetent, incapable, unable, inadequate, unequipped, unqualified**, ill-qualified, out of one's depth, outmatched, **unfit, unfitted**, unadapted, not equal *or* up to, not cut out for (*informal*); ineffective, **ineffectual**; unadjusted, maladjusted

20 **bungling, blundering**, blunderheaded, bumbling, flat-footed, fumbling, mistake-prone, accident-prone; **clumsy, awkward, uncoordinated**, maladroit, unhandy, left-hand, left-handed, heavy-handed, ham-fisted *and* cack-handed (*both informal*), butterfingered (*informal*), **all thumbs**, fingers all thumbs, with a handful of thumbs; stiff; **ungainly**, uncouth, **ungraceful**, graceless, inelegant, *gauche* (*French*); **gawky**, gawkish; **lubberly, loutish, oafish**, boorish, clownish, lumpish, slobbish

(*informal*); **sloppy, careless** *see* 340.11; **ponderous, cumbersome,** lumbering, hulking, hulky; **unwieldy**

21 botched, bungled, fumbled, muffed, spoiled, **butchered,** murdered; **ill-managed,** ill-done, ill-conducted, ill-devised, ill-contrived, ill-executed; mismanaged, misconducted, **misdirected, misguided;** impolitic, ill-considered, ill-advised; negligent *see* 340.10

22 (*informal terms*) **messed up, fouled-up, fucked-up,** screwed up, bollocksed-up, loused-up, gummed-up, buggered, buggered-up, snafued, goofed-up (*US*); half-arsed; arse-over-tit

adverbs

23 unskilfully, inexpertly, unproficiently, uncleverly; inefficiently; **incompetently, incapably,** inadequately, unfitly; **undexterously, undeftly, inadeptly,** unfacilely; **unaptly, inaptly,** ineptly, poorly

24 clumsily, awkwardly; **bunglingly, blunderingly; maladroitly,** unhandily; **ungracefully,** gracelessly, inelegantly, uncouthly; **ponderously, cumbersomely,** lumberingly, hulkingly, hulkily;

415 CUNNING

nouns

1 **cunning,** cunningness, **craft, craftiness,** callidity (*old*), **artfulness, art, artifice, wiliness,** wiles, guile, **slyness,** insidiousness, **foxiness,** slipperiness, shiftiness, trickiness; low cunning, animal cunning; gamesmanship *and* one-upmanship (*both informal*); **canniness, shrewdness,** sharpness, acuteness, astuteness, **cleverness** *see* 413.1; **resourcefulness, ingeniousness, wit,** inventiveness, readiness; subtlety, subtleness, Italian hand, fine Italian hand, finesse; acuteness, cuteness *and* cutification (*both informal*); Jesuitism, Jesuitry, **sophistry** *see* 935; "the ape of wisdom"—Locke; satanic cunning, the cunning of the serpent; sneakiness, **stealthiness, stealth** *see* 345.4; cageyness (*informal*), wariness *see* 494.2

2 Machiavellianism, Machiavellism; **politics,** diplomacy, diplomatics; jobbery, jobbing

3 **stratagem,** artifice, art (*old*), **craft, wile,** strategy, **device,** wily device, wheeze (*informal*), **contrivance, expedient, design, scheme, trick,** gimmick (*informal*), **ruse, red herring, shift,** tactic, **manoeuvre, stroke,** master stroke, **move,** coup, gambit, **ploy, dodge,** artful dodge; **plot,** conspiracy, **intrigue;** sleight, feint, jugglery; method in one's madness; **subterfuge,** blind, dust in the eyes; chicanery, knavery, deceit, jiggery-pokery, trickery *see* 356.4

4 **machination, manipulation, string-pulling** (*informal*); influence, political influence, behind-the-scenes influence *or* pressure; **manoeuvring,** manoeuvres, tactical manoeuvres; **tactics,** devices, expedients, gimmickry (*informal*)

5 **circumvention,** getting round *or* around; **evasion,** elusion, the slip (*informal*); the runaround *and* buck-passing *and* passing the buck (*all informal*); **frustration, foiling, thwarting** *see* 1011.3;

outwitting, outsmarting, outguessing, **outmanoeuvring**

6 **slyboots,** sly dog (*informal*), **fox,** Reynard (*old*), dodger, Artful Dodger (*Charles Dickens*), crafty rascal (*informal*), smooth operator, cool customer (*informal*), glib tongue, smooth *or* sweet talker, smoothie (*informal*), charmer; **trickster,** shyster (*informal*), shady character; horse trader; **swindler** *see* 357.3

7 **strategist, tactician; manoeuvrer, machinator, manipulator, string-puller** (*informal*); calculator, schemer, **intriguer**

8 **Machiavellian,** Machiavel, Machiavellianist; **diplomat,** diplomatist, **politician** *see* 610; political realist; influence peddler; powerbroker, kingmaker; power behind the throne, grey eminence, *éminence grise* (*French*)

verbs

9 **to live by one's wits,** play a deep game; use one's fine Italian hand, finesse; shift, dodge, twist and turn, zig and zag; have something up one's sleeve, hide one's hand, cover one's path, have a way out *or* an escape hatch; **trick, deceive** *see* 356.14

10 **to manoeuvre, manipulate,** pull strings; **machinate, contrive,** angle (*informal*), jockey, **engineer;** play games (*informal*); **plot, scheme, intrigue; finagle, wangle;** gerrymander

11 **to outwit, outfox, outsmart,** outguess, outfigure, **outmanoeuvre,** outgeneral, outflank, outplay; get the better *or* best of, go one better, know a trick worth two of that; play one's trump card; **overreach,** outreach; **circumvent,** get round *or* around, **evade,** stonewall (*informal*), **elude, frustrate, foil,** give the slip *or* runaround (*informal*); pass the buck (*informal*); pull a fast one (*informal*), steal a march on; make a fool of; be too much for, be too deep for; **deceive, victimize** *see* 356.18

adjectives

12 **cunning, crafty, artful, wily,** callid (*old*), **guileful, sly,** insidious, **shifty,** arch, **smooth,** slick (*both informal*), **slippery,** snaky, serpentine, **foxy,** vulpine, feline; **canny, shrewd,** knowing, sharp, razor-sharp, acute, astute, **clever;** resourceful, ingenious, inventive, ready; subtle; Jesuitical, **sophistical** *see* 935.10; **tricky,** trickish, tricksy (*old*), gimmicky (*informal*); **Machiavellian,** Machiavellic, politic, diplomatic; **strategic, tactical; deep, deep-laid;** cunning as a fox *or* serpent, crazy like a fox (*US informal*), slippery as an eel, too clever by half; sneaky, **stealthy** *see* 345.12; cagey (*informal*), wary *see* 494.9; **scheming, designing; manipulative,** manipulatory; **deceitful**

adverbs

13 **cunningly, craftily, artfully,** wilily, guilefully, insidiously, shiftily, foxily, trickily, smoothly, slick (*informal*); **slyly,** on the sly; **cannily, shrewdly,** knowingly, astutely, **cleverly;** subtlely; cagily (*informal*), warily *see* 494.13; diplomatically

416 ARTLESSNESS

nouns

1 artlessness, ingenuousness, guilelessness; **simplicity**, simpleness, plainness; simpleheartedness, simplemindedness; **unsophistication**, unsophisticatedness; *naïveté (French)*, naivety, naiveness, childlikeness; **innocence**; trustfulness, trustingness, unguardedness, unwariness, unsuspiciousness; **openness**, openheartedness, sincerity, **candour** *see* 644.4; **integrity**, single-heartedness, single-mindedness, singleness of heart; directness, bluffness, bluntness, outspokenness

2 **naturalness**, naturalism, nature; state of nature; unspoiledness; **unaffectedness**, unaffectation, **unassumingness**, unpretendingness, unpretentiousness, undisguise; **inartificiality**, unartificialness, genuineness

3 **simple soul**, unsophisticate, naïf, **ingenue**, **innocent**, **child**, mere child, infant, **babe**, baby, newborn babe, babe in the woods, lamb; child of nature, noble savage; primitive; yokel, hick; oaf, lout *see* 923.5; dupe *see* 358

verbs

4 to wear one's heart on one's sleeve, look one in the face

adjectives

5 **artless, simple,** plain, **guideless,** homely; simplehearted, simpleminded; **ingenuous,** *ingénu (French);* **unsophisticated, naive;** childlike, born yesterday; **innocent;** trustful, trusting, unguarded, unwary, unreserved, confiding, unsuspicious; **open,** openhearted, sincere, candid, **frank** *see* 644.17; single-hearted, single-minded; direct, bluff, blunt, outspoken, straight-talking

6 **natural,** naturelike, native; in the state of nature; primitive, primal, pristine, unspoiled, untainted, uncontaminated; **unaffected, unassuming, unpretending,** unpretentious, unfeigning, undisguising, undissimulating, undissembling, undesigning; **genuine, inartificial,** unartificial, unadorned, unvarnished, unembellished; homespun; **pastoral, rural,** Arcadian, bucolic

adverbs

7 artlessly, ingenuously, guilelessly; simply, plainly; naturally, genuinely; naïvely; openly, openheartedly

417 AUTHORITY

nouns

1 authority, prerogative, right, power, faculty, competence *or* competency; **mandate,** popular authority *or* mandate, people's mandate, electoral mandate; regality, royal prerogative; constituted authority, vested authority; inherent authority; legal *or* lawful *or* rightful authority, legitimacy; derived *or* delegated authority, vicarious authority, indirect authority; **the say** *and* **the say-so** *(both informal);* divine right, *jus divinum (Latin);* absolute power, absolutism *see* 612.9

2 authoritativeness, authority, power, powerfulness, magisterialness, **potency** *or* potence, puissance, **strength,** might, mightiness, clout *(informal)*

3 authoritativeness, masterfulness, lordliness, magistrality, magisterialness; **arbitrariness,** peremptoriness, imperativeness, **imperiousness,** autocraticalness, high-handedness, dictatorialness, overbearingness, overbearance, overbearing, domineering, domineeringness, tyrannicalness, authoritarianism, bossism *(informal)*

4 prestige, authority, influence, influentialness; pressure, **weight,** weightiness, moment, **consequence;** eminence, **stature,** rank, seniority, preeminence, priority, precedence; **greatness** *see* 247; **importance, prominence** *see* 996.2

5 governance, authority, jurisdiction, control, command, power, rule, reign, regnancy, dominion, sovereignty, empire, empery, raj *(India),* imperium, **sway; government** *see* 612; administration, disposition *see* 573.3; **control, grip,** claws, **clutches,** hand, hands, iron hand, talons

6 dominance *or* dominancy, dominion, domination; preeminence, supremacy, superiority *see* 249; ascendance *or* ascendancy; upper *or* whip hand, sway; sovereignty, suzerainty, suzerainship, overlordship; primacy, principality, **predominance** *or* predominancy, predomination, prepotence *or* prepotency, hegemony; preponderance; balance of power; eminent domain

7 mastership, masterhood, masterdom, **mastery; leadership, headship, lordship;** hegemony; supervisorship, directorship *see* 573.4; hierarchy, nobility, aristocracy, **ruling class** *see* 575.15; chair, chairmanship; chieftainship, chieftaincy, chieftainry, chiefery; presidentship, presidency; premiership, prime-ministership, prime-ministry; governorship; princeship, princedom, principality; rectorship, rectorate; suzerainty, suzerainship; regency, regentship; prefectship, prefecture; proconsulship, proconsulate; provostship, provostry; protectorship, protectorate; seneschalship, seneschalsy; pashadom, pashalic; sheikhdom; emirate, viziership, vizierate; magistrateship, magistrature, magistracy; mayorship, mayoralty; sheriffdom, sheriffcy, sheriffalty, shrievalty; consulship, consulate; chancellorship, chancellery, chancellorate; seigniory; tribunate, aedileship; deanship, decanal authority, deanery; patriarchate, patriarchy *(old);* bishopric, episcopacy; archbishopric, archiepiscopacy, archiepiscopate; metropolitanship, metropolitanate; popedom, popeship, popehood, papacy, pontificate, pontificality; dictatorship, dictature

8 sovereignty, royalty, regnancy, **majesty,** empire, empery, imperialism, **emperorship; kingship,** kinghood; queenship, queenhood; kaisership, kaiserdom; tsardom *or* czardom; rajaship; sultanship, sultanate; caliphate; the throne, the Crown, the purple; royal insignia *see* 647.3

9 **sceptre, rod, staff,** wand, staff *or* rod of office, baton, mace, truncheon, fasces; crosier, crook, cross-staff; caduceus; gavel; mantle; chain of office; portfolio

10 (*seat of authority*) **saddle** (*informal*), **helm, driver's seat** (*informal*); seat, **chair,** bench; woolsack; seat of state, seat of power; curule chair; dais
11 **throne,** royal seat; musnud *or* gaddi (*both India*); Peacock throne
12 (*acquisition of authority*) **accession; succession,** rightful *or* legitimate succession; **usurpation,** arrogation, assumption, taking over, seizure; anointment, anointing, consecration, coronation; **delegation,** deputation, assignment, **appointment;** election; **authorization,** empowerment

verbs

13 **to possess** *or* **wield authority, have power,** have the power, have in one's hands, have the right, have the say *or* say-so (*informal*), have the whip hand, wear the crown, hold the prerogative, have the mandate, wear the trousers (*informal*); exercise sovereignty; be vested *or* invested, carry authority, have clout (*informal*), have what one says go, have one's own way; show one's authority, crack the whip, throw one's weight around (*informal*); **rule** *see* 612.14, **control;** supervise *see* 573.10
14 **to take command, take charge, take over,** take the helm, take the reins of government, take the reins into one's hand, get the power into one's hands, gain *or* get the upper hand, take the lead; ascend *or* mount *or* succeed *or* accede to the throne; **assume command,** assume, **usurp,** arrogate, seize; usurp *or* seize the throne *or* crown *or* mantle, usurp the prerogatives of the crown; seize power, execute a *coup d'état*

adjectives

15 **authoritative,** clothed *or* vested *or* invested with authority, **commanding, imperative; governing, controlling, ruling** *see* 612.18; **preeminent, supreme,** leading, **superior** *see* 249.12; **powerful, potent,** puissant, mighty; dominant, ascendant, hegemonic, hegemonistic; **influential, prestigious, weighty,** momentous, consequential, eminent, substantial, considerable; great *see* 247.6; important, prominent; ranking, senior; authorized, empowered, duly constituted, competent; **official,** *ex officio* (*Latin*); authoritarian; absolute, autocratic, monocratic; **totalitarian**
16 **imperious,** imperial, **masterful,** authoritative, feudal, aristocratic, **lordly,** magistral, **magisterial;** arrogant *see* 141.9; **arbitrary, peremptory,** imperative; absolute, absolutist, absolutistic; **dictatorial, authoritarian; bossy** (*informal*), **domineering, high-handed, overbearing,** overruling; autocratic, monocratic, **despotic, tyrannical;** tyrannous, grinding, oppressive *see* 98.24; repressive, suppressive *see* 428.11; strict, severe *see* 425.6
17 **sovereign; regal, royal, majestic,** purple; **kinglike, kingly,**
   "every inch a king"—SHAKESPEARE; **imperial,** imperious *or* imperatorious (*both old*); imperatorial; monarchic *or* monarchical, monarchal, monarchial; tetrarchic; princely, princelike; **queenly,** queenlike; dynastic

adverbs

18 **authoritatively,** with authority, by virtue of office; **commandingly, imperatively; powerfully,** potently, puissantly, mightily; **influentially, weightily,** momentously, consequentially; **officially,** *ex cathedra* (*Latin*)
19 **imperiously, masterfully,** magisterially; **arbitrarily, peremptorily; autocratically, dictatorially, high-handedly, domineeringly,** overbearingly, despotically, tyrannically
20 **by authority of,** in the name of, in *or* by virtue of
21 **in authority,** in power, in charge, in control, in command, at the reins, at the head, **at the helm,** at the wheel, **in the saddle** *or* driver's seat (*informal*), on the throne;
   "drest in a little brief authority"—SHAKESPEARE

418 LAWLESSNESS
absence of authority

nouns

1 **lawlessness; licentiousness,** licence, uncontrol, anything goes, unrestraint *see* 430.3; indiscipline, insubordination, mutiny, disobedience *see* 327; permissiveness; **irresponsibility,** unaccountability; wilfulness, unchecked *or* rampant will; interregnum, power vacuum
2 **anarchy,** anarchism; **disorderliness, unruliness,** misrule, **disorder,** disruption, disorganization, confusion, **turmoil, chaos,** primal chaos, tohubohu; antinomianism; **nihilism;** lynch law, mob rule *or* law, mobocracy, ochlocracy; **law of the jungle;** revolution *see* 859; rebellion *see* 327.4
3 **anarchist,** anarch; antinomian; **nihilist;** revolutionist *see* 859.3; mutineer, rebel *see* 327.5

verbs

4 **to reject** *or* **defy authority,** enthrone one's own will; **take the law in one's own hands,** act on one's own responsibility; do *or* go as one pleases, indulge oneself; be a law unto oneself, answer to no man,
   "swear allegiance to the words of no master"—HORACE

adjectives

5 **lawless; licentious, ungoverned,** undisciplined, unrestrained; permissive; insubordinate, mutinous, disobedient *see* 327.8; **uncontrolled,** uncurbed, unbridled, unchecked, rampant, untrammeled, unreined, reinless, anything goes; **irresponsible,** wildcat, unaccountable; selfwilled, wilful, headstrong, heady, bolshie (*informal*)
6 **anarchic, anarchical,** anarchial, anarchistic; **unruly, disorderly,** disorganized, **chaotic;** antinomian; **nihilistic**

adverbs

7 **lawlessly,** licentiously; anarchically, chaotically

419 PRECEPT

nouns

1 **precept,** prescript, **prescription, teaching;**

instruction, direction, **charge**, commission, injunction, dictate; **order**, command *see* 420

2 **rule**, **law**, **canon**, **maxim**, dictum, moral, moralism; **norm**, **standard**; formula, form; rule of action *or* conduct, moral precept; commandment, *mitzvah* (*Hebrew*); **tradition**; ordinance, imperative, **regulation**, reg (*informal*), *règlement* (*French*); **principle**, principium, settled principle, general principle *or* truth, tenet, convention; **guideline**, ground rule, rubric, protocol, working rule, working principle, standard procedure; guiding principle, golden rule; **code**

3 **formula**, form (*old*), **recipe**, receipt; **prescription**; formulary

adjectives

4 **preceptive**, didactic, instructive, moralistic, **prescriptive**; prescript, prescribed, mandatory, hard-and-fast, binding, dictated; formulary, standard, regulation, official, authoritative, canonical, statutory, rubric, rubrical, protocolary, protocolic; **normative**; **conventional**; traditional

420 COMMAND

nouns

1 **command**, **commandment**, **order**, direct order, command decision, **bidding**, behest, hest (*old*), imperative, **dictate**, dictation, **will**, **pleasure**, say-so (*informal*), word, word of command, *mot d'ordre* (*French*); special order; **authority** *see* 417

2 **injunction**, **charge**, commission, **mandate**

3 **direction**, **directive**, **instruction**, **rule**, **regulation**; prescript, prescription, **precept** *see* 419; general order

4 **decree**, decreement (*old*), decretum, decretal, rescript, fiat, **edict**, *edictum* (*Latin*), order in council; law *see* 673.3; **rule**, **ruling**, dictum, ipse dixit; **ordinance**, *ordonnance* (*French*), appointment (*old*); **proclamation**, pronouncement, pronunciamento, **declaration**, ukase; bull, brevet (*old*); decree-law, *décret-loi* (*French*); *senatus consultum* (*Latin*), senatus consult; diktat

5 **summons**, bidding, beck, call, calling, nod, **beck and call**, preconization; **convocation**, convoking; evocation, calling forth, invocation; requisition, indent

6 **court order**, injunction, legal order, interdict (*Scottish*)

7 process server, summoner

verbs

8 **to command**, **order**, **dictate**, **direct**, **instruct**, mandate, **bid**, **enjoin**, **charge**, commission, call on *or* upon; issue a writ *or* an injunction; **decree**, **rule**, **ordain**, promulgate; give an order *or* a direct order, issue a command, say the word, give the word *or* word of command; call the shots *or* tune *or* signals *or* play (*informal*); order about *or* around; **speak**, **proclaim**, **declare**, pronounce *see* 352.12

9 **to prescribe**, **require**, **demand**, **dictate**, impose, lay down, set, fix, appoint, make obligatory *or* mandatory; decide once and for all, carve in stone, set in concrete (*informal*); authorize *see* 443.11

10 **to lay down the law**, put one's foot down (*informal*), read the riot act, set the record straight

11 **to summon**, **call**, demand, preconize; call for, send for *or* after, bid come; **cite**, **summons** (*informal*), **subpoena**, serve; page; convoke, convene, call together; call away; muster, invoke, conjure; order up, summon up, muster up, call up, conjure up, magic *or* magic up; evoke, call forth, summon forth, call out; recall, call back, call in; requisition, indent

adjectives

12 **mandatory**, mandated, **imperative**, **compulsory**, prescript, prescriptive, **obligatory**, must (*informal*); dictated, imposed, required, entailed, decretory; decisive, final, peremptory, absolute, eternal, written, hard-and-fast, carved in stone, set in concrete (*informal*), ultimate, conclusive, binding, irrevocable, without appeal

13 **commanding**, imperious, imperative, jussive, peremptory, abrupt; **directive**, **instructive**; **mandating**, dictating, compelling, obligating, **prescriptive**, preceptive; decretory, decretive, decretal; **authoritative** *see* 417.15

adverbs

14 **commandingly**, imperatively, peremptorily

15 **by order** *or* **command**, at the word of command, as ordered *or* required, to order; mandatorily, compulsorily, obligatorily

421 DEMAND

nouns

1 **demand**, **claim**, **call**; **requisition**, requirement, stated requirement, order, rush order, indent; seller's market, land-office business; strong *or* heavy demand, draft, drain, levy, tax, taxing; imposition, impost, tribute, duty, contribution; insistent demand, rush; exorbitant *or* extortionate demand, exaction, extortion, blackmail; **ultimatum**, nonnegotiable demand; notice, warning *see* 399

2 **stipulation**, **provision**, proviso, condition; **terms**; exception, reservation; **qualification** *see* 958

3 (*informal terms*) catch, Catch-22, snag; strings, strings attached; ifs, ands, and buts; whereases, however

4 **insistence**, **exigence**, **importunity**, importunateness, importunacy, **demandingness**, pertinaciousness, pertinacity; pressure, pressingness, **urgency**, **exigency** *see* 996.4; **persistence** *see* 360.1

verbs

5 **to demand**, **ask**, **ask for**, make a demand; **call for**, call on *or* upon one for, appeal to one for; call out for, cry *or* cry out for, clamour for; **claim**, **challenge**, **require**, **levy**, **impose**, impose on one for; **exact**, **extort**, squeeze, screw; blackmail; **requisition**, make *or* put in requisition, indent, **confiscate**; **order**, put in *or* place an order, order up; deliver *or* issue an ultimatum; warn *see* 399.5

6 **to claim**, **pretend to**, lay claim to, stake a claim (*informal*), put *or* have dibs on (*US informal*), assert *or* vindicate a claim *or* right *or* title to; have going for it *or* one (*informal*); **challenge**

7 to **stipulate**, stipulate for, specifically provide, set conditions *or* terms, make reservations; **qualify** *see* 958.3

8 to **insist**, insist on *or* upon, stick to (*informal*), set one's heart *or* mind upon; **take one's stand upon**, stand on *or* upon, put *or* lay it on the line (*informal*), make no bones about it; stand upon one's rights, **put one's foot down** (*informal*); brook *or* take no denial, not take no for an answer; **maintain, contend**, assert; urge, press *see* 375.14; **persist** *see* 360.2

adjectives

9 **demanding, exacting**, exigent; draining, taxing, exorbitant, extortionate, grasping; **insistent**, instant, **importunate**, urgent, pertinacious, pressing, loud, clamant, crying, clamorous; persistent

10 **claimed**, spoken for; requisitioned; requisitorial, requisitory

adverbs

11 **demandingly, exactingly**, exigently; exorbitantly, extortionately; **insistently, importunately, urgently**, pressingly, clamorously, loudly, clamantly

12 **on demand**, at demand, **on call**, upon presentation

422 ADVICE

nouns

1 **advice, counsel, recommendation, suggestion**; proposal; advising, advocacy; **direction, instruction**, guidance, briefing; **exhortation**, hortation (*old*), enjoinder, expostulation, remonstrance; **sermons**, sermonizing, preaching, preachiness; **admonition**, monition, monitory *or* monitory letter, caution, caveat, **warning** *see* 399; **idea**, thought, opinion *see* 952.6; **consultancy**, consultantship, **consultation**, parley *see* 541.6; council *see* 423; **counselling**; guidance counselling, educational counselling, vocational guidance

2 piece of advice, **word of advice, word to the wise**, *verbum sapienti* (*Latin*), verb *or* verbum sap (*informal*), word in the ear, **hint, broad hint, flea in the ear** (*informal*), **tip** (*informal*), a few words of wisdom, intimation, insinuation

3 **adviser, counsel, counsellor, consultant**, professional consultant, expert, boffin (*informal*), maven (*US*); instructor, guide, **mentor**, nestor, orienter; confidant, personal adviser; agony aunt, agony uncle; admonisher, monitor, Dutch uncle; Polonius (*Shakespeare*), preceptist; **teacher** *see* 571; meddler, backseat driver (*informal*)

4 **advisee**, counselee; client

verbs

5 to **advise, counsel, recommend, suggest, advocate**, propose, submit; **instruct**, coach, guide, direct, brief; prescribe; weigh in with advice (*informal*), give a piece of advice, give a hint *or* broad hint, hint at, intimate, insinuate, put a flea in one's ear (*informal*), have a word with one, speak words of wisdom; meddle; confer, consult with *see* 541.11

6 to **admonish, exhort**, expostulate, remonstrate, preach; **enjoin, charge**, call upon one to; caution, issue a caveat, wag one's finger (*informal*); warn away, warn off, **warn** *see* 399.5, 6; move, prompt, **urge, incite, encourage, induce, persuade** *see* 375.23; **implore** *see* 440.11

7 to **take** *or* **accept advice, follow advice**, follow, follow implicitly, go along with (*informal*), buy *or* buy into (*informal*); solicit advice, desire guidance, implore counsel; **be advised by**; have at one's elbow, take one's cue from

adjectives

8 **advisory**, recommendatory; **consultative**, consultatory; **directive**, instructive; **admonitory**, monitory, monitorial, cautionary, **warning** *see* 399.7; **expostulative**, expostulatory, **remonstrative**, remonstratory, remonstrant; **exhortative**, exhortatory, hortative, hortatory, preachy (*informal*), **didactic**, moralistic, sententious

phrases

9 too many cooks spoil the broth

423 COUNCIL

nouns

1 **council, conclave**, *concilium* (*Latin*), deliberative *or* advisory body, **assembly**; deliberative assembly, consultative assembly; chamber, house; **board**, court, bench; full assembly, plenum, plenary session; congress, diet, synod, senate, soviet; **legislature** *see* 613; **cabinet**, divan, council of ministers, council of state, British Cabinet, US Cabinet; kitchen cabinet, camarilla, star chamber; staff; junta, directory; Sanhedrin; privy council; county council, parish council, borough *or* town council, city *or* municipal council, village council, district council; brains trust (*informal*), group *or* corps *or* body of advisers, inner circle; council of war; wages council, works council; syndicate, **association** *see* 617; **conference** *see* 541.6; **assembly** *see* 769.2; **tribunal** *see* 595

2 **committee**, subcommittee, standing committee; select committee, special committee, ad hoc committee; committee of one

3 **forum, conference**, discussion group **round table, panel**; open forum, colloquium, symposium; town meeting; **powwow** (*informal*)

4 ecclesiastical council, chapter, classis, conclave, conference, congregation, consistory, convention, convocation, presbytery, session, synod, vestry; General Assembly, General Synod; parochial council, parochial church council; diocesan conference, diocesan court; provincial court, plenary council; ecumenical council; Council of Nicaea, Council of Trent, Lateran Council, Vatican Council, Vatican Two; conciliarism

adjectives

5 **conciliar**, council, councilmanic, aldermanic; **consultative, deliberative, advisory**; synodal, synodic, synodical

adverbs

6 in council, in conference, in consultation, in a huddle (*informal*), in conclave; in session, sitting

424 COMPULSION

nouns

1 compulsion, obligation, obligement; command *see* 420; necessity *see* 962; inevitability *see* 962.7; irresistibility, compulsiveness; forcing, enforcement; command performance; constraint, coaction; restraint *see* 428

2 force, *ultima ratio* (*Latin*); brute force, naked force, rule of might, big battalions, main force, physical force; the right of the strong, the law of the jungle; tyranny *see* 612.10

3 coercion, intimidation, scare tactics, arm-twisting (*informal*), duress; the strong arm *and* strong-arm tactics (*both informal*), a pistol *or* gun to one's head, the sword, the mailed fist, the bludgeon, the boot in the face, the jackboot, the big stick, the club, *argumentum baculinum* (*Latin*); pressure, high pressure, high-pressure methods; violence *see* 671

verbs

4 to compel, force, make; have, cause, cause to; constrain, bind, tie, tie one's hands; restrain *see* 428.7; enforce, drive, impel; dragoon, use force upon, force one's hand, hold a pistol *or* gun to one's head

5 to oblige, necessitate, require, exact, demand, dictate, impose, call for; take *or* brook no denial; leave no option *or* escape, admit of no option

6 to press; bring pressure to bear upon, put pressure on, bear down on, bear against, bear hard upon

7 to coerce, use violence, ride roughshod, intimidate, bully, bludgeon, blackjack (*US*); hijack, shanghai, dragoon

8 (*informal terms*) to twist one's arm, arm-twist, twist arms, knock *or* bang heads, knock *or* bang heads together, strong-arm, steamroller, bulldoze, pressure, lean on, squeeze; put the screws on *or* to, get one over a barrel *or* under one's thumb, put the heat on; pull rank; ram down one's throat

9 to be compelled, be coerced, have to *see* 962.10; be stuck with (*informal*), can't help but

adjectives

10 compulsory, compulsive, compulsatory, compelling; pressing, driving, imperative, imperious; constraining, coactive; restraining *see* 428.11; irresistible

11 obligatory, compulsory, imperative, mandatory, required, dictated, binding; involuntary; necessary *see* 962.12; inevitable *see* 962.15

12 coercive, forcible; steamroller *and* bulldozer *and* sledgehammer *and* strong-arm (*all informal*); violent

adverbs

13 compulsively, compulsorily, compellingly, imperatively, imperiously

14 forcibly, by force, by main force, by *force majeure*, by a strong arm; by force of arms, *vi et armis*

(*Latin*), at gunpoint, with a pistol *or* gun to one's head, at the point of a gun, at the point of the sword *or* bayonet, at bayonet point

15 obligatorily, compulsorily, mandatorily, by stress of, under press of; under the lash *or* gun; of necessity

425 STRICTNESS

nouns

1 strictness, severity, harshness, stringency, astringency, hard line; discipline, strict *or* tight *or* rigid discipline, regimentation, spit and polish; austerity, sternness, grimness, ruggedness, toughness (*informal*); belt-tightening; Spartanism; authoritarianism; demandingness, exactingness; meticulousness *see* 339.3

2 firmness, rigour, rigorousness, rigidness, rigidity, stiffness, hardness, obduracy, obdurateness, inflexibility, inexorability, unyieldingness, unbendingness, impliability, unrelentingness, relentlessness; uncompromisingness; stubbornness, obstinacy *see* 361; purism; precisianism, puritanism, fundamentalism, orthodoxy

3 firm hand, iron hand, heavy hand, strong hand, tight hand, tight rein; tight *or* taut ship

verbs

4 to hold *or* keep a tight hand upon, keep a firm hand on, keep a tight rein on, rule with an iron hand, rule with a rod of iron, knock *or* bang heads together (*informal*); regiment, discipline; run a tight *or* taut ship, ride herd, keep one in line; maintain the highest standards, not spare oneself nor anyone else, go out of one's way, go the extra mile (*informal*)

5 to deal harshly with, deal hard measure to, lay a heavy hand on, bear hard upon, take a hard line, not pull one's punches (*informal*)

adjectives

6 strict, exacting, exigent, demanding, not to be trifled with, stringent, astringent; disciplined, spit-and-polish; severe, harsh, dour, unsparing; stern, grim, austere, rugged, tough (*informal*); Spartan, Spartanic; hard-line, authoritarian *see* 417.16; meticulous *see* 339.12

7 firm, rigid, rigorous, rigorist, rigoristic, stiff, hard, iron, steel, steely, hard-shell, obdurate, inflexible, ironhanded, inexorable, dour, unyielding, unbending, impliable, relentless, unrelenting, procrustean; uncompromising; stubborn, obstinate *see* 361.8; purist, puristic; puritan, puritanic, puritanical, fundamentalist, orthodox; ironbound, rockbound, musclebound, ironclad (*informal*); straitlaced, hidebound

adverbs

8 strictly, severely, stringently, harshly; sternly, grimly, austerely, ruggedly, toughly (*informal*)

9 firmly, rigidly, rigorously, stiffly, stiff, hardly, obdurately, inflexibly, impliably, inexorably, unyieldingly, unbendingly; uncompromisingly, relentlessly, unrelentingly; ironhandedly, with a firm *or* a strong *or* a heavy *or* an iron hand

426 LAXNESS

nouns

1 **laxness, laxity, slackness, looseness,** relaxedness; loosening, relaxation; imprecision, sloppiness (*informal*), carelessness, remissness, negligence *see* 340.1; indifference *see* 102; weakness *see* 16; impotence *see* 19; unrestraint *see* 430.3

2 unstrictness, nonstrictness, undemandingness, unsevereness, unharshness; leniency *see* 427; **permissiveness,** overpermissiveness, overindulgence, **softness;** unsternness, unausfereness; easygoingness, easiness; **flexibility,** pliancy

verbs

3 to hold a loose rein, **give free rein to,** give the reins to, **give one his head,** give a free course to, give rope enough to; permit all *or* anything

adjectives

4 **lax, slack, loose,** relaxed; imprecise, sloppy (*informal*), careless, slipshod; remiss, negligent *see* 340.10; indifferent *see* 102.6; weak *see* 16.12; impotent *see* 19.13; untrammeled, unrestrained

5 unstrict, undemanding, **unexacting; unsevere, unharsh; unstern,** unaustere; lenient *see* 427.7; **permissive,** overpermissive, overindulgent, **soft;** easy, easygoing, laid-back (*informal*); **flexible,** pliant, yielding

427 LENIENCY

nouns

1 **leniency** *or* lenience, lenientness, lenity; **clemency,** clementness, **mercifulness,** mercy, **humaneness,** humanity, pity, **compassion** *see* 145.1; **mildness, gentleness,** tenderness, softness, moderateness; **easiness,** easygoingness; laxness *see* 426; **forebearance,** forebearing, patience *see* 134; acceptance, **tolerance** *see* 978.4

2 **compliance, complaisance,** obligingness, accommodatingness, **agreeableness;** affability, graciosity, graciousness, generousness, decency, amiability; kindness, kindliness, benignity, **benevolence** *see* 143

3 **indulgence, humouring,** obliging; favouring, gratification, pleasing; **pampering,** cosseting, **coddling,** mollycoddling, petting, **spoiling; permissiveness,** overpermissiveness, overindulgence; sparing the rod, wrapping up in cotton wool

4 **spoiled child** *or* **brat,** *enfant gâté* (*French*), pampered darling, mother's boy, mollycoddle, sissy; *enfant terrible* (*French*), naughty child

verbs

5 to **be easy on,** ease up on, handle with kid *or* velvet gloves, use a light hand *or* rein, slap one's wrist, spare the rod, wrap up in cotton wool; **tolerate,** bear with *see* 134.5

6 to **indulge, humour, oblige;** favour, please, gratify, satisfy, **cater to; give way to,** yield to, let one have his own way; **pamper,** cosset, **coddle,** mollycoddle, pet, make a lap dog of, **spoil;** spare the rod

adjectives

7 **lenient, mild, gentle,** mild-mannered, tender, humane, compassionate, **clement,** merciful *see* 145.7; soft, moderate, **easy,** easygoing; lax *see* 426.4; forgiving *see* 148.6; **forebearing, forebearant,** patient *see* 134.9; accepting, **tolerant** *see* 978.11

8 **indulgent, compliant,** complaisant, **obliging, accommodating, agreeable,** amiable, gracious, generous, benignant, affable, decent, kind, kindly, benign, benevolent *see* 143.15; **hands-off** (*informal*), permissive, overpermissive, overindulgent

9 **indulged, pampered, coddled, spoiled,** spoiled rotten (*informal*)

428 RESTRAINT

nouns

1 **restraint, constraint; inhibition;** legal restraint, injunction, enjoining, enjoinder, interdict; **control, curb, check,** rein, arrest, arrestation; **retardation,** deceleration, slowing down; cooling *and* cooling off *and* cooling down (*all informal*); retrenchment, curtailment; self-control *see* 359.5; **hindrance** *see* 1011; rationing; thought control; restraint of trade, monopoly, protection, protectionism, protective tariff, trade barrier, tariff wall; clampdown *and* crackdown (*both informal*), proscription, **prohibition** *see* 444

2 **suppression, repression; subdual,** quelling, putting down, shutting *or* closing down, smashing, crushing; quashing, squashing *and* squelching (*both informal*); smothering, stifling, suffocating, strangling, throttling; extinguishment, quenching; **censorship** *and* censoring, bleeping *or* bleeping out (*informal*)

3 **restriction, limitation, confinement;** Hobson's choice, no choice, zero option; circumscription *see* 210; stint, cramping, cramp; qualification *see* 958

4 **shackle,** restraint, **restraints, fetter, hamper,** trammel, trammels, **manacle,** gyves (*old*), bond, **bonds,** irons, chains, darbies (*informal*); **stranglehold; handcuffs,** cuffs; stocks, bilboes, pillory; **tether,** spancel, leash, choke chain, collar, lead, leading string; **rein;** hobble, hopple; strait-jacket; yoke, collar; bridle, halter; **muzzle, gag;** electronic tag, clamp *or* wheel clamp

5 **lock, bolt, bar,** padlock, catch, safety catch; barrier *see* 1011.5

6 **restrictionist, protectionist, monopolist;** censor

verbs

7 to **restrain, constrain, control, govern,** guard, contain, keep under control, put *or* lay under restraint; **inhibit,** straiten (*old*); enjoin, clamp *or* crack down on (*informal*), proscribe, prohibit *see* 444.3; **curb, check, arrest, bridle,** get under control, rein, snub, snub in; **retard,** slow down, decelerate; **cool** *and* cool off *and* cool down (*all informal*); retrench, curtail; hold, **hold in,** keep, withhold, hold up (*informal*), **keep from;** hinder *see* 1011.10; **hold back, keep back,** pull, set back; **hold in, keep in,** pull in, rein in; **hold** *or* **keep in check, hold at bay,** hold in leash, tie one down, tie one's hands; hold fast, keep a tight hand on; restrain

oneself, not go too far, not go off the deep end (*informal*)

8 **to suppress, repress,** stultify; **keep down,** hold down, keep under; **close** *or* shut down; **subdue, quell, put down,** smash, **crush; quash, squash** *and* **squelch** (*both informal*); **extinguish,** quench, stanch, damp down, pour water on, dash *or* pour cold water on, drown, kill; **smother, stifle,** suffocate, asphyxiate, strangle, throttle, choke off, muzzle, gag; censor, bleep *or* bleep out (*informal*), silence; sit on *and* sit down on (*both informal*); jump on *and* crack down on *and* clamp down on (*all informal*), put *or* keep the lid on (*informal*); bottle up, cork, cork up

9 **to restrict, limit, narrow, confine,** tighten; ground, restrict to home, barracks, bedroom, quarters, etc; circumscribe *see* 210.4; keep in *or* within bounds, keep from spreading, localize; **cage in,** hem, hem in, box, box in *or* up; **cramp,** stint; qualify *see* 958.3

10 **to bind, restrain, tie,** tie up, **strap,** lash, leash, pinion, fasten, secure, make fast; **hamper, trammel,** entrammel; rope; **chain, enchain; shackle, fetter, manacle,** gyve (*old*), put in irons; **handcuff,** tie one's hands; **tie hand and foot,** hog-tie (*US informal*); straitjacket; hobble, hopple, fetter, leash, put on a lead, spancel; tether, picket, moor, anchor; tie down, pin down, peg down; clamp; get a stranglehold on, put a half nelson on (*informal*); **bridle**

adjectives

11 **restraining, constraining; inhibiting,** inhibitive; **suppressive, repressive,** stultifying; controlling, on top of (*informal*)

12 **restrictive,** limitative, restricting, **narrowing,** limiting, **confining,** cramping; censorial

13 **restrained, constrained, inhibited,** pent-up; guarded; controlled, curbed, bridled; **under restraint,** under control, in check, under discipline; grounded, out of circulation; slowed-down, retarded, arrested, in remission; in *or* on leash, in leading strings

14 **suppressed, repressed; subdued,** quelled, put down, smashed, crushed; quashed, squashed *and* squelched (*both informal*); smothered, stifled, suffocated; censored

15 **restricted, limited, confined;** circumscribed *see* 210.6
"cabined, cribbed, confined"— SHAKESPEARE, hemmed in, hedged in *or* about, boxed in; landlocked; **shut-in,** stormbound, weatherbound, windbound, icebound, snowbound; cramped, stinted; qualified *see* 958.10

16 **bound, tied,** bound hand and foot, tied up, tied down, strapped, hampered, trammelled, shackled, handcuffed, fettered, manacled, tethered; **in bonds,** in irons *or* chains, ironbound

429 CONFINEMENT

nouns

1 **confinement,** locking-up, lockup, caging, penning, putting behind bars, impoundment, **restraint,** restriction; check, **restraint, constraint** *see* 428.1

2 **quarantine, isolation,** cordoning off, segregation, separation, sequestration, seclusion; walling in *or* up *or* off; sanitary cordon, *cordon sanitaire* (*French*), cordon; quarantine flag, yellow flag

3 **imprisonment, jailing,** incarceration, **internment,** immurement, immuration; **detention, captivity,** duress, durance (*old*); close arrest, house arrest; term of imprisonment; preventive detention; minimum- *or* maximum-security imprisonment *or* detention; lockdown

4 **commitment, committal,** consignment; recommitment, remand; mittimus (*law*); institutionalization

5 **custody,** custodianship, keep (*old*), **keeping, care, change, ward,** guarding, hold, protective *or* preventive custody, youth custody; protection, safekeeping *see* 1007.1

6 **arrest,** arrestment, arrestation, pinch (*informal*); **capture, apprehension, seizure,** netting (*informal*)

7 **place of confinement,** close quarters, not enough room to swing a cat; limbo, hell, purgatory; pound, pinfold; **cage; enclosure,** pen, coop *see* 212.3

8 **prison, penal institution,** prisonhouse, **penitentiary** (*US*), pen (*US informal*), keep, bastille; house of detention, detention centre, detention home; **jail** *or* **gaol,** jailhouse, lockup, tollbooth (*Scottish*), bridewell; maximum- *or* minimum-security prison, open prison; **military prison, guardhouse, stockade, brig,** glasshouse (*informal*); **dungeon,** oubliette, black hole, Black Hole of Calcutta; attendance centre, youth custody centre, remand centre, borstal (*old*), boot camp (*informal*); debtor's prison *and* sponging house (*both old*); **prison camp,** internment camp, detention camp, labour camp, forced-labour camp, gulag, **concentration camp;** prisoner-of-war camp *or* stockade, POW camp, stalag; **cell;** bullpen (*US informal*); solitary confinement, the hole (*informal*); **cell,** prison *or* jail cell; **detention cell,** holding cell, lockup; tank *and* drunk tank (*both US informal*); cellblock, cellhouse; condemned cell, death cell, death house *or* row; penal settlement *or* colony, Devil's Island

9 (*informal terms*) **nick, jug,** chokey, quod, pokey, clink, slammer, can, coop, cooler, big house; **porridge,** time, stir; **joint,** big school, big cage (*all US*)

10 **jailer** *or* **gaoler; keeper, warder,** prison guard, turnkey, screw (*informal*); **warden,** governor, commandant; custodian, guardian *see* 1007.6; **guard** *see* 1007.9

11 **prisoner, captive,** *détenu* (*French*), cageling; arrestee; **convict,** con (*informal*); **jailbird** *or* **gaolbird** (*informal*); detainee; internee; **prisoner of war** *or* **POW;** enemy prisoner of war *or* EPWS; political prisoner, prisoner of conscience; lifer (*informal*); trusty; parolee; ex-convict, ex-con (*informal*); **chain gang**

verbs

12 to **confine, shut in,** shut away, coop in, hem in, pen in, fence in *or* up, wall in *or* up, rail in; **shut up, coop up,** box up, bottle up, cork up, seal up, **impound;** pen, coop, pound *(old)*, crib, mew, cloister, immure, cage, cage in, encage; **enclose** *see* 212.5; **hold, keep in,** hold *or* keep in custody, **detain,** keep in detention, constrain, ground, **restrain,** hold in restraint; check, inhibit *see* 428.7; restrict *see* 428.9; shackle *see* 428.10

13 to **quarantine, isolate,** segregate, separate, seclude; **cordon, cordon off,** seal off, rope off; wall off, set up barriers, put behind barriers

14 to **imprison, incarcerate, intern,** immure; **jail** *or* **gaol,** jug *(informal)*, throw into jail *(informal)*; throw *or* cast in prison, clap up, clap in jail *or* prison, send up the river *(informal)*; **lock up,** lock in, bolt in, put *or* keep under lock and key, put behind bars; hold captive, hold prisoner, hold in captivity; hold under close *or* house arrest

15 to **arrest,** make an arrest, put under arrest, pick up; catch flat-footed; catch with one's pants down *or* hand in the till *(informal)*, catch one in the act *or* red-handed *or* in flagrante delicto, catch *or* have one bang to rights; run down, run to earth, **take captive, take prisoner, apprehend, capture,** seize, net *(informal)*, lay by the heels, **take into custody**

16 *(informal terms)* to **nick,** nab, pull in, **run in,** collar, **bust, pinch**

17 to **commit,** consign, commit to prison, send to jail, send down *and* send down the river *(both informal)*; commit to an institution, institutionalize; recommit, remit, remand

18 to **be imprisoned, do** *or* **serve time** *(informal)*, go down *(informal)*, do porridge *(informal)*; pay one's debt to society

adjectives

19 confined, in confinement, **shut-in,** pent, **pent-up,** kept in, under restraint;
"cabined, cribbed, confined"—SHAKESPEARE; impounded; grounded, out of circulation; **detained;** restricted *see* 428.15; cloistered, enclosed *see* 212.10

20 quarantined, isolated, segregated, separated; cordoned, cordoned *or* sealed *or* roped off

21 jailed, jugged *(informal)*, **imprisoned, incarcerated, interned,** immured; **in prison,** in stir *(informal)*, in captivity, **behind bars,** locked up, under lock and key, in durance

22 under arrest, in custody, in hold, under *or* in detention; under close arrest, under house arrest

430 FREEDOM

nouns

1 freedom, liberty; licence, loose *(old)*; run *and* the run of *(both informal)*,
"the right to live as we wish"—EPICTETUS, "the will to be responsible to ourselves"—NIETZSCHE, "political power divided into small fragments"—THOMAS HOBBES, "the choice of working or starving"—SAMUEL JOHNSON, "the recognition of necessity"—FRIEDRICH ENGELS; **civil liberty,** the Four Freedoms (F D Roosevelt):
freedom of speech and expression, freedom of worship, freedom from want, freedom from fear; constitutional freedom; academic freedom

2 right, rights, civil rights, civil liberties, constitutional rights, legal rights; Bill of Rights, Petition of Right, Declaration of Right, Declaration of the Rights of Man, Magna Charta *or* Carta; **unalienable rights, human rights,** natural rights, "life, liberty, and the pursuit of happiness"—THOMAS JEFFERSON

3 unrestraint, unconstraint, noncoercion, nonintimidation; **unreserve,** irrepressibleness, irrepressibility, uninhibitedness, exuberance *see* 109.4; **immoderacy, intemperance,** incontinence, uncontrol, unruliness, indiscipline; **abandon,** abandonment, **licentiousness,** wantonness, riotousness, wildness; permissiveness, unstrictness, laxness *see* 426

4 latitude, scope, room, range, way, field, manoeuvring space *or* room, room to swing a cat *(informal)*; **margin,** clearance, **space,** open space *or* field, elbowroom, breathing space, **leeway** *(informal)*, sea room, wide berth; **tolerance; free scope,** full *or* ample scope, **free hand,** free play, free course; **carte blanche,** blank cheque; no holds barred; swing, play, full swing; rope, long rope *or* tether, enough rope to hang oneself

5 independence, self-determination, self-government, self-direction, **autonomy,** home rule; **devolution,** subsidiarity, federalism; autarky, autarchy, self-containment, self-sufficiency; **individualism,** rugged individualism, individual freedom; **self-reliance,** self-dependence; inner-direction; Declaration of Independence

6 free will, free choice, discretion, option, choice, say, say-so *(informal)*, free decision; **full consent;** absolute *or* unconditioned *or* noncontingent free will

7 own free will, own account, own accord, own say-so *(informal)*, own discretion, own choice, **own initiative,** personal initiative, own responsibility, personal *or* individual responsibility, own volition, own authority, own power; own way, own sweet way *(informal)*; law unto oneself

8 exemption, exception, **immunity; release,** discharge; **franchise, licence,** charter, patent, liberty; diplomatic immunity, parliamentary immunity; special case *or* privilege; privilege; permission *see* 443

9 noninterference, nonintervention; isolationism; laissez-faireism, deregulation; *laissez-faire, laissez-aller (both French)*; liberalism, free enterprise, free competition, self-regulating market; capitalism *see* 611.9; free trade

10 liberalism, libertarianism, latitudinarianism; broad-mindedness, open-mindedness, toleration, tolerance; unbigotedness *see* 978.1; libertinism, **freethinking,** free thought; liberalization, **liberation** *see* 431

11 freeman, freewoman; citizen, free citizen, burgess; franklin; emancipated *or* manumitted slave, freedman, freedwoman; dediticism

12 free agent, independent, freelance; individualist, rugged individualist; free spirit; **liberal,** libertarian, latitudinarian; libertine, freethinker; free trader; **nonpartisan**, neutral, mugwump; isolationist

verbs

13 to liberalize, ease; **free, liberate** see 431.4

14 to exempt, free, release, discharge, **let go** and **let off** (both informal), set at liberty, spring (informal); **excuse**, spare, except, grant immunity, make a special case of; **dispense**, dispense from, give dispensation from; dispense with, save the necessity; remit, remise; absolve see 601.4

15 to give a free hand, let one have his head, **give one his head**; give the run of (informal), give the freedom of; give one leeway (informal), give full play; give one scope or space or room; **give rein** or **free rein to**, give the reins to, give bridle to, give one line, give one rope; **give one carte blanche, give one a blank cheque**; let go one's own way, let one go at will

16 to not interfere, **leave** or **let alone, let be**, leave or let well enough alone, let sleeping dogs lie; **keep hands off**, not tamper, not meddle, not involve oneself, not get involved, let it ride (informal), let nature take its course; live and let live, leave one to oneself, leave one in peace; mind one's own business; **deregulate**, decontrol

17 (informal terms) to get off one's back or one's case, get out of one's face or hair, **back off**, leave be, keep one's nose out, get lost, take a hike

18 to be free, feel free, feel free as a bird, feel at liberty; **go at large**, breathe free, breathe the air of freedom; **have free scope**, have a free hand, have the run of (informal); be at home, feel at home; be freed, be released; be exonerated, go or get off scot-free, walk

19 to let oneself go, let go, let loose and cut loose and let one's hair down (all informal), open up, let it all hang out (informal), chill out (informal); go all out, go flat out, pull out all the stops; go unrestrained, run wild, sow one's wild oats

20 to stand on one's own two feet, **shift for oneself, fend for oneself**, stand on one's own, strike out for oneself, look out for number one (informal); go it alone, be one's own man, pull a lone oar, play a lone hand (informal), **paddle one's own canoe** (informal); suffice to oneself, do for oneself, make or pay one's own way; ask no favours, ask no quarter; **be one's own boss** (informal), answer only to oneself, ask leave of no man; **go one's own way**, take one's own course; do on one's own, do on one's own initiative, do in one's own sweet way (informal); **have a will of one's own**, have one's own way, do what one likes or wishes or chooses, **do as one pleases**, go as one pleases, please oneself (informal), **suit oneself**; have a free mind; free-lance, be a free agent

adjectives

21 free; at liberty, at large, on the loose, **loose**, unengaged, disengaged, detached, unattached, uncommitted, uninvolved, clear, in the clear, go-as-you-please, easygoing, footloose, footloose and fancy-free,

"afoot and lighthearted"—WHITMAN, free and easy; free as air, free as a bird, free as the wind; scot-free; **freeborn; freed, liberated, emancipated**, manumitted, released, uncaged, sprung (informal)

22 independent, self-dependent; free-spirited, freewheeling, free-floating, free-standing; **self-determined**, self-directing, one's own man; inner-directed, **individualistic**; self-governed, **self-governing, autonomous**, sovereign; stand-alone, self-reliant, self-sufficient, self-subsistent, self-supporting, self-contained, autarkic, autarchic; nonpartisan, neutral, **nonaligned**

23 free-acting, free-going, free-moving, free-working; freehand, freehanded; **free-spoken**, outspoken, **plain-spoken, open, frank**, direct, candid, blunt see 644.17

24 unrestrained, unconstrained, unforced, uncompelled, uncoerced; unmeasured, uninhibited, **unsuppressed, unrepressed, unreserved**, unbuttoned (informal), exuberant see 109.14; **uncurbed, unchecked, unbridled**, unmuzzled; **unreined**, reinless; **uncontrolled**, unmastered, unsubdued, ungoverned, **unruly**; out of control, out of hand, out of one's power; **abandoned**, intemperate, immoderate, **incontinent, licentious**, loose, wanton, rampant, riotous, wild; irrepressible; lax see 426.4

25 nonrestrictive, unrestrictive; **permissive**, hands-off (informal); indulgent see 427.8; lax see 426.4; **liberal**, libertarian, latitudinarian; broad-minded, open-minded, tolerant; unbigoted see 978.8; libertine; freethinking

26 unhampered, untrammelled, unhandicapped, unimpeded, unhindered, unprevented, unclogged, unobstructed; clear, unencumbered, unburdened, unladen, unembarrassed, disembarrassed

27 unrestricted, unconfined, uncircumscribed, unbound (old), unbounded, unmeasured; **unlimited**, limitless, illimitable; unqualified, unconditioned, **unconditional**, without strings, no strings, no strings attached; **absolute**, perfect, unequivocal, full, plenary; open-ended, open, **wide-open** (informal); **deregulated**, decontrolled

28 unbound, untied, **unfettered**, unshackled, unchained; unmuzzled, ungagged; uncensored; declassified

29 unsubject, ungoverned, unenslaved, unenthralled; unvanquished, unconquered, unsubdued, unquelled, **untamed**, unbroken, undomesticated, unreconstructed

30 exempt, immune; exempted, **released, excused**, excepted, let off (informal), spared; **privileged**, licensed, favoured, chartered; permitted; dispensed; **unliable**, unsubject, irresponsible, unaccountable, unanswerable

31 quit, clear, free, rid; free of, clear of, rid of, shot or shut of (informal)

adverbs

32 freely, free; **without restraint**, without stint, unreservedly, with abandon; outright

33 independently, alone, by oneself, on one's tod (informal), under one's own power or steam, **on one's own** and **on one's own hook** (both informal), on one's own initiative; **on one's own account** *or* **responsibility**, on one's own say-so (*informal*); **of one's own free will, of one's own accord**, of one's own volition, at one's own discretion

431 LIBERATION

nouns

1 **liberation, freeing**, setting free, setting at liberty; **deliverance, delivery**; **rescue** *see* 398; **emancipation**, disenthralment, manumission; enfranchisement, affranchisement; Emancipation Proclamation; women's liberation; gay liberation; women's *or* gay lib (*informal*)

2 **release, freeing**, unhanding, **loosing**, unloosing; unbinding, untying, unbuckling, unshackling, unfettering, unlashing, unstrapping, untrussing *and* unpinioning (*both old*), unmanacling, **unleashing**, unchaining, untethering, unhobbling, unharnessing, unyoking, unbridling; unmuzzling, ungagging; unlocking, unlatching, unbolting, unbarring; unpenning, uncaging; **discharge, dismissal**; parole; convict release, springing (*informal*); demobilization, separation from the service

3 **extrication**, freeing, releasing, clearing; **disengagement, disentanglement**, untangling, unsnarling, unravelling, disentwining, disinvolvement, unknotting, disembarrassment, disembroilment; dislodgment, breaking out *or* loose, busting out *or* loose (*informal*)

verbs

4 **to liberate, free, deliver, set free**, set at liberty, set at large; **emancipate**, manumit, disenthral; enfranchise, affranchise; **rescue** *see* 398.3

5 **to release, unhand, let go, let loose, turn loose**, cast loose, let out, let off, let go free; **discharge, dismiss**; let out on bail, grant bail to; **parole**, put on parole; release from prison, spring (*informal*); demobilize, separate from the service

6 **to loose**, loosen, let loose, cut loose *or* free, unloose, unloosen; **unbind, untie**, unstrap, unbuckle, unlash, untruss *and* unpinion (*both old*); **unfetter, unshackle**, unmanacle, unchain, unhandcuff, untie one's hands; **unleash**, untether, unhobble; unharness, unyoke, unbridle; unmuzzle, ungag; unlock, unlatch, unbolt, unbar; unpen, uncage

7 **to extricate, free, release, clear**, get out; **disengage, disentangle**, untangle, unsnarl, unravel, disentwine, disinvolve, unknot, disembarrass, disembroil; dislodge, break out *or* loose, cut loose, tear loose

8 **to free oneself from**, deliver oneself from, **get free of, get rid of**, get clear of, **get out of**, get well out of, get around, extricate oneself, get out of a jam (*informal*); **throw off, shake off**; break out, bust out (*informal*), **escape** *see* 369.6; wriggle out of

9 **to go free**, go scot free, go at liberty, **get off**, get off scot-free, get out of, beat the rap *and* walk (*both informal*)

adjectives

10 **liberated, freed, emancipated, released**; delivered, rescued, ransomed, redeemed; extricated, unbound, untied, unshackled, etc; free *see* 430.20; on parole

432 SUBJECTION

nouns

1 **subjection, subjugation**; **domination** *see* 612.2; **restraint, control** *see* 428.1; **bondage, captivity**; **thrall, thraldom**, enthralment; **slavery**, enslavement, master-slave relationship; **servitude**, compulsory *or* involuntary servitude, servility, bond service, indentureship; **serfdom**, serfhood, villenage, **vassalage**; helotry, helotism; debt slavery, **peonage**; feudalism, feudality; absolutism, tyranny *see* 612.9, 10; deprivation of freedom, disenfranchisement, disfranchisement

2 **subservience** *or* subserviency, subjecthood, subordinacy, **subordination**, juniority, **inferiority**; lower status, subordinate role, satellite status; back seat *and* second fiddle (*both informal*); **service**, servitorship *see* 577.12

3 **dependence** *or* dependency, tutelage, chargeship, wardship; clientship, clientage

4 **subdual, quelling**, crushing, trampling *or* treading down, reduction, **humbling, humiliation**; **breaking, taming**, domestication, gentling; conquering *see* 412.1; **suppression** *see* 428.2

5 **subordinate**, junior, secondary, second-in-command, lieutenant, **inferior**; **underling**, understrapper, errand boy, flunky, fag, gofer (*informal*); assistant, personal assistant *or* PA, helper *see* 616.6; strong right arm, **right-hand man** *see* 616.7; **servant, employee** *see* 577

6 **dependent, charge, ward**, client, protégé, encumbrance; pensioner, pensionary; public charge, ward of the state; foster child; dependency *or* dependent state, client state, satellite *or* satellite state, puppet government, creature

7 **subject, vassal**, liege, liege man, liege subject, homager; **captive**; **slave**, servant, chattel, chattel slave, **bondsman**, bondman, **bondslave**, theow, thrall; indentured servant; labourer; bondwoman, bondswoman, bondmaid; odalisque, concubine; galley slave; **serf**, helot, villein, churl; debt slave, **peon**

verbs

8 **to subjugate, subject, subordinate**; **dominate** *see* 612.15; disfranchise, disenfranchise, divest *or* deprive of freedom; **enslave**, enthral, hold in thrall, make a chattel of; take captive, lead captive *or* into captivity; **hold in subjection**, hold in bondage, **hold captive**, hold in captivity; **hold down**, keep down, keep under; **keep** *or* **have under one's thumb**, have tied to one's apron strings, hold in leash, hold in leading strings, hold in swaddling clothes, hold *or* keep at one's beck and call; vassalize, make dependent *or* tributary; peonize

9 **to subdue, master**, overmaster, **quell, crush, reduce**, beat down, **break**, break down, overwhelm; tread underfoot, trample on *or* down, trample underfoot, roll in the dust, trample in the dust, drag at one's chariot wheel; **suppress** *see* 428.8; make one give in (*informal*), **conquer** *see* 412.10; kick around (*informal*), tyrannize *see* 612.16; unman *see* 19.12;

bring low, **bring to terms, humble,** humiliate, take down a notch *or* peg, bend, **bring one to his knees, bend to one's will**

10 **to have subject,** twist *or* turn *or* wind around one's little finger, make lie down and roll over, have eating out of one's hand, **lead by the nose,** make a puppet of, make a sport *or* plaything of; use as a doormat, treat like dirt under one's feet

11 **to domesticate, tame, break,** gentle, break in, break to harness; housebreak

12 **to depend on,** be at the mercy of, be putty in the hands of; not dare to say one's soul is one's own; eat out of one's hands; play second fiddle, take a back seat

adjectives

13 **subject, dependent,** tributary, client; **subservient, subordinate, inferior;** servile; liege, **vassal,** feudal, feudatory

14 **subjugated,** subjected, **enslaved, enthralled, in thrall,** captive, bond, unfree; disenfranchised, disfranchised, **oppressed, suppressed** see 428.14; **in subjection, in bondage, in captivity,** in slavery, in bonds, in chains; under the lash, under the heel; **in one's power,** in one's control, in one's hands *or* clutches, in one's pocket, **under one's thumb,** at one's mercy, under one's command *or* orders, at one's beck and call, at one's feet, at one's pleasure; **subordinated,** playing second fiddle; at the bottom of the ladder

15 **subdued, quelled,** crushed, broken, reduced, mastered, overmastered, humbled, humiliated, brought to one's knees, brought low, made to grovel; **tamed, domesticated,** broken to harness, gentled; housebroken

16 **downtrodden,** downtrod (*old*), kept down *or* under, ground down, overborne, trampled, **oppressed; abused,** misused; **henpecked, browbeaten,** led by the nose, in leading strings, tied to one's apron strings, ordered *or* kicked around (*informal*), regimented, tyrannized; slavish, servile, submissive see 433.12; unmanned see 19.19; treated like dirt under one's feet

prepositions

17 **under, below, beneath,** underneath, subordinate to; at the feet of; under the heel of; at the beck and call of, at the whim *or* pleasure of

433 SUBMISSION

nouns

1 **submission,** submittal, **yielding; compliance,** complaisance, **acquiescence, acceptance;** going along with (*informal*), **assent** see 332; **consent** see 441; **obedience** see 326; **subjection** see 432; **resignation,** resignedness, stoicism, philosophical attitude; **deference,** homage, kneeling, obeisance; **passivity, unassertiveness,** passiveness, supineness, longanimity, long-suffering, long-sufferance (*old*), nonresistance, nonopposition, nonopposal, quietness, nondissent, quietude, quietism; **cowardice** see 491

2 **surrender, capitulation;** renunciation, giving over, abandonment, relinquishment, **cession;** giving up *or*

in, backing off *or* down (*informal*), retreat, recession, recedence

3 **submissiveness, docility, tractability,** biddability, yieldingness, compliableness (*old*), pliancy, pliability, flexibility, malleability, mouldability, ductility, plasticity, facility; agreeableness, agreeability; subservience, **servility** see 138

4 **manageability, governability, controllability,** manipulability, manipulatability, corrigibility, untroublesomeness; **tameness,** housebrokenness; tamableness, domesticability; milk-toast, milquetoast, Caspar Milquetoast (*all US & Canadian*)

5 **meekness, gentleness, tameness, mildness,** mild-manneredness, peaceableness, lamblikeness, dovelikeness; **self-abnegation, humility** see 137

verbs

6 **to submit, comply, take, accept,** go along with (*informal*), suffer, bear, brook, **acquiesce,** be agreeable, accede, **assent** see 332.8; **consent** see 441.2; relent, **succumb,** resign, resign oneself, give oneself up, not resist; take one's medicine, swallow the pill, face the music; **bite the bullet; knuckle down** *or* **under,** knock under (*old*), take it, swallow it; jump through a hoop, dance to another's tune; take it lying down; put up with it, grin and bear it, make the best of it, take the rough with the smooth, shrug, shrug off, **live with it; obey** see 326.2

7 **to yield, cede, give way, give ground, back down, give up, give in,** cave in (*informal*), withdraw from *or* quit the field, break off combat, cease resistance, have no fight left

8 **to surrender, give up, capitulate,** acknowledge defeat, cry quits, cry pax, beg a truce, pray for quarter, implore mercy, **throw in the towel** *or* **sponge** (*informal*), show *or* wave the white flag, lower *or* haul down *or* strike one's flag *or* colours, throw down *or* lay down *or* deliver up one's arms, hand over one's sword, yield the palm, come to terms; renounce, abandon, relinquish, **cede,** give over, hand over

9 **to submit to, yield to, defer to,** bow to, give way to, knuckle under to, succumb to

10 **to bow down,** bow, bend, stoop, crouch, **bow one's head,** bend the neck, bow submission; genuflect, curtsy; **bow to, bend to,** knuckle to (*informal*), bend *or* bow to one's will, bend to one's yoke; kneel to, **bend the knee to, fall on one's knees before,** crouch before, **fall at one's feet,** throw oneself at the feet of, prostrate oneself before, **truckle to,** cringe to; **kowtow,** bow and scrape, grovel, do obeisance *or* homage

11 **to eat humble pie,** eat dirt, eat crow (*US & Canadian*), lick the dust

adjectives

12 **submissive, compliant,** compliable (*old*), complaisant, complying, **acquiescent,** consenting see 441.4; **assenting,** accepting, agreeable; subservient, abject, **obedient** see 326.3; servile; **resigned,** uncomplaining; unassertive; **passive,** supine, **unresisting,** nonresisting, unresistant, nonresistant, nonresistive, long-suffering, longanimous, nonopposing, nondissenting

13 docile, tractable, biddable, unmurmuring, **yielding,** pliant, pliable, flexible, malleable, mouldable, ductile, plastic, facile (*old*), like putty in one's hands

14 manageable, governable, controllable, manipulable, manipulatable, handleable, corrigible, restrainable, untroublesome; domitable, tamable, domesticable; milk-toast *or* milquetoast (*US & Canadian*)

15 meek, gentle, mild, mild-mannered, peaceable, pacific, quiet; subdued, chastened, tame, tamed, broken, housebroken, domesticated; lamblike, gentle as a lamb, dovelike; humble

16 deferential, obeisant; subservient, obsequious, servile see 138.13; crouching, prostrate, prone, on one's belly, on one's knees, on bended knee

adverbs

17 submissively, compliantly, complaisantly, acquiescently, agreeably; obediently *see* 326.6; resignedly, uncomplainingly, with resignation; passively, supinely, unresistingly, unresistantly, nonresistively

18 docilely, tractably, biddably, yieldingly, pliantly, pliably, malleably, flexibly, plastically, facilely (*old*)

19 meekly, gently, tamely, mildly, peaceably, pacifically, quietly, like a lamb

434 OBSERVANCE

nouns

1 observance, observation; keeping, adherence, heeding; compliance, conformance, conformity, accordance; faith, faithfulness, fidelity; respect, deference *see* 155.1; performance, practice, execution, discharge, carrying out *or* through; dutifulness *see* 641.2, acquittal, acquittance (*both old*), fulfilment, satisfaction; heed, care *see* 339.1

verbs

2 to observe, keep, heed, follow, keep the faith; regard, defer to, respect *see* 155.4, attend to, comply with, conform to; hold by, abide by, adhere to; live up to, act up to, practise what one preaches, be faithful to, keep faith with, do justice to, do the right thing by; fulfil, fill, meet, satisfy; make good, keep *or* make good one's word *or* promise, be as good as one's word, redeem one's pledge, stand to one's engagement

3 to perform, practise, do, execute, discharge, carry out *or* through, carry into execution, do one's duty *see* 641.10, do one's office, fulfil one's role, discharge one's function

adjectives

4 observant, respectful *see* 155.8, regardful, mindful; faithful, devout, devoted, true, loyal, constant; dutiful *see* 641.13, duteous; as good as one's word; practised, active; compliant, conforming; punctual, punctilious, scrupulous, meticulous, conscientious *see* 339.12

435 NONOBSERVANCE

nouns

1 nonobservance, inobservance, unobservance, nonadherence; nonconformity, disconformity, nonconformance, noncompliance; apostasy; inattention, indifference, disregard *see* 983.1; laxity *see* 426.1; nonfulfilment, nonperformance, nonfeasance, failure, dereliction, delinquency, omission, default, slight, oversight; negligence; neglect *see* 340; abandonment *see* 370

2 violation, infraction, breach, breaking; infringement, transgression, trespass, contravention; offence *see* 674.4; breach of promise, breach of contract, breach of trust *or* faith, bad faith, breach of privilege; breach of the peace

verbs

3 to disregard, lose sight of, pay no regard to; neglect *see* 340.6; renege, abandon *see* 370.5; defect *see* 857.13

4 to violate, break, breach; infringe, transgress, trespass, contravene, trample on *or* upon, trample, underfoot, do violence to, make a mockery of, outrage; defy, set at defiance, flout, set at naught, set naught by; take the law into one's own hands; break one's promise, break one's word

adjectives

5 nonobservant, inobservant, unobservant, nonadherent; nonconforming, unconforming, noncompliant, uncompliant; inattentive, disregardful *see* 983.6; negligent *see* 340.10; unfaithful, untrue, unloyal, inconstant, lapsed, renegade *see* 857.20, 363.11

436 PROMISE

nouns

1 promise, pledge, solemn promise, troth, plight, faith, parole, word, word of honour, solemn declaration *or* word; oath, vow; avouch, avouchment; assurance, guarantee, warranty; entitlement

2 obligation, commitment, agreement, engagement, undertaking, recognizance; understanding, gentlemen's agreement; verbal agreement, nonformal agreement, pactum (*law*); tacit *or* unspoken agreement; contract *see* 437.1; designation, committal, earmarking

3 betrothal, betrothment, espousal, engagement, handfasting *and* affiance (*both old*), troth, marriage contract *or* vow, plighted troth *or* faith *or* love; banns, banns of matrimony; prenuptial agreement *or* contract

verbs

4 to promise, give *or* make a promise, hold out an expectation; pledge, plight, troth, vow; give one's word, pledge one's word, give one's parole, give one's word of honour, plight one's troth *or* faith, pledge *or* plight one's honour; cross one's heart *and* cross one's heart and hope to die (*both informal*), swear; vouch, avouch, **warrant, guarantee, assure;** underwrite, countersign

5 **to commit, engage,** undertake, obligate, bind, **agree to,** answer for, be answerable for, take on oneself, be responsible for, be security for, accept obligation *or* responsibility, bind oneself to, put oneself down for; have an understanding; enter into a gentlemen's agreement; take the vows *or* marriage vows; shake hands on; contract; designate, commit, earmark

6 **to be engaged, affiance, betroth,** troth, plight one's troth, **contract,** contract an engagement, pledge *or* promise in marriage; publish the banns

adjectives

7 **promissory,** votive; under *or* upon oath, on one's word, on one's word of honour, on the Book, under hand and seal

8 **promised, pledged, bound, committed,** compromised, **obligated; sworn,** warranted, **guaranteed,** assured, underwritten; contracted *see* 437.12; **engaged, plighted, affianced, betrothed,** intended

adverbs

9 on one's honour *or* word *or* word of honour; solemnly

437 COMPACT

nouns

1 **compact, pact, contract,** legal contract, valid contract, **covenant,** convention, transaction, paction (*Scottish*), accord, **agreement,** mutual agreement, agreement between *or* among parties, signed *or* written agreement, formal agreement, legal agreement, undertaking, stipulation; adjustment, accommodation; **understanding, arrangement, bargain,** deal; **settlement,** negotiated settlement; **union agreement,** wage contract, employment contract, collective agreement; cartel, consortium; protocol; bond, binding agreement, ironclad agreement, covenant of salt; gentleman's *or* gentlemen's agreement; promise *see* 436

2 **treaty,** international agreement, *entente, entente cordiale* (*both French*), concord, concordat, cartel, convention, capitulation; **alliance, league;** nonaggression pact, mutual-defence treaty; NATO *or* North Atlantic Treaty Organization; SEATO *or* Southeast Asia Treaty Organization

3 **signing,** signature, sealing, closing, conclusion, solemnization; handshake

4 **execution, completion; transaction; carrying out, discharge, fulfilment,** prosecution, effectuation; enforcement; observance *see* 434

verbs

5 **to contract,** compact, **covenant, bargain, agree, engage,** undertake, commit, mutually commit, make a deal (*informal*), do a deal, stipulate, agree to, bargain for, contract for; preset, prearrange, **promise** *see* 436.4; subcontract, outsource

6 **to treat with, negotiate, bargain,** make terms, sit down with, sit down at the bargaining table

7 **to sign, shake hands** *or* shake (*informal*), seal, formalize, make legal and binding, solemnize, affix one's John Hancock (*US informal*); agree on terms, come to an agreement *see* 332.10; strike a bargain *see* 731.18; plea-bargain

8 **to arrange, settle; adjust,** fine-tune, accommodate, reshuffle, **compose,** fix, make up, straighten out, put *or* set straight, work out, sort out; **conclude,** close, **close with,** settle with

9 **to execute, complete, transact,** promulgate, **make;** make out, fill out; **discharge, fulfil,** render, administer; **carry out,** carry through, put through, prosecute; effect, effectuate, set in motion, implement; enforce, put in force; **abide by, honour, live up to,** adhere to, live by, **observe** *see* 434.2

adjectives

10 contractual, covenantal, conventional

11 **contracted,** compacted, **covenanted, agreed upon, bargained for,** agreed, stipulated; engaged, undertaken; **promised** *see* 436.8; arranged, settled; **signed, sealed;** signed, sealed and delivered

adverbs

12 **contractually, as agreed upon, as promised,** as contracted for, by the terms of the contract, according to the contract *or* bargain *or* agreement

438 SECURITY

thing given as a pledge

nouns

1 **security, surety,** indemnity, **guaranty, guarantee, warranty, insurance,** warrant, assurance; **obligation** *see* 436.2, full faith and credit; **bond,** tie; stocks and bonds *see* 738.1

2 **pledge, gage,** *pignus, vadium* (*both Latin*); undertaking; **earnest,** earnest money, god's penny, handsel (*old*); escrow; token payment; pawn, hock (*US & Canadian informal*); **bail,** bond, vadimonium; replevin, replevy, recognizance; mainprise (*old*); **hostage,** surety

3 **collateral,** collateral security *or* warranty; deposit, stake, forfeit; caution money, caution; margin; cosigned promissory note

4 **mortgage,** mortgage deed, deed of trust, lien, security agreement; vadium mortuum *or* mortuum vadium; vadium vivum, antichresis; hypothec, hypothecation, bottomry, bottomry bond; endowment mortgage, adjustment mortgage, blanket mortgage, chattel mortgage, closed mortgage, participating mortgage, instalment mortgage, leasehold mortgage, trust mortgage; first mortgage, second mortgage, third mortgage; adjustable-rate mortgage, variable-rate mortgage, fixed-rate mortgage; equity loan

5 **lien,** general lien, particular lien; pignus legale, common-law lien, statutory lien, judgment lien, pignus judiciale, tax lien, mechanic's lien; mortgage bond

6 **guarantor,** warrantor, guaranty, guarantee; mortgagor; insurer, underwriter; sponsor, surety; godparent, godfather, godmother; bondsman, bailsman, mainpernor

7 warrantee, mortgagee; insuree, policyholder; godchild, godson, goddaughter

8 guarantorship, sponsorship, sponsion

verbs

9 to secure, guarantee, guaranty, warrant, assure, insure, ensure, bond, **certify;** countersecure; **sponsor,** be sponsor for, sign for, sign one's note, **back,** stand behind *or* back of, stand up for; **endorse;** sign, cosign, **underwrite,** undersign, subscribe to; confirm, attest

10 to pledge, impignorate *and* handsel (*both old*), **deposit, stake,** post, put in escrow, **put up,** put up as collateral, lay out *or* down; **pawn,** put in pawn, soak (*informal*), hock *and* put in hock (*both US & Canadian informal*); mortgage, hypothecate, bottomry, bond; **put up bail,** bail out

adjectives

11 secured, covered, **guaranteed, warranted,** certified, **insured,** ensured, **assured;** certain, sure *see* 969.13

12 pledged, staked, posted, deposited, in escrow, **put up,** put up as collateral; on deposit, at stake; as earnest; **pawned,** in pawn, in hock (*US & Canadian informal*)

13 in trust, held in trust, held in pledge, fiduciary; in escrow

439 OFFER

nouns

1 offer, offering, proffer, presentation, **bid,** submission; **advance, overture,** approach, invitation; hesitant *or* tentative *or* preliminary approach, feeling-out, **feeler** (*informal*); asking price; **counteroffer, counterproposal**

2 proposal, proposition, suggestion, instance; **motion,** resolution; sexual advance *or* approach *or* invitation *or* overture, indecent proposal, pass (*informal*), improper suggestion; request *see* 440

3 ultimatum, last *or* final word *or* offer, firm bid *or* price, sticking point

verbs

4 to offer, proffer, present, tender, offer up, **put up, submit, extend,** prefer (*old*), **hold out,** hold forth, place in one's way, lay at one's feet, put *or* place at one's disposal, put one in the way of

5 to propose, submit, table, prefer; **suggest,** recommend, **advance,** commend to attention, **propound, pose, put forward,** bring forward, put *or* set forth, put it to, put *or* set *or* lay *or* bring before, dish up *and* come out *or* up with (*both informal*); put a bee in one's bonnet, put ideas into one's head; **bring up, broach, moot,** introduce, open up, launch, start, kick off (*informal*); **move, make a motion,** offer a resolution; postulate *see* 950.12

6 to bid, bid for, make a bid

7 to make advances, approach, overture, **make an overture,** throw *or* fling oneself at one (*informal*); **solicit, importune**

8 (*informal terms*) **to proposition, come on to,** hit on, put *or* make a move on, jump one's bones, make a pass, **make a play for,** play footsie with

9 to urge upon, press upon, ply upon, push upon, force upon, thrust upon; **press, ply;** insist

10 to volunteer, come *or* **step forward, offer** *or* **proffer** *or* **present oneself,** be at one's service, not wait to be asked, not wait for an invitation, need no prodding, step into the breach

440 REQUEST

nouns

1 request, asking; desire, wish, expressed desire; **petition,** petitioning, impetration, address; **application; requisition,** indent; demand *see* 421

2 entreaty, appeal, plea, bid, suit, call, cry, clamour, *cri du cœr* (*French*), beseeching, impetration, obtestation; **supplication, prayer,** rogation, **beseechment,** imploring, imploration, obsecration, obtestation, adjuration, imprecation; **invocation,** invocatory plea *or* prayer

3 importunity, importunateness, urgency, pressure, high pressure *and* hard sell (*both informal*); **urging, pressing, plying;** buttonholing; dunning; **teasing,** pestering, plaguing, nagging, nudging (*informal*); **coaxing,** wheedling, cajolery, cajolement, blandishment

4 invitation, invite *and* **bid** (*both informal*), engraved invitation, bidding, biddance, **call,** calling, **summons**

5 solicitation, canvass, canvassing; suit, addresses; **courting, wooing**

6 beggary, mendicancy, mendicity; **begging,** cadging, scrounging, bludging (*Australian & NZ informal*); panhandling (*informal*)

7 petitioner, supplicant, suppliant, suitor; **solicitor** *see* 730.7; **applicant,** solicitant, claimant; **aspirant,** seeker, wannabee (*informal*); **candidate,** postulant; bidder

8 beggar, mendicant, scrounger, cadger, bludger (*Australian & NZ informal*); panhandler (*informal*); *schnorrer* (*Yiddish*); tramp, down-and-out, vagabond, dosser (*informal*), vagrant, hobo *or* bum (*both US informal*) *see* 178.3; loafer *see* 331.8; mendicant friar; mendicant order

verbs

9 to request, ask, make a request, **beg leave,** make bold to ask; **desire,** wish, wish for, express a wish for, crave; **ask for,** order, put in an order for, bespeak, call for, trouble one for; whistle for (*informal*); **requisition,** make *or* put in a requisition, indent; make application, **apply for,** file for, **put in for;** demand *see* 421.4

10 to petition, present *or* prefer a petition, sign a petition, circulate a petition; **pray,** sue; **apply to, call on** *or* **upon;** memorialize

11 to entreat, implore, beseech, beg, crave, **plead, appeal, pray, supplicate,** impetrate, obtest; adjure, conjure; invoke, imprecate (*old*), **call on** *or* **upon,** cry on *or* upon, **appeal to,** cry to, run to; go cap *or* hat in hand; kneel to, go down on one's knees to, fall on one's knees to, go on bended knee to, throw oneself at the feet of, get *or* come down on one's marrow-bones (*informal*); **plead for**, clamour for, cry for, cry out for; call for help

12 **to importune, urge, press**, pressure (*informal*), prod, prod at, apply *or* exert pressure, push, ply; dun; **beset, buttonhole**, besiege, take *or* grasp by the lapels; work on (*informal*), **tease**, pester, plague, nag, nag at, chivvy (*informal*), make a pest *or* nuisance of oneself, try one's patience, bug (*informal*), nudge; **coax**, wheedle, cajole, blandish, flatter, soft-soap (*informal*)

13 **to invite, ask, call, summon, call in, bid come**, extend *or* issue an invitation, request the presence of, request the pleasure of one's company, send an engraved invitation

14 **to solicit, canvass; court, woo**, address, sue, sue for, pop the question (*informal*); **seek, bid for**, look for; **fish for**, angle for

15 **to beg, scrounge, cadge**, tap, bludge (*Australian & NZ informal*); panhandle (*informal*)

adjectives

16 **supplicatory, suppliant**, supplicant, supplicating, **prayerful**, precative; **petitionary; begging**, mendicant, cadging, scrounging; on one's knees *or* bended knees; with joined *or* folded hands

17 **imploring, entreating, beseeching, begging, pleading, appealing**, precatory, precative, adjuratory

18 **importunate; teasing**, pesty, pestering, plaguing, nagging, dunning, pesky (*US informal*); **coaxing**, wheedling, cajoling, flattering, soft-soaping (*informal*); **insistent, demanding, urgent**

19 **invitational**, inviting, invitatory

exclamations

20 **please**, prithee (*old*), pray, do, **pray do**; be so good as to, be good enough, have the goodness; will you, may it please you; **if you please**, *s'il vous plaît* (*French*); I beg you, *je vous en prie* (*French*); for God's *or* goodness *or* heaven's *or* mercy's sake; be my guest, feel free

441 CONSENT

nouns

1 **consent, assent, agreement**, accord, acceptance, approval, blessing, approbation, sanction, **endorsement**, ratification, backing; **affirmation**, affirmative, affirmative voice *or* vote, yea, aye, **nod** *and* **okay** *and* **OK** (*all informal*); **leave, permission** see 443; **willingness**, readiness, promptness, promptitude, eagerness, unreluctance, unloathness, ungrudgingness, tacit *or* unspoken *or* silent *or* implicit consent, **connivance; acquiescence, compliance**; submission see 433

verbs

2 **to consent, assent**, give consent, yield assent, be willing, be amenable, be persuaded, accede to, accord to *and* grant (*both old*), say yes *or* aye *or* yea, vote affirmatively, vote aye, **nod, nod assent; accept**, play *or* go along (*informal*), **agree to**, go along

with (*informal*); be in accord with, be in favour of, take kindly to, **approve of**, hold with; **approve**, give one's blessing to, **okay** *or* **OK** (*informal*); sanction, **endorse, ratify**; consent to silently *or* by implication *or* in petto (*Italian*); **wink at, connive at; be willing**, turn a willing ear; deign, condescend; have no objection, not refuse; permit see 443.9

3 **to acquiesce, comply, comply with**, fall in with, be persuaded, come round *or* around, come over, come to (*informal*), see one's way clear to; **submit** see 433.6, 9

adjectives

4 **consenting, assenting**, affirmative, amenable, persuaded, approving, agreeing, favourable, accordant, consentient, consentual; sanctioning, endorsing, ratifying; **acquiescent, compliant**, compliable (*old*); submissive see 433.12; **willing, agreeable**, content; ready, prompt, eager, unreluctant, unloath, nothing loath, unmurmuring, ungrudging, unrefusing; permissive see 443.14

adverbs

5 **consentingly, assentingly**, affirmatively, approvingly, favourably, positively, agreeably, accordantly; acquiescently, compliantly; willingly see 324.8; yes see 332.18

442 REFUSAL

nouns

1 **refusal, rejection**, turndown, turning down; thumbs down (*informal*), *pollice verso* (*Latin*); nonconsent, nonacceptance; **declining**, declination, declension, declinature; **denial**, disclamation, disclaimer, disallowance; decertification, disaccreditation; **repudiation** see 372.1; disagreement, dissent see 333; recantation see 363.3; contradiction see 335.2; negation, abnegation, negative, negative answer, nay, no, nix (*US & Canadian informal*); unwillingness see 325; disobedience see 327; noncompliance, nonobservance see 435; withholding, holding back, retention, deprivation

2 **repulse, rebuff**, peremptory *or* flat *or* point-blank refusal, summary negative; a flea in one's ear; slap in the face *and* kick in the teeth (*both informal*); short shrift

verbs

3 **to refuse, decline**, not consent, refuse consent, **reject, turn down** (*informal*), decline to accept, **not have**, not buy (*informal*); not hold with, not think *or* hear of; **say no**, say nay, vote nay, vote negatively *or* in the negative, side against, disagree, beg to disagree, dissent see 333.4; shake one's head, negative, negate; vote down, **turn thumbs down on; be unwilling** see 325.3; contract out, opt out; turn one's back on, turn a deaf ear to, set oneself against, set one's face against, be unmoved, harden one's heart, resist entreaty *or* persuasion; stand aloof, not lift a finger, have nothing to do with, wash one's hands of; hold out against; put *or* set one's foot down, refuse point-blank *or* summarily; decline

politely *or* with thanks, beg off; **repudiate**, disallow, disclaim *see* 372.2; decertify, disaccredit

4 **to deny, withhold,** hold back; grudge, begrudge; close the hand *or* purse; deprive one of

5 **to repulse, rebuff, repel,** slap one in the face *and* kick one in the teeth (*both informal*), send one away with a flea in one's ear, give one short shrift, shut *or* slam the door in one's face, turn one away; slap *or* smack one down (*informal*); deny oneself to, refuse to receive, not be at home to, **snub** *see* 157.5

adjectives

6 **unconsenting,** nonconsenting, **negative; unwilling** *see* 325.5; **uncompliant,** uncomplying, uncomplaisant, inacquiescent, uncooperative; disobedient; rejective, declinatory; deaf to, not willing to hear of

phrases

7 I refuse, I won't, I will not, I will do no such thing; over my dead body, far be it from me, not if I can help it, not likely, not on your life, count me out, include me out, I won't buy it, it's no go, like hell I will, I'll be hanged if I will, try and make me, you should live so long, I'll see you in hell first, nothing doing (*all informal*); out of the question, not to be thought of, impossible; **no,** by no means, **no way,** no way José, **there's no way**

443 PERMISSION

nouns

1 **permission, leave, allowance,** vouchsafement; **consent** *see* 441; permission to enter, admission, ticket, ticket of admission; **licence,** liberty *see* 430.1; okay *and* OK *and* nod *and* go-ahead *and* **green light** *and* **thumbs-up** (*all informal*); special permission, charter, patent, dispensation, release, waiver

2 **sufferance, tolerance,** toleration, **indulgence;** overlooking, connivance; permissiveness

3 **authorization, authority, sanction, licensing,** countenance, **warrant,** warranty, fiat; empowerment, enabling, entitlement, enfranchisement, certification; clearance, security clearance; ratification *see* 332.4; legalization, legitimation, decriminalization

4 **carte blanche,** blank cheque (*informal*), **full authority,** full power, free hand, open mandate

5 **grant, concession;** charter, franchise, liberty, diploma, patent, letters patent, brevet; royal charter, royal grant

6 **permit, licence, warrant;** planning permission, building permit; road-fund licence, driver's licence, special licence, marriage licence, hunting licence, fishing licence, etc; nihil obstat, imprimatur

7 **pass, passport,** visitor's passport, **safe-conduct,** safeguard, protection; visa, entry visa, exit visa; **clearance,** clearance papers; bill of health, clean bill of health, pratique, full pratique

8 **permissibility,** permissibleness, **allowableness; admissibility,** admissibleness; justifiableness, warrantableness, sanctionableness; **validity,** legitimacy, lawfulness, licitness, legality

verbs

9 **to permit, allow, admit, let,** leave (*informal*), give permission, give leave, make possible; **allow** *or* **permit of;** give *or* leave room for, open the door to; consent *see* 441.2; grant, accord, vouchsafe; okay *and* OK *and* give the nod *or* go-ahead *or* green light *or* thumbs up (*all informal*), say *or* give the word (*informal*); dispense, release, waive

10 **to suffer, countenance,** have, **tolerate, condone,** brook, endure, stomach, bear, bear with, put up with, stand for, hear of *and* go along with (*both informal*); indulge *see* 427.6; shut one's eyes to, **wink at,** blink at, overlook, connive at; leave the door *or* way open to

11 **to authorize, sanction, warrant;** give official sanction *or* warrant, legitimize, validate, legalize; empower, give power, enable, entitle; **license; privilege;** charter, patent, enfranchise, franchise; accredit, certificate, certify; ratify *see* 332.12; **legalize,** legitimate, legitimize, decriminalize

12 **to give carte blanche,** issue *or* accord *or* give a blank cheque (*informal*), give full power *or* authority, give an open mandate *or* invitation, give free rein, give a free hand, leave alone, leave it to one; permit all *or* anything, open the floodgates, remove all restrictions, deregulate

13 **may,** can, have permission, **be permitted** *or* **allowed**

adjectives

14 **permissive,** admissive, permitting, allowing; consenting *see* 441.4; **unprohibitive,** nonprohibitive; tolerating, obliging, **tolerant;** suffering, **indulgent, lenient** *see* 427.7; hands-off (*informal*); lax *see* 426.4

15 **permissible, allowable, admissible;** justifiable, warrantable, sanctionable; licit, **lawful, legitimate, legal,** legitimized, legalized, legitimated, decriminalized

16 **permitted, allowed,** admitted; tolerated, on sufferance; unprohibited, unforbidden, unregulated, deregulated, unchecked

17 **authorized,** empowered, entitled; **warranted, sanctioned; licensed, privileged;** chartered, patented; franchised, enfranchised; accredited, certificated

adverbs

18 **permissively,** admissively; **tolerantly, indulgently**

19 **permissibly, allowably,** admissibly; with permission, by one's leave; licitly, lawfully, legitimately, legally

phrases

20 **by your leave,** with your permission, if you please, with respect, may I?

444 PROHIBITION

nouns

1 **prohibition, forbidding,** forbiddance; **ruling out, disallowance,** denial, rejection *see* 372; refusal *see* 442; **repression,** suppression *see* 428.2; **ban, embargo, enjoinder, injunction,** prohibitory injunction, **proscription, court order,** inhibition, interdict, *interdictum* (*Latin*), interdiction; **index,** *Index Expurgatorius, Index Librorum Prohibitorum* (*both Latin*); **taboo;** thou-shalt-not *and* don't *and* no-no (*all informal*); law, statute *see* 673.3; preclusion, exclusion, **prevention** *see* 1011.2; forbidden fruit, contraband; sumptuary law *or* ordinance; restrictive convenant; forbidden territory *or* ground, no-man's-land (*informal*)

2 **veto,** negative (*old*); absolute veto, qualified *or* limited *or* negative veto, suspensive *or* suspensory veto, item veto, pocket veto; **thumbs down** (*informal*), *pollice verso* (*Latin*)

verbs

3 **to prohibit, forbid; disallow, rule out** *or* **against;** deny, **reject** *see* 372.2; say no to, **refuse** *see* 442.3; **bar,** debar, preclude, exclude, exclude from, shut out, shut *or* close the door on, **prevent** *see* 1011.14; **ban,** put under the ban, **outlaw; repress, suppress** *see* 428.8; **enjoin,** put under an injunction, issue an injunction against, issue a prohibitory injunction; **proscribe,** inhibit, **interdict,** put *or* lay under an interdict *or* interdiction; put on the Index; embargo, lay *or* put an embargo on; taboo

4 **to not permit** *or* **allow, not have, not suffer** *or* **tolerate,** not endure, not stomach, not bear, not bear with, **not countenance,** not brook, brook no, not condone, not accept, not put up with, not go along with (*informal*); not stand for *and* not hear of (*both informal*), put *or* set one's foot down on (*informal*)

5 **to veto,** put one's veto upon, decide *or* rule against, **turn thumbs down on** (*informal*), **negative, kill**

adjectives

6 **prohibitive,** prohibitory, prohibiting, **forbidding;** inhibitive, inhibitory, **repressive, suppressive** *see* 428.11; proscriptive, interdictive, interdictory; preclusive, exclusive, **preventive** *see* 1011.19

7 **prohibited, forbidden,** forbade, forbid, *verboten* (*German*), **barred;** vetoed; **unpermissible,** nonpermissible, not permitted *or* allowed, unchartered, **unallowed;** disallowed, ruled out, contraindicated; beyond the pale, off limits, out of bounds; unauthorized, **unsanctioned,** unlicensed; banned, under the ban, **outlawed,** contraband; taboo, tabooed, untouchable; **illegal,** unlawful, illicit

445 REPEAL

nouns

1 **repeal, revocation,** revoke, revokement; reneging, going back on *and* welshing (*both informal*), **rescindment,** rescindment, rescission, **reversal, striking down, abrogation,** cassation, reversal; suspension; waiving, **waiver, setting aside; countermand,** counterorder; **annulment,** nullification, withdrawal, **invalidation,** voiding, voidance, vacation, vacatur, defeasance; **cancellation,** cancelling, cancel, write-off; **abolition,** abolishment; **recall,** retraction, recantation *see* 363.3

verbs

2 **to repeal, revoke, rescind, reverse, strike down, abrogate;** renege, go back on *and* welsh (*both informal*); suspend; **waive, set aside; countermand,** counterorder; **abolish,** do away with; **cancel,** write off; **annul,** nullify, disannul, withdraw, **invalidate,** void, vacate, make void, declare null and void; **overrule,** override; **recall,** retract, recant; unwish

adjectives

3 **repealed, revoked, rescinded,** struck down, set aside; **invalid,** void, **null and void**

446 PROMOTION

nouns

1 **promotion, preferment, advancement, advance,** step-up *and* upping (*both informal*), rise, elevation, upgrading, jump, step-up, step up the ladder; kicking upstairs (*informal*); exaltation, aggrandizement; ennoblement, knighting; graduation, passing; pay rise

verbs

2 **to promote, advance,** prefer (*old*), elevate, upgrade, jump; kick upstairs (*informal*); **raise;** exalt, aggrandize; **ennoble,** knight; pass, graduate; raise one's pay

447 DEMOTION, DEPOSAL

nouns

1 **demotion,** degrading, degradation, disgrading, downgrading, debasement; abasement, humbling, humiliation, casting down; **reduction;** stripping of rank, depluming, displuming

2 **deposal, deposition, removal,** displacement, outplacement, supplanting, supplantation, replacement, deprivation, **ousting,** unseating; **cashiering, firing** (*informal*), **dismissal** *see* 908.5; forced resignation; kicking upstairs (*informal*); **superannuation,** pensioning off, putting out to pasture, **retirement,** the golden handshake *or* parachute (*informal*); **suspension;** impeachment; purge, liquidation; overthrow, overthrowal; **dethronement,** disenthronement, discrownment; **disbarment,** disbarring; unfrocking, defrocking, unchurching; deconsecration, expulsion, excommunication *see* 908.4

verbs

3 **to demote, degrade,** disgrade, downgrade, relegate, debase, abase, humble, humiliate, **lower, reduce;** strip of rank, cut off one's spurs, deplume, displume

4 **to depose, remove from office,** divest *or* deprive *or* strip of office, **remove,** displace, outplace, supplant, replace; **oust; suspend; cashier,** drum out, strip of rank, **break; dismiss** *see* 908.19; **purge, liquidate; overthrow; retire,** superannuate, pension, pension off, put out to pasture, give the golden handshake *or* parachute (*informal*); kick upstairs (*informal*); **unseat,** unsaddle; **dethrone,** disenthrone, unthrone, uncrown, discrown; **disbar;**

unfrock, defrock, unchurch; strike off the roll; **expel**, excommunicate *see* 908.17; deconsecrate

448 RESIGNATION, RETIREMENT

nouns

1 **resignation**, demission, **withdrawal, retirement**, pensioning, pensioning off, golden handshake *or* parachute (*informal*), retiral (*Scottish*), superannuation, emeritus status; **abdication**; voluntary resignation; forced resignation, deposal *see* 447; relinquishment *see* 370.3

verbs

2 **to resign**, demit, **quit**, leave, **vacate**, withdraw from; **retire**, superannuate, be superannuated, be pensioned *or* pensioned off, be put out to pasture, get the golden handshake *or* parachute (*informal*); relinquish, give up *see* 370.7; retire from office, stand down, stand *or* step aside, give up one's post, hang up one's spurs (*informal*); **tender** *or* **hand in one's resignation**, send in one's papers, turn in one's badge *or* uniform; **abdicate**, renounce the throne, give up the crown; pension off *see* 447.4; be invalided out

adjectives

3 **retired**, in retirement, superannuated, on pension, pensioned, pensioned off, emeritus, emerita (*feminine*)

449 AID

nouns

1 **aid, help, assistance, support**, succour, relief, comfort, ease, remedy; mutual help *or* assistance; **service**, benefit *see* 387.4; ministry, ministration, office, offices, good offices; yeoman's service; therapy *see* 91; protection *see* 1007; **bailout** (*informal*), rescue *see* 398

2 **assist, helping hand, hand, lift**; leg up (*informal*); help in time of need; **support group**, self-help group, Alcoholics Anonymous *or* AA, Gamblers Anonymous, etc, 12-step group

3 **support, maintenance, sustainment**, sustentation, **sustenance, subsistence**, provision, total support, meal ticket (*informal*); **keep, upkeep; livelihood, living**, meat, bread, daily bread; **nurture, fostering**, nurturance, nourishment, mothering, parenting, rearing, fosterage, foster-care, **care, caring**, care-giving, tender loving care *or* TLC (*informal*); manna, manna in the wilderness; economic support, price support, subsidy, subsidization, subvention, endowment; **social services, safety net**

4 **patronage, fosterage, tutelage, sponsorship, backing, auspices**, aegis, care, guidance, **championing, championship**, seconding; interest, advocacy, encouragement, **backing, abetment**; countenance, **favour, goodwill**, charity, **sympathy**

5 **furtherance, helping along, advancement**, advance, **promotion, forwarding**, facilitation, speeding, easing *or* smoothing of the way, clearing of the track, greasing of the wheels, expedition, expediting, rushing; special *or* preferential treatment

6 **self-help, self-support**, self-sustainment, self-improvement; independence *see* 430.5

7 **helper**, assistant *see* 616.6; benefactor *see* 592; facilitator, animator

8 **reinforcements, support, relief**, auxiliaries, reserves, reserve forces

9 **facility, accommodation, appliance, convenience**, amenity, appurtenance; advantage

10 **helpfulness**; serviceability, utility, **usefulness** *see* 387.3; **advantageousness**, profitability, favourableness, beneficialness *see* 998.1

verbs

11 **to aid, help, assist**, comfort, abet (*old*), **succour**, relieve, **ease**, doctor, remedy; be of some help, put one's oar in (*informal*); do good, do a world of good, **benefit**, avail *see* 998.10; favour, befriend; **give help**, render assistance, offer *or* proffer aid, come to the aid of, rush *or* fly to the assistance of, lend aid, give *or* hold out a helping hand, cater for; take by the hand, take in tow; **give a leg up** *or* lift (*informal*), help a lame dog over a stile; **save**, redeem, bail out (*informal*), rescue *see* 398.3; protect *see* 1007.18; set up, put on one's feet; give new life to, resuscitate, rally, reclaim, revive, **restore** *see* 396.11, 15; be the making of, set one up in business; see one through

12 **to support, lend support**, give *or* furnish *or* afford support; **maintain, sustain, keep**, upkeep; **uphold**, hold up, bear, upbear, **bear up**, bear out; reinforce, undergird, bolster, **bolster up**, buttress, shore, shore up, prop, prop up, crutch; **finance**, fund, subsidize, subvention, subventionize

13 **to back, back up, stand behind, stand back of** *or* in back of, get behind, get in behind, get in back of; **stand by**, stick by *and* **stick up for** (*both informal*), **champion**; second, **take the part of**, take up *or* adopt *or* espouse the cause of, take under one's wing, take up the cudgels for, **side with**, take sides with, associate oneself with, join oneself to, align oneself with, come down *or* range oneself on the side of, find time for

14 **to abet, aid and abet**, encourage, hearten, embolden, comfort (*old*); advocate, hold a brief for (*informal*), countenance, keep in countenance, **endorse, lend oneself to**, lend one's countenance to, lend one's favour *or* support to, lend one's offices, plump for *and* thump the tub for (*both informal*), lend one's name to, give one's support *or* countenance to, give moral support to, hold one's hand, make one's cause one's own, weigh in for (*informal*); subscribe, **favour**, go for (*informal*), smile upon, shine upon

15 **to patronize, sponsor**, take up

16 **to foster, nurture**, nourish, mother, care for, lavish care on, feed, parent, rear, fetch up, sustain, cultivate, **cherish**; pamper, coddle, cosset, fondle (*old*); **nurse**, suckle, cradle; dry-nurse, wet-nurse; spoon-feed

17 **to be useful, further, forward, advance, promote**, stand in good stead, encourage, favour, advantage, **facilitate**, set *or* put *or* push forward, give an impulse to; speed, expedite, quicken, hasten, lend wings to; conduce to, make for, contribute to

18 to **serve, lend** *or* **give oneself,** render service to, do service for, **work for, labour on behalf of; minister to,** cater to; attend *see* 577.13; pander to

19 to **oblige, accommodate, favour,** do a favour, do a service

adjectives

20 **helping,** assisting, serving; **assistant, auxiliary,** adjuvant, subservient, subsidiary, ancillary, accessory; ministerial, ministering, ministrant; fostering, nurtural; care, caring, care-giving; instrumental

21 **helpful, useful,** utile; **profitable, salutary,** good for, **beneficial** *see* 998.12; remedial, therapeutic; **serviceable, useful** *see* 387.18; **contributory,** contributing, conducive, **constructive, positive,** promotional; at one's service, at one's command, at one's beck and call

22 **favourable, propitious;** kind, kindly, kindly-disposed, all for (*informal*), **well-disposed,** well-affected, well-intentioned, well-meant, **well-meaning;** benevolent, beneficent, benign, benignant; friendly, amicable, neighbourly; cooperative

23 self-helpful, self-helping, self-improving; **self-supporting, self-sustaining;** self-supported, self-sustained; independent

adverbs

24 **helpfully,** helpingly; **beneficially,** favourably, profitably, advantageously, to advantage, to the good; serviceably, **usefully**

prepositions

25 helped by, with the help *or* assistance of, by the aid of; **by means of**

26 **for, on** *or* **in behalf of,** in aid of, in the name of, on account of, **for the sake of,** in the service of, in furtherance of, in favour of

27 **behind, back of** (*informal*), supporting, **in support of**

450 COOPERATION

nouns

1 **cooperation, collaboration, coaction,** concurrence, synergy, synergism; **consensus, commonality; community,** harmony, concordance, concord, fellowship, fellow feeling, solidarity, concert, **teamwork;** pulling *or* working together, communal *or* community activity, joining of forces, pooling, pooling of resources, joining of hands; bipartisanship, **mutualism,** mutuality, mutual assistance, coadjuvancy; **reciprocity;** joint effort, common effort, combined *or* joint operation, common enterprise *or* endeavour, collective *or* united action, mass action; job-sharing; coagency; coadministration, cochairmanship, codirectorship; duet, duumvirate; trio, triumvirate, troika; quartet, quintet, sextet; septet, octet; government by committee; symbiosis, commensalism; **cooperativeness,** collaborativeness, team spirit, morale, esprit, *esprit de corps* (*French*); communism, communalism, communitarianism, collectivism; ecumenism, ecumenicism, ecumenicalism; **collusion,** complicity

2 **affiliation, alliance, allying, alignment, association,** consociation, combination, **union,** unification, **coalition,** fusion, merger, coalescence, coadunation, amalgamation, **league, federation, confederation,** confederacy, consolidation, incorporation, inclusion, integration; tie-up *and* tie-in (*both informal*); **partnership,** copartnership, cahoots (*informal*); colleagueship, **collegialism, collegiality; fraternity,** confraternity, fraternization, fraternalism; sorority; **fellowship,** sodality; comradeship, camaraderie, freemasonry

verbs

3 to **cooperate, collaborate,** do business (*informal*), coact, concur; concert, harmonize, concord; **join,** band, league, **associate, affiliate,** ally, **combine, unite,** fuse, merge, coalesce, amalgamate, federate, confederate, consolidate; tie up *and* tie in (*both informal*); partner, be in league, **go into partnership with,** go *or* be in cahoots with; **join together,** club together, league together, band together; **work together,** get together *and* team up (*both informal*), work as a team, act together, act in concert, **pull together,** muck in (*informal*); **hold together, hang together,** keep together, **stand together,** stand shoulder to shoulder; lay *or* put *or* get heads together; **close ranks,** make common cause, unite efforts, join in; reciprocate; **conspire,** collude

4 to **side with,** take sides with, **unite with; join, join with,** join up with *and* get together with *and* team up with (*all informal*); go along with *and* string along with; **line up with** (*informal*), align with, align oneself with, range with, range oneself with, stand up with, stand in with; **join hands with,** be hand in glove with, go hand in hand with; act with, take part with, **go in with;** cast in one's lot with, join one's fortunes with, stand shoulder to shoulder with, be cheek by jowl with, sink or swim with, stand or fall with; **close ranks with,** fall in with, make common cause with, pool one's interests with; enlist under the banner of, rally round, flock to

adjectives

5 **cooperative, cooperating,** cooperant, **hand in glove; collaborative,** coactive, coacting, coefficient, synergetic, synergic, synergical, synergistic *or* synergistical; **fellow;** concurrent, concurring, concerted, **in concert; consensus,** consensual, agreeing, in agreement, of like mind; harmonious, harmonized, concordant, **common, communal,** collective; **mutual,** reciprocal; **joint, combined** *see* 804.5; coadjuvant, coadjutant; symbiotic, commensal; uncompetitive, noncompetitive, communalist, communalistic, communist, communistic, communitarian, collectivist, collectivistic, ecumenic *or* ecumenical; **conniving, collusive**

adverbs

6 **cooperatively,** cooperatingly, coactively, coefficiently, concurrently; in consensus, consensually; **jointly,** combinedly, **conjointly,** concertedly, in concert with; harmoniously, concordantly; communally, collectively, **together;** as one, with one voice, unanimously, in chorus, in unison, as one man, en masse; **side by side, hand in hand, hand in glove, shoulder to shoulder,** back to back,

"all for one, one for all"—DUMAS PÈRE

7 **in cooperation, in collaboration, in partnership, in cahoots** (*informal*), **in collusion, in league**

prepositions

8 **with, in cooperation with,** etc

451 OPPOSITION

nouns

1 **opposition, opposing, opposure, crossing,** oppugnancy, bucking (*informal*), standing against; contraposition *see* 778.1; **resistance** *see* 453; **noncooperation; contention** *see* 457; negation *see* 335; **rejection** *see* 372, refusal; **counteraction,** counterworking *see* 899.1; refusal *see* 442; **contradiction,** challenge, contravention, contraversion, rebutment, rebuttal, denial, impugnation, impugnment; countercurrent, head wind; crosscurrent, undercurrent, undertow

2 **hostility, antagonism,** oppugnancy, oppugnance *and* oppugnation (*both old*), **antipathy,** enmity, bad blood, inimicalness; **contrariness, contrariety,** orneriness (*US & Canadian informal*), repugnance *or* repugnancy, perverseness, **obstinacy** *see* 361; fractiousness, refractoriness, recalcitrance *see* 327.2; uncooperativeness, noncooperation, negativeness, **obstructionism,** traversal, bloody-mindedness, attitude (*informal*); **friction, conflict,** clashing, **collision,** cross-purposes, dissension, disaccord *see* 456; rivalry, vying, competition *see* 457.2

verbs

3 **to oppose, counter, cross,** go *or* act in opposition to, **go against,** run against, **run counter to,** fly in the face of, fly in the teeth of; kick out against, make waves (*informal*), **protest** *see* 333.5; set oneself against, set one's face *or* heart against; be at cross-purposes, **obstruct,** traverse, sabotage; **take issue with, take a stand against,** lift *or* raise a hand against, declare oneself against, stand and be counted against, side against, vote against, vote nay, veto; make a stand against, make a dead set against; join the opposition; not put up with, not abide, not be content with; counteract, counterwork, countervail *see* 899.6; **resist,** withstand *see* 453.3

4 **to contend against,** militate against, **contest, combat, battle,** clash with, **clash, fight against, strive against,** struggle against, labour against, **take on** (*informal*), grapple with, join battle with, close with, come to close quarters with, antagonize (*old*), **fight, counter;** buffet, beat against, beat up against, breast, stem, stem *or* breast the tide *or* current *or* flood, breast the wave, buffet the waves; rival, compete with *or* against, vie with *or* against; fight back, **resist, offer resistance** *see* 453.3

5 **to confront, affront,** front, go eyeball-to-eyeball *or* one-on-one *or* toe-to-toe with (*informal*), **meet, face, meet head-on;** encounter

6 **to contradict,** cross, traverse, contravene, controvert, rebut, deny, **gainsay;** challenge, contest; oppugn, call into question; **belie,** be contrary to, come in conflict with, negate *see* 335.3; **reject** *see* 372.2

7 **to be against,** be agin (*informal*); discountenance *see* 510.11; not hold with, not have anything to do with; have a bone to pick

adjectives

8 **oppositional, opponent, opposing, opposed; anti** (*informal*), contra, confrontational, confrontive; at odds, at loggerheads; **adverse, adversary,** adversarial, adversative, oppugnant, antithetic, antithetical, repugnant, con (*informal*), **set** *or* **dead set against; contrary, counter; negative; opposite,** oppositive, death on; overthwart (*old*), cross; **contradictory;** unfavourable, unpropitious *see* 133.17; **hostile, antagonistic,** unfriendly, enemy, inimical, alien, antipathetic, antipathetical; fractious, refractory, recalcitrant *see* 327.10; uncooperative, noncooperative, **obstructive,** bloody-minded, stroppy; ornery (*US & Canadian informal*), perverse, obstinate *see* 361.8; **conflicting, clashing,** dissentient, disaccordant *see* 456.15; rival, competitive

adverbs

9 **adversarial, in opposition, in confrontation,** eyeball-to-eyeball *and* one-on-one *and* toe-to-toe (*all informal*), head-on, **at variance, at cross-purposes, at odds,** at issue, at war with, up in arms, with crossed bayonets, at daggers drawn, at daggers, in hostile array, poised against one another; contra, contrariwise, counter, cross, athwart; against the tide *or* wind *or* grain

prepositions

10 **opposed to, adverse to,** counter to, **in opposition to,** in conflict with, at cross-purposes with; **against,** agin (*informal*), dead against, athwart; **versus,** vs; **con,** contra, face to face with, *vis-à-vis* (*French*)

452 OPPONENT

nouns

1 **opponent, adversary, antagonist, assailant, foe,** foeman, **enemy,** archenemy; adverse *or* opposing party, opposite camp, opposite *or* opposing side, **the opposition,** the loyal opposition; **combatant** *see* 461

2 **competitor, contestant, contender,** corrival, vier, player, entrant; **rival,** arch-rival; emulator; the field; finalist, semifinalist, etc

3 **oppositionist,** opposer; obstructionist, obstructive, negativist, naysayer; contra; **objector, protester,** dissident, dissentient; **resister;** noncooperator; **disputant,** litigant, plaintiff, defendant; quarreller, irritable man, scrapper (*informal*), wrangler, brawler; die-hard, bitter-ender, last-ditcher, intransigent, irreconcilable

453 RESISTANCE

nouns

1 **resistance**, withstanding, countering, renitence *or* renitency, repellence *or* repellency; **defiance** *see* 454; **opposing**, opposition *see* 451; **stand**; **repulsion**, repulse, rebuff; **objection**, **protest**, remonstrance, **dispute**, challenge, **demur**; **complaint**; dissentience, **dissent** *see* 333; reaction, hostile *or* combative reaction, **counteraction** *see* 899; revolt *see* 327.4; recalcitrance *or* recalcitrancy, recalcitration, fractiousness, refractoriness *see* 327.2; **reluctance** *see* 325.1; **obstinacy** *see* 361; passive resistance, noncooperation; uncooperativeness, negativism

verbs

2 **to resist**, withstand; **stand**; **endure** *see* 134.5; **stand up**, bear up, hold up, hold out; **defy** *see* 454.3, tell one where to get off (*informal*), throw down the gauntlet; be proof against, bear up against; **repel**, **repulse**, rebuff

3 **to offer resistance**, **fight back**, bite back, not turn the other cheek, show fight, lift *or* raise a hand, stand *or* hold one's ground, **withstand**, **stand**, **take one's stand**, make a stand, make a stand against, take one's stand against, square up to, put up one's dukes (*both informal*), **stand up to**, stand up against, stand at bay; front, **confront**, meet head-on, fly in the teeth *or* face of, **face up to**, face down, face out; **object**, **protest**, remonstrate, **dispute**, challenge, **complain**, complain loudly, exclaim at; **dissent** *see* 333.4; make waves (*informal*); make a determined resistance; kick against, kick out against, recalcitrate, "kick against the pricks"—BIBLE; put up a fight *or* struggle (*informal*), not take lying down, tough it out (*informal*); **revolt** *see* 327.7; **oppose** *see* 451.3; **contend with** *see* 457.18; **strive against** *see* 451.4

4 **to stand fast**, **stand** *or* **hold one's ground**, make a resolute stand, **hold one's own**, remain firm, stick *and* stuck fast (*both informal*), **stick to one's guns**, **stay it out**, stick it out (*informal*), **hold out**, not back down, not give up, not submit, **never say die**; fight to the last drop of blood, die hard, sell one's life dearly, go down with all guns blazing

adjectives

5 **resistant**, **resistive**, resisting, renitent, up against, **withstanding**, repellent; obstructive, retardant, retardative; **unyielding**, unsubmissive *see* 361.12; rebellious *see* 327.11; **proof against**; **objecting**, **protesting**, disputing, disputatious, complaining, dissentient, dissenting *see* 333.6; recalcitrant, fractious, refractory *see* 327.10; **reluctant** *see* 325.6; noncooperative, uncooperative; up in arms, on the barricades, not lying down

454 DEFIANCE

nouns

1 **defiance**, defying, defial (*old*); **daring**, daringness, **audacity**, boldness, bold front, brash bearing, brashness, brassiness (*informal*), brazenness, bravado, insolence; bearding, beard-tweaking, nose-tweaking; **arrogance** *see* 141; **sauciness**, **cheekiness**

(*informal*), pertness, impudence, impertinence; bumptiousness, cockiness; **contempt**, contemptuousness, derision, **disdain**, disregard, despite; **risk-taking**, tightrope walking, funambulism

2 **challenge**, **dare**, double dare; fighting words; defy; gage, gage of battle, gauntlet, glove, chip on one's shoulder, slap of the glove, invitation *or* bid to combat, call to arms; war cry, war whoop, battle cry, rebel yell

verbs

3 **to defy**, bid defiance, hurl defiance, snarl *or* shout *or* scream defiance; **dare**, double-dare, outdare; **challenge**, call out, throw *or* fling down the gauntlet *or* glove *or* gage, knock the chip off one's shoulder, cross swords; beard, beard the lion in his den, face, face out, look in the eye, stare down, stare out, **confront**, **affront**, front, say right to one's face, square up to, go eyeball-to-eyeball *or* one-on-one *or* toe-to-toe with (*informal*); tweak the nose, pluck by the beard, slap one's face, double *or* shake one's fist at; give the V-sign; **ask for it** (*informal*), ask *or* look for trouble, make something of it (*informal*), show fight, show one's teeth, bare one's fangs; dance the war dance (*US*); **brave** *see* 492.11

4 **to flout**, disregard, **slight**, slight over, treat with contempt, set at defiance, fly in the teeth *or* face of, **snap one's fingers at**; **thumb one's nose at**, cock a snook at; **disdain**, **despise**, **scorn** *see* 157.3; laugh at, laugh to scorn, laugh out of court, laugh in one's face; hold in derision, scout, scoff at, **deride** *see* 508.8

5 **to show** *or* **put up a bold front**, bluster, throw out one's chest, strut, crow, look big, stand with arms akimbo

6 **to take a dare**, accept a challenge, **take one up on** *and* **call one's bluff** (*both informal*); **start something**, take up the gauntlet

adjectives

7 **defiant**, defying, challenging; **daring**, **bold**, brash, brassy (*informal*), brazen, **audacious**, insolent; bumptious, arrogant *see* 141.9; saucy, cheeky (*informal*), pert, impudent, impertinent; cocky, gallus (*Scottish*); **contemptuous**, disdainful, derisive, disregardful, greatly daring, regardless of consequences

adverbs

8 **in defiance of**, in the teeth of, in the face of, under one's very nose

455 ACCORD

harmonious relationship

nouns

1 **accord**, accordance, **concord**, concordance, **harmony**, symphony; **rapport**; good vibrations (*informal*), good vibes (*informal*), good karma; amity *see* 587.1; frictionlessness; *rapprochement* (*French*); **sympathy**, empathy, identity, feeling of identity, fellow feeling, **fellowship**, kinship, togetherness, **affinity**; **agreement**, **understanding**, **like-mindedness**, **congruence**; congeniality,

compatibility; **oneness,** unity, unison, union;
community, communion, community of interests;
solidarity, team spirit, esprit, *esprit de corps* (*French*);
mutuality, sharing, reciprocity, mutual
supportiveness; bonds of harmony, ties of affection,
cement of friendship; happy family; peace *see* 464;
love, *agape* (*Greek*), charity, *caritas* (*Latin*), brotherly
love; correspondence *see* 787.1

verbs

2 **to get along,** harmonize, **agree with, agree, get
along with,** get on with, hit it off with (*informal*),
cotton to (*US & Canadian informal*), harmonize with,
be in harmony with, be in tune with, fall *or* chime
in with, blend in with, be well in with, go hand in
hand with, **be at one with;** sing in chorus, be on
the same wavelength (*informal*); **sympathize,**
empathize, identify with, respond to, understand one
another, enter into one's views, enter into the ideas
or feelings of; **accord,** correspond *see* 787.6;
reciprocate, interchange *see* 862.4

adjectives

3 **in accord,** accordant (*old*), **harmonious, in
harmony,** congruous, congruent, in tune, attuned,
agreeing, in concert, **in rapport,** *en rapport* (*French*),
amicable *see* 587.15, 18; frictionless; **sympathetic,**
simpatico (*informal*), empathic, empathetic,
understanding; like-minded, akin, of the same
mind, of one mind, at one, united, together;
concordant, corresponding *see* 787.9; agreeable,
congenial, **compatible; peaceful** *see* 464.9

456 DISACCORD
unharmonious relationship

nouns

1 **disaccord, discord,** discordance *or* discordancy,
asynchrony, **unharmoniousness,** inharmoniousness,
disharmony, inharmony, incongruence, disaffinity,
incompatibility, incompatibleness; culture gap,
generation gap, gender gap; noncooperation; **conflict,**
open conflict *or* war, **friction;** jar, **jarring,** jangle,
clash, clashing; touchiness, strained relations,
tension; bad blood; **unpleasantness;** mischief;
contention *see* 457; **enmity** *see* 589; Eris, Discordia;
the Apple of Discord

2 **disagreement, difficulty, misunderstanding,
difference,** difference of opinion, agreement to
disagree, **variance,** division, dividedness; cross-
purposes; polarity of opinion, polarization; **disparity**
see 788.1

3 **dissension, dissent,** dissidence, flak (*informal*);
bickering, infighting, faction, factiousness,
partisanship, partisan spirit; **divisiveness;
quarrelsomeness;** litigiousness; pugnacity,
bellicosity, combativeness, **aggressiveness,**
contentiousness, belligerence; feistiness (*informal*),
touchiness, irritability, shrewishness, irascibility *see*
110.2

4 **falling-out, breach of friendship,** parting of the
ways, bust-up (*informal*); **alienation, estrangement,
disaffection,** disfavour; **breach, break, rupture,
schism, split, rift,** cleft, **disunity, disunion,**

disruption, separation, cleavage, divergence,
division, dividedness; division in the camp, house
divided against itself; open rupture, breaking off of
negotiations, recall of ambassadors

5 **quarrel,** open quarrel, dustup, **dispute, argument,**
polemic, argy-bargy *and* slanging match, fliting (*old*),
lovers' quarrel, tug of love, **controversy,** altercation,
fight, squabble, contention, strife, **tussle,** bicker,
wrangle, snarl, **tiff, spat,** fuss; **breach of the
peace; fracas,** donnybrook; broil, embroilment,
imbroglio; words, sharp words, war of words,
logomachy; **feud,** blood feud, vendetta; brawl *see*
457.5

6 (*informal terms*) **row, rumpus,** spot of bother, argy-
bargy, ruck, ruckus, ruction, hoo-ha, barney, set-to,
run-in, **scrap,** rhubarb (*US & Canadian*)

7 **bone of contention,** apple of discord, sore point,
tender spot, delicate *or* ticklish issue, rub, beef
(*informal*); **bone to pick;** *casus belli* (*Latin*), grounds
for war

verbs

8 **to disagree, differ,** differ in opinion, hold opposite
views, disaccord, **be at variance,** not get along, pull
different ways, be at cross-purposes, have no
measures with, misunderstand one another; **conflict,
clash,** collide, jostle, jangle, jar; live like cat and
dog, live a cat-and-dog life

9 **to have a bone to pick with,** have a beef with
(*informal*)

10 **to fall out,** have a falling-out, **break with, split,**
separate, **diverge,** divide, agree to disagree, **part
company,** come to *or* reach a parting of the ways

11 **to quarrel, dispute,** oppugn, flite (*old*), altercate,
fight, squabble, tiff, spat, **bicker, wrangle,** spar,
broil, have words, set to, join issue, make the fur fly;
cross swords, **feud, battle;** brawl; **be quarrelsome**
or contentious, be thin-skinned, be touchy *or*
sensitive, be a bear with a sore head, get out of bed
on the wrong side

12 (*informal terms*) **to row, scrap,** kick up a row; mix it
up, lock horns, bump heads

13 **to pick a quarrel,** fasten a quarrel on, look for
trouble, pick a bone with, start on (*informal*); have a
chip on one's shoulder; add insult to injury

14 **to sow dissension,** stir up trouble, make *or* borrow
trouble; **alienate, estrange,** separate, **divide,
disunite,** disaffect, **come between;** irritate,
provoke, aggravate; **set at odds,** set at variance; **set
against,** pit against, sic on *or* at, **set on,** set by the
ears, set at one's throat; add fuel to the fire *or* flame,
fan the flame, pour oil on the blaze, light the fuse,
stir the pot (*informal*)

adjectives

15 **disaccordant, unharmonious,** inharmonious,
disharmonious, out of tune, asynchronous,
unsynchronized, out of sync (*informal*), **discordant,**
out of accord, dissident, dissentient, **disagreeing,
differing; conflicting,** clashing, colliding; like cats
and dogs; **divided,** faction-ridden, fragmented

16 **at odds, at variance, at loggerheads,** at square
(*old*), at cross-purposes; at war, at strife, at feud, at

swords' points, at daggers *or* at daggers drawn, up in arms

17 partisan, polarizing, **divisive**, factional, factious; **quarrelsome**, bickering, disputatious, wrangling, eristic, eristical, polemical; litigious, pugnacious, combative, **aggressive**, bellicose, belligerent; feisty (*informal*), touchy, irritable, shrewish, **irascible** *see* 110.19

457 CONTENTION

nouns

1 contention, contest, contestation, combat, **fighting, conflict, strife, war, struggle**, blood on the floor, cut and thrust; fighting at close quarters, infighting; **warfare** *see* 458; **hostility**, enmity *see* 589; **quarrel, altercation, controversy**, dustup (*informal*), polemic, debate, forensics, **argument, dispute, disputation**; litigation; words, war of words, paper war, logomachy; **fighting**, scrapping (*informal*); **quarrelling, bickering, wrangling, squabbling**; oppugnancy, contentiousness, disputatiousness, litigiousness, **quarrelsomeness** *see* 456.3; cat-and-dog life; Kilkenny cats; **competitiveness**, vying, rivalrousness, competitorship

2 competition, rivalry, trying conclusions *or* the issue, vying, emulation, jockeying (*informal*); cutthroat competition; run for one's money; **sportsmanship, gamesmanship**, lifemanship, one-upmanship, **competitive advantage**

3 contest, engagement, encounter, match, fixture, tie, meet, meeting, derby, **trial, test** *or* **test match**, *concours* and *rencontre* (*both French*); **close contest, hard contest**, closely fought contest, close *or* tight one; **fight, bout**; joust, tilt; **tournament**, tourney (*US & Canadian*); rally; **game** *see* 743.9; **games**, Olympic Games, Olympics, gymkhana

4 fight, battle, fray, affray, combat, action, conflict, embroilment; gun battle; **clash; brush, skirmish; tussle, scuffle, struggle**, scramble, shoving match; exchange of blows, *passage d'armes* (*French*), passage at *or* of arms, clash of arms; **quarrel** *see* 456.5; pitched battle; battle royal; unarmed combat; **fistfight**, punch-up, set-to; **hand-to-hand fight**, stand-up fight (*informal*), running fight *or* engagement; tug-of-war; bull-fight, tauromachy; dogfight, cockfight; street fight, rumble (*informal*), tear-up; air *or* aerial combat, sea *or* naval combat, ground combat, armoured combat, infantry combat, fire fight, hand-to-hand combat, house-to-house combat; **internal struggle**, intestine *or* internecine struggle *or* combat

5 free-for-all, brawl, broil, melee, **fracas**, riot, scrimmage

6 death struggle, life-and-death *or* **life-or-death struggle, struggle** *or* **fight** *or* **duel to the death**, *guerre à mort* and *guerre à outrance* (*both French*), all-out war, total war, last-ditch fight, fight to the last ditch, fight with no quarter given

7 duel, single combat, monomachy, satisfaction, **affair of honour**, *affaire d'honneur* (*French*)

8 fencing, swordplay; swordsmanship

9 boxing *see* 754, **fighting**, noble art of self-defence, **fisticuffs, pugilism, prize-fighting**, the ring; **boxing match, prizefight**, spar, bout; shadowboxing; close fighting, infighting; kick boxing, Thai boxing, savate

10 wrestling, grappling, rassling (*US informal*), sumo; **martial arts**; catch-as-catch-can; wrestling match, wrestling bout; Graeco-Roman wrestling, Cornish wrestling, Westmorland wrestling, Cumberland wrestling, sambo *or* sambo wrestling, freestyle *or* all-in wrestling, International freestyle; arm wrestling

11 racing, track, track sports; **horse racing** *see* 757, the turf, the sport of kings; dog racing, the dogs (*informal*), motor racing *see* 756

12 race, contest of speed; derby; **horse race; motor race; heat, lap**, bell lap, victory lap; footrace, run, running event; obstacle race, three-legged race, sack race, egg-and-spoon race; walk; endurance race, motorcycle race, bicycle race; boat race, yacht race, regatta; air race; dog race

verbs

13 to contend, contest, jostle; **fight, battle, combat, war, declare** *or* **go to war**, take *or* take up arms, put up a fight (*informal*); wage war; **strive, struggle**, scramble, go for the brass ring (*US informal*); make the fur *or* feathers fly, **tussle, scuffle; quarrel** *see* 456.11, 12; clash, collide; **wrestle**, grapple, grapple with, rassle (*US informal*); **come to blows**, close, try conclusions, **mix it up** *and* go toe-to-toe (*both informal*), exchange blows *or* fisticuffs, box, spar, give and take; cut and thrust, **cross swords, fence**, thrust and parry; **joust, tilt, tourney**, run a tilt *or* a tilt at, break a lance with; **duel**, fight a duel, give satisfaction; feud; skirmish; fight one's way; fight the good fight; **brawl; riot**

14 to lift *or* **raise one's hand against**; make war on; draw the sword against, take up the cudgels, couch one's lance; square up *or* off (*informal*); have at, jump; lay on, lay about one; **pitch into** *and* **sail into** *and* lay into (*all informal*), strike the first blow, draw first blood; **attack** *see* 459.15

15 to encounter, come *or* **go up against**, fall *or* run foul *or* afoul of; close with, come to close quarters, bring to bay, meet *or* fight hand-to-hand

16 to engage, take on (*informal*), go against *or* up against, enter the ring *or* arena with, put on the gloves with, match oneself against; **join issue** *or* **battle, do** *or* **give battle**, engage in battle *or* combat

17 to contend with, engage with, cope with, **fight with, strive with, struggle with**, wrestle with, grapple with, bandy with (*old*), try conclusions with, measure swords with, tilt with, **cross swords with**; exchange shots, shoot it out with (*informal*); **lock horns** *and* **bump heads** (*both informal*), go to loggerheads (*old*); **tangle with** *and* **mix it up with** (*both informal*), have a brush with; have it out, fight *or* battle it out, settle it; **fight** *or* **go at it hammer and tongs** *or* **tooth and nail**, fight it out, fight like devils, ask and give no quarter, make blood flow freely, battle *à outrance*, fight to the death, duke it out (*US informal*)

18 to compete, contend, vie, try conclusions *or* the issue, **jockey** (*informal*); **compete with** *or* **against, vie with, challenge,** cope (*old*), enter into competition with, give a run for one's money, **meet;** try *or* test one another; **rival,** emulate, outvie; keep up with the Joneses

19 to race, race with, run a race; horse-race, boat-race

20 to contend for, strive for, struggle for, fight for, vie for; stickle for, stipulate for, hold out for, make a point of

21 to dispute, contest, oppugn, take issue with; **fight over, quarrel over, wrangle over, squabble over,** bicker over, strive *or* contend about

adjectives

22 contending, contesting; **contestant,** disputant; striving, struggling; fighting, battling, warring; warlike; **quarrelsome** *see* 456.17

23 competitive, competitory, competing, **vying,** rivalling, **rival,** rivalrous, emulous, in competition, in rivalry; **cutthroat**

458 WARFARE

nouns

1 war, warfare, warring, warmaking, combat, fighting, *la guerre* (*French*); armed conflict, armed combat, military operations, the sword, arbitrament of the sword, appeal to arms *or* the sword, resort to arms, force *or* might of arms, bloodshed; **state of war, hostilities,** belligerence *or* belligerency, open war *or* warfare *or* hostilities; hot war, **shooting war;** total war, **all-out war;** cold war; phoney war; **wartime; battle** *see* 457.4; **attack** *see* 459; **war zone, theatre of operations;** trouble spot

2 "an epidemic insanity"—EMERSON, "a brain-spattering, windpipe-slitting art", "the feast of vultures, and the waste of life"—BOTH BYRON, "the business of barbarians"—NAPOLEON, "the trade of kings"—DRYDEN, "a by-product of the arts of peace"—AMBROSE BIERCE, "a conflict which does not determine who is right—but who is left"—ANON, "the continuation of politics by other means"—VON CLAUSEWITZ, "an emblem, a hieroglyphic, of all misery"—DONNE, "politics with bloodshed"—MAO TSE-TUNG

3 battle array, order of battle, **disposition, deployment, marshalling;** open order; close formation; echelon

4 campaign, war, **drive, expedition,** hostile expedition; **crusade,** holy war, jihad

5 operation, action; **movement; mission; operations,** military operations, naval operations; combined operations, joint operations, coordinated operations; active operations, amphibious operations, airborne operations, major operations, minor operations, night operations, overseas operations; war plans, staff work; logistic; war game, dry run, kriegspiel, manoeuvre, manoeuvres; **strategy, tactics; battle**

6 military science, art *or* rules *or* science of war; siegecraft; warcraft, war, **arms,** profession of arms;

generalship, soldiership; chivalry, knighthood, knightly skill

7 declaration of war, challenge; defiance *see* 454

8 call to arms, call-up, call to the colours, **rally; mobilization; muster,** levy; conscription, recruitment; **rallying cry,** slogan, watchword, catchword, exhortation; **battle cry,** war cry, war whoop, rebel yell; banzai, gung ho, St George, Montjoie, Geronimo; bugle call, trumpet call, clarion, clarion call

9 service, military service; active service *or* duty; military obligation; national service, selective service (*US*); reserved list

10 militarization, activation, **mobilization;** war *or* wartime footing, national emergency; **war effort, war economy;** martial law, suspension of civil rights; garrison state, military dictatorship; remilitarization, reactivation; arms race; war clouds, war scare

11 warlikeness, unpeacefulness, war *or* warlike spirit, ferocity, fierceness; **hard line; combativeness, contentiousness; hostility, antagonism;** unfriendliness *see* 589.1; aggression, **aggressiveness;** aggro; belligerence *or* belligerency, **pugnacity,** pugnaciousness, **bellicosity, bellicoseness, truculence,** fight (*informal*); chip on one's shoulder (*informal*); militancy, **militarism,** martialism, militaryism; sabre-rattling, gunboat diplomacy; **chauvinism, jingoism,** hawkishness (*informal*), **warmongering;** waving of the bloody shirt (*US*); warpath; oppugnancy, **quarrelsomeness** *see* 456.3

12 (*rallying devices and themes*) battle flag, banner, colours, gonfalon, bloody shirt (*US*), fiery cross *or* crostarie, atrocity story, enemy atrocities; martial music, war song, battle hymn, national anthem; national honour, face; foreign threat, totalitarian threat, Islamic threat, Communist threat, colonialist *or* neocolonialist *or* imperialist threat, Western imperialism, yellow peril; expansionism, Manifest Destiny (*US*); independence, self-determination

13 war-god, Mars, Ares, Odin *or* Woden *or* Wotan, Tyr *or* Tiu *or* Tiw; **war-goddess,** Athena, Minerva, Bellona, Enyo, Valkyrie

verbs

14 to war, wage war, make war, carry on war *or* **hostilities,** engage in hostilities, wield the sword; battle, **fight;** spill *or* shed blood

15 to make war on, levy war on, "let slip the dogs of war"—SHAKESPEARE; **attack** *see* 459.15, 17; **declare war, challenge,** throw *or* fling down the gauntlet; **defy** *see* 454.3; open hostilities, plunge the world into war; launch a holy war on, go on a crusade against

16 to go to war, break *or* breach the peace, take up the gauntlet, **go on the warpath, rise up in arms, take** *or* **resort to arms,** take arms, take up arms, take up the cudgels *or* sword, fly *or* appeal to the sword, unsheathe one's weapon, come to cold steel; take the field

17 to campaign, undertake operations, pursue a strategy, make an expedition, go on a crusade

18 to serve, do duty; fulfil one's military obligation, wear the uniform; **soldier,** see *or* do active duty;

bear arms, carry arms, shoulder arms, shoulder a gun; see action *or* combat, hear shots fired in anger

19 **to call to arms, call up,** call to the colours, **rally; mobilize; muster,** levy; **conscript, recruit;** sound the call to arms, give the battle cry, wave the bloody shirt (*US*), beat the drums, blow the bugle *or* clarion

20 **to militarize, activate, mobilize,** go on a wartime footing, gird *or* gird up one's loins, muster one's resources; reactivate, remilitarize, take out of mothballs *and* retread (*both informal*)

adjectives

21 **warlike, militant,** fighting, warring, battling; **martial, military,** soldierly, soldierlike; **combative, contentious,** gladiatorial; trigger-happy (*informal*); **belligerent, pugnacious, truculent, bellicose,** scrappy (*informal*), full of fight; **aggressive,** offensive; fierce, ferocious, savage, bloody, bloody-minded, bloodthirsty, sanguinary, sanguineous; **unpeaceful,** unpeaceable, unpacific; **hostile, antagonistic, enemy,** inimical; unfriendly *see* 589.9; quarrelsome *see* 456.17

22 **militaristic, warmongering,** sabre-rattling; **chauvinistic,** chauvinist, **jingoistic,** jingoist, jingoish, jingo; **hard-line, hawkish** (*informal*), of the war party

23 **embattled,** battled, **engaged,** at grips, in combat; **arrayed, deployed,** ranged, in battle array, in the field; **militarized; armed** *see* 460.14; war-ravaged, war-torn

adverbs

24 **at war, up in arms;** in the midst of battle, in the thick of the fray *or* combat; in the cannon's mouth, at the point of the gun; at swords' points, at the point of the bayonet *or* sword

25 **wars**

Afghanistan War	Korean War
Algerian War	Macedonian-Persian
American Revolution	War
Arab-Israeli War	Manchurian War
Balkan Wars	Mexican War
Boer War	Napoleonic Wars
Civil War (England)	Norman Conquest
Civil War (US)	Peloponnesian Wars
Civil War (Spain)	Persian Wars
Civil Wars (China)	Punic Wars
Civil Wars (Roman)	Russian Revolution
Crimean War	Russo-Japanese War
Crusades	Samnite Wars
Falklands War	Seven Weeks' War
Franco-Prussian War	Seven Years' War
French and Indian War	Sino-Japanese War
French Revolution	Six Day War
Gallic Wars	Southeast Asian War
Graeco-Persian Wars	Spanish-American War
Gulf War *or* Operation	Sri Lankan Civil War
Desert Storm	Thirty Years' War
Hundred Years' War	Vietnam War
Indian Wars	War Between the States
Indochina War	War of the Austrian
Iran-Iraq War	Succession
Italian Wars of	War of the Polish
Independence	Succession
War of the Spanish	World War I *or* Great
Succession	War
Wars of the French	World War II
Revolution	Yom Kippur War
Wars of the Roses	Yugoslav Civil War

459 ATTACK

nouns

1 **attack, assault,** assailing, assailment; **offence, offensive; aggression; onset, onslaught; strike;** surgical strike, first strike, preventive war; descent on *or* upon; **charge, rush,** dead set at, run at *or* against; **drive, push** (*informal*); **sally, sortie;** infiltration; *coup de main* (*French*); frontal attack *or* assault, head-on attack, flank attack; mass attack, kamikaze attack; banzai attack *or* charge, suicide attack *or* charge; hit-and-run attack; breakthrough; **counterattack, counteroffensive;** amphibious attack; gas attack; diversionary attack, diversion; assault and battery, simple assault, mugging (*informal*), aggravated assault, armed assault, unprovoked assault; **preemptive strike; blitzkrieg, blitz,** lightning attack, lightning war, panzer warfare, sudden *or* devastating *or* crippling attack, deep strike, shock tactics; atomic *or* thermonuclear attack, first-strike capacity, megadeath, overkill

2 **surprise attack,** surprise, surprisal, unforeseen, attack, sneak attack (*informal*); stab in the back

3 **thrust, pass, lunge, swing,** cut, stab, jab; **feint;** home thrust

4 **raid, foray,** razzia; **invasion, incursion,** inroad, irruption; **air raid, air strike,** air attack, fire raid, saturation raid, thousand-bomber raid; escalade, scaling, boarding, **tank** *or* **armoured attack,** panzer attack

5 **siege, besiegement, beleaguerment;** encompassment, investment, encirclement, envelopment; blockading, blockade; cutting of supply lines; vertical envelopment; pincer movement

6 **storm,** storming, taking by storm, overrunning

7 **bombardment, bombing, air bombing;** strafing

8 **gunfire, fire, firing,** musketry, **shooting,** gunplay (*informal*); gunfight, shoot-out; **firepower,** offensive capacity

9 **volley, salvo,** burst, spray, **fusillade,** drumfire, **cannonade,** cannonry, **broadside,** enfilade; **barrage, artillery barrage**

10 **stabbing,** piercing, sticking (*informal*); **knifing,** bayonetting; the sword; **impalement, transfixion**

11 **stoning,** lapidation

12 **assailant,** assailer, **attacker;** assaulter, mugger (*informal*); **aggressor;** invader, raider

13 **zero hour, H hour;** D-day, target day

verbs

14 **to attack, assault, assail,** harry, assume *or* take the offensive; commit an assault upon; **strike, hit, pound; go at, come at,** have at, **launch out against,** make a set *or* dead set at; **fall on** *or* **upon, set on** *or* **upon, descend on** *or* upon, come down on, swoop down on; pounce upon; **lift** *or* **raise** *or* **lift a hand against,** draw the sword against, take

up arms *or* the cudgels against; **lay hands on,** lay a hand on, bloody one's hands with; **gang up on,** attack in force; surprise, **ambush; blitz,** attack *or* hit like lightning

15 (*informal terms*) **to lambaste,** pile into, sail into, wade into, lay into; **let one have it,** let one have it with both barrels; **land on,** land on like a ton of bricks, climb all over, crack down on; **mug,** jump, sandbag, bushwhack (*US & Canadian*); swipe at, lay at, **go for, go at;** blindside, sucker-punch; **take a swing** *or* **crack** *or* **swipe** *or* **poke** *or* punch *or* **shot at**

16 **to lash out at, strike out at,** hit out at, let drive at, let fly at, strike out at; **strike at,** hit at, poke at, thrust at, **swing at,** swing on, make a thrust *or* pass at, lunge at, aim *or* deal a blow at, flail at, flail away at, take a fling *or* shy at; cut and thrust; feint

17 **to launch an attack,** kick off an attack, mount an attack, **push, thrust,** mount *or* open an offensive, **drive; advance against** *or* **upon, march upon** *or* **against,** bear down upon; **infiltrate; strike;** flank; press the attack, follow up the attack; **counterattack**

18 **to charge,** rush, **rush at, fly at,** run at, dash at, make a dash *or* rush at; tilt at, go full tilt at, ride full tilt against; **jump off,** go over the top (*informal*)

19 **to besiege, lay siege to,** encompass, surround, **encircle,** envelope, invest, set upon on all sides, get in a pincers, close the jaws of the pincers *or* trap; **blockade; beset, beleaguer, harry, harass,** drive *or* press one hard; soften up

20 **to raid,** foray, make a raid; **invade,** inroad, make an inroad; escalade, scale, scale the walls, board; storm, take by storm, overwhelm, inundate

21 **to pull a gun on,** draw a gun on; beat to the draw (*informal*)

22 **to pull the trigger, fire upon,** fire at, **shoot at,** pop at *and* take a pop at (*both informal*), take *or* fire *or* let off a shot at, blaze away at (*informal*); **open fire,** commence firing, open up on (*informal*); **aim at,** take aim at, level at (*old*), zero in on, take dead aim at, draw a bead on; **snipe,** snipe at; **bombard, blast, strafe, shell,** cannonade, mortar, barrage, blitz; pepper, fusillade, fire a volley; rake, enfilade; pour a broadside into; cannon; **torpedo; shoot**

23 **to bomb,** drop a bomb; dive-bomb, carpet-bomb, glide-bomb, area-bomb, pattern-bomb, etc; atom-bomb, hydrogen-bomb

24 **to mine,** plant a mine, trigger a mine

25 **to stab, stick** (*informal*), **pierce,** plunge in; **run through,** impale, spit, **transfix,** transpierce; **spear,** lance, poniard, bayonet, sabre, sword, put to the sword; **knife,** dirk, dagger, stiletto; spike

26 **to gore,** horn, tusk

27 **to pelt,** stone, lapidate (*old*), pellet

28 **to hurl at, throw at, cast at,** heave at, chuck at (*informal*), fling at, sling at, toss at, shy at, fire at, let fly at; hurl against, hurl at the head of

adjectives

29 **attacking,** assailing, assaulting, charging, driving, thrusting, advancing; **invading,** invasive, invasionary, incursive, incursionary, irruptive

30 **offensive, combative,** on the offensive *or* attack; **aggressive**

adverbs

31 **under attack, under fire;** under siege

exclamations

32 **attack!,** advance!, **charge!,** over the top!, up and at 'em!, have at them!, give 'em hell!, let 'em have it!, fire!, open fire!; banzai!, Geronimo!

460 DEFENCE

nouns

1 **defence, guard,** ward; **protection** *see* 1007; resistance *see* 453; self-defence, self-protection, self-preservation; deterrent capacity; defence in depth; the defensive; covering one's arse *or* rear-end (*informal*); defences, psychological defences, ego defences, defence mechanism, escape mechanism, avoidance reaction, negative taxis *or* tropism; bunker mentality

2 **military defence, national defence,** defence capability; **civil defence;** Fire and Civil Defence Authority; radar defences, close air defence systems *or* CADS, airborne warning and control system *or* AWACS, distant early warning *or* DEW Line (*US & Canadian*); antimissile missile, antiballistic-missile system *or* ABM, Patriot missile; strategic defence initiative *or* SDI *or* Star Wars

3 **armour,** armature; armour plate; body armour, suit of armour, plate armour; panoply, harness; **mail,** chain mail, chain armour; bulletproof vest; battledress; **protective covering,** cortex, **thick skin,** carapace, shell *see* 295.15; spines, needles

4 **fortification,** work, defence work, **bulwark, rampart, fence, barrier** *see* 1011.5; **enclosure** *see* 212.3

5 **entrenchment, trench,** ditch, fosse; **moat; dugout,** abri (*French*); **bunker; foxhole,** slit trench; approach trench, communication trench, fire trench, gallery, parallel, coupure; tunnel, fortified tunnel; undermining, sap, single *or* double sap, flying sap; mine, countermine

6 **stronghold,** hold, safehold, fasthold, strong point, **fastness,** keep, ward, **bastion,** donjon, **citadel, castle,** tower, tower of strength, strong point; mote *or* motte; **fort, fortress,** post; **bunker, pillbox,** blockhouse, garrison *or* trenches *or* barricades; garrison house; acropolis; peel, peel tower; rath (*Irish*); martello tower, martello; **bridgehead, beachhead**

7 **defender, champion, advocate; upholder; guardian angel, supporter** *see* 616.9; vindicator, apologist; **protector** *see* 1007.5; **guard** *see* 1007.9; paladin; guard dog, attack dog

verbs

8 **to defend, guard, shield,** screen, secure, guard against; defend tooth and nail *or* to the death *or* to the last breath; **safeguard, protect** *see* 1007.18; stand by the side of, flank; **advocate, champion** *see* 600.10; **defend oneself,** cover one's arse *or* rear-end (*informal*), cover your arse (*informal*)

9 **to fortify,** embattle *or* battle (*old*); arm; **armour,** armour-plate; **man;** garrison, man the garrison *or* trenches *or* barricades; **barricade, blockade;**

bulwark, wall, palisade, fence; castellate, crenellate; bank; entrench, **dig in**; mine

10 **to fend off, ward off, stave off, hold off, fight off**, keep off, beat off, parry, fend, counter, turn aside; **hold** or **keep at bay**, keep at arm's length; **hold the fort, hold the line**, stop, check, block, hinder, obstruct; **repel, repulse, rebuff, drive back**, put back, push back; go on the defensive, fight a holding or delaying action, fall back to prepared positions

adjectives

11 **defensive, defending, guarding**, shielding, screening; **protective** see 1007.23; self-defensive, self-protective, self-preservative

12 **fortified, battlemented, embattled** or **battled** (old); castellated, crenellated, casemated, machicolated

13 **armoured**, armour-plated; in armour, panoplied, armed cap-a-pie, armed at all points, in harness, "in complete steel"—SHAKESPEARE; mailed, mailclad, ironclad; loricate, loricated

14 **armed**, heeled and carrying and gun-toting (all informal); accoutred, **in arms**, bearing or wearing or carrying arms, under arms, sword in hand; **well-armed**, heavy-armed, fully-armed, bristling with arms, **armed to the teeth**; light-armed; **garrisoned**, manned

15 **defensible, defendable**, tenable

adverbs

16 **defensively, in defence**, in self-defence; **on the defensive**, on guard; **at bay**, aux abois (French), with one's back to the wall

461 COMBATANT

nouns

1 **combatant, fighter, battler**, scrapper (informal); **contestant, contender, competitor, rival**; disputant, wrangler, squabbler, bickerer, quarreller; struggler, tussler, scuffler; brawler, rioter; feuder; **belligerent**, militant; gladiator; jouster, tilter; **knight**, belted knight; swordsman, blade, sword, sabreur, beau sabreur (both French); fencer, foilsman, swordplayer (old); duelist; gamecock, fighting cock; **tough**, rough, rowdy, **ruffian**, thug, hooligan, streetfighter, bully, bullyboy, **hoodlum, hood** (informal), bravo; gorilla and goon (both informal); hatchet man (informal), enforcer (US informal), strong-arm man, strong arm, strong-armer; swashbuckler

2 **boxer, pugilist**, pug or palooka (both US informal); **street fighter**, scrapper, pit bull

3 **wrestler**, grunt-and-groaner (informal), grappler, scuffler

4 **bullfighter**, toreador, torero (Spanish); banderillero, picador, matador

5 **militarist, warmonger, hawk** (informal), war dog or hound, war hawk; **chauvinist, jingo**, jingoist

6 **military man** or **woman, serviceman, servicewoman**, navy man or woman; air service-man or woman; **soldier, warrior**, brave, fighting man, legionary, hoplite, **man-at-arms**, rifleman,

rifle; **cannon fodder**, food for powder; warrioress, Amazon; spearman, pikeman, halberdier

7 (common soldiers) **squaddie**, erk, bootie, bootneck, Tommy Atkins or **Tommy**, GI and GI Joe (both US informal), dough and doughboy (both US informal), grunt (US informal); redcoat; poilu (French); Aussie, Anzac, digger (all Australian); jock (Scottish); Fritz, Jerry, Hun, Boche, Kraut (German soldier); Janissary (Turkish soldier); sepoy (India); askari (Africa)

8 **enlisted man**, noncommissioned officer see 575.19; **common soldier, private, private soldier**, buck private (US informal); private first class or pfc

9 **infantryman, foot soldier**; light infantryman, chasseur, Jäger (German), Zouave; **rifleman**, rifle, musketeer; fusileer, carabineer; **sharpshooter**, marksman, expert rifleman, bersagliere (Italian); **sniper**; grenadier

10 **artilleryman**, artillerist, **gunner**, cannoneer, machine gunner; **bomber**, bomb thrower, bombardier

11 **cavalryman**, mounted infantryman, **trooper**; dragoon, light or heavy dragoon; lancer, lance, uhlan, hussar; cuirassier; spahi; cossack

12 **tanker**, tank corpsman, tank crewman

13 **engineer**, combat engineer, pioneer, Seabee (US); sapper, sapper and miner

14 **elite troops**, special troops, **shock troops**, storm troops, elite corps; Waffen SS; Republican Guard (Iraq); rapid reaction force; commandos, Special Air Service or SAS, Special Boat Service or SBS, Delta Force (US), marines, paratroops, Special Forces (US), Green Berets (US), Black Berets (Russia); guardsmen, guards, household troops; Life Guards, Horse Guards, Foot Guards, Grenadier Guards, Coldstream Guards, Scots Guards, Irish Guards; Swiss Guards

15 **irregular**, casual; **guerrilla**, partisan, franctireur; **bushfighter**, bushwhacker (US informal); underground, resistance, maquis; mujaheddin or the mujaheddin, SWAPO or South West African People's Organization; Shining Path or Sendero Luminoso; Contras; maquisard (French), underground or resistance fighter

16 **mercenary, hireling**, condottiere (Italian), freelance, free companion, **soldier of fortune**, adventurer; gunman, gun, hired gun, hired killer, professional killer

17 **recruit, rookie** (informal), **conscript**, drafted man, **draftee, inductee, selectee, enlistee**, enrollee, trainee, boot (US informal); **raw recruit**, tenderfoot; awkward squad (informal); draft, levy

18 **veteran**, campaigner, old campaigner, old soldier, old sweat (informal), war-horse (informal), Old Contemptible, vet (US informal)

19 **defence forces, the forces**, the services, **armed forces**, armed services, fighting machine; **the military**, the military establishment

20 **branch**, branch of the service, corps (see list); **service**, arm of the service, Air Force, Army, Navy, Royal Marines, Merchant Marine

21 (military units) **unit, organization**, tactical unit, **outfit** (informal); **army**, field army, army group,

corps, **division**, infantry division, armoured division, airborne division; **regiment, battle group,** battalion, garrison, **company**, troop, brigade, legion, phalanx, cohort, **platoon**, section, **battery**, maniple; **combat team**, combat command; **task force; squad**, squadron; detachment, detail, posse; column, flying column; rank, file; train, field train; cadre

22 **army**, this man's army (*informal*), **soldiery, forces, troops, host**, array, legions; ranks, rank and file; **standing army, regular army**, regulars, professional *or* career soldiers; the line, troops of the line; line of defence, first *or* second line of defence; ground forces, ground troops; storm troops; **airborne troops**, paratroops; ski troops, mountain troops; occupation force

23 **militia**, organized militia, national militia, mobile militia, territorial militia, reserve militia; home guard, Dad's Army (*informal*); National Guard, Air National Guard, state guard (*all US*); trainband, yeomanry, Minutemen (*US*)

24 **reserves**, reserved list, auxiliaries, **second line of defence**, landwehr, army reserves, home reserves, territorial reserves, Territorial Army *or* TA, supplementary reserves, organized reserves

25 **volunteers, enlistees**, volunteer army, volunteer militia, volunteer navy

26 **navy**, naval forces, **first line of defence**, senior service; **fleet**, flotilla, argosy, armada, squadron, escadrille, division, task force, task group; Royal Navy *or* RN; United States Navy *or* USN; marine, mercantile *or* merchant marine, merchant navy, merchant fleet; naval militia; naval reserve; coast guard

27 **marines**, sea soldiers, **Royal Marines**, Marine Corps (*US*); leathernecks (*US informal*)

28 **air force**, air corps, air service, air arm; **Royal Air Force** *or* **RAF**, Fleet Air Arm; Royal Flying Corps *or* RFC (*old*); Fighter Command, Bomber Command, Coastal Command (*all old*); US Air Force *or* USAF; strategic air force, tactical air force; squadron, escadrille, flight, wing

29 **war-horse, charger**, courser, trooper

30 Arms, Branches, and Corps of the British Armed Services

Army Air Corps	Royal Army Vetinary
Brigade of Gurkhas	Corps
Corps of Royal Engineers	Royal Auxiliary Air Force
Fleet Air Arm	Royal Corps of Signals
Guards Division	Royal Irish Regiment
Household Cavalry	Royal Logistics Corps
Intelligence Corps	Royal Marines
King's Division	Royal Marines Reserve
Light Division	Royal Naval Auxiliary
Parachute Regiment	Service
Prince of Wales's Division	Royal Naval Reserve
Queen's Division	Royal Regiment of
Royal Air Force Volunteer	Artillery
Reserve	Scottish Division
Royal Armoured Corps	Special Air Service
Royal Army Medical	Regiment
Corps	Territorial Army

462 ARMS

nouns

1 **arms, weapons**, deadly weapons, instruments of destruction, offensive weapons, **military hardware**, matériel, **weaponry, armament, munitions, ordnance**, munitions of war, *apparatus belli* (*Latin*); musketry; missilery; small arms; side arms; stand of arms; conventional weapons, nonnuclear weapons; **nuclear weapons**, atomic weapons, thermonuclear weapons, A-weapons; biological weapons; chemical weapons, binary weapons; weapons of mass destruction; arms industry, arms maker, military-industrial complex

2 **armoury, arsenal**, magazine, dump; ammunition depot, ammo dump (*informal*); park, gun park, artillery park, park of artillery; atomic arsenal, thermonuclear arsenal

3 **ballistics, gunnery**, musketry, artillery; rocketry, missilery; archery

4 **fist, clenched fist**; knuckle-dusters, knuckles; **club**, blunt instrument, cosh

5 **sword, blade**, good *or* trusty sword; steel, **cold steel**; Excalibur; **knife**, flick knife; **dagger**, skean-dhu (*Scottish*); **axe**

6 **arrow, shaft, dart**, reed, bolt; quarrel; chested arrow, footed arrow, bobtailed arrow, cloth yard shaft; arrowhead, barb; flight, volley

7 **bow**, longbow, carriage bow; **bow and arrow**; crossbow, arbalest

8 **spear**, throwing spear, javelin

9 **sling, slingshot**; throwing-stick, throw stick, spear-thrower, atlatl, woomera; **catapult**, arbalest, ballista, trebuchet

10 **gun, firearm**; shooter (*informal*), piece *and* tool (*both US informal*); shoulder weapon *or* gun *or* arm; gun make; gun part; stun gun; AK-47 *or* Kalshnikov, automatic, BB gun, blunderbuss (*old*), Bren *or* Bren gun, Browning automatic rifle, carbine, derringer, Enfield rifle, flintlock, forty-five *or* .45, forty-four *or* .44, Gatling gun, handgun, machine gun, musket, Luger, pistol, repeater, revolver, rifle, Saturday night special, sawn-off shotgun, service revolver, shotgun, six-gun *or* six-shooter (*US informal*), Sten gun, submachine gun, thirty-eight *or* .38, thirty-thirty *or* .30-30, thirty-two *or* .32, Thompson submachine gun *or* tommy gun (*informal*), twenty-two *or* .22, Uzi sub-machine gun, Webley, zip gun

11 **artillery, cannon**, cannonry, ordnance, engines of war, Big Bertha, howitzer, super gun; field artillery; heavy artillery, heavy field artillery; siege artillery, bombardment weapons; breakthrough weapons; siege engine; mountain artillery, coast artillery, trench artillery, anti-aircraft artillery, flak (*informal*); battery

12 **antiaircraft gun** *or* AA gun, ack-ack (*informal*), pom-pom (*informal*), *Fliegerabwehrkanone* (*German*), skysweeper, Bofors, Oerlikon

13 **ammunition, ammo** (*informal*), **powder and shot**, iron rations (*informal*)

14 **explosive**, high explosive; cellulose nitrate, cordite, dynamite, gelignite, guncotton, gunpowder, nitroglycerin, plastic explosive *or* plastique, powder, Semtex, trinitrotoluene *or* trinitrotoluol *or* TNT

15 **fuse, detonator,** exploder; **cap,** blasting cap, percussion cap, mercury fulminate, fulminating mercury; electric detonator *or* exploder; detonating powder; **primer,** priming; primacord

16 **charge, load;** blast; warhead, payload

17 **cartridge,** cartouche, **shell;** ball cartridge; blank cartridge, dry ammunition

18 **missile, projectile,** bolt; brickbat, stone, rock; boomerang; bola; throwing-stick, throw stick, waddy (*Australian*); **ballistic missile,** cruise missile, Exocet missile, intercontinental ballistic missile *or* ICBM, Patriot missile, Pershing missile, Scud missile, sea-launched cruise missile *or* SLCM, SS-20 *and* SS-22, submarine-launched ballistic missile *or* SLBM, surface-to-air missile *or* SAM, surface-to-surface missile; **rocket** *see* 1072.2-6,14; **torpedo**

19 **shot; ball,** cannonball, rifle ball, grapeshot, minié ball; **bullet,** slug, pellet, birdshot; copkiller (*US informal*), dumdum bullet, expanding bullet, explosive bullet, manstopping bullet, manstopper, Teflon bullet (*trademark*); tracer bullet, tracer; plastic bullet *or* baton round; **shell,** high-explosive shell, **shrapnel**

20 **bomb,** bombshell; antipersonnel bomb, atomic bomb *or* atom bomb *or* A-bomb, atomic warhead, blockbuster, depth charge *or* depth bomb *or* ash can (*informal*), fire bomb *or* incendiary bomb *or* incendiary, grenade, hand grenade, hydrogen bomb *or* H-bomb, letter bomb, Molotov cocktail, napalm bomb, neutron bomb, nuclear warhead, pipe bomb, plastic *or* plastique bomb, plutonium bomb, smart bomb, stench *or* stink bomb, time bomb, whiz-bang; clean bomb, dirty bomb; **mine**

21 **launcher,** projector, bazooka; rocket launcher, grenade launcher, hedgehog, mine thrower, *Minenwerfer* (*German*), **mortar**

463 ARENA

nouns

1 **arena, scene of action, site,** scene, setting, background, **field, ground,** terrain, sphere, place, locale, milieu, precinct, purlieu; course, range, walk (*old*); campus; **theatre,** stage, stage set *or* setting, scenery; **platform; forum,** agora, marketplace, open forum, public square; **amphitheatre,** circus, **hippodrome, coliseum,** colosseum, **stadium,** bowl (*US*); **hall, auditorium;** gymnasium, gym (*informal*), palaestra; **lists,** tiltyard, tilting ground; floor, **pit,** cockpit; bear garden; **ring,** prize ring, boxing ring, canvas, squared circle (*informal*), wrestling ring, mat, bull ring; parade ground; pitch, field, playing field, park; stamping ground, turf, bailiwick *see* 893.4

2 **battlefield, battleground,** battle site, **field,** combat area, **field of battle;** field of slaughter, field of blood *or* bloodshed, aceldama, killing ground *or* field, shambles; **battlefront, the front,** front line, **line,** enemy line *or* lines, firing line, battle line, line of battle; combat zone; **theatre, theatre of operations,** theatre *or* seat of war; communications zone, zone of communications; no-man's-land;

demilitarized zone *or* DMZ; jump area *or* zone, landing beach

3 campground, camp, encampment, bivouac, tented field

464 PEACE

nouns

1 **peace,** *pax* (*Latin*); **peacetime,** "piping time of peace"—SHAKESPEARE, the storm blown over; freedom from war, cessation of combat, exemption from hostilities, public tranquillity, "liberty in tranquillity"—CICERO; **harmony,** accord *see* 455

2 **peacefulness, tranquillity, serenity, calmness, quiet,** peace and quiet, quietude, quietness, quiet life, restfulness; order, orderliness, law and order

3 **peace of mind,** peace of heart, peace of soul *or* spirit, peace of God, "peace which passeth all understanding"—BIBLE; ataraxia, shanti

4 **peaceableness, unpugnaciousness,** uncontentiousness, nonaggression; irenicism, dovelikeness, dovishness (*informal*), **pacifism,** pacificism; peaceful coexistence; **nonviolence;** meekness, lamblikeness *see* 433.5

5 **noncombatant,** nonbelligerent, nonresistant, nonresister; **civilian,** citizen

6 **pacifist,** pacificist, peacenik (*informal*), **peace lover;** pacificator, peacemaker, bridgebuilder; peacekeeper; peacemonger; **conscientious objector,** conchie (*informal*)

verbs

7 **to keep the peace,** remain at peace, wage peace; refuse to shed blood, keep one's sword in its sheath; forswear violence, beat one's swords into ploughshares; pursue the arts of peace, pour oil on troubled waters; defuse

8 "be at peace among yourselves", "follow after the things which make for peace", "follow peace with all men", "as much as lieth in you, live peaceably with all men", "seek peace, and pursue it", "have peace one with another", "be of one mind, live in peace"—ALL BIBLE

adjectives

9 **pacific, peaceful, peaceable;** tranquil, serene; idyllic, pastoral; halcyon, soft, piping, **calm, quiet,** restful, **untroubled,** orderly, **at peace;** concordant *see* 455.3; bloodless; peacetime

10 **unbelligerent, unhostile,** unbellicose, **unpugnacious, uncontentious,** unmilitant, unmilitary, **nonaggressive,** noncombative, nonmilitant; noncombatant, civilian; **antiwar, pacific, peaceable,** peace-loving, dovish (*informal*); meek, lamblike *see* 433.15; **pacifistic,** pacifist, irenic; **nonviolent;** conciliatory *see* 465.12, peacekeeping

exclamations

11 **peace!, peace be with you!,** peace be to you!, *pax vobiscum!, pax tecum!* (*both Latin*); shalom!, shalom aleichem! (*both Hebrew*), salaam aleikum! (*Arabic*);

"peace be to this house!", "peace be within thy walls, and prosperity within thy palaces", "let the peace of God rule in your hearts"—ALL BIBLE; go in peace!, *vade in pace!* (*Latin*)

465 PACIFICATION

nouns

1 **pacification, peacemaking,** peacemongering, **conciliation, propitiation, placation, appeasement, mollification,** dulcification; **calming, soothing,** tranquillization; détente, relaxation of tension, easing of relations; mediation *see* 466; placability; peace-keeping force, United Nations troops

2 **peace offer,** offer of parley, parley; peace feelers; **peace offering,** propitiatory gift; **olive branch; white flag,** truce flag, flag of truce; calumet, peace pipe, **pipe of peace;** downing of arms, hand of friendship, empty hands, outstretched hand; **cooling off, cooling-off period**

3 **reconciliation,** reconcilement, *rapprochement* (*French*), **reunion,** shaking of hands, making up *and* kissing and making up (*both informal*)

4 **adjustment,** accommodation, resolution, composition of differences, compromise, arrangement, settlement, terms; consensus building, consensus seeking

5 **truce, armistice, peace; pacification,** treaty of peace, suspension of hostilities, **cease-fire,** stand-down, breathing spell, cooling-off period; Truce *or* Peace of God, Pax Dei, Pax Romana; temporary arrangement, *modus vivendi* (*Latin*); hollow truce, *pax in bello* (*Latin*); demilitarized zone, buffer zone, neutral territory

6 **disarmament,** reduction of armaments; peace dividend; unilateral disarmament, multilateral disarmament; **demilitarization,** deactivation, disbanding, disbandment, **demobilization,** mustering out, reconversion, decommissioning; civilian life, mufti *and* civvy street (*both informal*)

verbs

7 **to pacify, conciliate, placate, propitiate, appease, mollify,** dulcify; **calm, settle, soothe,** tranquillize *see* 670.7; smooth, smooth over *or* out, smooth down, smooth one's feathers; allay, lay, lay the dust; pour oil on troubled waters, pour balm on, take the edge off of, take the sting out of; cool (*informal*), defuse; clear the air

8 **to reconcile, bring to terms, bring together,** reunite, heal the breach; bring about a détente; **harmonize,** restore harmony, put in tune; **iron *or* sort out,** adjust, settle, compose, accommodate, arrange matters, settle differences, resolve, compromise; **patch things up,** fix up (*informal*), patch up a friendship *or* quarrel, smooth it over; weave peace between, mediate *see* 466.6

9 **to make peace,** cease hostilities, cease fire, stand down, raise a siege; **cool it** *and* **chill out** (*both informal*), **bury the hatchet, smoke the pipe of peace;** negotiate a peace, dictate peace; make a peace offering, hold out the olive branch, hoist *or* show *or* wave the white flag

10 **to make up** *and* **kiss and make up** *and* make it up *and* make matters up (*all informal*), **shake hands,** come round, come together, come to an understanding, **come to terms,** let the wound heal, let bygones be bygones, forgive and forget, put it all behind one, settle *or* compose one's differences, meet halfway

11 **to disarm, lay down one's arms,** unarm, turn in one's weapons, down *or* ground one's arms, sheathe the sword, turn swords into ploughshares; **demilitarize,** deactivate, **demobilize, disband,** reconvert, decommission

adjectives

12 **pacificatory, pacific,** irenic, **conciliatory,** reconciliatory, **propitiatory,** propitiative, **placative,** placatory, **mollifying, appeasing; pacifying, soothing** *see* 670.15, appeasable

13 **pacifiable, placable, appeasable,** propitiable

adverbs

14 **pacifically, peaceably; with no hard feelings**

466 MEDIATION

nouns

1 **mediation,** mediating, intermediation, **intercession; intervention,** interposition, putting oneself between, stepping in, declaring oneself in, involvement, interagency; interventionism

2 **arbitration,** arbitrament, compulsory arbitration, binding arbitration; nonbinding arbitration; umpirage, refereeship, mediatorship

3 **mediator,** intermediator, intermediate agent, intermediate, intermedium, **intermediary,** interagent, internuncio; **medium; intercessor,** interceder; ombudsman; ACAS; **intervener,** intervenor; interventionist; **go-between, middleman** *see* 576.4; connection (*informal*); front *and* front man (*both informal*); deputy, agent *see* 576; **spokesman, spokeswoman,** spokesperson, spokespeople; **mouthpiece; negotiator,** negotiant, negotiatress *or* negotiatrix

4 **arbitrator,** arbiter, impartial arbitrator, third party, unbiased observer; **moderator; umpire, referee, judge;** magistrate *see* 596.1

5 **peacemaker,** make-peace, reconciler, smoother-over; **pacifier,** pacificator; **conciliator,** propitiator, **appeaser;** marriage counsellor, family counsellor; patcher-up

verbs

6 **to mediate,** intermediate, **intercede, go between; intervene,** interpose, step in, step into the breach, declare oneself a party, involve oneself, put oneself between disputants, use one's good offices, act between; butt in *and* put one's nose in (*both informal*); represent *see* 576.14; **negotiate,** bargain, **treat with,** make terms, meet halfway; **arbitrate,** moderate; **umpire, referee,** judge

7 **to settle, arrange,** compose, patch up, adjust, straighten out, bring to terms *or* an understanding; make peace *see* 465.9

adjectives

8 **mediatory**, mediatorial, mediative, mediating, going *or* coming between; intermediatory, intermediary, intermedial, intermediate, **middle**, intervening, mesne, interlocutory; interventional, arbitrational, arbitrative; **intercessory**, intercessional; pacificatory *see* 465.12

467 NEUTRALITY

nouns

1 **neutrality, neutralism,** strict neutrality; noncommitment, noninvolvement; **independence, nonpartisanism, unalignment, nonalignment;** fence-sitting *or* straddling, mugwumpery, mugwumpism; **evasion, cop-out** (*informal*), abstention; **impartiality** *see* 649.4
2 **indifference,** indifferentness, Laodiceanism; passiveness *see* 329.1; apathy *see* 94.4
3 **middle course** *or* **way**, *via media* (*Latin*); **middle ground**, neutral ground *or* territory, centre; meeting ground, interface; grey area, penumbra; **middle of the road**, sitting on *or* straddling the fence (*informal*); medium, **happy medium**; mean, **golden mean**; moderation, moderateness *see* 670.1; compromise *see* 468; halfway measures, half measures, half-and-half measures
4 **neutral,** neuter; **independent, nonpartisan;** fence-sitter *or* straddler, mugwump; anythingarian *and* nothingarian (*both informal*)

verbs

5 **to remain neutral**, stand neuter, hold no brief, **keep in the middle of the road, straddle** *or* **sit on the fence** *and* sit out *and* sit on the sidelines (*all informal*); **evade**, evade the issue, duck the issue *and* waffle *and* cop out (*all informal*), abstain
6 **to steer a middle course**, hold *or* keep *or* preserve a middle course, walk a middle path, follow the *via media*, strike *or* preserve a balance, **strike** *or* **keep a happy medium**, keep the golden mean, steer between *or* avoid Scylla and Charybdis; be moderate *see* 670.5

adjectives

7 **neutral,** neuter; noncommitted, uncommitted, noninvolved, uninvolved; **indifferent,** Laodicean; passive *see* 329.6; apathetic *see* 94.13; neither one thing nor the other, neither fish nor fowl; even, half-and-half, fifty-fifty (*informal*), six and half a dozen; on the fence *or* sidelines (*informal*), **in the middle of the road**, centrist, moderate, midway; **independent, nonpartisan; unaligned, nonaligned;** impartial *see* 649.10

468 COMPROMISE

mutual concession

nouns

1 **compromise,** composition, adjustment, accommodation, settlement, mutual concession, give-and-take; abatement of differences; bargain, deal (*informal*), arrangement, understanding; **concession,**

giving way, yielding; surrender, desertion of principle, evasion of responsibility, cop-out (*informal*)

verbs

2 **to compromise,** make *or* reach a compromise, compound, compose, accommodate, adjust, settle, make an adjustment *or* arrangement, **make a deal** (*informal*), do a deal, come to an understanding, strike a bargain, do something mutually beneficial; plea-bargain; strike a balance, take the mean, **meet halfway,** split the difference, go fifty-fifty (*informal*), give and take; play politics; steer a middle course *see* 467.6; **make concessions**, give way, yield, wimp *or* chicken out (*informal*); **surrender** *see* 433.8, desert one's principles, evade responsibility, sidestep, duck responsibility *and* cop out (*both informal*)

phrases

3 half a loaf is better than none; you can't win them all

469 POSSESSION

nouns

1 **possession,** possessing, outright possession, free-and-clear possession; **owning,** having title to; seisin, nine tenths of the law, *de facto* possession, *de jure* possession, lawful *or* legal possession; property rights, proprietary rights; **title,** absolute title, free-and-clear title, original title; derivative title; adverse possession, squatting, squatterism, **squatter's right,** vacant possession; **claim, legal claim,** lien; usucapion, usucaption (*old*), prescription; **occupancy,** occupation; **hold, holding, tenure,** security of tenure; **tenancy,** tenantry, **lease,** leasehold, sublease, underlease, undertenancy; gavelkind; villenage, villein socage, villeinhold; socage, free socage; burgage; frankalmoign, lay fee; tenure in chivalry, knight service; fee fief, fiefdom, feud, feodum; freehold, alodium; fee simple, fee tail, fee simple absolute, fee simple conditional, fee simple defeasible *or* fee simple determinable; fee position; dependency, colony, mandate; prepossession (*old*), preoccupation, preoccupancy; chose in possession, bird in hand; **property** *see* 471
2 **ownership, title,** possessorship, *dominium* (*Latin*), **proprietorship,** proprietary, **property right** *or* rights; lordship, **overlordship,** seigniory; **dominion, sovereignty** *see* 417.5; landownership, landowning, landholding, land tenure
3 **monopoly,** monopolization; **corner** *and* cornering *and* a corner on (*all informal*); exclusive possession; engrossment, forestalment

verbs

4 **to possess, have, hold,** have and hold, possess outright *or* free and clear, **occupy, fill, enjoy,** boast; be possessed of, have tenure of, have in hand, be seized of, have in one's grip *or* grasp, have in one's possession, be enfeoffed of; **command,** have at one's command *or* pleasure *or* disposition *or* disposal, have going for one (*informal*); claim, usucapt; **squat,** squat on, claim squatter's right

5 to own, have title to, have for one's own *or* very own, have to one's name, call one's own, have the deed for, hold in fee simple, etc

6 to monopolize, hog *and* grab all of *and* gobble up (*all informal*), take it all, have all to oneself, have exclusive possession of *or* exclusive rights to; engross, forestall, tie up; **corner** *and* corner the market (*both informal*)

7 to belong to, pertain to, appertain to; vest in

adjectives

8 possessed, owned, held; in seisin, in fee, in fee simple, **free and clear;** own, of one's own; **in one's possession, in hand,** in one's grip *or* grasp, at one's command *or* disposal; on hand, by one, in stock, in store

9 possessing, having, holding, having and holding, occupying, owning; **in possession of, possessed of,** seized of, master of; tenured; enfeoffed; endowed with, blessed with; worth; propertied, property-owning, landed, landowning, landholding

10 possessive, possessory, **proprietary**

11 monopolistic, monopolist, monopolizing, hogging (*informal*)

adverbs

12 free and clear, outright; bag and baggage; by fee simple, etc

470 POSSESSOR

nouns

1 possessor, holder, keeper, haver, enjoyer

2 proprietor, proprietary, **owner;** *rentier* (*French*); titleholder, deedholder; proprietress, proprietrix; **master, mistress, lord,** laird (*Scottish*); **landlord, landlady;** hotelier; lord of the manor, mesne lord, mesne, feudatory, feoffee; squire, country gentleman; householder; beneficiary, cestui, cestui que trust, cestui que use

3 landowner, landholder, property owner, owner-occupier, propertied *or* landed person, man of property, freeholder; landed interests, landed gentry, slumlord, rent gouger; absentee landlord

4 tenant, occupant, sitting tenant, occupier, incumbent, **resident; lodger,** roomer, paying guest; **renter,** hirer, **lessee,** leaseholder; subtenant, sublessee, underlessee, undertenant; tenant at sufferance, tenant at will; tenant from year to year, tenant for years, tenant for life; squatter; homesteader (*US*)

5 trustee, fiduciary, holder of the legal estate; depository, depositary

471 PROPERTY

nouns

1 property, properties, possessions, holdings, havings, goods, chattels, goods and chattels, **effects,** estate and effects, what one can call one's own, what one has to one's name, all one owns *or* has, all one can lay claim to, one's all; household possessions *or* effects, lares and penates; hereditament, corporeal hereditament, incorporeal hereditament; acquest; acquisitions, receipts *see* 627; **inheritance** *see* 479.2

2 belongings, appurtenances, trappings, paraphernalia, appointments, accessories, perquisites, appendages, appanages, choses local; **things,** material things, mere things; consumer goods; choses, choses in possession, choses in action; **personal effects,** chattels personal, movables, choses transitory

3 impedimenta, luggage, baggage, bag and baggage, dunnage, traps, tackle, apparatus, truck, gear, kit, clobber (*informal*), outfit, duffel (*US & Canadian*)

4 estate, interest, equity, stake, part, percentage; **right, title** *see* 469.1, **claim,** holding; use, trust, benefit; absolute interest, vested interest, contingent interest, beneficial interest, equitable interest; easement, right of common, common, right of entry; limitation; settlement, strict settlement

5 freehold, estate of freehold; alodium, alod; frankalmoign, lay fee, tenure in *or* by free alms; mortmain, dead hand

6 real estate, realty, real property, land, land and buildings, chattels real, tenements; immoveables; *praedium* (*Latin*), landed property *or* estate, **land, lands,** property, grounds, acres; lot, lots, parcel, plot, plat, quadrat; demesne, domain (*old*); messuage, manor, honour, toft (*old*)

7 assets, means, resources, total assets *or* resources; stock, stock-in-trade; **worth,** net worth, what one is worth; circumstances, funds *see* 728.14; wealth *see* 618; **material assets,** tangible assets, tangibles; intangible assets, intangibles; current assets, deferred assets, fixed assets, frozen assets, liquid assets, quick assets, assets and liabilities, net assets; assessed valuation

adjectives

8 propertied, proprietary; **landed**

9 real, praedial; manorial, seignioral, seigneurial; feudal, feudatory, feodal

10 freehold, leasehold, copyhold; alodial

472 ACQUISITION

nouns

1 acquisition, gaining, getting, getting hold of (*informal*), coming by, **acquirement, obtainment,** obtention, **attainment,** securement, winning; trover; accession; addition *see* 253; **procurement,** procural, procurance, procuration; **earnings,** making, pulling *or* dragging *or* knocking down (*informal*), moneymaking, moneygetting, moneygrubbing

2 collection, gathering, gleaning, bringing together, assembling, putting *or* piecing together, **accumulation,** cumulation, **amassment,** grubbing

3 gain, profit, percentage (*informal*), take *or* take-in *and* slice *and* rakeoff (*all informal*); **gains, profits, earnings, winnings, return, returns, proceeds,** bottom line, makings; **income** *see* 624.4; **receipts** *see* 627; **fruits,** pickings, gleanings; **booty, spoils** *see* 482.11; pelf, lucre, filthy lucre; perquisite, perk *or* perks; **pile** *and* bundle *and* killing *and* mint (*all informal*); easy money; net profit, clean *or* clear profit, net; gross profit, gross; paper profits; capital gains; interest, dividends; hoard, store *see* 386; wealth *see* 618

4 **profitableness, profitability,** gainfulness, remunerativeness, rewardingness

5 **yield, output,** make, production; **proceeds,** produce, product; **crop, harvest,** fruit, vintage, bearing; second crop, aftermath; bumper crop

6 **find,** finding, **discovery; trove,** *trouvaille* (*French*); treasure trove, buried treasure; **windfall,** windfall money, windfall profit, found money, money in the bank, **bonus,** icing on the cake, gravy (*informal*), bunce (*informal*)

7 **godsend, boon, blessing;** manna, manna from heaven, loaves and fishes, gift from on high

verbs

8 **to acquire, get, gain, obtain, secure, procure; win,** score; **earn,** make; **reap, harvest;** contract; take, catch, capture; **net;** come *or* enter into possession of, **come into, come by,** come in for, be seized of; draw, derive

9 (*informal terms*) **to grab,** latch on to, bag, get *or* lay hold of, rake in *or* off, skim *or* skim off, catch, collar, cop, dig up, grub up, round up, drum up, get hold of, get *or* lay one's hands *or* mitts on, get one's fingers *or* hands on, get one's hooks into, snag, snaffle, grub up, hook, land, nab, pick up, nail; take home, pull in

10 **to take possession, appropriate, take up,** take over, make one's own, move in *or* move in on (*informal*), annex

11 **to collect, gather, glean, pick, pluck,** cull, **take up,** pick up, get *or* gather in, gather to oneself, bring *or* get together, scrape together; heap up, amass, assemble, accumulate *see* 386.11

12 **to profit, make** *or* **draw** *or* **realize** *or* **reap profit, come out ahead, make money;** rake it in *and* coin money *and* make a bundle *or* pile *or* killing *or* mint *and* clean up (*all informal*); gain by, **capitalize on,** commercialize, make capital out of, **cash in on** *and* make a good thing of (*both informal*), turn to profit *or* account, **realize on,** make money by, obtain a return, turn a penny *or* an honest penny; **gross, net; realize, clear;** kill two birds with one stone, turn to one's advantage; make a fast *or* quick buck (*informal*)

13 **to be profitable,** pay, repay, pay off (*informal*), yield a profit, show a percentage, be gainful, be worthwhile *or* worth one's while, be a good investment

adjectives

14 **obtainable, attainable, available,** accessible, to be had

15 **acquisitive,** acquiring; grasping, graspy; **greedy** *see* 100.27

16 **gainful,** productive, **profitable, remunerative, remuneratory,** lucrative, fat, **paying,** well-paying, high-yield, high-yielding; advantageous, worthwhile; banausic, moneymaking, breadwinning

adverbs

17 **profitably, gainfully,** remuneratively, lucratively, **at a profit,** in the black; for money; advantageously, to advantage, to profit, to the good

473 LOSS

nouns

1 **loss, losing, privation,** getting away, losing hold of; **deprivation, bereavement,** taking away, stripping, dispossession, despoilment, despoliation, spoliation, robbery; divestment, denudation; **sacrifice, forfeit, forfeiture,** giving up *or* over, denial; nonrestoration; **expense, cost, debit;** detriment, injury, damage; **destruction, ruin,** perdition, total loss, dead loss; losing streak (*informal*); **loser** *see* 412.5

2 **waste,** wastage, **exhaustion, depletion,** sapping, depreciation, dissipation, diffusion, **wearing, wearing away, erosion,** ablation, leaching away; moulting, shedding, casting *or* sloughing off; **using, using up, consumption, expenditure, drain;** stripping, clear-cutting; impoverishment, shrinkage; leakage, evaporation; decrement, decrease *see* 252

3 **losses,** losings; red ink; net loss, bottom line (*informal*)

verbs

4 **to lose,** incur loss, **suffer loss,** undergo privation *or* deprivation, be bereaved *or* bereft of, have no more, meet with a loss; kiss goodbye (*informal*); let slip, let slip through one's fingers; **forfeit,** default; **sacrifice; miss,** wander from, go astray from; **mislay,** misplace; lose out; **lose everything,** go broke *and* lose one's shirt *and* get cleaned out (*all informal*)

5 **to waste, deplete, depreciate,** dissipate, wear, wear away, erode, ablate, consume, drain, **shrink,** dribble away; **moult, shed,** cast *or* slough off; decrease *see* 252.6; squander *see* 486.3

6 **to go to waste,** come to nothing, come to naught, go up in smoke *and* go down the drain (*both informal*); run to waste, go to pot, go for a burton (*informal*), run *or* go to seed; dissipate, leak, leak away, scatter to the winds,

"waste its sweetness on the desert air"—Thomas Gray

adjectives

7 **lost, gone;** forfeited, forfeit; by the board, out the window *and* down the drain *or* tube (*all informal*); **nonrenewable;** long-lost; lost to; wasted, consumed, depleted, dissipated, diffused, **expended; worn away, eroded,** ablated, used, used up, shrunken; stripped, clear-cut; squandered *see* 486.9; irretrievable *see* 125.15

8 **bereft, bereaved,** divested, denuded, **deprived of,** shorn of, parted from, bereaved of, stripped of, dispossessed of, despoiled of, robbed of; **out of,** minus (*informal*), wanting, lacking; cut off, cut off without a penny; out of pocket; **penniless, destitute, broke** *and* stony-broke *and* flat broke *and* cleaned out *and* skint *and* on one's uppers (*all informal*)

adverbs

9 **at a loss, unprofitably,** to the bad (*informal*); in the red (*informal*); out, out of pocket

474 RETENTION

nouns

1 retention, retainment, **keeping, holding, maintenance, preservation;** prehension; keeping *or* holding in, **bottling** *or* corking up (*informal*), locking in, suppression, repression, inhibition, retentiveness, retentivity; **tenacity** *see* 802.3

2 **hold, purchase, grasp, grip, clutch, clamp, clinch, clench;** seizure *see* 480.2; bite, nip, toothhold; **cling,** clinging; toehold, foothold, footing; **clasp, hug, embrace,** bear hug; **grapple;** firm hold, tight grip, iron grip, grip of iron *or* steel, death grip

3 (*wrestling holds*) half nelson, full nelson, quarter nelson, three-quarter nelson, stranglehold, toehold, lock, hammerlock, headlock, scissors, bear hug

4 **clutches, claws, talons,** pounces, unguals; **nails,** fingernails; **pincers,** nippers, chelae; **tentacles; fingers,** digits; **hands,** paws *and* mitts (*both informal*); palm; prehensile tail; **jaws,** mandibles, maxillae; **teeth,** fangs

verbs

5 to **retain, keep, save,** save up, pocket *and* hippocket (*both informal*); **maintain, preserve;** keep *or* hold in, **bottle** *or* cork up (*both informal*), lock in, suppress, repress, inhibit, keep to oneself; persist in; hold one's own, hold one's ground

6 to **hold, grip, grasp, clutch,** clip, **clinch, clench;** bite, nip; grapple; **clasp, hug, embrace; cling, cling to,** cleave to, stick to, adhere to, freeze to; **hold on to,** hold fast *or* tight, hang on to, keep a firm hold upon; **hold on, hang on** (*informal*), stick like glue, stick like a leech, cling like a winkle, hang on for dear life; keep hold of, never let go; **seize** *see* 480.14

7 to **hold, keep, harbour,** bear, have, have and hold, hold on to; **cherish,** fondle, entertain, treasure, treasure up; **foster, nurture, nurse;** embrace, hug, cling to; bosom *or* embosom (*both old*), take to the bosom

adjectives

8 **retentive,** keeping, holding, gripping, grasping; **tenacious,** clinging; vicelike

9 **prehensile,** raptorial; fingered, digitate *or* digitated, digital; clawed, taloned, jawed, toothed, dentate, fanged

adverbs

10 **for keeps** (*informal*), to keep, **for good,** for good and all, for always; forever *see* 828.12

475 RELINQUISHMENT

nouns

1 **relinquishment, release,** giving up, letting go, dispensation; **disposal,** disposition, riddance, getting rid of, dumping *see* 390.3; **renunciation,** forgoing, forswearing, swearing off, resignation, abjuration, **abandonment** *see* 370; recantation, retraction *see* 363.3; **surrender,** cession, handover, turning over, **yielding;** sacrifice

2 **waiver,** quitclaim, deed of release

verbs

3 to **relinquish, give up,** render up, **surrender, yield,** cede, hand *or* turn over; take one's hands off, loose one's grip on; spare; resign, vacate; drop, **waive,** dispense with; **forgo,** do *or* go without, get along without, forswear, abjure, **renounce,** swear off; walk away from, **abandon** *see* 370.5; recant, retract; opt out, contract out; disgorge, throw up; have done with, wash one's hands of; **part with,** give away, dispose of, rid oneself of, get rid of, see the last of, dump *see* 390.7; kiss goodbye *or* off (*informal*); **sacrifice,** make a sacrifice; quitclaim; sell off

4 to **release, let go,** leave go (*informal*), **let loose of,** unhand, unclutch, unclasp, relax one's grip *or* hold

adjectives

5 **relinquished,** released, disposed of; waived, dispensed with; forgone, forsworn, renounced, abjured, **abandoned** *see* 370.8; recanted, retracted; **surrendered,** ceded, yielded; sacrificed

476 PARTICIPATION

nouns

1 **participation, partaking, sharing,** having a part *or* share *or* voice, contribution, association; **involvement,** engagement; complicity; **voting** *see* 609.18, **suffrage** *see* 609.17; **power-sharing;** partnership, copartnership, copartnery, joint control, cochairmanship, joint chairmanship; joint tenancy, cotenancy; joint ownership, condominium *or* condo, cooperative *or* coop *or* co-op; communal ownership, commune

2 **communion,** community, communal effort *or* enterprise, **cooperation,** cooperative society; social life, socializing; **collectivity,** collectivism, collective enterprise, collective farm, kibbutz, kolkhoz; **democracy,** participatory democracy, self-rule; community council, town meeting, collegiality; common ownership, public ownership, state ownership, communism, socialism *see* 611.7; profit sharing; sharecropping

3 **communization,** communalization, **socialization, nationalization,** collectivization

4 **participator, participant, partaker, player, sharer;** party, **a party to,** accomplice, accessory; partner, copartner; cotenant; shareholder

verbs

5 to **participate, take part, partake, contribute,** chip in, involve *or* engage oneself, get involved; **have** *or* **take a hand in,** get in on, have a finger in, have a finger in the pie, have to do with, have a part in, be an accessory to, be implicated in, be a party to, be a player in; **participate in,** partake of *or* in, **take part in,** take an active part in, **join, join in,** figure in, make oneself part of, join oneself to, buy into (*informal*), associate oneself with, play *or* perform a part in, play a role in, get in the act (*informal*); **join up,** sign on, enlist; climb on the bandwagon; **have a voice in,** help decide, be in on the decisions, **vote,** have suffrage, be enfranchised; **enter into,** go into; make the scene (*informal*); sit in,

sit on; bear a hand, pull an oar; come out of one's shell

6 **to share, share in,** come in for a share, **go shares,** be partners in, have a stake in, have a percentage *or* piece of (*informal*), **divide with, divvy up with** (*informal*), halve, go halves; go halvers *and* go fifty-fifty *and* go even steven (*all informal*), split the difference, **share and share alike;** do one's share *or* part, pull one's weight, muck in; cooperate *see* 450.3; apportion *see* 477.6

7 **to communize,** communalize, **socialize, collectivize, nationalize**

adjectives

8 **participating, participative,** participant, participatory; involved, engaged, **in** *or* **in on** (*informal*); implicated, accessory; **partaking, sharing**

9 **communal, common,** general, public, collective, popular, social, societal; **mutual,** commutual (*old*), reciprocal, associated, **joint,** conjoint, **in common,** share and share alike; **cooperative** *see* 450.5; power-sharing, profit-sharing; collectivistic, **communistic,** socialistic *see* 611.31

477 APPORTIONMENT

nouns

1 **apportionment, apportioning, portioning, division,** divvy (*informal*), **partition,** repartition, partitionment, partitioning, parcelling, budgeting, rationing, **dividing, sharing,** share-out, sharing out, splitting, cutting, slicing, cutting the cake *and* divvying up (*both informal*); reapportionment

2 **distribution,** dispersion, **disposal,** disposition; dole, doling, doling out, giving out, passing around; **dispensation,** administration, issuance; disbursal, disbursement, paying out; redistribution; maldistribution

3 **allotment, assignment, appointment,** setting aside, **earmarking,** tagging; underallotment, overallotment; appropriation; **allocation;** misallocation; reallocation

4 **dedication, commitment,** devoting, devotion, consecration

5 **portion, share, interest, part,** stake, stock, **piece,** bit, segment; **bite** *and* **cut** *and* **slice** *and* **chunk** *and* slice of the cake *and* piece of the action (*all informal*), lot, allotment, end (*informal*), **proportion, percentage,** measure, quantum, **quota,** deal *or* dole (*both old*), meed, moiety, mess, helping; contingent; dividend; **commission,** rake-off (*informal*); equal share, half; **lion's share,** bigger half; small share, modicum; **allowance, ration, budget; load,** work load; fate, destiny *see* 963.2

verbs

6 **to apportion, portion, parcel, partition, part, divide,** share; share with, cut *or* deal one in (*informal*), share and share alike, divide with, go halvers *or* fifty-fifty *or* even steven with (*informal*); divide into shares, **share out** *or* **around,** divide up, **divvy** *or* divvy up *or* out (*informal*), **split,** split up, carve, cut, slice, carve up, slice up, cut up, cut *or* slice the cake (*informal*); divide *or* split fifty-fifty

7 **to proportion,** proportionate, **prorate,** divide *pro rata*

8 **to parcel out, portion out,** measure out, serve out, spoon *or* ladle *or* dish out, **deal out, dole out, hand out, mete out,** ration out, give out, hand around, pass around; mete, dole, deal; **distribute,** disperse; **dispense,** dispose (*old*), issue, administer; disburse, pay out

9 **to allot,** lot, **assign, appoint, set,** detail; **allocate,** make assignments *or* allocations, schedule; **set apart** *or* **aside,** earmark, tag, mark out for; set off, mark off, portion off; assign to, appropriate to *or* for; reserve, restrict to, restrict *see* 210.5; **ordain, destine, fate**

10 **to budget, ration;** allowance, put on an allowance

11 **to dedicate, commit, devote, consecrate,** set apart

adjectives

12 **apportioned,** portioned out, parcelled, allocated, etc; **apportionable,** allocable, divisible, distributable, commitable, appropriable, dispensable, donable, severable

13 **proportionate,** proportional; prorated, *pro rata* (*Latin*); half; halvers *or* fifty-fifty *or* even steven (*all informal*), half-and-half, equal; **distributive,** distributional; **respective,** particular, per head, per capita, several

adverbs

14 **proportionately, in proportion,** *pro rata* (*Latin*); **distributively; respectively,** severally, each to each; share and share alike, in equal shares, half-and-half; fifty-fifty *and* even steven (*both informal*)

478 GIVING

nouns

1 **giving, donation,** bestowal, bestowment; **endowment,** gifting (*informal*), **presentation,** presentment; **award,** awarding; grant, granting; accordance, vouchsafement (*old*); conferment, conferral; investiture; **delivery,** deliverance, surrender; **concession,** communication, impartation, impartment; **contribution,** subscription; tithing; accommodation, supplying, furnishment, provision *see* 385; **offer** *see* 439; **liberality** *see* 485

2 **commitment, consignment,** assignment, **delegation,** relegation, commendation, remanding, **entrustment;** enfeoffment, infeudation *or* infeodation

3 **charity,** almsgiving; **philanthropy** *see* 143.4

4 **gift, present,** presentation, *cadeau* (*French*), **offering,** fairing (*old*); tribute, **award;** whip-round (*informal*); **free gift,** freebie, gimme (*US informal*); oblation *see* 696.7; handsel; box; **Christmas present** *or* **gift,** stocking filler, **birthday present** *or* **gift;** peace offering

5 **gratuity, largess, bounty,** liberality, donative, sportula; **perquisite,** perks (*informal*); consideration, fee (*old*), **tip,** *pourboire* (*French*), *Trinkgeld* (*German*), sweetener, inducement; grease *and* salve *and* palm oil (*all US informal*); **premium, bonus,** something extra, **gravy** (*informal*), bunce (*informal*), lagniappe;

baker's dozen; honorarium; incentive pay, time and a half, double time; bung (*informal*), bribe *see* 378.2

6 **donation**, donative; **contribution, subscription; alms**, pittance, **charity, dole, handout** (*informal*), alms fee, widow's mite; Peter's pence; **offering**, offertory, votive offering, collection; tithe

7 **benefit**, benefaction, benevolence, **blessing, favour, boon**, grace; manna, manna from heaven

8 **subsidy**, subvention, subsidization, support, price support, tax benefit *or* write-off, tax holiday; **grant**, grant-in-aid, bounty; **allowance, stipend**, allotment; pocket money; **aid**, assistance, financial assistance; **help**, pecuniary aid; scholarship, fellowship, exhibition; honorarium; **social security**, welfare, unemployment benefit, family credit, Earnings Related Supplement, child benefit, housing benefit, invalidity benefit; guaranteed annual income; maintenance, alimony, palimony (*US*); annuity; pension, retirement relief

9 **endowment**, investment, **settlement**, foundation; **dowry**, *dot* (*French*), portion, marriage portion; **dower**, widow's dower, widow's benefit; jointure, legal jointure, thirds; appanage

10 **bequest**, bequeathal, **legacy**, devise; inheritance *see* 479.2; **will, testament**, last will and testament; probate, attested copy; codicil

11 **giver, donor**, donator, gifter (*informal*), presenter, bestower, conferrer, grantor, awarder, imparter, vouchsafer; fairy godmother, Lady Bountiful, Santa Claus, sugar daddy (*informal*); cheerful giver; **contributor, subscriber**, supporter, backer, financer, funder, angel (*informal*); subsidizer; patron, patroness, Maecenas; tither; almsgiver, almoner; **philanthropist** *see* 143.8; assignor, consignor; settler; testate, testator, testatrix; feoffor

verbs

12 **to give, present, donate**, slip (*informal*), let have; **bestow, confer, award, allot, render**, bestow on; impart, let one know, communicate; **grant**, accord, **allow**, vouchsafe, yield, afford, make available; **tender**, proffer, offer, extend, come up with (*informal*); **issue, dispense**, administer; serve, help to; **distribute**; deal, dole, mete; **give out, deal out, dole out, mete out, hand** *or* dish out (*informal*), fork *or* shell out (*informal*); make a present of, gift (*informal*), give as a gift; **give generously**, give the shirt off one's back; be generous *or* liberal with, give freely; pour, shower, rain, snow, heap, lavish *see* 486.3; give in addition, give into the bargain

13 **to deliver, hand, pass**, reach, forward, render, put into the hands of; transfer; **hand over**, give over, deliver over, fork over (*informal*), **pass over, turn over**, come across with (*informal*); hand out, give out, pass out, distribute, circulate; hand in, give in; **surrender**, resign

14 **to contribute, subscribe, chip in** *and* **kick in** *and* **pay up** (*all informal*), give one's share *or* fair share; put oneself down for, pledge; contribute to, give to, **donate to, gift** *and* **gift with** (*both informal*); put something in the pot *or* kitty

15 **to furnish, supply, provide, afford**, provide for; **make available to**, put one in the way of; **accommodate with**, favour with, indulge with;

heap upon, pour on, shower down upon, **lavish upon**

16 **to commit, consign, assign, delegate**, relegate, confide, commend, remit, remand, give in charge; **entrust, trust**, give in trust; enfeoff, infeudate

17 **to endow**, invest, vest; endow with, favour with, bless with, grace with, vest with; **settle on** *or* **upon**; **dower**

18 **to bequeath, will**, will and bequeath, **leave, devise, will to**, hand down, hand on, pass on, transmit; **make a will**, draw up a will, execute a will, make a bequest, write one's last will and testament, write into one's will; add a codicil; entail

19 **to subsidize, finance**, bankroll (*informal*), fund; angel (*informal*); **aid, assist, support, help**, pay the bills, pick up the check *or* tab (*both US informal*); pension, pension off

20 **to thrust upon, force upon, press upon**, push upon, obtrude on, ram down one's throat

21 **to give away**, dispose of, part with, sacrifice, spare

adjectives

22 philanthropic, eleemosynary, **charitable** *see* 143.15; giving, generous to a fault, liberal, **generous** *see* 485.4

23 **giveable**, presentable, bestowable; impartable, communicable; bequeathable, devisable; allowable; committable; fundable

24 **given**, allowed, accorded, granted, vouchsafed, bestowed, etc; gratuitous *see* 634.5; God-given, providential

25 donative, contributory; concessive; testate, testamentary; intestate

26 endowed, dowered, invested; dower, dowry, dotal; subsidiary, stipendiary, pensionary

adverbs

27 as a gift, gratis, on one, on the house, free; to his heirs, to the heirs of his body, to his heirs and assigns, to his executors *or* administrators and assigns

479 RECEIVING

nouns

1 **receiving, reception**, receival, **receipt, getting, taking; acquisition** *see* 472; derivation; **assumption, acceptance**; admission, admittance; reception *see* 187

2 **inheritance**, heritance (*old*), **heritage, patrimony, birthright, legacy, bequest**, bequeathal; reversion; entail; heirship; **succession**, line of succession, mode of succession, law of succession; primogeniture, ultimogeniture, postremogeniture, borough-English, coheirship, coparcenary, gavelkind; hereditament, corporeal *or* incorporeal hereditament; **heritable; heirloom**

3 **recipient, receiver**, accepter, getter, taker, acquirer, obtainer, procurer; payee, endorsee; addressee, consignee; holder, trustee; **hearer**, viewer, beholder, audience, auditor, listener, looker, spectator; the receiving end

4 **beneficiary**, allottee, **donee, grantee**, patentee; **assignee, assign; devisee, legatee**, legatary (*old*);

feoffee; almsman, almswoman; stipendiary; pensioner, pensionary; annuitant

5 **heir**, heritor, inheritor, *heres* (*Latin*); **heiress**, inheritress, inheritrix; coheir, joint heir, fellow heir, coparcener; heir portioner (*Scottish*); heir expectant; **heir apparent**, apparent heir; **heir presumptive**, presumptive heir; statutory next of kin; legal heir, heir at law, heir general; heir of provision (*Scottish*), heir by destination; heir of the body; heir in tail, heir of entail; fideicommissary heir, fiduciary heir; reversioner; remainderman; **successor**, next in line

verbs

6 **to receive, get, gain, secure**, have, come by, be in receipt of, be on the receiving end; **obtain, acquire** *see* 472.8, 9; **admit, accept, take**, take off one's hands; **take in** *see* 187.10; assume, take on, take over; **derive, draw**, draw *or* derive from; have an income of, drag down *and* pull down *and* rake in (*all informal*), have coming in, take home

7 **to inherit**, be heir to, **come into**, come in for, come by, fall *or* step into; step into the shoes of, succeed to

8 **to be received, come in**, come to hand, pass *or* fall into one's hands, go into one's pocket, come *or* fall to one, fall to one's share *or* lot; **accrue**, accrue to

adjectives

9 **receiving**, on the receiving end; **receptive**, recipient *see* 187.16

10 **received, accepted, admitted, recognized, approved**

480 TAKING

nouns

1 **taking**, possession, taking possession, taking away; **claiming**, staking one's claim; **acquisition** *see* 472; **reception** *see* 479.1; **theft** *see* 482

2 **seizure, seizing, grab**, grabbing, snatching, snatch; **kidnapping, abduction**, forcible seizure; coup, coup d'état, seizure of power; hold *see* 474.2; **catch**, catching; **capture**, collaring (*informal*), nabbing (*informal*), a fair cop (*informal*); **apprehension**, prehension; **arrest**, arrestation, taking into custody; picking up *and* taking in *and* running in (*all informal*); dragnet

3 **sexual possession**, taking; sexual assault, ravishment, **rape**, violation, indecent assault, date rape *or* acquaintance rape, serial rape; statutory rape; defloration, deflowerment, devirgination

4 **appropriation, taking over, takeover** (*informal*), **adoption, assumption, usurpation**, arrogation; requisition, indent; preoccupation, prepossession, preemption; **conquest**, occupation, subjugation, enslavement, colonization

5 **attachment, annexation**, annexure, attachment of earnings; **confiscation**, sequestration; impoundment; **commandeering, impressment**; expropriation, nationalization, socialization, communalization, communization, collectivization; levy; distraint, distress; garnishment; execution; eminent domain, angary, right of eminent domain, right of angary

6 **deprivation, deprival**, privation, divestment, bereavement; relieving, disburdening, disburdenment; curtailment, abridgment (*old*); disentitlement

7 **dispossession**, disseisin, expropriation; reclaiming, repossessing, **repossession**, foreclosure; **eviction** *see* 908.2; disendowment; **disinheritance**, disherison, disownment

8 **extortion**, shakedown (*US informal*), **blackmail**, bloodsucking, vampirism; protection racket; badger game

9 **rapacity**, rapaciousness, ravenousness, sharkishness, wolfishness, **predaciousness**, predacity; pillaging, looting

10 **take, catch, bag**, capture, seizure, **haul**; booty *see* 482.11

11 **taker**; partaker; **catcher, captor**, capturer

12 **extortionist**, extortioner, **blackmailer**, racketeer, **bloodsucker**, leech, **vampire**; **predator**, raptor, bird of prey, beast of prey; harpy; **vulture**, shark; profiteer; rack-renter, Rachman

verbs

13 **to take**, possess, take possession; **get**, get into one's hold *or* possession; pocket, palm; draw off, drain off; skim *and* skim off (*both informal*); **claim**, stake one's claim, enforce one's claim; partake; **acquire** *see* 472.8, 9; **receive** *see* 479.6; **steal** *see* 482.13

14 **to seize**, take *or* get hold of, **lay hold of**, catch *or* grab hold of, latch on to (*informal*), **get** *or* **lay hands on**, clap hands on (*informal*), put one's hands on, get into one's grasp *or* clutches; get one's fingers *or* hands on; **grab, grasp, grip**, gripe (*old*), **grapple, snatch**, snatch up, nip, nail (*informal*), **clutch**, claw, clinch, clench; **clasp, hug, embrace**; snap up; pillage, loot; take by assault *or* storm; **kidnap, abduct**, snatch (*informal*), carry off; shanghai; take by the throat, throttle

15 **to possess sexually**, take; **rape**, commit rape, commit date *or* acquaintance rape, ravish, violate, assault sexually, lay violent hands on, have one's will of; deflower, deflorate, devirginate

16 **to seize on** *or* **upon**, fasten upon; spring *or* pounce upon, jump (*informal*), swoop down upon; **catch at, snatch at**, snap at, jump at, make a grab for, scramble for

17 **to catch, take**, catch flatfooted, land *and* nail (*both informal*), hook, **snag, snare**, sniggle, spear, harpoon; ensnare, enmesh, entangle, tangle, foul, tangle up with; **net**, mesh; **bag**, sack; **trap**, entrap; lasso, rope, noose

18 **to capture, apprehend, collar** (*informal*), run down, run to earth, **nab** (*informal*), grab (*informal*), lay by the heels, take prisoner; **arrest**, place *or* put under arrest, take into custody; pick up *or* take in *or* run in (*all informal*)

19 **to appropriate, adopt, assume, usurp**, arrogate, accroach; requisition, indent; **take possession of**, possess oneself of, take for oneself, arrogate to oneself, take up, **take over, help oneself to**, make use of, make one's own, make free with, dip one's hands into; take it all, take all of, hog (*informal*), monopolize, sit on, snaffle; preoccupy, prepossess, preempt; jump a claim (*US*); **conquer**, overrun, occupy, subjugate, enslave, colonize; squat on

20 to attach, annex; confiscate, sequester, sequestrate, impound; commandeer, press, impress; expropriate, nationalize, socialize, communalize, communize, collectivize; exercise the right of eminent domain, exercise the right of angary; levy, distrain, replevy, replevin; garnishee, garnish

21 to take from, take away from, deprive of, do out of (*informal*), relieve of, disburden of, lighten of, ease of; deprive, bereave, divest; tap, milk, mine, drain, bleed, curtail, abridge (*old*); cut off; disentitle

22 to wrest, wring, wrench, rend, rip; extort, exact, squeeze, screw, blackmail, levy blackmail; force from, wrest from, wrench from, wring from, tear from, rip from, rend from, snatch from, pry loose from

23 to dispossess, disseise, expropriate, foreclose; evict *see* 908.15; disendow; disinherit, disherison, disown, cut out of one's will, cut off, cut off without a penny

24 to strip, strip bare *or* clean, fleece (*informal*), shear, denude, skin (*informal*), flay, despoil, divest, pick clean, pick the bones of; deplume, displume; milk; bleed, bleed white; exhaust, drain, dry, suck dry; impoverish, beggar; clean out *and* take to the cleaners (*both informal*); eat out of house and home

adjectives

25 taking, catching; private, deprivative; confiscatory, annexational, expropriatory; thievish *see* 482.21

26 rapacious, ravenous, ravening, vulturous, vulturine, sharkish, wolfish, lupine, predacious, predatory, raptorial; vampirish, bloodsucking, parasitic; extortionate; grasping, graspy, grabby (*informal*), insatiable *see* 100.27; all-devouring, all-engulfing

481 RESTITUTION

nouns

1 restitution, restoration, restoring, giving back, sending back, remitting, remission, return; reddition (*old*); extradition, rendition; repatriation; recommitment, remandment, remand

2 reparation, recompense, paying back, squaring (*informal*), repayment, reimbursement, refund, remuneration, compensation, indemnification; retribution, atonement, redress, satisfaction, amends, making good, requital

3 recovery, regaining; retrieval, retrieve; recuperation, recoup, recoupment; retake, retaking, recapture; repossession, resumption, reoccupation; reclamation, reclaiming; redemption, ransom, salvage, trover; replevin, replevy; revival, restoration *see* 396, retro

verbs

4 to restore, return, give back, restitute, hand back, put back; take back, bring back; put the genie back into the bottle, put the toothpaste back into the tube; remit, send back; repatriate; extradite; recommit, remand

5 to make restitution, make reparation, make amends, make good, make up for, atone, give satisfaction, redress, recompense, pay back, square (*informal*), repay, reimburse, refund, remunerate,

compensate, requite, indemnify, make up for, make it up; pay damages, pay reparations; pay conscience money; overcompensate

6 to recover, regain, retrieve, recuperate, recoup, get back, come by one's own; redeem, ransom; reclaim; repossess, resume, reoccupy; retake, recapture, take back; replevin, replevy; revive, renovate, restore *see* 396.11, 15

adjectives

7 restitutive, restitutory, restorative; compensatory, indemnificatory, retributive, reparative; reversionary, reversional, revertible; redeeming, redemptive, redemptional; reimbursable

adverbs

8 in restitution, in reparation, in recompense, in compensation, to make up for, in return for, in retribution, in requital, in amends, in atonement, to atone for

482 THEFT

nouns

1 theft, thievery, stealage, stealing, thieving, purloining; swiping *and* lifting *and* snatching *and* pinching (*all informal*); conveyance (*old*), appropriation, conversion, liberation *and* annexation (*both informal*); pilfering, pilferage, filching, scrounging (*informal*); abstraction; sneak thievery; shoplifting; poaching; graft; embezzlement *see* 389.1; fraud, swindle *see* 356.8

2 petty theft, grand theft, petty larceny (*US*), grand larceny (*US*); car theft, twoccing *and* hotting (*both informal*)

3 theft, robbery, robbing; bank robbery; banditry, highway robbery; armed robbery, holdup, assault and robbery, mugging, steaming (*informal*); purse snatching; pocket picking; hijacking, asportation (*old*); cattle stealing, cattle rustling (*informal*); extortion *see* 480.8

4 (*informal terms*) blag, job, snatch, heist, stickup, stickup job, smash-and-grab raid

5 burglary, burglarizing, housebreaking, breaking and entering, break and entry, break-in, unlawful entry; safebreaking, safecracking, safeblowing

6 plundering, pillaging, looting, sacking, freebooting, ransacking, rifling, spoiling, despoliation, despoilment, despoiling; rapine, spoliation, depredation, direption (*old*), raiding, ravage, ravaging, ravagement, rape, ravishment; pillage, plunder, sack; brigandage, brigandism, banditry; marauding, foraging; raid, foray, razzia

7 piracy, buccaneering, privateering, freebooting; letters of marque, letters of marque and reprisal; air piracy, aeroplane hijacking, skyjacking

8 plagiarism, plagiarizing, plagiary, piracy, literary piracy, appropriation, borrowing, cribbing; infringement of copyright; autoplagiarism

9 abduction, kidnapping, snatching (*informal*); shanghaiing, impressment, crimping

10 grave-robbing, body-snatching (*informal*), resurrectionism

11 booty, spoil, **spoils**, loot, **swag** (*informal*), ill-gotten gains, **plunder**, prize, haul, take, pickings, stealings, stolen goods, hot goods *or* items (*informal*); perquisite, perks, spoils of office, public trough, pork barrel; till *or* public till (*both US*); blackmail

12 thievishness, larcenousness, taking ways (*informal*), light fingers, sticky fingers; kleptomania, bibliokleptomania, etc

verbs

13 to steal, thieve, purloin, **appropriate**, **take**, snatch, palm, **make off with**, walk off with, run off *or* away with, abstract, disregard the distinction between *meum* and *tuum*; have one's hand in the till; **pilfer**, **filch**; shoplift; poach; rustle; **embezzle** *see* 389.4; defraud, swindle; **extort** *see* 480.22

14 to rob, commit robbery; pick pockets; hold up

15 to **burglarize**, burgle (*informal*), commit burglary; crack *or* blow a safe

16 (*informal terms*) to swipe, pinch, half inch, nick, lift, blag, filch, pilfer, cabbage; **heist**, **knock off** *or* **over**, tip over; **stick up**; **mug**; hijack

17 to plunder, pillage, loot, **sack**, ransack, rifle, freeboot, spoil, spoliate, despoil, depredate, prey on *or* upon, **raid**, ravage, ravish, raven, sweep, gut; **fleece** *see* 480.24; maraud, foray, forage

18 to pirate, buccaneer, privateer, freeboot

19 to plagiarize, **pirate**, borrow *and* crib (*both informal*), appropriate; **pick one's brains**; infringe a copyright

20 to abduct, abduce, spirit away, **carry off** *or* **away**, magic away, run off *or* away with; **kidnap**, snatch (*informal*), hold for ransom; skyjack; carjack; **shanghai**, crimp, impress

adjectives

21 thievish, thieving, larcenous, **light-fingered**, **sticky-fingered**; kleptomaniacal, burglarious; brigandish, piratical, piratelike; fraudulent

22 plunderous, **plundering**, **looting**, pillaging, ravaging, marauding, spoliatory; predatory, predacious

23 stolen, pilfered, purloined; pirated, plagiarized; hot (*informal*), off the back of a lorry (*informal*)

483 THIEF

nouns

1 thief, robber, stealer, tea leaf (*informal*), purloiner, lifter (*informal*), ganef (*Yiddish*), **crook** (*informal*); larcenist *or* larcener (*both US*); pilferer, filcher, petty thief; sneak thief, prowler; shoplifter, booster (*informal*); poacher; jewel thief; **swindler**, con man *see* 357.3, 4; land pirate, land shark, land-grabber; grave robber, body snatcher, resurrectionist, ghoul; embezzler, peculator, white-collar thief; den of thieves

2 pickpocket, cutpurse; **purse snatcher**; light-fingered gentry

3 burglar, yegg *and* cracksman (*both US informal*); housebreaker, cat burglar; **safecracker**, safebreaker, safeblower

4 bandit, brigand, dacoit; **gangster** *and* mobster (*both informal*); racketeer; **thug, hoodlum** *see* 593.4

5 **robber**, **holdup man** *and* stickup man (*both informal*); highwayman, highway robber, footpad, road agent, bushranger (*Australian*); **mugger** (*informal*), sandbagger; train robber; bank robber, ram raider; **hijacker** *and* **carjacker** (*both informal*); twoccer *and* hotter (*both informal*)

6 **plunderer**, **pillager**, **looter**, **marauder**, rifler, sacker, spoiler, despoiler, spoliator, depredator, **raider**, moss-trooper, free-booter, forayer, forager, ravisher, ravager; wrecker

7 **pirate**, **corsair**, **buccaneer**, **privateer**, sea rover, rover, picaroon; viking, sea king; Blackbeard, Captain Kidd, Jean Lafitte, Captain Morgan; Captain Hook (*J M Barrie*), Long John Silver (*Stevenson*); air pirate, aeroplane hijacker, skyjacker; carjacker (*informal*)

8 cattle thief, abactor, rustler *and* **cattle rustler** (*both informal*)

9 plagiarist, plagiarizer, cribber (*informal*), **pirate**, literary pirate, copyright infringer

10 abductor, kidnapper; shanghaier, snatcher *and* baby-snatcher (*both informal*); crimp, crimper

11 (*famous thieves*) Barabbas, Robin Hood, Dick Turpin, Jesse James, John Dillinger; Autolycus, Macheath (*John Gay*), Thief of Baghdad, Jean Valjean (*Hugo*), Jimmy Valentine (*O Henry*), Raffles (*E W Hornung*), Bill Sikes (*Dickens*)

484 PARSIMONY

nouns

1 **parsimony**, parsimoniousness; frugality *see* 635.1; **stinting**, **pinching**, **scrimping**, skimping, cheeseparing; economy, economy of means, economy of assumption, law of parsimony, Ockham's razor, elegance

2 niggardliness, penuriousness, **meanness**, minginess, shabbiness, sordidness

3 stinginess, ungenerosity, illiberality, cheapness, chintziness *and* tightness *and* narrowness (*all informal*), tight purse strings, nearness, closeness, closefistedness, closehandedness (*old*), tightfistedness, hardfistedness, miserliness, penny-pinching, hoarding; avarice *see* 100.8

4 niggard, cheapskate (*informal*), **miser**, meanie (*informal*), **skinflint**, scrooge, penny pincher, pinchpenny, churl, curmudgeon, muckworm, save-all (*informal*), Harpagon (*Molière*), Silas Marner (*George Eliot*)

verbs

5 to stint, scrimp, skimp, scamp, scant, screw, pinch, starve, famish; **pinch pennies**; live upon nothing; grudge, begrudge

6 to **withhold**, hold back, hold out on (*informal*)

adjectives

7 **parsimonious**, careful, sparing, cheeseparing, stinting, scamping, scrimping, skimping; frugal *see* 635.6; too frugal, overfrugal, frugal to excess; penny-wise, penny-wise and pound-foolish

8 **niggardly**, niggard, pinchpenny, penurious, grudging, **mean**, mingy, shabby, sordid

9 stingy, illiberal, ungenerous, chintzy, miserly, save-all, **cheap** *and* **tight** (*both informal*), tight-arsed *and* tight as a duck's arse (*both informal*), **tightfisted**, hardfisted; near as the bark on a tree, "as close as a vice" —HAWTHORNE; pinching, **penny-pinching**; avaricious *see* 100.27

adverbs

10 parsimoniously, stintingly, scrimpingly, skimpingly
11 niggardly, **stingily**, illiberally, ungenerously, closefistedly, tightfistedly; meanly, shabbily, sordidly

485 LIBERALITY

nouns

1 liberality, liberalness, freeness, freedom; **generosity**, generousness, largeness, **unselfishness**, **munificence**, largess *or* largesse; bountifulness, bounteousness, **bounty**; hospitality, welcome, graciousness; **openhandedness**, freehandedness, open *or* free hand, easy purse strings; **givingness**; open-heartedness, bigheartedness, largeheartedness, greatheartedness, freeheartedness; open heart, big *or* large *or* great heart, heart of gold; **magnanimity** *see* 652.2
2 cheerful giver, free giver; Lady Bountiful; Santa Claus

verbs

3 to give freely, give cheerfully, give with an open hand, give with both hands, put one's hands in one's pockets, open the purse, loosen *or* untie the purse strings; **spare no expense**, spare nothing, not count the cost, let money be no object; **heap upon**, lavish upon, shower down upon; give the coat *or* shirt off one's back, give more than one's share, **give until it hurts**; give of oneself, give of one's substance, not hold back, offer oneself; keep the change!

adjectives

4 liberal, free, free with one's money, free-spending; **generous, munificent**, large, princely, handsome; **unselfish**, ungrudging; **unsparing, unstinting**, stintless, unstinted; **bountiful**, bounteous, **lavish**, profuse; hospitable, gracious; **openhanded**, freehanded, open; **giving**; openhearted, **bighearted**, largehearted, greathearted, freehearted; **magnanimous** *see* 652.6

adverbs

5 liberally, freely; generously, **munificently**, handsomely; unselfishly, ungrudgingly; **unsparingly, unstintingly; bountifully**, bounteously, **lavishly**, profusely; hospitably, graciously; **openhandedly**, freehandedly; openheartedly, bigheartedly, largeheartedly, greatheartedly, freeheartedly; with open hands, with both hands, with an unsparing hand, without stint

486 PRODIGALITY

nouns

1 prodigality, overliberality, overgenerousness, overgenerosity; profligacy, **extravagance**, pound-foolishness, recklessness, reckless spending *or* expenditure; incontinence, intemperance *see* 669; lavishness, profuseness, profusion; **wastefulness, waste; dissipation, squandering**, squandermania; *carpe diem* (*Latin*); loose purse strings, leaking purse; conspicuous consumption *or* waste
2 prodigal, wastrel, waster, **squanderer; spendthrift**, wastethrift, spender, spendall, big spender (*informal*); prodigal son

verbs

3 to squander, lavish, splash out, lash out, blow (*informal*), slather (*US informal*), play ducks and drakes with; **dissipate**, scatter (*old*), scatter to the winds; **run through**, go through; **throw away**, throw one's money away, throw money around, **spend money like water**, let slip *or* flow through one's fingers, spend as if money grew on trees, spend money as if it were going out of style, throw money around, spend like a drunken sailor; gamble away; burn the candle at both ends; seize the day, live for the day, let tomorrow take care of itself
4 to waste, consume, spend, expend, use up, exhaust; lose; spill, pour down the drain *or* sink; pour water into a sieve, cast pearls before swine, kill the goose that lays the golden egg, *manger son blé en herbe* (*French*), throw out the baby with the bath water
5 to fritter away, dally away; idle away, while away
6 to misspend, throw good money after bad, throw the helve after the hatchet, throw out the baby with the bathwater
7 to overspend, spend more than one has, spend what one hasn't got; overdraw, overdraw one's account, live beyond one's means, have champagne tastes on a beer budget

adjectives

8 prodigal, extravagant, lavish, profuse, **overliberal**, overgenerous, overlavish, **spendthrift, wasteful**, profligate, dissipative; incontinent, intemperate *see* 669.7; pound-foolish, penny-wise and pound-foolish; easy come, easy go
9 wasted, squandered, dissipated, consumed, spent, used, lost; **gone to waste**, run *or* gone to seed; down the drain *or* spout *or* sink (*informal*); misspent

487 CELEBRATION

nouns

1 celebration, celebrating; **observance**, formal *or* solemn *or* ritual observance, **solemnization**; marking *or* honouring the occasion; **commemoration**, memorialization, remembrance, memory; jubilee; red-letter day, **holiday** *see* 20.4; anniversaries; **festivity** *see* 743.3, 4; **revel** *see* 743.6; rejoicing *see* 116; **ceremony**, rite *see* 580.4; religious rites *see* 701; ovation, triumph; **tribute**; testimonial, testimonial banquet *or* dinner; toast; roast; **salute**; salvo; flourish of trumpets, fanfare, fanfaronade; dressing ship

verbs

2 to celebrate, observe, keep, mark, solemnly mark, honour; commemorate, memorialize; solemnize,

signalize, hallow, mark with a red letter; hold jubilee, jubilize, jubilate, maffick (*old*); **make merry**, push the boat out, paint the town red; kill the fatted calf; sound a fanfare, blow the trumpet, beat the drum, fire a salute; dress ship

adjectives

3 **celebrative**, celebratory, celebrating; **commemorative**, commemorating; memorial; solemn

adverbs

4 **in honour of, in commemoration of**, in memory *or* remembrance of, to the memory of

488 HUMOROUSNESS

nouns

1 **humorousness, funniness**, amusingness, laughableness, laughability, hilarity, hilariousness; wittiness *see* 489.2; **drollness**, drollery; **whimsicalness**, quizzicalness; **ludicrousness, ridiculousness, absurdity**, absurdness, quaintness, eccentricity, incongruity, bizarreness, bizarrerie; richness, pricelessness (*informal*); the funny side

2 **comicalness**, comicality, funiosity; farcicalness, **farcicality**, slapstick quality, broadness

3 bathos; anticlimax, comedown

adjectives

4 **humorous, funny, amusing**; witty *see* 489.15; **droll, whimsical**, quizzical; **laughable**, risible, good for a laugh; **ludicrous, ridiculous, hilarious, absurd**, quaint, eccentric, incongruous, bizarre

5 (*informal terms*) **funny ha-ha**, priceless, too funny *or* for words, side-splitting, rib-tickling, hysterical

6 **comic** *or* **comical; farcical**, slapstick, broad; **burlesque** *see* 508.14; tragicomic, serio-comic, mock-heroic

adverbs

7 **humorously, amusingly**, funnily, **laughably**; wittily *see* 489.18; drolly, whimsically, quizzically; **comically**, farcically, broadly; **ludicrously, ridiculously, absurdly**, quaintly, eccentrically, incongruously, bizarrely

489 WIT, HUMOUR

nouns

1 **wit, humour**, pleasantry, *esprit* (*French*), salt, spice *or* savour of wit; Attic wit *or* salt, Atticism; ready wit, quick wit, nimble wit, agile wit, pretty wit; dry wit, subtle wit; **comedy** *see* 704.6; black humour, sick humour, gallows humour; **satire**, sarcasm, irony; Varronnian satire, Menippean satire; **parody, lampoon**, lampoonery, travesty, **caricature, burlesque**, squib; **farce**, mere farce; **slapstick**, slapstick humour, broad humour, low comedy; visual humour

2 **wittiness, humorousness** *see* 488, **funniness; facetiousness**, pleasantry, **jocularity**, jocoseness, jocosity; **joking**, japery, joshing (*US informal*); smartness, cleverness, brilliance; pungency, saltiness;

keenness, sharpness; **keen-wittedness**, quick-wittedness, nimble-wittedness

3 **drollery**, drollness; **whimsicality**, whimsicalness, antic wit

4 **waggishness, waggery**; roguishness *see* 322.2; **playfulness**, sportiveness, **levity, frivolity**, flippancy, merriment *see* 109.5; **prankishness**, pranksomeness; trickery, trickiness, tricksiness, trickishness

5 **buffoonery**, buffoonism, clownery, clowning, clowning around, carrying-on, harlequinade; **clownishness**, buffoonishness; **foolery**, fooling, **tomfoolery**; horseplay; shenanigans *and* monkey tricks (*both informal*); **banter** *see* 490

6 **joke, jest, gag** *and* one-liner (*both informal*), wheeze, jape; **fun, sport, play**; story, yarn, **funny story**, good story; dirty story *or* joke, blue story *or* joke, *double entendre* (*French*); shaggy-dog story; sick joke (*informal*); ethnic joke; good one, laugh, belly laugh, rib tickler, sidesplitter, thigh-slapper, howler, hoot, giggle, gas, scream, riot; visual joke, sight gag (*informal*); **point**, punch line, gag line, tag line; sight gag

7 **witticism, pleasantry**, *plaisanterie, boutade* (*both French*); play of wit, *jeu d'esprit* (*French*); **crack** *and* **wisecrack** (*both informal*); **quip**, conceit, bright *or* happy thought, bright *or* brilliant idea; **mot, bon mot**, smart saying, stroke of wit, one-liner (*informal*), zinger (*US*); epigram, turn of thought, aphorism, apothegm; flash of wit, scintillation; **sally**, flight of wit; **repartee**, backchat, retort, riposte, snappy comeback (*informal*); facetiae (*plural*), quips and cranks; **gibe**; persiflage *see* 490.1

8 **wordplay, play on words**, *jeu de mots* (*French*), missaying, corruption, paronomasia, *calembour* (*French*), abuse of terms; **pun**, punning; equivoque, equivocality; anagram, logogram, logogriph, metagram; acrostic, double acrostic; amphiboly, amphibologism; palindrome; spoonerism; malapropism

9 **old joke, trite joke**, hoary-headed joke, joke with whiskers; **chestnut** *and* **corny joke** *and* **oldie** (*all informal*); twice-told tale, retold story, cauld kail het again (*Scottish*)

10 **prank, trick, practical joke**, wind-up, wheeze, leg-pull, ploy, waggish trick, *espièglerie* (*French*), antic, caper, frolic; monkey tricks *and* shenanigans (*both informal*)

11 **sense of humour**, risibility, funny bone

12 **humourist, wit**, funnyman, comic, *bel-esprit* (*French*), life and soul of the party; **joker**, jokester, gagman (*informal*), **jester, quipster, wisecracker** *and* gagster (*both informal*); wag, wagwit; zany, madcap, cutup (*informal*); **prankster; comedian**, stand-up comedian *or* comic, funnyman (*informal*); **clown** *see* 707.10; punster, punner, punnet; epigrammatist; satirist, ironist; burlesquer, caricaturist, parodist, lampooner; reparteeist; witling; gag writer (*informal*), jokesmith

verbs

13 **to joke, jest**, wisecrack (*informal*), utter a mot, quip, jape (*informal*), fun (*informal*), make fun, **kid** *or* **kid around** (*both informal*), josh (*US*); make a

funny (*US informal*); **crack a joke**, tell a good story; pun, play on words; scintillate, sparkle; **make fun of**, gibe at, fleer at, mock, scoff at, poke fun at, make the butt of one's humour, be merry with; ridicule *see* 508.8

14 **to trick, play a practical joke**, play tricks *or* pranks, **play a joke** *or* **trick on**, make merry with; **clown around**, pull a stunt *or* trick; pull one's leg *and* put one on (*both informal*)

adjectives

15 **witty, amusing**, *spirituel* (*French*); **humorous** *see* 488.4, 5, **comic, comical, farcical** *see* 488.6; **funny**; **jocular**, joky (*informal*), **joking, jesting**, **jocose, tongue-in-cheek**; **facetious** (*informal*), **whimsical, droll**, humoursome, joshing (*US*); smart, clever, brilliant, scintillating, sparkling, sprightly; keen, sharp, rapier-like, pungent, pointed, biting, mordant; satiric, **satirical, sarcastic, ironic**, ironical; salty, salt, Attic; **keen-witted, quick-witted, nimble-witted**

16 **clownish**, buffoonish

17 **waggish**; roguish *see* 322.6; **playful, sportive**; **prankish**, pranky, pranksome; **tricky**, trickish, tricksy

adverbs

18 **wittily, humorously**; **jocularly**, jocosely; **facetiously**; **whimsically**, drolly

19 **in fun, in sport, in play, in jest**, in joke, as a joke, jokingly, jestingly, with tongue in cheek; for fun, for sport

490 BANTER

nouns

1 **banter, badinage, persiflage, pleasantry, fooling, fooling around, kidding** *and* **kidding around** (*both informal*), **raillery**, rallying, repartee, **sport**, good-natured banter, harmless teasing; ridicule *see* 508; exchange, give-and-take; side-talk, **byplay**, asides; flyting, slanging, the dozens (*informal*)

2 **bantering, chaffing, joking, jesting**, japing, **fooling, teasing**, hazing (*US & Canadian*); playing the dozens (*informal*)

3 (*informal terms*) **kidding**, jollying, jiving, fooling around, joshing (*US*); **ribbing**, ragging, razzing, **roasting**

4 **banterer**, *persifleur* (*French*), **chaffer, twitter**; kidder (*informal*), josher (*US informal*)

verbs

5 **to banter, chaff**, rally, **joke, jest**, jape, rag, **tease**, wind up, haze (*US & Canadian*); have a slanging match, play the dozens (*informal*)

6 (*informal terms*) **to kid**, jolly, fool around, jive (*US*), rub, put on, josh (*US*); **roast**, ride, needle, **razz** (*US & Canadian*)

adjectives

7 **bantering, chaffing, twitting**; jollying *and* kidding (*both informal*), **fooling, teasing**, quizzical

491 COWARDICE

nouns

1 **cowardice, cowardliness; fear** *see* 127; **faintheartedness**, faintheart, weakheartedness, chickenheartedness, henheartedness, pigeonheartedness; **yellowness**, white-liveredness *and* lily-liveredness *and* chicken-liveredness (*all informal*), weak-kneedness; weakness, softness; unmanliness, unmanfulness; timidness, **timidity**, timorousness, milksoppiness, milksoppishness, milksopism

2 **uncourageousness, unvaliantness**, unvalorousness, unheroicness, ungallantness, unintrepidness; **plucklessness**, gritlessness *and* gutlessness (*both informal*), spiritlessness, heartlessness

3 **dastardliness**, pusillanimousness, **pusillanimity**, **poltroonery**, poltroonishness, poltroonism, baseness, **cravenness**; desertion under fire, skedaddling *and* scarpering (*both informal*)

4 **cold feet** (*informal*), weak knees, **faintheart**, chicken heart, **yellow streak** (*informal*), white feather

5 **coward**, jellyfish, invertebrate, **weakling**, milksop, milquetoast, mouse, **sissy**, wet, **wimp** (*informal*), baby, **big baby, chicken** (*informal*), weak sister (*US informal*); **yellow-belly**, *and* white-liver *and* lily-liver *and* chicken-liver (*all informal*), white feather; scaredy-cat (*informal*); funk *and* funker (*both informal*);
"one who in a perilous emergency thinks with his legs"—AMBROSE BIERCE

6 **dastard, craven, poltroon**, recreant, caitiff, arrant coward; **sneak**

verbs

7 **to dare not; have a yellow streak** (*informal*), **have cold feet** (*informal*), be unable to say 'boo' to a goose

8 **to lose one's nerve**, lose courage, **get cold feet** (*informal*), bottle out *and* lose one's bottle (*both informal*), **show the white feather**; falter, boggle, funk (*informal*); put one's tail between one's legs, back out, funk out (*informal*), **wimp** *or* **chicken out** (*both informal*); desert under fire, turn tail, scarper *and* skedaddle (*both informal*), **run scared** (*informal*), scuttle

9 **to cower, quail, cringe, crouch, skulk, sneak, slink**

adjectives

10 **cowardly**, coward; **afraid, fearful** *see* 127.32, 34; timid, timorous, overtimorous, overtimid; **fainthearted**, weakhearted, chicken-hearted, pigeonhearted; white-livered *and* lily-livered *and* chicken-livered (*all informal*); yellow *and* yellow-bellied *and* with a yellow streak (*all informal*); **weak-kneed, chicken** (*informal*), afraid of one's shadow; weak, soft, wet; **wimpy** *or* wimpish (*informal*), unmanly, unmanful, sissy, sissified; milksoppy, milksoppish; panicky, panic-prone, funking *and* funky (*both informal*); daunted, dismayed, unmanned, cowed, intimidated

11 **uncourageous, unvaliant, unvalorous, unheroic, ungallant, unintrepid, undaring**, unable to say

'boo' to a goose; unsoldierlike, unsoldierly; **pluckless, gutless** (*informal*), spiritless, heartless

12 **dastardly, dastard;** hit-and-run; **poltroonish,** poltroon; **pusillanimous,** base, craven, recreant, caitiff

13 **cowering, quailing, cringing; skulking, sneaking, slinking,** sneaky, slinky

adverbs

14 **cravenly,** poltroonishly, like a coward, **cowardly, uncourageously,** unvaliantly, unvalorously, unheroically, ungallantly, unintrepidly, undaringly; plucklessly, spiritlessly, heartlessly; faintheartedly, weakheartedly, chickenheartedly; wimpishly

492 COURAGE

nouns

1 **courage,** courageousness, **nerve,** pluck, **bravery,** braveness, ballsiness *and* gutsiness (*all informal*), **boldness, valour,** valorousness, valiance, valiancy, **gallantry,** conspicuous gallantry, gallantry under fire *or* beyond the call of duty, gallantness, **intrepidity,** intrepidness, **prowess,** virtue; doughtiness, stalwartness, stoutness, stoutheartedness, lionheartedness, greatheartedness; **heroism,** heroicalness; chivalry, chivalrousness, knightliness; military *or* martial spirit, soldierly quality *or* virtues; **manliness,** manfulness, **manhood,** virility, machismo; Dutch courage (*informal*), pot-valour

2 "fear that has said its prayers"—DOROTHY BERNARD, "fear holding on a minute longer"—GEORGE PATTON, "taking hard knocks like a man when occasion calls"—PLAUTUS, "doing without witnesses that which we would be capable of doing before everyone"—LA ROCHEFOUCAULD

3 **fearlessness,** dauntlessness, **undauntedness, unfearfulness,** unfearingness, unafraidness, **unapprehensiveness; confidence** see 969.5; untimidness, untimorousness, unshrinkingness, unshyness, unbashfulness

4 (*informal terms*) **balls, guts,** bottle, backbone, intestinal fortitude, spunk, brass balls, cojones (*Spanish*), moxie (*US & Canadian*), chutzpah

5 **daring,** derring-do, deeds of derring-do; **bravado,** bravura; **audacity,** audaciousness, overboldness; **venturousness,** venturesomeness, risk-taking, tightrope walking, funambulism; **adventurousness,** adventuresomeness, enterprise; foolhardiness see 493.3

6 **fortitude, hardihood,** hardiness; **pluckiness,** mettlesomeness; **gameness,** gaminess; grit, **stamina,** toughness, pith (*old*), **mettle,** bottom; **heart,** spirit, stout heart, heart of oak; **resolution** see 359, resoluteness, tenaciousness, tenacity, pertinaciousness, pertinacity, bulldog courage

7 **exploit, feat, deed, enterprise, achievement, adventure,** gest, **bold stroke,** heroic act *or* deed; aristeia

8 (*brave person*) **hero, heroine;** brave, stalwart, gallant, valiant, man *or* woman of courage *or* mettle, a man, valiant knight, good soldier; demigod, paladin; demigoddess; the brave; decorated hero; Hector, Achilles, Roland, David; lion, **tiger,** bulldog, fighting cock, gamecock

9 **encouragement, heartening, inspiration,** inspiriting, inspiritment, emboldening, assurance, reassurance, pat *or* clap on the back

verbs

10 **to dare, venture, make bold to,** make so bold as to, take risks, walk the tightrope, **have the nerve, have the guts** *or* the balls (*informal*), have the courage of one's convictions, be a man, "dare do all that may become a man"—SHAKESPEARE, "be strong, and quit yourselves like men"—BIBLE; defy see 454.3

11 **to brave, face, confront,** affront, front, look one in the eye, say to one's face, **face up to,** meet, **meet head-on** *or* boldly, square up to, stand up to *or* against, go eyeball-to-eyeball *or* one-on-one with (*informal*); set at defiance see 454.4; speak up, speak out, stand up and be counted; not flinch *or* shrink from, bite the bullet (*informal*), look full in the face, put a bold face upon, show *or* present a bold front; head into, face up, come to grips with, grapple with; face the music (*informal*); **brazen,** brazen out; beard, "beard the lion in his den"—SIR WALTER SCOTT; put one's head in the lion's mouth, fly into the face of danger, take the bull by the horns, march up to the cannon's mouth, bell the cat, go through fire and water, go in harm's way, throw caution to the wind, run the gauntlet, take one's life in one's hands, put one's life *or* neck on the line (*informal*)

12 **to outbrave, outdare; outface,** face down, face out; **outbrazen,** brazen out; **outlook, outstare,** stare down, stare out, stare out of countenance

13 **to steel oneself, get up nerve,** nerve oneself, muster *or* summon up *or* gather courage, pluck up heart, screw up one's nerve *or* courage, "screw your courage to the sticking place"—SHAKESPEARE, stiffen one's backbone (*informal*)

14 **to take courage, take heart,** pluck up courage, take heart of grace; **brace** *or* **buck up** (*informal*)

15 **to keep up one's courage,** bear up, **keep one's chin up** (*informal*), keep one's pecker up (*informal*), **keep a stiff upper lip** (*informal*), hold up one's head, take what comes; hang in *or* hang in there *or* hang tough *or* stick it out (*all informal*), stick to one's guns

16 **to encourage, hearten, embolden, nerve,** pat *or* clap on the back, **assure, reassure,** bolster, support, cheer on, root for; **inspire,** inspirit; buck *or* brace up (*informal*); put upon one's mettle, make a man of; cheer see 109.7

adjectives

17 **courageous, plucky, brave, bold, valiant, valorous, gallant, intrepid,** doughty, **hardy,** stalwart, stout, stouthearted, ironhearted, lionhearted, greathearted, bold-spirited, brave as a lion; **heroic,** herolike; **chivalrous,** chivalric, knightly, knightlike, soldierly, soldierlike; **manly,** manful, virile, macho

18 **resolute, tough, game; spirited,** spiritful, red-blooded, **mettlesome;** bulldoggish, tenacious, pertinacious

19 (*informal terms*) **ballsy, gutsy, gutty, stand-up, gritty,** spunky, nervy

20 unafraid, unfearing, unfearful; unapprehensive, undiffident; **confident** see 969.21; **fearless, dauntless,** aweless, dreadless; **unfrightened,** unscared, unalarmed, unterrified; **untimid,** untimorous, unshy, unbashful

21 undaunted, undismayed, uncowed, unintimidated, unappalled, unabashed, unawed; **unflinching, unshrinking,** unquailing, uncringing, unwincing, unblenching, unblinking

22 daring, audacious, overbold; **adventurous, venturous, venturesome,** adventuresome, enterprising; foolhardy see 493.9

adverbs

23 courageously, bravely, boldly, heroically, valiantly, valorously, **gallantly, intrepidly,** doughtily, stoutly, hardily, stalwartly; **pluckily, spunkily** (*informal*), gutsily (*informal*), **resolutely, gamely,** tenaciously, pertinaciously, bulldoggishly, **fearlessly,** unfearingly, unfearfully; **daringly,** audaciously; chivalrously, knightly, yeomanly; like a man, like a soldier

493 RASHNESS

nouns

1 rashness, brashness, brazen boldness, **incautiousness,** overboldness, **imprudence, indiscretion,** injudiciousness, improvidence; **unwariness,** unchariness; overcarelessness; overconfidence, oversureness, overweeningness; **impudence,** insolence see 142; **gall** *and* cheek *and* chutzpah (*all informal*); hubris; **temerity,** temerariousness; heroics

2 recklessness, devil-may-careness; heedlessness, **carelessness** see 340.2; **impetuousness** see 365.2, impetuosity, hotheadedness; **haste** see 401, **hastiness,** hurriedness, overeagerness, overzealousness, overenthusiasm; **furiousness,** desperateness, wantonness, wildness, wild oats; **precipitateness,** precipitousness, precipitance, precipitancy, precipitation

3 foolhardiness, harebrainedness; **audacity,** audaciousness; more guts than brains (*informal*), *courage fou* (*French*); forwardness, boldness, **presumption,** presumptuousness; **daring,** daredeviltry, daredevilry, fire-eating; playing with fire, flirting with death, courting disaster, stretching one's luck, going for broke (*informal*), brinkmanship, tightrope walking, funambulism; adventurousness

4 daredevil, devil, **madcap,** tearaway, wild man, hotspur, hellcat, rantipole, harumscarum *and* fire-eater (*both informal*); **adventurer,** adventuress, adventurist; brazen-face

verbs

5 to be rash, be reckless, carry too much sail, sail too near the wind, go out of one's depth, go too far, go to sea in a sieve, take a leap in the dark, buy a pig in a poke, count one's chickens before they are hatched, clutch at straws, lean on a broken reed, put all one's eggs in one basket, live in a glass house; go

out on a limb (*informal*), leave oneself wide open (*informal*), drop one's guard, stick one's neck out *and* ask for it (*both informal*)

6 to court danger, mock *or* defy danger, go in harm's way, thumb one's nose at the consequences, **tempt fate** *or* **the gods** *or* **Providence,** tweak the devil's nose, bell the cat, play a desperate game, ride for a fall; play with fire, flirt with death, stretch one's luck, march up to the cannon's mouth, put one's head in a lion's mouth, beard the lion in his den, sit on a barrel of gunpowder, sleep on a volcano, play Russian roulette, playing with a loaded pistol *or* gun, working without a net; **risk all,** go for broke (*informal*)

adjectives

7 rash, brash, incautious, overbold, **imprudent, indiscreet,** injudicious, improvident; **unwary, unchary;** overcareless; overconfident, oversure, overweening, **impudent,** insolent, brazenfaced, brazen; hubristic; temerarious

8 reckless, devil-may-care; **careless** see 340.11; **impetuous,** hotheaded; **hasty** see 401.9, hurried, overeager, overzealous, overenthusiastic; **furious,** desperate, mad, wild, wanton, harum-scarum (*informal*); precipitate, **precipitous, precipitant; headlong, breakneck;** slapdash, slap-bang; accident-prone

9 foolhardy, harebrained, madcap, wild, madbrain, madbrained; **audacious;** forward, bold, **presumptuous; daring,** daredevil, fire-eating, death-defying; adventurous

adverbs

10 rashly, brashly, incautiously, imprudently, indiscreetly, injudiciously, improvidently; **unwarily,** uncharily; overconfidently, overweeningly, **impudently,** insolently, **brazenly,** hubristically, temerariously

11 recklessly, happen what may; heedlessly, **carelessly** see 340.18; **impetuously,** hotheadedly; **hastily,** hurriedly, overeagerly, overzealously, overenthusiastically; **furiously,** desperately, wildly, wantonly, **madly,** like mad *or* crazy *and* like there was no tomorrow (*all informal*); **precipitately,** precipitiously, precipitantly; **headlong,** headfirst, headforemost, **head over heels,** heels over head, *à corps perdu* (*French*); slapdash, slap-bang (*informal*); helter-skelter, hurry-scurry, pell-mell, holus-bolus

12 foolhardily, daringly, audaciously, presumptuously, harebrainedly

494 CAUTION

nouns

1 caution, cautiousness; slowness to act *or* commit oneself *or* make one's move; **care, heed, solicitude; carefulness, heedfulness,** mindfulness, regardfulness, thoroughness; paying mind *or* attention; **guardedness;** uncommunicativeness see 344; **gingerliness, tentativeness,** hesitation, hesitancy, unprecipitateness; slow and careful steps, deliberate stages, wait-and-see attitude *or* policy; **prudence,** prudentialness, **circumspection,**

discretion, canniness (*Scottish*); **coolness, judiciousness** *see* 919.7; calculation, **deliberateness,** deliberation, careful consideration, prior consultation; **safeness,** safety first, no room for error; **hedge, hedging,** hedging one's bets, cutting one's losses

2 **wariness, chariness, cageyness** *and* **leeriness** (*both informal*); **suspicion,** suspiciousness; **distrust,** distrustfulness, mistrust, mistrustfulness

3 **precaution,** precautiousness; **forethought, foresight,** foresightedness, forehandedness, forethoughtfulness; **providence,** provision, forearming; precautions, steps, measures, steps and measures; **safeguard,** protection *see* 1007, preventive measure, safety net, safety valve, sheet anchor; **insurance**

4 **overcaution,** overcautiousness, overcarefulness, overwariness

verbs

5 **to be cautious, be careful,** mind out; think twice, give it a second thought; make haste slowly, take it easy *or* slow (*informal*); put the right foot forward, take one step at a time, pick one's steps, go step by step, feel one's ground *or* way; pussyfoot, tiptoe, go *or* walk on tiptoe, walk on eggs *or* eggshells *or* thin ice; pull *or* draw in one's horns

6 **to take precautions, take steps** *or* **measures,** take steps and measures; **prepare** *or* **provide for** *or* **against,** forearm; **guard against, make sure against,** make sure, "make assurance double sure"—SHAKESPEARE; **play safe** (*informal*), keep on the safe side; leave no stone unturned, forget *or* leave out nothing, overlook no possibility, leave no room *or* margin for error, leave nothing to chance, consider every angle; **look before one leaps;** see how the land lies *or* the wind blows, see how the cat jumps (*informal*); clear the decks, batten down the hatches, shorten sail, reef down, tie in *or* tuck in *or* take in a reef, get out a sheet-anchor, have an anchor to windward; **hedge,** provide a hedge, hedge one's bets, cut one's losses; take out insurance; keep something for a rainy day

7 **to beware, take care, have a care,** take heed, take heed at one's peril; keep at a respectful distance, keep out of harm's way; mind, mind one's business; **be on one's guard,** be on the watch *or* lookout, be on the *qui vive*; **look out, watch out** (*informal*); **look sharp,** keep one's eyes open, keep a weather eye out *or* open (*informal*), keep one's eye peeled (*informal*), **watch one's step** (*informal*), look about one, look over one's shoulder; stop, look and listen; not stick one's neck out (*informal*), not go out on a limb (*informal*), not expose oneself, not be too visible, **keep a low profile,** lie low, stay in the background, blend in with the scenery; not blow one's cover (*informal*); hold one's tongue *see* 51.5

adjectives

8 **cautious, careful,** heedful, mindful, regardful, **thorough; prudent, circumspect,** slow to act *or* commit oneself *or* make one's move, noncommittal, uncommitted; canny (*Scottish*); sly, crafty, scheming; **discreet, politic, judicious** *see* 919.19, Polonian, Machiavelian; unadventurous, unenterprising,

undaring; **gingerly; guarded,** on guard, on one's guard; uncommunicative *see* 344.8; **tentative,** hesitant, unprecipitate, cool; **deliberate;** safe, on the safe side, leaving no stone unturned, forgetting *or* leaving out nothing, overlooking no possibility, leaving no room *or* margin for error

9 **wary, chary, cagey** (*informal*), **leery** (*informal*), **suspicious,** suspecting, **distrustful,** mistrustful, shy

10 **precautionary,** precautious, precautional; **preventive,** preemptive, prophylactic; **forethoughtful,** forethoughted, **foresighted,** foreseeing, forehanded; **provident,** provisional

11 **overcautious, overcareful,** overwary

adverbs

12 **cautiously, carefully,** heedfully, mindfully, regardfully; **prudently, circumspectly,** cannily (*Scottish*), pawkily, **discreetly,** judiciously; **gingerly,** guardedly, easy (*informal*), with caution, with care

13 **warily, charily, cagily** (*informal*); **askance,** askant, suspiciously, leerily (*informal*), distrustfully

exclamations

14 careful!, be careful!, **take care!,** have a care!, **look out!, watch out!, watch your step!,** watch it!, take heed!, steady!, look sharp!, easy!, take it easy!, easy does it!, go easy!

495 FASTIDIOUSNESS

nouns

1 **fastidiousness, particularity,** particularness; **scrupulousness,** scrupulosity; **punctiliousness,** punctilio, spit and polish; **preciseness,** precision; **meticulousness, conscientiousness,** criticalness; **taste** *see* 496; **sensitivity, discrimination** *see* 943, discriminatingness, discriminativeness; **selectiveness,** selectivity, pickiness (*informal*), choosiness; **strictness** *see* 339.3, **perfectionism,** precisianism, **purism; puritanism, priggishness, prudishness, prissiness** (*informal*), propriety, strait-lacedness, censoriousness, judgmentalness

2 **finicalness,** finickiness, finickingness, finicality; **fussiness,** pernicketiness (*informal*); squeamishness, queasiness

3 **nicety,** niceness, **delicacy,** delicateness, daintiness, exquisiteness, fineness, refinement, **subtlety**

4 **overfastidiousness, overscrupulousness, overparticularity, overconscientiousness,** overmeticulousness, overniceness, **overnicety; overcriticalness,** hypercriticism, hairsplitting; overrefinement, oversubtlety, supersubtlety; oversqueamishness, oversensitivity, hypersensitivity, morbid sensibility

5 **exclusiveness,** exclusivity, selectness, selectiveness, selectivity; **cliquishness,** clannishness; **snobbishness,** snobbery, snobbism

6 **perfectionist,** precisian, precisianist, stickler, nitpicker, pedant, anal retentive (*informal*), captious critic *see* 945.7

7 **fusspot** (*informal*), fuss, fusser, **fuddy-duddy** (*informal*), granny, old woman, old maid

verbs

8 to be hard to please, want everything just so, **fuss,** fuss over; pick and choose; **turn up one's nose,** look down one's nose, disdain, scorn, spurn; not dirty *or* soil one's hands

adjectives

9 fastidious, particular, scrupulous, meticulous, conscientious, exacting, precise, punctilious, spit-and-polish; **sensitive, discriminating** see 943.7, discriminative; **selective,** picky (*informal*), choosy, choicy (*informal*); critical, "nothing if not critical"—SHAKESPEARE; **strict** see 339.12, perfectionistic, precisianistic, puristic; puritanic, puritanical, priggish, prudish, prissy, proper, strait-laced, censorious, judgmental

10 finical, finicky, finicking, finikin; **fussy,** fussbudgety (*informal*); **squeamish,** pernickety (*informal*), difficult, hard to please

11 nice, dainty, delicate, *délicat* (*French*), fine, refined, exquisite, **subtle**

12 overfastidious, queasy, **overparticular, overscrupulous, overconscientious,** overmeticulous, **overnice,** overprecise; **overcritical,** hypercritical, ultracritical, hairsplitting, pedantic; overrefined, oversubtle, supersubtle; oversqueamish, oversensitive, hypersensitive, morbidly sensitive; **compulsive,** anal-retentive

13 exclusive, selective, **select,** elect, elite; **cliquish,** clannish; **snobbish,** snobby

adverbs

14 fastidiously, particularly, scrupulously, meticulously, conscientiously, critically, punctiliously; discriminatingly, discriminatively, selectively; **finically,** finickily, finickingly; **fussily; squeamishly,** queasily; refinedly, subtly

496 TASTE, TASTEFULNESS

nouns

1 taste, good taste, sound critical judgment, discernment *or* appreciation of excellence, preference for the best, *goût raffiné* (*French*); **tastefulness,** quality, excellence, choiceness, **elegance,** grace, gracefulness, gracility, graciousness, graciosity; **refinement,** finesse, **polish, culture, cultivation,** civilizedness, refined *or* cultivated *or* civilized taste; niceness, nicety, delicacy, daintiness, **subtlety, sophistication; discrimination** see 943, fastidiousness see 495; acquired taste, "caviare to the general"—SHAKESPEARE

2 "good sense delicately put in force"—CHÉVIER, "the microscope of the judgment"—ROUSSEAU, "a fine judgment in discerning art"—HORACE, "the literary conscience of the soul"—JOSEPH JOUBERT, "the fundamental quality which sums up all other qualities"—LAUTRÉAMONT, "the enemy of creativeness"—PICASSO

3 decorousness, decorum, decency, properness, propriety, rightness, right thinking, **seemliness,** becomingness, fittingness, fitness, appropriateness,

suitability, meetness, happiness, felicity; gentility, genteelness; civility, urbanity see 504.1

4 restraint, restrainedness, **understatement,** unobtrusiveness, quietness, subduedness, quiet taste; simplicity see 499.1

5 aesthetic *or* **artistic taste,** virtuosity, virtu, **expertise,** expertism, connoisseurship; dilettantism; fine art of living; epicurism, epicureanism; gastronomy, *friandise* (*French*); aesthetics

6 aesthete, person of taste, lover of beauty

7 connoisseur, *connaisseur* (*French*), *cognoscente* (*Italian*); **judge,** good judge, **critic, expert,** authority, maven (*US informal*), arbiter, arbiter of taste, *arbiter elegantiarum* (*Latin*), tastemaker, trendsetter; **epicure,** epicurean; **gourmet, gourmand,** *bon vivant* (*French*), good *or* refined palate; virtuoso; dilettante, amateur; culture vulture (*informal*); collector

adjectives

8 tasteful, in good taste, in the best taste; excellent, of quality, of the best, of the first water; **aesthetic,** artistic, pleasing, well-chosen, choice, of choice; pure, chaste; classic *or* classical, Attic, restrained, understated, unobtrusive, quiet, subdued, simple, unaffected see 499.7

9 elegant, graceful, gracile, gracious; **refined, polished, cultivated,** civilized, **cultured;** nice, fine, delicate, dainty, **subtle, sophisticated, discriminating** see 943.7, fastidious see 495.9

10 decorous, decent, proper, right, right-thinking, **seemly, becoming,** fitting, appropriate, suitable, meet, happy, felicitous; genteel; civil, urbane see 504.14

adverbs

11 tastefully, with taste, in good taste, in the best taste; aesthetically, artistically; elegantly, gracefully; decorously, genteelly, decently, properly, seemly, becomingly; quietly, unobtrusively; simply see 499.10

497 VULGARITY

nouns

1 vulgarity, vulgarness, vulgarism, commonness, meanness; **inelegance** *or* inelegancy, indelicacy, **impropriety, indecency, indecorum,** indecorousness, unseemliness, unbecomingness, unfittingness, inappropriateness, unsuitableness, unsuitability; ungentility; **untastefulness,** tastelessness, unaestheticness, unaestheticism, tackiness (*informal*); low *or* bad *or* poor taste, *mauvais goût* (*French*); vulgar taste, bourgeois taste, philistinism, Babbittry (*US*); camp, campness, high *or* low camp; kitsch

2 coarseness, grossness, *grossièreté* (*French*), **rudeness, crudeness,** crudity, **crassness,** rawness, roughness, **earthiness;** ribaldness, ribaldry; raunchiness (*informal*), **obscenity** see 666.4; meretriciousness, **loudness** (*informal*), **gaudiness** see 501.3

3 unrefinement, uncouthness, uncultivation, uncultivatedness, unculturedness; uncivilizedness, wildness; impoliteness, incivility, ill breeding see

505.1; **barbarism**, barbarousness, barbarity, philistinism, Gothicism; **savagery**, savagism; **brutality**, brutishness, bestiality, animality, **mindlessness**; Neanderthalism, troglodytism

4 **boorishness, churlishness**, carlishness, **loutishness**, lubberliness, lumpishness, cloddishness, clownishness, yokelism; ruffianism, rowdyism, hooliganism; parvenuism, arrivism, upstartness

5 **commonness, commonplaceness**, ordinariness, homeliness; **lowness, baseness, meanness;** ignobility, plebeianism

6 **vulgarian**, low *or* vulgar *or* ill-bred fellow, guttersnipe, *épicier* (*French*); Philistine, bourgeois, Babbitt (*US*); *parvenu, arriviste, nouveau riche* (*all French*), upstart; bounder (*informal*), cad, **boor**, churl, oik (*informal*), yob *or* yobbo (*informal*), **lout**, yahoo, redneck (*US informal*), looby, peasant, groundling, yokel; rough, **ruffian**, roughneck (*informal*), **rowdy**, hooligan; vulgarist, ribald

7 **barbarian, savage**, Goth, animal, brute; Neanderthal, troglodyte, caveman

8 vulgarization, coarsening; popularization; *haute vulgarisation* (*French*); dumbing down (*US informal*)

verbs

9 to vulgarize, coarsen; popularize; dumb down (*US informal*); **pander**

adjectives

10 **vulgar, inelegant, indelicate, indecorous, indecent, improper, unseemly**, unbeseeming, unbecoming, unfitting, inappropriate, unsuitable, **ungenteel**, undignified; **untasteful**, tasteless, in bad *or* poor taste, tacky *and* naff *and* chintzy (*all informal*); **offensive**, offensive to gentle ears

11 **coarse, gross, rude, crude, crass**, raw, rough, **earthy**; ribald; raunchy (*informal*), **obscene** *see* 666.9; meretricious, loud (*informal*), gaudy *see* 501.20

12 **unrefined, unpolished, uncouth**, unkempt, uncombed, unlicked; **uncultivated, uncultured; uncivilized**, noncivilized; impolite, uncivil, ill-bred *see* 505.6; **wild**, untamed; **barbarous**, barbaric, barbarian; outlandish, Gothic; primitive; **savage, brutal**, brutish, bestial, animal, **mindless**; Neanderthal, troglodytic; wild-and-woolly, rough-and-ready

13 **boorish, churlish**, carlish, **loutish**, yobbish, redneck (*US informal*), lubberly, lumpish, cloddish, clownish, loobyish, yokelish; rowdy, **rowdyish, ruffianly**, roughneck (*informal*), hooliganish, raffish, raised in a barn

14 **common, commonplace, ordinary**; plebeian, non-U (*informal*); homely, homespun; **general, public, popular**, pop (*informal*); vernacular; Philistine, bourgeois, Biedermier, Babbittish (*US*); campy, high-camp, low-camp, kitsch

15 **low, base, mean, ignoble**, vile, scurvy, sorry, beggarly; low-minded, base-minded

adverbs

16 **vulgarly, uncouthly, inelegantly**, indelicately, indecorously, indecently, improperly, unseemly,

untastefully, offensively; **coarsely, grossly, rudely,** crudely, crassly, roughly; ribaldly

498 ORNAMENTATION

nouns

1 **ornamentation, ornament; decoration**, decor; **adornment, embellishment**, embroidery, elaboration; nonfunctional addition *or* adjunct; garnish, garnishment, garniture; trimming, trim; flourish; emblazonment, emblazonry; illumination; **colour**, colour scheme, colour pattern, colour compatibility, colour design, colour arrangement; **arrangement**, flower arrangement, floral decoration, furniture arrangement; table setting *or* decoration; window dressing; **interior decoration** *or* decorating, room decoration, interior design; **redecoration, refurbishment** *see* 396.4, redoing

2 **ornateness, elegance, fanciness**, fineness, **elaborateness; ostentation** *see* 501; richness, luxuriousness, luxuriance; **floweriness**, floridness, floridity; dizenment (*old*), **bedizenment; gaudiness, flashiness** *see* 501.3; flamboyance *or* flamboyancy; **overelegance**, overelaborateness, overornamentation, busyness; clutteredness; baroqueness, baroque, rococo, arabesque, moresque, chinoiserie

3 **finery, frippery**, gaudery, gaiety, bravery, trumpery, folderol, trickery, chiffon, trappings, festoons, superfluity; **frills**, frills and furbelows, bells and whistles *and* gimmickry *and* glitz (*all informal*), frillery, frilling, frilliness; fuss (*informal*), froufrou; gingerbread; **tinsel**, clinquant, pinchbeck, paste; gilt, gilding

4 **trinket**, gewgaw, **knickknack** *or* nicknack, knack (*old*), **gimcrack**, kickshaw, **bauble**, fribble, bibelot, toy, gaud; bric-a-brac

5 **jewellery**, bijouterie, ice (*informal*); costume jewellery, glass, paste, junk jewellery (*informal*)

6 **jewel**, bijou, **gem**, stone, precious stone; rhinestone; pin, brooch, stickpin, breastpin, scatter pin, chatelaine; cuff-link, tie clasp *or* clip, tie bar, tiepin; **ring**, band, wedding ring, engagement ring, eternity ring, mood ring, signet ring, school *or* class ring (*US*), circle, earring, nose ring, nipple ring; bracelet, wristlet, wristband, armlet, anklet; chain, necklace, torque, pendant; locket; beads, chaplet, wampum (*US*); bangle; charm; fob; crown, coronet, diadem, tiara

7 **motif**, ornamental motif, **figure, detail**, form, touch, repeated figure; **pattern, theme**, design, ornamental theme, ornamental *or* decorative composition; foreground detail, background detail; **background**, setting, foil, **style**, ornamental *or* decorative style, national style, **period style**

verbs

8 **to ornament, decorate, adorn, dress, trim**, garnish, array, **deck**, bedeck, dizen (*old*), bedizen; prettify, **beautify; redecorate**, refurbish, redo; **embellish, furbish**, embroider, enrich, grace, set off *or* out, paint, colour, blazon, emblazon, paint in glowing colours; **dress up; spruce up** *and* gussy up *and* doll up *and* tart up (*all informal*), **primp up**, prink up, prank up, trick up *or* out, deck out,

bedight (*old*); primp, prink, preen; smarten, smarten up, dandify, titivate

9 to figure, filigree; **spangle, bespangle;** bead; tinsel; jewel, bejewel, gem, diamond; ribbon, beribbon; flounce; flower, garland, wreathe; feather, plume; flag; illuminate; paint *see* 35.13; engrave

adjectives

10 ornamental, decorative, adorning, embellishing

11 ornamented, adorned, decorated, embellished, bedecked, decked out, tricked out, garnished, trimmed, dizened (*old*), bedizened; figured; flowered; festooned, befrilled, wreathed; spangled, bespangled, spangly; jewelled, bejewelled; beaded; studded; plumed, feathered; beribboned

12 ornate, elegant, fancy, fine, pretty-pretty; picturesque; **elaborate,** overornamented, overornate, overelegant, etc, laboured, high-wrought; **ostentatious** *see* 501.18; **rich, luxurious,** luxuriant; flowery, florid; flamboyant, fussy, frilly, frilled, flouncy, gingerbread; **overelegant,** overelaborate, overlabored, overworked, overwrought, overornamented, over the top, busy; cluttered; **baroque,** rococo, arabesque, moresque; tarted-up *or* gussied-up (*both informal*)

499 PLAINNESS
unaffectedness

nouns

1 plainness, simplicity *see* 797, **simpleness, ordinariness, commonness, commonplaceness,** homeliness, prosaicness, prosiness, matter-of-factness; **purity,** chasteness, classic *or* classical purity, Attic simplicity

2 naturalness, inartificiality; **unaffectedness,** unassumingness, **unpretentiousness;** directness, straightforwardness; innocence, naïveté

3 unadornment, unembellishment, unadornedness, unornamentation; **no frills,** no nonsense, back-to-basics; **uncomplexity,** uncomplication, uncomplicatedness, **unsophistication,** unadulteration; bareness, baldness, nakedness, nudity, undress, beauty unadorned

4 inornateness, unelaborateness, unfanciness, unfussiness; **austerity,** severity, starkness, Spartan simplicity

verbs

5 to simplify *see* 797.4; chasten, restrain, purify; put in words of one syllable, spell out

adjectives

6 simple *see* 797.6, **plain, ordinary, nondescript, common, commonplace, prosaic,** mumsy (*informal*), bog-standard (*informal*), **matter-of-fact, homely, homespun,** everyday, workday, workaday, household, garden, common- *or* garden-variety; pure, **pure and simple,** chaste, classic *or* classical, Attic

7 natural, native; **inartificial,** unartificial; **unaffected, unpretentious,** unpretending, unassuming, unfeigning, direct, straightforward, honest, candid; innocent, naive

8 unadorned, undecorated, unornamented, unembellished, ungarnished, unfurbished, unvarnished, untrimmed; olde *and* olde-worlde (*both informal*); back-to-basics, no-frills, no-nonsense, vanilla (*informal*); low-tech; back-to-nature; **uncomplex,** uncomplicated, **unsophisticated,** unadulterated; **undressed,** undecked, unarrayed; bare, bald, blank, naked, nude

9 inornate, unornate, **unelaborate,** unfancy, unfussy; austere, monkish, cloistral, severe, stark, Spartan

adverbs

10 plainly, simply, ordinarily, commonly, commonplacely, prosaically, matter-of-factly

11 unaffectedly, naturally, unpretentiously, unassumingly, directly, straightforwardly

500 AFFECTATION

nouns

1 affectation, affectedness; pretension, pretence, airs, putting on airs, put-on (*informal*); **show, false show,** mere show; front, false front (*informal*), **facade,** mere facade, **image,** public image; feigned belief, **hypocrisy** *see* 354.6; phoneyness (*informal*), sham *see* 354.3; artificiality, unnaturalness, insincerity; airs and graces, prunes and prisms; stylishness, mannerism

2 mannerism, *minauderie* (*French*), trick, **quirk,** habit, peculiarity, peculiar trait, idiosyncrasy, trademark

3 posing, pose, posturing, attitudinizing, attitudinarianism; peacockery, peacockishness

4 foppery, foppishness, dandyism, coxcombry, puppyism, conceit

5 overniceness, overpreciseness, **overrefinement, elegance,** exquisiteness, preciousness, preciosity; purism, formalism, formality, pedantry, precisionism, precisianism; euphuism; euphemism

6 prudery, prudishness, prissiness, priggishness, primness, smugness, stuffiness (*informal*), old-maidishness, **straitlacedness,** stiff-neckedness, narrowness, censoriousness, sanctimony, sanctimoniousness, **puritanism,** puritanicalness; **false modesty,** overmodesty, demureness, *mauvaise honte* (*French*)

7 phoney *and* **fake** *and* **fraud** (*all informal*) *see* 354.13; affecter; mannerist; **pretender,** actor, playactor (*informal*), performer; paper tiger, hollow man, straw man, man of straw, empty suit (*informal*)

8 poser, poseur, striker of poses, **posturer,** posturist, posture maker, attitudinarian, attitudinizer

9 dandy, fop, toff, coxcomb, macaroni, gallant, ponce (*informal*), exquisite, blood, fine gentleman, puppy, jackanapes, jack-a-dandy, fribble, clotheshorse, fashion plate; beau, Beau Brummel, spark, blade, ladies' man, lady-killer (*informal*), cocksman (*informal*); man-about-town, boulevardier

10 fine lady, *grande dame, précieuse* (*both French*); belle, toast

11 prude, prig, priss, puritan, schoolmarm, goody-goody (*informal*), old maid; Victorian, mid-Victorian

verbs

12 to affect, assume, put on, assume *or* put on airs, wear, **pretend, simulate, counterfeit, sham, fake** (*informal*), **feign,** make out like (*informal*), make a show of, play, playact (*informal*), act *or* play a part, play a scene, do a bit (*informal*), put up a front (*informal*), dramatize, histrionize, lay it on thick (*informal*), overact, mug *and* ham *and* ham it up *and* emote (*all informal*), tug at the heartstrings

13 to pose, posture, attitudinize, peacock, strike a pose, strike an attitude, pose for effect

14 to mince, mince it, prink; **simper,** smirk, bridle

adjectives

15 affected, pretentious, la-di-da, posy; **mannered,** *maniéré* (*French*); **artificial, unnatural,** insincere; theatrical, stagy, histrionic; overdone, overacted, hammed up (*informal*)

16 assumed, put-on, pretended, simulated, **phoney** *and* **fake** *and* **faked** (*all informal*), feigned, counterfeited; spurious, sham; hypocritical

17 foppish, dandified, dandy, coxcombical, conceited

18 (*affectedly nice*) **overnice,** twee, overprecise, precious, *précieuse* (*French*), exquisite, **overrefined, elegant,** mincing, simpering, namby-pamby; puristic, formalistic, pedantic, precisionistic, precisian, precisianistic, euphuistic, euphemistic

19 prudish, priggish, prim, prissy, smug, stuffy (*informal*), old-maidish, **overmodest,** demure, **straitlaced,** stiff-necked, hide-bound, narrow, censorious, po-faced, sanctimonious, **puritanical,** Victorian, mid-Victorian, holier than thou

adverbs

20 affectedly, pretentiously; elegantly, mincingly; for effect, for show

21 prudishly, priggishly, primly, smugly, stuffily (*informal*), straitlacedly, stiffneckedly, puritanically

501 OSTENTATION

nouns

1 ostentation, ostentatiousness, ostent; **pretentiousness, pretension, pretence;** loftiness, lofty affectations, **triumphalism**

2 pretensions, vain pretensions; **airs,** lofty airs, airs and graces, highfalutin *or* highfaluting ways (*informal*), side, swank (*informal*), Lord Muck *and* Lady Muck (*informal*)

3 showiness, flashiness, flamboyance, panache, dash, jazziness (*informal*), jauntiness, sportiness (*informal*), gaiety, glitter, glare, dazzle, dazzlingness; extravaganza; **gaudiness,** gaudery, glitz *and* gimmickry *and* razzmatazz *and* razzledazzle (*all informal*), **tawdriness,** meretriciousness; gorgeousness, colourfulness; **garishness,** loudness (*informal*), **blatancy,** flagrancy, shamelessness, brazenness, luridness, extravagance, sensationalism, obtrusiveness, vulgarness, crudeness, extravagation

4 display, show, demonstration, manifestation, **exhibition, parade,** *étalage* (*French*); **pageantry,** pageant, spectacle; vaunt, fanfaronade, blazon, flourish, flaunt, flaunting; daring, brilliancy, éclat, bravura, flair; dash *and* splash (*both informal*); figure;

exhibitionism, showing-off; theatrics, histrionics, dramatics, staginess; false front, **sham** *see* 354.3

5 grandeur, grandness, grandiosity, **magnificence,** gorgeousness, **splendour,** splendidness, splendiferousness, resplendence, brilliance, glory; nobility, proudness, **state, stateliness, majesty;** impressiveness, imposingness; **sumptuousness, elegance, elaborateness, lavishness,** luxuriousness; poshness *or* plushness *or* swankness *or* swankiness (*all informal*); **luxury,** barbaric *or* Babylonian splendour

6 pomp, circumstance, pride, **state,** solemnity, formality; **pomp and circumstance,** "pride, pomp, and circumstance"—Shakespeare; heraldry, "trump and solemn heraldry"—Coleridge

7 pompousness, pomposity, pontification, pontificality, **stuffiness** (*informal*), **self-importance,** inflation; grandiloquence, turgidity, orotundity

8 swagger, strut, swank (*informal*), bounce, brave show; swaggering, strutting; swash, **swashbucklery,** swashbuckling, swashbucklering; peacockishness, peacockery

9 stuffed shirt (*informal*), blimp (*informal*), Colonel Blimp; bloated aristocrat

10 strutter, swaggerer, swanker, swash, swasher, **swashbuckler,** peacock, miles gloriosus

11 show-off (*informal*), exhibitionist, flaunter, hot dog (*US informal*)

verbs

12 to put *or* **thrust oneself forward,** come forward, step to the front *or* fore, step into the limelight, take centre stage, attract attention, make oneself conspicuous

13 to cut a dash, make a show, put on a show, make one's mark, cut a swath, **cut** *or* **make a figure;** make a splash (*informal*); splash (*informal*); shine, glitter, glare, dazzle

14 to give oneself airs, put on airs, put on, put on side, put up a front (*informal* (*informal*)), act the grand seigneur, **swank** (*informal*), swell, ritz it, put on the dog (*US & Canadian informal*); pontificate, play the pontiff

15 to strut, swagger, swank, prance, stalk, peacock, swash, swashbuckle

16 to show off (*informal*), play to the gallery *or* galleries (*informal*), please the crowd, **grandstand** *and* hotdog *and* showboat (*all US informal*); exhibit *or* parade one's wares (*informal*), strut one's stuff (*informal*), go through one's paces, show what one has

17 to flaunt, vaunt, parade, display, demonstrate, manifest, make a great show of, **exhibit, air,** put forward, put forth, hold up, flash *and* sport (*both informal*); advertise; **flourish, brandish,** wave, troop the colour; dangle, dangle before the eyes; emblazon, blazon forth; trumpet, trumpet forth

adjectives

18 ostentatious, pretentious, posy; **ambitious,** vaunting, **lofty, highfalutin** *and* highfaluting (*both informal*), **high-flown,** high-flying; **fancy,** classy (*informal*)

19 showy, flaunting, flashy, snazzy, flashing, glittering, **jazzy** *and* **glitzy** *and* gimmicky (*all informal*); exhibitionistic, showoffy (*informal*), bravura; **gay**, jaunty, rakish, **dashing**; gallant, brave, braw (*Scottish*), daring; **sporty** *or* dressy (*both informal*); **frilly, flouncy,** frothy, chichi

20 gaudy, tawdry, tinsel; gorgeous, colourful; **garish, loud** (*informal*), **blatant, flagrant,** shameless, **brazen,** brazenfaced, lurid, extravagant, sensational, **spectacular,** glaring, flaring, flaunting, screaming (*informal*), tabloid, obtrusive, vulgar, crude, over the top *or* OTT; meretricious, low-rent *and* tacky (*both informal*)

21 grandiose, grand, magnificent, splendid, splendiferous, **glorious,** superb, fine, superfine, fancy, superfancy, swell (*informal*); **imposing, impressive,** larger than life, awful, awe-inspiring, awesome; **noble, proud, stately, majestic,** princely; **sumptuous, elegant, elaborate, luxurious,** extravagant, deluxe; executive *and* plush *and* posh *and* ritzy *and* swanky (*all informal*), Corinthian; palatial, Babylonian; barbaric

22 pompous, stuffy (*informal*), **self-important,** impressed with oneself, pontific, pontifical; **inflated, swollen,** bloated, tumid, turgid, flatulent (*informal*), stilted; grandiloquent, bombastic *see* 545.9; solemn *see* 111.3, formal

23 strutting, swaggering; swashing, **swashbuckling,** swashbucklering; peacockish, peacocky; too big for one's boots

24 theatrical, theatric, stagy, dramatic, histrionic; spectacular

adverbs

25 ostentatiously, pretentiously, loftily; with flourish of trumpet, with beat of drum, with flying colours

26 showily, **flauntingly,** flashily, with a flair, glitteringly; gaily, jauntily, **dashingly;** gallantly, bravely, daringly

27 gaudily, tawdrily; gorgeously, colourfully; **garishly, blatantly, flagrantly,** shamelessly, **brazenly,** brazenfacedly, luridly, sensationally, **spectacularly,** glaringly, flaringly, obtrusively

28 grandiosely, grandly, magnificently, **splendidly,** splendiferously, splendaciously (*informal*), gloriously, superbly; nobly, proudly, majestically; imposingly, impressively; **sumptuously, elegantly,** elaborately, luxuriously, **extravagantly;** palatially

29 pompously, pontifically, stuffily (*informal*), **self-importantly;** stiltedly; **bombastically** *see* 545.12

502 BOASTING

nouns

1 boasting, bragging, vaunting; **boastfulness, braggadocio, braggartism; boast, brag,** vaunt; side, bombast, bravado, vauntery, fanfaronade, blowing one's own trumpet (*informal*), gasconade, gasconism, rodomontade; bluster, swagger *see* 503.1; vanity, conceit *see* 140.4; jactation, jactitation; heroics

2 (*informal terms*) **big talk,** fine talk, fancy talk, tall talk, highfalutin *or* highfaluting, **hot air,** gas, bunk, bunkum, **bullshit;** tall story, fishy tale

3 **self-approbation,** self-praise, self-laudation, self-gratulation, self-applause, self-boosting, self-puffery, self-vaunting, self-advertising, self-advertisement, self-adulation, self-glorification, self-dramatizing, self-dramatization, self-promoting, self-promotion; **vainglory,** vaingloriousness

4 crowing, exultation, elation, triumph, jubilation; **gloating**

5 **braggart, boaster,** brag, braggadocio, hector, fanfaron, Gascon, gasconader, miles gloriosus; big mouth (*informal*); blusterer *see* 503.2; Braggadocchio (*Spenser*), Captain Bobadil (*Ben Jonson*), Thraso (*Terence*), Parolles (*Shakespeare*)

verbs

6 to boast, brag, make a boast of, vaunt, flourish, gasconade, vapour, puff, advertise oneself, **blow one's own trumpet, toot one's own horn,** sing one's own praises, exaggerate one's own merits; bluster, swagger *see* 503.3

7 (*informal terms*) to mouth off, **talk big,** sound off, **bullshit,** talk a good game, lay it on thick, bum (*Scottish informal*)

8 to flatter oneself, conceit oneself, **congratulate oneself,** hug oneself, shake hands with oneself, form a mutual admiration society with oneself, **pat oneself on the back,** take merit to oneself

9 to exult, triumph, glory, delight, joy, jubilate; **crow** *or* crow over; **gloat,** gloat over

adjectives

10 boastful, boasting, braggart, bragging, braggadocious, thrasonical, thrasonic, big-mouthed (*informal*), vaunting, gasconading, Gascon, fanfaronading, fanfaron; vain, conceited *see* 140.11; **vainglorious**

11 self-approving, self-approbatory, self-praising, self-gratulating, self-boosting, self-puffing, self-adulating, self-adulatory, self-glorifying, self-glorying, self-glorious, self-lauding, self-laudatory, self-congratulatory, self-applauding, self-praising, self-flattering, self-vaunting, self-advertising, self-dramatizing, self-promoting

12 inflated, swollen, bombastic, **high-flown, highfalutin** *and* highfaluting (*both informal*), **pretentious,** extravagant, big

13 crowing, exultant, exulting, elated, elate, jubilant, **triumphant, flushed,** cock-a-hoop, in high feather; **gloating**

adverbs

14 boastfully, boastingly, braggingly, vauntingly, vaingloriously; **self-approvingly,** self-praisingly, etc

15 exultantly, exultingly, elatedly, jubilantly, triumphantly, triumphally, in triumph; **gloatingly**

503 BLUSTER

nouns

1 **bluster,** blustering, hectoring, bullying, **swagger,** swashbucklery, side; **bravado,** rant, rodomontade, fanfaronade; fuss, bustle, fluster, flurry; bluff, bluster and bluff; intimidation *see* 127.6; **boastfulness** *see* 502.1

2 blusterer, swaggerer, swasher, swashbuckler, fanfaron, bravo, **bully**, bullyboy, bucko, roisterer, cock of the walk, vapourer, blatherskite (*informal*), swank (*informal*); ranter, raver, hectorer, hector, Herod; bluff, bluffer; **braggart** see 502.5

verbs

3 to bluster, hector; **swagger**, swashbuckle; bully; bounce, roister, rollick, gasconade; splutter; rant, rage, rave, rave on, storm, "out-herod Herod"—Shakespeare; bluff, bluster and bluff; intimidate; shoot off one's mouth, sound off, brag see 502.6

adjectives

4 blustering, blustery, blusterous, hectoring, **bullying, swaggering,** swashing, swashbuckling, boisterous, roisterous, roistering, rollicking; ranting, raging, raving, storming; tumultuous; noisy, "full of sound and fury"—Shakespeare

504 COURTESY

nouns

1 courtesy, courteousness, common courtesy, **politeness, civility,** *politesse* (*French*), amenity, agreeableness, urbanity, comity, affability; **graciousness,** gracefulness; complaisance; **thoughtfulness, considerateness** see 143.3, **tactfulness,** tact, consideration, **solicitousness, solicitude;** respect, respectfulness, deference; civilization, quality of life

2 gallantry, gallantness, **chivalry,** chivalrousness, knightliness; courtliness, courtly behaviour *or* politeness; *noblesse oblige* (*French*)

3 mannerliness, manners, **good manners,** excellent *or* exquisite manners, good *or* polite deportment, good *or* polite behaviour, *bienséance* (*French*); *savoir-faire, savoir-vivre* (*both French*); correctness, correctitude, **etiquette** see 580.3

4 good breeding, breeding; refinement, finish, polish, culture, cultivation; gentility, gentleness, genteelness, elegance; gentlemanliness, gentlemanlikeness, ladylikeness

5 suavity, suaveness, smoothness, smugness, blandness; **unctuousness,** oiliness, oleaginousness, smarm *or* smarminess (*informal*); **glibness,** slickness (*informal*), fulsomeness; sweet talk, fair words, soft words *or* tongue, sweet *or* honeyed words *or* tongue, incense; soft soap (*informal*)

6 courtesy, civility, amenity, urbanity, attention, polite act, act of courtesy *or* politeness, graceful gesture; old-fashioned courtesy *or* civility, courtliness

7 amenities, courtesies, civilities, gentilities, graces, elegancies; dignities; formalities, ceremonies, rites, rituals, observances

8 regards, compliments, respects, *égards, devoirs* (*both French*); **best wishes,** one's best, good wishes, best regards, kind *or* kindest regards, love, best love; greetings see 585.3; remembrances, kind remembrances; compliments of the season

9 gallant, cavalier, chevalier, **knight,** "a verray parfit gentil knight"—Chaucer

10 "the very pink of courtesy"—Shakespeare, "the very pineapple of politeness"—R B Sheridan, "the mirror of all courtesy"—Shakespeare

verbs

11 to mind one's manners, mind one's P's and Q's (*informal*); keep a civil tongue in one's head; mend one's manners; observe etiquette, observe *or* follow protocol

12 to extend courtesy, do the honours, pay one's respects, make one's compliments, present oneself, pay attentions to, do service, wait on *or* upon

13 to give one's regards *or* compliments *or* love, give one's best regards, give one's best, send one's regards *or* compliments *or* love; wish one joy, wish one luck, bid Godspeed

adjectives

14 courteous, polite, civil, urbane, gracious, graceful, agreeable, affable, fair; complaisant; obliging, accommodating; **thoughtful, considerate,** tactful, solicitous; respectful, deferential, attentive

15 gallant, chivalrous, chivalric, knightly; courtly; formal, ceremonious; old-fashioned, old-world

16 mannerly, well-mannered, good-mannered, well-behaved, well-spoken; correct, correct in one's manners *or* behaviour; housebroken (*informal*)

17 well-bred, highbred, well-brought-up; cultivated, cultured, polished, refined, genteel, gentle; gentlemanly, gentlemanlike, ladylike

18 suave, smooth, smug, bland, glib, unctuous, oily, oleaginous, smarmy (*informal*), fulsome, ingratiating, disarming; suave-spoken, fine-spoken, fair-spoken, soft-spoken, smooth-spoken, smooth-tongued, honey-tongued, honey-mouthed

adverbs

19 courteously, politely, civilly, urbanely, mannerly; gallantly, chivalrously, courtly, knightly; graciously, gracefully, with good grace; complaisantly, complacently; out of consideration *or* courtesy; obligingly, accommodatingly; respectfully, attentively, deferentially

505 DISCOURTESY

nouns

1 discourtesy, discourteousness; **impoliteness,** unpoliteness; **rudeness, incivility,** inurbanity, **ungraciousness, ungallantness,** uncourtesy, uncourtliness, ungentlemanliness, **unmannerliness,** mannerlessness, bad *or* ill manners, **ill breeding,** conduct unbecoming a gentleman, caddishness; inconsiderateness, inconsideration, unsolicitousness, unsolicitude, tactlessness, **insensitivity; crassness, grossness,** crass *or* gross behaviour, **boorishness, vulgarity, coarseness, crudeness,** offensiveness, loutishness, yobbishness, nastiness

2 disrespect, disrespectfulness see 156.1; **insolence** see 142

3 gruffness, brusqueness, *brusquerie* (*French*), curtness, shortness, sharpness, abruptness, bluntness, brashness; **harshness,** roughness, severity;

truculence, aggressiveness; **surliness,** crustiness, bearishness, beastliness, churlishness

adjectives

4 **discourteous,** uncourteous; **impolite,** unpolite; **rude, uncivil, ungracious, ungallant,** uncourtly, inaffable, uncomplaisant, unaccommodating; disrespectful; **insolent**

5 **unmannerly,** unmannered, mannerless, **ill-mannered, ill-behaved,** ill-conditioned

6 **ill-bred, ungenteel,** ungentle, caddish; **ungentlemanly,** ungentlemanlike; **unladylike,** unfeminine; **vulgar, boorish, unrefined** see 497.12, **inconsiderate, unsolicitous, tactless, insensitive; crass,** offensive, gross, **coarse, crude,** loutish, yobbish, nasty

7 **gruff, brusque, curt,** short, sharp, snippy *(informal),* abrupt, **blunt,** bluff, brash, cavalier; **harsh,** rough, severe; truculent, aggressive; **surly,** crusty, bearish, beastly, churlish

adverbs

8 **discourteously, impolitely, rudely,** uncivilly, ungraciously, ungallantly, ungenteelly, caddishly; inconsiderately, unsolicitously, tactlessly, insensitively

9 **gruffly, brusquely, curtly,** shortly, sharply, snippily *(informal),* abruptly, bluntly, bluffly, brashly, cavalierly; harshly, crustily, bearishly, churlishly, **boorishly,** nastily

506 RETALIATION

nouns

1 **retaliation, reciprocation,** exchange, interchange, give-and-take; **retort, reply,** return, comeback *(informal);* counter, counterblow, counterstroke, counterblast, recoil, boomerang, backlash

2 **reprisal, requital, retribution; recompense, compensation** see 338, **reward,** comeuppance *(informal),* desert, deserts, **just deserts,** what is merited, what is due *or* condign, what's coming to one *and* a taste of one's own medicine *(both informal);* quittance, return of evil for evil; **revenge** see 507; **punishment** see 604

3 **tit for tat, measure for measure,** like for like, quid pro quo, something in return, blow for blow, a Roland for an Oliver, a game two can play, **an eye for an eye,** a tooth for a tooth, "eye for eye, tooth for tooth, hand for hand, foot for foot"—BIBLE, law of retaliation *or* equivalent retaliation, *lex talionis (Latin),* talion

verbs

4 **to retaliate, retort,** counter, **strike back,** hit back at *(informal),* give in return; **reciprocate,** give in exchange, give and take; **get** *or* **come back at** *(informal),* turn the tables on

5 **to requite,** quit, make requital *or* reprisal *or* retribution, get satisfaction, recompense, compensate, make restitution, indemnify, reward, redress, make amends, **repay,** pay, **pay back,** pay off; **give one his comeuppance** *(informal),* give one his desserts *or* just desserts, serve one right, give one what is coming to him *(informal)*

6 **to give in kind,** cap, match, give as good as one gets *or* as was sent; repay in kind, **pay one in one's own coin** *or* **currency, give one a dose of one's own medicine** *(informal);* return the like, return the compliment; return like for like, **return evil for evil;** return blow for blow, **give one tit for tat,** give a quid pro quo, give as good as one gets, give measure for measure, give *or* get an eye for an eye and a tooth for a tooth, follow *or* observe the *lex talionis*

7 **to get even with** *(informal),* even the score, **settle** *or* **settle up with, settle** *or* **square accounts** *and* settle the score *(all informal),* pay off old scores, get one's own back, pay back in full measure, be quits; **take revenge** see 507.4; **punish** see 604.10, 11

adjectives

8 **retaliatory,** retaliative; **retributive,** retributory; reparative, compensatory, restitutive, recompensing, recompensive, reciprocal; punitive

adverbs

9 **in retaliation, in exchange,** in reciprocation; **in return,** in reply; **in requital, in reprisal,** in retribution, in reparation, in amends; **in revenge,** *en revanche (French)*

phrases

10 **what goes around comes around,** one's chickens come home to roost; the shoe is on the other foot

507 REVENGE

nouns

1 **revenge, vengeance, avengement,** sweet revenge, getting even, evening of the score; **wrath;** revanche, revanchism; **retaliation, reprisal** see 506.2; vendetta, feud, blood feud; the wrath of God

2 **revengefulness, vengefulness, vindictiveness,** rancour, grudgefulness, irreconcilableness, unappeasableness, implacableness, implacability

3 **avenger, vindicator;** revanchist; Nemesis, the Furies, the Erinyes, the Eumenides

verbs

4 **to revenge, avenge, take** *or* **exact revenge,** have one's revenge, wreak one's vengeance; **retaliate, even the score, get even with** see 506.4-7; launch a vendetta

5 **to harbour revenge,** breathe vengeance; have accounts to settle, have a bone to pick with; nurse one's revenge, brood over, dwell on *or* upon, keep the wound open, wave the bloody shirt *(US)*

6 **to reap** *or* **suffer** *or* **incur vengeance** *or* revenge; sow the wind and reap the whirlwind; live by the sword and die by the sword

adjectives

7 **revengeful, vengeful,** avenging; **vindictive,** vindicatory; revanchist; **punitive,** punitory; **wrathful,** rancorous, grudgeful, irreconcilable, unappeasable, implacable, unwilling to forgive and forget, unwilling to let bygones be bygones; **retaliatory** see 506.8

508 RIDICULE

nouns

1 **ridicule, derision, mockery, raillery,** rallying, chaffing; panning *and* roasting *and* ragging (*all informal*), **scoffing, jeering,** razzing (*US & Canadian informal*), piss-taking (*informal*), **sneering,** sniggering, snickering, smirking, grinning, leering, fleering, snorting, levity, flippancy, smartness, joshing (*US informal*), fooling, japery, twitting, taunting, booing, hooting, catcalling, hissing; **banter** *see* 490

2 **gibe, scoff, jeer,** fleer, flout, **mock,** barracking, **taunt,** quip, jest, jape, leg-pull (*informal*), foolery; **insult** *see* 156.2; scurrility, caustic remark; **cut,** cutting remark, verbal thrust; gibing retort, rude reproach, short answer, back answer, comeback (*informal*), parting shot, Parthian shot

3 **boo, booing, hoot, catcall,** slow handclap; raspberry (*informal*), Bronx cheer (*US informal*); **hiss, hissing,** the bird (*informal*)

4 scornful laugh *or* smile, snigger, snicker, **smirk,** sardonic grin, leer, fleer, **sneer,** snort

5 **sarcasm, irony, cynicism, satire,** satiric wit *or* humour, invective, innuendo; causticity *see* 144.8

6 **burlesque, lampoon,** squib, **parody, satire, farce,** mockery, imitation, wicked imitation *or* pastiche, takeoff *and* send-up (*both informal*), **travesty, caricature**

7 **laughingstock,** jestingstock, gazingstock, derision, mockery, **figure of fun,** byword, byword of reproach, jest, joke, **butt,** target, stock, toy, game, **fair game,** victim, Aunt Sally, dupe, fool, everybody's fool, monkey, mug

verbs

8 **to ridicule, deride,** ride (*informal*), make a laughingstock *or* a mockery of; roast (*informal*), **insult** *see* 156.5; **make fun** *or* **game of, poke fun at,** make merry with, put one on *and* pull one's leg (*both informal*); **laugh at,** laugh in one's face, grin at, smile at, snigger *or* snicker at; **laugh to scorn,** hold in derision, laugh out of court, hoot down; point at, point the finger of scorn; pillory; take the piss out of (*informal*)

9 **to scoff, jeer, gibe,** barrack, **mock, revile, rail at, rally,** chaff, **twit, taunt,** jape, flout, scout; cut at; jab, jab at, dig at, take a dig at; pooh, **pooh-pooh;** sneer, **sneer at,** fleer, curl one's lip

10 **to boo, hiss, hoot,** catcall, blow a raspberry (*informal*), give the bird (*informal*), whistle at, give the Bronx cheer (*US informal*)

11 **to burlesque, lampoon, satirize, parody, caricature,** travesty, take off *and* send up (*both informal*)

adjectives

12 **ridiculing, derisive, derisory; mocking, railing,** rallying, chaffing; panning *and* roasting *and* ragging (*all informal*), **scoffing,** jeering, sneering, snickering, sniggering, smirky, smirking, grinning, leering, fleering, snorting, flippant, smart, smart-arse (*informal*); fooling, japing, taunting, booing, hooting, catcalling, hissing, bantering, joshing (*US informal*), kidding, teasing, quizzical

13 **satiric, satirical; sarcastic, ironic, ironical,** sardonic, cynical, Rabelaisian, dry; caustic

14 **burlesque, farcical, broad,** slapstick; parodic, caricatural, macaronic, doggerel

adverbs

15 **derisively, mockingly, scoffingly,** jeeringly, sneeringly,
"with scoffs and scorns and contumelious taunts"—
SHAKESPEARE

509 APPROVAL

nouns

1 **approval, approbation;**
"Our polite recognition of another's resemblance to ourselves"—AMBROSE BIERCE, "the daughter of ignorance"—FRANKLIN; **sanction,** acceptance, countenance, **favour; admiration, esteem, respect** *see* 155; **yes,** endorsement, vote, favourable vote, yea vote, yea, voice, adherence, blessing, seal of approval, nod, stamp of approval, **OK** *see* 332.4

2 **applause,** plaudit, éclat, **acclaim, acclamation; popularity;** clap, handclap, **clapping,** handclapping, clapping of hands; **cheer** *see* 116.2; burst of applause, peal *or* thunder of applause; **round of applause, hand, big hand; ovation,** standing ovation

3 **commendation,** good word, acknowledgment, recognition, appreciation; **puff,** promotion; **blurb** *and* **plug** *and* promo *and* hype (*all informal*); honourable mention

4 **recommendation,** letter of recommendation; **advocacy,** advocating, advocation, patronage; **reference, credential,** letter of reference, voucher, **testimonial;** character reference, character, certificate of character, good character; letter of introduction

5 **praise,** bepraisement; **laudation,** laud; **glorification,** glory, exaltation, magnification, **honour; eulogy,** éloge *and* hommage (*both French*), eulogium; **encomium,** accolade, kudos, panegyric; paean; **tribute,** homage, meed of praise; congratulation *see* 149.1; flattery *see* 511; overpraise, excessive praise, idolizing, idolatry, deification, apotheosis, adulation, lionizing, hero worship

6 **compliment,** polite commendation, complimentary *or* flattering remark, stroke (*US & Canadian informal*); **bouquet** *and* posy (*both informal*)

7 **praiseworthiness, laudability,** laudableness, commendableness, estimableness, meritoriousness, exemplariness, admirability

8 **commender,** eulogist, eulogizer; **praiser,** lauder, extoller, encomiast, panegyrist, promoter; tout *and* touter (*both informal*); **applauder,** claqueur (*French*); claque; fan *and* buff (*both informal*), adherent; appreciator; **flatterer** *see* 138.3, 511.4

verbs

9 **to approve, approve of,** think well of, take kindly to; **sanction, accept; admire, esteem, respect** *see* 155.4; **endorse, bless,** sign off on (*informal*), **OK** *see* 332.12; **countenance,** keep in countenance; hold

with, uphold; **favour**, be in favour of, view favourably, take kindly to

10 **to applaud, acclaim, hail; clap,** clap one's hands, give a hand *or* big hand, have *or* hear a hand *or* big hand for, hear it for (*informal*); **cheer** see 116.6; root for (*informal*), cheer on; encore; cheer *or* applaud to the very echo

11 **to commend, speak well** *or* **highly of,** speak in high terms of, speak warmly of, have *or* say a good word for; promote, cry up; plug *and* tout *and* hype; pour *or* spread *or* lay it on thick (*all informal*); **recommend, advocate,** put in a word *or* good word for, support, back, lend one's name *or* support *or* backing to, make a pitch for (*informal*)

12 **to praise,** bepraise, talk one up (*informal*); **laud,** belaud; **eulogize,** panegyrize, pay tribute, salute, hand it to one (*informal*); **extol, glorify,** magnify, exalt, bless; cry up, puff up; boast of, brag about (*informal*), bum up (*Scottish informal*), make much of; celebrate, emblazon, sound *or* resound the praises of, ring one's praises, sing the praises of, trumpet; praise to the skies, *porter aux nues* (*French*); flatter see 511.5; overpraise, praise to excess, idolize, deify, apotheosize, adulate, lionize, hero-worship; put on a pedestal

13 **to espouse,** join *or* associate oneself with, take up, take for one's own; **campaign for, crusade for,** put on a drive for, take up the cudgels for, push for (*informal*); carry the banner of, march under the banner of; beat the drum for, thump the tub for; lavish oneself on, fight the good fight for; devote *or* dedicate oneself to, spend *or* give *or* sacrifice oneself for

14 **to compliment, pay a compliment,** make one a compliment, give a bouquet *or* posy (*informal*), say something nice about; hand it to *and* have to hand it to (*both informal*), pat on the back, take off one's hat to, doff one's cap to, congratulate see 149.2

15 **to meet with approval,** find favour with, **pass muster,** recommend itself, do credit to; redound to the honour of; sing with the praises of

adjectives

16 **approbatory, approbative, commendatory, complimentary, laudatory,** acclamatory, eulogistic, panegyric, panegyrical, encomiastic, **appreciative, appreciatory; admiring, regardful, respectful** see 155.8; flattering see 511.8

17 **approving, favourable,** favouring, in favour of, **pro,** well-disposed, well-inclined, supporting, backing, **advocating;** promoting, promotional; touting *and* hyping (*both informal*)

18 **uncritical,** uncriticizing, **uncensorious,** unreproachful; overpraising, overappreciative, unmeasured *or* excessive in one's praise, idolatrous, adulatory, lionizing, hero-worshipping, fulsome; knee-jerk (*informal*)

19 **approved,** favoured, backed, advocated, supported; favourite; **accepted,** received, admitted; **recommended,** bearing the seal of approval, highly touted (*informal*), **admired** see 155.11, **applauded,** well-thought-of, in good odour, **acclaimed,** cried up; **popular**

20 **praiseworthy,** worthy, **commendable,** estimable, **laudable,** admirable, meritorious, creditable; exemplary, model, unexceptionable; deserving, well-deserving; beyond all praise, *sans peur et sans reproche* (*French*); **good** see 998.12, 13

prepositions

21 **in favour of, for, pro,** all for

exclamations

22 **bravo!,** bravissimo!, **well done!,** ¡eole! (*Spanish*), bene! (*Italian*), beaut! (*Australian & NZ*), hear, hear!, aha!; hurrah!; **good!,** fine!, excellent!, super!, great!, beautiful!, swell!, good for you!, not bad!, now you're talking!; attaboy!, attagirl!, attagal!, good boy!, good girl!, way to go! (*US*); that's the idea!, that's the ticket!; encore!, bis!, take a bow!, three cheers!, one cheer more!, **congratulations!** see 149.4

23 **hail!,** all hail!, *ave!* (*Latin*), *vive!* (*French*), *viva!*, *evviva!* (*both Italian*), live live!, long life to!, glory be to!, honour be to!

510 DISAPPROVAL

nouns

1 **disapproval, disapprobation,** disfavour, disesteem, disrespect see 156; dim view, poor *or* low opinion, low estimation, adverse judgment; **displeasure,** distaste, **dissatisfaction,** discontent, discontentment, discontentedness, disgruntlement, indignation, **unhappiness;** disillusion, disillusionment, disenchantment, disappointment; disagreement, **opposition** see 451, opposure; rejection, thumbs down, exclusion, ostracism, blackballing, blackball, ban; **complaint, protest,** objection, **dissent** see 333

2 **deprecation,** discommendation, dispraise, denigration, disvaluation; **ridicule** see 508; depreciation, disparagement see 512; **contempt** see 157

3 **censure, reprehension,** stricture, reprobation, **blame, denunciation,** denouncement, decrying, decrial, bashing *and* trashing (*both informal*), impeachment, arraignment, indictment, **condemnation,** damnation, fulmination, anathema; castigation, flaying, skinning alive (*informal*), fustigation, excoriation; pillorying

4 **criticism,** adverse criticism, harsh *or* hostile criticism, flak (*informal*), bad notices, bad press, animadversion, imputation, reflection, **aspersion,** stricture, obloquy; **knock** *and* **swipe** *and* **slam** *and* **rap** *and* blast (*all informal*); minor *or* petty criticism, niggle, cavil, quibble, exception, nit (*informal*); **censoriousness,** reproachfulness, priggishness; **faultfinding,** taking exception, carping, cavilling, pettifogging, quibbling, captiousness, niggling, nitpicking, pestering, nagging; hypercriticism, hypercriticalness, overcriticalness, hairsplitting, trichoschistism

5 **reproof,** reproval, reprobation, a flea in one's ear; **rebuke, reprimand, reproach,** reprehension, **scolding, chiding,** rating, **upbraiding,** objurgation; **admonishment, admonition; correction,** castigation, chastisement, rap on the knuckles;

lecture, lesson, sermon; **disrecommendation,** low rating, adverse report

6 (*informal terms*) piece *or* bit of one's mind, **talking-to,** speaking-to, roasting, carpeting, raking-down, **raking-over,** raking over the coals, slating, dressing, dressing-down, set-down; **bawling-out,** wigging, rollicking, going-over, reaming, rocket, what-for, ticking-off

7 **berating,** rating, tongue-lashing, bollocking (*informal*), mouthful; **revilement, vilification,** blackening, **execration, abuse, vituperation,** invective, contumely, hard *or* cutting *or* bitter words; **tirade, diatribe,** jeremiad, screed, philippic; **attack, assault,** onslaught, assailing; **abusiveness;** acrimony

8 **reproving look,** dirty look (*informal*), black look, frown, scowl

9 **faultfinder,** *frondeur* (*French*), momus; **critic** *see* 945.7, captious critic, criticizer, **nitpicker** (*informal*), belittler, censor, censurer, carper, caviler, quibbler, petti-fogger; **scold,** common scold; kvetch, **complainer** *see* 108.3

verbs

10 **to disapprove, disapprove of,** not approve, raise an objection, go *or* side against, go contra; **disfavour,** view with disfavour, **raise one's eyebrows, frown at** *or* **on,** look black upon, look askance at, make a wry face at, grimace at, **turn up one's nose at,** shrug one's shoulders at; **take a dim view of** (*informal*), not think much of, think ill of, think little of, not take kindly to, not hold with, hold no brief for (*informal*); not hear of, not go for *and* not get all choked up over *and* be turned off by (*all informal*); not want *or* have any part of, wash one's hands of, dissociate oneself from; **object to,** take exception to; **oppose** *see* 451.3, set oneself against, set one's face *or* heart against; **reject,** categorically reject, disallow, not hear of; give the thumbs down (*informal*), vote down, veto, frown down, exclude, ostracize, blackball, ban; say no to, shake one's head at; **dissent from, protest, object** *see* 333.4, 5; turn over in one's grave

11 **to discountenance,** not countenance, **not tolerate,** not brook, not condone, not suffer, not abide, not endure, not bear with, not put up with, **not stand for** (*informal*)

12 **to deprecate,** discommend, dispraise, disvalue, not be able to say much for, denigrate, **fault,** faultfind, find fault with, put down (*informal*), pick at *or* on, pick holes in, pick to pieces, slate; **ridicule** *see* 508.8; **depreciate, disparage** *see* 512.8; **hold in contempt,** disdain, **despise** *see* 157.3

13 **to censure,** reprehend; **blame,** lay *or* cast blame upon; trash *and* rubbish (*both informal*); **reproach,** impugn; **condemn,** damn, take out after; damn with faint praise; fulminate against, anathematize, anathemize, put on the Index; **denounce,** denunciate, **accuse** *see* 599.7, 9, **decry,** cry down, impeach, arraign, indict, call to account, exclaim *or* declaim *or* inveigh against, peg away at, cry out against, cry out on *or* upon, cry shame upon, raise one's voice against, raise a hue and cry against, shake up (*old*); reprobate, hold up to reprobation;

animadvert on *or* upon, reflect upon, cast reflection upon, cast a reproach *or* slur upon, complain against; throw a stone at, cast *or* throw the first stone

14 **to criticize; pan** *and* **knock** *and* **slam** *and* **rap** *and* **blast** *and* **take a swipe at** (*all informal*), snipe at, strike out at, **rip into** *and* **open up on** *and* **plough into** (*all informal*)

15 **to find fault,** take exception, fault-find, pick holes, cut up, pick *or* pull *or* tear apart, **pick** *or* **pull** *or* **tear to pieces; tear down, carp, cavil,** quibble, **nitpick,** pick nits, pettifog, catch at straws

16 **to nag,** niggle, **carp at, fuss at, fret at, pester,** henpeck, pick on (*informal*), bug *and* hassle (*both informal*)

17 **to reprove, rebuke, reprimand,** reprehend, put a flea in one's ear, **scold, chide,** rate, **admonish, upbraid,** objurgate, have words with, tear someone off a strip, take a hard line with; **lecture,** read a lesson *or* lecture to; **correct,** rap on the knuckles, **chastise,** spank, turn over one's knees; **take to task,** call to account, bring to book, carpet (*informal*), read the riot act, give one a tongue-lashing, tonguelash; take down, set down, set straight, straighten out

18 (*informal terms*) to give someone a dressing-down *or* wigging *or* ticking off, **speak** *or* **talk to, tell off,** tell a thing or two, pin one's ears back, give a piece of one's mind, haul over the coals, rake up one side and down the other, give it to, let one have it, let one have it with both barrels, come down on *or* down hard on, jump on *or* all over *or* down one's throat; give one a hard time *or* what for; **bawl out,** give a bawling out, sit on *or* upon, lambaste, give a going-over, tell where to get off

19 **to berate,** rate, betongue, **tongue-lash, rail at,** rag, thunder *or* fulminate against, rave against, yell at, bark *or* yelp at; **revile, vilify,** blacken, **execrate, abuse,** vituperate, load with reproaches

20 (*criticize or reprove severely*) **to attack, assail; castigate, flay,** skin alive (*informal*), lash, slash, **excoriate,** fustigate, scarify, scathe, **roast** (*informal*), scorch, blister, trounce

adjectives

21 **disapproving, disapprobatory,** unapproving, turned-off, **displeased, dissatisfied,** less than pleased, discontented, disgruntled, indignant, **unhappy;** disillusioned, disenchanted, disappointed; **unfavourable,** low, poor, **opposed** *see* 451.8, **opposing, con,** against, agin (*informal*), dead set against, death on, down on, **dissenting** *see* 333.6; **uncomplimentary;** unappreciative

22 **condemnatory, censorious,** censorial, damnatory, **denunciatory, reproachful,** blameful, reprobative, objurgatory, po-faced, priggish, judgmental; deprecative, deprecatory; **derisive, ridiculing, scoffing** *see* 508.12; **depreciative, disparaging** *see* 512.13; **contemptuous** *see* 157.8; invective, inveighing; reviling, vilifying, blackening, execrating, execrative, execratory, abusive, vituperative

23 **critical, faultfinding,** carping, nitpicking (*informal*), cavilling, quibbling, pettifogging, captious, cynical; nagging, niggling; hypercritical, ultracritical, overcritical, hairsplitting, trichoschistic

24 unpraiseworthy, illaudable; **uncommendable,** discommendable; **objectionable,** exceptionable, unacceptable, not to be thought of, beyond the pale
25 **blameworthy,** blamable, to blame, at fault, much at fault; **reprehensible,** censurable, reproachable, reprovable, open to criticism *or* reproach; **culpable,** chargeable, impeachable, accusable, indictable, arraignable, imputable

adverbs

26 **disapprovingly, askance,** askant, **unfavourably;** censoriously, critically, reproachfully, rebukingly; captiously

exclamations

27 **God forbid!,** Heaven forbid!, Heaven forfend!, forbid it Heaven!; by no means!, not for the world!, not on your life!, over my dead body!, not if I know it!, nothing doing! (*US informal*), no way! *and* no way José! (*both informal*), perish the thought!, I'll be hanged *or* damned if!, **shame!,** for shame!, tut-tut!

511 FLATTERY

nouns

1 **flattery, adulation; praise** *see* 509.5; **blandishment,** palaver, **cajolery,** cajolement, flannel, wheedling; **blarney** *and* bunkum *and* **soft soap** (*all informal*), eyewash (*informal*); ego massage (*informal*), sweet talk, fair *or* sweet *or* honeyed words, soft *or* honeyed phrases, incense, pretty lies, sweet nothings; trade-last (*old informal*), **compliment** *see* 509.6; sucking up (*informal*), **fawning, sycophancy** *see* 138.2
2 **unction,** "that flattering unction"—SHAKESPEARE; **unctuousness,** oiliness; gush, smarm *and* smarminess (*both informal*); flattering tongue; insincerity *see* 354.5
3 **overpraise,** overprizing, excessive praise, overcommendation, overlaudation, overestimation; idolatry *see* 509.5
4 **flatterer,** *flatteur* (*French*), adulator, courtier; **cajoler, wheedler; backslapper,** back-scratcher; blarneyer *and* soft-soaper (*both informal*); boot-licker (*informal*), brown-noser (*informal*), crawler, **sycophant** *see* 138.3

verbs

5 **to flatter,** adulate, conceit; **cajole, wheedle, blandish,** palaver; slaver *or* slobber over, beslobber, beslubber; oil the tongue, lay the flattering unction to one's soul, make fair weather; **praise, compliment** *see* 509.14, praise to the skies; scratch one's back, kiss ass (*US & Canadian informal*), crawl, brown-nose, fawn upon *see* 138.9
6 (*informal terms*) **to flannel, soft-soap, butter up,** soften up; massage the ego (*informal*); **blarney,** jolly, pull one's leg; lay it on (*informal*), pour *or* spread *or* lay it on thick *or* with a trowel (*informal*), overdo it; string along; play up to, get around
7 **to overpraise,** overprize, overcommend, overlaud; overesteem, overestimate, overdo it, protest too much; idolize *see* 509.12, put on a pedestal

adjectives

8 **flattering, adulatory; complimentary** *see* 509.16; **blandishing, cajoling, wheedling,** blarneying *and* soft-soaping (*both informal*); fair-spoken, fine-spoken, smooth-spoken, smooth-tongued, **mealymouthed,** honey-mouthed, honey-tongued, honeyed, oily-tongued; fulsome, slimy, gushing, protesting too much, smarmy (*informal*), insinuating, **unctuous,** smooth, bland; insincere; courtly, courtierly; **fawning, sycophantic, obsequious;** brown-nosing *and* ass-kissing (*both informal*)

512 DISPARAGEMENT

nouns

1 **disparagement, faultfinding, depreciation, detraction,** deprecation, derogation, bad-mouthing *and* running down *and* knocking *and* putting down *and* doing down (*all informal*), **belittling;** sour grapes; slighting, minimizing, faint praise, lukewarm support, discrediting, decrying, decrial; **disapproval** *see* 510; **contempt** *see* 157; indignity, disgrace, comedown (*informal*)
2 **defamation,** malicious defamation, defamation of character, injury of *or* to one's reputation; **vilification,** revilement, defilement, blackening, denigration; **smear,** character assassination, *ad hominem* (*Latin*), *or* personal attack, name-calling, smear word, smear campaign; **muckraking, mudslinging**
3 **slander, scandal, libel,** traducement; calumny, calumniation; backbiting, cattiness *and* bitchiness (*both informal*)
4 **aspersion, slur, remark, reflection,** imputation, **insinuation,** suggestion, sly suggestion, innuendo, whispering campaign; disparaging *or* uncomplimentary remark; **personality,** personal
5 **lampoon,** send-up (*informal*), pasquinade, pasquin, pasquil, squib, lampoonery, **satire,** malicious parody, **burlesque** *see* 508.6; poison pen, hatchet job
6 **disparager, depreciator,** decrier, detractor, critic, belittler, debunker, deflater, slighter, derogator, **knocker** (*informal*), caustic critic, hatchet man; **slanderer,** libeler, defamer, backbiter; calumniator, traducer; **muckraker, mudslinger,** social critic; cynic, railer, Thersites, "A man who knows the price of everything, and the value of nothing"—OSCAR WILDE
7 **lampooner,** lampoonist, **satirist,** pasquinader; poison-pen writer

verbs

8 **to disparage, depreciate, belittle,** slight, minimize, make little of, degrade, debase, **run** *or* **knock down** (*informal*), **put down** (*informal*), do down; **discredit,** bring into discredit, reflect discredit upon, disgrace; detract from, derogate from, cut down to size (*informal*); **decry,** cry down; speak ill of; slag *or* slag off (*both informal*); criticize, speak slightingly of, not speak well of; disapprove of *see* 510.10; hold in contempt *see* 157.3; submit to indignity *or* disgrace, bring down, bring low

9 to defame, malign, bad-mouth (*informal*); asperse, cast aspersions on, cast reflections on, injure one's reputation, damage one's good name, give one a black eye (*informal*); slur, cast a slur on, do a number *or* a job on (*informal*), tear down

10 to vilify, revile, defile, sully, soil, smear, smirch, besmirch, bespatter, tarnish, blacken, denigrate, blacken one's good name, give a black eye (*informal*); call names, give a bad name, give a dog a bad name, stigmatize see 661.9; muckrake, throw mud at, mudsling, heap dirt upon, drag through the mud; engage in personalities

11 to slander, libel; calumniate, traduce; stab in the back, backbite, speak ill of behind one's back

12 to lampoon, satirize, pasquinade; parody, send up (*informal*); dip the pen in vitriol, burlesque see 508.11

adjectives

13 disparaging, derogatory, derogative, depreciatory, depreciative, deprecatory, slighting, belittling, minimizing, detractory, pejorative, back-biting, catty *and* bitchy (*both informal*), contumelious, contemptuous, derisive, derisory, ridiculing see 508.12; snide, insinuating; censorious; defamatory, vilifying, slanderous, scandalous, libellous; calumnious, calumniatory; abusive, scurrilous, scurrile (*old*)

513 CURSE

nouns

1 curse, malediction, malison, damnation, denunciation, commination, imprecation, execration; blasphemy; anathema, fulmination, thundering, excommunication; ban, proscription; hex, evil eye, *malocchio* (*Italian*)

2 vilification, abuse, revilement, vituperation, invective, opprobrium, obloquy, contumely, calumny, scurrility, blackguardism; disparagement see 512

3 cursing, cussing (*informal*), swearing, profanity, profane swearing, foul *or* profane *or* obscene *or* blue *or* bad *or* strong *or* unparliamentary *or* indelicate language, vulgar language, vile language, colourful language, effing and blinding (*informal*), unrepeatable expressions, dysphemism, billingsgate, ribaldry, evil speaking, dirty language *or* talk (*informal*), obscenity, scatology, coprology, filthy language, filth

4 oath, profane oath, curse; four-letter word *and* swearword, naughty word, no-no (*informal*), foul invective, expletive, epithet, dirty name (*informal*), dysphemism, obscenity

verbs

5 to curse, accurse, damn, darn, confound, blast, anathematize, fulminate *or* thunder against, execrate, imprecate; excommunicate; call down evil upon, call down curses on the head of; put a curse on; curse up hill and down dale; curse with bell, book, and candle; blaspheme; hex, give the evil eye, throw a whammy (*informal*)

6 to curse, swear, cuss (*informal*), curse and swear, execrate, take the Lord's name in vain; swear like a trooper, cuss like a sailor, make the air blue, swear till one is blue in the face; scatologize, coprologize, dysphemize, use strong language

7 to vilify, abuse, revile, vituperate, blackguard, call names, epithet, epithetize; swear at, damn

adjectives

8 cursing, maledictory, imprecatory, damnatory, denunciatory, epithetic, epithetical; abusive, vituperative, contumelious; calumnious, calumniatory; execratory, comminatory, fulminatory, excommunicative, excommunicatory; scurrilous, scurrile (*old*); blasphemous, profane, foul, foulmouthed, vile, thersitical, dirty (*informal*), obscene, dysphemistic, scatologic, scatological, coprological, toilet, sewer, cloacal; ribald, Rabelaisian, raw, risqué

9 cursed, accursed, bloody (*informal*), bleeding (*informal*), bally (*informal*), damned, damn, damnable, goddamned, goddamn, execrable

10 (*euphemisms*) confounded, deuced, blessed, blasted, dashed, ruddy, flipping, flaming, darned (*US*), danged (*US*), doggone *or* doggoned (*US*); blankety-blank

exclamations

11 damn!, damn it!, God damn it! *or* goddam it!, confound it!, hang it!, devil take!, a plague upon!, a pox upon!, *parbleu!* (*French*), *verdammt!* (*German*)

12 (*euphemistic oaths*) darn!, dash!, drat!, blast!, lumme!, blimey!, cor blimey!, cripes!, crikey!, crivvens! (*Scottish*), drat!, golly!, gosh!, heck!, dang! (*US*), doggone! (*US*)

514 THREAT

nouns

1 threat, menace, threateningness, threatfulness, promise of harm, knife poised at one's throat, arrow aimed at one's heart, sword of Damocles; imminent threat, powder keg, time bomb, imminence see 839; foreboding; warning see 399; sabre-rattling, muscle-flexing, bulldozing, scare tactics, intimidation see 127.6, arm-twisting (*informal*); denunciation, commination; veiled *or* implied threat, idle *or* hollow *or* empty threat

verbs

2 to threaten, menace, bludgeon, bulldoze, put the heat *or* squeeze on (*informal*), lean on (*informal*); hold a pistol to one's head, terrorize, intimidate, twist one's arm *and* arm-twist (*both informal*); utter threats against, shake *or* double *or* clench one's fist at; hold over one's head; denounce, comminate; lower, spell *or* mean trouble, look threatening, loom, loom up; be imminent see 839.2; forebode see 133.11; warn see 399.5

adjectives

3 threatening, menacing, threatful, minatory, minacious; lowering; imminent see 839.3; ominous, foreboding see 133.17; denunciatory, comminatory, abusive; fear-inspiring, intimidating, bludgeoning, muscle-flexing, sabre-rattling, bulldozing, browbeating, bullying, hectoring, blustering, terrorizing, terroristic

adverbs

4 under duress *or* threat, under the gun, at gunpoint *or* knifepoint

515 FASTING

nouns

1 **fasting,** abstinence from food; starvation; punishment of Tantalus; hunger strike

2 **fast,** lack of food; diet, spare *or* meagre diet, Lenten diet, Lenten fare,
"Lenten entertainment"—SHAKESPEARE; short commons *or* rations, starvation diet, water diet, bread and water, bare subsistence, portion control; xerophagy, xerophagia; Barmecide *or* Barmecidal feast

3 **fast day,** *jour maigre* (*French*); **Lent,** Quadragesima; Yom Kippur, Tishah B'Av *or* Ninth of Av; Ramadan

verbs

4 **to fast,** not eat, go hungry, dine with Duke Humphrey; eat sparingly

adjectives

5 **fasting,** uneating, unfed; **Lenten,** quadragesimal

516 SOBRIETY

nouns

1 **sobriety, soberness;** unintoxicatedness, uninebriatedness, undrunkenness; temperance *see* 668

verbs

2 **to sober up,** sober off; sleep it off; bring one down; dry out, go on the wagon

adjectives

3 **sober,** in one's sober senses, in one's right mind, in possession of one's faculties; clearheaded;
unintoxicated, uninebriated, uninebriate, uninebrious, undrunk, undrunken, untipsy, unbefuddled; cold *or* stone sober (*informal*), **sober as a judge,** on the wagon; dry, straight, temperate *see* 668.9

4 **unintoxicating,** nonintoxicating, uninebriating; **nonalcoholic,** soft, alcohol-free

517 SIGNS, INDICATORS

nouns

1 **sign,** telltale sign, sure sign, tip-off (*informal*), **index,** indicant, **indicator,** signal (*old*), measure; tip of the iceberg; **symptom;** note, keynote, **mark, earmark,** hallmark, **badge,** device, banner, stamp, signature, sigil, seal, trait, **characteristic,** character, peculiarity, idiosyncrasy, **property,** differentia; image, picture, **representation,** representative; insignia *see* 647

2 **symbol,** emblem, icon, token, cipher (*old*), type; **allegory; symbolism, symbology,** iconology, charactery; conventional symbol; symbolic system;

symbolization; ideogram, logogram, pictogram; **logo** (*informal*), logotype; **totem,** totem pole; love knot

3 **indication,** signification, identification, differentiation, denotation, **designation,** denomination; characterization, highlighting; **specification,** naming, pointing, pointing out *or* to, fingering (*informal*), picking out, selection; symptomaticness, indicativeness; **meaning** *see* 518; hint, suggestion *see* 551.4; **expression, manifestation** *see* 348; show, showing, disclosure *see* 351

4 **pointer,** index, **lead; direction, guide;** fist, index finger *or* mark; **arrow;** hand, hour hand, minute hand, **needle,** compass needle, lubber line; **signpost,** guidepost, finger post, direction post; milepost; blaze; guideboard, signboard *see* 352.7

5 **mark, marking;** watermark; **scratch,** scratching, engraving, graving, **score,** scotch, cut, hack, gash, blaze; bar code; nick, notch *see* 289; **scar,** cicatrix, scarification, cicatrization; **brand, earmark; stigma; stain, discolouration** *see* 1003.2; blemish, macula, **spot,** blotch, splotch, flick, patch, splash; mottle, dapple; **dot,** point; polka dot; tittle, jot; **speck, speckle,** fleck; tick, **freckle,** lentigo, mole; **birthmark,** strawberry mark, port-wine stain, vascular naevus, naevus, haemangioma; beauty mark *or* spot; caste mark; **check,** checkmark; prick, puncture; tattoo, tattoo mark

6 **line,** score, **stroke,** slash, virgule, diagonal, **dash, stripe, strip, streak, striation,** striping, streaking, bar, band; squiggle; hairline; dotted line; lineation, delineation; sublineation, **underline,** underlining, underscore, underscoring; hatching, cross-hatching, hachure

7 **print, imprint, impress, impression;** dint, dent, indent, indentation, indention, concavity; sitzmark; **stamp,** seal, sigil, signet; colophon; **fingerprint,** finger mark, thumbprint, thumbmark, dactylogram, dactylograph; **footprint,** footmark, footstep, step, vestige; hoofprint, hoofmark; pad, paw print, pawmark, pug, pugmark; claw mark; fossil print *or* footprint, ichnite, ichnolite; **bump,** boss, stud, pimple, lump, excrescence, convexity, embossment

8 **track, trail, path, course,** *piste* (*French*), **line, wake;** vapour trail, contrail, condensation trail; **spoor,** signs, traces, **scent**

9 **clue, cue, key,** tip-off (*informal*), telltale, smoking gun (*informal*), straw in the wind; **trace, vestige, spoor,** scent, whiff; **lead** *and* hot lead (*both informal*); catchword, cue word, key word; **evidence** *see* 956; **hint,** intimation, suggestion *see* 551.4

10 **marker,** mark; bookmark; **landmark,** seamark; bench mark; **milestone,** milepost; cairn, menhir, catstone; Catseye (*Trademark*), bollard; **lighthouse,** lightship, tower, Texas tower; platform, watchtower, pharos; **buoy,** aid to navigation, bell, gong, lighted buoy, nun, can, spar buoy, wreck buoy, junction buoy, special-purpose buoy; **monument** *see* 549.12

11 **identification,** identification mark; **badge,** identification badge, identification tag, dog tag (*military*), personal identification number *or* PIN number *or* PIN, **identity card** *or* **ID card** *or* **ID;**

card, business card, calling card, visiting card, *carte de visite* (*French*), press card; bus pass, railcard; letter of introduction; signature, initials, monogram, calligram; credentials; serial number; countersign, countermark; theme, theme tune *or* song; **criminal identification**, forensic tool, DNA print, genetic fingerprint, voiceprint; fingerprint *see* 517.7

12 password, watchword, countersign; token; open sesame; secret handshake; shibboleth

13 label, tag; ticket, docket, tally; **stamp, sticker;** seal, sigil, signet; cachet; stub, counterfoil; **token,** check; **brand, brand name, trade name,** trademark name; **trademark,** registered trademark; government mark, government stamp; **hallmark,** countermark; price tag; plate, bookplate, book stamp, colophon, *ex libris* (*Latin*), logotype *or* logo; International Standard Book Number *or* ISBN; masthead, imprint, title page; letterhead, billhead; running head *or* title

14 gesture, gesticulation; motion, movement; carriage, bearing, posture, poise, pose, stance, way of holding oneself; body language, kinesics; beck, beckon; shrug; charade, dumb show, **pantomime;** sign language *or* signing, gesture language, ticktack; dactylology; hand signal; peace sign, V-sign, chironomy

15 signal, sign; high sign *and* the wink *and* the nod (*all informal*); wink, flick of the eyelash, glance, leer; look in one's eyes, tone of one's voice; nod; nudge, elbow in the ribs, poke, kick, touch; **alarm** *see* 400; **beacon,** signal beacon, marker beacon, radio beacon; signal light, signal lamp *or* lantern; blinker, indicator; signal fire, beacon fire, watch fire, balefire; **flare,** parachute flare; rocket, signal rocket, Roman candle; signal gun, signal shot; signal siren *or* whistle, signal bell, bell, signal gong, **police whistle,** watchman's rattle; fog signal *or* alarm, fog bell, **foghorn,** diaphone, fog whistle, fog bell; **traffic signal,** traffic light, red light, amber light, green light; heliograph; signal flag; **semaphore,** semaphore telegraph, semaphore flag; wigwag, wigwag flag; international alphabet flag, international numeral pennant; red flag; white flag; yellow flag, quarantine flag; blue peter; Blue Ensign, Red Ensign, White Ensign; pilot flag *or* jack; signal post, signal mast, signal tower; telecommunications

16 call, summons; whistle; bird call, duck call, goose call, crow call, hawk call, dog whistle; **bugle call,** trumpet call; **reveille, taps,** last post, first post; alarm, alarum; **battle cry,** war cry, rebel yell (*US*), rallying cry; Angelus, Angelus bell

verbs

17 to signify, betoken, stand for, identify, differentiate, note (*old*), speak of, talk, **indicate,** be indicative of, be an indication of, be significant of, connote, denominate, argue, bespeak, be symptomatic *or* diagnostic of, symptomize, **characterize, mark,** highlight, be the mark *or* sign of, give token, **denote, mean** *see* 518.8; testify, give evidence; **show, express, display, manifest** *see* 348.5, **hint,** suggest *see* 551.10, reveal, **disclose** *see* 351.4; entail, involve *see* 771.4

18 to designate, specify; denominate, name, denote; stigmatize; **symbolize, stand for,** typify, be taken as, symbol, emblematize, figure (*old*); **point to,** refer to, advert to, allude to, make an allusion to; pick out, select; **point out,** point at, put *or* lay one's finger on, finger (*informal*)

19 to mark, make a mark, put a mark on, frank; pencil, chalk; mark out, demarcate, delimit, define; **mark off, check, check off,** tick, tick off, chalk up; punctuate, point; **dot, spot,** blotch, splotch, dash, **speck, speckle,** fleck, freckle; mottle, dapple; blemish; **brand,** stigmatize; **stain, discolour** *see* 1003.6; stamp, seal, punch, impress, imprint, **print, engrave; score, scratch,** gash, scotch, scar, scarify, cicatrize; nick, notch *see* 289.4; **blaze,** blaze a trail; **line, seam,** trace, **stripe, streak,** striate; hatch; **underline, underscore;** prick, puncture, tattoo, riddle, pepper

20 to label, tag, tab, ticket; stamp, seal; **brand, earmark;** hallmark; bar-code

21 to gesture, gesticulate; motion, motion to; beckon, wiggle the finger at; wave the arms, wig-wag, saw the air; shrug, shrug the shoulders; pantomime, mime, ape, take off; sign

22 to signal, signalize, sign, give a signal, make a sign; speak; flash; nod; nudge, poke, kick, dig one in the ribs, touch; wink, glance, raise one's eyebrows, leer; hold up the hand; **wave,** wave the hand, wave a flag, **flag,** flag down; **unfurl a flag,** hoist a banner, break out a flag; **show one's colours,** exchange colours; **salute,** dip; dip a flag, hail, hail and speak; half-mast; give *or* sound an alarm, raise a cry; beat the drum, sound the trumpet

adjectives

23 indicative, indicatory; connotative, indicating, signifying, signalizing; **significant,** significative, meaningful; symptomatic, symptomatologic, symptomatological, diagnostic, pathognomonic, pathognomonical; evidential, **designative,** denotative, denominative, naming; **suggestive,** implicative; **expressive,** demonstrative, exhibitive; representative; identifying, identificational; individual, peculiar, idiosyncratic; **emblematic, symbolic,** emblematical, symbolical; symbolistic, symbological, typical; figurative, figural, metaphorical; ideographic; semiotic, semantic

24 marked, designated, flagged; signed, signposted; monogrammed, individualized, personal; own-brand, own-label

25 gestural, gesticulative, gesticulatory; kinesic; pantomimic, **in pantomime,** in dumb show

518 MEANING

nouns

1 meaning, significance, signification, *significatum* (*Latin*), *signifié* (*French*), point, **sense,** idea, **purport, import,** where one is coming from (*informal*); **reference, referent;** intension, extension; denotation; dictionary meaning, lexical meaning; emotive *or* affective meaning, undertone, overtone, colouring; relevance, bearing, **relation,** pertinence *or* pertinency; **substance, gist,** pith, spirit, essence, gravamen, last word, name of the game *and* bottom line (*all informal*); **drift,** tenor; sum, sum and substance; **literal meaning, true** *or* **real meaning, unadorned meaning; secondary meaning, connotation** *see* 519.2; more than meets the eye, what is read between the lines; effect, force, impact, consequence, practical consequence, response; shifted *or* displaced meaning, implied meaning, **implication** *see* 519.2; Aesopian *or* Aesopic meaning, Aesopian *or* Aesopic language; totality of associations *or* references *or* relations, value; syntactic *or* structural meaning, grammatical meaning; symbolic meaning; metaphorical *or* transferred meaning; semantic field, semantic domain, semantic cluster; range *or* span of meaning, scope

2 intent, intention, purpose, aim, object, design, plan

3 explanation, definition, construction, sense-distinction, **interpretation** *see* 341

4 acceptation, acception, accepted *or* received meaning; **usage,** acceptance

5 meaningfulness, suggestiveness, expressiveness, pregnancy; **significance,** significancy, significantness; intelligibility, interpretability, readability; pithiness, meatiness, sententiousness

6 (*units*) sign, symbol, significant, significant, type, token, icon, verbal icon, lexeme, sememe, morpheme, glosseme, **word,** term, phrase, utterance, lexical form *or* item, linguistic form, semantic *or* semiotic *or* semasiological unit; text

7 semantics, semiotic, semiotics, significs, semasiology; lexicology

verbs

8 to mean, signify, denote, connote, import, spell, have the sense of, be construed as, have the force of; be talking *and* be talking about (*both informal*); **stand for, symbolize; imply,** suggest, argue, breathe, bespeak, betoken, **indicate; refer to; mean something,** mean a lot, have impact, come home, hit one close to home (*informal*)

9 to intend, have in mind, seek to communicate

adjectives

10 meaningful, meaning, **significant,** significative; **denotative, connotative,** denotational, connotational, intensional, extensional, associational; **referential; symbolic, metaphorical,** figurative, allegorical; transferred, extended; intelligible, interpretable, definable, readable; **suggestive,** indicative, **expressive; pregnant,** full of meaning, loaded *or* laden *or* fraught *or* freighted *or* heavy with significance; **pithy, meaty,** sententious, substantial, full of substance; pointed, full of point

11 meant, implied *see* 519.7, **intended**

12 semantic, semantological, semiotic, semasiological; lexological; **symbolic,** signific, iconic, lexemic, sememic, glossematic, morphemic, **verbal,** phrasal, lexical; structural

adverbs

13 meaningfully, meaningly, **significantly;** suggestively, indicatively; **expressively**

519 LATENT MEANINGFULNESS

nouns

1 latent meaningfulness, latency, latentness, delitescence, latent content; **potentiality,** virtuality, possibility; dormancy *see* 173.4

2 implication, connotation, import, latent *or* underlying *or* implied meaning, ironic suggestion *or* implication, more than meets the eye, what is read between the lines; meaning *see* 518; **suggestion,** allusion; coloration, tinge, undertone, overtone, undercurrent, more than meets the eye *or* ear, something between the lines, intimation, touch, nuance, innuendo; **code word,** weasel word; **hint** *see* 551.4; **inference, supposition,** presupposition, assumption, presumption; secondary *or* transferred *or* metaphorical sense; undermeaning, undermention, subsidiary sense, subsense, **subtext;** Aesopian *or* Aesopic meaning, cryptic *or* hidden *or* esoteric *or* arcane meaning, occult meaning; **symbolism, allegory**

verbs

3 to be latent, underlie, lie under the surface, lurk, lie hid *or* low, lie beneath, hibernate, lie dormant, smoulder; be read between the lines; make no sign, escape notice

4 to imply, implicate, involve, import, connote, entail *see* 771.4; mean *see* 518.8; **suggest,** lead one to believe, bring to mind; **hint, insinuate, infer, intimate** *see* 551.10; **allude to,** point to from afar, point indirectly to; write between the lines; allegorize; **suppose, presuppose,** assume, presume, take for granted; mean to say *or* imply *or* suggest

adjectives

5 latent, lurking, lying low, delitescent, **hidden** *see* 346.11, obscured, obfuscated, veiled, muffled, covert, occult, mystic (*old*), cryptic; esoteric; **underlying, under the surface,** submerged; **between the lines;** hibernating, sleeping, dormant *see* 173.14; **potential,** unmanifested, virtual, possible

6 suggestive, allusive, allusory, **indicative, inferential;** insinuating, insinuative, insinuatory; ironic; **implicative,** implicatory, implicational; referential

7 implied, implicated, involved; **meant,** indicated; **suggested, intimated, insinuated, hinted; inferred, supposed,** assumed, presumed, presupposed; subtextual, hidden, arcane, esoteric, **cryptic,** Aesopian *or* Aesopic

8 tacit, implicit, implied, understood, taken for granted

9 unexpressed, unpronounced, **unsaid, unspoken, unuttered,** undeclared, unbreathed, unvoiced, wordless, silent; **unmentioned,** untalked-of, **untold,** unsung, unproclaimed, unpublished; unwritten, unrecorded

10 symbolic, symbolical, allegoric, allegorical, figural, figurative, tropological, **metaphoric,** metaphorical, anagogic, anagogical

adverbs

11 latently, underlyingly; **potentially,** virtually

12 suggestively, allusively, inferentially, insinuatingly; impliedly; by suggestion, by allusion, etc

13 tacitly, implicitly, unspokenly, wordlessly, silently

520 MEANINGLESSNESS

nouns

1 **meaninglessness, unmeaningness, senselessness,** nonsensicality; **insignificance,** unsignificancy; **noise,** mere noise, static, empty sound, talking to hear oneself talk, phatic communion; inanity, emptiness, nullity;
"sounding brass and a tinkling cymbal"—BIBLE, "a tale told by an idiot, full of sound and fury, signifying nothing"—SHAKESPEARE; purposelessness, aimlessness, futility; dead letter

2 **nonsense, stuff and nonsense,** load of rubbish, **folderol, balderdash,** *niaiserie (French),* flummery, trumpery, **rubbish,** trash, fudge; **humbug,** gammon, hocus-pocus; rant, claptrap, fustian, rodomontade, bombast, absurdity *see* 922.3; stultiloquence, **twaddle,** twiddle-twaddle, fiddle-faddle, fiddledeedee, fiddlesticks, **blather, babble, gibber, jabber,** prate, **prattle,** palaver, rigmarole *or* rigamarole, galimatias, skimble-skamble, drivel; **gibberish,** jargon, mumbo jumbo, **double-talk,** amphigory, gobbledygook *(informal);* glossolalia, speaking in tongues

3 *(informal terms)* **bullshit,** shit, crap, cobblers, codswallop, horsefeathers, bull, poppycock, tosh, bunkum, bunk, garbage, guff, bilge, piffle, pish *(Scottish),* moonshine, a crock of shit, claptrap, tommyrot, rot, hogwash, malarkey, double Dutch, hokum, hooey, balls, bollocks, baloney, blarney, mince *(Scottish),* tripe, hot air, gas, wind, waffle, jive *(US),* applesauce *(US)*

verbs

4 **to be meaningless, mean nothing,** signify nothing, not mean a thing, not convey anything; not make sense, not figure *(informal),* not compute; **not register,** not ring any bells

5 **to talk nonsense, twaddle, piffle,** waffle, **blather, blabber, babble, jabber, gibber,** prate, **prattle;** talk through one's hat; **bullshit** *and* **shoot off one's mouth** *(both informal);* drivel, drool, run off at the mouth *(informal);* speak in tongues

adjectives

6 **meaningless, unmeaning, senseless,** purportless, importless, nondenotative, nonconnotative; **insignificant,** unsignificant; empty, inane, null; phatic, garbled, scrambled; **purposeless, aimless,** designless, **without rhyme or reason**

7 **nonsensical,** silly, poppycockish *(informal);* **foolish, absurd;** twaddling, twaddly; rubbishy, trashy; skimble-skamble; Pickwickian

adverbs

8 **meaninglessly,** unmeaningly, nondenotatively, nonconnotatively, **senselessly, nonsensically;** insignificantly, unsignificantly; **purposelessly,** aimlessly

521 INTELLIGIBILITY

nouns

1 **intelligibility, comprehensibility, apprehensibility,** prehensibility, graspability, **understandability,** knowability, cognizability, scrutability, penetrability, fathomableness, decipherability; recognizability, readability, interpretability; articulateness

2 **clearness, clarity; plainness, distinctness,** microscopical distinctness, explicitness, clear-cutness, definition; **lucidity,** limpidity, pellucidity, crystal *or* crystaline clarity, crystallinity, perspicuity, transpicuity, transparency; **simplicity,** straightforwardness, directness, literalness; unmistakableness, unequivocalness, unambiguousness; **coherence,** connectedness, consistency, structure; plain language, plain style, plain English, plain speech, unadorned style; clear, plain text, unencoded text

3 **legibility,** decipherability, **readability**

verbs

4 **to be understandable, make sense;** be plain *or* clear, be obvious, be self-evident, be self-explanatory; **speak for itself,** tell its own tale, speak volumes, have no secrets, put up no barriers; read easily

5 *(be understood)* **to get over** *or* **across** *(informal),* come through, **register** *(informal),* **penetrate, sink in,** soak in; dawn on, be glimpsed

6 **to make clear,** make it clear, **let it be understood,** make oneself understood, get *or* put over *or* across *(informal);* **simplify,** put in plain words *or* plain English, put in words of one syllable, spell out *(informal);* elucidate, **explain,** explicate, **clarify** *see* 341.10; put one in the picture; demystify, descramble; **decode, decipher;** make available to all, popularize, vulgarize

7 **to understand, comprehend, apprehend,** have, **know, conceive, realize,** appreciate, have no problem with, ken *(Scottish),* savvy *(informal),* sense, make sense out of, make something of; **fathom, follow; grasp, seize,** get hold of, grasp *or* seize the meaning, be seized of, take, **take in,** catch, **catch on,** get the meaning of, get the hang of; **master, learn** *see* 570.6–15, 551.14; **assimilate, absorb, digest**

8 *(informal terms)* **to read one loud and clear,** read, read one, get the idea, be with one, be with it, get the message, get the word, get the picture, get up to speed, get into *or* through one's head *or* thick head, get, get it, twig, catch *or* get the drift, have it taped, have it down pat, see where one is coming from, hear loud and clear, hear what one is saying, have hold of, have a fix on, know like the back *or* palm of one's hand, know inside out

9 **to perceive, see, discern, make out,** descry; see the light, see daylight *(informal),* wake up, wake up to, tumble to *(informal),* come alive; **see through,** see to the bottom of, penetrate, see into, pierce, plumb; see at a glance, see with half an eye; get *or* have someone's number *and* read someone like a book *(both informal)*

adjectives

10 intelligible, comprehensible, apprehensible,
prehensible, graspable, **knowable,** cognizable,
scrutable, **fathomable,** decipherable, plumbable,
penetrable, interpretable; **understandable,** easily
understood, easy to understand, exoteric; readable;
articulate

11 clear, crystal-clear, clear as crystal, clear as day,
clear as the nose on one's face; **plain, distinct,**
microscopically distinct, plain as a pikestaff; **definite,**
defined, well-defined, **clear-cut,** clean-cut, crisp;
direct, literal; simple, **straightforward; explicit,**
express; unmistakable, unequivocal, univocal,
unambiguous, unconfused; loud and clear (*informal*);
lucid, pellucid, limpid, crystal-clear, crystalline,
perspicuous, transpicuous, **transparent,** translucent,
luminous; **coherent,** connected, consistent

12 legible, decipherable, readable, fair; uncoded,
unenciphered, in the clear, clear, plaintext

adverbs

13 intelligibly, understandably, comprehensibly,
apprehensibly; articulately; **clearly, lucidly,**
limpidly, pellucidly, perspicuously, **simply, plainly,**
distinctly, definitely; **coherently; explicitly,**
expressly; unmistakably, unequivocally,
unambiguously; in plain terms *or* words, in plain
English, in no uncertain terms, in words of one
syllable

14 legibly, decipherably, readably, fairly

522 UNINTELLIGIBILITY

nouns

1 unintelligibility, incomprehensibility,
inapprehensibility, ungraspability, unseizability,
ununderstandability, unknowability, incognizability,
inscrutability, impenetrability, unfathomableness,
unsearchableness, numinousness; **incoherence,**
unconnectedness, ramblingness; inarticulateness;
ambiguity see 539

2 abstruseness, reconditeness; crabbedness,
crampedness, knottiness; **complexity,** intricacy,
complication see 798.1; **hardness, difficulty;**
profundity, profoundness, deepness; esotericism,
esotery

3 obscurity, obscuration, obscurantism, obfuscation,
mumbo jumbo (*informal*), mystification; perplexity;
unclearness, unclarity, unplainness, opacity;
vagueness, indistinctness, indeterminateness,
fuzziness, shapelessness, amorphousness; murkiness,
murk, mistiness, mist, fogginess, fog, darkness, dark

4 illegibility, unreadability; undecipherability,
indecipherability; scribble, scrawl, spidery handwriting

5 unexpressiveness, inexpressiveness,
expressionlessness, impassivity;
uncommunicativeness; straight face, dead pan
(*informal*), poker face (*informal*)

6 inexplicability, unexplainableness,
uninterpretability, indefinability, undefinability,
unaccountableness; insolvability, inextricability;
enigmaticalness, mysteriousness, mystery, strangeness,
weirdness

7 (*something unintelligible*) Greek, double Dutch;
gibberish, babble, jargon, garbage, gobbledygook,
noise, Babel; scramble, jumble, garble; argot, cant,
slang, secret language, Aesopian *or* Aesopic language,
code, cipher, cryptogram; glossolalia, gift of tongues

8 enigma, mystery, puzzle, puzzlement; Chinese
puzzle, crossword puzzle, jigsaw puzzle; **problem,**
puzzling *or* baffling problem, why; question, question
mark, vexed *or* perplexed question, enigmatic
question, sixty-four dollar question (*informal*);
perplexity; knot, knotty point, crux, point to be
solved; **puzzler,** poser, brain-teaser (*informal*);
mind-boggler; nut to crack, **hard** *or* **tough nut to**
crack; tough proposition (*informal*),
"a perfect nonplus and baffle to all human
understanding"—SOUTHEY, "a riddle wrapped in a
mystery inside an enigma"—WINSTON CHURCHILL

9 riddle, conundrum, charade, rebus; logogriph,
anagram; riddle of the Sphinx

verbs

10 to be incomprehensible, not make sense, be too
deep, go over one's head, be beyond one, beat one
(*informal*), elude *or* escape one, lose one, need
explanation *or* clarification *or* translation, be Greek
to, pass comprehension *or* understanding, not
penetrate; **baffle, perplex** see 970.13, riddle, be
sphinxlike, speak in riddles; speak in tongues; talk
double Dutch, babble, gibber, ramble, drivel

11 to not understand, be unable to comprehend,
not have the first idea, not get (*informal*), be unable
to get into *or* through one's head *or* thick skull; be
out of one's depth, be at sea, be lost; **not know**
what to make of, make nothing of, not be able to
account for, not make head or tail of; be unable to
see, not see the wood for the trees; go over one's
head, escape one; give up, pass (*informal*)

12 to make unintelligible, scramble, jumble, garble;
obscure, obfuscate, mystify, shadow; **complicate** see
798.3

adjectives

13 unintelligible, incomprehensible, inapprehensible,
ungraspable, unseizable, **ununderstandable,**
unknowable, incognizable; **unfathomable,**
inscrutable, impenetrable, unsearchable, numinous;
ambiguous; incoherent, unconnected, rambling;
inarticulate; past comprehension, beyond one's
comprehension, beyond understanding; Greek to one

14 hard to understand, difficult, hard, tough
(*informal*), beyond one, **over one's head,** beyond *or*
out of one's depth; knotty, cramp, crabbed; intricate,
complex, overtechnical, perplexed, **complicated** see
798.4; **scrambled,** jumbled, **garbled; obscure,**
obscured, obfuscated

15 obscure, vague, indistinct, indeterminate, fuzzy,
shapeless, amorphous; unclear, unplain, opaque,
muddy, **clear as mud** and clear as ditch water (*both*
informal); **dark,** dim, blind (*old*), shadowy; **murky,**
cloudy, foggy, fogbound, hazy, misty, nebulous

16 recondite, abstruse, abstract, transcendental;
profound, deep; hidden see 346.11; arcane,
esoteric, occult; **secret** see 345.11

17 enigmatic, enigmatical, cryptic, cryptical; sphinxlike; **perplexing, puzzling;** riddling; logogriphic, anagrammatic

18 inexplicable, unexplainable, uninterpretable, undefinable, indefinable, funny, funny peculiar (*informal*), **unaccountable; insolvable,** unsolvable, insoluble, inextricable; mysterious, mystic, mystical, shrouded *or* wrapped *or* enwrapped in mystery

19 illegible, unreadable, unclear; undecipherable, indecipherable

20 inexpressive, unexpressive, impassive, po-faced; uncommunicative; **expressionless; vacant, empty, blank;** glassy, glazed, glazed-over, fishy, wooden; deadpan, poker-faced (*informal*)

adverbs

21 unintelligibly, incomprehensibly, inapprehensibly, unununderstandably

22 obscurely, vaguely, indistinctly, indeterminately; **unclearly,** unplainly; illegibly

23 reconditely, **abstrusely;** esoterically, occultly

24 inexplicably, unexplainably, undefinably, bafflingly, **unaccountably, enigmatically; mysteriously,** mystically

25 expressionlessly, vacantly, blankly, emptily, woodenly, glassily, fishily

prepositions

26 beyond, past, above; **too deep for**

phrases

27 I don't understand, I can't see, I don't see how *or* why, **it beats me** (*informal*), you've got me (*informal*), **it's beyond me,** it's too deep for me, it has me guessing, I don't have the foggiest idea, it's Greek to me, I don't have a clue; **I give up, I pass** (*informal*)

523 LANGUAGE

nouns

1 language (*see list*), speech, tongue, *lingua* (*Latin*), spoken language, natural language; **talk, parlance, locution,** phraseology, **idiom, lingo** (*informal*); dialect; idiolect, personal usage, individual speech habits *or* performance, parole; code *or* system of oral communication, individual speech, competence, langue; **usage; language type; language family, subfamily, language group;** area language, regional language; world language, universal language

2 dead language, ancient language, lost language; parent language; classical language; living language, vernacular; sacred language *or* tongue

3 mother tongue, native language *or* tongue, natal tongue, native speech, vernacular, first language

4 standard language, standard *or* prestige dialect, acrolect; national language, official language; educated speech *or* language; literary language, written language, formal written language; classical language; correct *or* good English, **Standard English, the King's** *or* **Queen's English,** Received Standard English, Received Pronunciation *or* RP

5 nonformal language *or* **speech,** nonformal standard speech, **spoken language,** colloquial

language *or* speech, vernacular language *or* speech, vernacular; **slang;** colloquialism, colloquial usage, conversationalism, vernacularism; ordinary language *or* speech; nonformal English, conversational English, colloquial English, English as it is spoken

6 substandard *or* nonstandard language *or* **speech,** nonformal language *or* speech; vernacular language *or* speech, **vernacular,** demotic language *or* speech, vulgate, vulgar tongue, common speech; uneducated speech, illiterate speech; substandard usage; basilect; **nonformal**

7 dialect, idiom; class dialect; regional *or* local dialect; subdialect; folk speech *or* dialect, patois; **provincialism, localism, regionalism,** regional accent *see* 524.9; English accent; Northern accent; Southern accent; Scottish accent, Glaswegian, Doric, Morningside *and* Kelvinside; Welsh accent; Irish accent; Scouse; Geordie; West Country; Cockney; Estuary English; Yorkshire; Lancashire; Brummie; Anglo-Indian; Australian English, Strine (*informal*); dialect atlas, linguistic atlas; isogloss, bundle of isoglosses; speech community; linguistic community; linguistic ambience; speech *or* linguistic island, relic area

8 (*idioms*) Anglicism, Briticism, Englishism; Americanism; Gallicism, Frenchism; Irishism, Hibernicism; Canadianism, Scotticism, Germanism, Russianism, Latinism, etc

9 jargon, lingo (*informal*), **slang, cant, argot, patois, patter, vernacular;** vocabulary, phraseology; gobbledygook, mumbo jumbo, gibberish; **nonformal;** taboo language, vulgar language; obscene language, scatology; Newspeak (*George Orwell*), doublespeak, mediaspeak, technospeak

10 (*jargons*) Academese, cinemese, collegese, constablese, economese, sociologese, legalese, pedagese, telegraphese, journalese, newspaperese, officialese, medical Greek, medicalese, businessspeak, computerese, technobabble, psychobabble; Yinglish, Japlish, Franglais, Spanglish; Eurojargon; man-talk, woman-talk; shoptalk

11 lingua franca, jargon, **pidgin,** trade language; auxiliary language, interlanguage; creolized language, creole language, creole; koine; pidgin English, talkee-talkee; Kitchen Kaffir; Esperanto

12 linguistics, linguistic science, science of language; glottology, glossology (*old*); linguistic analysis; linguistic terminology, metalanguage; **philology;** paleography; speech origins, language origins, bowwow theory, dingdong theory, pooh-pooh theory; language study, foreign-language study

13 linguist, linguistic scientist, linguistician, linguistic scholar; philologist, philologer, philologian; philologaster; **grammarian,** grammatist; grammaticaster; **etymologist,** etymologer; **lexicologist; lexicographer,** glossographer, glossarist; phoneticist, phonetician, phonemicist, phonologist, orthoepist; dialectician, dialectologist; semanticist, semasiologist; paleographer

14 polyglot, linguist, **bilingual** *or* diglot, trilingual, multilingual

15 colloquializer; jargonist, jargoneer, jargonizer; slangster

verbs

16 to **speak, talk,** use language, communicate orally *or* verbally; use nonformal speech *or* style, colloquialize, vernacularize; jargon, jargonize, cant; patter

adjectives

17 **linguistic,** lingual, glottological; descriptive, structural, glottochronological, lexicostatistical, psycholinguistic, sociolinguistic, metalinguistic; **philological;** lexicological, lexicographic, lexicographical; syntactic, syntactical, **grammatical;** grammatic, semantic *see* 518.12; phonetic *see* 524.31, phonemic, phonological; morphological; morphophonemic, graphemic, paleographic, paleographical
18 **vernacular, colloquial, conversational, unliterary, nonformal,** demotic, spoken, vulgar, vulgate; unstudied, familiar, common, everyday; **substandard,** nonformal, uneducated
19 **jargonish,** jargonal; **slang,** slangy; taboo; scatological; rhyming slang
20 **idiomatic; dialect,** dialectal, dialectological; provincial, regional, local

word elements

21 lingu–, linguo–, lingui–, gloss–, glosso–, glott–, glotto–
22 types of language

affixing	monosyllabic
agglutinative	polysyllabic
analytic	polysynthetic
fusional	polytonic
incorporative	symbolic
inflectional	synthetic
isolating	tone

524 SPEECH
utterance

nouns

1 **speech, talk,** the power *or* faculty of speech, the verbal *or* oral faculty, talking, speaking, **discourse,** oral communication, vocal *or* voice *or* viva-voce communication, communication; **waffle, palaver, prattle, gab** *and* jaw-jaw (*both informal*); yakking *and* yakkety-yak (*both informal*); **words, accents;** chatter *see* 540.3; conversation *see* 541; elocution *see* 543.1; **language** *see* 523
2 "the mirror of the soul"—PUBLILIUS SYRUS, "the image of life"—DEMOCRITUS, "a faculty given to man to conceal his thoughts"—TALLEYRAND, "but broken light upon the depth of the unspoken"—GEORGE ELIOT
3 **utterance, speaking,** *parole* (*French*), locution (*old*), phonation; **speech act,** linguistic act *or* behaviour; string, utterance string, sequence of phonemes; **voice, tongue;** word of mouth, parol, the spoken word; vocable, **word** *see* 526
4 **remark, statement,** earful *and* tuppence worth (*both informal*), **word, say, saying,** utterance, observation, reflection, expression; note, thought, mention; assertion, averment, allegation, affirmation, pronouncement, position, dictum; **declaration;** interjection, exclamation; question *see*

937.10; answer *see* 938; address, greeting, apostrophe; sentence, phrase; subjoinder, Parthian shot
5 **articulateness,** articulacy, oracy, readiness *or* facility of speech; **eloquence** *see* 544
6 **articulation,** uttering, phonation, voicing, giving voice, **vocalization; pronunciation, enunciation,** utterance; **delivery, attack**
7 **intonation, inflection, modulation;** intonation pattern *or* contour, intonation *or* inflection of voice, speech tune *or* melody; suprasegmental, suprasegmental phoneme; **tone, pitch;** pitch accent, tonic accent
8 **manner of speaking,** way of saying, mode of expression; **tone of voice, voice,** *voce* (*Italian*), **tone;** voice quality, vocal style, **timbre;** voice qualifier; paralinguistic communication
9 **accent,** regional accent, brogue, twang, burr, drawl, broad accent; **foreign accent;** broken English
10 pause, juncture, open juncture, close juncture; terminal, clause terminal, rising terminal, falling terminal; sandhi; word boundary, clause boundary; pause
11 **accent,** accentuation, stress accent; **emphasis, stress, word stress;** ictus, beat, rhythmical stress; rhythm, rhythmic pattern, **cadence;** prosody, prosodics, metrics; stress pattern; level of stress; primary stress, secondary stress, tertiary stress, weak stress
12 vowel quantity, **quantity,** mora; long vowel, short vowel, full vowel, reduced vowel
13 **speech sound,** phone, vocable, phonetic unit *or* entity; puff of air, aspiration; stream of air, airstream, glottalic airstream; articulation, manner of articulation; **stop,** plosive, explosive, mute, check, occlusive, **affricate,** continuant, **liquid,** lateral, **nasal;** point *or* place of articulation; voice, voicing; sonority; aspiration, palatalization, labialization, pharyngealization, glottalization; surd, voiceless sound; sonant, voiced sound; **consonant; semivowel,** glide, transition sound; vocalic, syllabic nucleus, syllabic peak, peak; vocoid; **vowel;** monophthong, **diphthong,** triphthong; **syllable; phoneme,** segmental phoneme, morphophoneme; modification, assimilation, dissimilation; **allophone;** parasitic vowel, epenthetic vowel, svarabhakti vowel, prothetic vowel; vowel gradation, vowel mutation; doubletalk
14 **phonetics,** articulatory phonetics, acoustic phonetics; phonology; morphophonemics; orthoepy; sound *or* phonetic law; sound shift, *Lautverschiebung* (*German*); umlaut, mutation, ablaut, gradation; rhotacism, betacism; Grimm's law, Verner's law, Grassmann's law
15 **phonetician,** phonetist, phoneticist; orthoepist
16 **ventriloquism,** ventriloquy; **ventriloquist**
17 talking machine, sonovox, voder, vocoder
18 **talker, speaker,** sayer, utterer, patterer; chatterbox *see* 540.4; conversationalist *see* 541.8
19 **vocal** *or* **speech organ,** articulator; tongue, apex, tip, blade, dorsum, back; vocal cords *or* bands, vocal processes, vocal folds; voice box, larynx, Adam's apple; syrinx; arytenoid cartilages; glottis, vocal chink; lips, teeth, palate, hard palate, soft palate,

velum, alveolus, teeth ridge, alveolar ridge; nasal cavity, oral cavity; pharynx, throat *or* pharyngeal cavity

verbs

20 **to speak, talk; patter** *or* **gab** *or* **wag the tongue** (*all informal*); **mouth;** chatter *see* 540.5; converse *see* 541.9; declaim *see* 543.10

21 (*informal terms*) **to yak,** yap, yakkety-yak, gab, spiel, jaw, shoot one's mouth off, shoot the breeze (*US & Canadian*), bend one's ear, make chin music (*US & Canadian*), prattle away, talk someone's ear *or* head off, natter, spout off, sound off

22 **to speak up, speak out, say one's piece** *or* **speak one's mind, pipe up, open one's mouth,** open one's lips, say out, say loud and clear, say out loud, sound off, lift *or* raise one's voice, break silence, find one's tongue; take the floor; put in a word, get in a word edgeways; **have one's say,** put in one's tuppence worth (*informal*), get a load off one's mind (*informal*), give vent *or* voice to, pour one's heart out

23 **to say, utter, breathe,** sound, voice, vocalize, phonate, **articulate, enunciate, pronounce,** lip, give voice, give tongue, give utterance; whisper; **express,** give expression, verbalize, put in words, find words to express; **word,** formulate, put into words, couch, phrase *see* 532.4; **present,** deliver; **emit,** give, raise, **let out,** out with, come *or* give out with, put *or* set forth, pour forth; throw off, fling off; chorus, chime; **tell, communicate** *see* 343.6, 7; **convey, impart, disclose** *see* 351.4

24 **to state, declare, assert,** aver, affirm, asserverate, allege; **say,** make a statement, send a message; **announce,** tell the world, notify; **relate, recite;** quote; proclaim, nuncupate

25 **to remark, comment, observe, note; mention,** speak (*old*), let drop *or* fall, say by the way, make mention of; refer to, allude to, touch on, make reference to, call attention to; muse, reflect; opine (*informal*); interject; blurt, blurt out, exclaim

26 (*utter in a certain way*) **to murmur, mutter, mumble,** whisper, breathe, buzz, sigh; gasp, pant; exclaim, yell *see* 59.6, 8; sing, lilt, warble, chant, coo, chirp; pipe, flute; squeak; cackle, crow; bark, yelp, yap; growl, snap, snarl; hiss, sibilate; grunt, snort; roar, bellow, blare, trumpet, bray, blat, bawl, thunder, rumble, boom; scream, shriek, screech, squeal, squawk; whine, wail, blubber, sob; drawl, twang

27 **to address, speak to, talk to,** bespeak, beg the ear of; **appeal to,** invoke; apostrophize; **approach;** **buttonhole,** take by the button *or* lapel; take aside, talk to in private, closet oneself with; **accost, call to,** hail, halloo, greet, salute, speak, speak fair

28 **to pass one's lips, escape one's lips, fall from the lips** *or* **mouth**

29 to inflect, modulate, intonate

adjectives

30 **speech; language, linguistic, lingual; spoken, uttered, said,** vocalized, **voiced, verbalized, pronounced, sounded, articulated, enunciated;** vocal, voiceful; **oral, verbal, unwritten,** *viva voce* (*Latin*), nuncupative, parol

31 **phonetic,** phonic; articulatory, acoustic; intonated; pitched, pitch, **tonal,** tonic, oxytone, oxytonic, paroxytonic, barytone; **accented, stressed,** strong, heavy; unaccented, unstressed, weak, light, pretonic, atonic, posttonic; articulated; stopped, muted, checked, occlusive, nasal, nasalized, twangy, continuant, liquid, lateral, affricated; alveolabial, alveolar, alveolingual, etc; low, high, mid, open, broad, close; front, back, central; wide, lax, tense, narrow; voiced, sonant, voiceless, surd; rounded, unrounded, flat; aspirated; labialized; palatalized, soft, *mouillé* (*French*); unpalatalized, hard; pharyngealized, glottalized; **consonant,** consonantal, semivowel, glide, **vowel;** vowellike, vocoid, vocalic, syllabic; monophthongal, diphthongal, triphthongal; **phonemic,** allophonic; assimilated, dissimilated

32 **speaking, talking;** articulate, talkative *see* 540.9; **eloquent** *see* 544.8, well-spoken; true-speaking, clean-speaking, plain-speaking, plain-spoken, **outspoken,** free-speaking, free-spoken, loud-speaking, loud-spoken, soft-speaking, soft-spoken; English-speaking, etc

33 ventriloquial, ventriloquistic

adverbs

34 **orally, vocally, verbally, by word of mouth,** *viva voce* (*Latin*); from the lips of, from his own mouth

525 IMPERFECT SPEECH

nouns

1 **speech defect,** speech impediment, impairment of speech; dysarthria, dysphasia, dysphrasia; dyslalia, dyslogia; idioglossia, idiolalia; **broken speech,** cracked *or* broken voice, broken tones *or* accents; indistinct *or* blurred *or* muzzy speech; loss of voice, aphonia; **nasalization,** nasal tone *or* accent, **twang,** nasal twang, talking through one's nose; **falsetto,** childish treble, artificial voice; **shake, quaver,** tremor; **lisp,** lisping; **hiss,** sibilation; **croak,** choked voice, hawking voice; crow; harshness, dysphonia, hoarseness *see* 58.2

2 **inarticulateness,** inarticulacy; thickness of speech

3 **stammering, stuttering,** hesitation, faltering, traulism, dysphemia, *balbuties* (*Latin*); palilalia; stammer, stutter

4 **mumbling, muttering,** maundering; droning, drone; mumble, mutter; jabber, jibber, gibber, gibbering, gabble; whispering, whisper, susurration; mouthing; murmuring

5 **mispronunciation,** misspeaking, cacology, cacoepy; lallation, lambdacism, paralambdacism; rhotacism, pararhotacism; gammacism; mytacism; **corruption,** language pollution

6 **aphasia, agraphia;** aphrasia, aphrasia paranoica; **aphonia,** loss of speech, aphonia clericorum, hysterical aphonia, stage fright, aphonia paralytica, aphonia paranoica, spastic aphonia, mutism, muteness *see* 51.2

verbs

7 **to speak poorly,** talk incoherently, be unable to string two words together; have a bone in one's neck *or* throat; speak thickly; **croak; lisp; shake, quaver;**

drawl; mince, clip one's words; lose one's voice, get stage fright, freeze (*informal*)

8 **to stammer, stutter,** stammer out; have a speech impediment, hesitate, falter, halt, stumble; hem, haw, hum, **hum and haw, hem and haw**

9 **to mumble, mutter,** chunter, maunder; drone, drone on; swallow one's words, speak drunkenly *or* incoherently; jabber, gibber, gabble; splutter, sputter; blubber, sob; whisper, susurrate; murmur; mouth

10 **to nasalize,** whine, **speak through one's nose,** twang, snuffle

11 **to mispronounce,** misspeak, missay, murder the King's *or* Queen's English

adjectives

12 (*imperfectly spoken*) inarticulate, indistinct, blurred, muzzy; **mispronounced; shaky,** shaking, **quavering,** tremulous, titubant; **drawling,** drawly, **plummy; lisping; throaty, guttural,** thick, velar; stifled, choked, choking, strangled; **nasal, twangy,** breathy, adenoidal, snuffling; croaking, hawking; harsh, dysphonic, hoarse *see* 58.15

13 **stammering, stuttering,** halting, hesitating, faltering, stumbling, balbutient; **aphasic;** aphrasic; aphonic, dumb, **mute** *see* 51.12

526 WORD

nouns

1 **word,** free form, minimum free form, **term,** expression, locution, linguistic form, lexeme; content word, function word; *logos* (*Greek*), *verbum* (*Latin*); verbalism, vocable, utterance, articulation; **usage;** syllable, polysyllable; homonym, homophone, homograph; monosyllable; synonym; metonym; antonym

2 **root,** etymon, primitive; eponym; derivative, derivation; cognate; doublet

3 **morphology,** morphemics; morphophonemics; **morpheme;** morph, allomorph; bound morpheme *or* form, free morpheme *or* form; difference of form, formal contrast; accidence; **inflection,** conjugation, declension; paradigm; derivation, word-formation; formative; root, radical; theme, stem; word element, combining form; **affix, suffix, prefix,** infix; proclitic, enclitic; affixation, infixation, suffixation, prefixation; morphemic analysis, immediate constituent *or* IC analysis, cutting; morphophonemic analysis

4 **word form,** formation, construction; back formation; clipped word; spoonerism; **compound;** *tatpurusha, dvandva, karmadharaya, dvigu, avyayibhava, bahuvrihi* (*all Sanskrit*); endocentric compound, exocentric compound; acronym, acrostic; paronym, conjugate

5 **technical term,** technicality; jargon word; jargon *see* 523.9, 10

6 **barbarism, corruption, vulgarism, impropriety,** taboo word, swearword *and* four-letter word (*both informal*); **colloquialism, slang,** localism *see* 526.6

7 **loan word,** borrowing, borrowed word, paronym; loan translation, calque; foreignism

8 **neologism,** neology, neoterism, new word *or* term,

newfangled expression; **coinage;** new sense *or* meaning; **nonce word;** ghost word *or* name

9 **catchword,** catch phrase, shibboleth, slogan, cry; **pet expression,** byword, cliché; **buzzword,** vogue word, fad word, in-word; euphemism, **code word**

10 long word, hard word, jawbreaker (*informal*), polysyllable; sesquipedalian, sesquipedalia (*plural*); lexiphanicism, grandiloquence *see* 545

11 hybrid word, **hybrid;** macaronicism, macaronic; hybridism, contamination; blendword, blend, portmanteau word, portmanteau, portmantologism, telescope word, **counterword**

12 **archaism,** archaicism, antiquated word *or* expression; obsoletism, obsolete

13 **vocabulary, lexis, words, word stock,** wordhoard, stock of words; phraseology; **thesaurus,** Roget's; lexicon

14 **lexicology; lexicography,** lexigraphy, glossography; onomastics *see* 527.1, toponymics; **meaning** *see* 518, semantics, semasiology

15 **etymology, derivation, origin,** word origin, word history, semantic history; historical linguistics, comparative linguistics; eponymy; folk etymology

16 echoic word, onomatopoeic word, onomatope; onomatopoeia; bowwow theory

17 **neologist, word-coiner,** neoterist; phraser, phrasemaker, phrasemonger

adjectives

18 **verbal,** vocabular, vocabulary

19 lexical, lexicologic, lexicological; lexigraphic, lexigraphical, **lexicographical,** lexicographic; glossographic, glossographical; etymological, etymologic, derivational; onomastic, onomatologic; onomasiological; echoic, onomatopoeic; conjugate, paronymous, paronymic

20 neological, neoterical

21 **morphological,** morphemic; morphophonemic; inflective, inflectional, paradigmatic, derivational; affixal, prefixal, infixal, suffixal

word elements

22 log–, logo–, onomato–, –onym, –onymy

527 NOMENCLATURE

nouns

1 **nomenclature, terminology,** orismology, glossology (*old*); onomatology, onomastics; toponymics, toponymy, place-names, place-naming; antonomasia; polyonymy; **taxonomy,** classification, systematics, biosystematics, cytotaxonomy, binomial nomenclature, binomialism, Linnaean method, trinomialism; kingdom, phylum, class, order, family, genus, species

2 **naming, calling, denomination,** appellation, designation, designating, styling, terming, definition, identification; **christening,** baptism; dubbing; nicknaming

3 **name, appellation,** appellative, **denomination, designation, style,** *nomen* (*Latin*), **cognomen,** cognomination, full name; proper name *or* noun; moniker *and* handle (*both informal*); title, honorific; empty title *or* name; **label, tag; epithet,** byword; **scientific name,** trinomen, trinomial name,

binomen, binomial name; *nomen nudum* (*Latin*),
hyponym; tautonym; typonym; middle name;
eponym; namesake; secret name, cryptonym, euonym

4 **first name**, forename, **Christian name**, given name
(*US*), baptismal name; **middle name**

5 **surname, last name, family name, cognomen,**
byname; **maiden name**; married name; patronymic,
matronymic

6 (*Latin terms*) **praenomen, nomen, agnomen, cognomen**

7 **nickname, sobriquet**, byname, cognomen; epithet,
agnomen; pet name, diminutive, hypocoristic,
affectionate name

8 **alias, pseudonym**, anonym, **assumed name**, false
or fictitious name, *nom de guerre* (*French*); **pen
name, nom de plume**; stage name, *nom de théâtre*
(*French*), professional name; John Doe

9 **misnomer**, wrong name

10 **signature**, sign manual, **autograph, hand,** John
Hancock (*US & Canadian informal*); mark, mark of
signature, cross, christcross, X; initials; subscription;
countersignature, countersign, countermark,
counterstamp; endorsement; visa, *visé* (*French*);
monogram, cipher, device; seal, sigil, signet

verbs

11 **to name, denominate, nominate, designate, call,**
term, style, dub; specify; define, identify; **title,**
entitle; **label, tag; nickname; christen,** baptize

12 **to misname,** misnomer, **miscall,** misterm,
misdesignate

13 **to be called, be known by** *or* as, go by, go as, **go**
by the name of, go *or* pass under the name of,
bear the name of, rejoice in the name of; go under
an assumed *or* a false name, have an alias

adjectives

14 **named, called,** yclept (*old*), **styled, titled,**
denominated, denominate (*old*), **known as,** known by
the name of, designated, termed, dubbed, identified
as; christened, baptized; what one may well *or* fairly
or properly *or* fitly call

15 **nominal,** cognominal; **titular, in name only,**
nominative, formal; **so-called,** quasi; would-be, *soi-*
disant (*French*); **self-called, self-styled,** self-
christened; honorific; agnominal, epithetic,
epithetical; hypocoristic, diminutive; by name, by
whatever name, under any other name; **alias, a.k.a**
or AKA (*also known as*)

16 **denominative,** nominative, appellative; eponymous,
eponymic

17 **terminological,** nomenclatural, orismological;
onomastic; toponymic, toponymous; taxonomic,
classificatory, binomial, Linnaean, trinomial; double-
barrelled

word elements

18 log–, logo–, onomato–, –onym, –onymy

528 ANONYMITY

nouns

1 **anonymity, anonymousness, namelessness;**
incognito; cover, cover name; code name; anonym

2 what's-its-name *and* what's-his-name *and*
what's-his-face *and* what's-her-name *and* (*all*
informal); *je ne sais quoi* (*French*), I don't know what;
such-and-such; **so-and-so**, certain person, Mr X,
A.N. Other; you-know-who

adjectives

3 **anonymous, anon; nameless, unnamed,**
unidentified, undesignated, unspecified, innominate,
without a name, **unknown;** undefined;
unacknowledged; **incognito;** cryptonymous,
cryptonymic

529 PHRASE

nouns

1 **phrase, expression, locution, utterance,** usage,
term, verbalism; **word-group,** construction,
endocentric construction, headed group, syntagm;
syntactic structure; noun phrase, verb phrase, verb
complex, adverbial phrase, adjectival phrase,
prepositional phrase; **clause; sentence,** period,
periodic sentence; **paragraph; idiom,** idiotism,
phrasal verb; turn of phrase *or* expression, peculiar
expression, manner *or* way of speaking; set phrase *or*
term; conventional *or* common *or* standard phrase;
phraseogram, phraseograph

2 **diction, phrasing**

3 **phraser, phrasemaker,** phrasemonger, phraseman

adjectives

4 **phrasal, phrase**

5 in set phrases *or* terms, in good set terms, in round
terms

530 GRAMMAR

nouns

1 **grammar,** rules of language, linguistic structure,
syntactic structure;
"the rule and pattern of speech"—Horace;
grammaticalness, well-formedness, grammaticality,
grammatical theory; **traditional grammar, school**
grammar; descriptive grammar, **structural**
grammar; case grammar; phrase-structure grammar;
generative grammar, **transformational grammar,**
transformational generative grammar; tagmemic
analysis; glossematics; stratificational grammar;
parsing, grammatical analysis; **morphology** *see*
526.3; **phonology** *see* 524.14

2 **syntax, structure, syntactic structure,** word
order, word arrangement; syntactics, syntactic
analysis; immediate constituent analysis *or* IC
analysis, cutting; phrase structure; surface structure,
shallow structure, deep structure, underlying
structure; levels, ranks, strata; tagmeme, form-
function unit, slot, filler, slot and filler; **function,**
subject, predicate, complement, object, direct
object, indirect object, **modifier,** qualifier, sentence
or construction modifier, appositive, attribute,
attributive

3 **part of speech,** form class, major form class,
function class; function *or* empty *or* form word;
adjective, adjectival, attributive; **adverb,** adverbial;

preposition; verbal adjective, gerundive; **participle,** present participle, past participle, perfect participle; **conjunction,** subordinating conjunction, coordinating conjunction, conjunctive adverb, adversative conjunction, copulative, copulative conjunction, correlative conjunction, disjunctive, disjunctive conjunction; **interjection,** exclamatory noun *or* adjective; **particle**

4 **verb,** transitive, transitive verb, intransitive, intransitive verb, impersonal verb, neuter verb, deponent verb, defective verb; finite verb; linking verb, copula; verbal, verbid, nonfinite verb form; **infinitive; auxiliary verb,** auxiliary, modal auxiliary; phrasal verb; verb phrase

5 **noun, pronoun,** substantive, substantival, common noun, proper noun, concrete noun, abstract noun, collective noun, quotation noun, hypostasis, adherent noun, adverbial noun; verbal noun, gerund; nominal; noun phrase; mass noun, count noun

6 **article,** definite article, indefinite article; determiner, noun determiner, determinative, post-determiner

7 **person;** first person; second person, proximate; third person; fourth person, obviative

8 number; singular, dual, trial, plural

9 **case;** common case, subject case, nominative; object *or* objective case, accusative, dative, possessive case, genitive; local case, locative, essive, superessive, inessive, adessive, abessive, lative, allative, illative, sublative, elative, ablative, delative, terminative, approximative, prolative, perlative, translative; comitative, instrumental, prepositional, vocative; oblique case

10 **gender,** masculine, feminine, neuter, common gender; grammatical gender, natural gender; animate, inanimate

11 **mood,** mode; indicative, subjunctive, imperative, conditional, potential, obligative, permissive, optative, jussive

12 **tense; present;** historical present; **past,** preterite *or* preterit (*US*); aorist; imperfect; future; **perfect,** present perfect, future perfect; past perfect, **pluperfect;** progressive tense, durative; point tense

13 **aspect;** perfective, imperfective, inchoative, iterative, frequentative, desiderative

14 **voice;** active voice, active, passive voice, passive; middle voice, middle; medio-passive; reflexive

15 **punctuation,** punctuation marks (*see list*); diacritical mark *or* sign (*see list*); reference mark (*see list*), reference; point, tittle; stop, full stop, end stop

verbs

16 to grammaticize; **parse,** analyse; inflect, **conjugate, decline; punctuate,** mark, point; parenthesize, hyphenate, bracket; diagram, notate

adjectives

17 **grammatical, syntactical,** formal, structural; correct, well-formed; tagmemic, glossematic; **functional;** substantive, nominal, pronominal; verbal, transitive, intransitive; linking, copulative; attributive, adjectival, adverbial, participial; prepositional, post-positional; conjunctive

18 **punctuation marks**

ampersand (&)	parentheses *or* parens
angle brackets (<>)	(informal) (())
apostrophe (')	full stop, point, decimal
braces ({})	point, dot (.)
brackets ([])	question mark *or*
colon (:)	interrogation mark *or*
comma (,)	point (?)
dash (—, –)	quotation marks, quotes
ellipsis, suspension periods	("")
(...) *or* (***)	semicolon (;)
exclamation mark *or* point	single quotation marks,
(!)	single quotes ('')
hyphen (-)	virgule, diagonal, solidus,
interrobang (¡?)	slash mark, oblique (/)

19 **diacritical marks**

acute accent (´)	grave accent (`)
breve (˘)	háček (ˇ)
cedilla (¸)	macron (¯)
circumflex accent (^ *or* ˜)	tilde (˜)
diaeresis, umlaut (¨)	

20 **reference marks**

asterisk, star (*)	double prime (″)
asterism (***)	index *or* fist (☞)
bullet, centred dot (•)	leaders (.......)
caret (^)	paragraph (¶)
dagger *or* obelisk (†)	parallels (‖)
ditto mark (")	prime (′)
double dagger, diesis (‡)	section (§)

531 UNGRAMMATICALNESS

nouns

1 **ungrammaticalness,** bad *or* faulty grammar, faulty syntax; lack of concord *or* agreement, faulty reference, misplaced *or* dangling modifier, shift of tense, shift of structure, anacoluthon, faulty subordination, faulty comparison, faulty coordination, faulty punctuation, lack of parallelism, sentence fragment, comma fault, comma splice; abuse of terms, corruption of speech, broken speech

2 **solecism,** ungrammaticism, **misusage, missaying, misconstruction,** barbarism, infelicity; corruption; antiphrasis, malapropism *see* 974.7

verbs

3 to solecize, commit a solecism, use faulty *or* inadmissable *or* inappropriate grammar, ignore *or* disdain *or* violate grammar, murder the King's *or* Queen's English, break Priscian's head (*old*)

adjectives

4 **ungrammatic, ungrammatical,** solecistic, solecistical, **incorrect,** barbarous; faulty, erroneous *see* 974.16; infelicitous, improper *see* 788.7; careless, slovenly, slipshod *see* 809.15; loose, imprecise *see* 974.17

532 DICTION

nouns

1 **diction,** words, wordage, verbiage, word-usage, **usage,** *usus loquendi* (*Latin*), use *or* choice of words, formulation, way of putting *or* couching, word

garment, word dressing; **rhetoric**, speech, talk (*informal*); **language**, dialect, parlance, locution, expression, **grammar** *see* 530; **idiom**; composition

2 **style; mode, manner,** strain, vein; fashion, way; **rhetoric; manner of speaking,** mode of expression, literary style, style of writing, command of language *or* idiom, form of speech, expression of ideas; feeling for words *or* language, way with words, sense of language, *Sprachgefühl* (*German*); gift of gab *or* of the gab (*informal*), blarney *or* the blarney (*informal*); the power *or* grace of expression; linguistic tact *or* finesse; personal style; mannerism, trick, pecularity; affectation;

"the dress of thought"—CHARLES DICKENS, "a certain absolute and unique manner of expressing a thing"— WALTER PATER; inflation, exaggeration, grandiloquence *see* 545; the grand style, the sublime style, the sublime; the plain style; **stylistics,** stylistic analysis

3 **stylist,** master of style; rhetorician, rhetor, rhetorizer (*old*); mannerist

verbs

4 **to phrase, express,** find a phrase for, give expression *or* words to, **word,** state, **frame,** conceive, style, couch, **put in** *or* **into words,** clothe *or* embody in words, couch in terms, express by *or* in words, find words to express; put, present, set out; **formulate,** formularize; paragraph; rhetorize (*old*)

adjectives

5 **phrased,** expressed, worded, formulated, styled, put, presented, couched; stylistic

533 ELEGANCE
of language

nouns

1 **elegance,** elegancy; **grace,** gracefulness, gracility; **taste,** tastefulness, good taste; **correctness,** seemliness, comeliness, **propriety,** aptness, fittingness; **refinement,** precision, exactitude, lapidary quality, finish; **discrimination,** choice; **restraint; polish, finish,** terseness, neatness; smoothness, flow, **fluency; felicity,** felicitousness, **ease;** clarity, clearness, lucidity, limpidity, pellucidity, perspicuity; distinction, dignity; **purity,** chastity, chasteness; **plainness,** straightforwardness, directness, **simplicity,** naturalness, unaffectedness, Atticism, unadorned simplicity, gracility, Attic quality; classicism, classicalism; well-rounded *or* well-turned periods, flowing periods; the right word in the right place, mot juste (*French*); fittingness, appropriateness

2 **harmony, proportion,** symmetry, **balance,** equilibrium, order, orderedness, measure, measuredness, concinnity; rhythm; **euphony,** sweetness, beauty

3 (*affected elegance*) **affectation,** affectedness, studiedness, **pretentiousness, mannerism,** manneredness, artifice, artfulness, **artificiality,** unnaturalness; **euphuism,** Gongorism, Marinism; **preciousness,** preciosity; euphemism; purism;

overelegance, overelaboration, overniceness, overrefinement, hyperelegance, etc

4 **purist,** classicist, Atticist, plain stylist

5 **euphuist,** Gongorist, Marinist, *précieux* (*French*), *précieuse* (*French feminine*); phrasemaker, phrasemonger

adjectives

6 **elegant, tasteful, graceful, polished,** finished, round, terse; neat, trim, **refined, exact,** lapidary *or* lapidarian; **restrained; clear,** lucid, limpid, pellucid, perspicuous; **simple, unaffected, natural,** unlaboured, fluent, flowing, **easy; pure,** chaste; **plain,** straightforward, direct, unadorned, gracile, no-frills *and* vanilla (*both informal*); classic, classical; Attic, Ciceronian

7 **appropriate, fit, fitting,** just (*old*), **proper, correct, seemly,** comely; **felicitous,** happy, **apt, well-chosen; well-put,** well-expressed, inspired

8 **harmonious, balanced,** symmetrical, orderly, ordered, measured, concinnate, concinnous; **euphonious,** euphonic, euphonical (*old*), sweet; **smooth,** tripping, smooth-sounding, fluent, flowing

9 (*affectedly elegant*) **affected,** euphuistic, euphuistical; elaborate, elaborated; **pretentious, mannered, artificial, unnatural,** studied, plummy, posh (*informal*); precious, *précieux, précieuse* (*both French*), overnice, overrefined, overelegant, overelaborate, hyperelegant, etc; Gongoristic, Gongoresque, Marinistic

534 INELEGANCE
of language

nouns

1 **inelegance,** inelegancy; inconcinnity (*old*), infelicity; **clumsiness,** cumbrousness, leadenness, heavy-handedness, ham-fistedness, heavy-footedness, heaviness, stiltedness, **ponderousness,** unwieldiness, clunkiness *and* klutziness (*both US informal*); sesquipedalianism, sesquipedality; turgidity, bombasticness, pompousness *see* 545.1; **gracelessness,** ungracefulness; **tastelessness,** bad taste, **impropriety,** indecorousness, unseemliness; incorrectness, impurity; **vulgarity,** vulgarism, Gothicism (*old*), barbarism, barbarousness, **coarseness, unrefinement,** roughness, grossness, rudeness, crudeness, uncouthness; dysphemism; cacology, poor diction; cacophony, uneuphoniousness, harshness; loose *or* slipshod construction, ill-balanced sentences; lack of finish *or* polish

adjectives

2 **inelegant, clumsy,** heavy-handed, heavy-footed, ham-fisted, graceless, ungraceful, inconcinnate *and* inconcinnous (*both old*), infelicitous, unfelicitous, clunky *and* klutzy (*both US informal*); **tasteless,** in bad taste, naff (*informal*), offensive to sensitive ears; **incorrect, improper; indecorous, unseemly,** uncourtly, undignified; **unpolished, unrefined;** impure, unclassical; **vulgar,** barbarous, barbaric, rude, **crude, uncouth,** Doric, outlandish; low, gross, **coarse,** dysphemistic, doggerel; cacologic, cacological, cacophonous, uneuphonious, harsh, ill-sounding

3 stiff, stilted, formal, Latinate, *guindé* (*French*), **laboured,** ponderous, elephantine, lumbering, cumbrous, leaden, heavy, unwieldy, sesquipedalian, inkhorn, turgid, bombastic, pompous *see* 545.8; **forced,** awkward, cramped, halting; crabbed

535 PLAIN SPEECH

nouns

1 plain speech, plain speaking, plain-spokenness, plain style, unadorned style, gracility, **plain English,** plain words, common speech, vernacular, household words, words of one syllable; **plainness,** simpleness, simplicity;
"more matter with less art"—SHAKESPEARE; soberness, restraint; severity, austerity; spareness, leanness, baldness, bareness, starkness, unadornedness, naturalness, unaffectedness; **directness, straightforwardness,** calling a spade a spade, not mincing one's words, making no bones about it (*informal*); unimaginativeness, prosaicness, matter-of-factness, prosiness, unpoeticalness; homespun, rustic style; **candour,** frankness, openness

verbs

2 to speak plainly, waste no words, **call a spade a spade,** come to the point, lay it on the line, not beat about the bush, not mince one's words, make no bones about it (*informal*)

adjectives

3 plain-speaking, simple-speaking; **plain,** common; **simple,** unadorned, unvarnished, pure, neat; sober, severe, austere, ascetic, spare, lean, bald, bare, stark, Spartan; **natural, unaffected;** direct, straightforward, woman-to-woman, man-to-man, one-on-one; commonplace, homely, homespun, rustic; **candid,** up-front (*informal*), plain-spoken, frank, straight-out (*informal*), open; **prosaic,** prosing, prosy; unpoetical, unimaginative, dull, dry, **matter-of-fact**

adverbs

4 plainly, simply, naturally, unaffectedly, matter-of-factly; in plain words, plain-spokenly, **in plain English,** in words of one syllable; **directly,** point-blank, to the point; candidly, frankly

phrases

5 read my lips, I'll spell it out

536 FIGURE OF SPEECH

nouns

1 figure of speech (*see list*), **figure, image,** trope, turn of expression, manner *or* way of speaking, ornament, device, flourish, flower; purple passage; imagery, nonliterality, nonliteralness, figurativeness, figurative language; figured *or* florid *or* flowery style, Gongorism, floridity, euphuism

verbs

2 to metaphorize, figure (*old*); similize; personify, personalize; symbolize

adjectives

3 figurative, tropologic, tropological; **metaphorical,** trolatitious; allusive, referential; mannered, figured, ornamented, **flowery** *see* 545.11

adverbs

4 figuratively, tropologically; **metaphorically;** symbolically; **figuratively speaking,** so to say *or* speak, in a manner of speaking, **as it were**

5 figures of speech

agnomination	hysteron-proteron
alliteration	inversion
allusion	irony
anacoluthon	kenning
anadiplosis	litotes
analogy	malapropism
anaphora	meiosis
anastrophe	metalepsis
antiphrasis	metaphor
antithesis	metonymy
antonomasia	mixed metaphor
apophasis	onomatopoeia
aporia	oxymoron
aposiopesis	paradiastole
apostrophe	paralepsis
catachresis	paregmenon
chiasmus	parenthesis
circumlocution	periphrasis
climax	personification
conversion	pleonasm
ecphonesis	ploce
emphasis	polyptoton
enallage	polysyndeton
epanaphora	preterition
epanodos	prolepsis
epanorthosis	prosopopoeia
epidiplosis	regression
epiphora	repetition
eroteme	rhetorical question
exclamation	sarcasm
gemination	simile, similitude
hendiadys	spoonerism
hypallage	syllepsis
hyperbaton	symploce
hyperbole	synecdoche
hypozeugma	Wellerism
hypozeuxis	zeugma

537 CONCISENESS

nouns

1 conciseness, concision, briefness, brachylogy, **brevity,**
"the soul of wit"—SHAKESPEARE; shortness, compactness; **curtness,** brusqueness, **crispness, terseness,** summariness; taciturnity *see* 344.2, reserve *see* 344.3; **pithiness,** succinctness, pointedness, sententiousness; compendiousness

2 laconicness, laconism, laconicism, economy of language; laconics

3 aphorism, epigram *see* 973.1; **abridgment** *see* 557

4 abbreviation, shortening, clipping, cutting, pruning,

truncation; ellipsis, aposiopesis, contraction, syncope, apocope, elision, crasis, syneresis (*all rhetoric*)

verbs

5 **to be brief, come to the point,** get to the bottom, line *or* the nitty-gritty (*informal*), **cut a long story short,** cut the matter short, cut the crap (*informal*), be telegraphic, waste no words, put it in few words, give more matter and less art; shorten, condense, **abbreviate** *see* 268.6

adjectives

6 **concise, brief, short,**
"short and sweet"—THOMAS LODGE; **condensed, compressed,** tight, close, compact; compendious *see* 268.8; **curt,** brusque, **crisp, terse,** summary; taciturn *see* 344.9; reserved *see* 344.10; **pithy, succinct;** laconic, Spartan; **abridged, abbreviated,** vest-pocket, synopsized, shortened, clipped, cut, pruned, contracted, truncated, docked; elliptic, aposiopestic; sententious, epigrammatic, epigrammatical, gnomic, aphoristic(al), **pointed,** to the point

adverbs

7 **concisely, briefly,** shortly, standing on one leg; laconically; **curtly,** brusquely, **crisply, tersely,** summarily; **pithily, succinctly,** pointedly; sententiously, aphoristically, epigrammatically

8 **in brief, in short,** for short, *tout court* (*French*); in substance, in epitome, in outline; **in a nutshell,** in a capsule; **in a word,** in two words, in a few words, without wasting *or* mincing words; **to be brief,** to come to the point, to cut the matter short, **to cut a long story short**

538 DIFFUSENESS

nouns

1 **diffuseness,** diffusiveness, diffusion; shapelessness, **formlessness** *see* 263, amorphousness, blobbiness (*informal*), unstructuredness; obscurity *see* 522.3

2 **wordiness, verbosity,** verbiage, verbalism, verbality; **prolixity, long-windedness,** longiloquence; flow *or* flux of words, cloud of words; **profuseness,** profusiveness, profusion; **effusiveness,** effusion, gush, gushing; outpour, tirade; logorrhoea, verbal diarrhoea, diarrhoea of the mouth, **talkativeness** *see* 540; **copiousness, exuberance,** rampancy, amplitude, extravagance, prodigality, fertility, fecundity, rankness, teemingness, prolificity, prolificacy, productivity, abundance, overflow, fluency (*old*); superfluity, superflux, superabundance, overflow, inundation; **redundancy,** pleonasm, repetitiveness, reiterativeness, reiteration, iteration, tautology, macrology; repetition for effect *or* emphasis, palilogy

3 discursiveness, desultoriness, digressiveness, aimlessness; rambling, maundering, meandering, wandering, roving

4 **digression, departure,** deviation, **discursion,** excursion, excursus, sidetrack, side path, side road, byway, bypath; episode

5 **circumlocution, roundaboutness,** circuitousness, ambages (*old*); deviousness, obliqueness, **indirection;** periphrase, periphrasis

6 **amplification, expatiation, enlargement, expansion,** dilation, dilatation, dilating; **elaboration, labouring; development,** explication, unfolding, working-out, fleshing-out, detailing, filling in the empty spaces

verbs

7 **to amplify, expatiate, dilate, expand, enlarge, enlarge on,** expand on, **elaborate;** relate *or* rehearse in extenso; detail, particularize; **develop,** open out, fill in, flesh out, evolve, unfold; work out, explicate; descant, relate at large

8 **to protract, extend, spin out,** string out, draw out, stretch out, go on *or* be on about, **drag out,** run out, drive into the ground (*informal*); pad, fill out; perorate; **speak at length,** spin a long yarn, never finish; verbify, chatter, talk one to death *see* 540.5, 6

9 **to digress,** wander, **get off the subject, wander from the subject,** get sidetracked, excurse, ramble, maunder, stray, go astray; depart, **deviate,** turn aside, jump the track; **go off on a tangent,** go up blind alleys

10 **to circumlocute** (*informal*), say in a roundabout way, talk in circles, **go round about,** go around and around, **beat around** *or* **about the bush;** periphrase

adjectives

11 **diffuse,** diffusive; **formless** *see* 263.4, unstructured; **profuse,** profusive; **effusive,** gushing, gushy; copious, exuberant, extravagant, prodigal, fecund, teeming, prolific, productive, abundant, superabundant, overflowing; **redundant,** pleonastic, repetitive, reiterative, iterative, tautologous, parrotlike

12 **wordy, verbose; talkative** *see* 540.9; prolix, windy (*informal*), **long-winded,** longiloquent; **protracted,** extended, *de longue haleine* (*French*), lengthy, long, **long-drawn-out,** long-spun, spun-out, endless, unrelenting; padded, filled out

13 **discursive, aimless,** loose; **rambling, maundering, wandering,** peripatetic, roving; excursive, **digressive,** deviative, **desultory,** episodic; by-the-way

14 **circumlocutory,** circumlocutional, **roundabout, circuitous,** ambagious (*old*), oblique, indirect; periphrastic

15 **expatiating,** dilative, dilatative, enlarging, amplifying, expanding; **developmental**

adverbs

16 **at length,** *ad nauseam* (*Latin*), at large, in full, *in extenso* (*Latin*), in detail

539 AMBIGUITY

nouns

1 **ambiguity,** ambiguousness; **equivocalness,** equivocacy, equivocality; **double meaning,** amphibology, multivocality, polysemy, polysemousness; punning, paronomasia; double reference, double entendre; twilight zone, grey area;

six of one and half dozen of the other; inexplicitness, uncertainty *see* 970; irony, contradiction, oxymoron, enantiosis; levels of meaning, richness of meaning, complexity of meaning

2 (*ambiguous word or expression*) **ambiguity**, equivoque, equivocal, equivocality; equivocation, amphibology, double entendre; counterword, portmanteau word; polysemant; weasel word; squinting construction; pun *see* 489.8

verbs

3 to equivocate, weasel; ironize; have mixed feelings, be uncertain *see* 970.9

adjectives

4 **ambiguous, equivocal**, equivocatory; multivocal, polysemous, polysemantic, amphibolous, amphibological; two-edged, two-sided, either-or, betwixt and between; bittersweet, mixed; inexplicit, uncertain *see* 970.15; ironic; obscure, mysterious, funny, funny peculiar (*informal*), enigmatic *see* 522.17

540 TALKATIVENESS

nouns

1 **talkativeness**, loquacity, loquaciousness; overtalkativeness, loose tongue, big mouth (*informal*); **garrulousness**, garrulity; **long-windedness, prolixity, verbosity** *see* 538.2; multiloquence, multiloquy; **volubility, fluency, glibness**; fluent tongue, flowing tongue, **gift of gab** (*informal*); openness, candour, frankness *see* 644.4; effusion, gush, slush; gushiness, **effusiveness**; flow *or* flux *or* spate of words; *flux de bouche, flux de mots,* and *flux de paroles* (*all French*); **communicativeness** *see* 343.3; gregariousness, sociability, conversableness *see* 582

2 logomania, logorrhoea, diarrhoea of the mouth, verbal diarrhoea, *cacoëthes loquendi, furore loquendi* (*both Latin*)

3 **chatter, jabber, gibber, babble,** babblement, prate, **prating, prattle, palaver,** chat, natter, **gabble, gab** *and* jaw-jaw (*both informal*), blab, **blabber, blather,** blether, blethers (*Scottish*), waffle, clack, cackle, talkee-talkee; *caquet, caqueterie, bavardage* (*all French*), twaddle, twattle, **chitter-chatter, prittle-prattle, tittle-tattle,** mere talk, idle talk *or* chatter, "the hare-brained chatter of irresponsible frivolity"— DISRAELI; guff *and* gas *and* **hot air** *and* blah-blah *and* yakkety-yak (*all informal*); **gossip;** nonsense talk *see* 520.2

4 **chatterer, chatterbox, babbler, jabberer, prater, prattler, gabbler,** gibble-gabbler, **gabber** (*informal*), **blabberer, blabber,** blatherer, patterer, word-slinger, *moulin à paroles* (*French*), blab, waffler, "agreeable rattle"— GOLDSMITH; magpie, jay; **windbag** *and* gasbag *and* hot-air artist *and* motormouth *and* ratchet-jaw (*all informal*); idle chatterer, talkative person, **big** *or* **great talker** (*informal*), spendthrift of one's tongue

verbs

5 to **chatter, chat, prate, prattle, patter,** palaver, **babble, gab** (*informal*), natter, **gabble,** tittle-tattle,

jabber, gibber, **blab, blabber, blather,** blether, twaddle, twattle, rattle, gibber (*informal*), clack, waffle, rabbit (*informal*), natter *and* haver, dither, spout *or* **spout off** (*informal*), pour forth, **gush,** have a big mouth (*informal*), love the sound of one's own voice, talk to hear one's head rattle (*informal*); **jaw** *and* **gas** *and* yak yakkety-yak *and* run off at the mouth (*all informal*), shoot one's mouth off (*informal*); reel off; **talk on, talk away, go on** (*informal*), run on, rattle on, run on like a mill race; ramble on; talk oneself hoarse, talk till one is blue in the face, talk oneself out of breath; "varnish nonsense with the charms of sound"— CHARLES CHURCHILL; **talk too much; gossip;** talk nonsense *see* 520.5

6 (*informal terms*) to talk one to death, talk one's head *or* ear off, talk one deaf and dumb, talk one into a fever, talk the hind leg off a mule

7 to **outtalk, outspeak, talk down,** outlast; filibuster, talk out

8 to be loquacious *or* garrulous, be a windbag *or* gasbag (*informal*); have a big mouth (*informal*)

adjectives

9 **talkative, loquacious,** talky (*US & Canadian*), big-mouthed (*informal*), overtalkative, garrulous, chatty; gossipy, newsy; all mouth (*informal*); multiloquent, multiloquious; **longwinded, prolix, verbose** *see* 538.12; voluble, fluent; glib, smooth; candid, frank *see* 644.17; **effusive, gushy;** expansive, **communicative;** conversational; gregarious, sociable

10 **chattering, prattling, prating,** gabbling, jabbering, gibbering, babbling, blabbing, blabbering, blathering, waffling, rabbiting (*informal*)

adverbs

11 **talkatively, loquaciously,** garrulously; **volubly, fluently,** glibly; effusively, gushingly

541 CONVERSATION

nouns

1 **conversation, converse,** conversing; interlocution, colloquy; **exchange;** verbal intercourse, conversational interchange, interchange of speech, give-and-take, crosstalk, **repartee,** backchat; **discourse,** colloquial discourse; **communion, intercourse, communication** *see* 343

2 **the art of conversation,** "a game of circles", "our account of ourselves"— BOTH EMERSON, "the sweeter banquet of the mind", "the feast of reason and the flow of soul"— BOTH POPE

3 **talk, palaver, speech, words;** confabulation, **confab** (*informal*); chinwag *and* talkfest (*both informal*); **dialogue,** duologue, trialogue; **interview,** question-and-answer session

4 **chat,** cosy chat, friendly chat *or* talk, **little talk,** causerie, **visit** (*informal*), *tête-à-tête* (*French*), **heart-to-heart talk** *or* heart-to-heart; pillow-talk, intimate discourse

5 **chitchat, tittle-tattle, small talk,** cocktail-party chitchat, tea-table talk, table talk, idle chat, gossip backchat

6 conference, congress, convention, parley, palaver, confab (*informal*), confabulation, conclave, powwow, huddle (*informal*), consultation, *pourparler* (*French*), surgery, meeting, annual general meeting *or* AGM, extraordinary general meeting *or* EGM; session, sitting, sit-down (*informal*), séance; exchange *or* interchange of views; council, council of war; discussion; interview, audience; news conference, press conference; photo opportunity; high-level talk, conference at the summit, summit, summit conference; summitry; negotiations, bargaining, bargaining session; confrontation, eyeball-to-eyeball encounter (*informal*); teleconference; council fire; conference table, negotiating table

7 discussion, debate, debating, deliberation, nonformalogue, exchange of views, canvassing, ventilation, airing, review, treatment, consideration, investigation, examination, study, analysis, logical analysis; logical discussion, dialectic; brainstorming session *or* brainstorm; panel, panel discussion, open discussion, joint discussion, symposium, colloquium, conference, seminar; forum, open forum, town meeting

8 conversationalist, converser, conversationist; talker, discourser, verbalist, confabulator; colloquist, colloquialist, collocutor; conversational partner; interlocutor, interlocutress *or* interlocutrice *or* interlocutrix; parleyer, palaverer; dialogist; Dr Johnson

verbs

9 to converse, talk together, talk *or* speak with, converse with, strike up a conversation, visit with (*informal*), discourse with, commune with, communicate with, take counsel with, commerce with, have a talk with, have a word with, chinwag (*informal*), chew the fat (*informal*), shoot the breeze (*informal*), hold *or* carry on *or* join in *or* engage in a conversation; confabulate, confab (*informal*); colloque, colloquize;
"inject a few raisins of conversation into the tasteless dough of existence"—O Henry; bandy words; communicate *see* 343.6, 7

10 to chat, pass the time of day, have a friendly *or* cosy chat, touch base with (*US*); have a little talk, have a heart-to-heart talk, let one's hair down; talk with one in private, talk with one *tête-à-tête*, be closeted with, make conversation *or* talk, engage in small talk; prattle, tittle-tattle; gossip

11 to confer, hold a conference, parley, palaver, powwow, sit down together, meet around the conference table, go into a huddle (*informal*), deliberate, take counsel, counsel, lay *or* put heads together; collogue; confer with, sit down with, consult with, advise with, discuss with, take up with, reason with; discuss, talk over; consult, refer to, call in; compare notes, exchange observations *or* views; have conversations; negotiate, bargain

12 to discuss, debate, reason, deliberate, deliberate upon, exchange views *or* opinions, talk, talk over, hash over (*informal*), talk of *or* about, comment upon, reason about, discourse about, consider, treat, dissertate on, handle, deal with, take up, go into, examine, investigate, talk out, analyse, sift,

study, canvass, review, pass under review, controvert, ventilate, air, thresh out, reason the point, consider pros and cons; kick *or* knock around (*informal*)

adjectives

13 conversational, colloquial, confabulatory, interlocutory; communicative; chatty, cosy

adverbs

14 conversationally, colloquially; *tête-à-tête* (*French*)

542 SOLILOQUY

nouns

1 soliloquy, monology, self-address; monologue; aside; solo; monodrama; apostrophe

2 soliloquist, soliloquizer, Hamlet; monologist

verbs

3 to soliloquize, monologize; talk to oneself, say to oneself, tell oneself, think out loud *or* aloud; address the four walls; say aside; do all the talking, monopolize the conversation, hold forth without interruption

adjectives

4 soliloquizing, monologic, monological, self-addressing; apostrophic; soloistic; monodramatic

543 PUBLIC SPEAKING

nouns

1 public speaking, declamation, speechmaking, speaking, speechification (*informal*), lecturing, speeching; after-dinner speaking; oratory, platform oratory *or* speaking; campaign oratory, the stump, the hustings; the soap box, Speakers' corner; elocution; rhetoric, art of public speaking; eloquence *see* 544; forensics, debating; speechcraft, wordcraft; preaching, pulpit oratory, Bible-thumping (*informal*), the pulpit, homiletics; demagogism, demagogy, demagoguery, rabble-rousing; pyrotechnics

2 speech, speeching, speechification (*informal*), talk, oration, address, declamation, harangue; public speech *or* address, formal speech, set speech, prepared speech *or* text; campaign speech, stump speech (*US*); say; tirade, screed, diatribe, jeremiad, philippic, invective; after-dinner speech; funeral oration, eulogy; allocution, exhortation, hortatory address, forensic, forensic address; recitation, recital, reading; salutatory, salutatory address; valediction, valedictory, valedictory address; inaugural address, inaugural; chalk talk (*US & Canadian informal*); pep talk (*informal*); pitch, sales talk *see* 734.5; talkathon, filibuster; peroration; debate

3 lecture, prelection, discourse; sermon, sermonette, homily, religious *or* pulpit discourse; preachment, preaching, preachification (*informal*); evangelism, TV evangelism *or* televangelism; travel talk, travelogue

4 speaker, talker, public speaker, speechmaker, speecher, speechifier (*informal*); after-dinner speaker;

spokesman, spokeswoman; **demagogue**, rabble-rouser; declaimer, ranter, tub-thumper (*informal*), haranguer, spouter (*informal*); valedictorian, salutatorian; panellist, debater

5 lecturer, praelector, discourser, reader; **preacher**; sermonizer, sermonist, sermoner, homilist (*old*), pulpitarian, pulpiteer (*informal*), Boanerges, hellfire preacher; **evangelist**, televison *or* TV evangelist; **expositor**, expounder; chalk talker (*US & Canadian informal*)

6 orator, **public speaker**, platform orator *or* speaker; rhetorician, rhetor; silver-tongued orator, **spellbinder**; Demosthenes, Cicero, Winston Churchill, Nye Bevan, Martin Luther King; **soapbox orator**, soapboxer, stump orator (*US & Canadian*)

7 elocutionist, elocutioner; **recitationist**, reciter, diseur, diseuse; reader; improvisator, *improvvisatore* (*Italian*)

8 rhetorician, teacher of rhetoric, rhetor, elocutionist; speech-writer

verbs

9 to make a speech, give a talk, deliver an address, speechify (*informal*), **speak, talk,** discourse; address; stump (*informal*), go on *or* take the stump; platform, soapbox; take the floor

10 to declaim, hold forth, **orate**, elocute (*informal*), spout (*informal*), spiel (*informal*), mouth; **harangue, rant,**
"out-herod Herod"—Shakespeare, tub-thump, perorate, rodomontade; **recite**, read; debate; demagogue, rabble-rouse

11 to lecture, prelect, read *or* deliver a lecture; **preach**, Bible-thump *and* preachify (*both informal*), **sermonize**, read a sermon

adjectives

12 declamatory, elocutionary, oratorical, **rhetorical**, forensic; eloquent *see* 544.8; demagogic, demagogical

544 ELOQUENCE

nouns

1 eloquence, rhetoric, silver tongue, eloquent tongue, facundity; **articulateness**; gift of gab (*informal*), **glibness**, smoothness, slickness; **felicitousness**, felicity; oratory *see* 543.1; expression, **expressiveness**, command of words *or* language *or* English, gift of the gab (*informal*), gift of expression, vividness; pleasing *or* effective style; **meaningfulness** *see* 518.5

2 fluency, flow; **smoothness, facility, ease; grace,** gracefulness, poetry; **elegance** *see* 533

3 vigour, force, power, strength, vitality, drive, sinew, sinewiness, nervousness, nervosity, vigorousness, forcefulness, effectiveness, impressiveness, pizzazz *and* punch *and* clout (*all informal*); incisiveness, trenchancy, cuttingness, poignancy, bitingness, bite, mordancy; strong language,
"thoughts that breathe and words that burn"—Thomas Gray

4 spirit, pep (*informal*), liveliness, raciness, sparkle, vivacity, dash, verve, vividness; piquancy, poignancy, pungency

5 vehemence, **passion**, impassionedness, enthusiasm, **ardour**, ardency, **fervour**, fervency, fire, fieriness, glow, warmth

6 loftiness, elevation, sublimity; grandeur, **nobility**, stateliness, majesty, gravity, *gravitas* (*Latin*), solemnity, **dignity**

verbs

7 to have the gift of the gab (*informal*), have a tongue in one's head; **spellbind**; shine, "pour the full tide of eloquence along"—Pope

adjectives

8 eloquent, silver-tongued, silver; well-speaking, well-spoken, **articulate**, fecund; **glib, smooth,** smooth-spoken, smooth-tongued, **slick; felicitous;** facile, slick as a whistle (*informal*), spellbinding; Demosthenic, Demosthenian; Ciceronian, Tullian

9 fluent, flowing, tripping; **smooth**, pleasing, facile, easy, graceful, elegant *see* 533.6

10 expressive, graphic, vivid, suggestive, imaginative; well-turned; **meaningful** *see* 518.10

11 vigorous, strong, **powerful**, imperative, **forceful**, forcible, vital, driving, sinewy, sinewed, punchy *and* zappy (*both informal*), **striking, telling, effective**, impressive; incisive, trenchant, cutting, biting, piercing, poignant, penetrating, slashing, mordant, acid, corrosive; sensational

12 spirited, lively, peppy (*informal*), racy, sparkling, vivacious; piquant, poignant, pungent

13 vehement, emphatic, **passionate, impassioned**, enthusiastic, **ardent**, fiery, fervent, burning, glowing, warm; urgent, stirring, exciting, stimulating, provoking

14 lofty, elevated, sublime, grand, majestic, noble, stately, grave, solemn, dignified; serious, weighty; moving, inspiring

adverbs

15 eloquently; fluently, smoothly, glibly, trippingly on the tongue; **expressively**, vividly, graphically; **meaningfully** *see* 518.13; vigorously, powerfully, forcefully, spiritedly; tellingly, strikingly, effectively, impressively; **vehemently, passionately**, ardently, fervently, warmly, glowingly, in glowing terms

545 GRANDILOQUENCE

nouns

1 grandiloquence, magniloquence, lexiphanicism, **pompousness**, pomposity, orotundity; **rhetoric**, mere rhetoric, rhetoricalness; high-flown language, big talk (*informal*); grandioseness, grandiosity; loftiness, stiltedness; fulsomeness; **pretentiousness**, pretension, **affectation** *see* 533.3; ostentation; **flamboyancy**, showiness, flashiness, gaudiness, meretriciousness, bedizenment, **glitz** (*informal*), garishness; sensationalism, luridness, Barnumism; **inflation, inflatedness**, swollenness, turgidity, turgescence, flatulence *or* flatulency, tumidness, tumidity; sententiousness, pontification; swollen

phrase *or* diction, swelling utterance; platitudinous ponderosity, polysyllabic profundity, pompous prolixity; Johnsonese; prose run mad; convolution, tortuosity, tortuousness, ostentatious complexity *or* profundity

2 **bombast**, bombastry, **fustian**, **rant**, rodomontade; **hot air** (*informal*); balderdash, gobbledygook (*informal*)

3 high-sounding words, lexiphanicism, hard words; **sesquipedalian word**, big *or* long word, **jawbreaker**, jawtwister, mouthful; antidisestablishmentarianism, honorificabilitudinitatibus (*Shakespeare*), pneumonoultramicroscopicsilicovolcanoconiosis; polysyllabism, sesquipedalianism, sesquipedality; Latinate diction; technical jargon

4 **ornateness**, **floweriness**, floridness, floridity, lushness, luxuriance; flourish, flourish of rhetoric, flowers of speech *or* rhetoric, **purple patches *or* passages**, fine writing; **ornament**, ornamentation, **adornment**, **embellishment**, elegant variation, embroidery, frill, colours *or* colours of rhetoric (*both old*), figure, **figure of speech** *see* 536

5 **phrasemonger**, rhetorician; phraseman, phrasemaker, fine writer, wordspinner; euphuist, Gongorist, Marinist; pedant

verbs

6 **to talk big** (*informal*), phrasemake, **pontificate**; inflate, bombast, lay *or* pile it on (*informal*), lay it on thick *and* lay it on with a trowel (*both informal*); smell of the lamp (*US*)

7 **to ornament**, **decorate**, **adorn**, **embellish**, **embroider**, enrich; overcharge, overlay, overload, load with ornament, festoon, weight down with ornament, flourish (*old*); gild, gild the lily, trick out *or* up, varnish; paint in glowing colours, tell in glowing terms;
"to gild refined gold, to paint the lily, to throw a perfume on the violet"—SHAKESPEARE; elaborate, convolute, involve

adjectives

8 **grandiloquent**, magniloquent, **pompous**, **orotund**; **grandiose**; fulsome; lofty, elevated, tall (*informal*), **stilted**; **pretentious**, **affected** *see* 533.9; overdone, overwrought; **showy**, **flashy**, **ostentatious**, gaudy, glitzy (*informal*), meretricious, flamboyant, flaming, bedizened, flaunting, garish; lurid, sensational, sensationalistic; **high-flown**, **high-falutin** (*informal*), high-flying; high-flowing, **high-sounding**, **big-sounding**, great-sounding, grandisonant (*old*), sonorous; **rhetorical**, declamatory; **pedantic**, inkhorn, lexiphanic (*old*); sententious, Johnsonian; convoluted, tortuous, labyrinthine, overelaborate, overinvolved; euphuistic, Gongoresque

9 **bombastic**, fustian, **inflated**, **swollen**, swelling, turgid, turgescent, tumid, tumescent, flatulent; overadorned, fulsome

10 **sesquipedalian**, sesquipedal, polysyllabic, jawbreaking *and* jawtwisting (*both informal*)

11 **ornate**, purple (*informal*), coloured, **fancy**; adorned, **embellished**, **embroidered**, lavish, adorned, decorated, festooned, overcharged, overloaded,

befrilled; **flowery**, **florid**, lush, luxuriant; figured, **figurative** *see* 536.3

adverbs

12 **grandiloquently**, magniloquently, **pompously**, grandiosely, fulsomely, loftily, stiltedly, pretentiously; **ostentatiously**, showily; **bombastically**, turgidly, tumidly, flatulently, windily (*informal*)

13 **ornately**, fancily; **flowerily**, floridly

546 LETTER

nouns

1 **letter**, **written character**, **character**, **sign**, **symbol**, graph, digraph, grapheme, allograph, alphabetic character *or* symbol, phonetic character *or* symbol; diacritic, diacritical mark, vowel point; logographic *or* lexigraphic character *or* symbol; ideographic *or* ideogrammic *or* ideogrammatic character *or* symbol; syllabic character *or* symbol, syllabic, syllabogram; pictographic character *or* symbol; cipher, device; monogram; graphy, *mater lectionis* (*Latin*); **writing** *see* 547

2 (*phonetic and ideographic symbols*) **phonogram**; phonetic symbol; **logogram**, logograph, grammalogue; word letter; **ideogram**, ideograph, phonetic, radical, determinative; **pictograph**, pictogram; **hieroglyphic**, hieroglyph, hieratic symbol, demotic character; **rune**, runic character *or* symbol; **cuneiform**, **character**; wedge, arrowhead, ogham; kana, hiragana, katakana; **shorthand** *see* 547.8; hieroglyphics

3 **writing system**, **script**, **letters**; **alphabet**, letters of the alphabet, ABC's; christcross-row; **phonetic alphabet**, International Phonetic Alphabet *or* IPA; Initial Teaching Alphabet *or* ITA; phonemic alphabet; runic alphabet, futhark; alphabetism; **syllabary**; alphabetics, alphabetology, graphemics; paleography; **speech sound** *see* 524.13

4 **spelling**, orthography; phonetic spelling *or* respelling, phonetics, phonography; normalization; spelling reform; spelling bee; bad spelling, cacography; spelling pronunciation

5 **lettering**, initialling; **inscription**, epigraph, graffito; alphabetization; transliteration, romanization, Pinyin, Wade-Giles system; transcription

verbs

6 **to letter**, initial, inscribe, character, sign, mark; **capitalize**; **alphabetize**, alphabet; transliterate, transcribe

7 **to spell**, orthographize; spell *or* respell phonetically; spell out, write out, trace out; spell backward; outspell, spell down; syllabify, syllabize, syllable, syllabicate

adjectives

8 **literal**, **lettered**; **alphabetic**, **alphabetical**; abecedarian; graphemic, allographic; large-lettered, majuscule, majuscular, uncial; **capital**, capitalized, upper-case; small-lettered, minuscule, minuscular, lower-case; logographic, logogrammatic, lexigraphic, ideographic, ideogrammic, ideogrammatic, pictographic; transliterated, transcribed

547 WRITING

nouns

1 **writing,** scrivening *or* scrivenery (*both old*), inscription, lettering; engrossment; pen, **pen-and-ink; typing, typewriting;** macrography, micrography; stroke *or* dash of the pen, *coup de plume* (*French*); secret writing, cryptography *see* 345.6; **alphabet, writing system** *see* 546.3

2 **authorship, writing,** authorcraft, pencraft, wordsmanship, **composition,** the art of composition, inditing, inditement; one's pen; **creative writing,** literary art, verbal art, literary composition, literary production, verse-writing, short-story writing, novel-writing, playwriting, drama-writing, essay-writing; **expository writing;** technical writing; journalism, newspaper writing, editorial-writing, feature-writing, rewriting; magazine writing; songwriting, lyric-writing, libretto-writing; artistry, literary power, literary artistry, literary talent *or* flair, skill with words *or* language, facility in writing, ready pen; **writer's itch,** graphomania, scribblemania, graphorrhea, *cacoëthes scribendi* (*Latin*); automatic writing; writer's cramp, graphospasm

3 **handwriting, hand, script,** fist (*informal*), chirography, **calligraphy,** autography; **manuscript,** scrive (*Scottish*); **autograph,** holograph; **penmanship,** penscript, pencraft; stylography; graphology, graphanalysis, graphometry; paleography

4 **handwriting style; printing,** handprinting, block letter, **lettering; stationery; writing materials,** paper, foolscap, note paper, pad, papyrus, parchment, tracing paper, typing paper, vellum

5 (*good writing*) **calligraphy,** fine writing, elegant penmanship, **good hand,** fine hand, good fist (*informal*), fair hand, copybook hand

6 (*bad writing*) **cacography, bad hand,** poor fist (*informal*), cramped *or* crabbed hand, botched writing, childish scrawl, illegible handwriting, *griffonage* (*French*)

7 **scribbling,** scribblement; **scribble, scrabble, scrawl, scratch,** *barbouillage* (*French*)

8 **stenography, shorthand,** brachygraphy, tachygraphy; speedwriting; phonography, stenotype; contraction

9 **letter, written character** *see* 546.1; **alphabet, writing system** *see* 546.3; punctuation *see* 530.15,18-20

10 (*written matter*) **writing, the written word; piece;** piece of writing, text, screed; **copy, matter;** printed matter, literature, reading matter; the written word, *literae scriptae* (*Latin*); nonfiction; fiction *see* 722; **composition, work,** opus, production, literary production, literary artefact *or* artefact, lucubration, brainchild; essay, article *see* 556.1; poem; play *see* 704.4; letter *see* 553.2; **document** *see* 549.5, 8; **paper,** parchment, scroll; **script,** scrip, scrive (*Scottish*); **penscript, typescript; manuscript** *or* MS. *or* ms., holograph, autograph; **draft,** first draft, second draft, etc, recension, **version;** edited version, finished version, final draft; transcription, transcript, fair copy, engrossment; flimsy; original, author's copy; camera-ready copy; printout, computer printout, hard copy

11 (*ancient manuscript*) **codex;** scroll; palimpsest, *codex rescriptus* (*Latin*); papyrus, parchment

12 **literature, letters, belles lettres,** polite literature, humane letters, *litterae humaniores* (*Latin*), republic of letters; **work, literary work, text, literary text; works, complete works,** oeuvre, **canon, literary canon, author's canon;** serious literature; **classics,** ancient literature; medieval literature, Renaissance literature, etc; national literature, English literature, French literature, etc; contemporary literature; underground literature; pseudonymous literature; folk literature; travel literature; wisdom literature; erotic literature, erotica; pornographic literature, pornography, porn *and* hard porn *and* soft porn (*all informal*), obscene literature, scatological literature; popular literature, pop literature (*informal*); bumph *or* bumf (*informal*); kitsch

13 **writer, scribbler** (*informal*), **penman, pen,** penner; **pen pusher** (*informal*), knight of the plume *or* pen *or* quill (*informal*); **scribe, scrivener, amanuensis, secretary,** recording secretary, **clerk;** letterer; **copyist,** copier, transcriber; chirographer, calligrapher

14 **writing expert,** graphologist, handwriting expert, graphometrist; paleographer

15 **author, writer,** scribe (*informal*), composer, inditer; authoress, penwoman; **creative writer,** *littérateur* (*French*), literary artist, literary craftsman *or* artisan *or* journeyman, belletrist, man of letters, literary man; wordsmith, word painter; freelance, freelance writer; ghostwriter, ghost (*informal*); collaborator, coauthor; prose writer, logographer; fiction writer, fictioneer (*informal*); story writer, **short story writer;** storyteller; **novelist;** novelettist; diarist; **newspaperman; annalist; poet** *see* 720.13; **dramatist,** humorist *see* 489.12; scriptwriter, scenario writer, scenarist; nonfiction writer; article writer, magazine writer; **essayist;** monographer; reviewer, critic, literary critic, music critic, art critic, drama critic, dance critic; columnist; pamphleteer; technical writer; copywriter, advertising writer; compiler, encyclopedist, bibliographer

16 **hack writer,** hack, literary hack, Grub Street writer, **penny-a-liner, scribbler** (*informal*), **potboiler** (*informal*)

17 **stenographer,** brachygrapher, tachygrapher; phonographer, stenotypist

18 **typist;** printer

verbs

19 **to write, pen,** pencil, push the pen (*informal*); stain *or* spoil paper (*informal*), shed *or* spill ink (*informal*), scribe, scrivener (*old*); inscribe, scroll; superscribe; enface; take pen in hand; **put in writing,** put in black and white; **draw up, draft, write out, make out; write down, record** *see* 549.16; take down in shorthand; **type; transcribe,** copy out, engross, make a fair copy, copy; trace; **rewrite, revise, edit,** recense, make a recension, make a critical revision

20 **to scribble, scrabble, scratch, scrawl** (*informal*), doodle

21 **to write, author, compose, indite,** formulate, produce, prepare; dash off, knock off *or* out (*informal*), throw on paper, pound *or* crank *or* grind

or churn out; freelance; collaborate, coauthor; ghostwrite, ghost (*informal*); novelize; scenarize; pamphleteer; editorialize

adjectives

22 **written**, penned, pencilled; **inscribed**; engrossed; **in writing**, **in black and white**, on paper; scriptural, scriptorial, graphic; calligraphic, chirographic, chirographical; stylographic, stylographical; manuscript, autograph, autographic, holograph, holographic, holographical, in one's own hand, under one's hand; **longhand**, in longhand, in script; **shorthand**, in shorthand; italic, italicized; cursive, running, flowing; graphologic, graphological, graphometric, graphometrical; graphoanalytic, graphoanalytical; typewritten; printed
23 **scribbled**, scrabbled, **scratched, scrawled**; scribbly, scratchy, scrawly
24 **literary**, belletristic; classical
25 auctorial, authorial; polygraphic; graphomaniac, graphomaniacal, scribblemaniac, scribblemaniacal, scripturient (*old*)
26 **alphabetic**, ideographic, etc *see* 546.8
27 stenographic, stenographical; **shorthand**, in shorthand
28 clerical, secretarial

word elements

29 grapho–, –graphy, –graphia; –graph, –gram; –grapher

548 PRINTING

nouns

1 **printing**, publishing, publication, photographic reproduction, photochemical process, phototypography, phototypy; **photoengraving**; **letterpress**, relief printing, **typography**, letterpress photoengraving; zincography, photozincography; line engraving, halftone engraving; stereotypy; wood-block printing, xylotypography, chromoxylography; intaglio printing, **gravure**; rotogravure, rotary photogravure; planographic printing, planography, **lithography**, typolithography, photolithography, lithogravure, lithophotogravure; offset lithography, offset, dry offset, photo-offset; photogelatin process, albertype, collotype; electronography, electrostatic printing, onset, xerography, xeroprinting; stencil, mimeograph, silk-screen printing; colour printing, chromotypography, chromotypy, two-colour printing, three-colour printing, four-colour printing; book printing, job printing, sheetwork; history of printing, palaeotypography; photography *see* 714; **graphic arts, printmaking** *see* 713.1
2 **composition, typesetting, setting,** composing; hand composition, machine composition; hot-metal typesetting, cold-type typesetting, photosetting, photocomposition; imposition; justification; composing stick, galley chase, furniture, quoin; typesetting machine, phototypesetter, phototypesetting machine; computer composition, computerized typesetting; composition tape; line of type, slug; layout, dummy
3 **print, imprint, stamp, impression, impress,**

letterpress; reprint, reissue; offprint; offcut; offset, setoff, mackle
4 **copy**, printer's copy, manuscript, typescript; **camera-ready copy; matter**; composed matter, live matter, dead matter, standing matter
5 **proof**, proof sheet, pull, trial impression; galley, **galley proof**, slip; page proof, foundry proof, plate proof, stone proof, press proof, cold-type proof, colour proof, computer proof, engraver's proof, reproduction *or* repro proof, blueprint, vandyke, progressive proof; author's proof; revise
6 **type, print, stamp, letter;** type size; type body *or* shank *or* stem, body, shank, stem, shoulder, belly, back, bevel, beard, feet, groove, nick, face, counter; ascender, descender, serif; lower case, minuscule; upper case, majuscule; capital, cap (*informal*), small capital, small cap (*informal*); ligature, logotype; pi; type lice; **font; face**, typeface; type class, roman, sans serif, script, italic, black letter; case, typecase; point, pica; en, em; typefounders, typefoundry
7 **space**, spacing, patent space, justifying space, justification space; spaceband, slug; quadrat, quad; em quad, en quad; em, en; three-em space, thick space; four-em space, five-em space, thin space; hair space
8 **printing surface, plate**, printing plate, block; typeform, locked-up page; duplicate plate, electrotype, stereotype, plastic plate, rubber plate; zincograph, zincotype; **printing equipment**
9 **presswork**, makeready; **press, printing press,** printing machine; platen press, flatbed cylinder press, cylinder press, rotary press, web press, rotogravure press; bed, platen, web
10 **printed matter; reading matter, text**, letterpress; prelims, backmatter, appendices, index; advance sheets
11 **press**, printing office, print shop, printery, printers; publishers, **publishing house; pressroom**, composing room, caseroom, proofroom
12 **printer**, printworker; **compositor, typesetter,** typographer, Linotyper; keyboarder; proofer; stereotyper, stereotypist, electrotyper; apprentice printer, devil, printer's devil; **pressman**
13 **proofreader**, reader, printer's reader, copyholder; **copyreader**, copy editor

verbs

14 **to print**; imprint, impress, **stamp**, enstamp (*old*); engrave; run, run off, strike; **publish, issue, put in print, bring out, put out, get out**; pass for press, put to press, see through the press; prove, proof, prove up, make *or* pull a proof, pull; overprint; reprint, reissue; mimeograph, hectograph; multigraph
15 **to autotype**, electrotype, Linotype (*trademark*), monotype, palaeotype, stereotype, cliché; keyboard
16 **to compose**, set, set in print; **make up**, impose; justify, overrun; pi, pi a form
17 **to copy-edit**; proofread, read, read *or* correct copy
18 (*be printed*) to go to press, come off press, come out, appear in print

adjectives

19 **printed**, in print; typeset

20 typographic, typographical; phototypic, phototypographic; chromotypic, chromotypo- graphic; stereotypic, palaeotypographical; **boldface,** bold- faced, blackface, black-faced, full-faced; **lightface,** light-faced; **upper-case, lower-case**

549 RECORD

nouns

1 **record, recording,** documentation, written word; **chronicle, annals,** history, story; roll, **rolls,** pipe roll *or* the Great Roll of the Exchequer; **account; register, registry,** rota, roster, scroll, catalogue, inventory, table, list *see* 870; letters, correspondence; **vestige, trace,** memorial, token, relic, remains

2 **archives,** public records, government archives, government papers, historical documents, historical records, memorabilia; cartulary; biographical records, life records, biographical material, papers, ana; parish rolls *or* register *or* records

3 registry, registry *or* register office; archives, files; chancery; Somerset House, National Archives, Library of Congress (*both US*)

4 **memorandum, memo** (*informal*), memoir, *aide- mémoire* (*French*), memorial; **reminder** *see* 988.6; **note, notation,** annotation, jotting, docket, marginal note, marginalia, scholium, scholia, adversaria, footnote; **entry,** register, **registry,** item; **minutes**

5 **document,** official document, legal document, legal paper, legal instrument, **instrument,** writ, **paper,** parchment, scroll, roll, **writing,** script, scrip; holograph, chirograph; **papers,** ship's papers; docket, file, personal file, **dossier;** blank, form; bumph *or* bumf (*informal*)

6 **certificate, certification,** ticket; **authority,** authorization; **credential, voucher, warrant,** warranty, testimonial; note; **affidavit,** sworn statement, notarized statement, deposition, witness, attestation, *procès-verbal* (*French*); **visa,** *visé* (*French*); **bill of health,** clean bill of health; navicert; **diploma,** sheepskin (*informal*); certificate of proficiency, testamur; birth certificate, death certificate; registration document

7 **report, bulletin, brief, statement, account,** accounting; account rendered, *compte rendu* (*French*); **minutes,** the record, proceedings, transactions, acta; **yearbook,** annual; **returns,** census report *or* returns, election returns, tally

8 (*official documents*) state paper, white paper; blue book, green book, Red Book, white book, yellow book, *livre jaune* (*French*); gazette, official journal, Hansard, Congressional Record (*US*)

9 (*registers*) genealogy, pedigree, studbook; Social Register (*US*), blue book; directory; Who's Who; Almanach de Gotha; Burke's Peerage Baronetage and Knightage; Debrett's Peerage Baronetage Knightage and Companionage; Red Book; Lloyd's Register

10 (*recording media*) bulletin board, notice board; scoresheet, scorecard, scoreboard; **tape,** magnetic tape, videotape, digital audio tape *or* DAT; **computer disk,** diskette, floppy disk *or* floppy, hard disk, disk cartridge; memory; compact disc *or* CD, compact disc interactive *or* CDI, compact disc video

or CDV; video cassette, videodisc; phonograph record, **record,** disc, platter (*informal*), vinyl; film, motion-picture film; slip, card, index card, filing card; library catalogue, catalogue card; microcard, microfiche, microdot, microfilm; **file** *see* 870.3

11 (*record books*) **notebook, pocketbook,** pocket notebook; loose-leaf notebook, spiral notebook; **memorandum book,** memo book (*informal*), commonplace book, adversaria; address book; workbook, jotter; **blotter,** police blotter; docket, court calendar; **calendar,** desk calendar, appointment calendar, appointment schedule, engagement book, agenda, personal organizer, electronic organizer, Filofax (*Trademark*); tablet, table (*old*), writing tablet; diptych, triptych; pad, scratch pad (*US*); **scrapbook,** memory book, **album; diary, journal; log,** ship's log, **logbook;** account book, **ledger,** daybook; **cashbook,** petty cashbook; Domesday Book; catalogue, classified catalogue; yearbook, annual, almanac; guestbook, guest register, register

12 **monument,** monumental *or* memorial record, **memorial;** necrology, obituary, **memento,** remembrance, testimonial; cup, trophy, prize, ribbon, plaque; **marker;** inscription; **tablet,** stone, hoarstone, boundary stone, memorial stone; **pillar,** stele *or* stela, shaft, column, memorial column, rostral column, manubial column; cross; war memorial, cenotaph; arch, memorial arch, triumphal arch, Arc de Triomphe; memorial statue, bust; monolith, obelisk, **pyramid; tomb,** grave *see* 309.16; **gravestone, tombstone;** memorial tablet, brass; headstone, footstone; mausoleum; cenotaph; cairn, mound, barrow, cromlech, dolmen, megalith, menhir, cyclolith; **shrine,** reliquary, tope, stupa

13 recorder, registrar *see* 550.1

14 **registration, register, registry; recording,** record keeping, recordation; archiving; minuting, **enrolment,** matriculation, enlistment; impanelment; **listing, tabulation, cataloguing,** inventorying, indexing; chronicling; **entry,** insertion, entering, posting; docketing, inscribing, **inscription; booking, logging;** recording instruments

verbs

15 **to record,** put *or* place upon record; **inscribe,** enscroll; **register, enrol,** matriculate, check in; impanel; poll; **file,** index, **catalogue,** calendar, **tabulate, list,** docket; **chronicle;** minute, put in the minutes *or* on the record; commit to *or* preserve in an archive, archive; **write,** commit *or* reduce to writing, put in writing, put in black and white, put on paper; **write out; make out,** fill out; **write up,** chalk, chalk up; **write down, mark down, jot down, put down, set down, take down; note,** note down, make a note, make a memorandum; **post,** post up; **enter,** make an entry, insert, write in; **book, log;** cut, carve, grave, engrave, incise; put on tape, tape, tape-record; record, cut; videotape

adjectives

16 **recording,** recordative (*old*), registrational; certificatory

17 **recorded,** registered; inscribed, written down, down; **filed,** indexed, enrolled, **entered,** logged, booked,

posted; documented; minuted; **on record**, on file, on the books; official, legal, of record
18 **documentary**, documentational, documental, archival; epigraphic, inscriptional; necrological, obituary; testimonial

550 RECORDER

nouns

1 **recorder**, recordist; **registrar**, register, prothonotary; archivist, documentalist; Master of the Rolls, *custos rotulorum* (*Latin*); librarian; **clerk**, record clerk, penpusher (*informal*), filing clerk; town *or* municipal clerk, county clerk; bookkeeper, accountant; **scribe**, scrivener (*old*); **secretary**, amanuensis; **stenographer** *see* 547.17; notary, notary public; marker; scorekeeper, scorer, official scorer, timekeeper; engraver, stonecutter
2 **annalist**, genealogist, chronicler; cliometrician; historian

551 INFORMATION

nouns

1 **information**, info (*informal*), gen, **facts**, **data**, **knowledge** *see* 927; public knowledge, open secret, common knowledge; general information; factual information, hard information; **evidence**, **proof** *see* 956; **enlightenment**, light; incidental information, sidelight; **acquaintance**, familiarization, briefing; **instruction** *see* 568.1; **intelligence**; transmission, **communication** *see* 343; **report**, **word**, message, presentation, account, **statement**, mention; white paper, white book, blue book, command paper; dispatch, bulletin, communiqué, handout (*informal*), fact sheet, release; publicity, promotional material, broadsheet; **notice**, notification; notice board, bulletin board; announcement, **publication** *see* 352; directory, guidebook *see* 574.10
2 **inside information**, private *or* confidential information; hot tip (*informal*); insider; pipeline (*informal*); privileged information, classified information
3 **tip** *and* tip-off *and* **pointer** (*all informal*), clue, cue; steer (*informal*); **advice**; whisper, passing word, **word to the wise**, word in the ear, bee in the bonnet (*informal*); warning, caution, monition, alerting, sound bite
4 **hint**, gentle hint, **intimation**, **indication**, **suggestion**, mere *or* faint suggestion, **suspicion**, inkling, whisper, **glimmer**, **glimmering**; **cue**, **clue**, index, **symptom**, **sign**, spoor, track, scent, sniff, whiff, telltale, tip-off (*informal*); **implication**, **insinuation**, **innuendo**; broad hint, gesture, signal, nod, wink, look, nudge, kick, prompt
5 **informant**, **informer**, **source**, teller, interviewee, enlightener; **adviser**, monitor; **reporter**, notifier; **announcer**, annunciator; spokesperson, spokespeople, spokeswoman, spokesman, press secretary, press officer, information officer, mouthpiece; communicator, communicant, publisher; **authority**, witness, expert witness; **tipster** (*informal*), **tout** (*informal*); newsmonger, gossipmonger; **information**

medium *or* **media**, **mass media**, **print media**, electronic media, the press, radio, television; channel, the grapevine; information network, network; information centre; public relations officer
6 **informer**, betrayer, grass *and* supergrass (*both informal*), double-crosser (*informal*), delator (*old*); **snitch** *and* snitcher (*both informal*); whistle-blower (*informal*); tattler, tattletale, telltale, talebearer; **blab** *or* blabber *or* blabberer *or* blabbermouth (*all informal*); **squealer** *and* **stool pigeon** *and* nark (*all informal*), rat *and* fink (*both US informal*); **spy** *see* 576.9
7 **information technology**, information *or* communication theory; data storage *or* retrieval, EDP *or* electronic data processing; signal, noise; encoding, decoding; bit; redundancy, entropy; channel; information *or* communication explosion

verbs

8 **to inform**, **tell**, **speak on** *or* **for**, apprise, **advise**, **advertise**, advertise of, **give word**, mention to, acquaint, **enlighten**, familiarize, brief, verse, give the facts, give an account of, give by way of information; **instruct**; possess *or* seize one of the facts; **let know**, **have one to know**, **give** *or* **lead one to believe** *or* **understand**; tell once and for all; notify, give notice *or* notification, serve notice; **communicate** *see* 343.6, 7; bring *or* send *or* leave word; **report** *see* 552.11; **disclose** *see* 351.4; put in a new light, shed new *or* fresh light upon
9 **to post** *and* **keep one posted** (*both informal*); wise up *and* clue *or* fill in *and* bring up to speed *or* date *and* put in the picture (*all informal*)
10 **to hint**, **intimate**, **suggest**, **insinuate**, **imply**, **indicate**, adumbrate, lead *or* leave one to gather, justify one in supposing, give *or* drop *or* throw out a hint, give an inkling of, **hint at**; **leak**, let slip out; allude to, make an allusion to, glance at (*old*); **prompt**, give the cue, put onto; put in *or* into one's head, put a bee in one's bonnet
11 **to tip** *and* **tip off** *and* **give one a tip** (*all informal*), alert; **give a pointer to** (*informal*); tip the wink (*informal*), **let in on**, let in on the know (*informal*); **confide**, confide to, entrust with information, give confidential information, mention privately *or* confidentially, whisper, buzz, breathe, whisper in the ear
12 **to inform on** *or* **against**, **betray**; **tattle**; turn informer; testify against, **bear witness against**; turn queen's *or* king's evidence, turn state's evidence (*US*)
13 (*informal terms*) **to sell one out** *or* **down the river**, tell on, blab, snitch, grass, squeal, peach (*old*), sell out, sing, rat, nark, finger, put the finger on, blow the whistle, shop, spill one's guts, spill the beans, squawk, weasel, stool *and* fink *and* dime (*all US*)
14 **to learn**, **come to know**, **be informed** *or* **apprised of**, have it reported, get the facts, **get wise to** (*informal*); become conscious *or* aware of, become alive *or* awake to, awaken to, tumble to (*informal*), open one's eyes to
15 **to know** *see* 927.12, be informed *or* apprised, have the facts, be in the know (*informal*), **come to one's knowledge**, come to *or* reach one's ears; be told,

hear, overhear, hear tell of *and* hear say (*both informal*); get scent *or* wind of; **know well** *see* 927.13; have inside information, know where the bodies are buried (*informal*)

16 **to keep informed**, keep posted (*informal*), stay briefed, **keep up on**, keep up to date *or* au courant, keep abreast of the times; **keep track of**, keep count *or* account of, keep watch on, keep tab *or* tabs on (*informal*), keep a check on, keep an eye on; gen up on, clue up on (*both informal*)

adjectives

17 **informed** *see* 927.18-20; informed of, in the know *see* 927.16, clued-in *or* clued-up (*informal*)

18 **informative**, informing, informational; **instructive, enlightening**; educative, educational; advisory, monitory; **communicative**

19 **telltale**, tattletale, kiss-and-tell

adverbs

20 from information received, according to reports *or* rumour, from notice given, as a matter of general information, by common report, from what one can gather, as far as anyone knows

552 NEWS

nouns

1 **news**, tidings, intelligence, information, word, advice; newsiness (*informal*); newsworthiness; a nose for news; **journalism**, reportage, coverage, news coverage; **the press**, the fourth estate, the press corps, print journalism, electronic journalism, broadcast journalism, broadcast news, radio journalism, television journalism; **news medium** *or* **media**, newspaper, newsletter, newsmagazine, radio, television, press association, news service, news agency, press agency, wire service, telegraph agency; press box, press gallery; tabloid press, yellow press; pack journalism, chequebook journalism

2 **good news**, good word, **glad tidings**; gospel, evangel; bad news

3 **news item**, piece *or* budget of news; **article, story**, piece; copy; scoop (*informal*), exclusive; breaking story, newsbreak (*US*); stop press; follow-up, sidebar; spot news (*US*); outtake; sound bite

4 **message, dispatch, word, communication, communiqué**, advice, press release, release; express; embassy, embassage (*old*); **letter** *see* 553.2; **telegram** *see* 347.14; pneumatogram, *petit bleu* (*French*)

5 **bulletin**, news report, **newsflash** *or* **flash**

6 **report, rumour**, flying rumour, unverified *or* unconfirmed report, **hearsay**, *on-dit* (*French*), **scuttlebutt** *and* latrine rumour (*both US informal*); talk, whisper, buzz, rumble, bruit, cry; idea afloat, news stirring; **common talk**, town talk, **talk of the town**, topic of the day, *cause célèbre* (*French*); **grapevine**; canard, roorback

7 **gossip**, gossiping, gossipry, gossipmongering, newsmongering, mongering (*informal*), newsmongering; **talebearing**, taletelling; **tattle**, tittle-tattle, chitchat, **talk**, idle talk, small talk, by-talk, clishmaclaver (*Scottish*);

"putting two and two together, and making it five"—Pascal; piece of gossip, groundless rumour, tale, story

8 **scandal, dirt** (*informal*), **malicious gossip**, "gossip made tedious by morality"—Oscar Wilde; juicy morsel, titbit, dirt (*informal*); **scandalmongering**; gossip column; character assassination, **slander** *see* 512.3; whispering campaign

9 **newsmonger, rumourmonger, scandalmonger, gossip**, gossipmonger, gossiper, *yenta* (*Yiddish*), quidnunc, **busybody**, tabby (*informal*); **talebearer**, taleteller, telltale, **tattletale** (*informal*), tattler, tittle-tattler,
"a tale-bearing animal"—J Harrington; gossip columnist; reporter, newspaperman

10 (*secret news channel*) **grapevine, grapevine telegraph**, bush telegraph (*Australian*); **pipeline**; a little bird *or* birdie

verbs

11 **to report**, give a report, give an account of, notify, tell, relate, rehearse (*old*); write up, make out *or* write up a report; gather the news, newsgather; dig *or* dig up dirt (*informal*); bring word, tell the news, break the news, give tidings of; bring glad tidings, give the good word; announce *see* 352.12; put around, spread, **rumour** *see* 352.10; clue in *or* clue up (*informal*), **inform** *see* 551.8

12 **to gossip; tattle**, tittle-tattle; **talk**; retail gossip, **dish the dirt** (*informal*), tell idle tales

adjectives

13 **newsworthy**, front-page, with news value, newsy; reportorial

14 **gossipy**, gossiping, newsy; **talebearing**, taletelling

15 **reported, rumoured**, whispered; rumoured about, talked-about, whispered about, bruited about, bandied about; **in the news, in circulation, in the air, going around**, going about, **current, rife**, afloat, on everyone's lips, on all tongues, on the street, all over the town; made public *see* 352.17

adverbs

16 **reportedly**, allegedly, as they say, as it is said, **as the story goes** *or* runs, as the fellow says (*informal*), it is said

553 CORRESPONDENCE

nouns

1 **correspondence, letter writing**, written communication, exchange of letters, epistolary intercourse *or* communication; personal correspondence, business correspondence; **mailing**, mass mailing

2 **letter** (*see list*), **epistle, message, communication, dispatch, missive**, favour (*old*); personal letter, business letter; **note, line**, chit, billet (*old*); **reply, answer, acknowledgment**, rescript

3 **card, postcard**, postal card, lettercard; picture postcard

4 **post, mail, postal services**, letter bag; post day; mailing list, mailshot; junk mail (*informal*); direct mail, direct-mail advertising *or* selling, mail-order

selling; inertia selling; mail solicitation; fan mail; hate mail; electronic mail *or* email

5 **postage**; stamp, postage stamp; spif; frank; postmark, cancellation; recorded delivery, RMSD, Datapost, parcel post, registered post; Freepost

6 **postbox** *and* **letter box**, pillar box, mailbox (*US & Canadian*); letter drop *and* mail drop (*both US & Canadian*); mailing machine; postbag, mailbag

7 **postal service, postal system**; **post office** *or* **PO**, general post office *or* GPO, sub post office, sea post office; **postman** *or* **postwoman**, postmaster general, postmaster *or* postmistress, postie (*Scottish, Australian, & NZ informal*), mailman (*US & Canadian*); postbus; post-office *or* postal clerk

8 **correspondent, letter writer**, writer, communicator; pen pal (*informal*); addressee

9 **address**, name and address, direction (*old*), **destination**, superscription; **postcode**, zip code *or* zip (*US*), postal code (*Canadian*); letterhead

verbs

10 **to correspond**, correspond with, **communicate with, write, write to**, write a letter, send a letter to, send a note, **drop a line** (*informal*); keep up a correspondence, exchange letters

11 **to reply, answer, acknowledge**

12 **to mail, post**, dispatch, send; airmail

13 **to address, direct, superscribe**

adjectives

14 **epistolary; postal**, post; letter; mail-order, direct-mail; mailable; sendable; first-class, second-class

phrases

15 please reply, **RSVP** *or répondez s'il vous plaît* (*French*)

16 **kinds of letters**

aerogram	letter of introduction
air letter	letter of marque
airgraph	letter of request
apostolic *or* papal brief	letter of resignation
bull	letter overt
chain letter	letter patent
circular letter	letter rogatory
cover *or* covering letter	letter testamentary
dead letter	love letter *or billet doux*
dimissory letter *or*	(*French*)
dimissorial	market letter
drop letter	monitory *or* monitory
encyclical	letter
encyclical letter	newsletter
fan letter	open letter
form letter	paschal letter
letter credential	pastoral letter
letter of credence	poison-pen letter
letter of credit	round robin
letter of delegation	

554 BOOK

nouns

1 **book, volume, tome**; publication, writing, **work, opus, production**; title; opusculum, opuscule; **trade book**; textbook, schoolbook; **reference book**, playbook; songbook *see* 708.28; notebook *see* 549.11; storybook, **novel**; **best seller**; coffee-table book; nonbook; **children's book**, juvenile book, juvenile; picture book; colouring book, sketchbook; prayer book, psalter, psalmbook; **classic**, the book, the bible, magnum opus, great work, standard work, definitive work

2 **publisher, book publisher**; publishing house, press, small press, vanity press; **editor**, trade editor, reference editor, textbook editor, dictionary editor, school editor, line editor; commissioning editor, executive editor, managing editor, senior editior, editor-in-chief; picture editor; packager; copy editor, desk editor, production editor, permissions editor; **printer**, book printer; **bookbinder**, bibliopegist; **bookdealer, bookseller**, book agent, book salesman; book manufacturer, press

3 **book, printed book, bound book**, bound volume, cased book, casebound book, cloth-bound book, clothback, leather-bound book; manufactured book, finished book; packaged book; **hardcover**, hardcover book, hardbound, hardbound book, hard book; **paperback**, paper-bound book, limp book; pocket book, soft-cover, soft-bound book, vinyl-bound book

4 **volume, tome**; folio; quarto *or* 4to; octavo *or* 8vo; twelvemo *or* 12mo; sextodecimo *or* sixteenmo *or* 16mo; octodecimo *or* eighteenmo *or* 18mo; imperial, super, royal, medium, crown; trim size

5 **edition**, issue; volume, number; **printing**, impression, press order, print order, print run, reprint; copy; series, set, boxed set, collection, library; library edition; back number; **trade edition**, subscription edition, subscription book; school edition, text edition

6 **rare book**, early edition; first edition; Aldine, Aldine book *or* edition; manuscript, scroll, codex; incunabulum, cradle book

7 **compilation**, omnibus; compendium; symposium; collection, collectanea, miscellany; collected works, selected works, complete works, *œuvres* (*French*), canon; **miscellanea**, analects; ana; chrestomathy, delectus; **anthology**, garland, florilegium; flowers, beauties; garden; *Festschrift* (*German*); quotation book; album, photograph album; scrapbook

8 **handbook, manual**, enchiridion, vade mecum, gradus, how-to book (*informal*); **cookbook**, cookery book (*British*); nature book, field guide; travel book, **guidebook** *see* 574.10

9 **reference book**, work of reference; **encyclopedia**, cyclopedia; **concordance; catalogue**; calendar; index; classified catalogue, *catalogue raisonné* (*French*), dictionary catalogue; **directory**, city directory; telephone directory, telephone book, phone book (*informal*); **atlas, gazetteer**; studbook; source book, casebook; record book *see* 549.11; **language reference book** (*see list*); **dictionary**, lexicon, wordbook; glossary, gloss, **vocabulary**, onomasticon, nomenclator; **thesaurus, Roget's**, storehouse *or* treasury of words

10 **textbook, text, schoolbook, manual**, manual of instruction; **primer**, alphabet book, abecedary, abecedarium; hornbook, battledore; gradus, exercise book, workbook; **grammar, reader**; spelling book, speller, casebook

11 **booklet, pamphlet, brochure,** chapbook, **leaflet, folder, tract;** circular *see* 352.8; comic book, graphic novel

12 **makeup, design;** front matter, preliminaries, text, back matter; head, fore edge, back, tail; page, leaf, folio; type page; trim size; flyleaf, endpaper, endleaf, endsheet, signature; recto, verso *or* reverso; title page, half-title page; title, bastard title, binder's title, subtitle, running title; copyright page, imprint, printer's imprint, colophon; catchword, catch line; dedication, inscription; acknowledgments, preface, foreword, introduction; contents, contents page, table of contents; errata; bibliography; index, appendices

13 **part, section, book, volume;** article; serial, instalment, *livraison (French);* fascicle; **passage,** phrase, clause, verse, paragraph, chapter, column

14 **bookbinding,** bibliopegy; **binding, cover, book cover,** case, bookcase, hard binding, soft binding, mechanical binding, spiral binding, comb binding, plastic binding; library binding; headband, footband, tailband; **jacket, book jacket, dust jacket,** dust cover, wrapper; slipcase, slipcover; book cloth, binder's cloth, binder's board, binder board; folding, tipping, gathering, collating, sewing; **signature;** collating mark; Smyth sewing, side sewing, saddle stitching, wire stitching, stapling, perfect binding; smashing, gluing-off, trimming, rounding, backing, lining, lining-up; casemaking, stamping, casing-in

15 (*bookbinding styles*) Aldine, Arabesque, Byzantine, Canevari, cottage, dentelle, Etruscan, fanfare, Grolier, Harleian, Jansenist, Maioli, pointillé, Roxburgh

16 **bookstore, bookshop,** *librairie (French),* bookseller's; **bookstall,** bookstand; **book club**

17 **bookholder, bookrest,** book support, **book end; bookcase,** revolving bookcase *or* bookstand, bookrack, bookstand, **bookshelf,** spinner; stack, bookstack; book table, book tray, book truck; folder, folio; **portfolio**

18 **booklover,** philobiblist, bibliophile, bibliolater, book collector, bibliomane, bibliomaniac, bibliotaph; **bookworm,** bibliophage; book-stealer, biblioklept

19 **bibliology,** bibliography; bookcraft, bookmaking, book printing, book production, book manufacturing, bibliogenesis, bibliogony; bookselling, bibliopolism

adjectives

20 **bibliological,** bibliographical; bibliothecal, bibliothecary; bibliopolic; bibliopegic

21 **language reference books**

bilingual dictionary	geographical dictionary *or* gazetteer
biographical dictionary	
children's dictionary	glossary
college dictionary	idiom dictionary
desk dictionary	rhyming dictionary
dialect dictionary	Roget's Thesaurus
dictionary of quotations	school dictionary
dictionary of science, electronics, psychology, philosophy, etc	synonym dictionary spelling dictionary thesaurus
etymological dictionary *or* etymologicon	unabridged dictionary usage dictionary
foreign-language dictionary	

555 PERIODICAL

1 **periodical, serial, journal,** gazette; ephemeris; **magazine,** zine (*informal*); pictorial; review; organ, **house organ; trade journal,** trade magazine; daily, weekly, biweekly, bimonthly, fortnightly, monthly, quarterly; part work; annual, yearbook, almanac; daybook, diary *see* 549.11

2 **newspaper,** news, **paper,** sheet *or* rag (*both informal*), **gazette,** daily newspaper, daily, weekly newspaper, weekly, neighbourhood newspaper, national newspaper; newspaper of record; **tabloid,** extra, special, extra edition, special edition; colour supplement, business section, sports section, personal finance section, etc

3 **the press,** journalism, the public press, **the fourth estate;** print medium, the print media, print journalism, the print press, the public print; Fleet Street; **wire service,** newswire, Associated Press, AP; United Press International *or* UPI; Reuters; **publishing,** newspaper publishing, **magazine publishing;** the publishing industry, **communications,** mass media, the communications industry, public communication; satellite publishing

4 **journalist, newspaperman, newspaperwoman, newsman, newswoman,** journo (*informal*), newspeople, inkstained wretch, pressman, newswriter, gazetteer (*old*), gentleman *or* representative of the press; **reporter,** newshound *and* newshawk (*both US & Canadian informal*); leg man (*US & Canadian informal*); interviewer; investigative reporter; **cub reporter; correspondent, foreign correspondent,** war correspondent, special correspondent, own correspondent, stringer; publicist; rewriter; reviser, diaskeuast; **editor,** subeditor, managing editor, city editor, news editor, sports editor, woman's editor, feature editor, **copy editor,** copyman, copy chief; reader, **copyreader;** editorial writer, leader writer; **columnist,** paragrapher, paragraphist; **photographer, news photographer,** photojournalist; paparazzo

adjectives

5 **journalistic,** journalese (*informal*); **periodical, serial;** magazinish, magaziny; newspaperish, newspapery; **editorial; reportorial**

556 TREATISE

nouns

1 **treatise,** piece, treatment, handling, tractate, tract; contribution; examination, survey, **discourse, discussion,** disquisition, descant, exposition, screed; homily; memoir; dissertation, **thesis; essay,** theme; pandect; excursus; **study,** lucubration, étude; **paper,** research paper, term paper; **sketch,** outline, aperçu; causerie; **monograph,** research monograph; *morceau (French),* paragraph, **note;** preliminary study, introductory study, first approach, prolegomenon; **article,** feature, special article

2 **commentary,** commentation (*old*); **comment, remark; criticism,** critique, *compte-rendu critique (French),* analysis; **review,** critical review, **report,** notice, **write-up** (*informal*); **editorial,** leading article *or* leader; gloss, running commentary

3 discourser, discusser, disquisitor, expositor, descanter; symposiast, discussant; **essayist**; monographer, monographist; tractation, tractator (*old*); **writer, author** *see* 547.15

4 commentator, commenter; expositor, expounder; annotator, scholiast; glossarist, glossographer; **critic**; **reviewer, book reviewer; editor**; editorial writer, editorialist, leader writer; news analyst; publicist

verbs

5 to write upon, touch upon, **discuss, treat, treat of, deal with**, take up, handle, go into, inquire into, survey; discourse, dissert, dissertate, descant; **comment upon**, remark upon; **criticize, review, write up**

adjectives

6 dissertational, disquisitional, discursive; expository, expositorial, expositive; essayistic; monographic, commentative, commentatorial; critical

557 ABRIDGMENT

nouns

1 abridgment, compendium, compend, *abrégé* (*French*), **condensation**, short *or* shortened version, condensed version, abbreviation, abbreviature, brief, digest, **abstract**, epitome, **précis, capsule**, nutshell *or* capsule version, capsulization, encapsulation, sketch, thumbnail sketch, **synopsis, conspectus**, syllabus, *aperçu* (*French*), **survey, review**, overview, pandect, bird's-eye view; **outline**, skeleton, draft; topical outline; head, rubric

2 summary, résumé, recapitulation, recap (*informal*), rundown, run-through; **summation**; sum, substance, sum and substance, **wrapup** (*informal*); pith, meat, gist, core, essence, main point *see* 996.6

3 excerpt, extract, selection, extraction, excerption, snippet; passage, selected passage; **clip** (*informal*), film clip, outtake, sound bite (*informal*)

4 excerpts, *excerpta* (*Latin*), **extracts, gleanings**, cuttings, clippings, snippets; flowers, florilegium, **anthology**; fragments; analects; **miscellany**, miscellanea; **collection**, collectanea; ana

verbs

5 to abridge, shorten *see* 268.6, **condense, cut, clip**; summarize, synopsize, wrap up (*informal*); **outline**, sketch, sketch out; capsule, capsulize, encapsulate; put in a nutshell

adjectives

6 abridged, condensed; shortened, clipped; nutshell, compendious, **brief** *see* 268.8

adverbs

7 in brief, in summary, in sum, in a nutshell *see* 537.8

558 LIBRARY

nouns

1 library, book depository; learning centre; media centre, media resource centre, information centre; **public library**, town *or* city *or* municipal library, village library; school library, community college library, college library, university library; **special library**, medical library, law library, art library, etc; **circulating library, lending library; mobile library**; bookroom, bookery (*old*), *bibliothèque* (*French*), *bibliotheca* (*Latin*), athenaeum; reading room; **national library**, Bibliothèque Nationale, Bodleian Library, British Library, Deutsche Bücherei, Library of Congress, Vatican Library, Faculty of Advocates Library; Library Association, American Library Association

2 librarianship, professional librarianship; **library science**, information science, library services, library and information services, library and information studies

3 librarian, professional librarian, library professional; **director, head librarian, chief librarian**; head of service; library services director

4 bibliography (*see list*); **index** (*see list*); Books in Print, Paperbound Books in Print; **publisher's catalogue**, publisher's list, backlist; General Catalogue of Printed Books, Library of Congress Catalog (*US*); **library catalogue**, computerized catalogue, on-line catalogue, integrated online system; CD-ROM workstation

5 bibliographies

annotated bibliography	cumulative bibliography
annual bibliography	national bibliography
bibliography of bibliographies	period bibliography
critical bibliography	subject bibliography
	trade bibliography

6 indexes to periodicals

Art Index	Humanities Index
Bibliography Index	Index Medicus
Business Periodicals Index	PsycLIT
Cumulative Book Index	Reader's Guide to
Dissertation Abstracts Ondisc	Periodical Literature
	Religion Index
Education Index	Social Sciences Index
General Science Index	The Philosopher's Index

559 RELATIONSHIP BY BLOOD

nouns

1 blood relationship, blood, ties of blood, consanguinity, common descent *or* ancestry, biological *or* genetic relationship, **kinship**, kindred, **relation, relationship**, sibship; propinquity; cognation; agnation, enation; filiation, affiliation; alliance, connection, **family connection** *or* tie; motherhood, maternity; fatherhood, paternity; patrocliny, matrocliny; patrilineage, matrilineage; patriliny, matriliny; patrisib, matrisib; brotherhood, brothership, fraternity; sisterhood, sistership; cousinhood, cousinship; **ancestry** *see* 560

2 kinfolk *and* kinfolks (*both informal*), kinsmen, **kinsfolk**, kindred, kinnery (*informal*), kin, kith and kin, **family, relatives, relations, people**, folks (*informal*), connections; **blood relation** *or* **relative**, flesh, blood, flesh and blood, uterine kin, consanguinean; cognate; agnate, enate; kinsman, kinswoman, sib, sibling; german; near relation, distant relation; next of kin; collateral relative, collateral; distaff *or* spindle side, distaff *or* spindle kin; sword *or* spear side, sword *or* spear kin; **tribesman,** tribespeople, clansman *or* woman; **ancestry** *see* 560, **posterity** *see* 561

3 **brother,** frater; brethren *see* 700.1; **sister,** sis (*informal*); sistern (*informal*); kid brother *or* sister; blood brother *or* sister, uterine brother *or* sister, brother- *or* sister-german; half brother *or* sister, foster brother *or* sister, stepbrother *or* stepsister; **aunt,** auntie (*informal*); **uncle,** unc *and* uncs *and* nunks *and* nunky *and* nuncle (*all informal*), **nephew, niece; cousin,** cousin-german; first cousin, second cousin, etc; cousin once removed, cousin twice removed, etc; country cousin; great-uncle, granduncle; great-granduncle; great-aunt, grandaunt; great-grandaunt; grandnephew, grandniece; **father, mother,** mater (*informal*), pater (*informal*); **son, daughter** *see* 561.2

4 **race, people, folk, family, house, clan, tribe, nation,** *volk* (*German*); patriclan, matriclan, deme, sept, gens, phyle, phratry, totem; **lineage,** line, blood, strain, stock, stem, species, stirps, **breed,** brood, kind; plant *or* animal kingdom, class, order, etc *see* 808.5; **ethnicity,** tribalism, clannishness

5 **family,** brood, nuclear family, binuclear family, extended family, one-parent *or* single-parent family; **house, household,** hearth, hearthside, ménage, people, **folk,** homefolk, folks (*informal*); **children,** issue, descendants, progeny, **offspring,** get, kids (*informal*)

adjectives

6 **related, kindred, akin;** consanguineous *or* consanguinean *or* consanguineal, consanguine, by *or* of the blood; **biological,** genetic; **natural, birth,** by birth; cognate, uterine, agnate, enate; sib, sibling; allied, affiliated, congeneric; german, germane; collateral; foster, novercal; patrilineal, matrilineal; patroclinous, matroclinous; patrilateral, matrilateral; avuncular; intimately *or* closely related, remotely *or* distantly related

7 **racial, ethnic, tribal, national, family,** clannish, totemic, **lineal; ethnic;** phyletic, phylogenetic, genetic; gentile, gentilic

word elements

8 adelpho–, phyl–

560 ANCESTRY

nouns

1 **ancestry,** progenitorship; parentage, parenthood; grandparentage, grandfatherhood, grandmotherhood

2 **paternity, fatherhood,** fathership; natural *or* birth *or* biological fatherhood; fatherliness, paternalness; adoptive fatherhood

3 **maternity, motherhood,** mothership; natural *or* birth *or* biological motherhood; motherliness, maternalness; adoptive motherhood; surrogate motherhood

4 **lineage,** line, **bloodline, descent,** descendancy, line of descent, ancestral line, succession, **extraction,** derivation, birth, **blood,** breed, **family,** house, **strain,** sept, **stock,** race, stirps, seed; direct line, phylum; **branch,** stem; filiation, affiliation,

apparentation; side, father's side, mother's side; enate, agnate, cognate; male line, spear *or* sword side; female line, distaff *or* spindle side; consanguinity, common ancestry *see* 559.1

5 **genealogy, pedigree,** stemma, *Stammbaum* (*German*), genealogical tree, **family tree,** tree; genogram

6 **heredity, heritage, inheritance, birth;** patrocliny, matrocliny; endowment, inborn capacity *or* tendency *or* susceptibility *or* predisposition; diathesis; inheritability, heritability, hereditability; Mendel's law, Mendelism *or* Mendelianism; Weismann theory, Weismannism; Altmann theory, De Vries theory, Galtonian theory, Verworn theory, Wiesner theory; **genetics,** pharmacogenetics, genesiology, eugenics; **gene,** factor, inheritance factor, determiner, determinant; **character,** dominant *or* recessive character, allele *or* allelomorph; germ cell, germ plasm; **chromosome;** sex chromosome, X chromosome, Y chromosome; chromatin, chromatid; genetic code; DNA, RNA, replication

7 **ancestors, antecedents, predecessors,** ascendants, **fathers, forefathers, forebears,** progenitors, primogenitors; **grandparents,** grandfathers; patriarchs, elders

8 **parent, progenitor, ancestor,** procreator, begetter; natural *or* birth *or* biological parent; grandparent; ancestress, progenitress, progenitrix; stepparent; adoptive parent; surrogate parent

9 **father, sire,** genitor, paternal ancestor, pater (*informal*), the old man (*informal*), governor (*informal*); patriarch, paterfamilias; stepfather; foster father, adoptive father; birth *or* natural *or* biological father

10 (*informal terms*) **dad,** papa, pa, **daddy,** the old man, pater

11 **mother,** genetrix, dam, maternal ancestor, matriarch, materfamilias; stepmother; foster mother, adoptive mother; birth *or* **natural** *or* **biological mother;** surrogate mother

12 (*informal terms*) **mum,** mummy, mammy, mam, **ma, mama,** mater, the old woman, maw (*Scottish*), mom *and* mommy (*both US*)

13 **grandfather,** grandsire; old man *see* 304.2; **great-grandfather**

14 (*informal terms*) **grandpa,** grampa, grandpapa, **granddad,** granddaddy, grandpappy *and* gramps (*both US*)

15 **grandmother,** grandam; **great-grandmother**

16 (*informal terms*) gran, granny, **grandma,** granma, old woman *see* 304.3; grandmamma, grammy (*US*)

adjectives

17 **ancestral,** ancestorial, patriarchal; **parental,** parent; **paternal,** fatherly, fatherlike; **maternal,** motherly, motherlike; grandparental; grandmotherly, grandmaternal; grandfatherly, grandpaternal

18 **lineal, family,** genealogical; enate *or* enatic, agnate *or* agnatic, cognate *or* cognatic; direct, in a direct line; phyletic, phylogenetic; diphyletic

19 **hereditary,** patrimonial, **inherited, innate;** genetic, genic; patroclinous, matroclinous

20 **inheritable,** heritable, hereditable

561 POSTERITY

nouns

1 **posterity, progeny, issue, offspring,** fruit, seed, brood, breed, family; **descent,** succession; lineage *see* 560.4, blood, bloodline; **descendants,** heirs, inheritors, sons, **children, kids** (*informal*), little ones, little people (*informal*), treasures, hostages to fortune, youngsters, younglings; grandchildren, great-grandchildren; new *or* young *or* rising generation

2 (*of animals*) **young, brood, get, spawn,** spat, fry; **litter,** farrow (*of pigs*); clutch, hatch

3 **descendant;** offspring, child, scion; **son,** son and heir, a chip off the old block, sonny; **daughter,** heiress; grandchild, grandson, granddaughter; stepchild, stepson, stepdaughter; foster child

4 (*derived or collateral descendant*) **offshoot,** offset, **branch,** sprout, shoot, filiation

5 **bastard,** illegitimate, illegitimate *or* bastard child, whoreson, by-blow, child born out of wedlock *or* without benefit of clergy, natural *or* love child, *nullius filius* (*Latin*); illegitimacy, bastardy, bar *or* bend sinister; hellspawn

6 sonship, sonhood; daughtership, daughterhood

adjectives

7 **filial,** sonly, sonlike; **daughterly,** daughterlike

562 LOVEMAKING, ENDEARMENT

nouns

1 **lovemaking,** dalliance, amorous dalliance, billing and cooing; **fondling, caressing,** hugging, kissing; cuddling, snuggling, nestling, nuzzling; sexual intercourse *see* 75.7

2 (*informal terms*) **necking, petting,** snogging, smooching, canoodling, making out (*US*)

3 **embrace, hug, squeeze,** fond embrace, embracement, clasp, enfoldment, bear hug (*informal*)

4 **kiss,** smacker (*informal*), osculation; French kiss, soul kiss, snog (*informal*); lovebite

5 **endearment; caress,** pat; sweet talk, soft words, honeyed words, sweet nothings; blandishments, artful endearments; love call, mating call, wolf whistle

6 (*terms of endearment*) **darling, dear,** deary, ducky, **sweetheart, sweetie, sweet,** sweets, sweetkins, **honey,** hon, honeybun, honey-bunny, honeybunch, honey child, sugar, love, lover, precious, precious heart, pet, petkins, babe, **baby, doll,** baby-doll, cherub, angel, buttercup, duck, duckling, ducks, lamb, lambkin, snookums, poppet

7 **courtship, courting, wooing;** court, suit, suing, amorous pursuit, addresses; gallantry; serenade

8 **proposal,** marriage proposal, offer of marriage, popping of the question; engagement *see* 436.3

9 **flirtation, flirtiness, coquetry,** dalliance; flirtatiousness, coquettishness, coyness; sheep's eyes, amorous looks, coquettish glances, come-hither look; ogle, side-glance; bedroom eyes (*informal*)

10 **philandering,** philander, lady-killing (*informal*); lechery, licentiousness, unchastity *see* 665

11 **flirt, coquette,** gold digger *and* vamp (*both informal*); strumpet, whore *see* 665.14, 16

12 **philanderer,** philander, woman chaser, **ladies' man,** heartbreaker; masher, lady-killer, wolf, skirt chaser, man on the make (*both informal*); libertine, lecher, cocksman (*informal*), seducer *see* 665.12, Casanova, Don Juan

13 **love letter,** billet-doux; valentine

verbs

14 **to make love,** bill and coo; dally, toy, trifle, wanton; sweet-talk (*informal*), whisper sweet nothings; go steady, keep company; copulate

15 (*informal terms*) **to neck, pet,** snog, smooch, canoodle, get off with, winch (*Scottish*), make out (*US*)

16 **to caress, pet,** pat; feel *or* feel up (*informal*), touch up (*informal*), **fondle,** dandle, coddle, cocker, cosset; pat on the head *or* cheek, chuck under the chin

17 **to cuddle, snuggle, nestle,** nuzzle; lap; bundle

18 **to embrace, hug, clasp, press,** squeeze (*informal*), fold, **enfold,** bosom, embosom, put *or* throw one's arms around, take to *or* in one's arms, fold to the heart, press to the bosom

19 **to kiss, osculate,** smooch (*informal*); blow a kiss

20 **to flirt, coquet; philander,** gallivant, play the field (*informal*), run *or* play around, sow one's oats; **make eyes at, ogle,** eye, cast coquettish glances, make sheep's eyes at (*informal*), *faire les yeux doux* (*French*); play hard to get

21 **to court, woo, sue,** press one's suit, **pay court or suit to,** make suit to, cosy up to (*informal*), eye up *and* chat up (*informal*), pay one's court to, address, pay one's addresses to, pay attention to, lay siege to, fling oneself at, throw oneself at the head of; **pursue,** follow; chase (*informal*); set one's cap at *or* for (*informal*); serenade; squire, esquire, beau, sweetheart (*informal*), swain

22 **to propose, pop the question** (*informal*), ask for one's hand; become engaged

adjectives

23 **amatory,** amative; sexual *see* 75.28, 29; caressive; **flirtatious, flirty; coquettish,** coy, come-hither

563 MARRIAGE

nouns

1 **marriage, matrimony, wedlock, married status,** holy matrimony, holy wedlock, match, matching, match-up, splicing (*informal*), union, matrimonial union, alliance, "a world-without-end bargain"—SHAKESPEARE, "a dignified and commodious sacrament"—T S ELIOT, marriage sacrament, sacrament of matrimony, bond of matrimony, wedding knot, conjugal bond *or* tie *or* knot, nuptial bond *or* tie *or* knot; married state *or* status, wedded state *or* status, wedded bliss, weddedness, wifehood, husbandhood, spousehood; coverture, cohabitation; bed, marriage bed, bridebed; intermarriage, mixed marriage, interfaith marriage, interracial marriage; miscegenation; misalliance, *mésalliance* (*French*), ill-assorted marriage

2 **marriageability,** nubility, ripeness

3 **wedding, marriage,** marriage ceremony, nuptial mass; church wedding, civil wedding, civil ceremony; espousement, bridal; banns; **nuptials,** spousals,

espousals, hymeneal rites; *chuppah* (*Hebrew*), wedding canopy; white wedding; wedding song, marriage song, nuptial song, prothalamium, epithalamium, epithalamy, hymen, hymeneal; wedding veil, saffron veil *or* robe; bridechamber, bridal suite, nuptial apartment; **honeymoon;** forced marriage, shotgun wedding; Gretna Green wedding, elopement

4 **wedding party;** wedding attendant, usher; **best man,** bridesman, groomsman; paranymph; **bridesmaid,** bridemaiden, maid *or* matron of honour; flower girl, page

5 **newlywed; bridegroom, groom; bride,** plighted bride, blushing bride; war bride, GI bride (*informal*); honeymooner

6 **spouse, mate,** yokemate, partner, consort, **better half** (*informal*),
"bone of my bones, and flesh of my flesh"—BIBLE

7 **husband, married man,** man, benedict, goodman (*old*), old man (*informal*)

8 **wife, married woman,** wedded wife, goodwife *or* goody (*both old*), squaw, woman, lady, matron, old lady *and* old woman *and* little woman *and* ball and chain *and* her indoors (*all informal*), feme, feme covert, **better half** (*informal*), **helpmate,** helpmeet, rib, wife of one's bosom; wife in name only; wife in all but name, concubine, common-law wife

9 **married couple,** wedded pair, happy couple, **man and wife,** husband and wife, man and woman, *vir et uxor* (*Latin*), one flesh; newlyweds, **bride and groom**

10 **harem,** seraglio, serai, gynaeceum; zenana, purdah

11 **monogamist,** monogynist; **bigamist;** digamist, deuterogamist; trigamist; **polygamist,** polygynist, polyandrist; Bluebeard

12 **matchmaker, marriage broker,** matrimonial agent

13 (*god*) Hymen; (*goddesses*) Hera, Teleia; Juno, Pronuba; Frigg

verbs

14 (*join in marriage*) **to marry,** wed, nuptial, **join, unite, hitch** *and* **splice** (*both informal*), couple, match, match up, make *or* arrange a match, join together, **unite in marriage,** join *or* unite in holy wedlock, tie the knot, tie the nuptial *or* wedding knot, make one; give away, give in marriage; marry off, find a mate for, find a husband *or* wife for

15 (*get married*) **to marry, wed,** contract matrimony, mate, couple, espouse, wive, **take to wife,** take to oneself a wife, **get hitched** *or* **spliced** (*both informal*), tie the knot, become one, be made one, pair off, give one's hand to, bestow one's hand upon, lead to the altar, take for better *or* for worse; remarry, rewed; intermarry, interwed, miscegenate

16 **to honeymoon,** go on a honeymoon

17 **to cohabit,** live together, live as man and wife, share one's bed and board

adjectives

18 **matrimonial, marital, conjugal, connubial, nuptial,** wedded, married, hymeneal; epithalamic; **spousal;** husbandly, uxorious; bridal, wifely, uxorial

19 **monogamous,** monogynous, monandrous; **bigamous,** digamous; **polygamous,** polygynous, polyandrous; morganatic; miscegenetic

20 **marriageable,** nubile, ripe, of age, of marriageable age

21 **married, wedded,** one, one bone and one flesh, mated, matched, coupled, partnered, paired, hitched *and* spliced (*both informal*)

word elements

22 –gamy; –gamous

564 RELATIONSHIP BY MARRIAGE

nouns

1 **marriage relationship,** affinity, marital affinity; connection, family connection, marriage connection, matrimonial connection

2 **in-laws** (*informal*), **relatives-in-law;** brother-in-law, sister-in-law, father-in-law, mother-in-law, son-in-law, daughter-in-law

3 stepfather, stepmother; stepbrother, stepsister; stepchild, stepson, stepdaughter

adjectives

4 **affinal,** affined, by marriage

565 CELIBACY

nouns

1 **celibacy, singleness,** singlehood, single blessedness, single *or* unmarried *or* unwed state *or* condition; **bachelorhood,** bachelordom, bachelorism, bachelorship; **spinsterhood,** maidenhood, maidenhead, **virginity,** maiden *or* virgin state; **monasticism,** monachism; misogamy, misogyny; sexual abstinence *or* abstention, continence *see* 664.3

2 **celibate,** *célibataire* (*French*); monk, monastic, priest, nun; misogamist, misogynist; unmarried, single (*informal*)

3 **bachelor,** confirmed bachelor, **single man**

4 **single** *or* **unmarried woman,** spinster, spinstress, **old maid,** maid, maiden, bachelor girl, single girl, single woman, lone woman, maiden lady, feme sole; **virgin,** virgo intacta, cherry (*informal*); vestal, vestal virgin

verbs

5 **to be unmarried, be single,** live alone, enjoy single blessedness, keep bachelor quarters, keep one's freedom

adjectives

6 **celibate; monastic,** monachal, **monkish;** misogamic, misogynous; sexually abstinent *or* continent, abstinent, abstaining

7 **unmarried, unwedded, unwed, single,** sole, spouseless, wifeless, husbandless; **bachelorly,** bachelorlike; **spinsterly,** spinsterish, spinsterlike; **old-maidish,** old-maidenish; maiden, maidenly; virgin, virginal

566 DIVORCE, WIDOWHOOD

nouns

1 **divorce,** divorcement, grasswidowhood, civil divorce, **separation,** legal *or* judicial separation, separate

maintenance; interlocutory decree, decree absolute, decree nisi; dissolution of marriage; annulment, decree of nullity; broken marriage, broken home

2 **divorcé**, divorced person, divorced man, divorced woman, *divorcée* (*French*); divorcer; grass widow, grass widower

3 **widowhood**, viduity (*old*); **widowerhood**, widowership; weeds, widow's weeds

4 **widow**, widow woman (*informal*), relict; dowager, queen dowager, etc; **widower**, widowman (*informal*)

verbs

5 **to divorce, separate**, part, split up (*informal*), unmarry, put away, obtain a divorce, come to a parting of the ways, untie the knot, sue for divorce, file suit for divorce; grant a divorce, grant a final decree; grant an annulment, grant a decree of nullity, annul a marriage, put asunder

6 **to widow**, bereave

adjectives

7 widowly, widowish, widowlike; **widowed**, widowered; **divorced**; separated, legally separated

567 SCHOOL

nouns

1 **school** (*see list*), **educational institution**, teaching institution, academic *or* scholastic institution, teaching and research institution, **institute, academy**, seminary, *Schule* (*German*), *école* (*French*), *escuela* (*Spanish*); alternative school; magnet school

2 infant school, nursery, **nursery school**, preschool; day nursery, **day-care centre**, crèche; playschool, playgroup; **kindergarten**

3 **primary school**; junior school; elementary school *or* grade school *or* grammar school (*US*); folk school, *Volksschule* (*German*)

4 middle school; **academy**, *Gymnasium* (*German*); *lycée* (*French*), lyceum; **high school**; intermediate school; **preparatory school**, prep school (*informal*), seminary; boarding school; comprehensive *or* comprehensive school, state school, secondary school, secondary modern school, city technology college; grant-maintained school; private school, independent school, public school, grammar school (*old*); sixth-form college, tertiary college; Latin school; *Progymnasium* (*German*), *Realschule* (*German*), *Realgymnasium* (*German*), special school; village college *or* community college, community school

5 **college, university**, polytechnic (*old*), technical college, institution of higher education *or* learning, college of further education; teacher training college; single-sex school, coeducational school *or* co-ed; academe, academia, the groves of Academe, **the campus**, the halls of learning *or* ivy, ivied halls; alma mater

6 **service school, service academy** (*see list*), military academy, naval academy

7 **art school, performing arts school**, music school, conservatory, arts conservatory, dance school

8 **religious school** (*see list*), parochial school, church school; Sunday school

9 reform school, youth custody centre, borstal (*old*), remand centre

10 **schoolhouse**, school building; classroom building; hall; campus

11 **schoolroom, classroom**; recitation room; lecture room *or* hall; auditorium; theatre, amphitheatre

12 **board of governors**; board of education, school board; senate

adjectives

13 **scholastic, academic**, institutional, **school**, classroom; **collegiate**; **university**, varsity; Oxbridge, ancient, redbrick; preschool; interscholastic, intercollegiate, extramural; intramural; coeducational *or* co-ed

14 **schools**

adult-education school	playschool
alternative school	preparatory school *or* prep
boarding school	school (informal)
day school	primary school
finishing school	private school
junior school *or*	public school
intermediate school	summer school
military school *or* academy	technical school *or* tech
night school	(informal)

15 **service schools or academies**

École de l'Air (Salon-de-Provence)	Royal Military College of Canada (Kingston)
École Navale (Brest)	Royal Naval College
École Spéciale Militaire Interarmes (St Cyr)	(Dartmouth)
Royal Air Force College (Cranwell)	US Air Force Academy (Colorado Springs)
Royal Military Academy (Woolwich)	US Military Academy (West Point)
Royal Military College (Sandhurst)	US Naval Academy (Annapolis)

16 **religious schools**

Bible institute	religious *or* parochial
Bible school	school
church school	Sabbath school
convent school	seminary
denominational school	Sunday school
divinity school	Talmud Torah
Hebrew school *or* heder	theological seminary *or*
(Yiddish)	school
mesivta	vacation church school
parish school	yeshiva

568 TEACHING

nouns

1 **teaching, instruction, education, schooling, tuition**; **edification, enlightenment**, illumination; tutelage, tutorage, tutorship; tutoring, coaching, private teaching, teacher *see* 571; spoon-feeding; direction, guidance; **pedagogy**, pedagogics, didactics, didacticism; catechization; computer-aided instruction, programmed instruction; self-teaching, self-instruction; information *see* 551; reeducation *see* 857.4; **school** *see* 567; **formal education**, coursework, school-work, open learning, **further education**; part-time education, day release *or* block release, sandwich course

2 inculcation, **indoctrination**, catechization, inoculation, **implantation**, infixation, infixion, **impression, instilment,** instillation, impregnation, **infusion,** imbuement; absorption and regurgitation; dictation; conditioning, brainwashing; reindoctrination *see* 857.5

3 **training, preparation,** readying (*informal*), **conditioning, grooming,** cultivation, development, improvement; **discipline;** breaking, housebreaking; **upbringing, bringing-up,** fetching-up (*informal*), **rearing, raising, breeding, nurture,** nurturing, fostering; **practice,** rehearsal, **exercise, drill,** drilling; **apprenticeship,** in-service training, on-the-job training; work-study; military training, basic training, square bashing (*informal*); manual training; vocational training *or* education

4 preinstruction, pre-education; **priming,** cramming (*informal*)

5 elementary education; initiation, introduction, propaedeutic; **rudiments,** grounding, first steps, elements, **ABC's, basics;** reading, writing, and arithmetic, **three R's;** primer, hornbook, abecedarium, abecedary

6 **instructions, directions, orders; briefing,** final instructions

7 **lesson, teaching, instruction, lecture,** lecture-demonstration, harangue, **discourse,** disquisition, exposition, **talk,** homily, **sermon,** preachment; chalk talk (*US & Canadian informal*); **recitation,** recital; **assignment, exercise,** task, set task, homework; **moral,** morality, moralization, moral lesson; object lesson

8 **study,** branch of learning; **discipline,** subdiscipline; **field, speciality,** academic speciality, area; **course,** course of study, **curriculum; subject;** major (*US*), minor (*US*); requirement *or* required course, elective course, core curriculum, syllabus; **National Curriculum,** core curriculum, Basic Curriculum, core subjects, foundation subjects, programme of study; refresher course; summer course; **seminar,** proseminar

9 physical education *or* PE, physical training *or* PT, games (*informal*), physical culture, gymnastics *or* gym, callisthenics, eurhythmics

verbs

10 to teach, instruct, give instruction, give lessons in, **educate, school; edify, enlighten,** civilize, illumine; **direct, guide;** get across, **inform** *see* 551.8; **show,** show how, show the ropes, demonstrate; give an idea of; put in the right, set right; improve one's mind, enlarge *or* broaden the mind; sharpen the wits, open the eyes *or* mind; teach a lesson, give a lesson to; **ground,** teach the rudiments *or* elements *or* basics; catechize; teach an old dog new tricks; reeducate *see* 857.14

11 to tutor, coach; prime, cram (*informal*), cram with facts, stuff with knowledge

12 to inculcate, indoctrinate, catechize, inoculate, instil, infuse, imbue, impregnate, implant, infix, impress; impress upon the mind *or* memory, urge on the mind, beat into, beat *or* knock into one's head, grind in, drill into, drum into one's head *or* skull; condition, brainwash, programme

13 to train; drill, exercise; practise, rehearse; keep in practice, keep one's hand in; **prepare,** ready, **condition, groom,** fit, put in tune, form, **lick into shape** (*informal*); **rear, raise, bring up,** fetch up (*informal*), bring up by hand, **breed; cultivate,** develop, improve; **nurture, foster,** nurse; **discipline,** take in hand; put through the mill *or* grind (*informal*); break, break in, house-train; put to school, send to school, apprentice

14 to preinstruct, pre-educate; initiate, introduce

15 to give instructions, give directions; brief, give a briefing

16 to expound, exposit; explain *see* 341.10; lecture, discourse, harangue, hold forth, give *or* read a lesson; preach, sermonize; moralize, point a moral

17 to assign, give an assignment, give homework, set a task, set hurdles; lay out a course, make a syllabus

adjectives

18 educational, educative, educating, teaching, instructive, instructional, tuitional, tuitionary; cultural, edifying, enlightening, illuminating; informative; didactic, preceptive; self instructional, self-teaching, autodidactic; lecturing, preaching, hortatory, exhortatory, homiletic, homiletical; initiatory, introductory, propaedeutic; disciplinary; coeducational

19 scholastic, academic, schoolish, pedantic, donnish; scholarly; pedagogical; graduate, professional, graduate-professional, postgraduate; interdisciplinary, cross-disciplinary; curricular

20 extracurricular, extraclassroom, extramural; nonscholastic, noncollegiate

569 MISTEACHING

nouns

1 **misteaching,** misinstruction; **misguidance,** misdirection, misleading; sophistry *see* 935; perversion, corruption; mystification, obscuration, obfuscation, obscurantism; **misinformation,** misknowledge; the blind leading the blind; college of Laputa

2 propaganda; propagandism, indoctrination; brainwashing; **propagandist,** agitprop; **disinformation**

verbs

3 to misteach, misinstruct, miseducate; misinform; misadvise, misguide, misdirect, mislead; pervert, corrupt; mystify, obscure, obfuscate

4 to propagandize, carry on a propaganda; indoctrinate; disinform, brainwash

adjectives

5 mistaught, misinstructed; misinformed; misadvised, misguided, misdirected, misled

6 misteaching, misinstructive, miseducative, misinforming; misleading, misguiding, misdirecting; obscuring, mystifying, obfuscatory; propagandistic, indoctrinational; disinformational

570 LEARNING

nouns

1 **learning,** intellectual acquirement *or* acquisition *or* attainment, stocking *or* storing the mind, mental cultivation, mental culture, improving *or* broadening the mind; **mastery,** mastery of skills; **self-education,** self-instruction; **knowledge, erudition** *see* 927.5; education *see* 568.1; memorization *see* 988.4

2 **absorption,** ingestion, imbibing, assimilation, taking in, getting, getting hold of, getting the hang of (*informal*), soaking-up, digestion

3 **study, studying,** application, conning; **reading, perusal; revision,** restudy, restudying, brushing up, **review; contemplation** *see* 930.2; **inspection** *see* 937.3; **engrossment; brainwork, headwork,** lucubration, mental labour; exercise, **practice, drill;** cramming *and* swotting (*both informal*); extensive study, wide reading; **subject** *see* 568.8

4 **studiousness, scholarliness,** scholarship; bookishness, diligence *see* 330.6

5 **teachableness, teachability, educability,** trainableness; **aptness, aptitude,** quickness, **readiness; receptivity,** mind like a blotter, ready grasp, quick mind, quick study; **willingness, motivation,** hunger *or* thirst for learning; docility, **malleability,** mouldability, pliability, facility, plasticity, **impressionability,** susceptibility, formability; brightness, cleverness, **intelligence** *see* 919

verbs

6 **to learn,** get, get hold of (*informal*), get into one's head, get through one's thick skull (*informal*); **gain knowledge,** pick up information, gather *or* collect *or* glean knowledge *or* learning; stock *or* store the mind, improve *or* broaden the mind; stuff *or* cram the mind; burden *or* load the mind; **find out, ascertain, discover,** find, determine; **become informed,** gain knowledge *or* understanding of, acquire information *or* intelligence about, **learn about, find out about;** acquaint oneself with, make oneself acquainted with, become acquainted with; be informed *see* 551.14

7 **to absorb, acquire, take in,** ingest, imbibe, get by osmosis, **assimilate, digest, soak up,** drink in; **soak in, seep in,** percolate in

8 **to memorize** *see* 988.17, get by rote; fix in the mind *see* 988.18

9 **to master,** attain mastery of, make oneself master of, **gain command of, become adept in,** become familiar *or* conversant with, become versed *or* well-versed in, **get up in** *or* **on,** gain a good *or* thorough knowledge of, **learn all about, get off pat** (*informal*), get taped, get to the bottom *or* heart of; **get the hang** *or* **knack of; learn the ropes,** learn the ins and outs; know well *see* 927.13

10 **to learn by experience,** learn by doing, **live and learn,** go through the school of hard knocks, learn the hard way (*informal*); teach *or* school oneself; **learn a lesson,** be taught a lesson

11 **to be taught, receive instruction,** be tutored, undergo schooling, pursue one's education, attend classes, go to *or* attend school, take lessons, matriculate, enrol, register; **train,** prepare oneself, ready oneself, go into training; serve an

apprenticeship; apprentice oneself to; **study with,** read with, sit at the feet of, learn from, have as one's master; monitor, audit

12 **to study,** regard studiously, apply oneself to; **read, peruse,** go over, read up *or* read up on, gen up on (*informal*), have one's nose in a book (*informal*); **revise,** restudy, **review; contemplate** *see* 930.12; **examine** *see* 937.23; give the mind to *see* 982.5; **pore over;** be highly motivated, hunger *or* thirst for knowledge; bury oneself in, wade through, plunge into; swot (*informal*), cram (*informal*); lucubrate, elucubrate, **burn the midnight oil;** make a study of; **practise, drill**

13 **to browse, scan, skim, dip into,** thumb over *or* through, run over *or* through, glance *or* run the eye over *or* through, turn over the leaves, have a look at, rifle through

14 **to study up, mug up** (*informal*), study up on, read up on; **review, brush up,** polish up (*informal*), **cram** *or* cram up (*informal*)

15 **to study to be, study for, read for,** read law, etc; **specialize in, go in for,** make one's field; major in (*US*), minor in (*US*)

adjectives

16 **educated, learned** *see* 927.21, 22; self-taught, self-instructed, autodidactic

17 **studious,** devoted to studies, **scholarly,** scholastic, academic, professorial, tweedy, donnish; owlish; rabbinic, mandarin; pedantic, dry as dust; bookish *see* 927.22; diligent *see* 330.22

18 **teachable, instructable, educable,** schoolable, trainable; **apt, quick, ready,** ripe for instruction; **receptive, willing,** motivated; hungry *or* thirsty for knowledge; docile, **malleable, mouldable,** pliable, facile, plastic, **impressionable,** susceptible, formable; bright, clever, **intelligent** *see* 919.12

571 TEACHER

nouns

1 **teacher, instructor, educator,** preceptor, **mentor; master,** maestro; **pedagogue,** pedagogist, educationist; schoolman; **schoolteacher, schoolmaster,** schoolkeeper; dominie (*Scottish*); **professor, academic,** member of academy; don, fellow; guide *see* 574.7, docent; rabbi, *melamed* (*Hebrew*), pandit, pundit, guru, *mullah* (*Persian*), *starets* (*Russian*)

2 (*woman teachers*) instructress, educatress, preceptress, **mistress; schoolmistress; schoolma'am** *or* **schoolmarm,** dame, schooldame; **governess,** duenna

3 (*academic ranks*) professor, associate professor, assistant professor, instructor, tutor, associate, assistant, lecturer, reader; visiting professor; Regius professor; emeritus, professor emeritus, retired professor

4 teaching fellow, teaching assistant, supervisor; intern (*US & Canadian*); apprentice teacher, student teacher; monitor, proctor, prefect, prepositor *or* preposter; student assistant, graduate assistant

5 **tutor,** tutorer; **coach,** coacher; **private instructor,**

Privatdocent, Privatdozent (both German); crammer (*informal*)

6 trainer, handler, groom; drillmaster; **coach**

7 lecturer, lector, **reader**, prelector, **preacher**, homilist

8 principal, headmaster, head teacher, headmistress, beak (*informal*); president, chancellor, vice-chancellor, rector, provost, warden, master; **dean**, academic dean, dean of the faculty, dean of women *and* dean of men (*both US*); administrator, educational administrator; Chief Education Officer *or* Director of Education; administration

9 faculty, staff, faculty members, professorate, professoriate, professors, professordom, teaching staff; senate, court

10 instructorship, teachership, preceptorship, schoolmastery; **tutorship**, tutorhood, tutorage, tutelage; **professorship**, professorhood, professorate, professoriate; **chair**, endowed chair; lectureship, readership; fellowship

adjectives

11 pedagogic, pedagogical, preceptorial, tutorial; **teacherish**, teachery, teacherlike, teachy, **schoolteacherish**, schoolteachery, **schoolmasterish**, schoolmasterly, schoolmastering, schoolmasterlike; schoolmistressy, schoolmarmish (*informal*); **professorial**, professorlike, academic, tweedy, donnish; pedantic *see 927.22*

572 STUDENT

nouns

1 student, pupil, scholar, learner, studier, educatee, **trainee**, *élève (French)*; tutee; inquirer; mature student, adult-education *or* continuing *or* further education student; self-taught person, autodidact; auditor; **reader**, reading enthusiast, great reader, bookworm (*informal*)

2 disciple, follower, apostle; convert, proselyte *see 857.7*; **discipleship**, disciplehood, tutelage, studentship, followership

3 schoolchild; schoolboy; schoolgirl; day pupil, day boy, day girl, boarder; infant, preschool child, preschooler, nursery school child; schoolmate, schoolfellow, fellow student, classmate; sixth-former, senior pupil; head boy, head girl, prefect

4 special *or* **exceptional student**, gifted student; scholarship student, bursar (*Scottish & NZ*); special education *or* special ed (*informal*), student; student with learning difficulties; slow learner, underachiever; student with special needs; emotionally disturbed student; culturally disadvantaged student (*US*)

5 college student, collegian, collegiate, university student, **varsity student** (*informal*), college boy *or* girl

6 undergraduate, undergrad (*informal*); **fresher** (*informal*), first-year

7 commoner, sizar, exhibitioner, fellow commoner, sophister; wrangler, senior wrangler (*both Cambridge University*); (*US & Canadian terms*) freshman, sophomore, junior, senior

8 graduate, graduand; **alumnus**, alumni, alumna, alumnae; old boy, old girl; **graduate student**, master's degree candidate, doctoral candidate; **postgraduate**, postgrad (*informal*); degrees; university graduate, university man *or* woman, educated man *or* woman, educated class; meritocracy

9 novice, novitiate *or* noviciate, **tyro**, abecedarian, alphabetarian, **beginner** *see 817.2*, entrant, **neophyte**, tenderfoot *and* greenhorn (*both US informal*), fresher, **fledgling**; catechumen, initiate, debutant; new boy, newcomer *see 773.4*; ignoramus *see 929.8*; **recruit, raw recruit**, inductee, rookie (*informal*); **probationer**, probationist, postulant; **apprentice**

10 nerd (*informal*), swot *or* swotter (*both informal*), anorak (*informal*); bookworm *see 928.4*

11 class, form, grade, shell; track; year

adjectives

12 studentlike, schoolboyish, schoolgirlish; undergraduate, graduate, postgraduate; **collegiate**, college-bred; autodidactic; **studious** *see 570.17*; **learned, bookish** *see 927.22*; exceptional, gifted, special

13 probationary, probational, on probation; in detention

573 DIRECTION, MANAGEMENT

nouns

1 direction, management, managing, managery (*old*), handling, **running** (*informal*), **conduct**; governance, **command, control, chiefdom, government** *see 612*, controllership; **authority** *see 417*; **regulation**, ordering, husbandry; manipulation; **guidance, lead, leading; steering, navigation**, pilotage, conning, the con, the helm, the wheel

2 supervision, superintendence, intendance *or* intendancy, heading, heading up *and* **bossing** *and* running (*all informal*); **surveillance**, oversight, eye; **charge, care, auspices, jurisdiction; responsibility**, accountability *see 641.2*

3 administration, executive function *or* role, command function, say-so *and* last word (*both informal*); **decision-making; disposition**, disposal, **dispensation**; officiation

4 directorship, leadership, managership, directorate, headship, governorship, chairmanship, convenership, presidency, generalship, captainship; mastership *see 417.7*; dictatorship, sovereignty *see 417.8*; superintendence *or* **superintendency**, intendancy, foremanship, overseership, supervisorship; stewardship, custody, guardianship, shepherding, proctorship; collective leadership

5 helm, con, rudder, tiller, wheel, steering wheel; **reins**, reins of government

6 domestic management, housekeeping, homemaking, housewifery, ménage, husbandry (*old*); domestic economy, home economics

7 efficiency engineering, scientific management, bean-counting (*informal*), industrial engineering, management engineering, management consulting; management theory; management consultant, efficiency expert; time and motion study, time-motion study, time study

verbs

8 to **direct, manage, regulate, conduct, carry on, handle, run** (*informal*); **control, command, head, govern** *see* 612.12, **boss** *and* head up *and* pull the strings *and* **mastermind** (*all informal*); **order, prescribe**; lay down the law, make the rules, call the shots *or* tune (*informal*); **head**, head up, office, captain, skipper (*informal*); **lead**, take the lead, lead on; manipulate, manoeuvre, engineer; take command *see* 417.14; be responsible for

9 to **guide, steer, drive, run** (*informal*); herd, shepherd; channel; **pilot**, take the helm, be at the helm *or* wheel *or* tiller *or* rudder, hold the reins, **be in the driver's seat** (*informal*)

10 to **supervise, superintend, boss, oversee,** overlook, stand over, keep an eye on *or* upon, keep in order; take care of *see* 1007.19

11 to **administer,** administrate; **officiate; preside,** preside over, preside at the board; chair, chairman, occupy the chair

adjectives

12 **directing, directive,** directory, directorial; **managing, managerial; commanding, controlling, governing** *see* 612.18; regulating, regulative, regulatory; **head, chief;** leading, guiding

13 **supervising, supervisory,** overseeing, **superintendent, boss; in charge** *see* 417.21

14 **administrative, administrating;** ministerial, **executive;** officiating, presiding

adverbs

15 in the charge of, in the hands of, in the care of; **under the auspices of,** under the aegis of; in one's charge, on one's hands, under one's care, under one's jurisdiction

574 DIRECTOR

nouns

1 **director,** *directeur* (*French*), director general, **governor,** rector, **manager, administrator,** intendant, **conductor;** person in charge, responsible person; ship's husband, supercargo; impresario, producer; deputy, agent *see* 576

2 **superintendent; supervisor, foreman,** monitor, **head,** headman, overman, **boss,** chief, gaffer (*informal*), guv'nor *and* guv (*both informal*), taskmaster; sirdar (*India*), **overseer,** overlooker; inspector, surveyor, visitor; proctor; charge hand; slave driver; boatswain; floorman, floorwalker, floor manager; noncommissioned officer *see* 575.19; controller, comptroller, auditor

3 **executive,** officer, official; **president,** chief executive officer *or* CEO, chief executive, managing director; provost, prefect, warden, archon; policy-maker, agenda-setter; magistrate; **chairman of the board; chancellor,** vice-chancellor; vice-president; secretary; treasurer; dean; executive officer, executive director, executive secretary; **management,** the administration *see* 574.11

4 **steward,** bailiff, reeve (*old*), factor (*Scottish*), seneschal; majordomo, butler, housekeeper, *maître d'hôtel* (*French*); master of ceremonies *or* MC *and* emcee (*both informal*), master of the revels; proctor, procurator, attorney; guardian, custodian *see* 1007.6; curator, librarian; croupier

5 **chairman, chairwoman, chair,** convener, speaker, presiding officer; co-chairman, etc

6 **leader,** conductor (*old*); file leader, fugleman; pacemaker, pacesetter; bellwether, bell mare, bell cow, Judas goat; standard-bearer, torchbearer; **leader of men,** born leader, charismatic leader *or* figure, inspired leader; messiah, Mahdi; Führer, duce; forerunner *see* 815.1; ringleader *see* 375.11; precentor, coryphaeus, choragus, symphonic conductor, *kapellmeister* (*German*), choirmaster *see* 710.18

7 **guide,** guider; **shepherd,** herd, herdsman, drover, cowherd, goatherd, etc; tour guide, tour director *or* conductor, cicerone, mercury (*old*), courier, dragoman; **pilot,** river pilot, navigator, **helmsman,** timoneer, steersman, steerer, coxswain, boatsteerer, boatheader; automatic pilot, Gyropilot; pointer, finger post, guidepost *see* 517.4

8 **guiding star,** cynosure (*old*), **polestar,** polar star, lodestar, Polaris, **North Star**

9 **compass,** magnetic compass, gyrocompass, gyroscopic compass, gyrostatic compass, Gyrosin compass, surveyor's compass, mariner's compass; needle, magnetic needle; direction finder, radio compass, radio direction finder *or* RDF

10 **directory, guidebook,** handbook, Baedeker; city directory, business directory; telephone directory, telephone book, phone book (*informal*), classified directory, Yellow Pages (*Trademark*); **bibliography;** catalogue, index, handlist, checklist, finding list; itinerary, road map, A-Z, roadbook; gazetteer, reference book

11 **directorate,** directory, **management, the administration,** top brass (*informal*), the people upstairs (*informal*), executive hierarchy; the executive, executive arm *or* branch; middle management; **cabinet; board,** governing board *or* body, board of directors, board of trustees, board of regents; steering committee, executive committee, interlocking directorate; cadre, executive council; infrastructure; council *see* 423

575 MASTER

nouns

1 **master, lord, lord and master,** overlord, seigneur, paramount, lord paramount, liege, liege lord, *padrone* (*Italian*), *patron* and *chef* (*both French*), patroon; **chief, boss,** sahib (*India*), bwana (*Swahili*); employer; husband, man of the house, master of the house, goodman (*old or informal*), paterfamilias; patriarch, elder; teacher, rabbi, guru, starets; church dignitary, ecclesiarch

2 **mistress,** governess, dame (*old*), madam; **matron, housewife,** homemaker, goodwife (*old*), lady of the house, chatelaine; housemistress, housemother; rectoress, abbess, mother superior; great lady, first lady; matriarch, dowager

3 chief, principal; **master**, dean, doyen, doyenne; high priest (*informal*), superior, senior; **leader** *see* 574.6; important person, personage *see* 996.8

4 (*informal terms*) **top dog**, boss man, big cheese, kingpin, supremo, head honcho (*US*); queen bee

5 **figurehead**, nominal head, dummy, lay figure, front man *and* front (*both informal*), stooge (*informal*), puppet, creature

6 **governor, ruler; captain, master, commander,** commandant, commanding officer, intendant, castellan, chatelain, chatelaine; **director, manager, executive** *see* 574.3

7 **head of state, chief of state; premier, prime minister, chancellor,** grand vizier, dewan (*India*); doge; **president,** chief executive

8 **potentate, sovereign, monarch, ruler, prince,** dynast, **crowned head, emperor,** *imperator* (*Latin*), king-emperor, **king,** anointed king, majesty, royalty, royal, royal personage; petty king, tetrarch, kinglet; grand duke; paramount, lord paramount, suzerain, overlord, overking, high king; **chief, chieftain,** high chief; prince consort *see* 608.7

9 (*rulers*) **caesar,** kaiser, **czar;** Holy Roman Emperor; Dalai Lama; **pharaoh;** pendragon, rig, ardri; **mikado,** tenno; shogun, tycoon; khan *or* cham; shah, padishah; negus; bey; **sheikh;** sachem, sagamore; Inca; cacique; kaid

10 (*Muslim rulers*) **sultan,** Grand Turk, grand seignior; caliph, imam; hakim; khan *or* cham; nizam, nabab; emir; Great Mogul, Mogul

11 **sovereign queen, sovereign princess, princess, queen,** queen regent, queen regnant, **empress,** czarina, *Kaiserin* (*German*); rani, maharani (*both India*); grand duchess; queen consort

12 **regent,** protector, prince regent, queen regent

13 (*regional governors*) **governor,** governor-general, lieutenant governor; **viceroy,** vice-king, exarch, proconsul, khedive, stadtholder, vizier; nabob *and* nabab *and* subahdar (*all India*); gauleiter; eparch; palatine; tetrarch; burgrave; collector; hospodar, vaivode; dey, bey *or* beg, beglerbeg, wali *or* vali, satrap; provincial

14 **tyrant, despot,** warlord; **autocrat,** autarch; oligarch; absolute ruler *or* master *or* monarch, omnipotent *or* all-powerful ruler; **dictator,** duce, Führer, commissar, pharaoh, caesar, czar; usurper, arrogator; **oppressor, hard master,** driver, **slave driver;** martinet, disciplinarian, stickler

15 **the authorities, the powers that be,** ruling class *or* classes, the lords of creation, **the Establishment,** the interests, the power elite, **the power structure; they, them;** the inner circle; the ins *and* the in-group *and* those on the inside (*all informal*); **management, the administration;** higher echelons, **top brass** (*informal*), **the top** (*informal*), the corridors of power; prelacy, hierarchy; ministry; **bureaucracy, officialdom;** directorate *see* 574.11

16 **official, officer,** officiary, functionary, *fonctionnaire* (*French*), apparatchik; **public official,** public servant; officeholder, office-bearer; government *or* public employee; **civil servant; bureaucrat,** mandarin, red-tapist, *rond-de-cuir* (*French*), *apparatchik* (*Russian*); petty tyrant, jobsworth

17 (*ministers*) **minister,** Deputy Prime Minister, secretary of state, undersecretary of state, cabinet minister, minister of state, junior minister, minister without portfolio, Foreign Secretary, Home Secretary, Chancellor of the Exchequer, Chief Secretary to the Treasury, President of the Board of Trade, Chancellor of the Duchy of Lancaster; chancellor; warden; archon; magistrate, Justice of the Peace *or* JP, bailie (*Scottish*); syndic; commissioner; commissar; ombudsman, Parliamentary Commissioner; mayor, *maire* (*French*), lord mayor, burgomaster, city manager (*US*); headman, induna (*Africa*); **councillor,** elder, city father, alderman, provost (*Scottish*); reeve, portreeve; legislator *see* 610.3

18 **commissioned officer, officer;** top brass *and* brass hats (*both informal*); **commander in chief,** generalissimo; hetman, sirdar; **marshal,** *maréchal* (*French*), field marshal

19 (*air force ranks*) Marshal of the RAF, Air Chief Marshal, Air Marshal, Air Vice-Marshal, Air Commodore, Group Captain, Wing Commander, Squadron Leader, Flight Lieutenant, Flying Officer, Pilot Officer, Warrant Officer, Flight Sergeant, Chief Technician, Sergeant, Corporal, Aircraftsman

20 (*army ranks*) Field Marshal, General, Lieutenant-General, Major-General, Brigadier, Colonel, Lieutenant-Colonel, Major, Captain, Lieutenant, Second Lieutenant, Warrant Officer, Sergeant, Lance Corporal, Corporal, Private

21 (*naval ranks*) Admiral of the Fleet, Admiral, Vice-Admiral, Rear-Admiral, Commodore, Captain, Commander, Lieutenant, Sub-Lieutenant, Acting Sub-Lieutenant, Warrant Officer, Chief Petty Officer, Petty Officer, Midshipman, Able Rating, Ordinary Rating

22 (*heraldic officials*) herald, king of arms, king at arms, earl marshal; Garter, Garter King of Arms, Clarenceux, Clarenceux King of Arms, Norroy and Ulster, Norroy and Ulster King of Arms, Norroy, Norroy King of Arms, Lyon, Lyon King of Arms; College of Arms

576 DEPUTY, AGENT

nouns

1 **deputy, proxy, representative, substitute,** vice, vicegerent, **alternate,** backup *and* stand-in (*both informal*), alter ego, **surrogate,** procurator, secondary, understudy, the bench (*informal*); second in command, executive officer; exponent, advocate, pleader, paranymph, attorney, champion; **lieutenant;** vicar general; locum tenens *or* locum; amicus curiae; **puppet,** dummy, creature, cat's-paw, figurehead

2 **delegate,** legate; **commissioner,** commissary, *commissionaire* (*French*), commissar; **messenger,** herald, **emissary, envoy; minister,** secretary

3 **agent, instrument,** implement, implementer; expediter, facilitator; **tool; steward** *see* 574.4; **functionary; official** *see* 575.16; clerk, **secretary;** amanuensis; factor, consignee; puppet, cat's-paw; dupe *see* 358

4 go-between, middleman, intermediary, medium, intermedium, intermediate, interagent, internuncio, broker; connection (*informal*), contact; negotiator, negotiant; interpleader; arbitrator, mediator *see* 466.3

5 spokesman, spokeswoman, spokesperson, spokespeople, official spokesman *or* woman *or* person, press officer, speaker, voice, mouthpiece (*informal*); herald; proloctor, prolocutress *or* prolocutrix; reporter, rapporteur

6 diplomat, diplomatist, diplomatic agent, diplomatic (*old*); emissary, envoy, legate, minister, foreign service officer; ambassador, ambassadress, ambassador extraordinary and plenipotentiary, ambassador extraordinary, ambassador plenipotentiary, ambassador-at-large (*US*); envoy extraordinary, plentipotentiary, minister plenipotentiary; nuncio, internuncio, apostolic delegate; vice-legate; resident, minister resident; chargé d'affaires, chargé, chargé d'affaires ad interim; chancellor, secretary of legation; attaché, commercial attaché, military attaché, consul, consul general, vice-consul, consular agent; career diplomat

7 foreign office, foreign service, diplomatic service; diplomatic mission, diplomatic staff *or* corps, *corps diplomatique* (*French*); embassy, legation; consular service; chancery

8 vice-president, vice-chairman, vice-governor, vice-director, vice-master, vice-chancellor, vice-premier, vice-warden, vice-consul, vice-legate; vice-regent, viceroy, vicegerent, vice-king, vice-queen, vice-reine, etc

9 secret agent, operative, cloak-and-dagger operative, undercover man, inside man (*informal*); spy, espionage agent; counterspy, double agent; spotter; scout, reconnoitrer; intelligence agent *or* officer; MI5 man *or* woman, military-intelligence man, naval-intelligence man; spymaster; spy-catcher (*informal*), counterintelligence agent

10 detective, operative, investigator, sleuth, Sherlock Holmes (*A Conan Doyle*); police detective, CID man *or* woman, plain-clothes policeman *or* policewoman, Bow Street runner; private detective, private investigator *or* PI, dick *or* private dick (*US*), inquiry agent; hotel detective, house detective, store detective, house dick (*US informal*); arson investigator; narcotics agent *or* officer, narc (*informal*); Federal Bureau of Investigation *or* FBI

11 (*informal terms*) tec, dick, gumshoe, sleuthound, flatfoot, beagle (*old*); eye, private eye; skip tracer, spotter

12 secret service, intelligence service, intelligence bureau *or* department; intelligence, military intelligence, naval intelligence; counterintelligence

13 (*group of delegates*) delegation, deputation, commission, mission; committee, subcommittee

verbs

14 to represent, act for, act on behalf of, substitute for, appear for, answer for, speak for, be the voice of, give voice to, be the mouthpiece of (*informal*), hold the proxy of, hold a brief for, act in the place of, stand in the stead of, serve in one's stead; understudy, double for *and* stand in for *and* back up

(*all informal*); front for (*informal*); deputize, commission

adjectives

15 deputy, deputative; acting, representative

16 diplomatic, ambassadorial, consular, ministerial, plenipotentiary

adverbs

17 by proxy, indirectly; in behalf of *see* 861.12

577 SERVANT, EMPLOYEE

nouns

1 retainer, dependent, follower; myrmidon, yeoman; vassal, liege, liege man, feudatory, homager; inferior, underling, subordinate, understrapper; minion, creature, hanger-on, lackey, flunky, stooge (*informal*); peon, serf, slave *see* 432.7

2 servant, servitor, help; domestic, domestic help, domestic servant, house servant; live-in help, day help; menial, drudge, skivvy, dogsbody; scullion, turnspit

3 employee; pensioner, hireling, mercenary, myrmidon; hired man, hired hand, man *or* girl Friday, right-hand man, assistant, personal assistant *or* PA *see* 616.6; worker *see* 726

4 man, manservant, serving man, gillie (*Scottish*), boy, garçon (*French*), houseboy; butler; valet, *valet de chambre* (*French*), gentleman, gentleman's gentleman; driver, chauffeur, coachman; gardener; lord-in-waiting, lord of the bedchamber, equerry

5 attendant, tender, usher, squire, yeoman; errand boy *or* girl, gofer (*informal*), office boy *or* girl, copyboy; page *or* pageboy, buttons, footboy; bellboy *and* bellhop (*US & Canadian*); cabin boy, purser; printer's devil, fag, bedder, chore boy; caddie; bootblack, boots; trainbearer; cupbearer, Ganymede, Hebe; orderly, batman; cabin *or* flight attendant, steward, stewardess, hostess, air stewardess *or* hostess, purser

6 lackey, flunky, livery *or* liveried servant; footman, *valet de pied* (*French*)

7 waiter, waitress; busboy (*US & Canadian*); headwaiter, *maître d'hôtel* (*French*), maître d' (*informal*); hostess; wine waiter, sommelier; barman, barmaid, bartender, barkeeper *or* barkeep, tea lady

8 home help, daily, Mrs Mop (*informal*), charlady *and* charwoman *and* char, cleaning lady; maid, maidservant, servitress, girl, servant girl, *bonne* (*French*), serving girl, wench, hired girl; au pair girl, ayah (*India*), amah (*China*); live-in maid, live-out maid; handmaid, handmaiden; lady's maid, waiting maid *or* woman, gentlewoman, abigail, soubrette; lady-in-waiting, maid-in-waiting, lady of the bedchamber; companion; chaperon; betweenmaid, tweeny; duenna; parlour maid; kitchenmaid, scullery maid; cook; housemaid, chambermaid, *femme de chambre*, *fille de chambre* (*both French*), upstairs maid; nursemaid *see* 1007.8

9 factotum, do-all (*old*), general servant, man of all work; maid of all work, domestic drudge

10 major-domo, steward, house steward, butler,

chamberlain, *maître d'hôtel* (*French*), seneschal;
housekeeper
11 **staff, personnel, employees,** help, hired help,
crew, gang, men, force, servantry, retinue *see* 768.6
12 **service,** servanthood, servitude (*old*), servitorship,
servitium (*Latin*); **employment, employ; ministry,
ministration, attendance,** tendance; serfdom,
peonage, slavery *see* 432.1

verbs

13 **to serve, work for,** be in service with, serve one's
every need; minister *or* administer to, pander to, do
service to; **help** *see* 449.11; **care for,** do for
(*informal*), **look after,** wait on hand and foot, take
care of; **wait, wait on** *or* **upon, attend,** tend,
attend on *or* upon, dance attendance upon; lackey,
valet, maid, chore, fag; drudge *see* 725.14

adjectives

14 **serving,** servitorial, servitial, **ministering,** waiting,
attending, attendant; in the train of, in one's pay *or*
employ; helping *see* 449.20; **menial, servile**

adverbs

15 downstairs, below stairs

578 FASHION

nouns

1 **fashion, style, mode, vogue,** trend, prevailing
taste; proper thing, ton, bon ton; custom *see* 373;
convention *see* 579.1, 2; the swim (*informal*), current
or stream of fashion; height of fashion; the new look,
the season's look; high fashion, *haute couture*
(*French*), street fashion
2 **fashionableness,** ton, bon ton, fashionability,
stylishness, modishness, voguishness; with-itness
(*informal*); **popularity,** prevalence, currency *see* 863.2
3 **smartness, chic,** elegance; style-consciousness,
clothes-consciousness; **spruceness, nattiness,**
neatness, trimness, sleekness, **dapperness,** jauntiness;
sharpness *and* classiness (*both informal*); swankiness
(*informal*); foppery, foppishness, coxcombry,
dandyism; hipness (*informal*); street credibility *or*
cred (*informal*)
4 **the rage,** the thing, **the last word** (*informal*), *le
dernier cri* (*French*), **the latest thing,** the in thing
(*informal*)
5 **fad, craze, rage;** wrinkle (*informal*); novelty *see*
840.2; faddishness, faddiness (*informal*), faddism;
faddist; the bandwagon, me-tooism
6 **society,** *société* (*French*), fashionable society, **polite
society, high society,** high life, *beau monde, haut
monde* (*both French*), good society; best people,
people of fashion, right people; *monde* (*French*),
world of fashion, Vanity Fair; **smart set** (*informal*);
the Four Hundred (*US*), upper crust (*informal*);
cream of society, *crème de la crème* (*French*), elite,
carriage trade; café society, jet set, beautiful people,
in-crowd, the glitterati (*informal*); *jeunesse dorée*
(*French*); drawing room, salon; social register (*US*)
7 **person of fashion,** fashionable, man-about-town, man
or woman of the world, nob, *mondain, mondaine* (*both
French*); leader *or* arbiter of fashion, tastemaker,

trendsetter, tonesetter, *arbiter elegantiae* (*Latin*); ten
best-dressed, clotheshorse,
"the glass of fashion and the mould of form"—
SHAKESPEARE, Beau Brummel; fashion victim; fop,
blood, rake, dandy *see* 500.9; **socialite;
clubwoman,** clubman; salonist, salonnard; jet setter;
debutante, deb (*informal*)

verbs

8 **to catch on,** become popular, **become all the
rage,** catch *or* take fire
9 **to be fashionable, be the style, be all the rage,**
be the thing; have a run; cut a figure in society
(*informal*), give a tone to society, set the fashion *or*
style *or* tone; dress to kill
10 **to follow the fashion, get in the swim** (*informal*),
get *or* climb *or* jump on the bandwagon (*informal*),
join the parade, follow the crowd, go with the
stream *or* tide *or* current *or* flow; keep in step, do as
others do; keep up, **keep up appearances,** keep up
with the Joneses

adjectives

11 **fashionable, in fashion, smart, in style, in
vogue; all the rage,** all the thing; **popular,**
prevalent, current *see* 863.12; **up-to-date,** up-to-
datish, up-to-the-minute, cool *and* hip (*both
informal*), trendy (*informal*), swish (*informal*),
newfashioned, modern, new *see* 840.9,10,12-14; **in
the swim;** sought-after, much sought-after
12 **stylish, modish,** voguish, vogue; dressy (*informal*);
soigné or *soignée* (*both French*); *à la mode* (*French*), in
the mode
13 **chic, smart,** elegant; style-conscious, clothes-
conscious; **well-dressed,** well-groomed, *soignée* or
soignée (*both French*), dressed to advantage, all
dressed up, dressed to kill, dressed to the nines,
dolled up (*informal*), well-turned-out; **spruce, natty,**
neat, trim, sleek; **dapper,** dashing, jaunty; sharp *and*
classy *and* nifty *and* snazzy (*all informal*); **swank** *or*
swanky (*informal*), posh (*informal*), ritzy (*informal*);
genteel; exquisite, *recherché* (*French*); cosmopolitan,
sophisticated
14 **ultrafashionable,** ultrastylish, ultrasmart; foppish,
dandified, dandyish, dandiacal
15 **trendy** (*informal*), **faddish,** faddy (*informal*)
16 socially prominent, in society, high-society, elite;
café-society, jet-set; lace-curtain, silk-stocking

adverbs

17 **fashionably, stylishly, modishly,** *à la mode*
(*French*), in the latest style *or* mode
18 **smartly,** dressily, chicly, elegantly, exquisitely;
sprucely, nattily, neatly, trimly, sleekly; **dapperly,**
jauntily, dashingly, swankily (*informal*); foppishly,
dandyishly

579 SOCIAL CONVENTION

nouns

1 **social convention, convention,** conventional usage,
what is done, the done thing, what one does, **social
usage, form, formality; custom** *see* 373;
conformism, conformity *see* 866; **propriety,**

decorum, decorousness, correctness, *convenance,*
bienséance (*both French*), decency, seemliness, civility
(*old*), good form, etiquette *see* 580.3;
conventionalism, conventionality

2 **the conventions, the proprieties, the mores,** the
right things, accepted *or* sanctioned conduct, what is
done, civilized behaviour; **dictates of society**

3 conventionalist; conformist *see* 866.2

verbs

4 **to conform,** observe the proprieties, play the game,
follow the rules *see* 866.4, fall in *or* into line

adjectives

5 **conventional, decorous,** orthodox, **correct,** right,
right-thinking, proper, decent, seemly, meet;
accepted, recognized, acknowledged, received,
admitted, approved, being done; *comme il faut, de*
rigueur (*both French*); **traditional, customary;**
formal *see* 580.7; conformable *see* 866.5

adverbs

6 **conventionally,** decorously, orthodoxly;
customarily, traditionally; correctly, properly, as
is proper, as it should be, *comme il faut* (*French*);
according to use *or* custom, according to the dictates
of society

580 FORMALITY

nouns

1 **formality, form, formalness; ceremony,**
ceremonial, **ceremoniousness; the red carpet;**
ritual, rituality; extrinsicality, impersonality *see*
767.1; formalization, stylization, conventionalization;
stiffness, stiltedness, primness, prissiness,
rigidness, starchiness, **dignity,** gravity, weight,
gravitas (*Latin*), bottom, weighty dignity, staidness,
reverend seriousness, **solemnity** *see* 111; **pomp** *see*
501.6; pomposity *see* 501.7

2 **formalism, ceremonialism, ritualism;** legalism;
pedantry, pedantism, pedanticism; precisianism,
preciseness, preciousness, preciosity, purism;
punctiliousness, punctilio, scrupulousness

3 **etiquette,** social code, rules *or* code of conduct;
formalities, social procedures, social conduct, what
is done, what one does; **manners,** good manners,
exquisite manners, quiet good manners, **politeness,**
politesse (*French*), natural politeness, comity, civility
see 504.1; **amenities,** decencies, civilities, elegancies,
social graces, mores, proprieties; decorum, good
form; **courtliness,** elegance *see* 533; **protocol,**
diplomatic code; punctilio, point of etiquette;
convention, social usage; table manners

4 (*ceremonial function*) **ceremony,** ceremonial; **rite,**
ritual, formality; solemnity, service, function,
office, **observance,** performance; **exercise,** exercises;
celebration, solemnization; **liturgy,** religious
ceremony; **rite of passage,** *rite de passage* (*French*);
convocation; commencement, commencement
exercises; graduation, graduation exercises;
baccalaureate service; inaugural, inauguration;
initiation; formal; empty formality *or* ceremony,
mummery

verbs

5 **to formalize,** ritualize, solemnize, **celebrate,**
dignify; **observe;** conventionalize, stylize

6 **to stand on ceremony,** observe the formalities,
follow protocol

adjectives

7 **formal,** formulary; **formalist,** formalistic; legalistic;
pedantic, pedantical; stylized, conventionalized;
extrinsic, outward, impersonal *see* 767.3; surface,
superficial, nominal *see* 527.15

8 **ceremonious, ceremonial; red-carpet; ritualistic;**
ritual; hieratic, hieratical, sacerdotal, liturgic; **grave,**
solemn *see* 111.3; **pompous** *see* 501.22; **stately** *see*
501.21; **well-mannered** *see* 504.16; **conventional,**
decorous *see* 579.5

9 **stiff, stilted,** prim, prissy, rigid, starch, starchy,
starched

10 **punctilious, scrupulous, precise,** precisian,
precisionist, precious, puristic; by-the-book; exact,
meticulous *see* 339.12; **orderly, methodical** *see*
806.6

adverbs

11 **formally,** in due form, in set form;
ceremoniously, ritually, ritualistically; **solemnly**
see 111.4; for form's sake, *pro forma* (*Latin*), **as a**
matter of form; by the book

12 **stiffly,** stiltedly, starchly, primly, rigidly

581 INFORMALITY

nouns

1 **informality, informalness, unceremoniousness;**
casualness, offhandedness, **ease, easiness,**
easygoingness; **relaxedness;** affability, graciousness,
cordiality, sociability *see* 582; Bohemianism,
unconventionality *see* 867.2; **familiarity;**
naturalness, simplicity, plainness, homeliness,
common touch, **unaffectedness,** unpretentiousness
see 499.2; unconstraint, unconstrainedness, looseness;
irregularity

verbs

2 **to not stand on ceremony,** let one's hair down
(*informal*), be oneself, be at ease, come as you are;
relax, chill out (*informal*)

adjectives

3 **informal, unceremonious; casual, offhand,**
offhanded, throwaway (*informal*), unstudied, easy,
easygoing, free and easy; *dégagé* (*French*); **relaxed;**
affable, gracious, cordial, sociable; Bohemian,
unconventional *see* 867.6; **familiar; natural,** simple,
plain, homely, folksy (*informal*), downhome (*US*),
unaffected, unassuming *see* 499.7; unconstrained,
loose; irregular; unofficial

adverbs

4 **informally, unceremoniously,** without ceremony,
sans cérémonie, sans façon (*both French*); **casually,**
offhand, offhandedly; relaxedly; familiarly;
naturally, simply, plainly; **unaffectedly,**
unassumingly *see* 499.11; unconstrainedly,
unofficially; *en famille* (*French*)

582 SOCIABILITY

nouns

1 sociability, sociality, sociableness, fitness *or* fondness for society, socialmindedness, **gregariousness, affability,** companionability, compatibility, geniality, *Gemütlichkeit (German),* **congeniality;** hospitality *see* 585; clubbability *(informal),* clubbishness, clubbiness, clubbism; intimacy, familiarity; amiability, **friendliness** *see* 587.1; **communicativeness** *see* 343.3; social grace, civility, urbanity, courtesy *see* 504

2 camaraderie, comradery, comradeship, **fellowship, good-fellowship;** male bonding; consorting, hobnobbing, hanging *and* hanging out *(both informal)*

3 conviviality, joviality, jollity, gaiety, heartiness, cheer, good cheer, festivity, partying, merrymaking, merriment, revelry

4 social life, social intercourse, social activity, **intercourse, communication, communion,** intercommunion, **fellowship,** intercommunication, **community,** collegiality, commerce, congress, converse, conversation, social relations

5 social circle *or* set, social class, one's crowd *or* set, clique, coterie, crowd *(informal);* **association** *see* 617

6 association, consociation, affiliation, bonding, social bonding, **fellowship, companionship, company, society;** fraternity, **fraternization;** membership, participation, partaking, sharing, cooperation *see* 450

7 visit, social call, call; formal visit, duty visit, required visit; exchange visit; flying visit, look-in; visiting, visitation; round of visits; social round, social whirl, mad round

8 appointment, engagement, date *(informal),* double date *and* blind date *(both informal);* arrangement, interview; engagement book

9 rendezvous, tryst, assignation, meeting; trysting place, meeting place, place of assignation; assignation house; love nest *(informal)*

10 social gathering, social, sociable, social affair, social hour, hospitality hour, affair, gathering, get-together *(informal);* **reception,** at home, salon, levee, soiree; matinee; reunion, family reunion; wake

11 party *(see list),* **entertainment,** party time, festivity *see* 743.3, 4

12 *(informal terms)* **bash,** do, blast, bean-feast, knees-up, rave-up, bun fight, blowout, shindig, clambake *and* wingding *(both US)*

13 tea, afternoon tea, five-o'clock tea, high tea, cream tea

14 spelling bee, whist drive, beetle drive

15 debut, coming out *(informal),* presentation

16 *(sociable person)* joiner, mixer *and* **good mixer** *(both informal),* good *or* pleasant company, excellent companion, life and soul of the party, bon vivant, raver; man-about-town, playboy, social lion, nightclub habitué; clubman, clubwoman; salonnard, salonist

verbs

17 to associate with, assort with, sort with, consort with, hobnob with, fall in with, go around with, **mingle with, mix with,** rub shoulders with; **fraternize,** fellowship, join in fellowship; **keep company with,** bear one's company, walk hand in hand with; **join; flock together,** herd together, club together

18 *(informal terms)* **to hang with,** hang out *or* around with, clique, clique with, gang up with, run with, chum, chum together, pal, pal with, pal up *or* around with, run around with, run with; take *or* tie up with

19 to visit, make *or* pay a visit, **call on** *or* **upon, drop in,** run *or* stop in, look in, look one up, see, stop off *or* over *(informal),* drop *or* run *or* stop by, drop around *or* round; leave one's card; exchange visits

20 to have *or* **give a party, entertain**

21 *(informal terms)* **to throw a party; party,** have fun, live it up, have a ball, kick up one's heels, paint the town red, make whoopee, whoop it up

adjectives

22 sociable, social, social-minded, fit for society, fond of society, **gregarious, affable; companionable,** companionate, compatible, genial, *gemütlich (German),* **congenial;** hospitable *see* 585.11; clubby, clubbable *(both informal),* clubbish; **communicative** *see* 343.10; amiable, **friendly;** civil, urbane, courteous *see* 504.14

23 convivial, boon, free and easy, hail-fellow-well-met; **jovial, jolly,** hearty, festive

24 intimate, familiar, cosy, chatty, *tête-à-tête (French);* man-to-man, woman-to-woman

adverbs

25 sociably, socially, gregariously, affably; friendlily, companionably, arm in arm, hand in hand, hand in glove

26 types of parties

ball	masquerade party *or* mask
birthday party	*or* masque *or* masquerade
cocktail party	open house
coming-out party	pyjama party
dinner party	stag *or* stag party
fête champêtre (French)	(informal)
garden party	surprise party
house-warming	tea party
masked ball *or* bal masqué	thé dansante (French)
(French)	

583 UNSOCIABILITY

nouns

1 unsociability, insociability, unsociableness, dissociability, dissociableness; **ungregariousness,** uncompanionability; unclubbableness *or* unclubbability *(both informal),* ungeniality, **uncongeniality;** incompatibility, social incompatibility; **unfriendliness** *see* 589.1; **uncommunicativeness** *see* 344; sullenness, mopishness, moroseness; self-sufficiency, self-containment; autism, catatonia; bashfulness *see* 139.4

2 aloofness, standoffishness, offishness, withdrawnness, **remoteness,** distance, detachment; **coolness,** coldness, frigidity, chill, chilliness, iciness, frostiness; cold shoulder; inaccessibility, unapproachability

3 seclusiveness, seclusion *see* 584; exclusiveness, exclusivity

verbs

4 **to keep to oneself,** keep oneself to oneself, not mix *or* mingle, enjoy *or* prefer one's own company, stay at home, shun companionship, be a poor mixer, **stand aloof,** hold oneself aloof *or* apart, keep one's distance, keep at a distance, keep in the background, retire, retire into the shade, creep into a corner, seclude oneself; have nothing to do with *see* 586.5, be unfriendly, not give one the time of day

adjectives

5 **unsociable,** insociable, dissociable, unsocial; **ungregarious,** nongregarious; **uncompanionable,** ungenial, uncongenial; incompatible, socially incompatible; unclubbable (*informal*); **unfriendly** *see* 589.9; **uncommunicative** *see* 344.8; sullen, mopish, mopey, morose; self-sufficient, self-contained; autistic, catatonic; bashful *see* 139.12

6 **aloof, standoffish,** offish, standoff, **distant, remote,** withdrawn, removed, detached, Olympian; **cool,** cold, cold-fish, frigid, chilly, icy, frosty; seclusive; exclusive; inaccessible, unapproachable

584 SECLUSION

nouns

1 **seclusion,** reclusion, **retirement, withdrawal, retreat,** recess; renunciation *or* forsaking of the world; cocooning; **sequestration,** quarantine, separation, detachment, apartness; segregation, apartheid, Jim Crow (*US*); **isolation,** "splendid isolation"—Sir William Goschen; ivory tower, ivory-towerism, ivory-towerishness; **privacy,** privatism, **secrecy;** rustication; isolationism

2 **hermitism,** hermitry, eremitism, anchoritism, anchoretism, cloistered monasticism

3 **solitude,** solitariness, **aloneness,** loneness, singleness; **loneliness, lonesomeness**

4 **forlornness, desolation;** friendlessness, kithlessness, fatherlessness, motherlessness, homelessness, rootlessness; helplessness, defencelessness; abandonment, desertion

5 **recluse, loner,** solitaire, solitary, solitudinarian; **shut-in,** invalid, bedridden invalid; cloistered monk *or* nun; **hermit,** eremite, anchorite, anchoret; marabout; hermitess, anchoress; **ascetic;** closet cynic; stylite, pillarist, pillar saint; Hieronymite, Hieronymian; Diogenes, Timon of Athens, St Simeon Stylites, St Anthony, desert saints, desert fathers; outcast, pariah *see* 586.4; **stay-at-home,** homebody; **isolationist,** seclusionist; ivory-towerist, ivory-towerite

6 **retreat** *see* 1008.5, **hideaway, cell, ivory tower,** hidey-hole (*informal*), lair, sanctum, sanctum sanctorum, inner sanctum

verbs

7 **to seclude oneself, go into seclusion, retire, go into retirement,** retire from the world, abandon *or* forsake the world, live in retirement, lead a retired life, lead a cloistered life, sequester *or* sequestrate oneself, be *or* remain incommunicado, shut oneself up, live alone, live apart, retreat to one's ivory tower; stay at home; rusticate; take the veil; opt out *or* drop out of society

adjectives

8 **secluded, seclusive, retired, withdrawn; isolated,** shut off, insular, **separate,** separated, **apart,** detached, removed; segregated, quarantined; **remote, out-of-the-way,** up-country, in a backwater, out-of-the-world, back of beyond, out-back (*Australian*); **unfrequented,** unvisited, off the beaten track; untravelled

9 **private,** privatistic, reclusive; ivory-towered, ivory-towerish

10 **recluse, reclusive, sequestered, cloistered,** sequestrated, shut up *or* in; hermitlike, hermitic, hermitical, eremitic, eremitical, hermitish; anchoritic, anchoritical; stay-at-home, domestic; homebound

11 **solitary, alone; in solitude,** by oneself, all alone; **lonely, lonesome, lone;** lonely-hearts

12 **forlorn,** lorn; **abandoned, forsaken, deserted, desolate,** godforsaken (*informal*), friendless, unfriended, kithless, fatherless, motherless, homeless; helpless, defenceless; outcast *see* 586.10

adverbs

13 **in seclusion, in retirement,** in retreat, in solitude; in privacy, in secrecy;
"far from the madding crowd's ignoble strife"— Thomas Gray, "the world forgetting by the world forgot"—Pope

585 HOSPITALITY, WELCOME

nouns

1 **hospitality,** hospitableness, receptiveness; honours *or* freedom of the house; **cordiality,** amiability, graciousness, **friendliness,** neighbourliness, geniality, heartiness, bonhomie, **generosity,** liberality, openheartedness, warmth, warmness, warmheartedness; open door

2 **welcome,** welcoming, **reception,** accueil (*French*); cordial *or* warm *or* hearty welcome, pleasant *or* smiling reception, the glad hand (*informal*), **open arms; embrace, hug;** welcome mat

3 **greetings, salutations,** salaams; **regards,** best wishes *see* 504.8

4 **greeting, salutation,** salute; **hail, hello,** how-do-you-do; accost, address; nod, bow, bob; curtsy *see* 155.2; wave; handshake, handclasp; high five (*informal*); namaste; open arms, embrace, hug, kiss; smile, smile *or* nod of recognition, nod

5 **host,** mine host; hostess, receptionist, greeter; landlord *see* 470.2

6 **guest, visitor,** visitant; **caller,** company; invited guest, invitee; frequenter, habitué, haunter; uninvited guest, gate-crasher (*informal*); freeloader *and* ligger (*both informal*), moocher (*US & Canadian*)

verbs

7 **to receive, admit,** accept, take in, let in, open the door to; **be at home to,** have the latchstring out, keep a light in the window, put out the welcome mat, keep the door open, keep an open house, keep the home fires burning, keep a welcome in the hillside

8 **to entertain,** entertain guests, guest; host, preside, do the honours (*informal*); give a party, throw a party (*informal*); spread oneself (*informal*)

9 **to welcome,** make welcome, bid one welcome, bid one feel at home, make one feel welcome *or* at home *or* like one of the family, do the honours of the house, give one the freedom of the house, hold out the hand, extend the right hand of friendship; glad hand *and* give the glad hand *and* glad eye (*all informal*); **embrace, hug, receive** *or* **welcome with open arms;** give a warm reception to, "kill the fatted calf"—Bible, roll out the red carpet, give the red-carpet treatment, receive royally, make feel like a king *or* queen

10 **to greet, hail, accost,** address; **salute,** make one's salutations; **bid** *or* **say hello,** bid good day *or* good morning, etc; exchange greetings, **pass the time of day;** give one's regards *see* 504.13; shake hands, shake *and* give one some skin *and* give a high *or* a low five (*all informal*), press the flesh (*informal*), press *or* squeeze one's hand; nod to, bow to; curtsy *see* 155.6; tip the hat to, lift the hat, touch the hat *or* cap; take one's hat off to, uncover; pull *or* tug at the forelock; kiss, greet with a kiss, kiss hands *or* cheeks, air kiss

adjectives

11 **hospitable, receptive,** welcoming; **cordial,** amiable, gracious, **friendly,** neighbourly, genial, hearty, open, openhearted, warm, warmhearted; **generous,** liberal

12 **welcome,** welcome as the roses in May, wanted, desired, wished-for; **agreeable,** desirable, acceptable; **grateful,** gratifying, pleasing

adverbs

13 **hospitably, with open arms;** friendlily

exclamations

14 **welcome!,** *soyez le bienvenu!* (*French*), *¡bien venido!* (*Spanish*), *benvenuto!* (*Italian*), *Willkommen!* (*German*); glad to see you!

15 **greetings!, salutations!, hello!,** hullo!, hail!, hey! *or* heigh!, **hi!,** aloha!, *¡hola!* (*Spanish*); **how do you do?, how are you?,** *comment allez-vous?, comment ça va?* (*both French*), *¿cómo está Usted?* (*Spanish*), *come sta?* (*Italian*), *wie geht's?* (*German*); **good morning!,** top of the morning to you!, *guten Morgen!* (*German*); good day!, *bon jour!* (*French*), *¡buenos días!* (*Spanish*), *buon giorno!* (*Italian*), *guten Tag!* (*German*); **good afternoon!,** *¡buenas tardes!* (*Spanish*); **good evening!,** *bon soir!* (*French*), *buona sera!* (*Italian*), *guten Abend!* (*German*)

16 (*informal terms*) how you doing?, how's things?, how's tricks?, how goes it?, how's the world treating you?, yo!, ahoy!, hey!; long time no see!

586 INHOSPITALITY

nouns

1 **inhospitality,** inhospitableness, unhospitableness, unreceptiveness; **uncordialness,** ungraciousness,

unfriendliness, unneighbourliness; **nonwelcome,** nonwelcoming

2 **unhabitability,** uninhabitability, unlivability

3 **ostracism,** ostracization, thumbs down; **banishment** *see* 908.4; **proscription, ban; boycott,** boycottage; **blackball,** blackballing, blacklist; **rejection** *see* 442.1

4 **outcast,** social outcast, outcast of society, **castaway, derelict,** Ishmael; **pariah, untouchable,** leper; outcaste; *déclassé* (*French*); **outlaw;** expellee, evictee; displaced person *or* DP; exile, expatriate, expat (*informal*), man without a country; undesirable; *persona non grata* (*Latin*), unacceptable person

verbs

5 **to have nothing to do with,** have no truck with (*informal*), refuse to associate with, steer clear of (*informal*), **spurn, turn one's back upon,** not give one the time of day (*informal*); deny oneself to, refuse to receive, not be at home to; shut the door upon

6 **to ostracize,** turn thumbs down, disfellowship; **reject** *see* 442.3, **exile, banish** *see* 908.17; **proscribe, ban, outlaw** *see* 444.3, put under the ban; **boycott, blackball,** blacklist

adjectives

7 **inhospitable,** unhospitable; **unreceptive,** closed; **uncordial,** ungracious, **unfriendly,** unneighbourly

8 **unhabitable, uninhabitable,** nonhabitable, unoccupiable, untenantable, **unlivable, unfit to live in,** not fit for man or beast

9 **unwelcome, unwanted; unagreeable,** undesirable, unacceptable; **uninvited,** unasked, unbidden

10 **outcast, cast-off, castaway, derelict;** outlawed *see* 444.7, outside the pale, outside the gates; **rejected, disowned; abandoned, forsaken**

587 FRIENDSHIP

nouns

1 **friendship, friendliness; amicability,** amicableness, amity, peaceableness, unhostility; **amiability,** amiableness, **congeniality,** well-affectedness; **neighbourliness,** neighbourlikeness; sociability *see* 582; **affection, love** *see* 104; **loving kindness, kindness** *see* 143

2 **fellowship, companionship, comradeship,** colleagueship, chumship (*informal*), freemasonry, consortship, boon companionship; **comradery,** camaradery, male bonding; **brotherhood, fraternity,** fraternalism, sodality, confraternity; **sisterhood, sorority;** brotherliness, sisterliness; community of interest, *esprit de corps* (*French*)

3 **good terms, good understanding,** good footing, friendly relations; **harmony,** sympathy, fellow feeling, **rapport** *see* 455.1; **favour, goodwill, good graces, regard,** respect, mutual regard, favourable regard, the good *or* right side of (*informal*)

4 **acquaintance,** acquaintedness, close acquaintance; **introduction,** presentation, knockdown (*US & Australian informal*)

5 familiarity, intimacy, intimate acquaintance, closeness, nearness, inseparableness, inseparability; affinity, special affinity, mutual affinity; chumminess (*informal*), palliness *or* palsiness *or* palsy-walsiness (*informal*), mateyness (*informal*)

6 cordiality, geniality, heartiness, bonhomie, ardency, warmth, warmness, affability, warmheartedness; hospitality *see* 585

7 devotion, devotedness; dedication, commitment; fastness, steadfastness, firmness, constancy, staunchness; triedness, trueness, true-blueness, tried-and-trueness

8 cordial friendship, warm *or* ardent friendship, devoted friendship, bosom friendship, intimate *or* familiar friendship, sincere friendship, beautiful friendship, fast *or* firm friendship, staunch friendship, loyal friendship, lasting friendship, undying friendship

verbs

9 to be friends, have the friendship of, have the ear of; be old friends *or* friends of long standing, be long acquainted, go way back; **know, be acquainted with**; associate with; cotton to *and* hit it off (*both informal*), get on well with, hobnob with, fraternize with; be close friends with, be best friends, be inseparable; **be on good terms**, enjoy good *or* friendly relations with; keep on good terms, have an in with (*informal*)

10 to befriend, make friends with, gain the friendship of, **strike up a friendship**, get to know one another, take up with (*informal*), shake hands with, **get acquainted**, make acquaintance with, pick up an acquaintance with; win friends, win friends and influence people

11 (*informal terms*) to be buddy-buddy *or* palsy-walsy with, click, hit it off with, have good *or* great chemistry, team up; get palsy *or* palsy-walsy with, get cosy with, cosy *or* snuggle up to, get close to, get chummy with, buddy *or* pal up with, play footsie with

12 to cultivate, cultivate the friendship of, **court**, pay court to, pay addresses to, seek the company of, **run after** (*informal*), play up to *and* suck up to (*both informal*), hold out *or* extend the right of friendship *or* fellowship; **make advances**, approach, break the ice

13 to get on good terms with, get into favour, win the regard of, **get in the good graces of**, get in good with, get in with (*informal*), **get on the good** *or* **right side of** (*informal*); stay friends with, keep in with (*informal*)

14 to introduce, present, acquaint, make acquainted, give an introduction, give a knockdown (*US & Australian informal*), do the honours (*informal*)

adjectives

15 friendly, friendlike; **amicable, peaceable,** unhostile; **harmonious** *see* 455.3; **amiable, congenial,** *simpático* (*Spanish*), *simpatico* (*Italian*), *sympathique* (*French*), pleasant, agreeable, favourable, well-affected, well-disposed, well-intentioned, well-meaning, well-meant; brotherly, fraternal; sisterly; neighbourly, neighbourlike; sociable; **kind** *see* 143.13

16 cordial, genial, hearty, ardent, warm, warmhearted, affable; hospitable *see* 585.11

17 friends with, friendly with, at home with; acquainted

18 on good terms, on a good footing, on friendly *or* amicable terms, **on speaking terms,** on a first-name basis, on visiting terms; in with (*informal*), **in favour, in one's good graces,** in one's good books, on the good *or* right side of (*informal*)

19 familiar, intimate, close, near, inseparable, on familiar *or* intimate terms; just between the two, one-to-one, man-to-man, woman-to-woman; hand-in-hand, hand and glove *or* hand in glove; **thick as thieves** (*informal*)

20 chummy (*informal*), matey (*informal*); pally *and* palsy *and* palsy-walsy *and* buddy-buddy (*all informal*)

21 devoted, dedicated, committed, **fast,** steadfast, constant, faithful, staunch; tried, true, **tried and true,** true-blue, tested

adverbs

22 amicably, friendly, friendlily; **amiably, congenially,** pleasantly, agreeably, favourably; **cordially, genially,** heartily, ardently, warmly, with open arms; familiarly, intimately; arm in arm, hand in hand, hand in glove

588 FRIEND

nouns

1 friend, acquaintance, close acquaintance; confidant, confidante, repository; **intimate,** familiar, **close friend,** intimate *or* familiar friend; **bosom friend,** friend of one's bosom, inseparable friend, **best friend;** alter ego, other self; brother, fellow, fellow man, fellow creature, neighbour; **sympathizer,** well-wisher, partisan, advocate, favourer, backer, **supporter** *see* 616.9; casual acquaintance; pickup (*informal*); lover *see* 104.12; live-in lover, significant other, bidie-in (*Scottish*)

2 good friend, best friend, great friend, **devoted friend,** warm *or* ardent friend, **faithful friend,** trusted *or* trusty friend, *fidus Achates* (*Latin*), constant friend, staunch friend, fast friend, "a friend that sticketh closer than a brother"—BIBLE; **friend in need,** friend indeed

3 companion, fellow, fellow companion, **comrade,** *camarade* (*French*), amigo (*informal*), mate, company, associate *see* 616, consociate, compeer, confrere, consort, **colleague, partner,** copartner, side partner, **crony,** old crony; girlfriend (*informal*); **roommate,** chamberfellow; flatmate; bunkmate; bedfellow, bedmate; **schoolmate,** schoolfellow, classmate, classfellow, school companion, school chum, fellow student *or* pupil; **playmate,** playfellow; **teammate,** yokefellow, yokemate; workmate, workfellow *see* 616.5; shipmate; messmate; brother *or* comrade in arms

4 (*informal terms*) **mate, pal, chum,** buddy, china *and* old china, mucker, cock, bosom buddy, sidekick, cobber (*Australian*), main man, home boy *and* homey, bro, pardner *and* pard

5 **boon companion,** boonfellow; **good fellow,** jolly fellow, hearty, *bon vivant* (*French*); drinking buddy

6 (*famous friendships*) Achilles and Patroclus, Aeneas and Achates, Damon and Pythias, David and Jonathan, Diomedes and Sthenelus, Epaminondas and Pelopidas, Gary Lineker and Willie Thorne, Hercules and Iolaus, Nisus and Euryalus, Pylades and Orestes, Theseus and Pirithoüs, Christ and the beloved disciple; the Three Musketeers

589 ENMITY

nouns

1 **enmity, unfriendliness,** inimicality; **uncordiality,** unamiability, ungeniality, disaffinity, incompatibility, incompatibleness; personal conflict, strain, **tension;** coolness, coldness, chilliness, chill, frost, iciness, the freeze; inhospitality *see* 586, unsociability *see* 583

2 **disaccord** *see* 456; ruffled feelings, strained relations, alienation, **disaffection, estrangement** *see* 456.4

3 **hostility, antagonism, repugnance, antipathy,** spitefulness, spite, despitefulness, malice, malevolence, malignity, **hatred, hate** *see* 103; **conflict, contention** *see* 457, collision, clash, clashing, **friction;** quarrelsomeness *see* 456.3; belligerence

4 **animosity,** animus; **ill will,** ill feeling, bitter feeling, **hard feelings,** no love lost; **bad blood,** ill blood, feud, blood feud, vendetta; **bitterness,** sourness, soreness, **rancour,** acrimony, virulence, venom, vitriol

5 **grudge, spite,** bone to pick; peeve (*informal*)

6 **enemy, foe,** foeman, **adversary, antagonist;** bitter enemy; sworn enemy; open enemy; public enemy; archenemy, devil;

"my nearest and dearest enemy"—Thomas Middleton; the other side, the opposition; **bane** *see* 395.8, bête noire

verbs

7 **to antagonize,** set against, set at odds, set at each other's throat; aggravate, exacerbate, heat up, **provoke, envenom, embitter,** infuriate, madden; **alienate, estrange** *see* 456.14; be alienated *or* estranged, draw *or* grow apart

8 **to bear ill will,** bear malice, have it in for (*informal*), hold it against, be down on (*informal*); **bear** *or* **harbour** *or* **nurse a grudge,** owe a grudge, have a bone to pick with; no love is lost between; pick a quarrel; **hate** *see* 103.5

adjectives

9 **unfriendly, inimical, unamicable; uncordial,** unamiable, ungenial, incompatible; strained, tense; disaccordant, unharmonious; **cool, cold, chill, chilly, frosty, icy;** inhospitable *see* 586.7; unsociable *see* 583.5

10 **hostile, antagonistic,** repugnant, antipathetic, set against, snide, spiteful, despiteful, malicious, malevolent, malignant, hateful, full of hate *or* hatred; virulent, **bitter,** sore, rancorous, acrid, caustic, venomous, vitriolic; conflicting, clashing, colliding; quarrelsome *see* 456.17; **provocative,** off-putting; belligerent

11 **alienated, estranged,** out on a limb (*informal*), disaffected, separated, divided, disunited, torn; irreconcilable

12 **at outs,** at enmity, at variance, **at odds,** at loggerheads, at cross-purposes, at sixes and sevens, at each other's throats, at daggers drawn, at swords' points

13 **on bad terms,** not on speaking terms; in bad with (*informal*), in bad odour with, in one's bad *or* black books

adverbs

14 **unamicably,** inimically; **uncordially,** unamiably, ungenially; coolly, coldly, chillily, frostily; **hostilely, antagonistically**

590 MISANTHROPY

nouns

1 **misanthropy,** misanthropism, people-hating, Timonism, cynicism, antisociality, antisocial sentiments *or* attitudes; unsociability *see* 583; **man-hating,** misandry; **woman-hating,** misogyny; **sexism,** sex discrimination, sexual stereotyping, male *or* female chauvinism

2 **misanthrope,** misanthropist, people-hater, cynic, Timon, Timonist; **man-hater,** misandrist; **woman-hater,** misogynist; **sexist,** male *or* female chauvinist, chauvinist

adjectives

3 **misanthropic,** people-hating, Timonist, Timonistic, cynical, **antisocial;** unsociable *see* 583.5; **man-hating,** misandrist; **woman-hating,** misogynic, misogynistic, misogynous; **sexist,** male- *or* female-chauvinistic, chauvinistic

591 PUBLIC SPIRIT

nouns

1 **public spirit,** social consciousness *or* responsibility; **citizenship, good citizenship,** citizenism, civism; altruism

2 **patriotism,** love of country;

"the last refuge of a scoundrel"—Samuel Johnson; **nationalism,** nationality, ultranationalism; Briticism, Americanism, etc; **chauvinism, jingoism,** overpatriotism; patriotics, flag-waving; sabre-rattling

3 **patriot;** nationalist; ultranationalist; **chauvinist,** chauvin, **jingo,** jingoist; patrioteer (*informal*), flag waver, superpatriot, hard hat (*US informal*); hawk

adjectives

4 **public-spirited, civic; patriotic; nationalistic;** ultranationalist, ultranationalistic; overpatriotic, superpatriotic, flagwaving, **chauvinist, chauvinistic,** jingoist, jingoistic; hawkish

592 BENEFACTOR

nouns

1 **benefactor,** benefactress, **benefiter,** succourer, befriender; ministrant, ministering angel; Samaritan,

good Samaritan; **helper, aider, assister, help, aid,** helping hand,

"a very present help in time of trouble"—Bible; jack-at-a-pinch (*old informal*); angel (*informal*), **patron, backer** see 616.9, cash cow (*informal*); **good person** see 659

2 **saviour, redeemer,** deliverer, **liberator,** rescuer, freer, **emancipator,** manumitter

verbs

3 **to benefit, aid,** assist, succour; befriend, take under one's wing; back, support; save the day, save one's neck *or* skin *or* bacon

adjectives

4 benefitting, aiding, befriending, assisting; backing, supporting; saving, salving, salvational, redemptive, redeeming; liberating, freeing, emancipative, emancipating, manumitting

adverbs

5 by one's aid *or* good offices, with one's support, on one's shoulders *or* coattails

prepositions

6 with *or* by benefit of, with *or* by the aid of

593 EVILDOER

nouns

1 **evildoer, wrongdoer,** worker of ill *or* evil, **malefactor,** malfeasant, malfeasor, misfeasor, malevolent, public enemy, **sinner, villain,** villainess, transgressor, delinquent; bad guy *and* baddy *and* meany *and* black hat *and* bad hat (*all informal*), wrong'un (*informal*); **criminal,** outlaw, felon, **crook** (*informal*), lawbreaker, perpetrator, gangster *and* mobster (*both informal*), racketeer, thief; **bad person** see 660; deceiver see 357

2 **troublemaker, mischief-maker;** agitator see 375.11

3 **ruffian,** rough, bravo, **rowdy, yob** *or* **yobbo, thug,** casual, desperado, cutthroat, mad dog; gunman; bully, bullyboy; devil, hellcat, hell-raiser; killer

4 (*informal terms*) roughneck, tough, bruiser, mugger, ugly customer, **hoodlum, hood, hooligan,** gorilla, ape, plug-ugly, strong-arm man, muscle man, goon (*US*); gun, trigger man, rodman, hatchet man, gunsel (*US*), torpedo (*US*); hellion, terror, holy terror, ugly customer

5 **savage, barbarian, brute, beast, animal,** tiger, shark, hyena; wild man; cannibal, man-eater, anthropophagite; **wrecker, vandal,** nihilist, destroyer

6 **monster, fiend,** fiend from hell, **demon, devil,** devil incarnate, hellhound; **vampire,** lamia, **harpy, ghoul;** werewolf, ape-man; ogre, ogress; Frankenstein's monster

7 **witch, hag, vixen,** hellhag, hellcat, she-devil, virago, brimstone, termagant, grimalkin, Jezebel, beldam, she-wolf, tigress, wildcat, siren, fury

594 JURISDICTION
administration of justice

nouns

1 **jurisdiction,** legal authority *or* power *or* right *or* sway, the confines of the law; original *or* appellate jurisdiction, exclusive *or* concurrent jurisdiction, civil *or* criminal jurisdiction, common-law jurisdiction, *in rem* jurisdiction, *in personam* jurisdiction; voluntary jurisdiction

2 **judiciary,** judicial *or* legal *or* court system, judicature, judicatory, court, the courts; criminal-justice system; **justice,** the wheels of justice, judicial process; judgment see 945

3 **magistracy,** magistrature, magistrateship; **judgeship,** justiceship; mayoralty, mayorship

4 **bureau, office, department;** secretariat, ministry, commissariat; municipality, bailiwick; constabulary, constablery, sheriffry, sheriffalty, shrievalty; constablewick, sheriffwick

verbs

5 **to administer justice,** administer, administrate; preside, preside at the board; **sit in judgment** see 598.17; **judge** see 945.8

adjectives

6 **jurisdictional,** jurisdictive; **judicatory,** judicatorial, judicative, **juridic** *or* **juridical; judicial, judiciary;** magisterial

595 TRIBUNAL

nouns

1 **tribunal, forum, board,** curia, Areopagus; judicature, judicatory, judiciary see 594.2; council see 423; inquisition, the Inquisition

2 **court, law court, court of law** *or* **justice,** court of arbitration, legal tribunal, judicature; **British court** (*see list*), Crown court, Sherriff court (*Scottish*), **United States court** (*see list*), federal court

3 (*ecclesiastical courts*) Papal Court, Curia, Rota, Sacra Romana Rota, Court of Arches *and* Court of Peculiars

4 **military court, court-martial,** general *or* special *or* summary court-martial, drumhead court-martial; naval court, captain's mast

5 **seat of justice, judgment seat,** mercy seat, siege of justice (*old*); **bench;** woolsack

6 **courthouse, court;** county *or* town hall, town house; **courtroom;** chambers; jury box; witness stand *or* box, dock

adjectives

7 **tribunal, judicial,** judiciary, court, curial; appellate

8 **British courts**

Board of Green Cloth	Court of Criminal Appeal
Council	Court of Divorce and
court of admiralty	Matrimonial Causes
Court of Appeal	Court of Exchequer
court of attachments	Court of Exchequer
Court of Common	Chamber
Court of Common Bank	court of piepoudre *or*
Court of Common Pleas	dustyfoot

Court of Queen's *or* King's Bench
Court of Session *or* College of Justice (Scottish)
Court of the Duchy of Lancaster
Green Cloth
High Court
High Court of Appeal
High *or* Supreme Court of Judicature
High Court of Justiciary
House of Lords

Judicial Committee of the Privy Council
Lords Justices' Court
Palatine Court
Rolls Court
Sheriff Court (Scottish)
Stannary Court
superior courts of Westminster
Teind Court (Scottish)
Vice Chancellor's Court
Wardmote *or* Wardmote Court
Woodmote

9 United States courts

Court of Private Land Claims
Federal Court of Claims
Supreme Court *or* United States Supreme Court

Territorial court
United States Circuit Court of Appeals
United States District Court

596 JUDGE, JURY

nouns

1 **judge, magistrate, justice,** adjudicator, bencher, man *or* woman on the bench, beak (*informal*); circuit judge; **justice of the peace** *or* JP; arbiter, arbitrator, moderator; umpire, referee; his honour, his worship, his lordship; Mr Justice; critic *see* 945.7; **special judge** (*see list*)

2 (*historical*) tribune, praetor, ephor, archon, syndic, podesta; Areopagite; justiciar, justiciary; dempster, deemster, doomster, doomsman

3 (*Muslim*) mullah, ulema, hakim, mufti, cadi

4 Lord Chief Justice, Lord Justice, Lord Chancellor *or* Lord High Chancellor, Lord Advocate (*Scottish*), Lord of Appeal, Lord Justice of Appeal, Master of the Rolls, Baron of the Exchequer; Chief Justice, Associate Justice, Justice of the Supreme Court; judge advocate general

5 Pontius Pilate, Solomon, Minos, Rhadamanthus, Aeacus

6 **jury** (*see list*), **panel,** jury of one's peers, country, twelve men in a box; inquest; jury panel, jury list, venire facias; hung *or* deadlocked jury

7 **juror, juryman, jurywoman,** venire-man *or* woman, talesman; foreman of the jury, foreman, jury chancellor (*Scottish*); grand-juror, grand-juryman; petit-juror, petit-juryman; recognitor

8 **special judges**

amicus curiae	master
assessor *or* legal assessor	military judge
bankruptcy judge	ombudsman
barmaster	ordinary *or* judge ordinary
chancellor	police judge *or* justice *or*
coroner	magistrate
circuit judge	presiding judge
district judge	probate judge
judge advocate	procurator fiscal (Scottish)
judge *or* justice of assize	puisne judge *or* justice
jurat	recorder
justice in eyre	tax judge
lay judge	vice-chancellor

9 kinds of jury

blue-ribbon jury *or* panel	petit jury *or* petty jury *or*
common jury	traverse jury
coroner's jury	police jury
elisor jury	pyx jury
grand jury	special jury
jury of inquest	struck jury
jury of matrons *or* women	trial jury
jury of the vicinage	

597 LAWYER

nouns

1 **lawyer, barrister,** barrister-at-law, **solicitor,** advocate (*Scottish*), **attorney** (*US*), **attorney-at-law** (*US*), counsellor *or* counsellor-at-law (*both US*), **counsel,** legal counsel, legal adviser, legal expert, **pleader;** member of the bar, legal practitioner, officer of the court; Templar; smart lawyer, Philadelphia lawyer (*US*); friend at *or* in court, amicus curiae; deputy, agent *see* 576; intercessor *see* 466.3; sea lawyer, self-styled lawyer, legalist, barrack-room lawyer, bush lawyer (*Australian & NZ*)

2 legist, jurist, jurisprudent, jurisconsult; law member of a court-martial

3 (*informal terms*) brief, mouthpiece, ambulance chaser, fixer, legal eagle

4 **bar,** legal profession, members of the bar, inner bar; representation, counsel, pleading, attorneyship; **practice,** legal practice, criminal practice, corporate practice, etc; legal-aid *or* pro bono practice; **law firm,** legal firm, partnership

verbs

5 **to practice law,** practice at the bar; call to the bar; take silk

adjectives

6 **lawyerly,** lawyerlike, barristerial; representing, of counsel

598 LEGAL ACTION

nouns

1 **lawsuit, suit,** suit in *or* at law; countersuit (*US*); **litigation, prosecution, action, legal action,** proceedings, legal proceedings, legal process; legal remedy; **case, court case,** cause, cause in court, legal case; **judicial process**

2 **summons, subpoena,** writ of summons; **writ, warrant**

3 **arraignment, indictment, impeachment; complaint, charge** *see* 599.1; presentment; information; bill of indictment, true bill (*US*); **bail** *see* 438.2

4 court order, injunction, interdict (*Scottish*)

5 **jury selection,** impanelment, venire, venire facias, venire facias de novo

6 **trial, jury trial,** trial by jury, trial at the bar, **hearing, inquiry, inquisition,** inquest, assize; court-martial; **examination,** cross-examination; retrial; mistrial; change of venue

7 **pleadings,** arguments at the bar; **plea,** pleading, argument; **defence,** statement of defence; demurrer,

general *or* special demurrer; refutation *see* 957.2; rebuttal *see* 938.2

8 **declaration, statement,** allegation, allegation *or* statement of facts, procès-verbal; **deposition,** affidavit; claim; complaint; bill, bill of complaint; libel, narratio; nolle prosequi, nol pros; nonsuit

9 **testimony; evidence** *see* 956; **argument,** presentation of the case; resting of the case; **summing up,** summation, charge to the jury, charging of the jury

10 **judgment, decision,** landmark decision; **verdict,** open verdict, **sentence** *see* 945.5; rider; acquittal *see* 601; condemnation *see* 602, penalty *see* 603

11 **appeal,** appeal motion, application for retrial, appeal to a higher court; writ of error; certiorari, order *or* writ of certiorari

12 **litigant, litigator,** litigationist; suitor, **party,** party to a suit; injured *or* aggrieved party, **plaintiff** *see* 599.5; **defendant** *see* 599.6; witness; accessory, accessory before *or* after the fact; panel, parties litigant

verbs

13 **to sue, litigate, prosecute,** go into litigation, **bring suit,** put in suit, sue *or* prosecute at law, **go to law,** seek in law, appeal to the law, seek justice *or* legal redress, implead, **bring action against,** prosecute a suit against, take *or* institute legal proceedings against; law *or* have the law in (*both informal*); take to court, bring into court, haul *or* drag into court, bring a case before the court *or* bar, bring before a jury, bring to justice, bring to trial, **put on trial,** bring to the bar, take before the judge; set down for hearing

14 **to summons, issue a summons,** subpoena

15 **to arraign, indict, impeach,** find an indictment against, present a true bill, prefer *or* file a claim, have *or* pull up (*informal*), bring up for investigation; **prefer charges** *see* 599.7

16 **to obtain an injunction,** obtain a court order, obtain an interdict (*Scottish*)

17 **to select** *or* **impanel a jury,** impanel, panel

18 **to call to witness,** bring forward, put on the stand; swear in *see* 334.7; take oath; take the stand, testify

19 **to try,** try a case, conduct a trial, **hear,** give a hearing to, sit on; charge the jury, deliver one's charge to the jury; **judge, sit in judgment**

20 **to plead,** enter a plea *or* pleading, implead, conduct pleadings, argue at the bar; **plead** *or* **argue one's case,** present one's case, make a plea, tell it to the judge (*informal*); rest, rest one's case; sum up one's case; throw oneself on the mercy of the court

21 **to bring in a verdict, pass** *or* **pronounce sentence** *see* 945.13; acquit *see* 601.4; convict *see* 602.3; penalize *see* 603.4

adjectives

22 litigious, litigant, litigatory; causidical, lawyerly; litigable, actionable, prosecutable; prosecutorial; **moot,** sub judice; unactionable, unprosecutable, unlitigable, frivolous, without merit, inadmissable; guilty, not guilty, not proven (*Scottish*)

phrases

23 **in litigation,** in court, in chancery, in jeopardy, **at law,** at bar, at the bar, **on trial,** up for investigation *or* hearing, before the court *or* bar *or* judge

599 ACCUSATION

nouns

1 **accusation,** accusal, finger-pointing (*informal*), **charge, complaint,** plaint, count, **blame, imputation,** delation, reproach, taxing; **accusing, bringing of charges,** laying of charges, bringing to book; **denunciation,** denouncement; **impeachment, arraignment, indictment,** bill of indictment, true bill (*US*); **allegation,** allegement; **imputation,** ascription; **insinuation, implication, innuendo,** veiled accusation, unspoken accusation; information, information against, bill of particulars; charge sheet; specification; gravamen of a charge; prosecution, suit, lawsuit *see* 598.1

2 **incrimination,** crimination, **inculpation,** implication, **citation,** involvement, impugnment; attack, assault; **censure** *see* 510.3

3 **recrimination,** retort, countercharge

4 **trumped-up charge,** false witness; **put-up job** *and* **frame-up** *and* **fit-up** (*all informal*)

5 **accuser,** accusant, accusatrix; incriminator, delator, allegator, impugner; informer *see* 551.6; impeacher, indictor; **plaintiff, complainant,** claimant, appellant, petitioner, libellant, suitor, **party,** party to a suit; **prosecutor,** the prosecution

6 **accused, defendant,** respondent, codefendant, corespondent, libellee, suspect, prisoner

verbs

7 **to accuse,** bring accusation; **charge, press charges, prefer** *or* **bring charges,** lay charges; complain, **lodge a complaint,** lodge a plaint; **impeach, arraign, indict,** bring in *or* hand up an indictment, return a true bill (*US*), article, **cite,** cite on several counts; book; **denounce,** denunciate; **finger** *and* point the finger at *and* put *or* lay the finger on (*all informal*), **inform on** *or* **against** *see* 551.12, 13; impute, ascribe; allege, insinuate, imply; bring to book; tax, task, take to task *or* account; **reproach,** twit, taunt with; report, put on report

8 **to blame,** blame on *or* upon (*informal*), lay on, hold against, **put** *or* **place** *or* **lay the blame on,** lay *or* cast blame upon, place *or* fix the blame *or* responsibility for; fasten on *or* upon, pin *or* hang on (*informal*)

9 **to accuse of, charge with,** tax *or* task with, saddle with, lay to one's charge, place to one's account, lay at one's door, bring home to, cast *or* throw in one's teeth, throw up to one, throw *or* thrust in the face of

10 **to incriminate,** criminate, **inculpate,** implicate, involve; cry out against, cry out on *or* upon, cry shame upon, raise one's voice against; attack, assail, impugn; **censure** *see* 510.13; throw a stone at, cast *or* throw the first stone

11 **to recriminate,** countercharge, retort an accusation

12 to trump up a charge, bear false witness; **frame** *and* frame up *and* set up *and* **fit up** (*all informal*)

adjectives

13 accusing, **accusatory**, accusatorial, accusative; imputative, denunciatory; recriminatory; prosecutorial; **condemnatory**

14 incriminating, incriminatory, criminatory; delatorian; inculpative, inculpatory

15 accused, charged, blamed, tasked, taxed, reproached, **denounced, impeached, indicted, arraigned; under a cloud** *or* a cloud of suspicion; incriminated, inculpated, implicated, involved, in complicity; **cited,** impugned; under attack, under fire

600 JUSTIFICATION

nouns

1 justification, vindication; **clearing,** clearing of one's name *or* one's good name, clearance, purging, purgation, destigmatizing, destigmatization, **exculpation** *see* 601.1; no bill, failure to indict; explanation, rationalization; reinstatement, restoration, **rehabilitation**

2 defence, plea, pleading; argument, statement of defence; answer, reply, counterstatement, response, riposte; **refutation** *see* 957.2, **rebuttal** *see* 938.2; demurrer, general *or* special demurrer; denial, objection, exception; **special pleading;** self-defence, plea of self-defence, Nuremberg defence, the devil-made-me-do-it defence, blame-the-victim defence

3 apology, apologia, apologetic

4 excuse, **cop-out** *and* **alibi** *and* **out** (*all informal*); lame excuse, poor excuse, likely story; escape hatch, way out

5 extenuation, mitigation, palliation, softening; extenuative, palliative, saving grace; **whitewash, whitewashing,** decontamination; gilding, gloss, varnish; qualification, allowance; extenuating circumstances, diminished responsibility

6 warrant, reason, good reason, cause, call, right, basis, substantive *or* material basis, ground, grounds, foundation, substance

7 justifiability, vindicability, defensibility; explainability, explicability; excusability, pardonableness, forgivableness, remissibility, veniality; warrantableness, allowableness, admissibility, reasonableness, reasonability, legitimacy

8 justifier, vindicator; defender, pleader; **advocate,** successful advocate *or* defender, proponent, **champion;** apologist, apologizer, apologetic

verbs

9 to justify, vindicate, do justice to, make justice *or* right prevail; fail to indict, no-bill; **warrant,** account for, show sufficient grounds for, give good reasons for; **rationalize,** explain, cry sour grapes, "make a virtue of necessity"—Shakespeare; get off the hook (*informal*), **exculpate** *see* 601.4; **clear,** clear one's name *or* one's good name, purge, destigmatize, reinstate, restore, rehabilitate

10 to defend, offer *or* say in defence, allege in support *or* vindication, **support, uphold, sustain, maintain,** assert; **answer,** reply, respond, riposte,

counter; refute *see* 957.5, **rebut** *see* 938.5; **plead for,** make a plea, offer as a plea, plead one's case *or* cause, put up a front *or* a brave front; **advocate, champion,** espouse, join *or* associate oneself with, stand *or* stick up for, speak up for, contend for, speak for, argue for, urge reasons for, put in a good word for

11 to excuse, **alibi** (*informal*), offer excuse for, give as an excuse, cover with excuses, **explain,** offer an explanation; plead ignorance *or* insanity *or* diminished responsibility; **apologize for,** make apology for; alibi out of (*informal*), crawl *or* worm *or* squirm out of, lie out of, have an alibi *or* story (*both informal*)

12 to extenuate, mitigate, palliate, soften, lessen, diminish, **ease,** mince; **soft-pedal;** slur over, ignore, pass by in silence, give the benefit of the doubt, not hold it against one, **explain away, gloss** *or* **smooth over,** put a gloss upon, put a good face upon, varnish, **white-wash,** show to best advantage; **allow for,** make allowance for; give the Devil his due

adjectives

13 justifying, justificatory; **vindicative,** vindicatory, rehabilitative; refuting *see* 957.6; **excusing,** excusatory; **apologetic,** apologetical; **extenuating,** extenuative, **palliative**

14 justifiable, vindicable, defensible; excusable, pardonable, forgivable, expiable, remissible, exemptible, venial; **condonable,** dispensable; **warrantable,** allowable, admissible, reasonable, legitimate; innocuous, unobjectionable, inoffensive

601 ACQUITTAL

nouns

1 acquittal, acquittance; **exculpation,** disculpation, verdict of acquittal *or* not guilty; **exoneration, absolution, vindication, remission,** compurgation, purgation, purging; **clearing,** clearance, destigmatizing, destigmatization, quietus; **pardon, excuse, forgiveness,** Royal pardon, free pardon; **discharge, release, dismissal,** setting free; quashing of the charge *or* indictment

2 exemption, **immunity,** impunity; **amnesty,** indemnity, nonprosecution, non prosequitur, nolle prosequi; stay

3 reprieve, respite, grace

verbs

4 to acquit, clear, exculpate, exonerate, absolve, give absolution, bring in *or* return a verdict of not guilty; **vindicate,** justify; **pardon, excuse, forgive;** remit, grant remission, remit the penalty of; amnesty, grant *or* extend amnesty; **discharge, release, dismiss, free, set free,** let off (*informal*), let go; quash the charge *or* indictment, withdraw the charge; **exempt,** grant immunity, exempt from, dispense from; shrive, purge; blot out one's sins, wipe the slate clean; **whitewash,** decontaminate; destigmatize; non-pros

5 to reprieve, respite, give *or* grant a reprieve

602 CONDEMNATION

nouns

1 **condemnation, damnation, doom,** guilty verdict, verdict of guilty; proscription, excommunication, anathematizing; **denunciation,** denouncement; **censure** *see* 510.3; **conviction; sentence, judgment,** rap (*informal*); capital punishment, death penalty, death sentence, death warrant

2 attainder, attainture, attaintment; bill of attainder

verbs

3 **to condemn, damn, doom; denounce,** denunciate; **censure** *see* 510.13; **convict,** find guilty, bring home to; proscribe, excommunicate, anathematize; blacklist, put on the Index; pronounce judgment *see* 945.13; **sentence,** pronounce sentence, pass sentence on; penalize *see* 603.4; attaint; sign one's death warrant

4 **to stand condemned,** be convicted, be found guilty

adjectives

5 **condemnatory, damnatory,** denunciatory, proscriptive; **censorious**

603 PENALTY

nouns

1 **penalty,** penalization, penance, penal retribution; **sanctions,** penal *or* punitive measures; **punishment** *see* 604; **reprisal** *see* 506.2, retaliation *see* 506, compensation, price; the devil *or* hell to pay

2 **handicap,** disability, **disadvantage** *see* 1011.6

3 **fine,** monetary *or* financial penalty, mulct, amercement, sconce, **damages,** punitive damages, compensatory damages; distress, distraint; forfeit, forfeiture; escheat, escheatment

verbs

4 **to penalize,** put *or* impose *or* inflict a penalty *or* sanctions on; **punish** *see* 604.10; **handicap,** put at a disadvantage

5 **to fine,** mulct, amerce, sconce, estreat; distrain, levy a distress; award damages

adverbs

6 **on pain of,** under *or* upon pain of, **on** *or* **under penalty of**

604 PUNISHMENT

nouns

1 **punishment,** punition, **chastisement, chastening, correction, discipline,** disciplinary measure *or* action, **castigation,** infliction, scourge, what-for (*informal*); pains, pains and punishments; pay, payment; **retribution,** retributive justice, nemesis; judicial punishment; punishment that fits the crime, condign punishment, well-deserved punishment; **penalty,** penal retribution; penology; cruel and unusual punishment (*US*); judgment; what's coming to one, **just deserts, deserts**

2 (*forms of punishment*) penal servitude, jailing, imprisonment, incarceration, confinement; hard labour, chain gang, rock pile; galleys; torture, torment, martyrdom; the gauntlet, keelhauling, tar-

and-feathering, the rack, impalement, dismemberment; strappado, estrapade

3 **slap,** smack, whack, **cuff, box,** belt; blow *see* 901.4; **rap on the knuckles,** box on the ear, slap in the face; slap on the wrist, token punishment

4 **corporal punishment, whipping, beating, thrashing, spanking, caning, flogging,** flagellation, scourging, flailing, trouncing, basting, drubbing, buffeting, belabouring; **lashing, lacing,** stripes; horse-whipping, strapping, belting, rawhiding (*US*); **switching; clubbing,** cudgelling, caning, truncheoning, fustigation, bastinado; pistol-whipping; battery

5 (*informal terms*) larruping, walloping, lathering, leathering, **hiding, tanning, dressing-down,** larruping, licking (*US*)

6 **capital punishment, execution;** legal *or* judicial murder; **hanging,** the gallows, the rope *or* noose; summary execution; **lynching,** necktie party (*US informal*), vigilanteism, vigilante justice; the necklace; **crucifixion; electrocution,** the chair (*informal*), the hot seat (*informal*); gassing, the gas chamber; lethal injection; **decapitation,** decollation, beheading, the guillotine, the axe, the block; **strangling,** strangulation, garrote; **shooting,** fusillade, firing squad; **burning,** burning at the stake; **poisoning,** hemlock; stoning, lapidation; defenestration

7 **punisher,** discipliner, chastiser, chastener; **executioner,** executionist, deathsman, Jack Ketch (*old*); **hangman; lyncher;** electrocutioner; headsman, **beheader,** decapitator; strangler, garroter; sadist, torturer

8 **penologist;** jailer *see* 429.10

verbs

9 **to punish, chastise, chasten, discipline, correct, castigate, penalize;** take to task, bring to book, bring *or* call to account; deal with, settle with, settle *or* square accounts, **give one his deserts** *or* **just deserts,** serve one right; inflict upon, visit upon; teach *or* give one a lesson, make an example of; pillory; masthead

10 (*informal terms*) **to attend to,** do for, take care of, **give it to,** take *or* have it out of; pay, pay out, **fix, settle,** settle the score, make it hot for one, **give one his comeuppance;** put one through the wringer, come down on *or* down hard on, throw the book at, throw to the wolves; **give what-for,** give a going-over, let one have it, lay into, wipe up the floor with, skin alive, have one's hide

11 **to slap,** smack, whack, **cuff, box;** strike *see* 901.13; slap the face, box the ears, give a rap on the knuckles

12 **to whip,** give a whipping *or* beating *or* thrashing, **beat, thrash, spank, cane, flog,** scourge, flagellate, flail; **smite,** thump, trounce, baste, **pummel, drub, belabour,** lay on; **lash, lace,** cut, stripe; horsewhip; knout; **strap,** belt; **switch,** birch, give the stick; **club, cudgel,** cane, truncheon, fustigate, bastinado; pistol-whip

13 **to thrash soundly, batter,** bruise

14 (*informal terms*) **to beat up,** rough up, clobber, marmelize, work over, duff up, do over, bash up, larrup, wallop, beat one's brains out, beat *or* kick the

shit out of, beat to a pulp, **beat black and blue, knock one's lights out, nail,** welt, flax, lather, leather, **hide,** tan, **tan one's hide,** dress down, lick *and* whop (*both US*), give a dressing-down, sort out, knock heads together, kick ass (*US*); **lambaste, clobber,** dust one's jacket

15 **to torture,** put to the question; rack, put on *or* to the rack; dismember, tear limb from limb; draw and quarter, break on the wheel, tar and feather, keelhaul, impale, grill

16 **to execute, put to death,** inflict capital punishment; **electrocute,** burn *and* fry (*informal*); send to the gas chamber; **behead, decapitate,** decollate, guillotine, bring to the block; **crucify; shoot,** execute by firing squad; burn, **burn at the stake; strangle,** garrote, bowstring; stone, lapidate; defenestrate

17 **to hang,** hang by the neck; **string up** *and* stretch (*informal*); gibbet, noose, neck, bring to the gallows; **lynch;** hang, draw, and quarter

18 **to be hanged,** suffer hanging, **swing,** dance upon nothing, kick the air *or* wind *or* clouds

19 **to be punished, suffer,** suffer for, **suffer the consequences** *or* **penalty,** get it *and* **catch it** (*both informal*), get *or* catch it in the neck (*informal*), catch hell *or* the devil (*informal*); **get one's deserts** *or* **just deserts** *see* 639.6; get it coming and going (*informal*), be doubly punished, sow the wind and reap the whirlwind; get hurt, get one's fingers burned, have *or* get one's knuckles rapped

20 **to take one's punishment,** bow one's neck, take the consequences, **take one's medicine** *or* what is coming to one, swallow the bitter pill *or* one's medicine, pay the piper, face the music (*informal*), stand up to it, make one's bed and lie on it; take the rap (*informal*)

21 **to deserve punishment, have it coming** (*informal*), be for it *or* in for it, be heading for a fall *or* the high jump, be cruising for a bruising (*informal*)

adjectives

22 **punishing, chastising,** chastening, corrective, disciplinary; retributive; **penal, punitive,** punitory, inflictive; castigatory; baculine; penological

605 INSTRUMENTS OF PUNISHMENT

nouns

1 **whip, lash, scourge,** flagellum, strap, thong, rawhide, sjambok, belt, tawse (*Scottish*), razor strap, blacksnake (*US & Canadian*); knout; bullwhip, bullwhack; horsewhip; crop; quirt (*US*); rope's end; cat, cat-o'-nine-tails; whiplash

2 **rod, stick, switch; paddle,** ruler, ferule; birch, rattan; cane; club

3 (*devices*) **pillory, stocks,** finger pillory; ducking stool, trebuchet; whipping post, branks, wooden horse; treadmill

4 (*instruments of torture*) **rack,** wheel, Iron Maiden of Nuremberg; screw, thumbscrew; boot, iron heel, scarpines; Procrustean bed *or* bed of Procrustes

5 (*instruments of execution*) **scaffold; block, guillotine,** axe, maiden; **stake; cross; gallows,** gallows-tree, gibbet, tree, drop; **hangman's rope, noose,** rope, halter, hemp, hempen collar *or* necktie *or* bridle (*all US informal*); **electric chair,** death chair, the chair (*informal*), hot seat (*informal*); **gas chamber,** lethal chamber, death chamber; the necklace

606 THE PEOPLE
the population

nouns

1 **the people, the populace, the public,** the general public, people in general, everyone, everybody; **the population,** the citizenry, the whole people, the polity, the body politic; **the community, the commonwealth, society,** the society, the social order *or* fabric, the nation; the commonalty *or* commonality, commonage, commoners, commons, *demos* (*Greek*); **common people, ordinary people** *or* **folk, persons,** folk, folks, gentry; the common sort, plain people *or* folks, the common run (*informal*), the rank and file, "the unknown ranks" /Pm WOODROW WILSON, Brown Jones and Robinson, Middle England; Tom, Dick and Harry; the salt of the earth, Everyman, Everywoman, the man *or* woman in the street, the common man, you and me, Joe Bloggs *and* Joe Public (*both informal*), the man on the Clapham omnibus, Joe Sixpack (*US informal*), *vulgus* (*Latin*), the third estate; **the upper class; the middle class; the lower class;** demography, demographics; social anthropology

2 **the masses, the hoi polloi,** *hoi polloi* (*Greek*), the many, **the multitude,** the crowd, **the mob,** "the hateful, hostile mob"—PETRARCH, the horde, the million, **the majority,** the mass of the people, the herd, the great unnumbered, the great unwashed, **the vulgar** *or* **common herd;** *profanum vulgus, ignobile vulgus, mobile vulgus* (*all Latin*); "the multitude of the gross people"—ERASMUS, "many-headed multitude" —SIR PHILIP SIDNEY, "the beast with many heads", "the blunt monster with uncounted heads, the still-discordant wavering multitude"—BOTH SHAKESPEARE

3 **rabble,** rabblement, rout (*old*), ruck, common ruck, canaille, *racaille* (*French*), ragtag (*informal*), "the tagrag people"—SHAKESPEARE, **ragtag and bobtail;** rag, tag, and bobtail; **riffraff, trash,** raff, chaff, **rubbish,** dregs, sordes, offscourings, off-scum, **scum, scum of the earth, dregs** *or* **scum** *or* **offscum** *or* **offscourings of society,** swinish multitude, vermin, cattle

4 **the underprivileged,** the disadvantaged, the poor, slum-dwellers, chronic poor, underclass, depressed class, poverty subculture, the wretched of the earth, outcasts, the homeless, the dispossessed, the powerless, the unemployable, lumpen, the lumpenproletariat *or* lumpenprole (*informal*)

5 **common man, commoner,** little man, **little fellow, average man,** ordinary man, typical man, **man in the street,** one of the people, man of the people, Everyman; **plebeian,** pleb (*slang*);

proletarian, prole (*informal*), *roturier* (*French*); ordinary *or* average Joe (*US informal*), John Doe *and* John Q Public (*both US*)

6 **peasant, countryman,** countrywoman, **provincial,** son of the soil, tiller of the soil; **peon,** hind, fellah, muzhik;

"hewers of wood and drawers of water"—BIBLE; **farmer** *see 1067.5,* **hick** *and* yokel (*both informal*), **bumpkin,** country bumpkin, clod, **clodhopper** (*informal*), teuchter (*Scottish*), hillbilly *and* woodhick (*both US informal*)

7 **upstart, parvenu,** adventurer, sprout (*informal*), "an upstart crow beautified in our feathers"—ROBERT GREENE; *bourgeois gentilhomme* (*French*), would-be gentleman; *nouveau riche, nouveau roturier* (*both French*), *arriviste* (*French*), **newly-rich,** pig in clover (*informal*); **social climber,** climber, name-dropper, status seeker

adjectives

8 **populational,** population; **demographic,** demographical; national, societal; **popular,** public, mass, grass-roots, **common,** common as dirt, commonplace, **plain, ordinary, lowly,** low, mean, base; **humble,** homely; **lowborn,** lowbred, baseborn, earthborn, earthy,

"of the earth earthy"—BIBLE, plebeian; third-estate; ungenteel, shabby-genteel; **vulgar, rude,** coarse, below the salt; **parvenu, upstart,** risen from the ranks, jumped-up (*informal*); **newly-rich,** *nouveau-riche* (*French*)

607 SOCIAL CLASS AND STATUS

nouns

1 **class, social class, economic class,** social group *or* grouping, status group, accorded status, social category, order, grade, caste, estate, rank; **status, social status, economic status,** socioeconomic status *or* background, standing, footing, prestige, rank, ranking, place, station, position, level, degree, stratum; **social structure, hierarchy,** social system, social gamut, social differentiation, class structure, class distinction, status system, power structure, ranking, stratification, ordering, social scale, gradation, division, social inequality, inequality, haves and have-nots,

"the classes and the masses"—WILLIAM EWART GLADSTONE, "the Privileged and the People"—BENJAMIN DISRAELI; **social bias, class conflict,** class identity, class difference, class prejudice, class struggle, class politics; **mobility, social mobility,** upward mobility, downward mobility, vertical mobility, horizontal mobility

2 **upper class, upper classes, aristocracy,** patriciate, second estate, ruling class, ruling circles, elite, elect, the privileged, the better sort, upper circles, upper crust *and* cream (*both informal*), upper-income group *or* higher-income group, gentry, gentlefolk, lords of creation; **high society,** high life, the Four Hundred (*US*), bon ton, *haut monde* (*French*); nobility, gentry *see 608*

3 **aristocracy, aristocratic status,** aristocraticalness, aristocraticness, high status, high rank, quality, high estate, gentility, social distinction, social prestige; **birth,** high birth, distinguished ancestry *or* descent *or* heritage *or* blood, **blue blood**

4 **aristocrat, patrician,** Brahmin, blue-blood, thoroughbred, member of the upper class, socialite, debutante *and* deb (*informal*), toff *and* dandy (*both informal*), grandee, grand dame, dowager, magnifico, lord of creation; **gentleman, lady,** person of breeding

5 **middle class,** middle order *or* orders, lower middle class, upper middle class, bourgeoisie, educated class, professional class, abc1s, middle-income group, white-collar workers, salaried workers; **suburbia;** Middle England, silent majority

6 **bourgeois,** member of the middle class, white-collar worker *see 726.2,* salaried worker; pillar of society, solid citizen

7 **lower class, lower classes,** lower orders, plebs, workers, working class, working people, proletariat, proles (*informal*), labouring class *or* classes, toilers, toiling class *or* classes, the other half, low-income group, wage-earners, hourly worker, blue-collar workers

8 **the underclass, the underprivileged**

9 **worker** *see 726.2,* **workman, working man, working woman,** working girl, proletarian, prole (*informal*), labourer, labouring man, toiler, wage slave (*informal*), artisan, mechanic, industrial worker, factory worker

adjectives

10 **upper-class, aristocratic, patrician, upscale,** U (*informal*); gentle, genteel, of gentle blood; gentlemanly, gentlemanlike; ladylike, quite the lady; **wellborn, well-bred, blue-blooded,** of good breed; **thoroughbred,** purebred, pure-blooded, *pur sang* (*French*), full-blooded; **highborn,** highbred; born to the purple,

"to the manner born"—SHAKESPEARE, born with a silver spoon in one's mouth; **high-society,** socialite, hoity-toity (*informal*), posh; **middle-class, bourgeois,** *petit-bourgeois* (*French*), petty-bourgeois, suburban; **working class, blue collar,** proletarian, lower-class, born on the wrong side of the tracks; **class-conscious; mobile, socially mobile,** upwardly mobile, downwardly mobile, vertically mobile, horizontally mobile, *déclassé*

608 ARISTOCRACY, NOBILITY, GENTRY
noble rank or birth

nouns

1 **aristocracy, nobility,** titled aristocracy, hereditary nobility, noblesse, **aristocracy; elite,** upper class, elect, upper classes, upper crust (*informal*), upper ten thousand, the Four Hundred (*US*), high society, high life, *haut monde* (*French*); old nobility, *ancienne noblesse* (*French*), *noblesse de robe, noblesse d'épée* (*both French*); **peerage,** baronage, lords temporal and spiritual; baronetage; knightage, chivalry; royalty

2 nobility, nobleness, aristocracy, aristocraticalness; gentility, genteelness; quality, rank, distinction; birth, high *or* noble birth, ancestry, high *or* honourable descent; blood, blue blood; royalty *see* 417.8

3 gentry, gentlefolk, gentlefolks, gentlepeople, better sort; lesser nobility, *petite noblesse (French)*; *samurai (Japanese)*; landed gentry, squirearchy

4 nobleman, noble, gentleman; peer; aristocrat, patrician, Brahman, blue blood, thoroughbred, silk-stocking, lace-curtain, toff *and* nob *and* dandy *(all informal)*; grandee, magnifico, magnate, optimate; lord, laird *(Scottish)*, lordling; seignior, seigneur, *hidalgo (Spanish)*; duke, grand duke, archduke, marquis, earl, count, viscount, baron, daimio, baronet; squire; esquire, armiger; palsgrave, waldgrave, margrave, landgrave

5 knight, cavalier, chevalier, *caballero (Spanish)*, *Ritter (German)*,

"a verray parfit gentil knight"—CHAUCER; knight-errant, knight-adventurer; companion; bachelor, knight bachelor; baronet, knight baronet; banneret, knight banneret; Bayard, Gawain, Lancelot, Sidney, Sir Galahad, Don Quixote

6 noblewoman, peeress, gentlewoman; lady, dame, *doña (Spanish)*, khanum; duchess, grand duchess, archduchess, marchioness, viscountess, countess, baroness, margravine

7 prince, *Prinz*, *Fürst (both German)*, *dauphin (French)*, knez, atheling, sheikh, sherif, mirza, khan, emir, shahzada *(India)*; princeling, princelet; crown prince, heir apparent; heir presumptive; prince consort; prince regent; king; maharaja; Muslim rulers *see* 575.10

8 princess, *princesse (French)*, *infanta (Spanish)*, rani *and* maharani *and* begum *and* shahzadi *and* kumari *or* kunwari *and* raj-kumari *and* malikzadi *(all India)*; crown princess; queen *see* 575.11

9 *(rank or office)* lordship, ladyship; dukedom, marquisate, earldom, barony, baronetcy; viscountship, viscountcy, viscounty; knighthood, knight-errantship; seigniory, seigneury, seignioralty; pashaship, pashadom; princeship, princedom; kingship, queenship *see* 417.8

adjectives

10 noble, of rank, high, exalted; aristocratic, patrician; gentle, genteel, of gentle blood; gentlemanly, gentlemanlike; ladylike, quite the lady; knightly, chivalrous; ducal, archducal; princely, princelike; regal *see* 417.17, kingly, kinglike, "every inch a king"—SHAKESPEARE; queenly, queenlike; titled

11 wellborn, well-bred, blue-blooded, well-connected, of good breed; thoroughbred, purebred, pure-blooded, *pur sang (French)*, full-blooded; highborn, highbred; born to the purple

609 POLITICS

nouns

1 politics, polity, the art of the possible,
"economics in action"—ROBERT LA FOLLETTE, "the people's business, the most important business there is"—ADLAI STEVENSON; practical politics, *Realpolitik (German)*; empirical politics; party *or* partisan politics, partisanism; politicization; reform politics; multiparty politics; power politics, *Machtpolitik (German)*; machine politics, bossism *(informal)*, Tammany Hall *(US)*; confrontation *or* confrontational politics; interest politics, single-issue politics, interest-group politics, pressure-group politics, PAC *or* political action committee politics *(US)*; consensus politics; career politics; pork-barrel politics; party politics, domestic politics; world politics, international politics

2 political science, politics, government, civics; political philosophy, political theory; political behaviour; political economy, comparative government, international relations, public administration; political geography, geopolitics, *Geopolitik (German)*

3 statesmanship, statecraft, political *or* governmental leadership, national leadership; transpartisan *or* suprapartisan leadership; "the wise employment of individual meanness for the public good"—LINCOLN; kingcraft, queencraft; senatorship

4 policy, polity, public policy; line, party line, party principle *or* doctrine *or* philosophy, position; noninterference, nonintervention, *laissez-faire (French)*, laissez-faireism; free enterprise; government control, governmentalism, centralism; planned economy, command economy, managed currency, price supports, pump-priming *(informal)*; autarky, economic self-sufficiency; free trade; protection, protectionism; bimetallism; states' rights, nullification *(both US)*

5 foreign policy, foreign affairs; world politics; diplomacy, diplomatic *or* diplomatics *(both old)*; "the police in grand costume"—NAPOLEON; shuttle diplomacy; gunboat diplomacy; brinkmanship; nationalism, internationalism; expansionism, imperialism, colonialism, neocolonialism, manifest destiny *(US)*; spheres of influence; balance of power; containment; deterrence; militarism, preparedness; tough policy, the big stick *(informal)*, twisting the lion's tail; brinksmanship; nonresistance, isolationism, neutralism, coexistence, peaceful coexistence; détente; compromise, appeasement; peace offensive; good-neighbor policy *(Franklin D Roosevelt)*; open-door policy *(Deng Xiaoping)*; Monroe Doctrine *(US)*; Sinatra Doctrine *(Mikhail Gorbachev)*

6 programme; austerity plan, belt tightening; Beveridge Plan; social contract; Thatcherism; back to basics *(John Major)*; Square Deal *(Theodore Roosevelt)*, New Deal *(Franklin D Roosevelt)*, Fair Deal *(Harry S Truman)*, New Frontier *(John F Kennedy)*, Great Society *(Lyndon B Johnson)*, "A kinder, gentler nation"—GEORGE BUSH

7 platform, party platform, manifesto, programme, declaration of policy; plank; issue; keynote address, keynote speech; position paper

8 party conference; political convention, convention; conclave; constitutional convention; *(US*

conventions, etc) national convention, state convention, county convention, preliminary convention, nominating convention

9 caucus, legislative *or* congressional caucus, packed caucus; secret caucus (*all US*)

10 candidacy, candidature, **running,** standing *or* standing for office, **running for office,** throwing *or* tossing one's hat in the ring (*informal*)

11 nomination, selection; acceptance speech

12 electioneering, campaigning, politicking (*informal*), take to the hustings; **rally;** campaign dinner, fund-raising dinner

13 campaign; canvass, solicitation; grass-roots campaign; soap box campaign; TV *or* media campaign; campaign *or* election promises; campaign fund, campaign contribution

14 smear campaign, mudslinging campaign, negative campaign, dirty tricks campaign; **whispering campaign;** muckraking, mudslinging, character assassination

15 election, general election, by-election, local election, European *or* Euro election; **referendum,** plebiscite; (*US elections*) congressional election, presidential election, primary, primary election, direct primary, open primary, closed primary, nonpartisan primary, mandatory primary, optional primary, preference primary, presidential primary, runoff primary, caucus *see* 609.9

16 constituency, seat, ward; marginal, safe seat; pocket borough *and* rotten borough; precinct, borough (*both US*)

17 suffrage, franchise, the vote, right to vote; universal suffrage, manhood suffrage, woman *or* female suffrage; suffragism, suffragettism; suffragist, woman-suffragist, suffragette; one man one vote

18 voting, going to the polls, casting one's ballot; preferential voting, preferential system, alternative vote; proportional representation *or* PR, cumulative system *or* voting, Hare system, list system; single system *or* voting, single transferrable vote *or* STV; first-past-the-post system; single-member constituency *see* 609.16; tactical voting; absentee voting; proxy voting; voting machine (*US*); electoral fraud; card vote, block vote; spoiled ballot, **vote** *see* 371.6

19 ballot, slate, ticket

20 polls, poll, polling station, polling place (*US*); voting booth, polling booth; ballot box; voting machine (*US*); electoral roll

21 returns, election returns, **poll,** count, official count; **recount;** returning officer; majority, relative majority; landslide, tidal wave

22 electorate, electors; **constituency,** constituents; electoral college

23 voter, elector, balloter; registered voter; fraudulent voter; proxy

24 political party (*see list*), **party,** major party, minor party, third party, splinter party; "the madness of many for the gain of a few"—POPE; party in power, opposition party, loyal opposition; **faction, camp; machine,** political *or* party machine, Tammany Hall (*US*); city hall; one-party

system, two-party system, multiple party system, multiparty system

25 partisanism, partisanship, partisanry; Conservatism, Toryism; Liberalism; socialism; social democracy; Whiggism

26 nonpartisanism, independence, neutralism; mugwumpery, mugwumpism

27 partisan, party member, party man *or* woman; regular, stalwart, loyalist; **party hack;** party faithful

28 nonpartisan, independent, neutral, mugwump, undecided *or* floating voter, centrist; swing vote

29 political influence, wire-pulling (*informal*); **social pressure, public opinion, special-interest pressure,** group pressure; **influence peddling; lobbying,** lobbyism; **logrolling,** back scratching

30 wire-puller (*informal*); **influence peddler,** power broker, fixer

31 pressure group, interest group, special-interest group, single-issue group, political action committee *or* PAC (*US*); **special interest;** vested interest; financial interests, farm interests, trade union union interests, etc; minority interests, ethnic vote, Black vote, Asian vote, etc

32 lobby, parliamentary lobby, special-interest lobby; **lobbyist,** lobbyer

33 front, movement, coalition, political front; popular front, people's front, national front, etc; grass-roots movement, ground swell, the silent majority

34 (*political corruption*) **graft,** sleaze (*informal*), jobbery; pork-barrel politics; political intrigue

35 spoils of office; graft, boodle (*informal*); slush fund (*informal*); campaign fund, campaign contribution; public trough (*informal*); spoils system; cronyism, nepotism

36 political patronage, patronage, favours of office, pork barrel (*informal*)

37 political *or* **official jargon;** officialese *and* gobbledygook *and* Eurospeak (*all informal*); political doubletalk, doublespeak, bunkum, windbaggery; pussyfooting

verbs

38 to politick (*informal*), politicize; gerrymander

39 to run for office, run; **throw** *or* **toss one's hat in the ring** (*informal*), stand *and* stand for office, enter the lists *or* arena; contest a seat

40 to electioneer, campaign; stump *and* take to the stump *and* take to the hustings *and* hit the campaign trail (*all informal*); **canvass,** go to the voters *or* electorate, go *or* appeal to the country, solicit votes, ring doorbells; shake hands and kiss babies

41 to support, back *and* back up (*both informal*), come out for, **endorse;** go with the party, follow the party line; **get on the bandwagon** (*informal*); **nominate, elect, vote** *see* 371.18, 20

42 to hold office, hold *or* occupy a post, fill an office, be the incumbent, be in office

adjectives

43 political, politic; governmental, civic; geopolitical; statesmanlike; diplomatic; suffragist; politico-commercial, politico-diplomatic, politico-ecclesiastical, politico-economic, politico-ethical, politico-geographical, politico-judicial, politico-military,

politico-moral, politico-religious, politico-scientific,
politico-social, politico-theological

44 partisan, party; bipartisan, biparty, two-party
45 nonpartisan, independent, neutral, mugwumpian
and mugwumpish (*both informal*), **on the fence**

word elements

46 politico–
47 political parties (United Kingdom)

Alliance Party	Official Ulster Unionist
British National Party *or*	Party
BNP	Plaid Cymru
Communist Party of Great	Revolutionary Communist
Britain *or* CPGB	Party *or* RCP
Conservative and Unionist	Scottish National Party *or*
Party	SNP
Democratic Unionist Party	Sinn Féin
or DUP	Social Democratic and
Green Party	Labour Party *or* SDLP
Labour Party	Socialist Workers Party *or*
Liberal Democrats	SWP
Natural Law Party	

610 POLITICIAN

nouns

1 politician, politico, political leader, professional
politician; party leader, party boss; **political hack;**
old campaigner, war-horse; reform politician,
reformer
2 statesman, stateswoman, solon, public man *or*
woman, national leader;
"a politician who is held upright by equal pressure
from all directions"—ERIC JOHNSTON, "a successful
politician who is dead"—THOMAS B REED; elder
statesman
3 legislator, lawmaker, solon, lawgiver;
parliamentarian, Member of Parliament *or* MP,
Member of the European Parliament *or* MEP;
backbencher, backwoodsman; parliamentary private
secretary; frontbencher; crossbencher; Speaker,
Deputy Speaker; Father of the House; councillor,
mayor, provost (*Scottish*), alderman (*old*), city father
(*US politicians*) **congressman,** congresswoman,
Member of Congress, Senator, Representative,
Speaker of the House, majority leader, minority
leader, floor leader
4 (*petty politician*) **hack, party hack**
5 (*corrupt politician*) **dirty** *or* **crooked politician** (*both
informal*), placeman; **grafter,** boodler (*informal*);
spoilsman, spoilsmonger; influence peddler *see 609.30*
6 (*political intriguer*) strategist, machinator, gamesman,
wheeler-dealer (*informal*); operator *and* finagler *and*
wire-puller (*all informal*); pork-barrel politician;
Machiavellian; behind-the-scenes operator, grey
eminence, *éminence grise* (*French*), power behind the
throne, kingmaker (*informal*), **powerbroker** *see 893.6*
7 (*political leader*) **boss** (*informal*); policy maker;
standard-bearer; ringleader *see 375.11*; **big shot**
(*informal*) *see 996.9*
8 spin doctor (*informal*), PR man *or* woman, media
manager

9 candidate, aspirant, hopeful *and* political hopeful
and wannabee (*all informal*), office seeker *or* hunter,
baby kisser (*informal*); running mate; **dark horse;**
stalking-horse; favourite son; presidential timber;
defeated candidate, also-ran *and* dud (*both informal*)
10 campaigner, electioneer, soapbox speaker *or* orator
(*informal*)
11 officeholder, office-bearer, public servant, public
official, **incumbent;** lame duck, holdover (*US*); new
broom (*informal*); president-elect; the powers that be
12 political worker, fundraiser, leafleter, newspaper
seller; party chairman

verbs

13 to go into politics; **stand,** run; **campaign,** take to
the hustings

adjectives

14 statesmanlike, statesmanly

611 POLITICO-ECONOMIC PRINCIPLES

nouns

1 conservatism, conservativeness, rightism;
unprogressiveness, backwardness;
ultraconservatism, reaction, arch-conservative,
reactionism, reactionarism, reactionaryism,
reactionariness, die-hardism (*informal*)
2 moderatism, moderateness, moderatism, middle-
of-the-roadism; middle of the road, moderate
position, via media, **centre,** centrism; third force,
nonalignment
3 progressivism, leftism; left, left wing,
progressiveness, social democracy
4 One Nation Toryism, Christian Democracy; social
market, mixed economy, Butskellism, **Keynesianism**
5 radicalism, extremism, ultraism; radicalization;
revolutionism; ultraconservatism *see 611.1*; extreme
left, extreme left wing, left-wing extremism, loony
left (*informal*); New Left, Old Left; Jacobinism,
sans-culottism, *sans-culotterie* (*French*); **anarchism,
nihilism,** syndicalism *and* anarcho-syndicalism (*both
old*); extreme rightism, radical rightism; extreme
right, extreme right wing; social Darwinism; laissez-
faireism *see 329.1*; **royalism, monarchism;**
Toryism, Bourbonism
6 communism, Bolshevism, Marxism, Marxism-
Leninism, Leninism, Trotskyism, Stalinism, Maoism,
Titoism, Castroism, revisionism; Marxian socialism;
dialectical materialism; democratic centralism;
dictatorship of the proletariat; **Communist Party;**
Communist International, Comintern; Communist
Information Bureau, Cominform; iron curtain *see
1011.5*
7 socialism, collective ownership, collectivization,
public ownership; **collectivism;** creeping socialism;
state socialism, dirigisme, *Staatssozialismus* (*German*);
guild socialism; Fabian socialism, Fabianism; utopian
socialism; Marxian socialism, Marxism *see 611.6*;
phalansterism; Owenism; Saint-Simonianism, Saint-
Simonism; **nationalization**
8 welfarism, welfare statism; **cradle-to-grave
security,** womb-to-tomb security; social welfare;
social security, social insurance; unemployment

benefit, income support; national insurance; National Health Service, Medicaid (*US*); sickness insurance; **relief, welfare,** Family Credit, child benefit, retirement *or* state *or* old-age pension, sickness benefit, disability allowance; guaranteed income, guaranteed annual income; welfare state; welfare capitalism

9 **capitalism,** capitalistic system, **free enterprise,** private enterprise, free-enterprise economy, free-enterprise system, free economy; Thatcherism; laissez-faire, laissez-faireism; private sector; private ownership; **individualism**

10 **nationalism, fascism, National Socialism** *or* **Nazism,** Hitlerism, Falangism; authoritarianism, social authoritarianism; racism, racialism, apartheid; anti-Semitism; ethnic cleansing; Bonapartism; militarism

11 patriotism, jingoism, flag-waving, chauvinism; Little England, Britain First, "Britain first, Britain second, Britain third"— Norman Tebbit, Euroscepticism, Gaullism; America First; isolationism, autarky

12 internationalism, interdependence; Europhilicism, communitairism

13 **conservative,** conservatist, **rightist, right-winger;** dry, true blue, "a person who has something to conserve"— Edward Young, "the leftover progressive of an earlier generation"— Edmund Fuller; social Darwinist; ultraconservative, arch-conservative, extreme right-winger, **reactionary,** reactionarist, reactionist, die-hard, blimp; **royalist, monarchist,** Bourbon, Tory, imperialist; **right, right wing; radical right**

14 **moderate,** moderatist, moderationist, **centrist,** middle-of-the-roader (*informal*); independent; centre

15 **progressive,** progressivist, **leftist, left-winger,** social democrat; welfare stater; **left**

16 One Nation Tory, Christian Democrat; Keynesian, Butskellite

17 **radical, extremist,** ultra, ultraist; **revolutionary,** revolutionist; **subversive;** extreme left-winger, left-wing extremist, **red** (*informal*), Bolshevik; Jacobin, sansculotte; **anarchist,** nihilist; lunatic fringe

18 **Communist,** Bolshevist; Bolshevik, **Red** *and* commie *and* bolshie (*all informal*); Marxist, Leninist, Marxist-Leninist, Trotskyite *or* Trotskyist, Stalinist, Maoist, Titoist, Castroite, revisionist; card-carrying Communist, avowed Communist; fellow traveller, Communist sympathizer

19 **socialist,** collectivist; social democrat; state socialist, dirigiste; Fabian, Fabian socialist; Marxist *see* 611.18; utopian socialist; Fourierist, phalansterian; Saint-Simonian; Owenite

20 **capitalist;** Thatcherite; individualist; rich man *see* 618.7

21 **nationalist, fascist, National Socialist** *or* **Nazi,** Hitlerist, Falangist; authoritarian, social authoritarian; racist, racialist; Bonapartist; militarist

22 patriot, jingoist, flag waver, chauvinist; Little Englander, Eurosceptic; Gaullist; isolationist

23 internationalist; Europhile

verbs

24 **to politicize;** democratize, republicanize, socialize, communize; nationalize *see* 476.7; deregulate, privatize, denationalize; radicalize

adjectives

25 **conservative, right-wing,** right-of-centre, dry; old-line, die-hard, unreconstructed, unprogressive, nonprogressive; ultraconservative, **reactionary,** reactionist

26 **moderate,** centrist, middle-of-the-road (*informal*), independent

27 **progressive,** progressivistic, wet, bleeding-heart (*informal*); **leftist, left-wing,** on the left, left of centre

28 One-Nation Tory, Christian Democratic; Butskellite, Keynesian

29 **radical, extreme, extremist,** extremistic, ultraist, ultraistic; revolutionary, revolutionist; subversive; ultraconservative *see* 611.25; extreme left-wing, **red** (*informal*); anarchistic, nihilistic, syndicalist *and* anarcho-syndicalist (*both old*)

30 **Communist, communistic,** Bolshevik, Bolshevist, commie *and* bolshie *and* Red (*all informal*); **Marxist,** Leninist, Marxist-Leninist, Trotskyite *or* Trotskyist, Stalinist, Maoist, Titoist, Castroite; revisionist

31 **socialist, socialistic,** collectivistic; social-democratic; Fabian; welfarist; Fourieristic, phalansterian; Saint-Simonian

32 **capitalist, capitalistic,** bourgeois, individualistic, nonsocialistic, free-enterprise, private-enterprise, Thatcherite

33 **nationalist, fascist, National Socialist** *or* **Nazi,** Hitlerist, Falangist; authoritarian, racist, racialist; Bonapartist; militaristic

34 patriotic, jingoistic, flag-waving, chauvinistic, Eurosceptical; Gaullist

35 internationalist; Europhilic, Communitaire

612 GOVERNMENT

nouns

1 **government,** governance, **discipline, regulation; direction, management, administration,** dispensation, disposition, oversight, **supervision** *see* 573.2; **regime,** regimen; **rule, sway, sovereignty, reign,** regnancy; empire, empery; social order, civil government, political government; form *or* system of government, political organization, polity

2 **control, mastery, mastership, command, power, jurisdiction, dominion, domination; hold, grasp,** grip, gripe; hand, hands, iron hand, clutches; talons, claws; helm, reins of government

3 **the government, the authorities; the powers that be,** national government, central government, the Establishment; the corridors of power, government circles; the Crown, His *or* Her Majesty's Government, Downing Street, Whitehall, Uncle Sam, Washington

4 (*kinds of government*) central government, federal government, federation; **constitutional government; republic,** commonwealth;

democracy, representative government, representative democracy, direct *or* pure democracy; "government of the people, by the people, for the people"—LINCOLN, "the worst form of government except all those other forms that have been tried from time to time"—WINSTON CHURCHILL, "the recurrent suspicion that more than half of the people are right more than half of the time"—E B WHITE; **parliamentary government**; local government; social democracy, welfare state, nanny state (*informal*); mob rule, tyranny of the majority, mobocracy, ochlocracy; minority government; pantisocracy; aristocracy, hierarchy, oligarchy; feudal system; monarchy, absolute monarchy, constitutional monarchy, limited monarchy; dictatorship, tyranny, autocracy, autarchy; dyarchy, duarchy, duumvirate; triarchy, triumvirate; **totalitarian government** *or* regime, police state; **fascism, communism;** stratocracy, **military government**, militarism, garrison state; martial law, rule of the sword; regency; hierocracy, theocracy, thearchy; patriarchy, patriarchate; gerontocracy; technocracy, meritocracy; **autonomy, self-government**, self-rule, self-determination, home rule, independence, devolution; heteronomy, dominion rule, colonial government, colonialism, neocolonialism; provisional government; coalition government

5 matriarchy, matriarchate, gynarchy, gynocracy, gynaecocracy; petticoat government

6 (*other types of rule*) ergatocracy (*workers*), hagiocracy (*holy men*), hierocracy (*priests*), isocracy (*equals*), monocracy (*one person*), nomocracy (*rule of law*), plantocracy (*planters*), plutocracy (*wealthy*), pornocracy (*whores*), ptochocracy (*the poor*), slavocracy (*slaveholders*), squirearchy (*squires*), stratocracy (*the military*), technocracy (*experts*)

7 **supranational government**, supergovernment, **world government**; European Union *or* EU, **United Nations**, League of Nations (*old*) *see* 614

8 (*principles of government*) democratism, power-sharing, republicanism; constitutionalism, rule of law, parliamentarism, parliamentarianism; monarchism, royalism; feudalism, feudality; imperialism; fascism, neofascism, Nazism, national socialism; statism, governmentalism; collectivism, communism *see* 611.6, socialism *see* 611.7; federalism; centralism; pluralism; political principles *see* 611

9 absolutism, dictatorship, despotism, tyranny, autocracy, autarchy, monarchy, absolute monarchy; **authoritarianism**; totalitarianism; one-man rule, one-party rule; Caesarism, Stalinism, kaiserism, czarism, Bonapartism; benevolent despotism, paternalism

10 **despotism, tyranny, fascism**, domineering, domination, oppression; heavy hand, high hand, iron hand, iron heel *or* boot; big stick, *argumentum baculinum* (*Latin*); **terrorism**, reign of terror; thought control, Big Brother

11 officialism, bureaucracy; quangocracy; **red-tapeism** *and* red tape (*all informal*); official jargon *see* 609.37

verbs

12 to **govern, regulate; wield authority** *see* 417.13; **command**, officer, captain, **head, lead**, be master, be at the head of, **preside over**, chair; **direct, manage, supervise, administer**, administrate *see* 573.11; discipline; stand over

13 to **control, hold in hand**, have in one's power, gain a hold upon; hold the reins, hold the helm, call the shots *or* tune *and* be in the driver's seat *or* saddle (*all informal*); have control of, **have under control, have in hand** *or* **well in hand**; be master of the situation, have it all one's own way, have the game in one's own hands, hold all the aces (*informal*); pull the strings *or* wires

14 to **rule, sway, reign**, bear reign, have the sway, wield the sceptre, wear the crown, sit on the throne; rule over, overrule

15 to **dominate, predominate**, preponderate, prevail; **have the ascendancy, have the upper** *or* **whip hand**, get under control; **master**, have the mastery of; bestride; dictate, lay down the law; **rule the roost** *and* wear the trousers *and* crack the whip (*all informal*); take the lead, play first fiddle; **lead by the nose, twist** *or* **turn around one's little finger; keep under one's thumb**, bend to one's will

16 to **domineer**, domineer over, **lord it over**; browbeat, order around, henpeck (*informal*), intimidate, bully, cow, bulldoze (*informal*), walk over, walk all over; castrate, unman; daunt, terrorize; **tyrannize**, tyrannize over, push *or* kick around (*informal*), despotize; **grind**, grind down, break, **oppress**, suppress, repress, weigh *or* press heavy on; keep under, keep down, beat down, clamp down on (*informal*); overbear, overmaster, overawe; override, ride over, trample *or* stamp *or* tread upon, trample *or* tread down, **trample** *or* **tread underfoot**, keep down, crush under an iron heel, **ride roughshod over**; hold *or* keep a tight hand upon, rule with a rod of iron, rule with an iron hand *or* fist; enslave, subjugate *see* 432.8; compel, coerce *see* 424.7

adjectives

17 **governmental**, gubernatorial; **political, civil**, civic; **official**, bureaucratic; democratic, republican, fascist, fascistic, oligarchal, oligarchic, oligarchical, aristocratic, aristocratical, theocratic, **federal**, federalist, federalistic, **constitutional**, parliamentary, parliamentarian; monarchic *or* monarchical, monarchial, monarchal (*old*); autocratic, monocratic, absolute; **authoritarian**; despotic, **dictatorial; totalitarian**; pluralistic; paternalistic, patriarchal, patriarchic, patriarchical; matriarchal, matriarchic, matriarchical; heteronomous; autonomous, self-governing

18 **governing, controlling, regulating**, regulative, regulatory, **commanding; ruling, reigning, sovereign**, regnant; **master, chief**, general, **boss, head; dominant, predominant**, predominate, preponderant, preponderate, prepotent, prepollent, prevalent, **leading, paramount, supreme**, number one (*informal*), hegemonic, hegemonistic; ascendant, in the ascendant, in ascendancy; at the head, in chief; in charge *see* 417.21

19 executive, administrative, ministerial; official, bureaucratic; **supervisory, directing, managing** *see* 573.12

adverbs

20 under control, in hand, well in hand; **in one's power,** under one's control

word elements

21 –archy, –cracy, –ocracy

613 LEGISLATURE, GOVERNMENT ORGANIZATION

nouns

1 legislature (*see list*), legislative body; **parliament, congress, assembly,** general assembly, house of assembly, legislative assembly, **national assembly, chamber of deputies,** federal assembly, diet, soviet (*old*), court; unicameral legislature, bicameral legislature; legislative chamber, **upper chamber** *or* **house** (*see list*), **lower chamber** *or* **house** (*see list*); regional *or* state legislature, regional *or* state assembly; provincial legislature, provincial parliament; local authority, city council, county council, district council, commission; town hall

2 Her Majesty's Government; British Cabinet (*see list*)

3 cabinet, Privy Council, **council,** ministry, advisory council, council of state, divan; front bench, Treasury Bench; **Her Majesty's Loyal Opposition,** opposition, shadow cabinet; kitchen cabinet, Star Chamber, camarilla

4 legislation, lawmaking, legislature (*old*); **enactment,** enaction, royal assent, constitution, passage, passing; **resolution,** concurrent resolution, joint resolution; act *see* 673.3

5 (*legislative procedure*) introduction, first reading, select committee, tabling, filing, second reading, deliberation, **debate,** third reading, **vote,** free vote, division, roll call; **filibustering,** filibuster; closure, guillotine, cloture *and* gag rule (*both US*)

6 veto, executive veto, absolute veto, qualified *or* limited veto, item veto *and* pocket veto (*both US*)

7 referendum, constitutional referendum, statutory referendum, compulsory *or* mandatory referendum; **mandate; plebiscite,** plebiscitum; initiative, direct initiative, indirect initiative; recall

8 bill, private member's bill; statute, decree, order in council; **clause, proviso; rider; motion;** question, previous question; vote of no confidence

verbs

9 to legislate, make *or* enact laws, **enact, pass,** constitute, ordain, put in force, put on the statute book; **put through,** lobby through; table, pigeonhole; take the floor, get the floor, have the floor; yield the floor, give way; **filibuster,** talk out; logroll (*US*); **veto, pocket, kill; decree** *see* 420.8

adjectives

10 legislative, legislatorial, lawmaking; deliberative; **parliamentary, congressional;** senatorial; bicameral, unicameral

11 legislatures

Althing (Iceland)	Slovenia, Tanzania,
Chamber of Deputies	Thailand, Tunisia,
(Lebanon, Luxembourg)	Uganda, Burkina Faso,
Chamber of	North Vietnam, Zaïre,
Representatives	Zambia)
(Morocco)	National Congress (Brazil,
Congress (Chile, Colombia,	Dominican Republic,
Honduras, Liberia,	Ecuador, Georgia,
Mexico, USA,	Guatemala)
Venezuela)	National Council (Monaco,
Cortes (Spain)	Slovakia)
Council of Representatives	National People's Congress
(Ethiopia)	(People's Republic of
Council of the Valleys	China)
(Andorra)	People's Assembly
Diet (Japan)	(Myanmar, Mozambique)
Eduskunta (Finland)	Oireachtas (Ireland)
Federal Assembly (Czech	Parliament (Austria,
Republic, Russia,	Barbados, Belgium,
Switzerland)	Canada, Ethiopia,
Federal National Assembly	European Union, Fiji,
(Cameroon)	France, Germany, India,
Federal Parliament	Iran, Italy, Jamaica, Laos,
(Australia)	Liechtenstein, Malagasy
Folketing (Denmark)	Republic, Malaysia,
Grand National Assembly	Romania, Singapore,
(Bulgaria, Turkey)	South Africa, Swaziland,
Great and General Council	Trinidad and Tobago,
(San Marino)	United Kingdom)
Great Hural (Mongolia)	People's Assembly
House of Assembly	(Albania, Egypt,
(Zimbabwe)	Mozambique)
House of Representatives	People's Consultative
(Cyprus, Gambia, Malta,	Congress (Indonesia)
New Zealand, Sierra	People's Council (Maldive
Leone)	Islands, Syria)
Knesset (Israel)	Riigikogu (Estonia)
Legislative Assembly	Riksdag (Sweden)
(Costa Rica, Mauritius,	Saeíma (Latvia)
Nauru, Western Samoa,	Seimas (Lithuania)
Tonga)	Sejm (Poland)
Legislative Chamber	States General
(Haiti)	(Netherlands)
Loya Jerga (Afghanistan)	Storting (Norway)
Milli Majlis (Azerbaijan)	Supreme Assembly
National Assembly	(Tajikistan, Uzbekistan)
(Bhutan, Botswana,	Supreme Council
Cambodia, Republic of	(Ukraine)
China, El Salvador,	Supreme Kenges
Gabon, Guinea,	(Kazakhstan)
Equatorial Guinea,	Supreme People's
Guyana, Hungary, Ivory	Assembly (North Korea)
Coast, Jordan, Kenya,	Supreme Soviet (Armenia,
South Korea, Kuwait,	Belarus, Moldova)
Macedonia, Malawi,	Uluk Kenesh (Kyrgyzstan)
Mauritania, Pakistan,	
Rwanda, Senegal,	

12 upper houses

Bundesrat (Austria,	Chamber of Notables
Germany)	(Jordan)
Chamber of Districts	Chamber of Republics
(Croatia)	(Yugoslavia)

Corporative Chamber
(Portugal)
Council of Nationalities
(Russian Federation)
Council of States
(Switzerland)
Seanad Éireann (Ireland)
Federal Council (Russia)
First Chamber
(Netherlands)
House of Councillors
(Japan)
House of Elders
(Afghanistan)
House of Lords (United
Kingdom)
Khalk Maslakhaty
(Turkmenistan)
King's Council (Laos)
Lagting (Norway)
National Council

13 lower houses

Assembly of Deputies
(Romanaia)
Bundestag (Germany)
Chamber of Citizens
(Yugoslavia)
Chamber of Deputies
(Brazil, Chile, Croatia,
Czech Republic,
Dominican Republic,
Ecuador, Ethiopia, Italy,
Jordan, Mexico,
Nicaragua, Paraguay,
Venezuela)
Chamber of
Representatives (Belgium,
Colombia)
Chamber of the People
(Czechoslovakia)
Council of the Federation
(Russian Federation)
Dáil Éireann (Ireland)
House of Assembly
(Barbados, South Africa,
Swaziland)
House of Commons

14 The Cabinet

Chancellor of the Duchy
of Lancaster
Chancellor of the
Exchequer
Chief Secretary to the
Treasury
Deputy Prime Minister
Lord High Chancellor
Lord President of the
Council
Lord Privy Seal
President of the Board of
Trade and Secretary of
State for Trade and
Industry

(Namibia)
Rajya Sabha (India)
Republican Senate
(Turkey)
Senate (Australia,
Barbados, Belgium,
Brazil, Canada, Chile,
Colombia, Czech
Republic, Dominican
Republic, Ecuador, Fiji,
France, Iran, Ireland,
Italy, Jamaica, Liberia,
Malagasy Republic,
Malaysia, Mexico,
Nicaragua, Paraguay,
Philippines, Romania,
South Africa, Swaziland,
Trinidad and Tobago,
USA, Venezuela)
State Council (Slovenia)

(Canada, United
Kingdom)
House of Representatives
(Australia, Fiji, Jamaica,
Japan, Liberia, Malaysia,
Philippines, USA)
House of the People
(Afghanistan)
Lok Sabha (India)
Majlis (Iran,
Turkemenistan)
Nationalrat (Austria)
National Assembly
(France, Laos, Malagasy
Republic, Namibia,
Portugal, South Africa,
Turkey)
National Council
(Switzerland)
Odelsting (Norway)
Second Chamber
(Netherlands)
State Chamber (Slovenia)
State Duma (Russia)

Prime Minister, First Lord
of the Treasury, and
Minister of the Civil
Service
Secretary of State for
Defence
Secretary of State for
Education
Secretary of State for
Employment
Secretary of State for
Foreign and
Commonwealth Affairs
Secretary of State for
Health

Secretary of State for
National Heritage
Secretary of State for
Northern Ireland
Secretary of State for
Scotland
Secretary of State for
Social Security

15 Ministers of State

Agriculture, Fisheries, and
Food
Armed Forces
Construction and Planning
Consumer Affairs and
Small Firms
Defence Procurement
Economic Secretary
Education
Employment
Energy and Industry
Environment and
Countryside

Secretary of State for the
Environment
Secretary of State for the
Home Department
Secretary of State for
Transport
Secretary of State for
Wales

Europe
Financial Secretary
Health
Home Office
Local Government
Northern Ireland
Overseas Development
Paymaster-General
Scottish Office
Social Security and
Disabled People
Trade
Transport

614 UNITED NATIONS, INTERNATIONAL ORGANIZATIONS

nouns

1 **United Nations** *or* UN; League of Nations (*old*)
2 (*United Nations organs*) Secretariat; General
Assembly; Security Council; Trusteeship Council;
International Court of Justice; **United Nations
agency** (*see list*), Economic and Social Council *or*
ECOSOC
3 international organization, non-UN international
organization
4 **United Nations agencies**

Food and Agricultural
Organization *or* FAO
General Agreement on
Tariffs and Trade *or*
GATT
Intergovernmental
Maritime Consultative
Organization *or* IMCO
International Atomic
Energy Agency *or* IAEA
International Bank for
Reconstruction and
Development *or* World
Bank
International Civil Aviation
Organization *or* ICAO
International Development
Association *or* IDA
International Finance
Corporation *or* IFO
International Labour
Organization ILO
International Monetary
Fund *or* IMF

International
Telecommunication
Union *or* ITU
United Nations Children's
Fund *or* UNICEF
United Nations
Educational, Scientific
and Cultural
Organization *or*
UNESCO
United Nations Relief and
Works Agency *or*
UNRWA
Universal Postal Union *or*
UPU
World Health Organization
or WHO
World Intellectual Property
Organization *or* WIPO
World Meteorological
Organization *or* WMO
World Trade Organization
or WTO

615 COMMISSION

nouns

1 **commission, commissioning, delegation,** devolution, devolvement, vesting, investing, investment, investiture; **deputation;** commitment, entrusting, entrustment, **assignment,** consignment; **errand, task, office; care,** cure, **responsibility,** purview, jurisdiction; **mission,** legation, embassy; **authority** *see* 417; **authorization,** empowerment, power to act, full power, plenipotentiary power, vicarious *or* delegated authority; **warrant,** licence, **mandate, charge, trust,** brevet, exequatur; **agency,** agentship, factorship; regency, regentship; lieutenancy; trusteeship, executorship; **proxy,** procuration, **power of attorney**

2 **appointment, assignment,** designation, **nomination,** naming, selection; **ordainment,** ordination; posting, transferral, secondment

3 **installation,** instalment, **instatement,** induction, placement, **inauguration,** investiture, taking office; **accession,** accedence; coronation, enthronement

4 **engagement, employment, hiring, appointment,** taking on (*informal*), recruitment, recruiting; executive recruiting, executive search; retaining, retainment, briefing; preengagement, bespeaking; reservation, booking

5 executive search agency *or* firm; executive recruiter, executive recruitment consultant, executive development specialist; **headhunter** *and* body snatcher *and* talent scout (*all informal*)

6 **rental, rent; lease,** let; hire, hiring; sublease, subrent; **charter,** bareboat charter; lend-lease

7 **enlistment, enrolment; conscription,** national service, military service, draft, drafting, induction, impressment, press; call, call-up, summons, call to the colours; **recruitment,** recruiting; **muster,** mustering, mustering in, levy, levying; mobilization; selective service, compulsory military service

8 indenture, binding over; **apprenticeship**

9 assignee, appointee, selectee, nominee, candidate; licensee, licentiate; deputy, agent *see* 576

verbs

10 to **commission, authorize,** empower, accredit; **delegate,** devolute, devolve, devolve upon, vest, invest; depute, **deputize; assign,** consign, **commit, charge, entrust,** give in charge; license, charter, warrant; detail, detach, post, transfer, second, send out, mission, send on a mission

11 to **appoint, assign,** designate, **nominate,** name, select; **ordain,** ordinate (*old*)

12 to **install,** instate, induct, **inaugurate,** invest, put in, place, **place in office;** chair; crown, throne, enthrone, anoint

13 to **be instated, take office,** accede; take *or* mount the throne; attain to

14 to **employ, hire,** give a job to, wage, take into employment, take into one's service, take on (*informal*), recruit, headhunt (*informal*), **engage,** sign up *or* on (*informal*); retain; bespeak, preengage; sign up for (*informal*), **reserve,** book

15 to **rent, lease, let,** hire, job, **charter; sublease, sublet,** underlet

16 to **rent out,** rent; **lease,** lease out; let *and* let off *and* let out; **hire out,** hire; charter; **sublease, sublet,** underlet; lend-lease, lease-lend; lease-back; farm, farm out

17 to **enlist,** list (*old*), **enrol, sign up** *or* on (*informal*); conscript, **draft, induct,** press, impress, commandeer; detach, detach for service; summon, call up, call to the colours; **mobilize,** call to active duty; **recruit, muster,** levy, raise, muster in; join *see* 617.14

18 to indenture, article, bind, bind over; **apprentice**

adjectives

19 **commissioned, authorized, accredited;** delegated, deputized, appointed

20 **employed, hired, hireling, paid,** mercenary; rented, leased, let; sublet, underlet, subleased; chartered

21 **indentured,** articled, bound over; **apprenticed, apprentice,** prentice (*old*)

adverbs

22 **for hire,** for rent, to let, to lease

616 ASSOCIATE

nouns

1 **associate, confederate,** consociate, **colleague,** fellow member, **companion, fellow,** bedfellow, **crony,** consort, cohort, compeer, compatriot, confrere, brother, brother-in-arms, **ally,** adjunct, coadjutor; comrade in arms, **comrade** *see* 588.3

2 **partner,** copartner, buddy (*informal*), sidekick (*informal*), pardner *or* pard (*both US informal*); **mate; business partner,** nominal *or* ostensible, general partner, special partner, silent partner, secret partner, dormant *or* sleeping partner

3 **accomplice,** cohort, confederate, fellow conspirator, coconspirator, partner *or* accomplice in crime; *particeps criminis, socius criminis* (*both Latin*); **accessory,** accessory before the fact, accessory after the fact; **abettor**

4 **collaborator,** cooperator; coauthor; **collaborationist**

5 **co-worker,** workfellow, workmate, mate, **fellow worker;** teammate, yokefellow, yokemate; benchfellow, shopmate

6 **assistant, helper,** auxiliary, aider, **aid, aide,** paraprofessional; **help, helpmate, helpmeet;** deputy, **agent** *see* 576; **attendant, second,** acolyte; best man, groomsman, paranymph; **servant, employee** *see* 577; adjutant, aide-de-camp; lieutenant, executive officer; coadjutant, coadjutor; coadjutress, coadjutrix; sidesman; supporting actor *or* player; supporting instrumentalist, sideman

7 **right-hand man** *or* **woman, right hand,** strong right hand *or* arm, **man** *or* **girl Friday,** fidus Achates, second self, alter ego, confidant

8 **follower, disciple,** adherent, votary; **man, henchman,** camp follower, hanger-on, satellite, creature, lackey, flunky, stooge (*informal*), jackal, minion, myrmidon; yes-man (*informal*), sycophant *see*

138.3; goon (*US informal*), thug *see* 593.3; puppet, cat's-paw; dummy, figurehead

9 **supporter, upholder,** maintainer, sustainer; support, **mainstay, standby,** stalwart, reliance, dependence; **abettor, seconder,** second; endorser, sponsor; **backer, promoter; patron,** Maecenas; friend at *or* in court; **champion,** defender, apologist, **advocate,** exponent, **protagonist; well-wisher,** favourer, encourager, sympathizer; **partisan,** sider (*old*), sectary, votary; fan, aficionado, **admirer,** lover

617 ASSOCIATION

nouns

1 **association, society,** body; **alliance, coalition, league, union;** council; **bloc,** axis; **partnership; federation, confederation,** confederacy; **grouping,** assemblage *see* 769; **combination,** combine; *Bund, Verein* (*both German*); **unholy alliance, gang** *and* **ring** *and* mob (*all informal*); machine, **political machine;** economic community, common market, free trade area, customs union; credit union; cooperative, cooperative society, consumer cooperative, Rochdale cooperative; college, **group,** corps, band *see* 769.3; trade union *see* 727

2 **community, society, commonwealth;** body; **kinship group, clan,** sept, moiety, totemic *or* totemistic group, phyle, phratry *or* phratria, gens, caste, subcaste, endogamous group; **family,** extended family, nuclear family, binuclear family, one-parent family *or* single-parent family; order, **class, social class** *see* 607, economic class; colony, settlement; **commune,** ashram

3 **fellowship,** sodality; **society,** guild, order, livery company; **brotherhood, fraternity,** confraternity, confrerie, fraternal order *or* society; **sisterhood, sorority; club,** country club; secret society, **cabal**

4 **party, interest, camp, side;** interest group, pressure group, ethnic group; minority group, vocal minority; **silent majority; faction,** division, **sect,** wing, **caucus,** splinter, splinter group, breakaway group, offshoot; **political party** *see* 609.24

5 **school, sect,** class, order; **denomination, communion,** confession, faith, church; **persuasion, ism; disciples, followers,** adherents

6 **clique, coterie, set, circle,** ring, junto, junta, cabal, camarilla, **clan,** group; **crew** *and* mob *and* **crowd** *and* **bunch** *and* outfit (*all informal*); cell; cadre, inner circle; closed *or* charmed circle; ingroup; elite, elite group; leadership group; **old-boy network**

7 **team, outfit,** squad, string; eleven, nine, eight, five, etc; **crew,** rowing crew; varsity, first team, first string; bench, reserves, second team, second IX, second string, third string; platoon; complement; **cast,** company

8 **organization, establishment, foundation, institution,** institute

9 **company, firm, business firm, concern,** house, close *or* closed company, limited company, public corporation, *compagnie* (*French*), *compañía* (*Spanish*), *Aktiengesellschaft* (*German*), *aktiebolag* (*Swedish*); **business, industry, enterprise,** business establishment, commercial enterprise; **trust,**

syndicate, cartel, combine, pool, consortium; chamber of commerce, junior chamber of commerce; trade association

10 **branch, organ, division,** wing, arm, offshoot, **affiliate; chapter,** lodge, post; chapel; **local;** branch office

11 **member,** affiliate, belonger, insider, initiate, one of us, cardholder, card-carrier, card-carrying member; **enrollee,** enlistee; **associate,** socius, **fellow;** brother, sister; comrade; honorary member; life member; member in good standing, dues-paying member; charter member; clubman, clubwoman, clubber (*informal*); fraternity man, sorority woman; sorority sister, guildsman; committeeman; conventionist, conventioner, conventioneer

12 **membership,** members, associates, affiliates, body of affiliates, constituency

13 **partisanism,** partisanship, **partiality; factionalism, sectionalism,** faction; sectarianism, denominationalism; **cliquism,** cliquishness, cliqueyness; **clannishness,** clanship; exclusiveness, exclusivity; ethnocentricity; party spirit, *esprit de corps* (*French*)

verbs

14 **to join,** join up (*informal*), **enter,** go into, come into, get into, make oneself part of, swell the ranks of; **enlist, enrol, affiliate, sign up** *or* **on** (*informal*), take up membership, take out membership; inscribe oneself, put oneself down; associate oneself with, affiliate with, league with, team *or* team up with; sneak in, creep in, insinuate oneself into; **combine, associate** *see* 804.4

15 **to belong,** hold membership, be a member, be on the rolls, be inscribed, subscribe, hold *or* carry a card, be in (*informal*)

adjectives

16 **associated, corporate,** incorporated; **combined** *see* 804.5; non-profit-making, non-profit, not-for-profit

17 **associational, social, society, communal;** organizational; coalitional; sociable

18 **cliquish,** cliquey, **clannish;** ethnocentric; exclusive

19 **partisan,** party; **partial,** interested; **factional, sectional,** sectarian, sectary, denominational

adverbs

20 **in association, conjointly** *see* 450.6

618 WEALTH

nouns

1 **wealth, riches, opulence** *or* opulency *see* 990.2, **luxuriousness** *see* 501.5; richness, wealthiness; **prosperity,** prosperousness, **affluence,** comfortable *or* easy circumstances, independence; **money,** lucre, pelf, gold, mammon; **substance, property, possessions,** material wealth; **assets** *see* 728.14; **fortune, treasure,** handsome fortune; full *or* heavy *or* well-lined *or* bottomless *or* fat *or* bulging wallet, deep pockets (*informal*); *embarras de richesses* (*French*), money to burn (*informal*); high income, six-figure income; high tax bracket, upper bracket

2 large sum, good sum, tidy sum *and* pretty penny, king's ransom; heaps of gold; thousands, millions, cool million, billion, etc

3 (*informal terms*) bomb, bundle, big bucks, megabucks, big money, serious money, funny money, telephone numbers, heaps, heavy money, important money, packet, pot, potful, power, mint, barrel, **loads**, pile, wad, wads

4 (*rich source*) **mine**, mine of wealth, **gold mine**, bonanza, luau (*informal*), lode, rich lode, mother lode, Eldorado, Golconda, Seven Cities of Cibola; gravy train (*informal*); rich uncle; cash cow, money-spinner, moneymaker

5 **the golden touch**, Midas touch; philosophers' stone; Pactolus

6 **the rich, the wealthy**, the well-to-do, the haves (*informal*); **plutocracy**, timocracy

7 **rich man** *or* **woman**, wealthy man *or* woman, **moneyed man** *or* **woman**, man *or* woman of wealth, **man** *or* **woman of means** *or* **substance**, fat cat (*informal*), richling, moneybags (*informal*), Daddy Warbucks (*Harold Gray*), nabob; **capitalist**, **plutocrat**, bloated plutocrat; **millionaire**, multimillionaire, megamillionaire, millionairess, multibillionaire, multimillionairess, billionaire; parvenu

8 Croesus, Midas, Plutus, Dives, Timon of Athens, Danaë; Rockefeller, Vanderbilt, Ford, Getty, Rothschild, Onassis, Hughes, Trump

verbs

9 **to enrich**, richen

10 **to grow rich, get rich**, fill *or* line one's pockets, feather one's nest, **make** *or* **coin money**, have a gold mine, have the golden touch, **make a fortune**, make a mint, make one's pile (*informal*); **strike it rich**; come into money; make good, get on in the world, do all right by oneself *and* rake it in (*both informal*)

11 **to have money**, command money, **be loaded** *and* have deep pockets (*both informal*), have the wherewithal, have means, have independent means; **afford**, well afford

12 **to live well**, live high, **live in clover**, roll *or* wallow in wealth, roll *or* live in the lap of luxury; have all the money in the world, have money to burn (*informal*)

13 to worship mammon, worship the golden calf

adjectives

14 **wealthy, rich, affluent, moneyed** *or* **monied**, in funds *or* cash, **well-to-do**, well-to-do in the world, **well-off, well-situated, prosperous**, comfortable, provided for, well provided for, fat, **flush**, flush with *or* of money, abounding in riches, worth a great deal, frightfully rich, rich as Croesus; independent, independently rich, independently wealthy; **luxurious** *see* 501.21; **opulent** *see* 990.7; privileged, born with a silver spoon in one's mouth; higher-income, upper-income, well-paid

15 (*informal terms*) **loaded, well-heeled, filthy rich**, in the money, well-fixed, made of money, **rolling in money**, rolling *or* wallowing in it, disgustingly rich

619 POVERTY

nouns

1 **poverty, poorness**, impecuniousness, impecuniosity; **straits**, difficulties, **hardship** *see* 1010.1; financial distress *or* embarrassment, **embarrassed** *or* **reduced** *or* **straitened circumstances**, the pinch (*informal*), cash *or* credit squeeze; cash-flow crisis; slender *or* narrow means, insolvency, light purse; unprosperousness; broken fortune; genteel poverty; vows of poverty, voluntary poverty

2 **indigence, penury, pennilessness**, penuriousness, moneylessness; **pauperism**, pauperization, **impoverishment**, grinding *or* crushing poverty, chronic pauperism; **beggary**, beggarliness, mendicancy; homelessness; **destitution, privation, deprivation; neediness, want**, need, lack, pinch, necessity, disadvantagedness, necessitousness, **homelessness; hand-to-mouth existence**, bare subsistence, wolf at the door, bare cupboard, empty purse *or* pocket

3 **the poor, the needy**, the have-nots (*informal*), the down-and-out, the disadvantaged, the underprivileged, the distressed, the underclass, the long-term unemployed; the urban poor, ghetto-dwellers; welfare recipients; the homeless, the ranks of the homeless;
"wretched of the earth"—E POTTIER, "houseless heads and unfed sides"—SHAKESPEARE; the forgotten man, "the forgotten man at the bottom of the economic pyramid"—F D ROOSEVELT; depressed population, depressed area, deprived area, inner city; underdeveloped nation, third world

4 **poor man**, poorling, poor devil, down-and-out, **pauper**, indigent, penniless man, starveling; homeless person, dosser, bag woman *or* lady, homeless *or* street person (*informal*); **beggar** *see* 440.8; charity case, casual; bankrupt *see* 625.4

verbs

5 **to be poor**, be hard up (*informal*), find it hard going, have seen better days, be on one's uppers, be pinched *or* strapped, **be in want**, want, need, lack; **starve**, not know where one's next meal is coming from, **live from hand to mouth**, eke out *or* squeeze out a living; not have a penny, not have a brass farthing, not have two pennies to rub together; sign on

6 **to impoverish**, reduce, pauperize, beggar; eat out of house and home; **bankrupt** *see* 625.8

adjectives

7 **poor**, ill off, badly *or* poorly off, hard up (*informal*), downscale, impecunious, **unmoneyed; unprosperous**; reduced, in reduced circumstances; **straitened, in straitened circumstances**, narrow, in narrow circumstances, feeling the pinch, strapped, **financially embarrassed** *or* distressed, **pinched**, feeling the pinch, squeezed, at the end of one's rope, down to bedrock, in Queer Street; short, **short of money** *or* **funds** *or* **cash**, out of pocket; unable to make ends meet, unable to keep the wolf from the door; poor as a church mouse,
"poor as Job"—JOHN GOWER; dirt-poor

8 indigent, poverty-stricken; needy, necessitous, in need, in want, disadvantaged, deprived, underprivileged; beggared, beggarly, mendicant; impoverished, pauperized, starveling; ghettoized; bereft, bereaved; stripped, fleeced; down-at-heel, on *or* down on one's uppers, out at the heels, out at the elbows, in rags; on the dole, on relief, on welfare

9 destitute, down and out, in the gutter; penniless, moneyless, fortuneless, out of funds, without a sou, without a brass farthing, without two pennies to rub together; insolvent, in the red, bankrupt *see* 625.11; homeless; propertyless, landless

10 (*informal terms*) broke, flat broke, stone *or* stony broke, down for the count, strapped, skint; down to one's last penny, cleaned out, wasted, without a pot to piss in

620 LENDING

nouns

1 lending, loaning; moneylending, lending at interest; advance, advancing, advancement; usury, loan-sharking *and* shylocking (*both informal*); lend-lease; interest, interest rate, base rate, lending rate, the price of money

2 loan, advance, accommodation

3 lender, loaner; loan officer; commercial banker; moneylender, moneymonger; money broker; banker *see* 729.10; usurer, shylock *and* loan shark (*both informal*); pawnbroker; mortgagee, mortgage holder

4 lending institution, building society; savings and loan association *or* thrift *or* thrift institution *or* savings institution (*US*), finance company *or* corporation, loan office, mortgage company; commercial bank, bank *see* 729.13; credit union; pawnbroker, pawnshop, pawnbrokery, *mont-de-piété* (*French*), sign of the three balls

verbs

5 to lend, loan, advance, accommodate with; loan-shark (*informal*); float *or* negotiate a loan; lend-lease, lease-lend

adjectives

6 loaned, lent

adverbs

7 on loan, on security; in advance

621 BORROWING

nouns

1 borrowing, money-raising; financing, mortgaging; instalment buying, instalment plan, hire purchase *or* HP; debt, debtor *see* 623.4

2 adoption, appropriation, taking, deriving, derivation, assumption; imitation, simulation, copying, mocking; borrowed plumes; a leaf from someone else's book; plagiarism, plagiary, pastiche, pasticcio; infringement, pirating

verbs

3 to borrow, borrow the loan of, get on credit *or* trust, get on tick (*informal*), get on HP, get on the

never-never (*informal*); get a loan, float *or* negotiate a loan, go into the money market, raise money; run into debt *see* 623.6; pawn *see* 438.10

4 to adopt, appropriate, take, take on, take over, assume, make use of, take a leaf from someone's book, derive from; imitate, simulate, copy, mock, steal one's stuff (*informal*); plagiarize, steal; pirate, infringe

622 FINANCIAL CREDIT

nouns

1 credit, trust, tick (*informal*), the slate (*informal*); borrowing power *or* capacity; commercial credit, cash credit, bank credit, book credit, tax credit, investment credit; credit line, line of credit; instalment plan, instalment credit, consumer credit, store credit, hire purchase plan, never-never (*informal*); credit standing, standing, credit rating, Dun and Bradstreet rating, rating, solvency *see* 729.6; credit squeeze, insolvency; credit-reference agency; credit insurance; credit union, cooperative credit union

2 account, credit account, charge account; bank account, current account, savings account, deposit account; TESSA; bank balance; expense account

3 credit instrument; paper credit; letter of credit, *lettre de créance* (*French*), circular note; credit slip, credit memorandum, deposit slip, certificate of deposit; share certificate; negotiable instruments *see* 728.11; credit card, plastic, plastic money *or* credit, affinity card, debit card, cash card, store card, loyalty card, gold card, charge card

4 creditor, creditress; debtee; mortgagee, mortgage-holder; note-holder; credit man; bill collector, debt collector

verbs

5 to credit, credit with; credit to one's account, place to one's credit *or* account

6 to give *or* extend credit *or* a line of credit; sell on credit, trust, entrust; give tick (*informal*), put on the slate (*informal*); carry, carry on one's books

7 to receive credit, take credit, charge, charge to one's account, keep an account with, go on tick (*informal*), buy on credit, buy on the instalment plan; have one's credit good for

adjectives

8 creditworthy, credited, of good credit, well-rated

adverbs

9 to one's credit *or* account, to the credit *or* account of, to the good

10 on credit, on account, on trust, on tick (*informal*); on terms, on good terms, on easy terms, on budget terms, in instalments

623 DEBT

nouns

1 debt, indebtedness, indebtment, obligation, liability, financial commitment, due, dues, score, pledge, unfulfilled pledge, amount due, outstanding debt; **bill, bills,** chits (*informal*), **charges;** floating debt; funded debt, unfunded debt; accounts receivable; accounts payable; borrowing *see* 621; maturity; bad debts, uncollectibles; **national debt, public debt,** Public Sector Borrowing Requirement *or* PSBR; deficit, national deficit (*US*); debt explosion

2 **arrears,** arrear, arrearage, back debts, back payments; **deficit,** default, deferred payments; cash *or* credit squeeze (*informal*); overdraft, bouncing cheque, rubber cheque (*informal*); balance of payments deficit, trade deficit *or* gap; deficit financing

3 **interest, premium, price, rate;** interest rate, rate of interest, base rate, lending rate, borrowing rate, the price of money; discount rate; APR *or* annual percentage rate; **usury** *see* 620.1, excessive *or* exorbitant interest; simple interest, compound interest; net interest, gross interest; compensatory interest; lucrative interest; penal interest

4 **debtor,** borrower; mortgagor

verbs

5 **to owe, be indebted,** be obliged *or* obligated for, be financially committed, lie under an obligation, be bound to pay

6 **to go in debt,** get into debt, run into debt, plunge into debt, incur *or* contract a debt, be overextended, reschedule one's debt, run up a bill; run *or* show a deficit, operate at a loss; borrow

7 **to mature, accrue, fall due**

adjectives

8 **indebted, in debt,** plunged in debt, in difficulties, embarrassed, in embarrassed circumstances, in the red, encumbered, mortgaged, mortgaged to the hilt, tied up, involved; deep in debt, involved *or* deeply involved in debt, burdened with debt, head over heels *or* up to one's ears in debt (*informal*); cash poor

9 **chargeable, obligated, liable,** pledged, responsible, answerable for

10 **due, owed, owing, payable,** receivable, redeemable, mature, **outstanding, unpaid,** in arrear *or* arrears

624 PAYMENT

nouns

1 **payment, paying,** paying off, paying up (*informal*), payoff; **defrayment,** defrayal; paying out, doling out, disbursal *see* 626.1; **discharge, settlement, clearance, liquidation, amortization,** amortizement, retirement, satisfaction; quittance; acquittance *or* acquitment *or* acquittal (*all old*); **debt service, interest payment,** sinking-fund payment; **remittance;** instalment, instalment plan; hire purchase *or* hire purchase plan *or* never-never; regular payments, monthly payments, weekly payments, quarterly payments, etc; down payment, deposit, binder; god's penny; the King's shilling; **cash,** hard cash, cash payment, cash on the nail (*informal*); pay-as-you-go; prepayment; **postponed** *or* **deferred payment;** payment in kind

2 **reimbursement,** recoupment, recoup, return,

restitution; **refund,** refundment; kickback (*informal*); payback, chargeback, **repayment** *see* 481.2

3 **recompense, remuneration, compensation;** requital, requitement, quittance, **retribution, reparation, redress,** satisfaction, **atonement, amends,** return, restitution *see* 481; blood money, wergild (*old*); **indemnity,** indemnification; price, consideration; **reward,** meed (*old*), guerdon; honorarium; damages, settlement, solatium (*US*); salvage

4 **pay, payment, remuneration, compensation,** total compensation, wages plus fringe benefits, financial package, pay and allowances, financial remuneration; rate of pay; **salary, wage, wages, income, earnings,** hire; real wages, purchasing power; payday, pay envelope, pay packet, pay cheque; take-home pay *or* income, wages after taxes, pay *or* income *or* wages after deductions, net income *or* wages *or* pay *or* earnings, taxable income; gross income; living wage; minimum wage; severance pay, redundancy pay, discontinuance *or* dismissal wage; wage scale; escalator plan, escalator clause, sliding scale; guaranteed income, guaranteed annual income, negative income tax; fixed income; wage freeze, wage rollback, wage reduction, wage control; guaranteed annual wage, guaranteed income plan; overtime; danger money, combat pay, flight pay; back pay; strike pay; **payroll**

5 **fee, stipend, allowance,** emolument, tribute; **reckoning,** account, bill; assessment; initiation fee, footing (*old*); retainer, appearance money; boot money (*informal*), bung (*informal*); hush money, blackmail; blood money

6 (*extra pay or allowance*) **bonus, premium, fringe benefit** *or* **benefits,** bounty, perquisite, perquisites, perks (*informal*), lagniappe (*US*), solatium (*US*); **tip** *see* 478.5; overtime; bonus system; golden handshake, golden hello, golden handcuffs, golden parachute; share option

7 **dividend; royalty; commission,** rake-off *and* cut (*both informal*)

8 (*the bearing of another's expense*) **treat,** standing treat, picking up the check *or* tab (*US informal*); paying the bills, maintenance, support *see* 449.3; subsidy *see* 478.8

9 **payer,** remunerator, compensator, recompenser; paymaster, purser, bursar, cashier, treasurer *see* 729.11; defrayer; liquidator; **taxpayer, ratepayer**

verbs

10 **to pay,** render, tender; **recompense, remunerate, compensate, reward,** indemnify, satisfy, guerdon; salary, fee; remit; prepay; pay by *or* in instalments, pay on, pay in; make payments to *or* towards *or* on

11 **to repay,** pay back, service one's debt, restitute, **reimburse,** recoup; requite, quit, atone, redress (*old*), **make amends,** make good, make up for, make up to, make restitution, make reparation *see* 481.5; pay in kind, pay one in his own coin, give tit for tat; **refund,** kick back (*informal*)

12 **to settle with,** reckon with, account with (*old*), pay out, **settle** *or* **square accounts with,** square oneself with, get square with, **get even with,** get quits

with; even the score (*informal*), wipe *or* clear off old scores, pay old debts, clear the board

13 to **pay in full, pay off, pay up** (*informal*), **discharge, settle,** square, **clear, liquidate, amortize,** retire, take up, lift, take up and pay off, honour, acquit oneself of; satisfy; meet one's obligations *or* commitments, redeem, redeem one's pledge *or* pledges, tear up *or* burn one's mortgage, settle *or* square accounts, make accounts square, strike a balance; pay the bill

14 to **pay out, fork out** *or* **over** (*informal*), **shell out** (*informal*); **expend** *see* 626.5

15 to **pay over,** hand over; ante, **ante up,** put up; put down, lay down, lay one's money down, show the colour of one's money

16 (*informal terms*) to **kick in, fork out,** pay up, cough up, stump up, come across, come through with, come across with, come down with the needful, plank down, plunk down, grease the palm, cross one's palm with; pay to the tune of

17 to **pay cash,** make a cash payment, cash, **pay cash down,** pay cash on the nail (*informal*), put one's money on the line (*informal*); pay in advance; pay as you go; pay cash on delivery *or* pay COD

18 to **pay for,** pay *or* stand the costs, **bear the expense** *or* cost, pay the piper (*informal*); **finance, fund** *see* 729.15; **defray,** defray expenses; pay the bill, foot the bill, pick up the check *or* tab (*US*); honour a bill, acknowledge, redeem; pay one's way; pay one's share, chip in (*informal*), go Dutch (*informal*)

19 to **treat,** treat to, pay the bill; stand drinks; maintain, support *see* 449.12; subsidize *see* 478.19

20 to **be paid,** draw wages, be salaried, work for wages, be remunerated, collect for one's services, **earn,** get an income, earn a crust (*informal*)

adjectives

21 **paying,** remunerative, remuneratory; **compensating,** compensative, compensatory; retributive, retributory; **rewarding,** rewardful; lucrative, moneymaking, profitable; repaying, satisfying, reparative

22 **paid, paid-up** discharged, settled, liquidated, acquitted (*old*), paid in full, receipted, remitted; **spent, expended;** salaried, waged, hired; prepaid, postpaid

23 **unindebted,** unowing, **out of debt,** above water, out of the red (*informal*), **clear,** all clear, free and clear, all straight; solvent *see* 729.17

adverbs

24 **in compensation,** as compensation, in recompense, for services rendered, for professional services, **in reward,** in requital, in reparation, in retribution, in restitution, in exchange for, **in amends,** in atonement, to atone for

25 **cash,** cash on the nail (*informal*), strictly cash; **cash down, money down,** down; cash on delivery *or* **COD;** on demand, on call; pay-as-you-go

625 NONPAYMENT

nouns

1 **nonpayment, default, delinquency,** delinquence (*old*), nondischarge of debts, nonremittal, failure to pay; defection; protest, repudiation; dishonour, dishonouring; bad debt, uncollectible, dishonoured payment

2 **moratorium,** grace period; **write-off,** cancellation, obliteration *see* 395.7

3 **insolvency, bankruptcy,** receivership, **failure; crash,** collapse, bust (*informal*); run on a bank; insufficient funds, overdraft, overdrawn account, not enough to cover, bounced *or* bouncing cheque, dishonoured cheque, rubber cheque (*informal*)

4 **insolvent,** insolvent debtor; **bankrupt, failure; loser,** heavy loser, lame duck (*informal*)

5 **defaulter,** delinquent, nonpayer; **welsher** (*informal*), levanter; tax evader, tax dodger *or* cheat (*informal*)

verbs

6 to **not pay;** dishonour, repudiate, disallow, protest, stop payment, refuse to pay; **default, welsh** (*informal*), levant; tighten one's belt, draw the purse strings; **underpay;** bounce a cheque (*informal*)

7 to **go bankrupt, go bust,** go broke (*informal*), go into receivership, become insolvent *or* bankrupt, **fail,** break, bust (*informal*), crash, collapse, **fold, fold up,** belly up *and* go up *and* go belly up *and* **go under** (*all informal*), shut down, shut one's doors, go out of business, **be ruined,** go to ruin, go on the rocks, go to the wall, go to pot (*informal*), go to the dogs; be taken to the cleaners *and* be cleaned out *and* lose one's shirt (*all informal*)

8 to **bankrupt, ruin, break,** bust *and* wipe out (*both informal*); put out of business, drive to the wall, scuttle, sink; impoverish *see* 619.6

9 to **declare a moratorium; write off, forgive,** absolve, **cancel,** nullify, wipe the slate clean; wipe out, obliterate *see* 395.16

adjectives

10 **defaulting,** nonpaying, **delinquent;** behindhand, in arrear *or* arrears

11 **insolvent, bankrupt,** in receivership, in the hands of the receivers, belly-up (*informal*), broken, **broke** *and* busted (*both informal*), **ruined,** failed, out of business, unable to pay one's creditors, unable to meet one's obligations, on the rocks; destitute *see* 619.9

12 **unpaid, unremunerated,** uncompensated, unrecompensed, **unrewarded,** unrequited, unwaged; underpaid

13 **unpayable,** irredeemable, inconvertible

626 EXPENDITURE

nouns

1 **expenditure, spending,** expense, disbursal, **disbursement;** debit, debiting; budgeting, scheduling; costing, costing-out; **payment** *see* 624; deficit spending; **use** *see* 387; **consumption** *see* 388

2 **spendings,** disbursements, payments, outgoings, outgo, outflow, **outlay,** money going out

3 expenses, costs, charges, disbursals, **liabilities; expense, cost,** burden of expenditure; budget, budget item, budget line, line item; **overhead,** operating expense *or* expenses *or* costs *or* budget, oncost, general expenses; expense account, swindle sheet (*informal*); business expenses, overheads, nonremunerated business expenses, out-of-pocket expenses; direct costs, indirect costs; distributed costs, undistributed costs; material costs; labour costs; carrying charge; unit cost; replacement cost; prime cost; cost of living, cost-of-living index, **Retail Price Index**

4 **spender,** expender, expenditor, disburser

verbs

5 **to spend, expend, disburse, pay out,** fork out *or* over (*informal*), shell out (*informal*), **lay out,** lash out *and* splash out (*both informal*), outlay; go to the expense of; **pay** *see* 624.10; put one's hands in one's pocket, open the purse, loosen *or* untie the purse strings *and* throw money around (*both informal*), go on a spending spree, splurge, spend money like a drunken sailor *and* like water *and* as if it were confetti (*all informal*), go *or* run through, **squander** *see* 486.3; **invest,** sink money in (*informal*), put out; throw money at the problem; **incur costs** *or* **expenses;** budget, schedule, cost, cost out; **use** *see* 387.13; **consume**

6 **to be spent,** burn in one's pocket, burn a hole in one's pocket

7 **to afford,** well afford, spare, spare the price, bear, stand, support, endure, undergo, meet the expense of, swing

627 RECEIPTS

nouns

1 **receipts, receipt, income, revenue, profits, earnings, returns, proceeds,** avails (*old*), **take,** takings, intake, take *or* take-in (*informal*); credit, credits; gains *see* 472.3; gate receipts, gate money, gate, box office; net receipts, net; gross receipts, gross; national income; net income, gross income; earned income, unearned income; **dividend** *see* 738.7, dividends, payout, payback; royalties, commissions; receivables; disposable income; make, produce, **yield, output** *see* 892.2, fruits, first fruits

2 (*written acknowledgment*) **receipt, acknowledgment, voucher,** warrant, chit, chitty, paying-in slip; cancelled cheque; **receipt in full,** receipt in full of all demands, release, acquittance, quittance, discharge

verbs

3 **to receive** *see* 479.6, pocket, acquire *see* 472.8, 9; acknowledge receipt of, receipt, mark paid

4 **to yield, bring in,** afford, pay, pay off (*informal*), **return; gross, net**

628 ACCOUNTS

nouns

1 **accounts; outstanding accounts,** uncollected *or* unpaid accounts; **accounts receivable,** receipts, assets; **accounts payable,** expenditures, liabilities; **budget,** budgeting; costing out

2 **account, reckoning, audit, tally, rendering-up, score;** account current; account rendered, *compte rendu* (*French*), account stated; balance, trial balance

3 **statement, bill,** itemized bill, bill of account, **account, reckoning, cheque,** *l'addition* (*French*), score *or* tab (*both informal*); **dun; invoice,** manifest, bill of lading

4 **account book, ledger, journal,** daybook, **register,** registry, **record book,** books; inventory, catalogue; **log,** logbook; **cashbook; bankbook,** passbook; balance sheet; cost sheet, cost card

5 **entry, item,** line item, minute, note, notation; single entry, double entry; **credit, debit**

6 **accounting, accountancy, bookkeeping,** double-entry bookkeeping *or* accounting, single-entry bookkeeping *or* accounting; comptrollership *or* controllership; business *or* commercial *or* monetary arithmetic; cost accounting, costing, cost system, cost-accounting system; **audit, auditing;** stocktaking

7 **accountant, bookkeeper; clerk,** actuary (*old*), registrar, recorder, journalizer; calculator, reckoner; cost accountant, cost keeper; chartered accountant *or* CA; certified accountant; certified public accountant *or* CPA (*US*); **auditor,** bank examiner; bank accountant; accountant general; comptroller *or* controller

verbs

8 **to keep accounts, keep books,** make up *or* cast up *or* render accounts; make an entry, enter, post, post up, journalize, book, docket, log, note, minute; **credit, debit;** charge off, write off; capitalize; carry, carry on one's books; carry over; **balance,** balance accounts, balance the books, strike a balance; close the books, close out

9 **to take account of, take stock,** overhaul; **inventory; audit,** examine *or* inspect the books

10 **to falsify accounts,** cook *or* doctor accounts (*informal*), salt, engage in creative accounting, cook the books (*informal*); surcharge

11 **to bill,** send a statement; **invoice;** call, call in, demand payment, **dun**

adjectives

12 accounting, bookkeeping; budget, budgetary

629 TRANSFER OF PROPERTY OR RIGHT

nouns

1 **transfer,** transference; **conveyance,** conveyancing; **giving** *see* 478; delivery, deliverance; **assignment,** assignation; **consignment,** consignation; conferment, conferral, settling, settlement; vesting; bequeathal *see* 478.10; **sale** *see* 734; surrender, cession; transmission, transmittal; disposal, disposition, deaccession, deaccessioning; demise; alienation, abalienation; amortization, amortizement; enfeoffment; deeding; **exchange,** barter, trading; entailment

2 devolution, succession, reversion

verbs

3 to transfer, convey, deliver, hand, pass, negotiate; **give** *see* 478.12-14,16,21; **hand over, turn over, pass over; assign, consign,** confer, settle, settle on; cede, surrender; bequeath *see* 478.18; entail; **sell** *see* 734.8, 11, 12, sell off, deaccession; **make over, sign over,** sign away; transmit, **hand down, hand on, pass on,** devolve upon; demise; alienate, alien, abalienate, amortize; enfeoff; **deed,** deed over, give title to; **exchange,** barter, trade, trade away

4 to change hands, change ownership; devolve, pass on, descend, succeed (*old*)

adjectives

5 transferable, conveyable, negotiable, alienable; **assignable,** consignable; devisable, bequeathable; heritable, inheritable

630 PRICE, FEE

nouns

1 price, cost, expense, expenditure, **charge,** damage *and* score *and* tab (*all informal*); rate, figure, amount, tariff; **quotation,** quoted price, price tag *and* ticket *and* sticker (*all informal*), reserve price; **price list,** prices current; stock market quotations

2 worth, value, account, rate; face value, face; par value; market value; street value; net worth; conversion factor *or* value; money's worth, pennyworth, value received

3 valuation, evaluation, value-setting, value-fixing, pricing, price determination, **assessment, appraisal,** appraisement, estimation, rating; unit pricing, dual pricing

4 price index, business index; wholesale price index; consumer price *or* retail price index; cost-of-living index; price level; price ceiling, ceiling price, ceiling, top price; floor price, floor, bottom price; demand curve; rising prices, **inflation,** inflationary spiral

5 price controls, price-fixing, valorization; managed prices, fair-trading, fair trade, fair-trade agreement; **price supports,** rigid supports, flexible supports; price freeze; rent control

6 fee, dues, toll, charge, charges, subscription, demand, exaction, exactment, scot, shot, scot and lot; hire; **fare,** carfare; user fee; airport fee *or* charge; licence fee; entrance *or* entry *or* admission fee, admission; cover charge; portage, towage; wharfage, anchorage, dockage; pilotage; storage, cellarage; brokerage; murage; salvage

7 freightage, freight, haulage, carriage, cartage, drayage, expressage, lighterage; poundage, tonnage

8 rent, rental; rent-roll; rent charge; rack rent, quitrent; ground rent, wayleave rent

9 tax, taxation, duty, tribute, taxes, rates, contribution, **assessment, revenue enhancement,** cess, **levy, toll, impost,** imposition; tax code, tax law; **tithe;** indirect taxation, direct taxation; **tax burden,** overtaxation, undertaxation; bracket *or* tax-bracket; progressive taxation, graduated taxation; regressive taxation; tax withholding; tax return, separate returns, joint return; tax evasion *or* avoidance; tax haven *or* shelter; **tax deduction,**

deduction; **tax write-off,** write-off, tax relief, tax allowance; tax exemption, tax-exempt status; tax structure, tax base; taxable income *or* goods *or* land *or* property, ratables

10 tax collector, tax inspector, inspector of taxes, taxer, taxman, publican; collector of inland revenue, inland revenue agent; tax farmer, farmer; assessor, **tax assessor;** exciseman, revenuer; Inland Revenue *or* IR, Inland Revenue Office *or* IRO; Internal Revenue Service *or* IRS (*US*); **customs agent; customs,** Bureau of Customs and Excise; custom house *or* customs house

verbs

11 to price, set *or* name a price, fix the price of; place a value on, **value, evaluate,** valuate, **appraise, assess, rate,** prize, apprize; quote a price; set an arbitrary price on, control *or* manage the price of, valorize; mark up, mark down, **discount;** fair-trade; reassess

12 to charge, demand, ask, require; overcharge, undercharge; **exact, assess, levy, impose; tax,** assess a tax upon, slap a tax on (*informal*), lay *or* put a duty on, make dutiable, subject to a tax *or* fee *or* duty, collect a tax *or* duty on; tithe; prorate, assess *pro rata*; charge for, stick for (*informal*)

13 to cost, sell for, fetch, bring, bring in, stand one *and* set *or* knock one back (*all informal*); **come to,** run to *or* into, **amount to,** mount up to, come up to, total up to

adjectives

14 priced, valued, evaluated, assessed, appraised, rated, prized; **worth,** valued at; good for; ad valorem, pro rata

15 chargeable, taxable, ratable, assessable, dutiable, leviable, declarable; tithable

16 tax-free, nontaxable, nondutiable, tax-exempt, zero-rated; deductible, tax-deductible; duty-free

adverbs

17 at a price, for a consideration; to the amount of, to the tune of *and* in the neighbourhood of (*both informal*)

631 DISCOUNT

nouns

1 discount, cut, deduction, slash, abatement, reduction, price reduction, price-cutting, price-cut, rollback (*US informal*); underselling; **rebate,** rebatement; bank discount, cash discount, chain discount, time discount, trade discount; write-off, charge-off; **depreciation; allowance,** concession; setoff; drawback, **refund,** kickback (*informal*); **premium,** percentage, agio; trading stamp

verbs

2 to discount, cut, deduct, bate, abate; **take off,** write off, charge off; **depreciate,** reduce; sell at a loss; **allow,** make allowance; rebate, **refund,** kick back (*informal*); take a premium *or* percentage

adverbs

3 at a discount, at a reduction, at a reduced rate, at cost, below par, below *or* under cost

632 EXPENSIVENESS

nouns

1 expensiveness, costliness, dearness, high *or* great cost, highness, stiffness *or* steepness (*both informal*), priceyness; **richness, sumptuousness, luxuriousness**

2 preciousness, dearness, value, high *or* great value, **worth,** extraordinary worth, price *or* great price (*both old*), **valuableness; pricelessness, invaluableness**

3 high price, high *or* big price tag (*both informal*), big ticket *and* big sticker price (*both US informal*), **fancy price,** good price, steep *or* stiff price (*informal*), luxury price, a pretty penny *or* an arm and a leg (*both informal*), exorbitant *or* unconscionable *or* extortionate price; famine price, scarcity price; rack rent; inflationary prices, rising *or* soaring *or* spiralling prices, soaring costs; sellers' market; **inflation,** cost *or* cost-push inflation *or* cost-push, demand-pull inflation, inflationary trend *or* pressure, hot economy, overheated economy, inflationary spiral, inflationary gap; reflation; stagflation, slumpflation

4 exorbitance, exorbitancy (*old*), **extravagance,** excess, **excessiveness,** inordinateness, immoderateness, immoderation, undueness, unreasonableness, outrageousness, preposterousness; unconscionableness, extortionateness

5 overcharge, surcharge, overassessment; gouging *or* price-gouging (*US*); **extortion,** extortionate price, rip-off (*informal*); daylight robbery *and* armed robbery *and* highway robbery (*all informal*); profiteering

verbs

6 to cost much, cost money *and* cost you (*both informal*), cost a pretty penny *or* an arm and a leg *or* a packet *or* a bomb *or* a fortune (*informal*), **run into money;** be overpriced, price out of the market

7 to overprice, set the price tag too high; overcharge, surcharge, overtax; **hold up** *and* **stick** *and* **sting** *and* **clip** (*all informal*), **make pay through the nose,** gouge (*US*), soak (*US & Canadian*); victimize, swindle *see* 356.18; exploit, skin (*informal*), **fleece,** rip off, screw *and* put the screws to (*both informal*), bleed, bleed white; profiteer; rack *or* rack up the rents, rack rent

8 to overpay, overspend, pay too much, pay more than it's worth, **pay dearly,** pay exorbitantly, pay, **pay through the nose,** be had *or* taken (*both informal*)

9 to inflate, heat *or* heat up the economy; reflate

adjectives

10 precious, dear, valuable, worthy, rich, golden, of great price (*old*), worth a pretty penny (*informal*), worth a king's ransom, worth its weight in gold, good as gold, precious as the apple of one's eye; **priceless, invaluable,** inestimable, without *or*

beyond price, not to be had for love or money, not for all the tea in China

11 expensive, dear, costly, of great cost, dear-bought, **high, high-priced,** premium, at a premium, top; big money (*informal*), **fancy** *and* **stiff** *and* **steep** (*all informal*), pricey; beyond one's means, not affordable, more than one can afford; unpayable; up-market, upscale (*US informal*), rich, sumptuous, executive *and* posh (*both informal*), **luxurious** *see* 501.21, gold-plated

12 overpriced, grossly overpriced, **exorbitant, excessive, extravagant, inordinate, immoderate,** over the odds, undue, unwarranted, unreasonable, fancy, unconscionable, outrageous, preposterous, out of bounds, out of sight (*informal*), **prohibitive; extortionate,** cutthroat, gouging (*US*), **usurious,** exacting; **inflationary,** spiralling, skyrocketing; stagflationary, slumpflationary; reflationary

adverbs

13 dear, dearly; at a high price, at great cost, at a premium, at a great rate, at heavy cost, at great expense

14 preciously, valuably, worthily; pricelessly, invaluably, inestimably

15 expensively, richly, sumptuously, luxuriously

16 exorbitantly, excessively, grossly, **extravagantly, inordinately,** immoderately, unduly, unreasonably, unconscionably, outrageously, preposterously; **extortionately,** usuriously, gougingly (*US*)

633 CHEAPNESS

nouns

1 cheapness, inexpensiveness, affordableness, affordability, reasonableness, modestness, moderateness, nominalness; drug *or* glut on the market; shabbiness, shoddiness *see* 997.2

2 low price, nominal price, reasonable price, modest *or* manageable price, sensible price, moderate price; low *or* nominal *or* reasonable charge; bargain prices, budget prices, economy prices, easy prices, popular prices, rock-bottom prices; buyers' market; low *or* small price tag *and* low tariff (*all informal*), low sticker price (*US informal*); **reduced price,** cut price, sale price; cheap *or* reduced rates

3 bargain, advantageous purchase, **buy** (*informal*), **good buy,** steal *and* snip (*both informal*); money's worth, pennyworth, good pennyworth

4 cheapening, depreciation, devaluation, reduction, lowering; deflation, deflationary spiral, cooling *or* cooling off of the economy; **buyers' market; decline,** plummet, plummeting, plunge, dive, nose dive *and* slump *and* sag (*all informal*), free-fall; price fall; **price cut** *or* **reduction,** cut, slash, **markdown;** price war

verbs

5 to be cheap, cost little, not cost anything *and* cost nothing *and* next to nothing (*all informal*); **buy dirt cheap** *or* for a song *or* for pennies *or* for peanuts (*all informal*), buy at a bargain, buy for a mere nothing; get one's money's worth, get a good pennyworth; buy at wholesale prices *or* at cost

6 to **cheapen, depreciate, devaluate,** lower, reduce, **mark down, cut prices, cut,** slash, shave, trim, pare, underprice, knock the bottom out of (*informal*); deflate, cool *or* cool off the economy; beat down; come down *or* fall in price; **fall,** decline, plummet, dive, nose-dive (*informal*), drop, crash, head for the bottom, plunge, sag, slump; reach a new low

adjectives

7 **cheap,** cheapo (*informal*), **inexpensive,** unexpensive, **low, low-priced,** frugal, reasonable, sensible, manageable, modest, moderate, affordable, to suit the wallet, budget, easy, economy, economic, economical; within means, within reach *or* easy reach; nominal, token; worth the money, well worth the money; cheap *or* good at the price, cheap at half the price; shabby, shoddy; deflationary

8 **dirt cheap,** cheap as dirt (*informal*), **a dime a dozen,** bargain-basement

9 **reduced,** cut, cut-price, slashed, **marked down;** cut-rate, knockdown; half-price; giveaway (*informal*), sacrificial; **lowest,** rock-bottom, bottom, best

adverbs

10 **cheaply, cheap,** on the cheap; **inexpensively,** reasonably, moderately, nominally; **at a bargain,** *à bon marché* (*French*), for a song *or* mere song (*informal*), for pennies *or* peanuts (*both informal*), at small cost, at a low price, at budget prices, at piggy-bank prices, at a sacrifice; at cost *or* cost price, at prime cost, wholesale, at wholesale; at reduced rates

634 COSTLESSNESS
absence of charge

nouns

1 **costlessness,** gratuitousness, gratuity, **freeness,** expenselessness, complimentariness, no charge; free ride (*informal*); freebie *and* gimme (*both informal*); labour of love; **gift** *see* 478.4

2 **complimentary ticket, pass,** comp (*informal*), free pass *or* ticket, free admission, guest pass *or* ticket; discount ticket

3 **freeloader,** free rider, pass holder, ligger (*informal*), deadhead (*informal*)

verbs

4 to **give, present** *see* 478.12, comp (*informal*); freeload, sponge, lig (*informal*)

adjectives

5 **gratuitous, gratis,** buckshee, **free, free of charge,** for free, **for nothing,** free for nothing, free for the asking, free gratis *and* free gratis for nothing (*both informal*), for love, free as air; freebie *and* freebee *and* freeby (*all informal*); costless, expenseless, untaxed, without charge, free of cost *or* expense; no charge; unbought, unpaid-for; **complimentary, on the house, comp** (*informal*), given *see* 478.24; giftlike; eleemosynary, charitable *see* 143.15

adverbs

6 **gratuitously, gratis, free, free of charge,** for nothing, for the asking, at no charge, without charge,

with the compliments of the management *or* house, as our guest, on the house

635 THRIFT

nouns

1 **thrift, economy, thriftiness,** economicalness, savingness, sparingness, unwastefulness, **frugality,** frugalness; tight purse strings; parsimony, **parsimoniousness** *see* 484.1; false economy; carefulness, care, chariness, canniness, tightness (*informal*), closeness; **prudence,** providence, forehandedness; **husbandry,** management, good management *or* stewardship, custodianship, prudent *or* prudential administration; **austerity,** austerity programme, belt-tightening; economic planning; economy of means *see* 484.1

2 **economizing,** economization, reduction of spending *or* government spending; **cost-effectiveness; saving,** scrimping, skimping (*informal*), scraping, sparing, cheeseparing; **cuts,** cutbacks, cutting down, axing, the axe; **retrenchment, curtailment,** reduction of expenses, cutback, slowdown, rollback (*US*), cooling, cooling off *or* down, low growth rate

3 **economizer,** economist (*old*), **saver**

verbs

4 to **economize, save,** make *or* enforce economies; **scrimp, skimp** (*informal*), **scrape,** scrape and save; **manage, husband,** husband one's resources; live frugally, get along on a shoestring, get by on little; keep within compass (*old*), keep *or* stay within one's means *or* budget, balance income and expenditure, live within one's income, make ends meet, cut one's coat according to one's cloth, keep *or* stay ahead of the game; put something aside, **save up,** save for a rainy day, have a nest egg; supplement *or* eke out one's income

5 to **retrench, cut down,** cut *or* pare down expenses, **curtail expenses; cut corners, tighten one's belt,** cut back, roll back (*US*), slow down

adjectives

6 **economical, thrifty, frugal,** economic, unwasteful, conserving, **saving,** economizing, spare, **sparing; prudent,** prudential, provident, forehanded; careful, chary, canny, tight (*informal*), close; scrimping, skimping (*informal*), cheeseparing; penny-wise; **parsimonious** *see* 484.7; **cost-effective, cost-efficient; efficient,** labour-saving, time-saving, money-saving

adverbs

7 **economically, thriftily, frugally,** husbandly (*old*); **cost-effectively, cost-efficiently;** prudently, providently; carefully, charily, cannily; sparingly, with a sparing hand

636 ETHICS

nouns

1 **ethics, principles,** standards, norms, principles of conduct *or* behaviour, principles of professional practice, code of practice; **morals,** moral principles;

code, ethical *or* moral code, **ethic**, code of morals *or* ethics, ethical system, value system, axiology; **norm**, behavioural norm, normative system; moral climate, **ethos**, *Zeitgeist* (*German*); Ten Commandments, decalogue; social ethics, professional ethics, bioethics, medical ethics, legal ethics, business ethics, etc

2 ethical *or* moral philosophy, ethonomics, aretaics, eudaemonics, casuistry, deontology, empiricism, evolutionism, hedonism, ethical formalism, intuitionism, perfectionism, Stoicism, utilitarianism, categorical imperative, golden rule; egoistic ethics, altruistic ethics; Christian ethics; situation ethics; comparative ethics

3 **morality, morals,** morale; virtue *see* 653; ethicality, ethicalness

4 **amorality,** unmorality; amoralism

5 **conscience,** grace, **sense of right and wrong;** inward monitor, inner arbiter, moral censor, censor, ethical self, superego; **voice of conscience,** still small voice within, guardian *or* good angel; tender conscience; clear *or* clean conscience; social conscience; conscientiousness *see* 644.2; twinge of conscience *see* 113.2

adjectives

6 **ethical, moral,** moralistic; ethological; axiological

637 RIGHT

nouns

1 **right,** rightfulness, rightness; what is right *or* proper, what should be, what ought to be, the seemly, the thing *or* the done thing, the right *or* proper thing, the right *or* proper thing to do, what is done

2 **propriety, decorum, decency,** good behaviour *or* conduct, correctness, correctitude, rightness, properness, decorousness, goodness, goodliness, niceness, seemliness, cricket (*informal*), straight bat; fitness, fittingness, appropriateness, suitability *see* 994.1; normativeness, normality, proprieties, decencies; rightmindedness, **righteousness** *see* 653.1

adjectives

3 **right,** rightful; fit, suitable *see* 994.5; **proper, correct, decorous,** good, nice, decent, seemly, **due, appropriate,** fitting, condign, **right and proper,** as it should be, as it ought to be, *comme il faut* (*French*); kosher *and* according to Hoyle (*both informal*); in the right; normative, normal; rightminded, right-thinking, **righteous**

adverbs

4 **rightly, rightfully,** right; **by rights,** by right, with good right, **as is right** *or* **only right; properly,** correctly, as is proper *or* fitting, **duly, appropriately,** fittingly, condignly, **in justice,** in equity; in reason, in all conscience

638 WRONG

nouns

1 **wrong,** wrongfulness, wrongness; **impropriety, indecorum;** incorrectness, improperness, indecorousness, unseemliness; unfitness, unfittingness,

inappropriateness, unsuitability *see* 995.1; infraction, violation, delinquency, criminality, illegality, unlawfulness; abnormality, deviance *or* deviancy, aberrance *or* aberrancy; sinfulness, wickedness, unrighteousness; **dysfunction,** malfunction; maladaptation, maladjustment; malfeasance, malversation, malpractice; malformation

2 **abomination, horror,** terrible thing; **scandal, disgrace, shame, pity,** atrocity, profanation, desecration, violation, sacrilege, infamy, ignominy

adjectives

3 **wrong, wrongful; improper, incorrect, indecorous,** undue, unseemly; unfit, unfitting, inappropriate, unsuitable *see* 995.5; delinquent, criminal, illegal, unlawful; fraudulent, creative (*informal*); abnormal, deviant, aberrant; **dysfunctional; evil, sinful, wicked, unrighteous;** not the thing, hardly the thing, not done, not cricket; off-base *and* out-of-line *and* off-colour (*all informal*); abominable, terrible, scandalous, disgraceful, shameful, shameless, atrocious, sacrilegious, infamous, ignominious; maladapted, maladjusted

adverbs

4 **wrongly, wrongfully,** wrong; **improperly,** incorrectly, indecorously

word elements

5 mis–, dis–; dys–, caco–

639 DUENESS

nouns

1 **dueness, entitlement,** entitledness, deservingness, deservedness, meritedness, expectation, just *or* justifiable expectation, expectations, outlook, prospect, prospects; **justice** *see* 649

2 **due,** one's due, what one merits *or* is entitled to, what one has earned, what is owing, what one has coming, what is coming to one, acknowledgment, cognizance, recognition, credit, crediting; **right**

3 **deserts,** just deserts, deservings, merits, dues, due reward *or* punishment, **comeuppance** (*informal*), all that is coming to one; the wrath of God; retaliation *see* 506, vengeance *see* 507.1

verbs

4 **to be due,** be one's due, **be entitled to,** have a right or title to, have a rightful claim to *or* upon, claim as one's right, **have coming,** come by honestly

5 **to deserve, merit,** earn, rate *and* be in line for (*both informal*), **be worthy of,** be deserving, richly deserve

6 **to get one's deserts, get one's dues, get one's comeuppance** *and* get his *or* hers (*all informal*), get what is coming to one; get justice; serve one right, be rightly served; get for one's pains, reap the fruits *or* benefit of, reap where one has sown, come into one's own

adjectives

7 **due, owed, owing,** payable, redeemable, coming, coming to

8 **rightful,** condign, appropriate, proper; fit, becoming *see* 994.5; **fair, just** *see* 649.8

9 **warranted, justified, entitled,** qualified, worthy; **deserved, merited,** richly deserved, earned, well-earned

10 **due, entitled to,** with a right to; **deserving, meriting, meritorious, worthy of;** attributable, ascribable

adverbs

11 **duly,** rightfully, condignly, as is one's due *or* right

phrases

12 what's sauce for the goose is sauce for the gander; give the devil his due; give credit where credit is due; he's made his bed let him lie in it; let the punishment fit the crime

640 UNDUENESS

nouns

1 **undueness, undeservedness,** undeservingness, unentitledness, unentitlement, unmeritedness; disentitlement; lack of claim *or* title, false claim *or* title, invalid claim *or* title, no claim *or* title, empty claim *or* title; unearned increment; **inappropriateness** *see* 995.1; **impropriety** *see* 638.1; **excess** *see* 992

2 **presumption,** assumption, **imposition; licence,** licentiousness, **undue liberty,** liberties, familiarity, **presumptuousness,** freedom *or* liberty abused, hubris; lawlessness *see* 418; injustice *see* 650

3 **usurpation, arrogation,** seizure, unlawful seizure, **appropriation,** assumption, adoption, infringement, encroachment, invasion, trespass, trespassing; playing God

4 **usurper,** arrogator, pretender

verbs

5 to not be entitled to, have no right *or* title to, have no claim upon, not have a leg to stand on

6 to presume, assume, venture, hazard, dare, pretend, attempt, **make bold** *or* so bold, make free, **take the liberty,** take upon oneself, go so far as to

7 to presume on *or* upon, impose on *or* upon, encroach upon, obtrude upon; **take liberties,** take a liberty, overstep, overstep one's rights *or* bounds *or* prerogatives, make free with *or* of, abuse one's rights, abuse a privilege; **inconvenience,** bother, trouble, cause to go out of one's way

8 (*take to oneself unduly*) **to usurp, arrogate,** seize, grab *and* latch on to (*both informal*), **appropriate,** assume, adopt, take over, arrogate *or*, accroach to oneself, pretend to, infringe, encroach, invade, trespass; play God

adjectives

9 **undue,** unowed, unowing, not coming, not outstanding; **undeserved, unmerited,** unearned; **unwarranted, unjustified,** unprovoked; unentitled, undeserving, unmeriting, nonmeritorious, unworthy; preposterous, outrageous

10 **inappropriate** *see* 995.5; **improper** *see* 638.3; **excessive** *see* 992.16

11 **presumptuous, presuming,** licentious; hubristic *see* 493.7

phrases

12 give him an inch he'll take a mile; let a camel get his nose under the tent and he'll come in

641 DUTY

moral obligation

nouns

1 **duty, obligation,** charge, **onus, burden,** mission, devoir, must, ought, imperative, bounden duty, proper *or* assigned task, what ought to be done, what one is responsible for, where the buck stops (*informal*), "stern daughter of the voice of God"—WORDSWORTH, deference, respect *see* 155, fealty, allegiance, loyalty, homage; devotion, dedication, **commitment;** self-commitment, self-imposed duty; **business** *see* 724, function, province, place *see* 724.3; ethics *see* 636; line of duty; call of duty; duties and responsibilities, assignment, work-load

2 **responsibility,** incumbency; **liability, accountability,** accountableness, answerability, answerableness, amenability; product liability; **responsibleness, dutifulness,** duteousness, devotion *or* dedication to duty, sense of duty *or* obligation

verbs

3 **should, ought to,** had best, had better, be expedient

4 **to behove, become,** befit, beseem, be bound, be obliged *or* obligated, be under an obligation; **owe it to,** owe it to oneself

5 **to be the duty of,** be incumbent on *or* upon, be his *or* hers to, stand on *or* upon, be a must *or* an imperative for, duty calls one to

6 **to be responsible for,** answer for, stand responsible for, **be liable for,** be answerable *or* accountable for; be on the hook for *and* take the rap for (*both informal*), take the heat for (*US informal*)

7 **to be one's responsibility,** be one's office, be one's charge *or* mission, **rest with,** lie upon, devolve on, rest on the shoulders of, lie on one's head *or* at one's door *or* one's doorstep, fall to one *or* to one's lot

8 **to incur a responsibility,** become bound to, become a sponsor for

9 **to take** *or* **accept the responsibility,** take upon oneself, take upon one's shoulders, commit oneself; be where the buck stops (*informal*); **answer for,** respect *or* defer to one's duty; sponsor, be *or* stand sponsor for; do at one's own risk *or* peril; **take the blame,** be in the hot seat *or* on the spot *and* take the rap for (*all informal*), take the heat for (*US informal*)

10 **to do one's duty,** perform *or* fulfil *or* discharge one's duty, do what one has to do, pay one's dues (*informal*), **do what is expected,** do the needful, do the right thing, do justice to, **do** *or* **act one's part**, play one's proper role; answer the call of duty, do one's bit *or* part

11 **to meet an obligation,** satisfy one's obligations, stand to one's engagement, stand up to, **acquit oneself, make good,** redeem one's pledge

12 **to obligate, oblige, require,** make incumbent *or* imperative, tie, **bind,** pledge, commit, saddle with, put under an obligation; call to account, hold responsible *or* accountable *or* answerable

adjectives

13 **dutiful, duteous;** moral, ethical; conscientious, scrupulous, observant; obedient *see* 326.3; deferential, respectful *see* 155.8

14 **incumbent on** *or* **upon,** chargeable to, behoving

15 **obligatory, binding, imperative,** imperious, peremptory, mandatory, must, *de rigueur (French)*; **necessary,** required *see* 962.13

16 **obliged, obligated,** obligate, **under obligation; bound, duty-bound,** in duty bound, tied, pledged, committed, saddled, beholden, bounden; **obliged to,** beholden to, bound *or* bounden to, **indebted to**

17 **responsible, answerable; liable, accountable,** amenable, unexempt from, chargeable, on one's head, at one's doorstep, on the hook (*informal*); responsible for, at the bottom of; to blame

adverbs

18 **dutifully, duteously, in the line of duty,** as in duty bound; beyond the call of duty

642 PREROGATIVE

nouns

1 **prerogative, right, due,** droit; power, authority, prerogative of office; faculty, appurtenance; **claim,** proper claim, demand, **interest, title,** pretension, pretence, prescription; birthright; natural right, presumptive right, inalienable right; divine right; vested right *or* interest; property right; conjugal right

2 **privilege, licence, liberty, freedom, immunity;** franchise, patent, copyright, grant, warrant, blank cheque, carte blanche; favour, indulgence, **special favour,** dispensation

3 **human rights,** rights of man; constitutional rights, rights of citizenship, **civil rights** *see* 430.2, civil liberties; rights of minorities, minority rights; gay rights, gay liberation

4 **women's rights,** rights of women; **feminism, women's liberation,** women's lib (*informal*), womanism, women's movement *or* liberation movement, sisterhood

5 women's rightist, **feminist, women's liberationist,** women's liberation advocate *or* adherent *or* activist, womanist, **women's libber** *and* **libber** (*both informal*); **suffragette,** suffragist

verbs

6 to have *or* claim *or* assert a right, exercise a right; defend a right

643 IMPOSITION
a putting or inflicting upon

nouns

1 **imposition, infliction,** laying on *or* upon, charging, taxing, tasking; burdening, weighting *or* weighting down, freighting, loading *or* loading down, heaping on *or* upon, imposing an onus; **exaction, demand** *see* 421; unwarranted demand, obtrusiveness, presumptuousness *see* 142.1; inconvenience, trouble, bother; inconsiderateness *see* 144.3

2 administration, giving, bestowal; applying, application, dosing, dosage, meting out, prescribing; **forcing,** forcing on *or* upon, enforcing

3 **charge, duty, tax,** task; **burden,** weight, freight, cargo, load, onus

verbs

4 **to impose, impose on** *or* **upon, inflict on** *or* **upon, put on** *or* **upon, lay on** *or* **upon,** enjoin; **put, place, set, lay,** put down; **levy, exact, demand** *see* 421.4; tax, task, **charge,** burden with, weight *or* freight with, weight down with, yoke with, **fasten upon,** saddle with, stick with (*informal*), lumber with; subject to

5 **to inflict, wreak, do to,** bring, bring upon, bring down upon, bring on *or* down on one's head, visit upon

6 **to administer, give, bestow; apply, put on** *or* **upon,** lay on *or* upon, dose, dose with, dish out (*informal*), mete out, prescribe; **force, force upon,** impose by force *or* main force, strongarm (*informal*), force down one's throat, enforce upon

7 **to impose on** *or* **upon, take advantage of** *see* 387.16; **presume upon** *see* 640.7; **deceive,** play *or* work on, out on *or* upon, put over *or* across (*informal*); palm *or* pass *or* fob off on, fob *or* foist on; shift the blame *or* responsibility, **pass the buck** (*informal*)

adjectives

8 **imposed, inflicted,** piled *or* heaped on; burdened with, stuck with (*informal*), lumbered; self-inflicted; exacted, demanded

644 PROBITY

nouns

1 **probity,** assured probity, **honesty, integrity, rectitude, uprightness,** upstandingness, erectness, **virtue,** virtuousness, **righteousness, goodness;** cleanness, **decency; honour,** honourableness, worthiness, estimableness, reputability, nobility; unimpeachableness, unimpeachability, irreproachableness, irreproachability, blamelessness; immaculacy, unspottedness, stainlessness, pureness, purity; respectability; principles, high principles, high ideals, high-mindedness; **character,** good *or* sterling character, moral strength, moral excellence; **fairness,** justness, justice *see* 649

2 **conscientiousness, scrupulousness,** scrupulosity, **scruples,** punctiliousness, meticulousness; scruple, point of honour, punctilio; qualm *see* 325.2; twinge

of conscience *see* 113.2; overconscientiousness, overscrupulousness; fastidiousness *see* 495

3 **honesty, veracity,** veraciousness, verity, **truthfulness,** truth, veridicality, truth-telling, truth-speaking; truth-loving; credibility, absolute credibility

4 **candour, candidness, frankness,** plain dealing; sincerity, genuineness, authenticity; ingenuousness; artlessness *see* 416; **openness,** openheartedness; freedom, freeness; **unreserve,** unrestraint, unconstraint; **forthrightness, directness, straightforwardness;** outspokenness, plainness, plainspokenness, plain speaking, roundness, broadness; **bluntness,** bluffness, brusqueness

5 **undeceptiveness, undeceitfulness, guilelessness**

6 **trustworthiness,** faithworthiness, trustiness, trustability, **reliability, dependability,** dependableness, sureness; answerableness, responsibility *see* 641.2; unfalseness, unperfidiousness, untreacherousness; incorruptibility, inviolability

7 **fidelity, faithfulness, loyalty, faith; constancy, steadfastness,** staunchness, firmness; trueness, troth, true blue; good faith, *bona fides* (*Latin*), *bonne foi* (*French*); **allegiance, fealty, homage;** bond, tie; attachment, adherence, adhesion; devotion, devotedness

8 **person** *or* **man** *or* **woman of honour,** man of his word, woman of her word; gentleman, *gentilhomme* (*French*), *galantuomo* (*Italian*); **honest man,** good man; **lady, real lady; honest woman, good woman;** salt of the earth; square *or* straight shooter *and* straight arrow (*all informal*); true blue, truepenny; trusty, faithful

verbs

9 **to keep faith,** not fail, **keep one's word** *or* **promise,** keep troth, show good faith, be as good as one's word, have one's word as one's bond, redeem one's pledge, play by the rules, acquit oneself, make good; practise what one preaches

10 to shoot straight (*informal*), draw a straight furrow, **put one's cards on the table,** level with one (*informal*)

11 to speak *or* tell the truth, speak *or* tell true, paint in its true colours, tell the truth and shame the devil; tell the truth, the whole truth, and nothing but the truth

12 to be frank, speak plainly, speak out, speak one's mind, say what one thinks, **call a spade a spade,** tell it like it is

adjectives

13 honest, upright, uprighteous, **upstanding,** erect, right, **righteous, virtuous, good,** clean, squeaky-clean (*informal*), decent; **honourable,** full of integrity, **reputable,** estimable, creditable, worthy, noble, sterling, manly, yeomanly; Christian (*informal*); unimpeachable, irreproachable, blameless, immaculate, spotless, stainless, unstained, unspotted, unblemished, untarnished, unsullied, undefiled, pure; **respectable,** highly respectable; **ethical, moral; principled, high-principled,** high-minded, right-minded; uncorrupt, uncorrupted, inviolate; truehearted, true-souled, true-spirited; true-dealing,

true-disposing, true-devoted; **law-abiding,** law-loving, law-revering; **fair, just** *see* 649.8

14 **straight, square,** foursquare, straight-arrow (*informal*), honest and aboveboard, right as rain; **fair and square; square-dealing,** square-shooting, straight-shooting, up-and-up, **on the up-and-up** *and* **on the level** *and* on the square (*all informal*); **aboveboard, open and aboveboard;** bona fide, good-faith; authentic, all wool and a yard wide (*US & Canadian*), veritable, genuine; single-hearted; honest as the day is long

15 **conscientious,** tender-conscienced; **scrupulous,** careful *see* 339.10; punctilious, punctual, meticulous, religious, strict, nice; fastidious *see* 495.9; overconscientious, overscrupulous

16 **honest, veracious, truthful,** true, true to one's word, veridical; truth-telling, truth-speaking, truth-declaring, truth-passing, truth-bearing, truth-loving, truth-seeking, truth-desiring, truth-guarding, truth-filled; true-speaking, true-meaning, true-tongued

17 **candid, frank, sincere,** genuine, ingenuous, frankhearted; **open,** openhearted, transparent, open-faced; artless *see* 416.5; **straightforward, direct,** up-front *and* straight (*both informal*), **forthright,** downright, straight-out (*informal*); plain, broad, round; **unreserved,** unrestrained, unconstrained, unchecked; unguarded, uncalculating; free; **outspoken, plain-spoken,** free-spoken, free-speaking, free-tongued; explicit, unequivocal, full-frontal; **blunt,** bluff, brusque; heart-to-heart

18 **undeceptive, undeceitful, undissembling,** undissimulating, undeceiving, undesigning, uncalculating; **guileless,** unbeguiling, unbeguileful; unassuming, unpretending, unfeigning, undisguising, unflattering; undissimulated, undissembled; unassumed, unaffected, unpretended, unfeigned, undisguised, unvarnished, untrimmed

19 **trustworthy, trusty,** trustable, faithworthy, **reliable, dependable, responsible,** straight (*informal*), sure, to be trusted, **to be depended** *or* **relied upon,** to be counted *or* reckoned on, as good as one's word; tried, true, **tried and true,** tested, proven; unfalse, unperfidious, untreacherous; incorruptible, inviolable

20 **faithful, loyal,** devoted, allegiant; true, true-blue, true to one's colours; **constant, steadfast,** unswerving, steady, consistent, stable, unfailing, staunch, firm, solid, "marble-constant" — SHAKESPEARE

adverbs

21 **honestly, uprightly, honourably,** upstandingly, erectly, **virtuously, righteously, decently,** worthily, reputably, nobly; unimpeachably, irreproachably, blamelessly, immaculately, unspottedly, stainlessly, purely; high-mindedly, morally; **conscientiously, scrupulously,** punctiliously, meticulously, fastidiously *see* 495.14

22 **truthfully, truly,** veraciously; to tell the truth, to speak truthfully; in truth, in sooth (*old*), of a truth, with truth, in good *or* very truth, straight up

23 **candidly, frankly, sincerely,** genuinely, in all seriousness *or* soberness, from the heart, in all conscience; in plain words *or* English, straight from the shoulder, not to mince the matter, not to mince words, without equivocation, with no nonsense, all joking aside *or* apart; **openly,** openheartedly, **unreservedly,** unrestrainedly, unconstrainedly, **forthrightly, directly, straightforwardly,** outspokenly, **plainly,** plain-spokenly, broadly, roundly, **bluntly,** bluffly, brusquely

24 **trustworthily,** trustily, **reliably, dependably, responsibly;** undeceptively, undeceitfully, guilelessly; incorruptibly, inviolably

25 **faithfully, loyally,** devotedly; **constantly, steadfastly,** steadily, responsibly, consistently, unfailingly, unswervingly, staunchly, firmly; in *or* with good faith, *bona fide (Latin)*

645 IMPROBITY

nouns

1 **improbity, dishonesty,** dishonour; **unscrupulousness,** unconscientiousness; **corruption,** corruptness, corruptedness; **crookedness,** criminality, feloniousness, **fraudulence** *or* fraudulency, underhandedness, unsavouriness, fishiness *and* shadiness *(both informal),* indirection, shiftiness, slipperiness, deviousness, evasiveness, unstraightforwardness, trickiness

2 **knavery, roguery, rascality,** rascalry, **villainy,** reprobacy, scoundrelism; chicanery *see 356.4;* knavishness, roguishness, scampishness, villainousness; **baseness, vileness,** degradation, turpitude, moral turpitude

3 **deceitfulness; falseness** *see 354;* perjury, forswearing, untruthfulness *see 354.8,* credibility gap; **insincerity,** unsincereness, uncandidness, uncandour, unfrankness, disingenuousness; sharp practice *see 356.4;* fraud *see 356.8;* artfulness, craftiness *see 415.1;* intrigue

4 **untrustworthiness,** unfaithworthiness, untrustiness, **unreliability, undependability,** irresponsibility

5 **infidelity, unfaithfulness,** unfaith, faithlessness, trothlessness; **inconstancy, unsteadfastness,** fickleness; **disloyalty,** unloyalty; **falsity,** falseness, untrueness; disaffection, recreancy, dereliction; bad faith, *mala fides (Latin),* Punic faith; breach of promise, breach of trust *or* faith, barratry; breach of confidence

6 **treachery,** treacherousness; **perfidy,** perfidiousness, falseheartedness *see 354.4,* two-facedness, doubleness; **duplicity, double-dealing,** foul play, dirty work *and* dirty trick *and* dirty game *(all informal)*

7 **treason,** petty treason, misprision of treason, high treason; lese majesty, sedition; quislingism, fifth-column activity; collaboration, fraternization

8 **betrayal,** betrayment, letting down *(informal),* **double cross** *and* sellout *(both informal),* Judas kiss, kiss of death, stab in the back

9 **corruptibility, venality,** bribability, purchasability

10 criminal *see 660.10,* perpetrator, scoundrel *see 660.3,* traitor *see 357.10,* deceiver *see 357*

verbs

11 *(be dishonest)* to live by one's wits; shift, shift about, evade; deceive; cheat; falsify; lie; sail under false colours

12 **to be unfaithful,** not keep faith *or* troth, **go back on** *(informal),* **fail,** break one's word *or* promise, renege, go back on one's word *(informal),* break faith, perjure *or* forswear oneself; forsake, desert *see 370.5;* pass the buck *(informal);* shift the responsibility *or* blame

13 **to play one false,** prove false; **stab one in the back,** knife one *(informal);* bite the hand that feeds one; play dirty *(informal);* shift *or* move the goalposts *and* change the rules *(both informal)*

14 **to betray, double-cross** *and* two-time *(both informal),* sell out *and* sell down the river *(both informal),* turn in; **mislead,** lead one up the garden path; let down *and* let down one's side *(both informal);* inform on *see 551.12*

15 **to act the traitor,** turn against, go over to the enemy, turn one's coat, cross sides, sell oneself, sell out *(informal);* collaborate, fraternize

adjectives

16 **dishonest, dishonourable; unconscientious,** unconscienced, conscienceless, unconscionable, shameless, without shame *or* remorse, **unscrupulous, unprincipled,** unethical, immoral, amoral; **corrupt,** corrupted, rotten; **crooked, criminal,** felonious, **fraudulent,** creative *(informal),* underhand, underhanded; shady *(informal),* up to no good, not kosher *(informal),* unsavoury, dark, sinister, insidious, indirect, slippery, devious, rum, tricky, shifty, evasive, unstraightforward; fishy *and* dodgy *(both informal),* questionable, suspicious, doubtful, dubious, hooky *(informal);* ill-gotten, ill-got, off the back of a lorry

17 **knavish, roguish, scampish, rascally, scoundrelly,** blackguardly, villainous, reprobate, recreant, **base, vile,** degraded; **infamous, notorious**

18 **deceitful;** falsehearted; perjured, forsworn, untruthful *see 354.34;* **insincere,** unsincere, uncandid, unfrank, disingenuous; artful, crafty *see 415.12;* calculating, scheming; **tricky,** cute *and* dodgy *(both informal),* slippery as an eel

19 **untrustworthy,** unfaithworthy, untrusty, trustless, **unreliable, undependable,** fly-by-night, irresponsible, unsure, not to be trusted, not to be depended *or* relied upon

20 **unfaithful,** faithless, of bad faith, trothless; **inconstant, unsteadfast,** fickle; **disloyal,** unloyal; false, **untrue,** not true to; disaffected, recreant, derelict, barratrous

21 **treacherous, perfidious,** falsehearted; **shifty,** slippery, tricky; **double-dealing,** double, ambidextrous; **two-faced**

22 **traitorous,** turncoat, double-crossing *and* two-timing *(both informal),* betraying; Judas-like, Iscariotic; **treasonable,** treasonous; quisling, quislingistic, fifth-column, Trojan-horse

23 **corruptible, venal,** bribable, purchasable, on the pad *(informal),* mercenary, hireling

adverbs

24 **dishonestly, dishonourably; unscrupulously,**
unconscientiously; **crookedly,** criminally, feloniously,
fraudulently, underhandedly, like a thief in the
night, insidiously, deviously, shiftily, evasively, fishily
(*informal*), suspiciously, dubiously, by fair means or
foul; **deceitfully;** knavishly, roguishly, villainously;
basely, vilely; infamously, notoriously

25 **perfidiously,** falseheartedly; **unfaithfully,**
faithlessly; **treacherously;** traitorously, treasonably

646 HONOUR
token of esteem

nouns

1 **honour,** great honour, distinction, glory, credit,
ornament;
"blushing honours"—SHAKESPEARE

2 **award, reward, prize;** first prize, second prize, etc;
gold medal, silver medal, bronze medal; blue riband,
blue ribbon; consolation prize; booby prize, wooden
spoon; Nobel Prize, Pulitzer Prize, Booker Prize;
sweepstake; jackpot; Oscar, Academy Award;
BAFTA award; Grammy; Tony; Emmy; platinum
disc, gold disc, silver disc

3 **trophy,** laurel, **laurels,** bays, palm, palms, crown,
chaplet, wreath, garland, **feather in one's cap**
(*informal*); civic crown *or* garland *or* wreath; **cup,**
loving cup, pot (*informal*); **World Cup; belt,**
championship belt, Lonsdale Belt, black belt, brown
belt, etc; banner, flag

4 **citation,** eulogy, mention, honourable mention,
kudos, **accolade, tribute, praise** see 511.1

5 **decoration,** decoration of honour, order, ornament;
Order of the Garter, Order of the Thistle, Order of
the Bath, Order of Merit, Order of St Michael and
St George, Royal Victorian Order, Order of the
British Empire, Order of the Companions of
Honour; garter; star, gold star, riband, ribbon; blue
riband, blue ribbon, *cordon bleu* (*French*); red ribbon,
red ribbon of the Legion of Honor; cordon, grand
cordon

6 **medal, military honour** (*see list*), order, medallion,
gong (*informal*); military medal, service medal, war
medal, soldier's medal; lifesaving medal; police
citation, departmental citation

7 scholarship, fellowship

verbs

8 **to honour, do honour,** pay regard to, give *or* pay
or render honour to, **recognize; cite; decorate,** pin
a medal on; crown, crown with laurel; hand it to *or*
take off one's hat to one (*informal*), pay tribute,
praise see 511.5; give credit where credit is due; give
one the red carpet treatment, roll out the red carpet

adjectives

9 **honoured, distinguished;** laureate, crowned with
laurel

10 honorary, honorific, honourable

adverbs

11 **with honour,** with distinction; *cum laude, magna*

cum laude, summa cum laude, insigne cum laude,
honoris causa (all *Latin*)

12 **military honours**

Air Force Cross	Distinguished Service
Congressional Medal of	Medal
Honor (US)	Distinguished Service
Croix de Guerre (France)	Order
Distinguished Conduct	George Cross
Medal	Médaille Militaire (France)
Distinguished Flying Cross	Military Cross
Distinguished Flying	Order of the Purple Heart
Medal	(US)
Distinguished Service	Victoria Cross
Cross	

647 INSIGNIA

nouns

1 **insignia, regalia,** ensign, **emblem, badge,**
symbol, logo (*informal*), colophon, marking, flash,
attribute; badge of office, mark of office, chain, chain
of office, collar; wand, verge, *fasces* (*Latin*), **mace,**
staff, baton; livery, uniform, mantle, dress; tartan,
tie, old school tie, regimental tie; ring, school ring
and class ring (*both US*); pin, button, lapel pin *or*
button; cap and gown, mortarboard; cockade;
brassard; figurehead, eagle; cross see 170.4, skull and
crossbones, swastika, hammer and sickle, rose, thistle,
shamrock, fleur-de-lis; medal, **decoration** see 646.5;
heraldry, armory, blazonry, sigillography,
sphragistics

2 (*heraldry terms*) heraldic device, achievement,
bearings, coat of arms, arms, armorial bearings,
armory, blazonry, blazon; hatchment; shield,
escutcheon, scutcheon, lozenge; charge, field; crest,
torse, wreath, garland, bandeau, chaplet, mantling,
helmet; crown, coronet; device, motto; pheon, broad
arrow; animal charge, lion, unicorn, griffin, yale,
cockatrice, falcon, alerion, eagle, spread eagle;
marshalling, quartering, impaling, impalement,
dimidiating, differencing, difference; ordinary, bar,
bend, bar sinister, bend sinister, baton, chevron,
chief, cross, fess, pale, paly, saltire; subordinary,
billet, bordure, canton, flanch, fret, fusil, gyron,
inescutcheon, mascle, orle, quarter, rustre, tressure;
fess point, nombril point, honour point; cadency
mark, file, label, crescent, mullet, martlet, annulet,
fleur-de-lis, rose, cross moline, octofoil; tincture,
gules, azure, vert, sable, purpure, tenne; metal, or,
argent; fur, ermine, ermines, erminites, erminois,
pean, vair; heraldic officials see 575.21

3 (*royal insignia*) regalia; sceptre, rod, rod of empire;
orb; armilla; purple, ermine, robe of state *or* royalty;
purple pall; crown, royal crown, coronet, tiara,
diadem; cap of maintenance *or* dignity *or* estate,
triple plume, Prince of Wales's feathers; uraeus; seal,
signet, great seal, privy seal

4 (*ecclesiastical insignia*) tiara, triple crown; ring, keys;
mitre, crosier, crook, pastoral staff; pallium;
cardinal's hat, red hat

5 (*military insignia*) insignia of rank, grade insignia,
chevron, stripe, tape, tab; star, bar, eagle, spread
eagle (*informal*), pip, oak leaf; branch of service

insignia, insignia of branch *or* arm; shoulder patch, patch; badge, aviation badge *or* wings; parachute badge, submarine badge; service stripe; epaulette

6 **flag, banner,** oriflamme, **standard,** gonfalon *or* gonfanon, guidon, *vexillum* (*Latin*), *labarum* (*Latin*); **pennant,** pennon, pennoncel, banneret, banderole, swallowtail, burgee, **streamer; bunting;** coachwhip, long pennant; **national flag, colours;** royal standard; **ensign,** rag (*informal*), merchant flag, jack, Jolly Roger, black flag; house flag; (*Britain*) Union Jack, Union Flag, white *or* red *or* blue ensign, red duster (*informal*); (*US*) Old Glory, Stars and Stripes, Star-Spangled Banner, red, white and blue; (*US Confederacy*) Stars and Bars; (*France*) tricolour, *le drapeau tricolore* (*French*); (*Denmark*) Dannebrog; vexillology; signal flag *see* 517.15

648 TITLE
appellation of dignity or distinction

nouns

1 **title, honorific, honour,** title of honour; **handle** *and* handle to one's name (*both informal*); courtesy title

2 (*honorifics*) Excellency, Eminence, Reverence, Grace, Honour, Worship, Your *or* His *or* Her Excellency; Lord, My Lord, milord, Lordship, Your *or* His Lordship; Lady, My Lady, milady, Ladyship, Your *or* Her Ladyship; Highness, Royal Highness, Imperial Highness, Serene Highness, Your *or* His *or* Her Highness; Majesty, Royal Majesty, Imperial Majesty, Serene Majesty, Your *or* His *or* Her Majesty

3 Sir, sire, sirrah; Esquire; Master, Mister *see* 76.7; mirza, effendi, sirdar, emir, khan, sahib

4 Mistress, madame *see* 77.8

5 (*ecclesiastical titles*) Reverend, His Reverence, His Grace; Monsignor; Holiness, His Holiness; Dom, Brother, Sister, Father, Mother; Rabbi

6 **degree, academic degree** (*see list*); **bachelor,** baccalaureate, *baccalaureus* (*Latin*), bachelor's degree; **master,** master's degree; **doctor,** doctorate, doctor's degree; double first, first, upper second *or* 2:1, lower second *or* 2:2, Desmond (*informal*), third, honours degree, pass degree

adjectives

7 **titular,** titulary; honorific; honorary

8 the Noble, the Most Noble, the Most Excellent, the Most Worthy, the Most Worshipful; the Honourable, the Most Honourable, the Right Honourable; the Reverend, the Very Reverend, the Right Reverend, the Most Reverend

9 **academic degrees**

BA *or* Bachelor of Arts	Commerce
BAgr *or* Bachelor of Agriculture	BD *or* Bachelor of Divinity
BArch *or* Bachelor of Architecture	BDS *or* Bachelor of Dental Surgery
BCh *or* Bachelor of Surgery	BEd *or* Bachelor of Education
BCL *or* Bachelor of Civil Law	BEng *or* Bachelor of Engineering
BCom *or* Bachelor of	BL *or* Bachelor of Law

BLitt *or* Bachelor of Letters	HND *or* Higher National Diploma
BM *or* Bachelor of Medicine	LittD *or* Doctor of Letters
BMus *or* Bachelor of Music	LLB *or* Bachelor of Laws
	LLD *or* Doctor of Laws
BPharm *or* Bachelor of Pharmacy	LLM *or* Master of Laws
	MA *or* Master of Arts
BPhil *or* Bachelor of Philosophy	MArch *or* Master of Architecture
BS *or* Bachelor of Surgery	MB *or* Bachelor of Medicine
BSc *or* Bachelor of Science	MBA *or* Master of Business Administration
CertEd *or* Certificate in Education	MCh *or* MS *or* Master of Surgery
DipEd *or* Diploma in Education	MD *or* Doctor of Medicine
DD *or* Doctor of Divinity	
DLitt *or* Doctor of Letters	MDiv *or* Master of Divinity
DDS *or* Doctor of Dental Surgery	MEd *or* Master of Education
DDSc *or* Doctor of Dental Science	MLitt *or* Master of Letters
DEd *or* Doctor of Education	MMus *or* Master of Music
	MPhil *or* Master of Philosophy
DMin *or* Doctor of Ministry	MSc *or* Master of Science
DMus *or* Doctor of Music	MTech *or* Master of Technology
DO *or* Doctor of Osteopathy *or* Optometry	MusB *or* MusBac *or* Bachelor of Music
DPH *or* Diploma in Public Health	MusD *or* Doctor of Music
DPhil *or* Doctor of Philosophy	ONC *or* Ordinary National Certificate
DPM *or* Diploma in Psychological Medicine	OND *or* Ordinary National Diploma
DSc *or* Doctor of Science	PhD *or* Doctor of Philosophy
DSC *or* Doctor of Surgical Chiropody	ScD *or* Doctor of Science
EdD *or* Doctor of Education	STD *or* Doctor of Sacred Theology
JCD *or* Doctor of Canon Law	ThB *or* Bachelor of Theology
JD *or* Doctor of Jurisprudence	ThD *or* Doctor of Theology
HNC *or* Higher National Certificate	ThM *or* Master of Theology

649 JUSTICE

nouns

1 **justice, justness; equity,** equitableness, level playing field (*informal*); **evenhandedness,** measure for measure, give-and-take; balance, equality *see* 789; **right, rightness,** rightfulness, meetness, properness, propriety, what is right; dueness *see* 639; justification, **justifiableness,** justifiability, warrantedness, warrantability, defensibility; poetic justice; retributive justice, nemesis; summary justice, drumhead justice, rude justice; scales of justice; lawfulness, legality *see* 673

2 "truth in action"—DISRAELI, "right reason applied to command and prohibition"—CICERO, "the firm and

continuous desire to render to everyone that which is his due"—Justinian, "the ligament which holds civilized beings and civilized nations together"—Daniel Webster

3 fairness, fair-mindedness, candour; the fair thing, the right *or* proper thing, the handsome thing (*informal*); level playing field, **square deal** *and* **fair crack of the whip** (*both informal*); **fair play,** cricket (*informal*); sportsmanship, good sportsmanship, sportsmanliness, sportsmanlikeness

4 impartiality, detachment, **dispassion,** loftiness, Olympian detachment, **dispassionateness, disinterestedness,** disinterest, unbias, unbiasedness, a fair field and no favour; **neutrality** *see* 467; selflessness, unselfishness *see* 652

5 (*personifications*) Justice, Justitia, blind *or* blindfolded Justice; Rhadamanthus, Minos; (*deities*) Jupiter Fidius, Deus Fidius; Fides, Fides publica Romani, Fides populi Romani; Nemesis, Dike, Themis; Astraea

verbs

6 to be just, be fair, do the fair thing, do the handsome thing (*informal*), do right, be righteous, do it fair and square, do the right thing by; **do justice to,** see justice done, see one righted *or* redressed, redress a wrong *or* an injustice, remedy an injustice, serve one right, be straight with *and* **give a square deal** *or* **fair crack of the whip** (*all informal*); give the Devil his due; give and take; bend *or* lean over backwards, go out of one's way, go the extra mile (*informal*)

7 to play fair, play the game (*informal*), be a good sport, show a proper spirit; judge on its own merits, hold no brief

adjectives

8 just, fair, square, **fair and square; equitable,** balanced, level (*informal*), **even,** evenhanded; **right, rightful;** justifiable, justified, warranted, warrantable, defensible; **due** *see* 639.7, 10, deserved, merited; meet, meet and right, right and proper, fit, **proper, good,** as it should *or* ought to be; lawful, legal *see* 673.10

9 fair-minded; sporting, sportsmanly, sportsmanlike; square-dealing (*informal*)

10 impartial, impersonal, evenhanded, equitable, **dispassionate, disinterested,** detached, objective, lofty, Olympian; **unbiased,** uninfluenced, unswayed; **neutral** *see* 467.7; selfless, unselfish *see* 652.5

adverbs

11 justly, fairly, fair, in a fair manner; rightfully, rightly, duly, deservedly, meetly, properly; **equitably, equally, evenly,** upon even terms; justifiedly, justifiably, warrantably, warrantedly; **impartially, impersonally, dispassionately, disinterestedly,** without distinction, without regard *or* respect to persons, without fear or favour

12 in justice, in equity, in reason, in all conscience, in all fairness, **to be fair,** as is only fair *or* right, as is right *or* just *or* fitting *or* proper

650 INJUSTICE

nouns

1 injustice, unjustness; inequity, iniquity, inequitableness, iniquitousness; inequality *see* 790, inequality of treatment *or* dealing; **wrong, wrongness,** wrongfulness, unmeetness, improperness, **impropriety;** undueness *see* 640; what should not be, what ought not *or* must not be; unlawfulness, illegality *see* 674

2 unfairness; unsportsmanliness, unsportsmanlikeness; foul play, foul, a hit below the belt, dirty play

3 partiality, onesidedness; bias, leaning, inclination, tendentiousness; undispassionateness, undetachment, interest, involvement, **partisanism,** partisanship, *parti pris* (*French*), *Tendenz* (*German*); unneutrality; **slant,** angle, spin (*informal*); **favouritism,** preference, nepotism; unequal *or* preferential treatment, discrimination, unjust legal disability, inequality

4 injustice, wrong, injury, grievance, disservice; raw *or* rotten deal (*both informal*); imposition; mockery *or* miscarriage *or* travesty of justice; great wrong, grave *or* gross injustice; atrocity, outrage

5 unjustifiability, unwarrantability, indefensibility; **inexcusability,** unconscionableness, **unpardonability,** unforgivableness, inexpiableness, irremissibility

verbs

6 to not play fair, hit below the belt, give a raw deal *or* rotten deal (*informal*)

7 to do one an injustice, wrong, do wrong, do wrong by, **do one a wrong,** do a disservice; do a great wrong, do a grave *or* gross injustice, commit an atrocity *or* outrage

8 to favour, prefer, show preference, **play favourites,** treat unequally, discriminate; **slant,** angle, put a spin on (*informal*)

adjectives

9 unjust, inequitable, unequitable, iniquitous, **unbalanced, discriminatory, uneven, unequal** *see* 790.4; **wrong, wrongful,** unrightful; **undue** *see* 640.9, unmeet, undeserved, unmerited; unlawful, illegal *see* 674.6

10 unfair, not fair; **unsporting,** unsportsmanly, unsportsmanlike, not done, not kosher (*informal*), not cricket (*informal*), a bit thick; **dirty** (*informal*), foul, below the belt

11 partial, interested, involved, **partisan,** unneutral, **one-sided,** all on *or* way over to one side, undetached, interested, unobjective, subjective, **undispassionate, biased,** prejudiced, tendentious, tendential, warped, influenced, swayed, slanted

12 unjustifiable, unwarrantable, unallowable, unreasonable, indefensible; **inexcusable,** unconscionable, **unpardonable, unforgivable,** inexpiable, irremissible

adverbs

13 unjustly, unfairly; wrongfully, wrongly, undeservedly; inequitably, iniquitously, unequally, unevenly; partially, interestedly, one-sidedly, undispassionately; **unjustifiably, unwarrantably,** unallowably, unreasonably, indefensibly; inexcusably, unconscionably, unpardonably, unforgivably, inexpiably, irremissibly

651 SELFISHNESS

nouns

1 **selfishness,** selfism, **self-seeking,** self-serving, self-pleasing, **self-indulgence,** hedonism; self-advancement, self-promotion, self-advertisement; **careerism,** personal ambition; **narcissism, self-love,** self-devotion, self-jealousy, **self-consideration,** self-solicitude, self-sufficiency, self-absorption, ego trip, self-occupation; self-containment, self-isolation; autism, catatonia, remoteness *see* 583.2; **self-interest,** self-interestedness, interest; self-esteem, self-admiration *see* 140.1; **self-centredness, self-obsession,** narcissism, egotism *see* 140.3; **avarice, greed,** graspingness, grabbiness (*informal*), acquisitiveness, possessiveness; **individualism** *see* 430.5, personalism, privatism, private *or* personal desires, private *or* personal aims

2 **ungenerousness,** unmagnanimousness, **illiberality,** meanness, smallness, littleness, paltriness, minginess, pettiness; **niggardliness, stinginess** *see* 484.3

3 **self-seeker,** self-pleaser, self-advancer; member of the me generation; **narcissist, egotist** *see* 140.5; timepleaser, timeserver, temporizer; fortune hunter, name-dropper; self-server, careerist; monopolist, hog, road hog; dog in the manger; **individualist,** loner *and* lone wolf (*both informal*)

verbs

4 **to please oneself,** gratify oneself; ego-trip *and* be *or* go on an ego trip (*all informal*), be full of oneself; indulge *or* pamper *or* coddle oneself, consult one's own wishes, look after one's own interests, know which side one's bread is buttered on, take care of *or* look out for number one *or* numero uno (*informal*); want everything, have one's cake and eat it

adjectives

5 **selfish, self-seeking, self-serving,** self-advancing, self-promoting, self-advertising, careerist, ambitious for self, **self-indulgent,** self-pleasing, hedonistic, self-jealous, self-sufficient, **self-interested,** self-considerative, self-besotted, self-devoted, self-occupied, self-absorbed, wrapped up in oneself, self-contained, autistic, remote *see* 583.6; self-esteeming, self-admiring *see* 140.8; **self-centred, self-obsessed,** narcissistic, egotistical *see* 140.10; possessive; **avaricious, greedy,** grasping, graspy *and* grabby (*both informal*), acquisitive; **individualistic,** personalistic, privatistic

6 **ungenerous, illiberal,** unchivalrous, mean, small, little, paltry, mingy, petty; **niggardly, stingy** *see* 484.9

adverbs

7 **selfishly, for oneself,** in one's own interest, from selfish *or* interested motives, for private ends

652 UNSELFISHNESS

nouns

1 **unselfishness, selflessness;** self-subjection, self-subordination, self-suppression, self-abasement, self-effacement; **humility** *see* 137; modesty *see* 139; self-neglect, self-neglectfulness, self-forgetfulness; **self-renunciation,** self-renouncement; **self-denial,** self-abnegation; **self-sacrifice,** sacrifice, self-immolation, self-devotion, devotion, dedication, commitment, consecration; disinterest, disinterestedness; unpossessiveness, unacquisitiveness; **altruism** *see* 143.4

2 **magnanimity,** magnanimousness, greatness of spirit *or* soul, **generosity,** generousness, openhandedness, **liberality,** liberalness; **bigness, bigheartedness,** greatheartedness, largeheartedness, big *or* large *or* great heart, greatness of heart; noble-mindedness, **high-mindedness, idealism; benevolence** *see* 143.4; **nobleness,** nobility, princeliness, greatness, **loftiness,** elevation, exaltation, sublimity; chivalry, chivalrousness, knightliness, errantry, knight-errantry; heroism

verbs

3 to not have a selfish bone in one's body, think only of others; be generous to a fault; put oneself out, go out of the way, lean over backwards; sacrifice, make a sacrifice; subject oneself, subordinate oneself, abase oneself

4 to observe the golden rule, do as one would be done by, do unto others as you would have others do unto you

adjectives

5 **unselfish, selfless;** self-unconscious, self-forgetful, self-abasing, self-effacing; **altruistic** *see* 143.15, **humble; unpretentious, modest** *see* 139.9; self-neglectful, self-neglecting; **self-denying,** self-renouncing, self-abnegating, self-abnegatory; **self-sacrificing,** self-immolating, sacrificing, self-devotional, self-devoted, devoted, dedicated, committed, consecrated, unsparing of oneself, disinterested; unpossessive, unacquisitive

6 **magnanimous,** great-souled *or* spirited; **generous,** generous to a fault, openhanded, **liberal; big, bighearted,** greathearted, largehearted, great of heart *or* soul; noble-minded, **high-minded, idealistic; benevolent** *see* 143.15, **noble,** princely, handsome, great, high, elevated, **lofty,** exalted, sublime; chivalrous, knightly; heroic

adverbs

7 **unselfishly, altruistically,** forgetful of oneself; for others

8 **magnanimously, generously,** openhandedly, **liberally; bigheartedly,** greatheartedly, largeheartedly; **nobly,** handsomely; chivalrously

653 VIRTUE
moral goodness

nouns

1 **virtue, virtuousness, goodness, righteousness,** rectitude, right conduct *or* behaviour, the straight and narrow, the straight and narrow way, the right thing; probity *see* 644; **morality,** moral fibre *or* rectitude *or* virtue, morale; **saintliness,** saintlikeness; **godliness** *see* 692.2

2 "the health of the soul"—JOSEPH JOUBERT, "the fount whence honour springs"—MARLOWE, "the beauty of the soul", "the adherence in action to the nature of things"—BOTH EMERSON, "victorious resistance to one's vital desire to do this, that or the other"—JAMES BRANCH CABELL, "to do unwitnessed what we should be capable of doing before all the world"—LA ROCHEFOUCAULD

3 **purity,** immaculacy, immaculateness, spotlessness, unspottedness; **uncorruptness,** uncorruptedness, incorruptness; **unsinfulness, sinlessness,** unwickedness, uniniquitousness; undegenerateness, undepravedness, undissoluteness, undebauchedness; **chastity** *see* 664; guiltlessness, innocence *see* 657

4 **cardinal virtues,** natural virtues; prudence, justice, temperance, fortitude; theological virtues *or* supernatural virtues; faith, hope, charity *or* love

verbs

5 **to be good,** do no evil, do the right thing; keep in the right path, walk the straight path, follow the straight and narrow, keep on the straight and narrow way *or* path; fight the good fight

adjectives

6 **virtuous, good, moral; upright, honest** *see* 644.13, 14, 16; **righteous,** just, straight, rightminded, rightthinking; **angelic,** seraphic; **saintly,** saintlike; **godly** *see* 692.9

7 **chaste, immaculate, spotless, pure** *see* 664.4; **clean,** squeaky-clean (*informal*); guiltless, **innocent** *see* 657.6

8 **uncorrupt,** uncorrupted, incorrupt, incorrupted; **unsinful,** sinless; **unwicked,** uniniquitous, unerring, unfallen; undegenerate, undepraved, undemoralized, undissolute, undebauched

654 VICE
moral badness

nouns

1 **vice, viciousness; criminality, wrongdoing** *see* 655; **immorality,** unmorality, **evil; amorality** *see* 636.4; **unvirtuousness,** ungoodness; **unrighteousness, ungodliness,** unsaintliness; **uncleanness, impurity, unchastity** *see* 665, fallenness, fallen state, lapsed state; waywardness, wantonness, prodigality; delinquency, moral delinquency; peccability; backsliding, recidivism; **evil nature, carnality** *see* 663.2

2 **vice, weakness,** weakness of the flesh, **flaw,** moral flaw *or* blemish, **frailty, infirmity; failing,** failure; weak point, weak side, foible; bad habit, besetting sin; **fault, imperfection** *see* 1002

3 **iniquity, evil,** bad, wrong, error, obliquity, villainy, knavery, reprobacy, peccancy, **abomination, atrocity, infamy,** shame, disgrace, scandal, unforgiveable *or* cardinal *or* mortal sin, sin *see* 655.2

4 **wickedness, badness,** naughtiness, evilness, **viciousness, sinfulness, iniquitousness; baseness,** rankness, **vileness,** foulness, arrantness, nefariousness, **heinousness,** infamousness, villainousness, flagitiousness; fiendishness, hellishness; devilishness, devilry, deviltry

5 **turpitude, moral turpitude; corruption,** corruptedness, corruptness, rottenness, moral pollution *or* pollutedness, lack *or* absence of moral fibre; **decadence** *or* decadency, debasement, **degradation,** demoralization, abjection; **degeneracy,** degenerateness, degeneration, reprobacy, **depravity,** depravedness, depravation; **dissoluteness, profligacy;** abandonment, abandon

6 **obduracy, hardheartedness, hardness, callousness,** heartlessness, hardness of heart, heart of stone

7 **sewer, gutter, pit, sink, sink of corruption; den of iniquity,** den, **fleshpots,** hellhole; hole *and* joint *and* dive *and* the pits (*all informal*); Sodom, Gomorrah, Babylon; **brothel** *see* 665.9

verbs

8 **to do wrong, sin** *see* 655.5; misbehave, misdemean *and* misdo (*both old*)

9 **to go wrong,** stray, go astray, **err,** deviate, deviate from the path of virtue, leave the straight and narrow, step out of line, get or go off base (*informal*); **fall, lapse,** slip, trip; **degenerate; go to the bad** *see* 395.24; **relapse,** recidivate, backslide *see* 394.4

10 **to corrupt; sully, soil, defile;** demoralize, vitiate, drive to the dogs

adjectives

11 **vice-prone,** vice-laden, vicious, **steeped in vice; immoral,** unmoral; **amoral,** nonmoral; unethical

12 **unvirtuous,** virtueless, ungood; **unrighteous, ungodly,** unsaintly, unangelic; **unclean, impure,** spotted, flawed, blemished, maculate (*old*), **unchaste** *see* 665.23; fleshly, carnal *see* 663.6, wayward, wanton, prodigal; erring, **fallen, lapsed,** postlapsarian; frail, weak, infirm; Adamic; peccable; **relapsing, backsliding,** recidivist, recidivistic; of easy virtue *see* 665.26

13 **diabolic,** diabolical, devilish, demonic, demoniac, demoniacal, **satanic,** Mephistophelian; **fiendish,** fiendlike; **hellish,** hellborn, infernal

14 **corrupt,** corrupted, vice-corrupted, polluted, morally polluted, rotten, tainted, contaminated, vitiated; warped, perverted; **decadent,** debased, degraded, reprobate, **depraved, debauched, dissolute, degenerate,** profligate, abandoned, gone to the bad *or* dogs, sunk *or* steeped in iniquity, rotten at *or* to the core, in the sewer *or* gutter

15 **evil-minded,** evilhearted, **blackhearted; base-minded,** low-minded; low-thoughted, dirty *or* dirty-minded (*informal*)

16 wicked, evil, vicious, bad, naughty, wrong,
sinful, iniquitous, peccant, reprobate; dark, black;
base, low, vile, foul, rank, flagrant, arrant,
nefarious, heinous, villainous, criminal, up to no
good, knavish, flagitious; abominable, atrocious,
monstrous, unspeakable, execrable, damnable;
shameful, disgraceful, scandalous, infamous,
unpardonable, unforgivable; improper,
reprehensible, blamable, blameworthy, unworthy

17 hardened, hard, case-hardened, obdurate,
inured, indurated; callous, calloused, seared;
hardhearted, heartless; shameless, lost to shame,
blind to virtue, lost to all sense of honour,
conscienceless, unblushing, brazen, bare-faced

18 irreclaimable, irredeemable, unredeemable,
unregenerate, irreformable, incorrigible, past
praying for; shriftless, graceless; lost

adverbs

19 wickedly, evilly, sinfully, iniquitously, peccantly,
viciously; basely, vilely, foully, rankly, arrantly,
flagrantly, flagitiously

655 WRONGDOING

nouns

1 wrongdoing, evildoing, wickedness, misdoing
(*old*), wrong conduct, misbehaviour *see* 322,
misconduct, misdemeaning, misfeasance,
malfeasance, malversation, malpractice, evil courses,
machinations of the devil; sin,
"thou scarlet sin"—Shakespeare, "the transgression of
the law"—Bible; crime, criminality, lawbreaking,
feloniousness; criminal tendency; habitual criminality,
criminosis; viciousness, vice *see* 654; misprision,
negative *or* positive misprision, misprision of treason
or felony

2 misdeed, misdemeanour, misfeasance, malfeasance,
malefaction, criminal *or* guilty *or* sinful act, offence,
injustice, injury, wrong, iniquity, evil, peccancy,
malum (*Latin*); tort; error, fault, breach;
impropriety, slight *or* minor wrong, venial sin,
indiscretion, peccadillo, misstep, trip, slip, lapse;
transgression, trespass; sin,
"deed without a name"—Shakespeare; cardinal *or*
deadly *or* mortal sin, grave *or* heavy sin,
unutterable sin, unpardonable *or* unforgivable *or*
inexpiable sin; sin against the Holy Ghost; sin of
commission; sin of omission, nonfeasance, omission,
failure, dereliction, delinquency; crime, felony;
capital crime; white-collar crime, execu-crime,
corporate crime; computer crime, computer fraud;
copycat crime (*informal*); war crime, crime against
humanity, genocide; outrage, atrocity, enormity

3 original sin, fall from grace, fall, fall of man, fall of
Adam *or* Adam's fall, sin of Adam

verbs

4 to do wrong, do amiss, misdo (*old*), misdemean
oneself, misbehave *see* 322.4, err, offend; sin,
commit sin; transgress, trespass

adjectives

5 wrongdoing, evildoing, malefactory, malfeasant;
wrong, iniquitous, sinful, wicked *see* 654.16;
criminal, felonious, criminous (*old*); crime-infested,
crime-ridden

656 GUILT

nouns

1 guilt, guiltiness; criminality, peccancy; guilty *or*
wrongful *or* criminal involvement; culpability,
reprehensibility, blamability, blameworthiness;
chargeability, answerability, much to answer for;
censurability, censurableness, reproachability,
reproachableness, reprovability, reprovableness,
inculpation, implication, involvement, complicity,
impeachability, impeachableness, indictability,
indictableness, arraignability, arraignableness;
bloodguilt *or* guiltiness, red-handedness, dirty hands,
red *or* bloody hands,
"hangman's hands"—Shakespeare; much to answer for;
ruth, ruefulness, remorse, guilty conscience, guilt
feelings; onus, burden

verbs

2 to be guilty, look guilty, look like the cat that
swallowed the canary, blush, stammer; have on one's
hands *or* to one's discredit, have much to answer for;
have a red face; be caught in the act *or* flatfooted *or*
redhanded, be caught with one's pants down *or* with
one's hand in the till (*informal*), be caught with one's
hand in the cookie jar (*US informal*)

adjectives

3 guilty, guilty as hell, peccant, criminal, to blame,
at fault, faulty, on one's head; culpable,
reprehensible, censurable, reproachable, reprovable,
inculpated, implicated, involved, impeachable,
indictable, arraignable; red-handed, bloodguilty;
caught in the act *or* flatfooted *or* red-handed, caught
with one's pants down *or* with one's hand in the till
or with one's hand in the cookie jar (*informal*)

adverbs

4 red-handed, red-hand, in the act, in the very act,
in flagrante delicto (*Latin*)

5 guilty, shamefacedly, sheepishly, with a guilty
conscience

657 INNOCENCE

nouns

1 innocence, innocency, innocentness; unfallen *or*
unlapsed *or* prelapsarian state; unguiltiness,
guiltlessness, faultlessness, blamelessness,
reproachlessness, sinlessness, offencelessness;
spotlessness, stainlessness, taintlessness,
unblemishedness; purity, cleanness, cleanliness,
whiteness, immaculateness, immaculacy,
impeccability; clean hands, clean slate, clear
conscience, nothing to hide

2 childlikeness *see* 416.1; lamblikeness, dovelikeness,
angelicness; unacquaintance with evil,

uncorruptedness, incorruptness, pristineness, undefiledness

3 inculpability, unblamability, unblamableness, **unblameworthiness**, irreproachability, irreproachableness, impeccability, impeccableness, unexceptionability, unexceptionableness, **irreprehensibility**, irreprehensibleness, uncensurability, uncensurableness, unimpeachability, unimpeachableness, unindictableness, unarraignableness

4 **innocent**, baby, babe, babe in arms, newborn babe, infant, babe in the woods, child, mere child, lamb, dove, angel

verbs

5 to know no wrong, have clean hands, have a clear conscience, look as if butter would not melt in one's mouth

adjectives

6 **innocent**; unfallen, unlapsed, prelapsarian; **unguilty**, not guilty, **guiltless, faultless, blameless,** reproachless, **sinless**, offenceless, with clean hands, "blameless in life and pure of crime"—HORACE; clear, in the clear; without reproach, *sans reproche* (*French*); innocent as a lamb, lamblike, dovelike, angelic, childlike *see 416.5*; unacquainted with *or* untouched by evil, uncorrupted, incorrupt, pristine, undefiled

7 **spotless**, stainless, taintless, unblemished, unspotted, **untainted, unsoiled, unsullied, undefiled; pure, clean, immaculate**, impeccable, white, pure *or* white as driven snow, squeaky-clean (*informal*), "without unspotted, innocent within"—DRYDEN

8 **inculpable**, unblamable, unblameworthy, **irreproachable**, irreprovable, **irreprehensible**, uncensurable, unimpeachable, unindictable, unarraignable, unobjectionable, unexceptionable, above suspicion

adverbs

9 **innocently, guiltlessly, unguiltily**, with a clear conscience; **unknowingly**, unconsciously, unawares

658 ATONEMENT

nouns

1 **atonement, reparation, amends**, making amends, **restitution, propitiation, expiation, redress, recompense**, compensation, setting right, making right *or* good, making up, squaring, redemption, reclamation, satisfaction, quittance; making it quits; indemnity, indemnification; compromise, composition; expiatory offering *or* sacrifice, piaculum, peace offering

2 **apology, excuse**, regrets; acknowledgment, penitence, contrition, breast-beating, *mea culpa* (*Latin*), confession *see 351.3*; abject apology

3 **penance**, penitence, repentance; penitential act *or* exercise, **mortification**, maceration, flagellation, lustration; **asceticism** *see 667*, **fasting** *see 515*; **purgation**, purgatory, "cold purgatorial fires"—T S ELIOT; **sackcloth and ashes**; hair shirt; **Lent**; Day of Atonement, Yom Kippur

verbs

4 **to atone**, atone for, propitiate, expiate, compensate, restitute, recompense, redress, redeem, repair, satisfy, give satisfaction, **make amends, make reparation** *or* **compensation** *or* **expiation** *or* **restitution**, make good *or* right, set right, **make up for**, make matters up, square it, square things, make it quits, pay the forfeit *or* penalty, pay one's dues (*informal*), wipe off old scores; wipe the slate clean; set one's house in order; live down, unlive

5 **to apologize, beg pardon, ask forgiveness**, beg indulgence, express regret; take back; get *or* fall down on one's knees, get down on one's marrowbones (*informal*)

6 **to do penance**, flagellate oneself, mortify oneself, mortify one's flesh, make oneself miserable, shrive oneself, purge oneself, cleanse oneself of guilt, stand in a white sheet, repent in sackcloth and ashes, wear a hair shirt, wear sackcloth *or* sackcloth and ashes; receive absolution

adjectives

7 **atoning, propitiatory, expiatory**, piacular, reparative, reparatory, restitutive, restitutory, restitutional, redressing, recompensing, compensatory, compensational, righting, squaring; redemptive, redeeming, reclamatory, satisfactional; **apologetic, apologetical**; repentant, repenting; **penitential**, purgative, purgatorial; lustral, lustrative, lustrational, cleansing, purifying; ascetic

659 GOOD PERSON

nouns

1 good person, fine person, good *or* fine man *or* woman *or* child, worthy, prince, one of nature's gentlemen, man *or* woman after one's own heart; *persona grata* (*Latin*), acceptable person; **good fellow**, capital fellow, **good sort**, right sort, a decent sort of fellow, good lot (*informal*), no end of a fellow; real person, real man *or* woman, mensch (*US informal*); **gentleman**, perfect gentleman, a gentleman and a scholar; **lady**, perfect lady; **gem**, jewel, pearl, diamond; rough diamond, diamond in the rough; honest man *see 644.8*

2 (*informal terms*) **good guy**, crackerjack, brick, trump, good egg, stout fellow, nice guy, Mr Nice Guy, good Joe (*US*), likely lad, no slouch, doll, living doll, pussycat, **sweetheart, sweetie**

3 **good** *or* **respectable citizen**, excellent *or* exemplary citizen, good neighbour, burgher, taxpayer, **pillar of society**, pillar of the church, salt of the earth; Christian *and* true Christian (*both informal*)

4 **paragon, ideal**, beau ideal, nonpareil, person to look up to, *chevalier sans peur et sans reproche* (*French*), **good example, role model**, shining example; exemplar, epitome; **model, pattern, standard**, norm, mirror, "the observed of all observers"—SHAKESPEARE; *Übermensch* (*German; Nietzsche*); **standout**, one in a thousand *or* ten thousand *or* a million, man of men, a man among men, woman of women, a woman among women

5 hero, god, demigod, phoenix; heroine, goddess, demigoddess; idol

6 holy man; great soul, mahatma; guru, *rishi* (*Sanskrit*); *starets* (*Russian*); saint, angel *see* 679

660 BAD PERSON

nouns

1 bad person, bad man *or* woman *or* child, unworthy *or* disreputable person, unworthy, disreputable, **undesirable**, *persona non grata* (*Latin*), unacceptable *or* unwanted *or* objectionable person, baddy *and* bad news (*all informal*); bad example

2 **wretch**, mean *or* miserable wretch, **beggarly fellow**, **beggar**, **blighter** (*informal*); **bum** *and* bummer *and* lowlifer *and* lowlife *and* **mucker** (*all informal*), caitiff, budmash (*India*), pilgarlic; devil, **poor devil**, *pauvre diable* (*French*), poor creature, *mauvais sujet* (*French*); **sad case**; **good-for-nothing, good-for-naught, no-good** (*informal*), ne'er-do-well, wastrel, *vaurien* (*French*), worthless fellow; **down-and-out, derelict**, tramp, hobo (*US*), beachcomber, **drifter**, drunkard, vagrant, vag (*Australian informal*), vagabond, truant, skid-row bum *and* Bowery bum (*both US*), stiff *and* bindlestiff (*both US informal*), swagman *or* sundowner (*both Australian*); human wreck

3 **rascal**, precious rascal, rogue, knave, **scoundrel**, villain, blackguard, **scamp, scallywag** (*informal*), nasty piece of work, waster, spalpeen (*Irish*), rapscallion, **devil**; shyster; sneak

4 "a rascally yeaforsooth knave", "a foul-mouthed and calumnious knave", "poor cuckoldy knave", "a poor, decayed, ingenious, foolish, rascally knave", "an arrant, rascally, beggarly, lousy knave", "a slipper and subtle knave, a finder of occasions", "a whoreson, beetle-headed, flap-ear'd knave", "filthy, worsted-stocking knave", "a lily-livered, action-taking knave", "a knave; a rascal; an eater of broken meats; a base, proud, shallow, beggarly, three-suited, hundred-pound, filthy, worsted-stocking knave"—ALL SHAKESPEARE

5 **reprobate**, recreant, **miscreant**, bad *or* sorry lot (*informal*), bad egg *and* wrong number (*both informal*), bad'un *or* wrong'un (*both informal*); scapegrace, black sheep; lost soul, lost sheep, *âme damnée* (*French*), backslider, recidivist, fallen angel; degenerate, pervert; profligate, **lecher** *see* 665.11; trollop, **whore** *see* 665.14, 16; **pimp** *see* 665.18

6 (*informal terms*) **arsehole, prick, bastard, sod,** son of a bitch *or* SOB (*US & Canadian*), **jerk,** horse's ass (*US*), creep, git, motherfucker, mother, dork, **shit,** turd, birdturd, shithead, shitface, cuntface, dickhead, scumbag, fart, **louse,** meanie, **heel,** shitheel, toerag, tosser, **rat, stinker,** stinkard, pill, bugger, dirtbag, dork, geek, dweeb, twerp, sleaze, sleazoid, sleazebag, bad lot, bad hat; **yob** *or* **yobbo,** lager lout, hood (*US*), **hooligan** *see* 593.4

7 beast, **animal; cur,** dog, hound, whelp, mongrel; **reptile,** viper, serpent, snake; vermin, varmint (*informal*), hyena; **swine,** pig; **skunk,** polecat; insect, worm

8 cad, bounder *and* rotter (*informal*)

9 **wrongdoer, malefactor, sinner,** transgressor, delinquent; malfeasor, misfeasor, nonfeasor; misdemeanant, misdemeanist; **culprit, offender; evil person, evil man** *or* **woman** *or* **child, evildoer** *see* 593

10 criminal, felon, perpetrator, crook (*informal*), public enemy, **lawbreaker,** scofflaw (*US informal*); **gangster,** mobster *and* wiseguy (*both US informal*), **racketeer; swindler** *see* 357.3; **thief** *see* 483; **thug** *see* 593.3; **desperado,** desperate criminal; **outlaw,** fugitive, **convict,** jailbird, gaolbird; gallows bird (*informal*); **traitor,** betrayer, quisling, Judas, double-dealer, two-timer (*informal*), **deceiver** *see* 357

11 **the underworld,** gangland, gangdom, **organized crime,** organized crime family, the rackets, the mob, the syndicate, the Mafia, Cosa Nostra, Black Hand, Triad; **gangsterism; gangster,** ganglord, gangleader, caporegime *or* capo, button man, soldier, Yardie

12 **the wicked,** the bad, the evil, the unrighteous, the reprobate; sons of men, sons of Belial, sons *or* children of the devil, limbs *or* get *or* imps of Satan, children of darkness; **scum of the earth,** dregs of society

661 DISREPUTE

nouns

1 **disrepute, ill repute,** bad repute, bad *or* poor reputation, evil repute *or* reputation, ill fame, shady *or* unsavoury reputation, **bad name,** bad odour, bad report, bad character; **disesteem, dishonour,** public dishonour, **discredit; disfavour,** ill-favour; disapprobation *see* 510.1

2 **disreputability,** disreputableness, **notoriety;** discreditableness, dishonourableness, unsavouriness, **unrespectability;** disgracefulness, **shamefulness**

3 **baseness, lowness, meanness, crumminess** (*informal*), poorness, pettiness, paltriness, smallness, littleness, pokiness, cheesiness (*informal*), beggarliness, **shabbiness, shoddiness, squalor,** sleaze, sleaziness, scrubbiness, scumminess, scabbiness, scurviness, scruffiness, shittiness (*informal*); **abjectness, wretchedness,** miserableness, despicableness, contemptibleness, contemptibility, abominableness, execrableness, obnoxiousness; **vulgarity,** tastelessness, crudity, crudeness, tackiness *and* chintziness (*both informal*); **vileness** *see* 98.2, foulness, rankness, fulsomeness, grossness, nefariousness, heinousness, **atrociousness,** monstrousness, enormity; degradation, debasement, depravity

4 **infamy,** infamousness; **ignominy,** ignominiousness; ingloriousness, **ignobility,** odium, obloquy, opprobrium,

"a long farewell to all my greatness"—SHAKESPEARE; depluming, displuming, loss of honour *or* name *or* repute *or* face; degradation, comedown (*informal*), **demotion** *see* 447

5 **disgrace, scandal, humiliation; shame,** dirty shame *and* low-down dirty shame (*both informal*), crying or burning shame; **reproach,** byword, byword of reproach, a disgrace to one's name

6 **stigma,** stigmatism, onus; **brand,** badge of infamy; **slur,** reproach, censure, reprimand, imputation, aspersion, reflection or reflexion, stigmatization; pillorying; **black eye** (*informal*), black mark; **disparagement** see 512; **stain, taint,** attaint, **tarnish,** blur, **smirch,** smutch or smooch, smudge, **smear,** spot, blot, blot on or in one's escutcheon or scutcheon; bend or bar sinister (*heraldry*); baton, champain, point champain (*all heraldry*); mark of Cain; broad arrow

verbs

7 **to incur disgrace,** incur disesteem or dishonour or discredit, get a black eye (*informal*), be shamed, earn a bad name or reproach or reproof, forfeit one's good opinion, fall into disrepute, seal one's infamy; lose one's good name, **lose face,** lose countenance, lose credit, **lose caste; disgrace oneself,** lower oneself, demean oneself, drag one's banner in the dust, degrade or debase oneself, act beneath oneself, dirty or soil one's hands, get one's hands dirty, sully or lower oneself, derogate, stoop, descend, ride for a fall, fall from one's high estate, foul one's own nest; **scandalize,** make oneself notorious, put one's good name in jeopardy; compromise oneself; raise eyebrows, cause eyebrows to raise, cause tongues to wag

8 **to disgrace, dishonour, discredit,** reflect discredit upon, bring into discredit, reproach, cast reproach upon, be a reproach to; **shame, put to shame,** impute shame to, hold up to shame; hold up to public shame or public scorn or public ridicule, pillory, bring shame upon, **humiliate** see 137.4; **degrade, debase** see 447.3, deplume, displume, defrock, unfrock, bring low

9 **to stigmatize, brand; stain, besmirch,** smirch, tarnish, taint, attaint, blot, **blacken, smear,** **sully,** soil, defile, vilify, **slur,** cast a slur upon, blow upon; disapprove see 510.10; **disparage, defame** see 512.9; censure, reprimand, **give a black eye** (*informal*), give a black mark, put in one's bad or black books; give a bad name, give a dog a bad name; expose, expose to infamy; pillory, gibbet; burn or hang in effigy; **skewer,** impale, crucify

adjectives

10 **disreputable, discreditable, dishonourable,** unsavoury, shady, **seamy, sordid; unrespectable, ignoble, ignominious, infamous,** inglorious; notorious; unpraiseworthy; derogatory see 512.13

11 **disgraceful, shameful,** pitiful, deplorable, opprobrious, sad, sorry, too bad; degrading, debasing, demeaning, beneath one, beneath one's dignity, *infra dignitatem* (*Latin*), infra dig (*informal*), unbecoming, unworthy of one; cheap, gutter; **humiliating,** humiliative; **scandalous,** shocking, outrageous

12 **base, low,** low-rent and low-down (*both informal*), **mean,** crummy (*informal*), poor, petty, paltry, small, little, **shabby, shoddy, squalid,** sleazy, lumpen, scrubby, scummy, scabby, **scurvy,** scruffy, mangy (*informal*), measly and cheesy (*both informal*), poky,

beggarly, **wretched, miserable,** abject, **despicable, contemptible,** abominable, execrable, obnoxious, **vulgar,** tasteless, crude, **tacky** and chintzy (*both informal*); **disgusting, odious** see 98.18, vile, foul, **dirty,** rank, fulsome, gross, flagrant, grave, arrant, nefarious, heinous, reptilian, **atrocious,** monstrous, unspeakable, unmentionable; degraded, debased, depraved

13 **in disrepute,** in bad repute, in bad odour; **in disfavour,** in discredit, in one's bad or black books, out of favour, out of countenance, at a discount; **in disgrace, in the doghouse** (*informal*), under a cloud; scandal-plagued or ridden; stripped of reputation, disgraced, discredited, dishonoured, shamed, loaded with shame, unable to show one's face; **in trouble**

14 **unrenowned,** renownless, nameless, inglorious, **unnotable, unnoted,** unnoticed, unremarked, **undistinguished, unfamed,** uncelebrated, unsung, unhonoured, unglorified, unpopular; no credit to; **unknown,** little known, obscure, unheard-of, *ignotus* (*Latin*)

adverbs

15 **disreputably, discreditably, dishonourably,** unrespectably, ignobly, ignominiously, **infamously,** ingloriously

16 **disgracefully, scandalously,** shockingly, deplorably, outrageously; **shamefully,** to one's shame, to one's shame be it spoken

17 **basely, meanly,** poorly, pettily, **shabbily, shoddily,** scurvily, **wretchedly, miserably,** abjectly, **despicably, contemptibly,** abominably, execrably, obnoxiously, **odiously** see 98.26, **vilely,** foully, grossly, flagrantly, arrantly, nefariously, heinously, **atrociously,** monstrously

662 REPUTE

nouns

1 **repute, reputation,** "the bubble reputation"—SHAKESPEARE; **name,** character, figure; **fame, famousness, renown,** "that last infirmity of noble mind"—MILTON, **kudos,** report, **glory;** éclat, **celebrity, popularity,** recognition, a place in the sun; popular acceptance or favour, vogue; **acclaim, public acclaim,** réclame, **publicity;** notoriety, notoriousness, talk of the town; **exposure;** play and air-play (*both informal*)

2 **reputability,** reputableness; good reputation, good name, **good** or **high repute,** good report, good track record (*informal*), good odour, face, fair name, name to conjure with

3 **esteem,** estimation, **honour, regard, respect,** approval, approbation, account, favour, consideration, **credit,** points and Brownie points (*both informal*)

4 **prestige, honour; dignity; rank, standing,** stature, high place, position, station, face, **status**

5 **distinction, mark, note; importance, consequence,** significance; **notability, prominence, eminence, preeminence, greatness,** conspicuousness, outstandingness; **stardom;** elevation, exaltation, exaltedness, loftiness, high and

mightiness (*informal*); nobility, grandeur, sublimity; excellence *see* 998.1, supereminence *see* 998.2

6 **illustriousness, lustre,** brilliance *or* brilliancy, radiance, splendour, resplendence *or* resplendency, refulgence *or* refulgency, refulgentness, **glory,** blaze of glory, nimbus, halo, aura, envelope; charisma, mystique, glamour, numinousness, magic; cult of personality, personality cult

7 (*posthumous fame*) **memory, remembrance,** blessed *or* sacred memory, legend, heroic legend *or* myth; **immortality,** lasting *or* undying fame, niche in the hall of fame, secure place in history; immortal name,

"ghost of a great name"—Lucan

8 **glorification, ennoblement,** dignification, **exaltation,** elevation, enskying, enskyment, magnification, aggrandizement; enthronement; immortalization, enshrinement; beatification, canonization, sainting, sanctification; **deification, apotheosis;** lionization

9 **celebrity,** celeb (*informal*), man *or* woman of mark *or* note, person of note *or* consequence, **notable, notability, luminary, great man *or* woman,** master spirit, worthy, name, **big name,** figure, public figure, **somebody; important person, VIP** *and* standout (*both informal*), personage *see* 996.8, one in a hundred *or* thousand *or* million etc; cynosure, model, very model, ideal type,

"the observed of all observers"—Shakespeare, **idol,** popular idol, heart-throb, tin god *or* little tin god (*informal*); lion, social lion; hero, heroine, popular hero, folk hero, superhero, **star, superstar,** megastar, hot stuff (*informal*); cult figure; **immortal;** luminaries, galaxy, pleiad, constellation; semicelebrity

verbs

10 **to be somebody,** be something, **impress,** charismatize; **figure,** make *or* cut a figure, cut a dash *and* make a splash (*both informal*), make a noise in the world, make *or* leave one's mark; live, **flourish; shine,** glitter, gleam, glow

11 **to gain recognition,** be recognized, get a reputation, **make a name *or* make a name for oneself,** make oneself known, come into one's own, come to the front *or* fore, come into vogue; **burst onto the scene,** become an overnight success *or* sensation, come onto the scene (*informal*), come out of the woodwork *or* out of nowhere *or* out of the shadows (*all informal*); gain points *or* Brownie points (*informal*)

12 **to honour,** confer *or* bestow honour upon; **dignify,** adorn, grace; **distinguish,** signalize, confer distinction on, give credit where credit is due

13 **to glorify,** glamorize; **exalt,** elevate, ensky, raise, uplift, set up, **ennoble,** aggrandize, magnify, exalt to the skies; crown; throne, enthrone; immortalize, enshrine, hand one's name down to posterity, make legendary; beatify, canonize, saint, sanctify; **deify,** apotheosize, apotheose; **lionize**

14 **to reflect honour,** lend credit *or* distinction, shed a lustre, redound to one's honour, give one a reputation

adjectives

15 **reputable,** highly reputed, **estimable, esteemed,** much *or* highly esteemed, **honourable,** honoured; **meritorious,** worth one's salt, noble, worthy, creditable; respected, respectable, highly respectable; revered, reverend, venerable, venerated, worshipful; **well-thought-of,** highly regarded, held in esteem, in good odour, in favour, in high favour; in one's good books; prestigious

16 **distinguished,** distingué; **noted, notable,** marked, of note, of mark; **famous,** famed, honoured, **renowned, celebrated, popular,** acclaimed, much acclaimed, sought-after, hot *and* world-class (*both informal*), **notorious, well-known,** best-known, in everyone's mouth, on everyone's tongue *or* lips, talked-of, talked-about; far-famed, far-heard; fabled, legendary, mythical

17 **prominent, conspicuous, outstanding,** stickout (*informal*), much in evidence, to the front, in the limelight (*informal*); **important,** consequential, significant

18 **eminent, high, exalted,** elevated, enskyed, lofty, sublime, held in awe, awesome; immortal; **great,** big (*informal*), **grand;** excellent *see* 998.12, 13, 15, supereminent, mighty, high and mighty (*informal*); glorified, ennobled, magnified, aggrandized; enthroned, throned; immortalized, shrined, enshrined; beatified, canonized, sainted, sanctified; **idolized, godlike, deified,** apotheosized

19 **illustrious,** lustrous, glorious, brilliant, radiant, splendid, splendorous, splendrous, splendent, resplendent, bright, shining; charismatic, glamorous, numinous, magic, magical

adverbs

20 **reputably, estimably, honourably,** nobly, respectably, worthily, creditably

21 **famously, notably,** notedly, **notoriously,** popularly, celebratedly; **prominently, eminently,** conspicuously, outstandingly; **illustriously,** gloriously

663 SENSUALITY

nouns

1 **sensuality,** sensualness, sensualism; appetitiveness, appetite; **voluptuousness,** luxuriousness, luxury; **unchastity** *see* 665; **pleasure-seeking;** sybaritism; **self-indulgence, hedonism,** Cyrenaic hedonism, Cyrenaicism, ethical hedonism, psychological hedonism, hedonics, hedonic calculus; epicurism, epicureanism; pleasure principle, *Lustprinzip* (*German*); **instant gratification;** sensuousness *see* 24.1

2 **carnality,** carnal-mindedness; **fleshliness,** flesh; animal *or* carnal nature, the flesh, the beast, Adam, the Old Adam, the offending Adam, fallen state *or* nature, lapsed state *or* nature, postlapsarian state *or* nature; **animality, animalism, bestiality,** beastliness, brutishness, **brutality;** coarseness, grossness; swinishness; **earthiness,** unspirituality, nonspirituality, materialism

3 sensualist, voluptuary, pleasure-seeker, sybarite, Cyrenaic, Sardanapalus, Heliogabalus, hedonist, bon vivant (*French*), carpet knight; epicure, epicurean; gourmet, gourmand; swine

verbs

4 to sensualize, carnalize, coarsen, brutify; carpe diem (*L, seize the day*), live for the moment

adjectives

5 sensual, sensualist, sensualistic; appetitive; voluptuous, luxurious; unchaste see 665.23, hedonistic, pleasure-seeking, pleasure-bent, bent on pleasure, luxury-loving, hedonic, epicurean, sybaritic; Cyrenaic; sensory, sensuous

6 carnal, carnal-minded, fleshly, bodily, physical; Adamic, fallen, lapsed, postlapsarian; animal, animalistic; brutish, brutal, brute; bestial, beastly, beastlike; Circean; coarse, gross; swinish; orgiastic; earthy, unspiritual, nonspiritual, material, materialistic

664 CHASTITY

nouns

1 chastity, virtue, virtuousness, honour; purity, cleanness, cleanliness; whiteness, snowiness; immaculacy, immaculateness, spotlessness, stainlessness, taintlessness, blotlessness, unspottedness, unstainedness, unblottedness, untaintedness, unblemishedness, unsoiledness, unsulliedness, undefiledness, untarnishedness; uncorruptness; sexual innocence, innocence see 657

2 decency, seemliness, propriety, decorum, decorousness, elegance, delicacy; modesty, shame, pudicity, pudency

3 continence or continency; abstemiousness, abstaining, abstinence see 668.2; celibacy; virginity, intactness, maidenhood, maidenhead; Platonic love; marital fidelity or faithfulness

adjectives

4 chaste, virtuous; pure, purehearted, pure in heart; clean, cleanly; immaculate, spotless, blotless, stainless, taintless, white, snowy, pure or white as driven snow; unsoiled, unsullied, undefiled, untarnished, unstained, unspotted, untainted, unblemished, unblotted, uncorrupt;
"as chaste as Diana", "as chaste as unsunn'd snow"—BOTH SHAKESPEARE, "chaste as morning dew"— EDWARD YOUNG; sexually innocent, innocent see 657.6, 7

5 decent, modest, decorous, delicate, elegant, proper, becoming, seemly

6 continent; abstemious, abstinent see 668.10; celibate; virginal, virgin, maidenly, vestal, intact; Platonic

7 undebauched, undissipated, undissolute, unwanton, unlicentious

665 UNCHASTITY

nouns

1 unchastity, unchasteness; unvirtuousness; impurity, uncleanness, uncleanliness, taintedness, soiledness, sulliedness; indecency see 666

2 incontinence, uncontinence; intemperance see 669; unrestraint see 430.3

3 profligacy, dissoluteness, licentiousness, licence, unbridledness, wildness, fastness, rakishness, gallantry, libertinism, libertinage; dissipation, debauchery, debauchment; venery, wenching, whoring, womanizing

4 wantonness, waywardness; looseness, laxity, lightness, loose morals, easy virtue, whorishness, chambering, promiscuity, sleeping around *and* swinging (*both informal*)

5 lasciviousness, lechery, lecherousness, lewdness, bawdiness, dirtiness, salacity, salaciousness, carnality, animality, fleshliness, sexuality, sexiness, lust, lustfulness,
"an expense of spirit in a waste of shame is lust in action"—SHAKESPEARE; obscenity see 666.4; prurience *or* pruriency, sexual itch, concupiscence, lickerishness, libidinousness, randiness, horniness (*informal*), lubricity, lubriciousness, sensuality, eroticism, goatishness; satyrism, satyriasis, gynecomania; nymphomania, furor uterinus (*Latin*), hysteromania, uteromania, clitoromania; erotomania, eroticomania, aphrodisiomania

6 seduction, seducement, betrayal; violation, abuse; debauchment, defilement, ravishment, ravage, despoilment, fate worse than death; priapism; defloration, deflowering; rape, sexual *or* criminal assault; date *or* acquaintance rape

7 (*illicit sexual intercourse*) adultery, criminal conversation *or* congress *or* cohabitation, extramarital *or* premarital sex, extramarital *or* premarital relations, extracurricular sex *or* relations (*informal*), fornication; free love, free-lovism; incest; concubinage; cuckoldry

8 prostitution, harlotry, whoredom, street-walking; soliciting, solicitation; Mrs Warren's profession; whoremonging, whoremastery, pimping, pandering

9 brothel, house of prostitution, house of assignation, house of joy *or* ill repute *or* ill fame, whorehouse, bawdyhouse, massage parlour, knocking shop (*informal*), disorderly house, cathouse *and* sporting house (*both US*), bordello, bagnio, stew, dive, den of vice, den *or* sink of iniquity, crib, joint; red-light district, tenderloin (*US*), stews, street of fallen women

10 libertine, swinger (*informal*), profligate, rake, rakehell, rip (*informal*), roué, wanton, womanizer, cocksman (*informal*), walking phallus, debauchee, rounder (*old*), wolf (*informal*), woman chaser, skirt chaser (*informal*), gay dog, gay deceiver, gallant, philanderer, lover-boy (*informal*), lady-killer, Lothario, Don Juan, Casanova

11 lecher, satyr, goat, old goat, dirty old man; whorer *or* whoremonger (*both old*), whoremaster, whorehound (*informal*); Priapus; gynecomaniac; erotomaniac, eroticomaniac, aphrodisiomaniac

12 seducer, betrayer, deceiver; debaucher, ravisher, ravager, violator, despoiler, defiler; raper, rapist

13 adulterer, cheater, fornicator; adulteress, fornicatress, fornicatrix

14 strumpet, trollop, wench, hussy, slut, slag, scrubber, jade, baggage, cocotte (*French*), grisette;

tart *and* floozy (*both informal*), broad (*US & Canadian informal*), bitch, drab, trull, quean, harridan, Jezebel, wanton, whore (*informal*), bad woman, **loose woman**, easy woman (*informal*), easy lay (*informal*), woman of easy virtue, frail sister; pickup; nymphomaniac, nympho (*informal*), hysteromaniac, uteromaniac, clitoromaniac; nymphet

15 **demimonde**, demimondaine, demirep; **courtesan**, adventuress, **seductress**, femme fatale, vampire, vamp, temptress; hetaera, houri, harem girl, odalisque; Jezebel, Messalina, Delilah, Thais, Phryne, Aspasia, Lais

16 **prostitute, harlot, whore,** *fille de joie* (*French*), daughter of joy, call girl (*informal*), **scarlet woman**, unfortunate woman, painted woman, fallen woman, erring sister, **streetwalker**, hustler *and* **hooker** (*both US informal*), woman of the town, *poule* (*French*), stew, meretrix, Cyprian, Paphian; male prostitute, rent boy; white slave

17 **mistress**, woman, **kept woman**, kept mistress, **paramour**, concubine, doxy, playmate, spiritual *or* unofficial wife; **common-law wife**, live-in lover (*informal*)

18 **procurer**, pimp, pander *or* panderer, *maquereau* (*French*), mack *or* mackman, ponce (*informal*); **bawd; gigolo,** fancy man; procuress, **madam** (*informal*); white slaver

verbs

19 **to be promiscuous**, sleep around *and* swing (*both informal*); **debauch, wanton,** rake, chase women, womanize, whore, sow one's wild oats; **philander; dissipate** *see* 669.6; fornicate, **cheat, commit adultery**, have a bit on the side (*informal*)

20 **to seduce, betray, deceive**, mislead, lead astray, lead down the garden *or* the primrose path; **debauch, ravish**, ravage, despoil, ruin; **deflower,** pop one's cherry (*US informal*); **defile**, soil, sully; **violate**, abuse, interfere with; **rape, force**

21 **to prostitute oneself**, walk the streets, sell *or* peddle one's ass (*US informal*), streetwalk; pimp, procure, pander

22 **to cuckold**; wear horns, wear the horn

adjectives

23 **unchaste, unvirtuous**, unvirginal; **impure, unclean; indecent** *see* 666.5; soiled, sullied, smirched, besmirched, defiled, tainted, maculate

24 **incontinent**, uncontinent; **orgiastic**; intemperate *see* 669.7; unrestrained

25 **profligate, licentious**, unbridled, untrammelled, uninhibited, free; **dissolute, dissipated, debauched,** abandoned; **wild, fast,** gallant, gay, rakish; rakehell, rakehellish, rakehelly

26 **wanton, wayward,** Paphian; **loose,** lax, slack, loose-moraled, of loose morals, of easy virtue, easy (*informal*), **light,** no better than she should be, whorish, chambering, **promiscuous**

27 **freeloving; adulterous**, illicit, extramarital, premarital; incestuous

28 **prostitute**, prostituted, **whorish, harlot,** scarlet, fallen, meretricious, streetwalking, hustling (*informal*), on the town *or* streets, **on the game** (*informal*), on the *pavé*, in the life (*US*)

29 **lascivious, lecherous, sexy, salacious, carnal,** animal, **sexual, lustful,** ithyphallic, **hot,** horny (*informal*); prurient, itching, itchy (*informal*); concupiscent, lickerish, libidinous, randy, horny (*informal*), lubricious; **lewd, bawdy,** adult, X-rated, hard, pornographic, porno (*informal*), **dirty, obscene** *see* 666.9; erotic, **sensual,** fleshly; goatish, satyric, priapic, gynecomaniacal; nymphomaniacal, hysteromaniacal, uteromaniacal, clitoromaniacal; erotomaniacal, eroticomaniacal, aphrodisiomaniacal

666 INDECENCY

nouns

1 **indecency, indelicacy,** inelegance *or* inelegancy, **indecorousness**, indecorum, **impropriety** *see* 638.1, inappropriateness, unseemliness, indiscretion, indiscreetness; **unchastity** *see* 665

2 **immodesty**, unmodestness, impudicity; exhibitionism; **shamelessness**, unembarrassedness; **brazenness** *see* 142.2, brassiness, pertness, forwardness, boldness, procacity, bumptiousness; **flagrancy**, notoriousness, scandal, scandalousness

3 **vulgarity** *see* 497, **uncouthness, coarseness, crudeness, grossness,** rankness, rawness, raunchiness (*informal*); **earthiness,** frankness; **spiciness, raciness,** saltiness

4 **obscenity, dirtiness,** bawdry, raunch (*informal*), **ribaldry, pornography,** porno *and* porn (*both informal*), hard *or* hard-core pornography, soft *or* soft-core pornography, salacity, **smut, dirt, filth; lewdness, bawdiness,** salaciousness, **smuttiness, foulness, filthiness,** nastiness, vileness, offensiveness; scurrility, fescenninity; Rabelaisianism; erotic art *or* literature, pornographic art *or* literature; sexploitation; blue movie *and* dirty movie *and* porno film *and* skin flick (*all informal*), adult movie, stag film (*informal*), X-rated movie; pornographomania, erotographomania, iconolagny, erotology; **dirty talk, scatology** *see* 523.9

adjectives

5 **indecent, indelicate, inelegant, indecorous, improper,** inappropriate, **unseemly, unbecoming,** indiscreet

6 **immodest,** unmodest; exhibitionistic; **shameless,** unashamed, unembarrassed, unabashed, unblushing, **brazen,** brazenfaced, brassy; **forward,** bold, pert, procacious (*old*), bumptious; **flagrant,** notorious, scandalous

7 **risqué,** risky, **racy,** salty, spicy, **off-colour,** suggestive, scabrous

8 **vulgar, uncouth, coarse, gross,** rank, raw, broad, low, foul, gutter; **earthy,** frank, pulling no punches

9 **obscene, lewd,** adult, **bawdy,** ithyphallic, **ribald, pornographic, salacious,** sultry (*informal*), lurid, **dirty, smutty,** raunchy (*informal*), blue, smoking-room, impure, unchaste, unclean, **foul, filthy,** nasty, vile, fulsome, offensive, unprintable, unrepeatable, not fit for mixed company; scurrilous, scurrile, Fescennine; **foulmouthed,** foul-tongued, foul-spoken; Rabelaisian

667 ASCETICISM

nouns

1 asceticism, austerity, **self-denial**, self-abnegation, **rigour**; **puritanism**, eremitism, anchoritism, anchorite *or* anchoritic monasticism, monasticism, monachism; Sabbatarianism; Albigensianism, Waldensianism, Catharism; yoga; mortification, self-mortification, maceration, flagellation; **abstinence** *see* 668.2; belt-tightening, fasting *see* 515; voluntary poverty, mendicantism, Franciscanism; Trappism

2 ascetic, puritan, Sabbatarian; Albigensian, Waldensian, Catharist; **abstainer** *see* 668.4; anchorite, **hermit** *see* 584.5; yogi, yogin; sannyasi, bhikshu, dervish, fakir, flagellant, Penitente; mendicant, Franciscan, Discalced *or* barefooted Carmelite; Trappist

verbs

3 to deny oneself; abstain, tighten one's belt; flagellate oneself, wear a hair shirt, make oneself miserable

adjectives

4 ascetic, austere, self-denying, self-abnegating, **rigorous, rigoristic**; **puritanical**, eremitic, anchoritic, Sabbatarian; **penitential**; Albigensian, Waldensian, Catharist; **abstinent** *see* 668.10; mendicant, discalced, barefoot, wedded to poverty, Franciscan; Trappist; flagellant

668 TEMPERANCE

nouns

1 temperance, temperateness, **moderation**, moderateness, sophrosyne; golden mean, via media, *juste milieu (French)*; nothing in excess, sobriety, soberness, frugality, forbearance, abnegation; renunciation, renouncement, forgoing; denial, **self-denial**; restraint, constraint, **self-restraint**; **self-control**, self-reining, self-mastery, **discipline**, self-discipline

2 abstinence, abstention, abstainment, **abstemiousness**, refraining, refrainment, avoidance, eschewal, denying *or* refusing oneself, saying no to, passing up *(informal)*; **total abstinence, teetotalism**, nephalism, Rechabitism; the pledge; Encratism, Shakerism; Pythagorism, Pythagoreanism; sexual abstinence, celibacy *see* 565; chastity *see* 664; gymnosophy; Stoicism; vegetarianism, veganism, fruitarianism; plain living, spare diet, simple diet; Spartan fare, Lenten fare; fish day, Friday, banyan day; fast *see* 515.2, 3; **continence** *see* 664.3; asceticism *see* 667

3 prohibition, prohibitionism

4 abstainer, abstinent; **teetotaler**, teetotalist; nephalist, Rechabite, hydropot, water-drinker; vegetarian, vegan, fruitarian; banian, banya; gymnosophist; Pythagorean, Pythagorist; Encratite, Apostolici, Shaker; ascetic *see* 667.2; nonsmoker, nondrinker, etc

5 **prohibitionist, dry** *(informal)*

verbs

6 to restrain oneself, constrain oneself, curb oneself, hold back, **avoid excess; limit oneself, restrict oneself; control oneself**, control one's appetites, repress *or* inhibit one's desires, contain oneself, discipline oneself, master oneself, exercise self-control *or* self-restraint, keep oneself under control, keep in *or* within bounds, keep within compass *or* limits, know when one has had enough, **deny** *or* refuse oneself, **say no** *or* just say no; live plainly *or* simply *or* frugally; mortify oneself, mortify the flesh, control the fleshy lusts, control the carnal man *or* the old Adam,
"let the passions be amenable to reason"—Cicero; eat to live, not live to eat; eat sparingly

7 to abstain, abstain from, refrain, **refrain from, forbear, forgo**, spare, withhold, hold back, **avoid, shun**, eschew, **pass up** *(informal)*, **keep from**, keep *or* stand *or* hold aloof from, have nothing to do with, take no part in, have no hand in, **let alone**, let well enough alone, let go by, **deny oneself**, do without, go without, make do without, not *or* never touch, keep hands off

8 to swear off, renounce, forswear, give up, abandon, stop, discontinue; take the pledge, get on the wagon *(informal)*, get on the water wagon *(US informal)*; kick the habit *(informal)*, dry out

adjectives

9 temperate, moderate, sober, frugal, restrained; **sparing**, stinting, measured

10 abstinent, abstentious, **abstemious**; teetotal, sworn off, on the wagon *(informal)*, on the water wagon *(US informal)*; nephalistic, Rechabite; Encratic, Apostolic, Shaker; Pythagorean; sexually abstinent, celibate, chaste; Stoic; vegetarian, veganistic, fruitarian; Spartan, Lenten; maigre, meatless; **continent** *see* 664.6; ascetic

11 prohibitionist, antisaloon, dry *(informal)*

adverbs

12 temperately, moderately, sparingly, stintingly, frugally, in moderation, within compass *or* bounds

669 INTEMPERANCE

nouns

1 intemperance, intemperateness, **indulgence, self-indulgence; overindulgence**, overdoing; **unrestraint**, unconstraint, indiscipline, uncontrol; **immoderation**, immoderacy, immoderateness; inordinacy, inordinateness; **excess, excessiveness**, too much; prodigality, extravagance; crapulence *or* crapulency, crapulousness; **incontinence** *see* 665.2; **swinishness, gluttony** *see* 672; drunkenness *see* 88.1

2 dissipation, licentiousness; **riotous living**, free living, high living *(informal)*, fast *or* killing pace, burning the candle at both ends; **debauchery**, debauchment; **carousal** *see* 88.5, carousing, carouse; **debauch, orgy**, saturnalia

3 dissipater, rounder *(old)*, free liver, high liver *(informal)*; nighthawk *and* nightowl *(both informal)*; **playboy**, partyer, partygoer, party girl

verbs

4 **to indulge**, indulge oneself, indulge one's appetites, "indulge in easy vices"—SAMUEL JOHNSON, deny oneself nothing *or* not at all; **give oneself up to**, give free course to, give free rein to; live well *or* high, live high on the hog (*US informal*), live off the fat of the land; indulge in, luxuriate in, wallow in; roll in

5 **to overindulge**, **overdo**, **carry to excess**, carry too far, go the limit, go the whole hog (*informal*), know no limits, not know when to stop, bite off more than one can chew, spread oneself too thin; dine not wisely but too well; live above *or* beyond one's means

6 **to dissipate**, plunge into dissipation, **debauch**, **wanton**, **carouse**, run riot, live hard *or* fast, squander one's money in riotous living, burn the candle at both ends, keep up a fast *or* killing pace, live in the fast lane (*informal*), sow one's wild oats, have one's fling, **party** (*informal*), "eat, drink, and be merry"—BIBLE

adjectives

7 **intemperate**, **indulgent**, **self-indulgent**; **overindulgent**, overindulging, unthrifty, unfrugal, **immoderate**, inordinate, **excessive**, too much, prodigal, extravagant, extreme, unmeasured, unlimited; crapulous, crapulent; undisciplined, uncontrolled, unbridled, unconstrained, uninhibited, **unrestrained**; **incontinent** see 665.24; **swinish**, **gluttonous** see 672.6; bibulous

8 **licentious**, **dissipated**, **riotous**, **dissolute**, **debauched**; free-living, high-living (*informal*)

9 **orgiastic**, saturnalian, corybantic

adverbs

10 **intemperately**, prodigally, **immoderately**, inordinately, excessively, **in** *or* **to excess**, to extremes, beyond all bounds *or* limits, without restraint; high, high on the hog (*informal*)

670 MODERATION

nouns

1 **moderation**, moderateness; **restraint**, constraint, control; **judiciousness**, prudence; steadiness, evenness, balance, equilibrium, **stability** see 854; **temperateness**, temperance, sobriety; self-abnegation, self-restraint, self-control, self-denial; abstinence, continence, abnegation; **mildness**, lenity, gentleness; calmness, serenity, tranquillity, repose, calm, cool (*informal*); unexcessiveness, unextremeness, unextravagance, nothing in excess, *meden agan* (*Greek*); **happy medium**, **golden mean**, *juste-milieu* (*French*), middle way *or* path, *via media* (*Latin*), balancing act (*informal*); moderationism, **conservatism** see 852.3; **nonviolence**, pacifism; impartiality, neutrality, dispassion; irenics, ecumenism

2 **modulation**, **abatement**, remission, **mitigation**, diminution, defusing, de-escalation, **reduction**, lessening, falling-off; **relaxation**, relaxing, slackening, **easing**, loosening, letup *and* letdown (*both informal*); **alleviation**, assuagement, allayment,

palliation, leniency, relenting, lightening, **tempering**, **softening**, subdual; **deadening**, **dulling**, damping, blunting; drugging, narcotizing, sedating, sedation; **pacification**, **tranquillization**, tranquillizing, mollification, demulsion, dulcification, **quieting**, quietening, lulling, **soothing**, **calming**, hushing

3 **moderator**, **mitigator**, modulator, stabilizer, temperer, assuager; **mediator**, **bridge-builder**, calming *or* restraining hand, wiser head; **alleviator**, alleviative, palliative, lenitive; **pacifier**, **soother**, comforter, peacemaker, pacificator, dove of peace, mollifier; **drug**, anodyne, dolorifuge, soothing syrup, **tranquillizer**, calmative; **sedative** see 86.12; balm, salve; cushion, shock absorber

4 **moderate**, moderatist, moderationist, middle-of-the-roader, **centrist**, neutral, compromiser; **conservative** see 852.4

verbs

5 **to be moderate**, **keep within bounds**, keep within compass; practise self-control *or* self-denial, live within one's means, live temperately, do nothing in excess, strike a balance, strike *or* keep a happy medium, seek the golden mean, steer *or* preserve an even course, keep to the middle path *or* way, steer *or* be between Scylla and Charybdis; keep the peace, not resist, espouse *or* practise nonviolence, be pacifistic; not rock the boat *and* not make waves *or* static (*all informal*); cool it *and* keep one's cool (*both informal*), keep one's head *or* temper; sober down, settle down; remit, relent; take in sail; go out like a lamb; be conservative see 852.6

6 **to moderate**, **restrain**, constrain, control, **keep within bounds**; modulate, mitigate, defuse, abate, weaken, **diminish**, **reduce**, de-escalate, slacken, lessen, slow down; **alleviate**, assuage, allay, lay, lighten, palliate, extenuate, **temper**, attemper, lenify; **soften**, **subdue**, tame, hold in check, keep a tight rein, chasten, underplay, play down, downplay, de-emphasize, tone *or* tune down; turn down the volume, lower the voice; **drug**, narcotize, sedate, tranquillize, deaden, dull, blunt, obtund, take the edge off, take the sting *or* bite out; smother, suppress, stifle; **damp**, **dampen**, bank the fire, reduce the temperature, throw cold water on, throw a wet blanket on; sober, sober down *or* up; clear the air

7 **to calm**, calm down, **stabilize**, **tranquillize**, **pacify**, mollify, appease, dulcify; **quiet**, quieten, hush, still, rest, compose, **lull**, **soothe**, gentle, rock, cradle, rock to sleep; cool, **subdue**, quell; ease, steady, smooth, smoothen, smooth over, smooth down, even out; keep the peace, be the dove of peace, pour oil on troubled waters, pour balm into

8 **to cushion**, absorb the shock, **soften the blow**, break the fall, deaden, damp *or* dampen, soften, suppress, neutralize, offset; show pity *or* mercy *or* consideration *or* sensitivity, temper the wind to the shorn lamb

9 **to relax**, unbend; ease, **ease up**, ease off, **let up**, let down; abate, bate, remit, mitigate; **slacken**, slack, slake, slack off, slack up; loose, **loosen**; unbrace, unstrain, unstring

adjectives

10 **moderate, temperate,** sober; **mild,** soft, bland,
gentle, tame; mild as milk *or* mother's milk, mild as
milk and water, gentle as a lamb; **nonviolent,**
peaceable, peaceful, pacifistic; **judicious, prudent**

11 **restrained,** constrained, limited, controlled, **stable,**
in control, in hand; tempered, **softened,** hushed,
subdued, quelled, chastened

12 **unexcessive,** unextreme, unextravagant,
conservative; reasonable

13 **equable,** even, low-key *or* low-keyed, **cool,** even-
tempered, level-headed, dispassionate; tranquil,
reposeful, serene, calm *see* 173.12

14 **mitigating,** assuaging, abating, **diminishing,
reducing,** lessening, allaying, **alleviating, relaxing,
easing;** tempering, **softening,** chastening,
subduing; deadening, dulling, blunting, damping,
dampening, cushioning

15 **tranquillizing,** pacifying, mollifying, appeasing;
cooling-off; **calming,** lulling, gentling, rocking,
cradling, hushing, quietening, stilling; **soothing,**
soothful, restful; dreamy, drowsy

16 **palliative, alleviative,** alleviatory, assuasive,
lenitive, **calmative,** calmant, **narcotic, sedative,**
demulcent, anodyne; antiorgastic, anaphrodisiac

adverbs

17 **moderately, in moderation,** restrainedly,
subduedly, in *or* within reason, within bounds *or*
compass, in balance; **temperately,** soberly,
prudently, judiciously, dispassionately; composedly,
calmly, coolly, evenly, steadily, equably, tranquilly,
serenely; soothingly, conservatively

671 VIOLENCE
vehement action

nouns

1 **violence, vehemence, virulence, venom,
furiousness, force, rigour,** roughness, harshness,
ungentleness, extremity, impetuosity, inclemency,
severity, intensity, acuteness, **sharpness;**
acrimony *see* 17.5; fierceness, ferociousness,
furiousness, viciousness, insensateness, savagery,
destructiveness, **destruction, vandalism;**
terrorism, barbarity, brutality, atrocity,
inhumanity, bloodlust, killer instinct, murderousness,
malignity, mercilessness, pitilessness, mindlessness,
animality, brutishness; **rage,** raging, anger *see* 152

2 **turbulence, turmoil,** chaos, upset, **fury, furor,**
furore (Italian), **rage,** frenzy, **passion,** fanaticism,
zealousness, zeal, tempestuousness, storminess,
wildness, tumultuousness, **tumult, uproar,** racket,
cacophony, pandemonium, hubbub, **commotion,
disturbance, agitation,** bluster, broil, brawl,
embroilment, brouhaha, kerfuffle, fuss, flap
(informal), **row, rumpus,** ruckus *(informal),* foofaraw
(US informal), **ferment,** fume, boil, boiling,
seething, ebullition, fomentation

3 **unruliness, disorderliness,** obstreperousness; **riot,
rioting;** looting, pillaging, plundering, rapine;
wilding *(informal);* laying waste, sowing with salt,
sacking; scorched earth; **attack** *see* 459, **assault,**

onslaught, battering; **rape, violation,** forcible
seizure; **killing** *see* 308, butchery, massacre, slaughter

4 **storm, tempest,** squall, line squall, **tornado,
cyclone, hurricane,** tropical cyclone, typhoon,
storm-centre, tropical storm, eye of the storm *or*
hurricane, war of the elements,

"Nature's elemental din"—THOMAS CAMPBELL,
"tempestuous rage", "groans of roaring wind and
rain"—BOTH SHAKESPEARE; stormy weather, rough
weather, foul weather, dirty weather; rainstorm *see*
316.2; thunderstorm *see* 316.3; windstorm *see* 318.12;
snowstorm *see* 1022.8; **firestorm**

5 **upheaval, convulsion,** cataclysm, catastrophe,
disaster; **fit, spasm, paroxysm,** apoplexy, stroke;
climax; **earthquake,** quake, temblor *(US),*
diastrophism, epicentre, shock-wave; tidal wave,
tsunami (Japanese)

6 **outburst, outbreak, eruption,** debouchment,
eructation, belch, spew; **burst,** dissilience *or*
dissiliency; meltdown, atomic meltdown; **torrent,**
rush, gush, spate, cascade, spurt, jet, rapids,
volcano, volcan, burning mountain

7 **explosion, discharge, blowout,** blowup, detonation,
fulmination, **blast, burst, report** *see* 56.1; flash,
flash *or* flashing point, flare, flare-up, fulguration;
bang, boom *see* 56.4; backfire

8 **concussion, shock, impact,** crunch, smash;
percussion, repercussion

9 *(violent person)* berserk *or* berserker; **hothead,**
hotspur; **devil, demon, fiend, brute,** hellhound,
hellcat, hellion, hell-raiser; **beast,** wild beast, tiger,
dragon, mad dog, wolf, monster, mutant, savage;
rapist, mugger, killer; Mafioso, hit man *(informal),*
contract killer, hired killer, hired gun; **fury,** virago,
vixen, termagant, beldam, she-wolf, tigress, witch;
firebrand, revolutionary *see* 859.3, **terrorist,**
incendiary, bomber, guerrilla

10 *(informal terms)* goon, gorilla, ape, knuckle dragger,
muscle man, plug-ugly, cowboy, bozo, bruiser,
hardnose, tough guy, tough, hoodlum, hood, meat-
eater, gunsel *(US),* terror, holy terror, fire-eater,
spitfire, tough *or* ugly customer

verbs

11 **to rage, storm,** rant, rave, roar; **rampage,** ramp,
tear, tear around; go *or* carry on *(informal);* come in
like a lion; **destroy, wreck,** wreak havoc, ruin; sow
chaos *or* disorder; **terrorize,** sow terror, vandalize,
barbarize, brutalize; **riot,** loot, burn, pillage, sack, lay
waste; **slaughter, butcher; rape,** violate; **attack,
assault,** batter, savage, mug, maul, hammer; go for
the jugular

12 **to seethe, boil, fume,** foam, simmer, stew, ferment,
stir, churn

13 **to erupt, burst forth** *or* **out, break out, blow out**
or **open,** eruct, belch, **vomit,** spout, spew, disgorge,
discharge, eject, throw *or* hurl forth

14 **to explode, blow up, burst,** go off, go up, blow
out, blast, bust *(informal);* **detonate,** fulminate;
touch off, trigger, trip, set off, let off; **discharge,**
fire, shoot; backfire; melt down

15 **to run amok, go berserk, go on the rampage,**
cut loose, run riot, run wild

adjectives

16 violent, vehement, virulent, venomous, severe, rigorous, furious, fierce, intense, sharp, acute, keen, cutting, splitting, piercing; **destructive**; rough, bruising, tough (*informal*); **drastic**, extreme, outrageous, excessive, exorbitant, unconscionable, intemperate, immoderate, extravagant; acrimonious *see* 17.14

17 unmitigated, unsoftened, untempered, unallayed, unsubdued, unquelled; unquenched, unextinguished, unabated; unmixed, unalloyed; **total**

18 turbulent, tumultuous, raging, chaotic, hellish, anarchic, storming, stormy, tempestuous, troublous, frenzied, wild, wild-eyed, frantic, furious, infuriate, insensate, mad, demented, insane, raging, enraged, ravening, raving, slavering; angry; blustering, blustery, blusterous; uproarious, rip-roaring (*informal*); pandemoniac; orgastic, orgasmic

19 unruly, disorderly, obstreperous; **unbridled**; riotous, wild, rampant; terroristic, anarchic, nihilistic, revolutionary *see* 859.5

20 boisterous, rampageous, rambunctious (*informal*), rumbustious, roisterous, wild, rollicking, rowdy, rough, hoody (*US informal*), harum-scarum (*informal*); knockabout, rough-and-tumble, knock-down-and-drag-out (*US informal*)

21 savage, fierce, ferocious, vicious, murderous, cruel, atrocious, mindless, brutal, brutish, bestial, mindless, insensate, monstrous, mutant, inhuman, pitiless, ruthless, merciless, bloody, sanguinary, kill-crazy (*informal*); malign, malignant; feral, ferine; wild, untamed, tameless, undomesticated, ungentle; barbarous, barbaric; uncivilized, noncivilized

22 fiery, heated, inflamed, flaming, scorching, hot, red-hot, white-hot; fanatic, zealous, totally committed, hard-core, hard-line, ardent, passionate; hotheaded

23 convulsive, cataclysmic, disastrous, upheaving; seismic; spasmodic, paroxysmal, spastic, jerky; orgasmic

24 explosive, bursting, detonating, explosible, explodable, fulminating, fulminant, fulminatory; dissilient; volcanic, eruptive

adverbs

25 violently, vehemently, virulently, venomously, rigorously, severely, fiercely, drastically; furiously, wildly, madly, like mad, like fury (*informal*), like blazes; all to pieces, with a vengeance

26 turbulently, tumultuously, riotously, uproariously, stormily, tempestuously, troublously, frenziedly, frantically, furiously, ragingly, enragedly, madly; angrily *see* 152.33

27 savagely, fiercely, ferociously, atrociously, viciously, murderously, brutally *or* brutishly, mindlessly, bestially, barbarously, inhumanly, insensately, ruthlessly, pitilessly, mercilessly; **tooth and nail**, tooth and claw, *bec et ongles* (*French*)

672 GLUTTONY

nouns

1 gluttony, gluttonousness, **greed**, greediness, voraciousness, voracity, ravenousness, edacity, crapulence *or* crapulency, gulosity, rapacity, insatiability; omnivorousness; **piggishness, hoggishness**, swinishness, "swinish gluttony" —Milton; **overindulgence, overeating**; eating disorder, polyphagia, hyperphagia, bulimia, bulimia nervosa, binge-purge syndrome; **intemperance** *see* 669

2 epicurism, epicureanism, gourmandise; gastronomy

3 glutton, greedy eater, big eater (*informal*), hefty *or* husky eater (*US informal*), trencherman, trencherwoman, belly-god, gobbler, greedygut *or* greedyguts (*informal*), gorger, **gourmand**, gourmandizer, gormand, gormandizer, guttler, cormorant, gannet; animal, hog *and* pig (*both informal*), chow hound *and* khazer (*both US informal*)

verbs

4 to gluttonize, gormandize, **indulge one's appetite**, live to eat; gorge, engorge, glut, cram, **stuff**, batten, guttle, guzzle, **scoff, devour**, raven, bolt, gobble, gulp, **wolf**, gobble *or* gulp *or* bolt *or* wolf down, eat like a horse, stuff oneself *and* hog it down *and* eat one's head off *and* fork *or* shovel it in (*all informal*), eat one out of house and home

5 to overeat, overgorge, **overindulge, make a pig** *or* **hog of oneself, pig out** (*informal*), pork out *or* scarf out (*US informal*); stuff oneself

adjectives

6 gluttonous, greedy, voracious, ravenous, edacious, rapacious, insatiable, polyphagic, bulimic, hyperphagic, Apician; piggish, hoggish, swinish; crapulous, crapulent; intemperate *see* 669.7; omnivorous, all-devouring; gorging, cramming, glutting, guttling, stuffing, guzzling, wolfing, bolting, gobbling, gulping, gluttonizing

7 overfed, overgorged, overindulged

adverbs

8 gluttonously, greedily, voraciously, ravenously, edaciously; piggishly, hoggishly, swinishly

673 LEGALITY

nouns

1 legality, legitimacy, lawfulness, legitimateness, licitness, rightfulness, validity, scope, applicability; jurisdiction *see* 594; actionability, justiciability, constitutionality, constitutional validity; legal process, legal form, **due process**; legalism, constitutionalism; justice *see* 649

2 legalization, legitimation, legitimatization, decriminalization; money-washing *or* laundering; validation; authorization, sanction; legislation, enactment

3 law, *lex, jus* (*both Latin*), **statute**, rubric, **canon**, institution; **ordinance**; act, enactment, **measure**, legislation; rule, ruling; prescript, prescription;

regulation, *règlement* (*French*), reg (*informal*); **dictate**, dictation; form, formula, formulary, formality; standing order; bylaw; **edict, decree** *see* 420.4; **bill**

4 **law**, legal system, system of laws, legal branch *or* speciality

5 **code, digest**, pandect, capitulary, **body of law,** corpus juris, legal code, code of laws, digest of law; **codification; civil code, penal code;** Justinian Code; Napoleonic code, *Code Napoléon* (*French*); lawbook, statute book, compilation;

6 **constitution**, written constitution, unwritten constitution; constitutional amendment; Bill of Rights, constitutional guarantees; constitutional interpretation

7 **jurisprudence**, law, legal science; nomology, nomography; **forensic science**, forensic *or* legal medicine, medical jurisprudence, medico–legal medicine; forensic psychiatry; forensic *or* legal chemistry; criminology

verbs

8 **to legalize, legitimize**, legitimatize, legitimate, make legal, declare lawful, **decriminalize;** wash *or* launder money; validate; **authorize, sanction;** constitute, ordain, establish, put in force; prescribe, formulate; regulate, make a regulation; **decree; legislate, enact; enforce; litigate** *see* 598.12, take legal action

9 **to codify**, digest; compile, publish

adjectives

10 **legal, legitimate,** legit *and* kosher (*both informal*), competent, **licit, lawful,** rightful, according to law, within the law; **actionable,** litigable, justiciable, within the scope of the law; **enforceable,** legally binding; **judicial,** juridical; **authorized, sanctioned,** valid, applicable; **constitutional;** statutory, statutable; **legislative, lawmaking;** lawlike; **just** *see* 649.8

11 **jurisprudent**, jurisprudential; **legalistic; forensic;** nomistic, nomothetic; criminological

adverbs

12 **legally, legitimately,** licitly, lawfully, by law, *de jure* (*Latin*), in the eyes of the law

674 ILLEGALITY

nouns

1 **illegality, unlawfulness, illicitness, lawlessness,** wrongfulness; unauthorization, impermissibility, **unconstitutionality;** legal *or* technical flaw, legal irregularity; **outlawry; anarchy,** collapse *or* breakdown *or* paralysis of authority, anomie; illicit business *see* 732

2 **illegitimacy, illegitimateness**, illegitimation; **bastardy,** bastardism; bend *or* bar sinister, baton

3 **lawbreaking, violation,** breach *or* violation of law, infringement, contravention, infraction, **transgression,** trespass, trespassing; **criminality,** criminalism, habitual criminality, delinquency; flouting *or* making a mockery of the law

4 **offence, wrong**, illegality; **violation** *see* 435.2; **wrongdoing** *see* 655; much to answer for; **crime, felony; misdemeanour;** tort; delict, delictum

verbs

5 **to break** *or* **violate the law,** breach the law, infringe, contravene, infract, **violate** *see* 435.4, **transgress, trespass,** disobey the law, offend against the law, flout the law, make a mockery of the law, fly in the face of the law, set the law at defiance, snap one's fingers at the law, set the law at naught, circumvent the law, disregard the law, **take the law into one's own hands,** twist *or* torture the law to one's own ends *or* purposes; commit a crime; have much to answer for; live outside the law

adjectives

6 **illegal, unlawful, illegitimate, illicit,** nonlicit, nonlegal, lawless, wrongful, fraudulent, creative (*informal*), **against the law; unauthorized,** unallowed, impermissible, unwarranted, unwarrantable, unofficial; unstatutory; **unconstitutional,** nonconstitutional; flawed, irregular, contrary to law; actionable, chargeable, justiciable, litigable; triable, punishable; **criminal, felonious; outlaw, outlawed; contraband,** bootleg, black-market; under-the-table, under-the-counter; unregulated, unchartered; anarchic, anarchistic, anomic

7 **illegitimate, spurious,** false; **bastard,** misbegot, **misbegotten,** miscreated, baseborn, born out of wedlock, without benefit of clergy

adverbs

8 **illegally, unlawfully, illegitimately, illicitly;** impermissibly; criminally, feloniously; contrary to law, in violation of law

675 RELIGIONS, CULTS, SECTS

nouns

1 **religion**, religious belief *or* faith, **belief, faith,** teaching, doctrine, creed, credo, theology *see* 676, orthodoxy *see* 687; system of beliefs; tradition

2 **cult**, ism; cultism; **mystique**

3 **sect** (*see* list), sectarism, religious order, **denomination, persuasion,** faction, **church,** communion, community, group, fellowship, affiliation, order, school, party, society, body, organization; branch, variety, version, segment; offshoot; **schism,** division

4 **sectarianism**, sectarism, **denominationalism,** partisanism, the clash of creeds; schismatism; syncretism, eclecticism

5 **theism; monotheism; polytheism,** multitheism, myriotheism; **ditheism,** dyotheism, dualism; **tritheism,** tetratheism; **pantheism,** cosmotheism, theopantism, acosmism; physitheism, psychotheism, animotheism; physicomorphism; hylotheism; anthropotheism, anthropomorphism; anthropolatry; allotheism; monolatry, henotheism, autotheism; zootheism, theriotheism; **deism**

6 **animism, animistic religion** *or* cult; voodooism, voodoo, hoodoo, wanga, juju, jujuism, obeah,

obeahism; shamanism; fetishism, totemism; nature worship, naturism; primitive religion

7 Christianity (*see list*), Christianism, Christendom; Latin *or* Roman *or* Western Christianity; Eastern *or* Orthodox Christianity; Protestant Christianity; Judaeo-Christian religion *or* tradition *or* belief; fundamentalism, Christian fundamentalism

8 Catholicism, Catholicity; **Roman Catholicism,** Romanism, Rome; papalism; popery *and* popeism *and* papism *and* papistry (*all informal*); ultramontanism; Catholic Church, **Roman Catholic Church,** Church of Rome; Eastern Rites, Uniate Rites, Uniatism, Alexandrian *or* Antiochian *or* Byzantine Rite

9 Orthodoxy; Eastern Orthodox Church, Holy Orthodox Catholic Apostolic Church, Greek Orthodox Church, Russian Orthodox Church; patriarchate of Constantinople, patriarchate of Antioch, patriarchate of Alexandria, patriarchate of Jerusalem

10 Protestantism, Reform, Reformationism; **Nonconformism;** Evangelicalism; Zwinglianism; dissent *see* 333; apostasy *see* 363.2; new theology

11 Anglicanism; High-Churchism, Low-Churchism; Anglo-Catholicism; Church of England, Established Church; High Church, Low Church; Broad Church, Free Church

12 Judaism; Hebraism, Hebrewism; Israelitism; Orthodox Judaism, Conservative Judaism, Reform Judaism, Reconstructionism; Hasidism; rabbinism, Talmudism; Pharisaism; Sadduceeism; Karaism *or* Karaitism

13 Islam, Muslimism, Islamism, Moslemism; Sufism; Wahabiism, Sunnism, Shiism; Black Muslimism; Muslim fundamentalism, militant Muslimism

14 Christian Science; New Thought, Higher Thought, Practical Christianity, Mental Science, Divine Science Church

15 religionist, religioner; **believer** *see* 692.4; cultist

16 theist; monotheist; polytheist, multitheist, myriotheist; ditheist, dualist; tritheist; tetratheist; **pantheist,** cosmotheist; psychotheist; physitheist; hylotheist; anthropotheist; anthropolater; allotheist; henotheist; autotheist; zootheist, theriotheist; **deist**

17 Christian, Nazarene, Nazarite; Christian sectarian

18 sectarian, sectary, **denominationalist,** factionist, schismatic

19 Catholic, Roman Catholic, RC (*informal*), Romanist, papist (*informal*); ultramontane; Eastern-Rite Christian, Uniate

20 Protestant, non-Catholic, Reformed believer, Reformationist, Evangelical; **Nonconformist;** Zwinglian; dissenter *see* 333.3; apostate *see* 363.5

21 Jew, Hebrew, Judaist, Israelite; Orthodox *or* Conservative *or* Reform Jew, Reconstructionist; Hasid; Rabbinist, Talmudist; Pharisee; Sadducee; Karaite

22 Mormon, Latter-day Saint, Josephite (*informal*)

23 Muslim, Mussulman, Moslem, Islamite; Shiite, Shia, Sectary; Motazilite, Sunni, Sunnite, Wahabi, Sufi; dervish; abdal; Black Muslim; Muslim fundamentalist *or* militant

24 Christian Scientist, Christian Science Practitioner

adjectives

25 religious, theistic; monotheistic; polytheistic, ditheistic, tritheistic; **pantheistic,** cosmotheistic; physicomorphic; anthropomorphic, anthropotheistic; **deistic**

26 sectarian, sectary, **denominational,** schismatic, schismatical

27 nonsectarian, ecumenical, undenominational, nondenominational; interdenominational

28 Protestant, non-Catholic, Reformed, Reformationist, Nonconformist, Evangelical; Lutheran, Calvinist, Calvinistic, Zwinglian; dissentient *see* 333.6; apostate *see* 363.11

29 Catholic; Roman Catholic, RC (*informal*), Roman; Romish *and* popish *and* papish *and* papist *and* papistical (*all informal*); ultramontane

30 Jewish, Hebrew, Judaic, Judaical, Israelite, Israelitic, Israelitish; Orthodox, Conservative, Reform, Reconstructionist; Hasidic

31 Muslim, Islamic, Moslem, Islamitic, Islamistic; Shiite, Sunni, Sunnite

32 (*Oriental*) Buddhist, Buddhistic; Brahmanic, Brahmanistic; Vedic, Vedantic; Confucian, Confucianist; Taoist, Taoistic, Shintoist, Shintoistic; Zoroastrian, Zarathustrian, Parsee

33 religions and sects

anthroposophy	Rastafarianism
Babism *or* Babi	Reconstructionism
Bahhá'í *or* Bahaism	Reform Judaism
Brahmanism	reincarnationism
Brahmoism	Rosicrucianism
Buddhism	Sabaeanism
Ch'an Buddhism	Saivism
Chen Yen Buddhism	Shaivite Hinduism
Ching-t'u Buddhism	Shiite Muslimism
Christianity	Shin Buddhism
Confucianism	Shingon Buddhism
Conservative Judaism	Shinto *or* Shintoism
Dakshincharin Hinduism	Sikhism
Eleusinianism	Soka Gakkai Buddhism
Ethical Culture	Sufism
Gnosticism	Sunni Muslimism
gymnosophy	Taoism
Hinduism	Tendai Buddhism
Islam	Theosophy
Jainism	Theravada *or* Hinayana
Jodo Buddhism	Buddhism
Judaism	T'ien-t'ai Buddhism
Lamaism	Unitarianism
Lingayat Hinduism	Vaishnavite Hinduism
Magianism	Vajrayana Buddhism
Mahayana Buddhism	Vamacharin Hinduism
Mandaeism	Vedanta *or* Vedantism
Mithraism	Wahabiism
Nichiren Buddhism	Yoga *or* Yogism
Orphism	Zen *or* Zen Buddhism
Orthodox Judaism	Zoroastrianism *or*
Parsiism *or* Parsism	Zoroastrism

34 Christian denominations

Adventism *or* Second	Anglicanism
Adventism	Anglo-Catholicism
Amish	antinomianism
Anabaptism	Arianism

Athanasianism
Baptist Church
Boehmenism
Calvinism
Catholicism
Christian Science
Congregationalism
Eastern Orthodox
  Christianity
Episcopalianism
Erastianism
homoiousianism
homoousianism
Jansenism
latitudinarianism
Laudism *or* Laudianism
Liberal Catholicism
Lutheranism
Mennonitism
Methodism
Moral Rearmament
Mormonism
New Thought

Origenism
Orthodox Christianity
Oxford Movement
Practical Christianity
Presbyterianism
Puritanism
Puseyism
Quakerism
quietism
Roman Catholicism
Rosicrucianism
Sabellianism
Salvation Army
Socinianism
Stundism
Swedenborgianism
Tractarianism
Trinitarianism
Ubiquitarianism
Uniatism
Unitarianism
Universalism
Wesleyanism *or* Wesleyism

676 THEOLOGY

nouns

1 **theology** (*see list*), **religion, divinity**; theologism; doctrinism, doctrinalism

2 **doctrine, dogma** *see* 952.2; **creed**, credo; credenda, articles of religion *or* faith; Apostles' Creed, Nicene Creed, Athanasian Creed; Catechism

3 **theologian**, theologist, theologizer, theologer, theologician; **divine**; scholastic, schoolman (*US*); theological *or* divinity student, theological, theologue; canonist

adjectives

4 **theological, religious; divine**; doctrinal, doctrinary; canonic *or* canonical; physicotheological

5 **kinds and branches of theology**

apologetics
canonics
Christology
crisis theology
doctrinal theology
dogmatics *or* dogmatic
  theology
eschatology
existential theology
feminist theology
hagiology
hierography *or* hagiography
hierology
liberation theology
Mercersburg theology
natural *or* rational theology
neoorthodoxy *or*

neoorthodox theology
nonformalogical theology
patristics *or* patristic
  theology
phenomenological theology
philosophical theology
physicotheology
rationalism
school theology *or*
  scholastic theology
secularism
soteriology *or* Christology
  or logos theology *or* logos
  Christology
systematics *or* systematic
  theology
theological hermeneutics

677 DEITY

nouns

1 **deity, divinity**, divineness; **godliness**, godlikeness; **godhood**, godhead, godship, Fatherhood; heavenliness; **transcendence**

2 **God; Jehovah;** *Yahweh, Adonai, Elohim* (*all Hebrew*); **Allah;** the Great Spirit, Manitou

3 (*Hinduism*) **Brahma**, the Supreme Soul, the Essence of the Universe; **Atman**, the Universal Ego *or* Self; **Vishnu**, the Preserver; **Siva**, the Destroyer, the Regenerator

4 (*Buddhism*) **Buddha**, the Blessed One, the Teacher, **the Lord Buddha**, bodhisattva

5 (*Zoroastrianism*) **Ahura Mazda**, Ormazd, Mazda, the Lord of Wisdom, the Wise Lord, the Wise One, the King of Light, the Guardian of Mankind

6 (*Christian Science*) **Mind, Divine Mind**, Spirit, Soul Principle, Life, Truth, Love

7 **world spirit** *or* **soul**, *anima mundi* (*Latin*), universal life force, world principle, **world-self**, universal ego *or* self, infinite spirit, supreme soul *or* principle, **oversoul, nous, Logos**, World Reason

8 **Nature, Mother Nature**, Dame Nature, Natura, "Beldame Nature"—MILTON

9 **Godhead, Trinity;** Trimurti, Hindu trinity *or* triad

10 **Christ**

11 **the Word, Logos**, the Word Made Flesh, **the Incarnation**, the Hypostatic Union

12 **God the Holy Ghost, the Holy Ghost, the Holy Spirit**, the Spirit of God, the Spirit of Truth, the Paraclete, the Comforter, the Consoler, the Intercessor, the Dove

13 (*divine functions*) creation, preservation, dispensation; **providence, divine providence**, dealings *or* dispensations *or* visitations of providence

14 (*functions of Christ*) salvation, redemption; atonement, propitiation; mediation, intercession; judgment

15 (*functions of the Holy Ghost*) inspiration, unction, regeneration, sanctification, comfort, consolation, grace, witness

adjectives

16 **divine**, heavenly, celestial, empyrean; **godly, godlike** *see* 692.9; **transcendent**, superhuman, supernatural; self-existent; Christly, Christlike, redemptive, salvational, propitiative, propitiatory, mediative, mediatory, intercessive, intercessional; incarnate, incarnated, made flesh; messianic

17 **almighty, omnipotent**, all-powerful; creating, creative, making, shaping; **omniscient**, all-wise, all-knowing, all-seeing; **infinite**, boundless, limitless, unbounded, unlimited, undefined, omnipresent, ubiquitous; eternal, everlasting, timeless, perpetual, immortal, permanent; one; immutable, unchanging, changeless, eternally the same; supreme, sovereign, highest; holy, hallowed, sacred, numinous; glorious, radiant, luminous; majestic; good, just, loving, merciful; triune, tripersonal, three-personed, three-in-one

678 MYTHICAL AND POLYTHEISTIC GODS AND SPIRITS

nouns

1 **the gods,** the immortals; the major deities, the greater gods, *di majores* (*Latin*); the minor deities, the lesser gods, *di minores* (*Latin*); pantheon; theogony; **spirits,** animistic spirit *or* powers, manitou, huaca, nagual, mana, pokunt, tamanoas, wakan, zemi

2 **god,** *deus* (*Latin*); **deity, divinity,** immortal, heathen god, pagan deity *or* divinity; **goddess,** *dea* (*Latin*); deva, devi, the shining ones; **idol,** false god, devil-god

3 **godling,** godlet, godkin; **demigod,** half-god, hero; cult figure; demigoddess, heroine

4 **god, goddesses;** Greek and Roman deities (*see list*); **Norse and Germanic deities** (*see list*); **Celtic deities** (*see list*); **Hindu deities** (*see list*); **avatars of Vishnu; Egyptian deities** (*see list*); **Semitic deities; Chinese deities; Japanese deities; specialized** *or* **tutelary deities** (*see list*)

5 **spirit,** intelligence, supernatural being; **genius,** daemon, demon; atua; **spectre** *see* 987; **evil spirits** *see* 680

6 **elemental,** elemental spirit; **sylph,** spirit of the air; **gnome,** spirit of the earth, earth-spirit; **salamander,** fire-spirit; **undine,** water spirit, water-sprite

7 **fairyfolk,** elfenfolk, shee *or* sidhe (*Irish*), **the little people** *or* **men,** the good folk *or* people, denizens of the air; **fairyland,** faerie

8 **fairy,** sprite, fay, fairy man *or* woman; **elf, brownie, pixie, gremlin,** ouphe, hob, cluricaune, puca *or* pooka *or* pwca, kobold, nisse, peri; **imp, goblin** *see* 680.8; **gnome,** dwarf; **sylph,** sylphid; **banshee; leprechaun;** fairy queen; Ariel, Mab, Oberon, Puck, Titania, Béfind, Corrigan, Finnbeara

9 **nymph;** nymphet, nymphlin; **dryad,** hamadryad, wood nymph; vila *or* willi; tree nymph; **oread,** mountain nymph; limoniad, meadow *or* flower nymph; Napaea, glen nymph; Hyades; Pleiades, Atlantides

10 **water god,** water spirit *or* sprite *or* nymph; **undine,** nix, nixie, kelpie; **naiad,** limniad, fresh-water nymph; **Oceanid,** Nereid, sea nymph, ocean nymph, **mermaid,** sea-maid, sea-maiden, siren; Thetis; **merman,** man fish; **Neptune,**

"the old man of the sea"—HOMER; Oceanus, Poseidon, Triton; Davy Jones, Davy

11 **forest god,** sylvan deity, vegetation spirit *or* daemon, field spirit, fertility god, corn spirit, **faun, satyr,** silenus, panisc, paniscus, panisca; **Pan,** Faunus; Cailleac; Priapus; Vitharr *or* Vidar, the goat god; Jack-in-the-green, Green Man

12 **familiar spirit,** familiar; **genius, good genius,** daemon, demon, *numen* (*Latin*), totem; **guardian, guardian spirit, guardian angel,** angel, good angel, ministering angel, **fairy godmother;** guide, control, attendant godling *or* spirit, invisible helper, special providence; **tutelary** *or* **tutelar god** *or* **genius** *or* **spirit;** *genius tutelae, genius loci, genius domus, genius familiae* (*all Latin*); **household gods;** *lares familiaris, lares praestites, lares compitales, lares*

viales, lares permarini (*all Latin*); penates, lares and penates; ancestral spirits; manes, pitris

13 **Santa Claus,** Santa, Saint Nicholas, Saint Nick, Kriss Kringle, Father Christmas

14 **mythology,** mythicism; **legend, lore, folklore,** mythical lore; fairy lore, fairyism; mythologist

adjectives

15 **mythic, mythical, mythological; fabulous, legendary;** folkloric

16 **divine, godlike**

17 **fairy,** faery, **fairylike,** fairyish, fay; sylphine, sylphish, sylphy, sylphidine, sylphlike; **elfin,** elfish, elflike; gnomish, gnomelike; pixieish

18 **nymphic,** nymphal, nymphean, nymphlike

19 **Greek and Roman deities**

Apollo *or* Apollon *or* Phoebus *or* Phoebus Apollo	Mercury *or* Hermes
	Mithras
	Momus
Ate	Neptune *or* Poseidon
Athena *or* Minerva *or* Pallas Athena	Nike
	Olympic gods *or* Olympians
Bacchus *or* Dionysus	
Cronus	Persephone *or* Proserpina *or* Proserpine
Cupid *or* Amor *or* Eros	
Cybele *or* Agdistis *or* Great Mother *or* Magna Mater *or* Mater Turrita	Pluto *or* Hades *or* Dis *or* Orcus
	Rhea *or* Ops
Demeter *or* Ceres	Saturn
Despoina	Venus *or* Aphrodite
Diana *or* Artemis	Vesta
Ge *or* Gaea *or* Gaia *or* Tellus	Vulcan *or* Hephaestus
	Zeus *or* Jupiter *or* Jove *or*
Helios *or* Hyperion *or* Sol	Jupiter Fulgur *or*
Hestia	Fulminator *or* Jupiter
Hymen	Tonans *or* Jupiter
Juno *or* Hera *or* Here	Pluvius *or* Jupiter
Kore *or* Cora	Optimus Maximus *or*
Mars *or* Ares	Jupiter Fidius

20 **Norse and Germanic deities**

Aesir	Nerthus *or* Hertha
Balder	Njorth *or* Njord
Bor	Odin *or* Woden *or* Wotan
Bori	Reimthursen
Bragi	Sif
Forseti	Sigyn
Frey *or* Freyr	Thor *or* Donar
Freya *or* Freyja	Tyr *or* Tiu
Frigg *or* Frigga	Ull *or* Ullr
Heimdall	Vali
Hel	Vanir
Höder *or* Hödr	Vitharr *or* Vidar
Hoenir	Völund
Ing	Wayland
Ithunn *or* Idun	Weland
Loki	Wyrd
Nanna	Ymir

21 **Celtic deities**

Aine	Bóann
Amaethon	Bodb
Angus Og	Brigit
Arawn	Dagda
Arianrhod	Danu
Blodenwedd	Dôn

Dylan	Lug
Epona	Macha
Goibniu	Morrigan
Lir	Neman
Llew Llaw Gyffes	

22 Hindu deities

Aditi	Kala
Agni	Kali
Aryaman	Kama
Asapurna	Kamsa
Asvins	Karttikeya
Avalokita *or* Avalokitesvara	Lakshmi
Bhaga	Marut
Bhairava	Mitra
Bhairavi	Parjanya
Bhudevi	Parvati
Brahma	Pushan
Brihaspati	Rahu
Chandi	Rhibhus
Chitragupta	Rudra
Daksha	Sarasvati
Devaki	Savitar
Devi	Sita
Dharma	Siva
Dharti Mai	Soma
Durga	Surya
Dyaus	Uma
Ganesa *or* Ganesh *or*	Ushas
Ganesha *or* Ganapati	Vaja
Garuda	Varuna
Gauri	Varuni
Hanuman	Vayu
Himavat	Vibhu
Indra	Vishnu
Jaganmati	Yama
Ka	

23 Egyptian deities

Anubis	Nephthys
Bast	Nut
Horus	Osiris
Isis	Ptah
Khem	Ra *or* Amen-Ra
Min	Set
Neph	Thoth

24 specialized deities, tutelary deities

679 ANGEL, SAINT

nouns

1 **angel,** celestial, celestial *or* heavenly being; messenger of God; **seraph,** seraphim (*plural*), angel of love; **cherub, cherubim** (*plural*), angel of light; principality, archangel; recording angel; **saint,** beatified soul, canonized mortal; patron saint; martyr; redeemed *or* saved soul, soul in glory

2 **heavenly host,** host of heaven, choir invisible, angelic host, heavenly hierarchy, Sons of God, ministering spirits; Amesha Spentas

3 (*celestial hierarchy of Pseudo-Dionysius*) seraphim, cherubim, thrones; dominations *or* dominions, virtues, powers; principalities, archangels, angels; angelology

4 **Azrael,** angel of death, death's bright angel; Abdiel, Chamuel, Gabriel, Jophiel, Michael, Raphael, Uriel, Zadkiel

5 **the Madonna;** the Immaculate Conception; Mariology; Mariolatry

adjectives

6 **angelic, seraphic, cherubic; heavenly, celestial;** archangelic; **saintly, sainted,** beatified, canonized; martyred; saved, redeemed, glorified, in glory

680 EVIL SPIRITS

nouns

1 **evil spirits, demons, demonkind,** powers of darkness, spirits of the air, host of hell, hellish host, hellspawn, denizens of hell, inhabitants of Pandemonium, souls in hell, damned spirits, lost souls, the lost, the damned

2 **devil,** *diable* (*French*), *diablo* (*Spanish*), *diabolus* (*Latin*), deil (*Scottish*), *Teufel* (*German*)

3 **Satan** (*see list*), Satanas

4 Beelzebub, Belial, Eblis, Azazel, Ahriman *or* Angra Mainyu; Mephistopheles, Mephisto; Shaitan, Sammael, Asmodeus; Abaddon, Apollyon; Lilith; Aeshma, Pisacha, Putana, Ravana

5 (*gods of evil*) Set, Typhon, Loki; Nemesis; gods of the nether world

6 **demon, fiend,** fiend from hell, **devil,** Satan, daeva, rakshasa, dybbuk, shedu, gyre (*Scottish*), bad *or* evil *or* unclean spirit; **hellion** (*informal*), hellhound, hellkite (*old*), she-devil; cacodemon, incubus, succubus; **jinni,** genie, genius, jinniyeh, afreet; evil genius; barghest; **ghoul,** lamia, Lilith, yogini, Baba Yaga, **vampire,** the undead

7 **imp, pixie, sprite, elf, puck,** kobold, *diablotin* (*French*), tokoloshe, poltergeist, **gremlin,** Dingbelle, Fifinella, **bad fairy,** bad peri; little *or* young devil, devilkin, devilling; erlking; Puck, Robin Goodfellow, Hob, Hobgoblin

8 **goblin, hobgoblin,** hob, ouphe

9 **bugbear, bugaboo, bogey,** bogle, boggart; **booger, bugger,** bug (*old*), **booger-man, bogeyman, boogeyman;** bête noire, fee-faw-fum, Mumbo Jumbo

10 **Fury,** avenging spirit; the Furies, the Erinyes, the Eumenides, the Dirae; Alecto, Megaera, Tisiphone

11 **changeling,** elf child; shape-shifter

12 werefolk, were-animals; werewolf, lycanthrope, *loup-garou* (*French*); werejaguar, jaguar-man, uturuncu; wereass, werebear, werecalf, werefox, werehyena, wereleopard, weretiger, werelion, wereboar, werecrocodile, werecat, werehare

13 devilishness, demonishness, **fiendishness;** devilship, devildom; horns, the cloven hoof, the Devil's pitchfork

14 Satanism, diabolism, devil-worship, **demonism, devilry, diablerie, demonry;** demonomy, demonianism; black magic; Black Mass; sorcery *see* 690; demonolatry, demon *or* devil *or* chthonian worship; demonomancy; demonology, diabolology *or* diabology, demonography, devil lore

15 Satanist, Satan-worshipper, diabolist, devil-worshipper, **demonist;** demonomist, demoniast; demonologist, demonologer; demonolater, chthonian, demon worshipper; sorcerer *see* 690.5

verbs

16 to demonize, devilize, diabolize; possess, **obsess;** bewitch, bedevil

adjectives

17 demoniac *or* **demoniacal,** demonic *or* demonical, demonish, demonlike; **devilish,** devil-like; **satanic, diabolic, diabolical; hellish** *see* 682.8; **fiendish,** fiendlike; ghoulish, ogreish; foul, unclean, damned; inhuman

18 impish, puckish, elfish, elvish; mischievous *see* 322.6

19 designations of Satan

His Satanic Majesty	the Demon
Lucifer	the Deuce (informal)
Old *or* Auld Clootie	the Devil Incarnate
(Scottish informal)	the Dickens (informal)
Old Bendy (informal)	the Evil One
Old Gooseberry (informal)	the Evil Spirit
Old Harry (informal)	the Father of Lies
Old Horny (informal)	the Fiend
Old Ned (informal)	the Foul Fiend
Old Nick (informal)	the Lord of the Flies
Old Poker (informal)	the Old Enemy
Old Scratch (informal)	the Old Gentleman
the Adversary	(informal)
the Angel *or* Prince of	the Old Serpent
darkness	the Prince of the Devils
the Angel of the	the Prince of the power of
bottomless pit	the air
the Arch-fiend	the Prince of this world
the archenemy	the serpent
the Author *or* Father of	the Tempter
Evil	the Wicked One
the Common Enemy	

681 HEAVEN
abode of the deity and blessed dead

nouns

1 Heaven (*see list*);
"my Father's house"—BIBLE, "God's residence"—EMILY DICKINSON, "mansions in the sky"—ISAAC WATTS, "the bosom of our rest"—CARDINAL NEWMAN, "the treasury of everlasting joy"—SHAKESPEARE, "the great world of light, that lies behind all human destinies"—LONGFELLOW

2 the hereafter, the afterworld, the afterlife *see* 838.2, life after death

3 Holy City, **Zion,** New Jerusalem, Heavenly *or* Celestial City, City Celestial, Heavenly City of God, City of God, *Civitas Dei* (*Latin*), "heaven's high city"—FRANCIS QUARLES

4 heaven of heavens, seventh heaven, the empyrean, throne of God, God's throne, celestial throne, the great white throne

5 (*Christian Science*) bliss, harmony, spirituality, the reign of Spirit, the atmosphere of Soul

6 (*Mormon*) celestial kingdom, terrestrial kingdom, telestial kingdom

7 (*Muslim*) Alfardaws, Assama; Falak al aflak

8 (*Hindu, Buddhist, and Theosophical*) nirvana; Buddha-field; devaloka, land of the gods; kamavachara, kamaloka; devachan; samadhi

9 (*mythological*) Olympus, Mount Olympus; Elysium, Elysian fields; fields of Aalu; Islands *or* Isles of the Blessed, Happy Isles, Fortunate Isles *or* Islands; Avalon; garden of the Gods, garden of the Hesperides, Bower of Bliss; Tir-na-n'Og, Annwfn

10 (*Norse*) Valhalla, Asgard, Fensalir, Glathsheim, Vingolf, Valaskjalf, Hlithskjalf, Thruthvang *or* Thruthheim, Bilskirnir, Ydalir, Sökkvabekk, Breithablik, Folkvang, Sessrymnir, Noatun, Thrymheim, Glitnir, Himinbjorg, Vithi

11 (*removal to heaven*) **apotheosis, resurrection, translation,** gathering, **ascension,** the Ascension; **assumption,** the Assumption; removal to Abraham's bosom

adjectives

12 heavenly, heavenish; **paradisal, paradisaic, paradisaical,** paradisiac, paradisiacal, paradisic, paradisical; **celestial,** supernal, ethereal; **unearthly,** unworldly; **otherworldly,** extraterrestrial, extramundane, transmundane, transcendental; Elysian, Olympian; blessed, beatified, beatific *or* beatifical, glorified, in glory; from on high

adverbs

13 celestially, paradisally, supernally, ethereally; in heaven, in Abraham's bosom, *in sinu Abraham* (*Latin*), on high, among the blest, in glory

14 designations of Heaven

a better place	kingdom come (informal)
abode of the blessed	Land of the Leal
Abraham's bosom	(Scottish)
better world	my Father's house
Beulah	Paradise
Beulah Land	the happy land
eternal home	the heavenly kingdom
eternity	the kingdom of glory
glory	the kingdom of God
God's kingdom	the kingdom of heaven
God's presence	the otherworld
happy hunting ground	the place up there
heaven above	the presence of God
high heaven	the Promised Land
inheritance of the saints in	the realm of light
light	the world above

682 HELL

nouns

1 **hell, Hades,** Sheol, Gehenna, Tophet, Abaddon, Naraka, jahannan, avichi, **perdition,** Pandemonium, inferno, the pit, **the bottomless pit,** the abyss, "a vast, unbottom'd, boundless pit"—Robert Burns, **nether world,** lower world, under-world, infernal regions, abode *or* world of the dead, abode of the damned, place of torment, the grave, shades below; **purgatory; limbo**

2 **hellfire,** fire and brimstone, lake of fire and brimstone, everlasting fire *or* torment, "the fire that never shall be quenched"—Bible

3 (*mythological*) **Hades,** Orcus, Tartarus, Avernus, Acheron, pit of Acheron; Amenti, Aralu; Hel, Niflhel, Niflheim, Naströnd

4 (*rivers of Hades*) Styx, Stygian creek; Acheron, River of Woe; Cocytus, River of Wailing; Phlegethon, Pyriphlegethon, River of Fire; Lethe, River of Forgetfulness

5 (*deities of the nether world*) Pluto, Orcus, Hades *or* Aides *or* Aidoneus, Dis *or* Dis pater, Rhadamanthus, Minos, Aeacus, Erebus, Charon, Cerberus; Osiris; Persephone, Proserpine, Proserpina, Persephassa, Despoina, Kore *or* Cora; Hel, Loki; Satan *see* 680.3

verbs

6 **to damn,** doom, send *or* consign to hell, cast into hell, doom to perdition, condemn to hell *or* eternal punishment

7 **to go to hell** *or* to the devil, be damned, go the other way *or* to the other place (*informal*)

adjectives

8 **hellish, infernal,** sulphurous, brimstone, fire-and-brimstone; chthonic, chthonian; pandemonic, pandemoniac; devilish; Plutonic, Plutonian; Tartarean; Stygian; Lethean; Acherontic; purgatorial, hellborn

adverbs

9 **hellishly, infernally,** in hell, in hellfire, below, in torment

683 SCRIPTURE

nouns

1 **scripture, scriptures, sacred writings** *or* **texts, Bible;** canonical writings *or* books, sacred canon

2 **Bible, Holy Bible, Scripture, the Scriptures, Holy Scripture,** Holy Writ, the Book, the Good Book, the Book of Books, the Word, the Word of God; Vulgate, Septuagint, Douay Bible, Authorized *or* King James Version, Revised Version; Revised Standard Version, New English Bible, Good News Bible; Jerusalem Bible; Testament; canon

3 **Old Testament,** Tenach; Hexateuch, Octateuch; Pentateuch, Chumash, Five Books of Moses, **Torah,** the Law, the Jewish *or* Mosaic Law, Law of Moses; the Prophets, Nebiim, Major *or* Minor Prophets; the Writings, Hagiographa, Ketubim; Apocrypha, noncanonical writings

4 **New Testament; Gospels,** Evangels, the Gospel, Good News, Good *or* Glad Tidings; Synoptic Gospels, Epistles, Pauline Epistles, Catholic Epistles, Johannine Epistles; Acts, Acts of the Apostles; Apocalypse, Revelation

5 **Talmud,** Mishnah, Gemara; Masorah

6 **Koran** *or* **Qur'an,** Alkoran *or* Alcoran; sharia *or* sheria; Avesta, **Zend-Avesta;** Granth, Adigranth; Tripitaka, agama; Tao Tê Ching; Analects of Confucius; the Eddas; Arcana Caelestia; **Book of Mormon;** Science and Health with Key to the Scriptures

7 (*Hindu*) **the Vedas,** Veda, Rig-Veda, Yajur-Veda, Sama-Veda, Atharva-Veda, sruti; Brahmana, Upanishad, Aranyaka; Samhita; shastra, Smriti, Purana, Tantra, Agama; Bhagavad-Gita

8 (*Buddhist*) Vinaya Pitaka, Sutta Pitaka, Abhidamma Pitaka; Dhammapada, Jataka; The Diamond-Cutter, The Lotus of the True Law, Prajna-Paramita Sutra, Pure Land Sutras

9 **revelation, divine revelation; inspiration,** afflatus, divine inspiration; theopneusty, theopneustia; theophany, theophania, epiphany; **mysticism,** direct *or* immediate intuition *or* communication, mystical experience, mystical intuition, contemplation, ecstasy; **prophecy,** prophetic revelation, apocalypse

adjectives

10 **scriptural, Biblical,** Old-Testament, New-Testament, Gospel, Mosaic, Yahwist, Yahwistic, Elohist; **revealed, revelational;** prophetic, apocalyptic, apocalyptical; **inspired,** theopneustic; evangelic, evangelical, evangelistic, gospel; apostolic, apostolical; textual, textuary; canonical

11 Talmudic, Mishnaic, Gemaric, Masoretic; rabbinic

12 epiphanic, mystic, mystical

13 Koranic; Avestan; Eddic; Mormon

14 Vedic; tantrist

684 PROPHETS, RELIGIOUS FOUNDERS

nouns

1 **prophet** *see* 961.4, *vates sacer* (*Latin*); Old Testament prophets (*see list*)

2 (*Christian founders*) evangelist, apostle, disciple, saint; Matthew, Mark, Luke, John; Paul; Peter; **the Fathers, fathers of the church**

3 Martin Luther, John Calvin, John Wycliffe, Jan Hus, John Wesley, John Knox, George Fox (*Protestant reformers*); Emanuel Swedenborg (*Church of the New Jerusalem*); Mary Baker Eddy (*Christian Science*); Joseph Smith (*Church of Jesus Christ of Latter-day Saints*)

4 Buddha, Gautama Buddha (*Buddhism*); Mahavira *or* Vardhamana *or* Jina (*Jainism*); Mirza Ali Muhammad of Shiraz *or* the Bab (*Babism*); Muhammad *or* Mohammed (*Islam*); Confucius (*Confucianism*); Lao-tzu (*Taoism*); Zoroaster *or* Zarathustra (*Zoroastrianism*); Nanak (*Sikhism*); Ram Mohan Roy (*Brahmo-Samaj*)

5 **Old Testament prophets**

Abraham	Daniel
Amos	Ezekiel

Habakkuk	Joshua
Haggai	Malachi
Hosea	Micah
Isaac	Moses
Isaiah	Nahum
Jacob	Obadiah
Jeremiah	Samuel
Joel	Zechariah
Jonah	Zephaniah
Joseph	

685 SANCTITY
sacred quality

nouns

1 **sanctity,** sanctitude; **sacredness, holiness,** hallowedness, numinousness; sacrosanctness, sacrosanctity; heavenliness, transcendence, divinity, divineness *see* 677.1; venerableness, **venerability, blessedness;** awesomeness, awfulness; inviolableness, **inviolability;** ineffability, unutterability, unspeakability, inexpressibility, inenarrableness; godliness *see* 692.2; odour of sanctity

2 **the sacred,** the holy, the holy of holies, the numinous, the ineffable, the unutterable, the unspeakable, the inexpressible, the inenarrable, the transcendent

3 **sanctification, hallowing; purification;** beatitude, blessing; **glorification,** exaltation, enskying; **consecration,** dedication, devotion, setting apart; sainting, canonization, enshrinement; **sainthood, beatification; blessedness; grace,** state of grace; justification, justification by faith, justification by works

4 **redemption,** redeemedness, **salvation,** conversion, regeneration, new life, reformation, adoption; **rebirth, new birth, second birth;** circumcision, spiritual purification *or* cleansing

verbs

5 **to sanctify, hallow; purify,** cleanse, wash one's sins away; **bless,** beatify; **glorify,** exalt, ensky; **consecrate,** dedicate, devote, set apart; **beatify, saint, canonize;** enshrine

6 **to redeem,** regenerate, reform, convert, save, give salvation

adjectives

7 **sacred,** holy, numinous, **sacrosanct, religious, spiritual,** heavenly, divine; **venerable,** awesome, awful; inviolable, **inviolate,** untouchable; **ineffable,** unutterable, unspeakable, inexpressible, inenarrable

8 **sanctified, hallowed; blessed,** consecrated, devoted, dedicated, set apart; **glorified, exalted,** enskied; **saintly,** sainted, beatified, canonized

9 **redeemed, saved,** converted, regenerated, regenerate, justified, reborn, born-again, renewed; circumcised, spiritually purified *or* cleansed

word elements

10 sacr–, sacro–, hier–, hiero–, hagi–, hagio–

686 UNSANCTITY

nouns

1 **unsanctity,** unsanctitude; **unsacredness, unholiness,** unhallowedness, unblessedness; profanity, profaneness; unregenerateness, reprobation; **worldliness,** secularity, secularism; secular humanism

2 **the profane,** the unholy; the temporal, the secular, **the worldly,** the fleshly, the mundane; the world, the flesh and the devil

adjectives

3 **unsacred,** nonsacred, **unholy,** unhallowed, unsanctified, unblessed; profane, **secular, temporal, worldly,** fleshly, mundane; unsaved, unredeemed, unregenerate, reprobate

687 ORTHODOXY

nouns

1 **orthodoxy,** orthodoxness, orthodoxism; **soundness,** soundness of doctrine, rightness, right belief *or* doctrine; **authoritativeness,** authenticity, canonicalness, canonicity; traditionalism; the truth, religious truth, gospel truth

2 **the faith, true faith,** apostolic faith, primitive faith, "the faith once delivered unto the saints"—BIBLE; old-time religion, faith of our fathers

3 **the Church, the true church,** Holy Church, Church of Christ, the Bride of the Lamb, body of Christ, temple of the Holy Ghost, body of Christians, members in Christ, disciples *or* followers of Christ; apostolic church; universal church, the church universal; church visible, church invisible; church militant, church triumphant

4 **true believer,** orthodox Christian; Sunni Muslim; Orthodox Jew; orthodox, orthodoxian, orthodoxist; textualist, textuary; canonist; fundamentalist; the orthodox

5 **strictness,** strict interpretation, scripturalism, evangelicalism; hyperorthodoxy, puritanism, puritanicalness, purism; staunchness; straitlacedness, stiff-neckedness, hideboundness; hard line (*informal*); bigotry *see* 979.1; dogmatism *see* 969.6; **fundamentalism,** literalism, precisianism; bibliolatry; Sabbatarianism; sabbatism

6 **bigot** *see* 979.5; **dogmatist** *see* 969.7

adjectives

7 **orthodox,** orthodoxical; of the faith, of the true faith; **sound,** firm, faithful, true, true-blue, right-thinking; Christian; **evangelical; scriptural,** canonical; traditional, traditionalistic; literal, textual; standard, customary, conventional; **authoritative,** authentic, accepted, received, approved; correct, right, proper

8 **strict,** scripturalistic, evangelical; hyperorthodox, puritanical, purist *or* puristic, straitlaced; staunch; hidebound, hardline (*informal*), creedbound; **bigoted** *see* 979.10; **dogmatic** *see* 969.22; **fundamentalist,** precisianist *or* precisianistic, literalist *or* literalistic; Sabbatarian

688 UNORTHODOXY

nouns

1 **unorthodoxy, heterodoxy;** unorthodoxness, **unsoundness,** un-Scripturality; **unauthoritativeness,** unauthenticity, uncanonicalness, uncanonicity; **nonconformity** see 867

2 **heresy,** false doctrine, **misbelief; fallacy, error** see 974

3 **infidelity,** infidelism; unchristianity; gentilism; **atheism, unbelief** see 695.5

4 **paganism, heathenism;** paganry, heathenry; pagandom, heathendom; pagano-Christianism; allotheism; animism, animatism; idolatry see 697

5 **heretic, misbeliever;** heresiarch; nonconformist see 867.3; antinomian, Albigensian, Arian, Donatist, etc

6 **gentile;** non-Christian; **non-Jew,** goy, goyim, non-Jewish man or shegets (Yiddish), non-Jewish woman or shiksa (Yiddish); non-Muslim, non-Moslem, giaour (Turkish), kaffir; zendik, zendician, zendikite; non-Mormon; infidel; unbeliever see 695.11

7 **pagan, heathen;** allotheist; animist; idolater see 697.4

verbs

8 **to misbelieve, err,** stray, deviate, wander, go astray, stray from the path, step out of line (informal), go wrong, fall into error; be wrong, be mistaken, be in error; serve Mammon

adjectives

9 **unorthodox,** nonorthodox, **heterodox, heretical; unsound; unscriptural,** uncanonical, apocryphal; **unauthoritative,** unauthentic, unaccepted, unreceived, unapproved; **fallacious,** erroneous see 974.16; antinomian, Albigensian, Arian, Donatist, etc

10 **infidel,** infidelic, misbelieving; **atheistic,** unbelieving see 695.19; **unchristian,** non-Christian; gentile, non-Jewish, goyish, uncircumcised; non-Muslim, non-Moslem, non-Islamic; non-Mormon

11 **pagan, paganish,** paganistic; **heathen, heathenish;** pagano-Christian; allotheistic; animist, animistic; idolatrous see 697.7

689 OCCULTISM

nouns

1 **occultism, esoterics,** esotericism, esoterism, esotery; cabalism, cabala or kabala or kabballa; yoga, yogism, yogeeism; **theosophy,** anthroposophy; symbolics, symbolism; anagogics; anagoge; mystery; mystification, hocus-pocus, mumbo jumbo; mysticism see 683.9

2 **supernaturalism,** supranaturalism, preternaturalism, **transcendentalism; the supernatural,** the supersensible, the paranormal

3 **metaphysics,** hyperphysics, transphysical science, the first philosophy or theology

4 **psychics,** psychism, psychicism; **parapsychology, psychical research;** metapsychics, metapsychism; psychosophy; panpsychism; psychic monism

5 **spiritualism,** spiritism; mediumism; necromancy; séance, sitting; spirit see 987.1

6 **psychic** or psychical phenomena, spirit manifestation; materialization; spirit rapping, table tipping or turning; poltergeistism, poltergeist; telekinesis, psychokinesis, power of mind over matter, telaesthesia, teleportation; levitation; trance speaking; psychorrhagy; automatism, psychography, automatic or trance or spirit writing; Ouija board, Ouija; planchette

7 **ectoplasm,** exteriorized protoplasm; aura, emanation, effluvium; ectoplasy

8 **extrasensory perception** or **ESP; clairvoyance,** lucidity, second sight, insight, sixth sense; intuition see 933; foresight see 960; premonition see 133.1; clairsentience, clairaudience, crystal vision, psychometry, metapsychosis

9 **telepathy, mental telepathy, mind reading,** thought transference, telepathic transmission; telepathic dream, telepathic hallucination

10 **divination** see 961.2; **sorcery** see 690

11 **occultist,** esoteric, mystic, mystagogue, cabalist, supernaturalist, transcendentalist; adept, mahatma; yogi, yogin, yogist; theosophist, anthroposophist

12 **parapsychologist;** psychist, psychicist; **metapsychist;** panpsychist; **metaphysician,** metaphysicist

13 **psychic; spiritualist,** spiritist, **medium,** ecstatic, spirit rapper, automatist, psychographist; necromancer

14 **clairvoyant;** clairaudient; psychometer, psychometrist

15 **telepathist, mental telepathist, mind reader,** thought reader

16 **diviner** see 961.4; **sorcerer** see 690.5

17 **astral body,** astral, linga sharira, design body, subtle body, vital body, etheric body, bliss body, Buddhic body, spiritual body, soul body; kamarupa, desire or kamic body; causal body; mental or mind body

18 (seven principles of man, theosophy) spirit, atman; mind, manas; soul, buddhi; life principle, vital force, prana; astral body, linga sharira; physical or dense or gross body, sthula sharira; principle of desire, kama

19 **spiritualization,** etherealization, idealization; **dematerialization,** immaterialization, unsubstantialization; **disembodiment,** disincarnation

verbs

20 **to spiritualize,** spiritize; etherealize; idealize; **dematerialize,** immaterialize, unsubstantialize; **disembody,** disincarnate

21 **to practise spiritualism,** hold a séance or sitting; call up spirits see 690.11

22 **to telepathize, read one's mind**

adjectives

23 **occult, esoteric,** esoterical, **mysterious,** mystic, mystical, **New Age,** anagogic, anagogical; metaphysic, metaphysical; cabalic, cabalistic; **paranormal, supernatural** see 869.15; theosophical, theosophic, anthroposophical

24 **psychic, psychical, spiritual; spiritualistic,** spiritistic; mediumistic; **clairvoyant,** second-sighted, clairaudient, clairsentient, **telepathic; extrasensory,** psychosensory; supersensible, supersensual, pretersensual; telekinetic, psychokinetic; automatist

690 SORCERY

nouns

1 **sorcery, necromancy, magic,** sortilege, **wizardry,** theurgy, gramarye (*old*), rune, glamour; **witchcraft, spellcraft,** spellbinding, spellcasting; **witchery,** witchwork, bewitchery, **enchantment; voodooism, voodoo,** hoodoo, wanga, juju, jujuism, obeah, obeahism; shamanism; magism, magianism; fetishism; vampirism; thaumaturgy, thaumaturgia, thaumaturgics, thaumaturgism; alchemy; white *or* natural magic; sympathetic magic; **divination** *see* 961.2; spell, charm *see* 691

2 **black magic,** the black art; **diabolism, demonism,** Satanism

3 (*practices*) magic circle; ghost dance; Sabbath, witches' meeting *or* Sabbath, sabbat; ordeal, ordeal by battle *or* fire *or* water *or* lots

4 **conjuration,** conjurement, evocation, invocation; **exorcism,** exorcisation; exsufflation; **incantation** *see* 691.4

5 **sorcerer, necromancer, wizard, wonder-worker,** warlock, theurgist; warlock, male witch; thaumaturge, thaumaturgist, miracle- *or* wonder-worker; alchemist; **conjurer; diviner** *see* 961.4; dowser, water witch *or* diviner; diabolist; Faust, Comus

6 **magician, mage,** magus, magian; Merlin; prestidigitator, illusionist *see* 357.2

7 **shaman,** shamanist; **voodoo,** voodooist, wangateur, **witch doctor,** obeah doctor, **medicine man,** mundunugu, isangoma; witch-hunter, witch-finder; exorcist, exorciser; unspeller

8 **sorceress,** shamaness; **witch,** witchwoman (*informal*), witchwife (*Scottish*), hex (*US & Canadian informal*), **hag,** lamia; witch of Endor; coven, witches' coven, Weird Sisters (*Shakespeare*)

9 **bewitcher, enchanter, charmer, spellbinder; enchantress, siren,** vampire; Circe; Medusa, Medea, Gorgon, Stheno, Euryale

verbs

10 to sorcerize, shamanize; make *or* work magic, wave a wand, rub the ring *or* lamp; ride a broomstick; alchemize

11 **to conjure, conjure up,** evoke, invoke, raise, summon, call up; **call up spirits,** conjure *or* conjure up spirits, summon spirits, raise ghosts, evoke from the dead,

"call spirits from the vasty deep"—SHAKESPEARE

12 **to exorcise,** lay; lay ghosts, **cast out devils;** unspell

13 to cast a spell, bewitch *see* 691.9

adjectives

14 sorcerous, necromantic, **magic, magical,** magian, numinous, thaumaturgic, thaumaturgical, miraculous, cantrip *or* weird (*both Scottish*), wizardlike, wizardly; alchemical, alchemistic, alchemistical; shaman, shamanic, shamanist *or* shamanistic; witchlike, witchy, witch; voodoo, hoodoo (*informal*), voodooistic; incantatory, incantational; talismanic

691 SPELL, CHARM

nouns

1 **spell, magic spell, charm,** glamour, weird *or* cantrip (*both Scottish*), wanga; hand of glory; evil eye, malocchio (*Italian*), whammy (*US informal*); **jinx, curse,** hex (*US & Canadian informal*); **exorcism**

2 **bewitchment, witchery, bewitchery; enchantment, entrancement,** fascination, captivation; illusion, maya; bedevilment; **possession, obsession**

3 **trance, ecstasy,** ecstasis, transport, mystic transport; meditation, contemplation; **rapture;** yoga trance, dharana, dhyana, samadhi; hypnosis *see* 22.7

4 **incantation, conjuration,** magic words *or* formula; hocus-pocus, abracadabra, mumbo jumbo; open sesame; hey presto

5 **charm, amulet, talisman, fetish,** periapt, phylactery; **voodoo, hoodoo,** juju, obeah, mumbo jumbo; **good-luck charm,** good-luck piece, lucky piece, luckpenny, rabbit's-foot, lucky bean, **four-leaf clover,** whammy (*US informal*); mascot; madstone; love charm, philtre; scarab, scarabaeus, scarabee; veronica, sudarium; swastika, fylfot, gammadion

6 **wish-bringer,** wish-giver; **wand, magic wand,** Aaron's rod; Aladdin's lamp, magic ring, magic belt, magic spectacles, magic carpet, seven-league boots; wishing well, wishing stone, wishing cap, Fortunatus's cap; cap of darkness, Tarnkappe, Tarnhelm; fern seed; **wishbone,** wishing bone, merrythought

verbs

7 **to cast a spell,** spell, **spellbind; entrance,** trance, put in a trance; **hypnotize, mesmerize**

8 **to charm,** becharm, **enchant, fascinate,** captivate, glamour

9 **to bewitch,** witch, jinx, hex (*US & Canadian informal*); voodoo, hoodoo; **possess, obsess;** bedevil, diabolize, demonize; hagride; overlook, look on with the evil eye, cast the evil eye

10 **to put a curse on,** put a hex on (*US & Canadian informal*), put a juju on, put obeah on, give the evil eye, give the *malocchio*, give a whammy (*US informal*)

adjectives

11 **bewitching, witching;** illusory, illusive, illusionary; **charming, enchanting, entrancing, spellbinding,** fascinating, glamorous, Circean

12 **enchanted, charmed,** becharmed, charmstruck, charm-bound; **spellbound,** spell-struck, spell-caught; **fascinated,** captivated; **hypnotized, mesmerized;** under a spell, in a trance

13 **bewitched,** witched, witch-charmed, witch-held, witch-struck; hag-ridden; **possessed,** taken over, obsessed

692 PIETY

nouns

1 **piety, piousness,** pietism; **religion, faith; religiousness,** religiosity, religionism, religious-mindedness; theism; love of God, adoration;

devoutness, devotion, devotedness, worship *see* 696, worshipfulness, prayerfulness, cultism; faithfulness, dutifulness, observance, churchgoing, conformity *see* 866; **reverence**, veneration; discipleship, followership; daily communion

2 **godliness**, godlikeness; fear of God; **sanctity**, sanctitude; odour of sanctity, beauty of holiness; **righteousness, holiness, goodness; spirituality**, spiritual-mindedness, holy-mindedness, heavenly-mindedness, godly-mindedness; **purity**, pureness, pure-heartedness, pureness of heart; **saintliness**, saintlikeness; saintship, sainthood; angelicalness, seraphicalness; heavenliness, **unworldliness**, unearthliness, other-worldliness

3 **zeal**, zealousness, zealotry, zealotism; **evangelism, revival**, evangelicalism, revivalism; pentecostalism, charismatic movement; charismatic renewal, baptism in the spirit; charismatic gift, gift of tongues, glossolalia; **overreligiousness, religiosity**, overpiousness, overrighteousness, **overzealousness**, overdevoutness; bibliolatry; fundamentalism, militance, **fanaticism** *see* 925.11; **sanctimony** *see* 693

4 **believer**, truster, accepter, receiver; God-fearing man, pietist, religionist, saint, theist; **devotee**, devotionalist, votary; **zealot**, zealotist, fundamentalist, militant; **churchgoer**, churchman, churchite; pillar of the church; communicant, daily communicant; **convert**, proselyte, neophyte, catechumen; **disciple**, follower, servant, faithful servant; **fanatic**

5 **the believing, the faithful**, the righteous, the good; the elect, the chosen, the saved; the children of God, the children of light; Christendom, the Church *see* 687.3

verbs

6 **to be pious, be religious; have faith**, trust in God, love God, fear God; witness, bear witness, affirm, **believe** *see* 952.10; keep the faith, fight the good fight, let one's light shine, praise and glorify God, walk humbly with one's God; be observant, follow righteousness

7 **to be converted, get religion** (*informal*), receive *or* accept Christ, stand up for Jesus, be washed in the blood of the Lamb; be born again, see the light

adjectives

8 **pious**, pietistic; **religious**, religious-minded; theistic; **devout**, devoted, worshipful, prayerful, cultish, cultist, cultistic; **reverent**, reverential, venerative, venerational, adoring, solemn; faithful, dutiful; affirming, witnessing, believing *see* 952.21; **observant, practising**

9 **godly**, godlike; **God-fearing; righteous, holy, good; spiritual**, spiritual-minded, holy-minded, godly-minded, heavenly-minded; **pure**, purehearted, pure in heart; **saintly**, saintlike; **angelic, angelical**, seraphic, seraphical; heavenly; **unworldly**, unearthly, otherworldly, not of the earth, not of this world

10 **regenerate**, regenerated, **converted, redeemed, saved**, reborn, **born-again**; sanctified *see* 685.8

11 **zealous**, zealotical; **overreligious**, ultrareligious,

overpious, overrighteous, **overzealous**, overdevout; **fanatical** *see* 925.32; sanctimonious *see* 693.5

693 SANCTIMONY

nouns

1 **sanctimony, sanctimoniousness; pietism**, piety, **piousness**, pietisticalness, false piety; religionism, religiosity; **self-righteousness**; goodiness *and* goody-goodiness (*both informal*); pharisaism, pharisaicalness; Tartuffery, Tartuffism; **falseness, insincerity, hypocrisy** *see* 354.6; affectation *see* 500; **cant**, mummery, snivel, snuffle; unction, unctuousness, oiliness, smarm *and* smarminesss (*both informal*), mealymouthedness

2 **lip service**, mouth honour, mouthing, lip homage *or* worship *or* devotion *or* praise *or* reverence; formalism, solemn mockery; BOMFOG *or* brotherhood of man and fatherhood of God

3 **pietist**, religionist, **hypocrite**, religious hypocrite, canting hypocrite, pious fraud, religious *or* spiritual humbug, whited sepulchre, **pharisee**, Holy Willie (*Robert Burns*),
"a saint abroad and a devil at home"—Bunyan; bleeding heart (*informal*); **canter**, ranter, snuffler, sniveler; dissembler, dissimulator; affecter, poser *see* 500.8; **lip server**, lip worshipper, formalist; Pharisee, scribes and Pharisees; Tartuffe, Pecksniff, Mawworm, Joseph Surface

verbs

4 **to be sanctimonious**, be hypocritical; cant, snuffle, snivel; render *or* pay lip service, give mouth honour

adjectives

sanctimonious, sanctified, **pious**, pi (*informal*), pietistic, pietistical, **self-righteous**, pharisaic, pharisaical, **holier-than-thou**, holier-than-the-pope (*informal*); goody *and* goody-goody *and* goo-goo (*all informal*); **false, insincere, hypocritical** *see* 354.32; affected *see* 500.15; Tartuffish, Tartuffian; canting, snivelling, unctuous, mealymouthed, smarmy (*informal*)

694 IMPIETY

nouns

1 **impiety, impiousness; irreverence**, undutifulness; desertion, renegadism, apostasy, recreancy; backsliding, recidivism, lapse, fall *or* lapse from grace; **atheism, irreligion; unsanctity** *see* 686

2 **sacrilege, blasphemy**, blaspheming, impiety; **profanity**, profaneness; sacrilegiousness, blasphemousness; **desecration, profanation;** tainting, pollution, contamination

3 **sacrilegist, blasphemer**, Sabbath-breaker; deserter, renegade, apostate, recreant; backslider, recidivist; **atheist**, unbeliever *see* 695.11

verbs

4 **to desecrate, profane**, dishonour, unhallow, commit sacrilege

5 **to blaspheme**; vilify, abuse *see* 513.7; curse, swear *see* 513.6; take in vain; taint, pollute, contaminate

adjectives

6 impious, irreverent, undutiful; **profane,** profanatory; **sacrilegious, blasphemous;** renegade, apostate, recreant, backsliding, recidivist *or* recidivistic, lapsed, fallen, lapsed *or* fallen from grace; atheistic, **irreligious** *see* 695.17; unsacred *see* 686.3

695 NONRELIGIOUSNESS

nouns

1 **nonreligiousness, unreligiousness; undevoutness;** indevoutness, indevotion, undutifulness, nonobservance; adiaphorism, indifferentism, Laodiceanism, lukewarm piety; indifference *see* 102; **laicism, unconsecration; deconsecration, secularization,** laicization, desacralization

2 **secularism, worldliness,** earthliness, earthiness, mundaneness; **unspirituality,** carnality; worldly-mindedness, earthly-mindedness, carnal-mindedness; materialism, philistinism

3 **ungodliness, godlessness, unrighteousness, irreligion,** unholiness, unsaintliness, unangelicalness; unchristianliness, un-Christliness; impiety *see* 694; **wickedness, sinfulness** *see* 654.4

4 unregeneracy, unredeemedness, reprobacy, gracelessness, shriftlessness

5 **unbelief, disbelief** *see* 954.1; infidelity, infidelism, faithlessness; **atheism;** nullifidianism, minimifidianism

6 **agnosticism; scepticism, doubt, incredulity,** Pyrrhonism, Humism; scoffing *see* 508.1

7 **freethinking,** free thought, **latitudinarianism; humanism,** secular humanism

8 antireligion; antichristianism, antichristianity; antiscripturism

9 **iconoclasm,** iconoclasticism, image breaking

10 irreligionist; worldling, earthling; **materialist;** iconoclast, idoloclast; anti-Christian, antichrist

11 **unbeliever, disbeliever,** nonbeliever; **atheist, infidel, pagan, heathen;** nullifidian, minimifidian; secularist; **gentile** *see* 688.6

12 agnostic; sceptic, doubter, dubitante, **doubting Thomas,** scoffer, Pyrrhonist, Humist

13 freethinker, latitudinarian, *esprit fort (French)*; humanist, secular humanist

verbs

14 **to disbelieve,** doubt *see* 954.6; scoff *see* 508.9; laicize, deconsecrate, **secularize,** desacralize

adjectives

15 **nonreligious, unreligious,** having no religious preference; **undevout,** indevout, indevotional, undutiful, nonobservant, nonpractising; adiamorphic, indifferentist *or* indifferentistic, Laodicean, lukewarm, indifferent *see* 102.6; unconsecrated, **deconsecrated, secularized,** laicized, desacralized

16 **secularist, secularistic, worldly, earthly,** earthy, terrestrial, **mundane,** temporal; **unspiritual, profane,** carnal, **secular;** humanistic, secular-humanistic; worldly minded, earthly minded, carnal-minded; **materialistic,** material, Philistine

17 **ungodly, godless, irreligious, unrighteous, unholy,** unsaintly, unangelic, unangelical; impious *see* 694.6; **wicked, sinful** *see* 654.16

18 **unregenerate,** unredeemed, **unconverted,** godless, reprobate, graceless, shriftless, **lost, damned;** lapsed, fallen, recidivist, recidivistic

19 **unbelieving, disbelieving, faithless; infidel,** infidelic; **pagan, heathen; atheistic,** atheist; nullifidian, minimifidian

20 **agnostic; sceptic, sceptical, doubtful, dubious, incredulous,** Humean, Pyrrhonic; Cartesian

21 **freethinking, latitudinarian**

22 **antireligious;** antichristian; antiscriptural; **iconoclastic**

696 WORSHIP

nouns

1 **worship, worshipping, adoration, devotion, homage, veneration, reverence,** "transcendent wonder"—CARLYLE; cult, cultus, cultism; latria, dulia, hyperdulia; falling down and worshipping, prostration; co-worship; idolatry *see* 697

2 **glorification,** glory, **praise,** laudation, laud, exaltation, magnification

3 **paean,** laud; hosanna, hallelujah, alleluia; **hymn,** hymn of praise, **doxology, psalm, anthem,** motet, canticle, chorale; **chant,** versicle; mantra, Vedic hymn *or* chant; Introit, Miserere; Gloria, Gloria in Excelsis, Gloria Patri; Te Deum, Agnus Dei, Benedicite, Magnificat, Nunc Dimittis; response, responsory, report, answer; Trisagion; antiphon, antiphony; offertory, offertory sentence *or* hymn; hymnody, hymnology, hymnography, psalmody

4 **prayer, supplication, invocation,** imploration, impetration, entreaty, beseechment, appeal, petition, suit, aid prayer, bid *or* bidding prayer, orison, obsecration, obtestation, rogation, **devotions;** silent prayer, meditation, contemplation, communion; intercession; **grace, thanks, thanksgiving;** litany; breviary, canonical prayers; collect, collect of the Mass, collect of the Communion; Angelus; Paternoster, the Lord's Prayer; Hail Mary, Ave, Ave Maria; Kyrie Eleison; chaplet; rosary, beads, beadroll; Kaddish, Mourner's Kaddish; prayer wheel *or* machine

5 **benediction, blessing,** benison, invocation, benedicite; sign of the cross; laying on of hands

6 **propitiation,** appeasement *see* 465.1; atonement *see* 658

7 **oblation, offering, sacrifice, immolation,** incense; libation, drink offering; burnt offering, holocaust; thank offering, votive *or* ex voto offering; heave offering, peace offering, sacramental offering, sin *or* piacular offering, whole offering; human sacrifice, mactation, infanticide, hecatomb; self-sacrifice, self-immolation; sutteeism; scapegoat, suttee; offertory, collection

8 divine service, **service,** public worship, **liturgy** *see* 701.3, office, duty, exercises, **devotions;** meeting; church service, church; **revival,** revival meeting, camp meeting, tent meeting, praise meeting; watch meeting, watch-night service, watch night; **prayer**

meeting, prayers, prayer; morning devotions *or* services *or* prayers, matins, lauds; prime, prime song; tierce, undersong; sext; none, nones; novena; evening devotions *or* services *or* prayers, vesper, vespers, vigils, evensong; compline, night song *or* prayer; bedtime prayer; Mass

9 **worshipper,** adorer, venerator, votary, communicant, daily communicant, celebrant, churchgoer, chapelgoer; prayer, suppliant, supplicant, supplicator, petitioner; orans, orant; beadsman; revivalist, evangelist; congregation; **idolater** *see* 697.4

verbs

10 **to worship, adore, reverence, venerate, revere, honour,** do *or* pay homage to, pay divine honours to, do service, lift up the heart, bow down and worship, humble oneself before; **idolize** *see* 697.5

11 **to glorify, praise, laud, exalt, extol,** magnify, bless, celebrate; praise God, praise *or* glorify the Lord, bless the Lord, praise God from whom all blessings flow; praise Father, Son, and Holy Ghost; sing praises, sing the praises of, sound *or* resound the praises of; doxologize, hymn

12 **to pray, supplicate,** invoke, petition, make supplication, *daven* (*Yiddish*); **implore, beseech** *see* 440.11, obtest; offer a prayer, send up a prayer, commune with God; **say one's prayers;** tell one's beads, recite the rosary; **say grace, give** *or* **return thanks;** pray over

13 **to bless, give one's blessing,** give benediction, confer a blessing upon, invoke benefits upon; cross, make the sign of the cross over *or* upon; lay hands on

14 **to propitiate,** make propitiation; appease *see* 465.7; **offer sacrifice,** sacrifice, make sacrifice to, immolate before, offer up an oblation

adjectives

15 **worshipful,** worshipping; **adoring,** adorant; **devout,** devotional; **reverent,** reverential; **venerative,** venerational; solemn; at the feet of; **prayerful, supplicatory,** supplicant, suppliant, precatory, precative, imploring, on one's knees, on bended knee; prone *or* prostrate before, in the dust; blessing, benedictory, benedictional; propitiatory

exclamations

16 **hallelujah!,** alleluia!, **hosanna!, praise God!,** praise the Lord!, praise ye the Lord!,

"praise Him all His hosts!"—BIBLE, Heaven be praised!, glory to God!, glory be to God!, glory be to God in the highest!, bless the Lord!,

"bless the Lord, O my soul, and all that is within me, bless His holy name!", "hallowed be Thy Name!"—BOTH BIBLE; thanks be to God!, *Deo gratias!* (*Latin*); *sursum corda!* (*Latin*); (*Hinduism*) om!, om mani padme hum!

17 O Lord!, our Father which art in heaven!; God grant!, pray God that!; God bless!, God save!, God forbid!

697 IDOLATRY

nouns

1 **idolatry,** idolatrousness, idolism, idolodulia, **idol worship;** heathenism, paganism; image worship, iconolatry, iconoduly; **fetishism; demonism,** demonolatry, demon *or* devil worship, Satanism; animal worship, snake worship, fire worship, pyrolatry, Parsiism, Zoroastrianism; sun worship, star worship, Sabaism; tree worship, plant worship, Druidism, nature worship; phallic worship, phallicism; hero worship; idolomancy

2 **idolization,** fetishization; **deification,** apotheosis

3 **idol; fetish,** totem, joss; **graven image, golden calf;** devil-god,
"the god of my idolatry"—SHAKESPEARE; Baal, Jaganatha *or* Juggernaut; sacred cow

4 **idolater,** idolatress, idolizer, idolatrizer, idolist, idol worshipper, image-worshipper; fetishist, totemist; demon *or* devil worshipper, demonolater, chthonian; animal worshipper, zoolater, theriolater, therolater, snake worshipper, ophiolater; fire worshipper, pyrolater, Parsi, Zoroastrian; sun worshipper, heliolater; star worshipper, Sabaist; tree worshipper, arborolater, dendrolater, plant worshipper, Druid, nature worshipper; phallic worshipper; anthropolater, archaeolater, etc

verbs

5 **to idolatrize,** idolize, idolify, idol; fetishize, fetish; **make an idol of, deify,** apotheosize

6 **to worship idols,** worship the golden calf, *adorer le veau d'or* (*French*)

adjectives

7 **idolatrous,** idolatric *or* idolatrical, **idol worshipping;** idolistic, fetishistic, totemistic; heathen, pagan; demonolatrous, chthonian; heliolatrous; bibliolatrous; zoolatrous

698 THE MINISTRY

nouns

1 **the ministry, pastorate,** pastorage, pastoral care, cure *or* care of souls, **the Church,** the cloth, the pulpit, the desk; **priesthood,** priestship; apostleship; call, vocation, sacred calling; holy orders; rabbinate

2 ecclesiasticalism, ecclesiology, priestcraft

3 **clericalism,** sacerdotalism; priesthood; priestism; episcopalianism; ultramontanism

4 **monasticism,** monachism, monkery, **monkhood,** friarhood; celibacy *see* 565

5 ecclesiastical office (*see* list), church office, dignity

6 **papacy,** papality, **pontificate,** popedom, the Vatican, Apostolic See, See of Rome, Holy See, the Church

7 hierarchy, hierocracy; theocracy

8 **diocese, see,** archdiocese, bishopric, archbishopric; province; synod, conference; **parish**

9 **benefice, living, incumbency,** glebe, advowson; curacy, cure, charge, cure *or* care of souls; prelacy, rectory, vicarage

10 **holy orders, orders** *see* 699.4, major orders, apostolic orders, minor orders; calling, election,

nomination, appointment, preferment, induction, institution, installation, investiture; conferment, presentation; **ordination**, ordainment, consecration, canonization, reading in

verbs

11 **to be ordained, take holy orders,** take orders, take vows, read oneself in; **take the veil,** wear the cloth

12 **to ordain,** frock, **canonize, consecrate;** saint

adjectives

13 **ecclesiastic, ecclesiastical, churchly; ministerial, clerical,** sacerdotal, **pastoral; priestly,** priestish; prelatic, prelatical, prelatial; episcopal, episcopalian; archiepiscopal; primatal, primatial, primatical; canonical; capitular, capitulary; abbatical, abbatial; ultramontane; **evangelistic;** rabbinic, rabbinical; priest-ridden

14 **monastic,** monachal, **monasterial, monkish;** conventual

15 **papal, pontific, pontifical,** apostolic, apostolical; **popish** or papist or papistic or papistical or papish (*all informal*)

16 **hierarchical,** hierarchal; theocratic, theocratist

17 **ordained;** in orders, in holy orders, of the cloth

18 **ecclesiastical offices**

abbacy	deanery *or* deanship
archbishopric *or*	episcopate *or* episcopacy
archiepiscopate *or*	pastorate *or* pastorship
archiepiscopacy	prebend *or* prebendaryship
archdeaconry	*or* prebendal stall
bishopric *or* bishopdom	prelacy *or* prelature *or*
canonry *or* canonicate	prelateship *or* prelatehood
cardinalate *or* cardinalship	presbytery *or* presbyterate
chaplaincy *or* chaplainship	primacy *or* primateship
curacy	rectorate *or* rectorship
deaconry *or* deaconship	vicariate *or* vicarship

699 THE CLERGY

nouns

1 **clergy, ministry,** the cloth; clerical order, clericals; **priesthood;** priestery; presbytery; prelacy; Sacred College; rabbinate

2 **clergyman, clergywoman,** man *or* woman of the cloth, **divine, ecclesiastic, churchman, cleric,** clerical; clerk, clerk in holy orders, tonsured cleric; **minister, minister of the Gospel, parson, pastor,** abbé, curé (*both French*), **vicar, rector,** curate, man *or* woman of God, servant of God, shepherd, sky pilot *and* Holy Joe (*both informal*), reverend (*informal*); supply minister *or* preacher, supply clergy; rural dean; **chaplain;** military chaplain, padre (*informal*); the Reverend, the Very *or* Right *or* Most Reverend; Doctor of Divinity *or* DD

3 **preacher,** sermoner, sermonizer, sermonist, homilist; pulpiter, pulpiteer; predicant, predikant; preaching friar; circuit rider; televison *or* TV preacher, telepreacher (*informal*)

4 **holy orders, major orders,** priest *or* presbyter, deacon *or* diaconus, subdeacon *or* subdiaconus; minor orders, acolyte *or* acolytus, exorcist *or* exorcista, reader *or* lector, doorkeeper *or* ostiarius; ordinand, candidate for holy orders

5 **priest,** gallach (*Hebrew*), **father,** father in Christ, **padre,** cassock, presbyter; curé, parish priest; confessor, father confessor, spiritual father *or* director *or* leader, holy father; penitentiary

6 **evangelist,** revivalist, evangel, evangelicalist; hot-gospeller (*informal*), Bible-basher *and* Bible-thumper *and* Bible-pounder *and* Bible-puncher (*all informal*), **missionary,** missioner; missionary apostolic, missionary rector, colporteur; television *or* TV evangelist (*US*), televangelist (*US informal*)

7 **benefice-holder,** beneficiary, **incumbent;** resident, residentiary

8 **church dignitary,** ecclesiarch, ecclesiast, hierarch; minor *or* lay officer

9 (*Mormon*) deacon, teacher, priest, elder, Seventy, high priest, bishop, patriarch, apostle; Aaronic priesthood, Melchizedek priesthood

10 (*Jewish*) **rabbi,** rabbin; chief rabbi; baal kore (*Yiddish*); cantor, chazan (*Hebrew*), reader; priest, kohen (*Hebrew*), high priest; Levite; scribe

11 (*Muslim*) imam, qadi, sheikh, mullah, murshid, mufti, hajji, muezzin, dervish, abdal, fakir, santon

12 (*Hindu*) Brahman, pujari, purohit, pundit, guru, bashara, vairagi *or* bairagi, Ramwat, Ramanandi; sannyasi; swami; yogi, yogin; bhikshu, bhikhari

13 (*Buddhist*) bonze, bhikku, poonghie, talapoin; lama; Grand Lama, Dalai Lama, Panchen Lama

14 (*pagan*) Druid, Druidess; flamen; hierophant, hierodule, hieros, daduchus, mystes, epopt

15 **religious,** religieux (*French*); **monk,** monastic; brother, lay brother; cenobite, conventual; caloyer, hieromonach; **mendicant, friar;** pilgrim, palmer; stylite, pillarist, pillar saint; beadsman; prior, claustral *or* conventual prior, grand prior, general prior; abbot; lay abbot, abbacomes; hermit see 584.5; ascetic see 667.2; celibate see 565.2

16 **religious orders** (*see list*)

17 **nun,** sister, religieuse (*French*), clergywoman, conventual; abbess, prioress; **mother superior,** lady superior, superioress, the reverend mother, holy mother; canoness, regular *or* secular canoness; novice, postulant

18 **religious orders**

Augustinian *or* Austin	Friars Minor
Friars	Friars Preacher
Augustinian Hermit	Gilbertine
Benedictine *or* Black	Hospitaller
Monks	Jesuit *or* Loyolite
Bernardine	Lorettine
Bonhomme	Marist
Brigittine	Maryknoll
Capuchin	Maturine
Carmelite *or* White Friars	Minorite
Carthusian	Observant
Cistercian	Oratorian
Cluniac	preaching Friars *or*
Conventual	brothers
Crutched Friars *or* Crossed	Premonstratensian
Friars	Recollect *or* Recollet
Discalced Carmelite	Redemptorist
Dominican *or* Black Friars	Templar
Franciscan *or* Grey Friars	Trappist

700 THE LAITY

nouns

1 **the laity, lay persons,** laymen, laywomen,
noncleric, nonordained persons, seculars; brothers,
sisters, brethren, sistren (*informal*), people; flock,
fold, sheep; **congregation,** parishioners,
churchgoers, assembly; minyan (*Hebrew*); **parish,**
society; class

2 **layman,** laic, secular, churchman, **parishioner,**
church member; brother, sister, lay brother, lay
sister; laywoman, churchwoman; catechumen;
communicant

adjectives

3 lay, laic *or* laical; **nonecclesiastical,** nonclerical,
nonministerial, nonpastoral, nonordained;
nonreligious; **secular,** secularist; secularistic;
temporal, popular, civil; congregational

701 RELIGIOUS RITES

nouns

1 **ritualism,** rituality, **ceremonialism, formalism,**
liturgism; symbolism, symbolics; **cult,** cultus,
cultism; sacramentalism, sacramentarianism;
sabbatism, Sabbatarianism; ritualization,
solemnization, solemn observance, **celebration;**
liturgics, liturgiology

2 **ritualist, ceremonialist,** liturgist, **formalist,**
formulist, formularist; sacramentalist, sacramentarian;
sabbatist, Sabbatarian; High-Churchman, High-
Churchist

3 **rite** (*see list*), **ritual,** rituality, **liturgy,** holy rite;
order of service, order of worship; **ceremony,
ceremonial; observance,** ritual observance;
formality, solemnity; **form,** formula, formulary,
form of worship *or* service, mode of worship;
prescribed form; service, function, duty, office,
practice; **sacrament,** sacramental, mystery;
ordinance; institution

4 **seven sacraments,** mysteries: baptism, confirmation,
the Eucharist, penance, extreme unction, holy orders,
matrimony

5 **unction,** sacred unction, sacramental anointment,
chrism *or* chrisom, chrismation, chrismatory;
extreme unction, last rites, viaticum; ointment;
chrismal

6 **baptism,** baptizement; **christening; immersion,**
total immersion; **sprinkling,** aspersion, aspergation;
affusion, infusion; baptism for the dead; baptismal
regeneration; christening gown *or* dress *or* robe,
baptismal gown *or* dress *or* robe, chrismal; baptistery,
font; confirmation, bar *or* bat mitzvah (*both Jewish*)

7 **Eucharist, Lord's Supper, Last Supper,
Communion,** Holy Communion, **the Sacrament,**
the Holy Sacrament; intinction; consubstantiation,
impanation, subpanation, transubstantiation; real
presence; elements, consecrated elements, bread and
wine, body and blood of Christ; Host, wafer, loaf,
bread, altar bread, consecrated bread; Sacrament
Sunday

8 **Mass,** Missa (*Latin*), Eucharistic rites; **the Liturgy,**
the Divine Liturgy; **parts of the Mass**

9 **sacred object** *or* **article;** ritualistic manual, Book
of Common Prayer, breviary, canon, haggadah
(*Jewish*), missal *or* Mass book, prayer book, siddur
machazor (*Jewish*)

10 **psalter, psalmbook;** Psalm Book, Book of Common
Order; the Psalms, Book of Psalms, the Psalter, the
Psaltery

11 **holy day,** hallowday (*informal*), holytide; feast, fast;
Sabbath; Sunday, Lord's day; saint's day; church
calendar, ecclesiastical calendar

12 Christian holy days (*see list*); Jewish holy days (*see
list*)

13 (*Muslim holy days*) Ramadan (*month*), Bairam,
Muharram

verbs

14 **to celebrate, observe, keep, solemnize;** celebrate
Mass; communicate, administer Communion; attend
Communion, receive the Sacrament, partake of the
Lord's Supper; attend Mass

15 **to minister, officiate,** do duty, **perform a rite,**
perform service *or* divine service; administer a
sacrament, administer the Eucharist, etc; anoint,
chrism; confirm, impose, lay hands on; make the
sign of the cross

16 **to baptize, christen;** dip, immerse; sprinkle,
asperge; circumcise

17 **to confess,** make confession, receive absolution;
shrive, hear confession; **absolve,** administer
absolution; administer extreme unction

adjectives

18 **ritualistic,** ritual; **ceremonial,** ceremonious;
formal, formular, formulary; **liturgic, liturgical,**
liturgistic, liturgistical; High-Church; **sacramental,**
sacramentarian; eucharistic, eucharistical, baptismal;
paschal; Passover

19 **rites**

aspersion *or* asperges	invocation
celebration	invocation of saints
circumcision *and* bar	litany
mitzvah *and* bat mitzvah	love feast *or* agape
(all Jewish)	lustration
confession *or* auricular	pax *or* kiss of peace
confession *or* the	processional
confessional *or* the	reciting the rosary *or*
confessionary	telling one's beads
confirmation	sign of the cross *or* signing
greater *or* lesser litany	*or* crossing oneself *or*
high celebration	*signum crucis* (Latin)
imposition *or* laying on of	thurification *or* censing
hands	

20 **Christian holy days**

Advent	Easter *or* Eastertide
Annunciation *or*	Easter Saturday *or* Easter
Annunciation Day *or*	Sunday
Lady Day	Ember days
Ascension Day *or* Holy	Epiphany *or* Three Kings'
Thursday	Day
Ash Wednesday	Good Friday
Candlemas *or* Candlemas	Hallowmas *or*
Day	Allhallowmas *or*
Christmas	Allhallowtide *or*
Corpus Christi	Halloween *or* Allhallows

or All Saints' Day *or* All Souls' Day

Holy Week *or* Passion Week

Lammas *or* Lammas Day *or* Lammastide *or* Feast of St Peter's Chains

Lent *or* Lententide

Martinmas

Maundy Thursday

Michaelmas *or* Michaelmas Day *or* Michaelmastide

Palm Sunday

Pentecost *or* Whitsuntide

or Whitsun *or* Whitsunday

Quadragesima *or* Quadragesima Sunday

Quinquagesima

Septuagesima

Sexagesima

Shrove Tuesday *or* Pancake Day *or* Mardi Gras *or* Carnival

Trinity Sunday

Twelfth-night *or* Twelfth-tide *or* Twelfth-day

21 Jewish holy days

Fast of Av *or* Ninth of Av *or* Tishah b'Av

Hanukkah *or* Feast of the Dedication

High Holy Days

Lag b'Omer

Passover *or* Pesach

Purim

Rosh Hashanah *or* New Year

Shavuot *or* Shabuoth *or* Pentecost *or* Feast of Weeks

Simhath Torah *or* Rejoicing over the Law

Sukkoth *or* Feast of Tabernacles

Yom Kippur *or* Day of Atonement

702 ECCLESIASTICAL ATTIRE

nouns

1 **canonicals,** clericals (*informal*), robes, cloth; **vestments,** vesture; liturgical garments, ceremonial attire; pontificals, pontificalia, episcopal vestments

2 **robe,** frock, mantle, gown, cloak

3 **staff,** pastoral staff, **crosier, cross,** cross-staff, crook, paterissa

adjectives

4 vestmental, vestmentary

703 RELIGIOUS BUILDINGS

nouns

1 **church,** kirk (*Scottish*), bethel, **meetinghouse,** church house, **house of God,** place of worship, house of worship *or* prayer; conventicle; **mission;** basilica, major *or* patriarchal basilica, minor basilica; **cathedral,** cathedral church, **minster,** *duomo* (*Italian*); collegiate church

2 **temple,** fane; **tabernacle; synagogue,** *shul* (*Yiddish*); **mosque,** masjid; dewal, girja; pagoda; kiack; pantheon

3 **chapel,** chapel of ease, chapel royal, side chapel, school chapel, sacrament chapel, Lady chapel, oratory, oratorium; chantry; sacellum, sacrarium

4 **shrine,** holy place, dagoba, naos; sacrarium, delubrum; tope, stupa; reliquary, *reliquaire* (*French*)

5 **sanctuary, holy of holies, sanctum, sanctum sanctorum,** adytum, sacrarium

6 **cloister, monastery, house, abbey,** friary; priory, priorate; lamasery; **convent, nunnery**

7 **parsonage, pastorage,** pastorate, manse, **church house,** clergy house; presbytery, **rectory,** vicarage, deanery; glebe; chapter house

8 bishop's palace; **Vatican;** Lambeth, Lambeth Palace

9 (*church interior*) vestry, sacristy, sacrarium, diaconicon *or* diaconicum; baptistery; ambry, apse, blindstory, chancel, choir, choir screen, clerestory, cloisters, confessional, confessionary (*old*), crypt, Easter sepulchre, nave, porch, presbytery, rood loft, rood stair, rood tower *or* spire *or* steeple, transept, triforium; organ loft

10 (*church furnishings*) piscina; stoup, holy-water stoup *or* basin; baptismal font; patent; reredos; jube, rood screen, rood arch, chancel screen; altar cloth, cerecloth, chrismal; communion *or* sacrament cloth, corporal, fanon, oblation cloth; rood cloth; baldachin, *baldacchino* (*Italian*); kneeling stool, *prie-dieu* (*French*); prayer rug *or* carpet *or* mat

11 (*vessels*) cruet; chalice; ciborium, pyx; chrismal, chrismatory; monstrance, ostensorium; reliquary; font, holy-water font

12 **altar,** scrobis; bomos, eschara, hestia; **Lord's table,** holy table, **Communion table,** chancel table, table of the Lord, God's board; rood altar; altar desk, missal stand; credence, prothesis, table *or* altar of prothesis, predella; superaltar, retable, retablo, ancona, gradin; altarpiece, altar side, altar rail, altar carpet, altar stair; altar facing *or* front, frontal; altar slab, altar stone, mensal

13 **pulpit, rostrum,** ambo; **lectern,** desk, reading desk

14 (*seats*) **pew; stall;** mourners' bench, anxious bench *or* seat, penitent form; amen corner; sedilia

adjectives

15 **churchly,** churchish, **ecclesiastical;** churchlike, temple-like; cathedral-like, cathedralesque; tabernacular; synagogical, synagogal; pantheonic

16 **claustral, cloistered; monastic,** monachal, **monasterial; conventual,** conventical

704 SHOW BUSINESS, THEATRE

nouns

1 **show business,** show biz (*informal*), the entertainment industry; **the theatre, the footlights, the stage, the boards,** the bright lights, Broadway, the scenes (*old*), traffic of the stage; avant-garde theatre, contemporary theatre, experimental theatre, total theatre, epic theatre, theatre of the absurd, theatre of cruelty, guerrilla theatre, street theatre; stagedom, theatre world, stage world, stageland, playland; **drama,** legitimate stage *or* theatre, legit (*informal*), off Broadway, off-off-Broadway; music *or* musical theatre; café theatre, dinner theatre; regional theatre; repertory drama *or* theatre, stock (*US*); summer stock (*US*), straw hat *or* straw hat circuit (*US informal*); **music hall, variety,** vaudeville (*US & Canadian*); burlesque; **circus,** carnival; theatromania, theatrophobia

2 **dramatics;** dramatization, dramaticism, dramatism; **theatrics,** theatricism, **theatricalism,** theatricality, staginess; theatricals, amateur theatricals; **histrionics,** histrionism; dramatic *or* histrionic *or* Thespian art; dramatic stroke, *coup de théâtre* (*French*); **melodramatics,** sensationalism; **dramaturgy,** dramatic structure, play construction, dramatic form; dramatic irony, tragic irony

3 theatrecraft, stagecraft, stagery, scenecraft; **showmanship**

4 **stage show, show; play,** stage play, piece, vehicle, work; **hit** *or* hit show (*informal*), success, smash hit, critical success, audience success, word-of-mouth success, gasser (*US informal*); failure, **flop** *and* bomb *and* turkey (*all informal*)

5 **tragedy,** tragic drama; tragic flaw; buskin, cothurnus; tragic muse, Melpomene

6 **comedy; pantomime,** panto (*informal*); **farce;** comic relief, comedy relief; comic muse, Thalia; sock, coxcomb, cap and bells, motley, bladder, slapstick

7 **act, scene, number, turn,** bit *and* shtick (*both informal*), routine (*informal*); curtain raiser *or* lifter; introduction; expository scene; **prologue,** epilogue; **entr'acte,** intermezzo, interval, intermission, interlude, *divertissement* (*French*), *divertimento* (*Italian*); **finale,** afterpiece; exodus, exode; chaser (*informal*); curtain call, curtain; hokum *or* hoke act (*US informal*); song and dance; burlesque act (*US & Canadian*), striptease; stand-up comedy act; sketch, skit

8 **acting, playing,** playacting, performing, **performance,** taking a role *or* part; **representation, portrayal, characterization,** projection; **impersonation,** personation, miming, mimicking, mimicry, mimesis; pantomiming, mummery; ham *and* hammy acting *and* hamming *or* hamming up (*all informal*), overacting; stage presence; stage directions, **business,** stage business, *jeu de théâtre* (*French*), acting device; stunt *and* gag (*both informal*); hokum *or* hoke (*US informal*); buffoonery, slapstick; patter; stand-up comedy

9 **repertoire, repertory;** stock

10 **role, part,** piece (*informal*); cue, **lines,** side; cast; **character,** person, personage; lead, starring *or* lead *or* leading role, fat part, leading man, leading woman *or* lady, hero, heroine; antihero; title role, protagonist, principal character; supporting role, supporting character; ingenue, *jeune première or jeune premier* (*French*), romantic lead; soubrette; villain, heavy (*informal*), antagonist; bit, bit part, minor role; feeder, straight part; walking part, walk-on; top banana, second banana; **actor** *see* 707.2

11 **engagement,** playing engagement, booking; **run; stand,** one-night stand *or* one-nighter; **circuit,** variety circuit, pub circuit, club circuit; **tour,** bus-and-truck, **production tour;** date

12 **theatrical performance, performance, show, presentation,** presentment, **production,** entertainment, stage presentation *or* performance; bill; **exhibit, exhibition;** benefit performance, benefit; personal appearance, flesh show (*informal*); showcase, tryout; premiere, premier performance, debut; farewell performance, swan song (*informal*)

13 **production,** mounting, staging, putting on; stage management; **direction,** *mise-en-scène* (*French*); blocking; **rehearsal,** dress rehearsal, walk-through, run-through, technical *or* tech rehearsal *or* run, final dress, gypsy rehearsal *or* run-through *or* run

14 **theatre, playhouse, house,** theatron, odeum; **auditorium; opera house,** opera; **hall,** music hall, concert hall; **amphitheatre;** circle theatre, arena theatre, theatre-in-the-round; vaudeville theatre (*US*); burlesque theatre (*US*); **little theatre,** community theatre; open-air theatre, outdoor theatre; Greek theatre; children's theatre; Elizabethan theatre, Globe Theatre; showboat; dinner theatre; cabaret, nightclub, club, night spot, *boîte de nuit* (*French*)

15 **auditorium;** parquet, orchestra, **pit; orchestra circle,** parquet circle, parterre; **dress circle;** fauteuil *or* theatre stall *or* **stall; box,** box seat, **loge,** *baignoire* (*French*); stage box; proscenium boxes, parterre boxes; **gods,** balcony, gallery; standing room

16 **stage,** the boards; acting area, playing *or* performing area; thrust stage, three-quarter-round stage, theatre-in-the-round; apron, passerelle, apron stage, forestage; proscenium stage, proscenium arch, proscenium; bridge; revolving stage; orchestra, pit, orchestra pit; **bandstand,** shell, band shell; stage right, **R;** stage left, **L;** upstage, downstage, backstage; **wings,** coulisse; dressing room, greenroom; flies, fly gallery, fly floor; gridiron, grid (*informal*); board, lightboard, switchboard; dock; prompter's box; curtain, grand drape, safety curtain, asbestos curtain, fire curtain; stage door

17 (*stage requisites*) **property, prop;** practical piece *or* prop (*informal*); costume *see* 5.9; theatrical makeup, makeup, greasepaint, blackface, clown white; spirit gum

18 lights, instruments; **footlights,** foots (*informal*), floats; floodlight, flood; bunch light; **limelight,** follow spot, spotlight *or* spot (*informal*), arc light, arc, klieg *or* kleig light; colour filter, medium, gelatin *or* gel; dimmer; marquee; light plot

19 **setting, stage setting,** stage set, **set,** *mise-en-scène* (*French*); location, locale

20 **scenery,** decor; **scene;** screen, **flat;** cyclorama *or* cyc; batten; side scene, **wing,** coulisse; border; tormentor, **teaser;** wingcut, woodcut; transformation, transformation scene; flipper; counterweight; **curtain,** rag (*informal*), hanging; **drop,** drop scene, drop curtain, scrim, cloth; **backdrop,** back cloth; act drop *or* curtain; tab, tableau curtain

21 **playbook, script,** text, **libretto;** prompt-book; book; **score; scenario,** continuity, shooting script; scene plot; lines, actor's lines, cue, sides; stage direction; prompt book

22 **dramatist; playwright,** playwriter, dramaturge; doctor *and* play doctor *and* play fixer (*all informal*); dramatizer; **scriptwriter, scenario writer,** scenarist, **scenarioist, screenwriter; gagman,** joke writer, jokesmith; **librettist;** tragedian, comedian; farcist, *farceur, farceuse* (*both French*), farcer; melodramatist; monodramatist; mimographer; **choreographer**

23 **theatre man,** theatrician; **showman,** exhibitor, **producer, impresario; director,** auteur; stage director, **stage manager;** set designer, scenewright; costume designer, costumer, *costumier, costumière* (*both French*), wardrobe master *or* mistress; dresser; hair *or* wig maker *or* designer; makeup man *or* artist, visagiste; propsmaster *or* propsmistress; prompter; callboy; playreader; master of ceremonies, MC *or* emcee (*informal*); ticket collector; usher, usherer, usherette; ringmaster, equestrian director; barker, ballyhoo man *and* spieler (*both informal*)

24 stage technician, stagehand, machinist (*old*), sceneman, **sceneshifter;** flyman; carpenter; **electrician;** scene painter, scenic artist, scenewright

25 agent, actor's agent, playbroker, ten-percenter (*informal*); **booking agent;** advance agent, advance man; publicity man *or* agent

26 patron, patroness; backer, angel (*informal*); Dionysus

27 playgoer, theatregoer; attender *see* 221.5, spectator *see* 917, audience *see* 48.6; **filmgoer,** cinemagoer, moviegoer, **film buff** (*informal*); first-nighter; standee, groundling (*old*); *claqueur* (*French*), hired applauder; pass holder, deadhead (*informal*)

verbs

28 to dramatize, theatricalize; melodramatize; scenarize; **present, stage, produce, mount, put on,** put on the stage; **put on a show;** try out, preview; give a performance; premiere; **open,** open a show, open a show cold (*informal*); set the stage; ring up the curtain, ring down the curtain; **star, feature** (*informal*), bill, **headline,** give top billing to; succeed, make *or* be a hit *and* have legs (*all informal*), be a gas (*informal*), run out of gas (*US informal*); fail, flop *and* bomb *and* bomb out (*all informal*)

29 to act, perform, play, playact, tread the boards, strut one's stuff (*informal*); appear, **appear on the stage;** act like a trouper; register; emotionalize, emote (*informal*); pantomime, mime; patter; sketch; troupe, barnstorm (*informal*); steal the show, upstage, steal the spotlight; **debut,** make one's debut *or* bow, come out; act as foil *or* feeder, stooge (*informal*), be straight man for; **star,** play the lead, get top billing, have one's name in lights

30 to enact, act out; represent, depict, portray; act *or* play *or* perform a part *or* role, take a part, sustain a part, act *or* play the part of; create a role *or* character; **impersonate,** personate; play opposite, support

31 to overact, overdramatize, chew up the scenery (*informal*), act all over the stage; **ham** *and* ham it up (*both informal*); **mug** (*informal*), grimace; spout, rant, roar, declaim,

"out-herod Herod"—Shakespeare; milk a scene; **underact,** throw away (*informal*)

32 to rehearse, practise, go through, walk *or* run through, go over; go through one's part, read one's lines; con *or* study one's part; be a fast *or* slow study (*US*)

adjectives

33 dramatic, dramatical (*old*), **dramaturgic, dramaturgical; theatric, theatrical, histrionic, thespian;** scenic; **stagy;** theatre-like, stagelike; **spectacular; melodramatic;** ham *or* hammy (*informal*); overacted, overplayed, milked (*informal*); underacted, underplayed, thrown away; **operatic;** ballet, balletic; legitimate; stellar, all-star; stagestruck, starstruck; stageworthy, actor-proof

34 tragic, heavy; buskined, cothurned

35 comic, light; tragicomical, **farcical, slapstick;** camp *or* campy (*informal*)

adverbs

36 on the stage *or* boards, before an audience, before the footlights; **in the limelight** *or* spotlight; onstage; downstage, upstage; backstage, off stage, behind the scenes; down left *or* DL; down right *or* DR; up left *or* UL; up right *or* UR

705 DANCE

nouns

1 dancing (*see list*), terpsichore, **dance;** the light fantastic; **choreography;** dance drama, choreodrama; jigging (*Scottish*), **hoofing** (*informal*)

2 dance, knees-up (*informal*), **hop** (*informal*), dancing party, **shindig** *and* shindy (*both informal*); **ball,** *bal* (*French*); masked ball, masque, mask, masquerade ball, masquerade, *bal masqué* (*French*), *bal costumé* (*French*), fancy-dress ball, cotillion; formal ball, **formal** (*informal*), promenade, prom (*US informal*); barn dance, country dance, square dance, ceilidh; mixer (*US*); disco, rave (*informal*); dinner-dance, tea dance, *thé dansant* (*French*)

3 dancer, danseur, terpsichorean, **hoofer** (*informal*), step dancer, tap dancer, clog dancer, etc; **ballet dancer; ballerina,** danseuse, coryphée; prima ballerina, *première danseuse, danseur noble* (*both French*); **modern dancer;** *corps de ballet* (*French*); figurant, figurante; **chorus girl,** chorine (*US*), chorus boy *or* man; chorus line; geisha *or* geisha girl; nautch girl, bayadere; hula girl; taxi dancer; topless dancer, erotic dancer; burlesque dancer, strip-teaser, stripper *and* bump-and-grinder (*both informal*); choreographer

4 ballroom, dance hall, dancery; dance palace; casino; **disco,** discotheque; **dance floor**

verbs

5 to dance, trip the light fantastic,
"trip it as we go, on the light fantastic toe"—Milton, trip, skip, hop, foot, prance (*informal*), **hoof** (*informal*), boogie, clog, tap-dance, fold-dance, etc; shake, shimmy, shuffle; waltz, one-step, two-step, foxtrot, etc; choreograph

adjectives

6 dancing, dance, terpsichorean; balletic; choreographic

7 kinds of dancing

ballet	disco dancing
ballroom dancing	flamenco
belly dancing	folklorico
body popping	folk dancing
break dancing	ice dancing
character dancing	interpretive dancing
choral dancing	jazz dancing
classical ballet	jazz tap
clog dancing	modern ballet
comedy ballet	modern dance
country dancing	morris dancing
couple dancing	old-time dancing
dirty *or* touch dancing	robotic dancing

round dancing	square dancing
slam dancing	step dancing
social dancing	tap dancing
soft-shoe dancing	taxi dancing
solo dancing	

706 CINEMA

nouns

1 **cinema, films, movies, the movies, the pictures, motion pictures,** moving pictures, the film, the screen, the big screen, the silver screen, the flicks *and* the flickers (*both informal*); **film, movie, picture, motion picture,** flick *and* flicker (*both informal*), picture show, motion-picture show, moving-picture show, photoplay, photodrama; **sound film,** silent film *or* silent; cinéma vérité *or* direct cinema; vérité; magic realism; **documentary film** *or* **movie,** docudrama, docutainment; **feature,** feature film, feature-length film, main attraction; theatrical film, big-screen film; **film genre** *or* **type;** TV film *or* movie, made-for-television film *or* movie; **short,** short film, short subject; preview, sneak preview; **B-movie,** B-picture, Grade B movie, low-budget picture; **educational film** *or* **movie,** training film, promotional film, infomercial; **underground film** *or* **movie,** experimental film *or* movie, avant-garde film *or* movie, representational film, art film *or* movie, art-house film *or* movie, surrealistic film *or* movie, film noir; **cartoon,** animated cartoon, animation, cel animation, claymation, computer graphics; animatron, audioanimatron; **rated film** *or* **movie,** rating system, rating, U *or* universal audience, PG *or* parental guidance suggested, 15 *or* no one under 15 admitted, 18 *or* no one under 18 admitted, X *or* X-rating (*old*)

2 **script, screenplay,** film script, shooting script, storyboard, scenario, treatment, original screenplay; **dialogue, book; role,** lead, romantic lead, stock character, ingenue, soubrette, cameo, bit, silent bit

3 **film studio, movie studio,** motion-picture studio, dream factory (*informal*), animation studio, lot, back lot, sound stage, location; **set, motion-picture set, film set,** *mise-en-scène* (*French*), properties *or* props, set dressing; **film company,** motion-picture company, production company; **producer,** filmmaker, moviemaker, **director,** auteur, screenwriter *or* scriptwriter *or* scenarist, editor *or* film editor, **actor, actress, film actor, film actress, film star,** player, cinemactor, cinemactress, star, starlet, character actor, featured player, supporting actor *or* actress, supporting player, bit player, extra; **crew,** film crew

4 **cinematography, photography,** film photography, camera work, cinematics, camera angle, camera position, **shot, take,** footage, retake, wrap; screen test; **special effects,** rear-screen projection, mechanical effects, optical effects, process photography, FX; **colour photography,** Technicolor (*trade name*), black-and-white, colour, colourization; **cameraman** *or* **camerawoman, film cameraman** *or* **camerawoman,** cinematographer, director of photography *or* DP, first cameraman, lighting cameraman

5 **film editing,** motion-picture editing, **editing,** cutting; **transition,** fade, fade-out/fade-in, dissolve, lap *or* overlap dissolve, out-focus-dissolve, match dissolve, cross dissolve, mix

6 **cinema,** film theatre, motion-picture theatre (*US*), movie theatre (*US*), picture theatre (*US*), **multiplex,** multiscreen cinema, movie palace, picture palace, dream palace (*informal*), drive-in cinema *or* drive-in (*US*), fleapit (*informal*); **screen,** cinema screen, movie screen, silver screen, aspect ratio *or* format, screen proportion, wide-screen, Cinerama *and* Cinemascope *and* VistaVision *and* Todd-AO *and* Ultra-Panavision (*all trade names*)

verbs

7 **to film, shoot,** cinematize, filmmake; colourize

adjectives

8 **cinema, film, movie,** motion-picture, cinematic, filmistic, filmic; colourized; animated; animatronic, audioanimatronic

707 ENTERTAINER

nouns

1 **entertainer,** public entertainer, performer; artist, artiste; impressionist, impersonator, female impersonator, drag artist, drag queen, pantomime dame; variety performer, vaudevillian *and* vaudevillist (*both US & Canadian*); dancer see 705.3, hoofer (*informal*); song and dance man; chorus girl, show girl, chorine (*US*); coryphée; chorus boy *or* man; burlesque queen (*US & Canadian informal*), **stripteaser,** exotic dancer, ecdysiast; stripper, peeler *and* stripteuse *and* bump-and-grinder (*all US informal*); dancing girl, nautch girl, belly dancer; go-go dancer; geisha, geisha girl; mountebank; **magician,** conjurer, prestidigitator, sleight-of-hand artist; mummer, guiser (*Scottish*), guisard; singer, musician see 710; performance artist

2 **actor, actress, player,** stage player *or* performer, playactor, histrion, histrio, thespian, Roscius, theatrical (*informal*), trouper; child actor; mummer, pantomime, pantomimist; monologist, diseur, diseuse, reciter; dramatizer; mime, mimer, mimic; strolling player, stroller; barnstormer (*informal*); character actor *or* actress, character man *or* woman, character; **villain,** antagonist, **bad guy** *or* **heavy** *or* black hat (*all informal*), villainess; juvenile, ingenue; *jeune premier* *and* *jeune première* (*both French*); soubrette; principal boy; foil, feed *and* stooge (*both informal*), straight man *or* person; utility man *or* person; protean actor; matinee idol (*informal*); romantic lead

3 circus artist *or* performer; trapeze artist, aerialist, flier (*informal*); high-wire artist, tightrope walker, funambulist, equilibrist; acrobat, tumbler; bareback rider; juggler; lion tamer, sword swallower; snake charmer; clown; ringmaster, equestrian director

4 **film actor,** movie actor; **film star, movie star;** starlet

5 **ham** *or* ham actor (*both informal*); grimacer

6 **lead,** leading man *or* lady, leading actor *or* actress, principal, **star,** superstar, megastar, headliner, headline *or* feature attraction; costar; **hero, heroine,**

antihero, protagonist; juvenile lead, *jeune premier, jeune première* (*both French*); first tragedian, heavy lead (*informal*); **prima donna**, diva, singer *see* 710.13; première danseuse, prima ballerina, *danseur noble* (*French*)

7 **supporting actor** *or* **actress**; **support**, supporting cast; **supernumerary**, super *or* supe (*informal*), spear-carrier (*informal*), **extra**; bit player; walking gentleman *or* lady (*informal*), walk-on, mute; figurant, figurante; **understudy, stand-in**, standby, substitute, swing

8 **tragedian**, tragedienne

9 **comedian**, comedienne, **comic, funnyman**; farcist, farcer, *farceur, farceuse* (*both French*); stand-up comic *or* comedian (*informal*), light comedian, genteel comedian, low comedian, slapstick comedian, hokum *or* hoke comic (*US informal*)

10 **buffoon**, *buffo* (*Italian*), **clown, fool, jester, zany, merry-andrew**, jack-pudding, pickle-herring, **motley fool**, motley, wearer of the cap and bells; harlequin; Pierrot; Pantaloon, Pantalone; Punch, Punchinello, Pulcinella, Polichinelle; Punch and Judy; Hanswurst; Columbine; Harlequin; Scaramouch

11 **cast**, cast of characters, characters, persons of the drama, *dramatis personae* (*Latin*); supporting cast; **company**, acting company, **troupe**; repertory company, stock company (*US*); ensemble, chorus, *corps de ballet* (*French*); circus troupe

708 MUSIC

nouns

1 **music** (*see list*), harmonious sound, "the speech of angels"—CARLYLE, "the mosaic of the Air"—ANDREW MARVELL, "the harmonious voice of creation; an echo of the invisible world"—GIUSEPPE MAZZINI, "the only universal tongue"—SAMUEL ROGERS, "the universal language of mankind"—LONGFELLOW, "the poor man's Parnassus"—EMERSON, "the brandy of the damned"—G B SHAW, "nothing else but wild sounds civilized into time and tune"—THOMAS FULLER

2 **melody**, melodiousness, **tunefulness**, musicalness, musicality; **tune, tone**, musical sound, musical quality, tonality; sweetness, dulcetness, mellifluence, mellifluousness

3 **harmony, concord**, concordance, concert, consonance *or* consonancy, consort, accordance, **accord**, monochord, concentus, symphony, diapason; synchronism, synchronization; **attunement**, tune, attune; chime, chiming; unison, unisonance, homophony, monody; **euphony**; light *or* heavy harmony; two-part *or* three-part harmony, etc; harmony *or* music of the spheres; harmonics *see* 709

4 **air**, aria, **tune, melody**, line, melodic line, refrain, note, **song**, solo, solo part, soprano part, treble, lay, descant, lilt, **strain**, measure; canto, cantus

5 **piece**, opus, **composition**, production, work; **score; arrangement**, adaptation, orchestration, harmonization, setting; **form**

6 **classical music**, classic; concert music, serious music, longhair music (*informal*), symphonic music; semiclassic, semiclassical music

7 **popular music**, pop music, light music, popular song *or* air *or* tune, **ballad**; hit, hit song, hit tune; Tin Pan Alley

8 **dance music**, ballroom music, **dances**; syncopated music, **syncopation**; **ragtime** *or* rag

9 **jazz**; traditional jazz *or* trad, hot jazz, Dixieland; **swing**, jive (*informal*); bebop, bop (*informal*); mainstream jazz; avant-garde jazz; boogie *or* boogie-woogie; walking bass, stride *or* stride piano

10 **rock-and-roll, rock music**, rock'n'roll, rock, hard rock, jazz rock, acid rock, folk rock, country rock, full-tilt boogie

11 **folk music**, folk songs, folk, roots music, roots, ethnic music, ethnomusicology; folk ballads, balladry; border ballads; country music, hillbilly music; country-and-western music, western swing; old-time country music *or* old-timey music; bluegrass; the blues, talking blues, country blues, city blues, Delta blues

12 **march**, martial *or* military music; military march, quick *or* quickstep march; processional march, recessional march; funeral *or* dead march; wedding march

13 **vocal music**, song; **singing**, carolling, warbling, lyricism, vocalism, **vocalization**; operatic singing, bel canto, coloratura, bravura; choral singing; folk singing; croon, crooning; yodel, yodelling; scat, scat singing; intonation; hum, humming; solmization, tonic sol-fa, solfeggio, solfège, sol-fa, sol-fa exercise

14 **song**, lay, *Lied* (*German*), *chanson* (*French*), carol, ditty, canticle, lilt; **ballad**, ballade, *ballata* (*Italian*); *canzone* (*Italian*); canzonet, *canzonetta* (*Italian*)

15 **solo; aria**; operatic aria

16 (*Italian terms for arias*) arietta, arioso; aria buffa, aria da capo, aria d'agilità, aria da chiesa, aria d'imitazione, aria fugata, aria parlante; bravura, aria di bravura; coloratura, aria di coloratura; cantabile, aria cantabile; recitativo

17 **sacred music, church music**, liturgical music; **hymn**, hymn-tune, hymnody, hymnology; **psalm**, psalmody; **chorale**, choral fantasy, anthem; motet; **oratorio**; passion; **mass**; requiem mass, requiem, missa brevis, missa solemnis; offertory, offertory sentence *or* hymn; **cantata**; doxology, introit, canticle, paean, prosodion; recessional

18 **part music**, polyphonic music, part song, part singing, ensemble music, ensemble singing; **duet**, duo, *duettino* (*Italian*); **trio**, terzet, *terzetto* (*Italian*); **quartet; quintet; sextet**, sestet; **septet**, septuor; **octet**; cantata, lyric cantata; madrigal, *madrigaletto* (*Italian*); **chorus** *see* 710.16, chorale, glee club, choir; choral singing; four-part, soprano-alto-tenor-base *or* SATB

19 **round, rondo**, rondeau, **roundelay**, catch, troll; rondino, rondoletto; **fugue**, canon, fugato

20 **polyphony**, polyphonism; **counterpoint**, contrapunto; **plainsong**, Gregorian chant, Ambrosian chant; *faux-bourdon* (*French*); musica ficta, false music

21 monody, monophony, homophony

22 **part**, melody *or* voice part, **voice** *see* 709.5, **line**; descant, canto, cantus, cantus planus *or* firmus, plain song, plain chant; prick song, cantus figuratus; soprano, tenor, treble, alto, contralto, baritone, bass,

bassus; undersong; drone; **accompaniment;** continuo, basso continuo, figured bass, thorough bass; ground bass, basso ostinato; drone, drone bass, bourdon, burden

23 response, responsory report, answer; echo; antiphon, antiphony, antiphonal chanting *or* singing

24 passage, phrase, musical phrase, strain, part, motive, motif, theme, subject, figure; leitmotiv; **movement;** introductory phrase, anacrusis; statement, exposition, development, variation; division; period, musical sentence; section; **measure;** figure; **verse, stanza;** burden, bourdon; **chorus, refrain,** response; folderol, **ornament** *see* 709.18, cadence *see* 709.23, harmonic close, resolution; **coda,** tailpiece; ritornello; intermezzo, interlude; bass passage; tutti, tutti passage; bridge, bridge passage

25 (*fast, slow, etc passages*) presto, prestissimo; allegro, allegretto; scherzo, scherzando; adagio, adagietto; andante, andantino; largo, larghetto, larghissimo; crescendo; diminuendo, decrescendo; rallentando, ritardando; ritenuto; piano, pianissimo; forte, fortissimo; staccato, marcato, marcando; pizzicato; spiccato; legato; stretto

26 overture, prelude, *Vorspiel* (*German*), **introduction,** operatic overture, dramatic overture, concert overture, voluntary, descant, vamp; curtain raiser

27 impromptu, extempore, improvisation, interpolation; cadenza; **ornament** *see* 709.18, flourish, ruffles and flourishes, grace note, appoggiatura, mordent, upper mordent, inverted mordent; **run,** melisma; vamp; lick, hot lick, riff

28 score, musical score *or* copy, **music,** notation, musical notation, written music, copy, draft, transcript, transcription, version, edition, text, arrangement; part; full *or* orchestral score, compressed *or* short score, piano score, vocal score, instrumental score; tablature, lute tablature; opera score, opera; **libretto;** sheet music; **songbook,** songster; hymnbook, hymnal; music paper; music roll

29 stave, staff; line, ledger line; bar, bar line; space, degree; brace

30 execution, performance; rendering, rendition, music-making, **touch, expression;** fingering; pianism; intonation; repercussion; pizzicato, staccato, spiccato, parlando, legato, cantando, rubato, demilegato, mezzo staccato, slur; glissando

31 musicianship; musical talent *or* flair, musicality; virtuosity; pianism; musical ear, ear for music; musical sense, sense of rhythm; absolute *or* perfect pitch; relative pitch

32 musical occasion; choral service, carol service, service of lessons and carols, service of song, **singsong,** singalong, sing (*informal*), singing, community singing *or* sing, singfest, songfest, sing-in; singers' night, hootenanny (*US informal*); **festival,** music festival; opera festival; folk festival, jazz festival, rock festival; *Sängerfest* (*German*), *eisteddfod* (*Welsh*), *fleadh* (*Irish*); jam session (*informal*)

33 performance, musical performance, **programme,** musical programme, programme of music; **concert,** symphony concert, chamber concert; philharmonic concert, philharmonic; popular concert, pops *and* pop concert (*both informal*); promenade concert, prom

(*informal*); band concert; **recital;** service of music; concert performance (*of an opera*); **medley,** potpourri; swan song, farewell performance

34 musical theatre, music theatre, lyric theatre, musical stage, lyric stage; **music drama,** lyric drama; song-play, *Singspiel* (*German*); **opera,** grand opera, light opera, ballad opera; comic opera, *opéra bouffe* (*French*), *opera buffa* (*Italian*); **operetta; musical comedy; musical;** Broadway musical, West End musical; **ballet,** *opéra ballet* (*French*), comedy ballet, *ballet d'action* (*French*), *ballet divertissement* (*French*); dance drama; chorus show; **song-and-dance act;** minstrel, minstrel show

verbs

35 to harmonize, be harmonious, be in tune *or* concert, chord, **accord,** symphonize, synchronize, **chime, blend,** blend in; tune, attune, atone, sound together, sound in tune; assonate; melodize, musicalize

36 to tune, tune up, attune, atone, chord, **put in tune;** voice, string; tone up, tone down

37 to strike up, strike up a tune, **strike up the band,** break into music, pipe up, pipe up a song, **burst into song**

38 to sing, vocalize, carol, descant, lilt, troll, line out *and* belt out *and* tear off (*all informal*); **warble,** trill, tremolo, quaver, shake; **chirp,** chirrup, twit, **twitter;** pipe, whistle, tweedle, tweedledee; **chant; intone,** intonate; **croon; hum; yodel;** roulade; chorus, choir, sing in chorus; **hymn,** anthem, psalm, "make a joyful noise unto the Lord"—BIBLE; sing the praises of; minstrel; ballad; **serenade;** sol-fa, do-re-mi, solmizate

39 to play, perform, execute, render, do; interpret; make music; concertize; symphonize; chord; accompany; play by ear; play at, pound out *and* saw away at (*both informal*)

40 to strum, thrum, pluck, plunk, **pick,** twang, sweep the strings

41 to fiddle (*informal*), play violin *or* the violin; scrape *and* saw (*both informal*); double-stop

42 to blow a horn, sound *or* wind the horn, sound, blow, wind, **toot,** tootle, pipe, tweedle; bugle, carillon, clarion, fife, flute, trumpet, whistle; bagpipe, doodle (*informal*); lip, tongue, double-tongue, triple-tongue

43 to syncopate, play jazz, swing, jive (*informal*), rag (*informal*)

44 to beat time, keep time, tap, tap out the rhythm; count, count the beats; beat the drum, **drum** *see* 55.4, play drum *or* the drums, thrum, beat, thump, pound; tomtom; ruffle; beat *or* sound a tattoo

45 to conduct, direct, lead, wield the baton

46 to compose, write, arrange, score, set, set to music, put to music; musicalize, melodize, **harmonize; orchestrate;** instrument, instrumentate; **adapt,** make an adaptation; transcribe, transpose

adjectives

47 musical, musically inclined, musicianly, with an ear for music; virtuoso, virtuose, virtuosic; **music-loving,** music-mad, musicophile, philharmonic; absolute, aleatory

48 melodious, melodic; **musical,** music-like; **tuneful,** tunable; fine-toned, **pleasant-sounding,** agreeable-sounding, pleasant, appealing, agreeable, catchy, singable; **euphonious** or euphonic, **lyric, lyrical,** melic; **lilting,** songful, songlike; **sweet, dulcet,** sweet-sounding, achingly sweet, sweet-flowing; honeyed, mellifluent, mellifluous, mellisonant, music-flowing; rich, mellow; sonorous, canorous; golden, golden-toned; silvery, silver-toned; sweet-voiced, golden-voiced, silver-voiced, silver-tongued, golden-tongued, music-tongued; ariose, arioso, cantabile

49 harmonious, harmonic, symphonious; harmonizing, **chiming,** blending, well-blended, blended; **concordant,** consonant, accordant, according, **in accord,** in concord, in concert; synchronous, synchronized, in sync (informal), **in tune,** tuned, attuned, in unison, in chorus; unisonous, unisonant; homophonic, monophonic, monodic; assonant, assonantal

50 vocal, singing; **choral,** choric; four-part; operatic; hymnal; psalmic, psalmodic, psalmodial; sacred, liturgical; treble, soprano, tenor, alto, falsetto; coloratura, lyric, bravura, dramatic, heroic; baritone; bass

51 instrumental, orchestral, symphonic, concert; dramatico-musical; jazz, syncopated, jazzy, rock, swing

52 polyphonic, contrapuntal

adjectives, adverbs

53 (directions, style) legato; staccato; spiccato; pizzicato; forte, fortissimo; piano, pianissimo; sordo; crescendo, accrescendo; decrescendo, diminuendo, morendo; dolce; amabile; affettuoso, con affetto; amoroso, con amore lamentabile; agitato, con agitazione; leggiero; agilmente, con agilità; capriccioso, a capriccio; scherzando, scherzoso; appassionato, appassionatamente; abbandono; brillante; parlando; a cappella; trillando, tremolando, tremoloso; sotto voce; stretto

54 (slowly) largo, larghetto, allargando; adagio, adagietto; andante, andantino, andante moderato; calando; a poco; lento; ritardando, rallentando

55 (fast) presto, prestissimo; veloce; accelerando; vivace, vivacissimo; desto, con anima, con brio; allegro, allegretto; affrettando, moderato

56 varieties of music

absolute music	cajun
acid house or acid	calypso
Afro-beat	cathedral music
aleatory music	chamber music
AOR or adult-oriented	church music
rock	circus music
art music	classical music
art rock	country music
atonal music or atonalism	country-and-western music
ballet music	dance hall
baroque music	dance music
beach music	Delta blues
bhangra	ear candy (informal)
big band	easy listening music
bluegrass	electronic or synthesized
blues	music

elevator music or Muzak	programme music
(trademark)	progressive rock
ensemble music	progressive soul
field music	psychobilly
folk music	punkabilly
folk rock	punk rock
funk	ragga
fusion	ragtime music or ragtime
gangsta rap	rai
glam rock	rap music
gothic	reggae
gospel music	rhythm and blues or R
grunge	and B
hard rock	rockabilly
heavy metal	rock music
heavy rock	rock'n'roll
hillbilly music	rococo music
hip-hop	romantic music
house music or House	roots music or roots
indie	sacred music
inspirational music	salon music
instrumental music	salsa
jazz music or jazz	semiclassical music
jazz rock	ska
jungle	skiffle
Latin rock	soca
loft jazz	soukous
martial or military music	soul music or soul
minimalism	swing music or swing
MOR or middle-of-the-	technopop
road	thirdstream music
new age	thrash metal or thrash
new country	through-composed music
part music	twelve-tone music or
piped music	serialism
political rock	vocal music
pomp rock	wind music
polyphonic music	world music
pop-rock	Zopf music
popular or pop music	zydeco

709 HARMONICS, MUSICAL ELEMENTS

nouns

1 harmonics, harmony; melodics; rhythmics; musicality; music, **music theory,** theory; musicology; musicography

2 harmonization; orchestration, instrumentation; arrangement, setting, adaptation, transcription; chordal progression; phrasing, modulation, intonation, preparation, suspension, solution, resolution; tone painting

3 tone, tonality see 50.3

4 pitch, tuning, tune, **tone,** key, note, register, tonality; height, depth; pitch range, tessitura; classical pitch, high pitch, diapason or normal or French pitch, international or concert or new philharmonic pitch, standard pitch, low pitch, Stuttgart or Scheibler's pitch, philharmonic pitch, philosophical pitch; temperament

5 voice, voce (Italian); voce di petto (Italian), chest voice; voce di testa (Italian), head voice; **soprano,** mezzo-soprano, dramatic soprano, soprano spinto, lyric soprano, coloratura soprano; boy soprano; male soprano, castrato; alto, contralto; tenor, lyric tenor, operatic tenor, heldentenor *or* heroic tenor *or* Wagnerian tenor; countertenor *or* male alto; baritone, light *or* lyric baritone; **bass,** basso, basso profundo, basso cantante *or* lyric bass, basso buffo *or* comic bass; treble, falsetto

6 **scale, gamut,** register, compass, range, diapason; diatonic scale, chromatic scale, enharmonic scale, major scale, minor scale, natural *or* harmonic *or* melodic minor, whole-tone scale; great scale; octave scale, dodecuple scale, pentatonic scale; tetrachordal scale; twelve-tone *or* dodecuple scale, tone block, tone row, tone cluster

7 **sol-fa,** tonic sol-fa, do-re-mi; Guidonian syllables, ut, re, mi, fa, sol, la; sol-fa syllables, do, re, mi, fa, sol, la, ti *or* si, do; fixed-do system, movable-do system; solmization; bobization

8 (*diatonic series*) tetrachord, chromatic tetrachord, enharmonic tetrachord, Dorian tetrachord; hexachord, hard hexachord, natural hexachord, soft hexachord; pentachord

9 **octave,** *ottava (Italian),* eighth; *ottava alta (Italian), ottava bassa (Italian);* small octave, great octave; contraoctave, subcontraoctave, double contraoctave; one-line octave, two-line octave, four-line octave, two-foot octave, four-foot octave; tenor octave

10 **mode,** octave species; major mode, minor mode; Greek modes, Ionian mode, Dorian mode, Phrygian mode, Lydian mode, mixolydian mode, Aeolian mode, Locrian mode; hypoionian mode, hypodorian mode, hypophrygian mode, hypolydian mode, hypoaeolian mode, hypomixolydian mode, hypolocrian mode; Gregorian *or* ecclesiastical *or* church *or* medieval mode; plagal mode, authentic mode; Indian *or* Hindu mode, raga

11 **form,** arrangement, pattern, model, design; song *or* lied form, primary form; **sonata form,** sonata allegro, ternary form, symphonic form, canon form, toccata form, fugue form, rondo form

12 **notation,** character, mark, symbol, signature, sign, *segno (Italian);* dot; custos, direct; cancel; bar, measure; measure *or* time signature, key signature; tempo mark, metronome *or* metronomic mark; fermata, hold, pause; *presa (Italian),* lead; slur, tie, ligature, vinculum, enharmonic tie; swell; accent, accent mark, expression mark

13 **clef;** C clef, soprano clef, alto *or* viola clef, tenor clef; F *or* **bass clef,** G *or* **treble clef**

14 **note,** musical note, notes of a scale; **tone** *see* 50.2; **sharp, flat, natural; accidental;** breve, double whole note (*US*); semibreve, whole note (*US*); minim, half note (*US*); crotchet, quarter note (*US*); quaver, eighth note (*US*); semiquaver, sixteenth note (*US*); demisemiquaver, thirty-second note (*US*); hemidemisemiquaver, sixty-fourth note (*US*); triplet, tercet; sustained note, dominant, dominant note; enharmonic, enharmonic note; separation, hammering, staccato, spiccato; connectedness, smoothness, legato; responding note, report; shaped note, patent note

15 **key,** key signature, tonality, sharps and flats; **keynote,** tonic; tonic key; major, minor, major *or* minor key, tonic major *or* minor; supertonic, mediant, submediant, dominant, subdominant, subtonic; pedal point, organ point

16 **harmonic,** harmonic tone, overtone, upper partial tone; flageolet tone

17 **chord,** *concento (Italian),* combination of tones *or* notes; major *or* minor chord, tonic chord, dominant chord

18 **ornament,** grace, arabesque, embellishment, *fioritura (Italian);* **flourish,** roulade, flight, run; passage, division *see* 708.24; florid phrase *or* passage; coloratura; incidental, incidental note; grace note, appoggiatura; rubato; mordent, single mordent, double *or* long mordent; inverted mordent, pralltriller; turn, back *or* inverted turn; cadence, cadenza

19 **trill,** trillo; trillet, *trilleto (Italian);* **tremolo,** tremolant, tremolando; quaver, quiver, tremble, tremor, flutter, falter, shake; **vibrato,** *Bebung (German)*

20 **interval,** degree, **step,** note, tone; second, third, fourth, fifth, sixth, seventh, octave; prime *or* unison interval, major *or* minor interval, harmonic *or* melodic interval, enharmonic interval, diatonic interval; parallel *or* consecutive intervals, parallel fifths, parallel octaves; whole step, major second; half step, halftone, semitone, minor second; augmented interval; diminished interval; diatonic semitone, chromatic semitone, less semitone, quarter semitone, tempered *or* mean semitone; quarter step, enharmonic diesis; diatessaron, diapason; *tierce de Picardie (French) or* Picardy third; augmented fourth *or* tritone

21 **rest,** pause; breve rest, semibreve rest, whole rest (*US*), minim rest, half rest (*US*), crotchet rest, quarter rest (*US*), quaver rest, eighth rest (*US*), semiquaver rest, sixteenth rest (*US*), demisemiquaver rest, thirty-second rest (*US*), hemidemisemiquaver rest, sixty-fourth rest (*US*)

22 **rhythm, beat, metre, measure,** number *or* numbers, movement, **lilt, swing;** prosody, metrics; rhythmic pattern *or* phrase

23 **cadence** *or* cadency, authentic cadence, plagal cadence, mixed cadence, perfect *or* imperfect cadence, half cadence, deceptive *or* false cadence, interrupted *or* suspended cadence

24 **tempo, time, beat,** time pattern, timing; time signature; simple time *or* measure, compound time *or* measure; two-part *or* duple time, three-part *or* triple time, triplet, four-part *or* quadruple time, five-part *or* quintuple time, six-part *or* sextuple time, seven-part *or* septuple time, nine-part *or* nonuple time; two-four time, six-eight time, etc; tempo rubato, rubato; mixed times; **syncopation,** syncope; **ragtime,** rag (*informal*); waltz time, three-four *or* three-quarter time, andante tempo, march tempo, etc; largo, etc; presto, etc

25 **accent,** accentuation, rhythmical accent *or* accentuation, ictus, emphasis, stress arsis, thesis

26 **beat,** throb, pulse, pulsation; downbeat, upbeat, offbeat, backbeat; bar beat

adjectives

27 **tonal,** tonic; chromatic, enharmonic; semitonic

28 **rhythmic, rhythmical,** cadent, cadenced, **measured, metric, metrical;** in rhythm, in numbers; beating, throbbing, pulsing, pulsating, pulsative, pulsatory

29 **syncopated; ragtime,** ragtimey (*informal*); **jazz;** jazzy *and* jazzed *and* jazzed up (*all informal*), hot, swingy (*informal*)

adverbs

30 **in time,** in tempo *see* 709.24, *a tempo* (*Italian*)

710 MUSICIAN

nouns

1 **musician,** musico, **music maker,** professional musician, muso (*informal*); performer, executant, interpreter, tunester, artiste, artist, concert artist, **virtuoso,** virtuosa; maestro; recitalist; **soloist,** duettist; street musician, busker

2 **popular** *or* pop musician; ragtime musician; **jazz musician,** jazzman; swing musician; big-band musician; **rock** *or* **rock'n'roll musician,** rocker

3 **player, instrumentalist,** instrumental musician; bandman, bandsman; orchestral musician; symphonist; concertist; accompanist, accompanist

4 **wind player,** wind-instrumentalist, reedsman, reedman (*US*), horn player, French-horn player *or* hornist, horner, piper, tooter; bassoonist, bugler, clarinettist, cornettist, fifer, oboist, piccoloist, saxophonist, trombonist; trumpeter, trumpet major; fluegelhornist; flautist *or* flutist

5 **string musician,** strummer, picker (*informal*), thrummer, twanger; banjoist, banjo-picker (*informal*), citharist, guitarist, guitar-picker (*informal*), classical guitarist, folk guitarist, lute player, lutenist, lutist, lyrist, mandolinist, theorbist; violinist, fiddler (*informal*); bass violinist, bassist, bass player, contrabassist; violoncellist, cellist, celloist; violist; harpist, harper; zitherist, psalterer

6 xylophonist, marimbaist, vibist *or* vibraphonist

7 **pianist,** pianiste, pianofortist, piano player, ivory tickler *or* thumper (*informal*); keyboard player *or* keyboardist; harpsichordist, clavichordist, monochordist; accordionist, concertinist

8 **organist,** organ player

9 organ-grinder, hurdy-gurdist, hurdy-gurdyist, hurdy-gurdy man

10 **drummer, percussionist,** skinsman, tympanist, kettle-drummer; taborer

11 **cymbalist,** cymbaler; **bell-ringer,** carilloneur, campanologist, campanist

12 **orchestra, band, ensemble,** combo (*informal*), group; strings, woodwind *or* woodwinds, brass *or* brasses, string *or* woodwind *or* brass section, string *or* woodwind *or* brass choir; desks

13 **singer, vocalist,** vocalizer, voice, songster, songbird, warbler, lead singer, caroler *or* caroller, melodist, minstrel, cantor; songstress, singstress, cantatrice, chanteuse, song stylist, canary (*informal*); chanter, chantress; aria singer, lieder singer, opera singer, diva, prima donna; improvisator; rap singer; blues singer, torch singer (*informal*); crooner, rock *or* rock-and-roll singer; yodeler; country singer, folk

singer *or* folkie (*informal*); psalm singer, hymner; Meistersinger; **singing voice, voice** *see* 709.5

14 **minstrel, ballad singer,** balladeer, **bard,** rhapsode, rhapsodist; wandering *or* strolling minstrel, **troubadour,** trovatore, trouvère, minnesinger, scop, gleeman, fili, jongleur; street singer, wait; serenader; **folk singer,** folk-rock singer; country-and-western singer

15 **choral singer,** choir member, chorister, chorus singer, choralist; choirman, **choirboy; chorus girl,** chorine (*US*)

16 **chorus, chorale, choir,** choral group, choral society, oratorio society, chamber chorus *or* Kammerchor (*German*), chorale, men's *or* women's chorus, **male voice choir,** male chorus *or* Männerchor (*German*), mixed chorus, ensemble, voices; **glee club,** *Liedertafel* and *Liederkranz* (*both German*), singing club *or* society; *a cappella* choir; choral symphony

17 **conductor,** leader, symphonic conductor, **musical director,** director, *Kapellmeister* (*German*); **orchestra leader, band leader, bandmaster,** band major, drum major

18 **choirmaster,** choral director *or* conductor, song leader, *Kapellmeister* (*German*), *maestro di cappella* (*Italian*); choir chaplain, minister of music, precentor, cantor, chorister

19 **concertmaster,** concertmeister, *Konzertmeister* (*German*), first violinist; first chair

20 **composer, scorer, arranger,** musicographer; melodist, melodizer; harmonist, harmonizer; **orchestrator;** symphonist; tone poet; ballad maker *or* writer, balladeer, balladist, balladmonger; madrigalist; lyrist; hymnist, hymnographer, hymnologist; contrapuntist; song writer, songsmith, tunesmith; lyricist, librettist; musicologist, ethnomusicologist

21 **music lover,** philharmonic person, **music fan** *and* music buff (*both informal*), musicophile; musicmonger; concertgoer, operagoer; tonalist

22 (*patrons*) the Muses, the Nine, sacred Nine, tuneful Nine, Pierides; Apollo, Apollo Musagetes; Orpheus; Erato, Euterpe, Polymnia *or* Polyhymnia, Terpsichore, St Cecilia

23 **songbird,** singing bird, **songster,** feathered songster, warbler; nightingale, Philomel; bulbul, canary, cuckoo, lark, mavis, mockingbird, oriole, ringdove, song sparrow, thrush

711 MUSICAL INSTRUMENTS

1 **musical instrument,** instrument of music; electronic instrument, synthesizer, synth (*informal*), keyboard, Mellotron (*trademark*), Moog synthesizer (*trademark*), vocoder

2 **string** *or* **stringed instrument,** chordophone; strings, string choir

3 **harp, lyre**

4 **plucked stringed instrument** (*see list*)

5 **viol** *or* **violin family** (*see list*), chest of viols; Stradivarius, Stradivari, Strad (*informal*); Amati, Cremona, Guarnerius; bow, fiddlestick, fiddlebow; bridge, sound hole, soundboard, fingerboard, tuning peg, scroll; string, G string, D string, A string, E string

6 **wind instrument**, wind; aerophone; **horn**, pipe, tooter; mouthpiece, embouchure, lip, chops (*informal*); valve, bell, reed, double reed, key, slide

7 **brass** (*see list*), brass *or* brass-wind instrument; brasses, brass choir

8 **woodwind** (*see list*), wood *or* woodwind instrument; woods, woodwind choir; reed instrument, **reed**; double-reed instrument, **double reed; single-reed instrument**, single reed

9 **bagpipe** *or* bagpipes, pipes, uillean pipes, union pipes, war pipes, Irish pipes, Northumbrian pipes, doodlesack, *Dudelsack* (*German*); cornemuse, musette; sordellina; chanter, drone; pipe bag

10 **mouth organ**, mouth harp, harp, French harp (*informal*), **harmonica**, harmonicon; jaws *or* Jew's harp, mouth bow; kazoo

11 **accordion**, piano accordion; **concertina**; squeeze box (*informal*); mellophone; bandonion

12 keyboard instrument (*see list*), **piano, harpsichord, clavichord, player piano**; music roll, piano player roll

13 **organ**, keyboard wind instrument

14 **hurdy-gurdy**, vielle, **barrel organ**, hand organ, grind organ, street organ

15 **music box**, musical box; orchestrion, orchestrina

16 **percussion instrument** (*see list*), percussion, **drum; drum machine**, beatbox (*informal*); drumstick, jazz stick, tymp stick

17 **keyboard**, fingerboard; console, **keys**, manual, claviature; piano keys, ivories (*informal*), eighty-eight (*informal*), organ manual, great, swell, choir, solo, echo; pedals

18 **carillon**, chimes *see* 711.18, chime of bells; electronic carillon

19 **organ stop**, stop, rank, register

20 string, chord, steel string, wound string, nylon string; fiddlestring, catgut; horsehair; music wire, piano wire

21 plectrum, plectron, pick

22 (*aids*) metronome, rhythmometer; tone measurer, monochord, sonometer; tuning fork, tuning bar, diapason; pitch pipe, tuning pipe; mute; music stand, music lyre; baton, conductor's baton, stick (*informal*)

23 plucked stringed instruments

archlute	mando-bass
balalaika	mando-cello
bandore	mandolin *or* mandola
bandurria (Spanish)	mandolute
banjo	mandore
banjo-ukulele *or* banjuke *or*	oud
banjulele *or* banjo-uke	pandora
banjo-zither	samisen
banjorine	sarod
bass guitar	sitar
bouzouki	Spanish guitar
centrehole guitar	steel guitar
classical guitar	tamboura
concert guitar	theorbo
Dobro guitar (trademark)	troubadour fiddle
electric guitar	ukulele *or* uke (informal)
F-hole guitar	vina
Hawaiian guitar	

24 viol or violin family

alto *or* tenor viol	trumpet marine *or* tromba
baritone viol *or* viola	marina
d'amore	vielle
baryton	viol *or* viola da braccio
basso da camera (Italian)	viol *or* viola da spalla
bass viol *or* viola da gamba	viol *or* viola di bordone
contrabass	viol *or* viola di fagotto
crowd (old)	viola *or* tenor
descant viol	viola alta
double bass *or* violone *or*	viola bastarda
bass viol *or* bass *or*	viola pomposa
doghouse *or* bull fiddle	violette
(both informal)	violin *or* fiddle (informal)
kit	violinette
kit violin	violino piccolo
pocket *or* kit fiddle	violoncello *or* cello
rebec	violoncello piccolo
treble viol	violotta

25 brass instruments, brasses

alpenhorn *or* alphorn	lur
althorn *or* alto horn	mellophone
ballad horn	nyas taranga
baritone horn	ophicleide
bass horn	orchestral horn
bombardon	pocket trumpet
bugle *or* bugle horn	post horn
clarion	sackbut
cornet *or* cornet-à-pistons	saxcornet
cornopean	saxhorn
double-bell euphonium	saxtuba
E-flat horn	serpent
euphonium	slide trombone *or* sliphorn
F horn	(informal)
flugelhorn	sousaphone
French horn	tenor tuba
helicon	tromba
horn	trombone
hunting horn *or* *corno di*	trumpet
caccia (Italian)	tuba
key trumpet	valve trombone
lituus	valve trumpet

26 woodwinds

bass *or* basset oboe	nose-flute
basset horn	oaten reed
bassoon	oboe *or* hautboy *or*
bombard	hautbois
bombardon	oboe d'amore (Italian)
clarinet *or* liquorice stick	oboe da caccia (Italian)
(informal)	ocarina *or* sweet potato
contrabassoon *or*	(informal)
contrafagotto	Pandean pipe
cor anglais *or* English horn	panpipe
crumhorn *or* krummhorn	pibgorn
or cromorne *or* cromorna	piccolo
double bassoon	pipe
fife	pommer
fipple flute *or* pipe	recorder
flageolet	saxophone *or* sax
flute	(informal)
heckelphone	shawm
hornpipe	sonorophone
musette	syrinx *or* shepherd's pipe

tabor pipe	whistle
tenoroon	transverse flute
tin-whistle *or* penny-	whistle

27 keyboard stringed instruments

baby grand	manichord
cembalo	melodion
clarichord	melopiano
clavichord	monochord
clavicittern	pair of virginals
clavicymbal *or*	parlour grand
clavicembalo	pianette
clavicytherium	pianino
clavier	piano *or* pianoforte
concert grand	piano–violin
console piano	Pianola (trademark)
cottage piano	player *or* mechanical piano
couched harp	sostinente pianoforte
digital piano	spinet
dulcimer harpsichord	square piano
grand piano	street piano
hammer dulcimer	upright *or* upright piano
harmonichord	violin piano
harpsichord	virginal
lyrichord	

28 percussion instruments, drums

bass drum	metallophone
bells	nagara (India)
bodhrán	naker
bones	orchestral bells
bongo drum	rattle
carillon	rattlebones
castanets	ride cymbal
celesta	side drum
chime	sizzler
chimes	snappers
clappers	snare drum
conga	tabor
crash cymbal	tam-tam
cymbals *or* potlids	tambourine
(informal)	tenor drum
drumhead	timbrel
drumskin	timpani *or* kettledrums
finger cymbals	tintinnabula
gamelan	thumb piano
glockenspiel	tom-tom
gong	tonitruone
handbells	triangle
highhat cymbal (informal)	troll-drum
kettledrum *or* timbal	tubular bells
lyra	vibraphone *or* vibraharp *or*
maraca	vibes (informal)
marimba	war drum
mbira *or* kalimba	xylophone
membranophone	

712 VISUAL ARTS

nouns

1 **visual arts; art, artwork,** the arts; **fine arts,** *beaux arts* (*French*); arts of design, **design,** designing; art form; abstract art, representative art; **graphic arts** *see* 713; plastic art; **arts and crafts;** primitive art, cave art; folk art; calligraphy; commercial art, applied art; sculpture *see* 715; ceramics *see* 742; photography *see* 714; etching, engraving *see* 713.2; decoration *see* 498.1; artist *see* 716

2 "a treating of the commonplace with the feeling of the sublime"—J F MILLET, "the conveyance of spirit by means of matter"—SALVADOR DE MADARIAGA, "the expression of one soul talking to another"—RUSKIN, "an instant arrested in eternity"—JAMES HUNEKER, "a handicraft in flower"—GEORGE ILES, "science in the flesh"—JEAN COCTEAU, "life upon the larger scale"—E B BROWNING, "the perfection of nature"—SIR THOMAS BROWNE, "the conscious utterance of thought, by speech or action, to any end"—EMERSON, "the wine of life"—JEAN PAUL RICHTER, "a shadow of the divine perfection"—MICHELANGELO, "life seen through a temperament"—ZOLA, "a form of catharsis"—DOROTHY PARKER

3 **craft, manual art,** industrial art, **handicraft,** artisan work, craftwork, artisanship; industrial design; woodcraft, woodwork, metalcraft, stonecraft

4 (*act or art of painting*) **painting, colouring,** "a noble and expressive language"—RUSKIN; the brush

5 (*art of drawing*) **drawing, draughtsmanship, sketching, delineation; black and white,** charcoal; technical drawing, mechanical drawing, draughting; freehand drawing

6 scenography, ichnography, orthographic *or* orthogonal projection

7 **artistry, art, talent,** artistic skill, flair, artistic flair, artistic invention; artiness *and* arty-craftiness *and* artsy-craftsiness (*all informal*); artistic temperament; virtu, artistic quality

8 **style; lines; genre; school,** movement (*see list*); the grand style

9 **treatment; technique,** draughtsmanship, brushwork, painterliness; **composition, design,** arrangement; grouping, balance; **colour,** values; atmosphere, tone; shadow, shading; **line;** perspective

10 **work of art,** objet d'art, object of art, art object, art work, artistic production, piece, **work, study, design, composition;** creation, brainchild; virtu, article *or* piece of virtu; **masterpiece,** *chef d'œuvre* (*French*), masterwork, master (*old*), old master, classic; museum piece; grotesque; statue; mobile, stabile; nude, still life; pastiche, *pasticcio* (*Italian*); artware, artwork; bric-a-brac; kitsch

11 **picture; image, likeness, representation,** tableau; "a poem without words"—HORACE; photograph *see* 714.3; **illustration,** illumination; miniature; copy, reproduction; print, colour print; engraving *see* 713.2, stencil, block print; daub; abstraction, abstract; mural, fresco, wall painting; cyclorama, panorama; montage, collage, assemblage; still life, study in still life; tapestry, mosaic, stained glass, stained glass window, **icon,** altarpiece, diptych, triptych

12 **scene, view, scape; landscape;** waterscape, riverscape, seascape, seapiece; airscape, skyscape, cloudscape; snowscape; cityscape, townscape; farmscape; pastoral; treescape; diorama; exterior, interior

13 **drawing; delineation;** line drawing; **sketch, draft; black and white,** chiaroscuro; **charcoal, crayon,**

pen-and-ink, pencil drawing, charcoal drawing, pastel, pastel painting; silhouette; vignette; doodle; rough draft *or* copy, rough outline, cartoon, sinopia, **study**, design; *brouillon, ébauche, esquisse* (*all French*); diagram, graph; silver-print drawing, tracing

14 **painting, canvas, easel-picture,** "a pretty mocking of the life"—Shakespeare, "silent poetry"—Simonides, "the intermediate somewhat between a thought and a thing"—Coleridge; **oil painting,** oil; **watercolour,** water, aquarelle, wash, wash drawing; finger painting; tempera, egg tempera; *gouache* (*French*)

15 **portrait, portraiture, portrayal;** head; profile; silhouette, shadow figure; miniature

16 **cartoon, caricature; comic strip;** comic section, comics, funny paper *and* funnies (*both informal*); comic book; animated cartoon

17 **studio,** *atelier* (*French*); **gallery** *see* 386.9

18 (*art equipment*) palette; easel; paintbox; art paper, drawing paper; sketchbook, sketchpad; canvas, artists' canvas; canvas board; scratchboard; lay figure; camera obscura, camera lucida; maulstick; palette knife, spatula; brush, paintbrush; air brush, spray gun; pencil, drawing pencil; crayon, charcoal, chalk, pastel; stump; painter's cream; ground; pigments, medium; siccative, drier; fixative, varnish; **paint** *see* 35.8

verbs

19 **to portray, picture,** picturize, **depict, limn,** draw *or* paint a picture; **paint** *see* 35.13; brush, brush in; colour, tint; spread *or* lay on a colour; **daub** (*informal*); scumble; **draw, sketch, delineate; draft,** pencil, chalk, crayon, charcoal; draw in, pencil in; dash off, scratch (*informal*); doodle; design; diagram; cartoon; copy, trace; stencil; hatch, crosshatch, shade

adjectives

20 **artistic,** painterly; **arty** *or* **arty-crafty** *or* **artsy-craftsy** *or* **arty-farty** *or* **artsy-fartsy** (*informal*); **art-minded,** art-conscious; **aesthetic; tasteful; beautiful; decorative, ornamental** *see* 498.10; **well-composed,** well-grouped, well-arranged, well-varied; of consummate art; in the grand style

21 **pictorial,** pictural, **graphic, picturesque;** picturable; photographic *see* 714.17; scenographic; painty, pastose; scumbled; monochrome, polychrome; freehand

22 art schools, groups, movements

American	Flemish
Art Nouveau	Florentine
Ashcan school *or* the Eight	Fontainebleau
Barbizon	French
Bauhaus	Honfleur
Bolognese	Hudson River
British	Impressionism
classical abstraction	Italian
Cobra	L'Age d'or
Dada	letrist
De Stijl	Lombard
Der Blaue Reiter	Madinensor
Die Brücke	Madrid
Dutch	Mannerist
eclectic	Milanese
Modenese	Raphaelite
Momentum	Reflex
'N'	Restany
Neapolitan	Roman
Neonism	Scottish
New Objectivity	Sienese
New York	Spur
Origine	Suprematism
Paduan	surrealism
Parisian	The Ten
Phases	Tuscan
plein-air	Umbrian
pop art	Venetian
Pre-Raphaelite	Washington

713 GRAPHIC ARTS

nouns

1 **graphic arts, graphics; printmaking; painting; drawing; relief-carving; photography** *see* 714; **printing** *see* 548; graphic artist *see* 716.8

2 **engraving** (*see list*), engravement, graving, enchasing, **tooling,** chiselling, incising, incision, lining, scratching, slashing, scoring; **inscription,** inscript; type-cutting; **marking,** line, scratch, slash, score; hatching, cross-hatching; etch, etching; stipple, stippling; tint, demitint, half tint; burr; photoengraving *see* 548.1

3 **lithography,** planography, autolithography, artist lithography; chromolithography; photolithography, offset lithography *see* 548.1

4 stencil printing, stencil; silk-screen printing, serigraphy; monotype; glass printing, decal, decalcomania; cameography

5 **print,** numbered print, imprint, impression, first impression, impress; negative; colour print; **etching; lithograph;** autolithograph; chromolithograph; lithotype; crayon engraving, graphotype; **block, block print,** linoleum-block print, rubber-block print, wood engraving, **woodprint,** xylograph, **cut, woodcut,** woodblock; vignette

6 **plate,** steel plate, copperplate, chalcograph; zincograph; stone, lithographic stone; printing plate *see* 548.8

7 **proof,** artist's proof, proof before letter, open-letter proof, remarque proof

8 **engraving tool, graver,** burin, tint tool, style, point, etching point, needle, etching needle; etching ball; etching ground *or* varnish; scorper; rocker; **die,** punch, stamp, intaglio, seal

verbs

9 **to engrave, grave, tool, enchase, incise, sculpture, inscribe,** character, **mark,** line, crease, score, scratch, scrape, cut, carve, chisel; groove, furrow *see* 290.3; stipple, cribble; hatch, crosshatch; lithograph, autolithograph; **be a printmaker** *or* graphic artist; make prints *or* graphics; print *see* 548.14

10 **to etch,** eat, eat out, corrode, bite, bite in

adjectives

11 **engraved, graven,** graved, glypt- *or* glypto-; tooled, enchased, inscribed, incised, marked, lined, creased, cut, carved, glyphic, **sculptured**, insculptured, "insculp'd upon"—SHAKESPEARE; grooved, furrowed *see* 290.4; **printed, imprinted, impressed, stamped,** numbered

12 glyptic, glyptical, glyptographic, lapidary, lapidarian; xylographic, wood-block; lithographic, autolithographic, chromolithographic; aquatint, aquatinta, mezzotint

13 **kinds of engraving**

acid-blast	metal cut
aquatint	mezzotint
black-line engraving	photochemical engraving *or*
cerography	photoetching
chalcography	photoengraving
chalk engraving	plate engraving
copperplate engraving	pyrography *or* pyrogravure
crayon engraving	*or* pokerwork
cribbling *or* manière criblée	relief etching
(French)	relief method
drypoint *or* draw-point	soft-ground etching
engraving	steel engraving
eccentric engraving	stipple engraving
electric engraving	woodburning *or*
etching	xylopyrography
gem-engraving	woodcut *or* wood
glass-cutting	engraving
glyptics *or* glyptography	xylography
intaglio	zinc etching
line engraving	zincography *or* zinc
linocut	engraving

714 PHOTOGRAPHY

nouns

1 **photography** (*see list*), picture-taking; **cinematography**, cinema photography; colour photography; photochromy, heliochromy; **3-D**, three-dimensional photography; photofinishing; photogravure; radiography, X-ray photography; photogrammetry, phototopography

2 **photographer** *see* 716.5, shutter-bug (*US informal*), press photographer, lensman, paparazzo

3 **photograph, photo** (*informal*), heliograph, **picture,** pic (*informal*), shot (*informal*); **snapshot,** snap (*informal*); black-and-white photograph; colour photograph, colour print, heliochrome; slide, diapositive, transparency; Polaroid *or* Polaroid photograph (*trademark*); candid photograph; still, still photograph; photomural; montage, photomontage; aerial photograph, photomap; facsimile *or* fax transmission; telephotograph, Telephoto (*trademark*), Wirephoto (*trademark*); photomicrograph, microphotograph; metallograph; microradiograph; electron micrograph; photochronograph, chronophotograph; **portrait;** pinup (*informal*), cheesecake *and* beefcake (*both informal*); police photograph, mug *or* mug shot (*informal*); rogues' gallery; photobiography

4 tintype *or* ferrotype, ambrotype, **daguerreotype,** calotype *or* talbotype, collotype, photocollotype, autotype, vitrotype

5 **print,** photoprint, positive; glossy, matte, semi-matte; **enlargement, blowup;** photocopy, Photostat (*trademark*), photostatic copy, Xerox (*trademark*), Xerox copy; microprint, microcopy; blueprint, cyanotype; **slide,** transparency, lantern slide; contact printing, projection printing; photogravure; hologram

6 shadowgraph, shadowgram, skiagraph, skiagram; radiograph, radiogram, scotograph; **X-ray,** X-ray photograph, roentgenograph, roentgenogram; photofluorogram; photogram

7 spectrograph, spectrogram; spectroheliogram

8 (*cinema photography*) **shot; take, retake;** close-up, long shot, medium shot, full shot, group shot, deuce shot, matte shot, process shot, boom shot, travel shot, trucking shot, follow-focus shot, pan shot *or* panoramic shot, rap shot, reverse *or* reverse-angle shot, wild shot, zoom shot; film, motion picture; kinescope

9 **exposure,** time exposure; shutter speed; f-stop, lens opening; film rating, **film speed,** film gauge, ASA exposure index, **DIN** *or* *Deutsche Industrie Normen* number; exposure meter, light meter

10 **film; negative;** printing paper, photographic paper; **plate;** dry plate; vehicle; **cine film,** motion-picture film, panchromatic film, monochromatic film, orthochromatic film, black-and-white film, colour film, colour negative film, colour reversal film; Polaroid film (*trademark*); microfilm, bibliofilm; sound-on-film, sound film; sound track, soundstripe; roll, cartridge; pack, bipack, tripack; frame; emulsion, dope, backing

11 **camera,** Kodak (*trademark*); reflex camera, disc camera, instamatic (*trademark*); Polaroid camera (*trademark*); **cine camera,** film camera, motion-picture camera, cinematograph *or* kinematograph; **video camera, camcorder**

12 **projector;** film projector, motion-picture projector, cineprojector, cinematograph *or* kinematograph, vitascope; **slide projector,** magic lantern, stereopticon; slide viewer; overhead projector *or* OHP; epidiascope

13 **processing solution;** developer, soup (*informal*); fixer, fixing bath, sodium thiosulphate *or* sodium hyposulphite *or* hypo; stop bath, short-stop, short-stop bath

verbs

14 **to photograph, shoot** (*informal*), take a photograph, **take a picture,** take one's picture; **snap,** snapshot, snapshoot; **film,** get *or* capture on film; **mug** (*informal*); daguerreotype, talbotype, calotype; Photostat (*trademark*); Xerox (*trademark*); microfilm; photomap; pan; **X-ray,** radiograph, roentgenograph

15 **to process; develop; print;** blueprint; **blow up, enlarge**

16 **to project, show, screen**

adjectives

17 **photographic,** photo; **photogenic,** picturesome; photosensitive, photoactive; panchromatic; telephotographic, telephoto; tintype; three-dimensional, 3-D

18 types of photography

acoustical holography	miniature photography
aerophotography *or* aerial photography *or* air photography	phonophotography
	photoheliography
	photomacrography
animation photography	photomicrography
astrophotography	pyrophotography
available-light photography	radiation-field *or* Kirlian photography
candid photography	
chronophotography	radiography
cinematography	schlieren photography
cinephotomicrography	skiagraphy
colour photography	spectroheliography
electrophotography	spectrophotography
flash photography	stereophotography
heliophotography	stroboscopic photography
holography	telephotography
infrared photography	time-lapse photography
integral photography	uranophotography
laser photography	xerography
macrophotography	X-ray photography
microphotography	

715 SCULPTURE

nouns

1 **sculpture, sculpturing**; plastic art, **modelling; statuary; stonecutting**; gem-cutting, masonry; **carving**, bone-carving, cameo carving, scrimshaw, *taille directe* (*French*), whittling, woodcarving *or* xyloglyphy; embossing, **engraving** see 713.2, **chasing**, toreutics, founding, casting, moulding, plaster casting, lost-wax process, *cire perdue* (*French*); sculptor see 716.6

2 (*sculptured piece*) **sculpture; glyph; statue**; marble, bronze, terra cotta; mobile, stabile; cast see 784.6; found object, *objet trouvé* (*French*)

3 **relief**, relievo; **embossment**, boss; half relief, *mezzo-rilievo* (*Italian*); high relief, *alto-rilievo* (*Italian*); low relief, bas-relief, *basso-rilievo* (*Italian*), *rilievo stiacciato* (*Italian*); sunk relief, *cavo-rilievo* (*Italian*), coelanaglyphic sculpture, **intaglio**, *intaglio rilievo, intaglio rilevato* (*both Italian*); *repoussé* (*French*); glyph, anaglyph; glyptograph; **mask**; plaquette; **medallion; medal; cameo**, cameo glass, sculptured glass; cut glass

4 (*tools, materials*) chisel, point, mallet, modelling tool, spatula; cutting torch, welding torch, soldering iron; solder; modelling clay, Plasticine (*trademark*), sculptor's wax; plaster

verbs

5 **to sculpture**, sculp *or* sculpt (*informal*), insculpture (*old*); **carve**, chisel, cut, grave, engrave, chase; weld, solder; assemble; **model, mould**; cast, found

adjectives

6 **sculptural**, sculpturesque, sculptitory; **statuary; statuesque**, statuelike; **monumental**, marmoreal

7 **sculptured**, sculpted; sculptile; **moulded, modelled**, ceroplastic; **carved**, chiselled; **graven**, engraved; in relief, in high *or* low relief; **glyphic, glyptic**, anaglyphic, anaglyptic; anastatic; embossed, chased, hammered, toreutic; *repoussé* (*French*)

716 ARTIST

nouns

1 **artist**, *artiste* (*French*), "a dreamer consenting to dream of the actual world"—SANTAYANA; creator, maker; master, **old master**; dauber, daubster; copyist; **craftsman, artisan** see 726.6

2 **limner**, delineator, depicter, picturer, portrayer, imager; **illustrator**; illuminator; calligrapher; commercial artist

3 **draughtsman, sketcher, delineator**; drawer, architectural draughtsman; crayonist, charcoalist, pastelist; **cartoonist, caricaturist**

4 **painter**, *artiste-peintre* (*French*); **colourist**; luminist, luminarist; **oil painter**, oil-colourist; **watercolourist**; aquarellist; finger painter; monochromist, polychromist; genre painter, historical painter, landscapist, miniaturist, portrait painter, portraitist, marine painter, still-life painter; pavement artist; scene painter, scenewright, scenographer

5 **photographer**, photographist, lensman, **cameraman; cinematographer**; snapshotter, snap shooter, shutterbug (*informal*); daguerreotypist, calotypist, talbotypist; skiagrapher, shadowgraphist, radiographer, X-ray technician

6 **sculptor**, sculptress, sculpturer; earth artist, environmental artist; statuary; figurer, *figuriste* (*French*), **modeller**, moulder, wax modeller, clay modeller; graver, chaser, carver; stonecutter, mason, monumental mason, wood carver, xyloglyphic artist, whittler; ivory carver, bone carver, shell carver; gem carver, glyptic *or* glyptographic artist

7 **ceramist, ceramicist, potter**; china decorator *or* painter, tile painter, majolica painter; glassblower, glazer, glass decorator, pyroglazer, glass cutter; enamellist, enameller

8 **printmaker**, graphic artist; **engraver**, graver, burinist; inscriber, carver; **etcher**; line engraver; **lithographer**, autolithographer, chromolithographer; serigrapher, silk-screen artist; cerographer, cerographist; chalcographer; gem engraver, glyptographer, lapidary; wood engraver, xylographer; pyrographer, xylopyrographer; zincographer

9 **designer, stylist**, styler; costume designer, dress designer, *couturier* (*French*), *couturière* (*French feminine*); furniture designer, rug designer, textile designer

10 **architect**, civil architect; landscape architect, landscape gardener; city *or* urban planner, urbanist; functionalist

11 **decorator**, expert in decor, ornamentist, ornamentalist; **interior decorator** *or* designer, house decorator, room decorator, floral decorator, table decorator; window decorator *or* dresser; confectionery decorator

717 ARCHITECTURE, DESIGN

nouns

1 **architecture**, architectural design, building design, the art and technique of building,

"inhabited sculpture"—BRANCUSI, "frozen music"—GOETHE, "music in space"—SCHELLING, "the art of significant forms in space"—CLAUDE BRAGDON; **architectural science**, architectural engineering, structural engineering, architectural technology, building science, building technology; **architectural style** (*see list*); **architectural speciality** (*see list*); landscape architecture, landscape gardening *see* 1067.2

2 **architectural element; ornamentation, architectural ornamentation;** column order, Doric, Ionic, Corinthian, Tuscan, Composite; **type of construction** (*see list*), building type

3 **architect;** landscape architect, landscape gardener *see* 1067.6; city *or* urban planner, urbanist, urbanologist

4 **design, styling, patterning, planning, shaping,** "the conscious effort to impose meaningful order"—VICTOR PAPANEK; **design speciality** (*see list*)

5 **designer, stylist,** styler

adjectives

6 **architectural, design, designer**

7 **architectural styles and types**

absolute	German Renaissance
academic	Gothic
action	Graeco-Roman
additive	Great West Road
American colonial	Greek
American Georgian	Greek Revival
Art Deco *or* Art Moderne	hard
Art Nouveau	high Gothic
arts and crafts	high Renaissance
baroque	hi-tech
Bauhaus	indeterminate
Beaux Arts	international
brutalist	Islamic
Byzantine	Italian Gothic
Chicago School	Italian Mannerism
Chinese	Jacobean
churrigueresque *or*	Japanese
churrigueresco	Jesuit
Cistercian	kinetic
classical	mechanist
conceptual *or* invisible *or*	Mesopotamian
imaginary *or* nowhere	Mestizo
decorated Gothic	moderne
de Stijl	neo-Gothic
directed *or* programmed	neoclassical
duck	new brutalist
early English	Norman
early Gothic	organicist
early Renaissance	Palladian
earthwork	perpendicular
eclectic	Persian
ecological	pneumatic
Egyptian	postmodern
Elizabethan	Prairie
endless	Queen Anne
flamboyant Gothic	rayonnant Gothic
formalist	Renaissance
French Renaissance	rococo
functionalist	rococo Gothic
funk	Roman
Georgian	Romanesque

Romanesque Revival	Utopian *or* fantastic *or*
Romantic	visionary
Spanish	vernacular
tensile	Victorian
Tudor	Victorian Gothic

8 **architectural specialities**

church *or* religious *or*	industrial architecture
ecclesiastical architecture	institutional architecture
commercial architecture	library architecture
domestic architecture	museum architecture
governmental architecture	recreational architecture

9 **elements of architecture**

aesthetic quality *or*	facilitation
venustas (Latin)	fenestration
aesthetic unity	materials
applied ornament	mimetic ornament
circulation	organic ornament
columniation	proportions
commodity *or* *utilitas*	repetitions
(Latin)	scale
decoration *or* ornament *or*	strength *or* *firmitas* (Latin)
detail	

10 **design specialities**

accessory design	graphics design
appearance design	high-tech
architectural design	industrial *or* product
automotive design	design
book design	interior design
carpet design	jewellery design
clothing design	landscape architecture
costume design	lighting design
ergonomics *or* ergonomy *or*	package design
human engineering *or*	pottery design
human factors	special effects design
engineering	stage design
fashion design	textile design
furniture design	typographic design

718 LITERATURE

nouns

1 **literature, letters, belles lettres,** polite literature, humane letters, *litterae humaniores* (*Latin*), republic of letters; **work, literary work, text, literary text; works, complete works, oeuvre, canon, literary canon, author's canon;** serious literature; **classics,** ancient literature; medieval literature, Renaissance literature, etc; national literature, English literature, French literature, etc; ethnic literature; contemporary literature; underground literature; pseudonymous literature; folk literature; travel literature; wisdom literature; erotic literature, erotica; pornographic literature, pornography, porn *and* hard porn *and* soft porn (*all informal*), obscene literature, scatological literature; popular literature, pop literature (*informal*); kitsch

2 **authorship, writing,** authorcraft, pencraft, wordsmanship, **composition,** the art of composition, inditing, inditement; one's pen; **creative writing,** literary art, verbal art, literary composition, literary production, verse-writing, short-story writing, novel-writing, playwriting, drama-writing; essay-writing; **expository writing;** technical writing; journalism,

newspaper writing, editorial-writing, feature-writing, rewriting; magazine writing; songwriting, lyric-writing, libretto-writing; artistry, literary power, literary artistry, literary talent *or* flair, skill with words *or* language, facility in writing, ready pen; **writer's itch**, graphomania, scribblemania, graphorrhea, *cacoëthes scribendi* (*Latin*)

3 **writer**, **scribbler** (*informal*), **penman**, pen, penner; pen *or* pencil driver *or* pusher (*informal*), word-slinger, inkslinger *and* ink spiller *and* inkstained wretch (*all informal*), knight of the plume *or* pen *or* quill (*informal*)

4 **author**, **writer**, scribe (*informal*), composer, inditer; authoress, penwoman; **creative writer**, *littérateur* (*French*), literary artist, literary craftsman *or* artisan *or* journeyman, belletrist, man of letters, literary man; wordsmith, word painter; freelance, freelance writer; ghostwriter, ghost (*informal*); collaborator, coauthor; prose writer, logographer; fiction writer, fictioneer (*informal*); story writer, **short story writer**; storyteller; **novelist**; novelettist; diarist; **newspaperman**; **annalist**; **poet** *see* 720.13; **dramatist**, humorist *see* 489.12; scriptwriter, scenario writer, scenarist; nonfiction writer; article writer, magazine writer; **essayist**; monographer; reviewer, critic, literary critic, music critic, art critic, drama critic, dance critic; columnist; pamphleteer; technical writer; copywriter, advertising writer; compiler, encyclopedist, lexicographer, bibliographer

5 **hack writer**, hack, literary hack, Grub Street writer, **penny-a-liner**, **scribbler** (*informal*), **potboiler** (*informal*)

verbs

6 **to write**, author, pen, **compose**, **indite**, formulate, produce, prepare; dash off, knock off *or* out (*informal*), throw on paper, pound *or* crank *or* grind *or* churn out; freelance; collaborate, coauthor; ghostwrite, ghost (*informal*); novelize; scenarize; pamphleteer; editorialize

adjectives

7 **literary**, belletristic; classical
8 auctorial, authorial

719 HISTORY

nouns

1 **history**, the historical discipline, the investigation of the past, the record of the past, the story of mankind; historical research; **annals, chronicles,** memorabilia, chronology; chronicle, record *see* 549; historical method, historical approach, philosophy of history, **historiography**; cliometrics; narrative history, **oral history**, oral record, survivors' *or* witnesses' accounts; **biography, memoir,** memorial, life, story, **life story**, adventures, fortunes, experiences; curriculum vitae *or* CV, résumé, vita; life and letters; legend, saint's legend, hagiology, hagiography; **autobiography, memoirs,** memorials; **journal, diary,** confessions; **profile, biographical sketch**; obituary, necrology, martyrology; photobiography; case history; historiography, theory

of history; Clio, Muse of history; **the past** *see* 836; **record, recording** *see* 549

2 (*history*)
"a set of lies agreed upon"—Napoleon, "a voice forever sounding across the centuries the laws of right and wrong"—J A Froude, "a cyclic poem written by Time upon the memories of man"—Shelley, "the essence of innumerable biographies"—Carlyle, "philosophy learned from examples"—Dionysius of Halicarnassus, "a shallow village tale"—Emerson, "History is more or less bunk"—Henry Ford, "history is merely gossip"—Oscar Wilde, "a realm in which human freedom and natural necessity are curiously mingled"—Reinhold Niebuhr

3 **story, tale, yarn, account, narrative,** narration, chronicle; **anecdote**, anecdotage; **epic**, epos, **saga**

4 **historian**, cliometrician, historiographer; **chronicler**, annalist; **biographer**, memorialist, Boswell; autobiographer, autobiographist; diarist, Pepys

verbs

5 **to chronicle**, write history, historify; historicize; biograph, biography, biographize; immortalize; **record** *see* 549.16

6 **to narrate, tell, relate, recount,** report, **recite,** rehearse, give an account of

adjectives

7 **historical, historic,** historied, historically accurate; fact-based; historicized; historiographical; cliometric; **chronicled;** chronologic, chronological; **traditional, legendary;** biographical, autobiographic, autobiographical; hagiographic, hagiographical, martyrologic, martyrological; necrologic, necrological

8 **narrative,** narrational; **fictional**

adverbs

9 **historically**, historically speaking; as chronicled, as history tells us, according to *or* by all accounts; as the record shows

720 POETRY

nouns

1 **poetry**, poesy, verse, song, rhyme; "musical thought", "the harmonious unison of man with nature"—both Carlyle, "the supreme fiction"—Wallace Stevens, "the spontaneous overflow of powerful feelings recollected in tranquillity"—Wordsworth, "the rhythmical creation of beauty"—Poe, "painting with the gift of speech"—Simonides, "the poet's innermost feeling issuing in rhythmic language"—John Keble, "the record of the best and happiest moments of the happiest and best minds"—Shelley, "the journal of a sea animal living on land, wanting to fly in the air", "the achievement of the synthesis of hyacinths and biscuits"—both Sandburg, "the best words in the best order"—Coleridge, "the rhythmic, inevitably narrative, movement from an overclothed blindness to a naked vision"—Dylan Thomas, "not the thing said but a way of saying it"—A E Housman, "the art of uniting pleasure with truth, by calling imagination to the help of reason"—Samuel Johnson, "the emotion of life rhythmically remembering beauty"—Fiona MacLeod,

"the music of the soul, and above all of great and of feeling souls"—Voltaire, "adolescence fermented and thus preserved"—J Ortega y Gasset

2 **poetics**, poetcraft, versecraft, versification, versemaking, *ars poetica* (*Latin*);

"my craft and sullen art"—Dylan Thomas; **poetic language**, poeticism; **poetic licence, poetic justice**

3 **bad poetry**, doggerel, versemongering, poetastering, poetastery; poesy; crambo, crambo clink *or* jingle (*Scottish*), Hudibrastic verse; nonsense verse, amphigory; macaronics, macaronic verse; lame verses, limping metres, halting metres

4 **poem, verse, rhyme,**

"imaginary gardens with real toads in them"— Marianne Moore; verselet, versicle

5 **book of verse**, garland, **collection, anthology;** poetic works, poesy

6 **metrics, prosody, versification; scansion,** scanning; metrical pattern *or* form, prosodic pattern *or* form, metre, numbers, measure; quantitative metre, syllabic metre, accentual metre; free verse, *vers libre* (*French*); alliterative metre, *Stabreim* (*German*)

7 **metre, measure,** numbers; **rhythm, cadence,** movement, lilt, jingle, swing; sprung rhythm; **accent,** accentuation, metrical accent, stress, emphasis, ictus, **beat;** arsis, thesis; quantity, mora; metrical unit; **foot, metrical foot** (*see list*); triseme, tetraseme; metrical group, metron, colon, period; dipody, syzygy, tripody, tetrapody, pentapody, hexapody, heptapody; dimeter, trimeter, tetrameter, pentameter, hexameter, heptameter; **iambic pentameter, dactylic hexameter;** Alexandrine; Saturnian metre; elegiac, elegiac couplet *or* distich, elegiac pentameter; heroic couplet; counterpoint; caesura, diaeresis, masculine caesura, feminine caesura; catalexis; anacrusis

8 **rhyme;** clink, crambo; **consonance, assonance; alliteration;** eye rhyme; male *or* masculine *or* single rhyme; female *or* feminine *or* double rhyme; initial rhyme, end rhyme; tail rhyme, rhyme royal; near rhyme, slant rhyme; rhyme scheme; rhyming dictionary; unrhymed poetry, blank verse

9 (*poetic divisions*) **measure, strain; syllable; line;** verse; stanza, stave; strophe, antistrophe, epode; **canto, book; refrain, chorus,** burden; envoi; monostich, distich, tristich, tetrastich, pentastich, hexastich, heptastich, octastich; **couplet;** triplet, tercet, *terza rima* (*Italian*); **quatrain;** sextet, sestet; septet; octave, octet, *ottava rima* (*Italian*); rhyme royal; Spenserian stanza

10 **Muse;** the Muses, Pierides, *Camenae* (*Latin*); Apollo, Apollo Musagetes; Calliope, Polyhymnia, Erato, Euterpe; Helicon, Parnassus; Castilian Spring, Pierian Spring, Hippocrene; Bragi; **poetic genius,** poesy, afflatus, fire of genius, **creative imagination** *see* 985.2, **inspiration** *see* 919.8

11 **poet,** poetess, poetress (*old*), maker (*old*), makar (*Scottish*);

"the painter of the soul"—Disraeli, "a nightingale who sits in darkness and sings to cheer its own solitude with sweet sounds", "the unacknowledged legislators of the world"—both Shelley, "all who love, who feel

great truths, and tell them"—Philip James Bailey, "literalists of the imagination"—Marianne Moore; ballad maker, balladmonger; **bard, minstrel,** scop, fili, baird, skald, **jongleur, troubadour,** *trovatore* (*Italian*), trouveur, *trouvère* (*French*), *Meistersinger* (*German*), minnesinger; minor poet, major poet, arch-poet; laureate, **poet laureate;** occasional poet; **lyric poet;** epic poet; pastoral poet, pastoralist, idyllist, bucoliast (*old*); rhapsodist, rhapsode; verslibrist, *vers libriste* (*French*); elegist, librettist; lyricist, lyrist; odist; satirist; sonneteer; modernist, imagist, symbolist; Parnassian; beat poet

12 **bad poet;** rhymester, rhymer; metrist; versemaker, versesmith, versifier, verseman, versemonger; poetling, **poetaster,** poeticule; balladmonger

verbs

13 **to poetize, versify, verse, write** *or* **compose poetry,** build the stately rime, sing deathless songs, make immortal verse; tune one's lyre, climb Parnassus, mount Pegasus; **sing,**

"lisp in numbers"—Pope; elegize; poeticize

14 **to rhyme,** assonate, alliterate; **scan;** jingle; cap verses *or* rhymes

adjectives

15 **poetic, poetical,** poetlike; **lyrical, narrative,** dramatic, lyrico-dramatic; bardic; runic, skaldic; epic, heroic; mock-heroic, Hudibrastic; pastoral, bucolic, georgic, eclogic, idyllic, Theocritean; didactic; elegiac, elegiacal; dithyrambic, rhapsodic, rhapsodical, Alcaic, Anacreontic, Homeric, Pindaric, sapphic; Castalian, Pierian; poetico-mythological; poetico-mystical, poetico-philosophic

16 **metric, metrical, prosodic, prosodical; rhythmic, rhythmical, measured,** cadenced, scanning; iambic, dactylic, spondaic, pyrrhic, trochaic, anapaestic, antispastic, etc

17 **rhyming; assonant,** assonantal; **alliterative;** jingling; musical, lilting

adverbs

18 **poetically, lyrically; metrically, rhythmically,** in measure; musically

19 **metrical feet**

amphibrach	iamb *or* iambus *or* iambic
anapaest	ionic
antispast	molossus
bacchius	paeon
choriambus *or* choriamb	proceleusmatic
cretic *or* amphimacer	pyrrhic
dactyl	spondee
dochmiac	tribrach
epitrite	trochee

721 PROSE

nouns

1 **prose,**

"words in their best order"—Coleridge; prose fiction, nonfiction prose, expository prose; prose rhythm; prose style; poetic prose, polyphonic prose, prose poetry

2 **prosaism**, **prosaicism**, **prosaicness**, prosiness, pedestrianism, **unpoeticalness**; **matter-of-factness**, unromanticism, unidealism; **unimaginativeness** *see* 986; **plainness**, commonness, commonplaceness, unembellishedness; insipidness, flatness, vapidity; **dullness** *see* 117

verbs

3 **to prose**, write prose *or* in prose; pedestrianize

adjectives

4 **prose**, in prose; unversified, nonpoetic, nonmetrical
5 **prosaic**, **prosy**, **prosing**; unpoetical, poetryless; **plain**, **common**, **commonplace**, **ordinary**, unembellished, mundane; **matter-of-fact**, **unromantic**, **unidealistic**, unimpassioned; pedestrian, **unimaginative** *see* 986.5; insipid, vapid, flat; humdrum, tiresome, **dull** *see* 117.6

722 FICTION

nouns

1 **fiction**, narrative, narrative literature, imaginative narrative, prose fiction; **narration**, relation, relating, recital, rehearsal, telling, retelling, recounting, recountal, review, portrayal, graphic narration, description, delineation, presentation; **storytelling**, tale-telling, yarn-spinning *and* yarning (*both informal*); narrative poetry; operatic libretto; computer *or* interactive fiction
2 **narration**, **narrative**, **relation**, **recital**, rehearsal, telling, retelling, recounting, recountal, review; **storytelling**, tale-telling, yarn spinning *or* yarning (*both informal*)
3 **story** (*see list*), **short story**, tale, narrative, yarn, account, narration, chronicle, relation, version; **novel** (*see list*), roman (*French*)
4 (*story elements*) **plot**, fable, argument, story, line, story line, subplot, secondary plot, mythos; **structure**, plan, architecture, architectonics, scheme, design; **subject**, **topic**, **theme**, motif; thematic development, development, continuity; **action**, movement; incident, episode; **complication**; rising action, climax, falling action, *peripeteia* (*Greek*), switch (*informal*); *anagnorisis* (*Greek*), recognition; denouement, catastrophe; *deus ex machina* (*Latin*); device, contrivance, **gimmick** (*informal*); angle *and* slant *and* twist (*all informal*); **character**, characterization; **speech**, dialogue; **tone**, **atmosphere**, mood; **setting**, locale, world, milieu, background, region, local colour
5 **narrator**, relator, reciter, recounter, *raconteur* (*French*); **anecdotist**; **storyteller**, storier, taleteller, teller of tales, spinner of yarns *and* yarn spinner (*both informal*); word painter; **persona**, central consciousness, the I of the story; point-of-view (*see list*); **author**, **writer**, short-story writer, **novelist**, novelettist, fictionist; fabulist, fableist, fabler, mythmaker, mythopoet; romancer, romancist; sagaman

verbs

6 **to narrate**, tell, **relate**, **recount**, report, **recite**, rehearse, give an account of; tell a story, unfold a tale, a tale unfold, fable, fabulize; storify, fictionalize; romance; novelize; mythicize, mythify, mythologize, allegorize; retell

adjectives

7 **fictional**, fictionalized; **novelistic**, novelized, novelettish; mythical, mythological, **legendary**, **fabulous**; mythopoeic, mythopoetic *or* mythopoetical; **allegorical** *or* allegoric, parabolic *or* parabolical; **romantic**, romanticized; historical, historicized, fact-based
8 **narrative**, **narrational**; storied, storified; **anecdotal**, anecdotic; epic *or* epical
9 types of stories

adventure story	informal)
allegory	lai
apologue	legend
beast fable	love story
bedtime story	Milesian tale
chivalric romance	mystery *or* mystery story
classical detective story	myth *or* mythos
conte (*French*)	nursery tale
detective story *or* detective	parable
yarn *or* whodunit	penny dreadful (informal)
(informal)	romance
epic *or* epos	romantic adventure
exemplum *or* didactic tale	saga
or moral tale	saint's legend
fable	science fiction story *or*
fabliau	sci-fi story (informal)
fairy tale *or* fairy story *or*	short short story *or* short-
Märchen (German)	short
fantasy	short story
folktale *or* folk story	sketch
gest	suspense story
ghost story	thriller
hero tale	vignette
horror story *or* spine-	Western *or* Western story
chiller *or* chiller (both	*or* cowboy story

10 types of novels

adventure novel	novel of ideas
antinovel *or* anti-roman *or*	novel of incident
nouveau roman	novel of manners
Bildungsroman (German)	novel of sensibility
collage novel	novel of the soil
comic novel	novelette
detective novel	novella *or* nouvelle
dystopia *or* cacotopia	(French)
entertainment	picaresque novel
epistolary novel	political novel
erotic novel	pornographic novel
experimental novel	problem novel
fictional *or* fictionalized	proletarian novel
biography	propaganda novel
Gothic novel	psychological novel
graphic novel	realistic novel
historical novel	regional novel
historical romance *or*	roman à clef (French)
bodice-ripper (informal)	roman-fleuve (French)
Kunstlerroman (German)	satirical novel
lyrical novel	science-fiction novel
naturalistic novel	sentimental novel
nouveau roman	social melodrama
novel of character	sociological novel

stream-of-consciousness novel	techno-thriller
	thesis novel
surrealistic novel	utopia *or* utopian novel

11 narrative points of view

documentary *or* camera-eye observer	omniscient observer
	stream of consciousness *or* interior monologue
fallible observer	
first-person past narrator	third-person past narrator
first-person present narrator	third-person present narrator

723 CRITICISM OF THE ARTS

nouns

1 **criticism**, criticism of the arts, aesthetic *or* artistic criticism, aesthetic *or* artistic evaluation, aesthetic *or* artistic analysis, aesthetic *or* artistic interpretation, critical commentary, critique, critical analysis, critical interpretation, critical evaluation, metacriticism, exegetics, hermeneutics; **art criticism**, formalist criticism, expressionist criticism, neoformalist criticism; **music criticism**; dramatic criticism; dance criticism; aesthetics

2 **review**, critical notice, commentary, *compte rendu critique (French)*, critical treatment *or* treatise

3 **literary criticism**, Lit-Crit *(informal)*, literary analysis *or* evaluation *or* interpretation *or* exegetics *or* hermeneutics, poetics; **critical approach *or* school** *(see list)*; **literary theory**, theory of literature, critical theory, theory of criticism

4 **critic**, interpreter, exegete, analyst, explicator, theoretician, aesthetician; reviewer

verbs

5 **to criticize**, critique, evaluate, interpret, explicate, analyse, judge; theorize

adjectives

6 **critical**, evaluative, interpretive, exegetical, analytical, explicative

7 **literary critical approaches**

archetypal criticism	New Criticism
contextualist criticism	ontological approach
deconstruction *or* deconstructionism	post-structuralist criticism *or* post-structuralism
epistemological approach	practical criticism
ethical criticism	psychological *or* psychoanalytic criticism
feminist criticism	
formalist criticism	reader-response criticism
Freudian criticism	revisionist criticism
genre *or* generic criticism	rhetorical criticism
impressionistic criticism	sociological criticism
Jungian criticism	speech-act criticism
literary history	structuralist criticism *or* structuralism
Marxist criticism	
myth criticism	textual criticism

724 OCCUPATION

nouns

1 **occupation**, work, job, employment, business, employ, **activity**, function, enterprise, undertaking, **work**, **affairs**, labour; thing *and* bag *(both informal)*; **affair**, **matter**, concern, concernment, interest,

lookout *(informal)*; what one is doing *or* about; **commerce** *see* 731

2 **task**, **work**, **stint**, **job**, labour, piece of work, **chore**, chare, odd job; **assignment**, **charge**, project, errand, **mission**, commission, **duty**, service, exercise; things to do, matters in hand, irons in the fire, fish to fry; homework; busywork, makework

3 **function**, **office**, **duty**, **job**, province, place, **role**, *rôle (French)*, part; **capacity**, character, **position**

4 *(sphere of work or activity)* **field**, **sphere**, profession, province, bailiwick, turf *(informal)*, department, area, discipline, subdiscipline, orb, orbit, realm, arena, domain, walk; **speciality**, specialty *(US)*, line of country; beat, round; shop

5 **position**, **job**, employment, gainful employment, situation, **office**, **post**, **place**, station, berth, billet, **appointment**, engagement, gig *(informal)*; incumbency, tenure; opening, vacancy; second job, moonlighting *(informal)*

6 **vocation**, **occupation**, **business**, **work**, **line**, **line of work**, line of business *or* endeavour, number *(informal)*, walk, **walk of life**, **calling**, mission, **profession**, **practice**, **pursuit**, speciality, specialization, *métier (French)*, mystery *(old)*, **trade**, racket *and* game *(both informal)*; **career**, lifework, life's work; career path; **craft**, art, handicraft; careerism, career building

7 **avocation**, **hobby**, hobbyhorse *(old)*, sideline, by-line, side interest, pastime, spare-time activity; amateur pursuit, amateurism; unpaid work, volunteer work

8 **professionalism**, professional standing *or* status

9 **nonprofessionalism**, **amateurism**, amateur standing *or* status

verbs

10 **to occupy**, **engage**, **busy**, devote, spend, **employ**, occupy oneself, busy oneself, go about one's business, devote oneself; pass *or* employ *or* spend the time; occupy one's time, take up one's time; attend to business, attend to one's work; mind one's business, mind the store *(US informal)*, stick to one's last *or* knitting *(informal)*

11 **to busy oneself with**, **do**, occupy *or* engage oneself with, employ oneself in *or* upon, pass *or* employ *or* spend one's time in; **engage in**, **take up**, devote oneself to, apply oneself to, address oneself to, have one's hands in, turn one's hand to; concern oneself with, make it one's business; **be about**, **be doing**, be occupied with, be engaged *or* employed in, be at work on; practise, follow as an occupation

12 **to work**, work at, work for, have a job, be employed, **ply one's trade**, labour in one's vocation, do one's number *(informal)*, follow a trade, practise a profession, carry on a business *or* trade, keep up; **do** *or* **transact business**, carry on *or* conduct business; set up shop, set up in business, hang out one's shingle *(US informal)*; stay employed, hold down a job *(informal)*; moonlight *(informal)*; labour, toil *see* 725.13, 14

13 **to officiate**, function, serve; perform as, act as, act *or* play one's part, do duty, discharge *or* perform *or* exercise the office *or* duties *or* functions of, serve in the office *or* capacity of

14 **to hold office**, fill an office, occupy a post

adjectives

15 **occupied, busy,** working; **practical, realistic** *see* 986.6; banausic, moneymaking, breadwinning, utilitarian *see* 387.18; materialistic *see* 695.16; workaday, workday, prosaic *see* 117.8; **commercial** *see* 731.21

16 **occupational, vocational,** functional; **professional,** pro (*informal*); official; technical, industrial; all in the day's work

17 avocational, hobby, amateur, nonprofessional

adverbs

18 professionally, vocationally; as a profession *or* vocation; in the course of business

725 EXERTION

nouns

1 **exertion, effort, energy,** elbow grease; **endeavour** *see* 403; **trouble, pains;** great *or* mighty effort, might and main, muscle, one's back, nerve, and sinew, hard *or* strong *or* long pull,
"a long pull, a strong pull, and a pull all together"—DICKENS

2 **strain, straining, stress,** stressfulness, **stress and strain,** taxing, **tension,** stretch, rack; tug, pull, haul, heave; overexertion, overstrain, overtaxing, overextension, overstress

3 **struggle, fight, battle, tussle, scuffle, wrestle,** hassle (*informal*)

4 **work, labour,** employment, industry, **toil,** moil, travail, toil and trouble, sweat of one's brow; **drudgery, sweat,** slavery, skivvying, spadework, rat race (*informal*); treadmill; unskilled labour, hewing of wood and drawing of water; dirty work, grunt work (*US informal*), donkey work (*informal*); makework (*US*), tedious *or* stupid *or* idiot *or* tiresome work, humdrum toil, grind (*informal*), fag; **manual labour,** handwork, handiwork; hand's turn, stroke of work, stroke; lick *and* lick of work *and* stitch of work (*all informal*); man-hour; **workload,** work schedule; task *see* 724.2; fatigue *see* 21

5 **hard work** *or* **labour, backbreaking work,** warm work, uphill work, hard *or* tough grind (*informal*); **hard job** *see* 1012.2; labour of Hercules; **laboriousness, toilsomeness,** effortfulness, **strenuousness, arduousness,** operosity, operoseness; onerousness, oppressiveness, burdensomeness; troublesomeness

6 **exercise** *see* 84, exercising; **practice, drill, workout;** weight training, multigym; keep fit, aerobics, yoga; constitutional (*informal*), stretch; violent exercise; physical education

7 exerciser; horizontal bar, parallel bars, horse, side horse, long horse, rings; trapeze; trampoline; Indian club; medicine ball; punch bag; exercise bike; rowing machine; weight, dumbbell, barbell

verbs

8 **to exert, exercise, ply, employ, use, put forth,** put out (*informal*), make with (*US informal*); practise

9 **to exert oneself,** use some elbow grease (*informal*), spread oneself, put forth one's strength, bend every effort, bend might and main, spare no effort, tax one's energies, break sweat (*informal*); put *or* lay oneself out (*informal*), go all out (*informal*), get *or* pull one's finger out (*informal*); endeavour *see* 403.4; **do one's best; apply oneself,** come to grips with; lay to; lay to the oars, ply the oar

10 **to strain, tense, stress, stretch, tax,** press, rack; **pull, tug,** haul, **heave;** strain the muscles, strain every nerve *or* every nerve and sinew; put one's back into it (*informal*); sweat blood; take on too much, spread oneself too thin, overexert, overstrain, overtax, overextend; drive *or* whip *or* flog oneself

11 **to struggle, strive, contend, fight, battle,** buffet, scuffle, tussle, wrestle, hassle (*informal*), work *or* fight one's way, agonize, huff and puff, grunt and sweat, sweat it out (*informal*), make heavy weather of it

12 **to work, labour;** busy oneself *see* 724.10, 11; turn a hand, do a hand's turn, do a lick of work, earn one's keep; chore, do the chores, char *or* do chars, chare

13 **to work hard;** scratch *and* hustle *and* sweat (*all informal*), **slave, sweat and slave** (*informal*), slave away, toil away; pour it on (*informal*); work one's head off (*informal*), work one's fingers to the bone, break one's back, bust one's hump *or* ass (*both US informal*); beaver *or* beaver away (*informal*), work like a beaver, work like a horse *or* cart horse *or* dog, work like a slave *or* galley slave, work like a coal heaver, work like a Trojan; work overtime, be a workaholic (*informal*), do double duty, work double hours *or* tides, **work day and night,** work late, **burn the midnight oil;** lucubrate, elucubrate; overwork *see* 992.10

14 **to drudge,** skivvy, **grind** *and* **dig** (*both informal*), fag, **grub,** toil, moil, toil and moil, travail, **plod, slog, peg, plug** (*informal*), hammer, peg away *or* along, plug away *or* along (*informal*), hammer away, pound away, struggle along, struggle on, work away; **get** *or* **keep one's nose to the grindstone;** wade through

15 **to set to work, get rolling, get busy, get down to business** *or* **work,** roll up one's sleeves, spit on one's hands, gird up one's loins; fall to work, **fall to, buckle** *or* **knuckle down to** (*informal*), **turn to, set to** *or* **about,** put *or* set one's hand to, start in, set up shop, enter on *or* upon, launch into *or* upon; **get on the job** *and* **get going** (*both informal*); **go to it** *and* **get with it** *and* **get cracking** *and* **get one's teeth into it** (*all informal*); hop *or* jump to it (*informal*); **attack,** set at, **tackle** (*informal*); **plunge into, dive into; pitch in** *or* **into** (*informal*); light into *and* wade into *and* tear into *and* sail into (*all informal*), put *or* lay one's shoulder to the wheel, put one's hand to the plough; take on, undertake *see* 404.3

16 **to task, work, busy,** keep busy, fag, sweat (*informal*), **drive, tax;** overtask, overtax, **overwork,** overdrive; burden, oppress *see* 297.13

adjectives

17 **labouring, working; struggling, striving, straining; drudging, toiling,** slaving, sweating *and* grinding (*both informal*), grubbing, **plodding,** slogging, pegging, plugging (*informal*); hardworking

18 **laborious, toilsome, arduous, strenuous,** painful, effortful, operose, troublesome, onerous, oppressive, burdensome; wearisome; **heavy, hefty** (*informal*), tough (*informal*), uphill, **backbreaking,** gruelling, punishing, crushing, killing, Herculean; **laboured,** forced, strained; straining, tensive, **intensive;** hard-fought, hard-earned

adverbs

19 laboriously, arduously, toilsomely, strenuously, operosely; **effortfully,** with effort, **hard,** by the sweat of one's brow; the hard way; with all one's might, for all one is worth, with a will, **with might and main,** with a strong hand, manfully; **hammer and tongs, tooth and nail,** *bec et ongles* (*French*), heart and soul; **industriously** *see* 330.27

726 WORKER, DOER

nouns

1 **doer, agent,** actor, **performer, worker, practitioner,** perpetrator; **producer, maker,** creator, fabricator, **author,** mover, prime mover; architect; **agent,** medium; **executor,** executant, executrix; **operator,** operative, operant; subject *and* agent (*both grammar*)

2 **worker, labourer, toiler,** moiler; member of the working class, proletarian, prole (*informal*), blue-collar worker, labouring man, stiff *and* working stiff (*both US informal*); **workman, workingman; workwoman, workingwoman,** workfolk, workpeople; working girl, workgirl; **factory worker,** industrial worker; carworker, steelworker; construction worker, builder; **commuter;** home worker, telecommuter; **office worker, white-collar worker;** career woman, career girl; **jobholder,** wageworker, **wage earner,** salaried worker; **breadwinner;** wage slave; employee, servant *see* 577; **hand,** workhand; **labourer,** common labourer, **unskilled labourer,** navvy, day labourer, roustabout (*US & Canadian*); casual, casual labourer; **agricultural worker** *see* 1067.5; migrant worker, migrant; menial, flunky; piece-worker, jobber; full-time worker, part-time worker; temporary employee, temporary, office temporary, temp (*informal*); freelance worker, freelance, freelancer; self-employed person; **labour force, work force,** shop floor; labour market

3 **drudge,** skivvy, grub, **hack, fag, plodder, slave,** galley slave, **workhorse,** beast of burden, dogsbody, slogger;
"hewers of wood and drawers of water"—BIBLE; slave labour, sweatshop labour

4 **professional,** member of a learned profession, professional practitioner; pro *and* old pro (*both informal*), seasoned professional; gownsman; doctor, lawyer, member of the clergy, teacher, accountant; social worker; health-care professional, military professional; law-enforcement professional, etc

5 **amateur, nonprofessional, layman,** member of the laity, laic

6 **skilled worker,** skilled labourer, **journeyman,** mechanic, tradesman, time-served worker; **craftsman, handicraftsman;** craftswoman; craftsperson; craftspeople; **artisan,** artificer, artist

(*old*); **maker,** *fabbro* (*Italian*); **wright; technician;** apprentice, prentice (*informal*); **master,** master craftsman, master workman, master carpenter, etc

7 **engineer,** professional engineer; **technician,** technical worker, techie (*US informal*); engineering, technology

8 **smith,** blacksmith; farrier, forger, forgeman, metalworker; Vulcan, Hephaestus, Wayland *or* Völund

727 UNIONISM, TRADE UNION

nouns

1 **unionism,** trade unionism, trades unionism, labor unionism (*US*); **unionization; collective bargaining; arbitration,** nonbinding arbitration; ACAS; industrial relations, labour relations

2 trade union, trades union, labor union (*US*); Trades Council; organized labour; collective bargaining; **craft union,** horizontal union; **industrial union,** vertical union; company union

3 **union shop,** preferential shop, **closed shop;** open shop; nonunion shop; **labour contract, union contract,** sweetheart agreement, yellow-dog contract (*US*); maintenance of membership

4 **unionist, trade unionist, union member,** trades unionist, organized *or* unionized worker, cardholder, labor unionist (*US*); shop steward, bargainer, negotiator; business agent; union officer; union *or* labour organizer, organizer; union contractor

5 **strike, walkout,** tie-up (*US informal*), **industrial action,** action; work stoppage, sit-down strike, sit-down, wildcat strike, out-law strike; sympathy strike; **go-slow,** slowdown (*US & Canadian*), work-to-rule, rule-book slowdown (*US & Canadian*); general strike; **boycott,** boycottage; buyer's *or* consumer's strike; **lock-out;** revolt *see* 327.4

6 **striker;** sitdown striker; holdout (*US informal*)

7 (*strike enforcer*) **picket;** goon (*US informal*), strong-arm man; flying picket, secondary picket, goon squad (*US informal*)

8 **blackleg, strikebreaker, scab** (*informal*), rat *and* fink *and* scissorbill (*all US informal*)

verbs

9 **to organize, unionize;** bargain, bargain collectively; arbitrate; submit to arbitration

10 **to strike, go on strike, come out, go out, walk, walk out,** down tools; hit the bricks (*US informal*), shut it down; slow down; sit down; **boycott,** black; picket; hold out (*informal*); **lock out;** revolt *see* 327.7

11 **to break a strike; blackleg, scab** (*informal*), rat *and* fink (*both US informal*)

728 MONEY

nouns

1 **money, currency, legal tender, medium of exchange,** circulating medium, sterling, **cash,** hard cash, cold cash; specie, coinage, mintage, coin of the realm, gold; **silver;** pounds, shillings, and pence, l.s.d.; **the wherewithal,** the wherewith; lucre, **filthy**

lucre (*informal*), the almighty dollar (*US*), pelf, root of all evil, mammon;

"the sinews of war"—Libanius, "the sinews of affairs"—Laertius, "the ruling spirit of all things"—Publilius Syrus, "coined liberty"—Dostoyevsky; **hard currency**, soft currency; broad money, narrow money; fractional currency, postage currency, postal currency; managed currency; necessity money, scrip, emergency money

2 (*informal terms*) **dough, bread, dosh**, rhino, **lolly**, change, mazuma, mopus, gelt, gilt, coin, spondulics, wampum, moolah, dinero, brass, tin, shekels, bucks, green, green stuff, the needful, the necessary, **loot**

3 **wampum**, wampumpeag, peag, sewan, roanoke; cowrie

4 **specie**, hard money; coin, piece, piece of money, piece of silver *or* gold; roll of coins, rouleau; **gold piece**; guinea, sovereign, pound sovereign, crown, half crown; doubloon; ducat; napoleon, louis d'or; eagle, half eagle, double eagle; moidore

5 **paper money; note**, pound note, etc; negotiable note, legal-tender note; **bill; bank note**; national bank note; government note, treasury note; silver certificate; gold certificate; scrip; fractional note, shinplaster (*US & Canadian informal*); fiat money, assignat

6 (*informal terms*) **folding money**, green stuff, greenbacks

7 (*British denominations*) mite; farthing; halfpenny *or* ha'penny, bawbee (*informal*), mag *or* meg (*both informal*); penny, new penny; pence, p; new pence, np; two-pence *or* tuppence; threepence *or* thruppence, threepenny bit *or* piece; fourpence, fourpenny, groat; sixpence, tanner (*informal*), teston; shilling, bob (*informal*); florin; half crown, half-dollar (*informal*); crown, dollar (*informal*); pound, quid *and* knicker *and* oncer *and* single (*all informal*); guinea; five-pound note, fiver (*informal*); ten-pound note, tenner (*informal*); pony (£25), monkey (£500), grand (£1000), plum (£100 000), marigold (£1 000 000) (*all informal*)

8 (*US denominations*) mill; cent, penny, copper, red cent (*informal*); five cents, nickel; ten cents, dime; twenty-five cents, quarter, two bits (*informal*); fifty cents, half-dollar, four bits (*informal*); dollar, dollar bill; buck *and* smacker *and* frogskin *and* fish *and* skin (*all informal*); silver dollar, cartwheel *and* iron man (*both informal*); two-dollar bill, two-spot (*informal*); five-dollar bill, fiver *and* five-spot *and* fin (*all informal*); ten-dollar bill, tenner *and* ten-spot *and* sawbuck (*all informal*); twenty-dollar bill, double sawbuck (*informal*); fifty-dollar bill, half a C (*informal*); hundred-dollar bill, C *and* C-note *and* century *and* bill (*all informal*); five hundred dollars, half grand (*informal*), five-hundred-dollar bill, half G (*informal*); thousand dollars, G *and* grand (*both informal*), thousand-dollar bill, G-note *and* yard *and* big one (*all informal*)

9 **foreign money**, foreign denominations; **convertibility, foreign exchange**; rate of exchange *or* exchange rate; parity of exchange; agio

10 **counterfeit**, counterfeit money, funny *or* phoney *or* bogus money (*informal*), false *or* bad money, queer (*informal*), base coin, green goods (*informal*); **forgery**, bad cheque, rubber cheque *and* bounced cheque *and* kite (*all informal*)

11 **negotiable instrument** *or* **paper**, commercial paper, paper, bill; **bill of exchange**, bill of draft; certificate, certificate of deposit *or* CD; **cheque**, check (*US*); crossed cheque, open cheque; blank cheque; bank cheque, teller's cheque; treasury cheque; cashier's cheque, certified cheque; traveller's cheque *or* banker's cheque; letter of credit, commercial letter of credit; **money order** *or* **MO**; **postal order** *or* postoffice order; giro cheque, giro; draft, warrant, voucher, debenture; **promissory note, note, IOU**; note of hand; credit note; acceptance, acceptance bill, bank acceptance, trade acceptance; due bill; demand bill, sight bill, demand draft, sight draft; time bill, time draft; exchequer bill *or* treasury bill; chequebook

12 **token, counter**, slug (*US*); **scrip, coupon; receipt, ticket**, tag; cloakroom ticket; book token, record token; luncheon voucher

13 **sum**, amount of money; lump sum, round sum

14 **funds, finances, moneys**, exchequer, purse, budget, pocket; treasury, treasure, substance, **assets**, resources, total assets, worth, net worth, **pecuniary resources, means**, available means *or* resources *or* funds, cash flow, wherewithal, command of money; balance; pool, **fund, kitty** (*informal*); war chest; bank account, cheque account; Swiss bank account, unnumbered *or* unregistered bank account; reserves, cash reserves; savings, savings account, nest egg (*informal*); life savings; bottom dollar (*informal*)

15 **capital, fund**; moneyed capital; principal, corpus; circulating capital, floating capital; fixed capital, working capital, equity capital, **risk** *or* **venture capital**; capital structure; capital gains distribution; capitalization

16 **money market**, supply of short-term funds; tight money, cheap money; **borrowing** see 621; **lending** see 620; discounting, note discounting, note shaving (*US*), dealing in commercial paper

17 **bankroll**; roll *or* wad (*both informal*)

18 **cash, ready money** *or* **cash**, the ready *or* readies (*informal*), available funds, money in hand, cash in hand, balance in hand, immediate resources, **liquid assets**, cash supply, **cash flow**; treasury

19 **petty cash, pocket money, pin money**, spending money, mad money, **change**, small change; pennies, coppers, nickels and dimes (*US*), chicken feed *and* peanuts (*both informal*)

20 **precious metals; gold**, yellow stuff (*informal*); nugget, gold nugget; **silver, copper, nickel**, coin gold *or* silver; bullion, ingot, bar

21 **standard of value**, gold standard, silver standard; monometallism, bimetallism; money of account

22 (*science of coins*) **numismatics**, numismatology; numismatist, numismatologist

23 **monetization**; issuance, circulation; remonetization; demonetization; revaluation, devaluation

24 **coining, coinage**, mintage, striking, stamping; **counterfeiting, forgery**; coin-clipping

25 **coiner**, minter, mintmaster, moneyer; **counterfeiter, forger**; coin-clipper

verbs

26 to monetize; **issue**, utter, **circulate**; remonetize, reissue; demonetize; revalue, devalue, devaluate
27 to discount, discount notes, deal in commercial paper, shave (*US*); borrow, lend *see* 620.5
28 to coin, **mint**; **counterfeit, forge**; utter
29 to cash, cash in (*informal*), liquidate, convert into cash

adjectives

30 monetary, pecuniary, nummary, financial; capital; fiscal; sumptuary; numismatic; sterling
31 convertible, liquid, negotiable

729 FINANCE, INVESTMENT

nouns

1 finance, finances, money matters; world of finance, financial world, financial industry, high finance, investment banking, international banking, City of London *or* City, Square Mile, Lombard Street, Wall Street; the gnomes of Zurich; economics *see* 731
2 financing, funding, backing, financial backing, sponsorship, patronization, support, financial support; stake *and* grubstake (*both US informal*); subsidy *see* 478.8; capitalizing, capitalization, provision of capital; front-end funding; deficit financing
3 investment, venture, risk, plunge (*informal*), speculation; prime investment; ethical *or* conscience investment; pump priming; divestment, disinvestment
4 banking, money dealing, money changing; investment banking; banking industry
5 financial condition, state of the exchequer; credit rating
6 solvency, soundness, solidity; credit standing, creditworthiness; unindebtedness
7 crisis, financial crisis; sterling crisis, sterling gap, run on the pound
8 financier, moneyman, capitalist, finance capitalist; investor; financial expert, economist, authority on money and banking; international banker, merchant banker
9 financer, backer, funder, sponsor, patron, supporter, angel (*informal*), Maecenas; cash cow (*informal*), meal ticket (*informal*), staker *and* grubstaker (*both US informal*); fundraiser
10 banker, money dealer, moneymonger; money broker; discounter, note broker, bill broker; moneylender *see* 620.3; money changer, cambist; investment banker; bank chairman, bank manager, bank officer, loan officer, trust manager, banking executive; bank clerk, cashier, teller
11 treasurer, financial officer, bursar, purser, purse bearer, cashier, cashkeeper; accountant, auditor, controller *or* comptroller, bookkeeper; chamberlain, curator, steward, trustee; depositary, depository; receiver, liquidator; paymaster; Chancellor of the Exchequer, Secretary to the Treasury
12 treasury, treasure-house; subtreasury; depository, repository; storehouse *see* 386.6; gold depository,

Fort Knox; **strongbox, safe**, money chest, **coffer**, locker, chest, deed box; piggy bank, penny bank, bank; vault, strong room; safe-deposit *or* safety-deposit box *or* vault; cashbox, coin box, cash register, till; bursary; exchequer, fisc; consolidated fund, public treasury, public funds, public purse, taxpayer funds *or* money, pork barrel (*US informal*)
13 bank, banking house, lending institution, savings institution; cash dispenser, automated teller machine *or* ATM, cash machine; central bank, Bank of England *or* the Old Lady of Threadneedle Street, Bundesbank, Bank of France, Federal Reserve Bank *or* System, Bank of Japan; World Bank, International Monetary Fund; clearing house
14 purse, wallet, pocketbook (*US & Canadian*), bag, handbag, porte-monnaie, billfold (*US & Canadian*), money belt, money clip, poke (*informal*), pocket; moneybag; purse strings

verbs

15 to finance, back, fund, sponsor, patronize, support, provide for, capitalize, provide capital *or* money for, pay for, bankroll (*US & Canadian informal*), angel (*informal*), put up the money, raise the wind (*informal*); stake *or* grubstake (*both US informal*); subsidize *see* 478.19; set up, set up in business; refinance
16 to invest, place, put, sink; risk, venture; make an investment, lay out money, place out *or* put out at interest; reinvest, roll over, plough back into (*informal*); invest in, put money in, sink money in, pour money into, tie up one's money in; buy in *or* into, buy a piece *or* share of; disinvest; financier; plunge (*informal*), speculate *see* 737.23

adjectives

17 solvent, sound, substantial, solid, good, sound as a pound, creditworthy; able to pay, good for, unindebted *see* 624.23, out of the hole (*US*), out of the red
18 insolvent, unsound, indebted *see* 623.8

730 BUSINESSMAN, MERCHANT

nouns

1 businessman, businesswoman, businessperson, businesspeople; enterpriser, entrepreneur, man of commerce, intrapreneur; small *or* little businessman; big businessman, magnate, tycoon (*informal*), baron, king, top executive, business leader; director, manager *see* 574.1; big boss, industrialist, captain of industry; banker, financier; robber baron
2 merchant, merchandiser, marketer, trader, trafficker, dealer, monger, chandler; tradesman, tradeswoman; storekeeper, shopkeeper; regrater; wholesaler, jobber, middleman; importer, exporter; distributor; retailer, retail merchant, retail dealer *or* seller; dealership, distributorship; franchise; concession (*US & Canadian*)
3 salesman, seller, salesperson, salesclerk; saleswoman, saleslady, salesgirl; shop assistant, clerk *and* shop clerk *and* store clerk (*all US*); shopwalker, floorwalker (*US*); agent, sales agent, selling agent; sales engineer; sales manager;

salespeople, sales force, sales personnel; tout *and* ticket tout, scalper *and* ticket scalper (*both US informal*)

4 **travelling salesman, traveller, commercial traveller,** sales representative *or* rep, travelling agent, travelling man *or* woman, knight of the road, bagman, drummer (*old*); detail man; door-to-door salesman, canvasser

5 **vendor, pedlar, huckster, hawker,** butcher (*old*), higgler, cadger (*Scottish*), colporteur, chapman (*old*); cheap-jack (*informal*); **stallholder,** barrow boy, coster *or* costermonger, bummaree (*old*); fishmonger, fruiterer, ironmonger, chemist, newsagent; street vendor, sidewalk salesman (*US & Canadian*); news vendor

6 **solicitor,** canvasser

7 (*informal terms*) tout, touter, pitch-man *or* -woman *or* person (*all US*), barker, spieler, ballyhooer *and* ballyhoo man (*both US*)

8 **auctioneer,** auction agent

9 **broker,** note broker, bill broker, discount broker, cotton broker, hotel broker, insurance broker, mortgage broker, diamond broker, furniture broker, ship broker, grain broker; stockbroker *see* 737.10; pawnbroker *see* 620.3; money broker, money changer, cambist; land broker, real estate broker (*US*), realtor (*US*), real estate agent (*US*), estate agent *or* agent, house agent

10 **ragman,** old-clothesman, rag-and-bone man; **junkman,** junk dealer

11 **tradesmen, tradespeople,** tradesfolk, **merchantry**

adjectives

12 **business, commercial,** mercantile; entrepreneurial

731 COMMERCE, ECONOMICS

nouns

1 **commerce, trade, traffic,** truck, intercourse, **dealing, dealings; business,** business dealings *or* affairs *or* relations, commercial affairs *or* relations; the business world, the world of trade *or* commerce, the marketplace; merchantry, mercantile business; **market,** marketing, state of the market, buyers' market, sellers' market; **industry** *see* 725.4; big business, small business; fair trade, free trade, reciprocal trade, unilateral trade, multilateral trade; most favoured nation (*US*); balance of trade; restraint of trade, trade barriers

2 **trade, trading, doing business, trafficking;** barter, bartering, **exchange,** interchange, swapping (*informal*); give-and-take, horse trading (*informal*), **dealing, deal-making,** wheeling and dealing (*informal*); **buying and selling; wholesaling,** jobbing; brokerage, agency; **retailing,** merchandising *see* 734.2

3 **negotiation, bargaining, haggling,** higgling, **dickering, chaffering,** chaffer, haggle; hacking out *or* working out *or* hammering out a deal, coming to terms; collective bargaining, package bargaining, pattern bargaining

4 **transaction,** business *or* commercial transaction,

deal, business deal, negotiation (*old*), operation, turn; package deal

5 **bargain, deal** (*informal*), dicker; **trade, swap** (*informal*); horse trade (*informal*); trade-in; blind bargain, pig in a poke; hard bargain

6 **custom,** patronage, trade; **goodwill,** repute, good name

7 **economy, economic system,** capitalist *or* capitalistic economy, free-enterprise *or* private-enterprise economy, enterprise culture, market economy, socialist *or* socialistic economy, collectivized economy; hot *or* overheated economy; healthy *or* sound economy; **gross national product** *or* **GNP;** economic sector, public sector, private sector; economic self-sufficiency, autarky

8 **standard of living,** standard of life, standard of comfort; real wages, take-home pay *or* take-home; **cost of living;** cost-of-living index, consumer price index, retail price index *or* RPI

9 **business cycle, economic cycle,** business fluctuations; peak, peaking; low, bottoming out (*informal*); prosperity, boom (*informal*); boomlet *or* miniboom; crisis, **recession, depression,** slowdown, cooling off, slump *and* bust (*both informal*), downturn, downtick (*US informal*); upturn, uptick (*US informal*), expanding economy, recovery; **growth,** economic growth, business growth, sustainable growth, high growth rate, expansion, market expansion, **economic expansion; trade cycle;** trade deficit, trade gap, balance of payments; **monetary cycle; inflation,** deflation, stagflation, reflation

10 **economics,** eco *or* econ (*informal*), economic science, the dismal science; political economy; dynamic economics; theoretical economics, plutology; classical economics; Keynesian economics, Keynesianism; neoclassical economics; monetarism; supply side economics; econometrics; economism, economic determinism; economic man; rational expectations

11 **economist,** economic expert *or* authority; monetarist; political economist

12 **commercialism,** mercantilism; industrialism; mass marketing

13 **commercialization;** industrialization

verbs

14 **to trade, deal, traffic, truck, buy and sell, do business; barter; exchange,** change, interchange, give in exchange, take in exchange, **swap** (*informal*), switch; horse-trade (*informal*); trade off; trade in; trade sight unseen, make a blind bargain, sell a pig in a poke; **ply one's trade** *see* 724.12

15 **to deal in, trade in, traffic in, handle,** carry, be in; market, merchandise, **sell,** retail, wholesale, job

16 **to trade with, deal with, traffic with, do business with,** have dealings with, have truck with, transact business with; frequent as a customer, shop at, trade at, **patronize,** take one's business *or* trade to; open an account with, have an account with

17 **to bargain, drive a bargain, negotiate, haggle,** higgle, chaffer, huckster, **deal, dicker,** make a deal, do a deal, hack out *or* work out *or* hammer out a deal; **bid,** bid for, cheapen, beat down; underbid, outbid; drive a hard bargain

18 to strike a bargain, make a bargain, make a dicker, make a deal, get oneself a deal, put through a deal, shake hands, shake on it (*informal*); bargain for, agree to; come to terms *see* 332.10; be a bargain, be a go *and* be a deal (*both informal*), be on (*informal*)

19 to put on a business basis *or* footing, make businesslike; commercialize; industrialize

20 (*adjust the economy*) to cool *or* cool off the economy; heat *or* heat up the economy, overheat the economy

adjectives

21 commercial, business, trade, trading, mercantile, merchant; commercialistic, mercantilistic; industrial; wholesale, retail

22 economic; socio-economic, politico-economic *or* economical

732 ILLICIT BUSINESS

nouns

1 illicit business, illegitimate business, illegal operations, illegal commerce *or* traffic, shady dealings, racket (*informal*); the rackets (*informal*), the syndicate, organized crime, Mafia, Cosa Nostra; black market, grey market; drug *or* narcotics traffic; narcoterrorism; prostitution, streetwalking; pimping, traffic in women, white slavery; usury *see* 623.3, loan-sharking *and* shylocking (*both informal*); protection racket; bootlegging, moon-shining (*informal*); gambling *see* 759.7

2 smuggling, contrabandage, contraband; narcotics smuggling, dope smuggling (*informal*), jewel smuggling, cigarette smuggling; gunrunning, rumrunning

3 contraband, smuggled goods; narcotics, drugs, dope (*informal*), jewels, cigarettes; bootleg liquor; stolen goods *or* property, hot goods *or* items (*informal*)

4 racketeer; Mafioso; black marketeer, spiv, grey marketeer; bootlegger, moonshiner (*informal*); pusher *and* dealer (*both informal*), narcotics *or* dope *or* drug pusher (*informal*); drug lord; Medellin cartel

5 smuggler, contrabandist, runner; drug smuggler, mule (*informal*); gunrunner, rumrunner

6 fence, receiver, receiver of stolen goods, swagman *and* swagsman (*both informal*), bagman, bagwoman

verbs

7 (*deal in illicit goods*) to push (*informal*); sell under the counter; black-market, black-marketeer; bootleg, moonshine (*informal*); fence (*informal*), receive, reset (*Scottish*)

8 to smuggle, run, sneak

733 PURCHASE

nouns

1 purchase, buying, purchasing; shopping, marketing; shopping around, comparison shopping; window-shopping; one-stop shopping; impulse buying; shopping spree; repurchase, rebuying; mail-order buying, catalogue buying; instalment buying, hire purchase, never-never; shared ownership; layaway purchase; buying up, cornering, coemption (*old*); buying *or* purchasing power; consumerism;

consumer society, consumer sovereignty, consumer power, acquisitive society; retail *or* consumer price index; wholesale price index

2 option, first option, first refusal, refusal, preemption, right of preemption, prior right of purchase

3 market, public, purchasing public; urban market, rural market, youth market, suburban market, etc; clientele, customers, clientage, patronage, custom, trade; carriage trade

4 customer, client, punter (*informal*); patron, patronizer (*informal*), regular customer *or* buyer, regular; prospect; mark *or* mug *or* sucker (*all informal*)

5 buyer, purchaser, emptor, consumer, vendee; shopper, marketer; window-shopper, browser; purchasing agent, customer agent

6 by-bidder, decoy, come-on man *and* shill (*both informal*)

verbs

7 to purchase, buy, procure, make *or* complete a purchase, make a buy, make a deal for; buy up, regrate, corner, monopolize, engross; buy out; buy in, buy into, buy a piece of; repurchase, rebuy, buy back; buy on credit, buy on the instalment plan, buy on the never-never; buy sight unseen *or* blind; trade up

8 to shop, market, go shopping, go marketing; shop around; window-shop, comparison-shop, browse; impulse-buy

9 to bid, make a bid, offer, offer to buy, make an offer; give the asking price; by-bid, shill (*informal*); bid up; bid in

adjectives

10 purchasing, buying, in the market; cliental

11 bought, store-bought, boughten *or* store-boughten (*both informal*), purchased

734 SALE

nouns

1 sale; wholesale, retail; market, demand, outlet; buyers' market, sellers' market; mass market; conditional sale; tie-in sale, tie-in; turnover; bill of sale; cash sale, cash-and-carry

2 selling, merchandising, marketing; niche marketing; wholesaling, jobbing; retailing; direct selling; mail-order selling, direct-mail selling, catalogue selling; telesales *or* telemarketing *or* telephone selling, television *or* video selling; presale; vending, peddling, hawking, huckstering; hucksterism, inertia selling, sugging; market *or* marketing research, consumer research, consumer preference study, consumer survey; sales campaign, promotion, sales promotion, preselling; salesmanship, high-pressure salesmanship, hard sell (*informal*), low-pressure salesmanship, soft sell (*informal*); sellout

3 sale, closing-down sale, going-out-of-business sale, clearance sale *or* inventory-clearance sale, distress sale, fire sale, warrant sale (*Scottish*); bazaar; jumble sale, bring-and-buy sale, sale of work, rummage sale, white elephant sale, car-boot sale *or* boot sale, garage sale, flea market; party plan; tax sale

4 **auction**, auction sale, vendue, outcry, sale at *or* by auction, sale to the highest bidder; Dutch auction; **auction block, block**

5 **sales talk, sales pitch**, patter; **pitch** *or* spiel *or* ballyhoo (*all informal*)

6 **sales resistance**, consumer *or* buyer resistance

7 **saleability**, saleableness, commerciality, merchandisability, **marketability**, vendibility

verbs

8 **to sell**, flog (*informal*), **merchandise, market,** move, shift, turn over, sell off, make *or* effect a sale; convert into cash, turn into money; **sell out,** close out; sell up; **retail**, sell retail, sell over the counter; **wholesale**, sell wholesale, job, be jobber *or* wholesaler for; dump, unload, flood the market with; sacrifice, sell at a sacrifice *or* loss; resell, sell over; undersell, undercut, cut under; sell short; sell on consignment; presell

9 **to vend**, dispense, peddle, hawk, huckster

10 **to put up for sale**, put up, ask bids *or* offers for, offer for sale, offer at a bargain, put on the market

11 **to auction**, auction off, auctioneer, sell at auction, sell by auction, put up for auction, **put on the block**, bring under the hammer; knock down, sell to the highest bidder

12 **to be sold**, sell, bring, realize, sell for; sell like hot cakes

adjectives

13 **sales**, selling, market, **marketing, merchandising, retail,** retailing, wholesale, wholesaling

14 **saleable**, sellable, **marketable,** retailable, merchandisable, merchantable, commercial, vendible; in demand

15 **unsaleable**, nonsaleable, **unmarketable;** on one's hands, on the shelves, not moving, not turning over, unbought, unsold

adverbs

16 **for sale**, to sell, up for sale, in *or* on the market, in the marts of trade; at a bargain, marked down

17 **at auction**, at outcry, at public auction *or* outcry, by auction, **on the block**, under the hammer

735 MERCHANDISE

nouns

1 **merchandise, commodities, wares, goods,** effects, vendibles; **items**, oddments; **consumer goods,** consumer items, retail goods, goods for sale; **stock, stock-in-trade;** staples; **inventory; line**, line of goods; sideline; job lot; mail-order goods, catalogue goods; **luxury goods,** high-ticket *or* big-ticket *or* upscale items (*US*)

2 **commodity, ware,** vendible, **product, article, item**, article of commerce *or* merchandise; staple, staple item, standard article; special, feature, leader, lead item, loss leader; seconds; drug, drug on the market

3 **dry goods, soft goods;** textiles; yard goods (*US*), white goods, linens, napery; men's wear, ladies' wear,

children's wear, infants' wear; sportswear, sporting goods; leatherware, leather goods

4 **hard goods,** brown goods, **durables, durable goods,** consumer durables; fixtures, white goods, **appliances** *see* 385.4; tools and machinery *see* 1039; **hardware,** ironmongery; sporting goods, **housewares,** home furnishings, kitchenware; tableware, dinnerware; flatware (*US & Canadian*), hollow ware; metalware, brassware, copperware, silverware, ironware, tinware; woodenware; glassware; chinaware, earthenware, clayware, stoneware, graniteware; enamelware; ovenware

5 **furniture** *see* 229, furnishings, home furnishings

6 **haberdashery,** notions, **sundries,** novelties, knickknacks, odds and ends; toilet goods, toiletries; cosmetics; giftware

7 **groceries**, grocery, food items, edibles, victuals, baked goods, packaged goods, canned goods, tinned goods; greengroceries, green goods, **produce**, truck

736 MARKET
place of trade

nouns

1 **market, mart, store, shop**, salon, boutique, wareroom, emporium, house, establishment, *magasin* (*French*); **retail store; cash-and-carry, wholesale house, discount store, discount house, outlet store;** warehouse; mail-order house; **general store,** country store; **department store; co-op** (*informal*), cooperative; **variety store,** variety shop, dime store (*US & Canadian*); ten-cent store *or* five-and-ten *or* five-and-dime (*US informal*); chain store; concession (*US & Canadian*); **trading post,** post; **supermarket,** hypermarket, greengrocery; sweet shop, tuck shop; fish-and-chip shop, chippy (*informal*); **off-licence, off-sales,** bottle shop (*Australian*), bottle store (*New Zealand & South African*), package store (*US*), liquor store (*US & Canadian*); filling station *and* petrol station, gas station (*US & Canadian*); sex shop

2 **marketplace, mart, market, open market,** market overt; **covered market, shopping centre, shopping plaza** *or* **mall,** plaza, mall, arcade, shopping *or* shop *or* commercial complex, shambles (*dialect*); emporium, rialto; staple; **bazaar,** craft fair, **fair**, trade fair, show, car show, boat show, etc, exposition; flea market, flea fair, street market, *marché aux puces* (*French*)

3 **booth, stall, stand, pitch;** newsstand, kiosk, news kiosk

4 **vending machine**, vendor, coin machine, coin-operated machine, slot machine, **automat**

5 **saleroom**, wareroom; showroom; auction room

6 **counter,** shopboard (*old*); notions counter (*US & Canadian*); showcase; barrow, pedlar's cart, pushcart

737 STOCK EXCHANGE

nouns

1 **stock exchange, stock market, the market,** The City, Wall Street; ticker market (*US*); open market, competitive market; steady market, strong market,

hard *or* stiff market; unsteady market, spotty market; weak market; long market; top-heavy market; FT Share Index, Footsie (*informal*), market index, stock price index, Dow-Jones Industrial Average, Nikkei Stock Average, Hang Seng Index

2 active market, brisk market, lively market

3 inactive market, slow market, stagnant market, flat market, tired market, sick market; investors on the sidelines

4 rising market, booming market, buoyant market; **bull market**, bullish market, bullishness

5 declining market, sagging market, retreating market, off market, soft market; **bear market**, bearish market, bearishness; **slump**, sag; break, break in the market; profit-taking, selloff; **crash**, smash

6 rigged market, manipulated market, pegged market, put-up market; **insider dealing** *or* **trading**

7 stock exchange, exchange, change, **stock market**, bourse, **board**, Wall Street; the Stock Exchange, London International Stock Exchange; American Stock Exchange, Amex; kerb, kerb market, kerb exchange; over-the-counter market, telephone market, outside market; third market; USM *or* unlisted securities market; exchange floor; commodity exchange, pit, corn pit, wheat pit, etc; SEAQ *or* Stock Exchange Automatic Quotations system, quotation board; tape machine, ticker *or* stock ticker (*both US*); ticker tape

8 financial district, the City, Square Mile, Lombard Street; Wall Street, the Street (*US*)

9 stockbrokerage, brokerage, brokerage house, brokerage office; wire house (*US*); share shop; bucket shop (*informal*), boiler room (*US informal*)

10 stockbroker, sharebroker, **broker**, jobber, stockjobber, dealer, stock dealer; Wall Streeter (*US*); stock-exchange broker, *agent de bourse* (*French*); floor broker, floor trader, floorman, specialist, market maker; pit man (*US*); sales trader; interbroker dealer; kerb broker; broker's agent, customer's broker *or* customer's man, registered representative

11 speculator, adventurer, operator; big operator, smart operator; **plunger**, gunslinger; scalper; stag; lame duck; margin purchaser; **arbitrager** *or* arbitrageur *or* arb (*informal*); insider dealer *or* trader

12 bear, short, short seller; shorts, short interest, short side; short account, bear account

13 bull, long, longs, long interest, long side; long account, bull account

14 shareholder, shareowner, stockholder, stockowner; bondholder; stockholder of record

15 joint-stock company, stock company; **public company**, listed company; issuing company; stock insurance company

16 trust, investment company; investment trust, holding company; closed-end investment company, closed-end fund; open-end fund, mutual fund, money-market fund; issuing house, unit trust; load fund, no-load fund, low-load fund, back-end fund; growth fund, income fund, dual purpose fund; trust fund; blind trust

17 pool (*US*)

18 stockbroking, brokerage, stockbrokerage, jobbing, stockjobbing, stockjobbery, stock dealing; bucketing, legal bucketing

19 trading, stock-market trading, market-trading; computer *or* programmed selling; playing the market (*informal*); **speculation**, stockjobbing, stockjobbery; **venture**, flutter; flier, plunge; scalping; liquidation, profit taking; **arbitrage**, arbitraging; bed and breakfast; buying in, covering shorts; short sale; spot sale; round trade *or* transaction, turn; risk *or* venture capital, equity capital; money-market trading, foreign-exchange trading, agiotage; **buyout, takeover**, hostile takeover, takeover bid; leveraged buyout; greenmail; **leverage**

20 manipulation, rigging; raid, bear raid, bull raid; **corner**, corner in, corner on the market, monopoly; laundering

21 option, stock option, share option, right, **put, call**, put and call, right of put and call; straddle, spread; strip; strap

22 panic, bear panic, rich man's panic

verbs

23 to trade, speculate, venture, operate, **play the market**, buy *or* sell *or* deal in futures; **arbitrage**, bang; **plunge**, take a flier (*informal*); scalp; bucket, bucketshop; stag *or* stag the market; trade on margin; pyramid; be long, go long, be long of the market, be on the long side of the market; be short, be short of the market, be on the short side of the market; margin up, apply *or* deposit margin; wait out the market, hold on; be caught short, miss the market, overstay the market; scoop the market, make a scoop *or* killing *or* bundle *or* pile (*all informal*)

24 to sell, convert, liquidate; throw on the market, dump, unload; **sell short**, go short, make a short sale; cover one's short, fulfil a short sale; make delivery, clear the trade; close out, sell out, terminate the account

25 to manipulate the market, rig the market; bear, **bear the market**; bull, **bull the market**; raid the market; hold *or* peg the market; whipsaw (*US*); launder sales

26 to corner, get a corner on, **corner the market**; monopolize, engross; buy up, absorb

738 SECURITIES

nouns

1 securities (*see list*), **stocks and bonds**, investment securities

2 shares (*see list*), **stock**, equity, equity security, corporate stock; stock split, split; reverse split; stock list; stock ledger, share ledger; **holdings, portfolio**, investment portfolio

3 share, lot; ordinary share; preference share; preferred ordinary share; golden share; dummy share; holding, holdings, stockholding, stockholdings; block; round lot, full lot, even lot, board lot; odd lot, fractional lot

4 share certificate, stock certificate, certificate of stock; street certificate; interim certificate; **coupon**

5 bond (*see list*); nominal rate, coupon rate, current yield, yield to maturity

6 issue, issuance; **flotation**; share issue, secondary issue; bonus issue, scrip issue, rights issue, capitalization issue; bond issue; poison pill (*informal*)

7 dividend; regular dividend; extra dividend, special dividend, plum (*informal*), melon (*US & Canadian informal*); payout ratio; cumulative dividend, accumulated dividends, accrued dividends; interim dividend; cash dividend; stock dividend; optional dividend; scrip dividend; liquidating dividend; phoney dividend; **interest** *see* 623.3; **bonus, return, yield**, return on investment, payout, payback; bonus issue *or* scrip issue

8 assessment, Irish dividend

9 price, quotation; bid-and-asked prices, bid price, asked *or* asking *or* offering price; actual *or* delivery *or* settling price, put price, call price; opening price, closing price; high, low; market price, quoted price, flash price; issue price; fixed price; parity, **par**, issue par; par value, nominal value, face value; stated value; book value; market value; bearish prices, bullish prices; swings, fluctuations; flurry, flutter; rally, decline

10 margin; thin margin, shoestring margin; exhaust price

11 (*commodities*) spots, spot grain, etc; futures, future grain, etc

verbs

12 to issue, float, put on the market; issue shares, go public (*informal*); float a bond issue

13 to declare a dividend, cut a melon (*US & Canadian informal*)

adverbs

14 dividend off, ex dividend; dividend on, cum dividend; coupon off, ex coupon; coupon on, cum coupon; warrants off, ex warrants; warrants on, cum warrants; when issued

15 kinds of securities

asset-backed securities	securities *or* mediums
bullets	mortgage securities
consols *or* bank annuities	mortgage-backed securities
government securities	penny shares
listed securities	rente (French)
long-dated gilt-edged securities *or* longs	short-dated gilt-edged securities *or* shorts
long-term securities	short-term securities
medium-dated gilt-edged	unlisted securities

16 kinds of stock

alpha stock	loan stock
beta stock	ordinary shares
blue chip stock	preference shares
capital stock	preferred ordinary shares
convertible stock	recovery stock
delta stock	second-line stock
gamma stock	third-line stock
gilt-edged stock	Treasury stock
government stock	value stock
growth stock	voting stock

17 kinds of bond

bulldog	ecu bond
capital bond	eurobond
convertible bond	government bond
corporate bond	guaranteed-income bond
income bond	short-term bond
junk bond	TIGR *or* Treasury Investment Growth Receipt *or* Tiger (US)
long-term bond	
medium-term bond	
municipal bond	Treasury bond (US)
perpetual debenture	war bond
post-obit bond	warrant bond
premium bond	Yankee (US)
property bond	yearling
samurai bond	

739 WORKPLACE

nouns

1 workplace, worksite, workshop, shop; sweatshop; shop floor, workspace, working space, loft; **bench**, workbench, worktable; counter, worktop; **workstation; desk**, desktop; **workroom; studio**, *atelier* (*French*); parlour, beauty parlour, funeral parlour, etc; **establishment, facility**, installation; **company**, institution, house, firm, concern, agency, organization, **corporation; financial institution, stock exchange** *see* 737, **bank** *see* 729; **market, store** *see* 736, mall, shopping mall; **restaurant, eating place** *see* 8.17

2 hive, hive of industry, beehive; factory *or* mill *or* manufacturing town; hub of industry, centre of manufacture; smokestack industry, heavy industry; sunrise industry, sunset industry

3 plant, factory, works, manufactory (*old*), manufacturing plant, *usine* (*French*); main plant, assembly plant, subassembly plant, feeder plant; foreign-owned plant, transplant; push-button plant, automated *or* cybernated *or* automatic *or* robot factory; assembly *or* production line; defence plant, munitions plant, armoury, arsenal; **power plant** *see* 1031.18; atomic energy plant; **machine shop; mill**, sawmill, flour mill, etc; **yard**, yards, railroad yard, brickyard, shipyard, dockyard, boatyard; ropewalk; mint; refinery, oil refinery, sugar refinery, etc; distillery, brewery, winery; boilery; bindery, bookbindery; packinghouse; cannery; dairy, creamery; pottery; tannery; **factory district**, industrial zone, industrial park, industrial estate *or* trading estate, business park; factory belt, manufacturing quarter; enterprise zone

4 foundry, metalworks; steelworks, steel mill; forge, furnace, bloomery; smelter; smithy, smithery, stithy, blacksmith shop *or* blacksmith's shop

5 repair shop, fix-it shop (*informal*); garage; roundhouse; hangar

6 laboratory, lab (*informal*); research laboratory, research installation *or* facility *or* centre;

7 office, shop (*informal*); home *or* head *or* main office, headquarters, executive office, corporate headquarters; office suite, executive suite; closet, cabinet (*old*), study, den, carrell; embassy, consulate, legation, chancery, chancellery; box office, booking office, ticket office; branch, branch office, local office; office *or* executive park

740 WEAVING

nouns

1 **weaving**, weave, warpage, weftage, warp and woof *or* weft, texture, tissue; **fabric, web; interweaving**, interweavement, intertexture; **interlacing**, interlacement, interlacery; **intertwining**, intertwinement; intertieing, interknitting, interthreading, intertwisting; **lacing**, enlacement; **twining**, entwining, entwinement; wreathing, knitting, twisting; crocheting; **braiding**, plaiting

2 **braid**, plait, **wreath**, wreathwork

3 **warp**; **woof, weft**, filling; shoot, pick

4 **weaver**, interlacer, webster (*old*); weaverbird, weaver finch, whirligig beetle

5 **loom**, weaver; hand loom; Navajo loom; knitting machine; shuttle

verbs

6 **to weave**, loom, tissue; **interweave, interlace**, **intertwine**, interknit, interthread, intertissue, intertie, intertwist; inweave, intort; web, net; **lace**, enlace; **twine**, entwine; **braid**, plait, pleach, **wreathe**, raddle, **knit**, twist, mat, wattle; crochet; twill, loop, noose; splice

adjectives

7 **woven**, loomed, textile; **interwoven, interlaced**, interthreaded, **intertwined**, interknit, intertissued, intertied, intertwisted; handwoven; **laced**, enlaced; **wreathed**, fretted, raddled, knit; crocheted; **twined**, entwined; **braided**, plaited, platted, pleached

8 **weaving**, twining, entwining; **intertwining**, **interlacing**, interweaving

741 SEWING

nouns

1 **sewing, needlework**, stitchery, stitching; tack; suture; **fancywork**; tailoring, garment making *see* 5.31

2 **sewer, needleworker, seamstress**, sempstress, needlewoman; seamster, sempster, **tailor**, needleman (*old*), needler; embroiderer, embroideress; knitter; garmentmaker *see* 5.33

3 **sewing machine**, sewer, Singer (*trademark*); housewife

verbs

4 **to sew, stitch**, needle; stitch up, sew up; tack; **tailor**

742 CERAMICS

nouns

1 **ceramics** (*see list*), **pottery**; potting

2 **ceramic ware**, ceramics; **pottery, crockery**; **china, porcelain**; enamelware; refractory, cement; bisque, biscuit; pot, crock, vase, urn, jug, bowl; tile, tiling; brick, firebrick, refractory brick, adobe; glass *see* 1028.2

3 (*materials*) clay; potter's clay *or* earth, fireclay, refractory clay; porcelain clay, kaolin, china clay; china stone, feldspar, petuntse; flux; slip; glaze

4 **potter's wheel**, wheel; kick wheel, pedal wheel, power wheel

5 **kiln, oven, stove, furnace**; acid kiln, brick kiln, cement kiln, enamel kiln, muffle kiln, limekiln, reverberatory, reverberatory kiln; pyrometer, pyrometric cone, Seger cone

verbs

6 **to pot**, shape, **throw**, throw *or* turn a pot; mould; **fire**, bake; glaze

adjectives

7 **ceramic**, earthen, earthenware, clay, enamel, china, porcelain; fired, baked, glazed; refractory

8 **ceramics**

Albion ware	jasper *or* jasper ware
Allervale pottery	Kinkozan ware
Aretine ware	Leeds pottery
basalt *or* basaltes	Limoges *or* Limoges ware
Belleek ware	Lowestoft ware
Berlin ware	lustreware *or* lustre pottery
biscuit ware	majolica
blackware	Meissen ware
bone china	Nabeshima ware
Castleford ware	Old Worcester ware
Castor ware	Palissy ware
celadon	Parian ware
champlevé *or* champlevé enamel	porcelain
china *or* chinaware	queensware
clayware	refractory ware
cloisonné *or* cloisonné enamel	Rockingham ware
cottage china	salt-glazed ware
crackle *or* crackleware	Samian ware
crouch ware	sanda ware
Crown Derby ware	Satsuma ware
delft *or* delftware	Sèvres *or* Sèvres ware
Dresden china	Seto ware
earthenware	soft-paste porcelain
eggshell porcelain	Spode
enamel *or* enamelware	spongeware
faience	Staffordshire *or* Staffordshire ware
glassware	stoneware
glazed ware	terra cotta
gombroon	terra sigillata
hard-paste porcelain	ting ware *or* ting yao
Hirado ware	Toft ware
Hizen porcelain	Wedgwood *or* Wedgwood ware
Imari ware	whiteware *or* white pottery
ironstone *or* ironstone china	Worcester ware
Jackfield ware	yi-hsing ware *or* yi-hsing yao

743 AMUSEMENT

nouns

1 **amusement, entertainment, diversion**, solace, divertisement, *divertissement* (*French*), **recreation**, **relaxation**, regalement; **pastime**, *passe-temps* (*French*); **mirth** *see* 109.5; **pleasure, enjoyment** *see* 95

2 **fun**, action (*informal*); funmaking, fun and games, **play, sport**, game; **good time**, lovely time, pleasant

time; **big time** *and* **high time** *and* high old time (*all informal*), **picnic** *and* **laughs** *and* lots of laughs *and* **ball** (*all informal*), great fun, time of one's life; a short life and a merry one; wild oats

3 **festivity, merrymaking, merriment, gaiety, jollity,** jollification (*informal*), jolly (*informal*), **joviality, conviviality,** whoopee *and* hoopla (*both informal*), beano; larking (*informal*), cavorting, skylarking, racketing, mafficking (*informal*), holiday-making; **revelry, revelment, revelling, revels;** nightlife

4 **festival, festivity,** festive occasion, *fiesta* (*Spanish*), **fete, gala, gala affair,** blowout (*informal*), **jamboree** (*informal*); **high jinks,** do, great doings (*all informal*); *fête champêtre* (*French*); **feast, banquet** *see* 8.9; picnic *see* 8.6; party *see* 582.11; waygoose *or* wayzgoose (*informal*); **fair,** carnival; kermis; *Oktoberfest* (*German*); Mardi Gras; Saturnalia; Hocktide; harvest festival, harvest home; **field day;** gala day, feria

5 **frolic, play,** romp, rollick, frisk, gambol, caper, dido (*informal*)

6 **revel, lark, escapade,** ploy; **celebration** *see* 487; **party** *see* 582.11; **spree, bout, fling,** wingding (*US & Canadian informal*), randan (*informal*), rave, randy (*Scottish*); **carouse, drinking bout** *see* 88.5

7 **round of pleasure,** mad round, **whirl,** merry-go-round, the rounds, the dizzy rounds

8 **sports** *see* 744; **athletics,** agonistics; athleticism

9 **game;** card game; board game; parlour game; **play; contest** *see* 457.3; race *see* 457.12; **event, meet; bout, match,** go (*informal*); gambling *see* 759

10 **tournament,** tourney, gymkhana, **field day;** rally; **regatta**

11 **playground;** adventure playground; field, sports field, playing field; football ground, football pitch; cricket ground; square, outfield; rugby pitch, hockey pitch; archery ground, polo ground, croquet ground *or* lawn, bowling green; bowling alley; links, golf links, golf course; fairway, putting green; **gymnasium,** gym (*informal*); **court,** badminton court, basketball court, tennis court, squash court, racket court; poolroom, pool hall, snooker hall, billiard hall; racecourse, track, course; rink, glaciarium, ice rink, skating rink; **playroom** *see* 197.12

12 **swimming pool, pool,** swimming bath, baths, plunge, plunge bath, natatorium; swimming hole; paddling pool, wading pool (*US*)

13 **entertainment; entertainment industry, show business,** show biz (*informal*); **theatre;** dinner theatre; **cabaret, tavern, roadhouse;** café dansant, chantant; **nightclub,** night spot *or* niterie *and* hot spot (*all informal*), *boîte, boîte de nuit* (*both French*); juke joint (*US informal*), discothèque *or* disco (*informal*); dance hall, dancing pavilion, ballroom, dance floor; casino; amusement arcade; **resort** *see* 228.27

14 **park,** public park, pleasure garden *or* ground, pleasance, paradise, common, commons, lido; **amusement park,** Tivoli, carnival; fairground, funfair; **theme park,** safari park

15 merry-go-round, carousel, roundabout, ride, whirligig, whip, flying horses; Ferris wheel, big wheel; seesaw, teeter-totter (*US*); slide; helter-skelter; swing; roller coaster; chutes, chute-the-chutes (*US*)

16 **toy, plaything,** sport; bauble, knickknack, gimcrack, gewgaw, kickshaw, whim-wham (*old*), trinket; **doll,** paper doll, golliwog, rag doll, teddy bear, puppet, glove puppet, marionette *or* string puppet, toy soldier, tin soldier; **doll's house,** doll's pram; **hobbyhorse,** cockhorse, rocking horse; **hoop,** hula hoop; **top,** spinning top, teetotum; windmill, pinwheel (*US & Canadian*); **jack-in-the-box;** jacks, jackstones; **jackstraws,** pick-up sticks, spillikins; **blocks; chequerboard,** chessboard; **marble,** mig, agate, steelie, taw; pop-gun, BB gun (*US*), air gun; slingshot, catapult

17 **chessman,** man, piece; **bishop, knight, king, queen, pawn, rook** *or* castle

18 **player, frolicker,** frisker, **funmaker,** funster, gamboler; **pleasure-seeker,** pleasurer, pleasurist, **playboy** (*informal*); raver, **reveller, celebrant, merrymaker,** rollicker, skylarker, **carouser,** cutup (*US informal*); contestant *see* 452.2

19 **athlete,** jock (*US informal*), **player,** amateur athlete, professional athlete, competitor, sportsman

20 **master of ceremonies, MC** *or* **emcee** (*both informal*), compère, marshal; **toastmaster;** host, master of the revels, revel master; Lord of Misrule, Abbot of Unreason (*Scottish*); social director

verbs

21 to **amuse, entertain, divert,** regale, beguile, solace, recreate, refresh, enliven, exhilarate, put in good humour; **relax,** loosen up; **delight, tickle, titillate,** tickle pink *or* to death (*informal*), tickle the fancy; **make one laugh, strike one as funny,** raise a smile *or* laugh, convulse, set the table on a roar, be the death of; wow *and* slay *and* knock dead *and* kill *and* break one up *and* crack one up *and* have one in fits (*all informal*); have them rolling in the aisles; keep them in stitches

22 to **amuse oneself,** pleasure oneself, take one's pleasure, give oneself over to pleasure; get one's kicks *or* jollies (*both informal*); **relax,** let oneself go, loosen up; **have fun, have a good time,** have a ball *and* have lots of laughs (*both informal*), live it up *and* laugh it up (*both informal*); drown care, drive dull care away; beguile the time, kill time, while away the time; get away from it all

23 to **play, sport, disport; frolic, rollick, gambol, frisk, romp, caper,** cut capers (*informal*), lark about (*informal*), antic, curvet, cavort, caracole, flounce, trip, skip, dance; cut up (*US informal*), cut a dido (*informal*), horse around (*informal*), fool around, carry on (*informal*)

24 to **make merry, revel, roister,** jolly, lark (*informal*), skylark, **make whoopee** (*informal*), let oneself go, **blow** *or* **let off steam;** cut loose, let loose, let go, let one's hair down (*informal*), push the boat out, whoop it up, **kick up one's heels;** raise hell *and* blow off the lid (*both informal*), step out (*informal*), go places and do things, go on the town, see life, **paint the town red** (*informal*); go the dizzy rounds, go on the merry-go-round (*informal*);

celebrate *see* 487.2; spree, **go on a spree**, go on a bust *or* toot *or* bender *or* binge *or* rip *or* tear *or* the randan (*all informal*); **carouse**, jollify (*informal*), wanton, debauch, pub-crawl; **sow one's wild oats, have one's fling**

25 "eat, drink, and be merry"—BIBLE; to feast, banquet

adjectives

26 **amused**, entertained; diverted, **delighted**, tickled, tickled pink *or* to death (*informal*), titillated; "pleased with a rattle, tickled with a straw"—POPE

27 **amusing, entertaining, diverting**, beguiling; **fun**, funsome *and* more fun than a barrel of monkeys (*both informal*); recreative, recreational; **delightful**, titillative, titillating; humorous *see* 488.4

28 **festive**, festal; **merry, gay, jolly, jovial, joyous**, joyful, gladsome, convivial, gala, hilarious; merrymaking, on the loose (*informal*); on the town, out on the town

29 **playful, sportive**, sportful; **frolicsome**, gamesome, rompish, larkish, capersome; waggish *see* 322.6

30 **sporting**, sports; **athletic**, agonistic; **gymnastic**, palaestral; **acrobatic**

adverbs

31 **in fun**, for amusement, **for fun**, for the fun of it; for kicks *and* for laughs (*both informal*), for the devil *or* heck *or* hell of it (*all informal*); just to be doing

744 SPORTS

nouns

1 **sport, sports, athletics**, athletic competition, game, sports activity, play, contest; aeronautical *or* air sport (*see list*); animal sport (*see list*); water *or* aquatic sport (*see list*); **ball game; track and field** *see* 755; **gymnastics** (*see list*); **outdoor sport** (*see list*); **winter sport** (*see list*); **combat sport**, martial art (*see list*); decathlon; triathlon, biathlon; **bicycling**, bicycle touring, cross-country cycling, cyclo-cross, bicycle moto-cross, road racing, track racing; **motor sport**, automobile racing *see* 756, go-carting, jet skiing, water skiing, motorcycling, moto-cross, dirt-biking, snowmobiling, soapbox racing; **roller skating**, in-line skating *or* blading *or* Roller-blading (*trademark*), roller hockey, skateboarding; **target sport**, archery, field archery, darts, arrows (*informal*), marksmanship, target shooting, skeet shooting, trap shooting, clay pigeon shooting; **throwing sport** (*see list*); **weightlifting, bodybuilding**, iron-pumping (*informal*), Olympic lifting, powerlifting, weight training

verbs

2 **to play, compete**; practise, train, work out; try out; follow

3 **aeronautical** *or* **air sports**

ballooning	parachuting
flying	parasailing
gliding	parascending
hang gliding	sky-diving
hydroplane racing	soaring

4 **animal sports**

barrel racing	horseback riding
bronc riding *and* bronco busting	horsemanship
	hunting
bull riding	pack riding
bullfighting	point-to-point
calf roping	pole bending
camel racing	polo
cockfighting	pony trekking
cross-country riding	puissance
dog racing	rodeo
dressage	sheepdog trials
driving	show jumping
endurance riding	steeplechase
equestrian sport	three-day event
harness racing	trail riding
horse racing	vaulting

5 **aquatic** *or* **water sports**

boating	sailing
body surfing	scuba diving
canoeing	skin diving
canoe slalom	snorkelling
distance swimming	sprint swimming
diving	surfing
dragon boat racing	swimming
fishing	synchronized swimming
inner tube water polo	underwater diving
kayaking	underwater hockey
lifesaving	underwaterball
parasailing	water polo
powerboating *or* powerboat racing	water skiing
rafting	windsurfing *or* boardsailing *or* sailboarding
rowing	yachting

6 **gymnastics**

balance beam	rings
floor exercises	trampolining
horizontal bar	tumbling
mini-trampolining	vaulting
parallel bars	modern rhythmic gymnastics
asymmetric bars	
pommel horse	Swedish gymnastics

7 **outdoor sports**

backpacking	rock climbing
camping	speleology *or* spelunking (*informal*)
hiking	
mountaineering *or* alpinism	superalpinism
orienteering	wilderness survival

8 **winter sports**

Alpine skiing	luge
bandy	skating
biathlon	ski jumping
bobsleighing	skibobbing
bobsledding (US & Canadian)	skiing
	skijoring
cross-country skiing	slalom
curling	sledging
downhill skiing	snowboarding
figure skating	snowshoeing
freestyle skiing *or* hotdogging (*informal*)	snow tubing
	speed skating
hockey	tobogganing
ice boating *or* sailing	

9 combat sports, martial arts

aikido *or* aiki-jutsu	jukendo
arm *and* wrist wrestling	kalari payat
arnis	karate
bando	kendo
bersilat	kenjutsu
bojutsu	kiaijutsu
boxing	kobu-jutsu
capoeira	kung-fu
Cornish wrestling	kyujutsu
dumog	lua
escrima	main tindju
fencing	naginata-jutsu
glimae	ninjutsu
go-ti	pankation
Graeco-Roman wrestling	pentjak-silat
Greek boxing	pukulan
hapkido	sambo wrestling
hwarang-do	savate
Iaido	stick fighting
Iaijutsu	sumo wrestling
Icelandic wrestling	tae kwon do
jeet kune do	tegumi
jobajutsu	Thai kick boxing
jojutsu	Tukido (trademark)
jousting	wrestling
judo	wu shu
jujutsu	

10 throwing sports

boomeranging	hammer throw
caber tossing	horseshoe pitching
discus throw	javelin throw
Frisbee (trademark)	shot put

745 ASSOCIATION FOOTBALL

nouns

1 **football, soccer, association football,** footie *and* footer (*both informal*); Federation of International Football Associations *or* FIFA, Union of European Football Associations *or* UEFA, Football Association *or* FA, Scottish Football Association *or* SFA; **tournament,** competition (*see list*), championship, cup; **professional football,** pro football, **Football League; football pitch, pitch,** football field, field, the park (*informal*), goal line, touchline, by-line, halfway line, penalty area, penalty spot, goal area, goal, goalpost, crossbar, net, corner area, corner flag, centre spot, centre circle; **kit,** equipment, gear, ball, strip, shirt, shorts, socks, shin pads *or* guards, football boots

2 **team,** squad, side, forward, striker, centre forward, winger, outside right, inside right, inside left, outside left, midfielder, right half, left half, defender, back, full back, wing back, right back, centre back *or* centre half, left back, sweeper, back four, goalkeeper *or* keeper *or* goalie, substitute *or* sub, benchwarmer

3 **game, match,** tie; official, **referee,** linesman; **play,** 4-4-2 formation, 4-3-3 formation, 4-2-4 formation, 3-5-2 formation, sweeper system, Christmas tree formation, diamond formation, man-to-man marking, toss, kickoff, kick (*see list*), throw-in, goal kick, corner kick, offside, ball-control, dribble, pass, back-

heel, outside-of-the-foot pass, short pass, long ball, tackle, sliding tackle, block tackle, trap, chest trap, thigh trap, counterattack, breakaway, header, shot, save; **rule,** law; **foul** (*see list*); caution, red card, yellow card, direct free kick, indirect free kick, penalty, drop ball; **goal,** score; **half,** period, extra time, penalty shoot-out, shootout

verbs

4 **to play,** kick, kick off, trap, pass, dribble, shield, head, centre, shoot, score, clear, mark, tackle, save

5 **football competitions**

World Cup	African Nations Cup
European Championships	FA Cup
European Cup	Scottish Cup
Champions' League	League Cup
Cup Winners Cup	Charity Shield
UEFA Cup	Olympic Games
Copa America	Women's World Cup
Copa Libertadores	

6 **kicks**

bicycle kick	lofted kick
chip	low drive
flick	overhead kick
half-volley	punt
instep *or* inside-of-the-foot kick	scissors kick
	volley

7 **fouls**

charging dangerously	kicking an opponent
charging from behind	obstructing an opponent
charging the goalkeeper	offside
dangerous play	persistent foul play
dissenting from referee's decision	pushing an opponent
foul or abusive language	spitting at an opponent
handling the ball	striking an opponent
holding an opponent	time wasting
jumping at an opponent	tripping an opponent
	ungentlemanly conduct

746 RUGBY FOOTBALL

nouns

1 **rugby, rugby football,** rugger; **rugby union; rugby league,** rugby league football; tournament, competition, championship, cup, Five Nations Championship, Triple Crown, World Cup; rugby pitch, **pitch,** rugby field, field, goalposts, uprights, goal line, try line, dead ball line, in-goal area, twenty-two metre line, ten metre line, halfway line, five metre line; **kit,** equipment, gear, ball, strip, shirt, jersey, shorts, socks, shin pads *or* guards, scrum cap, rugby boots

2 **team, side,** fifteen, squad; forward, front-row forward, hooker, prop *or* prop forward, tight-head prop, loose-head prop, second-row forward, lock *or* lock forward, tight forward, back-row forward, number eight, wing forward, flanker *or* flank forward, loose forward, breakaway forward, back, half back, scrum half, outside half *or* fly half *or* stand-off half, five-eighth (*Australian* & *NZ*), three-quarter, winger *or* wing three-quarter, centre *or* centre three-quarter, full back, replacement

3 **game, match;** referee, official, touch judge; kick, place kick, drop kick, touch kick, scrummage *or*

scrum, line-out, drop-out, tackle, ruck, maul, mark, run, pass, try, score, conversion, drop goal, penalty goal, penalty try, offside, knock on, forward pass

verbs

4 **to play**, kick off, kick, run, pass, tackle, score, ruck, maul, hook

747 CRICKET

nouns

1 **cricket**; International Cricket Conference *or* ICC, Test and County Cricket Board *or* TCCB; **cricket pitch, pitch**, cricket field, ground, square, wicket, track, strip, stump, bail, crease, bowling crease, popping crease, return crease, infield, outfield, covers, boundary, pavilion, sightscreen; **kit**, equipment, gear, whites, flannels, shirt, sweater, bat, pads, batting gloves, wicketkeeping gloves, box, protector, helmet, cap, thigh pad, arm guard, chest protector, boots

2 **team**, side, eleven, batsman, batter, opener *or* opening batsman *or* opening bat, bowler, fast bowler, paceman, quick bowler, quickie *or* quick (*both informal*), medium-pace bowler *or* medium-pacer, seamer *or* seam bowler, swing bowler, slow bowler, spinner *or* spin bowler, off spinner, leg spinner, finger spinner, wrist spinner, all-rounder, wicketkeeper *or* keeper, fielder (*see list*)

3 **match**, game, Test Match, one-day match, limited-overs match; umpire, square-leg umpire, third umpire; **play**, toss, session, declaration, follow on; **batting**, shot, stroke (*see list*), run, single, four, six, boundary, extra, leg bye, bye, innings, fifty, half century, hundred, century, ton (*informal*), duck, pair, stand, partnership; **bowling**, ball, delivery (*see list*), no ball, wide, over, maiden over, spell, appeal, wicket, hat trick, wicket maiden; **fielding**, catch, drop, stop, misfield, throw, run out, overthrow

verbs

4 **to play**; bat, block, hit, drive, pull, cut, hook, strike, slog, edge, nick, snick; **bowl**, dismiss, pitch, turn, spin; field, catch, drop, stop, misfield, throw, run out, keep wicket, stump

adjectives

5 **not out**, in; **out**, bowled, caught, run out, leg-before-wicket *or* lbw, stumped, hit wicket; retired, declared

6 **fielding positions**

backward point	gully
backward short leg	leg gully
cover	leg slip
deep extra cover	long leg
deep fine leg	long off
deep mid off	long on
deep mid on	mid off
deep mid wicket	mid on
deep square leg	mid wicket
extra cover	point
fine leg	second slip
first slip	short extra cover
forward short leg	short fine leg
short leg	slip
short third man	square leg
silly mid off	sweeper
silly mid on	third man
silly point	third slip

7 **cricket strokes**

backward defensive	off drive
cut	on drive
drive	pull
forward defensive	reverse sweep
hook	square cut
late cut	square drive
leg glance	straight drive
lofted drive	sweep

8 **types of delivery**

arm ball	leg break
beamer	leg cutter
bouncer *or* bumper	long hop
chinaman	off break
flipper	off cutter
full toss *or* full pitch	outswinger
good-length ball	overpitched ball
googly	short ball
half-volley	top spinner
inswinger	yorker

748 GOLF

nouns

1 **golf**, the Royal and Ancient *or* R & A; **professional golf**, pro tour, American tour, European tour, Professional Golfers Association *or* PGA, Ladies' Professional Golfers' Association *or* LPGA; **amateur golf**, club, Royal and Ancient Golf Club; **tournament** (*see list*), championship, major championship *or* major, title, cup; **golf course**, course, links, green, tee, teeing ground, back *or* championship marker, middle *or* men's marker, front *or* womens' marker, hole, par-3 hole, par-4 hole, par-5 hole, front nine *or* side, back nine *or* side, water hole, fairway, dogleg, obstruction, rub of the green, casual water, rough, hazard, water hazard, bunker, sand hazard, sand trap, beach (*informal*), collar, apron, fringe, putting green, pin, flagstick, flag, lip, cup; **equipment** (*see list*), gear, club, club parts

2 **golfer**, player, scratch golfer *or* player, tiger, handicapped golfer, duffer *and* hacker *and* rabbit (*all informal*), **team**, twosome, threesome, foursome

3 **round**, 9 holes, 18 holes, 72 holes, match, stroke play, match play, medal play, medal matchplay, four-ball match, three-ball match, best ball, foursome, greensome; **official**, referee, official observer, marker; **play**, golfing grip, overlapping *or* Vardon grip, reverse overlap, interlocking grip, full-finger grip, address, stance, closed stance, square stance, open stance, waggle, swing, backswing, downswing, follow-through, pivot, body pivot, tee-off; **stroke**, shot (*see list*), backspin, bite, distance, carry, run, lie, plugged lie, blind, stymie; **score**, scoring, strokes, albatross, eagle, birdie, par, bogey, double bogey, penalty, hole-in-one, halved hole, gross, handicap, net

verbs

4 to play, **shoot,** tee up, tee off, drive, hit, sclaff, draw, fade, pull, push, hook, slice, shank, top, sky, loft, putt, can (*informal*), borrow, hole out, sink, eagle, albatross, birdie, par, bogey, double bogey; play through; concede, default

exclamations

5 **fore!**

6 **golf tournaments**

Alfred Dunhill Cup	Solheim Cup
Australian Masters	US Open
British Open *or* The Open	US Womens' Open
Curtis Cup	Walker Cup
Grand Slam	World Amateur Team
LPGA Championship	Championship
US Masters	World Cup
US PGA Championship	World Matchplay
Ryder Cup	Championship

7 **golf equipment**

1 iron *or* driving iron	middle iron
2 iron *or* midiron	number 1 wood *or* driver
3 iron *or* mid mashie	number 2 wood *or* brassie
4 iron *or* mashie iron	number 3 wood *or* spoon
5 iron *or* mashie	number 4 wood *or* baffy
6 iron *or* spade mashie	number 5 wood
7 iron *or* mashie niblick	pitching wedge
8 iron *or* pitching niblick	putter
9 iron *or* niblick	sand wedge
ball *or* pill (informal)	short iron
driver	tee
golf cart	Texas wedge
golf glove	utility iron
iron	wedge
lofting iron	wood
long iron	

8 **golf shots**

approach shot *or* approach	lob
blast	long iron shot
block	Mulligan
chip shot *or* chip	pitch
chip–and–run	pitch-and-run
cut shot	punch
draw	putt
drive	run-up
duck hook	sand shot
fade	shank
fairway wood shot	slice
full shot	snake
gimme (informal)	tee shot
hook	water shot
lag	

749 TENNIS

nouns

1 **tennis,** lawn tennis, indoor tennis, outdoor tennis, singles, doubles, mixed doubles, team tennis; court *or* real *or* royal tennis; **organized tennis,** Lawn Tennis Association *or* LTA, Association of Tennis Professionals *or* ATP, International Tennis Federation *or* ITF, Women's Tennis Association *or* WTA; **tournament,** tennis competition (*see list*),

championship, crown, match, trophy; **tennis ball, ball, tennis racket, racket** (*see list*), bat (*informal*), sweet spot; **tennis court, court,** sideline, alley, doubles sideline, baseline, centre line, service line, half court line, backcourt, forecourt, midcourt, net, band; **surface,** slow surface, fast surface, grass surface *or* grass, concrete surface, wood *or* wooden surface, synthetic fibre surface, competition court, all-weather court, clay court

2 **game,** strategy, serve-and-volley, power game, baseline game; **official, umpire,** baseline umpires *or* linesmen, line umpires *or* linesmen, service-line umpire *or* linesman, net-court judge; **play,** coin-toss, racket-flip, grip, Eastern grip, Continental grip, Western grip, two-handed grip, **stroke** (*see list*), **shot,** service *or* serve, return, spin, top-spin, let ball *or* let, net-cord ball, rally, fault, double fault, foot fault; **error,** unforced error; **score, point,** service ace *or* ace, love, deuce, advantage *or* ad, game point, service break, break point, set point, match point, tiebreaker

verbs

3 to play tennis, play, serve, return, drive, volley, smash, lob, place the ball, serve and volley, play serve-and-volley tennis, fault, foot-fault, double-fault, make an unforced error; **score** *or* **make a point,** score, ace one's opponent, break service, break back

4 **tennis competitions**

Australian Open	King's Cup
Federation Cup	Masters Tournament
French Open	Olympic Games
Grand Prix	South African Open
Grand Slam	US Open
International Lawn Tennis	Virginia Slims Circuit
Challenge Trophy *or*	German Open
Davis Cup	Wightman Cup
Italian Open	Wimbledon

5 **tennis rackets**

aluminium racket	graphite racket
Fiberglas racket	steel racket
(trademark)	wooden *or* wood racket
Prince racket (trademark)	

6 **tennis strokes**

backhand	lob
backhand drive	lob volley
chop	overhead
drive	passing shot
drop shot	slice
forehand	service *or* serve
forehand drive	smash
ground stroke	two-handed backhand
half-volley	volley

750 HOCKEY

nouns

1 **hockey, field hockey,** banty *or* bandy, hurley *or* hurling, shinty; International Hockey Board, International Federation of Women's Hockey Associations; **competition,** championship, cup; **hockey field,** field, pitch, goal line, centre line, centre mark, bully circle, sideline, 7-yard line, alley, 25-yard line, striking *or* shooting circle, goalpost, goal, goal mouth; **equipment,** gear, stick, ball, shin pads

2 **team,** attack, outside left, inside left, centre forward, inside right, outside right, defence, left halfback, centre halfback, right halfback, left fullback, right fullback, goalkeeper

3 **game,** match; **umpire,** timekeeper; **foul,** infraction, advancing, obstructing, sticks, undercutting, **penalty,** free hit, corner hit, long corner, short corner, penalty corner, defence hit, penalty stroke, penalty flick; **play, bully, bully-off,** pass-back, stroke (*see list*), marking, pass, tackle, circular tackle, out-of-bounds, roll-in *or* push-in, hit-in; **goal,** point, score; **period,** half

4 **ice hockey;** National Hockey League *or* NHL; International Ice Hockey Federation; Olympic Games, Stanley Cup; **rink,** hockey rink, boards, end zone, defending *or* defensive zone, attacking *or* offensive zone, neutral zone *or* centre ice, blue line, red line, goal line, crease, goal *and* net *and* cage, face-off spot, face-off circle, penalty box, penalty bench, players' bench; equipment, gear

5 ice hockey team, team, skaters, squad, bench; line, forward line, centre, right wingman, left wingman; **defence,** right defenceman, left defenceman, netminder *or* goaltender *or* goalie; playmaker, penalty killer, point *or* point man

6 **game,** match; **referee,** linesman, goal judge, timekeepers, scorer; **foul,** penalty, infraction, offside, icing *or* icing the puck; **play,** skating, stick *or* puck handling, checking, passing, shooting; **pass; shot,** slap shot; power play; **score,** point, assist, hat trick; **period,** overtime *or* overtime period, shoot-out

verbs

7 **to play,** pass, stick-handle, dribble, drive, flick, scoop, push, shoot, score, clear; tackle, mark

8 **hockey strokes**

clearing	lob
dribble	push
drive	right cut
flick	right drive
left drive	right-hand lunge
left-hand lunge	scoop

751 BASKETBALL

nouns

1 **basketball; tournament,** competition, championship, Olympic Games; **basketball court, court,** forecourt, midcourt, backcourt, end line *or* base line, sideline, basket *or* hoop, backboard, glass (*informal*), free throw line, key *and* keyhole (*both informal*), foul line

2 **basketball team,** team, squad; **basketball player,** centre, right forward, left forward, corner man, right guard, left guard, point guard, point player *or* playmaker

3 **basketball game,** game, play, strategy, defence, man-to-man defence, zone defence, offence, full-court press, half-court press; **official, referee,** umpire, official scorekeeper, timer; **foul,** violation (*see list*), infraction; **play, strategy,** running game, fast break, passing game; **jump,** centre jump, jump

ball, live ball; **pass,** passing, pass ball, assist, bounce pass; **tactics, action,** dribble, fake, hand-off, ball control, ball-handling, one-on-one, screening, turnover, steal *or* burn, out-of-bounds, dead ball, throw-in; **shot** (*see list*), **score, basket** *or* **field goal,** bucket (*informal*), three-point play *or* three-pointer, free throw *or* foul shot; **quarter,** half, overtime period *or* overtime

verbs

4 **to play,** play basketball, **dribble,** fake, pass, double-team, block, screen, steal, **shoot, score,** rebound; **foul,** commit a foul *or* violation, foul out

5 **basketball fouls**

blocking	intentional foul
charging	multiple foul
disqualifying foul	offensive foul
double dribble	palming
double foul	personal foul *or* personal
force-out	pushing off
goaltending	technical foul *or* technical
hacking	three-second violation
held ball	travelling

6 **basketball shots**

bank shot	pivot shot
dunk (informal)	penalty free throw
free throw	scoop shot
hook shot *or* hook	set shot
jump shot *or* jumper	slam dunk (informal)
lay-up	tip-in
one-and-one	

752 SNOOKER

nouns

1 **snooker, billiards;** World Professional Snooker and Billiards Association *or* WPSBA

2 **table,** pocket, spot, D, baulk, baulkline, baize, nap, cushion, headrail; **cue,** rest, cue extension, spider, half-butt; chalk, triangle *or* rack (*US & Canadian*); bridge, bouclée, stance, cueing action; **ball,** cue ball, object ball, spot ball, red, yellow, green, brown, blue, pink, black

3 match, **frame; shot,** break-off shot, pot, double, fluke, plant, safety shot; cannon, nursery cannon, drop cannon, in-off, bricole, massé, jenny, short jenny, long jenny, Whitechapel; fluke, miscue, kick; side *or* English (*US & Canadian*), screw, stun, top; **break,** clearance, century *or* century break, maximum break *or* 147; foul, free ball; safety

verbs

4 **to play,** cue, break, pot, pocket, score, foul, strike, kiss, kick, cannon, snooker, double, fluke, miscue, plant, stun, screw; require snookers, concede

753 SKIING

nouns

1 **skiing,** snow-skiing, Alpine skiing, downhill skiing, Nordic skiing, cross-country skiing *or* langlauf, ski-jumping, jumping, freestyle skiing *or* hotdog skiing *or* hotdogging, skijoring, pulk skiing, helicopter skiing *or* heli-skiing, grass skiing, dry skiing;

organized **skiing**, competition skiing, *Fédération Internationale de Ski or FIS*, International Freestyle Skiers Association, World Hot Dog Ski Association; **competition** (*see list*), **championship**, cup, race; **slope**, ski slope, ski run, nursery *or* beginner's slope, expert's slope, intermediate slope, expert's trail, course, trail, mogul; **ski lift, lift**, rope tow, J-bar, chair lift, T-bar; **racecourse**, downhill course, slalom course, giant slalom course, super giant slalom course, parallel *or* dual slalom course; **starting gate**, fall line, drop *or* vertical drop, control gate, obligatory gate, flagstick, open gate, closed *or* blind gate, hairpin, flush, H, men's course, women's course, **ski-jump**, ramp, inrun, outrun, hill rating, 60-point hill, normal hill, big hill, cross-country course; **equipment**, gear (*see list*)

2 **skier**, snow-skier, cross-country skier, ski-jumper, racer, downhill racer, forerunner, forejumper, skimeister

3 **race**, downhill race, slalom, giant slalom, super giant slalom *or* super G, parallel *or* dual slalom, cross-country race, biathlon; **technique**, style, Arlberg technique, Lilienfeld technique, wedeln, **position**, tuck *and* egg, Vorlage, sitting position, inrun position, fish position, flight position; **manoeuvre**, **turn** (*see list*)

verbs

4 **to ski**, run, schuss, traverse, turn, check

5 **skiing competitions**

Alpine Combined	Nordic Combined
FIS World Championship	Olympic Games

6 **skiing equipment**

aluminium alloy pole	jumping ski
Alpine boot	laminated wood ski
Arlberg *or* safety strap	metal ski
basket *or* snow basket	molded boot
bent pole	plastic ski
cross-country binding	pole *or* stick
cross-country pole	release binding
cross-country ski	ski-boot
double boot	slalom ski
downhill pole	steel pole
downhill ski	step-in binding
fibreglass pole	toe clamp

7 **skiing manoeuvres and turns**

check	sidestep
Christiania *or* christie	snap
diagonal stride	snowplough *or* double
double-pole stride	stem
double-poling	stem turn
edging	stem christie
Geländesprung	step acceleration
herringbone	step turn
jump turn	Telemark
kick turn	tempo
parallel turn	unweighting
sideslip	

754 BOXING

nouns

1 **boxing, prizefighting**, fighting, pugilism, noble *or* manly art of self-defence, the noble *or* sweet science, fisticuffs, the fistic sport, the fights *and* the fight game (*both informal*), the ring; **amateur boxing**, Olympic Games, International Amateur Boxing Association *or* AIBA, Amateur Boxing Association *or* ABA, Golden Gloves (*US*); **professional boxing**, World Boxing Council *or* WBC, World Boxing Association *or* WBA, World Boxing Organization *or* WBO, International Boxing Federation *or* IBF, European Boxing Union, British Boxing Board of Control, club boxing *or* fighting; Queensbury rules, Marquess of Queensbury rules; **boxing ring, ring**, prize ring, square circle *or* ring, canvas, corner; **equipment, gloves**, mitts *and* mittens (*both informal*), tape, bandages, gumshield, mouthpiece

2 **boxer, fighter**, pugilist, prize-fighter, pug (*informal*), palooka (*US informal*), slugger, mauler; **weight** (*see list*); division; **manager; trainer; handler**, second, sparring partner

3 **fight, match, bout**, battle, duel, slugfest (*US informal*); **official, referee**, ref (*informal*), judge, timekeeper; **strategy, fight-plan, style**, stance, footwork, attack, **punch** (*see list*), blow, belt *and* biff *and* sock (*all informal*); **defence**, blocking, ducking, parrying, slipping, feint, clinching; **foul** (*see list*); **win, knockout** *or* **KO**, technical knockout *or* TKO, decision, unanimous decision, split decision, win on points; **round**, canto *and* stanza (*both informal*)

verbs

4 **to fight, box**, punch, spar, mix it up (*informal*), clinch, break, block, catch, slip a punch, duck, feint, parry, heel, thumb, knock down, knock out, slug, maul, go down, go down for the count, hit the canvas (*informal*), shadow-box

5 **weight divisions**

strawweight	light welterweight
light flyweight	welterweight
flyweight	light middleweight
bantamweight	middleweight
super bantamweight	light heavyweight
featherweight	cruiserweight
junior lightweight	heavyweight
lightweight	super-heavyweight

6 **boxing punches**

backhand *or* backhander	mishit *or* mislick
backstroke	rabbit punch
body blow *or* body slam	right *or* right-hander
bolo punch	round-arm blow
chop	roundhouse
combination	short-arm blow
corkscrew punch	sideswipe
counter-punch	sidewinder
cross	sneak punch *or* sucker
flanker	punch
follow-up	solar-plexus punch
haymaker	straight punch
hook	swing
jab	swipe
left *or* left-hander *or*	the one-two *or* the old
portsider	one-two
Long Melford	uppercut

7 **boxing fouls**

backhanding	elbowing
butting	heeling

hitting below the belt
hitting downed opponent
hitting while breaking
hitting with open glove
holding

kidney punch
kneeing
pivot blow
rabbit punch
thumbing

javelin
long jump
8 triathlon
cycling
running

pole vault
shot put

swimming

755 ATHLETICS

nouns

1 **athletics, track and field,** track (*US*), light athletics (*Germany*); governing organization, International Athletic Federation *or* IAAF, British Athletics Federation, Amateur Athletics Association *or* AAA; **games,** competition (*see list*), cup; **stadium, arena,** oval; **track,** oval, lane, start line, starting block, finish line, bend, straight, back straight, finishing straight, **infield** (*see list*); lap, lap of honour, victory lap

2 **athletics meeting, meet, games, programme; track event, running event; field event** (*see list*); **all-around event,** decathlon (*see list*), heptathlon (*see list*); triathlon (*see list*); **walking, race walking,** the walk, heel-and-toe racing

3 **track and field competitions**

AAA Championships	Olympic Games
Asian Games	Pacific Games
Central American and Caribbean Games	Pan-American Games Special Olympics
Commonwealth Games	World Championships
European Championships	World Cup
European Cup	World Junior Championships
European Grand Prix	
International Paraplegic Games	World Student Games

4 **infield sites**

cinder track	long-jump runway *or* run-up
crossbar	
dirt track	pole-vault runway *or* run-up
discus-throw circle	
hammer-throw circle	shot-put circle
hammer-throw sector	shot-put sector
high-jump runway *or* run-up	shot-put stopboard take-off board
javelin-throw runway *or* run-up	take-off box triple-jump runway *or* run-up
javelin-throw sector	
landing area	weight-throw circle
landing pit	weight-throw sector

5 **field events**

discus	long jump
hammer	pole vault
high jump	shot put
javelin	triple jump

6 **heptathlon**

100-metre hurdles	javelin
200-metres	long jump
800-metres	shot put
high jump	

7 **decathlon**

100-metres	1500-metres
110-metre hurdles	discus
400-metres	high jump

756 MOTOR RACING

nouns

1 **motor racing, automobile racing, auto racing, car racing,** motor sport; **race,** competition, championship; **track, circuit,** speedway (*US*), closed course, road course *or* circuit, dirt track; **car, racing car** (*see list*), racer; **racing engine** (*see list*); **supercharger,** turbocharger *or* turbo; **tyres, racing tyres,** shoes (*US informal*), slicks, wet tyres, dry tyres; **body,** body work, chassis, spoiler, roll bar, roll cage; **wheel,** wire wheel *or* wire, magnesium wheel *or* mag; **fuel, racing fuel,** methanol, nitromethane *or* nitro, blend, pop *and* juice (*both informal*)

2 **race driving, racing driver, driver,** fast driver *or* leadfoot (*informal*), slow driver *or* balloon foot, novice driver *or* yellowtail

3 **race, driving, start,** Le Mans start, flying start, paced start, grid start; **position,** qualifying, qualifying heat, starting grid, inside position, pole *or* pole position, bubble; **track,** turn, curve, hairpin, switchback, banked turn, corner, chicane, straight, pit, pit lane, pit area; **signal,** black flag, white flag, chequered flag; **lap,** pace lap, lap of honour, victory lap

verbs

4 **to drive, race,** start, jump, rev, accelerate, put the hammer down (*informal*), slow down, back off, fishtail, shut the gate, spin, spin out, crash

adverbs

5 **at top speed,** flat out, full-bore, ten-tenths
6 **racing cars**

dragster	Indy car
Formula 3000	production car
Formula Ford	prototype
Formula One	sports-racing car
Formula Two	stock car
Formula Three	touring car
grand touring car *or* GT	

7 **racing engines**

big banger (*informal*)	supercharged engine *or* blown engine
non-supercharged engine with overhead cams	
normally aspirated engine	supercharged engine with overhead cams
Offenhauser engine *or* Offy	supercharged stock-block engine
production engine	
stock-block engine	turbine engine

757 HORSE RACING

nouns

1 **horse racing, the turf,** the sport of kings, the turf sport, the racing world *or* establishment; **flat racing; National Hunt racing;** trotting, pacing; **Jockey Club; Grand National, Derby,** 1000 Guineas, 2000 Guineas, St Leger, Oaks, Cheltenham Gold Cup;

Prix de l'Arc de Triomphe *or* the Arc; Triple Crown, Kentucky Derby; **racetrack, track,** racecourse, course, turf, oval (*US*), strip (*US*); rail, inside rail, infield, paddock, enclosure; turf track, all-weather track; stalls, gate *and* barrier; home stretch, run-in, winning post; **course conditions** (*see list*), going; racing equipment, tack; silks

2 **jockey,** jock, rider, race rider, pilot, bug boy (*US informal*), money rider; apprentice jockey, bug (*US informal*); breeder, owner; trainer; steward, racing secretary; punter, racing man, turf-man, railbird *and* race bird (*both US informal*); **racehorse, pony,** thoroughbred, standardbred, mount, flyer, running horse, trotter, pacer, quarter horse, filly *and* gee-gee (*both informal*), bangtail *and* daisy-cutter (*both US informal*); **sire, dam,** stallion, stud, stud horse, racing stud, mare, brood mare, gelding, ridgeling *or* rigling; **horse,** aged horse, three-year-old, sophomore (*US*), two-year-old, juvenile, colt, racing colt, filly, baby, foal, tenderfoot, bug (*US*), maiden *or* maiden horse, yearling, weanling; **favourite,** chalk, choice, odds-on favourite, public choice, top horse, nap; runner, front-runner, pacesetter; strong horse, router, stayer; winner *or* winning horse, placed horse, also-ran; **nag** *and* race-nag *and* plater *and* selling plater (*all informal*), hayburner *and* palooka *and* pelter *and* pig (*all US informal*); **rogue,** bad actor, cooler

3 **horse race, race;** race meeting, race card, scratch sheet; **starters,** field, weigh-in *or* weighing-in, post parade, post time, post position *or* PP; **start, break,** off; easy race, romp, shoo-in (*US*), armchair ride, hand ride; **finish,** dead heat, blanket finish, photo finish, Garison finish (*US*); **dishonest race,** boat race *and* fixed race (*both informal*)

4 **statistics, records,** condition book, chart, **form, racing form,** daily racing form, past performance, **track record,** dope *or* tip *or* tout sheet (*informal*), par time, parallel-time chart; **betting;** tote *or* totalizator *or* totalizer, pari-mutuel *see* 759.4; horse-racing bets

verbs

5 **to race, run; start, break,** be off; air *and* breeze; make a move, drive, extend, straighten out; fade, come back; screw in *or* through; ride out, run wide; win, romp *or* breeze in; **place, show,** be in the money; be out of the money

adjectives

6 **winning, in the money;** losing, out of the money; on the chinstrap; out in front

7 **course conditions**

firm	good to soft
good	soft
good to firm	

758 CARDPLAYING

nouns

1 **cardplaying,** shuffling, dealing; **card game,** game; gambling *see* 759, gambling games

2 **card,** playing card, board, pasteboard; **deck, pack; suit,** hearts, diamonds, spades, clubs; **face card,** court card, picture card; **king,** figure, one-eyed king, king of hearts *or* suicide king; **queen,** queen of spades; **jack,** knave, one-eyed jack, jack of trumps; **joker;** spot card, rank card, plain card; **ace,** ace of diamonds, ace of clubs; **two, deuce,** two-spot, duck (*informal*), two of spades; **three, trey,** three-spot; **four,** four-spot, four of clubs *or* devil's bedposts (*informal*); **five,** fivespot; **six,** six-spot; **seven,** seven-spot; **eight,** eight-spot; **nine,** nine-spot, nine of diamonds *or* curse of Scotland (*informal*); **ten,** ten-spot

3 **bridge,** auction bridge, contract bridge, rubber bridge, duplicate *or* tournament bridge; **bridge player,** partner, dummy, North and South, East and West, left hand opponent *or* LHO, bidder, responder, declarer, senior; **suit,** major suit, minor suit, trump suit, trump *or* trumps, lay suit *or* plain suit *or* side suit; **call, bid** (*see list*); pass; **hand** (*see list*); **play,** lead, opening lead, **trick,** quick trick *or* honour trick, high-card trick, overtrick, odd trick; **score,** adjusted score, grand slam, little slam *or* small slam, game, rubber, premium, honours, set *or* setback

verbs

4 **to shuffle,** make up, make up the pack, fan *and* wash (*both informal*); cut; **deal,** serve, pitch (*informal*)

5 **bridge bids**

asking bid	original bid
borderline bid	overbid *or* overcall
business double *or* penalty double	rebid
conventional bid	redouble
demand bid	response
double	sacrifice bid
forcing bid	score bid
forcing pass	shut-out bid
free bid	sign-off
insufficient bid	skip bid
jump bid	suit bid
no-trump bid	takeout double
opening bid	trial bid

6 **bridge hands**

balanced hand	powerhouse
doubleton	semibalanced hand
exposed hand	side strength
long trump	singleton
long suit	short suit
major tenace	tenace
minor tenace	unbalanced hand
offensive strength	void
perfect tenace	yarborough

759 GAMBLING

nouns

1 **gambling, playing, betting, action,** wagering, punting, hazarding, risking, staking, gaming, laying, taking *or* giving *or* laying odds, sporting (*old*); **speculation, play;** drawing *or* casting lots, tossing *or* flipping a coin, sortition

2 **gamble, chance,** risk, risky thing, hazard; **gambling** *or* **gambler's chance,** betting proposition, bet, matter of chance, sporting chance,

luck of the draw, hazard of the die, roll or cast or throw of the dice, turn or roll of the wheel, turn of the table, turn of the cards, fall of the cards, flip or toss of a coin, toss-up, toss; heads or tails, touch and go; blind bargain, pig in a poke; leap in the dark, shot in the dark; potshot, random shot, potluck; **speculation, venture**, flier and plunge (both informal); calculated risk; uncertainty see 970; fortune, luck see 971.1

3 **bet, flutter, wager, stake**, hazard, lay, play and shot (both informal); cinch bet or sure thing, cert or dead cert; long shot; **ante**; parlay, double or nothing; **dice bet, craps bet**, golf bet, **horse-racing bet, poker bet**, roulette bet, telebet

4 **betting system; pari-mutuel**, accumulator, off-track betting or OTB

5 **pot, jackpot, pool, stakes, kitty; bank**; office pool

6 **gambling odds**, odds, price; **even or square odds**, even break; **short odds, long odds**, long shot; even chance, good chance, small chance, no chance see 971.10; **handicapper**, odds maker, pricemaker

7 **gambling game** (see list), game of chance, game, friendly game; card games

8 **dice, bones**, ivories, cubes, **craps**, crap shooting, crap game, bank craps or casino craps, floating crap game, floating game; poker dice; **false** or crooked or loaded dice

9 (throw of dice) **throw, cast, rattle, roll, shot**, hazard of the die; dice points and rolls (see list)

10 **poker**, draw poker or draw or five-card draw or open poker, stud poker or stud or closed poker, five-card stud or seven-card stud, up card or open card, down card or closed card; common or community or communal card; highball, high-low, lowball; **straight** or **natural poker**, wild-card poker; **poker hand**, duke and mitt (both informal), good hand or cards; bad hand or cards, trash and rags (both informal); **openers**, progressive openers, bet, raise or kick or bump or pump or push, showdown

11 **pontoon** or **blackjack** or **twenty-one** or vingt-et-un; deal, card count, stiff, hard seventeen, hard eighteen, soft count, soft hand, soft eighteen, hit, blackjack or natural or snap or snapper, California blackjack; cut card or indicator card or sweat card; card-counting or ace-count or number count

12 **roulette**, American roulette, European roulette; **wheel**, American wheel, European wheel, wheel well, canoe, fret; **layout**, column, damnation alley, outside; zero, double zero, knotholes or house numbers

13 **cheating**, cheating scheme, cheating method, angle, con and move and racket and scam and sting (all informal), grift (US informal); deception see 356

14 **football pools** or the pools; coupon; treble chance; lottery, drawing, sweepstake or sweep, art union (Australian & NZ); draft lottery; **raffle; state lottery**, National Lottery, Lotto; tombola; number lottery, numbers pool, **numbers game** or **policy**, Chinese lottery (informal); interest lottery, Dutch or class lottery; tontine; lucky dip, grab bag or barrel or box

15 **bingo**, slow death (informal), keno (US & Canadian), lotto, housey-housey; bingo card, banker, counter

16 (gambling device) gambling wheel, wheel of fortune, big six wheel, Fortune's wheel, raffle wheel or paddle wheel; roulette wheel, American wheel, European wheel; raffle wheel; pinball machine; slot machine, slot, the slots, one-armed bandit (informal), fruit machine; **layout** or green cloth, gambling table, craps table, Philadelphia layout, roulette table; Ernie; **cheating device**, gaff and gimmick and tool (all informal)

17 totalizator, totalizer, tote and tote board (both informal), odds board; pari-mutuel, pari-mutuel machine

18 **chip, check, counter**

19 **casino, gambling house, house**, store and shop (both informal), gaming house, betting house, betting parlour, gambling club, gambling den, gambling hall, sporting house (old), gambling hell (informal); luxurious casino, carpet joint and rug joint (both informal); honest gambling house, right joint (informal); disreputable gambling house, crib and dive and joint and sawdust joint and store and toilet (all informal); illegal gambling house, cheating gambling house, clip joint and hell and low den (all informal); **book, betting shop**, sports book, bookie joint (informal), racebook, horse parlour, horse room, off-track betting parlour, OTB

20 **bookmaker, bookie** (informal), turf accountant; **tout**, turf consultant; numbers runner; bagman

21 **gambler, player**, gamester, sportsman or sporting man (both archaic), sport, hazarder (old); **speculator**, venturer, adventurer; better, wagerer, punter; high-stakes gambler, money player, high roller, plunger; petty gambler, low roller, piker and tinhorn and tinhorn gambler (all informal); **professional gambler**, pro (informal); **skilful gambler, sharp, shark**, sharper (all informal); **cardsharp** or cardshark, cardsharper; **card counter**, counter, caser, matrix player; crap shooter and boneshaker (both informal); compulsive gambler; **spectator, kibitzer** (US & Canadian)

22 **cheater**, cheat, grifter and hustler and rook (all informal), bunco artist (US informal); deceiver see 357; **dupe, victim**, mark and lamb and sucker (informal), john and patsy (US informal)

verbs

23 **to gamble**, game, sport (old), play, **try one's luck** or **fortune; speculate; run** or **bank a game**; draw lots, draw straws, lot, cut lots, **cast lots**; cut the cards or deck; match coins, toss, flip a coin, call, call heads or tails; shoot craps, play at dice, roll the bones (informal); play the ponies or gee-gees (informal); raffle off

24 **to chance, risk, hazard**, set at hazard, **venture, wager**, take a flier (informal); **gamble on**, take a gamble on; **take a chance**, take one's chance, take the chances of, try the chance, **chance it**, chance one's arm,

"stand the hazard of the die"—SHAKESPEARE; **take** or **run the risk**, run a chance; **take chances**, tempt fortune; **leave** or **trust to chance** or **luck**, rely on fortune, take a leap in the dark; buy a pig in a poke; take potluck

25 to bet, wager, gamble, hazard, stake, flutter, punt, lay, lay down, put up, **make a bet, lay a wager,** give *or* take *or* lay odds, make book, get a piece of the action (*informal*); plunge (*informal*); bet on *or* upon, back; bet *or* play against; play *or* follow the ponies (*informal*); double up, parlay (*US*); **ante, ante up; cover, call,** match *or* meet a bet, see, fade; **check, sandbag** (*informal*), **pass,** stand pat *or* stand stiff

26 to cheat, pluck *and* skin *and* rook (*all informal*); load the dice, mark the cards

adjectives

27 speculative, uncertain *see* 970.15; **hazardous, risky** *see* 1005.10, dicey (*informal*), chancy; **lucky,** winning, hot *and* red hot *and* on a roll (*all informal*); **unlucky,** losing, cold (*informal*)

28 gambling games

all fours	lottery
auction bridge	lotto
baccarat	lowball poker
banker	monte
bezique	numbers *or* policy
bingo	ombre
blind poker	paddle wheel *or* raffle
bridge	wheel
canasta	penny ante
casino	picquet
chemin de fer	pinball
chuck-a-luck *or* birdcage	pinochle
chuck-farthing	pitch and toss
contract bridge *or* contract	poker
crack-loo	poker dice
craps	quinze
cribbage	romesteq
draw poker	rouge et noir
écarté	roulette
euchre	rum
fan tan	rummy
faro	seven-up
gin	skat
gin rummy	straight poker
hazard	stud poker
hearts	three-card monte
high, low, jack and the	trente-et-quarante
game	pontoon *or* twenty-one *or*
keno	blackjack *or* vingt-et-un
liar dice	wheel of fortune *or* big six
liar's poker	wheel
loo	whist

29 dice points and rolls

blanket roll *or* soft-pad roll	little natural *or* slow crap
craps	number *or* point
doublet	seven *or* natural *or* little
drop shot	natural *or* pass *or* craps
dump over shot	three *or* cock-eyes
even roll	two *or* snake eyes
greek shot	

760 EXISTENCE

nouns

1 existence, being; subsistence, entity, essence, isness, absolute *or* transcendental essence, *l'être* (*French*),

pure being, *Ding-an-sich* (*German*), thing-in-itself, noumenon; **occurrence,** presence; **materiality** *see* 1050, **substantiality** *see* 762; **life** *see* 306

2 reality, actuality, factuality, empirical *or* demonstrable *or* objective existence, the here and now; historicity; **truth** *see* 972; **authenticity;** sober *or* grim reality, real life, the nitty-gritty (*informal*), not a dream, more truth than poetry

3 fact, the case, the truth of the matter, not opinion, not guesswork, what's what *and* where it's at (*both informal*); **matter of fact,** "plain, plump fact"—R BROWNING; **bare fact,** naked fact, bald fact, **simple fact,** sober fact, simple *or* sober truth; **cold fact,** hard fact, **stubborn fact, brutal fact,** painful fact, the nitty-gritty *and* the bottom line (*both informal*); **actual fact,** positive fact, absolute fact; **self-evident fact,** axiom, postulate, premise, accomplished fact, *fait accompli* (*French*); **accepted fact,** conceded fact, admitted fact, fact of experience, well-known fact, established fact, inescapable fact, irreducible fact, indisputable fact, undeniable fact; **demonstrable fact,** provable fact; empirical fact; protocol, protocol statement *or* sentence *or* proposition; given fact, given, donné datum, **circumstance** *see* 765; **salient fact,** significant fact

4 the facts, the information *see* 551, the particulars, the, details, the specifics, **the data;** the dope *and* the scoop *and* the score (*all informal*); the picture (*informal*), the gen (*informal*); the fact *or* facts *or* truth of the matter, the facts of the case, the whole story (*informal*); "irreducible and stubborn facts"—W JAMES; essentials, basic *or* essential facts, brass tacks (*informal*)

5 self-existence, uncreated being, noncontingent existence, aseity, innascibility

6 mere existence, simple existence, **vegetable existence, vegetation,** mere tropism

7 (philosophy of being) ontology, metaphysics, existentialism

verbs

8 to exist, be, be in existence, be extant, have being; breathe, **live** *see* 306.7; subsist, stand, obtain, hold, prevail, be the case; **occur,** be present, be there, be found, be met with, happen to be

9 to live on, continue to exist, persist, last, stand the test of time, endure *see* 826.6

10 to vegetate, merely exist, just be, pass the time

11 to exist in, consist in, subsist in, lie in, rest in, repose in, reside in, abide in, inhabit, dwell in, **inhere in,** be present in, be a quality of, be comprised in, be contained in, be constituted by, be coextensive with

12 to become, come to be, go, get, get to be, turn out to be; be converted into, turn into *see* 857.17; grow *see* 860.5; be changed

adjectives

13 existent, existing, in existence, de facto; **subsistent,** subsisting; **being,** in being; **living** *see* 306.11; **present, extant, prevalent, current,** in force *or* effect, afoot, on foot, under the sun, on the face of the earth

14 self-existent, self-existing, innascible; uncreated, increate

15 real, actual, factual, veritable, your actual (*informal*), for real (*informal*), de facto, simple, sober, **hard; absolute, positive; self-evident,** axiomatic; accepted, conceded, stipulated, given; admitted, well-known, **established, inescapable, indisputable, undeniable; demonstrable,** provable; empirical, **objective,** historical; **true** *see* 972.12; honest-to-God (*informal*), genuine, card-carrying (*informal*), **authentic; substantial** *see* 762.6

adverbs

16 really, actually; factually; **genuinely,** veritably, **truly; in reality,** in actuality, in effect, in fact, de facto, in point of fact, as a matter of fact; positively, absolutely; no buts about it (*informal*); no ifs, ands, or buts (*informal*); obviously, manifestly *see* 348.14

word elements

17 onto–

761 NONEXISTENCE

nouns

1 nonexistence, nonsubsistence; **nonbeing,** unbeing, not-being, nonentity; **nothingness,** nullity, nihility; vacancy, deprivation, emptiness, inanity, vacuity *see* 222.2; vacuum, void *see* 222.3; "the intense inane"—Shelley; negativeness, negation, negativity; nonoccurrence; **unreality,** nonreality, unactuality; nonpresence, absence *see* 222

2 nothing, nil, *nihil* (*Latin*), *nichts* (*German*), *nada* (*Spanish*), **naught,** nowt (*northern Eng*), **aught;** zero, cipher; nothing whatever, nothing at all, nothing on earth *or* under the sun, no such thing; thing of naught *see* 763.2

3 (*informal terms*) zilch (*US & Canadian*), zip (*US & Canadian*), zippo (*US & Canadian*), nix (*US & Canadian*), goose egg (*US & Canadian*), diddly (*US & Canadian*), shit, diddly squat (*US & Canadian*), a hill of beans, a hoot, **a fart,** a fuck, a flying fuck, fuck all *and* bugger all *and* sod all, f.a. *or* sweet F.A. *or* Sweet Fanny Adams, jack-shit (*US & Canadian*), a rat's ass (*US & Canadian*)

4 none, not any, none at all, not a one, not a blessed one (*informal*), never a one, ne'er a one, nary one (*informal*); **not a bit,** not a whit, not a hint, not a smitch *or* smidgen (*informal*), not a speck, not a mite, not a particle, not an iota, not a jot, not a scrap, not a sausage, not a trace, not a lick *or* a whiff (*informal*), not a shadow, not a suspicion, not a shadow of a suspicion, neither hide nor hair

verbs

5 to not exist, not be in existence, not be met with, not occur, not be found, found nowhere, be absent *or* lacking *or* wanting

6 to cease to exist *or* **be, be annihilated,** be destroyed, **be wiped out,** be extirpated, be eradicated; go, vanish, be no more, leave no trace, "leave not a rack behind"—Shakespeare; **vanish, disappear** *see* 34.3, evaporate, fade, fade away *or* out, fly, flee, dissolve, melt away, die out *or* away,

pass, pass away, pass out of the picture (*informal*), turn to nothing *or* naught, peter out (*informal*), come to an end, wind down, tail off *and* trail off (*both informal*); **perish, expire,** pass away, **die** *see* 307.19

7 to annihilate *see* 395.13, **exterminate** *see* 395.14, eradicate, extirpate, **eliminate,** liquidate, **wipe out, stamp out,** waste *and* take out *and* nuke *and* zap (*all informal*), put an end to *see* 395.12

adjectives

8 nonexistent, unexistent, inexistent, nonsubsistent, unexisting, without being, nowhere to be found; **minus, missing,** lacking, wanting; **null, void,** devoid, empty, inane, vacuous; **negative,** less than nothing

9 unreal, unrealistic, unactual, not real; merely nominal; **immaterial** *see* 1051.7; **unsubstantial** *see* 763.5; **imaginary,** imagined, **fantastic, fanciful, fancied** *see* 985.19-22; illusory

10 uncreated, unmade, unborn, unbegotten, unconceived, unproduced

11 no more, extinct, defunct, dead *see* 307.30, expired, passed away; vanished, gone glimmering; perished, annihilated; gone, all gone; all over with, had it (*informal*), finished *and* phut *and* pffft *and* kaput (*all informal*), down the tube *and* down the drain *and* up the spout (*all informal*), done for *and* dead and done for (*both informal*)

adverbs

12 none, no, not at all, in no way, to no extent

word elements

13 nulli–

762 SUBSTANTIALITY

nouns

1 substantiality, substantialness; **materiality** *see* 1050; **substance, body,** mass; **solidity,** density, concreteness, **tangibility,** palpability, ponderability; **sturdiness, stability,** soundness, firmness, steadiness, stoutness, toughness, **strength,** durability

2 substance, stuff, fabric, material, matter *see* 1050.2, medium, the tangible; **elements,** constituent elements, constituents, ingredients, components, atoms, building blocks, parts

3 something, thing, an existence; **being, entity,** unit, individual, entelechy, monad; **person,** persona, personality, body, soul; **creature,** created being, contingent being; **organism,** life form, living thing, life; **object** *see* 1050.4

4 embodiment, incarnation, materialization, substantiation, concretization, hypostasis, reification

verbs

5 to embody, incarnate, **materialize,** concretize, body forth, lend substance to, reify, entify, hypostatize

adjectives

6 substantial, substantive; **solid, concrete; tangible,** sensible, appreciable, palpable, ponderable; **material** *see* 1050.9; **real** *see* 760.15; **created,** creatural, organismic *or* organismal, contingent

7 **sturdy**, stable, **solid**, sound, firm, steady, tough, stout, **strong**, rugged,
"strong as flesh and blood"—WORDSWORTH; **durable**, lasting, enduring; **hard, dense**, unyielding, steely, adamantine; **well-made**, well-constructed, well-built, well-knit; **well-founded**, well-established, well-grounded; **massive**, bulky, heavy, chunky

adverbs

8 **substantially**, essentially, materially

word elements

9 stere–, ont–

763 UNSUBSTANTIALITY

nouns

1 **unsubstantiality**, insubstantiality, unsubstantialness; **immateriality** see 1051; bodilessness, incorporeality, unsolidity, unconcreteness; **intangibility**, impalpability, imponderability; **thinness, tenuousness**, attenuation, tenuity, evanescence, subtlety, subtility, fineness, airiness, mistiness, vagueness, ethereality; **fragility, frailness; flimsiness** see 16.2; **transience** see 827, ephemerality, ephemeralness, fleetingness, fugitiveness

2 thing of naught, nullity, zero; **nonentity, nobody** and nonstarter (both informal), nonperson, unperson, cipher, man of straw, jackstraw (old), lay figure, puppet, dummy, hollow man; flash in the pan, dud (informal); **trifle** see 997.5; nugae (Latin); nothing see 761.2

3 **spirit, air, thin air,**
"airy nothing"—SHAKESPEARE, breath, mere breath, smoke, vapour, mist, ether, **bubble,**
"such stuff as dreams are made on"—SHAKESPEARE, **shadow**, mere shadow;
"a spume that plays upon a ghostly paradigm of things"—YEATS; illusion see 975; phantom see 987.1

verbs

4 to spiritualize, disembody, dematerialize; etherealize, **attenuate**, subtilize, rarefy, fine, refine; **weaken**, enervate, sap

adjectives

5 **unsubstantial**, insubstantial, nonsubstantial, unsubstanced; intangible, impalpable, imponderable; **immaterial** see 1051.7; **bodiless**, incorporeal, unsolid, unconcrete; **weightless** see 298.10; **transient** see 827.7, ephemeral, fleeting, fugitive

6 **thin, tenuous**, subtile, subtle, evanescent, fine, overfine, refined, rarefied; **ethereal**, airy, windy, spirituous, vaporous, gaseous; air-built, cloud-built; **chimerical**, gossamer, gossamery, gauzy, shadowy, phantomlike see 987.7; dreamlike, **illusory, unreal;** fatuous, fatuitous, inane; **imaginary**, fanciful see 985.20

7 fragile, **frail** see 1048.4; **flimsy**, shaky, weak, papery, paper-thin, **unsound**, infirm see 16.15

8 **baseless, groundless**, ungrounded, **without foundation**, unfounded, built on sand,
"writ on water"—KEATS

word elements

9 pseudo–

764 STATE

nouns

1 **state**, mode, modality; **status, situation**, status quo or status in quo, position, standing, footing, location, bearings, spot; **rank**, estate, station, place, place on the ladder, **standing; condition**, circumstance see 765; **case, lot; predicament, plight**, pass, pickle and picklement and fix and jam and spot and bind (all informal)

2 **the state of affairs**, the nature or shape of things, the way it shapes up (informal), the way of the world, how things stack up (informal), **how things stand**, how things are, the state of play, the way of things, the way it is, like it/is, where it's at (informal), **the way things are**, the way of it, the way things go, how it goes, the way the cookie crumbles, **how it is**, the status quo or status in quo, the size of it (informal); how the land lies, the lay of the land

3 **good condition, bad condition**; adjustment, fettle, form, order, repair, **shape** (informal), trim

4 **mode, manner, way**, tenor, vein, fashion, style, lifestyle, way of life, preference, thing and bag (both informal), cup of tea (informal); **form, shape**, guise, complexion, makeup; **role**, capacity, character, part

verbs

5 to be in or have a certain state, be such or so or thus, **fare**, go on or along; **enjoy** or occupy a certain position; **get on** or along, come on or along (informal); **manage** (informal), **contrive, make out** (informal), come through, get by; **turn out**, come out, stack up (informal), shape up (informal)

adjectives

6 conditional, modal, formal, situational, statal

7 **in condition** or order or repair or shape; **out of order**, out of commission and out of kilter or kelter and out of whack (all informal)

765 CIRCUMSTANCE

nouns

1 **circumstance, occurrence, occasion, event** see 830, **incident**; juncture, conjuncture, contingency, eventuality; **condition** see 764.1

2 **circumstances**, circs (informal), total situation, existing conditions or situation, set of conditions, terms of reference, **environment** see 209, environing circumstances, context, frame, setting, surround, surrounding conditions, parameters, status quo or status in quo; **the picture**, the whole picture, full particulars, ins and outs, play-by-play description, blow-by-blow account

3 **particular, instance, item, detail**, point, count, case, fact, matter, article, datum, element, part, ingredient, factor, facet, aspect, thing; **respect,**

regard, angle; minutia, minutiae (*plural*), trifle, petty *or* trivial matter; incidental, minor detail

4 **circumstantiality,** particularity, specificity, thoroughness, minuteness of detail; accuracy

5 **circumstantiation,** itemization, particularization, specification, spelling-out, detailing, anatomization, atomization, analysis *see* 800

verbs

6 **to itemize, specify,** circumstantiate, particularize, **spell out, detail,** go *or* enter into detail, descend to particulars, give full particulars, atomize, anatomize; **analyse** *see* 800.6; **cite,** instance, adduce, document, give *or* quote chapter and verse; **substantiate**

adjectives

7 **circumstantial,** conditional, provisional; **incidental,** occasional, contingent, adventitious, **accidental, chance,** fortuitous, casual, aleatory, unessential *or* inessential *or* nonessential

8 **environmental,** environing, surrounding, conjunctive, conjoined, contextual, attending, attendant, limiting, determining, parametric

9 **detailed, minute, full, particular,** meticulous, fussy, finicky *or* finicking *or* finical, picayune (*US* & *Canadian informal*), picky (*informal*), nice (*old*), precise, exact, specific, special

adverbs

10 **thus, thusly** (*informal*), in such wise, thuswise, this way, this-a-way (*informal*), thus and thus, thus and so, **so,** just so, like so *and* yea (*both informal*), like this, like that, just like that; similarly *see* 783.18, precisely

11 **accordingly, in that case, in that event, at that rate,** that being the case, such being the case, that being so, **under the circumstances,** under the circs (*informal*), the condition being such, as it is, as matters stand, as the matter stands, **therefore** *see* 887.7, **consequently; as the case may be,** as it may be, according to circumstances; as it may happen *or* turn out, as things may fall; **by the same token,** equally

12 **circumstantially,** conditionally, provisionally; provided *see* 958.12

13 **fully, in full, in detail,** minutely, specifically, particularly, in particular, wholly *see* 791.13, *in toto* (*Latin*), completely *see* 793.14, **at length,** *in extenso* (*Latin*), *ad nauseam* (*Latin*)

766 INTRINSICALITY

nouns

1 **intrinsicality,** internality, innerness, **inwardness;** inbeing, indwelling, immanence; **innateness,** inherence, indigenousness, essentiality, fundamentality; **subjectivity,** internal reality, nonobjectivity

2 **essence, substance,** stuff, very stuff, inner essence, essential nature, quiddity; **quintessence, epitome,** embodiment, incarnation, model, pattern, purest type, typification, perfect example *or* exemplar, elixir, flower; **essential,** principle, essential principle, fundamental, hypostasis, postulate, axiom; **gist,**

gravamen, **nub** (*informal*), nucleus, centre, focus, kernel, **core, pith,** meat; **heart,** soul, heart and soul, spirit, sap, marrow

3 (*informal terms*) **meat and potatoes,** nuts and bolts, the nitty-gritty, the guts, the name of the game, the bottom line, where it's at, what it's all about, the ball game, the payoff, the score, where the rubber meets the road (*US*)

4 **nature, character, quality,** suchness; **constitution,** crasis (*old*), composition, **characteristics,** makeup, constituents; physique *see* 262.4, physio; **build,** body-build, somatotype, frame, constitution, genetic make-up, system; complexion (*old*), humour *and* humours (*both old*); **temperament,** temper, fibre, **disposition,** spirit, ethos, genius, dharma; **way, habit,** tenor, cast, hue, tone, grain, vein, streak, stripe, mould, brand, stamp; **kind** *see* 808.3, **sort, type,** ilk; **property, characteristic** *see* 864.4; **tendency** *see* 895; the way of it, the nature of the beast (*informal*)

5 **inner nature,** inside, insides (*informal*), internal *or* inner *or* esoteric *or* intrinsic reality, iniety, true being, essential nature, what makes one tick (*informal*), centre of life, vital principle, nerve centre; **spirit, indwelling spirit, soul, heart, heart and soul, breast, bosom, inner person,** heart of hearts, secret heart, inmost heart *or* soul, secret *or* innermost recesses of the heart, heart's core, bottom *or* cockles of the heart; vitals, the quick, depths of one's being, guts (*informal*), kishkes (*US informal*), where one lives (*US informal*); **vital principle,** archeus, life force, *élan vital* (*French* (*Henri Bergson*))

verbs

6 **to inhere,** indwell, belong to *or* permeate by nature, make one tick (*informal*); run in the blood, run in the family, inherit, be born so, have it in the genes, be made that way, be built that way (*informal*)

adjectives

7 **intrinsic,** internal, **inner,** inward; **inherent,** resident, implicit, immanent, indwelling; inalienable, unalienable, uninfringeable, unquestionable, unchallengeable, irreducible, qualitative; **ingrained,** in the very grain; infixed, implanted, inwrought, deep-seated; **subjective,** esoteric, private, secret

8 **innate, inborn,** born, congenital; **native, natural,** natural to, connatural, native to, indigenous; **constitutional,** bodily, physical, temperamental, organic; **inbred, genetic, hereditary,** inherited, bred in the bone, in the blood, running in the blood *or* race *or* strain, radical, rooted; connate, connatal, coeval; **instinctive,** instinctual, atavistic, primal

9 **essential,** of the essence, **fundamental; primary,** primitive, primal, elementary, elemental, simple, bare-bones *and* no-frills *and* bread-and-butter (*all informal*), original, *ab ovo* (*Latin*), **basic, gut** (*informal*), basal, underlying; **substantive,** substantial, material; constitutive, constituent

adverbs

10 **intrinsically, inherently,** innately; internally, inwardly, immanently; originally, primally,

primitively; **naturally, congenitally, genetically, by birth, by nature**
11 **essentially, fundamentally, primarily, basically;** at **bottom,** *au fond* (*French*), at heart; in essence, at the core, in substance, in the main; substantially, materially, most of all; per se, of *or* in itself, as such, qua

word elements
12 physi–, physic–

767 EXTRINSICALITY

nouns

1 **extrinsicality, externality, outwardness, extraneousness,** otherness, discreteness; foreignness; **objectivity, nonsubjectivity, impersonality**
2 **nonessential,** inessential *or* unessential, nonvitalness, carrying coals to Newcastle, gilding the lily; **accessory, extra,** collateral; the other, not-self; **appendage,** appurtenance, auxiliary, supernumerary, **supplement,** addition, addendum, superaddition, adjunct *see* 254; **subsidiary,** subordinate, secondary; **contingency,** contingent, incidental, accidental, accident, happenstance (*US & Canadian*), mere chance; **superfluity,** superfluousness; fifth wheel (*informal*)

adjectives

3 **extrinsic, external,** outward, outside, outlying; **extraneous,** foreign; **objective, nonsubjective,** impersonal, extraorganismic *or* extraorganismal
4 **unessential,** inessential *or* nonessential, unnecessary, nonvital, superfluous; **accessory, extra,** collateral; auxiliary, supernumerary; adventitious, appurtenant, adscititious; **additional, supplementary,** supplemental, superadded, supervenient, make-weight; **secondary,** subsidiary, subordinate; incidental, circumstantial, contingent; **accidental, chance,** fortuitous, casual, aleatory; **indeterminate, unpredictable,** capricious

768 ACCOMPANIMENT

nouns

1 **accompaniment,** concomitance *or* concomitancy, withness *and* togetherness (*both informal*); synchronism, **simultaneity** *see* 835, simultaneousness; coincidence, co–occurrence, **concurrence,** concurrency; parallelism
2 **company, association,** consociation, **society,** community; **companionship, fellowship,** consortship, partnership
3 **attendant,** concomitant, corollary, **accessory,** appendage; **adjunct** *see* 254
4 **accompanier,** accompanist; **attendant, companion,** fellow, **mate,** comate, consort, **partner;** companion piece
5 **escort, conductor, usher,** shepherd; **guide,** tourist guide, cicerone; **squire,** esquire, swain, cavalier; **chaperon** *or* **chaperone,** duenna; **bodyguard,** guard, minder, **convoy;** companion, sidekick (*informal*), fellow traveller, travel companion, satellite, outrider

6 **attendance, following,** cortege, retinue, **entourage,** suite, followers, followership, rout, train, body of retainers; **court,** cohort; parasite *see* 138.5

verbs

7 **to accompany,** bear *or* keep one company, **keep company with,** companion, go *or* travel *or* run with, go along for the ride (*informal*), **go along with, attend,** wait on *or* upon; **associate with,** assort with, sort with, **consort with,** couple with, hang around with *and* hang out with *and* hang with (*all informal*), go about *or* around with, go hand in hand with; **combine** *see* 804.3, **associate,** consociate, confederate, flock *or* band *or* herd together
8 **to escort, conduct,** have in tow (*informal*), marshal, **usher,** shepherd, **guide, lead; convoy,** guard; **squire,** esquire, **attend,** wait on *or* upon, **take out** (*informal*); **chaperon** *or* **chaperone**

adjectives

9 **accompanying, attending, attendant, concomitant,** accessory, collateral; **combined** *see* 804.5, **associated,** coupled, paired; **fellow, twin, joint, joined** *see* 799.13, conjoint, hand-in-hand, hand-in-glove, mutual; **simultaneous, concurrent,** coincident, synchronic, synchronized; correlative; parallel

adverbs

10 **hand in hand** *or* **glove,** arm in arm, side by side, cheek by jowl, shoulder to shoulder; therewith, therewithal, herewith
11 **together, collectively, mutually,** jointly, unitedly, in conjunction, conjointly, *en masse* (*French*), communally, corporately, **in a body,** all at once, *ensemble* (*French*), in association, in company; simultaneously, coincidentally, concurrently, at once

prepositions

12 **with, in company with, along with, together with,** in association with, coupled *or* paired *or* teamed *or* partnered with, in conjunction with

word elements

13 co–, con–, col–, com–, cor–, meta–, syn–, sym–

769 ASSEMBLAGE

nouns

1 **assemblage, assembly, collection, gathering,** ingathering, **congregation;** concourse, concurrence, conflux, confluence, convergence; collocation, juxtaposition, junction *see* 799.1; combination *see* 804; mobilization, call-up, muster, *attroupement* (*French*); roundup, rodeo, corralling; **comparison** *see* 942; canvass, census, data-gathering, survey, inventory
2 **assembly** (*of persons*), *assemblée* (*French*), **gathering,** forgathering, **congregation,** congress, conference, convocation, concourse, **meeting, meet, get-together** *and* turnout (*both informal*); convention, conventicle, synod, council, diet, **conclave,** levee; caucus; mass meeting, **rally,** sit-in, demonstration, demo (*informal*); **session,** séance, sitting, sit-down (*informal*); **panel,** forum, symposium, colloquium;

committee, commission; *eisteddfod* (*Welsh*); plenum, quorum; **party, festivity** see 743.4, fete, at home, housewarming, soiree, reception, **dance**, ball, bash (*informal*), prom (*US & Canadian informal*), do, lig (*informal*), shindig *and* brawl (*both informal*); rendezvous, date, assignation

3 **company, group**, grouping, groupment, network, **party, band, knot, gang, crew**, complement, cast, outfit, pack, cohort, troop, troupe, tribe, **body**, corps, stable, bunch *and* mob *and* crowd *and* shower (*all informal*); squad, platoon, battalion, regiment, brigade, division, fleet; **team**, squad, string; covey, bevy; posse, detachment, contingent, detail, *posse comitatus* (*Latin*); phalanx; **party, faction**, movement, wing, persuasion; in-group, old-boy network, out-group, peer group, age group; coterie, salon, clique, **set**; junta, cabal

4 **throng, multitude, horde**, host, heap (*informal*), army, panoply, legion; flock, cluster, galaxy; **crowd**, press, crush, flood, spate, deluge, mass; **mob**, rabble, rout, ruck, jam, *cohue* (*French*), the world and his wife *or* his dog (*informal*), everybody and his uncle *or* his brother (*informal*)

5 (*animals*) **flock, bunch, pack**, colony, host, troop, army, **herd, drove**, drive, drift, trip; pride (*of lions*), sloth (*of bears*), skulk (*of foxes*), gang (*of elk*), kennel (*of dogs*), clowder (*of cats*), pod (*of seals*), gam (*of whales*), **school** *or* shoal (*of fish*); (*animal young*) litter

6 (*birds, insects*) **flock**, flight, **swarm**, cloud; covey (*of partridges*), bevy (*of quail*), skein (*of geese in flight*), gaggle (*of geese on water*), watch (*of nightingales*), charm (*of finches*), murmuration (*of starlings*), spring (*of teal*); hive (*of bees*), plague (*of locusts*)

7 **bunch, group**, grouping, groupment, crop, **cluster, clump**, knot; grove, copse, thicket; **batch, lot**, slew (*US & Canadian informal*), **mess** (*informal*); tuft, wisp; tussock, hassock; shock, stook, wad, truss

8 **bundle, pack, package**, packet, deck, budget, **parcel**, fardel (*old*), sack, bag, poke (*informal*), ragbag (*informal*), bale, truss, **roll**, rouleau, bolt; faggot, fascine, fasces; quiver, sheaf; bouquet, nosegay, posy

9 **accumulation**, cumulation, gathering, **amassment**, congeries, acervation; agglomeration, conglomeration, glomeration, conglomerate, agglomerate; **aggregation**, aggregate; conglobation; **mass, lump**, gob (*informal*), chunk *and* hunk (*both informal*), wad; snowball; stockpile, stockpiling

10 **pile, heap, stack**, clamp; **mound, hill**; molehill, anthill; bank, embankment, dune; haystack, hayrick, haymow, haycock, cock, mow, rick; drift, snowdrift; pyramid

11 **collection**, collector's items, collectables *or* collectibles; **holdings**, fund, treasure; corpus, corpora, **body**, data, raw data; compilation, collectanea; ana; Americana, Africana, Australiana; anthology, florilegium, treasury; *Festschrift* (*German*); chrestomathy; **museum, library**, zoo, menagerie, aquarium

12 **set, suit, suite, series**, outfit *and* kit (*both informal*)

13 **miscellany**, miscellanea, collectanea; **assortment, medley, variety, mixture** see 796; hotchpotch *or* hodgepodge, conglomerate, **conglomeration**,

omnium-gatherum (*informal*); **sundries**, oddments, **odds and ends**, odds and sods

14 (*a putting together*) **assembly**, assemblage; assembly line, production line; assembly-line production

15 **collector**, gatherer, accumulator, connoisseur, fancier, enthusiast, magpie (*informal*); collection agent, bill collector, dunner; tax collector, tax man, exciseman, customs agent, *douanier* (*French*); **miser** see 484.4

verbs

16 to **come together, assemble, congregate, collect**, come from far and wide, come *or* arrive in a body; **league** see 804.4, ally; **unite** see 799.5; muster, **meet**, **gather**, forgather, gang up (*informal*), mass; **merge**, converge, flow together, fuse; flock together; herd together; **throng, crowd**, swarm, teem, hive, surge, seethe, mill, stream, horde; **be crowded**, be mobbed, be packed, burst at the seams, be full to overflowing; **cluster**, bunch, bunch up, clot; gather around; rally, rally around; **huddle**, go into a huddle, close ranks; rendezvous, date; **couple**, copulate, link, link up

17 to **convene, meet**, hold a meeting *or* session, sit; **convoke**, summon, call together

18 (*bring or gather together*) to **assemble, gather**; drum up, muster, rally, **mobilize; collect**, collect up, fund-raise, take up a collection, raise, take up; **accumulate**, cumulate, **amass**, mass, bulk, batch; agglomerate, conglomerate, aggregate; **combine** see 804.3, **network**, **join** see 799.5, **bring together**, get together, **gather together**, draw *or* lump *or* batch *or* bunch together, pack, pack in, cram, cram in; **bunch**, bunch up; **cluster**, clump; **group**, aggroup; **gather in**, get *or* whip in; scrape *or* scratch together, scrape up, rake *or* dredge *or* dig up; round up, corral (*US & Canadian*), drive together; **put together**, make up, compile, colligate; collocate, **juxtapose**, pair, match, partner, team, twin; hold up together, **compare** see 942.4

19 to **pile, pile on, heap, stack**, heap *or* pile *or* stack up; mound, hill, bank, bank up; rick; pyramid; drift

20 to **bundle, bundle up, package**, parcel, parcel up, **pack**, bag, sack, truss, truss up; bale; wrap, **wrap up**, do *or* tie *or* bind up; roll up

adjectives

21 **assembled, collected, gathered**; congregate, congregated; meeting, in session; quorate; **combined** see 804.5; **joined** see 799.13; joint, leagued see 804.6; **accumulated**, cumulate, massed, **amassed**; heaped, stacked, piled; glomerate, agglomerate, conglomerate, aggregate; **clustered**, bunched, lumped, clumped, knotted; bundled, packaged, wrapped up; fascicled, fasciculated

22 **crowded, packed, crammed**, chock-a-block; bumper-to-bumper (*informal*), jam-packed, packed *or* crammed like sardines (*informal*); **compact**, firm, solid, dense, close, serried; **teeming, swarming, crawling**, bristling, populous, full see 793.11

23 **cumulative**, accumulative, total, overall

770 DISPERSION

nouns

1 **dispersion** *or* **dispersal**, **scattering**, scatter, scatteration, diffraction; ripple effect; **distribution**, **spreading**, strewing, sowing, broadcasting, **broadcast**, **spread**, narrowcast, publication *see* 352, **dissemination**, propagation, dispensation; **radiation**, divergence *see* 171; expansion, splay; **diffusion**, circumfusion; **dilution**, attenuation, thinning, thinning-out, watering, watering-down, weakening; **evaporation**, volatilization, dissipation; fragmentation, shattering, pulverization; sprinkling, spattering; peppering, buckshot *or* shotgun pattern
2 **decentralization**, deconcentration
3 **disbandment**, dispersion *or* dispersal, diaspora, separation, parting; breakup, split-up (*informal*); **demobilization**, deactivation, **release**, detachment; dismissal *see* 908.5; dissolution, disorganization, disintegration *see* 805

verbs

4 **to disperse**, **scatter**, diffract; **distribute**, **broadcast**, **sow**, narrowcast, disseminate, propagate, pass around *or* out, publish *see* 352.10; **diffuse**, **spread**, dispread, circumfuse, strew, bestrew, dot; **radiate**, diverge *see* 171.5; expand, splay, branch *or* fan *or* spread out; **issue**, **deal out**, retail, utter, dispense; sow broadcast, scatter to the winds; overscatter, overspread, oversow
5 **to dissipate**, **dispel**, dissolve, attenuate, dilute, thin, thin out, water, water down, weaken; **evaporate**, volatilize; drive away, clear away, cast forth, blow off
6 **to sprinkle**, besprinkle, asperge, **spatter**, splatter, splash; **dot**, spot, speck, speckle, stud; **pepper**, powder, dust; flour, crumb, bread, dredge
7 **to decentralize**, deconcentrate
8 **to disband**, **disperse**, **scatter**, **separate**, **part**, break up, split up; part company, go separate ways; **demobilize**, demob (*informal*), deactivate, muster out, debrief, **release**, detach, discharge, let go; dismiss *see* 908.18; **dissolve**, disorganize, disintegrate *see* 805.3

adjectives

9 **dispersed**, **scattered**, **distributed**, dissipated, disseminated, strown, strewn, broadcast, **spread**, dispread; **widespread**, diffuse, discrete, sparse; **diluted**, thinned, thinned-out, watered, watered-down, weakened; **sporadic**; straggling, straggly; all over the place *or* shop (*informal*), from hell to breakfast (*US* & *Canadian informal*)
10 **sprinkled**, spattered, splattered, asperged, splashed, **peppered**, spotted, dotted, powdered, dusted, specked, speckled, **studded**
11 **dispersive**, **scattering**, **spreading**, diffractive *or* diffractional, **distributive**, disseminative, diffusive, dissipative, attenuative

adverbs

12 **scatteringly**, **dispersedly**, diffusely, sparsely, **sporadically**, *passim* (*Latin*), **here and there**; in places, **in spots** (*informal*); at large, everywhere, throughout, wherever you look *or* turn (*informal*), in all quarters

771 INCLUSION

nouns

1 **inclusion**, **comprisal**, **comprehension**, coverage, envisagement, embracement, encompassment, incorporation, embodiment, assimilation, reception; **membership**, participation, admission, admissibility, eligibility, legitimation, legitimization; **power-sharing**, enablement, enfranchisement; **completeness** *see* 793, **inclusiveness**, **comprehensiveness**, exhaustiveness; **whole** *see* 791; openness, toleration *or* tolerance
2 **entailment**, **involvement**, **implication**; assumption, presumption, presupposition, subsumption

verbs

3 **to include**, **comprise**, **contain**, **comprehend**, hold, **take in**; **cover**, cover a lot of ground (*informal*), occupy, take up, fill; fill in *or* out, build into, **complete** *see* 793.6; **embrace**, encompass, enclose, encircle, incorporate, assimilate, embody, admit, receive, envisage; **legitimize**, legitimatize; **share power**, enable, enfranchise, cut in *and* deal in *and* give a piece of the action (*all informal*); among, count in, work in; **number among**, take into account *or* consideration
4 (*include as a necessary circumstance or consequence*) **to entail**, **involve**, **implicate**, imply, assume, presume, presuppose, subsume, affect, take in, contain, comprise, **call for**, **require**, take, bring, lead to

adjectives

5 **included**, **comprised**, comprehended, envisaged, embraced, encompassed, added-in, covered, subsumed; bound up with, forming *or* making a part of, built-in, tucked-in; **involved** *see* 897.3
6 **inclusive**, **including**, **containing**, **comprising**, **covering**, **embracing**, encompassing, enclosing, encircling, assimilating, incorporating, envisaging; counting, numbering; broad-brush (*informal*), ballpark (*US* & *Canadian informal*)
7 **comprehensive**, **sweeping**, **complete** *see* 793.9; **whole** *see* 791.9; **all-comprehensive**, all-inclusive *see* 863.14; without omission *or* exception, **overall**, universal, global, wall-to-wall (*informal*), around-the-world, **total**, blanket, omnibus, across-the-board; encyclopedic, compendious; synoptic; bird's-eye, panoramic

772 EXCLUSION

nouns

1 **exclusion**, **barring**, debarring, debarment, preclusion, exception, omission, nonadmission, black-balling, cutting-out, leaving-out; **restriction**, **circumscription**, narrowing, demarcation; **rejection**, repudiation; **ban**, bar, taboo, injunction; relegation; prohibition, embargo, blockade; boycott, lockout; inadmissibility, excludability, exclusivity
2 **elimination**, **riddance**, culling, culling out, winnowing-out, shakeout, eviction, chasing, bum's rush (*informal*); **severance** *see* 801.2; withdrawal, **removal**, detachment, disjunction *see* 801.1; discard,

eradication, clearance, **ejection,** expulsion, suspension; **deportation, exile,** expatriation, ostracism, outlawing *or* outlawry; disposal, disposition; **liquidation, purge**

3 **exclusiveness, narrowness,** tightness; **insularity,** snobbishness, parochialism, ethnocentrism, ethnicity, xenophobia, know-nothingism; **segregation, separation, separationism,** division; **isolation,** insulation, seclusion; quarantine; racial segregation, apartheid, colour bar, Jim Crow, race hatred; **outgroup; outsider,** non-member, stranger, the other, they; **foreigner, alien** *see* 773.3, outcast *see* 586.4, outlaw; *persona non grata* (*Latin*)

verbs

4 **to exclude, bar,** debar, bar out, **lock out, shut out, keep out,** count out (*informal*), close the door on, close out, cut out, cut off, preclude; **reject, repudiate,** blackball *and* turn thumbs down on (*both informal*), drum out, read out (*US & Canadian*), ease *or* freeze out *and* leave *or* keep out in the cold (*all informal*), send to Coventry, ostracize, wave off *or* aside; **ignore,** turn a blind eye, turn a deaf ear, filter out, tune out; **ban,** prohibit, proscribe, taboo, **leave out,** omit, pass over, ignore; relegate; **blockade,** embargo; **tariff,** trade barrier

5 **to eliminate, get rid of,** rid oneself of, **get quit of,** get shut of (*informal*), **dispose of, remove,** abstract, eject, expel, turf out (*informal*), give the bum's rush (*informal*), kick downstairs, cast off *or* out, chuck (*informal*), throw over *or* overboard (*informal*); **deport, exile,** outlaw, expatriate; **clear,** clear out, clear away, clear the decks; **weed out,** pick out; **cut out,** strike off *or* out, elide; eradicate, root up *or* out; **purge, liquidate**

6 **to segregate, separate,** separate out *or* off, divide, cordon, cordon off; **isolate,** insulate, seclude; **set apart,** keep apart; **quarantine,** put in isolation; put beyond the pale, ghettoize; **set aside,** lay aside, put aside, keep aside; **sort** *or* **pick out,** cull out, sift, screen, sieve, bolt, riddle, winnow, winnow out; thresh, thrash, gin

adjectives

7 **excluded, barred,** debarred, precluded, kept-out, **shut out, left-out,** left out in the cold (*informal*), passed over; not included, not in it, not in the picture (*informal*); **ignored;** relegated; **banned,** prohibited, proscribed, tabooed; **expelled,** ejected, **purged,** liquidated; deported, exiled; **blockaded,** embargoed

8 **segregated, separated, cordoned off, divided; isolated,** insulated, secluded; **set apart,** sequestered; **quarantined; ghettoized,** beyond the pale

9 **exclusive, excluding,** exclusory; **seclusive,** preclusive, exceptional, inadmissible, prohibitive, preventive, prescriptive, restrictive; separative, segregative, closed-door; select, selective; narrow, insular, parochial, ethnocentric, xenophobic, snobbish

prepositions

10 **excluding, barring,** bar, exclusive of, precluding, omitting, without, absent, **leaving out; excepting, except, except for,** with the exception of, outside of (*informal*), **save,** saving, save and except, let alone; **besides,** beside, **aside from**

773 EXTRANEOUSNESS

nouns

1 **extraneousness, foreignness;** otherness, alienism, alienage, alienation; **extrinsicality** *see* 767; **exteriority** *see* 206; nonassimilation, nonconformity; intrusion

2 **intruder,** foreign body *or* element, foreign intruder *or* intrusion, interloper, encroacher; **impurity,** blemish *see* 1003; speck *see* 258.7, spot, macula, blot; mote, splinter *or* sliver, **weed,** misfit *see* 788.4; oddball *see* 869.4; black sheep

3 **alien, stranger, foreigner, outsider,** non-member, not one of us, not our sort, not the right sort, the other, outlander, *Uitlander* (*Afrikaans*), tramontane, ultramontane, barbarian, foreign devil (*China*), gringo (*Spanish American*), wog (*derogatory informal*); **exile,** outcast, outlaw, wanderer, refugee, émigré, displaced person *or* DP, *déraciné* (*French*); the Wandering Jew

4 **newcomer, new arrival,** *novus homo* (*Latin*); *arriviste* (*French*), Johnny-come-lately (*informal*), new boy; blow-in (*Australian informal*), **tenderfoot,** greenhorn; settler, emigrant, immigrant; recruit, rookie (*informal*); **intruder, squatter,** gate-crasher, stowaway

adjectives

5 **extraneous, foreign, alien,** strange, exotic, foreign-looking; unearthly, extraterrestrial *see* 1070.26; exterior, **external;** extrinsic *see* 767.3; ulterior, outside, outland, outlandish; barbarian, barbarous, barbaric; foreign-born; intrusive

adverbs

6 **abroad,** in foreign parts; oversea, **overseas,** beyond seas; on one's travels

word elements

7 ep–, epi–, eph–, ex–, exo–, ef–, xen–, xeno–

774 RELATION

nouns

1 **relation, relationship, connection;** relatedness, connectedness, **association** *see* 617, **affiliation,** filiation, bond, union, alliance, **tie, tie-in** (*informal*), link, linkage, linking, linkup, liaison, **addition** *see* 253, adjunct *see* 254, junction *see* 799.1, **combination** *see* 804, assemblage *see* 769; deduction *see* 255.1, disjunction *see* 801.1, **contrariety** *see* 778, **disagreement** *see* 788, negative *or* bad relation; **positive** *or* **good relation, affinity, rapport,** mutual attraction, sympathy, accord *see* 455; **closeness,** propinquity, **proximity,** approximation, contiguity, nearness *see* 223, intimacy; **relations, dealings,** affairs, business, transactions, doings *and* truck (*both informal*), intercourse; **similarity** *see* 783, homology

2 **relativity,** dependence, contingency; **relativism,** indeterminacy, uncertainty, variability, variance; **interrelation, correlation** *see* 776

3 kinship, common source *or* stock *or* descent *or* ancestry, consanguinity, agnation, cognation, enation, blood relationship *see* 559; family relationship, affinity *see* 564.1

4 relevance, pertinence, pertinency, cogency, relatedness, materiality, **appositeness,** germaneness; application, applicability, effect, appropriateness; **connection,** reference, **bearing,** concern, concernment, interest, respect, regard

verbs

5 to relate to, refer to, **apply to, bear on** *or* **upon,** respect, regard, **concern, involve,** touch, affect, interest; **pertain, pertain to,** appertain, appertain to, belong to, fit; be (someone's) pigeon (*informal*); **agree, agree with,** answer to, correspond to, chime with; **have to do with,** have a connection with, link with *or* link up with, connect, tie in with (*informal*), liaise with (*informal*), deal with, treat of, touch upon

6 to relate, associate, connect, interconnect, ally, link, link up, wed, marry, marry up, weld, bind, tie, couple, bracket, equate, identify; bring into relation with, bring to bear upon, apply; **parallel,** parallelize, draw a parallel; **interrelate,** relativize, **correlate** *see* 776.4

adjectives

7 relative, comparative, relational; **relativistic,** indeterminate, uncertain, variable; **connective, linking,** associative; **relating,** pertaining, appertaining, pertinent, referring, referable

8 approximate, approximating, approximative, proximate; **near, close** *see* 223.14; **comparable,** relatable, commensurable; **proportional,** proportionate, proportionable; correlative; **like,** homologous, **similar** *see* 783.10

9 related, connected; linked, tied, coupled, knotted, twinned, wedded, wed, married *or* married up, welded, conjugate, bracketed, bound, yoked, spliced, conjoined, conjoint, conjunct, joined *see* 799.13; **associated, affiliated,** filiated, **allied,** associate, affiliate; interlocked, **interrelated,** interlinked, involved, implicated, overlapping, interpenetrating, **correlated;** in the same category, of that kind *or* sort *or* ilk; parallel, collateral; **congenial,** *en rapport* (*French*), sympathetic, compatible, affinitive

10 kindred, akin, related, of common source *or* stock *or* descent *or* ancestry, agnate, cognate, enate, connate, connatural, congeneric *or* congenerous, consanguine *or* consanguineous, genetically related, related by blood *see* 559.6, affinal *see* 564.4

11 relevant, pertinent, appertaining, **germane, apposite,** cogent, material, admissible, applicable, applying, pertaining, belonging, involving, appropriate, **apropos,** *à propos* (*French*), to the purpose, to the point, in point, *ad rem* (*Latin*)

adverbs

12 relatively, comparatively, proportionately, not absolutely, to a degree, to an extent, to some extent; **relevantly,** pertinently, appositely, germanely

prepositions

13 with *or* **in relation to,** with *or* in reference to, **with** *or* **in regard to,** with respect to, in respect to

or of, in what concerns, relative to, **relating** *or* **pertaining to,** pertinent to, appertaining to, referring to, in relation with, **in connection with,** apropos of, speaking of; **as to,** as for, as respects, as regards; in the matter of, on the subject of, in point of, on the score of; re, *in re* (*Latin*); **about,** anent, of, on, upon, **concerning,** touching, respecting, **regarding**

775 UNRELATEDNESS

nouns

1 unrelatedness, irrelativeness, irrelation; **irrelevance,** irrelevancy, impertinence, inappositeness, uncogency, ungermaneness, immateriality, inapplicability; inconnection *or* disconnection, inconsequence, independence; **unconnectedness,** separateness, delinkage, discreteness, dissociation, disassociation, disjuncture, disjunction *see* 801.1

2 misconnection, misrelation, wrong *or* invalid linking, **mismatch,** mismatching, misalliance, *mésalliance* (*French*); misapplication, misapplicability, misreference

3 an irrelevance *or* irrelevancy, quite another thing, something else again *and* a whole different story *and* a whole different ball game (*all informal*)

verbs

4 to not concern, not involve, not imply, not implicate, not entail, not relate to, not connect with, have nothing to do with, have no business with, cut no ice (*informal*)

5 to foist, drag in *see* 213.6; impose on *see* 643.7

adjectives

6 unrelated, irrelative, unrelatable, unrelational, **unconnected,** unallied, unlinked, **unassociated,** unaffiliated *or* disaffiliated; disrelated, disconnected, dissociated, detached, discrete, disjunct, removed, **separated,** segregated, apart, other, independent, marked off, bracketed; **isolated,** insular; **foreign, alien,** strange, exotic, outlandish; incommensurable, incomparable; extraneous *see* 767.3

7 irrelevant, irrelative; **impertinent, inapposite,** ungermane, uncogent, inconsequent, inapplicable, immaterial, inappropriate, inadmissible; wide of *or* away from the point, *nihil ad rem* (*Latin*), **beside the point,** beside the mark, wide of the mark, **beside the question,** off the subject, not to the purpose, **nothing to do with the case,** not at issue, out-of-the-way; **unessential,** nonessential, extraneous, extrinsic *see* 767.3; incidental, parenthetical

8 farfetched, remote, distant, out-of-the-way, strained, forced, dragged in, neither here nor there, brought in from nowhere; **imaginary** *see* 985.19; improbable *see* 968.3

adverbs

9 irrelevantly, irrelatively, impertinently, inappositely, ungermanely, uncogently, amiss; without connection, without reference *or* regard

776 CORRELATION
reciprocal or mutual relation

nouns

1 **correlation**, corelation; correlativity, correlativism; **reciprocation**, reciprocity, reciprocality, two-edged sword, relativity *see* 774.2; **mutuality**, communion, community, commutuality; **common denominator**, common factor; proportionality, direct *or* inverse relationship, direct *or* inverse ratio, direct *or* inverse proportion, covariation; **equilibrium, balance**, symmetry *see* 264; **correspondence, equivalence**, equipollence, coequality

2 **interrelation**, interrelationship; **interconnection**, interlocking, interdigitation, intercoupling, interlinking, interlinkage, interalliance, interassociation, interaffiliation, interdependence, interdependency

3 **interaction**, interworking, intercourse, intercommunication, **interplay**; alternation, seesaw; **meshing**, intermeshing, mesh, engagement; **complementation**, complementary relation, complementary distribution; **interweaving**, interlacing, intertwining *see* 740.1; **interchange** *see* 862, tit for tat, trade-off, *quid pro quo* (*Latin*); **concurrence** *see* 898, coaction, **cooperation** *see* 450; codependency

4 **correlate**, correlative; **correspondent**, analogue, counterpart; reciprocator, reciprocatist; each other, one another

verbs

5 **to correlate**, corelate; **interrelate, interconnect**, interassociate, interlink, intercouple, interlock, interdigitate, interally, intertie, interjoin, interdepend

6 **to interact**, interwork, **interplay**; mesh, intermesh, engage, fit, fit like a glove, dovetail, mortise; **interweave**, interlace, intertwine; **interchange**; coact, **cooperate**; codepend

7 **to reciprocate, correspond**, correspond to, respond to, answer, answer to, go tit-for-tat; **complement**, coequal; **cut both ways**, cut two ways

adjectives

8 **correlative**, corelative, correlational, corelational; **correlated**, corelated; **interrelated, interconnected**, interassociated, interallied, interaffiliated, interlinked, interlocked, intercoupled, intertied, interdependent

9 **interacting**, interactive, interworking, interplaying; in gear, in mesh; dovetailed, mortised; **cooperative**, cooperating *see* 450.5

10 **reciprocal**, reciprocative, tit-for-tat, seesaw, seesawing; **corresponding**, correspondent, answering, analogous, homologous, equipollent, tantamount, equivalent, coequal; **complementary**, complemental

11 **mutual**, commutual, **common, joint, communal**, shared, sharing, conjoint; respective, two-way

adverbs

12 **reciprocally**, back and forth, backward and forward, backwards and forwards, alternately, seesaw, to and fro; vice versa

13 **mutually, commonly**, communally, **jointly**; respectively, each to each; *entre nous* (*French*), *inter se* (*Latin*)

word elements

14 equi–

777 SAMENESS

nouns

1 **sameness, identity**, identicalness, selfsameness, indistinguishability, undifferentiation, nondifferentiation, two peas in a pod; **coincidence**, correspondence, agreement, congruence; **equivalence, equality** *see* 789, coequality; **synonymousness**, synonymity, synonymy; **oneness, unity**, homogeneity, consubstantiality

2 **identification**, likening, unification, coalescence, combination, union, fusion, merger, blending, melding, synthesis

3 **the same, selfsame**, very same, one and the same, identical same, no other, none other, very *or* actual thing, a distinction without a difference, the same difference (*informal*); **equivalent** *see* 783.3; **synonym**; homonym, homograph, homophone; ditto (*informal*), *idem* (*Latin*), *ipsissima verba* (*Latin*, the very words); **duplicate**, double, clone (*informal*), *Doppelgänger* (*German*), twin, very image, lookalike, dead ringer (*informal*), the image of, the picture of, spitting image *and* spit and image *and* dead spit (*all informal*), **exact counterpart, copy** *see* 784.1,3-5, replica, facsimile, carbon copy

verbs

4 **to coincide, correspond**, agree, chime with, match, tally, go hand in glove with, twin

5 **to identify**, make one, **unify**, unite, join, combine, coalesce, synthesize, merge, blend, meld, fuse *see* 804.3

6 **to reproduce**, copy, reduplicate, **duplicate**, ditto (*informal*), clone

adjectives

7 **identical**, identic; **same, selfsame, one, one and the same**, all the same, all one, of the same kidney; **indistinguishable**, without distinction, without difference, undifferent, undifferentiated; **alike, all alike, like** *see* 783.10, just alike, exactly alike, like two peas in a pod; **duplicate**, reduplicated, twin; **homogeneous**, consubstantial

8 **coinciding**, coincident, coincidental; **corresponding**, correspondent, congruent; **synonymous**, equivalent, six of one and half a dozen of the other *or* six and two threes (*informal*), as broad as it is long (*informal*); **equal** *see* 789.7, coequal, coextensive, coterminous; in *or* at parity

adverbs

9 **identically**, synonymously, **alike**; coincidentally, correspondently, correspondingly, congruently; **equally** *see* 789.11, coequally, coextensively, coterminously; on the same footing; **likewise**, the same way, just the same, as is, ditto, same here (*informal*); *ibid* and *ibidem* (*both Latin*)

778 CONTRARIETY

nouns

1 **contrariety, oppositeness, opposition** *see* 451; **antithesis, contrast**, contraposition *see* 215, counterposition, contradiction, contraindication, contradistinction; **antagonism**, repugnance, oppugnance, oppugnancy, **hostility**, perversity, nay-saying, negativeness, orneriness (*US & Canadian informal*), inimicalness, **antipathy**, scunner (*informal*); **confrontation**, showdown, standoff, clashing, collision, cross-purposes *see* 456.2, conflict; polarity; discrepancy, inconsistency, **disagreement** *see* 788

2 **the opposite, the contrary, the antithesis, the reverse**, the other way round *or* around, the inverse, the converse, the obverse, the counter; **the other side**, the mirror *or* reverse image, the other side of the coin, the flip *or* B side (*informal*); the direct *or* polar opposite, the other *or* opposite extreme; antipode, antipodes; countercheck *or* counterbalance *or* counterpoise, offset, setoff, **opposite pole**, antipole, counterpole, counterpoint; opposite number (*informal*), vis-à-vis; **antonym**, opposite, opposite term, counterterm

3 (contrarieties when joined or coexisting) self-contradiction, **paradox** *see* 788.2, antinomy, oxymoron, ambivalence, **irony**, enantiosis, equivocation, **ambiguity**

verbs

4 **to go contrary to, run counter to**, counter, **contradict**, contravene, controvert, fly in the face of, be *or* play at cross-purposes, go against; **oppose**, be opposed to, go *or* run in opposition to, side against; **conflict with**, come in conflict with, oppugn, conflict, clash; contrast with, **offset**, set off, countercheck *or* counterbalance, countervail; **counteract**, counterwork; counterpose *or* contrapose, counterpoise, juxtapose in opposition

5 **to reverse**, transpose *see* 205.5, flip (*informal*)

adjectives

6 **contrary**; contrarious, perverse, **opposite**, antithetic, antithetical, **contradictory**, counter, contrapositive, contrasted; **converse, reverse**, obverse, inverse; **adverse**, adversative *or* adversive, adversarial, **opposing, opposed**, oppositive, oppositional; anti (*informal*), dead against; **antagonistic**, repugnant, oppugnant, perverse, contrarious, ornery (*US & Canadian informal*), nay-saying, negative, hostile, combative, bellicose, belligerent, inimical, antipathetic, antipathetical, discordant; inconsistent, discrepant, conflicting, clashing, at cross-purposes, confronting, **confrontational**, confrontive, squared off (*informal*), eyeball to eyeball *and* toe-to-toe (*both informal*), at loggerheads; contradistinct; antonymous; countervailing, counterpoised, balancing, counterbalancing, compensating

7 **diametric, diametrical, diametrically opposite**, at opposite poles, in polar opposition, antipodal *or* antipodean; opposite as black and white *or* light and darkness *or* day and night *or* fire and water *or* chalk and cheese *or* the poles, etc,

"Hyperion to a satyr"—SHAKESPEARE

8 **self-contradictory, paradoxical**, antinomic, oxymoronic, ambivalent, **ironic**; equivocal, **ambiguous**

adverbs

9 contrarily, contrariwise, counter, conversely, inversely, **vice versa**, topsy-turvy, upside down, arsy-versy (*informal*), **on the other hand**, *per contra* (*Latin*), **on** *or* **to the contrary**, *tout au contraire or au contraire* (*French*), at loggerheads, in flat opposition; rather, nay rather, quite the contrary, otherwise *see* 779.11, just the other way, just the other way around, **oppositely**, just the opposite *or* reverse; by contraries, by way of opposition; against the grain, *à rebours* (*French*); contrariously, perversely, ornerily (*US & Canadian informal*)

prepositions

10 **opposite**, over against, contra, in contrast with, contrary to, vis-à-vis

word elements

11 con–, contra–, counter–

779 DIFFERENCE

nouns

1 **difference**, otherness, separateness, discreteness, distinctness, **distinction**; unlikeness, **dissimilarity** *see* 786; **variation**, variance, variegation, variety, **mixture** *see* 796, **heterogeneity, diversity**; **deviation**, divergence *or* divergency, departure; **disparity**, gap, inequality *see* 790, odds; **discrepancy**, inconsistency, inconsonance, incongruity, discongruity, unconformity *or* nonconformity, disconformity, **strangeness** *see* 869, unorthodoxy *see* 688, incompatibility, irreconcilability; culture gap; **disagreement, dissent** *see* 333, disaccord *or* disaccordance, inaccordance, discordance, dissonance, inharmoniousness, inharmony; **contrast**, opposition, **contrariety** *see* 778; a far cry, a world of difference, a whale of a difference (*informal*)

2 **margin**, wide *or* narrow margin, **differential**; differentia, distinction, point of difference; **nicety, subtlety**, refinement, delicacy, nice *or* fine *or* delicate *or* **subtle distinction**, fine point; shade *or* particle of difference, **nuance**, hairline; **seeming difference**, distinction without a difference

3 **a different thing**, a different story (*informal*), **something else**, something else again (*informal*), *tertium quid* (*Latin*, a third something), *autre chose* (*French*), another kettle of fish (*informal*), horse of a different colour, another tune, different breed of cat (*informal*), bird of another feather; **nothing of the kind**, no such thing, **quite another thing; other, another**, tother *or* t'other (*dialect*), different ball game *and* whole different ball game (*both informal*)

4 **differentiation**, differencing, **discrimination**, distinguishing, **distinction**; demarcation, limiting, drawing the line; **separation, separateness**, discreteness *see* 801.1, division, atomization, anatomization, analysis, disjunction, segregation,

severance, severalization; **modification, alteration, change** see 851, variation, diversification, disequalization; **particularization**, specification, individualization, individuation, personalization, specialization

verbs

5 to **differ, vary,** diverge, stand apart, be distinguished *or* distinct; **deviate from,** diverge from, divaricate from, depart from; **disagree with,** disaccord with, conflict with, contrast with, clash with, jar with; not be like, bear no resemblance to see 786.2, not square with, not accord with

6 to **differentiate,** difference; **distinguish, make a distinction, discriminate,** secern; **separate,** sever, severalize, segregate, divide; **demarcate,** mark, mark out *or* off, set off, set apart, draw a line, set limits; **modify,** vary, diversify, disequalize, **change** see 851.5, 6; **particularize,** individualize, individuate, personalize, specify, specialize; atomize, analyse, dissect, anatomize, disjoin; split hairs, sharpen *or* refine a distinction, chop logic

adjectives

7 **different,** differing; unlike, not like, **dissimilar** see 786.4; **distinct,** distinguished, differentiated, discriminated, discrete, separated, separate, disjoined see 801.21, widely apart; **various,** variant, varying, varied, heterogeneous, multifarious, motley, assorted, variegated, diverse, divers, **diversified** see 782.4; **several,** many; **divergent,** deviative, diverging, deviating, departing; **disparate,** unequal see 790.4; **discrepant,** inconsistent, inconsonant, incongruous, incongruent, unconformable, incompatible, irreconcilable; **disagreeing,** in disagreement; **at odds,** at variance, clashing, inaccordant, disaccordant, discordant, dissonant, inharmonious, out of tune; **contrasting,** contrasted, poles apart, poles asunder, worlds apart; **contrary** see 778.6; **discriminable,** separable, severable

8 **other, another,** else, otherwise, other than *or* from; not the same, not the type (*informal*), not that sort, of another sort, of a sort *and* of sorts (*both informal*); **unique,** one of a kind, rare, **special,** peculiar, *sui generis* (*Latin,* of its own kind), in a class by itself

9 **differentiative,** differentiating, diacritic, diacritical, differential; **distinguishing,** discriminating, discriminative, discriminatory, characterizing, individualizing, individuating, personalizing, differencing, separative; diagnostic; **distinctive,** contrastive, characteristic, peculiar, idiosyncratic

adverbs

10 **differently,** diversely, variously; in a different manner, in another way, with a difference; differentiatingly, distinguishingly

11 **otherwise,** in other ways, **in other respects;** elsewise, else, or else; than; other than; **on the other hand;** contrarily see 778.9; alias

word elements

12 all–, de–, dis–, heter–, xen–

780 UNIFORMITY

nouns

1 **uniformity, evenness,** equability; **steadiness, stability** see 854, steadfastness, firmness, unbrokenness, seamlessness, constancy, unwaveringness, undeviatingness, persistence, perseverance, continuity, **consistency;** consonance, correspondence, accordance; unity, **homogeneity,** consubstantiality, monolithism; **equanimity,** equilibrium, unruffledness, serenity, tranquillity, calm, calmness, cool (*informal*)

2 **regularity, constancy,** invariability, unvariation, undeviation, even tenor *or* pace, smoothness, clockwork regularity; **sameness** see 777, **monotony,** monotonousness, undifferentiation, the same old thing (*informal*), the daily round *or* grind *or* routine, the treadmill; monotone, drone, dingdong, singsong, monologue

verbs

3 to **persist, prevail,** persevere, run true to form *or* type, continue the same; drag on *or* along; hum, drone

4 to **make uniform,** uniformize; **regulate,** regularize, normalize, stabilize, damp; **even, equalize,** symmetrize, harmonize, balance, balance up, equilibrize; **level,** level out *or* off, smooth, smooth out, even, even out, flatten; **homogenize, assimilate,** standardize, stereotype; clone (*informal*)

adjectives

5 **uniform, equable,** equal, **even; level,** flat, smooth; **regular, constant,** steadfast, persistent, continuous; **unvaried,** unruffled, unbroken, seamless, undiversified, undifferentiated, unchanged; invariable, unchangeable, immutable; **unvarying,** undeviating, unchanging, steady, stable; cloned *or* clonish (*informal*); **ordered,** balanced, measured; **orderly,** methodical, systematic, mechanical, faceless, robotlike, robotic, automatic; **consistent,** consonant, correspondent, accordant, homogeneous, **alike,** all alike, all of a piece, of a piece, consubstantial, monolithic

6 **same,** wall-to-wall, back-to-back; **monotonous, humdrum,** unrelieved, repetitive, drab, grey, ho-hum (*informal*), samey (*informal*), usual, as usual; tedious, boring

adverbs

7 **uniformly,** equably, **evenly;** monotonously, in a rut *or* groove, dully, tediously, routinely, unrelievedly

8 **regularly; constantly, steadily,** continually; **invariably,** without exception, at every turn, every time one turns around, all the time, all year round, week in week out, year in year out, day in day out, never otherwise; methodically, orderly, systematically; **always** see 828.11; like clockwork

word elements

9 equi–, hol–, hom–, is–, mon–

781 NONUNIFORMITY

nouns

1 **nonuniformity, unevenness, irregularity,** raggedness, choppiness, jerkiness, **disorder** *see* 809; **difference** *see* 779; inequality; **inconstancy, inconsistency,** variability, changeability, changeableness, mutability, capriciousness, mercuriality, wavering, **instability, unsteadiness; variation, deviation,** deviance, divergence, differentiation, divarication, ramification; versatility, **diversity,** diversification, nonformalization; **nonconformity,** nonconformism, unconformity, unconformism, **unorthodoxy; pluralism,** variegation, variety, variousness, motleyness, dappleness; multiculturalism, multiculturism

verbs

2 **to diversify, vary,** variegate *see* 47.7, chop and change, waver, mutate; **differentiate,** divaricate, diverge, ramify; **differ** *see* 779.5; dissent *see* 333.4; **disunify,** break up, break down, fragment, partition, **analyse** *see* 800.6

adjectives

3 **nonuniform,** ununiform, **uneven, irregular,** ragged, erose, choppy, jerky, jagged, rough, disorderly, unsystematic; **different** *see* 779.7, unequal, unequable; **inconstant, inconsistent, variable,** varying, **changeable,** changing, mutable, capricious, impulsive, mercurial, erratic, spasmodic, sporadic, wavery, wavering, **unstable, unsteady;** deviating, deviative, deviatory, divergent, divaricate, ramified; **diversified,** variform, diversiform, nonformal; **nonconformist,** unorthodox; **pluralistic,** variegated, various, motley *see* 47.9, 12; multicultural, multiracial

adverbs

4 **nonuniformly,** ununiformly, unequally, **unevenly, irregularly,** inconstantly, **inconsistently,** unsteadily, erratically, spasmodically, by fits and starts, capriciously, impulsively, sporadically; unsystematically, chaotically, helter-skelter, higgledy-piggledy; in all manner of ways, every which way (*US & Canadian informal*), all over the shop *and* all over the place (*both informal*); here there and everywhere

word elements

5 diversi–, vari–, heter–

782 MULTIFORMITY

nouns

1 **multiformity,** multifariousness, **variety,** nonuniformity *see* 781, **diversity,** diversification, variation, variegation *see* 47, variability, versatility, proteanism, manifoldness, multiplicity, heterogeneity; omniformity, omnifariousness, everything but the kitchen sink (*informal*), polymorphism, heteromorphism; allotropy *or* allotropism (*chemistry*); Proteus, shapeshifting, shapeshifter;

"God's plenty"—Dryden, "her infinite variety"—Shakespeare

verbs

2 **to diversify, vary,** change form, change shape, shift shape, ring the changes, cover the spectrum, **variegate** *see* 47.7

adjectives

3 **multiform,** diversiform, variable, versatile, "of every shape that was not uniform"—James Russell Lowell; **protean,** proteiform, chameleonic; **manifold,** multifold, multiplex, multiple, multifarious, multitudinous, multifaceted, many-sided, multiphase; polymorphous, polymorphic, heteromorphous, heteromorphic, metamorphic; omniform, omniformal, omnifarious, omnigenous; allotropic *or* allotropical (*chemistry*)

4 **diversified, varied, assorted,** heterogeneous; **various,** many and various, divers (*old*), diverse, sundry, **several, many;** of all sorts *or* conditions *or* kinds *or* shapes *or* descriptions *or* types, of 57 varieties

adverbs

5 **variously, severally,** sundrily, multifariously, diversely, manifoldly

word elements

6 allo–, diversi–, heter–, multi–, omni–, parti–, party–, poecil– *or* poikil–, poly–, vari–

783 SIMILARITY

nouns

1 **similarity, likeness,** alikeness, **sameness,** similitude; **resemblance,** semblance; **analogy, correspondence,** conformity, accordance, agreement, comparability, comparison, **parallelism, parity,** community, alliance, consimilarity; **approximation,** approach, closeness, nearness; assimilation, likening, **simile, metaphor; simulation, imitation,** copying, aping, mimicking, taking off, takeoff, burlesque, pastiche, *pasticcio* (*Italian*); identity *see* 777.1

2 **kinship,** affinity, family resemblance *or* likeness, family favour, generic *or* genetic resemblance; connaturality *or* connaturalness, connature, connateness, congeneracy

3 **likeness, like,** the like of *or* the likes of (*informal*); suchlike, such; **analogue, parallel;** cognate, congener; **counterpart, complement, correspondent,** pendant, similitude, tally; **approximation,** rough idea, sketch; coordinate, reciprocal, obverse, equivalent; correlate, correlative; **close imitation** *or* reproduction *or* copy *or* facsimile *or* replica, near duplicate, simulacrum; **close match, fellow, mate, pair;** soul mate, kindred spirit *or* soul, **companion, twin,** brother, sister; *mon semblable* (*French*), second self, alter ego, doppelganger; clone, a chip off the old block; **lookalike,** the image of, the picture of, spitting image *or* spit *or* spit and image (*all informal*)

4 **close** or **striking resemblance**, startling or marked or decided resemblance; good likeness, lifelikeness; **faint** or **remote resemblance**, mere hint or shadow

5 **set**, group, matching pair or set, his and hers (*informal*), couple, pair, twins, lookalikes, two of a kind, birds of a feather, peas in a pod

6 (of words or sounds) assonance, alliteration, rhyme, half rhyme or slant rhyme, near rhyme, eye rhyme, jingle, clink; pun, paronamasia, play on words

verbs

7 **to resemble**, be like, bear resemblance; put one in mind of (*informal*), remind one of, bring to mind, be reminiscent of, suggest, evoke, call up, call to mind; **look like**, favour (*informal*), mirror; **take after**, partake of, follow, appear or seem like, sound like; savour or smack of, be redolent of; **have all the hallmarks of**, have every appearance of, have all the features of, have all the signs of, have every sign or indication of; **approximate**, approach, near, come near, come close; **compare with**, stack up with (*US informal*); **correspond, match, parallel**; not tell apart, not tell one from the other; **imitate** *see* 336.5, simulate, copy, ape, mimic, take off, counterfeit; nearly reproduce or duplicate or reduplicate

8 **to similarize**, approximate, assimilate, bring near; connaturalize

9 **to assonate**, alliterate, rhyme, chime; pun

adjectives

10 **similar, like, alike**, something like, not unlike; **resembling**, resemblant, following, favouring (*informal*), savouring or smacking of, suggestive of, of or in the order of; consimilar; **simulated, imitated**, imitation, copied, aped, mimicked, taken off, fake or phoney (*both informal*), counterfeit, **mock**, synthetic, ersatz; nearly reproduced or duplicated or reduplicated, virtually identical; uniform with, homogeneous, identical *see* 777.7

11 **analogous**, comparable; **corresponding**, correspondent, equivalent; **parallel**, paralleling; **matching**, lookalike, cast in the same mould, of a kind, of a size, of a piece; duplicate, twin, of the same hue or stripe, of that ilk

12 **such as**, suchlike, so

13 **akin**, affinitive; connatural, connate, cognate, agnate, enate, conspecific, correlative; congenerous, congeneric, congenerical; brothers or sisters under the skin

14 **approximating**, approximative, approximate, approximable; **near, close**; much of a muchness (*informal*), much the same, just the same, nearly the same, nothing or little to choose between, same but different,
"like — but oh! how different"—WORDSWORTH; quasi

15 **very like**, uncommonly like, remarkably like, extraordinarily like, strikingly like, mighty like, powerful like (*informal*), **ridiculously like, for all the world like**, as like as can be; a lot alike, pretty much the same, same difference *and* damned little difference (*both informal*); as like as two peas in a pod,
"as lyke as one pease is to another"—JOHN LYLY, "as like as eggs"—SHAKESPEARE, *comme deux gouttes d'eau*

(*French*, like two drops of water); faintly or remotely like

16 **lifelike**, speaking, faithful, living, breathing, to the life, **true to life** or nature; **realistic, natural**

17 (of words or sounds) assonant, assonantal, alliterative, alliteral; **rhyming**, jingling, chiming, punning

adverbs

18 **similarly**, correspondingly, **like, likewise**, either; in the same manner, **in like manner**, in kind; in that way, like that, like this; **thus** *see* 765.10; so; by the same token, by the same sign; identically *see* 777.9

19 **so to speak**, in a manner of speaking, **as it were**, in a manner, in a way; kind of *and* sort of (*both informal*)

784 COPY

nouns

1 **copy, representation, facsimile, image, likeness** *see* 783.3, **resemblance**, semblance, similitude, picture, portrait, life mask, death mask, icon, simulacrum; ectype; pastiche, *pasticcio* (*Italian*); fair copy, faithful copy; certified copy; **imitation** *see* 336.3, **counterfeit** *see* 354.13, forgery, fake *and* phoney (*both informal*)

2 **reproduction**, duplication, reduplication; reprography; transcription; tracing, rubbing; mimeography; xerography, hectography

3 **duplicate**, duplication, ditto (*informal*); **double**, clone; representation, **reproduction, replica**, repro (*informal*), reduplication, facsimile, model, **counterpart**; a chip off the old block; triplicate, quadruplicate, etc; backup; repetition *see* 848

4 **transcript**, transcription, apograph, tenor (*law*); **transfer**, tracing, rubbing, **carbon copy**, carbon; manifold (*old*); microcopy, microform; microfiche, fiche; recording

5 **print**, offprint; **impression**, impress; **reprint**, proof, reproduction proof, repro proof *and* repro (*both informal*), second edition; photostatic copy, Photostat (*trademark*), stat (*informal*); mimeograph copy, Ditto copy (*trademark*), hectograph copy, xerographic copy, Xerox copy (*trademark*), or Xerox (*trademark*); **facsimile**, fax; **photograph**, positive, negative, print, enlargement, contact print, photocopy

6 **cast**, casting; mould, **moulding**, die, stamp, seal

7 **reflection**, reflexion, reflex; **shadow**, silhouette, outline *see* 211.2; **echo**

verbs

8 **to copy, reproduce**, replicate, **duplicate**; clone; reduplicate; **transcribe**; trace; double; triplicate, quadruplicate, etc; back up; manifold (*old*), multigraph, mimeograph, mimeo, Photostat (*trademark*), stat (*informal*), facsimile, fax (*informal*), hectograph, Xerox (*trademark*); microcopy, microfilm; photocopy

adverbs

9 in duplicate, in triplicate, etc

785 MODEL
thing copied

nouns

1 **model, pattern, standard, criterion,** classic example, rule, mirror, paradigm; showpiece, showplace; **original,** urtext, *locus classicus* (*Latin*); **type, prototype,** antetype, **archetype,** genotype, biotype, type specimen, type species; **precedent**

2 **example,** exemplar; **representative,** type, symbol, emblem, exponent; **exemplification,** illustration, demonstration, explanation; **instance,** relevant instance, **case,** typical example *or* case, case in point, object lesson

3 **sample, specimen;** piece, taste, swatch; instance, for-instance (*informal*)

4 **ideal,** beau ideal, ego ideal, ideal type, acme, highest *or* perfect *or* best type; cynosure, apotheosis, idol; **shining example,** role model, **hero, superhero; model,** the very model, role model, mirror, paragon, epitome,
"The glass of fashion and the mould of form, The observ'd of all observers"—SHAKESPEARE; cult figure

5 artist's model, dressmaker's model, photographer's model, mannequin, supermodel; dummy, lay figure; clay model, wood model, pilot model, mock-up, maquette

6 **mould, form** *see* 262, cast, template, matrix, negative; **die,** punch, stamp, intaglio, seal, mint; last, shoe last

verbs

7 **to set an example,** set the pace, lead the way; **exemplify,** epitomize, fit the pattern; **emulate,** follow, hold up as a model, model oneself on

adjectives

8 **model, exemplary,** precedential, typical, paradigmatic, representative, standard, normative, classic; ideal

9 **prototypal,** prototypic, prototypical, archetypal, archetypic, archetypical, antitypic, antitypical

786 DISSIMILARITY

nouns

1 **dissimilarity,** unsimilarity; **dissimilitude,** dissemblance, **unresemblance; unlikeness,** unsameness, unrelatedness; **disparity,** diversity, divergence, gap, **contrast, difference** *see* 779; nonuniformity *see* 781; incomparability, incomparableness, uncomparability, uncomparableness, incommensurability, incommensurableness, uncommensurability, uncommensurableness; culture gap; **disguise,** dissimilation, camouflage, masking; cosmetics; poor imitation, bad likeness *or* copy, botched copy, mere caricature *or* counterfeit

verbs

2 **to not resemble, bear no resemblance,** not look like, **not compare with; differ** *see* 779.5; have little *or* nothing in common

3 to disguise, dissimilate, camouflage; do a cosmetic job on; vary *see* 851.6

adjectives

4 **dissimilar,** unsimilar, unresembling, unresemblant, unrelated; **unlike, unalike,** unidentical; **disparate,** diverse, divergent, **contrasting, different** *see* 779.7; nonuniform *see* 781.3; scarcely like, hardly like, a bit *or* mite different; **off,** a bit on the off side, offbeat (*informal*); unmatched, odd, counter, out

5 **nothing like,** not a bit alike, not a bit of it, **nothing of the sort,** nothing of the kind, something else, something else again (*informal*), different as night from day, quite another thing, cast in a different mould, not the same thing at all; not so you could tell it *and* not that you would know it *and* **far from it** *and* far other (*all informal*), a far cry; way off, away off, a mile off, way out, no such thing, chalk and cheese;
"no more like than an apple to an oyster"—SIR THOMAS MORE

6 **uncomparable,** not comparable, not to be compared, not capable of comparison, incomparable; incommensurable, uncommensurable, uncommensurate, incommensurate

adverbs

7 **dissimilarly, differently** *see* 779.10, with a difference, disparately, contrastingly

787 AGREEMENT

nouns

1 **agreement, accord** *see* 455, accordance; **concord,** concordance; **harmony, cooperation** *see* 450, peace *see* 464, *rapport* (*French*), concert, consort, concinnity, **consonance,** unisonance, **unison,** union, chorus, oneness; **correspondence,** coincidence, intersection, overlap, parallelism, symmetry, tally, equivalence *see* 777.1; congeniality, compatibility, affinity; **conformity,** conformance, conformation, uniformity *see* 780; congruity, congruence, congruency; **consistency,** self-consistency, coherence; synchronism, sync (*informal*), timing; **assent** *see* 332

2 **understanding,** entente; mutual *or* cordial understanding, consortium, *entente cordiale* (*French*); **compact** *see* 437

3 (*general agreement*) consensus, consentaneity, consentaneousness, *consensus omnium* (*Latin,* consent of all), *and consensus gentium* (*Latin,* consent of the people), sense, **unanimity** *see* 332.5; **likemindedness,** meeting *or* intersection *or* confluence of minds, sense of the meeting

4 **adjustment, adaptation,** mutual adjustment, **compromise,** coaptation, arbitration, arbitrament; **regulation,** attunement, harmonization, **coordination,** accommodation, squaring, integration, assimilation; reconciliation, reconcilement, conciliation, synchronization; consensus-building *or* seeking

5 **fitness** *or* fittedness, **suitability, appropriateness,** propriety, admissibility; **aptness,** aptitude, qualification; **relevance** *see* 774.4, felicity, appositeness, applicability

verbs

6 **to agree, accord** see 455.2, **harmonize, concur** see 332.9, have no problem with, go along with (*informal*), **cooperate** see 450.3, **correspond, conform**, coincide, parallel, intersect, overlap, **match**, tally, register, lock, interlock, square, dovetail, jibe (*informal*); **be consistent**, cohere, stand *or* hold *or* hang together, fall in with, fit together, chime, chime with, chime in; **assent** see 332.8, come to an agreement see 332.10, be of one *or* the same *or* like mind, see eye to eye, sing in chorus, have a meeting of minds, be on the same wavelength, climb on the bandwagon; **go together**, go with, conform with, be uniform with, square with, sort *or* assort with, be consistent with, register with, answer *or* respond to

7 (*make agree*) **to harmonize**, coordinate, bring into line, accord, make uniform see 780.4, equalize see 789.6, similarize, assimilate, homologize; **adjust, set**, regulate, fine-tune, **accommodate, reconcile**, synchronize, sync (*informal*); adapt, fit, tailor, measure, proportion, adjust to, trim to, cut to, make to measure, gear to, key to; fix, **rectify**, true, true up, right, set right, make plumb; **tune**, attune, put in tune

8 **to suit**, fit, suit *or* fit to a T *or* tee, fit like a glove, fit like a second skin, **qualify, do**, serve, answer, be OK (*informal*), do the job *and* do the trick *and* fit the bill *and* fill the bill *and* cut the mustard (*all informal*)

adjectives

9 **agreeing, in agreement; in accord, concurring**, positive, affirmative, in rapport, *en rapport* (*French*), **in harmony**, in accordance, in sync (*informal*), **at one**, of one *or* the same *or* like mind, **like-minded**, consentient, consentaneous, **unanimous** see 332.15, unisonous *or* unisonant; **harmonious**, accordant, **concordant**, consonant; **consistent**, self-consistent; uniform, coherent, conformable, of a piece, equivalent, **coinciding** see 777.8, coincident, corresponding *or* correspondent; answerable, reconcilable; commensurate, proportionate; **congruous**, congruent; **agreeable**, congenial, compatible, cooperating *or* cooperative see 450.5, coexisting *or* coexistent, symbiotic; **synchronized**, synchronous, synchronic

10 **apt, apposite, appropriate, suitable**; applicable, relevant, likely, sortable, seasonable, opportune; **fitting**, befitting, **suiting**, becoming; **fit**, fitted, qualified, **suited**, adapted, geared, tailored, tailor-made, dovetailing, meshing; **right**, just right, well-chosen, **pat**, happy, felicitous, just what the doctor ordered (*informal*); to the point, to the purpose, *ad rem* (*Latin*), *à propos* (*French*), **apropos**, on the button (*informal*), spot-on (*informal*)

adverbs

11 **in step**, in concert, **in unison**, in chorus, in tune, **in phase**, in line, in conformity, in keeping, hand in glove, just right; with it (*informal*); **unanimously, as one, with one voice, harmoniously**, concordantly, consonantly, in synchronization, in sync (*informal*), **by consensus**; agreeably, congenially, compatibly; fittingly

prepositions

12 in agreement with, together with, with, right with, in there with, right in there with; in line with, in keeping with; together on

phrases

13 that's it, that's the thing, that's just the thing, that's the very thing, that's the idea *and* that's the ticket (*both informal*); right on (*informal*); touché

788 DISAGREEMENT

nouns

1 **disagreement, discord**, discordance *or* discordancy; **disaccord** see 456, disaccordance, inaccordance; disunity, disunion; **disharmony**, unharmoniousness; dissonance, dissidence; **jarring**, clashing; **difference** see 779, **variance**, divergence, diversity; **disparity**, discrepancy, inequality; antagonism, **opposition** see 451, **conflict**, controversy, faction, oppugnancy, repugnance, dissension see 456.3, argumentation see 934.4; **dissent** see 333, negation see 335, contradiction

2 **inconsistency, incongruity**, asymmetry, inconsonance, incoherence; **incompatibility**, irreconcilability, incommensurability; disproportion, disproportionateness, nonconformity *or* unconformity, nonconformability *or* unconformability, heterogeneity, heterodoxy, unorthodoxy, heresy; self-contradiction, paradox, antinomy, oxymoron, **ambiguity** see 539.2, ambivalence, equivocality, equivocalness, mixed message *or* signal

3 **unfitness, inappropriateness, unsuitability**, impropriety; **inaptness**, inaptitude, **inappositeness, irrelevance** *or* irrelevancy, infelicity, uncongeniality, inapplicability, inadmissibility; abnormality, anomaly; **maladjustment**, misjoining, misjoinder; mismatch, mismatchment; misalliance, *mésalliance* (*French*)

4 **misfit, nonconformist**, individualist, maverick, inner-directed person, oddball (*informal*), queer fish (*informal*); **freak**, sport, anomaly; dissident, dissenter, naysayer, crosspatch; a fish out of water, a square peg in a round hole (*informal*)

verbs

5 **to disagree, differ** see 779.5, vary, not see eye-to-eye, be at cross-purposes, **disaccord** see 456.8, **conflict**, clash, **jar**, jangle, jostle, collide, square off, cross swords, break, break off; **mismatch**, mismate, mismarry, misally; **dissent** see 333.4, agree to disagree, object, **negate** see 335.3, **contradict**, counter; be *or* march out of step, march to a different tune,
"hear a different drummer"—THOREAU

adjectives

6 **disagreeing, differing** see 779.7, **discordant** see 456.15, disaccordant; dissonant, dissident; **inharmonious**, unharmonious, disharmonious; discrepant, disproportionate; divergent, variant; at variance, **at odds**, in conflict, at war, at daggers drawn, at opposite poles, at loggerheads, at cross-purposes; **hostile**, antipathetic, antagonistic, repugnant; inaccordant, out of accord; **jarring**, clashing, grating, jangling; **contradictory, contrary**, contrarious; **disagreeable**, cross, cranky *and* ornery (*both US & Canadian informal*), negative, uncongenial, incompatible; immiscible (*chemistry*)

7 **inappropriate, inapt**, unapt, inapposite, misplaced, **irrelevant**, malapropos, *mal à propos* (*French*); **unsuited**, ill-suited; **unfitted**, ill-fitted; **maladjusted**, unadapted, ill-adapted; ill-sorted, ill-assorted, ill-chosen; ill-matched, ill-mated, mismatched, mismated, mismarried, misallied; **unfit**, inept, unqualified; unfitting, unbefitting; **unsuitable**, improper, **unbecoming**, unseemly; infelicitous, inapplicable, inadmissible; **unseasonable, untimely**, ill-timed; **out of place**, out of line, out of keeping, out of character, out of proportion, out of joint, out of tune, out of time, out of season, out of its element

8 **inconsistent, incongruous, inconsonant**, inconsequent, incoherent, **incompatible**, irreconcilable; incommensurable, incommensurate; disproportionate, out of proportion, self-contradictory, paradoxical, oxymoronic, **absurd**; **abnormal**, anomalous

9 **nonconformist**, individualistic, inner-directed, perverse; **unorthodox**, heterodox, heretical

prepositions

10 **in disagreement with, against**, agin (*informal*), counter to, clean counter to, **contrary to**, in defiance of, in contempt of, in opposition to, in conflict with; out of line with, not in keeping with

word elements

11 contra–, counter–, dis–, ill–, mal–, mis–

789 EQUALITY

nouns

1 **equality, parity**, egalitarianism, par, equation, identity *see* 777.1; equivalence *or* equivalency, convertibility, **correspondence**, parallelism, equipollence, coequality; **likeness**, levelness, evenness, coextension; **balance**, poise, equipoise, **equilibrium**, equiponderance; symmetry, proportion; level playing field; **justice** *see* 649, equity

2 **equating, equation; equalizing**, equilibration, evening, evening up; coordination, integration, accommodation, adjustment; positive discrimination, affirmative action, equal opportunity, fair do's (*informal*), fair crack of the whip (*informal*), fair shake of the dice *and* fair go (*both Australian informal*)

3 **the same** *see* 777.3; **tie, draw**, dead heat, stalemate, deadlock, impasse, neck-and-neck race, photo finish, even money, tied score, level pegging; a distinction without a difference, six of one and half a dozen of the other, Tweedledum and Tweedledee

4 **equal, match**, mate, twin, fellow, **like, equivalent**, opposite number, counterpart, answer (*informal*), vis à vis, equipollent, coequal, parallel, ditto (*informal*); **peer**, compeer, colleague, peer group

verbs

5 **to equal, match, rival, correspond**, be even-steven, be level pegging, be tantmount to, be equal to; **keep pace with, keep step with, run abreast; amount to**, come to, come down to, come up to, run to, reach, touch; **measure up to**, come up to, match up with; be on a level with, **balance, parallel**, ditto (*informal*); break even (*informal*); **tie, draw**

6 **to equalize; equate**; equipoise; **even**, equal out, even up, even off, square, level, level out, level off; **balance**, strike a balance, poise, balance out, balance the accounts, balance the books, make both ends meet; **compensate**, make up for, counterpoise; countervail, counterbalance, cancel out; coordinate, integrate, proportion; fit, accommodate, adjust

adjectives

7 **equal, equalized**, like, **alike**, evenly matched, **even**, level, par, **on a par**, level pegging, at par, at parity, commensurate, proportionate; on the same level, on the same plane, on the same *or* equal footing; on terms of equality, equal opportunities, **on even** *or* **equal terms**, on even ground; on a level, on a level playing field, on a footing, in the same boat; **square**, quits, zero-sum, even-steven (*informal*); half-and-half, **fifty-fifty; drawn, tied**, neck-and-neck, nip and tuck, too close to call, deadlocked, stalemated

8 **equivalent, tantamount**, equiparant, equipollent, coequal, coordinate; **identical** *see* 777.7; corresponding *or* correspondent; convertible, much the same, one and the same, as broad as long, neither more nor less, **all one**, all the same, neither here nor there, nothing to choose between

9 **balanced, poised**, apoise, **on an even keel**; equibalanced, equipoised, equiponderant *or* equiponderous

10 **equisized**, equidimensional, equiproportional, equispaced; equiangular, isogonic, isometric; equilateral, equisided

adverbs

11 **equally, correspondingly, proportionately**, equivalently, **evenly; identically** *see* 777.9; without distinction, indifferently; to the same degree, *ad eundem* (*Latin*); as, so; as well; to all intents and purposes, other things being equal, *ceteris paribus* (*Latin*); as much as to say

12 **to a standoff** (*informal*), to a tie *or* draw

word elements

13 co–, equi–, aequi–, homal–, is–, pari–

790 INEQUALITY

nouns

1 **inequality, disparity, unevenness, contrariety** *see* 778, **difference** *see* 779; **irregularity**, nonuniformity *see* 781, heterogeneity; **disproportion**, asymmetry; **unbalance**, imbalance, disequilibrium, overbalance, inclination of the balance, tipping the scales, overcompensation, tippiness; **inadequacy**, insufficiency, shortcoming; **odds**, handicap;

injustice, inequity, unfair discrimination, prejudice, second-class citizenship, untouchability

verbs

2 to **unequalize**, disproportion

3 to **unbalance**, disbalance, disequilibrate, overbalance, tip the scales, overcompensate, **throw off balance**, upset, skew

adjectives

4 **unequal**, disparate, **uneven**; **irregular** *see* 781.3; disproportionate, **out of proportion**, skew, skewed, asymmetric *or* asymmetrical; mismatched *or* ill-matched, ill-sorted *or* ill-assorted; **inadequate, insufficient**

5 **unbalanced, ill-balanced**, overbalanced, off-balance, tippy, listing, heeling, leaning, canted, top-heavy; **lopsided**, askew, awry, cockeyed (*informal*), skewwhiff (*informal*); **unstable**, unsteady, tender (*nautical*)

adverbs

6 **unequally**, disparately, disproportionately, variously, **unevenly**; nonuniformly *see* 781.4

791 WHOLE

nouns

1 **whole, totality, entirety**, collectivity; complex; integration, embodiment; **unity, integrity, wholeness**; organic unity, oneness; integer

2 **total, sum**, sum total, sum and substance, **the amount**, whole *or* gross amount, grand total

3 **all, the whole, the entirety, everything**, all the above *or* all of the above (*both informal*), the aggregate, the assemblage, one and all, all and sundry, each and every (*informal*); **package**, set, complement, package deal; **the lot**, the corpus, all she wrote (*US*), **the ensemble; be-all**, be-all and end-all, beginning and end, "alpha and omega"—Bible, A to Z, A to izzard, the whole range *or* spectrum, length and breadth; everything but the kitchen sink (*informal*)

4 (*informal terms*) **whole caboodle, the kit and caboodle, whole kit and caboodle**, whole bit *or* shtick, whole bunch, whole mess, whole boiling, whole megillah, **whole shooting match**, whole hog, whole animal (*old*), **whole deal, whole shebang**, whole works, the works, whole show

5 **wholeness**, totality, **completeness** *see* 793, **unity, fullness**, inclusiveness, exhaustiveness, comprehensiveness; holism, holistic *or* total approach; universality

6 **major part, best part**, better part, **most; majority**, generality, plurality; **bulk, mass**, body, main body; **lion's share; substance**, gist, meat, essence, thrust, gravamen

verbs

7 to **form** *or* **make a whole**, constitute a whole; **integrate**, unite, form a unity

8 to **total, amount to, come to, run to** *or* **into**, mount up to, add up to, tot *or* tot up to (*informal*), tote *or* tote up to (*informal*), reckon up to (*informal*), aggregate to; aggregate, unitize; **number, comprise, contain**, encompass

adjectives

9 (*not partial*) **whole, total, entire**, aggregate, gross, all; integral, integrated; **one**, one and indivisible; **inclusive, all-inclusive, exhaustive**, comprehensive, omnibus, all-embracing; holistic; universal

10 **intact**, untouched, undamaged *see* 1001.8, all in one piece (*informal*), unimpaired, virgin, pristine, unspoiled

11 **undivided**, uncut, unsevered, unclipped, uncropped, unshorn; **undiminished**, unreduced, complete

12 **unabridged**, uncondensed, unexpurgated, unbowdlerized

adverbs

13 (*not partially*) **wholly, entirely**, all; **totally**, *in toto* (*Latin*), from start to finish, from A to Z, from A to izzard, across the board; **altogether, all put together**, in its entirety, *tout ensemble* (*French*); **in all**, on all counts, in all respects, at large; **as a whole, in the aggregate**, in the lump, in the gross, in bulk, in the mass, *en masse* (*French*), *en bloc* (*French*); **collectively, corporately**, bodily, in a body, as a body; lock, stock, and barrel; hook, line, and sinker

14 **on the whole**, in the long run, over the long haul, **all in all**, to all intents and purposes, on balance, **by and large**, in the main, **mainly, mostly, chiefly**, substantially, essentially, effectually, **for the most part**, almost entirely, for all practical purposes, **virtually**; approximately, nearly, all but

word elements

15 pan–, pant–, panta–, coen–

792 PART

nouns

1 **part, portion, fraction**; percentage; **division** *see* 801.1; **share**, parcel, dole, quota, piece *or* piece of the action (*informal*); cut *and* slice (*both informal*); **section**, sector, **segment**; quarter, quadrant; **item**, detail, particular; instalment; **subdivision**, subset, subgroup, subspecies; detachment, contingent; **cross section**, sample, random sample, sampling; **component** *see* 795.2, module, constituent, ingredient; **adjunct** *see* 254; **remainder** *see* 256

2 (*part of writing*) section, front *or* back matter, prelims, subsidiaries, prologue, epilogue, foreword, preface, introduction, afterword, text, chapter, verse, article; sentence, clause, phrase, segment, string, constituent, paragraph, passage; number, book, fascicle; sheet, folio, page, signature, gathering

3 **piece, particle, bit, scrap** *see* 248.3, bite, **fragment, morsel, crumb**, shard, potsherd, snatch, snack; **cut**, cutting, clip, clipping, paring, shaving, rasher, snip, snippet, chip, slice, collop, dollop, scoop; **tatter, shred**, stitch; **splinter**, sliver; **shiver, smithereen** (*informal*); lump, gob (*informal*), gobbet, hunk, chunk, wodge; **stump**, butt, end, butt-end, fag-end, tail end; modicum *see* 248.2, moiety; sound bite, outtake

4 member, **organ**; appendage; **limb; branch**, bough,
twig, sprig, spray, switch; runner, tendril; **off-shoot**,
ramification, scion, spur; **arm** *see* 905.5, **leg**, tail;
hand *see* 474.4; **wing**, pinion; lobe, lobule,
hemisphere

5 **dose, portion**, tot; slug *and* shot *and* nip *and* snifter
and snorter *or* snort *and* dram (*all informal*)

verbs

6 to **separate**, apportion, share, share out, distribute,
cut, cut up, slice, slice up, divide *see* 801.18;
analyse *see* 800.6

adjectives

7 **partial**, part; **fractional**, sectional, componential;
segmentary, segmental, modular; **fragmentary**;
incomplete *see* 794.4, open-ended

adverbs

8 **partly, partially**, part, **in part**
9 **piece by piece, bit by bit**, part by part, **little by
little**, inch by inch, foot by foot, drop by drop;
piecemeal, inchmeal, by inchmeal; **by degrees**, by
inches; **by** *or* **in snatches**, by *or* in instalments, in
lots, in small doses, in driblets, in dribs and drabs;
in detail

word elements

10 organo–; chir–; ali–, pter–, pterus–, pteryg–

793 COMPLETENESS

nouns

1 **completeness, totality; wholeness** *see* 791.5,
entireness, **entirety; unity, integrity**, integrality,
undividedness, intactness, untouchedness,
unbrokenness; solidity, solidarity; **thoroughness**,
exhaustiveness, unstintedness, inclusiveness,
comprehensiveness, universality; pervasiveness,
ubiquity *or* ubiquitousness, omnipresence; **universe**,
cosmos, plenum

2 **fullness**, full; **amplitude, plenitude**; impletion,
repletion, plethora; saturation, saturation point,
satiety, congestion

3 **full measure, fill**, full house,
"good measure, pressed down, and shaken together,
and running over"—BIBLE; **load, capacity,
complement**, lading, **charge**; the whole bit
(*informal*); bumper, brimmer; bellyful (*informal*),
skinful *or* mouthful (*both informal*); **crush, cram**
(*informal*), jam

4 **completion, fulfilment, consummation**,
culmination, perfection, realization, actualization,
accomplishment *see* 407, topping-off, topping-out,
closure

5 **limit, end** *see* 819, **extremity**, extreme, **acme**,
apogee, climax, **maximum**, max (*informal*), ceiling,
peak, summit, **pinnacle**, crown, top, zenith;
utmost, uttermost, utmost extent, highest degree,
nth degree *or* power, *ne plus ultra* (*Latin*); **all, the
whole** *see* 791.3, 4

verbs

6 (*make whole*) to **complete**, bring to completion *or*
fruition, mature; **fill in, fill out**, piece out, top off,

top out, eke *or* eke out, round out; **make up**, make
good, replenish, refill; **accomplish** *see* 407.4, fulfil

7 to **fill, charge, load**, lade, freight, weight; **stuff,
wad**, pad, **pack**, crowd, **cram**, jam, jam-pack, ram
in, chock up, pun; **fill up**, fill to the brim, brim, top
up *or* top off, fill to overflowing, fill the measure of;
supercharge, saturate, satiate, congest; overfill *see*
992.15, make burst at the seams, surfeit

8 (*be thorough*) to **go to all lengths**, go all out, go
the limit (*informal*), go the whole way, **go the
whole hog** (*informal*), cover a lot of ground, make a
big deal of *and* do with a vengeance (*both informal*),
see it through (*informal*), follow through *or* up,
bring to a conclusion; leave nothing undone, use
every trick in the book (*informal*); **move heaven
and earth, leave no stone unturned**

adjectives

9 **complete, whole, total**, global, **entire**, intact, solid;
full, full-fledged, full-dress, **full-scale**; full-grown,
mature, matured, ripe, developed; **uncut**,
unabbreviated, undiminished, unexpurgated,
unbowdlerized

10 **thorough, thoroughgoing**, thoroughpaced,
exhaustive, intensive, broad-based, wall-to-wall
(*informal*), house-to-house *and* door-to-door (*both
informal*), A-to-Z, comprehensive, all-embracing, all-
encompassing, omnibus, radical, sweeping;
pervasive, all-pervading, ubiquitous, omnipresent,
**universal; unmitigated, unqualified,
unconditional**, unrestricted, unreserved, **all-out**,
wholesale, whole-hog (*informal*); **out-and-out,
through-and-through**, outright, downright, straight;
congenital, born, **consummate**, unmitigated,
unalloyed, perfect, veritable, egregious, deep-dyed,
dyed-in-the-wool; **utter, absolute, total; sheer**,
clear, clean, **pure**, plumb (*informal*), **plain**, regular
(*informal*)

11 **full, filled, replete**, plenary, capacity, flush, round;
brimful, brimming; **chock-full**, chock-a-block,
chocker (*informal*), chuck-full, **cram-full**, topfull;
jam-full, jam-packed, overcrowded; stuffed,
overstuffed, **packed, crammed**, *farci* (*French*);
swollen *see* 259.13, bulging, bursting, bursting at the
seams, ready to burst, full to bursting, fit to bust
(*informal*); packed tight, packed like sardines *or*
herrings; packed out, standing room only *or* SRO;
saturated, satiated, soaked; congested; overfull *see*
992.20, surfeited

12 **fraught**, freighted, **laden, loaded, charged**,
burdened; heavy-laden; full-laden, full-fraught, full-
charged, super-charged

13 **completing, fulfilling**, filling; completive *or*
completory, consummative *or* consummatory,
culminative, perfective; **complementary**,
complemental

adverbs

14 **completely, totally**, globally, **entirely, wholly,
fully**, integrally, roundly, **altogether**, hundred
percent, **exhaustively**, inclusively, comprehensively,
bag and baggage *and* lock, stock, and barrel (*both
informal*); **unconditionally**, unrestrictedly,
unreservedly, with no strings attached, no ifs, ands,

or buts; **one and all**; outright, *tout à fait* (*French*); **thoroughly**, inside out (*informal*); in full, in full measure; to the hilt

15 **absolutely**, **perfectly**, **quite**, right, stark, clean, sheer, plumb (*informal*), plain; irretrievably, unrelievedly, irrevocably

16 **utterly**, **to the utmost**, all the way, **all out**, flat out, *à outrance* (*French*), *à toute outrance* (*French*), hammer and tongs *and* tooth and nail (*both informal*), **to the full**, **to the limit**, to the max (*informal*), to the backbone, to the marrow, to the nth degree *or* power, to the sky *or* skies, to the top of one's bent, to a fare-thee-well, to a fare-you-well *or* fare-ye-well, to beat the band (*informal*), with a vengeance, all hollow (*informal*)

17 **throughout**, **all over**, overall, **inside and out**, **through and through**; through thick and thin, down to the ground (*informal*), from the ground up, from the word 'go' (*informal*); **to the end** *or* **bitter end**, to the death; **at full length**, *in extenso* (*Latin*), *ad infinitum* (*Latin*); every inch, every whit, every bit; root and branch, head and shoulders, heart and soul; to the brim, to the hilt, neck deep, up to the ears, up to the eyes; **in every respect**, in all respects, you name it (*informal*); **on all counts**, at all points, for good and all

18 **from beginning to end**, **from start to finish**, from end to end, **from first to last**, **from A to Z**, from cover to cover; **from top to bottom**, *de fond en comble* (*French*); from top to toe, **from head to foot**, *a capite ad calcem* (*Latin*), cap-a-pie; from stem to stern, from clew to earing, fore and aft; from soup to nuts (*informal*),
ab ovo usque ad mala—Horace (*Latin*, from eggs to apples)

word elements

19 hol–, integri–, pan–, per–, tel–, teleut–

794 INCOMPLETENESS

nouns

1 **incompleteness**, incompletion; **deficiency**, defectiveness, imperfection, **inadequacy**; underdevelopment, hypoplasia, **immaturity**, callowness, arrestment; **sketchiness**, scrappiness, patchiness; short measure *or* weight

2 (*part lacking*) **deficiency**, want, **lack**, **need**, **deficit**, defect, **shortage**, shortfall; ullage, outage, wantage (*US*); defalcation, arrearage; **omission**, gap, hiatus, hole, vacuum, break, lacuna, discontinuity, interval

verbs

3 **to lack** *see* 991.7, want, want for; fall short *see* 910.2; be arrested, underdevelop, undergrow

adjectives

4 **incomplete**, **uncompleted**, **deficient**, defective, unfinished, imperfect, unperfected, **inadequate**; **undeveloped**, underdeveloped, undergrown, stunted, hypoplastic, **immature**, callow, infant, arrested, embryonic, **wanting**, **lacking**, needing, missing, **partial**, part, failing; in default, in arrears; **in short**

supply, scanty; **short**, scant, shy (*US informal*); **sketchy**, patchy, scrappy

5 **mutilated**, garbled, hashed, **mangled**, **butchered**, docked, hacked, lopped, truncated, castrated, cut short

adverbs

6 **incompletely**, **partially**, by halves, by *or* in half measures, in instalments, in *or* by bits and pieces; **deficiently**, imperfectly, inadequately

word elements

7 semi–, parti–

795 COMPOSITION
manner of being composed

nouns

1 **composition**, **constitution**, **construction**, **formation**, fabrication, fashioning, shaping, organization; **embodiment**, incorporation, incarnation; **make**, **makeup**, setup (*informal*); **building**, build-up, structure, structuring, shaping-up; **assembly**, assemblage, putting *or* piecing together; synthesis, syneresis; **combination** *see* 804; **compound** *see* 796.5; **junction** *see* 799.1; **mixture** *see* 796

2 **component**, **constituent**, **ingredient**, integrand, makings *and* fixings (*both informal*), **element**, **factor**, **part** *see* 792, player, module, part and parcel; appurtenance, adjunct *see* 254; **feature**, aspect, speciality, circumstance, detail, item

verbs

3 **to compose**, **constitute**, construct, fabricate; **incorporate**, embody, incarnate; **form**, **organize**, structure, shape, shape up; **enter into**, go into, go to make up; **make**, **make up**, build, build up, assemble, put *or* piece together; **consist of**, be a feature of, form a part of, combine *or* unite in, merge in; **consist**, be made up of, be constituted of, contain; **synthesize**; **combine** *see* 804.3; join *see* 799.5; **mix**

adjectives

4 **composed of**, formed of, **made of**, made up of, made out of, consisting of; composing, comprising, constituting, including, inclusive of, containing, incarnating, embodying, subsuming; contained in, embodied in

5 **component**, constituent, modular, integrant, integral; **formative**, elementary

796 MIXTURE

nouns

1 **mixture**, mixing, blending; **admixture**, composition, commixture, immixture, intermixture, **mingling**, minglement, commingling *or* comminglement, intermingling *or* interminglement, interlarding *or* interlardment; **eclecticism**, syncretism; **pluralism**, melting pot, multiculturism *or* multiculturalism, ethnic *or* racial *or* cultural diversity; **fusion**, interfusion, conflation;

amalgamation, **integration**, alloyage, coalescence; **merger, combination** *see* 804

2 imbuement, **impregnation, infusion**, suffusion, decoction, infiltration, instilment, instillation, permeation, pervasion, interpenetration, penetration; saturation, steeping, soaking, marination

3 adulteration, corruption, contamination, denaturalization, **pollution, doctoring** (*informal*); fortifying, lacing, spiking (*informal*); **dilution**, cutting (*informal*), watering, watering down; debasement, bastardizing

4 crossbreeding, crossing, interbreeding, miscegenation; **hybridism**, hybridization, mongrelism, mongrelization

5 compound, mixture, admixture, intermixture, immixture, commixture, **composite, blend**, meld, composition, confection, concoction, **combination**, combo (*informal*), ensemble, marriage; amalgam, alloy; paste, magma

6 hotchpotch, hodgepodge (*US & Canadian*), hotchpot; **medley, miscellany**, mélange, pastiche, *pasticcio* (*Italian*), **conglomeration, assortment**, assemblage, mixed bag, ragbag, grab bag (*US*), olio, *olla podrida* (*Spanish*), scramble, **jumble**, mixter-maxter (*Scottish*), mingle-mangle, box (*Australian & NZ*), **mix**, mishmash, **mess**, can of worms (*informal*), dog's breakfast (*informal*), mare's nest, hash, patchwork, salad, gallimaufry, salmagundi, **potpourri**, stew, sauce, slurry, omnium-gatherum, Noah's ark, **odds and ends**, oddments, odds and sods (*informal*), all sorts, everything but the kitchen sink (*informal*), "God's plenty"—DRYDEN, broad spectrum, what you will

7 (*slight admixture*) **tinge, tincture, touch, dash, smack**, taint, tinct, tint, **trace**, vestige, hint, inkling, intimation, soupçon, suspicion, suggestion, whiff, thought, shade, tempering; sprinkling, seasoning, sauce, spice, infusion

8 hybrid, crossbreed, cross, mixed-blood, mixblood, **half-breed**, half-bred, half blood, half-caste; **mongrel**; *ladino* (*Spanish*); mustee *or* mestee, *mestizo* (*Spanish*), *mestiza* (*Spanish feminine*), *métis* (*French*), *métisse* (*French feminine*); Eurasian; **mulatto**, high yellow (*informal*), quadroon, quintroon, octoroon; sambo, zambo, *cafuso* (*Brazilian Portuguese*), Cape Coloured (*South African*), griqua (*South African*); griffe; zebrule, zebrass, cattalo, mule, hinny, liger, tigon; tangelo, citrange, plumcot, minneola, Ugli (*Trademark*)

9 mixer, blender, beater, agitator, food processor; cement mixer, eggbeater, churn; homogenizer, colloid mill, emulsifier; crucible, melting pot

verbs

10 to mix, admix, commix, immix, **intermix, mingle,** bemingle, commingle, immingle, **intermingle,** interlace, interweave, intertwine, interlard; syncretize; **blend,** interblend, stir in; **amalgamate, integrate,** alloy, coalesce, **fuse, merge,** meld, compound, compose, conflate, concoct; **combine** *see* 804.3; mix up, hash, stir up, **scramble,** conglomerate, shuffle, **jumble,** jumble up, mingle-mangle, throw *or* toss together; knead, work; homogenize, emulsify

11 to imbue, imbrue, **infuse**, suffuse, transfuse, breathe, **instil**, infiltrate, **impregnate, permeate,** pervade, penetrate, leaven; **tinge, tincture,** entincture, temper, colour, dye, flavour, season, dredge, besprinkle; **saturate**, steep, decoct, brew, brew up (*British & NZ informal*), mash (*northern dialect*), boil up (*Australian & NZ*), boil the billy (*Australian & NZ informal*)

12 to adulterate, corrupt, contaminate, **debase,** denaturalize, pollute, denature, bastardize, **tamper with,** doctor *and* doctor up (*both informal*); fortify, spike (*informal*), lace; **dilute,** cut (*informal*), water, water down (*informal*)

13 to hybridize, crossbreed, cross, interbreed, miscegenate, mongrelize

adjectives

14 mixed, mingled, blended, compounded, amalgamated; **combined** *see* 804.5; **composite,** compound, **complex,** many-sided, multifaceted, intricate; **conglomerate,** pluralistic, multiracial, multicultural, multiethnic, multinational, heterogeneous, varied, **miscellaneous,** medley, motley, dappled, patchy; promiscuous, indiscriminate, **scrambled, jumbled,** thrown together; half-and-half, fifty-fifty (*informal*); amphibious; equivocal, **ambiguous,** ambivalent, ironic; syncretic, eclectic

15 hybrid, mongrel, interbred, **crossbred,** crossed, cross; **half-breed,** half-bred, half-blooded, half-caste

16 miscible, mixable, assimilable, integrable

prepositions

17 among, amongst, 'mongst; **amid,** mid, amidst, midst, **in the midst of, in the thick of; with,** together with

797 SIMPLICITY
freedom from mixture or complexity

nouns

1 simplicity, purity, simpleness, **plainness,** no frills, starkness, severity; unmixedness, monism; **unadulteration,** unsophistication, unspoiledness, intactness, fundamentality, elementarity, primitiveness *or* primitivity, primariness; **singleness,** oneness, unity, integrity, homogeneity, uniformity *see* 780

2 simplification, streamlining, refinement, purification, distillation; **disentanglement,** disinvolvement; uncluttering, unscrambling, unsnarling, unknotting; stripping, stripping away *or* down, narrowing, confining, bracketing; **analysis** *see* 800

3 oversimplification, oversimplicity, oversimplifying; **simplism,** reductivism; intellectual childishness *or* immaturity, conceptual crudity

verbs

4 to simplify, streamline, **reduce,** reduce to elements *or* essentials, factorize; purify, refine, distil; strip, strip down; narrow, confine, bracket, zero in (*informal*); oversimplify; **analyse** *see* 800.6

5 to disinvolve, disintricate, unmix, disembroil, **disentangle,** untangle, **unscramble, unsnarl,** unknot, untwist, unbraid, unweave, untwine, unwind, uncoil, unthread, **unravel**, ravel; **unclutter**, clarify, clear up, disambiguate, sort out, get to the core *or* nub *or* essence

adjectives

6 **simple, plain,** bare, bare-bones *and* no-frills (*both informal*), mere; **single,** uniform, homogeneous, of a piece; **pure,** simon-pure, pure and simple; **essential,** elementary, indivisible, **primary,** primal, primitive, prime, pristine, **irreducible, fundamental,** basic; undifferentiable *or* undifferentiated, undifferenced, monolithic; **austere,** chaste, unadorned, uncluttered, spare, stark, severe; homely, homespun, grass-roots, bread-and-butter, vanilla *or* plain-vanilla (*both informal*), down-home *and* white-bread (*both US & Canadian informal*); beginning, entry-level

7 **unmixed, unmingled,** unblended, **uncombined,** uncompounded; unleavened; **unadulterated,** unspoiled, untouched, intact, virgin, uncorrupted, unsophisticated, unalloyed, untinged, undiluted, unfortified; **clear,** clarified, purified, refined, **distilled,** rectified; **neat, straight,** absolute, sheer, naked, bare

8 **uncomplicated, uninvolved,** incomplex, straightforward

9 **simplified,** streamlined, stripped down

10 **oversimplified,** oversimple; **simplistic,** reductive; intellectually childish *or* immature, conceptually crude

adverbs

11 **simply, plainly, purely;** merely, barely; **singly, solely,** only, **alone,** exclusively, just, simply and solely

word elements

12 hapl–

798 COMPLEXITY

nouns

1 **complexity, complication, involvement,** complexness, involution, convolution, tortuousness, Byzantinism, *chinoiserie* (*French*), tanglement, **entanglement,** perplexity, **intricacy,** intricateness, ramification, crabbedness, technicality, subtlety

2 **complex,** perplex (*informal*), **tangle,** tangled skein, **mess** *and* snafu *and* fuck-up (*all informal*), ravel, snarl, snarl-up; knot, Gordian knot; **maze,** meander, Chinese puzzle, **labyrinth;** webwork, mesh; **wilderness, jungle,** morass, quagmire; Heath Robinson device, Rube Goldberg contraption (*US & Canadian*), wheels within wheels; mare's nest, rat's nest, hurrah's nest (*nautical informal*), can of worms (*informal*), snake pit

verbs

3 **to complicate,** involve, **perplex,** ramify; **confound, confuse,** muddle, **mix up,** mess up *and* balls up *and* bollocks up *and* screw up *and* foul up *and* fuck up *and* bugger up *and* muck up *and* cock up *and* louse up (*all informal*), snafu (*US & Canadian informal*), implicate; **tangle,** entangle, embrangle, **snarl,** snarl up, ravel, knot, tie in knots

adjectives

4 **complex, complicated,** many-faceted, multifarious, ramified, perplexed, **confused,** confounded, **involved,** implicated, crabbed, **intricate,** elaborate, involuted, convoluted, multilayered, multilevel; **mixed-up,** ballsed up *and* bollocksed up *and* screwed up *and* loused up *and* fouled up *and* fucked up *and* mucked up *and* messed up *and* buggered up *and* cocked up (*all informal*), snafued (*US & Canadian informal*); **tangled,** entangled, tangly, embrangled, **snarled,** knotted, matted, twisted, ravelled; mazy, daedal, **labyrinthine,** labyrinthian, meandering; **devious,** roundabout, deep-laid, Byzantine, subtle

5 **inextricable,** irreducible, unknottable, unsolvable

799 JOINING

nouns

1 **joining, junction,** joinder, jointure, **connection, union,** unification, bond, bonding, connectedness *or* connectivity, conjunction, conjoining, conjugation, liaison, marriage, hookup (*informal*), splice, tie, tie-up *and* tie-in (*both informal*), knotting; merger, merging; symbiosis; **combination** *see* 804; conglomeration, **aggregation,** agglomeration, congeries; **coupling,** copulation, accouplement, coupledness, **bracketing,** yoking, pairing, splicing, wedding; **linking,** linkup, linkage, bridging, **concatenation,** chaining, articulation, agglutination; **meeting,** meeting place *or* point, confluence, convergence, concurrence, concourse, gathering, massing, clustering; communication, intercommunication, intercourse

2 **interconnection,** interjoinder, **interlinking,** interlocking, interdigitation; **interassociation,** interaffiliation

3 **fastening, attachment, affixation,** annexation; ligature, ligation, ligating; **binding,** bonding, gluing, sticking, tying, lashing, splicing, knotting, linking, trussing, girding, hooking, clasping, zipping, buckling, buttoning; knot (*see list*); adhesive *see* 802.4; splice, bond, fastener; **hook,** hitch; **clasp,** hasp, clip; **button,** popper, buckle, zip *or* zip fastener, zipper (*US & Canadian*), Velcro (*trademark*); lock, latch; **pin,** drawing pin, thumbtack (*US & Canadian*), panel pin, skewer, peg, nail, tack, staple, toggle, screw, bolt, rivet; hairgrip, kirby grip, bobby pin (*US, Canadian, Australian & NZ*), hair slide

4 **joint,** join, joining, **juncture, union, connection,** link, connecting link, **coupling, accouplement;** clinch, embrace; articulation (*anatomy and botany*), symphysis (*anatomy*); **pivot, hinge; knee; elbow; wrist; ankle; knuckle; hip; shoulder; neck,** cervix; ball-and-socket joint, pivot joint, hinged joint, gliding joint; toggle joint; connecting rod, tie rod; seam, suture, stitch, closure, mortise and tenon, mitre, butt, scarf, dovetail, rabbet, weld; boundary, interface

verbs

5 **to put together, join,** conjoin, **unite,** unify, bond, **connect,** associate, league, band, merge, **assemble,** accumulate; **join up,** become a part of, associate oneself, enter into, come aboard (*informal*); **gather,** mobilize, marshal, mass, amass, **collect,** conglobulate; **combine** *see* 804.3; **couple,** pair, accouple, copulate, conjugate, marry, wed, tie the knot (*informal*), get spliced *or* hitched (*informal*), **link,** link up, build bridges, yoke, knot, splice, tie, chain, bracket; **concatenate,** articulate, agglutinate; glue, tape, cement, solder, weld; **put together,** fix together, lay together, piece together, clap together, tack together, stick together, lump together, roll into one; bridge over *or* between, span; **include,** encompass, take in, cover, embrace, comprise

6 to **interconnect, interjoin,** intertie, interassociate, interaffiliate, **interlink,** interlock, interdigitate

7 to **fasten, fix, attach, affix,** annexe, put to, set to; graft, engraft; **secure,** anchor, moor; cement, knit, set, grapple, belay, **make fast;** clinch, clamp, cramp; tighten, trim, trice up, screw up; cinch *or* cinch up

8 to **hook,** hitch; **clasp,** hasp, clip, snap; **button,** buckle, zipper; lock, latch; **pin,** skewer, peg, nail, nail up, tack, staple, toggle, screw, bolt, rivet; **sew,** stitch; **wedge,** jam, stick; rabbet, butt, scarf, mortise, mitre, dovetail; batten, batten down; cleat; **hinge,** joint, articulate

9 to **bind, tie,** brace, truss, **lash,** leash, rope, strap, lace, wire, chain; **splice,** bend; **gird,** girt, belt, girth, girdle, band, cinch; **tie up,** bind up, do up; **wrap,** wrap up, bundle; shrink-wrap; **bandage,** bandage up, swathe, swaddle

10 to **yoke, hitch up,** hook up; harness, harness up; halter, bridle; saddle; tether, fetter

11 (*be joined*) to **join, connect, unite, meet,** meet up, link up, merge, converge, **come together;** communicate, intercommunicate; knit, grow together; cohere, adhere, hang *or* hold together, clinch, embrace

adjectives

12 **joint, combined,** joined, **conjoint,** conjunct, conjugate, corporate, compact, cooperative, cooperating; concurrent, coincident; inclusive, comprehensive

13 **joined, united, connected,** copulate, **coupled,** linked, knit, bridged, tight-knit, knitted, bracketed, associated, conjoined, incorporated, integrated, **merged,** gathered, assembled, accumulated, **collected; associated,** joined up, on board; **allied,** leagued, banded together; hand-in-hand, hand-in-glove, intimate; unseparated, undivided; **wedded,** matched, married, paired, yoked, mated; **tied, bound,** knotted, spliced, lashed

14 **fast, fastened, fixed,** secure, firm, close, tight, set; **bonded,** glued, cemented, taped; **jammed,** wedged, stuck, frozen, seized, seized up

15 **inseparable,** impartible, **indivisible,** undividable, indissoluble, inalienable, inseverable, bound up in *or* with

16 **joining, connecting,** meeting; **communicating,** intercommunicating; **connective,** connectional; conjunctive, combinative, combinatorial, copulative, linking, bridging, binding

17 jointed, articulate

adverbs

18 **jointly,** conjointly, corporately, **together; in common,** in partnership, mutually, in concord; **all together,** as one, in unison, in agreement, in harmony; concurrently, at once, at *or* in one fell swoop

19 **securely, firmly, fast,** tight; **inseparably,** indissolubly

20 **knots**

anchor knot	marling hitch
becket knot	Matthew Walker knot
Blackwall hitch	mesh knot
bow	midshipman's hitch
bowknot	netting knot
bowline	open hand knot
bowline knot	outside clinch
builder's knot	prolonge knot
carrick bend	reef knot
cat's-paw	reeving-line bend
clinch	rolling hitches
clove hitch	rope-yarn knot
cuckold's neck	round seizing
diamond knot	round turn and half hitch
double hitch	running bowline
Englishman's tie	running knot
figure-of-eight knot	sheepshank
fisherman's bend	Shelby knot
flat knot	shroud knot
Flemish knot	single knot
French shroud knot	slide knot
German knot	slipknot
granny knot	square knot
half crown	stevedore's knot
half hitch	stopper's knot
half-Windsor knot	studding-sail halyard bend
harness hitch	stunner hitch
hawser bend	surgeon's knot
hawser fastening	tack bend
heaving-line bend	timber knot *or* hitch
inside clinch	truckman's knot
lanyard knot	truelove knot
loop knot	wall knot
magnus hitch	weaver's knot *or* hitch
manrope knot	Windsor knot
marlinespike hitch	

800 ANALYSIS

nouns

1 **analysis,** analysation, **breakdown,** breaking down, breakup, breaking up; anatomy, anatomizing, dissection; separation, **division, subdivision,** segmentation, reduction to elements *or* parts; chemical analysis, **assay** *or* assaying, resolution, titration, docimasy (*old*), qualitative analysis, quantitative analysis, volumetric analysis, gravimetric analysis; ultimate analysis, proximate analysis; microanalysis, semimicroanalysis

2 **itemization,** enumeration, detailing, breakout, isolation; outlining, schematization, blocking, blocking out; resolution; scansion, parsing

3 **classification, categorization, sorting,** taxonomy, sorting out, sifting, sifting out, grouping, factoring,

winnowing, shakeout; **weighing, evaluation,** gauging, assessment, appraisal, **judgment** *see* 945

4 outline, structural outline, **plan,** scheme, schema, chart, flow chart, graph, process map; table, table of contents, index; **diagram,** block diagram, exploded view, **blueprint; catalogue,** *catalogue raisonné* (*French*)

5 analyst, analyser, examiner *see* 937.16; taxonomist

verbs

6 to analyse, break down, break up, anatomize, dissect, atomize, unitize; **divide, subdivide,** segment; assay, titrate; separate, make discrete, isolate, reduce, reduce to elements, resolve

7 to itemize, enumerate, factorize, number, detail, break out; **outline,** schematize, block out, diagram, graph, chart; resolve; scan, parse

8 to classify, class, **categorize,** catalogue, sort, sort out, sift, group, factor, winnow, thrash out; weigh, weigh up, **evaluate, judge,** gauge *see* 945.9, assess, appraise *see* 945.9

adjectives

9 analytical, analytic; segmental; classificatory, enumerative; schematic

adverbs

10 analytically, by parts *or* divisions *or* sections; by categories *or* types

801 SEPARATION

nouns

1 separation, disjunction, severalty, disjointure, disjointing, split-up, splitting-up, demerger, delinkage, disarticulation, **disconnection,** disconnectedness, discontinuity, incoherence, disengagement, disunion, nonunion, disassociation, segregation; **parting,** alienation, estrangement, **removal,** withdrawal, isolation, detachment, sequestration, abstraction; **subtraction** *see* 255; divorce, divorcement; **division,** subdivision, partition, compartmentalization, segmentation, marking off; districting, zoning; **dislocation,** luxation; separability, partibility, dividableness, divisibility; separatism; **separateness,** discreteness, singleness, monism, unitariness

2 severance, disseverment *or* disseverance, **sunderance,** scission, fission, cleavage, dichotomy; **cutting, slitting,** slashing, **splitting,** slicing; **rending, tearing,** ripping, laceration, hacking, chopping, butchering, mutilation; section, resection; **surgery**

3 disruption, dissolution, abruption, cataclysm; revolution *see* 859; **disintegration** *see* 805, breakup, crack-up, shattering, splintering, fragmentizing, fragmentation; **bursting,** dissilience *or* dissiliency; **scattering,** dispersal, diffusion; **stripping,** scaling, exfoliation

4 break, breakage, breach, burst, **rupture, fracture; crack,** cleft, **fissure, cut, split,** slit; slash, slice; **gap, rift,** rent, rip, tear; chip, splinter, scale

5 dissection, analysis *see* 800, vivisection, resolution, breakdown, diaeresis; anatomy

6 disassembly, dismantlement, taking down *or* apart, dismemberment, dismounting; undoing, unbuilding; **stripping,** stripping away *or* down, divestiture, divestment, defoliation, deprivation; disrobing, unclothing, doffing

7 separator, sieve, centrifuge, ultracentrifuge; creamer, cream separator; breaker, stripper, mincer; slicer, cutter, microtome; analyser

verbs

8 to separate, divide, disjoin, disunite, draw apart, dissociate, disassociate, grow apart, **disjoint,** disengage, disarticulate, **disconnect;** uncouple, unyoke; **part,** cut the knot, **divorce,** estrange; **alienate, segregate,** separate off, factor out, sequester, isolate, curtain off, shut off, set apart *or* aside, split off, cut off *or* out *or* loose *or* adrift; **withdraw, leave, depart,** take one's leave, cut out *and* split (*both informal*); pull out *or* away *or* back, stand apart *or* aside *or* aloof, step aside; subtract *see* 255.9; delete *see* 255.12; **expel,** eject, throw off *or* out, cast off *or* out

9 to come apart, spring apart, fly apart, come unstuck, come unglued, come undone, come apart at the seams, **come** *or* **drop** *or* fall to pieces, **disintegrate,** go to pieces, fall apart, fall apart at the seams, atomize, unitize, fragmentize, pulverize, break up, bust up (*informal*), unravel; come *or* fall off, peel off, carry away; get loose, give way, start

10 to detach, remove, disengage, take *or* lift off, doff; **unfasten, undo,** unattach, unfix; **free, release,** liberate, loose, unloose, unleash, unfetter; **unloosen,** loosen; cast off, weigh anchor; **unhook,** unhitch, unclasp, unclinch, unbuckle, unbutton, unsnap, unscrew, unpin, unbolt; **untie,** unbind, unknit, unbandage, unlace, unzip, unstrap, unchain; unstick, unglue

11 to sever, dissever, cut off *or* away *or* loose, shear off, hack through, hack off, axe, amputate; **cleave, split,** fissure; sunder, cut in two, dichotomize, halve, bisect; **cut,** incise, carve, **slice,** pare, prune, trim, trim away, resect, excise *see* 255.10; slit, snip, lance, scissor; **chop, hew,** hack, **slash;** gash, whittle, butcher; saw, jigsaw, break down (*NZ*); **tear, rend,** rive, rend asunder

12 to break, burst, bust (*informal*), breach; **fracture, rupture; crack,** split, check, craze, fissure; snap; chip, scale, exfoliate

13 to shatter, splinter, shiver, break to *or* into pieces, fragmentize, smash to *or* into smithereens (*informal*), break to *or* into smithereens (*informal*); **smash,** crush, crunch, squash, squelch, squish (*informal*); **disrupt,** demolish, break up, smash up; **scatter,** disperse, diffuse; **fragment,** fission, atomize; **pulverize** *see* 1049.9, grind, cut to pieces, mince, make mincemeat of, make hamburger of (*US informal*)

14 to tear *or* **rip apart,** take *or* pull apart, **pick** *or* **rip** *or* **tear to pieces,** tear to rags *or* tatters, **shred,** rip to shreds; **dismember,** tear limb from limb, draw and quarter; **mangle,** lacerate, mutilate, maim; skin, flay, strip, peel, denude; defoliate

15 to disassemble, take apart *or* down, tear down; **dismantle, demolish,** dismount, unrig (*nautical*)

16 to disjoint, unjoint, **unhinge**, disarticulate, **dislocate**, luxate, throw out of joint, unseat

17 to dissect, **analyse** *see* 800.6, vivisect, anatomize, break down

18 to apportion, **portion**, section, partition, compartmentalize, segment; **divide**, divide up, divvy *and* divvy up (*both informal*), **parcel**, parcel up *or* out, **split**, split up, cut up, subdivide; district, zone

19 to part company, **part**, **separate**, split up, dispel, disband, scatter, **disperse**, break up, break it up (*informal*), **go separate ways**, diverge

adjectives

20 **separate**, distinct, discrete; **unjoined**, **unconnected**, **unattached**, unaccompanied, unattended, unassociated; **apart**, asunder, **in two**; discontinuous, noncontiguous, divergent; **isolated**, insular, detached, detachable, free-standing, free-floating, autonomous; **independent**, self-contained, stand-alone (*informal*); noncohesive, noncohering, incoherent *see* 803.4; bipartite, dichotomous, multipartite, multisegmental; **subdivided**, partitioned, curtained-off, marked-off, compartmentalized

21 **separated**, disjoined, disjoint, disjointed, disjunct, **disconnected**, disengaged, detached, **disunited**, **divided**, removed, divorced, **alienated**, estranged, distanced, **segregated**, sequestered, isolated, cloistered, shut off; **scattered**, dispersed, helter-skelter; disarticulated, dislocated, luxated, out of joint

22 **unfastened**, **unbound**, uncaught, unfixed, **undone**, **loose**, **free**, loosened, unloosened, clear; **untied**, **unbound**, unknit, unleashed, unfettered, unchained, unlaced, unbandaged, unhitched; unstuck, unglued; unclasped, unclinched, unbuckled, unbuttoned, unzipped, unsnapped; unscrewed, unpinned, unbolted; **unanchored**, adrift, afloat, floating, free, free-floating

23 severed, cut, cleaved, cleft, cloven, riven, hewn, sheared; **splintered**, shivered, cracked, **split**, slit, reft; **rent**, **torn**; tattered, shredded, in shreds; quartered, **dismembered**, in pieces

24 **broken**, busted (*informal*), **burst**, **ruptured**, dissilient; sprung; **shattered**, broken up, broken to pieces *or* bits, fragmentized, fragmentary, fragmented, in shards, in smithereens (*informal*), in pieces

25 **separating**, **dividing**, parting, distancing; **separative**, disjunctive

26 **separable**, severable, **divisible**, alienable, cleavable, partible; **fissionable**, fissile, scissile; dissoluble, dissolvable

adverbs

27 separately, severally, piecemeal, one by one; **apart**, adrift, asunder, **in two**, in twain; apart from, away from, aside from; abstractly, in the abstract, objectively, impersonally

28 disjointedly, unconnectedly, sporadically, spasmodically, discontinuously, by bits and pieces, by fits and starts, in dribs and drabs

29 **to pieces**, all to pieces, **to bits**, **to smithereens** (*informal*), to splinters, to shards, to tatters, to shreds

802 COHESION

nouns

1 **cohesion**, cohesiveness, **coherence**, **adherence**, **adhesion**, **sticking**, sticking together, cling, clinging, binding, colligation, inseparability; cementation, conglutination, agglutination; concretion, condensation, accretion, solidification, set, congelation, congealment, clotting, coagulation; **conglomeration**, conglobation, compaction, agglomeration, consolidation; **clustering**, massing, bunching, nodality

2 **consistency** *see* 787.1, connection, **connectedness**; **junction** *see* 799.1; continuity, **seriality**, sequence *see* 814, sequentialness, **consecutiveness** *see* 811.1, orderliness

3 **tenacity**, tenaciousness, **adhesiveness**, cohesiveness, retention; **tightness**, snugness; stickiness, **tackiness**, gluiness, gumminess, gunginess (*informal*), **viscidity**, consistency, viscosity, glutinosity; persistence *or* persistency, stick-to-itiveness (*informal*), toughness, **stubbornness**, **obstinacy** *see* 361, bulldoggedness *or* bulldoggishness, bullheadedness

4 (*something adhesive or tenacious*) **adhesive**, adherent, adherer; **bulldog**, barnacle, leech, limpet, remora; burr, cocklebur, clotbur, bramble, brier, prickle, thorn; sticker, bumper sticker, decalcomania, decal (*informal*); **glue**, **superglue**, **cement**, mucilage, epoxy resin, paste, PVA *or* polyvinyl acetate, gunk (*informal*); Sellotape (*trademark*), Scotch tape (*trademark*); **plaster**, adhesive plaster, court plaster; syrup, molasses, honey, treacle

5 **conglomeration**, conglomerate, breccia (*geology*), agglomerate, agglomeration, cluster, bunch, mass, clot; concrete, concretion

verbs

6 to cohere, adhere, stick, cling, cleave, hold; **persist**, stay, stay put (*informal*); cling to, freeze to (*informal*); hang on, hold on; take hold of, clasp, grasp, hug, embrace, clinch; **stick together**, **hang** *or* **hold together**; grow to, grow together; **solidify**, **set**, conglomerate, agglomerate, conglobate; **congeal**, coagulate, **clot**; **cluster**, mass, bunch

7 to be consistent *see* 787.6, **connect**, connect with, follow; **join** *see* 799.11, link up

8 to hold fast, stick close, stick like glue, stick like a wet shirt *or* wet T-shirt *or* second skin, stick closer than a brother, stick like a barnacle *or* limpet *or* leech, cling like ivy *or* a burr, hold on like a bulldog

9 to **stick together**, cement, **bind**, colligate, **paste**, glue, agglutinate, conglutinate, gum; **weld**, fuse, solder, braze

adjectives

10 **cohesive**, cohering, coherent; adhering, **sticking**, **clinging**, inseparable, cleaving, holding together; **cemented**, stuck, agglutinative, agglutinated, agglutinate, conglutinate, conglutinated; **concrete**, **condensed**, **solidified**, **set**, **congealed**, clotted, coagulated; conglomerated, conglobate, **compacted**, **consolidated**, agglomerated; **clustered**, massed, bunched, nodal

11 consistent *see* 787.9, **connected**; continuous *see* 811.8, **serial**, uninterrupted, contiguous, sequential, sequent, **consecutive** *see* 811.9; orderly, tight; joined *see* 799.13

12 **adhesive, adherent**, stickable, self-adhesive, retentive; **tenacious**, clingy; **sticky, tacky**, gluey, gummy, gungy (*informal*), **viscid**, glutinous; **persistent**, tough, **stubborn, obstinate** *see* 361.8, bulldoggish *or* bulldogged *or* bulldoggy, bullheaded

803 NONCOHESION

nouns

1 **noncohesion**, uncohesiveness, incoherence, inconsistency, discontinuity *see* 812, nonadhesion, unadhesiveness, unadherence, untenacity; **separateness**, discreteness, aloofness, standoffishness (*informal*); **disjunction** *see* 801.1, unknitting, unravelling, dismemberment; **dislocation; dissolution, chaos** *see* 809.2, anarchy, **disorder** *see* 809, confusion, entropy; **scattering**, dispersion *or* dispersal; diffusion

2 **looseness**, slackness, bagginess, **laxness**, laxity, relaxation; sloppiness, shakiness, ricketiness

verbs

3 **to loosen, slacken, relax**; slack, slack off; ease, ease off, let up; **loose, free**, let go, unleash; **disjoin**, unknit, unravel, dismember; sow confusion, open Pandora's box, open a can of worms; unstick, unglue; **scatter**, disperse, diffuse

adjectives

4 **incoherent**, uncoherent, noncoherent, **inconsistent, uncohesive, unadhesive**, nonadhesive, noncohesive, nonadherent, like grains of sand, **untenacious, unconsolidated**, tenuous; unjoined *see* 801.20, disconnected, unconnected, unravelled, dismembered, gapped, open; **disordered** *see* 809.12, **chaotic**, anarchic, anomic, confused; **discontinuous** *see* 812.4, broken, detached, discrete, aloof, standoffish (*informal*)

5 **loose, slack, lax, relaxed**, easy, sloppy; shaky, rickety; flapping, streaming; hanging, drooping, dangling; bagging, baggy

804 COMBINATION

nouns

1 **combination**, combine, combo (*informal*), composition; **union, unification**, marriage, wedding, coupling, accouplement, linking, linkage, yoking; **incorporation**, aggregation, agglomeration, conglomeration, congeries; **amalgamation, consolidation**, assimilation, **integration**, solidification, **encompassment**, inclusion, ecumenism; **junction** *see* 799.1; conjunction, conjugation; **alliance**, affiliation, reaffiliation, **association** *see* 617, **merger**, league, hookup (*informal*), tie-up (*informal*); **taking** *see* 480, buyout, takeover, leveraged buyout; **federation, confederation**, confederacy; federalization, centralization, cartel; **fusion**, blend, blending, meld, melding; coalescence, coalition; **synthesis**,

syncretism, syneresis; syndication; **conspiracy**, cabal, junta; *enosis* (*Greek*), *Anschluss* (*German*); package, package deal; **agreement** *see* 787; **addition** *see* 253

2 **mixture** *see* 796, **compound** *see* 796.5

verbs

3 **to combine, unite, unify**, marry, wed, couple, link, yoke, yoke together; **incorporate, amalgamate, consolidate**, assimilate, **integrate**, solidify, coalesce, compound, put *or* lump together, roll into one, come together, make one, unitize; **connect, join** *see* 799.5; **mix; add** *see* 253.4; **merge**, meld, **blend**, stir in, merge *or* blend *or* meld *or* shade into, **fuse**, flux, melt into one, conflate; interfuse, interblend; **encompass**, include, comprise; **take**, take over, buy out; **synthesize**, syncretize; syndicate; reembody

4 **to league, ally, affiliate, associate**, consociate; unionize, organize, cement a union; **federate, confederate**, federalize, centralize; **join forces**, join *or* unite with, join *or* come together, join up with (*informal*), hook up with (*informal*), tie up *or* in with (*informal*), **throw in one's lot with**, throw in with (*informal*), stand up with, go *or* be in cahoots (*informal*), **pool one's interests, join fortunes with**, stand together, close ranks, make common cause with; **marry, wed, couple, yoke**, yoke together, link; **band together**, club together, bunch, bunch up (*informal*), gang up (*informal*), gang, club; team with, **team up with** (*informal*), couple, pair, double up, pair off, partner; go in partnership, go in partners (*informal*), chum up with (*informal*), pal up with (*informal*); **conspire, cabal**

adjectives

5 **combined, united, amalgamated, incorporated, consolidated, integrated**, assimilated, one, unitary, unitive, unitized, **joined** *see* 799.13, **joint** *see* 799.12, conjoint; conjunctive, combinative *or* combinatory, connective, conjugate; **merged**, blended, fused; **mixed; synthesized**, syncretized, syncretistic, eclectic

6 **leagued**, enleagued, **allied, affiliated**, affiliate, **associated**, associate, corporate; federated, confederated, federate, confederate; **in league**, in cahoots (*informal*), in with; **conspiratorial**, cabalistic; partners with, in partnership; teamed, coupled, paired, married, wed, wedded, coupled, yoked, yoked together, linked, linked up

7 **combining, uniting**, unitive, unitizing, incorporating; merging, blending, fusing; combinative, combinatory; recombinant; associative; federative, federal; corporative, incorporative, corporational

805 DISINTEGRATION

nouns

1 **disintegration, decomposition, dissolution, decay**, coming-apart, resolution, disorganization, degradation, breakup, breakdown, fragmentation, atomization; **ruination, destruction** *see* 395; **erosion**, corrosion, crumbling, dilapidation, wear, wear and tear, waste, wasting, wasting away, ablation, ravagement, ravages of time; **disjunction** *see* 801.1; incoherence *see* 803.1; **impairment** *see* 393

2 dissociation; catalysis, dialysis, hydrolysis, proteolysis, thermolysis, photolysis (*all chemistry*); catalyst, hydrolyst (*chemistry*); hydrolyte (*chemistry*); **decay,** fission (*physics*), splitting

verbs

3 **to disintegrate, decompose, decay,** dissolve, come apart, disorganize, **break up** *see* 395.22, go to rack and ruin *see* 395.24, crack up, disjoin, unknit, split, fission, atomize, **come** *or* **fall to pieces; erode,** corrode, ablate, consume, wear *or* waste away, moulder, moulder away, crumble, crumble into dust

4 (*chemical terms*) to dissociate; catalyse, dialyse, hydrolyse, electrolyse, photolyse

adjectives

5 **disintegrative,** decomposing, disintegrating, disruptive, disjunctive; **destructive, ruinous** *see* 395.26; erosive, corrosive, ablative; resolvent, solvent, separative; **dilapidated,** disintegrated, ruinous, shacky, worn-out, worn, clapped-out (*informal*), mouldering, ravaged, wrecked, totalled (*informal*); disintegrable, decomposable, degradable, biodegradable

6 (*chemical terms*) dissociative; catalytic, dialytic, hydrolytic, proteolytic, thermolytic, electrolytic, photolytic

word elements

7 –lysis, lyso–, lysi–, –lyte

806 ORDER

nouns

1 order, arrangement *see* 807; **organization** *see* 807.2; disposition, disposal, deployment, marshalling; **formation, structure, configuration,** array, makeup, lineup, setup, layout; system; routine, even tenor, standard operating procedure; **peace,** quiet, quietude, **tranquillity; regularity,** uniformity *see* 780; symmetry, proportion, concord, **harmony,** order, the music of the spheres, Tao *or* Dào; "the eternal fitness of things"—SAMUEL CLARKE, "Heav'n's first law"—POPE

2 continuity, logical order, serial order; **degree** *see* 245; **hierarchy, gradation,** subordination, superordination, rank, place; **sequence** *see* 814

3 orderliness, trimness, tidiness, neatness; good shape (*informal*), good condition, fine fettle, good trim, apple-pie order (*informal*), a place for everything and everything in its place; **discipline,** method, methodology, methodicalness, system, systematicness; anality, anal-retentiveness, compulsiveness, compulsive neatness (*all psychoanalysis*)

verbs

4 **to order, arrange** *see* 807.8, get it together (*informal*), **organize, regulate;** dispose, deploy, marshal; **form,** form up, configure, structure, array, pull it together, straighten it out, get *or* put one's house in order, line up, set up, lay out; **pacify,**

quiet, cool off *or* down (*informal*), **tranquillize; regularize,** harmonize; **systematize,** methodize, normalize, standardize, routinize; hierarchize, grade, rank

5 **to form, take form,** take order, **take shape,** crystallize, **shape up;** arrange *or* range itself, place itself, take its place, fall in, **fall** *or* **drop into place,** fall into line *or* order *or* series, fall into rank, take rank; come together, draw up, gather around, rally round

adjectives

6 **orderly,** ordered, **regular, well-regulated, well-ordered, methodical, formal,** regular as clockwork, uniform *see* 780.5, **systematic,** symmetrical, **harmonious;** businesslike, routine, steady, normal, habitual, usual, en règle, in hand; **arranged** *see* 807.14

7 **in order, in trim,** to rights *and* in apple-pie order (*both informal*); **in condition,** in good condition, in kilter *or* kelter (*informal*), **in shape,** in good shape (*informal*), **in good form,** in fine fettle, in good trim, in the pink (*informal*), in the pink of condition; **in repair,** in commission, in adjustment, in working order, fixed; up to scratch *or* snuff (*informal*)

8 **tidy, trim, natty, neat,** spruce, sleek, slick *and* slick as a whistle (*informal*), smart, trig, dinky (*informal*), snug, tight, **shipshape,** shipshape and Bristol fashion; **well-kept,** well-kempt, well-cared-for, well-groomed; neat as a button *or* pin (*informal*)

adverbs

9 **methodically, systematically, regularly,** through channels, uniformly, harmoniously, like clockwork

10 **in order, in turn, in sequence, in succession,** hierarchically, in series, seriatim (*Latin*); step by step, by stages

807 ARRANGEMENT
putting in order

nouns

1 **arrangement, ordering,** structuring, shaping, forming, configurating, configuration, constitution; **disposition, disposal, deployment,** placement, marshalling, **arraying; distribution,** collation, collocation, allocation, allotment, apportionment; **formation,** formulation, **configuration,** form, array; regimentation; syntax; **order** *see* 806

2 **organization, methodization,** ordering, planning, charting, codification, regulation, regularization, routinization, normalization, rationalization; **adjustment,** harmonization, tuning, fine-tuning, tune-up, tinkering, tweaking (*informal*); **systematization,** ordination, coordination

3 **grouping, classification** *see* 808, categorization, taxonomy; **gradation,** subordination, superordination, **ranking,** placement; **sorting,** sorting out, assortment, sifting, screening, triage, culling, selection, shakeout

4 **table,** code, digest, **index, inventory,** census; table of organization

5 **arranger, organizer,** coordinator, spreadsheet;

sorter, sifter, **sieve**, riddle, **screen**, bolter, colander, grate, grating

6 (*act of making neat*) **cleanup**, red-up (*informal*); tidy-up, trim-up

7 **rearrangement, reorganization**, reconstitution, **reordering, restructuring**, *perestroika* (*Russian*), shake-up (*informal*); **redeployment**, redisposition, realignment

verbs

8 **to arrange**, order *see* 806.4, reduce to order, **put** *or* **get** *or* **set in order**, right, prioritize, put first things first; **put** *or* **set to rights**, get it together (*informal*), **pull it together**, put in *or* into shape, whip into shape (*informal*), sort out, unsnarl, make sense out of (*informal*)

9 **to dispose, distribute, fix, place**, set out, collocate, allocate, **compose**, space, **marshal**, rally, array; align, line, **line up**, form up, range; regiment; **allot, apportion**, parcel out, deal, **deal out**

10 **to organize**, methodize, **systematize**, rationalize, regularize, get *or* put one's house in order; **harmonize**, synchronize, **tune**, tune up; **regularize**, routinize, normalize, standardize; **regulate**, adjust, coordinate, fix, settle; **plan**, chart, codify

11 **to classify** *see* 808.6, group, categorize; **grade**, gradate, rank, subordinate; **sort**, sort out, assort; **separate**, divide; collate; **sift**, size, sieve, **screen**, bolt, riddle

12 **to tidy, tidy up**, neaten, trim, **put in trim**, trim up, trig up, **straighten up**, fix up (*informal*), **clean up**, groom, spruce *and* spruce up (*both informal*), **clear up**, clear the decks

13 **to rearrange, reorganize**, reconstitute, **reorder, restructure**, reshuffle, rejigger (*informal*), tinker *or* tinker with, tune, tune up, fine-tune, tweak (*informal*); **shake up**, shake out; redispose, redistribute, reallocate, realign

adjectives

14 **arranged, ordered, disposed**, configured, composed, constituted, fixed, placed, aligned, ranged, arrayed, marshalled, grouped, ranked, **graded**; organized, methodized, **regularized**, routinized, normalized, standardized, **systematized**; regulated, harmonized, synchronized; **classified** *see* 808.8, categorized, **sorted**, assorted; **orderly** *see* 806.6

15 **organizational**, formational, structural

word elements

16 tax–, taxi–, –taxia, –taxis

808 CLASSIFICATION

nouns

1 **classification, categorization**, classing, placement, ranging, **pigeonholing, sorting, grouping; grading**, stratification, ranking, rating, classing; division, subdivision; **cataloguing**, codification, tabulation, rationalization, indexing, filing; **taxonomy**, typology; analysis *see* 800, **arrangement** *see* 807

2 **class, category, head, order, division**, branch, set, **group**, grouping, bracket, pigeonhole; stream,

banding, family grouping *or* vertical grouping; **section**, heading, rubric, **label**, title; **grade**, rank, rating, status, estate, stratum, level, station, position; **caste**, clan, race, strain, blood, kin, sept; **subdivision**, subgroup, suborder

3 **kind, sort, ilk, type**, breed of cat (*informal*), lot (*informal*), **variety, species, genus**, *genre* (*French*), phylum, denomination, designation, description, style, manner, **nature, character**, persuasion, the like *or* likes of (*informal*); **stamp, brand**, feather, colour, stripe, line, grain, kidney; **make**, mark, label, shape, cast, form, mould; tribe, clan, race, strain, blood, kin, breed

4 **hierarchy**, class structure, power structure, pyramid, establishment, pecking order; natural hierarchy, order *or* chain of being, domain, realm, **kingdom**, animal kingdom, vegetable kingdom, mineral kingdom

5 (*botanical and zoological classifications, in descending order*) **kingdom**; subkingdom, **phylum** (*zoology*), branch (*botany*); superclass, **class**, subclass, superorder, **order**, suborder, superfamily, **family**, subfamily, tribe, subtribe, **genus**, subgenus, series, section, superspecies, **species**; subspecies, **variety**; biotype, genotype

verbs

6 **to classify**, class, assign, designate; **categorize**, type, put down as, **pigeonhole**, place, **group, arrange** *see* 807.8, range; stream; **order** *see* 806.4, put in order, rank, rate, **grade; sort**, assort; **divide, analyse** *see* 800.6, subdivide, break down; **catalogue**, list, file, tabulate, rationalize, **index**, alphabetize, digest, codify

adjectives

7 **classificational**, classificatory; **categorical, taxonomic** *or* **taxonomical**, typologic *or* typological; ordinal; divisional, divisionary, subdivisional; **typical**, typal; **special**, specific, characteristic, particular, peculiar, denominative, differential, distinctive, defining, varietal

8 **classified, catalogued, pigeonholed**, indexed, sorted, assorted, **graded, grouped**, ranked, streamed, rated, stratified, hierarchic, pyramidal; placed; filed, on file; tabular

adverbs

9 **any kind** *or* sort, **of any description, at all**, whatever, soever, whatsoever

word elements

10 speci–, specie–, gen–

809 DISORDER

nouns

1 **disorder, disorderliness, disarrangement**, derangement, disarticulation, disjunction *see* 801.1, **disorganization**; discomposure, **dishevelment, disarray**, upset, disturbance, discomfiture, disconcertedness; **irregularity**, randomness, turbulence, perturbation, ununiformity *or* nonuniformity, unsymmetry *or* nonsymmetry, **disproportion, disharmony**; indiscriminateness, promiscuity, promiscuousness, haphazardness; **randomness**, randomicity, vagueness, trendlessness; entropy; **disruption** *see* 801.3, destabilization; **incoherence** *see* 803.1; untogetherness (*informal*); disintegration *see* 805;

"most admired disorder"—Shakespeare, "inharmonious harmony"—Horace

2 **confusion, chaos,** anarchy, misrule, licence; **Babel,** cognitive dissonance; **muddle,** morass, **mix-up** *and* foul-up *and* fuck-up *and* snafu *and* screw-up *and* cock-up (*all informal*), balls-up (*informal*), ball-up (*US informal*), hoo-ha *and* fine how-de-do (*all informal*), pretty kettle of fish, pretty piece of business, nice piece of work;

"Chaos and old Night"—Milton, "the seed of Chaos, and of Night"—Pope, "mere anarchy is loosed upon the world", "fabulous formless darkness"—both Yeats

3 **jumble, scramble, tumble, snarl-up, mess,** bloody *or* holy *or* unholy *or* god-awful mess (*informal*), shemozzle (*informal*), **turmoil, shambles,** welter, mishmash, hash, helter-skelter, farrago, crazy-quilt, higgledy-piggledy; **clutter, litter, hodgepodge** *see* 796.6, rat's nest, mare's nest, hurrah's nest (*nautical*); topsy-turviness *or* topsy-turvydom, arsy-varsiness, hysteron proteron

4 **commotion, hubbub, Babel, tumult,** turmoil, **uproar, carry-on** (*informal*), **racket,** riot, **disturbance, rumpus** (*informal*), breeze (*informal*), ruckus *and* ruction (*both informal*), **fracas, hassle,** hoo-ha (*informal*), shemozzle (*informal*), kerfuffle (*informal*), shindy (*informal*), rampage; **ado,** to-do (*informal*), trouble, **bother** *or* **spot of bother,** pother, dustup (*informal*), stir (*informal*), **fuss,** pantomime (*informal*), song and dance (*informal*), palaver, brouhaha; **row** *and* hassle (*both informal*), **brawl,** free-for-all (*informal*), bust-up (*informal*), punch-up (*informal*), rough-and-tumble, donnybrook *or* donnybrook fair, broil, embroilment, melee, scramble, scrum (*informal*); helter-skelter, pell-mell, **roughhouse, rough-and-tumble**

5 **pandemonium,**
"confusion worse confounded"—Milton, **hell, bedlam,** witches' Sabbath, Babel, confusion of tongues; **cacophony,** din, noise, static, racket

6 slovenliness, **slipshodness,** carelessness, negligence; **untidiness,** unneatness, looseness, **messiness** (*informal*), **sloppiness,** dowdiness, seediness, **shabbiness,** tawdriness, chintziness (*informal*), shoddiness, tackiness (*informal*), grubbiness (*informal*), frowziness, blowziness; **slatternliness,** frumpishness (*informal*), sluttishness; **squalor,** squalidness, sordidness

7 **slob** (*informal*), fleabag (*informal*), **slattern, sloven,** mawkin (*dialect*), frump (*informal*), sloppy Joe (*US informal*), schlep (*US informal*), *Strüwelpeter* (*German*); drab, **slut, trollop; pig,** swine; litter lout, **litterbug** (*US & Canadian*)

verbs

8 to lapse into disorder, come apart, come apart at the seams, dissolve into chaos, slacken *see* 803.3, come unstuck *or* unglued (*informal*), disintegrate *see* 805.3, degenerate, detune, untune

9 **to disorder, disarrange** *see* 810.2, **disorganize,** dishevel; **confuse** *see* 810.3, sow confusion, open Pandora's box, **muddle,** jumble, jumble up; **discompose** *see* 810.4, **upset,** destabilize, unsettle, **disturb,** perturb

10 **to riot, roister,** roil, carouse; **create a disturbance, make a commotion,** make trouble, cause a stir *or* commotion, **make an ado** *or* **to-do,** create a riot, **cut loose, run wild, run riot,** run amok, go on a rampage, go berserk

11 (*informal terms*) **to kick up a row,** kick up a shindy *or* a fuss *or* a storm, piss up a storm (*US & Canadian*), kick up bobsy-die *or* play bobsy-die (*NZ*), **raise the devil,** raise the deuce *or* dickens, raise a rumpus *or* a storm, raise a ruckus, raise Cain, **raise hell,** raise the roof, whoop it up, hell around (*US & Canadian*), horse around *or* about; **carry on,** go on, maffick; **cut up,** cut up rough, **roughhouse**

adjectives

12 **unordered, orderless, disordered, unorganized, random, entropic, unarranged,** ungraded, unsorted, unclassified; unstreamed; untogether (*informal*); **unmethodical,** immethodical; **unsystematic,** systemless, nonsystematic; disjunct, unjoined *see* 801.20; disarticulated, **incoherent** *see* 803.4; discontinuous; **formless,** amorphous, inchoate, shapeless; ununiform *or* nonuniform, unsymmetrical *or* nonsymmetrical, disproportionate, misshapen; **irregular, haphazard,** desultory, **erratic,** sporadic, spasmodic, fitful, promiscuous, indiscriminate, casual, frivolous, capricious, random, hit-or-miss, vague, dispersed, wandering, planless, undirected, **aimless,** straggling, straggly; senseless, meaningless, gratuitous

13 **disorderly, in disorder, disordered, disorganized, disarranged, discomposed,** dislocated, deranged, convulsed; **upset, disturbed,** perturbed, unsettled, discomfited, disconcerted; **turbulent,** turbid, roily; **out of order,** out of place, misplaced, shuffled; **out of kilter** *or* **kelter** (*informal*), out of whack (*informal*), out of gear, out of joint, out of tune, on the fritz (*US & Canadian informal*); cockeyed (*informal*), skew-whiff (*informal*), awry, amiss, askew, on the blink *and* haywire (*both informal*)

14 **dishevelled, mussed up** (*informal*), messed up (*informal*), slobby (*informal*), **rumpled,** tumbled, ruffled, snarled, snaggy; **tousled,** tously; uncombed, shaggy, matted

15 **slovenly, slipshod, careless, loose, slack,** nonformal, negligent; **untidy, unsightly,** unneat, slobby *and* scuzzy (*both informal*), **unkempt; messy** (*informal*), mussy (*US & Canadian informal*), **sloppy** (*informal*), scraggly, poky, seedy (*informal*), **shabby, scruffy,** tatty, shoddy, schlocky (*informal*), lumpen, chintzy, grubby (*informal*), **frowzy, blowzy,** tacky (*informal*); **slatternly, sluttish, frumpish,** frumpy, draggletailed, drabbletailed, draggled, bedraggled; down at the heel, out at the heels, out at the elbows, in rags, ragged, raggedy, tattered; **squalid,** sordid, dilapidated, ruinous, **beat-up** (*informal*)

16 **confused, chaotic,** anarchic, **muddled, jumbled,** scattered, helter-skelter (*informal*), higgledy-piggledy, hugger-mugger, skimble-skamble, in a mess, shambolic; **topsy-turvy,** arsy-varsy, upside-down,

ass-backwards (*US informal*); **mixed-up**, ballsed *or* bollocksed up (*informal*), **screwed up** (*informal*), mucked up (*informal*), **fouled up** *and* fucked up *and* snafu *and* buggered up *and* cocked up (*all informal*)

adverbs

17 **in disorder**, **in disarray**, **in confusion**, Katy bar the door (*US informal*), in a jumble, in a tumble, in a muddle, in a mess; **higgledy-piggledy**, **helter-skelter** (*informal*), hugger-mugger, skimble-skamble, harum-scarum (*informal*), willy-nilly (*informal*), all over, **all over the place**, **all over the shop** (*informal*)

18 **haphazardly**, **unsystematically**, unmethodically, irregularly, desultorily, **erratically**, capriciously, promiscuously, indiscriminately, **sloppily** (*informal*), **carelessly**, randomly, **fitfully**, any old way *and* any which way *and* any old how (*all informal*); by *or* at intervals, sporadically, spasmodically, by fits, **by fits and starts**, by *or* in snatches, in dribs and drabs, in spots (*informal*); every now and then *and* every once in a while (*both informal*); **at random**, at haphazard, by chance, hit or miss

19 **chaotically**, **anarchically**, turbulently, **riotously**; confusedly, dispersedly, vaguely, wanderingly, **aimlessly**, planlessly, senselessly

810 DISARRANGEMENT
bringing into disorder

nouns

1 **disarrangement**, **derangement**, misarrangement, convulsion, dislocation; **disorganization**, shuffling; **discomposure**, disturbance, perturbation; **disorder** *see* 809; insanity *see* 925

verbs

2 **to disarrange**, **derange**, misarrange; **disorder**, **disorganize**, throw out of order, put out of gear, dislocate, upset the apple-cart, **disarray**; **dishevel**, rumple, ruffle; tousle (*informal*), muss *and* **muss up** (*both US & Canadian informal*), mess *and* **mess up** (*both informal*); **litter**, **clutter**, scatter

3 **to confuse**, **muddle**, **jumble**, confound, garble, tumble, scramble, snarl, tie in knots, fumble, pi; **shuffle**, riffle; **mix up**, snarl up, **balls** *or* **bollocks up** (*informal*), foul up *and* fuck up *and* **screw up** *and* muck up *and* snafu *and* cock up (*all informal*); make a hash *or* mess *or* fist *or* cod of (*all informal*), raise *or* play hob with (*US informal*)

4 **to discompose**, throw into confusion, **upset**, **unsettle**, **disturb**, trip up, perturb, trouble, distract, throw (*informal*), throw into a tizzy *or* stew (*informal*), throw into a snit (*US & Australian informal*), agitate, convulse, embroil; **psych** *and* spook *and* bug (*all informal*)

adjectives

5 **disarranged** *see* 809.13, **confused** *see* 809.16, **disordered** *see* 809.12

811 CONTINUITY
uninterrupted sequence

nouns

1 **continuity**, **uninterruption**, **uninterruptedness**, featurelessness, unrelievedness, monotony, unintermittedness, unbrokenness, **uniformity** *see* 780, undifferentiation; fullness, plenitude; seamlessness, jointlessness, gaplessness, smoothness; **consecutiveness**, successiveness; continuousness, **endlessness**, **ceaselessness**, **incessancy**; **constancy** *see* 846.2, continualness, constant flow; steadiness, steady state, equilibrium, stability *see* 854

2 **series**, **succession**, run, **sequence**, consecution, progression, course, gradation; **continuum**, plenum; lineage, descent, filiation; **connection**, **concatenation**, catenation, catena, **chain**, chaining, linkup, articulation, reticulation, nexus; chain reaction, powder train; **train**, range, rank, **file**, **line**, **string**, thread, queue, **row**, bank, tier; windrow, swath; single file, Indian file; crocodile; array; **round**, **cycle**, rotation, routine, the daily grind (*informal*), recurrence, periodicity, flywheel effect, pendulum; endless belt *or* chain, Möbius band *or* strip, la ronde (*French*), endless round; gamut, spectrum, scale; drone, monotone, hum, buzz

3 **procession**, **train**, **column**, **line**, **string**, **cortege**; stream, steady stream; cavalcade, caravan, motorcade; **parade**, pomp; dress parade; progress; promenade, review, march-past, flyover, flypast, funeral, state funeral; skimmington; chain gang, coffel; mule train, pack train

verbs

4 **to continue**, be continuous, **connect**, **connect up**, **concatenate**, continuate, catenate, **join** *see* 799.5, link *or* link up, **string together**, string, thread, chain *or* chain up, link *or* link up, follow in *or* form a series, run on, maintain continuity

5 **to align**, **line**, **line up**, string out, rank, array, range, get *or* put in a row

6 **to line up**, get in *or* get on line, queue *or* queue up, make *or* form a line, get in formation, **fall in**, fall in *or* into line, fall into rank, take rank, take one's place

7 **to file**, defile, file off; **parade**, go on parade, promenade, march past, fly over, fly past

adjectives

8 **continuous**, continued, **continual**, continuing; **uninterrupted**, **unintermittent**, unintermitted, featureless, unrelieved, monotonous; **connected**, **joined** *see* 799.13, linked, chained, concatenated, catenated, articulated; **unbroken**, serried, **uniform** *see* 780.5, homogeneous, homogenized, cloned *or* clonish (*informal*), undifferentiated, wall-to-wall *and* back-to-back (*both informal*), seamless, jointless, gapless, smooth, unstopped; unintermitting, unremitting; **incessant**, **constant**, steady, stable, **ceaseless**, unceasing, **endless**, unending, never-ending, **interminable**, perennial; **cyclical**, repetitive, **recurrent**, periodic; straight, running, **nonstop**; **round-the-clock**, twenty-four-hour, all-hours; immediate, direct

9 **consecutive, successive,** successional, back-to-back (*informal*); progressive; **serial,** ordinal, seriate, catenary; sequent, **sequential;** linear, lineal, in line

adverbs

10 **continuously, continually; uninterruptedly, unintermittently; without cease,** without stopping, with every other breath, without a break, back to back *and* wall-to-wall (*both informal*), unbrokenly, gaplessly, seamlessly, jointlessly, **connectedly,** together, cumulatively, on end; unceasingly, **endlessly,** *ad infinitum* (*Latin*), perennially, **interminably,** again and again, repeatedly, time after time, time and again, time and time again, repetitively, cyclically, monotonously, unrelievedly, week in week out, year in year out, year-round, on and on, at *or* on a stretch; round the clock, all day long, all the livelong day

11 **consecutively, progressively,** sequentially, successively, **in succession,** one after the other, back to back (*informal*), **in turn,** turn about, turn and turn about; step by step; running; **serially,** in a series, *seriatim* (*Latin*); **in a line,** in a row, in column, in file, in a chain, in single file, in Indian file

812 DISCONTINUITY
interrupted sequence

nouns

1 **discontinuity,** discontinuousness, discontinuation, discontinuance, noncontinuance; **incoherence** *see* 803.1, **disconnectedness,** disconnection, delinkage, decoupling, discreteness, **disjunction** *see* 801.1; **nonuniformity** *see* 781; irregularity, **intermittence,** fitfulness *see* 850.1; brokenness; nonseriality, nonlinearity, non sequitur; incompleteness *see* 794; episode, parenthesis; broken thread

2 **interruption, suspension, break,** fissure, breach, gap, hiatus, lacuna, caesura; **interval, pause,** interim *see* 825, lull, cessation, letup (*informal*), **intermission**

verbs

3 **to discontinue, interrupt** *see* 856.10, **break,** break off, **disjoin; disarrange** *see* 810.2; intermit *see* 850.2

adjectives

4 **discontinuous,** noncontinuous, unsuccessive, **incoherent** *see* 803.4, nonserial, nonlinear, nonsequential, discontinued, **disconnected,** unconnected, unjoined *see* 801.20, delinked, decoupled, *décousu* (*French*), **broken;** nonuniform *see* 781.3, irregular; broken, broken off, fragmentary, **interrupted,** suspended; disjunctive, discrete, discretive; **intermittent, fitful** *see* 850.3; scrappy, snatchy, spotty, patchy, jagged; choppy, chopped-off, herky-jerky (*US & Canadian informal*), jerky, spasmodic; episodic, parenthetic

adverbs

5 **discontinuously,** disconnectedly, brokenly, fragmentarily; at intervals; **haphazardly** *see* 809.18, randomly, occasionally, infrequently, now and then, now and again, intermittently, fitfully, **by fits and**

starts, by fits, by snatches, by catches, by jerks, spasmodically, episodically, by skips, skippingly, *per saltum* (*Latin*); willy-nilly, **here and there,** in spots, sporadically, patchily

813 PRECEDENCE
in order

nouns

1 **precedence** *or* precedency, antecedence *or* antecedency, anteposition, anteriority, precession; the lead, front position, front seat, pole position, first chair; **priority,** preference, urgency; top priority; prefixation, prothesis; **superiority** *see* 249; **dominion** *see* 417.6; **precursor** *see* 815; prelude *see* 815.2; preliminaries, run-up (*informal*); preceding *see* 165.1

verbs

2 **to precede,** antecede, **come first,** come *or* go before, **go ahead of, go in advance,** stand first, stand at the head, **head,** head up (*informal*), front, **lead** *see* 165.2, take precedence, have priority; lead off, kick off, usher in; head the table *or* board, sit on the dais; rank, outrank, rate

3 (*place before*) **to prefix, preface,** premise, prelude, prologize, preamble, introduce

adjectives

4 **preceding,** precedent, **prior,** antecedent, anterior, precessional, **leading** *see* 165.3; **preliminary,** precursory, prevenient, prefatory, exordial, prelusive, preludial, proemial, preparatory, initiatory, propaedeutic, inaugural; **first, foremost,** headmost, **chief** *see* 249.14

5 **former,** foregoing; aforesaid, aforementioned, beforementioned, above-mentioned, aforenamed, forenamed, forementioned, said, named, same

adverbs

6 **before** *see* 216.12; above, hereinbefore, hereinabove, *supra* (*Latin*), *ante* (*Latin*)

814 SEQUENCE

nouns

1 **sequence,** logical sequence, **succession,** successiveness, consecution, **consecutiveness,** following, coming after; descent, lineage, line; **series** *see* 811.2; **order,** order of succession; **priority; progression,** procession, rotation; **continuity** *see* 811; **continuation,** prolongation, extension, posteriority; suffixation, subjunction, postposition

verbs

2 **to succeed, follow, ensue,** come *or* go after, **come next; inherit,** take the mantle of, step into the shoes *or* place of, take over

3 (*place after*) **to suffix,** append, subjoin

adjectives

4 **succeeding, successive, following, ensuing,** sequent, sequential, sequacious, posterior, **subsequent,** consequent; proximate, **next;** appendant, suffixed, postpositive, postpositional

815 PRECURSOR

nouns

1 **precursor, forerunner, foregoer,** *voorlooper* (*Dutch*), **vaunt-courier, avant-courier, front-** *or* **lead-runner;** **pioneer,** *voortrekker* (*Dutch*), **frontiersman, bushwhacker; scout, pathfinder, explorer, point, point man, trailblazer** *or* **trailbreaker, guide; leader** *see* 574.6, **leadoff man** *or* **woman, bellwether, fugleman; pacemaker; herald, announcer,** *buccinator* (*Latin*), **messenger, harbinger, stormy petrel; predecessor, forebear, precedent, antecedent, ancestor; vanguard, avant-garde, avant-gardist, innovator, groundbreaker**

2 **curtain raiser, countdown, run-up** (*informal*), **lead-in, warm-up, kickoff, opening gun** *or* **shot; opening episode, first episode, prequel; prelude, preamble, preface, prologue, foreword, introduction,** *avant-propos* (*French*), **protasis, proem, proemium, prolegomenon** *or* **prolegomena, exordium; prefix, prefixture; frontispiece; preliminary, front matter; overture, voluntary, verse; premise, presupposition, postulate, prolepsis; innovation, breakthrough** (*informal*), **leap**

verbs

3 **to go before, pioneer, blaze** *or* **break the trail, break new ground, be in the van** *or* **vanguard; guide; lead** *see* 165.2, **lead** *or* **show the way; precede** *see* 813.2; **herald, count down, run up, lead in, forerun, usher in, introduce**

adjectives

4 **preceding** *see* 813.4; **preliminary, exploratory, pioneering, trailblazing, door-opening, kickoff, inaugural; advanced, avant-garde, original** *see* 337.5

816 SEQUEL

nouns

1 **sequel, sequela** *or* **sequelae, sequelant, sequent, sequitur, consequence** *see* 886.1; **continuation, continuance, follow-up** *or* **follow-through** (*informal*); **caboose; supplement, addendum, appendix, back matter; postfix, suffix; postscript** *or* **PS, subscript, postface; postlude, epilogue, conclusion, peroration, codicil; refrain, chorus, coda; envoi, colophon, tag; afterthought, second thought, double take** (*informal*), *arrière-pensée* (*French*), *esprit d'escalier* (*French*); **parting** *or* **Parthian shot; last words, swan song, dying words, famous last words**

2 **afterpart, afterpiece; wake, trail, train, queue; tail, tailpiece, rear, rear end; tab, tag, trailer**

3 **aftermath, afterclap, afterglow, afterimage, aftereffect, side effect, by-product, spin-off, aftertaste; aftergrowth, aftercrop; afterbirth, placenta, secundines; afterpain**

4 **successor, replacement, backup, backup man** *or* **woman, substitute, stand-in; descendant, posterity, heir, inheritor**

verbs

5 **to succeed,** follow, come next, come after, come on

the heels of; **follow through,** carry through, take the next step

817 BEGINNING

nouns

1 **beginning, commencement, start,** start-up, running *or* flying start, starting point, square one (*informal*), **outset,** outbreak, **onset,** oncoming; dawn; **creation, foundation, establishment, establishing, institution, origin,** origination, establishment, setting-up, setting in motion; **launching,** launch, launch *or* launching pad, roll-out; alpha, A; **opening,** rising of the curtain; leadoff, kickoff *and* jump-off *and* send-off *and* start-off *and* take-off *and* blast-off *and* square one (*all informal*), the word 'go' (*informal*); fresh start, new departure; opening wedge, leading edge, cutting edge, thin end of the wedge; entry level, bottom rung, bottom of the ladder, low place on the totem pole

2 **beginner, neophyte, tyro;** newcomer *see* 773.4, new arrival, Johnny-come-lately (*informal*); entry-level employee, low man on the totem pole; entrant, **novice,** novitiate, probationer, catechumen; **recruit,** raw recruit, rookie (*informal*); **apprentice,** trainee, learner; baby, infant; nestling, fledging; freshman *see* 572.6; tenderfoot, greenhorn, greeny (*informal*), rabbit (*informal*); debutant, deb (*informal*)

3 **first,** first ever, prime, primal, primary, **initial,** alpha; **initiation,** initialization, first move, opening move, gambit, **first step,** baby step, *le premier pas* (*French*), openers, starters, first lap, first round, first inning, first stage; breaking-in, warming-up; first blush, first glance, first sight, first impression

4 **origin,** origination, **genesis, inception,** incipience *or* incipiency, inchoation; **divine creation,** creationism, creation science; **birth,** birthing, bearing, parturition, pregnancy, nascency *or* nascence, nativity; **infancy,** babyhood, childhood, youth; freshman year (*US & Canadian*); incunabula, beginnings, cradle

5 **inauguration,** installation *or* instalment, induction, **introduction,** initiation; embarkation *or* embarkment, **launching,** floating, flotation, unveiling; debut, first appearance, coming out (*informal*); opener (*informal*), preliminary, curtain raiser *or* lifter; maiden speech, inaugural address

6 **basics, essentials, rudiments, elements, nuts and bolts** (*informal*); **principles,** principia, first principles, first steps, **outlines, primer,** hornbook, grammar, alphabet, **ABC's,** abecedarium; introduction, induction

verbs

7 **to begin, commence, start; start up, kick** *or* **click in** (*US & Canadian informal*); **start in, start off, start out, set out,** set sail, set in, set to *or* about, go *or* swing into action, get to *or* down to, **turn to,** fall to, pitch in (*informal*), dive in (*informal*), plunge into, head into (*informal*), **go ahead,** let her rip (*informal*), fire *or* blast away (*informal*), take *or* jump *or* kick *or* tee *or* blast *or* send off (*all informal*), get the show on the road (*informal*), get *or* set *or* start the ball rolling (*informal*), roll it *and* let it roll (*both informal*)

8 **to make a beginning,** make a move (*informal*),
start up, get going (*informal*), get off, set forth, set
out, launch *or* launch forth, get off the ground
(*informal*), **get under way,** set up shop, get in there
(*informal*); set a course, **get squared away**
(*informal*); make an auspicious beginning, **get off to
a good start,** make a dent; get in on the ground
floor (*informal*); **break in, warm up,** get one's feet
wet (*informal*), cut one's teeth

9 **to enter, enter on** *or* **upon** *or* **into, embark in** *or*
on *or* **upon,** take up, go into, have a go at, take a
crack *or* whack *or* shot at (*informal*); **debut,** make
one's debut

10 **to initiate, originate, create,** invent; **precede** *see*
813.2, **take the initiative, take the first step,** take
the lead, pioneer *see* 815.3; **lead,** lead off, lead the
way; **ahead,** head up (*informal*), stand at the head,
stand first; **break the ice,** take the plunge, break
ground, cut the first turf, lay the first stone

11 **to inaugurate,** institute, **found, establish,** set up
(*informal*); **install,** initiate, induct; **introduce,**
broach, bring up, lift up, raise; **launch,** float, roll
out; christen (*informal*); **usher in,** ring in (*informal*);
set on foot, set abroach, set agoing, turn on, kick-
start *and* jump-start (*both informal*), start up, start
going, start the ball rolling (*informal*)

12 **to open,** open up, breach, open the door to; open
fire

13 **to originate, take** *or* **have origin,** be born, take
birth, come into the world, **become,** come to be, get
to be (*informal*), see the light of day, rise, **arise,** take
rise, take its rise, **come forth, issue,** issue forth,
come out, spring *or* crop up; burst forth, break out,
erupt, irrupt

14 **to engender, beget, procreate** *see* 78.8; **give birth
to, bear,** birth, bring to birth; father, mother, sire

adjectives

15 **beginning, initial,** initiatory *or* initiative; **incipient,**
inceptive, **introductory,** inchoative, inchoate;
inaugural *or* inauguratory; **prime,** primal, **primary,**
primitive, primeval; **original, first,** first ever, first of
all; aboriginal, autochthonous; **elementary,**
elemental, **fundamental,** foundational;
rudimentary, rudimental, abecedarian; **ancestral,**
primogenital *or* primogenitary; **formative, creative,**
procreative, inventive; embryonic, in embryo, in the
bud, budding, fetal, gestatory, parturient, pregnant,
in its infancy; infant, infantile, incunabular; **natal,**
nascent, prenatal, antenatal, neonatal

16 **preliminary, prefatory,** preludial, proemial; entry-
level, door-opening; prepositive, prefixed

17 **first, foremost,** front, up-front (*informal*), **head,
chief, principal,** premier, **leading, main,** flagship;
maiden

adverbs

18 **first,** firstly, **at first,** first off, first thing, for
openers *or* starters (*informal*), as a gambit, up front
(*informal*), **in the first place,** first and foremost,
before everything, *primo* (*Latin*); **principally,**
mainly, chiefly, most of all; **primarily,** initially;
originally, in the beginning, *in limine* (*Latin*), **at
the start,** at first glance *or* first blush, at the outset,

at the first go-off (*informal*); from the ground up,
from the foundations, from the beginning, **from
scratch** (*informal*), from the first, **from the word
'go'** (*informal*), *ab origine* (*Latin*), *ab initio* (*Latin*); *ab
ovo* (*Latin*)

word elements

19 acro–, arche–, eo–, ne–, neo–, proto–; *Ur–* (*German*)

818 MIDDLE

nouns

1 **middle,** median, midmost, **midst;** thick, thick of
things; **centre** *see* 208.2; **heart, core,** nucleus,
kernel; **mean** *see* 246; interior *see* 207.2; midriff,
diaphragm; **waist,** waistline, zone, girth, tummy *and*
belly girt (*both informal*); equator; diameter

2 **mid-distance,** middle distance; **equidistance; half,**
moiety; **middle ground,** middle of the road,
centrism; halfway point *or* place, midway, midcourse,
halfway house; bisection

verbs

3 **to seek the middle,** bisect; average *see* 246.2; double,
fold, middle (*nautical*)

adjectives

4 **middle, medial,** median, mesial, middling,
mediocre, average, **medium** *see* 246.3, **mezzo** (*music*),
mean, mid; **midmost,** middlemost; **central** *see*
208.11, core, nuclear; interior; **intermediate,**
intermediary; equidistant, halfway, midway, in-
between, equatorial; midland, mediterranean;
midships, amidships; centrist, moderate, middle-of-
the-road; centre-seeking, centripetal

adverbs

5 **midway, halfway, in the middle,** betwixt and
between (*informal*), halfway in the middle (*informal*);
plump *or* smack *or* slap- *or* smack-dab *or* slap-bang
in the middle (*informal*); half-and-half, neither here
nor there, *mezzo-mezzo* (*Italian*); medially,
mediumly; in the mean; *in medias res* (*Latin*); **in the
midst of,** in the thick of; midships, amidships

word elements

6 mid–, medi–, medio–, mes–, meso–, mesio–;
intermedi–, intermedio–

819 END

nouns

1 **end,** end point, ending, perfection, be-all and end-
all, **termination, terminus, terminal,** terminating,
term, period, **expiration,** expiry, phaseout,
phasedown, discontinuation, closeout, **cessation** *see*
856, ceasing, consummation, culmination,
conclusion, finish, finis, finale, the end, finishing,
finalizing *or* finalization, a wrap (*informal*), quietus,
stoppage, windup *and* payoff (*both informal*), curtain,
curtains (*informal*), all she wrote (*US & Canadian
informal*), fall of the curtain, end of the road *or* line
(*informal*); decease, taps, **death** *see* 307; **last,**

"latter end"—Bible, last gasp *or* breath, final twitch, last throe, last legs, last hurrah (*informal*); omega, Ω, izzard, Z; **goal**, destination, stopping place, resting place, finish line, tape *and* wire (*both informal*); denouement, catastrophe, final solution, resolution; last *or* final words, peroration, swan song, dying words, envoi, coda, epilogue; **fate, destiny**, last things, eschatology, last trumpet, Gabriel's trumpet, crack of doom, doom; **effect** see 886; **happy ending**, Hollywood ending, walking into the sunset

2 **extremity, extreme; limit** see 793.5, ultimacy, definitiveness, **boundary**, farthest bound, jumping-off place, Thule, *Ultima Thule* (*Latin*), **pole; tip**, point, nib; tail, **tail end**, butt end, tag, tag end, fag end; bitter end; stub, stump, butt; bottom dollar (*informal*), bottom of the barrel (*informal*)

3 **close**, closing, cessation; decline, lapse; **homestretch, last lap** *or* **round** *or* **inning** (*informal*), last stage; beginning of the end

4 **finishing stroke**, ender, **end-all**, quietus, stopper, **deathblow**, death stroke, *coup de grâce* (*French*), kiss of death; **finisher**, clincher, equalizer, crusher, **settler;** knockout *and* knockout blow (*both informal*); sockdolager (*US informal*), KO *or* kayo *and* kayo punch (*all informal*); final stroke, finishing *or* perfecting *or* crowning touch, last dab *or* lick (*informal*)

verbs

5 **to end, terminate**, determine, close, close out, close the books on, phase out *or* down, **finish, conclude,** finish with, resolve, finish *or* wind up (*informal*); **put an end to**, put a period to, put paid to, put *or* lay to rest, **make an end of**, bring to an end, bring to a close *or* halt, end up; **get it over**, get over with *or* through with (*informal*); bring down *or* drop the curtain; put the lid on (*informal*), fold up (*informal*), wrap *and* wrap up (*both informal*), sew up (*informal*); call off (*informal*), call all bets off (*informal*); **dispose of**, polish off (*informal*); kibosh *and* put the kibosh on (*both informal*), put the skids under (*informal*); **stop, cease** see 856.6; perorate; abort; scrap *and* scratch (*both informal*); **kill** see 308.13, extinguish, scrag *and* waste *and* take out *and* zap (*all informal*), **give the quietus**, put the finisher *or* settler on (*informal*), knock on *or* in the head, knock out (*informal*), kayo *or* KO (*both informal*), shoot down *and* shoot down in flames (*both informal*), stop dead in one's tracks, wipe out (*informal*); **cancel, delete,** expunge, censor, censor out, blank out, erase

6 **to come to an end, draw to a close**, expire, die see 307.19, come to rest, end up, land up; lapse, become void *or* extinct *or* defunct, run out, run its course, have its time *and* have it (*both informal*), pass, **pass away**, die away, wear off *or* away, go out, blow over, be all over, be no more

7 **to complete** see 793.6, perfect, finish, finish off, finish up, put the last *or* final *or* finishing touches on, finalize (*informal*)

adjectives

8 **ended, at an end, terminated, concluded, finished, complete** see 793.9, perfected, settled, decided, set at rest; **over, all over**, all up (*informal*);

all off (*informal*), all bets off (*informal*); **done**, done with, over with, over and done with, through *and* through with (*both informal*); wound up (*informal*), washed up (*informal*); all over bar the shouting (*informal*); **dead** see 307.30, **defunct**, extinct; **finished**, defeated, out of action, disabled, *hors de combat* (*French*); **cancelled, deleted**, expunged, censored *or* censored out, blanked *or* blanked out, bleeped *or* bleeped out

9 (*informal terms*) **belly-up, dead meat**, kaput, shot, done for, scragged, shot down, shot down in flames, down in flames, wasted, zapped, pffft *or* phut, wiped out, washed up, down and out, down the tubes, totalled

10 **ending, closing, concluding, finishing,** culminating *or* culminative, consummative *or* consummatory, **ultimate**, definitive, perfecting *or* perfective, terminating, crowning, capping

11 **final, terminal**, terminating *or* terminative, determinative, definitive, **conclusive; last**, last-ditch (*informal*), last but not least, eventual, farthest, extreme, boundary, border, limbic, limiting, polar, **endmost, ultimate;** caudal, tail, tail-end

adverbs

12 **finally**, in fine; **ultimately, eventually, as a matter of course; lastly, last, at last**, at the last *or* end *or* conclusion, at length, at long last; **in conclusion, in sum;** conclusively, once and for all

13 **to the end, to the bitter end, all the way**, to the last gasp, the last extremity, **to a finish**, *à outrance* (*French*), till hell freezes over (*informal*), "to the edge of doom", "to the last syllable of recorded time"—both Shakespeare

phrases

14 **that's all for, that's final, that's that**, that's all she wrote (*US & Canadian informal*), that wraps it up (*informal*), that's the end of the matter, so much for that, 'nuff said *and* enough said (*both informal*), that's all folks (*informal*); the subject is closed, the matter is ended, the deal is off (*informal*); "the rest is silence"—Shakespeare

word elements

15 acr–, acro–, tel–, telo–, tele–

820 TIME

nouns

1 **time, duration**, *durée* (*French*), lastingness, continuity see 811, term, while, tide, space; real time; psychological time; tense see 530.12; **period** see 823, time frame; time warp; cosmic time; kairotic time; space-time see 158.6; the past see 836, the present see 837, the future see 838; timebinding; **chronology** see 831.1

2 **Time, Father Time**, Cronus, Kronos; "Old Time, that greatest and longest established spinner of all"—Dickens, "that old bald cheater, Time"—Ben Jonson, "Old Time, the clocksetter, that bald sexton Time", "that old common arbitrator, Time", "the nurse and breeder of all good"—all Shakespeare, "the soul of the world"—Pythagoras, "the

author of authors"—, "the greatest innovator"—BOTH FRANCIS BACON, "the devourer of things"—OVID, "the illimitable, silent, never-resting thing called Time"—CARLYLE, "a short parenthesis in a long period"—DONNE, "a sandpile we run our fingers in"—SANDBURG

3 tract of time, corridors of time, whirligig of time, glass *or* hourglass of time, sands of time, ravages of time, noiseless foot of Time, scythe of Time, "the dark backward and abysm of time", "the tooth of time"—BOTH SHAKESPEARE

4 **passage of time, course of time, lapse of time,** progress of time, process of time, succession of time, time-flow, flow *or* flowing *or* flux of time, sweep of time, stream *or* current *or* tide of time, march *or* step of time, flight of time, time's caravan, "Time's revolving wheels"—PETRARCH, "Time's wingèd chariot"—ANDREW MARVELL

verbs

5 **to elapse,** lapse, **pass, expire,** run its course, run out, go *or* pass by; **flow,** tick away *or* by *or* on, run, proceed, advance, roll *or* press on, flit, fly, slip, slide, glide; **continue** see 811.4, last, **endure,** go *or* run *or* flow on

6 **to spend time, pass time, put in time,** employ *or* use time, fill *or* occupy time, kill time (*informal*), consume time, take time, take up time, while away the time; find *or* look for time; race with *or* against time, buy time, work against time, run out of time, make time stand still; weekend, winter, summer; keep time, measure time

adjectives

7 **temporal, chronological;** durational, durative; lasting, continuous see 811.8

adverbs

8 **when, at which time,** what time *and* whenas (*both old*), at which moment *or* instant, on which occasion, **upon which, whereupon,** at which, in which time, at what time, in what period, on what occasion, whenever

9 **at that time,** on that occasion, at the same time as, at the same time *or* moment that, then, concurrently, simultaneously, contemporaneously

10 in the meantime, meanwhile see 825.5; during the time; for the duration; at a stretch

11 **then,** thereat, thereupon, **at that time,** at that moment *or* instant, in that case *or* instance, on that occasion; **again,** at another time, at some other time, anon

12 **whenever,** whene'er, whensoever, whensoe'er, **at whatever time,** at any time, any time, no matter when; if ever, once

13 in the year of our Lord, *anno Domini* (*Latin*), AD, in the Common *or* Christian Era, CE; *ante Christum* (*Latin*), AC, before Christ, BC, before the Common *or* Christian era, BCE; *anno urbis conditae* (*Latin*), AUC; *anno regni* (*Latin*), AR

prepositions

14 **during,** pending, *durante* (*law*); **in the course of,** in the process of, in the middle of; **in the time of,** at the time of, in the age *or* era of; over, through,

throughout, throughout the course of, **for the period of;** until the conclusion of

15 until, till, to, unto, **up to,** up to the time of

conjunctions

16 when, while, whilst, the while; **during the time that,** at the time that, at the same time that, at *or* during which time; **whereas, as long as,** as far as

phrases

17 time flies, *tempus fugit* (*Latin*), time runs out, time marches on, "Time rolls his ceaseless course"—SIR WALTER SCOTT, "Time and tide stayeth for no man"—RICHARD BRAITHWAITE

word elements

18 chron–, chrono–, –chronous

821 TIMELESSNESS

nouns

1 timelessness, neverness, datelessness, eternity see 828.1, 2; no time, no time at all, running out of time; time out of mind, stopping time; everlasting moment

2 (*a time that will never come*) Greek calends *or* kalends, when hell freezes over, the thirtieth of February, "till Birnam Wood do come to Dunsinane"—SHAKESPEARE

adjectives

3 timeless, dateless

adverbs

4 never, ne'er, **not ever,** at no time, on no occasion, not at all; **nevermore;** never in the world, never on earth; not in donkey's years, never in all one's born days (*informal*), never in my life, *jamais de la vie* (*French*)

5 without date, *sine die* (*Latin*), open, open-ended

822 INFINITY

nouns

1 infinity, infiniteness, infinitude, the all, the be-all and end-all; **boundlessness, limitlessness, endlessness;** illimitability, interminability, termlessness; **immeasurability,** unmeasurability, immensity, incalculability, innumerability, incomprehensibility; measurelessness, countlessness, unreckonability, numberlessness; exhaustlessness, inexhaustibility; universality, "world without end"—BIBLE; **all-inclusiveness,** all-comprehensiveness; **eternity** see 828.1, 2, **perpetuity** see 828, forever; "a dark illimitable ocean, without bound"—MILTON

verbs

2 to have no limit *or* **bounds,** have *or* know no end, be without end, **go on and on,** go on forever, never cease *or* end

adjectives

3 **infinite, boundless, endless, limitless,** termless, shoreless; unbounded, uncircumscribed, **unlimited,** illimited, infinitely continuous *or* extended, stretching *or* extending everywhere, without bound, without limit *or* end, no end of *or* to; illimitable, **interminable,** interminate; **immeasurable,** incalculable, unreckonable, innumerable, incomprehensible, unfathomable; measureless, countless, sumless; **unmeasured,** unmeasurable, immense, unplumbed, untold, unnumbered, without measure *or* number *or* term; exhaustless, inexhaustible; **all-inclusive,** all-comprehensive *see* 863.14, **universal** *see* 863.14; **perpetual, eternal** *see* 828.7;

"as boundless as the sea"—SHAKESPEARE

adverbs

4 **infinitely, illimitably,** boundlessly, limitlessly, **interminably; immeasurably,** measurelessly, immensely, incalculably, innumerably, incomprehensibly; **endlessly,** without end *or* limit; *ad infinitum* (*Latin*), to infinity; **forever, eternally** *see* 828.10, in perpetuity,

"to the last syllable of recorded time"—SHAKESPEARE

823 PERIOD
portion or point of time

nouns

1 **period, point, juncture,** stage; **interval,** lapse of time, time frame, space, span, timespan, stretch, time-lag, time-gap; **time,** while, **moment,** minute, instant, hour, day, **season;** psychological moment; pregnant *or* fateful moment, fated moment, kairos, moment of truth; **spell** *see* 824;

"this bank and shoal of time"—SHAKESPEARE

2 (*periods*) **moment, second,** millisecond, microsecond, nanosecond; **minute;** hour, man-hour; **day,** sun; weekday; **week;** fortnight; **month,** moon, lunation; calendar month, lunar month; **quarter; semester,** trimester, term, session, academic year; Lent term, Hilary term, Michaelmas term; **year,** annum, sun, twelvemonth; common year, regular year, intercalary year, leap year, bissextile year, defective year, perfect *or* abundant year; solar year, lunar year, sidereal year; fiscal year, financial year; calendar year; quinquennium, lustrum, lustre; **decade,** decennium, decennary; **century; millennium**

3 **term,** time, duration, **tenure;** spell *see* 824

4 **age, generation,** time, day, date, cycle; **aeon** *or* eon; Platonic year, great year, *annus magnus* (*Latin*)

5 **era, epoch, age;** Golden Age, Silver Age; Ice Age, glacial epoch; stone Age, Bronze Age, Iron Age, steel Age; Middle Ages, Dark Ages; Elizabethan Period; Georgian Period; Age of Elegance; Directoire; Victorian Period; Reconstruction Era *and* Gilded Age (*1870s and '80s*); Gay Nineties *and* Naughty Nineties *and* Mauve Decade *and* Golden Age *and* Gilded Age (*1890s*); Roaring Twenties *and* Golden Twenties *and* Mad Decade *and* Age of the Red-Hot Mamas *and* Jazz Age *and* Flapper Era (*1920s*); Depression Era, Hungry Thirties (*1930s*); New Deal Era; Prohibition Era; McCarthy Era; Rock'n'Roll years; Swinging Sixties (*1960s*), Me generation

6 (*modern age*) Technological Age, Automobile Age, Air Age, Jet Age, Supersonic Age, Atomic Age, Electronic Age, Computer Age, Space Age, Age of Anxiety, Age of Aquarius

7 **geological time periods**

Algonkian	Mississippian
Archaean	Oligocene
Archaeozoic	Ordovician
Cambrian	Paleocene
Carboniferous	Paleozoic
Cenozoic	Pennsylvanian
Comanchean	Permian
Cretaceous	Pleistocene
Devonian *or* Old Red	Pliocene
Sandstone	Precambrian
Eocene	Proterozoic
Glacial	Quaternary
Holocene	Recent
Jurassic	Silurian
Lower Cretaceous	Tertiary
Lower Tertiary	Triassic
Mesozoic	Upper Cretaceous
Miocene	Upper Tertiary

824 SPELL
period of duty, etc

nouns

1 **spell,** fit, stretch, go (*informal*)

2 **turn, bout, round, inning,** innings, **time,** time at bat, place, say, whack *and* go *and* shot (*all informal*); opportunity, chance; **relief, spell;** one's turn, one's move (*informal*), one's say

3 **shift,** work shift, **tour,** tour of duty, stint, bit, **watch, trick,** time, **turn,** relay, spell *or* turn of work; day shift, back shift, night shift, swing shift, graveyard shift (*informal*), dogwatch, anchor watch; sunrise watch; split shift, split schedule; flextime *or* flexitime; halftime, part-time, full-time; **overtime**

4 **term,** time; **tenure,** continuous tenure, tenure in *or* of office; **enlistment,** hitch (*informal*), tour (*US & Canadian*); prison term, stretch (*informal*), porridge (*informal*)

verbs

5 **to take one's turn,** have a go (*informal*); **take turns,** alternate, turn and turn about; **relieve,** cover, **fill in for,** take over for; put in one's time, work one's shift; **stand one's watch,** keep a watch; have one's innings; do a stint; hold office, have tenure *or* tenure of appointment; **enlist,** sign up; reenlist, re-up (*informal*); do a hitch (*informal*), do a tour *or* tour of duty; serve *or* do time, do porridge (*informal*)

825 INTERIM
intermediate period

nouns

1 **interim, interval, interlude, intermission,** pause, break, **time out,** recess, playtime, coffee break, tea break, lunchbreak, dinner hour, halftime *or* halftime intermission, interruption, natural break; **lull,** quiet spell, resting point, point of repose, plateau, letup, relief, vacation, vac (*informal*), holiday, time off, off-time; downtime; **respite** *see* 20.2; **intermission,** interval, entr'acte; *intermezzo* (*Italian*); interregnum

2 **meantime, meanwhile,** while, the while

verbs

3 **to intervene,** interlude, interval; **pause,** break, **recess,** declare a recess; call a halt *or* break *or* intermission; **call time** *or* time-out; take five *and* ten, etc *and* take a break (*all informal*)

adjectives

4 **interim, temporary,** tentative, provisional, provisory

adverbs

5 **meanwhile, meantime, in the meanwhile** *or* **meantime,** in the interim, *ad interim* (*Latin*); between acts *or* halves *or* periods, betweenwhiles, betweentimes, between now and then; till *or* until then; *en attendant* (*French*), in the intervening time, during the interval, at the same time, for the nonce, for a time *or* season; *pendente lite* (*Latin*)

826 DURATION

nouns

1 **durability, endurance,** duration, durableness, **lastingness,** *longueur* (*French*), perenniality, abidingness, long-lastingness, perdurability; **continuance,** maintenance, **steadfastness,** constancy, **stability** *see* 854, **persistence, permanence** *see* 852, standing, long standing; **longevity,** long-livedness; **antiquity, age; survival,** survivability, viability, defiance *or* defeat of time; **service life,** serviceable life, useful life, shelf life, mean life; **perpetuity** *see* 828

2 **protraction, prolongation,** continuation, extension, lengthening, drawing- *or* stretching- *or* dragging- *or* spinning-out, lingering; procrastination *see* 845.5

3 **length of time,** distance of time, vista *or* stretch *or* desert of time,
"deserts of vast eternity"—Andrew Marvell, "the dark backward and abysm of time"—Shakespeare; corridor *or* tunnel of time

4 **long time,** long while, long; **age** *and* **ages** (*both informal*), **aeon** *or* **eon,** century, eternity, years, **years on end,** coon's age (*US informal*), donkey's years (*informal*), month of Sundays (*informal*), yonks (*informal*)

5 **lifetime, life,** life's duration, life expectancy, lifespan, expectation of life,
"threescore years and ten"—Bible, period of existence, all the days of one's life; **generation, age;** all one's born days *or* natural life (*informal*), man and boy

verbs

6 **to endure, last** *or* **last out, bide, abide,** dwell, perdure, **continue,** run, extend, **go on,** carry on, hold on, keep on, stay on, run on, stay the course, go the distance, go through with, grind *or* slog on,

grind *or* plug away; **live, live on,** continue to be, subsist, exist, tarry; get *or* keep one's head above water; **persist;** hang in *and* hang in there *and* hang tough (*all informal*); maintain, sustain, **remain, stay,** keep, hold, stand, prevail, last long, hold out; **survive,** defy *or* defeat time; live to fight another day; perennate; **survive,** live on, live through; wear, wear well

7 **to linger on,** linger, tarry, go on, **go on and on, wear on,** crawl, creep, drag, **drag on,** drag along, drag its slow length along, drag a lengthening chain

8 **to outlast, outstay,** last out, outwear, **outlive, survive**

9 **to protract, prolong,** continue, **extend, lengthen,** lengthen out, **draw out, spin out,** drag *or* stretch out; linger on, dwell on; dawdle, procrastinate, temporize, drag one's feet

adjectives

10 **durable,** perdurable, **lasting, enduring,** perduring, **abiding, continuing,** remaining, staying, **stable** *see* 854.12, persisting, **persistent,** perennial; inveterate, agelong; **steadfast, constant,** intransient, immutable, unfading, evergreen, sempervirent, **permanent** *see* 852.7, perennial, **long-lasting,** long-standing, of long duration *or* standing, diuturnal; long-term; **long-lived,** tough, hardy, vital, longevous *or* longeval; **ancient,** aged, antique; macrobiotic; chronic; **perpetual** *see* 828.7

11 **protracted, prolonged,** extended, lengthened; **long,** overlong, time-consuming, interminable, marathon, lasting, **lingering,** languishing; long-continued, long-continuing, long-pending; drawn- *or* stretched- *or* dragged- *or* spun-out, long-drawn, **long-drawn-out;** long-winded, prolix, verbose *see* 538.12

12 **daylong, nightlong,** weeklong, monthlong, yearlong

13 **lifelong,** livelong, lifetime, for life

adverbs

14 **for a long time, long, for long,** interminably, unendingly, undyingly, persistently, protractedly, enduringly; for ever so long (*informal*), for many a long day, for life *or* a lifetime, for an age *or* ages, for a coon's *or* dog's age (*US informal*), for a month of Sundays (*informal*), for donkey's years (*informal*), **forever and a day, forever and ever, for years on end, for days on end,** etc; all the year round, all the day long, the livelong day, as the day is long; morning, noon, and night; hour after hour, day after day, month after month, year after year; day in day out, month in month out, year in year out; till hell freezes over (*informal*), till you're blue in the face (*informal*), till the cows come home (*informal*), till doomsday, from now till doomsday, from here to eternity, till the end of time, to the crack of doom, "to the edge of doom"—Shakespeare; since time began, from way back, long ago, long since, time out of mind, time immemorial

827 TRANSIENCE
short duration

nouns

1 **transience** *or* transiency, transientness, **impermanence** *or* impermanency, transitoriness, changeableness *see 853*, rootlessness, **mutability, instability, temporariness,** fleetingness, momentariness; finitude; **ephemerality,** ephemeralness, short duration; evanescence, volatility, fugacity, **short-livedness; mortality,** death, perishability, corruptibility, caducity; **expedience** *see 994*, ad hoc, ad hockery *or* ad hocism, adhocracy

2 **brevity, briefness,** shortness; **swiftness** *see 174*, fleetness

3 **short time, little while,** little, **instant, moment** *see 829.3*, mo (*informal*), small space, span, spurt, **short spell,** tick (*informal*), half a mo (*informal*), stound (*old or dialect*); no time, less than no time; bit *or* **little bit,** a breath, the wink of an eye, pair of winks (*informal*); **two shakes** *and* two shakes of a lamb's tail (*both informal*)

4 **transient,** transient guest *or* boarder, temporary lodger; **sojourner;** passer, passerby; **wanderer; vagabond,** vagrant, drifter, derelict, homeless person, tramp, hobo, bum (*informal*)

5 **ephemeron,** ephemera, ephemeral; **ephemerid,** ephemeris, ephemerides (*plural*); mayfly; bubble, smoke; nine days' wonder, flash in the pan; snows of yesteryear, *neiges d'antan* (*French*)

verbs

6 (*be transient*) **to flit, fly,** fleet; pass, **pass away, vanish, evaporate,** dissolve, evanesce, disappear, fade, melt, sink; fade like a shadow *or* dream, vanish like a dream, burst like a bubble, **go up in smoke,** melt like snow;
"leave not a rack behind"—SHAKESPEARE

adjectives

7 **transient, transitory,** transitive; **temporary,** temporal; **impermanent,** unenduring, undurable, nondurable, nonpermanent; frail, brittle, fragile, insubstantial; changeable *see 853.6*, **mutable, unstable,** inconstant *see 853.7*; capricious, fickle, impulsive, impetuous; **short-lived, ephemeral,** fly-by-night, evanescent, volatile, **momentary;** deciduous; **passing,** fleeting, flitting, flying, fading, dying; fugitive, fugacious; perishable, mortal, corruptible;
"as transient as the clouds"—ROBERT GREEN INGERSOLL, here today and gone tomorrow; **expedient** *see 994.5*, ad hoc

8 **brief, short,** short-time, quick, brisk, swift, fleet, speedy,
"short and sweet"—THOMAS LODGE; meteoric, cometary, flashing, flickering; short-term, short-termed

adverbs

9 **temporarily,** for the moment, for the time, *pro tempore* (*Latin*), pro tem, for the nonce, **for the time being,** for a time, awhile

10 **transiently,** impermanently, evanescently, transitorily, changeably, mutably, ephemerally, fleetingly, flittingly, flickeringly, **briefly, shortly,** swiftly, quickly, **for a little while,** for a short time; **momentarily,** for a moment; **in an instant** *see 829.7*

phrases

11 "all flesh is grass"—BIBLE

828 PERPETUITY
endless duration

nouns

1 **perpetuity,** perpetualness; **eternity,** eternalness, sempiternity, infinite duration; everness, foreverness, **everlastingness, permanence** *see 852*, everduringness, duration *see 826*, perdurability, indestructibility; **constancy,** stability, immutability, continuance, continualness, perennialness *or* perenniality, **ceaselessness,** unceasingness, incessancy; timelessness *see 821*; **endlessness,** never-endingness, **interminability; infinity** *see 822*; coeternity

2 **forever, an eternity,** endless time, **time without end;**
"a moment standing still for ever"—JAMES MONTGOMERY, "a short parenthesis in a long period"—DONNE, "deserts of vast eternity"—ANDREW MARVELL

3 **immortality,** eternal life, **deathlessness,** imperishability, undyingness, incorruptibility *or* incorruption, athanasy *or* athanasia; eternal youth, fountain of youth

4 **perpetuation,** preservation, eternalization, immortalization; eternal re-creation, eternal return *or* recurrence; steady-state universe

verbs

5 **to perpetuate, preserve,** preserve from oblivion, keep fresh *or* alive, perennialize, **eternalize,** eternize, **immortalize;** monumentalize; freeze, embalm

6 to last *or* endure forever, **go on forever,** go on and on, live forever, **have no end,** have no limits *or* bounds *or* term, never cease *or* end *or* die *or* pass

adjectives

7 **perpetual, everlasting,** everliving, ever-being, ever-abiding, ever-during, ever-durable, permanent *see 852.7*, perdurable, indestructible; **eternal,** sempiternal, eterne (*old*), **infinite** *see 822.3*, aeonian *or* eonian; dateless, ageless, timeless, immemorial; **endless,** unending, never-ending, without end, **interminable,** nonterminous, nonterminating; **continual,** continuous, steady, **constant, ceaseless,** nonstop, unceasing, never-ceasing, **incessant,** unremitting, unintermitting, uninterrupted,
"continuous as the stars that shine"—WORDSWORTH; coeternal

8 **perennial,** indeciduous, **evergreen,** sempervirent, ever-new, ever-young; ever-blooming, ever-bearing

9 **immortal,** everlasting, **deathless,** undying, never-dying, **imperishable,** incorruptible, amaranthine; fadeless, **unfading,** never-fading, ever-fresh; frozen, embalmed

adverbs

10 **perpetually,** in perpetuity, **everlastingly,**
eternally, permanently *see* 852.9, perennially,
perdurably, indestructibly, **constantly,** continually,
steadily, **ceaselessly,** unceasingly, never-ceasingly,
incessantly, never-endingly, **endlessly,** unendingly,
interminably, without end, world without end, time
without end,
"from everlasting to everlasting"—Bible; **infinitely,** *ad*
infinitum (*Latin*) *see* 822.4

11 **always, all along, all the time,** all the while, at
all times, *semper et ubique* (*Latin,* always and
everywhere); ever and always, **invariably,** without
exception, never otherwise, *semper eadem* (*Latin,* ever
the same; Elizabeth I)

12 **forever, forevermore, for ever and ever,** forever
and aye; forever and a day (*informal*), now and
forever, *ora e sempre* (*Italian*),
"yesterday and today and forever"—Bible; **ever,**
evermore, ever and anon, ever and again; aye, for
aye; **for good,** for keeps (*informal*), for good and all,
for all time; throughout the ages, from age to age, in
all ages,
"for ages of ages"—Douay Bible; **to the end of time,**
till time stops *or* runs out,
"to the last syllable of recorded time"—Shakespeare, to
the crack of doom, to the last trumpet, till
doomsday; till you're blue in the face (*informal*), till
hell freezes over (*informal*), till the cows come home
(*informal*)

13 **for life,** for all one's natural life, for the term of
one's days, while life endures, while one draws
breath, in all one's born days (*informal*); from the
cradle to the grave, from the womb to the tomb; **till**
death, till death do us part

829 INSTANTANEOUSNESS
imperceptible duration

nouns

1 **instantaneousness** *or* **instantaneity,**
momentariness, **momentaneousness** (*old*),
immediateness *or* immediacy, near-simultaneity *or*
simultaneousness; simultaneity *see* 835

2 **suddenness, abruptness, precipitateness,**
precipitance *or* precipitancy; **unexpectedness,**
unanticipation, inexpectation *see* 131

3 **instant, moment, second,** sec (*informal*), split
second, millisecond, microsecond, nanosecond, half a
second, half a mo (*informal*), minute, **trice,** twinkle,
twinkling, twinkling *or* **twinkle of an eye,** twink,
wink, bat of an eye (*informal*), **flash,** crack, tick,
stroke, breath, twitch, stound (*old or dialect*); two
shakes of a lamb's tail *and* two shakes *and* shake *and*
half a shake *and* jiffy *and* jiff *and* half a jiffy (*all*
informal)

adjectives

4 **instantaneous,** instant, momentary, momentaneous
(*old*), **immediate,** presto, quick as thought *or*
lightning; lightning-like, lightning-swift; nearly
simultaneous; simultaneous

5 **sudden, abrupt,** precipitant, **precipitate,**
precipitous; hasty, headlong, impulsive, impetuous;
speedy, swift, quick; **unexpected** *see* 131.10,
unanticipated, unpredicted, unforeseen, unlooked-for;
surprising *see* 131.11, startling, electrifying,
shocking, nerve-shattering

adverbs

6 **instantly,** instanter, momentaneously (*old*),
momentarily, momently, **instantaneously,**
immediately, right off the bat (*informal*); on the
instant, on the dot (*informal*), on the nail, on the
spot

7 **quickly, in an instant, in a trice, in a second,** in
a moment, in a mo *or* half a mo (*informal*), in a bit
or little bit, in a jiff *or* jiffy *or* half a jiffy (*informal*),
in a flash, in a wink (*informal*), in a twink, **in a**
twinkling, in the twinkling of an eye, as quick
as a wink, as quick as greased lightning (*informal*),
in two shakes *or* a shake *or* half a shake (*informal*), in
two shakes of a lamb's tail (*informal*), before you can
say 'Jack Robinson' (*informal*); **in no time,** in less
than no time, in nothing flat (*informal*), in short
order; at the drop of a hat, like a shot; with the
speed of light

8 **at once,** at once and on the spot, **then and there,**
now, right now, right away, right off,
straightway, straightaway, forthwith, this minute, this
very minute, **without delay,** without the least delay,
in a hurry (*informal*), *pronto* (*Spanish*), *subito*
(*Italian*); **simultaneously,** at the same instant, in
the same breath; **all at once,** all together, at one
time, at a stroke, at one stroke, at a blow, at one
blow, at one swoop,
"at one fell swoop"—Shakespeare; at one jump, *per*
saltum (*Latin*), *uno saltu* (*Latin*)

9 **suddenly,** sudden, of a sudden, on a sudden, **all of**
a sudden, all at once: abruptly, sharp;
precipitously *or* precipitately, precipitantly,
impulsively, impetuously, hastily; dash; smack, slap-
bang, bang, slap, plop, plunk, plump, pop;
unexpectedly *see* 131.14, out of a clear blue sky,
when least expected, before you know it; at short
notice, without notice *or* warning, without further
ado, unawares, **surprisingly** *see* 131.15, startlingly,
like a thunderbolt *or* thunderclap, like a flash, like a
bolt from the blue

phrases

10 no sooner said than done

830 EVENT

nouns

1 **event, eventuality,** eventuation, effect *see* 886,
issue, outcome, result, aftermath, consequence;
realization, materialization, coming to be *or* pass,
incidence; contingency, contingent; accident *see* 971.6

2 **event, occurrence, incident, episode, experience,**
adventure, hap, **happening,** happenstance,
phenomenon, fact, matter of fact, reality, particular,
circumstance, **occasion,** turn of events; **nonevent,**
pseudo-event, media event *or* happening, photo
opportunity; what's happening

3 affair, concern, matter, thing, concernment, interest, business, job (*informal*), transaction, proceeding, doing; current affairs *or* events; cause célèbre, matter of moment

4 affairs, concerns, matters, circumstances, relations, dealings, proceedings, doings, goings-on (*informal*); course *or* run of events, run of things, the way of things, the way things go, what happens, current of events, march of events; the world, life, the times; order of the day; conditions, state of affairs, environing *or* ambient phenomena, state *or* condition of things

verbs

5 to occur, happen *see* 971.11, hap, eventuate, take place, come *or* go down (*informal*), go on, transpire, be realized, come, come off (*informal*), come about, come true, come to pass, pass, pass off, go off, fall, befall, betide; be found, be met with

6 to turn up, show up (*informal*), come along, come one's way, cross one's path, come into being *or* existence, chance, crop up, spring up, pop up (*informal*), arise, come forth, come *or* draw on, appear, approach, materialize, present itself, be destined for one

7 to turn out, result *see* 886.5

8 to experience, have, know, feel, taste; encounter, meet, meet with, meet up with (*informal*), run up against (*informal*); undergo, go through, pass through, be subjected to, be exposed to, stand under, labour under, endure, suffer, sustain, pay, spend

adjectives

9 happening, occurring, current, actual, passing, taking place, on, going on, ongoing (*informal*), prevalent, prevailing, that is, that applies, in the wind, afloat, afoot, under way, in hand, on foot, ado, doing; incidental, circumstantial, accompanying; accidental; occasional; resultant; eventuating

10 eventful, momentous, stirring, bustling, full of incident; phenomenal

11 eventual, coming, final, last, ultimate; contingent, collateral, secondary, indirect

adverbs

12 eventually, ultimately, finally, in the end, after all is said and done, in the long run, in *or* over the long haul; in the course of things, in the natural way of things, as things go, as times go, as the world goes, as the tree falls, the way the cookie crumbles (*informal*), as things turn out, as it may be *or* happen *or* turn out, as luck *or* fate *or* destiny wills

conjunctions

13 in the event that, if, in case, if it should happen that, just in case, in any case, in either case, in the contingency that, in case that; provided *see* 958.12

831 MEASUREMENT OF TIME

nouns

1 chronology, timekeeping, timing, clocking, horology, chronometry, horometry, chronoscopy; watch- *or*

clock-making; calendar-making; dating, carbon-14 dating, dendrochronology

2 time of day, time *see* 820, the time; hour, minute; stroke of the hour, time signal, bell

3 standard time, civil time, zone time, slow time (*informal*); mean time, solar time, mean solar time, sidereal time, apparent time, local time; universal time *or* Greenwich time *or* Greenwich mean time *or* GMT; daylight-saving time; fast time (*informal*), summer time, British Summer Time *or* BST; Eastern time, Central time, Mountain time, Pacific time; Atlantic time; Alaska time, Yukon time; time zone

4 date, point of time, time, day; postdate, antedate; datemark; date line, International Date Line

5 epact, annual epact, monthly *or* menstrual epact

6 timepiece, timekeeper, timer, pinger, chronometer, ship's watch; horologe, horologium; clock, Big Ben, ticker (*informal*), watch, turnip (*informal*); speaking clock, hourglass, sundial; watch *or* clock movement, clockworks, watchworks

7 almanac, The Old Farmer's Almanac, Old Moore's Almanac, Ephemeris and Nautical Almanac, Information Please Almanac, Nautical Almanac, Poor Richard's Almanac, Reader's Digest Almanac, Whitaker's Almanack, World Almanac

8 calendar, calends; calendar stone, chronogram; almanac *or* astronomical calendar, ephemeris; perpetual calendar; advent calendar; Chinese calendar, church *or* ecclesiastical calendar, Cotsworth calendar, Gregorian calendar, Hebrew *or* Jewish calendar, Hindu calendar, international fixed calendar, Julian calendar, Muslim calendar, Republican *or* Revolutionary calendar, Roman calendar

9 chronicle, chronology, register, registry, record; annals, journal, diary; time sheet, time book, log, daybook; timecard, time ticket, clock card, check sheet; bundy (*Australian & NZ*); datebook; date slip; timetable, schedule, timeline, time schedule, time chart; time scale; time study, motion study, time and motion study

10 chronologist, chronologer, chronographer, horologist, horologer; watchmaker *or* clockmaker; timekeeper, timer; chronicler, annalist, diarist; calendar maker, calendarist

verbs

11 to time, fix *or* set the time, mark the time; keep time, mark time, measure time, beat time; clock (*informal*)

12 to punch the clock *and* punch in *and* punch out *and* time in *and* time out (*all informal*); ring in, ring out; clock in *or* on, clock out *or* off; check in, check out; check off

13 to date, be dated, date at *or* from, date back, bear a date of, bear the date of; fix *or* set the date, make a date; predate, backdate, antedate; postdate; update, bring up to date; datemark; date-stamp; dateline

14 to chronologize, chronicle, calendar, intercalate

adjectives

15 **chronologic** *or* **chronological,** temporal, timekeeping; **chronometric** *or* **chronometrical,** chronoscopic, chronographic *or* chronographical, chronogrammatic *or* chronogrammatical, horologic *or* horological, horometric *or* horometrical, metronomic *or* metronomical, calendric *or* calendrical, intercalary *or* intercalated; dated; annalistic, diaristic; calendarial

adverbs

16 **o'clock,** of the clock, by the clock; half past, half *or* half after; a quarter to *or* of, a quarter past *or* after

832 ANACHRONISM
false estimation or knowledge of time

nouns

1 **anachronism,** chronological *or* historical error, **mistiming, misdating,** misdate, postdating, antedating; parachronism, metachronism, prochronism; prolepsis, anticipation; earliness, lateness, tardiness, unpunctuality

verbs

2 to **mistime, misdate;** antedate, foredate, postdate; lag

adjectives

3 **anachronous** *or* **anachronistical** *or* **anachronistic,** parachronistic, metachronistic, prochronistic, unhistorical, unchronological; **mistimed, misdated;** antedated, foredated, postdated; ahead of time, **beforehand, early;** behind time, **behindhand, late,** unpunctual, tardy; **overdue,** past due; unseasonable, out of season; **dated,** out-of-date

833 PREVIOUSNESS

nouns

1 **previousness, earliness** *see* 844, **antecedence** *or* antecedency, priority, anteriority, **precedence** *or* precedency *see* 813, precession; *status quo ante* (*Latin*), previous *or* prior state, earlier state; preexistence; **anticipation,** predating, antedating; antedate; **past time** *see* 836
2 antecedent, precedent, premise; forerunner, **precursor** *see* 815, ancestor

verbs

3 to **be prior,** be before *or* early *or* earlier, come on the scene *or* appear earlier, **precede, antecede, forerun,** come *or* go before, set a precedent; **herald,** usher in, proclaim, announce; **anticipate,** antedate, predate; **preexist**

adjectives

4 **previous, prior, early** *see* 844.7, **earlier,** *ci-devant* *or* *ci-dessus* (*French*), **former,** fore, prime, first, **preceding** *see* 165.3, foregoing, above, anterior, **anticipatory,** antecedent; **preexistent;** older, elder, senior
5 prewar, ante-bellum, before the war; prerevolutionary; premundane *or* antemundane; prelapsarian, before the Fall; antediluvian, before the

Flood; protohistoric, prehistoric *see* 836.10; precultural; pre-Aryan; pre-Christian; premillenarian, premillennial; anteclassical, preclassical, pre-Roman, pre-Renaissance, pre-Romantic, pre-Victorian, etc

adverbs

6 **previously,** priorly, **hitherto, heretofore,** thitherto, theretofore; **before, early** *see* 844.11, **earlier,** ere, erenow, ere then, or ever; already, yet; before all; **formerly** *see* 836.13

prepositions

7 **prior to, previous to, before,** in advance of, in anticipation of, in preparation for

word elements

8 ante–, anti–, fore–, pre–, pro–, prot–, proto–, proter–, protero–, supra–

834 SUBSEQUENCE
later time

nouns

1 **subsequence,** posteriority, **succession, ensuing, following** *see* 166, sequence, coming after, supervenience, supervention; **lateness** *see* 845; afterlife, next life; remainder *see* 256, hangover (*informal*); postdating; postdate; future time *see* 838
2 **sequel** *see* 816, **follow-up,** sequelae, **aftermath; consequence,** effect *see* 886; **posterity,** offspring, descendant, heir, inheritor; **successor;** replacement, line, **lineage,** dynasty, family

verbs

3 to **come** *or* **follow** *or* **go after, follow,** follow on *or* **upon, succeed,** replace, take the place of, displace, overtake, supervene; **ensue,** issue, emanate, attend, **result;** follow up, trail, track, come close on *or* tread on the heels of, "follow hard upon"—Shakespeare, dog the footsteps of; **step into** *or* **fill the shoes of,** don the mantle of, assume the robe of

adjectives

4 **subsequent,** after, later, after-the-fact, *post factum* and *ex post facto* (*both Latin*), posterior, **following, succeeding,** successive, sequent, lineal, consecutive, ensuing, attendant; **junior,** cadet, puisne (*law*), younger
5 **posthumous,** afterdeath; **postprandial,** postcibal, postcenal, after-dinner; **post-war,** *postbellum* (*Latin*), after the war; **postdiluvian,** postdiluvial, after the flood, postlapsarian, after the Fall, post-industrial, postmodern, post-millenial, etc

adverbs

6 **subsequently,** after, afterwards, after that, after all, **later, next,** since; **thereafter,** thereon, thereupon, therewith, **then;** in the process *or* course of time, as things worked out, in the sequel; at a subsequent *or* later time, in the aftermath; *ex post facto* (*Latin*); hard on the heels *or* on the heels
7 **after which,** on *or* **upon which, whereupon,** whereon, whereat, whereto, whereunto, wherewith, wherefore, on, upon; hereinafter

prepositions

8 after, following, subsequent to, later than, past, beyond, behind; below, farther down *or* along

word elements

9 ante–, anti–, fore–, pre–, pro–, prot–, proto–, proter–, protero–, supra–; epi–, eph–, infra–, meta–, post–

835 SIMULTANEITY

nouns

1 simultaneity *or* simultaneousness, coincidence, co-occurrence, concurrence *or* concurrency, concomitance *or* concomitancy; coexistence; contemporaneousness *or* contemporaneity, coetaneousness *or* coetaneity, coevalness *or* coevalneity; unison; synchronism, synchronization; isochronism; accompaniment *see* 768, agreement *see* 787

2 contemporary, coeval, concomitant

3 tie, dead heat, draw

verbs

4 to coincide, co-occur, concur; coexist; coextend; synchronize, isochronize, put *or* be in phase, be in time, keep time, time; contemporize; accompany *see* 768.7, agree *see* 787.6, match, go along with, go hand in hand, keep pace with, keep in step

adjectives

5 simultaneous, concurrent, co-occurring, coinstantaneous, concomitant; tied, neck-and-neck, drawn; coexistent, coexisting; contemporaneous, contemporary, coetaneous, coeval; coterminous, conterminous; unison, unisonous; isochronous, isochronal; coeternal; accompanying *see* 768.9, collateral; agreeing *see* 787.9

6 synchronous, synchronized, synchronic *or* synchronal, in sync (*informal*); in time, in step, in tempo, in phase, with *or* on the beat

adverbs

7 simultaneously, concurrently, coinstantaneously; together, all together, at the same time, at one and the same time, as one, as one man, in concert with, in chorus, with one voice, in unison, in a chorus, in the same breath; at one time; synchronously, synchronically, isochronously, in phase, in sync (*informal*), with *or* on the beat, on the downbeat

836 THE PAST

nouns

1 the past, past, foretime, former times, past times, times past, water under the bridge, days *or* times gone by, bygone times *or* days, yesterday, yesteryear; recent past, just *or* only yesterday; history, past history; dead past, dead hand of the past,
"the dead cold hand of the Past"—OLIVER WENDELL HOLMES; the years that are past,

"the days that are no more"—TENNYSON, "the irrevocable Past"—LONGFELLOW, "a bucket of ashes"—CARL SANDBURG

2 old *or* olden times, early times, old *or* olden days, the olden time, times of old, days of old, days *or* times of yore, yore, yoretime, eld (*old*), good old times *or* days, the way it was, lang syne *or* auld lang syne (*both Scottish*), the long ago, time out of mind, days beyond recall; the old story, the same old story

3 antiquity, ancient times, time immemorial, ancient history, remote age *or* time, remote *or* far *or* dim *or* distant past, distance of time,
"the dark backward and abysm of time"—SHAKESPEARE; ancientness *see* 841

4 memory *see* 988, remembrance, recollection, reminiscence, fond remembrance, retrospection, musing on the past, looking back;
"the remembrance of things past"—SHAKESPEARE, "*la recherche du temps perdu*"—PROUST; reliving, reexperiencing; revival *see* 396.3; youth *see* 301

5 (*grammatical terms*) past tense, preterite, perfect tense, past perfect tense, pluperfect, historical present tense, past progressive tense; aorist; perfective aspect; preterition

verbs

6 to pass, be past, be a thing of the past, elapse, lapse, slip by *or* away, be gone, fade, fade away, be dead and gone, be all over, have run its course, have run out, have had its day; disappear *see* 34.2; die *see* 307.19

adjectives

7 past, gone, by, gone-by, bygone, gone glimmering, bypast, ago, over, departed, passed, passed away, elapsed, lapsed, vanished, faded, no more, irrecoverable, never to return, not coming back; dead *see* 307.30, dead as a dodo, expired, extinct, dead and buried, defunct, deceased; run out, blown over, finished, forgotten, wound up; passé, obsolete, has-been, dated, antique, antiquated

8 reminiscent *see* 988.22, retrospective, remembered *see* 988.23, recollected; relived, reexperienced; restored, revived

9 (*grammatical terms*) past, preterite *or* preteritive, pluperfect, past perfect; aorist, aoristic; perfective

10 former, past, fore, previous, late, recent, once, onetime, sometime, erstwhile, then, quondam; prior *see* 833.4; ancient, immemorial, early, primitive, primeval, prehistoric; old, olden

11 foregoing, aforegoing, preceding *see* 813.4; last, latter

12 back, backward, into the past; early; retrospective, retroactive, *ex post facto* (*Latin*), *a priori* (*Latin*)

adverbs

13 formerly, previously, priorly *see* 833.6; earlier, before, before now, erenow, erst, whilom, erewhile, hitherto, heretofore, thitherto, aforetime, beforetime, in the past, in times past; then; yesterday, only yesterday, recently; historically, prehistorically, in historic *or* prehistoric times

14 once, once upon a time, one day, one fine morning, time was

15 **ago, since,** gone by; back, back when; backward, to *or* into the past; **retrospectively,** reminiscently, retroactively

16 **long ago,** long since, **a long while** *or* **time ago,** some time ago *or* since, some time back, a way *or* away back (*informal*), ages ago, **years ago,** donkey's years ago (*informal*), yonks ago (*informal*); **in times past,** in times gone by, in the old days, in the good old days; **anciently, of old, of yore,** in ancient times, in olden times, in the olden times, **in days of yore,** early, in the memory of man, time out of mind

17 **since,** ever since, until now; **since long ago, long since,** from away back (*informal*), since days of yore, ages ago, **from time immemorial,** from time out of mind, aeons ago, since the world was made, since the world was young, since time began, since the year one *or* since the year dot, since Hector was a pup *and* since God knows when *and* since Adam was a boy (*both informal*)

word elements

18 archae–, archaeo–, archeo–; pale–, paleo–, praeter–, preter–, retro–; –ed, y– (*old*)

837 THE PRESENT

nouns

1 **the present,** presentness, present time, the here and now; **now,** the present juncture *or* occasion, the present hour *or* moment, this instant *or* second *or* moment, **the present day** *or* **time** *or* hour *or* minute, etc; **the present age,**
"the living sum-total of the whole Past"—CARLYLE; **today,** this day, **this day and age; this point,** this stage, this hour, **now,** nowadays, the now, the way things are, the nonce, **the time being; the times,** our times, these days; **contemporaneousness** *or* contemporaneity, nowness, actuality, topicality; **newness** *see* 840, modernity; the Now Generation, the me generation; historical present, present tense (*both grammatical*)

adjectives

2 **present, immediate,** latest, current, running, extant, existent, **existing,** actual, topical, being, that is, as is, that be; **present-day,** present-time, present-age, **modern** *see* 840.13, modern-day; **contemporary,** contemporaneous; up-to-date, up-to-the-minute, fresh, **new** *see* 840.7

adverbs

3 **now, at present, at this point,** at this juncture, at this stage *or* at this stage of the game, on the present occasion, **at this time,** at this moment *or* instant, at the present time,
"upon this bank and shoal of time"—SHAKESPEARE; **today,** this day, in these days, **in this day and age,** in our time, **nowadays;** this night, **tonight;** here, hereat, **here and now,** *hic et nunc* (*Latin*), even now, but now, **just now,** as of now, as things are; on the spot; for the nonce, for the time being; for this occasion, just this once

4 **until now, hitherto,** till now, thitherto, **hereunto,** heretofore, until this time, by this time, **up to now,** up to the present, up to this time, to this day, to the present moment, to this very instant, **so far,** thus far, **as yet, to date,** yet, already, still, now *or* then as previously

word elements

5 ne–, neo–, nov–, novo–; cen–, ceno–, caen–, caeno–, –cene

838 THE FUTURE

nouns

1 **the future,** future, futurity, what is to come, imminence *see* 839, subsequence *see* 834, eventuality *see* 830.1, **hereafter,** aftertime, afteryears, **time to come,** years to come, etc; **futurism,** futuristics; **tomorrow,** the morrow, the morning after, *mañana* (*Spanish*); **immediate** *or* **near future,** time just ahead, immediate prospect, offing, next period; **distant future,** remote *or* deep *or* far future; **by-and-by,** the sweet by-and-by (*informal*); time ahead, course ahead, **prospect,** outlook, anticipation, expectation, project, probability, prediction, extrapolation, forward look, foresight, prevision, prevenience, envisionment, envisagement, prophecy, divination, clairvoyance, crystal ball, second sight; what is to be *or* come; determinism; future tense; futurism; the womb of time,
"the past again, entered through another gate"— PINERO, "an opaque mirror"—JIM BISHOP

2 **destiny** *see* 963.2, **fate,** doom, karma, kismet, what bodes *or* looms, what is fated *or* destined *or* doomed, what is written, what is in the books,
"whatever limits us"—EMERSON; the Fates, the Parcae *or* Parcae Fates, Lachesis, Clotho, Atropos, Moira, Moirai, **the hereafter,** the great hereafter,
"the good hereafter"—WHITTIER, a better place, Paradise, Heaven, Elysian Fields, Happy Isles, the Land of Youth *or* Tir na n'Og, Valhalla; Hades, the Underworld, Hell, Gehenna; **the afterworld,** the otherworld, **the next world,** the world to come, life *or* world beyond the grave, **the beyond,** the great beyond, the unknown, the great unknown, **the grave,** home *or* abode *or* world of the dead, eternal home;
"the world of light"—HENRY VAUGHAN, "the great world of light, that lies behind all human destinies"— LONGFELLOW; **afterlife, postexistence,** future state, **life to come,** life after death

3 **doomsday,** doom, day of doom, day of reckoning, crack of doom, trumpet *or* trump of doom; **Judgment Day,** Day of Judgment, the Judgment; eschatology, last things, **last days**

4 **futurity;** ultimateness, eventuality, finality

5 **advent, coming, approach of time,** time drawing on

verbs

6 **to come,** come on, **approach,** near, **draw on** *or* **near;** be to be *or* come; be fated *or* destined *or* doomed, be in the books, be in the cards; **loom,**

threaten, await, stare one in the face, be imminent
see 839.2; lie ahead *or* in one's course; **predict,**
foresee, envision, envisage, see ahead, previse,
foretell, prophesy; **anticipate, expect,** hope, hope
for, look for, look forward to, **project,** plot, plan,
scheme, think ahead, extrapolate

7 **to live on,** postexist, survive, get by *or* through,
make it (*informal*)

adjectives

8 **future, later,** hereafter; **coming, forthcoming,
imminent** *see* 839.3, approaching, nearing,
prospective; **eventual** *see* 830.11, ultimate, to-be,
to come; **projected,** plotted, planned, looked- *or*
hoped-for, desired, emergent, **predicted,** prophesied,
foreseen, anticipated, anticipatory, previsional,
prevenient, envisioned, envisaged, probable,
extrapolated; determined, fatal, fatidic, fated,
destinal, destined, doomed; eschatological; futuristic

adverbs

9 **in the future,** in aftertime, **afterward** *or*
afterwards, **later,** at a later time, after a time *or*
while, anon; **by and by,** in the sweet by-and-by
(*informal*); **tomorrow,** *mañana* (*Spanish*), the day
after tomorrow; *proximo* (*Latin*), prox, **in the near
or immediate future,** just around the corner,
imminently *see* 839.4, **soon, before long;** probably,
predictably, hopefully; fatally, by destiny *or* necessity

10 **in future, hereafter,** hereinafter, thereafter,
henceforth, henceforward *or* henceforwards,
thence, **thenceforth,** thenceforward *or*
thenceforwards, over the long haul *or* short haul
(*informal*), from this time forward, from this day on
or forward, from this point, from this *or* that time,
from then on, **from here** *or* **now on, from now on
in** (*informal*), from here in *or* out (*informal*), from
this moment on

11 **in time,** in due time, in due season *or* course, all
in good time, **in the fullness of time,** in God's
good time, in the course *or* process of time,
eventually *see* 830.12, ultimately, in the long run

12 **sometime, someday, some of these days,** one of
these days, some fine day *or* morning, one fine day
or morning, some sweet day, sometime or other,
somewhen, **sooner or later,** when all is said and
done

prepositions

13 **about to,** at *or* **on the point of,** on the eve of, on
the brink *or* edge *or* verge of, near to, close upon, in
the act of

839 IMMINENCE
future event

nouns

1 **imminence** *or* **imminency,** impendence *or*
impendency, forthcomingness; **forthcoming,** coming,
approach, loom; immediate *or* near future; futurity
see 838.1

verbs

2 **to be imminent, impend, overhang,** hang *or* lie
over, **loom,** hang over one's head, hover, **threaten,
menace,** lower; brew, gather; **come** *or* **draw on,**
draw near *or* nigh, rush up on one, forthcome,
approach, loom up, near, be on the horizon, be in
the offing, be upcoming, be just around the corner,
await, face, **confront, loom,** stare one in the face,
be in store, breathe down one's neck, be about to be
born

adjectives

3 **imminent, impending,** impendent, **overhanging,**
hanging over one's head, waiting, lurking,
threatening, looming, lowering, **menacing,** lying
in ambush,
"in danger imminent"—SPENSER; brewing, gathering,
preparing; **coming, forthcoming, upcoming, to
come,** about to be, about *or* going to happen,
approaching, nearing, looming, looming up,
looming in the distance *or* future; **near, close,**
immediate, instant, soon to be, **at hand,** near at
hand, close at hand; **in the offing,** on the horizon,
in prospect, already in sight, just around the
corner, in view, in one's eye, in store, in reserve, **in
the wind,** in the womb of time; in the lap of the
gods, on the cards (*informal*); whatever will be will
be; future *see* 838.8

adverbs

4 **imminently,** impendingly; **any time,** any time
now, any moment, any second, any minute, any
hour, any day; **to be expected,** as may be expected,
as may be

conjunctions

5 **on the point of, on the verge of,** on the eve of

840 NEWNESS

nouns

1 **newness,** freshness, maidenhood, dewiness,
pristineness, mint condition, new-mintedness,
newbornness, virginity, intactness, greenness,
immaturity, rawness, callowness, brand-newness;
presentness, nowness; **recentness,** recency, lateness;
novelty, gloss of novelty, newfangledness *or*
newfangleness; originality *see* 337.1;
uncommonness, unusualness, strangeness,
unfamiliarity

2 **novelty, innovation,** newfangled device *or*
contraption (*informal*), neoism, neonism, **new** *or*
latest wrinkle (*informal*), **the last word** *or* **the
latest thing** (*both informal*), *dernier cri* (*French*);
what's happening *and* what's in *and* the in thing *and*
where it's at (*all informal*); new ball game; new look,
latest fashion *or* fad; advance guard, vanguard,
avant-garde; neophilia, neophiliac

3 **modernity,** modernness; **modernism;** modernization,
updating, *aggiornamento* (*Italian*); postmodernism,
space age

4 **modern,** modern man; **modernist; modernizer;**
neologist, neoterist, neology, neologism, neoterism,
neoteric; modern *or* rising *or* new generation;

neonate, fledgling, stripling, *novus homo* (*Latin*), new man, upstart, *arriviste* (*French*), *nouveau riche* (*French*), parvenu; Young Turk, bright young thing, comer (*informal*)

verbs

5 **to innovate, invent,** make from scratch *or* from the ground up, coin, new-mint, mint, inaugurate, neologize, neoterize; **renew,** renovate *see* 396.17

6 **to modernize,** streamline; update, **bring up to date,** keep *or* stay current, move with the times

adjectives

7 **new,** young, **fresh,** fresh as a daisy, fresh as the morning dew; **unused, firsthand, original;** untried, untouched, unhandled, unhandselled (*old*), untrodden, unbeaten; virgin, virginal, intact, maiden, maidenly; green, vernal; dewy, pristine, ever-new, sempervirent, evergreen; **immature,** undeveloped, raw, callow, fledgling, unfledged, nestling

8 **fresh, additional, further,** other, another; **renewed**

9 **new-made,** new-built, new-wrought, new-shaped, new-mown, new-minted, new-coined, uncirculated, in mint condition, mint, new-begotten, new-grown, new-laid; **newfound;** newborn, neonatal, new-fledged; **new-model,** late-model, like new, factory-new, factory-fresh, in its original carton

10 (*informal terms*) **brand-new,** fire-new, **brand-spanking new,** spanking, **spanking new; just out;** hot, hottest, hot off the fire *or* griddle *or* spit, hot off the press; newfangled

11 **novel, original, unique, different;** strange, unusual, uncommon; unfamiliar, unheard-of; **first, first ever** *see* 817.15

12 **recent, late,** newly come, nouveau, of yesterday; latter, later

13 **modern, contemporary, present-day,** present-time, twentieth-century, latter-day, space-age, neoteric, now (*informal*), **newfashioned,** fashionable, designer, modish, mod, *à la mode* (*French*), **up-to-date,** up-to-datish, **up-to-the-minute,** happening (*informal*), **in,** abreast of the times; **advanced,** progressive, forward-looking, modernizing, **avant-garde;** ultramodern, ultra-ultra, ahead of its time, far out, way out, modernistic, modernized, streamlined; postmodern

14 **state-of-the-art, newest, latest,** the very latest, up-to-the-minute, last, most recent, newest of the new, farthest out, leading-edge

adverbs

15 **newly,** freshly, new, **anew,** once more, from the ground up, from scratch (*informal*), *ab ovo* (*Latin*), *de novo* (*Latin*), **afresh, again;** as new

16 **now, recently, lately,** latterly, **of late,** not long ago, a short time ago, the other day, only yesterday; just now, right now (*informal*); neoterically

841 OLDNESS

nouns

1 **oldness, age,** eld (*old*), hoary eld; elderliness, seniority, senior citizenship, senility, **old age** *see* 303.5; **ancientness, antiquity,** dust of ages, rust *or* cobwebs of antiquity; venerableness, eldership, primogeniture, great *or* hoary age, "the ancient and honourable"—BIBLE; old order, old style, *ancien régime* (*French*); **primitiveness,** primordialism *or* primordiality, aboriginality; atavism

2 **tradition, custom,** immemorial usage; Sunna (*Muslim*); Talmud, Mishnah (*both Jewish*), ancient wisdom, ways of the fathers; traditionalism *or* traditionality; myth, mythology, legend, lore, folklore, folktale, folk motif; racial memory, archetypal myth *or* image *or* pattern, "Spiritus Mundi"—YEATS

3 **antiquation, superannuation,** staleness, disuse; **old-fashionedness,** unfashionableness, out-of-dateness; **old-fogyishness,** fogyishness, stuffiness, stodginess, fuddy-duddiness

4 **antiquarianism;** classicism, medievalism, Pre-Raphaelitism, longing *or* yearning *or* nostalgia for the past; **archaeology;** Greek archaeology, Roman archaeology, etc, Assyriology, Egyptology, Sumerology; crisis archeology, industrial archeology, underwater *or* marine archeology, paleology, epigraphy, palaeontology, human palaeontology, palaeoethnology, palaeoanthropology, palaeoethnography; palaeozoology, palaeornithology

5 **antiquarian,** antiquary, *laudator temporis acti* (*Latin*); dryasdust, the Rev Dr Dryasdust, Jonathan Oldbuck (*both Sir Walter Scott*), Herr Teufelsdröckh (*Carlyle*); **archaeologist;** classicist, medievalist, Miniver Cheevy (*E A Robinson*), Pre-Raphaelite; antique dealer, antique collector, antique-car collector; archaist

6 **antiquity, antique,** archaism; **relic,** relic of the past; **remains,** survival, vestige, ruin *or* ruins; old thing, oldie *and* golden oldie (*informal*); **fossil;** petrification, petrified wood, petrified forest; **artefact** *or* **artifact,** eolith, mezzolith, microlith, neolith, paleolith, plateaulith; cave painting, petroglyph; ancient manuscript *see* 547.11

7 **ancient,** man *or* woman *or* person of old, old Homo, **prehistoric mankind** (*see list*); preadamite, antediluvian; anthropoid, humanoid, primate, fossil man, protohuman, prehuman, missing link, apeman, hominid; **primitive, aboriginal,** aborigine, bushman, autochthon; **caveman,** cave dweller, troglodyte; bog man, bog body, Pete Moss, Lindow man; Stone Age man, Bronze Age man, Iron Age man

8 (*antiquated person*) back number (*informal*); grandfather, grandad *or* grandaddy (*both informal*); pop *and* pops *and* dad (*all informal*), dodo *and* old dodo (*both informal*); fossil *and* antique *and* relic (*all informal*); mossback (*US & Canadian informal*), longhair *and* square (*both informal*), **mid-Victorian,** antediluvian; old liner, old believer, conservative, hard-shell, traditionalist, reactionary; has-been; **fogy** *or* **fogey,** old fogy, regular old fogy, old poop *or* crock (*informal*), **fuddy-duddy** (*informal*), buffer (*informal*); dinosaur; Young Fogey, granny (*informal*), **old woman,** matriarch; **old man,** patriarch, elder, *starets* (*Russian*), old-timer (*informal*), Methuselah; senior citizen, pensioner *or* old-age pensioner

verbs

9 to age, grow old *see* 303.10, grow *or* have whiskers; **antiquate**, fossilize, date, **superannuate**, outdate; obsolesce, go out of use *or* style, moulder, fust, rust, fade, perish; lose currency *or* novelty; become obsolete *or* extinct; belong to the past, be a thing of the past

adjectives

10 old, age-old, auld (*Scottish*), olden (*old*), old-time, old-timey (*informal*); **ancient, antique**, venerable, hoary; of old, of yore; dateless, timeless, ageless; **immemorial**, old as Methuselah *or* Adam, old as God, old as history, old as time, old as the hills; **elderly** *see* 303.16

11 primitive, prime, **primeval**, primogenial, primordial, pristine; atavistic; **aboriginal**, autochthonous; ancestral, patriarchal; **prehistoric**, protohistoric, preglacial, preadamite, antepatriarchal; prehuman, protohuman, humanoid

12 traditional; mythological, heroic; **legendary**, unwritten, oral, handed down; true-blue, tried and true; **prescriptive, customary**, conventional, understood, admitted, recognized, acknowledged, received; **hallowed, time-honoured**, immemorial; **venerable**, hoary, worshipful; **long-standing, of long standing**, long-established, established, fixed, inveterate, rooted; folk, of the folk, folkloric

13 antiquated, grown old, **superannuated, antique**, old, age-encrusted, of other times, old-world; vintage, veteran; Victorian, mid-Victorian; classical, medieval, Gothic; antediluvian; **fossil**, fossilized, petrified

14 stale, fusty, musty, rusty, dusty, mouldy, mildewed; **worn, timeworn**, time-scarred; **motheaten**, moss-grown, crumbling, mouldering, gone to seed, dilapidated, ruined, ruinous

15 obsolete, passé, extinct, gone out, gone-by, dead, past, run out, **outworn**

16 old-fashioned, old-fangled, old-timey (*informal*), **dated, out, out-of-date, outdated, outmoded**, out of style *or* fashion, out of use, disused, out of season, **unfashionable**, styleless, **behind the times**, of the old school, old hat *and* back-number *and* hasbeen (*all informal*), vieux jeu (*French*)

17 old-fogyish, fogyish, old-fogy; fuddy-duddy, square *and* corny (*both informal*); **stuffy, stodgy**; past one's sell-by date (*informal*); **aged** *see* 303.16, senile, bent *or* wracked *or* ravaged with age

18 secondhand, used, worn, previously owned, unnew, not new, pawed-over; hand-me-down *and* reach-medown (*both informal*)

19 older, senior, Sr, major, elder, dean; **oldest**, eldest; first-born, firstling, primogenitary; former *see* 836.10

20 archaeological, paleological; antiquarian; paleolithic, eolithic, neolithic, mezzolithic

adverbs

21 anciently *see* 836.16

22 Stone Age cultures

Abbevillian	Chellean
Acheulean	Combe-Capelle
Aurignacian	Cro-Magnon
Azilian	Eolithic
Magdalenian	Paleolithic
Mousterian	Pre-Chellean
Neolithic	Solutrean

23 prehistoric men and manlike primates

Aurignacian man	Lucy
Australanthropus	Meganthropus
Australopithecus	Neanderthal man
Australopithecus afarensis	neolithic man
Australopithecus africanus	Oreopithecus
Australopithecus boisei	paleolithic man
Australopithecus robustus	Paranthropus
Brünn race	Peking man
caveman	Piltdown man *or* Dawn
Cro-Magnon man	man (hoax)
eolithic man	Pithecanthropus
Florisbad man	Plesianthropus
Furfooz *or* Grenelle man	Rhodesian man
Galley Hill man	Sinanthropus
Gigantopithecus	Stone Age man
Grimaldi man	Swanscombe man
Heidelberg man	Zinjanthropus
Java man	

24 prehistoric animals

allosaurus	dipnoan
ammonite	diprotodon
anatosaurus	duck-billed dinosaur
ankylosaurus	edaphosaurid
apatosaurus	elasmosaurus
archaeohippus	eohippus
archaeopteryx	eryopsid
archaeornis	eurypterid
archaeotherium	eurypterus remipes
archelon	giant sloth
arthrodiran	glyptodont
atlantosaurus	gorgosaurus
aurochs	hadrosaurus
baryonyx Walker	hesperornis
bothriolepis	hoplophoneus
brachiosaurus	hyaenodon
brontops	hyracodont
brontosaurus	hyracothere
brontothere	ichthyornis
camarasaurus	ichthyosaurus
cantius trigonodus	iguanodon
ceratopsid	imperial mammoth *or*
ceratosaurus	elephant
cetiosaurus	labyrinthodont
coccostean	machairodont
coelodont	mamenchisaurus
compsognathus	mammoth
coryphodon	mastodon
cotylosaur	megalosaurus
creodont	megathere
crossopterygian	merodus
cynodictis	merychippus
deinonychus	merycoidodon
denversaurus	merycopotamus
diacodexis	mesohippus
diatryma	miacis
dimetrodon	mosasaurus
dinichthyid	nummulite
dinothere	ornithomimid
diplodocus	ornithopod

ostracoderm	sauropod
palaeodictyopteron	scelidosaurus
palaeomastodon	smilodon
palaeoniscid	stegocephalian
palaeophis	stegodon
palaeosaur	stegosaurus
palaeospondylus	struthiomimus
pelycosaur	teleoceras
phytosaur	therapsid
pinchosaurus	theriodont
plesiosaurus	theropod
protoceratops	thrinaxodon liorhinus
protohippus	titanosaurus
protylopus	titanothere
pteranodon	trachodon
pteraspid	triceratops
pterichthys	trilobite
pterodactyl	tyrannosaurus
pterosaur	uintathere
quetzalcoatlus northropii	urus
rhamphorhynchus	woolly *or* northern
sabre-toothed cat, formerly	mammoth
sabre-toothed tiger	

842 TIMELINESS

nouns

1 **timeliness, seasonableness, opportuneness,** convenience; **expedience** *or* **expediency**, meetness, fittingness, fitness, appropriateness, rightness, propriety, suitability,
"To everything there is a season, and a time to every purpose under the heaven"—BIBLE; **favourableness, propitiousness**, auspiciousness, felicitousness; **ripeness**, pregnancy, cruciality, criticality, criticalness, expectancy, loadedness, chargedness

2 **opportunity, chance, time, occasion; opening,** room, scope, space, place, liberty,
"world enough and time"—ANDREW MARVELL; clear stage, fair field, level playing field, fair game, fair shake *and* even break (*both informal*); **opportunism**; equal opportunity, nondiscrimination, affirmative action, positive discrimination; trump card; a leg up, stepping-stone, rung of the ladder; time's forelock

3 **good opportunity, good chance,** favourable opportunity, golden opportunity, well-timed opportunity, the chance of a lifetime, a once-in-a-lifetime chance,
"a tide in the affairs of men"—SHAKESPEARE; suitable occasion, proper occasion, suitable *or* proper time, **good time**, high time, due season; propitious *or* well-chosen moment

4 **crisis, critical point,** crunch, crucial period, climax, climacteric, flash point; **turning point,** hinge, turn, turn of the tide, cusp; **emergency, exigency,** juncture *or* conjuncture *or* convergence of events, critical juncture, crossroads; **pinch,** clutch (*informal*), rub, push, pass, strait, extremity, spot (*informal*); **emergency,** state of emergency, red alert, race against time

5 **crucial moment,** critical moment, loaded *or* charged moment, decisive moment, kairotic moment, kairos, pregnant moment, defining moment, turning

point, climax, **moment of truth,** crunch *and* when push comes to shove (*both informal*), when the balloon goes up (*informal*); **psychological moment,** right moment; nick of time, eleventh hour; **zero hour,** H-hour, D-day, A-day, target date, deadline

verbs

6 **to be timely,** suit *or* befit the time *or* season *or* occasion, come *or* fall just right

7 **to take** *or* **seize the opportunity,** use the occasion, take the chance; take the bit in the teeth, leap into the breach, take the bull by the horns, bite the bullet, **make one's move,** cross the Rubicon, *prendre la balle au bond* (*French*, take the ball on the rebound); **commit oneself,** make an opening, drive an entering wedge

8 **to improve the occasion,**
"improve each shining hour"—ISAAC WATTS, turn to account *or* good account, avail oneself of, **take advantage of,** put to advantage, profit by, **cash in** *or* **capitalize on**; take time by the forelock, seize the opportunity, seize the present hour, *carpe diem* (*Latin*, seize the day), make hay while the sun shines; strike while the iron is hot; not be caught flatfooted, not be behindhand, not be caught napping (*informal*), don't let the chance slip by, get going (*informal*)

adjectives

9 **timely, well-timed, seasonable, opportune,** convenient; **expedient,** meet, fit, fitting, befitting, suitable, sortable, appropriate; **favourable, propitious,** ripe, auspicious, lucky, providential, heaven-sent, fortunate, happy, felicitous

10 **critical, crucial,** pivotal, climactic, climacteric *or* climacterical, decisive; pregnant, kairotic, loaded, charged; exigent, emergent

11 **incidental, occasional, casual,** accidental; parenthetical, by-the-way

adverbs

12 **opportunely, seasonably, propitiously,** auspiciously, in proper time *or* season, in due time *or* course *or* season, in the fullness of time, **in good time,** all in good time; in the nick of time, just in time, at the eleventh hour; now or never

13 **incidentally, by the way,** by the by; while on the subject, speaking of, *à propos* (*French*), apropos *or* apropos of; **in passing,** *en passant* (*French*); parenthetically, by way of parenthesis, *par parenthèse* (*French*); for example, *par exemple* (*French*)

14 a bird in the hand is worth two in the bush, better late than never, every minute *or* moment counts; live for the moment, you can't take it with you

843 UNTIMELINESS

nouns

1 **untimeliness, unseasonableness,** inopportuneness, inopportunity, unripeness, inconvenience; **inexpedience,** irrelevance *or* irrelevancy; **awkwardness,** inappropriateness, impropriety, unfitness, unfittingness, wrongness, unsuitability; **unfavourableness,** unfortunateness, inauspiciousness, unpropitiousness, infelicity;

intrusion, interruption; **prematurity** *see* 844.2; lateness *see* 845, afterthought, thinking too late, *l'esprit de l'escalier* (*French*)

2 **wrong time, bad time,** wrong *or* bad *or* poor timing, unsuitable time, unfortunate time; evil hour, unlucky day *or* hour, off-year, *contretemps* (*French*)

verbs

3 **to ill-time,** mistime, miss the time; **lack the time,** not have time, have other *or* better things to do, be otherwise occupied, be engaged, be preoccupied, have other fish to fry (*informal*)

4 **to talk out of turn,** speak inopportunely, interrupt, **put one's foot in one's mouth** (*informal*), intrude, butt in *and* stick one's nose in (*both informal*), **go off half-cocked** (*informal*), open one's big mouth *or* big fat mouth (*informal*); blow it (*informal*), speak too late *or* too soon

5 **to miss an opportunity, miss the chance, miss out, miss the boat,** miss one's turn, lose the opportunity, ignore opportunity's knock, lose the chance, blow the chance (*informal*), throw away *or* waste *or* neglect the opportunity, allow the occasion to go by, let slip through one's fingers, be left at the starting gate *or* post, be caught napping (*informal*), oversleep, lock the stable door after the horse has bolted

adjectives

6 **untimely, unseasonable, inopportune, ill-timed,** ill-seasoned, mistimed, unripe, unready, ill-considered, too late *or* soon, out of phase *or* time *or* sync; **inconvenient,** unhandy; **inappropriate,** irrelevant, improper, unfit, wrong, out of line, off-base, unsuitable, **inexpedient,** unfitting, unbefitting, untoward, malapropos, *mal à propos* (*French*), intrusive; **unfavourable,** unfortunate, infelicitous, inauspicious, **unpropitious,** unhappy, unlucky, misfortuned; **premature** *see* 844.8; late *see* 845.16

adverbs

7 **inopportunely, unseasonably,** inconveniently, inexpediently; **unpropitiously,** inauspiciously, unfortunately, in an evil hour, at just the wrong time

844 EARLINESS

nouns

1 **earliness,** early hour, time to spare, crack of dawn; **head start,** running start, ground floor, first crack, beginnings, first *or* early stage, very beginning, preliminaries; **anticipation, foresight,** prevision, prevenience; advance notice, lead time, a stitch in time, readiness, preparedness, preparation

2 **prematurity,** prematureness; **untimeliness** *see* 843; precocity, **precociousness,** forwardness; precipitation, haste, hastiness, **overhastiness,** rush, impulse, impulsivity, impulsiveness

3 **promptness, promptitude, punctuality,** punctualness, readiness; instantaneousness *see* 829, immediateness *or* immediacy, summariness, decisiveness, **alacrity, quickness** *see* 174.1, speediness, swiftness, rapidity, expeditiousness, expedition, dispatch

4 **early bird** (*informal*), early riser, early comer, first arrival, first on the scene; **precursor** *see* 815

verbs

5 **to be early,** be ahead of time, take time by the forelock, be up and stirring, be beforehand, be up betimes, be ready and waiting, be off and running; gain time, draw on futurity *or* on the future

6 **to anticipate, foresee,** foreglimpse, previse, see the writing on the wall, foretaste, pave the way for, prevent (*old*); **forestall,** forerun, go before, **get ahead of,** win the start, break out ahead, get a head start, steal a march on, beat someone to the draw (*informal*); **jump the gun,** beat the gun, go off half-cocked (*informal*); take the words out of one's mouth

adjectives

7 **early,** bright and early *and* with the birds (*both informal*), **beforetime,** in good time *or* season; **forehand,** forehanded; foresighted, **anticipative** *or* **anticipatory,** prevenient, previsional

8 **premature, too early, too soon,** oversoon; preterm, prem (*informal*); previous *and* a bit previous (*both informal*); **untimely; precipitate,** hasty *see* 829.5, **overhasty,** too soon off the mark, too quick on the draw *or* trigger *or* uptake (*informal*); **unprepared,** unripe, impulsive, rushed, unmatured; unpremeditated, unmeditated, ill-considered, **half-cocked** *and* **half-baked** (*both informal*), unjelled, uncrystallized, not firm; **precocious, forward, advanced,** far ahead, born before one's time

9 **prompt, punctual, immediate, instant,** instantaneous *see* 829.4, **quick** *see* 174.19, speedy, swift, expeditious, summary, decisive, apt, alert, **ready,** on the spot (*informal*)

10 **earlier,** previous *see* 833.4

adverbs

11 **early,** bright and early, beforehand, beforetime, early on, betimes, precociously, **ahead of time,** foresightedly, in advance, in anticipation, ahead, before, **with time to spare**

12 **in time, in good time, soon enough,** time enough, early enough; just in time, **in the nick of time,** with no time to spare, without a minute to spare

13 **prematurely, too soon, oversoon,** untimely, too early, before its *or* one's time; preterm; **precipitately,** impulsively, in a rush, hastily, overhastily; at half cock (*informal*)

14 **punctually, precisely,** exactly, sharp; **on time,** on the minute *or* instant, to the minute *or* second, **on the dot** (*informal*), spot on *and* bang on (*informal*), at the gun

15 **promptly, without delay,** without further delay *or* ado, directly, **immediately,** immediately if not sooner (*informal*), **instantly** *see* 829.6, instanter, on the instant, on the spot, **at once,** right off, **right away, straightway,** straightaway, **forthwith,** *pronto* (*Spanish*), *subito* (*Italian*), chop chop, PDQ *or* pretty damned quick (*both informal*), a.s.a.p. (*informal*), **quickly,** swiftly, speedily, with all speed, **summarily,** decisively, smartly, expeditiously, apace,

in no time, in less than no time; no sooner said than done

16 soon, presently, directly, shortly, in a short time *or* while, **before long,** ere long, in no long time, in a while, **in a little while, after a while, by and by,** anon, betimes, *bientôt (French)*, in due time, in due course, at the first opportunity; in a moment *or* minute, *tout à l'heure (French)*

phrases

17 the early bird gets the worm

845 LATENESS

nouns

1 lateness, tardiness, belatedness, unpunctuality, African time *(South African informal)*; late hour, small hours; eleventh hour, last minute, high time; unreadiness, unpreparedness; untimeliness *see* 843

2 delay, stoppage, jam *and* logjam *(both informal)*, obstruction, tie-up *and* bind *(both informal)*, **block,** blockage, **hang-up** *(informal)*, snarl-up *(informal)*; delayed reaction, double take, afterthought; **retardation** *or* retardance, slowdown *and* slow-up *(both informal)*, slowness, lag, time lag, lagging, dragging, dragging one's feet *and* foot-dragging *(both informal)*; **detention,** suspension, holdup *(informal)*, **obstruction, hindrance;** delaying action; **wait, halt, stay, stop,** down-time, break, pause, interim *see* 825, respite; reprieve, stay of execution; moratorium; **red tape,** red-tapery, red-tapeism, bureaucratic delay, *paperasserie (French)*

3 waiting, cooling one's heels *(informal)*, **tarrying,** tarriance *(old)*; **lingering, dawdling,** dalliance, dallying, dillydallying

4 postponement, deferment *or* **deferral,** prorogation, putting-off, tabling, holding up, holding in suspension, carrying over; **prolongation,** protraction, continuation, extension of time; **adjournment** *or* adjournal, adjournment sine die

5 procrastination, "the thief of time"—EDWARD YOUNG, hesitation *see* 362.3; **temporization,** a play for time, **stall** *(informal)*; Micawberism, Fabian policy; **dilatoriness,** slowness, backwardness, remissness, slackness, laxness

6 latecomer, late arrival, Johnny-come-lately; slow starter, dawdler, dallier, dillydallier; late bloomer *or* developer; retardee; late riser, slug-abed

verbs

7 to be late, not be on time, be overdue, be behindhand, show up late, miss the boat; keep everyone waiting; **stay late,** stay up late *or* into the small hours, burn the midnight oil, keep late hours; get up late, keep banker's hours; oversleep

8 to delay, retard, detain, make late, slacken, lag, drag, drag one's feet *and* stonewall *(both informal)*, slow down, **hold up** *(informal)*, hold *or* keep back, check, **stay, stop,** arrest, impede, **block,** hinder, obstruct, throw a spanner in the works *(informal)*, throw a monkey wrench in the works *(US & Canadian informal)*, confine; tie up with red tape

9 to postpone, delay, defer, put off, give one a rain check *(informal)*, shift off, hold off *or* up *(informal)*,

prorogue, put on hold *or* ice *or* the back burner *(all informal)*, reserve, waive, **suspend,** hang up, stay, hang fire; protract, drag *or* stretch out *(informal)*, **prolong, extend,** spin *or* string out, continue, adjourn, recess, take a recess, prorogue; **hold over,** lay over, stand over, let the matter stand, **put aside,** lay *or* set *or* push aside, lay *or* set by, **table,** lay on the table, pigeonhole, **shelve,** put on the shelf, mothball, put on ice *(informal)*; consult one's pillow about, sleep on

10 to be left behind, be outrun *or* outdistanced, make a slow start, be slow *or* late *or* last off the mark, be left at the post *or* starting gate; bloom *or* develop late

11 to procrastinate, be dilatory, hesitate, let something slide, hang, hang back, hang fire; **temporize,** gain *or* make time, **play for time,** drag one's feet *(informal)*, hold off *(informal)*; **stall, stall for time;** talk out, filibuster

12 to wait, delay, stay, bide, abide, **bide one's time; take one's time,** take time, mark time; **tarry, linger, loiter,** dawdle, dally, dillydally; hang around *or* about *or* out *(informal)*, stick around *(informal)*; **hold on** *(informal)*, sit tight *(informal)*, hold one's breath; wait a minute *or* second, wait up; hold everything *and* hold your horses *and* hold your water *and* keep your shirt on *(all informal)*; wait *or* stay up, sit up; **wait and see,** bide the issue, see which way the cat jumps, see how the cookie crumbles *or* the ball bounces *(informal)*; wait for something to turn up; **await** *see* 130.8

13 to wait impatiently, tear one's hair *and* sweat it out *and* champ *or* chomp at the bit *(all informal)*

14 to be kept waiting, be stood up *(informal)*, be left; **cool one's heels** *(informal)*

15 to overstay, overtarry

adjectives

16 late, belated, tardy, slow, slow on the draw *or* uptake *or* trigger *(all informal)*, **behindhand,** never on time, backward, back, **overdue, long-awaited, untimely; unpunctual,** unready; latish; **delayed,** detained, **held up** *(informal)*, **retarded, arrested,** blocked, **hung up** *and* in a bind *(both informal)*, obstructed, stopped, jammed, congested; weather-bound; **postponed, in abeyance,** held up, put off, **on hold** *or* put on hold *(informal)*, on the back burner *or* put on the back burner *(informal)*; delayed-action; moratory

17 dilatory, delaying, Micawberish; slow *or* late *or* last off the mark; **procrastinating,** procrastinative *or* procrastinatory, go-slow; **obstructive,** obstructionist *or* obstructionistic, bloody-minded *(informal)*; **lingering,** loitering, lagging, dallying, dillydallying, **slow,** sluggish, laggard, foot-dragging, shuffling, backward; easygoing, **lazy, lackadaisical; remiss,** slack, work-shy, lax

18 later *see* 834.4; last-minute, last-gasp, eleventh-hour, deathbed

adverbs

19 late, behind, behindhand, belatedly, backward, slow, **behind time,** after time; far on, deep into;

late in the day, at the last minute, at the eleventh hour, none too soon, in the nick of time

20 **tardily, slow, slowly,** deliberately, dilatorily, sluggishly, lackadaisically, leisurely, at one's leisure, lingeringly; until all hours, into the night

846 FREQUENCY

nouns

1 **frequency,** frequence, oftenness; **commonness,** usualness, prevalence, **common occurrence,** routineness, habitualness; **incidence,** relative incidence

2 **constancy, continualness,** steadiness, sustainment, **regularity,** noninterruption *or* uninterruption, nonintermission *or* unintermission, incessancy, ceaselessness, constant flow, continuity *see* 811; perpetuity *see* 828; repetition *see* 848; **rapidity** *see* 174.1; rapid recurrence *or* succession, rapid *or* quick fire, tattoo, **staccato,** chattering, stuttering; **vibration,** shuddering, juddering, pulsation, **oscillation** *see* 915

verbs

3 to be frequent, occur often, have a high incidence, continue *see* 811.4, recur *see* 849.5; shudder, judder, vibrate, oscillate *see* 915.10

adjectives

4 **frequent,** oftentime, many, many times, **recurrent, oft-repeated,** thick-coming; **common,** of common occurrence, not rare, thick on the ground, **prevalent,** usual, routine, habitual, ordinary, everyday; frequentative (*grammar*)

5 **constant, continual** *see* 811.8, **perennial; steady,** sustained, **regular; incessant, ceaseless, unceasing,** unintermitting, unintermittent *or* unintermitted, unremitting, relentless, unrelenting, unchanging, unvarying, uninterrupted, unstopped, unbroken; **perpetual** *see* 828.7; repeated *see* 848.12; **rapid, staccato,** stuttering, chattering, machine gun; pulsating, juddering, vibrating, **oscillating** *see* 915.15

adverbs

6 **frequently, commonly,** usually, ordinarily, routinely, habitually; **often, oft, oftentimes,** oft times; **repeatedly** *see* 848.16, **again and again, time after time; most often** *or* frequently, in many instances, **many times,** many a time, full many a time, many a time and oft, as often as can be, as often as not, more often than not; **in quick** *or* **rapid succession;** often enough, not infrequently, not seldom, unseldom; as often as you wish *or* like, whenever you wish *or* like

7 **constantly, continually** *see* 811.10, **steadily,** sustainedly, **regularly,** as regular as clockwork, with every other breath, every time one turns around, right along (*informal*), unvaryingly, uninterruptedly, unintermittently, **incessantly,** unceasingly, ceaselessly, without cease *or* ceasing, perennially, all the time, at all times, ever, ever and anon, on and on, without letup *or* break *or* intermission, without stopping; **perpetually, always** *see* 828.11; **rapidly;** all year round, every day, every hour, every moment;

daily, hourly, daily and hourly; **night and day,** day and night; **morning, noon and night;** hour after hour, day after day, month after month, year after year; **day in day out,** month in month out, year in year out

847 INFREQUENCY

nouns

1 **infrequency,** infrequence, unfrequentness, seldomness; occasionalness; **rarity, scarcity, scarceness,** rareness, **uncommonness,** uniqueness, unusualness; **sparsity** *see* 884.1; **slowness** *see* 175

adjectives

2 **infrequent,** unfrequent, **rare,** scarce, scarce as hens' teeth, scarcer than hens' teeth, **uncommon,** unique, unusual, almost unheard-of, seldom met with, seldom seen, few and far between, **sparse** *see* 884.5; **one-off, one-time, one-shot,** once in a lifetime; **slow** *see* 175.10

3 **occasional,** casual, **incidental; odd,** sometime, extra, side, off, off-and-on, out-of-the-way, spare, sparetime, **part-time**

adverbs

4 **infrequently,** unfrequently, **seldom, rarely, uncommonly,** scarcely, hardly, **scarcely** *or* **hardly ever,** very seldom, not often, only now and then, at infrequent intervals, unoften, off and on; **sparsely** *see* 884.8

5 **occasionally,** on occasion, **sometimes, at times,** at odd times, every so often (*informal*), at various times, on divers occasions, **now and then,** every now and then (*informal*), now and again, **once in a while,** every once in a while (*informal*), every now and then, every now and again, once and again, once or twice, betweentimes, betweenwhiles, at intervals, **from time to time;** only occasionally, only when the spirit moves, only when necessary, only now and then, at infrequent intervals, once in a blue moon (*informal*); irregularly, sporadically

6 **once, one-time,** on one occasion, just *or* only once, just this once, once and no more, once for all, once and for all *or* always

848 REPETITION

nouns

1 **repetition, reproduction,** duplication *see* 873, reduplication, doubling, redoubling; **recurrence,** reoccurrence, cyclicality, return, reincarnation, rebirth, reappearance, renewal, resumption; resurfacing, reentry; echo, reecho, parroting; regurgitation, rehearsal, rote recitation; **quotation; imitation** *see* 336; plagiarism *see* 621.2; **reexamination,** second *or* another look

2 **iteration, reiteration, recapitulation,** recap *and* wrapup (*both informal*), retelling, recounting, recountal, **recital, rehearsal, restatement,** rehash (*informal*); reissue, reprint; review, summary, rundown, précis, résumé, summing up; going over *or* through, practising; reassertion, reaffirmation; elaboration, dwelling upon; **copy** *see* 784

3 redundancy, **tautology**, tautologism, pleonasm, macrology, battology; stammering, stuttering; padding, filling, expletive

4 **repetitiousness**, repetitiveness, stale *or* unnecessary repetition; harping; **monotony**, monotone, drone; **tedium** *see* 118, the daily round *or* grind; **humdrum**, dingdong, singsong, chime, jingle, jingle-jangle, trot, pitter-patter; **rhyme, alliteration**, assonance, half-rhyme, slant *or* near rhyme; **repeated sounds** *see* 55

5 repeat, repetend, bis, ditto (*informal*), echo; **refrain**, burden, chant, undersong, chorus, bob; bob wheel, bob and wheel; ritornel, *ritornello* (*Italian*)

6 encore, repeat performance, repeat, **reprise**; replay, replaying, return match

verbs

7 to repeat, redo, do again, do over, do a repeat, **reproduce, duplicate** *see* 873.3, reduplicate, double, redouble, ditto (*informal*), **echo, parrot**, reecho; **rattle off**, reel off, regurgitate; renew, reincarnate, revive; come again *and* run it by again (*both informal*), say again, repeat oneself, **quote**, repeat word for word *or* verbatim, repeat like a broken record; **copy, imitate** *see* 336.5; plagiarize *see* 621.4, 336.5; **reexamine**, take *or* have a second look, take *or* have another look

8 to iterate, reiterate, rehearse, recapitulate, recount, rehash (*informal*), **recite, retell**, retail, **restate**, reword, review, run over, sum up, summarize, précis, resume, encapsulate; reissue, reprint; do *or* say over again, **go over *or* through**, practice, say over, go over the same ground, give an encore, quote oneself, go the same round, fight one's battles over again; **tautologize**, battologize, pad, fill; **reaffirm**, reassert

9 to dwell on *or* upon, insist upon, **harp on**, flog *or* beat a dead horse, have on the brain, constantly recur *or* revert to, labour, belabour, hammer away at, always trot out, sing the same old song *or* tune, play the same old record, plug the same theme, never hear the last of; **thrash *or* thresh over**, cover the same ground, go over again and again, go over and over

10 to din, ding; drum *see* 55.4, beat, hammer, pound; **din in the ear**, din into, drum into, say over and over

11 (*be repeated*) **to repeat, recur**, reoccur, **come again**, come round again, go round again, come up again, resurface, reenter, **return, reappear, resume**; resound, reverberate, echo; revert, turn *or* go back; keep coming, come again and again, happen over and over, run through like King Charles's head

adjectives

12 repeated, reproduced, doubled, redoubled; **duplicated**, reduplicated; regurgitated, recited by rote; **echoed**, reechoed, parroted; **quoted**, plagiarized; **iterated, reiterated**, reiterate; retold, **twice-told**; warmed up *or* over, *réchauffé* (*French*)

13 recurrent, recurring, **returning**, reappearing, revenant, ubiquitous, ever-recurring, cyclical, periodic, yearly, monthly, weekly, daily, circadian, thick-coming, frequent, incessant, continuous *see* 811.8, year-to-year, month-to-month, week-to-week, etc; haunting, thematic

14 **repetitious**, repetitive, repetitional *or* repetitionary, repeating; **duplicative**, reduplicative; **imitative** *see* 336.9, parrotlike; echoing, reechoing, echoic; **iterative, reiterative**, reiterant; recapitulative, recapitulatory; battological, **tautological *or* tautologous, redundant**

15 monotonous, monotone; **tedious**; harping, laboured, belaboured, cliché-ridden; **humdrum**, singsong, chiming, chanting, dingdong (*informal*), jog-trot, jingle-jangle; **rhymed, rhyming, alliterative**, alliterating, assonant

adverbs

16 repeatedly, often, frequently, recurrently, **every time one turns around**, with every other breath, like a tolling bell, **again and again, over and over**, over and over again, many times over, time and again, **time after time**, times without number, **ad nauseam**; year in year out, week in week out, etc, year after year, day after day, day by day, "tomorrow and tomorrow and tomorrow"— SHAKESPEARE; **many times**, several times, a number of times, many a time, many a time and oft, full many a time and oft; every now and then, every once in a while

17 again, over, over again, **once more**, *encore*, *bis* (*both French*), two times, twice over, ditto; **anew**, *de novo* (*Latin*), afresh; from the beginning, *da capo* (*Italian*)

exclamations

18 encore!, *bis!* (*French*), once more!, again!

849 REGULARITY OF RECURRENCE

nouns

1 regularity, regularness, clockwork regularity, predictability, punctuality, smoothness, **steadiness, evenness**, unvariableness, **methodicalness**, systematicalness; **repetition** *see* 848; **uniformity** *see* 780; **constancy** *see* 846.2

2 periodicity, periodicalness; cyclical motion, piston motion, pendulum motion, regular wave motion, undulation, **pulsation**; **intermittence *or*** intermittency, alternation; rhythm *see* 709.22, metre, beat; **oscillation** *see* 915; **recurrence**, merry-go-round, reoccurrence, reappearance, return, the eternal return, **cyclicalness**, cyclicality, seasonality; resurfacing, reentry

3 round, revolution, rotation, cycle, circle, wheel, **circuit**; beat, upbeat, downbeat, thesis, arsis, **pulse**; systole, diastole; course, series, **bout, turn**, spell *see* 824

4 anniversary, commemoration; immovable feast, annual holiday; biennial, triennial, quadrennial, quinquennial, sextennial, septennial, octennial, nonennial, decennial, tricennial, jubilee, silver jubilee, golden jubilee, diamond jubilee; centenary, centennial (*US & Canadian*); quasquicentenary, quasquicentennial (*US & Canadian*); sesquicentenary, sesquicentennial (*US & Canadian*); bicentenary, bicentennial (*US & Canadian*); tercentenary, tricentenary, tercentennial (*US & Canadian*);

quatercentenary, quatercentennial (*US & Canadian*); quincentenary, quincentennial (*US & Canadian*); **wedding anniversary**, crystal wedding anniversary, silver wedding anniversary, ruby wedding anniversary, golden wedding anniversary, diamond wedding anniversary; **birthday**, birthdate, natal day; saint's day, name day; leap year, bissextile day; **religious holiday**, holy day

verbs

5 (*occur periodically*) **to recur, reoccur, return, repeat** see 848.7, reappear, **come again**, come up again, be here again, resurface, reenter, **come round** *or* **around**, come round again, come in its turn; **rotate, revolve**, turn, circle, wheel, cycle, **roll around**, roll about, wheel around, go around, go round; **intermit**, alternate, **come and go**; undulate see 915.11; **oscillate** see 915.10, pulse, pulsate see 915.12

adjectives

6 **regular, systematic** *or* systematical, methodical, ordered, orderly, regular as clockwork; **uniform** *see* 780.5; **constant** *see* 846.5

7 **periodic** *or* periodical, seasonal, epochal, **cyclic** *or* cyclical, serial, isochronal, metronomic; measured, steady, even, **rhythmic** *or* rhythmical *see* 709.28; **recurrent**, recurring, reoccurring; **intermittent**, reciprocal, alternate, every other; circling, wheeling, rotary, wavelike, undulant, undulatory, oscillatory *see* 915.15, pulsing, beating *see* 915.18

8 **momentary**, momently, **hourly; daily**, diurnal, quotidian, circadian; **weekly**, tertian, hebdomadal, hebdomadary; biweekly, semiweekly; fortnightly; **monthly**, menstrual, catamenial; bimonthly, semimonthly; quarterly; biannual, semiannual, semiyearly, half-yearly, semestral; **yearly, annual;** biennial, triennial, decennial, etc; centennial, centenary, secular

adverbs

9 **regularly, systematically, methodically**, like clockwork, at regular intervals, punctually, steadily; at stated times, at fixed *or* established periods; intermittently, every so often, every now and then; **uniformly** *see* 780.7; **constantly** *see* 846.7

10 **periodically, recurrently, seasonally**, cyclically, epochally; rhythmically, on the beat, in time, synchronously, **hourly, daily**, etc; every hour, every day, etc; hour by hour, day by day, etc; from hour to hour, from day to day, *de die in diem* (*Latin*)

11 **alternately, by turns, in turns, in rotation**, turn about, **turn and turn about**, reciprocally, every other, one after the other; to and fro, up and down, from side to side; off and on, round and round

phrases

12 **what goes around comes around**, *plus ça change plus c'est la même chose* (*French*)

850 IRREGULARITY OF RECURRENCE

nouns

1 **irregularity**, unmethodicalness, unsystematicness; **inconstancy, unevenness, unsteadiness**, uncertainty, desultoriness; **variability**, capriciousness, unpredictability, whimsicality, eccentricity; stagger, wobble, weaving, erraticness; roughness; **fitfulness, sporadicity** *or* sporadicalness, spasticity, jerkiness, fits and starts, patchiness, spottiness, choppiness, brokenness, disconnectedness, discontinuity *see* 812; **intermittence, fluctuation; nonuniformity** *see* 781; arrhythmia, fibrillation (*both medical*); blip

verbs

2 **to intermit, fluctuate, vary**, lack regularity, go by fits and starts

adjectives

3 **irregular**, unregular, unsystematic, unmethodical *or* immethodical; **inconstant, unsteady, uneven**, unrhythmical, unmetrical, rough, unequal, uncertain, unsettled; **variable**, deviative, heteroclite; **capricious, erratic**, off-again-on-again, eccentric; wobbly, wobbling, weaving, staggering, lurching, careening; **fitful, spasmodic** *or* spasmodical, spastic, spasmic, **jerky**, herky-jerky (*US & Canadian informal*), halting; **sporadic**, patchy, spotty, scrappy, snatchy, catchy, choppy, **broken, disconnected, discontinuous** *see* 812.4; **nonuniform** *see* 781.3; **intermittent**, intermitting, **desultory, fluctuating, wavering**, wandering, rambling, veering; flickering, guttering

adverbs

4 **irregularly**, unsystematically, unmethodically; **inconstantly, unsteadily, unevenly**, unrhythmically, roughly, uncertainly; **variably**, capriciously, unpredictably, whimsically, eccentrically, wobblingly, lurchingly, erratically; **intermittently, disconnectedly, discontinuously** *see* 812.5; **nonuniformly** *see* 781.4; brokenly, desultorily, patchily, spottily, in spots, in snatches; **by fits and starts**, by fits, by jerks, by snatches, by catches; **fitfully, sporadically, jerkily, spasmodically**, haltingly; **off and on**, at irregular intervals, sometimes and sometimes not; when the mood strikes, when the spirit moves, at random

851 CHANGE

nouns

1 **change, alteration, modification; variation**, variety, difference, diversity, diversification; **deviation**, diversion, aberrance *or* aberrancy, **divergence**; switch, switchover, changeover, **turn**, turnabout, about-face, **reversal**, flip-flop (*informal*); apostasy, defection, change of heart; **shift**, transition, **modulation**, qualification; **conversion**, **renewal**, revival, revivification, retro; remaking, reshaping, re-creation, redesign, restructuring, *perestroika* (*Russian*); realignment, **adaptation, adjustment**, accommodation, fitting; **reform**, reformation, **improvement**, amelioration,

melioration, mitigation, constructive change, **betterment**, change for the better; take *and* new take (*both US informal*); **social mobility**, vertical mobility, horizontal mobility, upward *or* downward mobility; gradual change, progressive change, **continuity** *see* 811; **degeneration, deterioration**, worsening, degenerative change, change for the worse, disorder *see* 809, entropy; changeableness *see* 853;

"the ever whirling wheels of Change"—Spenser, "Nature's mighty law"—Robert Burns, "a sea-change, Into something rich and strange"—Shakespeare, "the changes and chances of this mortal life"—Book of Common Prayer

2 **revolution, break**, break with the past, sudden change, radical *or* revolutionary *or* violent *or* total change, catastrophic change, **upheaval**, overthrow, **quantum leap** *or* jump, sea change; **discontinuity** *see* 812

3 **transformation**, transmogrification; **translation**; **metamorphosis**, metamorphism; **mutation**, transmutation, permutation; **mutant**, mutated form, sport; **transfiguration** *or* transfigurement; metathesis, transposition, translocation, **displacement**, metastasis, heterotopia; **transubstantiation**, consubstantiation; transanimation, transmigration, reincarnation, metempsychosis avatar; metasomatism, metasomatosis; catalysis; metabolism, anabolism, catabolism; metagenesis; transformism

4 **innovation, introduction**, discovery, invention, launching; neologism, neoterism, coinage; **breakthrough**, leap, quantum leap *or* jump, new phase; **novelty** *see* 840.2

5 **transformer**, transmogrifier, **innovator**, innovationist, introducer; precursor *see* 815; alterant, alterer, alterative, **agent**, catalytic agent, catalyst; the wind *or* winds of change; **leaven**, yeast, ferment; **modifier**, modificator

verbs

6 **to be changed, change, undergo a change**, go through a change, sing *or* dance to a different tune (*informal*), be converted into, turn into *see* 857.17; alter, mutate, modulate; **vary**, chequer, diversify; **deviate, diverge**, turn, take a turn, take a new turn, turn aside, turn the corner, **shift**, veer, jibe, tack, come about, come round *or* around, haul around, chop, chop and change, swerve, warp; change sides, change horses in midstream; **revive**, be renewed, feel like a new person; **improve**, ameliorate, meliorate, mitigate; **degenerate, deteriorate, worsen**; hit bottom, bottom out (*informal*), reach the nadir, flop (*informal*)

7 **to change, work** *or* **make a change, alter**, change someone's tune; **mutate; modify**; adapt; modulate, accommodate, adjust, fine-tune, fit, **qualify; vary, diversify; convert, renew, recast, revamp** (*informal*), change over, exchange, **revive**, remake, reshape, re-create, redesign, **rebuild**, reconstruct, restructure; realign; refit; **reform, improve**, better, ameliorate, meliorate, mitigate; **revolutionize**, turn upside down, subvert, overthrow, break up; worsen, deform, denature; ring the changes; give a turn to,

give a twist to, turn the tide, turn the tables, turn the scale *or* balance; shift the scene; shuffle the cards; move *or* shift the goalposts; turn over a new leaf, pull one's socks up (*informal*); **about-face**, do an about-face, do a 180 (*informal*), reverse oneself, turn one's coat, sing *or* dance to a different tune, flip-flop (*informal*)

8 **to transform, transfigure, transmute**, transmogrify; **translate**; transubstantiate, metamorphose; metabolize

9 **to innovate**, make innovations, invent, discover, make a breakthrough, make a quantum leap *or* jump, **pioneer** *see* 815.3, **revolutionize, introduce**, introduce new blood; neologize, neoterize, coin

adjectives

10 **changed, altered, modified**, qualified, **transformed**, transmuted, **metamorphosed**; translated, metastasized; deviant, aberrant, mutant; divergent; **converted, renewed**, revived, **rebuilt; reformed**, improved, **better**, ameliorative, ameliatory; before-and-after; **degenerate, worse**, unmitigated; subversive, **revolutionary**; changeable *see* 853.6, 7

11 **innovational**, innovative

12 **metamorphic, metabolic**, anabolic, catabolic; metastatic, **catalytic**

13 **presto**, presto chango, hey presto

phrases

14 the shoe is on the other foot

852 PERMANENCE

nouns

1 **permanence** *or* permanency, **immutability**, **changelessness**, unchangingness, invariableness *or* invariability; **unchangeableness**, unchangeability, unchangingness, inalterability *or* inalterableness, inconvertibility *or* inconvertibleness; **fixedness**, **constancy**, steadfastness, firmness, solidity, immovableness *or* immovability, persistence *or* persistency, faithfulness, **lastingness, abidingness**, **endurance**, duration, standing, long standing, inveteracy; durableness, durability *see* 826; **perpetualness** *see* 828.1; **stability** *see* 854; **unchangeability** *see* 854.4; **immobility**, stasis, frozenness, hardening, **rigidity; quiescence**, torpor, coma

2 **maintenance, preservation** *see* 397, **conservation**

3 **conservatism, conservativeness**, opposition *or* resistance to change, unprogressiveness, fogyism, fuddy-duddyism, backwardness, old-fashionedness; ultraconservatism, arch-conservatism; misocainea, misoneism; political conservatism, rightism *see* 611.1; laissez-faireism *see* 329.1; old school tie;

"adherence to the old and tried, against the new and untried"—Lincoln, "be not the first by whom the new is tried"—Pope

4 **conservative**, conservatist; conservationist; ultraconservative, arch-conservative, knee-jerk conservative (*informal*), **die-hard**, old fogy, fogy, stick-in-the-mud (*informal*), mossback (*US &*

Canadian *informal*), *laudator temporis acti* (*Latin*),
rightist, right-winger *see* 611.9
"the leftover progressive of an earlier generation"—
EDMUND FULLER; old school

verbs

5 **to remain, endure** *see* 826.6, last, stay, persist,
bide, abide, stand, hold, subsist; be ever the same
6 **to be conservative,** save, preserve, oppose change,
stand on ancient ways; stand pat *and* stand still (*both
informal*); **let things take their course,** leave things
as they are, let be, let *or* leave alone, stick with it
and let it ride (*both informal*), follow a hands-off
policy, let well enough alone, do nothing; stop *or*
turn back the clock

adjectives

7 **permanent, changeless, unchanging, immutable,**
unvarying, unshifting; **unchanged,** unchangeable,
unvaried, **unaltered,** inalterable, inviolate,
undestroyed, intact; **constant, persistent,** sustained,
fixed, firm, solid, steadfast, like the Rock of
Gibraltar, faithful; unchecked, unfailing, unfading;
lasting, enduring, abiding, remaining, staying,
continuing; **durable** *see* 826.10; **perpetual** *see* 828.7;
stable *see* 854.12; **unchangeable** *see* 854.17;
immobile, static, stationary, frozen, **rigid;**
quiescent, torpid, comatose, vegetable
8 **conservative, preservative,** old-line, **die-hard,**
opposed to change; backward, backward-looking,
old-fashioned, **unprogressive,** nonprogressive,
unreconstructed, status-quo, stuck-in-the-mud;
ultraconservative, misoneistic, fogyish, **old-fogyish;**
right-wing *see* 611.25; *laissez-faire* (*French*), hands-
off; noninvasive, noninterventionist

adverbs

9 **permanently,** abidingly, lastingly, steadfastly,
unwaveringly, changelessly, unchangingly;
enduringly, **perpetually,** invariably, **forever,**
always *see* 828.11; statically, rigidly, inflexibly
10 *in status quo* (*Latin*), as things are, **as is, as usual,**
as per usual (*informal*); at a stand *or* standstill,
without a shadow of turning

phrases

11 *plus ça change, plus c'est la même chose* (*French,* the
more it changes, the more it's the same thing); if it
isn't broken don't fix it, let sleeping dogs lie

853 CHANGEABLENESS

nouns

1 **changeableness,** changefulness, **changeability,**
alterability, convertibility, modifiability;
mutability, permutability, impermanence,
transience, transitoriness; mobility, motility,
movability; plasticity, malleability, workability,
rubberiness, fluidity; **resilience, adaptability,**
adjustability, **flexibility,** suppleness; **nonuniformity**
see 781
2 **inconstancy, instability,** changefulness,
unstableness, **unsteadiness,** unsteadfastness,
unfixedness, unsettledness, rootlessness; **uncertainty,**

undependability, inconsistency, shiftiness,
unreliability; **variability,** variation, variety,
restlessness, deviability; unpredictability, irregularity
see 850.1; **desultoriness,** waywardness, wantonness;
erraticism, eccentricity; freakishness, freakery;
flightiness, impulsiveness *or* impulsivity, mercuriality,
moodiness, whimsicality, **capriciousness, fickleness**
see 364.3
3 **changing, fluctuation,** vicissitude, **variation,**
shiftingness; alternation, oscillation, **vacillation,**
pendulation; **mood swings; wavering,** shifting,
shuffling, teetering, tottering, seesawing; **exchange,**
trading, musical chairs
4 (*comparisons*) Proteus, kaleidoscope, chameleon,
shifting sands, rolling stone, April showers, cloud
shapes, feather in the wind; water; wheel of fortune;
whirligig; mercury, quicksilver; the weather,
weathercock, weather vane; moon, phases of the
moon

verbs

5 **to change, fluctuate, vary; shift; alternate,**
vacillate, oscillate, pendulate, blow hot and cold
(*informal*); ebb and flow, wax and wane; go through
phases, waver, shuffle, swing, sway, wobble, wobble
about, flounder, stagger, teeter, totter, **seesaw;** back
and fill, turn, blow hot and cold, ring the changes,
have as many phases as the moon; **exchange,** trade,
play musical chairs

adjectives

6 **changeable, alterable,** alterative, modifiable;
mutable, permutable, impermanent, transient,
transitory; variable, chequered, ever-changing,
many-sided, kaleidoscopic; **movable,** mobile, motile;
plastic, malleable, rubbery, fluid; **resilient,**
adaptable, adjustable, **flexible,** supple, able to
adapt, able to roll with the punches *or* bend without
breaking; protean, proteiform; metamorphic;
nonuniform *see* 781.3
7 **inconstant, changeable, changeful, changing,**
shifting, uncertain, inconsistent; **shifty,** unreliable,
undependable; **unstable, unfixed,** infirm, restless,
unsettled, unstaid, **unsteady,** wishy-washy,
spineless, shapeless, amorphous, indecisive, irresolute,
blowing hot and cold (*informal*), like a feather in the
wind, unsteadfast, unstable as water; **variable,**
deviable, dodgy (*informal*); unaccountable,
unpredictable; vicissitudinous *or* vicissitudinary;
whimsical, **capricious, fickle** *see* 364.6, off-again-
on-again; **erratic, eccentric,** freakish; volatile, giddy,
dizzy, ditzy (*US & Canadian informal*),
scatterbrained, mercurial, moody, flighty, impulsive,
impetuous; **fluctuating,** alternating, **vacillating,**
wavering, wavery, wavy, mazy, flitting, flickering,
guttering, fitful, shifting, shuffling; irregular,
spasmodic *see* 850.3; **desultory,** rambling, roving,
vagrant, wanton, wayward, wandering, afloat, adrift;
unrestrained, undisciplined, irresponsible,
uncontrolled, fast and loose

adverbs

8 **changeably, variably, inconstantly,** shiftingly,
shiftily, uncertainly, **unsteadily,** unsteadfastly,

whimsically, capriciously, desultorily, erratically, waveringly; **impulsively, impetuously,** precipitately; back and forth, to and fro, in and out, off and on, on and off, round and round

854 STABILITY

nouns

1 **stability, firmness, soundness, substantiality, solidity; security,** secureness, securement; **rootedness,** fastness; reliability *see* 969.4; **steadiness,** steadfastness; constancy *see* 846.2, invariability, undeflectability; **imperturbability,** unflappability (*informal*), nerve, steady *or* unshakable nerves, unshakableness, unsusceptibility, unimpressionability, stolidness *or* stolidity, stoicism, **cool** (*informal*), *sang-froid* (*French*); **equilibrium, balance,** stable state, stable equilibrium, homeostasis; steady state; emotional stability, balanced personality; aplomb; **uniformity** *see* 780

2 **fixity,** fixedness, fixture, fixation; infixion, implantation, embedment; **establishment, stabilization,** confirmation, entrenchment; inveteracy, deep-rootedness, **deep-seatedness**

3 **immobility,** immovability, unmovability, immovableness, irremovability, immotility; inextricability; **firmness,** solidity, unyieldingness, rigidity, **inflexibility** *see* 1044.3; inertia, *vis inertiae* (*Latin*), inertness; immobilization

4 **unchangeableness, unchangeability,** unalterability, inalterability, unmodifiability, **immutability,** incommutability, inconvertibility; nontransferability; lastingness, **permanence** *see* 852; irrevocability, indefeasibility, **irreversibility;** irretrievability, unreturnableness, unrestorableness; intransmutability

5 **indestructibility, imperishability,** incorruptibility, inextinguishability, immortality, **deathlessness;** invulnerability, invincibility, inexpugnability, impregnability; ineradicability, indelibility, ineffaceability, inerasableness

6 (*comparisons*) rock, Rock of Gibraltar, bedrock, pillar *or* tower of strength, foundation; leopard's spots

verbs

7 **to stabilize,** stabilitate *or* stabilify (*old*); **firm, firm up** (*informal*); **steady, balance,** counterbalance, ballast; **immobilize,** freeze, keep, retain; **transfix,** stick, hold, pin *or* nail down (*informal*)

8 **to secure,** make sure *or* secure, tie, tie off *or* up, chain, tether; cleat, belay; **wedge, jam, seize; make fast, fasten,** fasten down; **anchor,** moor; batten *and* batten down; "build one's house upon a rock"—BIBLE; **confirm,** ratify

9 **to fix, define,** set, **settle; establish,** found, ground, lodge, seat, **entrench; root;** infix, ingrain, set in, plant, implant, engraft, bed, embed; **print,** imprint, **stamp,** inscribe, **etch,** engrave, impress; deep-dye, **dye in the wool;** stereotype

10 (*become firmly fixed*) **to root, take root,** strike root, **stick,** stick fast; seize, seize up, freeze; **catch, jam,** lodge, foul

11 **to stand fast,** stand *or* remain firm, stand pat (*informal*), stay put (*informal*), hold fast, not budge, not budge an inch, **stand** *or* **hold one's ground,** hold one's own, dig in one's heels, take one's stand, **stick to one's guns,** put one's foot down (*informal*); **hold out,** stick *or* gut *or* tough it out *and* hang tough (*all informal*), stay the course; **hold up; weather,** weather the storm, ride it out, get home free (*US & Canadian informal*); be imperturbable, be unflappable *and* not bat an eye *or* eyelash *and* keep one's cool *and* keep one's head (*all informal*)

adjectives

12 **stable, substantial, firm, solid, sound,** stabile; firm as the rock of Gibraltar, solid as a rock, rocklike, built on bedrock; **fast, secure; steady,** unwavering, steadfast; **balanced,** in equilibrium, in a stable state; **well-balanced; imperturbable,** unflappable (*informal*), unshakable, **cool** (*informal*), unimpressionable, unsusceptible, impassive, stolid, stoic; without nerves, without a nerve in one's body, unflinching; **reliable** *see* 969.17, predictable; fiducial

13 **established,** stabilized, **entrenched,** vested, firmly established; **well-established,** well-founded, **well-grounded,** on a rock, in *or* on bedrock; old-line, long-established; **confirmed,** inveterate; **settled, set;** well-settled, well-set, in place; **rooted,** well-rooted; **deep-rooted, deep-seated,** deep-set, deep-settled, deep-fixed, deep-dyed, deep-engraven, deep-grounded, deep-laid; **infixed, ingrained,** implanted, engrafted, embedded, ingrown, inwrought; impressed, indelibly impressed, imprinted; engraved, etched, graven, embossed; **dyed-in-the-wool**

14 **fixed,** fastened, anchored, riveted; **set, settled, stated;** staple

15 **immovable,** unmovable, **immobile,** immotile, unmoving, **irremovable, stationary,** frozen, not to be moved, at a standstill, on dead centre; **firm, unyielding,** adamant, adamantine, rigid, **inflexible** *see* 1044.12; pat

16 **stuck, fast,** stuck fast, fixed, **transfixed, caught,** fastened, tied, chained, tethered, anchored, moored, held, inextricable; **jammed,** impacted, congested, packed, wedged; seized, seized up, frozen; aground, grounded, stranded, high and dry

17 **unchangeable,** not to be changed, changeless, unchanged, unchanging, unvarying, unvariable, **unalterable,** unaltered, unalterative, **immutable,** incommutable, inconvertible, unmodifiable; insusceptible of change; **constant, invariable,** undeviating, undeflectable; lasting, unremitting, **permanent** *see* 852.7; irrevocable, indefeasible, **irreversible,** nonreversible, reverseless; irretrievable, unrestorable, unreturnable, nonreturnable; intransmutable, inert, noble (*chemistry*)

18 **indestructible,** undestroyable, **imperishable,** nonperishable, incorruptible; **deathless,** immortal, undying; **invulnerable, invincible,** inexpugnable, impregnable, indivisible; **ineradicable,** indelible, ineffaceable, inerasable; **inextinguishable,** unquenchable, quenchless, undampable

phrases

19 stet, let it stand; what's done is done

855 CONTINUANCE
continuance in action

nouns

1 **continuance, continuation, ceaselessness,** unceasingness, uninterruptedness, unremittingness, **continualness** *see* 811.1; **prolongation, extension, protraction, perpetuation,** lengthening, spinning *or* stringing out; **survival** *see* 826.1, holding out, hanging on *or* in; **maintenance,** sustenance, sustained action *or* activity; pursuance; run, way, straight *or* uninterrupted course; **progress,** progression; **persistence, perseverance** *see* 360; **endurance** *see* 826.1, **stamina,** staying power; **continuity** *see* 811; **repetition** *see* 848

2 **resumption, recommencement,** rebeginning, recommencement, reestablishment, revival, recrudescence, resuscitation, **renewal,** reopening, reentrance, reappearance; **fresh start,** new beginning; another try, another shot *or* crack *or* go *or* bash *or* stab (*informal*)

verbs

3 **to continue** *see* 811.4, keep *or* stay with it, keep *or* stay at it, carry on; **remain,** bide, **abide, stay,** tarry, linger; **go on,** go along, **keep on,** keep on keeping on, keep going, carry on, see it through, stay on, hold on, hold one's way *or* course *or* path, hold steady, run on, jog on, drag on, bash ahead *or* on (*informal*), slog on, soldier on, plug away (*informal*), grind away *or* on, stagger on, put one foot in front of the other; never cease, cease not; **endure** *see* 826.6

4 **to sustain, protract, prolong, extend,** perpetuate, lengthen, spin *or* string out; **maintain,** keep, hold, retain, preserve; **keep up,** keep going, keep alive, **survive** *see* 826.6

5 **to persist, persevere,** keep at it *see* 360.2, stick it out, stick to it, stick with it, never say die, see it through, hang in *and* hang tough *and* not know when one is beaten (*all informal*); survive, make out, manage, get along, get on, eke out an existence, keep the even tenor of one's way; go on, go on with, go on with the show (*informal*), press on; perseverate, iterate, reiterate, **harp,** go on about, chew one's ear off *and* run off at the mouth (*both informal*), flog a dead horse

6 **to resume, recommence,** rebegin, **renew,** reestablish; **revive,** resuscitate, recrudesce; reenter, reopen, **return to,** go back to, begin again, take up again, make a new beginning, make a fresh start, start all over, have another try, have another shot *or* crack *or* go *or* bash *or* stab (*informal*)

adjectives

7 **continuing, abiding** *see* 826.10; staying, remaining, sticking; **continuous** *see* 811.8, **ceaseless, unceasing,** unending, endless, incessant, unremitting, steady, sustained, protracted, undying, indefatigable, **persistent; repetitious, repetitive** *see* 848.14; **resumed,** recommenced, rebegun, renewed, reopened

856 CESSATION

nouns

1 **cessation, discontinuance,** discontinuation, phaseout, phasedown, scratching *and* scrubbing *and* breakoff (*all informal*); **desistance,** desinence, cease, surcease, **ceasing,** ending, halting, stopping, termination; **close,** closing, shutdown, closedown; sign-off; log-off *or* log-out; **relinquishment,** renunciation, abandonment

2 **stop, stoppage, halt, stay, arrest,** check, cutoff (*informal*); stand, **standstill;** full stop, dead stop, screaming *or* grinding *or* shuddering *or* squealing halt; **strike** *see* 727.7, walkout, work stoppage, sit-down strike, lockout; **end,** ending, endgame, final whistle, gun, bell, checkmate; **tie,** stalemate, deadlock, toss-up (*informal*), wash (*US & Canadian informal*), standoff *and* Mexican standoff (*both US & Canadian informal*); **terminal,** end of the line, rest stop, stopping place, terminus

3 **pause, rest, break,** caesura, **recess, intermission,** interim *see* 825, intermittence, interval, interlude, *intermezzo* (*Italian*); **respite,** letup (*informal*); **interruption, suspension,** time out, break in the action, breathing spell, cooling-off period; **postponement** *see* 845.4, rain-off; **remission;** abeyance, stay, drop, lull, lapse; truce, cease-fire, stand-down; **vacation, holiday,** time off, day off, recess, playtime, leisure; half day, early closing

4 (*grammatical terms*) pause, juncture, boundary, caesura; (*punctuation*) stop *or* point *or* period, comma, colon, semicolon

5 (*legislatures*) closure, cloture (*US*), *clôture* (*French*); closure by compartment, kangaroo closure; guillotine

verbs

6 **to cease, discontinue, end, stop, halt,** end-stop, terminate, close the books on, close the books, put paid to, abort, cancel, scratch *and* scrub (*both informal*), hold, **quit,** stay, belay; **desist, refrain,** leave off, lay off (*informal*), give over, **pack in** (*informal*), **have done with,** stow (*informal*); cut it out *and* drop it *and* knock it off (*all informal*), break it down (*Australian & NZ informal*), relinquish, renounce, abandon; **come to an end** *see* 819.6, draw to a close

7 **to stop, come to a stop** *or* halt, **halt,** stop in one's tracks, skid to a stop, stop dead, **stall; bring up, pull up,** pull in, head in, draw up, **fetch up; stop short,** come up short, bring up short, come to a screaming *or* squealing *or* grinding *or* shuddering halt, stop on a dime (*US & Canadian informal*), come to a full stop, come to a stand *or* standstill, grind to a halt, fetch up all standing; **stick,** jam, hang fire, seize, seize up, freeze; **cease fire,** stand down; run into a brick wall

8 (*stop work*) **to lay off, knock off** (*informal*), call it a day (*informal*), call it quits (*informal*); lay down one's tools, down tools, **shut up shop,** close shop, shut down, close down, secure (*nautical informal*); **strike,** walk out, call a strike, go *or* go out on strike, come out, bring out, stand down; work to rule

9 **to pause, rest,** let up *and* take it easy (*both informal*), **relax,** rest on one's oars; recess, take *or* call a recess; **take a break,** break, take five *or* ten

10 to interrupt, suspend, intermit, **break, break off,** take a break (*informal*), cut off, break *or* snap the thread

11 to put a stop to, call a halt to, get it over with, blow the whistle on (*informal*), **put an end to** *see* 819.5, put paid to (*informal*), call off the dogs (*informal*); stop, stay, **halt, arrest, check,** flag down, wave down; block, brake, dam, stem, stem the tide *or* current; pull up, draw rein, put on the brakes, hit the brake pedal; **bring to a stand** *or* **standstill,** bring to a close *or* halt, freeze, bring to, bring up short, **stop dead** *or* dead in one's tracks, set one back on his heels, stop cold, stop short, cut short, check in full career; checkmate, stalemate, deadlock

12 to turn off, shut off, shut, shut down, close; **phase out,** phase down, taper off, wind up *or* down; **kill, cut,** cut off short, switch off

exclamations

13 cease!, stop!, halt!, *halte!* (*French*), hold!, freeze!, stay!, desist!, quit it!; **let up!, easy!, take it easy!,** relax!, get off it!, **leave off!,** *arrêtez!* (*French*), stop it!, forget it!, no more!, have done!, *tenez!* (*French*), **hold everything!, hold it!,** hold to!, hold on!, whoa!, that's it!, that's enough!, that will do!, enough!, enough is enough!, genug!, all right already! (*US*), *basta!* (*Italian*)

14 (*informal terms*) cut it out!, cool it!, bag it!, chill out!, call it quits!, can it!, turn it off!, chuck it!, stow it!, drop it!, lay off!, nark it!, all right already!, come off it!, **knock it off!,** break it off!, break it up!

857 CONVERSION
change to something different

nouns

1 conversion, reconversion, **changeover,** turning into, becoming; convertibility; **change** *see* 851, sea change, **transformation,** transubstantiation, transmutation; **transition,** transit, **switch** *and* **switchover** (*both informal*), passage, **shift; reversal,** about-face *and* flip-flop (*both informal*), *volte-face* (*French*); **relapse,** lapse, descent; **breakthrough; growth,** progress, development; transcendence; **resolution** *see* 939.1; reduction, simplification; **assimilation,** naturalization, adoption, assumption; alchemy

2 **new start, new beginning,** fresh start, clean slate, new leaf, square one (*informal*); **reformation, reform, regeneration, revival, reclamation,** redemption, amendment, improvement *see* 392, renewal, recrudescence, **rebirth,** renascence, new birth, **change of heart;** change of mind *or* commitment *or* allegiance *or* loyalty *or* conviction

3 apostasy, renunciation, **defection, desertion,** treason, crossing-over, abandonment; degeneration *see* 393.3

4 **rehabilitation,** reconditioning, recovery, readjustment, reclamation, restoration; **reeducation,** reinstruction; **repatriation**

5 **indoctrination,** reindoctrination, counterindoctrination; **brainwashing,** menticide; subversion, alienation, corruption

6 **conversion,** proselytization, proselytism, evangelization, persuasion *see* 375.3

7 **convert, proselyte,** neophyte, catechumen, disciple

8 **apostate, defector,** turncoat, traitor, deserter, **renegade**

9 **converter, proselyter,** proselytizer, **missionary, apostle, evangelist,** televangelist

10 (*instruments*) philosopher's stone, melting pot, crucible, alembic, test tube, cauldron, retort, mortar; potter's wheel, anvil, lathe; converter, transformer, transducer, engine, motor, machine *see* 1039.4

verbs

11 to **convert,** reconvert; **change over,** switch *and* switch over (*both informal*), **shift; do over,** re-do, make over, rejig; **change, transform** *see* 851.5, 8, transmute; **change into, turn into, become,** resolve into, assimilate to, bring to, reduce to, naturalize; **make,** render; **reverse,** do an about-face; change one's tune, sing a different tune, dance to another tune, laugh on the other side of one's face; turn back *see* 858.5

12 to **re-form,** remodel, reshape, refashion, recast; regroup, redeploy, rearrange *see* 807.13; **renew,** new-model; be reborn, be born again, be a new person, feel like a new person; get it together *and* get one's act together (*both informal*), get one's shit together (*US informal*), sort one's life out (*informal*); **regenerate, reclaim,** redeem, amend, set straight; **reform, rehabilitate,** set on the straight and narrow, make a new man of, restore self-respect; mend *or* change one's ways, **turn over a new leaf,** put on the new man

13 to **defect,** renege, wimp *or* chicken *or* cop out (*informal*), turn one's coat, desert, apostatize, change one's colours, turn against, turn traitor; leave *or* desert a sinking ship; lapse, relapse; degenerate

14 to **rehabilitate,** recondition, reclaim, recover, restore, readjust; **reeducate,** reinstruct; **repatriate**

15 to **indoctrinate, brainwash,** reindoctrinate, counterindoctrinate; subvert, alienate, win away, corrupt

16 to **convince, persuade,** wean, bring over, sweep off one's feet (*informal*), **win over;** proselyte, **proselytize,** evangelize

17 to be converted into, **turn into** *or* to, **become** *see* 760.12, **change into,** alter into, run *or* fall *or* pass into, slide *or* glide into, **grow into,** ripen into, **develop** *or* **evolve into,** merge *or* blend *or* melt into, shift into, lapse into, open into, resolve itself *or* settle into, come round to

adjectives

18 **convertible,** changeable, resolvable, transmutable, **transformable, transitional, modifiable;** reformable, reclaimable, renewable

19 **converted, changed, transformed;** naturalized, assimilated; **reformed,** regenerated, renewed, redeemed, reborn, born-again

20 **apostate, treasonable, traitorous,** degenerate, **renegade**

858 REVERSION
change to a former state

nouns

1 **reversion**, reverting, retroversion, retrogradation, **retrogression**, retrocession, regress, **relapse** *see 394*, **regression, backsliding**, lapse, slipping back, backing, recidivism, recidivation; reconversion; **reverse, reversal**, turnabout, about-face, right about-face, 180-degree shift, three-point turn, flip-flop (*informal*), **turn; return**, returning; disenchantment; **reclamation, rehabilitation**, redemption, return to the fold; **reinstatement**, restitution, restoration

2 **throwback**, atavism

3 **returnee, repeater**; prodigal son, lost lamb; reversioner, reversionist; recidivist, habitual criminal *or* offender, two-time loser (*informal*); backslider

verbs

4 **to revert**, retrovert, **regress, retrogress**, retrograde, retrocede, **reverse, return**, return to the fold; backslide, slip back, recidivate, lapse, lapse back, relapse *see 394.4*

5 **to turn back, change back, go back, hark back**, cry back, break back, **turn**, turn around *or* about; do an about-face *and* flip-flop *and* do a flip-flop (*all informal*); put the genie back into the bottle, put the toothpaste back into the tube; go back to go *or* to square one *or* to the drawing board (*informal*)

6 **to revert to, return to**, recur to, go back to; hark *or* cry back to

adjectives

7 **reversionary**, reversional, **regressive**, recessive, **retrogressive, retrograde**; reactionary; recidivist *or* recidivistic, recidivous, lapsarian; retroverse, retrorse; atavistic; revertible, returnable, reversible, recoverable

word elements

8 retro–

859 REVOLUTION
sudden or radical change

nouns

1 **revolution, radical** *or* **total change, violent change**, striking alteration, sweeping change, clean sweep, clean slate, square one (*informal*), tabula rasa; transilience, quantum leap *or* jump; **overthrow**, overturn, upset, *bouleversement* (*French*), convulsion, spasm, subversion, coup d'état; breakup, breakdown; **cataclysm, catastrophe**, debacle, *débâcle* (*French*); **revolution**, revolutionary war, war of national liberation; bloodless revolution, palace revolution; technological revolution, electronic *or* communications *or* computer *or* information revolution; green revolution; counterrevolution; revolt *see 327.4*

2 **revolutionism**, revolutionariness, anarchism, syndicalism, terrorism; Bolshevism *or* Bolshevikism (*both Russia*), Carbonarism (*Italy*), Sinn Feinism (*Ireland*), Jacobinism (*France*); sans-culottism (*France*), *sans-culotterie* (*French*), Castroism (*Cuba*),

Maoism (*China*), Shining Path (*Peru*), Sandinistism (*Nicaragua*)

3 **revolutionist, revolutionary**, revolutionizer; **rebel** *see 327.5*; anarchist, anarch, syndicalist, criminal syndicalist, terrorist *see 671.9*; subversive; red; Red Republican (*France*), *bonnet rouge* (*French*); Jacobin (*France*), sans-culotte, sans-culottist; Yankee *or* Yankee Doodle *or* Continental (*all US*); Puritan *or* Roundhead; Bolshevik *or* Bolshevist *or* Bolshie (*all Russia*), Marxist, Leninist, Communist, Commie (*informal*), Red, Trotskyite *or* Trotskyist, Castroist *or* Castroite (*Cuba*), Guevarist, Maoist; Vietcong *or* VC, Cong, Charley (*all Vietnam*); Carbonaro (*Italy*), Carbonarist (*Italy*); Sinn Feiner, Fenian (*both Ireland*); revolutionary junta; Sandinista; Tamil Tiger

verbs

4 **to revolutionize, make a radical change**, make a clean sweep, break with the past; **overthrow, overturn**, throw the rascals out *and* let heads roll (*both informal*), *bouleverse* (*French*), upset; revolt *see 327.7*

adjectives

5 **revolutionary**; revulsive, revulsionary; transilient; cataclysmic, catastrophic; **radical**, sweeping *see 793.10*; **insurrectionary** *see 327.11*

6 **revolutionist, revolutionary**, anarchic *or* anarchical, syndicalist, terrorist *or* terroristic, agin the government (*informal*); Bolshevistic, Bolshevik; sans-culottic, sans-culottish; Jacobinic *or* Jacobinical, Carbonarist, Fenian, Marxist, Leninist, Communist, Trotskyist *or* Trotskyite, Guevarist, Castroist *or* Castroite, Maoist, Vietcong, Mau-Mau

860 EVOLUTION

nouns

1 **evolution, evolving**, evolvement; evolutionary change, gradual change, step-by-step change, peaceful *or* nonviolent change; **development, growth**, rise, incremental change, developmental change, natural growth *or* development; flowering, blossoming; ripening, coming of age, maturation *see 303.6*; accomplishment *see 407*; **advance**, advancement, furtherance; **progress**, progression; **elaboration**, enlargement, amplification, **expansion**; devolution, degeneration *see 393.3*

2 **unfolding**, unfoldment, unrolling, unfurling, unwinding; revelation, gradual revelation

3 (*biological terms*) **genesis**; phylogeny, phylogenesis; ontogeny, ontogenesis; physiogeny, physiogenesis; **biological evolution**; natural selection, adaptation; horotely, bradytely, tachytely

4 **evolutionism**, theory of evolution; **Darwinism**, Darwinianism, punctuated equilibrium, Neo-Darwinism, organic evolution, survival of the fittest; Haeckelism, Lamarckism *or* Lamarckianism, Neo-Lamarckism, Lysenkoism, Weismannism, Spencerianism; social Darwinism, social evolution

verbs

5 **to evolve; develop, grow**, wax, change gradually *or* step-by-step; **progress, advance**, come a long way;

accomplish *see* 407.4; ripen, mellow, mature *see* 303.9, maturate; flower, bloom, blossom, bear fruit; degenerate

6 to elaborate, develop, **work out**, enlarge, enlarge on *or* upon, amplify, **expand**, expand on *or* upon, detail, go *or* enter into detail, go into, flesh out, **pursue**, spell out (*informal*); complete *see* 407.6

7 to unfold, unroll, unfurl, unwind, unreel, uncoil, reveal, reveal *or* expose gradually

adjectives

8 **evolutionary**, evolutional, evolutionist *or* evolutionistic; **evolving, developing, unfolding; maturing**, maturational, maturative; **progressing, advancing**; devolutionary, degenerative; genetic, phylogenetic, ontogenetic, physiogenetic; horotelic, bradytelic, tachytelic

861 SUBSTITUTION
change of one thing for another

nouns

1 **substitution, exchange, change**, switch, switcheroo (*US informal*), commutation, subrogation; **surrogacy**; vicariousness, **representation**, deputation, **delegation**; deputyship, **agency, power of attorney**; **supplanting**, supplantation, successsion; **replacement**, displacement; provision, provisionalness *or* provisionality, adhocracy, ad hockery *or* ad hocery, ad hocism; superseding, supersession *or* supersedure; tit for tat, *quid pro quo* (*Latin*)

2 **substitute**, sub (*informal*), **substitution, replacement**, backup, second *or* third string (*informal*), secondary, utility player, succedaneum; **change, exchange**; ersatz, phoney *and* fake (*both informal*), counterfeit, imitation *see* 336, copy *see* 784; surrogate; reserves, bench (*informal*), backup, backup personnel, spares; **alternate**, alternative, next best thing; **successor**, supplanter, superseder, capper (*informal*); **proxy**, dummy, ghost; vicar, agent, representative; **deputy** *see* 576; locum tenens, vice, vice-president, vice-regent, etc; **relief**, fill-in, **stand-in, understudy**, pinch hitter *or* runner (*US & Canadian informal*); double; **equivalent**, equal; ringer (*informal*); ghostwriter; **analogy**, comparison; **metaphor**, metonymy, synecdoche (*all grammatical*); **symbol, sign**, token, icon; makeshift *see* 994.2

3 **scapegoat**, goat (*informal*), fall guy *and* can-carrier *and* patsy *and* stooge (*all informal*), **whipping boy**

verbs

4 to **substitute, exchange, change**, take *or* ask *or* offer in exchange, switch, ring in (*informal*), **put in the place of**, change for, make way for, give place to; commute, redeem, compound for; **pass off**, pawn *or* foist *or* fob off; rob Peter to pay Paul; dub in; make do with, shift with, put up with

5 to **substitute for**, sub for (*informal*), subrogate; **act for**, double for *or* as, stand *or* sit in for, understudy for, fill in for, don the mantle of, change places with, swap places with (*informal*), stand in the stead of, step into *or* fill the shoes of, pinch-hit *and* pinch-run (*both US & Canadian informal*); **relieve**,

cover for; ghost, ghostwrite; **represent** *see* 576.14; **supplant, supersede**, succeed, **replace**, displace, **take the place of**, crowd out, cut out (*informal*)

6 (*informal terms*) to **cover up for**, front for; **take the rap for**, *and* take the fall for (*both informal*), carry the can *and* be the goat *or* patsy *or* fall guy *or* stooge (*all informal*)

7 to **delegate, deputize, commission**, give the nod to (*informal*), designate an agent *or* a proxy

adjectives

8 **substitute, alternate, alternative**, other, tother (*informal*), equivalent, token, dummy, pinch, utility, backup, secondary; ad hoc, provisional; **vicarious**, ersatz, mock, phoney *and* fake *and* bogus (*all informal*), counterfeit, imitation *see* 336.8; **proxy**; makeshift, reserve, **spare**, stopgap, temporary, provisional, tentative

9 **substitutional**, substitutionary, substitutive, supersessive; **substituted**, substituent

10 **replaceable**, substitutable, supersedable, expendable

adverbs

11 **instead, rather**, *faute de mieux* (*French*); in its stead *or* place; in one's stead, in one's behalf, in one's place, in one's shoes; by proxy; as an alternative; *in loco parentis* (*Latin*)

prepositions

12 **instead of**, in the stead of, rather than, sooner than, **in place of**, in the place of, **in** *or* **on behalf of**, in lieu of; **for**, as proxy for, as a substitute for, as representing, in preference to, as an alternative to; **replacing**, as a replacement for, vice

word elements

13 pro–, vice–, quasi–, pseudo–

862 INTERCHANGE
double or mutual change

nouns

1 **interchange, exchange**, counterchange; **transposition**, transposal; mutual transfer *or* replacement; mutual admiration, mutual support; **cooperation** *see* 450; commutation, permutation, intermutation; alternation; **interplay, tradeoff, compromise, reciprocation** *see* 776.1, reciprocality, reciprocity, mutuality; **give-and-take**, something for something, *quid pro quo* (*Latin*), measure for measure, **tit for tat**, an eye for an eye, "an eye for an eye and a tooth for a tooth"—Bible; **retaliation**, *lex talionis* (*Latin*); cross fire; battledore and shuttlecock

2 **trading, swapping** (*informal*); trade, swap (*informal*), even trade, even-steven trade (*US & Canadian informal*), **switch**; barter *see* 731.2; logrolling (*US*), back scratching, pork barrel (*US informal*)

3 **interchangeability**, exchangeability, changeability, standardization; convertibility, commutability, permutability

verbs

4 to **interchange, exchange**, change, counterchange; alternate; **transpose**; convert, commute, permute,

permutate; **trade, swap** (*informal*), **switch**; bandy, bandy about, play at battledore and shuttlecock; **reciprocate, trade off**, compromise, settle, settle for, respond, keep a balance; **give and take**, give tit for tat, give a Roland for an Oliver, give as much as one takes, give as good as one gets, return the compliment *or* favour, pay back, compensate, **requite**, return; **retaliate**, get back at, get even with, be quits with; logroll (*US*), scratch each other's back, **cooperate** *see* 450.3

adjectives

5 **interchangeable, exchangeable,** changeable, standard; equivalent; **even,** equal; returnable, **convertible,** commutable, permutable; commutative; retaliatory, equalizing; **reciprocative** *or* **reciprocating, reciprocatory, reciprocal, traded-off; mutual,** give-and-take; **exchanged, transposed,** switched, **swapped** (*informal*), traded, **interchanged**

adverbs

6 **interchangeably, exchangeably; in exchange, in return; even, evenly,** *au pair* (*French*); **reciprocally,** mutually; **in turn,** each in its turn, every one in his turn, by turns, turn about, turn and turn about

phrases

7 one good turn deserves another; you scratch my back I scratch yours

863 GENERALITY

nouns

1 **generality, universality,** cosmicality, inclusiveness *see* 771.1; worldwideness, globality *or* globalism, globaloney (*US informal*), ecumenicity *or* ecumenicalism; catholicity; **internationalism,** cosmopolitanism; **generalization,** universalization, globalization, ecumenization, internationalization; **labelling,** stereotyping

2 **prevalence, commonness,** commonality, usualness, **currency,** occurrence; **extensiveness,** widespreadness, sweepingness, rifeness, rampantness; **normality,** normalness, averageness, ordinariness, routineness, habitualness, standardness

3 **average,** ruck, **run,** general *or* common *or* average *or* ordinary run, **run of the mill;** any Tom, Dick or Harry; Everyman; common *or* average man, the man in the street, the man on the Clapham omnibus, punter, Joe Bloggs (*informal*), Joe Public, John *or* Jane Doe, ordinary Joe, Joe Six-pack (*US informal*), Joe Soap (*informal*), Joe Blow (*US, Canadian & Australian informal*); girl next door, boy next door; everyman, everywoman; *homme moyen sensuel* (*French*)

4 **all, everyone, everybody, each and everyone, one and all,** all comers *and* all hands *and* every man Jack *and* every mother's son (*all informal*), every living soul, **all the world,** the world and his wife, *tout le monde* (*French*), the devil and all (*informal*), **whole,** totality *see* 791.1; **everything,** all kinds *or* all manner of things; you name it *and* what have you *and* all the above (*all informal*)

5 **any, anything,** any one, aught, either; **anybody, anyone**

6 **whatever,** whate'er, **whatsoever,** whatsoe'er, **what, whichever,** anything soever which, no matter what *or* which

7 **whoever,** whoso, **whosoever, whomever,** whomso, **whomsoever,** anyone, no matter who

8 (*idea or expression*) **generalization,** general idea, **abstraction,** generalized proposition; glittering generality, sweeping statement; **truism, platitude, conventional wisdom,** commonplace, *lieu commun* (*French*), *locus communis* (*Latin*); **cliché,** tired cliché, bromide, trite *or* hackneyed expression

verbs

9 **to generalize, universalize,** catholicize, ecumenicize, globalize, internationalize; **broaden, widen, expand,** extend, spread; make a generalization, deal in generalities *or* abstractions; **label,** stereotype

10 **to prevail, predominate, obtain,** dominate, reign, rule; be in force *or* effect; be the rule *or* fashion, be all the rage (*informal*), be the rage *or* thing (*informal*), be in (*informal*), be the in thing (*informal*)

adjectives

11 **general, generalized, nonspecific,** generic, **indefinite,** indeterminate, vague, abstract, nebulous, unspecified, undifferentiated, featureless, uncharacterized, bland, neutral

12 **prevalent, prevailing, common,** popular, **current,** running; regnant, reigning, **ruling, predominant,** predominating, **dominant; rife, rampant,** pandemic, epidemic, besetting; **ordinary, normal, average, usual,** routine, standard, par for the course (*informal*), stereotyped

13 **extensive, broad, wide,** liberal, diffuse, large-scale, broad-scale, broad-scope, broadly-based, wide-scale, **sweeping; cross-disciplinary,** interdisciplinary; widespread, far-spread, far-stretched, **far-reaching,** far-going, far-embracing, far-extending, far-spreading, far-flying, far-ranging, **far-flung,** wide-flung, wide-reaching, wide-extending, wide-extended, wide-ranging, wide-stretching; **wholesale, indiscriminate**

14 **universal,** cosmic *or* cosmical, heaven-wide, galactic, planetary, world-wide, transnational, planet-wide, **global; total,** allover, holistic; catholic, **all-inclusive,** all-including, **all-embracing,** all-encompassing, all-comprehensive, all-comprehending, all-filling, all-pervading, all-covering; nonsectarian, nondenominational, ecumenic *or* ecumenical; **cosmopolitan,** international; **national,** nation-wide, country-wide, state-wide

15 **every, all,** any, whichever, whichsoever; **each,** each one; every one, each and every, each and all, **one and all, all and sundry,** all and some

16 **trite, commonplace,** hackneyed, platitudinous, truistic, overworked, stereotyped, clichéd, bromidic

adverbs

17 **generally, in general; generally speaking,** speaking generally, **broadly,** broadly speaking, **roughly,** roughly speaking, as an approximation; **usually, as a rule,** ordinarily, commonly, normally, routinely, as a matter of course, in the usual course; **by and large,** at large, altogether, overall, over the long haul (*informal*), **all things considered,** taking one thing with another, taking all things together, on balance, **all in all,** taking all in all, taking it for all in all, **on the whole,** as a whole, **in the long run,** for the most part, for better or for worse; **prevailingly, predominantly, mostly,** chiefly, mainly

18 **universally, galactically, cosmically; everywhere, all over,** the world over, all over the world, internationally; in every instance, without exception, **invariably, always,** never otherwise

word elements

19 glob–, globo–, omn–, omni–, pan–, pano–, pant–, panto–, panta–

864 PARTICULARITY

nouns

1 **particularity, individuality, singularity, differentiation,** differentness, distinctiveness, uniqueness; **identity,** individual *or* separate *or* concrete identity; **personality,** personship, personal identity; soul; **selfness,** selfhood, **egohood,** self-identity, self-image,
   "a single separate person"—WHITMAN; oneness *see* 871.1, wholeness, integrity; personal equation, human factor; **nonconformity** *see* 867; **individualism,** particularism; nominalism

2 **speciality, specialness,** specialty (*US & Canadian*), specificality, **specificness,** definiteness; special case

3 **the specific,** the special, **the particular,** the concrete, the individual, the unique;
   "all things counter, original, spare, strange"—G M HOPKINS

4 **characteristic, peculiarity, singularity,** particularity, speciality, specialty (*US & Canadian*), individualism, **character,** nature, **trait,** quirk, point of character, bad point, good point, saving grace, redeeming feature, mannerism, keynote, trick, **feature,** distinctive feature, trademark, middle name, lineament; **mark,** marking, **earmark,** hallmark, index; badge, token; **brand,** cast, stamp, cachet, seal, mould, cut, figure, shape, configuration; impress, impression; differential, differentia; **idiosyncrasy,** idiocrasy; **quality, property, attribute;** savour, flavour, taste, gust, aroma, odour, smack, tang, taint

5 **self, ego;** oneself, **I,** myself, me, myself, my humble self, number one (*informal*), yours truly (*informal*), muggins (*informal*); yourself, himself, herself, itself; ourselves, yourselves; themselves; you, thou; he, she; him, her; they, them; it; inner self, inner man; subliminal *or* subconscious self; superego, better self, ethical self; other self, alter ego, alter, *alterum* (*Latin*)

6 **specification, designation, stipulation,** specifying, designating, stipulating, singling-out, featuring, highlighting, focusing on, denomination; **allocation,** attribution, fixing, selection, assignment, pinning down

7 **particularization, specialization;** individualization, peculiarization, personalization; localization; itemization *see* 765.5

8 **characterization,** distinction, **differentiation;** definition, description

verbs

9 **to particularize, specialize; individualize,** peculiarize, personalize; **descend to particulars,** get precise, get down to brass tacks *or* to cases (*informal*), get down to the nitty-gritty (*informal*), come to the point, cut to the chase (*US & Canadian informal*), lay it on the line (*informal*); **itemize** *see* 765.6, detail, spell out

10 **to characterize, distinguish, differentiate, define, describe; mark, earmark,** mark off, mark out, demarcate, **set apart,** make special *or* unique; keynote (*informal*), sound the keynote, set the tone *or* mood, set the pace; be characteristic, **be a feature** *or* **trait of**

11 **to specify,** specialize, **designate, stipulate,** determine, single out, feature, highlight, focus on, mention, select, pick out, fix, set, assign, pin down; **name,** denominate, state, mark, check, check off, **indicate, signify,** point out, put *or* lay one's finger on

adjectives

12 **particular, special,** especial, **specific,** express, precise, **concrete; singular, individual,** individualist *or* individualistic; **personal,** private, intimate, inner, solipsistic, esoteric; respective, several; **fixed, definite, defined,** distinct, different, different as night and day, determinate, certain, absolute; **distinguished,** noteworthy, **exceptional, extraordinary;** minute, detailed

13 **characteristic, peculiar, singular,** single, quintessential, intrinsic, unique, qualitative, **distinctive,** marked, distinguished, notable, nameable; appropriate, proper; idiosyncratic, idiocratic, **in character, true to form**

14 **this,** this and no other, this one, this single; **these; that,** that one; those

adverbs

15 **particularly, specially, especially, specifically,** expressly, concretely, exactly, precisely, **in particular,** to be specific; **definitely, distinctly;** minutely, in detail, item by item, singly, separately

16 **personally,** privately, idiosyncratically, **individually; in person,** in the flesh, *in propria persona* (*Latin*); as for me, for all of me, **for my part,** as far as I am concerned

17 **characteristically, peculiarly, singularly,** intrinsically, **uniquely,** markedly, **distinctively,** in its own way, like no other

18 **namely,** nominally, **that is to say,** *videlicet* (*Latin*), viz, *scilicet* (*Latin*), scil, sc, **to wit**

19 **each,** apiece; severally, respectively, one by one, each to each; *per annum, per diem, per capita* (all *Latin*)

prepositions

20 **per,** for each

word elements

21 –ness, –hood, –dom; aut–, auto–, idio–, self–;
–acean, –aceous, –ey, –y, –ious, –ous, –ish, –ist,
–istic, –istical, –itious, –itic, –ose, –some

865 SPECIALITY

object of special attention or preference

nouns

1 **speciality, specialty** (*US & Canadian*), **line,
pursuit, pet subject, business, line of business,
line of country, field,** area, main interest, territory;
vocation *see* 724.6; **forte, métier, strong point,**
long suit; **specialism, specialization; technicality; way,**
manner, **style,** type; **lifestyle,** way of life,
preferences; cup of tea *and* bag *and* thing *and*
weakness (*all informal*), thang (*US informal*)

2 **special, feature,** main feature; **leader,** lead item,
leading card

3 **specialist,** specializer, **expert, authority,** savant,
scholar, connoisseur, maven (*informal*); technical
expert, technician, techie (*informal*), nerd (*informal*);
pundit, critic; amateur, dilettante; **fan, buff, freak**
and nut (*both informal*), aficionado

verbs

4 **to specialize, feature; narrow, restrict,** limit,
confine; **specialize in, go in for,** be into (*informal*),
have a weakness *or* taste for, be strong in, follow,
pursue, **make one's business;** major in, minor in;
do one's thing (*informal*)

adjectives

5 **specialized,** specialist, specialistic; up one's street
(*informal*), made for one, fits one like a glove;
technical; **restricted, limited,** confined; **featured,**
feature; **expert, authoritative,** knowledgeable

866 CONFORMITY

nouns

1 **conformity; conformance,** conformation, other-
directedness; **compliance,** acquiescence, goose step,
lockstep, obedience, observance, traditionalism,
orthodoxy; strictness; **accordance, accord,
correspondence,** harmony, agreement, **uniformity**
see 780; **consistency,** congruity; **accommodation,**
adaptation, adaption, pliancy, malleability, flexibility,
adjustment; reconciliation, reconcilement;
conventionality *see* 579.1

2 **conformist,** conformer, sheep, trimmer, parrot,
yes-man, organization man, company man;
conventionalist, Mrs Grundy, Babbitt, Philistine,
middle-class type, **bourgeois,** burgher, Middle
American, plastic person *and* clone *and* square (*all
informal*), three-piecer *and* yuppie (*both informal*), suit
(*informal*), Barbie Doll (*trademark, informal*); model
child; teenybopper (*informal*); **formalist,**
methodologist, perfectionist, precisianist *or* precisian;
anal character, compulsive character; pedant

verbs

3 **to conform, comply, correspond,** accord,
harmonize; **adapt, adjust, accommodate,** bend,
meet, suit, fit, shape; **comply with,** agree with, tally
with, chime *or* fall in with, go by, be guided *or*
regulated by, observe, follow, bend, yield, take the
shape of; **adapt to,** adjust to, gear to, assimilate to,
accommodate to *or* **with; reconcile,** settle,
compose; rub off corners; **make conform,** shape,
lick into shape, mould, force into a mould;
straighten, rectify, correct, **discipline**

4 **to follow the rule, toe the mark** *or* **line,** do it
according to Hoyle *or* by the book (*informal*), play
the game (*informal*); go through channels; **fit in,
follow the crowd,** follow the fashion, swim *or* go
with the stream *or* tide *or* current, get on the
bandwagon, trim one's sails to the breeze, follow the
beaten path, **do as others do, get** *or* **stay in line,**
fall in *or* into line, fall in with; **keep in step,**
goose-step, walk in lockstep; keep up to standard,
pass muster, come up to scratch (*informal*)

adjectives

5 **conformable, adaptable,** adaptive, adjustable;
compliant, pliant, complaisant, malleable, flexible,
plastic, acquiescent, unmurmuring, other-directed,
submissive, tractable, obedient

6 **conformist, conventional** *see* 579.5, bourgeois,
plastic *and* square *and* straight (*all informal*), cloned
and clonish (*both informal*), cookie-cutter (*US
informal*); **orthodox,** traditionalist *or* traditionalistic;
kosher, pukka; **formalistic,** legalistic, precisianistic,
anal, compulsive; pedantic, stuffy *and* hidebound
(*both informal*), uptight (*informal*); in accord, in
keeping, in line, in step, in lockstep; **corresponding,**
accordant, concordant, harmonious

adverbs

7 conformably, conformingly, in conformity,
obediently, pliantly, flexibly, malleably,
complaisantly, yieldingly, **compliantly,** submissively;
conventionally, traditionally; anally, **compulsively;**
pedantically

8 **according to rule,** *en règle* (*French*), according to
regulations; **according to Hoyle** *and* **by the book**
and by the numbers (*all informal*)

prepositions

9 **conformable to, in conformity with, in
compliance with; according to, in accordance
with, consistent with, in harmony with,** in
agreement with, in correspondence to; adapted to,
adjusted to, accommodated to; proper to, suitable
for, agreeable to, agreeably to; answerable to, in
obedience to; congruent with, uniform with, in
uniformity with; **in line with,** in step with, in
lock-step with, **in keeping with; after, by, per, as
per**

phrases

10 **don't rock the boat, don't make waves, get in
line, shape up, shape up** *or* **ship out** (*all informal*);
when in Rome do as the Romans do

867 NONCONFORMITY

nouns

1 **nonconformity**, unconformity, nonconformism, **inconsistency**, incongruity; **inaccordance**, disaccord, disaccordance; originality *see* 337.1; **nonconformance**, disconformity; **nonobservance**, **noncompliance**, nonconcurrence, **dissent** *see* 333, **protest** *see* 333.2, disagreement, contrariety, recalcitrance, refractoriness, recusance *or* recusancy; **deviation** *see* 869.1, deviationism

2 **unconventionality**, **unorthodoxy** *see* 688, revisionism, heterodoxy, heresy, originality, Bohemianism, beatnikism, hippiedom, counterculture; alternative lifestyle *or* society

3 **nonconformist**, unconformist, **original**, eccentric, gonzo (*informal*), deviant, deviationist, maverick (*informal*), dropout, Bohemian, beatnik, hippie, hipster, freak (*informal*), fruitcake (*informal*), fruit (*informal*), flower child, alt (*Australian informal*), street people, yippie; **misfit**, square peg in a round hole, ugly duckling, fish out of water; **dissenter** *see* 333.3; **heretic** *see* 688.5; sectary, sectarian; nonjuror

verbs

4 **to not conform**, nonconform, not comply; **get out of line** *and* **rock the boat** *and* **make waves** (*all informal*), **leave the beaten path**, **go out of bounds**, upset the apple cart, break step, break bounds; drop out, opt out; **dissent** *see* 333.4, swim against the current *or* against the tide *or* upstream, **protest** *see* 333.5;
"*épater le bourgeois*" —Baudelaire, "hear a different drummer" —Thoreau

adjectives

5 **nonconforming**, unconforming, nonconformable, unadaptable, unadjustable; **uncompliant**, unsubmissive; **nonobservant**; contrary, recalcitrant, refractory, recusant; **deviant**, deviationist, atypic *or* atypical, unusual; **dissenting** *see* 333.6, **dissident**

6 **unconventional**, **unorthodox**, **eccentric**, gonzo (*informal*), heterodox, heretical, outré; unfashionable, not done, not kosher, not cricket (*informal*); offbeat (*informal*), way out *and* far out *and* kinky *and* out in left field *and* off-the-wall (*all informal*), fringy, breakaway, **out-of-the-way**; original, maverick, Bohemian, beat, hippie, counterculture; **nonformal**, free and easy (*informal*),
"at ease and lighthearted" —Whitman

7 **out of line**, **out of keeping**, out of order *or* place, misplaced, **out of step**, out of turn (*informal*), out of tune

868 NORMALITY

nouns

1 **normality**, normalness, typicality, normalcy (*US & Canadian*), **naturalness**; health, wholesomeness, propriety, **regularity**; naturalism, naturism, realism; **order** *see* 806

2 **usualness**, **ordinariness**, **commonness**, commonplaceness, averageness, mediocrity; **generality** *see* 863, **prevalence**, currency

3 **the normal**, **the usual**, **the ordinary**, **the common**, the commonplace, the day-to-day, the way things are, the normal order of things; common or garden variety, the run of the mill

4 **rule**, **law**, **principle**, **standard**, criterion, canon, code, code of practice, maxim, prescription, guideline, rulebook, the book (*informal*), regulation, reg *or* regs (*informal*); **norm**, **model**, rule of behaviour, ideal, ideal type, specimen type, exemplar; **rule** *or* **law** *or* **order of nature**, natural *or* universal law; **form**, **formula**, formulary, formality, prescribed *or* set form; standing order, standard operating procedure; **hard-and-fast rule**, Procrustean law

5 **normalization**, **standardization**, **regularization**; **codification**, formalization

verbs

6 **to normalize**, **standardize**, **regularize**; **codify**, formalize

7 **to do the usual thing**, **make a practice of**, carry on, carry on as usual, do business as usual

adjectives

8 **normal**, **natural**; **general** *see* 863.11; typical, unexceptional; **normative**, prescribed, model, ideal, desired; naturalistic, naturistic, realistic; **orderly** *see* 806.6

9 **usual**, **regular**; **customary**, habitual, accustomed, wonted, **normative**, prescriptive, standard, regulation, conventional; **common**, **commonplace**, **ordinary**, **average**, **everyday**, mediocre, familiar, household, vernacular, stock; **prevailing**, **predominating**, current, popular; **universal** *see* 863.14

adverbs

10 **normally**, **naturally**; **normatively**, prescriptively, **regularly**; **typically**, usually, commonly, ordinarily, customarily, habitually, generally; mostly, chiefly, mainly, for the most part, most often *or* frequently; **as a rule**, as a matter of course; **as usual**, as per usual (*informal*); **as may be expected**, to be expected, as things go

word elements

11 norm–, normo–

869 ABNORMALITY

nouns

1 **abnormality**, abnormity; **unnaturalness**, unnaturalism, strangeness; **anomaly**, anomalousness, anomalism; **aberration**, aberrance *or* aberrancy; **atypicality**, atypicalness; **irregularity**, **deviation**, divergence, **difference** *see* 779; **eccentricity**, erraticism, unpredictability, unpredictableness, randomness; **monstrosity**, teratism (*see list*), amorphism, heteromorphism; **subnormality**; **inferiority** *see* 250; **superiority** *see* 249; **derangement** *see* 810.1

2 **unusualness**, **uncommonness**, unordinariness, unwontedness, exceptionalness, exceptionality, extraordinariness; **rarity**, rareness, **uniqueness**;

prodigiousness, marvellousness, wondrousness, fabulousness, mythicalness, remarkableness, stupendousness; **incredibility** *see* 954.3, increditability, inconceivability, **impossibility** *see* 966

3 **oddity, queerness,** curiousness, quaintness, **peculiarity, absurdity** *see* 966.1, singularity; **strangeness,** outlandishness; bizarreness, *bizarrerie* (*French*); fantasticality, anticness; **freakishness, grotesqueness,** grotesquerie, strangeness, weirdness, gonzo (*informal*), monstrousness, monstrosity, malformation, deformity, teratism

4 (*odd person*) oddity, **character** (*informal*), type, **case** (*informal*), **fruit** (*informal*), fruitcake (*informal*), natural, original, odd fellow, queer specimen; **oddball** *and* **weirdo** (*both informal*), odd *or* queer fish, queer duck, rum one *or* rum customer (*informal*); **rare bird**, *rara avis* (*Latin*); eccentric *see* 926.3; *meshuggenah* (*Yiddish*); **freak** *and* **screwball** *and* **crackpot** *and* **nut** *and* bird *and* gonzo (*all informal*), kook (*US & Canadian informal*); **fanatic, crank,** zealot; **outsider, alien,** foreigner; **alien,** extraterrestrial, Martian, little green man, visitor from another planet; pariah, loner, lone wolf, solitary, hermit; hobo, tramp; maverick; **outcast,** outlaw, scapegoat; **nonconformist** *see* 867.3

5 (*odd thing*) oddity, **curiosity, wonder,** funny *or* peculiar *or* strange thing; **abnormality, anomaly; rarity,** improbability, exception, one in a thousand *or* million; **prodigy,** prodigiosity; curio, conversation piece; museum piece

6 **monstrosity, monster** (*see list*), miscreation, abortion, teratism, abnormal *or* defective birth, abnormal *or* defective fetus; **freak,** freak of nature, *lusus naturae* (*Latin*)

7 **supernaturalism,** supernaturalness, supernaturality, supranaturalism, supernormalness, **preternaturalism,** supersensibleness, superphysicalness, superhumanity; **the paranormal;** numinousness; **unearthliness,** unworldliness, **otherworldliness,** eeriness; transcendentalism; New Age; **the supernatural, the occult,** the supersensible; **paranormality;** supernature, supranature; **mystery,** mysteriousness, miraculousness, strangeness; faerie, witchery, elfdom

8 **miracle, sign, signs and portents, prodigy, wonder,** wonderwork, ferlie (*Scottish*); thaumatology, thaumaturgy; fantasy, enchantment

adjectives

9 **abnormal, unnatural; anomalous,** anomalistic; **irregular,** eccentric, erratic, deviative, divergent, **different** *see* 779.7; **aberrant,** stray, straying, wandering; heteroclite, heteromorphic; formless, shapeless, amorphous; **subnormal**

10 **unusual, unordinary, uncustomary,** unwonted, **uncommon, unfamiliar,** atypic *or* atypical, unheard-of, *recherché* (*French*); **rare, unique,** *sui generis* (*Latin,* of its own kind); **out of the ordinary,** out of this world, out-of-the-way, out of the common, beyond the pale, **off the beaten track,** offbeat, breakaway; unexpected, not to be expected, unthought-of, undreamed-of

11 **odd, queer, peculiar, absurd** *see* 966.7, **singular, curious, oddball** (*informal*), weird *and* kinky *and* freaky *and* freaked-out (*all informal*), kooky (*US & Canadian informal*), quaint, **eccentric,** gonzo (*informal*), funny, rum (*informal*), wacky (*informal*); **strange, outlandish,** off-the-wall (*informal*), surreal, not for real (*informal*), passing strange, "wondrous strange"—SHAKESPEARE; **weird,** unearthly; off, out

12 **fantastic,** fantastical, fanciful, antic, **unbelievable** *see* 954.10, **impossible, incredible,** logic-defying, incomprehensible, unimaginable, unexpected, unaccountable, inconceivable

13 **freakish,** freak *or* freaky (*informal*); **monstrous, deformed,** malformed, misshapen, **misbegotten,** teratogenic, teratoid; **grotesque, bizarre,** baroque, rococo

14 **extraordinary, exceptional, remarkable,** noteworthy, **wonderful, marvellous,** fabulous, mythical, legendary; **stupendous,** stupefying, prodigious, portentous, phenomenal; unprecedented, unexampled, unparalleled, not within the memory of man, not within living memory; indescribable, unspeakable, ineffable

15 **supernatural, supranatural, preternatural; supernormal,** hypernormal, preternormal, **paranormal; superphysical,** hyperphysical; numinous; **supersensible,** supersensual, pretersensual; **superhuman,** preterhuman, unhuman, nonhuman; **supramundane,** extramundane, transmundane, extraterrestrial; **unearthly, unworldly, otherworldly, eerie;** fey; psychical, **spiritual, occult; transcendental; mysterious,** arcane, esoteric

16 **miraculous, wondrous,** wonder-working, thaumaturgic *or* thaumaturgical, necromantic, **prodigious; magical,** enchanted, bewitched

adverbs

17 **unusually, uncommonly, incredibly, unnaturally,** abnormally, unordinarily, **uncustomarily,** unexpectedly; **rarely, seldom,** seldom if ever, once in a thousand years, once in a blue moon, hardly, hardly ever

18 **extraordinarily, exceptionally, remarkably, wonderfully, marvellously,** prodigiously, fabulously, unspeakably, ineffably, phenomenally, stupendously

19 **oddly, queerly, peculiarly, singularly, curiously,** quaintly, **strangely,** outlandishly, **fantastically,** fancifully; **grotesquely, monstrously; eerily, mysteriously,** supernaturally

word elements

20 terat–, terato–; medus–, medusi–, –pagus, anom–, anomo–, anomal–, anomalo–, anomali–, dys–, dis–, mal–, ne–, neo–, par–, para–, poly–, pseud–, pseudo–

21 **mythical and imaginary monsters**

abominable snowman *or* yeti	banshee
	basilisk
afreet *or* afrit	behemoth
androsphinx	Bigfoot *or* Sasquatch
Argus	Briareus

Brocken spectre	manticore
bunyip (Australian)	Medusa
Cacus	mermaid
Caliban	merman
centaur	Midgard serpent
Cerberus	Minotaur
Ceto	nixie
Charybdis	ogre
chimera or chimaera	ogress
cockatrice	opinicus
Cyclops	Orthos or Orthros
dipsas	Pegasus
dragon	Python
drake (old)	roc
Echidna	Sagittary
Fury	salamander
Geryon	satyr
Gigantes	Scylla
Gorgon	sea horse
Grendel	sea serpent
griffin, griffon or gryphon	simurgh
Harpy	siren
hippocampus	Sphinx
hippocentaur	Talos
hippocerf	tokoloshe
hippogriff or hippogryph	troll
hircocervus	Typhoeus
Hydra	Typhon
kelpie	unicorn
Kraken	vampire
kylin	werewolf
Ladon	windigo
lamia	wivern
leviathan	xiphopagus
Loch Ness monster or Nessie	zombie

870 LIST

nouns

1 **list**, **enumeration**, **itemization**, listing, shopping list *and* laundry list *and* want list *and* wish list *and* hit list *and* worry list (*all informal*), shit list *and* drop-dead list (*both US informal*), items, **schedule**, **register**, registry; **inventory**, repertory, tally; **spreadsheet**, electronic spreadsheet; **checklist**; tally sheet; active list, civil list, New Year's Honours List, retired list, sick list; Army List; waiting list; blacklist; short list, leet (*Scottish*)

2 **table**, contents, table of contents

3 **catalogue**; classified catalogue, *catalogue raisonné* (*French*); **card catalogue, bibliography**, finding list, handlist; publisher's catalogue *or* list, back list, front list; **file**, filing system, letter file, pigeonholes, dooket (*Scottish*)

4 **dictionary**, word list, **lexicon, glossary, thesaurus, Roget's, vocabulary**, terminology, nomenclator; promptorium, gradus; **gazetteer**

5 **bill**, statement, account, ledger, books; **bill of fare, menu**, carte; **bill of lading**, manifest, waybill, invoice

6 **roll, roster**, scroll, rota; **roll call**, muster, **census**, head count (*informal*), **poll**, questionnaire, returns,

census report *or* returns; property roll, tax roll, cadaster *or* cadastre; electoral register *or* roll; muster roll; checkroll, checklist; jury list *or* panel; cause list; order paper; **calendar**, docket, **agenda**, order of business; **programme**, dramatis personae, lineup, beadroll (*old*); honour roll, dean's list (*US & Canadian*)

7 **index, listing**, tabulation; **cataloguing, itemization**, filing, card file, card index, Rolodex (*trademark*), Filofax (*trademark*), thumb index, indexing; **registration**, registry, enrolment

verbs

8 **to list, enumerate, itemize, tabulate, catalogue**, tally; **register**, post, enter, **enrol, book**; impanel; **file**, pigeonhole; **index**; inventory; calendar; score, keep score; **schedule**, programme

adjectives

9 **listed, enumerated, entered, itemized, catalogued**, tallied, inventoried; filed, **indexed, tabulated; scheduled**, programmed; put on the agenda; inventorial, cadastral

871 ONENESS
state of being one

nouns

1 **oneness, unity, singleness**, singularity, **individuality**, identity, selfsameness; **particularity** *see* 864; **uniqueness**; intactness, inviolability, purity, simplicity *see* 797, irreducibility, **integrity**, integrality; **unification**, uniting, integration, fusion, combination *see* 804; **solidification**, solidity, solidarity, **indivisibility**, undividedness, **wholeness** *see* 791.5; univocity, organic unity; uniformity *see* 780;
"the sacredness of private integrity"—EMERSON

2 **aloneness**, loneness, **loneliness, lonesomeness**, soleness, singleness; **privacy**, solitariness, **solitude**; separateness, aloofness, detachment, seclusion, sequestration, **withdrawal, alienation**, standing *or* moving *or* keeping apart, **isolation**,
"splendid isolation"—SIR WILLIAM GOSCHEN; celibacy, single blessedness

3 **one**, I, **unit**, ace, atom, Kelly's eye (*bingo*); monad; one and only, none else, no other, nothing else, nought beside

4 **individual**, single, unit, **integer, entity**, singleton, **item**, article, point, module; person, wight (*old*), persona, soul, body, warm body (*informal*); **individuality**, personhood

verbs

5 **to unify**, reduce to unity, unitize, make one; **integrate, unite** *see* 804.3

6 **to stand alone**, stand *or* move *or* keep apart, keep oneself to oneself, withdraw, alienate *or* seclude *or* sequester *or* isolate oneself, feel out of place; individuate, become an individual

adjectives

7 **one, single, singular, individual**, sole, **unique**, a certain, **solitary, lone**; exclusive; **integral**,

indivisible, irreducible, monadic, monistic, unanalysable, noncompound, atomic, unitary, unitive, unary, undivided, solid, whole-cloth, seamless, uniform *see* 780.5, simple *see* 797.6, whole *see* 791.9; an, any, any one, either

8 **alone, solitary,** on one's tod (*informal*), solo, *solus* (*Latin*); **isolated,** insular, apart, separate, separated, alienated, withdrawn, aloof, standoffish, detached, removed, out on a limb; **lone, lonely, lonesome,** lonely-hearts; **private,** reserved, reticent, reclusive, shy, nonpublic, ungregarious; **friendless,** kithless, homeless, rootless, companionless, **unaccompanied,** unescorted, unattended; **unaided,** unassisted, unabetted, unsupported, unseconded; **single-handed,** solo, one-man, one-woman, one-person

9 **sole, unique,** singular, absolute, unrepeated, **alone,** lone, **only,** only-begotten, **one and only,** first and last; odd, unpaired, azygous; celibate

10 **unitary, integrated,** integral, integrant; **unified,** united, rolled into one, composite

11 **unipartite,** unipart, **one-piece;** monadic *or* monadal; **unilateral, one-sided;** unilateralist, uniangulate, unibivalent, unibranchiate, unicameral, unicellular, unicuspid, unidentate, unidigitate; **unidimensional, unidirectional;** uniflorous, unifoliate, unifoliolate, unigenital, uniglobular, unilinear, uniliteral, unilobed, unilobular, unilocular, unimodular, unimolecular, uninuclear, uniocular; unipolar, **univalent, univocal**

12 **unifying, uniting,** unific; **combining,** combinative *see* 804.5, 7, combinatory; connective, connecting, connectional; conjunctive *see* 799.16, conjunctival; coalescing, coalescent

adverbs

13 **singly, individually,** particularly, severally, one by one, one at a time; **singularly,** in the singular; **alone,** by itself, *per se* (*Latin*); **by oneself,** on *or* by one's lonesome (*informal*), on one's own, on one's tod (*informal*), under one's own steam, **single-handedly,** solo, unaided; separately, apart; **once** *see* 847.6

14 **solely, exclusively,** only, merely, **purely,** simply; **entirely,** wholly, totally; **integrally, indivisibly,** irreducibly, unanalysably, undividedly

872 DOUBLENESS

nouns

1 **doubleness, duality,** dualism, duplexity, **twoness;** twofoldness, biformity; polarity; conjugation, pairing, coupling, yoking; **doubling,** duplication *see* 873, twinning, bifurcation; **dichotomy,** bisection *see* 874, halving, splitting down the middle *or* fifty-fifty; **duplicity,** two-facedness, double-think, hypocrisy; **irony,** enantiosis, ambiguity, equivocation, equivocality, **ambivalence;** Janus

2 **two, twain** (*old*), little boy blue (*bingo*); **couple, pair, matching pair, twosome,** item (*informal*), set of two, duo, duet, brace, team, span, yoke, double harness; match, matchup, mates; **couplet,** distich, doublet; duad, dyad; the two, **both**

3 **deuce;** pair, doubleton; craps *and* snake eyes (*both crapshooting*)

4 **twins,** pair of twins (*informal*), identical twins, fraternal twins, exact mates, look-alikes, dead ringers (*informal*); Tweedledum and Tweedledee, Siamese twins; Twin stars, Castor and Pollux, Gemini

verbs

5 **to double,** duplicate, replicate, dualize, twin; **halve,** split down the middle *or* fifty fifty (*informal*), bifurcate, dichotomize, bisect; team, **yoke,** yoke together, span, double-team, double-harness; **mate, match,** couple, conjugate; **pair,** pair off, pair up, couple up, team up, match up, chum up, buddy up (*US & Canadian informal*)

adjectives

6 **two,** twain (*old*); **dual, double,** duplex, doubled, twinned, duplicated, replicated, dualized; **dualistic;** dyadic; duadic; biform; bipartite, bipartisan, bilateral, either-or, two-sided, double-sided; dichotomous; bifurcated, bisected, dichotomized, split down the middle *or* fifty fifty (*informal*); twin, identical, matched, twinned, duplicated; **two-faced,** duplicitous, hypocritical, double-faced, Janus-like

7 **both,** the two, the pair; for two, tête-à-tête, *à deux* (*French*)

8 **coupled, paired,** yoked, yoked together, matched, matched up, mated, paired off, paired up, teamed up, buddied up (*US & Canadian informal*); **bracketed;** conjugate, conjugated; biconjugate, bigeminate; bijugate

phrases

9 it takes two to tango *and* it's not a one-way street (*both informal*)

word elements

10 ambi–, amph–, amphi–, bi–, bin–, bis–, deut–, deuto–, deuter–, deutero–, di–, dis–, didym–, didymo–, duo–, dyo–, gem–, twi–, zyg–, zygo–

873 DUPLICATION

nouns

1 **duplication, reduplication,** replication, conduplication; **reproduction, repro** (*informal*), **doubling;** twinning, gemination, ingemination; **repetition** *see* 848, iteration, reiteration, echoing; **imitation** *see* 336, parroting; **copying** *see* 336.1; duplicate *see* 784.3

2 **repeat,** encore, repeat performance; echo

verbs

3 **to duplicate,** dupe (*informal*), ditto (*informal*); **double,** double up; multiply by two; twin, geminate, ingeminate; **reduplicate, reproduce,** replicate, redouble; **repeat** *see* 848.7; **copy**

adjectives

4 **double, doubled, duplicate,** duplicated, reproduced, replicated, cloned, twinned, geminate, geminated, dualized

adverbs

5 **doubly; twofold,** as much again, twice as much; two-ply; two-piece; twice, two times

6 **secondly,** second, secondarily, **in the second place** *or* instance
7 **again,** another time, **once more,** once again, over again, yet again, *encore, bis (both French);* **anew,** afresh, new, freshly, newly

word elements

8 bi–, bis–, deuter–, deutero–, di–, dis–, diphy–, diphyo–, dipl–, diplo–, diss–, disso–, twi–

874 BISECTION

nouns

1 **bisection,** halving, bipartition, bifidity; **dichotomy, halving, division, in half** *or* **by two,** splitting *or* dividing *or* cutting in two, splitting *or* dividing fifty-fifty *(informal);* subdivision; bifurcation, forking, ramification, branching
2 **half,** moiety; hemisphere, semisphere, semicircle, **fifty percent;** half-and-half *and* fifty-fifty *(both informal)*
3 bisector, diameter, equator, halfway mark, divider, partition *see* 213.5, line of demarcation, boundary *see* 211.3

verbs

4 **to bisect, halve, divide, in half** *or* **by two,** transect, subdivide; cleave, fission, **divide** *or* split *or* cut in two, share and share alike, go halfers *or* go Dutch *(both informal),* **dichotomize;** bifurcate, fork, ramify, branch

adjectives

5 **half,** part, partly, **partial,** halfway
6 **halved, bisected, divided;** dichotomous; bifurcated, forked *or* forking, ramified, branched, branching; riven, **split,** cloven, cleft
7 **bipartite,** bifid, biform, bicuspid, biaxial, bicameral, binocular, binomial, binominal, biped, bipetalous, bipinnate, bisexual, bivalent, unibivalent

adverbs

8 **in half,** in halves, **in two,** in twain, by two, down the middle; half-and-half *and* fifty-fifty *(both informal);* apart, asunder

word elements

9 bi–, demi–, dich–, dicho–, hemi–, semi–, sesqui–

875 THREE

nouns

1 **three, trio, threesome,** trialogue, set of three, tierce *(cards),* leash, troika; **triad,** trilogy, trine, **trinity,** triunity, ternary, ternion; **triplet,** tercet, terzetto; trefoil, shamrock, clover; tripod, trivet; **triangle,** tricorn, trihedron, trident, trisul, triennium, trimester, trinomial, trionym, triphthong, triptych, triplopy, trireme, triseme, triskelion, triumvirate; triple crown, triple threat; trey *and* threespot *(both cards),* deuce-ace *(dice)*
2 **threeness,** triplicity, triality, tripleness; triunity, trinity

adjectives

3 **three, triple,** triplex, trinal, trine, trial; triadic *(al);* triune, three-in-one, *tria juncta in uno (Latin);* triform; **triangular,** deltoid, fan-shaped

word elements

4 tri–, ter–, ternati–

876 TRIPLICATION

nouns

1 **triplication,** triplicity, trebleness, **threefoldness;** triplicate, second carbon

verbs

2 **to triplicate, triple, treble, multiply by three,** threefold; cube

adjectives

3 **triple,** triplicate, **treble, threefold,** triplex, trinal, trine, tern, ternary, ternal, ternate; three-ply; three-piece; trilogic *or* trilocial
4 **third,** tertiary

adverbs

5 **triply, trebly,** trinely; **threefold; thrice,** three times, again and yet again
6 **thirdly,** in the third place

word elements

7 cub–, cubo–, cubi–; ter–; tert–, trit–, trito–

877 TRISECTION

nouns

1 **trisection,** tripartition, trichotomy
2 **third,** tierce, third part, one-third; *tertium quid (Latin, a third something)*

verbs

3 **to trisect, divide in thirds** *or* **three,** third, trichotomize; trifurcate

adjectives

4 **tripartite,** trisected, triparted, **three-parted,** trichotomous; three-sided, trihedral, trilateral; **three-dimensional;** three-forked, three-pronged, trifurcate; trident, tridental, tridentate, trifid; tricuspid; three-footed, tripodic, tripedal; trifoliate, trifloral, triflorate, triflorous, tripetalous, triadelphous, triarch; trimerous, 3-merous; three-cornered, tricornered, tricorn; trigonal, trigonoid; triquetrous, triquetral; trigrammatic, triliteral; **triangular,** triangulate, deltoid

878 FOUR

nouns

1 **four,** tetrad, quatern, quaternion, quaternary, quaternity, **quartet, quadruplet, foursome;** quadrennium; tetralogy; tetrapody; tetraphony, four-part diaphony; quadrille, square dance; quatrefoil *or* quadrifoil, four-leaf clover; tetragram, tetragrammaton; quadrangle, quad *(informal),* rectangle; tetrahedron; tetragon, square; biquadrate; quadrinomial; quadrature, squaring; quadrilateral

2 **fourness**, quaternity, quadruplicity

verbs

3 to **square**, **quadrate**, form *or* make four; form fours *or* squares; **cube**, **dice**

adjectives

4 **four**; foursquare; quaternary, quartile, quartic, quadric, quadratic; tetrad, tetradic; quadrinomial, biquadratic; tetractinal, four-rayed, **quadruped**, four-legged; quadrivalent, tetravalent; quadrilateral *see* 278.9

word elements

5 quadr–, quadri–, quadru–, tetr–, tetra–, tessar–, tessara–, tri–, trip–, tripl–, triplo–, tris–

879 QUADRUPLICATION

nouns

1 **quadruplication**, quadruplicature

verbs

2 to **quadruple**, **quadruplicate**, fourfold, form *or* make four, multiply by four; biquadrate, quadruplex

adjectives

3 **quadruplicate**, **quadruple**, quadraple, **quadruplex**, **fourfold**, four-ply, four-part, tetraploid, quadrigeminal, biquadratic

word elements

4 quadr–, quadri–, quadru–, quater–, tetr–, tetra–, tetrakis–

880 QUADRISECTION

nouns

1 **quadrisection**, quadripartition, **quartering**
2 **fourth**, one-fourth, **quarter**, one-quarter, fourth part, twenty-five percent, twenty-five cents, two bits (*old or informal*); quartern; quart; farthing; quarto *or* 4to *or* 4°

verbs

3 to **divide by four** *or* **into four**; **quadrisect**, **quarter**

adjectives

4 **quadrisected**, **quartered**, quarter-cut; quadripartite, quadrifid, quadriform; quadrifoliate, quadrigeminal, quadripinnate, quadriplanar, quadriserial, quadrivial, quadrifurcate, quadrumanal *or* quadrumanous
5 **fourth**, **quarter**

adverbs

6 **fourthly**, in the fourth place; quarterly, by quarters

881 FIVE AND OVER

nouns

1 **five**, V, cinque (*cards and dice*); **quintet**, **fivesome**, quintuplets, quin, quint (*US & Canadian*), cinquain, quincunx, pentad; **five pounds**, fiver (*informal*), fin

and finniff *and* five bucks (*all US & Canadian informal*); pentagon, pentahedron, pentagram; pentapody, pentameter, pentastich; pentarchy; Pentateuch; pentachord; pentathlon; five-pointed star, pentacle, pentalpha, mullet (*heraldry*)

2 **six**, **half a dozen**, **sextet**, sestet, sextuplets, hexad; hexagon, hexahedron, hexagram, six-pointed star, estoile (*heraldry*), Jewish star, star of David, *Magen David* (*Hebrew*); hexameter, hexapody, hexastich; hexapod; hexarchy; Hexateuch; hexastyle; hexachord

3 **seven**, heptad; septet, heptad; heptagon, heptahedron; heptameter, heptastich; septemvir, heptarchy; Septuagint, Heptateuch; heptachord; **week**

4 **eight**, ogdoad, eightsome; octad, octonary; octagon, octahedron; octastylos *or* oktostylos; octave, octavo *or* 8vo; octachord; octet *or* octal, octameter; Octateuch

5 **nine**, niner (*radio communication*); ennead; nonagon *or* enneagon, enneahedron; novena; enneastylos

6 **ten**, X, cocklehen (*informal*), Downing Street (*bingo*); **decade**; decagon, decahedron; decagram, decigram, decalitre, decilitre, decare, decametre, decimetre, decastere; decapod; decastylos; decasyllable; decemvir, decemvirate, decurion; decennium, decennary; Ten Commandments *or* Decalogue

7 (*eleven to ninety*) **eleven**, legs eleven (*bingo*); **twelve**, **dozen**, one doz (*bingo*), duodecimo *or* twelvemo *or* 12mo; **teens**; **thirteen**, long dozen, baker's dozen, unlucky for some (*bingo*); **fourteen**, two weeks, fortnight; **fifteen**, quindecima, quindene, quindecim, quindecennial; **sixteen**, sixteenmo *or* 16mo; **twenty**, **score**, applecore (*informal*), blind twenty (*bingo*); **twenty-one**, key of the door (*bingo*), **twenty-two**, all the twos *and* two little ducks (*bingo*), **twenty-four**, four and twenty, two dozen, twenty-fourmo *or* 24mo; **twenty-five**, five and twenty, quarter of a hundred *or* century, pony (*informal*); **thirty**, blind thirty (*bingo*), **thirty-two**, thirty-twomo *or* 32mo; **thirty-three**, all the threes (*bingo*), **forty**, twoscore, blind forty (*bingo*); **forty-four**, all the fours (*bingo*), **fifty**, L, half a hundred, McGarrett (*informal*), nifty (*informal*), blind fifty (*bingo*); **fifty-five**, all the fives (*bingo*), **sixty**, sexagenary, blind sixty (*bingo*); Sexagesima; sexagenarian, threescore; **sixty-four**, sixty-fourmo *or* 64mo *or* sexagesimo–quarto; **sixty-six**, all the sixes *and* clickety-click (*both bingo*), **seventy**, septuagenarian, threescore and ten, blind seventy (*bingo*); **seventy-seven**, all the sevens (*bingo*), **eighty**, octogenarian, fourscore, blind eighty (*bingo*); **eighty-eight**, all the eights *and* two fat ladies (*bingo*), **ninety**, nonagenarian, four-score and ten, top of the house *and* blind ninety (*bingo*)

8 **hundred**, **century**, ton (*informal*), C, one C (*informal*); centennium, centennial, centenary; centenarian; cental, centigram, centilitre, centimetre, centare, centistere; hundredweight *or* cwt; hecatomb; centipede; centumvir, centumvirate, centurion; (*120*) great *or* long hundred; (*144*) gross; (*150*) sesquicentennial, sesquicentenary; (*200*) bicentenary, bicentennial (*US*); (*300*) tercentenary, tercentennial (*US*), etc

9 **two hundred**, bottle (*informal*); **three hundred**, carpet (*informal*); **four hundred**, rofe (*informal*); **five**

hundred, D, five centuries, five C's (*informal*), monkey (*informal*)

10 thousand, M, chiliad; **millennium; G** *and* grand *and* K *and* thou *and* yard (*all informal*); chiliagon, chiliahedron *or* chiliaëdron; chiliarchia *or* chiliarch; millipede; milligram, millilitre, millimetre, kilogram *or* kilo, kiloliter, kilometre; kilocycle, kilohertz; **ten thousand,** myriad; **one hundred thousand,** lakh (*India*)

11 million; ten million, crore (*India*)

12 billion, thousand million, gillion, milliard

13 trillion, quadrillion, quintillion, sextillion, septillion, octillion, nonillion, decillion, undecillion, duodecillion, tredecillion, quattuordecillion, quindecillion, sexdecillion, septendecillion, octodecillion, novemdecillion, vigintillion; googol, googolplex; zillion *and* jillion *and* squillion (*all informal*)

14 (*division into five or more parts*) quinquesection, quinquepartition, sextipartition, etc; decimation, decimalization; fifth, sixth, etc; **tenth, tithe,** decima

verbs

15 (*divide by five, etc*) to quinquesect; decimalize

16 (*multiply by five, etc*) to fivefold, sixfold, etc; quintuple, quintuplicate; sextuple, sextuplicate; centuple, centuplicate

adjectives

17 **fifth,** quinary; **fivefold, quintuple,** quintuplicate; quinquennial; quinquepartite, pentadic, quinquefid; quincuncial, pentastyle; pentad, pentavalent, quinquevalent

18 **sixth,** senary; **sixfold, sextuple;** sexpartite, hexadic, sextipartite, hexapartite; hexagonal, hexahedral, hexangular; hexad, hexavalent; sextuplex, hexastyle; sexennial

19 **seventh,** septimal; **sevenfold, septuple,** septenary; septempartite, heptadic, septemfid; heptagonal, heptahedral, heptangular; heptamerous

20 **eighth,** octonary; **eightfold, octuple,** eightsome; octadic; octal, octofid, octaploid; octagonal, octahedral, octan, octangular; octosyllabic; octastyle

21 **ninth,** novenary, nonary; **ninefold, nonuple,** enneadic; enneahedral, enneastyle

22 **tenth,** denary, **decimal,** tithe; **tenfold, decuple;** decagonal, decahedral; decasyllabic

23 **eleventh,** undecennial, undecennary

24 **twelfth,** duodenary, duodenal; duodecimal

25 **thirteenth,** fourteenth, etc; eleventeenth, umpteenth (*informal*); in one's teens

26 **twentieth,** vicenary, vicennial, vigesimal, vicesimal

27 **sixtieth,** sexagesimal, sexagenary

28 **seventieth,** septuagesimal, septuagenary

29 **hundredth,** centesimal, **centennial,** centenary, centurial; **hundredfold, centuple,** centuplicate; secular; centigrado

30 **thousandth,** millenary, **millennial; thousandfold**

31 **millionth;** billionth, quadrillionth, quintillionth, etc

word elements

32 pent–, penta–, pen–, quinqu–, quinque–, quintquinti–; hex–, hexa–, sex–, sexi–, sexti–; hept–, hepta–, sept–, septi–; oct–, octa–, octo–; non–nona–,

ennea–; deca–, deka–, deci–; undec–, hendec–, hendeca–; dodec–, dodeca–; icos–, icosa–, icosi–, eicos–, eicosa–, cent–, centi–; hect–, hecto–, hecato–, hecaton–; kilo–, milli–; meg–, mega–, micro–; giga–, nano–; pico–

882 PLURALITY
more than one

nouns

1 **plurality,** pluralness; a greater number, a certain number; **several,** some, a few *see* 884.2, more; plural number, the plural; compositeness, nonsingleness, nonuniqueness; **pluralism** *see* 781.1, variety; numerousness *see* 883

2 **majority,** plurality, more than half, the greater number, the greatest number, **most,** preponderance *or* preponderancy, **bulk, mass;** lion's share

3 pluralization, plurification (*old*)

4 **multiplication,** multiplying, proliferation, **increase** *see* 251; duplication *see* 873; multiple, multiplier, multiplicand; multiplication table

verbs

5 **to pluralize,** plurify (*old*); raise to *or* make more than one

6 **to multiply,** proliferate, **increase** *see* 251.4, 6, duplicate *see* 873.3

adjectives

7 **plural,** pluralized, more than one, more, several, severalfold; **some,** certain; not singular, composite, nonsingle, nonunique; plurative (*logic*); **pluralistic** *see* 781.3, various; many, beaucoup (*informal*), numerous *see* 883.6

8 **multiple,** multiplied, multifold, **manifold** *see* 883.6; **increased** *see* 251.7; multinomial, polynomial (*both mathematics*)

9 **majority, most,** the greatest number

adverbs

10 **in the majority;** and others, et al, et cetera *see* 253.14; plurally

word elements

11 multi–; –fold

883 NUMEROUSNESS

nouns

1 **numerousness, multiplicity, manyness,** manifoldness, multifoldness, multitudinousness, multifariousness, teemingness, swarmingness, rifeness, profuseness, profusion; **plenty, abundance** *see* 990.2; **countlessness,** innumerability, infinitude

2 (*indefinite number*) **a number,** a certain number, one or two, two or three, **a few, several,** parcel, passel (*US informal*); eleventeen *and* umpteen (*both informal*)

3 (*large number*) **multitude, throng** *see* 769.4; a many, numbers, quantities, lots *see* 247.4, flocks, **scores;** an abundance of, all kinds *or* sorts of, no end of, quite a few, tidy sum; muchness, any, number of, **large amount; host, army,** more than one can shake a stick at, fistful (*informal*), slew *and* shitload *and* shithouse full (*all US & Canadian informal*), legion, rout, ruck, mob, jam, clutter; **swarm, flock** *see* 769.5, flight, cloud, hail, bevy, covey, shoal, hive, nest, pack, litter, bunch *see* 769.7; a world of, a mass of, worlds of, masses of

4 (*immense number*) **a myriad**, a thousand, a **thousand and one**, a lakh (*India*), a crore (*India*), a million, a billion, a quadrillion, a nonillion, etc *see* 881.13; a zillion *or* jillion *or* squillion (*all informal*); googol, googolplex

verbs

5 **to teem with**, overflow with, **abound with**, burst with, bristle with, pullulate with, **swarm with**, throng with, creep with, **crawl with, be alive with**, have coming out of one's ears (*informal*); clutter, crowd, jam, pack, overwhelm, overflow; multiply *see* 882.6; outnumber

adjectives

6 **numerous, many, manifold**, not a few, no few; **very many**, full many, **ever so many**, considerable *and* quite some (*both informal*); **multitudinous**, multitudinal, multifarious, multifold, multiple, **myriad**, thousand, million, billion; zillion *and* jillion *and* squillion (*all informal*); heaped-up; numerous as the stars, numerous as the sands, numerous as the hairs on the head,
"numerous as glittering gems of morning dew"— Edward Young

7 **several**, divers, **sundry**, various; fivish, sixish, etc; some five or six, etc; upwards of

8 **abundant**, copious, ample, plenteous, **plentiful** *see* 990.7, thick on the ground

9 **teeming, swarming, crowding**, thronging, overflowing, overcrowded, overwhelming, bursting, **crawling, alive with**, lousy with (*informal*), populous, prolific, proliferating, crowded, packed, hoatching (*Scottish*), jammed, bumper-to-bumper (*informal*), jam-packed, like sardines in a tin (*informal*), thronged, studded, bristling, rife, lavish, prodigal, superabundant, **profuse**, in profusion, thick, **thick with**, thick-coming, thick as hail *or* flies;
"thick as autumnal leaves that strow the brooks in Vallombrose"—Milton

10 **innumerable, numberless**, unnumbered, **countless**, uncounted, uncountable, unreckonable, untold, incalculable, immeasurable, unmeasured, measureless, inexhaustible, endless, infinite, without end *or* limit, more than one can tell, more than you can shake a stick at (*informal*), no end of *or* to; countless as the stars *or* sands; **astronomical**, galactic; millionfold, trillionfold, etc

11 **and many more**, *cum multis aliis* (*Latin*), and what not, and heaven knows what

adverbs

12 **numerously**, multitudinously, **profusely**, swarmingly, teemingly, thickly, copiously, **abundantly, prodigally; innumerably**, countlessly, infinitely, incalculably, inexhaustibly, immeasurably;

in throngs, in crowds, in swarms, in heaps, *acervatim* (*Latin*); **no end** (*informal*)

word elements

13 multi–, myri–, myrio–, pluri–, poly–

884 FEWNESS

nouns

1 **fewness**, infrequency, **sparsity**, sparseness, **scarcity, paucity, scantiness, meagreness**, miserliness, niggardliness, tightness, thinness, stringency, restrictedness; stinginess (*informal*), scrimpiness *and* skimpiness (*both informal*); **rarity**, exiguity; smallness *see* 258.1

2 **a few**, too few, mere *or* piddling *or* piddly few, only a few, **small number**, limited *or* piddling *or* piddly number, not enough to count *or* matter, not enough to shake a stick at, **handful, scattering**, corporal's guard, sprinkling, trickle

3 **minority**, least; the minority, the few; minority group;
"we happy few"—Shakespeare

adjectives

4 **few, not many**; hardly *or* scarcely any, precious little *or* few, of small number, to be counted on one's fingers

5 **sparse**, scant, **scanty**, exiguous, **infrequent**, scarce, scarce as hen's teeth (*informal*), poor, piddling, piddly, thin, slim, **meagre**; miserly, niggardly, cheeseparing, tight; stingy (*informal*), scrimpy *and* skimpy (*both informal*), skimping *and* scrimping (*both informal*); **scattered**, sprinkled, spotty, **few and far between; rare**, seldom met with, seldom seen, not thick on the ground, thin on the ground

6 **fewer, less**, smaller, not so much *or* many

7 **minority**, least

adverbs

8 **sparsely**, *sparsim* (*Latin*), **scantily, meagrely**, exiguously, piddlingly; stingily *and* scrimpily *and* skimpily (*all informal*), thinly; **scarcely**, rarely, infrequently; **scatteringly**, scatterdly, spottily, patchily, in dribs and drabs *and* in bits and pieces (*both informal*), **here and there**, in places, in spots

885 CAUSE

nouns

1 **cause, occasion**, antecedents, **grounds**, ground, background, stimulus, base, **basis**, element, principle, factor; **determinant**, determinative; causation, causality, cause and effect; etiology

2 **reason**, reason why, rationale, reason for *or* behind, underlying reason, rational ground, **explanation, the why**, the wherefore, the whatfor *or* whyfor (*informal*), **the why and wherefore**, the idea (*informal*), the big idea (*informal*); stated cause, pretext, pretence, excuse

3 **immediate cause**, proximate cause, trigger, spark; **domino effect**, causal sequence, chain *or* nexus of cause and effect, ripple effect, slippery slope, contagion effect, knock-on *or* knock-on effect;

transient cause, occasional cause; formal cause; efficient cause; ultimate cause, immanent cause, remote cause, causing cause, *causa causans* (*Latin*), first cause; **final cause**, *causa finalis* (*Latin*), end, end in view, teleology; provocation, **last straw**, straw that broke the camel's back, match in the powder barrel; butterfly effect *or* strange attraction *or* sensitive dependence on initial conditions

4 **author**, agent, **originator**, generator, begetter, engenderer, producer, maker, beginner, **creator**, mover; **parent, mother, father**, sire; **prime mover**, *primum mobile* (*Latin*); causer, effector; inspirer, instigator, catalyst

5 **source, origin**, genesis, original, origination, **derivation, rise, beginning**, conception, inception, commencement, **head**; provenance, provenience (*US*), background; **root**, radix, radical, taproot, grass roots; stem, stock

6 **fountainhead**, headwater, headstream, riverhead, springhead, headspring, **mainspring**, wellspring, wellhead, well, **spring, fountain**, fount, font, *fons et origo* (*Latin*); mine, quarry

7 **vital force** *or* **principle**, *élan vital* (*French*), reproductive urge, a gleam in one's father's eye (*informal*); **egg**, ovum *see* 305.12, **germ**, germen (*old*), spermatozoon *see* 305.11, nucleus *see* 305.7, **seed**; embryo *see* 305.14; bud *see* 310.21; loins; **womb**, matrix, uterus

8 **birthplace, breeding place**, breeding ground, birthsite, rookery, hatchery; **hotbed**, forcing bed; hothouse; incubator, brooder; **nest**, nidus; **cradle**, nursery

9 (*a principle or movement*) **cause, principle**, interest, issue, burning issue, commitment, faith, great cause, lifework; reason for being, *raison d'être* (*French*); **movement**, mass movement, activity; **drive, campaign, crusade**; zeal, passion, fanaticism

verbs

10 **to cause**, be the cause of, lie at the root of; **bring about, bring to pass**, effectuate, **effect**, bring to effect, realize; **impact**, impact on, influence; **occasion, make, create, engender**, generate, **produce**, breed, work, do; **originate**, give origin to, give occasion to, **give rise to**, spark, spark off, set off, trigger, trigger off; **give birth to, beget**, bear, bring forth, labour *or* travail and bring forth, author, **father**, sire, sow the seeds of; gestate, **conceive**, have the idea, have a bright idea (*informal*); set up, set afloat, **set on foot**; found, establish, inaugurate, institute

11 **to induce**, lead, procure, get, obtain, contrive, **effect**, bring, **bring on**, draw on, **call forth, elicit, evoke, provoke**, inspire, influence, instigate, egg on, **motivate**; draw down, open the door to; suborn; superinduce

12 **to determine**, decide, turn the scale, have the last word; **necessitate**, entail, require; contribute to, lead to, conduce to; **advance, forward**, influence, subserve; **spin off**, hive off

adjectives

13 **causal**, causative; chicken-and-egg (*informal*); occasional; originative, institutive, constitutive; **at the**

bottom of, behind the scenes; **formative**, determinative, effectual, decisive, pivotal; etiological

14 **original, primary**, primal, primitive, pristine, primo (*informal*), primeval, aboriginal, **elementary**, elemental, **basic**, basal, **rudimentary**, crucial, central, radical, **fundamental**; embryonic, in embryo, *in ovo* (*Latin*), germinal, seminal, pregnant; **generative**, genetic, protogenic

word elements

15 uter–, utero–, metr–, metro–, –metrium, venter; etio–, aetio–, prot–, proto–; –facient, –factive, –fic, –ic, –ical, –etic

886 EFFECT

nouns

1 **effect, result**, resultant, **consequence**, consequent, sequent, sequence, sequel, sequela, sequelae; event, eventuality, eventuation, **upshot, outcome**, logical outcome, possible outcome, scenario; **outgrowth**, spin-off, offshoot, offspring, issue, aftermath, legacy; **product** *see* 892, precipitate, distillate *or* distillation, **fruit**, first fruits, crop, harvest; development, corollary; derivative, derivation, by-product

2 **impact**, force, **repercussion**, reaction; backwash, backlash, reflex, recoil, response; mark, print, imprint, impress, impression

3 **aftereffect, aftermath**, aftergrowth, aftercrop, **afterclap**, aftershock, afterimage, afterglow, aftertaste; wake, trail, track; fallout; domino effect

verbs

4 **to result**, ensue, issue, follow, attend, accompany; **turn out, come out**, fall out, redound, **work out**, pan out (*informal*), fare; have a happy result, turn out well, come up roses (*informal*); turn out to be, prove, prove to be; **become of**, come of, come about; **develop**, unfold; **eventuate**, terminate, end; **end up**, land up, come out, wind up

5 **to result from**, be the effect of, be due to, originate in *or* from, **come from**, come out of, grow from, **grow out of**, follow from *or* on, proceed from, descend from, emerge from, issue from, ensue from, emanate from, flow from, **derive from**, accrue from, rise *or* arise from, take its rise from, **spring from**, stem from, sprout from, bud from, germinate from; **spin off**; **depend on**, hinge *or* pivot *or* turn on, hang on, be contingent on

adjectives

6 **resultant, resulting, following, ensuing; consequent**, consequential, following, sequent, sequential, sequacious; necessitated, entailed, required; **final**; derivative, derivational

adverbs

7 **consequently, as a result**, as a consequence, in consequence, in the event, naturally, *naturellement* (*French*), necessarily, of necessity, inevitably, of course, as a matter of course, and so, it follows that; **therefore**, ergo; **accordingly** *see* 765.11; **finally**

conjunctions

8 resulting from, coming from, arising from, deriving *or* derivable from, consequent to, in consequence of; **owing to, due to;** attributed *or* attributable to, dependent *or* contingent on; **caused by,** occasioned by, **at the bottom of;** required by, entailed by, following from, following strictly from

phrases

9 one thing leads to another, *post hoc, ergo propter hoc* (*Latin*), what goes up must come down (*informal*), what goes around comes around (*informal*)

887 ATTRIBUTION
assignment of cause

nouns

1 attribution, assignment, assignation, **ascription, imputation,** arrogation, placement, application, attachment, saddling, **charge, blame; indictment; responsibility,** answerability; **credit,** honour; accounting for, reference to, derivation from, connection with; etiology

2 acknowledgment, citation, tribute; confession; reference; trademark, signature; **by-line,** credit line

verbs

3 to attribute, assign, ascribe, impute, give, place, put, apply, attach, refer

4 to attribute to, ascribe to, impute to, assign to, **lay to,** put *or* set down to, apply to, refer to, point to; **pin on,** pinpoint (*informal*), fix on *or* upon, attach to, acrete to, connect with, fasten upon, hang on (*informal*), **saddle on *or* upon,** place upon, **father upon,** settle upon, saddle with; blame, **blame for,** blame on *or* upon, charge on *or* upon, place *or* put the blame on, place the blame *or* responsibility for, indict, **fix the responsibility for,** point to one, put the finger on *and* finger (*both informal*), fix the burden of, **charge to,** lay to one's charge, place to one's account, set to the account of, account for, lay at the door of, bring home to; acknowledge, confess; **credit *or* accredit with;** put words in one's mouth

5 to trace to, follow the trail to; **derive from,** trace the origin *or* derivation of; affiliate to, filiate to, father, fix the paternity of

adjectives

6 attributable, assignable, ascribable, imputable, traceable, referable, accountable, explicable; **owing, due,** assigned *or* referred to, derivable from, derivative, derivational; **charged,** alleged, imputed, putative; **credited, attributed**

adverbs

7 hence, therefore, therefor (*old*), **wherefore,** wherefrom, whence, then, thence, *ergo* (*Latin*), for which reason; **consequently** *see* 886.7; **accordingly** *see* 765.11; **because of that,** for that, by reason of that, for that reason, for the reason that, in consideration of something, from *or* for that cause, **on that account,** on those grounds, thereat; **because of this, on this account,** for this cause,

on account of this, *propter hoc* (*Latin*), for this reason, hereat; thus, thusly (*informal*), thuswise; on someone's head, on *or* at someone's doorstep

8 why, whyever, whyfor *and* for why (*both informal*), how come (*informal*), how is it that, **wherefore, what for,** for which, **on what account,** on account of what *or* which, for what *or* whatever reason, from what cause, *pourquoi* (*French*)

prepositions

9 because of, by reason of, **as a result of,** by *or* in virtue of, **on account of,** on the score of, for the sake of, **owing to, due to,** thanks to; **considering,** in consideration of, **in view of;** after

conjunctions

10 because, *parce que* (*French*), **since, as, for, whereas, inasmuch as,** forasmuch as, **insofar as, insomuch as,** as things go; in that, for the cause that, for the reason that, in view of the fact that, taking into account that, **seeing that,** seeing as how (*informal*), being as how (*informal*); **resulting from** *see* 886.8

888 OPERATION

nouns

1 operation, functioning, action, performance, performing, **working, work,** workings, exercise, practice; agency; operations; **management** *see* 573, **direction, conduct, running, carrying-on *or* -out,** execution, seeing to, overseeing, oversight; **handling,** manipulation; responsibility *see* 641.2; **occupation** *see* 724

2 process, procedure, proceeding, course; what makes it tick; **act,** step, measure, initiative, *démarche* (*French*), move, manoeuvre, motion

3 workability, operability, operativeness, performability, negotiability (*informal*), manageability, compassability, manipulatability, manoeuvrability; **practicability, feasibility,** viability

4 operator, operative, operant; **handler,** manipulator; **manager** *see* 574.1, **executive** *see* 574.3; functionary, agent; driver

verbs

5 to operate, function, run, work; manage, direct *see* 573.8, **conduct;** carry on *or* out *or* through, make go *or* work, carry the ball (*informal*), perform; **handle, manipulate, manoeuvre;** deal with, see to, take care of; occupy oneself with *see* 724.10; be responsible for *see* 641.6

6 to operate on, act on *or* upon, work on, affect, **influence,** bear on, impact, impact on; have to do with, treat, focus *or* concentrate on; bring to bear on

7 (*be operative*) to operate, function, work, act, perform, go, run, be in action *or* operation *or* commission; percolate *and* perk *and* tick (*all informal*); be effective, go into effect, have effect, take effect, militate; have play, have free play

8 to function as, work as, **act as,** act *or* play the part of, have the function *or* role *or* job *or* mission of

adjectives

9 **operative, operational, go** (*informal*), **functional, practical; effective,** effectual, efficient, efficacious

10 **workable, operable,** operatable, **performable,** actable, **doable,** manageable, compassable, negotiable, manipulatable, manoeuvrable; **practicable, feasible,** practical, viable

11 **operating, operational, working, functioning,** operant, functional, acting, active, running, **going,** going on, ongoing; **in operation,** in action, **in practice, in force,** in play, in exercise, at work, on foot; **in process,** in the works, on the fire, in the pipe *or* pipeline (*informal*), in hand

12 operational, functional; **managerial** *see* 573.12; agential, agentive *or* agentival; hands-on; manipulational

word elements

13 –age, –al, –ance, –ence, –ation, –ing, –ion, –ism, –ization, –isation, –ment, –osis, –sis, –th, –ure

889 PRODUCTIVENESS

nouns

1 **productiveness, productivity,** productive capacity; **fruitfulness,** fructification, procreativeness, progenitiveness, **fertility,** fecundity, prolificness, prolificity, prolificacy; **pregnancy; luxuriance, exuberance,** generousness, bountifulness, plentifulness, plenteousness, richness, lushness, **abundance** *see* 990.2, superabundance, copiousness, teemingness, swarmingness; teeming womb *or* loins

2 **proliferation,** multiplication, fructification, pullulation, teeming; **reproduction** *see* 78, **production** *see* 891

3 **fertilization, enrichment,** fecundation; insemination, impregnation *see* 78.4

4 **fertilizer,** dressing, top dressing, enricher, richener; Gro-bag (*trademark*); organic fertilizer, manure, muck, night soil, dung, guano, compost, slurry, leaf litter, leaf mould, humus, peat moss, castor-bean meal (*US & Canadian*), bone meal; commercial fertilizer, inorganic fertilizer, chemical fertilizer, phosphate, superphosphate, ammonia, nitrogen, nitrate, potash

5 (*goddesses of fertility*) Demeter, Ceres, Isis, Astarte *or* Ashtoreth, Venus of Willenburg; (*gods*) Frey, Priapus, Dionysus, Pan, Baal

6 (*comparisons*) rabbit, Hydra, warren, seed plot, hotbed, rich soil, land flowing with milk and honey

verbs

7 **to produce, be productive, proliferate,** pullulate, fructify, be fruitful, **multiply,** spin off, hive off, engender, beget, teem; **reproduce** *see* 78.7, 8

8 **to fertilize, enrich,** richen, fatten, feed; fructify, fecundate, fecundify, prolificate; inseminate, impregnate *see* 78.10; cross-fertilize, cross-pollinate; dress, top-dress, manure, muckspread (*informal*)

adjectives

9 **productive, fruitful,** fructiferous, fecund; **fertile, pregnant,** seminal, **rich,** flourishing, thriving, blooming; **prolific,** proliferous, uberous, **teeming,** swarming, bursting, bursting out, plenteous,

plentiful, copious, generous, bountiful, **abundant** *see* 990.7, **luxuriant, exuberant, lush,** superabundant; creative

10 **bearing, yielding, producing;** fruitbearing, fructiferous

11 **fertilizing, enriching,** richening, fattening, fecundatory, fructificative, **seminal,** germinal

890 UNPRODUCTIVENESS

nouns

1 **unproductiveness,** unproductivity, ineffectualness *see* 19.3; **unfruitfulness, barrenness,** nonfruition, dryness, aridity, dearth, famine; sterileness, **sterility,** unfertileness, **infertility,** infecundity; wasted *or* withered loins, dry womb; **birth control, contraception,** family planning, planned parenthood; abortion; impotence *see* 19, incapacity

2 **wasteland, waste,** desolation, barren *or* **barrens,** barren land, "weary waste"—SOUTHEY, "Rock and no water and the sandy road", "An old man in a dry season"—BOTH T S ELIOT; heath; **desert,** Sahara, "a barren waste, a wild of sand"—ADDISON, karroo (*Africa*), badlands, dust bowl, salt flat, Death Valley, Arabia Deserta, lunar waste *or* landscape; desert island; **wilderness,** howling wilderness, wild, wilds; treeless plain; bush, brush, outback (*Australian*)

verbs

3 to be unproductive, **come to nothing,** come to naught, hang fire, flash in the pan, fizzle *or* peter out (*informal*); **lie fallow**

adjectives

4 **unproductive,** nonproductive *or* nonproducing; **infertile, sterile,** unfertile *or* nonfertile, **unfruitful,** unfructuous, acarpous (*botany*), infecund, unprolific *or* nonprolific; **impotent,** gelded *see* 19.19; **ineffectual** *see* 19.15; **barren, desert, arid,** dry, dried-up, sere, exhausted, drained, leached, sucked dry, wasted, gaunt, **waste,** desolate, jejune; **childless,** issueless, without issue, *sine prole* (*Latin*); fallow, unploughed, unsown, untilled, uncultivated, unfecundated; celibate; virgin; menopausal

5 **uncreative,** noncreative, nonseminal, nongerminal, unfructified, unpregnant; uninventive, unoriginal, derivative

891 PRODUCTION

nouns

1 **production, creation, making, origination, invention, conception,** originating, engenderment, engendering, genesis, beginning; **devising,** hatching, fabrication, **concoction,** coinage, mintage, **contriving,** contrivance; **authorship;** creative effort, **generation** *see* 78.6; improvisation, making do; **gross national product** *or* **GNP,** net national product *or* NNP, national production of goods and services

2 **production, manufacture** *or* **manufacturing, making, producing,** devising, design, fashioning,

framing, forming, formation, formulation; engineering, tooling-up; processing, conversion; casting, **shaping**, moulding; machining, milling, finishing; **assembly**, composition, elaboration; **workmanship, craftsmanship, skill** *see* 413; **construction, building**, erection, architecture; **fabrication**, prefabrication; system building; handiwork, handwork, handicraft, crafting; **mining**, extraction, smelting, **refining; growing**, cultivation, **raising**, harvesting

3 **industrial production, industry, mass production**, volume production, **assembly-line production**; production line, assembly line; modular production *or* assembly, standardization; division of labour, industrialization; **cottage industry**; piecework, farmed-out work

4 **establishment, foundation**, constitution, institution, installation, formation, **organization**, inauguration, **inception, setting-up**, realization, materialization, effectuation; spinning-off, hiving-off

5 **performance, execution, doing, accomplishment, achievement**, productive effort *or* effect, realization, bringing to fruition, fructification, effectuation, operation *see* 888; overproduction, glut; underproduction, scarcity; **productiveness** *see* 889, fructuousness

6 **bearing, yielding, birthing; fruition**, fruiting, fructification

7 **producer, maker**, craftsman, wright, smith; **manufacturer**, industrialist; **creator**, begetter, engenderer, **author**, mother, **father**, sire; **ancestors** *see* 560.7; **precursor** *see* 815; **originator**, initiator, establisher, inaugurator, introducer, institutor, beginner, mover, prime mover, motive force, instigator; **founder**, organizer, founding father, founding *or* founder member, founding partner, cofounder; **inventor**, discoverer, deviser; developer; engineer; **builder**, constructor, artificer, **architect**, planner, **conceiver**, designer, **shaper**, master *or* leading spirit; executor, executrix; facilitator, animator; **grower**, raiser; effector, realizer; **apprentice, journeyman, master**, master craftsman *or* workman, artist, past master; "*il miglior fabbro*"—T S ELIOT (*Italian*, the better craftsman, literally, the better smith)

verbs

8 **to produce, create, make, manufacture, form**, formulate, evolve, mature, elaborate, fashion, **fabricate**, prefabricate, cast, shape, configure, carve out, mould, extrude, frame; **construct, build**, erect, put up, set up, run up, raise, rear; make up, get up, prepare, compose, write, indite, devise, design, concoct, compound, churn out *and* crank out *and* pound out *and* hammer out *and* grind out *and* rustle up (*all informal*); **put together, assemble**, piece together, patch together, cobble together, slap up *or* together (*informal*), fudge together (*informal*), improvise *see* 365.8; **make to order**, custom-make, custom-build, purpose-build; make to measure

9 **to process**, convert *see* 857.11; mill, machine; carve, chisel; **mine**, extract, pump, smelt, **refine; raise**, rear, **grow**, cultivate, harvest

10 **to establish, found**, constitute, institute, install, form, **set up, organize**, equip, endow, inaugurate, realize, materialize, effect, effectuate

11 **to perform, do**, work, act, execute, **accomplish, achieve** *see* 407.4, **deliver**, come through with, realize, engineer, effectuate, **bring about**, bring to fruition *or* into being, cause; mass-produce, volume-produce, industrialize; overproduce; underproduce; **be productive** *see* 889.7

12 **to originate, invent, conceive**, discover, **make up, devise, contrive**, concoct, fabricate, coin, mint, frame, hatch, hatch *or* cook up, strike out; improvise, make do with; think up, think out, dream up, **design**, plan, set one's wits to work; **generate, develop**, mature, **evolve**; breed, engender, beget, spawn, hatch; bring forth, give rise to, give being to, bring *or* call into being; procreate *see* 78.8

13 **to bear, yield, produce**, furnish; **bring forth**, usher into the world; fruit, **bear fruit**, fructify

adjectives

14 **productional, creational**, formational; executional; **manufacturing**, manufactural, fabricational, **industrial**, smokestack

15 **constructional, structural**, building, housing, edificial; **architectural**, architectonic

16 **creative, originative**, causative, **productive** *see* 889.9, **constructive**, formative, fabricative, demiurgic; inventive; generative *see* 78.16

17 **produced, made, caused, brought about**; effectuated, executed, performed, done; grown, raised

18 **made**, man-made; **manufactured**, created, crafted, formed, shaped, moulded, cast, forged, machined, milled, fashioned, **built, constructed**, fabricated; **mass-produced**, volume-produced, assembly-line; **well-made**, well-built, well-constructed; **homemade**, homespun, **handmade**, handcrafted, handicrafted, self-made, DIY *or* do it yourself, self-assembly; machine-made; **processed; assembled**, put together; **custom-made**, custom-built, purpose-built, custom, made to order, made to measure, bespoke; **ready-made**, ready-formed, ready-prepared, ready-to-wear, off-the-peg, off-the-shelf, off-the-rack; prefabricated, prefab (*informal*); system-built; **mined**, extracted, smelted, **refined; grown, raised**, harvested, gathered

19 **invented**, originated, **conceived**, discovered, newfound; fabricated, coined, minted, new-minted; **made-up**, made out of whole cloth

20 **manufacturable, producible**, productible

adverbs

21 **in production**; in the works, in hand, on foot; under construction; in the pipeline; on-line

892 PRODUCT

nouns

1 **product**, end product, production, manufacture; **work**, *œuvre* (*French*), **handiwork**, artefact; **creation**; creature; **offspring**, child, fruit, fruit of one's loins; **result, effect** *see* 886, issue, outgrowth, outcome; **invention**, origination, coinage, mintage *or* new mintage, brainchild; **concoction**, composition;

opus, opuscule; apprentice work; journeyman work; **masterwork, masterpiece,** *chef d'œuvre (French)*, *Meisterstück (German)*, work of an artist *or* a master *or* a past master, crowning achievement; gross national product *see* 891.1

2 **production, produce,** proceeds, net, **yield, output,** throughput; **crop,** harvest, take *(informal)*, return, bang *(informal)*

3 **extract, distillation,** essence; **by-product,** secondary *or* incidental product, spin-off, outgrowth, offshoot; **residue,** leavings, waste, waste product, industrial waste, solid waste, lees, dregs, ash

4 *(amount made)* make, making; batch, lot, run, boiling

893 INFLUENCE

nouns

1 **influence,** influentiality; **power** *see* 18, force, clout *(informal)*, potency, pressure, effect, indirect *or* incidental power, **say,** the final say, the last word, say-so *and* a lot to do with *or* to say about *(all informal)*, veto power; **prestige,** favour, good feeling, credit, esteem, repute, personality, leadership, charisma, magnetism, charm, enchantment; **weight,** moment, consequence, importance, eminence; **authority** *see* 417, control, domination, hold; **sway** *see* 612.1, reign, rule; **mastery,** ascendancy, supremacy, dominance, predominance, preponderance; upper hand, whip hand, trump card; leverage, purchase; **persuasion** *see* 375.3, suasion, suggestion, subtle influence, insinuation

2 **favour,** special favour, **interest; pull** *and* drag *and* suction *(all informal)*; **connections,** the right people, inside track *(informal)*

3 **backstairs influence,** intrigues, deals, schemes, **games,** Machiavellian *or* Byzantine intrigues, ploys; **strings** *and* **wires** *and* ropes *(all informal)*; **string-pulling** *(informal)*; **influence peddling;** lobbying, lobbyism

4 **sphere of influence,** orbit, ambit; bailiwick, vantage, stamping ground, footing, **territory,** turf, home turf, constituency, **power base**

5 **influenceability,** swayableness, movability; **persuadability,** persuadableness, persuasibility, suasibility, openness, open-mindedness, get-at-ableness *(informal)*, perviousness, accessibility, receptiveness, responsiveness, amenableness; **suggestibility, susceptibility,** impressionability, malleability; weakness *see* 16; putty in one's hands

6 *(influential person or thing)* **influence,** good influence; bad influence, sinister influence; **person** *or* **woman** *or* **man of influence,** an influential, an affluential, a presence, a palpable presence, a mover and shaker *(informal)*, a person to be reckoned with, a player *or* player on the scene; heavyweight, big wheel *and* biggie *and* heavy *(all informal)*, very important person *or* VIP *(informal)*; wheeler-dealer *(informal)*, influencer, wire-puller *(informal)*; **powerbroker; power behind the throne,** grey eminence, *éminence grise (French)*, hidden hand, manipulator, friend at *or* in court, kingmaker; **influence peddler,** lobbyist; Svengali, Rasputin; **pressure group,** special-interest group, special interests, single-issue group, PAC *or*

political action committee; lobby; the Establishment, ingroup, court, powers that be *see* 575.15, lords of creation; **key,** key to the city, access, open sesame

verbs

7 **to influence,** make oneself felt, **affect,** weigh with, **sway,** bias, bend, incline, dispose, predispose, **move,** prompt, lead; colour, tinge, tone, slant, impart spin, spin *(informal)*; **induce, persuade** *see* 375.23, twist one's arm *(informal)*, work, work *or* bend to one's will; lead by the nose *(informal)*, wear down, soften up; win friends and influence people, ingratiate oneself

8 *(exercise influence over)* **to govern** *see* 612.12, **rule, control** *see* 612.13, order, **regulate,** direct, guide; **determine,** decide, dispose; have the say *or* say-so, have veto power over, have the last word, call the shots *and* be in the driver's seat *and* wear the trousers *(all informal)*; charismatize

9 **to exercise** *or* **exert influence,** use one's **influence, bring pressure to bear upon,** lean on *(informal)*, act on, **work on,** bear upon, throw one's weight around *or* into the scale, say a few words to the right person *or* in the right quarter; charismatize; draw, draw on, lead on, magnetize; **approach,** go up to with hat in hand, make advances *or* overtures, make up to *or* get cosy with *(both informal)*; get at *or* get the ear of *(informal)*; **pull strings** *or* **wires** *or* **ropes,** wire-pull *(informal)*; lobby, lobby through

10 **to have influence, be influential, carry weight, weigh, tell, count,** cut ice, throw a lot of weight *(informal)*, have a lot to do with *or* say about *(informal)*; be the decisive factor *or* the one that counts, have pull *or* leverage *(both informal)*; have a way with one, have personality *or* magnetism *or* charisma, charm the birds out of the trees, be persuasive; have an in *(informal)*, have the inside track *(informal)*; have full play

11 **to have influence** *or* **power** *or* **a hold over,** have pull *or* clout with *(informal)*; **lead by the nose, twist** *or* **turn** *or* **wind around one's little finger,** have in one's pocket, keep under one's thumb, make sit up and beg *or* lie down and roll over; wear the trousers *(informal)*; hypnotize, mesmerize, **dominate** *see* 612.15

12 **to gain influence, get in with** *(informal)*, ingratiate oneself with, get cosy with *(informal)*; make peace, **mend fences;** gain a footing, take hold, move in, take root, strike root in, make a dent in; gain a hearing, make one's voice heard, make one sit up and take notice, be listened to, be recognized; get the mastery *or* control of, get the inside track *(informal)*, gain a hold upon; change the preponderance, turn the scale *or* balance, turn the tables

adjectives

13 **influential, powerful** *see* 18.12, affluential, potent, strong, to be reckoned with; **effective,** effectual, efficacious, telling; **weighty,** momentous, important, consequential, substantial, **prestigious,** estimable, authoritative, reputable; **persuasive,** suasive, personable, **winning,** magnetic, charming, enchanting, charismatic

14 (*in a position of influence*) **well-connected,** favourably situated, near the seat of power; **dominant** *see* 612.18, **predominant,** preponderant, prepotent, prepollent, regnant, ruling, swaying, prevailing, on the throne, in the driver's seat (*informal*); **ascendant,** in the ascendant, in ascendancy

15 **influenceable, swayable, movable; persuadable,** persuasible, suasible, open, open-minded, pervious, accessible, receptive, responsive, amenable; **under one's thumb,** in one's pocket, on one's payroll; coercible, bribable, compellable, vulnerable; **plastic, pliant,** pliable, malleable; **suggestible, susceptible, impressionable,** weak *see* 16.12

894 ABSENCE OF INFLUENCE

nouns

1 **lack of influence** *or* power *or* force, uninfluentiality, **unauthoritativeness,** powerlessness, forcelessness, impotence *see* 19, impotency; **ineffectiveness,** inefficaciousness, inefficacy, ineffectuality; **no say,** no say-so, nothing to do with *or* say about (*informal*); unpersuasiveness, lack of personality *or* charm, lack of magnetism *or* charisma; **weakness** *see* 16, wimpiness *or* wimpishness (*informal*)

2 **uninfluenceability,** unswayableness, unmovability; **unpersuadability,** impersuadability, impersuasibility, unreceptiveness, imperviousness, unresponsiveness; unsuggestibility, **unsusceptibility,** unimpressionability; invulnerability; **obstinacy** *see* 361

adjectives

3 **uninfluential, powerless,** forceless, impotent *see* 19.13; **weak** *see* 16.12, wimpy *or* wimpish (*informal*); unauthoritative; **ineffective,** ineffectual, inefficacious; **of no account,** no-account, without any weight, featherweight, lightweight

4 **uninfluenceable, unswayable, unmovable; unpliable,** unyielding, inflexible; **unpersuadable** *see* 361.13, impersuadable, impersuasible, unreceptive, unresponsive, unamenable; impervious, closed to; **unsuggestible, unsusceptible,** unimpressionable; invulnerable; **obstinate** *see* 361.8

5 **uninfluenced, unmoved, unaffected, unswayed**

895 TENDENCY

nouns

1 **tendency, inclination, leaning,** penchant, proneness, conatus, weakness, susceptibility; liability *see* 896, readiness, willingness, eagerness, aptness, aptitude, **disposition,** proclivity, **propensity,** predisposition, **predilection,** a thing for (*informal*), affinity, prejudice, **liking,** delight, soft spot; **yen,** lech (*informal*), hunger, thirst; instinct *or* feeling for, sensitivity to; **bent, turn, bias,** slant, tilt, spin (*informal*), cast, warp, twist; probability *see* 967; diathesis (*medicine*), tropism (*biology*)

2 **trend, drift, course, current,** *Tendenz* (*German*), flow, stream, mainstream, main current, movement, glacial movement, motion, run, **tenor,** tone, **set,** set of the current, swing, bearing, line, direction, the general tendency *or* drift, the main course, the course of events, the way the wind blows, **the way things go,** trend of the times, spirit of the age *or* time, time spirit, *Zeitgeist* (*German*); the way it looks

verbs

3 **to tend,** have a tendency, **incline,** be disposed, **lean, trend,** have a penchant, set, **go,** head, lead, point, verge, turn, warp, tilt, bias, bend to, work *or* gravitate *or* set toward; show a tendency *or* trend *or* set *or* direction, swing toward, point to, look to; **conduce,** contribute, serve, redound to

adjectives

4 **tending;** tendentious *or* tendential; **leaning, inclining,** inclinatory, inclinational; **mainstream,** main-current, mainline

prepositions

5 **tending to, conducive to,** leading to, inclined toward, inclining toward, heading *or* moving *or* swinging *or* working toward

6 **inclined to, leaning to, prone to, disposed to,** drawn to, predisposed to, given to; **apt to, likely to, liable to** *see* 896.6, calculated to, minded to, ready to, in a fair way to

896 LIABILITY

nouns

1 **liability, likelihood** *or* likeliness; **probability** *see* 967, contingency, chance *see* 971, eventuality *see* 830.1; weakness, **proneness** *see* 895.1; **possibility** *see* 965; **responsibility** *see* 641.2, legal responsibility; **indebtedness** *see* 623.1, financial commitment, pecuniary obligation

2 **susceptibility, liability,** susceptivity, liableness, **openness, exposure; vulnerability** *see* 1005.4

verbs

3 **to be liable; be subjected** *or* subjected to, be a pawn *or* plaything of, be the prey of, lie under; **expose oneself to, lay** *or* **leave oneself open to,** open the door to; **gamble,** stand to lose *or* gain, stand a chance, **run the chance** *or* risk, let down one's guard *or* defences; **admit of,** open the possibility of, be in the way of, bid *or* stand fair to; **owe,** be in debt *or* indebted for

4 **to incur, contract, invite, welcome, run, bring on, bring down,** bring upon *or* down upon, bring upon *or* down upon oneself; **be responsible for** *see* 641.6; fall into, fall in with; get, gain, acquire

adjectives

5 **liable, likely, prone; probable; responsible,** legally responsible, answerable; **in debt, indebted,** financially burdened, heavily committed, overextended; **exposed, susceptible, at risk,** overexposed, open, like a sitting duck, **vulnerable**

6 **liable to, subject to,** standing to, in a position to, incident to, dependent on; **susceptible** *or* **prone to,** susceptive to, **open** *or* vulnerable *or* **exposed to,** naked to, in danger of, within range of, at the mercy of; **capable of**, ready for; **likely to, apt to** *see* 895.6; obliged to, responsible *or* answerable for

conjunctions

7 lest, that, for fear that

897 INVOLVEMENT

nouns

1 involvement, involution, **implication, entanglement**, enmeshment, engagement, involuntary presence *or* cooperation, embarrassment; relation *see* 774; **inclusion** *see* 771; **absorption** *see* 982.3

verbs

2 to involve, implicate, tangle, **entangle**, embarrass, enmesh, engage, **draw in**, drag *or* hook *or* suck into, catch up in, **make a party to**; interest, concern; absorb *see* 982.13

3 to be involved, be into (*informal*), partake, participate, take an interest, interest oneself, have a role *or* part

adjectives

4 involved, implicated; interested, concerned, a party to; included *see* 771.5

5 involved in, implicated in, tangled *or* entangled in, enmeshed in, **caught up in**, tied up in, wrapped up in, all wound up in, dragged *or* hooked *or* sucked into; in deep, deeply involved, **up to one's neck or ears in**, up to one's elbows *or* arse in (*informal*), head over heels in, **absorbed in** *see* 982.17, immersed *or* submerged in, far-gone

898 CONCURRENCE

nouns

1 concurrence, collaboration, coaction, co-working, collectivity, combined effort *or* operation, united *or* concerted action, concert, synergy; **cooperation** *see* 450; **agreement** *see* 787; me-tooism; **coincidence**, simultaneity *see* 835, synchronism; concomitance, accompaniment *see* 768; **union**, junction *see* 799.1, **conjunction**, combination *see* 804, association, alliance, consociation; conspiracy, collusion, cahoots (*informal*); concourse, confluence; **accordance** *see* 455.1, concordance, correspondence, consilience; symbiosis, parasitism; saprophytism

verbs

2 to concur, **collaborate**, coact, **co-work**, synergize; **cooperate** *see* 450.3; conspire, collude, connive, be in cahoots (*informal*); **combine** *see* 804.3, **unite, associate** *see* 804.4, coadunate, join, conjoin; harmonize; **coincide**, synchronize, happen together; **accord** *see* 455.2, correspond, **agree** *see* 787.6

3 to go with, **go along with, go hand in hand with**, be hand in glove with, team *or* join up with, buddy up with (*US & Canadian informal*); keep pace with, run parallel to

adjectives

4 concurrent, concurring; **coacting**, coactive, **collaborative**, collective, **co-working**, cooperant,

synergetic *or* synergic *or* synergistic; **cooperative** *see* 450.5; conspiratorial, collusive; **united, joint, conjoint, combined, concerted**, associated, associate, coadunate; **coincident**, synchronous, synchronic, in sync *or* in synch, coordinate; concomitant, accompanying *see* 768.9; meeting, uniting, combining; **accordant, agreeing** *see* 787.9, concordant, harmonious, consilient, at one with; symbiotic, parasitic, saprophytic

adverbs

5 concurrently, coactively, **jointly, conjointly, concertedly**, in concert, in harmony *or* unison with, synchronously, **together**; **with one accord**, with one voice, as one, as one man; hand in hand, hand in glove, shoulder to shoulder, cheek by jowl

899 COUNTERACTION

nouns

1 **counteraction, counterworking; opposition** *see* 451, opposure, counterposition *or* contraposition, confutation, **contradiction; antagonism**, repugnance, oppugnance *or* oppugnancy, **antipathy, conflict, friction**, interference, clashing, collision; reaction, repercussion, **backlash, recoil**, kick, backfire; resistance, recalcitrance, dissent *see* 333, revolt *see* 327.4, perverseness, nonconformity *see* 867, crankiness, crotchetiness, orneriness (*US & Canadian informal*), renitency; going against the current *or* against the tide, swimming upstream; **contrariety** *see* 778

2 **neutralization, nullification, annulment**, cancellation, voiding, invalidation, vitiation, frustration, thwarting, undoing; **offsetting**, counterbalancing, countervailing, balancing

3 **counteractant**, counteractive, **counteragent**; counterirritant; **antidote**, remedy, preventive *or* preventative, prophylactic; **neutralizer**, nullifier, offset; antacid, buffer

4 **counterforce**, countervailing force, counterinfluence, counterpressure; counterpoise, counterbalance, counterweight; countercurrent, crosscurrent, undercurrent; counterblast; head wind, foul wind, cross wind

5 **countermeasure, counterattack**, counterstep; **counterblow** *or* counterstroke *or* countercoup *or* counterblast, counterfire; counterrevolution, counterinsurgency; counterterrorism; counterculture; **retort**, comeback (*informal*); defence *see* 460

verbs

6 to counteract, counter, counterwork, counterattack, countervail; counterpose *or* contrapose, **oppose**, antagonize, go in opposition to, go *or* run counter to, go *or* work against, go clean counter to, go *or* fly in the face of, run against, beat against, militate against; **resist**, fight back, bite back, lift a hand against, defend oneself; **dissent**, dissent from; **cross**, confute, **contradict**, contravene, oppugn, **conflict**, be antipathetic *or* hostile *or* inimical, interfere *or* conflict with, come in conflict with, **clash**, collide, meet head-on, lock horns; rub *or* go against the grain; swim upstream *or* against the tide *or* against the current

7 to **neutralize, nullify, annul, cancel,** cancel out, negate, negative, negativate, invalidate, vitiate, void, frustrate, stultify, thwart, come *or* bring to nothing, undo; **offset, counterbalance** *see* 338.5; buffer

adjectives

8 counteractive *or* counteractant, **counteracting, counterworking, counterproductive,** countervailing; **opposing,** oppositional; contradicting, contradictory; **antagonistic,** hostile, antipathetic, inimical, oppugnant, repugnant, **conflicting, clashing;** reactionary; resistant, recalcitrant, dissentient, dissident, revolutionary, breakaway, nonconformist, perverse, cranky, crotchety, ornery (*US & Canadian informal*), renitent

9 **neutralizing, nullifying,** stultifying, annulling, cancelling, negating, invalidating, vitiating, voiding; **balanced,** counterbalanced, poised, in poise, offset, zero-sum; **offsetting,** counterbalancing, countervailing; antacid, buffering

adverbs

10 counteractively, antagonistically, opposingly, **in opposition to, counter to**

word elements

11 ant–, anti–, anth–, contra–, counter–

900 SUPPORT

nouns

1 **support, backing,** aid *see* 449; **upholding, upkeep,** carrying, carriage, maintenance, **sustaining,** sustainment, sustenance, sustentation; **reinforcement,** backup; subsidy, subvention; **support services, infrastructure; moral support;** emotional *or* psychological support, security blanket (*informal*); **power base, constituency, party;** supportive relationship, supportive therapy; **approval** *see* 509; **assent, concurrence** *see* 332; **reliance** *see* 952.1; life-support, life-sustainment

2 **supporter, support; upholder,** bearer, carrier, sustainer, maintainer; staff *see* 273.2, stave, cane, stick, walking stick, alpenstock, crook, crutch; **advocate** *see* 616.9; **stay, prop,** fulcrum, **bracket, brace,** bracer, guy, guyrope *or* guywire *or* guyline, shroud, rigging, standing rigging; buttress, shoulder, arm, good right arm; mast, sprit, yard, yardarm; **mainstay,** backbone, spine, neck, cervix; athletic support, jock *and* jockstrap (*both informal*), truss, G-string (*informal*); brassiere, bra (*informal*), bandeau, corset, corselet, girdle, foundation garment; **reinforcement,** reinforce, reinforcing, reinforcer, strengthener, stiffener; back, backing; rest, resting place

3 (*mythology*) Atlas, Hercules, Telamon, the tortoise that supports the earth

4 **buttress,** buttressing; abutment, shoulder, truss; **bulwark,** rampart; **embankment,** bank, retaining wall, bulkhead, bulkheading, plank buttress, piling; **breakwater,** seawall, mole, **jetty,** jutty, groyne; **pier,** pier buttress, buttress pier; flying buttress,

arc-boutant (*French*), arch buttress; hanging buttress; **beam**

5 **footing, foothold, toehold,** hold, perch, **purchase** *see* 905; **standing,** stand, stance, standing place, pou sto, *point d'appui* (*French*), *locus standi* (*Latin*); footrest, footplate, footrail

6 **foundation,** *fond* (*French*), firm foundation, **base, basis, footing,** basement, pavement, **ground,** grounds, **groundwork, seat,** sill, floor *or* flooring, fundament, lacing; bed, bedding; **substructure,** substruction, substratum; infrastructure; **understructure,** understruction, underbuilding, undergirding, undercarriage, underpinning, bearing wall; stereobate, stylobate; firm *or* solid ground, *terra firma* (*Latin*); solid rock *or* bottom, rock bottom, bedrock; hardpan; riprap; **fundamental** *see* 996.6, **principle, premise** *see* 956.1; root, radical; rudiment

7 **foundation stone,** footstone; **cornerstone, keystone,** headstone, first stone, quoin

8 **base, pedestal; stand,** standard; **shaft** *see* 273, **upright, column, pillar, post,** jack, pole, staff, batten (*NZ*), stanchion, pier, pile *or* piling, king-post, queen-post, pilaster, newel-post, banister, baluster, balustrade, colonnade, caryatid; dado, die; plinth, subbase; surbase; socle; **trunk,** stem, **stalk,** pedicel, peduncle, footstalk

9 **sill,** groundsel; mudsill; window sill; doorsill, threshold; doorstone

10 **frame,** underframe, infrastructure, chassis, **skeleton;** armature; **mounting,** mount, **backing, setting;** surround

11 **handle, hold,** grip, grasp, haft, helve

12 **scaffold,** scaffolding, *échafaudage* (*French*); **stage,** staging

13 **platform; stage,** estrade, dais, floor; **rostrum, podium, pulpit,** speaker's platform *or* stand, **soapbox** (*informal*); hustings, **stump;** tribune, tribunal; emplacement; catafalque; landing stage, landing; heliport, landing pad; launching pad; **terrace; balcony, gallery**

14 **shelf, ledge,** shoulder, corbel, beam-end; **mantel,** mantelshelf, mantelpiece, chimneypiece; retable, superaltar, gradin, *gradino* (*Italian*), predella; hob

15 **table,** board, **stand; bench,** workbench; **counter,** bar, buffet; **desk,** writing table, **secretary,** *secrétaire* (*French*), escritoire, bureau; **lectern,** reading stand, ambo, reading desk

16 **trestle, horse;** clotheshorse; trestle board *or* table, trestle and table; trestlework, trestling; A-frame

17 **seat, chair,** pew; carver; director's chair; saddle

18 (*saddle parts*) **pommel,** horn; jockey; **girth, girt,** surcingle, bellyband; cinch, stirrup

19 **sofa, bed,** sofa bed; **couch;** futon; **lounger;** the sack *and* the hay *and* kip *and* doss (*all informal*); bedstead; **litter, stretcher,** gurney (*US & Canadian*)

20 **bedding,** underbed, underbedding; **mattress,** palliasse, pallet; air mattress, Lilo (*trademark*), foam-rubber mattress, innerspring mattress, orthopaedic mattress; sleeping bag; pad, mat, rug; litter, bedstraw; **pillow,** cushion, bolster; **springs,** bedsprings, box springs

verbs

21 **to support, bear,** carry, **hold, sustain, maintain, bolster, reinforce,** back, back up, shoulder, give *or* furnish *or* afford *or* supply *or* lend support; bat for (*informal*); **hold up, bear up,** bolster up, keep up, buoy up, keep afloat, back up; **uphold,** upbear, upkeep; **brace, prop,** crutch, buttress; shore, **shore up;** stay, mainstay; underbrace, undergird, underprop, underpin, underset; **underlie,** be at the bottom of, form the foundation of; cradle; cushion, pillow; **subsidize;** subvene; assent *see* 332.8; concur *see* 332.9; **approve** *see* 509.9

22 **to rest on, stand on, lie on,** recline on, repose on, bear on, **lean on,** abut on; **sit on,** perch, ride, ride piggyback on; **straddle,** bestraddle, stride, bestride; be based on, rely on

adjectives

23 **supporting, supportive, bearing,** carrying, burdened; **holding,** upholding, maintaining, sustaining, sustentative, suspensory; bracing, propping, shoring, bolstering, buttressing; life-sustaining

24 **supported, borne,** upborne, held, buoyed-up, **upheld, sustained,** maintained; **braced,** guyed, stayed, propped, shored *or* shored up, bolstered, buttressed; based *or* founded *or* grounded on

adverbs

25 **on,** across, **astride, astraddle,** straddle, straddle-legged, straddleback, on the back of; horseback, on horseback; pickaback *or* piggyback

901 IMPULSE, IMPACT
driving and striking force

nouns

1 **impulse,** impulsion, impelling force, impellent; **drive,** driving force *or* power; **motive power, power** *see* 18; **force,** irresistible force; clout (*informal*); **impetus; momentum;** moment, moment of force; propulsion *see* 903.1; incitement *see* 375.4, incentive *see* 375.7, compulsion *see* 424

2 **thrust, push, shove,** boost (*informal*); **pressure; stress;** press; **prod, poke, punch, jab,** dig, nudge; **bump,** jog, joggle, jolt; **jostle,** hustle; **butt,** bunt; head (*of water, steam, etc*)

3 **impact, collision,** prang (*informal*), shunt (*informal*), bingle (*Australian informal*), **clash,** appulse, **encounter,** meeting, impingement, **bump, crash,** crump; carom, cannon; sideswipe (*informal*); smash *and* crunch (*both informal*); **shock, brunt; concussion,** percussion; **thrusting, ramming, bulldozing,** shouldering, muscling, steamrollering, railroading; hammering, smashing, mauling, sledgehammering; onslaught *see* 459.1

4 **hit, blow, stroke, knock, rap, pound,** slam, bang, crack, **whack, smack, thwack,** bash, smash, dash, swipe, swing, **punch, poke, jab,** dig, drub, thump, pelt, cut, chop, dint, slog, slosh (*informal*), clock (*informal*); drubbing, drumming, tattoo, fusillade; beating *see* 604.4

5 (*informal terms*) **sock,** bang, bash, bat, belt, fourpenny one, bust (*US & Canadian*), clip, clout,

swat, plunk, larrup, paste, lick, biff, clump, clunk, clonk, wallop, whop, bonk, slam, slug

6 **punch, boxing punch,** blow, belt, sock

7 **tap, rap, pat,** dab, chuck, touch, tip; love-tap; **snap, flick, flip,** fillip, flirt, whisk, brush; **peck,** pick

8 **slap, smack, flap; box, cuff,** buffet; **spank;** whip, **lash,** cut, stripe

9 **kick, boot;** punt, drop kick, place kick, kicking, calcitration (*old*); balloon

10 **stamp,** stomp (*informal*), drub, clump, clop

verbs

11 **to impel,** give an impetus, **set going** *or* agoing, put *or* set in motion, give momentum; **drive, move,** animate, actuate, forward; **thrust,** power; drive *or* whip on; goad; **propel;** motivate, incite *see* 375.17; compel *see* 424.4

12 **to thrust, push, shove,** boost (*informal*); press, stress, **bear,** bear upon, bring pressure to bear upon; **ram,** ram down, tamp, pile-drive, jam, crowd, cram, shoehorn; bulldoze, muscle, steamroller, railroad; **drive, force,** run; **prod, goad, poke, punch, jab,** dig, nudge; **bump,** jog, joggle, jolt, shake, rattle; **jostle,** hustle, hurtle; elbow, shoulder; **butt,** bunt, run *or* bump *or* butt against, bump up against, knock *or* run one's head against; assault

13 **to collide,** come into collision, be on a collision course, **clash,** meet, encounter, confront each other, impinge; percuss, concuss; **bump, hit, knock, bang; run into, bump into,** bang into, slam into, smack into, **crash into, impact,** smash into, dash into, carom into, cannon into; rear-end; **hit against,** strike against, knock against; foul, fall *or* run foul *or* afoul of; hurtle, barrel (*informal*); carom, cannon; sideswipe (*informal*); **crash,** smash, crump, whomp; smash up *or* crack up *or* crunch (*all informal*)

14 **to hit, strike, knock,** knock down *or* out, smite; land a blow, draw blood; **poke, punch, jab,** thwack, **smack,** clap, crack, clock (*informal*), swipe, **whack;** deal, fetch, swipe at, take a punch at, throw one at (*informal*), deal *or* fetch a blow, hit a clip (*informal*), let have it; **thump,** snap; strike at *see* 459.16

15 (*informal terms*) **to belt,** bat, clout, bang, slam, bash, biff, paste, wham, whop, clump, bonk, wallop, lam (*informal*), clip, cut, plunk, swat, soak, sock, slog, slug, slosh, clunk, clonk, fist

16 **to pound, beat, hammer, maul,** sledgehammer, **knock, rap, bang,** thump, **drub,** buffet, **batter,** pulverize, paste (*informal*), patter, pommel, pummel, pelt, baste, lambaste; thresh, thrash; flail; spank, flap; whip

17 (*informal terms*) **to clobber,** knock for a loop, marmelize, knock cold, dust off, bash up, punch out, rough up, slap down, smack down, sandbag, work over, deck, wallop, larrup

18 **to tap, rap, pat,** dab, chuck, touch, tip; **snap, flick, flip,** fillip, tickle, flirt, whisk, **graze,** brush; bunt; **peck,** pick, beak

19 **to slap, smack,** flap; **box, cuff,** buffet; **spank;** whip

20 **to club,** cudgel, blackjack, sandbag, cosh

21 to kick, boot, kick about *or* around, calcitrate (*old*); balloon; kick downstairs (*old*); kick out; knee
22 to stamp, stomp (*informal*), trample, tread, drub, clump, clop

adjectives

23 impelling, impellent; impulsive, pulsive, **moving,** motive, animating, actuating, **driving;** thrusting
24 concussive, percussive, crashing, smashing

902 REACTION

nouns

1 reaction, response, respondence, feedback; reply, answer *see* 939.1, **rise** (*informal*); **reflex,** reflection *or* reflexion, **reflex action;** echo, bounce-back, reverberation, resonance, sympathetic vibration; return; reflux, refluence; action and reaction; opposite response, negative response, retroaction, revulsion; predictable response, automatic *or* autonomic reaction, knee jerk *and* knee-jerk response (*both informal*), spontaneous *or* unthinking response, spur-of-the-moment response; conditioned reflex
2 recoil, rebound, resilience, repercussion, *contrecoup* (*French*); **bounce, bound, spring,** bounce-back; **repulse, rebuff; backlash,** backlashing, kickback, **kick,** a kick like a mule (*informal*), recalcitration (*old*); **backfire, boomerang;** ricochet, carom, cannon
3 (*a drawing back or aside*) **retreat,** recoil, fallback, pullout, pullback, contingency plan, backup plan; evasion, avoidance, sidestepping; **flinch,** wince, cringe; **side step,** shy; **dodge, duck** (*informal*)
4 reactionary, reactionist, recalcitrant

verbs

5 to react, respond, reply, answer, riposte, snap back, come back at (*informal*); rise to the fly, take the bait; go off half-cocked *or* at half cock
6 to recoil, rebound, resile; **bounce, bound, spring; spring** *or* **fly back,** bounce *or* bound back, snap back; repercuss, have repercussions; **kick,** kick back, kick like a mule (*informal*), recalcitrate (*old*); **backfire, boomerang;** backlash, lash back; ricochet, carom, cannon *and* cannon off
7 to pull *or* **draw back,** retreat, recoil, fade, **fall back,** reel back, hang back, start back, shrink back, give ground; **shrink, flinch, wince, cringe,** blink, blench, quail; **shy,** shy away, start *or* turn aside, evade, avoid, sidestep, weasel, weasel out, cop out (*informal*); **dodge, duck** (*informal*); jib, swerve, sheer off, give a wide berth
8 to get a reaction, get a response, evoke a response, ring a bell, strike a responsive chord, strike fire, strike *or* hit home, hit a nerve, get a rise out of (*informal*)

adjectives

9 reactive, reacting, merely reactive; **responsive,** respondent, responding, antiphonal; **quick on the draw** *or* trigger *or* uptake; **reactionary;** retroactionary, retroactive; revulsive; **reflex,** reflexive, knee-jerk (*informal*); refluent
10 recoiling, rebounding, **resilient; bouncing,** bouncy, bounding, springing, springy; repercussive; recalcitrant

adverbs

11 on the rebound, on the return, on the bounce; on the spur of the moment, off the top of the head

903 PUSHING, THROWING

nouns

1 pushing, propulsion, propelling; shoving, butting; **drive, thrust,** motive power, driving force, means of propulsion (*see list*); **push, shove;** butt, bunt; shunt, impulsion *see* 901.1
2 throwing, projection, jaculation, ejaculation, flinging, slinging, **pitching, tossing,** casting, hurling, lobbing, chucking, chunking (*informal*), heaving, firing (*informal*); bowling, rolling; **shooting,** firing, gunnery, gunning, musketry; trap-shooting, skeet *or* skeet shooting; archery
3 throw, toss, fling, sling, cast, hurl, chuck, chunk (*informal*), lob, **heave,** cockshy *or* shy, **pitch, toss,** peg (*informal*); **flip;** put, shot-put; (*football*) pass; (*tennis*) serve, service; (*cricket*) bowl; (*baseball*) pitch
4 shot, discharge; ejection *see* 908; detonation *see* 56.3; gunfire; gun, cannon; bullet; **salvo, volley,** fusillade, tattoo, spray; bowshot, gunshot, stoneshot, potshot
5 projectile, ejecta, ejectamenta; **missile;** ball; discus, quoit
6 propeller, prop (*informal*), airscrew, prop-fan; propellant, propulsor, driver; screw, wheel, screw propeller, twin screws; bow thruster; paddle wheel; turbine; fan, impeller, rotor; piston
7 thrower, pitcher, hurler, bowler (*cricket*), chucker, chunker (*informal*), **heaver, tosser,** flinger, slinger, caster, jaculator, ejaculator; bowler; shot-putter; javelin thrower; discus thrower, discobolus
8 shooter, shot; **gunner, gun, gunman; rifleman,** musketeer, carabineer; cannoneer, artilleryman; Nimrod, hunter *see* 382.5; trapshooter; archer, bowman, toxophilite; **marksman, markswoman,** targetshooter, **sharpshooter,** sniper; good shot, dead shot, deadeye, **crack shot**

verbs

9 to push, propel, impel, **shove,** thrust *see* 901.11; **drive, move,** forward, advance; sweep, sweep along; butt, bunt; shunt; pole, row; pedal, treadle; **roll,** troll, bowl, trundle
10 to throw, fling, sling, pitch, toss, cast, hurl, heave, bung (*informal*), **chuck,** chunk *and* peg (*both informal*), lob, shy, fire, pepper (*informal*), launch, dash, let fly, let go, let rip, let loose; catapult; **flip,** snap, jerk; bowl; pass; serve; put, put the shot; dart, lance, tilt; fork, pitchfork; pelt *see* 459.27
11 to project, jaculate, ejaculate
12 to shoot, fire, fire off, let off, let fly, **discharge,** eject *see* 908.13; detonate *see* 56.8; gun (*informal*), pistol; sharpshoot; shoot at *see* 459.22, gun for (*informal*); strike, hit, plug (*informal*); shoot down, fell, drop, stop in one's tracks; **riddle, pepper,** pelt, pump full of lead (*informal*); snipe, pick off; torpedo; pot; potshoot, potshot, take a potshot; load, prime, charge; cock

13 to start, start off, start up, give a start, crank up, give a push *or* shove (*informal*), jump-start, kick-start, **put** *or* **set in motion, set on foot,** set going *or* agoing, start going; **kick off** *and* **start the ball rolling** (*both informal*); get off the ground *or* off the mark, **launch,** launch forth *or* out, float, set afloat; send, send off *or* forth; bundle off

adjectives

14 propulsive, propulsory, **propellant,** propelling; **motive; driving, pushing, shoving**
15 projectile, trajectile, jaculatory, ejaculatory; **ballistic, missile;** ejective
16 jet-propelled, rocket-propelled, steam-propelled, gasoline-propelled, gas-propelled, diesel-propelled, wind-propelled, self-propelled, etc
17 means of propulsion

battery propulsion	ram-jet propulsion
diesel propulsion	reaction propulsion
diesel-electric propulsion	resojet propulsion
electric propulsion	rocket propulsion
gas propulsion	spring propulsion
gasoline propulsion	steam propulsion
gravity propulsion	turbofan propulsion
jet propulsion	turbojet propulsion
plasma-jet propulsion	turbopropeller *or*
prop-fan propulsion	turboprop propulsion
pulse-jet propulsion	wind propulsion

904 PULLING

nouns

1 pulling, traction, drawing, draught, dragging, heaving, tugging, towing; pulling *or* tractive power, **pull;** tug-of-war; towing, towage; towrope, towbar, towline, towing cable *or* hawser; tow car (*US & Canadian*), wrecker (*US & Canadian*); **hauling,** haulage, drayage; man-hauling, man-haulage; attraction *see* 906; extraction *see* 192
2 pull, draw, heave, haul, tug, a long pull and a strong pull, strain, drag
3 jerk, yank (*informal*), quick *or* sudden pull; **twitch,** tweak, pluck, hitch, wrench, snatch, start, bob; **flip,** flick, flirt, flounce; jig, **jiggle;** jog, joggle

verbs

4 to pull, draw, heave, haul, hump, hale, lug, **tug, tow,** take in tow; trail, train; **drag,** man-haul, draggle, snake (*US informal*); troll, trawl
5 to jerk, yerk (*informal*), **yank** (*informal*); **twitch,** tweak, pluck, snatch, hitch, wrench, snake (*US informal*); **flip,** flick, flirt, flounce; **jiggle,** jig, jog, joggle

adjectives

6 pulling, drawing, tractional, tractive, hauling, tugging, towing, towage; man-hauled

905 LEVERAGE, PURCHASE
mechanical advantage applied to moving or raising

nouns

1 leverage, fulcrumage; pry (*US & Canadian*), prise *or* prize
2 purchase, hold, advantage; **foothold,** toehold, footing; differential purchase; collier's purchase; traction
3 fulcrum, axis, pivot, bearing, rest, resting point, *point d'appui* (*French*); thole, tholepin, rowlock, oarlock (*US & Canadian*)
4 lever; pry (*US & Canadian*), prize; **bar,** pinch bar, **crowbar,** crow, pinchbar, iron crow, wrecking bar, ripping bar (*US & Canadian*), claw bar (*US & Canadian*); cant hook, peavey (*US & Canadian*); **jemmy;** handspike, marlinespike *or* marlinspike; boom, spar, beam, outrigger; pedal, treadle, crank; limb
5 arm; forearm; wrist; elbow; upper arm, biceps
6 tackle, purchase
7 windlass; capstan (*nautical*); **winch,** crab; reel; differential windlass, Chinese windlass, Spanish windlass

verbs

8 to get a purchase, get leverage, get a foothold; **pry,** prise *or* prize, **lever,** wedge; pry *or* prise *or* prize out; **jemmy,** crowbar, pinchbar
9 to reel in, wind in, bring in, draw in, pull in, crank in, trim, tighten, tauten, draw taut, take the strain; windlass, winch, crank, reel; tackle

906 ATTRACTION
a drawing toward

nouns

1 attraction, traction *see* 904.1, attractiveness, attractivity; mutual attraction *or* magnetism; pulling power, **pull,** drag, draw, tug; magnetism *see* 1031.7; gravity, gravitation; G-force; centripetal force; capillarity, capillary attraction; adduction; **affinity, sympathy;** allurement *see* 377
2 attractor, attractant, attrahent; adductor; cynosure, focus, centre, centre of attraction *or* attention; crowd-pleaser *or* drawer, charismatic figure; **lure** *see* 377.2
3 magnet, artificial magnet, field magnet, bar magnet, horseshoe magnet, electromagnet, solenoid, paramagnet, electromagnetic lifting magnet, magnetic needle; lodestone, magnetite; magnetic pole, magnetic north

verbs

4 to attract, pull, draw, drag, tug, pull *or* draw towards, have an attraction; **magnetize,** magnet, be magnetic; **lure;** adduct

adjectives

5 attracting, drawing, pulling, dragging, tugging; eye-catching; **attractive, magnetic;** charismatic; magnetized, attrahent; sympathetic; **alluring;** adductive, adducent

adverbs

6 attractionally, attractively; magnetically; charismatically

907 REPULSION
a thrusting away

nouns

1 **repulsion**, repellence *or* repellency, **repelling**; mutual repulsion, polarization; disaffinity; centrifugal force; magnetic repulsion, diamagnetism; antigravity; ejection *see* 908

2 **repulse, rebuff**; dismissal, cold shoulder, snub, spurning, brush–off, cut; kiss-off (*informal*); turn–off (*informal*); refusal; discharge *see* 908.5

verbs

3 **to repulse, repel, rebuff, turn back,** put back, beat back, drive *or* push *or* thrust back; drive away, chase, chase off *or* away; send off *or* away, send about one's business, **send packing,** pack off, dismiss; snub, cut, brush off, drop; kiss off (*informal*); spurn, refuse; **ward off,** hold off, keep off, fend off, fight off, push off, keep at arm's length; slap *or* smack down (*informal*); eject *see* 908.13, discharge *see* 908.19

adjectives

4 **repulsive,** repellent, **repelling**; diamagnetic, of opposite polarity

adverbs

5 repulsively, repellently

908 EJECTION

nouns

1 **ejection,** ejectment, throwing out, **expulsion, discharge,** extrusion, obtrusion, detrusion, **ousting, ouster,** removal, kicking *or* booting *or* chucking out (*all informal*); throwing *or* kicking downstairs; the boot *and* the bounce *and* the bum's rush *and* the old heave-ho (*all informal*), the chuck (*informal*); defenestration; **rejection** *see* 372; jettison

2 **eviction,** ousting, dislodgment, dispossession; **ouster**

3 **depopulation,** dispeoplement, unpeopling; devastation, desolation

4 **banishment,** relegation, exclusion *see* 772; **excommunication,** disfellowship; **disbarment,** unfrocking, defrocking; **expatriation, exile,** exilement; outlawing *or* outlawry, fugitation (*Scottish law*); **ostracism,** ostracization, thumbs down, thumbing down, *pollice verso* (*Latin*), blackballing, silent treatment, sending to Coventry, cold shoulder; **deportation,** transportation, **extradition;** rustication, sending down; degradation, **demotion** *see* 447, stripping, depluming, displuming; deprivation

5 **dismissal, discharge,** forced separation, *congé* (*French*); outplacement; **firing** *and* canning (*both informal*), **cashiering,** drumming out, dishonourable discharge, rogue's march; disemployment, **layoff,** removal, surplusing, displacing, furloughing; suspension; **retirement;** the bounce, **the sack** *and*

the chuck (*both informal*), the chop (*informal*), the bullet (*informal*), the push (*informal*), notice; the boot *and* the axe (*both informal*), the gate (*US & Canadian informal*); walking papers *or* ticket (*US & Canadian informal*), pink slip (*US informal*), jotters (*Scottish informal*), books (*informal*), P45; deposal *see* 447

6 **evacuation,** voidance, voiding; **elimination,** removal; **clearance, clearing,** clearage; unfouling, freeing; scouring *or* cleaning out, unclogging; exhaustion, exhausting, venting, emptying, depletion; **unloading,** off-loading, discharging cargo *or* freight; draining, drainage; egress *see* 190.2; **excretion,** defecation *see* 12.2, 4

7 **disgorgement,** disemboguement, **expulsion,** ejaculation, **discharge,** emission; **eruption,** eructation, extravasation, **blowout, outburst;** outpour, jet, spout, squirt, spurt

8 **vomiting,** vomition, **disgorgement, regurgitation,** egestion, emesis, the pukes *and* the heaves (*both informal*); **retching,** heaving, gagging; nausea; **vomit,** vomitus, puke *and* barf (*both informal*), spew, egesta; the dry heaves (*informal*), the boak *or* the dry boak (*Scottish*); vomiturition

9 **belch, burp** (*informal*), belching, wind, gas, eructation; **hiccup**

10 **fart** (*informal*), **flatulence** *or* flatulency, flatuosity, flatus, gas, wind, pump (*Scottish informal*)

11 **ejector,** expeller, fuge; **ouster,** evictor; **bouncer** *and* chucker (*both informal*), chucker-out (*informal*)

12 **dischargee,** expellee; ejectee; evictee

verbs

13 **to eject, expel, discharge,** extrude, obtrude, detrude, exclude, **reject,** cast, remove; frogmarch; **oust, bounce** (*informal*), give the hook (*US & Canadian informal*), **put out, turn out,** thrust out; **throw out,** run out (*informal*), cast out, chuck out, give the chuck to (*informal*), toss out, heave out, throw *or* kick downstairs; kick *or* boot out (*informal*); give the bum's rush *or* give the old heave-ho *or* throw out on one's ear (*all informal*); defenestrate; jettison, throw overboard, discard, junk, throw away; **be rid of,** be shut of, see the last of

14 **to drive out, run out,** chase out, chase away, run off, **rout out;** drum out, read out (*US & Canadian*); freeze out (*informal*), push out, force out, send packing, send about one's business; **hunt out,** harry out; **smoke out,** drive into the open; run out of town (*US & Canadian*), ride on a rail (*US & Canadian informal*)

15 **to evict, oust,** dislodge, dispossess, put out, turn out, **turn out of doors,** turn out of house and home, turn *or* put out bag and baggage, throw into the street; unhouse, unkennel

16 **to depopulate,** dispeople, unpeople; devastate, desolate

17 **to banish, expel, cast out,** thrust out, relegate, **ostracize,** disfellowship, exclude, send down, **blackball,** spurn, thumb down, turn thumbs down on, snub, cut, give the cold shoulder, send to Coventry, give the silent treatment; **excommunicate; exile, expatriate, deport,** transport, send away, **extradite; deport; outlaw,**

fugitate (*Scottish law*), ban, proscribe; rusticate, send down

18 **to dismiss, send off** *or* **away, turn off** *or* **away,** turf out (*informal*), bundle, bundle off *or* out, hustle out, pack off, **send packing,** send about one's business, send to the showers (*informal*); bow out, **show the door,** show the gate; give the gate *or* the air (*US & Canadian informal*)

19 **to dismiss, discharge, expel, cashier,** drum out, disemploy, outplace, separate forcibly *or* involuntarily, **lay off,** suspend, surplus, furlough (*US*), turn off, make redundant, turn out, release, let go, let out, remove, displace, replace, strike off the rolls, give the pink slip (*US*), downsize, rightsize; unfrock, defrock; degrade, demote, strip, deplume, displume, deprive; depose, disbar *see* 447.4; break, bust (*informal*); **retire,** put on the retired list; invalid; pension off, superannuate, put out to pasture; read out of (*US & Canadian*); kick upstairs

20 (*informal terms*) **to fire, can, sack, bump,** bounce, kick, boot, give the axe, give one one's books, give one one's jotters (*Scottish*), give one the sack *or* the axe *or* the boot *or* the bullet, give one the gate *or* the air *or* one's walking papers (*US & Canadian*), send one to the showers, show one the door *or* gate

21 **to do away with, exterminate, annihilate,** disappear; purge, liquidate; **shake off,** shoo, dispel; **throw off,** fling off, cast off; **eliminate, get rid of** *see* 772.5; throw away *see* 390.7

22 **to evacuate, void; eliminate,** remove; **empty,** empty out, deplete, **exhaust,** vent, drain; **clear, purge,** clean *or* scour out, clear off *or* out *or* away, clear, unfoul, unclog, flush out, blow, blow out, sweep out, make a clean sweep, clear the decks; defecate *see* 12.13

23 **to unload,** off-load, unlade, unpack, disburden, unburden, **discharge, dump;** unship, break bulk; pump out

24 **to let out, give vent to,** give out *or* off, throw off, blow off, **emit, exhaust,** evacuate, let go; **exhale,** expire, breathe out, let one's breath out, blow, puff, fume, steam, vapour, smoke, reek; open the sluices *or* floodgates, turn on the tap

25 **to disgorge,** debouch, disembogue, **discharge, exhaust, expel,** ejaculate, throw out, **cast forth,** send out *or* forth; **erupt,** eruct, **blow out,** extravasate; **pour out** *or* **forth,** pour, outpour, decant; **spew,** jet, spout, squirt, **spurt**

26 **to vomit,** spew, **disgorge, regurgitate,** egest, **throw up,** bring up, be sick, sick up (*informal*), cast *or* heave the gorge; **retch,** keck (*US*), heave, **gag;** reject; be seasick, feed the fish

27 (*informal terms*) **to puke,** honk, upchuck (*US & Canadian*), chuck up, chunder (*Australian*), urp (*US & Canadian*), oops *or* oops up (*US & Canadian*), shoot *or* blow *or* toss one's cookies *or* lunch (*US & Canadian*), barf (*US & Canadian*), ralph *or* ralph up (*US & Canadian*), blow grits (*US & Canadian*), boak (*Scottish*)

28 **to belch, burp** (*informal*), rift (*informal*), eruct, eructate; **hiccup**

29 **to fart** (*informal*), blow off (*informal*), let *or* lay *or*

cut a fart (*US & Canadian informal*), let *or* break wind, pump (*Scottish informal*)

adjectives

30 **ejective, expulsive,** ejaculative, emissive, extrusive; eliminant; vomitive, vomitory; eructative; flatulent, flatuous; **rejected** *see* 372.3, rejective

exclamations

31 **go away!,** begone!, get you gone!, go along!, get along!, **run along!, get along with you!,** away!, away with you!, **off with you!,** off you go!, on your way!, go about your business!, be off!, **get out of here!,** get out!, clear out!, leave!, *allez!* (*French*), *allez-vous-en!* (*French*), *va-t'-en!* (*French*), *raus mit dir!* (*German*), *heraus!* (*German*), *¡váyase!* (*Spanish*), *via!* *or* *va' via!* (*Italian*), shoo!, scat!, git! (*informal*), "stand not on the order of your going, but go at once"—SHAKESPEARE, "go and hang yourself"—PLAUTUS

32 (*informal terms*) **beat it!,** hop it!, **scram!,** buzz off!, bugger off!, sod off!, piss off!, naff off!, fuck off! (*taboo*), on your bike!, shoo!, skiddoo! (*US & Canadian*), skedaddle!, vamoose!, cheese it!, make yourself scarce!, **get lost!,** take a walk!, take a hike!, take a running jump!, go chase yourself!, go fuck yourself! (*taboo*), go play in the traffic!, get the hell out!, push off!, shove off!, take a powder! (*US & Canadian*), blow!

909 OVERRUNNING

nouns

1 **overrunning, overgoing, overpassing;** overrun, overpass; **overspreading,** overgrowth; inundation, whelming, overwhelming; burying, burial; seizure, taking *see* 480; overflowing *see* 238.6; exaggeration *see* 355; surplus, excess *see* 992; superiority *see* 249

2 **infestation,** infestment; **invasion,** swarming, swarm, teeming, ravage, plague; **overrunning, overswarming,** overspreading; lousiness, pediculosis

3 **overstepping, transgression, trespass,** inroad, usurpation, incursion, intrusion, **encroachment,** infraction, **infringement**

verbs

4 **to overrun, overgo, overpass,** overreach, go beyond; overstep, overstride; overleap, overjump; **overshoot,** overshoot the mark, overshoot the field; exaggerate *see* 355.3; superabound, exceed, **overdo** *see* 992.10

5 **to overspread,** bespread, spread over; **overgrow,** grow over, run riot, cover, swarm over, teem over

6 **to infest, beset,** invade, swarm, ravage, plague; **overrun, overswarm,** overspread; **creep with, crawl with,** swarm with; seize *see* 480.14

7 **to run over,** overrun; **ride over,** override, **run down,** ride down; **trample, trample on** *or* **upon,** trample down, tread upon, step on, walk on *or* over, trample underfoot, **ride roughshod over;** tread on someone's toes *or* corns (*informal*); hit-and-run; **inundate, whelm, overwhelm;** overflow *see* 238.17; shout down

8 **to pass, go** *or* **pass by,** get *or* shoot ahead of;

bypass; **pass over, cross,** go across, ford; step over, overstride, bestride, straddle

9 **to overstep, transgress, trespass,** intrude, break bounds, overstep the bounds, go too far, know no bounds, **encroach, infringe,** invade, irrupt, make an inroad *or* incursion *or* intrusion, advance upon; usurp

adjectives

10 **overrun, overspread,** overpassed, bespread; overgrown; inundated, whelmed, overwhelmed; buried

11 **infested,** beset, ravaged, teeming, plagued; lousy, pediculous, pedicular; wormy, grubby; ratty

910 SHORTCOMING
motion or action short of

nouns

1 **shortcoming,** falling short, not measuring up, coming up short, **shortfall; shortage,** short measure, underage, deficit; **inadequacy** *see* 794.1; insufficiency *see* 991; delinquency; **default,** defalcation; arrear, **arrears,** arrearage; decline, slump; defectiveness, imperfection *see* 1002; inferiority *see* 250; **undercommitment; failure** *see* 410

verbs

2 **to fall short, come short, run short,** stop short, not make the course, not reach; not measure up, not hack it *and* not make the grade (*both informal*), not make the cut (*US & Canadian informal*), not make it, not make out, not cut the mustard (*informal*); want, want for, lack, not have it (*informal*), **be found wanting,** not answer, not fill the bill, not suffice; not reach to, not stretch; decline, lag, lose ground, slump, collapse, fall away, run out of gas *or* steam; **lose out, fail** *see* 410.9

3 **to fall through,** fall down, **fall to the ground,** fall flat, **collapse,** break down; get bogged down, get mired, get mired down, get hung up, come to nothing, come to naught, end up *or* go up in smoke; **fizzle** *or* peter out (*both informal*); fall *or* drop by the wayside,
end "not with a bang but a whimper"—T S ELIOT

4 **to miss, miscarry,** go amiss, go astray, **miss the mark,** miss by a mile (*informal*); misfire; **miss out,** miss the boat *or* bus; miss stays, miss one's mooring

adjectives

5 **short of,** short, fresh *or* clean out of (*informal*), all out of (*informal*), not all *or* what it is cracked up to be; **deficient, inadequate** *see* 794.4; **insufficient** *see* 991.9; undercommitted; **inferior** *see* 250.6; **lacking,** wanting, minus, bankrupt of; unreached

adverbs

6 **behind,** behindhand, in arrears *or* arrear

7 **amiss, astray, beside the mark,** below the mark, beside the point, far from it, to no purpose, in vain, vainly, fruitlessly, bootlessly

911 ELEVATION
act of raising

nouns

1 **elevation, raising, lifting,** upping, boosting *and* hiking (*both informal*); **rearing,** escalation, **erection;** uprearing, uplifting; upbuoying; **uplift,** upheaval, upthrow, upcast, upthrust; **exaltation;** apotheosis, deification; beatification, canonization; enshrinement, assumption; *sursum corda* (*Latin*); height *see* 272; ascent *see* 193; increase *see* 251

2 **lift, boost** *and* **hike** (*both informal*), hoist, heave; a leg up

3 **lifter, erector;** crane, derrick, gantry crane, crab; **jack,** jackscrew, bottlejack (*NZ*); **hoist,** lift, hydraulic lift; forklift; hydraulic tailgate; lever *see* 905.4; windlass *see* 905.7; tackle

4 **lift, elevator,** *ascenseur* (*French*); escalator, moving staircase *or* stairway; dumbwaiter

verbs

5 **to elevate, raise, rear,** escalate, up, boost *and* hike (*both informal*); **erect, heighten, lift,** levitate, boost (*informal*), **hoist,** heist (*informal*), heft, heave; raise up, rear up, lift up, hold up, set up; stick up, cock up, perk up; buoy up, upbuoy; **upraise, uplift,** uphold, uprear, uphoist; upheave, upthrow, upcast; throw up, cast up; jerk up, hike (*informal*); knock up, lob, loft; sky (*informal*)

6 **to exalt,** elevate, ensky; deify, apotheosize; beatify, canonize; enshrine; put on a pedestal

7 **to give a lift,** give a boost, give a leg up (*informal*), **help up,** put on; mount, horse

8 **to pick up,** take up, pluck up, **gather up;** draw up, fish up, haul up, drag up; dredge, dredge up

adjectives

9 **raised, lifted, elevated;** upraised, **uplifted,** upcast; **reared,** upreared; rearing, rampant; upthrown, upflung; **exalted, lofty;** deified, apotheosized; canonized, sainted, beatified; enshrined, sublime; stilted, on stilts; erect, upright *see* 200.11; high *see* 272.19

10 **elevating,** elevatory, escalatory; lifting; **uplifting;** erective, erectile

912 DEPRESSION
act of lowering

nouns

1 **depression, lowering;** sinking; ducking, submergence, pushing *or* thrusting under, down-thrust, down-thrusting, detrusion, pushing *or* pulling *or* hauling down; reduction, de-escalation, diminution; demotion *see* 447, debasement, degradation; concavity, hollowness *see* 284.1; descent *see* 194; decrease *see* 252

2 **downthrow,** downcast; **overthrow,** overturn *see* 205.2; **precipitation,** fall, downfall; downpour, downpouring

3 **crouch, stoop,** bend, squat; **bow,** genuflection, kneeling, kowtow, kowtowing, salaam, reverence, obeisance, **curtsy;** bob, duck, nod; prostration, supination; crawling, grovelling; abasement, self-abasement

verbs

4 **to depress, lower,** let *or* take down, debase, de-escalate, **sink,** bring low, reduce, couch; pull *or* haul down, take down a peg (*informal*); bear down, downbear; thrust *or* press *or* push down, detrude; indent *see* 284.14

5 **to fell, drop, bring down,** fetch down, down (*informal*), take down, take down a peg, lay low; **raze** *or* **rase,** raze to the ground; **level,** lay level; pull down, pull about one's ears; **cut down,** chop down, hew down, whack down (*informal*), mow down; **knock down,** dash down, send headlong, **floor,** deck *and* lay out (*both informal*), lay by the heels, ground, **bowl down** *or* **over** (*informal*); trip, trip up, topple, tumble; **prostrate,** supinate; **throw,** throw *or* fling *or* cast down, **precipitate;** bulldog; spread-eagle (*informal*), pin, pin down; blow over *or* down

6 **to overthrow,** overturn *see* 205.6; depose *see* 447.4; demote *see* 447.3

7 **to drop, let go of,** let drop *or* fall

8 **to crouch, duck,** cringe, **cower; stoop, bend, stoop down, squat,** squat down, get down, hunker *and* hunker down *and* get down on one's hunkers (*all informal*); hunch, hunch down, hunch over

9 **to bow, bend, kneel,** genuflect, bend the knee, curtsy, make a low bow, make a leg, make a reverence *or* an obeisance, salaam, bob, duck; **kowtow,** prostrate oneself; crawl, grovel; wallow, welter

10 **to sit down,** seat oneself, **be seated** *see* 173.10

11 **to lie down,** couch, drape oneself, **recline** *see* 201.5; prostrate, supinate, prone (*informal*); flatten oneself, prostrate oneself; hit the ground *or* the dirt (*informal*)

adjectives

12 **depressed, lowered,** debased, reduced, **fallen;** sunk, **sunken,** submerged; downcast, downthrown; prostrated, prostrate *see* 201.8; low, at a low ebb

913 CIRCUITOUSNESS

nouns

1 **circuitousness,** circuity, circuition (*old*); **roundaboutness,** indirection, ambagiousness (*old*), meandering, deviance *or* deviancy, **deviation** *see* 164; deviousness, **digression,** circumlocution *see* 538.5; **excursion,** excursus; **circling, wheeling,** circulation, rounding, orbit, **orbiting; spiralling,** spiral, gyring, gyre; circumambulation, circumambience *or* circumambiency, circumflexion, circumnavigation, circummigration; turning, **turn** *see* 164.1; circularity *see* 280; convolution *see* 281

2 **circuit, round,** revolution, **circle,** full circle, go-round, **cycle,** orbit, ambit; pass; round trip, *aller-retour* (*French*); **beat,** rounds, **walk,** tour, turn, lap, loop; round robin; milk round

3 **detour, bypass, roundabout way,** roundabout, ambages (*old*), circuit, circumbendibus (*informal*), the long way around, digression, deviation, excursion

verbs

4 **to go roundabout,** meander, deviate, go around Robin Hood's barn, take *or* go the long way around, twist and turn; **detour,** make a detour, **go around,** go round about, go out of one's way, **bypass;** deviate *see* 164.3; digress *see* 538.9; **talk in circles,** say in a roundabout way; equivocate *see* 935.9, shilly-shally; dodge *see* 368.8

5 **to circle, circuit,** describe a circle, make a circuit, move in a circle, **circulate; go round** *or* **around,** go about; **wheel,** orbit, round; make a pass; come full circle, close the circle, make a round trip, return to the starting point; cycle; spiral, gyre; go around in circles, chase one's tail, go round and round; revolve *see* 914.9; **compass,** encompass, encircle, surround; skirt, flank; go the round, make the round of, make one's rounds, circuiteer (*old*); lap; circumambulate, circummigrate; circumnavigate, girdle, girdle the globe,
"put a girdle round about the earth"—SHAKESPEARE

6 **to turn, go around, round,** turn *or* round a corner, corner, round a bend, double *or* round a point

adjectives

7 **circuitous, roundabout, out-of-the-way, devious, oblique, indirect,** ambagious (*old*), **meandering,** backhanded; **deviative** *see* 164.7, **deviating,** digressive, discursive, excursive; equivocatory *see* 935.14; evasive *see* 368.15; vacillating *see* 362.10; **circular** *see* 280.11, **round,** wheel-shaped, O-shaped; spiral, helical; orbital; rotary *see* 914.15

8 circumambient, circumambulatory, circumforaneous, circumfluent, circumvolant, circumnavigatory, circumnavigable

adverbs

9 **circuitously, deviously, obliquely,** ambagiously (*old*), **indirectly, round about,** about it and about, round Robin Hood's barn, in a roundabout way, by a side door, by a side wind; circlewise, wheelwise

914 ROTATION

nouns

1 **rotation, revolution, roll,** gyration, **spin,** circulation; axial motion, rotational motion, angular motion, angular momentum, angular velocity; circumrotation, circumgyration, full circle; **turning, whirling,** swirling, **spinning,** wheeling, reeling, whir; **spiralling,** twisting upward *or* downward, gyring, volution, turbination; centrifugation; swivelling, pivoting, swinging; **rolling,** trolling, trundling, bowling, volutation (*old*)

2 **whirl, wheel, reel, spin, turn,** round; spiral, helix, helicoid, gyre; pirouette; **swirl, twirl, eddy,** gurge, surge; vortex, **whirlpool,** maelstrom, Charybdis; dizzy round, rat race; tourbillion, **whirlwind** *see* 318.14

3 revolutions, **revs** (*informal*); revolutions per minute *or* rpm

4 **rotator, rotor;** centrifuge; **roller,** rundle; **whirler,** whirligig, **top,** whirlabout; **merry-go-round,** carousel, roundabout; **wheel,** disc; Ixion's wheel; rolling stone

5 axle, axis; pivot, gudgeon, trunnion, **swivel**, **spindle**, arbor, pole, radiant; fulcrum *see* 900.2; pin, pintle; **hub**, nave; axle shaft, axle spindle, axle bar, axle-tree; distaff; mandrel; gimbal; **hinge**, hingle (*informal*); rowlock, oarlock

6 axle box, journal, journal box; hotbox

7 bearing, ball bearing, journal bearing, saw bearing, tumbler bearing, main bearing, needle bearing, roller bearing, thrust bearing, bevel bearing, bushing; jewel; headstock

8 (*science of rotation*) trochilics, gyrostatics

verbs

9 to rotate, revolve, spin, **turn**, round, **go round** *or* **around**, turn round *or* around; **spiral, gyrate**, gyre; circumrotate, circumvolute; circle, circulate; **swivel, pivot, wheel**, swing; pirouette, turn a pirouette; wheelie (*informal*), do a wheelie (*informal*); wind, twist, screw, crank; wamble

10 to roll, trundle, troll, **bowl**; roll up, **furl**

11 to whirl, whirligig, twirl, **wheel, reel, spin**, spin like a top *or* teetotum, whirl like a dervish; centrifuge, centrifugate; **swirl**, gurge, surge, **eddy**, whirlpool

12 (*move around in confusion*) **to seethe, mill**, mill around *or* about, stir, roil, moil, be turbulent

13 (*roll about in*) **to wallow, welter**, grovel, roll, flounder, tumble

adjectives

14 rotating, revolving, **turning**, gyrating, centrifugal; **whirling, swirling**, twirling, **spinning**, wheeling, **reeling; rolling**, trolling, bowling

15 rotary, **rotational**, rotatory, rotative; trochilic, vertiginous; circumrotatory, circumvolutory, circumgyratory; spiral, spiralling, helical, gyral, gyratory, gyrational, gyroscopic, gyrostatic; whirly, swirly, gulfy; whirlabout, whirligig; vortical, cyclonic, tornadic, whirlwindy, whirlwindish

adverbs

16 round, around, round about, **in a circle; round and round**, in circles, like a horse in a mill; in a whirl, in a spin; head over heels, heels over head; clockwise, deasil, counterclockwise, anticlockwise, withershins *or* widdershins

915 OSCILLATION
motion to and fro

nouns

1 oscillation, vibration, vibrancy; to-and-fro motion; harmonic motion, simple harmonic motion; libration, nutation; pendulation; **fluctuation**, vacillation, wavering *see* 362.2; libration of the moon, libration in latitude *or* longitude; vibratility; **frequency**, frequency band *or* spectrum; resonance, resonant *or* resonance frequency; **periodicity** *see* 849.2

2 waving, wave motion, **undulation**, undulancy; **brandishing, flourishing**, flaunting, shaking; brandish, flaunt, flourish; wave *see* 238.14

3 pulsation, pulse, beat, throb; beating, throbbing; systole, diastole; rat-a-tat, staccato, rataplan, drumming *see* 55.1; **rhythm, tempo** *see* 709.24;

palpitation, flutter, arrhythmia, pitter-patter, pit-a-pat; fibrillation, ventricular fibrillation, tachycardia, ventricular tachycardia (*all medicine*); **heartbeat, heartthrob**

4 wave, wave motion, **ray**; transverse wave, longitudinal wave; electromagnetic wave, electromagnetic radiation; **light** *see* 1024; **radio wave** *see* 1033.11; mechanical wave; acoustic wave, **sound wave** *see* 50.1; seismic wave, **shock wave**; de Broglie wave; diffracted wave, guided wave; one- *or* two- *or* three-dimensional wave; periodic wave; standing wave, node, antinode; surface wave, **tidal wave**, tsunami; travelling wave; bore; surge, storm surge; amplitude, crest, trough; scend; **surf**, roller, curler, comber, whitecap, white horse; tube, pipeline; wavelength; frequency, frequency band *or* spectrum; resonance, resonant *or* resonance frequency; period; wave number; diffraction; reinforcement, interference; in phase, out of phase; wave equation, Schrödinger equation; Huygens' principle

5 alternation, reciprocation; regular *or* rhythmic play, **coming and going**, to-and-fro, back-and-forth, ebb and flow, *va-et-vien* (*French*), flux and reflux, systole and diastole, ups and downs; sine wave, Lissajous figure *or* curve; **seesawing**, teetering, tottering, **teeter-tottering**; seesaw, teeter, teeter-totter, wigwag; zigzag, zigzagging, zig, zag

6 swing, swinging, **sway**, swag; **rock, lurch, roll, reel**, careen; wag, waggle; wave, waver

7 seismicity, seismism; seismology, seismography, seismometry

8 (*instruments*) oscilloscope, oscillograph, oscillometer; wavemeter; harmonograph; vibroscope, vibrograph; kymograph; seismoscope, seismograph, seismometer; wave gauge

9 oscillator, vibrator; pendulum, pendulum wheel; metronome; swing; seesaw, teeter, teeter-totter (*US & Canadian*), teeterboard, teetery-bender; rocker, rocking chair; rocking stone, logan stone, shuttle; shuttlecock

verbs

10 to oscillate, vibrate, librate, nutate; pendulate; **fluctuate**, vacillate, waver, wave; resonate; **swing, sway**, swag, dangle, **reel, rock, lurch, roll**, careen, toss, pitch; wag, waggle; **wobble**, coggle (*Scottish*), wamble; **bob**, bobble; shake, flutter *see* 916.10, 12

11 to wave, undulate; **brandish, flourish**, flaunt, shake, swing, wield; float, fly; **flap, flutter**; wag, wigwag

12 to pulsate, pulse, **beat, throb**, not miss a beat; **palpitate**, go pit-a-pat; miss a beat; beat time, beat out, tick, ticktock; drum *see* 55.4

13 to alternate, reciprocate, swing, **go to and fro**, to-and-fro, **come and go**, pass and re-pass, ebb and flow, wax and wane, back and fill; **seesaw**, teeter, **teeter-totter**; shuttle, shuttlecock, battledore and shuttlecock; **wigwag**, wibble-wabble; zigzag

14 (*move up and down*) **to pump, shake**, bounce

adjectives

15 oscillating, oscillatory; **vibrating**, vibratory, harmonic; vibratile; librational, libratory; nutational; **periodic**, pendular, pendulous; **fluctuating**, fluctuational, fluctuant; wavering; vacillating, vacillatory; resonant

16 waving, undulating, undulatory, undulant

17 swinging, swingy, **swaying,** dangling, **reeling, rocking, lurching,** careening, **rolling,** tossing, pitching

18 pulsative, pulsatory, pulsatile; **pulsating, pulsing, beating, throbbing, palpitating,** palpitant, pit-a-pat, staccato; rhythmic *see* 709.28

19 alternate, **reciprocal,** reciprocative; sine-wave; **back-and-forth, to-and-fro,** up-and-down, seesaw

20 seismatical, seismological, seismographic, seismometric; successive, successatory, sussultatory

adverbs

21 to and fro, back and forth, backward and forward, backwards and forwards, **in and out, up and down,** seesaw, shuttlewise, from side to side, from pillar to post, off and on, round and round, like buckets in a well

916 AGITATION
irregular motion

nouns

1 agitation, perturbation, hecticness, conturbation (*old*); **frenzy, excitement** *see* 105; **trepidation** *see* 127.5, trepidity, fidgets *and* jitters *and* ants in the pants (*all informal*), jitteriness (*informal*), antsiness (*US & Canadian informal*), jumpiness, nervousness, yips (*informal*), nerviness, nervosity, twitter, upset; **unrest, malaise, unease,** restlessness; fever, feverishness, febrility; **disquiet,** disquietude, inquietude, discomposure; **stir, churn, ferment,** fermentation, foment; **seethe,** seething, ebullition, boil, boiling; embroilment, roil, turbidity, fume, **disturbance, commotion,** moil, **turmoil, turbulence** *see* 671.2, **swirl, tumult,** tumultuation, hubbub, shemozzle (*informal*), rout, fuss, carry-on (*informal*), row, to-do, kerfuffle (*informal*), bluster, fluster, flurry, flutteration, hoo-ha *and* flap (*both informal*), bustle, brouhaha, bobbery, hurly-burly; maelstrom; **disorder** *see* 809

2 shaking, quaking, palsy, **quivering, quavering, shivering, trembling,** tremulousness, **shuddering, vibration;** juddering, judder, succussion; jerkiness, fits and starts, spasms; jactation, jactitation; joltiness, bumpiness, the shakes *and* the shivers *and* the cold shivers (*all informal*), ague, chattering; chorea, St Vitus's dance; delirium tremens *or* the DT's

3 shake, quake, quiver, quaver, falter, **tremor, tremble, shiver, shudder,** twitter, didder, dither; **wobble; bob,** bobble; **jog,** joggle; **shock, jolt,** jar, jostle; **bounce,** bump; **jerk, twitch,** tic, grimace, rictus; jig, jiggle

4 flutter, flitter, flit, **flicker, waver,** dance; shake, quiver *see* 916.3; **sputter, splutter; flap,** flop (*informal*); **beat,** beating; **palpitation,** throb, pit-a-pat, pitter-patter

5 twitching, jerking, vellication; **fidgets,** fidgetiness; itchiness, formication, pruritus

6 spasm, convulsion, cramp, **paroxysm,** throes; **orgasm,** sexual climax; epitasis, eclampsia; **seizure,**

grip, attack, **fit,** access, ictus; epilepsy, falling sickness; stroke, apoplexy

7 wiggle, wriggle; wag, waggle; writhe, **squirm**

8 flounder, flounce, stagger, totter, stumble, falter; wallow, welter; **roll, rock, reel, lurch,** careen, **swing, sway; toss, tumble,** pitch, plunge

9 (*instruments*) **agitator,** shaker, jiggler, vibrator; beater, stirrer, paddle, whisk, eggbeater; churn; blender

verbs

10 to agitate, shake, disturb, perturb, shake up, perturbate, **disquiet, discompose, upset, trouble, unsettle, stir,** swirl, flurry, flutter, put the cat among the pigeons, fret, roughen, ruffle, rumple, ripple, ferment, convulse; **churn,** whip, whisk, beat, paddle; **excite** *see* 105.11; **stir up,** cause a stir *or* commotion, shake up *or* stir up a hornet's nest (*informal*); work up, shake up, churn up, whip up, beat up; roil, rile (*informal*); disarrange *see* 810.2

11 to shake, quake, vibrate, judder, jactitate; **tremble, quiver, quaver,** falter, **shudder, shiver,** twitter, didder, chatter; shake in one's boots *or* shoes, quake *or*, shake *or* tremble like an aspen leaf, have the jitters *or* the shakes (*informal*), have ants in one's pants (*informal*); have an ague; **wobble; bob,** bobble; **jog,** joggle; **shock, jolt,** jar, jostle, hustle, jounce, **bounce,** jump, bump

12 to flutter, flitter, flit, flick, **flicker,** gutter, bicker, wave, **waver,** dance; **sputter, splutter; flap,** flop (*informal*), flip, beat, slat; **palpitate,** pulse, throb, pitter-patter, go pit-a-pat

13 to twitch, jerk, vellicate; itch; **jig, jiggle,** jigger *or* jigget (*US & Canadian informal*); **fidget,** have the fidgets

14 to wiggle, wriggle; wag, waggle; **writhe, squirm,** twist and turn; have ants in one's pants (*informal*)

15 to flounder, flounce, **stagger,** totter, stumble, falter, blunder, wallop; **struggle,** labour; **wallow, welter; roll, rock, reel, lurch,** careen, career, **swing, sway; toss, tumble,** thrash about, **pitch, plunge,** pitch and plunge, toss and tumble, toss and turn, be the sport of winds and waves; **seethe**

adjectives

16 agitated, disturbed, perturbed, disquieted, discomposed, troubled, upset, ruffled, flurried, flustered, unsettled; stirred up, shaken, shaken up, all worked up, all shook up (*informal*); troublous, feverish, fidgety *and* jittery (*informal*), antsy (*US & Canadian informal*), jumpy, nervous, nervy, restless, **uneasy,** unquiet, unpeaceful; all of a twitter (*informal*), all of a flutter; **turbulent;** excited *see* 105.18, 20, 22

17 shaking, vibrating, chattering; **quivering, quavering, quaking, shivering, shuddering, trembling, tremulous,** palsied, aspen; successive, successatory; **shaky,** quivery, quavery, shivery, trembly; wobbly

18 fluttering, flickering, wavering, guttering, dancing; sputtering, spluttering, sputtery; fluttery, flickery, bickering, flicky, wavery, unsteady, desultory

19 jerky, herky-jerky (*US & Canadian informal*), twitchy *or* twitchety, jerking, **twitching, fidgety,**

jumpy, vellicative; **spastic, spasmodic,** eclamptic, orgasmic, convulsive; fitful, saltatory

20 jolting, jolty, **joggling,** joggly, jogglety, jouncy, **bouncy, bumpy,** choppy, rough; **jarring,** bone-bruising

21 wriggly, wriggling, crawly, creepy-crawly (*informal*); **wiggly,** wiggling; squirmy, squirming; writhy, writhing, antsy (*US & Canadian informal*)

adverbs

22 agitatedly, troublously, restlessly, uneasily, unquietly, unpeacefully, nervously, feverishly; **excitedly**

23 shakily, quiveringly, quaveringly, quakingly, **tremblingly,** shudderingly, tremulously; flutteringly, waveringly, unsteadily, desultorily; **jerkily,** spasmodically, fitfully, by jerks, by snatches, saltatorily, by fits and starts, "with many a flirt and flutter"—POPE

917 SPECTATOR

nouns

1 spectator, observer; looker, **onlooker,** looker-on, **watcher,** gazer, gazer-on, gaper, goggler, **viewer,** seer, beholder, perceiver, percipient; spectatress, spectatrix; **witness, eyewitness; bystander,** passerby; innocent bystander; kibitzer (*US & Canadian informal*); girl-watcher, ogler; bird-watcher, birder, twitcher (*informal*); train spotter; **viewer,** television-viewer, televiewer, video-gazer, TV-viewer, couch potato (*informal*)

2 attender *see* 221.5, attendee; theatregoer; **audience** *see* 48.6, house, crowd, gate, fans, punters (*informal*)

3 sightseer, excursionist, **tourist,** holiday-maker, rubberneck *or* **rubbernecker** (*informal*); slummer; tour group; coach party

4 sight-seeing, rubbernecking (*informal*), lionism (*informal*); **tour,** walking tour, bus tour, sightseeing tour *or* excursion

verbs

5 to spectate (*informal*), witness, **see** *see* 27.12, look on, eye, **ogle, gape;** take in, **look at, watch;** attend *see* 221.8

6 to sight-see, see the sights, take in the sights, lionize *or* see the lions (*both informal*); **rubberneck** (*informal*); go slumming; go on a tour, join a tour

adjectives

7 spectating, spectatorial; **onlooking;** sight-seeing, rubberneck (*informal*); passing by, caught in the cross-fire *or* in the middle

918 INTELLECT
mental faculty

nouns

1 intellect, mind, *mens* (*Latin*); mental *or* intellectual faculty, nous, **reason, rationality,** rational *or* reasoning faculty, power of reason, *Vernunft* (*German*), *esprit* (*French*), *raison* (*French*), ratio, discursive reason,

"discourse of reason"—SHAKESPEARE, **intelligence,** mentality, mental capacity, **understanding,** reasoning, intellection, conception; **brain, brains,** brainpower, smarts *and* grey matter *and* little grey cells (*all informal*); **thought** *see* 930; head, headpiece

2 wits, senses, faculties, parts, capacities, intellectual gifts *or* talents, mother wit; intellectuals (*old*); consciousness *see* 927.2

3 inmost mind, inner recesses of the mind, mind's core, deepest mind, centre of the mind; inner man; subconscious, subconscious mind; inmost heart

4 psyche, spirit, spiritus, **soul,** *âme* (*French*), **heart, mind,** anima, *anima humana* (*Latin*); shade, shadow, manes; breath, pneuma, breath of life, divine breath; *atman and purusha and buddhi and jiva and jivatma* (*all Sanskrit*); *ba and khu* (*both Egyptian myth*); *ruach and nephesh* (*both Hebrew*); spiritual being, inner man, "the Divinity that stirs within us"—ADDISON; **ego,** the self, the I

5 life principle, vital principle, vital spirit *or* soul, *élan vital–* (Henri Bergson (*French*)), **vital force,** prana (*Hinduism*); essence *or* substance of life, individual essence, *ousia* (*Greek*); divine spark, vital spark *or* flame

6 brain *see* 2.13, seat *or* organ of thought; sensory, sensorium; encephalon; grey matter, head, pate *and* sconce *and* noddle (*all informal*), loaf (*informal*); noddle *or* noodle *or* noggin *or* bean *or* chump *or* upper storey (*all informal*); sensation *see* 24

adjectives

7 mental, intellectual, rational, reasoning, thinking, noetic, conceptive, conceptual, phrenic; intelligent *see* 919.12; noological; endopsychic, psychic, psychical, psychologic, psychological, spiritual; cerebral; subjective, internal

919 INTELLIGENCE, WISDOM
mental capacity

nouns

1 intelligence, understanding, *Verstand* (*German*), **comprehension,** apprehension, mental *or* intellectual grasp, prehensility of mind, intellectual power, brainpower, thinking power, power of mind *or* thought; ideation, conception; integrative power, esemplastic power; rationality, reasoning *or* deductive power, ratiocination; **sense, wit,** mother wit, natural *or* native wit; **intellect** *see* 918; **intellectuality,** intellectualism; capacity, mental capacity, **mentality,** calibre, reach *or* compass *or* scope of mind; **IQ** *or* intelligence quotient, mental ratio, mental age; sanity *see* 924; knowledge *see* 927

2 smartness, braininess, smarts *and* savvy (*both informal*), **brightness, brilliance, cleverness,** aptness, aptitude, native cleverness, mental alertness, nous, **sharpness, keenness,** acuity, acuteness; **mental ability** *or* **capability,** gift, gifts, giftedness, **talent, flair, genius;** quickness, nimbleness, quickness *or* nimbleness of wit, adroitness, dexterity; sharp-wittedness, keen-wittedness, quick-wittedness, nimble-wittedness; nimble mind, mercurial mind, quick parts, clear *or* quick thinking; ready wit, quick wit, sprightly wit, *esprit* (*French*)

3 **shrewdness, artfulness, cunning,** cunningness, canniness, **craft, craftiness,** wiliness, guilefulnes, slickness (*informal*), **slyness,** pawkiness, foxiness (*informal*), peasant *or* animal cunning, low cunning; subtility, subtilty, **subtlety;** insinuation, insidiousness, deviousness

4 **sagacity,** sagaciousness, **astuteness, acumen,** longheadedness; **foresight,** foresightedness, providence; **farsightedness,** farseeingness, longsightedness; **discernment, insight,** penetration, acuteness, acuity; perspicacity, perspicaciousness, perspicuity, perspicuousness; incisiveness, trenchancy, cogency; **percipience** *or* percipiency, **perception,** apperception; **sensibility** *see* 24.2

5 **wisdom,** ripe wisdom, seasoned understanding, mellow wisdom, wiseness, sageness, sapience, good *or* sound understanding; Sophia (*female personification of wisdom*); erudition *see* 927.5; **profundity,** profoundness, depth; broad-mindedness *see* 978; **conventional wisdom,** received wisdom, prudential judgment

6 **sensibleness, reasonableness,** reason, rationality, sanity, saneness, **soundness; practicality,** practical wisdom, practical mind; **sense,** good *or* common *or* plain sense, **horse sense** (*informal*), nous (*informal*), gumption (*informal*); due sense of; level head, cool head, **levelheadedness,** balance, coolheadedness, coolness; soberness, sobriety, **sober-mindedness**

7 **judiciousness, judgment,** good *or* sound judgment, cool judgment, soundness of judgment; **prudence,** prudentialism, providence, policy, polity; weighing, consideration, circumspection, circumspectness; reflection *or* reflexion, reflectiveness, **thoughtfulness; discretion,** discreetness; **discrimination**

8 **genius,** *Geist* (*German*), spirit, soul; daimonion, demon, daemon; **inspiration,** afflatus, divine afflatus; Muse; fire of genius; **creativity;** talent *see* 413.4; creative thought *see* 985.2

9 (*intelligent being*) **intelligence, intellect,** head, brain, mentality, consciousness; wise man *see* 920

verbs

10 **to have all one's wits about one,** have all one's marbles *and* have smarts *or* savvy (*all informal*), have a head on one's shoulders *and* have one's head screwed on right (*both informal*); have method in one's madness; use one's head *or* wits, get *or* keep one's wits about one; know what's what, be wise as a serpent *or* an owl; be reasonable, listen to reason

11 to be brilliant, **scintillate,** sparkle, coruscate

adjectives

12 **intelligent,** intellectual (*old*); ideational, conceptual, conceptive, discursive; sophic, noetic; **knowing, understanding, reasonable, rational, sensible, bright;** sane *see* 924.4; not so dumb (*informal*), strong-minded

13 **clear-witted,** clearheaded, clear-eyed, clear-sighted; no-nonsense; awake, **wide-awake,** alive, **alert,** on the ball (*informal*), slippy (*informal*)

14 **smart,** brainy (*informal*), **bright, brilliant,** scintillating; **clever,** apt, **gifted,** talented; **sharp,**

keen; **quick,** nimble, adroit, dexterous; **sharp-witted,** keen-witted, needle-witted, **quick-witted,** quick-thinking, steel-trap, nimble-witted, quick on the trigger *or* uptake (*informal*); smart as a whip, sharp as a tack (*informal*); nobody's fool *and* no dumbbell *and* not born yesterday (*all informal*); up to snuff (*informal*)

15 **shrewd, artful, cunning, knowing, crafty, wily,** guileful, canny, slick, sly, pawky (*dialect*), downy (*informal*), smart as a fox, foxy *and* crazy like a fox (*both informal*); **subtle,** subtile; insinuating, insidious, devious, Byzantine, calculating

16 **sagacious, astute,** longheaded, argute; **understanding, discerning,** penetrating, incisive, acute, trenchant, cogent, piercing; **foresighted,** foreseeing; forethoughted, forethoughtful, provident; **farsighted,** farseeing, longsighted; **perspicacious,** perspicuous; **perceptive, percipient,** apperceptive, apperceptient

17 **wise, sage,** sapient, seasoned, **knowing; learned** *see* 927.21; **profound,** deep; wise as an owl *or* a serpent, wise as Solomon; wise beyond one's years, in advance of one's age, wise in one's generation; broad-minded *see* 978.8

18 **sensible, reasonable, rational, logical; practical,** pragmatic; philosophical; commonsense, commonsensical (*informal*); **levelheaded,** balanced, coolheaded, cool, **sound, sane,** sober, **sober-minded,** well-balanced

19 **judicious,** judicial, judgmatic, judgmatical, **prudent,** prudential, politic, careful, provident, **considerate,** circumspect, **thoughtful,** reflective, reflecting; **discreet;** discriminative, discriminating; **well-advised,** well-judged, enlightened

adverbs

20 **intelligently, understandingly,** knowingly, discerningly; **reasonably,** rationally, sensibly; **smartly, cleverly; shrewdly,** artfully, cunningly; **wisely,** sagaciously, astutely; **judiciously, prudently,** discreetly, providently, considerately, circumspectly, thoughtfully

920 WISE PERSON

nouns

1 **wise man, wise woman, sage,** sapient, man *or* woman of wisdom; **master, mistress,** authority, mastermind, master spirit of the age, oracle; **philosopher,** thinker, lover of wisdom; "he who, seeing the furthest, has the deepest love for mankind"—Maurice Maeterlinck, "the mouth of a wise man is in his heart"—Benjamin Franklin; rabbi; doctor; great soul, mahatma, guru, rishi; *starets* (*Russian*), elder, wise old man, elder statesman; illuminate; seer; mentor; **intellect,** man of intellect; mandarin, **intellectual** *see* 928; savant, **scholar** *see* 928.3

2 Solomon, Socrates, Plato, Mentor, Nestor, Confucius, Buddha, Gandhi, Albert Schweitzer, Martin Luther King Jr

3 **the wise,** the intelligent, the sensible, the prudent, the knowing, the understanding

4 Seven Wise Men of Greece, Seven Sages, Seven Wise Masters; Solon, Chilon, Pittacus, Bias, Periander, Cleobulus, Thales

5 Magi, Three Wise Men, Wise Men of the East, Three Kings; Three Kings of Cologne; Gaspar *or* Caspar, Melchior, Balthasar

6 **knowall, wiseacre,** wisehead, wiseling, **witling,** wise guy, smart aleck (*informal*), smarty-pants *or* smarty-boots (*informal*), smartarse (*informal*); wise fool; Gothamite, wise man of Gotham, wise man of Chelm

921 UNINTELLIGENCE

nouns

1 **unintelligence,** unintellectuality (*old*), unwisdom, unwiseness, intellectual *or* mental weakness; **senselessness, witlessness, mindlessness,** brainlessness, primal stupidity, *Urdummheit* (*German*), reasonlessness, lackwittedness, lackbrainedness, slackwittedness, slackmindedness; **irrationality;** ignorance *see* 929; foolishness *see* 922; incapacity, ineptitude; low IQ

2 **unperceptiveness,** imperceptiveness, insensibility, impercipience *or* impercipiency, undiscerningness, unapprehendingness, **incomprehension,** nonunderstanding; **blindness,** mindblindness, purblindness; **unawareness,** lack of awareness, unconsciousness, lack of consciousness; **shortsightedness,** nearsightedness, dim-sightedness

3 **stupidity,** stupidness, *bêtise* (*French*), **dumbness** (*informal*), **doltishness,** boobishness, duncery (*old*), dullardism, blockishness, cloddishness, lumpishness, sottishness, **asininity,** ninnyism, simpletonianism; oafishness, oafdom, yokelism, loutishness; **density,** denseness, opacity; grossness, crassness, crudeness, boorishness; **dullness,** dopiness (*informal*), obtuseness, sluggishness, bovinity, cowishness, slowness, lethargy, stolidity, hebetude; **dim-wittedness,** dimness, **dull-wittedness,** slow-wittedness, beef-wittedness, dull-headedness, thick-wittedness, thick-headedness, unteachability, ineducability; wrongheadedness

4 (*informal terms*) **gormlessness, blockheadedness,** woodenheadedness, klutziness, dunderheadedness, goofiness, jolterheadedness *or* joltheadedness, chuckleheadedness, beetleheadedness, chumpiness, numskulledness *or* numskullery, cabbageheadedness, sapheadedness, muttonheadedness, meatheadedness, fatheadedness, boneheadedness, knuckleheadedness, blunderheadedness

5 **muddleheadedness,** addleheadedness, addlepatedness, puzzleheadedness

6 **empty-headedness,** empty-mindedness, absence of mind, airheadedness and bubbleheadedness (*both informal*); **vacuity,** vacuousness, vacancy, vacuum, emptiness, mental void, blankness, hollowness, inanity, vapidity, jejunity

7 **superficiality, shallowness, unprofundity,** lack of depth, unprofoundness, thinness; shallow-wittedness, shallow-mindedness; **frivolousness,** flightiness, lightness, fluffiness, frothiness, volatility, dizziness *and* ditziness (*both informal*)

8 **feeblemindedness,** weak-mindedness; infirmity, weakness, feebleness, softness, mushiness (*informal*)

9 **mental deficiency,** mental retardation, amentia, mental handicap, subnormality, mental defectiveness; **arrested development,** infantilism, retardation, retardment, backwardness; **simplemindedness,** simple-wittedness, simpleness, simplicity; **idiocy,** idiotism (*old*), profound idiocy, **imbecility, half-wittedness,** blithering idiocy; moronity, moronism, **cretinism;** mongolism, mongolianism, mongoloid idiocy, Down's syndrome; insanity *see* 925

10 **senility,** senilism, senile weakness, senile debility, caducity, decrepitude, senectude, decline; **childishness, second childhood, dotage, dotardism;** anility; senile dementia, senile psychosis, Alzheimer's disease

11 **puerility,** puerilism, immaturity, **childishness; infantilism,** babyishness

verbs

12 **to be stupid,** not have all one's marbles; drool, slobber, drivel, dither, blither, blather, maunder, dote, burble; not see an inch beyond one's nose, not have enough sense to come in out of the rain; lose one's mind *or* marbles

adjectives

13 **unintelligent,** unintellectual (*old*), **unthinking, unreasoning, irrational,** unwise, inept, **not bright;** ungifted, untalented; **senseless,** insensate; **mindless, witless, reasonless, brainless,** pin-brained, pea-brained, of little brain, headless; **lackwitted,** lackbrained, slackwitted, slackminded, lean-minded, lean-witted, short-witted; **foolish** *see* 922.8; **ignorant** *see* 929.12

14 **undiscerning, unperceptive,** imperceptive, impercipient, insensible, unapprehending, uncomprehending, nonunderstanding; **shortsighted,** myopic, nearsighted, dim-sighted; **blind,** purblind, mind-blind, blind as a bat; blinded, blindfold, blindfolded

15 **stupid, dumb,** gormless (*informal*), dozy (*informal*), dullard, **doltish,** blockish, klutzy *and* klutzish (*both informal*), duncish, duncical, cloddish, clottish, chumpish (*informal*), lumpish *or* lumpen, **oafish,** boobish, sottish, **asinine,** lamebrained, Boeotian; **dense,** thick (*informal*), opaque, gross, crass, fat; bovine, cowish, beef-witted, beef-brained, beefheaded; unteachable, ineducable; wrongheaded

16 **dull,** dull of mind, **dopey** (*informal*), **obtuse,** blunt, dim, wooden, heavy, sluggish, slow, **slow-witted,** hebetudinous, **dim-witted, dull-witted,** blunt-witted, dull-brained, dull-headed, dull-pated, thick-witted, thick-headed, thick-pated, thick-skulled, thick-brained, fat-witted, gross-witted, gross-headed

17 (*informal terms*) **blockheaded,** woodenheaded, stupidheaded, dumbheaded, dunderheaded, blunderheaded, clueless *or* jolterheaded *or* joltheaded *or* jingle-brained, chuckleheaded, beetleheaded, nitwitted, numskulled, gormless, cabbageheaded, pumpkin-headed, sapheaded, muttonheaded, meatheaded, fatheaded, boneheaded, knuckleheaded, clodpated; dead from the neck up, dead above *or* between the ears, muscle-bound between the ears;

featherheaded, airheaded, bubbleheaded, out to lunch, spastic, spazzy, three bricks short of a load, not playing with a full deck

18 **muddleheaded, fuddlebrained** *and* scramblebrained (*both informal*), mixed-up, muddled, addled, addleheaded, **addlepated**, addlebrained, muddybrained, puzzleheaded, blear-witted; dizzy (*informal*), muzzy, foggy

19 **empty-headed**, empty-minded, empty-noddled, empty-pated, empty-skulled; **vacuous, vacant,** empty, hollow, inane, vapid, jejune, blank, airheaded *and* bubbleheaded (*both informal*); **rattlebrained,** rattleheaded; scatterbrained *see* 984.16

20 **superficial, shallow, unprofound;** shallow-witted, shallow-minded, shallow-brained, shallow-headed, shallow-pated; **frivolous,** dizzy *and* ditzy (*both informal*), flighty, light, volatile, frothy, fluffy, **featherbrained, birdwitted, birdbrained**

21 **feebleminded, weak-minded,** weak, feeble, infirm, soft, soft in the head, weak in the upper storey (*informal*)

22 **mentally deficient,** mentally defective, mentally handicapped, retarded, **mentally retarded,** backward, arrested, subnormal, not right in the head, **not all there** (*informal*); **simpleminded,** simplewitted, simple, simpletonian; **half-witted,** half-baked (*informal*); **idiotic, moronic, imbecile,** imbecilic, cretinous, cretinistic, mongoloid, spastic (*informal*); crackbrained, cracked, crazy; babbling, drivelling, slobbering, drooling, blithering, dithering, maundering, burbling

23 **senile,** decrepit, doddering, doddery; **childish,** childlike, in one's second childhood, **doting,** doited (*Scottish*)

24 **puerile,** immature, **childish;** childlike; **infantile,** infantine; **babyish,** babish

adverbs

25 **unintelligently, stupidly;** insensately, foolishly

922 FOOLISHNESS

nouns

1 **foolishness,** folly, foolery, foolheadedness, stupidity, asininity, *niaiserie* (*French*); *bêtise* (*French*); inanity, fatuity, fatuousness; ineptitude; silliness; frivolousness, frivolity, giddiness; triviality, triflingness, nugacity, desipience; **nonsense,** tomfoolery, poppycock; **senselessness, insensateness, witlessness, thoughtlessness,** brainlessness, mindlessness; **idiocy, imbecility; craziness, madness,** lunacy, **insanity;** eccentricity, queerness, crankiness, crackpottedness; weirdness; screwiness *and* nuttiness *and* wackiness *and* goofiness *and* daffiness *and* battiness *and* sappiness (*all informal*); zaniness, zanyism, **clownishness, buffoonery,** clowning, fooling *or* horsing *or* dicking around (*informal*), carry-on *or* carrying-on

2 **unwiseness,** unwisdom, **injudiciousness, imprudence;** indiscreetness, **indiscretion,** inconsideration, thoughtlessness, witlessness, inattention, unthoughtfulness, lack of sensitivity; doziness (*informal*); **unreasonableness,**

unsoundness, unsensibleness, senselessness, reasonlessness, **irrationality, unreason,** inadvisability; recklessness; childishness, immaturity, puerility, callowness; gullibility, bamboozlability (*informal*); inexpedience *see* 995; unintelligence *see* 921; pompousness, stuffiness

3 **absurdity,** absurdness, **ridiculousness;** ludicrousness *see* 488.1; **nonsense,** nonsensicality, stuff and nonsense, codswallop (*informal*), horseshit *and* bullshit (*both informal*); **preposterousness,** fantasticalness, monstrousness, wildness, **outrageousness**

4 (*foolish act*) **folly, stupidity,** act of folly, absurdity, *sottise* (*French*), foolish *or* stupid thing, dumb thing to do (*informal*); fool *or* fool's trick, dumb trick (*informal*); **imprudence, indiscretion,** imprudent *or* unwise step; blunder *see* 974.5

5 **stultification;** infatuation; trivialization

verbs

6 **to be foolish;** be stupid *see* 921.12; **act** *or* **play the fool;** get funny; **fool,** tomfool (*informal*), **trifle,** frivol; **fool** *or* **horse around** (*informal*), arse around (*informal*), clown, clown around; **make a fool of oneself,** make a monkey of oneself (*informal*), stultify oneself, invite ridicule, put oneself out of court, play the buffoon *or* fool; **lose one's head, take leave of one's senses,** go haywire; go from the sublime to the ridiculous; strain at a gnat and swallow a camel; tilt at windmills

7 **to stultify,** infatuate, turn one's head, befool; gull, dupe; **make a fool of,** make a monkey of *and* play for a sucker *and* put on (*all informal*), take the piss out of (*informal*)

adjectives

8 **foolish,** fool (*informal*), foolheaded (*informal*), **stupid, dumb** (*informal*), gormless (*informal*), clueless (*informal*), **asinine,** wet; buffoonish; **silly,** apish, dizzy (*informal*); **fatuous,** fatuitous, inept, **inane;** futile; **senseless, witless, thoughtless,** insensate, brainless; **idiotic,** moronic, imbecile, imbecilic, spastic (*informal*); **crazy, mad,** daft, **insane;** infatuated, besotted, credulous, gulled, befooled, beguiled, fond, doting, gaga; sentimental, maudlin; dazed, fuddled

9 (*informal terms*) **screwy, nutty,** cockeyed, wacky, goofy, daffy, loony, batty, crackers, doolally, sappy, kooky, flaky, damn-fool, out of it, out to lunch, dippy, doodle-brained, lame, dizzy, loony, loony-tune, moony, dopey, fluffheaded, loopy, scatty

10 **unwise,** injudicious, **imprudent,** unpolitic, impolitic, contraindicated, **counterproductive;** indiscreet; inconsiderate, thoughtless, mindless, witless, unthoughtful, unthinking, unreflecting, unreflective; **unreasonable, unsound, unsensible,** senseless, insensate, reasonless, **irrational,** reckless, inadvisable; inexpedient *see* 995.5; **ill-advised, ill-considered,** ill-gauged, ill-judged, ill-imagined, ill-contrived, ill-devised, on the wrong track, unconsidered; unadvised, misadvised, misguided; undiscerning; unforeseeing, unseeing, shortsighted, myopic; suicidal, self-defeating

11 **absurd, nonsensical,** insensate, ridiculous, laughable, ludicrous *see* 488.4; **foolish, crazy;** preposterous, cockamamie (*US & Canadian informal*), fantastic, fantastical, grotesque, monstrous, wild, weird, **outrageous,** incredible, beyond belief, *outré* (*French*), extravagant, **bizarre;** high-flown

12 foolable, befoolable, gullible, bamboozlable (*informal*); naive, artless, guileless, inexperienced, impressionable; malleable, like putty; persuasible, biddable

adverbs

13 **foolishly, stupidly,** sillily, idiotically; **unwisely,** injudiciously, imprudently, indiscreetly, inconsiderately; myopically, blindly, senselessly, unreasonably, thoughtlessly, witlessly, imsensately, unthinkingly; absurdly, ridiculously

923 FOOL

nouns

1 **fool, damn fool,** tomfool, perfect fool, born fool; *schmuck* (*Yiddish*); **ass,** jackass, stupid ass, egregious ass; zany, **clown, buffoon,** doodle; sop, milksop; mome (*old*), mooncalf, softhead; figure of fun; **lunatic** *see* 925.15; **ignoramus** *see* 929.8

2 **stupid person, dolt, dunce,** clod, Boeotian, **dullard,** *niais* (*French*), donkey, yahoo, thickwit, **dope, nitwit,** nit, dimwit, lackwit, half-wit, daftie (*informal*), lamebrain, putz (*US & Canadian informal*), lightweight, witling

3 (*informal terms*) **chump, wally** (*taboo*), charlie, burk *or* berk, pillock, bloody fool *or* bf, boob, booby, muggins, josser, sap, prize sap, klutz, basket case, dingbat, dingdong, ding-a-ling, **ninny,** ninnyhammer, **nincompoop,** looby, noddy, saphead, mutt, jerk, jerk-off (*US & Canadian*), **wanker** (*taboo*), tosser, arsehole, goof, schlemiel (*US*), sawney, galoot, gonzo, dumbo, dweeb (*US & Canadian*), nerd *or* nurd, twerp, twit, yo-yo, alec *or* aleck (*Australian*), boofhead (*Australian*)

4 (*informal terms*) **blockhead, airhead, dickhead, thickie** *or* **thicko,** bimbo, bubblehead, fluffhead, featherhead, woodenhead, dolthead, dumbhead, dummy, dum-dum, dumbo, dumb cluck, dodo head, dumbbell, dumb bunny, stupidhead, dullhead, bufflehead, bonehead, jughead, thickhead, thickskull, numskull, numpty (*Scottish*), doolie (*Scottish*), putz (*US*), lunkhead (*US & Canadian*), chucklehead, knucklehead, headbanger *and* jolterhead, muttonhead, beefhead, meathead, noodlehead, thimblewit, pinhead, pinbrain, peabrain, cabbagehead, pumpkin head, fathead, prune, blubberhead, muddlehead, puzzlehead, addlebrain, addlehead, addlepate, tottyhead (*old*), puddinghead, stupe, mushhead, blunderhead, dunderhead, dunderpate, clodpate, clodhead, clodpoll, jobbernowl *and* gaby *and* gowk

5 **oaf, lout,** boor, lubber, oik, **gawk,** gawky, **lummox,** yokel, rube (*US & Canadian informal*), hick, hayseed, bumpkin, clod, clodhopper, tyke; Hooray Henry *or* Hooray

6 **silly,** silly Billy (*informal*), **silly ass, goose**

7 **scatterbrain,** scatterbrains *and* shatterbrain *or* shatterplate (*both old*), **rattlebrain,** rattlehead, rattlepate, **harebrain,** featherbrain, shallowbrain, shallowpate (*old*), featherhead, giddybrain, giddyhead, giddypate, **flibbertigibbet**

8 **idiot,** drivelling *or* blithering *or* adenoidal *or* congenital idiot; **imbecile, moron, half-wit,** natural, natural idiot, born fool, natural-born fool, mental defective, defective; cretin, mongolian *or* mongoloid idiot, basket case *and* spastic *and* spaz (*all informal*); **simpleton,** simp (*informal*), juggins *and* jiggins (*both informal*), clot *and* berk (*both informal*), golem

9 **dotard,** senile; fogy, **old fogy,** fuddy-duddy, old fart (*informal*), buffer *or* old buffer (*informal*)

924 SANITY

nouns

1 **sanity, saneness,** sanemindedness, soundness, **soundness of mind,** soundmindedness, sound mind, healthy mind, right mind (*informal*), senses, reason, **rationality,** reasonableness, lucidity, balance, wholesomeness; normalness, normality, normalcy (*US*); **mental health;** mental hygiene; mental balance *or* poise *or* equilibrium; sobriety, sober senses; a sound mind in a sound body, "*mens sana in corpore sano*"—Juvenal (*Latin,* a healthy mind in a healthy body); contact with reality; lucid interval; knowing right from wrong

verbs

2 **to come to one's senses,** sober down *or* up, recover one's sanity *or* balance *or* equilibrium, get things into proportion; see in perspective; have all one's marbles (*informal*); have a good head on one's shoulders

3 **to bring to one's senses,** bring to reason

adjectives

4 **sane,** sane-minded, **rational,** reasonable, sensible, **lucid,** normal, wholesome, clearheaded, clearminded, balanced, **sound,** mentally sound, of sound mind, *compos mentis* (*Latin*), sound-minded, healthy-minded, right, right in the head, **in one's right mind,** in possession of one's faculties *or* senses, together *and* all there (*both informal*); in touch with reality

925 INSANITY, MANIA

nouns

1 **insanity,** insaneness, unsaneness, **lunacy, madness,** *folie* (*French*), **craziness, daftness,** oddness, strangeness, queerness, abnormality; loss of touch *or* contact with reality, loss of mind *or* reason; dementedness, dementia, athymia, brainsickness, mindsickness, mental sickness, sickness; **criminal insanity,** homicidal mania, hemothymia; **mental illness, mental disease;** brain damage; rabidness, **mania,** furore; alienation, aberration, mental disturbance, **derangement,** distraction, disorientation, mental derangement *or* disorder, unbalance, mental instability, unsoundness, **unsoundness of mind;** unbalanced mind, diseased *or* unsound mind, **sick mind,** disturbed *or* troubled *or* clouded mind, shattered mind, mind overthrown

or unhinged, darkened mind, disordered mind *or* reason; senselessness, witlessness, reasonlessness, irrationality; possession, pixilation; mental deficiency *see* 921.9

2 (*informal terms*) **nuttiness**, craziness, daffiness, battiness, screwiness, goofiness, kookiness, wackiness, dottiness, pottiness, *mishegas* (*Yiddish*), looniness, lunchiness, barminess *or* balminess; bats in the belfry, a screw loose, one sandwich short of a picnic, a can short of a sixpack, not the full shilling, a wheel off the barrow, not playing with a full deck, a chop short of a barbie; lame brains

3 **psychosis**, psychopathy, psychopathology, psychopathic condition; certifiability; **neurosis**; psychopathia sexualis, sexual pathology *see* 75.18; pathological drunkenness *or* intoxication, dipsomania; pharmacopsychosis, drug addiction *see* 87.1; moral insanity, psychopathic personality, *folie du doute* (*French*), abulia *see* 362.4

4 **schizophrenia**, dementia praecox, mental dissociation, dissociation of personality; catatonic schizophrenia, catatonia, hebephrenia, hebephrenic schizophrenia; schizothymia; schizophasia; thought disorder; schizotypal personality; **paranoia**, paraphrenia, paranoiac *or* paranoid psychosis; paranoid schizophrenia

5 **depression, melancholia**, depressive psychosis, dysthymia, barythymia, lypothymia, "moping, melancholy and moonstruck madness" — Milton; melancholia hypochondriaca; involutional melancholia *or* psychosis; stuporous melancholia, melancholia attonita; flatuous melancholia; melancholia religiosa; postpartum depression; **manic-depressive disorder, bipolar disorder**; SAD *or* seasonal affective disorder, cyclothymia, poikilothymia, mood swings

6 **rabies, hydrophobia**, lyssa, canine madness; dumb *or* sullen rabies, paralytic rabies; furious rabies

7 **frenzy, furore**, fury, maniacal excitement, fever, **rage**; **seizure**, attack, acute episode, episode, **fit**, paroxysm, spasm, **convulsion**; **snit**, *crise* (*French*); amok, murderous insanity *or* frenzy, homicidal mania, hemothymia; psychokinesis; furore epilepticus

8 **delirium**, deliriousness, brainstorm; calenture of the brain, afebrile delirium, lingual delirium, delirium mussitans; incoherence, wandering, raving, ranting; exhaustion delirium *or* infection, exhaustion psychosis

9 **delirium tremens**, mania *or* dementia a potu, delirium alcoholicum *or* ebriositatis

10 (*informal terms*) **the DT's**, the horrors, the shakes, the heebie-jeebies, the jimjams, the screaming meemies; pink elephants, pink spiders

11 **fanaticism**, fanaticalness, **rabidness**, **overzealousness**, overenthusiasm, ultrazealousness, zealotry, zealotism, bigotry, perfervidness; extremism, extremeness, extravagance, excessiveness, overreaction; overreligiousness *see* 692.3

12 **mania** (*see lists*), **craze, infatuation, enthusiasm**, passion, thing (*informal*), fascination, crazy fancy, bug (*informal*), rage, furore; manic psychosis; megalomania

13 **obsession**, prepossession, preoccupation, **hang-up** (*informal*), **fixation**, tic, complex, thing (*informal*),

fascination; hypercathexis; **compulsion**, morbid drive, obsessive compulsion, irresistible impulse; **monomania**, ruling passion, fixed idea, *idée fixe* (*French*), one-track mind; **possession**

14 **insane asylum**, asylum, lunatic asylum, **madhouse**, mental institution, mental home, bedlam; **nuthouse** *and* laughing academy *and* **loonybin** *and* bughouse *and* funny farm (*all informal*), booby hatch (*US informal*); mental hospital, psychopathic hospital *or* ward, psychiatric hospital *or* ward; padded cell, rubber room

15 **lunatic, madman, madwoman** dement, phrenetic *and* fanatic (*both archaic*), *fou, aliéné* (*both French*), non compos, *bacayaro* (*Japanese*); bedlamite, Tom o' Bedlam; demoniac, energumen; **maniac**, raving lunatic; homicidal maniac, psychopathic killer, berserk *or* berserker; borderline case; mental defective, idiot *see* 923.8

16 (*informal terms*) **nut**, nutter, nutcase, nutter, nut job, loon, loony, bampot (*Scottish*), doolie (*Scottish*), headcase, headbanger, crazy, psycho, crackpot, screwball, weirdie, weirdo, kook, flake (*US & Canadian*), crackbrain, *meshugana* (*Yiddish*), fruitcake, fruit, schizo, wacko, sickie, sicko

17 **psychotic**, psycho (*informal*), mental, mental case, certifiable case, **psychopath**, psychopathic case; psychopathic personality; paranoiac, paranoid; schizophrenic, schizophrene, schizoid; schiz *and* schizy *and* schizo (*all informal*); catatoniac; hebephreniac; manic-depressive; megalomaniac

18 **fanatic**, infatuate, **bug** (*informal*), **nut** (*informal*), **buff** *and* **fan** (*both informal*), freak (*informal*), *fanatico, aficionado* (*both Spanish*), devotee, **zealot, enthusiast**, energumen; **monomaniac**, crank (*informal*); lunatic fringe

19 **psychiatry**, alienism; psychiatrist, alienist

verbs

20 **to be insane, be out of one's mind**, not be in one's right mind, not be right in the head, **not be all there** (*informal*), have a demon *or* devil; have bats in the belfry *and* have a screw loose, not have all one's marbles (*informal*), not play with a full deck *and* not have both oars in the water (*both informal*), have a slate loose (*informal*), not be the full shilling (*informal*), be one sandwich short of a picnic (*informal*), be a can short of a sixpack (*informal*), be a chop short of a barbie (*informal*), have a wheel off the barrow (*informal*); **wander, ramble**; **rave, rage, rant**, have a fit; dote, babble; drivel, drool, slobber, slaver; froth *or* foam at the mouth, run mad, run amok, go berserk

21 **to go mad, take leave of one's senses**, lose one's mind *or* senses *or* reason *or* wits, **crack up**, go off one's head (*informal*)

22 (*informal terms*) **to go crazy, go bats**, go cuckoo, go nuts, go out of one's skull *or* tree, go off one's nut *or* rocker, go off one's trolley, go off the deep end, blow one's top *or* stack, pop one's cork, flip one's lid *or* wig, go ape *or* apeshit, go ballistic, go bananas, go crackers *and* go bonkers, blow one's mind, freak out, flip out, go hog wild (*US & Canadian*), go round the bend, have a screw loose, have bats in one's belfry,

have rocks in one's head, lose one's marbles, do one's nut, do one's block (*Australian* & *NZ*)

23 to addle the wits, **affect one's mind, go to one's head**

24 to **madden**, dement, **craze**, mad (*old*), make mad, send mad, **unbalance**, unhinge, undermine one's reason, **derange**, distract, frenzy, shatter, **drive insane** *or* mad *or* crazy, put *or* send out of one's mind, overthrow one's mind *or* reason, drive one up the wall (*informal*), drive one round the bend (*informal*), drive one bonkers (*informal*), drive one scatty (*informal*), send one off one's rocker (*informal*)

25 to **obsess, possess**, beset, infatuate, **preoccupy**, be uppermost in one's thoughts, have a thing about (*informal*); grip, hold, get a hold on, not let go; **fixate**; drive, compel, impel

adjectives

26 **insane**, unsane, **mad**, stark-mad, mad as a hatter, mad as a march hare, **stark-staring mad**, maddened, **sick**, crazed, **lunatic**, moonstruck, **daft**, **non compos mentis**, non compos, *baca* (*Japanese*), **unsound**, of unsound mind, **demented, deranged**, deluded, disoriented, unhinged, **unbalanced**, unsettled, distraught, wandering, mazed, crackbrained, brainsick, sick *or* soft in the head, not right, not in one's right mind, **touched**, touched in the head, **out of one's mind**, out of one's senses *or* wits, bereft of reason, reasonless, irrational, deprived of reason, senseless, witless; hallucinated; manic; queer, queer in the head, odd, strange, off, flighty (*old*); abnormal *see* 869.9, mentally deficient *see* 921.22

27 (*informal terms*) **crazy, nutty**, daffy, doited (*Scottish*), dotty, dippy, crazy as a bedbug *or* coot *or* loon, loony, loony-tune (*US* & *Canadian*), goofy, wacky, barmy *or* balmy, flaky (*US* & *Canadian*), kooky, potty, batty, ape, apeshit, out to lunch, bats, nuts, nutty as a fruitcake, fruity, fruitcakey, screwy, screwball, crackers, bananas, bonkers, loopy, cuckoo, moony, wired to the moon, slaphappy, flipped, freaked-out, off-the-wall, gaga, glaikit (*Scottish*), haywire, off in the upper storey, off one's nut *or* rocker, off one's trolley, off the hinges, round the bend, round the twist, nobody home, with bats in the belfry, just plain nuts, loco, mental, psycho, cracked, not right in the head, tetched, off one's head, out of one's head, out of one's skull *or* tree, not all there, *meshuggah* (*Yiddish*), not tightly wrapped (*US* & *Canadian*), three bricks short of a load, rowing with one oar in the water, up the wall, off-the-wall, up the pole, schizy, schizoid, schizo

28 **psychotic, psychopathic, psychoneurotic, mentally ill**, mentally sick, certifiable; disturbed, neurotic; schizophrenic, schizoid, schiz *or* schizy (*informal*); depressive; manic; manic-depressive; paranoiac, **paranoid**; catatonic; brain-damaged, brain-injured

29 **possessed**, possessed with a demon *or* devil, **pixilated, bedevilled**, demonized, devil-ridden, demonic, demonical, demoniacal

30 **rabid, maniac** *or* **maniacal**, raving mad, stark-raving mad, **frenzied, frantic**, frenetic; **mad**, madding, **wild, furious, violent**; desperate; **beside oneself**, like one possessed, uncontrollable; **raving, raging**, ranting; frothing *or* foaming at the mouth; **amok, berserk**, running wild; maenadic, corybantic, bacchic, Dionysiac

31 **delirious**, out of one's head (*informal*), off one's head (*informal*), off; **giddy**, dizzy, lightheaded; **wandering, rambling, raving, ranting**, babbling, incoherent

32 **fanatic, fanatical, rabid; overzealous**, ultrazealous, **overenthusiastic**, zealotic, bigoted, perfervid; **extreme**, extremist, extravagant, inordinate; **unreasonable, irrational; wild-eyed**, wild-looking, haggard; overreligious

33 **obsessed, possessed**, prepossessed, **infatuated**, preoccupied, fixated, **hung up** (*informal*), besotted, gripped, held; monomaniac *or* monomaniacal

34 **obsessive**, obsessional; **obsessing, possessing, preoccupying**, gripping, holding; driving, impelling, **compulsive, compelling**

adverbs

35 **madly, insanely, crazily**; deliriously; fanatically, rabidly, etc

36 **manias by subject**

(a few subjects) oligomania	(demonic possession)
(a special food) opsomania	cacodemonomania
(activity) ergasiomania	(dogs) cynomania
(acute mania) hypermania	(drinking water)
(alcohol) alcoholomania	hydrodipsomania
(animals) zoomania	(drinking) potomania
(ballet) balletomania	(England) Anglomania
(Beatles) Beatlemania	(erotica) eroticomania
(becoming larger)	(erotic literature)
macromania	erotographomania
(becoming smaller)	(ether) etheromania
micromania	(falsities) pseudomania
(bed rest) clinomania	(female lust) nymphomania
(bees) apimania	(fires) pyromania
(being in vehicles)	(fish) ichthyomania
amaxomania	(flowers) anthomania
(birds) ornithomania	(food; eating) phagomania
(blushing) erythromania	(food) sitomania
(book theft)	(foreigners) xenomania
bibliokleptomania	(foul speech)
(books) bibliomania	coprolalomania
(bullets) ballistomania	(France) Francomania *or*
(buying) oniomania	Gallomania
(cats) ailuromania	(freedom) eleuthromania
(China) Chinamania	(fur) doramania
(cliffs) cremnomania	(gaiety) cheromania
(counting) arithmomania	(genitals) edeomania
(crossing bridges)	(Germany) Germanomania
gephyromania	*or* Teutonomania
(crowds) demomania *or*	(great wealth) cresomania
ochlomania	*or* plutomania
(dancing) choreomania	(Greece) Grecomania
(Dante) Dantomania	(grinding one's teeth)
(death; the dead)	bruxomania
necromania	(hair) trichomania
(death) thanatomania	(home) oikomania
(deep melancholy)	(homesickness)
lypemania	philopatridomania
(delirium tremens)	(horses) hippomania
tromomania	(hypnosis) mesmeromania

(icons) iconomania
(idols) idolomania
(imagined disease) nosomania
(incurable insanity) acromania
(insects) entomomania
(Italy) Italomania
(joy in complaints) paramania
(lies; exaggerations) mythomania
(light) photomania
(liquor) dipsomania
(lycanthropy) lycomania
(male lust) satyromania
(marriage) gamomania
(medicines) pharmacomania
(melancholia) tristimania
(men) andromania
(mice) musomania
(Mikhail S Gorbachev) Gorbymania
(mild mania) hypomania *or* submania
(money) chrematomania
(moral insanity) pathomania
(movement) kinesomania
(murder) homicidomania
(music) melomania *or* musicomania
(nakedness) gymnomania
(narcotics) letheomania
(night) noctimania
(noise) phonomania
(novelty) kainomania
(nudity) nudomania
(nymphomania) hysteromania *or* oestromania *or* uteromania
(one's own wisdom) sophomania
(one's self) egomania
(one subject) monomania
(open spaces) agoramania
(opium) opiomania
(own importance) megalomania
(penis) mentulomania
(picking at growths) phaneromania
(pinching off one's hair) trichorrhexomania
(plants) florimania
(pleasing delusions) amenomania
(pleasure) hedonomania
(plucking one's hair) trichotillomania
(politics) politicomania
(pornography) pornographomania

(postage stamps) timbromania
(priests) hieromania
(public employment) empleomania
(railroad travel) siderodromomania
(religion) entheomania
(reptiles) ophidiomania
(return home) nostomania
(running away) drapetomania
(Russia) Russomania
(satyriasis) gynecomania
(sea) thalassomania
(second coming of Christ) parousiamania
(sexual pleasure) aphrodisiomania *or* erotomania
(sin) hamartomania
(sitting) kathisomania
(sleep) hypnomania
(snow) chionomania
(solitude) automania
(speech) lalomania
(spending) squandermania
(stealing) kleptomania
(stillness) eremiomania
(suicide) autophonomania
(sun) heliomania
(surgery) tomomania
(symmetry) symmetromania
(talking) logomania
(testicles) orchidomania
(that one is God) theomania
(theatre) theatromania
(thinking) phronemomania
(travel) hodomania
(travelling) dromomania
(tuberculosis) phthisiomania
(Turkey) Turkomania
(United States) Americamania
(wandering) ecdemiomania
(wanderlust) poriomania
(washing, bathing) ablutomania
(water) hydromania
(wine) enomania *or* oinomania
(woods) hylomania
(women) gynomania
(words) verbomania
(work) ergomania
(writing for publication) typomania
(writing verse) metromania
(writing) graphomania *or* scribblemania *or* scribomania

37 manias by name

ablutomania (washing, bathing)
acromania (incurable insanity)
agoramania (open spaces)
agyiomania (streets)
ailuromania (cats)
alcoholomania (alcohol)
amaxomania (being in vehicles)
amenomania (pleasing delusions)
Americamania (United States)
andromania (men)
Anglomania (England)
anthomania (flowers)
aphrodisiomania *or* erotomania (sexual pleasure)
apimania (bees)
arithmomania (counting)
automania (solitude)
autophonomania (suicide)
ballistomania (bullets)
balletomania (ballet)
Beatlemania (the Beatles)
bibliomania (books)
bibliokleptomania (book theft)
bruxomania (grinding one's teeth)
cacodemonomania (demonic possession)
cheromania (gaiety)
Chinamania (China)
chionomania (snow)
choreomania (dancing)
chrematomania (money)
clinomania (bed rest)
coprolalomania (foul speech)
cremnomania (cliffs)
cresomania (great wealth)
cynomania (dogs)
Dantomania (Dante)
demomania (crowds)
dipsomania (liquor)
doramania (fur)
drapetomania (running away)
dromomania (travelling)
ecdemiomania (wandering)
edeomania (genitals)
egomania (one's self)
eleuthromania (freedom)
empleomania (public employment)
enomania (wine)
entheomania (religion)
entomomania (insects)
eremiomania (stillness)

ergasiomania (activity)
ergomania (work)
eroticomania (erotica)
erotographomania (erotic literature)
erythromania (blushing)
etheromania (ether)
florimania (plants)
Francomania (France)
Gallomania (France)
gamomania (marriage)
gephyromania (crossing bridges)
Germanomania (Germany)
Gorbymania (Mikhail S Gorbachev)
graphomania (writing)
Grecomania (Greece)
gymnomania (nakedness)
gynomania (women)
gynecomania (satyriasis)
hamartomania (sin)
hedonomania (pleasure)
heliomania (sun)
hieromania (priests)
hippomania (horses)
hodomania (travel)
homicidomania (murder)
hydrodipsomania (drinking water)
hydromania (water)
hylomania (woods)
hypermania (acute mania)
hypnomania (sleep)
hypomania (mild mania)
hysteromania (nymphomania)
ichthyomania (fish)
iconomania (icons)
idolomania (idols)
Italomania (Italy)
kainomania (novelty)
kathisomania (sitting)
kinesomania (movement)
kleptomania (stealing)
lalomania (speech)
letheomania (narcotics)
logomania (talking)
lycomania (lycanthropy)
lypemania (deep melancholy)
macromania (becoming larger)
megalomania (own importance)
melomania (music)
mentulomania (the penis)
mesmeromania (hypnosis)
metromania (writing verse)
micromania (becoming smaller)
monomania (one subject)

musicomania (music)
musomania (mice)
mythomania (lies; exaggerations)
necromania (death; the dead)
noctimania (night)
nosomania (imagined disease)
nostomania (return home)
nudomania (nudity)
nymphomania (female lust)
ochlomania (crowds)
oestromania (nymphomania)
oikomania (home)
oinomania (wine)
oligomania (a few subjects)
oniomania (buying)
ophidiomania (reptiles)
opiomania (opium)
opsomania (a special food)
orchidomania (testicles)
ornithomania (birds)
paramania (joy in complaints)
parousiamania (second coming of Christ)
pathomania (moral insanity)
phagomania (food; eating)
phaneromania (picking at growths)
pharmacomania (medicines)
philopatridomania (homesickness)
phonomania (noise)
photomania (light)
phronemomania (thinking)
phthisiomania (tuberculosis)
plutomania (great wealth)
politicomania (politics)
poriomania (wanderlust)

pornographomania (pornography)
potomania (drinking; delirium tremens)
pseudomania (falsities)
pyromania (fires)
Russomania (Russia)
satyromania (male lust)
scribblemania (writing)
scribomania (writing)
siderodromomania (railroad travel)
sitomania (food)
sophomania (one's own wisdom)
squandermania (spending)
submania (mild mania)
symmetromania (symmetry)
Teutonomania (Germany)
thalassomania (the sea)
thanatomania (death)
theatromania (theatre)
theomania (that one is God)
timbromania (postage stamps)
tomomania (surgery)
trichomania (hair)
trichorrhexomania (pinching off one's hair)
trichotillomania (plucking one's hair)
tristimania (melancholia)
tromomania (delirium tremens)
Turkomania (Turkey)
typomania (writing for publication)
uteromania (nymphomania)
verbomania (words)
xenomania (foreigners)
zoomania (animals)

926 ECCENTRICITY

nouns

1 **eccentricity, idiosyncrasy,** idiocrasy, **erraticism,** erraticness, **queerness, oddity, peculiarity,** strangeness, singularity, freakishness, freakiness, quirkiness, crotchetiness, dottiness, crankiness, crankism, crackpotism; whimsy, whimsicality; abnormality, anomaly, unnaturalness, irregularity, deviation, deviancy, differentness, divergence, aberration; **nonconformity,** unconventionality *see* 867.2

2 **quirk, twist,** kink, crank, quip, trick, mannerism, **crotchet,** conceit, whim, maggot, maggot in the brain, bee in one's bonnet *or* head (*informal*)

3 **eccentric,** erratic, character; odd person *see* 869.4; **nonconformist** *see* 867.3, recluse *see* 584.5

4 freak, character, crackpot, nut, screwball, weirdie, weirdo, kook, queer fish, oddball, flake (*US & Canadian*), strange duck, odd fellow, crank, bird, wacko

adjectives

5 **eccentric, erratic,** idiocratic, idiocratical, idiosyncratic, idiosyncratical, **queer,** queer in the head, **odd, peculiar,** strange, fey, singular, anomalous, freakish, funny, rum; unnatural, abnormal, irregular, divergent, deviative, deviant, different, exceptional; unconventional *see* 867.6; **crotchety,** quirky, dotty, maggoty, cranky, crank, crankish, whimsical, twisted; solitary, reclusive, antisocial

6 (*informal terms*) kooky, goofy, funny, kinky, loopy, haywire, screwy, screwball, nutty, wacky, flaky (*US & Canadian*), oddball, wacky, wacko, out to lunch, nobody home, weird

927 KNOWLEDGE

nouns

1 **knowledge,** knowing, knowingness, ken; **command,** reach; **acquaintance, familiarity,** intimacy; private knowledge, privity; **information,** data, database, datum, items, facts, gen (*informal*), info (*informal*), dope (*informal*), low-down (*informal*), factual base, corpus; **certainty, sure** *or* **certain knowledge** *see* 969; protocol, protocol statement *or* sentence *or* proposition; intelligence, inside information; practical knowledge, **experience, know-how, expertise;** technic, technics, technique; self-knowledge; *ratio cognoscendi* (*Latin*)

2 **cognizance;** cognition, noesis; **recognition, realization; perception,** insight, apperception, sudden insight, illumination, dawning, aha reaction, flashing (*informal*); **consciousness, awareness,** mindfulness, note, notice; altered state of consciousness *or* ASC; **sense,** sensibility; appreciation, appreciativeness

3 **understanding, comprehension, apprehension,** intellection, prehension; conception, conceptualization, ideation; hipness *and* savvy (*both informal*), street credibility *or* street cred; **grasp,** mental grasp, grip, **command,** mastery; precognition, foreknowledge *see* 960.3, clairvoyance *see* 689.8; intelligence, wisdom *see* 919

4 **learning, enlightenment, education, schooling, instruction,** edification, illumination; acquirements, acquisitions, attainments, accomplishments, skills; sophistication; store of knowledge; liberal education; acquisition of knowledge *see* 570

5 **scholarship, erudition,** eruditeness, **learnedness,** reading, letters; **intellectuality,** intellectualism; **literacy;** computer literacy, computeracy, numeracy; **culture, literary culture, high culture,** book learning, booklore; **bookishness,** bookiness, **pedantry,** pedantism, donnishness; bluestockingism; bibliomania, book madness, bibliolatry, bibliophilism; classicism, classical scholarship, humanism, humanistic scholarship

6 **profound knowledge,** deep knowledge, total command *or* mastery; specialism, specialized *or*

special knowledge; expertise, proficiency *see* 413.1; wide *or* vast *or* extensive knowledge, generalism, general knowledge, interdisciplinary *or* cross-disciplinary knowledge; **encyclopedic knowledge,** polymathy, polyhistory, pansophy; **omniscience,** all-knowingness

7 slight knowledge *see* 929.6

8 tree of knowledge, tree of knowledge of good and evil; forbidden fruit; bo *or* bodhi tree

9 **lore, body of knowledge,** corpus, body of learning, store of knowledge, system of knowledge, treasury of information; **canon;** literature, literature of the field, publications, materials; bibliography; encyclopedia, cyclopedia

10 **science,** ology (*see list*), **art, study, discipline; field,** field of inquiry, concern, province, domain, area, arena, sphere, branch *or* field of study, branch *or* department of knowledge, speciality, academic speciality, academic discipline, territory; **technology, technics,** technicology, high technology, high-tech *or* hi-tech (*informal*), low technology, low-tech (*informal*); social science, natural science; hard science, applied science, pure science, experimental science; Big Science

11 **scientist,** man of science; **technologist;** back-room boy, practical scientist, experimental scientist; boffin (*informal*); savant, **scholar** *see* 928.3; authority, expert, maven (*US*); technocrat; intellectual

verbs

12 **to know, perceive, apprehend,** prehend, cognize, recognize, discern, see, make out; conceive, conceptualize; **realize, appreciate, understand, comprehend,** fathom, twig (*informal*); dig *and* savvy (*both informal*); wot *or* wot of (*informal*), ken (*Scottish*); have, possess, **grasp,** seize, have hold of; have knowledge of, be informed, be apprised of, have a good command of, have information about, be acquainted with, be conversant with, be cognizant of, be conscious *or* aware of; know something by heart *or* by rote *or* from memory

13 **to know well, know full well,** know damn well *or* darn well (*informal*), have a good *or* thorough knowledge of, be well-informed, be learned in, **be up on** (*informal*), be master of, command, be thoroughly grounded in, **have down pat** *or* **cold** (*both informal*), have it taped (*informal*), have at one's fingers' ends *or* fingertips, have in one's head, **know by heart** *or* rote, **know like a book,** know like the back of one's hand, **know backwards,** know backwards and forwards, **know inside out,** know down to the ground (*informal*), **know one's stuff** *and* know one's onions (*both informal*), know a thing or two, know one's way around; be expert in; **know the ropes,** know all the ins and outs, know the score (*informal*), know all the answers (*informal*); know what's what

14 **to learn** (*acquire knowledge*) *see* 570.6,9-11; come to one's knowledge *see* 551.15

adjectives

15 **knowing, knowledgeable, informed; cognizant, conscious, aware, mindful, sensible;** right-on; intelligent *see* 919.12; **understanding,**

comprehending, apprehensive, apprehending; **perceptive,** insightful, apperceptive, percipient, perspicacious, appercipient, prehensile; shrewd, sagacious, wise *see* 919.17; omniscient, all-knowing

16 **cognizant of, aware of, conscious of, mindful of, sensible to** *or* **of, appreciative of,** appreciatory of, no stranger to, seized of; privy to, in the secret, let into, in the know (*informal*), behind the scenes *or* curtain; alive to, awake to; **wise to** (*informal*), hip to *and* on to (*both informal*); streetwise; apprised of, informed of; undeceived, undeluded

17 (*informal terms*) **hip, hep,** on the beam, go-go (*US & Canadian*), **with it,** into, really into, groovy; chic, clued-up, clued in, in the know, trendy

18 **informed, enlightened, instructed,** versed, well-versed, educated, schooled, **taught;** posted, briefed, primed, trained; **up on,** up-to-date, abreast of, *au courant* (*French*)

19 **versed in,** informed in, read *or* well-read in, up on, clued-up on (*informal*), strong in, at home in, master of, expert *or* authoritative in, proficient in, **familiar with,** at home with, **conversant with, acquainted with,** intimate with

20 **well-informed,** well-posted, well-educated, **well-grounded,** well-versed, **well-read,** widely read

21 **learned, erudite, educated, cultured,** cultivated, lettered, literate, civilized, **scholarly,** scholastic, studious; wise *see* 919.17; **profound,** deep, abstruse; **encyclopedic,** pansophic, polymath *or* polymathic, polyhistoric

22 **book-learned,** book-read, **literary,** book-taught, book-fed, book-wise, book-smart, **bookish,** booky, book-minded; book-loving, bibliophilic, bibliophagic; **pedantic,** donnish, scholastic, inkhorn; **bluestocking**

23 **intellectual,** intellectualistic; **highbrow** *and* highbrowed *and* highbrowish (*all informal*); elitist

24 **self-educated,** self-taught, autodidactic

25 **knowable,** cognizable, recognizable, **understandable, comprehensible,** apprehendable, apprehensible, prehensile, graspable, seizable, discernible, conceivable, appreciable, perceptible, distinguishable, ascertainable, discoverable

26 **known, recognized,** ascertained, conceived, grasped, apprehended, prehended, seized, perceived, discerned, appreciated, **understood, comprehended,** realized; pat *and* **down pat** (*both informal*)

27 **well-known,** weel-kent (*Scottish*), well-understood, well-recognized, **widely known,** commonly known, universally recognized, generally *or* universally admitted; **familiar,** familiar as household words, household, **common, current; proverbial;** public, notorious; known by every schoolboy; talked-of, talked-about, in everyone's mouth, **on everyone's tongue** *or* **lips;** commonplace, trite *see* 117.9, hackneyed, platitudinous, truistic

28 **scientific; technical, technological,** technicological; high-tech *or* hi-tech (*informal*), low-tech (*informal*); **scholarly;** disciplinary

adverbs

29 **knowingly, consciously, wittingly, with forethought,** understandingly, intelligently,

studiously, learnedly, eruditely, as every schoolboy knows

30 to one's knowledge, **to the best of one's knowledge,** as far as one can see *or* tell, as far as one knows, as well as can be said

31 ologies by name

abiology (inanimate things)
acarology (lice and ticks)
acology (therapeutic agents)
acrology (initial sounds or signs)
adenology (glands)
aesthology (sensory organs)
alethology (truth)
algology *or* phycology (seaweeds)
ambrology (amber)
anatripsology (friction)
andrology (male diseases)
angiology (blood vessels)
anorganology (inorganic things)
anthropology (mankind)
apiology *or* melittology (bees)
arachnology *or* araneology (spiders)
archeology (ancient or historical artefacts)
archology (government)
areology (the planet Mars)
argyrology (money boxes)
aristology (dining)
arthrology (joints)
asthenology (diseases of debility)
astrolithology (meteorites)
astrology (stellar and planetary influence)
atmology (water vapour)
audiology (hearing disorders)
auxology (growth)
azoology (inanimate things)
balneology (therapeutic baths)
barology (weight)
batology (brambles)
bibliology (books)
bioecology (biological interrelationships)
biology (life, living things)
biometeorology (organic-atmospheric interrelationships)
bromatology (food)
brontology (thunder)
bryology *or* muscology (mosses)
caliology (bird nests)
campanology (bells; bell-ringing)

carcinology (crustaceans)
cardiology (the heart)
carpology *or* pomology (fruits)
cartology (maps)
cephalology (the head)
cetology (whales and dolphins)
chology *or* choledology (bile)
chorology (geographical boundaries)
choreology (dance notation)
chrondrology (cartilage)
chronology (dates; dating)
coleopterology (beetles)
conchology (shells)
cosmology (the universe)
craniology (the skull)
crustaceology (crustaceans)
cryptology (codes and ciphers)
curiology (picture writing)
cyesiology (pregnancy)
cytology (cells)
cytopathology (cell pathology)
dactyliology (finger-rings)
dactylology (fingers)
deltiology (picture postcards)
demology (human activities)
dendrochronology (tree-ring dating)
dendrology (trees)
deontology (moral obligation)
dermatology (the skin)
desmology (ligaments)
diabiology (the devil, devils)
dipteriology (flies)
dittology (double interpretation)
docimology (metal assaying)
dolorology (pain)
dosiology (dosage)
dysteleology (purposelessness)
ecclesiology (churches; church history)
ecology *and* environmentology (the enviroment)

edaphology (soils)
eidology (mental imagery)
electrology (electricity)
embryology (embryos)
endocrinology (the endocrine glands)
enterology (internal organs)
entomology (insects)
epiphuytology (plant diseases)
epistemology (human knowledge)
eremology (deserts)
ergology (work and its effects)
eschatology (last things, esp death and final judgment)
ethnology (races and peoples)
ethology (animal behaviour)
etiology (the causes of disease)
etymology (derivation and history of linguistic forms)
exobiology (life on other planets)
faunology (animal distribution)
fetology (the fetus)
garbology *or* garbageology (garbage, refuse)
gastrology (the stomach)
geology (the crust of the Earth)
geratology (extinction)
gerontology (old age)
glossology (language)
gnomology (didactic literature)
gnotobiology (germ-free biology)
graphology (handwriting)
gynaecology (female health and disease)
hagiology (saints)
hamartiology (sin)
helcology (ulcers)
heliology (the sun)
helminthology (worms, esp parasitic worms)
haematology (the blood)
heortology (religious festivals)
hepatology (the liver)
heresiology (heresies)
herpetology (reptiles)
hierology (sacred things)
hippology (horses)
hippopathology (diseases of the horse)
histology *or* histiology

(tissues and organs)
historology (history)
horology (time, clocks)
hydrology (water)
hyetology (rainfall)
hygiology (health and hygiene)
hygrology (humidity)
hymenology (membranes)
hymenopterology (wasps, bees, ants)
hypnology (sleep)
hysterology (the uterus)
iatrology (healing, medicine)
ichnolithology *or* ichnology (fossil footprint)
ichthyology *or* piscology (fishes)
immunology (immunity to diseases)
irenology (peace)
journology (newspapers)
kalology (beauty)
laryngology (the larynx)
lexicology (words and meanings)
limnology (lakes and ponds)
lithology *or* lithoidology (rock, stone)
loimology (infectious diseases)
malacostracology (crustaceology)
mallacology (molluscs)
mantology (divination)
mastology (mammals)
meteorology (the atmosphere and weather)
metrology (weights and measures)
microbiology (microorganisms)
micrology (tiny things)
microseismology (earthquake tremors)
morphology (form, shape)
mycology (fungi)
myology (muscles)
myrmecology (ants)
naology (church buildings)
nasology *or* rhinology (the nose)
nephology (clouds)
neurology (the nervous system)
neuropathology (pathology of the nervous system)
neurophysology (physiology of the nervous system)
neurypnology (hypnotism)
nomology (law)

noology (intuition)

nosology (classification of diseases)

nostology (old age, geriatrics)

numismatology (coins)

odontology (the teeth)

oenology *or* enology (wine)

olfactology (smells)

ombrology (rain)

oncology (tumours)

oneirology (dreams)

onomatology (names, naming)

ontology (being, as such)

oology (eggs)

ophiology (snakes)

ophthalmology (the eyes)

organology (body organs)

orismology (terminology)

ornithology (birds)

orology *or* oreology (mountains)

oryctology (fossils)

osmology (odours)

osteology (bones)

otology (the ear)

paleobiology (fossil life)

paleoethnology (prehistoric mankind)

paleoichtyology (fossil fishes)

paleontology (early history of life)

paleoornithology (fossil birds)

paleopedology (early soils)

paleoetiology (explanation of past phenomena)

paleozoology *or* zoogeolology (fossil animals)

palynology (pollen)

paroemiology (proverbs)

pathology (diseases)

paedology (soils; children)

penology (punishment of crime)

petrology *or* stromatology (rocks)

pharmacology (drugs)

phenology (natural cycles)

philology (languages)

phitology (political economy)

phlebology (blood vessels)

phonology (vocal sounds)

photology (light and optics)

phrenology (skull shape)

physicotheology (natural theology)

physiology (the living body)

phytology (plants)

phytopathology (plant diseases)

phytophysiology (plant physiology)

phytoserology (plant viruses)

piscatology (fishing)

pistology (religious faith)

pleology (running water)

pneumatology (spirit)

ponerology (evil)

potamology (rivers)

proctology (anus, rectum)

promorphology (fundamental shapes and forms)

psephology (election statistics)

psychology (the mind)

psychonosology (mental diseases)

psychopathology (insanity)

psychophysiology (body and mind)

pteridology (ferns)

pterology (insect wings)

pterylology (feathers)

pyretology (fever)

pyrgology (towers)

pyrology (fire and heat)

radiology *or* Röntgenology (X-rays)

rheology (flow and deformation of matter)

runology (runes)

satanology (devil worship)

scatology (fossil excrement)

seismology (earthquakes)

selenology (the moon)

semasiology (language meaning)

sematology *or* semeiology (symptoms)

serology (serums)

silphology (larval forms)

sinology (China)

siphonapterology (fleas)

sitiology (diet)

sociology (society)

somatology (organic bodies)

sophiology (ideas)

soteriology (salvation)

speciology (species)

spectrology (spectroscopic analysis)

speleology (caves)

spermatology (sperm)

sphygmoology (the pulse)

splanchnology (the viscera)

splenology (the spleen)

stoichiology (fundamental laws)

stomatology (mouth diseases)

storiology (folklore)

suicidology (suicide)

synchronology (comparative chronology)

systematology (ordered arrangements)

taxology (scientific classification)

technology (mechanical and manufacturing arts)

tectology (structural morphology)

teleology (aims, determined ends)

teratology (monsters)

terminology (system of names or terms)

thanatology (death)

thaumatology (miracles)

theology (divinity)

thermology *or* thermatology (heat)

therology (mammals)

thremmatology (plant or animal breeding)

threpsology (nutrition)

tidology (tides)

timbrology (stamps, stamp-collecting)

timology (values)

tocology (obstetrics)

toxicology (poisons)

traumatology (wounds; shock)

tribology (interacting surfaces)

trichology (hair)

typhology (blindness)

uranology (astronomy)

urbanology (cities)

urology (urogenital organs and diseases)

vermiology (worms)

vexillology (flags)

victimology (victims)

vulcanology (volcanoes)

xyloology (the structure of wood)

zoology (animal life)

zoonosology (animal diseases)

zoophysiology (animal physiology)

zymology *or* zymotechnology (fermentation)

32 ologies by subject

(aims, determined ends) teleology

(amber) ambrology

(ancient or historical artefacts) archeology

(animal behaviour) ethology

(animal diseases) zoonosology

(animal distribution) faunology

(animal life) zoology

(animal physiology) zoophysiology

(ants) myrmecology

(anus, rectum) proctology

(astronomy) uranology

(beauty) kalology

(bees) apiology *or* melittology

(beetles) coleopterology

(being, as such) ontology

(bells; bell-ringing) campanology

(bile) chololody *or* choledology

(biological interrelationships) bioecology

(bird nests) caliology

(birds) ornithology

(blindness) typhology

(blood vessels) angiology

(blood vessels) phlebology

(body and mind) psychophysiology

(body organs) organology

(bones) osteology

(books) bibliology

(brambles) batology

(cartilage) chrondrology

(caves) speleology

(cell pathology) cytopathology

(cells) cytology

(China) sinology

(church buildings) naology

(churches; church history) ecclesiology

(cities) urbanology

(classification of diseases) nosology

(clouds) nephology

(codes and ciphers) cryptology

(coins) numismatology

(comparative chronology) synchronology

(crustaceans) carcinology *or* crustaceology

(crustaceology) malacostracology

(dance notation) choreology

(dates, dating) chronology

(death) thanatology

(derivation and history of linguistic forms) etymology
(deserts) eremology
(devil worship) satanology
(didactic literature) gnomology
(diet) sitiology
(dining) aristology
(diseases of debility) asthenology
(diseases of the horse) hippopathology
(diseases) pathology
(divination) mantology
(divinity) theology
(dosage) dosiology *or* dosology *or* posology
(double interpretation) dittology
(dreams) oneirology
(drugs) pharmacology
(early history of life) paleontology
(early soils) paleopedology
(earthquake tremors) microseismology
(earthquakes) seismology
(eggs) oology
(election statistics) psephology
(electricity) electrology
(embryos) embryology
(evil) ponerology
(explanation of past phenomena) paleoetiology
(extinction) geratology
(feathers) pterylology
(female health and disease) gynaecology
(fermentation) zymology *or* zymotechnology
(ferns) pteridology
(fever) pyretology
(finger-rings) dactyliology
(fingers) dactylology
(fire and heat) pyrology
(fishes) ichthyology *or* piscology
(fishing) piscatology
(flags) vexillology
(fleas) siphonapterology
(flies) dipteriology
(flow and deformation of matter) rheology
(folklore) storiology
(food) bromatology
(form, shape) morphology
(fossil animals) paleozoology *or* zoogeolology
(fossil birds) paleoornithology
(fossil excrement) scatology

(fossil fishes) paleoichtyology
(fossil footprint) ichnolithology *or* ichnology
(fossil life) paleobiology
(fossils) oryctology
(friction) anatripsology
(fruits) carpology *or* pomology
(fundamental laws) stoichiology
(fundamental shapes and forms) promorphology
(fungi) mycology
(garbage, refuse) garbology *or* garbageology
(geographical boundaries) chorology
(germ-free biology) gnotobiology
(glands) adenology
(government) archology
(growth) auxology
(hair) trichology
(handwriting) graphology
(healing, medicine) iatrology
(health and hygiene) hygiology
(hearing disorders) audiology
(heat) thermology *or* thermatology
(heresies) heresiology
(history) historology
(horses) hippology
(human activities) demology
(human knowledge) epistemology
(humidity) hygrology
(hypnotism) neurypnolohy
(ideas) sophiology
(immunity to diseases) immunology
(inanimate things) abiology
(inanimate things) azoology
(infectious diseases) loimology
(initial sounds or signs) acrology
(inorganic things) anorganology
(insanity) psychopathology
(insect wings) pterology
(insects) entomology
(interacting surfaces) tribology
(internal organs) enterology
(intuition) noology
(joints) arthrology
(lakes and ponds) limnology

(language meaning) semasiology
(language) glossology
(languages) philology
(larval forms) silphology
(last things, esp death and final judgment) eschatology
(law) nomology
(lice and ticks) acarology
(life on other planets) exobiology
(life, living things) biology
(ligaments) desmology
(light and optics) photology
(male diseases) andrology
(mammals) mastology
(mammals) therology
(mankind) anthropology
(maps) cartology
(mechanical and manufacturing arts) technology
(membranes) hymenology
(mental diseases) psychonosology
(mental imagery) eidology
(metal assaying) docimology
(meteorites) astrolithology
(microorganisms) microbiology
(miracles) thaumatology
(molluscs) mallacology
(money boxes) argyrology
(monsters) teratology
(moral obligation) deontology
(mosses) bryology *or* muscology
(mountains) orology *or* oreology
(mouth diseases) stomatology
(muscles) myology
(names, naming) onomatology
(natural cycles) phenology
(natural theology) physicotheology
(newspapers) journology
(nutrition) threpsology
(obstetrics) tocology
(odours) osmology
(old age, geriatrics) nostology
(old age) gerontology
(ordered arrangements) systematology
(organic bodies) somatology
(organic-atmospheric interrelationships)

biometeorology
(pain) dolorology
(pathology of the nervous system) neuropathology
(peace) irenology
(physiology of the nervous system) neurophysology
(picture postcards) deltiology
(picture writing) curiology
(plant diseases) epiphuytology
(plant diseases) phytopathology
(plant or animal breeding) thremmatology
(plant physiology) phytophysiology
(plant viruses) phytoserology
(plants) phytology
(poisons) toxicology
(political economy) phitology
(pollen) palynology
(pregnancy) cyesiology
(prehistoric mankind) paleoethnology
(proverbs) paroemiology
(punishment of crime) penology
(purposelessness) dysteleology
(races and peoples) ethnology
(rain) ombrology
(rainfall) hyetology
(religious faith) pistology
(religious festivals) heortology
(reptiles) herpetology
(rivers) potamology
(rock, stone) lithology *or* lithoidology
(rocks) petrology *or* stromatology
(runes) runology
(running water) pleology
(sacred things) hierology
(saints) hagiology
(salvation) soteriology
(scientific classification) taxology
(seaweeds) algology *or* phycology
(sensory organs) aesthology
(serums) serology
(shells) conchology
(sin) hamartiology
(skull shape) phrenology
(sleep) hypnology
(smells) olfactology
(snakes) ophiology
(society) sociology

(soils; children) paedology
(soils) edaphology
(species) speciology
(spectroscopic analysis) spectrology
(sperm) spermatology
(spiders) arachnology *or* araneology
(spirit) pneumatology
(stamps, stamp-collecting) timbrology
(stellar and planetary influence) astrology
(structural morphology) tectology
(suicide) suicidology
(symptoms) sematology *or* semeiology
(system of names or terms) terminology
(terminology) orismology
(the atmosphere and weather) meteorology
(the blood) haematology
(the causes of disease) etiology
(the crust of the Earth) geology
(the devil, devils) diabiology
(the ear) otology
(the endocrine glands) endocrinology
(the environment) ecology *or* environmentology
(the eyes) ophthalmology
(the fetus) fetology
(the head) cephalology
(the heart) cardiology
(the larynx) laryngology
(the liver) hepatology
(the living body) physiology
(the mind) psychology
(the moon) selenology
(the nervous system) neurology
(the nose) nasology *or* rhinology
(the planet Mars) areology
(the pulse) sphygmoology
(the skin) dermatology
(the skull) craniology

(the spleen) splenology
(the stomach) gastrology
(the structure of wood) xyloology
(the sun) heliology
(the teeth) odontology
(the universe) cosmology
(the uterus) hysterology
(the viscera) splanchnology
(therapeutic agents) acology
(therapeutic baths) balneology
(thunder) brontology
(tides) tidology
(time, clocks) horology
(tiny things) micrology
(tissues and organs) histology *or* histiology
(towers) pyrgology
(tree-ring dating) dendrochronology
(trees) dendrology
(truth) alethology
(tumours) oncology
(ulcers) helcology
(urogenital organs and diseases) urology
(values) timology
(victims) victimology
(vocal sounds) phonology
(volcanoes) vulcanology
(wasps, bees, ants) hymenopterology
(water vapour) atmology
(water) hydrology
(weight) barology
(weights and measures) metrology
(whales and dolphins) cetology
(wine) oenology *or* enology
(words and meanings) lexicology
(work and its effects) ergology
(worms, esp parasitic worms) helminthology
(worms) vermiology
(wounds, shock) traumatology
(X-rays) radiology *or* Röntgenology

928 INTELLECTUAL

nouns

1 **intellectual, intellect,** intellectualist, literate, member of the intelligentsia, white-collar intellectual; "someone whose mind watches itself"—CAMUS; brainworker, thinker; **brain** *and* rocket scientist *and* brain surgeon (*all informal*); **pundit, Brahmin,** mandarin, egg-head (*informal*); **highbrow** (*informal*); wise man *see* 920

2 **intelligentsia,** literati, illuminati; intellectual elite; clerisy; literati

3 **scholar,** scholastic (*old*), clerk *or* learned clerk (*both archaic*); a gentleman and a scholar; student *see* 572; **learned man,** man of learning, giant of learning, colossus of knowledge, mastermind, **savant,** pundit; genius *see* 413.12; polymath, polyhistor *or* polyhistorian, **mine of information, walking encyclopedia;** literary man, *littérateur* (*French*), *or* litterateur, **man of letters;** philologist, philologue; philomath, lover of learning; philosopher, philosophe; bookman; **academician,** schoolman; classicist, classicalist, Latinist, humanist

4 **bookworm,** bibliophage; **booklover, bibliophile,** bibliophilist, philobiblist, bibliolater, bibliolatrist; bibliomaniac, bibliomane

5 **pedant; formalist, precisionist,** precisian, purist, *précieux* (*French*), **bluestocking,** *bas bleu* (*French*), *précieuse* (*French feminine*); Dr Pangloss (*Voltaire*), Dryasdust (*Rev Dr Carlyle*)

6 **dilettante,** half scholar, sciolist, **dabbler,** dabster, amateur, trifler, smatterer; grammaticaster, philologaster, criticaster, philosophaster, Latinitaster

929 IGNORANCE

nouns

1 **ignorance,** ignorantness, **unknowingness,** unknowing, nescience; lack of information, knowledge-gap, hiatus of learning; empty-headedness, blankmindedness, vacuousness, vacuity, inanity; tabula rasa; **unintelligence** *see* 921; **unacquaintance, unfamiliarity; greenness,** greenhornism, rawness, callowness, unripeness, green in the eye, **inexperience** *see* 414.2; innocence, ingenuousness, simpleness, simplicity; crass *or* gross *or* primal *or* pristine ignorance; ignorantism, know-nothingism, obscurantism; agnosticism

2 "blind and naked Ignorance"—TENNYSON, "the mother of devotion"—ROBERT BURTON, "the mother of prejudice"—JOHN BRIGHT, "the dominion of absurdity"—J A FROUDE

3 **incognizance, unawareness, unconsciousness, insensibility,** unwittingness, nonrecognition; deniability; nonrealization, incomprehension; **unmindfulness;** mindlessness; blindness *see* 30, deafness *see* 49

4 **unenlightenment, benightedness,** benightment, dark, darkness; savagery, barbarism, paganism, heathenism, Gothicism; age of ignorance, dark age; rural idiocy

5 **unlearnedness,** inerudition, ineducation, unschooledness, unletteredness; **unscholarliness,** unstudiousness; **illiteracy,** illiterateness, functional illiteracy; **unintellectuality,** unintellectualism, philistinism, bold ignorance

6 **slight knowledge,** vague notion, imperfect knowledge, a little learning, glimmering, glimpse (*old*), smattering, **smattering of knowledge,** smattering of ignorance, **half-learning,** semi-learning, semi-ignorance, sciolism; **superficiality,**

shallowness, surface-scratching; **dilettantism,** dilettantship, amateurism

7 the unknown, the unknowable, the strange, the unfamiliar, the incalculable; **matter of ignorance,** sealed book, riddle, enigma, mystery, puzzle *see* 970.3; *terra incognita* (*Latin*), unexplored ground *or* territory; frontier, frontiers of knowledge, **unknown quantity,** x, y, z, n; dark horse

8 ignoramus, know-nothing; no scholar, puddinghead, dunce, fool *see* 923; **illiterate; lowbrow** (*informal*); unintelligentsia, illiterati; **greenhorn,** greeny (*informal*), tenderfoot, neophyte, novice; **dilettante,** dabbler *see* 928.6; **middlebrow** (*informal*)

verbs

9 to be ignorant, be green, have everything to learn, **know nothing,** know from nothing (*US & Canadian informal*); wallow in ignorance; not know any better; **not know what's what,** not know what it is all about, not know the score (*informal*), not be with it (*informal*), not know any of the answers; not know the time of day *or* what o'clock it is, not know the first thing about, not know one's arse from one's elbow (*informal*), not know the way home, not know enough to come in out of the rain, not know chalk from cheese, **not know up from down,** not know which way is up, not know whether it is New Year or New York, nonformal

10 to be in the dark, be blind, labour in darkness, walk in darkness, be benighted, grope in the dark, "see through a glass, darkly"—BIBLE

11 to not know, not rightly know (*informal*), know not, know not what, know nothing of, wot not of (*informal*), be innocent of, have no idea *or* notion *or* conception, **not have the first idea, not have the least** *or* **remotest idea,** be clueless *and* not have a clue (*both informal*), not have the foggiest (*informal*), **not pretend to say,** not take upon oneself to say; not know the half of it; not know from Adam, not know from the man in the moon; wonder, wonder whether; half-know, have a little learning, scratch the surface, know a little, smatter, dabble, toy with, coquet with; pass, give up

adjectives

12 ignorant, nescient, **unknowing,** uncomprehending, **know-nothing;** simple, **dumb** (*informal*), empty, empty-headed, blankminded, vacuous, inane, **unintelligent** *see* 921.13; ill-informed, **uninformed, unenlightened,** unilluminated, unapprized, unposted (*informal*), clueless *or* pig-ignorant (*both informal*); **unacquainted, unconversant,** unversed, uninitiated, **unfamiliar,** strange to; **inexperienced** *see* 414.17; **green,** callow, innocent, ingenuous, gauche, awkward, naive, unripe, raw; groping, tentative, unsure

13 unaware, unconscious, insensible, unknowing, incognizant; mindless, witless; unprehensive, unrealizing, nonconceiving, **unmindful,** unwitting, unsuspecting; unperceiving, impercipient, unhearing, unseeing, uninsightful; unaware of, in ignorance of, unconscious of, unmindful of, insensible to, out of it (*informal*), not with it (*informal*); **blind to, deaf to,**

dead to, a stranger to; asleep, napping, **off one's guard,** caught napping, caught tripping

14 unlearned, inerudite, unerudite, **uneducated,** unschooled, uninstructed, untutored, unbriefed, untaught, unedified, unguided; ill-educated, misinstructed, misinformed, mistaught, led astray; hoodwinked, deceived; **illiterate,** functionally illiterate, unlettered, grammarless; **unscholarly,** unscholastic, unstudious; **unliterary, unread,** unbookish, unbook-learned, bookless (*old*), unbooked; **uncultured,** uncultivated, unrefined, rude, Philistine; barbarous, pagan, heathen; Gothic; nonintellectual, **unintellectual; lowbrow** *and* lowbrowed *and* lowbrowish (*all informal*)

15 half-learned, half-baked (*informal*), half-cocked *and* half-arsed (*both informal*), sciolistic; **shallow, superficial;** immature, sophomoric, sophomorical; **dilettante,** dilettantish, smattering, dabbling, amateur, amateurish; **wise in one's own conceit**

16 benighted, dark, in darkness, in the dark

17 unknown, unbeknown (*informal*), unheard (*old*), **unheard-of,** unapprehended, unapparent, unperceived, unsuspected; unexplained, unascertained; uninvestigated, unexplored; unidentified, unclassified, uncharted, unfathomed, unplumbed, virgin, untouched; undisclosed, unrevealed, undivulged, undiscovered, unexposed, sealed; **unfamiliar,** strange; incalculable, **unknowable,** incognizable, undiscoverable; enigmatic *see* 522.17, mysterious, puzzling

adverbs

18 ignorantly, unknowingly, unmindfully, unwittingly, witlessly, unsuspectingly, **unawares;** unconsciously, insensibly; for anything *or* aught one knows, not that one knows

exclamations

19 God knows!, God only knows!, Lord knows!, Christ knows! (*taboo*), Heaven knows!, nobody knows!, damned if I know!, buggered if I know!, search me!, **beats me!,** beats the hell *or* heck *or* shit out of me!, your guess is as good as mine!, it has me guessing!, it's Greek to me!; **search me!,** you've got me!, I give up!, I pass!, I haven't a clue!, I haven't the foggiest!, don't ask me!, **who knows?,** how should I know?, I don't know what!

930 THOUGHT
exercise of the intellect

nouns

1 thought, thinking, cogitation, cerebration, ideation, noesis, mentation, intellection, intellectualization, ratiocination; using one's head *or* noddle (*informal*); workings of the mind; **reasoning** *see* 934; **brainwork, headwork,** mental labour *or* effort, mental act *or* process, act of thought, mental *or* intellectual exercise; deep-think (*informal*); **way of thinking,** habit of thought *or* mind, thought-pattern; heavy thinking, straight thinking; conception, conceit (*old*), conceptualization; abstract thought, imageless thought; excogitation, thinking out *or* through;

thinking aloud; **idea** *see* 931; creative thought *see* 985.2

2 **consideration, contemplation, reflection** *or* **reflexion, speculation, meditation, musing, rumination, deliberation,** lucubration, brooding, study, **pondering,** weighing, revolving, turning over in the mind, looking at from all angles; lateral thought *or* thinking; advisement, counsel

3 **thoughtfulness,** contemplativeness, speculativeness, reflectiveness; **pensiveness,** wistfulness, reverie, musing, melancholy; **preoccupation, absorption, engrossment,** abstraction, brown study, intense *or* deep *or* profound thought; **concentration,** study, close study

4 **thoughts,** burden of one's mind, mind's content; inmost *or* innermost thoughts *or* mind, secret thoughts, mind's core, one's heart of hearts; **train of thought,** current *or* flow of thought *or* ideas, succession *or* sequence *or* chain of thought *or* ideas; **stream of consciousness; association,** association of ideas

5 **mature thought,** developed thought, ripe idea; **afterthought,** *arrière-pensée* (French), *esprit d'escalier* (French), second thought *or* thoughts; **reconsideration,** reappraisal, revaluation, rethinking, re-examination, review, thinking over

6 **introspection,** self-communion, self-counsel, self-consultation, subjective inspection *or* speculation, head trip (*informal*)

7 subject for thought, food for thought, something to chew on, something to get one's teeth into

verbs

8 **to think, cogitate,** cerebrate, put on one's thinking *or* considering cap (*informal*), intellectualize, ideate, conceive, conceptualize, form ideas, entertain ideas; **reason** *see* 934.15; **use one's head,** use one's noddle *or* noggin (*informal*), use *or* exercise the mind, set the brain *or* wits to work, bethink oneself, have something on one's mind, have a lot on one's mind

9 **to think hard,** think one's head off, **rack** *or* **ransack one's brains, beat** *or* **cudgel one's brains,** do some heavy thinking, bend *or* apply the mind, knit one's brow; sweat *or* stew over (*informal*), hammer *or* hammer away at; puzzle, **puzzle over**

10 **to concentrate,** concentrate the mind *or* thoughts, concentrate on *or* upon, attend closely to, brood on, **focus on** *or* **upon,** give *or* devote the mind to, glue the mind to, cleave to the thought of, fix the mind *or* thoughts upon, bend the mind upon, bring the mind to bear upon; get to the point; gather *or* collect one's thoughts, pull one's wits together, focus *or* fix one's thoughts, marshal *or* arrange one's thoughts *or* ideas

11 **to think about,** cogitate, **give** *or* **apply the mind to,** put one's mind to, apply oneself to, bend *or* turn the mind *or* thoughts to, direct the mind upon, **give thought to, trouble one's head about,** occupy the mind *or* thoughts with; think through *or* out, puzzle out, sort out, reason out, excogitate

12 **to consider, contemplate, speculate, reflect, study, ponder,** perpend, **weigh, deliberate, debate, meditate, muse, brood, ruminate,** chew the cud (*informal*), digest; introspect, be abstracted;

wrinkle one's brow; fall into a brown study, retreat into one's mind *or* thoughts; **toy with, play with,** play around with, flirt *or* coquet with the idea

13 **to think over, ponder over, brood over, muse over, mull over, reflect over,** con over, **deliberate over,** run over, **meditate over,** ruminate over, chew over, digest, turn over, **revolve,** revolve *or* turn over in the mind, deliberate upon, meditate upon, muse on *or* upon, bestow thought *or* consideration upon

14 **to take under consideration,** entertain, take under advisement, take under active consideration, inquire into, **think it over,** have a look at *and* see about (*both informal*); **sleep on** *or* **upon,** consult with *or* advise with *or* take counsel of one's pillow

15 **to reconsider, re-examine,** review; revise one's thoughts, reappraise, revaluate, rethink; view in a new light, have second thoughts, think better of

16 **to think of,** bethink oneself of, seize on, flash on (*informal*); tumble to (*informal*); **entertain the idea of,** entertain thoughts of; have an idea of, have thoughts about; **have in mind, contemplate, consider, have under consideration;** take it into one's head; **bear in mind, keep in mind,** hold the thought; harbour an idea, keep *or* hold an idea, cherish *or* foster *or* nurse *or* nurture an idea

17 (*look upon mentally*) **to contemplate, look upon, view, regard,** see, view with the mind's eye, **envisage,** envision, **visualize** *see* 985.15, imagine, image

18 **to occur to,** occur to one's mind, occur, **come to mind,** rise to mind, rise in the mind, come into one's head, impinge on one's consciousness, claim one's mind *or* thoughts, pass through one's head *or* mind, dawn upon one, **enter one's mind,** come into one's head, pass in the mind *or* thoughts, **cross one's mind,** race *or* tumble through the mind, flash on *or* across the mind; **strike,** strike one, strike the mind, grab one (*informal*), **suggest itself,** present itself, offer itself, present itself to the mind *or* thoughts, give one pause

19 **to impress, make an impression, strike,** grab (*informal*), hit; catch the thoughts, arrest the thoughts, seize one's mind, sink *or* penetrate into the mind, embed itself in the mind, lodge in the mind, **sink in** (*informal*)

20 **to occupy the mind** *or* **thoughts,** engage the thoughts, monopolize the thoughts, fasten itself on the mind, seize the mind, fill the mind, take up one's thoughts; **preoccupy,** occupy, **absorb, engross,** absorb *or* enwrap *or* engross the thoughts, obsess the mind, run in the head; foster in the mind; come uppermost, be uppermost in the mind; have in *or* on one's mind, **have on the brain** (*informal*), have constantly in one's thoughts

adjectives

21 **cognitive,** prehensive, **thought,** conceptive, conceptual, conceptualized, ideative, ideational, noetic, **mental; rational** *see* 934.18, logical, ratiocinative; **thoughtful,** cogitative, **contemplative, reflective, speculative, deliberative, meditative, ruminative,** ruminant, museful (*old*); **pensive,** wistful; introspective; thinking, reflecting, contemplating, pondering, deliberating, excogitating,

excogitative, meditating, ruminating, musing; sober, serious, deepthinking; concentrating, concentrative

22 absorbed *or* engrossed in thought, **absorbed, engrossed,** introspective, rapt, **wrapped in thought, lost in thought,** abstracted, immersed in thought, buried in thought, engaged in thought, occupied, **preoccupied**

adverbs

23 thoughtfully, contemplatively, reflectively, meditatively, ruminatively, musefully (*old*); **pensively,** wistfully; on reconsideration, on second thought

24 on one's mind, on the brain *and* on one's chest (*both informal*), in the thoughts; in the heart, *in petto* (*Italian*), in one's inmost *or* innermost thoughts

931 IDEA

nouns

1 idea; thought, mental *or* intellectual object, **notion, concept,** conception, conceit, fancy; **perception, sense, impression,** mental impression, image, **mental image,** picture in the mind, mental picture, representation, recept; imago; memory trace; **sentiment,** apprehension; reflection *or* reflexion, observation; **opinion** *see* 952.6; supposition, **theory** *see* 950

2 (*philosophy*) ideatum, ideate; noumenon; universal, universal concept *or* conception; idée-force; Platonic idea *or* form, archetype, prototype, subsistent form, eternal object, transcendent universal, eternal universal, pattern, model, exemplar, ideal, transcendent idea *or* essence, universal essence, innate idea; Aristotelian form, form-giving cause, formal cause; complex idea, simple idea; percept; construct of memory and association; Kantian idea, supreme principle of pure reason, regulative first principle, highest unitary principle of thought, transcendent nonempirical concept; Hegelian idea, highest category, the Absolute, the Absolute Idea, the Self-determined, the realized ideal; logical form *or* category; noosphere (*Teilhard de Chardin*); history of ideas, *Geistesgeschichte* (*German*); **idealism** *see* 1051.3

3 abstract idea, abstraction, general idea, generality, abstract

4 main idea, intellectual *or* philosophical basis, leading *or* principal idea, fundamental *or* basic idea, *idée-maitresse* (*French*), guiding principle, crowning principle, **big idea** (*informal*)

5 novel idea, intellectual *or* conceptual breakthrough, new *or* **latest wrinkle** (*informal*), new slant *or* twist *or* take (*informal*)

6 good idea, great idea, not a bad idea; **bright thought,** bright *or* brilliant idea, **insight; brainchild** *and* **brainstorm** (*both informal*), **inspiration**

7 absurd idea, crazy idea, brainstorm (*informal*), fool notion (*US & Canadian informal*)

8 ideology, system of ideas, body of ideas, system of theories; world view, *Weltanschauung* (*German*); philosophy; **ethos**

adjectives

9 ideational, ideal, **conceptual, notional,** fanciful; **intellectual; theoretical** *see* 950.13; **ideological**

10 ideaed, notioned, thoughted

932 ABSENCE OF THOUGHT

nouns

1 thoughtlessness, thoughtfreeness; **vacuity,** vacancy, **emptiness of mind, empty-headedness,** blankness, mental blankness, blankmindedness; fatuity, inanity, foolishness *see* 922; tranquillity, calm of mind; **nirvana,** ataraxia, calm *or* tranquillity of mind; **oblivion,** forgetfulness, lack *or* loss of memory, amnesia; quietism, passivity, apathy; blank mind, fallow mind, tabula rasa; **unintelligence** *see* 921

verbs

2 to not think, make the mind a blank, let the mind lie fallow; **not think of,** not consider, be unmindful of; **not enter one's mind** *or* **head,** be far from one's mind *or* head *or* thoughts; pay no attention *or* mind

3 to get it off one's mind, get it off one's chest (*informal*), clear the mind, relieve one's mind; **put it out of one's thoughts,** dismiss from the mind *or* thoughts, push from one's thoughts, put away thought

adjectives

4 thoughtless, thoughtfree, incogitant, **unthinking,** unreasoning; unideaed; unintellectual; **vacuous,** vacant, blank, blankminded, relaxed, empty, **empty-headed,** fatuous, inane *see* 921.19; unoccupied; calm, tranquil; nirvanic; oblivious; quietistic, passive

5 unthought-of, undreamed-of, unconsidered, unconceived, unconceptualized; unimagined, unimaged; imageless

933 INTUITION, INSTINCT

nouns

1 intuition, intuitiveness, sixth sense; intuitive reason *or* knowledge, direct perception *or* apprehension, immediate apprehension *or* perception, unmediated perception *or* apprehension, subconscious perception, unconscious *or* subconscious knowledge, immediate cognition, knowledge without thought *or* reason, flash of insight;

"*l'esprit de tact*"—Pascal, intuitive understanding, tact, spontaneous sense; **revelation,** epiphany, moment of illumination; **insight,** inspiration, aperçu; anticipation, a priori knowledge; *satori* (*Japanese*), *buddhi* (*Sanskrit*); woman's intuition; second sight, second-sightedness, precognition *see* 960.3, clairvoyance *see* 689.8; intuitionism, intuitivism

2 instinct, natural instinct, unlearned capacity, innate *or* inborn proclivity, native *or* natural tendency, **impulse,** blind *or* unreasoning impulse, vital impulse; **libido, id,** primitive self; archetype, archetypal pattern *or* idea; unconscious *or* subconscious urge *or* drive; collective unconscious, race memory;

"the *not ourselves*, which is in us and all around us"—Matthew Arnold, "an unfathomable Somewhat, which is *Not we*"—Carlyle, "that which is imprinted upon the spirit of man by an inward instinct"—Francis Bacon; **reflex**, spontaneous reaction, unthinking response, knee jerk, knee-jerk reaction

3 **hunch** (*informal*), sense, **presentiment, premonition**, preapprehension, intimation, foreboding; suspicion, **impression**, intuition, intuitive impression, **feeling**, forefeeling, vague feeling *or* idea, funny feeling (*informal*), feeling in one's bones

verbs

4 to **intuit, sense, feel**, feel intuitively, **feel** *or* **know in one's bones** (*informal*), **have a feeling**, have a funny feeling (*informal*), **get** *or* **have the impression, have a hunch** (*informal*), just know, know instinctively

adjectives

5 **intuitive**, intuitional, sensing, feeling; second-sighted, precognitive *see* 960.7, clairvoyant

6 **instinctive**, natural, **inherent, innate**, unlearned; unconscious, subliminal; **involuntary, automatic,** spontaneous, impulsive; **instinctual**, libidinal

adverbs

7 **intuitively**, by intuition; **instinctively**, automatically, spontaneously, on *or* by instinct, **instinctually**

934 REASONING

nouns

1 **reasoning, reason**, logical thought, discursive reason, rationalizing, rationalization, ratiocination; the divine faculty,
"the homage we pay for not being beasts"—Sir Thomas Browne, "a harmony among irrational impulses"—Santayana; **rationalism, rationality**, discourse *or* discourse of reason (*both old*); sweet reason, reasonableness; demonstration, proof *see* 956; specious reasoning, sophistry *see* 935; philosophy *see* 951

2 **logic**, logics; **dialectics**, dialectic, dialecticism; art of reason, science of discursive thought,
"the art of making truth prevail"—La Bruyère, "the ruin of the spirit"—Saint-Exupéry; formal logic, material logic; doctrine of terms, doctrine of the judgment, doctrine of inference, traditional *or* Aristotelian logic, Ramist *or* Ramistic logic, modern *or* epistemological logic, pragmatic *or* instrumental *or* experimental logic; psychological logic, psychologism; symbolic *or* mathematical logic, logistic; propositional calculus, calculus of individuals, functional calculus, combinatory logic, algebra of relations, algebra of classes, set theory, Boolean algebra

3 (*methods*) a priori reasoning, a fortiori reasoning, a posteriori reasoning; discursive reasoning; **deduction, deductive reasoning**, syllogism, syllogistic reasoning; hypothetico-deductive method; **induction, inductive reasoning**, epagoge; philosophical induction, inductive *or* Baconian method; **inference**;

generalization, particularization; synthesis, analysis; hypothesis and verification

4 **argumentation, argument, controversy, dispute, disputation, polemic, debate**, disceptation (*old*), eristic; **contention, wrangling, bickering**, hubbub *see* 53.3, bicker, set-to (*informal*), rhubarb *and* hassle (*both informal*), passage of arms; war of words, verbal engagement *or* contest, logomachy, flyting; paper war, *guerre de plume* (*French*); adversarial procedure, confrontational occasion; academic disputation, defence of a thesis; defence, apology, apologia, apologetics; pilpul, casuistry; polemics; litigation; examination, cross-examination

5 **argument**, *argumentum* (*Latin*); **case, plea**, pleading, *plaidoyer* (*French*), brief; special pleading; **reason, consideration; refutation**, elenchus, ignoratio elenchi; pros, cons, **pros and cons**; talking point; **dialogue**, reasoning together, dialectic

6 **syllogism**; prosyllogism; mode; figure; mood; pseudosyllogism, paralogism; sorites, progressive *or* Aristotelian sorites, regressive *or* Goclenian sorites; categorical syllogism; enthymeme; dilemma; **rule**, rule of deduction, transformation rule; modus ponens, modus tollens

7 **premise, proposition, position**, assumed position, sumption, **assumption**, supposal, presupposition, **hypothesis, thesis, theorem**, lemma, **statement**, affirmation, categorical proposition, assertion, basis, ground, foundation; **postulate, axiom, postulation**, postulatum; data; major premise, minor premise; first principles; a priori principle, apriorism; philosophical proposition, philosopheme; hypothesis ad hoc; sentential *or* propositional function, truth-function, truth table, truth-value

8 **conclusion** *see* 945.4

9 **reasonableness**, reasonability, **logicalness**, logicality, **rationality, sensibleness, soundness**, justness, justifiability, admissibility, cogency; **sense**, common sense, sound sense, sweet reason, **logic, reason**; plausibility *see* 967.3

10 **good reasoning, right thinking**, sound reasoning, ironclad reasoning, irrefutable logic; cogent argument, **cogency**; strong argument, knockdown argument; good case, good reason, sound evidence, strong point

11 **reasoner**, ratiocinator, **thinker; rationalist**; rationalizer; synthesizer; **logician**, logistician; logicaster; dialectician; syllogist, syllogizer; sophist *see* 935.6; philosopher *see* 951.6

12 **arguer, controversialist, disputant, debater**, eristic, argufier (*informal*), advocate, wrangler, mooter, bush lawyer (*Australian & NZ*), disceptator (*old*), pilpulist, casuist; polemic, polemist, polemicist; logomacher, logomachist; apologist

13 **contentiousness**, litigiousness, **quarrelsomeness**, argumentativeness, disputatiousness, testiness, feistiness (*informal*), combativeness; ill humour *see* 110

14 **side**, interest; **the affirmative**, pro, yes, aye, yea; **the negative**, con, no, nay

verbs

15 to **reason**; logicalize, logicize; rationalize, provide a rationale; intellectualize; bring reason to bear, apply

or use reason, put two and two together; **deduce, infer, generalize; synthesize, analyse; theorize,** hypothesize; philosophize; syllogize

16 **to argue,** argufy (*informal*), **dispute,** discept (*old*), logomachize, polemize, polemicize, moot, **bandy words,** chop logic, **plead,** pettifog (*informal*), join issue, give and take, cut and thrust, try conclusions, cross swords, lock horns, **contend, contest,** spar, **bicker, wrangle,** hassle (*informal*), have it out; thrash out; take one's stand upon, **put up an argument** (*informal*); take sides, take up a side; argue to no purpose; **quibble, cavil** *see* 935.9

17 **to be reasonable, be logical, make sense,** figure (*informal*), **stand to reason,** be demonstrable, be irrefutable; hold good, hold water (*informal*); have a leg to stand on

adjectives

18 **reasoning, rational,** ratiocinative *or* ratiocinatory; analytic, analytical

19 **argumentative, argumental, dialectic, dialectical, controversial, disputatious, contentious, quarrelsome,** litigious, combative, testy, feisty (*informal*), ill-humoured *see* 110.18, eristic, eristical, polemic, polemical, logomachic, logomachical, pilpulistic, pro and con

20 **logical, reasonable, rational, cogent, sensible, sane, sound,** well-thought-out, legitimate, just, justifiable, admissible; credible *see* 952.24; plausible *see* 967.7; as it should be, as it ought to be; well-argued, **well-founded, well-grounded**

21 **reasoned, advised, considered, calculated,** meditated, contemplated, deliberated, studied, weighed, thought-out

22 dialectic, dialectical, maieutic; syllogistic, syllogistical, enthymematic, enthymematical, soritical, epagogic, inductive, deductive, inferential, synthetic, synthetical, analytic, analytical, discursive; a priori, a fortiori, a posteriori; categorical, hypothetical, conditional

23 **deducible, derivable, inferable;** sequential, following

adverbs

24 **reasonably, logically, rationally,** by the rules of logic, **sensibly,** sanely, soundly; syllogistically, analytically; **in reason,** in all reason, within reason, within the bounds *or* limits of reason, within reasonable limitations, **within bounds,** within the bounds of possibility, as far as possible, in all conscience

935 SOPHISTRY
specious reasoning

nouns

1 **sophistry,** sophistication, sophism, philosophism, **casuistry,** Jesuitry, Jesuitism, subtlety, oversubtlety; **false *or* specious reasoning, rationalization,** evasive reasoning, vicious reasoning, sophistical reasoning, special pleading; **fallacy,** fallaciousness; **speciousness,** speciosity, superficial *or* apparent soundness, plausibleness, plausibility; **insincerity, disingenuousness; equivocation,** equivocalness;

fudging *and* waffling (*both informal*), fudge and mudge (*informal*); perversion, distortion, misapplication; vicious circle, circularity; mystification, obfuscation, obscurantism; reduction, trivialization

2 **illogicalness,** illogic, illogicality, **unreasonableness, irrationality, reasonlessness, senselessness, unsoundness,** unscientificness, invalidity, untenableness, inconclusiveness; **inconsistency,** incongruity, antilogy

3 (*specious argument*) **sophism,** sophistry, insincere argument, mere rhetoric, philosophism, solecism; paralogism, pseudosyllogism; claptrap, moonshine, empty words, doubletalk, doublespeak, "sound and fury, signifying nothing"—SHAKESPEARE; bad case, weak point, flaw in an argument, "lame and impotent conclusion"—SHAKESPEARE; **fallacy,** logical fallacy, formal fallacy, material fallacy, verbal fallacy; *argumentum ad hominem, argumentum ad baculum, argumentum ad captandum, argumentum ad captandum vulgus* (*all Latin*), crowd-pleasing argument, argument by analogy, *tu quoque* (*Latin*), argument, *petitio principii* (*Latin*), begging the question, **circular argument,** undistributed middle, *non sequitur* (*Latin*), *hysteron proteron* (*Greek*), *post hoc, ergo propter hoc* (*both Latin*)

4 **quibble,** quiddity, quodlibet, quillet (*old*), Jesuitism, **cavil;** quip, quirk, shuffle, dodge

5 **quibbling, cavilling,** boggling, captiousness, nit-picking, **bickering; logic-chopping, hairsplitting,** trichoschistism; subterfuge, chicane, chicanery, pettifoggery; **equivocation,** tergiversation, prevarication, **evasion, hedging, pussyfooting** (*informal*), flannel (*informal*), waffle (*informal*), **sidestepping,** dodging, shifting, shuffling, fencing, parrying, boggling, paltering

6 **sophist,** sophister, philosophist (*old*), **casuist,** Jesuit; choplogic (*old*), logic-hopper; paralogist

7 **quibbler, caviler,** pettifogger, hairsplitter, captious critic, nitpicker; **equivocator,** Jesuit, mystifier, mystificator, obscurantist, prevaricator, palterer, tergiversator, shuffler, mudger (*informal*), flannel merchant (*informal*); **hedger;** pussyfoot *or* **pussyfooter** (*informal*)

verbs

8 **to reason speciously,** reason ill, paralogize, reason in a circle, argue insincerely, pervert, distort, misapply; explain away, rationalize; prove that black is white and white black; not have a leg to stand on

9 **to quibble, cavil, bicker,** boggle, chop logic, **split hairs,** nitpick, pick nits; Jesuitize; **equivocate,** mystify, obscure, prevaricate, tergiversate, doubletalk, doublespeak, tap-dance (*informal*), palter, fence, parry, shift, **shuffle, dodge,** shy, **evade,** sidestep, hedge, skate around (*informal*), pussyfoot (*informal*), evade the issue, flannel (*informal*), waffle (*informal*); **beat about *or* around the bush,** not come to the point, **beg the question;** pick holes in, pick to pieces; blow hot and cold; strain at a gnat and swallow a camel

adjectives

10 sophistical, sophistic, philosophistic, philosophistical (*old*), casuistic, casuistical, Jesuitic, Jesuitical, **fallacious, specious,** colourable, plausible, hollow, superficially *or* apparently sound; deceptive, illusive, empty; overrefined, oversubtle, **insincere, disingenuous**

11 illogical, unreasonable, irrational, reasonless, contrary to reason, **senseless,** without reason, **without rhyme or reason; unscientific,** nonscientific, unphilosophical; **invalid,** inauthentic, unauthentic, faulty, flawed, paralogical, fallacious; inconclusive, inconsequent, inconsequential, not following; **inconsistent,** incongruous, absonant (*old*), loose, unconnected; contradictory, **self-contradictory,** self-annulling, self-refuting, oxymoronic, paradoxical

12 unsound, unsubstantial, insubstantial, weak, feeble, poor, flimsy, unrigorous, inconclusive, unproved, unsustained, poorly argued

13 baseless, groundless, ungrounded, **unfounded,** ill-founded, unbased, **unsupported,** unsustained, **without foundation,** without basis *or* sound basis; **untenable, unsupportable,** unsustainable; **unwarranted,** idle, empty, vain

14 quibbling, cavilling, equivocatory, captious, nitpicky *and* nit-picking (*both informal*), bickering; picayune (*US & Canadian informal*), petty, trivial, trifling; paltering, shuffling, hedging, pussyfooting (*informal*), **evasive; hairsplitting,** trichoschistic, logic-chopping, choplogic *or* choplogical (*old*)

adverbs

15 illogically, unreasonably, irrationally, reasonlessly, senselessly; baselessly, groundlessly; untenably, unsupportably, unsustainably; out of all reason, out of all bounds

936 TOPIC

nouns

1 topic, subject, subject of thought, **matter, subject matter,** what it is about, **concern,** focus of interest *or* attention, discrete matter, category; **theme,** burden, **text,** motif, motive, business at hand, **case,** matter in hand, **question, problem, issue; point,** point at issue, point in question, main point, gist *see* 996.6; item on the agenda; head, heading, chapter, rubric; substance, meat, essence, material part, basis; living issue, topic of the day

2 caption, title, heading, head, superscription, rubric; **headline;** overline (*US & Canadian*); banner, banner head *or* line, streamer; scarehead (*US & Canadian*), screamer; spread, spreadhead; drop head, dropline, hanger; running head *or* title, jump head (*US & Canadian*); **subhead, subheading,** subtitle; legend, motto, epigraph; title page

verbs

3 to focus on, have regard to, distinguish, lift up, set forth, specify, zero in on (*informal*); caption, title, head, head up (*informal*); **headline;** subtitle, subhead

adjectives

4 topical, thematic

937 INQUIRY

nouns

1 inquiry, inquiring, probing, **inquest** *see* 307.18, inquirendo; inquisition; inquiring mind; analysis *see* 800

2 examination, school examination, examen, **exam** (*informal*), **test, quiz;** eleven-plus, Ordinary level, O level, Standard Grade (*Scottish*), Advanced level, A level, Higher (*Scottish*), GCSE; oral examination, oral, doctor's oral, master's oral, viva voce examination, viva (*informal*); catechesis, catchization; **audition, hearing;** multiple-choice test, multiple-guess test (*informal*); written examination, written (*informal*), test paper; course examination, midterm, midyear, midsemester; qualifying examination, preliminary examination, prelim (*informal*), mock (*informal*); take-home examination; unannounced examination, pop *or* shotgun *or* surprise quiz (*US & Canadian informal*); final examination, **final** (*informal*), comprehensive examination, comps (*informal*); honours, tripos (*Cambridge*)

3 examination, inspection, scrutiny; survey, review, perusal, look-over, once over *and* look-see (*both informal*), perlustration, **study,** look-through, scan, run-through; visitation; overhaul, overhauling; MOT *or* MOT test; quality control; confirmation, cross-check

4 investigation, indagation (*old*), **research,** legwork (*informal*), inquiry into; data-gathering, gathering *or* amassing evidence; perscrutation, **probe,** searching investigation, close inquiry, exhaustive study; court of inquiry; police inquiry *or* investigation, criminal investigation, detective work, detection, sleuthing; investigative bureau *or* agency, bureau *or* department of investigation; legislative investigation, Congressional investigation, hearing; witch-hunt, Inquisition

5 preliminary *or* tentative examination; quick *or* cursory inspection, glance, quick look, first look, once-over (*informal*)

6 checkup, check; spot check; physical examination, **physical,** physical checkup, health examination, medical; self-examination; exploratory examination; testing, drug testing, alcohol testing, random testing

7 re-examination, reinquiry, recheck, **review,** reappraisal, revaluation, rethinking, revision, rebeholding, second *or* further look

8 reconnaissance; recce *and* recco *and* recon (*all informal*); **reconnoitring,** reconnoitre, exploration, **scouting**

9 surveillance, shadowing, following, trailing, tailing (*informal*), 24-hour surveillance, observation, stakeout (*informal*); **spying, espionage,** espial, **intelligence,** military intelligence, intelligence work, cloak-and-dagger work (*informal*); intelligence agency, secret service, secret police; counterespionage, counterintelligence; wiretap, wiretapping, bugging (*informal*), electronic surveillance

10 question, query, inquiry, demand (*old*), **interrogation,** interrogatory; interrogative; **problem, issue, topic** *see* 936, case *or* point in question, bone of contention, controversial point, question before the house, debating point, question *or* point at issue, **moot point** *or* case, question mark, *quodlibet* (*Latin*); vexed *or* knotty question, burning question; leader, leading question; feeler; cross-question, rhetorical question; cross-interrogatory; catechism, catechizing

11 interview, press conference, press opportunity, photo opportunity, photo op (*informal*)

12 questioning, interrogation, querying, asking, seeking, pumping, probing, inquiring; **quiz, quizzing, examination;** challenge, dispute; interpellation, bringing into question; catechizing, catechization; catechetical method, Socratic method *or* induction

13 grilling, the grill (*informal*), inquisition; police interrogation; **the third-degree** (*informal*); direct examination, redirect examination, **cross-examination,** cross-interrogation, **cross-questioning,** positive vetting

14 canvass, survey, inquiry, questionnaire, questionary; exit poll; **poll, public-opinion poll,** opinion poll *or* survey, straw poll, MORI poll, Gallup poll, statistical survey, opinion sampling, voter-preference survey; consumer-preference survey, market-research survey; consumer research, market research

15 search, searching, **quest, hunt,** hunting, stalk, stalking, still hunt, dragnet, posse, search party; search warrant; search-and-destroy operation *or* mission; **rummage, ransacking,** turning over *or* upside down; **forage;** totting, scavenging, scouring, beach-combing; house-search, perquisition, domiciliary visit; exploration, probe; **body search,** frisk (*informal*), toss *and* shake *and* shakedown *and* skin-search *and* body-shake *and* pat-down search (*all US & Canadian informal*), strip search

16 inquirer, asker, prober, querier, querist, **questioner,** questionist, interrogator; interviewer; interrogatrix; interpellator; **quizzer,** examiner, catechist; inquisitor, inquisitionist; cross-questioner, cross-interrogator, **cross-examiner;** interlocutor; **pollster,** poller, sampler, opinion sampler; **interviewer; detective** *see* 576.10; **secret agent** *see* 576.9; quiz-master

17 examiner, examinant, **tester; inspector,** scrutinizer, scrutator, scrutineer, quality-control inspector, surveyor; **monitor,** reviewer; fact-checker; observer; visitor, visitator; **investigator,** indagator (*old*); editor, subeditor, copy editor, proofreader

18 seeker, hunter, searcher, perquisitor; rummager, ransacker; digger, delver; zetetic; **researcher, fact finder,** researchist, research worker

19 examinee, examinant, examinate, questionee, quizzee; interviewee; informant, subject, interviewee; witness

verbs

20 to inquire, ask, question, query; make inquiry, take up *or* institute *or* pursue *or* follow up *or* conduct *or* carry on an inquiry, ask after, inquire after, ask about, ask questions, put queries; inquire of, require an answer, ask a question, put a question to, pose *or* set *or* propose *or* propound a question; bring into question, interpellate; **demand** (*old*), **want to know**

21 to interrogate, question, query, quiz, test, examine; catechize; **pump,** pump for information, shoot questions at, pick the brains of, worm out of; interview; draw one out

22 to grill, put on the grill (*informal*), inquisition, make inquisition; roast (*informal*), put the pressure on *and* put the screws on *and* go over (*all informal*); **cross-examine, cross-question,** cross-interrogate; third-degree (*informal*), give *or* put through the third degree (*informal*), hammer (*informal*); put to the question; extract information, pry *or* prize out

23 to investigate, indagate (*old*), sift, **explore, look into,** peer into, **search into, go into, delve into,** dig into, poke into, pry into; **probe, sound, plumb, fathom; check into, check on, check out,** nose into, see into; poke about, root around *or* about, scratch around *or* about, cast about *or* around

24 to examine, inspect, scrutinize, survey, canvass, **look at,** peer at, eyeball (*informal*), **observe, scan, peruse, study; look over,** give the once-over (*informal*), run the eye over, cast *or* pass the eyes over, scope out (*US & Canadian informal*), have *or* take a gander *or* butcher's at (*informal*), check *or* check out; go over, run over, pass over, pore over; overlook, overhaul; **monitor, review,** pass under review; set an examination, give an examination; **take stock of,** size *or* size up, take the measure (*informal*), tape (*informal*); **check, check out, check over *or* through; check up on;** autopsy, postmortem *see* 307.18

25 to make a close study of, scrutinize, examine thoroughly, vet, **go deep into,** look closely at; examine point by point, go over with a fine-tooth comb, go over step by step, subject to close scrutiny, view *or* try in all its phases, get down to nuts and bolts (*informal*); perscrutate, perlustrate

26 to examine cursorily, take a cursory view of, give a quick *or* cursory look, give the once-over (*informal*), give a dekko (*informal*), **scan, skim, skim over *or* through,** slur, slur over, slip *or* skip over *or* through, **glance at,** pass over lightly, zip through, **dip into, touch upon,** touch upon lightly *or* in passing, **hit the high spots; thumb through,** flip through the pages, turn over the leaves, leaf *or* page *or* flick through, skim through

27 to re-examine, recheck, reinquire, **reconsider,** reappraise, revaluate, rethink, **review,** revise, rebehold, take another *or* a second *or* a further look; retrace, retrace one's steps, go back over; rejig (*informal*), rejigger (*US & Canadian informal*); go back to the drawing board

28 to reconnoitre, make a reconnaissance, case (*informal*), scout, **scout out,** spy, **spy out,** play the spy, peep; **watch,** put under surveillance, stake out (*informal*); bug (*informal*); check up on, check up

29 to canvass, survey, make a survey; **poll,** conduct a poll, sample, **questionnaire** (*informal*)

30 to seek, hunt, look (*old*), **quest, pursue,** go in pursuit of, follow, go in search of, prowl after, try to find; **look up, hunt up; look for,** look around *or* about for, look for high and low, look high and low, search out, **search for,** seek for, **hunt for,** cast *or* beat about for, rootle about *or* around for; shop around for; **fish for, angle for,** bob for, dig for, delve for; **ask for,** inquire for; **gun for,** go gunning for; still-hunt (*informal*)

31 to search, hunt, explore; research; read up on; **hunt through, search through, look through, go through;** dig, delve, burrow, root, rootle, pick over, poke, pry; look round *or* around, poke around, nose around, smell around; beat the bushes; forage; scavenge; frisk (*informal*); strip search

32 to grope, grope for, **feel for,** fumble, grabble, scrabble, feel around, poke around, pry around, beat about, grope in the dark; **feel** *or* **pick one's way**

33 to ransack, rummage, rake, scour, comb; rifle; **look everywhere,** look into every hole and corner, **look high and low,** look upstairs and downstairs, **look all over,** search high heaven, turn upside down, turn inside out, **leave no stone unturned**

34 to search out, hunt out, spy out, scout out, **ferret out,** fish out, pry out, winkle out (*informal*), dig out, root out, grub up

35 to trace, stalk, track, trail; follow, follow up, shadow, tail (*informal*), dog the footsteps of, have *or* keep an eye on; nose, nose out, **smell** *or* **sniff out,** follow the trail *or* scent *or* spoor of; follow a clue; **trace down, hunt down, track down, run down, run to earth**

adjectives

36 inquiring, questioning, querying, quizzing; **quizzical, curious; interrogatory,** interrogative, interrogational; **inquisitorial,** inquisitional; visitatorial, visitorial; catechistic, catechistical, catechetic, catechetical

37 examining, examinational; scrutatorial, examinatorial; **testing,** trying, **tentative;** groping, feeling; **inspectional;** inspectorial; **investigative,** indagative (*old*); zetetic; heuristic, investigatory, investigational; **exploratory,** explorative, explorational; fact-finding; analytic, analytical

38 searching, probing, prying, nosy (*informal*); poking, digging, fishing, delving; in search *or* quest of, looking for, **out for,** on the lookout for, **in the market for;** all-searching

adverbs

39 in question, at issue, in debate *or* dispute, **under consideration,** under active consideration, **under advisement,** *subjudice* (*Latin*), under examination, under investigation, under surveillance, up *or* open for discussion; **before the house,** on the docket, **on the agenda,** on the table, on the floor

938 ANSWER

nouns

1 answer, reply, response, responsion, replication; answering, respondence; riposte, **uptake** (*informal*), **retort, rejoinder,** reaction *see* 902, return, **comeback** (*informal*), back answer, short answer, backchat; **repartee,** backchat, clever *or* ready *or*

witty reply *or* retort, snappy comeback (*informal*); yes-and-no answer, evasive reply; **acknowledgment,** receipt; rescript, rescription; antiphon; **echo,** reverberation *see* 54.2

2 rebuttal, counterstatement, counterreply, counterclaim, counterblast, counteraccusation, countercharge, *tu quoque* (*Latin,* you too), contraremonstrance; **rejoinder,** replication, defence, rebutter, surrebutter *or* surrebuttal, surrejoinder; confutation, refutation

3 answerer, replier, responder, **respondent,** responser

verbs

4 to answer, make *or* give answer, return answer, return for answer, offer, proffer, **reply, respond,** say, say in reply; **retort,** riposte, **rejoin,** return, throw back, flash back; come back *and* come back at *and* come right back at (*all informal*), answer back *and* talk back *and* shoot back (*all informal*); **react; acknowledge,** make *or* give acknowledgement; echo, reecho, reverberate *see* 54.7

5 to rebut, make a rebuttal; **rejoin,** surrebut, surrejoin; counterclaim, countercharge; confute, refute

adjectives

6 answering, replying, responsive, respondent, responding; rejoining, returning; antiphonal; echoing, echoic, reechoing *see* 54.11; confutative, refutative

adverbs

7 in answer, in reply, in response, in return, in rebuttal

939 SOLUTION
answer to a problem

nouns

1 solution, resolution, **answer, reason, explanation** *see* 341.4; **finding,** conclusion, determination, ascertainment, verdict, judgment; **outcome, upshot,** denouement, **result,** issue, end *see* 819, end result; accomplishment *see* 407; **solving,** working, **working-out,** finding out, resolving, **clearing up,** cracking; **unriddling,** riddling, unscrambling, unravelling, sorting out, untwisting, unspinning, unweaving, untangling, disentanglement; **decipherment, deciphering, decoding,** decryption; interpretation *see* 341; **happy ending** *or* outcome, the answer to one's prayers, the light at the end of the tunnel; possible solution, **scenario**

verbs

2 to solve, resolve, find the solution *or* answer, **clear up,** get, get right, do, work, **work out, find out, figure out; straighten out, iron out,** sort out, puzzle out; debug; psych *and* psych out (*both informal*); **unriddle,** riddle, unscramble, undo, untangle, disentangle, untwist, unspin, unweave, **unravel,** ravel, ravel out; **decipher, decode,** decrypt, crack; **make out,** interpret *see* 341.9; **answer, explain** *see* 341.10; unlock, pick *or* open the lock; find the key of, find a clue to; **get to the**

bottom *or* heart of, **fathom**, plumb, bottom; have it, hit it, hit upon a solution, hit the nail on the head, hit it on the nose (*informal*); guess, divine, guess right; end happily, work out right *and* come up roses (*both informal*)

adjectives

3 solvable, soluble, **resolvable**, open to solution, capable of solution, workable, doable, answerable; explainable, explicable, determinable, ascertainable; **decipherable**, decodable

940 DISCOVERY

nouns

1 discovery, **finding**, **detection**, spotting, catching, catching sight of, sighting, espial; recognition, determination, distinguishment; **locating**, **location**; **disclosure**, **exposure**, revelation, **uncovering**, **unearthing**, digging up, exhumation, excavation, bringing to light *or* view; **find**, trove, treasure trove, *trouvaille* (*French*), strike, lucky strike; accidental *or* chance discovery, happening *or* stumbling upon, tripping over, casual discovery; serendipity; **learning**, **finding out**, determining, becoming conscious *or* cognizant of, becoming aware of; self-discovery; rediscovery; invention

verbs

2 to discover, **find**, get; strike, hit; put *or* lay one's hands on, lay one's fingers on, **locate** *see* 159.10; **hunt down**, search out, trace down, track down, **run down**, **run** *or* **bring to earth**; trace; **learn**, **find out**, determine, become cognizant *or* conscious of, become aware of; discover *or* find out the hard way, discover to one's cost; discover *or* find oneself; rediscover; invent

3 to come across, run across, meet with, meet up with (*informal*), fall in with, **encounter**, **run into**, bump into (*informal*), come *or* run up against (*informal*), **come on** *or* **upon**, hit on *or* upon, strike on, light on *or* upon, alight on *or* upon, fall on, tumble on *or* upon; **chance on** *or* **upon**, happen on *or* upon *or* across, **stumble on** *or* **upon** *or* **across** *or* **into**, stub one's toe on *or* upon, trip over, bump up against, blunder upon, discover serendipitously

4 to uncover, unearth, **dig up**, disinter, exhume, excavate; **disclose**, **expose**, **reveal**, blow the lid off, crack wide open, **bring to light**; **turn up**, root up, rootle up, fish up; worm out, ferret out, winkle out, pry out

5 to detect, spot (*informal*), **see**, **lay eyes on**, catch sight of, clock (*informal*), **spy**, espy, descry, sense, pick up, notice, discern, **perceive**, **make out**, **recognize**, distinguish, identify

6 to scent, catch the scent of, sniff, smell, get a whiff of (*informal*), **get wind of**; sniff *or* scent *or* smell out, nose out; be on the right scent, be near the truth, be warm (*informal*), be burning (*informal*), have a fix on

7 to catch, catch out; catch off side, catch off base; catch tripping, **catch napping**, **catch off-guard**, catch asleep at the switch; **catch at**, catch in the act, **catch red-handed**, catch in *flagrante delicto*,

catch with one's pants down (*informal*), catch flat-footed, have the goods on (*informal*)

8 (*detect the hidden nature of*) **to see through**, **penetrate**, see as it really is, see in its true colours, see the inside of, read between the lines, see the cloven hoof; open the eyes to, tumble to, catch on to, wise up to (*informal*), rumble (*informal*), suss *or* suss out (*informal*); **be on to**, **be wise to**, **be hep to** (*informal*), have one's measure, **have one's number**, have dead to rights *or* bang to rights (*informal*), read someone like a book

9 to turn up, show up, be found; discover itself, expose *or* betray itself; materialize, **come to light**, come out; come along, come to hand

adjectives

10 on the right scent, **on the right track**, on the trail of; **hot** *and* **warm** (*both informal*); **discoverable**, determinable, findable, **detectable**, spottable, disclosable, exposable, locatable, **discernible**

exclamations

11 eureka!, I have it!, at last!, at long last!, finally!, *thalassa!, thalatta!* (*both Greek*); ah hah!

941 EXPERIMENT

nouns

1 experiment, experimentation; experimental method; testing, trying, trying-out, **trial**; research and development *or* R and D; running it up the flagpole (*informal*), trying it on *or* out (*informal*); **trial and error**, hit and miss; empiricism, experimentalism, pragmatism, instrumentalism; **rule of thumb**; tentativeness, tentative method; control experiment, controlled experiment, **control**; experimental design; experimental proof *or* verification; noble experiment; single-blind experiment, double-blind experiment

2 test, trial, try; essay; docimasy (*old*), assay; determination, blank determination; **proof**, verification; touchstone, standard, criterion *see* 300.2; crucial test; acid test, litmus *or* litmus-paper test; ordeal, crucible; probation; **feeling out**, **sounding out**, try-on (*informal*); test case; first *or* rough draft, *brouillon* (*French*); rough sketch

3 tryout, workout, **rehearsal**, practice; pilot plan *or* programme, pilot study; **dry run**, dummy run; *Gedankenexperiment* (*German*); road test, test drive; **trial run**, practical test; bench test; flight test, test flight *or* run; audition, hearing

4 feeler, probe, sound, sounder; **trial balloon**, *ballon d'essai* (*French*), pilot balloon, barometer; weather vane, weathercock; straw to show the wind, straw poll; sample, random sample, experimental sample

5 laboratory, lab (*informal*), research laboratory, research establishment *or* facility *or* institute, experiment station, field station, research and development *or* R and D establishment, back room; **proving ground**; think tank (*informal*)

6 experimenter, experimentist, experimentalist, bench scientist, **researcher**, research worker, R and D worker, boffin (*informal*), back-room boy;

experimental engineer; **tester**, tryer-out, test driver, test pilot; essayer; assayer; analyst, analyser

7 **subject, experimental subject**, experimentee, testee, patient, sample; laboratory animal, experimental *or* test animal, **guinea pig**

verbs

8 **to experiment**, experimentalize, **research**, make an experiment, **run an experiment**, run a sample *or* specimen; **test, try**, essay, **test** *or* **try out**, have a dry run *or* dummy run *or* rehearsal *or* test run; run it up the flagpole and see who salutes (*informal*); put to the test, **put to the proof, prove, verify**, validate, substantiate, confirm, put to trial, bring to test, make a trial of, give a trial to; **give a try**, have a go, give it a go (*informal*), have *or* take a stab (*informal*), have a bash (*informal*), have a shot; sample, taste; assay; play around *or* fool around with (*informal*); try out under controlled conditions; give a tryout *or* workout (*informal*), **road-test**, test-drive; try one out, put one through his paces; experiment *or* practise upon; try it on; try on, try it for size (*informal*); try one's strength, see what one can do

9 **to sound out, feel out, sound**, get a sounding *or* reading *or* sense, probe, **feel the pulse**, read; **put** *or* **throw out a feeler**, put out feelers, send up a trial balloon, fly a kite; **see which way the wind blows**, see how the land lies, test out, test the waters; take a straw poll, take a random sample, use an experimental sample

10 **to stand the test, stand up, hold up, hold up in the wash**, pass, **pass muster**, get by (*informal*), make it *and* hack it *and* cut the mustard (*all informal*), meet *or* satisfy requirements

adjectives

11 **experimental, test, trial**; pilot; testing, proving, trying; probative, probatory, verificatory; probationary; **tentative**, provisional; empirical; trial-and-error, hit-or-miss; heuristic

12 **tried, well-tried, tested, proved**, verified, confirmed, tried and true

adverbs

13 **experimentally**, by rule of thumb, by trial and error, by hit and miss, hit or miss

14 **on trial**, under examination, **on** *or* **under probation**, under suspicion, **on approval**

942 COMPARISON

nouns

1 **comparison**, compare, examining side by side, matching, matchup (*US & Canadian*), holding up together, proportion (*old*), comparative judgment *or* estimate; **likening**, comparing, **analogy**; parallelism; comparative relation; weighing, balancing; opposing, opposition, **contrast**; contrastiveness, distinctiveness, distinction *see* 943.3; confrontment, confrontation; **relation** *see* 774, relating, relativism; correlation *see* 776; simile, similitude, metaphor, allegory, figure *or* trope of comparison; comparative degree; comparative method; comparative linguistics,

comparative grammar, comparative literature, comparative anatomy, etc

2 **collation**, comparative scrutiny, point-by-point comparison; **verification, confirmation, checking**; check, cross-check

3 **comparability**, comparableness, comparativeness; analogousness, equivalence, **commensurability**; proportionateness *or* proportionability (*both old*); ratio, proportion, balance; **similarity** *see* 783

verbs

4 **to compare, liken**, assimilate, similize, liken to, compare with; **make** *or* **draw a comparison**, run a comparison, do a comparative study, bring into comparison; **analogize**, bring into analogy; **relate** *see* 774.6; metaphorize; **draw a parallel**, parallel; **match**, match up; examine side by side, view together, hold up together; weigh *or* measure against; confront, bring into confrontation, **contrast, oppose**, set in opposition, set off against, set in contrast, **put** *or* **set over against**, set *or* place against, counterpose; compare and contrast, note similarities and differences; **weigh**, balance

5 **to collate**, scrutinize comparatively, compare point by point, painstakingly match; **verify, confirm, check, cross-check**

6 **to compare notes**, exchange views *or* observations, match data *or* findings, put heads together (*informal*)

7 **to be comparable, compare, compare to** *or* **with**, not compare with *see* 786.2, admit of comparison, be commensurable, be of the same order *or* class, be worthy of comparison, be fit to be compared; **measure up to, come up to**, match up with, stack up with (*informal*), hold a candle to (*informal*), touch (*informal*); **match, parallel**; vie, vie with, rival; **resemble** *see* 783.7

adjectives

8 **comparative, relative** *see* 774.7, **comparable**, commensurate, commensurable, parallel, matchable, **analogous**; analogical; collatable; **correlative**; much at one, much of a muchness (*informal*); **similar** *see* 783.10; something of the sort *or* to that effect

9 **incomparable**, incommensurable, not to be compared, of different orders; apples and oranges; **unlike, dissimilar** *see* 786.4

adverbs

10 **comparatively, relatively**; comparably; pound for pound, ounce for ounce, dollar for dollar, etc; on the one hand, on the other hand

prepositions

11 **compared to, compared with**, as compared with, by comparison with, **in comparison with, beside**, over against, taken with; than

943 DISCRIMINATION

nouns

1 **discrimination**, discriminateness, discriminatingness, discriminativeness; seeing *or* making distinctions, appreciation of differences; analytic power *or* faculty; **criticalness; finesse**, refinement, delicacy; niceness

of distinction, nicety, subtlety, refined discrimination, critical niceness; **tact, tactfulness,** feel, feeling, sense, **sensitivity** *see* 24.3, **sensibility** *see* 24.2; intuition, instinct *see* 933; appreciation, appreciativeness; judiciousness *see* 919.7; taste, discriminating taste, aesthetic *or* artistic judgment; palate, fine *or* refined palate; ear, good ear, educated ear; eye, good eye; connoisseurship, savvy (*informal*), selectiveness, fastidiousness *see* 495

2 **discernment,** critical discernment, penetration, **perception,** perceptiveness, **insight,** perspicacity; **flair; judgment,** acumen *see* 919.4; analysis *see* 800

3 **distinction,** contradistinction, distinctiveness (*old*); **distinguishment, differentiation** *see* 779.4, winnowing, shakeout, separation, separationism, division, segregation, segregationism, demarcation; nice *or* subtle *or* fine distinction, **nuance,** shade of difference, microscopic distinction; hairsplitting, trichoschistism

verbs

4 **to discriminate, distinguish,** draw *or* make distinctions, contradistinguish, secern, distinguish in thought, **separate,** separate out, divide, analyse *see* 800.6, subdivide, **segregate,** sever, severalize, **differentiate,** demark, demarcate, mark the interface, set off, **set apart,** sift, sift out, sieve, sieve out, winnow, screen, screen out, sort, classify, sort out; **pick out, select** *see* 371.14; separate the sheep from the goats, separate the men from the boys, separate the wheat from the tares *or* chaff, winnow the chaff from the wheat; **draw the line,** fix *or* set a limit; **split hairs,** draw *or* make a fine *or* overfine *or* nice *or* subtle distinction, subtilize

5 **to be discriminating,** discriminate, exercise discrimination, tell which is which; **be tactful,** show *or* exercise tact; be tasteful, use one's palate; shop around, pick and choose; use advisedly

6 **to distinguish between, make** *or* **draw a distinction,** appreciate differences, see nuances *or* shades of difference, see the difference, tell apart, tell one thing from another, know which is which, know what's what (*informal*), not confound *or* mix up;

"know a hawk from a handsaw"—SHAKESPEARE, know one's arse from one's elbow (*informal*)

adjectives

7 **discriminating, discriminate,** discriminative, selective; discriminatory; **tactful, sensitive;** appreciative, appreciatory; **critical;** distinctive (*old*), **distinguishing;** differential; precise, accurate, exact; nice, fine, delicate, subtle, subtile, refined; fastidious *see* 495.9; distinctive, contrastive

8 **discerning, perceptive,** perspicacious, insightful; **astute, judicious** *see* 919.19

9 **discriminable, distinguishable,** separable, differentiable, contrastable, opposable

adverbs

10 **discriminatingly,** discriminatively, discriminately; with finesse; **tactfully; tastefully**

944 INDISCRIMINATION

nouns

1 **indiscrimination,** indiscriminateness, undiscriminatingness, undiscriminativeness, unselectiveness, **uncriticalness, unparticularness;** syncretism; unfastidiousness; lack of refinement, coarseness *or* crudeness *or* crudity of intellect; **casualness,** promiscuousness, **promiscuity; indiscretion,** indiscreetness, **imprudence** *see* 922.2; **untactfulness,** tactlessness, lack of feeling, **insensitivity,** insensibility *see* 25, unmeticulousness, unpreciseness *see* 340.4; **generality** *see* 863, catholicity

2 **indistinction,** indistinctness, vagueness *see* 32.2; **indefiniteness** *see* 970.4; uniformity *see* 780; facelessness, impersonality; **indistinguishableness,** undistinguishableness, indiscernibility; a distinction without a difference

verbs

3 **to confound, confuse,** mix, mix up, muddle, tumble, jumble, jumble together, **blur,** blur distinctions, overlook distinctions, muzz (*informal*)

4 **to use loosely,** use unadvisedly

adjectives

5 **undiscriminating, indiscriminate,** indiscriminative, undiscriminative, undifferentiating, unselective; wholesale, **general** *see* 863.11, **blanket; uncritical,** uncriticizing, undemanding, nonjudgmental; **unparticular,** unfastidious; unsubtle; **casual, promiscuous;** unexacting, unmeticulous *see* 340.13; **indiscreet,** undiscreet, **imprudent; untactful,** tactless, insensitive

6 **indistinguishable,** undistinguishable, undistinguished, indiscernible, **indistinct,** indistinctive, **without distinction,** not to be distinguished, undiscriminated, unindividual, unindividualized, undifferentiated, **alike,** six of one and half a dozen of the other (*informal*); **indefinite;** faceless, impersonal; standard, interchangeable, stereotyped, uniform *see* 780.5

945 JUDGMENT

nouns

1 **judgment,** judging, adjudgment, adjudication, judicature, deeming (*old*); judgment call (*informal*); arbitrament, arbitration *see* 466.2; **resolution** *see* 359; good judgment *see* 919.7; **choice** *see* 371; **discrimination** *see* 943

2 **criticism; censure** *see* 510.3; **approval** *see* 509; **critique,** review, notice, critical notice, report, comment; book review, critical review, thumbnail review; literary criticism, art criticism, music criticism, etc, critical journal, critical bibliography

3 **estimate, estimation;** view, opinion *see* 952.6; **assessment,** assessing, **appraisal,** appraisement, appraising, appreciation, reckoning, **stocktaking,** valuation, valuing, **evaluation,** evaluating, value judgment, evaluative criticism, analysing, weighing, weighing up, gauging, ranking, rank-ordering, **rating;** measurement *see* 300; comparison *see* 942

4 conclusion, deduction, inference, consequence, consequent, corollary; derivation, illation; induction

5 verdict, decision, resolution (*old*), determination, finding, holding; diagnosis, prognosis; decree, ruling, consideration, order, pronouncement, deliverance; award, action, sentence; condemnation, doom; dictum; precedent

6 judge, judger, adjudicator, justice; arbiter *see* 596.1; referee, umpire

7 critic, criticizer; connoisseur, *cognoscente* (*Italian*); literary critic, man of letters; textual critic; editor; social critic, muckraker; captious critic, smellfungus, caviler, carper, faultfinder; criticaster, criticule, critickin; censor, censurer; reviewer, commentator, commenter; scholiast, annotator

verbs

8 to judge, exercise judgment *or* the judgment; make a judgment call (*informal*); adjudge, adjudicate; be judicious *or* judgmental; consider, regard, hold, deem, esteem, count, account, think of; allow (*informal*), suppose, presume *see* 950.10, opine, form an opinion, give *or* pass *or* express an opinion, weigh in *and* put in one's tuppence worth (*both informal*)

9 to estimate, form an estimate, make an estimation; reckon, call, guess, figure (*informal*); assess, appraise, give an appreciation, gauge, rate, rank, rank-order, put in rank order, class, mark, value, evaluate, valuate, place *or* set a value on, weigh, weigh up, prize, appreciate; size up *or* take one's measure (*informal*), measure *see* 300.11

10 to conclude, draw a conclusion, be forced to conclude, come to *or* arrive at a conclusion, come up with a conclusion *and* end up (*both informal*); find, hold; deduce, derive, take as proved *or* demonstrated, extract, gather, collect, glean, fetch; infer, draw an inference; induce; reason, reason that; put two and two together

11 to decide, determine; find, hold, ascertain; resolve *see* 359.7, settle, fix; make a decision, come to a decision, make up one's mind, settle one's mind, come down (*informal*)

12 to sit in judgment, hold the scales, hold court; hear, give a hearing to; try *see* 598.17; referee, umpire, officiate; arbitrate *see* 466.6

13 to pass judgment, pronounce judgment, utter a judgment, deliver judgment; agree on a verdict, return a verdict, hand down a verdict, bring in a verdict, find, find for *or* against; pronounce on, act on, pronounce, report, rule, decree, order; sentence, pass sentence, hand down a sentence, doom, condemn

14 to criticize, critique; censure *see* 510.13, pick holes in, pick to pieces; approve *see* 509.9; review; comment upon, annotate; moralize upon; pontificate

15 to rank, rate, count, be regarded, be thought of, be in one's estimation

adjectives

16 judicial, judiciary, judicative, judgmental; juridic, juridical, juristic, juristical; judicious *see* 919.19; evaluative; critical; approbatory *see* 509.16

adverbs

17 all things considered, on the whole, taking one thing with another, on balance, taking everything into consideration *or* account; everything being equal, other things being equal, *ceteris paribus* (*Latin*), taking into account, considering, after all, this being so; therefore, wherefore; on the one hand, on the other hand, having said that; *sub judice* (*Latin*), in court, before the bench *or* bar *or* court

946 PREJUDGMENT

nouns

1 prejudgment, prejudication, forejudgment; preconception, presumption, supposition, presupposition, presupposal, presurmise, preapprehension, prenotion, prepossession; predilection, predisposition; preconsideration, predetermination, predecision, preconclusion, premature judgment; ulterior motive, hidden agenda, *parti pris* (*French*), an axe to grind, prejudice *see* 979.3

verbs

2 to prejudge, forejudge; preconceive, presuppose, presume, presurmise; be predisposed; predecide, predetermine, preconclude, judge beforehand *or* prematurely, judge before the evidence is in, have one's mind made up; jump to a conclusion, go off half-cocked *or* at half cock *and* beat the gun *and* jump the gun *and* shoot from the hip (*all informal*)

adjectives

3 prejudged, forejudged, preconceived, preconceptual, presumed, presupposed, presurmised; predetermined, predecided, preconcluded, judged beforehand *or* prematurely; predisposed, predispositional; prejudicial, prejudging, prejudicative

947 MISJUDGMENT

nouns

1 misjudgment, poor judgment, error in judgment, warped *or* flawed *or* skewed judgment; miscalculation, miscomputation, misreckoning, misestimation, misappreciation, misperception, misevaluation, misvaluation, misconjecture, wrong impression; misreading, wrong construction, misconstruction, misinterpretation *see* 342; inaccuracy, error *see* 974; unmeticulousness *see* 340.4; injudiciousness *see* 922.2

verbs

2 to misjudge, judge amiss, miscalculate, misestimate, misreckon, misappreciate, misperceive, get a wrong impression, misevaluate, misvalue, miscompute, misdeem, misesteem, misthink, misconjecture; misread, misconstrue, put the wrong construction on things, misread the situation *or* case; misinterpret *see* 342.2; err *see* 974.9; fly in the face of facts

948 OVERESTIMATION

nouns

1 **overestimation,** overestimate, **overreckoning,** overcalculation, **overrating,** overassessment, overvaluation, overappraisal; overreaction; **overstatement, exaggeration** *see* 355

verbs

2 to **overestimate, overreckon,** overcalculate, overcount, overmeasure, see more than is there; **overrate,** overassess, overappraise, overesteem, **overvalue,** overprize, think *or* make too much of, put on a pedestal, idealize, see only the good points of; overreact to; **overstate, exaggerate** *see* 355.3; pump up *and* jump up *and* make a big deal *or* Federal case (*all informal*)

adjectives

3 **overestimated, overrated,** puffed up, pumped up (*informal*), overvalued, on the high side; **exaggerated** *see* 355.4

949 UNDERESTIMATION

nouns

1 **underestimation,** misestimation, underestimate, **underrating,** underreckoning, undervaluation, misprizing, misprizal, misprision; **belittlement, depreciation,** deprecation, **minimization,** disparagement *see* 512

verbs

2 to **underestimate,** misestimate, **underrate,** underreckon, **undervalue,** underprize, **misprize; make little of,** set at little, set at naught, set little by, attach little importance to, not do justice to, sell short, think little of, make *or* think nothing of, see less than is there, miss on the low side, set no store by, make light of, shrug off; **depreciate, deprecate,** minimize, belittle, bad-mouth *and* poor-mouth *and* put down *and* run down (*all informal*), take someone for an idiot *or* a fool; disparage *see* 512.8

adjectives

3 **underestimated, underrated,** undervalued, on the low side; unvalued, unprized, misprized

950 THEORY, SUPPOSITION

nouns

1 **theory,** theorization, *theoria* (*Greek*); theoretics, theoretic, theoric (*old*); **hypothesis,** hypothecation, hypothesizing; **speculation,** mere theory; doctrinairism, doctrinality, doctrinarity; analysis, **explanation,** abstraction; theoretical basis *or* justification; body of theory, theoretical structure *or* construct; unified theory

2 **theory, explanation,** proposed *or* tentative explanation, proposal, proposition, statement covering the facts or evidence; **hypothesis,** working hypothesis

3 **supposition,** supposal, supposing; **presupposition,** presupposal; **assumption, presumption, conjecture,** inference, **surmise, guesswork;**

postulate, postulation, *postulatum* (*Latin*), set of postulates; **proposition, thesis, premise** *see* 934.7; **axiom** *see* 973.2

4 **guess, conjecture,** unverified supposition, perhaps, speculation, guesswork, surmise, educated guess; guesstimate *and* hunch *and* shot *and* stab (*all informal*); rough guess, wild guess, blind guess, bold conjecture, shot in the dark (*informal*)

5 (*vague supposition*) **suggestion,** bare suggestion, **suspicion,** sus (*informal*), **inkling, hint, sense, feeling,** feeling in one's bones, **intuition** *see* 933, **intimation, impression, notion,** mere notion, hunch *and* sneaking suspicion (*both informal*), trace of an idea, half an idea, vague idea, hazy idea, **idea** *see* 931

6 **supposititiousness,** presumptiveness, presumableness, theoreticalness, hypotheticalness, conjecturableness, speculativeness

7 **theorist, theorizer,** theoretic, **theoretician,** notionalist (*old*); **speculator;** hypothesist, hypothesizer; doctrinaire, doctrinarian; synthesizer; armchair authority *or* philosopher

8 **supposer,** assumer, surmiser, **conjecturer, guesser,** guessworker

verbs

9 to **theorize, hypothesize, hypothecate, speculate,** have *or* entertain a theory, espouse a theory

10 to **suppose, assume, presume, surmise,** expect, **suspect, infer, understand, gather, conclude, deduce, consider,** reckon, divine, imagine, **fancy,** dream, conceive, **believe, deem,** repute, feel, **think,** be inclined to think, opine, say, daresay, be afraid (*informal*); take, take it, take it into one's head, take for, take to be, take for granted, take as a, precondition, **presuppose, presurmise,** prefigure; provisionally accept *or* admit *or* agree to, take one up on (*informal*), grant, stipulate, take it as given, let, let be, say *or* assume for argument's sake, say for the hell of it (*informal*)

11 to **conjecture, guess,** guesstimate (*informal*), give a guess, talk off the top of one's head (*informal*), hazard a conjecture, venture a guess, risk assuming *or* stating, tentatively suggest, go out on a limb (*informal*)

12 to **postulate, predicate, posit,** set forth, lay down, assert; pose, advance, **propose, propound** *see* 439.5

adjectives

13 **theoretical, hypothetical,** hypothetic; postulatory, notional; **speculative, conjectural;** impressionistic, intuitive *see* 933.5; general, generalized, abstract, ideal; merely theoretical, academic, moot; impractical, armchair

14 **supposed,** suppositive, **assumed, presumed, conjectured, inferred,** understood, deemed, **reputed,** putative, alleged, accounted as; suppositional, supposititious; assumptive, **presumptive;** given, granted, taken as *or* for granted, taken as read, agreed, stipulated; **postulated,** postulational, premised

15 **supposable, presumable,** assumable, conjecturable, surmisable, imaginable, premissable

adverbs

16 theoretically, hypothetically, *ex hypothesi* (*Latin*), ideally; **in theory,** in idea, in the ideal, in the abstract, on paper, in Never-Neverland (*informal*), in an ideal world

17 supposedly, supposably, presumably, presumedly, assumably, assumedly, presumptively, assumptively, reputedly; suppositionally, supposititiously; **seemingly,** in seeming, quasi; as it were

18 conjecturably, conjecturally; to guess, to make a guess, **as a guess,** as a rough guess *or* an approximation

conjunctions

19 supposing, supposing that, **assuming that,** allowing that, if we assume that, let's say that, granting *or* granted that, given that, on the assumption *or* supposition that; if, as if, as though, by way of hypothesis

951 PHILOSOPHY

nouns

1 philosophy,
"life's guide"—CICERO, "a handmaid to religion"—FRANCIS BACON; philosophical inquiry *or* investigation, philosophical speculation; inquiry *or* investigation into first causes; branch of philosophy (*see list*), department *or* division of philosophy; school of philosophy (*see list*), philosophic system, school of thought; philosophic doctrine, philosophic theory; philosophastry, philosophastering; sophistry *see* 935

2 Platonic philosophy, Platonism, philosophy of the Academy; Aristotelian philosophy, Aristotelianism, philosophy of the Lyceum, Peripateticism, Peripatetic school; Stoic philosophy, Stoicism, philosophy of the Porch *or* Stoa; Epicureanism, philosophy of the Garden

3 materialism; idealism *see* 1051.3

4 monism, philosophical unitarianism, mind-stuff theory; pantheism, cosmotheism; hylozoism

5 pluralism; dualism, mind-matter theory

6 philosopher, philosophizer, philosophe; philosophaster; **thinker,** speculator; casuist; metaphysician, cosmologist; sophist *see* 935.6

verbs

7 to **philosophize,** reason *see* 934.15, probe

adjectives

8 philosophical, philosophic, sophistical *see* 935.10; philosophicohistorical, philosophicolegal, philosophicojuristic, philosophicopsychological, philosophicoreligious, philosophicotheological

9 absurdist, acosmistic, aesthetic, African, agnostic, Alexandrian, analytic, animalistic, animist *or* animistic, atomistic, etc (*see list of schools and doctrines*)

10 Aristotelian, Peripatetic; Augustinian, Averroist *or* Averroistic, Bergsonian, Berkeleian, Cartesian, Comtian, Hegelian, Neo-Hegelian, Heideggerian, Heraclitean, Humean, Husserlian, Kantian, Leibnizian, Parmenidean, Platonic, Neoplatonic, pre-Socratic, Pyrrhonic, Pyrrhonian, Pythagorean, Neo-Pythagorean, Sartrian, Schellingian, Schopenhauerian, Scotist, Socratic, Spencerian, Thomist *or* Thomistic, Viconian, Wittgensteinian

11 branches or departments of philosophy

aesthetics *or* theory of beauty *or* philosophy of art
axiology *or* value theory
cosmology
ethics
logic
metaphysics *or* first philosophy
ontology *or* science of being
philosophy of biology
philosophy of education
philosophy of history
philosophy of law
philosophy of logic
philosophy of nature
philosophy of physics
philosophy of religion
philosophy of science
political philosophy
theory of knowledge *or* epistemology *or* gnosiology

12 schools and doctrines of philosophy

Augustinianism
Averroism
Bergsonism
Berkeleianism
Bonaventurism
Bradleianism
Buddhism
Cartesianism
Comtism
Confucianism
cosmotheism
criticism *or* critical philosophy
Cynicism
Cyrenaic hedonism *or* Cyrenaicism
deconstructionism
deism
dialectical materialism
dualism
eclecticism
egoism
egoistic hedonism
Eleaticism *or* the Elean school
empiricism
Epicureanism
Eretrian school
eristic school
essentialism
ethicism
ethics
eudaemonism
existentialism *or* existential philosophy
Fichteanism
hedonism
Hegelianism
Heideggerianism
Heracliteanism
Herbartianism
Hinduism
humanism
Humism
hylomorphism
hylotheism
hylozoism
idealism
immaterialism
individualism
instrumentalism
intuitionism
Ionian school
Jainism
Kantianism
Leibnizianism
linguistic philosophy
logical empiricism *or* logical positivism
Marxism
materialism
mechanism
Megarianism
mentalism
Mimamsa
monism
mysticism
naturalism
Neo-Hegelianism
Neo-Pythagoreanism
neo-scholasticism
neocriticism
Neoplatonism
new ethical movement
nominalism
noumenalism
Nyaya
ontologism
ontology
optimism
ordinary language philosophy
organic mechanism
organicism
panlogism
panpneumatism
panpsychism
pantheism
panthelism
Parmenidean school
patristic philosophy
patristicism
Peripateticism
pessimism

phenomenalism
phenomenology
philosophy of organism
philosophy of signs
philosophy of the ante-
  Nicene Fathers
philosophy of the post-
  Nicene Fathers
physicalism
physicism
Platonism
pluralism
positivism
pragmatism or
  pragmaticism
probabilism
psychism
psychological hedonism
Purva Mimamsa
Pyrrhonism
Pythagoreanism
rationalism
realism
Sankhya
Sartrianism
Schellingism
Scholasticism
Schopenhauerism

Scotism
secular humanism
semiotic or semiotics or
  semi-idiotics (informal)
sensationalism
sensism
Shinto
Sikhism
scepticism
Socratism
solipsism
Sophism or Sophistry
Spencerianism
Spinozism
Stoicism
substantialism
syncretism
theism
Thomism
Toaism
transcendentalism
universalistic hedonism
utilitarianism
Uttara Mimamsa
Valsheshika
vitalism
voluntarism
zetetic philosophy

952 BELIEF

nouns

1 **belief,** credence, credit, faith, trust; hope; **confidence,** assuredness, convincedness, persuadedness, **assurance;** sureness, surety, **certainty** *see* 969; **reliance, dependence,** reliance on *or* in, dependence on, stock *and* store (*both informal*); acceptation, acception, reception, acquiescence; full faith and credit; suspension of disbelief; fideism; **credulity** *see* 953

2 **a belief, tenet, dogma,** precept, **principle, principle** *or* **article of faith,** canon, maxim, axiom; **doctrine,** teaching

3 **system of belief; religion, faith** *see* 675.1, belief-system; **school, cult, ism, ideology,** *Weltanschauung* (*German*), world view; political faith *or* belief *or* philosophy; **creed, credo,** credenda; articles of religion, articles of faith, creedal *or* doctrinal statement, formulated *or* stated belief; gospel; catechism

4 **statement of belief** *or* **principles, manifesto,** position paper; solemn declaration; deposition, affidavit, sworn statement

5 **conviction, persuasion, certainty; firm belief,** moral certainty, implicit *or* staunch belief, settled judgment, mature judgment *or* belief, fixed opinion, unshaken confidence, steadfast faith, rooted *or* deep-rooted belief

6 **opinion, sentiment, feeling, sense, impression,** reaction, **notion, idea, thought,** mind, thinking, **way of thinking, attitude,** stance, posture, position, mindset, **view,** point of view, eye, sight, lights, observation, **conception,** concept, conceit,

estimation, estimate, consideration, **theory** *see* 950, assumption, presumption, **conclusion, judgment** *see* 945, personal judgment; **point of view** *see* 977.2; public opinion, public belief, general belief, prevailing belief *or* sentiment, *consensus gentium* (*Latin*), common belief, community sentiment, popular belief, conventional wisdom, vox pop, *vox populi* (*Latin*), climate of opinion; ethos; mystique

7 **profession, confession,** declaration, **profession** *or* **confession** *or* **declaration of faith**

8 **believability, persuasiveness** believableness, convincingness, **credibility, credit, trustworthiness, plausibility,** tenability, acceptability, conceivability; **reliability** *see* 969.4

9 **believer, truster;** religious believer; true believer; the assured, the faithful, the believing; fideist; ideologist, ideologue

verbs

10 **to believe, credit, trust, accept,** receive, buy (*informal*), wear (*informal*); give credit *or* credence to, give faith to, put faith in, take stock in *or* set store by (*informal*), take to heart, attach weight to; be led to believe; accept implicitly, believe without reservation, take for granted, take *or* accept for gospel, take as gospel truth (*informal*), take on faith, take on trust *or* credit, pin one's faith on; take at face value; **take one's word for,** trust one's word, take at one's word; **buy** *and* **buy into** (*both informal*), swallow *see* 953.6; be certain *see* 969.9

11 **to think, opine,** be of the opinion, be persuaded, be convinced; be afraid (*informal*), **have the idea,** have an idea, **suppose, assume, presume, judge** *see* 945.8, **guess, surmise, suspect,** have a hunch (*informal*), have an inkling, expect (*informal*), have an impression, be under the impression, have a sense *or* the sense, conceive, ween *and* trow (*both archaic*), **imagine, fancy,** daresay; **deem, esteem, hold, regard, consider, maintain,** reckon, estimate; hold as, account as, set down as *or* for, view as, look upon as, take for, take, take it

12 **to state, assert,** swear, swear to God (*informal*), declare, **affirm,** vow, avow, avouch, warrant, asseverate, confess, be under the impression, profess, express the belief, swear to a belief; depose, make an affidavit *or* a sworn statement

13 **to hold the belief, have the opinion,** entertain a belief *or* an opinion, adopt *or* embrace a belief, take as an article of faith; foster *or* nurture *or* cherish a belief, be wedded to *or* espouse a belief; get hold of an idea, get it into one's head, form a conviction

14 **to be confident,** have confidence, **be satisfied, be convinced, be certain,** be easy in one's mind about, be secure in the belief, **feel sure, rest assured,** rest in confidence; doubt not, **have no doubt,** have no misgivings *or* diffidence *or* qualms, have no reservations, have no second thoughts

15 **to believe in, have faith in,** pin one's faith to, confide in, **have confidence in,** place *or* repose confidence in, place reliance in, put onself in the hands of, **trust in,** put trust in, have simple *or* childlike faith in, rest in, repose in *or* hope in (*both old*); give *or* get the benefit of the doubt

16 **to rely on** *or* **upon, depend on** *or* **upon**, place reliance on, rest on *or* upon, repose on, lean on, **count on**, calculate on, reckon on, **bank on** *or* **upon** (*informal*); **trust to** *or* **unto, swear by**, take one's oath upon; **bet on** *and* gamble on *and* lay money on *and* bet one's bottom dollar on (*all informal*), make book on (*US & Canadian informal*); take one's word for

17 **to trust, confide in, rely on, depend on**, repose, place trust *or* confidence in, have confidence in, **trust in** *see* 952.15, trust utterly *or* implicitly, deem trustworthy, think reliable *or* dependable, take one's word, take at one's word

18 **to convince; convert, win over**, lead one to believe, bring over, bring round, talk over, talk around, bring to reason, bring to one's senses, **persuade, lead to believe, give to understand; satisfy, assure**; put one's mind at rest on; sell *and* sell one on (*both informal*); **make** *or* **carry one's point**, bring *or* drive home to; ram down one's throat *and* beat into one's head (*both informal*); be convincing, carry conviction; inspire belief *or* confidence

19 **to convince oneself, persuade oneself**, sell oneself (*informal*), make oneself easy about, make oneself easy on that score, satisfy oneself on that point, make sure of, make up one's mind

20 **to find credence, be believed**, be accepted, be received; be swallowed *and* **go down** *and* pass current (*all informal*); produce *or* carry conviction; have the ear of, gain the confidence of

adjectives

21 **belief**, of belief, preceptive, principled; attitudinal; **believing, undoubting, undoubtful**, doubtless (*old*); faithful (*old*), God-fearing, pious, pietistic, observant, **devout**; under the impression, impressed with; **convinced, confident**, positive, dogmatic, secure, **persuaded**, sold on, **satisfied, assured; sure, certain** *see* 969.13, 20; fideistic

22 **trusting, trustful**, trusty (*old*), **confiding, unsuspecting, unsuspicious**, without suspicion; childlike, innocent, guileless, naive *see* 416.5; **knee-jerk, credulous** *see* 953.8; relying, depending, reliant, dependent

23 **believed, credited, held, trusted, accepted**; received, of belief; **undoubted**, unsuspected, **unquestioned**, undisputed, uncontested

24 **believable, credible; tenable**, conceivable, **plausible**, colourable; worthy of faith, trustworthy, trusty; fiduciary; reliable *see* 969.17; unimpeachable, unexceptionable, **unquestionable** *see* 969.15

25 fiducial, fiduciary; convictional

26 **convincing**, convictional, well-founded, **persuasive**, assuring, impressive, satisfying, satisfactory, confidence-building; decisive, absolute, conclusive, determinative; authoritative

27 **doctrinal, creedal**, preceptive, canonical, dogmatic, confessional, mandatory, of faith

adverbs

28 **believingly, undoubtingly**, undoubtfully, without doubt *or* question *or* quibble, unquestioningly; **trustingly**, trustfully, unsuspectingly, unsuspiciously;

piously, devoutly; with faith; **with confidence**, on *or* upon trust, on faith, on one's say-so

29 **in one's opinion, to one's mind**, in one's thinking, **to one's way of thinking**, the way one thinks, **in one's estimation**, according to one's lights, **as one sees it, to the best of one's belief**; in the opinion of, in the eyes of

953 CREDULITY

nouns

1 **credulity, credulousness**, inclination *or* disposition to believe, ease of belief, will *or* willingness to believe, wishful belief *or* thinking; **blind faith**, unquestioning belief, knee-jerk response *or* agreement (*informal*); uncritical acceptance, premature *or* unripe acceptation, hasty *or* rash conviction; **trustfulness, trustingness, unsuspiciousness**, unsuspectingness; uncriticalness, unskepticalness; overcredulity, overcredulousness, overtrustfulness, overopenness to conviction *or* persuasion, gross credulity; infatuation, fondness, dotage; one's blind side

2 **gullibility, dupability**, bamboozlability (*informal*), cullibility (*old*), **deceivability**, seduceability, persuadability, hoaxability; biddability; easiness (*informal*), softness, weakness; **simpleness**, simplicity, **ingenuousness, unsophistication; greenness**, naïveness, **naïveté**, naivety

3 **superstition**, superstitiousness; popular belief, **old wives' tale**; tradition, lore, folklore; charm, spell *see* 691

4 trusting soul; **dupe** *see* 358; sucker *and* easy mark *and* pushover *and* mug (*all informal*), patsy (*US & Canadian informal*)

verbs

5 **to be credulous**, accept unquestioningly; not boggle at anything, **believe anything**, be easy of belief *or* persuasion, be uncritical, believe at the drop of a hat, be a dupe, think the moon is made of green cheese, buy a pig in a poke

6 (*informal* or *informal terms*) to kid oneself, fall for, swallow, swallow anything, swallow whole, not choke *or* gag on; swallow hook, line, and sinker; eat up, lap up, devour, gulp down, gobble up *or* down, buy, buy into, bite, nibble, rise to the fly, take the bait, swing at, go for, tumble for, be taken in, be suckered, be a sucker *or* an easy mark *or* a mug (*all informal*), be a patsy (*US & Canadian informal*)

7 **to be superstitious**; touch wood, keep one's fingers crossed

adjectives

8 **credulous**, knee-jerk (*informal*), easy of belief, ready *or* inclined to believe, easily taken in; **undoubting** *see* 952.21; **trustful, trusting; unsuspicious, unsuspecting**; unthinking, uncritical, unsceptical; overcredulous, overtrustful, overtrusting, overconfiding; fond, infatuated, doting; **superstitious**

9 **gullible, dupable**, bamboozlable (*informal*), cullible (*old*), **deceivable, foolable, deludable, exploitable**, victimizable, seduceable, persuadable, hoaxable, humbugable, hoodwinkable; biddable; soft,

easy (*informal*), **simple; ingenuous,
unsophisticated, green, naive** *see* 416.5

954 UNBELIEF

nouns

1 **unbelief, disbelief,** nonbelief, unbelievingness,
discredit; refusal *or* inability to believe; **incredulity**
see 955; **unpersuadedness,** unconvincedness, lack of
conviction; **denial** *see* 335.2, **rejection** *see* 372;
misbelief, heresy *see* 688.2; infidelity, atheism,
agnosticism *see* 695.6; minimifidianism,
nullifidianism

2 **doubt, doubtfulness, dubiousness,** dubiety; half-
belief; **reservation, question,** question in one's
mind; **scepticism,** scepticalness; total scepticism,
Pyrrhonism; **suspicion,** suspiciousness, wariness,
leeriness, **distrust, mistrust, misdoubt,**
distrustfulness, mistrustfulness; **misgiving,** self-
doubt, diffidence; scruple, scrupulousness (*both old*);
apprehension *see* 127.4; **uncertainty** *see* 970; shadow
of doubt

3 **unbelievability,** unbelievableness, **incredibility,**
implausibility, inconceivability, untenableness;
unpersuasiveness, unconvincingness; **doubtfulness,
questionableness;** credibility gap; unreliability *see*
970.6

4 **doubter,** doubting Thomas; scoffer, sceptic, cynic,
pooh-pooher, nay-sayer, **unbeliever** *see* 695.11

verbs

5 **to disbelieve,** unbelieve, misbelieve, **not believe,**
find hard to believe, not admit, refuse to admit, not
buy (*informal*), take no stock in *and* set no store by
(*both informal*); **discredit,** refuse to credit, refuse to
credit *or* give credence to, give no credit *or* credence
to; gag on, **not swallow** *see* 955.3; negate, **deny** *see*
335.4, nay-say, say nay; scoff at, pooh-pooh; **reject**
see 372.2

6 **to doubt, be doubtful, be dubious, be sceptical,**
doubt the truth of, beg leave to doubt, **have one's
doubts,** have *or* harbour *or* entertain doubts *or*
suspicions, half believe, have reservations, **take with
a grain of salt,** scruple (*old*), **distrust, mistrust,**
misgive, cross one's fingers; **be uncertain** *see* 970.9;
suspect, smell a rat *and* see something funny (*both
informal*), suss *or* suss it (*informal*); **question,** query,
challenge, contest, dispute, cast doubt on, greet
with scepticism, keep one's eye on, treat with
reserve, bring *or* call into question, raise a question,
throw doubt upon, awake a doubt *or* suspicion;
doubt one's word, give one the lie; doubt oneself,
be diffident

7 **to be unbelievable,** be incredible, be hard to
swallow, defy belief, pass belief, be beyond belief, be
hard to believe, strain one's credulity, **stagger
belief;** shake one's faith, undermine one's faith;
perplex, boggle the mind, stagger, fill with doubt

adjectives

8 **unbelieving, disbelieving,** nonbelieving; faithless,
without faith; unconfident, unconvinced,
unconverted; nullifidian, minimifidian, creedless;

incredulous *see* 955.4; repudiative; **heretical** *see*
688.9; **irreligious** *see* 695.17

9 **doubting, doubtful,** in doubt, **dubious;
questioning; sceptical,** Pyrrhonic; **distrustful,
mistrustful,** untrustful, mistrusting, untrusting;
suspicious, suspecting, scrupulous (*old*), shy, wary,
leery; **agnostic; uncertain**

10 **unbelievable, incredible,** unthinkable,
implausible, unimaginable, inconceivable, not to be
believed, **hard to believe,** hard of belief, beyond
belief, unworthy of belief, not meriting *or* not
deserving belief, tall (*informal*), steep (*informal*);
defying belief, staggering belief, passing belief;
mind-boggling, preposterous, absurd, ridiculous,
unearthly, ungodly; **doubtful, dubious,** doubtable,
dubitable, **questionable,** problematic, problematical,
unconvincing, open to doubt *or* suspicion;
suspicious, suspect, sus (*informal*), funny; thin *and* a
bit thin (*both informal*); thick *and* a bit thick *and* a
little too thick (*all informal*)

11 **under a cloud,** unreliable

12 **doubted, questioned,** disputed, contested, moot;
distrusted, mistrusted; **suspect,** suspected, **under
suspicion,** under a cloud, sus (*informal*);
discredited, exploded, rejected, **disbelieved**

adverbs

13 **unbelievingly,** doubtingly, **doubtfully, dubiously,**
questioningly, **sceptically,** suspiciously; **with a
grain of salt,** with reservations, with some
allowance, with caution

14 **unbelievably, incredibly,** unthinkably, implausibly,
inconceivably, unimaginably, staggeringly

955 INCREDULITY

nouns

1 **incredulity, incredulousness,** uncredulousness,
refusal *or* disinclination to believe, resistance *or*
resistiveness to belief, tough-mindedness,
hardheadedness, **inconvincibility,** unconvincibility,
unpersuadability, unpersuasibility; **suspiciousness,**
suspicion, wariness, leeriness, guardedness,
cautiousness, caution; **scepticism** *see* 954.2

2 **ungullibility,** uncullibility (*old*), **undupability,
undeceivability,** unhoaxability, unseduceability;
sophistication

verbs

3 **to refuse to believe,** resist believing, **not allow
oneself to believe,** be slow to believe *or* accept; not
kid oneself (*informal*); **disbelieve** *see* 954.5; **be
sceptical** *see* 954.6; **not swallow,** not be able to
swallow *or* down (*informal*), not go for *and* **not fall
for** (*both informal*), not be taken in by; **not accept,**
not buy *or* buy into (*informal*), **reject** *see* 372.2

adjectives

4 **incredulous,** uncredulous, **hard of belief,** shy of
belief, disposed to doubt, indisposed *or* disinclined to
believe, unwilling to accept; impervious to
persuasion, **inconvincible,** unconvincible,
unpersuadable, unpersuasible; **suspicious,**

suspecting, wary, leery, cautious, guarded; sceptical *see* 954.9

5 **ungullible**, uncullible (*old*), **undupable, undeceivable, unfoolable, undeludable,** unhoaxable, unseduceable, hoaxproof; **sophisticated, wise, hardheaded,** practical, realistic, tough-minded; nobody's fool, not born yesterday, nobody's sucker (*informal*), nobody's patsy (*US & Canadian informal*), up to snuff (*informal*)

956 EVIDENCE, PROOF

nouns

1 **evidence, proof; reason to believe,** grounds for belief; **ground, grounds,** material grounds, **facts, data,** premises, basis for belief; piece *or* item of evidence, **fact,** datum, relevant fact; **indication, manifestation, sign, symptom,** mark, token, mute witness; body of evidence, documentation; muniments, title deeds and papers; chain of evidence; **clue; exhibit**

2 **testimony, attestation,** attest (*old*), **witness;** testimonial, testimonium (*old*); **statement, declaration, assertion,** asseveration, affirmation *see* 334, avouchment, avowal, averment, allegation, admission, **disclosure** *see* 351, profession, word; **deposition,** legal evidence, sworn evidence *or* testimony; king's evidence, queen's evidence, state's evidence (*US*); *procès-verbal* (*French*); compurgation; affidavit, sworn statement; instrument in proof, *pièce justificative* (*French*)

3 **proof, demonstration,** ironclad proof, incontrovertible proof; **determination, establishment, settlement; conclusive evidence,** indisputable evidence, incontrovertible evidence, damning evidence, unmistakable sign, sure sign, absolute indication, smoking gun (*informal*); open-and-shut case; burden of proof, onus, *onus probandi* (*Latin*); the proof of the pudding

4 **confirmation, substantiation,** proof, proving, proving out, bearing out, affirmation, attestation, **authentication, validation, certification,** ratification, **verification; corroboration, support,** supporting evidence, corroboratory evidence, fortification, buttressing, bolstering, backing, backing up, reinforcement, undergirding, strengthening, circumstantiation, fact sheet; **documentation**

5 **citation, reference,** quotation; sound bite; **exemplification,** instance, example, case, case in point, particular, item, illustration, demonstration; cross reference

6 **witness, eyewitness,** spectator, earwitness; **bystander,** passerby; **deponent, testifier,** attestant, attester, attestator, voucher, swearer; **informant,** informer; character witness; cojuror, compurgator

7 **provability, demonstrability,** determinability; confirmability, supportability, verifiability

verbs

8 **to evidence, evince,** furnish evidence, **show, go to show,** mean, tend to show, witness to, testify to; **demonstrate, illustrate,** exhibit, manifest, display, express, set forth; approve; **attest; indicate, signify,** signalize, symptomatize, mark, **denote,** **betoken, point to,** give indication of, show signs of, bear on, touch on; **connote, imply, suggest,** involve; argue, breathe, tell, bespeak; **speak for itself,** speak volumes

9 **to testify, attest, give evidence,** witness, witness to, **give** *or* **bear witness; disclose** *see* 351.4; **vouch,** state one's case, **depose,** depone, **warrant, swear,** take one's oath, acknowledge, avow, **affirm,** avouch, aver, allege, asseverate, **certify, give one's word**

10 **to prove, demonstrate, show,** afford proof of, prove to be, prove true; **establish, fix, determine, ascertain,** make out, remove all doubt; **settle,** settle the matter; **set at rest;** clinch *and* cinch *and* nail down (*all informal*); **prove one's point,** make one's case, bring home to, make good, have *or* make out a case; hold good, hold water; follow, follow from, follow as a matter of course

11 **to confirm, affirm, attest,** warrant, uphold (*informal*), **substantiate, authenticate, validate, certify,** ratify, **verify;** circumstantiate, **corroborate, bear out,** support, buttress, **sustain,** fortify, bolster, back, back up, reinforce, undergird, strengthen; **document;** probate, prove

12 **to adduce,** produce, **advance, present,** bring to bear, **offer,** proffer, invoke, obtest, allege (*old*), plead, **bring forward,** bring on; rally, marshal, deploy, array; call to witness, call to *or* put in the witness box

13 **to cite, name,** call to mind; **instance,** cite a particular *or* particulars, cite cases *or* a case in point, itemize, particularize, produce an instance, give a for-instance (*informal*); **exemplify,** example (*old*), **illustrate,** demonstrate; **document; quote,** quote chapter and verse

14 **to refer to,** direct attention to, **appeal to,** invoke; make reference to; cross-refer, make a cross-reference; reference, cross-reference

15 **to have evidence** *or* **proof,** have a case, possess incriminating evidence, **have something on** (*informal*); have bang to rights *or* dead to rights (*both informal*), have the goods on (*US & Canadian informal*)

adjectives

16 **evidential,** evidentiary, **factual,** symptomatic, **significant, indicative,** attestative, attestive, probative; founded on, grounded on, based on; implicit, suggestive; material, telling, convincing, weighty; overwhelming, damning; **conclusive,** determinative, **decisive,** final, incontrovertible, irresistible, indisputable, irrefutable, sure, certain, absolute; documented, documentary; **valid, admissible;** adducible; firsthand, authentic, reliable *see* 969.17, eye-witness; hearsay, circumstantial, presumptive, nuncupative, cumulative, ex parte

17 **demonstrative,** demonstrating, demonstrational; evincive, apodictic

18 **confirming,** confirmatory, confirmative, certificatory; substantiating, **verifying,** verificative; **corroborating,** corroboratory, **corroborative,** supportive, **supporting**

19 **provable, demonstrable,** demonstratable, apodictic, evincible, attestable, **confirmable,** checkable,

substantiatable, establishable, supportable, sustainable, **verifiable**, validatable, authenticatable

20 **proved, proven, demonstrated,** shown; **established,** fixed, **settled, determined,** nailed down (*informal*), ascertained; **confirmed, substantiated,** attested, **authenticated, certified, validated, verified;** circumstantiated, **corroborated,** borne out

21 **unrefuted,** unconfuted, unanswered, uncontroverted, uncontradicted, **undenied; unrefutable** *see* 969.15

adverbs

22 **evidentially,** according to the evidence, on the evidence, as attested by, judging by; **in confirmation, in corroboration of, in support of;** at first hand, at second hand; dead to rights *or* bang to rights *and* with a smoking gun *and* with one's trousers down (*all informal*)

23 **to illustrate,** to prove the point, as an example, as a case in point, to name an instance, by way of example, **for example, for instance,** to cite an instance, as an instance, e.g., *exempli gratia* (*Latin*); as, **thus**

24 **which see,** q.v., *quod vide* (*Latin*); *loco citato* (*Latin*), loc cit; *opere citato* (*Latin*), op cit; quote-unquote

phrases

25 it is proven, *probatum est* (*Latin*), there is nothing more to be said, it must follow; I rest my case; QED, *quod erat demonstrandum* (*Latin*)

957 DISPROOF

nouns

1 **disproof,** disproving, disproval, **invalidation,** disconfirmation, explosion, negation, redargution (*old*); exposure, exposé; *reductio ad absurdum* (*Latin*)

2 **refutation, confutation,** confounding, refutal, **rebuttal, answer,** complete answer, crushing *or* effective rejoinder, squelch; discrediting; **overthrow,** overthrowal, upset, upsetting, subversion, undermining, demolition; **contradiction,** controversion, denial *see* 335.2

3 **conclusive argument, knockdown argument,** floorer, sockdologer (*informal*); **clincher** *or* crusher *or* **settler** *and* finisher *and* squelcher (*all informal*)

verbs

4 **to disprove, invalidate,** disconfirm, discredit, prove the contrary, belie, give the lie to, redargue (*old*); **negate,** negative; **expose, show up; explode,** blow up, blow sky-high, **puncture, deflate, shoot** *or* **poke full of holes,** shoot down *or* shoot down in flames (*informal*), **cut to pieces, cut the ground from under;** knock the bottom out of (*informal*), knock the props *or* chocks out from under, take the ground from under, undercut, cut the ground from under one's feet, pull the rug from under one's feet, take *or* knock the feet from under, not leave a leg to stand on, have the last word, leave nothing to say, put *or* lay to rest

5 **to refute, confute, confound, rebut,** parry, answer, **answer conclusively,** dismiss, dispose of; **overthrow,** overturn, overwhelm, upset, subvert,

defeat, demolish, undermine; argue down; floor *and* finish *and* settle *and* squash *and* squelch (*all informal*), crush, smash all opposition; silence, put *or* reduce to silence, shut up, stop the mouth of; nonplus, take the wind out of one's sails, put one's gas at a peep (*Scottish*); **contradict,** controvert, counter, run counter, **deny** *see* 335.4

adjectives

6 **refuting, confuting,** confounding, confutative, refutative, refutatory, discomfirmatory; asymptomatic; contradictory, contrary *see* 335.5

7 **disproved,** disconfirmed, **invalidated,** negated, negatived, discredited, belied; **exposed,** shown up; **punctured,** deflated, **exploded; refuted,** confuted, confounded; **upset, overthrown,** overturned; **contradicted,** disputed, denied, impugned; dismissed, discarded, rejected *see* 372.3

8 **unproved,** not proved, **unproven,** not proven, **undemonstrated,** unshown, not shown; **untried,** untested; **unestablished,** unfixed, **unsettled, undetermined,** unascertained; **unconfirmed, unsubstantiated,** unattested, **unauthenticated,** unvalidated, uncertified, **unverified; uncorroborated,** unsustained, **unsupported,** unsupported by evidence, **groundless,** without grounds *or* basis, **unfounded** *see* 935.13; **inconclusive,** indecisive; **moot,** sub judice; not following

9 **unprovable,** controvertible, **undemonstrable,** undemonstratable, unattestable, unsubstantiatable, **unsupportable,** unconfirmable, unsustainable, unverifiable

10 **refutable,** confutable, **disprovable,** defeasible

958 QUALIFICATION

nouns

1 **qualification, limitation, limiting, restriction,** circumscription, **modification,** hedge, hedging; setting conditions, conditionality, provisionality, circumstantiality; specification; **allowance, concession,** cession, grant; grain of salt; **reservation, exception,** waiver, exemption; **exclusion,** ruling out, including out (*informal*); specialness, special circumstance, special case, special treatment; **mental reservation,** salvo (*old*), *arrière-pensée* (*French*), crossing one's fingers; extenuating circumstances, mitigating circumstances

2 **condition, provision, proviso, stipulation,** whereas; **specification,** parameter, given, *donnée* (*French*), **limitation,** limiting condition, boundary condition; **contingency, circumstance** *see* 765; **catch** *and* string *and* a string to it *and* a string attached (*all informal*), joker *and* kicker (*US & Canadian informal*); **requisite, prerequisite,** obligation; *sine qua non* (*Latin*), *conditio sine qua non* (*Latin*); clause, escape clause, escapeway, escape hatch, get-out, saving clause, loophole; escalator clause; **terms,** provisions; grounds; small *or* fine print *and* fine print at the bottom (*all informal*); ultimatum

verbs

3 **to qualify, limit,** condition (*old*), **hedge,** hedge
about, **modify, restrict,** restrain, circumscribe, set
limits *or* conditions, **box in** (*informal*), narrow; adjust
to, regulate by; alter *see* 851.6; **temper, season,**
leaven, soften, modulate, moderate, assuage,
mitigate, palliate, abate, reduce, diminish

4 **to make conditional,** make contingent, **condition;**
make it a condition, attach a condition *or* proviso,
stipulate; insist upon, make a point of; **have a
catch** *and* have a string attached (*both informal*),
have a joker *or* have a joker in the deck *or* pack *and*
have a kicker (*US & Canadian informal*); cross one's
fingers behind one's back

5 **to allow for, make allowances for,** make room
for, provide for, open the door to, take account of,
take into account *or* **consideration, consider,**
consider the circumstances; allow, **grant, concede,**
admit, admit exceptions, see the special
circumstances; **relax,** relax the condition, **waive, set
aside,** ease, lift temporarily, pull one's punches
(*informal*); disregard, **discount,** leave out of account;
consider the source, take with a grain of salt

6 **to depend,** hang, rest, hinge; **depend on** *or* **upon,
hang on** *or* **upon, rest on** *or* **upon,** rest with,
repose upon, lie on, lie with, stand on *or* upon, be
based on, be, bounded *or* limited by, be dependent
on, be predicated on, **be contingent** *or* **conditional
on; hinge on** *or* **upon, turn on** *or* **upon, revolve
on** *or* **upon,** have as a fulcrum

adjectives

7 **qualifying,** qualificative, qualificatory, **modifying,**
modificatory, altering; **limiting, limitational,
restricting,** limitative, restrictive, bounding;
circumstantial, contingent; **extenuating,** extenuatory,
mitigating, mitigative, mitigatory, modulatory,
palliative, assuasive, lenitive, softening

8 **conditional, provisional,** provisory, stipulatory;
specificative; **specified, stipulated,** fixed, stated,
given; **temporary,** expedient

9 **contingent, dependent, depending;** contingent on,
dependent on, depending on, predicated on, based
on, hanging *or* hinging on, turning on, revolving on;
depending on circumstances; circumscribed by,
hedged *or* hedged about by; boxed in (*informal*);
subject to, incidental to, incident to

10 **qualified, modified, conditioned, limited,
restricted,** hedged, hedged about; **tempered,**
seasoned, leavened, softened, **mitigated,** modulated

adverbs

11 **conditionally, provisionally, with qualifications,**
with a string *or* catch to it (*both informal*), with a
joker *or* kicker to it (*both US & Canadian informal*);
with a reservation *or* an exception, with a grain of
salt; **temporarily,** for the time being

conjunctions

12 **provided,** provided that, provided always,
providing, with this proviso, it being provided; **on
condition,** on condition that, **with the stipulation,**
with the understanding, on the understanding,
according as, **subject to**

13 **granting, admitting, allowing,** admitting that,
allowing that, seeing that; **exempting, waiving**

14 **if,** an *or* an' (*both old*), if and when, only if, if only,
if and only if, if it be so, if it be true that, if it so
happens *or* turns out

15 **so,** just so, so that (*old*), so as, **so long as, as long
as**

16 **unless,** unless that, **if not, were it not,** were it not
that; **except, excepting,** except that, with the
exception that, save, **but; without,** absent

959 NO QUALIFICATIONS

nouns

1 **unqualifiedness,** unlimitedness, **unconditionality,**
unrestrictedness, **unreservedness,**
uncircumscribedness; categoricalness; **absoluteness,**
definiteness, **explicitness;** decisiveness

adjectives

2 **unqualified, unconditional,** unconditioned,
unrestricted, unhampered, **unlimited,**
uncircumscribed, unmitigated, **categorical,** straight,
unreserved, without reserve; unaltered,
unadulterated, intact; **implicit,** unquestioning,
undoubting, unhesitating; **explicit, express,
unequivocal,** clear, unmistakable; **peremptory,**
indisputable, inappealable; **without exception,**
admitting no exception, unwaivable; **positive,
absolute, flat,** definite, definitive, determinate,
decided, decisive, fixed, final, conclusive; **complete,
entire, whole, total,** global; **utter,** perfect,
downright, outright, out-and-out, straight-out
(*informal*), all-out, flat-out (*informal*)

adverbs

3 (*informal terms*) **no ifs, ands, or buts; no strings
attached,** no holds barred, no catch, no joker *or*
kicker *and* no joker in the deck (*all US & Canadian
informal*), no small print *or* fine print, no fine print
at the bottom; downright, that's that, what you see
is what you get

960 FORESIGHT

nouns

1 **foresight,** foreseeing, looking ahead, prevision,
divination *see* 961.2, forecast; **prediction** *see* 961;
foreglimpse, foreglance, foregleam; preview,
prepublication; **prospect,** prospection; **anticipation,**
contemplation, envisionment, envisagement;
foresightedness; farsightedness, longsightedness,
farseeingness; sagacity, providence, discretion,
preparation, provision, forehandedness, readiness,
prudence *see* 919.7

2 **forethought,** premeditation, predeliberation,
preconsideration *see* 380.3; caution *see* 494; lead time,
advance notice; run-up

3 **foreknowledge,** foreknowing, forewisdom,
precognition, prescience, presage, presentiment,
foreboding; clairvoyance *see* 689.8; foreseeability *see*
961.8

4 **foretaste,** antepast (*old*), prelibation

verbs

5 **to foresee,** see beforehand *or* ahead, foreglimpse, foretaste, **anticipate,** contemplate, envision, envisage, **look forward to,** look ahead, look beyond, look *or* pry *or* peep into the future; **predict** *see* 961.9; think ahead *or* beforehand

6 **to foreknow,** know beforehand, precognize; smell in the wind, scent from afar; **have a presentiment, have a premonition** *see* 133.11; see the handwriting on the wall, have a hunch *or* feel in one's bones (*informal*), feel in one's water (*informal*), just know, intuit *see* 933.4

adjectives

7 **foreseeing, foresighted; foreknowing, precognizant,** precognitive, prescient; divinatory *see* 961.11; **forethoughted,** forethoughtful; anticipant, anticipatory; **farseeing, farsighted,** longsighted; sagacious, provident, providential, forehanded, prepared, ready, prudent *see* 919.19; intuitive *see* 933.5; clairvoyant

8 **foreseeable** *see* 961.13; **foreseen** *see* 961.14; intuitable

adverbs

9 **foreseeingly, foreknowingly,** with foresight; against the time when, for a rainy day

961 PREDICTION

nouns

1 **prediction, foretelling,** foreshowing, forecasting, **prognosis,** prognostication, presage (*old*), presaging; **prophecy,** prophesying, vaticination; **soothsaying,** soothsay; prefiguration, prefigurement, prefiguring; preshowing, presignifying, presigning (*old*); **forecast, promise;** apocalypse; prospectus; foresight *see* 960; presentiment, foreboding; omen *see* 133.3, 6; **guesswork,** speculation, guestimation (*informal*); **probability** *see* 967, statistical prediction, actuarial prediction; improbability *see* 968

2 **divination,** divining; **augury,** haruspication, haruspicy, pythonism, mantic, mantology (*old*); **fortunetelling,** crystal gazing, palm-reading, palmistry; crystal ball; I Ching; runes; tarot; horoscopy, astrology *see* 1070.20; sorcery *see* 690; clairvoyance *see* 689.8

3 **dowsing,** witching, water witching; **divining rod** *or* stick, wand, witch *or* witching stick, dowsing rod, doodlebug; water diviner, dowser, water witch *or* witcher

4 **predictor, foreteller, prognosticator,** seer, foreseer, foreshower, foreknower, presager (*old*), prefigurer; **forecaster;** prophet, prophesier, soothsayer, *vates* (*Latin*); **diviner,** divinator; augur; psychic *see* 689.13; prophetess, seeress, divineress, pythoness, spaewife (*Scottish*); Druid; **fortuneteller;** crystal gazer; palmist; geomancer; haruspex *or* aruspex, astrologer *see* 1070.23; weather prophet *see* 317.6; prophet of doom, calamity howler, Cassandra, doomwatcher; religious prophets *see* 684

5 (*informal terms*) dopester, tipster, **tout** *or* touter

6 **sibyl;** Pythia, Pythian, Delphic sibyl; Babylonian *or* Persian sibyl, Cimmerian sibyl, Cumaean sibyl, Erythraean sibyl, Hellespontine *or* Trojan sibyl,

Libyan sibyl, Phrygian sibyl, Samian sibyl, Tiburtine sibyl

7 **oracle;** Delphic *or* Delphian oracle, Python, Pythian oracle; Delphic tripod, tripod of the Pythia; Dodona, oracle *or* oak of Dodona

8 **predictability,** divinability, foretellableness, calculability, foreseeability, foreknowableness

verbs

9 **to predict,** make a prediction, **foretell, soothsay,** prefigure, **forecast, prophesy, prognosticate,** call (*informal*), make a prophecy *or* prognosis, vaticinate, forebode, presage, see ahead, see *or* tell the future, read the future, see in the crystal ball; **foresee** *see* 960.5; call the turn *and* call one's shot (*both informal*); **divine;** witch *or* dowse for water; **tell fortunes,** fortune-tell, cast one's fortune; read one's hand, read palms, read tea leaves, read the cards, read the tarot, cast a horoscope *or* nativity; **guess,** speculate, guestimate (*informal*); **bet, bet on, gamble**

10 **to portend,** foretoken *see* 133.12

adjectives

11 **predictive,** predictory, predictional; **foretelling,** forewarning, forecasting; prefiguring, prefigurative, presignifying, presignificative; **prophetic,** prophetical, fatidic, fatidical, apocalyptic, apocalyptical; vatic, vaticinatory, vaticinal, mantic, sibyllic, sibylline; **divinatory, oracular,** auguring, augural; haruspical; **foreseeing** *see* 960.7; presageful, presaging; **prognostic,** prognosticative, prognosticatory; fortunetelling; weather-wise

12 **ominous,** premonitory, foreboding *see* 133.17

13 **predictable, divinable, foretellable, calculable,** anticipatable; **foreseeable, foreknowable,** precognizable; **probable** *see* 967.6; improbable *see* 968.3

14 **predicted,** prophesied, presaged, **foretold, forecast,** foreshown; foreseen, foreglimpsed, **foreknown**

962 NECESSITY

nouns

1 **necessity,** necessariness, necessitude (*old*), necessitation, entailment; mandatoriness, mandatedness, obligatoriness, **obligation,** obligement; compulsoriness, **compulsion, duress** *see* 424.3

2 **requirement, requisite,** requisition; **necessity, need, want,** occasion; need for, **call for, demand,** demand for; desideratum, desideration; **prerequisite,** prerequirement; **must,** must item; **essential,** indispensable; the necessary, the needful; necessities, necessaries, essentials, bare necessities

3 **needfulness,** requisiteness; **essentiality,** essentialness, vitalness; **indispensability,** indispensableness; irreplaceability; irreducibleness, irreducibility

4 **urgent need, dire necessity; exigency** *or* exigence, **urgency,** imperative, imperativeness, immediacy, pressingness, pressure; "necessity's sharp pinch"—SHAKESPEARE; matter of necessity, case of need *or* emergency, **matter of life and death**; **predicament** *see* 1012.4

5 **involuntariness**, unwilledness, **instinctiveness**; compulsiveness; reflex action, conditioning, automatism; echolalia, echopraxia; automatic writing; **instinct**, impulse *see* 365; blind impulse *or* instinct, sheer chemistry

6 **choicelessness**, no choice, no alternative, **Hobson's choice**, only choice, zero option; that or nothing; not a pin to choose, six of one and half a dozen of the other, distinction without a difference; indiscrimination *see* 944

7 **inevitability**, inevitableness, **unavoidableness**, necessity, inescapableness, inevasibleness, unpreventability, undeflectability, ineluctability; irrevocability, indefeasibility; uncontrollability; relentlessness, inexorability, unyieldingness, inflexibility; fatedness, fatefulness, **certainty**, sureness; *force majeure* (*French*), vis major, act of God, inevitable accident, unavoidable casualty; **predetermination**, fate *see* 963.2

verbs

8 **to necessitate, oblige, dictate, constrain**; insist upon, **compel** *see* 424.4

9 **to require, need, want**, feel the want of, miss, have occasion for, be in need of, be hurting for (*US & Canadian informal*), stand in need of, not be able to dispense with, not be able to do without; **call for**, cry for, cry out for, clamour for; **demand**, ask, claim, exact; prerequire (*old*); need *or* want doing, take doing (*US & Canadian informal*), be indicated

10 **to be necessary**, lie under a necessity, be one's fate; be a must (*informal*); can't be avoided, can't be helped; be under the necessity of, be in for; be obliged, **must**, need *or* needs must (*old*), **have to**, have got to (*informal*), should, need, **need to**, have need to; not able to keep from, not able to help, **cannot help but**, cannot do otherwise; be forced *or* driven

11 **to have no choice** *or* **alternative**, have one's options reduced *or* closed *or* eliminated, have no option but, cannot choose but, be robbed *or* relieved of choice; be pushed to the wall, be driven into a corner; take it or leave it *and* like it or lump it (*both informal*), have that or nothing

adjectives

12 **necessary, obligatory, compulsory**, entailed, mandatory; **exigent, urgent**, necessitous, importunate, **imperative**; choiceless, without choice, out of one's hands *or* control

13 **requisite, needful, required, needed**, necessary, **wanted, called for**, indicated; **essential, vital**, indispensable, unforgoable, irreplaceable; irreducible, irreductible; prerequisite

14 **involuntary, instinctive, automatic, mechanical**, reflex, reflexive, kneejerk (*informal*), conditioned; **unconscious**, unthinking, blind; **unwitting**, unintentional, independent of one's will, unwilling, unwilled, against one's will; **compulsive**; forced; **impulsive** *see* 365.9

15 **inevitable, unavoidable**, necessary, **inescapable**, inevasible, unpreventable, undeflectable, ineluctable,

irrevocable, indefeasible; uncontrollable, unstoppable; relentless, inexorable, unyielding, inflexible; irresistible, resistless; **certain**, fateful, **sure**, sure as fate, sure as death, sure as death and taxes; **destined, fated** *see* 963.9

adverbs

16 **necessarily, needfully**, requisitely; **of necessity**, from necessity, need *or* needs (*both old*), perforce; without choice; **willy-nilly**, *nolens volens* (*Latin*), willing or unwilling, *bon gré mal gré* (*French*), whether one will or not, like it or not; come what may; compulsorily

17 **if necessary, if need be**, if the worst comes to the worst, if push comes to shove; for lack *or* want of something better, *faute de mieux* (*French*)

18 **involuntarily, instinctively, automatically, mechanically**, by reflex, reflexively; blindly, **unconsciously**, unthinkingly, without premeditation; **unwittingly**, unintentionally; **compulsively**; **unwillingly** *see* 325.8

19 **inevitably, unavoidably**, necessarily, **inescapably**, come hell or high water (*informal*), inevasibly, unpreventably, ineluctably; irrevocably, indefeasibly; uncontrollably; relentlessly, inexorably, unyieldingly, inflexibly; fatefully, **certainly, surely**

phrases

20 **it is necessary, it must be**, it needs must be *or* it must needs be (*both old*), it will be, there's no two ways about it, it must have its way; it cannot be helped, there is no helping it *or* help for it, that's the way the cookie crumbles *or* the ball bounces (*informal*), that's the way it goes, those are the breaks, what will be will be, it's God's will; the die is cast; it is fated *see* 963.11

963 PREDETERMINATION

nouns

1 **predetermination, predestination**, foredestiny, **preordination**, foreordination, foreordainment; decree; foregone conclusion, par for the course (*informal*); **necessity** *see* 962; foreknowledge, prescience *see* 960.3

2 **fate**, fatality, **fortune, lot**, cup, **portion**, appointed lot, karma, kismet, weird, *moira* (*Greek*), future *see* 838; **destiny**, destination, **end**, final lot; **doom**, foredoom (*old*), God's will, will of Heaven; **inevitability** *see* 962.7;

"a tyrant's authority for crime and a fool's excuse for failure"—AMBROSE BIERCE; the handwriting on the wall; book of fate; Fortune's wheel, wheel of fortune *or* chance; astral influences, stars, planets, constellation, astrology *see* 1070.20; unlucky day, ides of March, Friday, Friday the thirteenth, *dies funestis* (*Latin*)

3 **Fates**, *Fata* (*Latin*), Parcae, *Moirai* (*Greek*), Clotho, Lachesis, Atropos; Nona, Decuma, Morta; Weird Sisters, Weirds; Norns; Urdur, Verthandi, Skuld; Fortuna, Lady *or* Dame Fortune, Lady Luck, *Tyche* (*Greek*); Providence, Heaven,

"a divinity that shapes our ends, rough-hew them how we will"—SHAKESPEARE

4 determinism, fatalism, necessitarianism, necessarianism, predeterminism; predestinarianism, Calvinism, election

5 determinist, fatalist, necessitarian, necessarian; predestinationist, predestinarian, Calvinist

verbs

6 to predetermine, predecide, preestablish; **predestine,** predestinate, **preordain,** foreordain

7 to destine, predestine, necessitate *see* 962.8, destinate (*old*), **ordain,** fate, mark, appoint; come with the territory (*informal*); have in store for; **doom,** foredoom

adjectives

8 determined, predetermined, predecided, preestablished, **predestined,** predestinate, **preordained,** foreordained; foregone

9 destined, fated, fateful, fatal (*old*), ordained, written, in the cards, marked, appointed (*old*), in store; **doomed,** foredoomed, devoted; inevitable *see* 962.15

10 deterministic, fatalistic, necessitarian, necessarian

phrases

11 it is fated, it is written, it's in the cards; what will be will be, *che sarà sarà (Italian), que sera sera (Spanish)*; that's the way it goes, those are the breaks; that's life, *c'est la vie* and *c'est la guerre (both French)*

964 PREARRANGEMENT

nouns

1 prearrangement, preordering, preconcertedness; premeditation, plotting, planning, scheming; directed verdict; **reservation,** booking; overbooking

2 (*informal terms*) **put-up job,** packed *or* rigged game *or* jury, fixed match, stacked deck; **frame-up,** frame, setup

3 schedule, programme, programma, **bill,** card, **calendar,** docket, slate; playbill; batting order, **lineup, roster,** rota; blueprint, budget; **prospectus;** schedule *or* programme of operation, **order of the day,** things to be done, **agenda,** list of agenda; order paper; protocol; laundry list *and* wish list (*both informal*); **bill of fare, menu,** *carte du jour (French)*

verbs

4 to prearrange, precontrive, predesign (*old*), preorder, preconcert; premeditate, plot, plan, scheme; **reserve,** book, overbook

5 (*informal terms*) **to fix, rig,** pack, cook, cook up; **stack the cards;** put in the bag, sew up; frame, frame-up, set up; **throw**

6 to schedule, line up (*informal*), **slate, book,** book in, bill, programme, calendar, docket, budget, put on the agenda

adjectives

7 prearranged, precontrived, predesigned (*old*), preordered, preconcerted, cut out; premeditated, plotted, planned, schemed; cut-and-dried, cut-and-dry

8 (*informal terms*) **fixed, rigged, put-up,** packed, stacked, cooked, cooked-up; **in the bag,** on ice, cinched, sewed up; **framed, framed-up,** set-up

9 scheduled, slated, booked, billed, booked-in, to come, forthcoming

965 POSSIBILITY

nouns

1 possibility, possibleness, **the realm of possibility,** the domain of the possible, conceivableness, **conceivability,** thinkability, thinkableness, imaginability; **probability, likelihood** *see* 967; what may be, what might be, what is possible, what one can do, what can be done, the possible, the attainable, the feasible; **potential, potentiality,** virtuality; contingency, eventuality; **chance, prospect; outside chance** (*informal*), off chance, remote possibility, ghost of a chance; hope, outside hope, small hope, slim odds; **good possibility, good chance,** even chance *see* 971.7; bare possibility *see* 971.9

2 practicability, practicality, feasibility; workability, operability, actability, performability, realizability, negotiability; **viability,** viableness; **achievability,** doability, compassability, **attainability;** surmountability, superability

3 accessibility, access, **approachability, openness,** reachableness, come-at-ableness *and* get-at-ableness (*both informal*); **penetrability,** perviousness; **obtainability,** obtainableness, **availability,** donability, **procurability,** procurableness, securableness, getableness, acquirability

verbs

4 to be possible, could be, might be, **have *or* stand a chance *or* good chance, bid fair to**

5 to make possible, enable, permit, permit of, clear the road *or* path for, smooth the way for, open the way for, open the door to, open up the possibility of

adjectives

6 possible, within the bounds *or* realm *or* range *or* domain of possibility, in one's power, in one's hands, humanly possible; **probable, likely** *see* 967.6; **conceivable,** conceivably possible, **imaginable, thinkable,** cogitable; plausible *see* 967.7; **potential;** contingent

7 practicable, practical, feasible; workable, actable, performable, effectible (*old*), realizable, compassable, operable, negotiable, doable, swingable, bridgeable; **viable; achievable, attainable;** surmountable, superable, overcomable

8 accessible, approachable, come-at-able *and* get-at-able (*both informal*), **reachable,** within reach; **open,** open to; **penetrable,** get-in-able (*informal*), pervious; **obtainable, attainable, available,** procurable, securable, findable, easy to come by, getable, to be had, donable

adverbs

9 possibly, conceivably, imaginably, feasibly; within the realm of possibility; **perhaps,** perchance, haply; **maybe,** it may be, for all *or* aught one knows

10 **by any possibility**, **by any chance**, by any means, **by any manner of means**; in any way, in any possible way, **at any cost**, **at all**, if at all, ever; on the bare possibility, on the off chance, by merest chance

11 **if possible**, if humanly possible, **God willing**, *Deo volente* (*Latin*), inshallah (*Islam*), wind and weather permitting

966 IMPOSSIBILITY

nouns

1 **impossibility**, impossibleness, the realm *or* domain of the impossible, **inconceivability**, unthinkability, unimaginability, what cannot be, what can never be, what cannot happen, hopelessness, Chinaman's chance *and* a snowball's chance in hell (*both informal*), **no chance** see 971.10; **self-contradiction**, absurdity, paradox, oxymoron, logical impossibility; **impossible**, the impossible, impossibilism

2 **impracticability**, unpracticability, **impracticality**, **unfeasibility**; **unworkability**, inoperability, unperformability; **unachievability**, **unattainability**; unrealizability, uncompassability; insurmountability, **insuperability**

3 **inaccessibility**, unaccessibility; **unapproachability**, un-come-at-ableness (*informal*), unreachableness; **impenetrability**, imperviousness; **unobtainability**, unobtainableness, **unattainability**, **unavailability**, unprocurableness, unsecurableness, ungettableness (*informal*), unacquirability; undiscoverability, unascertainableness

verbs

4 **to be impossible**, be an impossibility, **not have a chance**, be a waste of time; **contradict itself**, be a logical impossibility, be a paradox; fly in the face of reason

5 **to attempt the impossible**, try for a miracle, look for a needle in a haystack *or* in a bottle of hay, try to be in two places at once, try to fetch water in a sieve *or* catch the wind in a net *or* weave a rope of sand *or* get figs from thistles *or* gather grapes from thorns *or* make bricks from straw *or* make cheese of chalk *or* make a silk purse out of a sow's ear *or* change the leopard's spots *or* get blood from a turnip *or* get blood from a stone; ask the impossible, cry for the moon

6 **to make impossible**, **rule out**, disenable, disqualify, close out, **bar**, prohibit, put out of reach, leave no chance

adjectives

7 **impossible**, **not possible**, beyond the bounds of possibility *or* reason, contrary to reason, at variance with the facts; **inconceivable**, **unimaginable**, **unthinkable**, **not to be thought of**, **out of the question**; hopeless; **absurd**, ridiculous, preposterous; **self-contradictory**, paradoxical, oxymoronic, logically impossible; **ruled out**, excluded, closed-out, **barred**, prohibited

8 **impracticable**, **impractical**, **unpragmatic**, **unfeasible**; **unworkable**, unperformable, inoperable, undoable, unnegotiable, unbridgeable; **unachievable**,

unattainable, uneffectible (*old*); unrealizable, uncompassable; insurmountable, unsurmountable, **insuperable**, unovercomable; **beyond one**, beyond one's power, beyond one's control, out of one's depth, too much for

9 **inaccessible**, unaccessible; **unapproachable**, un-come-at-able (*informal*); **unreachable**, beyond reach, out of reach; **impenetrable**, impervious; closed to, denied to, lost to, closed forever to; **unobtainable**, **unattainable**, **unavailable**, unprocurable, unsecurable, ungettable (*informal*), unacquirable; not to be had, **not to be had for love or money**; undiscoverable, unascertainable

adverbs

10 **impossibly**, **inconceivably**, unimaginably, unthinkably; not at any price

phrases

11 no can do, no way, no way José (*informal*), no chance

967 PROBABILITY

nouns

1 **probability**, **likelihood**, likeliness, liability, aptitude, verisimilitude; **chance**, **odds**; **expectation**, **outlook**, prospect, lookout (*informal*); favourable prospect, well-grounded hope, some *or* reasonable hope, fair expectation; **good chance** see 971.8; presumption, presumptive evidence; tendency; probable cause, reasonable ground *or* presumption; probabilism; possibility see 965

2 **mathematical probability**, statistical probability, statistics, **predictability**; probability theory, game theory, theory of games; operations research; probable error, standard deviation; stochastic *or* statistical independence, stochastic variable; probability curve, frequency curve, frequency polygon, frequency distribution, probability function, probability density function, probability distribution, cumulative distribution function; **statistical mechanics**, quantum mechanics, uncertainty *or* indeterminancy principle, Maxwell-Boltzmann distribution law, Bose-Einstein statistics, Fermi-Dirac statistics; **mortality table**, actuarial table, life table, combined experience table, Commissioners Standard Ordinary table

3 **plausibility**; **reasonability** see 934.9; **credibility** see 952.8

verbs

4 **to be probable**, **seem likely**, could be, offer a good prospect, offer the expectation, have *or* run a good chance; **promise**, be promising, make fair promise, **bid fair to**, stand fair to, show a tendency, be on the cards, have the makings of, have favourable odds, lead one to expect; **make probable**, probabilize, make more likely, smooth the way for; increase the chances

5 **to think likely**, daresay, venture to say; **presume**, suppose see 950.10

adjectives

6 **probable, likely, liable, apt,** verisimilar, in the cards, odds-on; **promising, hopeful,** fair, in a fair way; foreseeable, **predictable; presumable,** presumptive; **statistical,** actuarial; mathematically *or* statistically probable, predictable within limits

7 **plausible,** colourable, apparent (*old*); **reasonable** *see* 934.20; credible *see* 952.24; **conceivable** *see* 965.6

adverbs

8 **probably,** in all probability *or* likelihood, likely, **most likely,** very likely; as likely as not, very like *and* like enough *and* like as not (*all informal*); **doubtlessly,** doubtless, **no doubt,** indubitably; **presumably,** presumptively; by all odds, ten to one, a hundred to one

phrases

9 there is reason to believe, I am led to believe, it can be supposed, it would appear, it stands to reason, it might be thought, one can assume, appearances are in favour of, the chances *or* odds are, you can bank on it, you can bet on it, you can bet your bottom dollar, you can just bet, you can't go wrong; I daresay, I venture to say

968 IMPROBABILITY

nouns

1 **improbability, unlikelihood,** unlikeliness; **doubtfulness,** dubiousness, **questionableness; implausibility,** incredibility *see* 954.3; little expectation, low order of probability, poor possibility, bare possibility, faint likelihood, poor prospect, poor outlook, a ghost of a chance, fat chance (*informal*); **small chance** *see* 971.9

verbs

2 **to be improbable, not be likely,** be a stretch of the imagination, strain one's credulity, go beyond reason, go far afield, go beyond the bounds of reason *or* probability, be far-fetched *or* fetched from afar

adjectives

3 **improbable, unlikely,** unpromising, hardly possible, logic-defying, scarcely to be expected *or* anticipated; statistically improbable; **doubtful,** dubious, **questionable,** doubtable, dubitable, more than doubtful; **implausible,** incredible *see* 954.10; unlooked-for, unexpected, unpredictable

phrases

4 not likely!, no fear!, never fear!, no chance!, no way!, I ask you!, you should live so long! (*US & Canadian informal*), don't hold your breath!, don't bet on it (*informal*)

969 CERTAINTY

nouns

1 **certainty, certitude,** certainness, **sureness,** surety, **assurance, assuredness,** certain knowledge; **positiveness, absoluteness, definiteness,** dead *or* moral *or* absolute certainty; unequivocalness,

unmistakableness, unambiguity, nonambiguity, univocity, univocality; **infallibility,** infallibilism, inerrability, inerrancy; **necessity,** determinacy, determinateness, noncontingency, Hobson's choice, ineluctability, predetermination, predestination, **inevitability** *see* 962.7; **truth** *see* 972; **proved fact,** probatum

2 (*informal terms*) **sure thing,** dead certainty, dead cert, dead-sure thing, sure bet, cinch, dead cinch, open-and-shut case

3 **unquestionability, undeniability,** indubitability, indubitableness, **indisputability,** incontestability, incontrovertibility, **irrefutability,** unrefutability, unconfutability, irrefragability, unimpeachability; **doubtlessness, questionlessness; demonstrability,** provability, verifiability, confirmability; factuality, **reality,** actuality *see* 760.2

4 **reliability, dependability, dependableness, validity, trustworthiness,** faithworthiness; unerringness; predictability, calculability; stability, substantiality, firmness, **soundness,** solidity, staunchness, steadiness, **steadfastness;** secureness, **security;** invincibility *see* 15.4; **authoritativeness, authenticity**

5 **confidence,** confidentness, conviction, belief *see* 952, fixed *or* settled belief, **sureness, assurance, assuredness,** surety, security, certitude; **faith,** subjective certainty; trust *see* 952.1; **positiveness, cocksureness; self-confidence, self-assurance, self-reliance;** poise *see* 106.3; courage *see* 492; **overconfidence, oversureness,** overweening (*old*), overweeningness, hubris; pride *see* 136, arrogance *see* 141, pomposity *see* 501.7, self-importance *see* 140.1

6 **dogmatism,** dogmaticalness, pontification, **positiveness,** positivism, peremptoriness, **opinionatedness,** self-opinionatedness; bigotry; infallibilism

7 **dogmatist,** dogmatizer, opinionist, doctrinaire, bigot; positivist; infallibilist

8 **ensuring, assurance;** reassurance, reassurement; **certification;** ascertainment, **determination,** establishment; **verification, corroboration,** substantiation, validation, collation, check, cross-check, double-check, checking; independent *or* objective witness; **confirmation**

verbs

9 **to be certain, be confident,** feel sure, rest assured, have sewed up (*informal*), **have no doubt,** doubt not; know, just know, know for certain; **bet on** *and* gamble on *and* bet one's bottom dollar on (*all informal*); admit of no doubt; **go without saying,** aller sans dire (*French*), be axiomatic *or* apodictic

10 **to dogmatize,** lay down the law, pontificate, oracle, oraculate, proclaim

11 **to make sure, make certain,** make sure of, make no doubt, make no mistake; remove *or* dismiss *or* expunge *or* erase all doubt; **assure, ensure,** insure, **certify; ascertain,** get a fix *or* lock on (*informal*); **find out,** get at, see to it, see that; **determine,** decide, **establish,** settle, fix, lock in *and* nail down *and* clinch *and* cinch (*all informal*), clear up, sort out, set at rest; assure *or* satisfy oneself, make oneself easy about *or* on that score; **reassure**

12 to verify, **confirm**, test, prove, audit, **collate,** validate, **check,** check up *or* on *or* out (*informal*), check over *or* through, **double-check,** triple-check, cross-check, recheck, check and doublecheck, check up and down, check over and through, check in and out,
"make assurance double sure"—Shakespeare, measure twice, cut once

adjectives

13 **certain, sure,** sure-enough (*informal*); bound; **positive, absolute, definite,** perfectly sure, apodictic; decisive, conclusive; clear, clear as day, clear and distinct, unequivocal, unmistakable, unambiguous, nonambiguous, univocal; **necessary,** determinate, ineluctable, predetermined, predestined, **inevitable** *see* 962.15; **true** *see* 972.12

14 (*informal terms*) dead sure, sure as death, sure as death and taxes, sure as fate, sure as can be, sure as God made little green apples, sure as hell *or* the devil, as sure as I live and breathe

15 **obvious, patent, unquestionable, unexceptionable, undeniable, self-evident,** axiomatic; indubitable, unarguable, indisputable, incontestable, **irrefutable,** unrefutable, unconfutable, incontrovertible, irrefragable, unanswerable, inappealable, unimpeachable, absolute; admitting no question *or* dispute *or* doubt *or* denial; **demonstrable,** demonstratable, provable, verifiable, testable, confirmable; well-founded, well-established, well-grounded; factual, **real,** historical, actual *see* 760.15

16 **undoubted,** not to be doubted, indubious, **unquestioned, undisputed, uncontested,** uncontradicted, unchallenged, uncontroverted, uncontroversial; **doubtless, questionless,** beyond a shade *or* shadow of doubt, past dispute, beyond question

17 **reliable, dependable, sure,** surefire (*informal*), **trustworthy, trusty,** faithworthy, **to be depended** *or* **relied upon,** to be counted *or* reckoned on; predictable, calculable; **secure, solid, sound, firm,** fast, **stable, substantial,** staunch, steady, **steadfast, faithful, unfailing;** true to one's word; invincible

18 **authoritative, authentic,** magisterial, **official;** cathedral, ex cathedra; standard, approved, accepted, received, pontific; from *or* straight from the horse's mouth

19 **infallible, inerrable,** inerrant, **unerring**

20 **assured,** made sure; **determined, decided, ascertained; settled, established,** fixed, cinched *and* sewed up *and* taped (*all informal*), set, stated, determinate, secure; **certified,** attested, guaranteed, warranted, tested, tried, proved; cinched *and* open-and-shut *and* nailed down *and* in the bag *and* on ice (*all informal*), wired (*US & Canadian informal*)

21 **confident, sure,** secure, **assured,** reassured, decided, determined; **convinced,** persuaded, positive, **cocksure; unhesitating,** unfaltering, unwavering; **undoubting** *see* 952.21; **self-confident, self-assured, self-reliant,** sure of oneself; poised *see* 106.13; unafraid; **overconfident, oversure,**

overweening, hubristic, uppish (*informal*); proud *see* 136.8, arrogant *see* 141.9, pompous *see* 501.22, self-important *see* 140.8

22 **dogmatic, dogmatical,** dogmatizing, pronunciative, didactic, **positive,** positivistic, peremptory, pontifical, oracular; **opinionated,** opinioned, opinionative, conceited *see* 140.11; **self-opinionated,** self-opinioned; doctrinarian, doctrinaire; bigoted

adverbs

23 **certainly, surely, assuredly, positively, absolutely, definitely,** decidedly; without batting an eye (*informal*); decisively, distinctly, clearly, unequivocally, unmistakably; **for certain,** for sure *and* for a fact (*both informal*), in truth, certes *or* forsooth (*both old*), and no mistake (*informal*); **for a certainty,** to a certainty, *à coup sûr* (*French*); **most certainly,** most assuredly; **indeed,** indeedy (*informal*); truly; **of course,** as a matter of course; **by all means,** by all manner of means; at any rate, at all events; nothing else but (*informal*), no two ways about it, no buts about it (*informal*); no ifs, ands, or buts

24 **surely, sure, to be sure,** sure enough, for sure (*informal*); sure thing (*informal*)

25 **unquestionably, without question, undoubtedly, beyond the shadow of a doubt, beyond a reasonable doubt, indubitably, admittedly, undeniably,** unarguably, indisputably, incontestably, incontrovertibly, irrefutably, irrefragably; **doubtlessly,** doubtless, **no doubt, without doubt,** beyond doubt *or* question, out of question

26 **without fail,** unfailingly, whatever may happen, **come what may,** come hell or high water (*informal*); cost what it may, *coûte que coûte* (*French*); rain or shine, live or die, sink or swim

phrases

27 **it is certain,** there is no question, there is not a shadow of doubt, that's for sure (*informal*), there is no question about it; that goes without saying, *cela va sans dire* (*French*); that is evident, that leaps to the eye, *cela saute aux yeux* (*French*), Blind Freddie could see that (*Australian*)

970 UNCERTAINTY

nouns

1 **uncertainty, incertitude, unsureness,** uncertainness; indemonstrability, unverifiability, unprovability, unconfirmability; **unpredictability,** unforeseeableness, incalculability, unaccountability; **indetermination,** indeterminacy, indeterminism; **relativity,** relativism, contingency, conditionality; **randomness, chance,** chanciness, hit-or-missness, **luck;** entropy; **indecision,** indecisiveness, undecidedness, undeterminedness; **hesitation, hesitancy; suspense,** suspensefulness, agony *or* state of suspense; **fickleness, capriciousness,** whimsicality, **erraticness,** erraticism, **changeableness** *see* 853; **vacillation, irresolution** *see* 362; trendlessness; Heisenberg *or* indeterminacy *or* uncertainty principle

2 doubtfulness, dubiousness, doubt, dubiety, dubitancy, dubitation (*old*); **questionableness, disputability,** contestability, controvertibility, refutability, confutability, deniability; disbelief *see* 954.1

3 bewilderment, disconcertion, disconcertedness, disconcert, disconcertment, **embarrassment, confoundment,** discomposure, unassuredness, **confusion,** cognitive dissonance; **perplexity, puzzlement,** baffle, **bafflement,** predicament, plight, **quandary, dilemma,** horns of a dilemma, nonplus; **puzzle,** problem, riddle, conundrum, mystery, enigma; fix *and* jam *and* pickle *and* scrape *and* stew (*all informal*); perturbation, **disturbance, upset, bother,** pother

4 vagueness, indefiniteness, indecisiveness, indeterminateness, indeterminableness, indefinableness, **unclearness, indistinctness,** haziness, fogginess, mistiness, murkiness, blurriness, fuzziness; **obscurity,** obscuration; **looseness, laxity, inexactness,** inaccuracy, imprecision; **broadness, generality,** sweepingness; ill-definedness, amorphousness, shapelessness, blobbiness; inchoateness, disorder, incoherence

5 equivocalness, equivocality, polysemousness, ambiguity *see* 539

6 unreliability, undependability, untrustworthiness, unfaithworthiness, treacherousness, treachery; **unsureness, insecurity, unsoundness, infirmity,** insolidity, unsolidity, **instability,** insubstantiality, unsubstantiality, **unsteadfastness,** unsteadiness, desultoriness, shakiness; **precariousness,** hazard, danger, risk, riskiness, diciness *and* dodginess (*informal*), knife-edge, moment of truth, tightrope walking, peril, perilousness, ticklishness, slipperiness, shiftiness, shiftingness; speculativeness; **unauthoritativeness,** unauthenticity

7 fallibility, errability, errancy, liability to error

8 (*an uncertainty*) **gamble, guess,** piece of guesswork, estimate, guesstimate *and* ballpark figure (*informal*); **chance, wager; toss-up** *and* **coin-toss** (*both informal*), **touch and go;** contingency, double contingency, possibility upon a possibility; **question, open question;** undecided issue, loose end; **grey area,** twilight zone, borderline case; blind bargain, pig in a poke, sight-unseen transaction; leap in the dark

verbs

9 to be uncertain, feel unsure; doubt, have one's doubts, **question,** puzzle over, agonize over; **wonder,** wonder whether, wrinkle one's brow; not know what to make of, not be able to make head or tail of; be at sea, float in a sea of doubt; be at one's wit's end, **not know which way to turn,** be of two minds, be at sixes and sevens, not know where one stands, have mixed feelings, not know whether one stands on one's head or one's heels, be in a dilemma *or* quandary, flounder, grope, beat about, thrash about, not know whether one is coming or going, go around in circles; go off in all directions at once

10 to hang in doubt, stop to consider, think twice; falter, dither, **hesitate,** swither (*Scottish*), **vacillate** *see* 362.8

11 to depend, all depend, be contingent *or* conditional on, hang on *or* upon; **hang, hang in the balance,** be touch and go, tremble in the balance, **hang in suspense; hang by a thread,** cliffhang, hang by a hair

12 to bewilder, disconcert, discompose, **upset,** perturb, **disturb, dismay,** tie one in knots; abash, **embarrass, put out,** pother, **bother,** moither *or* moider (*dialect*), flummox (*informal*), keep one on tenterhooks

13 to perplex, baffle, confound, daze, amaze (*old*), maze, addle, fuddle, muddle, **mystify, puzzle,** nonplus, put to one's wit's end; keep one guessing, keep in suspense

14 (*informal terms*) **to stump,** boggle, bamboozle, stick, floor, throw, get, beat, lick

15 to make uncertain, obscure, muddle, muddy, fuzz, muzz (*informal*), fog, **confuse** *see* 984.7

adjectives

16 uncertain, unsure; doubting, agnostic, **sceptical,** unconvinced, unpersuaded; chancy, dicey, touch-and-go; **unpredictable,** unforeseeable, incalculable, uncountable, unreckonable, unaccountable, undivinable; indemonstrable, unverifiable, unprovable, unconfirmable; **equivocal,** polysemous, inexplicit, imprecise, ambiguous; **fickle, capricious,** whimsical, **erratic,** variable, wavering, **changeable** *see* 853.6; **hesitant,** hesitating; **indecisive, irresolute** *see* 362.9

17 doubtful, iffy (*informal*); **in doubt,** *in dubio* (*Latin*); dubitable, doubtable, **dubious, questionable, problematic, problematical, speculative,** conjectural, suppositional; **debatable,** moot, arguable, disputable, contestable, controvertible, **controversial,** refutable, confutable, deniable; mistakable; **suspicious,** suspect, sus (*informal*); open to question *or* doubt; in question, in dispute, at issue

18 undecided, undetermined, unsettled, unfixed, unestablished; untold, uncounted; pendent, dependent, **pending,** depending, contingent, conditional, conditioned; **open,** in question, at issue, **in the balance, up in the air,** up for grabs (*informal*), **in suspense,** in a state of suspense, suspenseful

19 vague, indefinite, indecisive, indeterminate, indeterminable, **undetermined,** unpredetermined, undestined; **random,** stochastic, entropic, **chance,** chancy (*informal*), dicey *and* dodgy (*informal*), aleatory *or* aleatoric, hit-or-miss; indefinable, undefined, ill-defined, **unclear,** unplain, **indistinct,** fuzzy, **obscure, confused, hazy,** shadowy, shadowed forth, misty, foggy, fog-bound, murky, blurred, blurry, veiled; **loose, lax, inexact,** inaccurate, imprecise; nonspecific, unspecified; **broad, general,** sweeping; amorphous, shapeless, blobby; inchoate, disordered, orderless, chaotic, incoherent

20 unreliable, undependable, untrustworthy, unfaithworthy, treacherous, **unsure,** not to be depended *or* relied on; **insecure, unsound, infirm,** unsolid, **unstable,** unsubstantial, insubstantial, **unsteadfast,** unsteady, desultory, shaky;

precarious, hazardous, dangerous, perilous, risky, dodgy (*informal*), ticklish; shifty, shifting, slippery, slippery as an eel; provisional, tentative, temporary

21 **unauthoritative, unauthentic, unofficial,** nonofficial, apocryphal; **uncertified, unverified,** unchecked, unconfirmed, uncorroborated, unauthenticated, unvalidated, unattested, unwarranted; **undemonstrated, unproved**

22 **fallible, errable,** errant, liable *or* open to error, error-prone

23 **unconfident, unsure, unassured, insecure,** unsure of oneself; unselfconfident, unselfassured, unselfreliant

24 **bewildered, dismayed,** distracted, distraught, abashed, **disconcerted, embarrassed,** discomposed, **put-out, disturbed, upset,** perturbed, **bothered,** all hot and bothered (*informal*); **confused** *see* 984.12; clueless, without a clue, guessing, mazed, in a maze; turned around, going around in circles, like a chicken with its head cut off *or* like a headless chicken (*informal*); in a fix *or* stew *or* pickle *or* jam *or* scrape (*informal*); **lost,** astray, abroad, adrift, **at sea,** off the track, out of one's reckoning, out of one's bearings, disoriented, bushed (*Australian & NZ*), up the boohai (*NZ*)

25 **in a dilemma,** on the horns of a dilemma; **perplexed, confounded, mystified, puzzled, nonplussed, baffled,** bamboozled (*informal*), buffaloed (*US & Canadian informal*), bushed (*Australian & NZ*); **at a loss, at one's wit's end,** fuddled, addled, muddled, dazed; **on tenterhooks,** in suspense

26 (*informal terms*) **beat,** licked, stuck, floored, stumped, thrown, boggled

27 **bewildering, confusing, distracting, disconcerting,** discomposing, **dismaying, embarrassing,** disturbing, **upsetting,** perturbing, bothering, off-putting; **perplexing, baffling, mystifying, mysterious, puzzling,** funny, funny peculiar, confounding; **problematic** *or* problematical; intricate *see* 798.4; **enigmatic** *see* 522.17

adverbs

28 uncertainly, in an uncertain state, **unsurely; doubtfully, dubiously;** in suspense, at sea, on the horns of a dilemma, at sixes and sevens, not knowing whether one is Arthur or Martha (*Australian & NZ informal*); perplexedly, disconcertedly, confusedly, dazedly, mazedly, in a daze, in a maze, around in circles

29 vaguely, **indefinitely,** indeterminably, indefinably, **indistinctly,** indecisively, **obscurely; broadly, generally,** in broad *or* general terms

971 CHANCE
absence of assignable cause

nouns

1 **chance,** happenstance, hap, "heedless hap"—SPENSER; **luck;** good luck *or* fortune, serendipity, happy chance, dumb luck (*informal*), rotten *and* tough *and* hard luck (*all informal*); **fortune,** fate, **destiny,** whatever comes, *moira*

(*Greek*), lot *see* 963.2; **fortuity, randomness,** randomicity, fortuitousness, adventitiousness, indeterminateness *or* indeterminacy, problematicness, uncertainty *see* 970, flukiness (*informal*), casualness, flip of a coin, crazy quilt, patternlessness, trendlessness, accidentality; break (*informal*), the breaks (*informal*), run of luck, the luck of the draw, the rub of the green, run *or* turn of the cards, fall *or* throw of the dice, the way things fall, the way the cards fall, how they fall, the way the cookie crumbles *or* the ball bounces (*both informal*); uncertainty principle, principle of indeterminacy, Heisenberg's principle; **probability** *see* 967, stochastics, theory of probability, law of averages, statistical probability, actuarial calculation; random sample, **risk, risk-taking, chancing, gamble** *see* 759; **opportunity** *see* 842.2

2 Chance, Fortune, Lady *or* Dame Fortune, wheel of fortune, Fortuna, the fickle finger of fate (*informal*); Luck, Lady Luck;

"a nickname of Providence"—DE CHAMFORT, "blind Chance"—LUCAN, "fickle Chance"—MILTON, "that Power which erring men call Chance"—MILTON, "the pseudonym of God when He did not want to sign"—ANATOLE FRANCE

3 **purposelessness, causelessness,** aimlessness, randomness, dysteleology, **unpredictability** *see* 970.1, designlessness, **aimlessness**

4 **haphazard,** chance-medley (*law*), **random;** random shot; potluck

5 **vicissitudes,** vicissitudes of fortune, ins and outs, **ups and downs,** ups and downs of life, chapter of accidents, feast and famine,

"the various turns of chance"—DRYDEN; **chain of circumstances,** concatenation of events, chain reaction, vicious circle, causal nexus, **domino effect**

6 (*chance event*) **happening,** hap, happenstance; **fortuity, accident,** casualty, adventure, hazard; contingent, contingency; **fluke** (*informal*), freak, freak occurrence *or* accident; chance hit, lucky shot, long shot, one in a million, long odds

7 **even chance,** even break *and* fair shake (*both informal*), even *or* square odds, level playing field, touch and go, odds; **half a chance,** fifty-fifty; toss, **toss-up,** standoff (*informal*)

8 **good chance, sporting chance,** good opportunity, good possibility; odds-on, odds-on chance, **likelihood, possibility** *see* 965, probability *see* 967, favourable prospect, well-grounded hope; **sure bet,** sure thing (*informal*), dead cert (*informal*); **best bet,** main chance, winning chance

9 **small chance,** little chance, dark horse, **poor prospect** *or* prognosis, poor lookout (*informal*), little opportunity, poor possibility, **unlikelihood, improbability** *see* 968, hardly a chance, not half a chance; **off chance, outside chance** (*informal*), **remote possibility,** bare possibility, a ghost of a chance, slim chance, gambling chance, **fighting chance** (*informal*); poor bet, long odds, long shot (*informal*), hundred-to-one shot (*informal*)

10 **no chance,** not a Chinaman's chance *and* not a snowball's chance in hell (*both informal*), Buckley's chance *or* Buckley's (*Australian informal*), not a prayer, not a hope in hell (*informal*); **impossibility** *see* 966, hopelessness

verbs

11 **to chance,** bechance, betide, come *or* happen by chance, hap, hazard, **happen** *see* 830.5, happen *or* fall on, come, come *or* happen along, **turn up,** pop up (*informal*), **befall;** fall to one's lot, be one's fate

12 **to risk,** take a chance, run a risk, push *or* press one's luck, lay one's arse on the line *and* put one's money where one's mouth is (*both informal*), **gamble, bet** *see* 759.19; risk one's neck *and* go for broke (*both informal*); **predict** *see* 961.9, prognosticate; call someone's bluff

13 to have a chance *or* an opportunity, **stand a chance, run a good chance, bid** *or* **stand fair to,** admit of; be in it *or* in the running (*informal*); have *or* take a chance at, have a fling *or* shot at (*informal*); have a small *or* slight chance, be a dark horse, barely have a chance

14 **to not have** *or* **stand a chance,** have no chance *or* opportunity, not have a prayer, not have a Chinaman's chance (*informal*), not stand a snowball's chance in hell (*informal*), not have a hope in hell (*informal*); not be in it (*informal*), be out of it (*informal*), **be out of the running**

adjectives

15 **chance;** chancy (*informal*), dicey (*informal*), **risky** (*informal*), dodgy (*informal*); **fortuitous, accidental,** aleatory; **lucky,** fortunate, blessed by fortune, serendipitous; **casual,** adventitious, incidental, contingent, iffy (*informal*); **causeless,** uncaused; indeterminate, undetermined; **unexpected** *see* 131.10, **unpredictable,** unforeseeable, unlooked-for, **unforeseen; fluky** (*informal*); fatal, fatidic, destinal

16 **purposeless, causeless,** designless, **aimless,** driftless, undirected, objectless, unmotivated, mindless; **haphazard, random,** dysteleological, stochastic, stray, inexplicable, unaccountable, promiscuous, indiscriminate, casual, leaving much to chance

17 **unintentional,** unintended, **unmeant, unplanned,** undesigned, unpurposed, unthought-of; **unpremeditated,** unmeditated, unprompted, unguided, unguarded; **unwitting, unthinking,** unconscious, involuntary

18 **impossible** *see* 966.7; **improbable** *see* 968.3; **certain** *see* 969.13; **probable** *see* 967.6

adverbs

19 **by chance,** perchance, **by accident, accidentally, casually,** incidentally, by coincidence, **unpredictably, fortuitously, out of a clear blue sky;** by a piece of luck, by a fluke (*informal*), by good fortune; **as it chanced, as luck would have it,** by hazard, as it may happen, as it may be, as the case may be, as it may chance, as it may turn up *or* out; somehow, in some way, in some way or other, somehow or other, for some reason

20 **purposelessly, aimlessly; haphazardly, randomly,** dysteleologically, stochastically, inexplicably, unaccountably, promiscuously,

indiscriminately, casually, **at haphazard, at random,** at hazard

21 **unintentionally, without design, unwittingly,** unthinkingly, unexpectedly, unconsciously, involuntarily

exclamations

22 break a leg!, best of luck!, good luck!

972 TRUTH
conformity to fact or reality

nouns

1 **truth, trueness, verity,** veridicality, conformity to fact *or* reality *or* the evidence *or* the data, simple *or* unadorned truth, very truth, sooth *or* good sooth (*both archaic*); more truth than poetry; **unerroneousness, unfalseness,** unfallaciousness; historical truth, **objective truth, actuality,** historicity, impersonality; **fact, actuality, reality** *see* 760.2, the real world; the true, ultimate truth; eternal verities; truthfulness, veracity *see* 644.3

2 **a truth, a self-evident truth, an axiomatic truth, an axiom;** a premise, a given, a donnée *or* donné, an accomplished fact *or* fait accompli (*French*)

3 **the truth,** the truth of the matter, the case; the home truth, the unvarnished truth, the simple truth, the unadorned truth, the naked truth, the plain truth, the unqualified truth, the honest truth, the sober truth, the exact truth, the straight truth; the absolute truth, the intrinsic truth, the unalloyed truth, the cast-iron truth, the hard truth, the stern truth, gospel, gospel truth, Bible truth, revealed truth; the truth, the whole truth, and nothing but the truth

4 (*informal terms*) **what's what,** how it is, how things are, like it is, where it's at, dinkum oil (*Australian*), the honest-to-God truth, God's truth, God's honest truth, the real thing, the very model, the genuine article, the very thing, it, the article, the goods, the McCoy, the real McCoy, chapter and verse, the gospel, the gospel truth, the lowdown

5 **accuracy, correctness,** care for truth, attention to fact, right, subservience to the facts *or* the data, **rightness, rigour, rigorousness, exactness, exactitude; preciseness, precision;** mathematical precision, pinpoint accuracy *or* precision, scientific exactness *or* exactitude; **faultlessness,** perfection, absoluteness, flawlessness, impeccability, unimpeachability; **faithfulness, fidelity;** literalness, literality, literalism, textualism, the letter; strictness, severity, rigidity; niceness, nicety, delicacy, subtlety, fineness, refinement; **meticulousness** *see* 339.3; laboratory conditions

6 **validity, soundness,** solidity, substantiality, justness; authority, **authoritativeness; cogency,** weight, force, persuasiveness

7 **genuineness, authenticity,** bona fides, bona fideness, **legitimacy; realness, realism,** photographic realism, absolute realism, realistic representation, **naturalism,** naturalness, truth to nature, **lifelikeness,** truth to life, slice of life, *tranche de vie* (*French*), kitchen sink, true-to-lifeness, verisimilitude, *vraisemblance* (*French*), verism,

verismo; absolute likeness, **literalness,** literality, literalism, truth to the letter; socialist realism; inartificiality, unsyntheticness; **unspuriousness,** unspeciousness, unfictitiousness, artlessness, unaffectedness; **honesty, sincerity;** unadulteration *see* 797.1

verbs

8 to be true, be the case; conform to fact, square *or* chime with the facts *or* evidence; **prove true,** prove to be, **prove out,** be so in fact; **hold true, hold good, hold water** (*informal*), hold *or* stick together (*informal*), **hold up, hold up in the wash** (*informal*), wash (*informal*), **stand up,** stand the test, be consistent *or* self-consistent, **hold,** remain valid; **be truthful**

9 to seem true, ring true, sound true, **carry conviction,** convince, persuade, win over, hold *or* have the ring of truth

10 to be right, be correct, be just right, get it straight; be OK (*informal*), add up; **hit the nail on the head,** hit it on the nose *or* on the money (*both informal*), say a mouthful (*US & Canadian*), hit the bull's-eye, score a bull's-eye

11 to be accurate, dot one's i's and cross one's t's, draw *or* cut it fine (*informal*), be precise; make precise, precise, particularize

12 to come true, come about, attain fulfilment, **turn out, come to pass** *or* **to be,** happen as expected

adjectives

13 true, truthful; unerroneous, not in error, in conformity with the facts *or* the evidence *or* reality, on the up-and-up *or* strictly on the up-and-up (*informal*); gospel, **hard,** cast-iron; unfalse, unfallacious, unmistaken; **real, veritable,** sure-enough (*informal*), objective, true to the facts, in conformity with the facts *or* the evidence *or* the data *or* reality, **factual, actual** *see* 760.15, effectual, **historical,** documentary; objectively true; **certain,** undoubted, unquestionable *see* 969.15; unrefuted, unconfuted, undenied; **ascertained, proved, proven, verified,** validated, **certified,** demonstrated, confirmed, determined, established, attested, substantiated, **authenticated,** corroborated; true as gospel; substantially true, categorically true; **veracious** *see* 644.16

14 valid, sound, well-grounded, well-founded, conforming to the facts *or* the data *or* the evidence *or* reality, hard, solid, substantial; consistent, self-consistent, logical; **good, just,** sufficient; **cogent, weighty, authoritative; legal, lawful,** legitimate, binding

15 genuine, authentic, veridic, veridical, **real, natural, realistic, naturalistic,** true to reality, **true to nature, lifelike,** true to life, verisimilar, veristic, your actual (*informal*); literal, following the letter, letter-perfect, *au pied de la lettre* (*French*), true to the letter; verbatim, verbal, word-perfect, **word-for-word;** true to the spirit; **legitimate,** rightful, lawful; **bona fide,** card-carrying (*informal*), **good,** sure-enough (*informal*), **sincere, honest;** candid, honest-to-God (*informal*), dinkum (*Australian informal*); **inartificial, unsynthetic;** unspurious, unspecious,

unsimulated, unfaked, unfeigned, **undisguised, uncounterfeited, unpretended, unaffected, unassumed; unassuming, simple,** unpretending, unfeigning, undisguising; **unfictitious,** unfanciful, unfabricated, unconcocted, uninvented, unimagined; unromantic; **original,** unimitated, uncopied; unexaggerated, undistorted; unflattering, unvarnished, uncoloured, unqualified; **unadulterated** *see* 797.7; **pure,** simon-pure; **sterling,** twenty-four carat

16 accurate, correct, right, proper, just; all right *or* OK *or* okay (*all informal*), just right as rain, right, dead right, on target *and* on the money *and* on the nose (*all informal*), bang on (*informal*), spot-on (*informal*), straight, straight-up-and-down; **faultless,** flawless, impeccable, unimpeachable, unexceptionable; **absolute, perfect; meticulous** *see* 339.12

17 exact, precise, express; even, square; absolutely *or* definitely *or* positively right; **faithful;** direct; **unerring,** undeviating, constant; **infallible,** inerrant, inerrable; **strict,** close, severe, **rigorous,** rigid; mathematically exact, mathematical; mechanically *or* micrometrically precise; scientifically exact, scientific; religiously exact, religious; **nice,** delicate, subtle, **fine,** refined; pinpoint, microscopic

adverbs

18 truly, really, really-truly (*informal*), **verily,** veritably, forsooth *or* in very sooth (*both old*), **in truth,** in good *or* very truth, **actually,** historically, objectively, impersonally, rigorously, strictly, strictly speaking, unquestionably, without question, **in reality, in fact,** factually, technically, in point of fact, as a matter of fact, for that matter, for the matter of that, to tell the truth, if you want to know the truth, to state the fact *or* truth, of a truth, with truth; **indeed,** indeedy (*informal*); **certainly; indubitably, undoubtedly** *see* 969.25; no buts about it (*informal*), nothing else but

19 genuinely, authentically, really, naturally, **legitimately, honestly,** veridically; warts and all; unaffectedly, unassumedly, from the heart, in one's heart of hearts, with all one's heart and soul

20 accurately, correctly, rightly, properly, straight; **perfectly, faultlessly,** flawlessly, impeccably, unimpeachably, unexceptionably; **just right,** just so; so, sic

21 exactly, precisely, to a T, expressly; **just, dead, right,** straight, even, square, **plumb,** directly, squarely, point-blank, bang on (*informal*); unerringly, undeviatingly; verbatim, **literally,** *literatim* (*Latin*), verbally, word-perfectly, word for word, word by word, word for word and letter for letter, *verbatim et litteratim* (*Latin*), in the same words, *ipsissimis verbis* (*Latin*), to the letter, according to the letter, *au pied de la lettre* (*French*); **faithfully, strictly, rigorously,** rigidly; **definitely, positively, absolutely; in every respect,** in all respects, for all the world, neither more nor less

22 to be exact, to be precise, strictly, technically, **strictly speaking,** not to mince the matter, by the book

23 to a nicety, to a T *or* tittle, to a turn, to a hair, to *or* within an inch

phrases

24 **right!**, **that's right, that is so**, amen!, that's it,
that's just it, just so, it is that, *c'est ça* (*French*); **you
are right**, right you are, right as rain, it is for a
fact, you speak truly, as you say, **right**; believe it or
not; touché!

25 (*informal terms*) **right on!**, you better believe it!,
you've got something there, I'll say, I'll tell the
world, I'll drink to that, I'll second that, righto,
quite, rather!, you got it!, you said it, you said a
mouthful (*US & Canadian*), now you're talking, you
can say that again, you're not kidding, that's for
sure, ain't it the truth?, you're damn tootin' (*US &
Canadian*), don't I know it?, you're telling me?,
you're not just whistling Dixie (*US & Canadian*), bet
your life *or* boots, fucking ay (*US & Canadian*)

973 WISE SAYING

nouns

1 **maxim, aphorism, apothegm, epigram, dictum,
adage, proverb**, gnome, words of wisdom, **saw,
saying**, witticism, sentence, expression, phrase,
catchword, catchphrase, word, byword, mot, motto,
moral; **precept**, prescript, teaching, text, verse,
sutra, distich, sloka; golden saying, proverbial saying;
common *or* current saying, stock saying, pithy
saying, wise saying *or* expression, oracle, sententious
expression *or* saying; **conventional wisdom,
common knowledge; ana, analects, proverbs,
wisdom, wisdom literature, collected sayings**

2 **axiom, truth**, a priori truth, postulate, **truism**,
self-evident truth, general *or* universal truth, home
truth, obvious truth; theorem; **proposition**; brocard,
principle, *principium* (*Latin*), settled principle;
formula; rule, law, dictate (*old*), **dictum**; golden
rule

3 **platitude, cliché, saw, old saw, commonplace,
banality**, bromide, **chestnut** (*informal*), corn
(*informal*), triticism (*old*), tired phrase, trite saying,
hackneyed *or* stereotyped saying, commonplace
expression, *lieu commun* (*French*), *locus communis*
(*Latin*), **familiar tune** *or* **story, old song** *or* **story**,
old song and dance (*informal*), twice-told tale, retold
story; reiteration *see 848.2*; prosaicism, prosaism;
prose; old joke *see 489.9*

4 **motto, slogan**, watchword, catchword, catchphrase,
tag line (*US & Canadian*); **device**; epithet;
inscription, epigraph

verbs

5 to **aphorize**, apothegmatize, epigrammatize, coin a
phrase; proverb

adjectives

6 **aphoristic, proverbial**, epigrammatic,
epigrammatical, **axiomatical; sententious, pithy,**
gnomic, pungent, succinct, terse, crisp, pointed;
formulistic, formulaic; **clichéd**, hackneyed, banal,
tired, trite, tritical (*old*), **platitudinous** *see 117.9*

adverbs

7 **proverbially, as the saying is** *or* **goes**, as they say,
as the man says (*informal*), as it has been said, as it
was said of old

974 ERROR

nouns

1 **error, erroneousness; untrueness**, untruthfulness,
**untruth; wrongness, wrong; falseness, falsity;
fallacy, fallaciousness**, self-contradiction; **fault,
faultiness**, defectiveness; **sin** *see 655*, sinfulness,
peccancy, **flaw**, flawedness, *hamartia* (*Greek*);
misdoing, misfeasance; **errancy, aberrancy, aberration,
deviancy; heresy**, unorthodoxy, heterodoxy;
perversion, distortion; mistaking, misconstruction,
misapplication, misprision (*old*); **delusion, illusion**
see 975; misjudgment *see 947*; **misinterpretation** *see
342*

2 **inaccuracy**, inaccurateness, **incorrectness,
uncorrectness, inexactness**, unfactualness,
inexactitude, **unpreciseness**, imprecision,
unspecificity, looseness, laxity, unrigorousness;
tolerance, allowance; negligence; approximation;
deviation, standard deviation, probable error,
predictable error, range of error; uncertainty *see 970*

3 **mistake, error**, *erratum* (*Latin*), *corrigendum* (*Latin*);
fault, *faute* (*French*); gross error, bevue; human
error; **misconception, misapprehension,
misunderstanding**; misstatement, misquotation;
misreport; **misprint, typographical error**, typo
(*informal*), printer's error, typist's error; clerical
error; foot fault (*tennis*); misidentification;
misjudgment, miscalculation *see 947.1*; misplay;
misdeal; miscount; misuse; failure, miss, miscarriage

4 **slip**, slipup *and* miscue (*both informal*); **lapse**, *lapsus*
(*Latin*), **oversight**, omission, balk (*old*), inadvertence
or inadvertency, loose thread; **misstep**, trip, stumble,
false *or* wrong step, wrong *or* bad *or* false move;
false note; **slip of the tongue**, *lapsus linguae* (*Latin*);
slip of the pen, *lapsus calami* (*Latin*)

5 **blunder, faux pas**, gaffe, solecism; stupidity,
indiscretion *see 922.4*; **botch, bungle** *see 414.5*

6 (*informal terms*) **goof, boob, boo-boo**, bish, muff,
bloomer, bloop, blooper, dumb trick, fool mistake,
blue (*Australian & NZ*); howler, clanger, screamer;
fuck-up, screw-up, foul-up, snafu, muck-up, balls-up,
cockup, louse-up; pratfall (*US & Canadian*), whoops

7 **grammatical error, solecism**, anacoluthon,
misusage, missaying, mispronunciation; **bull, Irish
bull**, fluff, **malapropism**, malaprop, Mrs Malaprop
(*R B Sheridan*); Pickwickian sense; spoonerism,
marrow-sky; hypercorrection, hyperform; folk
etymology; catachresis

verbs

8 **to not hold water** *and* **not hold together** (*both
informal*), **not stand up**, not square, not figure
(*informal*), not add up, **not hold up, not hold up
in the wash** *and* **not wash** (*both informal*)

9 to **err**, fall into error, **go wrong, go amiss**, go
astray, go *or* get out of line, go awry, stray, get off-
base (*informal*), **deviate**, wander; **lapse, slip, slip
up**, trip, stumble; **miscalculate** *see 947.2*

10 to **be wrong**, **mistake oneself**, **be mistaken, be
in error, be at fault**, be out of line, be off the

track, be in the wrong, miss the truth, miss the point, miss by a mile (*informal*), have another think coming (*informal*); take wrong, receive a false impression, take the shadow for the substance, be misled, be misguided; deceive oneself, be deceived, delude oneself; labour under a false impression

11 **to bark up the wrong tree, back the wrong horse,** count one's chickens before they are hatched

12 **to misdo,** do amiss; **misuse, misemploy, misapply; misconduct, mismanage; miscall, miscount, misdeal,** misplay, misfield; **misprint,** miscite, **misquote, misread,** misreport, **misspell**

13 **to mistake, make a mistake;** miscue *and* make a miscue (*both informal*); **misidentify; misunderstand,** misapprehend, **misconceive, misinterpret** *see* 342.2; **confuse** *see* 810.3, mix up, not distinguish

14 **to blunder, make a blunder, make a faux pas,** blot one's copy book, make a colossal blunder, make a false *or* wrong step, make a misstep, boob (*informal*); **misspeak,** misspeak oneself, trip over one's tongue; embarrass oneself, have egg on one's face (*informal*); blunder into; **botch, bungle** *see* 414.11

15 (*informal terms*) **to make a boo-boo;** drop a brick, goof, boob, fluff, duff, blow, blow it, drop the ball; fuck-up, screw-up, foul-up, muck-up, louse-up, cock up; put *or* stick one's foot in it *or* in one's mouth; muff one's cue, muff *or* blow *or* fluff one's lines, fall flat on one's face *or* arse, step on one's dick (*US & Canadian*), trip up

adjectives

16 **erroneous, untrue,** not true, **not right;** unfactual, **wrong,** all wrong; peccant, perverse, corrupt; **false, fallacious,** self-contradictory; **illogical** *see* 935.11; **unproved** *see* 957.8; **faulty,** faultful, flawed, defective, **at fault;** out, off, all off, off the track *or* rails, off beam *or* off the beam; wide (*old*), wide of the mark, beside the mark; amiss, awry, askew, deviant, deviative, deviational; erring, errant, **aberrant;** straying, astray, adrift; **heretical,** unorthodox, heterodox; abroad, all abroad; perverted, **distorted; delusive,** deceptive, **illusory**

17 **inaccurate, incorrect, inexact,** unfactual, **unprecise,** imprecise, unspecific, loose, lax, unrigorous; negligent; **vague;** approximate, approximative; out of line, out of plumb, out of true, out of square; off-base (*informal*)

18 **mistaken, in error, erring,** under an error, **wrong, all wet** (*US & Canadian informal*), full of bull *or* shit *or* hot air *or* it *or* crap (*all informal*), full of prunes *or* beans (*both US & Canadian informal*); off *or* out in one's reckoning

19 **unauthentic** *or* **inauthentic, unauthoritative, unreliable** *see* 970.20; **misstated,** misreported, miscited, misquoted, **garbled; unfounded** *see* 935.13; spurious

adverbs

20 **erroneously, falsely,** by mistake, fallaciously; faultily, faultfully; **untrue** (*old*), untruly; **wrong,** wrongly; **mistakenly;** amiss, astray, on the wrong track

21 **inaccurately, incorrectly,** inexactly, unprecisely

exclamations

22 **whoops!** *and* sorry about that (*both informal*)

phrases

23 **you are wrong, you are mistaken,** you're way off *or* you have another think coming *or* don't kid yourself (*all informal*), you're all wet (*US & Canadian informal*)

975 ILLUSION

nouns

1 **illusion, delusion,** deluded belief; **deception** *see* 356, **trick;** self-deception, self-deceit, self-delusion; dereism, autism; **misconception, misbelief,** false belief, wrong impression, warped *or* distorted conception; **bubble, chimera,** vapour, "airy nothing"—SHAKESPEARE; *ignis fatuus* (*Latin*), will-o'-the-wisp; **dream,** dream vision; dreamworld, dreamland, dreamscape; **daydream;** pipe dream *and* trip (*informal*); fool's paradise, castle in the air dreamscape; maya

2 **illusoriness,** illusiveness, delusiveness; **falseness,** fallaciousness; **unreality,** unactuality; unsubstantiality, airiness, immateriality; **idealization** *see* 985.7; **seeming,** semblance, simulacrum, **appearance,** false *or* specious appearance, show, false show, false light; **magic, sorcery** *see* 690, illusionism, sleight of hand, prestidigitation, magic show, magic act; magician, **sorcerer** *see* 690.5, illusionist, Prospero (*Shakespeare*); Mahamaya (*Hinduism*)

3 **fancy, phantasy, imagination** *see* 985

4 **phantom, phantasm,** phantasma, wraith, spectre; shadow, shade; phantasmagoria; **fantasy,** wildest dream; **figment of the imagination** *see* 985.5, phantom of the mind; **apparition, appearance; vision,** waking dream, image (*old*); shape, form, figure, presence; eidolon, idolum; "such stuff as dreams are made on"—SHAKESPEARE

5 **optical illusion, trick of eyesight;** afterimage, spectrum, ocular spectrum

6 **mirage,** fata morgana, will-o'-the-wisp, looming

7 **hallucination;** hallucinosis; tripping (*informal*), mind-expansion; consciousness-expansion; delirium tremens *see* 925.9, 10; dream *see* 985.9

verbs

8 **to go on a trip** *and* **blow one's mind** (*both informal*), freak out (*informal*); **hallucinate;** expand one's consciousness; make magic, prestidigitate

adjectives

9 **illusory,** illusive; **illusional,** illusionary; **Barmecide** *or* Barmecidal; **delusory,** delusive; delusional, delusionary, deluding; dereistic, autistic; **dreamy, dreamlike; visionary; imaginary** *see* 985.19; **erroneous** *see* 974.16; **deceptive;** self-deceptive, self-deluding; **chimeric, chimerical, fantastic,** Alice-in-Wonderland; **unreal,** unactual, unsubstantial *see* 763.5, airy; **unfounded** *see* 935.13; **false, fallacious, misleading; specious, seeming,** apparent, ostensible, supposititious, all in the mind; spectral, apparitional, phantom, phantasmal; phantasmagoric, surreal

10 **hallucinatory**, hallucinative, hallucinational; hallucinogenic, psychedelic, consciousness-expanding, mind-expanding, mind-blowing (*informal*)

976 DISILLUSIONMENT

nouns

1 **disillusionment**, disillusion, **disenchantment**, undeception, unspelling, return to reality, loss of one's illusions, loss of innocence, cold light of reality, enlightenment, bursting of the bubble; awakening, rude awakening, bringing back to earth; disappointment *see* 132; debunking (*informal*)

verbs

2 **to disillusion**, disillude, disillusionize; **disenchant**, unspell, uncharm, break the spell *or* charm; **disabuse, undeceive**; correct, **set right** *or* **straight**, put straight, tell the truth, enlighten, let in on, put one wise (*informal*); clear the mind of; open one's eyes, awaken, wake up, unblindfold; disappoint *see* 132.2; dispel *or* dissipate one's illusions, rob *or* strip one of one's illusions; bring one back to earth, let down gently (*informal*); **burst** *or* **prick the bubble**, puncture one's balloon (*informal*); let the air out of, take the wind out of; knock the props out from under, take the ground from under; debunk (*informal*); expose, show up *see* 351.4

3 **to be disillusioned**, be disenchanted, get back to earth, get one's feet on the ground, come down to earth with a bump, have one's eyes opened, return to *or* embrace reality; charge to experience; have another think *or* guess coming (*informal*)

adjectives

4 **disillusioning**, disillusive, disillusionary, **disenchanting**, disabusing, undeceiving, enlightening

5 **disillusioned, disenchanted**, unspelled, uncharmed, **disabused**, undeceived, stripped *or* robbed of illusion, enlightened, set right, put straight; with one's eyes open, sophisticated, **blasé**; disappointed *see* 132.5

977 MENTAL ATTITUDE

nouns

1 **attitude**, mental attitude; psychology; **position, posture**, stance; **way of thinking; feeling, sentiment**, the way one feels; feeling tone, affect, affectivity, emotion, emotivity; opinion *see* 952.6

2 **outlook**, mental outlook; *Anschauung* (*German*), **point of view, viewpoint, standpoint, perspective**, *optique* (*French*); position, stand, place, situation; side; footing, basis; where one is *or* sits *or* stands; view, sight, light, eye; respect, regard; angle, angle of vision, slant, way of looking at things, slant on things, where one is coming from (*informal*); **frame of reference**, intellectual *or* ideational frame of reference, framework, arena, world, universe,

world *or* universe of discourse, system, reference system; phenomenology

3 **disposition, character, nature, temper, temperament**, mettle, constitution, complexion *and* humour (*both old*), makeup, stamp, type, stripe, kidney, make, mould; **turn of mind, inclination, mind, tendency**, grain, vein, set, mental set, mindset, **leaning**, animus, propensity, proclivity, predilection, preference, predisposition; **bent, turn, bias**, slant, cast, warp, twist; idiosyncrasy, eccentricity, individualism; diathesis, aptitude; strain, streak

4 **mood, humour, feeling, feelings, temper, frame of mind, state of mind, morale**, cue *or* frame (*both old*), tone, note, vein; **mind**, heart, spirit *or* **spirits**

5 (*pervading attitudes*) **climate**, mental *or* intellectual climate, spiritual climate, moral climate, mores, norms, climate of opinion, **ethos**, ideology, *Weltanschauung* (*German*), world view; *Zeitgeist* (*German*), spirit of the time *or* the age

verbs

6 **to take the attitude**, feel about it, look at it, **view**, look at in the light of; **be disposed to**, tend *or* incline toward, prefer, lean toward, be bent on

adjectives

7 **attitudinal; temperamental, dispositional**, inclinational, constitutional; emotional, affective; mental, intellectual, ideational, ideological; spiritual; characteristic *see* 864.13; innate

8 **disposed**, dispositioned, **predisposed, prone, inclined, given**, bent, bent on, apt, likely, **minded, in the mood** *or* **humour**

adverbs

9 **attitudinally; temperamentally, dispositionally**, constitutionally; emotionally; mentally, intellectually, ideationally, ideologically; morally, spiritually; **by temperament** *or* **disposition**, by virtue of mindset, by the logic of character *or* temperament; from one's standpoint *or* viewpoint *or* angle, from where one stands *or* sits, from where one is; within the frame of reference *or* framework *or* reference system *or* universe of discourse

978 BROAD-MINDEDNESS

nouns

1 **broad-mindedness**, wide-mindedness, large-mindedness,

"the result of flattening high-mindedness out" — GEORGE SAINTSBURY; **breadth**, broadness, broad gauge, latitude; **unbigotedness**, unhideboundness, unprovincialism, noninsularity, unparochialism, cosmopolitanism; antiracism, colour-blindness; ecumenicity, ecumenicism, ecumenicalism, ecumenism; broad mind, spacious mind

2 **liberalness, liberality**, catholicity, **liberalmindedness**; liberalism, libertarianism, latitudinarianism; freethinking, free thought

3 **open-mindedness, openness**, receptiveness,

receptivity; persuadableness, persuadability, persuasibility; open mind

4 tolerance, toleration; **indulgence,** lenience *or* leniency *see* 427, condonation, lenity; **forbearance, patience,** long-suffering; easiness, **permissiveness; charitableness,** charity, **generousness, magnanimity** *see* 652.2; **compassion** *see* 427.1, sympathy; sensitivity

5 unprejudicedness, unbiasedness; impartiality *see* 649.4, evenhandedness, equitability, **justice** *see* 649, **fairness** *see* 649.3, justness, **objectivity, detachment, dispassionateness, disinterestedness,** impersonality; indifference, neutrality; unopinionatedness

6 liberal, liberalist; libertarian; freethinker, latitudinarian, ecumenist, ecumenicist; antiracist; big person, broad-gauge person; bleeding heart, bleeding-heart liberal

verbs

7 to keep an open mind, be big (*informal*), judge not, not write off, suspend judgment, listen to reason, open one's mind to, see both sides, judge on the merits; **live and let live;** bend *or* lean over backwards, **tolerate** *see* 134.5; **accept,** be easy with, **view with indulgence, condone,** brook, abide with, be content with; **live with** (*informal*); shut one's eyes to, look the other way, wink at, blink at, **overlook, disregard, ignore;**
"swear allegiance to the words of no master"—HORACE

adjectives

8 broad-minded, wide-minded, large-minded, **broad, wide,** wide-ranging, broad-gauged, catholic, spacious of mind; **unbigoted,** unfanatical, **unhidebound,** unprovincial, cosmopolitan, noninsular, unparochial, antiracist, colour-blind; ecumenistic, ecumenical

9 liberal, liberal-minded, liberalistic; libertarian; freethinking, latitudinarian; bleeding-heart

10 open-minded, open, receptive, rational, admissive; **persuadable,** persuasible; **unopinionated,** unopinioned, unwedded to an opinion; **unpositive, undogmatic;** uninfatuated, unbesotted, unfanatical

11 tolerant *see* 134.9, tolerating; **indulgent, lenient** *see* 427.7, **condoning;** forbearing, forbearant (*old*), **patient,** long-suffering; **charitable, generous, magnanimous** *see* 652.6; compassionate *see* 427.7, sympathetic, sensitive

12 unprejudiced, unbiased, unprepossessed, unjaundiced; impartial, evenhanded, **fair, just** *see* 649.8, equitable, **objective, dispassionate, impersonal, detached, disinterested;** indifferent, neutral; **unswayed, uninfluenced,** undazzled

13 liberalizing, liberating, broadening, enlightening

979 NARROW-MINDEDNESS

nouns

1 narrow-mindedness, narrowness, illiberality, uncatholicity; little-mindedness, **small-mindedness, smallness,** littleness, **meanness, pettiness; bigotry,** bigotedness, fanaticism, *odium theologicum* (*Latin*); insularity, insularism, provincialism, parochialism; **hideboundness,** straitlacedness,

stuffiness (*informal*); authoritarianism; **shortsightedness,** nearsightedness, purblindness; blind side, blind spot, tunnel vision, blinkers; closed mind, mean mind, petty mind, shut mind; narrow views *or* sympathies, cramped ideas; *parti pris* (*French*), an axe to grind

2 intolerance, intoleration; **uncharitableness,** ungenerousness; unforbearance; noncompassion, insensitivity

3 prejudice, prejudgment, forejudgment, **predilection, prepossession,** preconception; **bias,** bent, leaning, inclination, twist; **jaundice,** jaundiced eye; **partiality,** partialism, partisanship, favouritism, onesidedness, undispassionateness, undetachment

4 discrimination, social discrimination, minority prejudice; xenophobia, know-nothingism; **chauvinism,** ultranationalism, superpatriotism; fascism; **class consciousness,** class prejudice, class distinction, class hatred, class war; anti-Semitism; **racism,** racialism, race hatred, **race prejudice,** race snobbery, racial discrimination; white *or* black supremacy, white *or* black power; **colour line,** colour bar; **social barrier,** Jim Crow (*US*), Jim Crow law (*US*); **segregation,** apartheid; sex discrimination, sexism, manism, masculism, male chauvinism, feminism, womanism, heterosexism; ageism, age discrimination; queer-bashing; class prejudice, class hatred, social prejudice

5 bigot, intolerant, illiberal, little person; **racist,** racialist, racial supremacist, white *or* black supremacist, pig (*informal*); **chauvinist,** ultranationalist, jingo, superpatriot; **sexist,** male chauvinist, male chauvinist pig *or* MCP (*informal*), manist, masculist, feminist, female chauvinist, womanist, **dogmatist,** heterosexist, **doctrinaire** *see* 969.7; ageist; fanatic

verbs

6 to close one's mind, shut the eyes of one's mind, take narrow views, put on blinkers, blind oneself, have a blind side *or* spot, have tunnel vision, constrict one's views; not see beyond one's nose *or* an inch beyond one's nose; **view with a jaundiced eye,** see but one side of the question, look only at one side of the shield

7 to prejudge, forejudge, judge beforehand, precondemn, prejudicate (*old*), take one's opinions ready-made, accede to prejudice

8 to discriminate against, draw the line, draw the colour line; **bait, bash**

9 to prejudice, prejudice against, prejudice the issue, prepossess, **jaundice, influence, sway, bias,** bias one's judgment; warp, twist, bend, distort

adjectives

10 narrow-minded, narrow, narrow-gauged, closed, closed-minded, cramped, constricted, po-faced, *borné* (*French*), little-minded, small-minded, mean-minded, petty-minded, narrow-hearted, narrow-souled, narrow-spirited, mean-spirited, small-souled; **small, little, mean, petty;** uncharitable, ungenerous; bigot, **bigoted,** fanatical; **illiberal,** unliberal, uncatholic; provincial, insular, parochial, parish pump; **hidebound,** creedbound, **straitlaced,** stuffy (*informal*); authoritarian; **shortsighted,** nearsighted, purblind; deaf, deaf-minded, deaf to reason

11 **intolerant,** untolerating; **unindulgent,** uncondoning, unforbearing

12 **discriminatory; prejudiced,** prepossessed, **biased, jaundiced,** coloured; **partial,** one-sided, partisan; influenced, swayed, warped, twisted; interested, nonobjective, **undetached,** undispassionate; xenophobic, know-nothing; **chauvinistic,** ultranationalist, superpatriotic; **racist,** racialist, anti-Negro, antiblack, antiwhite; anti-Semitic; sexist, heterosexist; ageist; dogmatic, doctrinaire, **opinionated** *see* 969.22

980 CURIOSITY

nouns

1 **curiosity,** curiousness, **inquisitiveness; interest,** interestedness, lively interest; thirst *or* desire *or* lust *or* itch for knowledge, mental acquisitiveness, inquiring *or* curious mind; **attention** *see* 982; **alertness, watchfulness,** vigilance; **nosiness** *and* snoopiness (*both informal*), prying; eavesdropping; officiousness, meddlesomeness *see* 214.2; **morbid curiosity,** ghoulishness; voyeurism, scopophilia, prurience, prurient interest

2 inquisitive person, quidnunc; **inquirer,** questioner, querier, querist, inquisitor, inquisitress; **busybody,** gossip, *yenta* (*Yiddish*), **pry,** Paul Pry, **snoop,** snooper, nosy Parker (*informal*); eavesdropper; sightseer; rubbernecker *or* rubberneck (*informal*); watcher, Peeping Tom, voyeur, scopophiliac; Lot's wife

verbs

3 **to be curious, want to know, take an interest in,** take a lively interest, burn with curiosity; be alert, alert oneself, watch, be watchful, be vigilant; prick up one's ears, keep one's ear to the ground; eavesdrop; interrogate, quiz, question, inquire, query; keep one's eyes open, keep one's eye on, stare, gape, peer, gawk, rubberneck (*informal*), rubber (*US & Canadian informal*); seek, dig up, dig around for, nose out, nose around for

4 **to pry, snoop,** peep, peek, spy, nose, nose into, have a long *or* big nose, poke *or* stick one's nose in; meddle *see* 214.7

adjectives

5 **curious, inquisitive,** inquiring, interested, quizzical; **alert,** tuned in (*informal*), **attentive** *see* 982.15; burning with curiosity, eaten up *or* consumed with curiosity, curious as a cat; agape, agog, all agog, openmouthed, open-eyed; gossipy; overcurious, supercurious; morbidly curious, **morbid, ghoulish; prurient,** itchy, voyeuristic, scopophiliac

6 **prying,** snooping, **nosy** *and* **snoopy** (*both informal*); meddlesome *see* 214.9

981 INCURIOSITY

nouns

1 **incuriosity,** incuriousness, **uninquisitiveness;** boredom; **inattention** *see* 983; **uninterestedness,**

disinterest, disinterestedness, **unconcern,** uninvolvement, **indifference** *see* 102, indifferentness, indifferentism, uncaring, **apathy,** passivity, passiveness, impassivity, impassiveness, listlessness, stolidity, **lack of interest;** carelessness, heedlessness, regardlessness, insouciance, unmindfulness; aloofness, detachment, withdrawal, reclusiveness; intellectual inertia; catatonia, autism

verbs

2 **to take no interest in, not care;** mind one's own business, pursue the even tenor of one's way, glance neither to the right nor to the left, keep one's nose out; be indifferent, not care less (*informal*)

adjectives

3 **incurious, uninquisitive,** uninquiring; bored; **inattentive** *see* 983.6; **uninterested,** unconcerned, disinterested, uninvolved, **indifferent, apathetic,** passive, impassive, stolid, phlegmatic, listless; careless, heedless, regardless, insouciant, mindless, unmindful; aloof, detached, distant, withdrawn, reclusive, sequestered, eremitic; catatonic, autistic

982 ATTENTION

nouns

1 **attention, attentiveness,** mindfulness, regardfulness, heedfulness; **attention span; heed,** ear; consideration, thought, mind; **awareness, consciousness, alertness** *see* 339.5; **observation,** observance, advertence, advertency, **note, notice,** remark, put one's finger on, **regard,** respect; **intentness,** intentiveness, concentration; diligence, assiduity, assiduousness, earnestness; **care** *see* 339.1; **curiosity** *see* 980

2 **interest, concern,** concernment; **curiosity** *see* 980; **enthusiasm,** passion, ardour, zeal; cathexis; matter of interest, special interest

3 **engrossment, absorption, intentness,** single-mindedness, **concentration, application,** study, studiousness, **preoccupation,** engagement, **involvement, immersion,** submersion; obsession, monomania; rapt attention, absorbed attention *or* interest; deep study, deep *or* profound thought, contemplation, meditation

4 **close attention,** close study, scrutiny, fixed regard, rapt *or* fascinated attention, whole *or* total *or* undivided attention; minute *or* meticulous attention, attention to detail, microscopic *or* microscopical scrutiny, finicalness, finickiness; constant *or* unrelenting attention, harping, strict attention; special consideration

verbs

5 **to attend to,** look to, **see to,** advert to, be aware of; **pay attention to,** pay regard to, give mind to, pay mind to (*informal*), not forget, spare a thought for, **give heed to;** bethink, bethink oneself; have a look at; **turn to,** give thought to, trouble one's head about; give one's mind to, direct one's attention to, turn *or* bend *or* set the mind *or* attention to; **devote oneself to,** devote the mind *or* thoughts to, fix *or* rivet *or* focus the mind *or* thoughts on, set one's

thoughts on, apply the mind *or* attention to, apply oneself to, **occupy oneself with, concern oneself with,** give oneself up to, be absorbed *or* engrossed in, be into (*informal*); sink one's teeth in, take an interest in, take hold of; **have a lot on one's mind *or* plate;** be preoccupied with; **lose oneself in; hang on one's words,** hang on the lips; **drink in,** drink in with rapt attention

6 **to heed, attend,** be heedful, tend, **mind, watch, observe, regard,** look, see, view, mark, remark, animadvert (*old*), **note, notice,** take note *or* notice, get a load of (*informal*)

7 **to hearken to,** hark, **listen, hear,** give ear to, lend an ear to, incline *or* bend an ear to, prick up the ears, strain one's ears, **keep one's ears open,** unstopper one's ears, have *or* keep an ear to the ground, listen with both ears, **be all ears**

8 **to pay attention *or* heed, take heed,** give heed, look out, **watch out** (*informal*), mind out, **take care** see 339.7; look lively *or* alive, **look sharp,** stay *or* be alert, sit up and take notice; be on the ball *or* keep one's eye on the ball *or* not miss a trick (*all informal*), not overlook a bet (*US & Canadian informal*), keep a weather eye out *or* on; miss nothing; get after, seize on, keep one's eyes open see 339.8; attend to business, mind one's business; pay close *or* strict attention, strain one's attention, not relax one's concern, give one's undivided attention, give special attention; keep in the centre of one's attention, keep uppermost in one's thought; **concentrate on,** focus *or* fix on; **study,** scrutinize; be obsessed with; cathect

9 **to take cognizance of,** take note *or* notice of, take heed of, **take account of, take into consideration *or* account, bear in mind,** keep *or* hold in mind, reckon with, keep in sight *or* view, not lose sight of, have in one's eye, have an eye to, have regard for

10 **to call attention to,** direct attention to, **bring under *or* to one's notice,** hold up to notice, bring to attention, **mention,** mention in passing, touch on; **single out,** pick out, lift up, focus on, call *or* bring to notice, direct to the attention, **feature,** highlight, brightline (*US & Canadian*); **direct to,** address to; **mention,** specify, mention in passing, touch on, cite, **refer to,** allude to; **alert one,** call to one's attention, put one wise *and* put one on (*both informal*); **point out, point to,** point at, put *or* lay one's finger on; **excite *or* stimulate attention,** drum up attention

11 **to meet with attention,** fall under one's notice; **catch the attention,** strike one, impress one, draw *or* hold *or* focus the attention, take *or* catch *or* meet *or* strike the eye, get *or* catch one's ear, attract notice *or* attention, arrest *or* engage attention, fix *or* rivet one's attention, arrest the thoughts, awaken the mind *or* thoughts, **excite notice,** arouse notice, arrest one's notice, invite *or* solicit attention, claim *or* demand attention

12 **to interest, concern,** involve in *or* with, affect the interest, give pause; **pique, titillate,** tantalize, tickle, tickle one's fancy, **attract,** invite, **fascinate, provoke, stimulate, arouse, excite,** pique one's

interest, excite interest, excite *or* whet one's interest, arouse one's passion *or* enthusiasm, turn one on (*informal*), light one's candle (*informal*), press one's buttons (*informal*)

13 **to engross, absorb,** immerse, **occupy, preoccupy, engage,** involve, monopolize, exercise, take up; **obsess; grip, hold, arrest, hold the interest, fascinate, enthral,** spellbind, **hold spellbound,** grab (*informal*), charm, enchant, mesmerize, hypnotize, catch; absorb the attention, claim one's thoughts, engross the mind *or* thoughts, engage the attention, involve the interest, occupy the attention, monopolize one's attention, engage the mind *or* thoughts

14 **to come to attention,** stand at attention

adjectives

15 **attentive, heedful, mindful, regardful,** advertent; **intent,** intentive, on top of (*informal*), diligent, assiduous, intense, earnest, concentrated; **careful** see 339.10; **observing,** observant; watchful, aware, conscious, **alert** see 339.14; **curious** see 980.5; agog, openmouthed; open-eared, open-eyed, **all eyes, all ears,** all eyes and ears; on the job (*informal*), on the ball *and* Johnny-on-the-spot (*both informal*); **meticulous** see 339.12, nice, finical, finicky, finicking, niggling

16 **interested,** concerned; **alert to, sensitive to, on the watch; curious** see 980.5; tantalized, piqued, titillated, tickled, **attracted,** fascinated, excited, turned-on (*informal*); keen on *or* about, enthusiastic, passionate; fixating, cathectic

17 **engrossed, absorbed,** totally absorbed, single-minded, **occupied, preoccupied, engaged,** devoted, devoted to, intent, intent on, monopolized, obsessed, monomaniacal, swept up, taken up with, **involved, caught up in,** wrapped in, **wrapped up in,** engrossed in, **absorbed in** *or* with *or* by, **lost in, immersed in,** submerged in, buried in; over head and ears in, head over heels in (*informal*), up to one's elbows in, up to one's ears in; contemplating, contemplative, studying, studious, meditative, meditating

18 **gripped, held, fascinated, enthralled, rapt, spellbound,** charmed, enchanted, mesmerized, **hypnotized,** fixed, caught, riveted, **arrested,** switched on (*informal*)

19 **interesting, stimulating, provocative,** provoking, thought-provoking, thought-challenging, thought-inspiring; **titillating,** tickling, **tantalizing, inviting, exciting; piquant,** lively, racy, juicy, succulent, spicy, rich; readable, unputdownable

20 **engrossing, absorbing,** consuming, **gripping,** riveting, holding, **arresting,** engaging, attractive, **fascinating, enthralling, spellbinding,** enchanting, magnetic, hypnotic, mesmerizing, mesmeric; obsessive, obsessing

adverbs

21 **attentively,** with attention; **heedfully,** mindfully, regardfully, advertently; observingly, observantly; **interestedly,** with interest; **raptly,** with rapt attention; engrossedly, absorbedly, preoccupiedly;

devotedly, **intently**, without distraction, **with undivided attention**

exclamations

22 **attention!**, **look!**, **see!**, look you!, look here!, looky! (*informal*), witness!; tah-dah! (*informal*), presto!, hey presto!, voilà!; lo!, behold!, lo and behold!; **hark!**, listen!, listen up! (*informal*), hark ye!, hear ye!, oyez!; *nota bene* (*Latin*, note well), NB; mark my words

23 **hey!**, **hail!**, **ahoy!**, **hello!**, hollo!, hallo!, halloo!, halloa!, ho!, heigh!, hi!, hist!; hello there!, ahoy there!, yo!

983 INATTENTION

nouns

1 **inattention**, inattentiveness, **heedlessness**, **unheedfulness**, **unmindfulness**, **thoughtlessness**, inconsideration; **incuriosity** *see* 981, **indifference** *see* 102; inadvertence *or* inadvertency; unintentness, unintentiveness; disregard, disregardfulness, regardlessness; **flightiness** *see* 984.5, giddiness *see* 984.4, lightmindedness, dizziness (*informal*), ditziness (*US & Canadian informal*), scattiness (*informal*); levity, frivolousness, flippancy; shallowness, superficiality; **inobservance**, unobservance, nonobservance; **unalertness**, unwariness, unwatchfulness; **obliviousness**, unconsciousness, unawareness; **carelessness**, negligence *see* 340.1; distraction, **absentmindedness**, **woolgathering**, **daydreaming** *see* 984.2

verbs

2 **to be inattentive**, **pay no attention**, pay no mind (*informal*), not attend, not notice, **take no note** *or* **notice of**, take no thought *or* account of, miss, not heed, give no heed, pay no regard to, not listen, hear nothing, not hear a word; **disregard, overlook, ignore**, pass over *or* by, have no time for, let pass *or* get by *or* get past; think little of, think nothing of, **slight**, make light of; **close** *or* **shut one's eyes to**, see nothing, be blind to, turn a blind eye, **look the other way, blink at, wink at**, connive at; stick *or* bury *or* hide one's head in the sand; **turn a deaf ear to**, stop one's ears, let come in one ear and go out the other, tune out (*informal*); let well enough alone; not trouble oneself with, not trouble one's head with *or* about; **be unwary**, be off one's guard, be caught out

3 **to wander, stray**, divagate, wander from the subject, ramble; have no attention span, have a short attention span, let one's attention wander, get off the track (*informal*); **fall asleep at the switch** (*informal*), woolgather, daydream *see* 984.9

4 **to dismiss**, dismiss *or* drive from one's thoughts; **put out of mind**, put out of one's head *or* thoughts, wean *or* force one's thoughts from, **think no more of, forget, forget it**, forget about it, **let it go** (*informal*), let slip, not give it another *or* a second thought, **drop the subject**, give it no more thought; turn one's back upon, turn away from, turn one's attention from, walk away, abandon, leave out in the cold (*informal*); put *or* set *or* lay aside, push *or* thrust aside *or* to one side, wave aside; put on the

back burner *or* on hold (*informal*); **turn up one's nose at**, sneeze at; **shrug off, brush off** *or* **aside** *or* **away**, blow off *and* laugh off *or* away (*both informal*), dismiss with a laugh; **slight** *see* 157.6, kiss off *and* slap *or* smack down (*all informal*)

5 **to escape notice** *or* **attention**, escape one, get by, be missed, pass one by, not enter one's head, never occur to one, fall on deaf ears, not register, go over one's head

adjectives

6 **inattentive, unmindful**, inadvertent, thoughtless, **incurious** *see* 981.3, **indifferent** *see* 102.6; **heedless**, unheeding, unheedful, regardless, *distrait* (*French*), **disregardful**, disregardant; **unobserving**, inobservant, unobservant, unnoticing, unnoting, unremarking, unmarking; **distracted** *see* 984.10; **careless, negligent** *see* 340.10; **scatterbrained, giddy** *see* 984.16, ditzy (*US & Canadian informal*), scatty (*informal*), flighty

7 **oblivious, unconscious**, insensible, dead to the world, out of it *and* not with it (*both informal*); blind, deaf; **preoccupied** *see* 984.11

8 **unalert, unwary, unwatchful, unvigilant**, uncautious, incautious; **unprepared**, unready; unguarded, **off one's guard**, off-guard, on the hop (*informal*); **asleep**, sleeping, nodding, napping, **asleep at the switch** *and* asleep on the job *and* **not on the job** *and* looking out the window (*all informal*), goofing off (*US & Canadian informal*); daydreaming, woolgathering

984 DISTRACTION, CONFUSION

nouns

1 **distraction**, distractedness, **diversion**, separation *or* withdrawal of attention, divided attention, competing stimuli; too much on one's mind *or* on one's plate, cognitive dissonance, sensory overload; **inattention** *see* 983

2 **abstractedness, abstraction, preoccupation, absorption**, engrossment, depth of thought, fit of abstraction; **absentmindedness, absence of mind; bemusement**, musing, musefulness (*old*); **woolgathering**, mooning (*informal*), moonraking (*old*), stargazing, **dreaming, daydreaming**, fantasying, pipe-dreaming (*informal*), castle-building; **brown study**, study, reverie, muse, dreamy abstraction, quiet *or* muted ecstasy, trance; dream, **daydream**, fantasy, pipe dream (*informal*); daydreamer, Walter Mitty

3 **confusion, fluster**, flummox (*informal*), **flutter**, flurry, ruffle; disorientation, **muddle, muddlement**, fuddle *and* fuddlement (*both informal*), befuddlement, muddleheadedness, daze, maze (*informal*); unsettlement, disorganization, **disorder**, chaos, **mess** *and* mix-up *and* snafu (*all informal*), balls-up *and* cock-up *and* screw-up *and* fuck-up *and* shemozzle (*all informal*), shuffle, jumble, guddle (*Scottish*), **discomfiture, discomposure, disconcertion**, discombobulation (*informal*), **bewilderment**, **embarrassment, disturbance**, perturbation, **upset**, frenzy, pother, bother, botheration *and* stew (*both informal*), pucker (*old*); tizzy *and* swivet *and* sweat

(*all informal*); haze, fog, mist, cloud; maze;
perplexity *see* 970.3

4 **dizziness, vertigo,** vertiginousness, spinning head,
swimming, swimming of the head, **giddiness,**
wooziness (*informal*), **lightheadedness;** tiddliness
(*informal*), **drunkenness** *see* 88.1, 3

5 **flightiness, giddiness,** volatility, mercuriality;
thoughtlessness, witlessness, brainlessness, empty-
headedness, frivolity, frivolousness, dizziness
(*informal*), ditziness (*US & Canadian informal*),
scattiness (*informal*), foolishness *see* 922;
scatterbrain, flibbertigibbet *see* 923.7

verbs

6 to **distract, divert,** detract, distract the attention,
divert *or* detract attention, divert the mind *or*
thoughts, draw off the attention, call away, take the
mind off of, relieve the mind of, cause the mind to
stray *or* wander, put off the track, derail, throw off
the scent, lead the mind astray, beguile; throw off
one's guard, catch off balance, put off one's stride,
trip up

7 to **confuse,** throw into confusion *or* chaos, entangle,
mix up, fluster; flummox (*informal*), **flutter,** put
into a flutter, **flurry, rattle, ruffle,** moither *or*
moider (*informal*); **muddle,** fuddle (*informal*),
befuddle, addle, addle the wits, **daze, maze,
dazzle, bedazzle; upset, unsettle,** raise hell,
disorganize; throw into a tizzy *or* swivet; **disconcert,
discomfit, discompose,** discombobulate (*informal*),
disorient, disorientate, **bewilder, embarrass, put
out, disturb, perturb, bother,** pother, bug
(*informal*); fog, mist, cloud, becloud, muzz (*informal*);
perplex *see* 970.13

8 to **dizzy, make one's head swim,** cause vertigo,
send one spinning, whirl the mind, swirl the senses,
make one's head reel *or* whirl *or* spin *or* revolve, go
to one's head; **intoxicate** *see* 88.22

9 to **muse, moon** (*informal*), **dream, daydream,**
pipe-dream (*informal*), fantasy; abstract oneself, be
lost in thought, let one's attention wander, let one's
mind run on other things, dream of *or* muse on
other things; **wander, stray, ramble,** divagate, let
one's thoughts *or* mind wander, give oneself up to
reverie, **woolgather, go woolgathering,** let one's
wits go bird's nesting, **be in a brown study,** be
absent, be somewhere else, stargaze, be out of it *and*
be not with it (*both informal*)

adjectives

10 **distracted, distraught,** *distrait* (*French*);
**wandering, rambling; wild, frantic, beside
oneself**

11 **abstracted, bemused,** museful (*old*), **musing,**
preoccupied, absorbed, engrossed, taken up;
absentminded, absent, faraway, elsewhere,
somewhere else, not there; pensive, meditative; lost,
lost in thought, wrapped in thought; rapt,
transported, ecstatic; dead to the world,
unconscious, oblivious; dreaming, dreamy,
drowsing, dozing, nodding, half-awake, betwixt sleep
and waking, napping; **daydreaming,** daydreamy,
pipe-dreaming (*informal*); **woolgathering,** mooning
and moony (*both informal*), moonraking (*old*), castle-
building, in the clouds, off in the clouds, stargazing,
in a reverie

12 **confused, mixed-up,** crazy mixed-up (*informal*);
flustered, fluttered, **ruffled, rattled,** fussed
(*informal*); **upset, unsettled,** off-balance, off one's
stride; **disorganized, disordered,** disoriented,
disorientated, chaotic, jumbled, in a jumble, shuffled;
shaken, shook (*informal*), **disconcerted,
discomposed,** discombobulated (*informal*),
embarrassed, put-out, disturbed, perturbed,
bothered, all hot and bothered (*informal*); in a stew
or botheration (*informal*), in a pucker (*old*); in a tizzy
or swivet *or* sweat (*informal*), in a pother; **perplexed**

13 **muddled,** in a muddle; fuddled (*informal*),
befuddled; muddleheaded, fuddlebrained (*informal*);
puzzleheaded, puzzlepated; **addled,** addleheaded,
addlepated, addlebrained; adrift, at sea, foggy,
fogged, in a fog, hazy, muzzy (*informal*), misted,
misty, cloudy, beclouded

14 **dazed,** mazed, **dazzled,** bedazzled, in a daze; **silly,**
knocked silly, cockeyed (*informal*); **groggy** (*informal*),
dopey (*informal*), woozy (*informal*); **punch-drunk**
and punchy *and* **slap-happy** (*all informal*)

15 **dizzy, giddy,** vertiginous, spinning, swimming,
turned around, going around in circles; lightheaded,
tiddly (*informal*), **drunk, drunken** *see* 88.31

16 **scatterbrained,** shatterbrained *or* shatterpated (*both
old*), rattlebrained, rattleheaded, rattlepated,
scramblebrained, harebrain, harebrained, **giddy,
dizzy** *and* **ditzy** *and* gaga (*all informal*), scatty
(*informal*), giddy-brained, giddy-headed, giddy-pated,
giddy-witted, giddy as a goose, fluttery, frivolous,
featherbrained, featherheaded; **thoughtless, witless,
brainless, empty-headed** *see* 921.19

17 **flighty,** volatile, mercurial

985 IMAGINATION

nouns

1 **imagination,** imagining, imaginativeness, **fancy,
fantasy,** conceit (*old*); **mind's eye,**
"that inward eye which is the bliss of solitude"—
WORDSWORTH, "the mad boarder"—MALEBRANCHE; flight of
fancy, fumes of fancy; fantasticism

2 **creative thought,** conception; lateral thinking;
productive *or* constructive *or* creative imagination,
creative power *or* ability, esemplastic imagination *or*
power, shaping imagination, poetic imagination,
artistic imagination; mythopoeia, *mythopoesis* (*Greek*);
mythification, mythicization; inspiration, muse;
Muses: Calliope (*epic poetry*), Clio (*history*), Erato
(*lyric and love poetry*), Euterpe (*music*), Melpomene
(*tragedy*), Polyhymnia (*sacred song*), Terpsichore
(*dancing and choral song*), Thalia (*comedy*), Urania
(*astronomy*); **genius** *see* 919.8

3 **invention, inventiveness, originality, creativity,
fabrication,** creativeness, **ingenuity;** productivity,
prolificacy, **fertility,** fecundity; rich *or* teeming
imagination, fertile *or* pregnant imagination, seminal
or germinal imagination, fertile mind; imagineering;
fiction, fictionalization

4 **lively imagination,** active fancy, **vivid
imagination,** colourful *or* highly coloured *or* lurid

imagination, warm *or* ardent imagination, fiery *or* heated imagination, excited imagination, bold *or* daring *or* wild *or* fervent imagination; verve, vivacity of imagination

5 **figment of the imagination**, creature of the imagination, creation *or* coinage of the brain, fiction of the mind, maggot, whim, whimsy, figment, imagination, invention; **brainchild**; **imagining**, fancy, idle fancy, vapour, "thick-coming fancies"—SHAKESPEARE, imagery; **fantasy, make-believe**; phantom, vision, apparition, insubstantial image, eidolon, **phantasm** *see* 975.4; **fiction**, myth, romance; wildest dreams, stretch of the imagination; **chimera, bubble, illusion** *see* 975; hallucination, delirium, sick fancy; trip *or* drug trip (*both informal*)

6 **visualization, envisioning**, envisaging, picturing, objectification, imaging, calling to *or* before the mind's eye, figuring *or* portraying *or* representing in the mind; depicting *or* delineating in the imagination; conceptualization; **picture, vision, image**, mental image, mental picture, visual image, vivid *or* lifelike image, eidetic image, concept, **conception**, mental representation *or* presentation, *Vorstellung* (*German*); **imagery**, word-painting; poetic image, poetic imagery; imagery study; imagism, imagistic poetry

7 **idealism, idealization**; **ideal**, ideality; rose-coloured glasses; visionariness, **utopianism**; flight of fancy, play of fancy, imaginative exercise; **romanticism**, romanticizing, romance; **quixotism**, quixotry; dreamery; **impracticality**, unpracticalness, **unrealism**, unreality; **wishful thinking**, wish fulfilment, wish-fulfilment fantasy, dream come true; autistic thinking, dereistic thinking, autism, dereism, autistic distortion

8 **dreaminess**, dreamfulness, musefulness, pensiveness; dreamlikeness; **dreaming, musing; daydreaming**, pipe-dreaming (*informal*), dreamery, fantasying, castlebuilding

9 **dream; reverie, daydream, pipe dream** (*informal*); **brown study** *see* 984.2; **vision**; nightmare, incubus, bad dream

10 **air castle, castle in the air**, castle in the sky *or* skies, castle in Spain; Xanadu *and* pleasure dome of Kubla Khan (*both Coleridge*)

11 **utopia** *or* Utopia (*Sir Thomas More*), **paradise, heaven** *see* 681, heaven on earth; millennium, kingdom come; dreamland, lotus land, land of dreams, land of enchantment, land of heart's desire, wonderland, cloudland, fairyland, land of faerie, faerie; Eden, Garden of Eden; the Promised Land, land of promise, land of plenty, land of milk and honey, Canaan, Goshen; Shangri-la, New Atlantis (*Francis Bacon*), Arcadia, Agapemone, Happy Valley (*Samuel Johnson*), land of Prester John, Eldorado, Seven Cities of Cibola, Quivira; Laputa (*Swift*); Cockaigne, Big Rock-Candy Mountain, Fiddler's Green, Never-Never land (*J M Barrie*), Never-land, Cloudcuckooland *or* Nephelococcygia (*Aristophanes*), Erewhon (*Samuel Butler*), Land of Youth, Tir-na-n'Og (*Irish*); dystopia *or* kakotopia; Pandemonium

12 **imaginer**, fancier, fantast; fantasist; mythmaker, mythopoet; mythifier, mythicizer; **inventor; creative artist**, poet; imagineer

13 **visionary, idealist**; prophet, seer; **dreamer, daydreamer**, dreamer of dreams, castle-builder, lotus-eater, **wishful thinker; romantic**, romanticist, romancer; Quixote, Don Quixote; utopian, utopianist, utopianizer; escapist; enthusiast, rhapsodist

verbs

14 **to imagine, fancy, conceive**, conceit (*old*), conceptualize, ideate, figure to oneself; **invent, create, originate, make**, think up, dream up, shape, mould, coin, hatch, concoct, fabricate, produce; **suppose** *see* 950.10; **fantasize; fictionalize**; give free rein to the imagination, let one's imagination riot *or* run riot *or* run wild, allow one's imagination to run away with one; experience imaginatively *or* vicariously

15 **to visualize, vision, envision, envisage, picture, image**, objectify; picture in one's mind, picture to oneself, **view with the mind's eye**, contemplate in the imagination, form a mental picture of, represent, **see**, just see, have a picture of; **call up**, summon up, conjure up, **call to mind**, realize

16 **to idealize**, utopianize, quixotize, rhapsodize; **romanticize**, romance; paint pretty pictures of, paint in bright colours; see through rose-coloured glasses; **build castles in the air** *or* Spain

17 **to dream**; dream of, dream on; **daydream**, pipe-dream (*informal*), get *or* have stars in one's eyes, have one's head in the clouds, indulge in wish fulfilment; fantasy, conjure up a vision, "see visions and dream dreams"—BIBLE; blow one's mind *and* go on a trip *and* trip *and* freak out (*all informal*)

adjectives

18 **imaginative**, conceptual, conceptive, ideational, ideative, notional; **inventive, original**, originative, esemplastic, shaping, **creative, ingenious; productive, fertile**, fecund, prolific, seminal, germinal, teeming, pregnant; **inspired**, visioned

19 **imaginary**, imaginational, notional; **imagined, fancied; unreal**, unrealistic, airy-fairy, unactual, nonexistent, never-never; visional, supposititious, **all in the mind**; illusory

20 **fanciful, notional**, notiony (*informal*), whimsical, maggoty; brain-born; fancy-bred, fancy-born, fancy-built, fancy-framed, fancy-woven, fancy-wrought; dream-born, dream-built, dream-created; **fantastic, fantastical**, fantasque, extravagant, preposterous, outlandish, wild, baroque, rococo, florid; Alice-in-Wonderland, bizarre, grotesque, Gothic

21 **fictitious, make-believe, figmental**, fictional, fictive, fabricated, fictionalized; nonhistorical, nonfactual, nonactual, nonrealistic; **fabulous, mythic, mythical**, mythological, legendary; mythified, mythicized

22 **chimeric, chimerical, aerial, ethereal**, phantasmal; vaporous, vapoury; gossamer; air-built, cloud-built, cloud-born, cloud-woven

23 **ideal, idealized**; utopian, Arcadian, Edenic, paradisal; pie in the sky (*informal*); heavenly, celestial; millennial; dystopian

24 visionary, idealistic, quixotic; **romantic,
romanticized**, romancing, romanticizing; poetic *or*
poetical; storybook; **impractical, unpractical,
unrealistic**; wish-fulfilling, autistic, dereistic; starry-
eyed, dewy-eyed; in the clouds, with one's head in
the clouds; airy, **otherworldly**, transmundane,
transcendental
25 dreamy, dreamful; **dreamy-eyed**, dreamy-minded,
dreamy-souled; dreamlike; day-dreamy, **dreaming,
daydreaming**, pipe-dreaming (*informal*), castle-
building; **entranced**, tranced, in a trance, dream-
stricken, enchanted, spellbound, spelled, charmed
26 imaginable, fanciable, conceivable, thinkable,
cogitable; **supposable** *see* 950.15

986 UNIMAGINATIVENESS

nouns

1 unimaginativeness, unfancifulness; **prosaicness,**
prosiness, prosaism, prosaicism, unpoeticalness;
staidness, stuffiness (*informal*); stolidity; **dullness,
dryness**; aridness, aridity, barrenness, infertility,
infecundity; **unoriginality**, uncreativeness,
uninventiveness, dearth of ideas
2 (*practical attitude*) **realism**, realisticness,
**practicalness, practicality, practical-
mindedness**, sober-mindedness, sobersidedness,
hardheadedness, matter-of-factness; down-to-
earthness, earthiness, worldliness, secularism; real
world, the here and now; nuts and bolts, no
nonsense, no frills; **pragmatism**, pragmaticism,
positivism, scientism; unidealism, unromanticalness,
unsentimentality; sensibleness, saneness,
reasonableness, rationality; freedom from illusion,
lack of sentimentality; lack of feelings *see* 94
3 realist, pragmatist, positivist, practical person,
hardhead

verbs

4 to keep both feet on the ground, stick to the
facts, call a spade a spade; **come down to earth,**
come down out of the clouds, know when the
honeymoon is over

adjectives

5 unimaginative, unfanciful; unidealized,
unromanticized; **prosaic**, prosy, prosing, unpoetic,
unpoetical; **literal**, literal-minded; earthbound,
mundane; **staid, stuffy** (*informal*); stolid; **dull, dry**;
arid, barren, infertile, infecund; **unoriginal**,
uninspired; hedged, undaring, unaspiring,
uninventive *see* 890.5
6 realistic, realist, **practical**; pragmatic, pragmatical,
scientific, scientist, positivistic; **unidealistic**,
unideal, **unromantic, unsentimental, practical-
minded**, sober-minded, sobersided, **hardheaded**,
straight-thinking, **matter-of-fact, down-to-earth**,
with both feet on the ground; worldly, earthy,
secular; sensible, sane, reasonable, rational, sound,
sound-thinking; **reductive, simplistic**

987 SPECTRE

nouns

1 spectre, ghost, spectral ghost, spook (*informal*),
phantom, phantasm, phantasma, **wraith, shade,**
shadow, fetch, **apparition**, appearance, presence,
shape, form, eidolon, idolum, revenant, larva; **spirit;**
sprite, shrouded spirit, disembodied spirit, departed
spirit, restless *or* wandering spirit *or* soul, soul of the
dead, dybbuk, oni; Masan; astral spirit, astral;
unsubstantiality, immateriality, incorporeal,
incorporeity, incorporeal being *or* entity; walking
dead man, zombie; duppy; vision, theophany;
materialization; haunt *or* hant (*both US & Canadian
informal*); banshee; poltergeist; control, guide; manes,
lemures; grateful dead
2 White Lady, White Lady of Avenel (*Scottish*), White
Ladies of Normandy; Brocken spectre; Wild Hunt;
Flying Dutchman
3 double, etheric double *or* self, co-walker,
Doppelgänger (*German*), doubleganger, fetch, wraith
4 eeriness, ghostliness, weirdness, uncanniness,
spookiness (*informal*)
5 possession, spirit control; obsession

verbs

6 to haunt, hant (*US & Canadian informal*), spook
(*informal*); **possess**, control; obsess

adjectives

7 spectral, spectrelike; **ghostly**, ghostish, ghosty,
ghostlike; **spiritual, psychic**, psychical;
phantomlike, phantom, phantomic *or* phantomical,
phantasmal, phantasmic, **wraithlike**, wraithy,
shadowy; etheric, ectoplasmic, astral, ethereal *see*
763.6; incorporeal *see* 1051.7; **occult, supernatural**
see 869.15
8 disembodied, bodiless, immaterial *see* 1051.7,
discarnate, decarnate, decarnated
9 weird, eerie, eldritch, **uncanny**, unearthly, macabre;
spooky *and* spookish *and* hairy (*all informal*)
10 haunted, spooked *and* spooky (*both informal*), spirit-
haunted, ghost-haunted, spectre-haunted; **possessed**,
ghost-ridden; obsessed

988 MEMORY

nouns

1 memory, remembrance, recollection, mind,
souvenir (*French*); memory trace, engram; mind's eye,
eye of the mind, mirror of the mind, tablets of the
memory; corner *or* recess of the memory, inmost
recesses of the memory; Mnemosyne, mother of the
Muses; short-term memory, long-term memory,
anterograde memory; computer memory, information
storage; group memory, collective memory, mneme,
race memory; atavism; cover *or* screen memory,
affect memory; eye *or* visual memory, kinaesthetic
memory; skill, verbal response, emotional response
2 "that inward eye"—WORDSWORTH, "the warder of the
brain"—SHAKESPEARE, "the treasury and guardian of all
things"—CICERO, "storehouse of the mind, garner of
facts and fancies"—M F TUPPER, "the hearing of deaf

actions, and the seeing of blind"—PLUTARCH, "the diary that we all carry around with us"—OSCAR WILDE

3 **retention, retentiveness,** retentivity, memory span; good memory, retentive memory *or* mind; total memory, eidetic memory *or* imagery, photographic memory, total recall; camera-eye

4 **remembering, remembrance, recollection,** recollecting, exercise of memory, **recall,** recalling; reflection *or* reflexion, reconsideration; **retrospect,** retrospection, hindsight, looking back; flashback, **reminiscence,** review, contemplation of the past, review of things past; **memoir; memorization,** memorizing, **rote,** rote memory, rote learning, learning by heart, commitment to memory

5 **recognition, identification, reidentification,** distinguishment; realization *see* 927.2

6 **reminder, remembrance,** remembrancer; **prompt,** prompter, tickler; prompting, cue, hint; jogger (*informal*), flapper; *aide-mémoire* (*French*), **memorandum** *see* 549.4

7 **memento, remembrance, token, trophy, souvenir, keepsake, relic,** favour, token of remembrance; commemoration, memorial *see* 549.12; *memento mori* (*Latin*); **memories, memorabilia,** memorials

8 memorability, rememberability

9 mnemonics, memory training, mnemotechny, mnemotechnics, mnemonization; mnemonic, mnemonic device, *aide-mémoire* (*French*)

verbs

10 **to remember, recall, recollect,** flash on *and* mind (*both informal*); have a good *or* ready memory, remember clearly, remember as if it were yesterday; have total recall, remember everything; reflect; **think of,** bethink oneself (*old*); **call** *or* **bring to mind,** recall to mind, call up, summon up, conjure up, evoke, reevoke, revive, recapture, call back, bring back,
"call back yesterday, bid time return"—SHAKESPEARE; **think back,** go back, **look back,** cast the eyes back, carry one's thoughts back, look back upon things past, use hindsight, retrospect, **see in retrospect,** go back over, hark back, retrace; review, review in retrospect

11 **to reminisce,** rake *or* dig up the past

12 **to recognize, know, tell, distinguish, make out; identify, place,** have; spot *and* nail *and* peg *and* cotton on (*all informal*), reidentify, know again, recover *or* recall knowledge of, know by sight; realize *see* 927.12

13 **to keep in memory, bear in mind,** keep *or* hold in mind, hold *or* retain the memory of, **keep in view,** have in mind, hold *or* carry *or* retain in one's thoughts, store in the mind, **retain, keep;** tax *or* burden the memory, **treasure, cherish,** treasure up in the memory, enshrine *or* embalm in the memory, cherish the memory of; keep up the memory of, keep the memory alive, keep alive in one's thoughts; brood over, dwell on *or* upon, fan the embers, let fester in the mind, let rankle in the breast

14 **to be remembered,** sink in, penetrate, make an impression; live *or* dwell in one's memory, be easy to recall, remain in one's memory, be green *or* fresh in

one's memory, stick in the mind, remain indelibly impressed on the memory, be stamped on one's memory, **never be forgotten; haunt one's thoughts,** obsess, run in the head, be in one's thoughts, be on one's mind; be burnt into one's memory, plague one; be like King Charles's head; **rankle,** rankle in the breast, fester in the mind

15 **to recur,** recur to the mind, return to mind, come back, resurface, reenter

16 **to come to mind,** pop into one's head, come to one, come into one's head, flash on the mind, pass in review

17 **to memorize, commit to memory,** con; study; **learn by heart,** get by heart, learn *or* get by rote, get word-perfect *or* letter-perfect, learn word for word, learn verbatim; know by heart *or* from memory, have by heart *or* rote, have at one's fingers' ends *or* tips; repeat by heart *or* rote, give word for word, recite, repeat, parrot, repeat like a parrot, say one's lesson, rattle *or* reel off; be a quick study

18 **to fix in the mind** *or* memory, instil, infix, inculcate, impress, imprint, stamp, inscribe, etch, grave, engrave; **impress on the mind, get into one's head,** drive *or* hammer into one's head, get across, get into one's thick head *or* skull (*informal*); **burden the mind with,** task the mind with, load *or* stuff *or* cram the mind with; inscribe *or* stamp *or* rivet in the memory, set in the tablets of memory, etch indelibly in the mind

19 **to refresh the memory, review,** restudy, **brush up, rub up,** polish up *and* bone up (*both informal*), get up on; **cram** (*informal*), swot up (*informal*), mug up (*informal*)

20 **to remind, put in mind,** remember, put in remembrance, bring back, bring to recollection, refresh the memory of; **remind one of, recall,** suggest, **put one in mind of; take one back,** carry back, carry back in recollection; **jog the memory,** awaken *or* arouse the memory, flap the memory, give a hint *or* suggestion; **prompt,** prompt the mind, give the cue, hold the promptbook; nudge, pull by the sleeve, nag

21 **to try to recall,** think hard, rack *or* ransack one's brains, **cudgel one's brains,** crack one's brains (*informal*); have on the tip of one's tongue, have on the edge of one's memory *or* consciousness

adjectives

22 **recollective, memoried;** mnemonic; retentive; **retrospective,** in retrospect; **reminiscent, mindful, remindful, suggestive,** redolent, evocative

23 **remembered, recollected, recalled;** retained, pent-up in the memory, kept in remembrance, enduring, lasting, **unforgotten;** present to the mind, lodged in one's mind, stamped on the memory; vivid, eidetic, fresh, green, alive

24 **remembering, mindful,** keeping *or* bearing in mind, holding in remembrance; unable to forget, haunted, plagued, obsessed, nagged, rankled

25 **memorable, rememberable, recollectable;** notable

26 **unforgettable, never to be forgotten,** never to be erased from the mind, **indelible,** indelibly impressed on the mind, fixed in the mind; haunting, persistent, recurrent, nagging, plaguing, rankling, festering; obsessing, obsessive

27 memorial, commemorative

adverbs

28 by heart, *par cœur* (*French*), **by rote, by** *or* **from memory**, without book; **memorably**; rememberingly

29 in memory of, to the memory of, in remembrance *or* commemoration, *in memoriam* (*Latin*); *memoria in aeterna* (*Latin*), in perpetual remembrance

989 FORGETFULNESS

nouns

1 forgetfulness, unmindfulness, absentmindedness, **memorylessness**; short memory, short memory span, little retentivity *or* recall, mind *or* memory like a sieve; loose memory, vague *or* fuzzy memory, dim *or* hazy recollection; **lapse of memory**, decay of memory; **obliviousness, oblivion**, nirvana; obliteration; Lethe, Lethe water, waters of Lethe *or* oblivion, river of oblivion; nepenthe; **forgetting**; heedlessness *see* 340.2; forgiveness *see* 148

2 loss of memory, **memory loss, amnesia**, failure; **memory gap**, blackout (*informal*); fugue; agnosia, unrecognition, body-image agnosia, ideational agnosia, astereognosis *or* astereocognosy; paramnesia, retrospective falsification, false memory, misremembrance; amnesiac

3 block, blocking, **mental block**, memory obstruction; repression, suppression, defence mechanism, conversion, sublimation, symbolization

verbs

4 to be forgetful, suffer memory loss, be absentminded, have a short memory, have a mind *or* memory like a sieve, have a short memory span, be unable to retain, have little recall, forget one's own name

5 to forget, clean forget (*informal*); **not remember**, disremember *and* disrecollect (*both informal*), fail to remember, forget to remember, **have no remembrance** *or* **recollection of**, be unable to recollect *or* recall, draw a blank (*informal*); lose, lose sight of, lose one's train of thought, lose track of what one was saying; have on the tip of the tongue; blow *or* fluff one's lines, go up in one's lines (*US*); misremember, misrecollect

6 to efface *or* **erase from the memory**, consign to oblivion, unlearn, obliterate, **dismiss from one's thoughts** *see* 983.4; forgive *see* 148.3, 5

7 to be forgotten, escape one, slip one's mind, fade *or* die away from the memory, slip *or* escape the memory, drop from one's thoughts; fall *or* sink into oblivion, go in one ear and out the other

adjectives

8 forgotten, clean forgotten (*informal*), **unremembered**, disremembered *and* disrecollected (*both informal*), **unrecollected, unretained, unrecalled**, past recollection *or* recall, out of the mind, lost, erased, effaced, obliterated, gone out of one's head *or* recollection, consigned to oblivion, buried *or* sunk in oblivion; out of sight out of mind; misremembered, misrecollected

9 forgetful, forgetting, inclined to forget, **memoryless, unremembering, unmindful**, absentminded, **oblivious**, insensible to the past, with a mind *or* memory like a sieve; suffering from *or* stricken with amnesia, amnesic, amnestic; blocked, repressed, suppressed, sublimated, converted; heedless *see* 340.11; Lethean

10 forgettable, unrememberable, unrecollectable; effaceable, eradicable, erasable

adverbs

11 forgetfully, forgettingly, unmindfully, absentmindedly, **obliviously**

990 SUFFICIENCY

nouns

1 sufficiency, sufficientness, **adequacy**, adequateness, **enough**, a competence *or* competency; satisfactoriness, satisfaction, satisfactory amount, enough to go around; good *or* adequate supply; exact measure, right amount, no more and no less; bare sufficiency, minimum, bare minimum, just enough, enough to get by on

2 plenty, plenitude, plentifulness, plenteousness, muchness (*old*); myriad, myriads, numerousness *see* 883; **amplitude**, ampleness; substantiality, substantialness; **abundance, copiousness**; exuberance, riotousness; **bountifulness**, bounteousness, liberalness, **liberality**, generousness, **generosity**; **lavishness, extravagance**, prodigality; luxuriance, fertility, teemingness, productiveness *see* 889; **wealth, opulence** *or* opulency, richness, affluence; more than enough; maximum; **fullness**, full measure, repletion, repleteness; **overflow, outpouring**, flood, inundation, flow, shower, spate, stream, gush, avalanche; landslide; **prevalence**, profuseness, **profusion**, riot; **superabundance** *see* 992.2; overkill; no end of, great abundance, great plenty, "God's plenty"—Dryden, quantities, much, as much as one could wish, more than one can shake a stick at, lots, a fistful (*informal*), **scads** *see* 247.4; bumper crop, rich harvest, foison (*old*); rich vein, bonanza, luau (*informal*); an ample sufficiency, enough and to spare, enough and then some; fat of the land

3 cornucopia, horn of plenty, horn of Amalthea, endless supply, bottomless well

verbs

4 to suffice, **do**, just do, serve, **answer**; work, be equal to, **avail**; answer *or* serve the purpose, do the trick (*informal*), **suit**; qualify, meet, fulfil, **satisfy**, meet requirements; **pass muster**, make the grade *and* hack it *and* cut the mustard *and* **fill the bill** (*all informal*), make the cut (*US & Canadian informal*); get by *and* scrape by (*both informal*), do it, do in a pinch, **pass**, pass in the dark (*informal*); hold, stand, stand up, take it, bear; stretch (*informal*), reach, go around

5 to abound, exuberate (*old*), teem, **teem with**, creep with, crawl with, swarm with, be lousy with (*informal*), bristle with; proliferate *see* 889.7; **overflow**, run over, flood; flow, stream, rain, **pour**, shower, gush

adjectives

6 **sufficient**, sufficing; **enough, ample**, substantial, **plenty, satisfactory, adequate**, decent, due; competent, up to the mark; commensurate, proportionate, corresponding *see* 787.9; suitable, fit *see* 787.10; good, **good enough**, plenty good enough (*informal*); sufficient for *or* to *or* unto, up to, equal to; barely sufficient, minimal, minimum

7 **plentiful**, plenty, **plenteous**, plenitudinous, "plenty as blackberries"—SHAKESPEARE; **galore** *and* a gogo *and* up to the arse in (*all informal*), in plenty, in quantity *or* quantities, aplenty (*informal*); numerous *see* 883.6; beaucoup (*informal*), much, many *see* 247.8; **ample**, all-sufficing; wholesale; well-stocked, well-provided, well-furnished, well-found; abundant, abounding, **copious**, exuberant, riotous; flush; **bountiful**, bounteous, **lavish**, **generous, liberal, extravagant, prodigal**, slap-up (*informal*); luxuriant, fertile, productive *see* 889.9, **rich**, fat, **wealthy, opulent, affluent**; maximal; **full**, replete, well-filled, running over, overflowing; inexhaustible, exhaustless, bottomless; **profuse**, profusive, effuse, diffuse; **prevalent**, prevailing, rife, rampant, epidemic; lousy with (*informal*), teeming *see* 883.9; **superabundant** *see* 992.19; ten a penny, a dime a dozen

adverbs

8 **sufficiently, amply**, substantially, **satisfactorily, enough**; competently, **adequately**; minimally

9 **plentifully**, plenteously, **aplenty** (*informal*), **in plenty**, in quantity *or* quantities, in good supply; **abundantly**, in abundance, copiously, no end (*informal*); **superabundantly** *see* 992.24; **bountifully**, bounteously, **lavishly, generously, liberally, extravagantly, prodigally**; maximally; fully, in full measure, to the full, overflowingly; inexhaustibly, exhaustlessly, bottomlessly; exuberantly, luxuriantly, riotously; richly, opulently, affluently; **profusely**, diffusely, effusely; beyond one's wildest dreams, beyond the dreams of avarice

991 INSUFFICIENCY

nouns

1 **insufficiency, inadequacy**, insufficientness, inadequateness; short supply, seller's market; none to spare; nonsatisfaction, nonfulfilment, coming *or* falling short *or* shy; **undercommitment**; too little too late; a band-aid (*US & Canadian informal*), a drop in the bucket *or* the ocean, a lick and a promise, a cosmetic measure; **incompetence**, incompetency, unqualification, unsuitability *see* 788.3

2 **meagreness**, exiguousness, exiguity, scrimpiness, skimpiness, scantiness, spareness; meanness, miserliness, niggardliness, narrowness (*informal*), stinginess, parsimony; smallness, slightness, puniness, paltriness; thinness, leanness, slimness, slim pickings (*informal*), slenderness, scrawniness; jejuneness,

jejunity; austerity; Lenten fare; skeleton crew, corporal's guard

3 **scarcity**, scarceness; **sparsity**, sparseness; **scantiness**, scant sufficiency; **dearth, paucity**, poverty; **rarity**, rareness, uncommonness

4 **want, lack, need, deficiency, deficit, shortage, shortfall**, wantage, **incompleteness**, defectiveness, shortcoming *see* 910, imperfection; **absence** *see* 222, omission; **destitution**, impoverishment, beggary, deprivation; starvation, famine, drought, drying up

5 **pittance**, dole, scrimption (*informal*); drop in the bucket *or* the ocean; **mite**, bit *see* 248.2; short allowance, short commons, half rations, cheeseparings and candle ends; mere subsistence, starvation wages; widow's mite

6 **dietary deficiency**, vitamin deficiency; undernourishment, undernutrition, **malnutrition**

verbs

7 **to want, lack, need, require**; miss, feel the want of, be sent away empty-handed; run short of

8 **to be insufficient**, not qualify, be found wanting, leave a lot to be desired, not make it *and* not hack it *and* not cut it *and* not cut the mustard (*all informal*), not make the cut (*US & Canadian informal*), be beyond one's depth *or* ken, be in over one's head, **fall short**, fall shy, come short, not come up to; run short; want, want for, lack, fail, fail of *or* in

adjectives

9 **insufficient**, unsufficing, **inadequate**; found wanting, defective, incomplete, imperfect, deficient, lacking, failing, wanting; **too few**, undersupplied; **too little**, not enough, precious little, a trickle *or* mere trickle; **unsatisfactory**, unsatisfying; cosmetic, merely cosmetic, surface, superficial, symptomatic, merely symptomatic; **incompetent**, unequal to, unqualified, not up to snuff, out of one's depth *or* in over one's head, outmatched; short-staffed, understaffed, short-handed; inquorate

10 **meagre, slight**, scrimpy, skimp, skimpy, exiguous; scant, **scanty**, spare; miserly, niggardly, stingy, narrow (*informal*), parsimonious, mean; austere, Lenten, Spartan, abstemious, ascetic; stinted, frugal, sparing; poor, impoverished; small, puny, paltry; thin, lean, slim, slender, scrawny; dwarfish, dwarfed, stunted, undergrown; straitened, limited; jejune, watered, watery, unnourishing, unnutritious; subsistence, starvation

11 **scarce, sparse, scanty**; **in short supply**, at a premium; **rare**, uncommon; scarcer than hen's teeth (*informal*); not to be had, not to be had for love or money, not to be had at any price; out of print, out of stock *or* season

12 **ill-provided**, ill-furnished, ill-equipped, ill-found, ill off; **unprovided**, unsupplied, unreplenished; barehanded; unfed, underfed, undernourished; shorthanded, undermanned; **empty-handed, poor**, pauperized, impoverished, beggarly; starved, half-starved, on short commons, starving, starveling, famished

13 **wanting, lacking, needing, missing, in want of**; for want of, in default of, in the absence of; short, **short of**, scant of; shy, **shy of** *or* on; out of, clean

or fresh out of (*informal*), destitute of, bare of, void of, empty of, devoid of, forlorn of, bereft of, deprived of, denuded of, unpossessed of, unblessed with, bankrupt in; out of pocket; at the end of one's rope *or* tether

adverbs

14 **insufficiently**; **inadequately**, unsubstantially, incompletely

15 **meagrely**, **slightly**, sparely, punily, scantily, poorly, frugally, sparingly

16 scarcely, **sparsely**, **scantily**, skimpily, scrimpily; **rarely**, uncommonly

prepositions

17 without, minus, less, sans, absent

word elements

18 hyp–, hypo–, under–, mal–, ill–, sub–

992 EXCESS

nouns

1 **excess**, **excessiveness**, **inordinance**, inordinateness, nimiety, **immoderateness**, immoderacy, immoderation, **extravagance** *or* extravagancy, intemperateness, incontinence, overindulgence, **intemperance** *see* 669; unrestrainedness, abandon; gluttony *see* 672; **extreme**, extremity, **extremes**; **boundlessness** *see* 822.1; overlargeness, overgreatness, monstrousness, enormousness *see* 247.1; overgrowth, overdevelopment, hypertrophy, gigantism, giantism, elephantiasis; **overmuch**, overmuchness, too much, too–muchness; **exorbitance** *or* exorbitancy, undueness, **outrageousness**, unconscionableness, unreasonableness; radicalism, extremism *see* 611.5; egregiousness; fabulousness, hyperbole, **exaggeration** *see* 355

2 **superabundance**, overabundance, superflux, **plethora**, redundancy, overprofusion, too many, too much, too much of a good thing, **overplentifulness**, overplenteousness, overplenty, **oversupply**, overstock, overaccumulation, **oversufficiency**, overmuchness, overcopiousness, overlavishness, overluxuriance, overbounteousness, overnumerousness; lavishness, **extravagance** *or* extravagancy, **prodigality**; **plenty** *see* 990.2; **more than enough**, **enough and to spare**, enough in all conscience; **overdose**, overmeasure, "enough, with over-measure"—SHAKESPEARE; too much of a good thing, egg in one's beer (*informal*); more than one knows what to do with, drug on the market; spate, avalanche, landslide, deluge, flood, inundation; *embarras de richesses* (*French*), money to burn (*informal*); overpopulation

3 **overfullness**, plethora, **surfeit**, **glut**; satiety *see* 993; engorgement, repletion, congestion; hyperaemia; **saturation**, supersaturation; **overload**, overburden, overcharge, surcharge, overfreight, overweight; **overflow**, overbrimming, overspill; **insatiability**, insatiableness

4 **superfluity**, superfluousness, fat; **redundancy**, redundance; unnecessariness, needlessness; fifth wheel

(*informal*), tits on a boar (*US & Canadian informal*); featherbedding, payroll padding; duplication, duplication of effort, reinventing the wheel, overlap; **luxury**, extravagance, frill *and* **frills** *and* bells and whistles *and* gimcrackery (*all informal*); frippery, froufrou, overadornment, bedizenment, gingerbread; **ornamentation**, **embellishment** *see* 498.1; expletive, **padding**, **filling**; pleonasm, tautology; verbosity, prolixity *see* 538.2; more than one really wants to know

5 **surplus**, surplusage, leftovers, plus, **overplus**, overstock, **overage**, overset, overrun, **overmeasure**, **oversupply**; margin; **remainder**, **balance**, **leftover**, **extra**, **spare**, something extra *or* to spare; bonus, dividend; lagniappe (*informal*); gratuity, tip, *pourboire* (*French*)

6 **overdoing**, overcarrying, **overreaching**, supererogation; **overkill**; piling on (*informal*), overimportance, overemphasis; overuse; overreaction; **overwork**, **overexertion**, overexercise, overexpenditure, overtaxing, overstrain, tax, strain; too much on one's plate, too many irons in the fire, too much at once; **overachievement**, overachieving

7 **overextension**, **overdrawing**, drawing *or* spreading too thin, **overstretching**, overstrain, overstraining, stretching, straining, stretch, strain, tension, extreme tension, snapping *or* breaking point; **overexpansion**; inflation, distension, overdistension, oedema, turgidity, swelling, bloat, bloating *see* 259.2

verbs

8 **to superabound**, overabound, **know no bounds**, **swarm**, pullulate, run riot, luxuriate, **teem**; overflow, flood, overbrim, overspill, spill over, overrun, overspread, overswarm, overgrow, fill; meet one at every turn; hang heavy on one's hands, remain on one's hands

9 **to exceed**, **surpass**, **pass**, **top**, **transcend**, **go beyond**; overpass, overstep, overrun, **overreach**, overshoot, overshoot the mark

10 **to overdo**, **go too far**, do it to death (*informal*), pass all bounds, know no bounds, overact, ham it up, nonformal, **carry too far**, overcarry, go to an extreme, **go to extremes**, go overboard, go *or* jump off the deep end; **run** *or* **drive into the ground**; **make a big deal of** *and* **make a Federal case of** (*both informal*), make a production (out) of (*informal*); pile on *or* put on *or* turn on the agony (*informal*); overemphasize, overstress; **overplay**, overplay one's hand (*informal*); **overreact**, protest too much; overreach oneself; **overtax**, overtask, overexert, overexercise, overstrain, overdrive, overspend, exhaust, overexpend, overuse; overtrain; **overwork**, overlabour; overelaborate, overdevelop, tell more than one wants to know; overstudy; burn the candle at both ends; **spread oneself too thin**, **take on too much**, bite off more than one can chew, have too much on one's plate, have too many irons in the fire, do too many things at once; **exaggerate** *see* 355.3; **overindulge** *see* 669.5

11 **to pile it on**, lay it on, **lay it on thick**, lay it on with a trowel (*informal*)

12 **to carry coals to Newcastle**, teach fishes to swim, teach one's grandmother to suck eggs, kill the slain, beat *or* flog a dead horse, labour the obvious, butter one's bread on both sides, preach to the converted, paint *or* gild the lily,

"to gild refined gold, to paint the lily, to throw a perfume on the violet"—SHAKESPEARE

13 to overextend, overdraw, overstretch, overstrain, stretch, strain; reach the breaking *or* snapping point; **overexpand**, overdistend, overdevelop, inflate, swell *see* 259.4

14 to oversupply, overprovide, overlavish, overfurnish, overequip; **overstock**; overprovision, overprovender; overdose; flood the market, oversell; **flood, deluge**, inundate, engulf, swamp, whelm, overwhelm; lavish with, be prodigal with

15 to overload, overlade, **overburden**, overweight, **overcharge**, surcharge; **overfill**, stuff, crowd, cram, jam, pack, jam-pack, **congest**, choke; **overstuff**, overfeed; gluttonize *see* 672.4; **surfeit, glut, gorge**, satiate *see* 993.4; **saturate**, soak, drench, supersaturate, supercharge

adjectives

16 excessive, inordinate, immoderate, overweening, hubristic, **intemperate, extravagant**, incontinent; unrestrained, unbridled, abandoned; gluttonous *see* 672.6; **extreme**; overlarge, overgreat, overbig, larger than life, monstrous, enormous, jumbo, elephantine, gigantic *see* 247.7; overgrown, overdeveloped, hypertrophied; **overmuch**, too much, a bit much, over the top *or* OTT, a bit thick; **exorbitant, undue, outrageous**, unconscionable, **unreasonable**; fancy *and* high *and* stiff *and* steep (*all informal*); **out of bounds** *or* **all bounds**, out of sight *and* out of this world (*both informal*), **boundless** *see* 822.3; egregious; fabulous, hyperbolic, hyperbolical, **exaggerated** *see* 355.4

17 superfluous, redundant; excess, in excess; unnecessary, unessential, nonessential, expendable, dispensable, **needless**, unneeded, gratuitous, uncalled-for; expletive; pleonastic, tautologous, tautological; verbose, prolix *see* 538.12; *de trop* (*French*), supererogatory, supererogative; spare, to spare; on one's hands

18 surplus, overplus; **remaining**, unused, **leftover**; over, **over and above; extra, spare**, supernumerary, for lagniappe (*informal*), as a bonus

19 superabundant, overabundant, plethoric, **overplentiful**, overplenteous, overplenty, **oversufficient, overmuch; lavish, prodigal**, overlavish, overbounteous, overgenerous, overliberal; overcopious, overluxuriant, riotous, overexuberant; overprolific, overnumerous; **swarming**, pullulating, **teeming**, overpopulated, overpopulous; plentiful *see* 990.7

20 overfull, overloaded, overladen, overburdened, overfreighted, overfraught, overweighted, **overcharged**, surcharged, **saturated**, drenched, soaked, supersaturated, supercharged; **surfeited, glutted**, gorged, overfed, bloated, replete, swollen, satiated *see* 993.6, **stuffed**, overstuffed, **crowded**, overcrowded, crammed, jammed, packed, jam-packed, like sardines in a can *or* tin, bumper-to-bumper (*informal*), chock-a-block, chocker (*Australian & NZ informal*); choked, **congested**, stuffed up;

overstocked, oversupplied; **overflowing**, in spate, running over, filled to overflowing; plethoric, hyperaemic; **bursting**, ready to burst, bursting at the seams, at the bursting point, overblown, distended, **swollen, bloated** *see* 259.13

21 overdone, overwrought; overdrawn, overstretched, overstrained; overwritten, overplayed, overacted

adverbs

22 excessively, inordinately, immoderately, intemperately, overweeningly, hubristically, **overly**, over, **overmuch**, too much; **too**, too-too (*informal*); **exorbitantly, unduly, unreasonably**, unconscionably, **outrageously**

23 in *or* to excess, to extremes, to the extreme, all out *and* to the max (*both informal*), flat out (*informal*), to a fault, too far, out of all proportion

24 superabundantly, overabundantly, **lavishly, prodigally, extravagantly**; more than enough, plentifully *see* 990.9; without measure, out of measure, beyond measure

25 superfluously, redundantly, supererogatorily; tautologously; unnecessarily, needlessly, beyond need, beyond reason, to a fare-thee-well (*informal*)

prepositions

26 in excess of, over, beyond, past, above, **over and above**, above and beyond

word elements

27 arch–, hyper–, over–, super–, sur–, ultra–, extra–

993 SATIETY

nouns

1 satiety, satiation, satisfaction, fullness, surfeit, glut, repletion, engorgement; contentment; **fill, bellyful** *and* skinful (*both informal*); **saturation**, oversaturation, saturatedness, supersaturation; saturation point; more than enough, enough in all conscience, all one can stand *or* take; too much of a good thing

2 satedness, surfeitedness, cloyedness, jadedness; overfullness

3 cloyer, surfeiter, sickener; **overdose**; a diet of cake; warmed-over cabbage,

"cabbage repeatedly"—JUVENAL

verbs

4 to satiate, sate, satisfy, slake, allay; **surfeit, glut, gorge**, engorge; cloy, jade, pall; **fill**, fill up; saturate, oversaturate, supersaturate; **stuff**, overstuff, cram, chock up; **overfill**, overgorge, overdose, overfeed

5 to have enough, have about enough of, have quite enough, **have one's fill**; have too much, have too much of a good thing, **have a bellyful** *or* skinful (*informal*), have an overdose, **be fed up** (*informal*), have all one can take *or* stand, have it up to here (*informal*), have had it

adjectives

6 satiated, sated, satisfied, slaked, allayed; **surfeited, gorged**, replete, engorged, **glutted**; cloyed, jaded; **full**, full up, full of, with one's fill of, **overfull**, saturated, oversaturated, supersaturated;

stuffed, stuffed full, overstuffed, crammed, overgorged, overfed; **fed up** *and* fed to the gills *or* fed to the teeth (*all informal*); **with a bellyful** *or* skinful (*informal*), with enough of; disgusted, **sick of,** tired of, sick and tired of, sickened with

7 **satiating,** sating, satisfying, filling; surfeiting, overfilling; jading, **cloying,** cloysome

exclamations

8 enough!, *basta* (*Italian*), genug! *and* genug shayn! (*both Yiddish*)

994 EXPEDIENCE

nouns

1 **expedience** *or* **expediency, advisability,** politicness, **desirability,** recommendability; **fitness, fittingness, appropriateness,** propriety, decency (*old*), seemliness, **suitability,** rightness, feasibility, **convenience;** seasonableness, timeliness, opportuneness; **usefulness** *see* 387.3; advantage, advantageousness, beneficialness, **profit,** profitability, percentage *and* mileage (*both informal*), worthwhileness, fruitfulness; wisdom, prudence *see* 919.7; temporariness, provisionality

2 **expedient, means,** means to an end, **provision, measure, step, action,** effort, **stroke,** stroke of policy, coup, **move,** countermove, **manoeuvre,** demarche, course of action; tactic, **device,** contrivance, artifice, stratagem, **shift;** gimmick *and* dodge *and* trick (*all informal*); **resort,** resource; answer, solution; quick-and-dirty solution (*informal*); working proposition, working hypothesis; **temporary expedient, improvisation,** ad hoc measure, ad hoc *or* ad hockery *or* ad hocism; **fix** *and* **quick fix** (*both informal*), jury-rigged expedient, **makeshift,** stopgap, shake-up, jury-rig; last expedient, **last resort** *or* resource, *pis aller* (*French*), last shift, trump

verbs

3 **to expedite one's affair,** work to one's advantage, not come amiss, come in handy, be just the thing, be just what the doctor ordered (*informal*), fit to a T *or* like a glove *or* like a second skin; forward, advance, promote, profit, advantage, benefit; **work, serve,** answer, answer *or* serve one's purpose, fit the bill *and* do the trick (*both informal*); suit the occasion, **be fitting,** fit, befit, be right

4 **to make shift, make do,** make out (*informal*), rub along, cope, manage, manage with, get along on, get by on, do with; do as well as *or* the best one can; use a last resort, scrape the bottom of the barrel

adjectives

5 **expedient, desirable,** to be desired, much to be desired, **advisable, politic,** recommendable; **appropriate, meet, fit, fitting,** befitting, **right, proper,** good, decent (*old*), **becoming,** seemly, likely, congruous, **suitable,** sortable, feasible, doable, swingable (*informal*), **convenient,** happy, heaven-sent, felicitous; timely, seasonable, opportune, well-timed, in the nick of time; **useful** *see* 387.18; **advantageous,** favourable; **profitable,** fructuous, worthwhile, worth one's while; **wise** *see* 919.17

6 **practical,** practicable, pragmatic *or* pragmatical, banausic; feasible, workable, operable, realizable; **efficient,** effective, **effectual**

7 **makeshift,** makeshifty, **stopgap,** band-aid (*US & Canadian informal*), improvised, improvisational, **jury-rigged; last-ditch,** last-gasp; **ad hoc;** quick and dirty (*informal*); temporary, provisional, tentative

adverbs

8 **expediently, fittingly,** fitly, **appropriately, suitably,** sortably, congruously, rightly, properly, decently (*old*), feasibly, conveniently; practically; seasonably, opportunely; desirably, advisably; advantageously, to advantage, all to the good; as a last resort

phrases

9 there's more than one way to skin a cat, where there's a will there's a way

995 INEXPEDIENCE

nouns

1 **inexpedience** *or* **inexpediency, undesirability, inadvisability,** impoliticness *or* impoliticalness; **unwiseness** *see* 922.2; **unfitness, unfittingness, inappropriateness, unaptness, unsuitability,** incongruity, **unmeetness,** wrongness, unseemliness; **inconvenience** *or* inconveniency, awkwardness; ineptitude, inaptitude; unseasonableness, untimeliness, inopportuneness; unfortunateness, infelicity; disadvantageousness, unprofitableness, unprofitability, diseconomy, worthlessness, futility, uselessness *see* 391

2 **disadvantage, drawback,** liability; detriment, impairment, prejudice, loss, damage, hurt, harm, mischief, injury; **a step back** *or* **backward,** a loss of ground; **handicap** *see* 1011.6, disability; drag, millstone around one's neck, albatross

3 **inconvenience,** discommodity, incommodity, disaccommodation (*old*), **trouble, bother;** inconvenientness, inconveniency, **unhandiness,** awkwardness, clumsiness, unwieldiness, troublesomeness, clunkiness (*informal*); gaucheness, gaucherie

verbs

4 **to inconvenience,** put to inconvenience, **put out, discommode,** incommode, disaccommodate (*old*), disoblige, **burden, embarrass; trouble, bother,** put to trouble, put to the trouble of, **impose upon;** harm, disadvantage *see* 999.6

adjectives

5 **inexpedient, undesirable, inadvisable, counterproductive,** impolitic, impolitical, unpolitic, not to be recommended, contraindicated; **impractical, impracticable,** dysfunctional, unworkable; **ill-advised, ill-considered, unwise; unfit, unfitting,** unbefitting, **inappropriate, unsuitable,** unmeet, inapt, inept, unseemly, **improper, wrong,** bad, out of place, out of order, incongruous, ill-suited; malapropos, *mal à propos* (*French*), inopportune, untimely, ill-timed, badly

timed, unseasonable; infelicitous, unfortunate,
unhappy; unprofitable *see* 391.12; futile *see* 391.13

6 **disadvantageous**, unadvantageous, **unfavourable**;
unprofitable, profitless, unrewarding, worthless,
useless *see* 391.9; **detrimental**, deleterious, injurious,
harmful, prejudicial, disserviceable

7 **inconvenient, incommodious**, discommodious;
unhandy, awkward, clumsy, unwieldy, troublesome;
gauche

adverbs

8 **inexpediently, inadvisably**, impoliticly *or*
impolitically, **undesirably; unfittingly,
inappropriately, unsuitably**, ineptly, inaptly,
incongruously; inopportunely, unseasonably;
infelicitously, unfortunately, unhappily

9 **disadvantageously**, unadvantageously, unprofitably,
unrewardingly; uselessly *see* 391.15; **inconveniently**,
unhandily, with difficulty, ill

996 IMPORTANCE

nouns

1 **importance, significance, consequence,**
consideration, **import**, note, mark, **moment,
weight, gravity**; materiality; concern, concernment,
interest; **first order**, high order, high rank; **priority,**
primacy, precedence, preeminence, paramountcy,
superiority, **supremacy**; value, worth, merit,
excellence *see* 998.1; self-importance *see* 140.1

2 **notability, noteworthiness**, remarkableness,
salience, memorability; **prominence, eminence,
greatness**, distinction; prestige, esteem, repute,
reputation, honour, glory, renown, dignity, **fame** *see*
662.1; **stardom**, celebrity, celebrity-hood,
superstardom; semicelebrity

3 **gravity, graveness, seriousness**, solemnity,
weightiness; *gravitas* (*Latin*); no joke, no laughing
matter

4 **urgency**, imperativeness, exigence *or* exigency;
momentousness, crucialness, cruciality;
consequentiality, consequentialness; **press**, pressure,
high pressure, **stress**, tension, **pinch**; crunch
(*informal*); **crisis, emergency**; moment of truth,
turning point, climax, defining moment

5 **matter of importance** *or* **consequence**, thing of
interest, point of interest, matter of concern, object
of note, one for the book *and* something to write
home about (*both informal*), something special, no tea
party, no picnic; vital concern *or* interest, matter of
life or death; notabilia, memorabilia, great doings

6 **salient point**, cardinal point, high point, great
point; important thing, chief thing, **the point, main
point**, main thing, essential matter, **essence**, the
name of the game *and* the bottom line *and* what it's
all about *and* where it's at (*all informal*), substance,
gravamen, *sine qua non* (*Latin*), issue, real issue,
front-burner issue (*informal*), prime issue; **essential,**
fundamental, substantive point, material point; **gist,
nub** (*informal*), **heart**, meat, pith, kernel, **core;
crux**, crucial *or* pivotal *or* critical point, pivot;
turning point, **climax, cusp, crisis**; keystone,
cornerstone; landmark, milestone, bench mark;
linchpin

7 **feature, highlight**, high spot, main attraction,
centrepiece, *pièce de résistance;* outstanding feature

8 **personage, important person**, person of
importance *or* consequence, **great man** *or* **woman,**
man *or* woman of mark *or* note, **somebody,
notable**, notability, figure; **celebrity**, famous person,
person of renown, personality; name, big name,
nabob, **mogul**, panjandrum, person to be reckoned
with, very important person, nob (*informal*);
sagamore, sachem; mover and shaker, lord of
creation; **worthy**, pillar of society, elder, father;
dignitary, dignity; **magnate**; tycoon (*informal*),
baron; power; power elite, Establishment; interests;
brass, top brass; top people, the great; ruling circle,
lords of creation,

"the choice and master spirits of the age"—
SHAKESPEARE; the top, the summit

9 (*informal terms*) **big shot**, wheel, **big wheel**, big boy,
big cat, big fish, big shot, biggie, big cheese, big
noise, big-timer, big-time operator, **bigwig**, big man,
big gun, high-muck-a-muck *or* high-muckety-muck,
lion, something, **VIP**, brass hat, high man on the
totem pole (*US*), suit; sacred cow, little tin god, tin
god; big man on campus *or* BMOC (*US &
Canadian*); queen bee

10 **chief, principal**, chief executive, chief executive
officer *or* CEO, president, chairman, paramount,
overlord, **king**, electronics king, etc; leading light,
luminary, master spirit, **star**, superstar, prima donna,
diva, leading lady, lead, front man (*informal*) *see*
707.6

11 (*informal terms*) **boss**, honcho (*US informal*), big
enchilada (*US & Canadian informal*), biggest frog in
the pond, top *or* high man on the totem pole, top
dog, Mr Big, head cheese, his nibs, himself, man
upstairs

verbs

12 **to matter**, import (*old*), signify, **count, tell, weigh,
carry weight**, cut ice *and* cut some ice (*both
informal*), be prominent, stand out, mean much; be
something, be somebody, amount to something; have
a key to the executive washroom; be featured, star,
get top billing

13 **to value, esteem, treasure, prize**, appreciate, **rate
highly**, think highly of, think well of, **think much
of**, set store by; give *or* attach *or* ascribe importance
to; make much of, make a fuss *or* stir about, make
an ado *or* much ado about; hold up as an example

14 **to emphasize, stress**, lay emphasis *or* stress upon,
feature, highlight, place emphasis on, give emphasis
to, **accent, accentuate, punctuate, point up**,
bring to the fore, put in the foreground; prioritize;
highlight, spotlight; **star, underline, underscore**,
italicize; overemphasize, overstress, overaccentuate,
rub in; harp on; dwell on, belabour; attach too much
importance to, make a big deal *or* Federal case of
(*informal*), make a mountain out of a molehill

15 **to feature**, headline (*informal*); **star**, give top billing
to

16 **to dramatize, play up** (*informal*), splash, make a
production of

adjectives

17 **important, major, consequential, momentous, significant, considerable,** substantial, material, **great,** grand, big; superior, world-shaking, earthshaking; big-time *and* big-league *and* major-league *and* heavyweight (*all informal*); high-powered (*informal*), double-barrelled (*informal*); bigwig *and* bigwigged (*both informal*); name *and* big-name (*both informal*), self-important *see* 140.8

18 **of importance, of significance, of consequence,** of note, of moment, of weight; of concern, of concernment, of interest, not to be overlooked *or* despised, not to be sneezed at *or* sniffed at (*informal*), not hay *and* not chopped liver (*both US & Canadian informal*); viable

19 **notable, noteworthy, celebrated, remarkable, marked,** standout (*US & Canadian informal*), of mark, signal, serious; **memorable,** rememberable, unforgettable, never to be forgotten; striking, telling, salient; **eminent, prominent,** conspicuous, noble, **outstanding, distinguished;** prestigious, esteemed, estimable, reputable *see* 662.15; **extraordinary,** *extraordinaire* (*French*), out of the ordinary, **exceptional, special,** rare

20 **weighty,** heavy, **grave,** sober, sobering, **solemn, serious,** earnest; portentous, fateful, fatal; formidable, awe-inspiring, imposing, larger than life

21 **emphatic, decided, positive, forceful,** forcible; **emphasized, stressed,** accented, accentuated, punctuated, pointed; underlined, underscored, starred, italicized; red-letter, in red letters, in letters of fire

22 **urgent, imperative,** imperious, **compelling, pressing,** high-priority, high-pressure, crying, clamorous, insistent, instant, exigent; crucial, critical, pivotal, acute

23 **vital, all-important,** crucial, of vital importance, life-and-death *or* life-or-death; earth-shattering, epoch-making, momentous; **essential,** fundamental, indispensable, basic, substantive, bedrock, material; **central,** focal; bottom-line *and* meat-and-potatoes *and* gut (*all informal*)

24 **paramount, principal, leading, foremost, main, chief,** number one (*informal*), premier, **prime, primary,** preeminent, **supreme,** capital (*old*), cardinal; highest, uppermost, topmost, toprank, ranking, of the first rank, world-class, **dominant,** predominant, master, controlling, **overruling,** overriding, all-absorbing

adverbs

25 **importantly, significantly,** consequentially, materially, momentously, greatly, grandly; eminently, prominently, conspicuously, outstandingly, saliently, signally, notably, markedly, remarkably

26 **at the decisive moment,** when the chips are down *and* when push comes to shove (*both informal*)

997 UNIMPORTANCE

nouns

1 **unimportance, insignificance, inconsequence,** inconsequentiality, indifference, **immateriality;** inessentiality; ineffectuality; unnoteworthiness, unimpressiveness; inferiority, secondariness, low order of importance, low priority, dispensability, expendability, marginality; **smallness,** littleness, slightness, inconsiderableness, negligibility; irrelevancy, meaninglessness; **pettiness,** puniness, pokiness, picayune, picayunishness; irrelevance *see* 775.1

2 **paltriness,** poorness, **meanness,** sorriness, sadness, pitifulness, contemptibleness, pitiableness, despicableness, miserableness, wretchedness, vileness, crumminess (*informal*), shabbiness, shoddiness, cheapness, cheesiness, beggarliness, worthlessness, unworthiness, meritlessness; tawdriness, meretriciousness, gaudiness *see* 501.3

3 **triviality,** trivialness, triflingness, nugacity, nugaciousness; **superficiality,** shallowness; slightness, slenderness, slimness, flimsiness; **frivolity,** frivolousness, lightness, levity; **foolishness,** silliness; inanity, emptiness, vacuity; triteness, vapidity; vanity, idleness, futility; **much ado about nothing,** storm in a teacup, tempest in a teapot (*US*), much cry and little wool, piss and wind *and* big deal (*both informal*)

4 **trivia, trifles; trumpery,** *nugae* (*Latin*), gimcrackery, knickknackery, bric-a-brac; **rubbish,** trash, chaff, junk; peanuts *and* chicken feed *and* Mickey Mouse (*all informal*), chickenshit (*US & Canadian informal*), small change; small beer; froth, "trifles light as air"—SHAKESPEARE; minutiae, details, minor details

5 **trifle, triviality, oddment, bagatelle,** fribble, **gimcrack, gewgaw,** frippery, **trinket,** bibelot, curio, **bauble,** gaud, toy, **knickknack,** knickknackery, kickshaw, minikin (*old*), whim-wham, folderol; pin, button, hair, straw, rush, feather, fig, bean, hill of beans (*informal*), molehill, row of pins *or* buttons (*informal*), sneeshing (*informal*), pinch of snuff; bit, snap; a curse, a hoot *and* a damn *and* a darn *and* a shit *and* a toss *and* a fuck (*all informal*), a tinker's damn *or* tinker's cuss; picayune (*US & Canadian*), rap, sou, halfpenny, farthing, brass farthing, cent, red cent, two cents, twopence *or* tuppence; peppercorn; drop in the ocean *or* the bucket; fleabite, pinprick; joke, jest, farce, mockery, child's play

6 **an insignificancy,** an inessential, a marginal matter *or* affair, a trivial *or* paltry affair, a small *or* trifling *or* minor matter, **no great matter,** no big deal (*informal*); a little thing, *peu de chose* (*French*), hardly *or* scarcely anything, matter of no importance *or* consequence, matter of indifference; **a nothing, a big nothing, a naught,** a mere nothing, nothing in particular, nothing to signify, nothing to speak *or* worth speaking of, nothing to think twice about, nothing to boast of, nothing to write home about, thing of naught, *rien du tout* (*French*), nullity, nihility; **technicality,** mere technicality

7 **a nobody, insignificancy,** hollow man, jackstraw (*old*), **nonentity,** empty suit *and* nebbish (*both informal*), an obscurity, a nothing, cipher, "an O without a figure"—SHAKESPEARE, little man, nobody one knows; lightweight, mediocrity; whippersnapper *and* whiffet *and* pip-squeak *and* squirt *and* shrimp *and* scrub *and* runt (*all informal*); squit (*informal*), punk (*informal*); small potato, small potatoes; **the little fellow,** the little guy (*informal*), **the man in the street;** common man *see* 863.3; man of straw, dummy, figurehead, puppet; **small fry,** Mr and Mrs Nobody, Joe Bloggs, John Doe and Richard Roe *or* Mary Roe (*US & Canadian*); Tom, Dick and Harry; Brown, Jones and Robinson

8 **trifling,** dallying, **dalliance,** flirtation, flirtiness, coquetry; toying, fiddling, playing, fooling, **pottering,** tinkering, pottering, piddling; dabbling, smattering; loitering, idling *see* 331.4

9 (*informal terms*) **monkeying, monkeying around,** buggering around, diddling around, fiddling around, frigging around, horsing around, fooling around, kidding around, messing around, pissing around, playing around, screwing around, mucking around, farting around, arsing around, fucking around, wanking around; jerking off (*US & Canadian*)

10 **trifler, dallier,** fribble; **potterer,** piddler, tinkerer, smatterer, dabbler; amateur, dilettante, Sunday painter; **flirt, coquet**

verbs

11 **to be unimportant,** be of no importance, not signify, **not matter,** not count, signify nothing, matter little, **not make any difference; cut no ice, not amount to anything,** not amount to a damn (*informal*), make no never mind *and* not amount to a hill of beans (*both US & Canadian informal*)

12 **to attach little importance to,** give little weight to; **make little of,** underplay, deemphasize, downplay, play down, **minimize, make light of,** think little of, throw away, **make** *or* **think nothing of,** take no account of, set little by, set no store by, set at naught; snap one's fingers at; not care a straw about; not give a shit *or* a hoot *or* two hoots for (*informal*), not give a damn about, not give a dime a dozen for (*US & Canadian informal*); bad-mouth (*informal*), deprecate, depreciate *see* 512.8; **trivialize**

13 **to make much ado about nothing,** make mountains out of molehills, have a storm *or* tempest in a teacup *or* teapot

14 **to trifle, dally;** flirt, coquet; toy, fribble, **play, fool,** play at, **potter,** tinker, **piddle; dabble,** smatter; toy with, fiddle with, fool with, play with; idle, loiter *see* 331.12, 13; nibble, niggle

15 (*informal terms*) **to monkey, monkey around,** fiddle, fiddle around, fiddle-faddle, frivol, horse around, fool around, play around, mess around, kid around, **screw around,** muck around, fart around, piss around, bugger around, diddle around, frig around, mess around, fuck around, arse around; jerk off (*US & Canadian*)

adjectives

16 **unimportant, of no importance,** of little *or* small importance, of no great importance, **of no account,** of no significance, of no concern, of no matter, of little *or* no consequence, no great shakes (*informal*); no skin off one's nose *or* elbow *or* arse (*informal*); inferior, secondary, of a low order of importance, low-priority, expendable; marginal; one-dimensional, two-dimensional

17 **insignificant** *see* 248.6, **inconsequential, immaterial;** nonessential, unessential, inessential, **not vital,** back-burner (*informal*), dispensable; unnoteworthy, unimpressive; **inconsiderable,** inappreciable, negligible; **small, little,** minute, footling, petit (*old*), minor, inferior; technical; irrelevant

18 (*informal terms*) **measly, small-time, tuppenny-ha'penny, two-bit,** Mickey Mouse, chickenshit (*US & Canadian*), nickel-and-dime, low-rent, piddly, dinky, poky, tinhorn, punk, not much cop; not worth tuppence *or* a dime *or* a red cent *or* shit *or* beans *or* a hill of beans (*US & Canadian*), not worth a button; **one-horse,** two-by-four

19 **trivial, trifling;** fribble, fribbling, nugacious, nugatory; catchpenny; **slight,** slender, flimsy; **superficial, shallow; frivolous, light,** windy, airy, frothy; idle, futile, vain, otiose; **foolish,** fatuous, asinine, **silly; inane,** empty, vacuous; trite, vapid; unworthy of serious consideration

20 **petty, puny, piddling,** piffling, niggling, pettifogging, picayune *or* picayunish (*US & Canadian*); small-beer

21 **paltry, poor,** common, **mean, sorry, sad,** pitiful, pitiable, pathetic, **despicable, contemptible,** beneath contempt, **miserable, wretched,** beggarly, vile, **shabby,** scrubby, scruffy, shoddy, scurvy, scuzzy (*informal*), scummy, **crummy** *and* cheesy (*both informal*), **trashy,** rubbishy, garbagey (*informal*), trumpery, gimcracky (*informal*); tinpot (*informal*); **cheap,** worthless, valueless, tuppenny *or* tuppenny-ha'penny, two-for-a-penny *or* cent, ten-a-penny, dime-a-dozen; tawdry, meretricious, gaudy *see* 501.20

22 **unworthy, worthless,** meritless, unworthy of regard *or* consideration, beneath notice

adverbs

23 **unimportantly, insignificantly, inconsequentially,** immaterially, unessentially; **pettily, paltrily; trivially,** triflingly; superficially, shallowly; frivolously, lightly, idly

phrases

24 **it does not matter,** it matters not, it does not signify, **it is of no consequence** *or* **importance, it makes no difference,** it makes no never mind (*informal*), it cannot be helped, it is all the same; *n'importe, de rien, ça ne fait rien* (*all French*); it will all come out in the wash (*informal*), it will be all the same a hundred years from now

25 **no matter, never mind,** think no more of it, do not give it another *or* a second thought, don't lose any sleep over it, let it pass, let it go (*informal*), ignore it, forget it (*informal*), skip it *and* drop it (*both informal*); fiddle-dee-dee

26 **what does it matter?, what matter?,** what difference does it make?, **what's the difference?,** what's the diff? (*informal*), what do I care?, what of it?, what boots it?, what's the odds?, so what?, what else is new?, so?; for aught *or* all one cares, big deal (*informal*)

998 GOODNESS
good quality or effect

nouns

1 goodness, excellence, quality, class (*informal*);
virtue, grace; **merit,** desert; **value, worth;**
fineness, goodliness, fairness, niceness; **superiority,**
first-rateness, **skilfulness** *see* 413.1; wholeness,
soundness, healthiness *see* 81.1; **virtuousness** *see*
653.1; **kindness, benevolence,** benignity *see* 143.1;
beneficialness, helpfulness *see* 449.10; favourableness,
auspiciousness *see* 133.9; expedience,
advantageousness *see* 994.1; **usefulness** *see* 387.3;
pleasantness, agreeableness *see* 97.1; cogency, validity;
profitableness, rewardingness *see* 472.4

2 superexcellence, supereminence, preeminence,
supremacy, primacy, paramountcy, peerlessness,
unsurpassedness, matchlessness, superfineness;
superbness, exquisiteness, **magnificence,**
splendidness, splendiferousness, marvellousness

3 tolerableness, tolerability, goodishness, passableness,
fairishness, **adequateness, satisfactoriness,**
acceptability, admissibility; sufficiency *see* 990

4 good, welfare, well-being, **benefit; interest,**
advantage; behalf, behoof; blessing, benison, boon;
profit, avail (*old*), gain; world of good

5 good thing, a thing to be desired,
"a consummation devoutly to be wish'd"—SHAKESPEARE;
treasure, gem, jewel, diamond, pearl; boast, pride,
pride and joy; prize, trophy, plum; winner *and* no
slouch *and* nothing to sneeze at *or* sniff at (*all
informal*); catch, find (*informal*), trouvaille (*French*);
godsend, windfall

6 first-rater, topnotcher, world-beater; **wonder,**
prodigy, genius, virtuoso, **star, superstar;**
luminary, leading light, one in a thousand *or* a
million; hard *or* tough act to follow (*informal*)

7 (*informal terms*) **dandy,** jim dandy, dilly (*US &
Canadian*), **humdinger,** pip (*US & Canadian*),
pippin (*US & Canadian*), **peach,** ace, beaut, **lulu,**
honey, sweetheart, dream, lollapalooza (*US*), bitch,
crackerjack, hot shit (*US & Canadian*), pistol (*US &
Canadian*), corker, whiz, cracker, scorcher, smasher,
snorter, beezer, bottler (*Australian & NZ informal*),
knockout, something else, something else again,
killer, the cat's pyjamas, whiz, whizbang, wow

8 the best, the very best, the best ever, the top of the
heap *or* the line *or* the range (*all informal*), the tops
(*informal*); **quintessence,** prime, optimum,
superlative; **choice, pick, select, elect, elite,** corps
d'élite (*French*), chosen; **cream, flower,** fat; cream of
the crop, crème de la crème (*French*), salt of the earth;
pièce de résistance (*French*); prize, champion, queen;
nonesuch, paragon, nonpareil; gem of the first water

9 harmlessness, hurtlessness, uninjuriousness,
innocuousness, benignity, benignancy;
unobnoxiousness, inoffensiveness; innocence; heart of
gold, kindness of heart, milk of human kindness

verbs

10 to do good, profit, avail; do a world of good;
benefit, help, serve, be of service, advance,
advantage, favour *see* 449.11, 14, 17, 19; be the
making of, make a man *or* woman of; do no harm,
break no bones

11 to excel, surpass, outdo, pass, do *or* go one better,
top; do with a vengeance; be as good as, equal,
emulate, rival, vie, vie with, challenge comparison,
go one-on-one with (*US & Canadian informal*);
make the most of, optimize; cream off, skim off
the cream

adjectives

12 good, excellent, bueno (*Spanish*), bon (*French*),
bonny, **fine, nice,** goodly, fair; **splendid, capital,
grand,** elegant (*informal*), braw (*Scottish*), famous
(*informal*), noble; royal, regal, fit for a king; very
good, très bon (*French*); commendable, laudable,
estimable *see* 509.20; skilful *see* 413.22; **sound,**
healthy *see* 81.5; virtuous; kind, benevolent *see*
143.15; beneficial, helpful *see* 449.21; profitable;
favourable, auspicious *see* 133.18; expedient,
advantageous *see* 994.5; useful *see* 387.18; pleasant *see*
97.6; cogent, valid *see* 972.13

13 (*informal terms*) **great,** swell, dandy, bitchin', jim
dandy (*US & Canadian*), neat, cool, super, super-
duper, bully (*old*), mean, heavy, bad, groovy, out of
sight, fab, fantabulous, marvy, gear, something else,
ducky, dynamite, keen, killer, crucial, def, mega, hot,
nifty, sexy, spiffy, spiffing, ripping, corking,
cracking, beezer, jammy, nobby, peachy, peachy-
keen, plum *or* plummy, delicious, scrumptious, not
too shabby, out of this world, hunky-dory,
crackerjack, boss, stunning, corking, smashing, solid,
bang on; rum *or* wizard, bonzer (*Australian & NZ*);
bang-up, jam-up, slap-up, ace-high, fine and dandy,
just dandy, but good (*US & Canadian*), OK, okay,
A-OK

14 superior, above par, head and shoulders above,
crack (*informal*); **high-grade, high-class,** high-
quality, high-calibre, high-test (*US & Canadian*),
world-class

15 superb, super (*informal*), **superexcellent,
supereminent,** superfine, **exquisite; magnificent,**
splendid, splendiferous, tremendous, immense,
marvellous, wonderful, glorious, divine, heavenly,
terrific, sensational; sterling, golden; gilt-edged *and*
gilt-edge, blue-chip; of the highest type, of the best
sort, of the first water, as good as good can be, as
good as they come, as good as they make 'em *and*
out of this world (*both informal*), out of the box
(*Australian informal*)

16 best, very best, greatest *and* top-of-the-line *and* top-
of-the-range (*all informal*), **prime,** optimum, optimal,
up-market; **choice, select, elect,** elite, **picked,**
handpicked; **prize, champion; supreme,**
paramount, **unsurpassed,** surpassing, unparalleled,
unmatched, unmatchable, matchless, makeless (*old*),
peerless; quintessential; for the best, all for the best

17 first-rate, first-class, in a class by itself; of the first
or highest degree; unmatched, matchless; champion,
record-breaking; top of the class, top-marks,
straight-A (*US & Canadian*)

18 (*informal terms*) **A1, A number one,** primo, first-
chop (*US*), tip-top, top-notch, topflight, top-drawer,
tops; topping *or* top-hole

19 up to par, up to standard, **up to snuff** (*informal*); **up to the mark,** up to the notch *and* **up to scratch** (*both informal*)

20 tolerable, goodish, fair, fairish, fair to middling, moderate, tidy (*informal*), **decent,** respectable, presentable, good enough, **pretty good, not bad,** not amiss, not half bad, not so bad, **adequate, satisfactory, all right,** OK *or* okay (*informal*), tickety-boo (*informal*); better than nothing; **acceptable,** admissible, **passable,** unobjectionable, unexceptionable; workmanlike; sufficient *see* 990.6

21 harmless, hurtless, unhurtful; well-meaning, well-meant; **uninjurious,** undamaging, **innocuous,** innoxious, innocent; unobnoxious, inoffensive; nonmalignant, **benign;** nonpoisonous, nontoxic, nonvirulent, nonvenomous

adverbs

22 excellently, nicely, finely, **capitally, splendidly, famously,** royally; **well,** very well, **fine** (*informal*), right, aright, bang on; one's best, at one's best, at the top of one's bent

23 superbly, exquisitely, **magnificently,** tremendously, immensely, terrifically, **marvellously, wonderfully,** gloriously, divinely

24 tolerably, fairly, fairishly, moderately, respectably, **adequately, satisfactorily,** passably, **acceptably,** unexceptionably, presentably, decently; fairly well, well enough, pretty well; **rather, pretty**

999 BADNESS
bad quality or effect

nouns

1 badness, evil, evilness, viciousness, damnability, reprehensibility; moral badness, dereliction, peccancy, iniquity, sinfulness, wickedness *see* 654.4; unwholesomeness, unhealthiness *see* 82.1; inferiority *see* 1004.3; unskilfulness *see* 414.1; unkindness, malevolence *see* 144; inauspiciousness, unfavourableness *see* 133.8; inexpedience *see* 995; unpleasantness *see* 98; invalidity *see* 19.3; inaccuracy *see* 974.2; improperness *see* 638.1

2 terribleness, dreadfulness, direness, **awfulness** (*informal*), horribleness; **atrociousness, outrageousness,** heinousness, nefariousness; **notoriousness, egregiousness,** scandalousness, shamefulness, **infamousness; abominableness,** odiousness, **loathsomeness, detestableness,** despicableness, contemptibleness, hatefulness; **offensiveness,** grossness, obnoxiousness; squalor, squalidness, sordidness, **wretchedness,** filth, **vileness,** fulsomeness, **nastiness,** rankness, **foulness,** noisomeness; disgustingness, repulsiveness; uncleanness *see* 80; beastliness, bestiality, brutality; **rottenness** *and* lousiness (*both informal*); the pits (*informal*); shoddiness, shabbiness; scurviness, **baseness** *see* 661.3; **worthlessness** *see* 997.2

3 evil, bad, wrong, ill; harm, hurt, injury, damage, detriment; **destruction** *see* 395; despoliation; mischief, havoc; outrage, atrocity; abomination, grievance, vexation, woe, crying evil; poison *see* 1000.3; blight, venom, toxin, **bane** *see* 1000; **corruption,** pollution, infection, befoulment, defilement; environmental pollution, fly in the ointment, worm in the apple *or* rose; skeleton in the cupboard; snake in the grass; "something rotten in the state of Denmark"—SHAKESPEARE; ills the flesh is heir to, "all ills that men endure"—ABRAHAM COWLEY; the worst

4 bad influence, malevolent influence, evil star, **ill wind;** evil genius, **hoodoo** *and* **jinx** (*both informal*), **Jonah; curse,** enchantment, whammy *and* double *or* triple whammy (*all informal*), spell, hex, voodoo; **evil eye,** *malocchio* (*Italian*)

5 harmfulness, hurtfulness, injuriousness, banefulness, balefulness, detrimentalness, deleteriousness, perniciousness, mischievousness, noxiousness, venomousness, poisonousness, toxicity, virulence, noisomeness, **malignance** *or* **malignancy, malignity, viciousness;** unhealthiness *see* 82.1; disease *see* 85; deadliness, lethality *see* 308.8; ominousness *see* 133.7

verbs

6 to work evil, do ill; **harm, hurt; injure,** scathe, wound, **damage; destroy** *see* 395.10; despoil, prejudice, disadvantage, impair, disserve, distress, **wrong,** do wrong, do wrong by, aggrieve, do evil, do a mischief, do an ill office to; **molest,** afflict; lay a hand on; get into trouble; **abuse,** bash (*informal*), batter, outrage, violate, maltreat, mistreat *see* 389.5; torment, **harass,** hassle (*informal*), persecute, savage, crucify, torture *see* 96.18; play mischief *or* havoc with, wreak havoc on, play hob with (*US informal*); **corrupt,** deprave, taint, pollute, infect, befoul, defile; poison, envenom, blight; **curse,** put a whammy on (*informal*), give the evil eye, hex, jinx, bewitch; spell *or* mean trouble, threaten, menace *see* 514.2; doom; condemn *see* 602.3

adjectives

7 bad, evil, ill, untoward, black, sinister; **wicked, wrong,** peccant, iniquitous, **vicious; sinful** *see* 654.16; criminal; unhealthy *see* 82.5; **inferior** *see* 1004.9; unskilful *see* 414.15; unkind, malevolent *see* 144.19; inauspicious, unfavourable *see* 133.17; inexpedient *see* 995.5; unpleasant *see* 98.17; invalid *see* 19.15; inaccurate *see* 974.17; improper *see* 638.3

8 (*informal terms*) lousy, punk, bum, badass (*US & Canadian*), shitty, crappy, naff, duff, cruddy, cheesy, gross, raunchy, piss-poor, **crummy,** grim, low-rent, putrid, filthy, icky, yucky *or* yukky, grotty, vomity, barfy (*US & Canadian*), stinking, stinky, creepy, hairy, god-awful, gosh-awful

9 terrible, dreadful, awful (*informal*), dire, horrible, horrid; atrocious, outrageous, heinous, villainous, nefarious; enormous, monstrous; **deplorable,** lamentable, regrettable, pitiful, pitiable, woeful, woesome (*old*), grievous, sad *see* 98.20; flagrant, **scandalous,** shameful, **shocking,** infamous, **notorious,** arrant, **egregious;** unclean *see* 80.20; shoddy, schlocky (*informal*), shabby, scurvy, **base** *see* 661.12; **odious, obnoxious,** offensive, gross, **disgusting,** repulsive, loathsome, **abominable, detestable, despicable, contemptible,** beneath contempt, hateful; blameworthy, **reprehensible;** rank, fetid, foul, filthy, vile, fulsome, noisome, nasty, squalid, sordid, **wretched**; beastly, brutal; as bad as they come, as bad as they make 'em (*informal*), as bad as bad can be; worst; too bad; below par, subpar, not up to scratch *or* snuff *or* the mark, poor-quality, **worthless**

10 **execrable, damnable**; damned, accursed, cursed *see* 513.9; infernal, hellish, devilish, fiendish, satanic, ghoulish, demoniac, demonic, demonical, diabolic, diabolical, unholy, ungodly

11 evil-fashioned, ill-fashioned, evil-shaped, ill-shaped, evil-qualitied, evil-looking, ill-looking, evil-favoured, ill-favoured, evil-hued, evil-faced, evil-minded, evil-eyed, ill-affected (*old*), evil-got, ill-got, ill-conceived

12 **harmful, hurtful**, scatheful, **baneful**, baleful, distressing, **injurious, damaging, detrimental**, deleterious, counterproductive, **pernicious**, mischievous; noxious, mephitic, venomous, venenate, poisonous, venenous, veneniferous, toxic, virulent, noisome; **malignant**, malign, malevolent, malefic, vicious; prejudicial, disadvantageous, disserviceable; corruptive, corrupting, corrosive, corroding; deadly, lethal; ominous *see* 133.17

adverbs

13 **badly**, bad (*informal*), **ill**, evil, evilly, wrong, wrongly, amiss; to one's cost

14 **terribly, dreadfully**, dreadful (*informal*), **horribly**, horridly, **awfully** (*informal*), **atrociously**, **outrageously**; flagrantly, scandalously, shamefully, shockingly, infamously, notoriously, egregiously, grossly, offensively, nauseatingly, fulsomely, odiously, vilely, obnoxiously, **disgustingly**, loathsomely; wretchedly, sordidly, shabbily, basely, abominably, detestably, despicably, contemptibly, foully, nastily; brutally, bestially, savagely, viciously; something fierce *or* terrible *or* awful *or* chronic (*informal*)

15 **harmfully, hurtfully, banefully**, balefully, **injuriously, damagingly, detrimentally**, deleteriously, counterproductively, **perniciously**, mischievously, venomously, poisonously, toxically, virulently, noisomely; **malignantly**, malignly, malevolently, malefically, **viciously**; prejudicially, disadvantageously, disserviceably; corrosively, corrodingly

1000 BANE

nouns

1 **bane, curse, affliction**, infliction, visitation, **plague, pestilence**, pest, calamity, scourge, **torment**, open wound, running sore, grievance, woe, burden, crushing burden; disease *see* 85; death *see* 307; evil, harm *see* 999.3; destruction *see* 395; vexation *see* 96.2; thorn, thorn in the flesh *or* side; bugbear, **bête noire**, bogy, bogeyman, nemesis, arch-nemesis

2 **blight**, blast; canker, cancer; mould, fungus, mildew, smut, must, rust; rot, dry rot; **pest**; worm, worm in the apple *or* rose; moth (*old*), "moth and rust"—Bible

3 **poison, venom**, venin, virus (*old*), toxic, toxin, toxicant; eradicant, **pesticide; insecticide**, insect powder, bug bomb (*US & Canadian informal*); roach

powder, roach paste; stomach poison, contact poison, systemic insecticide *or* systemic, fumigant, chemosterilant; chlorinated hydrocarbon insecticide, organic chlorine; organic phosphate insecticide; carbamate insecticide, sheepdip; termiticide, miticide, acaricide, vermicide, anthelminthic; rodenticide, rat poison; **herbicide**, defoliant, Agent Orange, paraquat, **weed killer**; fungicide; microbicide, germicide, antiseptic, disinfectant, antibiotic; **toxicology**; toxic waste, **environmental pollutant**; aflatoxin, cytotoxin, mycotoxin

4 **miasma, mephitis**, malaria (*old*); effluvium, exhaust, exhaust gas; coal gas, chokedamp, blackdamp, firedamp; air *or* atmospheric pollution, smog; fug

5 sting, stinger, dart; **fang**, tang (*informal*); beesting, snakebite

6 **poisonous plants**

aconite	mayapple
amanita	mescal bean
baneberry	monkshood
banewort	mountain laurel
bearded darnel	nightshade
belladonna	Noogoora burr
black bryony	nux vomica
black henbane	oleander
black nightshade	ordeal tree
castor-oil plant	poison bean
corn cackle	poisonberry
cowbane	poison bush
coyotillo	poison dogwood *or* elder
datura	poison hemlock *or* parsley
deadly nightshade	poison ivy
death camass	poison oak
death cap *or* angel	poison rye grass
dieffenbachia	poison sumach
dog's mercury	poison tobacco
ergot	poisonweed
fly agaric	pokeweed *or* pokeberry *or*
foxglove	pokeroot
gastrolobium	sassy *or* sasswood *or* sassy
hellebore	wood
hemlock	sheep laurel
henbane	staggerbush
horsetail	stavesacre
Indian liquorice *or*	thorn apple *or* jimsonweed
jequirity *or* jequirity bean	tutu
laburnum	upas
larkspur	water hemlock
liberty cap	white snakeroot
locoweed	wolfsbane
manchineel	woody nightshade

1001 PERFECTION

nouns

1 **perfection, faultlessness, flawlessness**, defectlessness, indefectibility, impeccability, absoluteness; infallibility; spotlessness, stainlessness, taintlessness, purity, immaculateness; sinlessness; chastity *see* 664

2 **soundness, integrity, intactness, wholeness**, entireness, completeness; **fullness**, plenitude; finish

3 **acme of perfection, pink, pink of perfection,**
culmination, perfection, height, top, acme, ultimate,
summit, pinnacle, peak, highest pitch, climax,
consummation, *ne plus ultra* (*Latin*), **the last word,**
a dream come true

4 pattern *or* standard *or* mould *or* norm of perfection,
very model, quintessence; archetype, prototype,
exemplar, mirror, **epitome**; perfect specimen,
highest type; **classic,** masterwork, masterpiece, *chef*
d'œuvre (*French*), showpiece; **ideal** *see* 785.4; role
model; **paragon** *see* 659.4

verbs

5 **to perfect,** develop, flesh out, ripen, mature;
improve *see* 392.7; crown, culminate; lick *or* whip
into shape, fine-tune; complete *see* 407.6; do to
perfection *see* 407.7

adjectives

6 **perfect, ideal, faultless, flawless,** unflawed,
defectless, not to be improved, **impeccable,**
absolute; **just right;** spotless, stainless, taintless,
unblemished, untainted, unspotted, immaculate,
pure, uncontaminated, unadulterated, unmixed;
sinless; chaste *see* 664.4; indefective (*old*),
indefectible, trouble-free; infallible; beyond all praise,
irreproachable, unfaultable, *sans peur et sans reproche*
(*French*), **matchless, peerless** *see* 249.15

7 **sound, intact, whole, entire, complete,** integral;
full; total, utter, unqualified *see* 959.2

8 **undamaged, unharmed, unhurt, uninjured,**
unscathed, **unspoiled,** undefiled, virgin, inviolate,
unimpaired; harmless, scatheless; **unmarred,**
unmarked, unscarred, unscratched, undefaced,
unbruised; **unbroken,** unshattered, untorn;
undemolished, undestroyed; undeformed,
unmutilated, unmangled, unmaimed; unfaded,
unworn, unwithered, bright, fresh, untouched,
pristine, mint; none the worse for wear

9 **perfected, finished,** polished, refined; done to a T
or to a turn; **classic, classical,** masterly, masterful,
expert, proficient; ripened, ripe, matured, mature,
developed, fully developed; thorough-going,
thorough-paced; **consummate,** quintessential,
archetypical, exemplary, model

adverbs

10 **perfectly,** ideally; **faultlessly, flawlessly,**
impeccably; just right; spotlessly; immaculately,
purely; infallibly; **wholly, entirely, completely,**
fully, thoroughly, totally, absolutely *see* 793.15

11 to perfection, to a turn, to a T, to a finish, to a
nicety; to a fare-thee-well *or* fare-you-well *or* fare-
ye-well (*informal*); to beat the band (*informal*)

1002 IMPERFECTION

nouns

1 imperfection, imperfectness; **unperfectedness;**
faultiness, defectiveness, defectibility;
shortcoming, deficiency, lack, want, shortage,
inadequacy, inadequateness; erroneousness,
fallibility; inaccuracy, inexactness, inexactitude *see*
974.2; **unsoundness,** incompleteness, patchiness,

sketchiness, unevenness; **impairment** *see* 393;
mediocrity *see* 1004; immaturity, undevelopment *see*
406.4; impurity, adulteration *see* 796.3

2 **fault,** *faute* (*French*), **defect, deficiency,**
inadequacy, imperfection, kink, defection (*old*);
flaw, hole, bug (*informal*); something missing; catch
(*informal*), fly in the ointment, problem, little
problem, curate's egg, snag, drawback; **crack,** rift,
weakness, frailty, infirmity, failure, **failing, foible,**
shortcoming; weak point, Achilles' heel, vulnerable
place, chink in one's armour, weak link; **blemish,**
taint *see* 1003; **malfunction,** glitch (*informal*)

verbs

3 **to fall short,** come short, miss, miss out, miss the
mark, miss by a mile (*informal*), not qualify, fall
down (*informal*), **not measure up,** not come up to
par, not come up to the mark, not come up to
scratch *or* to snuff (*informal*), not pass muster, not
bear inspection, not hack it *and* not make it *and* not
cut it (*all informal*), not make the cut (*US &*
Canadian informal); not make the grade

adjectives

4 imperfect, not perfect; unperfected; **defective,**
faulty, duff (*informal*), dud (*informal*), **inadequate,**
deficient, short, not all it's cracked up to be
(*informal*), lacking, wanting, found wanting,
"weighed in the balance and found wanting"—BIBLE;
off; erroneous, **fallible;** inaccurate, inexact, imprecise
see 974.17; **unsound, incomplete,** unfinished,
partial, patchy, sketchy, uneven, unthorough;
makeshift *see* 994.7; **damaged, impaired** *see* 393.27;
mediocre *see* 1004.7; **blemished** *see* 1003.8; half-
baked (*informal*), immature, undeveloped *see* 406.12;
impure, adulterated, mixed

adverbs

5 imperfectly, inadequately, deficiently;
incompletely, partially; **faultily, defectively**

1003 BLEMISH

nouns

1 blemish, disfigurement, disfiguration,
defacement; scar, keloid, cicatrix; needle scar, track
or crater (*both informal*); scratch; scab; blister, vesicle,
bulla, bleb; weal, wale, welt, wen, sebaceous cyst;
port-wine stain *or* mark, haemangioma, strawberry
mark; pock, pustule; pockmark, pit; stretchmarks;
naevus, birthmark, mole; freckle, lentigo; milium,
whitehead, blackhead, comedo, pimple, sty; wart,
verruca; **crack,** craze, check, rift, split; **deformity,**
deformation, warp, twist, kink, **distortion;** flaw,
defect, fault *see* 1002.2

2 **discolouration,** discolourment, discolour (*old*);
bruise; lovebite, hickey (*US & Canadian informal*)

3 **stain, taint, tarnish;** mark, brand, **stigma;**
maculation, macule, macula; **spot, blot,** blur,
blotch, patch, speck, speckle, fleck, flick, flyspeck;
daub, dab; **smirch, smudge,** smutch *or* smouch,
smut, **smear;** splotch, splash, splatter, spatter;
bloodstain; eyesore

verbs

4 to **blemish, disfigure,** deface, **flaw, mar;** scab; scar, cicatrize, scarify; **crack,** craze, check, split; **deform,** warp, twist, kink, **distort**

5 to **spot,** bespot, **blot, blotch, speck, speckle,** bespeckle, maculate (*old*); freckle; flyspeck; **spatter, splatter,** splash, splotch

6 to **stain,** bestain, **discolour,** smirch, besmirch, **taint,** attaint, **tarnish; mark, stigmatize,** brand; smear, besmear, daub, bedaub, slubber (*informal*); blur, slur (*informal*); **darken, blacken;** smoke, besmoke; scorch, singe, sear; dirty, **soil** *see* 80.16

7 to **bloodstain, bloody,** ensanguine

adjectives

8 **blemished, disfigured,** defaced, **marred,** scarred, keloidal, cicatrized, scarified, scabbed, scabby; pimpled, pimply; cracked, crazed, checked, split; deformed, warped, twisted, kinked, distorted; **faulty, flawed, defective** *see* 1002.4

9 **spotted, spotty,** maculate, maculated, macular, blotched, **blotchy,** splotched, splotchy; **speckled,** speckly, bespeckled; freckled, freckly, freckle-faced; spattered, splattered, splashed

10 **stained, discoloured,** foxed, foxy, **tainted, tarnished,** smirched, besmirched; stigmatized, stigmatic, stigmatiferous; darkened, blackened, murky, smoky, inky; **soiled** *see* 80.21

11 **bloodstained,** blood-spattered, **bloody,** sanguinary, **gory,** ensanguined

1004 MEDIOCRITY

nouns

1 **mediocrity,** mediocreness, fairishness, modestness, modesty, moderateness, middlingness, **indifference;** respectability, passableness, **tolerableness** *see* 998.3; **dullness,** lacklustre, tediousness *see* 117.1

2 **ordinariness,** averageness, normalness, normality, **commonness, commonplaceness;** unexceptionality, unremarkableness, unnoteworthiness; conventionality

3 **inferiority,** inferiorness, **poorness,** lowliness, humbleness, **baseness, meanness, commonness,** coarseness, tackiness, tack; **second-rateness,** third-rateness, fourth-rateness

4 **low grade,** low class, low quality, poor quality; second best, next best

5 **mediocrity, second-rater,** third-rater, fourth-rater, nothing *or* nobody special, no great shakes (*informal*), no prize, no prize package, no brain surgeon, no rocket scientist, not much of a bargain, small potatoes *and* small beer (*both informal*); tinhorn (*informal*); **nobody, nonentity** *see* 997.7; middle class, bourgeoisie, burgherdom; suburbia, the burbs (*US informal*); silent majority, moral majority, Middle America

6 **irregular,** second, third; schlock (*US informal*)

adjectives

7 **mediocre, middling, indifferent, fair, fairish, fair to middling** (*informal*), moderate, modest, medium, betwixt and between; respectable, passable, **tolerable; so-so,** *comme ci comme ça* (*French*); of a

kind, of a sort, of sorts (*informal*); nothing to brag about, not much to boast of, nothing to write home about, not much cop (*informal*); "not below mediocrity nor above it"—JOHNSON; bush-league (*US & Canadian*), second-division; dull, lacklustre, tedious *see* 117.6; insipid, vapid, wishy-washy, namby-pamby

8 **ordinary, average,** bog-standard, normal, **common, commonplace,** common or garden, garden *and* garden-variety (*both informal*), run-of-the-mill; **unexceptional, unremarkable, unnoteworthy,** unspectacular, nothing *or* nobody special *and* no great shakes (*all informal*), no prize, no prize package, no brain surgeon, no rocket scientist; conventional; middle-class, bourgeois, plastic (*informal*); suburban; usual, regular

9 **inferior, poor,** punk (*informal*), **base, mean, common,** coarse, cheesy *and* tacky (*both informal*), tinny, ropy *or* ropey (*informal*), duff (*informal*), naff (*informal*), not much cop (*informal*); shabby, seedy; cheap, cheapo (*informal*), tuppenny-ha'penny (*informal*), Mickey Mouse (*informal*), paltry, tinpot (*informal*); irregular; second-best; **second-rate,** third-rate, fourth-rate; **second-class,** third-class, fourth-class, etc; **low-grade, low-class,** low-quality, low-rent (*US & Canadian informal*)

10 **below par,** below standard, **below the mark** (*informal*), substandard, **not up to scratch** *or* snuff *or* the mark (*informal*), not up to sample *or* standard *or* specification, off

adverbs

11 **mediocrely, middlingly,** fairly, fairishly, middling well, fair to middling (*informal*), moderately, modestly, **indifferently, so-so;** passably, **tolerably**

12 **inferiorly, poorly,** basely, meanly, commonly

1005 DANGER

nouns

1 **danger, peril, endangerment, imperilment, jeopardy, hazard, risk,** cause for alarm, **menace, threat** *see* 514; **crisis, emergency,** hot spot, nasty *or* tricky spot, pass, pinch, strait, plight, predicament *see* 1012.4; powder keg, time bomb; dangerous *or* unpredictable *or* uncontrollable person, loose cannon (*informal*); rocks *or* breakers *or* white water ahead, gathering clouds, storm clouds; dangerous ground, yawning *or* gaping chasm, quicksand, thin ice; hornet's nest; house of cards, cardhouse; no tea party, no picnic

2 **dangerousness, hazardousness, riskiness, precariousness** *see* 970.6, chanciness, dodginess (*informal*), diceyness (*informal*), **perilousness; unsafeness,** unhealthiness (*informal*); criticalness; **ticklishness,** slipperiness, touchiness, delicacy, ticklish business *and* shaky ground (*both informal*); **insecurity,** unsoundness, instability, unsteadiness, shakiness, totteriness, wonkiness (*informal*); sword of Damocles; **unreliability,** undependability, untrustworthiness *see* 970.6; **unsureness,** unpredictability, **uncertainty,** doubtfulness, dubiousness *see* 970.2

3 exposure, openness, liability, nonimmunity, susceptibility; **unprotectedness, defencelessness,** nakedness, helplessness; lamb, sitting duck

4 vulnerability, pregnability, penetrability, assailability, vincibility; weakness *see* 16; vulnerable point, **weak link, weak point, soft spot,** heel of Achilles, chink, chink in one's armour, soft spot, "the soft underbelly"—Sir Winston Churchill

5 (*hidden danger*) snags, rocks, reefs, ledges; coral heads; shallows, shoals; sandbank, sandbar, sands; quicksands; crevasses; rockbound *or* ironbound coast, lee shore; undertow, undercurrent, crosscurrent; **pitfall;** snake in the grass; trap, booby trap, springe, snare, tripwire, pitfall

verbs

6 to endanger, imperil, peril; **risk, hazard, gamble, gamble with;** jeopardize, jeopard, jeopardy, compromise, put in danger, **put in jeopardy,** put on the spot *and* lay on the line (*both informal*); **expose,** lay open; incur danger, run into *or* encounter danger

7 to take chances, take a chance, chance, risk, gamble, hazard, press *or* push one's luck, **run the chance** *or* **risk** *or* **hazard;** risk one's neck, run a risk, go out on a limb, stick one's neck out (*informal*), **expose oneself,** bare one's breast, lower one's guard, **lay oneself open to,** leave oneself wide open, open the door to, let oneself in for; **tempt Providence** *or* **fate,** forget the odds, **defy danger,** skate on thin ice, court destruction, dance on the razor's edge, go in harm's way, hang by a hair *or* a thread, stand *or* sleep on a volcano, sit on a barrel of gunpowder, build a house of cards, put one's head in the lion's mouth, "beard the lion in his den"—Sir Walter Scott, march up to the cannon's mouth, play with fire, go through fire and water, go out of one's depth, go to sea in a sieve, carry too much sail, sail too near the wind; risk one's life, throw caution to the wind, **take one's life in one's hands,** dice with death, **dare, face up to, brave** *see* 492.11

8 to be in danger, be in peril, be *in extremis*, be in a desperate case, have one's name on the danger list, have the chances *or* odds against one, have one's back to the wall, have something hanging over one's head; be despaired of; hang by a thread; tremble on the verge, totter *or* teeter on the brink; feel the ground sliding from under one; have to run for it; race against time *or* the clock; be threatened, be on the spot *or* in a bind (*both informal*)

adjectives

9 **dangerous,** dangersome (*informal*), **perilous,** periculous, parlous, jeopardous, bad, ugly, hairy (*informal*), serious, critical, explosive, attended *or* beset *or* fraught with danger; alarming, too close for comfort *or* words, **menacing, threatening** *see* 514.3

10 **hazardous, risky, chancy,** dodgy (*informal*), dicey (*informal*), aleatory, riskful, full of risk, high-risk; **adventurous,** venturous, venturesome; **speculative,** wildcat

11 **unsafe,** unhealthy (*informal*); **unreliable, undependable, untrustworthy,** treacherous,

insecure, unsound, unstable, unsteady, shaky, tottery, wonky (*informal*), rocky; **unsure, uncertain,** unpredictable, doubtful, dubious

12 **precarious, ticklish, touchy,** touch-and-go, **critical, delicate;** slippery, slippy; on thin ice, on slippery ground; hanging by a thread, trembling in the balance

13 **in danger, in jeopardy, in peril, at risk,** in a bad way; **endangered, imperilled, jeopardized,** *in periculo* (*Latin*), at the last extremity, *in extremis* (*Latin*), in deadly peril, *in periculo mortis* (*Latin*), in, desperate case; threatened, up against it, on the spot *and* on *or* in the hot seat (*both informal*); sitting on a powder keg; between the hammer and the anvil, between Scylla and Charybdis, between two fires, between the devil and the deep blue sea, between a rock and a hard place (*informal*); in a predicament *see* 1012.21; cornered

14 **unprotected, unshielded, unsheltered,** uncovered, unscreened, **unguarded, undefended,** unattended, unwatched, unfortified; armourless, unarmoured, **unarmed,** bare-handed, weaponless; guardless, ungarrisoned, **defenceless, helpless;** unwarned, unsuspecting

15 **exposed, open,** out in the open, naked; out on a limb (*informal*); liable, susceptible, nonimmune

16 **vulnerable, pregnable,** penetrable, expugnable; assailable, attackable, surmountable; conquerable, beatable (*informal*), vincible; weak *see* 16.12-14

adverbs

17 **dangerously, perilously, hazardously, riskily,** critically, unsafely; **precariously,** ticklishly; at gunpoint

1006 SAFETY

nouns

1 safety, safeness, **security,** surety (*old*), assurance; risklessness, immunity, clear sailing; **protection, safeguard** *see* 1007.3; harmlessness *see* 998.9; airworthiness, crashworthiness, roadworthiness, seaworthiness; invulnerability *see* 15.4

verbs

2 to be safe, be on the safe side; **keep safe, come through;** weather, ride out, weather the storm; keep one's head above water, tide over; land on one's feet; save one's bacon (*informal*), save one's neck, save one's skin; lead a charmed life, have nine lives

3 to play safe (*informal*), **keep on the safe side,** give danger a wide berth, watch oneself, watch out, take precautions *see* 494.6; assure oneself, make sure, keep an eye *or* a weather eye out, look before one leaps; **save, protect** *see* 1007.18

adjectives

4 **safe, secure,** safe and sound; immune, immunized; insured; **protected** *see* 1007.21; on the safe side; unthreatened, unmolested; unhurt, unharmed, unscathed, intact, untouched, with a whole skin, undamaged

5 **unhazardous, undangerous, unperilous, unrisky,** riskless, **unprecarious;** fail-safe, trouble-free;

recession-proof; guaranteed, warranted; dependable, reliable, trustworthy, sound, stable, steady, firm *see* 969.17;

"founded upon a rock"—BIBLE; as safe as houses; harmless; invulnerable

6 **in safety, out of danger,** past danger, out of the meshes *or* toils *or* mire, in, home, out of the woods *and* over the hump (*both informal*), home free (*US & Canadian informal*), home and dry (*informal*), **in the clear, out of harm's reach** *or* **way;** under cover, under lock and key; in shelter, in harbour *or* port, at anchor *or* haven, in the shadow of a rock; on sure *or* solid ground, on *terra firma*, high and dry, above water

7 **snug, cosy;** crashworthy, roadworthy, airworthy, seaworthy, seakindly

adverbs

8 **safely, securely,** reliably, dependably; with safety, with impunity

exclamations

9 **all's well!,** all clear!, all serene!, A-OK!

phrases

10 the danger is past, the storm has blown over, the coast is clear

1007 PROTECTION

nouns

1 **protection, guard, shielding, safekeeping; policing, law enforcement; patrol, patroling,** community policing, professional *or* bureaucratic policing; eye, protectiveness, watchfulness, vigilance, watchful eye, shepherding; house-sitting (*informal*); protective custody; **safeguarding, security,** security industry, public safety, **safety** *see* 1006; **shelter, cover,** shade, shadow (*old*), windbreak, lee; **refuge** *see* 1008; preservation *see* 397; **defence** *see* 460; protective coating, Teflon coating (*trademark*)

2 **protectorship, guardianship,** stewardship, custodianship; **care, caring, charge, keeping, nurture, nurturing,** nurturance, **custody,** fostering, fosterage; **hands,** safe hands, wing; **auspices, patronage, tutelage, guidance; ward,** wardship, wardenship, watch and ward; cure, pastorship, pastorage, pastorate; **oversight,** jurisdiction, management, ministry, administration, government, governance; **child care,** infant care, day-care, family service; baby-sitting, baby-minding, childminding

3 **safeguard, palladium, guard; shield, screen,** aegis; umbrella, protective umbrella; patent, copyright; **bulwark** *see* 460.4; backstop; fender, mudguard, **bumper, buffer, cushion,** pad, padding; seat *or* safety belt; protective clothing; shin guard, knuckle guard, knee guard, nose guard, hand guard, arm guard, ear guard, head guard, finger guard, foot guard; goggles, mask, face mask, welder's mask, fencer's mask; safety shoes; helmet, hard hat (*informal*), crash helmet, sun helmet; cowcatcher (*US & Canadian*), pilot (*US & Canadian*); dashboard; windscreen, windshield; dodger *and* cockpit dodger;

life preserver *see* 397.6; lifeline, safety rail, guardrail, handrail; governor; safety, safety switch, interlock, panic button; safety valve, safety plug; fuse, circuit breaker; insulation; insulating tape; safety glass, laminated glass, toughened glass, shatterproof glass; lightning rod, lightning conductor; **anchor,** bower, sea anchor, sheet anchor, drogue; **parachute; safety net;** prophylactic, preventive *see* 86.20; contraceptive *see* 86.23

4 **insurance,** assurance, life assurance; national insurance, sickness benefit; **social security** *see* 611.8; pension scheme, company pension scheme, state earnings-related pension scheme *or* SERPS *or* Serps; **insurance company,** stock company, mutual company; friendly society, club (*informal*), benefit society (*US*), provident society; **insurance policy,** policy, certificate of insurance, cover note; deductible; **annuity,** variable annuity; excess; insurance man, underwriter, insurance broker, insurance agent, insurance adjuster, loss adjuster, actuary

5 **protector, keeper,** protectress, safekeeper; patron, patroness; tower, pillar, strong arm, tower of strength, rock; champion, **defender** *see* 460.7

6 **guardian, warden,** governor; **custodian,** steward, **keeper, caretaker,** warder, attendant; caregiver, carer; next friend, prochein ami, guardian *ad litem;* **curator,** conservator; janitor; castellan; seneschal; **shepherd,** herd, cowherd; **game warden,** gamekeeper; **ranger,** forest ranger, forester; lifeguard, lifesaver; lollipop man, lollipop lady, school crossing patrol; air warden; guardian angel

7 **chaperon,** duenna; **governess;** escort

8 **nurse, nursemaid,** nurserymaid, nanny, amah, ayah, mammy (*US informal*); dry nurse, wet nurse; **baby-sitter,** baby-minder, sitter (*informal*), childminder

9 **guard,** guarder, guardsman (*old*), warder; **outguard, outpost; picket,** outlying picket, inlying picket, outrider; advance guard, **vanguard,** van; **rear guard;** coast guard; armed guard, security guard; jailer *see* 429.10; bank guard; railway *or* train guard; goalkeeper, goalie (*informal*); **garrison;** cordon, *cordon sanitaire* (*French*)

10 **watchman, watch,** watcher; watchkeeper; **lookout,** lookout man, cave (*old*); **sentinel,** picket, **sentry; scout,** vedette; **point,** forward observer, spotter; **patrol, patrolman,** patroller, roundsman; night watchman, Charley (*informal*); fireguard, fire patrolman, fire warden; aeroplane spotter; Argus

11 **watchdog,** bandog, guard dog, attack dog; sheep dog; Cerberus

12 **doorkeeper, doorman, gatekeeper,** Cerberus, warden; **porter, janitor,** commissionaire, *concierge* (*French*), ostiary, usher; receptionist

13 **picket, picketer,** demonstrator, flying picket, secondary picket, picket line; counterdemonstrator

14 **bodyguard,** safeguard, minder (*informal*); **convoy, escort;** guards, praetorian guard; guardsman; yeoman *or* yeoman of the guard *or* beefeater, gentleman-at-arms, Life Guardsman

15 **policeman, constable, officer, police officer,** *flic* (*French informal*), *gendarme* (*French*), *carabiniere* (*Italian*); peace officer, law enforcement agent, arm

of the law; military policeman *or* MP; detective *see* 576.10; policewoman, woman police constable *or* WPC, police matron; police constable *or* PC, patrolman; trooper (*US & Australian*), mounted policeman, Mountie (*Canadian*); reeve, portreeve; **sheriff, marshal**; deputy sheriff, deputy, bound bailiff, catchpole, beagle (*informal*), bumbailiff (*informal*); sergeant, police sergeant; roundsman; lieutenant (*US*), police lieutenant (*US*); captain (*US*), police captain (*US*); inspector, police inspector; chief constable; superintendent, chief of police; commissioner (*US*), police commissioner (*US*); government man (*US*), federal (*US*), fed *and* G-man (*both US informal*); narc (*US informal*); **bailiff**, tipstaff, tipstaves (*plural*); mace-bearer, lictor, sergeant at arms; beadle; traffic warden, meter maid (*informal*), traffic officer, traffic cop

16 (*informal terms*) cop, copper, John Law, bluecoat, bluebottle, Old Bill *or* the Bill, bull, flatfoot, gumshoe, gendarme, dick, pig, flattie, bizzy *and* bobby *and* peeler, polis (*Scottish*), Dogberry (*Shakespeare*); the cops, the law, the fuzz; tec

17 **police, police force**, law enforcement agency; **constabulary**; state police (*US*), troopers *or* state troopers (*US*), highway patrol, traffic cops, county police, provincial police, Metropolitan police; community policing; security force; special police, Special Branch; tactical police, riot police, snatch squad, flying squad, the Sweeney (*informal*); SWAT *or* special weapons and tactics (*US*), SWAT team (*US*), **posse**, *posse comitatus* (*Latin*); **vigilantes**, vigilance committee; neighbourhood watch; secret police, political police; Federal Bureau of Investigation *or* FBI; Fraud Squad, military police *or* MP, redcaps; shore patrol *or* SP (*US*); Scotland Yard, the Yard (*informal*); Criminal Investigation Department *or* CID, Garda Síochána, Sûreté (*France*); Cheka, NKVD, MVD, OGPU (*all USSR*); Securitate Romania; Gestapo (*Germany*); Royal Canadian Mounted Police *or* RCMP, Mounties (*all Canadian*); Interpol, International Criminal Police Commission

verbs

18 **to protect, guard, safeguard, secure, keep**, bless, make safe, **police, enforce the law**; keep from harm; **insure**, underwrite, assure; ensure, guarantee *see* 438.9; patent, copyright, register; **cushion**; champion, go to bat for (*US informal*); ride shotgun (*informal*), fend, defend *see* 460.8; **shelter, shield, screen, cover**, cloak, shroud (*old*), temper the wind to the shorn lamb; **harbour, haven**; nestle; compass about, fence; arm, armour

19 **to care for, take care of**; preserve, conserve; provide for, support; take charge of, **take under one's wing**, make one a *protégé*; **look after**, see after, **attend to, minister to**, look *or* see to, look *or* watch out for (*informal*), have *or* keep an eye on *or* upon, keep a sharp eye on *or* upon, **watch over**, keep watch over, **watch, mind, tend**, see (someone) right; keep a tab *or* tabs on (*informal*); **shepherd; chaperon**, matronize; baby-sit (*informal*); **foster, nurture, cherish, nurse; mother**, be a mother *or* father to

20 **to watch, keep watch, keep guard**, keep watch over, keep vigil, keep watch and ward; stand guard, stand sentinel; be on the lookout *see* 339.8; mount guard; **police**, patrol, pound a beat (*informal*), go on one's beat

adjectives

21 **protected, guarded**, safeguarded, defended; safe *see* 1006.4-6; insured, assured, covered; patented, copyrighted; **sheltered, shielded**, screened, covered, cloaked; policed; armed *see* 460.14; invulnerable

22 **under the protection of**, under the shield of, under the auspices of, under the aegis of, **under one's wing**, under the wing of, under the shadow of one's wing

23 **protective, custodial**, guardian, tutelary; curatorial; vigilant, watchful, on the watch, on top of; prophylactic, preventive; immunizing; protecting, guarding, safeguarding, sheltering, **shielding**, screening, covering; fostering, parental; caring; defensive *see* 460.11; Teflon-coated (*trademark*)

1008 REFUGE

nouns

1 **refuge, sanctuary**, safehold, **asylum, haven, port**, harbourage, **harbour**; harbour of refuge, port in a storm, snug harbour, safe haven; game sanctuary, bird sanctuary, preserve, forest preserve, game preserve; stronghold *see* 460.6; **political asylum**

2 **recourse, resource, resort**; last resort *or* resource, *dernier ressort* and *pis aller* (*both French*); hope; expedient *see* 994.2

3 **shelter, cover, covert**, coverture; concealment *see* 346; *abri* (*French*), dugout, cave, earth, funk hole (*informal*), foxhole; **bunker**; trench; storm cellar, storm cave, cyclone cellar; air-raid shelter, bomb shelter, Anderson shelter, bombproof, fallout shelter, safety zone *or* isle *or* island

4 **asylum, home**, retreat; **poorhouse**, almshouse, workhouse, poor farm; **orphanage; hospice**, hospitium; old folks' home, rest home, nursing home, old soldiers' home; foster home; halfway house; retirement home *or* village *or* community, sheltered housing

5 **retreat**, recess, hiding place, **hideaway**, hideout, hidey-hole (*informal*); **sanctum, inner sanctum**, sanctum sanctorum, holy ground, holy of holies, adytum; private place, privacy (*old*), secret place; **den**, lair, mew; safe house; **cloister**, hermitage, ashram, cell; **ivory tower**; study, library

6 **harbour, haven, port**, outport, **seaport**, port of call, free port, treaty port, home port; hoverport; harbourage, **anchorage**, anchorage ground, protected anchorage, moorage, moorings; **roadstead**, road, roads; berth, slip; **dock**, dockage, marina, basin; dry dock; shipyard, dockyard; **wharf, pier**, quay; harbourside, dockside, pierside, quayside, landing, landing place *or* stage, jetty, jutty (*old*); breakwater, mole, groyne *or* groin *or* groin; seawall, embankment, bulkhead

verbs

7 to take refuge, take shelter, seek refuge, **claim sanctuary,** claim refugee status; run into port; fly to, throw oneself into the arms of; bar the gate, lock *or* bolt the door, raise the drawbridge, let the portcullis down; take cover *see* 346.8

8 to find refuge *or* sanctuary, make port, reach safety; seclude *or* sequester oneself, dwell *or* live in an ivory tower

1009 PROSPERITY

nouns

1 prosperity, prosperousness, thriving *or* flourishing condition; **success** *see* 409; **welfare, well-being,** weal, happiness, felicity; quality of life; comfortable *or* easy circumstances, **comfort, ease,** security; **life of ease,** the life of Riley (*informal*), **the good life; clover** *and* **velvet** (*both informal*), **bed of roses, luxury,** lap of luxury, Easy Street (*informal*), Fat City *and* hog heaven (*both US & Canadian informal*); the affluent life, gracious life, gracious living; fat of the land; fleshpots, fleshpots of Egypt; milk and honey, loaves and fishes; a chicken in every pot, a car in every garage; purple and fine linen; high standard of living; upward mobility; **affluence, wealth** *see* 618

2 good fortune *or* **luck,** happy fortune, **fortune, luck,** the breaks (*informal*); **fortunateness, luckiness,** felicity (*old*); blessing, smiles of fortune, fortune's favour

3 stroke of luck, piece of good luck; blessing; **fluke** *and* lucky strike *and* **break** (*all informal*), **good** *or* **lucky break** (*informal*); **run** *or* **streak of luck** (*informal*)

4 good times, piping times, bright *or* palmy *or* halcyon days, days of wine and roses, rosy era; heyday; prosperity, era of prosperity; fair weather, sunshine; golden era, **golden age,** golden time, Saturnian age, reign of Saturn, *Saturnia regna* (*Latin*), alcheringa, alchera, dream time; age of Aquarius, millennium; **utopia** *see* 985.11; **heaven** *see* 681

5 roaring trade, bullishness, bull market, seller's market; **boom,** booming economy, expanding economy

6 lucky dog (*informal*), fortune's favourite, favourite of the gods, fortune's child, destiny's darling

verbs

7 to prosper, enjoy prosperity, **fare well,** get on well, do well, have it made (*informal*), have a good thing going, have everything going one's way, get on swimmingly, go great guns (*informal*); **turn out well, go well,** take a favourable turn; **succeed;** come on *or* along (*informal*), come a long way, get on (*informal*); **advance,** progress, make progress, make headway, get ahead (*informal*); move up in the world, pull oneself up by one's own boot-straps

8 to thrive, flourish, boom; blossom, bloom, flower; batten, fatten, grow fat

9 to be prosperous, make good, make one's mark, rise *or* get on in the world, make a noise in the world (*informal*), do all right for oneself (*informal*), **make one's fortune;** grow rich; drive a roaring trade, rejoice in a seller's market

10 to live well, live in clover *or* on velvet (*informal*), **live a life of ease,** live *or* lead the life of Riley, **live high,** live high on the hog (*US & Canadian informal*), live on *or* off the fat of the land, ride the gravy train (*informal*), live in the lap of luxury; bask in the sunshine, have one's place in the sun; have a good *or* fine time of it

11 to be fortunate, be lucky, be in luck, luck out (*US & Canadian informal*), have all the luck, have one's moments (*informal*), **lead** *or* **have a charmed life;** fall in the sea and come out dry (*informal*); **get a break** *and* get the breaks (*both informal*); hold aces *and* turn up trumps (*both informal*), come up roses (*informal*); have a run of luck *and* hit a streak of luck (*both informal*); have a stroke of luck; strike it lucky *and* make a lucky strike *and* strike oil (*all informal*), **strike it rich** (*informal*), make it big (*informal*), strike a rich vein, come into money, be onto a good thing

adjectives

12 prosperous, in good case; **successful,** rags-to-riches; **well-paid, high-income,** higher-income, well-heeled *and* upscale (*both informal*); **affluent, wealthy; comfortable,** comfortably situated, **easy;** on Easy Street (*informal*), in Fat City *and* in hog heaven (*both US & Canadian informal*), **in clover** *and* **on velvet** (*both informal*), on a bed of roses, in luxury, high on the hog (*US & Canadian informal*); up in the world, on top of the heap (*informal*)

13 thriving, flourishing, prospering, booming (*informal*), on the up and up; vigorous, exuberant; in full swing, going strong (*informal*); halcyon, palmy, balmy, rosy, piping, clear, fair; blooming, blossoming, flowering, fruiting; fat, sleek, in good case

14 fortunate, lucky, providential; in luck; blessed, blessed with luck, favoured; born under a lucky star, born with a silver spoon in one's mouth, jammy (*informal*); out of the woods, over the hump; **auspicious**

adverbs

15 prosperously, thrivingly, flourishingly, boomingly, swimmingly (*informal*)

16 fortunately, luckily, providentially

1010 ADVERSITY

nouns

1 adversity, adverse circumstances, difficulties, hard knocks *and* rough going (*both informal*), **hardship, trouble,** troubles, "sea of troubles"—SHAKESPEARE, **rigour,** vicissitude, care, stress, pressure, stress of life; hard case *or* plight, **hard life,** dog's life, vale of tears; wretched *or* miserable *or* hard *or* unhappy lot, tough *or* hard row to hoe (*informal*), ups and downs of life, things going against one; bummer *and* downer (*both informal*); the bad part, the downside (*informal*); annoyance, irritation, aggravation; **difficulty** *see*

1012; **trial**, tribulation, cross, curse, blight, **affliction** *see* 96.8; plight, predicament *see* 1012.4

2 **misfortune, mishap**, ill hap, **misadventure, mischance**, *contretemps* (*French*), grief; **disaster, calamity, catastrophe**, meltdown, cataclysm, **tragedy; shock, blow**, hard *or* nasty *or* staggering blow; **accident**, casualty, collision, crash, plane *or* car crash; prang (*informal*), bingle (*Australian informal*); **wreck**, shipwreck; smash *and* smashup *and* pileup (*all informal*), crack-up (*US informal*)

3 **reverse, reversal**, reversal of fortune, **setback**, check, severe check; **comedown**, descent, down

4 **unfortunateness, unluckiness**, lucklessness, ill success; unprosperousness; starcrossed *or* ill-fated life;
"the slings and arrows of outrageous fortune"— SHAKESPEARE; inauspiciousness *see* 133.8

5 **bad luck**, ill luck, **hard luck**, hard lines, hard cheese (*informal*), **tough** *or* **rotten luck** (*informal*), raw deal (*informal*), bad *or* tough *or* rotten break (*informal*), devil's own luck; own goal (*informal*); **ill fortune**, bad fortune, evil fortune, evil star, ill wind, evil dispensation; frowns of fortune

6 **hard times**, bad times, sad times; evil day, ill day; rainy day; hard *or* stormy *or* heavy weather; **depression**, recession, **slump**, economic stagnation, bust (*informal*)

7 **unfortunate**, poor unfortunate, the plaything *or* toy *or* sport of fortune, fortune's fool; **loser** *and* sure loser *and* non-starter (*all informal*); schlemiel, schlimazel (*both Yiddish*); odd man out; the underclass, the dispossessed, the homeless, the wretched of the earth; victim *see* 96.11

verbs

8 **to go hard with**, go ill with; run one hard; **oppress, weigh on** *or* **upon**, weigh heavy on, weigh down, **burden**, overburden, load, overload, bear hard upon, lie on, lie hard *or* heavy upon; try one, put one out

9 **to have trouble**; be born to trouble, be born under an evil star,
be "born unto trouble, as the sparks fly upward"— BIBLE; **have a hard time of it**, be up against it (*informal*), make heavy weather of it, meet adversity, have a bad time, lead *or* live a dog's life, have a tough *or* hard row to hoe; bear the brunt, bear more than one's share; be put to one's wit's end, not know which way to turn; **be unlucky, have bad** *or* **rotten luck**, be misfortuned, get the short *or* shitty end of the stick (*US & Canadian informal*), draw the short straw

10 **to come to grief**, have a mishap, suffer a misfortune, fall, be stricken, be staggered, be shattered, be poleaxed, be felled, come a cropper (*informal*), be clobbered (*informal*); score an own goal (*informal*), shoot oneself in the foot, be hoist with one's own petard; run aground, go on the rocks *or* shoals, split upon a rock; sink, drown; **founder**

11 **to fall on evil days**, go *or* come down in the world, go downhill, slip, be on the skids (*informal*), come down, have a comedown, fall from one's high estate; **deteriorate**, degenerate, run *or* go to seed, sink, decline; **go to pot** (*informal*), go to the dogs;

reach the depths, touch bottom, hit rock bottom; have seen better days

12 **to bring bad luck**; hoodoo *and* hex *and* jinx *and* Jonah *and* put the jinx on (*all informal*); put the evil eye on, point the bone at, whammy (*informal*)

adjectives

13 **adverse, untoward, detrimental, unfavourable**; sinister; hostile, antagonistic, inimical; contrary, counter, counteractive, conflicting, opposing, opposed, opposite, in opposition; **difficult, troublesome, troublous, hard**, trying, rigorous, stressful; wretched, miserable *see* 96.26; **not easy**; harmful *see* 999.12

14 **unfortunate, unlucky, unprovidential, unblessed, unprosperous**, sad, unhappy, hapless, fortuneless, misfortuned, luckless, donsie (*informal*); **out of luck**, short of luck; **down on one's luck** (*informal*), badly *or* ill off, down in the world, in adverse circumstances; underprivileged, depressed; ill-starred, evil-starred, born under a bad sign, born under an evil star, planet-stricken, planet-struck, star-crossed; fatal, dire, doomful, funest (*old*), ominous, inauspicious *see* 133.17; **in a jam** *and* in a pickle *or* pretty pickle *and* in a tight spot *and* between a rock and a hard place (*all informal*), between the devil and the deep blue sea, caught in the crossfire *or* middle; up a tree *and* up the creek *or* up shit creek without a paddle *and* up to one's arse in alligators (*all informal*)

15 **disastrous, calamitous, catastrophic, cataclysmic**, cataclysmal, **tragic**, ruinous, wreckful (*old*), fatal, dire, black, woeful, sore, baneful, grievous, rough; destructive *see* 395.26; **life-threatening, terminal**

adverbs

16 **adversely, untowardly**, detrimentally, **unfavourably**; contrarily, conflictingly, opposingly, oppositely

17 **unfortunately, unluckily**, unprovidentially, sadly, unhappily, **as ill luck would have it**; by ill luck, by ill hap; in adverse circumstances, if the worst comes to the worst

18 **disastrously**, calamitously, catastrophically, cataclysmically, grievously, woefully, sorely, banefully, tragically, crushingly, shatteringly

exclamations

19 **tough luck!**, tough shit! *and* tough titty! (*both informal*)

1011 HINDRANCE

nouns

1 **hindrance, hindering, hampering**, let, let or hindrance; **check, arrest**, arrestment, arrestation; fixation; **impediment**, holdback; **resistance, opposition** *see* 451; suppression, **repression, restriction, restraint** *see* 428; obstruction, blocking, blockage, clogging, occlusion; **bottleneck**, traffic jam, gridlock, snarl-up; speed bump, sleeping policeman, road hump; **interruption**, interference; **retardation**, retardment, **detention**, detainment, delay, holdup, setback; **inhibition**; constriction, squeeze, stricture, cramp, stranglehold; **closure,** closing up *or* off; obstructionism, bloody-mindedness, negativism, foot-dragging (*informal*); nuisance value

2 **prevention, stop, stoppage, stopping,** arrestation, estoppel; stay, staying, halt, halting, **prohibition,** forbiddance; debarment; **determent,** deterrence, **discouragement; forestalling, preclusion, obviation,** foreclosure

3 **frustration, thwarting, balking, foiling;** discomfiture, disconcertion, bafflement, confounding; **defeat,** upset; check, checkmate, balk, foil (*old*); derailing, derailment

4 **obstacle, obstruction,** obstructer; **hang-up** (*informal*); **block,** blockade, cordon, curtain; **difficulty,** hurdle, hazard, facer; **deterrent,** determent; **drawback,** objection; **stumbling block,** stumbling stone, stone in one's path, spanner in the works; fly in the ointment, one small difficulty, **hitch, catch,** joker (*US informal*), a "but", a "however"

5 **barrier, bar;** gate, portcullis; **fence, wall,** stone wall, brick wall, impenetrable wall; seawall, jetty, groyne, mole, breakwater; **bulwark, rampart,** defence, buffer, bulkhead, parapet, breastwork, work, earthwork, mound; bank, embankment, levee, dike; ditch, moat; dam, weir, leaping weir, barrage, milldam, beaver dam, cofferdam, wicket dam, shutter dam, bear-trap dam, hydraulic-fill dam, rock-fill dam, arch dam, arch-gravity dam, gravity dam; boom, jam, logjam; roadblock; backstop; iron curtain, bamboo curtain

6 **impediment,** embarrassment, hamper; encumbrance, cumbrance; **trouble,** difficulty *see* 1012; **handicap,** disadvantage, inconvenience, penalty; white elephant; **burden,** burthen (*old*), imposition, onus, cross, weight, deadweight, ball and chain, millstone around one's neck; **load,** pack, cargo, freight, charge; impedimenta, lumber

7 **curb, check,** countercheck, arrest, **stay, stop,** damper, holdback; **brake,** clog, drag, drogue; clamp, wheelclamp; chock, scotch, spoke, spoke in one's wheel; doorstop; check-rein, bearing rein, martingale; bit, snaffle, pelham, curb bit; shackle, chain, fetter, trammel *see* 428.4; sea anchor, drift anchor, drift sail, drag sail *or* sheet

8 **hinderer,** impeder, **marplot,** obstructer; frustrater, thwarter; obstructionist, negativist; filibuster, filibusterer

9 **spoilsport, wet blanket, killjoy,** grouch, grump (*informal*), sourpuss (*informal*), malcontent, **dog in the manger** (*informal*)

verbs

10 **to hinder, impede, inhibit, arrest, check,** countercheck, scotch, **curb,** snub; **resist, oppose** *see* 451.3; stonewall (*informal*), stall, stall off; **suppress, repress** *see* 428.8; **interrupt,** intercept (*old*); intervene, interfere, intermeddle, meddle *see* 214.7; damp, dampen, pour *or* dash *or* throw cold water; **retard,** slacken, **delay,** detain, **hold back, keep back,** set back, hold up (*informal*); **restrain** *see* 428.7; keep *or* hold in check, bottle up, dam up

11 **to hamper, impede, cramp,** embarrass; trammel, entrammel, enmesh, entangle, ensnarl, entrap, entwine, involve, entoil, toil, net, lime, tangle, snarl; fetter, shackle; **handcuff,** tie one's hands; **encumber,** cumber, **burden,** lumber, **saddle with,** weigh *or* weight down, press down; hang like a millstone round one's neck; **handicap,** put at a disadvantage; lame, cripple, hobble, hamstring, clamp, wheelclamp

12 **to obstruct, get *or* stand in the way;** dog, **block,** block the way, put up a roadblock, blockade, block up, occlude; **jam,** crowd, pack; **bar,** barricade, bolt, lock; **debar,** shut out; shut off, **close,** close off *or* up, close tight, shut tight; constrict, squeeze, squeeze shut, **strangle,** strangulate, **stifle,** suffocate, **choke,** choke off, chock; stop up *see* 293.7

13 **to stop, stay, halt,** bring to a stop, put a stop *or* end to, bring to a shuddering *or* screeching halt (*informal*); **brake,** slow down, put on the brakes, hit the brakes (*informal*), slam on the brakes (*informal*), slam on the anchors (*informal*); **block, stall, stymie,** deadlock; nip in the bud

14 **to prevent, prohibit, forbid; bar,** estop; save, help, **keep from; deter, discourage,** dishearten; **avert, parry, keep off, ward off, stave off, fend off,** fend, repel, deflect, turn aside; **forestall,** foreclose, **preclude,** exclude, debar, **obviate,** anticipate; rule out

15 **to thwart, frustrate, foil, cross, balk;** spike, scotch, checkmate; **counter,** contravene, counteract, countermand, counterwork; stand in the way of, confront, brave, defy, challenge; **defeat** *see* 412.6, 8, 9; **discomfit,** upset, **disrupt, confound,** flummox (*informal*), discountenance, put out of countenance, **disconcert, baffle,** nonplus, perplex, stump (*informal*); throw on one's beam ends, trip one up, throw one for a loss (*US & Canadian informal*); **circumvent,** elude; sabotage, **spoil, ruin,** dish (*informal*), dash, blast; **destroy** *see* 395.10; **throw a spanner into the works** (*informal*), throw a monkey wrench into the works (*US & Canadian informal*), throw a wrench in the machinery (*US & Canadian informal*); put a spoke in one's wheel, scotch one's wheel, spike one's guns, put one's nose out of joint (*informal*), upset one's applecart, put the mockers on (*informal*), put the mock *or* mocks on (*Australian informal*), queer one's pitch (*informal*); **derail;** take the wind out of one's sails, steal one's thunder, cut the ground from under one, pull the rug from under one, knock the chocks *or* props from under one, knock the bottom out of (*informal*), put one's gas at a peep (*Scottish*); tie one's hands, clip one's wings

16 (*informal terms*) **to queer,** crab (*US*), **foul up, louse up,** snafu, bollocks *or* ballocks up, balls up, bugger, bugger up, fuck up, gum, **gum up,** gum up the works; cramp, cramp one's style; cook one's goose, cut one down to size; give one a hard time

adjectives

17 **hindering,** troublesome; **inhibitive,** inhibiting, suppressive, repressive; constrictive, strangling, stifling, choking; restrictive *see* 428.12; **obstructive,** obstructing, occlusive, obstruent (*old*); cantankerous

(*informal*), bloody-minded, thrawn (*dialect*), contrary, crosswise; interruptive, interrupting; in the way

18 **hampering, impeding, counterproductive,** impedimental, impeditive; onerous, oppressive, burdensome, cumbersome, cumbrous, encumbering

19 **preventive,** preventative, avertive, prophylactic; **prohibitive, forbidding; deterrent,** deterring, **discouraging;** preclusive, forestalling

20 **frustrating,** confounding, disconcerting, baffling, defeating

adverbs

21 under handicap, at a disadvantage, on the hip (*old*), with everything against one

1012 DIFFICULTY

nouns

1 **difficulty,** difficultness;
"the nurse of greatness"—WILLIAM CULLEN BRYANT; **hardness, toughness** (*informal*), the hard way (*informal*), **rigour,** rigorousness, ruggedness; **arduousness,** laboriousness, strenuousness, toilsomeness; **troublesomeness,** bothersomeness; onerousness, oppressiveness, burdensomeness; formidability, hairiness (*informal*); complication, intricacy, **complexity** *see* 798; abstruseness *see* 522.2

2 **tough proposition** *and* tough one *and* toughie (*all informal*), large *or* tall order (*informal*), **hard job, tough job** (*informal*), backbreaker, ballbreaker (*informal*), **chore,** man-sized job; brutal task, Herculean task, Augean task; **uphill work** *or* **going,** rough go (*informal*), hard pull (*informal*), dead lift (*old*); hard road to travel; hard *or* tough nut to crack *and* hard *or* tough row to hoe (*all informal*); bitch (*informal*), pig (*informal*), snorter (*informal*); **handful** (*informal*), all one can manage

3 **trouble, the matter;** headache (*informal*), problem, besetment, **inconvenience,** disadvantage; the bad part, the downside (*informal*); ado, great ado; peck of troubles,
"sea of troubles"—SHAKESPEARE; hornet's nest, Pandora's box, can of worms (*informal*); **evil** *see* 999.3; **bother, annoyance** *see* 98.7; **anxiety, worry** *see* 126.2

4 **predicament, plight,** spot of trouble, spot of bother, **strait,** straits, parlous straits, tightrope, knife-edge, thin edge; **pinch, bind,** pass, situation, emergency; pretty pass, nice *or* pretty predicament, pretty *or* fine state of affairs, **sorry plight;** slough, quagmire, morass, swamp, quicksand; **embarrassment,** embarrassing position *or* situation; **complication,** imbroglio; the devil to pay, hell to pay

5 (*informal terms*) pickle, crunch, hobble, pretty pickle, fine kettle of fish, how-do-you-do, fine how-do-you-do; **spot, tight spot; squeeze, tight squeeze,** ticklish *or* tricky spot, hot spot, hot seat, sticky wicket; **scrape, jam, hot water,** tail in a gate; **mess,** holy *or* unholy mess, mix, stew

6 **impasse, corner** *and* **box** *and* **hole** (*all informal*), cleft stick; **cul-de-sac, blind alley, dead end,** dead-end street; **extremity, end of one's rope** *or*

tether, wit's end, nowhere to turn; **stalemate,** deadlock; stand, standoff, standstill, halt, stop

7 **dilemma,** horns of a dilemma, double bind, damned-if-you-do-and-damned-if-you-don't, no-win situation, **quandary,** nonplus; **vexed question,** thorny problem, knotty point, knot, crux, node, nodus, Gordian knot, poser, teaser, facer, tickler, perplexity, puzzle, enigma *see* 522.8; paradox, oxymoron; asses' bridge, *pons asinorum* (*Latin*)

8 **crux, hitch, pinch, rub,** snag, catch, joker (*US informal*), where the shoe pinches

9 **unwieldiness, unmanageability; unhandiness,** inconvenience, impracticality; **awkwardness, clumsiness; cumbersomeness,** ponderousness, bulkiness, hulkiness

verbs

10 **to be difficult, present difficulties, take some doing** (*informal*)

11 **to have difficulty, have trouble,** have a rough time (*informal*), hit a snag, have a hard time of it, have one's hands full, get off to a bad start *or* on the wrong foot; be hard put, have much ado with; labour under difficulties, labour under a disadvantage, have the cards stacked against one (*informal*), have two strikes against one (*US & Canadian informal*); struggle, **flounder,** beat about, make heavy weather of it; have one's back to the wall, not know where to turn, come to a dead end *or* standstill, not know whether one is coming or going, go around in circles, swim against the current; walk a tightrope, walk on eggshells *or* hot coals, dance on a hot griddle

12 **to get into trouble,** plunge into difficulties; **let oneself in for,** put one's foot in it (*informal*); **get in a jam** *or* **hot water** *or* **the soup** (*informal*), **get into a scrape** (*informal*), get in a mess *or* hole *or* box *or* bind (*informal*); paint oneself into a corner (*informal*), put oneself in a spot (*informal*), put one's foot in one's mouth; have a tiger by the tail; burn one's fingers; get all tangled *or* snarled *or* wound up, get all balled *or* bollocksed up (*informal*)

13 **to trouble,** beset; **bother,** pother, get one down (*informal*), **disturb, perturb,** irk, plague, **torment,** drive one up the wall (*informal*), give one grey hair, make one lose sleep, lead one a dance; **harass, vex, distress** *see* 96.16; inconvenience, **put out,** put out of the way, discommode *see* 995.4; **concern, worry** *see* 126.3; **puzzle, perplex** *see* 970.13; put to it, give one trouble, complicate matters; give one a hard time *and* give one a bad time *and* make it tough for (*all informal*); be too much for; ail, be the matter

14 **to cause trouble, bring trouble,**
"sow the wind and reap the whirlwind"—BIBLE; ask for trouble, ask for it (*informal*), bring down upon one, bring down upon one's head, bring down around one's ears; **stir up a hornet's nest,** kick up a fuss *or* storm *or* row (*informal*); bring a hornet's nest about one's ears, open Pandora's box, open a can of worms (*informal*); **raise hell** (*informal*); raise merry hell *and* play hell (*both informal*), play the deuce *or* devil (*informal*)

15 **to put in a hole** (*informal*), put in a spot (*informal*); **embarrass; involve,** enmesh, entangle

16 to corner, run *and* drive into a corner (*both informal*), **tree** (*informal*), chase up a tree *or* stump (*informal*), drive *or* force to the wall, push one to the wall, put one's back to the wall, have one on the ropes (*informal*)

adjectives

17 difficult, difficile; **not easy,** no picnic; **hard, tough** *and* **rough** *and* **rugged** (*all informal*), rigorous, brutal, severe; **wicked** *and* **mean** *and* **hairy** (*all informal*), **formidable; arduous, strenuous, toilsome, laborious,** operose, Herculean; steep, uphill; hard-fought; hard-earned; jawbreaking; knotty, knotted; thorny, spiny, set with thorns; delicate, ticklish, tricky, sticky (*informal*), critical, easier said than done, like pulling teeth, fiddly; exacting, demanding; intricate, complex *see* 798.4; abstruse *see* 522.16

18 troublesome, besetting; **bothersome,** irksome, vexatious, painful, plaguey (*informal*), annoying *see* 98.22; **burdensome,** oppressive, onerous, heavy *and* hefty (*both informal*), crushing, backbreaking; **trying,** gruelling

19 unwieldy, unmanageable, unhandy; inconvenient, impractical; **awkward, clumsy, cumbersome,** unmanoeuvrable; contrary, perverse, crosswise; ponderous, bulky, hulky, hulking

20 troubled, trouble-plagued, beset, sore beset; **bothered, vexed,** irked, annoyed *see* 96.21; plagued, **harassed** *see* 96.24; distressed, perturbed *see* 96.22; inconvenienced, embarrassed; put to it *and* hard put to it (*both informal*); **worried, anxious** *see* 126.6, 7; puzzled

21 in trouble, in deep trouble, in a predicament, in a sorry plight, in a pretty pass; in deep water, out of one's depth

22 (*informal terms*) **in deep shit,** in a jam, in a pickle, in a pretty pickle, in a spot, in a tight spot, in a fix, in a hole, in a bind, in a box; in a mess, in a scrape, in hot water, in the soup; up a tree, up to one's arse in alligators, up the creek, up shit creek without a paddle, in Dutch, on the spot, behind the eight ball (*US & Canadian*), in Queer Street, out on a limb, in the hot seat

23 in a dilemma, on the horns of a dilemma, **in a quandary;** between two stools; between Scylla and Charybdis, between the devil and the deep blue sea, between a rock and a hard place (*informal*)

24 at an impasse, at one's wit's end, at a loss, at a stand *or* standstill; **nonplussed,** at a nonplus; **baffled, perplexed, bewildered,** mystified, stuck *and* stumped (*both informal*), stymied

25 cornered, in a corner, with one's back to the wall; **treed** *and* **up a tree** *and* up a stump (*all informal*); at bay, *aux abois* (*French*)

26 straitened, reduced to dire straits, in dire straits, in desperate straits, **pinched,** sore *or* sorely pressed, **hard-pressed, hard up** (*informal*), **up against it** (*informal*); driven from pillar to post; **desperate, in extremities,** *in extremis* (*Latin*), **at the end of one's rope** *or* **tether**

27 stranded, grounded, aground, **on the rocks,** high and dry; **stuck,** stuck *or* set fast; foundered, swamped; castaway, marooned, wrecked, shipwrecked

adverbs

28 with difficulty, difficultly, with much ado; at a stretch; hardly, painfully; the hard way, **arduously, strenuously, laboriously,** toilsomely

29 unwieldily, unmanageably, unhandily, inconveniently; **awkwardly, clumsily, cumbersomely;** ponderously

1013 FACILITY

nouns

1 facility, ease, easiness, facileness, **effortlessness;** lack of hindrance, **smoothness,** freedom; clear coast, clear road *or* course; smooth road, royal road, highroad; easy going, plain sailing, smooth *or* straight sailing; clarity, intelligibility *see* 521; uncomplexity, uncomplicatedness, **simplicity** *see* 797

2 handiness, wieldiness, wieldableness, handleability, **manageability,** manageableness, manoeuvrability; **convenience,** practicality, untroublesomeness; **flexibility, pliancy, pliability,** ductility, malleability; adaptability, feasibility

3 easy thing, mere child's play, simple matter, mere twist of the wrist; easy target, sitting duck (*informal*), easy meat (*informal*); sinecure

4 (*informal terms*) **cinch, snap,** pushover, breeze, doddle, walkover, scoosh (*Scottish*), waltz, duck soup (*US*), picnic, cakewalk, piece of cake, kid's stuff, no-brainer (*US*), setup, easy meat, ludge (*Australian & NZ informal*)

5 facilitation, facilitating, easing, smoothing, smoothing out, smoothing the way; **speeding,** expediting, expedition, quickening, hastening; streamlining; lubricating, greasing, oiling

6 disembarrassment, disentanglement, disencumbrance, disinvolvement, uncluttering, uncomplicating, unscrambling, unsnarling, disburdening, unhampering; **extrication,** disengagement, **freeing,** clearing; deregulation; **simplification** *see* 797.2

verbs

7 to facilitate, ease; grease the wheels (*informal*); **smooth, smooth** *or* **pave the way,** ease the way, prepare the way, **clear the way,** make all clear for, make way for; open the way, open the door to; **open up,** unclog, unblock, unjam, unbar, loose *see* 431.6; **lubricate,** make frictionless *or* dissipationless, remove friction, grease, oil; **speed, expedite,** quicken, hasten; **help along,** help on its way; **aid** *see* 449.11; **explain,** make clear *see* 521.6; **simplify** *see* 797.4

8 to do easily, make short work of, do with one's hands tied behind one's back, do with both eyes shut, do standing on one's head, do hands down, sail *or* dance *or* waltz through, wing it (*informal*)

9 to disembarrass, disencumber, unload, relieve, disburden, unhamper, get out from under; **disentangle,** disembroil, disinvolve, unclutter, unscramble, unsnarl; **extricate,** disengage, **free,** free up, clear; liberate *see* 431.4

10 to go easily, run smoothly, work well, work like a machine, go like clockwork *or* a sewing machine;

present no difficulties, give no trouble, be painless, be effortless; flow, roll, glide, slide, coast, sweep, sail

11 to have it easy, have it soft (*informal*), have it all one's own way, have the game in one's hands; win easily; breeze in (*informal*), walk over the course (*informal*), win in a walk *or* in a canter *or* hands down (*informal*)

12 to take it easy and **go easy** (*both informal*), swim with the stream, drift with the current, go with the tide; cool it *and* not sweat it (*both informal*); take it in one's stride, make little *or* light of, think nothing of

adjectives

13 easy, facile, effortless, smooth, painless; soft (*informal*), cushy (*informal*); plain, uncomplicated, straightforward, **simple** see 797.6, Mickey Mouse (*informal*), simple as ABC (*informal*), easy as pie *and* easy as falling off a log (*both informal*), easy-peasy (*informal*), patsy (*informal*), downhill all the way, like shooting fish in a barrel, like taking candy from a baby; **clear;** glib; **light,** unburdensome; nothing to it; casual, throwaway (*informal*)

14 smooth-running, frictionless, dissipationless, easy-running, easy-flowing; well-lubricated, well-oiled, well-greased

15 handy, wieldy, wieldable, handleable; tractable; flexible, pliant, yielding, malleable, ductile, pliable, **manageable,** manoeuvrable; **convenient,** foolproof, goofproof (*US & Canadian informal*), practical, untroublesome, user-friendly; adaptable, feasible

adverbs

16 easily, facilely, **effortlessly, readily, simply,** lightly, swimmingly (*informal*), without difficulty; no sweat *and* like nothing *and* slick as a whistle (*all informal*); hands down (*informal*), with one hand tied behind one's back, with both eyes closed, standing on one's head; like a duck takes to water; **smoothly,** frictionlessly, like clockwork; on easy terms

1014 UGLINESS

nouns

1 ugliness, unsightliness, unattractiveness, uncomeliness, unhandsomeness, unbeautifulness, unprettiness, unloveliness, unaestheticness, unpleasingness see 98.1; unprepossessingness, ill-favouredness, inelegance; **homeliness,** plainness; unshapeliness, shapelessness; ungracefulness, gracelessness, clumsiness, ungainliness see 414.3; **uglification, uglifying, disfigurement,** defacement; dysphemism; cacophony

2 hideousness, horridness, horribleness, frightfulness, dreadfulness, terribleness, awfulness (*informal*); **repulsiveness** see 98.2, repugnance, repugnancy, repellence, repellency, offensiveness, forbiddingness, loathsomeness; ghastliness, gruesomeness, grisliness; **deformity,** misshapenness

3 forbidding countenance, vinegar aspect, wry face, face that would stop a clock

4 eyesore, blot, blot on the landscape, blemish, **sight** (*informal*), **fright,** disaster, **horror, mess,** no beauty,

no beauty queen, no oil painting, ugly duckling; baboon; **scarecrow,** gargoyle, monster, **monstrosity,** teratism; witch, bag *and* dog (*both informal*), boot (*informal*), trout (*informal*), **hag,** harridan; Loathly Lady

verbs

5 to offend, offend the eye, offend one's aesthetic sensibilities, **look bad;** look something terrible *and* look like hell *and* look like shit *and* look like the devil *and* look a sight *or* a fright *or* a mess *or* like something the cat dragged in (*all informal*); **uglify, disfigure,** deface, blot, blemish, mar, spoil; dysphemize

adjectives

6 ugly, unsightly, unattractive, unhandsome, unpretty, unlovely, uncomely, **inelegant; unbeautiful,** unbeauteous, beautiless, unaesthetic, unpleasing see 98.17; **homely,** plain; not much to look at, not much for looks, short on looks (*informal*), hard on the eyes (*informal*); ugly as sin, ugly as the wrath of God, ugly as hell, ugly enough to sour milk, ugly enough to stop a clock, not fit to be seen; **uglified, disfigured,** defaced, blotted, blemished, marred, spoiled; dysphemized, dysphemistic; cacophonous, cacophonic

7 unprepossessing, ill-favoured, hard-favoured, evil-favoured, ill-featured; ill-looking, evil-looking; hard-featured, hard-visaged; grim, grim-faced, grim-visaged; hatchet-faced, horse-faced

8 unshapely, shapeless, **ill-shaped,** ill-made, ill-proportioned; **deformed,** misshapen, misproportioned, malformed, misbegotten; grotesque, scarecrowish, gargoylish; monstrous, teratic, cacogenic

9 ungraceful, ungraced, graceless; clumsy, clunky (*informal*), **ungainly** see 414.20

10 inartistic, unartistic, **unaesthetic; unornamental, undecorative**

11 hideous, horrid, horrible, frightful, dreadful, terrible, awful (*informal*); **repulsive** see 98.18, repellent, repelling, rebarbative, **repugnant,** offensive, foul, forbidding, loathsome, loathly (*old*), revolting; **ghastly,** gruesome, grisly

adverbs

12 uglily, homelily, uncomelily, **unattractively, unhandsomely, unbeautifully, unprettily**

13 hideously, horridly, horribly, frightfully, dreadfully, terribly, awfully (*informal*); **repulsively, repugnantly,** offensively, forbiddingly, loathsomely, revoltingly; gruesomely, ghastly

1015 BEAUTY

nouns

1 beauty, beautifulness, beauteousness, **prettiness, handsomeness, attractiveness** see 97.2, wellfavouredness, **loveliness, pulchritude, charm,** grace, elegance, exquisiteness; bloom, glow; the beautiful; source of aesthetic pleasure *or* delight; beauty unadorned

2 "truth's smile when she beholds her own face in a perfect mirror"—TAGORE, "the sensible image of the Infinite"—BANCROFT, "God's handwriting"—EMERSON, "a form of genius"—OSCAR WILDE, "the power by which a woman charms a lover and terrifies a husband"—AMBROSE BIERCE

3 comeliness, fairness, sightliness, personableness, becomingness, pleasingness see 97.1, goodliness, bonniness, agreeability, agreeableness

4 good looks, good appearance, good effect; good proportions, aesthetic proportions; shapeliness, good figure, good shape, belle tournure (French), nice body, lovely build, physical or bodily charm, curvaceousness, curves (informal), pneumaticness, sexy body; bodily grace, gracefulness, gracility; good points, beauties, charms, delights, perfections, good features

5 daintiness, delicacy, delicateness; cuteness or cunningness (both informal)

6 gorgeousness, ravishingness; gloriousness, heavenliness, sublimity; splendour, splendidness, splendiferousness, splendorousness or splendrousness, resplendence; brilliance, brightness, radiance, lustre; glamour see 377.1

7 thing of beauty, vision, picture (informal), poem, eyeful (informal), sight or treat for sore eyes (informal)

8 beauty, charmer, charmeuse (French); beauty queen, beauty contest winner, Miss World, bathing beauty; glamour girl, cover girl, model, supermodel; sex goddess; belle, reigning beauty, great beauty, lady fair; beau ideal, paragon; enchantress; "the face that launch'd a thousand ships"—MARLOWE

9 (informal terms) doll, dish, cutie, babe, angel, angelface, babyface, beaut, honey, dream, looker, good-looker, stunner, dazzler, dreamboat, fetcher, crumpet, peach, knockout, raving beauty, centrefold, pinup girl, pinup, bunny, cutie or cutesy pie, cute or slick chick, pussycat, sex kitten, ten

10 (famous beauties) Venus, Venus de Milo; Aphrodite, Hebe; Adonis, Apollo, Apollo Belvedere, Hyperion, Antinoüs, Narcissus; Astarte; Balder, Freya; Helen of Troy, Cleopatra; the Graces, houri, peri

11 beautification, prettification, cutification (informal), adornment; decoration see 498.1; beauty care, beauty treatment, cosmetology; facial (informal); manicure; hairdressing; cosmetic surgery, nose job, facelift, tummy tuck, liposuction

12 makeup, cosmetics, beauty products, beauty-care products; war paint (informal); pancake makeup; powder, talcum, talcum powder; rouge, paint; lip rouge, lipstick, lip gloss; nail polish; greasepaint, clown white; eye makeup, eyeliner, mascara, eye shadow, kohl; cold cream, hand cream or lotion, vanishing cream, foundation cream; foundation, base; mudpack, facepack, face mask; eyebrow pencil; puff, powder puff; compact, vanity case

13 beautician, beautifier, cosmetologist; hairdresser, coiffeur, coiffeuse (both French); barber; manicurist

14 beauty parlour or salon or shop, salon de beauté (French); barbershop

verbs

15 to beautify, prettify, cutify (informal), pretty up or doll up or tart up (all informal), gussy up (US & Canadian informal), grace, adorn; decorate see 498.8; set off, set off to advantage or good advantage, become one; glamourize; make up, paint and put on one's face (both informal), titivate, cosmetize, cosmeticize

16 to look good; look like a million and look fit to kill and knock dead and knock one's eyes out (all informal); take the breath away, beggar description; shine, beam, bloom, glow

adjectives

17 beautiful, beauteous, endowed with beauty; pretty, handsome, attractive see 97.7, pulchritudinous, lovely, graceful, gracile; elegant; aesthetic, aesthetically appealing; cute; pretty as a picture, "lovely as the day"—LONGFELLOW, "fair as is the rose in May"—CHAUCER; tall dark and handsome

18 comely, fair, good-looking, nice-looking, well-favoured, personable, presentable, agreeable, becoming, pleasing see 97.6, goodly, bonny, likely (informal), sightly, braw (Scottish); pleasing to the eye, lovely to behold; shapely, well-built, built, well-shaped, well-proportioned, well-made, well-formed, stacked or well-stacked (both informal), curvaceous, curvy (informal), pneumatic, amply endowed, built for comfort or built like a brick shithouse (both informal), buxom, callipygian, callipygous; Junoesque, statuesque, goddess-like; slender see 270.16; Adonis-like, hunky (informal)

19 fine, exquisite, flowerlike, dainty, delicate, elfin; mignon (French)

20 gorgeous, drop-dead gorgeous, ravishing; glorious, heavenly, divine, sublime; resplendent, splendorous or splendrous, splendiferous, splendid, resplendently beautiful; brilliant, bright, radiant, shining, beaming, glowing, blooming, abloom, sparkling, dazzling; glamorous

21 (informal terms) eye-catching, easy on the eyes, not hard to look at, long on looks, looking fit to kill, dishy, tasty; cutesy, cutesy-poo; raving, devastating, stunning, killing

22 beautifying, cosmetic; decorative see 498.10; cosmetized, cosmeticized, beautified, made-up, mascaraed, titivated

adverbs

23 beautifully, beauteously, prettily, handsomely, attractively, becomingly, comelily; elegantly, exquisitely; charmingly, enchantingly

24 daintily, delicately; cutely

25 gorgeously, ravishingly; ravingly and devastatingly and stunningly (all informal); gloriously, divinely, sublimely; resplendently, splendidly, splendorously or splendrously; brilliantly, brightly, radiantly, glowingly, dazzlingly

word elements

26 cal-, calo-, callo-, cali-, calli-

1016 MATHEMATICS

nouns

1 mathematics (*see list*), maths (*informal*), math (*US informal*), mathematic, **numbers, figures**; pure mathematics, abstract mathematics, applied mathematics, higher mathematics, elementary mathematics, new maths; algorithm; mathematical element (*see list*)

2 (*mathematical operations*) notation, **addition** *see* 253, **subtraction** *see* 255, **multiplication, division,** proportion, practice, equation, extraction of roots, inversion, reduction, involution, evolution, approximation, interpolation, extrapolation, transformation, differentiation, integration

3 number (*see list*), **numeral,** *numero* (*Spanish and Italian*), no *or* n, digit, binary digit *or* bit, **cipher,** character, symbol, sign, notation

4 (*number systems*) **Arabic numerals,** algorism *or* algorithm, Roman numerals; **decimal system,** binary system, octal system, duodecimal system, hexadecimal system

5 large number, astronomical number, zillion *and* jillion *or* squillion (*all informal*); googol, googolplex; infinity, infinitude *see* 822.1; billion, trillion, etc *see* 881.13

6 sum, summation, difference, product, **number, count,** x number, n number; account, cast, **score, reckoning, tally,** tale, the story *and* whole story (*both informal*), all she wrote (*US & Canadian informal*), the bottom line (*informal*), **aggregate, amount,** quantity *see* 244; **whole** *see* 791, **total** *see* 791.2

7 ratio, rate, proportion; quota, quotum; **percentage,** percent; **fraction,** proper fraction, improper fraction, compound fraction, continued fraction; geometric ratio *or* proportion, arithmetical proportion, harmonic proportion; rule of three

8 series, progression; arithmetical progression, geometrical progression, harmonic progression; Fibonacci numbers

9 numeration, enumeration, numbering, counting, accounting, census, inventorying, telling, tallying; page numbering, pagination, foliation; counting on the fingers, dactylonomy; **measurement** *see* 300; quantification, quantization

10 calculation, computation, estimation, reckoning, calculus; adding, footing, casting, ciphering, totalling, toting *or* totting (*informal*)

11 summation, summary, summing, summing up, **recount,** recounting, rehearsal, capitulation, **recapitulation,** recap *and* rehash (*both informal*), statement, **reckoning, count,** repertory, census, inventory, head count, nose count, body count; account, accounts; **table,** reckoner, ready reckoner

12 account of, count of, a reckoning of, **tab** *or* **tabs of** (*informal*), tally of, check of, track of

13 figures, statistics, indexes *or* indices; vital statistics

14 calculator (*see list*), **computer** *see* 1041.2, estimator, figurer, reckoner, abacist; statistician, actuary; accountant, bookkeeper *see* 628.7

15 mathematician, arithmetician; geometer, geometrician; algebraist, trigonometrician, statistician, geodesist, mathematical physicist

verbs

16 to number, numerate, number off, **enumerate, count, tell, tally,** give a figure to, put a figure on, call off, name, call over, run over; **count noses** *or* **heads** (*informal*), call the roll; census, poll; page, paginate, foliate; **measure** *see* 300.11; **round,** round out *or* off *or* down; quantify, quantitate, quantize

17 to calculate, compute, estimate, reckon, figure, reckon at, put at, cipher, cast, tally, score; **figure out,** work out, dope out (*US informal*); take account of, figure in *and* figure on (*both informal*); **add, subtract, multiply, divide,** multiply out, algebraize, extract roots; factor, factor out, factorize; **measure** *see* 300.11

18 to sum up, sum, summate, say it all (*informal*); **figure up,** cipher up, reckon up, **count up, add up,** foot up, cast up, score up, **tally up; total,** total up, tote *or* tot up (*informal*); **summarize, recapitulate,** recap *and* rehash (*both informal*), **recount,** rehearse, recite, relate; detail, itemize, inventory

19 to keep account of, keep count of, **keep track of, keep tab** *or* **tabs** (*informal*), keep tally, keep a check on *or* of

20 to check, verify *see* 969.12, double-check, check on *or* out; **prove,** demonstrate; balance, balance the books; **audit,** overhaul; take stock, inventory

adjectives

21 mathematical, numeric *or* numerical, numerary, arithmetic *or* arithmetical, algebraic *or* algebraical, geometric *or* geometrical, trigonometric *or* trigonometrical, analytic *or* analytical

22 numeric *or* **numerical,** numeral, numerary, numerative; **odd,** impair, **even,** pair; arithmetical, algorismic *or* algorithmic; **cardinal, ordinal;** figural, **figurate,** figurative, **digital;** aliquot, submultiple, **reciprocal,** prime, fractional, decimal, exponential, **logarithmic,** logometric, differential, integral; positive, negative; rational, irrational, transcendental; surd, radical; real, imaginary; possible, impossible, finite, infinite, transfinite

23 numerative, enumerative; calculative, computative, estimative; **calculating,** computing, computational, estimating; statistical; quantifying, quantizing

24 calculable, computable, reckonable, estimable, countable, numberable, enumerable, numerable; **measurable,** mensurable, quantifiable

25 kinds of mathematics

addition algebra	combinatorial topology
affine geometry	commutative algebra
algebra	complex *or* double algebra
algebraic geometry	denumerative geometry
analysis	descriptive geometry
analytic geometry	differential calculus
arithmetic	division algebra
associative algebra	elementary arithmetic
binary arithmetic	elementary *or* ordinary
Boolean algebra	algebra
calculus	equivalent algebras
calculus of differences	Euclidean geometry
circle geometry	Fourier analysis
combinatorial mathematics	game theory

geodesic geometry
geodesy
geometry
Gödel's proof
graphic algebra
group theory
higher algebra
higher arithmetic
hyperalgebra
hyperbolic geometry
infinitesimal calculus
integral calculus
intuitional geometry
invariant subalgebra
inverse geometry
Lagrangian function
Laplace's equation
linear algebra
line geometry
mathematical physics
matrix algebra
metageometry
modular arithmetic
multiple algebra
natural geometry
new maths
nilpotent algebra
noncommutative algebra
non-Euclidean geometry

n-tuple linear algebra
number theory
plane geometry
plane trigonometry
point-set topology
political arithmetic
projective geometry
proper subalgebra
quadratics
quaternian algebra
reducible algebra
Riemannian geometry
semisimple algebra
set theory
simple algebra
solid geometry
speculative geometry
sphere geometry
spherical trigonometry
statistics
subalgebra
systems analysis
topology
trigonometry *or* trig
  (informal)
universal algebra
universal geometry
vector algebra
zero algebra

26 mathematical elements

addend
algorithm
aliquot
antilogarithm
argument
auxiliary equation
base
Bessel function
binomial
characteristic
characteristic equation
characteristic function
characteristic polynomial
characteristic root *or*
  characteristic value *or*
  eigenvalue *or* latent root
  or proper value
characteristic vector
coefficient
combination
common divisor *or*
  measure
complement
congruence
constant
cosecant
cosine
cotangent
cube
cube root
decimal
denominator
derivative

determinant
difference *or* remainder
differential
discriminate
dividend
division sign
divisor
e
elliptical function
empty set *or* null set
equal sign
equation
exponent
exponential
factor
factorial
formula
fraction
function
greatest common divisor *or*
  GCD
haversine
hyperbolic
i
increment
index
integral
Laplace transform
least common denominator
  or LCD
least common multiple *or*
  LCM
logarithm

mantissa
matrix
minuend
minus sign
mixed decimal
modulus
monomial
multiple
multiplicand
multiplicator
multiplier
norm
numerator
parameter
part
permutation
pi (ρ)
plus sign
polynomial
power
quadratic equation
quaternion
quotient
radical

radix
reciprocal
repeating *or* circulating
  decimal
root
secant
set
simultaneous equations
sine
square root
submultiple
subtrahend
summand
tangent
tensor
topological group
topological space
variable
vector
vector product
vector sum
versed sine *or* versine
vulgar fraction

27 kinds of numbers

abundant number
algebraic number
cardinal number *or*
  cardinal
complex *or* Gaussian
  integer
complex number
composite *or* rectangular
  number
deficient *or* defective
  number
even number *or* pair
Fermat number
figurate number
finite number
fraction
imaginary number *or* pure
  imaginary
infinity

integer *or* whole number
irrational number *or*
  irrational
Mersenne number
mixed number
odd number *or* impair
ordinal number *or* ordinal
perfect number
polygonal number
prime *or* rectilinear
  number
pyramidal number
rational number *or* rational
real number *or* real
round *or* rounded number
serial number
surd *or* surd quantity
transcendental number
transfinite number

28 calculators

abacus
adding machine
analog computer
arithmograph
arithmometer
calculating machine
cash register
Comptometer (trademark)
computer *or* electronic
  computer
counter
difference engine

digital computer
listing machine
Napier's bones *or* rods
pari-mutuel machine
pocket calculator
quipu
rule
slide rule *or* sliding scale
suan pan (Chinese)
tabulator
totalizator
Turing machine

1017 PHYSICS

nouns

1 **physics;** natural *or* physical science; philosophy *or*
  second philosophy *or* natural philosophy *or* physic

(*all old*); **branch of physics** (*see list*); physical theory, quantum theory, relativity theory, special relativity theory, general relativity theory, unified field theory, grand unified theory *or* GUT, superunified theory *or* theory of everything *or* TOE, eightfold way, superstring theory

2 **physicist,** aerophysicist, astrophysicist, biophysicist, etc

adjectives

3 **physical;** aerophysical, astrophysical, biophysical, etc
4 **branches of physics**

acoustics	mathematical physics
aerophysics	mechanics
applied physics	medicophysics
astrophysics	microphysics
basic conductor physics	molecular physics
biophysics	morphophysics
chaos theory *or* chaos	myophysics
dynamics *or* chaology	nuclear physics
chemical physics *or*	optics
chemicophysics	organismic physics
classical physics *or*	physical chemistry *or*
Newtonian physics	physicochemistry
condensed-matter physics	physicomathematics
cryogenics	plasma physics
crystallography	psychophysics
cytophysics	quantum physics
electron optics	radiation physics
electronics *or* electron	radionics
physics	solar physics
electrophysics	solid-state physics
geophysics	statics
high-energy physics	stereophysics
hyperphysics	theoretical physics
hypophysics	thermodynamics
iatrophysics	X-ray crystallography
macrophysics	zoophysics

1018 HEAT

nouns

1 **heat, hotness,** heatedness; superheat, superheatedness; calidity *or* caloric (*both old*); **warmth,** warmness; incalescence; radiant heat, thermal radiation, induction heat, convector *or* convected heat, coal heat, gas heat, oil heat, hot-air heat, steam heat, electric heat, solar heat, dielectric heat, ultraviolet heat, atomic heat, molecular heat; animal heat, body heat, blood heat, hypothermia; fever heat, fever; heating, burning *see* 1019.5

2 (*metaphors*) **ardour,** ardency, **fervour,** fervency, fervidness, fervidity; eagerness *see* 101; excitement *see* 105; **anger** *see* 152.5, 8, 9; **sexual desire** *see* 75.5; love 104

3 **temperature,** temp (*informal*); room temperature, comfortable temperature; comfort index, temperature-humidity index *or* THI; flash point; boiling point; melting point, freezing point; dew point; recalescence point; zero, absolute zero; regulo

4 **lukewarmness,** tepidness, tepidity; tepidarium
5 **torridness,** torridity; extreme heat, intense heat, torrid heat, red heat, white heat, tropical heat,

sweltering heat, Afric heat, Indian heat, Bengal heat, summer heat, oppressive heat;

"where the sun beats, and the dead tree gives no shelter, the cricket no relief"—T S Eliot; **hot wind** *see* 318.7

6 **sultriness, stuffiness, closeness,** oppressiveness, fug; **humidity, humidness, mugginess,** stickiness (*informal*), swelter

7 **hot weather,** sunny *or* sunshiny weather; sultry weather, stuffy weather, humid weather, muggy weather, sticky weather (*informal*); summer, midsummer, high summer; Indian summer, **dog days,** canicular days, canicule; **heat wave,** hot wave; broiling sun, midday sun; vertical rays; warm weather, fair weather

8 **hot day,** summer day; **scorcher** *and* **roaster** *and* **broiler** *and* **sizzler** *and* swelterer (*all informal*)

9 **hot air,** superheated air; **thermal;** firestorm
10 **hot water,** boiling water; **steam,** vapour; volcanic water; hot *or* warm *or* thermal spring, thermae; geyser, Old Faithful

11 (*hot place*) **oven, furnace,** fiery furnace, inferno, hell; suntrap; steam bath; **tropics,** subtropics, Torrid Zone; equator

12 **glow,** incandescence, fieriness; **flush, blush, bloom,** redness *see* 41, rubicundity, rosiness; whiteness *see* 37; thermochromism; hectic, hectic flush

13 **fire; blaze, flame,** ingle, devouring element; **combustion, ignition,** ignition temperature *or* point, flash *or* flashing point; **conflagration;** flicker *see* 1024.8, wavering *or* flickering flame,

"lambent flame"—Dryden; smouldering fire, sleeping fire; marshfire, fen fire, ignis fatuus, will-o'-the-wisp; fox fire; witch fire, St Elmo's fire, corposant; **cheerful fire,** cosy fire, crackling fire,

"bright-flaming, heatfull fire"—Du Bartas; **roaring fire,** blazing fire; **raging fire,** sheet of fire, sea of flames,

"whirlwinds of tempestuous fire"—Milton; bonfire, balefire; beacon fire, beacon, signal beacon, watch fire; alarm fire, two-alarm fire, three-alarm fire, etc; wildfire, prairie fire, forest fire, bushfire; backfire; backdraught; brushfire; open fire; campfire; smudge fire; death fire, pyre, funeral pyre, crematory; burning ghat

14 **flare, flare-up, flash,** flash fire, **blaze,** burst, outburst; deflagration

15 **spark,** sparkle; **scintillation,** scintilla; ignescence
16 **coal,** live coal, brand, firebrand, **ember,** burning ember; **cinder**

17 **fireworks** (*see list*), **pyrotechnics** *or* pyrotechny
18 (*perviousness to heat*) transcalency; adiathermancy, athermancy

19 **thermal unit;** British thermal unit *or* BTU; Board of Trade unit *or* BOT; centigrade thermal unit; centigrade *or* Celsius scale, Fahrenheit scale; **calorie,** mean calorie, centuple *or* rational calorie, small calorie, large *or* great calorie, kilocalorie, kilogram calorie; therm

20 **thermometer,** thermal detector; mercury, glass; thermostat

21 (*science of heat*) thermochemistry, thermology, thermotics, thermodynamics; volcanology; pyrology,

pyrognostics; pyrotechnics *or* pyrotechny, ebulliometry; calorimetry

verbs

22 (*be hot*) **to burn** *see* 1019.24, **scorch**, parch, scald, **swelter, roast**, toast, cook, bake, fry, broil, boil, seethe, simmer, stew; **be in heat**; shimmer with heat, give off waves of heat, radiate heat; **blaze**, combust, spark, **catch fire, flame** *see* 1019.23, flame up, **flare**, flare up; **flicker** *see* 1024.25; **glow**, incandesce, flush, bloom; smoulder; steam; sweat *see* 12.16; gasp, pant; **suffocate, stifle**, smother, choke

23 **to smoke, fume**, reek; smudge

adjectives

24 **warm**, calid (*old*), **thermal**, thermic; **toasty** (*informal*), warm as toast; **sunny**, sunshiny; fair, mild, genial; summery, aestival; **temperate**, warmish; **tropical**, equatorial, subtropical; semitropical; **tepid, lukewarm**, luke; room-temperature; blood-warm, blood-hot; unfrozen

25 **hot, heated, torrid**; **sweltering**, sweltry, canicular; **burning**, parching, scorching, searing, scalding, blistering, baking, roasting, toasting, broiling, grilling, simmering; **boiling**, seething, ebullient; **piping hot**, scalding hot, burning hot, roasting hot, scorching hot, sizzling hot, smoking hot; **red-hot**, white-hot; ardent; flushed, sweating, sweaty, sudorific; overwarm, overhot, overheated; hot as fire, hot as hell *or* blazes, hot as the hinges of hell, hot enough to roast an ox, so hot you can fry eggs on the pavement (*informal*), like a furnace *or* an oven; feverish

26 **fiery**, igneous, firelike, pyric; combustive, conflagrative

27 **burning, ignited**, kindled, enkindled, **blazing**, ablaze, ardent, flaring, flaming, aflame, inflamed, alight, in, **afire, on fire**, in flames, in a blaze, flagrant (*old*); conflagrant, comburent; live, living; **glowing**, aglow, in a glow, incandescent, candescent, candent; sparking, scintillating, scintillant, ignescent; **flickering**, aflicker, guttering; unquenched, unextinguished; slow-burning; **smouldering**; **smoking**, fuming, reeking

28 **sultry, stifling, suffocating, stuffy, close**, oppressive; **humid, sticky** (*informal*), **muggy**

29 warm-blooded, hot-blooded

30 isothermal, isothermic; centigrade, Fahrenheit

31 diathermic, diathermal, transcalent; adiathermic, adiathermal, athermanous

32 pyrological, pyrognostic, pyrotechnic *or* pyrotechnical; pyrogenic *or* pyrogenous *or* pyrogenetic; thermochemical; thermodynamic, thermodynamical

word elements

33 igni–, pyr–, pyro–; therm–, thermo–, –thermous
34 fireworks

banger	cap
bunger (Australian informal)	Catherine wheel cherry bomb
bomb	cracker
candlebomb	cracker bonbon
cannon cracker	firecracker

fizgig	serpent
flare	skyrocket
flowerpot	snake
girandole	sparkler
ladyfinger	squib
pinwheel	torpedo
rocket	whiz-bang
Roman candle	

1019 HEATING

nouns

1 **heating, warming**, calefaction, torrefaction, increase *or* raising of temperature; superheating; pyrogenesis; decalescence, recalescence; preheating; **heating system** (*see list*), heating method; solar radiation, insolation; dielectric heating; induction heating; heat exchange; cooking *see* 11

2 **boiling**, seething, **stewing**, ebullition, ebullience *or* ebulliency, coction; decoction; **simmering**; boil; simmer

3 **melting, fusion**, liquefaction, liquefying, liquescence, running; **thawing**, thaw; liquation; fusibility; thermoplasticity

4 **ignition, lighting**, lighting up *or* off, **kindling**, firing; reaching flash point *or* flashing point

5 **burning, combustion**, blazing, flaming; **scorching**, parching, singeing; **searing**, branding; **blistering**, vesication; **cauterization**, cautery; **incineration**; **cremation**; suttee, self-cremation, self-immolation; the stake, burning at the stake, *auto da fé* (*Portuguese*); scorification; carbonization; oxidation, oxidization; calcination; cupellation; deflagration; distilling, distillation; refining, smelting; pyrolysis; cracking, thermal cracking, destructive distillation; **spontaneous combustion**, thermogenesis

6 **burn**, scald, scorch, singe; sear; brand; sunburn, sunscald; windburn; mat burn; first- *or* second- *or* third-degree burn

7 **incendiarism, arson**, torch job (*informal*), fire-raising; **pyromania**; pyrophilia; pyrolatry, fire worship

8 **incendiary, arsonist**, torcher (*informal*); pyromaniac, firebug (*informal*); pyrophile, fire buff (*informal*); pyrolater, fire worshipper

9 **flammability, inflammability**, combustibility

10 **heater, warmer**; **stove, furnace**; **cooker**, cookery; firebox; tuyere, tewel (*old*); burner, jet, gas jet, pilot light *or* burner, element, heating element; heating pipe, steam pipe, hot-water pipe; heating duct, caliduct; hot-water cylinder, immersion heater *or* immerser, geyser

11 **fireplace, hearth**, ingle, chimney; **fireside**, hearthside, ingleside, inglenook, ingle cheek (*Scottish*), chimney corner; hearthstone; hob, hub; fireguard, fireboard, fire screen, fender; chimney, chimney piece, chimney-breast, chimney-pot, chimney-stack, flue; smokehole

12 **fire iron; andiron**, firedog; tongs, pair of tongs, fire tongs, coal tongs; poker, stove poker, salamander, fire hook; lifter, stove lifter; pothook, crook, crane, chain; trivet, tripod; spit, turnspit; grate, grating; gridiron, grid, griddle, grill, griller; damper

13 incinerator, cinerator, burner; solid-waste incinerator, garbage incinerator; **crematory,** cremator, crematorium, burning ghat; calcinatory

14 blowtorch, blowlamp, blast lamp, torch, alcohol torch, butane torch; soldering torch; blowpipe; **burner; welder;** acetylene torch *or* welder, cutting torch *or* blowpipe, oxyacetylene blowpipe *or* torch, welding blowpipe *or* torch

15 cauterant, cauterizer, cauter, cautery, thermocautery, actual cautery; hot iron, **branding iron,** brand iron, brand; moxa; electrocautery; **caustic, corrosive,** mordant, escharotic, potential cautery; acid; lunar caustic; radium

16 (*products of combustion*) scoria, sullage, slag, dross; **ashes,** ash; **cinder,** clinker, coal, nut; coke, charcoal, brand, lava, carbon, calx; **soot,** smut, coom (*informal*); **smoke,** smudge, fume, reek

verbs

17 to heat, raise *or* increase the temperature, hot *or* hot up, **warm,** warm up, fire, fire up, stoke up; chafe; take the chill off; tepefy; gas-heat, oil-heat, hot-air-heat, hot-water-heat, steam-heat, electric-heat, solar-heat; superheat; overheat; preheat; **reheat,** recook, warm over; mull; steam; foment; cook *see* 11.4

18 (*metaphors*) **to excite,** inflame; incite, **kindle,** arouse *see* 375.17, 19; anger, **enrage**

19 to insolate, sun-dry; **sun,** bask, bask in the sun, sun oneself, sunbathe

20 to boil, stew, **simmer, seethe;** distil

21 to melt, melt down, liquefy; **run,** colliquate, **fuse,** flux; refine, smelt; render; **thaw,** thaw out, unfreeze; defrost, de-ice

22 to ignite, set fire to, fire, set on fire, kindle, enkindle, inflame, **light,** light up, strike a light, apply the match *or* torch to, torch (*informal*), touch off, **burn,** conflagrate; **build a fire;** rekindle, relight, relume; feed, feed the fire, **stoke,** stoke the fire, add fuel to the flame; bank; poke *or* stir the fire, blow up the fire, fan the flame

23 to catch fire, catch on fire, catch, take fire, **burn, flame,** combust, blaze, **blaze up, burst into flames**

24 to burn, torrefy, **scorch, parch, sear; singe,** swinge; **blister,** vesicate; **cauterize,** brand, burn in; **char,** coal, carbonize; scorify; calcine; pyrolyse, crack; solder, weld; vulcanize; cast, found; oxidize, oxidate; deflagrate; cupel; burn off; blaze, flame *see* 1018.22

25 to burn up, incendiarize, **incinerate, cremate,** consume, burn *or* reduce to ashes, **burn to a crisp,** burn to a cinder; **burn down,** burn to the ground, **go up in smoke**

adjectives

26 heating, warming, chafing, calorific; calefactory, calefactive, calefacient, calorifacient, calorigenic; fiery, burning *see* 1018.25, 27; cauterant, cauterizing; calcinatory

27 inflammatory, inflammative, **inflaming, kindling,** enkindling, lighting; **incendiary,** incendive; arsonous

28 flammable, inflammable, combustible, burnable

29 heated, het *or* het up (*both informal*), hotted up, **warmed,** warmed up, centrally heated, gas-heated,

oil-heated, paraffin-heated, kerosene-heated, hot-water-heated, hot-air-heated, steam-heated, solar-heated, electric-heated, baseboard-heated; superheated; overheated; **reheated,** recooked, **warmed-over,** *réchauffé* (*French*); hot *see* 1018.25

30 burned, burnt, burned to the ground, incendiarized, torched (*informal*), burned-out *or* down, gutted; **scorched, blistered, parched, singed, seared, charred,** pyrographic, adust; sunburned; **burnt-up,** incinerated, cremated, consumed, consumed by fire; ashen, ashy, carbonized, pyrolysed, pyrolytic

31 molten, melted, fused, liquefied; liquated; meltable, fusible; thermoplastic

32 heating systems

baseboard heating (US & Canadian)	paraffin heating
central heating	kerosene heating
electric heating	oil heating
furnace heating	panel heating
gas heating	radiant heating
heat pump	solar heating
hot-air heating	steam heating
hot-water heating	stove heating

1020 FUEL

nouns

1 fuel (*see list*), energy source; heat source, firing, combustible *or* inflammable *or* flammable material, burnable, combustible, inflammable, flammable; fossil fuel, nonrenewable energy *or* fuel source; alternate *or* alternative energy source, renewable energy *or* fuel source; solar energy, solar radiation, insolation; wind energy; geothermal energy, geothermal heat, geothermal gradient; synthetic fuels *or* synfuels; fuel additive, dope, fuel dope; propellant; oil *see* 1054; gas *see* 1065

2 slack, coal dust, coom *or* comb (*both informal*), culm

3 firewood, stovewood, wood; woodpile; **kindling,** kindlings, kindling wood; brush, brushwood; faggot, bavin; log, backlog, yule log *or* yule clog (*old*)

4 lighter, light, igniter, sparker; pocket lighter, cigar *or* cigarette lighter, butane lighter; **torch,** flambeau, taper, spill; brand, **firebrand;** portfire; **flint,** flint and steel; **detonator**

5 match, matchstick, lucifer; friction match, vesuvian *and* vesta *and* fusee *and* Congreve *or* Congreve match (*all old*), locofoco (*US old*); safety match; matchbook

6 tinder, touchwood; **punk,** spunk, German tinder, amadou; tinder fungus; pyrotechnic sponge; tinderbox

verbs

7 to fuel, fuel up; fill up, tank up, top off; refuel; coal, oil; **stoke, feed,** add fuel to the flame; detonate, explode

adjectives

8 fuel, energy, heat; fossil-fuel; alternate- *or* alternative-energy; oil-fired, coal-fired, etc; gas-powered, oil-powered, etc; coaly, carbonaceous, carboniferous; anthracite; clean-burning; bituminous; high-sulphur; lignitic; peaty

9 fuels

alcohol	high-octane petrol
anthracite *or* hard coal	isooctane
aviation gasoline *or* avgas (US & Canadian)	jet fuel
	paraffin
aviation spirit	kerosene
benzine	leaded petrol
bituminous *or* soft coal	lignite *or* brown coal
blind coal	lump coal
briquette	methane
broken coal	methanol
buckwheat coal (US & Canadian)	motor fuel
	mustard-seed coal
butane	natural gas
cannel *or* cannel coal	North-Sea gas
carbon	octane
charcoal	pea coal (US & Canadian)
chestnut coal *or* nut coal (US & Canadian)	peat *or* turf
	pentane
coal	petrol
coke	four-star *or* premium *or* high-test petrol
diesel fuel *or* diesel *or* diesel oil *or* derv	
	propane
egg coal	two-star *or* regular petrol
ethane	rocket fuel
ethanol	sea coal
ethyl petrol	steamboat coal
flaxseed coal	stove coal
gas carbon	town gas
gasohol	unleaded *or* lead-free petrol
gasoline (US & Canadian)	
glance coal	unleaded petrol
grate coal	white gasoline (US & Canadian)
heptane	
hexane	

1021 INCOMBUSTIBILITY

nouns

1 **incombustibility, uninflammability,** noninflammability, **nonflammability;** unburnableness; fire resistance
2 **extinguishing,** extinguishment, extinction, **quenching,** dousing (*informal*), **snuffing,** putting out; **choking, damping, stifling, smothering,** smotheration; controlling; fire fighting; going out, dying, burning out, flame-out, burnout
3 **extinguisher, fire extinguisher;** fire apparatus, fire engine, hook-and-ladder, ladder truck; ladder pipe, snorkel, deluge set, deck gun; pumper, superpumper; **foam,** carbon-dioxide foam, Foamite (*trademark*), foam extinguisher; drypowder extinguisher; carbon tetrachloride, carbon tet; water, soda, acid, wet blanket, fire blanket; sprinkler, automatic sprinkler, sprinkler system, sprinkler head; hydrant, fire hydrant, fireplug; fire hose
4 **fire fighter, fireman,** fire-eater (*US informal*); pumpman; forest fire fighter, fire warden, fire-chaser, smokechaser, smokejumper; volunteer fireman, vamp (*US informal*); fire brigade, fire department
5 **fireproofing;** fire resistance; fireproof *or* fire-resistant *or* fire-resisting *or* fire-resistive *or* fire-retardant material, fire retardant; asbestos; amianthus, earth flax, mountain flax; fireguard, firescreen; asbestos curtain, fire wall; fire break, fire line

verbs

6 **to fireproof,** flameproof
7 **to fight fire; extinguish, put out, quench,** out, douse (*informal*), **snuff,** snuff out, blow out, stamp out; stub out, dinch (*informal*); **choke, damp, smother, stifle,** slack; bring under control, contain
8 **to burn out, go out, die,** die out *or* down *or* away; fizzle *and* **fizzle out** (*both informal*); flame out

adjectives

9 **incombustible, noncombustible, uninflammable, noninflammable,** noncombustive, **nonflammable,** unburnable; asbestine, asbestous, asbestoid, asbestoidal; amianthine
10 **fireproof, flameproof,** fireproofed, fire-retarded, fire-resisting *or* resistant *or* resistive, fire-retardant
11 **extinguished,** quenched, snuffed, **out;** contained, under control

1022 COLD

nouns

1 **cold, coldness; coolness,** coolth, freshness; low temperature, arctic temperature, drop *or* decrease in temperature; **chilliness,** nippiness, crispness, briskness, sharpness, bite; **chill, nip,** sharp air; wind chill; **frigidity, iciness,** frostiness, extreme *or* intense cold, gelidity, algidity, algidness; **rawness,** bleakness, keenness, sharpness, bitterness, severity, inclemency, rigor, "a hard, dull bitterness of cold"—WHITTIER; freezing point; cryology; cryogenics; absolute zero
2 (*sensation of cold*) **chill,** chilliness, chilling; shivering, **shivers,** cold shivers, shakes, didders (*informal*), dithers, chattering of the teeth; creeps, cold creeps (*informal*); **gooseflesh, goose pimples,** goose bumps (*informal*), horripilation; **frostbite, chilblains,** kibe, cryopathy; ache, aching
3 **cold weather,** bleak weather, raw weather, bitter weather, wintry weather, arctic weather, **freezing weather,** zero weather, subzero weather; **cold wave,** snap, **cold snap; freeze,** frost, hard frost, deep freeze, arctic frost; winter, depth of winter, hard winter; "The ways deep and the weather sharp, / The very dead of winter"—T S ELIOT, "When icicles hang by the wall"—SHAKESPEARE, "Stern winter"—WORDSWORTH; wintry wind *see* 318.8
4 (*cold place*) Siberia, Hell, Novaya Zemlya, Alaska, Iceland, the Hebrides, Greenland, "Greenland's icy mountains"—REGINALD HEBER, the Yukon, Tierra del Fuego, Lower Slobbovia (*Al Capp*); North Pole, South Pole; Frigid Zones; the Arctic, Arctic Circle *or* Zone; Antarctica, the Antarctic; Antarctic Circle *or* Zone; tundra; the freezer, the deep freeze
5 **ice,** frozen water; ice needle *or* crystal; **icicle,** iceshockle (*informal*); cryosphere; ice sheet, ice field, ice barrier, ice front; **floe, ice floe,** sea ice, ice island, ice raft, ice pack; ice foot, ice belt; shelf ice, sheet ice, pack ice, bay ice, berg ice, field ice;

iceberg, berg, growler; calf; snowberg; **icecap,** *jokul* (*Iceland*); ice pinnacle, serac, nieve penitente; **glacier,** glacieret, glaciation, ice dyke, "motionless torrents, silent cataracts"—SAMUEL TAYLOR COLERIDGE; piedmont glacier; icefall; ice banner; ice cave; **sleet,** glaze, glazed frost, verglas, black ice; snow ice; névé, granular snow, firn; ground ice, anchor ice, frazil; lolly; sludge, **slob** *or* slob ice (*chiefly Canadian*); ice cubes; crushed ice; Dry Ice (*trademark*), solid carbon dioxide; icequake; ice storm, freezing rain

6 **hail,** hailstone; soft hail, graupel, snow pellets, tapioca snow; **hailstorm**

7 **frost,** Jack Frost; **hoarfrost,** hoar, rime, rime frost, white frost; black frost; hard frost, sharp frost; killing frost; frost smoke; frost line

8 **snow;** granular snow, corn snow (*US & Canadian*), spring corn (*US & Canadian*), spring snow, powder snow, wet snow, tapioca snow; "a pure and grandfather moss"—DYLAN THOMAS, "White petals from the flowers that grow in the cold atmosphere"—GEORGE W BUNGAY; **snowfall,** "feather'd rain"—WILLIAM STRODE, "the whitening shower"—JAMES THOMSON; **snowstorm,** snow blast, snow squall, snow flurry, flurry, blizzard, whiteout; **snowflake,** snow-crystal, flake, crystal; snow dust; **snowdrift,** snowbank, snow wreath (*informal*), driven snow, "the frolic architecture of the snow"—EMERSON; snowcap; snow banner; snow blanket; snow bed, snowpack, snowfield, mantle of snow; snowscape; snowland; snowshed; snow line; snowball, snowman; snowslide, snowslip, avalanche; snow slush, **slush,** slosh; snowbridge; snow fence; snowhouse, igloo; mogul

verbs

9 to freeze, be cold, grow cold, lose heat; **shiver, quiver,** shiver to death, quake, shake, tremble, shudder, didder (*informal*), dither; **chatter,** chitter (*dialect*); **chill,** have a chill, have the cold shivers; **freeze,** freeze to death, freeze one's balls off (*informal*), die *or* perish with the cold, horripilate, have goose pimples, have goose bumps (*informal*), starve (*old*); have chilblains

10 (*make cold*) **to freeze, chill,** chill to the bone *or* marrow, make one shiver, make one's teeth chatter, starve (*old*); **nip,** bite, cut, **pierce,** penetrate, penetrate to the bone, go through *or* right through; **freeze** see 1023.11; frost, frostbite; numb, benumb; **refrigerate** see 1023.10

11 to hail, sleet, snow; snow in; snow under; **frost,** ice, ice up, ice over, glaze, glaze over

adjectives

12 **cool,** coolish, temperate; chill, **chilly,** parky (*informal*); **fresh,** brisk, crisp, bracing, sharpish, **invigorating,** stimulating

13 **unheated,** unwarmed; unmelted, unthawed

14 **cold, freezing,** freezing cold, **crisp, brisk,** nipping, nippy, **snappy** (*informal*), raw, bleak, keen, **sharp,** bitter, biting, pinching, cutting, **piercing,** penetrating; inclement, severe, rigorous; snowcold; sleety; slushy; **icy,** icelike, **ice-cold,** glacial, ice-

encrusted; cryospheric; supercooled; **frigid,** bitter *or* bitterly cold, gelid, algid; below zero, subzero; numbing; **wintry,** wintery, winterlike, winterbound, hiemal, brumal, hibernal; **arctic,** Siberian, boreal, hyperborean; stone-cold, cold as death, cold as ice, cold as marble, cold as charity, "cold as the north side of a gravestone in winter"—ANON

15 (*informal terms*) **cold as hell,** cold enough to freeze the tail *or* balls off a brass monkey, colder than hell *or* the deuce *or* the devil

16 (*feeling cold*) **cold, freezing; cool, chilly; shivering,** shivery, shaky, dithery; algid, aguish, aguey; chattering, with chattering teeth; **frozen** see 1023.14, half-frozen, frozen to death, chilled to the bone, blue with cold, *figé de froid* (*French*), so cold one could spit ice cubes

17 **frosty,** frostlike; **frosted,** frosted-over, frost-beaded, frost-covered, frost-chequered, rimed, **hoary,** hoar-frosted, rime-frosted; frost-riven, frost-rent; frosty-faced, frosty-whiskered; frostbound, frost-fettered

18 **snowy,** snowlike, niveous, nival; snow-blown, snow-drifted, snow-driven; **snow-covered,** snow-clad, snow-mantled, snow-robed, snow-blanketed, snow-sprinkled, snow-lined, snow-encircled, snow-laden, snow-loaded, snow-hung; **snow-capped,** snow-peaked, snow-crested, snow-crowned, snow-tipped, snow-topped; snow-bearded; snow-feathered; snow-still

19 frozen out *or* in, **snowbound,** snowed-in, **icebound**

20 **cold-blooded,** hypothermic, heterothermic, poikilothermic; cryogenic; cryological

word elements

21 cryo— *or* kryo—, frigo—, psychro—; glacio—; chio—, chion—

1023 REFRIGERATION
reduction of temperature

nouns

1 **refrigeration,** infrigidation, reduction of temperature; **cooling, chilling; freezing,** glacification, glaciation, congelation, congealment; refreezing, regelation; mechanical refrigeration, electric refrigeration, electronic refrigeration, gas refrigeration; food freezing, quick freezing, deep freezing, sharp freezing, blast freezing, dehydrofreezing; adiabatic expansion, adiabatic absorption, adiabatic demagnetization; cryogenics; super-cooling; **air conditioning,** air cooling, *climatisation* (*French*); climate control

2 refrigeration anaesthesia, crymoanesthesia, hypothermia *or* hypothermy; crymotherapy, cryo-aerotherapy; cold cautery, cryocautery; cryopathy

3 **cooler,** chiller; water cooler, air cooler; ventilator; fan; surface cooler; ice cube, ice pail *or* bucket, wine cooler; ice bag, ice pack, cold pack; cool bag *or* box, Esky (*Australian trademark*)

4 **refrigerator,** refrigeratory, **icebox,** ice chest; Frigidaire (*trademark*), fridge (*informal*), electric refrigerator, electronic refrigerator, gas refrigerator;

refrigerator car, refrigerator truck, reefer (*informal*); freezer ship

5 **freezer, deep freeze,** deep-freezer, quick-freezer, fast-freeze, sharp-freezer; ice-cream freezer, ice-cream maker; ice machine, ice-cube machine, freezing machine, refrigerating machine *or* engine; **ice plant,** icehouse, refrigerating plant

6 **cold storage; frozen-food locker,** locker, freezer locker, locker plant; coolhouse; coolerman; frigidarium

7 (*cooling agent*) **coolant; refrigerant;** cryogen; ice, Dry Ice (*trademark*), ice cubes; freezing mixture, liquid air, ammonia, carbon dioxide, Freon (*trademark*), ether; ethyl chloride; liquid air, liquid oxygen *or* lox, liquid nitrogen, liquid helium, etc

8 **antifreeze,** coolant, radiator coolant, alcohol, ethylene glycol, diethylene glycol

9 refrigerating engineering, refrigerating engineer

verbs

10 **to refrigerate; cool, chill;** refresh, freshen; ice, ice-cool; water-cool, air-cool; **air-condition;** ventilate

11 to freeze *see* 1022.9, 10, ice, glaciate, congeal; **deep-freeze,** quick-freeze, fast-freeze, sharp-freeze, blast-freeze; freeze solid; freeze-dry; **nip,** blight, blast; refreeze, regelate

adjectives

12 **refrigerative,** refrigeratory, refrigerant, frigorific, algific; **cooling, chilling; freezing,** congealing; quick-freezing, fast-freezing, deep-freezing, sharp-freezing, blast-freezing; freezable, glaciable

13 **cooled, chilled; air-conditioned;** iced, ice-cooled; air-cooled, water-cooled; super-cooled

14 **frozen,** frozen solid, glacial, gelid, congealed; **icy,** ice-cold, icy-cold, ice, icelike; deep-frozen, quick-frozen, fast-frozen, sharp-frozen, blast-frozen; frostbitten, frostnipped

15 antifreeze, antifreezing

1024 LIGHT

nouns

1 **light,** radiant *or* luminous energy, visible radiation, radiation in the visible spectrum, **illumination, radiation, radiance** *or* radiancy, irradiance *or* irradiancy, irradiation, emanation; "God's first creature"—Francis Bacon, "God's eldest daughter"—Thomas Fuller, "offspring of Heav'n firstborn"—Milton, "the first of painters"—Emerson, "the prime work of God"—Milton, "the white radiance of eternity"—Shelley; highlight; sidelight; photosensitivity; light source *see* 1025; **invisible light,** black light, infrared light, ultraviolet light, UV-A, UV-B

2 **shine,** shininess, **lustre, sheen, gloss,** glint; **glow, gleam,** flush, sunset glow; lambency; **incandescence,** candescence; shining light; afterglow; skylight, air glow, night glow, day glow, twilight glow

3 **lightness, luminousness,** lightedness, luminosity; **lucidity,** lucence *or* lucency, translucence *or* translucency; backlight

4 **brightness, brilliance** *or* brilliancy, **splendour,** radiant splendour, **glory, radiance** *or* radiancy, resplendence *or* resplendency, **vividness,** flamboyance *or* flamboyancy; effulgence, refulgence *or* refulgency, fulgentness, fulgidity, fulgor *or* fulgour; **glare,** blare, blaze; bright light, brilliant light, blazing light, glaring light, dazzling light, blinding light; TV lights, Klieg light; streaming light, flood of light, burst of light

5 **ray, radiation** *see* 1036, **beam, gleam,** leam (*Scottish*), **stream, streak, pencil, patch,** ray of light, beam of light; "slant of light"—Emily Dickinson; ribbon, ribbon of light, streamer, stream of light; violet ray, ultraviolet ray, infrared ray, X-ray, gamma ray, invisible radiation; actinic ray *or* light, actinism; atomic beam, atomic ray; laser beam; solar rays; photon

6 **flash, blaze, flare, flame, gleam, glint, glance;** blaze *or* flash *or* gleam of light; green flash; solar flare, solar prominence, facula; Bailey's beads

7 **glitter, glimmer, shimmer, twinkle, blink; sparkle,** spark; **scintillation,** scintilla; coruscation; **glisten,** glister, spangle, tinsel, glittering, glimmering, shimmering, twinkling; "shining from shook foil"—G M Hopkins; stroboscopic *or* strobe light (*informal*), blinking; firefly, glowworm

8 **flicker, flutter, dance, quiver;** flickering, fluttering, bickering, guttering, dancing, quivering, lambency; wavering *or* flickering light, play, play of light, dancing *or* glancing light; light show; "the lambent easy light"—Dryden

9 **reflection** *or* **reflexion;** reflected *or* incident light; reflectance, albedo; blink, iceblink, ice sky, snowblink, waterblink, water sky

10 **daylight,** dayshine, day glow, light of day; day, daytime, daytide, **natural light; sunlight, sunshine,** shine; noonlight, white light, midday sun, noonday *or* noontide light, "the blaze of noon"—Milton; broad day *or* daylight, full sun; bright time; dusk, twilight *see* 315.3; the break *or* crack of dawn, cockcrow, dawn *see* 314.4; sunburst, sunbreak; **sunbeam,** sun spark, ray of sunshine; green flash

11 **moonlight, moonshine,** moonglow; **moonbeam**

12 **starlight,** starshine; earthshine

13 **luminescence;** luciferin, luciferase; phosphor, luminophor; **ignis fatuus, will-o'-the-wisp,** will-with-the-wisp, wisp, jack-o'-lantern, marshfire, spunkie (*Scottish*); friar's lantern; fata morgana; fox fire; St Elmo's light *or* fire, wild fire, witch fire, corposant; double corposant

14 **halo, nimbus,** aura, **aureole,** circle, ring, glory; **rainbow,** solar halo, lunar halo, ring around the sun *or* moon; white rainbow *or* fogbow; **corona,** solar corona, lunar corona; parhelion, parhelic circle *or* ring, mock sun, sun dog; anthelion, antisun, countersun; paraselene, mock moon, moon dog

15 (*nebulous light*) nebula *see* 1070.7; zodiacal light, gegenschein, counterglow

16 **polar lights, aurora; northern lights, aurora borealis,** merry dancers; southern lights, **aurora australis;** aurora polaris; aurora glory; streamer *or* curtain *or* arch aurora; polar ray

17 lightning, flash or **stroke of lightning,** fulguration, fulmination, bolt, lightning strike, **bolt of lightning,** bolt from the blue, **thunderbolt,** thunderstroke, thunderball, fireball, firebolt, levin bolt or brand;

"flying flame"—TENNYSON, "the lightning's gleaming rod"—JOAQUIN MILLER, "oak-cleaving thunderbolts"—SHAKESPEARE; fork or forked lightning, chain lightning, globular or ball lightning, summer or heat lightning, sheet lightning, dark lightning; Jupiter Fulgur or Fulminator; Thor

18 iridescence, opalescence, nacreousness, pearliness; **rainbow;** nacre, mother-of-pearl; nacreous or mother-of-pearl cloud

19 lighting, illumination, artificial light or lighting; arc light, calcium light, candlelight, electric light, fluorescent light, gaslight, incandescent light, mercury-vapour light, neon light, sodium light, strobe light, torchlight, floodlight, spotlight; tonality; light and shade, black and white, chiaroscuro, clairobscure, contrast, highlights

20 illuminant, luminant; electricity; gas, illuminating gas; oil, petroleum, benzine; petrol, gasoline (*US & Canadian*); paraffin, kerosene, coal oil; light source *see* 1025

21 (*measurement of light*) **candle power,** luminous intensity, luminous power, luminous flux, flux, intensity, light; quantum, **light quantum, photon;** unit of light (*see list*), unit of flux; lux, candle-metre, lumen metre, lumetre, lumen, candle lumen; **exposure meter,** light meter, ASA scale, Scheiner scale

22 (*science of light*) photics, photology, photometry; **optics,** geometrical optics, physical optics; dioptrics, catoptrics, fibre optics; actinology, actinometry; heliology, heliometry, heliography

verbs

23 to shine, shine forth, **burn, give light,** incandesce; **glow, beam, gleam,** glint, lustre, glance; **flash, flare, blaze, flame,** fulgurate; **radiate,** shoot, shoot out rays, send out rays; spread or diffuse light; be bright, shine brightly, beacon; **glare;** daze, blind, dazzle, bedazzle

24 to glitter, glimmer, shimmer, twinkle, blink, spangle, tinsel, coruscate; **sparkle,** spark, **scintillate;** glisten, glister, glisk (*Scottish*)

25 to flicker, bicker, gutter, **flutter, waver, dance,** play, quiver

26 to luminesce, phosphoresce, fluoresce; iridesce, opalesce

27 to grow light, grow bright, light, **lighten,** brighten; dawn, break

28 to illuminate, illumine, illume, luminate, **light, light up, lighten,** enlighten, brighten, brighten up, irradiate; bathe or flood with light; relumine, relume; **shed light upon,** cast or throw light upon, shed lustre on, shine upon, overshine; spotlight, highlight; floodlight; beacon

29 to strike a light, light, **turn** or **switch on the light,** put on the light (*informal*), make a light, shine a light

adjectives

30 luminous, luminant, luminative, luminificent, luminiferous, luciferous or lucific (*both old*), luciform, illuminant; **incandescent,** candescent; **lustrous,** orient; **radiant,** irradiative; **shining,** shiny, burning, lamping, streaming; **beaming,** beamy; **gleaming,** gleamy, glinting; **glowing,** aglow, suffused, blushing, flushing; rutilant, rutilous; **sunny, sunshiny,** bright and sunny, light as day; starry, starlike, starbright

31 light, lightish, lightsome; **lucid,** lucent, luculent, relucent; translucent, translucid, pellucid, diaphanous, transparent; **clear,** serene; **cloudless,** unclouded, unobscured

32 bright, brilliant, vivid, splendid, splendorous or splendrous, splendent, **resplendent,** bright and shining; fulgid (*old*), fulgent, effulgent, refulgent; **flamboyant,** flaming; **glaring,** glary, garish, Day-Glo (*trademark*); **dazzling,** bedazzling, blinding, pitiless; shadowless, shadeless

33 shiny, shining, **lustrous, glossy,** glassy, *glacé* (*French*), bright as a new penny, bright as a new pin, **sheeny, polished,** burnished, shined

34 flashing, flashy, **blazing, flaming, flaring, burning,** fulgurant, fulgurating; aflame, ablaze; meteoric

35 glittering, glimmering, shimmering, twinkling, blinking, glistening, glistering; glittery, glimmery, glimmerous, shimmery, twinkly, blinky, spangly, tinselly; **sparkling, scintillating,** scintillant, scintillescent, coruscating, coruscant

36 flickering, bickering, **fluttering, wavering, dancing,** playing, quivering, lambent; flickery, flicky (*informal*), aflicker, fluttery, wavery, quivery; blinking, flashing, stroboscopic

37 iridescent, opalescent, nacreous, pearly, pearl-like; rainbowlike

38 luminescent, photogenic; autoluminescent, bioluminescent

39 illuminated, luminous, **lightened,** enlightened, brightened, **lighted,** lit, **lit up,** flooded or bathed with light, floodlit; irradiated, irradiate; **alight, glowing,** aglow, lambent, suffused with light; ablaze, blazing, in a blaze, fiery; lamplit, lanternlit, candlelit, torchlit, gaslit, firelit; sunlit, moonlit, starlit; spangled, bespangled, tinselled, studded; star-spangled, star-studded

40 illuminating, illumining, **lighting, lightening,** brightening

41 luminary, photic; photologic or photological; photometric or photometrical; heliological, heliographic; actinic, photoactinic; catoptric or catoptrical; luminal

42 photosensitive; photophobic; phototropic

word elements

43 phot–, photo–, lumin–, lumino–, lumini–; fluoro– or fluori–; irido–; actino–, actini–

44 units of light and lighting

bougie décimale (French)	decimal candle
British candle (candela)	foot-candle
candle	Hefner candle
candle-foot	international candle
candle-hour	standard candle

lamp-hour   lumen-hour
lumen

1025 LIGHT SOURCE

nouns

1 **light source**, source of light, **luminary**, illuminator,
luminant, illuminant, incandescent body *or* point,
light, glim; **lamp**, light bulb, electric light bulb,
lantern, candle, taper, torch, flame; match;
fluorescent light, fluorescent tube, fluorescent
lamp; quartz-iodine lamp; illuminations; fairy lights;
starter, ballast;
"a lamp unto my feet, and a light unto my path"—
BIBLE; fire *see* 1018.13; sun, moon, stars *see* 1070.4
2 **candle**, taper; dip, farthing dip, tallow dip; tallow
candle; wax candle, bougie; bayberry candle; rush
candle, rushlight; corpse candle; votary candle
3 **torch**, flaming torch, flambeau, cresset, link (*old*);
flare, signal flare, fusee; beacon
4 **traffic light**, stop-and-go light; stop *or* red light, go
or green light, caution *or* amber light
5 **firefly**, lightning bug, lampyrid, **glowworm**,
fireworm; fire beetle; lantern fly, candle fly; luciferin,
luciferase; phosphor, luminophor
6 **chandelier**, gasolier, electrolier, hanging *or* ceiling
fixture, lustre; uplighter; corona, corona lucis, crown,
circlet; light holder, light fixture, candlestick
7 **wick**, taper; candlewick, lampwick

1026 DARKNESS, DIMNESS

nouns

1 **darkness, dark, lightlessness; obscurity**, obscure,
tenebrosity, tenebrousness; **night** *see* 315.4, dead of
night, deep night; sunlessness, moonlessness,
starlessness; **pitch-darkness**, pitch-blackness, pitchy
darkness, utter *or* thick *or* total darkness, intense
darkness, velvet darkness, Cimmerian *or* Stygian *or*
Egyptian darkness, Erebus;
"obscure darkness"—BIBLE, "the palpable obscure"—
MILTON, "darkness visible"—MILTON, "a fabulous,
formless darkness"—YEATS, "the suit of night"—
SHAKESPEARE, "darkness which may be felt"—BIBLE;
blackness, swarthiness *see* 38.2
2 **darkishness**, darksomeness, **duskiness**, duskness;
murkiness, murk; dimness, dim; **semidarkness,**
semidark, partial darkness, bad light, dim light,
half-light, *demi-jour* (*French*); gloaming, crepuscular
light, **dusk**, twilight *see* 314.4, 315.3
3 **shadow, shade, shadiness**; umbra, umbrage,
umbrageousness; thick *or* dark shade, gloom; mere
shadow,
"the shadow of a shade"—AESCHYLUS; penumbra;
silhouette; skiagram, skiagraph
4 **gloom, gloominess, sombreness,** sombrousness,
sombre; lowering, lower
5 **dullness, flatness,** lifelessness, **drabness,
deadness,** sombreness, **lacklustre, lustrelessness,**
lack of sparkle *or* sheen; mat *or* matt *or* matte, mat
finish *or* matt finish *or* matte finish
6 **darkening, dimming, bedimming; obscuration,**
obscurement, obumbration, obfuscation; eclipsing,

occulting, blocking the light; **shadowing, shading,**
overshadowing, overshading, overshadowment,
clouding, overclouding, obnubilation, gathering of
the clouds, overcast; blackening *see* 38.5;
extinguishment *see* 1021.2
7 **blackout**, dimout, brownout
8 **eclipse**, occultation; total eclipse, partial eclipse,
central eclipse, annular eclipse; solar eclipse, lunar
eclipse

verbs

9 **to darken**, bedarken; **obscure**, obfuscate,
obumbrate; **eclipse**, occult, occultate, block the light;
black out, brown out; black, brown; blot out;
overcast, darken over; **shadow, shade,** cast a
shadow, spread a shadow *or* shade over, encompass
with shadow, overshadow; **cloud**, becloud, encloud,
cloud over, overcloud, obnubilate; gloom, begloom,
sombre, cast a gloom over, murk; **dim, bedim,** dim
out; blacken *see* 38.7
10 **to dull**, mat, deaden; **tone down**
11 **to turn** *or* **switch off the light,** put out the light
(*informal*); extinguish *see* 1021.7
12 **to grow dark, darken,** darkle, lower; gloom (*old*),
gloam (*Scottish*); dusk; **dim, grow dim**

adjectives

13 **dark, black,** darksome, darkling; **lightless,**
beamless, rayless, unlighted, **unilluminated,** unlit;
obscure, caliginous, obscured, obfuscated, eclipsed,
occulted, clothed *or* shrouded *or* veiled *or* cloaked *or*
mantled in darkness; tenebrous, tenebrific,
tenebrious, tenebrose; Cimmerian, Stygian; **pitch-
dark,** pitch-black, pitchy, dark as pitch,
"dark as a wolf's mouth"—SIR WALTER SCOTT, dark as the
inside of a black cat; ebon, ebony; night-dark,
night-black, dark *or* black as night; night-clad,
night-cloaked, night-enshrouded, night-mantled,
night-veiled, night-hid, night-filled; sunless,
moonless, starless
14 **gloomy,** gloomful (*old*), glooming, dark and gloomy,
Acheronian, Acherontic, **sombre,** sombrous;
lowering; **funereal;** stormy, cloudy, clouded,
overcast; ill-lighted, ill-lit
15 **darkish,** darksome, **semidark; dusky,** dusk;
fuscous, subfuscous, subfusc; **murky,** murksome,
murk (*old*); **dim,** dimmed, bedimmed, dimmish,
dimpsy (*informal*); dark-coloured *see* 38.9
16 **shadowy, shady, shadowed, shaded,** darkling,
umbral, umbrageous; overshadowed, overshaded,
obumbrate, obumbrated; penumbral
17 **lacklustre,** lustreless; **dull, dead,** deadened,
lifeless, sombre, drab, wan, **flat,** mat *or* matt *or*
matte
18 obscuring, obscurant

adverbs

19 **in the dark,** darkling, in darkness; in the night, in
the dark of night, in the dead of night, at *or* by
night; dimly, wanly

1027 SHADE
a thing that shades

nouns

1 **shade**, shader, **screen**, **light shield**, **curtain**, drape, drapery, blind, veil; Venetian blind, Austrian blind, festoon blind; **awning**, sunblind; **sunshade**, parasol, **umbrella**, beach umbrella; cover *see* 295.2; shadow *see* 1026.3

2 **eyeshade**, eyeshield, visor, bill; goggles, coloured spectacles, smoked glasses, dark glasses, **sunglasses**, shades (*informal*), Raybans (*trademark*)

3 **lamp shade**; moonshade; globe, light globe

4 **light filter**, filter, diffusing screen; smoked glass, frosted glass, ground glass; stained glass; butterfly; gelatin filter, celluloid filter; frosted lens; lens cap, lens hood; sunscreen

verbs

5 **to shade, screen**, veil, curtain, shutter, draw the curtains, put up *or* close the shutters; cover *see* 295.19; **shadow** *see* 1026.9

adjectives

6 **shading, screening**, veiling, curtaining; shadowing; covering

7 **shaded, screened**, veiled, curtained; sunproof; visored; shadowed, shady *see* 1026.16

1028 TRANSPARENCY

nouns

1 **transparency**, transparence, transpicuousness, show-through, transmission *or* admission of light; **lucidity**, pellucidity, **clearness, clarity**, limpidity; nonopacity, uncloudedness; **crystallinity**, crystal-clearness; **glassiness**, glasslikeness, vitreousness, vitrescence; vitreosity, hyalescence; **diaphanousness**, diaphaneity, sheerness, thinness, **gossameriness**, filminess, gauziness

2 transparent substance, diaphane; **glass** (*see* list), glassware, glasswork; vitrics; stemware; pane, windowpane, light, windowlight, shopwindow; vitrine; showcase, display case; watch crystal *or* glass

verbs

3 to be transparent, show through; pass light; vitrify

adjectives

4 **transparent**, transpicuous, light-pervious; show-through, see-through, peekaboo, revealing; **lucid**, pellucid, **clear**, limpid; nonopaque, unclouded, **crystalline**, crystal, **crystal-clear**, clear as crystal; **diaphanous**, diaphane (*old*), sheer, thin; **gossamer**, gossamery, filmy, gauzy

5 **glass, glassy**, glasslike, clear as glass, vitric, vitreous, vitriform, hyaline, hyalescent; hyalinocrystalline

word elements

6 vitri–

7 glass

agate glass	basalt glass
antimony glass	Bilbao glass
arsenic glass	borax glass
lead glass	lead glass
barley-pattern glass	milk glass
blown glass	opal glass
bone glass	opaline
bottle glass	optical glass
bullet-proof glass	ornamental glass
bullet-resisting glass	Orrefors glass
camphor glass	Perspex (trademark)
carnival glass	photosensitive glass
Cel-o-Glass (trademark)	plastic glass
CM-glass	plate glass
coralene	porcelain glass
cranberry glass	pressed glass
CR-glass	prism glass
crown glass	Pyrex (trademark)
cryolite glass	quartz glass
crystal *or* crystal glass	rhinestone
custard glass	ruby glass
cut glass	safety glass
end-of-day glass	Sandwich glass
etched glass	satin glass
fibreglass *or* glass fibre	sheet glass
flashed glass	show glass
flat glass	stained glass
flint glass	Steuben glass
float glass	Swedish glass
frosted glass	Syracuse watch glass
fused quartz	tempered glass *or*
glass bead	tempered safety glass
glass brick	Triplex (trademark)
glass wool	uranium glass
ground glass	uviol glass
hobnail glass	Venetian glass
ice glass	Vitaglass (trademark)
lace glass	vitreous silica
Lalique glass	Waterford glass
laminated glass *or*	window glass
laminated safety glass	wire *or* wired glass

1029 SEMITRANSPARENCY

nouns

1 **semitransparency**, semipellucidity, semidiaphaneity; semiopacity

2 **translucence, translucency**, lucence, lucency, translucidity, pellucidity, lucidity; transmission *or* admission of light

verbs

3 **to frost**, frost over

adjectives

4 **semitransparent**, semipellucid, semidiaphanous, semiopaque; frosty, frosted

5 **translucent**, lucent, translucid, lucid, pellucid; semitranslucent, semipellucid

1030 OPAQUENESS

nouns

1 **opaqueness**, opacity, intransparency, nontranslucency, imperviousness to light, adiaphanousness; roil, roiledness, turbidity, turbidness; cloudiness; **darkness, obscurity, dimness** *see* 1026

verbs

2 to opaque, **darken, obscure** *see* 1026.9; **cloud,** becloud

adjectives

3 **opaque,** intransparent, nontranslucent, adiaphanous, impervious to light; **dark, obscure** *see* 1026.13, cloudy, roiled, roily, grumly (*Scottish*), turbid

1031 ELECTRICITY, MAGNETISM

nouns

1 **electricity; electrical science** (*see list*); **electrical** *or* **electric unit,** unit of measurement

2 **current, electric current** (*see list*), current flow, amperage, electric stream *or* flow, juice (*informal*)

3 **electric** *or* **electrical field,** static field, electrostatic field, field of electrical force; tube of electric force, electrostatic tube of force; **magnetic field,** magnetic field of currents; **electromagnetic field;** variable field

4 **circuit, electrical circuit,** path

5 **charge, electric** *or* **electrical charge,** positive charge, negative charge; live wire

6 **discharge, arc,** electric discharge; **shock,** electroshock, galvanic shock

7 **magnetism,** magnetic attraction; **electromagnetism;** magnetization; diamagnetism, paramagnetism, ferromagnetism; residual magnetism, magnetic remanence; magnetic memory, magnetic retentiveness; magnetic elements; magnetic dip *or* inclination, magnetic variation *or* declination; hysteresis, magnetic hysteresis, hysteresis curve, magnetic friction, magnetic lag *or* retardation, magnetic creeping; permeability, magnetic permeability, magnetic conductivity; magnetic circuit, magnetic curves, magnetic figures; magnetic flux, gilbert, weber, maxwell; magnetic moment; magnetic potential; magnetic viscosity; magnetics

8 **polarity,** polarization; **pole, positive pole, anode, negative pole, cathode,** magnetic pole, magnetic axis; north pole, N pole; south pole, S pole

9 **magnetic force** *or* **intensity,** magnetic flux density, gauss, oersted; magnetomotive force; magnetomotivity; magnetic tube of force; line of force; **magnetic field, electromagnetic field**

10 **electroaffinity,** electric attraction; electric repulsion

11 **voltage,** volt, **electromotive force** *or* **EMF,** electromotivity, potential difference; **potential, electric potential;** tension, high tension, low tension

12 **resistance,** ohm, ohms, ohmage, ohmic resistance, electric resistance; surface resistance, skin effect, volume resistance; insulation resistance; **reluctance,** magnetic reluctance *or* resistance; specific reluctance, reluctivity; **reactance,** inductive reactance, capacitive reactance; **impedance**

13 **conduction,** electric conduction; **conductance,** conductivity, mho; superconductivity; gas conduction, ionic conduction, metallic conduction, liquid conduction, photoconduction; **conductor,**

semiconductor, superconductor; **nonconductor,** dielectric, insulator

14 **induction;** electrostatic induction, magnetic induction, electromagnetic induction, electromagnetic induction of currents; self-induction, mutual induction; **inductance,** inductivity, henry

15 **capacitance,** capacity, farad; collector junction capacitance, emitter junction capacitance, resistance capacitance

16 **gain,** available gain, current gain, operational gain

17 **electric power, wattage,** watts; electric horsepower; hydroelectric power, hydroelectricity; power load

18 **powerhouse, power station, power plant,** central station; oil-fired power plant, coal-fired power plant; hydroelectric plant; nuclear *or* atomic power plant; power grid, distribution system, national grid

19 **blackout, power failure,** power cut, power loss; **brownout,** voltage drop, voltage loss

20 **electrical device,** electrical appliance; **battery** (*see list*), accumulator, storage battery, storage device; **electric meter,** meter; **wire, cable,** electric wire, electric cord, cord, power cord, power cable, flex; power point, point

21 **electrician, electrotechnician;** radio technician *see* 1033.24; wireman; lineman *or* linesman (*US & Canadian*); rigger; groundman; power worker

22 **electrotechnologist,** electrobiologist, electrochemist, electrometallurgist, electrophysicist, electrophysiologist, **electrical engineer**

23 **electrification,** electrifying, supplying electricity

24 **electrolysis;** ionization; galvanization, electrogalvanization; electrocoating, electroplating, electrogilding, electrograving, electroetching; ion, cation, anion; electrolyte, ionogen; nonelectrolyte

verbs

25 **to electrify, galvanize,** energize, **charge;** wire, wire up; shock; **generate,** step up, amplify, stiffen; step down; plug in, loop in; switch on *or* off, turn on *or* off, turn on *or* off the juice (*informal*); short-circuit, short

26 **to magnetize; electromagnetize;** demagnetize, degauss

27 **to electrolyse;** ionize; galvanize, electrogalvanize; electroplate, electrogild

28 **to insulate,** isolate; **ground**

adjectives

29 **electric, electrical, electrifying;** galvanic, voltaic; dynamoelectric, hydroelectric, photoelectric, piezoelectric, etc; electrothermal, electrochemical, electromechanical, electropneumatic, electrodynamic, static, electrostatic; electromotive; electrokinetic; electroscopic, galvanoscopic; electrometric, galvanometric, voltametric; **electrified,** electric-powered, battery-powered, cordless; solar-powered

30 **magnetic, electromagnetic;** diamagnetic, paramagnetic, ferromagnetic; **polar**

31 **electrolytic;** hydrolytic; ionic, anionic, cationic; ionogenic

32 **electrotechnical;** electroballistic, electrobiological, electrochemical, electrometallurgical, electrophysiological

33 charged, electrified, live, hot; high-tension, low-tension; rechargeable

34 positive, plus, electropositive; **negative,** minus, electronegative

35 nonconducting, nonconductive, insulating, dielectric

word elements

36 electr–, electro–; rheo–; magnet–, magneto–

37 electrical sciences

electrical engineering	electrophotomicrography
electroballistics	electrophysics
electrobiology	electrophysiology
electrochemistry	electrostatics
electrodynamics	electrotechnology *or*
electrokinematics	electrotechnics
electrokinetics	electrothermics
electromechanics	galvanism
electrometallurgy	magnetics
electrometry	magnetometry
electronics	thermionics
electrooptics	

38 electric currents

absorption current	ionization current
active current	low-frequency current
alternating current *or* AC	magnetizing current
conduction current	multiphase current
convection current	oscillating current
delta current	pulsating direct current
dielectric displacement current	reactive current
	rotary current
direct current *or* DC	single-phase alternating
displacement current	current
eddy current	stray current
emission current	thermionic current
exciting current	thermoelectric current
free alternating current	three-phase alternating
galvanic current	current
high-frequency current	voltaic current
induced current	watt current
induction current	wattless *or* idle current

39 batteries

accumulator	nickel-cadmium battery
alkaline cell	primary battery
atomic battery	secondary battery
cell	solar battery
dry battery	solar cell
dry cell	storage battery
electronic battery	storage cell
fuel cell	voltaic battery
lead-acid battery	voltaic cell
Leyden battery	voltaic pile
Leyden jar	wet cell
mercury cell	

1032 ELECTRONICS

nouns

1 electronics, radionics, radioelectronics; electron physics, electrophysics, electron dynamics; electron optics; semiconductor physics, transistor physics; photoelectronics, photoelectricity; microelectronics; electronic engineering; avionics; electron microscopy; nuclear physics *see* 1037; radio *see* 1033; television *see* 1034; radar *see* 1035; automation *see* 1040

2 (*electron theory*) electron theory of atoms, electron theory of electricity, electron theory of solids, free electron theory of metals, band theory of solids

3 electron (*see list*), negatron, cathode particle, beta particle; thermion; electron capture, electron transfer; electron spin; electron state, energy level; ground state, excited state; electron pair, lone pair, shared pair, electron-positron pair, duplet, octet; electron cloud; shells, electron layers, electron shells, valency shell, valency electrons, subvalent electrons; electron affinity, relative electron affinity

4 electronic effect; Edison effect, thermionic effect, photoelectric effect

5 electron emission; thermionic emission; photoelectric emission, photoemission; collision emission, bombardment emission, secondary emission; field emission; grid emission, thermionic grid emission; electron ray, electron beam, cathode ray, anode ray, positive ray, canal ray; glow discharge, cathode glow, cathodoluminescence, cathodofluorescence; electron diffraction

6 electron flow, electron stream, electron *or* **electronic current;** electric current *see* 1031.2; electron gas, electron cloud, space charge

7 electron volt; ionization potential; input voltage, output voltage; base signal voltage, collector signal voltage, emitter signal voltage; battery supply voltage; screen-grid voltage; inverse peak voltage; voltage saturation

8 electronic circuit (*see list*), transistor circuit, semiconductor circuit; vacuum-tube circuit, thermionic tube circuit; **printed circuit, microcircuit; chip, silicon chip,** microchip; **circuitry**

9 conductance, electronic conductance; **resistance,** electronic resistance

10 electron tube, vacuum tube, tube, valve, thermionic tube; radio tube, television tube; **special-purpose tube; vacuum tube component**

11 photoelectric tube *or* **cell, phototube,** photocell; electron-ray tube, electric eye; photosensitivity, **photosensitive devices**

12 transistor (*see list*), semiconductor *or* solid-state device

13 electronic device, electronic meter, electronic measuring device; **electronic tester,** electronic testing device

14 electronics engineer, electronics physicist

adjectives

15 electronic; photoelectronic, **photoelectric;** autoelectronic; microelectronic; thermoelectronic; thermionic; anodic, cathodic; transistorized

16 electrons

bonding electron	planetary electron
bound electron	positive electron
conduction electron	primary electron
excess electron	recoil electron
extranuclear electron	secondary electron
free electron	spinning electron
nuclear electron	surface-bound electron
orbital electron	valency electron
peripheral electron	wandering electron
photoelectron	

17 electronic circuits

amplifier circuit	rectifier circuit
astable circuit	shunt circuit
back-to-back switching	sinusoidal circuit
circuit	small signal hybrid open
bistable circuit	circuit
coupling circuit	small signal hybrid short
equivalent circuit	circuit
flip-flop circuit	small signal open circuit
gate *or* logic gate	small signal short circuit
monostable circuit	trigger circuit
mu circuit	tuned circuit
nonsinusoidal circuit	

18 transistors

base	melt-quench transistor
collector	meltback transistor
conductivity-modulation	mesa transistor
transistor	microalloy transistor
diffused-base transistor	phototransistor
diffusion transistor	point-contact transistor
drift transistor	point-junction transistor
emitter	power transistor
field-effect transistor	rate-grown transistor
filamentary transistor	spacistor
germanium crystal triode	symmetrical transistor
germanium diode	tandem transistor
germanium triode	tetrode transistor
hook transistor	unijunction transistor
hook-collector transistor	unipolar transistor
junction transistor	

1033 RADIO

nouns

1 **radio, wireless**; radiotelephony, radiotelegraphy; communications, telecommunication *see* 347.1

2 radiotechnology, radio engineering, communication engineering; radio electronics, radioacoustics; radiogoniometry

3 **radio, radio receiver** (*see list*); radio telescope; **radio set, receiver**, receiving set, **wireless** *and* wireless set, set; cabinet, console, housing; chassis; receiver part

4 **radio transmitter** (*see list*), **transmitter**; transmitter part; microphone *see* 50.9, radiomicrophone, **antenna**, aerial

5 radiomobile, mobile transmitter, remote-pickup unit

6 **radio station**, transmitting station, **studio**, studio plant; AM station, FM station, shortwave station, ultrahigh-frequency station, clear-channel station; direction-finder station, RDF station; relay station, radio relay station, microwave relay station; amateur station, ham station (*informal*), ham shack (*informal*); pirate radio station, offshore station; local radio station; BBC, British Broadcasting Corporation, Auntie Beeb *or* Auntie *or* the Beeb (*informal*)

7 **control room**, mixing room, monitor room, monitoring booth; **control desk**, console, master control desk, instrument panel, control panel *or* board, jack field, mixer (*informal*)

8 **network**, net, radio links, **hookup**, communications net, circuit, network stations, network affiliations, affiliated stations; coaxial network, circuit network, coast-to-coast hookup

9 **radio circuit**, radio-frequency circuit, audio-frequency circuit, superheterodyne circuit, amplifying circuit; electronic circuit *see* 1032.8

10 **radio signal**, radio-frequency *or* RF signal, direct signal, shortwave signal, AM signal, FM signal; reflected signal, bounce; unidirectional signal, beam; signal-noise ratio; **radio-frequency** *or* **RF amplifier**, radio-frequency *or* RF stage

11 **radio wave**, electric wave, electromagnetic wave, hertzian wave; shortwave, long wave, microwave, high-frequency wave, low-frequency wave; ground wave, sky wave; carrier, carrier wave; **wavelength**

12 **frequency**; radio frequency *or* RF, intermediate frequency *or* IF, audio frequency *or* AF; high frequency *or* HF; very high frequency *or* VHF; ultrahigh frequency *or* UHF; superhigh frequency *or* SHF; extremely high frequency *or* EHF; medium frequency *or* MF; low frequency *or* LF; very low frequency *or* VLF; upper frequencies, lower frequencies; **carrier frequency**; spark frequency; spectrum, frequency spectrum; cycles, CPS, hertz, Hz, **kilohertz, kilocycles**; **megahertz, megacycles**

13 **band**, frequency band, standard band, broadcast band, amateur band, citizens band *or* CB, police band, shortwave band, FM band; **channel**, radio channel, broadcast channel

14 **modulation**; amplitude modulation *or* AM; frequency modulation *or* FM; phase modulation *or* PM; sideband, side frequency, single sideband, double sideband

15 **amplification**, radio-frequency *or* RF amplification, audio-frequency *or* AF amplification, intermediate-frequency *or* IF amplification, high-frequency amplification

16 **radio broadcasting, broadcasting**, the air waves, radiocasting; **airplay, airtime**; commercial radio, public radio; AM broadcasting, FM broadcasting, shortwave broadcasting; **transmission, radio transmission**; direction *or* beam transmission, asymmetric *or* vestigial transmission; multipath transmission, multiplex transmission; mixing, volume control, sound *or* tone control, fade-in, fade-out; broadcasting regulation, Radio Authority

17 **pickup**, outside pickup, **remote pickup**, spot pickup

18 **radiobroadcast, broadcast**, radiocast, **radio programme**; rebroadcast, rerun; simulcast, simultaneous broadcast; electronic *or* broadcast journalism, broadcast news, newscast, newsbreak, newsflash; all-news radio *or* format; sportscast; **talk radio**; talk show, audience-participation show, call-in *or* phone-in show, interview show; vox pop; network show; commercial programme, commercial; sustaining programme *or* sustainer (*US & Canadian*); serial, soap opera (*informal*); taped programme, canned show (*informal*), recorded *or* pre-recorded programme, electrical transcription; sound effects; closedown

19 **signature, station identification**, jingle, call letters (*US & Canadian*); theme song *or* tune; station break, pause for station identification

20 commercial, commercial announcement, commercial message, message, spot announcement, spot *and* plug (*both informal*), **commercial break**

21 reception; fading, fade-out; **drift,** creeping, crawling; **interference,** noise interference, station interference; **static,** atmospherics, noise; blasting, blaring; blind spot; **jamming,** deliberate interference

22 radio listener, listener-in *and* tuner-inner (*both informal*); radio audience, listeners, **listenership**

23 broadcaster, radiobroadcaster, radiocaster; newsreader, newscaster, sportscaster; commentator, news commentator; anchor, news anchor, anchor man *or* woman; host, talk-show host, talk jockey (*informal*), shock jock (*informal*); announcer, continuity announcer *or* man, linkman; disc jockey *or* DJ *or* deejay (*both informal*); master of ceremonies, MC *or* emcee (*both informal*), presenter; question master; programme director, controller, programmer; sound-effects man, sound man

24 radioman, radio technician, radio engineer; radiotrician, radio electrician, radio repairman; **radio operator;** control engineer, volume engineer; mixer; **amateur radio operator, ham** *and* ham operator (*both informal*), radio amateur; monitor; radiotelegrapher *see* 347.16

verbs

25 to broadcast, radiobroadcast, radiocast, simulcast, **radio, wireless,** radiate, **transmit,** send, relay; narrowcast; shortwave; beam; newscast, sportscast, put *or* go on the air, sign on; go off the air, sign off

26 to monitor, check

27 to listen in, tune in; tune up, tune down, tune out, tune off

adjectives

28 radio, wireless; radiosonic; neutrodyne; heterodyne; superheterodyne; shortwave, medium wave, long wave; radio-frequency, audio-frequency; high-frequency, low-frequency, etc; radiogenic

29 radio receivers

all-wave receiver	radar receiver
AM receiver	radio direction finder *or*
AM tuner	RDF
AM-FM receiver	radio-phonograph
AM-FM tuner	radio-record player
auto radio *or* car radio	radiophone
aviation radio	railroad radio (US &
battery radio	Canadian)
citizens band *or* CB radio	receiver
or CB	rechargeable-battery radio
clock radio	regenerative receiver
communications receiver	relay receiver
crystal set	scanner
facsimile receiver *or* fax	ship-to-shore radio
FM receiver	shortwave receiver
FM tuner	single-signal receiver
ghetto box *or* blaster *or*	six-band receiver
beat box *or* box	stereo receiver
headband receiver	superheterodyne
mobile radio	table radio
multiplex receiver	three-way *or* three-power
pocket radio	receiver
portable radio	transceiver

trannie *or* tranny	universal receiver
(*informal*)	VHF-FM receiver
transistor radio	walkie-talkie
transmit-receiver	Walkman (trademark)
tuner	weather radio
two-way radio	

30 radio transmitters

AM transmitter	radio marker
amateur *or* ham	radio range beacon
transmitter *or* rig	radiometeorograph
(*informal*)	radiosonde
arc *or* spark transmitter	radiotelephone transmitter
continuous-wave *or* CW	relay transmitter
transmitter	RT transmitter
facsimile transmitter *or* fax	shortwave transmitter
fan marker	standby transmitter
FM transmitter	tape transmitter
link transmitter	television transmitter
picture transmitter	transmitter receiver *or*
portable transmitter	transceiver
pulse transmitter	vacuum-tube transmitter
radio beacon	VHF-FM transmitter

1034 TELEVISION

nouns

1 television, TV, video, telly (*informal*); the small screen *or* the tube (*both informal*), the boob tube (*informal*), the box (*informal*), goggle box (*informal*); **network television,** free television; the dream factory; subscription television, pay TV; cable television, cable TV, cable-television system *or* cable system; closed-circuit television *or* closed circuit TV; public-access television *or* public-access TV

2 television broadcast, telecast, TV show; direct broadcast, live show (*informal*); taped show, canned show (*informal*), recorded show *or* pre-recorded show; outside broadcast; prime time, prime-time show *or* attraction; television drama *or* play, teleplay; telefilm; dramatic series *or* drama series, miniseries; costume drama; situation comedy *or* sitcom (*informal*); game-show; chat show; **serial,** daytime serial, soap opera *or* soap (*informal*); quiz show; giveaway show; panel show; electronic *or* broadcast journalism, broadcast news, newscast, news show, news bulletin, newsflash; documentary, docudrama; epilogue; edutainment, infotainment; film pickup; colourcast; simulcast, simultaneous broadcast; closedown; childrens' television, kidvid (*informal*); television *or* TV performer, television *or* TV personality; compere, commère; presenter; question master; news anchor, anchor, anchor man, anchor woman, anchor person; linkman; continuity announcer *or* man; VJ, video jockey; talking head; vox pop; ratings, Nielsen rating (*US*); people meter; ITC, Independent Television Commission

3 televising, telecasting; facsimile broadcasting; monitoring, mixing, shading, blanking, switching; scanning, parallel-line scanning, interlaced scanning

4 (*transmission*) photoemission, audioemission; television channel, TV band; BBC1, BBC2, ITV, Independent Television, Channel Four; video *or* picture channel, audio *or* sound channel, video frequency; picture carrier, sound carrier; beam, scanning beam, return beam; triggering pulse, voltage pulse, output pulse, timing pulse, equalizing pulse; synchronizing pulse, vertical synchronizing pulse, horizontal synchronizing pulse; video signal, audio signal; IF video signal, IF audio signal; synchronizing signal, blanking signal

5 (*reception*) **picture, image**; pixel; **colour television,** dot-sequential *or* field-sequential *or* line-sequential colour television; **black-and-white television;** HDTV *or* high-definition television; definition, blacker than black synchronizing; image enhancement; shading, black spot, hard shadow; test pattern, scanning pattern, grid; vertical interference, rain; granulation, scintillation, snow, snowstorm; flare, bloom, woomp; picture shifts, blooping, rolling; double image, multiple image, ghost; video static, noise, picture noise; signal-to-noise ratio; fringe area

6 **television studio, TV station**; BBC, British Broadcasting Corporation, Auntie Beeb *or* Auntie *or* the Beeb (*informal*), ITV, Independent Television

7 **mobile unit, TV mobile**; video truck, audio truck, transmitter truck

8 **transmitter**, televisor; audio transmitter, video transmitter; transmitter part (*see list*)

9 **relay links, boosters**, booster amplifiers, relay transmitters, **booster** *or* **relay stations**; microwave link; aeronautical relay, stratovision; communication satellite, satellite relay; Telstar, Intelsat, Syncom; Comsat

10 **television camera**, telecamera, pickup camera, pickup; **camera tube** (*see list*); camcorder; mobile camera

11 **television receiver, television** *or* **TV set, TV,** telly (*informal*), televisor, boob tube *and* idiot box *and* goggle box *and* the box (*all informal*); **picture tube** (*see list*); receiver part (*see list*); portable television *or* TV set; **screen**, telescreen, videoscreen; dish aerial, satellite dish *or* satellite dish aerial; raster; **videocassette recorder** *or* **VCR,** videorecorder, videotape recorder *or* VTR; videotape, videocassette; video nasty; videophone, Picturephone (*trademark*)

12 **televiewer, viewer**; television *or* viewing audience; viewership

13 **television technician**, TV man *or* woman, television *or* TV repairman *or* repairwoman, television engineer; monitor, sound *or* audio monitor, picture *or* video monitor; pickup unit man, cameraman, camerawoman, sound man, sound woman, key grip, vision mixer

verbs

14 **to televise, telecast**; colourcast; simulcast

15 **to teleview**, watch television *or* TV; telerecord, record, tape

adjectives

16 **televisional**, televisual, televisionary, **video;** telegenic, videogenic; in synchronization, in sync (*informal*), locked in

word elements

17 **tele–, video–, TV–**

18 **transmitter parts**

adder	reproducing element
antenna filter	signal generator
camera deflection generator	sound unit
channel filter	synchronizing generator
encoder	Tel-Eye
exploring element	TV-Eye
monitor screen	

19 **camera tubes**

iconoscope	image orthicon
image converter	orthicon
image dissector *or* dissector	pickup tube
tube	Saticon (trademark)
image iconoscope	vidicon
image intensifier	

20 **picture tubes**

cathode-ray tube	monoscope
colour kinescope	Oscilight
direct-viewing tube	projection tube
kinescope	shadow-mask kinescope

21 **receiver parts**

audio amplifier	photoelectric cells
audio detector	picture control
audio-frequency detector	picture detector
blanking amplifier	radio units
contrast control	screen
converter	shading amplifier
deflection generator	signal separator
electron tubes	sound limiter
FM detector	synchronizing separator
horizontal deflector	vertical deflector
horizontal synchronizer	vertical synchronizer
limiter	video amplifier
mixer	video detector
photocathode	vision mixer

1035 RADAR, RADIOLOCATORS

nouns

1 **radar**, radio detection and ranging; **radar set**, radiolocator; radar part; oscilloscope, radarscope; radar antenna; radar reflector

2 **airborne radar**, aviation radar; **navar**, navigation and ranging; **teleran**, television radar air navigation; radar bombsight, K-1 bombsight; radar dome, radome

3 **loran**, long range aid to navigation; **shoran**, short range aid to navigation; GEE navigation, consolan

4 **radiolocator**; direction finder, radio direction finder *or* RDF; radiogoniometer, high-frequency direction finder *or* HFDF, huff-duff (*informal*); radio compass, wireless compass

5 **radar speed meter**, electronic cop (*informal*); radar highway patrol; radar detector, Fuzzbuster (*trademark*)

6 **radar station**, control station; Combat Information Center *or* CIC; Air Route Traffic Control Center *or* ARTCC; beacon station, display station; fixed station, home station; portable field unit, mobile trailer unit; tracking station; direction-finder station, radio compass station; triangulation stations

7 **radar beacon**, racon; transponder; radar beacon buoy, marker buoy, radar marked beacon, ramark

8 (*radar operations*) data transmission, scanning, scan conversion, flector tuning, signal modulation, triggering signals; phase adjustment, locking signals; triangulation, three-pointing; mapping; range finding; tracking, automatic tracking, locking on; precision focusing, pinpointing; radar-telephone relay; radar navigation

9 (*applications*) detection, interception, ranging, ground control of aircraft, air-traffic control, blind flying, blind landing, storm tracking, hurricane tracking; radar fence *or* screen; radar astronomy

10 pulse, radio-frequency *or* RF pulse, high-frequency *or* HF pulse, intermediate-frequency *or* IF pulse, trigger pulse, echo pulse

11 signal, radar signal; transmitter signal, output signal; return signal, echo signal, video signal, reflection *or* reflexion, picture, target image, display, signal display, trace, reading, return, **echo, bounces, blips, pips**; spot, CRT spot; three-dimensional *or* 3-D display, double-dot display; deflection-modulated *or* DM display, intensity-modulated *or* IM display; radio-frequency *or* RF echoes, intermediate-frequency *or* IF signal; beat signal, Doppler signal, local oscillator signal; beam, beavertail beam

12 radar interference, deflection, refraction, superrefraction; atmospheric attenuation, signal fades, blind spots, false echoes; clutter, ground clutter, sea clutter

13 (*radar countermeasure*) **jamming, radar jamming**; tinfoil, aluminium foil, chaff, window

14 radar technician, radar engineer, radarman; air-traffic controller; jammer

verbs

15 to **transmit, send**, radiate, beam; **jam**

16 to **reflect**, return, echo, bounce back

17 to **receive, tune in**, pick up, spot, home on; pinpoint; identify, trigger; lock on; sweep, scan; map

1036 RADIATION, RADIOACTIVITY

nouns

1 **radiation**, radiant energy; ionizing radiation; **radioactivity**, activity, radioactive radiation *or* emanation, atomic *or* nuclear radiation; natural radioactivity, artificial radioactivity; curiage; specific activity, high-specific activity; actinic radiation, ultra-violet *or* violet radiation; radiotransparency, radiolucence *or* radiolucency; radiopacity; radiosensitivity, radiosensibility; half-life; radiocarbon dating; contamination, decontamination; saturation point; absorbed dose, acute dose; hot spot; radiac *or* radioactivity detection identification and computation; fallout *see* 1037.16

2 **radioluminescence, autoluminescence**; cathode luminescence; Cerenkov radiation, synchrotron radiation

3 **ray, radiation** (*see list*), cosmic ray bombardment, electron shower; electron emission *see* 1032.5

4 **radioactive particle**; alpha particle, beta particle; heavy particle; high-energy particle; meson, mesotron; cosmic particle, solar particle, aurora particle, V-particle

5 (*radioactive substance*) **radiator**; alpha radiator, beta radiator, gamma radiator; fluorescent paint, radium paint; radium; fission products; radiocarbon, radiocopper, radioiodine, radiothorium, etc; mesothorium; **radioactive element** (*see list*), radioelement; radioisotope; tracer, tracer element, tracer atom; radioactive waste

6 **counter, radioscope**, radiodetector, **atom-tagger**; ionization chamber; ionizing event; X-ray spectrograph, X-ray spectrometer

7 **radiation physics**, radiological physics; radiobiology, radiochemistry, radiometallography, radiography, roentgenography, roentgenology, radiometry, spectroradiometry, radiotechnology, radiopathology; radiology; radiotherapy; radioscopy, curiescopy, roentgenoscopy, radiostereoscopy, fluoroscopy, photofluorography, orthodiagraphy; X-ray photometry, X-ray spectrometry; tracer investigation, atom-tagging; **unit of radioactivity** (*see list*); exposure, dose, absorbed dose

8 **radiation physicist**; radiobiologist, radiometallographer, radiochemist, etc; radiologist, radiographer

verbs

9 to **radioactivate**, activate, **irradiate**, charge; radiumize; **contaminate**, poison, infect, nuke (*informal*)

adjectives

10 **radioactive**, activated, radioactivated, irradiated, charged, **hot; contaminated**, infected, poisoned; exposed; radiferous; radioluminescent, autoluminescent

11 **radiable**; radiotransparent, radioparent, radiolucent; radiopaque, radium-proof; radiosensitive

12 rays, radiation

actinic ray	gamma ray *or* radiation
alpha ray *or* radiation	Grenz ray
anode ray	infraroentgen ray
Becquerel ray	Leonard ray
beta ray *or* radiation	nuclear radiation
canal ray	positive ray
cathode ray	Roentgen ray
cosmic ray *or* radiation	X-ray *or* radiation

13 radioactive elements

actinium	neptunium
americium	nobelium
astatine	plutonium
berkelium	polonium
californium	promethium
curium	protactinium
einsteinium	radium
fermium	radon *or* radium emanation
francium	technetium
hahnium	thorium
mendelevium	uranium

14 units of radioactivity

curie	microcurie
dose equivalent	millicurie
grey	multicurie
half-life	rad
megacurie	roentgen

1037 NUCLEAR PHYSICS

nouns

1 **nuclear physics,** particle physics, nucleonics, atomics, atomistics, atomology, atomic science; quantum mechanics, wave mechanics; molecular physics; thermionics; mass spectrometry, mass spectrography; radiology *see* 1036.7

2 (*atomic theory*) quantum theory, Bohr theory, Dirac theory, Rutherford theory, Schrödinger theory, Lewis-Langmuir *or* octet theory, Thomson's hypothesis; law of conservation of mass, law of definite proportions, law of multiple proportions, law of Dulong and Petit, law of parity, correspondence principle; Standard Model; supersymmetry theory, unified field theory; atomism; quark model

3 **atomic scientist, nuclear physicist,** particle physicist; radiologist *see* 1036.8

4 **atom** (*see lists*); tracer, tracer atom, tagger atom; atomic model, nuclear atom; nuclide; **ion; shell,** subshell, planetary shell, valency shell; **atomic unit;** atomic constant

5 **isotope;** protium, deuterium *or* heavy hydrogen *and* tritium (*all isotopes of hydrogen*); radioactive isotope, **radioisotope;** carbon *see* 14, strontium *see* 90, uranium *see* 235; artificial isotope; isotone; isobar, isomer, nuclear isomer

6 **elementary particle,** atomic particle, **subatomic particle** (*see list*), subnuclear particle, ultraelementary particle; **atomic nucleus, nucleus,** *Kern* (*German*); **nuclear particle,** nucleon; proton, neutron (*see list*); deuteron *or* deuterium nucleus, triton *or* tritium nucleus, alpha particle *or* helium nucleus; **nuclear force,** weak force *or* weak nuclear force, strong force *or* strong nuclear force; weak interaction, strong interaction; fifth force; nucleosynthesis; nuclear resonance, Mössbauer effect, nuclear magnetic resonance *or* NMR; strangeness; charm

7 atomic cluster, molecule; radical, simple radical, compound radical, chain, straight chain, branched chain, side chain; ring, closed chain, cycle; homocycle, heterocycle; benzene ring *or* nucleus, Kekulé formula; lattice, space-lattice

8 **fission, nuclear fission,** fission reaction; **atom-smashing,** atom-chipping, **splitting the atom;** atomic reaction; atomic disintegration *or* decay, alpha decay, beta decay, gamma decay; stimulation, dissociation, photodisintegration, ionization, nucleization, cleavage; neutron reaction, proton reaction, etc; reversible reaction, nonreversible reaction; thermonuclear reaction; **chain reaction;** exchange reaction; breeding; disintegration series; bombardment, atomization; bullet, target; proton gun

9 **fusion, nuclear fusion,** fusion reaction, thermonuclear reaction, thermonuclear fusion, laser-induced fusion, cold fusion

10 **fissionable material,** nuclear fuel; magnox; fertile material; **critical mass,** noncritical mass; parent element, daughter element; end product

11 **accelerator** (*see list*), **particle accelerator,** atomic accelerator, atom smasher, atomic cannon

12 mass spectrometer, mass spectrograph

13 **reactor** (*see list*), **nuclear reactor, pile,** atomic pile, reactor pile, chain-reacting pile, chain reactor, **furnace,** atomic *or* nuclear furnace, neutron factory; fast pile, intermediate pile, slow pile; lattice; bricks; rods; radioactive waste, nuclear waste; nuclear dumping; nuclear repository

14 atomic engine, **atomic** *or* **nuclear power plant,** reactor engine

15 **atomic energy, nuclear energy** *or* **power,** thermonuclear power; activation energy, binding energy, mass energy; energy level; atomic research, atomic project; Atomic Energy Commission *or* AEC; NIREX *or* Nuclear Industry Radioactive Waste Executive

16 **atomic explosion, atom blast, A-blast; thermonuclear explosion,** hydrogen blast, **H-blast;** ground zero; blast wave, Mach stem; Mach front; mushroom cloud; **fallout,** airborne radioactivity, fission particles, dust cloud, radioactive dust; flash burn; **atom bomb** *or* **atomic bomb** *or* **A-bomb, hydrogen bomb,** thermonuclear bomb, nuke (*informal*); scram; meltdown; A-bomb shelter, fallout shelter; nuclear winter

verbs

17 **to atomize,** nucleize; activate, accelerate; bombard, cross-bombard; cleave, fission, **split** *or* **smash the atom**

adjectives

18 **atomic;** atomistic; atomiferous; monatomic, diatomic, triatomic, tetratomic, pentatomic, hexatomic, heptatomic; heteratomic, heteroatomic; subatomic, subnuclear, ultraelementary; dibasic, tribasic; cyclic, isocyclic, homocyclic, heterocyclic; isotopic, isobaric, isoteric

19 **nuclear, N-, thermonuclear,** isonuclear, homonuclear, heteronuclear, extranuclear

20 **fissionable,** fissile, scissile

21 **atoms**

acceptor atom	isotopic isobar
asymmetric carbon atom	labelled atom
discrete atom	neutral atom
excited atom	normal atom
hot atom	nuclear isomer
impurity atom	radiation atom
isobar	recoil atom
isotere	stripped atom

22 **subatomic particles**

antibaryon	fermion
antielectron	flavour
antilepton	gauge boson
antimeson	gluino
antineutrino	gravitino
antineutron	graviton
antiparticle	hadron
antiproton	Higgs boson
antiquark	hyperon
b *or* bottom quark	intermediate-vector boson
baryon	J *or* J particle *or* psi
beta particle	particle
boson	kaon *or* K-meson *or* K-
electron	particle
energy particle	lambda particle

lepton
magnetic monopole
matter particle
meson *or* mesotron
muon *or* mu-meson
neutrino
neutron
omega *or* omega-zero *or*
  omega nought particle
phi-meson
photino
photon
pion *or* pi-meson
positron *or* positive
  electron
proton
quark
quarkonium
rho particle
s *or* strange quark
sigma particle
slepton

squark
strange particle
superstring
tachyon
tardyon
tau *or* tauon *or* tau lepton
tau-meson
tau neutrino *or* tauonic
  neutrino
technifermion
t *or* top quark
u *or* up quark
weakon
WIMP *or* weakly
  interactive massive
  particle
w particle
xi-particle
zino
z particle
z-zero

23 neutrons

fast neutron
monoenergetic neutron
photoneutron

resonance neutron
slow neutron
thermal neutron

24 accelerators

betatron
bevatron
cascade transformer
charge-exchange accelerator
Cockcroft-Walton voltage
  multiplier
collider
cosmotron
cyclotron
electron accelerator
electrostatic generator
induction accelerator

linear accelerator
microwave linear
  accelerator
positive-ion accelerator
superconducting
  supercollider *or* SSC
synchrocyclotron
synchrotron
tokamak
Van de Graaff generator
wake-field accelerator

25 reactors

boiling water reactor
breeder reactor
CANDU *or* Canada
  deuterium oxide-uranium
  reactor
fast-breeder reactor
gas-cooled reactor
heterogeneous reactor

homogeneous reactor
magnox reactor
plutonium reactor
power-breeder reactor
power reactor
pressurized-water reactor
stellarator
uranium reactor

1038 MECHANICS

nouns

1 **mechanics** (*see list*); leverage *see* 905; tools and
  machinery *see* 1039
2 **statics** (*see list*)
3 **dynamics** (*see list*), kinetics, energetics
4 **hydraulics, fluid dynamics,** hydromechanics,
  hydrokinetics, fluidics, hydrodynamics, hydrostatics;
  hydrology, hydrography, hydrometry, fluviology
5 **pneumatics,** pneumatostatics; aeromechanics,
  aerophysics, aerology, aerometry, aerography,
  aerotechnics, aerodynamics, aerostatics

6 **engineering,** mechanical engineering, jet
  engineering, etc; engineers

adjectives

7 **mechanical,** mechanistic; locomotive, locomotor;
  zoomechanical, biomechanical, aeromechanical,
  hydromechanical, etc
8 **static;** biostatic, electrostatic, geostatic, etc
9 **dynamic, dynamical, kinetic, kinetical,**
  kinematic, kinematical; geodynamic,
  radiodynamic, electrodynamic, etc
10 **pneumatic,** pneumatological; aeromechanical,
  aerophysical, aerologic, aerological, aerotechnical,
  aerodynamic, aerostatic, aerographic, aerographical
11 **hydrologic,** hydrometric, hydrometrical,
  hydromechanic, hydromechanical, hydrodynamic,
  hydrostatic, hydraulic
12 **kinds and branches of mechanics**

aeromechanics
animal mechanics
applied mechanics
atomechanics
auto mechanics (US &
  Canadian)
celestial mechanics
electromechanics
fluid mechanics
hydromechanics *or*
  hydrodynamics
kinematics
magnetohydrodynamics *or*
  MHD
matrix mechanics

mechanical arts
micromechanics
practical mechanics
pure *or* abstract mechanics
quantum mechanics
rational mechanics
servomechanics
statistical mechanics
telemechanics
theoretical *or* analytical
  mechanics
wave mechanics
zoomechanics *or*
  biomechanics

13 statics

aerostatics
biostatics
electrostatics
geostatics
gnathostatics
graphostatics
gyrostatics

haemastatics *or*
  haematostatics
hydrostatics
hygrostatics
rheostatics
stereostatics
thermostatics

14 dynamics

aerodynamics
astrodynamics
barodynamics
biodynamics
cardiodynamics
electrodynamics
fluid dynamics
geodynamics
gnathodynamics
haemadynamics *or*
  haematodynamics
hydrodynamics
kinesiology

magnetohydrodynamics
megadynamics
myodynamics
pharmacodynamics
photodynamics
phytodynamics
pneodynamics
pneumodynamics
radiodynamics
thermodynamics
trophodynamics
zoodynamics

1039 TOOLS, MACHINERY

nouns

1 **tool, instrument, implement, utensil; apparatus,**
  device, mechanical device, contrivance, contraption
  (*informal*), gadget, gizmo, waldo, gimcrack, gimmick
  (*informal*), means, mechanical means; gadgetry; **hand**

tool; hammer, sledgehammer, claw hammer, mallet; wrench, monkey wrench, bobbejaan spanner (*South African*); chisel, screwdriver, clippers, awl, file, pick, punch; **power tool**; machine tool; speed tool; precision tool *or* instrument; **mechanization,** mechanizing; motorizing

2 cutlery, edge tool; **knife, axe,** chopper, dagger, sword, blade, cutter, whittle; steel, cold steel, naked steel; chiv *and* shiv *and* pigsticker *and* toad stabber *and* toad sticker (*all informal*); cutthroat *or* cutthroat razor; perforator, piercer, puncturer, point; sharpener; saw; trowel; shovel, banjo (*Australian & NZ informal*); clink; plane, buzzer (*NZ*); drill; valve *see* 239.10

3 **machinery,** enginery; **machine, mechanism,** mechanical device; heavy machinery, earthmoving machinery, earthmover; farm machinery; mill; welder; pump; petrol pump, bowser (*Australian & NZ*); **engine,** motor, linear motor; engine part, big end, little end; power plant, **power source,** drive, motive power, prime mover; **appliance,** convenience, facility, utility, home appliance, mechanical aid; fixture; labour-saving device

4 **mechanism,** machinery, **movement,** movements, **action, motion, works,** workings, inner workings, what makes it work, innards, what makes it tick; drive train, power train; wheelwork, **wheelworks,** wheels, gear, wheels within wheels, epicyclic train; clockworks, watchworks, servomechanism *see* 1040.13

5 **gear,** gearing, gear train; gearwheel, cogwheel, rack; **gearshift;** low, intermediate, high, neutral, reverse; differential, differential gear *or* gearing; **transmission,** gearbox; automatic transmission; selective transmission; standard transmission, gear lever, gearstick, stick shift (*US & Canadian*); synchronized shifting, synchromesh

6 **clutch,** cone clutch, plate clutch, dog clutch, disc clutch, multiple-disc clutch, rim clutch, friction clutch, cone friction clutch, slip friction clutch, spline clutch, rolling-key clutch

7 **tooling,** tooling up; **retooling;** instrumentation, industrial instrumentation; servo instrumentation

8 **mechanic,** mechanician; grease monkey (*informal*), greaser (*informal*); artisan, artificer; **machinist,** machiner; car mechanic, auto mechanic (*US & Canadian*), aeromechanic, etc

verbs

9 to tool, tool up, instrument; retool; **machine,** mill; **mechanize,** motorize; sharpen

adjectives

10 **mechanical;** machinelike; power, powered, power-driven, motor-driven, motorized; **mechanized**

1040 AUTOMATION

nouns

1 **automation,** automatic control; robotization, cybernation; **self-action,** self-activity; **self-movement,** self-motion, **self-propulsion;** self-direction, self-determination, self-government, automatism, self-regulation; automaticity, automatization; servo instrumentation; computerization

2 autonetics, automatic *or* automation technology, automatic electronics, automatic engineering, automatic control engineering, servo engineering, **servomechanics,** system engineering, systems analysis, feedback system engineering; **cybernetics;** telemechanics; radiodynamics, radio control; systems planning, systems design; circuit analysis; bionics; communication *or* communications theory, information theory

3 **automatic control,** cybernation, servo control, robot control, robotization; cybernetic control; electronic control, electronic-mechanical control; feedback control, digital feedback control, analogue feedback control; cascade control, piggyback control (*informal*); supervisory control; action, control action; derivative *or* rate action, reset action; control agent; control means

4 semiautomatic control; **remote control,** push-button control, remote handling, tele-action; radio control; telemechanics; telemechanism; telemetry, telemeter, telemetering; transponder; bioinstrument, bioinstrumentation

5 control system, **automatic control system,** servo system, robot system; closed-loop system; open-sequence system; linear system, nonlinear system; carrier-current system; integrated system, complex control system; data system, data-handling system, data-reduction system, data-input system, data-interpreting system, digital data reducing system; process-control system, annunciator system, flow-control system, motor-speed control system; automanual system; automatic telephone system; electrostatic spraying system; automated factory, automatic *or* robot factory, push-button plant; servo laboratory, servolab

6 **feedback,** closed sequence, feedback loop, closed loop; multiple-feed closed loop; process loop, quality loop; feedback circuit, current-control circuit, direct-current circuit, alternating-current circuit, calibrating circuit, switching circuit, flip-flop circuit, peaking circuit; multiplier channels; open sequence, linear operation; positive feedback, negative feedback; reversed feedback, degeneration

7 (*functions*) accounting, analysis, automatic electronic navigation, automatic guidance, braking, comparison of variables, computation, coordination, corrective action, fact distribution, forecasts, impedance matching, inspection, linear *or* nonlinear calibrations, manipulation, measurement of variables, missile guidance, output measurement, processing, rate determination, record keeping, statistical communication, steering, system stabilization, ultrasonic *or* supersonic flow detection

8 **process control,** bit-weight control, colour control, density control, dimension control, diverse control, end-point control, flavour control, flow control, fragrance control, hold control, humidity control, light-intensity control, limit control, liquid-level control, load control, pressure control, precision-production control, proportional control, quality control, quantity control, revolution control, temperature control, time control, weight control

9 variable, process variable; simple variable, complex variable; manipulated variable; steady state, transient state

10 values, target values; set point; differential gap; proportional band; dead band, dead zone; neutral zone

11 time constants; time lead, gain; time delay, dead time; lag, process lag, hysteresis, holdup, output lag; throughput

12 automatic device (*see list*), automatic; semi-automatic; self-actor, self-mover; **robot, automaton,** mechanical man; cyborg; bionic man, bionic woman; Dalek

13 **servomechanism,** servo; cybernion, automatic machine; **servomotor;** synchro, selsyn, autosyn; synchronous motor, synchronous machine

14 **system component; control mechanism; regulator, control,** controller, **governor;** servo control, servo regulator; control element

15 **automatic detector;** automatic analyser; automatic indicator

16 **control panel,** console; coordinated panel, graphic panel; panelboard, set-up board

17 **computer, computer science** *see* 1041, electronic computer, electronic brain; information machine, thinking machine; computer unit, hardware, computer hardware

18 **control engineer,** servo engineer, system engineer, systems analyst, automatic control system engineer, feedback system engineer, automatic technician, robot specialist; computer engineer, computer technologist, computer technician, **computer programmer;** cybernetic technologist, cyberneticist

verbs

19 **to automate,** automatize, robotize; robot-control, servo-control; program; computerize

20 **to self-govern,** self-control, **self-regulate,** self-direct

adjectives

21 **automated,** cybernated, robotized; **automatic,** automatous, **spontaneous; self-acting,** self-active; **self-operating,** self-operative, self-working; **self-regulating,** self-regulative, self-regulatory, self-governing, self-directing; **self-regulated, self-controlled,** self-governed, self-directed, self-steered; self-adjusting, self-cleaning, self-closing, self-cocking, self-cooking, self-dumping, self-emptying, self-lighting, self-loading, self-opening, self-priming, self-rising, self-sealing, self-starting, self-winding, automanual; semiautomatic; computerized, computer-controlled

22 **self-propelled,** self-moved, horseless; **self-propelling,** self-moving, self-propellent; self-driven, self-drive; **automotive,** automobile, automechanical; **locomotive,** locomobile

23 **servomechanical,** servo-controlled; **cybernetic;** isotronic

24 **remote-control,** remote-controlled, telemechanic; telemetered, telemetric; by remote control

word elements

25 aut–, auto–, automat–, automato–, self–

26 automatic devices

airborne controls	automatic telephone
antiaircraft gun positioner	automatic telephone
artificial feedback kidney	exchange
automatic block signal	automaton
automatic gun	chess-playing machine
automatic gun director	guided missile
automatic heater	gyroscopic pilot
automatic iron	lever pilot
automatic piano	mechanical heart
automatic pilot *or* autopilot	multiple-stylus electronic
or automatic *or* gyropilot	printer
or robot	radar controls
automatic pinspotter	robot pilot
automatic pistol	robot plane
automatic printer	robot submarine
automatic rifle	self-starter
automatic sight	semiautomatic pistol *or*
automatic sprinkler	rifle
automatic stop	speedometer
automatic telegraph	

1041 COMPUTER SCIENCE

nouns

1 **computer science** (*see list*), computer systems and applications, computer hardware and software, computers, digital computers, computing, machine computation, number-crunching (*informal*); **computerization,** digitization; **data processing,** electronic data processing *or* EDP, data storage and retrieval; data bank; **information science,** information processing, **information technology** *or* IT, informatics; computer security; computer crime *or* fraud, computer virus *or* worm; hacking, hackery (*informal*), cracking (*informal*)

2 **computer,** electronic data processor, information processor, electronic brain, digital computer, general purpose computer, analogue computer, hybrid computer, machine, **hardware,** computer hardware, microelectronics device; **processor,** central processing unit *or* CPU, multiprocessor, microprocessor, word processor *or* WP, mainframe computer *or* mainframe, dataflow computer, work station, minicomputer, microcomputer, personal computer *or* PC, home computer, desktop computer *or* desktop, laptop computer *or* laptop, lapheld computer, palmtop computer *or* palmtop, briefcase computer, pocket computer, notebook, minisupercomputer, multi-user computer, superminicomputer, supermicrocomputer, supercomputer, graphoscope, array processor, neurocomputer; neural net *or* network, semantic net *or* network

3 **circuitry,** circuit, integrated circuit, logic circuit, **chip,** silicon chip, gallium arsenide chip, semiconductor chip, hybrid chip, wafer chip, superchip, microchip, neural network chip, transputer, **board,** printed circuit board *or* PCB, motherboard; smart card *or* laser card *or* intelligent card; magnetic stripe; **peripheral,** peripheral device *or* unit, input device, output device; **port,** channel interface, serial interface, serial port; read-write head; streamer

4 input device, keyboard *or* electronic keyboard, key pad, key; reader, tape reader, scanner, optical scanner, optical character reader, optical character recognition *or* OCR device, light pen, data pen, mouse

5 drive, disk drive, floppy disk drive, hard disk drive *or* Winchester drive, tape drive

6 disk, magnetic disk, floppy disk *or* floppy (*informal*), diskette, minifloppy, microfloppy, hard *or* fixed *or* Winchester disk, disk pack, CD-ROM, optical disk *or* video disk, WORM; magnetic tape *or* mag tape (*informal*), magnetic tape unit, magnetic drum

7 memory, storage, memory bank, memory chip, firmware; **main memory,** main storage *or* store, random access memory *or* RAM, core, core storage *or* store, disk pack, magnetic disk, primary storage, backing store, read/write memory, optical disk memory, bubble memory, virtual memory; read-only memory *or* ROM, programmable read-only memory *or* PROM, serial access memory *or* SAM, cache memory, virtual memory, volatile memory

8 retrieval, access, random access, sequential access, direct access, remote access

9 output device, terminal, workstation, video terminal, video display terminal *or* VDT, video display unit *or* VDU, visual display unit *or* VDU, graphics terminal, **monitor,** cathode ray tube *or* CRT, monochrome monitor, colour monitor, RGB monitor, **printer, serial printer,** character printer, impact printer, dot-matrix printer, daisy-wheel *or* printwheel printer, drum printer, **line printer,** line dot-matrix printer, chain printer, **page printer,** nonimpact printer, laser printer, electronic printer, graphics printer, colour graphics printer; **modem** *or* modulator-demodulator

10 forms, computer forms, computer paper, continuous stationery

11 software, program, computer program, source program, object program, binary file, binary program, software package, software support, courseware, groupware, shareware, freeware, routine, subroutine

12 systems program, operating system *or* OS, disk operating system *or* DOS (*trademark*), shell program; Microsoft (*trademark*), Windows (*trademark*), disk operating system *or* MS-DOS (*trademark*); UNIX (*trademark*); control program monitor *or* CPM; parser; **word processor,** text editor, editor, print formatter, WYSIWYG *or* what-you-see-is-what-you-get word processor, post-formatted word processor; spreadsheet, electronic spreadsheet, desktop publishing program, database management system *or* DBMS; **computer application** (*see list*), applications program, bootloader *or* bootstrap loader

13 language (*see list*), assembler *or* assemblage language, programming language, machine language, machine-readable language, conventional programming language, computer language, high-level language, interpreter, low-level language, application development language, assembly language, object code, job-control language *or* JCL, procedural

language, problem-oriented language, query language; **computer** *or* **electronic virus,** computer worm, phantom bug, Trojan horse, logic bomb

14 bit, binary digit, infobit, kilobit, megabit, gigabit, terbit; **byte,** kilobyte *or* Kbyte *or* KB, megabyte

15 data, information, database, data capture, database management, file, record, data bank, input, input-output *or* I/O; megaflop; **file,** data set, record, data record, data file, text file

16 network, computer network, communications network, local area network *or* LAN, workgroup computing, mesh; **on-line system,** interactive system, on-line service; Internet, the Net, the Web, the World Wide Web

17 liveware, programmer, systems programmer, system software specialist, application programmer, systems analyst, systems engineer, computer designer, computer architect, operator, technician, key puncher; hacker (*informal*), cracker (*informal*)

verbs

18 to computerize, digitize; **program,** boot, boot up, initialize, log in, log out, run, load, download, **compute,** crunch numbers (*informal*); **keyboard,** key in, input; hack (*informal*), crack (*informal*)

adjectives

19 computerized, smart, intelligent; machine-usable, computer-usable; computer-aided, computer-assisted; computer-driven, computer-guided, computer-controlled, computer-governed

20 branches of computer science

analysis of algorithms	machine learning
artificial intelligence *or* AI	machine organization
or machine intelligence	nonnumerical applications
automata theory	numerical analysis
combinatorial processes	numerical applications
compiler design	operating systems
computer applications	optimization
computer architecture	programming
computer graphics	programming languages
computer systems	robotics
information storage and	simulation
retrieval	switching theory
information technology *or*	symbol manipulation
IT	theory of computation
language processing	theory of formal languages
logical design	utility programs

21 computer applications

batch processing	computer graphics
computer-aided design	computer *or* interactive
computer-aided	fiction
engineering	computer *or* synthesized
computer-aided	music
manufacturer	computer typesetting
computer-aided radiology	desktop publishing *or*
computer art	DTP
computer-assisted	electronic publishing
instruction	image enhancement
computer bulletin boards	inventory control
computer conferencing	linguistic analysis
computer crime	quality control
computer games	sales report program

simulation
time-sharing

22 computer languages

ADA
ALGOL *or* algorithmic-
oriented language
APL *or* a programming
language
APT *or* automatic
programmed tools
assembly language
awk *or* Aho Weinberger
and Kernighan
BAL *or* basic assembly
language
BASIC *or* beginners all-
purpose symbolic
instruction code
BCPL
C
C++
COBOL *or* common
business-oriented
language
COMIT
COMPACT II
efl
eqn
FLOWMATIC
FORMAC
FORTH
FORTRAN *or* formula
translator
FORTRAN 77
GPSS

word wrapping
virtual reality

Haskell
IPL-V
JOSS
JOVIAL
lex
LISP *or* list-processing
LOGO
make
MUMPS
OCCAM
PASCAL
Perl
pic
PILOT *or* programmed
inquiry learning or
teaching
PL/1 *or* programming
language 1
PROLOG
Ratfor
RPG II
sh
Simula
Smalltalk
SML
SNOBOL *or* sno *or*
string-oriented symbolic
language
SOL
yacc *or* yet another
computer compiler

1042 FRICTION

nouns

1 **friction, rubbing,** rub, frottage; frication *and*
confrication *and* perfrication (*all old*); **drag,** skin
friction; **resistance,** frictional resistance

2 **abrasion, attrition, erosion, wearing away, wear,**
detrition, ablation; ruboff; erasure, erasing, rubbing
away *or* off *or* out; **grinding, filing,** rasping,
limation; fretting; galling; **chafing, chafe; scraping,**
grazing, scratching, scuffing; **scrape,** scratch, **scuff;**
scrubbing, scrub; scouring, scour; **polishing,**
burnishing, sanding, smoothing, dressing, buffing,
shining; sandblasting; abrasive; brass-rubbing,
heelball rubbing, graphite rubbing

3 **massage,** massaging, stroking, kneading; **rubdown;**
massotherapy, rolfing; whirlpool bath, Jacuzzi
(*trademark*); vibrator; facial massage, facial; exfoliation

4 massager, **masseur, masseuse;** massotherapist

5 (*mechanics*) force of friction; force of viscosity;
coefficient of friction; friction head; friction clutch,
friction drive, friction gearing, friction pile, friction
saw, friction welding

verbs

6 **to rub,** frictionize; **massage,** knead, rub down;
caress, pet, stroke *see* 73.8

7 **to abrade,** abrase, gnaw, gnaw away; **erode,** erode
away, ablate, wear, wear away; erase, rub away *or* off
or out; **grind, rasp, file, grate; chafe,** fret, gall;
scrape, graze, raze (*old*), **scuff,** bark, skin; **fray,**
frazzle; **scrub, scour,** exfoliate

8 **to buff, burnish, polish,** rub up, sandpaper, **sand,**
smooth, dress, shine, furbish, sandblast

adjectives

9 **frictional,** friction; **fricative; rubbing**

10 **abrasive,** abradant, attritive, gnawing, erosive,
ablative; scraping; **grinding, rasping;** chafing,
fretting, galling

1043 DENSITY

nouns

1 **density,** denseness, **solidity, solidness,** firmness,
compactness, closeness, spissitude (*old*);
congestion, congestedness, crowdedness,
jammedness; **impenetrability,** impermeability,
imporosity; hardness *see* 1044; incompressibility;
specific gravity, relative density; **consistency,**
consistence, thick consistency, thickness; viscidity,
viscosity, **viscousness, thickness,** gluiness, ropiness

2 **indivisibility, inseparability,** impartibility,
infrangibility, indiscerptibility; indissolubility;
cohesion, coherence *see* 802; unity *see* 791;
insolubility, infusibility

3 **densification, condensation, compression,**
concentration, inspissation, concretion,
consolidation, conglobulation; hardening,
solidification *see* 1044.5; agglutination, clumping,
clustering

4 **thickening,** inspissation; congelation, **congealment,**
coagulation, clotting, **setting,** concretion;
gelatinization, gelatination, jellification, jellying,
jelling, gelling; **curdling,** clabbering; **distillation**

5 **precipitation,** deposit, sedimentation; precipitate

6 **solid,** solid body, body, mass; lump, clump, cluster;
block, cake; node, knot; concrete, concretion;
conglomerate, conglomeration

7 **clot,** coagulum, coagulate; blood clot, grume,
embolus, crassamentum; **coagulant,** coagulator,
clotting factor, coagulase, coagulose, thromboplastin
or coagulin; casein, caseinogen, paracasein, legumin;
curd, clabber, loppered milk *and* bonnyclabber (*both*
informal), clotted cream, Devonshire cream

8 (*instruments*) densimeter, densitometer; aerometer,
hydrometer, lactometer, urinometer, pycnometer

verbs

9 **to densify,** inspissate, densen; **condense,**
compress, compact, **consolidate, concentrate,**
come to a head; **congest; squeeze, press, crowd,**
cram, jam, ram down; steeve; pack *or* jam in;
solidify *see* 1044.8

10 **to thicken,** thick (*old*); inspissate, incrassate;
congeal, coagulate, clot, set, concrete; gelatinize,
gelatinate, jelly, jellify, **jell, gel; curdle,** curd,
clabber, lopper (*informal*); cake, lump, clump, cluster,
knot

11 **to precipitate,** deposit, sediment, sedimentate

adjectives

12 dense, compact, close; close-textured, close-knit, close-woven, tight-knit; serried, **thick, heavy**, thickset, thick-packed, thick-growing, thick-spread, thick-spreading; **condensed, compressed,** compacted, concrete, consolidated, concentrated; **crowded, jammed,** packed, jam-packed, packed *or* jammed in, packed *or* jammed in like sardines, chock-a-block, chock-full; **congested,** crammed, crammed full; **solid,** firm, substantial, massive; impenetrable, impermeable, imporous, nonporous; hard *see* 1044.10; incompressible; viscid, viscous, ropy, gluey

13 indivisible, nondivisible, undividable, **inseparable,** impartible, infrangible, indiscerptible, indissoluble; cohesive, coherent *see* 802.10; unified; insoluble, indissolvable, infusible

14 thickened, inspissate *or* inspissated, incrassate; **congealed, coagulated, clotted,** grumous; **curdled,** curded, clabbered; **jellied,** jelled, gelatinized; lumpy, lumpish; caked, cakey; coagulant, coagulating

adverbs

15 densely, compactly, **close,** closely, **thick,** thickly, heavily; solidly, firmly

1044 HARDNESS, RIGIDITY

nouns

1 hardness, durity (*old*), induration; **callousness,** callosity; stoniness, rock-hardness, flintiness, steeliness; **strength, toughness** *see* 1047; solidity, impenetrability, density *see* 1043; restiveness, resistance *see* 453; obduracy *see* 361.1; hardness of heart *see* 94.3

2 rigidity, rigidness, rigor (*old*); **firmness,** renitence *or* renitency, incompressibility; nonresilience *or* nonresiliency, inelasticity; **tension,** tensity, **tenseness,** tautness, tightness

3 stiffness, inflexibility, unpliability, unmalleability, intractability, unbendingness, unlimberness, starchiness; **stubbornness,** unyieldingness *see* 361.2; **unalterability,** immutability; immovability *see* 854.3; inelasticity, irresilience *or* irresiliency; inextensibility *or* unextensibility, unextendibility, inductility

4 temper, tempering; chisel temper, die temper, razor temper, saw file temper, set temper, spindle temper, tool temper; precipitation hardening, heat treating; hardness test, Brinell test; hardness scale, Brinell number *or* Brinell hardness number *or* Bhn; indenter; hardener, hardening, hardening agent

5 hardening, toughening, induration, firming; **strengthening; tempering,** case hardening, steeling; seasoning; **stiffening,** rigidification, starching; **solidification, setting,** curing, caking, concretion; crystallization, granulation; callusing; sclerosis, arteriosclerosis, atherosclerosis; lithification; lapidification (*old*); **petrification,** fossilization, ossification; cornification, hornification; calcification; vitrification, vitrifaction

6 (*comparisons*) stone, rock *see* 1057, adamant, granite, flint, marble, diamond; steel, iron, nails; concrete, cement; brick; oak, heart of oak; bone

verbs

7 to harden, indurate, firm, **toughen** *see* 1047.3; **callous; temper,** anneal, oil-temper, heat-temper, **case-harden,** steel; season; **petrify,** lapidify (*old*), fossilize; lithify; vitrify; calcify; ossify; cornify, hornify

8 to solidify, concrete, **set,** take a set, cure, cake; condense, thicken *see* 1043.10; **crystallize,** granulate, candy

9 to stiffen, rigidify, starch; **strengthen, toughen** *see* 1047.3; back, brace, reinforce, shore up; **tense, tighten,** tense up, tension; trice up, screw up

adjectives

10 hard, solid, dure (*old*), lacking give, **tough** *see* 1047.4; resistive, resistant, steely, steellike, iron-hard, ironlike; **stony,** rocky, stonelike, rock-hard, rocklike, lapideous, lapidific, lapidifical, lithoid *or* lithoidal; diamondlike, adamant, adamantine; flinty, flintlike; marble, marblelike; granitic, granitelike; gritty; concrete, cement, cemental; horny, bony, osseous; hard-boiled; hard as nails *or* a rock, etc *see* 1044.6
"as firm as a stone; yea, as hard as a piece of the nether millstone"—Bible; dense *see* 1043.12; obdurate *see* 361.10; hard-hearted *see* 94.12

11 rigid, stiff, firm, renitent, incompressible; **tense, taut, tight,** unrelaxed; nonresilient, inelastic; **rodlike,** virgate; ramrod-stiff, ramrodlike, pokerlike; stiff as a poker *or* rod, stiff as a board, stiff as buckram; starched, starchy

12 inflexible, unflexible, **unpliable, unpliant, unmalleable, intractable,** untractable, intractile, **unbending,** unlimber, **unyielding** *see* 361.9, ungiving, **stubborn, unalterable,** immutable; **immovable** *see* 854.15; **adamant,** adamantine; **inelastic,** nonelastic, irresilient; inextensile, inextensible, unextensible, inextensional, unextendible, nonstretchable, inductile

13 hardened, toughened, steeled, indurate, indurated; **callous,** calloused; **solidified,** set; crystallized, granulated; petrified, lapidified (*old*), fossilized; vitrified; sclerotic; ossified; cornified, hornified; calcified; crusted, crusty, incrusted; **stiffened, strengthened,** rigidified, backed, reinforced

14 hardening, toughening, indurative; petrifying, petrifactive

15 tempered, case-hardened, heat-treated, **annealed,** oil-tempered, heat-tempered, tempered in fire; seasoned

1045 SOFTNESS, PLIANCY

nouns

1 softness, give, nonresistiveness, insolidity, unsolidity, nonrigidity; **gentleness,** easiness, delicacy, tenderness; *morbidezza* (*Italian*); lenity, leniency *see* 427; mellowness; fluffiness, flossiness, downiness, featheriness; velvetiness, plushiness, satininess, silkiness; sponginess, pulpiness

2 pliancy, pliability, plasticity, flexibility, flexility, flexuousness, bendability, ductility, ductibility (*old*), tensileness, tensility, tractility, **tractability,** amenability, adaptability, facility, give, **suppleness,**

willowiness, **litheness, limberness; elasticity** *see* 1046, **resilience,** springiness, resiliency; malleability, mouldability, fictility, sequacity (*old*); **impressionability,** susceptibility, responsiveness, receptiveness, sensibility, sensitiveness; formability, formativeness; extensibility, extendibility; agreeability *see* 324.1; submissiveness *see* 433.3

3 **flaccidity,** flaccidness, **flabbiness, limpness,** rubberiness, floppiness; **looseness,** laxness, laxity, laxation, relaxedness, relaxation

4 (*comparisons*) putty, clay, dough, blubber, rubber, wax, butter, pudding; velvet, plush, satin, silk; wool, fleece; pillow, cushion; kapok; baby's bottom; puff; fluff, floss, flue; down, feathers, feather bed, eiderdown, swansdown, thistledown; breeze, zephyr; foam

5 **softening,** softening-up; **easing,** padding, cushioning; mollifying, mollification; **relaxation,** laxation; mellowing; tenderizing

verbs

6 **to soften,** soften up; unsteel; **ease,** cushion; gentle, mollify, milden; **subdue,** tone *or* tune down; mellow; tenderize; **relax,** laxate, loosen; **limber,** limber up, supple; massage, knead, plump, plump up, fluff, fluff up, shake up; **mash, smash,** squash, pulp

7 **to yield, give,** relent, relax, bend, unbend, give way; submit *see* 433.6, 9

adjectives

8 **soft,** nonresistive, nonrigid; mild, **gentle, easy, delicate, tender;** complaisant *see* 427.8; mellow, mellowy (*old*); **softened,** mollified; whisper-soft, soft as putty *or* clay *or* dough, etc *see* 1045.4, soft as a kiss *or* a sigh *or* a baby's bottom,

"soft as sinews of the new-born babe"—SHAKESPEARE

9 **pliant, pliable, flexible,** flexile, flexuous, **plastic, elastic** *see* 1046.7, ductile, sequacious *or* facile (*both old*), tractile, **tractable, yielding,** giving, bending; adaptable, **malleable,** mouldable, shapable, fabricable, fictile; compliant *see* 324.5, submissive *see* 433.12; **impressionable,** impressible, susceptible, responsive, receptive, sensitive; **formable,** formative; **bendable,** bendy; **supple,** willowy, **limber; lithe,** lithesome, lissome,

"as lissome as a hazel wand"—TENNYSON, double-jointed, loose-limbed, whippy; **elastic,** resilient, springy; extensile, extensible, extendible; like putty *or* wax *or* dough, etc

10 **flaccid, flabby, limp,** rubbery, flimsy, floppy; **loose,** lax, relaxed

11 **spongy,** pulpy, pithy, medullary; edematous

12 **pasty, doughy;** loamy, clayey, argillaceous

13 **squashy,** squishy, squooshy, squelchy, squidgy

14 **fluffy,** flossy, **downy,** pubescent, feathery; fleecy, woolly, lanate; furry

15 **velvety,** velvetlike, velutinous; plushy, plush; **satiny,** satinlike; cottony; **silky,** silken, silklike, sericeous, soft as silk

16 **softening, easing;** subduing, mollifying, emollient; demulcent; **relaxing,** loosening

adverbs

17 **softly, gently,** easily, delicately, tenderly; compliantly *see* 324.9, submissively *see* 433.17

1046 ELASTICITY

nouns

1 **elasticity, resilience** *or* resiliency, **give;** snap, **bounce,** bounciness; **stretch, stretchiness,** stretchability; extensibility; tone, tonus, tonicity; **spring, springiness;** rebound *see* 902.2; **flexibility** *see* 1045.2; **adaptability,** responsiveness; **buoyancy** *or* buoyance; **liveliness** *see* 330.2

2 **stretching;** extension; distension *see* 259.2; **stretch, tension, strain**

3 **elastic;** elastomer; **rubber,** gum elastic, latex; stretch fabric, Lastex (*trademark*), spandex, Lycra (*trademark*); gum, chewing gum *see* 1060.6; whalebone, baleen; rubber band *or* elastic band, rubber ball, handball, tennis ball; spring; springboard; rebounder; trampoline; racket, battledore; jumping jack

verbs

4 **to stretch;** extend; distend *see* 259.4

5 **to give,** yield *see* 1045.7; bounce, spring, spring back *see* 902.6

6 **to elasticize;** rubberize, rubber; vulcanize

adjectives

7 **elastic, resilient, springy,** bouncy; **stretchable, stretchy,** stretch; extensile; **flexible** *see* 1045.9; flexile; **adaptable,** adaptive, responsive; buoyant; lively *see* 330.17

8 **rubber, rubbery,** rubberlike; rubberized

1047 TOUGHNESS

nouns

1 **toughness, resistance; strength, hardiness,** vitality, stamina *see* 15.1; stubbornness, **stiffness; unbreakableness** *or* **unbreakability,** infrangibility; cohesiveness, **tenacity,** viscidity *see* 802.3; **durability,** lastingness *see* 826.1; **hardness** *see* 1044; **leatheriness,** leatherlikeness; stringiness

2 (*comparisons*) leather, old boots; gristle, cartilage

verbs

3 **to toughen,** harden, stiffen, work-harden, **temper,** strengthen; season; be tough; **endure, hang tough** (*informal*)

adjectives

4 **tough, resistant;** shockproof, shock-resistant, impactproof, impact-resistant; stubborn, stiff; **heavy-duty;** hard *or* tough as nails; **strong, hardy,** vigorous; cohesive, **tenacious,** viscid; **durable,** hard-wearing, lasting *see* 826.10; untiring; **hard** *see* 1044.10; chewy (*informal*); leathery, leatherlike, coriaceous, tough as leather; sinewy, wiry; gristly, cartilaginous; stringy, fibrous

5 **unbreakable,** nonbreakable, infrangible, unshatterable, shatterproof, chip-proof, fractureproof

6 **toughened,** hardened, tempered, annealed; seasoned

1048 BRITTLENESS, FRAGILITY

nouns

1 **brittleness, crispness,** crispiness; **fragility, frailty,** damageability, delicacy *see* 16.2, flimsiness, **breakability,** breakableness, frangibility, fracturableness, crackability, crackableness, crunchability, crushability, crushableness; lacerability; fissility; friability, crumbliness *see* 1049; vulnerableness, **vulnerability** *see* 1005.4

2 (*comparisons*) eggshell, matchwood, old paper, piecrust, glass, glass jaw, china, porcelain, parchment, ice, bubble, glass house, house of cards, hothouse plant

verbs

3 **to break, shatter,** fragment, fragmentize, fragmentate, fall to pieces, shard, **disintegrate** *see* 805

adjectives

4 **brittle, crisp,** crispy; **fragile, frail,** delicate *see* 16.14, flimsy, **breakable,** frangible, crushable, crackable, crunchable, fracturable; lacerable; **shatterable,** shattery, shivery, splintery; friable, crumbly *see* 1049.13; fissile, scissile; brittle as glass; **vulnerable** *see* 1005.16

1049 POWDERINESS, CRUMBLINESS

nouns

1 **powderiness,** pulverulence, **dustiness;** chalkiness; **mealiness,** flouriness, branniness; efflorescence

2 **granularity, graininess,** granulation; **sandiness, grittiness,** gravelliness, sabulosity

3 **friability,** pulverableness, crispness, crumbliness; brittleness *see* 1048

4 **pulverization,** comminution, trituration, attrition, detrition; levigation; reduction to powder *or* dust, pestling; fragmentation, sharding; brecciation; atomization, micronization; **powdering, crumbling;** abrasion *see* 1042.2; **grinding,** milling, grating, shredding; granulation, granulization; **beating, pounding, shattering,** flailing, mashing, smashing, crushing; disintegration *see* 805

5 **powder, dust;** stour (*Scottish*); dust ball, pussies, kittens, slut's wool, lint; efflorescence; **crumb,** crumble; **meal,** bran, flour, farina; groats, grits; filings, raspings, sawdust; soot, smut; **particle, particulate,** particulates, airborne particles, air pollution; fallout; cosmic dust

6 **grain,** granule, granulet; **grit, sand; gravel,** shingle; detritus, debris; breccia, collapse breccia

7 **pulverizer,** comminutor, triturator, levigator; **crusher; mill; grinder;** granulator, pepper grinder, pepper mill, salt mill; **grater,** nutmeg grater, cheese grater; coffee grinder; **shredder;** pestle, **mortar and pestle; masher;** millstone, quern, quernstone; roller, steamroller

8 koniology; konimeter

verbs

9 **to pulverize, powder,** comminute, triturate, contriturate, levigate, bray, pestle, disintegrate, reduce to powder *or* dust, grind to powder *or* dust, grind up; **fragment,** shard, shatter; brecciate; atomize, micronize; **crumble,** crumb; **granulate,** granulize, grain; **grind, grate, shred,** abrade *see* 1042.7; **mill,** flour; **beat, pound, mash, smash, crush,** crunch, flail, squash, scrunch (*informal*)

10 (*be reduced to powder*) **to powder,** come *or* fall to dust, **crumble,** crumble to *or* into dust, **disintegrate** *see* 805, fall to pieces, break up; effloresce; granulate, grain

adjectives

11 **powdery, dusty,** powder, pulverulent, pulverous, lutose; **pulverized,** pulverant, powdered, disintegrated, comminute, gone to dust, reduced to powder; **particulate; ground, grated,** pestled, milled, stone-ground, comminuted, triturated, levigated; sharded, **crushed; fragmented; shredded; fine,** impalpable; **chalky,** chalklike; **mealy,** floury, farinaceous; branny; furfuraceous, scaly, scurfy; flaky *see* 296.7; detrited, detrital; scobiform, scobicular; efflorescent

12 **granular, grainy,** granulate, **granulated; sandy, gritty,** sabulous, arenarious, arenaceous; shingly, shingled, pebbled, pebbly; **gravelly;** breccial, brecciated

13 **pulverable, pulverizable,** pulverulent, triturable; **friable,** crimp (*old*), crisp, **crumbly**

1050 MATERIALITY

nouns

1 **materiality,** materialness; **corporeity,** corporality, corporeality, corporealness, bodiliness, embodiment; **substantiality** *see* 762, concreteness *see* 762.1; **physicalness,** physicality

2 **matter, material,** materiality, **substance** *see* 762, **stuff,** hyle; **primal matter,** initial substance, xylem; brute matter; **element;** chemical element *see* 1058.1; the four elements; earth, air, fire, water; elementary particle, fundamental particle; elementary unit, building block, unit of being, monad; constituent, component; **atom** *see* 1037.4; atomic particles *see* 1037.6; **molecule;** material world, physical world, nature, natural world; hypostasis, substratum; plenum; antimatter

3 **body,** physical body, material body, corpus (*informal*), anatomy (*informal*), person, **figure, form,** frame, **physique,** carcass (*informal*), bones, flesh, clay, clod, hulk; soma; **torso, trunk;** warm body (*informal*)

4 **object, article, thing,** material thing, affair, something; whatsit (*informal*), what's-its-name *see* 528.2; something or other, *etwas* (*German*), *eppes* (*Yiddish*), *quelque chose* (*French*); artefact

5 (*informal terms*) **gadget** *see* 1039.1; thingum, **thingumabob,** thingumadad, thingy, thingumadoodle, **thingumajig** *or* **thingummyjig,** thingumajigger, thingumaree, thingummy, **doodah,** dofunny, dojigger, dojiggy, domajig, domajigger, **dohickey** (*US & Canadian*), dowhacky (*US & Canadian*), doings, flumadiddle, gigamaree, **gimmick, gizmo,** dingus, hickey (*US & Canadian*),

jigger, hootmalalie, hootenanny (*US*), whatchy, widget, whatnot

6 **materialism**, physicism, epiphenomenalism, identity theory of mind, atomism, mechanism; physicalism, behaviourism, instrumentalism, pragmatism, pragmaticism; historical materialism, dialectical materialism, Marxism; **positivism**, logical positivism, positive philosophy, empiricism, **naturalism**; realism, natural realism, commonsense realism, commonsense philosophy, naïve realism, new realism, critical realism, representative realism, epistemological realism; substantialism; hylomorphism; hylotheism; hylozoism; worldliness, earthliness, animalism, secularism, temporality

7 **materialist**, physicist, atomist; historical *or* dialectical materialist, Marxist; **naturalist**; realist, natural realist, commonsense realist, commonsense philosopher, epistemological realist

8 **materialization**, corporealization; substantialization, substantiation; **embodiment, incorporation,** personification, **incarnation; reincarnation;** reembodiment, transmigration, metempsychosis

verbs

9 **to materialize** *see* 762.5, corporalize; substantialize, substantify, substantiate; **embody** *see* 762.5, body, **incorporate,** corporify, personify, **incarnate; reincarnate,** reembody, transmigrate

adjectives

10 **material**, materiate, hylic, **substantial** *see* 762.6; **corporeal**, corporeous, corporal, **bodily; physical,** somatic, somatical, somatous; **fleshly;** worldly, earthly, here-and-now, **secular,** temporal, **unspiritual,** nonspiritual

11 **embodied**, bodied, **incorporated, incarnate**

12 **materialist** *or* **materialistic**, atomistic, mechanist, mechanistic; Marxian, Marxist; **naturalist, naturalistic, positivist, positivistic;** commonsense, **realist,** realistic; hylotheistic; hylomorphous; hylozoic, hylozoistic

1051 IMMATERIALITY

nouns

1 **immateriality**, immaterialness; incorporeity, incorporeality, incorporealness, **bodilessness; unsubstantiality** *see* 763, unsubstantialness; **intangibility,** impalpability, imponderability; inextension, nonextension; nonexteriority, nonexternality; **unearthliness, unworldliness; supernaturalism** *see* 689.2; **spirituality,** spiritualness, spirituousness (*old*), otherworldliness, ghostliness, shadowiness; occultism *see* 689, the occult, occult phenomena; ghost-raising, ghost-hunting, ghost-busting (*informal*); psychism, psychics, psychic *or* psychical research, psychicism; spirit world, astral plane

2 incorporeal, incorporeity, immateriality, unsubstantiality *see* 763

3 **immaterialism, idealism,** philosophical idealism, metaphysical idealism; objective idealism; absolute idealism; epistemological idealism; monistic idealism, pluralistic idealism; critical idealism; transcendental

idealism; subjectivism; solipsism; subjective idealism; **spiritualism;** personalism; panpsychism, psychism, animism, hylozoism, animatism; Platonism, Platonic realism, Berkeleianism, Cambridge Platonism, Kantianism, Hegelianism, New England Transcendentalism; Neoplatonism; Platonic idea *or* ideal *or* form, pure form, form, universal; transcendental object; transcendental

4 immaterialist, **idealist;** Berkeleian, Platonist, Hegelian, Kantian; Neoplatonist; **spiritualist;** psychist, panpsychist, animist; **occultist** *see* 689.11; medium; ghost-raiser, ghost-hunter, ghost-buster (*informal*)

5 dematerialization; **disembodiment,** disincarnation; **spiritualization**

verbs

6 to dematerialize, immaterialize, unsubstantialize, insubstantialize, desubstantialize, **disembody,** disincarnate; **spiritualize,** spiritize

adjectives

7 **immaterial**, nonmaterial; **unsubstantial** *see* 763.5, insubstantial, **intangible,** impalpable, imponderable; unextended, extensionless; **incorporeal,** incorporate, incorporeous; **bodiless,** unembodied, without body, asomatous; **disembodied,** disbodied, discarnate, decarnate, decarnated; **unphysical,** nonphysical; **unfleshly;** airy, ghostly, spectral, phantom, shadowy, ethereal; **spiritual,** astral, psychic *or* psychical; **unearthly, unworldly, otherworldly,** extramundane, transmundane; supernatural; **occult**

8 **idealist, idealistic,** immaterialist, immaterialistic; solipsistic; spiritualist, spiritualistic; panpsychist, panpsychistic; animist, animistic; Platonic, Platonistic, Berkeleian, Hegelian, Kantian; Neoplatonic, Neoplatonistic

1052 MATERIALS

nouns

1 **materials**, substances, stuff; **raw material, staple, stock;** material resources *or* means; store, supply *see* 386; strategic materials; matériel

2 (*building materials*) sticks and stones, lath and plaster, bricks and mortar, wattle and daub; roughcast, pebble dash; **roofing,** roofage, tiles, shingles; walling, siding; **flooring,** pavement, paving material, paving, paving stone; masonry, stonework, flag, flagstone, ashlar, stone *see* 1057.1; covering materials; mortar, plasters; **cement, concrete,** cyclopean concrete, ferroconcrete, prestressed concrete, reinforced concrete, slag concrete, cinder concrete; **brick,** firebrick; airbrick; cinder block, concrete block, batt (*Australian & NZ*); clinker, adobe; **tile,** tiling

3 **wood** (*see list*), **lumber, timber,** forest-product; hardwood, softwood; stick, stick of wood, stave; billet; pole, post, beam *see* 273.3, **board,** plank; deal; two-by-four, three-by-four, etc; slab, puncheon; slat, splat, lath; boarding, timbering, timberwork, planking; lathing, lathwork; sheeting; panelling, panelboard, panelwork; plywood, plyboard; sheathing, sheathing board; siding, sideboard; weatherboard,

clapboard; shingle, shake; log; driftwood; firewood, stovewood; cordwood; cord

4 cane, bamboo, rattan

5 **paper,** paper stock, stock; sheet, leaf, page; quire, ream, stationery; cardboard

6 **plastic** (*see list*); thermoplastic; thermosetting plastic; resin plastic; cellulose plastic; protein plastic; cast plastic, moulded plastic, extruded plastic; moulding compounds; laminate; adhesive; plasticizer; polymer; **synthetic;** synthetic fabric *or* textile *or* cloth; synthetic rubber

verbs

7 to gather *or* procure materials; **store, stock,** stock up *see* 386.11, lay in, restock; **process,** utilize

8 **woods**

acacia	fruit wood
African mahogany	gaboon
afrormosia	gopher wood
alder	greenheart
alerce	guaiacum *or* guaiocum
amboyna *or* amboina	gumtree *or* gumwood
applewood	hackberry
ash	hardwood
assegai *or* assagai	hazel *or* hazelwood
balsa	hemlock
balsam	hickory
banyan	hornbeam
bass *or* basswood	incense wood
baywood	iroko
beech *or* beechwood	ironwood
beefwood	jacaranda
birch	jelutong
black walnut	juniper
bog oak	kauri
boxwood	kiaat
brazil, brasil *or* brazil	kingwood
wood	koa
brierwood	knotty pine
bulletwood	lancewood
burl	larch
butternut	lemonwood
buttonwood	lignum vitae
cade	linden
calamander	loblolly pine
camwood	locust
candlewood	logwood
cedar *or* cedarwood	magnolia
cherry	mahogany
chestnut	maple
citron wood	marblewood
coachwood	nutwood
cork *or* corkwood	oak
cottonwood	olive
crabwood	orangewood
cypress	padauk *or* padouk
dogwood	Paraná pine
durmast *or* durmast oak	partridge-wood
eaglewood	pear
ebony	peachwood
elm *or* elmwood	pecan
eucalyptus	persimmon
fiddlewood	Philippine mahogany
fir	pine

pitch pine	softwood
poon	spotted gum
poplar	spruce
Port Orford cedar	stinkwood
pulpwood	sumach
quassia	sumach
quebracho	sycamore
red cedar	tamarack
red fir	tamarind
red gum	teak *or* teakwood
red oak	thorn
redwood	toon
ribbonwood	torchwood
rosewood	tulipwood
sandalwood	tupelo
sandarac	walnut
sappanwood	western red cedar
sassy, sasswood *or* sassy	white cedar
wood	white pine
satinwood	whitewood
Scots pine	willow
shagbark *or* shellbark	yellowwood
sneezewood	yew
	zebrawood

9 **plastics**

acetate	nitrate
acetate nitrate	nylon
acrylic	Perspex (trademark)
alkyd	phenolic
aminoplast	phenolic urea
Bakelite (trademark)	Plexiglas (trademark)
Buna (trademark)	polyester
casein plastic	polyethylene
Cellophane (trademark)	polymeric amide
celluloid	polypropylene
cellulose acetate	polystyrene
cellulose ether	polyurethane
cellulose nitrate	polyvinyl chloride *or* PVC
cellulosic	polyvinyl-formaldehyde
coumarone-indene	resinoid
epoxy	silicone resin
fluorocarbon plastic	Styrofoam (trademark)
Formica (trademark)	Teflon (trademark)
furane	terpene
lignin	tetrafluoroethylene
Lucite (trademark)	urea
melamine	urea formaldehyde
multiresin	vinyl
Mylar (trademark)	Vinylite (trademark)
neoprene	

1053 INORGANIC MATTER

nouns

1 **inorganic matter,** nonorganic matter; inanimate *or* lifeless *or* nonliving matter, inorganized *or* unorganized matter, inert matter, dead matter, **brute matter;** mineral kingdom *or* world; matter, mere matter

2 **inanimateness,** inanimation, **lifelessness,** inertness; **insensibility,** insentience, insensateness, senselessness, unconsciousness, unfeelingness

3 inorganic chemistry; chemicals *see* 1058

adjectives

4 **inorganic,** unorganic, nonorganic; **mineral,** nonbiological; unorganized, inorganized; material *see* 1050.9

5 **inanimate,** inanimated, unanimated, exanimate, azoic, nonliving, dead, **lifeless,** soulless; inert; insentient, unconscious, nonconscious, **insensible,** insensate, senseless, unfeeling; dumb, mute

1054 OILS, LUBRICANTS

nouns

1 **oil,** *oleum* (*Latin*); **fat,** lipid, **grease;** sebum, tallow, vegetable oil, animal oil; **ester,** glyceryl ester; fixed oil, fatty oil, nonvolatile oil, volatile oil, essential oil; saturated fat, hydrogenated fat, unsaturated fat, polyunsaturated fat; drying oil, semidrying oil, nondrying oil

2 **lubricant,** lubricator, lubricating oil, lubricating agent, antifriction; graphite, plumbago, black lead; silicone; glycerin; wax, cerate; mucilage, mucus, synovia; Vaseline (*trademark*), petroleum jelly, K-Y (*trademark*)

3 **ointment, balm, salve, lotion, cream, unguent,** unguentum, inunction, inunctum, unction, chrism; soothing syrup, lenitive, embrocation, demulcent, emollient; spikenard, nard; balsam; **pomade,** pomatum, brilliantine; cold cream, hand lotion, face cream, moisturizer, night cream, sun-tan oil, baby oil, baby lotion, lanolin; eye-lotion, eyewash, collyrium; sun-block, sunscreen, sun-tan lotion, tanning cream

4 **petroleum,** rock oil, fossil oil; **fuel;** fuel oil; mineral oil; crude oil, crude; motor oil

5 **oiliness, greasiness, unctuousness,** unctiousness, unctuosity; **fattiness,** fatness, pinguidity; richness; sebaceousness; adiposis, adiposity; **soapiness,** saponacity *or* saponaceousness; smoothness, slickness, sleekness, **slipperiness,** lubricity

6 **lubrication,** lubricating, **oiling, greasing,** lubrification (*old*); grease *or* lube job (*informal*); **anointment,** unction, inunction; chrismatory, chrismation

7 lubritorium, lubritory; grease rack, grease pit

verbs

8 **to oil,** grease; **lubricate,** lubrify (*old*); **anoint,** salve, unguent, embrocate, dress, pour oil *or* balm upon; smear, daub; slick, slick on (*informal*); pomade; smarm (down); lard; glycerolate, glycerinate, glycerinize; wax, beeswax; smooth the way *and* soap the way *and* grease the wheels (*all informal*)

adjectives

9 **oily, greasy; unctuous,** unctional; unguinous; **oleaginous,** oleic; unguentary, **unguent,** unguentous; chrismal, chrismatory; **fat, fatty,** adipose; pinguid, pinguedinous, pinguescent; rich; sebaceous; blubbery, tallowy, suety; lardy, lardaceous; buttery, butyraceous; soapy, saponaceous; paraffinic; mucoid; smooth, slick, sleek, **slippery**

10 **lubricant,** lubricating, **lubricative,** lubricatory, lubricational; lenitive, emollient, soothing

word elements

11 ole-, oleo-, oli-; lip-, lipo-, lipar-, liparo-; cer-, cero-; sebo-, sebi-; steat-, steato-; petr-, petro-, petri-

1055 RESINS, GUMS

nouns

1 **resin; gum,** gum resin; oleoresin; hard *or* varnish resin, vegetable resin; synthetic resin, plastic, resinoid; resene; **rosin,** colophony, colophonium, colophonone, resinate

verbs

2 to resin, resinize, resinate; rosin

adjectives

3 **resinous,** resinic, resiny; resinoid; rosiny; **gummy,** gummous, gumlike; pitchy

1056 MINERALS, METALS

nouns

1 **mineral** (*see list*); inorganic substance, lifeless matter found in nature; extracted matter *or* material; **mineral world *or* kingdom;** mineral resources; mineraloid, gel mineral; mineralization

2 **ore** (*see list*), mineral; mineral-bearing material; unrefined *or* untreated mineral; natural *or* native mineral

3 **metal,** elementary metal (*see list*); metallics; native metals, alkali metals, earth metals, alkaline-earth metals, noble metals, precious metals, base metals, rare metals, rare-earth metals *or* elements; metalloid, semimetal, nonmetal; gold *or* silver bullion; gold dust; leaf metal, metal leaf, metal foil; metalwork, metalware; metallicity, metallity

4 **alloy** (*see list*), alloyage, fusion, compound; **amalgam**

5 **cast, casting; ingot, bullion;** pig, sow; sheet metal; button, gate, regulus

6 **mine,** pit; **quarry; diggings, workings;** open cut, opencast; bank; shaft; coal mine, colliery; strip mine; gold mine, silver mine, etc

7 **deposit,** mineral deposit, pay dirt; **vein, lode,** seam, dike, ore bed; shoot *or* chute, ore shoot *or* chute; chimney; stock; placer, placer deposit, placer gravel; country rock; lodestuff, gangue, matrix, veinstone

8 **mining;** coal mining, gold mining, etc; long-wall mining (*US & Canadian*); room-and-pillar mining (*US & Canadian*); opencast mining, strip mining, open-cut mining (*Australian & NZ*); placer mining (*US & Canadian*); hydraulic mining; prospecting; mining claim, lode claim, placer claim (*US & Canadian*); gold fever; gold rush

9 **miner,** mineworker, pitman; coal miner, collier; gold miner, gold digger; gold panner; placer miner (*US & Canadian*); quarry miner; **prospector;** wildcatter (*US & Canadian informal*); **forty-niner;** hand miner, rockman, powderman, driller, draw man; butty

10 **mineralogy;** mineralogical chemistry; crystallography; **petrology,** petrography,

micropetrography; **geology**; mining geology, mining engineering

11 metallurgy; metallography, metallurgical chemistry, metallurgical engineering, physical metallurgy, powder metallurgy, electrometallurgy, hydrometallurgy, pyrometallurgy

12 mineralogist; **metallurgist**, electrometallurgist, metallurgical engineer; **petrologist**, petrographer; **geologist**; mining engineer

verbs

13 to mineralize; petrify *see* 1044.7

14 to mine; quarry; pan, pan for gold; prospect; hit pay dirt; mine out

adjectives

15 mineral; inorganic *see* 1053.4; mineralized, petrified; asbestine, carbonous, graphitic, micaceous, alabastrine, quartzose, silicic; sulphurous, sulphuric; ore-bearing, ore-forming

16 metal, metallic, metallike, metalline, metalloid *or* metalloidal, metalliform; semimetallic; nonmetallic; metallo-organic *or* metallorganic, organometallic; bimetallic, trimetallic; metalliferous, metalbearing

17 brass, brassy, brazen; bronze, bronzy; copper, coppery, cuprous, cupreous; gold, golden, gilt, aureate; nickel, nickelic, nickelous, nickeline; silver, silvery; iron, ironlike, ferric, ferrous, ferruginous; steel, steely; tin, tinny; lead, leaden; pewter, pewtery; mercurial, mercurous, quicksilver; gold-filled, gold-plated, silver-plated, etc

18 mineralogical, metallurgical, petrological, crystallographic

19 minerals

actinolite	barytes	colemanite	kainite
agate	bastnaesite *or* bastnasite	columbite	kaolinite
alabaster	beryl	cordierite	kernite
albite	biotite	corundum	kieserite
allanite	bismuthinite *or* bismuth	cristobalite	kunzite
allophane	glance	crocidolite	kyanite
alunite	Boehmite	crocoite *or* crocoisite	labradorite
amalgam	boracite	cryolite	lapis lazuli
amblygonite	borax	cuprite	lazulite
amphibole	bornite	cyanite	lazurite
analcite *or* analcime	braunite	datolite	leucite
anatase	brookite	diallage	lignite
andalusite	brucite	diamond	magnesite
andesine	calaverite	diaspore	malachite
anglesite	calcite	diopside	maltha
anhydrite	carnallite	dioptase	manganite
ankerite	carnotite	diatomite	marcasite
annabergite	celestite *or* celestine	dolomite	margarite
anorthite	cerargyrite	dumortierite	marl
apatite	chabazite	emery	massicot
aplite	chalcanthite	enstatite	meerschaum
apophyllite	chalcedony	epidote	metamict
aragonite	chlorite	epsomite	mica
argillite	chromite	erythrite	microcline
asbestos	chrysoberyl	euxenite	millerite
augite	chrysotile	fayalite	mimetite
autunite	clay	feldspar *or* felspar	molybdenite
axinite	cleveite	feldspathoid	monazite
azurite	clinopyroxene	fluorapatite	monmorillonite
baddeleyite	cobaltite *or* cobaltine	fluorspar *or* fluor	monzonite
		fool's gold	mullite
		forsterite	muscovite
		franklinite	natrolite
		gahnite	nepheline *or* nephelite
		garnet	nephrite
		garnierite	niccolite
		gehlenite	norite
		germanite	oligoclase
		geyserite	olivenite
		gibbsite	olivine
		glauconite	opal
		graphite	orpiment
		greenockite	orthoclase
		gummite	ozocerite *or* ozokerite
		gypsum	pentlandite
		halite	periclase
		harmotome	perovskite
		hatchettine	petuntse *or* petuntze
		hemimorphite	phenacite *or* phenakite
		hessite	phosgenite
		heulandite	phosphorite
		hiddenite	piedmontite
		holosiderite	pinite
		hornblende	pitchblende
		hyacinth	pollucite
		hypersthene	polybasite
		illite	proustite
		ilmenite	psilomelane
		iolite	pumicite
		iron pyrites	pyrargite
		jadeite	pyrite
		jarosite	pyrolusite
		jasper	pyromorphite
		jet	pyrophyllite

pyroxene
pyroxenite
pyrrhotite *or* pyrrhotine
quartz
realgar
rhodochrosite
rhodonite
rutile
samarskite
saponite
sapphirine
scapolite
scheelite
scolecite
senarmontite
serpentine
silicate
sillimanite
smaltite
smaragdite
smectite
smithsonite
sodalite
spar
sperrylite
sphalerite
sphene
spinel
spodumene
stannite
staurolite
stilbite
strontianite
sylvanite
sylvite *or* sylvine
talc

tantalite
tenorite
tetradymite
tetrahedrite
thenardite
thorianite
thorite
tiemannite
topaz
torbenite
tourmaline
tremolite
triphylite
trona
troostite
tungstite
turquoise
uralite
uraninite
uranite
vanadinite
variscite
vermiculite
vesuvianite
wavellite
willemite
witherite
wolframite
wollastonite
wulfenite
zaratite
zeolite
zinkenite *or* zinckenite
zircon
zoisite

20 ores

argentite
arsenopyrite
bauxite
cassiterite
chalcocite
chalcopyrite
cinnabar
galena
göthite
hematite *or* haematite
iron ore

ironstone
limonite
lodestone
magnetite
mispickel
pyrite
siderite
stibnite
tinstone
turgite
zincite

21 elementary metals

actinium
aluminium
americium
antimony
barium
berkelium
beryllium
bismuth
cadmium
caesium
calcium
californium
cerium
chromium

cobalt
copper
curium
dysprosium
einsteinium
erbium
europium
fermium
francium
gadolinium
gallium
germanium
gold
hafnium

holmium
indium
iridium
iron
lanthanum
lawrencium
lead
lithium
lutetium
magnesium
manganese
mendelevium
mercury
molybdenum
neodymium
neptunium
nickel
niobium
nobelium
osmium
palladium
platinum
plutonium
polonium
potassium
praseodymium
promethium

protactinium
radium
rhenium
rhodium
rubidium
ruthenium
samarium
scandium
silver
sodium
strontium
tantalum
technetium
terbium
thallium
thorium
thulium
tin
titanium
tungsten *or* wolfram
uranium
vanadium
ytterbium
yttrium
zinc
zirconium

22 alloys

Alnico (trademark)
austenitic stainless steel
Babbit metal
bell bronze
bell metal
billon
brass
brazing solder
Britannia metal
bronze
chromel
constantan
cupronickel
Duralumin (trademark)
electrum
ferrochromium
ferromanganese
ferromolybdenum
ferronickel
ferrosilicon
Invar (trademark)
kamacite
magnolia metal
magnox
Manganin (trademark)

misch metal
Monel *or* Monell metal
Nichrome (trademark)
nickel silver
nimonic alloy
ormolu
oroide
osmiridium
permalloy
pewter
phosphor bronze
pinchbeck
platina
platiniridium
soft solder
speculum metal
steel
Stellite (trademark)
sterling silver
terne
tombac *or* tambac
type metal
white gold
zircalloy

1057 ROCK

nouns

1 **rock, stone** (*see list*); living rock; **igneous rock,**
plutonic *or* abyssal rock, hypabyssal rock; volcanic
rock, extrusive *or* effusive rock, scoria; magma,
intrusive rock; granite, basalt, porphyry, **lava,** aa *and*
pahoehoe (*both Hawaiian*); **sedimentary rock;**
limestone, sandstone; **metamorphic rock,** schist,

gneiss; conglomerate, pudding stone, breccia, rubble, rubblestone, scree, talus, tuff, tufa, brash; sarsen, sarsen stone, druid stone; monolith; crag, craig (*Scottish*); tor; bedrock; mantlerock, regolith; saprolite, geest, laterite; building stone

2 **sand**; grain of sand; sands of the sea; sand pile, sand dune, sand hill; sand reef, sandbar; full

3 **gravel**, shingle, chesil

4 **pebble**, pebblestone, gravelstone, chuckie *or* chuckie stane (*Scottish*), brinny (*Australian informal*); jackstone *and* checkstone (*both US & Canadian informal*); fingerstone; slingstone; drakestone; spall

5 **boulder**, river boulder, shore boulder, glacial boulder

6 **precious stone, gem, gemstone** (*see list*); stone, crystal; semiprecious stone; gem of the first water; birthstone

7 petrification, petrifaction, lithification, crystallization

8 geology, petrology, crystallography; petrochemistry

verbs

9 to petrify, lithify, crystallize, turn to stone; harden *see* 1044.7

adjectives

10 **stone, rock**, lithic; petrified; petrogenic, petrescent; adamant, adamantine; flinty, flintlike; marbly, marblelike; granitic, granitelike; slaty, slatelike

11 **stony, rocky**, lapideous; stonelike, rocklike, lithoid *or* lithoidal; sandy, gritty *see* 1049.12; gravelly, shingly, shingled; pebbly, pebbled; porphyritic, trachytic; crystal, crystalline; bouldery, rock- *or* boulder-strewn, rock-studded, rock-ribbed; craggy; monolithic

word elements

12 petr–, petro–, petri–, saxi–, lith–, litho–, –lith; grano–; blast–, blasto–, blast–, orth–, ortho–, par–; para–; –clast; –lithic, –litic; –clastic; crystall–, crystallo–

13 **stones**

andesite	dendrite
anorthosite	diabase
anthracite	diorite
anthraconite	dolerite
aplite	dolomite
arkose	dripstone
aventurine *or* goldstone	dunite
basalt	eaglestone
basanite	eclogite
Bath stone	emery rock
beetlestone	felsite *or* felstone
bluestone	fieldstone
breccia	flag *or* flagstone
brownstone	flint
buhr *or* buhrstone	floatstone
chalk	freestone
chert	gabbro
clay	geode
clinkstone	gneiss
coal	granite
conglomerate	granulite
corundophilite	granodiorite
Cotswold stone	gravel

greywacke	quartzite
greenstone	ragstone *or* rag *or* ragg
grit	rance
gritrock *or* gritstone	red sandstone
hairstone	rhyolite
hornblendite	rottenstone
hornfels *or* hornstone	sandstone
ironstone	schist
lamphrophyre	serpentine
lava	shale
lignite	skarn
limestone	slab
lodestone	slate
loess	smokestone
Lydian stone	snakestone
marble	soapstone *or* steatite
milkstone	stalactite
monzonite	stalagmite
mudstone	starstone
obsidian	stinkstone
pegmatite	stone
peridotite	syenite
perknite	tinstone
phonolite	touchstone
phyllite	trachyite
pitchstone	trap *or* traprock
porphyry	tufa *or* calc-tufa
pumice	wacke (old)
pyroxenite	whitestone
quarrystone	

14 **gemstones**

adamant (old)	cymophane
adder stone	demantoid
adularia	diamond
agate	diopside
alexandrite	emerald
almandine	fire opal
amazonite	garnet
amethyst	girasol *or* girosol *or* girasole
andalusite	
andradite	grossularite
aquamarine	harlequin opal
aventurine *or* aventurin *or* avanturine	hawk's-eye
	helidor
balas	heliotrope
beryl	hessonite
black opal	hiddenite
bloodstone	hyacinth
bone turquoise	indicolite *or* indigolite
brilliant	jacinth
cairngorm	jadeite *or* jade *or* jadestone
carbuncle	jargon *or* jargoon
carnelian	jasper
cat's-eye	jet
chalcedony	kunzite
chrysoberyl	lapis lazuli
chrysolite	liver opal
chrysoprase	Madagascar aquamarine
citrine	melanite
Colorado ruby	moonstone
Colorado topaz	morganite
coral	morion
corundum	moss agate

New Zealand greenstone
odontolite
onyx
opal
Oriental almandine
Oriental emerald
peridot
plasma
pyrope
quartz
rhodolite
rose quartz
rubellite
ruby
sapphire
sard *or* sardine
sardonyx

smoky quartz
Spanish topaz
spessartite
sphene
spinel *or* spinel ruby
spodumene
staurolite
sunstone
titanite
topaz
tourmaline
turquoise
uvarovite
vesuvianite
water sapphire
white sapphire
zircon

1058 CHEMISTRY, CHEMICALS

nouns

1 **chemistry,** chemical science, science of substances, science of matter; branch of chemistry (*see list*)

2 **element** (*see list*), chemical element; table of elements, periodic table; rare earth element, rare gas element; **radical** group; free radical, diradical, **ion,** anion, cation; atom *see* 1037.4; **molecule,** macromolecule; dimer; trace element, microelement, micronutrient, minor element; **chemical, chemical compound;** organic chemical, biochemical, inorganic chemical; fine chemicals, heavy chemicals; agent, **reagent**

3 **acid;** hydracid, oxyacid, sulfacid; acidity; **base, alkali,** nonacid; pH; neutralizer, antacid; alkalinity

4 **valency,** positive valency, negative valency; monovalence, univalence, bivalence, trivalence, tervalence, quadrivalence, tetravalence, etc, multivalence, polyvalence; covalency, electrovalence

5 **atomic weight,** atomic mass, atomic volume, mass number; **molecular weight,** molecular mass, molecular volume; atomic number, valency number

6 **chemicalization,** chemical process (*see list*), chemical action, chemism; **chemical apparatus,** beaker, Bunsen burner, burette, centrifuge, condenser, crucible, graduated cylinder *or* graduate, pipette, test tube

verbs

7 **to chemicalize,** chemical; alkalize, alkalinize, alkalify; acidify, acidulate, acetify; borate, carbonate, chlorinate, hydrate, hydrogenate, hydroxylate, nitrate, oxidize, reduce, pepsinate, peroxidize, phosphatize, sulphate, sulphatize, sulphonate; dimerize, isomerize, metamerize, polymerize, copolymerize, homopolymerize; ferment, work; catalyse *see* 805.4; electrolyse

adjectives

8 **chemical;** biochemical, chemicobiologic; physicochemical, physiochemical, chemicophysical, chemicobiological, chemicophysiologic *or* chemicophysiological, chemicodynamic, chemicoengineering, chemicomechanical, chemicomineralogical, chemicopharmaceutical,

chemurgic, electrochemical, iatrochemical, chemotherapeutic *or* chemotherapeutical, chemophysiologic *or* chemophysiological, macrochemical, microchemical, phytochemical, photochemical, radiochemical, thermochemical, zoochemical; elemental, elementary; acid; alkaline, alkali, nonacid, basic; isomeric, isomerous, metameric, metamerous, heteromerous, polymeric, polymerous, copolymeric, copolymerous, monomeric, monomerous, dimeric, dimerous, etc

9 valent; univalent, monovalent, monatomic, bivalent, trivalent, tervalent, quadrivalent, tetravalent, etc, multivalent, polyvalent; covalent, electrovalent

word elements

10 chem–, chemo–, chemi–, chemic–, chemico–; –mer, –merous, –meric; –valent

11 branches of chemistry

actinochemistry
alchemy *or* alchemistry
analytical chemistry
applied chemistry
astrochemistry
atomic chemistry
biochemistry
biogeochemistry
business chemistry
capillary chemistry
chemiatry
chemical dynamics
chemical engineering
chemicobiology
chemicoengineering
chemicophysics
chemophysiology
chemurgy
colloid chemistry
colorimetry *or* colorimetric analysis
crystallochemistry
cytochemistry
electrochemistry
engineering chemistry
galactochemistry
galvanochemistry
geological chemistry *or* geochemistry
histochemistry
hydrochemistry
iatrochemistry
immunochemistry
industrial chemistry
inorganic chemistry
kinetics
lithochemistry
macrochemistry

magnetochemistry
metachemistry
metallurgical chemistry
microchemistry
mineralogical chemistry
neurochemistry
nuclear chemistry
organic chemistry
pathological chemistry *or* pathochemistry
petrochemistry
pharmacochemistry
phonochemistry
photochemistry
physical chemistry *or* physiochemistry
physiological chemistry *or* physiochemistry
phytochemistry
piezochemistry
pneumatochemistry
psychobiochemistry *or* psychochemistry
pure chemistry
radiochemistry
soil chemistry
spectrochemistry
stereochemistry
stoichometry
structural chemistry
synthetic chemistry
technochemistry
theoretical chemistry
thermochemistry
topochemistry
ultramicrochemistry
zoochemistry *or* zoochemy
zyochemistry *or* zymurgy

12 chemical elements

actinium *or* Ac
aluminium *or* Al
americium *or* Am
antimony *or* Sb
argon *or* Ar
arsenic *or* As
astatine *or* At

barium *or* Ba
berkelium *or* Bk
beryllium *or* Be
bismuth *or* Bi
boron *or* B
bromine *or* Br
cadmium *or* Cd

caesium *or* Cs
calcium *or* Ca
californium *or* Cf
carbon *or* C
cerium *or* Ce
chlorine *or* Cl
chromium *or* Cr
cobalt *or* Co
copper *or* Cu
curium *or* Cm
dysprosium *or* Dy
einsteinium *or* Es
erbium *or* Er
europium *or* Eu
fermium *or* Fm
fluorine *or* F
francium *or* Fr
gadolinium *or* Gd
gallium *or* Ga
germanium *or* Ge
gold *or* Au
hafnium *or* Hf
hahnium *or* Ha *or*
  nielsbohrium *or*
  unnilpentium *or* Unp
helium *or* He
holmium *or* Ho
hydrogen *or* H
indium *or* In
iodine *or* I
iridium *or* Ir
iron *or* Fe
krypton *or* Kr
lanthanum *or* La
lawrencium *or* Lr
lead *or* Pb
lithium *or* Li
lutetium *or* Lu
magnesium *or* Mg
manganese *or* Mn
mendelevium *or* Md
mercury *or* Hg
molybdenum *or* Mo
neodymium *or* Nd
neon *or* Ne
neptunium *or* Np
nickel *or* Ni
niobium *or* Nb

nitrogen *or* N
nobelium *or* No
osmium *or* Os
oxygen *or* O
palladium *or* Pd
phosphorus *or* P
platinum *or* Pt
plutonium *or* Pu
polonium *or* Po
potassium *or* K
praseodymium *or* Pr
protactinium *or* Pa
promethium *or* Pm
radium *or* Ra
radon *or* Rn
rhenium *or* Re
rhodium *or* Rh
rubidium *or* Rb
ruthenium *or* Ru
rutherfordium *or* Rf *or*
  kurchatovium *or* Ku *or*
  unnilquadium *or* Unq
samarium *or* Sm
scandium *or* Sc
selenium *or* Se
silicon *or* Si
silver *or* Ag
sodium *or* Na
strontium *or* Sr
sulphur *or* S
tantalum *or* Ta
technetium *or* Tc
tellurium *or* Te
terbium *or* Tb
thallium *or* Tl
thorium *or* Th
thulium *or* Tm
tin *or* Sn
titanium *or* Ti
tungsten *or* wolfram *or* W
uranium *or* U
vanadium *or* V
xenon *or* Xe
ytterbium *or* Yb
yttrium *or* Y
zinc *or* Zn
zirconium *or* Zr

13 chemical processes

acetification
acidification *or* acidulation
alkalization *or* alkalinization
carbonation
catalysis
chlorination
copolymerization
dimerization
electrolysis
fermentation *or* ferment
geometric isomerization
homopolymerization
hydration

hydrogenation
hydroxylation
isomerization
metamerization
nitration
optical isomerization
oxidation
oxidization
phosphatization
polymerization
position isomerization
reduction
saturization

sulphation
sulphatization

sulphonation
tautoisomerization

1059 LIQUIDITY

nouns

1 **liquidity, fluidity,** fluidness, liquidness, liquefaction *see* 1062; wateriness; rheuminess; **juiciness,** sappiness, succulence; milkiness, lactescence; lactation; chylifaction, chylification; serosity; suppuration; **moisture, wetness** *see* 1063.1; **fluency,** flow, flowage, flux, fluxion, fluxility (*old*); **circulation;** turbulence, turbidity, turbulent flow; streamline flow

2 **fluid, liquid;** liquor *see* 10.47, drink, beverage; liquid extract, fluid extract; **juice, sap,** latex; milk, whey; water *see* 1063.3; **body fluid, blood;** semiliquid *see* 1060.5; fluid mechanics, hydraulics, etc *see* 1038.4

3 flowmeter, fluidmeter, hydrometer

adjectives

4 **fluid,** fluidal, fluidic, **fluent, flowing,** fluxible *or* fluxile (*both old*), fluxional, fluxionary, runny; **circulatory,** circulation, turbid; **liquid,** liquidy; watery *see* 1063.16; **juicy,** sappy, succulent; **wet** *see* 1063.15

5 **milky,** lacteal, lacteous, **lactic;** lactescent, lactiferous; milk, milch

1060 SEMILIQUIDITY

nouns

1 **semiliquidity,** semifluidity; butteriness, creaminess; pulpiness *see* 1061

2 **viscosity,** viscidity, viscousness, slabbiness, lentor (*old*); thickness, spissitude (*old*), heaviness, stodginess; **stickiness, tackiness,** glutinousness, glutinosity, toughness, tenaciousness, tenacity, **adhesiveness,** clinginess, clingingness, **gumminess,** gauminess (*informal*), gumlikeness; **ropiness, stringiness;** clamminess, sliminess, mucilaginousness; gooeyness *and* gunkiness (*both informal*), gunginess (*informal*); **glueiness,** gluelikeness; syrupiness, treacliness; gelatinousness, jellylikeness, gelatinity; colloidality; doughiness, pastiness; **thickening,** curdling, clotting, coagulation, incrassation, inspissation, clabbering *and* loppering (*both informal*), jellification

3 **mucosity,** mucidness, mucousness, pituitousness (*old*), snottiness (*informal*); **sliminess**

4 **muddiness,** muckiness, miriness, **slushiness,** sloshiness, sludginess, **sloppiness,** slobbiness, slabbiness (*old*), squashiness, squelchiness, squishiness, squidginess, **ooziness,** miriness; **turbidity,** turbidness, dirtiness

5 **semiliquid,** semifluid; **goo** *and* **goop** *and* **gook** *and* **gunk** *and* **glop** *and* **gloop** *and* **gunge** (*all informal*), sticky mess, gaum (*informal*); **paste,** pap, pudding, putty, **butter,** cream; **pulp** *see* 1061.2; jelly, gelatin, jell, gel, jam, rob; **glue;** size; **gluten;** mucilage; mucus; **dough,** batter; **syrup,** treacle, molasses; egg white, albumen, glair; starch, cornstarch; **curd,**

clabber, bonnyclabber; gruel, porridge, loblolly (*informal*); soup, gumbo, purée

6 **gum** *see* 1055, chewing gum, bubble gum; chicle, chicle gum

7 **emulsion**, emulsoid; emulsification; emulsifier; **colloid**, colloider

8 **mud, muck, mire, slush, slosh**, sludge, glaur (*Scottish*), slob (*Irish*), squash, swill, **slime; slop, ooze, mire**; clay, slip; gumbo

9 **mud puddle, puddle**, loblolly (*informal*), slop; **mudhole**, slough, muckhole

verbs

10 **to emulsify**, emulsionize; colloid, colloidize; cream; churn, whip, beat up; **thicken**, inspissate, incrassate, curdle, clot, coagulate, clabber *and* lopper (*both informal*), gunge up (*informal*); jell, jelly, jellify

adjectives

11 **semiliquid**, semifluid, semifluidic; buttery; creamy; emulsive, colloidal; **pulpy** *see* 1061.6; half-frozen, half-melted

12 **viscous, viscid**, viscose, slabby; **thick**, heavy, stodgy, soupy, thickened, inspissated, incrassated; curdled, clotted, grumous, coagulated, clabbered *and* loppered (*both informal*); **sticky, tacky**, tenacious, adhesive, clingy, clinging, tough; gluey, gluelike, glutinous, glutenous, glutinose; gumbo, gumbolike; **gummy**, gaumy (*informal*), gummous, gumlike, **syrupy**; treacly; ropy, stringy; mucilaginous, clammy, slimy, slithery; gooey *and* gunky *and* gloppy *and* gloopy *and* goopy *and* gooky *and* gungy (*all informal*); **gelatinous**, jellylike, jellied, jelled; tremelloid *or* tremellose; glairy; **doughy, pasty**; starchy, amylaceous

13 **mucous**, muculent, mucoid, mucinous, pituitous (*old*), phlegmy, snotty (*informal*); mucific, muciferous

14 **slimy; muddy**, miry, mucky, **slushy, sloshy**, sludgy, **sloppy**, slobby, slabby (*old*), splashy, **squashy**, squishy, squidgy, **squelchy**, oozy, soft, sloughy, plashy, sploshy (*informal*); **turbid, dirty**

1061 PULPINESS

nouns

1 **pulpiness**, pulpousness; **softness** *see* 1045; flabbiness; **mushiness**, mashiness, squashiness; **pastiness**, doughiness; **sponginess**, pithiness; fleshiness, succulence

2 **pulp, paste, mash, mush**, smash, squash, crush; tomato paste *or* pulp; pudding, porridge, sponge; sauce, butter; poultice, cataplasm, plaster; pith; paper pulp, wood pulp, sulphate pulp, sulphite pulp, rag pulp; pulpwood; pulp lead, white lead; dental *or* tooth pulp

3 **pulping**, pulpification, pulpefaction; blending; digestion; **maceration**, mastication

4 **pulper**, pulpifier, macerator, pulp machine *or* engine, digester; **masher**, smasher, potato masher, beetle

verbs

5 **to pulp**, pulpify; **macerate**, masticate, chew; regurgitate; **mash**, smash, squash, squish, crush

adjectives

6 **pulpy**, pulpous, pulpal, pulpar, pulplike, pulped; **pasty**, doughy; pultaceous; **mushy**; macerated, masticated, chewed; regurgitated; **squashy**, squelchy, squishy, squidgy; soft, flabby; fleshy, succulent; **spongy**, pithy

1062 LIQUEFACTION

nouns

1 **liquefaction**, liquefying, liquidizing, liquidization, fluidification, fluidization; liquescence *or* liquescency, deliquescence, deliquiation *and* deliquium (*both old*); **solution**, dissolution, dissolving; **infusion**, soaking, steeping, brewing; **melting**, thawing, running, fusing, fusion; decoagulation, unclotting; solubilization; colliquation; lixiviation, percolation, leaching

2 **solubility**, solubleness, dissolvability, dissolvableness, dissolubility, dissolubleness; meltability, fusibility

3 **solution**; decoction, infusion, mixture; chemical solution; lixivium, leach, leachate; **suspension**, colloidal suspension; **emulsion**, gel, aerosol

4 **solvent** (*see list*), dissolvent, dissolver, dissolving agent, resolvent, resolutive, **thinner**, diluent; anticoagulant; liquefier, liquefacient; menstruum; universal solvent, alkahest; flux

verbs

5 **to liquefy**, liquidize, liquesce, fluidify, fluidize; **melt, run**, thaw, colliquate; melt down; fuse, flux; deliquesce; **dissolve**, solve; thin, cut; solubilize; hold in solution; unclot, decoagulate; leach, lixiviate, percolate; **infuse**, decoct, steep, soak, brew

adjectives

6 **liquefied, melted, molten**, thawed; unclotted, decoagulated; in solution, in suspension, liquescent, deliquescent; colloidal

7 **liquefying**, liquefactive; colliquative, **melting**, fusing, thawing; **dissolving**, dissolutive, dissolutional

8 **solvent**, dissolvent, resolvent, resolutive, thinning, cutting, diluent; alkahestic

9 **liquefiable; meltable**, fusible, thawable; **soluble, dissolvable**, dissoluble; water-soluble

10 **solvents**

acetone	furfural
alcohol	gasoline
aqua regia	kerosene
benzene *or* benzol	naphtha
benzine	paraffin
carbolic acid	petrol
carbon disulphide	phenol
carbon tetrachloride *or*	toluene
carbon tet (informal)	turpentine
chloroform	water
ether	xylene *or* xylol
ethyl acetate	

1063 MOISTURE

nouns

1 **moisture,** damp, wet; **dampness, moistness,** moistiness, **wetness,** wettedness, wettishness, **wateriness,** humour *or* humectation (*both old*); soddenness, soppiness, soppingness, sogginess; swampiness, bogginess, marshiness; dewiness; mistiness, fogginess *see* 319.3; raininess, pluviosity, showeriness; rainfall; exudation *see* 190.6; secretion *see* 13

2 **humidity,** humidness, **dankness,** dankishness, **mugginess,** stickiness, sweatiness, closeness; absolute humidity, relative humidity; dew point; humidification

3 **water,** *aqua* (*Latin*), *agua* (*Spanish*), *eau* (*French*); Adam's ale *or* wine, H_2O; hydrol; hard water, soft water; heavy water; water supply, water system, waterworks; drinking water, tap water; rainwater, rain *see* 316; snowmelt, meltwater; **groundwater,** underground water; water table, aquifer; spring water, well water; seawater, salt water; limewater; mineral water *or* waters; steam, water vapour; hydrosphere; hydrometeor; head, hydrostatic head; hydrothermal water; wetting agent, wetting-out agent, liquidizer, moisturizer; humidifier; bottled water, commercially bottled water, designer water (*informal*), mineral water, spring water

4 **dew, dewdrops,** dawn *or* morning dew, night dew, evening damp; fog drip, false dew

5 **sprinkle, spray,** sparge, shower; spindrift, spume, froth, foam; **splash,** plash, swash, slosh; **splatter,** spatter

6 **wetting, moistening, dampening,** damping; humidification; dewing, bedewing; **watering, irrigation;** hosing, wetting *or* hosing down; **sprinkling, spraying,** spritzing (*informal*), sparging, aspersion, aspergation; **splashing,** swashing, splattering, spattering; affusion, baptism; bath, bathing, rinsing, laving; **flooding,** drowning, inundation, deluge; **immersion, submersion** *see* 367.2

7 **soaking,** soakage, soaking through, sopping, **drenching,** imbruement, sousing; ducking, dunking (*informal*); soak, drench, souse; **saturation,** permeation; waterlogging; **steeping,** maceration, seething, infusion, brewing, imbuement; injection, impregnation; infiltration, percolation, leaching, lixiviation; pulping *see* 1061.3

8 **sprinkler,** sparger, sparge, sprayer, speed sprayer, concentrate sprayer, mist concentrate sprayer, spray, spray can, atomizer, aerosol; nozzle; aspergil, aspergillum; **shower,** shower bath, shower head, needle bath; syringe, fountain syringe, douche, enema, clyster; sprinkling *or* watering can, watering pot, watercart; lawn sprinkler; sprinkling system, sprinkler head, rose

9 (*science of humidity*) hygrology, hygrometry, psychrometry

10 (*instruments*) hygrometer, hair hygrometer, hygrograph, hygrodeik, hygroscope, hygrothermograph; psychrometer, sling psychrometer; humidor; hygrostat

verbs

11 to be damp, not have a dry thread; **drip,** weep; **seep, ooze,** percolate; exude *see* 190.15; sweat; secrete *see* 13.5

12 **to moisten, dampen,** moisturize, damp, wet, wet down; humidify, humect *or* humectate (*both old*); **water, irrigate;** dew, bedew; **sprinkle,** besprinkle, **spray,** spritz (*informal*), sparge, asperge; bepiss; **splash,** dash, **swash, slosh, splatter, spatter,** bespatter; dabble, paddle; slop, slobber; hose, hose down; syringe, douche; sponge

13 **to soak, drench,** drouk (*Scottish*), imbrue, **souse, sop,** sodden; **saturate,** permeate; **bathe,** lave, wash, rinse, douche, flush, swill; water-soak, waterlog; **steep,** seethe, macerate, infuse, imbue, brew, impregnate, inject; infiltrate, percolate, leach, lixiviate

14 **to flood,** float, **inundate, deluge,** turn to a lake *or* sea, swamp, whelm, overwhelm, drown; duck, dip, dunk (*informal*); **submerge** *see* 367.7; sluice, pour on, flow on; rain *see* 316.9

adjectives

15 **moist,** moisty; **damp,** dampish; **wet,** wettish; undried, tacky; **humid, dank, muggy, sticky,** close; dewy, bedewed, roric *and* roriferous (*both old*); rainy *see* 316.10; marshy, swampy, fenny, boggy

16 **watery,** waterish, **aqueous, aquatic;** liquid; **splashy,** plashy, sloppy, swashy; hydrous, hydrated; hydraulic

17 **soaked, drenched,** soused, bathed, steeped, macerated; **saturated,** permeated; **watersoaked, waterlogged; soaking, sopping; wringing wet,** soaking wet, sopping wet, soaked to the skin, like a drowned rat; **sodden,** soppy, **soggy,** soaky; dripping, **dripping wet;** dribbling, seeping, weeping, oozing; flooded, overflowed, whelmed, swamped, engulfed, inundated, deluged, drowned, submerged, submersed, immersed, dipped, dunked (*informal*); awash, weltering

18 wetting, dampening, moistening, watering, humectant; **drenching, soaking,** sopping; **irrigational,** irriguous (*old*)

19 hygric, hygrometric, hygroscopic, hygrophilous, hygrothermal

word elements

20 hydr–, hydro–, hydrat–, hydrato–, aqui–, aqua–; hygr–, hygro–

1064 DRYNESS

nouns

1 **dryness, aridness,** aridity, waterlessness; **drought;** juicelessness, saplessness; **thirst,** thirstiness; corkiness; watertightness, watertight integrity

2 (*comparisons*) desert, dust, bone, parchment, stick, mummy, biscuit, cracker

3 **drying, desiccation,** drying up; **dehydration,** anhydration; evaporation; air-drying; blow-drying; freeze-drying; insolation; drainage; withering, mummification; dehumidification

4 **drier,** desiccator, desiccative, siccative, exsiccative, exsiccator, **dehydrator,** dehydrant; dehumidifier;

evaporator; hair-drier, blow-dryer; clothes-drier; tumbler dryer *or* tumble dryer *or* tumbler

verbs

5 to thirst; drink up, soak up, sponge up
6 **to dry, desiccate,** exsiccate, dry up, **dehydrate,** anhydrate; evaporate; dehumidify; air-dry; drip-dry; insolate, sun, sun-dry; spin-dry, tumble-dry; blow-dry; freeze-dry; smoke, smoke-dry; cure; torrefy, burn, fire, kiln, **bake, parch,** scorch, sear; **wither, shrivel;** wizen, weazen; mummify; sponge, blot, soak up; **wipe,** rub, swab, brush; towel; drain *see* 192.12

adjectives

7 **dry, arid; waterless,** unwatered, undamped, anhydrous; **bone-dry,** dry as dust, dry as a bone; like parchment; droughty; juiceless, sapless; **thirsty,** thirsting, athirst; high and dry; sandy, dusty; desert, Saharan
8 rainless, fine, fair, bright and fair, pleasant
9 **dried, dehydrated, desiccated,** dried-up, exsiccated; evaporated; **parched, baked,** sunbaked, burnt, scorched, **seared,** sere, sun-dried, adust; wind-dried, air-dried; drip-dried; blow-dried; freeze-dried; **withered, shrivelled,** wizened, weazened; corky; mummified
10 **drying, dehydrating, desiccative,** desiccant, exsiccative, exsiccant, siccative, siccant; evaporative
11 **watertight, waterproof,** moistureproof, dampproof, leakproof, seepproof, dripproof, stormproof, stormtight, rainproof, raintight, showerproof, floodproof

1065 VAPOUR, GAS

nouns

1 **vapour,** volatile; **fume, reek,** exhalation, breath, effluvium; fluid; **miasma,** mephitis, malaria (*old*), fetid air *or* foetid air; **smoke,** smudge; wisp *or* plume *or* puff of smoke; **damp,** chokedamp, blackdamp, firedamp, afterdamp; **steam,** water vapour; **cloud** *see* 319
2 **gas** (*see list*); rare *or* noble *or* inert gas, halogen gas; fluid; **atmosphere, air** *see* 317; pneumatics, aerodynamics *see* 1038.5
3 **vaporousness,** vaporosity, vaporiness; vapour pressure *or* tension; **aeriness; ethereality,** etherialism; **gaseousness,** gaseous state, gassiness, gaseity; **gas,** stomach gas, gassiness, flatulence, flatus, wind, windiness, farting (*informal*), flatuosity (*old*); fluidity
4 **volatility,** vapourability, vaporizability, evaporability
5 **vaporization, evaporation,** volatilization, gasification; sublimation; distillation, fractionation; etherification; aeration, aerification; fluidization; atomization; exhalation; fumigation; smoking; steaming; etherealization
6 **vaporizer, evaporator;** atomizer, aerosol, spray; still, retort
7 **vaporimeter,** manometer, pressure gauge; gas meter, gasometer, gasholder; pneumatometer, spirometer; aerometer, airometer; eudiometer

verbs

8 **to vaporize, evaporate,** volatilize, **gasify;** sublimate, sublime; distil, fractionate; etherify; **aerate,** aerify; carbonate, oxygenate, hydrogenate, chlorinate, halogenate, etc; atomize, spray; fluidize; **reek, fume;** exhale, give off, emit, send out; **smoke; steam;** fumigate, perfume; **etherize**

adjectives

9 **vaporous,** vapourish, vapoury, vapourlike; **airy, aerial, ethereal; gaseous,** in the gaseous state, gasified, gassy, gaslike, gasiform; vapouring; **reeking,** reeky; miasmic *or* miasmal *or* miasmatic, mephitic; **fuming,** fumy; smoky, smoking; steamy, steaming; ozonic; oxygenous; oxyacetylene; pneumatic, aerostatic, aerodynamic
10 **volatile,** volatilizable; **vapourable,** vaporizable, vaporescent; **evaporative,** evaporable

word elements

11 vapo–, vapori–, atm–, atmo–; aer–, aero–, mano–, pneum–, pneumo–, pneumat–, pneumato–
12 gases

acetylene *or* ethyne	krypton
air gas	lewisite
ammonia	marsh *or* swamp gas
argon	methane
asphyxiating gas	mustard gas
butane	natural gas
carbon dioxide	neon
carbon monoxide	nerve gas
carbonic-acid gas	nitric oxide
carburetted-hydrogen gas	nitrogen
chlorine	nitrogen dioxide
chlorofluorocarbon *or* CFC	nitrous oxide *or* laughing
coal gas	gas
ethane	North-sea gas
ether *or* ethyl ether	oil gas
ethyl chloride	oxygen
ethylene *or* ethene *or*	ozone
olefiant gas	phosgene *or* carbon
ethylene oxide	oxychloride
fluorocarbon	poison gas
fluorine	propane
formaldehyde	radon
Freon (trademark)	refrigerator gas
greenhouse gas	sewer gas
helium	sneeze gas
hydrogen	tear gas *or* lachrymatory
hydrogen bromide	gas
hydrogen chloride	tetrafluoroethylene
hydrogen cyanide	vesicatory gas
hydrogen fluoride	vomiting gas
hydrogen iodide	war gas
hydrogen sulphide	water gas
illuminating gas	xenon

1066 BIOLOGY

nouns

1 **biology** (*see list*), biological science, life science, the science of life, the study of living things; **botany** (*see list*), plant biology, phytobiology, phytology, plant science; **plant kingdom,** vegetable kingdom;

plants *see* 310, flora plantlife; **zoology** (*see* list), animal biology, animal science; **animal kingdom**, kingdom Animalia, phylum, class, order, family, genus, species; **animals** *see* 311, fauna, animal life

2 **biologist, naturalist,** life scientist; **botanist,** plant scientist, plant biologist, phytobiologist, phytologist; **zoologist,** animal biologist, animal scientist (*for other agent nouns add –ist or –er to names of branches listed*)

adjectives

3 **biological,** biologic; **botanical,** botanic, plant, phytological, phytologic, phytobiological; **zoological,** zoologic, faunal (*for other adjectives add –ic or –ical to the names of branches listed*)

4 **branches of biology**

actinobiology	bioscience
aerobiology	genetics
agrobiology	histology
anatomy	human ecology
aquatic biology	hydrobiology
aquatic microbiology	hydrology *or* hydrogeology
astrobiology	*or* geohydrology
autoecology	mathematical biology
bacteriology	microbiology
biobehavioral science	molecular biology
biochemical genetics	morphology
biochemistry	natural classification
biodynamics	natural history
biogeography	neurobiology
biometry *or* biometrics *or*	neurochemistry
biostatistics	neuroendocrinology
bionics	neurogenetics
biophysics	neuroscience
biotechnology *or* biotech	oceanography
(informal)	organography
biothermodynamics	organology
biostatics	palaeontology
botany	palynology
cell biology	parasitology
cell physiology	photobiology
chronobiology	photodynamics
cryobiochemistry	phylogenetic classification
cryobiology	*or* phyletic classification
cytogenetics	*or* phyletics
cytology	physiology
cytotaxonomy	radiobiology
ecology *or* bioecology *or*	sociobiology
bionomics	somatology
electrobiology	stoichiology
electrophysiology	synecology
embryology	taxonomy *or* systematics
enzymology	teratology
ethnobiology	virology
exobiology *or* astrobiology	zoogeography *or* animal
or bioastronautics *or*	geography
space biology *or* space	zoology

5 **branches of botany**

agriculture	archaeobotany *or*
agrobiology	archeobotany
agronomy	astrobotany
agrostology	botanical histochemistry
algology	bryology
applied botany	carpology
aquiculture	dendrology

economic botany	phytopathology
ethnobotany	phytosociology
floriculture	plant anatomy *or*
floristics	phytotomy
forestry	plant biochemistry *or*
fungology	phytochemistry
gnotobiology	plant cytology
histology	plant ecology *or*
horticulture	phytoecology
hydroponics	plant geography *or*
mycology	phytogeography
olericulture	plant morphology
palaeobotany	plant pathology *or*
palaeoethnobotany	phytopathology
palynology	plant physiology
phycology	pomology
phytogenesis	pteridology
phytogeography	seed biology
phytography	silviculture

6 **branches of zoology**

animal behaviour	herpetology
animal chemistry *or*	histology
zoochemistry	ichthyology
animal pathology *or*	invertebrate zoology
zoopathology	malacology
animal physiology *or*	mammalogy
zoonomy	marine biology
animal psychology	morphology
arachnology	myrmecology
archaeozoology	ophiology
behavioural ecology	ornithology
cetology	palaeontology
comparative anatomy *or*	palaeozoology
zootomy	parasitology
comparative embryology	primatology
comparative psychology	protozoology
conchology	sociobiology
cytogenetics	systematic zoology *or*
cytology	systematics *or* taxonomy
embryology	vertebrate zoology
entomology	zoogeography
ethology	zoography
evolution	zoometry
genetics	zootomy
helminthology	

1067 AGRICULTURE

nouns

1 **agriculture, farming** (*see* list), husbandry; cultivation, culture, geoponics, tillage, tilth; green revolution; agrology, agronomy, agronomics, agrotechnology; thremmatology; agroecosystem; agrogeology, agricultural geology; agrochemistry; agricultural engineering; agricultural economics; rural economy *or* economics, farm economy *or* economics, agrarian economy *or* economics, agrarianism; agribusiness *or* agrobusiness, agribiz (*informal*), agroindustry; sharecropping

2 **horticulture, gardening**; landscape gardening, landscape architecture, groundskeeping; truck gardening, market gardening, olericulture; flower gardening, flower-growing, floriculture; viniculture,

viticulture; orcharding, fruit-growing, pomiculture, citriculture

3 **forestry**, arboriculture, tree farming, silviculture, forest management; Christmas tree farming; forestation, afforestation, reforestation; lumbering, logging; deforestation; woodcraft

4 (*agricultural deities*) vegetation spirit *or* daemon, fertility god *or* spirit, year-daemon, forest god *or* spirit, green man, corn god, Ceres, Demeter, Gaea, Triptolemus, Dionysus, Persephone, Kore, Flora, Aristaeus, Pomona, Frey

5 **agriculturist**, agriculturalist; agrologist, agronomist; **farmer**, granger, husbandman, **yeoman**, cultivator, tiller, sodbuster, **tiller of the soil**; boutique farmer, contour farmer, crop-farmer, dirt farmer (*informal*), etc; gentleman-farmer; **peasant**, *campesino* (*Spanish*), *Bauer* (*German*), countryman, rustic; **grower**, raiser; **planter**, tea-planter, coffee-planter, etc; peasant holder *or* proprietor, *kulak, muzhik* (*both Russian*); tenant farmer, crofter; sharecropper, cropper, collective farm worker, *kolkhoznik* (*Russian*), *kibbutznik* (*Yiddish*); **agricultural worker, farm worker**, farmhand, farm labourer, cottager, hind, migrant *or* migratory worker *or* labourer, bracero, picker; ploughman, ploughboy; land girl; farmboy, farmgirl; planter, sower; reaper, harvester, harvestman; haymaker

6 **horticulturist, nurseryman, gardener**, plantsman, plantswoman; landscape gardener, landscapist, landscape architect; truck gardener, market gardener, olericulturist; **florist**, floriculturist; vinegrower, viniculturist, viticulturist, vintager; *vigneron* (*French*); vinedresser; orchardist, orchardman, fruit-grower

7 **forester**; arboriculturist, silviculturist, tree farmer; conservationist; **ranger**, forest ranger; woodsman, woodman, woodcraftsman; **logger, lumberman**, timberman, lumberjack; woodcutter, wood chopper, bushwhacker (*NZ*)

8 **farm**, farmplace, farmstead, farmhold (*old*), farmery, **grange**, location (*Australian*), pen (*Jamaica*); boutique farm, crop farm, dirt farm, tree farm, etc; **plantation**, cotton plantation, etc, *hacienda* (*Spanish*); croft, homecroft; **homestead**, steading; toft; mains (*informal*); demesne, home farm, demesne farm, manor farm; **barnyard**, farmyard, barton (*informal*); collective farm, *kolkhoz* (*Russian*), *kibbutz* (*Hebrew*); farmland, cropland, arable land, plowland, fallow; grassland, pasture see 310.8

9 **field, tract**, plat, **plot, patch, allotment**, piece *or* parcel of land; cultivated land; clearing; hayfield, corn field, wheat field, etc; paddy, paddy field, rice paddy

10 **garden**, *jardin* (*French*); bed, **flower bed**, border, ornamental border; window box; paradise; garden spot; winter garden, kitchen garden; **vineyard**, vinery, grapery, grape ranch; market garden

11 **nursery**; **conservatory, greenhouse**, glasshouse, forcing house, summerhouse, lathhouse, **hothouse**, coolhouse; potager; potting shed; force *or* forcing bed, forcing pit, **hotbed**, cold frame; seedbed; cloche; pinery, orangery

12 **growing, raising**, rearing, cultivation; **green fingers**, green thumb (*US*)

13 **cultivation**, cultivating, culture, **tilling**, dressing, working; harrowing, plowing, contour plowing, furrowing, listing, fallowing, weeding, hoeing, pruning, thinning, double digging; overcropping, overcultivation; irrigation, overirrigation

14 **planting**, setting; **sowing, seeding**, semination, insemination; breeding, hydridizing; **dissemination**, broadcast, broadcasting; transplantation, resetting; retimbering, reforestation

15 **harvest**, harvesting, **reaping, gleaning**, gathering, cutting; nutting; clamp; cash crop, root crop, **crop** *see* 472.5

verbs

16 **to farm, ranch**; grow, **raise**, rear; crop; dryfarm; sharecrop; **garden; have green fingers**, have a green thumb (*US*); bushwhack (*NZ*)

17 **to cultivate**, culture, **dress, work, till**, till the soil, dig, delve, spade; mulch; **plough**, plough in, plough under, plough up, list, fallow, backset (*Western US*); **harrow**, rake; **weed**, weed out, hoe, cut, prune, thin, thin out; force; overcrop, overcultivate; slash and burn; fertilize *see* 889.8

18 **to plant**, implant (*old*), set, put in; **sow, seed**, seed down, seminate, inseminate; **disseminate**, broadcast, sow broadcast, scatter seed; drill; bed; dibble; **transplant**, reset, pot; vernalize; **forest**, afforest; deforest; retimber, reforest

19 **to harvest, reap**, crop, **glean, gather**, gather in, bring in, get in the harvest, reap and carry; **pick**, pluck; dig, grabble (*Southern US*); mow, cut; hay; nut; crop herbs

adjectives

20 **agricultural, agrarian**, agro–, geoponic, geoponical, agronomic, agronomical; farm, **farming**; arable; **rural** *see* 233.6

21 **horticultural**; olericultural; vinicultural, viticultural; arboricultural, silvicultural

22 **types of farming**

boutique farming	hydroponics *or* tank farming
contour farming	intensive farming
crofting	mixed farming
crop-farming	slash-and-burn
dirt farming (informal)	strip farming
dry farming	stubble-mulch farming *or* trash farming
dryland farming	
fen farming	subsistence farming
fruit farming	truck farming
grain farming	

1068 ANIMAL HUSBANDRY

nouns

1 **animal husbandry**, animal rearing *or* raising *or* culture, stock raising, **ranching**; zooculture, zootechnics, zootechny; thremmatology; gnotobiotics; herding, grazing, keeping flocks and herds, running livestock; transhumance; breeding, stockbreeding, stirpiculture; horse training, dressage, manège; horsemanship; pisciculture, fish culture; apiculture, bee culture, beekeeping; cattle raising; sheepherding; stock farming, fur farming; factory farming; pig-keeping; dairy-farming, chicken-farming, pig-farming, etc; cattle-ranching, mink-ranching, etc

2 **stockman**, stock raiser, stockkeeper (*Australian*); breeder, stockbreeder; poultryman, poulterer; sheepman; cattleman, cow keeper, cowman, grazier; **rancher**, ranchman, ranchero; ranchhand; dairyman, dairy farmer; milkmaid; **stableman**, stableboy, stable lad, stable girl, **groom**, hostler, equerry, lad; trainer, breaker, tamer; broncobuster *and* buckaroo (*both informal*); **blacksmith**, horseshoer, farrier

3 **herder, drover, herdsman**, herdboy; **shepherd**, shepherdess, **sheepherder**, sheepman; goatherd; swineherd, pigman, pigherd, hogherd; gooseherd, gooseboy, goosegirl; swanherd; cowherd, neatherd; **cowboy, cowgirl, cowhand**, puncher *and* **cowpuncher** *and* cowpoke (*all informal*), waddy (*Western US*), cowman, cattleman, *vaquero* (*Spanish*), gaucho, bullocky (*Australian & NZ informal*); horseherd, **wrangler**, horse wrangler

4 **apiarist**, apiculturist, **beekeeper**, beeherd

5 **farm**, stock farm, animal farm; **ranch**, rancho, rancheria, station (*Australian*); horse farm, stable, stud farm; **cattle ranch**; dude ranch; stump ranch; pig farm, piggery; chicken farm *or* ranch, turkey farm, duck farm, goose farm, poultry farm; sheep farm *or* ranch; fur farm *or* ranch, mink farm *or* ranch; **dairy farm**; factory farm; animal enclosure; battery; perchery

verbs

6 **to raise, breed**, rear, fetch up, grow, hatch, feed, nurture, fatten; keep, run; ranch, farm; culture; back-breed

7 **to tend; groom**, rub down, brush, curry, currycomb, wisp; water, drench, feed, fodder; bed, bed down, litter; milk; harness, saddle, hitch, bridle, yoke; gentle, handle, manage; tame, train, break

8 **to drive, herd**, drove, herd up, punch cattle, shepherd, ride herd on; spur, goad, prick, lash, whip; wrangle, round up; corral, cage

1069 EARTH SCIENCE

nouns

1 **earth science, earth sciences** (*see list*); geoscience; geography, geology, rock hunting *and* rock hounding (*both informal*), geological science, oceanography, oceanographic science, meteorology, atmospheric science, planetary science, space science

2 **earth scientist**, geoscientist; **geologist**, rock hunter *and* rock hound (*both informal*), **geographer, oceanographer, astronomer**, star-gazer (*informal*), **meteorologist**, weather man (*for other agent nouns, add –ist or –er to names of branches listed below*)

3 **earth sciences**

aerology	geochronology
aeronomy	geochronometry
bathymetry	geodesy
biogeography	geodynamics
biostratigraphy	geography
chronostratigraphy	geological cartography
climatology	geology
crystallography	geomagnetism
geochemistry	geomorphology
geophysics	palaeopedology
glaciology	pedology *or* soil science
historical geology	petrochemistry
hydrography	petrogenesis
hydrology *or* geohydrology *or* hydrogeology	petrography
	petrology *or* lithology
lithostratigraphy	physical climatology
magnetostratigraphy	physical geography *or* physiography
meteorology	
mineralogy	planetology
mining geology	plate *or* global tectonics
oceanography	sedimentology
oceanology	seismology
palaeobiogeography	submarine geology
palaeoclimatology	tectonic *or* geotectonic *or* structural geology
palaeogeography	
palaeogeophysics	tectonophysics
palaeolimnology	thalassography
palaeomagnetism	topography
palaeontology	volcanology

1070 THE UNIVERSE, ASTRONOMY

nouns

1 **universe, world, cosmos**; creation, created universe, created nature, all, **all creation**, all *or* everything that is, all being, totality, totality of being, sum of things; omneity, allness; nature, system; wide world, whole wide world, "world without end"—BIBLE; plenum; **macrocosm**, macrocosmos, megacosm; metagalaxy; open universe, closed universe, oscillating universe, steady-state universe, expanding universe, pulsating universe; Einsteinian universe, Newtonian universe, Friedmann universe; Ptolemaic universe, Copernican universe; sidereal universe

2 **the heavens**, heaven, **sky, firmament**; empyrean, welkin, *caelum* (*Latin*), lift *or* lifts (*Scottish*); **the blue**, blue sky, azure, cerulean, the blue serene; **ether, air**, hyaline, "the clear hyaline, the glassy sea"—MILTON, "an infinite grace"—ALBERT CAMUS; vault, cope, canopy, vault *or* canopy of heaven, "the arch of heaven"—VERGIL, "that inverted bowl they call the sky"—OMAR KHAYYÁM, "heaven's ebon vault"—SHELLEY, starry sphere, celestial sphere, starry heaven *or* heavens, "this majestical roof fretted with golden fire"—SHAKESPEARE; Caelus

3 **space, outer space**, cosmic space, empty space, ether space, pressureless space, celestial spaces, interplanetary *or* interstellar *or* intergalactic *or* intercosmic space, metagalactic space, **the void**, the void above, ocean of emptiness; chaos; outermost reaches of space; astronomical unit, light-year, parsec; interstellar medium

4 **stars**, fixed stars, starry host, "living sapphires"—MILTON, "all the fire-folk sitting in the air"—G M HOPKINS, "the burning tapers of the sky"—SHAKESPEARE, "the mystical jewels of God"—ROBERT BUCHANAN, "golden fruit upon a tree all out of reach"—GEORGE ELIOT, "bright sentinels of the sky"—WILLIAM HABINGTON, "the pale populace of Heaven"—R

BROWNING; music *or* harmony of the spheres; orb, sphere; **heavenly body**, celestial body *or* sphere; **comet; comet cloud; morning star,** daystar, Lucifer, Phosphor, Phosphorus; **evening star,** Vesper, Hesper, Hesperus, Venus; **North Star,** polestar, polar star, lodestar, Polaris; Dog Star, Sirius, Canicula; Bull's Eye, Aldebaran

5 **constellation** (*see list*), **configuration,** asterism; zodiacal constellation; **star cluster,** galactic cluster, open cluster, globular cluster, stellar association, supercluster; Magellanic clouds

6 **galaxy, island universe,** galactic nebula; spiral galaxy *or* nebula, spiral; barred spiral galaxy *or* nebula, barred spiral; elliptical *or* spheroidal galaxy; disc galaxy; irregular galaxy; radio galaxy; **the Local Group; the Galaxy, the Milky Way,** the galactic circle, *Via Lactea* (*Latin*); galactic cluster, supergalaxy; great attractor; chaotic attractor; continent of galaxies, great wall *or* sheet of galaxies; galactic coordinates, galactic pole, galactic latitude, galactic longitude; galactic noise, cosmic noise; galactic nucleus, active galactic nucleus; cosmic string

7 **nebula,** nebulosity; gaseous nebula; hydrogen cloud; dark nebula; dust cloud; dark matter, degenerate matter; planetary nebula; whirlpool nebula; cirronebula; ring nebula; diffuse nebula; bright diffuse nebula; dark nebula, dark cloud, coalsack; Nebula of Lyra *or* Orion, Crab Nebula, the Coalsack, Black Magellanic Cloud; nebulous stars; nebular hypothesis

8 **star** (*see list*); **quasar,** quasi-stellar radio source; **pulsar,** pulsating star, eclipsing binary X-ray pulsar; Nemesis, the Death Star; **black hole,** gravitational collapse, giant black hole, mini-black hole, starving black hole, supermassive black hole, frozen black hole, white hole, active galactic nucleus; Hawking radiation; **magnitude,** stellar magnitude, visual magnitude; relative magnitude, absolute magnitude; star *or* stellar populations; mass-luminosity law; spectrum-luminosity diagram, Hertzsprung-Russell diagram; star catalogue, star chart, sky atlas, Messier catalogue, Dreyer's New General Catalog *or* NGC; star cloud, star cluster, globular cluster, open cluster; Pleiades *or* Seven Sisters, Hyades, Beehive

9 **planet,** wanderer, terrestrial planet, inferior planet, superior planet, secondary planet, major planet; minor planet, planetoid, asteroid; asteroid belt; Earth; Jupiter; Mars, the Red Planet; Mercury; Neptune; Pluto; Saturn; Uranus; Venus; solar system

10 **Earth, the world,** *terra* (*Latin*); **globe,** terrestrial globe, Spaceship Earth, the blue planet; geosphere, biosphere, magnetosphere; vale, vale of tears; "this pendent world, "the little O, the earth", "this goodly frame, the earth", "a stage where every man must play a part"—ALL SHAKESPEARE, "a seat where gods might dwell"—MILTON; Mother Earth, Ge *or* Gaea *or* Gaia, Tellus *or* Terra; whole wide world, four corners of the earth, "the round earth's imagined corners"—DONNE, the length and breadth of the land; geography; Gaia hypothesis

11 **moon, satellite;** orb of night, queen of heaven, queen of night,

"that orbèd maiden"—SHELLEY, "the wat'ry star", "the governess of floods", "sovereign mistress of the true melancholy"—ALL SHAKESPEARE, "a ghostly galleon tossed upon cloudy seas"—ALFRED NOYES, "Maker of sweet poets"—KEATS, "the wandering Moon"—MILTON, "bright wanderer, fair coquette of Heaven"—SHELLEY, "Queen and huntress, chaste and fair"—BEN JONSON, "a ruined world, a globe burnt out, a corpse upon the road of night"—ROBERT BURTON; silvery moon; **new moon,** wet moon; **crescent moon,** crescent, increscent moon, increscent, waxing moon, waxing crescent moon; decrescent moon, decrescent, waning moon, waning crescent moon; gibbous moon; **half-moon,** demilune; **full moon, harvest moon,** hunter's moon; **eclipse,** lunar eclipse, eclipse of the moon; artificial satellite *see* 1073.6, 14

12 (*moon goddess, the moon personified*) Diana, Phoebe, Cynthia, Artemis, Hecate, Selene, Luna, Astarte, Ashtoreth; man in the moon

13 **sun;** orb of day, daystar;

"the glorious lamp of Heav'n, the radiant sun"—DRYDEN, "that orbed continent, the fire that severs day from night"—SHAKESPEARE, "of this great world both eye and soul"—MILTON, "the God of life and poesy and light"—BYRON; photosphere, chromosphere, corona; sunspot; sunspot cycle; solar flare, solar prominence; solar wind; **eclipse,** eclipse of the sun, solar eclipse, total eclipse, partial eclipse, central eclipse, annular eclipse; corona, solar corona, Baily's beads

14 (*sun god or goddess, the sun personified*) Sol, Helios, Hyperion, Titan, Phaëthon, Phoebus, Phoebus Apollo, Apollo, Ra *or* Amen-Ra, Shamash, Surya, Savitar, Amaterasu

15 **meteor;** falling *or* shooting star, meteoroid, fireball, bolide; **meteorite,** meteorolite; micrometeoroid, micrometeorite; aerolite; chondrite; siderite; siderolite; tektite; meteor dust, cosmic dust; meteor trail, meteor train; meteor swarm; meteor *or* meteoric shower; radiant, radiant point; meteor crater

16 **orbit, circle, trajectory;** circle of the sphere, great circle, small circle; **ecliptic; zodiac;** zone; meridian, celestial meridian; colures, equinoctial colure, solstitial colure; equator, celestial equator, equinoctial, equinoctial circle *or* line; equinox, vernal equinox, autumnal equinox; longitude, celestial longitude, geocentric longitude, heliocentric longitude, galactic longitude, astronomical longitude, geographic *or* geodetic longitude; apogee, perigee; aphelion, perihelion; period

17 **observatory,** astronomical observatory; radio observatory, orbiting astronomical observatory *or* OAO, orbiting solar observatory *or* OSO; **planetarium;** orrery; **telescope,** astronomical telescope; reflector, refractor, Newtonian telescope, Cassegrainian telescope; **radio telescope,** radar telescope; **spectroscope,** spectrograph; spectrohelioscope, spectroheliograph; coronagraph; heliostat, coelostat; **observation;** seeing, bright time, dark time

18 **cosmology,** cosmography, **cosmogony;** stellar cosmogony, astrogony; cosmism, cosmic philosophy, cosmic evolution; nebular hypothesis; **big bang** *or*

expanding universe theory, oscillating *or* pulsating universe theory, steady state *or* continuous creation theory, plasma theory; creationism, creation science

19 astronomy, stargazing, uranology, astrognosy, astrography, uranography, uranometry; astrophotography, stellar photometry; spectrography, spectroscopy, radio astronomy, radar astronomy, X-ray astronomy; **astrophysics,** solar physics; celestial mechanics, gravitational astronomy; astrolithology; meteoritics; astrogeology

20 astrology, astromancy, **horoscopy;** astrodiagnosis; natural astrology; judicial *or* mundane astrology; genethliacism, genethlialogy, genethliacs, genethliac astrology; **horoscope,** nativity; zodiac, **signs of the zodiac; house,** mansion; house of life, mundane house, planetary house *or* mansion; aspect

21 cosmologist; cosmogonist, cosmogoner; cosmographer, cosmographist; cosmic philosopher, cosmist

22 astronomer, stargazer, uranologist, uranometrist, uranographer, uranographist, astrographer, astrophotographer; radio astronomer, radar astronomer; **astrophysicist,** solar physicist; astrogeologist

23 astrologer, astrologian, astromancer, stargazer, Chaldean, astroalchemist, horoscoper, horoscopist, genethliac (*old*)

adjectives

24 cosmic, cosmical, **universal;** cosmologic *or* cosmological, cosmogonal, cosmogonic *or* cosmogonical; cosmographic, cosomographical

25 celestial, heavenly, empyrean, empyreal; uranic; **astral, starry, stellar,** stellary, sphery; star-spangled, star-studded; sidereal; zodiacal; equinoctial; **astronomic** *or* **astronomical,** astrophysical, astrologic *or* astrological, astrologistic, astrologous; **planetary,** planetarian, planetal, circumplanetary; planetoidal, planetesimal, asteroidal; **solar,** heliacal; terrestrial; **lunar,** lunular, lunate, lunulate, lunary, cislunar, translunar, Cynthian; semilunar; meteoric, meteoritic; extragalactic, anagalactic; galactic; nebular, nebulous, nebulose; interstellar, intersidereal; interplanetary; intercosmic

26 extraterrestrial, exterrestrial, extraterrene, extramundane, alien, space; **transmundane, otherworldly,** transcendental; extra-solar

adverbs

27 universally, everywhere

28 star types

A star	early-type star
binary star	eclipsing binary
black dwarf	eclipsing variable
blaze star	eruptive variable
brown dwarf	F star
C star	fixed star
carbon star	flare star
Cepheid *or* Cepheid variable	giant star
	gravity star
comparison star	Greenwich star
dark star	G star
double star	hydrogen star
dwarf star	intrinsic variable

irregular star	red giant
K star	red supergiant
late-type star	RR Lyrae star
long-period variable	runaway star
M star	semiregular variable
main sequence star	silicon star
multiple star	solar *or* sun star
N star	spectroscopic binary
nautical star	standard star
nebulous star	supermassive star
neutron star	supernova
nova	variable star
O-type star	visible binary
R star	white dwarf
radio star	x-ray star
red dwarf	zenith star

29 constellations

Andromeda *or* the Chained Lady	Wreath *or* the Southern Crown
Antlia *or* Antlia Pneumatica *or* the Air Pump	Corona Borealis *or* the Northern Crown
Apus *or* the Bird of Paradise	Corvus *or* the Crow
	Crater *or* the Cup
Aquarius *or* the Water Bearer	Crux *or* the Cross
	Cygnus *or* the Swan
Aquila *or* the Eagle	Delphinus *or* the Dolphin
Ara *or* the Altar	Dorado *or* the Dorado Fish
Argo *or* Argo Navis *or* the Ship Argo	Draco *or* the Dragon
Aries *or* the Ram	Equuleus *or* the Foal
Auriga *or* the Charioteer	Eridanus *or* the River Po
Big Dipper *or* Ursa Major *or* Charles' Wain	Fornax *or* the Furnace
	Gemini *or* the Twins
Boötes *or* the Herdsman	Grus *or* the Crane
Caelum *or* Caela Sculptoris *or* the Sculptor's Tool	Hercules
	Horologium *or* the Clock
Camelopardalis *or* Camelopardus *or* the Giraffe	Hydra *or* the Sea Serpent
	Hydrus *or* the Water Snake
Cancer *or* the Crab	Indus *or* the Indian
Canes Venatici *or* the Hunting Dogs	Lacerta *or* the Lizard
	Leo *or* the Lion
Canis Major the Larger Dog *or* Orion's Hound	Leo Minor *or* the Lesser Lion
Canis Minor *or* the Lesser Dog	Lepus *or* the Hare
	Libra *or* the Balance
Capricorn *or* the Horned Goat	Little Dipper *or* Ursa Minor
Carina *or* the Keel	Lupus *or* the Wolf
Cassiopeia *or* the Lady in the Chair	Lynx *or* the Lynx
	Lyra *or* the Lyre
Centaurus *or* the Centaur	Malus *or* the Mast
Cepheus *or* the Monarch	Mensa *or* the Table
Cetus *or* the Whale	Microscopium *or* the Microscope
Chamaeleon *or* the Chameleon	Monoceros *or* the Unicorn
	Musca *or* the Fly
Circinus *or* the Compasses	Norma *or* the Rule
Columba *or* Columba Noae *or* Noah's Dove	Northern Cross
	Octans *or* the Octant
Coma Berenices *or* Berenice's Hair	Ophiuchus *or* the Serpent Bearer
Corona Australis *or* the	Orion *or* the Giant Hunter

Orion's Belt
Orion's Sword
Pavo *or* the Peacock
Pegasus *or* the Winged
 Horse
Perseus
Phoenix *or* the Phoenix
Pictor *or* the Painter
Pisces *or* the Fishes
Piscis Austrinus *or* the
 Southern Fish
Plough
Puppis *or* the Stern
Pyxis *or* the Mariner's
 Compass
Reticulum *or* the Net
Sagitta *or* the Arrow
Sagittarius *or* the Archer
Scorpio *or* Scorpius *or* the
 Scorpion
Sculptor *or* the Sculptor
Scutum *or* the Shield

Serpens *or* the Serpent
Sextans *or* the Sextant
Southern Cross
Taurus *or* the Bull
Telescopium *or* the
 Telescope
Triangulum *or* the
 Triangle
Triangulum Australe *or*
 the Southern Triangle
Tucana *or* the Toucan
Ursa Major *or* the Great
 Bear *or* the Plough *or*
 the Big Dipper
Ursa Minor *or* the Lesser
 Bear *or* the Little Dipper
Vela *or* the Sails
Virgo *or* the Virgin
Volans *or* Piscis Volans *or*
 the Flying Fish
Vulpecula *or* the Little
 Fox

1071 THE ENVIRONMENT

nouns

1 **the environment,** the natural world, the ecology, global ecology, ecosystem, global ecosystem, the biosphere, the ecosphere, the balance of nature, macroecology, microecology; **ecology,** bioregion; **environmental protection,** environmental policy; **environmental control,** environmental management; environmental assessment, environmental auditing, environmental monitoring, environmental impact analysis; emission control; **environmental science** (*see list*), environmentology

2 **environmental destruction,** ecocide, ecocatastrophe; environmental pollution, pollution, contamination; **air pollution,** atmospheric pollution, air quality; **water pollution,** stream pollution, lake pollution, ocean pollution, groundwater pollution, pollution of the aquifer; **environmental pollutant** (*see list*); eutrophication; **biodegradation,** biodeterioration, microbial degradation

3 **environmentalist,** conservationist, preservationist, nature-lover, environmental activist, doomwatcher, duck-squeezer *and* ecofreak *and* tree-hugger *and* eagle freak (*all informal*), ecoterrorist; Friends of the Earth, Greenpeace, Green Panther

4 **environmental sciences**

autecology
bioecology *or* bionomics
ecology
environmental archaeology
environmental biology
environmental chemistry
environmental engineering

environmental health
human ecology
land management
synecology
wildlife management
zoo-ecology

5 **environmental pollutants**

aerosol sprays
Agent Orange
aircraft noise
aldrin
arsenic

asbestos
automobile exhaust
azo compounds
benzene
beryllium

bromo compounds
calcium carbonates
captan
carbon dioxide
carbon monoxide
carbon tetrachloride
carcinogens
chemical waste
chlordane
chlorine
chlorobenzenes
chloroethanes
chlorofluorocarbons
chlorohydrocarbons
chloromethane
chlorophenol
chloropropanones
chlorpropham
chromium
coal smoke
dibromochloropropane *or*
 DBCP
dichlorides
dichloroacetate
dichlorobenzenes
dichlorodiphenyltrichloro-
 ethane *or* DDT
dichloroethanes
dichlorophenol
dichloropropane
dieldrin
dioxin
dioxins
endosulphan
endrin
ethanes
ethylene
ethylene dibromide *or* EDB
ethylene glycol
ethylene oxide
fenoxaprop ethyl
fluorenes
fluorides
fluorocarbons
fluorohydrocarbons
formaldehyde
fungicides
greenhouse gases
heptachlor
herbicides

hexachlorethane
hexone
hydrocarbons
industrial particulate matter
isocyanuric acid
kepone
lead
lead paint
leaded petrol
leptophos
malathion
mercury
metalaxyl
methyl ethyl ketone
methyl parathion
mining waste
mirex
nabam
naphthalene
nitro compounds
nitrogen oxides
nitroso compounds
noise
nuclear waste
paraquat dichloride
parathion
pentachloraphenol *or* PCP
pesticides
petrol
polybrominated biphenyls *or*
 PBBs
polychlorinated biphenyls *or*
 PCBs
radionuclides
sewage
sewage sludge
solid waste
sulphur oxides
tobacco smoke
toxaphene
toxic waste
trichloroacetic acid
trichlorobenzene
trichloroethylene *or* TCE
trimethylbenzenes
triphenyltin hydroxide *or*
 DuTer (trademark)
ultraviolet radiation
vinyl chloride
wood smoke

1072 ROCKETRY, MISSILERY

nouns

1 **rocketry,** rocket science *or* engineering *or* research *or* technology; **missilery,** missile science *or* engineering *or* research *or* technology; rocket *or* missile testing; ground test, firing test, static firing; rocket *or* missile project *or* programme; instrumentation; telemetry

2 **rocket, rocket engine** *or* **motor,** reaction engine *or* motor; rocket thruster, thruster; retrorocket; rocket exhaust; plasma jet, plasma engine; ion engine; jetavator

3 rocket, missile (*see list*), **ballistic missile, guided missile; torpedo;** projectile rocket, ordnance rocket, combat *or* military *or* war rocket; bird (*informal*); **payload; warhead,** nuclear *or* thermonuclear warhead, atomic warhead; multiple *or* multiple-missile warhead

4 **rocket bomb,** flying bomb *or* torpedo, cruising missile; **robot bomb,** robomb, *Vergeltungswaffe* (*German*), V-weapon, V-1, V-2, P-plane; **buzzbomb,** bumblebomb, doodle-bug

5 **multistage rocket, step rocket;** two- *or* three-stage rocket, two- *or* three-step rocket; single-stage rocket, single-step rocket, one-step rocket; **booster,** booster unit, booster rocket, takeoff booster *or* rocket; piggyback rocket

6 **test rocket,** research rocket, high-altitude research rocket, registering rocket, instrument rocket, instrument carrier, test instrument vehicle, rocket laboratory; probe

7 **proving ground,** testing ground; firing area; impact area; control centre, mission control, bunker; radar tracking station, tracking station, visual tracking station; meteorological tower

8 **rocket propulsion,** reaction propulsion, jet propulsion, blast propulsion; **fuel, propellant,** solid fuel, liquid fuel, hydrazine, liquid oxygen *or* lox; charge, propelling *or* propulsion charge, powder charge *or* grain, high-explosive charge; **thrust,** constant thrust; **exhaust,** jet blast, backflash

9 **rocket launching** *or* **firing,** ignition, launch, shot, shoot; countdown; **lift-off,** blast-off; guided *or* automatic control, programming; flight, trajectory; **burn; burnout,** end of burning; velocity peak, *Brennschluss* (*German*); altitude peak, ceiling; descent; airburst; impact

10 **rocket launcher,** projector; **launching** *or* **launch pad,** launching platform *or* rack, firing table; **silo;** takeoff ramp; tower projector, launching tower; launching mortar, launching tube, projector tube, firing tube; rocket gun, bazooka, antitank rocket, *Panzerfaust* (*German*); superbazooka; multiple projector, calliope, Stalin organ, Katusha; antisubmarine projector, Mark *see* 10, hedgehog (*informal*); Minnie Mouse launcher, mousetrap (*informal*); Meilewagon

11 rocket scientist *or* technician, rocketeer *or* rocketer, rocket *or* missile man, rocket *or* missile engineer

verbs

12 to rocket, skyrocket
13 to launch, project, shoot, fire, blast off; abort
14 rockets, missiles

AAM *or* air-to-air missile	missile
AA target rocket	ATA missile *or* air-to-air
ABM *or* antiballistic missile	ATG rocket *or* air-to-ground
airborne rocket	atom-rocket
anchor rocket	ATS *or* air-to-ship
antiaircraft rocket	AUM *or* air-to-underwater missile
antimine rocket	barrage rocket
antimissile	bat bomb
antiradar rocket	bazooka rocket
antisubmarine *or* antisub rocket	bombardment rocket
antitank rocket	chemical rocket
ASM *or* air-to-surface	combat high-explosive
rocket	SAM *or* surface-to-air missile
Congreve rocket	Scud
countermissile	signal rocket
cruise missile	skyrocket
demolition rocket	SLBM *or* submarine-launched ballistic missile
Exocet	SLCM *or* sea-launched cruise missile
fin-stabilized rocket	
fireworks rocket	smart rocket
flare rocket	smokeless powder rocket
flying tank	smoke rocket
GAPA *or* ground-to-air pilotless aircraft	snake *or* antimine
	solid-fuel rocket
glide bomb	space rocket
GTA rocket *or* ground-to-air	spinner
	spin-stabilized rocket
GTG rocket *or* ground-to-ground	SS-18
	SS-20
guided missile	SSM *or* surface-to-surface missile
harpoon rocket	
high-altitude rocket	STS rocket *or* ship-to-shore standoff missile
homing rocket	
HVAR *or* high velocity aircraft rocket	submarine killer
	supersonic rocket
ICBM *or* intercontinental ballistic missile	target missile
	torpedo rocket
incendiary antiaircraft rocket	training rocket *or* missile
incendiary rocket	trajectory missile
ion rocket	transoceanic rocket
IRBM *or* intermediate range ballistic missile	Trident
	ullage rocket
line-throwing rocket	vernier *or* vernier rocket
liquid-fuel rocket	window rocket *or* antiradar
long-range rocket	winged rocket
Minuteman	wire-guided missile
MIRV *or* multiple independently targetable re-entry vehicle	XAAM *or* experimental air-to-air missile
MRV *or* multiple re-entry vehicle	XASM *or* experimental air-to-surface missile
Patriot	XAUM *or* experimental air-to-underwater missile
Pershing	
Polaris	XSAM *or* experimental surface-to-air missile
ram rocket	
retro-float light	XSSM *or* experimental surface-to-surface missile
retro-rocket	
rockoon	

1073 SPACE TRAVEL

nouns

1 **space travel, astronautics,** cosmonautics, **space flight,** navigation of empty space; interplanetary travel, space exploration; space walk; space navigation, astrogation; **space science,** space technology *or* engineering; **aerospace science,** aerospace technology *or* engineering; space *or* aerospace research; space *or* aerospace medicine, bioastronautics; astrionics; escape velocity; rocketry *see* 1072; multistage flight, step flight, shuttle flights; trip to the moon, trip to Mars, grand tour; space terminal, target planet; science fiction

2 **spacecraft** (*see list*), **spaceship, space rocket,** rocket ship, manned rocket, interplanetary rocket;

rocket *see* 1072.2; orbiter; **shuttle**, space shuttle; **capsule**, space capsule, ballistic capsule; **nose cone**, **heat shield**, heat barrier, thermal barrier; module, command module, lunar excursion module *or* LEM, lunar module *or* LM; moon ship, Mars ship, etc; deep-space ship; exploratory ship, reconnaissance rocket; ferry rocket, tender rocket, tanker ship, fuel ship; **multistage rocket** *see* 1072.5, shuttle rocket, retrorocket, rocket thruster *or* thruster, attitude-control rocket, main rocket; **burn**; space docking, docking, docking manoeuvre; **orbit**, parking orbit, geostationary orbit; earth orbit, apogee, perigee; lunar *or* moon orbit, apolune, perilune, apocynthion, pericynthion; **guidance system**, terrestrial guidance; soft landing, hard landing; injection, insertion, lunar insertion, Earth insertion; **reentry**, **splashdown**

3 **flying saucer**, unidentified flying object *or* UFO

4 **rocket engine** *see* 1072.2; atomic power plant; solar battery; power cell

5 **space station**, astro station, **space island**, island base, cosmic stepping-stone, halfway station, advance base; manned station; inner station, outer station, transit station, space airport, **spaceport**, spaceport station, space dock, launching base, research station, space laboratory, space observatory; tracking station, radar tracking station; radar station, radio station; radio relay station, radio mirror; space mirror, solar mirror; moon station, moon base, lunar base, lunar city, observatory on the moon

6 **artificial satellite** (*see list*), **satellite**, space satellite, robot satellite, unmanned satellite, sputnik; communications satellite, active communications satellite, communications relay satellite, weather satellite, orbiting observatory, geophysical satellite, navigational satellite, geodetic satellite, research satellite, interplanetary monitoring satellite, automated satellite; **probe**, **space probe**, geo probe, interplanetary explorer

7 (*satellite telemetered recorders*) micro-instrumentation; aurora particle counter, cosmic ray counter, gamma ray counter, heavy particle counter, impulse recorder, magnetometer, solar ultraviolet detector, solar X-ray detector, telecamera, Hubble telescope

8 **astronaut**, astronavigator, cosmonaut, **spaceman**, **spacewoman**, space crew member, shuttle crew member, space traveller, space cadet, rocketeer, rocket pilot; space doctor; space crew; planetary colony, lunar colony; extraterrestrial visitor *or* extraterrestrial, ET, alien, saucerman, man from Mars, Martian, little green man

9 **rocket society**, British Interplanetary Society, American Rocket Society, American Interplanetary Society, German Society for Space Research, NASA *or* National Aeronautics and Space Administration (*US*)

10 (*space hazards*) cosmic particles, intergalactic matter, aurora particles, radiation, cosmic ray bombardment; rocket *or* satellite debris, space junk (*informal*); meteors, meteorites; asteroids; meteor dust impacts, meteoric particles, space bullets; extreme temperatures; the bends, blackout, weightlessness, zero gravity, microgravity

11 **space suit**, pressure suit, G suit, anti-G suit; space helmet

verbs

12 to travel in space, go into outer space; orbit the earth, go into orbit, orbit the moon, etc; navigate in space, astrogate; escape earth, break free, leave the atmosphere, shoot into space; rocket to the moon, park in space, hang *or* float in space, space-walk

adjectives

13 **astronautical**, cosmonautical, spacetravelling, spacefaring; astrogational; rocketborne, spaceborne

14 **spacecraft, artificial satellites, space probes**

A-1	Lunik
Alouette	Mariner
Anik	Mars probes
Anna	Mercury
Apollo	Midas
Ariane	Mir
Ariel	Molniya
ATDA	Nimbus
Atlas-Score	OAO *or* orbiting
ATS	astronomical observatory
Aurora 7 (Mercury)	OGO *or* orbiting
Biosatellite	geophysical observatory
communications satellites	orbiter
or comsats	OSO *or* orbiting solar
Comsat	observatory
cosmic background	OV1
explorer *or* COBE	OV3
Cosmos	Pageos
Courier	Pegasus
D1-C	Pioneer
D2-D	Polyot
Diapason	Proton
Discoverer	Ranger
Early Bird	Relay
Echo	Samos
Elektron	San Marco
ERS	Secor
ESSA *or* environmental	shuttle *or* space shuttle
survey satellite	Sigma 7 (Mercury)
Explorer	Skylab
Explorer 760	skylab
Faith 7 (Mercury)	Solar Max
FR-1	Soyuz
Freedom 7 (Mercury)	Spacelab
Friendship 7 (Mercury)	space station
Galileo	Sputnik
GATV	Surveyor
Gemini	Syncom
Geostationary Operational	Telstar
Environmental Satellite	TIROS *or* television and
or GOES	infrared observation
Greb	satellite
Injun	Transit
Intelsat	Vanguard
killersat	Venus probes
Lageos *or* laser	Viking
geodynamic satellite	Voskhod
Lani Bird	Vostok
Liberty Bell 7 (Mercury)	Voyager
Lofti	WRESAT
Luna	Zond
Lunar Orbiter	

INDEX

Numbers after index entries refer to categories and paragraphs in the front section of this book, not to page numbers. The part of the number before the decimal point refers to the category in which synonyms and related words to the words you are looking up are found. The part of the number after the decimal point refers to the paragraph or paragraphs within the category. Look at the index entry for **abdomen** on the next page:

abdomen 2.16

This entry listing tells you that you can find words related to **abdomen** in paragraph 16 of category 2.

Words, of course, frequently have more than one meaning. Each of those meanings may have synonyms or associated related words. Look at the entry for **abhor**:

abhor dislike 99.3

hate 103.5

This tells you that you will find synonyms for **abhor** in the sense meaning "dislike" in category 99, paragraph 3. It also tells you that you will find synonyms for **abhor**, meaning "hate", in category 103, paragraph 5.

In many cases, words are spelled the same as nouns, verbs, adjectives, etc. Look at the entry for **abandon** and notice that here you are directed to **abandon** when it is used as a noun and when it is used as a verb in a variety of meanings. Here, as in the examples above, you are referred to the category and paragraph number.

Not all words in the main part of the book are included in the index. Many adverbs ending with **-ly** have been left out of the index; but you will find the common adverbs ending in **-ly** here, such as **lightly** or **easily**. If you can't find the adverb ending in **-ly** that you are looking for, look up the word in its adjective form and go to that category. Frequently, you can use the words in the adjective paragraphs you find and convert them into the adverb you are looking for by simply adding **-ly** to the adjective.

To make it easier to find phrases, we have indexed them according to their first word, unless that first word is an article such as **a, the** or **an**. You do not have to guess what the main word of the phrase is to find it in the index. Simply look up the first word in the phrase. For example, **hot air** will be found in the Hs, **fat cat** in the Fs and **let go** in the Ls.

A superior 249.4
  beginning 817.1

a 244.5

A1 seaworthy 180.18
  superlative 249.13
  number one 998.18

AB 183.1

aback 217.14

abandon
  noun zeal 101.2
  fury 105.8
  carelessness 340.2
  unrestraint 430.3
  turpitude 654.5
  excess 992.1
  verb quit 188.9
  leave undone 340.7
  desert 370.5
  break the habit 374.3
  discard 390.7
  surrender 433.8
  disregard 435.3
  relinquish 475.3
  swear off 668.8
  cease 856.6
  dismiss 983.4

abandoned zealous
  101.9
  frenzied 105.25
  available 222.15
  neglected 340.14
  forsaken 370.8
  disused 390.10
  unrestrained 430.24
  relinquished 475.5
  forlorn 584.12
  outcast 586.10
  corrupt 654.14
  profligate 665.25
  excessive 992.16

abandonment
  departure 188.1
  forsaking 370.1
  discontinuance 390.2
  unrestraint 430.3
  surrender 433.2
  nonobservance 435.1
  relinquishment 475.1
  forlornness 584.4
  turpitude 654.5
  cessation 856.1
  apostasy 857.3

abate weaken 16.10
  relieve 120.5
  decrease 252.6
  bate 252.8
  subtract 255.9
  discount 631.2
  moderate 670.6
  relax 670.9
  qualify 958.3

abated 252.10

abating 670.14

abattoir 308.11

abbey 703.6

abbot 699.15

abbreviated short
  268.8

shortened 268.9
  concise 537.6

abbreviation deletion
  255.5
  contraction 260.1
  shortening 268.3,
  537.4
  abridgment 557.1

abdicate give up 370.7
  cease to use 390.4
  resign 448.2

abdication
  relinquishment 370.3
  discontinuance 390.2
  resignation 448.1

abdomen 2.16

abdominal 2.29

abduct seize 480.14
  abduce 482.20

abduction seizure
  480.2
  kidnapping 482.9

abductor 483.10

aberration deviation
  164.1
  obliquity 204.1
  abnormality 869.1
  insanity 925.1
  eccentricity 926.1
  error 974.1

abeyance inertness
  173.4
  discontinuance 390.2
  pause 856.3

abhor dislike 99.3
  hate 103.5

abhorrence hostility
  99.2
  hate 103.1
  anathema 103.3

abhorrent offensive
  98.18
  unlikable 99.7
  hating 103.7

abide await 130.8
  endure 134.5, 826.6
  inhabit 225.7
  wait 845.12
  remain 852.5
  continue 855.3

abide by assent 332.8
  observe 434.2
  execute 437.9

abiding
  noun habitation 225.1
  adj resident 225.13
  durable 826.10
  permanent 852.7
  continuing 855.7

abigail 577.8

ability capability 18.2
  means 384.2
  preparedness 405.4
  skill 413.1
  talent 413.4

abject penitent 113.9

humble-hearted
  137.11
  obsequious 138.14
  submissive 433.12
  base 661.12

A-blast 1037.16

ablaze fervent 93.18
  burning 1018.27
  flashing 1024.34
  illuminated 1024.39

able capable 18.14
  fitted 405.17
  competent 413.24

able-bodied 15.16

able to pay 729.17

ably capably 18.16
  skilfully 413.31

abnormal wrong 638.3
  inconsistent 788.8
  unnatural 869.9
  insane 925.26
  eccentric 926.5

abnormality disease
  85.1
  wrong 638.1
  unfitness 788.3
  abnormity 869.1
  oddity 869.5
  insanity 925.1
  eccentricity 926.1

abnormally 869.17

aboard here 159.23
  on board 182.62

abode location 159.1
  habitation 225.1,
  228.1

abolish nullify 395.13
  repeal 445.2

abolition extinction
  395.6
  repeal 445.1

abominable offensive
  98.18
  wrong 638.3
  wicked 654.16
  base 661.12
  terrible 999.9

abomination
  defilement 80.4
  hostility 99.2
  hate 103.1
  anathema 103.3
  horror 638.2
  iniquity 654.3
  evil 999.3

aboriginal
  noun native 227.3
  ancient 841.7
  adj native 226.5
  beginning 817.15
  primitive 841.11
  original 885.14

abort miscarry 410.15
  end 819.5
  cease 856.6
  launch 1072.13

abortion miscarriage
  410.5
  monstrosity 869.6
  unproductiveness
  890.1

abortive fruitless
  391.12
  unsuccessful 410.18

abound 990.5

about
  adv around 209.12
  near 223.20
  approximately 244.6
  prep around 223.26

about to 405.16

about to be 839.3

about-turn 163.3,
  363.1

above
  adj superior 249.12
  higher 272.19
  previous 833.4
  adv additionally
  253.11
  on high 272.21
  before 813.6
  prep on 295.37
  beyond 522.26
  in excess of 992.26

above all 249.17

above and beyond
  992.26

above-ground 306.11

above water
  unindebted 624.23
  in safety 1006.6

abrasion trauma 85.37
  subtraction 255.1
  roughness 288.1
  attrition 1042.2
  pulverization 1049.4

abrasive
  noun smoother 287.4
  abrasion 1042.2
  adj unpleasant 98.17
  out of humour 110.17
  rugged 288.7
  abradant 1042.10

abreast
  adv in parallel 203.7
  prep beside 218.11

abreast of 927.18

abridged shortened
  268.9
  concise 537.6
  condensed 557.6

abroad
  adj nonresident 222.12
  bewildered 970.24
  erroneous 974.16
  adv extensively 158.11
  outdoors 206.11
  far and wide 261.16
  wide 261.19
  in foreign parts 773.6

abrupt steep 204.18
  blunt 286.3

precipitate 401.10
  commanding 420.13
  gruff 505.7
  sudden 829.5

abruptly short 268.13
  precipitately 401.15
  gruffly 505.9

abscess anaemia 85.9
  sore 85.36

absconded 222.11

absence nonpresence
  222.1
  nonattendance 222.4
  nonexistence 761.1
  want 991.4

absent
  adj not present 222.11
  abstracted 984.11
  prep lacking 222.19
  excluding 772.10
  without 991.17
  conj unless 958.16

absentee 222.5

absenteeism 222.4

absently 222.16

Absolute 931.2

absolute omnipotent
  18.13
  downright 247.12
  affirmative 334.8
  authoritative 417.15
  imperious 417.16
  mandatory 420.12
  unrestricted 430.27
  governmental 612.17
  musical 708.47
  real 760.15
  thorough 793.10
  unmixed 797.7
  particular 864.12
  sole 871.9
  convincing 952.26
  evidential 956.16
  unqualified 959.2
  certain 969.13
  obvious 969.15
  accurate 972.16
  perfect 1001.6

absolutely
  adv extremely 247.22
  affirmatively 334.10
  really 760.16
  perfectly 793.15,
  1001.10
  certainly 969.23
  exactly 972.21
  exclam yes 332.18

absolutely no 335.8

absolute power 417.1

absolution pardon
  148.2
  acquittal 601.1

absolved 148.7

absorb digest 7.16
  adsorb 187.13
  consume 388.3
  understand 521.7
  acquire 570.7

accommodations 385.3
compact 437.1
facility 449.9
adjustment 465.4, 787.4
compromise 468.1
giving 478.1
loan 620.2
equating 789.2
change 851.1
conformity 866.1

accompaniment
adjunct 254.1
part 708.22
concurrence 898.1

accompany play 708.39
coincide 835.4
result 886.4

accompanying
attending 768.9
happening 830.9
simultaneous 835.5
concurrent 898.4

accomplice participator 476.4
cohort 616.3

accomplish arrive 186.6
do 328.6
perform 328.9, 891.11
achieve 407.4
succeed with 409.11
complete 793.6
evolve 860.5

accomplished achieved 407.10
skilled 413.26

accomplishment
noun arrival 186.1
superiority 249.1
performance 328.2, 891.5
act 328.3
success 409.1
acquirement 413.8
completion 793.4
evolution 860.1
solution 939.1
adj achievement 407.1

accomplishments 927.4

accord
noun unanimity 332.5
compact 437.1
consent 441.1
accordance 455.1
peace 464.1
harmony 708.3
relation 774.1
agreement 787.1
conformity 866.1
verb concur 332.9, 898.2
permit 443.9
get along 455.2
give 478.12
harmonize 708.35, 787.7

agree 787.6
conform 866.3

accordance unanimity 332.5
observance 434.1
accord 455.1
giving 478.1
harmony 708.3
uniformity 780.1
similarity 783.1
agreement 787.1
conformity 866.1
concurrence 898.1

accorded 478.24

according 708.49

accordingly in that case 765.11
consequently 886.7
hence 887.7

according to 866.9

accordion 711.11

account
noun recounting 349.3
record 549.1
report 549.7
information 551.1
credit account 622.2
fee 624.5
reckoning 628.2
statement 628.3
worth 630.2
esteem 662.3
story 719.3, 722.3
bill 870.5
sum 1016.6
summation 1016.11
verb judge 945.8

accountability
supervision 573.2
responsibility 641.2

accountable
interpretable 341.17
responsible 641.17
attributable 887.6

accountancy 628.6

accountant recorder 550.1
bookkeeper 628.7
professional 726.4
treasurer 729.11
calculator 1016.14

account as 952.11

account for explain 341.10
justify 600.9
attribute to 887.4

accounting
noun report 549.7
accountancy 628.6
numeration 1016.9
analysis 1040.7
adj bookkeeping 628.12

accounting for 887.1

account of 1016.12

accounts outstanding
accounts 628.1
summation 1016.11

account with 624.12

accoutrements
wardrobe 5.2
equipment 385.4

accredited authorized 443.17
commissioned 615.19

accrue grow 251.6
be received 479.8
mature 623.7

accumulate grow 251.6
store up 386.11
collect 472.11
assemble 769.18
put together 799.5

accumulated stored 386.14
assembled 769.21
joined 799.13

accumulation increase 251.1
store 386.1
collection 472.2
cumulation 769.9

accumulator betting system 759.4
collector 769.15
electrical device 1031.20

accuracy
meticulousness 339.3
circumstantiality 765.4
correctness 972.5

accurate meticulous 339.12
discriminating 943.7
correct 972.16

accurately meticulously 339.16
correctly 972.20

accusation 599.1

accuse censure 510.13
bring accusation 599.7

accused
noun defendant 599.6
adj charged 599.15

accusing
noun accusation 599.1
adj accusatory 599.13

accustomed wont 373.16
usual 868.9

AC-DC 75.29

ace military pilot 185.3
short distance 223.2
modicum 248.2
superior 249.4
star 413.14
card 758.2
one 871.3
dandy 998.7

acerbic bitter 64.6
sour 67.5
pungent 68.6
caustic 144.23
resentful 152.26

ache
noun aching 26.5
pain 96.5
chill 1022.2
verb suffer 26.8, 96.19
grieve 112.17

aches and pains 26.1

achievable 965.7

achieve arrive 186.6
do 328.6
accomplish 407.4
succeed with 409.11
perform 891.11

achieved 407.10

achievement
noun arrival 186.1
performance 328.2, 891.5
act 328.3
exploit 492.7
heraldic device 647.2
adj accomplishment 407.1

Achilles 492.8

Achilles' heel 1002.2

aching
noun ache 26.5
pain 96.5
yearning 100.5
chill 1022.2
adj achy 26.12
pained 96.23

achy 26.12

acid
noun sour 67.2
big D 87.9
bitterness 152.3
cauterant 1019.15
extinguisher 1021.3
hydracid 1058.3
adj acrimonious 17.14
acidulous 67.6
pungent 68.6
out of humour 110.17
caustic 144.23
resentful 152.26
vigorous 544.11
chemical 1058.8

acidic caustic 144.23
resentful 152.26

acidity acrimony 17.5
sourness 67.1
pungency 68.1
causticity 144.8
bitterness 152.3
acid 1058.3

acid test 941.2

acknowledge thank 150.4
admit 332.11
confess 351.7
reply 553.11
pay for 624.18
attribute to 887.4
answer 938.4
testify 956.9

acknowledged accepted 332.14

conventional 579.5
traditional 841.12

acknowledging 150.5

acknowledgment
thanks 150.2
recognition 332.3
confession 351.3
commendation 509.3
letter 553.2
receipt 627.2
due 639.2
apology 658.2
citation 887.2
answer 938.1

acne 85.34

acoustic
noun sound 50.1
adj auditory 48.13
acoustical 50.17
phonetic 524.31

acoustics 50.5

acquaintance
information 551.1
acquaintedness 587.4
friend 588.1
knowledge 927.1

acquainted 587.17

acquainted with 927.19

acquiesce be willing 324.3
assent 332.8
submit 433.6
comply 441.3

acquiescence
resignation 134.2
willingness 324.1
assent 332.1
submission 433.1
consent 441.1
conformity 866.1
belief 952.1

acquire get 472.8
receive 479.6, 627.3
take 480.13
absorb 570.7
incur 896.4

acquiring 472.15

acquisition gaining 472.1
receiving 479.1
taking 480.1

acquisitions property 471.1
learning 927.4

acquisitive greedy 100.27
acquiring 472.15
selfish 651.5

acquit bring in a verdict 598.21
clear 601.4

acquittal observance 434.1
judgment 598.10
acquittance 601.1

acquitted forgiven
148.7
paid 624.22

acre 247.3

acreage 158.1

acres land 234.1
real estate 471.6

acrid acrimonious
17.14
bitter 64.6
pungent 68.6
caustic 144.23
sharp 285.8
hostile 589.10

acrimonious acrid
17.14
caustic 144.23
resentful 152.26
violent 671.16

acrimony acridity 17.5
causticity 144.8
bitterness 152.3
berating 510.7
animosity 589.4
violence 671.1

acrobatic 743.30

acronym 526.4

across
adj transverse 170.9,
204.19
adv transversely
204.24
on 900.25
prep opposite to 215.7
beyond 261.21

across the board
791.13

across-the-board
771.7

across the sea 240.10

act
noun action 328.1,
328.3
legislation 613.4
law 673.3
scene 704.7
process 888.2
verb behave 321.4
serve 328.4
impersonate 349.12
sham 354.21
perform 704.29,
891.11
operate 888.7

act as impersonate
349.12
officiate 724.13
function as 888.8

act for be instrumental
384.7
represent 576.14
substitute for 861.5

acting
noun action 328.1
impersonation 349.4
sham 354.3
playing 704.8
adj performing 328.10

deputy 576.15
operating 888.11

acting-out 92.25

action behaviour 321.1
activity 328.1, 330.1
act 328.3
undertaking 404.1
fight 457.4
operation 458.5, 888.1
lawsuit 598.1
plot 722.4
strike 727.5
fun 743.2
basketball game 751.3
gambling 759.1
verdict 945.5
expedient 994.2
mechanism 1039.4
automatic control
1040.3

actions 321.1

activate reactivate
17.12
militarize 458.20
radioactivate 1036.9
atomize 1037.17

activated 1036.10

activating 17.15

activation reactivation
17.9
militarization 458.10

active
noun voice 530.14
adj energetic 17.13
moving 172.7
lively 330.17
effectual 387.21
observant 434.4
operating 888.11

actively energetically
17.16
busily 330.25

activism action 328.1
activity 330.1

activist energetic 17.13
active 330.17
enterprising 330.23

activity animation 17.4
motion 172.1
behaviour 321.1
action 328.1, 330.1
occupation 724.1
cause 885.9
radiation 1036.1

act on 945.13

actor deceiver 357.1
phoney 500.7
role 704.10
film studio 706.3
actress 707.2
doer 726.1

act out impersonate
349.12
enact 704.30

actress film studio
706.3
actor 707.2

Acts 683.4

acts 321.1

act together 450.3

actual real 760.15
happening 830.9
present 837.2
obvious 969.15
true 972.13

actual fact 760.3

actuality reality 760.2
present 837.1
unquestionability
969.3
truth 972.1

actually positively
247.19
really 760.16
truly 972.18

act with 450.4

acumen sagacity 919.4
discernment 943.2

acupuncture 292.3

acute energetic 17.13
exquisite 24.13
painful 26.10
shrill 58.14
deep-felt 93.24
sharp 285.8
pointed 285.9
cunning 415.12
violent 671.16
sagacious 919.16
urgent 996.22

acutely 247.20

AD 820.13

ad 352.6

adage 973.1

adagio
noun presto 708.25
adj, adv largo 708.54

Adam human nature
312.6
carnality 663.2

adamant
noun stone 1044.6
adj unyielding 361.9
immovable 854.15
hard 1044.10
inflexible 1044.12
stone 1057.10

adamantly 361.15

adapt orient 161.11
accustom 373.10
fit 405.8
compose 708.46
harmonize 787.7
change 851.7
conform 866.3

adaptability versatility
413.3
changeableness 853.1
handiness 1013.2
pliancy 1045.2
elasticity 1046.1

adaptable handy
387.20, 1013.15
versatile 413.25
changeable 853.6

conformable 866.5
pliant 1045.9
elastic 1046.7

adaptation orientation
161.4
fitting 405.2
piece 708.5
harmonization 709.2
adjustment 787.4
change 851.1
genesis 860.3
conformity 866.1

adapted accustomed
373.16
fitted 405.17
apt 787.10

adapted to 866.9

adapting 134.10

adaptive resigned
134.10
conformable 866.5
elastic 1046.7

adapt to 866.3

A-day 842.5

add plus 253.4
combine 804.3
calculate 1016.17

added 253.9

added-in 771.5

added to 253.12

adder 311.26

addict drug addict
87.20
desirer 100.12
enthusiast 101.4
addiction 373.9

addicted 87.24

addiction substance
abuse 87.1
addict 373.9

adding 1016.10

addition increase 251.1
accession 253.1
adjunct 254.1
wing 254.3
expansion 259.1
acquisition 472.1
nonessential 767.2
relation 774.1
combination 804.1
notation 1016.2

additional additive
253.8
supplementary 253.10
unessential 767.4
fresh 840.8

additionally 253.11

additive
noun adjunct 254.1
adj additional 253.8

addled intoxicated
88.31
muddleheaded 921.18
in a dilemma 970.25
muddled 984.13

add-on
noun addition 253.1

adjunct 254.1
adj added 253.9

address
noun abode 228.1
behaviour 321.1
skill 413.1
request 440.1
remark 524.4
speech 543.2
name and address
553.9
greeting 585.4
round 748.3
verb solicit 440.14
speak to 524.27
make a speech 543.9
direct 553.13
court 562.21
greet 585.10

address book 549.11

addresses solicitation
440.5
courtship 562.7

address to 982.10

add to increase 251.4
augment 253.5
enlarge 259.4

add up compute 253.6
be right 972.10
sum up 1016.18

add up to 791.8

adept
noun expert 413.11
occultist 689.11
adj skilful 413.22

adequacy ability 18.2
satisfactoriness 107.3
mean 246.1
sufficiency 990.1

adequate able 18.14
satisfactory 107.11
sufficient 990.6
tolerable 998.20

adequately ably 18.16
satisfactorily 107.15
sufficiently 990.8
tolerably 998.24

adhere join 799.11
cohere 802.6

adherence observance
434.1
approval 509.1
fidelity 644.7
cohesion 802.1

adherents 617.5

adhere to observe
434.2
execute 437.9
hold 474.6

adhering 802.10

adhesive
noun fastening 799.3
adherent 802.4
plastic 1052.6
adj adherent 802.12
viscous 1060.12

ad hoc extemporaneous
365.12
  transient 827.7
  substitute 861.8
  makeshift 994.7
adjacent 223.16
adjective 530.3
adjoining 223.16
adjourn 845.9
adjudication 945.1
adjunct
  noun addition 253.1,
    254.1
  expansion 259.1
  associate 616.1
  nonessential 767.2
  attendant 768.3
  relation 774.1
  part 792.1
  component 795.2
  adj added 253.9
adjust orient 161.11
  size 257.15
  accustom 373.10
  fit 405.8
  arrange 437.8
  reconcile 465.8
  settle 466.7
  compromise 468.2
  harmonize 787.7
  equalize 789.6
  organize 807.10
  change 851.7
  conform 866.3
adjustable versatile
  413.25
  changeable 853.6
  conformable 866.5
adjusted accustomed
  373.16
  fitted 405.17
adjusted to 866.9
adjusting 134.10
adjustment adjustive
  reaction 92.27
  orientation 161.4
  habituation 373.8
  fitting 405.2
  compact 437.1
  accommodation 465.4
  compromise 468.1
  good condition 764.3
  adaptation 787.4
  equating 789.2
  organization 807.2
  change 851.1
  conformity 866.1
adjust to harmonize
  787.7
  conform 866.3
  qualify 958.3
adjutant 616.6
ad lib at will 323.5
  extemporaneously
    365.15
ad-lib
  noun improvisation
    365.5

unpreparedness 406.1
  verb improvise 365.8
  adj extemporaneous
    365.12
administer execute
  437.9
  parcel out 477.8
  give 478.12, 643.6
  administrate 573.11
  administer justice
    594.5
  govern 612.12
administration
  performance 328.2
  governance 417.5
  distribution 477.2
  principal 571.8
  executive 574.3
  directorate 574.11
  authorities 575.15
  government 612.1
  giving 643.2
  protectorship 1007.2
administrative
  administrating 573.14
  executive 612.19
administrator principal
  571.8
  director 574.1
admirable endearing
  104.25
  praiseworthy 509.20
Admiral 575.21
admiration love 104.1
  wonder 122.1
  respect 155.1
  approval 509.1
admire cherish 104.21
  respect 155.4
  approve 509.9
admired beloved
  104.24
  respected 155.11
  approved 509.19
admirer enthusiast
  101.4
  lover 104.12
  supporter 616.9
admiring reverent
  155.9
  approbatory 509.16
admissible acceptable
  107.12
  receptive 187.16
  eligible 371.24
  permissible 443.15
  justifiable 600.14
  relevant 774.11
  logical 934.20
  evidential 956.16
  tolerable 998.20
admission admittance
  187.2
  entrance 189.1
  naturalization 226.3
  acknowledgment 332.3
  confession 351.3
  permission 443.1
  receiving 479.1

fee 630.6
  inclusion 771.1
  testimony 956.2
admit receive 187.10,
  479.6, 585.7
  enter 189.7
  naturalize 226.4
  acknowledge 332.11
  confess 351.7
  permit 443.9
  include 771.3
  allow for 958.5
admittance admission
  187.2
  receiving 479.1
admitted accepted
  332.14
  disclosive 351.10
  permitted 443.16
  received 479.10
  approved 509.19
  conventional 579.5
  real 760.15
  traditional 841.12
admittedly 969.25
admitting 958.13
admitting that 958.13
ado
  noun agitation 105.4
  bustle 330.4
  commotion 809.4
  trouble 1012.3
  adj happening 830.9
adolescence 301.6
adolescent
  noun youngster 302.1
  adj grown 14.3
  pubescent 301.13
  immature 406.11
Adonis 1015.10
adopt naturalize 226.4
  approve 371.15
  use 384.5
  appropriate 480.19,
    621.4
  usurp 640.8
adopted naturalized
  226.6
  chosen 371.26
adoption naturalization
  226.3
  embracement 371.4
  appropriation 480.4,
    621.2
  usurpation 640.3
  redemption 685.4
  conversion 857.1
adoptive 371.23
adorable desirable
  100.30
  endearing 104.25
adoration love 104.1
  respect 155.1
  piety 692.1
  worship 696.1
adore enjoy 95.12
  cherish 104.21
  respect 155.4

worship 696.10
adored beloved 104.24
  respected 155.11
adoring loving 104.27
  reverent 155.9
  pious 692.8
  worshipful 696.15
adorn ornament 498.8,
  545.7
  honour 662.12
  beautify 1015.15
adorned ornamented
  498.11
  ornate 545.11
adorning 498.10
adornment
  ornamentation 498.1
  ornateness 545.4
  beautification 1015.11
adrenal 13.8
Adrenalin 86.9
adrenalin vim 17.2
  liveliness 330.2
adrenaline 86.9
adrift
  adj afloat 182.61
  unfastened 801.22
  inconstant 853.7
  bewildered 970.24
  erroneous 974.16
  muddled 984.13
  adv separately 801.27
adroit skilful 413.22
  smart 919.14
adroitly 413.31
adulation praise 509.5
  flattery 511.1
adult
  noun grownup 304.1
  adj grown 14.3
  mature 303.12
  lascivious 665.29
  obscene 666.9
adulterous 665.27
adultery copulation
  75.7
  love affair 104.6
adulthood 303.2
advance
  noun progression
    162.1
  approach 167.1
  course 172.2
  increase 251.1
  improvement 392.1
  offer 439.1
  promotion 446.1
  furtherance 449.5
  lending 620.1
  loan 620.2
  evolution 860.1
  verb progress 162.2
  further 162.5
  approach 167.3
  move 172.5
  grow 251.6
  be instrumental 384.7

improve 392.7, 392.9
  make good 409.10
  propose 439.5
  promote 446.2
  be useful 449.17
  lend 620.5
  elapse 820.5
  evolve 860.5
  determine 885.12
  push 903.9
  postulate 950.12
  adduce 956.12
  expedite one's affair
    994.3
  do good 998.10
  prosper 1009.7
advanced front 216.10
  aged 303.16
  improved 392.13
  preceding 815.4
  modern 840.13
  premature 844.8
advancement
  progression 162.1
  improvement 392.1
  promotion 446.1
  furtherance 449.5
  lending 620.1
  evolution 860.1
advance warning
  405.1
advancing
  noun progression
    162.1
  lending 620.1
  game 750.3
  adj progressive 162.6
  approaching 167.4
  improving 392.15
  attacking 459.29
  evolutionary 860.8
advantage
  noun vantage 249.2
  benefit 387.4
  facility 449.9
  purchase 905.2
  good 998.4
  verb avail 387.17
  be useful 449.17
  expedite one's affair
    994.3
  do good 998.10
advantageous useful
  387.18
  gainful 472.16
  expedient 994.5
  good 998.12
advent approach 167.1
  arrival 186.1
  coming 838.5
adventure act 328.3
  emprise 404.2
  exploit 492.7
  event 830.2
  happening 971.6
adventurer traveller
  178.1
  mercenary 461.16
  daredevil 493.4

upstart 606.7
speculator 737.11
gambler 759.21

adventures 719.1

adventurous
enterprising 330.23,
404.8
daring 492.22
foolhardy 493.9
hazardous 1005.10

adversarial
adj contrapositive
215.5
oppositional 451.8
contrary 778.6
adv in opposition
451.9

adversary
noun opponent 452.1
enemy 589.6
adj oppositional 451.8

adverse oppositional
451.8
contrary 778.6
untoward 1010.13

adversely 1010.16

adversity 1010.1

advert 352.6

advertise publish
352.10
publicize 352.15
flaunt 501.17
inform 551.8

advertisement 352.6

advertiser 352.9

advertising 352.5

advertising agency
352.5

advertising campaign
352.5

advice counsel 422.1
tip 551.3
news 552.1
message 552.4

advisable 994.5

advise warn 399.5
counsel 422.5
inform 551.8

advised intentional
380.8
reasoned 934.21

adviser counsel 422.3
informant 551.5

advising 422.1

advisory
recommendatory
422.8
conciliar 423.5
informative 551.18

advisory council 613.3

advocacy promotion
352.5
advice 422.1
patronage 449.4
recommendation 509.4

advocate

noun defender 460.7
deputy 576.1
friend 588.1
lawyer 597.1
justifier 600.8
supporter 616.9,
900.2
arguer 934.12
verb urge 375.14
advise 422.5
abet 449.14
defend 460.8, 600.10
commend 509.11

advocated 509.19

advocating
noun promotion 352.5
recommendation 509.4
adj approving 509.17

aegis patronage 449.4
safeguard 1007.3

aerial
noun radio transmitter
1033.4
adj aviation 184.49
high 272.14
airy 317.11
chimeric 985.22
vaporous 1065.9

aerobic exercise 84.2

aerobics 84.2, 725.6

aerodrome 184.22

aerodynamic aviation
184.49
pneumatic 1038.10
vaporous 1065.9

aerodynamics
pneumatics 1038.5
gas 1065.2

aeronautical 184.49

aeronautics 184.1

aeroplane
noun aircraft 181.1
verb fly 184.36

aerosol solution 1062.3
sprinkler 1063.8
vaporizer 1065.6

aerospace
noun airspace 184.32
adj aviation 184.49

aesthetic tasteful 496.8
artistic 712.20
absurdist 951.9
beautiful 1015.17

aesthetically 496.11

aesthetics 723.1

afar 261.15

affable pleasant 97.6
good-natured 143.14
indulgent 427.8
courteous 504.14
informal 581.3
sociable 582.22
cordial 587.16

affair love affair 104.6
undertaking 404.1
social gathering
582.10

occupation 724.1
concern 830.3
object 1050.4

affairs action 328.1
occupation 724.1
relation 774.1
concerns 830.4

affect
noun feeling 93.1
attitude 977.1
verb wear 5.43
touch 93.14
impress 93.15
move 145.5
imitate 336.5
manifest 348.5
sham 354.21
assume 500.12
entail 771.4
relate to 774.5
operate on 888.6
influence 893.7

affectation behaviour
321.1
sham 354.3
affectedness 500.1,
533.3
style 532.2
grandiloquence 545.1
sanctimony 693.1

affected moved 93.23
spurious 354.26
pretentious 500.15
euphuistic 533.9
grandiloquent 545.8
be sanctimonious
693.4

affecting touching
93.22
distressing 98.20
pitiful 145.8

affection disease 85.1
feeling 93.1
liking 100.2
love 104.1
amorousness 104.3
friendship 587.1

affectionate loving
104.27
kind 143.13

affectionately 104.32

affections 93.1

affective emotional
93.17
attitudinal 977.7

affidavit deposition
334.3
certificate 549.6
declaration 598.8
testimony 956.2

affiliate
noun branch 617.10
member 617.11
verb naturalize 226.4
adopt 371.15
cooperate 450.3
join 617.14
league 804.4
adj related 774.9

leagued 804.6

affiliated related 559.6,
774.9
leagued 804.6

affiliates 617.12

affiliation
naturalization 226.3
adoption 371.4
alliance 450.2
blood relationship
559.1
lineage 560.4
association 582.6
sect 675.3
relation 774.1
combination 804.1

affinity inclination
100.3
preference 371.5
accord 455.1
marriage relationship
564.1
familiarity 587.5
relation 774.1
kinship 774.3, 783.2
agreement 787.1
tendency 895.1
attraction 906.1

affirm ratify 332.12
assert 334.5
announce 352.12
state 524.24, 952.12
be pious 692.6
testify 956.9
confirm 956.11

affirmation ratification
332.4
affirmance 334.1
deposition 334.3
consent 441.1
remark 524.4
premise 934.7
testimony 956.2
confirmation 956.4

affirmative
noun yes 332.2
consent 441.1
side 934.14
adj affirming 334.8
consenting 441.4
agreeing 787.9

affirmative action
dilemma 371.3
equating 789.2
opportunity 842.2

affirmed accepted
332.14
asserted 334.9
published 352.17

affirming affirmative
334.8
pious 692.8

affix
noun postscript 254.2
morphology 526.3
verb add 253.4
fasten 799.7

afflict pain 26.7
disorder 85.49

distress 96.16
aggrieve 112.19
work evil 999.6

afflicted pained 26.9
fuddled 88.33
distressed 96.22

afflicting 98.20

affliction disease 85.1
infliction 96.8
bane 1000.1
adversity 1010.1

affluence flow 238.4
wealth 618.1
plenty 990.2
prosperity 1009.1

affluent
noun tributary 238.3
adj flowing 238.24
wealthy 618.14
plentiful 990.7
prosperous 1009.12

afford provide 385.7
give 478.12
furnish 478.15
have money 618.11
well afford 626.7
yield 627.4

affordable 633.7

affray 457.4

affront
noun provocation
152.11
indignity 156.2
verb offend 152.21,
156.5
confront 216.8, 451.5
defy 454.3
brave 492.11

afghan 295.10

afield 261.19

afloat
adj floating 182.60
adrift 182.61
flooded 238.25
reported 552.15
unfastened 801.22
happening 830.9
inconstant 853.7
adv on board 182.62
at sea 240.9
adj, adv afoot 405.23

afoot
adj astir 330.19
existent 760.13
happening 830.9
adv on foot 177.43
adj, adv on foot
405.23

aforementioned 813.5

aforesaid 813.5

afraid scared 127.22
weak-willed 362.12
cowardly 491.10

A-frame 900.16

afresh newly 840.15
again 848.17, 873.7

Africa 231.6, 235.1

African 951.9
African-American
312.3
aft abaft 182.69
after 217.14
After 318.3
after
adj subsequent 834.4
adv behind 166.6
aft 217.14
subsequently 834.6
prep like 336.12
following 834.8
conformable to 866.9
because of 887.9
after all
adv subsequently
834.6
all things considered
945.17
adv, conj
notwithstanding 338.8
after a while 844.16
after-dinner 834.5
afterlife hereafter
681.2
subsequence 834.1
destiny 838.2
aftermath yield 472.5
afterclap 816.3
event 830.1
sequel 834.2
effect 886.1
aftereffect 886.3
afternoon 315.7
afternoon tea 582.13
aftertaste taste 62.1
aftermath 816.3
aftereffect 886.3
after that 834.6
after the Fall 834.5
after the war 834.5
afterthought sequel
816.1
untimeliness 843.1
delay 845.2
mature thought 930.5
after time 845.19
afterwards 834.6
again
adv additionally
253.11
then 820.11
newly 840.15
over 848.17
another time 873.7
adv, conj
notwithstanding 338.8
again and again
continuously 811.10
frequently 846.6
repeatedly 848.16
against
adj disapproving
510.21
prep toward 161.26
opposite to 215.7

up against 223.25
in preparation for
405.24
opposed to 451.10
in disagreement with
788.10
against the clock
401.14
against the grain
adj unlikable 99.7
adv backwards 163.13
cross-grained 288.12
contrarily 778.9
against the law 674.6
against the wind
182.65
against time 401.14
agate 743.16
age
noun years 303.1
generation 823.4
era 823.5
durability 826.1
lifetime 826.5
oldness 841.1
verb grow old 303.10,
841.9
aged mature 303.13,
304.7
elderly 303.16
durable 826.10
old-fogyish 841.17
age group 769.3
ageism 979.4
ageless perpetual 828.7
old 841.10
agency instrumentality
384.3
commission 615.1
trade 731.2
workplace 739.1
substitution 861.1
operation 888.1
agenda notebook
549.11
roll 870.6
schedule 964.3
agent intermediary
213.4
instrument 384.4,
576.3
mediator 466.3
director 574.1
lawyer 597.1
assignee 615.9
assistant 616.6
actor's agent 704.25
doer 726.1
salesman 730.3
transformer 851.5
substitute 861.2
author 885.4
operator 888.4
element 1058.2
age of consent 303.2
age-old 841.10
ages ago long ago
836.16

since 836.17
aggravate annoy 96.13
irritate 96.14
vex 98.15
worsen 119.2
provoke 152.24
intensify 251.5
impair 393.9
sow dissension 456.14
antagonize 589.7
aggravated annoyed
96.21
worsened 119.4
provoked 152.27
impaired 393.27
aggravating annoying
98.22
aggravative 119.5
aggravation annoyance
96.2
irritation 96.3
vexatiousness 98.7
excitation 105.11
worsening 119.1
resentment 152.1
intensification 251.2
adversity 1010.1
aggregate
noun accumulation
769.9
all 791.3
sum 1016.6
verb assemble 769.18
total 791.8
adj assembled 769.21
whole 791.9
aggression enterprise
330.7
warlikeness 458.11
attack 459.1
aggressive energetic
17.13
enterprising 330.23
partisan 456.17
warlike 458.21
offensive 459.30
gruff 505.7
aggressiveness vim
17.2
enterprise 330.7
dissension 456.3
warlikeness 458.11
gruffness 505.3
aggressor 459.12
aggrieved pained 96.23
sorrowful 112.26
aggro annoyance 96.2
misbehaviour 322.1
warlikeness 458.11
aghast wondering
122.9
terrified 127.26
agile fast 174.15
quick 330.18
alert 339.14
nimble 413.23
agility quickness 330.3
alertness 339.5

nimbleness 413.2
aging 303.6
agitated distressed
96.22
perturbed 105.23
anxious 126.7
jittery 128.12
bustling 330.20
disturbed 916.16
agitating 105.30
agitation perturbation
105.4, 916.1
excitation 105.11
anxiety 126.1
trepidation 127.5
nervousness 128.1
bustle 330.4
incitement 375.4
turbulence 671.2
agnostic
noun sceptic 695.12
adj sceptic 695.20
absurdist 951.9
doubting 954.9
uncertain 970.16
ago
adj past 836.7
adv since 836.15
agog eager 101.8
excited 105.20
wondering 122.9
expectant 130.11
curious 980.5
attentive 982.15
agonized pained 26.9
affected 93.23
tortured 96.25
agonizing painful
26.10
excruciating 98.23
agony anguish 26.6
wretchedness 96.6
harshness 98.4
sorrow 112.10
moribundity 307.9
agony aunt 422.3
agrarian rustic 233.6
agricultural 1067.20
agree be willing 324.3
assent 332.8
concur 332.9, 898.2
come to an agreement
332.10
contract 437.5
get along 455.2
relate to 774.5
coincide 777.4, 835.4
accord 787.6
agreeable tasty 63.8
pleasant 97.6
desirable 100.30
acceptable 107.12
good-natured 143.14
considerate 143.16
willing 324.5
indulgent 427.8
submissive 433.12
consenting 441.4

in accord 455.3
courteous 504.14
welcome 585.12
friendly 587.15
melodious 708.48
agreeing 787.9
comely 1015.18
agreeable to 866.9
agreeably pleasantly
97.12
satisfactorily 107.15
favourably 324.9
submissively 433.17
consentingly 441.5
amicably 587.22
in step 787.11
agreed
adj assenting 332.13
contracted 437.11
supposed 950.14
phrase so be it 332.20
agreed upon 437.11
agreeing assenting
332.13
unanimous 332.15
consenting 441.4
cooperative 450.5
in accord 455.3
in agreement 787.9
simultaneous 835.5
concurrent 898.4
agreement assent
332.1
unanimity 332.5
obligation 436.2
compact 437.1
consent 441.1
accord 455.1, 787.1
sameness 777.1
similarity 783.1
combination 804.1
conformity 866.1
concurrence 898.1
agreement in
principle 332.1
agree to commit 436.5
contract 437.5
consent 441.2
strike a bargain 731.18
agree with make for
health 81.4
concur 332.9
come to an agreement
332.10
get along 455.2
relate to 774.5
conform 866.3
agricultural rustic
233.6
agrarian 1067.20
agriculture 1067.1
agro- 1067.20
aground
adj stuck 854.16
stranded 1012.27
adv on the rocks
182.73
ahead

verb initiate 817.10
adj front 216.10
superior 249.12
adv forward 162.8
before 216.12
early 844.11

ahead of time 844.11

aid
noun remedy 86.1
help 449.1
subsidy 478.8
benefactor 592.1
assistant 616.6
support 900.1
verb advance 162.5
help 449.11
subsidize 478.19
benefit 592.3
facilitate 1013.7

aide 616.6

aiding 592.4

ailing 85.55

ailment 85.1

aim
noun direction 161.1
motive 375.1
intention 380.1
objective 380.2
intent 518.2
verb direct 161.5
bear 161.7
intend 380.4
endeavour 403.5

aim at desire 100.14
direct 161.5
intend 380.4
pull the trigger 459.22

aimed directable
161.13
intentional 380.8

aimed at 380.8

aimless useless 391.9
meaningless 520.6
discursive 538.13
unordered 809.12
purposeless 971.16

aimlessly uselessly
391.15
meaninglessly 520.8
chaotically 809.19
purposelessly 971.20

aim to 403.8

air
noun looks 33.4
milieu 209.3
aether 298.2
ether 317.1
breeze 318.5
behaviour 321.1
aria 708.4
spirit 763.3
matter 1050.2
gas 1065.2
heavens 1070.2
verb air out 317.10
divulge 351.5
publish 352.10
make public 352.11

flaunt 501.17
discuss 541.12

air attack 459.4

air base 184.22

airborne 184.50

Air Chief Marshal
575.19

Air Commodore
575.19

air-conditioned
1023.13

air conditioning
ventilation 317.8
refrigeration 1023.1

air-cooled 1023.13

air cover 184.11

aircraft vehicle 179.1
aeroplane 181.1

aircraft carrier
warship 180.6
carrier 180.8

aircrew 185.4

airfield 184.22

Air Force 461.20

air force military
aircraft 181.9
military pilot 185.3
air corps 461.28

airhead vanguard 216.2
blockhead 923.4

airily cheerfully 109.17
carelessly 340.18

airing ride 177.7
walk 177.10
ventilation 317.8
publication 352.1
discussion 541.7

airing cupboard
197.15

airless 173.16

airlift
noun flight 184.9
verb fly 184.36
phrase transportation
176.3

airline 184.10

airmail send 176.15
mail 553.12

airman 185.1

Air Marshal 575.19

air out 317.10

airplane 181.1

air pollution powder
1049.5
environmental
destruction 1071.2

airport airfield 184.22
destination 186.5

air raid mission 184.11
raid 459.4

airs contempt 157.1
affectation 500.1
pretensions 501.2

air service air travel
184.10
air force 461.28

airship 181.11

air show 184.1

airspace space 158.1
open space 158.4
navigable airspace
184.32
region 231.1
plot 231.4

air strike 459.4

airstrip 184.23

air support 184.11

airtight resistant 15.20
close 293.12

airtime 1033.16

air traffic 184.1

air-traffic control
aviation 184.1
detection 1035.9

air transport 184.10

air travel 184.10

Air Vice-Marshal
575.19

airy lighthearted 109.12
thin 270.16, 763.6
high 272.14
light 298.10
rare 299.4
aery 317.11
windy 318.22
careless 340.11
illusory 975.9
visionary 985.24
trivial 997.19
immaterial 1051.7
vaporous 1065.9

aisle 383.3

ajar clashing 61.5
gaping 292.18

akin in accord 455.3
related 559.6
kindred 774.10
affinitive 783.13

alabaster
noun bone 37.2
smooth 287.3
adj whitish 37.8

alacrity eagerness
101.1
willingness 324.1
quickness 330.3
hastiness 401.2
promptness 844.3

alarm
noun fear 127.1
warning 399.1
alarum 400.1
signal 517.15
call 517.16
verb frighten 127.15
alert 400.3

alarm clock 400.1

alarmed frightened
127.25
aroused 400.4

alarming frightening
127.28
dangerous 1005.9

alarmingly 127.34

alarmist 127.8

Alaska 1022.4

albatross
noun round 748.3
disadvantage 995.2
verb play 748.4

albeit 338.8

albino
noun whiteness 37.1
adj albinic 37.10

Albion 232.3

album notebook 549.11
compilation 554.7

alchemical 690.14

alchemy sorcery 690.1
conversion 857.1

alcohol sedative 86.12
antiseptic 86.21
spirits 88.13
antifreeze 1023.8

alcohol abuse 87.1

alcohol-free 516.4

alcoholic
noun addict 87.20
drinker 88.11
adj spirituous 88.37

alcoholic drink 10.47

alcoholism substance
abuse 87.1
dipsomania 88.3

alcove nook 197.3
summerhouse 228.12
recess 284.7

alderman minister
575.17
legislator 610.3

ale 88.16

alert
noun warning sign
399.3
alarm 400.1
verb warn 399.5
alarm 400.3
tip 551.11
adj awake 23.8
on the alert 339.14
prepared 405.16
prompt 844.9
clear-witted 919.13
curious 980.5
attentive 982.15

alerted 400.4

alert for 405.18

alerting informing
343.2
preparation 405.1
tip 551.3

alertness wakefulness
23.1
attentiveness 339.5
curiosity 980.1
attention 982.1

alert to 982.16

alfresco
adj outdoor 206.8
airy 317.11
adv outdoors 206.11

algae 310.4

alias
noun pseudonym
527.8
adj nominal 527.15
adv otherwise 779.11

alibi
noun pretext 376.1
verb excuse 600.11

Alice-in-Wonderland
illusory 975.9
fanciful 985.20

alien
noun exclusiveness
772.3
stranger 773.3
oddity 869.4
astronaut 1073.8
verb transfer 629.3
adj extraterritorial
206.9
oppositional 451.8
extraneous 773.5
unrelated 775.6
extraterrestrial
1070.26

alienate sow dissension
456.14
antagonize 589.7
transfer 629.3
separate 801.8
indoctrinate 857.15

alienated dissenting
333.6
estranged 589.11
separated 801.21
alone 871.8

alienation defence
mechanism 92.23
dissent 333.1
falling-out 456.4
disaccord 589.2
transfer 629.1
extraneousness 773.1
separation 801.1
indoctrination 857.5
aloneness 871.2
insanity 925.1

alight
verb land 184.43,
186.8
get down 194.7
adj burning 1018.27
illuminated 1024.39

align level 201.6
parallelize 203.5
dispose 807.9
line 811.5

aligned parallel 203.6
arranged 807.14

alignment orientation
161.4
parallelism 203.1
affiliation 450.2

alike
adj identical 777.7
uniform 780.5
similar 783.10
equal 789.7
indistinguishable 944.6
adv identically 777.9

alimony 478.8

alive living 306.11
active 330.17
alert 339.14
clear-witted 919.13
remembered 988.23

alive and kicking in the pink 83.9
living 306.11

alive and well well 83.10
living 306.11

alive to sensible 24.11
cognizant of 927.16

alive with 883.9

alkali
noun acid 1058.3
adj chemical 1058.8

alkaline 1058.8

all
noun whole 791.3
limit 793.5
infinity 822.1
everyone 863.4
universe 1070.1
adj whole 791.9
every 863.15
adv wholly 791.13

all about 209.13

Allah 677.2

all alone 584.11

all along 828.11

all and sundry
noun all 791.3
adj every 863.15

all at once together 768.11
at once 829.8

allay gratify 95.7
relieve 120.5
pacify 465.7
moderate 670.6
satiate 993.4

allayed 993.6

all being 1070.1

all but nearly 223.22
on the whole 791.14

all clear
noun alarm 400.1
adj unindebted 624.23

all-consuming 395.27

all day long 811.10

all dressed up 578.13

allegation affirmation 334.1
claim 376.2
remark 524.4
declaration 598.8

accusation 599.1
testimony 956.2

allege affirm 334.5
pretext 376.3
state 524.24
accuse 599.7
testify 956.9
adduce 956.12

alleged affirmed 334.9
pretexted 376.5
attributable 887.6
supposed 950.14

allegedly ostensibly 376.6
reportedly 552.16

allegiance duty 641.1
fidelity 644.7

allegorical meaningful 518.10
symbolic 519.10

allegory symbol 517.2
implication 519.2
comparison 942.1

allegro
noun presto 708.25
adv actively 330.25
adj, adv presto 708.55

all-embracing whole 791.9
thorough 793.10
universal 863.14

all-encompassing
thorough 793.10
universal 863.14

allergen allergy 85.33
antitoxin 86.27

allergenic 85.60

allergic sensitive 24.12
anaemic 85.60
averse 99.8

allergy sensitivity 24.3
allergic disorder 85.33
hostility 99.2

alleviate relieve 120.5
abate 252.8
lighten 298.6
moderate 670.6

alleviated 298.11

alleviating relieving 120.9
lightening 298.16
mitigating 670.14

alleviation relief 120.1
decrease 252.1
lightening 298.3
modulation 670.2

alley passageway 383.3
tennis 749.1
hockey 750.1

all eyes vigilant 339.13
attentive 982.15

all for
adj favourable 449.22
prep in favour of 509.21

all fours 177.17

all gone 761.11

all-hours 811.8

alliance treaty 437.2
affiliation 450.2
blood relationship 559.1
marriage 563.1
association 617.1
relation 774.1
similarity 783.1
combination 804.1
concurrence 898.1

allied related 559.6, 774.9
joined 799.13
leagued 804.6

alligator 311.25

all-important 996.23

all in 21.8

all in all on the average 246.5
on the whole 791.14
generally 863.17

all-inclusive
comprehensive 771.7
whole 791.9
infinite 822.3
universal 863.14

all in the mind
illusory 975.9
imaginary 985.19

all night 315.11

all-night 315.9

allocate locate 159.11
allot 477.9
dispose 807.9

allocated 477.12

allocation placement 159.6
allotment 477.3
arrangement 807.1
specification 864.6

all of 244.7

all of a sudden short 268.13
suddenly 829.9

all off ended 819.8
erroneous 974.16

all one identical 777.7
equivalent 789.8

allotment rations 10.6
amount 244.2
assignment 477.3
portion 477.5
subsidy 478.8
arrangement 807.1
field 1067.9

all out actively 330.25
utterly 793.16

all-out thorough 793.10
unqualified 959.2

all out of 910.5

all-out war death struggle 457.6
war 458.1

all over
adj ended 819.8

adv everywhere 158.12
throughout 793.17
in disorder 809.17
universally 863.18
prep over 159.28

all over the place 809.17

all over the world
everywhere 158.12
universally 863.18

all over with
completed 407.11
no more 761.11

allow acknowledge 332.11
permit 443.9
give 478.12
discount 631.2
judge 945.8
allow for 958.5

allowable permissible 443.15
giveable 478.23
justifiable 600.14

allowance
noun rations 10.6
acknowledgment 332.3
permission 443.1
portion 477.5
subsidy 478.8
extenuation 600.5
fee 624.5
discount 631.1
qualification 958.1
inaccuracy 974.2
verb budget 477.10

allowed accepted 332.14
permitted 443.16
given 478.24

allow for condone 148.4
extenuate 600.12
make allowances for 958.5

allowing
adj permissive 443.14
conj granting 958.13

alloy
noun compound 796.5
alloyage 1056.4
verb corrupt 393.12
mix 796.10

all-pervading thorough 793.10
universal 863.14

all-powerful
omnipotent 18.13
almighty 677.17

all-present 221.13

all-purpose 387.20

all ready 405.16

all right
adj well 83.10
tolerable 998.20
exclam yes 332.18

all round everywhere 158.12
in every direction 161.25
all about 209.13

all-round handy 387.20
versatile 413.25

all-rounder 747.2

all sorts 796.6

all-star 704.33

all the more 249.17

all the rage 578.11

all the same
adj identical 777.7
equivalent 789.8
adv, conj notwithstanding 338.8

all the time regularly 780.8
always 828.11
constantly 846.7

all the way through
thick and thin 360.10
utterly 793.16
to the end 819.13

all the way to 261.20

all the while 828.11

all the world 863.4

all the year round 826.14

all through over 159.28
through 161.27

all together
unanimously 332.17
jointly 799.18
at once 829.8
simultaneously 835.7

all up 819.8

allure
noun allurement 377.1
attractiveness 377.2
verb enamour 104.23
trap 356.20
lure 377.5

alluring provocative 375.27
fascinating 377.8
attracting 906.5

allusion 519.2

all wrong 974.16

ally
noun country 232.1
associate 616.1
verb cooperate 450.3
come together 769.16
relate 774.6
league 804.4

all year round
regularly 780.8
constantly 846.7

almanac
noun notebook 549.11
The Old Farmer's Almanac 831.7
adj periodical 555.1

almighty 18.13, 677.17

almost 223.22

almost entirely 791.14

alms 478.6

aloft on board 182.62
   on high 272.21

alone
   adj solitary 584.11,
   871.8
   sole 871.9
   adv independently
   430.33
   simply 797.11
   singly 871.13

along 162.8

along by 218.11

alongside
   adj side 218.6
   adv board and board
   182.70
   in parallel 203.7
   aside 218.10
   prep beside 218.11

along these lines
   384.9

along the side of
   218.11

along the way 176.20

along with 768.12

aloof
   adj apathetic 94.13
   standoffish 141.12,
   583.6
   reticent 344.10
   incoherent 803.4
   alone 871.8
   incurious 981.3
   adv at a distance
   261.14
   on high 272.21

aloofness apathy 94.4
   standoffishness 141.4,
   583.2
   noncohesion 803.1
   aloneness 871.2
   incuriosity 981.1

alopecia 6.4

aloud audibly 50.18
   loudly 53.14

alp 237.6

alpha beginning 817.1
   first 817.3

alphabet
   noun representation
   349.1
   writing system 546.3
   writing 547.1
   letter 547.9
   basics 817.6
   verb letter 546.6

alphabetical 546.8

alpine 237.8, 272.18

already previously
   833.6
   until now 837.4

also

adv additionally
   253.11
   conj and 253.13

also not 335.7

also-ran loser 410.8,
   412.5
   jockey 757.2

altar 703.12

altarpiece altar 703.12
   picture 712.11

alter
   noun self 864.5
   verb be changed 851.6
   change 851.7
   qualify 958.3

alteration
   differentiation 779.4
   change 851.1

altercation quarrel
   456.5
   contention 457.1

altered 851.10

alter ego deputy 576.1
   friend 588.1
   likeness 783.3
   self 864.5

altering 958.7

alternate
   noun deputy 576.1
   substitute 861.2
   verb vacillate 362.8
   take one's turn 824.5
   recur 849.5
   change 853.5
   interchange 862.4
   reciprocate 915.13
   adj substitute 861.8
   reciprocal 915.19

alternately reciprocally
   776.12
   by turns 849.11

alternating 853.7

alternative
   noun loophole 369.4
   option 371.2
   substitute 861.2
   adj elective 371.22
   substitute 861.8

alternatively 371.27

although 338.8

altitude height 272.1
   coordinates 300.5

alto
   noun soprano 58.6
   part 708.22
   voice 709.5
   adj high 58.13
   vocal 708.50

altogether additionally
   253.11
   wholly 791.13
   completely 793.14
   generally 863.17

altruism benevolence
   143.4
   public spirit 591.1
   unselfishness 652.1

altruistic benevolent
   143.15
   unselfish 652.5

alum 260.6

aluminium foil
   wrapper 295.18
   jamming 1035.13

alumni 572.8

always regularly 780.8
   all along 828.11
   constantly 846.7
   permanently 852.9
   universally 863.18

Alzheimer's disease
   921.10

amalgam compound
   796.5
   alloy 1056.4

amalgamated mixed
   796.14
   combined 804.5

amalgamation
   affiliation 450.2
   mixture 796.1
   combination 804.1

amass store up 386.11
   collect 472.11
   assemble 769.18
   put together 799.5

amassed stored 386.14
   assembled 769.21

amateur
   noun enthusiast 101.4
   connoisseur 496.7
   nonprofessional 726.5
   specialist 865.3
   dilettante 928.6
   trifler 997.10
   adj avocational 724.17
   half-learned 929.15

amateurish unskilled
   414.16
   half-learned 929.15

amateurism
   inexperience 414.2
   avocation 724.7
   nonprofessionalism
   724.9
   slight knowledge
   929.6

amaze
   noun wonder 122.1
   verb astonish 122.6
   perplex 970.13

amazed 122.9

amazement wonder
   122.1
   marvel 122.2

amazing 122.12

amazingly
   astonishingly 122.16
   intensely 247.20

amazon virago 76.9
   giant 257.13

ambassador 576.6

ambassadorial 576.16

ambience environment
   209.1
   milieu 209.3

ambient 209.8

ambiguity
   unintelligibility 522.1
   ambiguousness 539.1
   equivoque 539.2
   inconsistency 788.2
   doubleness 872.1
   equivocalness 970.5

ambiguous
   unintelligible 522.13
   equivocal 539.4
   self-contradictory
   778.8
   mixed 796.14
   uncertain 970.16

ambition ambitiousness
   100.10
   desire 100.11
   motive 375.1
   intention 380.1

ambitious aspiring
   100.28
   enterprising 330.23
   ostentatious 501.18

ambivalence
   psychological stress
   92.17
   irresolution 362.1
   inconsistency 788.2
   doubleness 872.1

ambivalent irresolute
   362.9
   self-contradictory
   778.8
   mixed 796.14

amble
   noun walk 177.10
   gait 177.12
   verb stroll 177.28
   go on horseback
   177.34

ambling
   noun walking 177.8
   adj slow 175.10

ambush
   noun ambushment
   346.3
   verb surprise 131.7
   ambuscade 346.10
   attack 459.14

amen
   noun affirmative 332.2
   verb ratify 332.12
   phrase so be it 332.20
   exclam yes 332.18

amenable resigned
   134.10
   willing 324.5
   consenting 441.4
   responsible 641.17
   influenceable 893.15

amend improve 392.7,
   392.9
   revise 392.12
   remedy 396.13
   re-form 857.12

amendment
   improvement 392.1
   revision 392.4
   new start 857.2

amends compensation
   338.1
   reparation 396.6,
   481.2
   recompense 624.3
   atonement 658.1

amenities creature
   comforts 121.3
   courtesies 504.7
   etiquette 580.3

amenity pleasantness
   97.1
   facility 449.9
   courtesy 504.1, 504.6

America continent
   231.6
   United States 232.4

Americana 769.11

American dream
   100.11

American Indian
   312.3

Americanism
   Anglicism 523.8
   patriotism 591.2

American tour 748.1

Amex 737.7

amiable pleasant 97.6
   good-natured 143.14
   indulgent 427.8
   sociable 582.22
   hospitable 585.11
   friendly 587.15

amiably pleasantly
   97.12
   good-naturedly 143.19
   amicably 587.22

amicable pleasant 97.6
   favourable 449.22
   in accord 455.3
   friendly 587.15

amicably pleasantly
   97.12
   friendly 587.22

amid between 213.12
   among 796.17

amidships
   adj middle 818.4
   adv midway 818.5

amidst between 213.12
   among 796.17

amies 87.4

amiss
   adj disorderly 809.13
   erroneous 974.16
   adv irrelevantly 775.9
   astray 910.7
   erroneously 974.20
   badly 999.13

ammonia fertilizer
   889.4
   coolant 1023.7

ammunition 462.13

amnesia trance 92.19
　thoughtlessness 932.1
　loss of memory 989.2
amnesty
　noun pardon 148.2
　exemption 601.2
　verb forgive 148.3
　acquit 601.4
amok
　noun frenzy 925.7
　adj frenzied 105.25
　rabid 925.30
among
　verb include 771.3
　prep at 159.27
　between 213.12
　amongst 796.17
among other things
　253.11
amongst between
　213.12
　among 796.17
amoral dishonest
　645.16
　vice-prone 654.11
amorous sexual 75.24
　amatory 104.26
amorphous formless
　263.4
　obscure 522.15
　unordered 809.12
　inconstant 853.7
　abnormal 869.9
　vague 970.19
amount quantity 244.1,
　244.2
　degree 245.1
　price 630.1
　total 791.2
　sum 1016.6
amount of money
　728.13
amount to cost 630.13
　equal 789.5
　total 791.8
amour 104.6
amp 50.10
amphibious versatile
　413.25
　mixed 796.14
amphitheatre hall
　197.4
　arena 463.1
　schoolroom 567.11
　theatre 704.14
ample satisfactory
　107.11
　spacious 158.10
　much 247.8
　voluminous 257.17
　broad 269.6
　abundant 883.8
　sufficient 990.6
　plentiful 990.7
amplification
　aggravation 119.1
　increase 251.1
　expansion 259.1

translation 341.3
　exaggeration 355.1
　expatiation 538.6
　evolution 860.1
amplified aggravated
　119.4
　increased 251.7
　expanded 259.10
　exaggerated 355.4
amplifier listening
　device 48.8
　audio amplifier 50.10
amplify aggravate
　119.2
　increase 251.4
　enlarge 259.4
　exaggerate 355.3
　expatiate 538.7
　elaborate 860.6
　electrify 1031.25
amplitude sound 50.1
　loudness 53.1
　spaciousness 158.5
　quantity 244.1
　greatness 247.1
　size 257.1
　breadth 269.1
　wordiness 538.2
　fullness 793.2
　wave 915.4
　plenty 990.2
amply satisfactorily
　107.15
　intensely 247.20
　sufficiently 990.8
amputation 255.3
amuse 743.21
amused 743.26
amusement pleasure
　95.1
　merriment 109.5
　entertainment 743.1
amusing humorous
　488.4
　witty 489.15
　entertaining 743.27
amusingly 488.7
an quantitative 244.5
　one 871.7
ana archives 549.2
　compilation 554.7
　excerpts 557.4
　collection 769.11
　maxim 973.1
anabolic digestive 2.29
　metamorphic 851.12
anaemia weakness 16.1
　paleness 36.2
　ankylosis 85.9
anaemic weak 16.12
　colourless 36.7
　chlorotic 85.60
anaesthesia
　insensibility 25.1, 94.2
　unfeeling 94.1
　relief 120.1
anaesthetic

noun sleep-inducer
　22.10
　general anaesthetic
　25.3
　adj deadening 25.9,
　86.47
　relieving 120.9
anaesthetist 90.11
anagram wordplay
　489.8
　riddle 522.9
anal 866.6
analgesic
　noun anaesthetic 25.3
　sedative 86.12
　adj deadening 25.9
　sedative 86.45
　relieving 120.9
analogous parallel
　203.6
　reciprocal 776.10
　comparable 783.11
　comparative 942.8
analogue correlate
　776.4
　likeness 783.3
analogy parallelism
　203.1
　similarity 783.1
　substitute 861.2
　comparison 942.1
anal sex 75.7
analyse grammaticize
　530.16
　discuss 541.12
　criticize 723.5
　itemize 765.6
　differentiate 779.6
　diversify 781.2
　separate 792.6
　simplify 797.4
　break down 800.6
　dissect 801.17
　classify 808.6
　reason 934.15
　discriminate 943.4
analysing 945.3
analysis psychoanalysis
　92.6
　discussion 541.7
　commentary 556.2
　circumstantiation
　765.5
　differentiation 779.4
　simplification 797.2
　analysation 800.1
　dissection 801.5
　classification 808.1
　priori reasoning 934.3
　inquiry 937.1
　discernment 943.2
　theory 950.1
　accounting 1040.7
analyst psychologist
　92.10
　critic 723.4
　analyser 800.5
　experimenter 941.6

analytic analytical
　800.9
　reasoning 934.18
　dialectic 934.22
　examining 937.37
　absurdist 951.9
analytical critical
　723.6
　analytic 800.9
　reasoning 934.18
　dialectic 934.22
　examining 937.37
analytically 934.24
anarchic formless
　263.4
　anarchical 418.6
　turbulent 671.18
　unruly 671.19
　illegal 674.6
　incoherent 803.4
　confused 809.16
anarchism anarchy
　418.2
　radicalism 611.5
　revolutionism 859.2
anarchist anarch 418.3
　radical 611.17
　revolutionist 859.3
anarchy formlessness
　263.1
　anarchism 418.2
　illegality 674.1
　noncohesion 803.1
　confusion 809.2
anathema abomination
　103.3
　censure 510.3
　curse 513.1
anatomical 266.6
anatomy body 2.1,
　1050.3
　figure 262.4
　structure 266.1
　anthropology 312.10
　analysis 800.1
　dissection 801.5
ancestor parent 560.8
　precursor 815.1
　antecedent 833.2
ancestors antecedents
　560.7
　producer 891.7
ancestral ancestorial
　560.17
　beginning 817.15
　primitive 841.11
ancestry blood
　relationship 559.1
　kinfolk 559.2
　progenitorship 560.1
　nobility 608.2
anchor
　noun mooring 180.16
　safeguard 1007.3
　broadcaster 1033.23
　television broadcast
　1034.2
　verb settle 159.17

come to anchor
　182.15
　land 186.8
　bind 428.10
　fasten 799.7
　secure 854.8
anchorage
　establishment 159.7
　anchor 180.16
　destination 186.5
　fee 630.6
　harbour 1008.6
anchored fixed
　854.14
　stuck 854.16
ancient aged 303.16
　scholastic 567.13
　durable 826.10
　former 836.10
　old 841.10
ancient history 836.3
ancient times 836.3
ancillary additional
　253.10
　helping 449.20
ancona 703.12
and 253.13
and all
　adv additionally
　253.11
　phrase et cetera 253.14
and also
　adv additionally
　253.11
　conj and 253.13
and everything else
　253.14
and many more
　883.11
and not 335.7
and others
　adv in the majority
　882.10
　phrase et cetera 253.14
and other things
　253.14
androgynous 75.30
androgyny
　intersexuality 75.12
　effeminacy 77.2
and so additionally
　253.11
　consequently 886.7
and so forth 253.14
and so on 253.14
and the following
　253.14
and the like 253.14
and then some 253.11
and the rest 253.14
anecdotal 722.8
anecdote 719.3
anew newly 840.15
　again 848.17, 873.7
angel

noun doll 104.15, 1015.9
giver 478.11
darling 562.6
benefactor 592.1
innocent 657.4
holy man 659.6
familiar spirit 678.12
celestial 679.1
patron 704.26
financer 729.9
verb subsidize 478.19
finance 729.15

angelic endearing 104.25
virtuous 653.6
innocent 657.6
seraphic 679.6
godly 692.9

angels 679.3

anger
noun darkness 38.2
ill humour 110.1
wrath 152.5
violence 671.1
ardour 1018.2
verb lose one's temper 152.17
make angry 152.22
excite 1019.18

angered 152.28

angina 26.5

angle
noun viewpoint 27.7
aspect 33.3
station 159.2
point 278.2
partiality 650.3
cheating 759.13
particular 765.3
outlook 977.2
verb deviate 164.3
oblique 204.9
go sideways 218.5
crook 278.5
plot 381.9
fish 382.10
manoeuvre 415.10
favour 650.8

angler 382.6

angling 382.3

angrily indignantly 152.33
turbulently 671.26

angry sore 26.11
dark 38.9
annoyed 96.21
out of humour 110.17
angered 152.28
stormy 318.23
turbulent 671.18

angst unpleasure 96.1
anxiety 126.1

anguish
noun agony 26.6
unpleasure 96.1
wretchedness 96.6
sorrow 112.10
verb suffer 26.8, 96.19

pain 96.17
aggrieve 112.19

anguished pleasureless 96.20
pained 96.23
sorrowful 112.26

angular 278.6

anima psyche 92.28, 918.4
life force 306.3

animal
noun beast 144.14, 660.7
creature 311.2
barbarian 497.7
savage 593.5
glutton 672.3
adj cruel 144.26
animalian 311.38
unrefined 497.12
carnal 663.6
lascivious 665.29

animal kingdom
animal life 311.1
hierarchy 808.4
biology 1066.1

animals 1066.1

animate
noun gender 530.10
verb refresh 9.2
energize 17.10
stimulate 105.13
cheer 109.7
vivify 306.9
motivate 375.12
inspire 375.20
impel 901.11
adj organic 305.17
living 306.11

animated refreshed 9.4
energetic 17.13
eager 101.8
gay 109.14
living 306.11
active 330.17
moved 375.30
cinema 706.8

animatedly
energetically 17.16
eagerly 101.13
gaily 109.18
actively 330.25

animation vivacity 17.4
energizing 17.8
eagerness 101.1
excitation 105.11
gaiety 109.4
life 306.1
vivification 306.5
liveliness 330.2
motivation 375.2
inspiration 375.9
cinema 706.1

animosity bad feeling 93.7
enmity 103.2
bitterness 152.3
animus 589.4

animus will 323.1
inspiration 375.9
intention 380.1
animosity 589.4
disposition 977.3

ankle member 2.7
leg 177.14
joint 799.4

annals record 549.1
history 719.1
chronicle 831.9

annex add 253.4
take possession 472.10
attach 480.20

annexation addition 253.1
adjunct 254.1
attachment 480.5
fastening 799.3

annexe
noun adjunct 254.1
wing 254.3
verb fasten 799.7

annexed 253.9

annihilate excise 255.10
kill 308.12
abolish 395.13
exterminate 395.14, 761.7
do away with 908.21

annihilated 761.11

annihilation excision 255.3
death 307.1
extinction 395.6

anniversaries 487.1

anniversary 849.4

announce herald 133.14
affirm 334.5
annunciate 352.12
state 524.24
report 552.11
be prior 833.3

announced affirmed 334.9
published 352.17

announcement
affirmation 334.1
informing 343.2
annunciation 352.2
information 551.1

announcer harbinger 133.5
annunciator 353.3
informant 551.5
precursor 815.1
broadcaster 1033.23

annoy irk 96.13
vex 98.15
excite 105.12
aggravate 119.2
provoke 152.24

annoyance vexation 96.2
vexatiousness 98.7
aggravation 119.1

resentment 152.1
adversity 1010.1
trouble 1012.3

annoyed irritated 96.21
aggravated 119.4
provoked 152.27
troubled 1012.20

annoying irritating 98.22
aggravating 119.5
troublesome 126.10, 1012.18

annual
noun plant 310.3
report 549.7
notebook 549.11
adj periodical 555.1
momentary 849.8

annuity subsidy 478.8
insurance 1007.4

annul abolish 395.13
repeal 445.2
neutralize 899.7

annulment denial 335.2
extinction 395.6
repeal 445.1
divorce 566.1
neutralization 899.2

annum 823.2

anodyne
noun anaesthetic 25.3
sedative 86.12
relief 120.1
moderator 670.3
adj sedative 86.45
relieving 120.9
palliative 670.16

anomalous inconsistent 788.8
abnormal 869.9
eccentric 926.5

anomaly unfitness 788.3
misfit 788.4
abnormality 869.1
oddity 869.5
eccentricity 926.1

anon
adj anonymous 528.3
adv then 820.11
in the future 838.9
soon 844.16

anonymity privacy 345.2
anonymousness 528.1

anonymous private 345.13
anon 528.3

anorak 572.10

another
noun different thing 779.3
adj additional 253.10
other 779.8
fresh 840.8

another time 873.7

answer

noun communication 343.1
remark 524.4
letter 553.2
defence 600.2
paean 696.3
response 708.23
equal 789.4
reaction 902.1
reply 938.1
solution 939.1
refutation 957.2
expedient 994.2
verb communicate with 343.8
avail 387.17
reply 553.11
defend 600.10
reciprocate 776.7
suit 787.8
react 902.5
solve 939.2
refute 957.5
suffice 990.4
expedite one's affair 994.3

answerable responsible 641.17
agreeing 787.9
liable 896.5
solvable 939.3

answerable to 866.9

answer back 142.8

answer for commit 436.5
represent 576.14
be responsible for 641.6

answering
noun answer 938.1
adj communicational 343.9
reciprocal 776.10
replying 938.6

answer to relate to 774.5
reciprocate 776.7

ant 311.32

antagonism hostility 99.2, 451.2, 589.3
warlikeness 458.11
contrariety 778.1
disagreement 788.1
counteraction 899.1

antagonist opponent 452.1
enemy 589.6
role 704.10
actor 707.2

antagonistic
oppositional 451.8
warlike 458.21
hostile 589.10
contrary 778.6
disagreeing 788.6
adverse 1010.13

Antarctic 1022.4

antarctic 161.14

Antarctica continent
235.1
Siberia 1022.4

ante
noun bet 759.3
verb pay over 624.15
bet 759.25
adv before 813.6

antecedent
noun precursor 815.1
precedent 833.2
adj leading 165.3
preceding 813.4
previous 833.4

antecedents ancestors
560.7
cause 885.1

antelope lightning
174.6
deer 311.5

antenatal 817.15

antenna tactile process
3.10
feeler 73.4
radio transmitter
1033.4

anterior front 216.10
preceding 813.4
previous 833.4

anthem
noun paean 696.3
sacred music 708.17
verb sing 708.38

anthology compilation
554.7
excerpts 557.4
book of verse 720.5
collection 769.11

anthrax 85.40

anthropological
312.13

anthropologist 312.10

anthropology 312.10

anti oppositional 451.8
contrary 778.6

antibiotic
noun ampicillin 86.29
poison 1000.3
adj antidotal 86.41

antibody blood 2.23
immunity 83.4
antitoxin 86.27

anticipate expect 130.5
be prior 833.3
come 838.6
foresee 844.6, 960.5
prevent 1011.14

anticipated expected
130.13
future 838.8

anticipating 130.11

anticipation
expectation 130.1
carefulness 339.1
anachronism 832.1
previousness 833.1
future 838.1

earliness 844.1
intuition 933.1
foresight 960.1

anticlimax 488.3

antidote counterpoison
86.26
counteractant 899.3

antigen blood 2.23
immunity 83.4
antitoxin 86.27

anti-inflammatory
86.45

antipathy hostility
99.2, 451.2, 589.3
hate 103.1
anathema 103.3
refusal 325.1
contrariety 778.1
counteraction 899.1

antipodean 261.9

antiquarian
noun antiquary 841.5
adj archaeological
841.20

antiquated disused
390.10
past 836.7
grown old 841.13

antique
noun antiquity 841.6
adj disused 390.10
durable 826.10
past 836.7
old 841.10
antiquated 841.13

antique collector
841.5

antique dealer 841.5

antiquity durability
826.1
ancient times 836.3
oldness 841.1
antique 841.6

anti-Semitic 979.12

anti-Semitism hate
103.1
nationalism 611.10
discrimination 979.4

antiseptic
noun disinfectant
86.21
poison 1000.3
adj sanitary 79.27
disinfectant 86.43

antisocial misanthropic
590.3
eccentric 926.5

antispasmodic 86.32

antithesis
contraposition 215.1
contrariety 778.1
opposite 778.2

anus mouth 2.16
arsehole 292.5

anvil ear 2.10
philosopher's stone
857.10

anxiety unpleasure 96.1
eagerness 101.1
anxiousness 126.1
apprehension 127.4
suspense 130.3
impatience 135.1
trouble 1012.3

anxious pleasureless
96.20
eager 101.8
concerned 126.7
apprehensive 127.24
in suspense 130.12
impatient 135.6
troubled 1012.20

anxiously eagerly
101.13
concernedly 126.11
impatiently 135.8

any
noun some 244.3
anything 863.5
multitude 883.3
adj quantitative 244.5
every 863.15
one 871.7

anybody 863.5

any day 839.4

anyhow 384.10

any minute 839.4

any moment 839.4

any one
noun any 863.5
adj one 871.7

anyone any 863.5
whoever 863.7

anything some 244.3
any 863.5

anything goes
noun lawlessness 418.1
adj lawless 418.5

any time whenever
820.12
imminently 839.4

anyway 384.10

anywhere 159.22

AP 555.3

apace swiftly 174.17
hastily 401.12
promptly 844.15

apache 308.10

apart
adj distant 261.8
secluded 584.8
unrelated 775.6
separate 801.20
alone 871.8
adv away 261.17
privately 345.19
separately 801.27
singly 871.13
in half 874.8

apart from 801.27

apartheid seclusion
584.1
nationalism 611.10
exclusiveness 772.3

discrimination 979.4

apartment 228.13

apathetic insensible
25.6
indifferent 94.13
unconcerned 102.7
hopeless 125.12
inert 173.14
reluctant 325.6
languid 331.20
neutral 467.7
incurious 981.3

apathy insensibility
25.1
indifference 94.4,
467.2
unconcern 102.2
despair 125.2
inertness 173.4
languor 331.6
thoughtlessness 932.1
incuriosity 981.1

ape
noun hunk 15.7
bear 311.23
imitator 336.4
roughneck 593.4
goon 671.10
verb mimic 336.6
impersonate 349.12
gesture 517.21
resemble 783.7
adj crazy 925.27

aperture opening 292.1
passageway 383.3

apex summit 198.2
height 272.2
angle 278.2

aphrodisiac
noun love potion 75.6
adj aphroditous 75.25

Aphrodite Love 104.8
Venus 1015.10

apiece 864.19

aplenty
adj plentiful 990.7
adv plentifully 990.9

aplomb equanimity
106.3
verticalness 200.1
self-control 359.5
stability 854.1

Apocalypse 683.4

apocalypse disclosure
351.1
revelation 683.9
prediction 961.1

apocalyptic ominous
133.17
scriptural 683.10
predictive 961.11

apocryphal spurious
354.26
unorthodox 688.9
unauthoritative 970.21

apogee summit 198.2
boundary 211.3
long way 261.2

limit 793.5
orbit 1070.16
spacecraft 1073.2

Apollo Muses 710.22
Muse 720.10
Venus 1015.10
Sol 1070.14

apologetic
noun apology 600.3
justifier 600.8
adj penitent 113.9
justifying 600.13
atoning 658.7

apologetically 113.12

apologies 113.1

apologist defender
460.7
justifier 600.8
supporter 616.9
arguer 934.12

apologize repent 113.7
beg pardon 658.5

apologize for 600.11

apology penitence
113.4
pretext 376.1
apologia 600.3
excuse 658.2
argumentation 934.4

apoplectic
noun sick person 85.42
adj anaemic 85.60

apostle disciple 572.2
evangelist 684.2
deacon 699.9
converter 857.9

Apostolic 668.10

apostolic scriptural
683.10
papal 698.15

apotheosis respect
155.1
praise 509.5
glorification 662.8
resurrection 681.11
idolization 697.2
ideal 785.4
elevation 911.1

appalled 127.26

appalling horrid 98.19
terrible 127.30
remarkable 247.10

appallingly horridly
98.27
frightfully 127.34

apparatus equipment
385.4
impedimenta 471.3
tool 1039.1

apparel
noun clothing 5.1
verb clothe 5.38

apparent visible 31.6
appearing 33.11
exterior 206.7
manifest 348.8
specious 354.27

plausible 967.7
illusory 975.9

apparently visibly 31.8
seemingly 33.12
externally 206.10
manifestly 348.14
falsely 354.35

apparition appearance
33.1, 33.5
phantom 975.4
figment of the
imagination 985.5
spectre 987.1

appeal
noun delightfulness
97.2
desirability 100.13
loveableness 104.7
allurement 377.1
entreaty 440.2
appeal motion 598.11
prayer 696.4
match 747.3
verb attract 377.6
entreat 440.11

appealing delightful
97.7
alluring 377.8
imploring 440.17
melodious 708.48

appeal to entreat
440.11
address 524.27
refer to 956.14

appear show 31.4
become visible 33.8
appear to be 33.10
attend 221.8
come out 348.6,
352.16
be revealed 351.8
act 704.29
turn up 830.6

appearance appearing
33.1
exterior 33.2
apparition 33.5
arrival 186.1
exteriority 206.1
lineaments 262.3
manifestation 348.1
sham 354.3
illusoriness 975.2
phantom 975.4
spectre 987.1

appearance money
624.5

appear for 576.14

appearing
noun appearance 33.1
adj apparent 33.11
manifesting 348.9

appear to be 33.10

appease gratify 95.7
relieve 120.5
pacify 465.7
calm 670.7
propitiate 696.14

appeasement relief
120.1
pacification 465.1
foreign policy 609.5
propitiation 696.6

appeasing pacificatory
465.12
tranquillizing 670.15

appellant 599.5

appellation naming
527.2
name 527.3

appendage member
2.7, 792.4
hanger-on 138.6
follower 166.2
adjunct 254.1
nonessential 767.2
attendant 768.3

appended 253.9

appendix mouth 2.16
postscript 254.2
sequel 816.1

appetite eating 8.1
craving 100.6
stomach 100.7
eagerness 101.1
will 323.1
sensuality 663.1

applaud cheer 116.6
congratulate 149.2
assent 332.8
acclaim 509.10

applauded 509.19

applause cheer 116.2
congratulation 149.1
plaudit 509.2

appliance instrument
384.4
use 387.1
facility 449.9
machinery 1039.3

appliances equipment
385.4
hard goods 735.4

applicable usable
387.23
legal 673.10
relevant 774.11
apt 787.10

applicant 440.7

application dressing
86.33
industry 330.6
perseverance 360.1
use 387.1
request 440.1
study 570.3
administration 643.2
relevance 774.4
attribution 887.1
engrossment 982.3

applied 387.24

apply administer 643.6
relate 774.6
attribute 887.3

apply for 440.9

applying
noun administration
643.2
adj relevant 774.11

apply to cover 295.19
petition 440.10
relate to 774.5
attribute to 887.4

appoint elect 371.20
equip 385.8
prescribe 420.9
allot 477.9
assign 615.11
destine 963.7

appointed chosen
371.26
commissioned 615.19
destined 963.9

appointee 615.9

appointing 371.23

appointment election
371.9
accession 417.12
decree 420.4
allotment 477.3
engagement 582.8,
615.4
assignment 615.2
holy orders 698.10
position 724.5

appointments
equipment 385.4
belongings 471.2

apportion quantify
244.4
share 476.6
portion 477.6, 801.18
separate 792.6
dispose 807.9

apposite relevant
774.11
apt 787.10

appraisal measurement
300.1
valuation 630.3
classification 800.3
estimate 945.3

appraised measured
300.13
priced 630.14

appraising 945.3

appreciable weighable
297.19
measurable 300.14
substantial 762.6
knowable 927.25

appreciably to a degree
248.10
measurably 300.15

appreciate savour 63.5
enjoy 95.12
be grateful 150.3
respect 155.4
grow 251.6
measure 300.10
understand 521.7
know 927.12
estimate 945.9

value 996.13

appreciated respected
155.11
known 927.26

appreciation gratitude
150.1
respect 155.1
increase 251.1
acknowledgment 332.3
commendation 509.3
cognizance 927.2
discrimination 943.1
estimate 945.3

appreciative grateful
150.5
approbatory 509.16
discriminating 943.7

appreciative of 927.16

apprehend sense 24.6
fear 127.10
forebode 133.11
arrest 429.15
capture 480.18
understand 521.7
know 927.12

apprehended 927.26

apprehension anxiety
126.1
apprehensiveness
127.4
suspense 130.3
foreboding 133.2
arrest 429.6
seizure 480.2
intelligence 919.1
understanding 927.3
idea 931.1
doubt 954.2

apprehensive anxious
126.7
misgiving 127.24
nervous 128.11
in suspense 130.12
knowing 927.15

apprentice
noun novice 572.9
skilled worker 726.6
beginner 817.2
producer 891.7
verb train 568.13
indenture 615.18
adj indentured 615.21

apprenticed 615.21

apprenticeship training
568.3
indenture 615.8

approach
noun approaching
167.1
convergence 169.1
landing 184.18
arrival 186.1
entrance 189.5
nearness 223.1
plan 381.1
manner 384.1
attempt 403.2
offer 439.1
similarity 783.1

verb near 167.3, 223.7
converge 169.2
arrive 186.6
communicate with
343.8
bribe 378.3
use 384.5
attempt 403.6
make advances 439.7
address 524.27
cultivate 587.12
resemble 783.7
turn up 830.6
come 838.6
be imminent 839.2

approachable
accessible 167.5, 965.8
communicative 343.10
bribable 378.4

approaches 182.10

approaching
noun approach 167.1
adj nearing 167.4
converging 169.3
arriving 186.9
near 223.14
future 838.8
imminent 839.3

approbation respect
155.1
ratification 332.4
consent 441.1
approval 509.1
esteem 662.3

appropriate
verb take possession
472.10
adopt 480.19, 621.4
steal 482.13
plagiarize 482.19
usurp 640.8
adj useful 387.18
decorous 496.10
fit 533.7
right 637.3
rightful 639.8
relevant 774.11
apt 787.10
timely 842.9
characteristic 864.13
expedient 994.5

appropriately rightly
637.4
expediently 994.8

appropriateness
decorousness 496.3
elegance 533.1
propriety 637.2
relevance 774.4
timeliness 842.1

appropriation
allotment 477.3
taking over 480.4
theft 482.1
plagiarism 482.8
adoption 621.2
usurpation 640.3

approval respect 155.1
ratification 332.4

consent 441.1
approbation 509.1
esteem 662.3
support 900.1
criticism 945.2

approve ratify 332.12
adopt 371.15
consent 441.2
approve of 509.9
support 900.21
criticize 945.14
evidence 956.8

approved accepted
332.14
chosen 371.26
received 479.10
favoured 509.19
conventional 579.5
orthodox 687.7
authoritative 969.18

approve of consent
441.2
approve 509.9

approving consenting
441.4
favourable 509.17

approvingly 441.5

approximate
verb approach 167.3
imitate 336.5
resemble 783.7
similarize 783.8
adj approaching 167.4
approximating 774.8,
783.14
inaccurate 974.17

approximately
approximatively
223.23
nearly 244.6
on the whole 791.14

approximation
approach 167.1
nearness 223.1
measurement 300.1
reproduction 336.3
relation 774.1
similarity 783.1
likeness 783.3
inaccuracy 974.2
notation 1016.2

apricot 42.2

apron tablier 5.17
runway 184.23
stage 704.16
golf 748.1

apropos relevant
774.11
apt 787.10

apt skilful 413.22
appropriate 533.7
teachable 570.18
apposite 787.10
prompt 844.9
smart 919.14
probable 967.6
disposed 977.8

aptitude teachableness
570.5

tendency 895.1
smartness 919.2
probability 967.1
disposition 977.3

aptly 413.31

apt to
adj liable to 896.6
prep inclined to 895.6

aqua 1063.3

aquarium vivarium
228.24
collection 769.11

Aquarius 176.7

aquatic
noun vertebrate 311.3
adj water-dwelling
182.58
watery 1063.16

aqueous 1063.16

AR 820.13

Arab 178.4

arable 1067.20

arable land country
233.1
land 234.1
farm 1067.8

arbiter arbitrator 466.4
connoisseur 496.7
judge 596.1, 945.6

arbitrarily capriciously
364.7
imperiously 417.19

arbitrary voluntary
324.7
capricious 364.5
unthinking 365.10
imperious 417.16

arbitrate mediate 466.6
organize 727.9
sit in judgment 945.12

arbitration arbitrament
466.2
unionism 727.1
adjustment 787.4
judgment 945.1

arbitrator arbiter 466.4
go-between 576.4
judge 596.1

arbor 914.5

arboretum 310.11

arbour 228.12

arc
noun curve 279.2
lights 704.18
discharge 1031.6
verb curve 279.6

arcade corridor 197.18
fence 212.4
pillar 273.5
arch 279.4
passageway 383.3
marketplace 736.2

Arcadian rustic 233.6
natural 416.6
ideal 985.23

arcane

noun secret 345.5
adj secret 345.11
implied 519.7
recondite 522.16
supernatural 869.15

Arc de Triomphe
549.12

arch
noun foot 199.5
span 279.4
monument 549.12
verb curve 279.6
adj chief 249.14
mischievous 322.6
cunning 415.12

archaeological 841.20

archaeologist 841.5

archaeology 841.4

archangel 679.1

archduke 608.4

arched bowed 279.10
convex 283.13

archer 903.8

archery ballistics 462.3
sport 744.1
throwing 903.2

archetypal unimitated
337.6
prototypal 785.9

archetype engram
92.29
form 262.1
original 337.2
model 785.1
ideatum 931.2
instinct 933.2

arching 279.1

archipelago 235.2

architect planner 381.6
civil architect 716.10
landscape architect
717.3
doer 726.1
producer 891.7

architectural structural
266.6
design 717.6
constructional 891.15

architecture structure
266.1
architectural design
717.1
plot 722.4
production 891.2

archival 549.18

archive 549.15

archives storehouse
386.6
preserve 397.7
public records 549.2
registry 549.3

archivist 550.1

arch-rival 452.2

archway 279.4

Arctic 1022.4

arctic unfeeling 94.9

northern 161.14
seasonal 313.9
cold 1022.14

ardent alcoholic 88.37
fervent 93.18
zealous 101.9
amorous 104.26
willing 324.5
industrious 330.22
vehement 544.13
cordial 587.16
fiery 671.22
hot 1018.25
burning 1018.27

ardour animation 17.4
passion 93.2
desire 100.1
zeal 101.2
love 104.1
willingness 324.1
industry 330.6
vehemence 544.5
interest 982.2
ardency 1018.2

arduous laborious
725.18
difficult 1012.17

area space 158.1
location 159.1
region 231.1
size 257.1
study 568.8
field 724.4
speciality 865.1
science 927.10

arena space 158.1
hall 197.4
setting 209.2
enclosure 212.3
sphere 231.2
scene of action 463.1
field 724.4
athletics 755.1
science 927.10
outlook 977.2

argent
noun heraldic device
647.2
adj white 37.7

argentine 37.7

arguable 970.17

argue affirm 334.5
signify 517.17
mean 518.8
argufy 934.16
evidence 956.8

argue for 600.10

argument quarrel
456.5
contention 457.1
pleadings 598.7
testimony 598.9
defence 600.2
plot 722.4
argumentation 934.4
argumentum 934.5
sophism 935.3

argumentation
disagreement 788.1

argument 934.4

argumentative
contentious 110.26
argumental 934.19

Argus eagle 27.11
watchman 1007.10

aria air 708.4
solo 708.15

Arian
noun heretic 688.5
adj unorthodox 688.9

arid dull 117.6
unproductive 890.4
unimaginative 986.5
dry 1064.7

Ariel 678.8

arise get up 23.6
appear 33.8
emerge 190.11
ascend 193.8
rise 200.8
revolt 327.7
originate 817.13
turn up 830.6

arising
noun appearance 33.1
adj emerging 190.18

arising from 886.8

arista 3.9

aristocracy best 249.5
mastership 417.7
upper class 607.2
aristocratic status
607.3
aristocracy 608.1
nobility 608.1, 608.2
central government
612.4

aristocrat patrician
607.4
nobleman 608.4

aristocratic dignified
136.12
lordly 141.11
imperious 417.16
upper-class 607.10
noble 608.10
governmental 612.17

ark 180.1

arm
noun member 2.7,
792.4
inlet 242.1
branch 617.10
supporter 900.2
forearm 905.5
verb empower 18.10
equip 385.8
fortify 460.9
protect 1007.18

armada 461.26

armament provision
385.1
equipment 385.4
arms 462.1

armchair 950.13

armed provided 385.13

prepared 405.16
embattled 458.23
heeled 460.14
protected 1007.21
armed conflict 458.1
armed forces 461.19
armed guard 1007.9
armed robbery 482.3
armed services 461.19
armiger 608.4
arm in arm
  adj near 223.14
  adv sociably 582.25
  amicably 587.22
armistice 465.5
armour
  noun callousness 94.3
  shell 295.15
  armature 460.3
  verb fortify 460.9
  protect 1007.18
armoured covered
  295.31
  armour-plated 460.13
armoured division
  461.21
armour-plated 460.13
armoury storehouse
  386.6
  arsenal 462.2
  plant 739.3
armpit 284.2
arms military science
  458.6
  weapons 462.1
  heraldic device 647.2
arms race 458.10
Army 461.20
army unit 461.21
  this man's army
  461.22
  throng 769.4
  flock 769.5
  multitude 883.3
army group 461.21
aroma odour 69.1
  fragrance 70.1
  characteristic 864.4
aromatic
  noun perfumery 70.2
  adj odorous 69.9
  fragrant 70.9
around
  adv in every direction
  161.25
  round 209.12, 914.16
  near 223.20
  prep through 161.27
  about 223.26
around-the-world
  771.7
arousal awakening 23.2
  excitement 105.1
  excitation 105.11
  elicitation 192.5
  incitement 375.4

arouse energize 17.10
  awaken 23.5
  excite 105.12, 1019.18
  provoke 152.24
  elicit 192.14
  incite 375.17
  rouse 375.19
  alarm 400.3
  interest 982.12
aroused excited 105.20
  alarmed 400.4
arousing
  noun excitation 105.11
  adj aphrodisiac 75.25
  extractive 192.17
arrange plan 381.8
  prepare 405.6
  settle 437.8, 466.7
  compose 708.46
  order 806.4, 807.8
  classify 808.6
arranged planned
  381.12
  contracted 437.11
  orderly 806.6
  ordered 807.14
arrange for 405.11
arrangement form
  262.1, 709.11
  structure 266.1
  plan 381.1
  preparation 405.1
  compact 437.1
  adjustment 465.4
  compromise 468.1
  ornamentation 498.1
  appointment 582.8
  piece 708.5
  score 708.28
  harmonization 709.2
  treatment 712.9
  order 806.1
  ordering 807.1
  classification 808.1
arranger composer
  710.20
  organizer 807.5
array
  noun clothing 5.1
  army 461.22
  order 806.1
  arrangement 807.1
  series 811.2
  verb clothe 5.38
  ornament 498.8
  order 806.4
  dispose 807.9
  align 811.5
  adduce 956.12
arrayed clothing 5.44
  embattled 458.23
  arranged 807.14
arrears arrear 623.2
  shortcoming 910.1
arrest
  noun seizure 85.6,
  480.2
  slowing 175.4
  restraint 428.1

arrestment 429.6
  stop 856.2
  hindrance 1011.1
  curb 1011.7
  verb slow 175.9
  restrain 428.7
  make an arrest 429.15
  capture 480.18
  delay 845.8
  put a stop to 856.11
  engross 982.13
  hinder 1011.10
arrested retarded
  175.12
  undeveloped 406.12
  restrained 428.13
  incomplete 794.4
  late 845.16
  mentally deficient
  921.22
  gripped 982.18
arrested development
  fixation 92.21
  mental deficiency
  921.9
arresting 982.20
arrival landing 184.18
  coming 186.1
  incomer 189.4
arrive appear 33.8
  arrive at 186.6
  make good 409.10
arrive at arrive 186.6
  come at 186.7
arrive in 186.6
arriving 186.9
arrogance pride 136.1,
  140.2
  arrogantness 141.1
  insolence 142.1
  contempt 157.1
  defiance 454.1
  confidence 969.5
arrogant vain 136.9
  proud 140.9
  overbearing 141.9
  insolent 142.9
  contemptuous 157.8
  imperious 417.16
  defiant 454.7
  confident 969.21
arrogantly haughtily
  141.15
  insolently 142.12
arrondissement 231.5
arrow
  noun lightning 174.6
  shaft 462.6
  pointer 517.4
  verb be straight 277.4
arrowhead arrow 462.6
  phonogram 546.2
arrows 744.1
arse 217.5
arsehole prick 660.6
  chump 923.3

arsenal storehouse
  386.6
  armoury 462.2
  plant 739.3
arson 1019.7
art representation 349.1
  knack 413.6
  science 413.7, 927.10
  cunning 415.1
  stratagem 415.3
  visual arts 712.1
  artistry 712.7
  vocation 724.6
art critic 547.15, 718.4
artefact product 892.1
  object 1050.4
Artemis 1070.12
arterial 2.31
artery duct 2.21
  passageway 383.3
art form form 262.1
  visual arts 712.1
artful falsehearted
  354.31
  deceitful 356.22,
  645.18
  cunning 415.12
  shrewd 919.15
artfully skilfully 413.31
  cunningly 415.13
  intelligently 919.20
art gallery 386.9
arthritic
  noun sick person 85.42
  adj anaemic 85.60
article
  noun definite article
  530.6
  writing 547.10
  news item 552.3
  part 554.13
  treatise 556.1
  commodity 735.2
  particular 765.3
  section 792.2
  individual 871.4
  what's what 972.4
  object 1050.4
  verb accuse 599.7
  indenture 615.18
articulate
  verb say 524.23
  put together 799.5
  hook 799.8
  adj audible 50.16
  intelligible 521.10
  speaking 524.32
  eloquent 544.8
  jointed 799.17
articulated speech
  524.30
  phonetic 524.31
  continuous 811.8
articulation uttering
  524.6
  speech sound 524.13
  word 526.1
  joining 799.1

joint 799.4
  series 811.2
artifice falseheartedness
  354.4
  chicanery 356.4
  trick 356.6
  intrigue 381.5
  cunning 415.1
  stratagem 415.3
  affectation 533.3
  expedient 994.2
artificial spurious
  354.26
  affected 500.15, 533.9
artificial insemination
  78.3
artificially 354.35
artillery ballistics 462.3
  cannon 462.11
artisan expert 413.11
  worker 607.9
  artist 716.1
  skilled worker 726.6
  mechanic 1039.8
artist expert 413.11
  entertainer 707.1
  musician 710.1
  visual arts 712.1
  artiste 716.1
  skilled worker 726.6
  producer 891.7
artiste entertainer
  707.1
  musician 710.1
  artist 716.1
artistic skilful 413.22
  tasteful 496.8
  painterly 712.20
artistically skilfully
  413.31
  tastefully 496.11
artistry skill 413.1
  authorship 547.2,
  718.2
  art 712.7
artless natural 406.13
  unskilful 414.15
  simple 416.5
  candid 644.17
  foolable 922.12
arts 712.1
arts and crafts 712.1
art school 567.7
artwork visual arts
  712.1
  work of art 712.10
arvo 315.1
as
  adv how 384.9
  equally 789.11
  to illustrate 956.23
  conj because 887.10
as a body 791.13
as a bonus 992.18
as a consequence
  886.7
as a gift 478.27

in half 874.8

as usual
  adj same 780.6
  adv in status quo
  852.10
  normally 868.10

as well additionally
  253.11
  equally 789.11

as well as 253.12

as yet 837.4

asylum hiding place
  346.4
  insane asylum 925.14
  refuge 1008.1
  home 1008.4

asymmetric 265.10

as you say
  phrase right! 972.24
  exclam yes 332.18

at 159.27, 207.13

at about 159.28

at a disadvantage
  poorly 250.9
  under handicap
  1011.21

at a discount
  adj in disrepute
  661.13
  adv at a reduction
  631.3

at a distance
  adj distant 261.8
  adv away 261.14

at a glance 27.22

at all anyhow 384.10
  by any possibility
  965.10

at all costs 338.9

at all times always
  828.11
  constantly 846.7

at a loss
  adj in a dilemma
  970.25
  at an impasse 1012.24
  adv unprofitably 473.9

at an angle 204.21

at anchor
  adj motionless 173.13
  adv riding at anchor
  182.71

at an end 819.8

at any cost
  adv by any possibility
  965.10
  adv, prep in spite of
  338.9

at any rate
  adv to a degree 248.10
  anyhow 384.10
  certainly 969.23
  adv, conj
  notwithstanding 338.8

at any time 820.12

at a premium

adj expensive 632.11
  scarce 991.11
  adv dear 632.13

at a price 630.17

at a profit 472.17

at arm's length 261.14

at a standstill
  motionless 173.13
  inactive 331.17
  immovable 854.15

at a stroke 829.8

at auction 734.17

atavistic inverted 205.7
  innate 766.8
  primitive 841.11
  reversionary 858.7

at bar 598.23

at bay
  adj cornered 1012.25
  adv defensively 460.16

at best 248.10

at bottom deep 275.16
  essentially 766.11

at close quarters
  223.20

at close range 223.20

at dawn 314.8

at ease
  adj content 107.7
  at one's ease 121.12
  adv at rest 20.11

at every turn in every
  direction 161.25
  regularly 780.8

at fault blameworthy
  510.25
  guilty 656.3
  erroneous 974.16

at first 817.18

at first hand 956.22

at first light 314.8

at first sight 27.22

at full speed 174.20

at gunpoint forcibly
  424.14
  dangerously 1005.17

at hand
  adj present 221.12
  handy 387.20
  imminent 839.3
  adv near 223.20

at heart 766.11

atheism infidelity
  688.3
  impiety 694.1
  unbelief 695.5, 954.1

atheist
  noun sacrilegist 694.3
  unbeliever 695.11
  adj unbelieving 695.19

Athena 458.13

athenaeum 558.1

atherosclerosis 1044.5

athlete 743.19

athletic able-bodied
  15.16
  sporting 743.30

athleticism 743.8

athletics sports 743.8
  sport 744.1
  track and field 755.1

at home
  noun social gathering
  582.10
  assembly 769.2
  adj at ease 121.12
  adv in the bosom of
  one's family 225.16

at home in skilled in
  413.27
  versed in 927.19

at home with friends
  with 587.17
  versed in 927.19

at intervals
  discontinuously 812.5
  occasionally 847.5

at issue
  adj doubtful 970.17
  undecided 970.18
  adv adversarial 451.9
  in question 937.39

at it 330.21

at large
  adj escaped 369.11
  free 430.21
  adv at length 538.16
  scatteringly 770.12
  wholly 791.13
  generally 863.17

Atlas strong man 15.6
  Hercules 900.3

atlas pillar 273.5
  reference book 554.9

at last 819.12

at least 248.10

at leisure
  adj idle 331.18
  adv at one's leisure
  402.7

at length lengthily
  267.10
  ad nauseam 538.16
  fully 765.13
  finally 819.12

at liberty idle 331.18
  free 430.21

at loggerheads
  adj contrapositive
  215.5
  oppositional 451.8
  at odds 456.16
  at outs 589.12
  contrary 778.6
  disagreeing 788.6
  adv contrarily 778.9

at long last 819.12

at midday 314.9

atmosphere milieu
  209.3
  aerosphere 317.2

treatment 712.9
  plot 722.4
  gas 1065.2

atmospheric 317.11

atmospherics 1033.21

at most 248.10

at noon 314.9

at no time 821.4

at odds
  adj unwilling 325.5
  oppositional 451.8
  at variance 456.16
  at outs 589.12
  different 779.7
  disagreeing 788.6
  adv adversarial 451.9

at odds with 333.6

atoll 235.2

atom modicum 248.2
  atomy 258.8
  one 871.3
  tracer 1037.4
  matter 1050.2
  element 1058.2

atom-bomb 459.23

atomic infinitesimal
  258.14
  one 871.7
  atomistic 1037.18

atoms 762.2

at once hastily 401.12
  together 768.11
  jointly 799.18
  at once and on the
  spot 829.8
  promptly 844.15

at one unanimous
  332.15
  in accord 455.3
  agreeing 787.9

atone compensate 338.4
  make restitution 481.5
  repay 624.11
  atone for 658.4
  harmonize 708.35
  tune 708.36

atone for 658.4

atonement
  compensation 338.1
  reparation 481.2,
  658.1
  recompense 624.3
  salvation 677.14
  propitiation 696.6

at one time at once
  829.8
  simultaneously 835.7

at one with unanimous
  332.15
  concurrent 898.4

atop
  adv on top 198.15
  prep on 198.16

A to Z 791.3

A-to-Z 793.10

at peace 464.9

at present 837.3

at random haphazardly
  809.18
  irregularly 850.4
  purposelessly 971.20

at regular intervals
  849.9

at rest
  adj at ease 121.12
  quiescent 173.12
  dead 307.30
  adv at ease 20.11
  beneath the sod
  309.23

at right angles 200.14

at risk liable 896.5
  in danger 1005.13

atrocious painful 26.10
  horrid 98.19
  cruel 144.26
  insulting 156.8
  wrong 638.3
  wicked 654.16
  base 661.12
  savage 671.21
  terrible 999.9

atrocity dreadfulness
  98.3
  act of cruelty 144.12
  indignity 156.2
  mistreatment 389.2
  abomination 638.2
  injustice 650.4
  iniquity 654.3
  misdeed 655.2
  violence 671.1
  evil 999.3

at rock bottom 275.16

atrophy
  noun anaemia 85.9
  shrinking 260.3
  emaciation 270.6
  waste 393.4
  verb waste 393.19

at sea
  adj bewildered 970.24
  muddled 984.13
  adv under way 182.63
  on the high seas 240.9
  uncertainly 970.28

at short notice
  extemporaneously
  365.15
  suddenly 829.9

at square 456.16

at stake 438.12

attach add 253.4
  annex 480.20
  fasten 799.7
  attribute 887.3

attached 253.9

attached to 104.30

attachment love 104.1
  addition 253.1
  adjunct 254.1
  annexation 480.5
  fidelity 644.7
  fastening 799.3

auditory
noun audience 48.6
adj audio 48.13

auger
noun point 285.3
verb perforate 292.15

augment aggravate
119.2
increase 251.4
add to 253.5
enlarge 259.4

augmented aggravated
119.4
increased 251.7

augur
noun predictor 961.4
verb hint 133.12

august dignified 136.12
venerable 155.12
eminent 247.9

auld 841.10

aunt 559.3

auntie homo 75.15
brother 559.3

au pair 862.6

aura milieu 209.3
illustriousness 662.6
ectoplasm 689.7
halo 1024.14

aural eye 2.26
auditory 48.13

Aurora 314.2

aurora dawn 314.3
foredawn 314.4
polar lights 1024.16

Auschwitz 308.11

auspices patronage
449.4
supervision 573.2
protectorship 1007.2

auspicious promising
124.13
of good omen 133.18
timely 842.9
good 998.12
fortunate 1009.14

Aussie dago 232.7
squaddie 461.7

austere harsh 144.24
strict 425.6
inornate 499.9
plain-speaking 535.3
ascetic 667.4
simple 797.6
meagre 991.10

austerity harshness
144.9
strictness 425.1
inornateness 499.4
plain speech 535.1
thrift 635.1
asceticism 667.1
meagreness 991.2

austerity programme
635.1

Australasia 231.6

Australia 235.1

auteur theatre man
704.23
film studio 706.3

authentic original
337.5
straight 644.14
orthodox 687.7
real 760.15
evidential 956.16
authoritative 969.18
genuine 972.15

authentically 972.19

authenticated accepted
332.14
proved 956.20
true 972.13

authenticity
nonimitation 337.1
candour 644.4
orthodoxy 687.1
reality 760.2
reliability 969.4
genuineness 972.7

author
noun writer 547.15,
718.4
discourser 556.3
narrator 722.5
doer 726.1
agent 885.4
producer 891.7
verb write 547.21,
718.6
cause 885.10

authorial 547.25,
718.8

authoritarian
noun nationalist
611.21
adj authoritative
417.15
imperious 417.16
strict 425.6
nationalist 611.33
governmental 612.17
narrow-minded 979.10

authoritarianism
authoritativeness 417.3
strictness 425.1
nationalism 611.10
absolutism 612.9
narrow-mindedness
979.1

authoritative powerful
18.12
skilful 413.22
imperious 417.16
preceptive 419.4
commanding 420.13
orthodox 687.7
specialized 865.5
influential 893.13
convincing 952.26
authentic 969.18
valid 972.14

authorities powers that
be 575.15
government 612.3

authority power 18.1

supremacy 249.3
expert 413.11
prerogative 417.1,
642.1
authoritativeness 417.2
prestige 417.4
governance 417.5
command 420.1
authorization 443.3
connoisseur 496.7
certificate 549.6
informant 551.5
direction 573.1
commission 615.1
specialist 865.3
influence 893.1
wise man 920.1
scientist 927.11
validity 972.6

authorization
ratification 332.4
accession 417.12
authority 443.3
certificate 549.6
commission 615.1
legalization 673.2

authorized
authoritative 417.15
empowered 443.17
commissioned 615.19
legal 673.10

authorship writing
547.2, 718.2
production 891.1

autistic unfeeling 94.9
unsociable 583.5
selfish 651.5
illusory 975.9
incurious 981.3
visionary 985.24

auto 179.9

autobiographical
719.7

autobiography 719.1

autocratic authoritative
417.15
imperious 417.16
governmental 612.17

autograph
noun holograph 337.3
signature 527.10
handwriting 547.3
writing 547.10
verb ratify 332.12
adj written 547.22

automated 1040.21

automatic
noun gun 462.10
automatic device
1040.12
adj unpremeditated
365.11
habitual 373.15
uniform 780.5
instinctive 933.6
involuntary 962.14
automated 1040.21

automatically
intuitively 933.7

involuntarily 962.18

**automatic
transmission** 1039.5

automation electronics
1032.1
automatic control
1040.1

automobile
noun car 179.9
adj self-propelled
1040.22

automotive vehicular
179.23
self-propelled 1040.22

**autonomic nervous
system** 2.12

autonomous voluntary
324.7
independent 430.22
governmental 612.17
separate 801.20

autonomy voluntariness
324.2
independence 430.5
central government
612.4

autopsy
noun postmortem
307.18
verb examine 937.24

autumn
noun fall 313.4
adj seasonal 313.9

autumnal 313.9

auxiliary
noun verb 530.4
assistant 616.6
nonessential 767.2
adj additional 253.10
helping 449.20
unessential 767.4

avail
noun utility 387.3
benefit 387.4
good 998.4
verb be of use 387.17
aid 449.11
suffice 990.4
do good 998.10

availability presence
221.1
utility 387.3
accessibility 965.3

available present
221.12
open 222.15
idle 331.18
handy 387.20
prepared 405.16
obtainable 472.14
accessible 965.8

avalanche
noun slide 194.4
plenty 990.2
superabundance 992.2
snow 1022.8
verb slide 194.9

Avalon 681.9

avant-garde
noun vanguard 216.2
precursor 815.1
novelty 840.2
adj original 337.5
preceding 815.4
modern 840.13

avarice greed 100.8
stinginess 484.3
selfishness 651.1

Ave 696.4

avenge 507.4

avenger 507.3

avenging 507.7

avenue outlet 190.9
passageway 383.3

average
noun mean 246.1
ruck 863.3
verb average out 246.2
seek the middle 818.3
adj medium 246.3
middle 818.4
prevalent 863.12
usual 868.9
ordinary 1004.8

average man 606.5

averaging 246.1

averse allergic 99.8
unwilling 325.5

averse to 103.7

aversion hostility 99.2
hate 103.1
anathema 103.3
refusal 325.1

avert avoid 164.6
prevent 1011.14

avian 311.47

aviary 228.23

aviation
noun aeronautics 184.1
adj aeronautic 184.49

aviator 185.1

avid greedy 100.27
eager 101.8

avidly greedily 100.32
eagerly 101.13

avoid avoid like the
plague 157.7
evade 164.6
shun 368.6
abstain 668.7

avoidable 368.14

avoidance shunning
368.1
abstinence 668.2
retreat 902.3

avowed accepted
332.14
affirmed 334.9
pretexted 376.5

avuncular 559.6

await wait 130.8,
845.12
come 838.6
be imminent 839.2

awaited 130.13

awaiting 130.11

awake
verb awaken 23.4, 23.5
excite 105.12
come to life 306.8
adj conscious 23.8
alert 339.14
clear-witted 919.13

awaken awake 23.4
waken 23.5
excite 105.12
come to life 306.8
rouse 375.19
disillusion 976.2

awakening wakening 23.2
disillusionment 976.1

award
noun giving 478.1
gift 478.4
reward 646.2
verdict 945.5
verb give 478.12

awarding 478.1

award winner 413.15

aware sensible 24.11
knowing 927.15
attentive 982.15

awareness sensation 24.1
cognizance 927.2
attention 982.1

aware of 927.16

awash floating 182.60
flooded 238.25
soaked 1063.17

away
adj gone 34.5
absent 222.11
distant 261.8
adv backwards 163.13
hence 188.20
aside 218.10
elsewhere 222.18
at a distance 261.14
apart 261.17

away from
adv separately 801.27
prep from 188.21

away from home 222.12

awe
noun wonder 122.1
fear 127.1
respect 155.1
verb astonish 122.6
terrify 127.17
daunt 127.18
command respect 155.7

awed wondering 122.9
terrified 127.26
reverent 155.9

awe-inspiring awesome 122.11
terrible 127.30

venerable 155.12
grandiose 501.21
weighty 996.20

awesome awful 122.11
terrible 127.30
venerable 155.12
large 247.7
grandiose 501.21
eminent 662.18
sacred 685.7

awestruck wondering 122.9
terrified 127.26
reverent 155.9

awful awesome 122.11
terrible 127.30, 999.9
venerable 155.12
terrific 247.11
grandiose 501.21
sacred 685.7
hideous 1014.11

awfully awesomely 122.15
frightfully 127.34
distressingly 247.21
terribly 999.14
hideously 1014.13

awhile 827.9

awkward mortifying 98.21
bulky 257.19
bungling 414.20
stiff 534.3
ignorant 929.12
inconvenient 995.7
unwieldy 1012.19

awkwardly clumsily 414.24
unwieldily 1012.29

awkwardness
mortification 98.6
bulkiness 257.9
clumsiness 414.3
untimeliness 843.1
inconvenience 995.3
unwieldiness 1012.9

awning 1027.1

awry
adj askew 204.14
unbalanced 790.5
disorderly 809.13
erroneous 974.16
adv askew 204.22

axe
noun sword 462.5
capital punishment 604.6
scaffold 605.5
economizing 635.2
cutlery 1039.2
verb reduce 252.7
sever 801.11

axe to grind
prejudgment 946.1
narrow-mindedness 979.1

axial flowing 172.8
central 208.11

axing 635.2

axiom fact 760.3
essence 766.2
premise 934.7
supposition 950.3
belief 952.2
truth 972.2, 973.2

axiomatic manifest 348.8
real 760.15
obvious 969.15

axis centre 208.2
straight line 277.2
stem 310.19
association 617.1
fulcrum 905.3
axle 914.5

axle 914.5

aye
noun affirmative 332.2
vote 371.6
consent 441.1
side 934.14
adv forever 828.12
exclam yes 332.18

A-Z 574.10

azure
noun blueness 45.1
heraldic device 647.2
heavens 1070.2
verb blue 45.2
adj blue 45.3

babble
noun nonsense 520.2
Greek 522.7
chatter 540.3
verb ripple 52.11
betray 351.6
talk nonsense 520.5
be incomprehensible 522.10
chatter 540.5
be insane 925.20

babbling
noun divulgence 351.2
adj rippling 52.19
chattering 540.10
mentally deficient 921.22
delirious 925.31

babe gal 77.6
infant 302.9
dupe 358.1
simple soul 416.3
darling 562.6
innocent 657.4
doll 1015.9

Babel clash 61.2
Greek 522.7
confusion 809.2
commotion 809.4
pandemonium 809.5

baboon 1014.4

baby
noun weakling 16.6
sweetie 104.11
doll 104.15
miniature 258.6
youngster 302.1

infant 302.9
simple soul 416.3
coward 491.5
darling 562.6
innocent 657.4
jockey 757.2
beginner 817.2
adj miniature 258.12
infant 301.12

baby boom 251.2

baby clothes 5.30

baby-doll doll 104.15
darling 562.6

Babylon 654.7

Babylonian 501.21

baby oil 1054.3

baby-sitting 1007.2

Bacchus 88.2

bachelor confirmed
bachelor 565.3
knight 608.5
degree 648.6

back
noun exterior 206.2
setting 209.2
rear 217.1
dorsum 217.3
type 548.6
makeup 554.12
team 745.2, 746.2
supporter 900.2
verb reverse 163.7
move 172.5
backwater 182.34
mount 193.12
bring up the rear 217.8
secure 438.9
back up 449.13
commend 509.11
benefit 592.3
finance 729.15
bet 759.25
support 900.21
confirm 956.11
stiffen 1044.9
adj backward 163.12, 836.12
flowing 172.8
rear 217.9
hinterland 233.9
phonetic 524.31
late 845.16
adv backwards 163.13
in compensation 338.7
in reserve 386.17
ago 836.15

backache ache 26.5
anaemia 85.9

back and forth
reciprocally 776.12
changeably 853.8
to and fro 915.21

back-and-forth
noun alternation 915.5
adj alternate 915.19

backbeat 709.26

backbencher 610.3

backbone pluck 359.3
balls 492.4
supporter 900.2

back-burner 997.17

back door rear 217.1
secret passage 346.5
byway 383.4

back down hesitate 362.7
yield 433.7

backdrop setting 209.2
scenery 704.20

backed approved 509.19
hardened 1044.13

backer giver 478.11
friend 588.1
benefactor 592.1
supporter 616.9
patron 704.26
financer 729.9

backfire
noun explosion 671.7
counteraction 899.1
recoil 902.2
fire 1018.13
verb explode 671.14
recoil 902.6

back four 745.2

background setting 209.2
distance 261.3
experience 413.9
arena 463.1
motif 498.7
plot 722.4
cause 885.1
source 885.5

backhand insulting 156.8
oblique 204.13

back home 225.16

backing
noun reverse 163.3
course 172.2
means 384.2
consent 441.1
patronage 449.4
bookbinding 554.14
film 714.10
financing 729.2
reversion 858.1
support 900.1
supporter 900.2
frame 900.10
confirmation 956.4
adj approving 509.17
benefitting 592.4

backing up reverse 163.3
confirmation 956.4

backlash
noun retaliation 506.1
impact 886.2
counteraction 899.1
recoil 902.2
verb recoil 902.6

backlog

dance 705.2
football 745.1
rugby 746.1
match 747.3
tennis 749.1
hockey 750.1
table 752.2
assembly 769.2
projectile 903.5
verb snowball 282.7

ballad
noun popular music
708.7
song 708.14
verb sing 708.38

ballast
noun counterbalance
297.4
offset 338.2
light source 1025.1
verb trim ship 182.49
weight 297.12
stabilize 854.7

ballerina 705.3

ballet
noun musical theatre
708.34
adj dramatic 704.33

ballet dancer 705.3

balletic dramatic
704.33
dancing 705.6

ball game sport 744.1
meat and potatoes
766.3

ballistic 903.15

ballistic missile
missile 462.18
rocket 1072.3

ballistics 462.3

balloon
noun aerostat 181.11
bag 195.2
sphere 282.2
bubble 320.1
kick 901.9
verb grow 14.2, 251.6
fly 184.36
enlarge 259.5
ball 282.7
bulge 283.11
kick 901.21

ballooning
noun aviation 184.1
increase 251.1
adj drooping 202.10
bulging 283.15

ballot
noun vote 371.6
slate 609.19
verb vote 371.18

ballot box vote 371.6
polls 609.20

balloting 371.6

ballroom hall 197.4
dance hall 705.4
entertainment 743.13

balls pluck 359.3

guts 492.4
bullshit 520.3

ball-up 809.2

bally 513.9

balm anaesthetic 25.3
perfumery 70.2
remedy 86.1
medicine 86.4
lotion 86.11
condolence 147.1
moderator 670.3
ointment 1054.3

balmy fragrant 70.9
palliative 86.40
bright 97.11
relieving 120.9
thriving 1009.13

balsa 180.11

balsamic palliative
86.40
relieving 120.9

balustrade fence 212.4
post 273.4
base 900.8

bamboo grass 310.5
cane 1052.4

ban
noun prohibition 444.1
disapproval 510.1
curse 513.1
ostracism 586.3
exclusion 772.1
verb excise 255.10
prohibit 444.3
disapprove 510.10
ostracize 586.6
exclude 772.4
banish 908.17

banal trite 117.9
medium 246.3
aphoristic 973.6

banality triteness 117.3
platitude 973.3

bananas 925.27

band
noun stripe 47.5
dressing 86.33
strip 271.4
belt 280.3
layer 296.1
jewel 498.6
line 517.6
association 617.1
orchestra 710.12
tennis 749.1
company 769.3
frequency band
1033.13
verb variegate 47.7
encircle 209.7
cooperate 450.3
put together 799.5
bind 799.9

bandage
noun dressing 86.33
strip 271.4
wrapper 295.18
verb blind 30.7

treat 91.24
bind 799.9

bandages 754.1

Band-Aid 86.33

band-aid
noun pretext 376.1
insufficiency 991.1
adj makeshift 994.7

banded 47.15

bandied about 552.15

banding 808.2

bandit military aircraft
181.9
brigand 483.4

bandstand 704.16

band together
cooperate 450.3
league 804.4

bandwagon 578.5

bane death 307.1
killing 308.1
end 395.2
destroyer 395.8
enemy 589.6
evil 999.3
curse 1000.1

bang
noun tuft 3.6
pep 17.3
noise 53.3
report 56.1
detonation 56.3
dose 87.19
kick 105.3
explosion 671.7
production 892.2
hit 901.4
sock 901.5
verb din 53.7
crack 56.6
blast 56.8
close 293.6
trade 737.23
collide 901.13
belt 901.15
pound 901.16
adv suddenly 829.9

banger sausage 10.20
jalopy 179.10

banging crashing 56.11
whopping 257.21

bang on
adj accurate 972.16
great 998.13
adv exactly 972.21
excellently 998.22

bangs 3.6

banish ostracize 586.6
expel 908.17

banishment ostracism
586.3
relegation 908.4

banjo 1039.2

bank
noun incline 204.4
border 211.4
side 218.1

shore 234.2
slope 237.2
shoal 276.2
storehouse 386.6
preserve 397.7
lending institution
620.4
treasury 729.12
banking house 729.13
workplace 739.1
pot 759.5
pile 769.10
series 811.2
buttress 900.4
barrier 1011.5
mine 1056.6
verb stunt 184.40
incline 204.10
store 386.10
fortify 460.9
pile 769.19
ignite 1019.22

bank account account
622.2
funds 728.14

bank balance 622.2

bank clerk 729.10

banker lender 620.3
money dealer 729.10
businessman 730.1
bingo 759.15

bank holiday 20.4

banking 729.4

banking industry
729.4

bank manager 729.10

Bank of France 729.13

Bank of Japan 729.13

bank on 124.7

bank robber 483.5

bankrupt
noun failure 410.7
poor man 619.4
insolvent 625.4
verb impoverish 619.6
ruin 625.8
adj ruined 395.28
destitute 619.9
insolvent 625.11

bankruptcy impairment
393.1
failure 410.1
insolvency 625.3

bankrupt in 991.13

banned prohibited
444.7
excluded 772.7

banner
noun poster 352.7
battle flag 458.12
sign 517.1
trophy 646.3
flag 647.6
caption 936.2
adj chief 249.14

banquet
noun feast 8.9

festival 743.4
verb feast 8.24, 743.25

banshee fairy 678.8
spectre 987.1

Bantam 311.29

bantam
noun runt 258.4
adj miniature 258.12

bantamweight
noun cruiserweight
297.3
adj lightweight 298.13

banter
noun buffoonery 489.5
badinage 490.1
ridicule 508.1
verb chaff 490.5

baptism admission
187.2
submergence 367.2
naming 527.2
baptizement 701.6
wetting 1063.6

baptized 527.14

bar
noun stripe 47.5
barroom 88.20
island 235.2
line 267.3, 517.6
shaft 273.1
shoal 276.2
obstruction 293.3
lock 428.5
legal profession 597.4
heraldic device 647.2
insignia of rank 647.5
stave 708.29
notation 709.12
precious metals 728.20
exclusion 772.1
table 900.15
lever 905.4
barrier 1011.5
verb variegate 47.7
cross 170.6
fence 212.7
excise 255.10
close 293.6
stop 293.7
prohibit 444.3
exclude 772.4
make impossible 966.6
obstruct 1011.12
prevent 1011.14
prep excluding 772.10

barb
noun tactile process
3.10
quill 3.18
bristle 288.3
arrow 462.6
verb sharpen 285.7

barbarian
noun savage 497.7,
593.5
alien 773.3
adj unrefined 497.12
extraneous 773.5

barbaric cruel 144.26

unrefined 497.12
grandiose 501.21
inelegant 534.2
savage 671.21
extraneous 773.5
barbarism
unrefinement 497.3
corruption 526.6
solecism 531.2
inelegance 534.1
unenlightenment
929.4
barbarous cruel 144.26
unrefined 497.12
ungrammatic 531.4
inelegant 534.2
savage 671.21
extraneous 773.5
unlearned 929.14
barbecue
noun breakfast 8.6
meat 10.12
verb dine 8.21
cook 11.4
barbecued 11.6
barbed 285.9
barbel tactile process
3.10
feeler 73.4
bristle 288.3
barber 1015.13
barbican 272.6
barbiturates 87.4
barbs 87.4
bard minstrel 710.14
poet 720.11
bardic 720.15
bare
verb divest 6.5
unclose 292.12
disclose 351.4
adj naked 6.14
vacant 222.14
mere 248.8
open 292.17, 348.10
worn 393.31
unadorned 499.8
plain-speaking 535.3
simple 797.6
unmixed 797.7
bare bones 199.2
bare-bones 248.8
bared 6.12
barefoot barefooted
6.15
ascetic 667.4
barely nakedly 6.19
scarcely 248.9
narrowly 270.22
simply 797.11
barely audible 52.16
bare minimum 990.1
bargain
noun compact 437.1
compromise 468.1
advantageous purchase
633.3

deal 731.5
verb contract 437.5
treat with 437.6
mediate 466.6
confer 541.11
organize 727.9
drive a bargain 731.17
bargain-basement
633.8
bargained for 437.11
bargain for plan 380.6
contract 437.5
strike a bargain 731.18
bargaining conference
541.6
negotiation 731.3
bargain prices 633.2
barge haul 176.13
stroll 177.28
baring unclothing 6.1
disclosure 351.1
baritone
noun part 708.22
voice 709.5
adj deep 54.10
vocal 708.50
bark
noun detonation 56.3
cry 59.1
animal noise 60.1
ship 180.1
skin 295.3
hull 295.16
verb peel 6.8
blast 56.8
cry 59.6, 60.2
injure 393.13
murmur 524.26
abrade 1042.7
barker publicist 352.9
theatre man 704.23
tout 730.7
barking 60.1
barley 10.4
barmaid off-licence
owner 88.19
waiter 577.7
barman off-licence
owner 88.19
waiter 577.7
barmy leavening
298.17
foamy 320.7
barn 228.20
barney 456.6
barometer measure
300.2
weather instrument
317.7
feeler 941.4
baron nobleman 608.4
businessman 730.1
personage 996.8
baroness 608.6
baronet nobleman
608.4
knight 608.5

barons 249.5
baroque
noun ornateness 498.2
adj ornate 498.12
freakish 869.13
fanciful 985.20
barrack 508.9
barracks 428.9
barrage
noun staccato 55.1
volley 459.9
barrier 1011.5
verb pull the trigger
459.22
barred striped 47.15
netlike 170.11
enclosed 212.10
closed 293.9
prohibited 444.7
excluded 772.7
impossible 966.7
barrel
noun quill 3.18
quantity 247.3
cylinder 282.4
bomb 618.3
verb clip 174.9
package 212.9
collide 901.13
barren ineffective 19.15
dull 117.6
vacant 222.14
fruitless 391.12
unproductive 890.4
unimaginative 986.5
barricade close 293.6
fortify 460.9
obstruct 1011.12
barrier boundary 211.3
fence 212.4
partition 213.5
obstruction 293.3
lock 428.5
fortification 460.4
bar 1011.5
barring
noun exclusion 772.1
prep off 255.14
excluding 772.10
barrio 230.6
barrister 597.1
barrow cart 179.3
hill 237.4
tomb 309.16
swine 311.9
monument 549.12
counter 736.6
bartender off-licence
owner 88.19
waiter 577.7
barter
noun transfer 629.1
trade 731.2
trading 862.2
verb transfer 629.3
trade 731.14
bartering 731.2
barton 1067.8

basal basic 199.8
essential 766.9
original 885.14
basalt 1057.1
base
noun station 159.2
point of departure
188.5
basement 199.2
bottom 274.4
cause 885.1
foundation 900.6
pedestal 900.8
makeup 1015.12
acid 1058.3
verb establish 159.16
adj offensive 98.18
servile 138.13
inadequate 250.7
dastardly 491.12
low 497.15, 661.12
populational 606.8
knavish 645.17
wicked 654.16
terrible 999.9
inferior 1004.9
based on evidential
956.16
contingent 958.9
baseless 763.8, 935.13
baseline point of
departure 188.5
tennis 749.1
basement cellar 197.17
base 199.2
storehouse 386.6
foundation 900.6
base on 199.6
base rate lending 620.1
interest 623.3
bash
noun try 403.3
do 582.12
assembly 769.2
hit 901.4
sock 901.5
verb injure 393.13
belt 901.15
discriminate against
979.8
work evil 999.6
bashful fearful 127.23
shy 139.12
demurring 325.7
reticent 344.10
unsociable 583.5
bashing 389.3
basic basal 199.8
essential 766.9
simple 797.6
original 885.14
vital 996.23
chemical 1058.8
basically 766.11
basics elementary
education 568.5
essentials 817.6

basic training
preparation 405.1
training 568.3
basilica 703.1
basin washbasin 79.12
container 195.1
bed 199.4
plain 236.1
valley 237.7
cavity 284.2
harbour 1008.6
basis point of departure
188.5
motive 375.1
warrant 600.6
cause 885.1
foundation 900.6
premise 934.7
topic 936.1
outlook 977.2
bask 1019.19
basket
noun container 195.1
verb package 212.9
basketball 751.1
basketball player
751.2
bask in 95.12
bass
noun part 708.22
voice 709.5
adj deep 54.10
vocal 708.50
bassist 710.5
bass player 710.5
bastard
noun guy 76.5
illegitimate 561.5
arsehole 660.6
adj spurious 354.26
illegitimate 674.7
baste cook 11.4
whip 604.12
pound 901.16
bastille 429.8
basting cooking 11.1
corporal punishment
604.4
bastion 460.6
bat
noun blind 30.4
cricket 747.1
tennis 749.1
sock 901.5
verb play 747.4
belt 901.15
batch
noun bread 10.27
amount 244.2
lot 247.4
lump 257.10
bunch 769.7
make 892.4
verb assemble 769.18
bate decrease 252.6
abate 252.8
subtract 255.9

blunt 286.2
discount 631.2
relax 670.9

bath
noun bathe 79.8
dip 79.9
bathing place 79.10
washbasin 79.12
wetting 1063.6
verb wash 79.19

bathe
noun bath 79.8
aquatics 182.11
verb wash 79.19
treat 91.24
swim 182.56
soak 1063.13

bathed 1063.17

bathing balneation 79.7
aquatics 182.11
wetting 1063.6

bathroom latrine 12.10
bathing place 79.10
lavatory 197.26

baths bathing place
79.10
health resort 91.23
resort 228.27
swimming pool 743.12

bathtub 79.12

batman 577.5

baton staff 273.2
sceptre 417.9
insignia 647.1
heraldic device 647.2
stigma 661.6
illegitimacy 674.2
metronome 711.22

bat out of hell 174.6

bats 925.27

batsman 747.2

battalion unit 461.21
company 769.3

batten
noun strip 271.4
scenery 704.20
base 900.8
verb close 293.6
gluttonize 672.4
hook 799.8
thrive 1009.8

batter
noun team 747.2
semiliquid 1060.5
verb mistreat 389.5
injure 393.13
thrash soundly 604.13
rage 671.11
pound 901.16
work evil 999.6

battered 393.33

battering trauma 85.37
unruliness 671.3

battery coop 228.22
unit 461.21
artillery 462.11

corporal punishment
604.4
electrical device
1031.20
farm 1068.5

battery-powered
1031.29

batting 747.3

battle
noun fight 457.4,
754.3
war 458.1
operation 458.5
struggle 725.3
verb contend against
451.4
quarrel 456.11
contend 457.13
war 458.14
struggle 725.11

battle cry cry 59.1
challenge 454.2
call to arms 458.8
call 517.16

battled 458.23

battlefield 463.2

battleground 463.2

battleship warship
180.6
capital ship 180.7

battling contending
457.22
warlike 458.21

batty screwy 922.9
crazy 925.27

Bauer 1067.5

bawdy lascivious
665.29
obscene 666.9

bawling
noun weeping 115.2
adj vociferous 59.10
howling 60.6

bay
noun blare 53.5
nook 197.3
shore 234.2
ocean 240.3
inlet 242.1
recess 284.7
appaloosa 311.11
railway 383.7
storehouse 386.6
verb blare 53.10
cry 60.2
adj reddish-brown
40.4

bayonet 459.25

bays 646.3

bay window 2.17

bazaar sale 734.3
marketplace 736.2

BBC radio station
1033.6
television studio
1034.6

BBC1 1034.4

BBC2 1034.4

BC 820.13

be exist 760.8
depend 958.6

be able 18.11

be about 724.11

be about to 405.10

be above 157.3

be absent stay away
222.7
muse 984.9

be accepted 952.20

be accurate 972.11

beach
noun shore 234.2
golf 748.1
verb shipwreck 182.42

beacon
noun flying and
landing guides marker
184.19
alarm 400.1
signal 517.15
fire 1018.13
torch 1025.3
verb lead 165.2
shine 1024.23
illuminate 1024.28

bead
noun drop 282.3
verb ball 282.7
figure 498.9

be added 253.7

beaded beady 282.10
ornamented 498.11

beading 211.7

beadle 1007.15

be admitted 189.7

beads jewel 498.6
prayer 696.4

beady 282.10

be afraid fear 127.10
suppose 950.10
think 952.11

be after 380.4

be against 451.7

beagle tec 576.11
policeman 1007.15

beak
noun prow 216.3
spout 239.8
nose 283.8
principal 571.8
judge 596.1
verb tap 901.18

beaker 1058.6

be alert 980.3

be-all 791.3

be-all and end-all
supremacy 249.3
all 791.3
end 819.1
infinity 822.1

beam
noun smile 116.3

flying and landing
guides marker 184.19
side 218.1
breadth 269.1
timber 273.3
buttress 900.4
lever 905.4
ray 1024.5
radio signal 1033.10
photoemission 1034.4
signal 1035.11
wood 1052.3
verb be pleased 95.11
exude cheerfulness
109.6
smile 116.7
look good 1015.16
shine 1024.23
broadcast 1033.25
transmit 1035.15

be a man 492.10

be a member 617.15

beaming happy 95.15
cheerful 109.11
gorgeous 1015.20
luminous 1024.30

bean guy 76.5
legume 310.4
trifle 997.5

be angry 105.16

beano treat 95.3
festivity 743.3

beans vegetables 10.34
big chief 87.12

beanstalk 270.8

bear
noun sorehead 110.11
guinea pig 311.23
short 737.12
verb give birth 1.3
endure 134.5
head 161.7
transport 176.12
submit 433.6
suffer 443.10
support 449.12,
900.21
hold 474.7
afford 626.7
manipulate the market
737.25
engender 817.14
cause 885.10
yield 891.13
thrust 901.12
suffice 990.4

bearable 107.13

beard
noun genitals 2.11
whiskers 3.8
type 548.6
verb defy 454.3
brave 492.11

bearded 3.26

bearer
noun mourner 309.7
supporter 900.2
phrase carrier 176.7

bear fruit ripen 407.8
evolve 860.5
bear 891.13

bearing
noun looks 33.4
direction 161.1
behaviour 321.1
yield 472.5
gesture 517.14
meaning 518.1
relevance 774.4
origin 817.4
yielding 891.6
trend 895.2
fulcrum 905.3
ball bearing 914.7
adj born 1.4
yielding 889.10
supporting 900.23
phrase transportation
176.3

bearings location 159.1
orientation 161.4
heraldic device 647.2
state 764.1

bear in mind think of
930.16
take cognizance of
982.9
keep in memory
988.13

bearish irascible 110.19
ursine 311.42
gruff 505.7

bear on operate on
888.6
rest on 900.22
evidence 956.8

bear out support
449.12
confirm 956.11

be arrested 794.3

bear the brunt endure
134.5
have trouble 1010.9

bear with endure 134.5
condone 148.4
be easy on 427.5
suffer 443.10

bear witness 692.6

be as good as 998.11

be ashamed 137.9

be a sign of 133.12

beast animal 144.14,
311.2, 660.7
savage 593.5
carnality 663.2

beastly hoggish 80.24
offensive 98.18
cruel 144.26
animal 311.38
gruff 505.7
carnal 663.6
terrible 999.9

be a success 409.10

be at 221.8

beat

noun staccato 55.1
sphere 231.2
routine 373.6
route 383.1
accent 524.11
rhythm 709.22
tempo 709.24
throb 709.26
metre 720.7
field 724.4
periodicity 849.2
round 849.3
circuit 913.2
pulsation 915.3
flutter 916.4
verb poop 21.6
drum 55.4
sail near the wind
182.25
change course 182.30
best 249.7
foam 320.5
gyp 356.19
hunt 382.9
injure 393.13
defeat 411.5
clobber 412.9
whip 604.12
beat time 708.44
din 848.10
pound 901.16
pulsate 915.12
agitate 916.10
flutter 916.12
stump 970.14
pulverize 1049.9
adj bushed 21.8
clobbered 412.15
unconventional 867.6
licked 970.26

beaten burnt-out 21.10
bubbly 320.6
habitual 373.15
defeated 412.14

beaten up 393.33

beater hunter 382.5
mixer 796.9
agitator 916.9

be a thing of the past
pass 836.6
age 841.9

be at home 430.18

beatific happy 95.15
blissful 97.9

beating
noun staccato 55.1
defeat 412.1
corporal punishment
604.4
hit 901.4
pulsation 915.3
flutter 916.4
pulverization 1049.4
adj staccato 55.7
rhythmic 709.28
pulsative 915.18

beat it split 188.7,
222.10
blow 368.11

beatnik 867.3

beat off 460.10

beat out best 249.7
pulsate 915.12

be attractive 377.6

beat up injure 393.13
rough up 604.14
agitate 916.10
emulsify 1060.10

beat-up beat 21.8
screwed up 393.29
dilapidated 393.33
slovenly 809.15

beau
noun inamorato 104.13
dandy 500.9
verb court 562.21

beautician 1015.13

beauties compilation
554.7
good looks 1015.4

beautiful
noun beauty 1015.1
adj artistic 712.20
beauteous 1015.17

beautifully 1015.23

beautiful people 578.6

beauty harmony 533.2
beautifulness 1015.1
charmer 1015.8

beauty products
1015.12

beauty queen 1015.8

beaux arts 712.1

beaver 3.8

be aware of 982.5

be based on rest on
900.22
depend 958.6

be believed 952.20

be big 978.7

bebop 708.9

be born have birth 1.2
originate 817.13

be bound 641.4

be brief 537.5

be brilliant 919.11

be busy 330.10

becalmed 173.17

be careful 494.5

because 887.10

because of 887.9

because of that 887.7

because of this 887.7

be cautious 339.7,
494.5

be certain believe
952.10
be confident 952.14,
969.9

be changed become
760.12
change 851.6

be cheap 633.5

beck stream 238.1
summons 420.5
gesture 517.14

beckon
noun gesture 517.14
verb attract 377.6
gesture 517.21

be cold 1022.9

become behove 641.4
come to be 760.12
originate 817.13
convert 857.11
be converted into
857.17

become a part of
799.5

become aware of
940.2

become known 351.8

become of 886.4

become one marry
563.15
beautify 1015.15

become popular 578.8

becoming
noun conversion 857.1
adj decorous 496.10
rightful 639.8
decent 664.5
apt 787.10
expedient 994.5
comely 1015.18

be compelled 424.9

be concerned 339.6

be confident have
confidence 952.14
be certain 969.9

be confined 1.3

be consistent agree
787.6
connect 802.7

be consistent with
787.6

be construed as 518.8

be consumed disappear
34.3
be used up 388.4

be content 107.5

be content with 978.7

be converted 692.7

be converted into
become 760.12
be changed 851.6

be convicted 602.4

be convinced think
952.11
be confident 952.14

be correct 972.10

be cross 110.13

be crushed 137.9

bed
noun bottom 199.1,
199.4
furniture 229.1

watercourse 239.2
layer 296.1
accommodations 385.3
presswork 548.9
marriage 563.1
foundation 900.6
sofa 900.19
garden 1067.10
verb rest 20.6
go to bed 22.17
put to bed 22.19
house 225.10
fix 854.9
plant 1067.18
tend 1068.7

bed and breakfast inn
228.15
trading 737.19

bedchamber 197.7

bedclothes 295.10

bedding blanket 295.10
layer 296.1
foundation 900.6
underbed 900.20

be dead 307.27

bedecked clothing 5.44
ornamented 498.11

be dependent on 958.6

be determined be
resolved 359.8
endeavour 403.5

bedevilled tormented
96.24
possessed 925.29

be difficult 1012.10

bed in 191.5

be disappointed not
realize one's
expectations 132.4
neglect 408.2

be disposed 895.3

be divided 362.7

bedlam noise 53.3
pandemonium 809.5
insane asylum 925.14

bed linen 295.10

be doing 724.11

bed on 199.6

be done for 395.23

Bedouin 178.4

bedraggled soiled
80.21
slovenly 809.15

bedridden 85.58

bedrock
noun bottom 199.1
base 274.4
rock 854.6, 1057.1
foundation 900.6
adj bottom 199.7
deepest 275.15
vital 996.23

bedroom
noun boudoir 197.7
verb restrict 428.9

be drunk 88.27

bedsit 228.13

bedspread 295.10

bedtime sleep 22.2
night 315.4

be due 639.4

be due to 886.5

be dying 307.26

bee 311.33

beef
noun bœuf 10.13
muscularity 15.2
power 18.1
kick 115.5
cattle 311.6
bone of contention
456.7
verb bitch 108.6,
115.16

beefed-up increased
251.7
expanded 259.10

be effective 888.7

beef up strengthen
15.13
intensify 251.5
add to 253.5

beefy 257.18

Beehive 1070.8

beehive nest 228.25
hive 739.2

beekeeping 1068.1

be employed 724.12

be engaged affiance
436.6
ill-time 843.3

be entitled to 639.4

beep
noun blare 53.5
verb blare 53.10

beer 88.16

beery 88.31

beeswax 1054.8

beetle
noun insect 311.31
pulper 1061.4
verb overhang 202.7
adj overhanging
202.11

be exposed 31.5

be exposed to 830.8

be fair 649.6

befall occur 830.5
chance 971.11

be featured 996.12

befitting apt 787.10
timely 842.9
expedient 994.5

be foolish 922.6

before
adv in front 165.4
ahead 216.12
preferably 371.28
above 813.6
previously 833.6
formerly 836.13

sock 901.5
punch 901.6
verb encircle 209.7
whip 604.12
bind 799.9
bat 901.15
belted 209.11
belt in 209.7
belting 604.4
be lucky 1009.11
belvedere 89.4
be made up of 795.3
be met with be present
221.6
exist 760.8
occur 830.5
be misled 974.10
be mistaken misbelieve
688.8
be wrong 974.10
bemoaning
noun lamentation
115.1
adj lamenting 115.18
be moved 93.11
bemused intoxicated
88.31
abstracted 984.11
ben 272.4
bench fitness 84.1
plateau 272.4
combe 284.8
saddle 417.10
council 423.1
deputy 576.1
seat of justice 595.5
team 617.7
workplace 739.1
ice hockey team 750.5
substitute 861.2
table 900.15
bencher 596.1
bend
noun obeisance 155.2
deviation 164.1
bias 204.3
diagonal 204.7
angle 278.2
bending 279.3
heraldic device 647.2
athletics 755.1
crouch 912.3
verb bow 155.6, 912.9
direct 161.5
deviate 164.3
deflect 164.5
oblique 204.9
distort 265.5
angle 278.5
curve 279.6
conquer 412.10
subdue 432.9
bow down 433.10
bind 799.9
conform 866.3
influence 893.7
crouch 912.8
prejudice 979.9

yield 1045.7
bender 88.6
bending
noun deflection 164.2
bend 279.3
deliberate falsehood
354.9
adj pliant 1045.9
bends 1073.10
bend to bow down
433.10
tend 895.3
beneath below 274.11
under 432.17
be necessary 962.10
benedict 563.7
benefactor helper
449.7
benefactress 592.1
beneficent benevolent
143.15
favourable 449.22
beneficial healthful
81.5
useful 387.18
helpful 449.21
good 998.12
beneficiary proprietor
470.2
allottee 479.4
benefice-holder 699.7
benefit
noun act of kindness
143.7
use 387.4
aid 449.1
estate 471.4
benefaction 478.7
theatrical performance
704.12
good 998.4
verb do a favour
143.12
avail 387.17
aid 449.11, 592.3
expedite one's affair
994.3
do good 998.10
benefit from 387.15
benefitting 592.4
benevolence
auspiciousness 133.9
benevolentness 143.4
act of kindness 143.7
pity 145.1
forgiveness 148.1
compliance 427.2
benefit 478.7
magnanimity 652.2
goodness 998.1
benevolent charitable
143.15
forgiving 148.6
indulgent 427.8
favourable 449.22
magnanimous 652.6
good 998.12
be nice 321.5

benighted blind 30.9
night-overtaken
315.10
dark 929.16
benign healthful 81.5
auspicious 133.18
kind 143.13
indulgent 427.8
favourable 449.22
harmless 998.21
benignly 143.18
be no more be dead
307.27
perish 395.23
come to an end 819.6
bent
noun inclination 100.3
direction 161.1
bias 204.3
preference 371.5
aptitude 413.5
tendency 895.1
disposition 977.3
prejudice 979.3
adj high 87.23
fuddled 88.33
distorted 265.10
angular 278.6
curved 279.7
disposed 977.8
bent on determined
upon 359.16
disposed 977.8
benz 87.3
be obliged be grateful
150.3
be necessary 962.10
be obvious 521.4
be off depart 188.6
set out 188.8
race 757.5
be of use 387.17
be OK suit 787.8
be right 972.10
be on use 87.21
strike a bargain 731.18
be on hand 221.8
be on the cards 967.4
be on the safe side
1006.2
be open to 324.3
be optimistic 124.9
be packed 769.16
be paid 624.20
be patient 134.4
be persuaded persuade
oneself 375.24
consent 441.2
acquiesce 441.3
think 952.11
be pleased feel happy
95.11
be content 107.5
be pleased with 95.12
be poor 619.5
be possible 965.4

be precise 972.11
be pregnant 78.12
be prepared 405.14
be present 760.8
be present at 221.8
be present in 760.11
be profitable 472.13
be proud 136.4
be proud of 136.5
be punished 604.19
bequest bequeathal
478.10
inheritance 479.2
berate 510.19
berating 510.7
be ready be willing
324.3
be prepared 405.14
be ready for 130.6
be realized 830.5
be reasonable have all
one's wits about one
919.10
be logical 934.17
bereaved bereft 307.35,
473.8
indigent 619.8
bereavement loss
473.1
deprivation 480.6
be reborn 857.12
be received arrive
186.6
come in 479.8
find credence 952.20
be recognized gain
recognition 662.11
gain influence 893.12
be reflected 54.7
bereft bereaved 307.35,
473.8
indigent 619.8
bereft of 991.13
be regarded 945.15
be relaxed 121.8
be released 430.18
be relieved 120.8
be remembered
988.14
be renewed 851.6
be resolved 359.8
be responsible for
commit 436.5
direct 573.8
answer for 641.6
operate 888.5
incur 896.4
be revealed show 31.4
become known 351.8
berg plateau 272.4
ice 1022.5
be rid of 908.13

be right be correct
972.10
expedite one's affair
994.3
Berlin wall 211.5
berry 310.29
berserk frenzied 105.25
rabid 925.30
berth
noun anchor 180.16
quarters 228.4
position 724.5
harbour 1008.6
verb inhabit 225.7
house 225.10
be ruined 625.7
be safe 1006.2
be satisfied 952.14
be seated sit 173.10
sit down 912.10
be seen 31.4
be sensitive to 24.6
be sent back 54.7
beset
verb annoy 96.13
worry 126.5
enclose 212.5
persecute 389.7
importune 440.12
besiege 459.19
infest 909.6
obsess 925.25
trouble 1012.13
adj distressed 96.22
tormented 96.24
worried 126.8
enclosed 212.10
infested 909.11
troubled 1012.20
besetting prevalent
863.12
troublesome 1012.18
be short 737.23
be sick 908.26
beside
adj side 218.6
adv in juxtaposition
223.21
additionally 253.11
prep alongside 218.11
excluding 772.10
compared to 942.11
besides
adv additionally
253.11
prep excluding 772.10
beside the point
adj irrelevant 775.7
adv amiss 910.7
besieged 212.10
besieging 212.1
be single 565.5
be sold 734.12
be somebody be
something 662.10
matter 996.12

be something be
somebody 662.10
matter 996.12

besotted intoxicated
88.31
foolish 922.8
obsessed 925.33

be spared 306.10

bespectacled 29.11

be spent 626.6

bespoke tailored 5.47
made 891.18

best
noun creature comforts
121.3
top of the line 249.5
very best 998.8
verb excel 249.6
beat 249.7
defeat 411.5, 412.6
adj superlative 249.13
reduced 633.9
very best 998.16

best bet 971.8

best ever 998.8

best friend friend
588.1
good friend 588.2

bestial cruel 144.26
animal 311.38
unrefined 497.12
carnal 663.6
savage 671.21

be still keep quiet
173.7
do nothing 329.2

best-known 662.16

best man wedding
party 563.4
assistant 616.6

bestow spend 387.13
give 478.12
administer 643.6

bestowed 478.24

best part 791.6

best people best 249.5
society 578.6

best-quality 249.13

be strong 15.9

best seller great success
409.3
book 554.1

be stupid not have all
one's marbles 921.12
be foolish 922.6

best wishes
congratulation 149.1
regards 504.8
greetings 585.3

be subjected to 830.8

be successful 409.7

bet
noun gamble 759.2
flutter 759.3
poker 759.10
verb wager 759.25

predict 961.9
risk 971.12

be taken as 517.18

be taken in 953.6

be taught 570.11

be thankful 150.3

be that as it may
338.8

be the case exist 760.8
be true 972.8

be the cause of 885.10

be there have place
159.9
be present 221.6
exist 760.8

be thought of 945.15

be threatened 1005.8

betide occur 830.5
chance 971.11

be told 551.15

bet on 961.9

be too much for defeat
412.6
outwit 415.11
trouble 1012.13

be tough 1047.3

betray inform 351.6
deceive 356.14
defect 370.6
double-cross 645.14
seduce 665.20

betrayal divulgence
351.2
apostasy 363.2
desertion 370.2
betrayment 645.8
seduction 665.6

betrayed 132.5

betraying disclosive
351.10
traitorous 645.22

betrothed
noun fiancé 104.17
adj promised 436.8

be true 972.8

be truthful 972.8

better
noun gambler 759.21
verb excel 249.6
improve 392.9
change 851.7
adj superior 249.12
preferable 371.25
better off 392.14
changed 851.10

bettered 392.13

better for 392.14

betterment
improvement 392.1
change 851.1

better off 392.14

better part 791.6

better place 838.2

better than nothing
998.20

betting statistics 757.4
gambling 759.1

betting shop 759.19

between 213.12

between the lines
519.5

between us 345.14

be unwilling 325.3,
442.3

be up for 324.3

be up to 18.11

be used to 373.12

be useful 449.17

be useless 391.8

bevel
noun incline 204.4
goniometer 278.4
type 548.6
adj inclining 204.15

beverage drink 8.4,
10.47
spirits 88.13
fluid 1059.2

be vigilant keep awake
23.3
be watchful 339.8
be curious 980.3

be visible 31.4

bevy company 769.3
flock 769.6
multitude 883.3

beware 494.7

be warm 940.6

bewildered wondering
122.9
dismayed 970.24
at an impasse 1012.24

bewildering wonderful
122.10
confusing 970.27

bewilderment wonder
122.1
disconcertion 970.3
confusion 984.3

be willing be game
324.3
consent 441.2

be wise to 940.8

bewitched enamoured
104.28
wondering 122.9
witched 691.13
miraculous 869.16

bewitching delightful
97.7
alluring 377.8
witching 691.11

be wrong misbelieve
688.8
mistake oneself 974.10

beyond
noun destiny 838.2
adv additionally
253.11
prep past 261.21,
522.26

after 834.8
in excess of 992.26

beyond belief absurd
922.11
unbelievable 954.10

beyond the pale
prohibited 444.7
unpraiseworthy 510.24
segregated 772.8
unusual 869.10

Bias 920.4

bias
noun inclination 100.3
deviation 164.1
bend 204.3
diagonal 204.7
preference 371.5
partiality 650.3
tendency 895.1
disposition 977.3
prejudice 979.3
verb deflect 164.5
oblique 204.9
pervert 265.6
influence 893.7
tend 895.3
prejudice 979.9
adj inclining 204.15
transverse 204.19
adv diagonally 204.25

biased inclining 204.15
transverse 204.19
falsified 265.11
partial 650.11
discriminatory 979.12

bib
noun apron 5.17
verb drink 8.29
tipple 88.24

Bible scripture 683.1
Holy Bible 683.2

bible 554.1

Biblical 683.10

bibliography makeup
554.12
bibliology 554.19
index 558.4
directory 574.10
catalogue 870.3
lore 927.9

bicentenary
anniversary 849.4
hundred 881.8

biceps member 2.7
arm 905.5

bickering
noun dissension 456.3
contention 457.1
argumentation 934.4
quibbling 935.5
flicker 1024.8
adj partisan 456.17
fluttering 916.18
quibbling 935.14
flickering 1024.36

bicycle
noun cycle 179.8
verb exercise 84.4

ride 177.33

bicycling riding 177.6
sport 744.1

bid
noun attempt 403.2
offer 439.1
entreaty 440.2
bridge 758.3
verb command 420.8
bid for 439.6
bargain 731.17
make a bid 733.9

bidder petitioner 440.7
bridge 758.3

bidding command
420.1
summons 420.5
invitation 440.4

biddy gal 77.6
hen 77.9
poultry 311.29

bide await 130.8
endure 134.5, 826.6
be still 173.7
wait 845.12
remain 852.5
continue 855.3

bid for try for 403.9
bid 439.6
solicit 440.14
bargain 731.17

bid in 733.9

biennial
noun plant 310.3
anniversary 849.4
adj momentary 849.8

big arrogant 141.9
large 257.16
adult 303.12
inflated 502.12
magnanimous 652.6
eminent 662.18
important 996.17

Big Ben 831.6

big boy 996.9

Big Brother 612.10

big bucks 618.3

big business 731.1

big cat jungle cat
311.22
big shot 996.9

big deal 997.26

big fish 996.9

big game animal life
311.1
quarry 382.7

big gun 996.9

big head 140.4

big house 429.9

bight inlet 242.1
angle 278.2

big idea reason 885.2
main idea 931.4

big man 996.9

big money
noun bomb 618.3

adj expensive 632.11

big mouth braggart
502.5
talkativeness 540.1

big name celebrity
662.9
personage 996.8

bigot
noun hater 103.4
mule 361.6
dogmatist 687.6,
969.7
intolerant 979.5
adj narrow-minded
979.10

bigoted obstinate 361.8
strict 687.8
fanatic 925.32
dogmatic 969.22
narrow-minded 979.10

bigotry hate 103.1
obstinacy 361.1
strictness 687.5
fanaticism 925.11
dogmatism 969.6
narrow-mindedness
979.1

big screen 706.1

big stick coercion
424.3
foreign policy 609.5
despotism 612.10

big top 295.8

bigwigs 249.5

bijou 498.6

bike 179.8

biker 178.11

biking 177.6

bikini 5.29

bilateral sided 218.7
two 872.6

bile digestion 2.15, 7.8
ill humour 110.1
bitterness 152.3

bilge
noun offal 80.9
bulge 283.3
bullshit 520.3
verb bulge 283.11

bilious anaemic 85.60
sour 110.23

bill
noun point 283.9
poster 352.7
advertising matter
352.8
declaration 598.8
private member's bill
613.8
debt 623.1
fee 624.5
statement 628.3,
870.5
law 673.3
theatrical performance
704.12
paper money 728.5

schedule 964.3
eyeshade 1027.2
verb publicize 352.15
send a statement
628.11
dramatize 704.28
schedule 964.6

billboard 352.7

billed hooked 279.8
scheduled 964.9

billet
noun letter 553.2
heraldic device 647.2
position 724.5
wood 1052.3
verb house 225.10

billeted 225.14

billiards 752.1

billion
noun large sum 618.2
thousand million
881.12
myriad 883.4
large number 1016.5
adj numerous 883.6

bill of health pass
443.7
certificate 549.6

Bill of Rights right
430.2
constitution 673.6

billowing curved 279.7
wavy 281.10
bulging 283.15

bills 623.1

billy 76.8

bimbo hunk 15.7
blockhead 923.4

bin 386.6

bind
noun predicament
1012.4
verb border 211.10
stop 293.7
compel 424.4
restrain 428.10
commit 436.5
indenture 615.18
obligate 641.12
relate 774.6
tie 799.9
stick together 802.9

binder dressing 86.33
wrapper 295.18
payment 624.1

binding
noun edging 211.7
wrapper 295.18
bookbinding 554.14
fastening 799.3
cohesion 802.1
adj preceptive 419.4
mandatory 420.12
obligatory 424.11,
641.15
joining 799.16
valid 972.14

binge 88.6

bingo 759.15

binoculars 29.4

biochemical
noun element 1058.2
adj chemical 1058.8

biodegradable
degradable 393.47
disintegrative 805.5

biographer 719.4

biographical 719.7

biography
noun history 719.1
verb chronicle 719.5

biological organic
305.17
related 559.6
biologic 1066.3

biological weapons
462.1

biologist 1066.2

biology organic matter
305.1
animal life 311.1
biological science
1066.1

bionic strong 15.15
powerful 18.12
hale 83.12

biopsy 91.12

biosphere organic
matter 305.1
ecosphere 306.6
atmosphere 317.2
Earth 1070.10
environment 1071.1

birch
noun rod 605.2
verb whip 604.12

bird fowl 10.21, 311.28
guy 76.5
gal 77.6, 302.7
boo 508.3
freak 926.4
rocket 1072.3

birdie
noun round 748.3
verb play 748.4

birdies 50.13

bird's-eye 771.7

birds of a feather
783.5

birth
noun genesis 1.1
generation 78.6
life 306.1
lineage 560.4
heredity 560.6
aristocracy 607.3
nobility 608.2
origin 817.4
verb engender 817.14
adj related 559.6

birth certificate 549.6

birth control 890.1

birthday 849.4

birthing birth 1.1

origin 817.4
bearing 891.6

birthplace fatherland
232.2
breeding place 885.8

birth rate 78.1

birthright inheritance
479.2
prerogative 642.1

bis
noun repeat 848.5
adv again 848.17,
873.7

biscuit sinker 10.29
cookie 10.41
ceramic ware 742.2
desert 1064.2

bisexual
noun homosexual
75.14
adj homosexual 75.29
bipartite 874.7

bisexuality sexuality
75.2
sexual preference
75.10

bishop deacon 699.9
chessman 743.17

bison 311.6

bistro restaurant 8.17
bar 88.20

bit
noun short distance
223.2
modicum 248.2
point 285.3
portion 477.5
information technology
551.7
role 704.10
script 706.2
piece 792.3
shift 824.3
pittance 991.5
trifle 997.5
curb 1011.7
binary digit 1041.14
adv to a degree 245.7
scarcely 248.9

bit by bit by degrees
245.6
piece by piece 792.9

bitch
noun gal 77.6
hen 77.9
shrew 110.12
beef 115.5
dog 311.17
strumpet 665.14
dandy 998.7
tough proposition
1012.2
verb beef 108.6,
115.16

bitching
noun beef 115.5
adj grouchy 108.8,
115.20

bitchy crabby 110.20
peevish 110.22
spiteful 144.21

bite
noun morsel 8.2
bite 8.2
light meal 8.7
acrimony 17.5
pang 26.2
sip 62.2
zest 68.2
modicum 248.2
minutia 258.7
hold 474.2
vigour 544.3
round 748.3
piece 792.3
cold 1022.1
verb chew 8.27
pain 26.7
nip 68.5
hold 474.6
etch 713.10
kid oneself 953.6
freeze 1022.10

biting acrimonious
17.14
painful 26.10
pungent 68.6
penetrating 105.31
caustic 144.23
witty 489.15
vigorous 544.11
cold 1022.14

bit much 992.16

bit part 704.10

bitter
noun beer 88.16
verb sour 110.16
adj acrimonious 17.14
flavoured 62.9
pungent 68.6
unpleasant 98.17
distressing 98.20
sour 110.23
caustic 144.23
resentful 152.26
hostile 589.10
cold 1022.14

bitter end 819.2

bitterly caustically
144.32
distressingly 247.21

bitterness acrimony
17.5
taste 62.1
acridness 64.2
pungency 68.1
wretchedness 96.6
distressfulness 98.5
enmity 103.2
regret 113.1
causticity 144.8
bitter resentment
152.3
animosity 589.4
cold 1022.1

bitter pill acridness
64.2

affliction 96.8

bittersweet flavoured
62.9
sweet 66.4
ambiguous 539.4

bitter taste 64.2

bivouac
noun camp 228.29
campground 463.3
verb settle 159.17
camp 225.11

bizarre awesome
122.11
humorous 488.4
freakish 869.13
absurd 922.11
fanciful 985.20

bizarrely awesomely
122.15
humorously 488.7

black
noun blackness 38.1
mourning 115.7
Caucasian 312.3
table 752.2
verb blacken 38.7
soil 80.16
object 333.5
strike 727.10
darken 1026.9
adj dark-skinned
38.10
sullen 110.24
gloomy 112.24
ominous 133.17
wicked 654.16
bad 999.7
disastrous 1010.15
dark 1026.13

black and blue 38.12

black and white
opposites 215.2
drawing 712.5, 712.13
lighting 1024.19

black-and-white 706.4

Black Berets 461.14

black cat 133.6

Black Country 231.7

blacken cook 11.4
black 38.7
soil 80.16
berate 510.19
vilify 512.10
stigmatize 661.9
stain 1003.6
darken 1026.9

blackened cooked 11.6
stained 1003.10

black eye trauma 85.37
stigma 661.6

black flag flag 647.6
race 756.3

black hole prison 429.8
star 1070.8

black humour 489.1

blackjack coerce 424.7
club 901.20

blacklist
noun ostracism 586.3
list 870.1
verb reject 372.2
ostracize 586.6
condemn 602.3

black magic Satanism
680.14
black art 690.2

blackmail
noun demand 421.1
extortion 480.8
booty 482.11
fee 624.5
verb demand 421.5
wrest 480.22

blackmailer 480.12

black market 732.1

black-market
verb push 732.7
adj illegal 674.6

blackness nigritude
38.1
Caucasian 312.3
night 315.4
darkness 1026.1

black out faint 25.5
grey out 184.46
cover up 345.8
darken 1026.9

blackout
unconsciousness 25.2
disappearance 34.1
greyout 184.21
veil of secrecy 345.3
loss of memory 989.2
dimout 1026.7
power failure 1031.19
cosmic particles
1073.10

Black Power 18.1

black pudding 10.20

black sheep reprobate
660.5
intruder 773.2

blacksmith smith
726.8
stockman 1068.2

black spot 1034.5

blackwater 85.40

bladder bag 195.2
sphere 282.2
bubble 320.1
comedy 704.6

blade sledge 179.20
leaf 310.17
combatant 461.1
sword 462.5
dandy 500.9
cutlery 1039.2

blag
noun job 482.4
verb swipe 482.16

blah apathetic 94.13
tedious 118.9

blame
noun censure 510.3

accusation 599.1
attribution 887.1
verb censure 510.13
attribute to 887.4

blamed 599.15

blame for 887.4

blameless honest
644.13
innocent 657.6

blanch cook 11.4
suffer 26.8
decolour 36.5
lose colour 36.6
whiten 37.5
change colour 105.19

blanched bleached 36.8
terrified 127.26
weatherworn 393.34

blanching decoloration
36.3
whitening 37.3

Blanco
noun whitening agent
37.4
verb whitewash 37.6

bland wishy-washy
16.17
insipid 65.2
vacant 222.14
suave 504.18
flattering 511.8
moderate 670.10
general 863.11

blandishments 562.5

blandness insipidness
65.1
suavity 504.5

blank
noun absence 222.1
void 222.3
document 549.5
adj dull 117.6
vacant 222.14
closed 293.9
reticent 344.10
unadorned 499.8
inexpressive 522.20
empty-headed 921.19
thoughtless 932.4

blanket
noun coverlet 295.10
coating 295.12
verb cover 295.19
conceal 346.6
adj comprehensive
771.7
undiscriminating
944.5

blankly absently 222.16
expressionlessly
522.25

blaring
noun reception
1033.21
adj noisy 53.13

blasphemous cursing
513.8
impious 694.6

blasphemy curse 513.1
sacrilege 694.2

blast
noun noise 53.3
blare 53.5
detonation 56.3
kick 105.3
gust 318.6
smash 409.4
charge 462.16
bash 582.12
explosion 671.7
blight 1000.2
verb din 53.7
blare 53.10
detonate 56.8
waste 308.13
blow 318.20
blow up 395.18
pull the trigger 459.22
curse 513.5
explode 671.14
thwart 1011.15
freeze 1023.11

blasted high 87.23
disappointed 132.5
blighted 393.42
ruined 395.28
confounded 513.10

blasting
noun reception
1033.21
adj banging 56.11

blatant noisy 53.13
vociferous 59.10
howling 60.6
conspicuous 348.12
gaudy 501.20

blatantly distressingly
247.21
conspicuously 348.16
gaudily 501.27

blaze
noun outburst 105.9
notch 289.1
pointer 517.4
mark 517.5
fire 1018.13
flare 1018.14
brightness 1024.4
flash 1024.6
verb notch 289.4
proclaim 352.13
mark 517.19
burn 1018.22,
1019.24
catch fire 1019.23
shine 1024.23

blazed 289.5

blazing
noun burning 1019.5
adj burning 1018.27
flashing 1024.34
illuminated 1024.39

bleach
noun decoloration 36.3
bleacher 36.4
verb decolour 36.5
lose colour 36.6

whiten 37.5
clean 79.18

bleached decoloured
36.8
clean 79.25
vacant 222.14
weatherworn 393.34

bleaching decoloration
36.3
whitening 37.3

bleak distressing 98.20
gloomy 112.24
hopeless 125.12
windblown 318.24
cold 1022.14

bleakly 112.31

bleakness
distressfulness 98.5
gloom 112.7
vacancy 222.2
cold 1022.1

bleary 32.6

bleary-eyed 28.13

bleed haemorrhage
12.17
let blood 91.27
suffer 96.19
grieve 112.17
pity 145.3
exude 190.15
draw off 192.12
exploit 387.16
take from 480.21
strip 480.24
overprice 632.7

bleeding
noun haemorrhage
12.8
decoloration 36.3
anaemia 85.9
bloodletting 91.20
drawing 192.3
adj bloody 12.23
pained 96.23
pitying 145.7
cursed 513.9

blemish
noun mark 517.5
intruder 773.2
fault 1002.2
disfigurement 1003.1
eyesore 1014.4
verb deform 265.7
injure 393.13
mark 517.19
disfigure 1003.4
offend 1014.5

blend
noun hybrid word
526.11
motor racing 756.1
compound 796.5
combination 804.1
verb harmonize 708.35
identify 777.5
mix 796.10
combine 804.3

blended harmonious
708.49

mixed 796.14
combined 804.5

blender mixer 796.9
agitator 916.9

blend in 708.35

blending
noun identification
777.2
mixture 796.1
combination 804.1
pulping 1061.3
adj harmonious 708.49
combining 804.7

bless gladden 95.8
congratulate 149.2
thank 150.4
approve 509.9
praise 509.12
sanctify 685.5
glorify 696.11
give one's blessing
696.13
protect 1007.18

blessed happy 95.15
confounded 513.10
heavenly 681.12
sanctified 685.8
fortunate 1009.14

blessed with 469.9

blessing
noun act of kindness
143.7
congratulation 149.1
consent 441.1
godsend 472.7
benefit 478.7
approval 509.1
sanctification 685.3
benediction 696.5
good 998.4
stroke of luck 1009.3
adj worshipful 696.15

blight
noun disease 85.1
evil 999.3
blast 1000.2
adversity 1010.1
verb spoil 393.10
work evil 999.6
freeze 1023.11

blighted disappointed
132.5
blasted 393.42
ruined 395.28

Blighty 232.3

blind
noun sightless 30.4
trick 356.1
pretext 376.1
stratagem 415.3
round 748.3
shade 1027.1
verb blind the eyes
30.7
accelerate 174.10
conceal 346.6
hoodwink 356.17
shine 1024.23
adj insensible 25.6

poor-sighted 28.11
sightless 30.9
high 87.23
fuddled 88.33
closed 293.9
concealed 346.11
unpersuadable 361.13
obscure 522.15
undiscerning 921.14
involuntary 962.14
oblivious 983.7

blinded excecate 30.10
undiscerning 921.14

blind faith 953.1

blindfold
noun eye patch 30.5
verb blind 30.7
hoodwink 356.17
adj blinded 30.10
undiscerning 921.14

blindfolded blinded
30.10
undiscerning 921.14

blinding
noun blindness 30.1
adj obscuring 30.11
garish 35.19
rainy 316.10
bright 1024.32

blindly foolishly 922.13
involuntarily 962.18

blind man 30.4

blindness insensibility
25.1
faulty eyesight 28.1
sightlessness 30.1
carelessness 340.2
unpersuadableness
361.5
unperceptiveness
921.2
incognizance 929.3

blinds 30.5

blind side blindness
30.1
narrow-mindedness
979.1

blind to insensible
94.10
unaware 929.13

blink
noun glance 27.4
glitter 1024.7
verb wink 28.10
flinch 127.13
slight 340.8
glitter 1024.24

blinkered poor-sighted
28.11
blinded 30.10

blinkers spectacles 29.3
blindfold 30.5
narrow-mindedness
979.1

blinking
noun winking 28.7
glitter 1024.7
adj poor-sighted 28.11

glittering 1024.35
flickering 1024.36

blip 850.1

bliss happiness 95.2
pleasantness 97.1
harmony 681.5

blissful happy 95.15
pleasant 97.6
beatific 97.9

blissfully happily 95.18
pleasantly 97.12

blister
noun sore 85.36
bulge 283.3
bubble 320.1
blemish 1003.1
verb attack 510.20
burn 1019.24

blistered bubbly 320.6
burned 1019.30

blistering
noun burning 1019.5
adj bubbly 320.6
hot 1018.25

blithe 109.11

blithely 109.17

blitz
noun attack 459.1
verb blow up 395.18
attack 459.14
pull the trigger 459.22

blitzkrieg 459.1

blizzard windstorm
318.12
snow 1022.8

bloated puffed up
136.10
increased 251.7
corpulent 257.18
distended 259.13
deformed 265.12
bulging 283.15
pompous 501.22
overfull 992.20

bloating increase 251.1
distension 259.2
overextension 992.7

blob sphere 282.2
bulge 283.3

bloc 617.1

block
noun suppression
92.24
boundary 211.3
plot 231.4
lump 257.10
obstruction 293.3
printing surface 548.8
capital punishment
604.6
scaffold 605.5
print 713.5
auction 734.4
share 738.3
delay 845.2
blocking 989.3
obstacle 1011.4
solid 1043.6

verb stop 293.7,
1011.13
cover 295.19
fend off 460.10
play 747.4, 751.4
fight 754.4
delay 845.8
put a stop to 856.11
obstruct 1011.12

blockade
noun enclosure 212.1
closure 293.1
obstruction 293.3
siege 459.5
exclusion 772.1
obstacle 1011.4
verb enclose 212.5
stop 293.7
besiege 459.19
fortify 460.9
exclude 772.4
obstruct 1011.12

blockaded enclosed
212.10
excluded 772.7

blockading enclosure
212.1
siege 459.5

blockage seizure 85.6
suppression 92.24
obstruction 293.3
delay 845.2
hindrance 1011.1

blockbuster surprise
131.2
bomb 462.20

blocked stopped 293.11
late 845.16
forgetful 989.9

blocking disappearance
34.1
suppression 92.24
covering 295.1
production 704.13
fight 754.3
itemization 800.2
block 989.3
hindrance 1011.1

block of flats 228.14

block out form 262.7
itemize 800.7

blocks 743.16

block vote vote 371.6
voting 609.18

blond
noun brunette 35.9
adj flaxen-haired 37.9
yellow-haired 43.5

blonde 35.9

blood
noun whole blood 2.23
life force 306.3
killing 308.1
dandy 500.9
blood relationship
559.1
kinfolk 559.2
race 559.4

lineage 560.4
posterity 561.1
person of fashion
578.7
nobility 608.2
class 808.2
kind 808.3
fluid 1059.2
adj circulatory 2.31

bloodbath carnage
308.4
destruction 395.1

blood clot 1043.7

bloodied 96.25

bloodless weak 16.12
colourless 36.7
dull 117.6
pacific 464.9

blood pressure 2.23

blood-red 41.7

bloodshed killing 308.1
war 458.1

bloodstained 1003.11

bloodstream 2.23

blood test 91.12

bloodthirsty cruel
144.26
murderous 308.23
warlike 458.21

blood transfusion
91.18

blood vessel 2.21

bloody
verb bleed 12.17
torture 96.18
injure 393.13
bloodstain 1003.7
adj circulatory 2.31
bleeding 12.23
sanguine 41.7
cruel 144.26
murderous 308.23
warlike 458.21
cursed 513.9
savage 671.21
bloodstained 1003.11

bloody-minded
malevolent 144.19
cruel 144.26
murderous 308.23
perverse 361.11
oppositional 451.8
warlike 458.21
dilatory 845.17
hindering 1011.17

bloom
noun reddening 41.3
health 83.1
youth 301.1
flower 310.22
flowering 310.24
beauty 1015.1
glow 1018.12
picture 1034.5
verb enjoy good health
83.6
mature 303.9
flower 310.32

ripen 407.8
evolve 860.5
thrive 1009.8
look good 1015.16
burn 1018.22

blooming
noun maturation 303.6
flowering 310.24
adj grown 14.3,
259.12
red-complexioned
41.9
fresh 83.13
young 301.9
floral 310.35
ripe 407.13
productive 889.9
thriving 1009.13
gorgeous 1015.20

blossom
noun flower 310.22
flowering 310.24
verb grow 14.2, 259.7
mature 303.9
flower 310.32
ripen 407.8
evolve 860.5
thrive 1009.8

blossoming
noun maturation 303.6
flowering 310.24
evolution 860.1
adj grown 14.3,
259.12
increasing 251.8
floral 310.35
thriving 1009.13

blot
noun soil 80.5
obliteration 395.7
stigma 661.6
intruder 773.2
stain 1003.3
eyesore 1014.4
verb blacken 38.7
absorb 187.13
obliterate 395.16
stigmatize 661.9
spot 1003.5
offend 1014.5
dry 1064.6

blotchy dingy 38.11
spotted 47.13, 1003.9

blot out waste 308.13
obliterate 395.16
darken 1026.9

blotted forgiven 148.7
ugly 1014.6

blotter acid 87.9
sorption 187.6
notebook 549.11

blotting
noun sorption 187.6
obliteration 395.7
adj sorbent 187.17

blouse 5.15

blow
noun basuco 87.6
Acapulco gold 87.10

pain 96.5
surprise 131.2
disappointment 132.1
flower 310.22
flowering 310.24
gust 318.6
windstorm 318.12
act 328.3
slap 604.3
fight 754.3
hit 901.4
punch 901.6
misfortune 1010.2
verb burn out 21.5
blare 53.10
use 87.21
flower 310.32
waft 318.20
beat it 368.11
ripen 407.8
cock up 414.12
squander 486.3
blow a horn 708.42
evacuate 908.22
let out 908.24
make a boo-boo
974.15

blow away 308.13
blow-dry 1064.6
blower ventilator 317.9
bellows 318.18
fan 318.19
blow in 186.6
blow-in 773.4
blowing 310.24
blowing up
intensification 251.2
distension 259.2
exaggeration 355.1
blow it cock up 414.12
talk out of turn 843.4
make a boo-boo
974.15
blown windblown
318.24
tainted 393.41
blighted 393.42
blown up 259.13
blow out run out
190.13
explode 671.14
evacuate 908.22
disgorge 908.25
fight fire 1021.7
blow up excite 105.12
work oneself up
105.17
enlarge 259.4
strike dead 308.17
blow 318.20
misrepresent 350.3
blast 395.18
come to nothing
410.13
explode 671.14
process 714.15
disprove 957.4
bludgeon
noun coercion 424.3

verb intimidate 127.20
coerce 424.7
threaten 514.2
bludgeoning 514.3
blue
noun blueness 45.1
table 752.2
goof 974.6
heavens 1070.2
verb azure 45.2
adj bluish 45.3
melancholy 112.23
deathly 307.29
obscene 666.9
blue-chip 998.15
blue collar 607.10
blue-green 44.4
blue peter 517.15
blueprint
noun representation
349.1
plan 381.1
diagram 381.3
proof 548.5
print 714.5
outline 800.4
schedule 964.3
verb plot 381.10
process 714.15
blue riband award
646.2
decoration 646.5
blues sulks 110.10
folk music 708.11
blue sky 1070.2
blue water 240.1
blue-water 275.14
bluff
noun precipice 200.3
slope 237.2
sham 354.3
trick 356.6
impostor 357.6
bluster 503.1
blusterer 503.2
verb sham 354.21
deceive 356.14
bluster 503.3
adj impudent 142.10
steep 204.18
blunt 286.3
artless 416.5
gruff 505.7
candid 644.17
bluffing sham 354.3
deception 356.1
bluish 45.3
blunder
noun bungle 414.5
folly 922.4
faux pas 974.5
verb miss 410.14
bungle 414.11
flounder 916.15
make a blunder
974.14
blundering
noun bungling 414.4

adj bungling 414.20
blunt
verb weaken 16.10
deaden 25.4
dull 94.7, 286.2
disincline 379.4
moderate 670.6
adj unfeeling 94.9
dull 286.3, 921.16
artless 416.5
free-acting 430.23
gruff 505.7
candid 644.17
blunted 286.3
bluntly gruffly 505.9
candidly 644.23
blur
noun
inconspicuousness
32.2
stigma 661.6
stain 1003.3
verb dim 32.4
deform 263.3
confound 944.3
stain 1003.6
blurb 352.4
blurred inconspicuous
32.6
inarticulate 525.12
vague 970.19
blurred vision 28.1
blurry inconspicuous
32.6
vague 970.19
blush
noun warmth 35.2
reddening 41.3
blushing 139.5
glow 1018.12
verb redden 41.5
change colour 105.19
flush 139.8
be guilty 656.2
blushing
noun reddening 41.3
flushing 139.5
adj reddening 41.11
humiliated 137.14
blushful 139.13
luminous 1024.30
bluster
noun boasting 502.1
blustering 503.1
turbulence 671.2
agitation 916.1
verb intimidate 127.20
burn 152.15
blow 318.20
boast 502.6
hector 503.3
blustery windy 318.22
blustering 503.4
turbulent 671.18
B-movie 706.1
boa 311.26
boar cock 76.8
swine 311.9

board
noun meal 8.5
food 10.1
rations 10.6
accommodations 385.3
council 423.1
directorate 574.11
tribunal 595.1
stage 704.16
stock exchange 737.7
card 758.2
table 900.15
circuitry 1041.3
wood 1052.3
verb feed 8.18
dine 8.21
lay 182.48
embark 188.15
mount 193.12
face 295.23
provision 385.9
accommodate 385.10
raid 459.20
boarder eater 8.16
lodger 227.8
schoolchild 572.3
board game 743.9
boarding embarkation
188.3
raid 459.4
wood 1052.3
boarding school 567.4
board of directors
574.11
board of governors
567.12
boards show business
704.1
stage 704.16
ice hockey 750.4
boardwalk 383.2
boast
noun boasting 502.1
good thing 998.5
verb be stuck on
oneself 140.6
possess 469.4
brag 502.6
boastful vain 136.9
proud 140.9
boasting 502.10
boasting
noun bragging 502.1
adj boastful 502.10
boast of 509.12
boat
noun ship 180.1
verb navigate 182.13
boathouse 197.27
boating 182.1
boatman 183.5
boat race 457.12
boat-race 457.19
boat show 736.2
boatyard 739.3
bob
noun obeisance 155.2

float 180.11
square 200.6
weight 297.6
greeting 585.4
mite 728.7
repeat 848.5
jerk 904.3
crouch 912.3
shake 916.3
verb bow 155.6, 912.9
excise 255.10
shorten 268.6
caper 366.6
fish 382.10
oscillate 915.10
shake 916.11
bobbed 268.9
bobble
noun shake 916.3
verb oscillate 915.10
shake 916.11
boca 242.1
bode 133.11
bodhisattva 677.4
bodice 5.15
bodied 1050.11
bodily
adj carnal 663.6
innate 766.8
material 1050.10
adv in person 221.17
wholly 791.13
body
noun person 2.1, 312.5
guy 76.5
population 227.1
size 257.1
figure 262.4
thickness 269.2
corpse 307.16
type 548.6
association 617.1
community 617.2
sect 675.3
motor racing 756.1
substantiality 762.1
something 762.3
company 769.3
collection 769.11
major part 791.6
individual 871.4
solid 1043.6
physical body 1050.3
verb materialize 1050.9
body count obituary 307.14
summation 1016.11
bodyguard escort 768.5
safeguard 1007.14
body heat 1018.1
body language 517.14
body of evidence 956.1
body politic population 227.1

country 232.1
people 606.1
body weight 297.1
boffin expert 413.11
adviser 422.3
scientist 927.11
experimenter 941.6
bog
noun sink 80.12
marsh 243.1
verb mire 243.2
bogey
noun frightener 127.9
military aircraft 181.9
bugbear 680.9
round 748.3
verb play 748.4
boggle
noun demur 325.2
verb astonish 122.6
start 127.12
demur 325.4
object 333.5
not know one's own mind 362.6
lose one's nerve 491.8
quibble 935.9
stump 970.14
boggling
noun demur 325.2
bungling 414.4
quibbling 935.5
adj demurring 325.7
bogle 680.9
bogus 354.26
Bohemian
noun nomad 178.4
nonconformist 867.3
adj informal 581.3
unconventional 867.6
boil
noun sore 85.36
swelling 283.4
turbulence 671.2
agitation 916.1
boiling 1019.2
verb cook 11.4
sanitize 79.24
burn 152.15, 1018.22
bubble 320.4
seethe 671.12
stew 1019.20
boiled cooked 11.6
sanitary 79.27
fuddled 88.33
boiled eggs 10.25
boiling
noun cooking 11.1
bubbling 320.3
turbulence 671.2
make 892.4
agitation 916.1
seething 1019.2
adj heated 105.22
burning 152.29
mad 152.30
hot 1018.25
boiling point 1018.3

boiling water 1018.10
boil over anger 152.17
bubble 320.4
boisterous noisy 53.13
turbulent 105.24
blustering 503.4
rampageous 671.20
bold insolent 142.9
brazen 142.11
seaworthy 180.18
steep 204.18
protruding 283.14
in relief 283.18
conspicuous 348.12
defiant 454.7
courageous 492.17
foolhardy 493.9
immodest 666.6
boldly brazenly 142.14
conspicuously 348.16
courageously 492.23
boldness insolence 142.1
conspicuousness 348.4
defiance 454.1
courage 492.1
foolhardiness 493.3
immodesty 666.2
bollocks 520.3
Bolshevik
noun radical 611.17
Communist 611.18
adj Communist 611.30
revolutionist 859.6
Bolshevism 611.6
bolster
noun bedding 900.20
verb comfort 121.6
support 449.12, 900.21
encourage 492.16
confirm 956.11
bolstered 900.24
bolstering
noun confirmation 956.4
adj supporting 900.23
bolt
noun length 267.2
apostasy 363.2
flight 368.4
desertion 370.2
lock 428.5
arrow 462.6
missile 462.18
bundle 769.8
fastening 799.3
lightning 1024.17
verb gobble 8.23
refine 79.22
speed 174.8
close 293.6
flee 368.10
defect 370.6
gluttonize 672.4
segregate 772.6
hook 799.8
classify 807.11
obstruct 1011.12

bolting
noun refinement 79.4
absence 222.4
apostasy 363.2
adj gluttonous 672.6
bolt upright 200.11
bomb
noun Acapulco gold 87.10
surprise 131.2
lightning 174.6
jalopy 179.10
lot 247.4
flop 410.2
bombshell 462.20
bundle 618.3
verb blow up 395.18
lose out 410.10
drop a bomb 459.23
bombard blow up 395.18
pull the trigger 459.22
atomize 1037.17
bombardment
bombing 459.7
fission 1037.8
bombast
noun boasting 502.1
nonsense 520.2
bombastry 545.2
verb talk big 545.6
bombastic pompous 501.22
inflated 502.12
stiff 534.3
fustian 545.9
bombed 88.33
bombed out 87.23
bomber alarmist 127.8
destroyer 395.8
artilleryman 461.10
Bomber Command 461.28
bombing mission 184.11
bombardment 459.7
bombshell surprise 131.2
bomb 462.20
bon 998.12
bona fide
adj straight 644.14
genuine 972.15
adv faithfully 644.25
bonanza source of supply 386.4
mine 618.4
plenty 990.2
bond
noun shackle 428.4
compact 437.1
security 438.1
pledge 438.2
fidelity 644.7
nominal rate 738.5
relation 774.1
joining 799.1
fastening 799.3

verb secure 438.9
pledge 438.10
put together 799.5
adj subjugated 432.14
bondage 432.1
bonded 799.14
bonding association 582.6
joining 799.1
fastening 799.3
bond issue 738.6
bonds 428.4
bone
noun skeleton 2.2
alabaster 37.2
stone 1044.6
desert 1064.2
adj skeleton 2.24
bone of contention
apple of discord 456.7
question 937.10
bones skeleton 2.2
heart 93.3
corpse 307.16
refuse 391.4
dice 759.8
body 1050.3
bonfire 1018.13
bonhomie good nature 143.2
hospitality 585.1
cordiality 587.6
bonk
noun sock 901.5
verb belt 901.15
bonkers 925.27
bonne 577.8
bonnet cloak 5.39
top 295.21
bonny good 998.12
comely 1015.18
bonus extra 254.4
find 472.6
gratuity 478.5
premium 624.6
dividend 738.7
surplus 992.5
bony skeleton 2.24
lean 270.17
hard 1044.10
boo
noun Acapulco gold 87.10
booing 508.3
verb hiss 508.10
boobs 283.7
booby 923.3
booby trap ambush 346.3
trap 356.12
snags 1005.5
boogie 705.5
booing
noun ridicule 508.1
boo 508.3
adj ridiculing 508.12

Book 683.2
book
  noun publication 352.1
  volume 554.1
  book 554.1
  printed book 554.3
  part 554.13
  playbook 704.21
  script 706.2
  measure 720.9
  casino 759.19
  section 792.2
  rule 868.4
  verb curse 513.5
  record 549.15
  accuse 599.7
  employ 615.14
  keep accounts 628.8
  list 870.8
  prearrange 964.4
  schedule 964.6
bookbinding 554.14
bookcase storehouse
  386.6
  bookbinding 554.14
  bookholder 554.17
book club 554.16
booked recorded
  549.17
  scheduled 964.9
booked-in 964.9
Booker Prize 646.2
bookie 759.20
book in arrive 186.6
  schedule 964.6
booking registration
  549.14
  engagement 615.4,
  704.11
  prearrangement 964.1
bookish studious
  570.17
  studentlike 572.12
  book-learned 927.22
booklet 554.11
bookmaker 759.20
bookmark 517.10
book review 945.2
books account book
  628.4
  bill 870.5
  dismissal 908.5
bookseller 554.2
bookshelf 554.17
bookshop 554.16
bookstore 554.16
book value 738.9
boom
  noun noise 53.3
  reverberation 54.2
  booming 56.4
  float 180.11
  intensification 251.2
  explosion 671.7
  business cycle 731.9
  lever 905.4
  roaring trade 1009.5

barrier 1011.5
  verb hum 52.13
  din 53.7
  reverberate 54.7
  thunder 56.9
  lay 182.48
  grow 251.6
  murmur 524.26
  thrive 1009.8
boomerang
  noun missile 462.18
  retaliation 506.1
  recoil 902.2
  verb recoil 902.6
booming
  noun hum 52.7
  reverberation 54.2
  boom 56.4
  adj humming 52.20
  loud 53.11
  reverberating 54.11
  thundering 56.12
  thriving 1009.13
boon
  noun godsend 472.7
  benefit 478.7
  good 998.4
  adj convivial 582.23
boorish insensible 25.6
  countrified 233.7
  bungling 414.20
  churlish 497.13
  ill-bred 505.6
boost
  noun thrust 901.2
  verb cheer 109.7
  increase 251.4
  publicize 352.15
  improve 392.9
  thrust 901.12
  elevate 911.5
boosted 251.7
booster dose 86.6
  inoculation 91.16
  fan 101.5
  publicist 352.9
  thief 483.1
  multistage rocket
  1072.5
boot
  noun kick 105.3, 901.9
  navy man 183.4
  recruit 461.17
  rack 605.4
  eyesore 1014.4
  verb cloak 5.39
  kick 901.21
  fire 908.20
  computerize 1041.18
booted 5.44
booth compartment
  197.2
  hut 228.9
  stall 736.3
bootleg
  verb distil 88.30
  push 732.7
  adj illegal 674.6
boots footwear 5.27

attendant 577.5
  cricket 747.1
booty gain 472.3
  take 480.10
  spoil 482.11
booze
  noun spirits 88.13
  verb drink 8.29
  swig 88.25
boozy 88.33
bop 708.9
border
  noun exterior 206.2
  limbus 211.4
  frontier 211.5
  partition 213.5
  side 218.1
  sphere 231.2
  size 257.1
  scenery 704.20
  garden 1067.10
  verb edge 211.10
  side 218.4
  adjoin 223.9
  adj final 819.11
border-crossing 189.3
bordered 211.12
bordering
  noun edging 211.7
  adj environing 209.8
  fringing 211.11
  adjacent 223.16
borderline 211.11
borders environment
  209.1
  South 231.7
bore
  noun annoyance 96.2
  crashing bore 118.4
  wave 238.14, 915.4
  diameter 269.3
  hole 292.3
  verb leave one cold
  118.7
  excavate 284.15
  perforate 292.15
bored pleasureless
  96.20
  uninterested 118.12
  languid 331.20
  incurious 981.3
boredom unpleasure
  96.1
  weariness 118.3
  languor 331.6
  incuriosity 981.1
boring
  noun hole 292.3
  adj irritating 26.13
  dull 117.6
  wearying 118.10
  same 780.6
born given birth 1.4
  innate 766.8
  thorough 793.10
born-again redeemed
  685.9
  regenerate 692.10

converted 857.19
borne 900.24
borne out 956.20
borough town 230.1
  state 231.5
  constituency 609.16
borrow imitate 336.5
  find means 384.6
  borrow the loan of
  621.3
  go in debt 623.6
  discount 728.27
  play 748.4
borrower 623.4
borrowing plagiarism
  482.8
  loan word 526.7
  money-raising 621.1
  debt 623.1
  money market 728.16
borstal prison 429.8
  reform school 567.9
bosom
  noun heart 93.3
  interior 207.2
  breast 283.6
  inner nature 766.5
  verb keep secret 345.7
  secrete 346.7
  embrace 562.18
boss
  noun superior 249.4
  bulge 283.3
  print 517.7
  superintendent 574.2
  master 575.1
  policy maker 610.7
  relief 715.3
  honcho 996.11
  verb emboss 283.12
  roughen 288.4
  supervise 573.10
  adj supervising 573.13
  governing 612.18
  great 998.13
bossy
  noun hen 77.9
  adj in relief 283.18
  imperious 417.16
bosun 183.7
Boswell 719.4
botanic vegetable
  310.33
  biological 1066.3
botanical vegetable
  310.33
  biological 1066.3
botanist 1066.2
botany plants 310.1
  biology 1066.1
botched slipshod
  340.12
  bungled 414.21
both
  noun two 872.2
  adj two 872.7
bother

noun annoyance 96.2
  dither 105.6
  bustle 330.4
  imposition 643.1
  bewilderment 970.3
  confusion 984.3
  inconvenience 995.3
  trouble 1012.3
  verb annoy 96.13
  distress 96.16
  vex 98.15
  concern 126.4
  bewilder 970.12
  confuse 984.7
  inconvenience 995.4
  trouble 1012.13
bothered annoyed
  96.21
  distressed 96.22
  anxious 126.7
  bewildered 970.24
  confused 984.12
  troubled 1012.20
bothering annoying
  98.22
  bewildering 970.27
bottle
  noun spirits 88.13
  container 195.1
  pluck 359.3
  balls 492.4
  two hundred 881.9
  verb package 212.9
  put up 397.10
bottled 212.12
bottled water 1063.3
bottleneck convergence
  169.1
  contraction 260.1
  narrow 270.3
  obstruction 293.3
  hindrance 1011.1
bottling packaging
  212.2
  food preservation
  397.2
bottom
  noun ship 180.1
  bottom side 199.1
  bed 199.4
  buttocks 217.4
  marsh 243.1
  base 274.4
  valley 284.9
  pluck 359.3
  fortitude 492.6
  formality 580.1
  verb base on 199.6
  solve 939.2
  adj bottommost 199.7
  reduced 633.9
bottomless greedy
  100.27
  abysmal 275.11
  plentiful 990.7
bottom line gain 472.3
  losses 473.3
  meat and potatoes
  766.3

sum 1016.6

bottoms ships 180.10
   marsh 243.1

bottom up 205.8

boudoir 197.7

bouffant 259.13

bough branch 310.18
   member 792.4

bought 733.11

boulder 1057.5

bounce
   noun lightheartedness
   109.3
   impudence 142.2
   leap 366.1
   swagger 501.8
   recoil 902.2
   dismissal 908.5
   shake 916.3
   radio signal 1033.10
   elasticity 1046.1
   verb leap 366.5
   caper 366.6
   bluster 503.3
   recoil 902.6
   eject 908.13
   fire 908.20
   pump 915.14
   shake 916.11
   give 1046.5

bounce back
   reverberate 54.7
   reflect 1035.16

bounce-back reaction
   902.1
   recoil 902.2

bounces 1035.11

bouncing
   noun leaping 366.3
   adj strong 15.15
   hale 83.12
   active 330.17
   leaping 366.7
   recoiling 902.10

bouncy active 330.17
   recoiling 902.10
   jolting 916.20
   elastic 1046.7

bound
   noun boundary 211.3
   leap 366.1
   recoil 902.2
   verb speed 174.8
   circumscribe 210.4,
   211.8
   limit 210.5
   border 211.10
   enclose 212.5
   leap 366.5
   recoil 902.6
   adj limited 210.7
   enclosed 212.10
   stopped 293.11
   tied 428.16
   promised 436.8
   obliged 641.16
   related 774.9
   joined 799.13

certain 969.13

boundaries
   environment 209.1
   bounds 211.1

boundary
   noun limitation 210.2
   boundary 211.3
   bound 211.3
   fence 212.4
   size 257.1
   cricket 747.1
   match 747.3
   joint 799.4
   extremity 819.2
   pause 856.4
   bisector 874.3
   adj bordering 211.11
   final 819.11

bounded 210.7

bounder 497.6

bound for 161.26

bounding
   noun circumscription
   210.1
   leaping 366.3
   adj bordering 211.11
   leaping 366.7
   recoiling 902.10
   qualifying 958.7

boundless large 247.7
   almighty 677.17
   infinite 822.3
   excessive 992.16

bounds limitation 210.2
   limits 211.1

bound up with 771.5

bountiful liberal 485.4
   productive 889.9
   plentiful 990.7

bounty gratuity 478.5
   subsidy 478.8
   liberality 485.1
   bonus 624.6

bouquet fragrance 70.1
   nosegay 310.23
   bundle 769.8

Bourbon 611.13

bourgeois
   noun townsman 227.6
   vulgarian 497.6
   member of the middle
   class 607.6
   conformist 866.2
   adj common 497.14
   upper-class 607.10
   capitalist 611.32
   conformist 866.6
   ordinary 1004.8

bourgeoisie middle
   class 607.5
   mediocrity 1004.5

bourn destination 186.5
   boundary 211.3
   stream 238.1

bourse 737.7

bout spree 88.5
   contest 457.3

boxing 457.9
   revel 743.6
   game 743.9
   fight 754.3
   turn 824.2
   round 849.3

boutique 736.1

bovine
   noun cattle 311.6
   adj unconcerned 102.7
   inexcitable 106.10
   complacent 107.10
   ungulate 311.44
   stupid 921.15

bow
   noun obeisance 155.2
   prow 216.3
   curve 279.2
   bend 279.3
   bulge 283.3
   longbow 462.7
   greeting 585.4
   crouch 912.3
   verb fawn 138.7
   make obeisance 155.6
   curve 279.6
   lose 412.12
   bow down 433.10
   bend 912.9

bowed distorted 265.10
   embowed 279.10
   convex 283.13

bowed-out 283.13

bowels mouth 2.16
   insides 207.4
   depths 275.3

bower summerhouse
   228.12
   safeguard 1007.3

bowing 279.3

bowl
   noun tableware 8.12
   cavity 284.2
   arena 463.1
   ceramic ware 742.2
   throw 903.3
   verb sink 284.12
   hollow 284.13
   play 747.4
   push 903.9
   throw 903.10
   roll 914.10

bowled 747.5

bowler team 747.2
   thrower 903.7

bowling
   noun match 747.3
   throwing 903.2
   rotation 914.1
   adj rotating 914.14

bowling green
   horizontal 201.3
   green 310.7
   playground 743.11

bowls 8.12

bowman 903.8

bow out quit 188.9
   absent oneself 222.8

croak 307.20
   dismiss 908.18

bowsprit 216.3

bow to respect 155.4
   hand it to 250.5
   submit to 433.9
   bow down 433.10
   greet 585.10

box
   noun genitals 2.11
   container 195.1
   compartment 197.2
   cottage 228.8
   coffin 309.11
   storehouse 386.6
   gift 478.4
   slap 604.3, 901.8
   auditorium 704.15
   cricket 747.1
   hotchpotch 796.6
   television 1034.1
   verb package 212.9
   wrap 295.20
   restrict 428.9
   contend 457.13
   slap 604.11, 901.19
   fight 754.4

boxed packed 212.12
   covered 295.31

boxed in restricted
   428.15
   contingent 958.9

boxed set 554.5

Boxer 311.15

boxer pugilist 461.2
   fighter 754.2

box in enclose 212.5
   qualify 958.3

boxing packaging 212.2
   fighting 457.9
   prizefighting 754.1

boxing ring arena
   463.1
   boxing 754.1

box office receipts
   627.1
   office 739.7

boy big H 87.8
   lad 302.5
   man 577.4

boycott
   noun objection 333.2
   ostracism 586.3
   strike 727.5
   exclusion 772.1
   verb object 333.5
   ostracize 586.6
   strike 727.10

boyhood childhood
   301.2
   young people 302.2

boyish thin 270.16
   childish 301.11
   immature 406.11

bra brassiere 5.24
   supporter 900.2

brace

noun dressing 86.33
   verticalness 200.1
   stave 708.29
   two 872.2
   supporter 900.2
   verb refresh 9.2
   strengthen 15.13
   stand 200.7
   bind 799.9
   support 900.21
   stiffen 1044.9

braced
   adj supported 900.24
   adv vertically 200.13

bracelet band 280.3
   jewel 498.6

braces 202.5

bracing
   noun refreshment 9.1
   adj refreshing 9.3
   energizing 17.15
   healthful 81.5
   tonic 86.44
   supporting 900.23
   cool 1022.12

bracken 310.4

bracket
   noun boundary 211.3
   class 808.2
   supporter 900.2
   verb parenthesize
   212.8
   grammaticize 530.16
   relate 774.6
   simplify 797.4
   put together 799.5

bracketed related 774.9
   unrelated 775.6
   joined 799.13
   coupled 872.8

brackets 211.3

brackish nasty 64.7
   salty 68.9

brag
   noun boasting 502.1
   braggart 502.5
   verb boast 502.6
   bluster 503.3

bragging
   noun boasting 502.1
   adj boastful 502.10

Brahman cattle 311.6
   nobleman 608.4
   pujari 699.12

braid
   noun plait 3.7, 740.2
   cord 271.2
   verb spin 271.6
   weave 740.6

braided 740.7

braille 30.6

brain
   noun encephalon 2.13
   intellect 918.1
   intelligence 919.9
   verb strike dead
   308.17
   adj nerve 2.28

brainchild writing
547.10
  work of art 712.10
  product 892.1
  figment of the
  imagination 985.5
brain damage 925.1
brain-damaged 925.28
brain disease 92.14
brain-injured 925.28
brains kidneys 10.19
  intellect 918.1
brainstorm caprice
364.1
  impulse 365.1
  delirium 925.8
  absurd idea 931.7
brainy 919.14
braised 11.6
brake
  noun thicket 310.13
  curb 1011.7
  verb slow 175.9
  put a stop to 856.11
  stop 1011.13
braking 1040.7
bramble thorn 285.5
  shrubbery 310.9
  adhesive 802.4
bran feed 10.4
  hull 295.16
  powder 1049.5
branch
  noun fork 171.4,
  310.18
  stream 238.1
  tributary 238.3
  branch of the service
  461.20
  lineage 560.4
  offshoot 561.4
  organ 617.10
  sect 675.3
  office 739.7
  member 792.4
  class 808.2
  kingdom 808.5
  verb fork 171.7
  spread 259.6
  angle 278.5
  bisect 874.4
branched forked
171.10
  leafy 310.38
  halved 874.6
branching
  noun forking 171.3
  bisection 874.1
  adj forked 171.10
  leafy 310.38
  halved 874.6
branch out 259.6
brand
  noun mark 517.5
  label 517.13
  stigma 661.6
  nature 766.4
  kind 808.3

characteristic 864.4
  stain 1003.3
  coal 1018.16
  burn 1019.6
  cauterant 1019.15
  scoria 1019.16
  lighter 1020.4
  verb mark 517.19
  label 517.20
  stigmatize 661.9
  stain 1003.6
  burn 1019.24
branding 1019.5
brandishing 915.2
brand name 517.13
brand-new unused
390.12
  fire-new 840.10
brandy 88.15
brash
  noun rock 1057.1
  adj impudent 142.10
  defiant 454.7
  rash 493.7
  gruff 505.7
brass
  noun cheek 142.3
  monument 549.12
  dough 728.2
  personage 996.8
  adj brassy 1056.17
brassy noisy 53.13
  raucous 58.15
  brazen 142.11
  defiant 454.7
  immodest 666.6
  brass 1056.17
brat 302.4
bravado defiance 454.1
  daring 492.5
  boasting 502.1
  bluster 503.1
brave
  noun hero 492.8
  verb endure 134.5
  confront 216.8
  defy 454.3
  face 492.11
  take chances 1005.7
  thwart 1011.15
  adj courageous 492.17
  showy 501.19
brave face 216.1
bravely courageously
492.23
  showily 501.26
bravery courage 492.1
  finery 498.3
bravo killer 308.10
  combatant 461.1
  blusterer 503.2
  ruffian 593.3
bravura
  noun skill 413.1
  daring 492.5
  display 501.4
  vocal music 708.13
  arietta 708.16

adj skilful 413.22
  showy 501.19
  vocal 708.50
brawl
  noun noise 53.3
  quarrel 456.5
  free-for-all 457.5
  turbulence 671.2
  commotion 809.4
  verb be noisy 53.9
  quarrel 456.11
  contend 457.13
brawling noisy 53.13
  vociferous 59.10
brawn muscularity 15.2
  organic matter 305.1
bray
  noun blare 53.5
  rasp 58.3
  verb blare 53.10
  jangle 58.9
  cry 60.2
  murmur 524.26
  pulverize 1049.9
brazen
  verb brave 492.11
  adj reddish-brown
  40.4
  noisy 53.13
  raucous 58.15
  brazenfaced 142.11
  defiant 454.7
  rash 493.7
  gaudy 501.20
  hardened 654.17
  immodest 666.6
  brass 1056.17
brazenly brazenfacedly
142.14
  rashly 493.10
  gaudily 501.27
breach
  noun crack 224.2
  violation 435.2
  falling-out 456.4
  misdeed 655.2
  break 801.4
  interruption 812.2
  verb cleave 224.4
  rupture 292.14
  violate 435.4
  break 801.12
  open 817.12
breach of contract
435.2
breach of the peace
  violation 435.2
  quarrel 456.5
bread
  noun food 10.1
  pain 10.27
  support 449.3
  Eucharist 701.7
  dough 728.2
  verb sprinkle 770.6
bread and butter 10.1
bread-and-butter
797.6
breadth space 158.1

size 257.1
  width 269.1
  extent 300.3
  broad-mindedness
  978.1
breadwinner 726.2
break
  noun respite 20.2
  trauma 85.37
  act of kindness 143.7
  start 188.2
  boundary 211.3
  crack 224.2
  escape 369.1
  falling-out 456.4
  declining market
  737.5
  match 752.3
  horse race 757.3
  deficiency 794.2
  breakage 801.4
  interruption 812.2
  interim 825.1
  delay 845.2
  revolution 851.2
  pause 856.3
  chance 971.1
  verb weaken 16.9
  take a rest 20.8
  change course 182.30
  set out 188.8
  cleave 224.4
  billow 238.22
  come out 352.16
  accustom 373.10
  injure 393.13
  break up 393.23
  conquer 412.10
  subdue 432.9
  domesticate 432.11
  violate 435.4
  depose 447.4
  train 568.13
  domineer 612.16
  go bankrupt 625.7
  bankrupt 625.8
  play 752.4
  fight 754.4
  race 757.5
  disagree 788.5
  burst 801.12
  discontinue 812.3
  intervene 825.3
  pause 856.9
  interrupt 856.10
  dismiss 908.19
  grow light 1024.27
  shatter 1048.3
  tend 1068.7
break away revolt
327.7
  escape 369.6
  defect 370.6
breakaway
  noun apostasy 363.2
  desertion 370.2
  game 745.3
  adj rebellious 327.11
  dissenting 333.6
  repudiative 363.12
  unconventional 867.6

unusual 869.10
breakaway group
617.4
break down burn out
21.5
  aggrieve 112.19
  weep 115.12
  founder 393.24
  get out of kilter
  393.26
  raze 395.19
  subdue 432.9
  diversify 781.2
  analyse 800.6
  sever 801.11
  dissect 801.17
  classify 808.6
  fall through 910.3
breakdown exhaustion
21.2
  collapse 85.8, 410.3
  impairment 393.1
  debacle 395.4
  analysis 800.1
  dissection 801.5
  disintegration 805.1
  revolution 859.1
breaker separator 801.7
  stockman 1068.2
breakers wave 238.14
  foam 320.2
break even 789.5
breakfast
  noun breakfast 8.6
  petit déjeuner 8.6
  verb dine 8.21
break for 161.9
break free 1073.12
break in intrude 214.5
  interrupt 214.6
  breach 292.14
  accustom 373.10
  domesticate 432.11
  train 568.13
  make a beginning
  817.8
break-in 482.5
breaking habituation
373.8
  subdual 432.4
  violation 435.2
  training 568.3
breaking down 800.1
breaking-in habituation
373.8
  first 817.3
breaking out 85.35
breaking up debacle
395.4
  analysis 800.1
break into 292.14
breakneck fast 174.15
  steep 204.18
  precipitate 401.10
  reckless 493.8
break off disaccustom
374.2

noun brownness 40.1
big H 87.8
table 752.2
verb cook 11.4
embrown 40.2
darken 1026.9
adj brownish 40.3

browned 11.6

brownie apple-polisher
138.4
dwarf 258.5
fairy 678.8

browning 40.1

brownish 40.3

brows 3.12

browse scan 570.13
shop 733.8

browsing 8.1

bruise
noun trauma 85.37
discolouration 1003.2
verb pain 96.17
mistreat 389.5
injure 393.13
thrash soundly 604.13

bruised 96.23

bruising 671.16

Brummie 523.7

brunch 8.6

brunette
noun blonde 35.9
adj black-haired 38.13
brown 40.3
brown-haired 40.5

brunt 901.3

brush
noun awn 3.9
touch 73.1
tail 217.6
contact 223.5
hinterland 233.2
scrub 310.14
fight 457.4
painting 712.14
palette 712.18
wasteland 890.2
tap 901.7
firewood 1020.3
verb touch lightly 73.7
sweep 79.23
barrel 174.9
contact 223.10
portray 712.19
tap 901.18
dry 1064.6
tend 1068.7

brushing 223.17

brush off sweep 79.23
repulse 907.3

brush-off rejection
372.1
repulse 907.2

brush up groom 79.20
perfect 392.11
study up 570.14
refresh the memory
988.19

brusque taciturn 344.9
gruff 505.7
concise 537.6
candid 644.17

brusquely gruffly 505.9
concisely 537.7
candidly 644.23

brutal cruel 144.26
deadly 308.22
animal 311.38
unrefined 497.12
carnal 663.6
savage 671.21
terrible 999.9
difficult 1012.17

brutality cruelty
144.11
act of cruelty 144.12
unrefinement 497.3
carnality 663.2
violence 671.1
terribleness 999.2

brutally cruelly 144.35
terribly 999.14

brute
noun beast 144.14
animal 311.2
barbarian 497.7
savage 593.5
adj cruel 144.26
animal 311.38
carnal 663.6

brute force 424.2

brutish cruel 144.26
animal 311.38
unrefined 497.12
carnal 663.6
savage 671.21

Brutus 357.10

bubble
noun airy hope 124.5
structure 266.2
sphere 282.2
bulge 283.3
air 298.2
bleb 320.1
race 756.3
spirit 763.3
ephemeron 827.5
illusion 975.1
figment of the
imagination 985.5
eggshell 1048.2
verb ripple 52.11
weep 115.12
bubble up 320.4

bubbling
noun bubbliness 320.3
adj rippling 52.19
bubbly 320.6

bubbly light 298.10
burbly 320.6
active 330.17

buccaneer
noun mariner 183.1
pirate 483.7
verb pirate 482.18

buck
noun cock 76.8

boy 302.5
deer 311.5
goat 311.8
hare 311.24
leap 366.1
verb leap 366.5

bucket
noun basketball game
751.3
verb ladle 176.17
trade 737.23

bucking 451.1

Buckingham Palace
228.5

buckle
noun distortion 265.1
fastening 799.3
verb distort 265.5
hook 799.8

buckled 265.10

buckling 799.3

bucks 728.2

bucolic rustic 233.6
natural 416.6
poetic 720.15

bud
noun burgeon 310.21
verb graft 191.6
vegetate 310.31

Buddha Blessed One
677.4
Gautama Buddha
684.4
Solomon 920.2

Buddhist 675.32

budding
noun growth 259.3
vegetation 310.30
adj grown 14.3,
259.12
immature 301.10
beginning 817.15

buddy mate 588.4
partner 616.2

budge 172.5

budget
noun amount 244.2
store 386.1
portion 477.5
expenses 626.3
accounts 628.1
funds 728.14
bundle 769.8
schedule 964.3
verb ration 477.10
spend 626.5
schedule 964.6
adj accounting 628.12
cheap 633.7

budgetary 628.12

budgeting
apportionment 477.1
expenditure 626.1
accounts 628.1

buff
noun fan 101.5
skin 295.3

specialist 865.3
verb polish 287.7
burnish 1042.8
adj yellow 43.4

buffalo 311.6

buffer
noun partition 213.5
back number 841.8
counteractant 899.3
safeguard 1007.3
barrier 1011.5
verb neutralize 899.7

buffer zone 465.5

buffet
noun restaurant 8.17
disappointment 132.1
table 900.15
slap 901.8
verb mistreat 389.5
contend against 451.4
struggle 725.11
pound 901.16
slap 901.19

buffeting 604.4

buffoon mischief-maker
322.3
buffo 707.10
fool 923.1

bug
noun microphone 50.9
germ 85.41
fan 101.5
insect 311.31
bugbear 680.9
jockey 757.2
mania 925.12
fanatic 925.18
fault 1002.2
verb listen 48.10
annoy 96.13
bulge 283.11
importune 440.12
reconnoitre 937.28
confuse 984.7

bugged annoyed 96.21
tormented 96.24

bugger
noun sexual pervert
75.16
guy 76.5
arsehole 660.6
bugbear 680.9
verb screw up 393.11
cock up 414.12
queer 1011.16

buggered screwed up
393.29
messed up 414.22

buggery 75.7

bugging audition 48.2
surveillance 937.9

buggy
noun jalopy 179.10
adj insectile 311.50

bugle blare 53.10
blow a horn 708.42

build
noun muscularity 15.2

form 262.1
figure 262.4
structure 266.1
nature 766.4
verb establish 159.16
increase 251.4
enlarge 259.4
construct 266.5
compose 795.3
produce 891.8

builder worker 726.2
producer 891.7

build in 159.16

building
noun house 228.5
structure 266.1, 266.2
composition 795.1
production 891.2
adj constructional
891.15

building blocks 196.5,
762.2

building society 620.4

build on 199.6

build up aggravate
119.2
increase 251.4
enlarge 259.4
publicize 352.15
exaggerate 355.3
compose 795.3

build-up increase 251.1
composition 795.1

build up to 405.13

built made 891.18
comely 1015.18

built-in 771.5

built-up 259.10

bulb sphere 282.2
bulge 283.3
root 310.20

bulbous spherical 282.9
bulging 283.15
vegetable 310.33

bulge
noun tum 2.17
advantage 249.2
intensification 251.2
bilge 283.3
verb bilge 283.11

bulged 283.16

bulging
noun convexity 283.1
adj rotund 282.8
spherical 282.9
swelling 283.15
full 793.11

bulimia 672.1

bulk
noun quantity 244.1
greatness 247.1
size 257.1
bulkiness 257.9
thickness 269.2
major part 791.6
majority 882.2
verb loom 247.5

size 257.15
enlarge 259.5
assemble 769.18

bulkhead partition
213.5
buttress 900.4
harbour 1008.6
barrier 1011.5

bulky large 247.7
hulky 257.19
thick 269.8
sturdy 762.7
unwieldy 1012.19

bull
noun cock 76.8
centre 208.2
cattle 311.6
decree 420.4
bullshit 520.3
long 737.13
grammatical error
974.7
cop 1007.16
verb manipulate the
market 737.25
adj masculine 76.11

bulldog
noun hero 492.8
adhesive 802.4
verb fell 912.5

bulldozer strong man
15.6
tractor 179.18

bullet lightning 174.6
shot 462.19, 903.4
dismissal 908.5
fission 1037.8

bulletin
noun press release
352.3
report 549.7
information 551.1
news report 552.5
verb publicize 352.15

bulletin board
announcement 352.2
notice board 549.10
information 551.1

bullion precious metals
728.20
cast 1056.5

bullish 311.44

bullock cock 76.8
cattle 311.6

bull ring 463.1

bullshit
noun big talk 502.2
shit 520.3
verb mouth off 502.7

bully
noun hunk 15.7
tormentor 96.10
combatant 461.1
blusterer 503.2
ruffian 593.3
game 750.3
verb intimidate 127.20
coerce 424.7

bluster 503.3
domineer 612.16
adj great 998.13

bullying
noun frightening 127.6
bluster 503.1
adj blustering 503.4
threatening 514.3

bulwark
noun fortification
460.4
buttress 900.4
safeguard 1007.3
barrier 1011.5
verb fortify 460.9

bum
noun arse 217.5
stiff 331.9
transient 827.4
verb mouth off 502.7
adj lousy 999.8

bumblebee 311.33

bumbling 414.20

bump
noun thud 52.3
report 56.1
airspace 184.32
bulge 283.3
swelling 283.4
print 517.7
thrust 901.2
impact 901.3
shake 916.3
verb crack 56.6
thrust 901.12
collide 901.13
fire 908.20
shake 916.11

bumped 283.15

bumper
noun drink 8.4
cigarette 89.5
partition 213.5
full measure 793.3
safeguard 1007.3
adj large 257.16

bumping 257.21

bump into collide
901.13
come across 940.3

bumpy bulging 283.15
rough 288.6
nappy 294.7
jolting 916.20

bun braid 3.7
roll 10.30

bunce find 472.6
gratuity 478.5

bunch
noun amount 244.2
bulge 283.3
flock 769.5
group 769.7
conglomeration 802.5
multitude 883.3
verb come together
769.16
assemble 769.18

cohere 802.6
league 804.4

bunched bulging
283.15
assembled 769.21
cohesive 802.10

bunches 3.7

Bundesbank 729.13

bundle
noun bomb 618.3
pack 769.8
verb snuggle 121.10
stroll 177.28
package 212.9
hasten 401.4
make haste 401.5
cuddle 562.17
bundle up 769.20
bind 799.9
dismiss 908.18

bundled packed 212.12
assembled 769.21

bung
noun stopper 293.4
bribe 378.2
gratuity 478.5
fee 624.5
verb place 159.12
clap 159.13
stop 293.7
throw 903.10
adj dead 307.30

bungalow 228.8

bungle
noun fiasco 410.6
blunder 414.5, 974.5
verb do carelessly
340.9
miss 410.14
blunder 414.11,
974.14

bungled 414.21

bungling
noun slipshodness
340.3
blundering 414.4
adj slipshod 340.12
blundering 414.20

bunk
noun humbug 354.14
big talk 502.2
bullshit 520.3
verb inhabit 225.7
house 225.10

bunker
noun cellar 197.17
cave 284.5
storehouse 386.6
entrenchment 460.5
stronghold 460.6
golf 748.1
shelter 1008.3
proving ground
1072.7
verb provision 385.9

bunny 1015.9

bunting 647.6

buoy

noun float 180.11
life jacket 397.6
marker 517.10
verb buoy up 298.8

buoyancy
lightheartedness 109.3
lightness 298.1

buoyant lighthearted
109.12
floaty 298.14
recuperative 396.23
elastic 1046.7

buoyed-up 900.24

burden
noun affliction 96.8
load 196.2
capacity 257.2
burthen 297.7
duty 641.1
charge 643.3
guilt 656.1
part 708.22
passage 708.24
measure 720.9
repeat 848.5
topic 936.1
bane 1000.1
impediment 1011.6
verb distress 96.16
oppress 98.16
load 159.15
add 253.4
burthen 297.13
task 725.16
inconvenience 995.4
go hard with 1010.8
hamper 1011.11

burdened weighted
297.18
fraught 793.12
supporting 900.23

burdened with 643.8

burden of proof 956.3

burdensome oppressive
98.24
onerous 297.17
laborious 725.18
hampering 1011.18
troublesome 1012.18

bureau office 594.4
table 900.15

bureaucracy routine
373.6
authorities 575.15
officialism 612.11

bureaucrat 575.16

bureaucratic
governmental 612.17
executive 612.19

burg 230.1

burgee 647.6

burgeoning
noun growth 259.3
vegetation 310.30
adj grown 14.3,
259.12
increasing 251.8

burger 10.31

burgess townsman
227.6
freeman 430.11

burgh 230.1

burglar 483.3

burglar alarm 400.1

burglary 482.5

burial interment 309.1
funeral 309.5
tomb 309.16
concealment 346.1
submergence 367.2
overrunning 909.1

buried underground
275.12
underwater 275.13
concealed 346.11
overrun 909.10

buried in 982.17

burke 308.18

burlesque
noun imitation 336.1
reproduction 336.3
bad likeness 350.2
exaggeration 355.1
wit 489.1
lampoon 508.6, 512.5
show business 704.1
similarity 783.1
verb misrepresent
350.3
exaggerate 355.3
lampoon 508.11,
512.12
adj farcical 508.14

burly able-bodied 15.16
corpulent 257.18

burn
noun smart 26.3
trauma 85.37
stream 238.1
scald 1019.6
spacecraft 1073.2
verb pain 26.7
brown 40.2
seethe 152.15
cremate 309.20
gyp 356.19
injure 393.13
execute 604.16
rage 671.11
scorch 1018.22
ignite 1019.22
catch fire 1019.23
torrefy 1019.24
shine 1024.23
dry 1064.6

burn down raze 395.19
burn up 1019.25

burned impaired
393.27
burnt 1019.30

burned-out weakened
16.18
apathetic 94.13

burner destroyer 395.8
heater 1019.10
incinerator 1019.13

blowtorch 1019.14

burn in 1019.24

burning
noun smart 26.3
cremation 309.2
discard 390.3
capital punishment
604.6
heat 1018.1
combustion 1019.5
adj sore 26.11
colourful 35.18
zestful 68.7
in heat 75.27
feverish 85.57
fervent 93.18
zealous 101.9
heated 105.22
seething 152.29
vehement 544.13
hot 1018.25
ignited 1018.27
heating 1019.26
luminous 1024.30
flashing 1024.34

burnished sleek 287.10
shiny 1024.33

burn off 1019.24

burn out fatigue 21.4
burn out 21.5
get tired 21.5
go out 1021.8

burnt red-complexioned
41.9
burned 1019.30
dried 1064.9

burnt-out exhausted
21.10
overtired 21.11

burn up consume 388.3
incendiarize 1019.25

burp
noun belch 908.9
verb belch 908.28

burr
noun rasp 58.3
bulge 283.3
thorn 285.5
seed vessel 310.28
accent 524.9
engraving 713.2
adhesive 802.4
verb hum 52.13
jangle 58.9

burrow
noun lair 228.26
cave 284.5
verb settle 159.17
excavate 284.15
hide 346.8
search 937.31

bursar payer 624.9
treasurer 729.11

bursary 729.12

burst
noun report 56.1
detonation 56.3

outburst 105.9, 152.9,
671.6
run 174.3
bustle 330.4
volley 459.9
explosion 671.7
break 801.4
flare 1018.14
verb blast 56.8
break 393.23, 801.12
explode 671.14
adj impaired 393.27
broken 801.24

burst in intrude 214.5
breach 292.14

bursting
noun disruption 801.3
adj banging 56.11
excited 105.20
explosive 671.24
full 793.11
teeming 883.9
productive 889.9
overfull 992.20

burst into flames
1019.23

burst into tears
115.12

burst out exclaim 59.7
laugh 116.8

burst out laughing
116.8

bury inter 309.19
secrete 346.7
submerge 367.7

burying interment
309.1
funeral 309.5
concealment 346.1
overrunning 909.1

bus
noun jalopy 179.10
commercial vehicle
179.13
verb haul 176.13
ride 177.33

bus driver 178.10

bush Acapulco gold
87.10
lining 196.3
hinterland 233.2
shrubbery 310.9
woodland 310.11
brush 310.14
wasteland 890.2

bushel 247.3

bushy hairy 3.25
arboreal 310.36
sylvan 310.37

busily 330.25

business
noun action 328.1
activity 330.1
undertaking 404.1
company 617.9
duty 641.1
acting 704.8
occupation 724.1

vocation 724.6
commerce 731.1
relation 774.1
affair 830.3
speciality 865.1
adj commercial
730.12, 731.21

business cycle 731.9

business letter 553.2

businesslike 806.6

businessman 730.1

business park 739.3

business partner 616.2

businesswoman
woman 77.5
businessman 730.1

business world 731.1

bus pass 517.11

bust
noun binge 88.6
breast 283.6
figure 349.6
monument 549.12
insolvency 625.3
sock 901.5
hard times 1010.6
verb nick 429.16
go bankrupt 625.7
explode 671.14
break 801.12
dismiss 908.19

busted impaired 393.27
broken 801.24

bustle
noun agitation 105.4,
916.1
fuss 330.4
haste 401.1
bluster 503.1
verb fuss 330.12
hasten 401.4
make haste 401.5

bustling fussing 330.20
eventful 830.10

bust up 801.9

bust-up falling-out
456.4
commotion 809.4

busty corpulent 257.18
pectoral 283.19

busy
verb occupy 724.10
task 725.16
adj meddlesome 214.9
full of business 330.21
ornate 498.12
occupied 724.15

but
conj unless 958.16
adv, conj
notwithstanding 338.8

butcher
noun killer 308.10
vendor 730.5
verb slaughter 308.16
misdraw 350.4
bungle 414.11

rage 671.11
sever 801.11

butchered botched
414.21
mutilated 794.5

butchery butchering
308.3
aceldama 308.11
unruliness 671.3

but good 998.13

butler steward 574.4
man 577.4
major-domo 577.10

but now 837.3

butt
noun cigarette 89.5
objective 380.2
laughingstock 508.7
piece 792.3
joint 799.4
extremity 819.2
thrust 901.2
pushing 903.1
verb adjoin 223.9
hook 799.8
thrust 901.12
push 903.9

butter
noun putty 1045.4
semiliquid 1060.5
pulp 1061.2
verb coat 295.24

buttercup 562.6

butterflies 128.2

butterfly spectrum 47.6
aquatics 182.11
light filter 1027.4

Buttermilk 311.15

buttery
noun restaurant 8.17
dining room 197.11
storehouse 386.6
larder 386.8
adj slippery 287.11
oily 1054.9
semiliquid 1060.11

butt in 214.7

butting juxtaposition
223.3
pushing 903.1

buttocks bottom 199.1
rump 217.4

button
noun chin 216.6
runt 258.4
bulge 283.3
insignia 647.1
fastening 799.3
trifle 997.5
cast 1056.5
verb close 293.6
hook 799.8

buttonhole
noun bouquet 310.23
verb bore 118.7
importune 440.12
address 524.27

buttons beans 87.12
bad seed 87.16
attendant 577.5

buttress
noun supporter 900.2
buttressing 900.4
verb strengthen 15.13
support 449.12,
900.21
confirm 956.11

buttressed 900.24

buxom merry 109.15
corpulent 257.18
comely 1015.18

buy
noun bargain 633.3
verb assent 332.8
purchase 733.7
believe 952.10
kid oneself 953.6

buy and sell 731.14

buy back 733.7

buyer 733.5

buy in 733.7

buying
noun purchase 733.1
adj purchasing 733.10

buying and selling
731.2

buying in 737.19

buying up 733.1

buy into participate
476.5
purchase 733.7
kid oneself 953.6

buy out purchase 733.7
combine 804.3

buyout trading 737.19
combination 804.1

buy time 820.6

buy up purchase 733.7
corner 737.26

buzz
noun sibilation 57.1
rasp 58.3
tingle 74.1
kick 105.3
report 552.6
series 811.2
verb hum 52.13
sibilate 57.2
jangle 58.9
flathat 184.42
telephone 347.18
publish 352.10
murmur 524.26
tip 551.11

buzzed 87.23

buzzer alarm 400.1
cutlery 1039.2

buzzing
noun hum 52.7
flathatting 184.17
adj humming 52.20

by
adj past 836.7
adv in reserve 386.17

prep at 159.27
through 161.27
beside 218.11
by means of 384.13
conformable to 866.9

by accident 971.19

by all means
adv certainly 969.23
exclam yes 332.18

by and large
approximately 244.6
on the whole 791.14
generally 863.17

by any chance 965.10

by any means anyhow
384.10
by any possibility
965.10

by birth
adj related 559.6
adv intrinsically
766.10

by-blow 561.5

by bus 176.19

by chance haphazardly
809.18
perchance 971.19

by choice 324.10

by coincidence 971.19

by comparison with
942.11

by consensus 787.11

by design 380.10

by dint of
adv usefully 387.26
prep by virtue of
18.18
by means of 384.13

bye 747.3

by-election 609.15

by far 247.17

by fax 401.13

by force 424.14

bygone 836.7

by hand 176.19

by heart 988.28

by horse 177.44

by itself 871.13

by land 234.8

by law 673.12

by-line avocation 724.7
football 745.1
acknowledgment 887.2

by mail 176.19

by marriage 564.4

by means of 449.25

by mistake 974.20

by name 527.15

by nature 766.10

by no means
adv noway 248.11
phrase I refuse 442.7
exclam by no manner
of means 335.9

by one 469.8

bypass
noun byway 383.4
detour 913.3
verb pass 909.8
go roundabout 913.4

by-product aftermath
816.3
effect 886.1
extract 892.3

by proxy indirectly
576.17
instead 861.11

by rail 176.19

byre 228.20

by reason of 887.9

by remote control
1040.24

by right 637.4

by rights 637.4

by sea 240.9

by sight 27.22

bystander neighbour
223.6
spectator 917.1
witness 956.6

by storm 18.17

by surprise 131.14

by the board
adj lost 473.7
adv overboard 182.74

by the book formally
580.11
to be exact 972.22

by-the-book 580.10

by the by 842.13

by the same token
additionally 253.11
accordingly 765.11
similarly 783.18

by the side of 218.11

by the way 842.13

by-the-way discursive
538.13
incidental 842.11

by the wind 182.65

by this time 837.4

by turns alternately
849.11
interchangeably 862.6

by two 874.8

by use of
adv usefully 387.26
prep by means of
384.13

by virtue of 18.18

by water 240.9

by way of through
161.27
by means of 384.13

byword laughingstock
508.7
catchword 526.9
name 527.3

disgrace 661.5
maxim 973.1

by word of mouth
adj communicatively
343.12
adv orally 524.34

Byzantine
noun Aldine 554.15
adj convolutional
281.6
scheming 381.13
complex 798.4
shrewd 919.15

C basuco 87.6
hundred 881.8

c 223.26

cab 179.13

cabal
noun intrigue 381.5
fellowship 617.3
clique 617.6
company 769.3
combination 804.1
verb plot 381.9
league 804.4

caballero beau 104.13
rider 178.8
knight 608.5

cabaret bar 88.20
theatre 704.14
entertainment 743.13

cabbage
noun vegetables 10.34
verb swipe 482.16

cabin
noun stateroom 197.9
cottage 228.8
verb confine 212.6

cabinet container 195.1
sanctum 197.8
furniture 229.1
council 423.1
directorate 574.11
Privy Council 613.3
office 739.7
radio 1033.3

cabinet minister
575.17

cable
noun cord 271.2
telegram 347.14
line 347.17
electrical device
1031.20
verb telegraph 347.19

cable television 1034.1

cable TV 1034.1

cache
noun hiding place
346.4
reserve 386.3
verb secrete 346.7
store 386.10

cachet label 517.13
characteristic 864.4

cackle
noun rasp 58.3

laughter 116.4
chatter 540.3
verb jangle 58.9
warble 60.5
laugh 116.8
murmur 524.26

cacophony raucousness
58.2
discord 61.1
inelegance 534.1
turbulence 671.2
pandemonium 809.5
ugliness 1014.1

cactus beans 87.12
bad seed 87.16
thorn 285.5

cad vulgarian 497.6
bounder 660.8

caddie
noun attendant 577.5
phrase carrier 176.7

caddy 195.1

cadence sinkage 194.2
accent 524.11
passage 708.24
ornament 709.18
metre 720.7

cadet
noun navy man 183.4
adj subsequent 834.4

cadre frame 266.4
unit 461.21
directorate 574.11
clique 617.6

caesar kaiser 575.9
tyrant 575.14

cafeteria restaurant
8.17
dining room 197.11

caffeine 86.9

cage
noun enclosure 212.3
place of confinement
429.7
verb enclose 212.5
confine 429.12
drive 1068.8

cage bird 311.28

caged 212.10

cagey evasive 368.15
cunning 415.12
wary 494.9

Cain 308.10

cairn marker 517.10
monument 549.12

cajole deceive 356.14
urge 375.14
lure 377.5
importune 440.12
flatter 511.5

cajoling persuasive
375.29
alluring 377.8
importunate 440.18
flattering 511.8

cake
noun gâteau 10.40

solid 1043.6
verb thicken 1043.10
solidify 1044.8

caked 1043.14

calamitous destructive
395.26
disastrous 1010.15

calamity fatality 308.7
bane 1000.1
misfortune 1010.2

calculate measure
300.10
plan 380.6, 381.8
premeditate 380.7
compute 1016.17

calculated intentional
380.8
planned 381.12
reasoned 934.21

calculated to 895.6

calculating deceitful
356.22, 645.18
scheming 381.13
shrewd 919.15
numerative 1016.23

calculation
measurement 300.1
intentionality 380.3
plan 381.1
caution 494.1
computation 1016.10

calculator adding
253.3
strategist 415.7
accountant 628.7
computer 1016.14

calculus 1016.10

calendar
noun notebook 549.11
reference book 554.9
calends 831.8
roll 870.6
schedule 964.3
verb record 549.15
chronologize 831.14
list 870.8
schedule 964.6

calf member 2.7
leg 177.14
fledgling 302.10
cattle 311.6
ice 1022.5

calibrated 245.5

calibre ability 18.2
degree 245.1
size 257.1
diameter 269.3
talent 413.4
intelligence 919.1

calico 47.12

caliph 575.10

call
noun audition 48.2
cry 59.1
animal noise 60.1
telephone call 347.13
summons 420.5,
517.16

noun sore 85.36
blight 1000.2
verb corrupt 393.12
corrode 393.21
decay 393.22

canned fuddled 88.33
packed 212.12

cannibal
noun eater 8.16
killer 308.10
vertebrate 311.3
savage 593.5
adj eating 8.31

cannibalism eating 8.1
cruelty 144.11

canning packaging
212.2
food preservation
397.2

cannon
noun artillery 462.11
match 752.3
impact 901.3
recoil 902.2
shot 903.4
verb pull the trigger
459.22
play 752.4
collide 901.13

cannonball lightning
174.6
plunge 367.1
shot 462.19

cannot 19.8

cannot help but
962.10

canny cunning 415.12
cautious 494.8
economical 635.6
shrewd 919.15

canoe
noun ship 180.1
roulette 759.12
verb navigate 182.13

canoeing 182.1

can of worms
hotchpotch 796.6
complex 798.2
trouble 1012.3

canon round 280.9,
708.19
measure 300.2
rule 419.2, 868.4
literature 547.12,
718.1
compilation 554.7
law 673.3
Bible 683.2
lore 927.9
belief 952.2

canopy
noun heavens 1070.2
verb cover 295.19

cant
noun inclination 204.2
angle 278.2
hypocrisy 354.6
Greek 522.7

jargon 523.9
sanctimony 693.1
verb change course
182.30
careen 182.43
incline 204.10
be hypocritical 354.23
speak 523.16
be sanctimonious
693.4

cantankerous crabby
110.20
perverse 361.11
hindering 1011.17

cantata sacred music
708.17
part music 708.18

canteen restaurant 8.17
dining room 197.11

canter
noun run 174.3
hypocrite 357.8
pietist 693.3
verb speed 174.8
go on horseback
177.34

can't help but 424.9

canton state 231.5
heraldic device 647.2

canvas sail 180.14
tent 295.8
arena 463.1
painting 712.14
palette 712.18
boxing 754.1

canvass
noun vote 371.6
solicitation 440.5
campaign 609.13
assemblage 769.1
survey 937.14
verb vote 371.18
solicit 440.14
discuss 541.12
electioneer 609.40
examine 937.24
survey 937.29

canvassing vote 371.6
solicitation 440.5
discussion 541.7

canyon 237.7

cap
noun headdress 5.25
acid 87.9
summit 198.2
head 198.4
architectural topping
198.5
cover 295.5
fuse 462.15
type 548.6
cricket 747.1
verb cloak 5.39
top 198.9, 295.21
excel 249.6
complete 407.6
give in kind 506.6

capability ability 18.2
preparedness 405.4

skill 413.1
talent 413.4

capable able 18.14
fitted 405.17
competent 413.24

capable of 896.6

capacious spacious
158.10
voluminous 257.17

capacities 918.2

capacity
noun ability 18.2
spaciousness 158.5
volume 257.2
means 384.2
skill 413.1
talent 413.4
function 724.3
mode 764.4
full measure 793.3
intelligence 919.1
capacitance 1031.15
adj full 793.11

capacity for 413.5

cape 283.9

caper
noun dido 366.2
prank 489.10
frolic 743.5
verb exude
cheerfulness 109.6
rejoice 116.5
cut capers 366.6
play 743.23

capillary
noun duct 2.21
adj circulatory 2.31
hairlike 3.24
threadlike 271.7

capital
noun architectural
topping 198.5
metropolis 208.7
capital city 230.4
means 384.2
supply 386.2
type 548.6
fund 728.15
adj top 198.10
chief 249.14
literal 546.8
monetary 728.30
paramount 996.24
good 998.12

capital city 230.4

capital gains 472.3

capital goods 386.2

capitalism
noninterference 430.9
capitalistic system
611.9

capitalist
noun Thatcherite
611.20
financier 729.8
adj capitalistic 611.32

capitalize letter 546.6
keep accounts 628.8

finance 729.15

capital punishment
condemnation 602.1
execution 604.6

capitulate 433.8

capitulation surrender
433.2
treaty 437.2
summation 1016.11

capped clothing 5.44
topped 198.12

cappella 708.53

capping topping 198.11
superior 249.12
ending 819.10

caprice whim 364.1
capriciousness 364.2
thoughtlessness 365.3

capricious irresolute
362.9
whimsical 364.5
unthinking 365.10
unessential 767.4
nonuniform 781.3
unordered 809.12
transient 827.7
irregular 850.3
inconstant 853.7
uncertain 970.16

capsize
noun overturn 205.2
verb upset 182.44
tumble 194.8
overturn 205.6

capsized 205.7

capsule
noun pill 86.7
hull 295.16
seed vessel 310.28
abridgment 557.1
spacecraft 1073.2
verb package 212.9
abridge 557.5
adj shortened 268.9

Captain Field Marshal
575.20
Admiral of the Fleet
575.21

captain
noun aviator 185.1
governor 575.6
policeman 1007.15
verb direct 573.8
govern 612.12

caption
noun title 936.2
verb focus on 936.3

captivated enamoured
104.28
wondering 122.9
enchanted 691.12

captivating delightful
97.7
alluring 377.8

captive
noun prisoner 429.11
subject 432.7
adj subjugated 432.14

captivity imprisonment
429.3
subjection 432.1

captor 480.11

capture
noun arrest 429.6
seizure 480.2
take 480.10
verb triumph 411.3
arrest 429.15
acquire 472.8
apprehend 480.18

car automobile 179.9
railway carriage
179.15
motor racing 756.1

caravan wagon 179.2
trailer 179.19
mobile home 228.17
procession 811.3

carbon radium 91.8
transcript 784.4
scoria 1019.16
isotope 1037.5

carbonate chemicalize
1058.7
vaporize 1065.8

carbon copy same
777.3
transcript 784.4

carbon dioxide 1023.7

carboniferous 1020.8

carcass wreck 393.8
body 1050.3

carcinogen 85.41

carcinogenic 85.60

carcinoma 85.38

card
noun identification
517.11
bulletin board 549.10
postcard 553.3
playing card 758.2
schedule 964.3
verb comb 79.21

cardboard 1052.5

cardiac arrest 85.19

cardinal red 41.6
chief 249.14
paramount 996.24

cardiovascular disease
85.19

care
noun medicine 90.1
affliction 96.8
sorrow 112.10
anxiety 126.1
carefulness 339.1
usage 387.2
custody 429.5
observance 434.1
support 449.3
patronage 449.4
caution 494.1
supervision 573.2
commission 615.1
thrift 635.1

attention 982.1
protectorship 1007.2
adversity 1010.1
verb mind 339.6
adj helping 449.20
care about 93.11
career
  noun progression
  162.1
  course 172.2
  vocation 724.6
  verb flounder 916.15
  adj skilled 413.26
career woman woman
  77.5
  worker 726.2
care for treat 91.24,
  387.12
  love 104.19
  foster 449.16
  serve 577.13
  take care of 1007.19
carefree content 107.7
  lighthearted 109.12
careful heedful 339.10
  parsimonious 484.7
  cautious 494.8
  economical 635.6
  conscientious 644.15
  judicious 919.19
  attentive 982.15
careful consideration
  494.1
carefully heedfully
  339.15
  cautiously 494.12
  economically 635.7
careless unconcerned
  102.7
  heedless 340.11
  unthinking 365.10
  bungling 414.20
  lax 426.4
  reckless 493.8
  ungrammatic 531.4
  slovenly 809.15
  incurious 981.3
  inattentive 983.6
carelessly
  unconcernedly 102.10
  heedlessly 340.14
  on impulse 365.14
  recklessly 493.11
  haphazardly 809.18
carelessness unconcern
  102.2
  heedlessness 340.2
  thoughtlessness 365.3
  bungling 414.4
  laxness 426.1
  recklessness 493.2
  slovenliness 809.6
  incuriosity 981.1
  inattention 983.1
carer 1007.6
caress
  noun touch 73.1
  contact 223.5
  endearment 562.5

verb stroke 73.8
  contact 223.10
  pet 562.16
  rub 1042.6
caressing touching
  73.2
  lovemaking 562.1
caretaker paramedic
  90.11
  guardian 1007.6
cargo
  noun load 196.2
  burden 297.7
  charge 643.3
  impediment 1011.6
  phrase freight 176.6
cargo ship 180.1
caricature
  noun bad likeness
  350.2
  exaggeration 355.1
  wit 489.1
  burlesque 508.6
  cartoon 712.16
  verb misrepresent
  350.3
  exaggerate 355.3
  burlesque 508.11
caries 85.39
caring
  noun sympathy 93.5
  love 104.1
  carefulness 339.1
  support 449.3
  protectorship 1007.2
  adj careful 339.10
  helping 449.20
  protective 1007.23
carman 178.9
carmine
  verb redden 41.4
  adj red 41.6
carnage massacre 308.4
  destruction 395.1
carnal sexual 75.24
  unvirtuous 654.12
  carnal-minded 663.6
  lascivious 665.29
  secularist 695.16
carnation 41.6
carnival treat 95.3
  show business 704.1
  festival 743.4
  park 743.14
carnivorous 8.31
carol
  noun song 708.14
  verb warble 60.5
  rejoice 116.5
  sing 708.38
carousel merry-go-
  round 743.15
  rotator 914.4
carp 510.15
carp at 510.16
carpenter 704.24
carpet

noun ground covering
  199.3
  rug 295.9
  two hundred 881.9
  verb floor 295.22
  reprove 510.17
carpeting 295.9
car phone 347.4
carping
  noun criticism 510.4
  adj critical 510.23
carr 243.1
car racing 756.1
carriage
  noun looks 33.4
  vehicle 179.1
  four-wheeler 179.4
  railway carriage
  179.15
  behaviour 321.1
  gesture 517.14
  freightage 630.7
  support 900.1
  phrase transportation
  176.3
carriageway 383.5
carried 371.26
carried away overjoyed
  95.16
  excited 105.20
  frenzied 105.25
carrier infection 85.4
  vector 85.43
  vehicle 179.1
  aircraft carrier 180.8
  messenger 353.1
  carrier pigeon 353.6
  supporter 900.2
  radio wave 1033.11
carrion
  noun filth 80.7
  offal 80.9
  corpse 307.16
  rot 393.7
  adj dead 307.30
carrot 375.7
carry
  noun range 158.2
  round 748.3
  verb be pregnant
  78.12
  extend 158.8
  transport 176.12
  adopt 371.15
  induce 375.22
  triumph 411.3
  keep accounts 628.8
  deal in 731.15
  support 900.21
  phrase transportation
  176.3
carrying
  noun support 900.1
  adj pregnant 78.18
  supporting 900.23
  phrase transportation
  176.3
carrying-on 489.5

carrying out
  performance 328.2
  execution 437.4
carry it 411.3
carry off carry out
  328.7
  bring about 407.5
  succeed with 409.11
  seize 480.14
carry on be patient
  134.4
  practice 328.8
  keep going 330.15
  persevere 360.2
  direct 573.8
  play 743.23
  kick up a row 809.11
  endure 826.6
  continue 855.3
  do the usual thing
  868.7
carry-on agitation
  105.4, 916.1
  bustle 330.4
  commotion 809.4
carry out reach out
  261.5
  carry through 328.7
  apply 387.11
  bring about 407.5
  execute 437.9
carry-out 8.17
carry through be
  patient 134.4
  carry out 328.7
  not hesitate 359.10
  prosecute to a
  conclusion 360.5
  bring about 407.5
  execute 437.9
  succeed 816.5
cart
  noun two-wheeler
  179.3
  verb haul 176.13
carte menu 8.14
  bill 870.5
carte blanche latitude
  430.4
  blank cheque 443.4
  privilege 642.2
cartel compact 437.1
  treaty 437.2
  company 617.9
  combination 804.1
carter
  noun driver 178.9
  phrase carrier 176.7
Cartesian agnostic
  695.20
  Aristotelian 951.10
car theft 482.2
cartilage
  noun skeleton 2.2
  muscles 2.3
  leather 1047.2
  adj skeleton 2.24
carton 212.9

cartoon
  noun diagram 381.3
  cinema 706.1
  drawing 712.13
  caricature 712.16
  verb portray 712.19
cartoonist 716.3
cartridge record 50.12
  cartouche 462.17
  film 714.10
carve form 262.7
  furrow 290.3
  apportion 477.6
  record 549.15
  engrave 713.9
  sculpture 715.5
  sever 801.11
  process 891.9
carved formative 262.9
  engraved 713.11
  sculptured 715.7
carve out 891.8
carver sculptor 716.6
  printmaker 716.8
  seat 900.17
carve up 477.6
carving figure 349.6
  sculpture 715.1
casa 228.5
Casanova beau 104.13
  deceiver 357.1
  philanderer 562.12
  libertine 665.10
cascade
  noun descent 194.1
  waterfall 238.11
  outburst 671.6
  verb descend 194.5
  hang 202.6
  overflow 238.17
cascading 202.9
case
  noun sick person 85.42
  container 195.1
  frame 266.4
  blanket 295.10
  hull 295.16
  casing 295.17
  common case 530.9
  type 548.6
  bookbinding 554.14
  lawsuit 598.1
  fact 760.3
  state 764.1
  particular 765.3
  example 785.2
  oddity 869.4
  argument 934.5
  topic 936.1
  citation 956.5
  truth 972.3
  verb package 212.9
  wrap 295.20
  reconnoitre 937.28
case history medical
  history 91.10
  history 719.1

case in point example
785.2
citation 956.5

casement frame 266.4
window 292.7

case study 349.3

cash
noun payment 624.1
money 728.1
verb pay cash 624.17
cash in 728.29
adv cash on the nail
624.25

cash flow supply 386.2
funds 728.14
cash 728.18

cashier
noun payer 624.9
banker 729.10
treasurer 729.11
verb depose 447.4
dismiss 908.19

cash in croak 307.20
cash 728.29

cash in on 387.15

casing frame 266.4
case 295.17

casino resort 228.27
ballroom 705.4
entertainment 743.13
gambling house
759.19

cask
noun container 195.1
cylinder 282.4
verb package 212.9

casket
noun coffin 309.11
verb confine 212.6

Cassandra pessimist
125.7
warner 399.4
predictor 961.4

casserole 10.7

cassette 50.12

cassock 699.5

cast
noun slough 2.5
glance 27.4
strabismus 28.5
looks 33.4
colour 35.1
dressing 86.33
hint 248.4
form 262.1
team 617.7
role 704.10
cast of characters
707.11
sculpture 715.2
throw 759.9, 903.3
nature 766.4
company 769.3
casting 784.6, 1056.5
mould 785.6
kind 808.3
characteristic 864.4
tendency 895.1

disposition 977.3
sum 1016.6
verb give birth 1.3
shed 6.10
clap 159.13
change course 182.30
form 262.7
plan 381.8
discard 390.7
sculpture 715.5
produce 891.8
throw 903.10
eject 908.13
calculate 1016.17
burn 1019.24
adj born 1.4
formative 262.9
made 891.18

cast a shadow 1026.9

cast doubt on 954.6

caste rank 245.2
class 607.1, 808.2
community 617.2

caster 903.7

casting sculpture 715.1
cast 784.6, 1056.5
production 891.2
throwing 903.2
calculation 1016.10

cast-iron strong 15.15
unyielding 361.9
true 972.13

castle estate 228.7
stronghold 460.6

cast off take off 6.6
detach 801.10
do away with 908.21

cast-off adrift 182.61
outcast 586.10

cast out eject 908.13
banish 908.17

castrated unmanned
19.19
unsexual 75.28
crippled 393.30
mutilated 794.5

castration emasculation
19.5
gelding 255.4

casual
noun irregular 461.15
ruffian 593.3
poor man 619.4
worker 726.2
adj dressed up 5.45
in dishabille 5.46
unconcerned 102.7
nonchalant 106.15
careless 340.11
unpremeditated
365.11
informal 581.3
circumstantial 765.7
unessential 767.4
unordered 809.12
incidental 842.11
occasional 847.3
undiscriminating
944.5

chance 971.15
purposeless 971.16
easy 1013.13

casually nonchalantly
106.18
carelessly 340.18
informally 581.4
by chance 971.19
purposelessly 971.20

casual sex 75.7

casualty fatality 308.7
happening 971.6
misfortune 1010.2

casualty list 307.14

Cat 179.18

cat eagle 27.11
guy 76.5
bitch 110.12
feline 311.21
whip 605.1

cataclysm overflow
238.6
debacle 395.4
upheaval 671.5
disruption 801.3
revolution 859.1
misfortune 1010.2

cataclysmic destructive
395.26
convulsive 671.23
revolutionary 859.5
disastrous 1010.15

catacombs 309.16

catalogue
noun description 349.2
record 549.1
notebook 549.11
reference book 554.9
directory 574.10
account book 628.4
outline 800.4
classified catalogue
870.3
verb record 549.15
classify 800.8, 808.6
list 870.8

catalogued classified
808.8
listed 870.9

cataloguing description
349.2
registration 549.14
classification 808.1
index 870.7

catalyst instigator
375.11
dissociation 805.2
transformer 851.5
author 885.4

catalytic dissociative
805.6
metamorphic 851.12

catapult
noun takeoff 184.8
sling 462.9
toy 743.16
verb throw 903.10

cataract

noun blindness 30.1
eye disease 85.14
descent 194.1
waterfall 238.11
verb descend 194.5
overflow 238.17

catastrophe debacle
395.4
upheaval 671.5
plot 722.4
end 819.1
revolution 859.1
misfortune 1010.2

catastrophic
destructive 395.26
revolutionary 859.5
disastrous 1010.15

catch
noun desire 100.11
lover 104.12
surprise 131.2
trick 356.6
Catch-22 421.3
lock 428.5
seizure 480.2
take 480.10
round 708.19
match 747.3
good thing 998.5
fault 1002.2
obstacle 1011.4
crux 1012.8
verb hear 48.11
jump at 101.6
trap 356.20
acquire 472.8
grab 472.9
take 480.17
understand 521.7
play 747.4
fight 754.4
root 854.10
catch out 940.7
engross 982.13
catch fire 1019.23

Catch-22 421.3

catch at 940.7

catcher 480.11

catch fire be excitable
105.16
succeed 409.7
burn 1018.22
catch on fire 1019.23

catching
noun seizure 480.2
discovery 940.1
adj poisonous 82.7
contagious 85.61
alluring 377.8
taking 480.25

catch on understand
521.7
become popular 578.8

catchphrase maxim
973.1
motto 973.4

catch up 174.13

catch up with 174.13

catchy deceptive
356.21
melodious 708.48
irregular 850.3

Catechism 676.2

catechism question
937.10
system of belief 952.3

categorical
classificational 808.7
dialectic 934.22
unqualified 959.2

category class 808.2
topic 936.1

cater 385.9

catered 385.13

caterer 385.6

cater for toady to
138.8
aid 449.11

catering cooking 11.1
provision 385.1

Caterpillar 179.18

caterpillar larva 302.12
insect 311.31

cater to toady to 138.8
indulge 427.6
serve 449.18

cat food 10.4

catharsis defecation
12.2
cleansing 79.2
purgation 92.25
release 120.2

cathartic
noun cleanser 79.17
laxative 86.17
adj cleansing 79.28
laxative 86.48
relieving 120.9

cathedral
noun church 703.1
adj authoritative
969.18

catheter 239.6

Catholic
noun Roman Catholic
675.19
adj Roman Catholic
675.29

catholic universal
863.14
broad-minded 978.8

Catholic Church
675.8

Catholicism 675.8

cathouse 228.28

cattle animal life 311.1
kine 311.6
rabble 606.3

catwalk 383.2

caucus election 609.15
party 617.4
assembly 769.2

caught not out 747.5
stuck 854.16

gripped 982.18
caught up in involved in 897.5
engrossed 982.17
cauldron 857.10
causal motivating 375.25
causative 885.13
causality 885.1
causation 885.1
cause
noun motive 375.1
lawsuit 598.1
warrant 600.6
occasion 885.1
principle 885.9
verb prompt 375.13
compel 424.4
be the cause of 885.10
perform 891.11
cause and effect 885.1
caused 891.17
caused by 886.8
cause for alarm 1005.1
cause to 424.4
cause trouble 1012.14
causeway 295.22
caustic
noun curve 279.2
cauterant 1019.15
adj acrimonious 17.14
bitter 64.6
pungent 68.6
penetrating 105.31
out of humour 110.17
mordant 144.23
resentful 152.26
satiric 508.13
hostile 589.10
caution
noun carefulness 339.1
hesitation 362.3
dissuasion 379.1
warning 399.1
advice 422.1
collateral 438.3
cautiousness 494.1
tip 551.3
game 745.3
incredulity 955.1
forethought 960.2
verb dissuade 379.3
warn 399.5
admonish 422.6
cautionary dissuasive 379.5
warning 399.7
advisory 422.8
cautioning
noun dissuasion 379.1
adj warning 399.7
cautious slow 175.10
careful 339.10, 494.8
hesitant 362.11
incredulous 955.4
cautiously slowly 175.13
carefully 339.15, 494.12
cavalcade 811.3
cavalier
noun beau 104.13
rider 178.8
gallant 504.9
knight 608.5
escort 768.5
adj disdainful 141.13
gruff 505.7
cave
noun observation 27.2
lair 228.26
cavern 284.5
debacle 395.4
watchman 1007.10
shelter 1008.3
verb sink 194.6
collapse 260.10
hollow 284.13
caveat dissuasion 379.1
warning 399.1
advice 422.1
cave in weaken 16.9
sink 194.6
collapse 260.10
hollow 284.13
breach 292.14
yield 433.7
cave-in collapse 260.4
debacle 395.4
caveman real man 76.6
barbarian 497.7
ancient 841.7
cavendish 89.7
cavern 284.5
cavernous abysmal 275.11
concave 284.16
caviar fish 10.23
egg 305.15
cavity compartment 197.2
crack 224.2
pit 275.2
concavity 284.2
opening 292.1
cavorting leaping 366.3
festivity 743.3
CD-ROM 1041.6
CE 820.13
cease
noun cessation 856.1
verb disappear 34.3
quiet 173.8
close shop 293.8
give up 370.7
perish 395.23
end 819.5
discontinue 856.6
cease fire make peace 465.9
stop 856.7
cease-fire truce 465.5
pause 856.3
ceaseless continuous 811.8
perpetual 828.7
constant 846.5
continuing 855.7
ceaselessly perpetually 828.10
constantly 846.7
cease to be 34.3
cease to exist 34.3
ceasing end 819.1
cessation 856.1
cede give up 370.7
yield 433.7
surrender 433.8
relinquish 475.3
transfer 629.3
ceded 475.5
ceding 370.3
ceiling distinctness 31.2
airspace 184.32
boundary 211.3
height 272.1
roof 295.6
price index 630.4
limit 793.5
celeb 662.9
celebrate observe 487.2, 701.14
praise 509.12
formalize 580.5
glorify 696.11
make merry 743.24
celebrated distinguished 662.16
notable 996.19
celebrating
noun celebration 487.1
adj celebrative 487.3
celebration spree 88.5
treat 95.3
rejoicing 116.1
celebrating 487.1
ceremony 580.4
ritualism 701.1
revel 743.6
celebratory 487.3
celebrity glory 247.2
publicity 352.4
repute 662.1
celeb 662.9
notability 996.2
personage 996.8
celestial
noun angel 679.1
adj divine 677.16
angelic 679.6
heavenly 681.12, 1070.25
ideal 985.23
celibacy singleness 565.1
abstinence 668.2
monasticism 698.4
aloneness 871.2
celibate
noun célibataire 565.2
religious 699.15
adj monastic 565.6
continent 664.6
abstinent 668.10
sole 871.9
unproductive 890.4
cell compartment 197.2
bioplast 305.4
prison 429.8
retreat 584.6, 1008.5
clique 617.6
cellar cellarage 197.17
storehouse 386.6
cell division 305.16
cellist 710.5
Cellnet 347.4
cellular 305.19
cellulose 305.6
cement
noun pavement 383.6
ceramic ware 742.2
adhesive 802.4
stone 1044.6
sticks and stones 1052.2
verb floor 295.22
plaster 295.25
put together 799.5
fasten 799.7
stick together 802.9
adj hard 1044.10
cemented fast 799.14
cohesive 802.10
cemetery 309.15
cenotaph tomb 309.16
monument 549.12
censor
noun restrictionist 428.6
faultfinder 510.9
conscience 636.5
critic 945.7
verb delete 255.12
cover up 345.8
suppress 428.8
end 819.5
censored secret 345.11
suppressed 428.14
censorious averse 99.8
fastidious 495.9
prudish 500.19
condemnatory 510.22, 602.5
disparaging 512.13
censorship suppression 92.24
veil of secrecy 345.3
censure
noun reprehension 510.3
incrimination 599.2
condemnation 602.1
stigma 661.6
criticism 945.2
verb reprehend 510.13
incriminate 599.10
condemn 602.3
stigmatize 661.9
criticize 945.14
census
noun contents 196.1
population 227.1
assemblage 769.1
table 807.4
roll 870.6
numeration 1016.9
summation 1016.11
verb number 1016.16
cent mill 728.8
trifle 997.5
centenary
noun anniversary 849.4
hundred 881.8
adj momentary 849.8
hundredth 881.29
centigrade 1018.30
centimetre 881.8
centipede insect 311.31
hundred 881.8
central interior 207.6
centric 208.11
medium 246.3
chief 249.14
phonetic 524.31
middle 818.4
original 885.14
vital 996.23
Central America 231.6
central bank 729.13
central government
government 612.3
federal government 612.4
centralism
centralization 208.8
policy 609.4
democratism 612.8
centrality 208.1
centralization centring 208.8
combination 804.1
centralized 208.11
centrally internally 207.9
mediumly 246.4
central station 1031.18
centre
noun interior 207.2
centrum 208.2
mean 246.1
moderatism 611.2
moderate 611.14
ice hockey team 750.5
basketball team 751.2
essence 766.2
middle 818.1
attractor 906.2
verb converge 169.2
centralize 208.9
play 745.4

centre forward 745.2, 750.2

centrepiece focus 208.4
feature 996.7

centric 208.11

centrifugal diverging 171.8
rotating 914.14

centring 208.8

centrist
noun nonpartisan 609.28
moderate 611.14, 670.4
adj neutral 467.7
moderate 611.26
middle 818.4

century match 747.3
moment 823.2
long time 826.4
hundred 881.8

ceramic 742.7

ceramics visual arts 712.1
pottery 742.1
ceramic ware 742.2

cereal
noun breakfast food 10.33
grass 310.5
adj vegetable 310.33

cerebral nerve 2.28
mental 918.7

ceremonial
noun formality 580.1
ceremony 580.4
rite 701.3
adj ceremonious 580.8
ritualistic 701.18

ceremonies 504.7

ceremony celebration 487.1
formality 580.1
ceremonial 580.4
rite 701.3

certain expectant 130.11
quantitative 244.5
secured 438.11
particular 864.12
one 871.7
plural 882.7
belief 952.21
evidential 956.16
inevitable 962.15
sure 969.13
impossible 971.18
true 972.13

certain knowledge 969.1

certainly
adv positively 247.19
inevitably 962.19
surely 969.23
truly 972.18
exclam yes 332.18

certainly not 335.8

certain number
plurality 882.1
number 883.2

certainty expectation 130.1
knowledge 927.1
belief 952.1
conviction 952.5
inevitability 962.7
certitude 969.1

certificate
noun certification 549.6
verb authorize 443.11

certification ratification 332.4
deposition 334.3
authorization 443.3
certificate 549.6
confirmation 956.4
ensuring 969.8

certified accepted 332.14
affirmed 334.9
secured 438.11
proved 956.20
assured 969.20
true 972.13

certify ratify 332.12
depose 334.6
secure 438.9
authorize 443.11
testify 956.9
confirm 956.11
make sure 969.11

cervical 2.27

cervical smear 91.12

cervix genitals 2.11
contraction 260.1
joint 799.4
supporter 900.2

cessation standstill 173.3
abandonment 370.1
discontinuance 390.2, 856.1
interruption 812.2
end 819.1
close 819.3

chaff
noun remainder 256.1
hull 295.16
air 298.2
refuse 391.4
rabble 606.3
trivia 997.4
jamming 1035.13
verb banter 490.5
scoff 508.9

chafing
noun impatience 135.1
abrasion 1042.2
adj irritating 26.13
troublesome 126.10
impatient 135.6
heating 1019.26
abrasive 1042.10

chagrin
noun distress 96.4

humiliation 137.2
verb embarrass 96.15

chain
noun mountain 237.6
jewel 498.6
insignia 647.1
series 811.2
curb 1011.7
fire iron 1019.12
atomic cluster 1037.7
verb bind 428.10, 799.9
put together 799.5
secure 854.8

chained continuous 811.8
stuck 854.16

chain reaction series 811.2
vicissitudes 971.5
fission 1037.8

chains 428.4

chain smoking 87.1

chain store 736.1

chair
noun furniture 229.1
mastership 417.7
saddle 417.10
instructorship 571.10
chairman 574.5
capital punishment 604.6
scaffold 605.5
seat 900.17
verb administer 573.11
govern 612.12
install 615.12

chairman
noun chairwoman 574.5
chief 996.10
verb administer 573.11

chairman of the board 574.3

chairmanship
mastership 417.7
directorship 573.4

chairwoman 574.5

chaise 179.4

chalet 228.8

chalice 703.11

chalk
noun alabaster 37.2
palette 712.18
table 752.2
jockey 757.2
verb whiten 37.5
mark 517.19
record 549.15
portray 712.19

chalky white 37.7
powdery 1049.11

challenge
noun objection 333.2
opposition 451.1
resistance 453.1
dare 454.2

declaration of war 458.7
questioning 937.12
verb confront 216.8
object 333.5
demand 421.5
claim 421.6
contradict 451.6
offer resistance 453.3
defy 454.3
compete 457.18
make war on 458.15
doubt 954.6
thwart 1011.15

challenging provocative 375.27
defiant 454.7

chamber
noun toilet 12.11
room 197.1
compartment 197.2
bedroom 197.7
council 423.1
verb enclose 212.5

chamberlain major-domo 577.10
treasurer 729.11

chambermaid 577.8

chamber of commerce 617.9

chambers flat 228.13
courthouse 595.6
office 739.7

chameleon spectrum 47.6
timeserver 363.4
Proteus 853.4

champ
noun bite 8.2
champion 413.15
verb chew 8.27

Champion 311.15

champion
noun superior 249.4
victor 411.2
champ 413.15
defender 460.7
deputy 576.1
justifier 600.8
supporter 616.9
best 998.8
protector 1007.5
verb back 449.13
defend 460.8, 600.10
protect 1007.18
adj peerless 249.15
best 998.16
first-rate 998.17

championing 449.4

championship
supremacy 249.3
victory 411.1
patronage 449.4
football 745.1
rugby 746.1
golf 748.1
tennis 749.1
hockey 750.1
basketball 751.1

skiing 753.1
motor racing 756.1

Chance 971.2

chance
noun gamble 759.2, 970.8
turn 824.2
opportunity 842.2
liability 896.1
possibility 965.1
probability 967.1
uncertainty 970.1
happenstance 971.1
verb attempt 403.6
risk 759.24
turn up 830.6
bechance 971.11
take chances 1005.7
adj circumstantial 765.7
unessential 767.4
vague 970.19
chancy 971.15

chanced 404.7

chance it 759.24

chancel 703.9

chancellor principal 571.8
executive 574.3
head of state 575.7
minister 575.17
diplomat 576.6

Chancellor of the Exchequer minister 575.17
treasurer 729.11

chancery registry 549
foreign office 576.7
office 739.7

chandelier 1025.6

chandler provider 385.6
merchant 730.2

chandlery 385.1

change
noun custody 429.5
dough 728.2
petty cash 728.19
stock exchange 737.7
differentiation 779.4
alteration 851.1
conversion 857.1
substitution 861.1
substitute 861.2
verb don 5.42
move 172.5
vacillate 362.8
trade 731.14
differentiate 779.6
be changed 851.6
fluctuate 853.5
convert 857.11
substitute 861.4
interchange 862.4

changeable wishy-washy 16.17
irresolute 362.9
fickle 364.6
nonuniform 781.3

make haste 401.5
court 562.21
sculpture 715.5
repulse 907.3

chased in relief 283.18
sculptured 715.7

chaser drink 88.9
pursuer 382.4
act 704.7
sculptor 716.6

chasing following 166.1
sculpture 715.1
elimination 772.2

chasm crack 224.2
pit 275.2, 284.4
opening 292.1

chassis base 199.2
frame 266.4, 900.10
motor racing 756.1
radio 1033.3

chaste tasteful 496.8
simple 499.6, 797.6
elegant 533.6
immaculate 653.7
virtuous 664.4
abstinent 668.10
perfect 1001.6

chastened meek 433.15
restrained 670.11

chastity elegance 533.1
purity 653.3
virtue 664.1
abstinence 668.2
perfection 1001.1

chat
noun chatter 540.3
cosy chat 541.4
verb chatter 540.5
pass the time of day
541.10

chat show 1034.2

chatter
noun rattle 55.3
speech 524.1
jabber 540.3
verb rattle 55.6
warble 60.5
speak 524.20
protract 538.8
chat 540.5
shake 916.11
freeze 1022.9

chattering
noun constancy 846.2
shaking 916.2
adj rattly 55.8
prattling 540.10
constant 846.5
shaking 916.17
cold 1022.16

chatty talkative 540.9
conversational 541.13
intimate 582.24

chat up 377.5

chauffeur
noun driver 178.10
man 577.4
verb ride 177.33

chauvinism warlikeness
458.11
patriotism 591.2,
611.11
discrimination 979.4

chauvinist
noun militarist 461.5
misanthrope 590.2
patriot 591.3, 611.22
bigot 979.5
adj militaristic 458.22
public-spirited 591.4

chauvinistic militaristic
458.22
misanthropic 590.3
public-spirited 591.4
patriotic 611.34
discriminatory 979.12

cheap
adj worthless 391.11
cheapo 633.7
disgraceful 661.11
paltry 997.21
inferior 1004.9
adv cheaply 633.10

cheaply 633.10

cheat
noun fake 354.13
fraud 356.8
cheater 357.3, 759.22
verb victimize 356.18
live by one's wits
645.11
be promiscuous
665.19
pluck 759.26

cheating sham 354.3
fraud 356.8
cheating scheme
759.13

check
noun chequer 47.4
trauma 85.37
slowing 175.4
crack 224.2
opening 292.1
measure 300.2
discomfiture 412.2
restraint 428.1
confinement 429.1
mark 517.5
label 517.13
speech sound 524.13
chip 759.18
stop 856.2
checkup 937.6
collation 942.2
ensuring 969.8
blemish 1003.1
reverse 1010.3
hindrance 1011.1
frustration 1011.3
curb 1011.7
verb variegate 47.7
slow 175.9
cleave 224.4
injure 393.13
thwart 412.11
restrain 428.7
confine 429.12

fend off 460.10
mark 517.19
ski 753.4
bet 759.25
break 801.12
delay 845.8
put a stop to 856.11
specify 864.11
examine 937.24
collate 942.5
verify 969.12, 1016.20
blemish 1003.4
hinder 1011.10
monitor 1033.26
adj checked 47.14

checked chequered
47.14
retarded 175.12
impaired 393.27
phonetic 524.31
blemished 1003.8

check in arrive 186.6
croak 307.20
record 549.15
punch the clock
831.12

checking check 47.4
game 750.6
collation 942.2
ensuring 969.8

checklist directory
574.10
list 870.1
roll 870.6

check of 1016.12

check on 937.23

check out beat it 188.7
clock out 188.13
croak 307.20
qualify 405.15
punch the clock
831.12
investigate 937.23
examine 937.24

checks 47.4

check up 937.28

check up on examine
937.24
reconnoitre 937.28

cheek face 142.3
side 218.1

cheek by jowl
adv concurrently
898.5
phrase side by side
218.12

cheek-by-jowl 223.14

cheeks 217.5

cheeky 454.7

cheer
noun food 10.1
cry 59.1
happiness 95.2
cheerfulness 109.1
hurrah 116.2
applause 509.2
conviviality 582.3
verb refresh 9.2

cry 59.6
gladden 95.8, 109.7
give a cheer 116.6
comfort 121.6
give hope 124.10
assent 332.8
encourage 492.16
applaud 509.10

cheerful happy 95.15
pleasant 97.6
cheery 109.11
cheering 109.16
optimistic 124.12
homelike 228.33

cheerfully pleasantly
97.12
cheerily 109.17
hopefully 124.14

cheerfulness happiness
95.2
brightness 97.4
cheeriness 109.1
optimism 124.3
auspiciousness 133.9

cheerily 109.17

cheering refreshing 9.3
gladdening 109.16
comforting 121.13
promising 124.13

cheer up 109.9

cheery cheerful 109.11
cheering 109.16

cheese 10.46

cheesy 999.8

cheetah spectrum 47.6
big cat 311.22

chef 11.2

**Cheltenham Gold
Cup** 757.1

chemical
noun element 1058.2
verb chemicalize
1058.7
adj biochemical
1058.8

chemicals 1053.3

chemical weapons
462.1

chemist pharmacist
86.35
vendor 730.5

chemistry 1058.1

cheque 628.3

chequered checked
47.14
changeable 853.6

cherish hold dear
104.21
foster 449.16
hold 474.7
keep in memory
988.13
care for 1007.19

cherished 104.24

cherry 41.6

cherub child 302.3

darling 562.6
angel 679.1

cherubic 679.6

chest
noun breast 283.6
storehouse 386.6
treasury 729.12
adj pectoral 283.19

chested 283.19

chestnut
noun appaloosa 311.11
platitude 973.3
adj reddish-brown
40.4
redheaded 41.10

chevalier rider 178.8
gallant 504.9
knight 608.5

chevron zigzag 204.8
angle 278.2
heraldic device 647.2
insignia of rank 647.5

chew
noun bite 8.2
chewing tobacco 89.7
verb chew up 8.27
smoke 89.14
pulp 1061.5

chewed 1061.6

chewing
noun eating 8.1
smoking 89.10
adj masticatory 8.32
tobacco 89.15

chewing gum elastic
1046.3
gum 1060.6

chewy 1047.4

chic
noun smartness 578.3
adj dressed up 5.45
smart 578.13
hip 927.17

chicane chicanery
356.4
race 756.3
quibbling 935.5

chick gal 77.6, 302.7
fledgling 302.10
bird 311.28
poultry 311.29

chicken
noun weakling 16.6
mollycoddle 77.10
poultry 311.29
coward 491.5
adj effeminate 77.14
cowardly 491.10

chief
noun superior 249.4
superintendent 574.2
master 575.1
principal 575.3,
996.10
potentate 575.8
heraldic device 647.2
adj leading 165.3
top 198.10

front 216.10
main 249.14
directing 573.12
governing 612.18
preceding 813.4
first 817.17
paramount 996.24

chief constable
1007.15

chief engineer 183.7

chief executive
executive 574.3
head of state 575.7
chief 996.10

Chief Justice 596.4

chiefly mainly 249.17
on the whole 791.14
first 817.18
generally 863.17
normally 868.10

chief of police 1007.15

chief rabbi 699.10

**Chief Secretary to the
Treasury** 575.17

chieftain 575.8

chiffon
noun finery 498.3
adj bubbly 320.6

child nipper 302.3
person 312.5
simple soul 416.3
descendant 561.3
innocent 657.4
product 892.1

child abuse 144.11

childbearing 1.1

child benefit subsidy
478.8
welfarism 611.8

childbirth 1.1

child care 1007.2

childhood boyhood
301.2
young people 302.2
origin 817.4

childish childlike
301.11
senile 921.23
puerile 921.24

childless 890.4

childlike childish
301.11
artless 416.5
innocent 657.6
senile 921.23
puerile 921.24
trusting 952.22

childminder 1007.8

children young people
302.2
family 559.5
posterity 561.1

children's book 554.1

child's play 997.5

chill
noun anaemia 85.9

unfeeling 94.1
indifference 102.1
dejection 112.3
deterrent 379.2
aloofness 583.2
enmity 589.1
cold 1022.1
chilliness 1022.2
verb disincline 379.4
freeze 1022.9, 1022.10
refrigerate 1023.10
adj unfeeling 94.9
unfriendly 589.9
cool 1022.12

chilled reticent 344.10
cooled 1023.13

chilling
noun chill 1022.2
refrigeration 1023.1
adj frightening 127.28
refrigerative 1023.12

chill out relax 20.7
let oneself go 430.19
not stand on ceremony
581.2

chills 85.9

chilly unfeeling 94.9
aloof 141.12, 583.6
reticent 344.10
unfriendly 589.9
cool 1022.12
cold 1022.16

chime
noun ringing 54.3
harmony 708.3
repetitiousness 848.4
verb ring 54.8
say 524.23
harmonize 708.35
assonate 783.9
agree 787.6

chimera airy hope
124.5
illusion 975.1
figment of the
imagination 985.5

chimes bell 54.4
carillon 711.18

chiming
noun ringing 54.3
harmony 708.3
adj ringing 54.12
harmonious 708.49
monotonous 848.15

chimney valley 237.7
flue 239.14
fireplace 1019.11
deposit 1056.7

chimp 311.23

chimpanzee 311.23

chin 216.6

China 261.4

china
noun tableware 8.12
ceramic ware 742.2
eggshell 1048.2
adj ceramic 742.7

Chinatown 230.6

chine ridge 237.5
bulge 283.3

Chink 232.7

chink
noun thud 52.3
ringing 54.3
crack 224.2
furrow 290.1
vulnerability 1005.4
verb thud 52.15
ring 54.8
open 292.11
stop 293.7

chinook 318.7

chip
noun trauma 85.37
scrap 248.3
flake 296.3
air 298.2
check 759.18
piece 792.3
break 801.4
electronic circuit
1032.8
circuitry 1041.3
verb injure 393.13
break 801.12

chip in participate
476.5
pay for 624.18

chipped 393.27

chippy restaurant 8.17
market 736.1

chips 183.6

chiropractic 90.15

chiropractor 90.4

chirpy 109.13

chisel
noun point 715.4
tool 1039.1
verb form 262.7
furrow 290.3
gyp 356.19
engrave 713.9
sculpture 715.5
process 891.9

chiselled formative
262.9
sculptured 715.7

chit runt 258.4
child 302.3
gal 302.7
letter 553.2
receipt 627.2

chivalrous courageous
492.17
gallant 504.15
noble 608.10
magnanimous 652.6

chivalry military
science 458.6
courage 492.1
gallantry 504.2
aristocracy 608.1
magnanimity 652.2

chloroform
noun anaesthetic 86.15
verb deaden 25.4

kill 308.12

chlorophyll 44.1

chock
noun curb 1011.7
verb obstruct 1011.12

chocolate 40.3

choice
noun will 323.1
loophole 369.4
selection 371.1
free will 430.6
elegance 533.1
jockey 757.2
judgment 945.1
best 998.8
adj tasteful 496.8
best 998.16

choir
noun vestry 703.9
part music 708.18
chorus 710.16
keyboard 711.17
verb sing 708.38

choke
noun violent death
307.6
suffocation 308.6
verb silence 51.8
contract 260.7
close 293.6
stop 293.7
die a natural death
307.24
strangle 308.18
extinguish 395.15
overload 992.15
obstruct 1011.12
burn 1018.22
fight fire 1021.7

choked raucous 58.15
wretched 96.26
disappointed 132.5
resentful 152.26
contracted 260.12
closed 293.9
stopped 293.11
inarticulate 525.12
overfull 992.20

choking
noun contraction 260.1
obstruction 293.3
violent death 307.6
suffocation 308.6
extinction 395.6
extinguishing 1021.2
adj inarticulate 525.12
hindering 1011.17

cholesterol 7.7

chomp
noun bite 8.2
verb chew 8.27

choose desire 100.14
will 323.2
elect 371.13

choose to want to
100.15
will 323.2

choosing
noun choice 371.1

adj selective 371.23

choosy selective 371.23
fastidious 495.9

chop
noun feed 10.4
cutlet 10.18
side 218.1
wave 238.14
rough 288.2
hit 901.4
dismissal 908.5
verb reduce 252.7
notch 289.4
sever 801.11
be changed 851.6

chopped 289.5

chopped-off 812.4

chopper cycle 179.8
cutlery 1039.2

chopping 801.2

choppy rough 288.6
nonuniform 781.3
discontinuous 812.4
irregular 850.3
jolting 916.20

chops mouth 292.4
wind instrument 711.6

chopsticks 8.12

choral 708.50

chord
noun sympathy 93.5
straight line 277.2
concento 709.17
string 711.20
verb harmonize 708.35
tune 708.36
play 708.39

chore
noun task 724.2
tough proposition
1012.2
verb serve 577.13
work 725.12

choreographer
dramatist 704.22
dancer 705.3

choreography
representation 349.1
dancing 705.1

chorus
noun unanimity 332.5
cast 707.11
part music 708.18
passage 708.24
chorale 710.16
measure 720.9
agreement 787.1
sequel 816.1
repeat 848.5
verb imitate 336.5
say 524.23
sing 708.38

chorus line 705.3

chosen
noun elect 371.12
believing 692.5
best 998.8
adj superior 249.12

adj unbelligerent
464.10

civilian life 465.6

civility cultivation
392.3
decorousness 496.3
courtesy 504.1, 504.6
social convention
579.1
etiquette 580.3
sociability 582.1

civilization culture
373.3
cultivation 392.3
courtesy 504.1

civilized improved
392.13
elegant 496.9
learned 927.21

civil liberties right
430.2
human rights 642.3

civil list 870.1

civil rights right 430.2
human rights 642.3

civil servant 575.16

clack
noun noisemaker 53.6
rattle 55.3
snap 56.2
chatter 540.3
verb rattle 55.6
snap 56.7
warble 60.5
chatter 540.5

clad 5.44

cladding exterior 206.2
plating 295.13
lamina 296.2

claim
noun extortion 192.6
profession 376.2
demand 421.1
possession 469.1
estate 471.4
declaration 598.8
prerogative 642.1
verb extort 192.15
pretext 376.3
demand 421.5
pretend to 421.6
possess 469.4
take 480.13
require 962.9

claimant petitioner
440.7
accuser 599.5

claimed pretexted
376.5
spoken for 421.10

claiming 480.1

clairvoyance future
838.1
understanding 927.3
intuition 933.1
foreknowledge 960.3
divination 961.2

clairvoyant

noun clairaudient
689.14
adj psychic 689.24
intuitive 933.5
foreseeing 960.7

clam
noun marine animal
311.30
man of few words
344.5
verb fish 382.10

clamber
noun ascent 193.1
verb climb 193.11

clammy sweaty 12.22
viscous 1060.12

clamour
noun noise 53.3
outcry 59.4
clash 61.2
entreaty 440.2
verb be noisy 53.9
vociferate 59.8
complain 115.15

clamour for wish for
100.16
demand 421.5
entreat 440.11
require 962.9

clamp
noun contractor 260.6
hold 474.2
pile 769.10
curb 1011.7
harvest 1067.15
verb squeeze 260.8
bind 428.10
fasten 799.7
hamper 1011.11

clamp down on
612.16

clamped 260.12

clan race 559.4
community 617.2
clique 617.6
class 808.2
kind 808.3

clandestine 345.12

clang
noun ringing 54.3
rasp 58.3
animal noise 60.1
verb ring 54.8
jangle 58.9

clanging
noun ringing 54.3
adj noisy 53.13

clanking 54.3

clap
noun noise 53.3
report 56.1
applause 509.2
verb crack 56.6
slap 159.13
applaud 509.10
hit 901.14

clapped-out screwed
up 393.29

dilapidated 393.33
disintegrative 805.5

clapping 509.2

clarification refinement
79.4
explanation 341.4

clarified 797.7

clarify refine 79.22
explain 341.10
make clear 521.6
disinvolve 797.5

clarifying 341.15

clarion
noun call to arms
458.8
verb blare 53.10
blow a horn 708.42

clarity distinctness 31.2
clearness 521.2
elegance 533.1
facility 1013.1
transparency 1028.1

clash
noun report 56.1
rasp 58.3
jangle 61.2
disaccord 456.1
fight 457.4
hostility 589.3
impact 901.3
verb conflict 35.14
crack 56.6
jangle 58.9
contrapose 215.4
contend against 451.4
disagree 456.8, 788.5
contend 457.13
go contrary to 778.4
counteract 899.6
collide 901.13

clashing
noun hostility 451.2,
589.3
disaccord 456.1
contrariety 778.1
disagreement 788.1
counteraction 899.1
adj off-colour 35.20
jarring 61.5
oppositional 451.8
disaccordant 456.15
hostile 589.10
contrary 778.6
different 779.7
disagreeing 788.6

clash with contend
against 451.4
differ 779.5

clasp
noun hold 474.2
embrace 562.3
fastening 799.3
verb stay near 223.12
hold 474.6
seize 480.14
embrace 562.18
hook 799.8
cohere 802.6

clasping 799.3

class
noun rank 245.2
nomenclature 527.1
race 559.4
form 572.11
social class 607.1
community 617.2
school 617.5
laity 700.1
category 808.2
kingdom 808.5
goodness 998.1
biology 1066.1
verb classify 800.8,
808.6
estimate 945.9

class conflict 607.1

classic
noun book 554.1
classical music 708.6
work of art 712.10
adj elegant 533.6
model 785.8
perfected 1001.9

classical downright
247.12
elegant 533.6
literary 547.24, 718.7
antiquated 841.13
perfected 1001.9

classical music 708.6

classic example 785.1

classicism elegance
533.1
antiquarianism 841.4
scholarship 927.5

classics 547.12, 718.1

classification veil of
secrecy 345.3
nomenclature 527.1
categorization 800.3,
808.1
grouping 807.3

classified secret 345.11
arranged 807.14
catalogued 808.8

classify keep secret
345.7
class 800.8, 808.6
group 807.11
discriminate 943.4

classmate schoolchild
572.3
companion 588.3

classroom
noun schoolroom
567.11
adj scholastic 567.13

class structure class
607.1
hierarchy 808.4

class struggle 607.1

class war 979.4

classy 501.18

clatter
noun noise 53.3
rattle 55.3
verb rattle 55.6

clattering 55.8

clause phrase 529.1
part 554.13
bill 613.8
section 792.2
condition 958.2

claw torture 96.18
injure 393.13
seize 480.14

clawed tortured 96.25
pedal 199.9
prehensile 474.9

clawing 96.7

claws governance 417.5
clutches 474.4
control 612.2

clay
noun pipe 89.6
land 234.1
corpse 307.16
humankind 312.1
person 312.5
putty 1045.4
body 1050.3
mud 1060.8
adj ceramic 742.7

clay court 749.1

clean
verb cleanse 79.18
adj pure 79.25
shapely 264.5
skilful 413.22
honest 644.13
chaste 653.7, 664.4
spotless 657.7
thorough 793.10
adv cleanly 79.29
absolutely 793.15

clean bill of health
healthiness 83.2
pass 443.7
certificate 549.6

clean-cut distinct 31.7
shapely 264.5
clear 521.11

cleaned 79.26

cleaned out 619.10

cleaned up 79.26

cleaner cleaner-up
79.14
cleanser 79.17

cleaning
noun cleansing 79.2
adj cleansing 79.28

cleaning lady 577.8

cleaning up 79.2

cleanliness cleanness
79.1
innocence 657.1
chastity 664.1

cleanly
adj clean 79.25
chaste 664.4
adv clean 79.29

cleanse clean 79.18
release 120.6
sanctify 685.5

cleansed 79.26

cleanser 79.17

clean-shaven 6.17

cleansing
noun cleaning 79.2
release 120.2
adj cleaning 79.28
relieving 120.9
atoning 658.7

clean sweep 859.1

clean up 807.12

clear
noun clearness 521.2
verb refine 79.22
take off 184.38
rise above 272.11
unclose 292.12
leap 366.5
manage 409.12
extricate 431.7
profit 472.12
justify 600.9
acquit 601.4
pay in full 624.13
play 745.4, 750.7
eliminate 772.5
evacuate 908.22
disembarrass 1013.9
adj distinct 31.7
audible 50.16
vacant 222.14
open 292.17
manifest 348.8
free 430.21
unhampered 430.26
quit 430.31
crystal-clear 521.11
legible 521.12
elegant 533.6
unindebted 624.23
innocent 657.6
thorough 793.10
unmixed 797.7
unfastened 801.22
unqualified 959.2
certain 969.13
thriving 1009.13
easy 1013.13
light 1024.31
transparent 1028.4
adv wide 261.19

clearance room 158.3
open space 158.4
altitude of flight 184.35
interval 224.1
distance 261.1
latitude 430.4
authorization 443.3
pass 443.7
justification 600.1
acquittal 601.1
payment 624.1
match 752.3
elimination 772.2
evacuation 908.6

clear away dissipate 770.5
eliminate 772.5

clear conscience 657.1

clear-cut distinct 31.7
lost 473.7
clear 521.11

cleared 292.17

clearing open space 158.4
opening 292.1
extrication 431.3
justification 600.1
acquittal 601.1
evacuation 908.6
disembarrassment 1013.6
field 1067.9

clearing house 729.13

clearing up 939.1

clearly visibly 31.8
audibly 50.18
positively 247.19
manifestly 348.14
intelligibly 521.13
certainly 969.23

clear of 430.31

clear out disappear 34.3
clean 79.18
beat it 188.7, 368.11
eliminate 772.5

clear the air explain 341.10
pacify 465.7
moderate 670.6

clear the way prepare the way 405.12
facilitate 1013.7

clear up explain 341.10
disinvolve 797.5
tidy 807.12
solve 939.2
make sure 969.11

cleavage falling-out 456.4
severance 801.2
fission 1037.8

clef 709.13

cleft
noun crack 224.2
notch 289.1
opening 292.1
falling-out 456.4
break 801.4
adj cut 224.7
severed 801.23
halved 874.6

clemency 145.1

clement pitying 145.7
lenient 427.7

clench
noun hold 474.2
verb hold 474.6
seize 480.14

clenched fist 462.4

Cleopatra 1015.10

clergy 699.1

clergyman 699.2

cleric 699.2

clerical
noun clergyman 699.2
adj secretarial 547.28
ecclesiastic 698.13

clerk writer 547.13
recorder 550.1
agent 576.3
accountant 628.7
clergyman 699.2

clever skilful 413.22
well-laid 413.30
cunning 415.12
witty 489.15
teachable 570.18
smart 919.14

cleverly skilfully 413.31
cunningly 415.13
intelligently 919.20

cleverness skill 413.1
cunning 415.1
wittiness 489.2
teachableness 570.5
smartness 919.2

click
noun thud 52.3
snap 56.2
verb thud 52.15
snap 56.7

clicking
noun ticking 55.2
adj staccato 55.7

client
noun advisee 422.4
dependent 432.6
customer 733.4
adj subject 432.13

clientele 733.3

cliff precipice 200.3
slope 237.2

climactic top 198.10
critical 842.10

climate milieu 209.3
weather 317.3

climatic 317.12

climax
noun copulation 75.7
summit 198.2
upheaval 671.5
plot 722.4
limit 793.5
crisis 842.4
crucial moment 842.5
urgency 996.4
salient point 996.6
acme of perfection 1001.3
verb come 75.23
top 198.9
complete 407.6
adj finishing touch 407.3

climb
noun ascent 193.1
acclivity 204.6
verb move 172.5
ascend 184.39
climb up 193.11

incline 204.10

climb down get down 194.7
recant 363.8

climber traveller 178.1
ascender 193.6
legume 310.4
upstart 606.7

climbing
noun ambition 100.10
course 172.2
ascent 193.1
adj ascending 193.14
uphill 204.17

climb on 193.12

climb over 193.11

climb up 193.11

clinch
noun hold 474.2
joint 799.4
verb hold 474.6
seize 480.14
fight 754.4
fasten 799.7
join 799.11
cohere 802.6

clinching 754.3

cling
noun hold 474.2
cohesion 802.1
verb hold 474.6
cohere 802.6

clingfilm 295.18

clinging
noun hold 474.2
cohesion 802.1
adj retentive 474.8
cohesive 802.10
viscous 1060.12

cling to stay near 223.12
hold 474.6, 474.7
cohere 802.6

clingy adhesive 802.12
viscous 1060.12

clinic hospital 91.21
hospital room 197.25

clinical 90.15

clinical psychologist 92.10

clink
noun thud 52.3
ringing 54.3
nick 429.9
rhyme 720.8
cutlery 1039.2
verb thud 52.15
ring 54.8

Clio history 719.1
creative thought 985.2

clip
noun excerpt 557.3
piece 792.3
fastening 799.3
sock 901.5
verb barrel 174.9
excise 255.10

shorten 268.6
perforate 292.15
gyp 356.19
hold 474.6
abridge 557.5
hook 799.8
belt 901.15

clipped shortened 268.9
concise 537.6
abridged 557.6

clipper 181.8

clippers 1039.1

clipping abbreviation 537.4
piece 792.3

clippings 557.4

clique
noun coterie 617.6
company 769.3
verb hang with 582.18

clitoral 2.27

clitoris 2.11

cloak
noun overgarment 5.12
cover 295.2
pretext 376.1
robe 702.2
verb mantle 5.39
cover 295.19
conceal 346.6
protect 1007.18

cloaked clothing 5.44
covered 295.31
protected 1007.21

cloakroom latrine 12.10
wardrobe 197.15
bathroom 197.26

clobber
noun impedimenta 471.3
verb trim 412.9
beat up 604.14
knock for a loop 901.17

clobbered 412.15

cloche 1067.11

clock
noun looks 33.4
furniture 229.1
timepiece 831.6
hit 901.4
verb see 27.12
time 831.11
hit 901.14
detect 940.5

clocking 831.1

clockwise
adj right 219.4
adv rightward 161.24
round 914.16

clog
noun obstruction 293.3
curb 1011.7
verb stop 293.7
dance 705.5

clogged 293.11

clogging 1011.1

cloister
noun corridor 197.18
enclosure 212.3
passageway 383.3
monastery 703.6
retreat 1008.5
verb confine 212.6,
429.12

cloistered quiescent
173.12
enclosed 212.10
enclosing 212.11
confined 429.19
recluse 584.10
claustral 703.16
separated 801.21

cloisters 703.9

clone
noun same 777.3
likeness 783.3
duplicate 784.3
verb reproduce 777.6
make uniform 780.4
copy 784.8

cloned 873.4

clos 231.4

close
noun enclosure 212.3
plot 231.4
closing 819.3
cessation 856.1
verb approach 167.3
converge 169.2
surround 209.6
shut 293.6
arrange 437.8
contend 457.13
end 819.5
turn off 856.12
obstruct 1011.12
adj stuffy 173.16
near 223.14
narrow 270.14
tight 293.12
meticulous 339.12
taciturn 344.9
secret 345.11
secretive 345.15
concealed 346.11
completion 407.2
phonetic 524.31
concise 537.6
familiar 587.19
economical 635.6
crowded 769.22
approximate 774.8
approximating 783.14
fast 799.14
imminent 839.3
exact 972.17
sultry 1018.28
dense 1043.12
moist 1063.15
adv around 209.12
near 223.20
nearly 223.22
densely 1043.15

close at hand 839.3

close attention 982.4

close by 223.20

closed shut 293.9
secret 345.11
inhospitable 586.7
narrow-minded 979.10

closed-door closed
293.9
private 345.13
exclusive 772.9

closed-in 212.10

close down 856.8

closed shop 727.3

closed to
uninfluenceable 894.4
inaccessible 966.9

closed to the public
293.9

close friend 588.1

close in approach 167.3
converge 169.2
enclose 212.5

close-in 223.14

close in on 167.3

closely nearly 223.22
narrowly 270.22
densely 1043.15

closeness stuffiness
173.6
nearness 223.1
narrowness 270.1
uncommunicativeness
344.1
secrecy 345.1
stinginess 484.3
familiarity 587.5
thrift 635.1
relation 774.1
similarity 783.1
sultriness 1018.6
density 1043.1
humidity 1063.2

close quarters 429.7

closer 223.18

close season 313.1

closest 223.19

closet
noun sanctum 197.8
wardrobe 197.15
bathroom 197.26
storehouse 386.6
office 739.7
verb confine 212.6
adj secret 345.11

close to 223.24

close up converge
169.2
close 293.6
heal 396.21

close-up 714.8

close with approach
167.3
converge 169.2
sail for 182.35

concur 332.9
arrange 437.8
contend against 451.4
encounter 457.15

closing
noun closure 293.1
signing 437.3
close 819.3
cessation 856.1
adj ending 819.10

closure closing 293.1
introduction 613.5
completion 793.4
joint 799.4
cloture 856.5
hindrance 1011.1

clot
noun bungler 414.8
conglomeration 802.5
coagulum 1043.7
verb come together
769.16
cohere 802.6
thicken 1043.10
emulsify 1060.10

cloth material 4.1
sail 180.14
ministry 698.1
clergy 699.1
canonicals 702.1
scenery 704.20

clothe enclothe 5.38
empower 18.10
cover 295.19
equip 385.8

clothed 5.44

clothes clothing 5.1
blanket 295.10

clothing
noun clothes 5.1
adj dress 5.44

clotted cohesive 802.10
thickened 1043.14
viscous 1060.12

clotted cream 1043.7

clotting cohesion 802.1
thickening 1043.4
viscosity 1060.2

cloud
noun high fog 319.1
flock 769.6
multitude 883.3
confusion 984.3
vapour 1065.1
verb cover 295.19
becloud 319.6
conceal 346.6
confuse 984.7
darken 1026.9
opaque 1030.2

clouded mottled 47.12
covered 295.31
cloudy 319.7
concealed 346.11
gloomy 1026.14

cloudless 1024.31

cloud over cloud 319.6
darken 1026.9

cloudy stormy 318.23
nebulous 319.7
obscure 522.15
muddled 984.13
gloomy 1026.14
opaque 1030.3

clout
noun authoritativeness
417.2
influence 893.1
impulse 901.1
sock 901.5
verb belt 901.15

clover feed 10.4
comfort 121.1
three 875.1

clown
noun bungler 414.8
humourist 489.12
buffoon 707.10
fool 923.1
verb be foolish 922.6

clowning buffoonery
489.5
foolishness 922.1

cloying nasty 64.7
oversweet 66.5
sentimental 93.21
satiating 993.7

club
noun resort 228.27
coercion 424.3
fist 462.4
rod 605.2
fellowship 617.3
theatre 704.14
golf 748.1
insurance 1007.4
verb whip 604.12
league 804.4
cudgel 901.20

clubbing 604.4

clubhouse 228.27

clubs 758.2

clue cue 517.9
tip 551.3
hint 551.4
evidence 956.1

clueless foolish 922.8
bewildered 970.24

clump
noun thud 52.3
lump 257.10
bulge 283.3
growth 310.2
bunch 769.7
sock 901.5
stamp 901.10
solid 1043.6
verb thud 52.15
stroll 177.28
assemble 769.18
belt 901.15
stamp 901.22
thicken 1043.10

clumsily carelessly
340.18
awkwardly 414.24
unwieldily 1012.29

clumsiness bulkiness
257.9
awkwardness 414.3
inelegance 534.1
inconvenience 995.3
unwieldiness 1012.9
ugliness 1014.1

clumsy bulky 257.19
slipshod 340.12
bungling 414.20
inelegant 534.2
inconvenient 995.7
unwieldy 1012.19
ungraceful 1014.9

clunk
noun thud 52.3
sock 901.5
verb thud 52.15
belt 901.15

cluster
noun throng 769.4
bunch 769.7
conglomeration 802.5
solid 1043.6
verb come together
769.16
assemble 769.18
cohere 802.6
thicken 1043.10

clustered assembled
769.21
cohesive 802.10

clustering joining
799.1
cohesion 802.1
densification 1043.3

clutch
noun amount 244.2
hold 474.2
young 561.2
crisis 842.4
cone clutch 1039.6
verb hold 474.6
seize 480.14

clutches governance
417.5
claws 474.4
control 612.2

clutter
noun jumble 809.3
multitude 883.3
radar interference
1035.12
verb disarrange 810.2
teem with 883.5

cluttered 498.12

coach
noun railway carriage
179.15
preparer 405.5
tutor 571.5
trainer 571.6
verb advise 422.5
tutor 568.11

coached prepared
405.16
skilled 413.26

coaching riding 177.6
teaching 568.1

coal
noun live coal 1018.16
scoria 1019.16
verb provision 385.9
burn 1019.24
fuel 1020.7

coal-fired 1020.8

coalition affiliation
450.2
front 609.33
association 617.1
combination 804.1

coalition government
612.4

coal mine 1056.6

coal mining 1056.8

coarse raucous 58.15
bitter 64.6
offensive 98.18
thick 269.8
rough 288.6, 294.6
undeveloped 406.12
gross 497.11
ill-bred 505.6
inelegant 534.2
populational 606.8
carnal 663.6
vulgar 666.8
inferior 1004.9

coarse-fish 382.10

coarsely 497.16

coast
noun slide 194.4
border 211.4
side 218.1
shore 234.2
verb be still 173.7
glide 177.35
navigate 182.13
sail coast-wise 182.39
slide 194.9
do nothing 329.2
take it easy 331.15
go easily 1013.10

coastal bordering
211.11
littoral 234.7

coaster 180.1

coast guard rescuer
398.2
navy 461.26
guard 1007.9

coasting gliding 177.16
water travel 182.1

coastline 234.2

coat
noun hair 3.2
outerwear 5.13
colour 35.8
cover 295.2
blanket 295.12
lamina 296.2
verb cloak 5.39
colour 35.13
spread on 295.24

coated covered 295.31
layered 296.6

coating

noun colour 35.8
painting 35.12
covering 295.1
blanket 295.12
lamina 296.2
adj covering 295.35

coat of arms 647.2

coat of paint colour
35.8
pretext 376.1

coax
noun line 347.17
prompter 375.10
verb urge 375.14
lure 377.5
importune 440.12

coaxing
noun inducement
375.3
importunity 440.3
adj alluring 377.8
importunate 440.18

cob ear 310.27
race horse 311.14

cobalt
noun radium 91.8
adj blue 45.3

cobbler shoemaker 5.37
mender 396.10

cobblers 520.3

cobra 311.26

co-chairman 574.5

cock
noun rooster 76.8
valve 239.10
stopper 293.4
poultry 311.29
weather vane 318.17
mate 588.4
pile 769.10
verb prime 405.9
shoot 903.12

cocked 405.16

cocker wrinkle 291.6
caress 562.16

cockerel cock 76.8
poultry 311.29

Cockney 523.7

cockpit 463.1

cockroach 311.35

cocktail 88.9

cock up upturn 193.13
rise 200.8
protrude 283.10
screw up 393.11
muck up 414.12
elevate 911.5
make a boo-boo
974.15

cocky 454.7

cocoa 40.3

cocoon 302.12

cod
noun genitals 2.11
seed vessel 310.28
trick 356.6

verb deceive 356.14
adj imitation 336.8
spurious 354.26

coda adjunct 254.1
postscript 254.2
passage 708.24
sequel 816.1
end 819.1

code
noun cryptography
345.6
telegraph 347.2
rule 419.2, 868.4
Greek 522.7
ethics 636.1
digest 673.5
table 807.4
verb encode 345.10

coded 345.16

code name
cryptography 345.6
anonymity 528.1

code-named 346.11

code of practice ethics
636.1
rule 868.4

coefficient 450.5

coerce use violence
424.7
domineer 612.16

coercion 424.3

coercive 424.12

coexist 835.4

coexistence 609.5

coffee 40.3

coffee bar 8.17

coffee-pot 8.17

coffee shop 8.17

coffin
noun casket 309.11
verb confine 212.6
inter 309.19

cog
noun inferior 250.2
projection 285.4
verb cheat 356.18

cogent powerful 18.12
relevant 774.11
sagacious 919.16
logical 934.20
valid 972.14
good 998.12

cognition 927.2

cognitive 930.21

cohabitation copulation
75.7
habitation 225.1
marriage 563.1

coherence clearness
521.2
agreement 787.1
cohesion 802.1
indivisibility 1043.2

coherent clear 521.11
agreeing 787.9
cohesive 802.10

indivisible 1043.13

cohesion cohesiveness
802.1
indivisibility 1043.2

cohesive cohering
802.10
indivisible 1043.13
tough 1047.4

cohort hanger-on 138.6
unit 461.21
associate 616.1
accomplice 616.3
attendance 768.6
company 769.3

coil
noun braid 3.7
length 267.2
whorl 281.2
verb curl 281.5

coiled 281.7

coin
noun angle 278.2
dough 728.2
specie 728.4
verb mint 728.28
innovate 840.5, 851.9
originate 891.12
imagine 985.14

coinage neologism
526.8
money 728.1
coining 728.24
innovation 851.4
production 891.1
product 892.1

coincide concur 332.9,
898.2
correspond 777.4
agree 787.6
co-occur 835.4

coincidence
accompaniment 768.1
sameness 777.1
agreement 787.1
concurrence 898.1

coincidental 777.8

coincidentally together
768.11
identically 777.9

coinciding coincident
777.8
agreeing 787.9

coined 891.19

coital 75.24

coke basuco 87.6
scoria 1019.16

col ridge 237.5
valley 237.7

colander refinery 79.13
porousness 292.8
arranger 807.5

cold
noun coldness 1022.1
adj unconscious 25.8
chromatic 35.15
unsexual 75.28
unfeeling 94.9

indifferent 102.6
dull 117.6
insolent 142.9
heartless 144.25
stone-dead 307.31
reticent 344.10
aloof 583.6
unfriendly 589.9
speculative 759.27
freezing 1022.14,
1022.16

cold blood 94.1

cold-blooded unfeeling
94.9
heartless 144.25
hypothermic 1022.20

cold comfort 108.1

cold feet 491.4

cold frame 1067.11

coldly unfeelingly
94.14
indifferently 102.9
inertly 173.20
unamicably 589.14

coldness sexuality 75.2
unfeeling 94.1
indifference 102.1
heartlessness 144.10
aloofness 583.2
enmity 589.1
cold 1022.1

cold storage storage
386.5
frozen-food locker
1023.6

Coldstream Guards
461.14

cold sweat sweat 12.7
hostility 99.2
trepidation 127.5
jitters 128.2

cold war 458.1

cold water 379.2

cold weather weather
317.3
bleak weather 1022.3

colic ache 26.5
anaemia 85.9
gastrointestinal disease
85.29

coliseum 463.1

colitis 85.29

collaborate be willing
324.3
cooperate 450.3
write 547.21, 718.6
act the traitor 645.15
concur 898.2

collaborating 363.11

collaboration
cooperation 450.1
treason 645.7
concurrence 898.1

collaborative
cooperative 450.5
concurrent 898.4

collaborator subversive
357.11
apostate 363.5
author 547.15, 718.4
cooperator 616.4

collage 712.11

collapse
noun weakness 16.1
exhaustion 21.2
breakdown 85.8
descent 194.1
decline 252.2
prostration 260.4
impairment 393.1
debacle 395.4
crash 410.3
defeat 412.1
insolvency 625.3
verb weaken 16.9
burn out 21.5
descend 194.5
cave 260.10
break down 393.24
fall 410.12
go bankrupt 625.7
fall short 910.2
fall through 910.3

collapsible 260.11

collapsing 194.11

collar
noun band 280.3
foam 320.2
shackle 428.4
insignia 647.1
golf 748.1
verb nick 429.16
grab 472.9
capture 480.18

collate classify 807.11
scrutinize
comparatively 942.5
verify 969.12

collateral
noun kinfolk 559.2
nonessential 767.2
adj parallel 203.6
additional 253.10
related 559.6, 774.9
unessential 767.4
accompanying 768.9
eventual 830.11
simultaneous 835.5

collating 554.14

colleague companion
588.3
associate 616.1
equal 789.4

collect
noun prayer 696.4
verb store up 386.11
gather 472.11
come together 769.16
assemble 769.18
put together 799.5
conclude 945.10

collected composed
106.13
stored 386.14
assembled 769.21

joined 799.13

collected works 554.7

collection store 386.1
gathering 472.2
donation 478.6
edition 554.5
compilation 554.7
excerpts 557.4
oblation 696.7
book of verse 720.5
assemblage 769.1
collector's items
769.11

collective cooperative
450.5
communal 476.9
concurrent 898.4

collective bargaining
unionism 727.1
trade union 727.2
negotiation 731.3

collective leadership
573.4

collectively
cooperatively 450.6
together 768.11
wholly 791.13

collective unconscious
psyche 92.28
instinct 933.2

collectivism
cooperation 450.1
communion 476.2
socialism 611.7
democratism 612.8

collectivist
noun socialist 611.19
adj cooperative 450.5

collector desirer 100.12
enthusiast 101.4
connoisseur 496.7
governor 575.13
gatherer 769.15

colleen 302.6

college university 567.5
association 617.1

collegiate
noun college student
572.5
adj scholastic 567.13
studentlike 572.12

collide clash 35.14
sail into 182.41
disagree 456.8, 788.5
contend 457.13
counteract 899.6
come into collision
901.13

colliding off-colour
35.20
disaccordant 456.15
hostile 589.10

collier ship 180.1
miner 1056.9

colliery 1056.6

collision crash 184.20
hostility 451.2, 589.3

contrariety 778.1
counteraction 899.1
impact 901.3
misfortune 1010.2

collision course
convergence 169.1
meeting 223.4

collocate locate 159.11
assemble 769.18
dispose 807.9

colloquial vernacular
523.18
conversational 541.13

collude plot 381.9
cooperate 450.3
concur 898.2

collusion chicanery
356.4
intrigue 381.5
cooperation 450.1
concurrence 898.1

cologne 70.3

colon mouth 2.16
metre 720.7
pause 856.4

Colonel 575.20

colonial 227.9

colonialism foreign
policy 609.5
central government
612.4

colonization
establishment 159.7
peopling 225.2
appropriation 480.4

colonized 225.12

colony country 232.1
possession 469.1
community 617.2
flock 769.5

colorado 89.4

coloration colour 35.1
colouring 35.11
implication 519.2

colossal large 247.7
huge 257.20
high 272.14
giant 272.16

colossus strong man
15.6
giant 257.13
tower 272.6

colour
noun dye 3.16
looks 33.4
hue 35.1
colourfulness 35.4
colouring 35.8
redness 41.1
timbre 50.3
milieu 209.3
sham 354.3
pretext 376.1
ornamentation 498.1
cinematography 706.4
treatment 712.9
kind 808.3

verb hue 35.13
redden 41.5, 152.14
change colour 105.19
blush 139.8
pervert 265.6
misrepresent 350.3
falsify 354.16
ornament 498.8
portray 712.19
imbue 796.11
influence 893.7

colour-blind blind 30.9
broad-minded 978.8

coloured hued 35.16
dark-skinned 38.10
spurious 354.26
specious 354.27
ornate 545.11
discriminatory 979.12

colourful variegated
47.9
gaudy 501.20

colourfully 501.27

colouring
noun colour 35.1, 35.8
coloration 35.11
reddening 41.3
timbre 50.3
blushing 139.5
misrepresentation
350.1
sham 354.3
deliberate falsehood
354.9
meaning 518.1
painting 712.4
adj chromatic 35.15
reddening 41.11

colourist 716.4

colourless hueless 36.7
dull 117.6

colour print picture
712.11
print 713.5
photograph 714.3

colours battle flag
458.12
flag 647.6

colour scheme colour
35.1
ornamentation 498.1

colour television
1034.5

colt boy 302.5
fledgling 302.10
horse 311.10
jockey 757.2

Columbia 232.4

column tower 272.6
pillar 273.5
cylinder 282.4
unit 461.21
monument 549.12
part 554.13
roulette 759.12
procession 811.3
base 900.8

columnist

noun author 547.15,
718.4
adj journalist 555.4

coma stupor 22.6
unconsciousness 25.2
apathy 94.4

comatose sleepy 22.21
asleep 22.22
unconscious 25.8
apathetic 94.13
permanent 852.7

comb
noun ridge 237.5
wave 238.14
projection 285.4
verb curry 79.21
billow 238.22
ransack 937.33

combat
noun contention 457.1
fight 457.4
war 458.1
verb contend against
451.4
contend 457.13

combatant opponent
452.1
fighter 461.1

combative partisan
456.17
warlike 458.21
offensive 459.30
contrary 778.6
argumentative 934.19

combe valley 237.7
cwm 284.8

combination cycle
179.8
concoction 405.3
affiliation 450.2
association 617.1
assemblage 769.1
relation 774.1
identification 777.2
composition 795.1
mixture 796.1
compound 796.5
joining 799.1
combine 804.1
oneness 871.1
concurrence 898.1

combine
noun association 617.1
company 617.9
combination 804.1
verb cooperate 450.3
join 617.14
accompany 768.7
assemble 769.18
identify 777.5
compose 795.3
mix 796.10
put together 799.5
unite 804.3
concur 898.2

combined cooperative
450.5
associated 617.16
accompanying 768.9

coming from 886.8
coming in 184.18
coming of age growth
259.3
  development 392.2
  evolution 860.1
coming out emergence
190.1
  debut 582.15
  inauguration 817.5
coming to 639.7
coming to terms
731.3
Comintern 611.6
comma 856.4
command
  noun field of view 31.3
  supremacy 249.3
  will 323.1
  skill 413.1
  governance 417.5
  precept 419.1
  commandment 420.1
  compulsion 424.1
  direction 573.1
  control 612.2
  knowledge 927.1
  understanding 927.3
  verb rule 249.11
  rise above 272.11
  will 323.2
  order 420.8
  possess 469.4
  direct 573.8
  govern 612.12
  know well 927.13
commandant 575.6
command economy
609.4
Commander 575.21
commander captain
183.7
  superior 249.4
  governor 575.6
commander in chief
575.18
commanding
  authoritative 417.15
  imperious 420.13
  directing 573.12
  governing 612.18
commanding officer
575.6
commandos 461.14
commemorate 487.2
commemorating
487.3
commemoration
  celebration 487.1
  anniversary 849.4
  memento 988.7
commemorative
  celebrative 487.3
  memorial 988.27
commence 817.7
commencement
  ceremony 580.4

beginning 817.1
source 885.5
commend 478.16
commendable
  praiseworthy 509.20
  good 998.12
commendation
  commitment 478.2
  good word 509.3
commensurate
  satisfactory 107.11
  agreeing 787.9
  equal 789.7
  comparative 942.8
  sufficient 990.6
comment
  noun word of
  explanation 341.5
  commentary 556.2
  criticism 945.2
  verb remark 524.25
commentary postscript
254.2
  comment 341.5
  commentation 556.2
  review 723.2
commentator
  interpreter 341.7
  commenter 556.4
  critic 945.7
  broadcaster 1033.23
commerce copulation
75.7
  communication 343.1
  social life 582.4
  occupation 724.1
  trade 731.1
commercial
  noun advertisement
  352.6
  radiobroadcast
  1033.18
  commercial
  announcement
  1033.20
  adj occupied 724.15
  business 730.12,
  731.21
  saleable 734.14
commercial bank
620.4
commercialism
731.12
commercial radio
1033.16
commission
  noun performance
  328.2
  precept 419.1
  injunction 420.2
  portion 477.5
  delegation 576.13
  legislature 613.1
  commissioning 615.1
  dividend 624.7
  task 724.2
  assembly 769.2
  verb repair 396.14
  command 420.8

represent 576.14
authorize 615.10
delegate 861.7
commissioned 615.19
commissioner minister
575.17
  delegate 576.2
  policeman 1007.15
commissioning 615.1
commissions 627.1
commit do 328.6
  consign 429.17,
  478.16
  engage 436.5
  commit 436.5
  contract 437.5
  dedicate 477.11
  commission 615.10
  obligate 641.12
commitment zeal
101.2
  resolution 359.1
  undertaking 404.1
  committal 429.4
  obligation 436.2
  dedication 477.4
  consignment 478.2
  devotion 587.7
  commission 615.1
  duty 641.1
  unselfishness 652.1
  cause 885.9
commit suicide
308.21
committal commitment
429.4
  obligation 436.2
committed zealous
101.9
  resolute 359.11
  promised 436.8
  devoted 587.21
  obliged 641.16
  unselfish 652.5
committee
  subcommittee 423.2
  delegation 576.13
  assembly 769.2
commodities 735.1
commodity 735.2
Commodore 575.21
common
  noun green 310.7
  estate 471.4
  park 743.14
  normal 868.3
  adj trite 117.9
  medium 246.3
  inferior 250.6, 1004.9
  public 312.16
  cooperative 450.5
  communal 476.9
  commonplace 497.14
  simple 499.6
  vernacular 523.18
  plain-speaking 535.3
  populational 606.8
  prosaic 721.5

mutual 776.11
frequent 846.4
prevalent 863.12
usual 868.9
well-known 927.27
paltry 997.21
ordinary 1004.8
common denominator
776.1
commoner sizar 572.7
  common man 606.5
commoners 606.1
common factor 776.1
common knowledge
  noun information
  551.1
  maxim 973.1
  adj published 352.17
commonly tritely
117.11
  plainly 499.10
  mutually 776.13
  frequently 846.6
  generally 863.17
  normally 868.10
  inferiorly 1004.12
commonly known
927.27
common man people
606.1
  commoner 606.5
  nobody 997.7
common market
617.1
common people 606.1
commonplace
  noun generalization
  863.8
  normal 868.3
  platitude 973.3
  adj trite 117.9, 863.16
  common 497.14
  simple 499.6
  plain-speaking 535.3
  populational 606.8
  prosaic 721.5
  usual 868.9
  well-known 927.27
  ordinary 1004.8
common practice
373.5
commons nutriment
10.3
  rations 10.6
  dining room 197.11
  people 606.1
  park 743.14
common sense 934.9
commonsense 919.18
Commonwealth 232.3
commonwealth
  population 227.1
  country 232.1
  people 606.1
  central government
  612.4
  community 617.2

commotion noise 53.3
  agitation 105.4, 916.1
  bustle 330.4
  turbulence 671.2
  hubbub 809.4
communal public
312.16
  cooperative 450.5
  common 476.9
  associational 617.17
  mutual 776.11
commune state 231.5
  participation 476.1
  community 617.2
communicate transfer
176.10
  impart 343.7
  give 478.12
  say 524.23
  converse 541.9
  inform 551.8
  celebrate 701.14
  join 799.11
communicate with
  converse 541.9
  correspond 553.10
communicating
  communicational
  343.9
  joining 799.16
communication
  noun communion
  343.1
  passageway 383.3
  giving 478.1
  speech 524.1
  conversation 541.1
  information 551.1
  message 552.4
  letter 553.2
  social life 582.4
  joining 799.1
  adj communicational
  347.20
  phrase transference
  176.1
communications
  noun electronic
  communications 343.5
  signalling 347.1
  radio 1033.1
  adj communicational
  347.20
  press 555.3
communicative
  talkative 343.10, 540.9
  conversational 541.13
  informative 551.18
  sociable 582.22
communicator
  informant 551.5
  correspondent 553.8
Communion 701.7
communion
  communication 343.1
  accord 455.1
  community 476.2
  conversation 541.1
  social life 582.4

school 617.5
sect 675.3
prayer 696.4
correlation 776.1

communism
cooperation 450.1
communion 476.2
Bolshevism 611.6
central government
612.4
democratism 612.8

Communist
noun Bolshevist
611.18
revolutionist 859.3
adj communistic
611.30
revolutionist 859.6

communist
noun left side 220.1
adj left 220.4
cooperative 450.5

Communist Party
611.6

community population
227.1
humankind 312.1
cooperation 450.1
accord 455.1
communion 476.2
social life 582.4
people 606.1
society 617.2
sect 675.3
company 768.2
correlation 776.1
similarity 783.1

community centre
metropolis 208.7
town hall 230.5

commute travel 177.18
substitute 861.4
interchange 862.4

commuter traveller
178.1
worker 726.2

commuter train
179.14

comp
noun complimentary
ticket 634.2
verb give 634.4
adj gratuitous 634.5

compact
noun pact 437.1
understanding 787.2
makeup 1015.12
verb contract 260.7,
437.5
densify 1043.9
adj miniature 258.12
short 268.8
close 293.12
concise 537.6
crowded 769.22
joint 799.12
dense 1043.12

compacted contracted
437.11

cohesive 802.10
dense 1043.12

companion
noun lover 104.12
stairs 193.3
image 349.5
home help 577.8
fellow 588.3
knight 608.5
associate 616.1
accompanier 768.4
escort 768.5
likeness 783.3
verb accompany 768.7

companionable 582.22

companionship
association 582.6
fellowship 587.2
company 768.2

companionway
entrance 189.5
stairs 193.3

company unit 461.21
association 582.6,
768.2
guest 585.6
companion 588.3
team 617.7
firm 617.9
cast 707.11
workplace 739.1
group 769.3

comparable
approximate 774.8
analogous 783.11
comparative 942.8

comparative 774.7,
942.8

comparatively to a
degree 248.10
relatively 774.12,
942.10

compare
noun comparison
942.1
verb assemble 769.18
liken 942.4
be comparable 942.7

compared to 942.11

compared with 942.11

compare with resemble
783.7
compare 942.4

comparing 942.1

comparison assemblage
769.1
similarity 783.1
substitute 861.2
compare 942.1
estimate 945.3

compartment 197.2

compass
noun range 158.2
environment 209.1
bounds 211.1
boundary 211.3
degree 245.1
distance 261.1

magnetic compass
574.9
scale 709.6
verb surround 209.6
enclose 212.5
accomplish 407.4
succeed with 409.11
circle 913.5

compassion sensitivity
24.3
kindness 143.1
pity 145.1
tolerance 978.4

compassionate
verb pity 145.3
adj sensitive 24.12
kind 143.13
pitying 145.7
lenient 427.7
tolerant 978.11

compatibility
pleasantness 97.1
accord 455.1
sociability 582.1
agreement 787.1

compatible pleasant
97.6
in accord 455.3
sociable 582.22
related 774.9
agreeing 787.9

compatriot fellow
citizen 227.5
associate 616.1

compel motivate
375.12
force 424.4
domineer 612.16
impel 901.11
obsess 925.25
necessitate 962.8

compelling motivating
375.25
commanding 420.13
compulsory 424.10
obsessive 925.34
urgent 996.22

compendium
compilation 554.7
abridgment 557.1

compensate
symmetrize 264.3
make compensation
338.4
remedy 396.13
make restitution 481.5
requite 506.5
pay 624.10
atone 658.4
equalize 789.6
interchange 862.4

compensating
compensatory 338.6
paying 624.21
contrary 778.6

compensation defence
mechanism 92.23
symmetrization 264.2

recompense 338.1,
624.3
reparation 396.6,
481.2
reprisal 506.2
penalty 603.1
pay 624.4
atonement 658.1

compensatory
compensating 338.6
restitutive 481.7
retaliatory 506.8
paying 624.21
atoning 658.7

compere 1034.2

compete contend
457.18
play 744.2

competence ability
18.2
skill 413.1
language 523.1

competency 18.2

competent able 18.14
fitted 405.17
capable 413.24
authoritative 417.15
legal 673.10
sufficient 990.6

competently ably
18.16
skilfully 413.31
sufficiently 990.8

competing 457.23

competition hostility
451.2
rivalry 457.2
football 745.1
rugby 746.1
hockey 750.1
basketball 751.1
skiing 753.1
athletics 755.1
motor racing 756.1

competitive
oppositional 451.8
competitory 457.23

**competitive
advantage** 457.2

competitive market
737.1

competitiveness 457.1

competitor contestant
452.2
combatant 461.1
athlete 743.19

compilation omnibus
554.7
code 673.5
collection 769.11

compile codify 673.9
assemble 769.18

compiler 547.15, 718.4

complacency
complacence 107.2
vanity 140.1

complacent bovine
107.10
vain 140.8

complacently
contentedly 107.14
courteously 504.19

complain dissatisfy
108.5
groan 115.15
object 333.5
offer resistance 453.3
accuse 599.7

complainant
malcontent 108.3
accuser 599.5

complaining
noun complaint 115.4
adj discontented 108.7
plaintive 115.19
resistant 453.5

complain of 85.45

complaint disease 85.1
grievance 115.4
objection 333.2
resistance 453.1
disapproval 510.1
arraignment 598.3
declaration 598.8
accusation 599.1

complement
noun hand 183.6
adjunct 254.1
syntax 530.2
team 617.7
company 769.3
likeness 783.3
all 791.3
full measure 793.3
verb reciprocate 776.7

complementary
reciprocal 776.10
completing 793.13

complete
verb perform 328.9
perfect 407.6, 819.7,
1001.5
execute 437.9
include 771.3
elaborate 860.6
adj downright 247.12
perfect 407.12
skilful 413.22
comprehensive 771.1
undivided 791.11
whole 793.9
ended 819.8
unqualified 959.2
sound 1001.7

completed 407.11

completely extremely
247.22
fully 765.13
totally 793.14
perfectly 1001.10

completeness inclusion
771.1
wholeness 791.5
totality 793.1
soundness 1001.2

complete works
literature 547.12,
718.1
compilation 554.7

completing completion
407.2
completive 407.9
fulfilling 793.13

completion
noun performance
328.2
execution 437.4
fulfilment 793.4
adj completing 407.2

complex
noun inferiority
complex 92.22
culture 373.3
whole 791.1
perplex 798.2
obsession 925.13
adj hard to understand
522.14
mixed 796.14
complicated 798.4
difficult 1012.17

complexion
noun looks 33.4
colour 35.1
personality tendency
92.11
mode 764.4
nature 766.4
verb colour 35.13

complexity convolution
281.1
abstruseness 522.2
complication 798.1
difficulty 1012.1

compliance resignation
134.2
willingness 324.1
assent 332.1
complaisance 427.2
submission 433.1
observance 434.1
consent 441.1
conformity 866.1

compliant resigned
134.10
willing 324.5
obedient 326.3
assenting 332.13
usable 387.23
indulgent 427.8
submissive 433.12
observant 434.4
consenting 441.4
conformable 866.5
pliant 1045.9

complicate intensify
251.5
add 253.4
make unintelligible
522.12
involve 798.3

complicated hard to
understand 522.14
complex 798.4

complication disease
85.1
abstruseness 522.2
plot 722.4
complexity 798.1
difficulty 1012.1
predicament 1012.4

complicity intrigue
381.5
cooperation 450.1
participation 476.1
guilt 656.1

compliment
noun congratulation
149.1
polite commendation
509.6
flattery 511.1
verb congratulate
149.2
pay a compliment
509.14
flatter 511.5

complimentary
congratulatory 149.3
approbatory 509.16
flattering 511.8
gratuitous 634.5

compliments 504.8

comply obey 326.2
assent 332.8
submit 433.6
acquiesce 441.3
conform 866.3

complying obedient
326.3
submissive 433.12

comply with observe
434.2
acquiesce 441.3
conform 866.3

component
noun part 792.1
constituent 795.2
matter 1050.2
adj constituent 795.5

components contents
196.1
substance 762.2

compose make up
405.7
arrange 437.8
reconcile 465.8
settle 466.7
compromise 468.2
write 547.21, 708.46,
718.6
set 548.16
calm 670.7
constitute 795.3
mix 796.10
dispose 807.9
conform 866.3
produce 891.8

composed collected
106.13
content 107.7
unastonished 123.3
arranged 807.14

composed of 795.4

composer author
547.15, 718.4
scorer 710.20

composing
noun composition
548.2
adj composed of 795.4

Composite 717.2

composite
noun compound 796.5
adj mixed 796.14
unitary 871.10
plural 882.7

composition contents
196.1
form 262.1
structure 266.1
concoction 405.3
compromise 468.1
diction 532.1
authorship 547.2,
718.2
writing 547.10
typesetting 548.2
atonement 658.1
piece 708.5
treatment 712.9
work of art 712.10
nature 766.4
constitution 795.1
mixture 796.1
compound 796.5
combination 804.1
production 891.2
product 892.1

compost 889.4

compost heap 80.10

composure
countenance 106.2
contentment 107.1
unastonishment 123.1
self-control 359.5

compote 10.38

compound
noun word form 526.4
composition 795.1
mixture 796.5, 804.2
alloy 1056.4
verb make up 405.7
compromise 468.2
mix 796.10
combine 804.3
produce 891.8
adj mixed 796.14

compounded 796.14

comprehend
understand 521.7
include 771.3
know 927.12

comprehensible
intelligible 521.10
knowable 927.25

comprehension
inclusion 771.1
intelligence 919.1
understanding 927.3

comprehensive great
247.6
voluminous 257.17
broad 269.6
sweeping 771.7
whole 791.9
thorough 793.10
joint 799.12

comprehensively
793.14

compress
noun dressing 86.33
verb reduce 252.7
contract 260.7
squeeze 260.8
shorten 268.6
densify 1043.9

compressed contracted
260.12
shortened 268.9
concise 537.6
dense 1043.12

compression
contraction 260.1
squeezing 260.2
shortening 268.3
densification 1043.3

compressor 260.6

comprise internalize
207.5
include 771.3
entail 771.4
total 791.8
put together 799.5
combine 804.3

comprised 771.5

comprising inclusive
771.6
composed of 795.4

compromise
noun adjustment
465.4, 787.4
composition 468.1
foreign policy 609.5
atonement 658.1
interchange 862.1
verb reconcile 465.8
interchange 862.4
endanger 1005.6

compromised 436.8

comptroller 574.2

compulsion power
18.1
urge 375.6
obligation 424.1
impulse 901.1
obsession 925.13
necessity 962.1

compulsive compulsory
424.10
overfastidious 495.12
conformist 866.6
obsessive 925.34
involuntary 962.14

compulsively
compulsorily 424.13
conformably 866.7
involuntarily 962.18

compulsorily
compulsively 424.13
obligatorily 424.15
necessarily 962.16

compulsory mandatory
420.12
compulsive 424.10
obligatory 424.11
necessary 962.12

compunction qualm
113.2
demur 325.2
objection 333.2

computer calculator
1016.14
computer science
1040.17
electronic data
processor 1041.2

computer-aided
1041.19

computer-controlled
automated 1040.21
computerized 1041.19

computer graphics
706.1

computerized
automated 1040.21
smart 1041.19

computer program
1041.11

**computer
programmer**
1040.18

computers 1041.1

computer science
computer 1040.17
computer systems and
applications 1041.1

computing
noun computer science
1041.1
adj numerative
1016.23

comrade companion
588.3
associate 616.1
member 617.11

comradeship affiliation
450.2
camaraderie 582.2
fellowship 587.2

con
noun prisoner 429.11
direction 573.1
helm 573.5
side 934.14
verb cheat 356.18
persuade 375.23
memorize 988.17
adj oppositional 451.8
disapproving 510.21
prep opposed to
451.10

concave
noun cavity 284.2
verb hollow 284.13
adj bowed 279.10

concaved 284.16

conceal keep secret
345.7
hide 346.6

concealed invisible
32.5
secret 345.11
hidden 346.11

concealing 346.15

concealment
invisibility 32.1
secrecy 345.1
hiding 346.1
hiding place 346.4
shelter 1008.3

concede acknowledge
332.11
confess 351.7
play 748.4, 752.4
allow for 958.5

conceded accepted
332.14
real 760.15

conceding 332.13

conceit
noun pride 136.1
conceitedness 140.4
caprice 364.1
witticism 489.7
foppery 500.4
boasting 502.1
quirk 926.2
thought 930.1
idea 931.1
opinion 952.6
imagination 985.1
verb flatter 511.5
imagine 985.14

conceited vain 136.9
self-conceited 140.11
contemptuous 157.8
foppish 500.17
boastful 502.10
dogmatic 969.22

conceivable knowable
927.25
believable 952.24
possible 965.6
plausible 967.7
imaginable 985.26

conceivably 965.9

conceive get in the
family way 78.11
vivify 306.9
understand 521.7
phrase 532.4
cause 885.10
originate 891.12
know 927.12
think 930.8, 952.11
suppose 950.10
imagine 985.14

conceived invented
891.19
known 927.26

conceiving 78.4

concentrate
noun extract 192.8

verb converge 169.2
focus 208.10
intensify 251.5
contract 260.7
densify 1043.9

concentrated central
208.11
contracted 260.12
attentive 982.15
dense 1043.12

concentrating 930.21

concentration
convergence 169.1
squeezing 192.7
extract 192.8
centralization 208.8
intensification 251.2
contraction 260.1
industry 330.6
firmness 359.2
perseverance 360.1
thoughtfulness 930.3
attention 982.1
engrossment 982.3
densification 1043.3

concentration camp
camp 228.29
aceldama 308.11
prison 429.8

concentric 208.14

concept idea 931.1
opinion 952.6
visualization 985.6

conception conceiving
78.4
plan 381.1
source 885.5
production 891.1
intellect 918.1
intelligence 919.1
understanding 927.3
thought 930.1
idea 931.1
opinion 952.6
creative thought 985.2
visualization 985.6

conceptual mental
918.7
intelligent 919.12
cognitive 930.21
ideational 931.9
imaginative 985.18

conceptualization
understanding 927.3
thought 930.1
visualization 985.6

concern
noun sensitivity 24.3
sympathy 93.5
anxiety 126.1
considerateness 143.3
carefulness 339.1
undertaking 404.1
company 617.9
occupation 724.1
workplace 739.1
relevance 774.4
affair 830.3
science 927.10

topic 936.1
interest 982.2
importance 996.1
verb give concern
126.4
relate to 774.5
involve 897.2
interest 982.12
trouble 1012.13

concerned anxious
126.7
involved 897.4
interested 982.16

concerns worry 126.2
affairs 830.4

concert
noun unanimity 332.5
cooperation 450.1
harmony 708.3
performance 708.33
agreement 787.1
concurrence 898.1
verb plan 381.8
cooperate 450.3
adj instrumental
708.51

concerted cooperative
450.5
concurrent 898.4

concert hall hall 197.4
theatre 704.14

concession
acknowledgment 332.3
confession 351.3
grant 443.5
compromise 468.1
giving 478.1
discount 631.1
merchant 730.2
market 736.1
qualification 958.1

concierge 1007.12

conciliation pacification
465.1
adjustment 787.4

conciliatory forgiving
148.6
unbelligerent 464.10
pacificatory 465.12

concise short 268.8
taciturn 344.9
brief 537.6

conclude resolve 359.7
complete 407.6
arrange 437.8
end 819.5
draw a conclusion
945.10
suppose 950.10

concluded completed
407.11
ended 819.8

concluding completing
407.9
ending 819.10

conclusion
noun affirmation 334.1
signing 437.3

sequel 816.1
end 819.1
solution 939.1
deduction 945.4
opinion 952.6
adj completion 407.2

conclusive completing
407.9
mandatory 420.12
final 819.11
convincing 952.26
evidential 956.16
unqualified 959.2
certain 969.13

conclusive evidence
956.3

conclusively 819.12

concocted 354.29

concoction fabrication
354.10
decoction 405.3
compound 796.5
production 891.1
product 892.1

concomitant
noun adjunct 254.1
attendant 768.3
contemporary 835.2
adj accompanying
768.9
simultaneous 835.5
concurrent 898.4

concord
noun unanimity 332.5
treaty 437.2
cooperation 450.1
accord 455.1
harmony 708.3
agreement 787.1
order 806.1
verb cooperate 450.3

Concorde 181.3

concourse convergence
169.1
flow 238.4
assemblage 769.1
assembly 769.2
joining 799.1
concurrence 898.1

concrete
noun ground covering
199.3
pavement 383.6
conglomeration 802.5
specific 864.3
solid 1043.6
stone 1044.6
sticks and stones
1052.2
verb floor 295.22
plaster 295.25
thicken 1043.10
solidify 1044.8
adj substantial 762.6
cohesive 802.10
particular 864.12
dense 1043.12
hard 1044.10

concubine subject
432.7
wife 563.8
mistress 665.17

concur accord 332.9
cooperate 450.3
agree 787.6
coincide 835.4
collaborate 898.2
support 900.21

concurrent converging
169.3
parallel 203.6
unanimous 332.15
cooperative 450.5
accompanying 768.9
joint 799.12
simultaneous 835.5
concurring 898.4

concurrently
unanimously 332.17
cooperatively 450.6
together 768.11
jointly 799.18
at that time 820.9
simultaneously 835.7
coactively 898.5

concurring
noun assent 332.1
adj cooperative 450.5
agreeing 787.9
concurrent 898.4

concussion trauma
85.37
shock 671.8
impact 901.3

condemn destroy
395.10
censure 510.13
damn 602.3
pass judgment 945.13
work evil 999.6

condemnation censure
510.3
judgment 598.10
damnation 602.1
verdict 945.5

condensation trickle
238.7
intensification 251.2
contraction 260.1
shortening 268.3
abridgment 557.1
cohesion 802.1
densification 1043.3

condense trickle 238.18
intensify 251.5
contract 260.7
shorten 268.6
be brief 537.5
abridge 557.5
densify 1043.9
solidify 1044.8

condensed contracted
260.12
shortened 268.9
concise 537.6
abridged 557.6
cohesive 802.10

dense 1043.12

condescending 141.9

condescension
condescendence 137.3
arrogance 141.1

condition
noun fitness 84.1
disease 85.1
rank 245.2
preparedness 405.4
stipulation 421.2
state 764.1
circumstance 765.1
provision 958.2
verb limit 210.5
accustom 373.10
repair 396.14
fit 405.8
inculcate 568.12
train 568.13
qualify 958.3
make conditional
958.4

conditional
noun mood 530.11
adj modal 764.6
circumstantial 765.7
dialectic 934.22
provisional 958.8
undecided 970.18

conditionally
circumstantially
765.12
provisionally 958.11

conditioned limited
210.7
accustomed 373.16
qualified 958.10
involuntary 962.14
undecided 970.18

conditioning
noun habituation 373.8
fitting 405.2
inculcation 568.2
training 568.3
involuntariness 962.5
adj healthful 81.5

conditions 830.4

condolence consolation
121.4
pity 145.1
condolences 147.1

condolences pity 145.1
condolence 147.1

condom 86.23

condone accept 134.7
overlook 148.4
suffer 443.10
keep an open mind
978.7

condoned 148.7

condoning
noun forgiveness 148.1
adj tolerant 978.11

conducive modal 384.8
helpful 449.21

conducive to 895.5

conduct

noun behaviour 321.1
performance 328.2
direction 573.1
operation 888.1
verb transport 176.12
channel 239.15
practice 328.8
perform 328.9
direct 573.8, 708.45
escort 768.8
operate 888.5

conductive 176.18

conductor railwayman
178.13
director 574.1
leader 574.6, 710.17
escort 768.5
conduction 1031.13

conduit channel 239.1
passageway 383.3

cone
noun loudspeaker 50.8
conoid 282.5
raceme 310.25
verb round 282.6

confection sweets
10.38
concoction 405.3
compound 796.5

confectionery 10.38

confederate
noun associate 616.1
accomplice 616.3
verb cooperate 450.3
accompany 768.7
league 804.4
adj leagued 804.6

confederation
affiliation 450.2
association 617.1
combination 804.1

confer advise 422.5
give 478.12
hold a conference
541.11
transfer 629.3

conference audition
48.2
council 423.1
forum 423.3
ecclesiastical council
423.4
congress 541.6
discussion 541.7
diocese 698.8
assembly 769.2

conference table 541.6

confess acknowledge
332.11
break down and
confess 351.7
make confession
701.17
attribute to 887.4
state 952.12

confessed accepted
332.14
disclosive 351.10

confessing 351.3

confession
acknowledgment
332.3, 887.2
confessing 351.3
school 617.5
apology 658.2
profession 952.7

confessional
noun vestry 703.9
adj admissive 351.11
doctrinal 952.27

confessions 719.1

confessor penitent
113.5
priest 699.5

confetti 47.6

confidant adviser 422.3
friend 588.1

confidante 588.1

confide hope 124.7
divulge 351.5
commit 478.16
tip 551.11

confide in believe in
952.15
trust 952.17

confidence equanimity
106.3
hope 124.1
expectation 130.1
secret 345.5
fearlessness 492.3
belief 952.1
confidentness 969.5

confidence-building
952.26

confident composed
106.13
hopeful 124.11
expectant 130.11
unafraid 492.20
belief 952.21
sure 969.21

confidential 345.14

confidentiality 345.2

confidentially 345.20

confidently 124.14

confiding artless 416.5
trusting 952.22

configuration aspect
33.3
gestalt 92.32
environment 209.1
outline 211.2
form 262.1
forming 262.5
structure 266.1
order 806.1
arrangement 807.1
characteristic 864.4
constellation 1070.5

confine
noun boundary 211.3
enclosure 212.3
verb limit 210.5
immure 212.6

narrow 270.11
restrict 428.9
shut in 429.12
simplify 797.4
delay 845.8
specialize 865.4

confined laid up 85.58
limited 210.7
enclosed 212.10
local 231.9
narrow 270.14
restricted 428.15
in confinement 429.19
specialized 865.5

confinement birth 1.1
limitation 210.2
enclosure 212.1
narrowness 270.1
restriction 428.3
locking-up 429.1
penal servitude 604.2

confines bounds 211.1
nearness 223.1
region 231.1

confining
noun simplification
797.2
adj limiting 210.9
enclosing 212.11
restrictive 428.12

confirm strengthen
15.13
ratify 332.12
accustom 373.10
secure 438.9, 854.8
minister 701.15
experiment 941.8
collate 942.5
affirm 956.11
verify 969.12

confirmation
ratification 332.4
seven sacraments
701.4
baptism 701.6
fixity 854.2
examination 937.3
collation 942.2
substantiation 956.4
ensuring 969.8

confirmed accepted
332.14
inveterate 373.19
established 854.13
tried 941.12
proved 956.20
true 972.13

confirming 956.18

confiscate demand
421.5
attach 480.20

confiscation 480.5

conflagration 1018.13

conflict
noun psychological
stress 92.17
hostility 451.2, 589.3
disaccord 456.1
contention 457.1

fight 457.4
contrariety 778.1
disagreement 788.1
counteraction 899.1
verb clash 35.14
disagree 456.8, 788.5
go contrary to 778.4
counteract 899.6

conflicting off-colour
35.20
clashing 61.5
oppositional 451.8
disaccordant 456.15
hostile 589.10
contrary 778.6
adverse 1010.13

conflict with go
contrary to 778.4
differ 779.5

confluence convergence
169.1
flow 238.4
assemblage 769.1
joining 799.1
concurrence 898.1

conform obey 326.2
observe the proprieties
579.4
agree 787.6
comply 866.3

conformation form
262.1
forming 262.5
structure 266.1
agreement 787.1
conformity 866.1

conforming obedient
326.3
observant 434.4

conformist
noun imitator 336.4
conventionalist 579.3
conformer 866.2
adj customary 373.14
conventional 866.6

conformity symmetry
264.1
custom 373.1
observance 434.1
social convention
579.1
piety 692.1
similarity 783.1
agreement 787.1
conformance 866.1

conform to concur
332.9
observe 434.2

conform with 787.6

confound chagrin
96.15
astonish 122.6
dismay 127.19
corrupt 393.12
destroy 395.10
overwhelm 412.8
curse 513.5
complicate 798.3
confuse 810.3, 944.3

refute 957.5
perplex 970.13
thwart 1011.15

confounded wondering
122.9
defeated 412.14
deuced 513.10
complex 798.4
disproved 957.7
in a dilemma 970.25

confounding
noun refutation 957.2
frustration 1011.3
adj astonishing 122.12
refuting 957.6
bewildering 970.27
frustrating 1011.20

confront approach
167.3
contrapose 215.4
front 216.8
meet 223.11
affront 451.5
offer resistance 453.3
defy 454.3
brave 492.11
be imminent 839.2
compare 942.4
thwart 1011.15

confrontation
contraposition 215.1
meeting 223.4
conference 541.6
contrariety 778.1
comparison 942.1

confrontational
contrapositive 215.5
front 216.10
oppositional 451.8
contrary 778.6

confronting
adj contrapositive
215.5
front 216.10
contrary 778.6
prep opposite to 215.7

confuse chagrin 96.15
deform 263.3
complicate 798.3
disorder 809.9
muddle 810.3
confound 944.3
make uncertain 970.15
mistake 974.13

confused inconspicuous
32.6
clashing 61.5
distressed 96.22
shy 139.12
formless 263.4
complex 798.4
incoherent 803.4
chaotic 809.16
disarranged 810.5
vague 970.19
bewildered 970.24
mixed-up 984.12

confusing 970.27

confusion chagrin 96.4

shyness 139.4
formlessness 263.1
discomfiture 412.2
anarchy 418.2
noncohesion 803.1
chaos 809.2
bewilderment 970.3
fluster 984.3

Cong 859.3

congealed cohesive
802.10
frozen 1023.14
thickened 1043.14

congenial pleasant 97.6
in accord 455.3
sociable 582.22
friendly 587.15
related 774.9
agreeing 787.9

congenital innate 766.8
thorough 793.10

congested diseased
85.59
stopped 293.11
full 793.11
late 845.16
stuck 854.16
overfull 992.20
dense 1043.12

congestion obstruction
293.3
fullness 793.2
overfullness 992.3
density 1043.1

conglomerate
noun accumulation
769.9
miscellany 769.13
conglomeration 802.5
solid 1043.6
rock 1057.1
verb assemble 769.18
mix 796.10
cohere 802.6
adj assembled 769.21
mixed 796.14

congratulate gratulate
149.2
compliment 509.14

congratulation
congratulations 149.1
praise 509.5

congratulations 149.1

congratulatory 149.3

congregate
verb come together
769.16
adj assembled 769.21

congregated 769.21

congregation audience
48.6
ecclesiastical council
423.4
worshipper 696.9
laity 700.1
assemblage 769.1
assembly 769.2

congress copulation
75.7
convergence 169.1
communication 343.1
council 423.1
conference 541.6
social life 582.4
legislature 613.1
assembly 769.2

congressional 613.10

congressman 610.3

conical 282.12

conifer 310.10

conjecture
noun supposition
950.3
guess 950.4
verb guess 950.11

conjugal loving 104.27
matrimonial 563.18

conjunction
juxtaposition 223.3
part of speech 530.3
joining 799.1
combination 804.1
concurrence 898.1

conjunctivitis 85.33

conjure deceive 356.14
summon 420.11
entreat 440.11
conjure up 690.11

conjure up summon
420.11
conjure 690.11
visualize 985.15
remember 988.10

con man gyp 357.4
thief 483.1

connect converge 169.2
adjoin 223.9
relate to 774.5
relate 774.6
put together 799.5
join 799.11
be consistent 802.7
combine 804.3
continue 811.4

connected clear 521.11
related 774.9
joined 799.13
consistent 802.11
continuous 811.8

connecting adjacent
223.16
joining 799.16
unifying 871.12

connection copulation
75.7
addict 87.20
intermediary 213.4
juxtaposition 223.3
communication 343.1
passageway 383.3
mediator 466.3
blood relationship
559.1
marriage relationship
564.1

go-between 576.4
relation 774.1
relevance 774.4
joining 799.1
joint 799.4
consistency 802.2
series 811.2

connections kinfolk
559.2
favour 893.2

connection with 887.1

connective relative
774.7
joining 799.16
combined 804.5
unifying 871.12

connective tissue
muscles 2.3
skin 2.4

connect with be
consistent 802.7
attribute to 887.4

conner 183.8

conning deception
356.1
inducement 375.3
study 570.3
direction 573.1

connivance chicanery
356.4
intrigue 381.5
consent 441.1
sufferance 443.2

conniving scheming
381.13
cooperative 450.5

connoisseur expert
413.11
connaisseur 496.7
collector 769.15
specialist 865.3
critic 945.7

connotation meaning
518.1
implication 519.2

conquer vanquish
412.10
subdue 432.9
appropriate 480.19

conquered 412.17

conquering
noun defeat 412.1
subdual 432.4
adj victorious 411.7

conqueror 411.2

conquest lover 104.12
victory 411.1
defeat 412.1
appropriation 480.4

cons 934.5

conscience psyche
92.28
grace 636.5

conscientious
meticulous 339.12
observant 434.4
fastidious 495.9

dutiful 641.13
tender-conscienced
644.15

conscientiously
meticulously 339.16
fastidiously 495.14
honestly 644.21

conscious awake 23.8
sensible 24.11
shy 139.12
living 306.11
intentional 380.8
knowing 927.15
attentive 982.15

consciously
intentionally 380.10
knowingly 927.29

consciousness
wakefulness 23.1
sensation 24.1
wits 918.2
intelligence 919.9
cognizance 927.2
attention 982.1

conscious of 927.16

conscript
noun recruit 461.17
verb call to arms
458.19
enlist 615.17

conscription call to
arms 458.8
enlistment 615.7

consecrated unselfish
652.5
sanctified 685.8

consecration accession
417.12
dedication 477.4
unselfishness 652.1
sanctification 685.3
holy orders 698.10

consecutive following
166.5
consistent 802.11
successive 811.9
subsequent 834.4

consensual assenting
332.13
cooperative 450.5

consensus
noun unanimity 332.5
cooperation 450.1
consentaneity 787.3
adj cooperative 450.5

consent
noun willingness 324.1
assent 332.1, 441.1
unanimity 332.5
submission 433.1
permission 443.1
verb be willing 324.3
assent 332.8, 441.2
submit 433.6
permit 443.9

consenting willing
324.5
obedient 326.3

constitutional rights
right 430.2
human rights 642.3

constrain compel 424.4
restrain 428.7
confine 429.12
moderate 670.6
necessitate 962.8

constrained reserved
139.11
reticent 344.10
restrained 428.13,
670.11

constraint reserve
139.3
self-control 359.5
urge 375.6
compulsion 424.1
restraint 428.1
confinement 429.1
temperance 668.1
moderation 670.1

constricted contracted
260.12
narrow 270.14
closed 293.9
narrow-minded 979.10

constriction contraction
260.1
narrowing 270.2
hindrance 1011.1

construct
noun structure 266.2
verb build 266.5
compose 795.3
produce 891.8

constructed 891.18

construction structure
266.1, 266.2
interpretation 341.1
explanation 518.3
word form 526.4
phrase 529.1
composition 795.1
production 891.2

constructive
interpretative 341.14
helpful 449.21
creative 891.16

consul 576.6

consular 576.16

consulate house 228.5
mastership 417.7
office 739.7

consul general 576.6

consult 541.11

consultancy 422.1

consultant doctor 90.4
expert 413.11
adviser 422.3

consultation advice
422.1
conference 541.6

consultative advisory
422.8
conciliar 423.5

consult with advise
422.5
confer 541.11

consume devour 8.22
decrease 252.6
shrink 260.9
spend 387.13, 388.3,
626.5
waste 393.19, 473.5,
486.4
destroy 395.10
disintegrate 805.3
burn up 1019.25

consumed reduced
252.10
shrunk 260.13
used up 388.5
lost 473.7
wasted 486.9
burned 1019.30

consumer eater 8.16
user 387.9
buyer 733.5

consumer credit 622.1

consumer durables
735.4

consumer goods
belongings 471.2
merchandise 735.1

consumerism 733.1

consuming
noun consumption
388.1
adj agonizing 98.23
destructive 395.26
engrossing 982.20

consummate
verb top 198.9
accomplish 407.4
adj top 198.10
downright 247.12
complete 407.12
thorough 793.10
perfected 1001.9

consummated 407.10

consummation
noun completion 793.4
end 819.1
acme of perfection
1001.3
adj accomplishment
407.1

consumption eating
8.1
decrement 252.3
shrinking 260.3
use 387.1
consuming 388.1
waste 393.4, 473.2
destruction 395.1
expenditure 626.1

contact
noun touch 73.1,
223.5
addict 87.20
communication 343.1
go-between 576.4
verb be heard 48.12

come in contact
223.10
communicate with
343.8

contacting 223.17

contact lenses 29.3

contacts 29.3

contagion
noun infection 85.4
phrase transference
176.1

contagious poisonous
82.7
infectious 85.61
transferable 176.18
communicable 343.11

contain internalize
207.5
limit 210.5
enclose 212.5
close 293.6
restrain 428.7
include 771.3
entail 771.4
total 791.8
compose 795.3
fight fire 1021.7

contained 1021.11

contained in 795.4

container receptacle
195.1
enclosure 212.3
cavity 284.2

containing
noun enclosure 212.1
adj inclusive 771.6
composed of 795.4

containment
surrounding 209.5
enclosure 212.1
foreign policy 609.5

contaminate defile
80.17
infect 85.50
corrupt 393.12
blaspheme 694.5
adulterate 796.12
radioactivate 1036.9

contaminated unclean
80.20
unhealthful 82.5
diseased 85.59
corrupt 654.14
radioactive 1036.10

contamination
defilement 80.4
unhealthfulness 82.1
infection 85.4
corruption 393.2
hybrid word 526.11
sacrilege 694.2
adulteration 796.3
radiation 1036.1
environmental
destruction 1071.2

contemplate scrutinize
27.14
expect 130.5

meditate 380.5
study 570.12
consider 930.12
think of 930.16
look upon 930.17
foresee 960.5

contemplated
intentional 380.8
reasoned 934.21

contemplating
cognitive 930.21
engrossed 982.17

contemplation scrutiny
27.6
expectation 130.1
inaction 329.1
study 570.3
revelation 683.9
trance 691.3
prayer 696.4
consideration 930.2
foresight 960.1
engrossment 982.3

contemplative passive
329.6
cognitive 930.21
engrossed 982.17

contemporary
noun coeval 835.2
adj simultaneous
835.5
present 837.2
modern 840.13

contempt hate 103.1
insolence 142.1
indignity 156.2
disdain 157.1
rejection 372.1
defiance 454.1
deprecation 510.2
disparagement 512.1

contemptible offensive
98.18
hateful 103.8
base 661.12
paltry 997.21
terrible 999.9

contemptuous hating
103.7
disdainful 141.13,
157.8
insolent 142.9
insulting 156.8
rejective 372.4
defiant 454.7
condemnatory 510.22
disparaging 512.13

contemptuously
arrogantly 141.15
impudently 142.13
scornfully 157.9

contend contrapose
215.4
affirm 334.5
insist 421.8
contest 457.13
compete 457.18
struggle 725.11
argue 934.16

contender competitor
452.2
combatant 461.1

contending 457.22

contend with treat
387.12
offer resistance 453.3
engage with 457.17

content
noun pleasure 95.1
contentment 107.1
contents 196.1
capacity 257.2
verb satisfy 107.4
adj pleased 95.14
contented 107.7
willing 324.5
assenting 332.13
consenting 441.4

contented pleased
95.14
content 107.7
comfortable 121.11

contentedly 107.14

contention
contraposition 215.1
opposition 451.1
disaccord 456.1
quarrel 456.5
contest 457.1
hostility 589.3
argumentation 934.4

contentious
quarrelsome 110.26
aggravating 119.5
warlike 458.21
argumentative 934.19

contentment pleasure
95.1
content 107.1
comfort 121.1
satiety 993.1

contents content 196.1
makeup 554.12
table 870.2

contest
noun contention 457.1
engagement 457.3
game 743.9
sport 744.1
verb deny 335.4
contend against 451.4
contradict 451.6
contend 457.13
dispute 457.21
argue 934.16
doubt 954.6

contestant
noun competitor 452.2
combatant 461.1
player 743.18
adj contending 457.22

contested 954.12

contesting 457.22

context environment
209.1
circumstances 765.2

continent

noun landmass 231.6
mainland 235.1
adj abstemious 664.6
abstinent 668.10

continental
noun mainlander 235.3
adj mainland 235.6

contingency
circumstance 765.1
nonessential 767.2
relativity 774.2
event 830.1
liability 896.1
condition 958.2
possibility 965.1
uncertainty 970.1
gamble 970.8
happening 971.6

contingent
noun portion 477.5
nonessential 767.2
company 769.3
part 792.1
event 830.1
happening 971.6
adj in contact 223.17
substantial 762.6
circumstantial 765.7
unessential 767.4
eventual 830.11
qualifying 958.7
dependent 958.9
possible 965.6
undecided 970.18
chance 971.15

continual continuous
811.8
perpetual 828.7
constant 846.5

continually regularly
780.8
continuously 811.10
perpetually 828.10
constantly 846.7

continuance sequel
816.1
durability 826.1
perpetuity 828.1
continuation 855.1

continuation adjunct
254.1
sequence 814.1
sequel 816.1
protraction 826.2
postponement 845.4
continuance 855.1

continue lengthen
267.6
persevere 360.2
be continuous 811.4
elapse 820.5
endure 826.6
protract 826.9
postpone 845.9
be frequent 846.3

continued 811.8

continue to be 826.6

continuing persevering
360.8

continuous 811.8
durable 826.10
permanent 852.7
abiding 855.7

continuity playbook
704.21
plot 722.4
uniformity 780.1
consistency 802.2
logical order 806.2
uninterruption 811.1
sequence 814.1
time 820.1
constancy 846.2
change 851.1
continuance 855.1

continuous
omnipresent 221.13
uniform 780.5
consistent 802.11
continued 811.8
temporal 820.7
perpetual 828.7
recurrent 848.13
continuing 855.7

continuously 811.10

continuum space 158.1
omnipresence 221.2
series 811.2

contorted 265.10

contour
noun outline 211.2
tournure 262.2
verb outline 211.9

contra
noun oppositionist
452.3
adj negative 335.5
oppositional 451.8
adv adversarial 451.9
prep opposed to
451.10
opposite 778.10

contraband
noun prohibition 444.1
smuggling 732.2
smuggled goods 732.3
adj prohibited 444.7
illegal 674.6

contraception 890.1

contraceptive birth
control device 86.23
safeguard 1007.3

contract
noun undertaking
404.1
obligation 436.2
compact 437.1
verb make small 258.9
compress 260.7
shorten 268.6
narrow 270.11
close 293.6
commit 436.5
be engaged 436.6
compact 437.5
acquire 472.8
incur 896.4

contracted reduced
252.10
compressed 260.12
closed 293.9
promised 436.8
compacted 437.11
concise 537.6

contract for 437.5

contraction decrease
252.1
contracture 260.1
narrowing 270.2
abbreviation 537.4
stenography 547.8

contractor 260.6

contractual 437.10

contradict deny 335.4
reject 372.2
cross 451.6
go contrary to 778.4
disagree 788.5
counteract 899.6
refute 957.5

contradicted 957.7

contradicting 335.5

contradiction denial
335.2
rejection 372.1
refusal 442.1
opposition 451.1
ambiguity 539.1
contrariety 778.1
disagreement 788.1
counteraction 899.1
refutation 957.2

contradictory negative
335.5
oppositional 451.8
contrary 778.6
disagreeing 788.6
illogical 935.11
refuting 957.6

contraption 1039.1

contrary
noun opposite 778.2
adj negative 335.5
perverse 361.11
oppositional 451.8
contrarious 778.6
different 779.7
disagreeing 788.6
nonconforming 867.5
refuting 957.6
adverse 1010.13
hindering 1011.17
unwieldy 1012.19
adv opposite 215.6

contrary to opposite
778.10
in disagreement with
788.10

Contras 461.15

contrast
noun contraposition
215.1
contrariety 778.1
difference 779.1
dissimilarity 786.1

comparison 942.1
lighting 1024.19
verb contrapose 215.4
compare 942.4

contrasted contrary
778.6
different 779.7

contrasting different
779.7
dissimilar 786.4

contrast with go
contrary to 778.4
differ 779.5

contravene deny 335.4
violate 435.4
contradict 451.6
go contrary to 778.4
counteract 899.6
thwart 1011.15

contravention denial
335.2
violation 435.2
opposition 451.1
lawbreaking 674.3

contribute provide
385.7
participate 476.5
subscribe 478.14
tend 895.3

contribute to advance
162.5
be useful 449.17
contribute 478.14
determine 885.12

contributing 449.21

contribution demand
421.1
participation 476.1
giving 478.1
donation 478.6
treatise 556.1
tax 630.9

contributor 478.11

contributory additional
253.10
helpful 449.21
donative 478.25

contrite 113.9

contrition regret 113.1
apology 658.2

contrivance plan 381.1
intrigue 381.5
instrument 384.4
stratagem 415.3
plot 722.4
production 891.1
expedient 994.2
tool 1039.1

contrive plan 381.8
manage 409.12
manoeuvre 415.10
induce 885.11
originate 891.12

contrived 381.12

control
noun supremacy 249.3
self-control 359.5
skill 413.1

governance 417.5
restraint 428.1
subjection 432.1
direction 573.1
mastery 612.2
moderation 670.1
familiar spirit 678.12
influence 893.1
experiment 941.1
spectre 987.1
system component
1040.14
verb pilot 184.37
restrain 428.7
direct 573.8
hold in hand 612.13
moderate 670.6
govern 893.8
haunt 987.6

control centre nerve
centre 208.5
proving ground
1072.7

controllable 433.14

controlled strong-willed
359.15
restrained 428.13,
670.11

controller
superintendent 574.2
broadcaster 1033.23
system component
1040.14

controlling
noun extinguishing
1021.2
adj authoritative
417.15
restraining 428.11
directing 573.12
governing 612.18
paramount 996.24

control panel 1040.16

control room 1033.7

control system 1040.5

control tower 184.22

controversial
contentious 110.26
argumentative 934.19
doubtful 970.17

controversy quarrel
456.5
contention 457.1
disagreement 788.1
argumentation 934.4

conundrum riddle
522.9
bewilderment 970.3

convalescence 396.8

convalescent 396.23

convene summon
420.11
meet 769.17

convener 574.5

convenience latrine
12.10
comfortableness 121.2
benefit 387.4

leisure 402.1
facility 449.9
timeliness 842.1
handiness 1013.2
machinery 1039.3
conveniences creature
comforts 121.3
equipment 385.4
convenient comfortable
121.11
nearby 223.15
handy 387.20,
1013.15
timely 842.9
expedient 994.5
conveniently
comfortably 121.14
usefully 387.26
expediently 994.8
convent 703.6
convention custom
373.1
rule 419.2
ecclesiastical council
423.4
compact 437.1
treaty 437.2
conference 541.6
fashion 578.1
social convention
579.1
etiquette 580.3
party conference 609.8
assembly 769.2
conventional
customary 373.14
preceptive 419.4
contractual 437.10
decorous 579.5
ceremonious 580.8
orthodox 687.7
traditional 841.12
conformist 866.6
usual 868.9
ordinary 1004.8
conventionally
customarily 373.20
decorously 579.6
conformably 866.7
conventional weapons
462.1
conventional wisdom
generalization 863.8
wisdom 919.5
opinion 952.6
maxim 973.1
conventions 579.2
converge come together
169.2, 769.16
focus 208.10
near 223.7
join 799.11
convergence
converging 169.1
centralization 208.8
nearness 223.1
assemblage 769.1
joining 799.1
converging

noun convergence
169.1
adj convergent 169.3
focal 208.13
conversation
communication 343.1
speech 524.1
converse 541.1
social life 582.4
conversational
communicational
343.9
vernacular 523.18
talkative 540.9
colloquial 541.13
converse
noun inverse 205.4
opposite side 215.3
communication 343.1
conversation 541.1
social life 582.4
opposite 778.2
verb communicate
343.6
speak 524.20
talk together 541.9
adj contrapositive
215.5
contrary 778.6
conversely inversely
205.8
contrarily 778.9
conversing 541.1
conversion misuse
389.1
reform 392.5
theft 482.1
redemption 685.4
game 746.3
change 851.1
reconversion 857.1
proselytization 857.6
production 891.2
block 989.3
convert
noun apostate 363.5
disciple 572.2
believer 692.4
proselyte 857.7
verb invert 205.5
misuse 389.4
redeem 685.6
sell 737.24
change 851.7
reconvert 857.11
interchange 862.4
process 891.9
convince 952.18
converted improved
392.13
redeemed 685.9
regenerate 692.10
changed 851.10,
857.19
forgetful 989.9
converter proselyter
857.9
philosopher's stone
857.10

convertibility foreign
money 728.9
equality 789.1
changeableness 853.1
conversion 857.1
interchangeability
862.3
convertible liquid
728.31
equivalent 789.8
changeable 857.18
interchangeable 862.5
convex
noun bulge 283.3
adj bowed 279.10
rotund 282.8
convexed 283.13
convey transport
176.12
channel 239.15
communicate 343.7
say 524.23
transfer 629.3
conveyancing 629.1
conveyor belt 176.5
convict
noun prisoner 429.11
criminal 660.10
verb bring in a verdict
598.21
condemn 602.3
conviction hope 124.1
condemnation 602.1
persuasion 952.5
confidence 969.5
convince persuade
375.23, 857.16
convert 952.18
seem true 972.9
convinced belief
952.21
confident 969.21
convincing convictional
952.26
evidential 956.16
convivial boon 582.23
festive 743.28
convoluted
grandiloquent 545.8
complex 798.4
convoy
noun escort 768.5
bodyguard 1007.14
verb manoeuvre
182.46
escort 768.8
convulsion seizure 85.6
anaemia 85.9
outburst 105.9
laughter 116.4
fit 152.8
fall 395.3
upheaval 671.5
disarrangement 810.1
revolution 859.1
spasm 916.6
frenzy 925.7

convulsive cataclysmic
671.23
jerky 916.19
coo murmur 52.10,
524.26
warble 60.5
cook
noun chef 11.2
home help 577.8
verb prepare food 11.4
fix 964.5
burn 1018.22
heat 1019.17
cookbook 554.8
cooked heated 11.6
fixed 964.8
cooked-up fabricated
354.29
fixed 964.8
cooker kitchen 11.3
heater 1019.10
cookery cooking 11.1
kitchen 11.3
heater 1019.10
cookery book 554.8
cookie biscuit 10.41
guy 76.5
cooking
noun cookery 11.1
heating 1019.1
adj culinary 11.5
cookware 11.3
cool
noun composure 106.2
unastonishment 123.1
moderation 670.1
uniformity 780.1
stability 854.1
verb disincline 379.4
pacify 465.7
calm 670.7
refrigerate 1023.10
adj chromatic 35.15
unfeeling 94.9
indifferent 102.6
calm 106.12
unastonished 123.3
aloof 141.12, 583.6
insolent 142.9
quiescent 173.12
reticent 344.10
cautious 494.8
unfriendly 589.9
equable 670.13
stable 854.12
sensible 919.18
great 998.13
coolish 1022.12
cold 1022.16
coolant refrigerant
1023.7
antifreeze 1023.8
cool down 106.7
cooled 1023.13
cooler nick 429.9
jockey 757.2
chiller 1023.3
coolie 176.7

cooling
noun economizing
635.2
refrigeration 1023.1
adj refrigerative
1023.12
cooling off peace offer
465.2
business cycle 731.9
cooling-off 670.15
cooling-off period
peace offer 465.2
truce 465.5
pause 856.3
coolly indifferently
102.9
inexcitably 106.16
quiescently 173.18
unamicably 589.14
moderately 670.17
coolness unfeeling 94.1
indifference 102.1
composure 106.2
unastonishment 123.1
aloofness 141.4, 583.2
caution 494.1
enmity 589.1
sensibleness 919.6
cold 1022.1
cool off 106.7
coon 311.23
co-op 736.1
coop
noun enclosure 212.3
place of confinement
429.7
nick 429.9
verb enclose 212.5
confine 429.12
cooped 212.10
cooperate be willing
324.3
collaborate 450.3
share 476.6
interact 776.6
agree 787.6
interchange 862.4
concur 898.2
cooperating cooperative
450.5
interacting 776.9
joint 799.12
cooperation
collaboration 450.1
communion 476.2
association 582.6
interaction 776.3
agreement 787.1
interchange 862.1
concurrence 898.1
cooperative
noun association 617.1
market 736.1
adj willing 324.5
favourable 449.22
cooperating 450.5
communal 476.9
interacting 776.9

letter writing 553.1
correlation 776.1
sameness 777.1
uniformity 780.1
similarity 783.1
agreement 787.1
equality 789.1
conformity 866.1
concurrence 898.1

correspondent
noun letter writer
553.8
correlate 776.4
likeness 783.3
adj journalist 555.4
reciprocal 776.10
coinciding 777.8
uniform 780.5
analogous 783.11

corresponding in
accord 455.3
reciprocal 776.10
coinciding 777.8
analogous 783.11
conformist 866.6
sufficient 990.6

correspondingly
identically 777.9
similarly 783.18
equally 789.11

correspond to relate to
774.5
reciprocate 776.7

correspond with
553.10

corridor airway 184.33
entrance 189.5
hall 197.18
region 231.1
passageway 383.3

corridors of power
authorities 575.15
government 612.3

Corrigan 678.8

corroborated proved
956.20
true 972.13

corroboration
confirmation 956.4
ensuring 969.8

corroded 393.43

corrosion decrement
252.3
decay 393.6
disintegration 805.1

corrosive
noun cauterant
1019.15
adj out of humour
110.17
caustic 144.23
corrupting 393.44
vigorous 544.11
disintegrative 805.5
harmful 999.12

corrugated rough
288.6
rugged 288.7

furrowed 290.4
wrinkled 291.8

corrupt
verb defile 80.17
bribe 378.3
debase 393.12
decay 393.22
misteach 569.3
sully 654.10
adulterate 796.12
indoctrinate 857.15
work evil 999.6
adj bribable 378.4
decayed 393.40
dishonest 645.16
corrupted 654.14
erroneous 974.16

corrupted unclean
80.20
dishonest 645.16
corrupt 654.14

corrupting corruptive
393.44
harmful 999.12

corruption filth 80.7
perversion 265.2
bribery 378.1
pollution 393.2
decay 393.6
wordplay 489.8
mispronunciation
525.5
barbarism 526.6
solecism 531.2
misteaching 569.1
improbity 645.1
turpitude 654.5
adulteration 796.3
indoctrination 857.5
evil 999.3

corset stays 5.23
supporter 900.2

cortege funeral 309.5
attendance 768.6
procession 811.3

cortex exterior 206.2
skin 295.3
shell 295.15
armour 460.3

corvette 180.6

Cosa Nostra
underworld 660.11
illicit business 732.1

cosily 121.14

cosiness pleasure 95.1
comfortableness 121.2

cosmetic exterior 206.7
shallow 276.5
hasty 401.9
insufficient 991.9
beautifying 1015.22

cosmetics appearance
33.2
exteriority 206.1
pretext 376.1
haberdashery 735.6
dissimilarity 786.1
makeup 1015.12

cosmetic surgery
1015.11

cosmic large 247.7
cosmical 1070.24

cosmology 1070.18

cosmopolitan
noun citizen 227.4
sophisticate 413.17
adj travelled 177.40
public 312.16
experienced 413.28
chic 578.13
universal 863.14
broad-minded 978.8

cosmos completeness
793.1
universe 1070.1

cossack 461.11

cost
noun loss 473.1
expenses 626.3
price 630.1
verb spend 626.5
sell for 630.13

cost-effective 635.6

cost-effectiveness
635.2

costing expenditure
626.1
accounting 628.6

costly 632.11

cost of living expenses
626.3
standard of living
731.8

costs 626.3

costume
noun clothing 5.1
suit 5.6
costumery 5.9
property 704.17
verb outfit 5.40

costumed 5.44

costume drama
1034.2

cosy pleased 95.14
comfortable 121.11
homelike 228.33
conversational 541.13
intimate 582.24
snug 1006.7

cote 212.3

coterie clique 617.6
company 769.3

Cotswolds 231.7

cottage 554.15

cottage industry 891.3

cotton 86.33

cotton wool 86.33

couch
noun psychoanalysis
92.6
lair 228.26
sofa 900.19
verb rest 20.6
lie low 274.5

lurk 346.9
say 524.23
phrase 532.4
depress 912.4
lie down 912.11

couched 532.5

cough 2.19

coughing 85.9

cough up 624.16

could be be possible
965.4
be probable 967.4

council
noun advice 422.1
conclave 423.1
conference 541.6
directorate 574.11
tribunal 595.1
cabinet 613.3
association 617.1
assembly 769.2
adj conciliar 423.5

**Council for the
Protection of Rural
England** 397.5

council housing 228.1

councillor minister
575.17
legislator 610.3

council of ministers
423.1

council of state council
423.1
cabinet 613.3

counsel
noun advice 422.1
adviser 422.3
lawyer 597.1
bar 597.4
consideration 930.2
verb advise 422.5
confer 541.11

counselling 422.1

counselling service
92.10

counsellor psychologist
92.10
adviser 422.3

count
noun amount 244.2
accusation 599.1
nobleman 608.4
returns 609.21
particular 765.3
sum 1016.6
summation 1016.11
verb quantify 244.4
beat time 708.44
have influence 893.10
judge 945.8
rank 945.15
matter 996.12
number 1016.16

countdown 815.2

counted on 130.14

countenance
noun looks 33.4

composure 106.2
face 216.4
authorization 443.3
patronage 449.4
approval 509.1
verb accept 134.7
encourage 375.21
suffer 443.10
abet 449.14
approve 509.9

counter
noun stern 217.7
retaliation 506.1
type 548.6
token 728.12
shopboard 736.6
workplace 739.1
bingo 759.15
chip 759.18
gambler 759.21
opposite 778.2
table 900.15
radioscope 1036.6
verb deny 335.4
oppose 451.3
contend against 451.4
fend off 460.10
retaliate 506.4
defend 600.10
go contrary to 778.4
disagree 788.5
counteract 899.6
refute 957.5
thwart 1011.15
adj backward 163.12
oppositional 451.8
contrary 778.6
dissimilar 786.4
adverse 1010.13
adv opposite 215.6
adversarial 451.9
contrarily 778.9

counteract contrapose
215.4
offset 338.5
oppose 451.3
go contrary to 778.4
counter 899.6
thwart 1011.15

counterbalance
noun makeweight
297.4
offset 338.2
counterforce 899.4
verb weigh 297.10
offset 338.5
equalize 789.6
stabilize 854.7
neutralize 899.7

counterfeit
noun fake 354.13
counterfeit money
728.10
copy 784.1
substitute 861.2
verb imitate 336.5
fabricate 354.18
sham 354.21
affect 500.12
coin 728.28
resemble 783.7

noun jellyfish 491.5
adj cowardly 491.10

cowardice frailty 16.2
fear 127.1
weak will 362.4
submission 433.1
cowardliness 491.1

cowardly
adj weak 16.12
fearful 127.23
weak-willed 362.12
coward 491.10
adv cravenly 491.14

cowboy rider 178.8
goon 671.10
herder 1068.3

cowed terrified 127.26
cowardly 491.10

cowering obsequious
138.14
quailing 491.13

cowling 295.2

cox 183.8

coxswain
noun steersman 183.8
guide 574.7
verb pilot 182.14

coy shy 139.12
amatory 562.23

coyly 139.15

coyote 311.20

CPS 1033.12

crab
noun grouch 108.4,
115.9
marine animal 311.30
vermin 311.35
windlass 905.7
lifter 911.3
verb beef 108.6,
115.16
stunt 184.40
queer 1011.16
adj sour 67.5

crack
noun stripe 47.5
report 56.1
snap 56.2
detonation 56.3
trauma 85.37
basuco 87.6
cleft 224.2
furrow 290.1
opening 292.1
try 403.3
break 801.4
instant 829.3
hit 901.4
fault 1002.2
blemish 1003.1
verb clap 56.6
snap 56.7
blast 56.8
crack up 128.8
cleave 224.4
furrow 290.3
open 292.11
unclose 292.12

explain 341.10
injure 393.13
break 393.23, 801.12
hit 901.14
solve 939.2
blemish 1003.4
burn 1019.24
computerize 1041.18
adj superior 998.14

crack down on 459.15

cracked raucous 58.15
dissonant 61.4
cleft 224.7
gaping 292.18
impaired 393.27
severed 801.23
mentally deficient
921.22
crazy 925.27
blemished 1003.8

cracker biscuit 10.29
noisemaker 53.6
dandy 998.7
liveware 1041.17
desert 1064.2

crackers screwy 922.9
crazy 925.27

cracking
noun snap 56.2
explanation 341.4
solution 939.1
burning 1019.5
computer science
1041.1
adj snapping 56.10
banging 56.11
deteriorating 393.45
great 998.13

crackle
noun snap 56.2
trauma 85.37
verb snap 56.7

crackling
noun snap 56.2
adj snapping 56.10

crackpot nut 925.16
freak 926.4

cradle
noun refinery 79.13
fatherland 232.2
infancy 301.5
origin 817.4
birthplace 885.8
verb put to bed 22.19
foster 449.16
calm 670.7
support 900.21

cradling 670.15

craft ship 180.1
deceit 356.3
skill 413.1
art 413.7
cunning 415.1
stratagem 415.3
manual art 712.3
vocation 724.6
shrewdness 919.3

crafted 891.18

craftsman expert
413.11
artist 716.1
skilled worker 726.6
producer 891.7

craftsmanship skill
413.1
production 891.2

craftspeople 726.6

crafty falsehearted
354.31
deceitful 356.22,
645.18
cunning 415.12
cautious 494.8
shrewd 919.15

crag precipice 200.3
mountain 237.6
projection 285.4
rock 1057.1

craggy rugged 288.7
stony 1057.11

craig precipice 200.3
rock 1057.1

cram
noun full measure
793.3
verb stuff 8.25
tutor 568.11
study 570.12
gluttonize 672.4
assemble 769.18
fill 793.7
thrust 901.12
refresh the memory
988.19
overload 992.15
satiate 993.4
densify 1043.9

crammed crowded
769.22
full 793.11
overfull 992.20
satiated 993.6
dense 1043.12

cramming
noun preinstruction
568.4
adj gluttonous 672.6

cramp
noun seizure 85.6
pain 96.5
restriction 428.3
spasm 916.6
hindrance 1011.1
verb weaken 16.10
confine 212.6
contract 260.7
squeeze 260.8
restrict 428.9
fasten 799.7
hamper 1011.11
queer 1011.16
adj hard to understand
522.14

cramped limited 210.7
enclosed 212.10
little 258.10
contracted 260.12

narrow 270.14
restricted 428.15
stiff 534.3
narrow-minded 979.10

cramping
noun restriction 428.3
adj painful 26.10
restrictive 428.12

crane
noun lifter 911.3
fire iron 1019.12
verb gaze 27.15
be long 267.5
demur 325.4

cranial 198.14

cranium 198.7

crank
noun bennies 87.3
grouch 108.4, 115.9
sorehead 110.11
angle 278.2
caprice 364.1
oddity 869.4
lever 905.4
fanatic 925.18
quirk 926.2
freak 926.4
verb angle 278.5
reel in 905.9
rotate 914.9
adj eccentric 926.5

cranky grouchy 108.8,
115.20
irascible 110.19
capricious 364.5
eccentric 926.5

cranny nook 197.3
crack 224.2
furrow 290.1
hiding place 346.4

crap big H 87.8
bullshit 520.3

crappy 999.8

crash
noun noise 53.3
report 56.1
prang 184.20
descent 194.1
decline 252.2
debacle 395.4
collapse 410.3
defeat 412.1
insolvency 625.3
declining market
737.5
impact 901.3
misfortune 1010.2
verb snooze 22.14
hit the hay 22.18
din 53.7
crack 56.6
prang 184.44
penetrate 189.8
descend 194.5
inhabit 225.7
billow 238.22
break down 393.24
fall 410.12
go bankrupt 625.7

cheapen 633.6
drive 756.4
collide 901.13

crash helmet 1007.3

crash in 214.5

crashing loud 53.11
banging 56.11
concussive 901.24

crash into 901.13

crass downright 247.12
thick 269.8
coarse 497.11
ill-bred 505.6
stupid 921.15

crate
noun jalopy 179.10
storehouse 386.6
verb package 212.9
wrap 295.20

crater valley 237.7
pit 275.2
cavity 284.2

cravat 86.33

crave covet 100.18
request 440.9
entreat 440.11

craven
noun dastard 491.6
adj dastardly 491.12

craving
noun coveting 100.6
adj coveting 100.24

crawl
noun slow motion
175.2
creeping 177.17
verb feel creepy 74.7
fawn 138.7
creep 177.26
lie 201.5
lie low 274.5
flatter 511.5
linger on 826.7
bow 912.9

crawling
noun obsequiousness
138.2
creeping 177.17
crouch 912.3
reception 1033.21
adj obsequious 138.14
slow 175.10
creeping 177.39
recumbent 201.8
permeated 221.15
reptile 311.46
crowded 769.22
teeming 883.9

crayfish 311.30

crayon
noun drawing 712.13
palette 712.18
verb portray 712.19

craze
noun stripe 47.5
trauma 85.37
greed 100.8
eagerness 101.1

fury 105.8
crack 224.2
caprice 364.1
fad 578.5
mania 925.12
blemish 1003.1
verb cleave 224.4
injure 393.13
break 801.12
madden 925.24
blemish 1003.4

crazed cleft 224.7
impaired 393.27
insane 925.26
blemished 1003.8

crazily 925.35

crazy
noun nut 925.16
adj variegated 47.9
distorted 265.10
mentally deficient
921.22
foolish 922.8
absurd 922.11
nutty 925.27

crazy about 101.11

creak
noun screech 58.4
stridulation 58.5
verb stridulate 58.7
screech 58.8

creaking
noun stridulation 58.5
adj shrill 58.14

creaky 58.14

cream
noun alabaster 37.2
cleanser 79.17
best 249.5, 998.8
ointment 1054.3
semiliquid 1060.5
verb foam 320.5
emulsify 1060.10
adj whitish 37.8
yellow 43.4

cream-coloured 43.4

creamed 412.15

creamy soft-coloured
35.21
whitish 37.8
yellow 43.4
semiliquid 1060.11

crease
noun fold 291.1
wrinkle 291.3
cricket 747.1
ice hockey 750.4
verb fold 291.5
wrinkle 291.6
engrave 713.9

creased folded 291.7
wrinkled 291.8
engraved 713.11

create complain 115.15
form 262.7
originate 337.4
initiate 817.10
cause 885.10

produce 891.8
imagine 985.14

created substantial
762.6
made 891.18

creating 677.17

creation forming 262.5
structure 266.1
preservation 677.13
work of art 712.10
beginning 817.1
production 891.1
product 892.1
universe 1070.1

creative original 337.5
falsehearted 354.31
wrong 638.3
dishonest 645.16
illegal 674.6
almighty 677.17
beginning 817.15
productive 889.9
originative 891.16
imaginative 985.18

creative writing 547.2,
718.2

creativity nonimitation
337.1
genius 919.8
invention 985.3

creator artist 716.1
doer 726.1
author 885.4
producer 891.7

creature sycophant
138.3
inferior 250.2
organism 305.2
animal 311.2
person 312.5
assenter 332.6
instrument 384.4
dependent 432.6
figurehead 575.5
deputy 576.1
retainer 577.1
follower 616.8
something 762.3
product 892.1

creature comforts
pleasure 95.1
comforts 121.3

credence altar 703.12
belief 952.1

credentials
preparedness 405.4
identification 517.11

credibility honesty
644.3
believability 952.8
plausibility 967.3

credible logical 934.20
believable 952.24
plausible 967.7

credit
noun thanks 150.2
difference 255.8
trust 622.1

receipts 627.1
entry 628.5
due 639.2
honour 646.1
esteem 662.3
attribution 887.1
influence 893.1
belief 952.1
believability 952.8
verb thank 150.4
credit with 622.5
keep accounts 628.8
believe 952.10

creditable praiseworthy
509.20
honest 644.13
reputable 662.15

credit card 622.3

credited creditworthy
622.8
attributable 887.6
believed 952.23

creditor 622.4

credit rating credit
622.1
financial condition
729.5

credits 627.1

credit union association
617.1
lending institution
620.4
credit 622.1

credo religion 675.1
doctrine 676.2
system of belief 952.3

credulity belief 952.1
credulousness 953.1

creed affirmation 334.1
policy 381.4
religion 675.1
doctrine 676.2
system of belief 952.3

creek stream 238.1
inlet 242.1

creep
noun slow motion
175.2
creeping 177.17
arsehole 660.6
verb feel creepy 74.7
fawn 138.7
crawl 177.26
lurk 346.9
linger on 826.7

creeper 310.4

creep in intrude 214.5
join 617.14

creeping
noun slowness 175.1
crawling 177.17
expansion 259.1
reception 1033.21
adj slow 175.10
crawling 177.39
permeated 221.15
reptile 311.46

creeps jitters 128.2

chill 1022.2

creepy crawly 74.11
spooky 127.31
lousy 999.8

cremated 1019.30

cremation incineration
309.2
burning 1019.5

crematorium mortuary
309.9
incinerator 1019.13

creole 523.11

crescendo
noun loudness 53.1
increase 251.1
expansion 259.1
presto 708.25
verb din 53.7
grow 251.6
enlarge 259.4, 259.5
adj, adv legato 708.53

crescent
noun circus 230.9
semicircle 279.5,
280.8
heraldic device 647.2
moon 1070.11
adj grown 14.3,
259.12
increasing 251.8
crescent-shaped
279.11

crest
noun feather 3.17
summit 198.2
head 198.4
mountain 237.6
notching 289.2
heraldic device 647.2
wave 915.4
verb top 198.9

crested tufted 3.30
topped 198.12

crestfallen glum
112.25
disappointed 132.5
humiliated 137.14

cretinous 921.22

crevice 224.2

crew aircrew 185.4
staff 577.11
team 617.7
film studio 706.3
company 769.3

crewman mariner
183.1
crew 185.4

crib
noun compartment
197.2
hut 228.9
infancy 301.5
translation 341.3
storehouse 386.6
garner 386.7
brothel 665.9
verb confine 212.6,
429.12

imitate 336.5
cheat 356.18

crick
noun pang 26.2
stridulation 58.5
stream 238.1
verb stridulate 58.7

cricket noisemaker 53.6
locust 311.34
propriety 637.2
fairness 649.3

cricket ground 743.11

cricket pitch 747.1

crime wrongdoing
655.1
misdeed 655.2
offence 674.4

criminal
noun evildoer 593.1
perpetrator 645.10
felon 660.10
adj wrong 638.3
dishonest 645.16
wicked 654.16
wrongdoing 655.5
guilty 656.3
illegal 674.6
bad 999.7

criminal investigation
937.4

criminality wrong
638.1
improbity 645.1
vice 654.1
wrongdoing 655.1
guilt 656.1
lawbreaking 674.3

**criminal-justice
system** 594.2

criminally dishonestly
645.24
illegally 674.8

criminology 673.7

crimson
verb redden 41.4, 41.5
change colour 105.19
blush 139.8
adj red 41.6

cringe
noun retreat 902.3
verb shake 16.8
flinch 127.13
fawn 138.7
retract 168.3
cower 491.9
crouch 912.8

cringing
noun obsequiousness
138.2
adj obsequious 138.14
cowering 491.13

crinkled rugged 288.7
wrinkled 291.8

crinkly 291.8

cripple
noun defective 85.44
verb weaken 16.10
disable 19.9

philosopher's stone
857.10
test 941.2
chemicalization 1058.6

crucified pained 26.9
tortured 96.25

crucifix 170.4

crucifixion agony 26.6
torment 96.7
capital punishment
604.6

crude
noun raw material
406.5
petroleum 1054.4
adj garish 35.19
offensive 98.18
raw 406.10
undeveloped 406.12
coarse 497.11
gaudy 501.20
ill-bred 505.6
inelegant 534.2
base 661.12

crudely 497.16

crude oil 1054.4

cruel painful 26.10
cruel-hearted 144.26
pitiless 146.3
murderous 308.23
savage 671.21

cruelly brutally 144.35
pitilessly 146.4
distressingly 247.21

cruelty cruelness
144.11
act of cruelty 144.12
pitilessness 146.1

cruise
noun journey 177.5
voyage 182.6
verb journey 177.21
navigate 182.13
fly 184.36

cruise missile 462.18

cruiser traveller 178.1
motorboat 180.4
warship 180.6
battleship 180.7

cruiserweight 297.3

cruise ship ship 180.1
liner 180.5

cruising water travel
182.1
aviation 184.1

crumb
noun scrap 248.3
minutia 258.7
piece 792.3
powder 1049.5
verb sprinkle 770.6
pulverize 1049.9

crumble
noun powder 1049.5
verb weaken 16.9
decrease 252.6
decay 393.22
fall 395.22

disintegrate 805.3
pulverize 1049.9
powder 1049.10

crumbling
noun disintegration
805.1
pulverization 1049.4
adj unsound 16.15
deteriorating 393.45
stale 841.14

crumbly frail 16.14
brittle 1048.4
pulverable 1049.13

crumple
noun wrinkle 291.3
verb distort 265.5
ruffle 288.5
wrinkle 291.6

crumpled distorted
265.10
rugged 288.7
wrinkled 291.8

crunch
noun rasp 58.3
concussion 671.8
crisis 842.4
urgency 996.4
pickle 1012.5
verb grate 58.10
shatter 801.13
pulverize 1049.9

crunched 265.10

crusade campaign
458.4
cause 885.9

crush
noun liking 100.2
squeezing 260.2
throng 769.4
full measure 793.3
pulp 1061.2
verb sadden 112.18
aggrieve 112.19
unnerve 128.10
abase 137.5
squeeze 260.8
conquer 412.10
suppress 428.8
subdue 432.9
shatter 801.13
refute 957.5
pulverize 1049.9
pulp 1061.5

crushed wretched
96.26
overcome 112.29
unnerved 128.14
disappointed 132.5
humiliated 137.14
conquered 412.17
suppressed 428.14
subdued 432.15
powdery 1049.11

crushing
noun wretchedness
96.6
suppression 428.2
subdual 432.4
pulverization 1049.4

adj mortifying 98.21
oppressive 98.24
humiliating 137.15
laborious 725.18
troublesome 1012.18

crushing defeat 412.3

crust
noun bread 10.27
cheek 142.3
exterior 206.2
land 234.1
incrustation 295.14
verb incrust 295.27

crusty crabby 110.20
gruff 505.7
hardened 1044.13

crutch
noun genitals 2.11
fork 171.4
staff 273.2
supporter 900.2
verb support 449.12,
900.21

crux cross 170.4
enigma 522.8
salient point 996.6
dilemma 1012.7
hitch 1012.8

cry
noun call 59.1
animal noise 60.1
lament 115.3
cheer 116.2
publicity 352.4
entreaty 440.2
catchword 526.9
report 552.6
verb call 59.6, 60.2
weep 115.12
wail 115.13
cheer 116.6
proclaim 352.13

cry for wish for 100.16
entreat 440.11
require 962.9

crying
noun weeping 115.2
adj vociferous 59.10
howling 60.6
tearful 115.21
demanding 421.9
urgent 996.22

cry out vociferate 59.8
wail 115.13
proclaim 352.13

crypt compartment
197.2
understructure 266.3
cavity 284.2
tomb 309.16
vestry 703.9

cryptic secret 345.11
latent 519.5
implied 519.7
enigmatic 522.17

crypto 357.11

crystal
noun bennies 87.3
snow 1022.8

precious stone 1057.6
adj transparent 1028.4
stony 1057.11

crystal ball future
838.1
divination 961.2

crystal-clear distinct
31.7
manifest 348.8
clear 521.11
transparent 1028.4

crystalline clear 521.11
transparent 1028.4
stony 1057.11

cub
noun boy 302.5
fledgling 302.10
adj unaccustomed
374.4
immature 406.11

cube triplicate 876.2
square 878.3

cubed 278.9

cubes acid 87.9
dice 759.8

cubic 158.9

cubicle nook 197.3
bedroom 197.7

cuckoo
noun imitator 336.4
songbird 710.23
verb warble 60.5
adj crazy 925.27

cud bite 8.2
chewing tobacco 89.7

cuddle 121.10, 562.17

cuddling 562.1

cuddly 104.25

cue
noun braid 3.7
clue 517.9
tip 551.3
hint 551.4
role 704.10
playbook 704.21
table 752.2
reminder 988.6
verb play 752.4

cuff
noun slap 604.3, 901.8
verb slap 604.11,
901.19

cuffs 428.4

cuisine food 10.1
cooking 11.1
kitchen 11.3

cul-de-sac obstruction
293.3
impasse 1012.6

culinary 11.5

cull excise 255.10
select 371.14
collect 472.11

culling elimination
772.2
grouping 807.3

culminate top 198.9
complete 407.6
perfect 1001.5

culminating topping
198.11
completing 407.9

culmination
noun summit 198.2
completion 793.4
end 819.1
acme of perfection
1001.3
adj completion 407.2

culpability 656.1

culpable blameworthy
510.25
guilty 656.3

culprit 660.9

cult ism 675.2
worship 696.1
ritualism 701.1
system of belief 952.3

cult figure celebrity
662.9
godling 678.3
ideal 785.4

cultivate sensitize 24.7
develop 392.10
foster 449.16
train 568.13
cultivate the friendship
of 587.12
process 891.9
culture 1067.17

cultivated improved
392.13
elegant 496.9
well-bred 504.17
learned 927.21

cultivating 1067.13

cultivation culture
392.3
taste 496.1
good breeding 504.4
training 568.3
production 891.2
agriculture 1067.1
growing 1067.12
cultivating 1067.13

cultural 568.18

cultural centre 208.7

culture
noun humankind 312.1
society 373.3
cultivation 392.3,
1067.13
taste 496.1
good breeding 504.4
scholarship 927.5
agriculture 1067.1
verb cultivate 1067.17
raise 1068.6

cultured improved
392.13
elegant 496.9
well-bred 504.17
learned 927.21

culture shock 226.3

culvert 239.2

cumbersome bulky
257.19
onerous 297.17
bungling 414.20
hampering 1011.18
unwieldy 1012.19

cumulative additive
253.8
accumulative 769.23
evidential 956.16

cunning
noun falseheartedness
354.4
deceit 356.3
skill 413.1
cunningness 415.1
shrewdness 919.3
adj falsehearted
354.31
deceitful 356.22
skilful 413.22
well-laid 413.30
crafty 415.12
shrewd 919.15

cunningly skilfully
413.31
craftily 415.13
intelligently 919.20

cup
noun spirits 88.13
container 195.1
cupful 196.4
cavity 284.2
victory 411.1
monument 549.12
trophy 646.3
football 745.1
rugby 746.1
golf 748.1
hockey 750.1
skiing 753.1
athletics 755.1
fate 963.2
verb bleed 91.27
ladle 176.17
sink 284.12
hollow 284.13

cupboard container
195.1
wardrobe 197.15
storehouse 386.6

Cupid 104.8

cupid 104.9

cup of tea 764.4

cuppa 8.4

cupped 284.16

cups 8.12

curable 396.25

curate 699.2

curative remedial 86.39
tonic 396.22

curator steward 574.4
treasurer 729.11
guardian 1007.6

curb
noun kerb 211.6
restraint 428.1

check 1011.7
verb slow 175.9
restrain 428.7
hinder 1011.10

curbed 428.13

curd
noun clot 1043.7
semiliquid 1060.5
verb thicken 1043.10

curdling thickening
1043.4
viscosity 1060.2

cure
noun remedy 86.1
treatment 91.14
curing 396.7
commission 615.1
benefice 698.9
protectorship 1007.2
verb remedy 86.38
treat 91.24
disaccustom 374.2
work a cure 396.15
preserve 397.9
prepare 405.6
solidify 1044.8
dry 1064.6

cure-all 86.3

cured 405.16

curfew 315.5

curing cure 396.7
food preservation
397.2
hardening 1044.5

curiosity desire 100.1
marvel 122.2
oddity 869.5
curiousness 980.1
attention 982.1
interest 982.2

curious careful 339.10
odd 869.11
inquiring 937.36
inquisitive 980.5
attentive 982.15
interested 982.16

curiously 869.19

curl
noun lock 3.5
exercise 84.2
curve 279.2
coil 281.2
verb curve 279.6
coil 281.5

curled 281.9

curl up rest 20.6
snuggle 121.10

curly 281.9

currency publicity
352.4
fashionableness 578.2
money 728.1
prevalence 863.2
usualness 868.2

current
noun direction 161.1
course 172.2
flow 238.4

wind 318.1
trend 895.2
electric current 1031.2
adj published 352.17
customary 373.14
reported 552.15
fashionable 578.11
existent 760.13
happening 830.9
present 837.2
prevalent 863.12
usual 868.9
well-known 927.27

current account 622.2

curricular 568.19

curriculum 568.8

curried cooked 11.6
zestful 68.7

curry
noun stew 10.11
verb cook 11.4
comb 79.21
tend 1068.7

curse
noun menstruation
12.9
affliction 96.8
malediction 513.1
oath 513.4
spell 691.1
trifle 997.5
bad influence 999.4
bane 1000.1
adversity 1010.1
verb accurse 513.5
swear 513.6
blaspheme 694.5
work evil 999.6

cursed accursed 513.9
execrable 999.10

cursing
noun cussing 513.3
adj maledictory 513.8

cursory insignificant
248.6
shallow 276.5
unwilling 325.5
careless 340.11
hasty 401.9

curt short 268.8
taciturn 344.9
gruff 505.7
concise 537.6

curtail reduce 252.7
subtract 255.9
contract 260.7
shorten 268.6
restrain 428.7
take from 480.21

curtailed reduced
252.10
shortened 268.9

curtain
noun cover 295.2
veil of secrecy 345.3
veil 346.2
act 704.7
stage 704.16
scenery 704.20

end 819.1
obstacle 1011.4
shade 1027.1
verb cover 295.19
conceal 346.6
shade 1027.5

curtained covered
295.31
shaded 1027.7

curtain raiser overture
708.26
countdown 815.2

curtains death 307.1
end 819.1

curtly shortly 268.12
gruffly 505.9
concisely 537.7

curvaceous curved
279.7
comely 1015.18

curvature 279.1

curve
noun deviation 164.1
angle 278.2
sinus 279.2
trick 356.6
race 756.3
verb deviate 164.3
deflect 164.5
angle 278.5
turn 279.6
adj curved 279.7

curved 279.7

curves 1015.4

curving
noun curvature 279.1
adj curved 279.7

curvy crooked 204.20
curved 279.7
comely 1015.18

cushion
noun silencer 51.4
partition 213.5
moderator 670.3
table 752.2
bedding 900.20
safeguard 1007.3
putty 1045.4
verb muffle 51.9
relieve 120.5
absorb the shock
670.8
support 900.21
protect 1007.18
soften 1045.6

cushioned 121.11

cushioning
noun softening 1045.5
adj mitigating 670.14

custard 10.44

custodial vigilant
339.13
preservative 397.11
protective 1007.23

custodian cleaner
79.14
steward 574.4
guardian 1007.6

custody vigilance 339.4
storage 386.5
preservation 397.1
custodianship 429.5
directorship 573.4
protectorship 1007.2

custom
noun behaviour 321.1
convention 373.1
habit 373.4
fashion 578.1
social convention
579.1
patronage 731.6
market 733.3
tradition 841.2
adj made 891.18

customarily
conventionally 373.20,
579.6
normally 868.10

customary wonted
373.14
conventional 579.5
orthodox 687.7
traditional 841.12
usual 868.9

custom-built 891.18

customer guy 76.5
client 733.4

customers 733.3

custom-made tailored
5.47
made 891.18

customs 630.10

customs union 617.1

cut
noun trauma 85.37
pain 96.5
indignity 156.2
snub 157.2
absence 222.4
crack 224.2
degree 245.1
curtailment 252.4
form 262.1
shortcut 268.5
notch 289.1
furrow 290.1
trench 290.2
lamina 296.2
thrust 459.3
gibe 508.2
mark 517.5
discount 631.1
cheapening 633.4
print 713.5
piece 792.3
break 801.4
characteristic 864.4
hit 901.4
slap 901.8
repulse 907.2
verb dilute 16.11
pain 26.7, 96.17
bite 68.5
offend 152.21
cleave 224.4
reduce 252.7

censure 510.3
curse 513.1
condemnation 602.1

damned
noun evil spirits 680.1
adj cursed 513.9
unregenerate 695.18
execrable 999.10

damning 956.16

damp
noun silencer 51.4
killjoy 112.14
deterrent 379.2
moisture 1063.1
vapour 1065.1
verb muffle 51.9
sadden 112.18
reduce 252.7
disincline 379.4
moderate 670.6
make uniform 780.4
hinder 1011.10
fight fire 1021.7
moisten 1063.12
adj moist 1063.15

dampen muffle 51.9
sadden 112.18
reduce 252.7
disincline 379.4
moderate 670.6
hinder 1011.10
moisten 1063.12

dampened 52.17

dampening
noun decrease 252.1
wetting 1063.6
adj mitigating 670.14
wetting 1063.18

damper silencer 51.4
killjoy 112.14
deterrent 379.2
curb 1011.7
fire iron 1019.12

damping
noun weakening 16.5
decrease 252.1
modulation 670.2
extinguishing 1021.2
wetting 1063.6
adj mitigating 670.14

dampness 1063.1

damp squib 410.5

damsel 302.6

dance
noun dancing 705.1
knees-up 705.2
assembly 769.2
flutter 916.4
flicker 1024.8
verb exude
cheerfulness 109.6
rejoice 116.5
trip the light fantastic
705.5
play 743.23
flutter 916.12
flicker 1024.25
adj dancing 705.6

dance floor ballroom
705.4
entertainment 743.13

dance hall hall 197.4
ballroom 705.4
entertainment 743.13

dance music 708.8

dancer danseur 705.3
entertainer 707.1

dances 708.8

dancing
noun terpsichore 705.1
flicker 1024.8
adj happy 95.15
dance 705.6
fluttering 916.18
flickering 1024.36

dander 152.6

dandruff filth 80.7
flake 296.3

dandy
noun fop 500.9
person of fashion
578.7
jim dandy 998.7
adj foppish 500.17
great 998.13

danger unreliability
970.6
peril 1005.1

dangerous unreliable
970.20
dangersome 1005.9

dangerously 1005.17

dangerousness 1005.2

dangle
noun hang 202.2
verb attach oneself to
138.11
hang 202.6
manifest 348.5
flaunt 501.17
oscillate 915.10

dangling pendent
202.9
loose 803.5
swinging 915.17

dank 1063.15

dapper 578.13

dapple
noun spottiness 47.3
mark 517.5
verb variegate 47.7
mark 517.19
adj mottled 47.12

dappled mottled 47.12
mixed 796.14

dare
noun challenge 454.2
verb have the audacity
142.7
confront 216.8
defy 454.3
venture 492.10
presume 640.6
take chances 1005.7

daredevil

noun devil 493.4
adj foolhardy 493.9

dare not 491.7

daresay suppose 950.10
think 952.11
think likely 967.5

dare to 403.8

daring
noun defiance 454.1
derring-do 492.5
foolhardiness 493.3
display 501.4
adj defiant 454.7
audacious 492.22
foolhardy 493.9
showy 501.19

daringly courageously
492.23
foolhardily 493.12
showily 501.26

dark
noun secrecy 345.1
obscurity 522.3
unenlightenment
929.4
darkness 1026.1
adj blind 30.9
inconspicuous 32.6
black 38.8, 1026.13
dark-coloured 38.9
sullen 110.24
gloomy 112.24
ominous 133.17
cloudy 319.7
secret 345.11
secretive 345.15
obscure 522.15
dishonest 645.16
wicked 654.16
benighted 929.16
opaque 1030.3

Dark Ages 823.5

dark-blue 45.3

darken blind 30.7
blacken 38.7
change colour 105.19
sadden 112.18
cloud 319.6
stain 1003.6
bedarken 1026.9
grow dark 1026.12
opaque 1030.2

darkened blinded
30.10
stained 1003.10

darkening blackening
38.5
concealment 346.1
dimming 1026.6

dark glasses spectacles
29.3
eyeshade 1027.2

dark horse candidate
610.9
unknown 929.7
small chance 971.9

dark matter 1070.7

darkness blindness
30.1
inconspicuousness
32.2
blackness 38.1
darkishness 38.2
gloom 112.7
night 315.4
obscurity 522.3
unenlightenment
929.4
dark 1026.1
opaqueness 1030.1

dark-skinned 38.10

darling
noun sweetheart
104.10
favourite 104.16
child 302.3
dear 562.6
adj beloved 104.24

darn repair 396.14
curse 513.5

darned 513.10

dart
noun lightning 174.6
arrow 462.6
sting 1000.5
verb speed 174.8
throw 903.10

darts 744.1

Darwinism 860.4

dash
noun vim 17.2
disappointment 132.1
run 174.3
hint 248.4
haste 401.1
showiness 501.3
line 517.6
spirit 544.4
tinge 796.7
hit 901.4
verb sadden 112.18
unnerve 128.10
disappoint 132.2
speed 174.8
billow 238.22
make haste 401.5
thwart 412.11,
1011.15
mark 517.19
throw 903.10
moisten 1063.12
adv suddenly 829.9

dashboard 1007.3

dashed dejected 112.22
unnerved 128.14
disappointed 132.5
confounded 513.10

dashing fast 174.15
showy 501.19
chic 578.13

dastardly 491.12

data information 551.1,
1041.15
facts 760.4
collection 769.11
knowledge 927.1

premise 934.7
evidence 956.1

database knowledge
927.1
data 1041.15

date
noun appointment
582.8
engagement 704.11
assembly 769.2
age 823.4
point of time 831.4
verb come together
769.16
be dated 831.13
age 841.9

date back 831.13

dated past 836.7
old-fashioned 841.16

dateline 831.13

dating 831.1

daughter brother 559.3
descendant 561.3

daughter-in-law 564.2

daunt deter 127.18
dissuade 379.3
domineer 612.16

daunted frightened
127.25
cowardly 491.10

daunting 127.28

dauphin 608.7

David 492.8

Davy spirit of the sea
240.4
water god 678.10

dawn
noun dawn of day
314.3
beginning 817.1
daylight 1024.10
verb grow light
1024.27
adj morning 314.6

dawning
noun dawn 314.3
cognizance 927.2
adj morning 314.6

day period 823.1
moment 823.2
age 823.4
date 831.4
daylight 1024.10

day after day for a
long time 826.14
constantly 846.7
repeatedly 848.16

day and night 846.7

daybreak 314.3

day by day repeatedly
848.16
periodically 849.10

day-care 1007.2

daydream
noun wistfulness 100.4
illusion 975.1

abstractedness 984.2
dream 985.9
verb wander 983.3
muse 984.9
dream 985.17

daydreaming
noun trance 92.19
wistfulness 100.4
inattention 983.1
abstractedness 984.2
dreaminess 985.8
adj unalert 983.8
abstracted 984.11
dreamy 985.25

Day-Glo
noun colourfulness
35.4
adj garish 35.19
bright 1024.32

day in day out
regularly 780.8
for a long time 826.14
constantly 846.7

daylight dawn 314.3
publicity 352.4
dayshine 1024.10

day off holiday 20.3,
20.4
absence 222.4
pause 856.3

daytime 1024.10

day-to-day 868.3

day trip 177.5

daze
noun trance 92.19
confusion 984.3
verb blind 30.7
astonish 122.6
perplex 970.13
confuse 984.7
shine 1024.23

dazed stupefied 25.7
blinded 30.10
foolish 922.8
in a dilemma 970.25
mazed 984.14

dazzle
noun showiness 501.3
verb blind 30.7
astonish 122.6
cut a dash 501.13
confuse 984.7
shine 1024.23

dazzled blinded 30.10
dazed 984.14

dazzler 1015.9

dazzling blinding 30.11
gorgeous 1015.20
bright 1024.32

dazzlingly 1015.25

D-day zero hour
459.13
crucial moment 842.5

dea 678.2

deacon 699.9

dead
noun silence 51.1

corpse 307.16
majority 307.17
adj beat 21.8
asleep 22.22
insensible 25.6
unconscious 25.8
colourless 36.7
muffled 52.17
insipid 65.2
dull 117.6
inert 173.14
closed 293.9
lifeless 307.30
languid 331.20
no more 761.11
ended 819.8
past 836.7
obsolete 841.15
lacklustre 1026.17
inanimate 1053.5
adv directly 161.23
extremely 247.22
exactly 972.21

dead and buried 836.7

dead body 307.16

dead end obstruction
293.3
impasse 1012.6

dead-end 293.9

dead heat horse race
757.3
same 789.3
tie 835.3

deadline boundary
211.3
plan 381.1
crucial moment 842.5

deadlock
noun standstill 173.3
same 789.3
stop 856.2
impasse 1012.6
verb put a stop to
856.11
stop 1011.13

deadlocked 789.7

deadly
adj poisonous 82.7
terrific 247.11
deathly 307.29,
308.22
destructive 395.26
harmful 999.12
adv distressingly
247.21
deathly 307.37

dead of night midnight
315.6
darkness 1026.1

deadpan
adj inexpressive
522.20
adv unfeelingly 94.14

dead right 972.16

dead ringer image
349.5
same 777.3

dead to insensible
94.10
unaware 929.13

deaf
noun hard-of-hearing
49.2
adj hard-of-hearing
49.6
unpersuadable 361.13
narrow-minded 979.10
oblivious 983.7

deaf ears 49.1

deafening intense
15.22
loud 53.11

deafness hardness of
hearing 49.1
ear disease 85.15
unpersuadableness
361.5
incognizance 929.3

deaf to insensible 94.10
unconsenting 442.6
unaware 929.13

deal
noun amount 244.2
lot 247.4
lamina 296.2
act 328.3
compact 437.1
compromise 468.1
transaction 731.4
bargain 731.5
wood 1052.3
verb parcel out 477.8
give 478.12
trade 731.14
bargain 731.17
shuffle 758.4
dispose 807.9
hit 901.14
adv greatly 247.15

deal by 321.6

dealer merchant 730.2
stockbroker 737.10

dealership 730.2

deal in 731.15

dealing act 328.3
communication 343.1
commerce 731.1
trade 731.2
cardplaying 758.1

dealings act 328.3
communication 343.1
commerce 731.1
relation 774.1
affairs 830.4

deals 893.3

deal with treat 321.6,
387.12
perform 328.9
communicate 343.6
accomplish 407.4
discuss 541.12
write upon 556.5
punish 604.9
trade with 731.16
relate to 774.5

operate 888.5

dean
noun superior 249.4
senior 304.5
principal 571.8
executive 574.3
chief 575.3
adj older 841.19

dear
noun sweetheart
104.10
darling 562.6
adj beloved 104.24
precious 632.10
expensive 632.11
adv dearly 632.13

dearly lovingly 104.32
dear 632.13

dearly love 104.21

dearly love to 100.15

dearth
unproductiveness
890.1
scarcity 991.3

Death 307.3

death fatal disease 85.2
dying 307.1
end 395.2, 819.1
bane 1000.1

deathbed
noun moribundity
307.9
adj later 845.18

death certificate 549.6

death knell dirge 115.6
death 307.1
end 395.2

deathly
adj deathlike 307.29
deadly 308.22
adv distressingly
247.21
deadly 307.37

death on averse 99.8
hating 103.7
oppositional 451.8
disapproving 510.21

death penalty 602.1

death rate 307.13

death sentence 602.1

death squad 308.10

death throes 307.9

death toll death rate
307.13
obituary 307.14

death wish 112.3

deb person of fashion
578.7
beginner 817.2

debacle descent 194.1
disaster 395.4
defeat 412.1
revolution 859.1

debased low 274.7
corrupt 654.14
base 661.12

depressed 912.12

debatable 970.17

debate
noun contention 457.1
discussion 541.7
speech 543.2
introduction 613.5
argumentation 934.4
verb hesitate 362.7
discuss 541.12
declaim 543.10
consider 930.12

debating discussion
541.7
public speaking 543.1

debauched corrupt
654.14
profligate 665.25
licentious 669.8

debauchery profligacy
665.3
dissipation 669.2

debilitated weak 16.12
ineffective 19.15
unmanned 19.19
tired 21.7
unhealthy 85.53
stricken in years
303.18
languid 331.20

debilitating 16.20

debility weakness 16.1
fatigue 21.1
unhealthiness 85.3
old age 303.5

debit
noun loss 473.1
expenditure 626.1
entry 628.5
verb keep accounts
628.8

debonair 109.12

debriefing 184.3

debris
noun remainder 256.1
rubbish 391.5
grain 1049.6
phrase deposit 176.9

debt borrowing 621.1
indebtedness 623.1

debtor borrowing 621.1
borrower 623.4

debunking 976.1

debut
noun coming out
582.15
theatrical performance
704.12
inauguration 817.5
verb act 704.29
enter 817.9

debutant novice 572.9
beginner 817.2

debutante 578.7

decade moment 823.2
ten 881.6

decadence 393.3

decadent deteriorating
393.45
corrupt 654.14

decathlon sport 744.1
athletics meeting
755.2

decay
noun filth 80.7
decomposition 393.6
rot 393.7
disintegration 805.1
dissociation 805.2
verb decompose
393.22
disintegrate 805.3

decayed 393.40

deceased
noun corpse 307.16
adj dead 307.30
past 836.7

deceit deceitfulness
356.3
stratagem 415.3

deceitful falsehearted
354.31, 645.18
false 356.22
cunning 415.12

deceive lie 354.19
beguile 356.14
live by one's wits
415.9, 645.11
outwit 415.11
seduce 665.20

deceived 929.14

deceiving
noun deception 356.1
adj deceptive 356.21

decency kindness 143.1
compliance 427.2
decorousness 496.3
social convention
579.1
propriety 637.2
probity 644.1
seemliness 664.2

decent kind 143.13
indulgent 427.8
decorous 496.10
conventional 579.5
right 637.3
honest 644.13
modest 664.5
sufficient 990.6
expedient 994.5
tolerable 998.20

decently tastefully
496.11
honestly 644.21
expediently 994.8
tolerably 998.24

decentralization 770.2

deception concealment
346.1
sham 354.3
calculated deception
356.1
hoax 356.7
cheating 759.13

illusion 975.1

deceptive deceiving
356.21
sophistical 935.10
erroneous 974.16
illusory 975.9

deceptively 356.23

decibel 50.7

decide will 323.2
resolve 359.7
induce 375.22
determine 885.12,
945.11
govern 893.8
make sure 969.11

decide between 371.14

decided downright
247.12
affirmative 334.8
resolute 359.11
ended 819.8
unqualified 959.2
assured 969.20
confident 969.21
emphatic 996.21

decidedly positively
247.19
affirmatively 334.10
resolutely 359.17
certainly 969.23

decided upon 359.16

deciduous descending
194.11
arboreal 310.36
perennial 310.41
transient 827.7

decimal 881.22

decipher explain
341.10
make clear 521.6
solve 939.2

deciphering 939.1

decision will 323.1
resolution 359.1
choice 371.1
judgment 598.10
fight 754.3
verdict 945.5

decision-making 573.3

decisive resolute
359.11
mandatory 420.12
critical 842.10
prompt 844.9
causal 885.13
convincing 952.26
evidential 956.16
unqualified 959.2
certain 969.13

decisively resolutely
359.17
promptly 844.15
certainly 969.23

decisiveness strength
15.1
resolution 359.1
promptness 844.3
unqualifiedness 959.1

deck
noun ground covering
199.3
layer 296.1
card 758.2
bundle 769.8
verb clothe 5.38
overcome 412.7
ornament 498.8
clobber 901.17

decked clothing 5.44
rigged 180.17
low 274.7

decked out clothing
5.44
ornamented 498.11

declaration
acknowledgment 332.3
affirmation 334.1
announcement 352.2
decree 420.4
remark 524.4
statement 598.8
match 747.3
profession 952.7
testimony 956.2

**Declaration of
Independence** 430.5

declaration of war
458.7

declare affirm 334.5
announce 352.12
command 420.8
state 524.24, 952.12

declared affirmed
334.9
published 352.17
not out 747.5

declarer 758.3

declare war 458.15

decline
noun sinkage 194.2
declivity 204.5
declension 252.2
deterioration 393.3
cheapening 633.4
price 738.9
close 819.3
shortcoming 910.1
senility 921.10
verb weaken 16.9
fail 85.47
recede 168.2
sink 194.6, 393.17
incline 204.10
decrease 252.6
age 303.10
reject 372.2
refuse 442.3
grammaticize 530.16
cheapen 633.6
fall short 910.2
fall on evil days
1010.11

declined downhill
204.16
rejected 372.3

declining
noun rejection 372.1

refusal 442.1
adj languishing 16.21
receding 168.5
descending 194.11
downhill 204.16
decreasing 252.11
deteriorating 393.45

decode make clear
521.6
solve 939.2

decoder 341.7

decoding translation
341.3
explanation 341.4
information technology
551.7
solution 939.1

decommissioning
465.6

decomposed 393.40

decomposing 805.5

decomposition decay
393.6
rot 393.7
disintegration 805.1

decor furniture 229.1
ornamentation 498.1
scenery 704.20

decorate add 253.4
ornament 498.8, 545.7
honour 646.8
beautify 1015.15

decorated ornamented
498.11
ornate 545.11

decoration extra 254.4
ornamentation 498.1
decoration of honour
646.5
insignia 647.1
visual arts 712.1
beautification 1015.11

decorative ornamental
498.10
artistic 712.20
beautifying 1015.22

decorator 716.11

decorous solemn 111.3
decent 496.10, 664.5
conventional 579.5
ceremonious 580.8
right 637.3

decorum decorousness
496.3
social convention
579.1
etiquette 580.3
propriety 637.2
decency 664.2

decoy
noun trap 356.12
shill 357.5
lure 377.3
by-bidder 733.6
verb trap 356.20
lure 377.5

decrease
noun descent 194.1

decrescence 252.1
reduction 255.2
contraction 260.1
deterioration 393.3
waste 473.2
depression 912.1
verb quantify 244.4
graduate 245.4
diminish 252.6
reduce 252.7
subtract 255.9
contract 260.7
waste 473.5

decreased 252.10

decreasing 252.11

decree
noun decreement
420.4
bill 613.8
law 673.3
verdict 945.5
predetermination
963.1
verb will 323.2
command 420.8
legislate 613.9
legalize 673.8
pass judgment 945.13

decrepit unsound 16.15
stricken in years
303.18
dilapidated 393.33
senile 921.23

decry censure 510.13
disparage 512.8

dedicate commit
477.11
sanctify 685.5

dedicated zealous
101.9
resolute 359.11
devoted 587.21
unselfish 652.5
sanctified 685.8

dedication zeal 101.2
resolution 359.1
commitment 477.4
makeup 554.12
devotion 587.7
duty 641.1
unselfishness 652.1
sanctification 685.3

deduce elicit 192.14
reason 934.15
conclude 945.10
suppose 950.10

deduct reduce 252.7
subtract 255.9
discount 631.2

deduction decrease
252.1
subtraction 255.1
decrement 255.7
tax 630.9
discount 631.1
relation 774.1
priori reasoning 934.3
conclusion 945.4

deed

noun act 328.3
exploit 492.7
verb transfer 629.3

deem judge 945.8
suppose 950.10
think 952.11

deemed 950.14

deep
noun ocean 240.1
pit 275.2
ocean depths 275.4
secret 345.5
adj coloured 35.16
deep-toned 54.10
deep-felt 93.24
spacious 158.10
interior 207.6
great 247.6
broad 269.6
profound 275.10
cunning 415.12
recondite 522.16
wise 919.17
learned 927.21
adv beyond one's
depth 275.16

deep-blue 45.3

deep breathing 2.19

deep-down 275.10

deepen aggravate 119.2
intensify 251.5
broaden 269.4
lower 275.8

deepened 251.7

deepening aggravation
119.1
intensification 251.2
lowering 275.7

deepest bottom 199.7
deepmost 275.15

deep freeze cold
weather 1022.3
Siberia 1022.4
freezer 1023.5

deep-freeze 1023.11

deep into 845.19

deeply 207.9

deeply involved 897.5

deep-rooted deep
275.10
confirmed 373.19
established 854.13

deeps space 158.1
depths 275.3
ocean depths 275.4

deep sea ocean 240.1
ocean depths 275.4

deep-sea aquatic
182.58
oceanic 240.8
deep-water 275.14

deep-seated deep
275.10
confirmed 373.19
intrinsic 766.7
established 854.13

deep-set deep 275.10

confirmed 373.19
established 854.13

deep sleep 22.5

deep water 240.1

deep-water 275.14

deer 311.5

def 998.13

defaced deformed
265.12
blemished 1003.8
ugly 1014.6

de facto
adj existent 760.13
real 760.15
adv really 760.16

defamation 512.2

defamatory 512.13

default
noun absence 222.4
disobedience 327.1
neglect 340.1
nonobservance 435.1
arrears 623.2
nonpayment 625.1
shortcoming 910.1
verb be absent 222.7
neglect 340.6
lose 473.4
not pay 625.6
play 748.4

defeat
noun disappointment
132.1
failure 410.1
beating 412.1
frustration 1011.3
verb disappoint 132.2
best 249.7
do for 395.11
triumph over 411.5
worst 412.6
refute 957.5
thwart 1011.15

defeated disappointed
132.5
worsted 412.14
ended 819.8

defeating victorious
411.7
frustrating 1011.20

defeatism 125.6

defeatist
noun pessimist 125.7
adj pessimistic 125.16

defect
noun disease 85.1
deficiency 794.2
fault 1002.2
blemish 1003.1
verb leave home
188.17
emigrate 190.16
deny 335.4
secede 370.6
disregard 435.3
renege 857.13

defection departure
188.1

emigration 190.7
denial 335.2
apostasy 363.2, 857.3
desertion 370.2
nonpayment 625.1
change 851.1
fault 1002.2

defective
noun cripple 85.44
idiot 923.8
adj incomplete 794.4
erroneous 974.16
insufficient 991.9
imperfect 1002.4
blemished 1003.8

defector goer 190.10
apostate 363.5, 857.8

defence guard 460.1
pleadings 598.7
plea 600.2
team 750.2
ice hockey team 750.5
basketball game 751.3
fight 754.3
countermeasure 899.5
argumentation 934.4
rebuttal 938.2
protection 1007.1
barrier 1011.5

defence forces 461.19

defenceless helpless
19.18
forlorn 584.12
unprotected 1005.14

defence mechanism
defence reaction 92.23
avoidance 368.1
defence 460.1
block 989.3

defences 460.1

defend guard 460.8
protect 1007.18

defendant oppositionist
452.3
litigant 598.12
accused 599.6

defended 1007.21

defender champion
460.7
justifier 600.8
supporter 616.9
team 745.2
protector 1007.5

defending 460.11

defensible defendable
460.15
justifiable 600.14
just 649.8

defensive
noun defence 460.1
adj defending 460.11
protective 1007.23

defensively 460.16

defer retreat 163.6
retract 168.3
postpone 845.9

deference respect 155.1
submission 433.1

observance 434.1
courtesy 504.1
duty 641.1

deferential respectful
155.8
obedient 326.3
obeisant 433.16
courteous 504.14
dutiful 641.13

defer to respect 155.4
obey 326.2
submit to 433.9
observe 434.2

defiance impenitence
114.2
refractoriness 327.2
ungovernability 361.4
resistance 453.1
defying 454.1
declaration of war
458.7

defiant impenitent
114.5
disobedient 327.8
refractory 327.10
ungovernable 361.12
defying 454.7

defiantly 327.12

deficiency inadequacy
250.3
incompleteness 794.1
want 794.2, 991.4
imperfection 1002.1
fault 1002.2

deficient inadequate
250.7
slipshod 340.12
incomplete 794.4
short of 910.5
insufficient 991.9
imperfect 1002.4

deficit difference 255.8
debt 623.1
arrears 623.2
deficiency 794.2
shortcoming 910.1
want 991.4

define circumscribe
210.4
interpret 341.9
mark 517.19
name 527.11
fix 854.9
characterize 864.10

defined distinct 31.7
circumscribed 210.6
clear 521.11
particular 864.12

defining limiting 210.9
classificational 808.7

definite distinct 31.7
audible 50.16
circumscribed 210.6
resolute 359.11
clear 521.11
particular 864.12
unqualified 959.2
certain 969.13

definitely visibly 31.8

intelligibly 521.13
particularly 864.15
certainly 969.23
exactly 972.21

definition distinctness
31.2
circumscription 210.1
interpretation 341.1
explanation 518.3
clearness 521.2
naming 527.2
characterization 864.8
picture 1034.5

definitive limiting
210.9
downright 247.12
ending 819.10
final 819.11
unqualified 959.2

deflate paralyse 19.10
humiliate 137.4
reduce 252.7
collapse 260.10
cheapen 633.6
disprove 957.4

deflated reduced
252.10
punctured 260.14
disproved 957.7

deflation humiliation
137.2
decrease 252.1
collapse 260.4, 410.3
cheapening 633.4
business cycle 731.9

deflationary contractive
260.11
cheap 633.7

deflect deviate 164.5
oblique 204.9
curve 279.6
disincline 379.4
prevent 1011.14

deflected 164.8

deflection bending
164.2
obliquity 204.1
angle 278.2
bend 279.3
radar interference
1035.12

deforestation 1067.3

deformed malformed
265.12
freakish 869.13
blemished 1003.8
unshapely 1014.8

defraud cheat 356.18
steal 482.13

defrost 1019.21

deft 413.22

deftly 413.31

defunct
noun corpse 307.16
adj dead 307.30
no more 761.11
ended 819.8
past 836.7

defuse relieve 120.5
keep the peace 464.7
pacify 465.7
moderate 670.6

defusing relief 120.1
modulation 670.2

defy
noun challenge 454.2
verb confront 216.8
disobey 327.6
violate 435.4
resist 453.2
bid defiance 454.3
make war on 458.15
dare 492.10
thwart 1011.15

defying
noun defiance 454.1
adj defiant 454.7

degenerate
noun reprobate 660.5
verb corrupt 393.12
deteriorate 393.16
go wrong 654.9
lapse into disorder 809.8
be changed 851.6
defect 857.13
evolve 860.5
fall on evil days 1010.11
adj deteriorating 393.45
corrupt 654.14
changed 851.10
apostate 857.20

degeneration
deterioration 393.3
turpitude 654.5
change 851.1
apostasy 857.3
evolution 860.1
feedback 1040.6

degenerative impaired 393.27
evolutionary 860.8

degradation
deterioration 393.3
decay 393.6
demotion 447.1
knavery 645.2
turpitude 654.5
baseness 661.3
infamy 661.4
disintegration 805.1
banishment 908.4
depression 912.1

degrade abase 137.5
corrupt 393.12
demote 447.3
disparage 512.8
disgrace 661.8
dismiss 908.19

degraded knavish 645.17
corrupt 654.14
base 661.12

degrading
noun demotion 447.1

adj insulting 156.8
disgraceful 661.11

degree grade 245.1
measure 300.2
extent 300.3
class 607.1
academic degree 648.6
stave 708.29
interval 709.20
continuity 806.2

degrees points of the compass 161.3
graduate 572.8

dehydrated 1064.9

dehydration food preservation 397.2
drying 1064.3

deity divinity 677.1
god 678.2

dejected sullen 110.24
depressed 112.22

de jure 673.12

delay
noun slowing 175.4
stoppage 845.2
hindrance 1011.1
verb dawdle 175.8
slow 175.9
do nothing 329.2
put away 390.6
retard 845.8
postpone 845.9
wait 845.12
hinder 1011.10

delayed retarded 175.12
late 845.16

delaying dawdling 175.11
dilatory 845.17

delectable tasty 63.8
delicious 97.10

delegate
noun legate 576.2
verb commit 478.16
commission 615.10
deputize 861.7

delegated 615.19

delegation accession 417.12
commitment 478.2
deputation 576.13
commission 615.1
substitution 861.1

delete erase 255.12
obliterate 395.16
separate 801.8
end 819.5

deleted absent 222.11
ended 819.8

deliberate
verb hesitate 362.7
confer 541.11
discuss 541.12
consider 930.12
adj slow 175.10
intentional 380.8
leisurely 402.6

cautious 494.8

deliberately slowly 175.13
intentionally 380.10
tardily 845.20

deliberation slowness 175.1
intentionality 380.3
leisureliness 402.2
caution 494.1
discussion 541.7
introduction 613.5
consideration 930.2

delicacy dainty 10.8
frailty 16.2
sensitivity 24.3
unhealthiness 85.3
sensibility 93.4
tenderness 93.6
considerateness 143.3
insignificance 248.1
thinness 270.4
smoothness 294.3
lightness 298.1
meticulousness 339.3
nicety 495.3
taste 496.1
decency 664.2
margin 779.2
discrimination 943.1
accuracy 972.5
dangerousness 1005.2
daintiness 1015.5
softness 1045.1
brittleness 1048.1

delicate frail 16.14
sensitive 24.12, 93.20
soft-coloured 35.21
tasty 63.8
considerate 143.16
dainty 248.7
thin 270.16
smooth 294.8
light 298.12
meticulous 339.12
nice 495.11
elegant 496.9
decent 664.5
discriminating 943.7
exact 972.17
precarious 1005.12
difficult 1012.17
fine 1015.19
soft 1045.8
brittle 1048.4

delicately weakly 16.22
daintily 1015.24
softly 1045.17

delicious edible 8.33
tasty 63.8
delightful 97.7
delectable 97.10
great 998.13

deliciously 97.14

delight
noun happiness 95.2
tendency 895.1
verb delectate 95.9
be pleased 95.11
rejoice 116.5

exult 502.9
amuse 743.21

delighted pleased 95.14
amused 743.26

delightedly 95.18

delightful tasty 63.8
exquisite 97.7
amusing 743.27

delightfully 97.13

delight in savour 63.5
enjoy 95.12

delighting 116.10

delights 1015.4

delinquency
misbehaviour 322.1
disobedience 327.1
nonobservance 435.1
nonpayment 625.1
wrong 638.1
vice 654.1
misdeed 655.2
lawbreaking 674.3
shortcoming 910.1

delinquent
noun evildoer 593.1
defaulter 625.5
wrongdoer 660.9
adj defaulting 625.10
wrong 638.3

delirious feverish 85.57
fervent 93.18
overzealous 101.12
frenzied 105.25
out of one's head 925.31

deliriously frenziedly 105.35
madly 925.35

delirium fever 85.7
psychosomatic symptom 92.18
fury 105.8
deliriousness 925.8
figment of the imagination 985.5

deliver release 120.6
transfer 176.10, 629.3
do 328.6
rescue 398.3
accomplish 407.4
succeed 409.7
liberate 431.4
hand 478.13
say 524.23
perform 891.11

deliverance release 120.2
escape 369.1
rescue 398.1
liberation 431.1
giving 478.1
transfer 629.1
verdict 945.5

delivered 431.10

delivery
noun birth 1.1
escape 369.1
rescue 398.1

liberation 431.1
giving 478.1
articulation 524.6
transfer 629.1
match 747.3
phrase transportation 176.3

delivery room 197.25

dell 237.7, 284.9

delta fork 171.4
plain 236.1
point 283.9

deluded 925.26

deluding 975.9

Deluge 238.6

deluge
noun torrent 238.5
overflow 238.6
rainstorm 316.2
throng 769.4
superabundance 992.2
wetting 1063.6
verb overflow 238.17
submerge 367.7
oversupply 992.14
flood 1063.14

deluged flooded 238.25
soaked 1063.17

delusion psychosomatic symptom 92.18
sham 354.3
deception 356.1
error 974.1
illusion 975.1

deluxe 501.21

delve excavate 284.15
search 937.31
cultivate 1067.17

delve into 937.23

delving 937.38

demagogue
noun instigator 375.11
speaker 543.4
verb declaim 543.10

demand
noun extortion 192.6
claim 421.1
request 440.1
fee 630.6
prerogative 642.1
imposition 643.1
sale 734.1
question 937.10
requirement 962.2
verb extort 192.15
prescribe 420.9
summon 420.11
ask 421.5
oblige 424.5
request 440.9
charge 630.12
impose 643.4
inquire 937.20
require 962.9

demand curve 630.4

demanded 643.8

demand for 962.2

demanding meticulous 339.12
exacting 421.9
strict 425.6
importunate 440.18
difficult 1012.17

demarcation
circumscription 210.1
exclusion 772.1
differentiation 779.4
distinction 943.3

demeaning inferior 250.6
disgraceful 661.11

demeanour looks 33.4
behaviour 321.1

demented turbulent 671.18
insane 925.26

dementia 925.1

demerger 801.1

Demeter 889.5

demise
noun death 307.1
transfer 629.1
verb transfer 629.3

demo objection 333.2
assembly 769.2

demob 770.8

democracy communion 476.2
central government 612.4

democratic 612.17

demographic human 312.13
populational 606.8

demolish wreck 395.17
shatter 801.13
disassemble 801.15
refute 957.5

demolishing 395.26

demolition
demolishment 395.5
refutation 957.2

demon fan 101.5
monster 593.6
spirit 678.5
familiar spirit 678.12
fiend 680.6
genius 919.8

demonic frenzied 105.25
diabolic 654.13
possessed 925.29
execrable 999.10

demons 680.1

demonstrably 247.19

demonstrate object 333.5
explain 341.10
manifest 348.5
image 349.11
flaunt 501.17
teach 568.10
evidence 956.8
prove 956.10

cite 956.13
check 1016.20

demonstrated
manifested 348.13
proved 956.20
true 972.13

demonstrating
manifesting 348.9
demonstrative 956.17

demonstration
objection 333.2
explanation 341.4
display 348.2, 501.4
representation 349.1
assembly 769.2
example 785.2
reasoning 934.1
proof 956.3
citation 956.5

demonstrative
emotional 93.17
loving 104.27
explanatory 341.15
communicative 343.10
manifesting 348.9
indicative 517.23
demonstrating 956.17

demonstrator
interpreter 341.7
picket 1007.13

demoralized 128.14

demos 606.1

demoted 274.7

demotion deterioration 393.3
degrading 447.1
infamy 661.4
banishment 908.4
depression 912.1

dempster 596.2

demure solemn 111.3
shy 139.12
prudish 500.19

den sanctum 197.8
lair 228.26
dive 228.28
hiding place 346.4
sewer 654.7
office 739.7
retreat 1008.5

dene 237.7

denial disavowal 335.2
recantation 363.3
rejection 372.1
refusal 442.1
prohibition 444.1
opposition 451.1
loss 473.1
defence 600.2
temperance 668.1
unbelief 954.1
refutation 957.2

denied rejected 372.3
disproved 957.7

denied to 966.9

denigrate blacken 38.7
deprecate 510.12
vilify 512.10

denigration blackening 38.5
deprecation 510.2
defamation 512.2

denominated 527.14

denomination
indication 517.3
naming 527.2
name 527.3
school 617.5
sect 675.3
kind 808.3
specification 864.6

denominational
partisan 617.19
sectarian 675.26

denote signify 517.17
designate 517.18
mean 518.8
evidence 956.8

denouement plot 722.4
end 819.1
solution 939.1

denounce censure 510.13
threaten 514.2
accuse 599.7
condemn 602.3

denounced 599.15

dense thick 269.8
luxuriant 310.40
sturdy 762.7
crowded 769.22
stupid 921.15
compact 1043.12
hard 1044.10

densely 1043.15

density substantiality 762.1
stupidity 921.3
denseness 1043.1
hardness 1044.1

dent
noun indentation 284.6
print 517.7
verb indent 284.14

dental 90.15

dented 284.17

dentist 90.6

dentistry 90.3

denuded divested 6.12
bereft 473.8

denunciation censure 510.3
curse 513.1
threat 514.1
accusation 599.1
condemnation 602.1

deny not admit 335.4
recant 363.8
reject 372.2
withhold 442.4
prohibit 444.3
contradict 451.6
disbelieve 954.5
refute 957.5

denying 335.5

deodorant
noun deodorizer 72.3
adj deodorizing 72.6

depart disappear 34.3
make off 188.6
exit 190.12
absent oneself 222.8
die 307.19
flee 368.10
digress 538.9
separate 801.8

departed
noun corpse 307.16
adj left 188.19
absent 222.11
dead 307.30
past 836.7

depart from deviate 164.3
abandon 370.5
differ 779.5

departing deviative 164.7
leaving 188.18
different 779.7

department region 231.1
sphere 231.2
bureau 594.4
field 724.4

department store 736.1

departure
disappearance 34.1
deviation 164.1
leaving 188.1
leave-taking 188.4
egress 190.2
absence 222.4
death 307.1
digression 538.4
difference 779.1

depend hang 202.6, 958.6
all depend 970.11

dependable trustworthy 644.19
reliable 969.17
unhazardous 1006.5

dependence hope 124.1
supporter 616.9
relativity 774.2
belief 952.1

dependence on 952.1

dependency 469.1

dependent
noun hanger-on 138.6
follower 166.2
charge 432.6
retainer 577.1
adj pendent 202.9
subject 432.13
trusting 952.22
contingent 958.9
undecided 970.18

dependent on liable to 896.6

contingent 958.9

depending pendent 202.9
trusting 952.22
contingent 958.9
undecided 970.18

depending on 958.9

depend on be at the mercy of 432.12
result from 886.5
trust 952.17

depict represent 349.8
describe 349.9
enact 704.30
portray 712.19

depiction
representation 349.1
description 349.2

deplete consume 388.3
waste 473.5
evacuate 908.22

depleted used up 388.5
lost 473.7

depletion decrement 252.3
reduction 255.2
consumption 388.1
waste 473.2
evacuation 908.6

deplorable distressing 98.20
regrettable 113.10
disgraceful 661.11
terrible 999.9

deplore regret 113.6
lament 115.10

deploy locate 159.11
diverge 171.5
spread 259.6
prepare 405.6
order 806.4
adduce 956.12

deployed located 159.18
embattled 458.23

deployment placement 159.6
expansion 259.1
battle array 458.3
order 806.1
arrangement 807.1

deport transfer 176.10
emigrate 190.16
eliminate 772.5
banish 908.17

deportation
noun emigration 190.7
elimination 772.2
banishment 908.4
phrase transference 176.1

deported 772.7

depose dislodge 160.6
depone 334.6
remove from office 447.4
dismiss 908.19
overthrow 912.6

state 952.12
testify 956.9

deposed 334.9

deposit
noun placement 159.6
collateral 438.3
payment 624.1
precipitation 1043.5
mineral deposit 1056.7
verb lay 78.9
repose 159.14
secrete 346.7
store 386.10
pledge 438.10
precipitate 1043.11
phrase sediment 176.9

deposit account 622.2

deposited 438.12

deposition placement
159.6
dregs 256.2
sworn statement 334.3
deposal 447.2
certificate 549.6
declaration 598.8
testimony 956.2

deposits 256.2

depot 386.6

depraved corrupt
654.14
base 661.12

depravity turpitude
654.5
baseness 661.3

deprecation
discommendation
510.2
disparagement 512.1
underestimation 949.1

depreciation decrease
252.1
reduction 255.2
deterioration 393.3
waste 473.2
deprecation 510.2
disparagement 512.1
discount 631.1
cheapening 633.4
underestimation 949.1

depress sadden 112.18
reduce 252.7
lower 274.6, 912.4
deepen 275.8
indent 284.14

depressant
noun sedative 86.12
drug 87.2
adj sedative 86.45
depressing 112.30

depressed pleasureless
96.20
dejected 112.22
low 274.7
indented 284.17
lowered 912.12
unfortunate 1010.14

depressing distressing
98.20

depressive 112.30

depressingly 112.31

depression mental
disorder 92.14
wretchedness 96.6
distressfulness 98.5
dejection 112.3
decrease 252.1
lowness 274.1
deepening 275.7
concavity 284.1
cavity 284.2
notch 289.1
business cycle 731.9
lowering 912.1
melancholia 925.5
hard times 1010.6

depressive
noun sourpuss 112.13
adj distressing 98.20
depressing 112.30
psychotic 925.28

deprivation absence
222.1
refusal 442.1
deposal 447.2
loss 473.1
deprival 480.6
indigence 619.2
nonexistence 761.1
disassembly 801.6
banishment 908.4
want 991.4

deprive take from
480.21
dismiss 908.19

deprived limited 210.7
bereaved 307.35
indigent 619.8

deprived of bereft
473.8
wanting 991.13

depth space 158.1
interiority 207.1
size 257.1
thickness 269.2
deepness 275.1
pit 275.2
pitch 709.4
wisdom 919.5

depths deeps 275.3
ocean depths 275.4

deputation accession
417.12
delegation 576.13
commission 615.1
substitution 861.1

deputy
noun mediator 466.3
director 574.1
proxy 576.1
lawyer 597.1
assignee 615.9
assistant 616.6
substitute 861.2
policeman 1007.15
adj deputative 576.15

**Deputy Prime
Minister** 575.17

Deputy Speaker 610.3

derail miscarry 410.15
distract 984.6
thwart 1011.15

deranged disorderly
809.13
insane 925.26

Derby 757.1

derby contest 457.3
race 457.12

deregulated
unrestricted 430.27
permitted 443.16

deregulation
noninterference 430.9
disembarrassment
1013.6

derelict
noun bum 331.9
castoff 370.4
outcast 586.4
wretch 660.2
transient 827.4
adj negligent 340.10
abandoned 370.8
dilapidated 393.33
outcast 586.10
unfaithful 645.20

dereliction
disobedience 327.1
neglect 340.1
desertion 370.2
nonobservance 435.1
infidelity 645.5
misdeed 655.2
badness 999.1

deride have the
audacity 142.7
disdain 157.3
flout 454.4
ridicule 508.8

de rigueur conventional
579.5
obligatory 641.15

derision impudence
142.2
defiance 454.1
ridicule 508.1
laughingstock 508.7

derisive impudent
142.10
disrespectful 156.7
defiant 454.7
ridiculing 508.12
condemnatory 510.22
disparaging 512.13

derisory ridiculing
508.12
disparaging 512.13

derivation receiving
479.1
root 526.2
morphology 526.3
etymology 526.15
lineage 560.4
adoption 621.2
source 885.5
effect 886.1

conclusion 945.4

derivative
noun root 526.2
effect 886.1
adj resultant 886.6
attributable 887.6
uncreative 890.5

derive elicit 192.14
acquire 472.8
receive 479.6
conclude 945.10

derive from adopt
621.4
result from 886.5
trace to 887.5

deriving 621.2

dermatitis 85.34

derogatory disparaging
512.13
disreputable 661.10

derrick tower 272.6
lifter 911.3

dervish ascetic 667.2
Muslim 675.23
imam 699.11

descend condescend
137.8
give oneself airs 141.8
move 172.5
land 184.43
incline 204.10
gravitate 297.15
change hands 629.4
incur disgrace 661.7

descendant
noun offspring 561.3
successor 816.4
sequel 834.2
adj descending 194.11

descendants family
559.5
posterity 561.1

descending
noun course 172.2
descent 194.1
adj flowing 172.8
descendant 194.11
downhill 204.16

descent humiliation
137.2
course 172.2
descending 194.1
declivity 204.5
deterioration 393.3
lineage 560.4
posterity 561.1
series 811.2
sequence 814.1
conversion 857.1
depression 912.1
reverse 1010.3

describe interpret
341.9
portray 349.9
characterize 864.10

description
interpretation 341.1
portrayal 349.2

fiction 722.1
kind 808.3
characterization 864.8

descriptive
interpretative 341.14
depictive 349.14
linguistic 523.17

desecration misuse
389.1
abomination 638.2
sacrilege 694.2

desert
noun open space 158.4
plain 236.1
reprisal 506.2
wasteland 890.2
goodness 998.1
dust 1064.2
verb quit 188.9
flee 368.10
abandon 370.5
be unfaithful 645.12
defect 857.13
adj unproductive
890.4
dry 1064.7

deserted available
222.15
neglected 340.14
abandoned 370.8
disused 390.10
forlorn 584.12

deserter apostate 363.5,
857.8
desertion 370.2
sacrilegist 694.3

desertion departure
188.1
apostasy 363.2, 857.3
flight 368.4
defection 370.2
forlornness 584.4
impiety 694.1

desert island 890.2

deserts reprisal 506.2
punishment 604.1
just deserts 639.3

deserve 639.5

deserved warranted
639.9
just 649.8

deservedly 649.11

deserving praiseworthy
509.20
due 639.10

desiccated wasted
393.35
dried 1064.9

design
noun trick 356.6
intention 380.1
plan 381.1
diagram 381.3
stratagem 415.3
motif 498.7
intent 518.2
makeup 554.12
form 709.11

visual arts 712.1
treatment 712.9
work of art 712.10
drawing 712.13
styling 717.4
plot 722.4
production 891.2
verb intend 380.4
plan 381.8
portray 712.19
produce 891.8
originate 891.12
adj architectural 717.6

designate nominate
371.19
commit 436.5
specify 517.18, 864.11
name 527.11
appoint 615.11
classify 808.6

designated chosen
371.26
marked 517.24
named 527.14

designation nomination
371.8
obligation 436.2
indication 517.3
naming 527.2
name 527.3
appointment 615.2
kind 808.3
specification 864.6

designed intentional
380.8
planned 381.12

designer
noun planner 381.6
stylist 716.9, 717.5
producer 891.7
adj architectural 717.6
modern 840.13

designing
noun visual arts 712.1
adj scheming 381.13
cunning 415.12

desirability agreeability
100.13
loveableness 104.7
eligibility 371.11

desirable sexual 75.24
pleasant 97.6
sought-after 100.30
eligible 371.24
welcome 585.12
expedient 994.5

desire
noun sexual desire
75.5
wish 100.1
heart's desire 100.11
love 104.1
hope 124.1
will 323.1
intention 380.1
request 440.1
verb lust 75.20
desiderate 100.14
jump at 101.6

hope 124.7
will 323.2
intend 380.4
request 440.9

desired wanted 100.29
welcome 585.12
future 838.8
normal 868.8

desist cease to use
390.4
cease 856.6

desk furniture 229.1
ministry 698.1
pulpit 703.13
workplace 739.1
table 900.15

desks 710.12

desktop 739.1

Desmond 648.6

desolate
verb agonize 98.12
aggrieve 112.19
destroy 395.10
depopulate 908.16
adj wretched 96.26
distressing 98.20
disconsolate 112.28
forlorn 584.12
unproductive 890.4

desolation
wretchedness 96.6
harshness 98.4
disconsolateness
112.12
destruction 395.1
forlornness 584.4
wasteland 890.2
depopulation 908.3

despair
noun wretchedness
96.6
dejection 112.3
desperation 125.2
verb lose heart 112.16
despair of 125.10

despaired of 307.33

despairing dejected
112.22
hopeless 125.12

despairingly 112.33

despair of 125.10

desperate hopeless
125.12
reckless 493.8
rabid 925.30
straitened 1012.26

desperately hopelessly
125.17
violently 247.23
recklessly 493.11

desperation 125.2

despicable offensive
98.18
base 661.12
paltry 997.21
terrible 999.9

despise hate 103.5

disdain 157.3
reject 372.2
flout 454.4
deprecate 510.12

despised disliked 99.9
rejected 372.3

despising
noun hate 103.1
rejection 372.1
adj hating 103.7
rejective 372.4

despite
noun hate 103.1
spite 144.6
indignity 156.2
contempt 157.1
defiance 454.1
adv, prep in spite of
338.9

despondency
noun wretchedness
96.6
despair 125.2
verb lose heart 112.16

despondent dejected
112.22
hopeless 125.12

despot 575.14

despotic imperious
417.16
governmental 612.17

despotism absolutism
612.9
tyranny 612.10

dessert serving 8.10
delicacy 10.8

destination goal 186.5
objective 380.2
address 553.9
end 819.1
fate 963.2

destined future 838.8
inevitable 962.15
fated 963.9

destiny portion 477.5
end 819.1
fate 838.2, 963.2
chance 971.1

destitute bereft 473.8
down-and-out 619.9
insolvent 625.11

destitution indigence
619.2
want 991.4

destroy excise 255.10
kill 308.12
spoil 393.10
defeat 412.6
rage 671.11
work evil 999.6
thwart 1011.15

destroyed 395.28

Destroyer 677.3

destroyer warship
180.6
battleship 180.7
ruiner 395.8

savage 593.5

destroying 395.26

destruction excision
255.3
killing 308.1
impairment 393.1
ruin 395.1
defeat 412.1
loss 473.1
violence 671.1
disintegration 805.1
evil 999.3
bane 1000.1

destructive poisonous
82.7
deadly 308.22
destroying 395.26
violent 671.16
disintegrative 805.5
disastrous 1010.15

destructiveness
poisonousness 82.3
violence 671.1

desultory deviative
164.7
discursive 538.13
unordered 809.12
irregular 850.3
inconstant 853.7
fluttering 916.18
unreliable 970.20

detach commission
615.10
enlist 615.17
disband 770.8
remove 801.10

detachable 801.20

detached apathetic
94.13
reticent 344.10
free 430.21
aloof 583.6
secluded 584.8
impartial 649.10
unrelated 775.6
separate 801.20
separated 801.21
incoherent 803.4
alone 871.8
unprejudiced 978.12
incurious 981.3

detached house 228.5

detachment apathy
94.4
unconcern 102.2
unit 461.21
aloofness 583.2
seclusion 584.1
impartiality 649.4
company 769.3
disbandment 770.3
elimination 772.2
part 792.1
separation 801.1
aloneness 871.2
unprejudicedness
978.5
incuriosity 981.1

detail

noun meticulousness
339.3
unit 461.21
motif 498.7
particular 765.3
company 769.3
part 792.1
component 795.2
verb allot 477.9
amplify 538.7
commission 615.10
itemize 765.6, 800.7
elaborate 860.6
particularize 864.9
sum up 1016.18

detailed meticulous
339.12
minute 765.9
particular 864.12

detailing amplification
538.6
circumstantiation
765.5
itemization 800.2

details description
349.2
facts 760.4
trivia 997.4

detain slow 175.9
confine 429.12
delay 845.8
hinder 1011.10

detained retarded
175.12
confined 429.19
late 845.16

detainee 429.11

detect 940.5

detectable visible 31.6
on the right scent
940.10

detection investigation
937.4
discovery 940.1
interception 1035.9

detective operative
576.10
inquirer 937.16
policeman 1007.15

detective work 937.4

detention slowing
175.4
imprisonment 429.3
delay 845.2
hindrance 1011.1

detention centre 429.8

deter daunt 127.18
disincline 379.4
prevent 1011.14

detergent
noun cleanser 79.17
adj cleansing 79.28

deteriorate aggravate
119.2
impair 393.9
sicken 393.16
be changed 851.6

fall on evil days
1010.11

deteriorated aggravated
119.4
impaired 393.27

deteriorating 393.45

deterioration
aggravation 119.1
decadence 393.3
change 851.1

determinant boundary
211.3
heredity 560.6
cause 885.1

determination
circumscription 210.1
measurement 300.1
will 323.1
resolution 359.1
obstinacy 361.1
intention 380.1
endeavour 403.1
solution 939.1
discovery 940.1
test 941.2
verdict 945.5
proof 956.3
ensuring 969.8

determine direct 161.5
circumscribe 210.4
will 323.2
resolve 359.7
induce 375.22
intend 380.4
learn 570.6
end 819.5
specify 864.11
decide 885.12, 945.11
govern 893.8
discover 940.2
prove 956.10
make sure 969.11

determined
circumscribed 210.6
resolute 359.11
trial 403.16
future 838.8
proved 956.20
predetermined 963.8
assured 969.20
confident 969.21
true 972.13

determinedly 359.17

determining
noun discovery 940.1
adj limiting 210.9
environmental 765.8

determinism future
838.1
fatalism 963.4

deterrence dissuasion
379.1
foreign policy 609.5
prevention 1011.2

deterrent
noun determent 379.2
obstacle 1011.4
adj frightening 127.28
dissuasive 379.5

warning 399.7
preventive 1011.19

deterring frightening
127.28
preventive 1011.19

detest dislike 99.3
hate 103.5

detonate blast 56.8
explode 671.14
shoot 903.12
fuel 1020.7

detonation blast 56.3
explosion 671.7
shot 903.4

detour
noun deviation 164.1
byway 383.4
bypass 913.3
verb deviate 164.3
go roundabout 913.4

detract subtract 255.9
distract 984.6

detract from minimize
252.9
disparage 512.8

detriment impairment
393.1
loss 473.1
disadvantage 995.2
evil 999.3

detrimental
disadvantageous 995.6
harmful 999.12
adverse 1010.13

detritus
noun remainder 256.1
grain 1049.6
phrase deposit 176.9

deva 678.2

devaluation cheapening
633.4
monetization 728.23

devalue corrupt 393.12
monetize 728.26

devaluing 252.5

devastate destroy
395.10
depopulate 908.16

devastated 395.28

devastating destructive
395.26
eye-catching 1015.21

devastation destruction
395.1
depopulation 908.3

develop grow 14.2,
251.6, 259.7
enlarge 259.4, 259.5
mature 303.9
manifest 348.5
disclose 351.4
improve 392.7
elaborate 392.10,
860.6
amplify 538.7
train 568.13
process 714.15

evolve 860.5
result 886.4
originate 891.12
perfect 1001.5

developed grown 14.3,
259.12
mature 303.13
improved 392.13
complete 793.9
perfected 1001.9

developer planner
381.6
processing solution
714.13
producer 891.7

developing 860.8

development birth
78.6
increase 251.1
growth 259.3
maturation 303.6
refinement 392.2
amplification 538.6
training 568.3
passage 708.24
plot 722.4
conversion 857.1
evolution 860.1
effect 886.1

developmental 538.15

devi 678.2

deviance obliquity
204.1
nonuniformity 781.1

deviant
noun sexual pervert
75.16
nonconformist 867.3
adj homosexual 75.29
deviative 164.7
oblique 204.13
wrong 638.3
changed 851.10
nonconforming 867.5
eccentric 926.5
erroneous 974.16

deviate
noun sexual pervert
75.16
verb depart from
164.3
deflect 164.5
oblique 204.9
digress 538.9
go wrong 654.9
misbelieve 688.8
be changed 851.6
go roundabout 913.4
err 974.9

deviate from 779.5

deviation orientation
161.4
obliquity 204.1
distortion 265.1
digression 538.4
difference 779.1
nonuniformity 781.1
change 851.1
nonconformity 867.1

abnormality 869.1
circuitousness 913.1
detour 913.3
eccentricity 926.1
inaccuracy 974.2

device surgery 91.19
trick 356.6
pretext 376.1
plan 381.1
instrumentality 384.3
instrument 384.4
stratagem 415.3
sign 517.1
signature 527.10
figure of speech 536.1
letter 546.1
heraldic device 647.2
plot 722.4
motto 973.4
expedient 994.2
tool 1039.1

devices means 384.2
machination 415.4

devil
noun beast 144.14
dust storm 318.13
mischief-maker 322.3
daredevil 493.4
printer 548.12
enemy 589.6
ruffian 593.3
monster 593.6
wretch 660.2
rascal 660.3
diable 680.2
demon 680.6
verb cook 11.4
annoy 96.13

devilish cruel 144.26
mischievous 322.6
diabolic 654.13
hellish 682.8
execrable 999.10

devious deviative 164.7
oblique 204.13
dishonest 645.16
complex 798.4
circuitous 913.7
shrewd 919.15

devise
noun bequest 478.10
verb plan 381.8
bequeath 478.18
produce 891.8
originate 891.12

devised 381.12

devising 891.1, 891.2

devoid vacant 222.14
nonexistent 761.8

devoid of 991.13

devolution inversion
205.1
deterioration 393.3
relapse 394.1
independence 430.5
central government
612.4
commission 615.1
succession 629.2

evolution 860.1

devote spend 387.13
dedicate 477.11
sanctify 685.5
occupy 724.10

devoted zealous 101.9
loving 104.27
obedient 326.3
resolute 359.11
observant 434.4
dedicated 587.21
faithful 644.20
unselfish 652.5
sanctified 685.8
pious 692.8
destined 963.9
engrossed 982.17

devoted to fond of
104.30
engrossed 982.17

devotee desirer 100.12
enthusiast 101.4
lover 104.12
believer 692.4
fanatic 925.18

devoting 477.4

devotion zeal 101.2
love 104.1
resolution 359.1
dedication 477.4
devotedness 587.7
duty 641.1
fidelity 644.7
unselfishness 652.1
sanctification 685.3
piety 692.1
worship 696.1

devotional 696.15

devour swallow 8.22
enjoy 95.12
ingest 187.11
destroy 395.10
gluttonize 672.4
kid oneself 953.6

devouring
noun eating 8.1
adj greedy 100.27

devout zealous 101.9
observant 434.4
pious 692.8
worshipful 696.15
belief 952.21

devoutly zealously
101.14
believingly 952.28

dew
noun dewdrops 1063.4
verb moisten 1063.12

dewy young 301.9
immature 301.10
new 840.7
moist 1063.15

dewy-eyed 985.24

dexter
adj right 219.4
adv rightward 219.7

dexterity rightness
219.2

skill 413.1
smartness 919.2

dey 575.13

dharma 766.4

diabetes 85.21

diabetic 85.60

diablo 680.2

diabolical cruel 144.26
diabolic 654.13
execrable 999.10

diagnose treat 91.24
interpret 341.9

diagnosis examination 91.12
interpretation 341.1
verdict 945.5

diagnostic
interpretative 341.14
indicative 517.23
differentiative 779.9

diagonal
noun crosspiece 170.5
oblique 204.7
straight line 277.2
line 517.6
adj transverse 204.19

diagonally 204.25

diagram
noun representation 349.1
plot 381.3
drawing 712.13
outline 800.4
verb represent 349.8
plot 381.10
grammaticize 530.16
portray 712.19
itemize 800.7

dial 33.4

dialect
noun language 523.1
idiom 523.7
diction 532.1
adj idiomatic 523.20

dialectic
noun discussion 541.7
logic 934.2
argument 934.5
adj argumentative 934.19
dialectical 934.22

dialectical
argumentative 934.19
dialectic 934.22

dialogue talk 541.3
script 706.2
plot 722.4
argument 934.5

dialysis 805.2

diameter size 257.1
bore 269.3
straight line 277.2
middle 818.1
bisector 874.3

diamond
noun good person 659.1

good thing 998.5
stone 1044.6
verb figure 498.9

diamonds 758.2

Diana hunter 382.5
Phoebe 1070.12

diaphanous dainty 248.7
thin 270.16
light 1024.31
transparent 1028.4

diaphragm mouth 2.16
loudspeaker 50.8
contraceptive 86.23
partition 213.5
middle 818.1

diarist author 547.15, 718.4
historian 719.4
chronologist 831.10

diarrhoea defecation 12.2
anaemia 85.9

diary
noun notebook 549.11
history 719.1
chronicle 831.9
adj periodical 555.1

diaspora 770.3

diatribe berating 510.7
speech 543.2

dibble 1067.18

dice
noun bones 759.8
verb square 878.3

diced 278.9

dicey speculative 759.27
uncertain 970.16
chance 971.15
hazardous 1005.10

dichotomy severance 801.2
doubleness 872.1
bisection 874.1

dick tec 576.11
cop 1007.16

dicky 16.16

dictate
noun precept 419.1
command 420.1
law 673.3
axiom 973.2
verb command 420.8
prescribe 420.9
oblige 424.5
dominate 612.15
necessitate 962.8

dictated preceptive 419.4
mandatory 420.12
obligatory 424.11

dictating 420.13

dictator 575.14

dictatorial lordly 141.11
imperious 417.16

governmental 612.17

dictatorship mastership 417.7
directorship 573.4
central government 612.4
absolutism 612.9

diction phrasing 529.2
words 532.1

dictionary reference book 554.9
word list 870.4

dictum affirmation 334.1
rule 419.2
decree 420.4
remark 524.4
verdict 945.5
maxim 973.1
axiom 973.2

didactic preceptive 419.4
advisory 422.8
educational 568.18
poetic 720.15
dogmatic 969.22

dido caper 366.2
frolic 743.5

die
noun engraving tool 713.8
cast 784.6
mould 785.6
base 900.8
verb disappear 34.3
decease 307.19
decline 393.17
perish 395.23
stall 410.16
come to an end 819.6
pass 836.6
burn out 1021.8

die for 100.14

die hard be determined 359.8
die trying 360.6
balk 361.7
stand fast 453.4

die-hard
noun mule 361.6
oppositionist 452.3
conservative 611.13, 852.4
adj conservative 611.25, 852.8

die out 307.26

diet
noun dieting 7.11
council 423.1
fast 515.2
legislature 613.1
assembly 769.2
verb go on a diet 7.17
eat 8.20
slenderize 270.13

dietary
noun diet 7.11
adj dietetic 7.21

dieting diet 7.11
eating 8.1

differ dissent 333.4
disagree 456.8, 788.5
vary 779.5
diversify 781.2
not resemble 786.2

difference
noun remainder 255.8
dissent 333.1
disagreement 456.2, 788.1
heraldic device 647.2
otherness 779.1
nonuniformity 781.1
dissimilarity 786.1
inequality 790.1
change 851.1
abnormality 869.1
sum 1016.6
verb differentiate 779.6

difference of opinion 456.2

different differing 779.7
nonuniform 781.3
dissimilar 786.4
novel 840.11
particular 864.12
abnormal 869.9
eccentric 926.5

differential
noun margin 779.2
characteristic 864.4
gear 1039.5
adj differentiative 779.9
classificational 808.7
discriminating 943.7

differentiate signify 517.17
difference 779.6
diversify 781.2
characterize 864.10
discriminate 943.4

differentiated 779.7

differentiating 779.9

differentiation
indication 517.3
differencing 779.4
nonuniformity 781.1
particularity 864.1
characterization 864.8
distinction 943.3
notation 1016.2

differently diversely 779.10
dissimilarly 786.7

different story 779.3

different thing 779.3

differing unwilling 325.5
dissenting 333.6
disaccordant 456.15
different 779.7
disagreeing 788.6

difficult perverse 361.11
finical 495.10
hard to understand 522.14
adverse 1010.13
difficile 1012.17

difficulties poverty 619.1
adversity 1010.1

difficulty annoyance 96.2
disagreement 456.2
abstruseness 522.2
adversity 1010.1
obstacle 1011.4
impediment 1011.6
difficultness 1012.1

diffidence fearfulness 127.3
self-effacement 139.2
demur 325.2
hesitation 362.3
doubt 954.2

diffident fearful 127.23
self-effacing 139.10
demurring 325.7
hesitant 362.11

diffuse
verb deflect 164.5
radiate 171.6
transfer 176.10
pervade 221.7
rarefy 299.3
publish 352.10
disperse 770.4
shatter 801.13
loosen 803.3
adj deflective 164.8
rare 299.4
diffusive 538.11
dispersed 770.9
extensive 863.13
plentiful 990.7

diffused deflective 164.8
rare 299.4
published 352.17
lost 473.7

diffusion
noun deflection 164.2
radiation 171.2
permeation 221.3
rarefaction 299.2
publication 352.1
waste 473.2
diffuseness 538.1
disruption 801.3
noncohesion 803.1
phrase transference 176.1

dig
noun put-down 156.3
pit 284.4
thrust 901.2
hit 901.4
verb deepen 275.8
excavate 284.15
thrust 901.12
search 937.31

cultivate 1067.17
harvest 1067.19

dig at bad-mouth 156.6
scoff 508.9

digest
noun abridgment
557.1
code 673.5
table 807.4
verb assimilate 7.16
take 134.8
absorb 187.13, 570.7
consume 388.3
understand 521.7
codify 673.9
classify 808.6
consider 930.12
think over 930.13

digested 268.9

digestible 7.19

digestion ingestion
2.15, 7.8
sorption 187.6
consumption 388.1
absorption 570.2
pulping 1061.3

digestive
noun digestant 7.9
adj stomachal 2.29
assimilative 7.20
sorbent 187.17

digestive system 2.15,
7.8

dig for 937.30

digger excavator 284.10
squaddie 461.7
seeker 937.18

digging
noun deepening 275.7
excavation 284.11
adj searching 937.38

digging out 192.2

digging up 940.1

dig in remain firm
359.9
fortify 460.9

dig into 937.23

digit finger 73.5
foot 199.5
number 1016.3

digital 474.9

digits 474.4

dignified solemn 111.3
stately 136.12
lofty 544.14

dignity solemnity 111.1
proud bearing 136.2
elegance 533.1
loftiness 544.6
formality 580.1
prestige 662.4
ecclesiastical office
698.5
notability 996.2
personage 996.8

dig out excavate 284.15
search out 937.34

dig up disinter 192.11
grab 472.9
uncover 940.4
be curious 980.3

dilapidated unsteady
16.16
ramshackle 393.33
disintegrative 805.5
slovenly 809.15
stale 841.14

dilate enlarge 259.4,
259.5
bulge 283.11
amplify 538.7

dilated 259.13

dilemma Scylla and
Charybdis 371.3
syllogism 934.6
bewilderment 970.3
horns of a dilemma
1012.7

dilettante
noun enthusiast 101.4
connoisseur 496.7
specialist 865.3
half scholar 928.6
ignoramus 929.8
trifler 997.10
adj half-learned
929.15

diligence industry
330.6
painstakingness 339.2
perseverance 360.1
studiousness 570.4
attention 982.1

diligent industrious
330.22
painstaking 339.11
persevering 360.8
studious 570.17
attentive 982.15

diligently industriously
330.27
carefully 339.15
perseveringly 360.9

dilly 998.7

dilute
verb cut 16.11
abate 252.8
thin 270.12
rarefy 299.3
dissipate 770.5
adulterate 796.12
adj insipid 65.2
rare 299.4

diluted cut 16.19
insipid 65.2
thin 270.16
rare 299.4
dispersed 770.9

dilution weakening
16.5
thinness 270.4
rarefaction 299.2
adulteration 796.3

dim
noun darkishness
1026.2

verb blind 30.7
blur 32.4
decolour 36.5
darken 1026.9
grow dark 1026.12
adj dim-sighted 28.13
inconspicuous 32.6
colourless 36.7
faint 52.16
obscure 522.15
dull 921.16
darkish 1026.15

dime 728.8

dimension space 158.1
size 257.1

dimensional 158.9

dimensions 257.1

diminish relieve 120.5
abase 137.5
recede 168.2
decrease 252.6
reduce 252.7
subtract 255.9
narrow 270.11
languish 393.18
extenuate 600.12
moderate 670.6
qualify 958.3

diminished humbled
137.13
reduced 252.10

**diminished
responsibility** 600.5

diminishing receding
168.5
decreasing 252.11
mitigating 670.14

diminution relief 120.1
decrease 252.1
reduction 255.2
modulation 670.2
depression 912.1

diminutive
noun runt 258.4
nickname 527.7
adj miniature 258.12
nominal 527.15

dim light 1026.2

dimly faintly 52.21
in the dark 1026.19

dimmed colourless
36.7
darkish 1026.15

dimness
inconspicuousness
32.2
paleness 36.2
faintness 52.1
stupidity 921.3
darkishness 1026.2
opaqueness 1030.1

dimpled 284.17

dim view 510.1

din
noun noise 53.3
pandemonium 809.5
verb boom 53.7
ding 848.10

dine feed 8.18
sup 8.21

diner breakfast 8.6
eater 8.16
restaurant 8.17
railway carriage
179.15

ding
noun ringing 54.3
verb ring 54.8
din 848.10

dingle ringing 54.3
valley 237.7, 284.9

dingy colourless 36.7
grimy 38.11
grey 39.4
dirty 80.22

dining
noun eating 8.1
adj eating 8.31

dining room restaurant
8.17
salle à manger 197.11

dinky little 258.10
tidy 806.8
measly 997.18

dinner 8.6

dinosaur behemoth
257.14
reptile 311.25
back number 841.8

dint
noun power 18.1
indentation 284.6
print 517.7
hit 901.4
verb indent 284.14

diocese state 231.5
see 698.8

dip
noun bath 79.9
declivity 204.5
cavity 284.2
submergence 367.2
candle 1025.2
verb colour 35.13
ladle 176.17
stunt 184.40
incline 204.10
submerge 367.7
signal 517.22
baptize 701.16
flood 1063.14

dip into browse 570.13
examine cursorily
937.26

diploma grant 443.5
certificate 549.6

diplomacy skill 413.1
Machiavellianism
415.2
foreign policy 609.5

diplomat expert 413.11
Machiavellian 415.8
diplomatist 576.6

diplomatic
noun diplomat 576.6
adj skilful 413.22

cunning 415.12
ambassadorial 576.16
political 609.43

diplomatically 415.13

diplomatic mission
576.7

diplomatic service
576.7

dipped 1063.17

dipping
noun submergence
367.2
adj downhill 204.16

dippy screwy 922.9
crazy 925.27

dire horrid 98.19
terrible 127.30, 999.9
ominous 133.17
unfortunate 1010.14
disastrous 1010.15

direct
noun notation 709.12
verb point 161.5
pilot 182.14
focus 208.10
channel 239.15
command 420.8
advise 422.5
address 553.13
teach 568.10
manage 573.8
govern 612.12, 893.8
conduct 708.45
operate 888.5
adj directional 161.12
straight 277.6
artless 416.5
free-acting 430.23
natural 499.7
clear 521.11
elegant 533.6
plain-speaking 535.3
lineal 560.18
candid 644.17
continuous 811.8
exact 972.17
adv directly 161.23

direct access 1041.8

direct action 328.1

directed 161.13

directeur 574.1

directing directive
573.12
executive 612.19

direction directionality
161.1
motivation 375.2
precept 419.1
directive 420.3
advice 422.1
pointer 517.4
address 553.9
teaching 568.1
management 573.1
government 612.1
production 704.13
operation 888.1
trend 895.2

directional azimuthal 161.12
directable 161.13
directions 568.6
directive
noun direction 420.3
adj directable 161.13
motivating 375.25
commanding 420.13
advisory 422.8
directing 573.12
direct line straight line 277.2
line 347.17
lineage 560.4
directly direct 161.23
straight 277.7
unaffectedly 499.11
plainly 535.4
candidly 644.23
promptly 844.15
soon 844.16
exactly 972.21
direct mail 553.4
direct-mail 553.14
directness straightness 277.1
artlessness 416.1
naturalness 499.2
clearness 521.2
elegance 533.1
plain speech 535.1
candour 644.4
director librarian 558.3
directeur 574.1
governor 575.6
theatre man 704.23
film studio 706.3
conductor 710.17
businessman 730.1
directorate directorship 573.4
directory 574.11
authorities 575.15
director general 574.1
directorial 573.12
directorship supremacy 249.3
mastership 417.7
leadership 573.4
directory
noun council 423.1
genealogy 549.9
information 551.1
reference book 554.9
guidebook 574.10
directorate 574.11
adj directing 573.12
direct to give directions to 161.6
call attention to 982.10
dirge
noun last offices 309.4
funeral 309.5
verb lament 115.10
dirk 459.25
dirt

noun grime 80.6
land 234.1
scandal 552.8
obscenity 666.4
verb dirty 80.15
dirt track 756.1
dirty
verb dirty up 80.15
stain 1003.6
adj dingy 38.11
grimy 80.22
stormy 318.23
cloudy 319.7
cursing 513.8
unfair 650.10
base 661.12
lascivious 665.29
obscene 666.9
slimy 1060.14
dirty tricks campaign 609.14
dirty work 725.4
dis 156.6
disability inability 19.2
disease 85.1
handicap 603.2
disadvantage 995.2
disabled weakened 16.18
incapacitated 19.16
crippled 393.30
ended 819.8
disablement inability 19.2
impairment 393.1
disadvantage
noun handicap 603.2
drawback 995.2
impediment 1011.6
trouble 1012.3
verb inconvenience 995.4
work evil 999.6
disadvantaged
noun underprivileged 606.4
poor 619.3
adj inferior 250.6
indigent 619.8
disaffected averse 99.8
alienated 589.11
unfaithful 645.20
disaffection dislike 99.1
falling-out 456.4
disaccord 589.2
infidelity 645.5
disagree dissent 333.4
refuse 442.3
differ 456.8, 788.5
disagreeable unsavoury 64.5
unpleasant 98.17
irascible 110.19
unkind 144.16
disagreeing 788.6
disagreeing unwilling 325.5

dissenting 333.6
disaccordant 456.15
different 779.7
differing 788.6
disagreement refusal 325.1, 442.1
dissent 333.1
difficulty 456.2
disapproval 510.1
relation 774.1
contrariety 778.1
difference 779.1
discord 788.1
nonconformity 867.1
disagree with not be good for 82.4
dissent 333.4
differ 779.5
disallowed 444.7
disappear vanish 34.3
quit 188.9
absent oneself 222.8
hide 346.8
perish 395.23
flit 827.6
pass 836.6
do away with 908.21
disappearance
invisibility 32.1
disappearing 34.1
absence 222.4
flight 368.4
disappeared gone 34.5
absent 222.11
disappearing
noun disappearance 34.1
adj vanishing 34.4
fugitive 368.16
disappoint dissatisfy 108.5
shatter one's hopes 125.11
disillusion 976.2
disappointed
discontented 108.7
unaccomplished 408.3
disapproving 510.21
disillusioned 976.5
disappointing
unsatisfactory 108.9
not up to expectation 132.6
disappointment
discontent 108.1
dashed hopes 125.5
nonaccomplishment 408.1
collapse 410.3
disapproval 510.1
disillusionment 976.1
disapproval dislike 99.1
resentment 152.1
dissent 333.1
rejection 372.1
disapprobation 510.1
disparagement 512.1
disapprove reject 372.2

disapprove of 510.10
stigmatize 661.9
disapproved 372.3
disapprove of dislike 99.3
shudder at 99.5
disapprove 510.10
disparage 512.8
disapproving averse 99.8
disapprobatory 510.21
disarm disable 19.9
lay down one's arms 465.11
disarmament 465.6
disarmed 19.16
disarming 504.18
disarray
noun disorder 809.1
verb undress 6.7
disarrange 810.2
disassociate 801.8
disaster fatality 308.7
debacle 395.4
upheaval 671.5
misfortune 1010.2
eyesore 1014.4
disastrous destructive 395.26
convulsive 671.23
calamitous 1010.15
disastrously 1010.18
disband disarm 465.11
disperse 770.8
part company 801.19
disbanding 465.6
disbelief unbelief 695.5, 954.1
doubtfulness 970.2
disbelieve doubt 695.14
unbelieve 954.5
refuse to believe 955.3
disbelieving 695.19, 954.8
disc record 50.12
circle 280.2
lamina 296.2
bulletin board 549.10
rotator 914.4
discard
noun derelict 370.4
rejection 372.1
discarding 390.3
elimination 772.2
verb abandon 370.5
reject 372.2, 390.7
eject 908.13
discarded abandoned 370.8
rejected 372.3, 390.11
disproved 957.7
discarding 390.3
discern see 27.12
perceive 521.9
know 927.12
detect 940.5

discerned 927.26
discernible visible 31.6
manifest 348.8
knowable 927.25
on the right scent 940.10
discerning sagacious 919.16
perceptive 943.8
discernment vision 27.1
sagacity 919.4
critical discernment 943.2
discharge
noun humour 2.22
excretion 12.1
excrement 12.3
detonation 56.3
release 120.2, 431.2
emergence 190.1
outflow 190.4
performance 328.2
exemption 430.8
observance 434.1
execution 437.4
acquittal 601.1
payment 624.1
receipt 627.2
explosion 671.7
shot 903.4
repulse 907.2
ejection 908.1
dismissal 908.5
disgorgement 908.7
arc 1031.6
verb excrete 12.12
blast 56.8
exude 190.15
perform 328.9, 434.3
accomplish 407.4
exempt 430.14
release 431.5
execute 437.9
acquit 601.4
pay in full 624.13
erupt 671.13
explode 671.14
disband 770.8
shoot 903.12
repulse 907.3
eject 908.13
dismiss 908.19
unload 908.23
disgorge 908.25
adj accomplishment 407.1
discharged 407.10
disciple enthusiast 101.4
follower 166.2, 572.2, 616.8
evangelist 684.2
believer 692.4
convert 857.7
disciples 617.5
disciplinarian 575.14
disciplinary
educational 568.18

punishing 604.22
scientific 927.28

discipline
noun limitation 210.2
self-control 359.5
strictness 425.1
training 568.3
study 568.8
punishment 604.1
government 612.1
temperance 668.1
field 724.4
orderliness 806.3
science 927.10
verb limit 210.5
train 568.13
punish 604.9
govern 612.12
conform 866.3

disciplined patient
134.9
limited 210.7
strict 425.6

disclaimer denial
335.2
recantation 363.3
refusal 442.1

disclose unclose 292.12
manifest 348.5
reveal 351.4
signify 517.17
say 524.23
inform 551.8
uncover 940.4
testify 956.9

disclosed visible 31.6
open 292.17, 348.10
revealed 351.9

disclosing
noun disclosure 351.1
adj disclosive 351.10

disclosure appearance
33.1
opening 292.1
informing 343.2
manifestation 348.1
disclosing 351.1
indication 517.3
discovery 940.1
testimony 956.2

disco dance 705.2
ballroom 705.4

discoloured colourless
36.7
stained 1003.10

discomfiture chagrin
96.4
disappointment 132.1
rout 412.2
disorder 809.1
confusion 984.3
frustration 1011.3

discomfort
noun pain 26.1
unpleasure 96.1
distressfulness 98.5
verb distress 96.16,
98.14

disconcerted distressed
96.22
disorderly 809.13
bewildered 970.24
confused 984.12

disconcerting
mortifying 98.21
frightening 127.28
bewildering 970.27
frustrating 1011.20

disconcertingly 127.34

disconnected unrelated
775.6
separated 801.21
incoherent 803.4
discontinuous 812.4
irregular 850.3

disconsolate wretched
96.26
inconsolable 112.28
hopeless 125.12

discontent
noun unpleasure 96.1
discontentment 108.1
ill humour 110.1
unhappiness 112.2
resentment 152.1
disapproval 510.1
verb dissatisfy 108.5

discontented
dissatisfied 108.7
out of humour 110.17
unhappy 112.21
disapproving 510.21

discontinue break the
habit 374.3
cease to use 390.4
swear off 668.8
interrupt 812.3
cease 856.6

discontinued disused
390.10
discontinuous 812.4

discord noise 53.3
raucousness 58.2
disaccord 456.1
disagreement 788.1

discordant off-colour
35.20
dissonant 61.4
disaccordant 456.15
contrary 778.6
different 779.7
disagreeing 788.6

discotheque 705.4

discount
noun cut 631.1
verb reject 372.2
price 630.11
cut 631.2
discount notes 728.27
allow for 958.5

discounted 372.3

discounting
noun rejection 372.1
money market 728.16
prep off 255.14

discount rate 623.3

discourage sadden
112.18
daunt 127.18
disincline 379.4
prevent 1011.14

discouraged 112.22

discouraging
depressing 112.30
frightening 127.28
dissuasive 379.5
preventive 1011.19

discourse
noun speech 524.1
conversation 541.1
lecture 543.3
treatise 556.1
lesson 568.7
verb make a speech
543.9
write upon 556.5
expound 568.16

discover see 27.12
disclose 351.4
learn 570.6
innovate 851.9
originate 891.12
find 940.2

discovered 891.19

discoverer 891.7

discovering 351.1

discovery disclosure
351.1
find 472.6
innovation 851.4
finding 940.1

discredit
noun disrepute 661.1
unbelief 954.1
verb disparage 512.8
disgrace 661.8
disbelieve 954.5
disprove 957.4

discredited in disrepute
661.13
doubted 954.12
disproved 957.7

discrediting
disparagement 512.1
refutation 957.2

discreet reticent 344.10
secretive 345.15
cautious 494.8
judicious 919.19

discreetly cautiously
494.12
intelligently 919.20

discrepancy difference
255.8, 779.1
contrariety 778.1
disagreement 788.1

discrete dispersed
770.9
unrelated 775.6
different 779.7
separate 801.20
incoherent 803.4
discontinuous 812.4

discretion will 323.1

secrecy 345.1
option 371.2
free will 430.6
caution 494.1
judiciousness 919.7
foresight 960.1

discretionary 324.7

discriminate
verb favour 650.8
differentiate 779.6
distinguish 943.4
be discriminating
943.5
adj discriminating
943.7

discriminate against
979.8

discriminated 779.7

discriminating
selective 371.23
fastidious 495.9
elegant 496.9
differentiative 779.9
judicious 919.19
discriminate 943.7

discrimination
selectivity 371.10
fastidiousness 495.1
taste 496.1
elegance 533.1
partiality 650.3
differentiation 779.4
judiciousness 919.7
discriminateness 943.1
judgment 945.1
social discrimination
979.4

discriminatory unjust
650.9
differentiative 779.9
discriminating 943.7
prejudiced 979.12

discursive deviative
164.7
wandering 177.37
aimless 538.13
circuitous 913.7
intelligent 919.12
dialectic 934.22

discus circle 280.2
projectile 903.5

discuss confer 541.11
debate 541.12
write upon 556.5

discussion conference
541.6
debate 541.7
treatise 556.1

discussion group
423.3

discuss with 541.11

disdain
noun disdainfulness
141.5
insolence 142.1
contempt 157.1
rejection 372.1
defiance 454.1

verb scorn 157.3
reject 372.2
flout 454.4
be hard to please
495.8
deprecate 510.12

disdainful dismissive
141.13
insolent 142.9
contemptuous 157.8
rejective 372.4
defiant 454.7

disdainfully arrogantly
141.15
insolently 142.12
contemptuously 157.9

disease
noun illness 85.1
harmfulness 999.5
bane 1000.1
verb infect 85.50

diseased unwholesome
85.54
morbid 85.59

disembodied bodiless
987.8
immaterial 1051.7

disenchanted averse
99.8
disapproving 510.21
disillusioned 976.5

disenchantment
disapproval 510.1
reversion 858.1
disillusionment 976.1

disenfranchised
432.14

disengaged idle 331.18
escaped 369.11
free 430.21
separated 801.21

disengagement retreat
163.2
extrication 431.3
separation 801.1
disembarrassment
1013.6

disentangle extract
192.10
straighten 277.5
extricate 431.7
disinvolve 797.5
solve 939.2
disembarrass 1013.9

disfigured deformed
265.12
blemished 1003.8
ugly 1014.6

disgrace
noun humiliation
137.2
disparagement 512.1
abomination 638.2
iniquity 654.3
scandal 661.5
verb humiliate 137.4
disparage 512.8
dishonour 661.8

disgraced 661.13

disgraceful wrong
638.3
wicked 654.16
shameful 661.11

disgracefully 661.16

disgruntled
discontented 108.7
disapproving 510.21

disguise
noun costume 5.9
veil 346.2
sham 354.3
cover 356.11
dissimilarity 786.1
verb conceal 346.6
misrepresent 350.3
falsify 354.16
dissimilate 786.3

disguised clothing 5.44
invisible 32.5
camouflaged 346.13

disgust
noun hostility 99.2
verb repel 64.4, 99.6
offend 98.11

disgusted pleasureless
96.20
hating 103.7
satiated 993.6

disgusting filthy 80.23
offensive 98.18
horrid 98.19
base 661.12
terrible 999.9

disgustingly
unpleasantly 98.26
terribly 999.14

dish
noun serving 8.10
tableware 8.12
cooking 11.1
doll 1015.9
verb ladle 176.17
sink 284.12
hollow 284.13
thwart 1011.15

disharmony discord
61.1
disaccord 456.1
disagreement 788.1
disorder 809.1

disheartened 112.22

disheartening
unsatisfactory 108.9
depressing 112.30
frightening 127.28

dished disappointed
132.5
concave 284.16

dishes 8.12

dishevelled 809.14

dishing 284.16

dishonest falsehearted
354.31
insincere 354.32
untruthful 354.34

dishonourable 645.16

dishonestly 645.24

dishonesty
falseheartedness 354.4
untruthfulness 354.8
fraud 356.8
improbity 645.1

dishonour
noun disrespect 156.1
nonpayment 625.1
improbity 645.1
disrepute 661.1
verb offend 156.5
not pay 625.6
disgrace 661.8
desecrate 694.4

dishonourable
dishonest 645.16
disreputable 661.10

dishwasher washbasin
79.12
washer 79.15

dishy fun 97.8
desirable 100.30
alluring 377.8
eye-catching 1015.21

disillusion
noun disapproval
510.1
disillusionment 976.1
verb disappoint 132.2
disillude 976.2

disillusioned
disappointed 132.5
disapproving 510.21
disenchanted 976.5

disillusionment
disappointment 132.1
disapproval 510.1
disillusion 976.1

disincentive 379.2

disinclined averse 99.8
unwilling 325.5

disinfectant
noun antiseptic 86.21
poison 1000.3
adj antiseptic 86.43

disinfected 79.27

disinformation
misrepresentation
350.1
deliberate falsehood
354.9
fabrication 354.10
propaganda 569.2

disingenuous insincere
354.32
deceitful 645.18
sophistical 935.10

disintegrate weaken
16.9
strike dead 308.17
decay 393.22
break 393.23, 1048.3
demolish 395.17
fall 395.22
disband 770.8
come apart 801.9

decompose 805.3
lapse into disorder
809.8
pulverize 1049.9
powder 1049.10

disintegrated
disintegrative 805.5
powdery 1049.11

disintegrating unsound
16.15
deteriorating 393.45
disintegrative 805.5

disintegration frailty
16.2
decay 393.6
destruction 395.1
disbandment 770.3
disruption 801.3
decomposition 805.1
disorder 809.1
pulverization 1049.4

disinterest
noun apathy 94.4
unconcern 102.2
impartiality 649.4
unselfishness 652.1
incuriosity 981.1
verb disincline 379.4

disinterested apathetic
94.13
unconcerned 102.7
impartial 649.10
unselfish 652.5
unprejudiced 978.12
incurious 981.3

disjointed dislocated
160.9
separated 801.21

disk 1041.6

diskette bulletin board
549.10
disk 1041.6

dislike
noun unpleasure 96.1
distaste 99.1
hate 103.1
verb mislike 99.3
have it in for 103.6

disliked 99.9

dislocated displaced
160.9
separated 801.21
disorderly 809.13

dislocation
displacement 160.1
separation 801.1
noncohesion 803.1
disarrangement 810.1

dislodge unplace 160.6
remove 176.11
extricate 431.7
evict 908.15

disloyal apostate
363.11
unfaithful 645.20

disloyalty apostasy
363.2
infidelity 645.5

dismal grey 39.4
distressing 98.20
gloomy 112.24
dull 117.6
hopeless 125.12
pessimistic 125.16
funereal 309.22

dismally sadly 112.31
dully 117.10

dismantle demolish
395.17
disassemble 801.15

dismay
noun fear 127.1
verb distress 98.14
disconcert 127.19
bewilder 970.12

dismayed frightened
127.25
cowardly 491.10
bewildered 970.24

dismembered severed
801.23
incoherent 803.4

dismemberment penal
servitude 604.2
disassembly 801.6
noncohesion 803.1

dismiss slight 157.6
reject 372.2
release 431.5
depose 447.4
acquit 601.4
play 747.4
disband 770.8
repulse 907.3
discharge 908.19
refute 957.5

dismissal snub 157.2
rejection 372.1
release 431.2
deposal 447.2
acquittal 601.1
disbandment 770.3
repulse 907.2
discharge 908.5

dismissed rejected
372.3
disproved 957.7

dismissive disdainful
141.13
rejective 372.4

disobedience refusal
325.1, 442.1
nonobedience 327.1
lawlessness 418.1

disorder
noun disease 85.1
formlessness 263.1
misbehaviour 322.1
anarchy 418.2
nonuniformity 781.1
noncohesion 803.1
disorderliness 809.1
disarrangement 810.1
change 851.1
agitation 916.1
vagueness 970.4
confusion 984.3

verb afflict 85.49
deform 263.3
disarrange 809.9,
810.2

disordered neurotic
92.38
incoherent 803.4
unordered 809.12
disorderly 809.13
disarranged 810.5
vague 970.19
confused 984.12

disorderly formless
263.4
misbehaving 322.5
anarchic 418.6
unruly 671.19
nonuniform 781.3
in disorder 809.13

disorganized anarchic
418.6
disorderly 809.13
confused 984.12

disorientated 984.12

disorientation
psychosomatic
symptom 92.18
orientation 161.4
insanity 925.1
confusion 984.3

disoriented insane
925.26
bewildered 970.24
confused 984.12

disown deny 335.4
recant 363.8
reject 372.2
dispossess 480.23

disowned rejected
372.3
outcast 586.10

disparaging
disrespectful 156.7
condemnatory 510.22
derogatory 512.13

disparate different
779.7
dissimilar 786.4
unequal 790.4

disparity dissent 333.1
disagreement 456.2,
788.1
difference 779.1
dissimilarity 786.1
inequality 790.1

dispassionate unfeeling
94.9
unconcerned 102.7
inexcitable 106.10
impartial 649.10
equable 670.13
unprejudiced 978.12

dispassionately
unfeelingly 94.14
unconcernedly 102.10
inexcitably 106.16
justly 649.11
moderately 670.17

dispatch
noun velocity 174.1
killing 308.1
performance 328.2
quickness 330.3
information 551.1
message 552.4
letter 553.2
promptness 844.3
verb send 176.15
kill 308.12
perform 328.9
hasten 401.4
accomplish 407.4
mail 553.12
adj accomplishment 407.1

dispatched 407.10

dispel disappear 34.3
dissipate 770.5
part company 801.19
do away with 908.21

dispensation
permission 443.1
relinquishment 475.1
distribution 477.2
administration 573.3
government 612.1
privilege 642.2
creation 677.13

dispense exempt 430.14
permit 443.9
parcel out 477.8
give 478.12
vend 734.9
disperse 770.4

dispensed 430.30

dispensed with 475.5

dispenser 86.35

dispense with not use 390.5
exempt 430.14
relinquish 475.3

dispersal 801.3

disperse disappear 34.3
deflect 164.5
radiate 171.6
spread 259.6
rarefy 299.3
parcel out 477.8
scatter 770.4
disband 770.8
shatter 801.13
part company 801.19
loosen 803.3

dispersed deflective 164.8
rare 299.4
scattered 770.9
separated 801.21
unordered 809.12

dispersion
disappearance 34.1
deflection 164.2
radiation 171.2
expansion 259.1
rarefaction 299.2
distribution 477.2

dispirited dejected 112.22
weary 118.11

dispiriting 112.30

displace dislocate 160.5
remove 176.11
depose 447.4
substitute for 861.5
dismiss 908.19

displaced 160.9

displacement
noun defence mechanism 92.23
dislocation 160.1
draught 275.6
deposal 447.2
transformation 851.3
substitution 861.1
phrase moving 176.4

displacing 908.5

display
noun appearance 33.2
spectacle 33.7
externalization 206.4
front 216.1
demonstration 348.2
publication 352.1
show 501.4
signal 1035.11
verb externalize 206.5
manifest 348.5
make public 352.11
flaunt 501.17
signify 517.17
evidence 956.8

displayed 348.13

displaying
noun externalization 206.4
adj manifesting 348.9

displeased averse 99.8
discontented 108.7
disapproving 510.21

displeasure unpleasure 96.1
unpleasantness 98.1
dislike 99.1
unhappiness 112.2
resentment 152.1
disapproval 510.1

disposable 388.6

disposable income 627.1

disposal placement 159.6
discard 390.3
relinquishment 475.1
distribution 477.2
administration 573.3
transfer 629.1
elimination 772.2
order 806.1
arrangement 807.1

dispose locate 159.11
bear 161.7
induce 375.22
parcel out 477.8
order 806.4

distribute 807.9
influence 893.7
govern 893.8

disposed willing 324.5
arranged 807.14
dispositioned 977.8

disposed of
accomplished 407.10
relinquished 475.5

disposed to 895.6

dispose of kill 308.12
perform 328.9
discard 390.7
put an end to 395.12
accomplish 407.4
relinquish 475.3
give away 478.21
eliminate 772.5
end 819.5
refute 957.5

disposition placement 159.6
will 323.1
plan 381.1
governance 417.5
battle array 458.3
relinquishment 475.1
distribution 477.2
administration 573.3
government 612.1
transfer 629.1
nature 766.4
elimination 772.2
order 806.1
arrangement 807.1
tendency 895.1
character 977.3

dispossessed
underprivileged 606.4
unfortunate 1010.7

disproportionate
exaggerated 355.4
disagreeing 788.6
inconsistent 788.8
unequal 790.4
unordered 809.12

disproportionately 790.6

disprove deny 335.4
invalidate 957.4

disproved 957.7

dispute
noun resistance 453.1
quarrel 456.5
contention 457.1
argumentation 934.4
questioning 937.12
verb object 333.5
deny 335.4
offer resistance 453.3
quarrel 456.11
contest 457.21
argue 934.16
doubt 954.6

disputed doubted 954.12
disproved 957.7

disputing 453.5

disqualification
inability 19.2
unpreparedness 406.1

disqualified disabled 19.16
unfitted 406.9

disqualify invalidate 19.11
make impossible 966.6

disquiet
noun unpleasure 96.1
trepidation 105.5, 127.5
anxiety 126.1
nervousness 128.1
impatience 135.1
agitation 916.1
verb distress 96.16
agitate 105.14, 916.10
concern 126.4
frighten 127.15

disquieting exciting 105.30
troublesome 126.10
frightening 127.28

disregard
noun unconcern 102.2
forgiveness 148.1
snub 157.2
neglect 340.1
rejection 372.1
nonobservance 435.1
defiance 454.1
inattention 983.1
verb take 134.8
condone 148.4
slight 157.6
disobey 327.6
neglect 340.6
reject 372.2
lose sight of 435.3
flout 454.4
allow for 958.5
keep an open mind 978.7
be inattentive 983.2

disregarded forgiven 148.7
neglected 340.14

disrepair uselessness 391.1
impairment 393.1

disreputable
noun bad person 660.1
adj discreditable 661.10

disrepute 661.1

disrespect
noun impudence 142.2
disrespectfulness 156.1, 505.2
disobedience 327.1
disapproval 510.1
verb not respect 156.4

disrespectful impudent 142.10
irreverent 156.7
discourteous 505.4

disrupt shatter 801.13

thwart 1011.15

disruption
misbehaviour 322.1
destruction 395.1
anarchy 418.2
falling-out 456.4
dissolution 801.3
disorder 809.1

disruptive misbehaving 322.5
disintegrative 805.5

dissatisfaction
unpleasure 96.1
discontent 108.1
disappointment 132.1
resentment 152.1
dissent 333.1
disapproval 510.1

dissatisfied
discontented 108.7
disappointed 132.5
disapproving 510.21

dissect differentiate 779.6
analyse 800.6, 801.17

dissection 800.1, 801.5

disseminate transfer 176.10
communicate 343.7
publish 352.10
disperse 770.4
plant 1067.18

disseminated
published 352.17
dispersed 770.9

dissemination
noun manifestation 348.1
publication 352.1
planting 1067.14
phrase transference 176.1

dissension dissent 333.1, 456.3
hostility 451.2
disagreement 788.1

dissent
noun complaint 115.4
refusal 325.1, 442.1
dissidence 333.1
resistance 453.1
dissension 456.3
disapproval 510.1
Protestantism 675.10
difference 779.1
disagreement 788.1
nonconformity 867.1
counteraction 899.1
verb dissent from 333.4
refuse 442.3
offer resistance 453.3
diversify 781.2
disagree 788.5
not conform 867.4
counteract 899.6

dissenting dissident 333.6
resistant 453.5

anxious 126.7
disorderly 809.13
psychotic 925.28
bewildered 970.24
confused 984.12

disturbing mortifying
98.21
annoying 98.22
exciting 105.30
troublesome 126.10
bewildering 970.27

disunity falling-out
456.4
disagreement 788.1

disused abandoned
370.8, 390.10
old-fashioned 841.16

ditch
noun crack 224.2
channel 239.1
trench 290.2
entrenchment 460.5
barrier 1011.5
verb land 184.43
cleave 224.4
furrow 290.3
discard 390.7

ditched 290.4

dithering
noun vacillation 362.2
adj mentally deficient
921.22

ditto
noun same 777.3
duplicate 784.3
equal 789.4
repeat 848.5
verb concur 332.9
imitate 336.5
reproduce 777.6
equal 789.5
repeat 848.7
duplicate 873.3
adv identically 777.9
again 848.17

ditty 708.14

diuretic
noun cleanser 79.17
laxative 86.17
adj cleansing 79.28
cathartic 86.48

diva lead 707.6
singer 710.13
chief 996.10

divan council 423.1
cabinet 613.3

dive
noun bar 88.20
surfacing 182.8
tumble 194.3
den 228.28
decline 252.2
plunge 367.1
cheapening 633.4
brothel 665.9
verb surface 182.47
swim 182.56
nose-dive 184.41
decrease 252.6

deepen 275.8
plunge 367.6
cheapen 633.6

dived 311.28

dive in 817.7

dive into rush into
401.7
set to work 725.15

diver swimmer 182.12
plunger 367.4

diverge deviate 164.3
deflect 164.5
divaricate 171.5
oblique 204.9
fall out 456.10
disperse 770.4
differ 779.5
diversify 781.2
part company 801.19
be changed 851.6

divergence deviation
164.1
obliquity 204.1
distance 261.1
falling-out 456.4
nonuniformity 781.1
dissimilarity 786.1
disagreement 788.1
change 851.1
abnormality 869.1
eccentricity 926.1

divergent diverging
171.8
oblique 204.13
different 779.7
nonuniform 781.3
dissimilar 786.4
disagreeing 788.6
separate 801.20
changed 851.10
abnormal 869.9
eccentric 926.5

divers different 779.7
diversified 782.4
several 883.7

diverse different 779.7
diversified 782.4
dissimilar 786.4

diversification
differentiation 779.4
nonuniformity 781.1
multiformity 782.1
change 851.1

diversified different
779.7
nonuniform 781.3
varied 782.4

diversify differentiate
779.6
vary 781.2, 782.2
be changed 851.6
change 851.7

diversion deviation
164.1
byway 383.4
misuse 389.1
attack 459.1
amusement 743.1
change 851.1

distraction 984.1

diversity dissent 333.1
difference 779.1
nonuniformity 781.1
multiformity 782.1
dissimilarity 786.1
disagreement 788.1
change 851.1

divert deflect 164.5
disincline 379.4
misuse 389.4
amuse 743.21
distract 984.6

diverted 743.26

diverting 743.27

Dives 618.8

divide
noun watershed 272.5
verb diverge 171.5
bound 211.8
partition 213.8
quantify 244.4
open 292.11
measure 300.10
vote 371.18
fall out 456.10
sow dissension 456.14
apportion 477.6,
801.18
segregate 772.6
differentiate 779.6
separate 792.6, 801.8
analyse 800.6
classify 807.11, 808.6
bisect 874.4
discriminate 943.4
calculate 1016.17

divided disaccordant
456.15
alienated 589.11
segregated 772.8
separated 801.21
halved 874.6

dividend portion 477.5
royalty 624.7
receipts 627.1
regular dividend 738.7
surplus 992.5

dividends gain 472.3
receipts 627.1

dividing
noun apportionment
477.1
adj separating 801.25

dividing line boundary
211.3
partition 213.5

divination sorcery
689.10, 690.1
future 838.1
foresight 960.1
divining 961.2

divinatory foreseeing
960.7
predictive 961.11

divine
noun theologian 676.3
clergyman 699.2

verb augur 133.12
solve 939.2
suppose 950.10
predict 961.9
adj blissful 97.9
theological 676.4
heavenly 677.16
godlike 678.16
sacred 685.7
superb 998.15
gorgeous 1015.20

divinely superbly
998.23
gorgeously 1015.25

divine right authority
417.1
prerogative 642.1

diving aquatics 182.11
plunging 367.3

divining 961.2

divinity theology 676.1
deity 677.1
god 678.2
sanctity 685.1

division partition 213.5
region 231.1
vote 371.6
disagreement 456.2
falling-out 456.4
unit 461.21
navy 461.26
apportionment 477.1
class 607.1, 808.2
introduction 613.5
party 617.4
branch 617.10
sect 675.3
passage 708.24
ornament 709.18
boxer 754.2
company 769.3
exclusiveness 772.3
differentiation 779.4
part 792.1
analysis 800.1
separation 801.1
classification 808.1
bisection 874.1
distinction 943.3
notation 1016.2

divisional 808.7

division of labour
891.3

divisions 196.1

divisive 456.17

divorce
noun divorcement
566.1
separation 801.1
verb separate 566.5,
801.8

divorced widowly
566.7
separated 801.21

divulge manifest 348.5
divulgate 351.5
make public 352.11

dizziness weakness
16.1
anaemia 85.9
ear disease 85.15
inattention 983.1
vertigo 984.4
flightiness 984.5

dizzy
verb make one's head
swim 984.8
adj weak 16.12
intoxicated 88.31
inconstant 853.7
muddleheaded 921.18
foolish 922.8
screwy 922.9
delirious 925.31
giddy 984.15

DNA 560.6

do
noun bash 582.12
sol-fa 709.7
festival 743.4
assembly 769.2
verb cook 11.4
be satisfactory 107.6
go 177.19
traverse 177.20
average 246.2
behave 321.4
effect 328.6
practice 328.8
imitate 336.5
impersonate 349.12
gyp 356.19
avail 387.17
accomplish 407.4
perform 434.3, 891.11
play 708.39
busy oneself with
724.11
suit 787.8
cause 885.10
solve 939.2
suffice 990.4
exclam please 440.20

do a 180 851.7

do a bit 500.12

do a deal contract
437.5
compromise 468.2
bargain 731.17

do-all 577.9

do away with kill
308.12
put an end to 395.12
repeal 445.2
exterminate 908.21

do business cooperate
450.3
trade 731.14

do business with
731.16

do by 321.6

doc 90.4

docile willing 324.5
tractable 433.13
teachable 570.18

dock
  noun hangar 184.24
  tail 217.6
  storehouse 386.6
  courthouse 595.6
  stage 704.16
  harbour 1008.6
  verb anchor 182.15
  land 186.8
  excise 255.10
  shorten 268.6
docked shortened 268.9
  concise 537.6
  mutilated 794.5
docking landing 186.2
  spacecraft 1073.2
dockside 1008.6
dockyard plant 739.3
  harbour 1008.6
doctor
  noun doc 90.4
  degree 648.6
  professional 726.4
  wise man 920.1
  verb practice medicine 90.14
  treat 91.24
  undergo treatment 91.29
  aid 449.11
doctorate 648.6
doctored 265.11
doctoring 796.3
doctrinaire
  noun theorist 950.7
  dogmatist 969.7
  bigot 979.5
  adj dogmatic 969.22
  discriminatory 979.12
doctrinal theological 676.4
  creedal 952.27
doctrine religion 675.1
  dogma 676.2
  belief 952.2
document
  noun writing 547.10
  official document 549.5
  verb itemize 765.6
  confirm 956.11
  cite 956.13
documentary
  noun television broadcast 1034.2
  adj documentational 549.18
  evidential 956.16
  true 972.13
documentation record 549.1
  evidence 956.1
  confirmation 956.4
documented recorded 549.17
  evidential 956.16
doddle 1013.4
dodge

noun trick 356.6
  fraud 356.8
  avoidance 368.1
  stratagem 415.3
  retreat 902.3
  quibble 935.4
  verb avoid 157.7, 164.6
  slight 340.8
  prevaricate 344.7
  duck 368.8
  shirk 368.9
  live by one's wits 415.9
  go roundabout 913.4
  quibble 935.9
dodger neglecter 340.5
  deceiver 357.1
  slyboots 415.6
dodging
  noun prevarication 344.4
  shirking 368.2
  quibbling 935.5
  adj avertive 164.9
dodgy avertive 164.9
  inconstant 853.7
  unreliable 970.20
  chance 971.15
  hazardous 1005.10
doe hen 77.9
  deer 311.5
  goat 311.8
  hare 311.24
do for kill 308.12
  fix 395.11
  serve 577.13
  attend to 604.10
dog
  noun cock 76.8
  foot 199.5
  canine 311.17
  beast 660.7
  verb annoy 96.13
  worry 126.5
  follow 166.3
  pursue 382.8
  hunt 382.9
  obstruct 1011.12
dog-eared eared 48.15
  folded 291.7
  worn 393.31
dog food 10.4
dogged tormented 96.24
  worried 126.8
  persevering 360.8
  obstinate 361.8
doggedly perseveringly 360.9
  obstinately 361.14
doggy 311.40
doghouse kennel 228.21
  tight spot 258.3
dog it 222.9
dogma doctrine 676.2
  belief 952.2

dogmatic obstinate 361.8
  unpersuadable 361.13
  strict 687.8
  belief 952.21
  doctrinal 952.27
  dogmatical 969.22
  discriminatory 979.12
dogmatism obstinacy 361.1
  unpersuadableness 361.5
  strictness 687.5
  dogmaticalness 969.6
do good do a favour 143.12
  aid 449.11
  profit 998.10
dogs 457.11
do in fatigue 21.4
  beat 21.6
  waste 308.13
  do for 395.11
  put an end to 395.12
doing
  noun behaviour 321.1
  action 328.1
  act 328.3
  affair 830.3
  performance 891.5
  adj happening 830.9
doing business 731.2
doings behaviour 321.1
  act 328.3
  activity 330.1
  affairs 830.4
  gadget 1050.5
do it 990.4
do justice to feast 8.24
  savour 63.5
  enjoy 95.12
  observe 434.2
  justify 600.9
  do one's duty 641.10
  be just 649.6
dolce 708.53
doldrums blues 112.6
  calm 173.5
  prevailing wind 318.10
dole
  noun welfare 143.5
  modicum 248.2
  distribution 477.2
  donation 478.6
  part 792.1
  pittance 991.5
  verb parcel out 477.8
  give 478.12
doleful sorrowful 112.26
  pitiful 145.8
do like 336.5
doll gal 77.6, 302.7
  angel 104.15
  miniature 258.6
  figure 349.6
  darling 562.6

good guy 659.2
  toy 743.16
  dish 1015.9
dollar mite 728.7
  mill 728.8
dollar bill 728.8
dollop 792.3
dolls bennies 87.3
  amies 87.4
doll's house tight spot 258.3
  toy 743.16
dolly gal 77.6
  figure 349.6
dolphin 311.30
Dom 648.5
domain sphere 231.2
  country 232.1
  real estate 471.6
  field 724.4
  hierarchy 808.4
  science 927.10
dome
  noun hall 197.4
  highlands 237.1
  mountain 237.6
  tower 272.6
  arch 279.4
  verb curve 279.6
  top 295.21
domed 295.31
domestic
  noun servant 577.2
  adj residential 228.32
  recluse 584.10
domesticated tame 228.34
  subdued 432.15
  meek 433.15
domestic economy 573.6
domesticity 228.3
domestic politics 609.1
domicile
  noun abode 228.1
  verb inhabit 225.7
  house 225.10
dominance 893.1
dominant
  noun note 709.14
  key 709.15
  adj chief 249.14
  victorious 411.7
  authoritative 417.15
  governing 612.18
  prevalent 863.12
  well-connected 893.14
  paramount 996.24
dominate show 31.4
  rise above 272.11
  subjugate 432.8
  predominate 612.15
  prevail 863.10
dominating 272.14
domination field of view 31.3

subjection 432.1
  control 612.2
  despotism 612.10
  influence 893.1
domineering
  noun arrogance 141.1
  authoritativeness 417.3
  despotism 612.10
  adj arrogant 141.9
  imperious 417.16
dominion sphere 231.2
  country 232.1
  supremacy 249.3
  governance 417.5
  ownership 469.2
  control 612.2
domino 356.11
don
  noun Mister 76.7
  teacher 571.1
  verb put on 5.42
donate provide 385.7
  give 478.12
donation giving 478.1
  donative 478.6
done
  adj well-done 11.7
  beat 21.8
  completed 407.11
  ended 819.8
  produced 891.17
  phrase so be it 332.20
done for dead 307.30
  dying 307.33
  screwed up 393.29
  shot 395.29
  defeated 412.14
  belly-up 819.9
done in beat 21.8, 412.15
  shot 395.29
done up 21.8
done with disused 390.10
  completed 407.11
  ended 819.8
dong 54.8
Don Juan beau 104.13
  deceiver 357.1
  tempter 377.4
  philanderer 562.12
  libertine 665.10
donkey ass 311.16
  stupid person 923.2
donna woman 77.5
  Ms 77.8
do no harm 998.10
donor provider 385.6
  giver 478.11
donor insemination 78.3
do nothing not stir 329.2
  idle 331.12
  be conservative 852.6
do-nothing 329.6

Don Quixote knight
608.5
visionary 985.13

doodle
noun drawing 712.13
fool 923.1
verb waste time 331.13
dally 331.14
scribble 547.20
blow a horn 708.42
portray 712.19

doom
noun death 307.1
end 395.2, 819.1
condemnation 602.1
destiny 838.2
doomsday 838.3
verdict 945.5
fate 963.2
verb condemn 602.3
damn 682.6
pass judgment 945.13
destine 963.7
work evil 999.6

doomed futile 125.13
future 838.8
destined 963.9

doomsday 838.3

door entrance 189.5
porch 189.6
outlet 190.9
doorway 292.6

doorman 1007.12

doormat 358.2

doorstep 193.5

doorway porch 189.6
door 292.6

do over beat up 604.14
repeat 848.7
convert 857.11

dope
noun anaesthetic 25.3
drug 87.2
film 714.10
contraband 732.3
stupid person 923.2
knowledge 927.1
fuel 1020.1
verb put to sleep
22.20
deaden 25.4
medicate 91.25

doped 22.21

dopey inert 173.14
languid 331.20
dull 921.16
screwy 922.9
dazed 984.14

do right behave oneself
321.5
be just 649.6

dorm 228.15

dormant asleep 22.22
inert 173.14
passive 329.6
languid 331.20
latent 519.5

dormitory bedroom
197.7
inn 228.15

dosage 643.2

dose
noun draught 86.6
hit 87.19
amount 244.2
portion 792.5
radiation physics
1036.7
verb medicate 91.25
administer 643.6

dosh 728.2

do something 328.5

do something about
328.5

do something about it
216.8

dossier 549.5

dot
noun spottiness 47.3
modicum 248.2
minutia 258.7
endowment 478.9
mark 517.5
notation 709.12
verb variegate 47.7
interspace 224.3
mark 517.19
disperse 770.4
sprinkle 770.6

do the right thing do
one's duty 641.10
be good 653.5

do the trick do 328.6
accomplish 407.4
succeed with 409.11
suffice 990.4

doting senile 921.23
foolish 922.8
credulous 953.8

do to do 328.6
inflict 643.5

dots 87.9

dotted spotted 47.13
interspaced 224.6
sprinkled 770.10

dotted line 517.6

dotty spotted 47.13
crazy 925.27
eccentric 926.5

double
noun deviation 164.1
fold 291.1
image 349.5
match 752.3
same 777.3
duplicate 784.3
substitute 861.2
verb turn back 163.8
intensify 251.5
fold 291.5
play 752.4
copy 784.8
seek the middle 818.3
repeat 848.7
duplicate 872.5, 873.3

adj falsehearted
354.31
treacherous 645.21
two 872.6
doubled 873.4

double agent traitor
357.10
secret agent 576.9

double bogey
noun round 748.3
verb play 748.4

double-check
noun ensuring 969.8
verb verify 969.12
check 1016.20

doubled folded 291.7
repeated 848.12
two 872.6
double 873.4

double-decker 179.13

double-edged
acrimonious 17.14
sharp 285.8

double fault 749.2

double-fault 749.3

doubles 749.1

double-sided 872.6

double standard 354.4

double take sequel
816.1
delay 845.2

double up bet 759.25
league 804.4
duplicate 873.3

double vision 28.1

doubling lining 196.3
fold 291.1
repetition 848.1
doubleness 872.1
duplication 873.1

doubly 873.5

doubt
noun apprehension
127.4
suspiciousness 153.2
agnosticism 695.6
doubtfulness 954.2,
970.2
verb suffer pangs of
jealousy 153.3
disbelieve 695.14
be doubtful 954.6
be uncertain 970.9

doubted 954.12

doubtful dishonest
645.16
agnostic 695.20
doubting 954.9
unbelievable 954.10
improbable 968.3
iffy 970.17
unsafe 1005.11

doubtfully
unbelievingly 954.13
uncertainly 970.28

doubting doubtful
954.9

uncertain 970.16

doubtless
adj belief 952.21
undoubted 969.16
adv probably 967.8
unquestionably 969.25

douche
noun washing 79.5
bathe 79.8
sprinkler 1063.8
verb wash 79.19
moisten 1063.12
soak 1063.13

dough bread 728.2
putty 1045.4
semiliquid 1060.5

doughnut 10.42

doughty strong 15.15
courageous 492.17

do up beat 21.6
repair 396.14
put up 397.10
bind 799.9

dour sullen 110.24
harsh 144.24
unyielding 361.9
strict 425.6
firm 425.7

Dove 677.12

dove left side 220.1
innocent 657.4

do very well 409.7

dovetail
noun joint 799.4
verb interact 776.6
agree 787.6
hook 799.8

dowager woman 77.5
old woman 304.3
widow 566.4
mistress 575.2
aristocrat 607.4

dowdy
noun pastry 10.39
adj shabby 393.32

dowel 283.3

do well 1009.7

do with use 387.10
treat 387.12
make shift 994.4

do without not use
390.5
abstain 668.7

**Dow-Jones Industrial
Average** 737.1

down
noun beard 3.8
fluff 3.20
descent 194.1
plain 236.1
hill 237.4
smoothness 294.3
air 298.2
reverse 1010.3
putty 1045.4
verb devour 8.22
tipple 88.24

take 134.8
descend 194.5
thin 270.12
fell 912.5
adj ill 85.55
laid up 85.58
dejected 112.22
motionless 173.13
descending 194.11
lower 274.8
defeated 412.14
recorded 549.17
adv downward 194.13
cash 624.25

down and out ruined
395.28
destitute 619.9
belly-up 819.9

down-and-out beggar
440.8
poor 619.3
poor man 619.4
wretch 660.2

down-at-heel shabby
393.32
indigent 619.8

downbeat
noun beat 709.26
round 849.3
adj depressing 112.30
pessimistic 125.16

down below 274.10

downcast
noun downthrow 912.2
adj dejected 112.22
downturned 194.12
depressed 912.12

downfall descent 194.1
rainstorm 316.2
fall 395.3
collapse 410.3
defeat 412.1
downthrow 912.2

downgrade
noun descent 194.1
declivity 204.5
verb reduce 252.7
demote 447.3
adj downhill 204.16
adv down 194.13
slantingly 204.23

downgrading 447.1

downhill
noun declivity 204.5
adj descending 194.11
downgrade 204.16
adv down 194.13
slantingly 204.23

down home 225.16

down-home 233.8

Downing Street
government 612.3
ten 881.6

down on averse 99.8
disapproving 510.21

down payment 624.1

downpour descent
194.1

flow 238.4
rainstorm 316.2
downthrow 912.2

downright
adj vertical 200.11
outright 247.12
candid 644.17
thorough 793.10
unqualified 959.2
adv down 194.13
extremely 247.22
no ifs 959.3

downs amies 87.4
plain 236.1
highlands 237.1,
272.3

downside bottom 199.1
adversity 1010.1
trouble 1012.3

down south 194.13

Down's syndrome
921.9

downstairs down
194.13
below 274.10
below stairs 577.15

downstream 194.13

downswing 748.3

down the middle
874.8

down-to-earth 986.6

down to the ground
793.17

downtown
noun East End 230.6
adj urban 230.11
adv down 194.13

downtrodden 432.16

downturn descent
194.1
decline 252.2
deterioration 393.3
business cycle 731.9

down under 231.6

downward
adj flowing 172.8
descending 194.11
adv down 194.13

downwards 194.13

downward trend
descent 194.1
deterioration 393.3

downwind
verb land 184.43
adv leeward 182.68,
218.9

downy feathery 3.28
smooth 287.9, 294.8
light 298.10
shrewd 919.15
fluffy 1045.14

dowry
noun talent 413.4
endowment 478.9
adj endowed 478.26

dowsing 961.3

doyen senior 304.5
chief 575.3

doyenne senior 304.5
chief 575.3

doze
noun sleep 22.2
verb sleep 22.13

dozen 881.7

dozens 490.1

dozing 984.11

dozy sleepy 22.21
stupid 921.15

drab
noun strumpet 665.14
slob 809.7
adj brown 40.3
same 780.6
lacklustre 1026.17

drabble draggle 80.19
hang 202.6

Draconian 144.26

Dracula 127.9

draft
noun diagram 381.3
demand 421.1
recruit 461.17
writing 547.10
abridgment 557.1
score 708.28
drawing 712.13
verb outline 381.11
write 547.19
enlist 615.17
portray 712.19

drafting drawing 192.3
enlistment 615.7

drag
noun smoking 89.10
drip 118.5
slowing 175.4
gait 177.12
resistance 184.27
burden 297.7
pull 904.2
attraction 906.1
disadvantage 995.2
curb 1011.7
friction 1042.1
verb use 87.21
smoke 89.14
lag 166.4
dawdle 175.8
stroll 177.28
hang 202.6
smooth 287.5
linger on 826.7
delay 845.8
pull 904.4
attract 906.4

dragged in 775.8

dragged-out lengthened
267.8
worn-out 393.36

dragging
noun delay 845.2
pulling 904.1
adj dawdling 175.11

attracting 906.5

drag on be tedious
118.6
linger on 826.7
continue 855.3

dragon 110.11

dragoon
noun cavalryman
461.11
verb intimidate 127.20
compel 424.4
coerce 424.7

drag queen homo
75.15
entertainer 707.1

drain
noun sink 80.12
outflow 190.4
sough 239.5
consumption 388.1
demand 421.1
waste 473.2
verb disable 19.9
decolour 36.5
run out 190.13
draw off 192.12
subtract 255.9
exploit 387.16
consume 388.3
waste 473.5
take from 480.21
strip 480.24
evacuate 908.22
dry 1064.6

drainage outflow 190.4
drawing 192.3
evacuation 908.6
drying 1064.3

drained weakened
16.18
burnt-out 21.10
bleached 36.8
unhealthy 85.53
used up 388.5
unproductive 890.4

draining
noun exhaustion 21.2
drawing 192.3
evacuation 908.6
adj weakening 16.20
fatiguing 21.13
deteriorating 393.45
demanding 421.9

drake cock 76.8
poultry 311.29

dram
noun drink 8.4, 88.7
modicum 248.2
verb tipple 88.24

drama representation
349.1
show business 704.1

dramatic emotionalistic
93.19
theatrical 501.24
dramatical 704.33
vocal 708.50
poetic 720.15

dramatics
emotionalism 93.9
display 501.4
dramatization 704.2

dramatist author
547.15, 718.4
playwright 704.22

drape
noun pendant 202.4
cover 295.2
shade 1027.1
verb clothe 5.38
hang 202.6

draped 201.8

draper 5.32

drastic 671.16

drastically 671.25

draught
noun drink 8.4, 88.7
dose 86.6
submergence 275.6
wind 318.1
pulling 904.1
verb draw off 192.12

draughtsman 716.3

draughty 318.22

draw
noun valley 237.7
lure 377.3
same 789.3
tie 835.3
pull 904.2
attraction 906.1
verb smoke 89.14
extract 192.10
draw off 192.12
contract 260.7
lengthen 267.6
represent 349.8
describe 349.9
lure 377.5
acquire 472.8
receive 479.6
hang 604.17
portray 712.19
play 748.4
equal 789.5
pull 904.4
attract 906.4

draw a line 779.6

drawback discount
631.1
disadvantage 995.2
fault 1002.2
obstacle 1011.4

drawer storehouse
386.6
draughtsman 716.3

draw from 192.12

draw in suck 187.12
narrow 270.11
lure 377.5
portray 712.19
involve 897.2
reel in 905.9

drawing
noun extraction 192.1
drafting 192.3

representation 349.1
diagram 381.3
draughtsmanship
712.5
delineation 712.13
graphic arts 713.1
pulling 904.1
adj pulling 904.6
attracting 906.5

drawing out 192.1

drawing room
stateroom 197.10
society 578.6

drawl
noun slowness 175.1
accent 524.9
verb murmur 524.26
speak poorly 525.7

drawn tired-looking
21.9
lengthened 267.8
equal 789.7
simultaneous 835.5

drawn-out 267.8

drawn to
adj approaching 167.4
prep inclined to 895.6

draw on enamour
104.23
lure 377.5
induce 885.11

draw out extract
192.10
protract 538.8, 826.9

draw the line limit
210.5
discriminate 943.4
discriminate against
979.8

draw up write 547.19
form 806.5
stop 856.7
pick up 911.8

dread
noun unpleasure 96.1
anxiety 126.1
fear 127.1
suspense 130.3
verb fear 127.10
expect 130.5
adj terrible 127.30

dreaded 127.30

dreadful
adj horrid 98.19
terrible 127.30, 999.9
venerable 155.12
terrific 247.11
hideous 1014.11
adv terribly 999.14

dreadfully horridly
98.27
frightfully 127.34
distressingly 247.21
terribly 999.14
hideously 1014.13

dream
noun aspiration 100.9
airy hope 124.5

illusion 975.1
hallucination 975.7
abstractedness 984.2
reverie 985.9
dandy 998.7
doll 1015.9
verb suppose 950.10
muse 984.9
dream of 985.17

dream come true
idealism 985.7
acme of perfection
1001.3

dreamer 985.13

dreaming
noun abstractedness
984.2
dreaminess 985.8
adj abstracted 984.11
dreamy 985.25

dreamland sleep 22.2
illusion 975.1

dreamlike thin 763.6
illusory 975.9
dreamy 985.25

dream of 985.17

dream on 985.17

dream up originate
891.12
imagine 985.14

dreamy sleepy 22.21
tranquillizing 670.15
illusory 975.9
abstracted 984.11
dreamful 985.25

dreary grey 39.4
distressing 98.20
gloomy 112.24
dull 117.6
tedious 118.9
ominous 133.17

dredge
noun excavator 284.10
verb extract 192.10
excavate 284.15
sprinkle 770.6
imbue 796.11
pick up 911.8

dredging 192.1

dregs grounds 256.2
refuse 391.4
rabble 606.3
extract 892.3

drenched intoxicated
88.31
overfull 992.20
soaked 1063.17

drenching
noun soaking 1063.7
adj wetting 1063.18

dress
noun clothing 5.1
suit 5.6
gown 5.16
insignia 647.1
verb clothe 5.38
groom 79.20
smooth 287.5

equip 385.8
prepare 405.6
ornament 498.8
fertilize 889.8
buff 1042.8
oil 1054.8
cultivate 1067.17
adj clothing 5.44

dressage 1068.1

dressed clothing 5.44
prepared 405.16

dressed up 354.26

dresser paramedic
90.11
theatre man 704.23

dress in 5.42

dressing clothing 5.1
stuffing 10.26
application 86.33
fertilizer 889.4
abrasion 1042.2
cultivation 1067.13

dressing-down 604.5

dressing room
wardrobe 197.15
stage 704.16

dressmaker 5.35

dressmaking 5.31

dress rehearsal 704.13

dress up get up 5.41
falsify 354.16
ornament 498.8

dribble
noun saliva 13.3
leakage 190.5
trickle 238.7
modicum 248.2
game 745.3
basketball game 751.3
verb salivate 13.6
leak 190.14
trickle 238.18
play 745.4, 750.7,
751.4

dribbling 1063.17

dried 1064.9

dried-up shrunk 260.13
wasted 393.35
unproductive 890.4
dried 1064.9

drier colour 35.8
palette 712.18
desiccator 1064.4

drift
noun direction 161.1
deviation 164.1
course 172.2
drift angle 184.28
flow 238.4
meaning 518.1
flock 769.5
pile 769.10
trend 895.2
reception 1033.21
verb stray 164.4
wander 177.23
drift off course 182.29

float 182.54
fly 184.36
do nothing 329.2
take it easy 331.15
pile 769.19
phrase deposit 176.9

drift away 168.2

drifter bum 331.9
fisher 382.6
wretch 660.2
transient 827.4

drifting
noun deviation 164.1
wandering 177.3
adj flowing 172.8
wandering 177.37

driftwood 1052.3

drill
noun exercise 84.2,
725.6
point 285.3
action 328.1
rule 373.5
manner 384.1
training 568.3
study 570.3
cutlery 1039.2
verb deepen 275.8
excavate 284.15
perforate 292.15
train 568.13
study 570.12
plant 1067.18

drilling extraction
192.1
deepening 275.7
training 568.3

drink
noun potation 8.4
beverage 10.47
dram 88.7
cocktail 88.9
spirits 88.13
fluid 1059.2
verb drink in 8.29
tipple 88.24
ingest 187.11
absorb 187.13

drinkable
noun beverage 10.47
adj potable 8.34

drinker 88.11

drink in drink 8.29
absorb 570.7
attend to 982.5

drinking
noun imbibing 8.3,
88.4
ingestion 187.4
adj bibulous 88.35

drinking water 1063.3

drink to drink 8.29
toast 88.29

drip
noun weakling 16.6
drag 118.5
leakage 190.5
trickle 238.7

verb leak 190.14
trickle 238.18
be damp 1063.11

dripping
noun leakage 190.5
trickle 238.7
adj soaked 1063.17

drive
noun vim 17.2
power 18.1
desire 100.1
acceleration 174.4
ride 177.7
enterprise 330.7
impulse 365.1, 901.1
urge 375.6
haste 401.1
campaign 458.4
attack 459.1
vigour 544.3
flock 769.5
cause 885.9
pushing 903.1
machinery 1039.3
disk drive 1041.5
verb set in motion
172.6
ride 177.33
drift off course 182.29
pilot 184.37
excavate 284.15
hustle 330.13
hunt 382.9
compel 424.4
launch an attack
459.17
guide 573.9
task 725.16
play 747.4, 748.4,
750.7
play tennis 749.3
race 756.4, 757.5
impel 901.11
thrust 901.12
push 903.9
obsess 925.25
herd 1068.8

drive at 380.4

drive away dissipate
770.5
repulse 907.3

drive back 460.10

drive in 191.7

drive-in 8.17

drivel
noun saliva 13.3
nonsense 520.2
verb salivate 13.6
talk nonsense 520.5
be incomprehensible
522.10
be stupid 921.12
be insane 925.20

drive on hustle 330.13
hasten 401.4

drive out 908.14

driver reinsman 178.9
motorist 178.10
tyrant 575.14

man 577.4
race driving 756.2
operator 888.4
propeller 903.6

driver's seat 417.10

driving
noun riding 177.6
race 756.3
adj moving 172.7
rainy 316.10
enterprising 330.23
motivating 375.25
compulsory 424.10
attacking 459.29
vigorous 544.11
impelling 901.23
propulsive 903.14
obsessive 925.34

driving force 903.1

drizzle
noun rain 316.1
verb rain 316.9

Dr Johnson 541.8

droll humorous 488.4
witty 489.15

drone
noun slowcoach 175.5
bee 311.33
nonworker 331.11
mumbling 525.4
part 708.22
regularity 780.2
series 811.2
repetitiousness 848.4
verb hum 52.13
mumble 525.9
persist 780.3

droning
noun hum 52.7
mumbling 525.4
adj sounding 50.15
humming 52.20

drooling 921.22

droop
noun gait 177.12
sinkage 194.2
hang 202.2
verb weaken 16.9
burn out 21.5
fail 85.47
lose heart 112.16
sink 194.6
hang 202.6
languish 393.18

drooping weak 16.12
languishing 16.21
tired 21.7
dejected 112.22
descending 194.11
droopy 202.10
deteriorating 393.45
loose 803.5

droopy weak 16.12
tired 21.7
dejected 112.22
drooping 202.10
languid 331.20

drop
noun drink 88.7

leakage 190.5
descent 194.1
declivity 204.5
trickle 238.7
modicum 248.2
decline 252.2
minutia 258.7
droplet 282.3
plunge 367.1
deterioration 393.3
scaffold 605.5
scenery 704.20
match 747.3
pause 856.3
verb give birth 1.3
take off 6.6
weaken 16.9
burn out 21.5
faint 25.5
lay 78.9
snub 157.5
leak 190.14
descend 194.5
incline 204.10
trickle 238.18
decrease 252.6
gravitate 297.15
strike dead 308.17
plunge 367.6
give up 370.7
break the habit 374.3
cease to use 390.4
relinquish 475.3
cheapen 633.6
play 747.4
shoot 903.12
repulse 907.3
fell 912.5
let go of 912.7

drop dead 307.22

drop-dead 249.13

drop goal 746.3

drop in enter 189.7
visit 582.19

drop it 106.7

drop off go to sleep
22.16
descend 194.5
decrease 252.6
croak 307.20

drop on 194.10

drop out dissent 333.4
abandon 370.5
not conform 867.4

drop-out 746.3

dropout 867.3

dropped born 1.4
reduced 252.10

dropping
noun descent 194.1
adj descending 194.11
downhill 204.16

dropping out dissent
333.1
relinquishment 370.3

droppings 12.4

drops 86.4

dross dregs 256.2

refuse 391.4
scoria 1019.16

drought appetite 100.7
want 991.4
dryness 1064.1

drove
noun flock 769.5
verb drive 1068.8

drown die a natural
death 307.24
strangle 308.18
submerge 367.7
suppress 428.8
come to grief 1010.10
flood 1063.14

drowned flooded
238.25
gulfy 242.2
underwater 275.13
soaked 1063.17

drowning violent death
307.6
suffocation 308.6
wetting 1063.6

drowsiness sleepiness
22.1
languor 331.6

drowsy sleepy 22.21
tranquillizing 670.15

drubbing defeat 412.1
corporal punishment
604.4
hit 901.4

drudgery 725.4

drug
noun anaesthetic 25.3
medicine 86.4
narcotic drug 86.5
narcotic 87.2
moderator 670.3
commodity 735.2
verb put to sleep
22.20
deaden 25.4
medicate 91.25
numb 94.8
moderate 670.6

drug abuse 87.1

drug addict 87.20

drug addiction
substance abuse 87.1
psychosis 925.3

drugged sleepy 22.21
unconscious 25.8
unfeeling 94.9
languid 331.20

drugs 732.3

drugstore 86.36

drug testing 937.6

drug use 87.1

drug user 87.20

Druid idolater 697.4
Druidess 699.14
predictor 961.4

Druidism 697.1

drum
noun staccato 55.1

cylinder 282.4
percussion instrument
711.16
verb thrum 55.4
warble 60.5
rain 316.9
beat time 708.44
din 848.10
pulsate 915.12

drum machine 711.16

drummer percussionist
710.10
travelling salesman
730.4

drumming
noun staccato 55.1
hit 901.4
pulsation 915.3
adj staccato 55.7
rainy 316.10

drum up grab 472.9
assemble 769.18

drunk
noun binge 88.6
drinker 88.11
lush 88.12
adj intoxicated 88.31
fervent 93.18
dizzy 984.15

drunken intoxicated
88.31
bibulous 88.35
dizzy 984.15

drunkenness drinking
8.3
intoxication 88.1
intemperance 669.1
dizziness 984.4

dry
noun conservative
611.13
prohibitionist 668.5
verb preserve 397.9
strip 480.24
desiccate 1064.6
adj raucous 58.15
sour 67.5
thirsty 100.26
dull 117.6
tedious 118.9
right 219.4
satiric 508.13
sober 516.3
plain-speaking 535.3
conservative 611.25
prohibitionist 668.11
unproductive 890.4
unimaginative 986.5
arid 1064.7

Dry Ice ice 1022.5
coolant 1023.7

dry ice 316.5

drying
noun food preservation
397.2
desiccation 1064.3
adj dehydrating
1064.10

drying out 87.1

drying up want 991.4
drying 1064.3

dry land 234.1

dryly 117.10

dryness raucousness
58.2
sourness 67.1
appetite 100.7
dullness 117.1
unproductiveness
890.1
unimaginativeness
986.1
aridness 1064.1

dry out use 87.21
sober up 516.2
swear off 668.8

dry rot rot 393.7
blight 1000.2

dry up shrink 260.9
be consumed 388.4
languish 393.18
dry 1064.6

dual
noun number 530.8
adj two 872.6

dualism theism 675.5
doubleness 872.1
pluralism 951.5

duality 872.1

dub smooth 287.5
name 527.11

dubbed 527.14

dubbing 527.2

dubious deceptive
356.21
irresolute 362.9
dishonest 645.16
agnostic 695.20
doubting 954.9
unbelievable 954.10
improbable 968.3
doubtful 970.17
unsafe 1005.11

duce leader 574.6
tyrant 575.14

duchess 608.6

duchy state 231.5
country 232.1

duck
noun guy 76.5
poultry 311.29
submergence 367.2
avoidance 368.1
darling 562.6
match 747.3
card 758.2
retreat 902.3
crouch 912.3
verb avoid 164.6
retract 168.3
prevaricate 344.7
submerge 367.7
dodge 368.8
shirk 368.9
fight 754.4
crouch 912.8
bow 912.9

flood 1063.14

ducking submergence
367.2
shirking 368.2
fight 754.3
depression 912.1
soaking 1063.7

duckling fledgling
302.10
poultry 311.29
darling 562.6

ducks doll 104.15
darling 562.6

duct vessel 2.21
channel 239.1

dud
noun flop 410.2
abortion 410.5
loser 410.8
thing of naught 763.2
adj imperfect 1002.4

dude 76.5

due
noun debt 623.1
one's due 639.2
prerogative 642.1
adj expected 130.13
owed 623.10, 639.7
right 637.3
entitled to 639.10
just 649.8
attributable 887.6
sufficient 990.6
adv directly 161.23

duel
noun single combat
457.7
fight 754.3
verb contend 457.13

dues debt 623.1
fee 630.6
deserts 639.3

duet cooperation 450.1
part music 708.18
two 872.2

due to
prep because of 887.9
conj resulting from
886.8

duff
verb make a boo-boo
974.15
adj lousy 999.8
imperfect 1002.4
inferior 1004.9

duffel equipment 385.4
impedimenta 471.3

dugout cave 284.5
hiding place 346.4
entrenchment 460.5
shelter 1008.3

duke 608.4

dull
verb weaken 16.10
deaden 25.4
decolour 36.5
muffle 51.9
blunt 94.7, 286.2

relieve 120.5
moderate 670.6
mat 1026.10
adj weak 16.12
insensible 25.6
colourless 36.7
grey 39.4
muffled 52.17
unfeeling 94.9
apathetic 94.13
inexcitable 106.10
dry 117.6
tedious 118.9
inert 173.14
blunt 286.3
languid 331.20
plain-speaking 535.3
prosaic 721.5
dull of mind 921.16
unimaginative 986.5
mediocre 1004.7
lacklustre 1026.17

dulled muffled 52.17
blunt 286.3

dullness weakness 16.1
insensibility 25.1
colourlessness 36.1
paleness 36.2
greyness 39.1
muffled tone 52.2
unfeeling 94.1
apathy 94.4
unpleasure 96.1
inexcitability 106.1
dryness 117.1
tediousness 118.2
bluntness 286.1
languor 331.6
prosaism 721.2
stupidity 921.3
unimaginativeness
986.1
mediocrity 1004.1
flatness 1026.5

dully apathetically
94.15
dryly 117.10
tediously 118.13
inertly 173.20
uniformly 780.7

duly rightly 637.4
rightfully 639.11
justly 649.11

dumb mute 51.12
animal 311.38
taciturn 344.9
stammering 525.13
stupid 921.15
foolish 922.8
ignorant 929.12
inanimate 1053.5

dumbfounded mute
51.12
wondering 122.9

dummy
noun mute 51.3
reproduction 336.3
figure 349.6
fake 354.13
instrument 384.4

composition 548.2
figurehead 575.5
deputy 576.1
follower 616.8
bridge 758.3
thing of naught 763.2
artist's model 785.5
substitute 861.2
blockhead 923.4
nobody 997.7
adj spurious 354.26
substitute 861.8

dump
noun sink 80.12
put-down 156.3
slum 228.11
derelict 370.4
store 386.1
storehouse 386.6
rubbish heap 391.6
armoury 462.2
verb place 159.12
load 159.15
abandon 370.5
discard 390.7
relinquish 475.3
sell 734.8, 737.24
unload 908.23

dumping placement
159.6
discard 390.3
relinquishment 475.1

dumps sulks 110.10
blues 112.6

dumpy corpulent
257.18
dwarf 258.13
stubby 268.10

dun
noun appaloosa 311.11
statement 628.3
verb importune 440.12
bill 628.11
adj brown 40.3

dunce stupid person
923.2
ignoramus 929.8

dune hill 237.4
pile 769.10

dung
noun faeces 12.4
fertilizer 889.4
verb defecate 12.13

dungeon 429.8

dunk submerge 367.7
flood 1063.14

dunning
noun importunity
440.3
adj importunate
440.18

duo part music 708.18
two 872.2

duodenal 881.24

duomo 703.1

dupe
noun sycophant 138.3
gull 358.1

instrument 384.4
simple soul 416.3
laughingstock 508.7
agent 576.3
cheater 759.22
trusting soul 953.4
verb deceive 356.14
duplicate 873.3
stultify 922.7

duplicate
noun image 349.5
same 777.3
duplication 784.3,
873.1
verb reproduce 78.7,
777.6
copy 784.8
repeat 848.7
double 872.5
dupe 873.3
multiply 882.6
adj identical 777.7
analogous 783.11
double 873.4

duplicated repeated
848.12
two 872.6
double 873.4

duplication
reproduction 78.1,
336.3, 784.2
duplicate 784.3
repetition 848.1
doubleness 872.1
reduplication 873.1
multiplication 882.4
superfluity 992.4

duplicity
falseheartedness 354.4
deceit 356.3
treachery 645.6
doubleness 872.1

durability substantiality
762.1
endurance 826.1
toughness 1047.1

durable sturdy 762.7
perdurable 826.10
permanent 852.7
tough 1047.4

durables 735.4

duration time 820.1
term 823.3
durability 826.1
perpetuity 828.1

duress power 18.1
coercion 424.3
imprisonment 429.3
necessity 962.1

during 820.14

during the time
820.10

dusk
noun daylight 1024.10
darkishness 1026.2
verb grow dark
1026.12
adj dark 38.9
evening 315.8

darkish 1026.15

dusky dark 38.9
evening 315.8
darkish 1026.15

dust
noun dirt 80.6
basuco 87.6
angel dust 87.17
land 234.1
air 298.2
corpse 307.16
refuse 391.4
rubbish 391.5
powder 1049.5
desert 1064.2
verb clean 79.18
dirty 80.15
sprinkle 770.6

dustbin 391.7

dusted 770.10

dusty grey 39.4
dirty 80.22
dull 117.6
tedious 118.9
wayworn 177.41
stale 841.14
powdery 1049.11
dry 1064.7

duties 155.3

dutiful respectful 155.8
obedient 326.3
observant 434.4
duteous 641.13
pious 692.8

dutifully respectfully
155.13
obediently 326.6
duteously 641.18

duty respect 155.1
function 387.5, 724.3
demand 421.1
tax 630.9
obligation 641.1
charge 643.3
divine service 696.8
rite 701.3
task 724.2

duty-bound 641.16

duty-free 630.16

duvet 295.10

duvet cover 295.10

dwarf
noun modicum 248.2
dwarfling 258.5
fairy 678.8
verb minimize 252.9
adj dwarfed 258.13

dwarfed dwarf 258.13
deformed 265.12
meagre 991.10

dwell inhabit 225.7
endure 826.6

dweller 227.2

dwellers 227.1

dwelling
noun habitation 225.1
abode 228.1

house 228.5
adj resident 225.13

dwell on protract 826.9
emphasize 996.14

dwindle disappear 34.3
fail 85.47
recede 168.2
quiet 173.8
decrease 252.6

dwindling
noun decline 252.2
adj receding 168.5
quiescent 173.12
decreasing 252.11
deteriorating 393.45

dye
noun tint 3.16
colour 35.8
verb colour 35.13
imbue 796.11

dyed 35.16

dyeing 35.11

dying
noun decrease 252.1
death 307.1
terminal case 307.15
deterioration 393.3
extinguishing 1021.2
adj unhealthy 85.53
impatient 135.6
receding 168.5
terminal 307.33
transient 827.7

dying to desirous
100.21
eager 101.8

dyke 75.15

Dylan mariner 183.1
spirit of the sea 240.4

dynamic energetic
17.13
powerful 18.12
enterprising 330.23
dynamical 1038.9

dynamics statics 18.7
motion 172.1
kinetics 1038.3

dynamism energy 17.1
enterprise 330.7

dynamite
noun explosive 462.14
adj great 998.13

dynastic 417.17

dynasty 834.2

dysentery defecation
12.2
anaemia 85.9

dysfunction 638.1

dysfunctional wrong
638.3
inexpedient 995.5

dyspepsia 85.9

E 161.17

each
adj every 863.15
adv apiece 864.19

each and every
noun all 791.3
adj every 863.15

each one 863.15

each other 776.4

eager desirous 100.21
anxious 101.8
expectant 130.11
impatient 135.6
willing 324.5
active 330.17
enterprising 404.8
prepared 405.16
consenting 441.4

eagerly anxiously
101.13
willingly 324.8

eagerness vim 17.2
desire 100.1
enthusiasm 101.1
impatience 135.1
willingness 324.1
hastiness 401.2
consent 441.1
tendency 895.1
ardour 1018.2

eagle
noun hawk 27.11
lightning 174.6
rocket 193.7
bird 311.28
insignia 647.1
heraldic device 647.2
insignia of rank 647.5
specie 728.4
round 748.3
verb play 748.4

ear
noun auditory
apparatus 2.10
hearing 48.1
audition 48.2
lug 48.7
bulge 283.3
spike 310.27
discrimination 943.1
attention 982.1
adj eye 2.26

earache ache 26.5
ear disease 85.15

eared 48.15

ear for good hearing
48.3
aptitude 413.5

earl 608.4

earlier
adj lower 274.8
previous 833.4,
844.10
adv previously 833.6
formerly 836.13

earliest 216.10

early
adj previous 833.4
former 836.10
back 836.12
bright and early 844.7
adv previously 833.6

long ago 836.16
bright and early
844.11

early death 307.5

early enough 844.12

early on 844.11

early-season 313.9

early years 301.1

earn acquire 472.8
be paid 624.20
deserve 639.5

earned 639.9

earnest
noun pledge 438.2
adj zealous 101.9
solemn 111.3
resolute 359.11
attentive 982.15
weighty 996.20

earnestly zealously
101.14
solemnly 111.4
resolutely 359.17

earnestness zeal 101.2
solemnity 111.1
resolution 359.1
attention 982.1

earnings acquisition
472.1
gain 472.3
pay 624.4
receipts 627.1

earring band 280.3
jewel 498.6

earshot earreach 48.4
short distance 223.2

Earth planet 1070.9
world 1070.10

earth
noun ground covering
199.3
horizontal 201.3
lair 228.26
land 234.1
corpse 307.16
shelter 1008.3
matter 1050.2
adj terrestrial 234.4

earthbound terrestrial
234.4
unimaginative 986.5

earthen earthy 234.5
ceramic 742.7

earthenware
noun hard goods 735.4
adj ceramic 742.7

earthly terrestrial 234.4
secularist 695.16
material 1050.10

earthquake 671.5

earth's crust 234.1

earth-shattering
996.23

earthy earthen 234.5
human 312.13
coarse 497.11

populational 606.8
carnal 663.6
vulgar 666.8
secularist 695.16
realistic 986.6

ease
noun rest 20.1
pleasure 95.1
contentment 107.1
relief 120.1
comfort 121.1
leisure 402.1
aid 449.1
elegance 533.1
fluency 544.2
informality 581.1
prosperity 1009.1
facility 1013.1
verb relax 20.7, 670.9
relieve 120.5
release 120.6
comfort 121.6
abate 252.8
lighten 298.6
liberalize 430.13
aid 449.11
extenuate 600.12
calm 670.7
loosen 803.3
allow for 958.5
facilitate 1013.7
soften 1045.6

eased retarded 175.12
lightened 298.11

ease in 191.3

easel 712.18

ease of 480.21

easier said than done
1012.17

easily comfortably
121.14
slowly 175.13
facilely 1013.16
softly 1045.17

easing
noun relief 120.1
decrease 252.1
lightening 298.3
modulation 670.2
facilitation 1013.5
softening 1045.5
adj relieving 120.9
lightening 298.16
mitigating 670.14
softening 1045.16

East 231.6

east
noun points of the
compass 161.3
adj northern 161.14
adv E 161.17

East and West 758.3

East Anglia 231.7

East coast 231.7

East End 230.6

easter
noun north wind 318.9
verb go west 161.8

easterly
noun north wind 318.9
adj northern 161.14
adv east 161.17

eastern 161.14

East Midlands 231.7

eastward
noun points of the
compass 161.3
adv east 161.17

eastwards 161.17

easy
adj pleased 95.14
nonchalant 106.15
content 107.7
comfortable 121.11
at ease 121.12
good-natured 143.14
slow 175.10
light 298.12
indolent 331.19
leisurely 402.6
unstrict 426.5
lenient 427.7
elegant 533.6
fluent 544.9
informal 581.3
cheap 633.7
wanton 665.26
loose 803.5
gullible 953.9
prosperous 1009.12
facile 1013.13
soft 1045.8
adv cautiously 494.12

easy going 1013.1

easygoing unconcerned
102.7
nonchalant 106.15
content 107.7
careless 340.11
unstrict 426.5
lenient 427.7
free 430.21
informal 581.3
dilatory 845.17

easy money 472.3

easy target 1013.3

easy thing 1013.3

easy to find 167.5

easy to understand
521.10

easy victory 411.1

eat feed 8.20
take 134.8
ingest 187.11
consume 388.3
corrode 393.21
etch 713.10

eaten 393.43

eaten up 388.5

eater 8.16

eating
noun feeding 8.1
ingestion 187.4
adj feeding 8.31

eating disorder 672.1

eat out dine 8.21
etch 713.10

eats 10.2

eat up devour 8.22
feast 8.24
enjoy 95.12
consume 388.3
kid oneself 953.6

eau 1063.3

eau de Cologne 70.3

eaves 295.6

eavesdrop listen 48.10
be curious 980.3

eavesdropping audition
48.2
curiosity 980.1

ebb
noun standstill 173.3
tide 238.13
decline 252.2
deterioration 393.3
verb recede 168.2
move 172.5
quiet 173.8
flow 238.16
decrease 252.6
decline 393.17

ebb and flow
noun tide 238.13
alternation 915.5
verb billow 238.22
change 853.5
alternate 915.13

ebbing
noun course 172.2
standstill 173.3
adj receding 168.5
quiescent 173.12
deteriorating 393.45

ebony
noun blackness 38.1
adj black 38.8
dark 1026.13

ebullient excited
105.20
bubbly 320.6
active 330.17
hot 1018.25

eccentric
noun nonconformist
867.3
oddity 869.4
erratic 926.3
adj off-centre 160.12
humorous 488.4
irregular 850.3
inconstant 853.7
unconventional 867.6
abnormal 869.9
odd 869.11
erratic 926.5

eccentricity
humorousness 488.1
irregularity 850.1
inconstancy 853.2
abnormality 869.1
foolishness 922.1
idiosyncrasy 926.1

disposition 977.3

ecclesiastical
ecclesiastic 698.13
churchly 703.15

echelon flight formation
184.12
rank 245.2
battle array 458.3

echo
noun reverberation
54.2
sympathy 93.5
imitator 336.4
response 708.23
keyboard 711.17
reflection 784.7
repetition 848.1
repeat 848.5, 873.2
reaction 902.1
answer 938.1
signal 1035.11
verb reverberate 54.7
respond 93.11
concur 332.9
imitate 336.5
repeat 848.7, 848.11
answer 938.4
reflect 1035.16

echoed 848.12

echoing
noun duplication 873.1
adj resonant 54.9
reverberating 54.11
repetitious 848.14
answering 938.6

eclampsia seizure 85.6
spasm 916.6

eclectic mixed 796.14
combined 804.5

eclecticism selectivity
371.10
sectarianism 675.4
mixture 796.1

eclipse
noun disappearance
34.1
covering 295.1
occultation 1026.8
moon 1070.11
sun 1070.13
verb blind 30.7
overshadow 249.8
cover 295.19
conceal 346.6
darken 1026.9

eclipsed covered
295.31
concealed 346.11
dark 1026.13

ecological 209.9

ecology 1071.1

economic cheap 633.7
economical 635.6
socio-economic 731.22

economical cheap
633.7
thrifty 635.6

economically shortly
268.12
thriftily 635.7

economic community
617.1

economic cycle 731.9

economic expansion
731.9

economic growth
731.9

economic planning
635.1

economics 729.1

economic support
449.3

economic system
731.7

economist economizer
635.3
financier 729.8

economy
noun parsimony 484.1
thrift 635.1
economic system
731.7
adj cheap 633.7

ecosystem 1071.1

ecstasy bennies 87.3
passion 93.2
happiness 95.2
amorousness 104.3
fury 105.8
revelation 683.9
trance 691.3

ecstatic
noun psychic 689.13
adj overjoyed 95.16
frenzied 105.25
abstracted 984.11

ecumenical
nonsectarian 675.27
broad-minded 978.8

eczema allergy 85.33
skin diseases 85.34

eddies 184.29

eddy
noun agitation 105.4
back stream 238.12
whirl 914.2
verb gurge 238.21
whirl 914.11

edge
noun acrimony 17.5
pungency 68.1
summit 198.2
border 211.4
advantage 249.2
straight line 277.2
sharpness 285.1
cutting edge 285.2
verb border 211.10
side 218.4
go sideways 218.5
sharpen 285.7
play 747.4

edged acrimonious
17.14

bordered 211.12
sharp 285.8

edge in enter 189.7
interpose 213.6
intrude 214.5

edge off 164.6

edges 211.1

edging 211.7

edgy excitable 105.28
nervous 128.11
impatient 135.6

edible 8.33

edict announcement
352.2
decree 420.4
law 673.3

edifice house 228.5
structure 266.2

edifying 568.18

edit delete 255.12
comment upon 341.11
revise 392.12
write 547.19

editing deletion 255.5
explanation 341.4
revision 392.4
film editing 706.5

edition rendering 341.2
issue 554.5
score 708.28

editor
noun interpreter 341.7
publisher 554.2
commentator 556.4
examiner 937.17
critic 945.7
systems program
1041.12
adj journalist 555.4

editorial
noun commentary
556.2
adj explanatory 341.15
journalistic 555.5

editor-in-chief 554.2

educate improve 392.9
teach 568.10

educated improved
392.13
learned 570.16,
927.21
informed 927.18

educating 568.18

education cultivation
392.3
teaching 568.1
learning 570.1, 927.4

educational informative
551.18
educative 568.18

educator 571.1

eel 10.23

eerie awesome 122.11
creepy 127.31
deathly 307.29
supernatural 869.15

weird 987.9

eerily awesomely
122.15
oddly 869.19

effect
noun power 18.1
aspect 33.3
intention 380.1
meaning 518.1
relevance 774.4
end 819.1
event 830.1
sequel 834.2
result 886.1
product 892.1
influence 893.1
verb do 328.6
use 384.5
accomplish 407.4
execute 437.9
cause 885.10
induce 885.11
establish 891.10

effected 407.10

effective powerful
18.12
able 18.14
effectual 387.21
vigorous 544.11
operative 888.9
influential 893.13
practical 994.6

effectively powerfully
18.15
ably 18.16
usefully 387.26
eloquently 544.15

effectiveness power
18.1
supremacy 249.3
utility 387.3
vigour 544.3

effects equipment
385.4
property 471.1
merchandise 735.1

effeminate
noun mollycoddle
77.10
verb feminize 77.12
adj frail 16.14
homosexual 75.29
womanish 77.14

effervescent sibilant
57.3
excited 105.20
bubbly 320.6
active 330.17

effete weak 16.12
weakened 16.18
ineffective 19.15
dull 117.6
used up 388.5
worn-out 393.36
deteriorating 393.45

efficacious able 18.14
effectual 387.21
operative 888.9
influential 893.13

efficacy ability 18.2
utility 387.3

efficiency ability 18.2
utility 387.3
skill 413.1

efficient able 18.14
effectual 387.21
competent 413.24
economical 635.6
operative 888.9
practical 994.6

efficiently ably 18.16
usefully 387.26
skilfully 413.31

effigy 349.5

effluent
noun excrement 12.3
tributary 238.3
refuse 391.4
adj outgoing 190.19

effort act 328.3
endeavour 403.1
attempt 403.2
undertaking 404.1
exertion 725.1
expedient 994.2

effortless 1013.13

effortlessly 1013.16

effrontery 142.1

effusive outgoing
190.19
communicative 343.10
diffuse 538.11
talkative 540.9

e.g. 956.23

egalitarianism 789.1

egg ovum 305.12
ovule 305.15

egg on 885.11

eggs 10.25

eggshell
noun egg 305.15
matchwood 1048.2
adj soft-coloured
35.21
whitish 37.8

egg white egg 305.15
semiliquid 1060.5

ego psyche 92.28, 918.4
egotism 140.3
self 864.5

egocentric
noun egotist 140.5
adj unfeeling 94.9
egotistic 140.10

egotism egoism 140.3
selfishness 651.1

egotistical egotistic
140.10
selfish 651.5

eight team 617.7
card 758.2
ogdoad 881.4

eighth
noun octave 709.9
adj octonary 881.20

eighty 881.7

eighty-eight keyboard
711.17
eleven 881.7

eisteddfod musical
occasion 708.32
assembly 769.2

either
noun any 863.5
adj one 871.7
adv similarly 783.18

either-or ambiguous
539.4
two 872.6

either . . . or 371.29

ejaculate exclaim 59.7
climax 75.23
project 903.11
disgorge 908.25

ejaculation excretion
12.1
exclamation 59.2
throwing 903.2
disgorgement 908.7

eject erupt 671.13
eliminate 772.5
separate 801.8
shoot 903.12
repulse 907.3
expel 908.13

ejected 772.7

ejection excretion 12.1
excrement 12.3
outburst 190.3
elimination 772.2
shot 903.4
repulsion 907.1
ejectment 908.1

eke out 385.12

el 179.14

elaborate
verb develop 392.10,
860.6
amplify 538.7
ornament 545.7
produce 891.8
adj painstaking 339.11
ornate 498.12
grandiose 501.21
affected 533.9
complex 798.4

elaborated 533.9

elaborately 501.28

elaboration
development 392.2
ornamentation 498.1
amplification 538.6
iteration 848.2
evolution 860.1
production 891.2

elapse lapse 820.5
pass 836.6

elapsed 836.7

elastic
noun elastomer 1046.3
adj expansive 259.9
recuperative 396.23

pliant 1045.9
resilient 1046.7

elasticity muscularity
15.2
pliancy 1045.2

elated overjoyed 95.16
cheerful 109.11
rejoicing 116.10
puffed up 136.10
crowing 502.13

elation happiness 95.2
rejoicing 116.1
crowing 502.4

elbow
noun member 2.7
angle 278.2
joint 799.4
arm 905.5
verb angle 278.5
thrust 901.12

elder
noun old man 304.2
senior 304.5
master 575.1
minister 575.17
deacon 699.9
back number 841.8
wise man 920.1
personage 996.8
adj previous 833.4
older 841.19

elderly aged 303.16
old 841.10

elders 560.7

elder statesman expert
413.11
statesman 610.2
wise man 920.1

eldest
noun senior 304.5
adj older 841.19

Eldorado 618.4

eldritch 987.9

elect
noun elite 371.12
upper class 607.2
aristocracy 608.1
believing 692.5
best 998.8
verb choose 371.13
vote in 371.20
support 609.41
adj chosen 371.26
exclusive 495.13
best 998.16

elected 371.26

election choice 371.1
appointment 371.9
accession 417.12
general election
609.15
holy orders 698.10
determinism 963.4

electioneering 609.12

elective voluntary
324.7
volitional 371.22
selective 371.23

electoral 371.23

electoral college
609.22

electoral fraud 609.18

electorate population
227.1
state 231.5
selector 371.7
electors 609.22

electors 609.22

electric exciting 105.30
provocative 375.27
electrical 1031.29

electrical 1031.29

electric chair 605.5

electric current
current 1031.2
electron flow 1032.6

electrician stage
technician 704.24
electrotechnician
1031.21

electricity lightning
174.6
telegraph 347.2
illuminant 1024.20
electrical science
1031.1

electric light 1024.19

electric power
manpower 18.4
wattage 1031.17

electrification
excitation 105.11
electrifying 1031.23

electrified startled
131.13
electric 1031.29
charged 1031.33

electrifying
noun electrification
1031.23
adj surprising 131.11
sudden 829.5
electric 1031.29

electromagnetic
1031.30

electron atom 258.8
negatron 1032.3

electronic 1032.15

electronics radio 347.3
radionics 1032.1

elegance parsimony
484.1
taste 496.1
ornateness 498.2
overniceness 500.5
grandeur 501.5
good breeding 504.4
elegancy 533.1
fluency 544.2
smartness 578.3
etiquette 580.3
decency 664.2
beauty 1015.1

elegant graceful 496.9
ornate 498.12

overnice 500.18
grandiose 501.21
tasteful 533.6
fluent 544.9
chic 578.13
decent 664.5
good 998.12
beautiful 1015.17

elegantly tastefully
496.11
affectedly 500.20
grandiosely 501.28
smartly 578.18
beautifully 1015.23

elegiac
noun metre 720.7
adj dirgelike 115.22
poetic 720.15

elegy 115.6

element medium 209.4
particular 765.3
component 795.2
cause 885.1
heater 1019.10
matter 1050.2
chemical element
1058.2

elemental
noun elemental spirit
678.6
adj basic 199.8
climatal 317.12
essential 766.9
beginning 817.15
original 885.14
chemical 1058.8

elementary basic 199.8
essential 766.9
component 795.5
simple 797.6
beginning 817.15
original 885.14
chemical 1058.8

elements contents
196.1
weather 317.3
elementary education
568.5
Eucharist 701.7
substance 762.2
basics 817.6

elephant
noun angel dust 87.17
behemoth 257.14
pachyderm 311.4
phrase beast of burden
176.8

elevate elate 109.8
erect 200.9
heighten 272.13
improve 392.9
promote 446.2
glorify 662.13
raise 911.5
exalt 911.6

elevated
noun train 179.14
adj fuddled 88.33
lofty 136.11, 544.14

eminent 247.9, 662.18
increased 251.7
high 272.14
grandiloquent 545.8
magnanimous 652.6
raised 911.9

elevating 911.10

elevation ascent 193.1
erection 200.4
increase 251.1
height 272.1, 272.2
diagram 381.3
promotion 446.1
loftiness 544.6
magnanimity 652.2
distinction 662.5
glorification 662.8
raising 911.1

elevator
noun garner 386.7
lift 911.4
phrase people mover
176.5

eleven team 617.7,
747.2
legs eleven 881.7

eleven-plus 937.2

eleventh 881.23

eleventh hour curfew
315.5
crucial moment 842.5
lateness 845.1

eleventh-hour 845.18

elf dwarf 258.5
brat 302.4
mischief-maker 322.3
fairy 678.8
imp 680.7

elfin dwarf 258.13
fairy 678.17
fine 1015.19

elicit educe 192.14
prompt 375.13
induce 885.11

eligibility qualification
371.11
inclusion 771.1

eligible
noun eligibility 371.11
adj qualified 371.24

eliminate excrete 12.12
excise 255.10
murder 308.15
discard 390.7
exterminate 395.14
annihilate 761.7
get rid of 772.5
do away with 908.21
evacuate 908.22

elimination excretion
12.1
disappearance 34.1
excision 255.3
homicide 308.2
discard 390.3
extinction 395.6
riddance 772.2
evacuation 908.6

elite
  noun best 249.5, 998.8
  elect 371.12
  society 578.6
  upper class 607.2
  aristocracy 608.1
  clique 617.6
  adj exclusive 495.13
  socially prominent
    578.16
  best 998.16
elitism 141.3
elitist
  noun snob 141.7
  adj lordly 141.11
  intellectual 927.23
elixir panacea 86.3
  medicine 86.4
  extract 192.8
  substance 196.5
  essence 766.2
elk 311.5
ell 278.2
elliptical oblong 267.9
  shortened 268.9
  parabolic 279.13
elongated lengthened
    267.8
  oblong 267.9
eloquence articulateness
    524.5
  public speaking 543.1
  rhetoric 544.1
eloquent speaking
    524.32
  declamatory 543.12
  silver-tongued 544.8
eloquently 544.15
else
  adj other 779.8
  adv additionally
    253.11
  otherwise 779.11
elsewhere
  adj abstracted 984.11
  adv away 222.18
elude evade 368.7
  outwit 415.11
  thwart 1011.15
elusive 368.15
em type 548.6
  space 548.7
emaciated shrunk
    260.13
  haggard 270.20
  wasted 393.35
emanate radiate 171.6
  emerge 190.11
emanate from 886.5
emanating 190.18
emancipation 431.1
emasculated
  unmanned 19.19
  unsexual 75.28
  crippled 393.30
embalmed 828.9

embankment shore
    234.2
  railway 383.7
  pile 769.10
  buttress 900.4
  harbour 1008.6
  barrier 1011.5
embargo
  noun closure 293.1
  prohibition 444.1
  exclusion 772.1
  verb stop 293.7
  prohibit 444.3
  exclude 772.4
embargoed 772.7
embark send 176.15
  get under way 182.19
  go aboard 188.15
embarrass chagrin
    96.15
  mortify 98.13
  humiliate 137.4
  involve 897.2
  bewilder 970.12
  confuse 984.7
  inconvenience 995.4
  hamper 1011.11
  put in a hole 1012.15
embarrassed distressed
    96.22
  humiliated 137.14
  blushing 139.13
  indebted 623.8
  bewildered 970.24
  confused 984.12
  troubled 1012.20
embarrassing
  mortifying 98.21
  humiliating 137.15
  bewildering 970.27
embarrassment
  chagrin 96.4
  mortification 98.6
  humiliation 137.2
  shyness 139.4
  involvement 897.1
  bewilderment 970.3
  confusion 984.3
  impediment 1011.6
  predicament 1012.4
embassy house 228.5
  message 552.4
  foreign office 576.7
  commission 615.1
  office 739.7
embattled 458.23
embedded 854.13
embellish falsify
    354.16
  develop 392.10
  ornament 498.8, 545.7
embellished spurious
    354.26
  improved 392.13
  ornamented 498.11
  ornate 545.11
embellishment
  development 392.2
  ornamentation 498.1

ornateness 545.4
  ornament 709.18
  superfluity 992.4
embezzlement misuse
    389.1
  theft 482.1
embittered sour
    110.23
  aggravated 119.4
  resentful 152.26
  impaired 393.27
emblem symbol 517.2
  insignia 647.1
  example 785.2
emblematic 517.23
embodied 1050.11
embodied in 795.4
embodiment
  manifestation 348.1
  impersonation 349.4
  representative 349.7
  incarnation 762.4
  essence 766.2
  inclusion 771.1
  whole 791.1
  composition 795.1
  materiality 1050.1
  materialization 1050.8
embody manifest 348.5
  image 349.11
  incarnate 762.5
  include 771.3
  compose 795.3
  materialize 1050.9
embodying
  representational
    349.13
  composed of 795.4
embossed in relief
    283.18
  sculptured 715.7
  established 854.13
embrace
  noun hold 474.2
  hug 562.3
  welcome 585.2
  greeting 585.4
  joint 799.4
  verb surround 209.6
  wrap 295.20
  adopt 371.15
  hold 474.6, 474.7
  seize 480.14
  hug 562.18
  welcome 585.9
  include 771.3
  put together 799.5
  join 799.11
  cohere 802.6
embraced chosen
    371.26
  included 771.5
embracing environing
    209.8
  inclusive 771.6
embroidered spurious
    354.26
  ornate 545.11

embroidery
  ornamentation 498.1
  ornateness 545.4
embryo 305.14
embryonic infinitesimal
    258.14
  germinal 305.22
  undeveloped 406.12
  incomplete 794.4
  beginning 817.15
  original 885.14
emerald 44.4
emerald-green 44.4
emerge show 31.4
  appear 33.8
  come out 190.11
  find vent 369.10
emerge from 886.5
emergence appearance
    33.1
  coming out 190.1
  escape 369.1
emergency hospital
  room 197.25
  crisis 842.4
  urgency 996.4
  danger 1005.1
  predicament 1012.4
emergent emerging
    190.18
  future 838.8
  critical 842.10
emerging 190.18
emeritus
  noun professor 571.3
  adj retired 448.3
emery 287.8
emigrate migrate
    177.22
  leave home 188.17
  out-migrate 190.16
emigration migration
    177.4
  out-migration 190.7
Eminence 648.2
eminence hill 237.4
  glory 247.2
  height 272.1, 272.2
  prestige 417.4
  distinction 662.5
  influence 893.1
  notability 996.2
eminent prominent
    247.9
  superior 249.12
  high 272.14, 662.18
  protruding 283.14
  authoritative 417.15
  notable 996.19
eminently intensely
    247.20
  superlatively 249.16
  famously 662.21
  importantly 996.25
emir sultan 575.10
  prince 608.7
  Sir 648.3

emirate 417.7
emissary messenger
    353.1
  delegate 576.2
  diplomat 576.6
emission excretion
    12.1
  emergence 190.1
  disgorgement 908.7
emit excrete 12.12
  exude 190.15
  issue 352.14
  say 524.23
  let out 908.24
  vaporize 1065.8
emitting 190.1
Emmy 646.2
emotion feeling 93.1
  excitement 105.1
  attitude 977.1
emotional affective
    93.17
  sensitive 93.20
  excitable 105.28
  attitudinal 977.7
emotional life 93.1
emotionally feelingly
    93.25
  attitudinally 977.9
emotive emotional
    93.17
  emotionalistic 93.19
  affecting 93.22
empathy sensitivity
    24.3
  sympathy 93.5
  accord 455.1
emperor 575.8
emphasis accent
    524.11, 709.25
  metre 720.7
emphasize 996.14
emphasized 996.21
emphatic affirmative
    334.8
  vehement 544.13
  decided 996.21
emphatically intensely
    247.20
  affirmatively 334.10
empire country 232.1
  governance 417.5
  sovereignty 417.8
  government 612.1
empirical real 760.15
  experimental 941.11
employ
  noun use 387.1
  service 577.12
  occupation 724.1
  verb practice 328.8
  use 387.10
  spend 387.13
  hire 615.14
  occupy 724.10
  exert 725.8
employed busy 330.21

used 387.24
hired 615.20
employee subordinate
432.5
pensioner 577.3
assistant 616.6
worker 726.2
employees 577.11
employer user 387.9
master 575.1
employing 387.8
employment action
328.1
use 387.1
utilization 387.8
service 577.12
engagement 615.4
occupation 724.1
position 724.5
work 725.4
emporium market
736.1
marketplace 736.2
empower enable 18.10
authorize 443.11
commission 615.10
empowered
authoritative 417.15
authorized 443.17
empowerment
enablement 18.8
accession 417.12
authorization 443.3
commission 615.1
empress 575.11
emptied 393.36
emptiness unpleasure
96.1
appetite 100.7
dullness 117.1
space 158.1
vacancy 222.2
void 222.3
concavity 284.1
insincerity 354.5
futility 391.2
meaninglessness 520.1
nonexistence 761.1
empty-headedness
921.6
triviality 997.3
empty
verb run out 190.13
draw off 192.12
evacuate 908.22
adj ineffective 19.15
hungry 100.25
dull 117.6
vacant 222.14
concave 284.16
insincere 354.32
vain 391.14
meaningless 520.6
inexpressive 522.20
nonexistent 761.8
empty-headed 921.19
ignorant 929.12
thoughtless 932.4
sophistical 935.10

baseless 935.13
trivial 997.19
empty-handed 991.12
emptying drawing
192.3
evacuation 908.6
empty of
adj wanting 991.13
prep absent 222.19
empty space space
158.1, 1070.3
airspace 184.32
void 222.3
empty stomach 100.7
emulate follow 336.7
compete 457.18
set an example 785.7
excel 998.11
emulation imitation
336.1
competition 457.2
emulsion film 714.10
emulsoid 1060.7
solution 1062.3
en type 548.6
space 548.7
enable empower 18.10
fit 405.8
authorize 443.11
include 771.3
make possible 965.5
enabling 443.3
enact perform 328.9
manifest 348.5
impersonate 349.12
accomplish 407.4
legislate 613.9
legalize 673.8
act out 704.30
enacting 349.4
enactment performance
328.2
display 348.2
impersonation 349.4
legislation 613.4
legalization 673.2
law 673.3
enamel
noun blanket 295.12
verb colour 35.13
coat 295.24
adj ceramic 742.7
enamelled 35.16
enamoured 104.28
enamoured of 104.30
encampment camping
225.4
camp 228.29
campground 463.3
encapsulate shorten
268.6
wrap 295.20
abridge 557.5
iterate 848.8
encapsulated 268.9
encased packed 212.12
covered 295.31

enchanted overjoyed
95.16
enamoured 104.28
wondering 122.9
charmed 691.12
miraculous 869.16
gripped 982.18
dreamy 985.25
enchanting delightful
97.7
alluring 377.8
bewitching 691.11
influential 893.13
engrossing 982.20
enchantment happiness
95.2
delightfulness 97.2
amorousness 104.3
allurement 377.1
sorcery 690.1
bewitchment 691.2
miracle 869.8
influence 893.1
bad influence 999.4
encircled circled
209.11
circumscribed 210.6
encircling environing
209.8
inclusive 771.6
enclave enclosure 212.3
plot 231.4
enclose internalize
207.5
surround 209.6
circumscribe 210.4
bound 211.8
close in 212.5
confine 429.12
include 771.3
enclosed
noun enclosure 196.6
adj surrounded 209.10
closed-in 212.10
confined 429.19
enclosing environing
209.8
confining 212.11
inclusive 771.6
enclosure enclosed
196.6
surrounding 209.5
confinement 212.1
close 212.3
place of confinement
429.7
fortification 460.4
horse racing 757.1
encoded 345.16
encompass extend
158.8
surround 209.6
enclose 212.5
circle 280.10, 913.5
wrap 295.20
besiege 459.19
include 771.3
total 791.8
put together 799.5

combine 804.3
encompassed
surrounded 209.10
included 771.5
encompassing
noun surrounding
209.5
adj environing 209.8
inclusive 771.6
encore
noun repeat
performance 848.6
repeat 873.2
verb applaud 509.10
adv again 848.17,
873.7
encounter
noun meeting 223.4
contest 457.3
impact 901.3
verb approach 167.3
confront 216.8, 451.5
meet 223.11
experience 830.8
collide 901.13
come across 940.3
encourage cheer 109.7
comfort 121.6
hearten 375.21,
492.16
admonish 422.6
abet 449.14
be useful 449.17
encouragement
consolation 121.4
urging 375.5
incentive 375.7
patronage 449.4
heartening 492.9
encouraging cheering
109.16
comforting 121.13
promising 124.13
provocative 375.27
encouragingly 121.16
encroachment
intrusion 214.1
impairment 393.1
usurpation 640.3
overstepping 909.3
encumbered weighted
297.18
indebted 623.8
encyclopedia reference
book 554.9
lore 927.9
encyclopedic
comprehensive 771.7
learned 927.21
end
noun boundary 211.3
remainder 256.1
death 307.1
motive 375.1
objective 380.2
fate 395.2, 963.2
portion 477.5
piece 792.3
limit 793.5

end 819.1
end point 819.1
stop 856.2
immediate cause 885.3
solution 939.1
verb kill 308.12
put an end to 395.12
perish 395.23
complete 407.6
terminate 819.5
cease 856.6
result 886.4
adj completion 407.2
end-all 819.4
endanger 1005.6
endangered 1005.13
endear 104.23
endearing delightful
97.7
lovable 104.25
endeavour
noun act 328.3
effort 403.1
attempt 403.2
exertion 725.1
verb strive 403.5
undertake 404.3
exert oneself 725.9
endeavour to 403.8
ended completed
407.11
at an end 819.8
endemic contagious
85.61
native 226.5
ender 819.4
ending
noun death 307.1
end 819.1
cessation 856.1
stop 856.2
adj completion 407.2
closing 819.10
end in itself 380.2
endless wordy 538.12
continuous 811.8
infinite 822.3
perpetual 828.7
continuing 855.7
innumerable 883.10
endlessly tediously
118.13
continuously 811.10
infinitely 822.4
perpetually 828.10
endocrine 13.8
end of the line
destination 186.5
railway 383.7
stop 856.2
endorse ratify 332.12
adopt 371.15
secure 438.9
consent 441.2
abet 449.14
approve 509.9
support 609.41

endorsed 332.14

endorsement
ratification 332.4
consent 441.1
approval 509.1
signature 527.10

endorsing 441.4

endow empower 18.10
provide 385.7
invest 478.17
establish 891.10

endowed provided
385.13
talented 413.29
dowered 478.26

endowed with 469.9

endowment
empowerment 18.8
provision 385.1
talent 413.4
support 449.3
giving 478.1
investment 478.9
heredity 560.6

end product product
892.1
fissionable material
1037.10

end result 939.1

end-to-end 223.16

end up arrive 186.6
end 819.5
come to an end 819.6
result 886.4

endurance strength
15.1
patience 134.1
perseverance 360.1
durability 826.1
continuance 855.1

endure bear 134.5
condone 148.4
keep alive 306.10
persevere 360.2
suffer 443.10
resist 453.2
afford 626.7
live on 760.9
elapse 820.5
experience 830.8
remain 852.5
continue 855.3
toughen 1047.3

enduring patient 134.9
persevering 360.8
sturdy 762.7
durable 826.10
permanent 852.7
remembered 988.23

enema washing 79.5
cleanser 79.17
clyster 86.19
sprinkler 1063.8

enemy
noun opponent 452.1
foe 589.6
adj oppositional 451.8
warlike 458.21

energetic vigorous
17.13
powerful 18.12
active 330.17
industrious 330.22

energetically
vigorously 17.16
powerfully 18.15
actively 330.25
industriously 330.27

energy
noun strength 15.1
vigour 17.1
power 18.1
liveliness 330.2
industry 330.6
exertion 725.1
adj fuel 1020.8

energy level electron
1032.3
atomic energy 1037.15

energy source energy
17.1
fuel 1020.1

enfant terrible brat
302.4
mischief-maker 322.3

enfeebled weakened
16.18
tired 21.7

enforce apply 387.11
compel 424.4
execute 437.9
legalize 673.8

enforceable 673.10

enforcement
compulsion 424.1
execution 437.4

enforcing 643.2

engage induce 375.22
attract 377.6
attempt 403.6
commit 436.5
contract 437.5
take on 457.16
employ 615.14
occupy 724.10
interact 776.6
involve 897.2
engross 982.13

engaged busy 330.21
promised 436.8
contracted 437.11
embattled 458.23
participating 476.8
engrossed 982.17

engage in practice
328.8
undertake 404.3
busy oneself with
724.11

engagement
inducement 375.3
undertaking 404.1
obligation 436.2
betrothal 436.3
contest 457.3
participation 476.1

proposal 562.8
appointment 582.8
employment 615.4
playing engagement
704.11
position 724.5
interaction 776.3
involvement 897.1
engrossment 982.3

engagement ring
498.6

engage with 457.17

engaging delightful
97.7
alluring 377.8
engrossing 982.20

engagingly delightfully
97.13
alluringly 377.9

engender procreate
78.8
beget 817.14
cause 885.10
produce 889.7
originate 891.12

engine philosopher's
stone 857.10
machinery 1039.3

engineer
noun train driver
178.12
planner 381.6
combat engineer
461.13
professional engineer
726.7
producer 891.7
verb plot 381.9
manage 409.12
manoeuvre 415.10
direct 573.8
perform 891.11

engineered 354.30

engineering intrigue
381.5
engineer 726.7
production 891.2
mechanical engineering
1038.6

engineers 1038.6

English breakfast 8.6

English Heritage
397.5

English literature
547.12, 718.1

English-speaking
524.32

engraved indented
284.17
furrowed 290.4
graven 713.11
sculptured 715.7
established 854.13

engraver recorder
550.1
printmaker 716.8

engraving excavation
284.11

furrow 290.1
mark 517.5
visual arts 712.1
picture 712.11
engravement 713.2
sculpture 715.1

engrossed written
547.22
absorbed 982.17
abstracted 984.11

engrossed in 982.17

engrossing 982.20

engulf ingest 187.11
overflow 238.17
submerge 367.7
overwhelm 395.21
oversupply 992.14

engulfed flooded
238.25
underwater 275.13
soaked 1063.17

enhance aggravate
119.2
intensify 251.5
improve 392.9

enhanced aggravated
119.4
increased 251.7
improved 392.13

enhancement
aggravation 119.1
intensification 251.2
exaggeration 355.1
improvement 392.1

enigma secret 345.5
mystery 522.8
unknown 929.7
bewilderment 970.3
dilemma 1012.7

enigmatic wonderful
122.10
secret 345.11
enigmatical 522.17
ambiguous 539.4
unknown 929.17
bewildering 970.27

enigmatically
wonderfully 122.14
inexplicably 522.24

enjoy savour 63.5
pleasure in 95.12
possess 469.4

enjoyable 97.6

enjoyment pleasure
95.1
amusement 743.1

enlarge aggravate 119.2
increase 251.4
size 257.15
expand 259.4, 259.5
amplify 538.7
process 714.15
elaborate 860.6

enlarged aggravated
119.4
increased 251.7
expanded 259.10

furrow 290.1
mark 517.5
visual arts 712.1
picture 712.11
engravement 713.2
sculpture 715.1

enlargement
aggravation 119.1
increase 251.1
expansion 259.1
exaggeration 355.1
amplification 538.6
print 714.5, 784.5
evolution 860.1

enlarging 538.15

enlighten explain
341.10
improve 392.9
inform 551.8
teach 568.10
disillusion 976.2
illuminate 1024.28

enlightened judicious
919.19
informed 927.18
disillusioned 976.5
illuminated 1024.39

enlightening
explanatory 341.15
informative 551.18
educational 568.18
disillusioning 976.4
liberalizing 978.13

enlightenment
explanation 341.4
cultivation 392.3
information 551.1
teaching 568.1
learning 927.4
disillusionment 976.1

enlist install 191.4
induce 375.22
participate 476.5
list 615.17
join 617.14
take one's turn 824.5

enliven refresh 9.2
energize 17.10
stimulate 105.13
cheer 109.7
inspire 375.20
amuse 743.21

enlivened 306.11

en masse cooperatively
450.6
together 768.11
wholly 791.13

enmeshed in 897.5

enmity hostility 99.2,
451.2
bitterness 103.2
disaccord 456.1
contention 457.1
unfriendliness 589.1

ennui unpleasure 96.1
weariness 118.3
languor 331.6

enormity indignity
156.2
hugeness 257.7
misdeed 655.2
baseness 661.3

enormous large 247.7
huge 257.20

excessive 992.16
terrible 999.9

enormously 247.16

enough
noun sufficiency 990.1
adj satisfactory 107.11
sufficient 990.6
adv satisfactorily
107.15
sufficiently 990.8

enough said 399.1

enraged infuriated
152.32
turbulent 671.18

enraptured overjoyed
95.16
enamoured 104.28
frenzied 105.25
wondering 122.9

enrich vitaminize 7.18
improve 392.9
ornament 498.8, 545.7
richen 618.9
fertilize 889.8

enriched 392.13

enriching 889.11

enrichment
vitaminization 7.12
improvement 392.1
fertilization 889.3

enrol install 191.4
record 549.15
be taught 570.11
enlist 615.17
join 617.14
list 870.8

enrolled 549.17

enrolment admission
187.2
registration 549.14
enlistment 615.7
index 870.7

en route 176.20

en route to 161.26

ensconced 159.18

ensemble
noun furniture 229.1
cast 707.11
orchestra 710.12
chorus 710.16
all 791.3
compound 796.5
adv together 768.11

enshrine enclose 212.5
inter 309.19
glorify 662.13
sanctify 685.5
exalt 911.6

enshrined eminent
662.18
raised 911.9

ensign insignia 647.1
flag 647.6

enslaved 432.14

enslavement subjection
432.1
appropriation 480.4

ensue succeed 814.2
result 886.4

ensuing
noun subsequence
834.1
adj succeeding 814.4
subsequent 834.4
resultant 886.6

ensure secure 438.9
make sure 969.11
protect 1007.18

ensured 438.11

ensuring 969.8

entail
noun inheritance 479.2
verb bequeath 478.18
signify 517.17
imply 519.4
transfer 629.3
involve 771.4
determine 885.12

entailed mandatory
420.12
resultant 886.6
necessary 962.12

entangled 798.4

entente treaty 437.2
understanding 787.2

enter appear 33.8
insert 191.3
record 549.15
join 617.14
keep accounts 628.8
list 870.8

entered recorded
549.17
listed 870.9

entering
noun registration
549.14
adj arriving 186.9
ingressive 189.12

enter into participate
476.5
compose 795.3
put together 799.5

enterprise vim 17.2
act 328.3
enterprisingness 330.7
plan 381.1
endeavour 403.1
undertaking 404.1
daring 492.5
exploit 492.7
company 617.9
occupation 724.1

enterprising energetic
17.13
aggressive 330.23
venturesome 404.8
daring 492.22

entertain hold 474.7
entertain guests 585.8
amuse 743.21
take under
consideration 930.14

entertained 743.26

entertainer 707.1

entertaining 743.27

entertainment meal
8.5
pleasure 95.1
party 582.11
theatrical performance
704.12
amusement 743.1
entertainment industry
743.13

**entertainment
industry** show
business 704.1
entertainment 743.13

enthralled wondering
122.9
subjugated 432.14
gripped 982.18

enthralling delightful
97.7
alluring 377.8
engrossing 982.20

enthroned 662.18

enthronement
installation 615.3
glorification 662.8

enthusiasm animation
17.4
eagerness 101.1
willingness 324.1
vehemence 544.5
mania 925.12
interest 982.2

enthusiast zealot 101.4
collector 769.15
fanatic 925.18
visionary 985.13

enthusiastic energetic
17.13
fervent 93.18
enthused 101.10
willing 324.5
vehement 544.13
interested 982.16

enthusiastic about
101.10

enthusiastically
fervently 93.26
eagerly 101.13
willingly 324.8

entice 377.5

enticing 377.8

entire
noun cock 76.8
horse 311.10
adj whole 791.9
complete 793.9
unqualified 959.2
sound 1001.7

entirely wholly 791.13
completely 793.14
solely 871.14
perfectly 1001.10

entirety whole 791.1
all 791.3
completeness 793.1

entitle authorize 443.11
name 527.11

entitled authorized
443.17
warranted 639.9

entitled to 639.10

entitlement promise
436.1
authorization 443.3
dueness 639.1

entity existence 760.1
something 762.3
individual 871.4

entourage follower
166.2
environment 209.1
attendance 768.6

entrails mouth 2.16
insides 207.4

entrance
noun entree 187.3
entry 189.1, 189.5
insertion 191.1
vestibule 197.19
intrusion 214.1
channel 239.1
door 292.6
verb put to sleep
22.20
delight 95.9
fascinate 377.7
cast a spell 691.7

entranced overjoyed
95.16
wondering 122.9
dreamy 985.25

entrance hall 197.19

entrancing delightful
97.7
alluring 377.8
bewitching 691.11

entrant incomer 189.4
competitor 452.2
novice 572.9
beginner 817.2

entree serving 8.10
dish 10.7
entrée 187.3
entrance 189.1

entrenched 854.13

entrepreneur 730.1

entrepreneurial 730.12

entropy inertness 173.4
formlessness 263.1
information technology
551.7
noncohesion 803.1
disorder 809.1
change 851.1
uncertainty 970.1

entrust commit 478.16
commission 615.10

entry entree 187.3
entrance 189.1, 189.5
vestibule 197.19
door 292.6
memorandum 549.4
registration 549.14
item 628.5

entwined 740.7

enunciated affirmed
334.9
speech 524.30

envelope
noun exterior 206.2
wrapper 295.18
illustriousness 662.6
verb besiege 459.19

enveloped surrounded
209.10
covered 295.31

enveloping environing
209.8
covering 295.35

enviable 100.30

envious discontented
108.7
jealous 153.5
envying 154.4

environment
surroundings 209.1
element 209.4
surrounding 209.5
circumstances 765.2
natural world 1071.1

environmental
environal 209.9
environing 765.8

environmentalist
1071.3

**environmental
pollution**
unhealthfulness 82.1
evil 999.3
environmental
destruction 1071.2

**environmental
protection** 1071.1

environs environment
209.1
nearness 223.1
region 231.1

envisage expect 130.5
contemplate 380.5,
930.17
include 771.3
come 838.6
foresee 960.5
visualize 985.15

envisaged intentional
380.8
included 771.5
future 838.8

envisioned intentional
380.8
future 838.8

envoy delegate 576.2
diplomat 576.6

envy discontent 108.1
jealousy 153.1
enviousness 154.1

enzyme 7.9

Eos 314.2

ephemera 827.5

ephemeral
noun plant 310.3

ephemeron 827.5
adj mortal 307.34
perennial 310.41
unsubstantial 763.5
transient 827.7

epic
noun story 719.3
adj huge 257.20
poetic 720.15

epicentre 671.5

epidemic
noun plague 85.5
adj contagious 85.61
prevalent 863.12
plentiful 990.7

epidemiology hygiene
81.2
infection 85.4

epilepsy seizure 85.6
spasm 916.6

epileptic
noun sick person 85.42
adj anaemic 85.60

epilogue postscript
254.2
act 704.7
section 792.2
sequel 816.1
end 819.1
television broadcast
1034.2

epiphany visibility 31.1
appearance 33.1
manifestation 348.1
revelation 683.9
intuition 933.1

episcopal 698.13

episode interjection
213.2
digression 538.4
plot 722.4
discontinuity 812.1
event 830.2
frenzy 925.7

episodic interjectional
213.9
discursive 538.13
discontinuous 812.4

epitaph 309.18

epithet
noun oath 513.4
name 527.3
nickname 527.7
motto 973.4
verb vilify 513.7

epitome shortening
268.3
abridgment 557.1
paragon 659.4
essence 766.2
ideal 785.4

epoch 823.5

eponymous 527.16

equal
noun match 789.4
substitute 861.2
verb parallel 203.4
match 789.5

excel 998.11
adj parallel 203.6
symmetric 264.4
proportionate 477.13
coinciding 777.8
uniform 780.5
equalized 789.7
interchangeable 862.5

equality symmetry
264.1
justice 649.1
sameness 777.1
parity 789.1

equally justly 649.11
accordingly 765.11
identically 777.9
correspondingly
789.11

equal opportunities
789.7

equal opportunity
equating 789.2
opportunity 842.2

equal to able 18.14
satisfactory 107.11
prepared for 405.18
competent 413.24
sufficient 990.6

equanimity
equilibrium 106.3
uniformity 780.1

equate parallelize 203.5
relate 774.6
equalize 789.6

equating 789.2

equation equality 789.1
equating 789.2
notation 1016.2

equator zone 231.3
band 280.3
middle 818.1
bisector 874.3
oven 1018.11
orbit 1070.16

equatorial middle
818.4
warm 1018.24

equerry man 577.4
stockman 1068.2

equestrian
noun rider 178.8
adj ungulate 311.44

equilibrium
equanimity 106.3
symmetry 264.1
inaction 329.1
harmony 533.2
moderation 670.1
correlation 776.1
uniformity 780.1
equality 789.1
continuity 811.1
stability 854.1

equine
noun horse 311.10
adj ungulate 311.44

equinox vernal equinox
313.7

orbit 1070.16

equip outfit 5.40
furnish 385.8
fit 405.8
establish 891.10

equipment provision
385.1
matériel 385.4
preparation 405.1
fitting 405.2
talent 413.4
football 745.1
rugby 746.1
cricket 747.1
golf 748.1
hockey 750.1
ice hockey 750.4
skiing 753.1
boxing 754.1

equipped provided
385.13
prepared 405.16

equitable just 649.8
impartial 649.10
unprejudiced 978.12

equity estate 471.4
justice 649.1
shares 738.2
equality 789.1

equivalence correlation
776.1
sameness 777.1
agreement 787.1
comparability 942.3

equivalent
noun offset 338.2
same 777.3
likeness 783.3
equal 789.4
substitute 861.2
adj reciprocal 776.10
coinciding 777.8
analogous 783.11
agreeing 787.9
tantamount 789.8
substitute 861.8
interchangeable 862.5

equivocal
noun ambiguity 539.2
adj prevaricating
344.11
untruthful 354.34
ambiguous 539.4
self-contradictory
778.8
mixed 796.14
uncertain 970.16

era 823.5

eradicate extract
192.10
excise 255.10
exterminate 395.14
annihilate 761.7
eliminate 772.5

eradication extraction
192.1
excision 255.3
extinction 395.6
elimination 772.2

erase delete 255.12
waste 308.13
obliterate 395.16
end 819.5
abrade 1042.7

erased 989.8

erasure disappearance
34.1
excision 255.3
deletion 255.5
obliteration 395.7
abrasion 1042.2

ere 833.6

erect
verb elevate 200.9,
911.5
produce 891.8
adj proud 136.8
vertical 200.11
honest 644.13
raised 911.9

erecting 200.4

erection sexual desire
75.5
erecting 200.4
house 228.5
structure 266.2
production 891.2
elevation 911.1

ergo consequently
886.7
hence 887.7

ermine heraldic device
647.2
regalia 647.3

Ernie 759.16

erode disappear 34.3
recede 168.2
decrease 252.6
subtract 255.9
consume 388.3
wear 393.20
corrode 393.21
waste 473.5
disintegrate 805.3
abrade 1042.7

eroded reduced 252.10
used up 388.5
weatherworn 393.34
corroded 393.43
lost 473.7

eroding receding 168.5
corrupting 393.44

erogenous 75.24

Eros love 104.1
Love 104.8

erosion decrement
252.3
subtraction 255.1
consumption 388.1
wear 393.5
waste 473.2
disintegration 805.1
abrasion 1042.2

erotic sexual 75.24
amorous 104.26
lascivious 665.29

erotica 547.12, 718.1

eroticism sexual desire
75.5
lasciviousness 665.5

err stray 164.4
miss 410.14
go wrong 654.9
do wrong 655.4
misbelieve 688.8
misjudge 947.2
fall into error 974.9

errand commission
615.1
task 724.2

errant deviative 164.7
wandering 177.37
fallible 970.22
erroneous 974.16

erratic
noun eccentric 926.3
adj deviative 164.7
nonuniform 781.3
unordered 809.12
irregular 850.3
inconstant 853.7
abnormal 869.9
eccentric 926.5
uncertain 970.16

erratically
nonuniformly 781.4
haphazardly 809.18
irregularly 850.4
changeably 853.8

erroneous false 354.25
ungrammatic 531.4
unorthodox 688.9
untrue 974.16
illusory 975.9
imperfect 1002.4

erroneously 354.35,
974.20

error misinterpretation
342.1
miss 410.4
bungle 414.5
iniquity 654.3
misdeed 655.2
heresy 688.2
game 749.2
misjudgment 947.1
erroneousness 974.1
mistake 974.3

ersatz
noun substitute 861.2
adj imitation 336.8
spurious 354.26
similar 783.10
substitute 861.8

erstwhile 836.10

erudite 927.21

erudition learning
570.1
wisdom 919.5
scholarship 927.5

erupt burst forth 33.9
emerge 190.11
find vent 369.10
originate 817.13
disgorge 908.25

eruption skin eruption
85.35
outburst 105.9, 152.9,
671.6
disgorgement 908.7

escalate 911.5

escalation 911.1

escalator
noun lift 911.4
phrase people mover
176.5

escapade 743.6

escape
noun defence
mechanism 92.23
departure 188.1
outlet 190.9
absence 222.4
avoidance 368.1
getaway 369.1
verb absent oneself
222.8
evade 368.7
free oneself from
431.8

escaped 369.11

escape route 346.5

escapism defence
mechanism 92.23
escape 369.1

escapist escapee 369.5
visionary 985.13

escarpment precipice
200.3
slope 237.2

eschew 668.7

escort
noun lover 104.12
conductor 768.5
chaperon 1007.7
bodyguard 1007.14
verb conduct 768.8

esoteric
noun occultist 689.11
adj secret 345.11
confidential 345.14
latent 519.5
implied 519.7
recondite 522.16
occult 689.23
intrinsic 766.7
particular 864.12
supernatural 869.15

ESP 343.1

especial 864.12

especially chiefly
249.17
particularly 864.15

espionage observation
27.2
surveillance 937.9

esplanade 383.2

espouse adopt 371.15
marry 563.15
defend 600.10

espoused 371.26

esprit heart 93.3

gaiety 109.4
cooperation 450.1
accord 455.1
wit 489.1
intellect 918.1
smartness 919.2

Esquire 648.3

esquire
noun beau 104.13
nobleman 608.4
escort 768.5
verb court 562.21
escort 768.8

essay
noun attempt 403.2
writing 547.10
treatise 556.1
test 941.2
verb attempt 403.6
experiment 941.8

essence odour 69.1
perfumery 70.2
extract 192.8, 892.3
substance 196.5, 766.2
meaning 518.1
summary 557.2
existence 760.1
major part 791.6
topic 936.1
salient point 996.6

essential
noun essence 766.2
requirement 962.2
salient point 996.6
adj quintessential
192.18
basic 199.8
of the essence 766.9
simple 797.6
requisite 962.13
vital 996.23

essentially extremely
247.22
substantially 762.8
fundamentally 766.11
on the whole 791.14

essential nature
essence 766.2
inner nature 766.5

essential oil 1054.1

essentials facts 760.4
basics 817.6
requirement 962.2

establish fix 159.16,
854.9
publicize 352.15
accustom 373.10
legalize 673.8
inaugurate 817.11
cause 885.10
found 891.10
prove 956.10
make sure 969.11

established located
159.18
customary 373.14
confirmed 373.19
real 760.15
traditional 841.12

stabilized 854.13
proved 956.20
assured 969.20
true 972.13

establishing 817.1

Establishment
authorities 575.15
government 612.3
influence 893.6
personage 996.8

establishment
foundation 159.7,
891.4
best 249.5
structure 266.2
organization 617.8
market 736.1
workplace 739.1
hierarchy 808.4
beginning 817.1
fixity 854.2
proof 956.3
ensuring 969.8

estate mansion 228.7
rank 245.2
interest 471.4
class 607.1, 808.2
state 764.1

esteem
noun respect 155.1
approval 509.1
estimation 662.3
influence 893.1
notability 996.2
verb cherish 104.21
respect 155.4
approve 509.9
judge 945.8
think 952.11
value 996.13

esteemed beloved
104.24
respected 155.11
reputable 662.15
notable 996.19

estimate
noun measurement
300.1
estimation 945.3
opinion 952.6
gamble 970.8
verb measure 300.10
form an estimate
945.9
think 952.11
calculate 1016.17

estimating 1016.23

estimation respect
155.1
measurement 300.1
valuation 630.3
esteem 662.3
estimate 945.3
opinion 952.6
calculation 1016.10

estranged alienated
589.11
separated 801.21

estrangement falling-
out 456.4
disaccord 589.2
separation 801.1

estuary outlet 190.9
inlet 242.1

ET 1073.8

et al
adv in the majority
882.10
phrase et cetera 253.14

et cetera
adv in the majority
882.10
phrase and so forth
253.14

etched 854.13

etching visual arts
712.1
engraving 713.2
print 713.5

eternal mandatory
420.12
almighty 677.17
infinite 822.3
perpetual 828.7

eternal life 828.3

eternally infinitely
822.4
perpetually 828.10

eternity timelessness
821.1
infinity 822.1
long time 826.4
perpetuity 828.1
forever 828.2

ether anaesthetic 86.15
air 317.1
spirit 763.3
coolant 1023.7
heavens 1070.2

ethereal thin 270.16,
763.6
high 272.14
light 298.10
rare 299.4
airy 317.11
heavenly 681.12
chimeric 985.22
spectral 987.7
immaterial 1051.7
vaporous 1065.9

etheric 987.7

ethic 636.1

ethical moral 636.6
dutiful 641.13
honest 644.13

ethics principles 636.1
duty 641.1

ethnic
noun person 312.5
adj racial 559.7

ethnic cleansing
611.10

ethnic group
humankind 312.1
party 617.4

ethnicity humankind
312.1
race 559.4
exclusiveness 772.3

ethnographic 312.13

ethnography 312.10

ethos culture 373.3
ethics 636.1
nature 766.4
ideology 931.8
opinion 952.6
climate 977.5

etiquette good
behaviour 321.2
custom 373.1
mannerliness 504.3
social convention
579.1
social code 580.3

Etruscan 554.15

Eucharist seven
sacraments 701.4
Lord's Supper 701.7

eulogy dirge 115.6
last offices 309.4
praise 509.5
speech 543.2
citation 646.4

eunuch impotent 19.6
sexlessness 75.9

euphemism
overniceness 500.5
catchword 526.9
affectation 533.3

euphoria pleasure 95.1
contentment 107.1

euphoric pleased 95.14
content 107.7
cheerful 109.11

Eurasian 796.8

Europe 231.6, 235.1

European tour 748.1

euthanasia natural
death 307.7
killing 308.1

evacuate defecate
12.13
quit 188.9
abandon 370.5
void 908.22
let out 908.24

evacuation defecation
12.2
departure 188.1
abandonment 370.1
voidance 908.6

evade avoid 164.6
prevaricate 344.7
elude 368.7
escape 369.6
outwit 415.11
remain neutral 467.5
live by one's wits
645.11
quibble 935.9

evaluate measure
300.10

price 630.11
criticize 723.5
classify 800.8
estimate 945.9
evaluated 630.14
evaluating 945.3
evaluation
measurement 300.1
valuation 630.3
classification 800.3
estimate 945.3
Evangelical
noun Protestant 675.20
adj Protestant 675.28
evangelical scriptural
683.10
orthodox 687.7
strict 687.8
evangelism lecture
543.3
zeal 692.3
evangelist herald 353.2
lecturer 543.5
apostle 684.2
worshipper 696.9
revivalist 699.6
converter 857.9
evaporate disappear
34.3
preserve 397.9
dissipate 770.5
flit 827.6
dry 1064.6
vaporize 1065.8
evaporated 1064.9
evaporating 34.4
evaporation
disappearance 34.1
food preservation
397.2
waste 473.2
drying 1064.3
vaporization 1065.5
evasion prevarication
344.4
secrecy 345.1
avoidance 368.1
escape 369.1
circumvention 415.5
neutrality 467.1
retreat 902.3
quibbling 935.5
evasive avertive 164.9
prevaricating 344.11
secretive 345.15
elusive 368.15
dishonest 645.16
circuitous 913.7
quibbling 935.14
Eve 77.5
eve 315.2
even
noun evening 315.2
verb level 201.6
symmetrize 264.3
smooth 287.5
make uniform 780.4
equalize 789.6

adj horizontal 201.7
parallel 203.6
symmetric 264.4
straight 277.6
smooth 287.9
neutral 467.7
just 649.8
equable 670.13
uniform 780.5
equal 789.7
interchangeable 862.5
exact 972.17
adv chiefly 249.17
interchangeably 862.6
exactly 972.21
adv, conj
notwithstanding 338.8
evening
noun symmetrization
264.2
eve 315.2
equating 789.2
adj evensong 315.8
evening dress 5.11
evening wear 5.11
evenly horizontally
201.9
smoothly 287.12
justly 649.11
moderately 670.17
uniformly 780.7
equally 789.11
interchangeably 862.6
even money 789.3
even more 253.11
even now 837.3
even out calm 670.7
make uniform 780.4
even so 338.8
event game 743.9
circumstance 765.1
eventuality 830.1
occurrence 830.2
effect 886.1
eventful 830.10
eventual final 819.11
coming 830.11
future 838.8
eventuality
circumstance 765.1
event 830.1
future 838.1
futurity 838.4
effect 886.1
liability 896.1
possibility 965.1
eventually finally
819.12
ultimately 830.12
in time 838.11
even up symmetrize
264.3
equalize 789.6
even with 338.9
ever forever 828.12
constantly 846.7
by any possibility
965.10

ever-being 828.7
ever-changing 853.6
evergreen
noun plant 310.3
tree 310.10
adj arboreal 310.36
perennial 310.41,
828.8
durable 826.10
new 840.7
everlasting tedious
118.9
almighty 677.17
perpetual 828.7
immortal 828.9
ever more 251.9
ever since 836.17
ever so greatly 247.15
chiefly 249.17
ever so much 247.15
evert 205.5
every 863.15
every bit 793.17
everybody people
606.1
all 863.4
every day constantly
846.7
periodically 849.10
everyday customary
373.14
simple 499.6
vernacular 523.18
frequent 846.4
usual 868.9
every hour constantly
846.7
periodically 849.10
every inch 793.17
Everyman people
606.1
common man 606.5
average 863.3
everyman 863.3
every moment 846.7
every now and again
847.5
every now and then
occasionally 847.5
repeatedly 848.16
regularly 849.9
every once in a while
occasionally 847.5
repeatedly 848.16
every one 863.15
everyone people 606.1
all 863.4
every other 849.11
every so often
occasionally 847.5
regularly 849.9
everything 791.3,
863.4
everywhere

adj omnipresent
221.13
adv everywheres
158.12
from everywhere
158.13
in every direction
161.25
scatteringly 770.12
universally 863.18,
1070.27
evict dislodge 160.6
dispossess 480.23
oust 908.15
evicted 160.10
eviction dislocation
160.1
dispossession 480.7
elimination 772.2
ousting 908.2
evidence
noun distinctness 31.2
manifestation 348.1
manifestness 348.3
clue 517.9
information 551.1
testimony 598.9
proof 956.1
verb manifest 348.5
evince 956.8
evident visible 31.6
distinct 31.7
manifest 348.8
evidently visibly 31.8
manifestly 348.14
evil
noun vice 654.1
iniquity 654.3
misdeed 655.2
wicked 660.12
badness 999.1
bad 999.3
bane 1000.1
trouble 1012.3
adj ominous 133.17
wrong 638.3
wicked 654.16
bad 999.7
adv badly 999.13
evil spirits spirit 678.5
demons 680.1
evocation elicitation
192.5
description 349.2
summons 420.5
conjuration 690.4
evocative extractive
192.17
recollective 988.22
evoke elicit 192.14
describe 349.9
prompt 375.13
summon 420.11
conjure 690.11
resemble 783.7
induce 885.11
remember 988.10
evolution development
392.2

evolving 860.1
notation 1016.2
evolutionary 860.8
evolve extract 192.10
develop 392.10, 860.5
amplify 538.7
produce 891.8
originate 891.12
evolving
noun evolution 860.1
adj evolutionary 860.8
ewe hen 77.9
sheep 311.7
ex 190.22
exacerbate pain 26.7
irritate 96.14
sour 110.16
aggravate 119.2
intensify 251.5
impair 393.9
antagonize 589.7
exacerbated aggravated
119.4
impaired 393.27
exact
verb extort 192.15
demand 421.5
oblige 424.5
wrest 480.22
charge 630.12
impose 643.4
require 962.9
adj meticulous 339.12
elegant 533.6
punctilious 580.10
detailed 765.9
discriminating 943.7
precise 972.17
exacted 643.8
exacting extractive
192.17
meticulous 339.12
demanding 421.9
strict 425.6
fastidious 495.9
overpriced 632.12
difficult 1012.17
exactly
adv meticulously
339.16
punctually 844.14
particularly 864.15
precisely 972.21
exclam yes 332.18
exaggerate intensify
251.5
misrepresent 350.3
lie 354.19
hyperbolize 355.3
overrun 909.4
overestimate 948.2
overdo 992.10
exaggerated
hyperbolical 355.4
overestimated 948.3
excessive 992.16
exaggerating

noun exaggeration
355.1
adj exaggerative 355.5

exaggeration
intensification 251.2
misrepresentation
350.1
deliberate falsehood
354.9
lie 354.11
exaggerating 355.1
style 532.2
overrunning 909.1
overestimation 948.1
excess 992.1

exaltation happiness
95.2
height 272.1
promotion 446.1
praise 509.5
magnanimity 652.2
distinction 662.5
glorification 662.8,
696.2
sanctification 685.3
elevation 911.1

exalted overjoyed 95.16
cheerful 109.11
eminent 247.9, 662.18
high 272.14
noble 608.10
magnanimous 652.6
sanctified 685.8
raised 911.9

exam 937.2

examination scrutiny
27.6
diagnosis 91.12
discussion 541.7
treatise 556.1
trial 598.6
argumentation 934.4
school examination
937.2
inspection 937.3
questioning 937.12

examine scrutinize
27.14
discuss 541.12
study 570.12
interrogate 937.21
inspect 937.24

examiner analyst 800.5
inquirer 937.16
examinant 937.17

examining 937.37

example
noun sample 62.4
representative 349.7
warning 399.1
exemplar 785.2
citation 956.5
verb cite 956.13

exasperated annoyed
96.21
aggravated 119.4
provoked 152.27

exasperating annoying
98.22

aggravating 119.5

exasperation
annoyance 96.2
vexatiousness 98.7
excitation 105.11
aggravation 119.1
resentment 152.1
incitement 375.4

Excalibur 462.5

excavation extraction
192.1
crack 224.2
deepening 275.7
pit 284.4
digging 284.11
discovery 940.1

exceed loom 247.5
excel 249.6
overrun 909.4
surpass 992.9

exceeding 249.12

exceedingly very
247.18
superlatively 249.16

excel 249.6, 998.11

excellence superiority
249.1
taste 496.1
distinction 662.5
importance 996.1
goodness 998.1

Excellency 648.2

excellent superior
249.12
skilful 413.22
tasteful 496.8
eminent 662.18
good 998.12

excellently skilfully
413.31
nicely 998.22

except
verb excise 255.10
reject 372.2
exempt 430.14
prep excluding 772.10
conj unless 958.16

excepted rejected 372.3
exempt 430.30

except for 772.10

excepting
prep excluding 772.10
conj unless 958.16

exception marvel 122.2
objection 333.2
rejection 372.1
stipulation 421.2
exemption 430.8
criticism 510.4
defence 600.2
exclusion 772.1
oddity 869.5
qualification 958.1

exceptional wonderful
122.10
remarkable 247.10
studentlike 572.12
exclusive 772.9

particular 864.12
extraordinary 869.14
eccentric 926.5
notable 996.19

exceptionally
wonderfully 122.14
intensely 247.20
extraordinarily 869.18

except that 958.16

excerpt
noun extract 557.3
verb select 371.14

excerpts 557.4

excess
noun surplus 256.4
exaggeration 355.1
exorbitance 632.4
undueness 640.1
intemperance 669.1
overrunning 909.1
excessiveness 992.1
insurance 1007.4
adj superfluous 992.17

excessive exaggerated
355.4
overpriced 632.12
inappropriate 640.10
intemperate 669.7
violent 671.16
inordinate 992.16

excessive force 144.11

excessively
distressingly 247.21
exorbitantly 632.16
intemperately 669.10
inordinately 992.22

exchange
noun communication
343.1
telephone number
347.12
banter 490.1
retaliation 506.1
conversation 541.1
transfer 629.1
trade 731.2
stock exchange 737.7
changing 853.3
substitution 861.1
substitute 861.2
interchange 862.1
verb transfer 629.3
trade 731.14
change 851.7, 853.5
substitute 861.4
interchange 862.4

exchanged 862.5

exchange of letters
553.1

exchange of views
541.7

exchequer storehouse
386.6
funds 728.14
treasury 729.12

excise extract 192.10
cut out 255.10
sever 801.11

excitable emotional
105.28
irascible 110.19
nervous 128.11

excite sensitize 24.7
impassion 105.12
incite 375.17
agitate 916.10
interest 982.12
inflame 1019.18

excited fervent 93.18
affected 93.23
impassioned 105.20
impatient 135.6
agitated 916.16
interested 982.16

excitedly fervently
93.26
agitatedly 105.33,
916.22

excitement passion
93.2
emotion 105.1
excitation 105.11
impatience 135.1
incitement 375.4
agitation 916.1
ardour 1018.2

exciting desirable
100.30
thrilling 105.30
provocative 375.27
alluring 377.8
vehement 544.13
interesting 982.19

exclaim give an
exclamation 59.7
remark 524.25
murmur 524.26

exclamation ejaculation
59.2
remark 524.4

exclude excise 255.10
close 293.6
reject 372.2
prohibit 444.3
disapprove 510.10
bar 772.4
eject 908.13
banish 908.17
prevent 1011.14

excluded closed 293.9
rejected 372.3
barred 772.7
impossible 966.7

excluding
adj exclusive 772.9
prep off 255.14
barring 772.10

exclusion excision
255.3
closure 293.1
rejection 372.1
prohibition 444.1
disapproval 510.1
barring 772.1
banishment 908.4
qualification 958.1

exclusive

noun news item 552.3
adj contemptuous
157.8
limiting 210.9
closed 293.9
selective 371.23,
495.13
prohibitive 444.6
aloof 583.6
cliquish 617.18
excluding 772.9
one 871.7

exclusively simply
797.11
solely 871.14

exclusivity contempt
157.1
exclusiveness 495.5
seclusiveness 583.3
partisanism 617.13
exclusion 772.1

excrement dejection
12.3
filth 80.7

excrete egest 12.12
secrete 13.5
exude 190.15

excretion egestion 12.1
secretion 13.1
exuding 190.6
evacuation 908.6

excruciating exquisite
24.13
painful 26.10
agonizing 98.23

excruciatingly 98.28,
247.21

excursion deviation
164.1
journey 177.5
obliquity 204.1
digression 538.4
circuitousness 913.1
detour 913.3

excuse
noun pardon 148.2
pretext 376.1
cop-out 600.4
acquittal 601.1
apology 658.2
reason 885.2
verb forgive 148.3
exempt 430.14
alibi 600.11
acquit 601.4

excused forgiven 148.7
exempt 430.30

execute kill 308.12
perform 328.9, 434.3,
891.11
accomplish 407.4
complete 437.9
put to death 604.16
play 708.39

executed accomplished
407.10
produced 891.17

execution
noun killing 308.1

performance 328.2,
708.30, 891.5
observance 434.1
completion 437.4
attachment 480.5
capital punishment
604.6
operation 888.1
adj accomplishment
407.1

executioner killer
308.10
punisher 604.7

executive
noun officer 574.3
directorate 574.11
governor 575.6
operator 888.4
adj administrative
573.14, 612.19

executive committee
574.11

executive council
574.11

executive director
574.3

executive officer
executive 574.3
deputy 576.1
assistant 616.6

executive secretary
574.3

executor doer 726.1
producer 891.7

exemplar representative
349.7
paragon 659.4
example 785.2
rule 868.4
ideatum 931.2

exemplary typical
349.15
warning 399.7
praiseworthy 509.20
model 785.8
perfected 1001.9

exemplify explain
341.10
image 349.11
set an example 785.7
cite 956.13

exempt
verb free 430.14
acquit 601.4
adj immune 430.30

exempted 430.30

exempt from 601.4

exemption pardon
148.2
exception 430.8
immunity 601.2
qualification 958.1

exercise
noun motion 84.2
action 328.1
use 387.1
training 568.3
lesson 568.7

study 570.3
ceremony 580.4
task 724.2
exercising 725.6
operation 888.1
verb work out 84.4
annoy 96.13
practice 328.8
use 387.10
train 568.13
exert 725.8
engross 982.13

exercise book 554.10

exercised 387.24

exercises ceremony
580.4
divine service 696.8

exercising 725.6

exert use 387.10
exercise 725.8

exerted 387.24

exertion use 387.1
endeavour 403.1
effort 725.1

ex gratia volitional
323.4
voluntary 324.7

exhalation breathing
2.19
murmur 52.4
odour 69.1
outflow 190.4
vapour 1065.1
vaporization 1065.5

exhale smell 69.6
let out 908.24
vaporize 1065.8

exhaust
noun wash 184.30
outflow 190.4
outlet 190.9
miasma 1000.4
rocket propulsion
1072.8
verb weaken 16.10
unman 19.12
fatigue 21.4
oppress 98.16
run out 190.13
draw off 192.12
spend 387.13
consume 388.3
strip 480.24
waste 486.4
evacuate 908.22
let out 908.24
disgorge 908.25
overdo 992.10

exhausted weakened
16.18
burnt-out 21.10
unhealthy 85.53
used up 388.5
worn-out 393.36
unproductive 890.4

exhausting
noun use 387.1
consumption 388.1
evacuation 908.6

adj weakening 16.20
fatiguing 21.13
oppressive 98.24

exhaustion weakness
16.1
weakening 16.5
exhaustedness 21.2
unhealthiness 85.3
collapse 85.8
decrement 252.3
consumption 388.1
waste 473.2
evacuation 908.6

exhaustive great 247.6
broad 269.6
complete 407.12
whole 791.9
thorough 793.10

exhaustively 793.14

exhibit
noun spectacle 33.7
display 348.2
theatrical performance
704.12
evidence 956.1
verb externalize 206.5
manifest 348.5
flaunt 501.17
evidence 956.8

exhibited 348.13

exhibition spectacle
33.7
display 348.2, 501.4
subsidy 478.8
theatrical performance
704.12

exhibitionist sexual
pervert 75.16
show-off 501.11

exhibitor 704.23

exhilarated refreshed
9.4
pleased 95.14
excited 105.20
cheerful 109.11

exhilarating refreshing
9.3
energizing 17.15
exciting 105.30
cheering 109.16
inspiring 375.26

exhilaration
refreshment 9.1
energizing 17.8
happiness 95.2
excitement 105.1
excitation 105.11
good humour 109.2
inspiration 375.9

exhortation
inducement 375.3
advice 422.1
call to arms 458.8
speech 543.2

exile
noun migrant 178.5
emigration 190.7
outcast 586.4
elimination 772.2

alien 773.3
banishment 908.4
verb emigrate 190.16
ostracize 586.6
eliminate 772.5
banish 908.17

exiled unplaced 160.10
excluded 772.7

exist be present 221.6
live 306.7
be 760.8
endure 826.6

existence presence
221.1
life 306.1
being 760.1
something 762.3

existent living 306.11
existing 760.13
present 837.2

existentialism 760.7

exist in 760.11

existing existent 760.13
present 837.2

exit
noun departure 188.1
egress 190.2
outlet 190.9
channel 239.1
death 307.1
flight 368.4
passageway 383.3
verb disappear 34.3
depart 188.6
make an exit 190.12
absent oneself 222.8
find vent 369.10

exit poll vote 371.6
canvass 937.14

exodus departure 188.1
egress 190.2
act 704.7

exonerated 148.7

exorbitant exaggerated
355.4
demanding 421.9
overpriced 632.12
violent 671.16
excessive 992.16

exorcise 690.12

exorcism conjuration
690.4
spell 691.1

exorcist 690.7

exotic
noun plant 310.3
adj colourful 35.18
distant 261.8
alluring 377.8
extraneous 773.5
unrelated 775.6

expand increase 251.4
enlarge 259.4, 259.5
spread 259.6
broaden 269.4
rarefy 299.3
amplify 538.7
disperse 770.4

elaborate 860.6
generalize 863.9

expanded increased
251.7
extended 259.10

expanding increasing
251.8
expatiating 538.15

expand on 538.7

expanse space 158.1
range 158.2
spaciousness 158.5
greatness 247.1
size 257.1
breadth 269.1

expansion space 158.1
increase 251.1
size 257.1
extension 259.1
exaggeration 355.1
amplification 538.6
business cycle 731.9
evolution 860.1

expansionism battle
flag 458.12
foreign policy 609.5

expansive spacious
158.10
voluminous 257.17
extensive 259.9
broad 269.6
communicative 343.10
talkative 540.9

ex parte 956.16

expatriate
noun migrant 178.5
outcast 586.4
verb migrate 177.22
leave home 188.17
emigrate 190.16
eliminate 772.5
banish 908.17

expect hope 124.7
be expectant 130.5
come 838.6
suppose 950.10
think 952.11

expectancy 842.1

expectant hopeful
124.11
expecting 130.11

expectantly hopefully
124.14
expectingly 130.15

expectation
unastonishment 123.1
hope 124.1
dueness 639.1
future 838.1
probability 967.1

expectations prospects
130.4
dueness 639.1

expected unastonished
123.3
anticipated 130.13

expected of 130.14

expecting pregnant
78.18
 unastonished 123.3
 expectant 130.11
expectorant 86.32
expect to 130.9
expedient
 noun instrumentality
 384.3
 stratagem 415.3
 means 994.2
 recourse 1008.2
 adj useful 387.18
 transient 827.7
 timely 842.9
 conditional 958.8
 desirable 994.5
 good 998.12
expedition velocity
174.1
 journey 177.5
 quickness 330.3
 adventure 404.2
 furtherance 449.5
 campaign 458.4
 promptness 844.3
 facilitation 1013.5
expeditionary 177.36
expel transfer 176.10
 depose 447.4
 eliminate 772.5
 separate 801.8
 eject 908.13
 banish 908.17
 dismiss 908.19
 disgorge 908.25
expelled 772.7
expend spend 387.13,
626.5
 consume 388.3
 waste 486.4
 pay out 624.14
expendable consumable
388.6
 replaceable 861.10
 superfluous 992.17
 unimportant 997.16
expended lost 473.7
 paid 624.22
expenditure use 387.1
 consumption 388.1
 waste 473.2
 spending 626.1
 price 630.1
expenditures 628.1
expense loss 473.1
 expenditure 626.1
 expenses 626.3
 price 630.1
expenses 626.3
expensive 632.11
expensively 632.15
experience
 noun sensation 24.1
 practice 413.9
 event 830.2
 knowledge 927.1
 verb sense 24.6

feel 93.10
 have 830.8
experienced
 accustomed 373.16
 practised 413.28
experiences 719.1
experiment
 noun attempt 403.2
 experimentation 941.1
 verb see what one can
 do 403.10
 experimentalize 941.8
experimental trial
403.16
 test 941.11
experimentally 941.13
experimentation 941.1
experimenter 941.6
expert
 noun adept 413.11
 adviser 422.3
 connoisseur 496.7
 specialist 865.3
 scientist 927.11
 adj skilful 413.22
 specialized 865.5
 perfected 1001.9
expert at 413.27
expertise skill 413.1
 knowledge 927.1
 profound knowledge
 927.6
expertly 413.31
expire die 307.19
 perish 395.23
 come to an end 819.6
 elapse 820.5
 let out 908.24
expired no more
761.11
 past 836.7
expiry 819.1
explain explicate
341.10
 make clear 521.6
 expound 568.16
 justify 600.9
 excuse 600.11
 solve 939.2
 facilitate 1013.7
explain away explain
341.10
 extenuate 600.12
 reason speciously
 935.8
explaining 341.15
explanation explication
341.4
 definition 518.3
 justification 600.1
 example 785.2
 reason 885.2
 solution 939.1
 theory 950.1, 950.2
explanatory 341.15
expletive
 noun exclamation 59.2

oath 513.4
 redundancy 848.3
 superfluity 992.4
 adj superfluous 992.17
explicit manifest 348.8
 clear 521.11
 candid 644.17
 unqualified 959.2
explicitly manifestly
348.14
 intelligibly 521.13
explode burst forth
33.9
 blast 56.8
 be excitable 105.16
 grow 251.6
 blow up 395.18,
 671.14
 come to nothing
 410.13
 disprove 957.4
 fuel 1020.7
exploded doubted
954.12
 disproved 957.7
exploding 56.11
exploit
 noun act 328.3
 feat 492.7
 verb take advantage of
 387.15, 387.16
 overprice 632.7
exploitation 387.8
exploitative 387.19
exploration adventure
404.2
 reconnaissance 937.8
 search 937.15
exploratory preceding
815.4
 examining 937.37
explore investigate
937.23
 search 937.31
explorer traveller 178.1
 precursor 815.1
explosion detonation
56.3
 outburst 105.9, 152.9
 intensification 251.2
 discharge 671.7
 disproof 957.1
explosive
 noun high explosive
 462.14
 speech sound 524.13
 adj banging 56.11
 excitable 105.28
 hot-tempered 110.25
 bursting 671.24
 dangerous 1005.9
exponent interpreter
341.7
 representative 349.7
 deputy 576.1
 supporter 616.9
 example 785.2
export

noun exporting 190.8
 verb transfer 176.10
 send 176.15
 send abroad 190.17
 phrase transference
 176.1
exporter 730.2
exporting 190.8
expose divest 6.5
 unclose 292.12
 disclose 351.4
 stigmatize 661.9
 uncover 940.4
 disprove 957.4
 disillusion 976.2
 endanger 1005.6
exposed divested 6.12
 visible 31.6
 open 292.17, 348.10,
 1005.15
 airy 317.11
 windblown 318.24
 liable 896.5
 disproved 957.7
 radioactive 1036.10
exposing
 noun unclothing 6.1
 adj disclosive 351.10
exposition spectacle
33.7
 explanation 341.4
 display 348.2
 disclosure 351.1
 treatise 556.1
 lesson 568.7
 passage 708.24
 marketplace 736.2
exposure unclothing
6.1
 visibility 31.1
 distinctness 31.2
 appearance 33.1
 navigation 159.3
 display 348.2
 disclosure 351.1
 publicity 352.4
 repute 662.1
 time exposure 714.9
 susceptibility 896.2
 discovery 940.1
 disproof 957.1
 openness 1005.3
 radiation physics
 1036.7
expound explain
341.10
 exposit 568.16
expounding 341.4
express
 noun train 179.14
 messenger 353.1
 message 552.4
 verb send 176.15
 affirm 334.5
 manifest 348.5
 describe 349.9
 signify 517.17
 say 524.23
 phrase 532.4

evidence 956.8
 adj fast 174.15
 manifest 348.8
 clear 521.11
 particular 864.12
 unqualified 959.2
 exact 972.17
 adv posthaste 401.13
 phrase carrier 176.7
expressed 532.5
expressing 192.1
expression extraction
192.1
 squeezing 192.7
 manifestation 348.1
 indication 517.3
 remark 524.4
 word 526.1
 phrase 529.1
 diction 532.1
 eloquence 544.1
 execution 708.30
 maxim 973.1
expressionism 350.1
expressionless reticent
344.10
 inexpressive 522.20
expressive manifesting
348.9
 descriptive 349.14
 indicative 517.23
 meaningful 518.10
 graphic 544.10
expressly manifestly
348.14
 intelligibly 521.13
 particularly 864.15
 exactly 972.21
express train lightning
174.6
 train 179.14
expulsion
 noun deposal 447.2
 elimination 772.2
 ejection 908.1
 disgorgement 908.7
 phrase transference
 176.1
exquisite
 noun dandy 500.9
 adj poignant 24.13
 painful 26.10
 tasty 63.8
 delightful 97.7
 meticulous 339.12
 nice 495.11
 overnice 500.18
 chic 578.13
 superb 998.15
 fine 1015.19
exquisitely delightfully
97.13
 intensely 247.20
 meticulously 339.16
 smartly 578.18
 superbly 998.23
 beautifully 1015.23
extant remaining 256.7
 existent 760.13

present 837.2

extend reach 158.8
increase 251.4
enlarge 259.4, 259.5
spread 259.6
reach out 261.5
be long 267.5
lengthen 267.6
broaden 269.4
straighten 277.5
offer 439.4
give 478.12
protract 538.8, 826.9
race 757.5
endure 826.6
postpone 845.9
sustain 855.4
generalize 863.9
stretch 1046.4

extended spacious
158.10
increased 251.7
expanded 259.10
lengthened 267.8
meaningful 518.10
wordy 538.12
protracted 826.11

extended family
family 559.5
community 617.2

extending 158.10

extend to 261.6

extension space 158.1
increase 251.1
adjunct 254.1
wing 254.3
size 257.1
expansion 259.1
length 267.1
lengthening 267.4
telephone 347.4
meaning 518.1
sequence 814.1
protraction 826.2
continuance 855.1
stretching 1046.2

extensive spacious
158.10
large 247.7
voluminous 257.17
expansive 259.9
long 267.7
broad 269.6, 863.13

extensively widely
158.11
lengthily 267.10

extent space 158.1
spaciousness 158.5
quantity 244.1, 300.3
degree 245.1
size 257.1
distance 261.1
length 267.1
breadth 269.1

exterior
noun appearance 33.2
external 206.2
scene 712.12
adj external 206.7

extraneous 773.5

exterminate kill
308.12
eliminate 395.14
annihilate 761.7
do away with 908.21

extermination killing
308.1
extinction 395.6

external
noun exterior 206.2
adj exterior 206.7
extrinsic 767.3
extraneous 773.5

externally 206.10

extinct gone 34.5
no more 761.11
ended 819.8
past 836.7
obsolete 841.15

extinction
disappearance 34.1
excision 255.3
death 307.1
extermination 395.6
extinguishing 1021.2

extinguish overshadow
249.8
excise 255.10
quench 395.15
suppress 428.8
end 819.5
fight fire 1021.7

extinguished 1021.11

extinguisher 1021.3

extortion exaction
192.6
demand 421.1
shakedown 480.8
theft 482.3
overcharge 632.5

extortionate extractive
192.17
demanding 421.9
rapacious 480.26
overpriced 632.12

extra
noun bonus 254.4
film studio 706.3
match 747.3
nonessential 767.2
surplus 992.5
adj additional 253.10
unused 390.12
newspaper 555.2
unessential 767.4
occasional 847.3
surplus 992.18
adv additionally
253.11

extract
noun perfumery 70.2
extraction 192.8
excerpt 557.3
distillation 892.3
verb refine 79.22
take out 192.10
subtract 255.9
select 371.14

rescue 398.3
process 891.9
conclude 945.10

extracted 891.18

extraction refinement
79.4
egress 190.2
withdrawal 192.1
extract 192.8
reduction 255.2
excerpt 557.3
lineage 560.4
production 891.2
pulling 904.1

extractor 192.9

extracts 557.4

extradite transfer
176.10
restore 481.4
banish 908.17

extradition
noun restitution 481.1
banishment 908.4
phrase transference
176.1

extraneous extrinsic
767.3
foreign 773.5
unrelated 775.6
irrelevant 775.7

extraordinaire 996.19

extraordinarily
wonderfully 122.14
intensely 247.20
exceptionally 869.18

extraordinary
wonderful 122.10
unexpected 131.10
remarkable 247.10
particular 864.12
exceptional 869.14
notable 996.19

extra time 745.3

extravagance
exaggeration 355.1
prodigality 486.1
showiness 501.3
wordiness 538.2
exorbitance 632.4
intemperance 669.1
fanaticism 925.11
plenty 990.2
superfluity 992.4

extravagant
exaggerated 355.4
prodigal 486.8
gaudy 501.20
grandiose 501.21
inflated 502.12
diffuse 538.11
overpriced 632.12
intemperate 669.7
violent 671.16
absurd 922.11
fanatic 925.32
fanciful 985.20
plentiful 990.7
excessive 992.16

extravagantly
distressingly 247.21
grandiosely 501.28
exorbitantly 632.16
plentifully 990.9
superabundantly
992.24

extravaganza
fabrication 354.10
showiness 501.3

extreme
noun exaggeration
355.1
limit 793.5
extremity 819.2
excess 992.1
adj exquisite 24.13
bordering 211.11
radical 247.13, 611.29
farthest 261.12
rebellious 327.11
exaggerated 355.4
intemperate 669.7
violent 671.16
final 819.11
fanatic 925.32
excessive 992.16

extreme left 611.5

extreme left wing
611.5

extreme left-wing
611.29

extremely to a degree
245.7
utterly 247.22

extreme right 611.5

extreme right wing
611.5

extremes 992.1

extremism
rebelliousness 327.3
reform 392.5
radicalism 611.5
fanaticism 925.11
excess 992.1

extremist
noun rebel 327.5
reformer 392.6
radical 611.17
adj radical 611.29
fanatic 925.32

extremity wretchedness
96.6
summit 198.2
foot 199.5
boundary 211.3
moribundity 307.9
violence 671.1
limit 793.5
extreme 819.2
crisis 842.4
excess 992.1
impasse 1012.6

extricate extract 192.10
rescue 398.3
free 431.7
disembarrass 1013.9

extrovert

noun introvert 92.12
adj extroverted 92.40

exuberance happiness
95.2
gaiety 109.4
unrestraint 430.3
wordiness 538.2
productiveness 889.1
plenty 990.2

exuberant fervent
93.18
gay 109.14
luxuriant 310.40
unrestrained 430.24
diffuse 538.11
productive 889.9
plentiful 990.7
thriving 1009.13

exude excrete 12.12
sweat 12.16
exudate 190.15
be damp 1063.11

exuding
noun exudation 190.6
adj exudative 190.20

exultant overjoyed
95.16
rejoicing 116.10
crowing 502.13

eye
noun visual organ 2.9,
27.9
vision 27.1
look 27.3
circlet 280.5
supervision 573.2
tec 576.11
discrimination 943.1
opinion 952.6
outlook 977.2
protection 1007.1
verb look 27.13
scrutinize 27.14
gaze 27.15
flirt 562.20
spectate 917.5
adj optic 2.26
visual 27.20

eyeball
noun eye 2.9, 27.9
verb look 27.13
examine 937.24
adj visual 27.20

eyebrows 3.12

eye-catching alluring
377.8
attracting 906.5
easy on the eyes
1015.21

eye contact 27.5

eye for 413.5

eyelashes 3.12

eyelid 2.9, 27.9

eyeliner 1015.12

eye-opener drink 88.9
surprise 131.2

eye shadow 1015.12

eyesight vision 27.1

field of view 31.3
eyes-only secret 345.11
  confidential 345.14
eyesore stain 1003.3
  blot 1014.4
eye-witness 956.16
eyewitness spectator
  917.1
  witness 956.6
fa 709.7
fab 998.13
Fabian
  noun reformer 392.6
  socialist 611.19
  adj emendatory 392.16
  socialist 611.31
fable
  noun fabrication
  354.10
  plot 722.4
  verb narrate 722.6
fabled 662.16
fabric material 4.1
  substance 196.5, 762.2
  house 228.5
  structure 266.1, 266.2
  frame 266.4
  weaving 740.1
fabricated invented
  354.29, 891.19
  made 891.18
  fictitious 985.21
fabrication structure
  266.1
  invention 354.10,
  985.3
  composition 795.1
  production 891.1,
  891.2
fabulous wonderful
  122.10
  remarkable 247.10
  fabricated 354.29
  mythic 678.15
  fictional 722.7
  extraordinary 869.14
  fictitious 985.21
  excessive 992.16
fabulously wonderfully
  122.14
  extraordinarily 869.18
facade appearance 33.2
  exterior 206.2
  front 216.1
  sham 354.3
  pretext 376.1
  affectation 500.1
face
  noun looks 33.4
  pride 136.1
  cheek 142.3
  precipice 200.3
  exterior 206.2
  front 216.1
  facies 216.4
  slope 237.2
  sham 354.3
  battle flag 458.12

type 548.6
  worth 630.2
  reputability 662.2
  prestige 662.4
  verb colour 35.13
  expect 130.5
  fill 196.7
  contrapose 215.4
  confront 216.8, 451.5
  veneer 295.23
  plaster 295.25
  defy 454.3
  brave 492.11
  be imminent 839.2
faced 296.6
face down offer
  resistance 453.3
  outbrave 492.12
faceless uniform 780.5
  indistinguishable
  944.6
face-lift 396.17
facelift 1015.11
face mask safeguard
  1007.3
  makeup 1015.12
facet aspect 33.3
  exterior 206.2
  front 216.1
  particular 765.3
facetious 489.15
face-to-face
  adj adjacent 223.16
  adv opposite 215.6
  openly 348.15
face to face with
  451.10
face up 492.11
face up to offer
  resistance 453.3
  brave 492.11
  take chances 1005.7
face value worth 630.2
  price 738.9
face with 216.8
facial beautification
  1015.11
  massage 1042.3
facile docile 433.13
  eloquent 544.8
  fluent 544.9
  teachable 570.18
  easy 1013.13
facilitate advance
  162.5
  be instrumental 384.7
  be useful 449.17
  ease 1013.7
facilitating
  noun facilitation
  1013.5
  adj modal 384.8
facilities
  accommodations 385.3
  equipment 385.4
facility ability 18.2
  equipment 385.4

skill 413.1
  submissiveness 433.3
  accommodation 449.9
  fluency 544.2
  teachableness 570.5
  workplace 739.1
  ease 1013.1
  machinery 1039.3
  pliancy 1045.2
facing
  noun lining 196.3
  blanket 295.12
  adj contrapositive
  215.5
  fronting 216.11
  adv frontward 216.13
  prep opposite to 215.7
facsimile
  noun reproduction
  336.3
  fax 347.15
  same 777.3
  copy 784.1
  duplicate 784.3
  print 784.5
  verb copy 784.8
  adj communicational
  347.20
fact case 760.3
  particular 765.3
  event 830.2
  evidence 956.1
  truth 972.1
fact-finding 937.37
faction dissension
  456.3
  political party 609.24
  party 617.4
  partisanism 617.13
  sect 675.3
  company 769.3
  disagreement 788.1
factional 456.17,
  617.19
factionalism 617.13
factor
  noun heredity 560.6
  steward 574.4
  agent 576.3
  particular 765.3
  component 795.2
  cause 885.1
  verb classify 800.8
  calculate 1016.17
factory 739.3
factory worker 607.9,
  726.2
facts information 551.1,
  760.4
  knowledge 927.1
  evidence 956.1
fact sheet information
  551.1
  confirmation 956.4
factual real 760.15
  evidential 956.16
  obvious 969.15
  true 972.13

faculties 918.2
faculty ability 18.2
  talent 413.4
  authority 417.1
  staff 571.9
  prerogative 642.1
fad caprice 364.1
  great success 409.3
  craze 578.5
fade
  noun film editing
  706.5
  verb weaken 16.9
  disappear 34.3
  decolour 36.5
  lose colour 36.6
  fail 85.47
  recede 168.2
  age 303.10, 841.9
  decline 393.17
  languish 393.18
  play 748.4
  race 757.5
  bet 759.25
  flit 827.6
  pass 836.6
  adj insipid 65.2
fade away recede 168.2
  languish 393.18
  perish 395.23
  pass 836.6
faded colourless 36.7
  weatherworn 393.34
  past 836.7
fade in 33.8
fade-in 1033.16
fade out 36.6
fade-out decrease 252.1
  radio broadcasting
  1033.16
  reception 1033.21
fading
  noun disappearance
  34.1
  decoloration 36.3
  deterioration 393.3
  reception 1033.21
  adj languishing 16.21
  vanishing 34.4
  receding 168.5
  deteriorating 393.45
  transient 827.7
faecal excremental
  12.20
  malodorous 71.5
  filthy 80.23
faeces feculence 12.4
  dregs 256.2
fag
  noun homo 75.15
  subordinate 432.5
  attendant 577.5
  work 725.4
  drudge 726.3
  verb beat 21.6
  serve 577.13
  drudge 725.14
  task 725.16

faggot homo 75.15
  bundle 769.8
  firewood 1020.3
Fahrenheit 1018.30
fail weaken 16.9, 85.47
  be inferior 250.4
  age 303.10
  neglect 340.6, 408.2
  decline 393.17
  be unsuccessful 410.9
  go bankrupt 625.7
  be unfaithful 645.12
  dramatize 704.28
  fall short 910.2
  be insufficient 991.8
failed useless 391.9
  unsuccessful 410.18
  insolvent 625.11
failing
  noun deterioration
  393.3
  vice 654.2
  fault 1002.2
  adj languishing 16.21
  unhealthy 85.53
  deteriorating 393.45
  unsuccessful 410.18
  incomplete 794.4
  insufficient 991.9
failure ineffectiveness
  19.3
  disappointment 132.1
  inadequacy 250.3
  neglect 340.1
  deterioration 393.3
  nonaccomplishment
  408.1
  unsuccessfulness 410.1
  flash in the pan 410.7
  defeat 412.1
  nonobservance 435.1
  insolvency 625.3
  insolvent 625.4
  vice 654.2
  misdeed 655.2
  stage show 704.4
  shortcoming 910.1
  mistake 974.3
  loss of memory 989.2
  fault 1002.2
faint
  noun unconsciousness
  25.2
  verb weaken 16.9
  burn out 21.5
  swoon 25.5
  adj weak 16.12
  tired 21.7
  inconspicuous 32.6
  colourless 36.7
  low 52.16
  ill 85.55
  weak-willed 362.12
fainting
  noun anaemia 85.9
  adj tired 21.7
faintly weakly 16.22
  softly 52.21
  scarcely 248.9

fair
noun marketplace 736.2
festival 743.4
adj light 36.9
whitish 37.8
clean 79.25
pleasant 97.6
bright 97.11
auspicious 133.18
courteous 504.14
legible 521.12
rightful 639.8
honest 644.13
just 649.8
probable 967.6
unprejudiced 978.12
good 998.12
tolerable 998.20
mediocre 1004.7
thriving 1009.13
comely 1015.18
warm 1018.24
rainless 1064.8
adv pleasantly 97.12
justly 649.11

Fair Deal 609.6

fair game
laughingstock 508.7
opportunity 842.2

fairground 743.14

fair-haired 37.9

fairly to a degree 245.7, 248.10
legibly 521.14
justly 649.11
tolerably 998.24
mediocrely 1004.11

fairly well 998.24

fair-minded 649.9

fairness paleness 36.2
whiteness 37.1
probity 644.1
fair-mindedness 649.3
unprejudicedness 978.5
goodness 998.1
comeliness 1015.3

fair play 649.3

fair-trading 630.5

fairway seaway 182.10
runway 184.23
green 310.7
playground 743.11
golf 748.1

fair weather
cheerfulness 97.4
weather 317.3
good times 1009.4
hot weather 1018.7

fairy
noun homo 75.15
air 298.2
sprite 678.8
adj faery 678.17

fairy godmother giver 478.11
familiar spirit 678.12

fairyland 678.7

fairy tale 354.11

fairy-tale 354.29

fait accompli
noun act 328.3
fact 760.3
adj accomplishment 407.1

faith zeal 101.2
hope 124.1
observance 434.1
promise 436.1
school 617.5
fidelity 644.7
cardinal virtues 653.4
religion 675.1
true faith 687.2
piety 692.1
cause 885.9
belief 952.1
system of belief 952.3
confidence 969.5

faithful
noun believing 692.5
believer 952.9
adj zealous 101.9
loving 104.27
obedient 326.3
descriptive 349.14
persevering 360.8
observant 434.4
devoted 587.21
loyal 644.20
orthodox 687.7
pious 692.8
lifelike 783.16
permanent 852.7
belief 952.21
reliable 969.17
exact 972.17

faithfully obediently 326.6
descriptively 349.16
perseveringly 360.9
loyally 644.25
exactly 972.21

faithfulness zeal 101.2
observance 434.1
fidelity 644.7
piety 692.1
accuracy 972.5

faithless falsehearted 354.31
apostate 363.11
unfaithful 645.20
unbelieving 695.19, 954.8

fake
noun put-up job 354.13
basketball game 751.3
verb imitate 336.5
tamper with 354.17
fabricate 354.18
sham 354.21
improvise 365.8
affect 500.12
play 751.4
adj spurious 354.26

faked 354.26

fake fur 4.2

faking 354.3

falcon
noun bird 311.28
heraldic device 647.2
verb hunt 382.9

falconer 382.5

falconry 382.2

fall
noun false hair 3.13
descent 194.1
tumble 194.3
hang 202.2
declivity 204.5
waterfall 238.11
decline 252.2
autumn 313.4
rain 316.1
plunge 367.1
deterioration 393.3
backsliding 394.2
downfall 395.3
collapse 410.3
defeat 412.1
original sin 655.3
downthrow 912.2
verb descend 194.5
tumble 194.8
hang 202.6
incline 204.10
decrease 252.6
die 307.19
rain 316.9
plunge 367.6
decline 393.17
relapse 394.4
fall to the ground 395.22
fall down 410.12
lose 412.12
cheapen 633.6
go wrong 654.9
occur 830.5
come to grief 1010.10

fallacy falseness 354.1
deception 356.1
heresy 688.2
sophistry 935.1
sophism 935.3
error 974.1

fall apart break 393.23
come apart 801.9

fall asleep go to sleep 22.16
die 307.19

fall away decrease 252.6
decline 393.17
fall short 910.2

fall back retreat 163.6
bring up the rear 217.8
deteriorate 393.16
relapse 394.4

fall behind 217.8

fall down drift off course 182.29
tumble 194.8

fall 410.12
fall through 910.3
fall short 1002.3

fallen reduced 252.10
dead 307.30
ruined 395.28
defeated 412.14
unvirtuous 654.12
carnal 663.6
prostitute 665.28
impious 694.6
unregenerate 695.18
depressed 912.12

fall for 953.6

fall from grace
noun backsliding 394.2
original sin 655.3
verb relapse 394.4

fall guy 358.2

fallible errable 970.22
imperfect 1002.4

fall in collapse 260.10
obey 326.2
fall 410.12
form 806.5
line up 811.6

falling
noun descent 194.1
adj descending 194.11
pendent 202.9
downhill 204.16
deteriorating 393.45

falling back 394.1

falling-off deterioration 393.3
modulation 670.2

falling-out 456.4

fall in love 104.22

fall into undertake 404.3
incur 896.4

fall off descend 194.5
decrease 252.6
decline 393.17

fall on light upon 194.10
come across 940.3

fallopian tube 2.21

fall out have a falling-out 456.10
result 886.4

fallout aftereffect 886.3
radiation 1036.1
atomic explosion 1037.16
powder 1049.5

fall over 194.8

fallow
noun farm 1067.8
verb cultivate 1067.17
adj colourless 36.7
yellow 43.4
idle 331.18
untilled 406.14
unproductive 890.4

falls 238.11

fall short fall 410.12

lack 794.3
come short 910.2, 1002.3
be insufficient 991.8

fall through fall 410.12
fall down 910.3

fall to eat 8.20
undertake 404.3
set to work 725.15
begin 817.7

false untrue 354.25
falsehearted 354.31
deceptive 356.21
deceitful 356.22
unfaithful 645.20
illegitimate 674.7
be sanctimonious 693.4
erroneous 974.16
illusory 975.9

false alarm cry of wolf 400.2
loser 410.8

falsehood falseness 354.1
untruthfulness 354.8
lie 354.11

falsely untruly 354.35
deceptively 356.23
erroneously 974.20

falsetto
noun soprano 58.6
speech defect 525.1
voice 709.5
adj high 58.13
vocal 708.50

falsified perverted 265.11
spurious 354.26

falter
noun demur 325.2
hesitation 362.3
trill 709.19
shake 916.3
flounder 916.8
verb despair 125.10
dawdle 175.8
demur 325.4
hesitate 362.7
lose one's nerve 491.8
stammer 525.8
shake 916.11
flounder 916.15
hang in doubt 970.10

faltering
noun demur 325.2
hesitation 362.3
stammering 525.3
adj slow 175.10
demurring 325.7
hesitant 362.11
stammering 525.13

fame glory 247.2
publicity 352.4
repute 662.1
notability 996.2

famed 662.16

familiar
noun friend 588.1

familiar spirit 678.12
adj trite 117.9
insolent 142.9
customary 373.14
vernacular 523.18
informal 581.3
intimate 582.24,
587.19
usual 868.9
well-known 927.27
familiarity informality
581.1
sociability 582.1
intimacy 587.5
presumption 640.2
knowledge 927.1
familiar with used to
373.17
versed in 927.19
family
noun nomenclature
527.1
kinfolk 559.2
race 559.4
brood 559.5
lineage 560.4
posterity 561.1
community 617.2
kingdom 808.5
sequel 834.2
biology 1066.1
adj racial 559.7
lineal 560.18
Family Credit 611.8
family credit 478.8
family doctor 90.4
family home 228.2
family name 527.5
family planning 890.1
family room 197.12
family tree 560.5
famine
unproductiveness
890.1
want 991.4
famished hungry
100.25
ill-provided 991.12
famous eminent 247.9
distinguished 662.16
good 998.12
famously intensely
247.20
notably 662.21
excellently 998.22
fan
noun buff 101.5
fork 171.4
ventilator 317.9
flabellum 318.19
supporter 616.9
specialist 865.3
propeller 903.6
cooler 1023.3
verb excite 105.12
spread 259.6
air 317.10
incite 375.17

fanatic
noun enthusiast 101.4
mule 361.6
believer 692.4
oddity 869.4
infatuate 925.18
bigot 979.5
adj obstinate 361.8
fiery 671.22
fanatical 925.32
fanatical overzealous
101.12
obstinate 361.8
zealous 692.11
fanatic 925.32
narrow-minded 979.10
fanaticism
overzealousness 101.3
obstinacy 361.1
turbulence 671.2
zeal 692.3
cause 885.9
fanaticalness 925.11
narrow-mindedness
979.1
fancied fabricated
354.29
unreal 761.9
imaginary 985.19
fancier desirer 100.12
enthusiast 101.4
collector 769.15
imaginer 985.12
fanciful capricious
364.5
unreal 761.9
thin 763.6
fantastic 869.12
ideational 931.9
notional 985.20
fan club 101.5
fancy
noun desire 100.1
inclination 100.3
love 104.1
will 323.1
caprice 364.1
impulse 365.1
preference 371.5
idea 931.1
phantasy 975.3
imagination 985.1
figment of the
imagination 985.5
verb lust 75.20
desire 100.14
love 104.19
suppose 950.10
think 952.11
imagine 985.14
adj edible 8.33
skilful 413.22
ornate 498.12, 545.11
ostentatious 501.18
grandiose 501.21
overpriced 632.12
fancy dress 5.10
fanfare blare 53.5
celebration 487.1

Aldine 554.15
fang teeth 2.8
sting 1000.5
fangs 474.4
fan mail 553.4
fanned 259.11
fanning 259.11
fans 917.2
fantasize fabricate
354.18
imagine 985.14
fantastic wonderful
122.10
remarkable 247.10
fabricated 354.29
unreal 761.9
fantastical 869.12
absurd 922.11
illusory 975.9
fanciful 985.20
fantastical fantastic
869.12
absurd 922.11
fanciful 985.20
fantastically
wonderfully 122.14
oddly 869.19
fantasy
noun defence
mechanism 92.23
desire 100.1
caprice 364.1
miracle 869.8
phantom 975.4
abstractedness 984.2
imagination 985.1
figment of the
imagination 985.5
verb muse 984.9
dream 985.17
fanzine 101.5
far
adj distant 261.8
adv by far 247.17
far off 261.15
far afield 261.19
far ahead 844.8
far and away by far
247.17
superlatively 249.16
far and wide
extensively 158.11
by far 247.17
far and near 261.16
far away 261.15
faraway distant 261.8
abstracted 984.11
farce wit 489.1
burlesque 508.6
comedy 704.6
trifle 997.5
farcical witty 489.15
burlesque 508.14
comic 704.35
far cry
noun long way 261.2
difference 779.1

adj nothing like 786.5
fare
noun food 10.1
traveller 178.1
fee 630.6
verb eat 8.20
travel 177.18
journey 177.21
result 886.4
Far East 231.6
farewell
noun leave-taking
188.4
adj departing 188.18
far-flung long 267.7
extensive 863.13
far from home 222.12
far from it
adv amiss 910.7
exclam no 335.8
by no means 335.9
far-gone intoxicated
88.31
worn-out 393.36
involved in 897.5
farina 1049.5
farm
noun house 228.5
farmplace 1067.8
stock farm 1068.5
verb ruralize 233.5
rent out 615.16
ranch 1067.16
raise 1068.6
adj rustic 233.6
agricultural 1067.20
farmer peasant 606.6
tax collector 630.10
agriculturist 1067.5
farmhouse 228.5
farming
noun agriculture
1067.1
adj agricultural
1067.20
farmland country
233.1
farm 1067.8
farm machinery
1039.3
farmyard 1067.8
far off 261.15
far-off 261.8
far on 845.19
far out 840.13
farrago lie 354.11
jumble 809.3
far-reaching spacious
158.10
long 267.7
extensive 863.13
farrier smith 726.8
stockman 1068.2
farrow
noun young 561.2
verb give birth 1.3

fart
noun stinker 71.3
arsehole 660.6
zilch 761.3
verb blow off 908.29
farther
adj additional 253.10
thither 261.10
adv additionally
253.11
farthest furthest 261.12
final 819.11
farthing modicum
248.2
mite 728.7
fourth 880.2
trifle 997.5
farting 1065.3
fascia horizontal 201.3
front 216.1
strip 271.4
band 280.3
fascinate delight 95.9
enamour 104.23
thrill 105.15
captivate 377.7
charm 691.8
interest 982.12
engross 982.13
fascinated enamoured
104.28
wondering 122.9
enchanted 691.12
interested 982.16
gripped 982.18
fascinating delightful
97.7
wonderful 122.10
alluring 377.8
bewitching 691.11
engrossing 982.20
fascination
delightfulness 97.2
inclination 100.3
eagerness 101.1
wonder 122.1
wonderfulness 122.3
allurement 377.1
bewitchment 691.2
mania 925.12
obsession 925.13
fascism nationalism
611.10
central government
612.4
democratism 612.8
despotism 612.10
discrimination 979.4
fascist
noun nationalist
611.21
adj nationalist 611.33
governmental 612.17
fash 96.13
fashion
noun clothing 5.1
aspect 33.3
form 262.1
structure 266.1

custom 373.1
manner 384.1
style 532.2, 578.1
mode 764.4
verb form 262.7
produce 891.8

fashionable
noun person of fashion 578.7
adj in fashion 578.11
modern 840.13

fashionably 578.17

fashioned formative 262.9
made 891.18

fashioning forming 262.5
structure 266.1
composition 795.1
production 891.2

fast
noun lack of food 515.2
abstinence 668.2
holy day 701.11
verb not eat 515.4
adj deep-dyed 35.17
swift 174.15
close 293.12
confirmed 373.19
devoted 587.21
profligate 665.25
fastened 799.14
stable 854.12
stuck 854.16
reliable 969.17
adv swiftly 174.17
securely 799.19

fast asleep 22.22

fast bowler 747.2

fasten close 293.6
bind 428.10
fix 799.7
secure 854.8

fastened fast 799.14
fixed 854.14
stuck 854.16

fastening 799.3

fast food 10.1

fast-forward
noun run 174.3
hastening 401.3
verb progress 162.2

fast-growing grown 14.3, 259.12
increasing 251.8

fastidious clean 79.25
particular 495.9
elegant 496.9
conscientious 644.15
discriminating 943.7

fasting
noun abstinence from food 515.1
penance 658.3
asceticism 667.1
adj hungry 100.25
uneating 515.5

fast time 831.3

fat
noun glyceride 7.7
superfluity 992.4
best 998.8
oil 1054.1
verb fatten 259.8
adj corpulent 257.18
distended 259.13
stubby 268.10
thick 269.8
heavy 297.16
gainful 472.16
wealthy 618.14
stupid 921.15
plentiful 990.7
thriving 1009.13
oily 1054.9

fatal deadly 308.22
destructive 395.26
future 838.8
destined 963.9
chance 971.15
weighty 996.20
unfortunate 1010.14
disastrous 1010.15

fatal accident 308.7

fatalism composure 106.2
resignation 134.2
determinism 963.4

fatalistic 963.10

fatality ominousness 133.7
inauspiciousness 133.8
fatal accident 308.7
deadliness 308.8
fate 963.2

fatally 838.9

fate
noun end 395.2, 819.1
portion 477.5
destiny 838.2
inevitability 962.7
fatality 963.2
chance 971.1
verb allot 477.9
destine 963.7

fated future 838.8
inevitable 962.15
destined 963.9

fateful ominous 133.17
destructive 395.26
inevitable 962.15
destined 963.9
weighty 996.20

Fates destiny 838.2
Fata 963.3

Father 648.5

father
noun senior 304.5
brother 559.3
sire 560.9
priest 699.5
author 885.4
producer 891.7
personage 996.8
verb procreate 78.8
engender 817.14

cause 885.10
trace to 887.5

Father Christmas 678.13

father figure 92.31

Fatherhood 677.1

fatherhood blood relationship 559.1
paternity 560.2

father-in-law 564.2

fatherland 232.2

fatherless helpless 19.18
bereaved 307.35
forlorn 584.12

fatherly 560.17

Fathers 684.2

fathers 560.7

fathom sound 275.9
measure 300.10
understand 521.7
know 927.12
investigate 937.23
solve 939.2

fatigue
noun weakness 16.1
weakening 16.5
tiredness 21.1
anaemia 85.9
languor 331.6
work 725.4
verb tire 21.4
burn out 21.5
be tedious 118.6

fatigued weakened 16.18
tired 21.7
worn-out 393.36

fatigues 5.1

fattening
noun increase 251.1
adj fertilizing 889.11

fatty 1054.9

fatty acid 7.7

fatuous ineffective 19.15
vain 391.13
thin 763.6
foolish 922.8
thoughtless 932.4
trivial 997.19

fault
noun crack 224.2
vice 654.2
misdeed 655.2
game 749.2
error 974.1
mistake 974.3
faute 1002.2
blemish 1003.1
verb complain 115.15
deprecate 510.12
play tennis 749.3

faultless innocent 657.6
accurate 972.16
perfect 1001.6

faulty ungrammatic 531.4
guilty 656.3
illogical 935.11
erroneous 974.16
imperfect 1002.4
blemished 1003.8

fauna animal life 311.1
biology 1066.1

Faust 690.5

favour
noun looks 33.4
inclination 100.3
act of kindness 143.7
pity 145.1
respect 155.1
face 216.4
superiority 249.1
preference 371.5
patronage 449.4
benefit 478.7
approval 509.1
letter 553.2
good terms 587.3
privilege 642.2
esteem 662.3
influence 893.1
special favour 893.2
memento 988.7
verb desire 100.14
be kind 143.9
respect 155.4
prefer 371.17, 650.8
improve 392.9
indulge 427.6
aid 449.11
abet 449.14
be useful 449.17
oblige 449.19
approve 509.9
resemble 783.7
do good 998.10

favourable promising 124.13
auspicious 133.18
willing 324.5
consenting 441.4
propitious 449.22
approving 509.17
friendly 587.15
timely 842.9
expedient 994.5
good 998.12

favourably auspiciously 133.21
kindly 143.18
advantageously 249.19
agreeably 324.9
consentingly 441.5
helpfully 449.24
amicably 587.22

favoured preferable 371.25
exempt 430.30
approved 509.19
fortunate 1009.14

favouring
noun indulgence 427.3
adj auspicious 133.18
preferable 371.25

modal 384.8
approving 509.17
similar 783.10

favourite
noun preference 104.16
jockey 757.2
adj beloved 104.24
approved 509.19

favouritism partiality 650.3
prejudice 979.3

favour with furnish 478.15
endow 478.17

fawn
noun fledgling 302.10
deer 311.5
verb give birth 1.3
truckle 138.7
adj brown 40.3

fawning
noun obsequiousness 138.2
flattery 511.1
adj obsequious 138.14
flattering 511.8

fax
noun facsimile 347.15
print 784.5
verb copy 784.8
adj communicational 347.20

fay
noun fairy 678.8
adj fairy 678.17

fear
noun anxiety 126.1
fright 127.1
nervousness 128.1
weak will 362.4
cowardice 491.1
verb be afraid 127.10
hesitate 362.7

fear for 133.11

fearful anxious 126.7
fearing 127.23
frightening 127.28
nervous 128.11
terrific 247.11
cowardly 491.10

fearfully apprehensively 127.32
frightfully 127.34

fearing 127.23

fearless 492.20

fearlessly 492.23

fearsome fearful 127.23
frightening 127.28

feasibility workability 888.3
practicability 965.2
handiness 1013.2

feasible
noun possibility 965.1
adj workable 888.10
practicable 965.7

expedient 994.5
practical 994.6
handy 1013.15

feast
noun banquet 8.9
food 10.1
holiday 20.4
treat 95.3
holy day 701.11
festival 743.4
verb banquet 8.24,
743.25
gratify 95.7

feast day 20.4

feasting 8.1

feat act 328.3
masterpiece 413.10
exploit 492.7

feather
noun plume 3.17
plumage 3.19
air 298.2
kind 808.3
trifle 997.5
verb fledge 3.22
row 182.53
stunt 184.40
fill 196.7
figure 498.9

feathered plumaged
3.29
ornamented 498.11

feathering 3.19

feathers plumage 3.19
clothing 5.1
putty 1045.4

featherweight
noun runt 258.4
bantamweight 297.3
adj lightweight 298.13
uninfluential 894.3

feathery plumy 3.28
light 298.10
fluffy 1045.14

feature
noun aspect 33.3
looks 33.4
treatise 556.1
cinema 706.1
commodity 735.2
component 795.2
characteristic 864.4
special 865.2
highlight 996.7
verb manifest 348.5
dramatize 704.28
specify 864.11
specialize 865.4
call attention to
982.10
emphasize 996.14
headline 996.15
adj specialized 865.5

featured conspicuous
348.12
specialized 865.5

feature film 706.1

featureless vacant
222.14
formless 263.4
continuous 811.8
general 863.11

features looks 33.4
outline 211.2
face 216.4
appearance 262.3

featuring
conspicuousness 348.4
specification 864.6

febrile feverish 85.57
fervent 93.18
overzealous 101.12
heated 105.22

feckless ineffective
19.15
useless 391.9
improvident 406.15

federal
noun policeman
1007.15
adj governmental
612.17
combining 804.7

federal assembly
613.1

federal court 595.2

federal government
612.4

federalism
independence 430.5
democratism 612.8

federalist 612.17

federated 804.6

federation affiliation
450.2
central government
612.4
association 617.1
combination 804.1

fed up 118.11

fee
noun gratuity 478.5
stipend 624.5
dues 630.6
verb pay 624.10

feeble weak 16.12
impotent 19.13
inconspicuous 32.6
faint 52.16
unhealthy 85.53
stricken in years
303.18
weak-willed 362.12
feebleminded 921.21
unsound 935.12

feebly weakly 16.22
faintly 52.21
scarcely 248.9

feed
noun fodder 10.4
verb nourish 7.15
dine 8.18
eat 8.20
gratify 95.7
encourage 375.21

provision 385.9
foster 449.16
fertilize 889.8
ignite 1019.22
fuel 1020.7
raise 1068.6
tend 1068.7

feedback audio
distortion 50.13
reaction 902.1
closed sequence
1040.6

feeder eater 8.16
tributary 238.3
role 704.10

feeding
noun nutrition 7.1
eating 8.1
adj eating 8.31

feed on 138.12

feel
noun touch 73.1
milieu 209.3
texture 294.1
knack 413.6
discrimination 943.1
verb sense 24.6
appear to be 33.10
touch 73.6
contact 223.10
experience 830.8
intuit 933.4
suppose 950.10

feel about it 977.6

feel at home be at ease
121.8
be free 430.18

feel better about
120.8

feel confident 124.7

feel for pity 145.3
grope 937.32

feel free
verb be free 430.18
exclam please 440.20

feel good enjoy good
health 83.6
be pleased 95.11

feel happy 95.11

feel ill 85.45

feeling
noun sensation 24.1
touch 73.1
touching 73.2
emotion 93.1
pity 145.1
milieu 209.3
hunch 933.3
discrimination 943.1
suggestion 950.5
opinion 952.6
attitude 977.1
mood 977.4
adj emotional 93.17
intuitive 933.5
examining 937.37

feelings feeling 93.1
mood 977.4

feel of 73.6

feel pain 26.8

feel sure be confident
952.14
be certain 969.9

feel with 147.2

fee simple 469.1

feet 548.6

feign sham 354.21
affect 500.12

feigned spurious
354.26
assumed 500.16

feigning 354.3

feisty crabby 110.20
hot-tempered 110.25
perverse 361.11
partisan 456.17
argumentative 934.19

felicitous pleasant 97.6
decorous 496.10
appropriate 533.7
eloquent 544.8
apt 787.10
timely 842.9
expedient 994.5

felicity happiness 95.2
aptitude 413.5
decorousness 496.3
elegance 533.1
eloquence 544.1
prosperity 1009.1

feline
noun vertebrate 311.3
cat 311.21
adj felid 311.41
covert 345.12
cunning 415.12

fell
noun fur 4.2
plain 236.1
plateau 237.3
skin 295.3
verb level 201.6
strike dead 308.17
raze 395.19
conquer 412.10
shoot 903.12
drop 912.5
adj terrible 127.30
cruel 144.26

fellah 606.6

felled 412.17

feller 76.5

fellow
noun guy 76.5
doctor 90.4
boy 302.5
person 312.5
image 349.5
teacher 571.1
friend 588.1
companion 588.3
associate 616.1
member 617.11
accompanier 768.4
likeness 783.3
equal 789.4

adj cooperative 450.5
accompanying 768.9

fellow countryman
227.5

fellowship
noun cooperation
450.1
affiliation 450.2
accord 455.1
subsidy 478.8
instructorship 571.10
camaraderie 582.2
social life 582.4
association 582.6
companionship 587.2
sodality 617.3
scholarship 646.7
sect 675.3
company 768.2
verb associate with
582.17

fellow student 572.3

felt 4.1

female
noun female being
77.4
adj feminine 77.13

female sex 77.3

Femidom 86.23

feminine
noun gender 530.10
adj female 77.13

femininity sex 75.1
feminality 77.1
womankind 77.3
maturity 303.2

feminism effeminacy
77.2
women's rights 642.4
discrimination 979.4

feminist women's
rightist 642.5
bigot 979.5

femme 77.5

femme fatale tempter
377.4
demimonde 665.15

fen 243.1

fence
noun wall 212.4
fortification 460.4
receiver 732.6
barrier 1011.5
verb wall 212.7
dodge 368.8
contend 457.13
fortify 460.9
push 732.7
quibble 935.9
protect 1007.18

fenced 212.10

fence in enclose 212.5
fence 212.7

fencing prevarication
344.4
swordplay 457.8
quibbling 935.5

fend fend off 460.10
protect 1007.18
prevent 1011.14

fender partition 213.5
safeguard 1007.3
fireplace 1019.11

fend off ward off
460.10
repulse 907.3
prevent 1011.14

fenland 243.1

Fens 231.7

feral frenzied 105.25
cruel 144.26
deadly 308.22
funereal 309.22
animal 311.38
savage 671.21

ferment
noun bread 10.27
agitation 105.4, 916.1
dudgeon 152.7
leavening 298.4
bubbling 320.3
bustle 330.4
turbulence 671.2
transformer 851.5
verb sour 67.4
leaven 298.7
bubble 320.4
incite 375.17
seethe 671.12
agitate 916.10
chemicalize 1058.7

fermentation souring
67.3
agitation 105.4, 916.1
leavening 298.4
bubbling 320.3

fermenting 298.17

fern 310.4

ferocious frenzied
105.25
cruel 144.26
warlike 458.21
savage 671.21

ferociously cruelly
144.35
savagely 671.27

ferocity cruelty 144.11
warlikeness 458.11

ferret eagle 27.11
bear 311.23

ferrous 1056.17

ferry
noun passageway 383.3
verb haul 176.13
fly 184.36

fertile productive 889.9
imaginative 985.18
plentiful 990.7

fertility wordiness
538.2
productiveness 889.1
invention 985.3
plenty 990.2

fertilization
fecundation 78.3
enrichment 889.3

fertilizer 889.4

fervent fervid 93.18
zealous 101.9
heated 105.22
industrious 330.22
vehement 544.13

fervently fervidly 93.26
zealously 101.14
heatedly 105.34
industriously 330.27
eloquently 544.15

fervour passion 93.2
zeal 101.2
love 104.1
industry 330.6
vehemence 544.5
ardour 1018.2

fester
noun sore 85.36
verb suppurate 12.15
pain 26.7
idle 331.12
decay 393.22

festering
noun pus 12.6
soreness 26.4
sore 85.36
corruption 393.2
adj suppurative 12.21
sore 26.11
decayed 393.40
unforgettable 988.26

festival musical
occasion 708.32
festivity 743.4

festive convivial 582.23
festal 743.28

festooned ornamented
498.11
ornate 545.11

fetal embryonic 305.22
undeveloped 406.12
beginning 817.15

fetch
noun range 158.2
trick 356.6
spectre 987.1
double 987.3
verb bring 176.16
travel 177.18
sail for 182.35
arrive 186.6
attract 377.6
cost 630.13
hit 901.14
conclude 945.10

fetching delightful 97.7
alluring 377.8

fete treat 95.3
festival 743.4
assembly 769.2

fetid nasty 64.7
malodorous 71.5
filthy 80.23
offensive 98.18

terrible 999.9

fetish
noun charm 691.5
idol 697.3
verb idolatrize 697.5

feud
noun quarrel 456.5
possession 469.1
revenge 507.1
animosity 589.4
verb quarrel 456.11
contend 457.13

feudal imperious
417.16
subject 432.13
real 471.9

feudalism subjection
432.1
democratism 612.8

fever feverishness 85.7
anaemia 85.9
fever of excitement
105.7
agitation 916.1
frenzy 925.7
heat 1018.1

fevered feverish 85.57
fervent 93.18

feverish fevered 85.57
fervent 93.18
overzealous 101.12
heated 105.22
hasty 401.9
agitated 916.16
hot 1018.25

feverishly heatedly
105.34
hastily 401.12
agitatedly 916.22

fever pitch 105.7

few
noun plurality 882.1
number 883.2
too few 884.2
minority 884.3
adj insignificant 248.6
least 250.8
not many 884.4

few and far between
infrequent 847.2
sparse 884.5

fewer 884.6

fey supernatural 869.15
eccentric 926.5

fiasco disappointment
132.1
botch 410.6

fiat decree 420.4
authorization 443.3

fibre nutrient 7.3
filament 271.1
organic matter 305.1
nature 766.4

fibreglass 295.23

fibrillation anaemia
85.9
irregularity 850.1

pulsation 915.3

fibroid 271.7

fibrous threadlike 271.7
tough 1047.4

fickle irresolute 362.9
flighty 364.6
unfaithful 645.20
transient 827.7
inconstant 853.7
uncertain 970.16

fiction fabrication
354.10
lie 354.11
writing 547.10
narrative 722.1
invention 985.3
figment of the
imagination 985.5

fictional fabricated
354.29
narrative 719.8
fictionalized 722.7
fictitious 985.21

fictitious spurious
354.26
fabricated 354.29
make-believe 985.21

fiddle
noun gyp 356.9
verb repair 396.14
monkey 997.15

fiddler 710.5

fiddle with 997.14

fiddling 997.8

fiddly 1012.17

fidelity zeal 101.2
perseverance 360.1
observance 434.1
faithfulness 644.7
accuracy 972.5

fidgeting 128.12

fiefdom 469.1

field
noun space 158.1
airport 184.22
setting 209.2
enclosure 212.3
sphere 231.2, 724.4
plot 231.4
latitude 430.4
competitor 452.2
arena 463.1
battlefield 463.2
study 568.8
heraldic device 647.2
playground 743.11
football 745.1
rugby 746.1
hockey 750.1
horse race 757.3
speciality 865.1
science 927.10
tract 1067.9
verb play 747.4

field day festival 743.4
tournament 743.10

fielder 747.2

fielding 747.3

Field Marshal 575.20

field marshal 575.18

field of vision vision
27.1
field of view 31.3

fiend fan 101.5
monster 593.6
demon 680.6

fiendish cruel 144.26
diabolic 654.13
execrable 999.10

fiendishly 144.35

fierce acrimonious
17.14
frenzied 105.25
passionate 105.29
cruel 144.26
infuriated 152.32
warlike 458.21
violent 671.16
savage 671.21

fiercely frenziedly
105.35
cruelly 144.35
violently 247.23,
671.25
savagely 671.27

fiery sore 26.11
red 41.6
feverish 85.57
fervent 93.18
zealous 101.9
heated 105.22, 671.22
passionate 105.29
hot-tempered 110.25
vehement 544.13
igneous 1018.26
heating 1019.26
illuminated 1024.39

fiesta treat 95.3
festival 743.4

fife 708.42

fifteen team 746.2
eleven 881.7

fifth
noun interval 709.20
quinquesection 881.14
adj quinary 881.17

fifty match 747.3
eleven 881.7

fifty-fifty
noun even chance
971.7
adj symmetric 264.4
neutral 467.7
equal 789.7
mixed 796.14

fifty-five 881.7

fifty percent 874.2

fig 997.5

fight
noun quarrel 456.5
contest 457.3
battle 457.4
warlikeness 458.11
struggle 725.3

match 754.3
verb clash 35.14
contend against 451.4
quarrel 456.11
contend 457.13
war 458.14
struggle 725.11
box 754.4

fight against 451.4

fight back contend
against 451.4
offer resistance 453.3
counteract 899.6

fighter military aircraft
181.9
combatant 461.1
boxer 754.2

fighter pilot 185.3

fight for 457.20

fighting
noun contention 457.1
boxing 457.9, 754.1
war 458.1
adj contending 457.22
warlike 458.21

fighting force 18.9

fight it out 457.17

fight off fend off
460.10
repulse 907.3

fight over 457.21

fight with 457.17

figment fabrication
354.10
figment of the
imagination 985.5

figurative
representational
349.13
indicative 517.23
meaningful 518.10
symbolic 519.10
tropologic 536.3
ornate 545.11

figuratively 536.4

figure
noun aspect 33.3
apparition 33.5
gestalt 92.32
outline 211.2
form 262.1, 262.4
figurine 349.6
diagram 381.3
motif 498.7
display 501.4
figure of speech 536.1
ornateness 545.4
price 630.1
repute 662.1
celebrity 662.9
passage 708.24
card 758.2
characteristic 864.4
syllogism 934.6
phantom 975.4
personage 996.8
body 1050.3
verb form 262.7

image 349.11
plan 381.8
filigree 498.9
designate 517.18
metaphorize 536.2
be somebody 662.10
be reasonable 934.17
estimate 945.9
calculate 1016.17

figured planned 381.12
ornamented 498.11
figurative 536.3
ornate 545.11

figurehead prow 216.3
figure 349.6
nominal head 575.5
deputy 576.1
follower 616.8
insignia 647.1
nobody 997.7

figure in 476.5

figure on 380.6

figure out plan 380.6
solve 939.2
calculate 1016.17

figures mathematics
1016.1
statistics 1016.13

figuring 381.1

file
noun gyp 357.4
unit 461.21
document 549.5
bulletin board 549.10
heraldic device 647.2
series 811.2
catalogue 870.3
tool 1039.1
data 1041.15
verb march 177.30
sharpen 285.7
grind 287.8
store 386.10
record 549.15
classify 808.6
defile 811.7
list 870.8
abrade 1042.7

filed recorded 549.17
classified 808.8
listed 870.9

file for 440.9

files 549.3

filial loving 104.27
sonly 561.7

filigree
noun network 170.3
extra 254.4
verb figure 498.9

filing introduction
613.5
classification 808.1
index 870.7
abrasion 1042.2

fill
noun full measure
793.3
satiety 993.1

verb load 159.15
pack 196.7
top 198.9
pervade 221.7
stop 293.7
provide 385.7
observe 434.2
possess 469.4
include 771.3
charge 793.7
iterate 848.8
superabound 992.8
satiate 993.4

filled 793.11

filled out 538.12

filled with 221.15

filler lining 196.3
syntax 530.2

fillet strip 271.4
band 280.3

fill in injure 393.13
amplify 538.7
complete 793.6

fill-in 861.2

filling
noun lining 196.3
extra 254.4
warp 740.3
redundancy 848.3
superfluity 992.4
adj completing 793.13
satiating 993.7

fillip
noun extra 254.4
incentive 375.7
tap 901.7
verb stimulate 105.13
tap 901.18

fill out increase 251.4
enlarge 259.5
round 282.6
execute 437.9
protract 538.8
record 549.15
complete 793.6

fill up stop 293.7
provide 385.7
provision 385.9
fill 793.7
satiate 993.4
fuel 1020.7

filly hen 77.9
gal 302.7
horse 311.10
jockey 757.2

film
noun blanket 295.12
lamina 296.2
fog 319.2
bulletin board 549.10
cinema 706.1
shot 714.8
negative 714.10
verb blur 32.4
cover 295.19
shoot 706.7
photograph 714.14
adj cinema 706.8

film actor film studio
706.3
movie actor 707.4

film company 706.3

film crew 706.3

filmed 295.31

filmmaker 706.3

film noir 706.1

films 706.1

film set 706.3

film speed 714.9

film star film studio
706.3
film actor 707.4

film theatre 706.6

filo 10.39

Filofax notebook
549.11
index 870.7

filter
noun refinery 79.13
light filter 1027.4
verb refine 79.22
exude 190.15
trickle 238.18

filtering refinement
79.4
exuding 190.6

filth muck 80.7
cursing 513.3
obscenity 666.4
terribleness 999.2

filthy foul 80.23
obscene 666.9
lousy 999.8
terrible 999.9

filtration refinement
79.4
exuding 190.6

fin 182.11

final
noun examination
937.2
adj departing 188.18
completing 407.9
mandatory 420.12
terminal 819.11
eventual 830.11
resultant 886.6
evidential 956.16
unqualified 959.2

final draft 547.10

finale act 704.7
end 819.1

finalist 452.2

finality 838.4

finally in fine 819.12
eventually 830.12
consequently 886.7

final say 893.1

final solution carnage
308.4
end 819.1

final touch 407.3

final whistle 856.2

finance
noun finances 729.1
verb support 449.12
subsidize 478.19
pay for 624.18
back 729.15

finances funds 728.14
finance 729.1

financial 728.30

financial assistance
478.8

financial backing
729.2

financial crisis 729.7

financial institution
739.1

financial support
729.2

financial world 729.1

financial year 823.2

financier
noun moneyman 729.8
businessman 730.1
verb invest 729.16

financing borrowing
621.1
funding 729.2

find
noun finding 472.6
discovery 940.1
good thing 998.5
verb arrive 186.6
provide 385.7
learn 570.6
discover 940.2
conclude 945.10
decide 945.11
pass judgment 945.13

find a way 384.6

finder 29.5

finding provision 385.1
find 472.6
solution 939.1
discovery 940.1
verdict 945.5

finding out solution
939.1
discovery 940.1

find out learn 570.6
solve 939.2
discover 940.2
make sure 969.11

find out about 570.6

fine
verb mulct 603.5
spiritualize 763.4
adj edible 8.33
healthy 83.8
pleasant 97.6
tiny 258.11
thin 270.16, 763.6
sharp 285.8
smooth 294.8
rare 299.4
meticulous 339.12
nice 495.11
elegant 496.9

noun fishery 382.3
adj pursuing 382.11
searching 937.38

fishing fleet 180.10

fishmonger 730.5

fish out 937.34

fishy fishlike 311.48
deceptive 356.21
inexpressive 522.20

fissure
noun crack 224.2
break 801.4
interruption 812.2
verb open 292.11
break 393.23, 801.12
sever 801.11

fist
noun clenched fist
462.4
pointer 517.4
handwriting 547.3
verb belt 901.15

fistful multitude 883.3
plenty 990.2

fisticuffs 457.9, 754.1

fit
noun seizure 85.6
outburst 105.9
fit of anger 152.8
bustle 330.4
fitting 405.2
upheaval 671.5
spell 824.1
spasm 916.6
frenzy 925.7
verb outfit 5.40
have place 159.9
equip 385.8
condition 405.8
train 568.13
relate to 774.5
interact 776.6
harmonize 787.7
suit 787.8
equalize 789.6
change 851.7
conform 866.3
expedite one's affair
994.3
adj healthy 83.8
hale 83.12
eligible 371.24
fitted 405.17
competent 413.24
appropriate 533.7
right 637.3
rightful 639.8
just 649.8
apt 787.10
timely 842.9
sufficient 990.6
expedient 994.5

fitful unordered 809.12
discontinuous 812.4
irregular 850.3
inconstant 853.7
jerky 916.19

fitfully haphazardly
809.18

discontinuously 812.5
irregularly 850.4
shakily 916.23

fit in have place 159.9
implant 191.8
follow the rule 866.4

fitness ability 18.2
health 83.1
physical fitness 84.1
eligibility 371.11
preparedness 405.4
decorousness 496.3
propriety 637.2
timeliness 842.1

fitted eligible 371.24
provided 385.13
adapted 405.17
competent 413.24
apt 787.10

fitted out 385.13

fitter 5.34

fitting
noun checking the fit
405.2
change 851.1
adj useful 387.18
decorous 496.10
appropriate 533.7
right 637.3
apt 787.10
timely 842.9
expedient 994.5

fittingly rightly 637.4
in step 787.11
expediently 994.8

fitting out 385.1

fittings 385.4

fit together 787.6

five team 617.7
card 758.2
V 881.1

five centuries 881.9

five hundred 881.9

**Five Nations
Championship** 746.1

five pounds 881.1

fiver mite 728.7
five 881.1

fix
noun navigation 159.3
celestial navigation
182.2
verb locate 159.11
establish 159.16
direct 161.5
circumscribe 210.4
quantify 244.4
form 262.7
perforate 292.15
waste 308.13
resolve 359.7
accustom 373.10
bribe 378.3
perfect 392.11
do for 395.11
repair 396.14
prepare 405.6
clobber 412.9

prescribe 420.9
arrange 437.8
attend to 604.10
harmonize 787.7
fasten 799.7
dispose 807.9
organize 807.10
define 854.9
specify 864.11
decide 945.11
prove 956.10
rig 964.5
make sure 969.11

fixated 925.33

fixation establishment
159.7
motionlessness 173.2
fixity 854.2
obsession 925.13
hindrance 1011.1

fixed located 159.18
motionless 173.13
circumscribed 210.6
firm 359.12
confirmed 373.19
beat 412.15
fast 799.14
in order 806.7
arranged 807.14
traditional 841.12
permanent 852.7
fastened 854.14
stuck 854.16
particular 864.12
proved 956.20
conditional 958.8
unqualified 959.2
rigged 964.8
assured 969.20
gripped 982.18

fixed assets 471.7

fixed capital 728.15

fixed price 738.9

fixed-rate mortgage
438.4

fixer mender 396.10
brief 597.3
wire-puller 609.30
processing solution
714.13

fixing hole 292.3
reparation 396.6
specification 864.6

fix on direct 161.5
decide upon 371.16

fixture adjunct 254.1
contest 457.3
fixity 854.2
machinery 1039.3

fixtures equipment
385.4
hard goods 735.4

fizz
noun sibilation 57.1
bubbling 320.3
verb sibilate 57.2
bubble 320.4

fizzy 320.6

fjord 242.1

flabbergasted 122.9

flabby weak 16.12
impotent 19.13
out of practice 414.18
flaccid 1045.10
pulpy 1061.6

flaccid weak 16.12
flabby 1045.10

flack appearance 33.2
promotion 352.5

flag
noun leaf 310.17
pavement 383.6
trophy 646.3
banner 647.6
golf 748.1
sticks and stones
1052.2
verb weaken 16.9
fatigue 21.4
burn out 21.5
fail 85.47
dawdle 175.8
floor 295.22
languish 393.18
figure 498.9
signal 517.22

flagged 517.24

flagging
noun slowing 175.4
pavement 383.6
adj languishing 16.21
tired 21.7
slow 175.10
deteriorating 393.45

flagrant downright
247.12
conspicuous 348.12
gaudy 501.20
wicked 654.16
base 661.12
immodest 666.6
terrible 999.9
burning 1018.27

flagship 817.17

flag-waving
noun patriotism 591.2,
611.11
adj patriotic 611.34

flail whip 604.12
pound 901.16
pulverize 1049.9

flailing corporal
punishment 604.4
pulverization 1049.4

flair ability 18.2
talent 413.4
aptitude 413.5
display 501.4
artistry 712.7
smartness 919.2
discernment 943.2

flak dissension 456.3
artillery 462.11
criticism 510.4

flake
noun basuco 87.6

flock 296.3
nut 925.16
freak 926.4
snow 1022.8
verb scale 6.11
variegate 47.7
layer 296.5

flaky flocculent 296.7
screwy 922.9
crazy 925.27
kooky 926.6
powdery 1049.11

flamboyance 501.3

flamboyant ornate
498.12
grandiloquent 545.8
bright 1024.32

flame
noun love 104.1
fire 1018.13
flash 1024.6
light source 1025.1
verb redden 41.5
burn 1018.22,
1019.24
catch fire 1019.23
shine 1024.23

flameproof
verb fireproof 1021.6
adj resistant 15.20
fireproof 1021.10

flaming
noun burning 1019.5
adj red 41.6
fervent 93.18
zealous 101.9
heated 105.22
confounded 513.10
grandiloquent 545.8
fiery 671.22
burning 1018.27
bright 1024.32
flashing 1024.34

flan 10.44

flank
noun side 218.1
verb side 218.4
launch an attack
459.17
defend 460.8
circle 913.5

flanked 218.7

flanking 218.6

flannel
noun humbug 354.14
flattery 511.1
quibbling 935.5
verb prevaricate 344.7
soft-soap 511.6
quibble 935.9

flannels underclothes
5.22
cricket 747.1

flap
noun row 53.4
report 56.1
dither 105.6
bulge 283.3
overlayer 295.4

lamina 296.2
turbulence 671.2
slap 901.8
flutter 916.4
verb crack 56.6
hang 202.6
pound 901.16
slap 901.19
wave 915.11
flutter 916.12

flapping banging 56.11
loose 803.5

flare
noun expansion 259.1
alarm 400.1
signal 517.15
explosion 671.7
flare-up 1018.14
flash 1024.6
torch 1025.3
picture 1034.5
verb spread 259.6
burn 1018.22
shine 1024.23

flared 259.11

flare up burst forth
33.9
be excitable 105.16
blaze up 152.19
burn 1018.22

flare-up outburst 105.9
explosion 671.7
flare 1018.14

flaring garish 35.19
spread 259.11
gaudy 501.20
burning 1018.27
flashing 1024.34

flash
noun glance 27.4
kick 105.3
lightning 174.6
impulse 365.1
ace 413.14
insignia 647.1
explosion 671.7
instant 829.3
flare 1018.14
blaze 1024.6
verb undress 6.7
burst forth 33.9
telegraph 347.19
signal 517.22
shine 1024.23

flashback 988.4

flashing
noun unclothing 6.1
cognizance 927.2
adj showy 501.19
brief 827.8
flashy 1024.34
flickering 1024.36

flash in the pan
noun impotent 19.6
false alarm 400.2
great success 409.3
abortion 410.5
failure 410.7
thing of naught 763.2

ephemeron 827.5
verb come to nothing
410.13
be unproductive 890.3

flashy garish 35.19
showy 501.19
grandiloquent 545.8
flashing 1024.34

flat
noun floor 197.23
horizontal 201.3
apartment 228.13
plain 236.1
shoal 276.2
smooth 287.3
scenery 704.20
note 709.14
adj soft-coloured
35.21
colourless 36.7
muffled 52.17
dissonant 61.4
insipid 65.2
dull 117.6
spatial 158.9
inert 173.14
horizontal 201.7
recumbent 201.8
champaign 236.2
deflated 260.14
lean 270.17
low 274.7
straight 277.6
smooth 287.9
phonetic 524.31
prosaic 721.5
uniform 780.5
unqualified 959.2
lacklustre 1026.17
adv horizontally 201.9

flatfish 10.23

flatly 201.9

flatmate 588.3

flatness faintness 52.1
muffled tone 52.2
discord 61.1
insipidness 65.1
unpleasure 96.1
dullness 117.1, 1026.5
horizontalness 201.1
straightness 277.1
bluntness 286.1
smoothness 287.1
prosaism 721.2

flat out at full speed
174.20
at top speed 756.5
utterly 793.16

flat-out 959.2

flat racing 757.1

flats tenement 228.14
plain 236.1

flatten level 201.6
straighten 277.5
smooth 287.5
raze 395.19
conquer 412.10
make uniform 780.4

flattened horizontal
201.7
conquered 412.17

flattening 395.5

flatter fawn 138.7
congratulate 149.2
importune 440.12
praise 509.12
adulate 511.5

flattering obsequious
138.14
congratulatory 149.3
importunate 440.18
approbatory 509.16
adulatory 511.8

flattery congratulation
149.1
praise 509.5
adulation 511.1

flatulence 1065.3

flaunt
noun display 501.4
waving 915.2
verb manifest 348.5
vaunt 501.17
wave 915.11

flaunting
noun display 501.4
waving 915.2
adj garish 35.19
showy 501.19
gaudy 501.20
grandiloquent 545.8

flavour
noun taste 62.1
flavouring 63.3
odour 69.1
characteristic 864.4
verb savour 63.7
imbue 796.11

flavoured 62.9

flavouring 63.3

flavoursome flavourful
63.9
delectable 97.10

flaw
noun crack 224.2
gust 318.6
vice 654.2
error 974.1
fault 1002.2
blemish 1003.1
verb blemish 1003.4

flawed unvirtuous
654.12
illegal 674.6
illogical 935.11
erroneous 974.16
blemished 1003.8

flawless accurate
972.16
perfect 1001.6

flax 604.14

flea vermin 311.35
jumper 366.4

fleadh 708.32

flea market sale 734.3

marketplace 736.2

fleck
noun tuft 3.6
spottiness 47.3
modicum 248.2
minutia 258.7
mark 517.5
stain 1003.3
verb variegate 47.7
mark 517.19

flecked 47.13

fled 369.11

fledgling
noun youngster 302.1
boy 302.5
birdling 302.10
bird 311.28
novice 572.9
modern 840.4
adj immature 406.11
new 840.7

flee disappear 34.3
fly 368.10
escape 369.6

fleece
noun hair 3.2
head of hair 3.4
fur 4.2
alabaster 37.2
skin 295.3
putty 1045.4
verb divest 6.5
cheat 356.18
strip 480.24
plunder 482.17
overprice 632.7

fleeing 222.4

fleet
noun ships 180.10
inlet 242.1
navy 461.26
company 769.3
verb speed 174.8
flit 827.6
adj fast 174.15
agile 413.23
brief 827.8

fleeting vanishing 34.4
receding 168.5
unsubstantial 763.5
transient 827.7

fleetingly 827.10

Fleet Street 555.3

flesh meat 10.12
sexuality 75.2
skin 295.3
organic matter 305.1
humankind 312.1
kinfolk 559.2
carnality 663.2
body 1050.3

flesh and blood 559.2

fleshy corpulent 257.18
pulpy 1061.6

flex
noun bend 279.3
electrical device
1031.20

verb curve 279.6

flexed deflective 164.8
angular 278.6
curved 279.7

flexibility versatility
413.3
unstrictness 426.2
submissiveness 433.3
changeableness 853.1
conformity 866.1
handiness 1013.2
pliancy 1045.2
elasticity 1046.1

flexible folded 291.7
versatile 413.25
unstrict 426.5
docile 433.13
changeable 853.6
conformable 866.5
handy 1013.15
pliant 1045.9
elastic 1046.7

flexibly docilely 433.18
conformably 866.7

flick
noun thud 52.3
touch 73.1
mark 517.5
tap 901.7
jerk 904.3
stain 1003.3
verb touch 73.6
play 750.7
tap 901.18
jerk 904.5
flutter 916.12

flicker
noun flutter 916.4,
1024.8
fire 1018.13
verb flutter 916.12
burn 1018.22
bicker 1024.25

flickering
noun flicker 1024.8
adj brief 827.8
irregular 850.3
inconstant 853.7
fluttering 916.18
burning 1018.27
bickering 1024.36

flier speeder 174.5
aviator 185.1
advertising matter
352.8
trading 737.19

flies 704.16

flight defence
mechanism 92.23
course 172.2
velocity 174.1
migration 177.4
aviation 184.1
trip 184.9
departure 188.1
fugitation 368.4
escape 369.1
air force 461.28
arrow 462.6

ornament 709.18
flock 769.6
multitude 883.3
flight deck 184.23
flighted 3.29
Flight Lieutenant
575.19
flight of stairs 193.3
flight path airway
184.33
route 383.1
flight test 941.3
flighty fickle 364.6
inconstant 853.7
superficial 921.20
insane 925.26
inattentive 983.6
volatile 984.17
flimsy
noun writing 547.10
adj frail 16.14
thin 270.16
rare 299.4
fragile 763.7
unsound 935.12
trivial 997.19
flaccid 1045.10
brittle 1048.4
flinch
noun retreat 902.3
verb shrink 127.13
be startled 131.5
retract 168.3
demur 325.4
hesitate 362.7
fling
noun try 403.3
revel 743.6
throw 903.3
verb clap 159.13
speed 174.8
throw 903.10
flinging 903.2
flint lighter 1020.4
stone 1044.6
flip
noun tap 901.7
throw 903.3
jerk 904.3
verb work oneself up
105.17
crack 128.8
reverse 778.5
tap 901.18
throw 903.10
jerk 904.5
flutter 916.12
adj impudent 142.10
flippant impudent
142.10
careless 340.11
ridiculing 508.12
flipped 925.27
flipper aquatics 182.11
scenery 704.20
flipping 513.10
flirt

noun lover 104.12
tempter 377.4
coquette 562.11
tap 901.7
jerk 904.3
trifler 997.10
verb lure 377.5
coquet 562.20
tap 901.18
jerk 904.5
trifle 997.14
flirtation love affair
104.6
allurement 377.1
flirtiness 562.9
trifling 997.8
flirtatious fickle 364.6
alluring 377.8
amatory 562.23
flirt with 377.5
flit
noun homo 75.15
velocity 174.1
departure 188.1
flutter 916.4
verb speed 174.8
travel 177.18
migrate 177.22
wander 177.23
glide 177.35
quit 188.9
elapse 820.5
fly 827.6
flutter 916.12
flitting
noun wandering 177.3
adj wandering 177.37
transient 827.7
inconstant 853.7
float
noun raft 180.11
life jacket 397.6
verb haul 176.13
ride 182.54
swim 182.56
take off 193.10
buoy 298.8
levitate 298.9
issue 738.12
inaugurate 817.11
start 903.13
wave 915.11
flood 1063.14
floating
noun aquatics 182.11
inauguration 817.5
adj wandering 177.37
afloat 182.60
buoyant 298.14
unfastened 801.22
floats 704.18
floaty 298.14
flock tuft 3.6
flake 296.3
laity 700.1
throng 769.4
bunch 769.5
flight 769.6
multitude 883.3

flocks 883.3
flock to 450.4
flog urge 375.14
whip 604.12
sell 734.8
flogging inducement
375.3
corporal punishment
604.4
Flood 238.6
flood
noun torrent 238.5
overflow 238.6
tide 238.13
quantity 247.3
increase 251.1
high tide 272.8
rainstorm 316.2
lights 704.18
throng 769.4
plenty 990.2
superabundance 992.2
verb flow 238.16
overflow 238.17
abound 990.5
superabound 992.8
oversupply 992.14
float 1063.14
flooded deluged 238.25
underwater 275.13
soaked 1063.17
flooding 1063.6
floodlit 1024.39
flood tide tide 238.13
high tide 272.8
floor
noun storey 197.23
ground covering 199.3
bed 199.4
horizontal 201.3
boundary 211.3
layer 296.1
arena 463.1
price index 630.4
platform 900.13
verb carpet 295.22
overcome 412.7
fell 912.5
stump 970.14
floorboards 295.9
floor covering 199.3
floored covered 295.31
defeated 412.14
beat 970.26
flooring ground
covering 199.3
rug 295.9
sticks and stones
1052.2
flop
noun report 56.1
tumble 194.3
clinker 410.2
loser 410.8
flutter 916.4
verb hit the hay 22.18
hang 202.6
lose out 410.10

be changed 851.6
flutter 916.12
floppy weak 16.12
drooping 202.10
flaccid 1045.10
flora 310.1
flora and fauna 305.1
floral 310.35
florid red-complexioned
41.9
floral 310.35
ornate 498.12, 545.11
fanciful 985.20
florin 728.7
florist 1067.6
floss down 3.20
putty 1045.4
flotation issue 738.6
inauguration 817.5
flotilla ships 180.10
navy 461.26
flotsam 370.4
flounder
noun fish 10.23
flounce 916.8
verb pitch 182.55
tumble 194.8
bungle 414.11
change 853.5
wallow 914.13
flounce 916.15
be uncertain 970.9
have difficulty
1012.11
flour
noun cereal 10.33
alabaster 37.2
powder 1049.5
verb sprinkle 770.6
pulverize 1049.9
flourish
noun extra 254.4
ornamentation 498.1
display 501.4
figure of speech 536.1
ornateness 545.4
impromptu 708.27
ornament 709.18
waving 915.2
verb grow 14.2, 259.7
have energy 17.11
enjoy good health 83.6
mature 303.9
vegetate 310.31
manifest 348.5
ripen 407.8
flaunt 501.17
boast 502.6
ornament 545.7
be somebody 662.10
wave 915.11
thrive 1009.8
flourishing
noun maturation 303.6
waving 915.2
adj grown 14.3,
259.12
increasing 251.8

luxuriant 310.40
productive 889.9
thriving 1009.13
flout
noun indignity 156.2
gibe 508.2
verb offend 156.5
disobey 327.6
violate 435.4
disregard 454.4
scoff 508.9
flouting 156.2
flow
noun excretion 12.1
course 172.2
gliding 177.16
air flow 184.29
flowing 238.4
tide 238.13
elegance 533.1
fluency 544.2
trend 895.2
plenty 990.2
liquidity 1059.1
verb move 172.5
travel 177.18
glide 177.35
run out 190.13
hang 202.6
stream 238.16
elapse 820.5
abound 990.5
go easily 1013.10
flower
noun posy 310.22
figure of speech 536.1
essence 766.2
best 998.8
verb mature 303.9
be in flower 310.32
figure 498.9
evolve 860.5
thrive 1009.8
flowered floral 310.35
ornamented 498.11
flowering
noun florescence
310.24
evolution 860.1
adj grown 14.3,
259.12
young 301.9
floral 310.35
thriving 1009.13
flower power power
18.1
benevolence 143.4
flowers menstruation
12.9
compilation 554.7
excerpts 557.4
flowery fragrant 70.9
floral 310.35
ornate 498.12, 545.11
figurative 536.3
flow from 886.5
flow in inpour 189.9
flow 238.16
flowing

noun gliding 177.16
flow 238.4
adj fluent 172.8, 544.9
pendent 202.9
streaming 238.24
elegant 533.6
harmonious 533.8
written 547.22
fluid 1059.4

flow into 238.16

flown 369.11

flow of blood 308.1

fluctuate vacillate
362.8
blow hot and cold
364.4
intermit 850.2
change 853.5
oscillate 915.10

fluctuating vacillating
362.10
irregular 850.3
inconstant 853.7
oscillating 915.15

fluctuation vacillation
362.2
irregularity 850.1
changing 853.3
oscillation 915.1

fluctuations 738.9

flue down 3.20
chimney 239.14
air 298.2
fireplace 1019.11
putty 1045.4

fluency flow 238.4,
544.2
elegance 533.1
wordiness 538.2
talkativeness 540.1
liquidity 1059.1

fluent flowing 172.8,
238.24, 544.9
elegant 533.6
harmonious 533.8
talkative 540.9
fluid 1059.4

fluently talkatively
540.11
eloquently 544.15

fluff
noun down 3.20
smoothness 294.3
air 298.2
bungle 414.5
grammatical error
974.7
putty 1045.4
verb make a boo-boo
974.15
soften 1045.6

fluffy feathery 3.28
smooth 294.8
light 298.10
superficial 921.20
flossy 1045.14

fluid
noun liquid 1059.2

vapour 1065.1
gas 1065.2
adj changeable 853.6
fluidal 1059.4

fluidity changeableness
853.1
liquidity 1059.1
vaporousness 1065.3

fluke
noun fish 10.23
match 752.3
happening 971.6
verb play 752.4

flurry
noun agitation 105.4,
916.1
velocity 174.1
rain 316.1
gust 318.6
bustle 330.4
haste 401.1
bluster 503.1
price 738.9
confusion 984.3
snow 1022.8
verb agitate 105.14,
916.10
confuse 984.7

flush
noun warmth 35.2
reddening 41.3
washing 79.5
health 83.1
fever 85.7
thrill 105.2
blushing 139.5
jet 238.9
skiing 753.1
glow 1018.12
shine 1024.2
verb redden 41.5,
152.14
wash 79.19
change colour 105.19
elate 109.8
make proud 136.6
blush 139.8
level 201.6
flow 238.16
hunt 382.9
burn 1018.22
soak 1063.13
adj red-complexioned
41.9
hale 83.12
fresh 83.13
horizontal 201.7
wealthy 618.14
full 793.11
plentiful 990.7
adv horizontally 201.9

flushed red-
complexioned 41.9
fresh 83.13
feverish 85.57
fervent 93.18
overjoyed 95.16
heated 105.22
cheerful 109.11
rejoicing 116.10

puffed up 136.10
blushing 139.13
crowing 502.13
hot 1018.25

flushing
noun reddening 41.3
washing 79.5
blushing 139.5
adj reddening 41.11
luminous 1024.30

flush out wash 79.19
evacuate 908.22

flustered intoxicated
88.31
agitated 105.23,
916.16
confused 984.12

flute
noun furrow 290.1
verb furrow 290.3
fold 291.5
murmur 524.26
blow a horn 708.42

fluted furrowed 290.4
folded 291.7

flutter
noun audio distortion
50.13
staccato 55.1
trepidation 105.5
dither 105.6
bustle 330.4
haste 401.1
trill 709.19
trading 737.19
price 738.9
bet 759.3
pulsation 915.3
flitter 916.4
confusion 984.3
flicker 1024.8
verb drum 55.4
agitate 105.14, 916.10
thrill 105.18
bet 759.25
oscillate 915.10
wave 915.11
flitter 916.12
confuse 984.7
flicker 1024.25

fluttered 984.12

fluttering
noun audio distortion
50.13
flicker 1024.8
adj staccato 55.7
flying 184.50
flickering 916.18,
1024.36

flux
noun excretion 12.1
defecation 12.2
anaemia 85.9
course 172.2
flow 238.4
tide 238.13
clay 742.3
candle power 1024.21
liquidity 1059.1

solvent 1062.4
verb treat 91.24
combine 804.3
melt 1019.21
liquefy 1062.5

fly
noun rig 179.5
overlayer 295.4
insect 311.31
snare 356.13
verb disappear 34.3
speed 174.8
transport 176.12
glide 177.35
be airborne 184.36
pilot 184.37
take off 193.10
flee 368.10
elapse 820.5
flit 827.6
wave 915.11

fly at 459.18

flyer 757.2

flying
noun aviation 184.1
adj vanishing 34.4
high 87.23
flowing 172.8
fast 174.15
airborne 184.50
hasty 401.9
transient 827.7

flying boat 181.8

flying start 756.3

fly off 164.6

fly on the wall
viewpoint 27.7
listener 48.5

fly over 811.7

flyover crossing 170.2
passageway 383.3
bridge 383.9
procession 811.3

fly past 811.7

fly to 1008.7

flyweight 297.3

foal
noun fledgling 302.10
horse 311.10
jockey 757.2
verb give birth 1.3

foam
noun saliva 13.3
alabaster 37.2
air 298.2
froth 320.2
extinguisher 1021.3
putty 1045.4
sprinkle 1063.5
verb bubble 320.4
froth 320.5
seethe 671.12

foaming 320.3

fob
noun bag 195.2
jewel 498.6
verb cheat 356.18

focal converging 169.3
confocal 208.13
chief 249.14
vital 996.23

focal point 208.4

focus
noun convergence
169.1
focal point 208.4
centralization 208.8
essence 766.2
attractor 906.2
verb focalize 208.10

focused 169.3

focusing
noun centralization
208.8
adj converging 169.3

focusing on 864.6

focus of attention
208.4

focus on specify 864.11
have regard to 936.3
call attention to
982.10

fodder
noun feed 10.4
verb feed 8.18
tend 1068.7

foe opponent 452.1
enemy 589.6

fog
noun airspace 184.32
grass 310.5
pea soup 319.2
obscurity 522.3
confusion 984.3
verb blur 32.4
cover 295.19
cloud 319.6
make uncertain 970.15
confuse 984.7

foggy inconspicuous
32.6
obscure 522.15
muddleheaded 921.18
vague 970.19
muddled 984.13

foil
noun lamina 296.2
discomfiture 412.2
motif 498.7
actor 707.2
frustration 1011.3
verb disappoint 132.2
outwit 415.11
thwart 1011.15

foiled 132.5

fold
noun enclosure 212.3
cavity 284.2
double 291.1
lamina 296.2
laity 700.1
verb collapse 260.10
fold on itself 291.5
lose out 410.10
embrace 562.18

go bankrupt 625.7
seek the middle 818.3
folded 291.7
folder advertising
matter 352.8
booklet 554.11
bookholder 554.17
fold in 291.5
folding
noun mountain 237.6
creasing 291.4
bookbinding 554.14
adj folded 291.7
fold up collapse 260.10
fold 291.5
lose out 410.10
go bankrupt 625.7
end 819.5
foliage 310.16
folie 925.1
folk
noun population 227.1
race 559.4
family 559.5
people 606.1
folk music 708.11
adj traditional 841.12
folk art 712.1
folk hero 662.9
folklore mythology
678.14
tradition 841.2
superstition 953.3
folk music 708.11
folks kinfolk 559.2
family 559.5
people 606.1
folk singer 710.14
folk songs 708.11
folksy 581.3
follicle 310.28
follow
noun pursuit 382.1
verb look 27.13
attach oneself to
138.11
parallelize 203.5
bring up the rear
217.8
be inferior 250.4
practice 328.8
emulate 336.7
pursue 382.8
observe 434.2
understand 521.7
court 562.21
play 744.2
resemble 783.7
set an example 785.7
be consistent 802.7
succeed 814.2, 816.5
specialize 865.4
conform 866.3
result 886.4
seek 937.30
trace 937.35
prove 956.10

follower enthusiast
101.4
lover 104.12
hanger-on 138.6
successor 166.2
inferior 250.2
pursuer 382.4
disciple 572.2, 616.8
retainer 577.1
believer 692.4
followers school 617.5
attendance 768.6
follow from 956.10
following
noun heeling 166.1
follower 166.2
imitation 336.1
pursuit 382.1
attendance 768.6
sequence 814.1
subsequence 834.1
surveillance 937.9
adj trailing 166.5
pursuing 382.11
similar 783.10
succeeding 814.4
subsequent 834.4
resultant 886.6
deducible 934.23
prep after 834.8
follow on 747.3
follow suit 336.7
follow the example of
336.7
follow through
prosecute to a
conclusion 360.5
succeed 816.5
follow-through 748.3
follow up pursue 382.8
trace 937.35
follow-up case history
91.10
pursuit 382.1
news item 552.3
sequel 834.2
folly foolishness 922.1
stupidity 922.4
fond
noun foundation 900.6
adj loving 104.27
hopeful 124.11
foolish 922.8
credulous 953.8
fondling touch 73.1
touching 73.2
favourite 104.16
lovemaking 562.1
fondly lovingly 104.32
hopefully 124.14
fondness tenderness
93.6
liking 100.2
love 104.1
credulity 953.1
fond of 104.30
font jet 238.9
source of supply 386.4

type 548.6
baptism 701.6
cruet 703.11
fountainhead 885.6
food nutrient 7.3
foodstuff 10.1
food and drink 10.1
food for thought 930.7
food intake 7.1
food items 735.7
food poisoning 85.31
food preparation 11.1
food processor 796.9
food supply 10.5
fool
noun sweets 10.38
dupe 358.1
laughingstock 508.7
buffoon 707.10
damn fool 923.1
ignoramus 929.8
verb befool 356.15
be foolish 922.6
trifle 997.14
adj foolish 922.8
foolhardy daring
492.22
harebrained 493.9
fooling
noun deception 356.1
buffoonery 489.5
banter 490.1
bantering 490.2
ridicule 508.1
trifling 997.8
adj bantering 490.7
ridiculing 508.12
foolish mischievous
322.6
nonsensical 520.7
unintelligent 921.13
fool 922.8
absurd 922.11
trivial 997.19
foolishly unintelligently
921.25
stupidly 922.13
foolishness mischief
322.2
unintelligence 921.1
folly 922.1
thoughtlessness 932.1
flightiness 984.5
triviality 997.3
foolproof resistant
15.20
handy 1013.15
foot
noun member 2.7
sail 180.14
base 199.2
extremity 199.5
metre 720.7
verb speed 174.8
walk 177.27
stroll 177.28
make way 182.21
float 182.54

dance 705.5
footage length 267.1
cinematography 706.4
football 745.1
football field 745.1
football ground
743.11
Football League 745.1
football pitch
playground 743.11
football 745.1
footballs 87.3
football season 313.1
footbridge 383.9
footed 199.9
foothills country 233.1
highlands 237.1
foothold hold 474.2
footing 900.5
purchase 905.2
footing station 159.2
base 199.2
rank 245.2
hold 474.2
class 607.1
fee 624.5
state 764.1
sphere of influence
893.4
foothold 900.5
foundation 900.6
purchase 905.2
outlook 977.2
calculation 1016.10
foot it 177.27
footlights show
business 704.1
lights 704.18
footman 577.6
footnote comment
341.5
memorandum 549.4
footpath 383.2
footprint 517.7
Footsie 737.1
foot the bill 624.18
footwear 5.27
footwork 754.3
for
prep in preparation for
405.24
in favour of 509.21
instead of 861.12
conj because 887.10
prep, conj to 380.11
forage
noun feed 10.4
search 937.15
verb feed 8.18
provision 385.9
plunder 482.17
search 937.31
foraging 482.6
for a little while
827.10

for all that 338.8
for all the world
972.21
for all the world like
783.15
for all time 828.12
for all to see
adj distinct 31.7
adv openly 348.15
for a long time 826.14
for a moment 827.10
for a short time
827.10
for a time 827.9
foray
noun raid 459.4
plundering 482.6
verb raid 459.20
plunder 482.17
forbade 444.7
forbid
verb prohibit 444.3
prevent 1011.11
adj prohibited 444.7
forbidden 444.7
forbidding
noun prohibition 444.1
adj offensive 98.18
reticent 344.10
prohibitive 444.6
preventive 1011.19
hideous 1014.11
force
noun strength 15.1
energy 17.1
power 18.1
waterfall 238.11
quantity 244.1
enterprise 330.7
ultima ratio 424.2
meaning 518.1
vigour 544.3
staff 577.11
violence 671.1
impact 886.2
influence 893.1
impulse 901.1
validity 972.6
verb motivate 375.12
compel 424.4
administer 643.6
seduce 665.20
thrust 901.12
cultivate 1067.17
forced unwilling 325.5
stiff 534.3
laborious 725.18
farfetched 775.8
involuntary 962.14
force from 480.22
forceful strong 15.15
energetic 17.13
powerful 18.12
enterprising 330.23
vigorous 544.11
emphatic 996.21

forcefully strongly
15.23
  energetically 17.16
  powerfully 18.15
  eloquently 544.15
force in 191.7
forceps 192.9
for certain 969.23
forces work force 18.9
  defence forces 461.19
  army 461.22
forcible strong 15.15
  energetic 17.13
  powerful 18.12
  coercive 424.12
  vigorous 544.11
  emphatic 996.21
forcibly strongly 15.23
  energetically 17.16
  powerfully 18.15
  by force 18.17, 424.14
forcing compulsion
424.1
  administration 643.2
Ford 618.8
ford
  noun shoal 276.2
  passageway 383.3
  verb pass 909.8
fore
  noun front 216.1
  adj front 216.10
  previous 833.4
  former 836.10
for each 864.20
fore and aft aft 182.69
  from beginning to end
793.18
forearm
  noun member 2.7
  arm 905.5
  verb prepare for
405.11
  take precautions 494.6
forebears 560.7
foreboding
  noun feeling 93.1
  anxiety 126.1
  apprehension 127.4
  boding 133.2
  forewarning 399.2
  threat 514.1
  hunch 933.3
  foreknowledge 960.3
  prediction 961.1
  adj anxious 126.7
  ominous 133.17,
961.12
  forewarning 399.8
  threatening 514.3
forecast
  noun foresight 960.1
  prediction 961.1
  verb plan 381.8
  predict 961.9
  adj predicted 961.14
forecaster 961.4

forecasting
  noun meteorology
317.5
  prediction 961.1
  adj predictive 961.11
forecasts 1040.7
forecourt tennis 749.1
  basketball 751.1
foredeck 216.3
forefathers 560.7
for effect 500.20
forefinger 73.5
forefront leading 165.1
  border 211.4
  front 216.1
  vanguard 216.2
foregoing
  noun leading 165.1
  adj leading 165.3
  former 813.5
  previous 833.4
  aforegoing 836.11
foregone 963.8
foregone conclusion
  sure success 409.2
  predetermination
963.1
foreground front 216.1
  nearness 223.1
forehand
  noun front 216.1
  adj front 216.10
  early 844.7
forehead 216.5
foreign extraterritorial
206.9
  extrinsic 767.3
  extraneous 773.5
  unrelated 775.6
foreign affairs 609.5
foreign correspondent
555.4
foreigner exclusiveness
772.3
  alien 773.3
  oddity 869.4
foreign exchange
728.9
foreign office 576.7
foreign policy 609.5
Foreign Secretary
575.17
foreign service 576.7
foreknowledge
  understanding 927.3
  foreknowing 960.3
  predetermination
963.1
foreman superintendent
574.2
  juror 596.7
foremost
  adj leading 165.3
  front 216.10
  chief 249.14
  preceding 813.4

first 817.17
  paramount 996.24
  adv before 165.4,
216.12
forensic
  noun speech 543.2
  adj declamatory
543.12
  jurisprudent 673.11
forensic science 673.7
foreplay 75.7
forerunner harbinger
133.5
  herald 353.2
  preparer 405.5
  leader 574.6
  skier 753.2
  precursor 815.1
  antecedent 833.2
foresee expect 130.5
  look forward to 130.6
  come 838.6
  anticipate 844.6
  predict 961.9
foreseeable foreseen
960.8
  predictable 961.13
  probable 967.6
foreseen expected
130.13
  future 838.8
  foreseeable 960.8
  predicted 961.14
foreshadowed 133.15
foreshore 234.2
foresight plan 381.1
  precaution 494.3
  future 838.1
  earliness 844.1
  sagacity 919.4
  foreseeing 960.1
  prediction 961.1
forest
  noun woodland 310.11
  verb plant 1067.18
  adj sylvan 310.37
forestall look forward
to 130.6
  deceive 356.14
  monopolize 469.6
  anticipate 844.6
  prevent 1011.14
forested 310.37
forester guardian
1007.6
  arboriculturist 1067.7
forestry woodland
310.11
  arboriculture 1067.3
forests 233.2
foretaste
  noun appetizer 10.9
  antepast 960.4
  verb anticipate 844.6
  foresee 960.5
forethought carefulness
339.1

intentionality 380.3
  plan 381.1
  precaution 494.3
  premeditation 960.2
foretold 961.14
forever
  noun infinity 822.1
  eternity 828.2
  adv for keeps 474.10
  infinitely 822.4
  forevermore 828.12
  permanently 852.9
forewarned 130.11
foreword front 216.1
  makeup 554.12
  section 792.2
  curtain raiser 815.2
for example
  incidentally 842.13
  to illustrate 956.23
for fear of 127.32
for fear that 896.7
forfeit
  noun collateral 438.3
  loss 473.1
  fine 603.3
  verb lose 473.4
  adj lost 473.7
forfeited 473.7
for free 634.5
for fun 489.19, 743.31
forge
  noun foundry 739.4
  verb form 262.7
  imitate 336.5
  fabricate 354.18
  coin 728.28
forged formative 262.9
  imitation 336.8
  fabricated 354.29
  made 891.18
forger imitator 336.4
  deceiver 357.1
  smith 726.8
  coiner 728.25
forgery imitation 336.1
  fabrication 354.10
  fake 354.13
  counterfeit 728.10
  coining 728.24
  copy 784.1
forget forgive and
forget 148.5
  dismiss 983.4
  clean forget 989.5
forget about it 983.4
forgetful inconsiderate
144.18
  careless 340.11
  forgetting 989.9
forgetfulness
  inconsiderateness
144.3
  carelessness 340.2
  thoughtlessness 932.1
  unmindfulness 989.1
forget it

  verb compose oneself
106.7
  dismiss 983.4
  phrase no matter
997.25
  exclam nope 335.10
forgettable 989.10
forgetting
  noun forgetfulness
989.1
  adj forgetful 989.9
forging 266.1
forgive have pity 145.4
  pardon 148.3
  acquit 601.4
  declare a moratorium
625.9
forgiven 148.7
forgiveness pity 145.1
  forgivingness 148.1
  acquittal 601.1
  forgetfulness 989.1
forgiving sparing 148.6
  lenient 427.7
forgo refrain 329.3
  give up 370.7
  not use 390.5
  relinquish 475.3
  abstain 668.7
for good for keeps
474.10
  forever 828.12
forgotten forgiven
148.7
  unthanked 151.5
  past 836.7
  clean forgotten 989.8
for hire 615.22
for instance 956.23
for-instance 785.3
fork
  noun prong 171.4
  tributary 238.3
  angle 278.2
  branch 310.18
  verb furcate 171.7
  ladle 176.17
  angle 278.5
  bisect 874.4
  throw 903.10
forked forking 171.10
  angular 278.6
forking
  noun furcation 171.3
  bisection 874.1
  adj forked 171.10
fork out 624.16
forks 8.12
for life
  adj lifelong 826.13
  adv for all one's
natural life 828.13
for long 826.14
forlorn disconsolate
112.28
  hopeless 125.12
  lorn 584.12

nurture 449.16
hold 474.7
train 568.13
care for 1007.19
adj related 559.6

fostering
noun accommodations
385.3
support 449.3
training 568.3
protectorship 1007.2
adj helping 449.20
protective 1007.23

foster mother 560.11

fou
noun lunatic 925.15
adj intoxicated 88.31

foul
noun unfairness 650.2
game 745.3, 750.3,
750.6
basketball game 751.3
match 752.3
fight 754.3
verb defile 80.17
stop 293.7
misuse 389.4
catch 480.17
play 751.4, 752.4
root 854.10
collide 901.13
adj nasty 64.7
malodorous 71.5
filthy 80.23
unhealthful 82.5
offensive 98.18
inert 173.14
stopped 293.11
stormy 318.23
decayed 393.40
cursing 513.8
unfair 650.10
wicked 654.16
base 661.12
vulgar 666.8
obscene 666.9
terrible 999.9
hideous 1014.11
adv afoul 182.72

fouled soiled 80.21
stopped 293.11

fouling misuse 389.1
corruption 393.2

foul play homicide
308.2
chicanery 356.4
treachery 645.6
unfairness 650.2

found establish 159.16,
891.10
form 262.7
sculpture 715.5
inaugurate 817.11
fix 854.9
cause 885.10
burn 1019.24

foundation
establishment 159.7,
891.4

base 199.2
preparation 405.1
endowment 478.9
warrant 600.6
organization 617.8
beginning 817.1
rock 854.6
fond 900.6
premise 934.7
makeup 1015.12

foundation stone
900.7

founded 262.9

founded on 956.16

founder
noun producer 891.7
verb go lame 85.48
capsize 182.44
sink 194.6, 367.8,
410.11
break down 393.24
come to grief 1010.10

foundered 1012.27

founding 715.1

founding father 891.7

found on 199.6

foundry 739.4

found wanting
insufficient 991.9
imperfect 1002.4

fount jet 238.9
source of supply 386.4
fountainhead 885.6

fountain
noun ascent 193.1
jet 238.9
source of supply 386.4
fountainhead 885.6
verb shoot up 193.9

four
noun match 747.3
card 758.2
tetrad 878.1
adj foursquare 878.4

four elements 1050.2

fourfold
verb quadruple 879.2
adj quadruplicate
879.3

Four Hundred society
578.6
upper class 607.2
aristocracy 608.1

four hundred 881.9

four-legged 878.4

four-part
noun part music
708.18
adj vocal 708.50
quadruplicate 879.3

foursome golfer 748.2
round 748.3
four 878.1

fourteen 881.7

fourteenth 881.25

fourth

noun interval 709.20
one-fourth 880.2
adj quarter 880.5

fourth estate
noun news 552.1
adj press 555.3

fourthly 880.6

fowl
noun bird 10.21,
311.28
poultry 311.29
verb hunt 382.9

fox reynard 311.20
slyboots 415.6

fox hunting 382.2

foxy reddish-brown
40.4
canine 311.40
cunning 415.12
stained 1003.10

foyer vestibule 197.19
home 228.2

fracas noise 53.3
quarrel 456.5
free-for-all 457.5
commotion 809.4

fraction part 792.1
ratio 1016.7

fractionally by degrees
245.6
scarcely 248.9
small 258.16

fractious irascible
110.19
unwilling 325.5
defiant 327.10
ungovernable 361.12
oppositional 451.8
resistant 453.5

fracture
noun trauma 85.37
crack 224.2
break 801.4
verb cleave 224.4
injure 393.13
break 393.23, 801.12

fragile frail 16.14,
763.7
transient 827.7
brittle 1048.4

fragility frailty 16.2
unhealthiness 85.3
unsubstantiality 763.1
brittleness 1048.1

fragment
noun modicum 248.2
piece 792.3
verb demolish 395.17
diversify 781.2
shatter 801.13
break 1048.3
pulverize 1049.9

fragmentary unsound
16.15
partial 792.7
broken 801.24
discontinuous 812.4

fragmentation
disruption 801.3
disintegration 805.1
pulverization 1049.4

fragmented unsound
16.15
disaccordant 456.15
broken 801.24
powdery 1049.11

fragments 557.4

fragrance odour 69.1
fragrancy 70.1

fragrant odorous 69.9
aromatic 70.9

frail
noun gal 302.7
adj slight 16.14
unhealthy 85.53
thin 270.16
human 312.13
weak-willed 362.12
unvirtuous 654.12
fragile 763.7
transient 827.7
brittle 1048.4

frailty slightness 16.2
unhealthiness 85.3
thinness 270.4
humanness 312.8
weak will 362.4
vice 654.2
fault 1002.2
brittleness 1048.1

frame
noun body 2.1, 1050.3
base 199.2
border 211.4
form 262.1
figure 262.4
structure 266.1
framing 266.4
film 714.10
match 752.3
circumstances 765.2
nature 766.4
underframe 900.10
put-up job 964.2
verb border 211.10
form 262.7
plan 381.8
phrase 532.4
produce 891.8
originate 891.12
fix 964.5

framed formative 262.9
fixed 964.8

frame of mind 977.4

frame of reference
977.2

framework skeleton
2.2
outline 211.2
frame 266.4
outlook 977.2

framing frame 266.4
production 891.2

franchise
noun vote 371.6
exemption 430.8

grant 443.5
suffrage 609.17
privilege 642.2
merchant 730.2
verb authorize 443.11

franchised 443.17

Franciscan
noun ascetic 667.2
adj ascetic 667.4

frank
noun postage 553.5
verb mark 517.19
adj communicative
343.10
artless 416.5
free-acting 430.23
plain-speaking 535.3
talkative 540.9
candid 644.17
vulgar 666.8

Frankenstein 127.9

franklin 430.11

frankly plainly 535.4
candidly 644.23

frankness
communicativeness
343.3
plain speech 535.1
talkativeness 540.1
candour 644.4
vulgarity 666.3

frantic overzealous
101.12
frenzied 105.25
overactive 330.24
turbulent 671.18
rabid 925.30
distracted 984.10

frantically frenziedly
105.35
violently 247.23
turbulently 671.26

frater 559.3

fraternal kind 143.13
friendly 587.15

fraternity affiliation
450.2
blood relationship
559.1
association 582.6
fellowship 587.2,
617.3

Frau woman 77.5
Ms 77.8

fraud sham 354.3
fake 354.13
impostor 357.6
theft 482.1
deceitfulness 645.3

Fraud Squad 1007.17

fraudulent deceitful
356.22
thievish 482.21
wrong 638.3
dishonest 645.16
illegal 674.6

fraught weighted
297.18

freighted 793.12

fray
noun trauma 85.37
fight 457.4
verb injure 393.13
wear 393.20
abrade 1042.7

frayed 393.32

frazzled beat 21.8
shabby 393.32
worn-out 393.36

freak
noun desirer 100.12
fan 101.5
caprice 364.1
misfit 788.4
nonconformist 867.3
monstrosity 869.6
fanatic 925.18
character 926.4
happening 971.6
verb crack 128.8

freaked-out wild about
101.11
crazy 925.27

freakish capricious
364.5
inconstant 853.7
eccentric 926.5

freak out crack 128.8
go crazy 925.22
go on a trip 975.8

freckled 47.13, 1003.9

free
verb release 120.6
unclose 292.12
rescue 398.3
liberalize 430.13
exempt 430.14
liberate 431.4
extricate 431.7
acquit 601.4
detach 801.10
loosen 803.3
disembarrass 1013.9
adj available 222.15
open 292.17
voluntary 324.7
idle 331.18
communicative 343.10
escaped 369.11
leisure 402.5
at liberty 430.21
quit 430.31
liberated 431.10
liberal 485.4
gratuitous 634.5
candid 644.17
profligate 665.25
unfastened 801.22
adv freely 430.32
as a gift 478.27
gratuitously 634.6

free admission 634.2

free and easy
nonchalant 106.15
lighthearted 109.12
careless 340.11
free 430.21

informal 581.3
convivial 582.23
unconventional 867.6

freebie 478.4

free choice will 323.1
choice 371.1
free will 430.6

freed free 430.21
liberated 431.10

freedman 430.11

freedom leisure 402.1
liberty 430.1
liberality 485.1
privilege 642.2
candour 644.4
facility 1013.1

free enterprise
noninterference 430.9
policy 609.4
capitalism 611.9

free-enterprise 611.32

free-fall
noun descent 194.1
plunge 367.1
deterioration 393.3
cheapening 633.4
verb plunge 367.6

free-floating
independent 430.22
separate 801.20
unfastened 801.22

free-for-all row 53.4
brawl 457.5
commotion 809.4

free form 526.1

free from 120.6

free gift 478.4

free hand latitude
430.4
carte blanche 443.4

freehold
noun land 234.1
possession 469.1
estate of freehold
471.5
adj leasehold 471.10

freeing
noun release 120.2,
431.2
escape 369.1
rescue 398.1
liberation 431.1
extrication 431.3
evacuation 908.6
disembarrassment
1013.6
adj benefitting 592.4

freelance
noun free agent 430.12
mercenary 461.16
author 547.15, 718.4
worker 726.2
verb write 547.21,
718.6

freelance writer
547.15, 718.4

free love sexology
75.18
love 104.1
adultery 665.7

freely voluntarily
324.10
free 430.32
liberally 485.5

freeman 430.11

freemasonry affiliation
450.2
fellowship 587.2

free of
adj quit 430.31
prep absent 222.19

free of charge
adj gratuitous 634.5
adv gratuitously 634.6

Freepost 553.5

freer 592.2

free radical 1058.2

free spirit 430.12

free-standing
independent 430.22
separate 801.20

freestyle 182.11

free time 402.1

free trade
noninterference 430.9
policy 609.4
commerce 731.1

free trade area 617.1

free vote 613.5

freewheeling 430.22

free will will 323.1
voluntariness 324.2
choice 371.1
free choice 430.6

freeze
noun enmity 589.1
cold weather 1022.3
verb deaden 25.4
numb 94.8
take fright 127.11
terrify 127.17
be still 173.7
preserve 397.9
speak poorly 525.7
perpetuate 828.5
stabilize 854.7
root 854.10
stop 856.7
put a stop to 856.11
be cold 1022.9
freeze 1022.9, 1022.10
chill 1022.10
ice 1023.11

freeze-dried 1064.9

freezer Siberia 1022.4
deep freeze 1023.5

freezing
noun food preservation
397.2
refrigeration 1023.1
adj cold 1022.14,
1022.16
refrigerative 1023.12

freezing cold 1022.14

freight
noun train 179.14
load 196.2
burden 297.7
freightage 630.7
charge 643.3
impediment 1011.6
verb load 159.15
transport 176.12
send 176.15
burden 297.13
fill 793.7
phrase transportation
176.3
freightage 176.6

freighter
noun train 179.14
ship 180.1
phrase carrier 176.7

freight train 179.14

frenetic overzealous
101.12
overactive 330.24
rabid 925.30

frenzied overzealous
101.12
frantic 105.25
overactive 330.24
turbulent 671.18
rabid 925.30

frenzy
noun seizure 85.6
overzealousness 101.3
fury 105.8
turbulence 671.2
agitation 916.1
furore 925.7
confusion 984.3
verb excite 105.12
enrage 152.25
madden 925.24

frequency tone 50.2
frequence 846.1
oscillation 915.1
wave 915.4

frequent
verb haunt 221.10
adj habitual 373.15
oftentime 846.4
recurrent 848.13

frequently habitually
373.21
commonly 846.6
repeatedly 848.16

fresco
noun painting 35.12
picture 712.11
verb colour 35.13

fresh
noun stream 238.1
torrent 238.5
adj refreshing 9.3
clean 79.25
green 83.13
additional 253.10,
840.8
windy 318.22
original 337.5

unused 390.12
inexperienced 414.17
present 837.2
new 840.7
remembered 988.23
undamaged 1001.8
cool 1022.12

freshen refresh 9.2
clean 79.18
air 317.10
blow 318.20
perfect 392.11
refrigerate 1023.10

fresher undergraduate
572.6
novice 572.9

fresh-faced fresh 83.13
young 301.9

freshly newly 840.15
again 873.7

freshman commoner
572.7
beginner 817.2

freshness cleanness
79.1
impudence 142.2
immaturity 301.3
nonimitation 337.1
newness 840.1
cold 1022.1

fresh start beginning
817.1
resumption 855.2
new start 857.2

fret
noun ache 26.5
irritation 96.3
dither 105.6
dudgeon 152.7
network 170.3
heraldic device 647.2
roulette 759.12
verb pain 26.7
irritate 96.14
sulk 110.14
grieve 112.17
complain 115.15
worry 126.5, 126.6
be impatient 135.4
burn 152.15
provoke 152.24
injure 393.13
wear 393.20
agitate 916.10
abrade 1042.7

fretful peevish 110.22
plaintive 115.19
impatient 135.6
bustling 330.20

fretted worried 126.8
woven 740.7

fretting
noun worry 126.2
impatience 135.1
abrasion 1042.2
adj irritating 26.13
troublesome 126.10
impatient 135.6
abrasive 1042.10

fretwork 170.3

Frey 889.5

Freya Love 104.8
Venus 1015.10

friar 699.15

friction
noun touching 73.2
hostility 451.2, 589.3
disaccord 456.1
counteraction 899.1
rubbing 1042.1
adj frictional 1042.9

Friday abstinence 668.2
fate 963.2

fridge 1023.4

fried cooked 11.6
high 87.23
fuddled 88.33

friend 588.1

friendless helpless
19.18
forlorn 584.12
alone 871.8

friendliness
comfortableness 121.2
sociability 582.1
hospitality 585.1
friendship 587.1

friendly
adj comfortable
121.11
homelike 228.33
favourable 449.22
sociable 582.22
hospitable 585.11
friendlike 587.15
adv amicably 587.22

friendly relations
587.3

friendly with 587.17

friendship 587.1

Friends of the Earth
1071.3

friends with 587.17

frigate 180.6

fright
noun fear 127.1
eyesore 1014.4
verb frighten 127.15

frighten fright 127.15
startle 131.8
alarm 400.3

frightened frightened
to death 127.25
nervous 128.11
alarmed 400.4

frightening
noun intimidation
127.6
adj frightful 127.28

frightful frightening
127.28
terrific 247.11
hideous 1014.11

frightfully fearfully
127.34

distressingly 247.21
hideously 1014.13

frigid unsexual 75.28
unfeeling 94.9
reticent 344.10
aloof 583.6
cold 1022.14

frill
noun edging 211.7
extra 254.4
fold 291.1
ornateness 545.4
verb fold 291.5

frilled 498.12

frills 498.3

frilly ornate 498.12
showy 501.19

fringe
noun tuft 3.6
exterior 206.2
border 211.4
edging 211.7
golf 748.1
adj exterior 206.7

fringed 211.12

fringes 211.1

fringing 211.11

frisk
noun caper 366.2
frolic 743.5
search 937.15
verb rejoice 116.5
go on horseback
177.34
caper 366.6
play 743.23
search 937.31

frisky gay 109.14
active 330.17

frith thicket 310.13
undergrowth 310.15

Fritz 461.7

frivolity merriment
109.5
lightness 298.1
waggishness 489.4
foolishness 922.1
flightiness 984.5
triviality 997.3

frivolous merry 109.15
light 298.10
litigious 598.22
unordered 809.12
superficial 921.20
scatterbrained 984.16
trivial 997.19

frizz
noun lock 3.5
verb cook 11.4

frizzy 281.9

fro 163.13

frock
noun garment 5.3
suit 5.6
dress 5.16
robe 702.2
verb cloak 5.39

ordain 698.12

frog dago 232.7
amphibian 311.27
jumper 366.4

frolic
noun prank 489.10
play 743.5
verb exude
cheerfulness 109.6
rejoice 116.5
play 743.23

from at 159.27
away from 188.21
out of 190.22
off 255.14

from bad to worse
119.6

from beginning to
end 793.18

from day to day
849.10

from head to foot
793.18

from on high 681.12

from scratch first
817.18
newly 840.15

from side to side
alternately 849.11
to and fro 915.21

from start to finish
wholly 791.13
from beginning to end
793.18

from the beginning
first 817.18
again 848.17

from the first 817.18

from the heart
adj deep-felt 93.24
adv fervently 93.26
candidly 644.23
genuinely 972.19

from then on 838.10

from this point 838.10

from time to time
847.5

from top to bottom
793.18

front
noun appearance 33.2
cheek 142.3
leading 165.1
airspace 184.32
exteriority 206.1
exterior 206.2
fore 216.1
vanguard 216.2
weather map 317.4
sham 354.3
pretext 376.1
battlefield 463.2
affectation 500.1
movement 609.33
verb contrapose 215.4
confront 216.8, 451.5
offer resistance 453.3

defy 454.3
brave 492.11
precede 813.2
adj frontal 216.10
phonetic 524.31
first 817.17

frontage navigation
159.3
front 216.1

frontal
noun front 216.1
altar 703.12
adj front 216.10

front bench 613.3

front for represent
576.14
cover up for 861.6

frontier
noun boundary 211.3
border 211.5
front 216.1
hinterland 233.2
jumping-off place
261.4
unknown 929.7
adj bordering 211.11

fronting
adj facing 216.11
prep opposite to 215.7

front line border 211.4
vanguard 216.2
battlefield 463.2

front man front 216.1
chief 996.10

front on 216.9

front page 216.1

front-page 552.13

front room 197.5

front-runner vanguard
216.2
jockey 757.2

frost
noun enmity 589.1
cold weather 1022.3
Jack Frost 1022.7
verb whiten 37.5
top 198.9
freeze 1022.10
hail 1022.11
frost over 1029.3

frostbite
noun chill 1022.2
verb freeze 1022.10

frosted white 37.7
unfeeling 94.9
frosty 1022.17
semitransparent
1029.4

frosting sweets 10.38
whitening 37.3
topping 198.3

frosty white 37.7
unfeeling 94.9
reticent 344.10
aloof 583.6
unfriendly 589.9
frostlike 1022.17

semitransparent
1029.4

froth
noun saliva 13.3
dregs 256.2
air 298.2
foam 320.2
trivia 997.4
sprinkle 1063.5
verb bubble 320.4
foam 320.5

frothing 320.3

frothy light 298.10
foamy 320.7
showy 501.19
superficial 921.20
trivial 997.19

frown
noun scowl 110.9
offence 152.2
reproving look 510.8
verb look sullen
110.15
redden 152.14

frowning sullen 110.24
solemn 111.3

frozen unfeeling 94.9
terrified 127.26
fast 799.14
immortal 828.9
permanent 852.7
immovable 854.15
stuck 854.16
cold 1022.16
frozen solid 1023.14

frozen foods 10.5

frugal parsimonious
484.7
cheap 633.7
economical 635.6
temperate 668.9
meagre 991.10

fruit
noun produce 10.36
homo 75.15
guy 76.5
seed 310.29
yield 472.5
posterity 561.1
nonconformist 867.3
oddity 869.4
effect 886.1
product 892.1
nut 925.16
verb bear 891.13

fruitful 889.9

fruiting
noun bearing 891.6
adj thriving 1009.13

fruition
noun pleasure 95.1
bearing 891.6
adj accomplishment
407.1

fruitless ineffective
19.15
gainless 391.12
unsuccessful 410.18

entrenchment 460.5
auditorium 704.15
studio 712.17
platform 900.13

galley kitchen 11.3
sailboat 180.3
proof 548.5

galling
noun abrasion 1042.2
adj irritating 26.13
annoying 98.22
abrasive 1042.10

gallop
noun run 174.3
gait 177.12
verb speed 174.8
go on horseback
177.34

galloping 174.15

gallows capital
punishment 604.6
scaffold 605.5

Gallup poll 937.14

galore 247.15

galvanized 295.33

gambit trick 356.6
attempt 403.2
stratagem 415.3
first 817.3

gamble
noun chance 759.2,
971.1
guess 970.8
verb game 759.23
bet 759.25
be liable 896.3
predict 961.9
risk 971.12
endanger 1005.6
take chances 1005.7

gamble on 759.24

gambler 759.21

gambling illicit
business 732.1
game 743.9
cardplaying 758.1
playing 759.1

game
noun meat 10.12
desire 100.11
sweetheart 104.10
animal life 311.1
objective 380.2
plan 381.1
quarry 382.7
contest 457.3
laughingstock 508.7
fun 743.2
card game 743.9
sport 744.1
match 745.3, 746.3,
747.3, 750.3, 750.6
strategy 749.2
basketball game 751.3
cardplaying 758.1
bridge 758.3
gambling game 759.7
verb gamble 759.23

adj willing 324.5
plucky 359.14
crippled 393.30
resolute 492.18

gamekeeper hunter
382.5
guardian 1007.6

gamely pluckily 359.18
courageously 492.23

game plan plan 381.1
project 381.2

games contest 457.3
athletics 755.1
athletics meeting
755.2
backstairs influence
893.3

game-show 1034.2

gamesmanship 457.2

gaming 759.1

gammon
noun humbug 354.14
nonsense 520.2
verb sham 354.21
deceive 356.14

gamut range 158.2
scale 709.6
series 811.2

gander cock 76.8
poultry 311.29

Gandhi 920.2

gang
noun staff 577.11
company 769.3
flock 769.5
verb league 804.4

gangland 660.11

gangrene
noun filth 80.7
mortification 85.39
verb decay 393.22

gangster criminal
660.10
underworld 660.11

gangway 189.5

gannet 672.3

gap
noun interval 224.1
crack 224.2
ridge 237.5
valley 284.9
opening 292.1
difference 779.1
dissimilarity 786.1
deficiency 794.2
break 801.4
interruption 812.2
verb cleave 224.4
open 292.11

gape
noun gaze 27.5
crack 224.2
opening 292.1
gaping 292.2
verb gaze 27.15
wonder 122.5
yawn 292.16

spectate 917.5
be curious 980.3

gaping
noun yawning 292.2
adj wondering 122.9
expectant 130.11
cleft 224.7
spread 259.11
abysmal 275.11
yawning 292.18

garage carport 197.27
repair shop 739.5

garb
noun clothing 5.1
looks 33.4
verb clothe 5.38

garbage offal 80.9
big H 87.8
refuse 391.4
bullshit 520.3
Greek 522.7

garbled falsified 265.11
misinterpreted 342.3
spurious 354.26
meaningless 520.6
hard to understand
522.14
mutilated 794.5

garden
noun compilation
554.7
jardin 1067.10
verb farm 1067.16
adj floral 310.35
simple 499.6

garden city 230.1

gardener man 577.4
horticulturist 1067.6

gardening flower
310.22
horticulture 1067.2

garden path route
383.1
path 383.2

Gargantuan large
247.7
huge 257.20

gargle
noun dentifrice 86.22
drink 88.7
verb wash 79.19
tipple 88.24

garish lurid 35.19
gaudy 501.20
grandiloquent 545.8
bright 1024.32

garland
noun circle 280.2
bouquet 310.23
compilation 554.7
trophy 646.3
heraldic device 647.2
book of verse 720.5
verb figure 498.9

garment
noun vestment 5.3
verb clothe 5.38

garments 5.1

garner
noun granary 386.7
verb store up 386.11

garnered 386.14

garnish
noun ornamentation
498.1
verb attach 480.20
ornament 498.8

garnished 498.11

garret 197.16

garrison
noun unit 461.21
guard 1007.9
verb fortify 460.9

garrulous 540.9

Garter 575.22

garter 646.5

gas
noun anaesthetic 86.15
joke 489.6
big talk 502.2
bullshit 520.3
belch 908.9
fart 908.10
fuel 1020.1
illuminant 1024.20
vaporousness 1065.3
verb provision 385.9

gas chamber aceldama
308.11
capital punishment
604.6
scaffold 605.5

gash
noun trauma 85.37
crack 224.2
notch 289.1
furrow 290.1
mark 517.5
verb cleave 224.4
notch 289.4
furrow 290.3
injure 393.13
mark 517.19
sever 801.11

gashed notched 289.5
furrowed 290.4

gasoline 1024.20

gasp
noun breathing 2.19
verb burn out 21.5
murmur 524.26
burn 1018.22

gasping 21.3

gas station 736.1

gastric 2.29

gastroenteritis 85.31

gastronomy
gastronomics 8.15
epicurism 672.2

gate entrance 189.5
porch 189.6
ingate 239.4
valve 239.10
floodgate 239.11
receipts 627.1

dismissal 908.5
attender 917.2
barrier 1011.5
cast 1056.5

gatehouse 228.9

gatekeeper 1007.12

gate receipts 627.1

gateway 189.6

gather
noun fold 291.1
verb grow 14.2, 259.7
fold 291.5
blow 318.20
collect 472.11
come together 769.16
assemble 769.18
put together 799.5
be imminent 839.2
conclude 945.10
suppose 950.10
harvest 1067.19

gathered folded 291.7
stored 386.14
assembled 769.21
joined 799.13
made 891.18

gather in assemble
769.18
harvest 1067.19

gathering
noun sore 85.36
collection 472.2
bookbinding 554.14
social gathering
582.10
apotheosis 681.11
assemblage 769.1
assembly 769.2
accumulation 769.9
section 792.2
joining 799.1
harvest 1067.15
adj imminent 839.3

gather together 769.18

gather up 911.8

gauche bungling
414.20
ignorant 929.12
inconvenient 995.7

gaudy garish 35.19
coarse 497.11
tawdry 501.20
grandiloquent 545.8
paltry 997.21

gauge
noun size 257.1
measure 300.2
verb size 257.15
measure 300.10
classify 800.8
estimate 945.9

gauged 300.13

gauging measurement
300.1
classification 800.3
estimate 945.3

Gaullist
noun patriot 611.22

adj patriotic 611.34

gaunt lean 270.17
unproductive 890.4

gauntlet challenge
454.2
penal servitude 604.2

gauze dressing 86.33
fog 319.2

Gawain 608.5

gawky
noun oaf 923.5
adj lean 270.17
bungling 414.20

gay colourful 35.18
homosexual 75.29
intoxicated 88.31
happy 95.15
gay as a lark 109.14
showy 501.19
profligate 665.25
festive 743.28

gay bar 88.20

gay liberation
liberation 431.1
human rights 642.3

gay rights 642.3

gaze
noun stare 27.5
verb gloat 27.15
wonder 122.5

gazebo 228.12

gazelle lightning 174.6
deer 311.5
jumper 366.4

gazette
noun state paper 549.8
adj periodical 555.1
newspaper 555.2

gazing 122.9

GCSE 937.2

gear
noun clothing 5.1
drug 87.2
rigging 180.12
cordage 271.3
equipment 385.4
impedimenta 471.3
football 745.1
rugby 746.1
cricket 747.1
golf 748.1
hockey 750.1
ice hockey 750.4
skiing 753.1
mechanism 1039.4
gearing 1039.5
verb equip 385.8
adj great 998.13

gearbox 1039.5

geared high 87.23
apt 787.10

geared up 87.23

gearing 1039.5

gear to harmonize
787.7
conform 866.3

gee 164.6

geek 660.6

geest 1057.1

geezer 76.5

gel
noun semiliquid
1060.5
solution 1062.3
verb thicken 1043.10

gelatin sweets 10.38
semiliquid 1060.5

gelding impotent 19.6
sexlessness 75.9
castration 255.4
horse 311.10
jockey 757.2

gem
noun jewel 498.6
good person 659.1
good thing 998.5
precious stone 1057.6
verb figure 498.9

Gemini 872.4

gemma 310.21

gen information 551.1
facts 760.4
knowledge 927.1

gendarme policeman
1007.15
cop 1007.16

gender sex 75.1
masculine 530.10

gene genetic material
305.9
heredity 560.6

genealogy 549.9, 560.5

General 575.20

general public 312.16
communal 476.9
common 497.14
governing 612.18
generalized 863.11
normal 868.8
undiscriminating
944.5
theoretical 950.13
vague 970.19

general agreement
assent 332.1
unanimity 332.5

general anaesthetic
25.3

General Assembly
ecclesiastical council
423.4
Secretariat 614.2

general assembly
613.1

general election
609.15

general hospital 91.21

general idea
generalization 863.8
abstract idea 931.3

general information
551.1

generalization custom
373.1
generality 863.1
general idea 863.8
priori reasoning 934.3

generalize universalize
863.9
reason 934.15

generalized general
863.11
theoretical 950.13

general knowledge
927.6

generally approximately
223.23
on the average 246.5
in general 863.17
normally 868.10
vaguely 970.29

generally accepted
373.14

generally speaking
approximately 223.23
generally 863.17

general practice 90.13

general public
population 227.1
people 606.1

general-purpose
387.20

general strike revolt
327.4
strike 727.5

General Synod 423.4

generate procreate 78.8
cause 885.10
originate 891.12
electrify 1031.25

generation procreation
78.2
birth 78.6
age 823.4
lifetime 826.5
production 891.1

generation gap 456.1

generative genetic
78.16
original 885.14
creative 891.16

generative grammar
530.1

generator 885.4

generic 863.11

generosity benevolence
143.4
liberality 485.1
hospitality 585.1
magnanimity 652.2
plenty 990.2

generous benevolent
143.15
forgiving 148.6
much 247.8
voluminous 257.17
indulgent 427.8
philanthropic 478.22
liberal 485.4

hospitable 585.11
magnanimous 652.6
productive 889.9
tolerant 978.11
plentiful 990.7

generously intensely
247.20
liberally 485.5
magnanimously 652.8
plentifully 990.9

genesis birth 1.1, 78.6
origin 817.4
phylogeny 860.3
source 885.5
production 891.1

genetic generative
78.16
protoplasmic 305.18
related 559.6
racial 559.7
hereditary 560.19
innate 766.8
evolutionary 860.8
original 885.14

genetically 766.10

genetic engineering
305.9

genetic make-up
766.4

genetic material 305.9

genetics 560.6

genial genetic 78.16
pleasant 97.6
cheerful 109.11
good-natured 143.14
sociable 582.22
hospitable 585.11
cordial 587.16
warm 1018.24

genie 680.6

genital phallic 2.27
genetic 78.16

genitalia genitals 2.11
sex 75.1

genitals genitalia 2.11
sex 75.1

genius ability 18.2
superior 249.4
inspiration 375.9
talent 413.4
talented person 413.12
master 413.13
spirit 678.5
familiar spirit 678.12
demon 680.6
nature 766.4
smartness 919.2
Geist 919.8
scholar 928.3
creative thought 985.2
first-rater 998.6

genius for 413.5

genocidal 308.23

genocide killing 308.1
carnage 308.4
misdeed 655.2

genome 305.8

genre form 262.1
style 712.8
kind 808.3

gent male 76.4
guy 76.5

genteel decorous
496.10
well-bred 504.17
chic 578.13
upper-class 607.10
noble 608.10

gentile
noun non-Christian
688.6
unbeliever 695.11
adj racial 559.7
infidel 688.10

gentility decorousness
496.3
good breeding 504.4
aristocracy 607.3
nobility 608.2

gentle
verb accustom 373.10
domesticate 432.11
calm 670.7
soften 1045.6
tend 1068.7
adj faint 52.16
good-natured 143.14
pitying 145.7
slow 175.10
light 298.12
lenient 427.7
meek 433.15
well-bred 504.17
upper-class 607.10
noble 608.10
moderate 670.10
soft 1045.8

gentleman male 76.4
man 577.4
aristocrat 607.4
nobleman 608.4
good person 659.1

gentlemanly masculine
76.11
well-bred 504.17
upper-class 607.10
noble 608.10

gentleness faintness
52.1
tenderness 93.6
good nature 143.2
pity 145.1
compassionateness
145.2
lightness 298.1
meekness 433.5
good breeding 504.4
moderation 670.1
softness 1045.1

gently faintly 52.21
slowly 175.13
meekly 433.19
softly 1045.17

gentry people 606.1
upper class 607.2
gentlefolk 608.3

gents 12.10

genuine natural 416.6
straight 644.14
candid 644.17
real 760.15
authentic 972.15

genuine article 972.4

genuinely artlessly
416.7
candidly 644.23
really 760.16
authentically 972.19

genus nomenclature
527.1
kind 808.3
kingdom 808.5
biology 1066.1

geographic 159.19

geographical 231.8

geography topography
159.8
earth science 1069.1
Earth 1070.10

geologist mineralogist
1056.12
earth scientist 1069.2

geology mineralogy
1056.10
petrology 1057.8
earth science 1069.1

Geordie 523.7

geriatric
noun old man 304.2
adj aged 303.16
stricken in years
303.18

germ pathogen 85.41
minutia 258.7
embryo 305.14

german
noun kinfolk 559.2
adj related 559.6

germinate grow 14.2,
259.7
vegetate 310.31

germination growth
259.3
vegetation 310.30

Geronimo 458.8

Gestapo 1007.17

gestation 78.5

gesture
noun gesticulation
517.14
hint 551.4
verb gesticulate 517.21

gestures 321.1

get
noun family 559.5
young 561.2
verb hear 48.11
procreate 78.8
annoy 96.13
barrel 174.9
fetch 176.16
waste 308.13
acquire 472.8

receive 479.6
take 480.13
read one loud and
clear 521.8
learn 570.6
become 760.12
induce 885.11
incur 896.4
solve 939.2
discover 940.2
stump 970.14

get across be heard
48.12
teach 568.10

get ahead progress
162.2
outdistance 249.10
grow 251.6
make good 409.10
prosper 1009.7

get along progress
162.2
improve 392.7
harmonize 455.2
persist 855.5

get along with 455.2

get around deceive
356.14
evade 368.7
know backwards and
forwards 413.19
free oneself from
431.8
flannel 511.6

get at arrive at 186.7
persecute 389.7
make sure 969.11

get away set out 188.8
escape 369.6

getaway acceleration
174.4
departure 188.1

get away from 368.7

get away from it all
holiday 20.9
amuse oneself 743.22

get away with 369.7

get back 481.6

get back to 343.8

get behind lag 166.4
bring up the rear
217.8
back 449.13

get better 396.19

get by get off 369.7
support oneself 385.12
manage 409.12
stand the test 941.10

get done 407.6

get down devour 8.22
alight 194.7
crouch 912.8

get drunk 88.26

get excited be excitable
105.16
be impatient 135.4

get free 369.6

get from 192.14

get going beat it 188.7
undertake 404.3
make a beginning
817.8
improve the occasion
842.8

get high 88.26

get hold of
communicate with
343.8
grab 472.9
understand 521.7
learn 570.6

get hurt 604.19

get in arrive 186.6
enter 189.7
mount 193.12
intrude 214.5

get in on intrude 214.5
participate 476.5

get in there 817.8

get into penetrate
189.8
join 617.14

get into trouble work
evil 999.6
plunge into difficulties
1012.12

get involved 476.5

get it 521.8

get it over complete
407.6
end 819.5

get it over with
complete 407.6
put a stop to 856.11

get killed 308.20

get lost 188.7

get off climax 75.23
set out 188.8
get down 194.7
go free 369.7, 431.9
make a beginning
817.8

get off the ground
817.8

get on use 87.21
depart 188.6
mount 193.12
age 303.10
make good 409.10
persist 855.5
prosper 1009.7

get on well 1009.7

get on well with 587.9

get on with 455.2

get out beat it 188.7
exit 190.12
extract 192.10
be revealed 351.8
issue 352.14
escape 369.6
extricate 431.7
print 548.14

get-out 958.2

get out of elicit 192.14
evade 368.7
shirk 368.9
escape 369.6
free oneself from
431.8
go free 431.9

get out of bed 23.6

get over move 172.5
rally 392.8
recover 396.20

get over it 83.7

get ready 405.13

get ready to 405.10

get rich 618.10

get rid of murder
308.15
discard 390.7
put an end to 395.12
free oneself from
431.8
relinquish 475.3
eliminate 772.5
do away with 908.21

get right 939.2

get smart 142.7

get the hell out 188.7,
368.11

get the idea 521.8

get the message 521.8

get the picture 521.8

get there arrive 186.6
make good 409.10

get through penetrate
189.8
carry out 328.7
bring about 407.5
complete 407.6

get through to be
heard 48.12
communicate with
343.8

getting acquisition
472.1
receiving 479.1
absorption 570.2

getting around 368.1

getting away 473.1

getting hold of
acquisition 472.1
absorption 570.2

getting off 186.2

getting rid of 475.1

get tired 21.5

get to be heard 48.12
worry 126.5
extend to 261.6
communicate with
343.8

get to be become
760.12
originate 817.13

get together come to
an agreement 332.10
assemble 769.18

get-together 582.10

get to grips with
endeavour 403.5
attempt 403.6

get to the bottom
537.5

get to the point
930.10

get tough exert
strength 15.12
remain firm 359.9

Getty 618.8

get under way depart
188.6
undertake 404.3
make a beginning
817.8

get up dress up 5.41
awake 23.4
get out of bed 23.6
rise 200.8
make up 405.7
produce 891.8

get-up-and-go pep
17.3
enterprise 330.7

get up early 330.16

get used to 373.12

get well 83.7, 396.20

get worse 393.16

ghastly
adj colourless 36.7
terrible 127.30
deathly 307.29
hideous 1014.11
adv hideously 1014.13

ghetto
noun sty 80.11
East End 230.6
adj urban 230.11

ghost
noun frightener 127.9
author 547.15, 718.4
substitute 861.2
spectre 987.1
picture 1034.5
verb float 182.54
write 547.21, 718.6
substitute for 861.5

ghostly deathly 307.29
spectral 987.7
immaterial 1051.7

ghost town 230.1

ghoulish terrible
127.30
curious 980.5
execrable 999.10

giant
noun strong man 15.6
giantess 257.13
longlegs 272.7
adj huge 257.20
gigantic 272.16

giant slalom 753.3

gibbering
noun mumbling 525.4
adj chattering 540.10

transparent substance
1028.2
eggshell 1048.2
verb face 295.23
adj glassy 1028.5

glasses tableware 8.12
spectacles 29.3

glasshouse
summerhouse 228.12
prison 429.8
nursery 1067.11

glassware hard goods
735.4
transparent substance
1028.2

glassy sleek 287.10
inexpressive 522.20
shiny 1024.33
glass 1028.5

Glaswegian 523.7

glaucoma blindness
30.1
eye disease 85.14

glaze
noun sweets 10.38
polish 287.2
clay 742.3
ice 1022.5
verb colour 35.13
sweeten 66.3
polish 287.7
face 295.23
pot 742.6
hail 1022.11

glazed sleek 287.10
inexpressive 522.20
ceramic 742.7

glazing 35.12

gleam
noun hint 248.4
shine 1024.2
ray 1024.5
flash 1024.6
verb burst forth 33.9
be somebody 662.10
shine 1024.23

gleaming sleek 287.10
luminous 1024.30

glean select 371.14
collect 472.11
conclude 945.10
harvest 1067.19

glee happiness 95.2
merriment 109.5

gleeful 109.15

gleefully 109.19

glen 237.7, 284.9

glib suave 504.18
talkative 540.9
eloquent 544.8
easy 1013.13

glide
noun gliding 177.16
slide 194.4
speech sound 524.13
verb coast 177.35
float 182.54

fly 184.36
slide 194.9
elapse 820.5
go easily 1013.10
adj phonetic 524.31

glider 181.12

gliding
noun sliding 177.16
aviation 184.1
adj flying 184.50

glimmer
noun hint 551.4
glitter 1024.7
verb glitter 1024.24

glimmering
noun hint 551.4
slight knowledge
929.6
glitter 1024.7
adj glittering 1024.35

glimpse
noun glance 27.4
slight knowledge
929.6
verb see 27.12
glance 27.17

glint
noun shine 1024.2
flash 1024.6
verb glance 27.17
shine 1024.23

glinting 1024.30

glistening 1024.35

glitter
noun showiness 501.3
glimmer 1024.7
verb cut a dash 501.13
be somebody 662.10
glimmer 1024.24

glitterati best 249.5
society 578.6

glittering
noun glitter 1024.7
adj showy 501.19
glimmering 1024.35

glittery 1024.35

glitz garishness 35.5
grandiloquence 545.1

glitzy garish 35.19
grandiloquent 545.8

gloat gaze 27.15
exult 502.9

gloating
noun crowing 502.4
adj crowing 502.13

global spherical 282.9
comprehensive 771.7
complete 793.9
universal 863.14
unqualified 959.2

globally 793.14

globe
noun sphere 282.2
lamp shade 1027.3
Earth 1070.10
verb ball 282.7

globe-trotting

noun travel 177.1
adj travelling 177.36

globular 282.9

gloom
noun gloominess
112.7, 1026.4
shadow 1026.3
verb look sullen
110.15
darken 1026.9
grow dark 1026.12

gloomily 112.31

gloomy dismal 112.24
pessimistic 125.16
ominous 133.17
cloudy 319.7
gloomful 1026.14

Gloria 696.3

glorification praise
509.5
ennoblement 662.8
sanctification 685.3
glory 696.2

glorified eminent
662.18
angelic 679.6
heavenly 681.12
sanctified 685.8

glorify praise 509.12,
696.11
glamorize 662.13
sanctify 685.5

glorious intoxicated
88.31
eminent 247.9
grandiose 501.21
illustrious 662.19
almighty 677.17
superb 998.15
gorgeous 1015.20

gloriously grandiosely
501.28
famously 662.21
superbly 998.23
gorgeously 1015.25

glory
noun radiation 171.2
eminence 247.2
circle 280.2
grandeur 501.5
praise 509.5
honour 646.1
repute 662.1
illustriousness 662.6
glorification 696.2
notability 996.2
brightness 1024.4
halo 1024.14
verb rejoice 116.5
exult 502.9

glory in 136.5

gloss
noun shallowness
276.1
polish 287.2
translation 341.3
comment 341.5
misinterpretation
342.1

sham 354.3
pretext 376.1
reference book 554.9
commentary 556.2
extenuation 600.5
shine 1024.2
verb colour 35.13
polish 287.7
coat 295.24
comment upon 341.11
misinterpret 342.2
falsify 354.16
adj soft-coloured
35.21

glossary translation
341.3
reference book 554.9
dictionary 870.4

gloss over neglect
340.6
conceal 346.6
falsify 354.16

glossy
noun print 714.5
adj sleek 287.10
shiny 1024.33

glove 454.2

glover 5.32

gloves 754.1

glow
noun animation 17.4
warmth 35.2
reddening 41.3
health 83.1
foredawn 314.4
vehemence 544.5
beauty 1015.1
incandescence 1018.12
shine 1024.2
verb redden 41.5
enjoy good health 83.6
thrill 105.18
change colour 105.19
exude cheerfulness
109.6
be somebody 662.10
look good 1015.16
burn 1018.22
shine 1024.23

glowering 110.24

glowing chromatic
35.15
red 41.6
red-complexioned
41.9
fervent 93.18
happy 95.15
overjoyed 95.16
enthusiastic 101.10
heated 105.22
cheerful 109.11
vehement 544.13
gorgeous 1015.20
burning 1018.27
luminous 1024.30
illuminated 1024.39

glue
noun adhesive 802.4
semiliquid 1060.5

verb put together
799.5
stick together 802.9

glued 799.14

gluing 799.3

glum sullen 110.24
grum 112.25

glumly sullenly 110.30
grumly 112.35

glut
noun performance
891.5
overfullness 992.3
satiety 993.1
verb stuff 8.25
be tedious 118.6
gluttonize 672.4
overload 992.15
satiate 993.4

gluten 1060.5

glutinous adhesive
802.12
viscous 1060.12

gnarled studded 283.17
gnarly 288.8

gnat 258.7

gnaw chew 8.27
pain 26.7
corrode 393.21
abrade 1042.7

gnawing
noun pang 26.2
ache 26.5
adj painful 26.10
abrasive 1042.10

gnome dwarf 258.5
elemental 678.6
fairy 678.8
maxim 973.1

go
noun act 328.3
enterprise 330.7
try 403.3
game 743.9
spell 824.1
verb disappear 34.3
have place 159.9
bear 161.7
progress 162.2
recede 168.2
move 172.5
travel 177.18
go at 177.19
depart 188.6
die 307.19
take action 328.5
perish 395.23
succeed 409.7
become 760.12
operate 888.7
tend 895.3
adj operative 888.9

go about use 384.5
undertake 404.3
circle 913.5

go-about 178.2

go abroad 177.21

go across 909.8

goad
noun spur 375.8
verb prod 375.15
impel 901.11
thrust 901.12
drive 1068.8

go after fetch 176.16
pursue 382.8

go against oppose 451.3
go contrary to 778.4

go ahead progress 162.2
hustle 330.13
begin 817.7

go-ahead
noun progression 162.1
enterprise 330.7
adj progressive 162.6

go ahead with 328.5

goal destination 186.5
motive 375.1
objective 380.2
score 409.5
football 745.1
game 745.3, 750.3
hockey 750.1
end 819.1

goalie 1007.9

goalkeeper team 750.2
guard 1007.9

goal line football 745.1
rugby 746.1
hockey 750.1
ice hockey 750.4

go all the way copulate 75.21
prosecute to a conclusion 360.5

go along progress 162.2
travel 177.18
continue 855.3

go along with concur 332.9
acknowledge 332.11
submit 433.6
consent 441.2
accompany 768.7
agree 787.6
coincide 835.4
go with 898.3

goalposts 746.1

go and do 328.6

go and get 176.16

go around recur 849.5
go roundabout 913.4
turn 913.6
suffice 990.4

go as 527.13

go at go 177.19
undertake 404.3
attack 459.14
lambaste 459.15

goat he-goat 311.8
jumper 366.4

lecher 665.11
scapegoat 861.3

goatee 3.8

go away disappear 34.3
recede 168.2
depart 188.6

gob
noun bite 8.2
sphere 282.2
mouth 292.4
accumulation 769.9
piece 792.3
verb salivate 13.6

go back retreat 163.6
bring up the rear 217.8
turn back 858.5
remember 988.10

go back on abandon 370.5
be unfaithful 645.12

go back to revisit 221.9
resume 855.6
revert to 858.6

go bankrupt fail 410.9
go bust 625.7

gobble gulp 8.23
warble 60.5
ingest 187.11
consume 388.3
destroy 395.10
gluttonize 672.4

go before lead 165.2
pioneer 815.3
anticipate 844.6

go between interpose 213.6
be instrumental 384.7
mediate 466.6

go-between
intermediary 213.4
interpreter 341.7
messenger 353.1
instrument 384.4
mediator 466.3
middleman 576.4

go beyond overrun 909.4
exceed 992.9

gobsmacked 122.9

go bust 625.7

go by be called 527.13
conform 866.3

go-by 157.2

go crazy 925.22

God 677.2

god hero 659.5
deus 678.2
goddesses 678.4

goddamn 513.9

goddamned 513.9

goddess hero 659.5
god 678.2

goddesses 678.4

godfather 438.6

God-fearing godly 692.9
belief 952.21

God forbid 335.9

God-given 478.24

Godhead 677.9

godhead 677.1

go directly 161.10

godless ungodly 695.17
unregenerate 695.18

godlike eminent 247.9, 662.18
divine 677.16, 678.16
godly 692.9

godly virtuous 653.6
divine 677.16
godlike 692.9

godmother 438.6

go down capsize 182.44
sink 194.6, 367.8, 410.11
decline 393.17
lose 412.12
be imprisoned 429.18
fight 754.4

gods immortals 678.1
auditorium 704.15

godsend boon 472.7
good thing 998.5

God's will 963.2

go easy 175.15

goer speeder 174.5
traveller 178.1
outgoer 190.10

Goethe 77.1

go far 409.10

go fishing 382.10

go for head for 161.9
fetch 176.16
intend 380.4
abet 449.14
lambaste 459.15
kid oneself 953.6

go for a walk 177.29

go for it tackle 403.7
knock oneself out 403.14

go forward 392.7

go free get off 369.7
go scot free 431.9

go get 176.16

goggle
noun gaze 27.5
verb gaze 27.15
squint 28.9
bulge 283.11
adj bulged 283.16

goggles spectacles 29.3
safeguard 1007.3
eyeshade 1027.2

go-go energetic 17.13
hip 927.17

go hand in hand 835.4

go home 307.21

go hungry 515.4

go in 270.11

go in for practice 328.8
adopt 371.15
undertake 404.3
study to be 570.15
specialize 865.4

going
noun disappearance 34.1
progression 162.1
motion 172.1
travel 177.1
departure 188.1
death 307.1
horse racing 757.1
adj flowing 172.8
travelling 177.36
dying 307.33
operating 888.11

going about 552.15

going around 552.15

going forward 162.1

going on
adj happening 830.9
operating 888.11
adv in progress 162.7
adj, adv in preparation 405.22

going out egress 190.2
extinguishing 1021.2

going over 363.2

goings-on behaviour 321.1
activity 330.1
affairs 830.4

going strong
unweakened 15.21
thriving 1009.13

going to the polls 609.18

go into undertake 404.3
participate 476.5
discuss 541.12
write upon 556.5
join 617.14
compose 795.3
enter 817.9
elaborate 860.6
investigate 937.23

go in with 450.4

go it alone 430.20

goitre 85.21

gold
noun yellowness 43.1
wealth 618.1
money 728.1
precious metals 728.20
adj yellow 43.4
brass 1056.17

gold card 622.3

gold dust basuco 87.6
metal 1056.3

golden yellow 43.4
auspicious 133.18
precious 632.10
melodious 708.48
superb 998.15

brass 1056.17

Golden Age 823.5

golden age 1009.4

golden opportunity 842.3

golden rule rule 419.2
axiom 973.2

golden-yellow 43.4

gold medal 646.2

gold mine source of supply 386.4
mine 618.4, 1056.6

gold-plated plated 295.33
expensive 632.11
brass 1056.17

gold rush 1056.8

gold standard 728.21

golf course playground 743.11
golf 748.1

golfer 748.2

Goliath 15.6

go mad 925.21

gondola 180.1

gone weak 16.12
beat 21.8
burnt-out 21.10
away 34.5
past hope 125.15
departed 188.19
absent 222.11
dead 307.30
used up 388.5
lost 473.7
no more 761.11
past 836.7

gone away 34.5

gone by 836.15

gone-by past 836.7
obsolete 841.15

gone on wild about 101.11
crazy about 104.31

gone out 841.15

gong
noun bell 54.4
marker 517.10
medal 646.6
verb ring 54.8

good
noun utility 387.3
believing 692.5
welfare 998.4
adj tasty 63.8
healthful 81.5
pleasant 97.6
auspicious 133.18
kind 143.13
skilful 413.22
praiseworthy 509.20
right 637.3
honest 644.13
just 649.8
virtuous 653.6
almighty 677.17

godly 692.9
solvent 729.17
valid 972.14
genuine 972.15
sufficient 990.6
expedient 994.5
excellent 998.12
adv kindly 143.18
exclam yes 332.18
good at 413.27
good behaviour 321.2
Good Book 683.2
good buy 633.3
good-bye 188.4
good case 934.10
good chance gambling
  odds 759.6
  good opportunity
  842.3
  possibility 965.1
  probability 967.1
  sporting chance 971.8
good character 509.4
good condition
  healthiness 83.2
  bad condition 764.3
  orderliness 806.3
good effect 1015.4
good enough
  adj acceptable 107.12
  sufficient 990.6
  tolerable 998.20
  exclam yes 332.18
good example 659.4
good eye 943.1
good faith 644.7
good-faith 644.14
good feeling pleasure
  95.1
  influence 893.1
good for healthful 81.5
  useful 387.18
  helpful 449.21
  priced 630.14
  solvent 729.17
good form social
  convention 579.1
  etiquette 580.3
good friend 588.2
good guy 659.2
good health 83.2
good hope 124.1
good humour good
  spirits 109.2
  good nature 143.2
good-humoured
  143.14
good idea 931.6
good life 1009.1
good-looking 1015.18
good looks 1015.4
goodly pleasant 97.6
  large 257.16
  good 998.12
  comely 1015.18

goodman husband
  563.7
  master 575.1
good manners good
  behaviour 321.2
  mannerliness 504.3
  etiquette 580.3
good name reputability
  662.2
  custom 731.6
good nature 143.2
good-natured 143.14
goodness savouriness
  63.1
  healthfulness 81.1
  pleasantness 97.1
  kindness 143.1
  propriety 637.2
  probity 644.1
  virtue 653.1
  godliness 692.2
  excellence 998.1
Good News 683.4
good news 552.2
good night's sleep
  22.4
good offices 449.1
good omen 133.9
good one 489.6
good opportunity
  842.3, 971.8
good point 864.4
good points 1015.4
good price 632.3
good reason warrant
  600.6
  good reasoning 934.10
good reputation 662.2
goods
  noun material 4.1
  property 471.1
  merchandise 735.1
  what's what 972.4
  phrase freight 176.6
good Samaritan 592.1
good shape healthiness
  83.2
  orderliness 806.3
  good looks 1015.4
good shot 903.8
good-sized 257.16
good soldier 492.8
good spirits 109.2
good story 489.6
good taste savouriness
  63.1
  taste 496.1
  elegance 533.1
good terms 587.3
good thing 998.5
good time fun 743.2
  good opportunity
  842.3
good times 1009.4

good turn 143.7
good use 387.1
good way 261.2
good weather 317.3
goodwill benevolence
  143.4
  willingness 324.1
  patronage 449.4
  good terms 587.3
  custom 731.6
good wishes
  congratulation 149.1
  regards 504.8
good word
  commendation 509.3
  good news 552.2
good works 143.6
goody
  noun delicacy 10.8
  exclam goody! 95.20
go off blast 56.8
  dislike 99.3
  avoid 164.6
  depart 188.6
  decline 393.17
  decay 393.22
  succeed 409.7
  explode 671.14
  occur 830.5
goofy protruding
  283.14
  screwy 922.9
  crazy 925.27
  kooky 926.6
go on progress 162.2
  depart 188.6
  behave 321.4
  persevere 360.2
  manage 409.12
  chatter 540.5
  kick up a row 809.11
  endure 826.6
  linger on 826.7
  occur 830.5
  continue 855.3
  persist 855.5
goon hunk 15.7
  roughneck 593.4
  follower 616.8
  gorilla 671.10
  picket 727.7
go on about 855.5
go on and on 826.7
go one better excel
  249.6
  outwit 415.11
go on forever 118.6
go on holiday 20.9
go on strike 727.10
go on with 855.5
goose
  noun poultry 311.29
  silly 923.6
  verb goad 375.15
go out exit 190.12
  die 307.19
  obsolesce 390.9

  strike 727.10
  come to an end 819.6
  burn out 1021.8
go out of business
  close shop 293.8
  go bankrupt 625.7
go over study 570.12
  rehearse 704.32
  examine 937.24
go over the top 459.18
go public 738.12
gore
  noun blood 2.23
  insert 191.2
  killing 308.1
  verb perforate 292.15
  horn 459.26
gorge
  noun mouth 2.16
  valley 237.7
  obstruction 293.3
  verb stuff 8.25
  gluttonize 672.4
  overload 992.15
  satiate 993.4
gorgeous colourful
  35.18
  gaudy 501.20
  drop–dead gorgeous
  1015.20
gorgeously gaudily
  501.27
  ravishingly 1015.25
gorilla hunk 15.7
  killer 308.10
  roughneck 593.4
  goon 671.10
goring 292.3
gormless stupid 921.15
  blockheaded 921.17
  foolish 922.8
go round 849.5
go-round 913.2
gory circulatory 2.31
  sanguine 41.7
  murderous 308.23
  bloodstained 1003.11
go shopping 733.8
gosling fledgling 302.10
  poultry 311.29
go so far as to 640.6
Gospel
  noun New Testament
  683.4
  adj scriptural 683.10
gospel
  noun good news 552.2
  system of belief 952.3
  truth 972.3
  what's what 972.4
  adj scriptural 683.10
  true 972.13
Gospels 683.4
gossamer
  noun filament 271.1
  air 298.2
  adj dainty 248.7

  thin 270.16, 763.6
  threadlike 271.7
  smooth 294.8
  chimeric 985.22
  transparent 1028.4
gossip
  noun chatter 540.3
  gossiping 552.7
  newsmonger 552.9
  inquisitive person
  980.2
  verb chatter 540.5
  chat 541.10
  tattle 552.12
gossiping
  noun gossip 552.7
  adj gossipy 552.14
gossipy communicative
  343.10
  talkative 540.9
  gossiping 552.14
  curious 980.5
go straight go directly
  161.10
  be straight 277.4
  improve 392.9
Goth 497.7
Gothic unrefined
  497.12
  antiquated 841.13
  unlearned 929.14
  fanciful 985.20
go through carry out
  328.7
  squander 486.3
  rehearse 704.32
  experience 830.8
  search 937.31
go through with take
  action 328.5
  endure 826.6
go through with it
  360.5
go to repair to 177.25
  extend to 261.6
go to bed rest 20.6
  retire 22.17
go to bed with 75.21
go together 787.6
go to hell 395.24
go too far be rash
  493.5
  overstep 909.9
  overdo 992.10
go to sleep 22.16
gouache 712.14
gouge
  noun indentation 284.6
  furrow 290.1
  verb blind 30.7
  excavate 284.15
  furrow 290.3
  perforate 292.15
  overprice 632.7
gouged 290.4
go under go to ruin
  395.24

sink 410.11
lose 412.12

go up ascend 193.8
grow 251.6
go to ruin 395.24
explode 671.14

go up and up 193.8

gourmet
noun eater 8.16
connoisseur 496.7
sensualist 663.3
adj edible 8.33
tasty 63.8

gout 85.22

govern restrain 428.7
direct 573.8
regulate 612.12
rule 893.8

governance authority
417.5
direction 573.1
government 612.1
protectorship 1007.2

governess instructress
571.2
mistress 575.2
chaperon 1007.7

governing authoritative
417.15
directing 573.12
controlling 612.18

government state
231.5
governance 417.5,
612.1
direction 573.1
political science 609.2
authorities 612.3
protectorship 1007.2

governmental political
609.43
gubernatorial 612.17

government control
609.4

governor father 560.9
director 574.1
ruler 575.6
governor-general
575.13
safeguard 1007.3
guardian 1007.6
system component
1040.14

governor-general
575.13

governorship
mastership 417.7
directorship 573.4

go well 1009.7

go west wester 161.8
croak 307.20

go wild 101.6

go with stay near
223.12
take action 328.5
concur 332.9
choose 371.13

undertake 404.3
agree 787.6
go along with 898.3

go without 668.7

gown
noun garment 5.3
dress 5.16
robe 702.2
verb cloak 5.39

go wrong be
disappointing 132.3
get out of order
393.25
go to ruin 395.24
miscarry 410.15
stray 654.9
misbelieve 688.8
err 974.9

grab
noun seizure 480.2
verb jump at 101.6
latch on to 472.9
seize 480.14
capture 480.18
impress 930.19
engross 982.13

grabbing 480.2

Grace 648.2

grace
noun delightfulness
97.2
benevolence 143.4
act of kindness 143.7
pity 145.1
pardon 148.2
thanks 150.2
skill 413.1
benefit 478.7
taste 496.1
elegance 533.1
fluency 544.2
reprieve 601.3
conscience 636.5
inspiration 677.15
sanctification 685.3
prayer 696.4
ornament 709.18
goodness 998.1
beauty 1015.1
verb ornament 498.8
honour 662.12
beautify 1015.15

graceful skilful 413.22
agile 413.23
elegant 496.9, 533.6
courteous 504.14
fluent 544.9
beautiful 1015.17

gracefully tastefully
496.11
courteously 504.19

Graces 1015.10

graces 504.7

gracious pleasant 97.6
kind 143.13
indulgent 427.8
liberal 485.4
elegant 496.9
courteous 504.14

informal 581.3
hospitable 585.11

graciously pleasantly
97.12
good-naturedly 143.19
liberally 485.5
courteously 504.19

grade
noun incline 204.4
degree 245.1
class 572.11, 607.1,
808.2
verb level 201.6
incline 204.10
graduate 245.4
size 257.15
smooth 287.5
order 806.4
classify 807.11, 808.6

graded arranged 807.14
classified 808.8

gradient rising 200.5
incline 204.4

grading gradation
245.3
classification 808.1

gradual slow 175.10
gradational 245.5

gradually little by little
175.14
by degrees 245.6

graduate
noun expert 413.11
graduand 572.8
verb grade 245.4
size 257.15
measure 300.10
improve 392.7
succeed 409.7
promote 446.2
adj scholastic 568.19
studentlike 572.12

graduated 245.5

graduate student
572.8

graduation gradation
245.3
promotion 446.1
ceremony 580.4

graft
noun insertion 191.1
insert 191.2
fraud 356.8
bribery 378.1
theft 482.1
sleaze 609.34
spoils of office 609.35
verb engraft 191.6
fasten 799.7

grafting 191.1

grain
noun feed 10.4
modicum 248.2
minutia 258.7
texture 294.1
grass 310.5
seed 310.29
nature 766.4

kind 808.3
disposition 977.3
granule 1049.6
verb colour 35.13
coarsen 294.4
pulverize 1049.9
powder 1049.10

grained 294.6

grain of 258.7

grainy rough 288.6,
294.6
granular 1049.12

grammar rules of
language 530.1
diction 532.1
textbook 554.10
basics 817.6

grammar school 567.4

grammatical linguistic
523.17
syntactical 530.17

Grammy 646.2

grammy 560.16

gramophone 50.11

gran 560.16

granary 386.7

grand
noun mite 728.7
adj dignified 136.12
great 247.6
large 257.16
grandiose 501.21
lofty 544.14
eminent 662.18
important 996.17
good 998.12

grandchild 561.3

grandchildren 561.1

granddad 560.14

granddaughter 561.3

grandeur proud bearing
136.2
greatness 247.1
sizableness 257.6
grandness 501.5
loftiness 544.6
distinction 662.5

grandfather old man
304.2
grandsire 560.13
back number 841.8

grandfathers 560.7

grandiose grand 501.21
grandiloquent 545.8

grandly dignifiedly
136.14
grandiosely 501.28
importantly 996.25

grandma 560.16

grandmaster 413.15

grandmother old
woman 304.3
grandam 560.15

Grand National 757.1

grandpa 560.14

grandparent 560.8

grandparents 560.7

grand slam score
409.5
victory 411.1
bridge 758.3

grandson 561.3

grand tour journey
177.5
space travel 1073.1

grange farmstead 228.6
farm 1067.8

granger 1067.5

granite stone 1044.6
rock 1057.1

granny old woman
304.3
fusspot 495.7
gran 560.16
back number 841.8

grant
noun concession 443.5
giving 478.1
subsidy 478.8
privilege 642.2
qualification 958.1
verb acknowledge
332.11
confess 351.7
permit 443.9
give 478.12
suppose 950.10
allow for 958.5

granted accepted
332.14
given 478.24
supposed 950.14

granting
noun giving 478.1
conj admitting 958.13

granular infinitesimal
258.14
rough 294.6
grainy 1049.12

granulated rough
288.6, 294.6
hardened 1044.13
granular 1049.12

grapevine legume
310.4
informant 551.5
report 552.6
grapevine telegraph
552.10

graph
noun diagram 381.3
letter 546.1
drawing 712.13
outline 800.4
verb plot 381.10
itemize 800.7

graphic representational
349.13
descriptive 349.14
expressive 544.10
written 547.22
pictorial 712.21

graphically
  descriptively 349.16
  eloquently 544.15

graphics 713.1

graphite 1054.2

graphology 547.3

grapple
  noun hold 474.2
  verb contend 457.13
  hold 474.6
  seize 480.14
  fasten 799.7

grapple with contend
  against 451.4
  contend 457.13
  contend with 457.17
  brave 492.11

grappling 457.10

grasp
  noun hold 474.2
  control 612.2
  handle 900.11
  understanding 927.3
  verb hold 474.6
  seize 480.14
  understand 521.7
  cohere 802.6
  know 927.12

grasped 927.26

grasping
  noun greed 100.8
  adj greedy 100.27
  demanding 421.9
  acquisitive 472.15
  retentive 474.8
  rapacious 480.26
  selfish 651.5

grass
  noun Acapulco gold
  87.10
  grassland 310.8
  verb feed 8.18

grass court 310.7

grasshopper
  noun locust 311.34
  jumper 366.4
  adj improvident
  406.15

grassland country
  233.1
  land 234.1
  plain 236.1
  grass 310.8
  farm 1067.8

grass-roots basic 199.8
  populational 606.8
  simple 797.6

grass roots bottom
  199.1
  country 233.1
  source 885.5

grassy green 44.4
  verdant 310.39

grate
  noun network 170.3
  arranger 807.5
  fire iron 1019.12
  verb pain 26.7

rasp 58.10
  irritate 96.14
  net 170.7
  abrade 1042.7
  pulverize 1049.9

grated netlike 170.11
  powdery 1049.11

grateful pleasant 97.6
  thankful 150.5
  welcome 585.12

grateful dead 987.1

grater 1049.7

gratification pleasure
  95.1
  bribe 378.2
  indulgence 427.3

gratified 95.14

gratifying pleasant
  97.6
  welcome 585.12

grating
  noun network 170.3
  arranger 807.5
  fire iron 1019.12
  pulverization 1049.4
  adj irritating 26.13
  jarring 58.16
  dissonant 61.4
  clashing 61.5
  unnerving 128.15
  disagreeing 788.6

gratitude 150.1

gratuitous impudent
  142.10
  voluntary 324.7
  given 478.24
  gratis 634.5
  unordered 809.12
  superfluous 992.17

gratuitously voluntarily
  324.10
  gratis 634.6

grave
  noun death 307.1
  tomb 309.16
  monument 549.12
  hell 682.1
  destiny 838.2
  verb record 549.15
  engrave 713.9
  sculpture 715.5
  adj painful 26.10
  dark 38.9
  deep 54.10
  sedate 106.14
  solemn 111.3
  gloomy 112.24
  dignified 136.12
  great 247.6
  heavy 297.16
  lofty 544.14
  ceremonious 580.8
  base 661.12
  weighty 996.20

gravel pavement 383.6
  grain 1049.6
  shingle 1057.3

gravelly rugged 288.7

rough 294.6
  granular 1049.12
  stony 1057.11

gravely solemnly 111.4
  sadly 112.31
  dignifiedly 136.14

graver engraving tool
  713.8
  sculptor 716.6
  printmaker 716.8

graveside 309.22

gravestone 309.17,
  549.12

graveyard 309.15

gravitas sedateness
  106.4
  solemnity 111.1
  proud bearing 136.2
  loftiness 544.6
  formality 580.1
  gravity 996.3

gravitational 297.20

gravity sedateness
  106.4
  solemnity 111.1
  gloom 112.7
  proud bearing 136.2
  weight 297.1
  gravitation 297.5
  loftiness 544.6
  formality 580.1
  attraction 906.1
  importance 996.1
  graveness 996.3

gravy find 472.6
  gratuity 478.5

gravy train 618.4

graze
  noun touch 73.1
  contact 223.5
  verb feed 8.18
  touch lightly 73.7
  contact 223.10
  tap 901.18
  abrade 1042.7

grazing
  noun eating 8.1
  touch 73.1
  grassland 310.8
  abrasion 1042.2
  animal husbandry
  1068.1
  adj in contact 223.17

grease
  noun oil 1054.1
  verb smooth 287.5
  facilitate 1013.7
  oil 1054.8

greased 287.11

greasing facilitation
  1013.5
  lubrication 1054.6

greasy slippery 287.11
  oily 1054.9

great
  noun ace 413.14
  keyboard 711.17
  personage 996.8

adj pregnant 78.18
  grand 247.6
  chief 249.14
  large 257.16
  authoritative 417.15
  magnanimous 652.6
  eminent 662.18
  important 996.17
  swell 998.13

great-aunt 559.3

great beauty 1015.8

great big 257.20

Great Britain 232.3

great deal 247.15

great distance 261.2

Great Divide
  jumping-off place
  261.4
  watershed 272.5

greater superior 249.12
  higher 272.19

Greater London 231.7

greater number
  plurality 882.1
  majority 882.2

greatest extreme
  247.13
  superlative 249.13

greatest number
  noun majority 882.2
  adj majority 882.9

great expectations
  124.1

great friend 588.2

great fun 743.2

great-grandfather
  560.13

great-grandmother
  560.15

great honour 646.1

great idea 931.6

greatly largely 247.15
  importantly 996.25

great majority 307.17

greatness pregnancy
  78.5
  magnitude 247.1
  superiority 249.1
  size 257.1
  sizableness 257.6
  prestige 417.4
  magnanimity 652.2
  distinction 662.5
  notability 996.2

great outdoors 206.3

great respect 155.1

great satisfaction 95.1

Great Spirit 677.2

great success 409.3

great-uncle 559.3

great work 554.1

greed greediness 100.8
  selfishness 651.1
  gluttony 672.1

greedily avariciously
  100.32
  gluttonously 672.8

greedy avaricious
  100.27
  acquisitive 472.15
  selfish 651.5
  gluttonous 672.6

Greek 522.7

**Greek Orthodox
Church** 675.9

green
  noun greenness 44.1
  lawn 310.7
  dough 728.2
  golf 748.1
  table 752.2
  verb verdigris 44.3
  adj virid 44.4
  sour 67.5
  fresh 83.13
  jealous 153.5
  immature 301.10,
  406.11
  preservative 397.11
  inexperienced 414.17
  new 840.7
  ignorant 929.12
  gullible 953.9
  remembered 988.23

green belt 397.7

greenery 310.1

greenhouse
  summerhouse 228.12
  nursery 1067.11

greenish 44.4

Greenland continent
  235.1
  jumping-off place
  261.4
  Siberia 1022.4

green light start 188.2
  signal 517.15

Green Man 678.11

Greenpeace 1071.3

green revolution
  revolution 859.1
  agriculture 1067.1

greens vegetables 10.34
  salad 10.35
  plants 310.1

greet weep 115.12
  address 524.27
  hail 585.10

greeting weeping 115.2
  remark 524.4
  salutation 585.4

greetings welcome
  186.4
  regards 504.8
  salutations 585.3

gregarious talkative
  540.9
  sociable 582.22

grenade 462.20

grenadier 461.9

grey

groundless baseless
763.8, 935.13
unproved 957.8

ground on 199.6

grounds nearness 223.1
dregs 256.2
green 310.7
real estate 471.6
warrant 600.6
cause 885.1
foundation 900.6
evidence 956.1
condition 958.2

ground troops 461.22

groundwater 1063.3

groundwork
preparation 405.1
foundation 900.6

group
noun amount 244.2
association 617.1
clique 617.6
sect 675.3
orchestra 710.12
company 769.3
bunch 769.7
set 783.5
class 808.2
verb size 257.15
assemble 769.18
classify 800.8, 807.11,
808.6

Group Captain 575.19

grouped arranged
807.14
classified 808.8

groupie fan 101.5
follower 166.2

grouping association
617.1
treatment 712.9
company 769.3
bunch 769.7
classification 800.3,
807.3, 808.1
class 808.2

grouse
noun beef 115.5
verb beef 108.6,
115.16

grove valley 284.9
woodlet 310.12
bunch 769.7

grovelling
noun obsequiousness
138.2
crouch 912.3
adj obsequious 138.14
recumbent 201.8

grow develop 14.2,
259.7
increase 251.6
grow up 272.12
mature 303.9
vegetate 310.31
become 760.12
evolve 860.5
process 891.9

farm 1067.16
raise 1068.6

grower producer 891.7
agriculturist 1067.5

grow from 886.5

growing
noun production 891.2
raising 1067.12
adj grown 14.3,
259.12
increasing 251.8
immature 301.10

growing season 313.3

growing up 259.3

grow into 857.17

growl
noun reverberation
54.2
boom 56.4
rasp 58.3
verb boom 56.9
jangle 58.9
snarl 60.4
complain 115.15
redden 152.14
sigh 318.21
murmur 524.26

growling
noun reverberation
54.2
adj reverberating
54.11
discontented 108.7
irascible 110.19

grown full-grown 14.3,
259.12
adult 303.12
produced 891.17
made 891.18

grown-up grown 14.3,
259.12
adult 303.12

grow old age 303.10,
841.9
mature 304.6

grow out of grow 14.2,
259.7
result from 886.5

growth anaemia 85.9
neoplasm 85.38
increase 251.1
development 259.3
maturation 303.6
stand 310.2
vegetation 310.30
business cycle 731.9
conversion 857.1
evolution 860.1

grow to 802.6

grow up grow 14.2,
259.7, 272.12
ascend 193.8
mature 303.9
ripen 407.8

grub
noun eats 10.2
vagabond 178.3
larva 302.12

drudge 726.3
verb excavate 284.15
drudge 725.14

grubby dirty 80.22
slovenly 809.15
infested 909.11

grudge
noun hostility 99.2
spite 589.5
verb envy 154.3
refuse 325.3
deny 442.4
stint 484.5

grudging
noun envy 154.1
adj envious 154.4
reluctant 325.6
niggardly 484.8

grudgingly 325.9

gruel
noun kitten 16.7
paper 270.7
semiliquid 1060.5
verb weaken 16.10

gruelling weakening
16.20
fatiguing 21.13
laborious 725.18
troublesome 1012.18

gruesome terrible
127.30
deathly 307.29
hideous 1014.11

gruff raucous 58.15
irascible 110.19
brusque 505.7

gruffly 505.9

grumble
noun reverberation
54.2
boom 56.4
rasp 58.3
verb boom 56.9
jangle 58.9
growl 60.4
complain 115.15

grumbling
noun reverberation
54.2
complaint 115.4
adj discontented 108.7
irascible 110.19

grumpy 108.7

grungy 80.22

grunt
noun animal noise 60.1
squaddie 461.7
verb oink 60.3
complain 115.15
murmur 524.26

G-string waistband
5.19
supporter 900.2

guano faeces 12.4
fertilizer 889.4

guarantee
noun oath 334.4
promise 436.1

security 438.1
guarantor 438.6
verb depose 334.6
promise 436.4
secure 438.9
protect 1007.18

guaranteed promised
436.8
secured 438.11
assured 969.20
unhazardous 1006.5

guarantor endorser
332.7
warrantor 438.6

guard
noun railwayman
178.13
vigilance 339.4
defence 460.1
defender 460.7
escort 768.5
protection 1007.1
safeguard 1007.3
guarder 1007.9
verb preserve 397.8
restrain 428.7
defend 460.8
escort 768.8
protect 1007.18

guard against defend
460.8
take precautions 494.6

guarded vigilant 339.13
reticent 344.10
restrained 428.13
cautious 494.8
incredulous 955.4
protected 1007.21

guarded secret 345.5

guardian
noun steward 574.4
familiar spirit 678.12
warden 1007.6
adj protective 1007.23

guardian angel
penitence 113.4
defender 460.7
familiar spirit 678.12
guardian 1007.6

guardianship vigilance
339.4
storage 386.5
usage 387.2
preservation 397.1
directorship 573.4
protectorship 1007.2

guarding
noun custody 429.5
adj defensive 460.11
protective 1007.23

guards elite troops
461.14
bodyguard 1007.14

guardsman guard
1007.9
bodyguard 1007.14

guardsmen 461.14

gudgeon dupe 358.1

axle 914.5

guerrilla 461.15

guess
noun conjecture 950.4
gamble 970.8
verb solve 939.2
estimate 945.9
conjecture 950.11
think 952.11
predict 961.9

guessing 970.24

guesswork supposition
950.3
guess 950.4
prediction 961.1

guest
noun visitor 585.6
verb entertain 585.8

guest house 228.15

guest room 197.7

guff 520.3

guidance navigation
159.3
advice 422.1
patronage 449.4
teaching 568.1
direction 573.1
protectorship 1007.2

guide
noun gutter 239.3
interpreter 341.7
adviser 422.3
pointer 517.4
teacher 571.1
guider 574.7
familiar spirit 678.12
escort 768.5
precursor 815.1
spectre 987.1
verb lead 165.2
pilot 182.14
advise 422.5
teach 568.10
steer 573.9
escort 768.8
go before 815.3
govern 893.8

guidebook information
551.1
handbook 554.8
directory 574.10

guided 161.13

guideline plan 381.1
rule 419.2, 868.4

guidelines 381.1

guiding 573.12

guiding principle rule
419.2
main idea 931.4

guild 617.3

guile deceit 356.3
cunning 415.1

guillotine
noun capital
punishment 604.6
scaffold 605.5
introduction 613.5

closure 856.5
verb execute 604.16

guilt 656.1

guilty
 adj litigious 598.22
 guilty as hell 656.3
 adv shamefacedly
 656.5

guilty verdict 602.1

guinea specie 728.4
 mite 728.7

guinea pig bear 311.23
 subject 941.7

guise clothing 5.1
 aspect 33.3
 looks 33.4
 cover 295.2
 behaviour 321.1
 pretext 376.1
 manner 384.1
 mode 764.4

guitarist 710.5

gulag 429.8

gulf crack 224.2
 eddy 238.12
 ocean 240.3
 inlet 242.1
 pit 275.2, 284.4
 opening 292.1

gull
 noun dupe 358.1
 verb deceive 356.14
 cheat 356.18
 stultify 922.7

gullet 2.16

gullible foolable 922.12
 dupable 953.9

Gulliver 178.2

gully
 noun valley 237.7
 watercourse 239.2
 verb furrow 290.3

gulp
 noun breathing 2.19
 drink 8.4
 ingestion 187.4
 verb gobble 8.23
 ingest 187.11
 gluttonize 672.4

gulping
 noun drinking 8.3
 ingestion 187.4
 adj gluttonous 672.6

gum
 noun elastic 1046.3
 resin 1055.1
 chewing gum 1060.6
 verb chew 8.27
 stick together 802.9
 queer 1011.16

gumbo
 noun semiliquid
 1060.5
 mud 1060.8
 adj earthy 234.5
 viscous 1060.12

gun

noun mercenary
 461.16
 firearm 462.10
 roughneck 593.4
 stop 856.2
 shot 903.4
 shooter 903.8
 verb hunt 382.9
 shoot 903.12

gun battle 457.4

gunfire fire 459.8
 shot 903.4

gun for shoot 903.12
 seek 937.30

gung ho
 noun call to arms
 458.8
 adj enthusiastic 101.10

gunman killer 308.10
 mercenary 461.16
 ruffian 593.3
 shooter 903.8

gunner hand 183.6
 crew 185.4
 artilleryman 461.10
 shooter 903.8

gunnery ballistics 462.3
 throwing 903.2

gunning hunting 382.2
 throwing 903.2

gunpowder 462.14

gunshot detonation
 56.3
 short distance 223.2
 shot 903.4

gurgling 52.19

gurney 900.19

guru teacher 571.1
 master 575.1
 holy man 659.6
 Brahman 699.12
 wise man 920.1

gush
 noun outflow 190.4
 ascent 193.1
 flow 238.4
 jet 238.9
 increase 251.1
 unction 511.2
 wordiness 538.2
 talkativeness 540.1
 outburst 671.6
 plenty 990.2
 verb be enthusiastic
 101.7
 run out 190.13
 shoot up 193.9
 flow 238.16
 jet 238.20
 chatter 540.5
 abound 990.5

gushing
 noun wordiness 538.2
 adj flowing 238.24
 flattering 511.8
 diffuse 538.11

gust taste 62.1
 outburst 105.9

wind gust 318.6
 characteristic 864.4

gustation 62.6

gusto vim 17.2
 animation 17.4
 savour 63.2
 passion 93.2
 pleasure 95.1
 liking 100.2
 eagerness 101.1
 gaiety 109.4

gusty 318.22

gut
 noun tum 2.17
 inlet 242.1
 verb eviscerate 192.13
 destroy 395.10
 plunder 482.17
 adj emotional 93.17
 interior 207.6
 unpremeditated
 365.11
 essential 766.9

gut reaction 93.1

guts tum 2.17
 zest 68.2
 contents 196.1
 insides 207.4
 pluck 359.3
 balls 492.4
 meat and potatoes
 766.1
 inner nature 766.5

gutsy 492.19

gutted disappointed
 132.5
 burned 1019.30

gutter
 noun trough 239.3
 drain 239.5
 trench 290.2
 pavement 383.6
 sewer 654.7
 verb flutter 916.12
 flicker 1024.25
 adj disgraceful 661.11
 vulgar 666.8

guttural raucous 58.15
 inarticulate 525.12

guy fellow 76.5
 supporter 900.2

guzzling
 noun drinking 88.4
 adj gluttonous 672.6

gym fitness 84.1
 arena 463.1
 playground 743.11

gymkhana contest
 457.3
 tournament 743.10

Gymnasium 567.4

gymnasium fitness
 84.1
 playroom 197.12
 arena 463.1
 playground 743.11

gymnastic 743.30

gymnastics exercise
 84.2
 sport 744.1

gypsy 178.4

H big H 87.8
 skiing 753.1

habit
 noun clothing 5.1
 suit 5.6
 substance abuse 87.1
 habitude 373.4
 mannerism 500.2
 nature 766.4
 verb outfit 5.40

habitable 225.15

habitat environment
 209.1
 habitation 225.1
 home 228.18

habitation inhabiting
 225.1
 abode 228.1

habitual regular 373.15
 orderly 806.6
 frequent 846.4
 usual 868.9

habitually regularly
 373.21
 frequently 846.6
 normally 868.10

hacienda farmstead
 228.6
 farm 1067.8

hack
 noun breathing 2.19
 commercial vehicle
 179.13
 notch 289.1
 nag 311.12
 hunter 311.13
 mark 517.5
 hack writer 547.16,
 718.5
 party hack 610.4
 drudge 726.3
 verb go on horseback
 177.34
 sever 801.11
 computerize 1041.18

hacked mad 152.30
 mutilated 794.5

hacker 1041.17

hacking severance
 801.2
 computer science
 1041.1

hackle feather 3.17
 plumage 3.19

hackman 178.9,
 178.10

hackney
 noun commercial
 vehicle 179.13
 hunter 311.13
 adj trite 117.9

hackneyed trite 117.9,
 863.16
 habitual 373.15

well-known 927.27
 aphoristic 973.6

had better 641.3

Hades hell 682.1
 Orcus 682.3
 destiny 838.2

had it 761.11

haemoglobin 2.23

haemorrhage
 noun haemorrhoea
 12.8
 anaemia 85.9
 verb bleed 12.17

haemorrhaging 12.23

haemorrhoids 85.36

hag old woman 304.3
 witch 593.7
 sorceress 690.8
 eyesore 1014.4

haggard tired-looking
 21.9
 colourless 36.7
 frenzied 105.25
 dejected 112.22
 poor 270.20
 deathly 307.29
 fanatic 925.32

haggle
 noun negotiation 731.3
 verb bargain 731.17

haggling 731.3

ha-ha
 noun laughter 116.4
 verb laugh 116.8

hail
 noun greeting 585.4
 multitude 883.3
 hailstone 1022.6
 verb cry 59.6
 assent 332.8
 applaud 509.10
 signal 517.22
 address 524.27
 greet 585.10
 sleet 1022.11

hair pile 3.2
 short distance 223.2
 modicum 248.2
 narrowness 270.1
 filament 271.1
 skin 295.3
 trifle 997.5

haircut 3.15

hairdo 3.15

hairdresser 1015.13

hairdressing 1015.11

hairless depilous 6.17
 mad 152.30

hairline line 517.6
 margin 779.2

hairpin
 noun deviation 164.1
 zigzag 204.8
 skiing 753.1
 race 756.3
 verb deflect 164.5
 adj crooked 204.20

hair-raising 127.29

hairstyle 3.15

hairy hirsute 3.25
threadlike 271.7
bristly 288.9
nappy 294.7
cutaneous 295.32
lousy 999.8
dangerous 1005.9

hajj 177.5

hakim sultan 575.10
mullah 596.3

halcyon bright 97.11
quiescent 173.12
pacific 464.9
thriving 1009.13

halcyon days 317.3

hale
verb pull 904.4
adj strong 15.15
hearty 83.12

half
noun portion 477.5
game 745.3, 750.3
basketball game 751.3
mid-distance 818.2
moiety 874.2
adj proportionate
477.13
part 874.5

half a chance 971.7

half a dozen 881.2

half-and-half
adj neutral 467.7
proportionate 477.13
equal 789.7
mixed 796.14
adv proportionately
477.14
midway 818.5

half a second 829.3

half asleep 22.21

half back 746.2

half-baked immature
406.11
mentally deficient
921.22
half-learned 929.15
imperfect 1002.4

half board 385.3

half century 747.3

half day 856.3

half-hardy 310.41

half inch 482.16

half-light foredawn
314.4
darkishness 1026.2

half-moon crescent
279.5
moon 1070.11

half-open 292.18

half past 831.16

half-pint 258.10

half-price 633.9

half term 20.3

halfway
adj middle 818.4
half 874.5
adv midway 818.5

hall entrance 189.5
assembly hall 197.4
corridor 197.18
house 228.5
inn 228.15
arena 463.1
schoolhouse 567.10
theatre 704.14

hallelujah cheer 116.2
paean 696.3

hallmark
noun sign 517.1
label 517.13
characteristic 864.4
verb label 517.20

hallow celebrate 487.2
sanctify 685.5

hallowed almighty
677.17
sanctified 685.8
traditional 841.12

hallucination
psychosomatic
symptom 92.18
deception 356.1
hallucinosis 975.7
figment of the
imagination 985.5

hallucinatory deceptive
356.21
hallucinative 975.10

hallucinogenic
psychochemical 86.46
hallucinatory 975.10

hallway entrance 189.5
corridor 197.18

halo radiation 171.2
circle 280.2
illustriousness 662.6
nimbus 1024.14

halt
noun respite 20.2
standstill 173.3
delay 845.2
stop 856.2
prevention 1011.2
impasse 1012.6
verb shake 16.8
quiet 173.8
dawdle 175.8
stroll 177.28
stammer 525.8
cease 856.6
stop 856.7, 1011.13
put a stop to 856.11
adj crippled 393.30

halter
noun shackle 428.4
scaffold 605.5
verb yoke 799.10

halting
noun cessation 856.1
prevention 1011.2
adj slow 175.10
crippled 393.30

stammering 525.13
stiff 534.3
irregular 850.3

halve share 476.6
sever 801.11
double 872.5
bisect 874.4

halved 874.6

halving doubleness
872.1
bisection 874.1

ham member 2.7
leg 177.14

hamburger beef 10.13
sandwich 10.31

Hamlet 542.2

hamlet village 230.2
state 231.5

hammer
noun ear 2.10
tool 1039.1
verb rage 671.11
drudge 725.14
din 848.10
pound 901.16
grill 937.22

hammered 715.7

hammered-out 262.9

hammering note
709.14
impact 901.3

hammock 237.4

hamper
noun shackle 428.4
impediment 1011.6
verb package 212.9
burden 297.13
bind 428.10
impede 1011.11

hampered weighted
297.18
bound 428.16

hampering
noun hindrance 1011.1
adj impeding 1011.18

hamstring disable 19.9
paralyse 19.10
cripple 393.14
hamper 1011.11

hamstrung disabled
19.16
crippled 393.30

hand
noun member 2.7,
792.4
deck hand 183.6
side 218.1
person 312.5
act 328.3
skill 413.1
governance 417.5
assist 449.2
applause 509.2
pointer 517.4
signature 527.10
handwriting 547.3
control 612.2

worker 726.2
bridge 758.3
verb deliver 478.13
transfer 629.3

hand back 481.4

handbag 729.14

handball 1046.3

handbook manual
554.8
directory 574.10

handcuffed 428.16

handcuffs 428.4

hand down bequeath
478.18
transfer 629.3

handed 218.7

handed down 841.12

handedness 218.1

hand for 413.5

handful modicum
248.2
few 884.2
tough proposition
1012.2

hand grenade 462.20

handgun 462.10

handicap
noun disease 85.1
burden 297.7
disability 603.2
round 748.3
inequality 790.1
disadvantage 995.2
impediment 1011.6
verb burden 297.13
penalize 603.4
hamper 1011.11

handicapped
noun cripple 85.44
adj crippled 393.30

handicapper 759.6

hand in 478.13

handing over 370.3

hand in hand
cooperatively 450.6
sociably 582.25
amicably 587.22
concurrently 898.5

hand-in-hand near
223.14
familiar 587.19
accompanying 768.9
joined 799.13

handiwork act 328.3
work 725.4
production 891.2
product 892.1

handkerchief 5.25

handle
noun bulge 283.3
pretext 376.1
hold 900.11
verb touch 73.6
pilot 182.14
treat 321.6, 387.12
perform 328.9

use 387.10
discuss 541.12
write upon 556.5
direct 573.8
deal in 731.15
operate 888.5
tend 1068.7

handler trainer 571.6
boxer 754.2
operator 888.4

handling touching 73.2
performance 328.2
usage 387.2
utilization 387.8
treatise 556.1
direction 573.1
operation 888.1

handmade 891.18

hand of friendship
465.2

hand on transfer
176.10, 629.3
communicate 343.7
bequeath 478.18

hand out parcel out
477.8
deliver 478.13

handout press release
352.3
advertising matter
352.8
donation 478.6
information 551.1

hand over transfer
176.10, 629.3
give up 370.7
surrender 433.8
deliver 478.13
pay over 624.15

handover 475.1

hands work force 18.9
governance 417.5
clutches 474.4
control 612.2
protectorship 1007.2

hands down 1013.16

handshake signing
437.3
greeting 585.4

hands-off indulgent
427.8
nonrestrictive 430.25
permissive 443.14
conservative 852.8

handsome liberal 485.4
magnanimous 652.6
beautiful 1015.17

handsomely liberally
485.5
magnanimously 652.8
beautifully 1015.23

hands-on 888.12

hand-to-mouth 406.15

handwriting 547.3

handy nearby 223.15
miniature 258.12
modal 384.8

convenient 387.20
skilful 413.22
wieldy 1013.15

hang
noun droop 202.2
declivity 204.5
knack 413.6
verb bear 161.7
take off 193.10
hang down 202.6
suspend 202.8
inhabit 225.7
hang 604.17
hang by the neck
604.17
procrastinate 845.11
depend 958.6, 970.11

hangar housing 184.24
garage 197.27
repair shop 739.5

hanger pendant 202.4
suspender 202.5
woodland 310.11
caption 936.2

hang in tough it out
15.11
take it 134.6
keep alive 306.10

hanging
noun pendency 202.1
pendant 202.4
declivity 204.5
cover 295.2
capital punishment
604.6
scenery 704.20
adj downcast 194.12
pendent 202.9
loose 803.5

hanging out 31.6

hangman 604.7

hang on keep alive
306.10
stay with it 360.4
hold 474.6
cohere 802.6
result from 886.5
attribute to 887.4

hang on to 474.6

hang out be exposed
31.5
overhang 202.7
inhabit 225.7

hang over overhang
202.7
overlie 295.30

hangover intoxication
88.1
subsequence 834.1

Hang Seng Index
737.1

hang up suspend 202.8
telephone 347.18
postpone 845.9

hang-up delay 845.2
obsession 925.13
obstacle 1011.4

hank 271.2

hankering
noun yearning 100.5
adj wistful 100.23

Hansard 549.8

haphazard
noun chance-medley
971.4
adj slipshod 340.12
unprepared 406.8
unordered 809.12
purposeless 971.16

haphazardly carelessly
340.18
unsystematically
809.18
discontinuously 812.5
purposelessly 971.20

hapless 1010.14

happen occur 830.5
chance 971.11

happening
noun event 830.2
hap 971.6
adj occurring 830.9
modern 840.13

happen to be 760.8

happily gladly 95.18
cheerfully 109.17
auspiciously 133.21

happiness felicity 95.2
contentment 107.1
cheerfulness 109.1
decorousness 496.3
prosperity 1009.1

happy intoxicated
88.31
glad 95.15
content 107.7
cheerful 109.11
auspicious 133.18
decorous 496.10
appropriate 533.7
apt 787.10
timely 842.9
expedient 994.5

happy couple 563.9

happy ending 819.1

happy family 455.1

happy-go-lucky 406.15

happy hour 20.2

harass fatigue 21.4
annoy 96.13
vex 98.15
worry 126.5
intimidate 127.20
persecute 389.7
besiege 459.19
work evil 999.6
trouble 1012.13

harassed tormented
96.24
worried 126.8
troubled 1012.20

harassing annoying
98.22
troublesome 126.10

harassment annoyance
96.2
vexatiousness 98.7
worry 126.2
persecution 389.3

harbinger
noun forerunner 133.5
herald 353.2
precursor 815.1
verb herald 133.14

harbour
noun destination 186.5
inlet 242.1
refuge 1008.1
haven 1008.6
verb house 225.10
hold 474.7
protect 1007.18

hard
adj strong 15.15
painful 26.10
bitter 64.6
alcoholic 88.37
callous 94.12
impenitent 114.5
harsh 144.24
heartless 144.25
pitiless 146.3
industrious 330.22
unyielding 361.9
obdurate 361.10
firm 425.7
hard to understand
522.14
phonetic 524.31
hardened 654.17
lascivious 665.29
real 760.15
sturdy 762.7
true 972.13
valid 972.14
adverse 1010.13
difficult 1012.17
dense 1043.12
solid 1044.10
tough 1047.4
adv near 223.20
laboriously 725.19

hard act to follow
413.11

hard and fast 182.73

hard-and-fast
preceptive 419.4
mandatory 420.12

hard at work 330.21

hard-boiled firm 15.18
hard 1044.10

hard by 223.20

hard cash payment
624.1
money 728.1

hard-core unyielding
361.9
fiery 671.22

hard currency 728.1

hard disk 549.10

hard drinking 88.4

hard-drinking 88.35

hard-earned laborious
725.18
difficult 1012.17

harden strengthen
15.13
callous 94.6
accustom 373.10
indurate 1044.7
toughen 1047.3
petrify 1057.9

hardened callous 94.12
impenitent 114.5
heartless 144.25
accustomed 373.16
hard 654.17
toughened 1044.13,
1047.6

hardening
noun strengthening
15.5
habituation 373.8
densification 1043.3
temper 1044.4
toughening 1044.5
adj toughening
1044.14

hard feelings bad
feeling 93.7
bitterness 152.3
animosity 589.4

hard-fought laborious
725.18
difficult 1012.17

hard labour 604.2

hard life 1010.1

hard line
unyieldingness 361.2
strictness 425.1, 687.5
warlikeness 458.11

hard-line unyielding
361.9
strict 425.6
militaristic 458.22
fiery 671.22

hardline 687.8

hard look 27.14

hard luck 1010.5

hardly scarcely 248.9
narrowly 270.22
firmly 425.9
infrequently 847.4
unusually 869.17
with difficulty 1012.28

hardly anything 248.5

hardly ever 869.17

hardness firmness 15.3,
425.2
callousness 94.3
impenitence 114.2
harshness 144.9
heartlessness 144.10
pitilessness 146.1
roughness 294.2
abstruseness 522.2
obduracy 654.6
difficulty 1012.1
density 1043.1
durity 1044.1

toughness 1047.1

hard-pressed 1012.26

hard rock 708.10

hard sell inducement
375.3
selling 734.2

hardship poverty 619.1
adversity 1010.1

hard times 1010.6

hard to believe 954.10

hard to understand
522.14

hard up poor 619.7
straitened 1012.26

hardware hard goods
735.4
computer 1040.17,
1041.2

hard way
noun difficulty 1012.1
adv laboriously 725.19
with difficulty 1012.28

hard-wearing 1047.4

hardwood
noun wood 1052.3
adj arboreal 310.36

hardworking
industrious 330.22
labouring 725.17

hardy strong 15.15
hale 83.12
insolent 142.9
perennial 310.41
courageous 492.17
durable 826.10
tough 1047.4

hare
noun lightning 174.6
leveret 311.24
verb barrel 174.9

harem 563.10

hark listen 48.10
hearken to 982.7

hark back turn back
858.5
remember 988.10

Harlequin 707.10

harlequin
noun check 47.4
spectrum 47.6
buffoon 707.10
verb variegate 47.7
adj variegated 47.9

harlot
noun prostitute 665.16
adj prostitute 665.28

harm
noun impairment
393.1
disadvantage 995.2
evil 999.3
bane 1000.1
verb impair 393.9
inconvenience 995.4
work evil 999.6

harmed 393.27

harmful unhealthful
82.5
malicious 144.20
disadvantageous 995.6
hurtful 999.12
adverse 1010.13

harmless hurtless
998.21
undamaged 1001.8
unhazardous 1006.5

harmonic
noun tone 50.2
harmonic tone 709.16
adj harmonious 708.49
oscillating 915.15

harmonica 711.10

harmonics 708.3,
709.1

harmonious chromatic
35.15
pleasant 97.6
symmetric 264.4
cooperative 450.5
in accord 455.3
balanced 533.8
friendly 587.15
harmonic 708.49
agreeing 787.9
orderly 806.6
conformist 866.6
concurrent 898.4

harmoniously
cooperatively 450.6
in step 787.11
methodically 806.9

harmony symmetry
264.1
unanimity 332.5
cooperation 450.1
accord 455.1
peace 464.1
proportion 533.2
good terms 587.3
bliss 681.5
concord 708.3
harmonics 709.1
agreement 787.1
order 806.1
conformity 866.1

harness
noun wardrobe 5.2
parachute 181.13
caparison 385.5
armour 460.3
verb yoke 799.10
tend 1068.7

harp
noun lyre 711.3
mouth organ 711.10
verb persist 855.5

harper 710.5

harping
noun repetitiousness
848.4
close attention 982.4
adj tedious 118.9
monotonous 848.15

harpsichord 711.12

harried tormented
96.24
worried 126.8

harrier 96.10

harrow
noun projection 285.4
verb pain 26.7
torture 96.18
smooth 287.5
cultivate 1067.17

harrowing
noun cultivation
1067.13
adj painful 26.10
agonizing 98.23

harry annoy 96.13
worry 126.5
persecute 389.7
attack 459.14
besiege 459.19

harsh acrimonious
17.14
painful 26.10
off-colour 35.20
raucous 58.15
dissonant 61.4
clashing 61.5
bitter 64.6
pungent 68.6
distressing 98.20
oppressive 98.24
rough 144.24
pitiless 146.3
rugged 288.7
strict 425.6
gruff 505.7
inarticulate 525.12
inelegant 534.2

harshly roughly 144.33
pitilessly 146.4
strictly 425.8
gruffly 505.9

harshness acrimony
17.5
raucousness 58.2
clash 61.2
pungency 68.1
agony 98.4
distressfulness 98.5
oppressiveness 98.8
roughness 144.9,
288.1
pitilessness 146.1
strictness 425.1
gruffness 505.3
speech defect 525.1
inelegance 534.1
violence 671.1

hart cock 76.8
deer 311.5

harvest
noun autumn 313.4
yield 472.5
effect 886.1
production 892.2
harvesting 1067.15
verb acquire 472.8
process 891.9
reap 1067.19

harvested 891.18

harvester 1067.5

harvesting production
891.2
harvest 1067.15

harvest moon 1070.11

harvest time 313.4

has-been
noun back number
841.8
adj past 836.7

hash
noun meat 10.12
black hash 87.7
fiasco 410.6
hotchpotch 796.6
jumble 809.3
verb mix 796.10

Hasidic 675.30

hassle
noun struggle 725.3
commotion 809.4
verb vex 98.15
struggle 725.11
argue 934.16
work evil 999.6

haste
noun impatience 135.1
velocity 174.1
impulsiveness 365.2
hurry 401.1
recklessness 493.2
prematurity 844.2
verb speed 174.8
hasten 401.4

hasten be impatient
135.4
advance 162.5
speed 174.8
accelerate 174.10
haste 401.4
make haste 401.5
be useful 449.17
facilitate 1013.7

hastening hurrying
401.3
facilitation 1013.5

hastily swiftly 174.17
impulsively 365.13
hurriedly 401.12
recklessly 493.11
suddenly 829.9
prematurely 844.13

hasty hot-tempered
110.25
impatient 135.6
fast 174.15
impulsive 365.9
hurried 401.9
unprepared 406.8
reckless 493.8
sudden 829.5
premature 844.8

hat
noun headdress 5.25
verb cloak 5.39
top 295.21

hatch

harvested 891.18

noun porch 189.6
young 561.2
verb be born 1.2
be pregnant 78.12
fabricate 354.18
plot 381.9
mark 517.19
portray 712.19
engrave 713.9
originate 891.12
imagine 985.14
raise 1068.6

hatched born 1.4
fabricated 354.29

hatching birth 1.1
network 170.3
line 517.6
engraving 713.2
production 891.1

hatchway 189.6

hate
noun hostility 99.2,
589.3
hatred 103.1
anathema 103.3
verb have deep feelings
93.12
dislike 99.3
detest 103.5
bear ill will 589.8

hateful offensive 98.18
loathesome 103.8
malicious 144.20
hostile 589.10
terrible 999.9

hate mail 553.4

hater 103.4

hating 103.7

hatred hostility 99.2,
589.3
hate 103.1

hatted 5.44

hatter 5.36

hat trick match 747.3
game 750.6

haughty vain 136.9
arrogant 141.9
contemptuous 157.8
high 272.14

haul
noun distance 261.1
take 480.10
booty 482.11
strain 725.2
pull 904.2
verb cart 176.13
sail against the wind
182.24
lay 182.48
strain 725.10
pull 904.4

haulage
noun freightage 630.7
pulling 904.1
phrase transportation
176.3

hauling
noun pulling 904.1

adj pulling 904.6
phrase transportation
176.3

haunches 217.4

haunt
noun resort 228.27
verb oppress 98.16
worry 126.5
frequent 221.10
hant 987.6

haunted worried 126.8
spooked 987.10
remembering 988.24

haunting recurrent
848.13
unforgettable 988.26

haute couture 578.1

Havana 89.4

have give birth 1.3
affirm 334.5
gyp 356.19
compel 424.4
suffer 443.10
possess 469.4
hold 474.7
receive 479.6
understand 521.7
experience 830.8
know 927.12
recognize 988.12

have a baby 1.3

have a feeling 933.4

have a go take action
328.5
tackle 403.7
take one's turn 824.5
experiment 941.8

have a go at practice
328.8
enter 817.9

have a good time
enjoy oneself 95.13
amuse oneself 743.22

have a job 724.12

have a look 27.13

have a look at browse
570.13
attend to 982.5

have an idea 952.11

have at 459.14

have a tendency 895.3

have a word with
541.9

have been around
413.19

have confidence
952.14

have confidence in
believe in 952.15
trust 952.17

have difficulty
1012.11

have done with give
up 370.7
cease to use 390.4
relinquish 475.3

cease 856.6

have enough lose
412.12
have about enough of
993.5

have faith 692.6

have faith in 952.15

have fun throw a party
582.21
amuse oneself 743.22

have got to 962.10

have had it have no
patience with 135.5
have enough 993.5

have in mind
contemplate 380.5
intend 518.9
think of 930.16
keep in memory
988.13

have it 939.2

have money 618.11

haven
noun destination 186.5
refuge 1008.1
harbour 1008.6
verb protect 1007.18

have no doubt be
confident 952.14
be certain 969.9

have no more 473.4

have nothing to do
331.16

**have nothing to do
with** let alone 329.4
avoid 368.6
refuse 442.3
keep to oneself 583.4
have no truck with
586.5
abstain 668.7
not concern 775.4

have-nots 619.3

have on 5.43

have plenty of time
402.3

have run out 836.6

haves 618.6

have sex 75.21

have the nerve 492.10

have time 402.3

have to be compelled
424.9
be necessary 962.10

have to do with
participate 476.5
relate to 774.5
operate on 888.6

have too much 993.5

have trouble be born
to trouble 1010.9
have difficulty
1012.11

having 469.9

having a baby 1.1

having said that
945.17

having sex 75.7

havoc
noun destruction 395.1
evil 999.3
verb destroy 395.10

haw avoid 164.6
stammer 525.8

hawk
noun eagle 27.11
bird 311.28
militarist 461.5
patriot 591.3
verb salivate 13.6
hunt 382.9
vend 734.9

hawker 730.5

hawking
noun inducement
375.3
hunting 382.2
selling 734.2
adj inarticulate 525.12

hawkish right 219.4
militaristic 458.22
public-spirited 591.4

hay
noun feed 10.4
Acapulco gold 87.10
verb harvest 1067.19

hay fever 85.33

haystack 769.10

haywire crazy 925.27
kooky 926.6

hazard
noun golf 748.1
gamble 759.2
bet 759.3
unreliability 970.6
happening 971.6
danger 1005.1
obstacle 1011.4
verb presume 640.6
chance 759.24, 971.11
bet 759.25
endanger 1005.6
take chances 1005.7

hazardous speculative
759.27
unreliable 970.20
risky 1005.10

haze
noun acid 87.9
fog 319.2
confusion 984.3
verb cloud 319.6
banter 490.5

hazel 40.3

hazy inconspicuous
32.6
formless 263.4
foggy 319.9
obscure 522.15
vague 970.19
muddled 984.13

he male 76.4
self 864.5

he— 76.11

head
noun member 2.7
head of hair 3.4
latrine 12.10
fan 101.5
sail 180.14
heading 198.4
architectural topping
198.5
headpiece 198.6
front 216.1
headwaters 238.2
superior 249.4
point 283.9
raceme 310.25
person 312.5
foam 320.2
makeup 554.12
abridgment 557.1
superintendent 574.2
portrait 712.15
class 808.2
source 885.5
thrust 901.2
intellect 918.1
brain 918.6
intelligence 919.9
topic 936.1
caption 936.2
water 1063.3
verb bear 161.7
lead 165.2
top 198.9
gravitate 297.15
direct 573.8
govern 612.12
play 745.4
precede 813.2
tend 895.3
focus on 936.3
adj top 198.10
front 216.10
directing 573.12
governing 612.18
first 817.17

headache ache 26.5
annoyance 96.2
drag 118.5
trouble 1012.3

head and shoulders
793.17

**head and shoulders
above** superlative
249.13
superior 998.14

headband 554.14

head chef 11.2

headdress hairdo 3.15
headgear 5.25

headed 198.12

headed for 161.26

header tumble 194.3
plunge 367.1
game 745.3

head for 161.9

headgear 5.25

head in 856.7

heading
noun direction 161.1
leading 165.1
course 184.34
head 198.4
front 216.1
supervision 573.2
class 808.2
topic 936.1
caption 936.2
adj leading 165.3
topping 198.11

head into brave 492.11
begin 817.7

headland 283.9

headless topless 198.13
unintelligent 921.13

headline
noun caption 936.2
verb dramatize 704.28
focus on 936.3
feature 996.15

headliner lure 377.3
lead 707.6

headlong
adj fast 174.15
steep 204.18
impulsive 365.9
precipitate 401.10
reckless 493.8
sudden 829.5
adv impulsively
365.13
precipitately 401.15
recklessly 493.11

headman
superintendent 574.2
minister 575.17

headmaster 571.8

headmistress 571.8

head off 164.6

head of hair 3.4

head of state 575.7

head-on
adj front 216.10
adv adversarial 451.9

head over heels
inversely 205.8
precipitately 401.15
recklessly 493.11
round 914.16

head-over-heels 205.7

headquarters 739.7

headroom 158.3

heads 215.3

headset loudspeaker
50.8
radiophone 347.5

head start 844.1

headstock 914.7

headstone monument
549.12
foundation stone
900.7

headstrong obstinate
361.8

lawless 418.5

head teacher 571.8

head-to-head 216.10

head up direct 573.8
precede 813.2
initiate 817.10
focus on 936.3

headway progression
162.1
way 182.9
improvement 392.1

heady intoxicating
88.36
exciting 105.30
foamy 320.7
lawless 418.5

heal treat 91.24
cure 396.15
heal over 396.21

healer nonmedical
therapist 90.9
healer 90.9

healing
noun therapy 91.1
nonmedical therapy
91.2
cure 396.7
adj remedial 86.39

health
noun well-being 83.1
normality 868.1
adj medical 90.15

health and fitness
83.1

health care 90.1

health centre hospital
91.21
metropolis 208.7

health club 84.1

health-conscious
83.14

health food nutrient
7.3
food 10.1

health hazard 82.1

health insurance 90.1

health spa 84.1

health visitor 90.10

healthy healthful 81.5,
83.8
large 257.16
good 998.12

heap
noun jalopy 179.10
amount 244.2
lot 247.4
store 386.1
throng 769.4
pile 769.10
verb load 159.15
give 478.12
pile 769.19

heaped 769.21

heaps 618.3

hear
verb sense 24.6

listen 48.10
catch 48.11
know 551.15
try 598.19
sit in judgment 945.12
hearken to 982.7
exclam bravo! 509.22

hear hear 332.18

hearing
noun senses 24.5
audition 48.1, 48.2
earshot 48.4
trial 598.6
examination 937.2
investigation 937.4
tryout 941.3
adj auditory 48.13

hearing aid 48.8

hear nothing 983.2

hear of 48.11

hearsay
noun report 552.6
adj evidential 956.16

hearse 309.19

heart viscera 2.14
kidneys 10.19
passion 93.2
soul 93.3
love 104.1
substance 196.5
interior 207.2
centre 208.2
life force 306.3
fortitude 492.6
essence 766.2
inner nature 766.5
middle 818.1
psyche 918.4
mood 977.4
salient point 996.6

heartache wretchedness
96.6
aching heart 112.9

heart and soul
noun essence 766.2
inner nature 766.5
adv fervently 93.26
resolutely 359.17
laboriously 725.19
throughout 793.17

heart attack 85.19

heartbeat life force
306.3
pulsation 915.3

heartbreak harshness
98.4
heartache 112.9

heartbreaking 98.23

heartbroken 112.29

heartburn ache 26.5
jealousy 153.1

heart condition 85.19

heart disease 85.19

heartening
noun encouragement
492.9
adj cheering 109.16

comforting 121.13

heart failure 85.19

heartfelt 93.24

hearth home 228.2
family 559.5
fireplace 1019.11

heartily strongly 15.23
energetically 17.16
fervently 93.26
zealously 101.14
gaily 109.18
amicably 587.22

heartland inland 207.3
region 231.1

heartless unfeeling
94.9, 144.25
apathetic 94.13
dejected 112.22
pitiless 146.3
uncourageous 491.11
hardened 654.17

heart of gold kindness
143.1
liberality 485.1
harmlessness 998.9

heart of hearts heart
93.3
interior 207.2
inner nature 766.5

hearts bennies 87.3
card 758.2

heart-shaped 279.15

heart-throb sweetie
104.11
celebrity 662.9

heart-to-heart 644.17

heartwarming pleasant
97.6
delightful 97.7
cheering 109.16

hearty
noun mariner 183.1
boon companion 588.5
adj strong 15.15
energetic 17.13
hale 83.12
fervent 93.18
zealous 101.9
gay 109.14
convivial 582.23
hospitable 585.11
cordial 587.16

heat
noun sexual desire
75.5
fever 85.7
passion 93.2
zeal 101.2
fever of excitement
105.7
anger 152.5
race 457.12
hotness 1018.1
verb cook 11.4
excite 105.12
incite 375.17
adj fuel 1020.8

heated cooked 11.6

fervent 93.18
zealous 101.9
passionate 105.22
fiery 671.22
hot 1018.25

heater 1019.10

heath plain 236.1
wasteland 890.2

heathen
noun pagan 688.7
unbeliever 695.11
adj pagan 688.11
unbelieving 695.19
idolatrous 697.7
unlearned 929.14

heating
noun heat 1018.1
warming 1019.1
adj warming 1019.26

heating system 1019.1

heat up incite 375.17
antagonize 589.7

heave
noun wave 238.14
strain 725.2
throw 903.3
pull 904.2
lift 911.2
verb feel disgust 99.4
thrill 105.18
lay 182.48
pitch 182.55
billow 238.22
strain 725.10
throw 903.10
pull 904.4
vomit 908.26
elevate 911.5

Heaven river of death
307.4
destiny 838.2
Fates 963.3

heaven happiness 95.2
good times 1009.4
heavens 1070.2

heavenly blissful 97.9
divine 677.16
angelic 679.6
heavenish 681.12
sacred 685.7
godly 692.9
ideal 985.23
superb 998.15
gorgeous 1015.20
celestial 1070.25

heavens 1070.2

heaven-sent timely
842.9
expedient 994.5

heavily sadly 112.31
dully 117.10
inertly 173.20
heavy 297.21
densely 1043.15

heaviness sleepiness
22.1
pregnancy 78.5
harshness 98.8

sadness 112.1
dullness 117.1
weight 297.1
languor 331.6
inelegance 534.1
viscosity 1060.2

heaving
noun trepidation 105.5
throwing 903.2
pulling 904.1
vomiting 908.8
adj respiratory 2.30

heavy
noun beer 88.16
heavyweight 257.12
role 704.10
adj underdone 11.8
sleepy 22.21
deep 54.10
pregnant 78.18
oppressive 98.24
sad 112.20
dull 117.6, 921.16
inert 173.14
great 247.6, 998.13
thick 269.8
ponderous 297.16
luxuriant 310.40
cloudy 319.7
languid 331.20
phonetic 524.31
stiff 534.3
tragic 704.34
laborious 725.18
sturdy 762.7
weighty 996.20
dense 1043.12
viscous 1060.12
adv heavily 297.21

heavy artillery 462.11

heavy drinking 88.3

heavy duty 387.1

heavy-duty 1047.4

heavy-handed
insensible 25.6
bungling 414.20
inelegant 534.2

heavy industry 739.2

heavy rain 316.2

heavyweight
noun pig 257.12
bantamweight 297.3
influence 893.6
adj heavy 297.16

Hebe
noun attendant 577.5
Venus 1015.10
phrase carrier 176.7

Hebrew
noun Jew 675.21
adj Jewish 675.30

Hebrides South 231.7
Siberia 1022.4

heckled 96.24

heckler 96.10

hectic
noun reddening 41.3
glow 1018.12

adj red-complexioned
41.9
feverish 85.57
overzealous 101.12
heated 105.22
overactive 330.24

Hector 492.8

hector
noun braggart 502.5
blusterer 503.2
verb annoy 96.13
intimidate 127.20
bluster 503.3

hedge
noun boundary 211.3
caution 494.1
qualification 958.1
verb limit 210.5
fence 212.7
dodge 368.8
take precautions 494.6
quibble 935.9
qualify 958.3

hedged limited 210.7
enclosed 212.10
qualified 958.10
unimaginative 986.5

hedgehog bear 311.23
launcher 462.21
rocket launcher
1072.10

hedging
noun limitation 210.2
caution 494.1
quibbling 935.5
qualification 958.1
adj demurring 325.7
quibbling 935.14

hedonism pleasure-
loving 95.4
selfishness 651.1
sensuality 663.1

hedonistic pleasure-
loving 95.17
selfish 651.5
sensual 663.5

heed
noun carefulness 339.1
observance 434.1
caution 494.1
attention 982.1
verb listen 48.10
obey 326.2
care 339.6
observe 434.2
attend 982.6

heel
noun foot 199.5
rear 217.1
stern 217.7
arsehole 660.6
verb deviate 164.3
follow 166.3
careen 182.43
equip 385.8
fight 754.4

heeled 385.13

hefty corpulent 257.18
heavy 297.16

laborious 725.18

hegemonic
authoritative 417.15
governing 612.18

hegemony superiority
249.1
supremacy 249.3
mastership 417.7

height space 158.1
mountain 237.6
degree 245.1
supremacy 249.3
size 257.1
heighth 272.1
elevation 272.2, 911.1
pitch 709.4
acme of perfection
1001.3

heighten aggravate
119.2
intensify 251.5
elevate 272.13, 911.5

heightened aggravated
119.4
increased 251.7

heightening
aggravation 119.1
intensification 251.2
exaggeration 355.1

heights highlands 237.1
height 272.2

heinous offensive 98.18
wicked 654.16
base 661.12
terrible 999.9

heir survivor 256.3
heritor 479.5
successor 816.4
sequel 834.2

heir apparent heir
479.5
prince 608.7

heiress heir 479.5
descendant 561.3

heirs 561.1

held reserved 386.15
possessed 469.8
stuck 854.16
supported 900.24
obsessed 925.33
believed 952.23
gripped 982.18

held back reserved
386.15
unused 390.12

held out 390.12

held up 845.16

helicopter 181.5

helix coil 281.2
whirl 914.2

Hell river of death
307.4
destiny 838.2
Siberia 1022.4

hell torment 96.7
depths 275.3

place of confinement
429.7
Hades 682.1
pandemonium 809.5
oven 1018.11

hell-bent on 359.16

hellfire 682.2

hellish frightening
127.28
cruel 144.26
diabolic 654.13
turbulent 671.18
infernal 682.8
execrable 999.10

hello 585.4

helm
noun saddle 417.10
direction 573.1
con 573.5
control 612.2
verb pilot 182.14

helmet heraldic device
647.2
cricket 747.1
safeguard 1007.3

helmsman steersman
183.8
guide 574.7

help
noun serving 8.10
remedy 86.1
aid 449.1
subsidy 478.8
servant 577.2
staff 577.11
benefactor 592.1
assistant 616.6
verb do a favour
143.12
aid 449.11
subsidize 478.19
serve 577.13
do good 998.10
prevent 1011.14

helper subordinate
432.5
assistant 449.7, 616.6
benefactor 592.1

helpful considerate
143.16
modal 384.8
useful 387.18, 449.21
good 998.12

helpfully 449.24

helping
noun serving 8.10
portion 477.5
adj assisting 449.20
serving 577.14

helping hand assist
449.2
benefactor 592.1

helpless defenceless
19.18
dead-drunk 88.32
forlorn 584.12
unprotected 1005.14

helplessness
defencelessness 19.4
forlornness 584.4
exposure 1005.3

helpline 347.13

help to 478.12

helter-skelter
noun haste 401.1
merry-go-round
743.15
jumble 809.3
commotion 809.4
adj separated 801.21
confused 809.16
adv hastily 401.12
recklessly 493.11
nonuniformly 781.4
in disorder 809.17

hem
noun border 211.4
edging 211.7
verb border 211.10
fence 212.7
restrict 428.9
stammer 525.8

hemisphere sphere
231.2
member 792.4
half 874.2

hemmed 212.10

hemmed in 428.15

hemp Acapulco gold
87.10
scaffold 605.5

hen gal 77.6
Partlet 77.9
poultry 311.29

hence thence 188.20
therefore 887.7

henceforth 838.10

henchman hanger-on
138.6
follower 166.2, 616.8

henna
verb redden 41.4
adj reddish-brown
40.4

henry big H 87.8
induction 1031.14

her female 77.4
basuco 87.6
self 864.5

herald
noun harbinger 133.5,
353.2
leading 165.1
king of arms 575.22
delegate 576.2
spokesman 576.5
precursor 815.1
verb harbinger 133.14
proclaim 352.13
go before 815.3
be prior 833.3

heraldic 352.18

herb cooking 11.1
Acapulco gold 87.10

legume 310.4

herbaceous 310.33

herbal 310.33

herbicide 1000.3

herbs 86.4

Herculean Briarean
15.17
huge 257.20
laborious 725.18
difficult 1012.17

Hercules strong man
15.6
Al Borak 311.15
Atlas 900.3

herd
noun guide 574.7
masses 606.2
flock 769.5
guardian 1007.6
verb guide 573.9
drive 1068.8

here hereat 159.23
there 221.16
now 837.3

hereabouts 159.23

hereafter
noun afterworld 681.2
future 838.1
destiny 838.2
adj future 838.8
adv in future 838.10

here and now
noun reality 760.2
present 837.1
realism 986.2
adv now 837.3

here-and-now 1050.10

here and there in
places 159.25
scatteringly 770.12
discontinuously 812.5
sparsely 884.8

hereby 384.12

hereditary protoplasmic
305.18
patrimonial 560.19
innate 766.8

heredity genetic
material 305.9
heritage 560.6

herein 207.10

heresy false doctrine
688.2
inconsistency 788.2
unconventionality
867.2
unbelief 954.1
error 974.1

heretic misbeliever
688.5
nonconformist 867.3

heretical unorthodox
688.9
nonconformist 788.9
unconventional 867.6
unbelieving 954.8
erroneous 974.16

heritage inheritance
479.2
heredity 560.6

Hermes 353.1

hermetic resistant
15.20
close 293.12
secret 345.11

hermit recluse 584.5
ascetic 667.2
religious 699.15
oddity 869.4

Hermitage 386.9

hermitage 1008.5

hero victor 411.2
heroine 492.8
god 659.5
celebrity 662.9
godling 678.3
role 704.10
lead 707.6
ideal 785.4

heroic eminent 247.9
huge 257.20
courageous 492.17
magnanimous 652.6
vocal 708.50
poetic 720.15
traditional 841.12

heroically pluckily
359.18
courageously 492.23

heroics rashness 493.1
boasting 502.1

heroine hero 492.8,
659.5
celebrity 662.9
godling 678.3
role 704.10
lead 707.6

heroism glory 247.2
courage 492.1
magnanimity 652.2

hero worship love
104.1
respect 155.1
praise 509.5
idolatry 697.1

hero-worship respect
155.4
praise 509.12

herpes 85.34

Herr 76.7

herself 864.5

hertz 1033.12

hesitancy hesitation
362.3
caution 494.1
uncertainty 970.1

hesitant demurring
325.7
hesitating 362.11
uncertain 970.16

hesitantly 362.13

hesitate demur 325.4
pause 362.7
stammer 525.8

procrastinate 845.11
hang in doubt 970.10

hesitating
  noun hesitation 362.3
  adj demurring 325.7
  hesitant 362.11
  stammering 525.13
  uncertain 970.16

hesitation demur 325.2
  hesitance 362.3
  caution 494.1
  stammering 525.3
  procrastination 845.5
  uncertainty 970.1

heterogeneous different
  779.7
  diversified 782.4
  mixed 796.14

heterosexual 75.13

heterosexuality
  sexuality 75.2
  sexual preference
  75.10

hew form 262.7
  sever 801.11

hewn formative 262.9
  severed 801.23

hex
  noun curse 513.1
  sorceress 690.8
  spell 691.1
  bad influence 999.4
  verb curse 513.5
  bewitch 691.9
  work evil 999.6

hexagonal pentagonal
  278.10
  sixth 881.18

heyday 1009.4

hey presto
  noun incantation 691.4
  adj presto 851.13

hiatus interval 224.1
  opening 292.1
  deficiency 794.2
  interruption 812.2

hibernation sleep 22.2
  inactivity 331.1

hiccup
  noun breathing 2.19
  belch 908.9
  verb belch 908.28

hick
  noun simple soul
  416.3
  oaf 923.5
  adj hicky 233.8

hickey discolouration
  1003.2
  gadget 1050.5

hid 346.11

hidalgo 608.4

hidden invisible 32.5
  secret 345.11
  concealed 346.11
  latent 519.5
  implied 519.7

hidden agenda 946.1

hide
  noun fur 4.2
  lamina 296.2
  ambush 346.3
  verb disappear 34.3
  conceal 346.6
  conceal oneself 346.8
  store up 386.11
  clobber 412.9
  beat up 604.14

hideaway hiding place
  346.4
  retreat 584.6, 1008.5

hideous horrid 98.19,
  1014.11
  terrible 127.30

hideously 98.27,
  1014.13

hideout hiding place
  346.4
  retreat 1008.5

hiding
  noun covering 295.1
  concealment 346.1
  hiding place 346.4
  larruping 604.5
  adj concealing 346.15

hiding place hideaway
  346.4
  retreat 1008.5

hierarchical gradual
  245.5
  hierarchal 698.16

hierarchy rank 245.2
  mastership 417.7
  authorities 575.15
  class 607.1
  central government
  612.4
  hierocracy 698.7
  continuity 806.2
  class structure 808.4

hi-fi 50.16

high
  noun stupor 22.6
  intoxication 88.1
  excitement 105.1
  weather map 317.4
  price 738.9
  gear 1039.5
  adj high-pitched 58.13
  nasty 64.7
  strong 68.8
  malodorous 71.5
  bent 87.23
  fuddled 88.33
  excited 105.20
  cheerful 109.11
  lofty 136.11
  spacious 158.10
  eminent 247.9, 662.18
  high-reaching 272.14
  tainted 393.41
  phonetic 524.31
  noble 608.10
  expensive 632.11
  magnanimous 652.6

raised 911.9
  adv on high 272.21
  intemperately 669.10

high and dry stuck
  854.16
  in safety 1006.6
  stranded 1012.27
  dry 1064.7

high and low 158.12

high blood pressure
  85.9

highbrow 928.1

high-class 998.14

high culture 927.5

Higher 937.2

higher 249.12, 272.19

higher-income wealthy
  618.14
  prosperous 1009.12

higher-up 249.4

highest
  noun supremacy 249.3
  adj top 198.10
  superlative 249.13
  higher 272.19
  almighty 677.17
  paramount 996.24

highest level 198.10

highest point 198.2

highest-quality 249.13

highest-ranking
  249.14

high explosive 462.14

high fashion 578.1

high-flying aspiring
  100.28
  ostentatious 501.18
  grandiloquent 545.8

high-frequency
  1033.28

high-grade 998.14

high-handed 417.16

high hopes 124.1

high income 618.1

high-income 1009.12

high jinks 743.4

high jump 366.1

high jumper 366.4

highland
  noun highlands 237.1,
  272.3
  adj rustic 233.6
  upland 272.17

Highlander 227.11

Highlands 231.7

highlands country
  233.1
  uplands 237.1
  highland 272.3

Highlands and Islands
  231.7

high life society 578.6
  upper class 607.2
  aristocracy 608.1

highlight
  noun feature 996.7
  light 1024.1
  verb manifest 348.5
  signify 517.17
  specify 864.11
  call attention to
  982.10
  emphasize 996.14
  illuminate 1024.28

highlighted 348.12

highlighting
  conspicuousness 348.4
  indication 517.3
  specification 864.6

highlights dye 3.16
  lighting 1024.19

highly 247.15

highly regarded
  662.15

highly strung excitable
  105.28
  touchy 110.21
  nervous 128.11

high-minded lofty
  136.11
  honest 644.13
  magnanimous 652.6

Highness 648.2

highness stridency 58.1
  strength 68.3
  height 272.1
  expensiveness 632.1

high noon summit
  198.2
  noon 314.5

high-performance
  18.12

high-pitched 58.13,
  272.14

high point 996.6

high-powered powerful
  18.12
  important 996.17

high pressure
  inducement 375.3
  coercion 424.3
  urgency 996.4

high-pressure
  verb urge 375.14
  adj powerful 18.12
  climatal 317.12
  urgent 996.22

high-priced 632.11

high priest chief 575.3
  deacon 699.9
  rabbi 699.10

high-priority 996.22

high profile 31.2

high-profile 31.7

high-quality 998.14

high regard 155.1

high resolution 31.2

high-rise
  noun tower 272.6
  adj high 272.14

high-risk 1005.10

high school 567.4

high seas 240.1

high season journey
  177.5
  season 313.1

high society society
  578.6
  upper class 607.2
  aristocracy 608.1

high-society socially
  prominent 578.16
  upper-class 607.10

high-speed 174.16

high-spirited excitable
  105.28
  mischievous 322.6

high spirits happiness
  95.2
  good humour 109.2
  gaiety 109.4
  mischief 322.2

high spot 996.7

high status 607.3

high summer 1018.7

high technology
  927.10

high tide tide 238.13
  high water 272.8

high time good
  opportunity 842.3
  lateness 845.1

high treason 645.7

high up 272.21

high-up 272.14

high-velocity 174.16

high water tide 238.13
  high tide 272.8

highway 383.5

hijack coerce 424.7
  swipe 482.16

hijacking 482.3

hike
  noun walk 177.10
  verb march 177.30
  elevate 911.5

hiked increased 251.7
  expanded 259.10

hiker 178.6

hiking walking 177.8
  expansion 259.1

hilarious merry 109.15
  humorous 488.4
  festive 743.28

hilariously 109.19

hilarity merriment
  109.5
  laughter 116.4
  humorousness 488.1

hill
  noun down 237.4
  plateau 272.4
  bulge 283.3
  pile 769.10
  verb pile 769.19

hills 237.1

hillside incline 204.4
slope 237.2

hilly rolling 237.8
knobby 272.18

him male 76.4
big H 87.8
self 864.5

himself self 864.5
boss 996.11

hind
noun hen 77.9
deer 311.5
peasant 606.6
agriculturist 1067.5
adj rear 217.9

hinder
verb restrain 428.7
fend off 460.10
delay 845.8
impede 1011.10
adj rear 217.9

hindering
noun hindrance 1011.1
adj troublesome
1011.17

hind legs 177.15

hindrance restraint
428.1
delay 845.2
hindering 1011.1

hindsight 988.4

hinge
noun joint 799.4
crisis 842.4
axle 914.5
verb hook 799.8
depend 958.6

hingle 914.5

hint
noun tinge 62.3, 796.7
soupçon 248.4
remainder 256.1
warning 399.1
piece of advice 422.2
indication 517.3
clue 517.9
implication 519.2
gentle hint 551.4
suggestion 950.5
reminder 988.6
verb augur 133.12
promise 133.13
signify 517.17
imply 519.4
intimate 551.10

hint at advise 422.5
hint 551.10

hinted 519.7

hinterland
noun inland 207.3
setting 209.2
region 231.1
back country 233.2
adj inland 207.7
back 233.9

hip
noun side 218.1

joint 799.4
adj hep 927.17

hippie
noun nonconformist
867.3
adj unconventional
867.6

hippo heavyweight
257.12
behemoth 257.14
pachyderm 311.4

hippodrome 463.1

hippy 257.18

hire
noun rental 615.6
pay 624.4
fee 630.6
verb employ 615.14
rent 615.15
rent out 615.16

hired employed 615.20
paid 624.22

hire purchase 733.1

hiring engagement
615.4
rental 615.6

hirsute hairy 3.25
feathery 3.28
bristly 288.9
nappy 294.7

his male 76.4
big H 87.8

His Holiness 648.5

his honour 596.1

his lordship 596.1

hiss
noun sibilation 57.1
boo 508.3
speech defect 525.1
verb sibilate 57.2
growl 60.4
bubble 320.4
boo 508.10
murmur 524.26

hissing
noun audio distortion
50.13
sibilation 57.1
ridicule 508.1
boo 508.3
adj sibilant 57.3
ridiculing 508.12

historian annalist 550.2
cliometrician 719.4

historic 719.7

historical historic
719.7
fictional 722.7
real 760.15
obvious 969.15
true 972.13

historically historically
speaking 719.9
formerly 836.13
truly 972.18

historical research
719.1

history
noun record 549.1
historical discipline
719.1
past 836.1
adj shot 395.29

histrionic emotionalistic
93.19
affected 500.15
theatrical 501.24
dramatic 704.33

histrionics
emotionalism 93.9
display 501.4
dramatics 704.2

hit
noun kick 105.3
smash 409.4
score 409.5
popular music 708.7
blow 901.4
verb impress 93.15,
930.19
go 177.19
arrive 186.6
contact 223.10
waste 308.13
attack 459.14
play 747.4, 748.4
collide 901.13
strike 901.14
shoot 903.12
discover 940.2

hit and miss 941.1

hit-and-miss 340.12

hit-and-run
verb run over 909.7
adj dastardly 491.12

hit at 459.16

hit back at 506.4

hitch
noun pang 26.2
gait 177.12
fastening 799.3
term 824.4
jerk 904.3
obstacle 1011.4
crux 1012.8
verb stroll 177.28
hook 799.8
jerk 904.5
tend 1068.7

hither 159.23

hitherto previously
833.6
formerly 836.13
until now 837.4

hit-in 750.3

hit it score a success
409.9
solve 939.2

hit man 308.10

hit on 439.8

hit out at 459.16

hit the jackpot 409.9

hit upon 186.7

hive

noun nest 228.25
hive of industry 739.2
flock 769.6
multitude 883.3
verb settle 159.17
come together 769.16

hives allergy 85.33
skin diseases 85.34
skin eruption 85.35

hoar
noun frost 1022.7
adj white 37.7
grey 39.4
grey-haired 39.5
aged 303.16

hoard
noun store 386.1
gain 472.3
verb store up 386.11
not use 390.5

hoarding poster 352.7
stinginess 484.3

hoarse raucous 58.15
inarticulate 525.12

hoary white 37.7
grey 39.4
grey-haired 39.5
aged 303.16
old 841.10
traditional 841.12
frosty 1022.17

hoax
noun fake 354.13
deception 356.7
verb deceive 356.14

Hob 680.7

hob fairy 678.8
goblin 680.8
shelf 900.14
fireplace 1019.11

hobble
noun slow motion
175.2
gait 177.12
shackle 428.4
pickle 1012.5
verb paralyse 19.10
stroll 177.28
cripple 393.14
bind 428.10
hamper 1011.11

hobbled 175.10

hobbling
noun impairment
393.1
adj slow 175.10
crippled 393.30

hobby
noun avocation 724.7
adj avocational 724.17

hock leg 177.14
pledge 438.2

hockey 750.1

hoe 1067.17

hoeing 1067.13

hog
noun pig 80.13

angel dust 87.17
cycle 179.8
swine 311.9
self-seeker 651.3
verb appropriate
480.19

hogan 228.10

hogging 469.11

ho-ho
noun laughter 116.4
verb laugh 116.8

hoist
noun lift 911.2
lifter 911.3
verb elevate 911.5
phrase people mover
176.5

hold
noun cellar 197.17
storehouse 386.6
custody 429.5
stronghold 460.6
possession 469.1
purchase 474.2, 905.2
seizure 480.2
control 612.2
notation 709.12
influence 893.1
footing 900.5
handle 900.11
verb extend 158.8
refrain 329.3
affirm 334.5
store up 386.11
restrain 428.7
confine 429.12
possess 469.4
grip 474.6
keep 474.7
exist 760.8
include 771.3
cohere 802.6
endure 826.6
remain 852.5
stabilize 854.7
sustain 855.4
cease 856.6
support 900.21
obsess 925.25
judge 945.8
conclude 945.10
decide 945.11
think 952.11
be true 972.8
engross 982.13
suffice 990.4

hold back slow 175.9
restrain 428.7
deny 442.4
withhold 484.6
restrain oneself 668.6
abstain 668.7
hinder 1011.10

hold down suppress
428.8
subjugate 432.8

holder container 195.1
possessor 470.1
recipient 479.3

real estate 471.6
praise 509.5
probity 644.1
great honour 646.1
title 648.1
esteem 662.3
prestige 662.4
chastity 664.1
attribution 887.1
notability 996.2
verb respect 155.4
execute 437.9
celebrate 487.2
pay in full 624.13
do honour 646.8
worship 696.10

Honourable 648.8

honourable venerable
155.12
honest 644.13
honorary 646.10
reputable 662.15

honourably honestly
644.21
reputably 662.20

honoured respected
155.11
distinguished 646.9,
662.16
reputable 662.15

honours bridge 758.3
examination 937.2

honours degree 648.6

hoo 60.5

hood
noun cover 295.2
mischief-maker 322.3
combatant 461.1
roughneck 593.4
arsehole 660.6
goon 671.10
verb cloak 5.39
cover 295.19
top 295.21

hooded clothing 5.44
covered 295.31

hoof
noun foot 199.5
verb dance 705.5

hook
noun angle 278.2
curve 279.2
point 283.9
snare 356.13
fastening 799.3
verb angle 278.5
curve 279.6
trap 356.20
grab 472.9
catch 480.17
play 746.4, 747.4,
748.4
hitch 799.8

hooked angular 278.6
crooked 279.8

hooker 746.2

hook in 356.20

hooking 799.3

hooky
noun absence 222.4
adj dishonest 645.16

hooligan mischief-
maker 322.3
combatant 461.1
vulgarian 497.6
roughneck 593.4
arsehole 660.6

hooliganism
misbehaviour 322.1
boorishness 497.4

hoop band 280.3
toy 743.16

hooray
noun cheer 116.2
verb cheer 116.6

hoot
noun blare 53.5
cry 59.1
joke 489.6
boo 508.3
zilch 761.3
verb blare 53.10
cry 59.6
warble 60.5
boo 508.10

hooter noisemaker 53.6
alarm 400.1

hooting
noun ridicule 508.1
adj ridiculing 508.12

hoover 79.23

hop
noun black pills 87.15
step 177.11
leap 366.1
dance 705.2
verb barrel 174.9
stroll 177.28
fly 184.36
leap 366.5
dance 705.5

hope
noun desire 100.1,
100.11
hopefulness 124.1
cardinal virtues 653.4
belief 952.1
possibility 965.1
recourse 1008.2
verb expect 130.5
come 838.6

hoped-for desired
100.29
expected 130.13

hope for wish for
100.16
hope 124.7
come 838.6

hope for the best
124.8

hopeful
noun optimist 124.6
youngster 302.1
adj cheerful 109.11
hoping 124.11
expectant 130.11

probable 967.6

hopefully cheerfully
109.17
hopingly 124.14
expectantly 130.15
in the future 838.9

hope in 124.7

hopeless apathetic
94.13
unhopeful 125.12
dying 307.33
unskilful 414.15
impossible 966.7

hopelessly 125.17

hopelessness apathy
94.4
dejection 112.3
unhopefulness 125.1
impossibility 966.1
no chance 971.10

hopes hope 124.1
expectations 130.4

hoping
noun hope 124.1
adj desirous 100.21
hopeful 124.11

hopper locust 311.34
jumper 366.4

hopping
noun leaping 366.3
adj leaping 366.7

horde
noun masses 606.2
throng 769.4
verb come together
769.16

horizon vision 27.1
field of view 31.3
skyline 201.4
distance 261.3

horizontal
noun plane 201.3
adj level 201.7
straight 277.6

horizontally 201.9

hormone 86.32

horn
noun loudspeaker 50.8
noisemaker 53.6
mountain 237.6
projection 285.4
alarm 400.1
wind instrument 711.6
pommel 900.18
verb gore 459.26

horned crescent-shaped
279.11
pointed 285.9

horner 710.4

hornet 311.33

horns 680.13

horny pointed 285.9
lascivious 665.29
hard 1044.10

horoscope 1070.20

horrendous horrid
98.19

terrible 127.30

horrendously 127.34

horrible horrid 98.19
terrible 127.30, 999.9
terrific 247.11
hideous 1014.11

horribly horridly 98.27
frightfully 127.34
distressingly 247.21
terribly 999.14
hideously 1014.13

horrid horrible 98.19
terrible 127.30, 999.9
hideous 1014.11

horrific horrid 98.19
terrible 127.30

horrified 127.26

horrifying horrid 98.19
terrible 127.30

horror torment 96.7
hostility 99.2
fear 127.1
frighteningness 127.2
frightener 127.9
abomination 638.2
eyesore 1014.4

horrors 925.10

horse
noun ox 15.8
big H 87.8
pony 311.10
exerciser 725.7
jockey 757.2
trestle 900.16
verb give a lift 911.7
phrase beast of burden
176.8

horseback
noun ridge 237.5
adv on horseback
177.44
on 900.25

Horse Guards 461.14

horsehair hair 3.2
string 711.20

horseman 178.8

horsemanship riding
177.6
skill 413.1
animal husbandry
1068.1

horsepower 18.4

horse race 457.12,
757.3

horse-race 457.19

horse racing racing
457.11
turf 757.1

horse-riding 177.6

horseshoe 279.5

horse trading 731.2

horst 237.5

horticultural floral
310.35
olericultural 1067.21

terrible 127.30

horticulture flower
310.22
gardening 1067.2

hose
noun hosiery 5.28
tube 239.6
verb moisten 1063.12

hosepipe 239.6

hosiery 5.28

hospice hospital 91.21
inn 228.15
asylum 1008.4

hospitable comforting
121.13
receptive 187.16,
585.11
liberal 485.4
sociable 582.22
cordial 587.16

hospital 91.21

hospitality
comfortableness 121.2
receptivity 187.9
housing 225.3
liberality 485.1
sociability 582.1
hospitableness 585.1
cordiality 587.6

Host 701.7

host
noun army 461.22
mine host 585.5
master of ceremonies
743.20
throng 769.4
flock 769.5
multitude 883.3
broadcaster 1033.23
verb entertain 585.8

hostage 438.2

hostel 228.15

hostelry 228.15

hostess crew 185.4
attendant 577.5
waiter 577.7
host 585.5

hostile dark 38.9
unpleasant 98.17
averse 99.8
oppositional 451.8
warlike 458.21
antagonistic 589.10
contrary 778.6
disagreeing 788.6
adverse 1010.13

hostilities 458.1

hostility darkness 38.2
bad feeling 93.7
unpleasantness 98.1
antagonism 99.2,
451.2, 589.3
contraposition 215.1
contention 457.1
warlikeness 458.11
contrariety 778.1

hot red 41.6
zestful 68.7
lustful 75.26

in heat 75.27
feverish 85.57
fervent 93.18
zealous 101.9
heated 105.22,
1018.25, 1019.29
hot-tempered 110.25
mad 152.30
fugitive 368.16
stolen 482.23
lascivious 665.29
fiery 671.22
syncopated 709.29
brand-new 840.10
great 998.13
charged 1031.33
radioactive 1036.10

hot air big talk 502.2
bullshit 520.3
bombast 545.2
superheated air 1018.9

hot bath 91.4

hotbed birthplace 885.8
rabbit 889.6
nursery 1067.11

hot day 1018.8

hot dog 501.11

hotel 228.15

hotelier 470.2

hothouse birthplace
885.8
nursery 1067.11

hotline telephone call
347.13
line 347.17

hotly heatedly 105.34
violently 247.23

hot pursuit 382.1

hot seat capital
punishment 604.6
scaffold 605.5
pickle 1012.5

hot spot danger 1005.1
pickle 1012.5
radiation 1036.1

hotspur sorehead
110.11
daredevil 493.4

hotter 178.10

hottest 840.10

hot water pickle
1012.5
boiling water 1018.10

hot weather 317.3

Houdini 369.5

hound
noun fan 101.5
beast 660.7
verb annoy 96.13
worry 126.5
follow 166.3
pursue 382.8
hunt 382.9
persecute 389.7

hounded tormented
96.24
worried 126.8

hounding annoyance
96.2
following 166.1
persecution 389.3

hour period 823.1
moment 823.2
time of day 831.2

hour after hour for a
long time 826.14
constantly 846.7

hourly
adj momentary 849.8
adv constantly 846.7
periodically 849.10

house
noun audience 48.6
cabin 197.9
dwelling 228.5
structure 266.2
council 423.1
race 559.4
family 559.5
lineage 560.4
company 617.9
cloister 703.6
theatre 704.14
market 736.1
workplace 739.1
casino 759.19
attender 917.2
astrology 1070.20
verb domicile 225.10
accommodate 385.10

house arrest 429.3

houseboat 228.5

housebound 85.53

housed domiciled
225.14
covered 295.31

household
noun home 228.2
family 559.5
adj residential 228.32
simple 499.6
usual 868.9
well-known 927.27

householder
homeowner 227.7
proprietor 470.2

household goods 229.1

house in 212.5

housekeeper steward
574.4
major-domo 577.10

housekeeping
domesticity 228.3
domestic management
573.6

houseman 90.4

house of cards kitten
16.7
danger 1005.1
eggshell 1048.2

housewife mistress
575.2
sewing machine 741.3

housing

noun hangar 184.24
domiciliation 225.3
abode 228.1
quarters 228.4
cover 295.2
horsecloth 295.11
radio 1033.3
adj constructional
891.15

housing association
225.3

housing benefit 478.8

housing development
225.3

housing estate 225.3

housing scheme 225.3

hover fly 184.36
take off 193.10
levitate 298.9
hesitate 362.7
be imminent 839.2

Hovercraft 181.7

hovering 184.50

how 384.1

how are you? 585.15

how come 887.8

how-do-you-do
greeting 585.4
pickle 1012.5

how do you do?
585.15

however
noun catch 421.3
adv anyhow 384.10
adv, conj
notwithstanding 338.8

how is it that 887.8

how it goes 764.2

how it is state of affairs
764.2
what's what 972.4

howl
noun noise 53.3
screech 58.4
cry 59.1
animal noise 60.1
lament 115.3
beef 115.5
verb screech 58.8
cry 59.6, 60.2
weep 115.12
wail 115.13
beef 115.16
sigh 318.21

howling
noun audio distortion
50.13
animal noise 60.1
lamentation 115.1
adj shrill 58.14
yowling 60.6
frenzied 105.25
plaintive 115.19
terrific 247.11

how things are state of
affairs 764.2
what's what 972.4

how-to 384.1

hub convergence 169.1
centre 208.2
axle 914.5
fireplace 1019.11

hubbub noise 53.3
outcry 59.4
bustle 330.4
turbulence 671.2
commotion 809.4
agitation 916.1
argumentation 934.4

hubris
presumptuousness
141.2
insolence 142.1
rashness 493.1
presumption 640.2
confidence 969.5

huddle
noun conference 541.6
verb stay near 223.12
come together 769.16

hue
noun colour 35.1
colour quality 35.6
nature 766.4
verb colour 35.13

hue and cry noise 53.3
outcry 59.4
publicity 352.4
pursuit 382.1
alarm 400.1

hued 35.16

huff
noun dudgeon 152.7
verb intimidate 127.20
provoke 152.24
enlarge 259.4
blow 318.20

huffing 2.30

hug
noun hold 474.2
embrace 562.3
welcome 585.2
greeting 585.4
verb stay near 223.12
hold 474.6, 474.7
seize 480.14
embrace 562.18
welcome 585.9
cohere 802.6

huge Herculean 15.17
large 247.7
immense 257.20

hugely 247.16

hugging 562.1

huggy 257.18

Hughes 618.8

hulk ship 180.1
whopper 257.11
wreck 393.8
body 1050.3

hull
noun ship 180.1
shell 295.16
seed vessel 310.28
verb husk 6.9

hum
noun audio distortion
50.13
humming 52.7
vocal music 708.13
series 811.2
verb thrum 52.13
stammer 525.8
sing 708.38
persist 780.3

human
noun person 312.5
adj kind 143.13
pitying 145.7
hominal 312.13

human behaviour
321.3

human being 312.5

human beings 312.1

humane kind 143.13
pitying 145.7
lenient 427.7

humanely kindly
143.18
pitifully 145.10

human error 974.3

human interest 93.9

humanism naturalistic
humanism 312.11
freethinking 695.7
scholarship 927.5

humanist freethinker
695.13
scholar 928.3

humanistic human
312.13
secularist 695.16

humanitarian
noun philanthropist
143.8
adj benevolent 143.15

humanity kindness
143.1
pity 145.1
humankind 312.1
human nature 312.6
humanness 312.8

humankind 312.1

humanly kindly 143.18
mortally 312.17

human nature
humanity 312.6
humanness 312.8

humanoid
noun ancient 841.7
adj manlike 312.14
primitive 841.11

human race 312.1

human resources 18.9

human rights right
430.2
rights of man 642.3

human sacrifice 696.7

humble
verb humiliate 137.4
conquer 412.10
subdue 432.9

demote 447.3
adj penitent 113.9
resigned 134.10
lowly 137.10
modest 139.9
inferior 250.6
meek 433.15
populational 606.8
unselfish 652.5

humbled penitent
113.9
reduced 137.13
humiliated 137.14
conquered 412.17
subdued 432.15

humblest 137.10

humbling
noun subdual 432.4
demotion 447.1
adj humiliating 137.15

humbly penitently
113.12
meekly 137.16
modestly 139.14

humbug
noun sham 354.3
quackery 354.7
humbuggery 354.14
hoax 356.7
impostor 357.6
nonsense 520.2
verb deceive 356.14

humdrum
noun tedium 118.1
repetitiousness 848.4
adj tedious 118.9
prosaic 721.5
same 780.6
monotonous 848.15

humid sultry 1018.28
moist 1063.15

humidity sultriness
1018.6
humidness 1063.2

humiliate mortify
98.13
humble 137.4
offend 156.5
subdue 432.9
demote 447.3
disgrace 661.8

humiliated humbled
137.14
subdued 432.15

humiliating mortifying
98.21
humiliative 137.15
insulting 156.8
disgraceful 661.11

humiliation chagrin
96.4
mortification 98.6,
137.2
indignity 156.2
snub 157.2
subdual 432.4
demotion 447.1
disgrace 661.5

humility resignation
134.2
humbleness 137.1
modesty 139.1
inferiority 250.1
meekness 433.5
unselfishness 652.1

humming
noun hum 52.7
vocal music 708.13
adj thrumming 52.20

humorous funny 488.4
witty 489.15
amusing 743.27

humour
noun lymph 2.22
blood 2.23
personality tendency
92.11
caprice 364.1
wit 489.1
mood 977.4
verb indulge 427.6

humourless 112.21

hump
noun blues 112.6
mountain 237.6
bulge 283.3
verb curve 279.6
break one's neck
330.14
pull 904.4

humped humpbacked
265.13
bowed 279.10
convex 283.13

humpty dumpty
257.12

humus 889.4

Hun dago 232.7
squaddie 461.7

hun 395.8

hunch
noun feeling 93.1
premonition 133.1
bulge 283.3
sense 933.3
verb curve 279.6
crouch 912.8

hunched 279.10

hundred state 231.5
match 747.3
century 881.8

hundred percent
793.14

hundredth 881.29

hung 202.9

hunger
noun eating 8.1
craving 100.6
appetite 100.7
tendency 895.1
verb eat 8.20
hunger for 100.19

hunger for 100.19

hunger strike 515.1

hungrily 100.31

hungry craving 100.24
hungering 100.25

hung up distressed
96.22
obsessed 925.33

hunk strong man 15.6
powerhouse 15.7
real man 76.6
piece 792.3

hunky 1015.18

hunt
noun hunting 382.2
search 937.15
verb pursue 382.8
go hunting 382.9
persecute 389.7
seek 937.30
search 937.31

hunt down hunt 382.9
trace 937.35
discover 940.2

hunted 382.7

hunter stalking-horse
311.13
sporting dog 311.18
pursuer 382.4
huntsman 382.5
shooter 903.8
seeker 937.18

hunt for 937.30

hunting
noun pursuit 382.1
gunning 382.2
search 937.15
adj pursuing 382.11

huntsman 382.5

hurdle
noun leap 366.1
obstacle 1011.4
verb leap 366.5

hurdler 366.4

hurdles 366.3

hurdling 366.3

hurl
noun ride 177.7
throw 903.3
verb clap 159.13
throw 903.10

hurling 903.2

hurly-burly 105.4,
916.1

hurrah
noun cry 59.1
cheer 116.2
verb cheer 116.6

hurricane outburst
105.9
windstorm 318.12
storm 671.4

hurried hasty 401.9
rushed 401.11
reckless 493.8

hurriedly hastily
401.12
recklessly 493.11

hurry
noun agitation 105.4

hungry craving 100.24

velocity 174.1
haste 401.1
verb move 172.5
speed 174.8
hasten 401.4
make haste 401.5

hurrying 401.3

hurry up accelerate
174.10
hasten 401.4
make haste 401.5

hurst 310.12

hurt
noun pain 26.1, 96.5
impairment 393.1
disadvantage 995.2
evil 999.3
verb pain 26.7, 96.17
suffer 26.8, 96.19
offend 152.21
impair 393.9
injure 393.13
work evil 999.6
adj pained 26.9, 96.23
impaired 393.27

hurtful painful 26.10
harmful 999.12

hurting
noun pain 26.1
impairment 393.1
adj pained 26.9
painful 26.10

hurtle speed 174.8
thrust 901.12
collide 901.13

husband
noun married man
563.7
master 575.1
verb reserve 386.12
economize 635.4

husband and wife
563.9

husbandry direction
573.1
domestic management
573.6
thrift 635.1
agriculture 1067.1

hush
noun silence 51.1
sibilation 57.1
verb fall silent 51.7
silence 51.8
sibilate 57.2
cover up 345.8
calm 670.7

hushed silent 51.10
quiescent 173.12
restrained 670.11

hush-hush
verb silence 51.8
cover up 345.8
adj secret 345.11

husk
noun hull 295.16
seed vessel 310.28
verb hull 6.9

husks remainder 256.1
refuse 391.4

husky
adj raucous 58.15
phrase beast of burden
176.8

hussar 461.11

hustings public
speaking 543.1
platform 900.13

hustle
noun enterprise 330.7
haste 401.1
thrust 901.2
verb drive 330.13
gyp 356.19
hasten 401.4
make haste 401.5
thrust 901.12
shake 916.11

hustler 357.4

hustling fast 174.15
prostitute 665.28

hut 228.9

hutch
noun hut 228.9
verb store 386.10

hybrid
noun hybrid word
526.11
crossbreed 796.8
adj mongrel 796.15

Hydra 889.6

hydraulic hydrologic
1038.11
watery 1063.16

hydro 91.23

hydrotherapy 91.3

hygiene sanitation 79.3
hygienics 81.2

hygienic sanitary 79.27
healthful 81.5

hymn
noun thanks 150.2
paean 696.3
sacred music 708.17
verb glorify 696.11
sing 708.38

hype 375.14

hyper overwrought
105.26
overactive 330.24

hyperactive 330.24

hyperactivity 330.9

hyperbole
misrepresentation
350.1
exaggeration 355.1
excess 992.1

Hyperion Venus
1015.10
Sol 1070.14

hypertension 85.9

hyperventilation 2.19

hypnosis 691.3

hypnotherapy 22.7

premature 844.8
unwise 922.10
inexpedient 995.5

ill-defined
inconspicuous 32.6
vague 970.19

illegal prohibited 444.7
wrong 638.3
unjust 650.9
unlawful 674.6

illegality wrong 638.1
injustice 650.1
unlawfulness 674.1
offence 674.4

illegally 674.8

illegible 522.19

illegitimate
noun bastard 561.5
adj spurious 354.26,
674.7
illegal 674.6

ill-equipped unfitted
406.9
ill-provided 991.12

ill-fated 133.17

ill feeling 589.4

ill health 85.3

illicit prohibited 444.7
freeloving 665.27
illegal 674.6

ill-informed 929.12

illiteracy 929.5

illiterate
noun ignoramus 929.8
adj unlearned 929.14

ill-judged 922.10

illness 85.1

illogical unreasonable
935.11
erroneous 974.16

I'll say 972.25

ill-tempered 110.18

ill-treatment 389.2

illuminate
noun wise man 920.1
verb colour 35.13
explain 341.10
manifest 348.5
figure 498.9
illumine 1024.28

illuminated fuddled
88.33
luminous 1024.39

illuminating
explanatory 341.15
educational 568.18
illumining 1024.40

illumination colouring
35.11
explanation 341.4
ornamentation 498.1
teaching 568.1
picture 712.11
cognizance 927.2
learning 927.4
light 1024.1

lighting 1024.19

illuminations 1025.1

illusion deception
356.1
bewitchment 691.2
spirit 763.3
error 974.1
delusion 975.1
figment of the
imagination 985.5

illusory deceptive
356.21
bewitching 691.11
unreal 761.9
thin 763.6
erroneous 974.16
illusive 975.9
imaginary 985.19

illustrate explain
341.10
image 349.11
evidence 956.8
cite 956.13

illustrating 349.13

illustration explanation
341.4
representation 349.1
picture 712.11
example 785.2
citation 956.5

illustrative explanatory
341.15
representational
349.13

illustrator 716.2

illustrious 662.19

ill will malevolence
144.4
animosity 589.4

image
noun appearance 33.2
aspect 33.3
apparition 33.5
engram 92.29
description 349.2
likeness 349.5
affectation 500.1
sign 517.1
figure of speech 536.1
picture 712.11, 1034.5
copy 784.1
idea 931.1
phantom 975.4
visualization 985.6
verb mirror 349.11
contemplate 930.17
visualize 985.15

image of same 777.3
likeness 783.3

imagery representation
349.1
description 349.2
figure of speech 536.1
figment of the
imagination 985.5
visualization 985.6

imaginable supposable
950.15

possible 965.6
fanciable 985.26

imaginary unreal
761.9
thin 763.6
farfetched 775.8
illusory 975.9
imaginational 985.19

imagination fancy
975.3
imagining 985.1
figment of the
imagination 985.5

imaginative original
337.5
expressive 544.10
conceptual 985.18

imagine contemplate
930.17
suppose 950.10
think 952.11
fancy 985.14

imagined unreal 761.9
imaginary 985.19

imaging catharsis
92.25
representation 349.1
visualization 985.6

imagining imagination
985.1
figment of the
imagination 985.5

imam sultan 575.10
qadi 699.11

imbalance distortion
265.1
inequality 790.1

imbecile
noun cripple 85.44
idiot 923.8
adj weak 16.12
mentally deficient
921.22
foolish 922.8

imbued 35.16

imbued with 93.23

imitate copy 336.5
adopt 621.4
resemble 783.7
repeat 848.7

imitated 783.10

imitation
noun reproduction
78.1, 336.3
copying 336.1
impersonation 349.4
fake 354.13
burlesque 508.6
adoption 621.2
similarity 783.1
copy 784.1
repetition 848.1
substitute 861.2
duplication 873.1
adj mock 336.8
spurious 354.26
similar 783.10
substitute 861.8

imitative simulative
336.9
representational
349.13
repetitious 848.14

immaculate clean
79.25
honest 644.13
chaste 653.7, 664.4
spotless 657.7
perfect 1001.6

immaculately cleanly
79.29
honestly 644.21
perfectly 1001.10

immanent present
221.12
intrinsic 766.7

immaterial unreal
761.9
unsubstantial 763.5
irrelevant 775.7
disembodied 987.8
insignificant 997.17
nonmaterial 1051.7

immature unadult
301.10
unripe 406.11
inexperienced 414.17
incomplete 794.4
new 840.7
puerile 921.24
half-learned 929.15
imperfect 1002.4

immaturity
undevelopment 301.3,
406.4
inexperience 414.2
incompleteness 794.1
newness 840.1
puerility 921.11
unwiseness 922.2
imperfection 1002.1

immeasurable large
247.7
infinite 822.3
innumerable 883.10

immeasurably
extremely 247.22
infinitely 822.4
numerously 883.12

immediacy presence
221.1
nearness 223.1
urgent need 962.4

immediate present
221.12, 837.2
adjacent 223.16
nearest 223.19
hasty 401.9
continuous 811.8
instantaneous 829.4
imminent 839.3
prompt 844.9

immediately hastily
401.12
instantly 829.6
promptly 844.15

immemorial perpetual
828.7
former 836.10
old 841.10
traditional 841.12

immense large 247.7
huge 257.20
infinite 822.3
superb 998.15

immensely vastly
247.16
infinitely 822.4
superbly 998.23

immerse submerge
367.7
baptize 701.16
engross 982.13

immersed underwater
275.13
soaked 1063.17

immersed in 982.17

immersion
submergence 367.2
baptism 701.6
engrossment 982.3
wetting 1063.6

immigrant migrant
178.5
incomer 189.4
citizen 227.4
settler 227.9
newcomer 773.4

immigration migration
177.4
in-migration 189.3

imminent expected
130.13
approaching 167.4
threatening 514.3
future 838.8
impending 839.3

immobile motionless
173.13
passive 329.6
permanent 852.7
immovable 854.15

immobility
motionlessness 173.2
inaction 329.1
inactivity 331.1
immovability 854.3

immoral dishonest
645.16
vice-prone 654.11

immorality 654.1

immortal
noun celebrity 662.9
god 678.2
adj peerless 249.15
eminent 662.18
almighty 677.17
everlasting 828.9
indestructible 854.18

immortality life 306.1
memory 662.7
eternal life 828.3
indestructibility 854.5

immortals 678.1

immovable unfeeling
94.9
firm 359.12
unyielding 361.9
unmovable 854.15
inflexible 1044.12
immune resistant
83.14
exempt 430.30
safe 1006.4
immune response
83.14
immunity resistance
83.4
immunization 91.15
pardon 148.2
exemption 430.8,
601.2
privilege 642.2
safety 1006.1
immutable persevering
360.8
unyielding 361.9
almighty 677.17
uniform 780.5
durable 826.10
permanent 852.7
unchangeable 854.17
inflexible 1044.12
imp
noun brat 302.4
mischief-maker 322.3
fairy 678.8
pixie 680.7
verb graft 191.6
impact
noun power 18.1
meaning 518.1
concussion 671.8
force 886.2
collision 901.3
verb thrust in 191.7
cause 885.10
operate on 888.6
collide 901.13
impacted 854.16
impact on cause
885.10
operate on 888.6
impair subtract 255.9
damage 393.9
work evil 999.6
impaired damaged
393.27
imperfect 1002.4
impairment reduction
255.2
damage 393.1
disintegration 805.1
disadvantage 995.2
imperfection 1002.1
impaled 96.25
impart transfer 176.10
communicate 343.7
disclose 351.4
give 478.12
say 524.23
impartial neutral 467.7

impersonal 649.10
unprejudiced 978.12
impartiality neutrality
467.1
detachment 649.4
moderation 670.1
unprejudicedness
978.5
impartially 649.11
imparting 343.2
impassable 293.13
impasse obstruction
293.3
same 789.3
corner 1012.6
impassioned fervent
93.18
zealous 101.9
amorous 104.26
excited 105.20
vehement 544.13
impassive unfeeling
94.9
inexcitable 106.10
quiescent 173.12
reticent 344.10
inexpressive 522.20
stable 854.12
incurious 981.3
impassively
apathetically 94.15
inexcitably 106.16
inertly 173.20
impatience eagerness
101.1
impatientness 135.1
impulsiveness 365.2
impatient eager 101.8
unpatient 135.6
impulsive 365.9
impatiently eagerly
101.13
breathlessly 135.8
impeachment deposal
447.2
censure 510.3
arraignment 598.3
accusation 599.1
impeccable spotless
657.7
accurate 972.16
perfect 1001.6
impeccably accurately
972.20
perfectly 1001.10
impede slow 175.9
delay 845.8
hinder 1011.10
hamper 1011.11
impeded 175.12
impediment
obstruction 293.3
hindrance 1011.1
embarrassment 1011.6
impeding 1011.18
impelled 375.30

impending overhanging
202.11
imminent 839.3
impenetrable
impregnable 15.19
impervious 293.13
luxuriant 310.40
unintelligible 522.13
inaccessible 966.9
dense 1043.12
imperative
noun rule 419.2
command 420.1
mood 530.11
duty 641.1
urgent need 962.4
adj authoritative
417.15
imperious 417.16
mandatory 420.12
commanding 420.13
compulsory 424.10
obligatory 424.11,
641.15
vigorous 544.11
necessary 962.12
urgent 996.22
imperceptible invisible
32.5
infinitesimal 258.14
imperfect
noun tense 530.12
adj inadequate 250.7
impaired 393.27
incomplete 794.4
insufficient 991.9
not perfect 1002.4
imperfection
inadequacy 250.3
vice 654.2
incompleteness 794.1
shortcoming 910.1
want 991.4
imperfectness 1002.1
fault 1002.2
imperfectly scarcely
248.9
incompletely 794.6
inadequately 1002.5
imperial
noun beard 3.8
volume 554.4
adj imperious 417.16
sovereign 417.17
imperialism
sovereignty 417.8
foreign policy 609.5
democratism 612.8
imperialist 611.13
imperious lordly
141.11
imperial 417.16
commanding 420.13
compulsory 424.10
obligatory 641.15
urgent 996.22
imperiously arrogantly
141.15
masterfully 417.19

compulsively 424.13
impersonal reticent
344.10
formal 580.7
impartial 649.10
extrinsic 767.3
indistinguishable
944.6
unprejudiced 978.12
impersonation
imitation 336.1
personation 349.4
acting 704.8
impersonator imitator
336.4
impostor 357.6
masquerader 357.7
entertainer 707.1
impertinence
impudence 142.2
meddling 214.2
defiance 454.1
unrelatedness 775.1
impertinent impudent
142.10
meddlesome 214.9
defiant 454.7
irrelevant 775.7
imperturbable
inexcitable 106.10
stable 854.12
impervious resistant
15.20
callous 94.12
impenetrable 293.13
uninfluenceable 894.4
inaccessible 966.9
impetuous energetic
17.13
passionate 105.29
impatient 135.6
impulsive 365.9
precipitate 401.10
reckless 493.8
transient 827.7
sudden 829.5
inconstant 853.7
impetus animation 17.4
acceleration 174.4
impulse 901.1
impinge intrude 214.5
contact 223.10
collide 901.13
impish mischievous
322.6
puckish 680.18
implacable unyielding
361.9
revengeful 507.7
implacably 361.15
implant graft 191.6
transplant 191.8
inculcate 568.12
fix 854.9
plant 1067.18
implantation insertion
191.1
inculcation 568.2

fixity 854.2
implanted confirmed
373.19
intrinsic 766.7
established 854.13
implausible
unbelievable 954.10
improbable 968.3
implement
noun instrument 384.4
agent 576.3
tool 1039.1
verb carry out 328.7
bring about 407.5
execute 437.9
implementation
noun performance
328.2
adj accomplishment
407.1
implemented 407.10
implicate imply 519.4
incriminate 599.10
entail 771.4
complicate 798.3
involve 897.2
implicated
participating 476.8
implied 519.7
accused 599.15
guilty 656.3
related 774.9
complex 798.4
involved 897.4
implicated in 897.5
implication meaning
518.1
connotation 519.2
hint 551.4
accusation 599.1
incrimination 599.2
guilt 656.1
entailment 771.2
involvement 897.1
implicit tacit 51.11,
519.8
intrinsic 766.7
evidential 956.16
unqualified 959.2
implicitly 519.13
implied meant 518.11
implicated 519.7
tacit 519.8
imploring
noun entreaty 440.2
adj entreating 440.17
worshipful 696.15
imply promise 133.13
mean 518.8
implicate 519.4
hint 551.10
accuse 599.7
entail 771.4
evidence 956.8
impolite unrefined
497.12
discourteous 505.4
import

noun introduction
187.7
entrance 189.1
meaning 518.1
implication 519.2
importance 996.1
verb transfer 176.10
bring in 187.14
mean 518.8
imply 519.4
matter 996.12
phrase transference
176.1

importance prestige
417.4
distinction 662.5
influence 893.1
significance 996.1

important authoritative
417.15
prominent 662.17
influential 893.13
major 996.17

importantly 996.25

important message
352.6

important person
chief 575.3
celebrity 662.9
personage 996.8

important thing 996.6

importation
noun introduction
187.7
entrance 189.1
phrase transference
176.1

importer 730.2

importing introduction
187.7
entrance 189.1

impose intrude 214.5
prescribe 420.9
demand 421.5
oblige 424.5
compose 548.16
charge 630.12
minister 701.15

imposed mandatory
420.12
inflicted 643.8

impose on 775.5

imposing dignified
136.12
corpulent 257.18
grandiose 501.21
weighty 996.20

imposition intrusion
214.1
fraud 356.8
demand 421.1
composition 548.2
tax 630.9
presumption 640.2
infliction 643.1
injustice 650.4
impediment 1011.6

impossibility
hopelessness 125.1
unusualness 869.2
impossibleness 966.1
no chance 971.10

impossible
noun impossibility
966.1
adj unacceptable
108.10
out of the question
125.14
fantastic 869.12
not possible 966.7
improbable 971.18
phrase I refuse 442.7

impossibly hopelessly
125.17
inconceivably 966.10

imposter 336.4

impotence sexuality
75.2
sexlessness 75.9
futility 391.2
laxness 426.1
unproductiveness
890.1

impotent
noun weakling 19.6
adj weak 16.12
powerless 19.13
unsexual 75.28
useless 391.9
lax 426.4
unproductive 890.4
uninfluential 894.3

impounded 429.19

impoverished used up
388.5
indigent 619.8
meagre 991.10
ill-provided 991.12

impoverishment
consumption 388.1
waste 473.2
indigence 619.2
want 991.4

impracticable
impractical 966.8
inexpedient 995.5

impractical theoretical
950.13
impracticable 966.8
visionary 985.24
inexpedient 995.5
unwieldy 1012.19

imprecise lax 426.4
ungrammatic 531.4
uncertain 970.16
vague 970.19
inaccurate 974.17
imperfect 1002.4

impregnable
impenetrable 15.19
indestructible 854.18

impregnated 78.17

impresario director
574.1

theatre man 704.23

impress
noun indentation 284.6
print 517.7, 548.3,
713.5, 784.5
characteristic 864.4
impact 886.2
verb affect 93.15
indent 284.14
attract 377.6
avail oneself of 387.14
attach 480.20
abduct 482.20
mark 517.19
print 548.14
inculcate 568.12
enlist 615.17
be somebody 662.10
fix 854.9
make an impression
930.19

impressed affected
93.23
engraved 713.11
established 854.13

impressed with 952.21

impression aspect 33.3
feeling 93.1
form 262.1
concavity 284.1
indentation 284.6
imitation 336.1
description 349.2
print 517.7, 548.3,
713.5, 784.5
edition 554.5
inculcation 568.2
characteristic 864.4
impact 886.2
idea 931.1
hunch 933.3
suggestion 950.5
opinion 952.6

impressionable
sensible 24.11
sensitive 93.20
teachable 570.18
influenceable 893.15
foolable 922.12
pliant 1045.9

impressionist 707.1

impressionistic 950.13

impressive sensible
24.11
exciting 105.30
grandiose 501.21
vigorous 544.11
convincing 952.26

impressively intensely
247.20
grandiosely 501.28
eloquently 544.15

impress upon 93.16

imprint
noun indentation 284.6
print 517.7, 548.3,
713.5
label 517.13
makeup 554.12

impact 886.2
verb indent 284.14
mark 517.19
print 548.14
fix 854.9

imprinted engraved
713.11
established 854.13

imprisoned enclosed
212.10
jailed 429.21

imprisonment
enclosure 212.1
jailing 429.3
penal servitude 604.2

improbable unexpected
131.10
farfetched 775.8
predictable 961.13
unlikely 968.3
impossible 971.18

improbably 131.14

impromptu
noun improvisation
365.5
extempore 708.27
adj extemporaneous
365.12
unprepared 406.8
adv extemporaneously
365.15

improper misbehaving
322.5
vulgar 497.10
ungrammatic 531.4
inelegant 534.2
wrong 638.3
inappropriate 640.10,
788.7
wicked 654.16
indecent 666.5
untimely 843.6
inexpedient 995.5
bad 999.7

improperly
distressingly 247.21
vulgarly 497.16
wrongly 638.4

impropriety
misbehaviour 322.1
vulgarity 497.1
barbarism 526.6
inelegance 534.1
injustice 650.1
misdeed 655.2
indecency 666.1
unfitness 788.3
untimeliness 843.1

improve take advantage
of 387.15
grow better 392.7
better 392.9
recuperate 396.19
train 568.13
be changed 851.6
change 851.7
perfect 1001.5

improved bettered
392.13
changed 851.10

improvement
progression 162.1
betterment 392.1
restoration 396.1
training 568.3
change 851.1
new start 857.2

improve on 249.6

improving 392.15

improvisation
extemporization 365.5
unpreparedness 406.1
impromptu 708.27
production 891.1
expedient 994.2

improvise extemporize
365.8
produce 891.8
originate 891.12

improvised
extemporaneous
365.12
unprepared 406.8
makeshift 994.7

improvising 365.5

impulse manpower
18.4
natural impulse 365.1
urge 375.6
prematurity 844.2
impulsion 901.1
instinct 933.2
involuntariness 962.5

impulsive fickle 364.6
impetuous 365.9
motivating 375.25
precipitate 401.10
nonuniform 781.3
transient 827.7
sudden 829.5
premature 844.8
inconstant 853.7
impelling 901.23
instinctive 933.6
involuntary 962.14

impulsively
impetuously 365.13
precipitately 401.15
nonuniformly 781.4
suddenly 829.9
prematurely 844.13
changeably 853.8

impunity 601.2

impure unclean 80.20
inelegant 534.2
unvirtuous 654.12
unchaste 665.23
obscene 666.9
imperfect 1002.4

in
noun entree 187.3
entrance 189.5
adj entering 189.12
not out 747.5
modern 840.13
in danger 1005.13

in safety 1006.6
burning 1018.27
adv inward 189.13
inside 207.10
prep at 159.27
into 189.14, 207.13

in a bad way ill 85.55
worn-out 393.36
in danger 1005.13

in a big way 257.25

inability incapability
19.2
unskilfulness 414.1

in a blaze burning
1018.27
illuminated 1024.39

in a box 1012.22

in abundance 990.9

inaccessible out-of-
the-way 261.9
reticent 344.10
aloof 583.6
unaccessible 966.9

in accord accordant
455.3
harmonious 708.49
agreeing 787.9
conformist 866.6

in accordance 787.9

in accordance with
866.9

inaccuracy
unmeticulousness
340.4
misrepresentation
350.1
misjudgment 947.1
vagueness 970.4
inaccurateness 974.2
badness 999.1
imperfection 1002.1

inaccurate
unmeticulous 340.13
vague 970.19
incorrect 974.17
bad 999.7
imperfect 1002.4

in a circle 914.16

in a corner
adj cornered 1012.25
adv secretly 345.17

in action acting 328.10
operating 888.11

inaction motionlessness
173.2
passiveness 329.1
inactivity 331.1

inactive inert 173.14
passive 329.6
unactive 331.17
leisurely 402.6

inactivity rest 20.1
motionlessness 173.2
inaction 329.1, 331.1
leisureliness 402.2

in a daze
adj dazed 984.14

adv uncertainly 970.28

in addition 253.11

in addition to 253.12

inadequacy inability
19.2
unsatisfactoriness
108.2
mediocrity 250.3
unskilfulness 414.1
inequality 790.1
incompleteness 794.1
shortcoming 910.1
insufficiency 991.1
imperfection 1002.1
fault 1002.2

inadequate ineffective
19.15
unsatisfactory 108.9
mediocre 250.7
incompetent 414.19
unequal 790.4
incomplete 794.4
short of 910.5
insufficient 991.9
imperfect 1002.4

inadequately
unsatisfactorily 108.12
poorly 250.9
unskilfully 414.23
incompletely 794.6
insufficiently 991.14
imperfectly 1002.5

in a dilemma 970.25,
1012.23

in admiration 122.18

inadmissible
unacceptable 108.10
exclusive 772.9
irrelevant 775.7
inappropriate 788.7

in advance before
165.4, 216.12
on loan 620.7
early 844.11

in advance of 833.7

inadvertent negligent
340.10
unthinking 365.10
unpremeditated
365.11
inattentive 983.6

inadvertently
negligently 340.17
on impulse 365.14

in a flash in no time
174.19
quickly 829.7

in a flurry 105.21

in a good mood 324.5

in agreement
adj unanimous 332.15
cooperative 450.5
agreeing 787.9
adv jointly 799.18

in agreement with
together with 787.12
conformable to 866.9

in a hole 1012.22

in a hurry in haste
401.14
at once 829.8

in aid of 449.26

in alarm 127.33

inalienable intrinsic
766.7
inseparable 799.15

in a line
adj straight 277.6
adv consecutively
811.11

in all 791.13

in all directions
161.25

in a manner to a
degree 248.10
so to speak 783.19

in amazement 122.18

in a mess
adj confused 809.16
in deep shit 1012.22
adv in disorder 809.17

in a moment 829.7

in ancient times
836.16

in and out windingly
281.11
changeably 853.8
to and fro 915.21

inane ineffective 19.15
insipid 65.2
dull 117.6
vacant 222.14
vain 391.11
meaningless 520.6
nonexistent 761.8
thin 763.6
empty-headed 921.19
foolish 922.8
ignorant 929.12
thoughtless 932.4
trivial 997.19

in anger 152.33

in an ideal world
950.16

inanimate
noun gender 530.10
adj dead 307.30
languid 331.20
inanimated 1053.5

in an instant
transiently 827.10
quickly 829.7

in another way 779.10

in answer 938.7

in anticipation
adv early 844.11
adj, adv in readiness
405.21

in anticipation of
833.7

in a nutshell small
258.16
shortly 268.12

in brief 537.8, 557.7

in any case
adv anyhow 384.10
conj in the event that
830.13
adv, conj
notwithstanding 338.8

in any event
adv anyhow 384.10
adv, conj
notwithstanding 338.8

in any way anyhow
384.10
by any possibility
965.10

in a panic 127.27

in a position to 896.6

inappropriate vulgar
497.10
wrong 638.3
improper 640.10
indecent 666.5
irrelevant 775.7
inapt 788.7
untimely 843.6
inexpedient 995.5

inappropriately 995.8

in arms infant 301.12
prepared 405.16
armed 460.14

in a row 811.11

in arrears 794.4

inarticulate mute
51.12
shy 139.12
unintelligible 522.13
indistinct 525.12

in a rush 844.13

in a second 829.7

in a series 811.11

in a small way 258.16

inasmuch as 887.10

in a spot 1012.22

in association
conjointly 617.20
together 768.11

in association with
768.12

in astonishment
122.18

inaudible 51.10

inaugural
noun speech 543.2
ceremony 580.4
adj preceding 813.4,
815.4

inaugural address
speech 543.2
inauguration 817.5

inaugurate install
191.4, 615.12
institute 817.11
innovate 840.5
cause 885.10
establish 891.10

inauguration
establishment 159.7,
891.4
admission 187.2
ceremony 580.4
installation 615.3

inauspicious ominous
133.17
untimely 843.6
bad 999.7
unfortunate 1010.14

in authority 417.21

in a way to a degree
245.7, 248.10
so to speak 783.19

in awe
adj wondering 122.9
reverent 155.9
adv in wonder 122.18
in fear 127.33

in awe of 122.9

in a while 844.16

in a whisper in an
undertone 52.22
secretly 345.17

in a word 537.8

in balance 670.17

in bed 20.11

in being 760.13

in-between 818.4

in black and white
547.22

in bloom 310.35

inborn 766.8

inbred bred 78.17
innate 766.8

in brief in short 537.8
in summary 557.7

in broad daylight
348.15

in bulk 791.13

Inca 575.9

incalculable
noun unknown 929.7
adj infinite 822.3
innumerable 883.10
unknown 929.17
uncertain 970.16

in camera 345.19

in-camera 293.9

incandescent burning
1018.27
luminous 1024.30

incapable
noun cripple 85.44
incompetent 414.7
adj unable 19.14
unfitted 406.9
incompetent 414.19

incapacitated
weakened 16.18
disabled 19.16
crippled 393.30

incapacity infirmity
16.3

inability 19.2
unskilfulness 414.1
unproductiveness 890.1
unintelligence 921.1
in captivity jailed 429.21
subjugated 432.14
incarcerated enclosed 212.10
jailed 429.21
incarceration enclosure 212.1
imprisonment 429.3
penal servitude 604.2
incarnate
verb manifest 348.5
image 349.11
embody 762.5
compose 795.3
materialize 1050.9
adj divine 677.16
embodied 1050.11
Incarnation 677.11
incarnation appearance 33.1
manifestation 348.1
impersonation 349.4
embodiment 762.4
essence 766.2
composition 795.1
materialization 1050.8
in case 830.13
incendiary
noun instigator 375.11
arsonist 1019.8
adj incitive 375.28
inflammatory 1019.27
incense
noun fragrance 70.1
joss stick 70.4
suavity 504.5
flattery 511.1
oblation 696.7
verb perfume 70.8
excite 105.12
provoke 152.24
incite 375.17
incensed 152.28
incentive
noun inducement 375.7
impulse 901.1
adj incitive 375.28
inception origin 817.4
source 885.5
establishment 891.4
incessant continuous 811.8
perpetual 828.7
constant 846.5
recurrent 848.13
continuing 855.7
incessantly perpetually 828.10
constantly 846.7
incest perversion 75.11
adultery 665.7

incestuous 665.27
inch
noun short distance 223.2
verb creep 177.26
in chains 432.14
in character to be expected 130.14
characteristic 864.13
in charge
adj supervising 573.13
governing 612.18
adv in authority 417.21
in check 428.13
in chief
adj governing 612.18
adv chiefly 249.17
incidence event 830.1
frequency 846.1
incident plot 722.4
circumstance 765.1
event 830.2
incidental
noun ornament 709.18
particular 765.3
nonessential 767.2
adj circumstantial 765.7
unessential 767.4
irrelevant 775.7
happening 830.9
occasional 842.11, 847.3
chance 971.15
incidentally by the way 842.13
by chance 971.19
incident to liable to 896.6
contingent 958.9
incineration cremation 309.2
discard 390.3
burning 1019.5
incinerator 1019.13
incipient 817.15
in circles 914.16
in circulation
published 352.17
reported 552.15
incision trauma 85.37
crack 224.2
notch 289.1
furrow 290.1
engraving 713.2
incisive energetic 17.13
acrimonious 17.14
caustic 144.23
vigorous 544.11
sagacious 919.16
incite excite 105.12, 1019.18
instigate 375.17
admonish 422.6
impel 901.11

incitement excitation 105.11
incitation 375.4
incentive 375.7
impulse 901.1
inciting 375.28
inclement harsh 144.24
pitiless 146.3
cold 1022.14
inclination penchant 100.3
obeisance 155.2
direction 161.1
descent 194.1
leaning 204.2
incline 204.4
will 323.1
preference 371.5
aptitude 413.5
partiality 650.3
tendency 895.1
disposition 977.3
prejudice 979.3
incline
noun stairs 193.3
inclination 204.4
slope 237.2
verb bear 161.7
lean 204.10
gravitate 297.15
be willing 324.3
induce 375.22
influence 893.7
tend 895.3
inclined inclining 204.15
willing 324.5
moved 375.30
disposed 977.8
inclined to 895.6
include internalize 207.5
enclose 212.5
comprise 771.3
put together 799.5
combine 804.3
included comprised 771.5
involved 897.4
including
adj inclusive 771.6
composed of 795.4
prep with 253.12
inclusion surrounding 209.5
enclosure 212.1
affiliation 450.2
comprisal 771.1
combination 804.1
involvement 897.1
inclusive including 771.6
whole 791.9
joint 799.12
inclusive of
adj composed of 795.4
prep with 253.12
incognito

noun privacy 345.2
cover 356.11
masquerader 357.7
anonymity 528.1
adj private 345.13
disguised 346.13
anonymous 528.3
incoherence dislocation 160.1
unintelligibility 522.1
inconsistency 788.2
separation 801.1
noncohesion 803.1
disintegration 805.1
disorder 809.1
discontinuity 812.1
delirium 925.8
vagueness 970.4
incoherent
unintelligible 522.13
inconsistent 788.8
separate 801.20
uncoherent 803.4
unordered 809.12
discontinuous 812.4
delirious 925.31
vague 970.19
in cold blood
unfeelingly 94.14
heartlessly 144.34
intentionally 380.10
in collaboration 450.7
in colour 35.16
in combat 458.23
income entrance 189.1
gain 472.3
pay 624.4
receipts 627.1
income support 611.8
in comfort 121.15
incoming
noun entrance 189.1
adj arriving 186.9
entering 189.12
in command 417.21
in common
adj communal 476.9
adv jointly 799.18
in company 768.11
in company with 768.12
incomparable peerless 249.15
unrelated 775.6
uncomparable 786.6
incommensurable 942.9
in comparison with 942.11
incompatibility
disaccord 456.1
unsociability 583.1
enmity 589.1
difference 779.1
inconsistency 788.2
incompatible
unsociable 583.5

unfriendly 589.9
different 779.7
disagreeing 788.6
inconsistent 788.8
in compensation in return 338.7
in restitution 481.8
as compensation 624.24
incompetence 991.1
incompetent
noun impotent 19.6
incapable 414.7
adj unable 19.14
inadequate 250.7
unfitted 406.9
incapable 414.19
insufficient 991.9
in competition 457.23
incomplete partial 792.7
uncompleted 794.4
insufficient 991.9
imperfect 1002.4
incomprehensible
wonderful 122.10
unintelligible 522.13
infinite 822.3
fantastic 869.12
incomprehension
unperceptiveness 921.2
incognizance 929.3
inconceivable
wonderful 122.10
fantastic 869.12
unbelievable 954.10
impossible 966.7
in concert
adj cooperative 450.5
in accord 455.3
harmonious 708.49
adv unanimously 332.17
in step 787.11
concurrently 898.5
in concert with
cooperatively 450.6
simultaneously 835.7
in conclusion 819.12
inconclusive illogical 935.11
unsound 935.12
unproved 957.8
in confidence 345.20
in conflict irresolute 362.9
disagreeing 788.6
in conflict with
opposed to 451.10
in disagreement with 788.10
in confusion 809.17
incongruity
humorousness 488.1
difference 779.1
inconsistency 788.2
nonconformity 867.1

illogicalness 935.2

incongruous off-colour 35.20
humorous 488.4
different 779.7
inconsistent 788.8
illogical 935.11
inexpedient 995.5

incongruously
humorously 488.7
inexpediently 995.8

in conjunction in juxtaposition 223.21
together 768.11

in conjunction with 253.12, 768.12

in consequence 886.7

inconsequential
insignificant 248.6, 997.17
illogical 935.11

inconsiderable 248.6, 997.17

inconsiderate
unthoughtful 144.18
careless 340.11
unthinking 365.10
ill-bred 505.6
unwise 922.10

inconsistency
contrariety 778.1
difference 779.1
nonuniformity 781.1
incongruity 788.2
noncohesion 803.1
inconstancy 853.2
nonconformity 867.1
illogicalness 935.2

inconsistent contrary 778.6
different 779.7
nonuniform 781.3
incongruous 788.8
incoherent 803.4
inconstant 853.7
illogical 935.11

inconsolable sorrowful 112.26
disconsolate 112.28

inconspicuous 32.6

in consultation 423.6

in contact 223.17

in contact with 223.25

incontinence greed 100.8
unrestraint 430.3
prodigality 486.1
uncontinence 665.2
intemperance 669.1
excess 992.1

incontinent
unrestrained 430.24
prodigal 486.8
uncontinent 665.24
intemperate 669.7
excessive 992.16

in contrast with 778.10

in control
adj restrained 670.11
adv in authority 417.21

incontrovertible
evidential 956.16
obvious 969.15

inconvenience
noun imposition 643.1
untimeliness 843.1
discommodity 995.3
impediment 1011.6
trouble 1012.3
unwieldiness 1012.9
verb put to inconvenience 995.4
trouble 1012.13

inconvenient untimely 843.6
incommodious 995.7
unwieldy 1012.19

incorporate
verb include 771.3
compose 795.3
combine 804.3
materialize 1050.9
adj immaterial 1051.7

incorporated associated 617.16
joined 799.13
combined 804.5
embodied 1050.11

incorporating inclusive 771.6
combining 804.7

incorporation
affiliation 450.2
inclusion 771.1
composition 795.1
combination 804.1
materialization 1050.8

incorrect ungrammatic 531.4
inelegant 534.2
wrong 638.3
inaccurate 974.17

incorrectly wrongly 638.4
inaccurately 974.21

incorrigible past hope 125.15
ungovernable 361.12
confirmed 373.19
irreclaimable 654.18

in council 423.6

in court
adv all things considered 945.17
phrase in litigation 598.23

increase
noun aggravation 119.1
ascent 193.1
gain 251.1
gains 251.3

addition 253.1
adjunct 254.1
expansion 259.1
improvement 392.1
multiplication 882.4
elevation 911.1
verb grow 14.2, 251.6, 259.7
aggravate 119.2
quantify 244.4
graduate 245.4
enlarge 251.4, 259.4, 259.5
add to 253.5
multiply 882.6

increased aggravated 119.4
heightened 251.7
expanded 259.10
multiple 882.8

increasing 251.8

increasingly 251.9

incredible wonderful 122.10
remarkable 247.10
fantastic 869.12
absurd 922.11
unbelievable 954.10
improbable 968.3

incredibly wonderfully 122.14
intensely 247.20
unusually 869.17
unbelievably 954.14

incredulity agnosticism 695.6
unbelief 954.1
incredulousness 955.1

incredulous agnostic 695.20
unbelieving 954.8
uncredulous 955.4

incremental 251.8

incriminating 599.14

incubation 78.5

incubator 885.8

incumbent
noun inhabitant 227.2
tenant 470.4
officeholder 610.11
benefice-holder 699.7
adj overhanging 202.11
overlying 295.36

incur 896.4

incurable
noun sick person 85.42
adj past hope 125.15

incursion influx 189.2
intrusion 214.1
raid 459.4
overstepping 909.3

in custody 429.22

in danger ill 85.55
in jeopardy 1005.13

in danger of 896.6

in darkness

adj blind 30.9
benighted 929.16
adv secretly 345.17
in the dark 1026.19

in debt indebted 623.8
liable 896.5

indebted in debt 623.8
insolvent 729.18
liable 896.5

indebtedness debt 623.1
liability 896.1

indebted to grateful 150.5
obliged 641.16

indecency sexual desire 75.5
vulgarity 497.1
unchastity 665.1
indelicacy 666.1

indecent vulgar 497.10
unchaste 665.23
indelicate 666.5

indecent assault 480.3

indecently 497.16

indecent proposal 439.2

indecipherable 522.19

indecision irresolution 362.1
uncertainty 970.1

indecisive wishy-washy 16.17
formless 263.4
irresolute 362.9
inconstant 853.7
unproved 957.8
uncertain 970.16
vague 970.19

indeed
adv positively 247.19
chiefly 249.17
certainly 969.23
truly 972.18
exclam yes 332.18

in deep 897.5

in deep trouble 1012.21

in deep water 1012.21

indefatigable
industrious 330.22
persevering 360.8
continuing 855.7

in default 794.4

in defence 460.16

indefensible
unacceptable 108.10
unjustifiable 650.12

in deference to 155.14

in defiance of
adv in the teeth of 454.8
prep in disagreement with 788.10

indefinable
indescribable 122.13

inexplicable 522.18
vague 970.19

indefinite
inconspicuous 32.6
formless 263.4
general 863.11
indistinguishable 944.6
vague 970.19

indefinitely extremely 247.22
vaguely 970.29

indelible deep-dyed 35.17
deep-felt 93.24
indestructible 854.18
unforgettable 988.26

in demand desired 100.29
saleable 734.14

indemnity pardon 148.2
compensation 338.1
security 438.1
exemption 601.2
recompense 624.3
atonement 658.1

independence pride 136.1
nationhood 232.6
voluntariness 324.2
self-control 359.5
self-determination 430.5
self-help 449.6
battle flag 458.12
neutrality 467.1
nonpartisanism 609.26
central government 612.4
wealth 618.1
unrelatedness 775.1

independent
noun free agent 430.12
neutral 467.4
nonpartisan 609.28
moderate 611.14
adj proud 136.8
voluntary 324.7
strong-willed 359.15
self-dependent 430.22
self-helpful 449.23
neutral 467.7
nonpartisan 609.45
moderate 611.26
wealthy 618.14
unrelated 775.6
separate 801.20

independently proudly 136.13
voluntarily 324.10
alone 430.33

independent school 567.4

Independent Television
photoemission 1034.4
television studio 1034.6

Independent Television Commission 1034.2

in-depth 269.6

indescribable ineffable 122.13
extraordinary 869.14

in despair 125.12

indestructible
perpetual 828.7
undestroyable 854.18

in detail meticulously 339.16
at length 538.16
fully 765.13
piece by piece 792.9
particularly 864.15

in detention 572.13

indeterminate formless 263.4
obscure 522.15
unessential 767.4
relative 774.7
general 863.11
vague 970.19
chance 971.15

index
noun finger 73.5
map 159.5
contents 196.1
prohibition 444.1
sign 517.1
pointer 517.4
printed matter 548.10
hint 551.4
reference book 554.9
makeup 554.12
bibliography 558.4
directory 574.10
outline 800.4
table 807.4
characteristic 864.4
listing 870.7
verb record 549.15
classify 808.6
list 870.8

indexed recorded 549.17
classified 808.8
listed 870.9

index finger 73.5

indexing registration 549.14
classification 808.1
index 870.7

India 235.1

Indian 312.3

Indian summer St Martin's summer 313.5
hot weather 1018.7

indicate augur 133.12
manifest 348.5
signify 517.17
mean 518.8
hint 551.10
specify 864.11
evidence 956.8

indicated augured 133.15
implied 519.7
requisite 962.13

indicating 517.23

indication omen 133.3
manifestation 348.1
signification 517.3
hint 551.4
evidence 956.1

indicative
noun mood 530.11
adj premonitory 133.16
manifesting 348.9
indicatory 517.23
meaningful 518.10
suggestive 519.6
evidential 956.16

indicator sign 517.1
signal 517.15

indicted 599.15

indictment censure 510.3
arraignment 598.3
accusation 599.1
attribution 887.1

indifference apathy 94.4
indifferentness 102.1, 467.2
nonchalance 106.5
inertness 173.4
languor 331.6
carelessness 340.2
laxness 426.1
nonobservance 435.1
nonreligiousness 695.1
unprejudicedness 978.5
incuriosity 981.1
inattention 983.1
unimportance 997.1
mediocrity 1004.1

indifferent insipid 65.2
apathetic 94.13
halfhearted 102.6
nonchalant 106.15
reluctant 325.6
careless 340.11
lax 426.4
neutral 467.7
nonreligious 695.15
unprejudiced 978.12
incurious 981.3
inattentive 983.6
mediocre 1004.7

indifferently
apathetically 94.15
with indifference 102.9
equally 789.11
mediocrely 1004.11

in difficulties 623.8

indigenous native 226.5
innate 766.8

indigestible 82.6

indigestion 85.9

indignant angry 152.28
disapproving 510.21

indignantly 152.33

indignation indignant
displeasure 152.4
disapproval 510.1

indignity affront 156.2
disparagement 512.1

indigo 45.3

indirect deviative 164.7
oblique 204.13
deceitful 356.22
circumlocutory 538.14
dishonest 645.16
eventual 830.11
circuitous 913.7

indirectly obliquely 204.21
deceitfully 356.24
by proxy 576.17
circuitously 913.9

in disarray 809.17

indiscipline
disobedience 327.1
lawlessness 418.1
unrestraint 430.3
intemperance 669.1

indiscreet rash 493.7
indecent 666.5
unwise 922.10
undiscriminating 944.5

indiscretion divulgence 351.2
rashness 493.1
misdeed 655.2
indecency 666.1
unwiseness 922.2
folly 922.4
indiscrimination 944.1
blunder 974.5

indiscriminate mixed 796.14
unordered 809.12
extensive 863.13
undiscriminating 944.5
purposeless 971.16

indiscriminately
haphazardly 809.18
purposelessly 971.20

in disgrace 661.13

in disguise
adj disguised 346.13
adv deceptively 356.23

indispensable
noun requirement 962.2
adj requisite 962.13
vital 996.23

indisputable manifest 348.8
real 760.15
evidential 956.16
unqualified 959.2
obvious 969.15

indisputably 969.25

in dispute 970.17

indistinct
inconspicuous 32.6
faint 52.16
obscure 522.15
inarticulate 525.12
indistinguishable 944.6
vague 970.19

indistinguishable
inconspicuous 32.6
identical 777.7
undistinguishable 944.6

in distress 26.9

individual
noun organism 305.2
person 312.5
something 762.3
specific 864.3
single 871.4
adj personal 312.15
indicative 517.23
particular 864.12
one 871.7

individual freedom 430.5

individualism egotism 140.3
independence 430.5
capitalism 611.9
selfishness 651.1
particularity 864.1
characteristic 864.4
disposition 977.3

individualist egotist 140.5
free agent 430.12
capitalist 611.20
self-seeker 651.3
misfit 788.4

individualistic
independent 430.22
capitalist 611.32
selfish 651.5
nonconformist 788.9

individuality person 312.5
particularity 864.1
oneness 871.1
individual 871.4

individually personally 864.16
singly 871.13

indivisible simple 797.6
inseparable 799.15
indestructible 854.18
one 871.7
nondivisible 1043.13

indoctrination
inculcation 568.2
propaganda 569.2
reindoctrination 857.5

indolence inertness 173.4
slowness 175.1
inaction 329.1
laziness 331.5

indolent
noun lazybones 331.7
adj slow 175.10
lazy 331.19

indomitable
impregnable 15.19
persevering 360.8
ungovernable 361.12

indoor
adj interior 207.6
adv indoors 207.12

indoors 207.12

in doubt doubting 954.9
doubtful 970.17

induce elicit 192.14
prompt 375.22
admonish 422.6
lead 885.11
influence 893.7
conclude 945.10

inducement enlistment 375.3
incentive 375.7
allurement 377.1
gratuity 478.5

induction admission 187.2
installation 615.3
enlistment 615.7
holy orders 698.10
inauguration 817.5
basics 817.6
priori reasoning 934.3
conclusion 945.4
electrostatic induction 1031.14

in due course 844.16

indulge humour 427.6
suffer 443.10
indulge oneself 669.4

indulged forgiven 148.7
pampered 427.9

indulge in enjoy 95.12
indulge 669.4

indulgence patience 134.1
considerateness 143.3
forgiveness 148.1
humouring 427.3
sufferance 443.2
privilege 642.2
intemperance 669.1
tolerance 978.4

indulgent patient 134.9
considerate 143.16
compliant 427.8
nonrestrictive 430.25
permissive 443.14
intemperate 669.7
tolerant 978.11

indulgently patiently 134.11
permissively 443.18

industrial occupational 724.16
commercial 731.21

productional 891.14

industrial action
727.5

industrialism 731.12

industrialist
businessman 730.1
producer 891.7

industrialization
commercialization
731.13
industrial production
891.3

industrial production
891.3

industrial relations
727.1

industrial waste refuse
391.4
extract 892.3

industrious assiduous
330.22
painstaking 339.11
persevering 360.8

industry
industriousness 330.6
painstakingness 339.2
perseverance 360.1
company 617.9
work 725.4
commerce 731.1
industrial production
891.3

in earnest
adj zealous 101.9
adv resolutely 359.17

inedible 64.8

ineffable
noun sacred 685.2
adj indescribable
122.13
sacred 685.7
extraordinary 869.14

in effect
adj in use 387.25
adv really 760.16

ineffective unable
19.14
ineffectual 19.15
useless 391.9
unsuccessful 410.18
incompetent 414.19
uninfluential 894.3

ineffectual ineffective
19.15
useless 391.9
unsuccessful 410.18
incompetent 414.19
unproductive 890.4
uninfluential 894.3

inefficiency inability
19.2
unskilfulness 414.1

inefficient unable
19.14
unskilful 414.15

in either case 830.13

inept unable 19.14

unskilful 414.15
inappropriate 788.7
unintelligent 921.13
foolish 922.8
inexpedient 995.5

ineptitude inability
19.2
unintelligence 921.1
foolishness 922.1

inequality roughness
288.1
class 607.1
injustice 650.1
partiality 650.3
difference 779.1
nonuniformity 781.1
disagreement 788.1
disparity 790.1

in error false 354.25
mistaken 974.18

inert inactive 173.14
passive 329.6
languid 331.20
unchangeable 854.17
inanimate 1053.5

inertia inertness 173.4
slowness 175.1
inaction 329.1
inactivity 331.1
indolence 331.5
immobility 854.3

inescapable real
760.15
inevitable 962.15

inescapably 962.19

in essence 766.11

in every direction
161.25

in every respect
throughout 793.17
exactly 972.21

in evidence 31.6

inevitability
compulsion 424.1
inevitableness 962.7
fate 963.2
certainty 969.1

inevitable obligatory
424.11
unavoidable 962.15
destined 963.9
certain 969.13

inevitably consequently
886.7
unavoidably 962.19

in excess 992.17

in excess of 992.26

in exchange in
retaliation 506.9
interchangeably 862.6

in exchange for
624.24

inexcusable 650.12

in exercise 888.11

inexhaustible infinite
822.3
innumerable 883.10

plentiful 990.7

in existence 760.13

inexorable pitiless
146.3
unyielding 361.9
firm 425.7
inevitable 962.15

inexorably pitilessly
146.4
unyieldingly 361.15
firmly 425.9
inevitably 962.19

inexpensive 633.7

inexperience
immaturity 301.3
unaccustomedness
374.1
unexperience 414.2
ignorance 929.1

inexperienced
immature 301.10
unaccustomed 374.4
unexperienced 414.17
foolable 922.12
ignorant 929.12

inexplicable
unexplainable 522.18
purposeless 971.16

inexplicably
unexplainably 522.24
purposelessly 971.20

in fact really 760.16
truly 972.18

infallible inerrable
969.19
exact 972.17
perfect 1001.6

infamous wrong 638.3
knavish 645.17
wicked 654.16
disreputable 661.10
terrible 999.9

infamy abomination
638.2
iniquity 654.3
infamousness 661.4

infancy inability 19.2
immaturity 301.3
babyhood 301.5
origin 817.4

infant
noun youngster 302.1
baby 302.9
simple soul 416.3
schoolchild 572.3
innocent 657.4
beginner 817.2
adj infantile 301.12
incomplete 794.4
beginning 817.15

infantile infant 301.12
beginning 817.15
puerile 921.24

infant school 567.2

in fashion 578.11

infatuated overzealous
101.12

enamoured 104.28
foolish 922.8
obsessed 925.33
credulous 953.8

infatuated with 101.10

infatuation liking
100.2
overzealousness 101.3
infatuatedness 104.4
stultification 922.5
mania 925.12
credulity 953.1

in favour on good
terms 587.18
reputable 662.15

in favour of
adj approving 509.17
prep for 449.26,
509.21

in fear
adj fearful 127.23
adv in terror 127.33

infect defile 80.17
disease 85.50
inspire 375.20
corrupt 393.12
work evil 999.6
radioactivate 1036.9

infected unclean 80.20
diseased 85.59
radioactive 1036.10

infection defilement
80.4
contagion 85.4
infectious disease
85.13
inspiration 375.9
corruption 393.2
evil 999.3

infectious poisonous
82.7
contagious 85.61

infective poisonous
82.7
contagious 85.61

infer imply 519.4
reason 934.15
conclude 945.10
suppose 950.10

inference implication
519.2
priori reasoning 934.3
conclusion 945.4
supposition 950.3

inferior
noun underling 250.2
subordinate 432.5
retainer 577.1
adj unable 19.14
subordinate 250.6
lower 274.8
subject 432.13
short of 910.5
unimportant 997.16
insignificant 997.17
bad 999.7
poor 1004.9

inferiority inability
19.2
subordinacy 250.1
abnormality 869.1
shortcoming 910.1
unimportance 997.1
badness 999.1
inferiorness 1004.3

inferiority complex
complex 92.22
self-effacement 139.2

infernal cruel 144.26
diabolic 654.13
hellish 682.8
execrable 999.10

inferno hell 682.1
oven 1018.11

inferred implied 519.7
supposed 950.14

infertile unproductive
890.4
unimaginative 986.5

infertility
unproductiveness
890.1
unimaginativeness
986.1

infestation 909.2

infested 909.11

infidelity love affair
104.6
unfaithfulness 645.5
infidelism 688.3
unbelief 695.5, 954.1

infighting dissension
456.3
contention 457.1
boxing 457.9

infiltrate absorb 187.13
filter in 189.10
intrude 214.5
launch an attack
459.17
imbue 796.11
soak 1063.13

infiltration sorption
187.6
entrance 189.1
intrusion 214.1
attack 459.1
imbuement 796.2
soaking 1063.7

in fine 819.12

infinite spacious 158.10
omnipresent 221.13
large 247.7
huge 257.20
almighty 677.17
boundless 822.3
perpetual 828.7
innumerable 883.10

infinitely extensively
158.11
extremely 247.22
illimitably 822.4
perpetually 828.10
numerously 883.12

infinity omnipresence
221.2
  greatness 247.1
  distance 261.1
  length 267.1
  infiniteness 822.1
  perpetuity 828.1
  large number 1016.5
infirm
  noun sick person 85.42
  adj unsound 16.15
  unhealthy 85.53
  stricken in years
  303.18
  weak-willed 362.12
  unvirtuous 654.12
  fragile 763.7
  inconstant 853.7
  feebleminded 921.21
  unreliable 970.20
infirmary 91.21
inflame energize 17.10
  pain 26.7
  redden 41.4
  excite 105.12, 1019.18
  provoke 152.24
  incite 375.17
  ignite 1019.22
inflamed sore 26.11
  red 41.6
  feverish 85.57
  diseased 85.59
  excited 105.20
  fiery 671.22
  burning 1018.27
in flames 1018.27
inflammable
  noun fuel 1020.1
  adj excitable 105.28
  flammable 1019.28
inflammation soreness
26.4
  anaemia 85.9
  inflammatory disease
  85.10
  excitation 105.11
  incitement 375.4
inflammatory exciting
105.30
  incitive 375.28
  inflammative 1019.27
inflammatory disease
85.10
inflatable 259.9
inflate puff up 140.7
  increase 251.4
  enlarge 259.4
  exaggerate 355.3
  talk big 545.6
  overextend 992.13
inflated increased
251.7
  distended 259.13
  exaggerated 355.4
  pompous 501.22
  swollen 502.12
  bombastic 545.9
inflation increase 251.1
  distension 259.2

  exaggeration 355.1
  pompousness 501.7
  style 532.2
  grandiloquence 545.1
  price index 630.4
  high price 632.3
  business cycle 731.9
  overextension 992.7
inflationary expansive
259.9
  overpriced 632.12
inflection angle 278.2
  bend 279.3
  intonation 524.7
  morphology 526.3
inflexibility firmness
359.2, 425.2
  unyieldingness 361.2
  immobility 854.3
  inevitability 962.7
  stiffness 1044.3
inflexible firm 359.12,
425.7
  unyielding 361.9
  immovable 854.15
  uninfluenceable 894.4
  inevitable 962.15
  unflexible 1044.12
inflict do 328.6
  wreak 643.5
inflicted 643.8
in flight 368.16
inflow influx 189.2
  flow 238.4
  wind 318.1
in flower 310.35
influence
  noun power 18.1
  supremacy 249.3
  motivation 375.2
  machination 415.4
  prestige 417.4
  influentiality 893.1
  good influence 893.6
  verb induce 375.22,
  885.11
  cause 885.10
  determine 885.12
  operate on 888.6
  make oneself felt
  893.7
  prejudice 979.9
influenced partial
650.11
  discriminatory 979.12
influential
  noun influence 893.6
  adj authoritative
  417.15
  powerful 893.13
influx inflow 189.2
  intrusion 214.1
info information 551.1
  knowledge 927.1
in focus 31.7
in force powerful 18.12
  in use 387.25
  operating 888.11

inform
  verb pervade 221.7
  betray 351.6
  inspire 375.20
  tell 551.8
  report 552.11
  teach 568.10
  adj formless 263.4
informal 581.3
informality 581.1
informally 581.4
informant informer
551.5
  examinee 937.19
  witness 956.6
information
  communication 343.1
  info 551.1
  news 552.1
  teaching 568.1
  arraignment 598.3
  accusation 599.1
  facts 760.4
  knowledge 927.1
  data 1041.15
information centre
  informant 551.5
  library 558.1
information officer
551.5
information storage
988.1
informative informing
551.18
  educational 568.18
informed prepared
405.16
  informed of 551.17
  knowing 927.15
  enlightened 927.18
informed of informed
551.17
  cognizant of 927.16
informer traitor 357.10
  informant 551.5
  betrayer 551.6
  accuser 599.5
  witness 956.6
informing
  noun telling 343.2
  adj informative 551.18
infra 274.10
infrared 41.6
infrastructure
  understructure 266.3
  directorate 574.11
  support 900.1
  foundation 900.6
  frame 900.10
infrequent unfrequent
847.2
  sparse 884.5
infrequently
  discontinuously 812.5
  unfrequently 847.4
  sparsely 884.8
infringe intrude 214.5

  violate 435.4
  adopt 621.4
  usurp 640.8
  overstep 909.9
infringement intrusion
214.1
  disobedience 327.1
  impairment 393.1
  violation 435.2
  adoption 621.2
  usurpation 640.3
  lawbreaking 674.3
  overstepping 909.3
in front
  adj front 216.10
  adv before 165.4,
  216.12
in front of 215.7
in full at length 538.16
  fully 765.13
  completely 793.14
in full swing
  adj astir 330.19
  thriving 1009.13
  adv actively 330.25
in full view 31.6
infuriate
  verb excite 105.12
  enrage 152.25
  antagonize 589.7
  adj infuriated 152.32
  turbulent 671.18
infuriated 152.32
infuse insert 191.3
  inspire 375.20
  inculcate 568.12
  imbue 796.11
  liquefy 1062.5
  soak 1063.13
infusion insertion
191.1
  squeezing 192.7
  extract 192.8
  inspiration 375.9
  inculcation 568.2
  baptism 701.6
  imbuement 796.2
  tinge 796.7
  liquefaction 1062.1
  solution 1062.3
  soaking 1063.7
in future 838.10
in gear 776.9
in general 863.17
ingenious skilful
413.22
  cunning 415.12
  imaginative 985.18
ingeniously 413.31
ingenue simple soul
416.3
  role 704.10
  script 706.2
  actor 707.2
ingenuity skill 413.1
  invention 985.3

ingenuous immature
301.10
  artless 416.5
  candid 644.17
  ignorant 929.12
  gullible 953.9
ingestion digestion
2.15, 7.8
  eating 8.1, 187.4
  consumption 388.1
  absorption 570.2
ingle home 228.2
  fire 1018.13
  fireplace 1019.11
inglorious humble
137.10
  disreputable 661.10
  unrenowned 661.14
in good condition
806.7
in good form 806.7
in good health 83.8
in good shape 806.7
in good spirits 109.11
in good time
  opportunely 842.12
  in time 844.12
ingrained deep-dyed
35.17
  confirmed 373.19
  intrinsic 766.7
  established 854.13
ingratiating obsequious
138.14
  suave 504.18
ingredient particular
765.3
  part 792.1
  component 795.2
ingredients contents
196.1
  substance 762.2
in-group 769.3
inhabit settle 159.17
  occupy 225.7
  people 225.9
  exist in 760.11
inhabitant 227.2
inhabitants 227.1
inhabited 225.12
inhabiting habitation
225.1
  peopling 225.2
inhalation breathing
2.19
  suction 187.5
inhale smell 69.8
  smoke 89.14
  draw in 187.12
in half 874.8
in hand
  adj unused 390.12
  undertaken 404.7
  possessed 469.8
  restrained 670.11
  orderly 806.6

happening 830.9
operating 888.11
adv under control
612.20
in production 891.21
adj, adv in preparation
405.22
in harmony
adj in accord 455.3
agreeing 787.9
adv jointly 799.18
in harmony with
866.9
in harness busy 330.21
armoured 460.13
in haste 401.14
in health 83.8
in heat 75.27
in heaven
adj overjoyed 95.16
adv celestially 681.13
in hell 682.9
inherent present
221.12
intrinsic 766.7
instinctive 933.6
inherently 766.10
inherit be heir to 479.7
inhere 766.6
succeed 814.2
inheritance property
471.1
bequest 478.10
heritance 479.2
heredity 560.6
inherited hereditary
560.19
innate 766.8
inhibit suppress 106.8
restrain 428.7
confine 429.12
prohibit 444.3
retain 474.5
hinder 1011.10
inhibited 428.13
inhibiting restraining
428.11
hindering 1011.17
inhibition suppression
92.24
restraint 428.1
prohibition 444.1
retention 474.1
hindrance 1011.1
in hiding 346.14
in high 174.17
in high spirits 109.11
in honour of 487.4
inhospitable unkind
144.16
unhospitable 586.7
unfriendly 589.9
in hospital 85.58
in hot pursuit 382.11
in hot water 1012.22
inhuman cruel 144.26

savage 671.21
inhumane 144.26
inhumanity cruelty
144.11
act of cruelty 144.12
violence 671.1
inimical oppositional
451.8
warlike 458.21
unfriendly 589.9
contrary 778.6
adverse 1010.13
inimitable 249.15
in intensive care 85.55
iniquitous malicious
144.20
unjust 650.9
wicked 654.16
wrongdoing 655.5
bad 999.7
initial
noun first 817.3
verb ratify 332.12
letter 546.6
adj beginning 817.15
initially 817.18
initials identification
517.11
signature 527.10
initiate
noun novice 572.9
member 617.11
verb install 191.4
preinstruct 568.14
originate 817.10
inaugurate 817.11
adj skilled 413.26
initiated 413.26
initiation establishment
159.7
admission 187.2
elementary education
568.5
ceremony 580.4
first 817.3
inauguration 817.5
initiative
noun vim 17.2
act 328.3
enterprise 330.7
undertaking 404.1
referendum 613.7
process 888.2
adj introductory
187.18
in its entirety 791.13
in its infancy 817.15
in its own way 864.17
inject use 87.21
insert 191.3
inspire 375.20
soak 1063.13
injection dose 86.6,
87.19
inoculation 91.16
entrance 189.1
insertion 191.1

interjection 213.2
intrusion 214.1
soaking 1063.7
spacecraft 1073.2
in jeopardy
adj in danger 1005.13
phrase in litigation
598.23
injunction precept
419.1
charge 420.2
court order 420.6,
598.4
restraint 428.1
prohibition 444.1
exclusion 772.1
injure mistreat 389.5
impair 393.9
hurt 393.13
work evil 999.6
injured pained 96.23
impaired 393.27
injurious unhealthful
82.5
impaired 393.27
corrupting 393.44
disadvantageous 995.6
harmful 999.12
injury pain 96.5
indignity 156.2
mistreatment 389.2
impairment 393.1
loss 473.1
injustice 650.4
misdeed 655.2
disadvantage 995.2
evil 999.3
injustice
misrepresentation
350.1
presumption 640.2
unjustness 650.1
wrong 650.4
misdeed 655.2
inequality 790.1
ink 38.7
in keeping
adj conformist 866.6
adv in step 787.11
in keeping with in
agreement with 787.12
conformable to 866.9
in kind 783.18
inkling hint 551.4
tinge 796.7
suggestion 950.5
inky black 38.8
stained 1003.10
inland
noun inlands 207.3
adj interior 207.7
adv inward 207.11
in-laws 564.2
inlay
noun insert 191.2
lining 196.3
verb inset 191.5
implant 191.8

fill 196.7
in layers 296.6
in league
adj leagued 804.6
adv in cooperation
450.7
inlet entrance 189.5
cove 242.1
opening 292.1
passageway 383.3
in lieu of 861.12
in line
adj consecutive 811.9
conformist 866.6
adv in step 787.11
in line with
adv directly 161.23
prep in agreement with
787.12
conformable to 866.9
in lots 792.9
in love 104.29
in love with 104.30
in luxury 1009.12
in many instances
846.6
inmate 227.2
in memory of 988.29
in miniature 258.16
in moderation
temperately 668.12
moderately 670.17
in motion
adj moving 172.7
adv under way 172.9
in mourning 115.18
inn 228.15
innards viscera 2.14
contents 196.1
insides 207.4
mechanism 1039.4
innate hereditary
560.19
inborn 766.8
instinctive 933.6
attitudinal 977.7
in need 619.8
inner
noun interior 207.2
adj interior 207.6
intrinsic 766.7
particular 864.12
inner circle council
423.1
authorities 575.15
clique 617.6
inner city sty 80.11
East End 230.6
poor 619.3
inner-city 230.11
inner ear 2.10
inner life 207.2
innermost interior
207.6
private 345.13

inner sanctum 584.6,
1008.5
inner self interior
207.2
self 864.5
innings match 747.3
turn 824.2
innocence artlessness
416.1
naturalness 499.2
purity 653.3
innocency 657.1
chastity 664.1
ignorance 929.1
harmlessness 998.9
innocent
noun child 302.3
dupe 358.1
simple soul 416.3
baby 657.4
adj immature 301.10
artless 416.5
natural 499.7
chaste 653.7, 664.4
unfallen 657.6
ignorant 929.12
trusting 952.22
harmless 998.21
innocently 657.9
innocuous humble
137.10
justifiable 600.14
harmless 998.21
in no time
instantaneously 174.19
quickly 829.7
promptly 844.15
in no uncertain terms
521.13
innovate originate
337.4
invent 840.5
make innovations
851.9
innovation
nonimitation 337.1
original 337.2
curtain raiser 815.2
novelty 840.2
introduction 851.4
innovative 851.11
innovator precursor
815.1
transformer 851.5
in no way 761.12
innuendo sarcasm
508.5
aspersion 512.4
implication 519.2
hint 551.4
accusation 599.1
in numbers 709.28
innumerable infinite
822.3
numberless 883.10
in-off 752.3

inoffensive odourless 72.5
justifiable 600.14
harmless 998.21

in operation in use 387.25
operating 888.11

in opposition
adj dissenting 333.6
adverse 1010.13
adv adversarial 451.9

in opposition to
adv counteractively 899.10
prep opposite to 215.7
opposed to 451.10
in disagreement with 788.10

in order
adj in trim 806.7
adv in turn 806.10

in orders 698.17

in order to 405.24

inordinate exaggerated 355.4
overpriced 632.12
intemperate 669.7
fanatic 925.32
excessive 992.16

inordinately
distressingly 247.21
exorbitantly 632.16
intemperately 669.10
excessively 992.22

inorganic unorganic 1053.4
mineral 1056.15

in other respects 779.11

in other ways 779.11

in other words 341.18

in our time 837.3

in pain 26.9

in paradise 95.16

in parallel parallelwise 203.7
aside 218.10

in part to a degree 248.10
partly 792.8

in particular fully 765.13
particularly 864.15

in partnership
adj leagued 804.6
adv in cooperation 450.7
jointly 799.18

in passing on the way 176.20
hastily 401.12
incidentally 842.13

in peril 1005.13

in perpetuity infinitely 822.4
perpetually 828.10

in person 221.17, 864.16

in pieces impaired 393.27
severed 801.23
broken 801.24

in place
adj located 159.18
present 221.12
provided 385.13
established 854.13
adv in position 159.20

in place of 861.12

in places here and there 159.25
scatteringly 770.12
sparsely 884.8

in play
adj operating 888.11
adv in fun 489.19

in plenty
adj plentiful 990.7
adv plentifully 990.9

in point 774.11

in poor health 85.53

in position 159.20

in possession of 469.9

in power
adj powerful 18.12
adv in authority 417.21

in practice in use 387.25
operating 888.11

in preference 371.28

in preference to 861.12

in preparation 405.22

in preparation for
against 405.24
prior to 833.7

in print published 352.17
printed 548.19

in prison 429.21

in private 345.19

in production
adv in the works 891.21
adj, adv in preparation 405.22

in progress 162.7

in proportion 477.14

in prospect expected 130.13
imminent 839.3

in public openly 348.15
publicly 352.19

in pursuit 382.11

input
noun entrance 189.1
data 1041.15
verb computerize 1041.18

inquest autopsy 307.18
jury 596.6
trial 598.6
inquiry 937.1

in question
adj doubtful 970.17
undecided 970.18
adv at issue 937.39

inquire ask 937.20
be curious 980.3

inquiring
noun inquiry 937.1
questioning 937.12
adj questioning 937.36
curious 980.5

inquiry trial 598.6
inquiring 937.1
question 937.10
canvass 937.14

inquiry into 937.4

Inquisition tribunal 595.1
investigation 937.4

inquisition
noun tribunal 595.1
trial 598.6
inquiry 937.1
grilling 937.13
verb grill 937.22

inquisitive meddlesome 214.9
curious 980.5

in readiness 405.21

in reality really 760.16
truly 972.18

in relief conspicuous 348.12
sculptured 715.7

in reply in retaliation 506.9
in answer 938.7

in reserve
adj imminent 839.3
adv back 386.17
adj, adv in readiness 405.21

in residence 225.13

in response 938.7

in retaliation 506.9

in retirement
adj retired 448.3
adv in seclusion 584.13

in retreat 584.13

in retrospect 988.22

in return in compensation 338.7
in retaliation 506.9
interchangeably 862.6
in answer 938.7

in return for 481.8

in revenge 506.9

in reverse 163.13

in ruins dilapidated 393.33
ruined 395.28

in safety 1006.6

ins and outs
circumstances 765.2
vicissitudes 971.5

insane overzealous 101.12
turbulent 671.18
foolish 922.8
unsane 925.26

insanely 925.35

insanity mental disorder 92.14
disarrangement 810.1
mental deficiency 921.9
foolishness 922.1
insaneness 925.1

insatiable greedy 100.27
rapacious 480.26
gluttonous 672.6

inscribed written 547.22
recorded 549.17
engraved 713.11

inscription epitaph 309.18
lettering 546.5
writing 547.1
monument 549.12
registration 549.14
makeup 554.12
engraving 713.2
motto 973.4

inscrutable 522.13

in search of 382.12

in secrecy 584.13

in secret 345.17

insect bug 311.31
insect 311.31
beast 660.7

insecticide 1000.3

insectivorous 8.31

insecure unreliable 970.20
unconfident 970.23
unsafe 1005.11

insecurity unreliability 970.6
dangerousness 1005.2

in self-defence 460.16

insemination
fertilization 78.3, 889.3
planting 1067.14

insensitive insensible 25.6
callous 94.12
inconsiderate 144.18
heartless 144.25
ill-bred 505.6
undiscriminating 944.5

insensitivity
insensibility 25.1
callousness 94.3
unconcern 102.2

heartlessness 144.10
discourtesy 505.1
indiscrimination 944.1
intolerance 979.2

inseparable familiar 587.19
impartible 799.15
cohesive 802.10
indivisible 1043.13

in sequence 806.10

insert
noun insertion 191.2
interjection 213.2
verb enter 189.7
introduce 191.3
record 549.15

insertion entrance 189.1
introduction 191.1
insert 191.2
interjection 213.2
registration 549.14
spacecraft 1073.2

in service 387.25

in session
adj assembled 769.21
adv in council 423.6

inset
noun map 159.5
insert 191.2
verb inlay 191.5

in shape healthy 83.8
in order 806.7

inshore 207.11

in short 537.8

in short supply
incomplete 794.4
scarce 991.11

inside
noun interior 207.2
inner nature 766.5
adj interior 207.6
confidential 345.14
adv in 207.10
prep in 207.13

inside and out
everywhere 158.12
throughout 793.17

inside information
secret 345.5
knowledge 927.1

inside of 207.13

inside out
adj inverted 205.7
adv completely 793.14

insider inside information 551.2
member 617.11

insider-trading 356.8

insides viscera 2.14
contents 196.1
innards 207.4
inner nature 766.5

insidious deceitful 356.22
cunning 415.12
dishonest 645.16

shrewd 919.15

in sight 31.6

insight sagacity 919.4
cognizance 927.2
good idea 931.6
intuition 933.1
discernment 943.2

insightful knowing
927.15
discerning 943.8

insignia sign 517.1
regalia 647.1

insignificance
inconsiderableness
248.1
meaninglessness 520.1
unimportance 997.1

insignificant small
248.6
meaningless 520.6
inconsequential 997.17

in silence 51.13

insincere uncandid
354.32
affected 500.15
flattering 511.8
deceitful 645.18
be sanctimonious
693.4
sophistical 935.10

insinuating flattering
511.8
disparaging 512.13
suggestive 519.6
shrewd 919.15

insipid wishy-washy
16.17
tasteless 65.2
dull 117.6
vacant 222.14
prosaic 721.5
mediocre 1004.7

insist affirm 334.5
urge 375.14
urge upon 439.9

insistence urging 375.5
exigence 421.4

insistent persevering
360.8
demanding 421.9
importunate 440.18
urgent 996.22

insistently
perseveringly 360.9
demandingly 421.11

in situ 159.20

in slow motion 175.13

in society 578.16

insofar as 887.10

insolence impenitence
114.2
presumptuousness
141.2
presumption 142.1
disrespect 156.1,
505.2
defiance 454.1

rashness 493.1

insolent impenitent
114.5
presumptuous 141.10
insulting 142.9, 156.8
disrespectful 156.7
defiant 454.7
rash 493.7
discourteous 505.4

insoluble inexplicable
522.18
indivisible 1043.13

insolvency poverty
619.1
credit 622.1
bankruptcy 625.3

insolvent
noun insolvent debtor
625.4
adj destitute 619.9
bankrupt 625.11
unsound 729.18

in some way somehow
384.11
by chance 971.19

insomnia wakefulness
23.1
anaemia 85.9

insouciance apathy
94.4
unconcern 102.2
carelessness 340.2
incuriosity 981.1

inspect scrutinize 27.14
examine 937.24

inspection scrutiny
27.6
study 570.3
examination 937.3
accounting 1040.7

inspector
superintendent 574.2
examiner 937.17
policeman 1007.15

inspiration breathing
2.19
suction 187.5
impulse 365.1
motive 375.1
infusion 375.9
encouragement 492.9
unction 677.15
revelation 683.9
Muse 720.10
genius 919.8
good idea 931.6
intuition 933.1
creative thought 985.2

inspirational 375.26

inspire cheer 109.7
give hope 124.10
draw in 187.12
prompt 375.13
inspirit 375.20
encourage 492.16
induce 885.11

inspired fired 375.31
appropriate 533.7

scriptural 683.10
imaginative 985.18

inspiring cheering
109.16
promising 124.13
inspirational 375.26
lofty 544.14

in spite 144.30

in spite of 338.9

in sport 489.19

instability infirmity
16.3
irresolution 362.1
nonuniformity 781.1
inconstancy 853.2
unreliability 970.6
dangerousness 1005.2

install locate 159.11
establish 159.16,
891.10
instate 191.4, 615.12
inaugurate 817.11

installation
establishment 159.7,
891.4
admission 187.2
instalment 615.3
holy orders 698.10
workplace 739.1

installations 385.4

installed 159.18

instalment
establishment 159.7
admission 187.2
part 554.13, 792.1
installation 615.3
payment 624.1

instance
noun urging 375.5
proposal 439.2
particular 765.3
example 785.2
sample 785.3
citation 956.5
verb itemize 765.6
cite 956.13

instant
noun period 823.1
short time 827.3
moment 829.3
adj hasty 401.9
ready-made 405.19
demanding 421.9
instantaneous 829.4
imminent 839.3
prompt 844.9
urgent 996.22

instantaneous short
268.8
instant 829.4
prompt 844.9

instantaneously in no
time 174.19
instantly 829.6

instantly hastily 401.12
instanter 829.6
promptly 844.15

instead 861.11

instead of 861.12

in step
adj synchronous 835.6
conformist 866.6
adv in concert 787.11

in step with 866.9

instigate incite 375.17
induce 885.11

instigating 375.28

instigation 375.4

instigator inciter
375.11
author 885.4
producer 891.7

instil inculcate 568.12
imbue 796.11

instilled 373.19

instinct feeling 93.1
impulse 365.1
talent 413.4
natural instinct 933.2
discrimination 943.1
involuntariness 962.5

instinctive innate
766.8
natural 933.6
involuntary 962.14

instinctively intuitively
933.7
involuntarily 962.18

instinctual innate
766.8
instinctive 933.6

institute
noun school 567.1
organization 617.8
verb inaugurate 817.11
cause 885.10
establish 891.10

institution organization
617.8
law 673.3
holy orders 698.10
rite 701.3
workplace 739.1
beginning 817.1
establishment 891.4

institutional 567.13

in stock
adj possessed 469.8
adv in store 386.16

in store
adj possessed 469.8
imminent 839.3
destined 963.9
adv in stock 386.16
adj, adv in readiness
405.21

instruct command
420.8
advise 422.5
inform 551.8
teach 568.10

instructed 927.18

instruction precept
419.1
direction 420.3

advice 422.1
information 551.1
teaching 568.1
lesson 568.7
learning 927.4

instructional 568.18

instructions 568.6

instructive preceptive
419.4
commanding 420.13
advisory 422.8
informative 551.18
educational 568.18

instructor aviator
185.1
preparer 405.5
adviser 422.3
teacher 571.1
professor 571.3

instrument
noun surgery 91.19
sycophant 138.3
measure 300.2
tool 384.4, 1039.1
document 549.5
agent 576.3
verb compose 708.46
tool 1039.9

instrumental
noun case 530.9
adj modal 384.8
helping 449.20
orchestral 708.51

instrumentation
measurement 300.1
harmonization 709.2
tooling 1039.7
rocketry 1072.1

instrument panel
1033.7

instruments 704.18

in style 578.11

in substance in brief
537.8
essentially 766.11

insubstantial thin
270.16
unsubstantial 763.5
transient 827.7
unsound 935.12
unreliable 970.20
immaterial 1051.7

in succession in order
806.10
consecutively 811.11

insufferable 98.25

insufficient
unsatisfactory 108.9
inadequate 250.7
unequal 790.4
short of 910.5
unsufficing 991.9

insufficiently
unsatisfactorily 108.12
inadequately 991.14

insular
noun islander 235.4
adj local 231.9

interposition 213.1
obtrusion 214.1
extraneousness 773.1
untimeliness 843.1
overstepping 909.3

intrusive entering
189.12
obtrusive 214.8
overactive 330.24
extraneous 773.5
untimely 843.6

in trust 438.13

in truth truthfully
644.22
certainly 969.23
truly 972.18

intuition intuitiveness
933.1
hunch 933.3
discrimination 943.1
suggestion 950.5

intuitive premonitory
133.16
intuitional 933.5
theoretical 950.13
foreseeing 960.7

intuitively 933.7

in tune
adj in accord 455.3
harmonious 708.49
adv in step 787.11

in turn in order 806.10
consecutively 811.11
interchangeably 862.6

in turns 849.11

in two
adj separate 801.20
adv separately 801.27
in half 874.8

inundated overcome
112.29
flooded 238.25
underwater 275.13
overrun 909.10
soaked 1063.17

in unison
adj harmonious 708.49
adv unanimously
332.17
cooperatively 450.6
in step 787.11
jointly 799.18
simultaneously 835.7

inured callous 94.12
accustomed 373.16
hardened 654.17

in use 387.25

invade intrude 214.5
raid 459.20
usurp 640.8
infest 909.6
overstep 909.9

invader intruder 214.3
assailant 459.12

invading 459.29

in vain unsuccessfully
410.19

amiss 910.7

invalid
noun impotent 19.6
sick person 85.42
recluse 584.5
verb afflict 85.49
dismiss 908.19
adj ineffective 19.15
unhealthy 85.53
repealed 445.3
illogical 935.11
bad 999.7

invalidate disqualify
19.11
abolish 395.13
repeal 445.2
neutralize 899.7
disprove 957.4

invalidity
ineffectiveness 19.3
unhealthiness 85.3
illogicalness 935.2
badness 999.1

invalidity benefit
478.8

invaluable 632.10

invariable tedious
118.9
uniform 780.5
unchangeable 854.17

invariably regularly
780.8
always 828.11
permanently 852.9
universally 863.18

invasion intrusion
214.1
raid 459.4
usurpation 640.3
infestation 909.2

invasive entering
189.12
intrusive 214.8
attacking 459.29

invective
noun sarcasm 508.5
berating 510.7
vilification 513.2
speech 543.2
adj condemnatory
510.22

invent originate 337.4,
891.12
fabricate 354.18
initiate 817.10
innovate 840.5, 851.9
discover 940.2
imagine 985.14

invented fabricated
354.29
originated 891.19

invention fabrication
354.10
innovation 851.4
production 891.1
product 892.1
discovery 940.1
inventiveness 985.3

figment of the
imagination 985.5

inventive cunning
415.12
beginning 817.15
creative 891.16
imaginative 985.18

inventiveness
nonimitation 337.1
cunning 415.1
invention 985.3

inventor producer
891.7
imaginer 985.12

inventory
noun contents 196.1
store 386.1
record 549.1
account book 628.4
merchandise 735.1
assemblage 769.1
table 807.4
list 870.1
summation 1016.11
verb take account of
628.9
list 870.8
sum up 1016.18
check 1016.20

inverse
noun reverse 205.4
opposite side 215.3
opposite 778.2
verb invert 205.5
adj contrapositive
215.5
contrary 778.6

inversion 1016.2

inverted 205.7

invest clothe 5.38
empower 18.10
establish 159.16
install 191.4, 615.12
surround 209.6
wrap 295.20
provide 385.7
besiege 459.19
endow 478.17
commission 615.10
spend 626.5
place 729.16

invested clothing 5.44
provided 385.13
endowed 478.26

investigate discuss
541.12
indagate 937.23

investigation
discussion 541.7
indagation 937.4

investigative 937.37

investigator detective
576.10
examiner 937.17

invest in 729.16

investing 615.1

investiture clothing 5.1
establishment 159.7

admission 187.2
giving 478.1
commission 615.1
installation 615.3
holy orders 698.10

investment clothing
5.1
empowerment 18.8
provision 385.1
siege 459.5
endowment 478.9
commission 615.1
venture 729.3

investment banking
finance 729.1
banking 729.4

investment company
737.16

investment trust
737.16

investor 729.8

inveterate confirmed
373.19
durable 826.10
traditional 841.12
established 854.13

invidious malicious
144.20
jealous 153.5
envious 154.4

in view visible 31.6
expected 130.13
present 221.12
imminent 839.3

in view of 887.9

**in view of the fact
that** 887.10

invigorated 9.4

invigorating refreshing
9.3
energizing 17.15
healthful 81.5
tonic 86.44
cheering 109.16
cool 1022.12

invincibility
impregnability 15.4
indestructibility 854.5
reliability 969.4

invincible impregnable
15.19
peerless 249.15
persevering 360.8
indestructible 854.18
reliable 969.17

invisibility
imperceptibility 32.1
infinitesimalness 258.2
concealment 346.1

invisible
noun invisibility 32.1
adj imperceptible 32.5
infinitesimal 258.14
unrevealed 346.12

invitation incentive
375.7
allurement 377.1
offer 439.1

invite 440.4

invitational 440.19

invite encourage 375.21
attract 377.6
ask 440.13
incur 896.4
interest 982.12

inviting delightful 97.7
receptive 187.16
provocative 375.27
alluring 377.8
invitational 440.19
interesting 982.19

invitingly 97.13

invocation summons
420.5
entreaty 440.2
conjuration 690.4
prayer 696.4
benediction 696.5

in vogue 578.11

invoice
noun statement 628.3
bill 870.5
verb bill 628.11

invoke summon 420.11
entreat 440.11
address 524.27
conjure 690.11
pray 696.12
adduce 956.12
refer to 956.14

involuntarily
unwillingly 325.8
on impulse 365.14
instinctively 962.18
unintentionally 971.21

involuntary unwilling
325.5
unpremeditated
365.11
obligatory 424.11
instinctive 933.6,
962.14
unintentional 971.17

involve surround 209.6
signify 517.17
imply 519.4
ornament 545.7
incriminate 599.10
entail 771.4
relate to 774.5
complicate 798.3
implicate 897.2
evidence 956.8
engross 982.13
hamper 1011.11
put in a hole 1012.15

involved participating
476.8
implied 519.7
accused 599.15
indebted 623.8
partial 650.11
guilty 656.3
included 771.5
related 774.9
complex 798.4
implicated 897.4

engrossed 982.17

involved in 897.5

involvement sympathy
93.5
surrounding 209.5
mediation 466.1
participation 476.1
incrimination 599.2
partiality 650.3
guilt 656.1
entailment 771.2
complexity 798.1
involution 897.1
engrossment 982.3

involving 774.11

inward
noun interior 207.2
adj entering 189.12
interior 207.6
private 345.13
intrinsic 766.7
adv in 189.13
inwards 207.11

inwardly in 189.13
internally 207.9
inward 207.11
intrinsically 766.10

inwards
noun viscera 2.14
insides 207.4
adv in 189.13
inward 207.11

in waves 281.11

in with on good terms
587.17
leagued 804.6

in wonder 122.18

in working order
806.7

in writing 547.22

ion atom 258.8, 1037.4
electrolysis 1031.24
element 1058.2

iota modicum 248.2
minutia 258.7

I pass 522.27

irascible excitable
105.28
irritable 110.19
perverse 361.11
partisan 456.17

irate 152.28

ire 152.5

I refuse 442.7

iridescent soft-coloured
35.21
iridal 47.10
opalescent 1024.37

Iris 353.1

iris eye 2.9, 27.9
spectrum 47.6

Irish accent 523.7

irked annoyed 96.21
weary 118.11
troubled 1012.20

irksome annoying
98.22
wearying 118.10
troublesome 1012.18

iron
noun horse 15.8
stone 1044.6
verb press 287.6
adj unyielding 361.9
firm 425.7
brass 1056.17

Iron Age 823.5

iron curtain frontier
211.5
veil of secrecy 345.3
communism 611.6
barrier 1011.5

ironic witty 489.15
satiric 508.13
suggestive 519.6
ambiguous 539.4
self-contradictory
778.8
mixed 796.14

ironical witty 489.15
satiric 508.13

iron maiden 96.7

iron out 939.2

irons 428.4

irony wit 489.1
sarcasm 508.5
ambiguity 539.1
doubleness 872.1

irrational unintelligent
921.13
unwise 922.10
insane 925.26
fanatic 925.32
illogical 935.11

irrationality
unintelligence 921.1
unwiseness 922.2
insanity 925.1
illogicalness 935.2

irreconcilable
noun oppositionist
452.3
adj unyielding 361.9
revengeful 507.7
alienated 589.11
different 779.7
inconsistent 788.8

irredeemably 125.18

irrefutable evidential
956.16
obvious 969.15

irregular
noun casual 461.15
second 1004.6
adj distorted 265.10
rough 288.6
informal 581.3
illegal 674.6
nonuniform 781.3
unequal 790.4
unordered 809.12
discontinuous 812.4
unregular 850.3

inconstant 853.7
abnormal 869.9
eccentric 926.5
inferior 1004.9

irregularity distortion
265.1
roughness 288.1,
294.2
informality 581.1
nonuniformity 781.1
inequality 790.1
disorder 809.1
discontinuity 812.1
unmethodicalness
850.1
inconstancy 853.2
abnormality 869.1
eccentricity 926.1

irregularly roughly
288.11
nonuniformly 781.4
haphazardly 809.18
occasionally 847.5
unsystematically 850.4

irrelevance
unrelatedness 775.1
irrelevancy 775.3
unimportance 997.1

irrelevant irrelative
775.7
inappropriate 788.7
untimely 843.6
insignificant 997.17

irreparable 125.15

irreparably 125.18

irreplaceable used up
388.5
requisite 962.13

irrepressible cheerful
109.11
ungovernable 361.12
unrestrained 430.24

irresistible impregnable
15.19
powerful 18.12
delightful 97.7
great 247.6
alluring 377.8
overpowering 412.18
compulsory 424.10
evidential 956.16
inevitable 962.15

irresistibly strongly
15.23
alluringly 377.9

irrespective of 338.9

irresponsibility
lawlessness 418.1
untrustworthiness
645.4

irresponsible lawless
418.5
exempt 430.30
untrustworthy 645.19
inconstant 853.7

irreverence disrespect
156.1
impiety 694.1

irreverent disrespectful
156.7
impious 694.6

irreversible past hope
125.15
directional 161.12
confirmed 373.19
unchangeable 854.17

irrevocable past hope
125.15
mandatory 420.12
unchangeable 854.17
inevitable 962.15

irrevocably
irreclaimably 125.18
absolutely 793.15
inevitably 962.19

irrigation washing 79.5
wetting 1063.6
cultivation 1067.13

irritability sensitivity
24.3
excitability 105.10
irascibility 110.2
dissension 456.3

irritable sensitive 24.12
excitable 105.28
irascible 110.19
nervous 128.11
partisan 456.17

irritably 110.27

irritant
noun irritation 96.3
adj irritating 26.13

irritate pain 26.7
aggravate 96.14, 119.2
get on one's nerves
128.9
provoke 152.24
impair 393.9
sow dissension 456.14

irritated sore 26.11
annoyed 96.21
aggravated 119.4
provoked 152.27
impaired 393.27

irritating irritative
26.13
pungent 68.6
annoying 98.22
aggravating 119.5

irritatingly 98.29

irritation soreness 26.4
aggravation 96.3,
119.1
excitation 105.11
resentment 152.1
incitement 375.4
adversity 1010.1

ish 223.26

Isis 889.5

Islam 675.13

Islamic 675.31

island
noun airport 184.22
isle 235.2
verb insulate 235.5

adj insular 235.7

islander 235.4

isle 235.2

islet 235.2

ism school 617.5
cult 675.2
system of belief 952.3

isolate insulate 235.5,
1031.28
excise 255.10
quarantine 429.13
segregate 772.6
analyse 800.6
separate 801.8

isolated quiescent
173.12
insular 235.7
private 345.13
quarantined 429.20
secluded 584.8
segregated 772.8
unrelated 775.6
separate 801.20
separated 801.21
alone 871.8

isolation defence
mechanism 92.23
privacy 345.2
quarantine 429.2
seclusion 584.1
exclusiveness 772.3
itemization 800.2
separation 801.1
aloneness 871.2

isolationism
noninterference 430.9
seclusion 584.1
foreign policy 609.5
patriotism 611.11

isolationist free agent
430.12
recluse 584.5
patriot 611.22

isometric
noun weather map
317.4
adj climatal 317.12
equisized 789.10

issue
noun emergence 190.1
amount 244.2
publication 352.1
escape 369.1
edition 554.5
family 559.5
posterity 561.1
platform 609.7
issuance 738.6
event 830.1
cause 885.9
effect 886.1
product 892.1
topic 936.1
question 937.10
solution 939.1
salient point 996.6
verb appear 33.8
set out 188.8
emerge 190.11

chump 923.3
verb thrill 105.18
preserve 397.9
throw 903.10
yerk 904.5
twitch 916.13

jerking
noun food preservation 397.2
twitching 916.5
adj jerky 916.19

jerky
noun meat 10.12
beef 10.13
adj convulsive 671.23
nonuniform 781.3
discontinuous 812.4
irregular 850.3
herky-jerky 916.19

Jerry dago 232.7
squaddie 461.7

jerry
noun toilet 12.11
adj frail 16.14

jersey 746.1

jest
noun joke 489.6
gibe 508.2
laughingstock 508.7
trifle 997.5
verb joke 489.13
banter 490.5

jester humourist 489.12
buffoon 707.10

Jesuit sophist 935.6
quibbler 935.7

jet
noun jet plane 181.3
ascent 193.1
spout 238.9
outburst 671.6
disgorgement 908.7
heater 1019.10
verb fly 184.36
run out 190.13
shoot up 193.9
spout 238.20
disgorge 908.25

jet-black 38.8

jet fighter 181.9

jet-lagged 177.41

jet set traveller 178.1
society 578.6

jet-set 578.16

jetstream 184.32

jettison
noun abandonment 370.1
discard 390.3
ejection 908.1
verb abandon 370.5
discard 390.7
eject 908.13

jettisoned 370.8

jetty
noun buttress 900.4
harbour 1008.6

barrier 1011.5
adj black 38.8

Jew 675.21

jewel
noun favourite 104.16
bijou 498.6
good person 659.1
bearing 914.7
good thing 998.5
verb figure 498.9

jewelled 498.11

jewellery 498.5

jewels 732.3

Jewish 675.30

jib start 127.12
avoid 164.6
refuse 325.3
hesitate 362.7

jibe agree 787.6
be changed 851.6

jig
noun snare 356.13
leap 366.1
jerk 904.3
shake 916.3
verb fish 382.10
jerk 904.5
twitch 916.13

jigsaw 801.11

jigsaw puzzle 522.8

jihad 458.4

jill ladylove 104.14
gal 302.7

jilted 99.10

jingle
noun ringing 54.3
metre 720.7
repetitiousness 848.4
signature 1033.19
verb ring 54.8
rhyme 720.14

jingoistic militaristic 458.22
public-spirited 591.4
patriotic 611.34

jinx
noun spell 691.1
verb bewitch 691.9
work evil 999.6

jitters 128.2

jittery 128.12

jive
noun bullshit 520.3
jazz 708.9
verb kid 490.6
syncopate 708.43

Job 134.3

job
noun act 328.3
blag 482.4
occupation 724.1
task 724.2
function 724.3
position 724.5
affair 830.3
verb rent 615.15
deal in 731.15

sell 734.8

jobbing
Machiavellianism 415.2
trade 731.2
selling 734.2
stockbroking 737.18

jobless 331.18

joblessness 331.3

Job-like 134.9

job lot 735.1

Jock 232.7

jock squaddie 461.7
athlete 743.19
jockey 757.2

jockey
noun speeder 174.5
rider 178.8
jock 757.2
pommel 900.18
verb manoeuvre 415.10
compete 457.18

Jockey Club 757.1

jockeying 457.2

jocular merry 109.15
witty 489.15

Joe 76.5

jog
noun slow motion 175.2
gait 177.12
bulge 283.3
notch 289.1
thrust 901.2
jerk 904.3
shake 916.3
verb exercise 84.4
stroll 177.28
thrust 901.12
jerk 904.5
shake 916.11

jogger 988.6

jogging 84.2

John 684.2

joie de vivre animation 17.4
pleasure 95.1

join
noun joint 799.4
verb adjoin 223.9
juxtapose 223.13
flow 238.16
cooperate 450.3
side with 450.4
participate 476.5
marry 563.14
associate with 582.17
enlist 615.17
join up 617.14
assemble 769.18
identify 777.5
compose 795.3
put together 799.5
connect 799.11
be consistent 802.7
combine 804.3

continue 811.4
concur 898.2

joined adjacent 223.16
accompanying 768.9
assembled 769.21
related 774.9
joint 799.12
united 799.13
consistent 802.11
combined 804.5
continuous 811.8

joined up 799.13

joiner 582.16

join forces 804.4

join in cooperate 450.3
participate 476.5

joining
noun meeting 223.4
addition 253.1
junction 799.1
joint 799.4
adj connecting 799.16

joint
noun meat 10.12
joy stick 87.11
crack 224.2
nick 429.9
brothel 665.9
join 799.4
verb hook 799.8
adj cooperative 450.5
communal 476.9
accompanying 768.9
assembled 769.21
mutual 776.11
combined 799.12, 804.5
concurrent 898.4

jointed 799.17

jointly cooperatively 450.6
together 768.11
mutually 776.13
conjointly 799.18
concurrently 898.5

join together cooperate 450.3
marry 563.14

joint-stock company 737.15

join up participate 476.5
join 617.14
put together 799.5

join with flow 238.16
side with 450.4

joke
noun jest 489.6
laughingstock 508.7
trifle 997.5
verb jest 489.13
banter 490.5

joker guy 76.5
surprise 131.2
mischief-maker 322.3
trick 356.6
deceiver 357.1
humourist 489.12

card 758.2
obstacle 1011.4
crux 1012.8

joking
noun wittiness 489.2
bantering 490.2
adj witty 489.15

jokingly 489.19

jolly
noun journey 177.5
festivity 743.3
verb kid 490.6
flannel 511.6
make merry 743.24
adj intoxicated 88.31
merry 109.15
convivial 582.23
festive 743.28
adv very 247.18

jolt
noun drink 88.7
kick 105.3
start 131.3
thrust 901.2
shake 916.3
verb agitate 105.14
startle 131.8
stroll 177.28
thrust 901.12
shake 916.11

jolted 131.13

Jonah 999.4

jones 87.8

Jordan 307.4

josh joke 489.13
kid 490.6

joss 697.3

jostle
noun thrust 901.2
shake 916.3
verb disagree 456.8, 788.5
contend 457.13
thrust 901.12
shake 916.11

jostling 61.5

jot modicum 248.2
minutia 258.7
mark 517.5

jot down 549.15

journal
noun notebook 549.11
account book 628.4
history 719.1
chronicle 831.9
axle box 914.6
adj periodical 555.1

journalism
noun authorship 547.2, 718.2
news 552.1
adj press 555.3

journalist 555.4

journalistic 555.5

journey
noun trip 177.5
verb travel 177.21

accurately 972.20
  perfectly 1001.10
just see 985.15
just so
  adv how 384.9
  thus 765.10
  accurately 972.20
  conj so 958.15
  phrase right! 972.24
  exclam yes 332.18
just the same
  adj approximating
  783.14
  adv identically 777.9
  adv, conj
  notwithstanding 338.8
jut overhang 202.7
  overlie 295.30
jutting
  noun overhang 202.3
  adj overhanging
  202.11
  protruding 283.14
juvenal
  noun youngster 302.1
  adj young 301.9
juvenile
  noun youngster 302.1
  book 554.1
  actor 707.2
  jockey 757.2
  adj young 301.9
  immature 406.11
juxtaposed 223.16
juxtaposition
  apposition 223.3
  addition 253.1
  assemblage 769.1
kaiser 575.9
kaleidoscope 853.4
kaleidoscopic
  chromatic 35.15
  variegated 47.9
  formless 263.4
  changeable 853.6
Kama 104.8
kama 689.18
kamikaze 181.9
kangaroo 366.4
karma destiny 838.2
  fate 963.2
kayak 180.1
keel
  noun ship 180.1
  base 199.2
  verb capsize 182.44
  incline 204.10
keen
  noun screech 58.4
  lament 115.3
  dirge 115.6
  verb screech 58.8
  lament 115.10
  adj energetic 17.13
  acrimonious 17.14
  exquisite 24.13
  shrill 58.14

pungent 68.6
  fervent 93.18
  deep-felt 93.24
  eager 101.8
  penetrating 105.31
  caustic 144.23
  sharp 285.8
  willing 324.5
  active 330.17
  alert 339.14
  enterprising 404.8
  prepared 405.16
  witty 489.15
  violent 671.16
  smart 919.14
  great 998.13
  cold 1022.14
keener 309.7
keen eye 27.10
keening
  noun lamentation
  115.1
  adj shrill 58.14
keen interest 101.1
keenly energetically
  17.16
  fervently 93.26
  eagerly 101.13
  caustically 144.32
keenness vim 17.2
  acrimony 17.5
  pungency 68.1
  eagerness 101.1
  causticity 144.8
  sharpness 285.1
  willingness 324.1
  alertness 339.5
  wittiness 489.2
  smartness 919.2
  cold 1022.1
keep
  noun nutriment 10.3
  accommodations 385.3
  custody 429.5
  prison 429.8
  support 449.3
  stronghold 460.6
  verb obey 326.2
  provide 385.7
  store up 386.11
  reserve 386.12
  preserve 397.8
  restrain 428.7
  observe 434.2
  support 449.12
  retain 474.5
  hold 474.7
  celebrate 487.2,
  701.14
  endure 826.6
  stabilize 854.7
  sustain 855.4
  keep in memory
  988.13
  protect 1007.18
  raise 1068.6
keep alive keep body
  and soul together
  306.10
  preserve 397.8

sustain 855.4
keep an eye on look
  27.13
  keep informed 551.16
keep an eye out look
  27.13
  be vigilant 339.8
keep at 360.2
keep away be absent
  222.7
  keep one's distance
  261.7
keep away from keep
  one's distance 261.7
  avoid 368.6
keep calm 106.9
keep coming 848.11
keep down suppress
  428.8
  subjugate 432.8
  domineer 612.16
keeper preserver 397.5
  possessor 470.1
  protector 1007.5
  guardian 1007.6
keep fit
  noun exercise 725.6
  verb enjoy good health
  83.6
keep from refrain
  329.3
  keep secret 345.7
  avoid 368.6
  restrain 428.7
  abstain 668.7
  prevent 1011.14
keep going keep on
  330.15
  persevere 360.2
  continue 855.3
  sustain 855.4
keep in restrain 428.7
  confine 429.12
keeping
  noun symmetry 264.1
  preservation 397.1
  custody 429.5
  observance 434.1
  retention 474.1
  protectorship 1007.2
  adj preservative
  397.11
  retentive 474.8
keep in mind 930.16
keep it up 134.5
keep moving 330.15
keep off fend off
  460.10
  repulse 907.3
  prevent 1011.14
keep on keep going
  330.15
  persevere 360.2
  endure 826.6
  continue 855.3
keep out 772.4

keep pace with keep
  up with 174.14
  equal 789.5
  coincide 835.4
  go with 898.3
keep quiet 173.7
keep the peace remain
  at peace 464.7
  be moderate 670.5
  calm 670.7
keep track of keep
  informed 551.16
  keep account of
  1016.19
keep trying 360.2
keep up not weaken
  15.10
  persevere 360.2
  preserve 397.8
  follow the fashion
  578.10
  work 724.12
  sustain 855.4
  support 900.21
keep up with 174.14
keep within 207.5
kelp 310.4
ken
  noun vision 27.1
  field of view 31.3
  knowledge 927.1
  verb see 27.12
  understand 521.7
  know 927.12
kennel
  noun doghouse 228.21
  drain 239.5
  trench 290.2
  dog 311.17
  pavement 383.6
  flock 769.5
  verb enclose 212.5
Kentucky Derby 757.1
kept reserved 386.15
  preserved 397.12
kept in 429.19
kept-out 772.7
kerb kerbing 211.6
  pavement 383.6
  stock exchange 737.7
Kern 1037.6
kernel nut 10.37
  substance 196.5
  centre 208.2
  seed 310.29
  essence 766.2
  middle 818.1
  salient point 996.6
kerosene 1024.20
key
  noun colour 35.1
  island 235.2
  opener 292.10
  translation 341.3
  telegraph 347.2
  clue 517.9
  pitch 709.4

key signature 709.15
  wind instrument 711.6
  influence 893.6
  input device 1041.4
  verb close 293.6
  adj central 208.11
keyboard
  noun musical
  instrument 711.1
  fingerboard 711.17
  verb autotype 548.15
  computerize 1041.18
key in 1041.18
Keynesian
  noun One Nation Tory
  611.16
  adj One-Nation Tory
  611.28
keynote
  noun sign 517.1
  key 709.15
  characteristic 864.4
  verb characterize
  864.10
keynote speech 609.7
keys tiara 647.4
  keyboard 711.17
keystone arch 279.4
  foundation stone
  900.7
  salient point 996.6
key to 787.7
key word 517.9
khaki 40.3
khan prince 608.7
  Sir 648.3
kibbutz communion
  476.2
  farm 1067.8
kick
  noun pep 17.3
  zest 68.2
  charge 105.3
  beef 115.5
  signal 517.15
  hint 551.4
  game 745.3, 746.3
  match 752.3
  counteraction 899.1
  boot 901.9
  recoil 902.2
  verb beef 108.6,
  115.16
  signal 517.22
  play 745.4, 746.4,
  752.4
  boot 901.21
  recoil 902.6
  fire 908.20
kickback bribe 378.2
  reimbursement 624.2
  discount 631.1
  recoil 902.2
kicker grouch 108.4,
  115.9
  surprise 131.2
kick in provide 385.7
  fork out 624.16

kicking beef 115.5
  kick 901.9
kick it 307.20
kick off propose 439.5
  play 745.4, 746.4
  precede 813.2
kick out 901.21
kicks 95.1
kick-start 903.13
kid
  noun fledgling 302.10
  goat 311.8
  verb jolly 490.6
kidding
  noun jollying 490.3
  adj ridiculing 508.12
kidnap seize 480.14
  abduct 482.20
kidnapper 483.10
kidnapping seizure
  480.2
  abduction 482.9
kidney viscera 2.14
  kind 808.3
  disposition 977.3
kidney disease 85.24
kidneys viscera 2.14
  heart 10.19
kids family 559.5
  posterity 561.1
kill
  noun stream 238.1
  killing 308.1
  quarry 382.7
  verb excise 255.10
  delete 255.12
  slay 308.12
  cover up 345.8
  put an end to 395.12
  obliterate 395.16
  suppress 428.8
  veto 444.5
  legislate 613.9
  end 819.5
  turn off 856.12
killer
  noun slayer 308.10
  ruffian 593.3
  dandy 998.7
  adj great 998.13
killing
  noun violent death
  307.6
  slaying 308.1
  unruliness 671.3
  adj fatiguing 21.13
  deadly 308.22
  laborious 725.18
  eye-catching 1015.21
killing fields 308.11
kill off excise 255.10
  kill 308.12
  put an end to 395.12
kiln
  noun oven 742.5
  verb dry 1064.6
kilometre 881.10

kin kinfolk 559.2
  class 808.2
  kind 808.3
kind
  noun race 559.4
  nature 766.4
  sort 808.3
  adj kindly 143.13
  forgiving 148.6
  indulgent 427.8
  favourable 449.22
  friendly 587.15
  good 998.12
kindergarten 567.2
kindled 1018.27
kindling
  noun ignition 1019.4
  firewood 1020.3
  adj inflammatory
  1019.27
kindly
  adj kind 143.13
  indulgent 427.8
  favourable 449.22
  adv fervently 93.26
  pleasantly 97.12
  benignly 143.18
kindness kindliness
  143.1
  act of kindness 143.7
  pity 145.1
  forgiveness 148.1
  compliance 427.2
  friendship 587.1
  goodness 998.1
kind of 245.7
kindred
  noun blood
  relationship 559.1
  kinfolk 559.2
  adj related 559.6
  akin 774.10
kinetic energetic 17.13
  dynamic 1038.9
king potentate 575.8
  prince 608.7
  businessman 730.1
  chessman 743.17
  card 758.2
  chief 996.10
kingdom country 232.1
  biological classification
  305.3
  nomenclature 527.1
  hierarchy 808.4
  subkingdom 808.5
kingmaker
  Machiavellian 415.8
  strategist 610.6
  influence 893.6
kingpin 575.4
kingship supremacy
  249.3
  sovereignty 417.8
  lordship 608.9
king size 257.4
king-size large 247.7,
  257.16

huge 257.20
  oversize 257.23
kink
  noun pang 26.2
  perversion 75.11
  coil 281.2
  caprice 364.1
  quirk 926.2
  fault 1002.2
  blemish 1003.1
  verb curl 281.5
  blemish 1003.4
kinky curly 281.9
  capricious 364.5
  kooky 926.6
kinship accord 455.1
  blood relationship
  559.1
  affinity 783.2
kiosk hut 228.9
  summerhouse 228.12
  telephone 347.4
  booth 736.3
kipper
  noun fish 10.23
  marine animal 311.30
  verb preserve 397.9
kirk 703.1
kiss
  noun touch 73.1
  contact 223.5
  smacker 562.4
  greeting 585.4
  verb touch lightly 73.7
  contact 223.10
  osculate 562.19
  greet 585.10
  play 752.4
kiss and tell 351.6
kiss-and-tell disclosive
  351.10
  telltale 551.19
kissing
  noun lovemaking 562.1
  adj in contact 223.17
kiss of life 2.19
kit fledgling 302.10
  cat 311.21
  equipment 385.4
  impedimenta 471.3
  football 745.1
  rugby 746.1
  cricket 747.1
kitchen
  noun restaurant 8.17
  cookroom 11.3
  storeroom 197.14
  adj cooking 11.5
kitchener 11.2
kitchen sink washbasin
  79.12
  genuineness 972.7
kitchenware 735.4
kite
  noun aircraft 181.1
  box kite 181.14
  verb take off 193.10

kitsch
  noun vulgarity 497.1
  literature 547.12,
  718.1
  work of art 712.10
  adj common 497.14
kitten
  noun reed 16.7
  child 302.3
  fledgling 302.10
  cat 311.21
  verb give birth 1.3
kittens 1049.5
kitty funds 728.14
  pot 759.5
knack art 413.6
  trinket 498.4
knackered beat 21.8
  worn-out 393.36
knead stroke 73.8
  form 262.7
  mix 796.10
  rub 1042.6
  soften 1045.6
kneading 1042.3
knee
  noun member 2.7
  leg 177.14
  angle 278.2
  joint 799.4
  verb kick 901.21
knee-deep deep 275.10
  shallow 276.5
knee-high little 258.10
  low 274.7
knee jerk impulse
  365.1
  habit 373.4
  instinct 933.2
knee-jerk
  unpremeditated
  365.11
  habitual 373.15
  uncritical 509.18
  reactive 902.9
  trusting 952.22
  credulous 953.8
knee-jerk reaction
  933.2
kneel fawn 138.7
  bow 155.6, 912.9
kneeling obeisance
  155.2
  submission 433.1
  crouch 912.3
knees-up bash 582.12
  dance 705.2
knell
  noun ringing 54.3
  dirge 115.6
  death 307.1
  passing bell 309.6
  verb ring 54.8
  lament 115.10
knife
  noun surgery 91.19
  sword 462.5

cutlery 1039.2
  verb stab 459.25
knife-edge edge 285.2
  unreliability 970.6
  predicament 1012.4
knight
  noun rider 178.8
  combatant 461.1
  gallant 504.9
  cavalier 608.5
  chessman 743.17
  verb promote 446.2
knighthood military
  science 458.6
  lordship 608.9
knightly
  adj courageous 492.17
  gallant 504.15
  noble 608.10
  magnanimous 652.6
  adv courageously
  492.23
  courteously 504.19
knit
  verb contract 260.7
  wrinkle 291.6
  heal 396.21
  weave 740.6
  fasten 799.7
  join 799.11
  adj woven 740.7
  joined 799.13
knitted contracted
  260.12
  wrinkled 291.8
  joined 799.13
knitting contraction
  260.1
  weaving 740.1
knives 8.12
knob
  noun hill 237.4
  sphere 282.2
  bulge 283.3
  verb roughen 288.4
knobbly 288.8
knock
  noun report 56.1
  hit 901.4
  verb crack 56.6
  collide 901.13
  hit 901.14
  pound 901.16
knockabout 671.20
knock down sadden
  112.18
  auction 734.11
  fight 754.4
  fell 912.5
knockdown
  noun acquaintance
  587.4
  adj reduced 633.9
knocked out beat 21.8
  formative 262.9
knocker 512.6
knocking 56.11

knock off take a rest
20.8
waste 308.13
improvise 365.8
accomplish 407.4
clobber 412.9
lay off 856.8

knock on 746.3

knock out paralyse
19.10
beat 21.6
deaden 25.4
do carelessly 340.9
do for 395.11
fight 754.4
end 819.5

knockout dandy 998.7
doll 1015.9

knoll 237.4

knot
noun braid 3.7
distortion 265.1
sphere 282.2
bulge 283.3
enigma 522.8
company 769.3
bunch 769.7
complex 798.2
fastening 799.3
dilemma 1012.7
solid 1043.6
verb distort 265.5
complicate 798.3
put together 799.5
thicken 1043.10

knots velocity 174.1
air speed 184.31

knotted studded 283.17
gnarled 288.8
wrinkled 291.8
assembled 769.21
related 774.9
complex 798.4
joined 799.13
difficult 1012.17

knotty studded 283.17
gnarled 288.8
hard to understand
522.14
difficult 1012.17

know understand 521.7
be friends 587.9
experience 830.8
perceive 927.12
be certain 969.9
recognize 988.12

know a little 929.11

know for certain 969.9

know-how 927.1

knowing
noun wise 920.3
knowledge 927.1
adj intentional 380.8
experienced 413.28
cunning 415.12
intelligent 919.12
shrewd 919.15
wise 919.17
knowledgeable 927.15

knowingly intentionally
380.10
cunningly 415.13
intelligently 919.20
consciously 927.29

know it all 140.6

knowledge information
551.1
learning 570.1
intelligence 919.1
knowing 927.1

knowledgeable
specialized 865.5
knowing 927.15

known 927.26

known as 527.14

know not 929.11

know nothing 929.9

know-nothing
noun ignoramus 929.8
adj ignorant 929.12
discriminatory 979.12

know well know
551.15
master 570.9
know full well 927.13

know what's what
know backwards and
forwards 413.19
have all one's wits
about one 919.10
know well 927.13
distinguish between
943.6

know which is which
943.6

knuckle 799.4

knuckles 462.4

Kodak 714.11

kohl 1015.12

kooky odd 869.11
screwy 922.9
crazy 925.27
goofy 926.6

kop 237.4

kosher edible 8.33
clean 79.25
conformist 866.6

kudos praise 509.5
citation 646.4
repute 662.1

kyle 242.1

L acid 87.9
angle 278.2
stage 704.16
eleven 881.7

la 709.7

lab 739.6, 941.5

label
noun tag 517.13
name 527.3
heraldic device 647.2
class 808.2
kind 808.3
verb tag 517.20
name 527.11

generalize 863.9

labelling custom 373.1
generality 863.1

laboratory hospital
room 197.25
lab 739.6, 941.5

laborious industrious
330.22
toilsome 725.18
difficult 1012.17

laboriously
industriously 330.27
arduously 725.19
with difficulty 1012.28

labour
noun birth 1.1
occupation 724.1
task 724.2
work 725.4
verb give birth 1.3
be busy 330.10
endeavour 403.5
work 724.12, 725.12
flounder 916.15

labour camp 429.8

labour costs 626.3

laboured ornate 498.12
stiff 534.3
laborious 725.18
monotonous 848.15

labourer subject 432.7
worker 607.9, 726.2

labour force 726.2

labouring
noun interpretation
341.1
amplification 538.6
adj working 725.17

labour market 726.2

labour of love act of
kindness 143.7
costlessness 634.1

labour relations 727.1

labour-saving 635.6

labyrinth 798.2

labyrinthine deviative
164.7
distorted 265.10
curved 279.7
convolutional 281.6
grandiloquent 545.8
complex 798.4

lace
noun network 170.3
strip 271.4
verb whip 604.12
weave 740.6
adulterate 796.12
bind 799.9

laced netlike 170.11
woven 740.7

lacing network 170.3
corporal punishment
604.4
weaving 740.1
adulteration 796.3
foundation 900.6

lack
noun absence 222.1
indigence 619.2
deficiency 794.2
want 991.4
imperfection 1002.1
verb be poor 619.5
want 794.3, 991.7
fall short 910.2
be insufficient 991.8

lacking
adj absent 222.11
bereft 473.8
nonexistent 761.8
incomplete 794.4
short of 910.5
insufficient 991.9
wanting 991.13
imperfect 1002.4
prep absent 222.19

lacklustre
noun colourlessness
36.1
mediocrity 1004.1
dullness 1026.5
adj colourless 36.7
mediocre 1004.7
lustreless 1026.17

lack of food 515.2

lack of information
929.1

lack of interest 981.1

lack of respect 156.1

laconic
noun man of few
words 344.5
adj taciturn 344.9
concise 537.6

lacquer
noun blanket 295.12
verb colour 35.13
coat 295.24

lacquered 287.10

lactation humour 2.22
secretion 13.1
liquidity 1059.1

lactic 1059.5

lacy netlike 170.11
thin 270.16

lad guy 76.5
boy 302.5
stockman 1068.2

ladder 193.4

laddie 302.5

laden weighted 297.18
fraught 793.12

ladies 12.10

ladies' man beau
104.13
dandy 500.9
philanderer 562.12

ladle
noun container 195.1
verb dip 176.17

Lady 648.2

lady woman 77.5
Ms 77.8

basuco 87.6
ladylove 104.14
wife 563.8
aristocrat 607.4
noblewoman 608.6
good person 659.1

lady-in-waiting 577.8

ladylike feminine 77.13
well-bred 504.17
upper-class 607.10
noble 608.10

Ladyship 648.2

ladyship 608.9

lag
noun dawdling 175.3
slowing 175.4
delay 845.2
time constants
1040.11
verb lag behind 166.4
dawdle 175.8
dally 331.14
mistime 832.2
delay 845.8
fall short 910.2

lag behind lag 166.4
bring up the rear
217.8

Lager 228.29

lagging
noun dawdling 175.3
delay 845.2
adj dawdling 175.11
dilatory 845.17

lagoon 241.1

laid-back at ease
121.12
quiescent 173.12
negligent 340.10
leisurely 402.6
unstrict 426.5

laid low ill 85.55
low 274.7
worn-out 393.36

laid-out 262.9

laid up invalided 85.58
stored 386.14

lair den 228.26
dive 228.28
cave 284.5
hiding place 346.4
retreat 584.6, 1008.5

laird proprietor 470.2
nobleman 608.4

laissez-faire
noun inaction 329.1
neglect 340.1
noninterference 430.9
policy 609.4
capitalism 611.9
adj passive 329.6
negligent 340.10
conservative 852.8

laity 700.1

lake 241.1

Lake District 231.7

laker 241.2

lastly 819.12

last minute 845.1

last-minute hasty
401.9

later 845.18

last name 527.5

last out keep alive
306.10
stay with it 360.4
outlast 826.8

last rites last offices
309.4
unction 701.5

last stage 819.3

last stop 186.5

last straw straw that
breaks the camel's
back 135.3
immediate cause 885.3

Last Supper 701.7

last word meaning
518.1
rage 578.4
influence 893.1
acme of perfection
1001.3

last words 816.1

latch
noun fastening 799.3
verb close 293.6
hook 799.8

latch on to grab 472.9
seize 480.14

late
adj retarded 175.12
dead 307.30
former 836.10
recent 840.12
untimely 843.6
belated 845.16
adv behind 845.19

late arrival 845.6

late in the day 845.19

lately 840.16

lateness anachronism
832.1
subsequence 834.1
newness 840.1
untimeliness 843.1
tardiness 845.1

latent invisible 32.5
inert 173.14
secret 345.11
concealed 346.11
lurking 519.5

later
adj subsequent 834.4
future 838.8
recent 840.12
last-minute 845.18
adv subsequently
834.6
in the future 838.9

lateral
noun speech sound
524.13
adj side 218.6

sided 218.7
phonetic 524.31

laterally 218.8

lateral thinking 985.2

later than 834.8

latest present 837.2
state-of-the-art 840.14

latex elastic 1046.3
fluid 1059.2

lathe 857.10

lather
noun sweat 12.7
foam 320.2
verb wash 79.19
work oneself up
105.17
foam 320.5
clobber 412.9
beat up 604.14

Latin America 231.6

latitude room 158.3
map 159.5
zone 231.3
breadth 269.1
coordinates 300.5
scope 430.4
broad-mindedness
978.1

latter foregoing 836.11
recent 840.12

latter-day 840.13

latterly 840.16

lattice
noun network 170.3
frame 266.4
atomic cluster 1037.7
reactor 1037.13
verb net 170.7

laudable praiseworthy
509.20
good 998.12

lauded 247.9

lauder 509.8

laugh
noun laughter 116.4
joke 489.6
verb be pleased 95.11
exude cheerfulness
109.6
burst out laughing
116.8

laughable humorous
488.4
absurd 922.11

laugh at flout 454.4
ridicule 508.8

laughing
noun laughter 116.4
adj happy 95.15
cheerful 109.11

laughingly 109.19

laughter merriment
109.5
laughing 116.4

launch
noun motorboat 180.4

beginning 817.1
verb issue 352.14
propose 439.5
inaugurate 817.11
throw 903.10
start 903.13
project 1072.13

launcher 462.21

launching beginning
817.1
inauguration 817.5
innovation 851.4

launder 79.19

laundering laundry
79.6
manipulation 737.20

laundry laundering
79.6
washery 79.11

laureate
noun superior 249.4
champion 413.15
poet 720.11
adj honoured 646.9

laurel 646.3

laurels supremacy
249.3
victory 411.1
trophy 646.3

lava scoria 1019.16
rock 1057.1

lavatory latrine 12.10
bathing place 79.10
washbasin 79.12
bathroom 197.26

lavender 46.3

lavish
verb give 478.12
squander 486.3
adj liberal 485.4
prodigal 486.8
ornate 545.11
teeming 883.9
plentiful 990.7
superabundant 992.19

lavishly liberally 485.5
plentifully 990.9
superabundantly
992.24

Law 683.3

law rule 419.2, 868.4
decree 420.4
prohibition 444.1
lex 673.3
legal system 673.4
jurisprudence 673.7
game 745.3
axiom 973.2
cop 1007.16

law-abiding obedient
326.3
honest 644.13

law and order 464.2

law enforcement
1007.1

law firm 597.4

lawful permissible
443.15
just 649.8
legal 673.10
valid 972.14
genuine 972.15

lawfully permissibly
443.19
legally 673.12

lawless disobedient
327.8
licentious 418.5
illegal 674.6

lawlessness
disobedience 327.1
licentiousness 418.1
presumption 640.2
illegality 674.1

lawn 310.7

lawn tennis 749.1

lawsuit suit 598.1
accusation 599.1

lawyer barrister 597.1
professional 726.4

lax indolent 331.19
negligent 340.10
slack 426.4
lenient 427.7
unrestrained 430.24
nonrestrictive 430.25
permissive 443.14
phonetic 524.31
wanton 665.26
loose 803.5
dilatory 845.17
vague 970.19
inaccurate 974.17
flaccid 1045.10

laxative
noun cathartic 86.17
adj cathartic 86.48

lay
noun navigation 159.3
direction 161.1
air 708.4
song 708.14
bet 759.3
verb deposit 78.9,
159.14
relieve 120.5
place 159.12
lay aloft 182.48
lie 201.5
level 201.6
smooth 287.5
pacify 465.7
impose 643.4
moderate 670.6
exorcise 690.12
bet 759.25

lay at 459.15

lay by 405.11

lay claim to 421.6

lay down deposit
159.14
layer 296.5
affirm 334.5
give up 370.7

store 386.10
prescribe 420.9
pay over 624.15
bet 759.25
postulate 950.12

layer
noun thickness 296.1
verb lay down 296.5

layered 296.6

lay in 386.10

laying 759.1

layman laic 700.2
amateur 726.5

laymen 700.1

lay off take a rest 20.8
circumscribe 210.4
measure off 300.11
plot 381.10
cease to use 390.4
cease 856.6
knock off 856.8
dismiss 908.19

lay on establish 159.16
cover 295.19
coat 295.24
blame 599.8
whip 604.12

lay out form 262.7
measure off 300.11
waste 308.13
embalm 309.21
plot 381.10
spend 626.5
order 806.4

làyout form 262.1
plan 381.1
composition 548.2
roulette 759.12
order 806.1

lay to exert oneself
725.9
attribute to 887.4

lay up afflict 85.49
layer 296.5
store up 386.11

lazily 175.13

laziness slowness 175.1
indolence 331.5
carelessness 340.2

lazing 331.4

lazy
verb idle 331.12
adj slow 175.10
indolent 331.19
careless 340.11
dilatory 845.17

lea 310.8

leach
noun solution 1062.3
verb refine 79.22
exude 190.15
trickle 238.18
subtract 255.9
liquefy 1062.5
soak 1063.13

lead
noun leading 165.1

abandoned 370.8
adv leftward 220.6

left back 745.2

left field 220.1

left hand 220.1

left-hand left 220.4
bungling 414.20

left-handed insulting
156.8
oblique 204.13
southpaw 220.5
bungling 414.20

left-hander 220.3

left-hand side 220.1

leftist
noun progressive
611.15
adj progressive 611.27

left of centre 611.27

left-of-centre 220.4

left-out 772.7

leftover
noun surplus 992.5
adj remaining 256.7
surplus 992.18

leftovers remainder
256.1
surplus 992.5

left side 220.1

left wing left side
220.1
progressivism 611.3

left-wing left 220.4
progressive 611.27

left-winger left side
220.1
progressive 611.15

leg
noun member 2.7,
792.4
drumstick 10.22
limb 177.14
voyage 182.6
shank 273.6
verb walk 177.27

legacy bequest 478.10
inheritance 479.2
effect 886.1

legal permissible
443.15
recorded 549.17
just 649.8
legitimate 673.10
valid 972.14

legal action 598.1

legal adviser 597.1

legality permissibility
443.8
justice 649.1
legitimacy 673.1

legalized 443.15

legally permissibly
443.19
legitimately 673.12

legally binding 673.10

legal proceedings
598.1

legal process lawsuit
598.1
legality 673.1

legal profession 597.4

legal rights 430.2

legal system 673.4

legal tender 728.1

legation foreign office
576.7
commission 615.1
office 739.7

legend map 159.5
memory 662.7
mythology 678.14
history 719.1
tradition 841.2
caption 936.2

legendary fabricated
354.29
distinguished 662.16
mythic 678.15
historical 719.7
fictional 722.7
traditional 841.12
extraordinary 869.14
fictitious 985.21

leggings 5.18

leggy 272.16

legible 521.12

legion unit 461.21
throng 769.4
multitude 883.3

legions 461.22

legislate 673.8

legislation lawmaking
613.4
legalization 673.2
law 673.3

legislative legislatorial
613.10
legal 673.10

legislature council
423.1
legislative body 613.1
legislation 613.4

legitimacy authority
417.1
permissibility 443.8
justifiability 600.7
legality 673.1
genuineness 972.7

legitimate
verb authorize 443.11
legalize 673.8
adj permissible 443.15
justifiable 600.14
legal 673.10
dramatic 704.33
logical 934.20
valid 972.14
genuine 972.15

legitimately
permissibly 443.19
legally 673.12
genuinely 972.19

legitimation
authorization 443.3
legalization 673.2
inclusion 771.1

legless 88.33

leg of lamb 10.15

legs 2.7

leg spinner 747.2

leg up assist 449.2
opportunity 842.2
lift 911.2

lei 310.23

leisure
noun idleness 331.2
ease 402.1
pause 856.3
adj idle 331.18
leisured 402.5

leisurely
adj slow 175.10
unhurried 402.6
adv slowly 175.13
tardily 845.20

lemon
noun sour 67.2
adj yellow 43.4

lemony 67.5

lend loan 620.5
discount 728.27

lender 620.3

lending loaning 620.1
money market 728.16

lending rate lending
620.1
interest 623.3

length size 257.1
distance 261.1
longness 267.1
piece 267.2
extent 300.3

length and breadth
791.3

lengthen increase 251.4
prolong 267.6
protract 826.9
sustain 855.4

lengthened prolonged
267.8
protracted 826.11

lengthening
noun prolongation
267.4
protraction 826.2
continuance 855.1
adj increasing 251.8

length of time 826.3

lengthways 201.9

lengthwise 201.9

lengthy long 267.7
giant 272.16
wordy 538.12

leniency patience 134.1
considerateness 143.3
pity 145.1
unstrictness 426.2
modulation 670.2

lenient patient 134.9
considerate 143.16
pitying 145.7
unstrict 426.5
mild 427.7
permissive 443.14
tolerant 978.11

leniently 134.11

Leninism 611.6

Leninist
noun Communist
611.18
revolutionist 859.3
adj Communist 611.30
revolutionist 859.6

lens eye 2.9
glass 29.2

Lent fast day 515.3
penance 658.3

lent 620.6

lentil 310.4

Leo 311.22

leopard spectrum 47.6
big cat 311.22

leotard 5.9

leper 586.4

lesbian
noun homosexual
75.14
amazon 76.9
adj homosexual 75.29

lesbianism 75.10

lesion sore 85.36
trauma 85.37
pain 96.5

less
adj inferior 250.6
reduced 252.10
fewer 884.6
adv decreasingly
252.12
prep off 255.14
without 991.17

less and less 252.12

lessen relieve 120.5
decrease 252.6
reduce 252.7
subtract 255.9
extenuate 600.12
moderate 670.6

lessening
noun relief 120.1
decrease 252.1
deterioration 393.3
modulation 670.2
adj decreasing 252.11
mitigating 670.14

lesser inferior 250.6
reduced 252.10

lesson warning 399.1
reproof 510.5
teaching 568.7

lest 896.7

let
noun rental 615.6

softness 1045.1

lenient patient 134.9
considerate 143.16
pitying 145.7
unstrict 426.5
mild 427.7
permissive 443.14
tolerant 978.11

hindrance 1011.1
verb draw off 192.12
permit 443.9
rent 615.15
suppose 950.10
adj employed 615.20

let alone
verb leave alone 329.4
avoid 368.6
not use 390.5
abstain 668.7
adv additionally
253.11
prep with 253.12
excluding 772.10

let down
verb relax 20.7, 670.9
disappoint 132.2
deceive 356.14
deteriorate 393.16
adj discontented 108.7
disappointed 132.5

let go let pass 329.5
neglect 340.6
leave undone 340.7
cease to use 390.4
let oneself go 430.19
release 431.5, 475.4
acquit 601.4
make merry 743.24
disband 770.8
loosen 803.3
throw 903.10
dismiss 908.19
let out 908.24

let go of 912.7

lethal deadly 308.22
harmful 999.12

lethal injection 604.6

lethargic sleepy 22.21
apathetic 94.13
languid 331.20

lethargy sleepiness
22.1
stupor 22.6
apathy 94.4
languor 331.6
stupidity 921.3

let in 187.10, 585.7

let into 927.16

let it go
verb compose oneself
106.7
forget 148.5
dismiss 983.4
phrase no matter
997.25

let loose release 431.5
loose 431.6
make merry 743.24
throw 903.10

let off
verb release 431.5
acquit 601.4
explode 671.14
shoot 903.12
adj exempt 430.30

let on confess 351.7

sham 354.21
let out draw off 192.12
  lengthen 267.6
  disclose 351.4
  divulge 351.5
  release 431.5
  say 524.23
  dismiss 908.19
  give vent to 908.24
let rip 903.10
let slip let go 329.5
  neglect 340.6
  betray 351.6
  lose 473.4
  dismiss 983.4
letter
  noun representation
  349.1
  written character
  546.1, 547.9
  writing 547.10
  type 548.6
  message 552.4
  epistle 553.2
  accuracy 972.5
  verb initial 546.6
  adj epistolary 553.14
lettering initialling
546.5
  writing 547.1
  handwriting style
  547.4
letters writing system
546.3
  literature 547.12,
  718.1
  record 549.1
  scholarship 927.5
letter writer 553.8
letter writing 553.1
letting go 475.1
let up relax 20.7, 670.9
  decrease 252.6
  loosen 803.3
level
  noun floor 197.23
  horizontal 201.3
  plain 236.1
  degree 245.1
  rank 245.2
  smooth 287.3
  layer 296.1
  class 607.1, 808.2
  examination 937.2
  verb flatten 201.6
  smooth 287.5
  raze 395.19
  make uniform 780.4
  equalize 789.6
  fell 912.5
  adj horizontal 201.7
  straight 277.6
  smooth 287.9
  just 649.8
  uniform 780.5
  equal 789.7
  adv horizontally 201.9
level at 459.22
level-headed 670.13

levelling 395.5
level playing field
  justice 649.1
  fairness 649.3
  equality 789.1
  opportunity 842.2
  even chance 971.7
levels 530.2
lever
  noun instrument 384.4
  pry 905.4
  lifter 911.3
  verb get a purchase
  905.8
leverage trading 737.19
  influence 893.1
  fulcrumage 905.1
  mechanics 1038.1
Leviathan 311.30
leviathan ship 180.1
  behemoth 257.14
levitation ascent 193.1
  lightness 298.1
levy
  noun demand 421.1
  call to arms 458.8
  recruit 461.17
  attachment 480.5
  enlistment 615.7
  tax 630.9
  verb demand 421.5
  call to arms 458.19
  attach 480.20
  enlist 615.17
  charge 630.12
  impose 643.4
lewd lascivious 665.29
  obscene 666.9
lex 673.3
lexical semantic 518.12
  lexicologic 526.19
lexicon vocabulary
  526.13
  reference book 554.9
  dictionary 870.4
liabilities expenses
  626.3
  accounts 628.1
liability debt 623.1
  responsibility 641.2
  tendency 895.1
  susceptibility 896.2
  probability 967.1
  disadvantage 995.2
  exposure 1005.3
liable chargeable 623.9
  responsible 641.17
  likely 896.5
  probable 967.6
  exposed 1005.15
liable to
  adj subject to 896.6
  prep inclined to 895.6
liaise interpose 213.6
  be instrumental 384.7
liaise with 774.5
liaison love affair 104.6

intermediary 213.4
instrument 384.4
relation 774.1
joining 799.1
liar 357.9
libel
  noun monstrous lie
  354.12
  slander 512.3
  declaration 598.8
  verb slander 512.11
libellous 512.13
liberal
  noun left side 220.1
  free agent 430.12
  liberalist 978.6
  adj left 220.4
  nonrestrictive 430.25
  philanthropic 478.22
  free 485.4
  hospitable 585.11
  magnanimous 652.6
  extensive 863.13
  liberal-minded 978.9
  plentiful 990.7
Liberalism 609.25
liberalism
  noninterference 430.9
  libertarianism 430.10
  liberalness 978.2
liberalization 430.10
liberally freely 485.5
  magnanimously 652.8
  plentifully 990.9
liberate rescue 398.3
  liberalize 430.13
  free 431.4
  detach 801.10
  disembarrass 1013.9
liberated free 430.21
  freed 431.10
liberating benefitting
  592.4
  liberalizing 978.13
liberation escape 369.1
  rescue 398.1
  liberalism 430.10
  freeing 431.1
liberator 592.2
libertarian
  noun free agent 430.12
  liberal 978.6
  adj nonrestrictive
  430.25
  liberal 978.9
liberties 640.2
liberty holiday 20.3
  freedom 430.1
  exemption 430.8
  permission 443.1
  grant 443.5
  privilege 642.2
  opportunity 842.2
libido sexuality 75.2
  psyche 92.28
  desire 100.1
  love 104.1
  amorousness 104.3

instinct 933.2
librarian recorder
  550.1
  professional librarian
  558.3
  steward 574.4
library stacks 197.6
  storehouse 386.6
  preserve 397.7
  edition 554.5
  book depository 558.1
  collection 769.11
  retreat 1008.5
Library of Congress
  registry 549.3
  library 558.1
libretto playbook
  704.21
  score 708.28
licence lawlessness
  418.1
  freedom 430.1
  exemption 430.8
  permission 443.1
  permit 443.6
  commission 615.1
  presumption 640.2
  privilege 642.2
  profligacy 665.3
  confusion 809.2
licence fee 630.6
license authorize
  443.11
  commission 615.10
licensed exempt 430.30
  authorized 443.17
licensing 443.3
lichen 310.4
lick
  noun sip 62.2
  touch 73.1
  hint 248.4
  impromptu 708.27
  sock 901.5
  verb lap up 8.30
  taste 62.7
  lap 73.9
  clobber 412.9
  stump 970.14
licked 412.15, 970.26
licking eating 8.1
  larruping 604.5
lid eye 2.9, 27.9
  stopper 293.4
  cover 295.5
lido shore 234.2
  park 743.14
lie
  noun navigation 159.3
  direction 161.1
  falsehood 354.11
  round 748.3
  verb extend 158.8
  ride at anchor 182.16
  lie down 201.5
  be present 221.6
  tell a lie 354.19

live by one's wits
  645.11
lie back 20.7
Lied 708.14
lie down rest 20.6
  lie 201.5
  couch 912.11
liege
  noun subject 432.7
  master 575.1
  retainer 577.1
  adj subject 432.13
lie in give birth 1.3
  exist in 760.11
lie on rest on 900.22
  depend 958.6
  go hard with 1010.8
lieu location 159.1
  place 159.4
Lieutenant Field
  Marshal 575.20
  Admiral of the Fleet
  575.21
lieutenant subordinate
  432.5
  deputy 576.1
  assistant 616.6
  policeman 1007.15
Lieutenant-Colonel
  575.20
Lieutenant-General
  575.20
lie with copulate 75.21
  depend 958.6
Life 677.6
life animation 17.4
  energizer 17.6
  eagerness 101.1
  gaiety 109.4
  living 306.1
  person 312.5
  liveliness 330.2
  history 719.1
  existence 760.1
  something 762.3
  lifetime 826.5
  affairs 830.4
life after death
  hereafter 681.2
  destiny 838.2
life assurance 1007.4
lifeblood blood 2.23
  life force 306.3
lifeboat ship 180.1
  bolt-hole 369.3
  life jacket 397.6
  rescuer 398.2
life cycle 306.3
life expectancy age
  303.1
  life 306.1
  lifetime 826.5
life force animation
  17.4
  soul 306.3
  inner nature 766.5

life-giving reproductive 78.15
  animating 306.12

lifeguard rescuer 398.2
  guardian 1007.6

life jacket 397.6

lifeless dull 117.6
  inert 173.14
  dead 307.30
  languid 331.20
  lacklustre 1026.17
  inanimate 1053.5

lifelike descriptive 349.14
  speaking 783.16
  genuine 972.15

lifeline bolt-hole 369.3
  life jacket 397.6
  safeguard 1007.3

lifelong 826.13

lifer 429.11

life savings 728.14

life size 257.3

lifespan age 303.1
  life 306.1
  lifetime 826.5

life story 719.1

lifestyle behaviour 321.1
  preference 371.5
  custom 373.1
  mode 764.4
  speciality 865.1

life-support 900.1

life's work 724.6

life-threatening
  disease-causing 85.52
  deadly 308.22
  disastrous 1010.15

lifetime
  noun life 306.1, 826.5
  adj lifelong 826.13

lift
  noun kick 105.3
  ride 177.7
  lift ratio 184.26
  wave 238.14
  height 272.2
  improvement 392.1
  assist 449.2
  skiing 753.1
  boost 911.2
  lifter 911.3
  elevator 911.4
  verb elate 109.8
  transport 176.12
  billow 238.22
  imitate 336.5
  improve 392.9
  swipe 482.16
  pay in full 624.13
  elevate 911.5
  phrase people mover 176.5

lifted 911.9

lifting
  noun elevation 911.1

adj elevating 911.10

lift up inaugurate 817.11
  elevate 911.5
  focus on 936.3
  call attention to 982.10

ligament 271.2

light
  noun aspect 33.3
  beer 88.16
  lightning 174.6
  window 292.7
  dawn 314.3
  explanation 341.4
  information 551.1
  wave 915.4
  outlook 977.2
  lighter 1020.4
  candle power 1024.21
  light source 1025.1
  transparent substance 1028.2
  verb land 184.43
  get down 194.7
  ignite 1019.22
  grow light 1024.27
  illuminate 1024.28
  strike a light 1024.29
  adj frail 16.14
  soft-coloured 35.21
  fair 36.9
  whitish 37.8
  lighthearted 109.12
  thin 270.16
  shallow 276.5
  unheavy 298.10
  gentle 298.12
  airy 317.11
  fickle 364.6
  agile 413.23
  phonetic 524.31
  wanton 665.26
  comic 704.35
  superficial 921.20
  trivial 997.19
  easy 1013.13
  lightish 1024.31

light and shade 1024.19

light at the end of the tunnel desire 100.11
  solution 939.1

light-blue 45.3

light bulb 1025.1

light-coloured 36.9

lighted 1024.39

lighten disburden 120.7
  moderate 670.6
  grow light 1024.27
  illuminate 1024.28

lightened bleached 36.8
  eased 298.11
  illuminated 1024.39

lightening
  noun decoloration 36.3
  disburdening 120.3

easing 298.3
  modulation 670.2
  adj easing 298.16
  illuminating 1024.40

lighter
  noun light 1020.4
  verb haul 176.13

lighthearted 109.12

light heavyweight 297.3

lighthouse tower 272.6
  alarm 400.1
  marker 517.10

lighting
  noun ignition 1019.4
  illumination 1024.19
  adj inflammatory 1019.27
  illuminating 1024.40

light lunch 8.7

lightly cheerfully 109.17
  scarcely 248.9
  negligently 340.17
  capriciously 364.7
  unimportantly 997.23
  easily 1013.16

light middleweight 297.3

lightness frailty 16.2
  colour quality 35.6
  paleness 36.2
  whiteness 37.1
  lightheartedness 109.3
  thinness 270.4
  levity 298.1
  fickleness 364.3
  agility 413.2
  wantonness 665.4
  superficiality 921.7
  triviality 997.3
  luminousness 1024.3

lightning 174.6

light of day 1024.10

lights lungs 2.20
  instruments 704.18
  opinion 952.6

light show spectacle 33.7
  iridescence 47.2
  flicker 1024.8

light source light 1024.1
  illuminant 1024.20
  source of light 1025.1

lights-out 315.4

light touch touch 73.1
  lightness 298.1

light up excite 105.12
  cheer up 109.9
  ignite 1019.22
  illuminate 1024.28

lightweight
  noun weakling 16.6
  inferior 250.2
  runt 258.4
  bantamweight 297.3

stupid person 923.2
  nobody 997.7
  adj frail 16.14
  bantamweight 298.13
  uninfluential 894.3

light welterweight 297.3

light-years 261.1

likable tasty 63.8
  pleasant 97.6
  desirable 100.30
  endearing 104.25

like
  noun love 104.1
  likeness 783.3
  equal 789.4
  verb savour 63.5
  enjoy 95.12
  desire 100.14
  love 104.19
  adj approximate 774.8
  identical 777.7
  similar 783.10
  equal 789.7
  adv how 384.9
  similarly 783.18
  prep in imitation of 336.12

like a man pluckily 359.18
  courageously 492.23

like for like 506.3

like it is state of affairs 764.2
  what's what 972.4

likelihood possibility 965.1
  probability 967.1
  good chance 971.8

likely
  adj apt 787.10
  liable 896.5
  possible 965.6
  probable 967.6
  disposed 977.8
  expedient 994.5
  comely 1015.18
  adv probably 967.8

likely to
  adj liable to 896.6
  prep inclined to 895.6

like mad 247.23, 671.25

like-minded unanimous 332.15
  in accord 455.3
  agreeing 787.9

liken 942.4

likeness aspect 33.3
  image 349.5
  picture 712.11
  similarity 783.1
  like 783.3
  copy 784.1
  equality 789.1

like new 840.9

like no other 864.17

like that thus 765.10

similarly 783.18

like this thus 765.10
  similarly 783.18

like to 100.15

likewise
  adv additionally 253.11
  identically 777.9
  similarly 783.18
  exclam yeah 332.19

liking love 100.2, 104.1
  will 323.1
  tendency 895.1

lilac 46.3

lilt
  noun air 708.4
  song 708.14
  rhythm 709.22
  metre 720.7
  verb exude cheerfulness 109.6
  rejoice 116.5
  murmur 524.26
  sing 708.38

lilting melodious 708.48
  rhyming 720.17

lily alabaster 37.2
  mollycoddle 77.10

limb member 2.7, 792.4
  leg 177.14
  border 211.4
  brat 302.4
  branch 310.18
  lever 905.4

limber
  verb soften 1045.6
  adj pliant 1045.9

limbo place of confinement 429.7
  hell 682.1

lime
  noun alabaster 37.2
  sour 67.2
  snare 356.13
  verb trap 356.20
  hamper 1011.11

limelight 704.18

limestone 1057.1

limit
  noun last straw 135.3
  summit 198.2
  limitation 210.2
  boundary 211.3
  capacity 257.2
  end 793.5
  extremity 819.2
  verb restrict 210.5, 428.9
  bound 211.8
  narrow 270.11
  specialize 865.4
  qualify 958.3
  adj bordering 211.11

limitation limiting 210.2
  boundary 211.3

listlessly weakly 16.22
  apathetically 94.15
  unconcernedly 102.10
lists 463.1
lit fuddled 88.33
  illuminated 1024.39
litany 696.4
literacy 927.5
literal clear 521.11
  lettered 546.8
  orthodox 687.7
  genuine 972.15
  unimaginative 986.5
literally 972.21
literary belletristic
  547.24, 718.7
  book-learned 927.22
literary critic author
  547.15, 718.4
  critic 945.7
literary criticism
  exegetics 341.8
  Lit-Crit 723.3
  criticism 945.2
literate
  noun intellectual 928.1
  adj learned 927.21
literature advertising
  matter 352.8
  writing 547.10
  letters 547.12, 718.1
  lore 927.9
lithe 1045.9
litigation contention
  457.1
  lawsuit 598.1
  argumentation 934.4
litter
  noun fledgling 302.10
  bier 309.13
  rubbish 391.5
  young 561.2
  flock 769.5
  jumble 809.3
  multitude 883.3
  sofa 900.19
  bedding 900.20
  verb give birth 1.3
  disarrange 810.2
  tend 1068.7
littering 1.1
little
  noun short distance
  223.2
  modicum 248.2
  short time 827.3
  adj insignificant 248.6,
  997.17
  inadequate 250.7
  small 258.10
  short 268.8
  ungenerous 651.6
  base 661.12
  narrow-minded 979.10
  adv by degrees 245.6
  to a degree 245.7
  scarcely 248.9
  small 258.16

little at a time 245.6
little by little gradually
  175.14
  by degrees 245.6
  piece by piece 792.9
little chance 971.9
little fellow common
  man 606.5
  nobody 997.7
little finger 73.5
little known 661.14
little man common
  man 606.5
  nobody 997.7
little one 302.3
little ones 561.1
little people 561.1
little problem 1002.2
little thing 997.6
little while 827.3
lit up fuddled 88.33
  illuminated 1024.39
liturgical ritualistic
  701.18
  vocal 708.50
Liturgy 701.8
liturgy ceremony 580.4
  divine service 696.8
  rite 701.3
live
  verb inhabit 225.7
  be somebody 662.10
  exist 760.8
  endure 826.6
  adj living 306.11
  active 330.17
  burning 1018.27
  charged 1031.33
live alone be unmarried
  565.5
  seclude oneself 584.7
live by 437.9
lived-in 121.11
live down 658.4
live in 225.7
live-in interior 207.6
  resident 225.13
livelihood 449.3
liveliness animation
  17.4, 330.2
  zest 68.2
  passion 93.2
  eagerness 101.1
  gaiety 109.4
  life 306.1
  spirit 544.4
  elasticity 1046.1
lively
  adj energetic 17.13
  zestful 68.7
  fervent 93.18
  eager 101.8
  gay 109.14
  fast 174.15
  active 330.17
  spirited 544.12

interesting 982.19
  elastic 1046.7
  adv actively 330.25
liven energize 17.10
  cheer 109.7
liven up refresh 9.2
  energize 17.10
  stimulate 105.13
live on continue to exist
  760.9
  endure 826.6
  postexist 838.7
liver viscera 2.14
  digestion 2.15, 7.8
  kidneys 10.19
liver disease 85.23
liveried 5.44
livery wardrobe 5.2
  uniform 5.7
  insignia 647.1
live show 1034.2
livestock 311.1
live through win
  through 409.13
  endure 826.6
live together inhabit
  225.7
  cohabit 563.17
live up to observe
  434.2
  execute 437.9
live with endure 134.5
  keep an open mind
  978.7
live with it stay with it
  360.4
  submit 433.6
livid colourless 36.7
  black and blue 38.12
  grey 39.4
  blue 45.3
  purple 46.3
  angry 152.28
  deathly 307.29
living
  noun habitation 225.1
  life 306.1
  living and breathing
  306.4
  animal 311.2
  support 449.3
  benefice 698.9
  adj energetic 17.13
  resident 225.13
  organic 305.17
  alive 306.11
  existent 760.13
  lifelike 783.16
  burning 1018.27
living in 225.13
living quarters housing
  225.3
  quarters 228.4
living room 197.5
living space open space
  158.4
  abode 228.1

living thing 762.3
living together 225.1
lizard 311.25
load
  noun affliction 96.8
  lading 196.2
  quantity 247.3
  burden 297.7
  charge 462.16, 643.3
  portion 477.5
  full measure 793.3
  impediment 1011.6
  verb lade 159.15
  fill 196.7, 793.7
  burden 297.13
  tamper with 354.17
  prime 405.9
  shoot 903.12
  go hard with 1010.8
  computerize 1041.18
  phrase freight 176.6
loaded fuddled 88.33
  weighted 297.18
  prepared 405.16
  well-heeled 618.15
  fraught 793.12
  critical 842.10
loader 183.9
loading placement
  159.6
  burden 297.7
load of rubbish 520.2
loads lot 247.4
  bomb 618.3
loaf
  noun lump 257.10
  Eucharist 701.7
  brain 918.6
  verb idle 331.12
loaf of bread 10.27
loan
  noun advance 620.2
  verb lend 620.5
loaned 620.6
loath 325.6
loathe dislike 99.3
  hate 103.5
loathing
  noun hostility 99.2
  hate 103.1
  adj hating 103.7
loathsome offensive
  98.18
  terrible 999.9
  hideous 1014.11
lob
  noun throw 903.3
  verb play tennis 749.3
  throw 903.10
  elevate 911.5
lobbing 903.2
lobby
  noun vestibule 197.19
  parliamentary lobby
  609.32
  influence 893.6
  verb urge 375.14

lobbying inducement
  375.3
  political influence
  609.29
  backstairs influence
  893.3
lobbyist lobby 609.32
  influence 893.6
lobe ear 2.10
  pendant 202.4
  member 792.4
lobster 311.30
local
  noun bar 88.20
  train 179.14
  branch 617.10
  adj localized 231.9
  idiomatic 523.20
local anaesthetic 25.3
local authority 613.1
local election 609.15
local government
  612.4
locality location 159.1
  habitat 228.18
localized 231.9
local radio station
  1033.6
local time 831.3
locate situate 159.11
  settle 159.17
  discover 940.2
located 159.18
locating placement
  159.6
  discovery 940.1
location situation 159.1
  placement 159.6
  setting 704.19
  film studio 706.3
  state 764.1
  discovery 940.1
  farm 1067.8
loch lake 241.1
  inlet 242.1
Loch Ness monster
  311.30
lock
  noun tress 3.5
  standstill 173.3
  floodgate 239.11
  bolt 428.5
  half nelson 474.3
  fastening 799.3
  verb close 293.6
  agree 787.6
  hook 799.8
  obstruct 1011.12
locked in 1034.16
locked up 429.21
locker storehouse 386.6
  treasury 729.12
  cold storage 1023.6
lock in enclose 212.5
  imprison 429.14
  retain 474.5

ascend 193.8
bulk 247.5
threaten 514.2
weave 740.6
come 838.6
be imminent 839.2

loomed 740.7

looming
noun mirage 975.6
adj ominous 133.17
imminent 839.3

loom large show 31.4
loom 247.5

loon 925.16

loony
noun nut 925.16
adj screwy 922.9
crazy 925.27

loop
noun spiral loop
184.16
circle 280.2
bulge 283.3
circuit 913.2
verb stunt 184.40
encircle 209.7
curve 279.6
weave 740.6

loophole outlet 190.9
way out 369.4
condition 958.2

loopy screwy 922.9
crazy 925.27
kooky 926.6

loose
noun freedom 430.1
verb loosen 431.6,
803.3
relax 670.9
detach 801.10
facilitate 1013.7
adj adrift 182.61
drooping 202.10
negligent 340.10
escaped 369.11
lax 426.4
free 430.21
unrestrained 430.24
ungrammatic 531.4
discursive 538.13
informal 581.3
wanton 665.26
unfastened 801.22
slack 803.5
slovenly 809.15
illogical 935.11
vague 970.19
inaccurate 974.17
flaccid 1045.10

loose ends slipshodness
340.3
nonaccomplishment
408.1

loose forward 746.2

loosely 340.17

loosen loose 431.6
relax 670.9
detach 801.10
slacken 803.3

soften 1045.6

loosened 801.22

looseness neglect 340.1
laxness 426.1
informality 581.1
wantonness 665.4
slackness 803.2
slovenliness 809.6
vagueness 970.4
inaccuracy 974.2
flaccidity 1045.3

loosening
noun laxness 426.1
modulation 670.2
adj softening 1045.16

loosen up amuse
743.21
amuse oneself 743.22

loot
noun booty 482.11
dough 728.2
verb seize 480.14
plunder 482.17
rage 671.11

looting
noun rapacity 480.9
plundering 482.6
unruliness 671.3
adj plunderous 482.22

lop
noun wave 238.14
rough 288.2
verb hang 202.6
excise 255.10
adj drooping 202.10

lopped 794.5

lopsided distorted
265.10
unbalanced 790.5

loquacious 540.9

Lord 648.2

lord proprietor 470.2
master 575.1
nobleman 608.4

Lord Advocate 596.4

Lord Chief Justice
596.4

Lord Justice 596.4

lord mayor 575.17

Lordship 648.2

lordship supremacy
249.3
mastership 417.7
ownership 469.2
ladyship 608.9

Lord's Prayer 696.4

lore mythology 678.14
tradition 841.2
body of knowledge
927.9
superstition 953.3

Lorelei 377.4

lorry 179.12

lorry driver
noun driver 178.10
phrase carrier 176.7

lose fail 410.9
lose out 412.12
incur loss 473.4
waste 486.4
forget 989.5

lose it 128.8

lose one 522.10

lose out get left 410.10
lose 412.12, 473.4
fall short 910.2

loser flop 410.2
non-starter 410.8
defeatee 412.5
loss 473.1
insolvent 625.4

lose sight of neglect
340.6
disregard 435.3
forget 989.5

losing
noun loss 473.1
adj winning 757.6
speculative 759.27

loss disappearance 34.1
decrement 252.3
impairment 393.1
losing 473.1
disadvantage 995.2

losses 473.3

loss of life 307.1

lost
noun evil spirits 680.1
adj gone 34.5, 473.7
past hope 125.15
unwon 412.13
wasted 486.9
irreclaimable 654.18
unregenerate 695.18
bewildered 970.24
abstracted 984.11
forgotten 989.8

lost cause 125.8

lost in 982.17

lost to insensible 94.10
lost 473.7
inaccessible 966.9

lot
noun plot 231.4
amount 244.2
lots 247.4
real estate 471.6
portion 477.5
film studio 706.3
share 738.3
state 764.1
bunch 769.7
all 791.3
kind 808.3
make 892.4
fate 963.2
chance 971.1
verb allot 477.9
gamble 759.23
adv greatly 247.15

lotion toilet water 70.3
cleanser 79.17
balm 86.11
ointment 1054.3

lots lot 247.4
real estate 471.6
multitude 883.3
plenty 990.2

lotto 759.15

loud
adj intense 15.22
garish 35.19
loud-sounding 53.11
demanding 421.9
coarse 497.11
gaudy 501.20
adv loudly 53.14

loud and clear
adj affirmative 334.8
clear 521.11
adv affirmatively
334.10

loudly strongly 15.23
aloud 53.14
affirmatively 334.10
demandingly 421.11

loudspeaker 50.8

lough 241.1

lounge
noun parlour 197.5
anteroom 197.20
verb rest 20.6
lie 201.5
idle 331.12

lounging
noun recumbency
201.2
idling 331.4
adj recumbent 201.8

louse vermin 311.35
arsehole 660.6

lousy infested 909.11
punk 999.8

lout mischief-maker
322.3
bungler 414.8
simple soul 416.3
vulgarian 497.6
oaf 923.5

Louvre 386.9

louvre 239.13

lovable desirable
100.30
endearing 104.25

Love Cupid 104.8
Mind 677.6

love
noun sexuality 75.2
liking 100.2
affection 104.1
sweetheart 104.10
benevolence 143.4
accord 455.1
regards 504.8
darling 562.6
friendship 587.1
game 749.2
ardour 1018.2
verb savour 63.5
have deep feelings
93.12
enjoy 95.12

desire 100.14
be fond of 104.19

love affair 104.6

love at first sight
104.4

lovebirds 104.18

loved 104.24

loved one sweetheart
104.10
corpse 307.16

love interest 93.9

loveless unloved 99.10
undesirous 102.8

love-life 75.2

loveliness
delightfulness 97.2
loveableness 104.7
beauty 1015.1

lovelock 3.5

lovelorn unloved 99.10
loving 104.27

lovely delightful 97.7
endearing 104.25
beautiful 1015.17

lovely time 743.2

lovemaking sexuality
75.2
copulation 75.7
love 104.1
dalliance 562.1

love of God 692.1

lover desirer 100.12
admirer 104.12
darling 562.6
friend 588.1
supporter 616.9

lovesick 104.27

love to 100.15

loving lovesome 104.27
kind 143.13
careful 339.10
almighty 677.17

loving care 339.1

lovingly fondly 104.32
carefully 339.15

low
noun weather map
317.4
business cycle 731.9
price 738.9
gear 1039.5
verb cry 60.2
adj faint 52.16
deep 54.10
dejected 112.22
humble 137.10
insignificant 248.6
inferior 250.6
short 268.8
unelevated 274.7
dying 307.33
base 497.15, 661.12
disapproving 510.21
phonetic 524.31
inelegant 534.2
populational 606.8
cheap 633.7

wicked 654.16
vulgar 666.8
depressed 912.12
adv faintly 52.21
near the ground 274.9
low blood pressure
85.9
low-cut 6.13
low-down 927.1
lowdown 972.4
lower
noun scowl 110.9
gloom 1026.4
verb look sullen
110.15
sadden 112.18
forebode 133.11
abase 137.5
redden 152.14
sink 194.6
reduce 252.7
debase 274.6
deepen 275.8
excavate 284.15
demote 447.3
threaten 514.2
cheapen 633.6
be imminent 839.2
depress 912.4
grow dark 1026.12
adj inferior 250.6,
274.8
reduced 252.10
lower class people
606.1
lower classes 607.7
lower-class 607.10
lower classes 607.7
lowered humbled
137.13
reduced 252.10
low 274.7
depressed 912.12
lowering
noun sinkage 194.2
decrease 252.1
deepening 275.7
cheapening 633.4
depression 912.1
gloom 1026.4
adj sullen 110.24
ominous 133.17
overhanging 202.11
threatening 514.3
imminent 839.3
gloomy 1026.14
lower middle class
607.5
lower orders 607.7
lowest humble 137.10
bottom 199.7
least 250.8
lower 274.8
reduced 633.9
lowest point 274.4
low grade 1004.4
low-grade 1004.9
low key 139.3

low-key 344.10
lowland
noun plain 236.1
lowlands 274.3
adj rustic 233.6
lowlands South 231.7
country 233.1
plain 236.1
lowland 274.3
low-level 274.7
lowly disliked 99.9
humble 137.10
inferior 250.6
populational 606.8
low-lying rustic 233.6
low 274.7
low-pressure 317.12
low price 633.2
low priority 997.1
low-priority 997.16
low profile distinctness
31.2
inconspicuousness
32.2
reserve 139.3
low-profile 32.6
low quality 1004.4
low-quality 1004.9
low-rent worthless
391.11
measly 997.18
lousy 999.8
inferior 1004.9
low season journey
177.5
season 313.1
low self-esteem 139.2
low temperature
1022.1
low tide tide 238.13
low water 274.2
low voice 52.4
low water tide 238.13
low tide 274.2
loyal zealous 101.9
obedient 326.3
firm 359.12
persevering 360.8
observant 434.4
faithful 644.20
loyalist 609.27
loyally obediently
326.6
perseveringly 360.9
faithfully 644.25
loyalty zeal 101.2
firmness 359.2
perseverance 360.1
duty 641.1
fidelity 644.7
lubricant
noun smoother 287.4
lubricator 1054.2
adj lubricating
1054.10

lubricated fuddled
88.33
slippery 287.11
lubricating
noun facilitation
1013.5
lubrication 1054.6
adj lubricant 1054.10
lubrication 1054.6
lucid clear 521.11
elegant 533.6
sane 924.4
light 1024.31
transparent 1028.4
translucent 1029.5
lucidity distinctness
31.2
clearness 521.2
elegance 533.1
sanity 924.1
lightness 1024.3
transparency 1028.1
translucence 1029.2
Lucifer 1070.4
lucifer 1020.5
Luck 971.2
luck gamble 759.2
uncertainty 970.1
chance 971.1
luckily auspiciously
133.21
fortunately 1009.16
luckless 1010.14
lucky auspicious 133.18
speculative 759.27
timely 842.9
chance 971.15
fortunate 1009.14
lucrative gainful
472.16
paying 624.21
ludicrous humorous
488.4
absurd 922.11
ludicrously 488.7
luff
noun sail 180.14
verb sail near the wind
182.25
lug
noun ear 2.10
verb pull 904.4
luggage
noun container 195.1
impedimenta 471.3
phrase freight 176.6
lugubrious sorrowful
112.26
pessimistic 125.16
Luke 684.2
luke 1018.24
lukewarm unfeeling
94.9
indifferent 102.6
nonreligious 695.15
warm 1018.24
lull

noun respite 20.2
silence 51.1
calm 173.5
inactivity 331.1
interruption 812.2
interim 825.1
pause 856.3
verb relieve 120.5
quiet 173.8
calm 670.7
lullaby 22.10
lulu 998.7
lumbar 217.10
lumber
noun impediment
1011.6
wood 1052.3
verb plod 175.7
stroll 177.28
burden 297.13
bungle 414.11
hamper 1011.11
lumbered 643.8
lumbering
noun walking 177.8
forestry 1067.3
adj slow 175.10
bulky 257.19
bungling 414.20
stiff 534.3
lumberjack 1067.7
luminaries 662.9
luminosity 1024.3
luminous clear 521.11
almighty 677.17
luminant 1024.30
illuminated 1024.39
lump
noun clump 257.10
bulge 283.3
swelling 283.4
bonehead 414.9
print 517.7
accumulation 769.9
piece 792.3
solid 1043.6
verb thicken 1043.10
lumped 769.21
lumpen
noun underprivileged
606.4
adj countrified 233.7
idle 331.18
base 661.12
slovenly 809.15
lump sum 728.13
lumpy bulky 257.19
formless 263.4
gnarled 288.8
nappy 294.7
thickened 1043.14
Luna 1070.12
lunacy foolishness
922.1
insanity 925.1
lunar crescent-shaped
279.11

celestial 1070.25
lunatic
noun fool 923.1
madman 925.15
adj insane 925.26
lunch
noun breakfast 8.6
verb dine 8.21
lunch break 20.2
luncheon 8.6
lunch hour 20.2
lung
noun viscera 2.14
adj respiratory 2.30
lunge
noun thrust 459.3
verb stroll 177.28
lungs viscera 2.14
bellows 2.20
lurch
noun gait 177.12
bias 204.3
swing 915.6
flounder 916.8
verb stroll 177.28
pitch 182.55
tumble 194.8
oscillate 915.10
flounder 916.15
lurching irregular
850.3
swinging 915.17
lure
noun snare 356.13
incentive 375.7
charm 377.3
attractor 906.2
verb trap 356.20
induce 375.22
allure 377.5
attract 906.4
lurid garish 35.19
colourless 36.7
brown 40.3
red 41.6
sensational 105.32
deathly 307.29
gaudy 501.20
grandiloquent 545.8
obscene 666.9
lurk couch 346.9
be latent 519.3
lurking in hiding
346.14
latent 519.5
imminent 839.3
luscious tasty 63.8
oversweet 66.5
delectable 97.10
lush
noun drunk 88.12
verb booze 88.25
adj tasty 63.8
luxuriant 310.40
ornate 545.11
productive 889.9
lust

noun sexual desire 75.5
craving 100.6
greed 100.8
will 323.1
lasciviousness 665.5
verb lust after 75.20
desire 100.14

lust for 100.16

lustful prurient 75.26
desirous 100.21
lascivious 665.29

lustre
noun polish 287.2
illustriousness 662.6
moment 823.2
gorgeousness 1015.6
shine 1024.2
chandelier 1025.6
verb polish 287.7
shine 1024.23

lustrous illustrious 662.19
luminous 1024.30
shiny 1024.33

lusty strong 15.15
energetic 17.13
hale 83.12
corpulent 257.18

Lutheran 675.28

lux 1024.21

luxuriant flourishing 310.40
ornate 498.12, 545.11
productive 889.9
plentiful 990.7

luxuries 121.3

luxurious delightful 97.7
comfortable 121.11
ornate 498.12
grandiose 501.21
wealthy 618.14
expensive 632.11
sensual 663.5

luxuriously delightfully 97.13
comfortably 121.14
grandiosely 501.28
expensively 632.15

luxury pleasure 95.1
delightfulness 97.2
grandeur 501.5
sensuality 663.1
superfluity 992.4
prosperity 1009.1

luxury goods 735.1

lyceum hall 197.4
middle school 567.4

Lycra 1046.3

lying
noun recumbency 201.2
lowness 274.1
untruthfulness 354.8
adj recumbent 201.8
untruthful 354.34

lying down 274.1

lying-in 1.1

lying in wait 346.14

lying to 182.71

lymph 2.22

lymphatic
noun duct 2.21
adj circulatory 2.31
secretory 13.7
languid 331.20

lynch kill 308.12
hang 604.17

lynx eagle 27.11
big cat 311.22

Lyon 575.22

lyric melodious 708.48
vocal 708.50

lyrical melodious 708.48
poetic 720.15

lyrically 720.18

lyricism 708.13

lyricist composer 710.20
poet 720.11

lyse 395.10

M Mister 76.7
big M 87.13
thousand 881.10

ma 560.12

macabre terrible 127.30
deathly 307.29
weird 987.9

macaroni noodles 10.32
dandy 500.9

mace sceptre 417.9
insignia 647.1

Mach 174.2

Machiavelli 357.1

Machiavellian
noun deceiver 357.1
schemer 381.7
Machiavel 415.8
strategist 610.6
adj falsehearted 354.31
scheming 381.13
cunning 415.12

machine
noun automobile 179.9
political party 609.24
association 617.1
philosopher's stone 857.10
machinery 1039.3
computer 1041.2
verb process 891.9
tool 1039.9

machined 891.18

machine gun
noun gun 462.10
adj constant 846.5

machinegun 308.17

machinery
instrumentality 384.3

equipment 385.4
enginery 1039.3
mechanism 1039.4

machine tool 1039.1

machismo male sex 76.2
courage 492.1

macho virile 76.12
courageous 492.17

mackerel 47.6

macro 257.20

mad
noun anger 152.5
verb madden 925.24
adj frenzied 105.25
sore 152.30
reckless 493.8
turbulent 671.18
foolish 922.8
insane 925.26
rabid 925.30

mad about 101.11

madam mistress 575.2
procurer 665.18

madame Ms 77.8
Mistress 648.4

madcap
noun humourist 489.12
daredevil 493.4
adj foolhardy 493.9

mad cow disease 85.40

madden excite 105.12
enrage 152.25
antagonize 589.7
dement 925.24

maddening 105.30

madder 41.4

mad dog 593.3

made formative 262.9
successful 409.14
produced 891.17
man-made 891.18

made for 413.29

made homeless 160.10

mademoiselle Ms 77.8
girl 302.6

made of 795.4

made out of 795.4

made public published 352.17
reported 552.15

made sure 969.20

made to measure 891.18

made to order 891.18

made-up fabricated 354.29
invented 891.19
beautifying 1015.22

made up of 795.4

madly frenziedly 105.35

violently 247.23, 671.25
recklessly 493.11
turbulently 671.26
insanely 925.35

madman 925.15

madness fury 105.8
foolishness 922.1
insanity 925.1

Madonna 679.5

Maelstrom 238.12

maelstrom eddy 238.12
bustle 330.4
whirl 914.2
agitation 916.1

maestro teacher 571.1
musician 710.1

Mae West 397.6

Mafia underworld 660.11
illicit business 732.1

Mafioso 732.4

magazine
noun storehouse 386.6
armoury 462.2
adj periodical 555.1

Magdalen 113.5

magenta 46.3

maggot alabaster 37.2
larva 302.12
insect 311.31
caprice 364.1
quirk 926.2
figment of the imagination 985.5

magic
noun illustriousness 662.6
sorcery 690.1
illusoriness 975.2
adj illustrious 662.19
sorcerous 690.14

magical illustrious 662.19
sorcerous 690.14
miraculous 869.16

magically 247.20

magic circle circle 280.2
ghost dance 690.3

magician trickster 357.2
master 413.13
mage 690.6
entertainer 707.1
illusoriness 975.2

magic wand 691.6

magisterial dignified 136.12
lordly 141.11
chief 249.14
skilful 413.22
imperious 417.16
jurisdictional 594.6
authoritative 969.18

magistrate arbitrator 466.4
executive 574.3
minister 575.17
judge 596.1

magma compound 796.5
rock 1057.1

magnanimity ambition 100.10
forgiveness 148.1
glory 247.2
liberality 485.1
magnanimousness 652.2
tolerance 978.4

magnanimous
forgiving 148.6
eminent 247.9
liberal 485.4
tolerant 978.11

magnate nobleman 608.4
businessman 730.1
personage 996.8

magnet
noun desire 100.11
focus 208.4
artificial magnet 906.3
verb attract 906.4

magnetic influential 893.13
attracting 906.5
engrossing 982.20
electromagnetic 1031.30

magnetism desirability 100.13
allurement 377.1
influence 893.1
attraction 906.1
magnetic attraction 1031.7

magnification
aggravation 119.1
intensification 251.2
expansion 259.1
exaggeration 355.1
praise 509.5
glorification 662.8, 696.2

magnificence grandeur 501.5
superexcellence 998.2

magnificent eminent 247.9
grandiose 501.21
superb 998.15

magnificently intensely 247.20
grandiosely 501.28
superbly 998.23

magnified aggravated 119.4
increased 251.7
exaggerated 355.4
eminent 662.18

magnify aggravate 119.2

intensify 251.5
enlarge 259.4
exaggerate 355.3
praise 509.12
glorify 662.13, 696.11

magnitude quantity
244.1
greatness 247.1
size 257.1
star 1070.8

magnox 1037.10

magpie bird of ill omen
133.6
chatterer 540.4
collector 769.15

magus 690.6

mahatma master
413.13
holy man 659.6
occultist 689.11
wise man 920.1

Mahdi 574.6

mahogany
noun smooth 287.3
adj reddish-brown
40.4

maid
noun girl 302.6
home help 577.8
verb serve 577.13

maiden
noun girl 302.6
scaffold 605.5
adj childish 301.11
unmarried 565.7
first 817.17
new 840.7

maidenhead 565.1

maiden name 527.5

mail
noun plumage 3.19
shell 295.15
armour 460.3
post 553.4
verb send 176.15
post 553.12

mailbag 553.6
mailbox 553.6
mailed 460.13
mailer 353.6
mailing 553.1
mailing list 553.4
mail-order 553.14
maim disable 19.9
injure 393.13
cripple 393.14
maimed 393.30
main
noun continent 235.1
water main 239.7
adj great 247.6
chief 249.14
first 817.17
paramount 996.24
main attraction
cinema 706.1

feature 996.7
main body 791.6
main course 895.2
main feature 865.2
main features 211.2
main force power 18.1
force 424.2
main interest 865.1
mainland
noun continent 235.1
adj continental 235.6
mainline
verb use 87.21
adj tending 895.4
mainly chiefly 249.17
on the whole 791.14
first 817.18
generally 863.17
normally 868.10
main man 588.4
main point summary
557.2
topic 936.1
salient point 996.6
mains 1067.8
mainstay
noun supporter 616.9,
900.2
verb support 900.21
mainstream
noun trend 895.2
adj tending 895.4
maintain affirm 334.5
provide 385.7
preserve 397.8
insist 421.8
support 449.12,
900.21
retain 474.5
defend 600.10
treat 624.19
endure 826.6
sustain 855.4
think 952.11
maintained 900.24
maintaining 900.23
maintenance
reparation 396.6
preservation 397.1,
852.2
support 449.3, 900.1
retention 474.1
subsidy 478.8
treat 624.8
durability 826.1
continuance 855.1
main thing 996.6
maire 575.17
maisonette 228.13
majestic dignified
136.12
eminent 247.9
sovereign 417.17
grandiose 501.21
lofty 544.14
almighty 677.17

majestically dignifiedly
136.14
grandiosely 501.28
Majesty 648.2
majesty proud bearing
136.2
glory 247.2
sovereignty 417.8
grandeur 501.5
loftiness 544.6
potentate 575.8
Major 575.20
major
noun adult 304.1
senior 304.5
study 568.8
key 709.15
adj older 841.19
important 996.17
Major-General 575.20
major in study to be
570.15
specialize 865.4
majority
noun maturity 303.2
dead 307.17
masses 606.2
returns 609.21
major part 791.6
plurality 882.2
adj most 882.9
major part 791.6
make
noun form 262.1
structure 266.1
yield 472.5
receipts 627.1
composition 795.1
kind 808.3
making 892.4
disposition 977.3
verb go 177.19
sail for 182.35
arrive 186.6
flow 238.16
act 328.4
do 328.6
perform 328.9
make up 405.7
accomplish 407.4
compel 424.4
execute 437.9
acquire 472.8
compose 795.3
convert 857.11
cause 885.10
produce 891.8
imagine 985.14
make a comeback
396.20
make a decision
945.11
make a fortune 618.10
make a fuss 330.12
make amends
compensate 338.4
make restitution 481.5
requite 506.5

repay 624.11
atone 658.4
make a mistake
974.13
make a move race
757.5
make a beginning
817.8
make an appearance
348.7
make an impression
be heard 48.12
impress 93.15, 930.19
be remembered
988.14
make a note 549.15
make a point of
resolve 359.7
contend for 457.20
make conditional
958.4
make arrangements
381.8
make a speech 543.9
make a statement
announce 352.12
state 524.24
make a success 409.10
make at 182.35
make available
provide 385.7
give 478.12
make believe 354.21
make-believe
noun figment of the
imagination 985.5
adj spurious 354.26
fictitious 985.21
make better 396.15
make certain 969.11
make clear explain
341.10
manifest 348.5
make it clear 521.6
facilitate 1013.7
make concessions
468.2
make contact with
343.8
make do 994.4
make do with
substitute 861.4
originate 891.12
make ends meet
support oneself 385.12
economize 635.4
make for head for
161.9
be useful 449.17
make friends with
587.10
make fun 489.13
make fun of 489.13
make good compensate
338.4

come through 409.10
observe 434.2
make restitution 481.5
grow rich 618.10
repay 624.11
meet an obligation
641.11
keep faith 644.9
complete 793.6
prove 956.10
be prosperous 1009.9
make it arrive 186.6
make good 409.10
manage 409.12
live on 838.7
make it clear 521.6
make it up 481.5
make love copulate
75.21
procreate 78.8
bill and coo 562.14
make money 472.12
make much of be
enthusiastic 101.7
exaggerate 355.3
praise 509.12
value 996.13
make music 708.39
make no difference
not matter to 102.5
be useless 391.8
make no mistake
969.11
make of 341.10
make one marry
563.14
identify 777.5
combine 804.3
unify 871.5
make out see 27.12
copulate 75.21
support oneself 385.12
manage 409.12
execute 437.9
perceive 521.9
write 547.19
record 549.15
neck 562.15
persist 855.5
know 927.12
solve 939.2
detect 940.5
prove 956.10
recognize 988.12
make shift 994.4
make over transfer
176.10, 629.3
convert 857.11
make peace cease
hostilities 465.9
settle 466.7
gain influence 893.12
make-peace 466.5
make progress
progress 162.2
improve 392.7
prosper 1009.7
make public 352.11

maker artist 716.1
poet 720.11
doer 726.1
skilled worker 726.6
author 885.4
producer 891.7
make room 292.13
make room for 958.5
make sense be
understandable 521.4
be reasonable 934.17
make sense of 341.10
makeshift
noun improvisation 365.5
substitute 861.2
expedient 994.2
adj extemporaneous 365.12
unprepared 406.8
substitute 861.8
makeshifty 994.7
imperfect 1002.4
make small 258.9
make something of 521.7
make sure take
precautions 494.6
make certain 969.11
play safe 1006.3
make sure of persuade oneself 375.24
convince oneself 952.19
make sure 969.11
make the best of 387.15
make the grade 409.12
make the most of take advantage of 387.15
excel 998.11
make the most of it 134.7
make time 174.8
make trouble 809.10
make up fabricate 354.18
improvise 365.8
get up 405.7
arrange 437.8
compose 548.16, 795.3
shuffle 758.4
assemble 769.18
complete 793.6
produce 891.8
originate 891.12
beautify 1015.15
makeup form 262.1
structure 266.1
design 554.12
property 704.17
mode 764.4
nature 766.4
composition 795.1
order 806.1
disposition 977.3

cosmetics 1015.12
make up for
compensate 338.4
make restitution 481.5
repay 624.11
atone 658.4
equalize 789.6
make up for lost time
progress 162.2
hustle 330.13
improve 392.7
make haste 401.5
make up to curry favour 138.9
head for 161.9
communicate with 343.8
repay 624.11
make use of use 387.10
avail oneself of 387.14
exploit 387.16
appropriate 480.19
adopt 621.4
make war 458.14
make way gather way 182.21
make an opening 292.13
make way for avoid 164.6, 368.6
substitute 861.4
facilitate 1013.7
make with 725.8
making
noun reproduction 78.1
forming 262.5
structure 266.1
acquisition 472.1
production 891.1, 891.2
make 892.4
adj almighty 677.17
making good 481.2
making out 562.2
makings 472.3
making up forming 262.5
atonement 658.1
making use of 387.8
malady 85.1
malaise pain 26.1
disease 85.1
unpleasure 96.1
discontent 108.1
dejection 112.3
anxiety 126.1
nervousness 128.1
agitation 916.1
malaria miasma 1000.4
vapour 1065.1
malarial 85.60
male
noun male being 76.4
adj masculine 76.11

male bonding
camaraderie 582.2
fellowship 587.2
male chauvinist 979.5
maleness sex 75.1
masculinity 76.1
maturity 303.2
male sex 76.2
male sexuality 76.2
malevolence hate 103.1
ill will 144.4
hostility 589.3
badness 999.1
malevolent
noun evildoer 593.1
adj ill-disposed 144.19
hostile 589.10
bad 999.7
harmful 999.12
malfunction
noun impairment 393.1
abortion 410.5
wrong 638.1
fault 1002.2
verb get out of order 393.25
malice hate 103.1
maliciousness 144.5
hostility 589.3
malicious maleficent 144.20
hostile 589.10
maliciously 144.30
malign
verb defame 512.9
adj poisonous 82.7
malicious 144.20
deadly 308.22
savage 671.21
harmful 999.12
malignant poisonous 82.7
anaemic 85.60
malicious 144.20
deadly 308.22
hostile 589.10
savage 671.21
harmful 999.12
mall path 383.2
marketplace 736.2
workplace 739.1
malleable docile 433.13
teachable 570.18
changeable 853.6
conformable 866.5
influenceable 893.15
foolable 922.12
handy 1013.15
pliant 1045.9
mallet chisel 715.4
tool 1039.1
malnutrition 991.6
malpractice misuse 389.1
mismanagement 414.6

wrong 638.1
wrongdoing 655.1
maltreatment 389.2
mam 560.12
mama 560.12
mammal 311.3
mammalian pectoral 283.19
vertebrate 311.39
mammoth
noun behemoth 257.14
pachyderm 311.4
adj large 247.7
huge 257.20
mammy mum 560.12
nurse 1007.8
man
noun mankind 76.3
male 76.4
beau 104.13
hanger-on 138.6
adult 304.1
humankind 312.1
person 312.5
hero 492.8
husband 563.7
manservant 577.4
follower 616.8
chessman 743.17
verb equip 385.8
fortify 460.9
mana power 18.1
gods 678.1
manage pilot 182.14
perform 328.9
support oneself 385.12
use 387.10
treat 387.12
accomplish 407.4
contrive 409.12
direct 573.8
govern 612.12
economize 635.4
persist 855.5
operate 888.5
make shift 994.4
tend 1068.7
manageable governable 433.14
cheap 633.7
workable 888.10
handy 1013.15
management
supremacy 249.3
performance 328.2
usage 387.2
utilization 387.8
direction 573.1
executive 574.3
directorate 574.11
authorities 575.15
government 612.1
thrift 635.1
operation 888.1
protectorship 1007.2
management consultant 573.7
manager director 574.1

governor 575.6
businessman 730.1
boxer 754.2
operator 888.4
managerial directing 573.12
operational 888.12
managing
noun direction 573.1
adj directing 573.12
executive 612.19
managing director 574.3
managing editor
noun publisher 554.2
adj journalist 555.4
man and wife 563.9
man and woman 563.9
mandarin
noun snob 141.7
official 575.16
wise man 920.1
intellectual 928.1
adj studious 570.17
mandate
noun country 232.1
authority 417.1
injunction 420.2
possession 469.1
referendum 613.7
commission 615.1
verb command 420.8
mandated 420.12
mandatory
noun country 232.1
adj preceptive 419.4
mandated 420.12
obligatory 424.11, 641.15
doctrinal 952.27
necessary 962.12
mane hair 3.2
head of hair 3.4
manfully pluckily 359.18
laboriously 725.19
mange 85.40
manger 197.2
mangled impaired 393.27
mutilated 794.5
manhood masculinity 76.1
mankind 76.3
maturity 303.2
courage 492.1
mania craving 100.6
overzealousness 101.3
insanity 925.1
craze 925.12
maniac
noun lunatic 925.15
adj frenzied 105.25
maniacal 105.25
manic excited 105.20
insane 925.26

psychotic 925.28

manic-depressive
noun psychotic 925.17
adj psychotic 925.28

manicure
noun beautification 1015.11
verb groom 79.20

manifest
noun statement 628.3
bill 870.5
verb unclose 292.12
show 348.5
disclose 351.4
flaunt 501.17
signify 517.17
evidence 956.8
adj visible 31.6
apparent 348.8

manifestation visibility 31.1
appearance 33.1, 348.1
disclosure 351.1
display 501.4
indication 517.3
evidence 956.1

manifested 348.13

manifesting 348.9

manifest itself 351.8

manifestly visibly 31.8
positively 247.19
apparently 348.14
really 760.16

manifesto
noun affirmation 334.1
announcement 352.2
platform 609.7
verb affirm 334.5

manifold
noun transcript 784.4
verb copy 784.8
adj multiform 782.3
multiple 882.8
numerous 883.6

man in the street
common man 606.5
average 863.3
nobody 997.7

manipulate touch 73.6
pilot 184.37
tamper with 354.17
use 387.19
exploit 387.16
manoeuvre 415.10
direct 573.8
operate 888.5

manipulated 354.30

manipulation touching 73.2
masturbation 75.8
intrigue 381.5
utilization 387.8
machination 415.4
direction 573.1
rigging 737.20
operation 888.1
accounting 1040.7

manipulative scheming 381.13
using 387.19
cunning 415.12

manipulator strategist 415.7
operator 888.4
influence 893.6

mankind man 76.3
humankind 312.1

manliness masculinity 76.1
maturity 303.2
courage 492.1

manly masculine 76.11
courageous 492.17
honest 644.13

man-made spurious 354.26
made 891.18

manna delicacy 10.8
support 449.3
godsend 472.7
benefit 478.7

manned provided 385.13
armed 460.14

mannequin 785.5

manner aspect 33.3
exteriority 206.1
behaviour 321.1
custom 373.1
way 384.1
style 532.2
mode 764.4
kind 808.3
speciality 865.1

mannered behavioural 321.7
affected 500.15, 533.9
figurative 536.3

manners behaviour 321.1
custom 373.1
mannerliness 504.3
etiquette 580.3

mannish homosexual 75.29
masculine 76.11
mannified 76.13

manoeuvrability
workability 888.3
handiness 1013.2

manoeuvre
noun exercise 84.2
act 328.3
stratagem 415.3
operation 458.5
race 753.3
process 888.2
expedient 994.2
verb execute a manoeuvre 182.46
take action 328.5
plot 381.9
manipulate 415.10
direct 573.8
operate 888.5

manoeuvres
machination 415.4
operation 458.5

manoeuvring intrigue 381.5
machination 415.4

man of the people 606.5

manor sphere 231.2
real estate 471.6

manor farm 1067.8

manor house 228.5

manpower 18.4

manse house 228.5
parsonage 703.7

mansion estate 228.7
flats 228.14
astrology 1070.20

manslaughter 308.2

mantel 900.14

mantelpiece 900.14

mantle
noun cover 295.2
sceptre 417.9
insignia 647.1
robe 702.2
verb cloak 5.39
redden 41.5, 152.14
change colour 105.19
blush 139.8
cover 295.19
foam 320.5

man-to-man plain-speaking 535.3
intimate 582.24
familiar 587.19

mantra 696.3

manual handbook 554.8
textbook 554.10
keyboard 711.17

manual labour 725.4

manufacture
noun structure 266.1
preparation 405.1
product 892.1
verb fabricate 354.18
produce 891.8

manufactured
fabricated 354.29
made 891.18

manufacturer 891.7

manufacturing 891.14

manure
noun faeces 12.4
fertilizer 889.4
verb fertilize 889.8

manuscript
noun handwriting 547.3
copy 548.4
rare book 554.6
adj written 547.22

many
noun masses 606.2
multitude 883.3

adj much 247.8
different 779.7
diversified 782.4
frequent 846.4
plural 882.7
numerous 883.6
plentiful 990.7

many times
adj frequent 846.4
adv frequently 846.6
repeatedly 848.16

many times over 848.16

Maoist
noun Communist 611.18
revolutionist 859.3
adj Communist 611.30
revolutionist 859.6

map
noun chart 159.5
representation 349.1
diagram 381.3
verb locate 159.11
represent 349.8
plot 381.10
receive 1035.17

maple syrup 66.2

map out 381.10

mapped 300.13

mapping plan 381.1
data transmission 1035.8

maquis 461.15

mar deform 265.7
spoil 393.10
bungle 414.11
blemish 1003.4
offend 1014.5

marais 243.1

marathon 826.11

marauding
noun plundering 482.6
adj plunderous 482.22

marble
noun spectrum 47.6
smooth 287.3
sculpture 715.2
toy 743.16
stone 1044.6
verb variegate 47.7
adj white 37.7
hard 1044.10

marbled mottled 47.12
striped 47.15

marcel 3.15

march
noun progression 162.1
walk 177.10
boundary 211.3
frontier 211.5
sphere 231.2
objection 333.2
verb mush 177.30
border 211.10
object 333.5

marches bounds 211.1
frontier 211.5

marching 177.8

marchioness 608.6

march on 162.3

march past 811.7

march-past 811.3

march with 223.12

Mardi Gras treat 95.3
festival 743.4

mare hen 77.9
plain 236.1
horse 311.10
jockey 757.2

margin
noun room 158.3
border 211.4
interval 224.1
distance 261.1
latitude 430.4
collateral 438.3
thin margin 738.10
surplus 992.5
verb border 211.10

marginal
noun constituency 609.16
adj bordering 211.11
unimportant 997.16

marginally 211.15

marigold 728.7

marina 1008.6

marinating 397.2

marine
noun navy man 183.4
navy 461.26
adj nautical 182.57
oceanic 240.8

mariner traveller 178.1
seaman 183.1

marines elite troops 461.14
sea soldiers 461.27

marital 563.18

maritime nautical 182.57
oceanic 240.8

Mark evangelist 684.2
rocket launcher 1072.10

mark
noun boundary 211.3
degree 245.1
sucker 358.2
objective 380.2
sign 517.1
marking 517.5
marker 517.10
signature 527.10
distinction 662.5
notation 709.12
game 746.3
kind 808.3
characteristic 864.4
impact 886.2
evidence 956.1
importance 996.1

mass-produced 891.18

mass production
889.3

mast spar 180.13
tower 272.6
supporter 900.2

Master Mister 76.7
Sir 648.3

master
noun captain 183.7
superior 249.4
boy 302.5
victor 411.2
past master 413.13
proprietor 470.2
teacher 571.1
principal 571.8
lord 575.1
chief 575.3
governor 575.6
degree 648.6
work of art 712.10
artist 716.1
skilled worker 726.6
producer 891.7
wise man 920.1
verb conquer 412.10
subdue 432.9
understand 521.7
attain mastery of
570.9
dominate 612.15
adj chief 249.14
governing 612.18
paramount 996.24

master bedroom
197.7

mastered conquered
412.17
subdued 432.15

masterful lordly
141.11
skilful 413.22
imperious 417.16
perfected 1001.9

masterly skilful 413.22
perfected 1001.9

mastermind master
413.13
wise man 920.1
scholar 928.3

master of skilled in
413.27
possessing 469.9
versed in 927.19

Master of the Rolls
recorder 550.1
Lord Chief Justice
596.4

masterpiece
masterwork 413.10
work of art 712.10
product 892.1

master plan 381.1

master's degree 648.6

mastership supremacy
249.3
skill 413.1

masterhood 417.7
directorship 573.4
control 612.2

mastery supremacy
249.3
preparedness 405.4
victory 411.1
defeat 412.1
skill 413.1
mastership 417.7
learning 570.1
control 612.2
influence 893.1
understanding 927.3

masthead
noun label 517.13
verb punish 604.9

masturbation
autoeroticism 75.8
vanity 140.1

mat
noun head of hair 3.4
border 211.4
partition 213.5
rug 295.9
arena 463.1
bedding 900.20
verb weave 740.6
dull 1026.10

matador killer 308.10
bullfighter 461.4

match
noun image 349.5
contest 457.3
marriage 563.1
game 743.9, 745.3,
746.3, 747.3, 750.3,
750.6
round 748.3
tennis 749.1
frame 752.3
fight 754.3
equal 789.4
two 872.2
matchstick 1020.5
light source 1025.1
verb parallel 203.4
parallelize 203.5
contrapose 215.4
size 257.15
give in kind 506.6
marry 563.14
assemble 769.18
coincide 777.4, 835.4
resemble 783.7
agree 787.6
equal 789.5
double 872.5
compare 942.4
be comparable 942.7

matched married
563.21
joined 799.13
two 872.6
coupled 872.8

matching
noun marriage 563.1
comparison 942.1
adj chromatic 35.15
analogous 783.11

matchless peerless
249.15
best 998.16
first-rate 998.17
perfect 1001.6

matchmaker 563.12

match play 748.3

match point 749.2

matchstick 1020.5

match up marry
563.14
double 872.5
compare 942.4

match-up 563.1

mate
noun captain 183.7
image 349.5
spouse 563.6
companion 588.3
pal 588.4
partner 616.2
co-worker 616.5
accompanier 768.4
likeness 783.3
equal 789.4
verb copulate 75.21
marry 563.15
double 872.5

mated married 563.21
joined 799.13
coupled 872.8

mater brother 559.3
mum 560.12

material
noun fabric 4.1
material 4.1
substance 196.5, 762.2
store 386.1
matter 1050.2
adj carnal 663.6
secularist 695.16
substantial 762.6
essential 766.9
relevant 774.11
evidential 956.16
important 996.17
vital 996.23
materiate 1050.10
inorganic 1053.4

materialism carnality
663.2
secularism 695.2
idealism 951.3
physicism 1050.6

materialist irreligionist
695.10
physicist 1050.7

materialistic carnal
663.6
secularist 695.16
occupied 724.15

materiality existence
760.1
substantiality 762.1
relevance 774.4
importance 996.1
materialness 1050.1
matter 1050.2

materialize show 31.4
appear 33.8
form 262.8
manifest 348.5
come out 348.6
embody 762.5
turn up 830.6, 940.9
establish 891.10
corporalize 1050.9

materially substantially
762.8
essentially 766.11
importantly 996.25

materials store 386.1
lore 927.9
substances 1052.1

material world 1050.2

maternal loving 104.27
native 226.5
ancestral 560.17

maternity blood
relationship 559.1
motherhood 560.3

mates 872.2

matey 587.20

math 1016.1

mathematical 972.17

mathematician
1016.15

mathematics 1016.1

maths 1016.1

matinee 582.10

mating copulation 75.7
fertilization 78.3

matriarch mother
560.11
mistress 575.2
back number 841.8

matriarchal 612.17

matrimonial 563.18

matrimony marriage
563.1
seven sacraments
701.4

matrix form 262.1
mould 785.6
deposit 1056.7

matron woman 77.5
wife 563.8
mistress 575.2

matt 36.7

matte 714.5

matted hairy 3.25
complex 798.4
dishevelled 809.14

matter
noun humour 2.22
excrement 12.3
pus 12.6
substance 196.5, 762.2
quantity 244.1
motive 375.1
undertaking 404.1
writing 547.10
copy 548.4
occupation 724.1

particular 765.3
affair 830.3
topic 936.1
trouble 1012.3
material 1050.2
inorganic matter
1053.1
verb fester 12.15
import 996.12

matter of course
373.5

matter of fact
prosaicness 117.2
fact 760.3
event 830.2

matter-of-fact prosaic
117.8, 721.5
simple 499.6
plain-speaking 535.3
realistic 986.6

matter-of-factly
499.10, 535.4

matters 830.4

Matthew 684.2

mattress 900.20

maturation
noun growth 259.3
adolescence 301.6
development 303.6,
392.2
evolution 860.1
adj completion 407.2

mature
verb grow 14.2, 259.7
grow up 303.9
grow old 304.6
develop 392.10
ripen 407.8
accrue 623.7
complete 793.6
evolve 860.5
produce 891.8
originate 891.12
perfect 1001.5
adj grown 14.3,
259.12
adult 303.12
ripe 303.13, 407.13
middle-aged 304.7
prepared 405.16
experienced 413.28
due 623.10
complete 793.9
perfected 1001.9

matured ripe 407.13
experienced 413.28
complete 793.9
perfected 1001.9

mature student 572.1

maturing
noun growth 259.3
adj evolutionary 860.8

maturity
noun adulthood 303.2
preparedness 405.4
debt 623.1
adj completion 407.2

maudlin intoxicated
88.31
sentimental 93.21
foolish 922.8

maul
noun game 746.3
verb mistreat 389.5
injure 393.13
rage 671.11
play 746.4
fight 754.4
pound 901.16

mauled 96.23

mauling 901.3

mausoleum tomb
309.16
monument 549.12

mauve 46.3

maverick
noun rebel 327.5
mule 361.6
misfit 788.4
nonconformist 867.3
oddity 869.4
adj unconventional
867.6

mavis 710.23

maw mouth 2.16,
292.4
mum 560.12

max
noun supremacy 249.3
limit 793.5
adj extreme 247.13

maxim rule 419.2,
868.4
belief 952.2
aphorism 973.1

maximize 251.4

maximum
noun summit 198.2
supremacy 249.3
limit 793.5
plenty 990.2
adj top 198.10
great 247.6
superlative 249.13

maximum speed
174.3

maxwell 1031.7

may be able 18.11
can 443.13

maya bewitchment
691.2
illusion 975.1

maybe 965.9

Mayday 400.1

mayfly 827.5

mayhem 393.1

may I? 443.20

mayor minister 575.17
legislator 610.3

Maypole 273.1

Mazda 677.5

maze
noun complex 798.2

confusion 984.3
verb perplex 970.13
confuse 984.7

McCoy 972.4

me 864.5

mead 310.8

meadow marsh 243.1
grassland 310.8

meagre insignificant
248.6
dwarf 258.13
narrow 270.14
lean 270.17
sparse 884.5
slight 991.10

meal repast 8.5
feed 10.4
cereal 10.33
powder 1049.5

meals 10.6

mealy colourless 36.7
powdery 1049.11

mean
noun median 246.1
middle 818.1
verb augur 133.12
manifest 348.5
intend 380.4
signify 517.17, 518.8
imply 519.4
evidence 956.8
adj crabby 110.20
humble 137.10
servile 138.13
cruel 144.26
envious 154.4
intervening 213.10
medium 246.3
insignificant 248.6
inadequate 250.7
niggardly 484.8
low 497.15
populational 606.8
ungenerous 651.6
base 661.12
middle 818.4
narrow-minded 979.10
meagre 991.10
paltry 997.21
great 998.13
inferior 1004.9

mean a lot 518.8

mean business 359.8

meander
noun bend 279.3
convolution 281.1
complex 798.2
verb stray 164.4
wander 177.23
convolve 281.4
go roundabout 913.4

meandering
noun convolution
281.1
discursiveness 538.3
circuitousness 913.1
adj deviative 164.7
wandering 177.37
flowing 238.24

curved 279.7
convolutional 281.6
complex 798.4
circuitous 913.7

meaning
noun ominousness
133.7
interpretation 341.1
intention 380.1
indication 517.3
significance 518.1
implication 519.2
lexicology 526.14
adj meaningful 518.10

meaningful
premonitory 133.16
indicative 517.23
meaning 518.10
expressive 544.10

meaningfully
ominously 133.19
meaningly 518.13
eloquently 544.15

meaningless
uncommunicative
344.8
useless 391.9
unmeaning 520.6
unordered 809.12

mean much 996.12

meanness crabbiness
110.3
humility 137.1
servility 138.1
envy 154.1
insignificance 248.1
inadequacy 250.3
niggardliness 484.2
vulgarity 497.1
commonness 497.5
ungenerousness 651.2
baseness 661.3
narrow-mindedness
979.1
meagreness 991.2
paltriness 997.2
inferiority 1004.3

mean nothing 520.4

means manner 384.1
ways 384.2
supply 386.2
assets 471.7
funds 728.14
expedient 994.2
tool 1039.1

means of transport
179.1

mean something
518.8

means to an end
means 384.2
expedient 994.2

mean streets 230.6

meant intentional
380.8
implied 518.11, 519.7

mean time 831.3

meantime

noun meanwhile 825.2
adv meanwhile 825.5

meanwhile
noun meantime 825.2
adv in the meantime
820.10
meantime 825.5

measly anaemic 85.60
small-time 997.18

measurable mensurable
300.14
calculable 1016.24

measure
noun space 158.1
quantity 244.1
amount 244.2
degree 245.1
size 257.1
capacity 257.2
length 267.1
measurement 300.1
measuring instrument
300.2
act 328.3
portion 477.5
sign 517.1
harmony 533.2
law 673.3
air 708.4
passage 708.24
notation 709.12
rhythm 709.22
metrics 720.6
metre 720.7
strain 720.9
process 888.2
expedient 994.2
verb traverse 177.20
quantify 244.4
size 257.15
gauge 300.10
harmonize 787.7
estimate 945.9
number 1016.16
calculate 1016.17

measured quantitative
244.5
gauged 300.13
harmonious 533.8
temperate 668.9
rhythmic 709.28
metric 720.16
uniform 780.5

measurement quantity
244.1
size 257.1
measure 300.1
estimate 945.3
numeration 1016.9

measures layer 296.1
precaution 494.3

measure up 405.15

measure up to equal
789.5
be comparable 942.7

measuring
noun measurement
300.1
adj metric 300.12

meat meal 8.5
breakfast 8.6
food 10.1
flesh 10.12
nut 10.37
substance 196.5
support 449.3
summary 557.2
essence 766.2
major part 791.6
topic 936.1
salient point 996.6

meat loaf 10.12

meaty corpulent 257.18
meaningful 518.10

mecca desire 100.11
focus 208.4

mechanic aircraftsman
185.6
mender 396.10
worker 607.9
skilled worker 726.6
mechanician 1039.8

mechanical uniform
780.5
involuntary 962.14
mechanistic 1038.7
machinelike 1039.10

**mechanical
engineering** 1038.6

mechanically 962.18

mechanics art 413.7
leverage 1038.1

mechanism
instrumentality 384.3
instrument 384.4
art 413.7
machinery 1039.3,
1039.4
materialism 1050.6

mechanistic 1038.7

mechanization 1039.1

mechanized 1039.10

medal military honour
646.6
insignia 647.1
relief 715.3

medallion medal 646.6
relief 715.3

medallist 413.15

medal winner 413.15

meddle intermeddle
214.7
advise 422.5
pry 980.4
hinder 1011.10

meddling
noun intermeddling
214.2
adj meddlesome 214.9

Medea 690.9

Medellin cartel 732.4

media 343.5, 347.1

medial intervening
213.10
medium 246.3
middle 818.4

median
noun mean 246.1
middle 818.1
adj intervening 213.10
medium 246.3
middle 818.4

mediate interpose
213.6
be instrumental 384.7
reconcile 465.8
intermediate 466.6

mediating
noun mediation 466.1
adj modal 384.8
mediatory 466.8

mediation
instrumentality 384.3
pacification 465.1
mediating 466.1
salvation 677.14

mediator intermediary
213.4
instrument 384.4
intermediator 466.3
go-between 576.4
moderator 670.3

medical
noun checkup 937.6
adj iatric 90.15

medical history 91.10

medical practice
medicine 90.1
practice of medicine
90.13

medical practitioner
90.4

medication medicine
86.4
therapy 91.1
treatment 91.14

medicinal
noun medicine 86.4
adj remedial 86.39

medicine
noun medicament 86.4
juice 88.14
medical practice 90.1
verb medicate 91.25

medicine man 690.7

medicines 91.1

medieval 841.13

mediocre medium
246.3
inadequate 250.7
unskilful 414.15
middle 818.4
usual 868.9
imperfect 1002.4
middling 1004.7

mediocrity mean 246.1
inadequacy 250.3
unskilfulness 414.1
incompetent 414.7
usualness 868.2
nobody 997.7
imperfection 1002.1
mediocreness 1004.1
second-rater 1004.5

meditate contemplate
380.5
consider 930.12

meditating cognitive
930.21
engrossed 982.17

meditation inaction
329.1
trance 691.3
prayer 696.4
consideration 930.2
engrossment 982.3

meditative passive
329.6
cognitive 930.21
engrossed 982.17
abstracted 984.11

mediterranean inland
207.7
middle 818.4

medium
noun colour 35.8
substance 196.5, 762.2
element 209.4
intermediary 213.4
mean 246.1
instrument 384.4
mediator 466.3
volume 554.4
go-between 576.4
psychic 689.13
lights 704.18
palette 712.18
doer 726.1
immaterialist 1051.4
adj done 11.7
intervening 213.10
mean 246.3
middle 818.4
mediocre 1004.7

medley
noun performance
708.33
miscellany 769.13
hotchpotch 796.6
adj variegated 47.9
mixed 796.14

Medusa 690.9

meek resigned 134.10
humble-hearted
137.11
modest 139.9
gentle 433.15
unbelligerent 464.10

meekly resignedly
134.12
humbly 137.16
modestly 139.14
gently 433.19

meet
noun contest 457.3
game 743.9
athletics meeting
755.2
assembly 769.2
verb converge 169.2
confront 216.8, 451.5
encounter 223.11
concur 332.9

observe 434.2
compete 457.18
brave 492.11
come together 769.16
convene 769.17
join 799.11
experience 830.8
conform 866.3
collide 901.13
suffice 990.4
adj approachable
167.5
decorous 496.10
conventional 579.5
just 649.8
timely 842.9
expedient 994.5

meeting
noun convergence
169.1
meeting up 223.4
contest 457.3
conference 541.6
rendezvous 582.9
divine service 696.8
assembly 769.2
joining 799.1
impact 901.3
adj converging 169.3
in contact 223.17
assembled 769.21
joining 799.16
concurrent 898.4

meeting of minds
332.5

meeting place resort
228.27
rendezvous 582.9

meet up meet 223.11
join 799.11

meet up with meet
223.11
experience 830.8
come across 940.3

meet with meet 223.11
experience 830.8
come across 940.3

mega huge 257.20
great 998.13

megalomaniac 925.17

megaphone 48.8

megastar celebrity
662.9
lead 707.6

melancholia mental
disorder 92.14
wretchedness 96.6
melancholy 112.5
depression 925.5

melancholic
noun introvert 92.12
sourpuss 112.13
adj melancholy 112.23
weary 118.11

melancholy
noun wretchedness
96.6
sullenness 110.8
melancholia 112.5

weariness 118.3
thoughtfulness 930.3
adj sullen 110.24
melancholic 112.23
weary 118.11

melee free-for-all 457.5
commotion 809.4

mellifluous sweet 66.4
pleasant 97.6
melodious 708.48

mellow
verb mature 303.9
ripen 407.8
evolve 860.5
soften 1045.6
adj soft-coloured
35.21
resonant 54.9
intoxicated 88.31
pleasant 97.6
ripe 407.13
melodious 708.48
soft 1045.8

melodic 708.48

melodious 708.48

melodrama 93.9

melodramatic
emotionalistic 93.19
sensational 105.32
dramatic 704.33

melody melodiousness
708.2
air 708.4

melon 738.7

melt disappear 34.3
affect 93.14
have pity 145.4
move 145.5
flit 827.6
melt down 1019.21
liquefy 1062.5

melt away disappear
34.3
decrease 252.6

meltdown outburst
671.6
misfortune 1010.2
atomic explosion
1037.16

melted penitent 113.9
molten 1019.31
liquefied 1062.6

melting
noun disappearance
34.1
fusion 1019.3
liquefaction 1062.1
adj vanishing 34.4
loving 104.27
pitying 145.7
liquefying 1062.7

melting pot United
States 232.4
mixture 796.1
mixer 796.9
philosopher's stone
857.10

member appendage 2.7

affiliate 617.11
organ 792.4

members 617.12

membership
association 582.6
members 617.12
inclusion 771.1

membrane membrana
2.6
lamina 296.2

memento monument
549.12
remembrance 988.7

memo 549.4

memoir memorandum
549.4
treatise 556.1
history 719.1
remembering 988.4

memoirs 719.1

memorabilia archives
549.2
history 719.1
memento 988.7

memorable
rememberable 988.25
notable 996.19

memorably 988.28

memorandum memo
549.4
reminder 988.6

memorial
noun record 549.1
memorandum 549.4
monument 549.12
history 719.1
memento 988.7
adj celebrative 487.3
commemorative
988.27

memorials history
719.1
memento 988.7

memories 988.7

memorize get by rote
570.8
commit to memory
988.17

memory engram 92.29
celebration 487.1
bulletin board 549.10
remembrance 662.7,
836.4, 988.1
storage 1041.7

memory loss 989.2

men work force 18.9
mankind 76.3
staff 577.11

menace
noun threat 514.1
danger 1005.1
verb forebode 133.11
threaten 514.2
be imminent 839.2
work evil 999.6

menacing ominous
133.17

threatening 514.3
imminent 839.3
dangerous 1005.9

menacingly 133.19

menagerie zoo 228.19
collection 769.11

mend
noun improvement
392.1
verb get well 83.7
improve 392.7, 392.9
repair 396.14

mending
noun improvement
392.1
reparation 396.6
adj improving 392.15

menfolk 76.3

menial
noun servant 577.2
worker 726.2
adj servile 138.13
serving 577.14

menopausal 890.4

menopause 303.7

mens 918.1

menstrual catamenial
12.24
momentary 849.8

menswear 5.1

mental
noun psychotic 925.17
adj intellectual 918.7
crazy 925.27
cognitive 930.21
attitudinal 977.7

mental attitude 977.1

mental disorder 92.14

mental handicap
921.9

mental health health
83.1
sanity 924.1

mental hospital
925.14

mental illness mental
disorder 92.14
insanity 925.1

mentality intellect
918.1
intelligence 919.1,
919.9

mentally 977.9

mentally handicapped
921.22

mentally ill 925.28

mentally retarded
921.22

mental picture idea
931.1
visualization 985.6

mention
noun remark 524.4
information 551.1
citation 646.4
verb remark 524.25

specify 864.11
call attention to
982.10

Mentor 920.2

mentor preparer 405.5
adviser 422.3
teacher 571.1
wise man 920.1

menu bill of fare 8.14
bill 870.5
schedule 964.3

mercantile business
730.12
commercial 731.21

mercenary
noun hireling 461.16
employee 577.3
adj greedy 100.27
employed 615.20
corruptible 645.23

mercer 5.32

merchandise
noun provisions 385.2
commodities 735.1
verb deal in 731.15
sell 734.8

merchandising
noun trade 731.2
selling 734.2
adj sales 734.13

merchant
noun provider 385.6
merchandiser 730.2
adj commercial 731.21

merchant banker
729.8

merchant navy 461.26

Mercia 231.7

merciful kind 143.13
pitying 145.7
lenient 427.7
almighty 677.17

mercifully 145.10

merciless pitiless 146.3
savage 671.21

mercilessly pitilessly
146.4
savagely 671.27

mercurial fast 174.15
active 330.17
irresolute 362.9
fickle 364.6
nonuniform 781.3
inconstant 853.7
flighty 984.17
brass 1056.17

Mercury messenger
353.1
planet 1070.9

mercury lightning
174.6
guide 574.7
Proteus 853.4
thermometer 1018.20

mercy kindness 143.1
act of kindness 143.7
pity 145.1

mere
noun lake 241.1
adj sheer 248.8
simple 797.6

merely to a degree
248.10
simply 797.11
solely 871.14

merge converge 169.2
submerge 367.7
cooperate 450.3
come together 769.16
identify 777.5
mix 796.10
put together 799.5
join 799.11
combine 804.3

merged joined 799.13
combined 804.5

merger convergence
169.1
affiliation 450.2
identification 777.2
mixture 796.1
joining 799.1
combination 804.1

merging
noun joining 799.1
adj converging 169.3
combining 804.7

meridian
noun map 159.5
summit 198.2
zone 231.3
noon 314.5
orbit 1070.16
adj top 198.10
noon 314.7

meringue sweets 10.38
foam 320.2

merit
noun importance 996.1
goodness 998.1
verb deserve 639.5

merited warranted
639.9
just 649.8

merits 639.3

Merlin 690.6

mermaid swimmer
182.12
spirit of the sea 240.4
water god 678.10

merrily 109.19

merriment merriness
109.5
rejoicing 116.1
waggishness 489.4
conviviality 582.3
festivity 743.3

merry intoxicated
88.31
mirthful 109.15
festive 743.28

merry-go-round round
of pleasure 743.7
carousel 743.15
periodicity 849.2

rotator 914.4

mesh
noun network 170.3,
1041.16
interaction 776.3
complex 798.2
verb net 170.7
trap 356.20
catch 480.17
interact 776.6

mesmeric hypnotic
22.24
alluring 377.8
engrossing 982.20

mesmerized wondering
122.9
enchanted 691.12
gripped 982.18

mess
noun meal 8.5
rations 10.6
filth 80.7
amount 244.2
lot 247.4
formlessness 263.1
fiasco 410.6
portion 477.5
bunch 769.7
hotchpotch 796.6
jumble 809.3
pickle 1012.5
eyesore 1014.4
verb feed 8.18

message
communication 343.1
advertisement 352.6
information 551.1
dispatch 552.4
letter 553.2
commercial 1033.20

mess around 997.15

messed up screwed up
393.29
fouled-up 414.22
dishevelled 809.14

messenger
noun harbinger 133.5
message-bearer 353.1
delegate 576.2
precursor 815.1
verb send 176.15

messiah 574.6

messianic 677.16

messing 8.1

messing around 997.9

Messrs 76.7

mess up deform 263.3
screw up 393.11
cock up 414.12

mess with 8.21

messy dirty 80.22
slovenly 809.15

metabolic digestive
2.29
plasmatic 262.10
metamorphic 851.12

metabolism metabolic
process 2.18
basal metabolism 7.10
transformation 851.3

metal
noun heraldic device
647.2
elementary metal
1056.3
verb floor 295.22
adj metallic 1056.16

metallic raucous
58.15
metal 1056.16

metalwork 1056.3

metamorphosed
851.10

metamorphosis 851.3

metaphor similarity
783.1
substitute 861.2
comparison 942.1

metaphorical
indicative 517.23
meaningful 518.10
symbolic 519.10
figurative 536.3

metaphorically 536.4

metaphysical 689.23

metaphysics
hyperphysics 689.3
ontology 760.7

meteoric increasing
251.8
brief 827.8
flashing 1024.34
celestial 1070.25

meteorite 1070.15

meteorites 1073.10

meteorological 317.12

meteors 1073.10

meter
noun measure 300.2
measurer 300.9
electrical device
1031.20
verb measure 300.10

meth 87.3

methanol 756.1

method behaviour
321.1
plan 381.1
manner 384.1
means 384.2
art 413.7
orderliness 806.3

methodical punctilious
580.10
uniform 780.5
orderly 806.6
regular 849.6

methodically regularly
780.8, 849.9
systematically 806.9

methodology behaviour
321.1
plan 381.1

manner 384.1
orderliness 806.3

methods 321.1

meticulous exacting
339.12
strict 425.6
observant 434.4
fastidious 495.9
punctilious 580.10
conscientious 644.15
detailed 765.9
accurate 972.16
attentive 982.15

meticulously exactingly
339.16
fastidiously 495.14
honestly 644.21

me-too 336.9

metre rhythm 709.22
metrics 720.6
measure 720.7
periodicity 849.2

metric measuring
300.12
rhythmic 709.28
metrical 720.16

metro 230.11

metronome
rhythmometer 711.22
oscillator 915.9

metropolis capital
208.7
town 230.1
state 231.5

metropolitan 230.11

Metropolitan Museum
386.9

Metropolitan police
1007.17

mettle animation 17.4
pluck 359.3
fortitude 492.6
disposition 977.3

mew
noun lair 228.26
retreat 1008.5
verb cry 60.2
enclose 212.5
confine 429.12

mews 228.20

mezzanine 197.23

mezzo 818.4

mi 709.7

Michael 679.4

Mick 232.7

Mickey 232.7

mickey 87.5

Mickey Mouse
insignificant 248.6
measly 997.18
inferior 1004.9
easy 1013.13

micro 258.12

microchip electronic
circuit 1032.8
circuitry 1041.3

microcosm 258.6

microfilm
noun bulletin board
549.10
film 714.10
verb photograph
714.14
copy 784.8

microphone mike 50.9
radio transmitter
1033.4

microprocessor 1041.2

microscope 29.1

microscopic telescopic
29.10
infinitesimal 258.14
exact 972.17

Microsoft 1041.12

microwave
noun radio wave
1033.11
verb cook 11.4

'mid 213.12

mid
adj phonetic 524.31
middle 818.4
prep between 213.12
among 796.17

mid-air 272.15

Midas 618.8

Midas touch 618.5

midday
noun noon 314.5
adj noon 314.7

middle
noun centre 208.2
mean 246.1
voice 530.14
median 818.1
verb centralize 208.9
seek the middle 818.3
adj central 208.11
intervening 213.10
mediatory 466.8
medial 818.4

middle age 303.4

middle-aged mid-life
303.14
mature 304.7

Middle Ages 823.5

Middle America
1004.5

middle class people
606.1
mediocrity 1004.5

middle-class upper-
class 607.10
ordinary 1004.8

middle distance short
distance 223.2
mid-distance 818.2

middle finger 73.5

middle ground 818.2

middle management
574.11

middle name name
527.3
first name 527.4
characteristic 864.4

middle of the road
mean 246.1
moderatism 611.2
mid-distance 818.2

middle-of-the-road
medium 246.3
moderate 611.26
middle 818.4

middle school 567.4

middleweight 297.3

middling medium
246.3
middle 818.4
mediocre 1004.7

middy 183.4

midfielder 745.2

midge dwarf 258.5
minutia 258.7

midget
noun dwarf 258.5
adj dwarf 258.13

midland
noun inland 207.3
adj inland 207.7
middle 818.4

Midlands 231.7

midlands 207.3

mid-life 303.14

midnight
noun dead of night
315.6
adj black 38.8
nocturnal 315.9

midriff mouth 2.16
partition 213.5
middle 818.1

mid-season 313.9

'midst 213.12

midst
noun middle 818.1
prep between 213.12
among 796.17

midsummer
noun summer 313.3
hot weather 1018.7
adj seasonal 313.9

mid Wales 231.7

midway
noun mid-distance
818.2
adj neutral 467.7
middle 818.4
adv mediumly 246.4
halfway 818.5

midwife health-care
professional 90.8
instrument 384.4

midwinter
noun winter 313.6
adj seasonal 313.9

mien looks 33.4
exteriority 206.1

behaviour 321.1

mig 743.16

might strength 15.1
power 18.1
greatness 247.1
authoritativeness 417.2

might be 965.4

mightily strongly 15.23
powerfully 18.15
very 247.18
authoritatively 417.18

mighty
noun strong man 15.6
adj strong 15.15
powerful 18.12
great 247.6
huge 257.20
authoritative 417.15
eminent 662.18

migraine 26.5

migrant migrator 178.5
bird 311.28
worker 726.2

migrate 177.22

migration
noun transmigration
177.4
departure 188.1
phrase transference
176.1

migrations 177.2

migratory 177.37

mike
noun microphone 50.9
verb idle 331.12

mild
noun beer 88.16
adj insipid 65.2
bright 97.11
good-natured 143.14
lenient 427.7
meek 433.15
moderate 670.10
warm 1018.24
soft 1045.8

mildew
noun fetidness 71.2
decay 393.6
blight 1000.2
verb decay 393.22

mildly to a degree
248.10
meekly 433.19

mild-mannered good-
natured 143.14
lenient 427.7
meek 433.15

mileage distance 261.1
length 267.1

mile long 267.7

mile off 786.5

miles per hour 174.1

milestone marker
517.10
salient point 996.6

milieu environment
209.1

ambience 209.3
region 231.1
arena 463.1
plot 722.4

militancy activity
330.1
warlikeness 458.11

militant
noun combatant 461.1
believer 692.4
adj active 330.17
warlike 458.21

militarism warlikeness
458.11
foreign policy 609.5
nationalism 611.10
central government
612.4

military
noun defence forces
461.19
adj warlike 458.21

military academy
567.6

military aircraft 181.9

military court 595.4

military dictatorship
458.10

military
establishment
461.19

military government
612.4

military hardware
462.1

military-industrial
complex 462.1

military intelligence
secret service 576.12
surveillance 937.9

military operations
war 458.1
operation 458.5

military service
service 458.9
enlistment 615.7

military training
568.3

militia 461.23

milk
noun humour 2.22
alabaster 37.2
fluid 1059.2
verb draw off 192.12
exploit 387.16
take from 480.21
strip 480.24
tend 1068.7
adj milky 1059.5

milked 704.33

milking 192.3

milk products 10.46

milky wishy-washy
16.17
white 37.7
lacteal 1059.5

mirth merriment 109.5
amusement 743.1

mirza prince 608.7
Sir 648.3

misadventure 1010.2

misapprehension
misinterpretation
342.1
mistake 974.3

misbehaviour good
behaviour 321.2
misconduct 322.1
wrongdoing 655.1

miscalculation
misjudgment 947.1
mistake 974.3

miscarriage abortion
410.5
mistake 974.3

miscarried 410.18

miscellaneous 796.14

mischief
mischievousness 322.2
mischief-maker 322.3
impairment 393.1
disaccord 456.1
disadvantage 995.2
evil 999.3

mischievous mischief-
loving 322.6
impish 680.18
harmful 999.12

mischievously
roguishly 322.7
harmfully 999.15

misconceived 342.3

misconception
misinterpretation
342.1
mistake 974.3
illusion 975.1

misconduct
noun misbehaviour
322.1
misuse 389.1
mismanagement 414.6
wrongdoing 655.1
verb mismanage
414.13
misdo 974.12

misdemeanour
misbehaviour 322.1
misdeed 655.2
offence 674.4

misdirected botched
414.21
mistaught 569.5

miserable wretched
96.26
unhappy 112.21
base 661.12
paltry 997.21
adverse 1010.13

miserably distressingly
247.21
basely 661.17

miserly greedy 100.27

stingy 484.9
sparse 884.5
meagre 991.10

misery pain 26.1
wretchedness 96.6
unhappiness 112.2
sorrow 112.10
grouch 115.9

misfit intruder 773.2
nonconformist 788.4,
867.3

misfortune 1010.2

misguided botched
414.21
mistaught 569.5
unwise 922.10

mishap 1010.2

misinformation
deliberate falsehood
354.9
misleading 356.2
misteaching 569.1

misinformed mistaught
569.5
unlearned 929.14

misinterpretation
perversion 265.2
misunderstanding
342.1
misjudgment 947.1
error 974.1

misinterpreted 342.3

misjudgment
misinterpretation
342.1
poor judgment 947.1
error 974.1
mistake 974.3

mislaid 160.11

mislead lie 354.19
misguide 356.16
misteach 569.3
betray 645.14
seduce 665.20

misleading
noun misguidance
356.2
misteaching 569.1
adj deceptive 356.21
misteaching 569.6
illusory 975.9

misleadingly 356.23

misled 569.5

mismanaged 414.21

mismanagement
misuse 389.1
mishandling 414.6

mismatch
noun misconnection
775.2
unfitness 788.3
verb disagree 788.5

mismatched 788.7

misnomer
noun wrong name
527.9
verb misname 527.12

misogynist hater 103.4
celibate 565.2
misanthrope 590.2

misogyny hate 103.1
celibacy 565.1
misanthropy 590.1

misplaced mislaid
160.11
inappropriate 788.7
disorderly 809.13
out of line 867.7

misquoted 265.11

misread
verb misinterpret
342.2
misjudge 947.2
misdo 974.12
adj misinterpreted
342.3

misreading
misinterpretation
342.1
misjudgment 947.1

misrepresentation
perversion 265.2,
350.1
deliberate falsehood
354.9

misrepresented 265.11

Miss 77.8

miss
noun girl 302.6
near miss 410.4
mistake 974.3
verb leave undone
340.7
miss the mark 410.14
lose 473.4
miscarry 910.4
require 962.9
be inattentive 983.2
want 991.7
fall short 1002.3

missed 340.14

misshapen deformed
265.12
unordered 809.12
freakish 869.13
unshapely 1014.8

missile
noun projectile 462.18,
903.5
rocket 1072.3
adj projectile 903.15

missing gone 34.5
absent 222.11
nonexistent 761.8
incomplete 794.4
wanting 991.13

missing link 841.7

mission
noun flight operation
184.11
adventure 404.2
operation 458.5
delegation 576.13
commission 615.1
duty 641.1

church 703.1
task 724.2
vocation 724.6
verb commission
615.10

missionary evangelist
699.6
converter 857.9

missive 553.2

miss out miss an
opportunity 843.5
miss 910.4
fall short 1002.3

miss the point
misinterpret 342.2
be wrong 974.10

Miss World 1015.8

missy 302.6

mist
noun rain 316.1
fog 319.2
obscurity 522.3
spirit 763.3
confusion 984.3
verb blur 32.4
cloud 319.6
confuse 984.7

mistake
noun miss 410.4
bungle 414.5
error 974.3
verb misinterpret
342.2
make a mistake 974.13

mistaken
misinterpreted 342.3
in error 974.18

mistakenly 974.20

mistaking
misinterpretation
342.1
error 974.1

misted 984.13

Mister Mr 76.7
Sir 648.3

mistral 318.9

mistreatment 389.2

Mistress Ms 77.8
madame 648.4

mistress ladylove
104.14
proprietor 470.2
instructress 571.2
governess 575.2
woman 665.17
wise man 920.1

mistrust
noun suspiciousness
153.2
wariness 494.2
doubt 954.2
verb suffer pangs of
jealousy 153.3
doubt 954.6

mistrusted 954.12

misty inconspicuous
32.6

formless 263.4
thin 270.16
rainy 316.10
foggy 319.9
obscure 522.15
vague 970.19
muddled 984.13

misunderstand
misinterpret 342.2
mistake 974.13

misunderstanding
misinterpretation
342.1
disagreement 456.2
mistake 974.3

misunderstood disliked
99.9
misinterpreted 342.3

misuse
noun perversion 265.2
use 387.1
misusage 389.1
corruption 393.2
mistake 974.3
verb pervert 265.6
exploit 387.16
misemploy 389.4
corrupt 393.12
misdo 974.12

misused 432.16

mite modicum 248.2
minutia 258.7
child 302.3
insect 311.31
vermin 311.35
farthing 728.7
pittance 991.5

mitigate weaken 16.10
relieve 120.5
abate 252.8
extenuate 600.12
moderate 670.6
relax 670.9
be changed 851.6
change 851.7
qualify 958.3

mitigated lightened
298.11
qualified 958.10

mitigating relieving
120.9
assuaging 670.14
qualifying 958.7

mitigation weakening
16.5
relief 120.1
pity 145.1
decrease 252.1
extenuation 600.5
modulation 670.2
change 851.1

mitre
noun tiara 647.4
joint 799.4
verb hook 799.8

mix
noun film editing
706.5
hotchpotch 796.6

pickle 1012.5
verb make up 405.7
compose 795.3
admix 796.10
combine 804.3
confound 944.3

mixed ambiguous 539.4
mingled 796.14
combined 804.5
imperfect 1002.4

mixed bag 796.6

mixed doubles 749.1

mixed economy 611.4

mixed-up complex
798.4
confused 809.16,
984.12
muddleheaded 921.18

mixer dance 705.2
blender 796.9
control room 1033.7
radioman 1033.24

mixing mixture 796.1
radio broadcasting
1033.16
televising 1034.3

mixture medicine 86.4
concoction 405.3
miscellany 769.13
difference 779.1
composition 795.1
mixing 796.1
compound 796.5,
804.2
solution 1062.3

mix up mix 796.10
complicate 798.3
confuse 810.3, 984.7
confound 944.3
mistake 974.13

mix with 582.17

MM 76.7

Mme 77.8

mo 827.3

moan
noun lament 115.3
verb sigh 52.14,
318.21
beef 108.6, 115.16
lament 115.10
wail 115.13

moaning
noun sigh 52.8
lamentation 115.1
adj lamenting 115.18

moat crack 224.2
trench 290.2
entrenchment 460.5
barrier 1011.5

mob masses 606.2
underworld 660.11
throng 769.4
multitude 883.3

mobile
noun telephone 347.4
work of art 712.10
sculpture 715.2

adj moving 172.7
upper-class 607.10
changeable 853.6

mobile home trailer
179.19
caravan 228.17

mobility motivity
172.3
class 607.1
changeableness 853.1

mobilization motion
172.1
utilization 387.8
preparation 405.1
call to arms 458.8
militarization 458.10
enlistment 615.7
assemblage 769.1

mobilize set in motion
172.6
prepare 405.6
call to arms 458.19
militarize 458.20
enlist 615.17
assemble 769.18
put together 799.5

mobilized 405.16

mobilizing 387.8

mock
noun indignity 156.2
fake 354.13
gibe 508.2
examination 937.2
verb offend 156.5
impersonate 349.12
deceive 356.14
joke 489.13
scoff 508.9
adopt 621.4
adj imitation 336.8
spurious 354.26
similar 783.10
substitute 861.8

mockery indignity
156.2
mimicry 336.2
insincerity 354.5
ridicule 508.1
burlesque 508.6
laughingstock 508.7
trifle 997.5

mocking
noun adoption 621.2
adj ridiculing 508.12

mockingly 508.15

mock-up reproduction
336.3
artist's model 785.5

mod 840.13

modal instrumental
384.8
conditional 764.6

mode form 262.1
manner 384.1, 764.4
mood 530.11
style 532.2
fashion 578.1
octave species 709.10

state 764.1
syllogism 934.6

model
noun form 262.1,
709.11
measure 300.2
reproduction 336.3
original 337.2
image 349.5
figure 349.6
paragon 659.4
celebrity 662.9
essence 766.2
duplicate 784.3
pattern 785.1
ideal 785.4
rule 868.4
ideatum 931.2
beauty 1015.8
verb form 262.7
sculpture 715.5
adj praiseworthy
509.20
exemplary 785.8
normal 868.8
perfected 1001.9

modelled formative
262.9
sculptured 715.7

modelling forming
262.5
imitation 336.1
sculpture 715.1

moderate
noun moderatist
611.14, 670.4
verb slow 175.9
limit 210.5
mediate 466.6
restrain 670.6
qualify 958.3
adj sedate 106.14
slow 175.10
medium 246.3
lenient 427.7
neutral 467.7
centrist 611.26
cheap 633.7
temperate 668.9,
670.10
middle 818.4
tolerable 998.20
mediocre 1004.7

moderated 210.7

moderately slowly
175.13
to a degree 248.10
cheaply 633.10
temperately 668.12
in moderation 670.17
tolerably 998.24
mediocrely 1004.11

moderation sedateness
106.4
limitation 210.2
temperance 668.1
moderateness 670.1

modern
noun modern man
840.4

adj fashionable 578.11
present 837.2
contemporary 840.13

modern-day 837.2

modernism 840.3

modernist poet 720.11
modern 840.4

modernity present
837.1
modernness 840.3

modernization 840.3

modernize 840.6

modernized 840.13

modernizing 840.13

modern man 840.4

modest humble 137.10
meek 139.9
inferior 250.6
demurring 325.7
reticent 344.10
cheap 633.7
unselfish 652.5
decent 664.5
mediocre 1004.7

modestly humbly
137.16
meekly 139.14
to a degree 248.10
mediocrely 1004.11

modesty humility
137.1
meekness 139.1
demur 325.2
unselfishness 652.1
decency 664.2
mediocrity 1004.1

modicum minim 248.2
portion 477.5
piece 792.3

modification speech
sound 524.13
differentiation 779.4
change 851.1
qualification 958.1

modified changed
851.10
qualified 958.10

modify differentiate
779.6
change 851.7
qualify 958.3

modifying 958.7

modish dressed up
5.45
stylish 578.12
modern 840.13

modular partial 792.7
component 795.5

modulated 958.10

module part 792.1
component 795.2
individual 871.4
spacecraft 1073.2

modus operandi 384.1

Mogul 575.10

mogul skiing 753.1

personage 996.8
snow 1022.8

Moira 838.2

moira fate 963.2
chance 971.1

moist 1063.15

moisten 1063.12

moisture rain 316.1
liquidity 1059.1
damp 1063.1

mojo 87.8

molasses sweetening
66.2
adhesive 802.4
semiliquid 1060.5

mole blind 30.4
growth 85.38
bulge 283.3
mark 517.5
buttress 900.4
blemish 1003.1
harbour 1008.6
barrier 1011.5

molecular 258.14

molecule modicum
248.2
atom 258.8
atomic cluster 1037.7
matter 1050.2
element 1058.2

molester 96.10

molesting 389.2

mollified 1045.8

molten melted 1019.31
liquefied 1062.6

moment prestige 417.4
period 823.1
second 823.2
short time 827.3
instant 829.3
influence 893.1
impulse 901.1
importance 996.1

momentarily
transiently 827.10
instantly 829.6

momentary transient
827.7
instantaneous 829.4
momently 849.8

moment of truth
period 823.1
crucial moment 842.5
unreliability 970.6
urgency 996.4

momentous
authoritative 417.15
eventful 830.10
influential 893.13
important 996.17
vital 996.23

momentum motion
172.1
course 172.2
impulse 901.1

monarch 575.8

monarchist 611.13

monarchy central
government 612.4
absolutism 612.9

monastery 703.6

monastic
noun celibate 565.2
religious 699.15
adj celibate 565.6
monachal 698.14
claustral 703.16

monde 578.6

monetarism 731.10

monetarist 731.11

monetary 728.30

money wealth 618.1
currency 728.1

money in the bank
472.6

money market 728.16

money matters 729.1

money's worth worth
630.2
bargain 633.3

mongering 552.7

Mongolian 312.3

mongrel
noun cur 311.19
beast 660.7
hybrid 796.8
adj hybrid 796.15

monitor
noun warner 399.4
adviser 422.3
informant 551.5
teaching fellow 571.4
superintendent 574.2
examiner 937.17
radioman 1033.24
television technician
1034.13
output device 1041.9
verb be taught 570.11
examine 937.24
check 1033.26

monitoring vigilance
339.4
televising 1034.3

monk celibate 565.2
religious 699.15

monkey
noun temper 152.6
bear 311.23
imitator 336.4
dupe 358.1
laughingstock 508.7
mite 728.11
two hundred 881.9
verb monkey around
997.15

mono 50.11

monochrome
noun colour system
35.7
adj chromatic 35.15
pictorial 712.21

monogamous 563.19

monogram
identification 517.11
signature 527.10
letter 546.1

monogrammed 517.24

monograph 556.1

monolith monument
549.12
rock 1057.1

monolithic uniform
780.5
simple 797.6
stony 1057.11

monologue soliloquy
542.1
regularity 780.2

monopolist
noun restrictionist
428.6
self-seeker 651.3
adj monopolistic
469.11

monopolistic 469.11

monopoly restraint
428.1
monopolization 469.3
manipulation 737.20

monotone
noun tone 50.2
regularity 780.2
series 811.2
repetitiousness 848.4
adj sounding 50.15
monotonous 848.15

monotonous tedious
118.9
same 780.6
continuous 811.8
monotone 848.15

monotony tone 50.2
tedium 118.1
regularity 780.2
continuity 811.1
repetitiousness 848.4

monsieur 76.7

Monsignor 648.5

monsoon season 313.1
wet weather 316.4

monster
noun frightener 127.9
beast 144.14
whopper 257.11
behemoth 257.14
fiend 593.6
monstrosity 869.6
eyesore 1014.4
adj large 247.7
huge 257.20

monstrosity hugeness
257.7
deformity 265.3
abnormality 869.1
oddity 869.3
monster 869.6
eyesore 1014.4

monstrous large 247.7
huge 257.20
deformed 265.12

wicked 654.16
base 661.12
savage 671.21
freakish 869.13
absurd 922.11
excessive 992.16
terrible 999.9
unshapely 1014.8

monstrously basely
661.17
oddly 869.19

montage picture
712.11
photograph 714.3

month 823.2

monthly periodical
555.1
recurrent 848.13
momentary 849.8

monthly payments
624.1

monument tower
272.6
gravestone 309.17
figure 349.6
marker 517.10

monumental large
247.7
huge 257.20
high 272.14
sculptural 715.6

mood mode 530.11
plot 722.4
syllogism 934.6
humour 977.4

moodily sullenly
110.30
glumly 112.35

mood swings changing
853.3
depression 925.5

moody sullen 110.24
glum 112.25
capricious 364.5
inconstant 853.7

moon
noun jumping-off place
261.4
moment 823.2
Proteus 853.4
light source 1025.1
satellite 1070.11
verb undress 6.7
idle 331.12
muse 984.9

moonlight
noun moonshine
1024.11
verb distil 88.30
work 724.12

moonlighting 724.5

moonlit 1024.39

moonshine
noun juice 88.14
bootleg alcohol 88.18
humbug 354.14
bullshit 520.3
sophism 935.3

moonlight 1024.11
verb distil 88.30
push 732.7

moor
noun plain 236.1
highlands 237.1
plateau 237.3
marsh 243.1
verb settle 159.17
anchor 182.15
land 186.8
bind 428.10
fasten 799.7
secure 854.8

moored 854.16

mooring establishment
159.7
anchor 180.16
landing 186.2

moorings anchor
180.16
harbour 1008.6

moorish 243.3

moorland plain 236.1
highlands 237.1,
272.3
marsh 243.1

moors country 233.1
highlands 272.3

moose 311.5

moot
verb propose 439.5
argue 934.16
adj litigious 598.22
theoretical 950.13
doubted 954.12
unproved 957.8
doubtful 970.17

mop
noun head of hair 3.4
verb wash 79.19
grimace 265.8

moped 179.8

mopping 79.5

mop up 79.19

mora vowel quantity
524.12
metre 720.7

moral
noun warning 399.1
rule 419.2
lesson 568.7
maxim 973.1
adj ethical 636.6
dutiful 641.13
honest 644.13
virtuous 653.6

morale cooperation
450.1
morality 636.3
virtue 653.1
mood 977.4

moralistic preceptive
419.4
advisory 422.8
ethical 636.6

morality lesson 568.7

morals 636.3
virtue 653.1

morally honestly
644.21
attitudinally 977.9

morals ethics 636.1
morality 636.3

moral support 900.1

moral victory 411.1

morass marsh 243.1
complex 798.2
confusion 809.2
predicament 1012.4

moratorium grace
period 625.2
delay 845.2

morbid unwholesome
85.54
diseased 85.59
terrible 127.30
curious 980.5

more
noun plurality 882.1
adj additional 253.10
plural 882.7
adv increasingly 251.9
additionally 253.11

more and more 251.9

more desirable 371.25

more distant 261.10

more often than not
846.6

more of the same
118.1

moreover 253.11

mores custom 373.1
culture 373.3
conventions 579.2
etiquette 580.3
climate 977.5

more so 253.11

more than enough
noun plenty 990.2
superabundance 992.2
satiety 993.1
adv superabundantly
992.24

more than ever 249.17

more than half 882.2

more than one 882.7

morgue 309.9

moribund unhealthy
85.53
dying 307.33
languid 331.20

MORI poll 937.14

Mormon
noun Latter-day Saint
675.22
adj Koranic 683.13

Morning 314.2

morning
noun morn 314.1
adj matin 314.6
adv for a long time
826.14

morning after
  intoxication 88.1
  future 838.1

mornings 314.8

morning sickness 85.9

morning star 1070.4

moron 923.8

moronic mentally
  deficient 921.22
  foolish 922.8

morose sullen 110.24
  glum 112.25
  unsociable 583.5

morosely sullenly
  110.30
  glumly 112.35

morphine sleep-inducer
  22.10
  sedative 86.12

morris 366.1

morrow morning 314.1
  future 838.1

morsel bite 8.2
  delicacy 10.8
  scrap 248.3
  piece 792.3

mortal
  noun person 312.5
  adj perishable 307.34
  deadly 308.22
  human 312.13
  transient 827.7

mortality death rate
  307.13
  deadliness 308.8
  humankind 312.1
  humanness 312.8

mortally 312.17

mortals 312.1

mortar
  noun launcher 462.21
  philosopher's stone
  857.10
  sticks and stones
  1052.2
  verb plaster 295.25
  pull the trigger 459.22

mortgage
  noun mortgage deed
  438.4
  verb pledge 438.10

mortgaged 623.8

mortified diseased
  85.59
  distressed 96.22
  humiliated 137.14
  decayed 393.40

mortuary
  noun morgue 309.9
  adj deathly 307.29
  funereal 309.22

Mosaic 683.10

mosaic
  noun check 47.4
  picture 712.11
  adj checked 47.14

Moslem
  noun Muslim 675.23
  adj Muslim 675.31

mosque 703.2

mosquito 311.36

moss marsh 243.1
  legume 310.4

mossy 310.39

most
  noun supremacy 249.3
  major part 791.6
  majority 882.2
  adj extreme 247.13
  superlative 249.13
  majority 882.9
  adv extremely 247.22
  superlatively 249.16

most certainly 969.23

Most Excellent 648.8

most favoured nation
  731.1

most likely 967.8

mostly chiefly 249.17
  on the whole 791.14
  generally 863.17
  normally 868.10

most of all essentially
  766.11
  first 817.18

most recent 840.14

mot witticism 489.7
  maxim 973.1

motel 228.16

moth 1000.2

Mother 648.5

mother
  noun brother 559.3
  genetrix 560.11
  arsehole 660.6
  author 885.4
  producer 891.7
  verb procreate 78.8
  foster 449.16
  engender 817.14
  care for 1007.19
  adj native 226.5

Mother Earth 1070.10

motherfucker 660.6

motherhood blood
  relationship 559.1
  maternity 560.3

mothering 449.3

mother-in-law 564.2

motherland 232.2

motherly 560.17

Mother Nature 677.8

mother-of-pearl
  noun spectrum 47.6
  iridescence 1024.18
  adj soft-coloured
  35.21
  iridescent 47.10

mother's side 560.4

motif edging 211.7

ornamental motif
  498.7
  passage 708.24
  plot 722.4
  topic 936.1

motion
  noun faeces 12.4
  exercise 84.2
  movement 172.1
  travel 177.1
  activity 330.1
  proposal 439.2
  gesture 517.14
  bill 613.8
  process 888.2
  trend 895.2
  mechanism 1039.4
  verb gesture 517.21

motionless unmoving
  173.13
  passive 329.6
  inactive 331.17

motion picture cinema
  706.1
  shot 714.8

motion-picture 706.8

motions 321.1

motion to 517.21

motivate set in motion
  172.6
  move 375.12
  induce 885.11
  impel 901.11

motivated moved
  375.30
  teachable 570.18

motivating 375.25

motivation motion
  172.1
  moving 375.2
  teachableness 570.5

motivational moving
  172.7
  motivating 375.25

motivator energizer
  17.6
  prompter 375.10

motive
  noun reason 375.1
  intention 380.1
  passage 708.24
  topic 936.1
  adj moving 172.7
  motivating 375.25
  impelling 901.23
  propulsive 903.14

motley
  noun costume 5.9
  comedy 704.6
  buffoon 707.10
  verb variegate 47.7
  adj variegated 47.9
  mottled 47.12
  different 779.7
  nonuniform 781.3
  mixed 796.14

motor
  noun automobile 179.9

philosopher's stone
  857.10
  machinery 1039.3
  verb ride 177.33
  adj moving 172.7

motorboat
  noun ship 180.1
  powerboat 180.4
  verb navigate 182.13

motorcade 811.3

motorcycle
  noun cycle 179.8
  verb ride 177.33

motorcycling riding
  177.6
  sport 744.1

motorcyclist 178.11

motoring 177.6

motorist 178.10

motorized 1039.10

motor racing racing
  457.11
  automobile racing
  756.1

motor sport sport
  744.1
  motor racing 756.1

motor vehicle 179.9

mottled 47.12

motto heraldic device
  647.2
  caption 936.2
  maxim 973.1
  slogan 973.4

mould
  noun germ 85.41
  land 234.1
  form 262.1, 785.6
  structure 266.1
  legume 310.4
  original 337.2
  decay 393.6
  nature 766.4
  cast 784.6
  kind 808.3
  characteristic 864.4
  disposition 977.3
  blight 1000.2
  verb form 262.7
  decay 393.22
  sculpture 715.5
  pot 742.6
  conform 866.3
  produce 891.8
  imagine 985.14

moulded formative
  262.9
  sculptured 715.7
  made 891.18

moulding forming
  262.5
  structure 266.1
  sculpture 715.1
  cast 784.6
  production 891.2

mouldy malodorous
  71.5
  blighted 393.42

stale 841.14

moult shed 6.10
  waste 473.5

moulting disrobing 6.2
  waste 473.2

mound
  noun hill 237.4
  monument 549.12
  pile 769.10
  barrier 1011.5
  verb pile 769.19

mount
  noun ascent 193.1
  mountain 237.6
  horse 311.10
  hunter 311.13
  jockey 757.2
  frame 900.10
  verb copulate 75.21
  move 172.5
  go on horseback
  177.34
  ascend 184.39, 193.8
  climb 193.11
  get on 193.12
  rise 200.8
  grow 251.6, 272.12
  tower 272.10
  dramatize 704.28
  give a lift 911.7

mountain mount 237.6
  quantity 247.3
  plateau 272.4
  bulge 283.3

mountain bike 179.8

mountaineer traveller
  178.1
  climber 193.6

mountainous hilly
  237.8, 272.18
  large 247.7
  huge 257.20

mountain range
  mountain 237.6
  plateau 272.4

mountains 237.1

mountainside 237.2

mounted 177.44

Mounties 1007.17

mounting
  noun course 172.2
  ascent 193.1
  increase 251.1
  production 704.13
  frame 900.10
  adj flowing 172.8
  ascending 193.14
  high 272.14

mourn distress 98.14
  grieve 112.17
  lament 115.10

mournful distressing
  98.20
  sorrowful 112.26
  plaintive 115.19
  funereal 309.22

mournfully sorrowfully
  112.36

lamentingly 115.23

mourning
noun lamentation
115.1
weeds 115.7
adj lamenting 115.18

mouse shrinking violet
139.6
runt 258.4
coward 491.5
input device 1041.4

mousetrap trap 356.12
rocket launcher
1072.10

mousse sweets 10.38
pudding 10.44
foam 320.2

moustache 3.11

mouth
noun maw 2.16, 292.4
eater 8.16
inlet 242.1
verb chew 8.27
lick 73.9
grimace 265.8
be hypocritical 354.23
speak 524.20
mumble 525.9
declaim 543.10

mouthful bite 8.2
berating 510.7
high-sounding words
545.3

mouthing hypocrisy
354.6
mumbling 525.4
lip service 693.2

mouthpiece telephone
347.4
mediator 466.3
informant 551.5
spokesman 576.5
brief 597.3
wind instrument 711.6
boxing 754.1

mouthwash cleanser
79.17
dentifrice 86.22

mouth-watering
noun saliva 13.3
adj appetizing 63.10
desirable 100.30
alluring 377.8

mouton 10.15

movable transferable
176.18
changeable 853.6
influenceable 893.15

move
noun act 328.3
attempt 403.2
stratagem 415.3
process 888.2
expedient 994.2
verb affect 93.14
excite 105.12
touch 145.5
settle 159.17

progress 162.2
budge 172.5
set in motion 172.6
remove 176.11
travel 177.18
behave 321.4
act 328.4
motivate 375.12
admonish 422.6
propose 439.5
sell 734.8
influence 893.7
impel 901.11
push 903.9

move back 163.6

moved affected 93.23
excited 105.20
motivated 375.30

move in settle 159.17
gain influence 893.12

move into 404.3

movement
noun defecation 12.2
faeces 12.4
exercise 84.2
motion 172.1
travel 177.1
act 328.3
activity 330.1
operation 458.5
gesture 517.14
front 609.33
passage 708.24
rhythm 709.22
style 712.8
metre 720.7
plot 722.4
company 769.3
cause 885.9
trend 895.2
mechanism 1039.4
phrase moving 176.4

movements behaviour
321.1
mechanism 1039.4

move out 188.6

move over 172.5

move quickly 401.5

mover wanderer 178.2
prompter 375.10
doer 726.1
author 885.4
producer 891.7

moves 321.1

movie
noun cinema 706.1
adj cinema 706.8

movies 706.1

movie star 707.4

moving
noun motion 172.1
travel 177.1
motivation 375.2
adj affecting 93.22
distressing 98.20
exciting 105.30
pitiful 145.8
progressive 162.6

stirring 172.7
travelling 177.36
motivating 375.25
lofty 544.14
impelling 901.23
phrase removal 176.4

movingly feelingly
93.25
excitingly 105.36

moving pictures 706.1

mow
noun scowl 110.9
grimace 265.4
garner 386.7
pile 769.10
verb grimace 265.8
shorten 268.6
smooth 287.5
harvest 1067.19

mowed 268.9

mown 268.9

Mr 76.7

Mr Big 996.11

Mr Justice 596.1

Mrs 77.8

Mr X 528.2

Ms 77.8

much
noun quantity 247.3
plenty 990.2
adj many 247.8
plentiful 990.7
adv greatly 247.15

much-admired 155.11

**much ado about
nothing** overreaction
355.2
triviality 997.3

much in evidence
distinct 31.7
remarkable 247.10
manifest 348.8
prominent 662.17

much sought-after
desirable 100.30
fashionable 578.11

much the same
approximating 783.14
equivalent 789.8

muck
noun filth 80.7
slime 80.8
refuse 391.4
fertilizer 889.4
mud 1060.8
verb dirty 80.15

mucky filthy 80.23
slimy 1060.14

mucous 1060.13

mucus filth 80.7
lubricant 1054.2
semiliquid 1060.5

mud dirt 80.6
marsh 243.1
muck 1060.8

muddle

noun formlessness
263.1
fiasco 410.6
confusion 809.2,
984.3
verb deform 263.3
bungle 414.11
complicate 798.3
disorder 809.9
confuse 810.3, 984.7
confound 944.3
perplex 970.13
make uncertain 970.15

muddled intoxicated
88.31
confused 809.16
muddleheaded 921.18
in a dilemma 970.25
in a muddle 984.13

muddy
verb dirty 80.15
make uncertain 970.15
adj colourless 36.7
dingy 38.11
dirty 80.22
marshy 243.3
obscure 522.15
slimy 1060.14

muffin 10.30

muffled muted 52.17
covered 295.31
latent 519.5

mufti mullah 596.3
imam 699.11

mug
noun sucker 358.2
laughingstock 508.7
verb lambaste 459.15
swipe 482.16
rage 671.11
overact 704.31
photograph 714.14

mugger assailant
459.12
robber 483.5
roughneck 593.4

mugging attack 459.1
theft 482.3

mulberry 46.3

mulch 1067.17

mule
noun spinner 271.5
ass 311.16
smuggler 732.5
hybrid 796.8
phrase beast of burden
176.8

mull
noun point 283.9
verb sweeten 66.3
heat 1019.17

mullah teacher 571.1
ulema 596.3
imam 699.11

mullet heraldic device
647.2
five 881.1

multicoloured 47.9

multicultural
nonuniform 781.3
mixed 796.14

multilateral sided
218.7
multiangular 278.11

multinational 796.14

multiple
noun multiplication
882.4
adj multiform 782.3
multiplied 882.8
numerous 883.6

multiplication
procreation 78.2
multiplying 882.4
proliferation 889.2
notation 1016.2

multiplicity
multiformity 782.1
numerousness 883.1

multiplied increased
251.7
multiple 882.8

multiplier 882.4

multiply procreate 78.8
grow 251.6
proliferate 882.6
teem with 883.5
produce 889.7
calculate 1016.17

multiplying
noun multiplication
882.4
adj increasing 251.8

multiracial nonuniform
781.3
mixed 796.14

multitude quantity
247.3
masses 606.2
throng 769.4, 883.3

mum
noun silence 51.1
mummy 560.12
adj mute 51.12
taciturn 344.9

mumble
noun murmur 52.4
mumbling 525.4
verb chew 8.27
murmur 52.10, 524.26
mutter 525.9

mumbling
noun murmur 52.4
muttering 525.4
adj murmuring 52.18

Mumbo Jumbo 680.9

mumbo jumbo
juggling 356.5
nonsense 520.2
obscurity 522.3
jargon 523.9
occultism 689.1
incantation 691.4
charm 691.5

mummery hypocrisy
354.6

cover 356.11
ceremony 580.4
sanctimony 693.1
acting 704.8

mummified 1064.9

mummy corpse 307.16
mum 560.12
desert 1064.2

mumps sulks 110.10
blues 112.6

munch
  noun bite 8.2
  verb chew 8.27

munching 8.1

mundane
  noun profane 686.2
  adj unsacred 686.3
  secularist 695.16
  prosaic 721.5
  unimaginative 986.5

municipal 230.11

municipality town
  230.1
  bureau 594.4

munitions equipment
  385.4
  store 386.1
  arms 462.1

mural
  noun picture 712.11
  adj partitioned 213.11

murder
  noun homicide 308.2
  verb commit murder
  308.15
  bungle 414.11

murdered 414.21

murderer 308.10

murderous cruel
  144.26
  slaughterous 308.23
  savage 671.21

murk
  noun gloom 112.7
  obscurity 522.3
  darkishness 1026.2
  verb blacken 38.7
  darken 1026.9
  adj darkish 1026.15

murky dingy 38.11
  gloomy 112.24
  obscure 522.15
  vague 970.19
  stained 1003.10
  darkish 1026.15

murmur
  noun murmuring 52.4
  lament 115.3
  verb mutter 52.10,
  524.26
  complain 115.15
  sigh 318.21
  mumble 525.9

murmured 52.16

murmuring
  noun murmur 52.4
  complaint 115.4

mumbling 525.4
  adj murmurous 52.18
  discontented 108.7

muscle
  noun muscularity 15.2
  exertion 725.1
  verb thrust 901.12
  adj skeleton 2.24

muscle-bound 15.16

muscle in 214.5

muscles 2.3

muscular skeleton 2.24
  able-bodied 15.16

Muse Muses 720.10
  genius 919.8

muse
  noun inspiration 375.9
  abstractedness 984.2
  creative thought 985.2
  verb remark 524.25
  consider 930.12
  moon 984.9

Muses inspiration 375.9
  Nine 710.22
  Muse 720.10

museum gallery 386.9
  preserve 397.7
  collection 769.11

**Museum of Modern
Art** 386.9

mush
  noun looks 33.4
  pulp 1061.2
  verb march 177.30

mushroom
  noun magic mushroom
  87.18
  legume 310.4
  verb grow 14.2, 259.7
  ball 282.7

mushrooming 251.8

mushy wishy-washy
  16.17
  pulpy 1061.6

music harmonious
  sound 708.1
  score 708.28
  harmonics 709.1

musical
  noun musical theatre
  708.34
  adj musically inclined
  708.47
  melodious 708.48
  rhyming 720.17

musical chairs 853.3

musical director
  710.17

musical instrument
  711.1

musically 720.18

musical theatre
  708.34

music box 711.15

music critic 547.15,
  718.4

music festival 708.32

music hall hall 197.4
  show business 704.1
  theatre 704.14

musician entertainer
  707.1
  musico 710.1

music-like 708.48

music-making 708.30

music theatre 708.34

musing
  noun consideration
  930.2
  thoughtfulness 930.3
  abstractedness 984.2
  dreaminess 985.8
  adj cognitive 930.21
  abstracted 984.11

musk 70.2

musket 462.10

musky 70.9

Muslim
  noun Mussulman
  675.23
  adj Islamic 675.31

muslin 180.14

muso 710.1

mussel 311.30

must
  noun fetidness 71.2
  wine 88.17
  duty 641.1
  requirement 962.2
  blight 1000.2
  verb be necessary
  962.10
  adj in heat 75.27
  mandatory 420.12
  obligatory 641.15

mustang 311.10

muster
  noun call to arms
  458.8
  enlistment 615.7
  assemblage 769.1
  roll 870.6
  verb avail oneself of
  387.14
  summon 420.11
  call to arms 458.19
  enlist 615.17
  come together 769.16
  assemble 769.18

musty malodorous 71.5
  in heat 75.27
  trite 117.9
  blighted 393.42
  stale 841.14

mutant
  noun transformation
  851.3
  adj savage 671.21
  changed 851.10

mutate diversify 781.2
  be changed 851.6
  change 851.7

mutation phonetics
  524.14
  transformation 851.3

mute
  noun dummy 51.3
  silencer 51.4
  mourner 309.7
  speech sound 524.13
  metronome 711.22
  verb muffle 51.9
  adj mum 51.12
  taciturn 344.9
  stammering 525.13
  inanimate 1053.5

muted muffled 52.17
  phonetic 524.31

mutilated deformed
  265.12
  impaired 393.27
  garbled 794.5

mutilation trauma
  85.37
  excision 255.3
  deformity 265.3
  impairment 393.1
  severance 801.2

mutiny
  noun revolt 327.4
  lawlessness 418.1
  verb revolt 327.7

mutt cur 311.19
  chump 923.3

mutter
  noun murmur 52.4
  lament 115.3
  mumbling 525.4
  verb murmur 52.10,
  524.26
  complain 115.15
  sigh 318.21
  mumble 525.9

muttering
  noun murmur 52.4
  mumbling 525.4
  adj murmuring 52.18
  discontented 108.7

mutton mouton 10.15
  sheep 311.7

mutual cooperative
  450.5
  communal 476.9
  accompanying 768.9
  commutual 776.11
  interchangeable 862.5

mutually together
  768.11
  commonly 776.13
  jointly 799.18
  interchangeably 862.6

mutual support 862.1

mutual understanding
  332.5

muzzle
  noun silencer 51.4
  nose 283.8
  mouth 292.4
  shackle 428.4
  verb paralyse 19.10

silence 51.8
  suppress 428.8

My Lady 648.2

My Lord 648.2

myopia 28.3

myopic poor-sighted
  28.11
  undiscerning 921.14
  unwise 922.10

myriad
  noun thousand 881.10,
  883.4
  plenty 990.2
  adj numerous 883.6

myrrh 70.2

myself 864.5

mysterious awesome
  122.11
  secret 345.11
  concealed 346.11
  inexplicable 522.18
  ambiguous 539.4
  occult 689.23
  supernatural 869.15
  unknown 929.17
  bewildering 970.27

mysteriously
  awesomely 122.15
  inexplicably 522.24
  oddly 869.19

mystery wonderfulness
  122.3
  secret 345.5
  inexplicability 522.6
  enigma 522.8
  occultism 689.1
  rite 701.3
  vocation 724.6
  supernaturalism 869.7
  unknown 929.7
  bewilderment 970.3

mystic
  noun occultist 689.11
  adj latent 519.5
  inexplicable 522.18
  epiphanic 683.12
  occult 689.23

mystical inexplicable
  522.18
  epiphanic 683.12
  occult 689.23

mysticism revelation
  683.9
  occultism 689.1

mystified in a dilemma
  970.25
  at an impasse 1012.24

mystifying misteaching
  569.6
  bewildering 970.27

mystique illustriousness
  662.6
  cult 675.2
  opinion 952.6

myth fabrication 354.10
  tradition 841.2
  figment of the
  imagination 985.5

mythic mythical 678.15
　fictitious 985.21
mythical fabricated
　354.29
　distinguished 662.16
　mythic 678.15
　fictional 722.7
　extraordinary 869.14
　fictitious 985.21
mythological mythic
　678.15
　fictional 722.7
　traditional 841.12
　fictitious 985.21
mythology mythicism
　678.14
　tradition 841.2
N 161.15
N- 1037.19
n 929.7
nab nick 429.16
　grab 472.9
　capture 480.18
nadir bottom 199.1
　boundary 211.3
　base 274.4
naff inelegant 534.2
　lousy 999.8
　inferior 1004.9
nag
　noun tormentor 96.10
　horse 311.10
　hack 311.12
　verb annoy 96.13
　urge 375.14
　importune 440.12
　niggle 510.16
　remind 988.20
nagged 988.24
nagging
　noun importunity
　440.3
　criticism 510.4
　adj peevish 110.22
　importunate 440.18
　critical 510.23
　unforgettable 988.26
nail
　noun fastening 799.3
　verb grab 472.9
　seize 480.14
　beat up 604.14
　hook 799.8
nail-biting
　noun nervousness
　128.1
　adj anxious 126.7
　nervous 128.11
nail polish 1015.12
nails horse 15.8
　clutches 474.4
　stone 1044.6
naive immature 301.10
　artless 416.5
　natural 499.7
　foolable 922.12
　ignorant 929.12
　trusting 952.22

gullible 953.9
naivety artlessness
　416.1
　gullibility 953.2
naked nude 6.14
　visible 31.6
　open 292.17, 348.10
　unadorned 499.8
　unmixed 797.7
　exposed 1005.15
naked eye eye 2.9,
　27.9
　field of view 31.3
nakedness nudity 6.3
　unadornment 499.3
　exposure 1005.3
naked truth 972.3
name
　noun appellation 527.3
　repute 662.1
　celebrity 662.9
　personage 996.8
　verb nominate 371.19
　designate 517.18
　denominate 527.11
　appoint 615.11
　specify 864.11
　cite 956.13
　number 1016.16
name and address
　553.9
named chosen 371.26
　called 527.14
　former 813.5
nameless anonymous
　528.3
　unrenowned 661.14
namely by
　interpretation 341.18
　nominally 864.18
name of the game
　766.3
namesake 527.3
naming
　noun nomination 371.8
　indication 517.3
　calling 527.2
　appointment 615.2
　adj indicative 517.23
nanny 1007.8
nap
　noun snooze 22.3
　texture 294.1
　table 752.2
　jockey 757.2
　verb sleep 22.13
napkin waistband 5.19
　table linen 8.13
napoleon 728.4
napping sleepy 22.21
　unaware 929.13
　unalert 983.8
　abstracted 984.11
nappy
　noun waistband 5.19
　adj feathery 3.28
　intoxicated 88.31

pily 294.7
narcissism perversion
　75.11
　vanity 140.1
　selfishness 651.1
narcissistic vain 140.8
　egotistic 140.10
　selfish 651.5
Narcissus egotist 140.5
　Venus 1015.10
narcotic
　noun anaesthetic 25.3
　drug 87.2
　adj sleep-inducing
　22.23
　deadening 25.9
　sedative 86.45
　palliative 670.16
narcotics 732.3
nares olfactory organ
　69.5
　nose 283.8
narration description
　349.2
　story 719.3, 722.3
　fiction 722.1
　narrative 722.2
narrative
　noun story 719.3,
　722.3
　fiction 722.1
　narration 722.2
　adj narrational 719.8,
　722.8
　poetic 720.15
narrator 722.5
narrow
　noun narrows 270.3
　verb limit 210.5
　contract 260.7
　constrict 270.11
　restrict 428.9
　simplify 797.4
　specialize 865.4
　qualify 958.3
　adj limited 210.7
　slender 270.14
　meticulous 339.12
　prudish 500.19
　phonetic 524.31
　poor 619.7
　exclusive 772.9
　narrow-minded 979.10
　meagre 991.10
narrow escape 369.2
narrowing
　noun contraction 260.1
　tapering 270.2
　exclusion 772.1
　simplification 797.2
　adj restrictive 428.12
narrowly 270.22
narrow-minded
　979.10
narrowness slenderness
　270.1
　prudery 500.6
　exclusiveness 772.3

narrow-mindedness
　979.1
　meagreness 991.2
narrows 270.3
nasal
　noun speech sound
　524.13
　adj respiratory 2.30
　phonetic 524.31
　inarticulate 525.12
nascent 817.15
nastiness foulness 64.3
　filthiness 80.2
　offensiveness 98.2
　malice 144.5
　discourtesy 505.1
　obscenity 666.4
　terribleness 999.2
nasty offensive 64.7,
　98.18
　filthy 80.23
　malicious 144.20
　ill-bred 505.6
　obscene 666.9
　terrible 999.9
natal native 226.5
　beginning 817.15
nation population
　227.1
　country 232.1
　humankind 312.1
　race 559.4
　people 606.1
national
　noun citizen 227.4
　adj public 312.16
　racial 559.7
　populational 606.8
　universal 863.14
national anthem
　458.12
national assembly
　613.1
national convention
　609.8
National Curriculum
　568.8
national debt 623.1
national defence 460.2
national emergency
　458.10
national flag 647.6
national front 609.33
National Gallery
　386.9
national government
　612.3
national grid 1031.18
National Guard
　461.23
**National Health
Service** 611.8
national holiday 20.4
national income 627.1
national insurance
　welfarism 611.8

insurance 1007.4
nationalism
　nationhood 232.6
　patriotism 591.2
　foreign policy 609.5
　fascism 611.10
nationalist
　noun patriot 591.3
　fascist 611.21
　adj fascist 611.33
nationalistic 591.4
nationality nativeness
　226.1
　country 232.1
　nationhood 232.6
　humankind 312.1
　patriotism 591.2
nationalization
　naturalization 226.3
　communization 476.3
　attachment 480.5
　socialism 611.7
national leader 610.2
national library 558.1
national newspaper
　555.2
national park 397.7
national service
　service 458.9
　enlistment 615.7
national socialism
　612.8
National Trust 397.5
nationhood 232.6
nation-state 232.1
nation-wide 863.14
native
　noun indigene 227.3
　adj natal 226.5
　natural 406.13, 416.6,
　499.7
　innate 766.8
native land 232.2
native to 766.8
Nativity 1.1
nativity birth 1.1
　nativeness 226.1
　origin 817.4
　astrology 1070.20
natty chic 578.13
　tidy 806.8
natural
　noun talented person
　413.12
　note 709.14
　oddity 869.4
　idiot 923.8
　adj typical 349.15
　native 406.13, 499.7
　naturelike 416.6
　elegant 533.6
　plain-speaking 535.3
　related 559.6
　informal 581.3
　innate 766.8
　lifelike 783.16
　normal 868.8

instinctive 933.6
genuine 972.15

natural colour 35.1

naturalism naturalness
416.2
normality 868.1
genuineness 972.7
materialism 1050.6

naturalist materialist
1050.7
biologist 1066.2

naturalistic descriptive
349.14
typical 349.15
normal 868.8
genuine 972.15

natural light 1024.10

naturally
adv artlessly 416.7
unaffectedly 499.11
plainly 535.4
informally 581.4
intrinsically 766.10
normally 868.10
consequently 886.7
genuinely 972.19
exclam yes 332.18

naturalness
inartificiality 406.3,
499.2
naturalism 416.2
elegance 533.1
plain speech 535.1
informality 581.1
normality 868.1
genuineness 972.7

naturals 413.4

natural science 927.10

natural selection
860.3

natural state 406.3

natural to 766.8

natural world matter
1050.2
environment 1071.1

Nature 677.8

nature naturalness
406.3, 416.2
character 766.4
kind 808.3
characteristic 864.4
disposition 977.3
matter 1050.2
universe 1070.1

nature reserve 397.7

naught nothing 761.2
insignificancy 997.6

naughty misbehaving
322.5
disobedient 327.8
wicked 654.16

nausea anaemia 85.9
nauseation 85.30
unpleasure 96.1
hostility 99.2
vomiting 908.8

nauseated nauseous
85.56
pleasureless 96.20

nauseating nasty 64.7
filthy 80.23
offensive 98.18

nauseous nasty 64.7
nauseated 85.56
pleasureless 96.20

nautical marine 182.57
oceanic 240.8

naval 182.57

naval forces 461.26

naval officer 183.7

nave centre 208.2
vestry 703.9
axle 914.5

navel 208.2

navigate locate 159.11
journey 177.21
sail 182.13
pilot 182.14
fly 184.36

navigating 182.1

navigation guidance
159.3
topography 159.8
direction 161.1, 573.1
water travel 182.1
avigation 184.6

navigational locational
159.19
nautical 182.57

navigator mariner
183.1
hand 183.6
captain 183.7
crew 185.4
guide 574.7

Navy 461.20

navy
noun ships 180.10
naval forces 461.26
adj blue 45.3

navy blue 45.3

nay
noun negation 335.1
vote 371.6
refusal 442.1
side 934.14
exclam no 335.8

Nazism 612.8

NB 982.22

Neanderthal
noun barbarian 497.7
adj unrefined 497.12

near
verb approach 167.3
come near 223.7
resemble 783.7
come 838.6
be imminent 839.2
adj approaching 167.4
left 220.4
close 223.14
narrow 270.14
familiar 587.19

approximate 774.8
approximating 783.14
imminent 839.3
adv nigh 223.20
nearly 223.22
prep at 159.27
nigh 223.24

nearby
adj handy 223.15
adv aside 218.10
near 223.20

near death 307.33

Near East 231.6

near enough to 223.26

nearer 223.18

nearest 223.19

nearing
noun approach 167.1
adj approaching 167.4
near 223.14
future 838.8
imminent 839.3

nearly near 223.22
approximately 244.6
narrowly 270.22
on the whole 791.14

near miss crash 184.20
meeting 223.4
narrow escape 369.2
miss 410.4

nearside 220.4

near to near 223.24
about to 838.13

neat
noun cattle 311.6
adj shipshape 180.20
shapely 264.5
skilful 413.22
elegant 533.6
plain-speaking 535.3
chic 578.13
unmixed 797.7
tidy 806.8
great 998.13

neath 274.11

neatly skilfully 413.31
smartly 578.18

neatness elegance
533.1
smartness 578.3
orderliness 806.3

neb olfactory organ
69.5
nose 283.8
point 285.3

nebulous cloudy 319.7
obscure 522.15
general 863.11
celestial 1070.25

necessarily
consequently 886.7
needfully 962.16
inevitably 962.19

necessary
noun dough 728.2
requirement 962.2

adj obligatory 424.11,
641.15, 962.12
requisite 962.13
inevitable 962.15
certain 969.13

necessitate oblige
424.5, 962.8
determine 885.12
destine 963.7

necessitated 886.6

necessities 962.2

necessity compulsion
424.1
indigence 619.2
necessariness 962.1
requirement 962.2
inevitability 962.7
predetermination
963.1
certainty 969.1

neck
noun leg 10.22
contraction 260.1
narrow 270.3
joint 799.4
supporter 900.2
verb pet 562.15
hang 604.17

neck-and-neck equal
789.7
simultaneous 835.5

necklace
noun band 280.3
jewel 498.6
capital punishment
604.6
scaffold 605.5
verb strike dead
308.17

nectar delicacy 10.8
sweetening 66.2

ned 302.4

need
noun desire 100.1
indigence 619.2
deficiency 794.2
requirement 962.2
want 991.4
verb be poor 619.5
require 962.9
be necessary 962.10
want 991.7

needed 962.13

need for 962.2

needful
noun dough 728.2
requirement 962.2
adj requisite 962.13

needing desirous
100.21
incomplete 794.4
wanting 991.13

needle
noun energizer 17.6
sound reproduction
system 50.11
mountain 237.6
point 285.3

thorn 285.5
leaf 310.17
pointer 517.4
compass 574.9
engraving tool 713.8
verb annoy 96.13
perforate 292.15
goad 375.15
kid 490.6
sew 741.4

needles 460.3

needless unnecessary
391.10
superfluous 992.17

needlessly uselessly
391.15
superfluously 992.25

needlework 741.1

need to 962.10

needy
noun poor 619.3
adj indigent 619.8

negate abnegate 335.3
abolish 395.13
refuse 442.3
contradict 451.6
disagree 788.5
neutralize 899.7
disbelieve 954.5
disprove 957.4

negated 957.7

negation negating
335.1
extinction 395.6
refusal 442.1
opposition 451.1
nonexistence 761.1
disagreement 788.1
disproof 957.1

negative
noun subtrahend 255.6
negation 335.1
refusal 442.1
veto 444.2
print 713.5, 784.5
film 714.10
mould 785.6
side 934.14
verb negate 335.3
abolish 395.13
refuse 442.3
veto 444.5
neutralize 899.7
disprove 957.4
adj pessimistic 125.16
negatory 335.5
unconsenting 442.6
oppositional 451.8
nonexistent 761.8
contrary 778.6
disagreeing 788.6
positive 1031.34
exclam no 335.8

negative attitude
335.1

negatively 335.6

negativity negation
335.1
nonexistence 761.1

New Left 611.5
new life 685.4
new look fashion 578.1
  novelty 840.2
newly freshly 840.15
  again 873.7
newlyweds 563.9
new man 840.4
new-model
  verb re-form 857.12
  adj new-made 840.9
new moon 1070.11
newness nonimitation
  337.1
  unaccustomedness
  374.1
  present 837.1
  freshness 840.1
new phase 851.4
news
  noun tidings 552.1
  adj newspaper 555.2
news agency 552.1
newsagent 730.5
news bulletin 1034.2
newscaster 1033.23
news conference 541.6
news coverage 552.1
news editor 555.4
newsletter 552.1
newsman 555.4
newspaper
  noun news 552.1
  adj news 555.2
newspaper publishing
  555.3
newsreader 1033.23
news report 552.5
news service 552.1
new start 857.2
newsworthy 552.13
newt 311.27
New Testament 683.4
New-Testament
  683.10
new to unaccustomed
  374.4
  inexperienced 414.17
new town 230.1
New World 231.6
next
  adj adjacent 223.16
  nearest 223.19
  succeeding 814.4
  adv subsequently
  834.6
next best 1004.4
next best thing 861.2
next-door 223.20
next door to 223.24
next in line 479.5
next of kin 559.2

next to 159.27
next to nothing 248.5
next world 838.2
nexus 811.2
Niagara 238.11
nibble
  noun bite 8.2
  verb feed 8.18
  pick 8.26
  chew 8.27
  kid oneself 953.6
  trifle 997.14
nibbling 8.1
nice tasty 63.8
  pleasant 97.6
  kind 143.13
  meticulous 339.12
  dainty 495.11
  elegant 496.9
  right 637.3
  conscientious 644.15
  detailed 765.9
  discriminating 943.7
  exact 972.17
  attentive 982.15
  good 998.12
nice guy 659.2
nice-looking 1015.18
nicely kindly 143.18
  meticulously 339.16
  excellently 998.22
niceness pleasantness
  97.1
  kindness 143.1
  meticulousness 339.3
  nicety 495.3
  taste 496.1
  propriety 637.2
  accuracy 972.5
  goodness 998.1
niche nook 197.3
  recess 284.7
  hiding place 346.4
nick
  noun town hall 230.5
  notch 289.1
  jug 429.9
  mark 517.5
  type 548.6
  verb notch 289.4
  nab 429.16
  swipe 482.16
  mark 517.19
  play 747.4
nicked 289.5
nickel
  noun mill 728.8
  precious metals 728.20
  adj brass 1056.17
nickname
  noun sobriquet 527.7
  verb name 527.11
nick of time 842.5
nicotine 89.9
nicotinic 89.15
niece 559.3
nifty

noun eleven 881.7
  adj great 998.13
niggling
  noun criticism 510.4
  adj insignificant 248.6
  critical 510.23
  attentive 982.15
  petty 997.20
nigh
  verb near 223.7
  adj left 220.4
  near 223.14
  adv near 223.20
  nearly 223.22
  prep near 223.24
night
  noun nighttime 315.4
  darkness 1026.1
  adj nocturnal 315.9
night and day
  noun opposites 215.2
  adv constantly 846.7
nightcap sleep-inducer
  22.10
  drink 88.9
nightclub bar 88.20
  theatre 704.14
  entertainment 743.13
nightdress 5.21
nightfall 315.2
nightgown 5.21
nightingale 710.23
nightlife 743.3
nightly
  adj nocturnal 315.9
  adv nights 315.11
nightmare torment
  96.7
  frightener 127.9
  dream 985.9
nightmarish 127.28
nights 315.11
night shift 824.3
night vision 27.1
nihilism pessimism
  125.6
  anarchy 418.2
  radicalism 611.5
nihilistic pessimistic
  125.16
  destructive 395.26
  anarchic 418.6
  radical 611.29
  unruly 671.19
nil 761.2
nimble fast 174.15
  quick 330.18
  alert 339.14
  agile 413.23
  smart 919.14
nimbus illustriousness
  662.6
  halo 1024.14
Nimrod hunter 382.5
  shooter 903.8
Nine 710.22

nine team 617.7
  card 758.2
  niner 881.5
nine-to-five
  noun routine 373.6
  adj habitual 373.15
ninety 881.7
ninth 881.21
nip
  noun bite 8.2
  drink 8.4, 88.7
  pang 26.2
  zest 68.2
  scrap 248.3
  squeezing 260.2
  hold 474.2
  cold 1022.1
  verb pain 26.7
  bite 68.5
  tipple 88.24
  converge 169.2
  barrel 174.9
  excise 255.10
  squeeze 260.8
  shorten 268.6
  put an end to 395.12
  hold 474.6
  seize 480.14
  freeze 1022.10,
  1023.11
nipped contracted
  260.12
  shortened 268.9
nipping
  noun drinking 8.3
  adj cold 1022.14
nipple tube 239.6
  breast 283.6
nirvana
  unconsciousness 25.2
  undesirousness 102.3
  Buddha-field 681.8
  thoughtlessness 932.1
  forgetfulness 989.1
nisse 678.8
nit vermin 311.35
  criticism 510.4
  stupid person 923.2
nitrate
  noun fertilizer 889.4
  verb chemicalize
  1058.7
nitrogen 889.4
nitty-gritty reality
  760.2
  meat and potatoes
  766.3
NKVD 1007.17
no
  noun negation 335.1
  vote 371.6
  refusal 442.1
  side 934.14
  adv none 761.12
  phrase I refuse 442.7
  exclam nay 335.8
no-account worthless
  391.11

uninfluential 894.3
Noah's ark 796.6
no alternative 962.6
no ball 747.3
nobby 998.13
Nobel Prize 646.2
no big deal 997.6
nobility proud bearing
  136.2
  glory 247.2
  best 249.5
  mastership 417.7
  grandeur 501.5
  loftiness 544.6
  upper class 607.2
  aristocracy 608.1
  nobleness 608.2
  probity 644.1
  magnanimity 652.2
  distinction 662.5
Noble 648.8
noble
  noun nobleman 608.4
  adj dignified 136.12
  eminent 247.9
  grandiose 501.21
  lofty 544.14
  of rank 608.10
  honest 644.13
  magnanimous 652.6
  reputable 662.15
  unchangeable 854.17
  notable 996.19
  good 998.12
nobleman 608.4
nobly dignifiedly
  136.14
  intensely 247.20
  grandiosely 501.28
  honestly 644.21
  magnanimously 652.8
  reputably 662.20
nobody no one 222.6
  insignificancy 997.7
  mediocrity 1004.5
no chance
  noun gambling odds
  759.6
  impossibility 966.1
  not a Chinaman's
  chance 971.10
  phrase no can do
  966.11
no charge
  noun costlessness
  634.1
  adj gratuitous 634.5
no choice dilemma
  371.3
  restriction 428.3
  choicelessness 962.6
no contest 412.3
nocturnal 315.9
nod
  noun stupor 22.6
  obeisance 155.2
  affirmative 332.2

summons 420.5
approval 509.1
signal 517.15
hint 551.4
greeting 585.4
crouch 912.3
verb bow 155.6
hang 202.6
assent 332.8
neglect 340.6
consent 441.2
signal 517.22

nodding sleepy 22.21
intoxicated 87.22
drooping 202.10
languid 331.20
unalert 983.8
abstracted 984.11

noddy
noun chump 923.3
adj high 87.23

node nodule 283.5
wave 915.4
dilemma 1012.7
solid 1043.6

no doubt probably
967.8
unquestionably 969.25

nod to 585.10

no end greatly 247.15
chiefly 249.17
numerously 883.12
plentifully 990.9

no end of
noun lot 247.4
multitude 883.3
plenty 990.2
adv greatly 247.15

no frills unadornment
499.3
simplicity 797.1
realism 986.2

no-frills reduced
252.10
unadorned 499.8

no future 125.1

no go
noun failure 410.1
adj useless 391.9

no-good
noun wretch 660.2
adj worthless 391.11

no holds barred
noun latitude 430.4
adv no ifs 959.3

no hope 125.1

noise
noun sound 50.1
loud noise 53.3
clash 61.2
meaninglessness 520.1
Greek 522.7
information technology
551.7
pandemonium 809.5
reception 1033.21
picture 1034.5
verb sound 50.14

be noisy 53.9

noisily 53.14

noisy noiseful 53.13
vociferous 59.10
blustering 503.4

no joke 996.3

no less than 244.7

nomad
noun Bedouin 178.4
adj wandering 177.37

nomadic 177.37

no man 222.6

no-man's-land
prohibition 444.1
battlefield 463.2

no matter 997.25

no matter how 384.11

no matter what 335.9

no matter who 863.7

no mean 413.22

nomenclature 527.1

nominal
noun noun 530.5
adj cognominal 527.15
grammatical 530.17
formal 580.7
cheap 633.7

nominally falsely
354.35
cheaply 633.10
namely 864.18

nominate name
371.19, 527.11
support 609.41
appoint 615.11

nominated 371.26

nomination designation
371.8
selection 609.11
appointment 615.2
holy orders 698.10

nominee 615.9

no more gone 34.5
dead 307.30
extinct 761.11
past 836.7

non 335.8

Nona 963.3

nonchalance apathy
94.4
unconcern 102.2
casualness 106.5

nonchalant apathetic
94.13
unconcerned 102.7
blasé 106.15

nonchalantly
unconcernedly 102.10
casually 106.18

nondescript formless
263.4
simple 499.6

none
noun divine service
696.8

not any 761.4
adv no 761.12

none at all 761.4

none other 777.3

nonetheless
adv anyhow 384.10
adv, conj
notwithstanding 338.8

non-Muslim
noun gentile 688.6
adj infidel 688.10

no-no 513.4

no nonsense
unadornment 499.3
realism 986.2

no-nonsense unadorned
499.8
clear-witted 919.13

nonplussed in a
dilemma 970.25
at an impasse 1012.24

non-profit 617.16

non-profit-making
617.16

nonsense stuff and
nonsense 520.2
foolishness 922.1
absurdity 922.3

nonsensical silly 520.7
absurd 922.11

non-starter flop 410.2
loser 410.8

nonstop continuous
811.8
perpetual 828.7

noodles 10.32

nook corner 197.3
angle 278.2
recess 284.7
hiding place 346.4

noon
noun summit 198.2
noonday 314.5
adj noonday 314.7
adv for a long time
826.14

no one 222.6

noose
noun circle 280.2
snare 356.13
scaffold 605.5
verb trap 356.20
catch 480.17
hang 604.17
weave 740.6

no other same 777.3
one 871.3

nope 335.10

nor 335.7

nor'
noun points of the
compass 161.3
adv north 161.15

norm mean 246.1
measure 300.2

rule 373.5, 419.2,
868.4
ethics 636.1
paragon 659.4

normal
noun vertical 200.2
mean 246.1
straight line 277.2
usual 868.3
adj medium 246.3
right-angled 278.7
typical 349.15
customary 373.14
right 637.3
orderly 806.6
prevalent 863.12
natural 868.8
sane 924.4
ordinary 1004.8

normality propriety
637.2
prevalence 863.2
normalness 868.1
sanity 924.1
ordinariness 1004.2

normally customarily
373.20
generally 863.17
naturally 868.10

normative customary
373.14
preceptive 419.4
right 637.3
model 785.8
normal 868.8
usual 868.9

norms ethics 636.1
climate 977.5

North 231.7

north
noun points of the
compass 161.3
adj northern 161.14
adv N 161.15

North America 231.6,
235.1

North and South
758.3

northbound 161.14

North Country 231.7

Northeast 231.7

northeast
noun points of the
compass 161.3
adj northern 161.14

northeastern 161.14

northerly
adj northern 161.14
adv north 161.15

northern 161.14

Northerner 227.11

Northern Hemisphere
231.6

North Pole opposites
215.2
jumping-off place
261.4

Siberia 1022.4

north pole 1031.8

Northumbria 231.7

North Wales 231.7

Northwest 231.7

northwest
noun points of the
compass 161.3
adj northern 161.14

northwestern 161.14

nose
noun olfactory organ
69.5, 283.8
prow 216.3
nozzle 239.9
person 312.5
verb smell 69.8
stroke 73.8
trace 937.35
pry 980.4

nose out trace 937.35
scent 940.6
be curious 980.3

nosing 69.3

nostalgia sentimentality
93.8
wistfulness 100.4
yearning 100.5
melancholy 112.5

nostalgic sentimental
93.21
wistful 100.23
melancholy 112.23

nostalgically 112.34

no stranger to used to
373.17
cognizant of 927.16

nostril 239.13

nostrils olfactory organ
69.5
nose 283.8

no strings 430.27

no such thing
noun nothing 761.2
different thing 779.3
adj nothing like 786.5
exclam no 335.8

nosy 937.38

not 335.8

not a bit
noun none 761.4
adv noway 248.11

not a bit of it
adj nothing like 786.5
adv noway 248.11
exclam nope 335.10

notable
noun celebrity 662.9
personage 996.8
adj remarkable 247.10
conspicuous 348.12
distinguished 662.16
characteristic 864.13
memorable 988.25
noteworthy 996.19

notably intensely 247.20
  conspicuously 348.16
  famously 662.21
  importantly 996.25
not absolutely 774.12
not accept deny 335.4
  refuse to believe 955.3
not admit deny 335.4
  disbelieve 954.5
not a few 883.6
not affect 94.5
not agree 333.4
not a little 247.15
not answer 910.2
not any 761.4
not appreciate 151.3
not approve 510.10
not at all
  adv noway 248.11
  none 761.12
  never 821.4
  exclam by no means 335.9
notation comment 341.5
  representation 349.1
  memorandum 549.4
  entry 628.5
  score 708.28
  character 709.12
  addition 1016.2
  number 1016.3
not attend 983.2
not bad 998.20
not be able 19.8
not be found 761.5
not-being 761.1
not believe 954.5
not buy refuse 442.3
  disbelieve 954.5
not care not mind 102.4
  take no interest in 981.2
not care for dislike 99.3
  neglect 340.6
notch
  noun crack 224.2
  ridge 237.5
  degree 245.1
  indentation 284.6
  nick 289.1
  mark 517.5
  verb indent 284.14
  nick 289.4
  mark 517.19
notched indented 284.17
  nicked 289.5
notching 289.2
not come 222.7
not coming 640.9
not complain 107.5

not comply 867.4
not concern 775.4
not conform disobey 327.6
  nonconform 867.4
not consider 932.2
not considered 372.3
not count 997.11
not counting 255.14
not destroy 397.8
not done underdone 11.8
  wrong 638.3
  unfair 650.10
  unconventional 867.6
note
  noun observation 27.2
  animal noise 60.1
  milieu 209.3
  postscript 254.2
  comment 341.5
  sign 517.1
  remark 524.4
  memorandum 549.4
  certificate 549.6
  letter 553.2
  treatise 556.1
  entry 628.5
  distinction 662.5
  air 708.4
  pitch 709.4
  musical note 709.14
  interval 709.20
  paper money 728.5
  cognizance 927.2
  mood 977.4
  attention 982.1
  importance 996.1
  verb signify 517.17
  remark 524.25
  record 549.15
  keep accounts 628.8
  heed 982.6
not easy adverse 1010.13
  difficult 1012.17
not eat 515.4
notebook pocketbook 549.11
  book 554.1
  computer 1041.2
noted 662.16
note down 549.15
not enough 991.9
not ever 821.4
noteworthy remarkable 247.10
  particular 864.12
  extraordinary 869.14
  notable 996.19
not exist 761.5
not expect 131.4
not fail 644.9
not fair 650.10
not far from 223.24
not foresee 131.4

not forget 982.5
not found 222.11
not get 522.11
not give up not weaken 15.10
  stay with it 360.4
  stand fast 453.4
not good enough 108.9
not guilty litigious 598.22
  innocent 657.6
not half 247.18
not have 442.3
not have it 910.2
not have time 843.3
not here 222.18
not hesitate 359.10
not hesitate to 324.3
nothing void 222.3
  nil 761.2
  thing of naught 763.2
  insignificancy 997.6
  nobody 997.7
nothing at all 761.2
nothing else 871.3
nothing like 786.5
nothingness
  unconsciousness 25.2
  space 158.1
  void 222.3
  nonexistence 761.1
nothing of the kind
  noun different thing 779.3
  adj nothing like 786.5
nothing of the sort 786.5
nothing to do 331.2
nothing to hide 657.1
nothing whatever 761.2
notice
  noun observation 27.2
  announcement 352.2
  press release 352.3
  publicity 352.4
  advertisement 352.6
  warning 399.1
  demand 421.1
  information 551.1
  commentary 556.2
  dismissal 908.5
  cognizance 927.2
  criticism 945.2
  attention 982.1
  verb see 27.12
  detect 940.5
  heed 982.6
noticeable visible 31.6
  remarkable 247.10
  measurable 300.14
  manifest 348.8
  conspicuous 348.12
noticeably visibly 31.8
  positively 247.19

measurably 300.15
  manifestly 348.14
  conspicuously 348.16
notice board
  announcement 352.2
  bulletin board 549.10
  information 551.1
notification informing 343.2
  announcement 352.2
  warning 399.1
  information 551.1
notify herald 133.14
  warn 399.5
  state 524.24
  inform 551.8
  report 552.11
no time timelessness 821.1
  short time 827.3
no time at all 821.1
not imply 775.4
not included 772.7
not in the least
  adv noway 248.11
  exclam by no means 335.9
not in the mood 325.5
not involve 775.4
notion caprice 364.1
  impulse 365.1
  intention 380.1
  plan 381.1
  idea 931.1
  suggestion 950.5
  opinion 952.6
notional capricious 364.5
  ideational 931.9
  theoretical 950.13
  imaginative 985.18
  imaginary 985.19
  fanciful 985.20
notions 735.6
not know 929.11
not know how 414.10
not like
  verb dislike 99.3
  adj different 779.7
not likely 442.7
not listen 983.2
not long ago 840.16
not look like 786.2
not make it lose out 410.10
  fall short 910.2
not many 884.4
not matter 997.11
not mind not care 102.4
  disobey 327.6
not moving 734.15
not much
  adv noway 248.11
  exclam nope 335.10

not nearly 248.11
not new 841.18
not notice 983.2
not occur 761.5
not often 847.4
not one 222.6
notoriety
  conspicuousness 348.4
  publicity 352.4
  disreputability 661.2
  repute 662.1
notorious conspicuous 348.12
  knavish 645.17
  disreputable 661.10
  distinguished 662.16
  immodest 666.6
  well-known 927.27
  terrible 999.9
notoriously
  conspicuously 348.16
  dishonestly 645.24
  famously 662.21
  terribly 999.14
not out 747.5
not pass 410.9
not pay 625.6
not perfect 1002.4
not possible 966.7
not present 222.11
not proved 957.8
not proven litigious 598.22
  unproved 957.8
not qualify be insufficient 991.8
  fall short 1002.3
not quite 223.22
not quite right 85.55
not reach 910.2
not real 761.9
not really 335.8
not receive 157.5
not refuse 441.2
not remember 989.5
not resist submit 433.6
  be moderate 670.5
not rest 403.15
not right insane 925.26
  erroneous 974.16
not see 30.8
not-self 767.2
not shown 957.8
not so 335.8
not so bad 998.20
not stand 103.5
not stand for 510.11
not suffer 510.11
not surprised 130.11
not tell 345.7
not there 984.11
not the same 779.8

not the type 779.8
not think 932.2
not think of not expect
  131.4
  not think 932.2
not tolerate 510.11
not to mention
  adv additionally
  253.11
  prep with 253.12
not touch avoid 368.6
  not use 390.5
not true false 354.25
  erroneous 974.16
not understand 522.11
not unlike 783.10
not use 390.5
not waste 397.8
notwithstanding 338.8
not worry 107.5
noun 530.5
nourish feed 7.15
  nurture 8.19
  encourage 375.21
  foster 449.16
nourishing
  noun nutrition 7.1
  adj nutritious 7.19
  eating 8.31
nourishment nutrition
  7.1
  nutriment 10.3
  support 449.3
nous intellect 918.1
  smartness 919.2
  sensibleness 919.6
nouveau 840.12
novel
  noun book 554.1
  story 722.3
  adj original 337.5,
  840.11
novelist author 547.15,
  718.4
  narrator 722.5
novelties 735.6
novelty nonimitation
  337.1
  fad 578.5
  newness 840.1
  innovation 840.2,
  851.4
novice nun 699.17
  beginner 817.2
  ignoramus 929.8
now
  noun present 837.1
  adj modern 840.13
  adv at once 829.8
  at present 837.3
  recently 840.16
nowadays
  noun present 837.1
  adv now 837.3
now and again
  discontinuously 812.5

occasionally 847.5
now and then
  discontinuously 812.5
  occasionally 847.5
no water 276.1
no way
  noun despair 125.2
  phrase I refuse 442.7
  no can do 966.11
  exclam nope 335.10
no way out 125.2
nowhere
  noun jumping-off place
  261.4
  adv in no place 222.17
nowhere near 248.11
no-win 410.18
nowt 761.2
noxious nasty 64.7
  malodorous 71.5
  unhealthful 82.5
  poisonous 82.7
  offensive 98.18
  malicious 144.20
  harmful 999.12
nozzle bib nozzle 239.9
  nose 283.8
  sprinkler 1063.8
np 728.7
nuance degree 245.1
  implication 519.2
  margin 779.2
  distinction 943.3
nub substance 196.5
  centre 208.2
  bulge 283.3
  texture 294.1
  essence 766.2
  salient point 996.6
nubile grown 14.3
  adolescent 301.13
  adult 303.12
  marriageable 563.20
nuclear nucleate 208.12
  nucleal 305.21
  middle 818.4
  N- 1037.19
nuclear energy 17.1
nuclear family family
  559.5
  community 617.2
nuclear fuel 1037.10
nuclear power 18.4
nuclear reactor
  1037.13
nuclear waste 1037.13
nuclear weapons
  462.1
nucleus centre 208.2
  cell nucleus 305.7
  essence 766.2
  middle 818.1
  elementary particle
  1037.6
nude
  noun nudity 6.3

work of art 712.10
  adj naked 6.14
  unadorned 499.8
nudge
  noun contact 223.5
  signal 517.15
  hint 551.4
  thrust 901.2
  verb set in motion
  172.6
  contact 223.10
  goad 375.15
  importune 440.12
  signal 517.22
  thrust 901.12
  remind 988.20
nudging
  noun importunity
  440.3
  adj in contact 223.17
nudist
  noun nudity 6.3
  adj naked 6.14
nudity nakedness 6.3
  unadornment 499.3
nugget lump 257.10
  precious metals 728.20
nuisance annoyance
  96.2
  tormentor 96.10
  bore 118.4
null vacant 222.14
  meaningless 520.6
  nonexistent 761.8
null and void vacant
  222.14
  repealed 445.3
numb
  verb deaden 25.4
  benumb 94.8
  relieve 120.5
  freeze 1022.10
  adj insensible 25.6
  apathetic 94.13
  unconcerned 102.7
  languid 331.20
numbed insensible 25.6
  apathetic 94.13
number
  noun amount 244.2
  superior 249.4
  singular 530.8
  edition 554.5
  act 704.7
  vocation 724.6
  section 792.2
  certain number 883.2
  numeral 1016.3
  sum 1016.6
  verb quantify 244.4
  total 791.8
  itemize 800.7
  numerate 1016.16
  adj superlative 249.13
numbered 713.11
number eight 746.2
numbering

noun numeration
  1016.9
  adj inclusive 771.6
number of 883.3
number of times
  848.16
number one
  noun urine 12.5
  self 864.5
  adj governing 612.18
  paramount 996.24
  A1 998.18
numbers quantity
  244.1
  metrics 720.6
  metre 720.7
  multitude 883.3
  mathematics 1016.1
Number Ten 228.5
number two 12.2
numbing
  noun relief 120.1
  adj deadening 25.9
  anaesthetic 86.47
  relieving 120.9
  cold 1022.14
numbness insensibility
  25.1
  apathy 94.4
numeracy 927.5
numerous much 247.8
  large 257.16
  plural 882.7
  many 883.6
  plentiful 990.7
nun marker 517.10
  celibate 565.2
  sister 699.17
nunnery 703.6
nuptial
  verb marry 563.14
  adj sexual 75.24
  matrimonial 563.18
nurse
  noun health-care
  professional 90.8
  charge nurse 90.10
  nursemaid 1007.8
  verb nourish 8.19
  treat 91.24
  foster 449.16
  hold 474.7
  train 568.13
  care for 1007.19
nursemaid home help
  577.8
  nurse 1007.8
nursery bedroom 197.7
  hospital room 197.25
  infancy 301.5
  infant school 567.2
  birthplace 885.8
  conservatory 1067.11
nursery school 567.2
nursing home hospital
  91.21
  asylum 1008.4

nurture
  noun nutrition 7.1
  nutriment 10.3
  support 449.3
  training 568.3
  protectorship 1007.2
  verb nourish 7.15,
  8.19
  look after 339.9
  encourage 375.21
  improve 392.9
  foster 449.16
  hold 474.7
  train 568.13
  care for 1007.19
  raise 1068.6
nurturing training
  568.3
  protectorship 1007.2
nut
  noun noix 10.37
  fan 101.5
  seed 310.29
  nutter 925.16
  fanatic 925.18
  freak 926.4
  scoria 1019.16
  verb harvest 1067.19
nutrient
  noun nutritive 7.3
  adj nutritious 7.19
nutrition nourishment
  7.1
  eating 8.1
  cooking 11.1
nutritionist 7.13
nutritious nutritive
  7.19
  eating 8.31
nutritive
  noun nutrient 7.3
  adj nutritious 7.19
nuts 925.27
nuts and bolts meat
  and potatoes 766.3
  basics 817.6
  realism 986.2
nutshell
  noun modicum 248.2
  adj shortened 268.9
  abridged 557.6
nutter 925.16
nutting 1067.15
nutty flavourful 63.9
  screwy 922.9
  crazy 925.27
  kooky 926.6
nymph larva 302.12
  embryo 305.14
  insect 311.31
  nymphet 678.9
O black pills 87.15
  circle 280.2
oak horse 15.8
  stone 1044.6
Oaks 757.1
oar remi- 180.15

boatman 183.5

oasis 241.1

oath vow 334.4
promise 436.1
profane oath 513.4

oats 10.4

obdurate insensible
25.6
impenitent 114.5
heartless 144.25
tough 361.10
firm 425.7
hardened 654.17
hard 1044.10

obedience resignation
134.2
submission 433.1
conformity 866.1

obedient resigned
134.10
compliant 326.3
submissive 433.12
dutiful 641.13
conformable 866.5

obediently compliantly
326.6
submissively 433.17
conformably 866.7

obelisk tower 272.6
monument 549.12

Oberon 678.8

obese corpulent 257.18
oversize 257.23

obesity oversize 257.5
corpulence 257.8

obey accept 134.7
mind 326.2
submit 433.6

obituary
noun obit 307.14
monument 549.12
history 719.1
adj funereal 309.22
documentary 549.18

object
noun objective 380.2
intent 518.2
syntax 530.2
something 762.3
article 1050.4
verb protest 333.5
offer resistance 453.3
disapprove 510.10
disagree 788.5

objecting protesting
333.7
resistant 453.5

objection demur 325.2
protest 333.2
resistance 453.1
disapproval 510.1
defence 600.2
obstacle 1011.4

objectionable offensive
98.18
unacceptable 108.10
unpraiseworthy 510.24

objective
noun will 323.1
object 380.2
adj unfeeling 94.9
impartial 649.10
real 760.15
extrinsic 767.3
true 972.13
unprejudiced 978.12

objectively separately
801.27
truly 972.18

objectivity unfeeling
94.1
extrinsicality 767.1
unprejudicedness
978.5

objector dissenter
333.3
oppositionist 452.3

object to refuse 325.3
disapprove 510.10

obligation act of
kindness 143.7
gratitude 150.1
undertaking 404.1
compulsion 424.1
commitment 436.2
security 438.1
debt 623.1
duty 641.1
condition 958.2
necessity 962.1

obligatory mandatory
420.12
compulsory 424.11
binding 641.15
necessary 962.12

oblige be kind 143.9
necessitate 424.5,
962.8
indulge 427.6
accommodate 449.19
obligate 641.12

obliged grateful 150.5
obligated 641.16

obliged to obliged
641.16
liable to 896.6

obliging
noun indulgence 427.3
adj considerate 143.16
indulgent 427.8
permissive 443.14
courteous 504.14

obligingly 504.19

oblique
noun diagonal 204.7
verb deviate 204.9
adj transverse 170.9
devious 204.13
circumlocutory 538.14
circuitous 913.7

obliquely deviously
204.21
circuitously 913.9

obliterate expunge
395.16

declare a moratorium
625.9

obliterated 989.8

oblivion
unconsciousness 25.2
insensibility 94.2
carelessness 340.2
thoughtlessness 932.1
forgetfulness 989.1

oblivious asleep 22.22
unconscious 25.8,
983.7
insensible 94.10
careless 340.11
thoughtless 932.4
abstracted 984.11
forgetful 989.9

oblong oblongated
267.9
quadrangular 278.9

obnoxious offensive
98.18
base 661.12
terrible 999.9

obscene offensive 98.18
coarse 497.11
cursing 513.8
lascivious 665.29
lewd 666.9

obscenity filth 80.7
offensiveness 98.2
coarseness 497.2
cursing 513.3
oath 513.4
lasciviousness 665.5
dirtiness 666.4

obscure
noun darkness 1026.1
verb blind 30.7
deform 263.3
cover 295.19
cloud 319.6
conceal 346.6
make unintelligible
522.12
misteach 569.3
quibble 935.9
make uncertain 970.15
darken 1026.9
opaque 1030.2
adj inconspicuous 32.6
formless 263.4
concealed 346.11
hard to understand
522.14
vague 522.15, 970.19
ambiguous 539.4
unrenowned 661.14
dark 1026.13
opaque 1030.3

obscured blinded 30.10
covered 295.31
concealed 346.11
latent 519.5
hard to understand
522.14
dark 1026.13

obscurely 522.22,
970.29

obscuring
noun covering 295.1
adj blinding 30.11
covering 295.35
concealing 346.15
misteaching 569.6
obscurant 1026.18

obscurity
inconspicuousness
32.2
formlessness 263.1
obscuration 522.3
diffuseness 538.1
vagueness 970.4
nobody 997.7
darkness 1026.1
opaqueness 1030.1

observable visible 31.6
manifest 348.8

observance observation
27.2, 434.1
vigilance 339.4
custom 373.1
execution 437.4
celebration 487.1
ceremony 580.4
piety 692.1
rite 701.3
conformity 866.1
attention 982.1

observant vigilant
339.13
respectful 434.4
dutiful 641.13
pious 692.8
belief 952.21
attentive 982.15

observation observance
27.2, 434.1
remark 524.4
idea 931.1
surveillance 937.9
opinion 952.6
attention 982.1
observatory 1070.17

observatory 1070.17

observe see 27.12
look 27.13
obey 326.2
keep 434.2
execute 437.9
celebrate 487.2,
701.14
remark 524.25
formalize 580.5
conform 866.3
examine 937.24
heed 982.6

observer military pilot
185.3
spectator 917.1
examiner 937.17

observing 982.15

obsessed affected 93.23
bewitched 691.13
possessed 925.33
engrossed 982.17
haunted 987.10
remembering 988.24

obsession bewitchment
691.2
prepossession 925.13
engrossment 982.3
possession 987.5

obsessional 925.34

obsessive obsessional
925.34
engrossing 982.20
unforgettable 988.26

obsolete
noun archaism 526.12
adj out of action 19.17
disused 390.10
past 836.7
passé 841.15

obstacle 293.3, 1011.4

obstetric 90.15

obstinacy strength 15.1
refusal 325.1
defiance 327.2
resolution 359.1
perseverance 360.1
obstinateness 361.1
firmness 425.2
hostility 451.2
resistance 453.1
tenacity 802.3
uninfluenceability
894.2

obstinate strong 15.15
disobedient 327.8
resolute 359.11
persevering 360.8
stubborn 361.8
firm 425.7
oppositional 451.8
adhesive 802.12
uninfluenceable 894.4

obstinately resolutely
359.17
stubbornly 361.14

obstruct slow 175.9
stop 293.7
oppose 451.3
fend off 460.10
delay 845.8

obstructed stopped
293.11
late 845.16

obstructing
noun game 750.3
adj hindering 1011.17

obstruction slowing
175.4
clog 293.3
golf 748.1
delay 845.2
hindrance 1011.1
obstacle 1011.4

obstructive
noun oppositionist
452.3
adj oppositional 451.8
resistant 453.5
dilatory 845.17
hindering 1011.17

obtain fetch 176.16

elicit 192.14
acquire 472.8
receive 479.6
exist 760.8
prevail 863.10
induce 885.11

obtainable attainable
472.14
accessible 965.8

obtaining 373.14

obtrusive conceited
140.11
insolent 142.9
intrusive 214.8
conspicuous 348.12
gaudy 501.20

obtuse insensible 25.6
unfeeling 94.9
blunt 286.3
negative 335.5
dull 921.16

obvious distinct 31.7
manifest 348.8
patent 969.15

obviously visibly 31.8
positively 247.19
manifestly 348.14
really 760.16

occasion
noun pretext 376.1
circumstance 765.1
event 830.2
opportunity 842.2
cause 885.1
requirement 962.2
verb cause 885.10

occasional
circumstantial 765.7
happening 830.9
incidental 842.11
casual 847.3
causal 885.13

occasionally
discontinuously 812.5
on occasion 847.5

occasioned by 886.8

occidental 161.14

occult
noun secret 345.5
supernaturalism 869.7
immateriality 1051.1
verb cover 295.19
conceal 346.6
darken 1026.9
adj secret 345.11
concealed 346.11
latent 519.5
recondite 522.16
esoteric 689.23
supernatural 869.15
spectral 987.7
immaterial 1051.7

occultism esoterics
689.1
immateriality 1051.1

occupancy habitation
225.1
possession 469.1

occupant inhabitant
227.2
tenant 470.4

occupation habitation
225.1
action 328.1
possession 469.1
appropriation 480.4
work 724.1
vocation 724.6
operation 888.1

occupational 724.16

occupied inhabited
225.12
busy 330.21, 724.15
engrossed 982.17

occupier inhabitant
227.2
tenant 470.4

occupy pervade 221.7
inhabit 225.7
possess 469.4
appropriate 480.19
engage 724.10
include 771.3
engross 982.13

occupying 469.9

occur be present 221.6
exist 760.8
happen 830.5
occur to 930.18

occurrence appearance
33.1
presence 221.1
existence 760.1
circumstance 765.1
event 830.2
prevalence 863.2

occurring 830.9

occur to 930.18

ocean sea 240.1, 240.3
quantity 247.3

Oceania 231.6

oceanic nautical 182.57
marine 240.8

ocean liner 180.5

o'clock 831.16

octagon 881.4

octagonal pentagonal
278.10
eighth 881.20

octave ottava 709.9
interval 709.20
measure 720.9
eight 881.4

octogenarian old man
304.2
eleven 881.7

OD 183.1

od 22.8

odd remaining 256.7
dissimilar 786.4
occasional 847.3
queer 869.11
sole 871.9
insane 925.26
eccentric 926.5

oddball
noun intruder 773.2
misfit 788.4
freak 926.4
adj odd 869.11
kooky 926.6

oddity queerness 869.3
character 869.4
curiosity 869.5
eccentricity 926.1

oddly 869.19

odd man out 1010.7

odds advantage 249.2
gambling odds 759.6
difference 779.1
inequality 790.1
probability 967.1
even chance 971.7

odds and ends
remainder 256.1
haberdashery 735.6
miscellany 769.13
hotchpotch 796.6

odds-on
noun good chance
971.8
adj probable 967.6

odds-on favourite
757.2

odious filthy 80.23
offensive 98.18
unlikable 99.7
base 661.12
terrible 999.9

odour smell 69.1
fragrance 70.1
characteristic 864.4

odyssey 177.2

oedema distension
259.2
swelling 283.4
overextension 992.7

o'er
adv on high 272.21
prep on 295.37

oesophagus 2.16

oeuvre 547.12, 718.1

of 57 varieties 782.4

of age adult 303.12
marriageable 563.20

of a kind analogous
783.11
mediocre 1004.7

of a piece unanimous
332.15
uniform 780.5
analogous 783.11
agreeing 787.9
simple 797.6

of a place 231.9

of a sort 1004.7

of a sudden 829.9

of belief belief 952.21
believed 952.23

of choice superior
249.12

tasteful 496.8

of concern 996.18

of course
adv consequently
886.7
certainly 969.23
exclam yes 332.18

of design 380.8

off
noun horse race 757.3
adj dissonant 61.4
right 219.4
idle 331.18
tainted 393.41
dissimilar 786.4
occasional 847.3
odd 869.11
insane 925.26
delirious 925.31
erroneous 974.16
imperfect 1002.4
below par 1004.10
adv hence 188.20
oceanward 240.11
at a distance 261.14
prep from 255.14

of faith 952.27

offal slough 80.9
refuse 391.4

off and on infrequently
847.4
alternately 849.11
irregularly 850.4
changeably 853.8
to and fro 915.21

off-and-on 847.3

off-balance eccentric
160.12
unbalanced 790.5
confused 984.12

offbeat
noun beat 709.26
adj dissimilar 786.4
unconventional 867.6
unusual 869.10

off Broadway 704.1

off-centre eccentric
160.12
distorted 265.10

off-colour off-tone
35.20
ill 85.55
risqué 666.7

off duty
adj idle 331.18
adv on holiday 20.12

of feeling 93.17

offence umbrage 152.2
provocation 152.11
indignity 156.2
violation 435.2
attack 459.1
misdeed 655.2
wrong 674.4
basketball game 751.3

offend give offence
98.11, 152.21
affront 156.5

do wrong 655.4
offend the eye 1014.5

offender 660.9

offensive
noun attack 459.1
adj nasty 64.7
malodorous 71.5
objectionable 98.18
insulting 156.8
warlike 458.21
combative 459.30
vulgar 497.10
ill-bred 505.6
obscene 666.9
terrible 999.9
hideous 1014.11

offer
noun attempt 403.2
offering 439.1
giving 478.1
verb put to choice
371.21
attempt 403.6
proffer 439.4
give 478.12
bid 733.9
answer 938.4
adduce 956.12

offered 324.7

offering offer 439.1
gift 478.4
donation 478.6
oblation 696.7

offer up 439.4

off-guard negligent
340.10
unalert 983.8

offhand
adj nonchalant 106.15
careless 340.11
unpremeditated
365.11
extemporaneous
365.12
informal 581.3
adv carelessly 340.18
extemporaneously
365.15
informally 581.4

office
noun act of kindness
143.7
library 197.6
function 387.5, 724.3
aid 449.1
ceremony 580.4
bureau 594.4
commission 615.1
divine service 696.8
rite 701.3
position 724.5
shop 739.7
verb direct 573.8

officer
noun executive 574.3
official 575.16
commissioned officer
575.18
policeman 1007.15

verb govern 612.12
offices 449.1
office worker 726.2
official
  noun executive 574.3
  officer 575.16
  agent 576.3
  game 745.3, 746.3,
    749.2
  round 748.3
  basketball game 751.3
  fight 754.3
  adj authoritative
    417.15, 969.18
  preceptive 419.4
  recorded 549.17
  governmental 612.17
  executive 612.19
  occupational 724.16
officialdom 575.15
official language
  523.4
officially 417.18
official residence
  228.5
Official Secrets Act
  345.3
officiating 573.14
offing distance 261.3
  future 838.1
off-licence 736.1
off limits restricted
  210.8
  prohibited 444.7
off-off-Broadway
  704.1
off-peak 252.10
off-putting exciting
  105.30
  dissuasive 379.5
  hostile 589.10
  bewildering 970.27
off-season 313.9
offset
  noun setoff 338.2
  printing 548.1
  print 548.3
  offshoot 561.4
  opposite 778.2
  counteractant 899.3
  verb set off 338.5
  cushion 670.8
  go contrary to 778.4
  neutralize 899.7
  adj neutralizing 899.9
offsetting
  noun compensation
    338.1
  neutralization 899.2
  adj compensating
    338.6
  neutralizing 899.9
offshoot fork 171.4
  adjunct 254.1
  branch 310.18, 617.10
  offset 561.4
  party 617.4

sect 675.3
  effect 886.1
  extract 892.3
offshore 240.11
off-side 219.4
offside right side 219.1
  game 745.3, 746.3,
    750.6
off spinner 747.2
offspring child 302.3
  family 559.5
  posterity 561.1
  descendant 561.3
  sequel 834.2
  effect 886.1
  product 892.1
off the beaten track
  secluded 584.8
  unusual 869.10
off the field 19.17
off-the-peg ready-made
  405.19
  made 891.18
off the record
  adj confidential 345.14
  adv confidentially
    345.20
off-the-shelf 891.18
off the track 970.24
off-the-wall unexpected
  131.10
  odd 869.11
  crazy 925.27
off-time 825.1
off-white 37.8
off with 6.6
off work 331.18
of heart 93.17
of help 387.18
of importance 996.18
of interest 996.18
of late 840.16
of long standing
  841.12
of mark remarkable
  247.10
  distinguished 662.16
  notable 996.19
of necessity obligatorily
  424.15
  consequently 886.7
  necessarily 962.16
of note distinguished
  662.16
  of importance 996.18
of no use 391.9
of old
  adj old 841.10
  adv long ago 836.16
of one's own 469.8
of promise promising
  124.13
  auspicious 133.18
of quality 496.8

of rank 608.10
of record 549.17
of sentiment 93.17
of service 387.18
of significance 996.18
of sorts 1004.7
of soul 93.17
oft 846.6
often frequently 846.6
  repeatedly 848.16
often enough 846.6
of the best 496.8
of the cloth 698.17
of the earth 312.13
of the essence 766.9
of the faith 687.7
of the old school
  841.16
of use 387.18
of value 387.22
of vital importance
  996.23
of weight 996.18
of yesterday 840.12
of yore
  adj old 841.10
  adv long ago 836.16
ogle
  noun gaze 27.5
  flirtation 562.9
  verb scrutinize 27.14
  gaze 27.15
  flirt 562.20
  spectate 917.5
ogre frightener 127.9
  monster 593.6
oh 122.21
oil
  noun balm 86.11
  painting 712.14
  fuel 1020.1
  illuminant 1024.20
  oleum 1054.1
  verb medicate 91.25
  smooth 287.5
  provision 385.9
  facilitate 1013.7
  fuel 1020.7
  grease 1054.8
oiled fuddled 88.33
  slippery 287.11
oilfield 386.4
oiling facilitation
  1013.5
  lubrication 1054.6
oil painting 712.14
oil refinery 739.3
oil rig 386.4
oil slick blanket 295.12
  lamina 296.2
oily slippery 287.11
  insincere 354.32
  suave 504.18
  greasy 1054.9

ointment anaesthetic
  25.3
  balm 86.11, 1054.3
  unction 701.5
Oisin 178.2
OK
  noun approval 509.1
  verb approve 509.9
  adj great 998.13
  exclam yeah 332.19
okay
  adj great 998.13
  exclam yeah 332.19
old aged 303.16
  disused 390.10
  experienced 413.28
  former 836.10
  age-old 841.10
  antiquated 841.13
old age 303.5, 841.1
old boy guy 76.5
  old man 304.2
  graduate 572.8
old chap 304.2
old clothes 5.5
old country continent
  231.6
  fatherland 232.2
older
  noun senior 304.5
  adj mature 304.7
  previous 833.4
  senior 841.19
oldest
  noun senior 304.5
  adj older 841.19
old-fashioned disused
  390.10
  gallant 504.15
  old-fangled 841.16
  conservative 852.8
old girl gal 77.6
  graduate 572.8
old hand 413.16
old hat 117.9
old lady doll 104.15
  old woman 304.3
Old Left 611.5
Old Man 183.7
old man guy 76.5
  beau 104.13
  elder 304.2
  father 560.9
  dad 560.10
  grandfather 560.13
  husband 563.7
  back number 841.8
old master work of art
  712.10
  artist 716.1
old order 841.1
old school 852.4
old soldier shirker
  368.3
  veteran 461.18
old style 841.1

Old Testament 683.3
Old-Testament 683.10
old thing 841.6
old-time 841.10
old wife 304.3
old woman
  mollycoddle 77.10
  old lady 304.3
  fusspot 495.7
  mum 560.12
  gran 560.16
  back number 841.8
Old World 231.6
old-world gallant
  504.15
  antiquated 841.13
O level 937.2
olfactory 69.12
oligarchy 612.4
olive 44.4
olive branch 465.2
olive-green 44.4
Olympian apathetic
  94.13
  aloof 141.12, 583.6
  high 272.14
  reticent 344.10
  impartial 649.10
  heavenly 681.12
Olympic Games
  contest 457.3
  ice hockey 750.4
  basketball 751.1
  boxing 754.1
Olympics 457.3
Olympus 681.9
ombudsman mediator
  466.3
  minister 575.17
omega 819.1
omelette 10.25
omen
  noun portent 133.3
  warning sign 399.3
  prediction 961.1
  verb foreshow 133.10
ominous portentous
  133.17
  threatening 514.3
  premonitory 961.12
  harmful 999.12
  unfortunate 1010.14
ominously 133.19
omission deletion
  255.5
  neglect 340.1
  nonaccomplishment
    408.1
  mismanagement 414.6
  nonobservance 435.1
  misdeed 655.2
  exclusion 772.1
  deficiency 794.2
  slip 974.4
  want 991.4
omit delete 255.12

leave undone 340.7
exclude 772.4

omitted absent 222.11
neglected 340.14

omitting 772.10

omnibus
noun commercial
vehicle 179.13
compilation 554.7
adj comprehensive
771.7
whole 791.9
thorough 793.10

omnipotence 18.3

omnipotent 18.13,
677.17

omnipresent all-
present 221.13
almighty 677.17
thorough 793.10

on
adj addicted 87.24
happening 830.9
adv forward 162.8
after which 834.7
across 900.25
prep at 159.27
toward 161.26
atop 198.16
against 223.25
upon 295.37

on account 622.10

on account of for
449.26
because of 887.9

on a large scale greatly
247.15
largely 257.25

on a level
adj equal 789.7
adv horizontally 201.9

on all fours
adj creeping 177.39
adv humbly 137.16

on all sides extensively
158.11
all round 209.13

on and off 853.8

on and on increasingly
251.9
continuously 811.10
constantly 846.7

on an even keel trim
180.19
balanced 789.9

on a par 789.7

on a rock 854.13

on a small scale
scarcely 248.9
small 258.16

Onassis 618.8

on a string 326.5

on balance on the
average 246.5
on the whole 791.14
generally 863.17

all things considered
945.17

on board
adj present 221.12
joined 799.13
adv here 159.23
on shipboard 182.62

on call
adj handy 387.20
adv on demand 421.12
cash 624.25

once
adj former 836.10
adv whenever 820.12
once upon a time
836.14
one-time 847.6
singly 871.13

once again 873.7

once and for all
819.12

once in a lifetime
847.2

once in a while 847.5

once more newly
840.15
again 848.17, 873.7

once-over 27.6

once upon a time
836.14

oncoming
noun approach 167.1
beginning 817.1
adj progressive 162.6
approaching 167.4

on condition 958.12

on condition that
958.12

on credit 622.10

on deck
adj present 221.12
adv on board 182.62

on demand at demand
421.12
cash 624.25

on deposit 438.12

on duty 330.21

one
noun person 312.5
I 871.3
adj quantitative 244.5
married 563.21
almighty 677.17
identical 777.7
whole 791.9
combined 804.5
single 871.7

one after the other
consecutively 811.11
alternately 849.11

one and all
noun all 791.3, 863.4
adj every 863.15
adv unanimously
332.17
completely 793.14

one and one 87.21

one and only
noun one 871.3
adj sole 871.9

one and the same
noun same 777.3
adj identical 777.7
equivalent 789.8

one another 776.4

one at a time 871.13

one by one separately
801.27
each 864.19
singly 871.13

one day 836.14

on edge nervous 128.11
in suspense 130.12
impatient 135.6

one-dimensional
997.16

one-eyed 28.12

one-horse little 258.10
measly 997.18

one hundred thousand
881.10

one in a million
superior 249.4
happening 971.6

one-man 871.8

on end vertically
200.13
continuously 811.10

oneness accord 455.1
sameness 777.1
agreement 787.1
whole 791.1
simplicity 797.1
particularity 864.1
unity 871.1

one-night stand 75.7

one-off unimitated
337.6
infrequent 847.2

one of the people
606.5

one of these days
838.12

one of us 617.11

one on one 215.6

one-on-one
noun basketball game
751.3
adj contrapositive
215.5
personal 312.15
plain-speaking 535.3

one-party rule 612.9

one-party system
609.24

one-person 871.8

one-piece 871.11

one-quarter 880.2

onerous oppressive
98.24, 297.17
laborious 725.18
hampering 1011.18

troublesome 1012.18

oneself 864.5

one-shot 847.2

one-sided sided 218.7
distorted 265.10
partial 650.11
unipartite 871.11
discriminatory 979.12

one-step 705.5

one-third 877.2

one-time
adj infrequent 847.2
adv once 847.6

one-to-one personal
312.15
familiar 587.19

one-up 216.10

one-upmanship 457.2

one-way 161.12

one-woman 871.8

on file recorded 549.17
classified 808.8

on fire fervent 93.18
zealous 101.9
inspired 375.31
burning 1018.27

on foot
adj astir 330.19
existent 760.13
happening 830.9
operating 888.11
adv afoot 177.43
in production 891.21
adj, adv afoot 405.23

on-go 162.1

ongoing
noun progression
162.1
course 172.2
adj progressive 162.6
improving 392.15
happening 830.9
operating 888.11

on good terms
adj on a good footing
587.18
adv on credit 622.10

on guard
adj vigilant 339.13
cautious 494.8
adv defensively 460.16

on hand
adj present 221.12
handy 387.20
possessed 469.8
adv in store 386.16

on high high up 272.21
celestially 681.13

on holiday 20.12

on horseback
horseback 177.44
on 900.25

on ice 964.8

on impulse 365.14

on its side 218.8

on land 234.8

on leave 20.12

on-line 891.21

on loan 620.7

onlooker neighbour
223.6
spectator 917.1

only
adj sole 871.9
adv to a degree 248.10
simply 797.11
solely 871.14

only a few 884.2

only human 312.13

only if 958.14

only just scarcely 248.9
narrowly 270.22

only occasionally
847.5

only too 247.18

only yesterday
formerly 836.13
now 840.16

on no account
adv noway 248.11
exclam by no means
335.9

on occasion 847.5

on one 478.27

on one hand 218.10

on one occasion 847.6

on one side 218.10

on opposite sides
215.5

on paper
adj written 547.22
adv theoretically
950.16

on parole 431.10

on probation 572.13

on purpose 380.10

on record 549.17

on schedule 130.14

on security 620.7

onset attack 459.1
printing 548.1
beginning 817.1

onshore 234.8

onslaught attack 459.1
berating 510.7
unruliness 671.3
impact 901.3

on song 413.26

on speaking terms
587.18

on stilts
adj raised 911.9
adv on high 272.21

on stream 405.22

on tap 387.20

on terms 622.10

on that occasion at
that time 820.9
then 820.11

on the agenda
adj planned 381.12
undertaken 404.7
adv in question 937.39

on the alert 339.14

on the average 246.5

on the back of 900.25

on the ball 919.13

on the beat 849.10

on the block 734.17

on the Book 436.7

on the books 549.17

on the brink 211.15

on the cards 839.3

on the cheap 633.10

on the decline 393.46

on the defensive
460.16

on the dole 619.8

on the edge 211.15

on the edge of 223.24

on the eve of
prep about to 838.13
conj on the point of
839.5

on the evidence
956.22

on the face of it 33.12

on the fence 609.45

on the fire
adj operating 888.11
adj, adv in preparation
405.22

on the floor 937.39

on the game 665.28

on the go 330.21

on the high seas under
way 182.63
at sea 240.9

on the hook 641.17

on the hop busy
330.21
unalert 983.8

on the horizon
adj expected 130.13
imminent 839.3
adv yonder 261.13

on the house
adj gratuitous 634.5
adv as a gift 478.27
gratuitously 634.6

on the increase 251.8

on the job busy 330.21
attentive 982.15

on the left
adj progressive 611.27
adv leftward 220.6

on the lines of 384.9

on the lookout 339.13

on the lookout for
adj searching 937.38
prep after 382.12

on the loose escaped
369.11
free 430.21
festive 743.28

on the make
adj aspiring 100.28
adv out for 403.17

on the mend 392.15

on the move 330.21

on the one hand aside
218.10
comparatively 942.10
all things considered
945.17

on the other hand
adv laterally 218.8
aside 218.10
contrarily 778.9
otherwise 779.11
comparatively 942.10
all things considered
945.17
adv, conj
notwithstanding 338.8

on the outside 206.10

on the point 211.15

on the point of 839.5

on the rack pained
26.9
tortured 96.25

on the receiving end
479.9

on the return 902.11

on the right 219.7

on the right track
940.10

on the rise 251.8

on the road 222.12

on the rocks
adj insolvent 625.11
stranded 1012.27
adv aground 182.73

on the run 330.21

on the safe side
cautious 494.8
safe 1006.4

on the same level
789.7

on the shelf neglected
340.14
disused 390.10

on the shelves 734.15

on the shoulders of
272.21

on the side aside
218.10
additionally 253.11

on the spot
adj hasty 401.9
prompt 844.9
in deep shit 1012.22
adv here 159.23
instantly 829.6
now 837.3
promptly 844.15

**on the spur of the
moment** on impulse
365.14
hastily 401.12
on the rebound
902.11

on the straight 277.7

on the street 552.15

on the surface
apparently 33.12
externally 206.10

on the table openly
348.15
in question 937.39

on the throne
adj well-connected
893.14
adv in authority
417.21

on the town 743.28

on the trail of 940.10

on the understanding
958.12

on the up 392.15

on the verge 211.15

on the verge of 839.5

on the wane decreasing
252.11
on the decline 393.46

on the way
adv along the way
176.20
adj, adv in preparation
405.22

on the way out 393.46

on the way to
adv forward 162.8
prep toward 161.26

on the whole on the
average 246.5
in the long run 791.14
generally 863.17
all things considered
945.17

on the wind 182.65

on the wing 176.20

on time 844.14

on tiptoe
adj in suspense 130.12
creeping 177.39
in hiding 346.14
adv on high 272.21

on top
adj successful 409.14
adv atop 198.15

on top of
adj restraining 428.11
attentive 982.15
protective 1007.23
adv additionally
253.11
prep atop 198.16
on 295.37

on top of the world
overjoyed 95.16
cheerful 109.11

on tour travelling
177.36
nonresident 222.12

on trial
adv under examination
941.14
phrase in litigation
598.23

on trust 622.10

onus duty 641.1
charge 643.3
guilt 656.1
stigma 661.6
proof 956.3
impediment 1011.6

on vacation 20.12

onward
adj progressive 162.6
adv forward 162.8
frontward 216.13

onwards forward 162.8
frontward 216.13

on welfare 619.8

on wheels 287.12

oomph 17.3

ooze
noun slime 80.8
exuding 190.6
mud 1060.8
verb exude 190.15
be damp 1063.11

oozing
noun exuding 190.6
adj soaked 1063.17

opal 47.6

opaline 47.10

opaque
verb darken 1030.2
adj obscure 522.15
stupid 921.15
intransparent 1030.3

op cit 956.24

ope 292.11

open
noun outdoors 206.3
verb cleave 224.4
spread 259.6
ope 292.11
disclose 351.4
dramatize 704.28
open up 817.12
adj visible 31.6
approachable 167.5
receptive 187.16
exterior 206.7
available 222.15
champaign 236.2
spread 259.11
unclosed 292.17
communicative 343.10
overt 348.10
published 352.17
leisure 402.5
artless 416.5
free-acting 430.23
unrestricted 430.27
liberal 485.4
phonetic 524.31

plain-speaking 535.3
hospitable 585.11
candid 644.17
incoherent 803.4
influenceable 893.15
liable 896.5
accessible 965.8
undecided 970.18
open-minded 978.10
exposed 1005.15
adv without date
821.5

open air 206.3

open-air outdoor 206.8
airy 317.11

open arms entree
187.3
welcome 585.2
greeting 585.4

open country open
space 158.4
plain 236.1

open discussion 541.7

open door entree 187.3
hospitality 585.1

open-ended
unaccomplished 408.3
unrestricted 430.27
partial 792.7
adv without date
821.5

opener tin opener
292.10
inauguration 817.5

openers poker 759.10
first 817.3

open fire
noun fire 1018.13
verb pull the trigger
459.22
open 817.12

open heart 485.1

opening appearance
33.1
entree 187.3
entrance 189.5
outlet 190.9
vacancy 222.2
crack 224.2
aperture 292.1
display 348.2
passageway 383.3
position 724.5
beginning 817.1
opportunity 842.2

opening up 292.1

openly externally
206.10
distressingly 247.21
overtly 348.15
publicly 352.19
artlessly 416.7
candidly 644.23

open market
marketplace 736.2
stock exchange 737.1

open mind 978.3

open-minded
nonrestrictive 430.25
influenceable 893.15
open 978.10

openness
approachability 167.2
receptivity 187.9
exteriority 206.1
communicativeness
343.3
manifestness 348.3
artlessness 416.1
plain speech 535.1
talkativeness 540.1
candour 644.4
inclusion 771.1
influenceability 893.5
susceptibility 896.2
accessibility 965.3
open-mindedness
978.3
exposure 1005.3

open out open 292.11
amplify 538.7

open prison 429.8

open question 970.8

open road 177.3

open sea 240.1

open season 389.3

open space 158.4

open the door to
receive 187.10, 585.7
prepare the way
405.12
permit 443.9
open 817.12
induce 885.11
be liable 896.3
allow for 958.5
make possible 965.5
take chances 1005.7
facilitate 1013.7

open the way prepare
the way 405.12
facilitate 1013.7

open the way for
965.5

open to 965.8

open to all 348.10

open to the public
352.17

open up spread 259.6
open 292.11, 817.12
come out 348.6
disclose 351.4
make public 352.11
let oneself go 430.19
propose 439.5
facilitate 1013.7

opera theatre 704.14
score 708.28
musical theatre 708.34

opera house 704.14

opera singer 710.13

operate treat 91.24
pilot 182.14
act 328.4

plot 381.9
use 387.10
trade 737.23
function 888.5, 888.7

operate on 91.24

operatic dramatic
704.33
vocal 708.50

operating
noun motion 172.1
adj acting 328.10
operational 888.11

operating theatre hall
197.4
hospital room 197.25

operation surgery 90.2,
91.19
motion 172.1
action 328.1, 458.5
act 328.3
function 387.5
utilization 387.8
undertaking 404.1
transaction 731.4
functioning 888.1
performance 891.5

operational acting
328.10
operative 888.9
operating 888.11
functional 888.12

operations action 328.1
operation 458.5, 888.1

operative
noun secret agent
576.9
detective 576.10
doer 726.1
operator 888.4
adj powerful 18.12
acting 328.10
effectual 387.21
operational 888.9

operator surgeon 90.5
telephone operator
347.9
schemer 381.7
doer 726.1
speculator 737.11
operative 888.4
liveware 1041.17

operetta 708.34

opinion advice 422.1
idea 931.1
estimate 945.3
sentiment 952.6
attitude 977.1

opinionated obstinate
361.8
dogmatic 969.22
discriminatory 979.12

opium 22.10

opponent
noun adversary 452.1
adj oppositional 451.8

opportune apt 787.10
timely 842.9
expedient 994.5

opportunism ambition
100.10
opportunity 842.2

opportunist
noun timeserver 363.4
schemer 381.7
adj scheming 381.13

opportunistic
contagious 85.61
repudiative 363.12
scheming 381.13

opportunity turn 824.2
chance 842.2, 971.1

oppose contrapose
215.4
dissent 333.4
deny 335.4
counter 451.3
offer resistance 453.3
disapprove 510.10
go contrary to 778.4
counteract 899.6
compare 942.4
hinder 1011.10

opposed contrapositive
215.5
unwilling 325.5
oppositional 451.8
disapproving 510.21
contrary 778.6
adverse 1010.13

opposed to 451.10

opposing
noun contraposition
215.1
opposition 451.1
resistance 453.1
comparison 942.1
adj contrapositive
215.5
dissenting 333.6
negative 335.5
oppositional 451.8
disapproving 510.21
contrary 778.6
adverse 1010.13

opposite
noun inverse 205.4
opposite 778.2
contrary 778.2
adj contrapositive
215.5
fronting 216.11
oppositional 451.8
contrary 778.6
adverse 1010.13
adv poles apart 215.6
prep against 223.25
over against 778.10

opposite number
opposite 778.2
equal 789.4

opposites 215.2

opposite side 215.3

opposite to 215.7

opposition
contraposition 215.1
refusal 325.1
dissent 333.1

opposing 451.1
opponent 452.1
resistance 453.1
disapproval 510.1
enemy 589.6
cabinet 613.3
contrariety 778.1
difference 779.1
disagreement 788.1
counteraction 899.1
comparison 942.1
hindrance 1011.1

opposition party
609.24

oppress burden 98.16,
297.13
sadden 112.18
aggrieve 112.19
persecute 389.7
domineer 612.16
task 725.16
go hard with 1010.8

oppressed sad 112.20
weighted 297.18
subjugated 432.14
downtrodden 432.16

oppression affliction
96.8
dejection 112.3
stuffiness 173.6
burden 297.7
persecution 389.3
despotism 612.10

oppressive burdensome
98.24
depressing 112.30
stuffy 173.16
onerous 297.17
imperious 417.16
laborious 725.18
hampering 1011.18
troublesome 1012.18
sultry 1018.28

oppressor 575.14

opt 371.13

opt for 371.13

optic
noun eye 2.9, 27.9
adj eye 2.26
visual 27.20
optical 29.9

optical visual 27.20
optic 29.9

optician 29.8

optics optical physics
29.7
photics 1024.22

optimal 998.16

optimism cheerfulness
109.1
optimisticalness 124.3

optimist 124.6

optimistic cheerful
109.11
upbeat 124.12
expectant 130.11

optimistically
cheerfully 109.17

hopefully 124.14

optimum
noun best 998.8
adj best 998.16

option discretion 371.2
free will 430.6
first option 733.2
stock option 737.21

optional voluntary
324.7
elective 371.22

opt out refuse 442.3
relinquish 475.3
not conform 867.4

opulent wealthy 618.14
plentiful 990.7

opus writing 547.10
book 554.1
piece 708.5
product 892.1

or
noun yellowness 43.1
heraldic device 647.2
adj yellow 43.4
conj either . . . or
371.29

oracle
noun wise man 920.1
maxim 973.1
verb dogmatize 969.10

oral
noun examination
937.2
adj mouthlike 292.22
communicational
343.9
speech 524.30
traditional 841.12

orally
adj communicatively
343.12
adv vocally 524.34

oral sex 75.7

orange
noun orangeness 42.1
adj orangeish 42.2

orange-red 42.2

orangery 1067.11

orator 543.6

oratorio 708.17

oratory public speaking
543.1
eloquence 544.1
chapel 703.3

orb
noun eye 2.9, 27.9
sphere 231.2, 282.2
regalia 647.3
field 724.4
stars 1070.4
adj spherical 282.9

orbit
noun sphere 231.2,
282.2
rank 245.2
circle 280.2, 1070.16
route 383.1

field 724.4
sphere of influence
893.4
circuitousness 913.1
circuit 913.2
spacecraft 1073.2
verb circle 280.10,
913.5

orbital 913.7

orbiting 913.1

orchard 310.12

orchestra audience
48.6
auditorium 704.15
stage 704.16
band 710.12

orchestral 708.51

orchestration piece
708.5
harmonization 709.2

orchid 46.3

ordained in orders
698.17
destined 963.9

ordeal trial 96.9
magic circle 690.3
test 941.2

order
noun rank 245.2
manner 384.1
precept 419.1
command 420.1
demand 421.1
peacefulness 464.2
nomenclature 527.1
harmony 533.2
race 559.4
class 607.1, 808.2
community 617.2
fellowship 617.3
school 617.5
decoration 646.5
medal 646.6
sect 675.3
good condition 764.3
arrangement 806.1,
807.1
order 806.1
kingdom 808.5
sequence 814.1
normality 868.1
verdict 945.5
biology 1066.1
verb outfit 5.40
command 420.8
demand 421.5
request 440.9
direct 573.8
arrange 806.4, 807.8
classify 808.6
govern 893.8
pass judgment 945.13

ordered harmonious
533.8
uniform 780.5
orderly 806.6
arranged 807.14
regular 849.6

ordering direction
573.1
class 607.1
arrangement 807.1
organization 807.2

orderly
noun paramedic 90.11
attendant 577.5
adj pacific 464.9
harmonious 533.8
punctilious 580.10
uniform 780.5
consistent 802.11
ordered 806.6
arranged 807.14
regular 849.6
normal 868.8
adv regularly 780.8

Order of Merit 646.5

order of the day affairs
830.4
schedule 964.3

orders instructions
568.6
holy orders 698.10

ordinance rule 419.2
decree 420.4
law 673.3
rite 701.3

ordinarily plainly
499.10
frequently 846.6
generally 863.17
normally 868.10

ordinariness
commonness 497.5
plainness 499.1
prevalence 863.2
usualness 868.2
averageness 1004.2

ordinary
noun service 8.11
heraldic device 647.2
normal 868.3
adj medium 246.3
inferior 250.6
customary 373.14
common 497.14
simple 499.6
populational 606.8
prosaic 721.5
frequent 846.4
prevalent 863.12
usual 868.9
average 1004.8

ordinary man 606.5

ordinary person 312.5

ordinate
noun coordinates 300.5
verb appoint 615.11

ordination admission
187.2
appointment 615.2
holy orders 698.10
organization 807.2

ordnance arms 462.1
artillery 462.11

ore raw material 406.5

mineral 1056.2

or else 779.11

organ
noun instrument 384.4
branch 617.10
keyboard wind
instrument 711.13
member 792.4
adj periodical 555.1

organic structural
266.6
organismic 305.17
innate 766.8

organism body 2.1
structure 266.1
organization 305.2
something 762.3

organist 710.8

organization contour
262.2
structure 266.1
organism 305.2
plan 381.1
unit 461.21
establishment 617.8,
891.4
sect 675.3
workplace 739.1
composition 795.1
order 806.1
methodization 807.2

organizational
associational 617.17
formational 807.15

organize form 262.7
construct 266.5
plan 381.8
unionize 727.9
compose 795.3
league 804.4
order 806.4
methodize 807.10
establish 891.10

organized fuddled
88.33
organic 305.17
planned 381.12
arranged 807.14

organizer planner
381.6
unionist 727.4
arranger 807.5
producer 891.7

orgasm copulation 75.7
fury 105.8
spasm 916.6

orgasmic lustful 75.26
frenzied 105.25
turbulent 671.18
convulsive 671.23
jerky 916.19

orgy spree 88.5
fury 105.8
dissipation 669.2

oriel 197.3

Orient 231.6

orient

noun points of the
compass 161.3
verb orientate 161.11
accustom 373.10
adj luminous 1024.30

Oriental 312.3

oriental 161.14

orientated 373.16

orientation navigation
159.3
direction 161.1
bearings 161.4
habituation 373.8

oriented 373.16

origin etymology
526.15
beginning 817.1
origination 817.4
source 885.5

original
noun model 337.2,
785.1
writing 547.10
nonconformist 867.3
oddity 869.4
source 885.5
adj basic 199.8
native 226.5
novel 337.5, 840.11
unused 390.12
essential 766.9
preceding 815.4
beginning 817.15
new 840.7
unconventional 867.6
primary 885.14
genuine 972.15
imaginative 985.18

originality nonimitation
337.1
newness 840.1
nonconformity 867.1
unconventionality
867.2
invention 985.3

originally intrinsically
766.10
first 817.18

original sin 655.3

originate invent 337.4,
891.12
initiate 817.10
cause 885.10
imagine 985.14

originated 891.19

originating 891.1

originator author 885.4
producer 891.7

ornament
noun extra 254.4
ornamentation 498.1
figure of speech 536.1
ornateness 545.4
honour 646.1
decoration 646.5
passage 708.24
impromptu 708.27
grace 709.18

verb add 253.4
decorate 498.8, 545.7

ornamental decorative
498.10
artistic 712.20

ornamentation
ornament 498.1
ornateness 545.4
architectural element
717.2
superfluity 992.4

ornate elegant 498.12
purple 545.11

or not 335.7

orphan
noun survivor 256.3
derelict 370.4
verb bereave 307.28
adj bereaved 307.35

orphanage 1008.4

orphaned 307.35

Orpheus 710.22

Orthodox 675.30

orthodox
noun true believer
687.4
adj firm 425.7
conventional 579.5
orthodoxical 687.7
conformist 866.6

Orthodoxy 675.9

orthodoxy firmness
425.2
religion 675.1
orthodoxness 687.1
conformity 866.1

orthopaedic 90.15

Oscar 646.2

Osiris 682.5

osmosis
noun sorption 187.6
phrase transference
176.1

ostensible apparent
33.11
conspicuous 348.12
specious 354.27
pretexted 376.5
illusory 975.9

ostensibly apparently
33.12
conspicuously 348.16
falsely 354.35
allegedly 376.6

ostentation display
348.2
conspicuousness 348.4
sham 354.3
ornateness 498.2
ostentatiousness 501.1
grandiloquence 545.1

ostentatious ornate
498.12
pretentious 501.18
grandiloquent 545.8

ostentatiously
pretentiously 501.25

inexpedient 995.5

out of pocket
adj bereft 473.8
poor 619.7
wanting 991.13
adv at a loss 473.9

out of print 991.11

out of proportion
inappropriate 788.7
inconsistent 788.8
unequal 790.4

out of range 261.18

out of reach
adj out-of-the-way
261.9
inaccessible 966.9
adv beyond reach
261.18

out of season
inappropriate 788.7
old-fashioned 841.16

out of shape 265.12

out of sight
adj invisible 32.5
gone 34.5
absent 222.11
overpriced 632.12
great 998.13
adv far 261.15
out of reach 261.18

out of sorts ill 85.55
out of humour 110.17
unhappy 112.21

out of steam weak
16.12
impotent 19.13

out of step 867.7

out of the blue
adj unexpected 131.10
adv unexpectedly
131.14

out of the closet
348.10

out of the ordinary
unusual 869.10
notable 996.19

out of the question
adj impossible 125.14,
966.7
rejected 372.3
phrase I refuse 442.7
exclam by no means
335.9

out of the running out
of action 19.17
disappointing 132.6

out-of-the-way
adj unexpected 131.10
deviative 164.7
godforsaken 261.9
secluded 584.8
irrelevant 775.7
farfetched 775.8
occasional 847.3
unconventional 867.6
unusual 869.10
circuitous 913.7

adv out of reach
261.18

out of the woods
1009.14

out of the world
307.30

out-of-the-world 584.8

out of this world
extreme 247.13
unusual 869.10
great 998.13

out of time 788.7

out of tune dissonant
61.4
disaccordant 456.15
different 779.7
inappropriate 788.7
disorderly 809.13
out of line 867.7

out of work 331.18

out on a limb alienated
589.11
alone 871.8
exposed 1005.15
in deep shit 1012.22

out on the town
743.28

outpost frontier 211.5
vanguard 216.2
hinterland 233.2
jumping-off place
261.4
guard 1007.9

outposts 209.1

outpouring
noun outflow 190.4
plenty 990.2
adj outgoing 190.19

output yield 472.5
receipts 627.1
production 892.2

outrage
noun indignity 156.2
mistreatment 389.2
injustice 650.4
misdeed 655.2
evil 999.3
verb offend 152.21,
156.5
mistreat 389.5
violate 435.4
work evil 999.6

outrageous insulting
156.8
overpriced 632.12
undue 640.9
disgraceful 661.11
violent 671.16
absurd 922.11
excessive 992.16
terrible 999.9

outrageously
exorbitantly 632.16
disgracefully 661.16
excessively 992.22
terribly 999.14

outreach outdo 249.9
be long 267.5

deceive 356.14
outwit 415.11

outright
adj downright 247.12
thorough 793.10
unqualified 959.2
adv freely 430.32
free and clear 469.12
completely 793.14

outrun
noun skiing 753.1
verb overtake 174.13
outdo 249.9
defeat 412.6

outset
noun beginning 817.1
verb set out 188.8

outside
noun appearance 33.2
exterior 206.2
outdoors 206.3
roulette 759.12
adj exterior 206.7
outdoor 206.8
extrinsic 767.3
extraneous 773.5
adv externally 206.10
outdoors 206.11

outside chance
possibility 965.1
small chance 971.9

outside in 205.7

outside of 772.10

outsider exclusiveness
772.3
alien 773.3
oddity 869.4

outsize
noun oversize 257.5
adj large 247.7
oversize 257.23

outskirts environment
209.1
bounds 211.1
frontier 211.5
town 230.1
East End 230.6
jumping-off place
261.4

outspoken
communicative 343.10
artless 416.5
free-acting 430.23
speaking 524.32
candid 644.17

outstanding exterior
206.7
eminent 247.9
remarkable 247.10
superior 249.12
superlative 249.13
remaining 256.7
protruding 283.14
conspicuous 348.12
due 623.10
prominent 662.17
notable 996.19

outstandingly
conspicuously 348.16

famously 662.21
importantly 996.25

outstretched 259.11

outstrip lead 165.2
overtake 174.13
loom 247.5
outdo 249.9

out to 403.17

out to lunch
blockheaded 921.17
screwy 922.9
crazy 925.27
kooky 926.6

outward
adj apparent 33.11
exterior 206.7
formal 580.7
extrinsic 767.3
adv forth 190.21

outward-bound
departing 188.18
outgoing 190.19

outwardly apparently
33.12
forth 190.21
externally 206.10

outwards forth 190.21
externally 206.10

outweigh excel 249.6
overweigh 297.14

outwit outdo 249.9
deceive 356.14
outfox 415.11

out with 524.23

oval
noun ovule 280.6
athletics 755.1
horse racing 757.1
adj ovate 280.12

ovarian genital 2.27
glandular 13.8

ovary 2.11

ovation celebration
487.1
applause 509.2

oven kiln 742.5
furnace 1018.11

over
noun match 747.3
adj superior 249.12
remaining 256.7
higher 272.19
ended 819.8
past 836.7
surplus 992.18
adv inversely 205.8
additionally 253.11
on high 272.21
again 848.17
excessively 992.22
prep all over 159.28
through 161.27
beyond 261.21
on 295.37
during 820.14
in excess of 992.26

over again 848.17,
873.7

overall
noun clothing 5.1
adj cumulative 769.23
comprehensive 771.7
adv throughout 793.17
generally 863.17

overalls 5.1

over and above
adj surplus 992.18
prep with 253.12
in excess of 992.26

over and done with
819.8

over and over 848.16

over and over again
848.16

overarching topping
198.11
high 272.14
overlying 295.36

overbearing
noun authoritativeness
417.3
adj arrogant 141.9
imperious 417.16

overblown past one's
prime 303.15
overfull 992.20

overburdened careworn
126.9
weighted 297.18
overfull 992.20

overcast
noun airspace 184.32
cloudiness 319.3
darkening 1026.6
verb cloud 319.6
darken 1026.9
adj cloudy 319.7
gloomy 1026.14

overcharged exciting
105.30
weighted 297.18
ornate 545.11
overfull 992.20

overcoat 5.13

overcome
verb unnerve 128.10
excel 249.6
defeat 411.5
surmount 412.7
adj dead-drunk 88.32
overwrought 105.26
crushed 112.29
unnerved 128.14
defeated 412.14

overcoming
noun defeat 412.1
adj exciting 105.30
victorious 411.7
irresistible 412.18

overcooked 11.7

overcrowded full
793.11
teeming 883.9
overfull 992.20

overdo exaggerate
355.3
overindulge 669.5
overrun 909.4
go too far 992.10

overdoing intemperance
669.1
overcarrying 992.6

overdo it flannel 511.6
overpraise 511.7

overdone done 11.7
exaggerated 355.4
affected 500.15
grandiloquent 545.8
overwrought 992.21

overdose
noun superabundance
992.2
cloyer 993.3
verb oversupply
992.14
satiate 993.4

overdraft arrears 623.2
insolvency 625.3

overdrawn exaggerated
355.4
overdone 992.21

overdrive task 725.16
overdo 992.10

overdue expected
130.13
late 845.16

overeating eating 8.1
gluttony 672.1

overestimate
noun overestimation
948.1
verb exaggerate 355.3
overpraise 511.7
overreckon 948.2

overestimated
exaggerated 355.4
overrated 948.3

overflow
noun spillage 238.6
wordiness 538.2
plenty 990.2
overfullness 992.3
verb flow over 238.17
teem with 883.5
run over 909.7
abound 990.5
superabound 992.8

overflowed 1063.17

overflowing
noun overflow 238.6
overrunning 909.1
adj much 247.8
diffuse 538.11
teeming 883.9
plentiful 990.7
overfull 992.20

overgrown grown 14.3,
259.12
large 247.7
oversize 257.23
luxuriant 310.40
overrun 909.10

excessive 992.16

overhang
noun overhanging
202.3
verb hang over 202.7
overlie 295.30
be imminent 839.2

overhanging
noun overhang 202.3
adj overhung 202.11
imminent 839.3

overhaul
noun reparation 396.6
examination 937.3
verb overtake 174.13
repair 396.14
take account of 628.9
examine 937.24
check 1016.20

overhauling reparation
396.6
examination 937.3

overhead
noun roof 295.6
expenses 626.3
adv on high 272.21

overheads 626.3

overhear hear 48.11
know 551.15

overheated hot
1018.25
heated 1019.29

overjoyed 95.16

overkill exaggeration
355.1
attack 459.1
plenty 990.2
overdoing 992.6

overland 234.8

overlap
noun overlayer 295.4
agreement 787.1
superfluity 992.4
verb overlie 295.30
agree 787.6

overlapping
noun overlayer 295.4
adj overlying 295.36
related 774.9

overlay
noun overlayer 295.4
verb cover 295.19
ornament 545.7

overload
noun burden 297.7
overfullness 992.3
verb burden 297.13
ornament 545.7
overlade 992.15
go hard with 1010.8

overloaded weighted
297.18
ornate 545.11
overfull 992.20

overlook accept 134.7
condone 148.4
slight 157.6
front on 216.9

rise above 272.11
neglect 340.6
suffer 443.10
supervise 573.10
bewitch 691.9
examine 937.24
keep an open mind
978.7
be inattentive 983.2

overlooked forgiven
148.7
neglected 340.14

overlooking
noun forgiveness 148.1
neglect 340.1
sufferance 443.2
adj high 272.14

overlord master 575.1
potentate 575.8
chief 996.10

overly 992.22

overnight 315.11

overpower be strong
15.9
drown out 53.8
overcome 412.7

overpowered
overwrought 105.26
defeated 412.14

overpowering
impregnable 15.19
exciting 105.30
irresistible 412.18

overpriced 632.12

overproduction 891.5

overrated 948.3

override outdo 249.9
overlie 295.30
conquer 412.10
repeal 445.2
domineer 612.16
run over 909.7

overriding 996.24

overrule repeal 445.2
rule 612.14

overrun
noun overrunning
909.1
surplus 992.5
verb pervade 221.7
overflow 238.17
spread 259.6
vegetate 310.31
appropriate 480.19
compose 548.16
overgo 909.4
infest 909.6
run over 909.7
superabound 992.8
exceed 992.9
adj luxuriant 310.40
overspread 909.10

overseas
adj nonresident 222.12
transoceanic 261.11
adv oversea 240.10
abroad 773.6

oversee 573.10

overseeing
noun operation 888.1
adj supervising 573.13

overshadow eclipse
249.8
rise above 272.11
cloud 319.6
darken 1026.9

overshadowed 1026.16

overshadowing 1026.6

oversight neglect 340.1
nonobservance 435.1
supervision 573.2
government 612.1
operation 888.1
slip 974.4
protectorship 1007.2

oversize
noun outsize 257.5
adj oversized 257.23

oversized 257.23

overspend spend more
than one has 486.7
overpay 632.8
overdo 992.10

overspill
noun overfullness
992.3
verb superabound
992.8

overstated 355.4

overstretched 992.21

overt 348.10

overtake plaster 88.23
outstrip 174.13

overtaken 88.33

over the hill 303.15

over the odds 632.12

over the top 498.12

over the water 240.10

overthrow
noun overturn 205.2
fall 395.3
defeat 412.1
deposal 447.2
match 747.3
revolution 851.2,
859.1
downthrow 912.2
refutation 957.2
verb overturn 205.6,
395.20, 912.6
revolt 327.7
overcome 412.7
depose 447.4
change 851.7
revolutionize 859.4
refute 957.5

overthrown ruined
395.28
defeated 412.14
disproved 957.7

overtime pay 624.4
bonus 624.6
shift 824.3

overtly 348.15

overture

noun offer 439.1
prelude 708.26
curtain raiser 815.2
verb make advances
439.7

overturn
noun upset 205.2
fall 395.3
defeat 412.1
revolution 859.1
downthrow 912.2
verb capsize 182.44
turn over 205.6
overthrow 395.20,
912.6
overcome 412.7
revolutionize 859.4
refute 957.5

overturned defeated
412.14
disproved 957.7

overuse
noun overdoing 992.6
verb overdo 992.10

overvalued 948.3

overview scrutiny 27.6
abridgment 557.1

overweight
noun oversize 257.5
weight 297.1
overfullness 992.3
verb burden 297.13
outweigh 297.14
overload 992.15
adj corpulent 257.18
oversize 257.23
heavy 297.16

overwhelm be strong
15.9
drown out 53.8
aggrieve 112.19
astonish 122.6
pervade 221.7
overflow 238.17
submerge 367.7
whelm 395.21, 412.8
subdue 432.9
raid 459.20
teem with 883.5
run over 909.7
refute 957.5
oversupply 992.14
flood 1063.14

overwhelmed
overwrought 105.26
overcome 112.29
wondering 122.9
flooded 238.25
defeated 412.14
overrun 909.10

overwhelming
noun permeation 221.3
overflow 238.6
overrunning 909.1
adj impregnable 15.19
exciting 105.30
astonishing 122.12
irresistible 412.18
teeming 883.9

evidential 956.16

overwinter 313.8

over with 819.8

overwork
noun overdoing 992.6
verb work hard 725.13
task 725.16
overdo 992.10

overworked ornate
498.12
trite 863.16

overwrought
overexcited 105.26
exaggerated 355.4
ornate 498.12
grandiloquent 545.8
overdone 992.21

ovulation 305.12

owe be indebted 623.5
be liable 896.3

owed 623.10, 639.7

owe it to 641.4

owing due 623.10,
639.7
attributable 887.6

owing to
prep because of 887.9
conj resulting from
886.8

owl bird of ill omen
133.6
bird 311.28

own
verb acknowledge
332.11
confess 351.7
have title to 469.5
adj possessed 469.8

own accord 430.7

own account 430.7

own authority 430.7

own-brand 517.24

own choice 430.7

owned 469.8

owner proprietor 470.2
jockey 757.2

ownership 469.2

own free will 430.7

own goal 1010.5

owning
noun confession 351.3
possession 469.1
adj possessing 469.9

own initiative 430.7

own-label 517.24

own power 430.7

own up 351.7

own volition 430.7

own way 430.7

ox
noun horse 15.8
cattle 311.6
bungler 414.8

phrase beast of burden
176.8

Oxbridge 567.13

oxen 311.6

oxidation decay 393.6
burning 1019.5

oyster leg 10.22
marine animal 311.30

ozone 317.1

P 87.16

p 728.7

pa 560.10

pace
noun velocity 172.4
step 177.11
gait 177.12
verb lead 165.2
walk 177.27
stroll 177.28
go on horseback
177.34
row 182.53
measure 300.10

pacemaker leader
574.6
precursor 815.1

paceman 747.2

pacific quiescent
173.12
meek 433.15
peaceful 464.9
unbelligerent 464.10
pacificatory 465.12

pacifism inaction 329.1
peaceableness 464.4
moderation 670.1

pacifist
noun pacificist 464.6
adj unbelligerent
464.10

pacify quiet 173.8
conciliate 465.7
calm 670.7
order 806.4

pacing 757.1

pack
noun parachute 181.13
amount 244.2
lot 247.4
stopping 293.5
film 714.10
card 758.2
company 769.3
flock 769.5
bundle 769.8
multitude 883.3
impediment 1011.6
verb load 159.15
transport 176.12
fill 196.7, 793.7
package 212.9
stop 293.7
wrap 295.20
tamper with 354.17
assemble 769.18
bundle 769.20
teem with 883.5
fix 964.5

overload 992.15
obstruct 1011.12
phrase freight 176.6

package
noun packaging 212.2
bundle 769.8
all 791.3
combination 804.1
verb pack 212.9
wrap 295.20
bundle 769.20

packaged packed
212.12
covered 295.31
assembled 769.21

package deal
transaction 731.4
all 791.3
combination 804.1

packaging 212.2

packed packaged
212.12
stopped 293.11
tampered with 354.30
crowded 769.22
full 793.11
stuck 854.16
teeming 883.9
fixed 964.8
overfull 992.20
dense 1043.12

packed-up 393.29

packet dose 87.19
ship 180.1
bomb 618.3
bundle 769.8

pack in enter 189.7
thrust in 191.7
assemble 769.18
cease 856.6

packing
noun placement 159.6
lining 196.3
packaging 212.2
stopping 293.5
phrase transportation
176.3

pack on 182.20

pack up 393.26

pact 437.1

pad
noun thud 52.3
foot 199.5
partition 213.5
race horse 311.14
print 517.7
handwriting style
547.4
notebook 549.11
bedding 900.20
safeguard 1007.3
verb thud 52.15
relieve 120.5
creep 177.26
walk 177.27
fill 196.7, 793.7
protract 538.8
iterate 848.8

padded 538.12

padding creeping
177.17
lining 196.3
extra 254.4
stopping 293.5
redundancy 848.3
superfluity 992.4
safeguard 1007.3
softening 1045.5

paddle
noun gait 177.12
oar 180.15
rod 605.2
agitator 916.9
verb stroll 177.28
row 182.53
agitate 916.10
moisten 1063.12

paddock 757.1

Paddy 232.7

paddy 1067.9

padlock
noun lock 428.5
verb close 293.6

padre clergyman 699.2
priest 699.5

pads 747.1

paean cheer 116.2
thanks 150.2
praise 509.5
laud 696.3
sacred music 708.17

paediatric 90.15

paella 10.11

pagan
noun heathen 688.7
unbeliever 695.11
adj paganish 688.11
unbelieving 695.19
idolatrous 697.7
unlearned 929.14

paganism heathenism
688.4
idolatry 697.1
unenlightenment
929.4

page
noun makeup 554.12
wedding party 563.4
section 792.2
paper 1052.5
verb summon 420.11
number 1016.16

pageant spectacle 33.7
display 501.4

pageantry spectacle
33.7
display 501.4

pagoda tower 272.6
temple 703.2

paid employed 615.20
paid-up discharged
624.22

pain
noun bread 10.27
suffering 26.1

anaemia 85.9
annoyance 96.2
distress 96.5
distressfulness 98.5
verb grieve 96.17
distress 98.14

pained in pain 26.9
grieved 96.23

painful hurtful 26.10
distressing 98.20
laborious 725.18
troublesome 1012.18

painfully distressingly
98.28, 247.21
with difficulty 1012.28

painless 1013.13

pains painstakingness
339.2
punishment 604.1
exertion 725.1

painstaking
noun painstakingness
339.2
adj diligent 339.11

painstakingly 339.15

paint
noun colour 35.8
blanket 295.12
appaloosa 311.11
palette 712.18
makeup 1015.12
verb colour 35.13
represent 349.8
describe 349.9
ornament 498.8
figure 498.9
portray 712.19

paintbrush 712.18

painted 35.16

painter 716.4

painterly 712.20

painting paint-work
35.12
colouring 712.4
canvas 712.14
graphic arts 713.1

pair
noun rig 179.5
match 747.3
likeness 783.3
set 783.5
two 872.2
deuce 872.3
verb assemble 769.18
put together 799.5
league 804.4
double 872.5
adj both 872.7

paired married 563.21
accompanying 768.9
joined 799.13
leagued 804.6
coupled 872.8

pairing joining 799.1
doubleness 872.1

Paki 232.7

pal

noun mate 588.4
verb hang with 582.18
palace 228.7
palais 228.7
palatable edible 8.33
    tasty 63.8
    desirable 100.30
palate taste 62.1
    discrimination 943.1
palatial residential
    228.32
    grandiose 501.21
palazzo 228.7
pale
    noun bounds 211.1
    enclosure 212.3
    sphere 231.2
    plot 231.4
    leg 273.6
    heraldic device 647.2
    verb blur 32.4
    decolour 36.5
    lose colour 36.6
    change colour 105.19
    take fright 127.11
    fence 212.7
    adj inconspicuous 32.6
    soft-coloured 35.21
    colourless 36.7
    whitish 37.8
    unhealthy 85.53
    dull 117.6
    deathly 307.29
pale-blue 45.3
paled beat 21.8
    enclosed 212.10
palette 712.18
pale-yellow 43.4
pall
    noun cover 295.2
    grave clothes 309.14
    veil of secrecy 345.3
    verb be tedious 118.6
    satiate 993.4
palladium 1007.3
pallid colourless 36.7
    dull 117.6
    terrified 127.26
pallor colour 35.1
    paleness 36.2
    dullness 117.1
    deathliness 307.12
palm
    noun clutches 474.4
    trophy 646.3
    verb touch 73.6
    take 480.13
    steal 482.13
palmer traveller 178.1
    religious 699.15
palm oil 375.7
palms supremacy 249.3
    trophy 646.3
palpable touchable
    73.11
    weighable 297.19
    manifest 348.8

substantial 762.6
palpably 348.14
palsy
    noun paralysis 85.27
    shaking 916.2
    verb deaden 25.4
paltry ungenerous
    651.6
    base 661.12
    meagre 991.10
    poor 997.21
    inferior 1004.9
pamper indulge 427.6
    foster 449.16
pampered 427.9
pampering 427.3
pamphlet advertising
    matter 352.8
    booklet 554.11
Pan forest god 678.11
    Demeter 889.5
pan
    noun toilet 12.11
    container 195.1
    verb cook 11.4
    photograph 714.14
    mine 1056.14
panacea 86.3
panache feather 3.17
    showiness 501.3
pancake
    noun crumpet 10.43
    verb land 184.43
Panchen Lama 699.13
pancreas viscera 2.14
    digestion 2.15, 7.8
pancreatic 13.8
Pandemonium 682.1
pandemonium noise
    53.3
    turbulence 671.2
    hell 809.5
pander vulgarize 497.9
    prostitute oneself
    665.21
pandering 665.8
pander to toady to
    138.8
    serve 449.18, 577.13
pandit 571.1
Pandora's box
    affliction 96.8
    trouble 1012.3
pane bread 10.27
    window 292.7
    lamina 296.2
    transparent substance
    1028.2
panel partition 213.5
    lamina 296.2
    forum 423.3
    discussion 541.7
    jury 596.6
    litigant 598.12
    assembly 769.2
panelling 1052.3

pang throe 26.2
    pain 96.5
    compunction 113.2
pangs 113.2
panic
    noun fear 127.1
    nervousness 128.1
    bear panic 737.22
    verb start 127.12
    put in fear 127.16
    overwhelm 412.8
panicked panicky
    127.27
    defeated 412.14
panicky panic-prone
    127.27
    nervous 128.11
    cowardly 491.10
panic-stricken 127.27
panoply armour 460.3
    throng 769.4
panorama view 33.6
    spectacle 33.7
    picture 712.11
panoramic 771.7
pansy 75.15
pant
    noun breathing 2.19
    verb burn out 21.5
    thrill 105.18
    murmur 524.26
    burn 1018.22
pantheon gods 678.1
    temple 703.2
panther 311.22
panting
    noun breathlessness
    21.3
    trepidation 105.5
    adj respiratory 2.30
    breathless 21.12
    eager 101.8
    precipitate 401.10
panto 704.6
pantomime
    noun impersonation
    349.4
    gesture 517.14
    comedy 704.6
    actor 707.2
    commotion 809.4
    verb impersonate
    349.12
    gesture 517.21
    act 704.29
pantry wardrobe
    197.15
    larder 386.8
pants 5.18
pap diet 7.11
    nutriment 10.3
    breast 283.6
    semiliquid 1060.5
papa 560.10
papacy mastership
    417.7
    papality 698.6

papal 698.15
paper
    noun alabaster 37.2
    wafer 270.7
    handwriting style
    547.4
    writing 547.10
    document 549.5
    treatise 556.1
    paper stock 1052.5
    verb face 295.23
    adj newspaper 555.2
paperback 554.3
paper over conceal
    346.6
    falsify 354.16
papers naturalization
    226.3
    archives 549.2
    document 549.5
paper-thin 763.7
par
    noun mean 246.1
    price 738.9
    round 748.3
    equality 789.1
    verb play 748.4
    adj equal 789.7
par-4 hole 748.1
par-5 hole 748.1
parabola 279.2
parachute
    noun chute 181.13
    life jacket 397.6
    safeguard 1007.3
    verb bail out 184.47
    descend 194.5
    plunge 367.6
parade
    noun spectacle 33.7
    walk 177.10
    path 383.2
    display 501.4
    procession 811.3
    verb go for a walk
    177.29
    march 177.30
    manifest 348.5
    flaunt 501.17
    file 811.7
parade ground 463.1
paradigm morphology
    526.3
    model 785.1
Paradise 838.2
paradise happiness
    95.2
    preserve 397.7
    park 743.14
    garden 1067.10
paradox inconsistency
    788.2
    impossibility 966.1
    dilemma 1012.7
paradoxical self-
    contradictory 778.8
    inconsistent 788.8
    illogical 935.11

impossible 966.7
paraffin 1024.20
paragon superior 249.4
    ideal 659.4, 785.4
    best 998.8
    beauty 1015.8
paragraph
    noun phrase 529.1
    part 554.13
    treatise 556.1
    section 792.2
    verb phrase 532.4
parallel
    noun map 159.5
    paralleler 203.2
    zone 231.3
    entrenchment 460.5
    likeness 783.3
    equal 789.4
    verb be parallel 203.4
    relate 774.6
    resemble 783.7
    agree 787.6
    equal 789.5
    compare 942.4
    be comparable 942.7
    adj paralleling 203.6
    side 218.6
    accompanying 768.9
    related 774.9
    analogous 783.11
    comparative 942.8
paralyse prostrate
    19.10
    deaden 25.4
    numb 94.8
    astonish 122.6
    terrify 127.17
paralysed disabled
    19.16
    fuddled 88.33
    terrified 127.26
    passive 329.6
paralysing 127.29
paralysis anaemia 85.9
    paralysation 85.27
    inaction 329.1
paramedic 90.11
parameter measure
    300.2
    condition 958.2
parameters bounds
    211.1
    circumstances 765.2
paramount
    noun master 575.1
    potentate 575.8
    chief 996.10
    adj top 198.10
    chief 249.14
    governing 612.18
    principal 996.24
    best 998.16
paranoia mental
    disorder 92.14
    dissociation 92.20
    schizophrenia 925.4
paranoid

noun psychotic 925.17
adj psychotic 925.28
paranormal
noun supernaturalism
689.2, 869.7
adj occult 689.23
supernatural 869.15
parapet 1011.5
paraphernalia
equipment 385.4
belongings 471.2
paraphrase
noun reproduction
336.3
translation 341.3
verb imitate 336.5
rephrase 341.13
parapsychology 689.4
parasite barnacle 138.5
follower 166.2
legume 310.4
vermin 311.35
bloodsucker 311.36
nonworker 331.11
attendance 768.6
parasitic obsequious
138.14
indolent 331.19
rapacious 480.26
concurrent 898.4
parasol umbrella 295.7
shade 1027.1
paratrooper parachutist
185.8
diver 367.4
paratroops elite troops
461.14
army 461.22
parcel
noun amount 244.2
real estate 471.6
bundle 769.8
part 792.1
number 883.2
verb package 212.9
quantify 244.4
apportion 477.6,
801.18
bundle 769.20
parched thirsty 100.26
shrunk 260.13
burned 1019.30
dried 1064.9
parchment handwriting
style 547.4
writing 547.10
codex 547.11
document 549.5
eggshell 1048.2
desert 1064.2
pardon
noun pity 145.1
excuse 148.2
acquittal 601.1
verb have pity 145.4
forgive 148.3
acquit 601.4
pardoned 148.7

pare peel 6.8
reduce 252.7
excise 255.10
cheapen 633.6
sever 801.11
parent
noun progenitor 560.8
author 885.4
verb foster 449.16
adj ancestral 560.17
parentage 560.1
parental loving 104.27
ancestral 560.17
protective 1007.23
parenthood 560.1
parenting 449.3
par excellence 249.16
par for the course
noun rule 373.5
predetermination
963.1
adj medium 246.3
typical 349.15
prevalent 863.12
parfum 70.2
pariah recluse 584.5
outcast 586.4
oddity 869.4
paring flake 296.3
piece 792.3
parish state 231.5
diocese 698.8
laity 700.1
parish council 423.1
parishioners 700.1
parish priest 699.5
parity price 738.9
similarity 783.1
equality 789.1
park
noun enclosure 212.3
green 310.7
woodland 310.11
preserve 397.7
armoury 462.2
arena 463.1
public park 743.14
football 745.1
verb place 159.12
settle 159.17
parkin 10.42
parkland grassland
310.8
woodland 310.11
parlance language
523.1
diction 532.1
parliament 613.1
parliamentarian
noun legislator 610.3
adj governmental
612.17
parliamentary
governmental 612.17
legislative 613.10

**parliamentary
immunity** 430.8
**parliamentary private
secretary** 610.3
parlour living room
197.5
workplace 739.1
parlous 1005.9
parochial local 231.9
exclusive 772.9
narrow-minded 979.10
parody
noun imitation 336.1
reproduction 336.3
bad likeness 350.2
wit 489.1
burlesque 508.6
verb imitate 336.5
misrepresent 350.3
burlesque 508.11
lampoon 512.12
parole
noun release 431.2
promise 436.1
language 523.1
utterance 524.3
verb release 431.5
parquet check 47.4
ground covering 199.3
rug 295.9
auditorium 704.15
parr 311.30
parrot
noun tedium 118.1
imitator 336.4
conformist 866.2
verb mimic 336.6
repeat 848.7
memorize 988.17
parry prevaricate 344.7
dodge 368.8
fend off 460.10
fight 754.4
quibble 935.9
refute 957.5
prevent 1011.14
parsimony
parsimoniousness
484.1
thrift 635.1
meagreness 991.2
parson 699.2
parsonage house 228.5
pastorage 703.7
part
noun contents 196.1
region 231.1
amount 244.2
length 267.2
function 387.5, 724.3
estate 471.4
portion 477.5, 792.1
section 554.13
role 704.10
passage 708.24
score 708.28
mode 764.4
particular 765.3

component 795.2
verb interspace 224.3
open 292.11
die 307.19
apportion 477.6
divorce 566.5
disband 770.8
separate 801.8
part company 801.19
adj partial 792.7
incomplete 794.4
half 874.5
adv to a degree 248.10
partly 792.8
partake eat 8.20
participate 476.5
take 480.13
be involved 897.3
part and parcel 795.2
part company fall out
456.10
disband 770.8
part 801.19
parted 224.6
parted from 473.8
partial
noun tone 50.2
adj partisan 617.19
interested 650.11
part 792.7
incomplete 794.4
half 874.5
discriminatory 979.12
imperfect 1002.4
partiality inclination
100.3
love 104.1
preference 371.5
partisanism 617.13
onesidedness 650.3
prejudice 979.3
partially to a degree
248.10
unjustly 650.13
partly 792.8
incompletely 794.6
imperfectly 1002.5
partial to 104.30
participant
noun participator
476.4
adj participating 476.8
participate take part
476.5
be involved 897.3
participate in 476.5
participating 476.8
participation partaking
476.1
association 582.6
inclusion 771.1
participatory 476.8
particle modicum
248.2
minutia 258.7
part of speech 530.3
piece 792.3
powder 1049.5

particular
noun instance 765.3
part 792.1
event 830.2
specific 864.3
citation 956.5
adj meticulous 339.12
selective 371.23
proportionate 477.13
fastidious 495.9
detailed 765.9
classificational 808.7
special 864.12
particularly intensely
247.20
chiefly 249.17
fastidiously 495.14
fully 765.13
specially 864.15
singly 871.13
particulars 760.4
parting
noun departure 188.1
leave-taking 188.4
death 307.1
disbandment 770.3
separation 801.1
adj departing 188.18
separating 801.25
parting shot 508.2
partisan
noun follower 166.2
irregular 461.15
friend 588.1
party member 609.27
supporter 616.9
adj polarizing 456.17
party 609.44, 617.19
partial 650.11
discriminatory 979.12
partition
noun dividing wall
213.5
apportionment 477.1
separation 801.1
bisector 874.3
verb set apart 213.8
apportion 477.6,
801.18
diversify 781.2
partitioned walled
213.11
separate 801.20
partly
adj half 874.5
adv to a degree 248.10
partially 792.8
partner
noun participator
476.4
spouse 563.6
companion 588.3
copartner 616.2
bridge 758.3
accompanier 768.4
verb cooperate 450.3
assemble 769.18
league 804.4
partnered 563.21

payoff bribe 378.2
  payment 624.1
  meat and potatoes
  766.3
pay on 624.10
pay out parcel out
  477.8
  attend to 604.10
  settle with 624.12
  spend 626.5
payout receipts 627.1
  dividend 738.7
pay over 624.15
pay packet 624.4
pay rise 446.1
payroll 624.4
pay the bill pay in full
  624.13
  pay for 624.18
  treat 624.19
pay the bills 478.19
pay tribute praise
  509.12
  honour 646.8
pay up pay in full
  624.13
  kick in 624.16
PCP 87.17
pea 310.4
peace silence 51.1
  angel dust 87.17
  comfortableness 121.2
  accord 455.1
  pax 464.1
  truce 465.5
  agreement 787.1
  order 806.1
peace and quiet 464.2
peace dividend 465.6
peaceful calm 106.12
  comfortable 121.11
  quiescent 173.12
  homelike 228.33
  in accord 455.3
  pacific 464.9
  moderate 670.10
peacefully comfortably
  121.14
  quiescently 173.18
peacekeeping 464.10
peace-keeping force
  465.1
peace-loving 464.10
peacemaker pacifist
  464.6
  make-peace 466.5
  moderator 670.3
peace of mind
  contentment 107.1
  peace of heart 464.3
peacetime
  noun peace 464.1
  adj pacific 464.9
peach
  noun smooth 287.3
  dandy 998.7

doll 1015.9
  adj orange 42.2
peachy feathery 3.28
  great 998.13
peacock
  noun spectrum 47.6
  cock 76.8
  bird 311.28
  strutter 501.10
  verb pose 500.13
  strut 501.15
peak
  noun summit 198.2
  mountain 237.6
  wave 238.14
  plateau 272.4
  projection 285.4
  speech sound 524.13
  business cycle 731.9
  limit 793.5
  acme of perfection
  1001.3
  verb fail 85.47
  top 198.9
  billow 238.22
Peak District 231.7
peaked 198.12
peaking 731.9
peaks 237.1
peal
  noun blare 53.5
  ringing 54.3
  boom 56.4
  verb din 53.7
  blare 53.10
  ring 54.8
  boom 56.9
pearl
  noun alabaster 37.2
  drop 282.3
  good person 659.1
  good thing 998.5
  adj whitish 37.8
  grey 39.4
pearly soft-coloured
  35.21
  whitish 37.8
  grey 39.4
  iridescent 47.10,
  1024.37
pear-shaped 279.14
peart 413.23
peasant vulgarian
  497.6
  countryman 606.6
  agriculturist 1067.5
peaty 1020.8
pebble
  noun modicum 248.2
  pebblestone 1057.4
  verb floor 295.22
peck
  noun quantity 247.3
  lot 247.4
  tap 901.7
  verb pick 8.26
  tap 901.18
pecking 8.1

pecking order 808.4
peculiar personal
  312.15
  indicative 517.23
  other 779.8
  differentiative 779.9
  classificational 808.7
  characteristic 864.13
  odd 869.11
  eccentric 926.5
peculiarity habit 373.4
  mannerism 500.2
  sign 517.1
  characteristic 864.4
  oddity 869.3
  eccentricity 926.1
peculiarly intensely
  247.20
  chiefly 249.17
  characteristically
  864.17
  oddly 869.19
pedal
  noun lever 905.4
  verb push 903.9
  adj plantar 199.9
pedalling 177.6
pedals 711.17
pedantic overfastidious
  495.12
  overnice 500.18
  grandiloquent 545.8
  scholastic 568.19
  studious 570.17
  pedagogic 571.11
  formal 580.7
  conformist 866.6
  book-learned 927.22
peddle 734.9
peddling 734.2
pedestal 900.8
pedestrian
  noun walker 178.6
  adj dull 117.6
  travelling 177.36
  unskilful 414.15
  prosaic 721.5
pedigree 549.9, 560.5
pee 12.14
peek
  noun glance 27.4
  verb look 27.13
  pry 980.4
peel
  noun skin 295.3
  lamina 296.2
  stronghold 460.6
  verb pare 6.8
  excise 255.10
peeled 6.14
peeling disrobing 6.2
  skin 295.3
peel off pilot 184.37
  come apart 801.9
peep
  noun glance 27.4
  verb look 27.13

warble 60.5
  reconnoitre 937.28
  pry 980.4
peer
  noun nobleman 608.4
  equal 789.4
  verb look 27.13
  be curious 980.3
peerage 608.1
peer group company
  769.3
  equal 789.4
peerless matchless
  249.15
  best 998.16
  perfect 1001.6
peg
  noun teeth 2.8
  drink 8.4, 88.7
  degree 245.1
  leg 273.6
  bulge 283.3
  stopper 293.4
  fastening 799.3
  throw 903.3
  verb plod 175.7
  stroll 177.28
  drudge 725.14
  hook 799.8
Pegasus 311.15
pegging 725.17
pejorative 512.13
pelham 1011.7
pellet
  noun sphere 282.2
  shot 462.19
  verb pelt 459.27
pelmet 295.2
pelt
  noun hair 3.2
  fur 4.2
  skin 295.3
  hit 901.4
  verb speed 174.8
  rain 316.9
  stone 459.27
  pound 901.16
  throw 903.10
  shoot 903.12
pelting 316.10
pelvis 2.11
pen
  noun enclosure 212.3
  place of confinement
  429.7
  prison 429.8
  writing 547.1
  writer 547.13, 718.3
  farm 1067.8
  verb enclose 212.5
  confine 429.12
  write 547.19, 718.6
penal 604.22
penal code 673.5
penalty judgment
  598.10
  penalization 603.1

punishment 604.1
  game 745.3, 750.3,
  750.6
  round 748.3
  impediment 1011.6
penalty area 745.1
penalty goal 746.3
penalty shoot-out
  745.3
penalty spot 745.1
penalty try 746.3
penance penitence
  113.4, 658.3
  penalty 603.1
  seven sacraments
  701.4
pence 728.7
penchant inclination
  100.3
  preference 371.5
  tendency 895.1
pencil
  noun palette 712.18
  ray 1024.5
  verb mark 517.19
  write 547.19
  portray 712.19
pencil in 712.19
pencilled 547.22
pendant hanger 202.4
  adjunct 254.1
  jewel 498.6
  likeness 783.3
pending
  adj pendent 202.9
  overhanging 202.11
  undecided 970.18
  prep during 820.14
pendragon 575.9
pendulum series 811.2
  oscillator 915.9
penetrate bite 68.5
  affect 93.14
  interpenetrate 189.8
  insert 191.3
  pervade 221.7
  perforate 292.15
  perceive 521.9
  imbue 796.11
  see through 940.8
  be remembered
  988.14
  freeze 1022.10
penetrating intense
  15.22
  acrimonious 17.14
  shrill 58.14
  pungent 68.6
  strong 69.10
  deep-felt 93.24
  piercing 105.31
  caustic 144.23
  vigorous 544.11
  sagacious 919.16
  cold 1022.14
penetration entrance
  189.1

insertion 191.1
permeation 221.3
hole 292.3
imbuement 796.2
sagacity 919.4
discernment 943.2

penicillin 86.29

penile 2.27

pen in 429.12

peninsula continent
235.1
point 283.9

peninsular 283.20

penis 2.11

penitentiary
noun prison 429.8
priest 699.5
adj penitent 113.9

penman 547.13, 718.3

pennant 647.6

penned enclosed 212.10
written 547.22

pennies 728.19

penniless bereft 473.8
destitute 619.9

penny mite 728.7
mill 728.8

pen pal 553.8

pension
noun inn 228.15
subsidy 478.8
verb depose 447.4
subsidize 478.19

pensioner old man
304.2
dependent 432.6
beneficiary 479.4
employee 577.3

pension scheme
1007.4

pensive melancholy
112.23
cognitive 930.21
abstracted 984.11

pent 429.19

pentagon 881.1

pentathlon 881.1

penthouse house 228.5
flat 228.13
roof 295.6

pent-up enclosed
212.10
restrained 428.13
confined 429.19

penury 619.2

people
noun population 227.1
humankind 312.1
populace 312.4, 606.1
kinfolk 559.2
race 559.4
family 559.5
laity 700.1
verb settle 159.17
empeople 225.9

peopled 225.12

people's republic
232.1

pep bang 17.3
spirit 544.4

pepper variegate 47.7
flavour 63.7
pull the trigger 459.22
mark 517.19
sprinkle 770.6
throw 903.10
shoot 903.12

peppered spotted 47.13
apertured 292.19
sprinkled 770.10

peppery zestful 68.7
hot-tempered 110.25

peptic 7.20

Pepys 719.4

per by means of 384.13
for each 864.20
conformable to 866.9

per annum 864.19

per capita
adj proportionate
477.13
adv each 864.19

perceive sense 24.6
see 27.12, 521.9
feel 93.10
know 927.12
detect 940.5

perceived 927.26

percent 1016.7

percentage incentive
375.7
benefit 387.4
estate 471.4
gain 472.3
portion 477.5
discount 631.1
part 792.1
ratio 1016.7

perceptible visible 31.6
measurable 300.14
manifest 348.8
knowable 927.25

perceptibly visibly
31.8
measurably 300.15
manifestly 348.14

perception sensation
24.1
vision 27.1
sagacity 919.4
cognizance 927.2
idea 931.1
discernment 943.2

perceptive sensible
24.11
sagacious 919.16
knowing 927.15
discerning 943.8

perch
noun birdhouse 228.23
footing 900.5
verb settle 159.17
sit 173.10

get down 194.7
rest on 900.22

percipient
noun spectator 917.1
adj sagacious 919.16
knowing 927.15

percussion noise 53.3
concussion 671.8
percussion instrument
711.16
impact 901.3

percussionist 710.10

percussive 901.24

Percy 77.10

peregrine
noun wanderer 178.2
adj travelling 177.36

perennial
noun plant 310.3
adj ephemeral 310.41
continuous 811.8
durable 826.10
indeciduous 828.8
constant 846.5

perennially
continuously 811.10
perpetually 828.10
constantly 846.7

perestroika
reproduction 78.1
reconstruction 396.5
rearrangement 807.7
change 851.1

perfect
noun tense 530.12
verb excel 249.6
touch up 392.11
complete 407.6, 819.7
develop 1001.5
adj downright 247.12
complete 407.12
unrestricted 430.27
thorough 793.10
unqualified 959.2
accurate 972.16
ideal 1001.6

perfected improved
392.13
ended 819.8
finished 1001.9

perfecting
noun revision 392.4
adj topping 198.11

perfection
noun development
392.2
completion 793.4
end 819.1
accuracy 972.5
faultlessness 1001.1
acme of perfection
1001.3
adj completion 407.2

perfectionism
optimism 124.3
fastidiousness 495.1

perfectionist
noun optimist 124.6

precisian 495.6
conformist 866.2
adj optimistic 124.12

perfectly extremely
247.22
absolutely 793.15
accurately 972.20
ideally 1001.10

perforated 292.19

perform execute 328.9
manifest 348.5
impersonate 349.12
accomplish 407.4
practise 434.3
act 704.29
play 708.39
operate 888.5, 888.7
do 891.11

performance
noun execution 328.2,
708.30, 891.5
act 328.3
display 348.2
impersonation 349.4
observance 434.1
ceremony 580.4
acting 704.8
theatrical performance
704.12
musical performance
708.33
operation 888.1
adj accomplishment
407.1

perform as 724.13

performed 891.17

performer phoney
500.7
entertainer 707.1
musician 710.1
doer 726.1

performing
noun impersonation
349.4
acting 704.8
operation 888.1
adj acting 328.10

perfume
noun fragrance 70.1
perfumery 70.2
verb odorize 69.7
scent 70.8
vaporize 1065.8

perfumed 70.9

perfumery 70.2

perfunctory indifferent
102.6
unwilling 325.5
reluctant 325.6
careless 340.11

pergola corridor 197.18
summerhouse 228.12

perhaps
noun guess 950.4
adv possibly 965.9

per head 477.13

peri fairy 678.8
Venus 1015.10

peril
noun unreliability
970.6
danger 1005.1
verb endanger 1005.6

perilous unreliable
970.20
dangerous 1005.9

perilously 1005.17

perimeter environment
209.1
bounds 211.1

period menstruation
12.9
degree 245.1
season 313.1
phrase 529.1
passage 708.24
metre 720.7
game 745.3, 750.3,
750.6
end 819.1
time 820.1
point 823.1
wave 915.4
orbit 1070.16

periodic continuous
811.8
recurrent 848.13
oscillating 915.15

periodical
noun publication 352.1
adj serial 555.1
journalistic 555.5

periodically 849.10

Peripatetic 951.10

peripatetic
noun wanderer 178.2
pedestrian 178.6
adj travelling 177.36
discursive 538.13

peripheral
noun circuitry 1041.3
adj exterior 206.7
environing 209.8
outlining 211.14

periphery exterior
206.2
environment 209.1
bounds 211.1
size 257.1

perish disappear 34.3
die 307.19
expire 395.23
age 841.9

perishable mortal
307.34
transient 827.7

perished 761.11

perjury deliberate
falsehood 354.9
deceitfulness 645.3

perk 140.11

perks gratuity 478.5
booty 482.11
bonus 624.6

perky lighthearted
109.12
conceited 140.11

perm 3.15

permanence
perseverance 360.1
durability 826.1
perpetuity 828.1
unchangeableness
854.4

permanent
noun hairdo 3.15
adj persevering 360.8
almighty 677.17
durable 826.10
perpetual 828.7
changeless 852.7
unchangeable 854.17

permanently
perpetually 828.10
abidingly 852.9

permeable exudative
190.20
pervious 292.21

permeate pervade
221.7
imbue 796.11
soak 1063.13

permeated saturated
221.15
soaked 1063.17

permissible 443.15

permission ratification
332.4
exemption 430.8
consent 441.1
leave 443.1

permissive
noun mood 530.11
adj negligent 340.10
lawless 418.5
unstrict 426.5
indulgent 427.8
nonrestrictive 430.25
consenting 441.4
admissive 443.14

permit
noun licence 443.6
verb ratify 332.12
consent 441.2
allow 443.9
make possible 965.5

permitted exempt
430.30
allowed 443.16

permitting 443.14

pernicious deadly
308.22
harmful 999.12

peroxide 36.5

perpendicular
noun vertical 200.2
straight line 277.2
adj plumb 200.12
right-angled 278.7

perpetrator evildoer
593.1

criminal 645.10,
660.10
doer 726.1

perpetual almighty
677.17
infinite 822.3
durable 826.10
everlasting 828.7
constant 846.5
permanent 852.7

perpetually in
perpetuity 828.10
constantly 846.7
permanently 852.9

perpetuate preserve
828.5
sustain 855.4

perpetuation
preservation 828.4
continuance 855.1

perpetuity length
267.1
infinity 822.1
durability 826.1
perpetualness 828.1
constancy 846.2

perplexed hard to
understand 522.14
complex 798.4
in a dilemma 970.25
confused 984.12
at an impasse 1012.24

perplexing enigmatic
522.17
bewildering 970.27

perplexity obscurity
522.3
enigma 522.8
complexity 798.1
bewilderment 970.3
confusion 984.3
dilemma 1012.7

per se essentially
766.11
singly 871.13

persecute annoy 96.13
worry 126.5
oppress 389.7
work evil 999.6

persecuted tormented
96.24
worried 126.8

persecution annoyance
96.2
torment 96.7
oppression 389.3

Persephone 682.5

perseverance patience
134.1
resolution 359.1
obstinacy 361.1
uniformity 780.1
continuance 855.1

persevere endure 134.5
persist 360.2, 780.3,
855.5
balk 361.7
win through 409.13

persevering patient
134.9
resolute 359.11
perseverant 360.8

persist keep alive
306.10
persevere 360.2, 855.5
insist 421.8
live on 760.9
prevail 780.3
cohere 802.6
endure 826.6
remain 852.5

persistence resolution
359.1
insistence 421.4
uniformity 780.1
durability 826.1
continuance 855.1

persistent reverberating
54.11
resolute 359.11
persevering 360.8
habitual 373.15
demanding 421.9
uniform 780.5
adhesive 802.12
durable 826.10
permanent 852.7
continuing 855.7
unforgettable 988.26

persistently resolutely
359.17
perseveringly 360.9
habitually 373.21
for a long time 826.14

persist in 474.5

persisting persevering
360.8
durable 826.10

person body 2.1,
1050.3
figure 262.4
human 312.5
first person 530.7
role 704.10
something 762.3
individual 871.4

persona psyche 92.28
narrator 722.5
something 762.3
individual 871.4

personable influential
893.13
comely 1015.18

personage person
312.5
chief 575.3
celebrity 662.9
role 704.10
important person
996.8

personal
noun aspersion 512.4
adj individual 312.15
private 345.13
marked 517.24
particular 864.12

personal appearance
704.12

personal best 249.3

personal choice 371.5

personality psyche
92.28
person 312.5
aspersion 512.4
something 762.3
particularity 864.1
influence 893.1
personage 996.8

personality disorder
92.15

personally in person
221.17
privately 864.16

personal space 158.7

personal stereo 50.11

personal style 532.2

personification
impersonation 349.4
materialization 1050.8

personnel work force
18.9
staff 577.11

persons 606.1

person-to-person
312.15

perspective field of
view 31.3
view 33.6
station 159.2
distance 261.1
treatment 712.9
outlook 977.2

perspiration humour
2.22
sweat 12.7

perspiring 12.22

persuade admonish
422.6
convince 857.16,
952.18
influence 893.7
seem true 972.9

persuaded consenting
441.4
belief 952.21
confident 969.21

persuading 375.29

persuasion inducement
375.3
school 617.5
sect 675.3
company 769.3
kind 808.3
conversion 857.6
influence 893.1
conviction 952.5

persuasive
noun incentive 375.7
adj suasive 375.29
influential 893.13
convincing 952.26

pert chirrupy 109.13
conceited 140.11

impudent 142.10
active 330.17
defiant 454.7
immodest 666.6

pertaining relative
774.7
relevant 774.11

pertinent relative 774.7
relevant 774.11

perturbed distressed
96.22
agitated 105.23,
916.16
anxious 126.7
disorderly 809.13
bewildered 970.24
confused 984.12
troubled 1012.20

pervading deep-felt
93.24
pervasive 221.14

pervasive deep-felt
93.24
pervading 221.14
thorough 793.10

perverse irascible
110.19
negative 335.5
contrary 361.11, 778.6
oppositional 451.8
nonconformist 788.9
erroneous 974.16
unwieldy 1012.19

perversely ill-
humouredly 110.27
contrarily 361.16,
778.9

perversion sexual
deviation 75.11
corruption 265.2,
393.2
misinterpretation
342.1
misrepresentation
350.1
deliberate falsehood
354.9
misuse 389.1
misteaching 569.1
sophistry 935.1
error 974.1

perversity irascibility
110.2
negation 335.1
perverseness 361.3
contrariety 778.1

pervert
noun sexual pervert
75.16
reprobate 660.5
verb falsify 265.6,
354.16
misinterpret 342.2
misrepresent 350.3
misuse 389.4
corrupt 393.12
misteach 569.3
reason speciously
935.8

perverted homosexual
75.29
falsified 265.11
misinterpreted 342.3
spurious 354.26
corrupt 654.14
erroneous 974.16

pessimism dejection
112.3
cynicism 125.6
suspense 130.3

pessimist
noun killjoy 112.14
cynic 125.7
adj pessimistic 125.16

pessimistic dejected
112.22
pessimist 125.16

pest epidemic 85.5
annoyance 96.2
tormentor 96.10
bore 118.4
bane 1000.1
blight 1000.2

pestered 96.24

pestering
noun importunity
440.3
criticism 510.4
adj annoying 98.22
importunate 440.18

pesticide killer 308.10
poison 1000.3

pestle
noun pulverizer 1049.7
verb pulverize 1049.9

pet
noun doll 104.15
favourite 104.16
dudgeon 152.7
darling 562.6
verb stroke 73.8
indulge 427.6
neck 562.15
caress 562.16
rub 1042.6
adj beloved 104.24

petal leaf 310.17
perianth 310.26

Peter 684.2

peter 87.5

pet food 10.4

petit 997.17

petite 258.10

petition
noun request 440.1
prayer 696.4
verb pray 696.12

petrified terrified
127.26
antiquated 841.13
hardened 1044.13
mineral 1056.15
stone 1057.10

petrol 1024.20

petroleum illuminant
1024.20

rock oil 1054.4

petticoat 77.13

petting touching 73.2
indulgence 427.3
necking 562.2

petty insignificant
248.6
inadequate 250.7
ungenerous 651.6
base 661.12
quibbling 935.14
narrow-minded 979.10
puny 997.20

Petty Officer 575.21

petulant discontented
108.7
peevish 110.22
plaintive 115.19
capricious 364.5

pew compartment 197.2
stall 703.14
seat 900.17

pewter 1056.17

P-funk 87.8

pH 1058.3

phalanx unit 461.21
company 769.3

phallic 2.27

phallus 2.11

phantom
noun apparition 33.5
alabaster 37.2
frightener 127.9
spirit 763.3
phantasm 975.4
figment of the
imagination 985.5
spectre 987.1
adj illusory 975.9
spectral 987.7
immaterial 1051.7

pharaoh caesar 575.9
tyrant 575.14

pharmacist 86.35

pharmacy
pharmacology 86.34
chemist 86.36
hospital room 197.25

phase 33.3

phased 245.5

phase in 245.4

phase out graduate
245.4
cease to use 390.4
turn off 856.12

phasing 245.3

phenomenal wonderful
122.10
eventful 830.10
extraordinary 869.14

phenomenally
wonderfully 122.14
extraordinarily 869.18

phenomenon
apparition 33.5
marvel 122.2

event 830.2

philandering 562.10

philanthropic
benevolent 143.15
eleemosynary 478.22

philanthropist altruist
143.8
giver 478.11

philanthropy
benevolence 143.4
charity 478.3

philharmonic
noun performance
708.33
adj musical 708.47

Philistine
noun vulgarian 497.6
conformist 866.2
adj callous 94.12
common 497.14
secularist 695.16
unlearned 929.14

philistinism callousness
94.3
vulgarity 497.1
unrefinement 497.3
secularism 695.2
unlearnedness 929.5

philosopher wise man
920.1
scholar 928.3
reasoner 934.11
philosophizer 951.6

philosophical calm
106.12
patient 134.9
sensible 919.18
philosophic 951.8

philosophically 134.11

philosophy composure
106.2
ideology 931.8
reasoning 934.1

phlegm humour 2.22
apathy 94.4
languor 331.6

phlegmatic
noun introvert 92.12
adj apathetic 94.13
inert 173.14
languid 331.20
incurious 981.3

phobia anathema 103.3
fear 127.1

phobic neurotic 92.38
afraid 127.22

Phoebe 1070.12

phoenix 659.5

phon 50.7

phone
noun sound 50.1
speech sound 524.13
verb telephone 347.18

phone book telephone
number 347.12
reference book 554.9
directory 574.10

phone call 347.13

phone in 347.18

phone number 347.12

phonetic
noun phonogram 546.2
adj linguistic 523.17
phonic 524.31

phonetics otology 48.9
articulatory phonetics
524.14
spelling 546.4

phoney
noun imitator 336.4
fake 354.13
hypocrite 357.8
adj spurious 354.26

phoney war 458.1

phonogram 546.2

phosphate 889.4

Phosphorus 1070.4

photo
noun photograph
714.3
adj photographic
714.17

photocopy
noun print 714.5,
784.5
verb copy 784.8

photo finish horse race
757.3
same 789.3

photogenic
photographic 714.17
luminescent 1024.38

photograph
noun description 349.2
image 349.5
picture 712.11
photo 714.3
print 784.5
verb shoot 714.14

photographer
noun shutter-bug
714.2
photographist 716.5
adj journalist 555.4

photographic pictorial
712.21
photo 714.17

photography optics
29.7
printing 548.1
cinematography 706.4
visual arts 712.1
graphic arts 713.1
picture-taking 714.1

photo opportunity
publicity 352.4
conference 541.6
event 830.2
interview 937.11

phrase
noun sign 518.6
remark 524.4
expression 529.1
part 554.13

passage 708.24
section 792.2
maxim 973.1
verb say 524.23
express 532.4
adj phrasal 529.4

phrased 532.5

phraseology language
523.1
jargon 523.9
vocabulary 526.13

phrasing diction 529.2
harmonization 709.2

physic
noun medicine 86.4
laxative 86.17
verb treat 91.24

physical
noun checkup 937.6
adj carnal 663.6
innate 766.8
aerophysical 1017.3
material 1050.10

physical body 1050.3

physical condition
83.1

physical education
725.6

physical examination
diagnosis 91.12
checkup 937.6

physical fitness health
83.1
fitness 84.1

physicality 1050.1

physical world 1050.2

physician doctor 90.4
health-care
professional 90.8

physicist aerophysicist
1017.2
materialist 1050.7

physio 766.4

physiological 305.17

physiotherapist 90.11

physique body 2.1,
1050.3
muscles 2.3
muscularity 15.2
figure 262.4
structure 266.1
nature 766.4

pi
noun type 548.6
verb compose 548.16
confuse 810.3
adj be sanctimonious
693.4

piaffe stroll 177.28
go on horseback
177.34

pianist 710.7

piano
noun presto 708.25
keyboard instrument
711.12
adj faint 52.16

arrest 429.6
poverty 619.1
indigence 619.2
crisis 842.4
urgency 996.4
danger 1005.1
predicament 1012.4
crux 1012.8
verb pain 26.7
converge 169.2
sail near the wind
182.25
squeeze 260.8
nick 429.16
swipe 482.16
stint 484.5
adj substitute 861.8
pinched limited 210.7
haggard 270.20
poor 619.7
straitened 1012.26
pinching
noun parsimony 484.1
adj stingy 484.9
cold 1022.14
pin down bind 428.10
specify 864.11
fell 912.5
pine weaken 16.9
fail 85.47
grieve 112.17
languish 393.18
ping 54.3
pink
noun pinkness 41.2
table 752.2
acme of perfection
1001.3
verb notch 289.4
perforate 292.15
adj pinkish 41.8
fresh 83.13
pinkie 73.5
pinkish 41.8
pinky 41.8
pinnacle summit 198.2
mountain 237.6
tower 272.6
limit 793.5
acme of perfection
1001.3
pinpoint
noun location 159.1
minutia 258.7
verb locate 159.11
attribute to 887.4
receive 1035.17
adj exact 972.17
pins 177.15
pinstripe
noun stripe 47.5
adj striped 47.15
pint 88.7
pinto
noun appaloosa 311.11
adj mottled 47.12
pioneer
noun traveller 178.1

vanguard 216.2
settler 227.9
engineer 461.13
precursor 815.1
verb go before 815.3
initiate 817.10
innovate 851.9
adj original 337.5
pioneering front
216.10
preceding 815.4
pious pietistic 692.8
be sanctimonious
693.4
belief 952.21
pip
noun anthrax 85.40
seed 310.29
insignia of rank 647.5
dandy 998.7
verb warble 60.5
pipe
noun screech 58.4
tobacco pipe 89.6
tube 239.6
cylinder 282.4
wind instrument 711.6
verb blare 53.10
screech 58.8
warble 60.5
channel 176.14,
239.15
sigh 318.21
murmur 524.26
sing 708.38
blow a horn 708.42
piped 239.16
pipeline
noun tube 239.6
inside information
551.2
grapevine 552.10
wave 915.4
verb channel 176.14
piper 710.4
pipes 183.7
piping
noun tube 239.6
adj shrill 58.14
pacific 464.9
thriving 1009.13
piping hot 1018.25
pips 1035.11
piquant appetizing
63.10
pungent 68.6
exciting 105.30
provocative 375.27
alluring 377.8
spirited 544.12
interesting 982.19
pique
noun offence 152.2
dudgeon 152.7
verb annoy 96.13
stimulate 105.13
provoke 152.24
incite 375.17
rouse 375.19

interest 982.12
piracy buccaneering
482.7
plagiarism 482.8
pirate
noun mariner 183.1
corsair 483.7
plagiarist 483.9
verb buccaneer 482.18
plagiarize 482.19
adopt 621.4
piss
noun humour 2.22
urine 12.5
verb urinate 12.14
pissed 88.33
piss off tick off 152.23
beat it 188.7
split 222.10
piste path 383.2
track 517.8
pistol
noun gun 462.10
dandy 998.7
verb strike dead
308.17
shoot 903.12
piston 903.6
pit
noun audience 48.6
deep 275.2
cavity 284.2
well 284.4
indentation 284.6
texture 294.1
tomb 309.16
seed 310.29
arena 463.1
sewer 654.7
hell 682.1
auditorium 704.15
stage 704.16
stock exchange 737.7
race 756.3
blemish 1003.1
mine 1056.6
verb indent 284.14
pit bull sorehead
110.11
boxer 461.2
pitch
noun tone 50.2
summit 198.2
inclination 204.2
incline 204.4
degree 245.1
plunge 367.1
arena 463.1
intonation 524.7
speech 543.2
tuning 709.4
booth 736.3
football 745.1
rugby 746.1
cricket 747.1
hockey 750.1
throw 903.3
flounder 916.8
verb establish 159.16

toss 182.55
descend 194.5
tumble 194.8
erect 200.9
incline 204.10
camp 225.11
plunge 367.6
play 747.4
shuffle 758.4
throw 903.10
oscillate 915.10
flounder 916.15
adj phonetic 524.31
pitch-black black 38.8
dark 1026.13
pitched inclining
204.15
phonetic 524.31
pitcher 903.7
pitch in eat 8.20
begin 817.7
pitching
noun throwing 903.2
adj swinging 915.17
pith substance 196.5
centre 208.2
pluck 359.3
fortitude 492.6
meaning 518.1
summary 557.2
essence 766.2
salient point 996.6
pulp 1061.2
pithy meaningful
518.10
concise 537.6
aphoristic 973.6
spongy 1045.11
pulpy 1061.6
pitiful pitiable 145.8
disgraceful 661.11
paltry 997.21
terrible 999.9
pitifully 145.10
pitiless unpitying 146.3
savage 671.21
bright 1024.32
pit lane 756.3
pitman 1056.9
pits bottom 199.1
terribleness 999.2
pittance modicum
248.2
donation 478.6
dole 991.5
pitted indented 284.17
rough 288.6
nappy 294.7
pity
noun kindness 143.1
sympathy 145.1
abomination 638.2
verb condole with
147.2
pitying sympathetic
145.7
condoling 147.3

pivot
noun centre 208.2
round 748.3
joint 799.4
fulcrum 905.3
axle 914.5
salient point 996.6
verb rotate 914.9
pivotal central 208.11
critical 842.10
causal 885.13
urgent 996.22
pixie mischief-maker
322.3
fairy 678.8
imp 680.7
placard
noun poster 352.7
verb publicize 352.15
placate 465.7
place
noun serving 8.10
location 159.1
stead 159.4
abode 228.1
square 230.8
region 231.1
rank 245.2
arena 463.1
class 607.1
duty 641.1
function 724.3
position 724.5
state 764.1
continuity 806.2
turn 824.2
opportunity 842.2
outlook 977.2
verb locate 159.11
put 159.12
install 615.12
impose 643.4
invest 729.16
race 757.5
dispose 807.9
classify 808.6
attribute 887.3
recognize 988.12
placebo 86.4
placed located 159.18
arranged 807.14
classified 808.8
placement location
159.1
positioning 159.6
installation 615.3
arrangement 807.1
grouping 807.3
classification 808.1
attribution 887.1
place-names 527.1
placenta 816.3
place of worship 703.1
place to live 228.1
placid calm 106.12
quiescent 173.12
placing 159.6
plage 234.2

component 795.2

playful gay 109.14
mischievous 322.6
waggish 489.17
sportive 743.29

playfully 322.7

playfulness gaiety
109.4
mischief 322.2
waggishness 489.4

play games deceive
356.14
manoeuvre 415.10

playground 743.11

playgroup 567.2

playhouse tight spot
258.3
theatre 704.14

playing
noun impersonation
349.4
acting 704.8
gambling 759.1
trifling 997.8
adj flickering 1024.36

playing around 997.9

playing field arena
463.1
playground 743.11

playmaker 750.5

playmate companion
588.3
mistress 665.17

play off 264.3

play out 21.5

playroom recreation
room 197.12
playground 743.11

play safe take
precautions 494.6
keep on the safe side
1006.3

play tennis 749.3

play the game conform
579.4
play fair 649.7
follow the rule 866.4

playtime interim 825.1
pause 856.3

play up get out of kilter
393.26
dramatize 996.16

play with consider
930.12
trifle 997.14

playwright 704.22

plaza square 230.8
marketplace 736.2

plea entreaty 440.2
pleadings 598.7
defence 600.2
argument 934.5

plead entreat 440.11
argue 934.16
adduce 956.12

plead for entreat
440.11
defend 600.10

plead guilty repent
113.7
confess 351.7

pleading
noun bar 597.4
pleadings 598.7
defence 600.2
argument 934.5
adj imploring 440.17

plead with 375.14

pleasance pleasantness
97.1
park 743.14

pleasant pleasing 97.6
cheerful 109.11
friendly 587.15
melodious 708.48
good 998.12
rainless 1064.8

pleasantly pleasingly
97.12
cheerfully 109.17
amicably 587.22

please
verb pleasure 95.5
prefer 371.17
indulge 427.6
exclam prithee 440.20

pleased delighted 95.14
content 107.7

pleased with 95.14

pleasing
noun indulgence 427.3
adj tasty 63.8
pleasant 97.6
desirable 100.30
tasteful 496.8
fluent 544.9
welcome 585.12
comely 1015.18

pleasingly 97.12

pleasurable 97.6

pleasure
noun enjoyment 95.1
pleasantness 97.1
desire 100.1
will 323.1
option 371.2
command 420.1
amusement 743.1
verb please 95.5

pleasure in 95.12

pleat
noun trench 290.2
pleating 291.2
verb furrow 290.3
fold 291.5

pleated furrowed 290.4
folded 291.7

plebiscite vote 371.6
election 609.15
referendum 613.7

pledge
noun toast 88.10

oath 334.4
promise 436.1
gage 438.2
debt 623.1
abstinence 668.2
verb drink 8.29
drink to 88.29
promise 436.4
impignorate 438.10
contribute 478.14
obligate 641.12

pledged affirmed 334.9
promised 436.8
staked 438.12
chargeable 623.9
obliged 641.16

Pleiades 678.9

plenary great 247.6
unrestricted 430.27
full 793.11

plenitude greatness
247.1
quantity 247.3
store 386.1
fullness 793.2
continuity 811.1
plenty 990.2
soundness 1001.2

plentiful much 247.8
abundant 883.8
productive 889.9
plenty 990.7
superabundant 992.19

plenty
noun quantity 247.3
store 386.1
numerousness 883.1
plenitude 990.2
superabundance 992.2
adj sufficient 990.6
plentiful 990.7
adv greatly 247.15

plenty to do 330.5

plenum omnipresence
221.2
council 423.1
assembly 769.2
completeness 793.1
series 811.2
matter 1050.2
universe 1070.1

plethora fullness 793.2
superabundance 992.2
overfullness 992.3

plexus nervous system
2.12
network 170.3

pliable folded 291.7
weak-willed 362.12
usable 387.23
docile 433.13
teachable 570.18
influenceable 893.15
handy 1013.15
pliant 1045.9

pliers 192.9

plight
noun promise 436.1
state 764.1

bewilderment 970.3
danger 1005.1
adversity 1010.1
predicament 1012.4
verb promise 436.4

plinth 900.8

plod
noun slow motion
175.2
verb plug 175.7
stroll 177.28
keep doggedly at
360.3
drudge 725.14

plodding
noun perseverance
360.1
adj dull 117.6
persevering 360.8
labouring 725.17

plonk 88.17

plot
noun house 228.5
diagram 381.3
intrigue 381.5
stratagem 415.3
real estate 471.6
fable 722.4
field 1067.9
verb premeditate 380.7
scheme 381.9
map 381.10
manoeuvre 415.10
come 838.6
prearrange 964.4

plotted measured
300.13
planned 381.12
future 838.8
prearranged 964.7

plotter traitor 357.10
schemer 381.7

plotting
noun intrigue 381.5
prearrangement 964.1
adj scheming 381.13

plough stunt 184.40
furrow 290.3
fail 410.9
cultivate 1067.17

ploy trick 356.6
stratagem 415.3
prank 489.10
revel 743.6

ploys 893.3

pluck
noun spunk 359.3
courage 492.1
jerk 904.3
verb divest 6.5
collect 472.11
strum 708.40
jerk 904.5
harvest 1067.19

plucky enterprising
404.8
courageous 492.17

plug

noun hydrant 239.12
stopper 293.4
nag 311.12
publicity 352.4
snare 356.13
verb plod 175.7
stop 293.7
top 295.21
publicize 352.15
keep doggedly at
360.3
drudge 725.14
shoot 903.12

plugged 293.11

plugging
noun perseverance
360.1
adj persevering 360.8
labouring 725.17

plug in 1031.25

plum desire 100.11
mite 728.7
dividend 738.7
good thing 998.5

plumage 3.19

plumb
noun vertical 200.2
square 200.6
weight 297.6
verb plumb-line
200.10
sound 275.9
measure 300.10
perceive 521.9
investigate 937.23
solve 939.2
adj perpendicular
200.12
thorough 793.10
adv perpendicularly
200.14
absolutely 793.15
exactly 972.21

plumbing 385.4

plume
noun feather 3.17
verb groom 79.20
figure 498.9

plumed feathered 3.29
topped 198.12
ornamented 498.11

plummet
noun square 200.6
weight 297.6
cheapening 633.4
verb descend 194.5
decrease 252.6
plunge 367.6
cheapen 633.6

plummeting
noun descent 194.1
cheapening 633.4
adj descending 194.11

plummy fun 97.8
inarticulate 525.12
affected 533.9

plump
noun thud 52.3
verb clap 159.13

sink 194.6
fatten 259.8
plunge 367.6
soften 1045.6
adj corpulent 257.18
adv suddenly 829.9

plunder
noun plundering 482.6
booty 482.11
verb pillage 482.17

plundering
noun pillaging 482.6
unruliness 671.3
adj plunderous 482.22

plunge
noun run 174.3
tumble 194.3
decline 252.2
dive 367.1
deterioration 393.3
cheapening 633.4
investment 729.3
trading 737.19
swimming pool 743.12
flounder 916.8
verb move 172.5
pitch 182.55
descend 194.5
decrease 252.6
gravitate 297.15
dive 367.6
make haste 401.5
rush into 401.7
cheapen 633.6
invest 729.16
trade 737.23
bet 759.25
flounder 916.15

plunge in thrust in
191.7
stab 459.25

plunge into be willing
324.3
rush into 401.7
undertake 404.3
study 570.12
set to work 725.15
begin 817.7

plunger diver 367.4
speculator 737.11
gambler 759.21

plunging
noun course 172.2
diving 367.3
adj flowing 172.8
descending 194.11
perpendicular 200.12
steep 204.18
abysmal 275.11

plural
noun number 530.8
plurality 882.1
adj pluralized 882.7

pluralism democratism
612.8
nonuniformity 781.1
mixture 796.1
plurality 882.1
dualism 951.5

pluralistic
governmental 612.17
nonuniform 781.3
mixed 796.14
plural 882.7

plurality major part
791.6
pluralness 882.1
majority 882.2

plus
noun plus sign 253.2
surplus 992.5
verb add 253.4
adj additional 253.10
positive 1031.34
adv additionally
253.11
prep with 253.12

plush
noun putty 1045.4
adj velvety 1045.15

Pluto Orcus 682.5
planet 1070.9

ply
noun fold 291.1
lamina 296.2
verb touch 73.6
traverse 177.20
navigate 182.13
sail near the wind
182.25
change course 182.30
fold 291.5
use 387.10
urge upon 439.9
importune 440.12
exert 725.8

plying 440.3

plywood lamina 296.2
wood 1052.3

pneumatic bulging
283.15
airy 317.11
comely 1015.18
pneumatological
1038.10
vaporous 1065.9

poach cook 11.4
steal 482.13

poached 11.6

poacher 483.1

poaching cooking 11.1
theft 482.1

pocket
noun airspace 184.32
bag 195.2
cavity 284.2
funds 728.14
purse 729.14
table 752.2
verb take 134.8,
480.13
load 159.15
enclose 212.5
legislate 613.9
receive 627.3
play 752.4
adj miniature 258.12
shortened 268.9

pocket money subsidy
478.8
petty cash 728.19

pod
noun Acapulco gold
87.10
hull 295.16
seed vessel 310.28
flock 769.5
verb husk 6.9

podium 900.13

poem writing 547.10
verse 720.4
thing of beauty 1015.7

poet author 547.15,
718.4
poetess 720.11
imaginer 985.12

poetic 720.15

poetical 720.15

poetic justice justice
649.1
poetics 720.2

poet laureate 720.11

poetry fluency 544.2
poesy 720.1

po-faced averse 99.8
prudish 500.19
condemnatory 510.22
inexpressive 522.20
narrow-minded 979.10

pogrom 308.4

poignancy acrimony
17.5
pungency 68.1
distressfulness 98.5
vigour 544.3
spirit 544.4

poignant acrimonious
17.14
exquisite 24.13
painful 26.10
pungent 68.6
deep-felt 93.24
distressing 98.20
vigorous 544.11
spirited 544.12

poignantly 93.25

point
noun acrimony 17.5
location 159.1
direction 161.1
leading 165.1
summit 198.2
mountain 237.6
degree 245.1
modicum 248.2
minutia 258.7
angle 278.2
hook 283.9
tip 285.3
intention 380.1
railway 383.7
benefit 387.4
joke 489.6
mark 517.5
meaning 518.1
punctuation 530.15

type 548.6
engraving tool 713.8
chisel 715.4
game 749.2, 750.3,
750.6
particular 765.3
precursor 815.1
extremity 819.2
period 823.1
individual 871.4
topic 936.1
salient point 996.6
watchman 1007.10
electrical device
1031.20
cutlery 1039.2
verb direct 161.5
bear 161.7
sharpen 285.7
gravitate 297.15
mark 517.19
grammaticize 530.16
tend 895.3

point at ridicule 508.8
designate 517.18
call attention to
982.10

point-blank plainly
535.4
exactly 972.21

pointed angular 278.6
pointy 285.9
witty 489.15
meaningful 518.10
concise 537.6
aphoristic 973.6
emphatic 996.21

pointedly intensely
247.20
intentionally 380.10
concisely 537.7

pointer index 517.4
guide 574.7

pointing 517.3

pointless dull 117.6
blunt 286.3
useless 391.9

point of reference
159.2

point of view
viewpoint 27.7
opinion 952.6
outlook 977.2

point-of-view 722.5

point out designate
517.18
specify 864.11
call attention to
982.10

point out to 161.6

point to augur 133.12
designate 517.18
attribute to 887.4
tend 895.3
evidence 956.8
call attention to
982.10

pointy 285.9

poise
noun looks 33.4
equanimity 106.3
behaviour 321.1
gesture 517.14
equality 789.1
confidence 969.5
verb take off 193.10
equalize 789.6

poised composed
106.13
balanced 789.9
neutralizing 899.9
confident 969.21

poison
noun poisonousness
82.3
juice 88.14
killer 308.10
evil 999.3
venom 1000.3
verb empoison 85.51
kill 308.12
corrupt 393.12
work evil 999.6
radioactivate 1036.9

poisoned diseased
85.59
radioactive 1036.10

poisoning intoxication
85.31
killing 308.1
corruption 393.2
capital punishment
604.6

poisonous nasty 64.7
toxic 82.7
harmful 999.12

poke
noun bag 195.2
signal 517.15
purse 729.14
bundle 769.8
thrust 901.2
hit 901.4
verb dally 331.14
goad 375.15
signal 517.22
thrust 901.12
hit 901.14
search 937.31

poker 1019.12

pokey 429.9

poking slow 175.10
searching 937.38

polar contrapositive
215.5
final 819.11
magnetic 1031.30

Polaris guiding star
574.8
stars 1070.4

polarity contraposition
215.1
symmetry 264.1
contrariety 778.1
doubleness 872.1
polarization 1031.8

Polaroid 29.3

pole
noun spar 180.13
oar 180.15
summit 198.2
jumping-off place 261.4
tower 272.6
shaft 273.1
beam 273.3
extremity 819.2
base 900.8
axle 914.5
polarity 1031.8
wood 1052.3
verb push 903.9

polemic
noun quarrel 456.5
contention 457.1
argumentation 934.4
arguer 934.12
adj contentious 110.26
argumentative 934.19

polemical contentious 110.26
partisan 456.17
argumentative 934.19

polemics 934.4

poles 215.2

pole vault 366.1

police
noun police force 1007.17
verb protect 1007.18
watch 1007.20

police car 179.11

police commissioner 1007.15

policed 1007.21

police force 1007.17

police inspector 1007.15

policeman 1007.15

police officer 1007.15

police sergeant 1007.15

police state 612.4

police station 230.5

police van 179.11

policewoman 1007.15

policing 1007.1

policy polity 381.4, 609.4
judiciousness 919.7
insurance 1007.4

polio 85.27

polish
noun gloss 287.2
smoother 287.4
cultivation 392.3
taste 496.1
good breeding 504.4
elegance 533.1
verb shine 287.7
perfect 392.11
buff 1042.8

polished sleek 287.10

improved 392.13
complete 407.12
elegant 496.9, 533.6
well-bred 504.17
perfected 1001.9
shiny 1024.33

polishing revision 392.4
abrasion 1042.2

polite 504.14

politely 504.19

politeness sensitivity 24.3
courtesy 504.1
etiquette 580.3

politic skilful 413.22
cunning 415.12
cautious 494.8
political 609.43
judicious 919.19
expedient 994.5

political politic 609.43
governmental 612.17

political asylum 1008.1

political economy
political science 609.2
economics 731.10

political influence
machination 415.4
wire-pulling 609.29

political leader 610.1

political organization 612.1

political party 609.24, 617.4

political philosophy 609.2

political prisoner 429.11

political science 609.2

political theory 609.2

politician expert 413.11
Machiavellian 415.8
politico 610.1

politicking 609.12

politico 610.1

politics
Machiavellianism 415.2
polity 609.1
political science 609.2

polity country 232.1
policy 381.4, 609.4
people 606.1
politics 609.1
government 612.1
judiciousness 919.7

polka dot spottiness 47.3
mark 517.5

polka-dot 47.13

poll
noun head 198.6
vote 371.6

polls 609.20
returns 609.21
roll 870.6
canvass 937.14
verb shorten 268.6
vote 371.18
record 549.15
canvass 937.29
number 1016.16

pollard
noun tree 310.10
verb shorten 268.6

polled 268.9

pollen
noun sperm 305.11
verb fertilize 78.10

pollination 78.3

polling 371.6

polling station 609.20

polls 609.20

pollute defile 80.17
plaster 88.23
misuse 389.4
corrupt 393.12
blaspheme 694.5
adulterate 796.12
work evil 999.6

polluted unclean 80.20
unhealthful 82.5
fuddled 88.33
corrupt 654.14

pollution defilement 80.4
unhealthfulness 82.1
misuse 389.1
corruption 393.2
sacrilege 694.2
adulteration 796.3
evil 999.3
environmental destruction 1071.2

polymer 1052.6

polymer 1052.6

polytechnic 567.5

pomp spectacle 33.7
circumstance 501.6
formality 580.1
procession 811.3

pomposity
pompousness 501.7
grandiloquence 545.1
formality 580.1
confidence 969.5

pompous stuffy 501.22
stiff 534.3
grandiloquent 545.8
ceremonious 580.8
confident 969.21

ponce mollycoddle 77.10
dandy 500.9
procurer 665.18

pond 241.1

ponder hesitate 362.7
consider 930.12

pondering
noun consideration 930.2

adj cognitive 930.21

ponderous dull 117.6
bulky 257.19
heavy 297.16
bungling 414.20
stiff 534.3
unwieldy 1012.19

pontoon 180.11

pony
noun runt 258.4
horse 311.10
mite 728.7
jockey 757.2
eleven 881.7
adj miniature 258.12

ponytail 3.5

pooh 508.9

pool lake 241.1
company 617.9
funds 728.14
swimming pool 743.12
pot 759.5

pooling centralization 208.8
cooperation 450.1

poop
noun stern 217.7
verb beat 21.6

poor
noun underprivileged 606.4
needy 619.3
adj unsound 16.15, 935.12
humble 137.10
haggard 270.20
unskilful 414.15
disapproving 510.21
ill off 619.7
base 661.12
sparse 884.5
meagre 991.10
ill-provided 991.12
paltry 997.21
inferior 1004.9

poor health 85.3

poorly incompetently 250.9
unskilfully 414.23
basely 661.17
meagrely 991.15
inferiorly 1004.12

poor man 619.4

poor quality 1004.4

poor-quality 999.9

pop
noun beverage 10.47
thud 52.3
detonation 56.3
verb thud 52.15
blast 56.8
bulge 283.11
adj common 497.14
adv suddenly 829.9

pop in 191.3

pop music 708.7

popper 799.3

poppers 87.4

popping 56.11

poppy 22.10

populace population 227.1
humankind 312.1
people 312.4, 606.1

popular desired 100.29
beloved 104.24
customary 373.14
communal 476.9
common 497.14
approved 509.19
fashionable 578.11
populational 606.8
distinguished 662.16
lay 700.3
prevalent 863.12
usual 868.9

popular belief opinion 952.6
superstition 953.3

popular front 609.33

popularity love 104.1
applause 509.2
fashionableness 578.2
repute 662.1

popularly 662.21

popular music 708.7

populated 225.12

population
noun establishment 159.7
peopling 225.2
inhabitants 227.1
people 312.4, 606.1
adj populational 606.8

populous inhabited 225.12
crowded 769.22
teeming 883.9

pop up burst forth 33.9
shoot up 193.9
turn up 830.6
chance 971.11

porcelain
noun ceramic ware 742.2
eggshell 1048.2
adj ceramic 742.7

porch propylaeum 189.6
stoop 197.21
vestry 703.9

porcupine 311.23

pore
noun duct 2.21
outlet 190.9
opening 292.1
verb scrutinize 27.14

pork 10.16

porky 257.18

porno 665.29

pornographic lascivious 665.29
obscene 666.9

pornography literature
547.12, 718.1
obscenity 666.4

porous exudative
190.20
porose 292.20

porridge nick 429.9
term 824.4
semiliquid 1060.5
pulp 1061.2

port
noun looks 33.4
airport 184.22
destination 186.5
outlet 190.9
left side 220.1
behaviour 321.1
refuge 1008.1
harbour 1008.6
circuitry 1041.3
adj left 220.4
adv leftward 220.6

portable 176.18

portal entrance 189.5
porch 189.6
vestibule 197.19

portent omen 133.3
ominousness 133.7
forewarning 399.2

portentous ominous
133.17
forewarning 399.8
extraordinary 869.14
weighty 996.20

porter
noun railwayman
178.13
doorkeeper 1007.12
phrase carrier 176.7

portfolio sceptre 417.9
bookholder 554.17
shares 738.2

portico vestibule
197.19
pillar 273.5
passageway 383.3

portion
noun serving 8.10
dose 86.6, 87.19,
792.5
amount 244.2
length 267.2
share 477.5
endowment 478.9
part 792.1
fate 963.2
verb apportion 477.6,
801.18

portly 257.18

port of call 1008.6

portrait description
349.2
image 349.5
portraiture 712.15
photograph 714.3
copy 784.1

portraiture
representation 349.1

description 349.2
portrait 712.15

portray represent 349.8
describe 349.9
enact 704.30
picture 712.19

portrayal
representation 349.1
description 349.2
impersonation 349.4
acting 704.8
portrait 712.15
fiction 722.1

portraying 349.13

pose
noun behaviour 321.1
sham 354.3
posing 500.3
gesture 517.14
verb place 159.12
propose 439.5
posture 500.13
postulate 950.12

pose as impersonate
349.12
masquerade as 354.22

poser impostor 357.6
poseur 500.8
enigma 522.8
pietist 693.3
dilemma 1012.7

posh affected 533.9
chic 578.13
upper-class 607.10

posing impersonation
349.4
sham 354.3
pose 500.3

position
noun location 159.1
navigation 159.3
rank 245.2
affirmation 334.1
remark 524.4
class 607.1, 808.2
policy 609.4
prestige 662.4
function 724.3
job 724.5
race 753.3, 756.3
state 764.1
premise 934.7
opinion 952.6
attitude 977.1
outlook 977.2
verb locate 159.11

positional 159.19

positioned 159.18

positioning 159.6

positive
noun print 714.5,
784.5
adj downright 247.12
affirmative 334.8
unpersuadable 361.13
helpful 449.21
real 760.15
agreeing 787.9
belief 952.21

unqualified 959.2
certain 969.13
confident 969.21
dogmatic 969.22
emphatic 996.21
plus 1031.34

**positive
discrimination**
dilemma 371.3
equating 789.2
opportunity 842.2

positively
adv decidedly 247.19
affirmatively 334.10
consentingly 441.5
really 760.16
certainly 969.23
exactly 972.21
exclam yes 332.18

positivism dogmatism
969.6
realism 986.2
materialism 1050.6

posse unit 461.21
company 769.3
search 937.15
police 1007.17

possess have 469.4
take 480.13
demonize 680.16
bewitch 691.9
obsess 925.25
know 927.12
haunt 987.6

possessed overjoyed
95.16
frenzied 105.25
owned 469.8
bewitched 691.13
obsessed 925.33
haunted 987.10

possessed of 469.9

possessing
noun possession 469.1
adj having 469.9
obsessive 925.34

possession equanimity
106.3
country 232.1
self-control 359.5
possessing 469.1
taking 480.1
bewitchment 691.2
insanity 925.1
obsession 925.13
spirit control 987.5

possessions property
471.1
wealth 618.1

possessive possessory
469.10
selfish 651.5

possessiveness 651.1

possessor 470.1

possibility latent
meaningfulness 519.1
liability 896.1
possibleness 965.1

probability 967.1
good chance 971.8

possible
noun possibility 965.1
adj latent 519.5

possible solution
939.1

possibly 965.9

post
noun station 159.2
standard 273.4
pillar 273.5
messenger 353.1
stronghold 460.6
mail 553.4
branch 617.10
position 724.5
market 736.1
base 900.8
wood 1052.3
verb place 159.12
speed 174.8
send 176.15
publicize 352.15
make haste 401.5
pledge 438.10
record 549.15
mail 553.12
commission 615.10
keep accounts 628.8
list 870.8
adj epistolary 553.14
adv swiftly 174.17
posthaste 401.13

postage 553.5

postage stamp 553.5

postal 553.14

postal service 553.7

postbag 553.6

postcard 553.3

postcode 553.9

posted located 159.18
pledged 438.12
recorded 549.17
informed 927.18

poster bill 352.7
carrier pigeon 353.6

posterior
noun rear 217.1
buttocks 217.4
adj rear 217.9
succeeding 814.4
subsequent 834.4

posterity kinfolk 559.2
progeny 561.1
successor 816.4
sequel 834.2

postgraduate
noun graduate 572.8
adj scholastic 568.19
studentlike 572.12

posthumous
postmortem 307.36
afterdeath 834.5

post-industrial 834.5

posting placement
159.6

registration 549.14
appointment 615.2

postman 353.5

postmaster 353.5

postmodern
posthumous 834.5
modern 840.13

post office 353.1

postpone put away
390.6
delay 845.9

postponed 845.16

postponement 856.3

postscript 254.2

postulate
noun fact 760.3
essence 766.2
curtain raiser 815.2
premise 934.7
supposition 950.3
axiom 973.2
verb propose 439.5
predicate 950.12

postulated 950.14

posture
noun looks 33.4
behaviour 321.1
sham 354.3
gesture 517.14
opinion 952.6
attitude 977.1
verb pose 500.13

posturing 500.3

post-war 834.5

posy
noun flower 310.22
bouquet 310.23
bundle 769.8
adj affected 500.15
ostentatious 501.18

pot
noun tum 2.17
Acapulco gold 87.10
container 195.1
lot 247.4
bomb 618.3
trophy 646.3
ceramic ware 742.2
match 752.3
jackpot 759.5
verb package 212.9
put up 397.10
shape 742.6
play 752.4
shoot 903.12
plant 1067.18

potash 889.4

potato 10.34

potency strength 15.1
energy 17.1
sexuality 75.2
influence 893.1

potent strong 15.15
powerful 18.12
sexual 75.24
virile 76.12
authoritative 417.15

influential 893.13
potential
  noun talent 413.4
  mood 530.11
  possibility 965.1
  voltage 1031.11
  adj latent 519.5
  possible 965.6
potentially 519.11
potion drink 8.4, 88.7
  dose 86.6
pots and pans 11.3
potted 88.33
potter
  noun ceramist 716.7
  verb waste time 331.13
  trifle 997.14
Potteries 231.7
pottering 997.8
pottery plant 739.3
  ceramics 742.1
  ceramic ware 742.2
potting food
  preservation 397.2
  ceramics 742.1
potty
  noun toilet 12.11
  adj crazy 925.27
pouch 283.11
poultry 311.29
pounce
  noun descent 194.1
  leap 366.1
  plunge 367.1
  verb descend 194.5
  leap 366.5
  plunge 367.6
pound
  noun staccato 55.1
  kennel 228.21
  avoirdupois weight
  297.8
  place of confinement
  429.7
  mite 728.7
  hit 901.4
  verb suffer 26.8
  drum 55.4
  pitch 182.55
  injure 393.13
  confine 429.12
  attack 459.14
  beat time 708.44
  din 848.10
  beat 901.16
  pulverize 1049.9
pound for pound
  942.10
pound in 191.7
pounding
  noun staccato 55.1
  pulverization 1049.4
  adj staccato 55.7
pound note 728.5
pour
  noun torrent 238.5
  rainstorm 316.2

verb ladle 176.17
  run out 190.13
  flow 238.16
  rain 316.9
  give 478.12
  disgorge 908.25
  abound 990.5
pour in 189.9
pouring flowing 238.24
  rainy 316.10
pour on coat 295.24
  furnish 478.15
  flood 1063.14
pour out 190.13
pout
  noun scowl 110.9
  grimace 265.4
  verb look sullen
  110.15
  grimace 265.8
  bulge 283.11
poverty poorness 619.1
  scarcity 991.3
poverty-stricken 619.8
powder
  noun medicine 86.4
  explosive 462.14
  makeup 1015.12
  dust 1049.5
  verb beat it 188.7
  sprinkle 770.6
  pulverize 1049.9
  adj powdery 1049.11
powdered sprinkled
  770.10
  powdery 1049.11
powdery 1049.11
power
  noun strength 15.1
  energy 17.1
  country 232.1
  greatness 247.1
  supremacy 249.3
  will power 359.4
  means 384.2
  talent 413.4
  authority 417.1
  authoritativeness 417.2
  governance 417.5
  vigour 544.3
  control 612.2
  bomb 618.3
  prerogative 642.1
  influence 893.1
  impulse 901.1
  personage 996.8
  verb impel 901.11
  adj mechanical
  1039.10
power base means
  384.2
  sphere of influence
  893.4
  support 900.1
powerboat 180.4
power cut 1031.19
powered 1039.10
powerful strong 15.15

potent 18.12
  great 247.6
  authoritative 417.15
  vigorous 544.11
  influential 893.13
powerfully strongly
  15.23
  potently 18.15
  authoritatively 417.18
  eloquently 544.15
powerhouse hunk 15.7
  power station 1031.18
power-hungry 100.28
powerless
  noun underprivileged
  606.4
  adj weak 16.12
  impotent 19.13
  uninfluential 894.3
power plant rocket
  propulsion 184.25
  plant 739.3
  powerhouse 1031.18
  machinery 1039.3
power play 750.6
power politics 609.1
powers talent 413.4
  seraphim 679.3
power-sharing
  noun participation
  476.1
  democratism 612.8
  inclusion 771.1
  adj communal 476.9
power station 1031.18
powers that be
  authorities 575.15
  officeholder 610.11
  government 612.3
  influence 893.6
power structure power
  18.1
  rank 245.2
  best 249.5
  authorities 575.15
  class 607.1
  hierarchy 808.4
power struggle 18.1
power vacuum 418.1
PR 33.2
practicable workable
  888.10
  practical 965.7, 994.6
practical useful 387.18
  usable 387.23
  occupied 724.15
  operative 888.9
  workable 888.10
  sensible 919.18
  ungullible 955.5
  practicable 965.7,
  994.6
  realistic 986.6
  handy 1013.15
practicality utility
  387.3
  sensibleness 919.6

practicability 965.2
  realism 986.2
  handiness 1013.2
practically
  approximately 223.23
  usefully 387.26
  expediently 994.8
practice
  noun behaviour 321.1
  action 328.1
  custom 373.1
  habit 373.4
  manner 384.1
  experience 413.9
  observance 434.1
  training 568.3
  study 570.3
  bar 597.4
  rite 701.3
  vocation 724.6
  exercise 725.6
  operation 888.1
  tryout 941.3
  notation 1016.2
  verb act 328.4
  put into practice 328.8
  iterate 848.8
practise use 384.5,
  387.10
  perform 434.3
  train 568.13
  study 570.12
  rehearse 704.32
  busy oneself with
  724.11
  exert 725.8
  play 744.2
practised skilled
  413.26
  experienced 413.28
  observant 434.4
practising
  noun iteration 848.2
  adj acting 328.10
  pious 692.8
practitioner health-care
  professional 90.8
  doer 726.1
Prado 386.9
prado 383.2
pragmatic sensible
  919.18
  realistic 986.6
pragmatism
  functionalism 387.6
  experiment 941.1
  realism 986.2
  materialism 1050.6
pragmatist 986.3
prairie
  noun open space 158.4
  horizontal 201.3
  plain 236.1
  grassland 310.8
  adj rustic 233.6
praise
  noun congratulation
  149.1
  thanks 150.2

bepraisement 509.5
  flattery 511.1
  citation 646.4
  glorification 696.2
  verb congratulate
  149.2
  bepraise 509.12
  flatter 511.5
  honour 646.8
  glorify 696.11
praiseworthy 509.20
pram 179.6
prancing
  noun leaping 366.3
  adj leaping 366.7
prank 489.10
prankster mischief-
  maker 322.3
  humourist 489.12
praxis behaviour 321.1
  action 328.1
  custom 373.1
  habit 373.4
pray
  verb petition 440.10
  entreat 440.11
  supplicate 696.12
  exclam please 440.20
prayer entreaty 440.2
  supplication 696.4
  divine service 696.8
  worshipper 696.9
prayer book 554.1
prayers 696.8
preach admonish 422.6
  lecture 543.11
  expound 568.16
preacher lecturer
  543.5, 571.7
  sermoner 699.3
preaching
  noun inducement
  375.3
  advice 422.1
  public speaking 543.1
  lecture 543.3
  adj educational 568.18
preamble
  noun curtain raiser
  815.2
  verb prefix 813.3
precarious unreliable
  970.20
  ticklish 1005.12
precariously 1005.17
precaution
  noun precautiousness
  494.3
  verb forewarn 399.6
precautionary
  forewarning 399.8
  precautious 494.10
precautions 494.3
precede lead 165.2
  rule 249.11
  antecede 813.2
  go before 815.3

initiate 817.10
be prior 833.3
precedence leading
165.1
rank 245.2
superiority 249.1
prestige 417.4
importance 996.1
precedent
noun model 785.1
precursor 815.1
antecedent 833.2
verdict 945.5
adj leading 165.3
preceding 813.4
preceding
noun leading 165.1
adj leading 165.3
precedent 813.4
preliminary 815.4
previous 833.4
foregoing 836.11
precinct enclosure
212.3
nearness 223.1
sphere 231.2
state 231.5
arena 463.1
constituency 609.16
precincts environment
209.1
region 231.1
precious
noun darling 562.6
adj beloved 104.24
downright 247.12
overnice 500.18
affected 533.9
punctilious 580.10
dear 632.10
precious little 991.9
precious metals gold
728.20
metal 1056.3
precipice cliff 200.3
slope 237.2
precipitate
noun dregs 256.2
effect 886.1
precipitation 1043.5
verb descend 194.5
gravitate 297.15
rain 316.9
hasten 401.4
fell 912.5
deposit 1043.11
adj fast 174.15
impulsive 365.9
precipitant 401.10
unprepared 406.8
reckless 493.8
sudden 829.5
premature 844.8
precipitation velocity
174.1
dregs 256.2
rain 316.1
impulsiveness 365.2
hastiness 401.2

recklessness 493.2
prematurity 844.2
downthrow 912.2
deposit 1043.5
precipitous
perpendicular 200.12
steep 204.18
precipitate 401.10
reckless 493.8
sudden 829.5
precise
verb be accurate
972.11
adj meticulous 339.12
fastidious 495.9
punctilious 580.10
detailed 765.9
particular 864.12
discriminating 943.7
exact 972.17
precisely
adv meticulously
339.16
thus 765.10
punctually 844.14
particularly 864.15
exactly 972.21
exclam yes 332.18
precision
meticulousness 339.3
fastidiousness 495.1
elegance 533.1
accuracy 972.5
preclude prohibit 444.3
exclude 772.4
prevent 1011.14
precluded 772.7
precocious 844.8
precognition
understanding 927.3
intuition 933.1
foreknowledge 960.3
preconceived 946.3
precondition 950.10
precursor harbinger
133.5
leading 165.1
vanguard 216.2
settler 227.9
warning sign 399.3
forerunner 815.1
antecedent 833.2
early bird 844.4
transformer 851.5
producer 891.7
predator 480.12
predators 311.1
predatory rapacious
480.26
plunderous 482.22
predecessor 815.1
predecessors 560.7
predetermined
premeditated 380.9
prejudged 946.3
determined 963.8
certain 969.13

predicament state
764.1
urgent need 962.4
bewilderment 970.3
danger 1005.1
adversity 1010.1
plight 1012.4
predicated 334.9
predict look forward to
130.6
foreshow 133.10
come 838.6
foresee 960.5
make a prediction
961.9
risk 971.12
predictability
expectation 130.1
regularity 849.1
divinability 961.8
mathematical
probability 967.2
reliability 969.4
predictable stable
854.12
divinable 961.13
probable 967.6
reliable 969.17
predictably 838.9
predicted expected
130.13
augured 133.15
future 838.8
prophesied 961.14
prediction premonition
133.1
future 838.1
foresight 960.1
foretelling 961.1
predictive premonitory
133.16
predictory 961.11
predictor 961.4
predilection inclination
100.3
love 104.1
preference 371.5
tendency 895.1
prejudgment 946.1
disposition 977.3
prejudice 979.3
predisposed willing
324.5
prejudged 946.3
disposed 977.8
predisposition
preference 371.5
tendency 895.1
prejudgment 946.1
disposition 977.3
predominance 893.1
predominant chief
249.14
governing 612.18
prevalent 863.12
well-connected 893.14
paramount 996.24

predominantly chiefly
249.17
generally 863.17
predominate
verb excel 249.6
dominate 612.15
prevail 863.10
adj governing 612.18
prefab
noun house 228.5
structure 266.2
adj ready-made 405.19
made 891.18
prefabricated ready-
made 405.19
made 891.18
preface
noun front 216.1
makeup 554.12
section 792.2
curtain raiser 815.2
verb prefix 813.3
prefect teaching fellow
571.4
schoolchild 572.3
executive 574.3
prefecture 417.7
prefer desire 100.14
have preference
371.17
offer 439.4
propose 439.5
promote 446.2
favour 650.8
take the attitude 977.6
preference inclination
100.3
favourite 104.16
choice 371.1
predilection 371.5
partiality 650.3
mode 764.4
disposition 977.3
preferences 865.1
preferential 371.25
preferred 371.25
preferring 371.25
prefer to 371.17
prefix
noun front 216.1
postscript 254.2
morphology 526.3
curtain raiser 815.2
verb add 253.4
preface 813.3
pregnancy gestation
78.5
meaningfulness 518.5
origin 817.4
timeliness 842.1
productiveness 889.1
pregnant enceinte
78.18
meaningful 518.10
beginning 817.15
critical 842.10
original 885.14
productive 889.9

imaginative 985.18
preheat 1019.17
prehistoric prewar
833.5
former 836.10
primitive 841.11
prejudice
noun preference 371.5
inequality 790.1
tendency 895.1
prejudgment 946.1,
979.3
disadvantage 995.2
verb prejudice against
979.9
work evil 999.6
prejudice against
979.9
prejudiced partial
650.11
discriminatory 979.12
prejudicial prejudged
946.3
disadvantageous 995.6
harmful 999.12
preliminaries
preparation 405.1
makeup 554.12
earliness 844.1
preliminary
noun preparation
405.1
curtain raiser 815.2
inauguration 817.5
adj preceding 813.4,
815.4
prefatory 817.16
prelude
noun overture 708.26
curtain raiser 815.2
verb prefix 813.3
prem 844.8
premature untimely
843.6
too early 844.8
premature death
307.5
prematurely 844.13
premeditated
predeliberated 380.9
prearranged 964.7
premier
noun head of state
575.7
adj first 817.17
paramount 996.24
premiere
noun theatrical
performance 704.12
verb dramatize 704.28
premiership 417.7
premise
noun fact 760.3
curtain raiser 815.2
antecedent 833.2
foundation 900.6
proposition 934.7

supposition 950.3
truth 972.2
verb prefix 813.3

premises region 231.1
evidence 956.1

premium
noun extra 254.4
gratuity 478.5
interest 623.3
bonus 624.6
discount 631.1
bridge 758.3
adj expensive 632.11

premonition
presentiment 133.1
forewarning 399.2
hunch 933.3

prenatal 817.15

prentice
noun skilled worker 726.6
adj indentured 615.21

preoccupation
perseverance 360.1
possession 469.1
appropriation 480.4
obsession 925.13
thoughtfulness 930.3
engrossment 982.3
abstractedness 984.2

preoccupied
persevering 360.8
obsessed 925.33
engrossed 982.17
oblivious 983.7
abstracted 984.11

preparation medicine 86.4
provision 385.1
preparing 405.1
training 568.3
harmonization 709.2
earliness 844.1
foresight 960.1

preparatory preparative 405.20
preceding 813.4

preparatory school 567.4

prepare cook 11.4
provide 385.7
equip 385.8
write 547.21, 718.6
train 568.13
produce 891.8

prepared expectant 130.11
provided 385.13
ready 405.16
skilled 413.26
foreseeing 960.7

prepared for 405.18

preparedness
carefulness 339.1
readiness 405.4
foreign policy 609.5
earliness 844.1

prepare for 405.11

prepare the ground 405.12

prepare the way pave the way 405.12
facilitate 1013.7

prepare to 405.10

preparing
noun preparation 405.1
adj imminent 839.3

preponderance
superiority 249.1
influence 893.1

preposterous
overpriced 632.12
undue 640.9
absurd 922.11
unbelievable 954.10
impossible 966.7
fanciful 985.20

prep school 567.4

Pre-Raphaelite 841.5

prerequisite
noun preparation 405.1
condition 958.2
requirement 962.2
adj preparatory 405.20
requisite 962.13

prerogative superiority 249.1
authority 417.1
right 642.1

prescience
foreknowledge 960.3
predetermination 963.1

prescient 960.7

prescribe remedy 86.38
require 420.9
advise 422.5
direct 573.8
administer 643.6
legalize 673.8

prescribed limited 210.7
customary 373.14
preceptive 419.4
normal 868.8

prescribing 643.2

prescription remedy 86.1
limitation 210.2
custom 373.1
precept 419.1
formula 419.3
direction 420.3
possession 469.1
prerogative 642.1
law 673.3
rule 868.4

prescriptive customary 373.14
preceptive 419.4
mandatory 420.12
commanding 420.13
exclusive 772.9
traditional 841.12

usual 868.9

presence looks 33.4
apparition 33.5
behaviour 321.1
existence 760.1
influence 893.6
phantom 975.4
spectre 987.1

present
noun gift 478.4
tense 530.12
time 820.1
presentness 837.1
verb manifest 348.5
put to choice 371.21
provide 385.7
offer 439.4
give 478.12, 634.4
say 524.23
phrase 532.4
introduce 587.14
dramatize 704.28
adduce 956.12
adj attendant 221.12
existent 760.13
immediate 837.2

presentable giveable 478.23
tolerable 998.20
comely 1015.18

presentation
appearance 33.1
spectacle 33.7
display 348.2
offer 439.1
giving 478.1
gift 478.4
information 551.1
debut 582.15
acquaintance 587.4
holy orders 698.10
theatrical performance 704.12
fiction 722.1

present-day present 837.2
modern 840.13

present difficulties 1012.10

presented 532.5

presenter giver 478.11
broadcaster 1033.23
television broadcast 1034.2

present itself turn up 830.6
occur to 930.18

presently 844.16

present time 837.1

present-time present 837.2
modern 840.13

present to 216.8

preservation storage 386.5
conservation 397.1
retention 474.1
creation 677.13

perpetuation 828.4
maintenance 852.2
protection 1007.1

preservative
noun preservative medium 397.4
adj preservatory 397.11
conservative 852.8

preserve
noun sweets 10.38
reserve 397.7
refuge 1008.1
verb reserve 386.12
conserve 397.8
cure 397.9
retain 474.5
perpetuate 828.5
be conservative 852.6
sustain 855.4
care for 1007.19

preserved reserved 386.15
conserved 397.12

preserving 397.11

preset 437.5

preside administer 573.11
entertain 585.8
administer justice 594.5

presidency supremacy 249.3
mastership 417.7
directorship 573.4

president principal 571.8
executive 574.3
head of state 575.7
chief 996.10

president-elect 610.11

presidential election 609.15

President of the Board of Trade 575.17

preside over administer 573.11
govern 612.12

presiding 573.14

press
noun extractor 192.9
squeezing 260.2
urge 375.6
presswork 548.9
printing office 548.11
informant 551.5
news 552.1
publisher 554.2
enlistment 615.7
throng 769.4
thrust 901.2
urgency 996.4
verb squeeze 260.8
hot-press 287.6
urge 375.14
hasten 401.4
insist 421.8

bring pressure to bear upon 424.6
urge upon 439.9
importune 440.12
attach 480.20
embrace 562.18
enlist 615.17
strain 725.10
thrust 901.12
densify 1043.9
adj journalism 555.3

press agency 552.1

press association 552.1

press box 552.1

press charges 599.7

press conference
publicity 352.4
conference 541.6
interview 937.11

press corps 552.1

press down sadden 112.18
hamper 1011.11

pressed 401.11

press in thrust in 191.7
intrude 214.5
indent 284.14

pressing
noun squeezing 192.7
urging 375.5
importunity 440.3
adj motivating 375.25
demanding 421.9
compulsory 424.10
urgent 996.22

pressman
noun printer 548.12
adj journalist 555.4

press officer informant 551.5
spokesman 576.5

press on hustle 330.13
hasten 401.4
persist 855.5

press release release 352.3
advertising matter 352.8
message 552.4

press secretary 551.5

pressure
noun touching 73.2
tension 128.3
squeezing 260.2
burden 297.7
urging 375.5
urge 375.6
prestige 417.4
insistence 421.4
coercion 424.3
importunity 440.3
influence 893.1
thrust 901.2
urgent need 962.4
urgency 996.4
adversity 1010.1
verb urge 375.14

author 885.4
producer 891.7
machinery 1039.3

primer colour 35.8
fuse 462.15
textbook 554.10
elementary education
568.5
basics 817.6

prime time 1034.2

primeval beginning
817.15
former 836.10
primitive 841.11
original 885.14

priming colour 35.8
painting 35.12
fuse 462.15
preinstruction 568.4

primitive
noun native 227.3
simple soul 416.3
root 526.2
ancient 841.7
adj basic 199.8
native 226.5
unimitated 337.6
natural 416.6
unrefined 497.12
essential 766.9
simple 797.6
beginning 817.15
former 836.10
prime 841.11
original 885.14

primo
adj original 885.14
A1 998.18
adv first 817.18

primordial 841.11

primp 498.8

primrose 43.4

prince potentate 575.8
Prinz 608.7
good person 659.1

Prince Charming
104.13

princely dignified
136.12
sovereign 417.17
liberal 485.4
grandiose 501.21
noble 608.10
magnanimous 652.6

princess sovereign
queen 575.11
princesse 608.8

principal
noun superior 249.4
headmaster 571.8
chief 575.3, 996.10
lead 707.6
capital 728.15
adj chief 249.14
first 817.17
paramount 996.24

principality state 231.5
country 232.1

mastership 417.7
angel 679.1

principally chiefly
249.17
first 817.18

principle motive 375.1
rule 419.2, 868.4
essence 766.2
cause 885.1, 885.9
foundation 900.6
belief 952.2
axiom 973.2

principled honest
644.13
belief 952.21

principles policy 381.4
ethics 636.1
probity 644.1
basics 817.6

print
noun indentation 284.6
imprint 517.7, 548.3
type 548.6
picture 712.11
numbered print 713.5
photoprint 714.5
offprint 784.5
print 784.5
impact 886.2
verb represent 349.8
mark 517.19
imprint 548.14
engrave 713.9
process 714.15
fix 854.9

printed written 547.22
in print 548.19
engraved 713.11

printer typist 547.18
printworker 548.12
publisher 554.2
output device 1041.9

printers 548.11

printing representation
349.1
publication 352.1
handwriting style
547.4
publishing 548.1
edition 554.5
graphic arts 713.1

printout 547.10

print run 554.5

prior
noun religious 699.15
adj leading 165.3
preceding 813.4
previous 833.4
former 836.10

priori back 836.12
dialectic 934.22

priority leading 165.1
front 216.1
superiority 249.1
prestige 417.4
sequence 814.1
previousness 833.1
importance 996.1

prior to 833.7

priory 703.6

prism 29.2

prison 429.8

prison camp 429.8

prisoner captive 429.11
accused 599.6

prison term 824.4

prissy effeminate 77.14
meticulous 339.12
fastidious 495.9
prudish 500.19
stiff 580.9

pristine unimitated
337.6
unused 390.12
natural 406.13, 416.6
innocent 657.6
intact 791.10
simple 797.6
new 840.7
primitive 841.11
original 885.14
undamaged 1001.8

privacy retirement
345.2
seclusion 584.1
aloneness 871.2
retreat 1008.5

Private 575.20

private
noun enlisted man
461.8
adj interior 207.6
closed 293.9
personal 312.15
privy 345.13
taking 480.25
privatistic 584.9
intrinsic 766.7
particular 864.12
alone 871.8

private detective
576.10

private enterprise
611.9

private-enterprise
611.32

private eye 576.11

private hospital 91.21

private housing 228.1

privately privily 345.19
personally 864.16

private member's bill
613.8

private ownership
611.9

private parts 2.11

private practice 91.21

private room 197.25

private school 567.4

private sector
capitalism 611.9
economy 731.7

privilege
noun superiority 249.1

exemption 430.8
licence 642.2
verb authorize 443.11

privileged
noun upper class 607.2
adj private 345.13
confidential 345.14
exempt 430.30
authorized 443.17
wealthy 618.14

privy
noun latrine 12.10
hut 228.9
adj covert 345.12
private 345.13

Privy Council 613.3

privy council 423.1

privy to 927.16

prize
noun desire 100.11
booty 482.11
monument 549.12
award 646.2
lever 905.4
good thing 998.5
best 998.8
verb cherish 104.21
respect 155.4
measure 300.10
price 630.11
estimate 945.9
value 996.13
adj best 998.16

prized beloved 104.24
respected 155.11
priced 630.14

prizewinner 413.15

pro
noun expert 413.11
gambler 759.21
side 934.14
adj approving 509.17
occupational 724.16
prep in favour of
509.21

proactive energetic
17.13
enterprising 330.23

probabilities 130.4

probability expectation
130.1
future 838.1
tendency 895.1
liability 896.1
prediction 961.1
possibility 965.1
likelihood 967.1
chance 971.1
good chance 971.8

probable expected
130.13
future 838.8
liable 896.5
predictable 961.13
possible 965.6
likely 967.6
impossible 971.18

probably 838.9

probation 941.2

probationary
probational 572.13
experimental 941.11

probe
noun investigation
937.4
search 937.15
feeler 941.4
test rocket 1072.6
artificial satellite
1073.6
verb measure 300.10
investigate 937.23
sound out 941.9
philosophize 951.7

probing
noun deepening 275.7
inquiry 937.1
questioning 937.12
adj searching 937.38

probity assured probity
644.1
virtue 653.1

problem annoyance
96.2
enigma 522.8
topic 936.1
question 937.10
bewilderment 970.3
fault 1002.2
trouble 1012.3

problematic
unbelievable 954.10
doubtful 970.17

problematical
unbelievable 954.10
doubtful 970.17

procedure behaviour
321.1
rule 373.5
plan 381.1
policy 381.4
manner 384.1
process 888.2

proceed progress 162.2
behave 321.4
act 328.4
take action 328.5
use 384.5
elapse 820.5

proceeding
noun behaviour 321.1
act 328.3
manner 384.1
affair 830.3
process 888.2
adj progressive 162.6

proceedings activity
330.1
report 549.7
lawsuit 598.1
affairs 830.4

proceeds gain 472.3
yield 472.5
receipts 627.1
production 892.2

proceed to 404.3

proceed with 328.5

process
noun manner 384.1
procedure 888.2
verb prepare 405.6
develop 714.15
convert 891.9

processed prepared
405.16
made 891.18

processing preparation
405.1
production 891.2
accounting 1040.7

procession train 811.3
sequence 814.1

processor 1041.2

proclaim herald 133.14
affirm 334.5
cry 352.13
command 420.8
state 524.24
be prior 833.3
dogmatize 969.10

proclaimed 352.17

proclamation
affirmation 334.1
announcement 352.2
decree 420.4

procrastination
dawdling 175.3
inaction 329.1
neglect 340.1
protraction 826.2
hesitation 845.5

procreation copulation
75.7
reproduction 78.2
birth 78.6
growth 259.3

proctor teaching fellow
571.9
superintendent 574.2
steward 574.4

procurator steward
574.4
deputy 576.1

procure fetch 176.16
elicit 192.14
induce 375.22, 885.11
acquire 472.8
prostitute oneself
665.21
purchase 733.7

procurement provision
385.1
acquisition 472.1

prod
noun goad 375.8
thrust 901.2
verb touch 73.6
goad 375.15
importune 440.12
thrust 901.12

prodding 375.5

prodigal
noun wastrel 486.2
adj exaggerated 355.4

improvident 406.15
extravagant 486.8
diffuse 538.11
unvirtuous 654.12
intemperate 669.7
teeming 883.9
plentiful 990.7
superabundant 992.19

prodigious wonderful
122.10
large 247.7
huge 257.20
extraordinary 869.14
miraculous 869.16

prodigy marvel 122.2
superior 249.4
talented person 413.12
master 413.13
oddity 869.5
miracle 869.8
first-rater 998.6

produce
noun vegetables 10.34
fruit 10.36
yield 472.5
receipts 627.1
groceries 735.7
production 892.2
verb secrete 13.5
lengthen 267.6
do 328.6
manifest 348.5
accomplish 407.4
write 547.21, 718.6
dramatize 704.28
cause 885.10
be productive 889.7
create 891.8
bear 891.13
adduce 956.12
imagine 985.14

produced formative
262.9
made 891.17

producer director
574.1
theatre man 704.23
film studio 706.3
doer 726.1
author 885.4
maker 891.7

producing
noun production 891.2
adj bearing 889.10

product yield 472.5
commodity 735.2
effect 886.1
end product 892.1
sum 1016.6

production
noun structure 266.1
lengthening 267.4
act 328.3
display 348.2
yield 472.5
writing 547.10
book 554.1
theatrical performance
704.12
mounting 704.13

piece 708.5
proliferation 889.2
creation 891.1
product 892.1
produce 892.2
adj accomplishment
407.1

production company
706.3

production line
assembly 769.14
industrial production
891.3

productive able 18.14
gainful 472.16
diffuse 538.11
fruitful 889.9
creative 891.16
imaginative 985.18
plentiful 990.7

productively 18.15

productivity power
18.1
wordiness 538.2
productiveness 889.1
invention 985.3

profane
noun unholy 686.2
verb misuse 389.4
desecrate 694.4
adj cursing 513.8
unsacred 686.3
impious 694.6
secularist 695.16

profess affirm 334.5
sham 354.21
pretext 376.3
state 952.12

professed accepted
332.14
affirmed 334.9
pretexted 376.5

profession
acknowledgment 332.3
affirmation 334.1
claim 376.2
field 724.4
vocation 724.6
confession 952.7
testimony 956.2

professional
noun expert 413.11
member of a learned
profession 726.4
adj skilful 413.22
skilled 413.26
scholastic 568.19
occupational 724.16

professional football
745.1

professionally 724.18

professor expert 413.11
teacher 571.1
associate professor
571.3

professorial studious
570.17
pedagogic 571.11

professors 571.9

proffered 324.7

proficiency ability 18.2
preparedness 405.4
skill 413.1
profound knowledge
927.6

proficient
noun expert 413.11
adj able 18.14
fitted 405.17
skilful 413.22
perfected 1001.9

profile
noun outline 211.2
side 218.1
contour 262.2
description 349.2
diagram 381.3
portrait 712.15
history 719.1
verb outline 211.9

profit
noun incentive 375.7
benefit 387.4
gain 472.3
good 998.4
verb avail 387.17
expedite one's affair
994.3
do good 998.10

profitability utility
387.3
helpfulness 449.10
profitableness 472.4

profitable useful
387.18
valuable 387.22
helpful 449.21
gainful 472.16
paying 624.21
expedient 994.5
good 998.12

profitably usefully
387.26
helpfully 449.24
gainfully 472.17

profit by take advantage
of 387.15
improve the occasion
842.8

profiteering 632.5

profits gains 251.3
gain 472.3
receipts 627.1

profit sharing 476.2

profit-sharing 476.9

profit taking 737.19

profit-taking 737.5

profligacy prodigality
486.1
turpitude 654.5
dissoluteness 665.3

profligate
noun reprobate 660.5
libertine 665.10
adj prodigal 486.8
corrupt 654.14

licentious 665.25

profound deep-felt
93.24
downright 247.12
huge 257.20
deep 275.10
recondite 522.16
wise 919.17
learned 927.21

profoundly 207.9

profundity sizableness
257.6
depth 275.1
abstruseness 522.2
wisdom 919.5

profuse exaggerated
355.4
liberal 485.4
prodigal 486.8
diffuse 538.11
teeming 883.9
plentiful 990.7

profusely intensely
247.20
liberally 485.5
numerously 883.12
plentifully 990.9

profusion quantity
247.3
prodigality 486.1
wordiness 538.2
numerousness 883.1
plenty 990.2

progeny family 559.5
posterity 561.1

prognosis
prognostication 91.13
verdict 945.5
prediction 961.1

program
noun software 1041.11
verb automate 1040.19
computerize 1041.18

programme
noun exercise 84.2
announcement 352.2
plan 381.1
undertaking 404.1
austerity plan 609.6
platform 609.7
performance 708.33
athletics meeting
755.2
roll 870.6
schedule 964.3
verb plan 381.8
inculcate 568.12
list 870.8
schedule 964.6

programmed 870.9

programmer
broadcaster 1033.23
liveware 1041.17

progress
noun progression
162.1
course 172.2
travel 177.1
journey 177.5

proper downright
247.12
useful 387.18
fastidious 495.9
decorous 496.10
appropriate 533.7
conventional 579.5
right 637.3
rightful 639.8
just 649.8
decent 664.5
orthodox 687.7
characteristic 864.13
accurate 972.16
expedient 994.5

properly tastefully
496.11
conventionally 579.6
rightly 637.4
justly 649.11
accurately 972.20
expediently 994.8

properties 471.1

proper to 866.9

property supply 386.2
possession 469.1
properties 471.1
real estate 471.6
sign 517.1
wealth 618.1
prop 704.17
nature 766.4
characteristic 864.4

property-owning
469.9

property rights 469.1

prophecy revelation
683.9
future 838.1
prediction 961.1

prophesied future
838.8
predicted 961.14

prophet vates sacer
684.1
predictor 961.4
visionary 985.13

prophetic scriptural
683.10
predictive 961.11

Prophets 683.3

propitious promising
124.13
auspicious 133.18
favourable 449.22
timely 842.9

proponent 600.8

proportion
noun space 158.1
degree 245.1
size 257.1
symmetry 264.1
portion 477.5
harmony 533.2
equality 789.1
order 806.1
comparison 942.1
comparability 942.3

notation 1016.2
ratio 1016.7
verb size 257.15
symmetrize 264.3
proportionate 477.7
harmonize 787.7
equalize 789.6

proportional spatial
158.9
proportionate 477.13
approximate 774.8

**proportional
representation** 371.6

proportionate
verb symmetrize 264.3
proportion 477.7
adj satisfactory 107.11
proportional 477.13
approximate 774.8
agreeing 787.9
equal 789.7
sufficient 990.6

proportionately in
proportion 477.14
relatively 774.12
equally 789.11

proportioned 264.4

proportions 257.1

proposal nomination
371.8
intention 380.1
project 381.2
advice 422.1
proposition 439.2
marriage proposal
562.8
theory 950.2

propose nominate
371.19
intend 380.4
advise 422.5
submit 439.5
pop the question
562.22
postulate 950.12

proposed 380.8

proposition
noun affirmation 334.1
project 381.2
proposal 439.2
premise 934.7
theory 950.2
supposition 950.3
axiom 973.2
verb come on to 439.8

propped 900.24

propping 900.23

proprietary
noun medicine 86.4
ownership 469.2
proprietor 470.2
adj possessive 469.10
propertied 471.8

proprietor householder
227.7
proprietary 470.2

propriety fastidiousness
495.1

decorousness 496.3
elegance 533.1
social convention
579.1
decorum 637.2
justice 649.1
decency 664.2
timeliness 842.1
normality 868.1

propulsion manpower
18.4
impulse 901.1
pushing 903.1

prop up 449.12

pros 934.5

prosaic prose 117.8
simple 499.6
plain-speaking 535.3
prosy 721.5
occupied 724.15
unimaginative 986.5

pros and cons 934.5

proscribed limited
210.7
excluded 772.7

prose
noun prosaicness 117.2
prose fiction 721.1
platitude 973.3
verb platitudinize
117.5
adj prosaic 117.8
in prose 721.4

prosecute practice
328.8
pursue 382.8
execute 437.9
sue 598.13

prosecution pursuit
382.1
execution 437.4
lawsuit 598.1
accusation 599.1
accuser 599.5

prosecutor 599.5

prospect
noun look 27.3
field of view 31.3
view 33.6
hope 124.1
expectation 130.1
dueness 639.1
customer 733.4
future 838.1
foresight 960.1
possibility 965.1
probability 967.1
verb mine 1056.14

prospecting 1056.8

prospective expected
130.13
future 838.8

prospector 1056.9

prospects expectations
130.4
dueness 639.1

prospectus intention
380.1

project 381.2
prediction 961.1
schedule 964.3

prosper succeed 409.7
enjoy prosperity
1009.7

prosperity success
409.1
wealth 618.1
business cycle 731.9
prosperousness 1009.1
good times 1009.4

Prospero 975.2

prosperous auspicious
133.18
successful 409.14
wealthy 618.14
in good case 1009.12

prostitute
noun harlot 665.16
verb misuse 389.4
corrupt 393.12
adj prostituted 665.28

prostitution misuse
389.1
corruption 393.2
harlotry 665.8
illicit business 732.1

prostrate
verb paralyse 19.10
fatigue 21.4
aggrieve 112.19
unnerve 128.10
raze 395.19
conquer 412.10
fell 912.5
lie down 912.11
adj disabled 19.16
burnt-out 21.10
laid up 85.58
unnerved 128.14
obsequious 138.14
obeisant 155.10
recumbent 201.8
deferential 433.16
depressed 912.12

protagonist supporter
616.9
role 704.10
lead 707.6

protect preserve 397.8
aid 449.11
defend 460.8
play safe 1006.3
guard 1007.18

protected limited 210.7
private 345.13
preserved 397.12
safe 1006.4
guarded 1007.21

protecting 1007.23

protection bribe 378.2
preservation 397.1
restraint 428.1
custody 429.5
pass 443.7
aid 449.1
defence 460.1
precaution 494.3

policy 609.4
safety 1006.1
guard 1007.1

protectionism restraint
428.1
policy 609.4

protectionist 428.6

protective
noun prophylactic
86.20
adj prophylactic 86.42
preservative 397.11
defensive 460.11
custodial 1007.23

protective clothing
1007.3

protector defender
460.7
regent 575.12
cricket 747.1
keeper 1007.5

protectorate country
232.1
mastership 417.7

protest
noun complaint 115.4
demur 325.2
objection 333.2
affirmation 334.1
resistance 453.1
disapproval 510.1
nonpayment 625.1
nonconformity 867.1
verb object 333.5
affirm 334.5
oppose 451.3
offer resistance 453.3
disapprove 510.10
not pay 625.6
not conform 867.4

Protestant
noun non-Catholic
675.20
adj non-Catholic
675.28

protestant
noun dissenter 333.3
adj protesting 333.7

Protestantism 675.10

protester dissenter
333.3
oppositionist 452.3

protesting protestant
333.7
resistant 453.5

protocol treatment
91.14
rule 419.2
compact 437.1
etiquette 580.3
fact 760.3
knowledge 927.1
schedule 964.3

proton atom 258.8
elementary particle
1037.6

prototype form 262.1
original 337.2

model 785.1
ideatum 931.2

protracted tedious
118.9
lengthened 267.8
wordy 538.12
prolonged 826.11
continuing 855.7

protruding 283.14

proud
noun proudling 136.3
adj prideful 136.8
arrogant 140.9, 141.9
grandiose 501.21
confident 969.21

proudly pridefully
136.13
arrogantly 141.15
grandiosely 501.28

prove print 548.14
result 886.4
experiment 941.8
demonstrate 956.10
confirm 956.11
verify 969.12
check 1016.20

proved tried 941.12
proven 956.20
assured 969.20
true 972.13

proven trustworthy
644.19
proved 956.20
true 972.13

provenance 885.5

proverb
noun maxim 973.1
verb aphorize 973.5

proverbial well-known
927.27
aphoristic 973.6

proverbs 973.1

prove to be result
886.4
prove 956.10
be true 972.8

provide supply 385.7
prepare 405.6
furnish 478.15

provided
adj supplied 385.13
prepared 405.16
adv circumstantially
765.12
conj in the event that
830.13
provided that 958.12

provided for 618.14

provided that 958.12

provide for provide
385.7
prepare for 405.11
furnish 478.15
finance 729.15
allow for 958.5
care for 1007.19

Providence 963.3

providence precaution
494.3
thrift 635.1
creation 677.13
sagacity 919.4
judiciousness 919.7
foresight 960.1

provident preparatory
405.20
precautionary 494.10
economical 635.6
sagacious 919.16
judicious 919.19
foreseeing 960.7

provider 385.6

providing
noun provision 385.1
conj provided 958.12

province sphere 231.2
state 231.5
country 232.1
duty 641.1
diocese 698.8
function 724.3
field 724.4
science 927.10

provincial
noun governor 575.13
peasant 606.6
adj local 231.9
rustic 233.6
idiomatic 523.20
narrow-minded 979.10

proving
noun confirmation
956.4
adj experimental
941.11

provision
noun food 10.1
providing 385.1
preparation 405.1
stipulation 421.2
support 449.3
giving 478.1
precaution 494.3
substitution 861.1
condition 958.2
foresight 960.1
expedient 994.2
verb feed 8.18
provender 385.9

provisional preparatory
405.20
precautionary 494.10
circumstantial 765.7
interim 825.4
substitute 861.8
experimental 941.11
conditional 958.8
unreliable 970.20
makeshift 994.7

**provisional
government** 612.4

provisionally
circumstantially
765.12
conditionally 958.11

provisions groceries
10.5
supplies 385.2
store 386.1
condition 958.2

proviso stipulation
421.2
bill 613.8
condition 958.2

provocation irritation
96.3
vexatiousness 98.7
excitation 105.11
aggravation 119.1
affront 152.11
incitement 375.4
incentive 375.7
immediate cause 885.3

provocative appetizing
63.10
desirable 100.30
exciting 105.30
aggravating 119.5
provoking 375.27
alluring 377.8
hostile 589.10
interesting 982.19

provocatively
excitingly 105.36
alluringly 377.9

provoke annoy 96.13
irritate 96.14
vex 98.15
stimulate 105.13
aggravate 119.2
sauce 142.8
incense 152.24
prompt 375.13
incite 375.17
sow dissension 456.14
antagonize 589.7
induce 885.11
interest 982.12

provoked annoyed
96.21
aggravated 119.4
vexed 152.27

provoking annoying
98.22
exciting 105.30
provocative 375.27
vehement 544.13
interesting 982.19

provost principal 571.8
executive 574.3
minister 575.17
legislator 610.3

prowess skill 413.1
courage 492.1

prowl
noun stealth 345.4
verb wander 177.23
creep 177.26
lurk 346.9

prowling
noun creeping 177.17
stealth 345.4
adj in hiding 346.14

proximity nearness
223.1
relation 774.1

proxy
noun vote 371.6
deputy 576.1
voter 609.23
commission 615.1
substitute 861.2
adj substitute 861.8

prudence vigilance
339.4
caution 494.1
thrift 635.1
cardinal virtues 653.4
moderation 670.1
judiciousness 919.7
foresight 960.1

prudent
noun wise 920.3
adj vigilant 339.13
cautious 494.8
economical 635.6
moderate 670.10
judicious 919.19
foreseeing 960.7

prudential economical
635.6
judicious 919.19

prudently vigilantly
339.17
cautiously 494.12
economically 635.7
moderately 670.17
intelligently 919.20

prudish fastidious
495.9
priggish 500.19

prune
noun blockhead 923.4
verb excise 255.10
shorten 268.6
sever 801.11
cultivate 1067.17

pruned shortened 268.9
concise 537.6

pruning abbreviation
537.4
cultivation 1067.13

prurient lustful 75.26
craving 100.24
lascivious 665.29
curious 980.5

pry
noun interventionist
214.4
leverage 905.1
lever 905.4
inquisitive person
980.2
verb look 27.13
meddle 214.7
get a purchase 905.8
search 937.31
snoop 980.4

prying
noun curiosity 980.1
adj meddlesome 214.9
searching 937.38

snooping 980.6

psalm
noun paean 696.3
sacred music 708.17
verb sing 708.38

Psalms 701.10

pseudo imitation 336.8
spurious 354.26

pseudonym 527.8

psoriasis 85.34

psyche psychic
apparatus 92.28
spirit 918.4

psychedelic
noun psychoactive
drug 86.13
drug 87.2
adj psychochemical
86.46
hallucinatory 975.10

psychiatric
psychological 92.36
psychotherapeutic
92.37

psychiatrist
psychologist 92.10
psychiatry 925.19

psychiatry
psychological medicine
92.3
alienism 925.19

psychic
noun spiritualist
689.13
predictor 961.4
adj psychical 689.24
mental 918.7
spectral 987.7

psychical psychic
689.24
supernatural 869.15
mental 918.7
spectral 987.7

psychical research
689.4

psychics psychism
689.4
immateriality 1051.1

psycho
noun nut 925.16
psychotic 925.17
adj crazy 925.27

psychoanalysis 92.6

psychoanalyst 92.10

psychoanalytic 92.37

psychological
psychiatric 92.36
mental 918.7

psychologist 92.10

psychology science of
the mind 92.1
anthropology 312.10
attitude 977.1

psychopath 925.17

psychopathic
psychological 92.36

punctuation marks
530.15
 letter 547.9

puncture
 noun trauma 85.37
 hole 292.3
 mark 517.5
 verb collapse 260.10
 perforate 292.15
 injure 393.13
 mark 517.19
 disprove 957.4

punctured deflated
260.14
 disproved 957.7

puncturing 292.3

pundit expert 413.11
 teacher 571.1
 Brahman 699.12
 specialist 865.3
 intellectual 928.1
 scholar 928.3

pungent intense 15.22
 painful 26.10
 bitter 64.6
 sour 67.5
 piquant 68.6
 strong 69.10
 witty 489.15
 spirited 544.12
 aphoristic 973.6

punish torture 96.18
 get even with 506.7
 penalize 603.4
 chastise 604.9

punishable 674.6

punishing fatiguing
21.13
 chastising 604.22
 laborious 725.18

punishment reprisal
506.2
 penalty 603.1
 punition 604.1

punitive retaliatory
506.8
 revengeful 507.7
 punishing 604.22

punk
 noun homosexual
75.14
 nobody 997.7
 tinder 1020.6
 adj measly 997.18
 lousy 999.8
 inferior 1004.9

punt
 noun kick 901.9
 verb row 182.53
 bet 759.25

punter boatman 183.5
 customer 733.4
 jockey 757.2
 gambler 759.21
 average 863.3

punters 917.2

puny frail 16.14
 little 258.10

haggard 270.20
 meagre 991.10
 petty 997.20

pup
 noun malapert 142.5
 boy 302.5
 fledgling 302.10
 dog 311.17
 verb give birth 1.3

pupil eye 2.9, 27.9
 student 572.1

puppet sycophant
138.3
 miniature 258.6
 figure 349.6
 instrument 384.4
 figurehead 575.5
 deputy 576.1
 agent 576.3
 follower 616.8
 toy 743.16
 thing of naught 763.2
 nobody 997.7

puppy malapert 142.5
 boy 302.5
 fledgling 302.10
 dog 311.17
 dandy 500.9

purchase
 noun hold 474.2,
905.2
 buying 733.1
 influence 893.1
 footing 900.5
 tackle 905.6
 verb bribe 378.3
 buy 733.7

purchased 733.11

purchaser 733.5

purchasing
 noun purchase 733.1
 adj buying 733.10

purchasing power
624.4

purdah 563.10

pure clean 79.25
 essential 192.18
 tasteful 496.8
 simple 499.6, 797.6
 elegant 533.6
 plain-speaking 535.3
 honest 644.13
 chaste 653.7, 664.4
 spotless 657.7
 godly 692.9
 thorough 793.10
 genuine 972.15
 perfect 1001.6

pure and simple
499.6, 797.6

purely cleanly 79.29
 extremely 247.22
 to a degree 248.10
 honestly 644.21
 simply 797.11
 solely 871.14
 perfectly 1001.10

pure white 37.7

purgatory torment
96.7
 place of confinement
429.7
 penance 658.3
 hell 682.1

purge
 noun defecation 12.2
 cleansing 79.2
 cleanser 79.17
 laxative 86.17
 release 120.2
 homicide 308.2
 extinction 395.6
 deposal 447.2
 elimination 772.2
 verb clean 79.18
 treat 91.24
 release 120.6
 kill 308.12
 murder 308.15
 exterminate 395.14
 depose 447.4
 justify 600.9
 acquit 601.4
 eliminate 772.5
 do away with 908.21
 evacuate 908.22

purged cleaned 79.26
 excluded 772.7

purging
 noun cleansing 79.2
 release 120.2
 homicide 308.2
 justification 600.1
 acquittal 601.1
 adj cleansing 79.28

purification cleansing
79.2
 refinement 79.4
 extract 192.8
 subtraction 255.1
 sanctification 685.3
 simplification 797.2

purified cleaned 79.26
 unmixed 797.7

purify clean 79.18
 refine 79.22
 subtract 255.9
 simplify 499.5, 797.4
 sanctify 685.5

purifying
 noun cleansing 79.2
 adj cleansing 79.28
 atoning 658.7

purist
 noun mule 361.6
 classicist 533.4
 pedant 928.5
 adj firm 425.7

puritan
 noun prude 500.11
 ascetic 667.2
 adj firm 425.7

puritanical firm 425.7
 fastidious 495.9
 prudish 500.19
 ascetic 667.4
 strict 687.8

puritanism firmness
425.2
 fastidiousness 495.1
 prudery 500.6
 asceticism 667.1
 strictness 687.5

purity colour quality
35.6
 cleanness 79.1
 plainness 499.1
 elegance 533.1
 probity 644.1
 immaculacy 653.3
 innocence 657.1
 chastity 664.1
 godliness 692.2
 simplicity 797.1
 oneness 871.1
 perfection 1001.1

purple
 noun purpleness 46.1
 sovereignty 417.8
 regalia 647.3
 verb empurple 46.2
 adj purpure 46.3
 sovereign 417.17
 ornate 545.11

purplish 46.3

purport
 noun meaning 518.1
 verb pretext 376.3
 intend 380.4

purported 376.5

purpose
 noun resolution 359.1
 intention 380.1
 function 387.5
 intent 518.2
 verb resolve 359.7
 intend 380.4

purpose-built 891.18

purposeful resolute
359.11
 intentional 380.8

purposefully resolutely
359.17
 intentionally 380.10

purposely 380.10

purr hum 52.13
 be pleased 95.11

purring
 noun hum 52.7
 adj humming 52.20
 happy 95.15

purse
 noun funds 728.14
 wallet 729.14
 verb contract 260.7
 wrinkle 291.6

pursed contracted
260.12
 wrinkled 291.8

purser hand 183.6
 attendant 577.5
 payer 624.9
 treasurer 729.11

purse strings 729.14

pursue follow 166.3

practice 328.8
 prosecute 382.8
 persecute 389.7
 court 562.21
 elaborate 860.6
 specialize 865.4
 seek 937.30

pursuer enthusiast
101.4
 lover 104.12
 follower 166.2
 pursuant 382.4

pursuing
 noun pursuit 382.1
 adj pursuant 382.11

pursuit following 166.1
 intention 380.1
 pursuing 382.1
 vocation 724.6
 speciality 865.1

purveyor 385.6

pus humour 2.22
 matter 12.6
 filth 80.7

push
 noun pep 17.3
 power 18.1
 enterprise 330.7
 urge 375.6
 attack 459.1
 crisis 842.4
 thrust 901.2
 pushing 903.1
 dismissal 908.5
 verb set in motion
172.6
 hustle 330.13
 urge 375.14
 hasten 401.4
 try hard 403.12
 importune 440.12
 launch an attack
459.17
 sell under the counter
732.7
 play 748.4, 750.7
 thrust 901.12
 propel 903.9

push ahead 162.2

push back 460.10

pushchair 179.6

pushed 401.11

pusher addict 87.20
 propeller plane 181.2

push for urge 375.14
 espouse 509.13

push in thrust in 191.7
 intrude 214.5

pushing
 noun urging 375.5
 propulsion 903.1
 adj meddlesome 214.9
 enterprising 330.23
 propulsive 903.14
 prep about 223.26

push on 401.4

pushover weakling 16.6
 sucker 358.2

qualitative intrinsic
766.7
characteristic 864.13

quality milieu 209.3
taste 496.1
aristocracy 607.3
nobility 608.2
nature 766.4
characteristic 864.4
goodness 998.1

quality control
examination 937.3
process control 1040.8

quality of life
contentment 107.1
courtesy 504.1
prosperity 1009.1

qualms compunction
113.2
nervousness 128.1

quandary bewilderment
970.3
dilemma 1012.7

quantified quantitative
244.5
measured 300.13

quantify quantize
244.4
measure 300.10
number 1016.16

quantitative quantitive
244.5
measuring 300.12

quantities quantity
247.3
multitude 883.3
plenty 990.2

quantity quantum
244.1
amount 244.2
numerousness 247.3
capacity 257.2
lump 257.10
measure 300.2
extent 300.3
vowel quantity 524.12
metre 720.7
sum 1016.6

quantum atomerg 17.7
quantity 244.1
portion 477.5
candle power 1024.21

quantum leap 392.1

quantum mechanics
mathematical
probability 967.2
nuclear physics 1037.1

quarantine
noun enclosure 212.1
isolation 429.2
seclusion 584.1
exclusiveness 772.3
verb enclose 212.5
isolate 429.13
segregate 772.6

quark 258.8

quarrel

noun open quarrel
456.5
contention 457.1
fight 457.4
arrow 462.6
verb dispute 456.11
contend 457.13

quarrelling 457.1

quarrelsome
contentious 110.26
partisan 456.17
contending 457.22
warlike 458.21
hostile 589.10
argumentative 934.19

quarry
noun desire 100.11
sweetheart 104.10
pit 284.4
objective 380.2
game 382.7
source of supply 386.4
fountainhead 885.6
mine 1056.6
verb extract 192.10
excavate 284.15
mine 1056.14

quarrying 192.1

quart 880.2

quarter
noun pity 145.1
direction 161.1
side 218.1
region 231.1
heraldic device 647.2
mill 728.8
basketball game 751.3
part 792.1
moment 823.2
fourth 880.2
verb house 225.10
adj fourth 880.5

quartered housed
225.14
severed 801.23
quadrisected 880.4

quarterly
adj periodical 555.1
momentary 849.8
adv fourthly 880.6

quartermaster captain
183.7
steersman 183.8
provider 385.6

quarters
noun living quarters
228.4
verb restrict 428.9

quartet cooperation
450.1
part music 708.18
four 878.1

quasar 1070.8

quash cover up 345.8
extinguish 395.15
suppress 428.8

quashed 428.14

quashing 428.2

quasi
adj imitation 336.8
spurious 354.26
nominal 527.15
approximating 783.14
adv imitatively 336.11
supposedly 950.17

quaver
noun trepidation 105.5
speech defect 525.1
note 709.14
trill 709.19
shake 916.3
verb shake 16.8,
916.11
thrill 105.18
tremble 127.14
speak poorly 525.7
sing 708.38

quay 1008.6

quayside 1008.6

queasy nauseated 85.56
overfastidious 495.12

queen homo 75.15
ant 311.32
bee 311.33
sovereign queen
575.11
princess 608.8
chessman 743.17
card 758.2
best 998.8

queer
noun homo 75.15
counterfeit 728.10
verb crab 1011.16
adj spurious 354.26
odd 869.11
insane 925.26
eccentric 926.5

quell extinguish 395.15
conquer 412.10
suppress 428.8
subdue 432.9
calm 670.7

quelled conquered
412.17
suppressed 428.14
subdued 432.15
restrained 670.11

quench gratify 95.7
disincline 379.4
extinguish 395.15
suppress 428.8
fight fire 1021.7

querulous discontented
108.7
peevish 110.22
plaintive 115.19

query
noun question 937.10
verb inquire 937.20
interrogate 937.21
doubt 954.6
be curious 980.3

quest
noun intention 380.1
pursuit 382.1
adventure 404.2

search 937.15
verb pursue 382.8
seek 937.30

questing 382.11

question
noun enigma 522.8
remark 524.4
bill 613.8
topic 936.1
query 937.10
doubt 954.2
gamble 970.8
verb communicate with
343.8
inquire 937.20
interrogate 937.21
doubt 954.6
be uncertain 970.9
be curious 980.3

questionable deceptive
356.21
dishonest 645.16
unbelievable 954.10
improbable 968.3
doubtful 970.17

**question-and-answer
session** 541.3

questioned 954.12

questioner inquirer
937.16
inquisitive person
980.2

questioning
noun interrogation
937.12
adj communicational
343.9
inquiring 937.36
doubting 954.9

questioningly 954.13

question mark enigma
522.8
question 937.10

questionnaire
noun roll 870.6
canvass 937.14
verb canvass 937.29

queue braid 3.7
tail 217.6
series 811.2
afterpart 816.2

quibble
noun criticism 510.4
quiddity 935.4
verb find fault 510.15
argue 934.16
cavil 935.9

quick
noun sore spot 24.4
provocation 152.11
living 306.4
inner nature 766.5
adj eager 101.8
hot-tempered 110.25
fast 174.15
living 306.11
willing 324.5
swift 330.18
alert 339.14

impulsive 365.9
hasty 401.9
skilful 413.22
teachable 570.18
brief 827.8
sudden 829.5
prompt 844.9
smart 919.14
adv swiftly 174.17

quicken refresh 9.2
energize 17.10
sensitize 24.7
stimulate 105.13
accelerate 174.10
come to life 306.8
vivify 306.9
hasten 401.4
be useful 449.17
facilitate 1013.7

quickening
noun energizing 17.8
acceleration 174.4
vivification 306.5
hastening 401.3
facilitation 1013.5
adj energizing 17.15
life-giving 306.12

quickie copulation 75.7
drink 88.7

quickly eagerly 101.13
swiftly 174.17, 330.26
impulsively 365.13
hastily 401.12
transiently 827.10
in an instant 829.7
promptly 844.15

quickness eagerness
101.1
velocity 174.1
swiftness 330.3
alertness 339.5
impulsiveness 365.2
hastiness 401.2
skill 413.1
teachableness 570.5
promptness 844.3
smartness 919.2

quicksand marsh 243.1
danger 1005.1
predicament 1012.4

quicksilver
noun lightning 174.6
Proteus 853.4
adj active 330.17
fickle 364.6
brass 1056.17

quick-thinking 919.14

quick time 177.13

quick-witted witty
489.15
smart 919.14

quid bite 8.2
chewing tobacco 89.7

quid pro quo offset
338.2
tit for tat 506.3
interaction 776.3
substitution 861.1
interchange 862.1

quiet
noun rest 20.1
silence 51.1
composure 106.2
peacefulness 464.2
order 806.1
verb fall silent 51.7
silence 51.8
quieten 173.8
calm 670.7
order 806.4
adj vacational 20.10
soft-coloured 35.21
silent 51.10
calm 106.12
reserved 139.11
quiescent 173.12
taciturn 344.9
covert 345.12
meek 433.15
pacific 464.9
tasteful 496.8

quieten fall silent 51.7
silence 51.8
quiet 173.8
calm 670.7

quiet life 464.2

quietly silently 51.13
inexcitably 106.16
modestly 139.14
quiescently 173.18
meekly 433.19
tastefully 496.11

quietness silence 51.1
taciturnity 344.2
submission 433.1
peacefulness 464.2
restraint 496.4

quill
noun feather 3.17
calamus 3.18
thorn 285.5
verb fold 291.5

quilt 295.10

quintessential essential
192.18
typical 349.15
characteristic 864.13
best 998.16
perfected 1001.9

quintet cooperation
450.1
part music 708.18
five 881.1

quip
noun witticism 489.7
gibe 508.2
quirk 926.2
quibble 935.4
verb joke 489.13

quirk distortion 265.1
caprice 364.1
mannerism 500.2
characteristic 864.4
twist 926.2
quibble 935.4

quirkiness
capriciousness 364.2
eccentricity 926.1

quirky capricious 364.5
eccentric 926.5

Quisling 357.10

quisling
noun traitor 357.10
apostate 363.5
criminal 660.10
adj traitorous 645.22

quit
verb vacate 188.9
abandon 370.5
cease to use 390.4
resign 448.2
requite 506.5
repay 624.11
cease 856.6
adj clear 430.31

quite
adv to a degree 245.7
very 247.18
positively 247.19
absolutely 793.15
phrase right on!
972.25
exclam yes 332.18

quite a few 883.3

quite the contrary
adv contrarily 778.9
exclam no 335.8
by no means 335.9

quits 789.7

quiver
noun thrill 105.2
trepidation 105.5
trill 709.19
bundle 769.8
shake 916.3
flutter 916.4
flicker 1024.8
verb shake 16.8,
916.11
thrill 105.18
tremble 127.14
freeze 1022.9
flicker 1024.25

quivering
noun trepidation 105.5
shaking 916.2
flicker 1024.8
adj jittery 128.12
in suspense 130.12
shaking 916.17
flickering 1024.36

Quixote 985.13

quixotic 985.24

quiz
noun examination
937.2
questioning 937.12
verb interrogate
937.21
be curious 980.3

quiz show 1034.2

quizzical humorous
488.4
bantering 490.7
ridiculing 508.12
inquiring 937.36

curious 980.5

quizzically 488.7

quota portion 477.5
part 792.1
ratio 1016.7

quotation price 630.1,
738.9
repetition 848.1
citation 956.5

quote state 524.24
repeat 848.7
cite 956.13

quoted 848.12

R 704.16

Rabbi 648.5

rabbi teacher 571.1
master 575.1
rabbin 699.10
wise man 920.1

rabbit
noun hare 311.24
beginner 817.2
Hydra 889.6
verb chatter 540.5

rabble rabblement
606.3
throng 769.4

rabble-rousing
noun incitement 375.4
public speaking 543.1
adj incitive 375.28

rabid frenzied 105.25
infuriated 152.32
fanatic 925.32

rabies anthrax 85.40
hydrophobia 925.6

race
noun run 174.3
stream 238.1
flow 238.4
watercourse 239.2
humankind 312.1
haste 401.1
contest of speed
457.12
people 559.4
lineage 560.4
game 743.9
skiing 753.1
downhill race 753.3
motor racing 756.1
driving 756.3
horse race 757.3
class 808.2
kind 808.3
verb speed 174.8
accelerate 174.10
make haste 401.5
race with 457.19
drive 756.4
run 757.5

race against time
842.4

racecourse playground
743.11
skiing 753.1
horse racing 757.1

racehorse 757.2

race meeting 757.3

racer speeder 174.5
skier 753.2
motor racing 756.1

racetrack 757.1

race with 457.19

racial 559.7

racial discrimination
979.4

racialism hate 103.1
nationalism 611.10
discrimination 979.4

racial segregation
772.3

racing
noun track 457.11
adj flowing 238.24

racing car 756.1

racing driver 756.2

racism hate 103.1
nationalism 611.10
discrimination 979.4

racist
noun hater 103.4
nationalist 611.21
bigot 979.5
adj nationalist 611.33
discriminatory 979.12

rack
noun agony 26.6
torment 96.7
slow motion 175.2
gait 177.12
storehouse 386.6
destruction 395.1
penal servitude 604.2
wheel 605.4
strain 725.2
gear 1039.5
verb pain 26.7
torture 96.18, 604.15
stroll 177.28
strain 725.10

racked pained 26.9
affected 93.23
tortured 96.25

racket
noun noise 53.3
rattle 55.3
fraud 356.8
turbulence 671.2
illicit business 732.1
tennis 749.1
commotion 809.4
pandemonium 809.5
elastic 1046.3
verb be noisy 53.9

rackets underworld
660.11
illicit business 732.1

racking painful 26.10
agonizing 98.23

raconteur 722.5

racy zestful 68.7
spirited 544.12
risqué 666.7
interesting 982.19

radar celestial
navigation 182.2
navigation 184.6
electronics 1032.1
radio detection and
ranging 1035.1

radial 171.9

radiance cheerfulness
109.1
radiation 171.2
illustriousness 662.6
gorgeousness 1015.6

radiant
noun axle 914.5
meteor 1070.15
adj happy 95.15
cheerful 109.11
illustrious 662.19
almighty 677.17
gorgeous 1015.20
luminous 1024.30

radiate
verb exude
cheerfulness 109.6
radiate out 171.6
disperse 770.4
shine 1024.23
broadcast 1033.25
transmit 1035.15
adj radiating 171.9

radiated 171.9

radiating 171.9

radiation ray 171.2,
1024.5, 1036.3
light 1024.1
radiant energy 1036.1
cosmic particles
1073.10

radiator 1036.5

radical
noun left side 220.1
reformer 392.6
morphology 526.3
phonogram 546.2
extremist 611.17
source 885.5
foundation 900.6
atomic cluster 1037.7
adj basic 199.8
left 220.4
extreme 247.13,
611.29
emendatory 392.16
innate 766.8
thorough 793.10
revolutionary 859.5
original 885.14

radicalism reform
392.5
extremism 611.5
excess 992.1

radically 247.22

radical reform 392.5

radical right 611.13

radio
noun radiotelephony
347.3
informant 551.5

news 552.1
electronics 1032.1
wireless 1033.1
radio receiver 1033.3
verb telegraph 347.19
broadcast 1033.25
adj communicational 347.20
wireless 1033.28

radioactive 1036.10

radioactive waste
radiator 1036.5
reactor 1037.13

radioactivity 1036.1

Radio Authority
1033.16

radio programme
1033.18

radio station
transmitting station 1033.6
space station 1073.5

radiotherapy radiation
therapy 91.6
radiation physics 1036.7

radius range 158.2
convergence 169.1
radiation 171.2
size 257.1
diameter 269.3
straight line 277.2
circle 280.2

raff 606.3

Raffles 483.11

raft
noun float 180.11
lot 247.4
verb haul 176.13

rag
noun material 4.1
garment 5.3
sail 180.14
rabble 606.3
flag 647.6
scenery 704.20
tempo 709.24
verb banter 490.5
berate 510.19
syncopate 708.43

rage
noun fury 105.8
fit 152.8
passion 152.10
thing 578.4
fad 578.5
violence 671.1
turbulence 671.2
frenzy 925.7
mania 925.12
verb be excitable 105.16
burn 152.15
blow 318.20
bluster 503.3
storm 671.11
be insane 925.20

ragged raucous 58.15

tormented 96.24
rugged 288.7
shabby 393.32
nonuniform 781.3
slovenly 809.15

raging
noun violence 671.1
adj frenzied 105.25
infuriated 152.32
stormy 318.23
blustering 503.4
turbulent 671.18
rabid 925.30

rags material 4.1
clothing 5.1
tatters 5.5
remainder 256.1
refuse 391.4

rags-to-riches 1009.12

raid
noun foray 459.4
plundering 482.6
manipulation 737.20
verb foray 459.20
plunder 482.17

raider assailant 459.12
plunderer 483.6

raiding 482.6

rail
noun fence 212.4
paper 270.7
railway 383.7
horse racing 757.1
verb fence 212.7

railcard 517.11

railed 212.10

railing
noun fence 212.4
adj ridiculing 508.12

railroad
noun railway 383.7
verb thrust 901.12

railway 383.7

rain
noun rainfall 316.1
picture 1034.5
water 1063.3
verb descend 194.5
precipitate 316.9
give 478.12
abound 990.5
flood 1063.14

rainbow
noun spectrum 47.6
bird of ill omen 133.6
halo 1024.14
iridescence 1024.18
adj chromatic 35.15

raincoat 5.13

rainfall rain 316.1
moisture 1063.1

rains 316.4

rainstorm scud 316.2
storm 671.4

rainwater rain 316.1
water 1063.3

rainy showery 316.10

stormy 318.23
moist 1063.15

rainy day wet weather 316.4
hard times 1010.6

raise
noun height 272.2
verb erect 200.9
increase 251.4
enlarge 259.4
emboss 283.12
leaven 298.7
communicate with 343.8
rouse 375.19
improve 392.9
promote 446.2
say 524.23
train 568.13
enlist 615.17
glorify 662.13
conjure 690.11
assemble 769.18
inaugurate 817.11
produce 891.8
process 891.9
elevate 911.5
farm 1067.16
breed 1068.6

raised increased 251.7
expanded 259.10
in relief 283.18
produced 891.17
made 891.18
lifted 911.9

raise money 621.3

raiser producer 891.7
agriculturist 1067.5

raising
noun erection 200.4
expansion 259.1
training 568.3
production 891.2
elevation 911.1
growing 1067.12
adj leavening 298.17

raison 918.1

raj 417.5

rake
noun inclination 204.2
paper 270.7
projection 285.4
person of fashion 578.7
libertine 665.10
verb comb 79.21
incline 204.10
pull the trigger 459.22
be promiscuous 665.19
ransack 937.33
cultivate 1067.17

raking 204.15

rally
noun objection 333.2
recovery 396.8
contest 457.3
call to arms 458.8
electioneering 609.12

price 738.9
tournament 743.10
game 749.2
assembly 769.2
verb object 333.5
incite 375.17
recuperate 396.19
recover 396.20
aid 449.11
call to arms 458.19
banter 490.5
scoff 508.9
come together 769.16
assemble 769.18
dispose 807.9
adduce 956.12

rallying
noun banter 490.1
ridicule 508.1
adj ridiculing 508.12

rallying cry cry 59.1
call to arms 458.8
call 517.16

rallying point 228.27

rally round side with 450.4
form 806.5

ram
noun cock 76.8
sheep 311.7
verb sail into 182.41
thrust 901.12

Ramadan fast day 515.3
Bairam 701.13

ramble
noun wandering 177.3
walk 177.10
verb stray 164.4
wander 177.23, 983.3
be incomprehensible 522.10
digress 538.9
be insane 925.20
muse 984.9

rambler wanderer 178.2
pedestrian 178.6

rambling
noun deviation 164.1
wandering 177.3
discursiveness 538.3
adj deviative 164.7
wandering 177.37
unintelligible 522.13
discursive 538.13
irregular 850.3
inconstant 853.7
delirious 925.31
distracted 984.10

ramming 901.3

ramp
noun stairs 193.3
incline 204.4
gyp 356.9
skiing 753.1
verb be excitable 105.16
climb 193.11

rise 200.8
gyp 356.19
rage 671.11

rampage
noun commotion 809.4
verb rage 671.11

rampant ascending 193.14
vertical 200.11
lawless 418.5
unrestrained 430.24
unruly 671.19
prevalent 863.12
raised 911.9
plentiful 990.7

ramshackle unsteady 16.16
dilapidated 393.33

ranch
noun farmstead 228.6
farm 1068.5
verb farm 1067.16
raise 1068.6

rancid nasty 64.7
malodorous 71.5
tainted 393.41

rancour virulence 144.7
bitterness 152.3
revengefulness 507.2
animosity 589.4

random
noun haphazard 971.4
adj unordered 809.12
vague 970.19
purposeless 971.16

randomly haphazardly 809.18
discontinuously 812.5
purposelessly 971.20

randy
noun revel 743.6
adj lustful 75.26
lascivious 665.29

range
noun vision 27.1
field of view 31.3
earshot 48.4
scope 158.2
direction 161.1
habitat 228.18
highlands 237.1
mountain 237.6
degree 245.1
size 257.1
distance 261.1
grassland 310.8
latitude 430.4
arena 463.1
scale 709.6
series 811.2
verb extend 158.8
traverse 177.20
wander 177.23
size 257.15
dispose 807.9
classify 808.6
align 811.5

ruckle 55.6
agitate 105.14
chatter 540.5
thrust 901.12
confuse 984.7

rattled 984.12

rattling
noun rattle 55.3
adj rattly 55.8

ratty crabby 110.20
rodent 311.43
shabby 393.32
infested 909.11

raucous raucid 58.15
dissonant 61.4

raunchy coarse 497.11
obscene 666.9
lousy 999.8

ravaged tired-looking
21.9
blighted 393.42
ruined 395.28
disintegrative 805.5
infested 909.11

rave
noun dance 705.2
revel 743.6
verb enjoy oneself
95.13
be enthusiastic 101.7
be excitable 105.16
burn 152.15
bluster 503.3
rage 671.11
be insane 925.20

ravel
noun complex 798.2
verb disinvolve 797.5
complicate 798.3
solve 939.2

raven
noun bird of ill omen
133.6
bird 311.28
verb hunger 100.19
plunder 482.17
gluttonize 672.4
adj black 38.8

ravenous hungry
100.25
greedy 100.27
rapacious 480.26
gluttonous 672.6

ravine 237.7, 284.9

raving
noun delirium 925.8
adj frenzied 105.25
infuriated 152.32
blustering 503.4
turbulent 671.18
rabid 925.30
delirious 925.31
eye-catching 1015.21

ravioli 10.32

ravishing delightful
97.7
exciting 105.30
alluring 377.8

gorgeous 1015.20

raw
noun nudity 6.3
sore spot 24.4
adj naked 6.14
sore 26.11
garish 35.19
immature 301.10,
406.11
windblown 318.24
crude 406.10
inexperienced 414.17
coarse 497.11
cursing 513.8
vulgar 666.8
new 840.7
ignorant 929.12
cold 1022.14

raw deal 1010.5

raw material diamond
in the rough 263.2
crude 406.5
materials 1052.1

ray
noun radiation 171.2,
1024.5, 1036.3
wave 915.4
verb radiate 171.6

rayed 171.9

razor-sharp sharp
285.8
cunning 415.12

RC
noun Catholic 675.19
adj Catholic 675.29

re 709.7

reach
noun earshot 48.4
range 158.2
inlet 242.1
degree 245.1
size 257.1
distance 261.1
length 267.1
knowledge 927.1
verb be heard 48.12
move 145.5
extend 158.8
go 177.19
sail for 182.35
arrive 186.6
arrive at 186.7
communicate with
343.8
deliver 478.13
equal 789.5
suffice 990.4

reaching 186.1

reach out stretch out
261.5
be long 267.5

react respond 93.11,
902.5
answer 938.4

reacting 902.9

reaction mental
disorder 92.14
feeling 93.1

regression 163.1
rocket propulsion
184.25
resistance 453.1
conservatism 611.1
impact 886.2
counteraction 899.1
response 902.1
answer 938.1
opinion 952.6

reactionary
noun malcontent 108.3
right side 219.1
conservative 611.13
back number 841.8
reactionist 902.4
adj regressive 163.11
right 219.4
conservative 611.25
reversionary 858.7
reactive 902.9

reactive 902.9

reactor 1037.13

read interpret 341.9
read one loud and
clear 521.8
declaim 543.10
copy-edit 548.17
study 570.12
sound out 941.9

readable meaningful
518.10
intelligible 521.10
legible 521.12
interesting 982.19

reader
noun lecturer 543.5,
571.7
elocutionist 543.7
proofreader 548.13
textbook 554.10
professor 571.3
student 572.1
rabbi 699.10
input device 1041.4
adj journalist 555.4

readers 29.3

readership 571.10

read for 570.15

readily eagerly 101.13
willingly 324.8
quickly 330.26
easily 1013.16

readiness eagerness
101.1
willingness 324.1
quickness 330.3
alertness 339.5
preparedness 405.4
skill 413.1
cunning 415.1
consent 441.1
teachableness 570.5
earliness 844.1
promptness 844.3
tendency 895.1
foresight 960.1

reading measure 300.2
interpretation 341.1

rendering 341.2
speech 543.2
elementary education
568.5
study 570.3
scholarship 927.5
signal 1035.11

reading in 698.10

reading room 558.1

read into interpret
341.9
explain 341.10

readjust 857.14

readjustment
adjustment 92.27
rehabilitation 857.4

readmission 187.8

read my lips 535.5

read one 521.8

read out exclude 772.4
drive out 908.14

read with 570.11

ready
verb repair 396.14
prepare 405.6
train 568.13
adj eager 101.8
expectant 130.11
willing 324.5
quick 330.18
alert 339.14
handy 387.20
prepared 405.16
skilful 413.22
cunning 415.12
consenting 441.4
teachable 570.18
prompt 844.9
foreseeing 960.7

ready for
adj prepared for
405.18
liable to 896.6
prep in preparation for
405.24

ready-made tailored
5.47
ready-mixed 405.19
made 891.18

ready to 895.6

ready-to-eat 405.19

ready-to-wear
noun ready-mades 5.4
adj tailored 5.47
ready-made 405.19
made 891.18

reaffirm 848.8

reaffirmation 848.2

real praedial 471.9
actual 760.15
substantial 762.6
obvious 969.15
true 972.13
genuine 972.15

real estate plot 231.4
land 234.1
realty 471.6

realignment
rearrangement 807.7
change 851.1

realism normality
868.1
genuineness 972.7
realisticness 986.2
materialism 1050.6

real issue 996.6

realist
noun pragmatist 986.3
materialist 1050.7
adj realistic 986.6

realistic descriptive
349.14
typical 349.15
occupied 724.15
lifelike 783.16
normal 868.8
ungullible 955.5
genuine 972.15
realist 986.6

realistically 349.16

reality actuality 760.2
event 830.2
unquestionability
969.3
truth 972.1

realization
noun appearance 33.1
externalization 206.4
representation 349.1
completion 793.4
event 830.1
establishment 891.4
performance 891.5
cognizance 927.2
recognition 988.5
adj accomplishment
407.1

realize externalize
206.5
do 328.6
image 349.11
accomplish 407.4
profit 472.12
understand 521.7
be sold 734.12
cause 885.10
establish 891.10
perform 891.11
know 927.12
visualize 985.15
recognize 988.12

realized accomplished
407.10
known 927.26

real life 760.2

really
adv very 247.18
positively 247.19
actually 760.16
truly 972.18
genuinely 972.19
exclam yes 332.18

really into 927.17

really something
122.2

recession regression
163.1
recedence 168.1
recess 284.7
surrender 433.2
business cycle 731.9
hard times 1010.6

recessionary 168.4

recessive regressive
163.11
recessional 168.4
reversionary 858.7

recharge activate 17.12
revive 396.16

rechargeable 1031.33

recipe remedy 86.1
formula 419.3

recipient
noun receiver 479.3
adj receptive 187.16
receiving 479.9

reciprocal
noun likeness 783.3
adj cooperative 450.5
communal 476.9
retaliatory 506.8
reciprocative 776.10
interchangeable 862.5
alternate 915.19

reciprocate cooperate
450.3
get along 455.2
retaliate 506.4
correspond 776.7
interchange 862.4
alternate 915.13

reciprocity cooperation
450.1
accord 455.1
correlation 776.1
interchange 862.1

recital speech 543.2
lesson 568.7
performance 708.33
fiction 722.1
narration 722.2
iteration 848.2

recitation speech 543.2
lesson 568.7

recite state 524.24
declaim 543.10
narrate 719.6, 722.6
iterate 848.8
memorize 988.17
sum up 1016.18

reckless unconcerned
102.7
fast 174.15
careless 340.11
impulsive 365.9
devil-may-care 493.8
unwise 922.10

recklessly
unconcernedly 102.10
carelessly 340.18
impulsively 365.13
happen what may
493.11

recklessness unconcern
102.2
carelessness 340.2
impulsiveness 365.2
prodigality 486.1
devil-may-careness
493.2
unwiseness 922.2

reckon plan 380.6
estimate 945.9
suppose 950.10
think 952.11
calculate 1016.17

reckoning amount
244.2
fee 624.5
account 628.2
statement 628.3
estimate 945.3
sum 1016.6
calculation 1016.10
summation 1016.11

reclaim redeem 396.12
aid 449.11
recover 481.6
re-form 857.12
rehabilitate 857.14

reclaiming
dispossession 480.7
recovery 481.3

reclamation recovery
396.2, 481.3
atonement 658.1
new start 857.2
rehabilitation 857.4
reversion 858.1

reclining
noun recumbency
201.2
lowness 274.1
adj recumbent 201.8

recluse
noun loner 584.5
eccentric 926.3
adj reclusive 584.10

reclusive private 584.9
recluse 584.10
alone 871.8
eccentric 926.5
incurious 981.3

recognition thanks
150.2
acknowledgment 332.3
commendation 509.3
due 639.2
repute 662.1
plot 722.4
cognizance 927.2
discovery 940.1
identification 988.5

recognizable visible
31.6
knowable 927.25

recognize see 27.12
thank 150.4
acknowledge 332.11
honour 646.8
know 927.12, 988.12
detect 940.5

recognized accepted
332.14
received 479.10
conventional 579.5
traditional 841.12
known 927.26

recoil
noun demur 325.2
retaliation 506.1
impact 886.2
counteraction 899.1
rebound 902.2
retreat 902.3
verb shudder at 99.5
flinch 127.13
demur 325.4
dodge 368.8
rebound 902.6

recollect 988.10

recollection memory
836.4, 988.1
remembering 988.4

recommend urge
375.14
advise 422.5
propose 439.5
commend 509.11

recommendation
advice 422.1
letter of
recommendation 509.4

recommended 509.19

recompense
noun compensation
338.1
reparation 396.6,
481.2
reprisal 506.2
remuneration 624.3
atonement 658.1
verb compensate 338.4
remedy 396.13
make restitution 481.5
requite 506.5
pay 624.10
atone 658.4

reconcile bring to
terms 465.8
harmonize 787.7
conform 866.3

reconciled content
107.7
resigned 134.10

reconciliation
contentment 107.1
reconcilement 465.3
adjustment 787.4
conformity 866.1

reconnaissance mission
184.11
recce 937.8

reconsider 930.15,
937.27

reconsideration mature
thought 930.5
remembering 988.4

reconstruct reproduce
78.7

remake 396.18
change 851.7

reconstruction
reproduction 78.1
re-creation 396.5

reconstructive 78.14

record
noun phonograph
record 50.12
supremacy 249.3
preparedness 405.4
recording 549.1
report 549.7
bulletin board 549.10
history 719.1
chronicle 831.9
data 1041.15
verb sound 50.14
write 547.19
record 549.15
chronicle 719.5
teleview 1034.15

record-breaker 249.4

record-breaking
998.17

recorded 549.17

recorder registrar
549.13
recordist 550.1
accountant 628.7

record holder 413.15

recording
noun record 50.12,
549.1
registration 549.14
history 719.1
transcript 784.4
adj recordative 549.16

record player 50.11

records 757.4

recount
noun returns 609.21
summation 1016.11
verb narrate 719.6,
722.6
iterate 848.8
sum up 1016.18

recounting account
349.3
fiction 722.1
narration 722.2
iteration 848.2
summation 1016.11

recoup
noun recovery 481.3
reimbursement 624.2
verb redeem 396.12
recover 481.6
repay 624.11

recourse
instrumentality 384.3
resource 1008.2

recover get well 83.7
rally 392.8, 396.20
redeem 396.12
rescue 398.3
regain 481.6
rehabilitate 857.14

recovery improvement
392.1
reclamation 396.2
rally 396.8
rescue 398.1
regaining 481.3
business cycle 731.9
rehabilitation 857.4

re-create reproduce
78.7
remake 396.18
change 851.7

recreate refresh 9.2
amuse 743.21

recreated 9.4

recreation refreshment
9.1
amusement 743.1

recreational 743.27

recrimination 599.3

recruit
noun rookie 461.17
novice 572.9
newcomer 773.4
beginner 817.2
verb add to 253.5
provide 385.7
avail oneself of 387.14
restore 396.11
revive 396.16
recuperate 396.19
call to arms 458.19
employ 615.14
enlist 615.17

recruiting utilization
387.8
engagement 615.4
enlistment 615.7

recruitment utilization
387.8
call to arms 458.8
engagement 615.4
enlistment 615.7

rectangle 878.1

rectangular oblong
267.9
right-angled 278.7
quadrangular 278.9

rectified 797.7

rectify refine 79.22
straighten 277.5
compensate 338.4
revise 392.12
remedy 396.13
harmonize 787.7
conform 866.3

rectifying 338.6

rectitude probity 644.1
virtue 653.1

rector principal 571.8
director 574.1
clergyman 699.2

rectory house 228.5
benefice 698.9
parsonage 703.7

rectum 2.16

registration 549.14
recorder 550.1
account book 628.4
pitch 709.4
scale 709.6
organ stop 711.19
chronicle 831.9
list 870.1
verb be heard 48.12
limit 210.5
represent 349.8
preserve 397.8
record 549.15
be taught 570.11
act 704.29
agree 787.6
list 870.8
protect 1007.18

registered limited
210.7
recorded 549.17

register with 787.6

registrar doctor 90.4
recorder 549.13, 550.1
accountant 628.7

registration register
549.14
index 870.7

registry record 549.1
memorandum 549.4
registration 549.14
account book 628.4
chronicle 831.9
list 870.1
index 870.7

regress
noun regression 163.1
reversion 858.1
verb go backwards
163.5
move 172.5
bring up the rear
217.8
deteriorate 393.16
relapse 394.4
revert 858.4

regression fixation
92.21
regress 163.1
course 172.2
deterioration 393.3
relapse 394.1
reversion 858.1

regressive recessive
163.11
flowing 172.8
deteriorating 393.45
relapsing 394.5
reversionary 858.7

regret
noun regrets 113.1
verb deplore 113.6

regretful remorseful
113.8
disappointed 132.5

regretfully 113.11

regrets regret 113.1
apology 658.2

regrettable distressing
98.20
much to be regretted
113.10
terrible 999.9

regrettably 98.29

regretting 113.1

regroup 857.12

regular
noun partisan 609.27
customer 733.4
adj gradual 245.5
downright 247.12
symmetric 264.4
smooth 287.9
typical 349.15
customary 373.14
habitual 373.15
uniform 780.5
thorough 793.10
orderly 806.6
constant 846.5
usual 868.9
ordinary 1004.8

regular army 461.22

regularity symmetry
264.1
smoothness 287.1
constancy 780.2,
846.2
order 806.1
regularness 849.1
normality 868.1

regularly smoothly
287.12
habitually 373.21
constantly 780.8,
846.7
methodically 806.9
systematically 849.9
normally 868.10

regulars 461.22

regulate direct 573.8
govern 612.12, 893.8
legalize 673.8
make uniform 780.4
harmonize 787.7
order 806.4
organize 807.10

regulated 807.14

regulating directing
573.12
governing 612.18

regulation
noun rule 419.2, 868.4
direction 420.3, 573.1
government 612.1
law 673.3
adjustment 787.4
organization 807.2
adj customary 373.14
preceptive 419.4
usual 868.9

regulative directing
573.12
governing 612.18

regulator 1040.14

regulatory directing
573.12
governing 612.18

rehabilitate restore
396.11
justify 600.9
re-form 857.12
recondition 857.14

rehabilitation
adjustment 92.27
restoration 396.1
justification 600.1
reconditioning 857.4
reversion 858.1

rehearsal training
568.3
production 704.13
fiction 722.1
narration 722.2
repetition 848.1
iteration 848.2
tryout 941.3
summation 1016.11

rehearse report 552.11
train 568.13
practise 704.32
narrate 719.6, 722.6
iterate 848.8
sum up 1016.18

reheat 1019.17

reheated 1019.29

reign
noun governance 417.5
government 612.1
influence 893.1
verb rule 612.14
prevail 863.10

reigning governing
612.18
prevalent 863.12

reign of terror
terrorization 127.7
despotism 612.10

reimburse make
restitution 481.5
repay 624.11

reimbursement
reparation 481.2
recoupment 624.2

rein
noun restraint 428.1
shackle 428.4
verb restrain 428.7

reincarnation
repetition 848.1
transformation 851.3
materialization 1050.8

reindeer
noun deer 311.5
phrase beast of burden
176.8

reinforce
noun supporter 900.2
verb strengthen 15.13
intensify 251.5
add to 253.5
support 449.12,
900.21

confirm 956.11
stiffen 1044.9

reinforced increased
251.7
hardened 1044.13

reinforcement
strengthening 15.5
conditioning 92.26
intensification 251.2
addition 253.1
adjunct 254.1
provision 385.1
support 900.1
supporter 900.2
wave 915.4
confirmation 956.4

reinforcements 449.8

reinforcing 900.2

rein in slow 175.9
restrain 428.7

reins 573.5

reinstate restore 396.11
justify 600.9

reinstatement
restoration 396.1
justification 600.1
reversion 858.1

reinvest restore 396.11
invest 729.16

reissue
noun reproduction
78.1
print 548.3
iteration 848.2
verb reproduce 78.7
print 548.14
monetize 728.26
iterate 848.8

reiterate
verb iterate 848.8
persist 855.5
adj repeated 848.12

reiterated 848.12

reject
noun derelict 370.4
discard 390.3
verb repudiate 372.2
discard 390.7
refuse 442.3
prohibit 444.3
contradict 451.6
disapprove 510.10
ostracize 586.6
exclude 772.4
eject 908.13
vomit 908.26
disbelieve 954.5
refuse to believe 955.3

rejected unloved 99.10
repudiated 372.3
discarded 390.11
outcast 586.10
ejective 908.30
doubted 954.12
disproved 957.7

rejection snub 157.2
dissent 333.1
repudiation 372.1

discard 390.3
refusal 442.1
prohibition 444.1
opposition 451.1
disapproval 510.1
ostracism 586.3
exclusion 772.1
ejection 908.1
unbelief 954.1

rejoice cheer 109.7
jubilate 116.5

rejoice in 95.12

rejoicing
noun jubilation 116.1
celebration 487.1
adj merry 109.15
delighting 116.10

rejoin answer 938.4
rebut 938.5

rejoining 938.6

rejuvenate make young
301.8
revive 396.16

rejuvenation 396.3

rekindle revive 396.16
ignite 1019.22

relapse
noun regression 163.1
apostasy 363.2
lapse 394.1
conversion 857.1
reversion 858.1
verb regress 163.5
invert 205.5
deteriorate 393.16
lapse 394.4
go wrong 654.9
defect 857.13
revert 858.4

relate state 524.24
report 552.11
narrate 719.6, 722.6
associate 774.6
compare 942.4
sum up 1016.18

related kindred 559.6,
774.10
connected 774.9

relate to communicate
with 343.8
refer to 774.5

relating
noun sympathy 93.5
fiction 722.1
comparison 942.1
adj relative 774.7

relation meaning 518.1
blood relationship
559.1
fiction 722.1
narration 722.2
story 722.3
relationship 774.1
involvement 897.1
comparison 942.1

relations copulation
75.7
kinfolk 559.2

relation 774.1
affairs 830.4

relationship blood
relationship 559.1
relation 774.1

relative 774.7, 942.8

relatively to a degree
248.10
comparatively 774.12,
942.10

relatives 559.2

relativism relativity
774.2
comparison 942.1
uncertainty 970.1

relativity fourth
dimension 158.6
dependence 774.2
correlation 776.1
uncertainty 970.1

relax unbend 20.7,
670.9
compose oneself 106.7
relieve 120.5
release 120.6
be at ease 121.8
have pity 145.4
slow 175.9
not stand on ceremony
581.2
amuse 743.21
amuse oneself 743.22
loosen 803.3
pause 856.9
allow for 958.5
soften 1045.6
yield 1045.7

relaxation weakening
16.5
rest 20.1
relief 120.1
decrease 252.1
idleness 331.2
laxness 426.1
modulation 670.2
amusement 743.1
looseness 803.2
flaccidity 1045.3
softening 1045.5

relaxed nonchalant
106.15
relieved 120.10
at ease 121.12
unnervous 129.2
quiescent 173.12
slow 175.10
negligent 340.10
leisurely 402.6
lax 426.4
informal 581.3
loose 803.5
thoughtless 932.4
flaccid 1045.10

relaxing
noun weakening 16.5
relief 120.1
modulation 670.2
adj relieving 120.9
comfortable 121.11

mitigating 670.14
softening 1045.16

relay
noun shift 824.3
verb transfer 176.10
broadcast 1033.25

release
noun deliverance 120.2
death 307.1
press release 352.3
escape 369.1
rescue 398.1
exemption 430.8
freeing 431.2
permission 443.1
relinquishment 475.1
information 551.1
message 552.4
acquittal 601.1
receipt 627.2
disbandment 770.3
verb free 120.6
rescue 398.3
exempt 430.14
unhand 431.5
extricate 431.7
permit 443.9
let go 475.4
acquit 601.4
disband 770.8
detach 801.10
dismiss 908.19

released dead 307.30
free 430.21
exempt 430.30
liberated 431.10
relinquished 475.5

release from prison
431.5

releasing 431.3

relegated 772.7

relegation commitment
478.2
exclusion 772.1
banishment 908.4

relent have pity 145.4
submit 433.6
be moderate 670.5
yield 1045.7

relentless pitiless 146.3
industrious 330.22
resolute 359.11
persevering 360.8
unyielding 361.9
firm 425.7
constant 846.5
inevitable 962.15

relentlessly pitilessly
146.4
industriously 330.27
resolutely 359.17
perseveringly 360.9
unyieldingly 361.15
firmly 425.9
inevitably 962.19

relevance meaning
518.1
pertinence 774.4

relevant pertinent
774.11
apt 787.10

reliability
trustworthiness 644.6
stability 854.1
believability 952.8
dependability 969.4

reliable trustworthy
644.19
stable 854.12
believable 952.24
evidential 956.16
dependable 969.17
unhazardous 1006.5

reliably trustworthily
644.24
safely 1006.8

reliance hope 124.1
expectation 130.1
supporter 616.9
support 900.1
belief 952.1

reliant 952.22

relic record 549.1
antiquity 841.6
memento 988.7

relics remainder 256.1
corpse 307.16

relief remedy 86.1
easement 120.1
consolation 121.4
welfare 143.5
pity 145.1
outline 211.2
lightening 298.3
aid 449.1
reinforcements 449.8
welfarism 611.8
relievo 715.3
turn 824.2
interim 825.1
substitute 861.2

relieve give relief 120.5
comfort 121.6
lighten 298.6
aid 449.11
take one's turn 824.5
substitute for 861.5
disembarrass 1013.9

relieved 298.11

relieving
noun deprivation 480.6
adj easing 120.9
comforting 121.13
lightening 298.16

religion theology 676.1
piety 692.1
system of belief 952.3

religious
noun religieux 699.15
adj meticulous 339.12
conscientious 644.15
theistic 675.25
theological 676.4
sacred 685.7
pious 692.8
exact 972.17

religiously 339.16

relinquish give up
370.7, 475.3
cease to use 390.4
surrender 433.8
resign 448.2
cease 856.6

relinquished disused
390.10
released 475.5

relish
noun taste 62.1
savour 63.2
flavouring 63.3
zest 68.2
passion 93.2
pleasure 95.1
liking 100.2
appetite 100.7
verb eat 8.20
savour 63.5
enjoy 95.12

relishing 8.1

relived 836.8

reliving 836.4

relocate settle 159.17
remove 176.11

relocation 176.4

reluctance slowness
175.1
refusal 325.1
resistance 453.1,
1031.12

reluctant slow 175.10
renitent 325.6
resistant 453.5

reluctantly slowly
175.13
grudgingly 325.9

relying 952.22

rely on hope 124.7
rest on 900.22
trust 952.17

remain be still 173.7
be present 221.6
inhabit 225.7
endure 826.6, 852.5
continue 855.3

remain anonymous
346.8

remainder difference
255.8
remains 256.1
part 792.1
subsequence 834.1
surplus 992.5

remaining resident
225.13
surviving 256.7
durable 826.10
permanent 852.7
continuing 855.7
surplus 992.18

remains remainder
256.1
corpse 307.16
record 549.1

antiquity 841.6

remake reproduce 78.7
reconstruct 396.18
change 851.7

remaking reproduction
78.1
reconstruction 396.5
change 851.1

remand
noun commitment
429.4
restitution 481.1
verb commit 429.17,
478.16
restore 481.4

remand centre prison
429.8
reform school 567.9

remark
noun interjection 213.2
aspersion 512.4
statement 524.4
commentary 556.2
attention 982.1
verb comment 524.25
heed 982.6

remarkable wonderful
122.10
outstanding 247.10
extraordinary 869.14
notable 996.19

remarkably
wonderfully 122.14
intensely 247.20
extraordinarily 869.18
importantly 996.25

remarkably like
783.15

remarry 563.15

remedial curative
86.39
relieving 120.9
tonic 396.22
helpful 449.21

remedy
noun cure 86.1, 396.7
relief 120.1
reparation 396.6
aid 449.1
counteractant 899.3
verb cure 86.38,
396.15
treat 91.24
rectify 396.13
aid 449.11

remember recall
988.10
remind 988.20

remembered
reminiscent 836.8
recollected 988.23

remembering
noun remembrance
988.4
adj mindful 988.24

remembrance
celebration 487.1
monument 549.12

memory 662.7, 836.4,
988.1
remembering 988.4
reminder 988.6
memento 988.7

remind 988.20

reminder memorandum
549.4
remembrance 988.6

reminiscence memory
836.4
remembering 988.4

reminiscent
retrospective 836.8
recollective 988.22

remission relief 120.1
pardon 148.2
decline 252.2
reduction 255.2
restitution 481.1
acquittal 601.1
modulation 670.2
pause 856.3

remit relieve 120.5
have pity 145.4
forgive 148.3
send 176.15
abate 252.8
commit 429.17,
478.16
exempt 430.14
restore 481.4
acquit 601.4
pay 624.10
be moderate 670.5
relax 670.9

remittance 624.1

remnant
noun remainder 256.1
adj remaining 256.7

remorse regret 113.1
guilt 656.1

remorseless unregretful
114.4
pitiless 146.3

remorselessly
unregretfully 114.7
pitilessly 146.4

remote aloof 141.12,
583.6
distant 261.8
reticent 344.10
secluded 584.8
selfish 651.5
farfetched 775.8

remote control 1040.4

remote-control
1040.24

remotely 261.14

remoteness aloofness
141.4, 583.2
distance 261.1
selfishness 651.1

remotest 261.12

removable 176.18

removal
noun unclothing 6.1

release 120.2
dislocation 160.1
departure 188.1
extraction 192.1
subtraction 255.1
homicide 308.2
discard 390.3
deposal 447.2
elimination 772.2
separation 801.1
ejection 908.1
dismissal 908.5
evacuation 908.6
phrase moving 176.4

remove
noun degree 245.1
verb divest 6.5
take off 6.6
release 120.6
move 176.11
quit 188.9
extract 192.10
subtract 255.9
murder 308.15
discard 390.7
exterminate 395.14
depose 447.4
eliminate 772.5
detach 801.10
eject 908.13
dismiss 908.19
evacuate 908.22

removed distant 261.8
reticent 344.10
aloof 583.6
secluded 584.8
unrelated 775.6
separated 801.21
alone 871.8

remuneration
reparation 481.2
recompense 624.3
pay 624.4

renaissance 396.3

render do 328.6
translate 341.12
communicate 343.7
represent 349.8
describe 349.9
execute 437.9
give 478.12
deliver 478.13
pay 624.10
play 708.39
convert 857.11
melt 1019.21

rendering squeezing
192.7
rendition 341.2
representation 349.1
description 349.2
execution 708.30

rendezvous
noun tryst 582.9
assembly 769.2
verb come together
769.16

rending
noun extortion 192.6
severance 801.2

adj agonizing 98.23

rendition squeezing
192.7
rendering 341.2
representation 349.1
description 349.2
restitution 481.1
execution 708.30

renegade
noun apostate 363.5,
857.8
sacrilegist 694.3
adj apostate 363.11,
857.20
nonobservant 435.5
impious 694.6

renege recant 363.8
abandon 370.5
disregard 435.3
repeal 445.2
be unfaithful 645.12
defect 857.13

renew refresh 9.2
stimulate 105.13
revive 396.16
renovate 396.17
innovate 840.5
repeat 848.7
change 851.7
resume 855.6
re-form 857.12

renewable remediable
396.25
convertible 857.18

renewal refreshment
9.1
relapse 394.1
revival 396.3
renovation 396.4
repetition 848.1
change 851.1
resumption 855.2
new start 857.2

renewed refreshed 9.4
renascent 396.24
redeemed 685.9
fresh 840.8
changed 851.10
continuing 855.7
converted 857.19

renounce deny 335.4
recant 363.8
give up 370.7
reject 372.2
cease to use 390.4
surrender 433.8
relinquish 475.3
swear off 668.8
cease 856.6

renounced rejected
372.3
disused 390.10
relinquished 475.5

renovate reproduce
78.7
perfect 392.11
renew 396.17
recover 481.6
innovate 840.5

renovation
reproduction 78.1
renewal 396.4

renown glory 247.2
repute 662.1
notability 996.2

renowned eminent
247.9
distinguished 662.16

rent
noun trauma 85.37
crack 224.2
rental 615.6, 630.8
break 801.4
verb cleave 224.4
inhabit 225.7
open 292.11
lease 615.15
rent out 615.16
adj cleft 224.7
impaired 393.27
severed 801.23

rental 615.6, 630.8

rent boy 665.16

rented 615.20

renunciation denial
335.2
recantation 363.3
relinquishment 370.3,
475.1
discontinuance 390.2
surrender 433.2
temperance 668.1
cessation 856.1
apostasy 857.3

reopen 855.6

reopened 855.7

reopening 855.2

reorganization
reproduction 78.1
rearrangement 807.7

repair
noun reparation 396.6
good condition 764.3
verb perfect 392.11
mend 396.14
atone 658.4

repairing 396.6

reparation
compensation 338.1
repair 396.6
recompense 481.2,
624.3
atonement 658.1

repartee witticism
489.7
banter 490.1
conversation 541.1
answer 938.1

repatriate restore
481.4
rehabilitate 857.14

repatriation restitution
481.1
rehabilitation 857.4

repay compensate
338.4

be profitable 472.13
make restitution 481.5
requite 506.5
pay back 624.11

repaying 624.21

repayment
compensation 338.1
reparation 481.2
reimbursement 624.2

repeal
noun revocation 445.1
verb abolish 395.13
revoke 445.2

repealed 445.3

repeat
noun repetend 848.5
encore 848.6, 873.2
verb reproduce 78.7
imitate 336.5
publish 352.10
redo 848.7
recur 848.11, 849.5
duplicate 873.3
memorize 988.17

repeated constant
846.5
reproduced 848.12

repeatedly continuously
811.10
frequently 846.6
often 848.16

repeating 848.14

repeat performance
encore 848.6
repeat 873.2

repel disgust 64.4, 99.6
offend 98.11
reject 372.2
disincline 379.4
repulse 442.5, 907.3
resist 453.2
fend off 460.10
prevent 1011.14

repelled 96.20

repellent offensive
98.18
resistant 453.5
repulsive 907.4
hideous 1014.11

repent
verb think better of
113.7
adj creeping 177.39
reptile 311.46

repentance penitence
113.4
penance 658.3

repentant penitent
113.9
atoning 658.7

repertoire store 386.1
repertory 704.9

repertory store 386.1
storehouse 386.6
repertoire 704.9
list 870.1
summation 1016.11

repetition reproduction
78.1, 848.1
triteness 117.3
tediousness 118.2
imitation 336.1
duplicate 784.3
constancy 846.2
regularity 849.1
continuance 855.1
duplication 873.1

repetitive habitual
373.15
diffuse 538.11
same 780.6
continuous 811.8
repetitious 848.14
continuing 855.7

replace restore 396.11
depose 447.4
substitute for 861.5
dismiss 908.19

replacement
restoration 396.1
deposal 447.2
team 746.2
successor 816.4
sequel 834.2
substitution 861.1
substitute 861.2

replacing 861.12

replant 91.24

replay 848.6

replenish provide
385.7
restore 396.11
complete 793.6

replete full 793.11
plentiful 990.7
overfull 992.20
satiated 993.6

replica reproduction
336.3
same 777.3
duplicate 784.3

replicate copy 784.8
double 872.5
duplicate 873.3

replicated two 872.6
double 873.4

replication heredity
560.6
duplication 873.1
answer 938.1
rebuttal 938.2

reply
noun communication
343.1
retaliation 506.1
letter 553.2
defence 600.2
reaction 902.1
answer 938.1
verb answer 553.11,
938.4
defend 600.10
react 902.5

replying 938.6

report

noun crash 56.1
account 349.3
announcement 352.2
publicity 352.4
bulletin 549.7
information 551.1
rumour 552.6
commentary 556.2
repute 662.1
explosion 671.7
paean 696.3
note 709.14
criticism 945.2
verb present oneself
221.11
communicate 343.7
announce 352.12
inform 551.8
give a report 552.11
accuse 599.7
narrate 719.6, 722.6
pass judgment 945.13

reportage 552.1

reported published
352.17
rumoured 552.15

reportedly publicly
352.19
allegedly 552.16

reporter
noun informant 551.5
newsmonger 552.9
spokesman 576.5
adj journalist 555.4

repose
noun rest 20.1
sleep 22.2
recumbency 201.2
leisure 402.1
moderation 670.1
verb rest 20.6
deposit 159.14
be still 173.7
lie 201.5
trust 952.17

repository storehouse
386.6
friend 588.1
treasury 729.12

repossess 481.6

repossession
dispossession 480.7
recovery 481.3

reprehensible
blameworthy 510.25
wicked 654.16
guilty 656.3
terrible 999.9

represent manifest
348.5
delineate 349.8
describe 349.9
mediate 466.6
act for 576.14
enact 704.30
substitute for 861.5
visualize 985.15

representation
spectacle 33.7

reproduction 336.3
display 348.2
delineation 349.1
description 349.2
representative 349.7
sham 354.3
vote 371.6
sign 517.1
bar 597.4
acting 704.8
picture 712.11
copy 784.1
duplicate 784.3
substitution 861.1
idea 931.1

representational
349.13

Representative 610.3

representative
noun representation
349.7
sign 517.1
deputy 576.1
example 785.2
substitute 861.2
adj representational
349.13
descriptive 349.14
indicative 517.23
deputy 576.15
model 785.8

**representative
government** 612.4

representing
representational
349.13
lawyerly 597.6

repress suppress 106.8,
428.8
blunt 286.2
cover up 345.8
prohibit 444.3
retain 474.5
domineer 612.16
hinder 1011.10

repressed reticent
344.10
suppressed 428.14
forgetful 989.9

repression suppression
92.24, 428.2
veil of secrecy 345.3
prohibition 444.1
retention 474.1
block 989.3
hindrance 1011.1

repressive imperious
417.16
restraining 428.11
prohibitive 444.6
hindering 1011.17

reprieve
noun release 120.2
pity 145.1
pardon 148.2
respite 601.3
delay 845.2
verb release 120.6
have pity 145.4

respite 601.5

reprieved 148.7

reprimand
noun reproof 510.5
stigma 661.6
verb reprove 510.17
stigmatize 661.9

reprint
noun print 548.3,
784.5
edition 554.5
iteration 848.2
verb reproduce 78.7
print 548.14
iterate 848.8

reprisal requital 506.2
revenge 507.1
penalty 603.1

reprise 848.6

reproach
noun reproof 510.5
accusation 599.1
disgrace 661.5
stigma 661.6
verb censure 510.13
accuse 599.7
disgrace 661.8

reproached 599.15

reproduce grow 14.2,
259.7
remake 78.7
copy 777.6, 784.8
repeat 848.7
duplicate 873.3
produce 889.7

reproduced repeated
848.12
double 873.4

reproduction making
78.1
procreation 78.2
growth 259.3
duplication 336.3,
784.2, 873.1
picture 712.11
duplicate 784.3
repetition 848.1
proliferation 889.2

reproductive re-
creative 78.14
procreative 78.15

reproductive organs
2.11

reptile
noun vertebrate 311.3
reptilian 311.25
beast 660.7
adj creeping 177.39
reptilian 311.46

reptilian
noun reptile 311.25
adj reptile 311.46
base 661.12

republic country 232.1
central government
612.4

republican 612.17

Republican Guard
461.14

republicanism 612.8

repudiate deny 335.4
recant 363.8
reject 372.2
refuse 442.3
not pay 625.6
exclude 772.4

repudiated 372.3

repudiation dissent
333.1
denial 335.2
recantation 363.3
rejection 372.1
refusal 442.1
nonpayment 625.1
exclusion 772.1

repugnant offensive
98.18
negative 335.5
oppositional 451.8
hostile 589.10
contrary 778.6
disagreeing 788.6
hideous 1014.11

repulsed 372.3

repulsive malodorous
71.5
filthy 80.23
offensive 98.18
repellent 907.4
terrible 999.9
hideous 1014.11

reputable honest
644.13
highly reputed 662.15
influential 893.13
notable 996.19

reputation repute
662.1
notability 996.2

repute
noun reputation 662.1
custom 731.6
influence 893.1
notability 996.2
verb suppose 950.10

reputed 950.14

reputedly 950.17

request
noun proposal 439.2
asking 440.1
verb ask 440.9

requiem dirge 115.6
last offices 309.4
sacred music 708.17

require prescribe 420.9
demand 421.5
oblige 424.5
charge 630.12
obligate 641.12
entail 771.4
determine 885.12
need 962.9
want 991.7

required mandatory
420.12

respective
proportionate 477.13
mutual 776.11
particular 864.12

respectively
proportionately 477.14
mutually 776.13
each 864.19

respects 155.3, 504.8

respiration 2.19

respirator 91.19

respiratory 2.30

respite
noun recess 20.2
release 120.2
reprieve 601.3
interim 825.1
delay 845.2
pause 856.3
verb reprieve 601.5

resplendent illustrious
662.19
gorgeous 1015.20
bright 1024.32

respond sense 24.6
react 93.11, 902.5
defend 600.10
interchange 862.4
answer 938.4

respondent
noun accused 599.6
answerer 938.3
adj reactive 902.9
answering 938.6

responding reactive
902.9
answering 938.6

respond to respond
93.11
treat 321.6
get along 455.2
reciprocate 776.7

response sensation 24.1
feeling 93.1
sympathy 93.5
communication 343.1
meaning 518.1
defence 600.2
paean 696.3
responsory report
708.23
passage 708.24
impact 886.2
reaction 902.1
answer 938.1

responsibility
supervision 573.2
commission 615.1
incumbency 641.2
trustworthiness 644.6
attribution 887.1
operation 888.1
liability 896.1

responsible chargeable
623.9
answerable 641.17
trustworthy 644.19
liable 896.5

responsible for 641.17

responsibly
trustworthily 644.24
faithfully 644.25

responsive sensitive
24.12, 93.20
willing 324.5
communicational
343.9
influenceable 893.15
reactive 902.9
answering 938.6
pliant 1045.9
elastic 1046.7

responsiveness
sensitivity 24.3
sympathy 93.5
willingness 324.1
influenceability 893.5
pliancy 1045.2
elasticity 1046.1

rest
noun repose 20.1
respite 20.2
silence 51.1
step 193.5
remainder 256.1
death 307.1
leisure 402.1
pause 709.21, 856.3
table 752.2
supporter 900.2
fulcrum 905.3
verb repose 20.6
deposit 159.14
be still 173.7
ride at anchor 182.16
remain 256.5
do nothing 329.2
plead 598.20
calm 670.7
pause 856.9
depend 958.6

rest assured hope
124.7
be confident 952.14
be certain 969.9

restatement translation
341.3
iteration 848.2

restaurant eating place
8.17
dining room 197.11
workplace 739.1

restful vacational 20.10
comfortable 121.11
quiescent 173.12
pacific 464.9
tranquillizing 670.15

rest in exist in 760.11
believe in 952.15

resting 173.12

resting place tomb
309.16
end 819.1
supporter 900.2

rest in peace 309.24

restitution
compensation 338.1

restoration 396.1,
481.1
reimbursement 624.2
recompense 624.3
atonement 658.1
reversion 858.1

restive restless 105.27
discontented 108.7
impatient 135.6
reluctant 325.6
defiant 327.10
obstinate 361.8
ungovernable 361.12

restless wakeful 23.7
restive 105.27
discontented 108.7
impatient 135.6
bustling 330.20
inconstant 853.7
agitated 916.16

restlessly impatiently
135.8
agitatedly 916.22

restlessness
wakefulness 23.1
trepidation 105.5
discontent 108.1
impatience 135.1
motion 172.1
bustle 330.4
inconstancy 853.2
agitation 916.1

rest on 900.22

restoration
vitaminization 7.12
reproduction 78.1
improvement 392.1
restitution 396.1,
481.1
recovery 481.3
justification 600.1
rehabilitation 857.4
reversion 858.1

restorative
noun energizer 17.6
remedy 86.1
tonic 86.8
adj reproductive 78.14
remedial 86.39
tonic 86.44, 396.22
restitutive 481.7

restore vitaminize 7.18
reproduce 78.7
put back 396.11
aid 449.11
return 481.4
recover 481.6
justify 600.9
rehabilitate 857.14

restored refreshed 9.4
reminiscent 836.8

restorer 396.10

restoring 481.1

restrain limit 210.5
compel 424.4
constrain 428.7
bind 428.10
confine 429.12
simplify 499.5

moderate 670.6
qualify 958.3
hinder 1011.10

restrained reserved
139.11
enclosed 212.10
reticent 344.10
constrained 428.13,
670.11
tasteful 496.8
elegant 533.6
temperate 668.9

restraining compulsory
424.10
constraining 428.11

restraint suppression
92.24
equanimity 106.3
reserve 139.3
limitation 210.2
self-control 359.5
compulsion 424.1
constraint 428.1
shackle 428.4
confinement 429.1
subjection 432.1
restrainedness 496.4
elegance 533.1
plain speech 535.1
temperance 668.1
moderation 670.1
hindrance 1011.1

restraints 428.4

restrict limit 210.5,
428.9
narrow 270.11
confine 429.12
allot 477.9
specialize 865.4
qualify 958.3

restricted limited
210.7, 428.15
out of bounds 210.8
narrow 270.14
secret 345.11
confined 429.19
specialized 865.5
qualified 958.10

restricting
noun limitation 210.2
adj limiting 210.9
restrictive 428.12
qualifying 958.7

restriction limitation
210.2, 428.3
narrowness 270.1
confinement 429.1
exclusion 772.1
qualification 958.1
hindrance 1011.1

restrictive limiting
210.9
limitative 428.12
exclusive 772.9
qualifying 958.7
hindering 1011.17

restructure reproduce
78.7
rearrange 807.13

change 851.7

restructuring
reproduction 78.1
reconstruction 396.5
rearrangement 807.7
change 851.1

rest with be one's
responsibility 641.7
depend 958.6

result
noun event 830.1
effect 886.1
product 892.1
solution 939.1
verb turn out 830.7
ensue 886.4

resultant
noun effect 886.1
adj happening 830.9
resulting 886.6

result from 886.5

resulting 886.6

resulting from coming
from 886.8
because 887.10

resume recover 481.6
iterate 848.8
repeat 848.11
recommence 855.6

resumed 855.7

resumption recovery
481.3
repetition 848.1
recommencement
855.2

resurface floor 295.22
repeat 848.11
recur 849.5, 988.15

resurgence 396.3

resurgent reproductive
78.14
renascent 396.24

resurrect reproduce
78.7
revive 396.16

resurrected 396.24

resurrection
reproduction 78.1
revival 396.3
apotheosis 681.11

resuscitate stimulate
105.13
come to life 306.8
revive 396.16
aid 449.11
resume 855.6

resuscitation revival
396.3
resumption 855.2

retail
noun sale 734.1
verb publish 352.10
deal in 731.15
sell 734.8
disperse 770.4
iterate 848.8
adj commercial 731.21

sales 734.13

retailer provider 385.6
merchant 730.2

retailing
noun provision 385.1
trade 731.2
selling 734.2
adj sales 734.13

Retail Price Index
626.3

retain reserve 386.12
keep 474.5
employ 615.14
stabilize 854.7
sustain 855.4
keep in memory
988.13

retained reserved
386.15
remembered 988.23

retainer hanger-on
138.6
dependent 577.1
fee 624.5

retaining 615.4

retake
noun recovery 481.3
cinematography 706.4
shot 714.8
verb recover 481.6

retaliate compensate
338.4
retort 506.4
revenge 507.4
interchange 862.4

retaliation
compensation 338.1
reciprocation 506.1
revenge 507.1
penalty 603.1
deserts 639.3
interchange 862.1

retaliatory
compensating 338.6
retaliative 506.8
revengeful 507.7
interchangeable 862.5

retard slow 175.9
restrain 428.7
delay 845.8
hinder 1011.10

retardation slowing
175.4
restraint 428.1
mental deficiency
921.9
hindrance 1011.1

retarded slowed-down
175.12
restrained 428.13
late 845.16
mentally deficient
921.22

retching 908.8

retelling fiction 722.1
narration 722.2
iteration 848.2

retention refusal 442.1

retainment 474.1
tenacity 802.3
retentiveness 988.3

retentive keeping 474.8
adhesive 802.12
recollective 988.22

rethink reconsider
930.15
re-examine 937.27

rethinking mature
thought 930.5
re-examination 937.7

reticent reserved
344.10
alone 871.8

retina 2.9

retinue staff 577.11
attendance 768.6

retire go to bed 22.17
efface oneself 139.7
retreat 163.6
recede 168.2
quit 188.9
sink 284.12
keep to oneself 344.6,
583.4
scrap 390.8
depose 447.4
resign 448.2
seclude oneself 584.7
pay in full 624.13
dismiss 908.19

retired private 345.13
disused 390.10
leisure 402.5
in retirement 448.3
secluded 584.8
not out 747.5

retirement retreat
163.2
recession 168.1
departure 188.1
privacy 345.2
disuse 390.1
leisure 402.1
deposal 447.2
resignation 448.1
seclusion 584.1
payment 624.1
dismissal 908.5

retiring reserved
139.11
receding 168.5
concave 284.16
reticent 344.10

retort
noun witticism 489.7
retaliation 506.1
recrimination 599.3
philosopher's stone
857.10
countermeasure 899.5
answer 938.1
vaporizer 1065.6
verb retaliate 506.4
answer 938.4

retrace re-examine
937.27
remember 988.10

retract withdraw 168.3
deny 335.4
recant 363.8
repeal 445.2
relinquish 475.3

retractable 168.6

retracted 475.5

retraction recession
168.1
reduction 255.2
denial 335.2
recantation 363.3
repeal 445.1
relinquishment 475.1

retreat
noun reculade 163.2
recession 168.1
departure 188.1
sanctum 197.8
summerhouse 228.12
decline 252.2
evening 315.2
hiding place 346.4
surrender 433.2
seclusion 584.1
hideaway 584.6
recoil 902.3
asylum 1008.4
recess 1008.5
verb recede 168.2
quit 188.9
incline 204.10
sink 284.12
hesitate 362.7

retreating receding
168.5
concave 284.16

retrenchment
curtailment 252.4
reduction 255.2
shortening 268.3
restraint 428.1
economizing 635.2

retrial 598.6

retribution reparation
481.2
reprisal 506.2
punishment 604.1
recompense 624.3

retrieval reclamation
396.2
rescue 398.1
recovery 481.3
access 1041.8

retrieve
noun recovery 481.3
verb fetch 176.16
redeem 396.12
rescue 398.3
recover 481.6

retro improvement
392.1
revival 396.3
recovery 481.3
change 851.1

retrograde
verb regress 163.5
deteriorate 393.16
revert 858.4

adj regressive 163.11
rear 217.9
deteriorating 393.45
reversionary 858.7

retrospect
noun remembering
988.4
verb remember 988.10

retrospective
noun display 348.2
adj reminiscent 836.8
back 836.12
recollective 988.22

retrospectively 836.15

return
noun regression 163.1
homecoming 186.3
relapse 394.1
recovery 396.8
gain 472.3
restitution 481.1
retaliation 506.1
reimbursement 624.2
recompense 624.3
dividend 738.7
game 749.2
repetition 848.1
periodicity 849.2
reversion 858.1
production 892.2
reaction 902.1
answer 938.1
signal 1035.11
verb reverberate 54.7
regress 163.5
turn back 163.8
restore 396.11, 481.4
yield 627.4
play tennis 749.3
repeat 848.11
recur 849.5
revert 858.4
interchange 862.4
answer 938.4
reflect 1035.16

returning
noun reversion 858.1
adj recurrent 848.13
answering 938.6

returns gain 472.3
report 549.7
election returns
609.21
receipts 627.1
roll 870.6

return to revisit 221.9
relapse 394.4
resume 855.6
revert to 858.6

reunion reconciliation
465.3
social gathering
582.10

reunite 465.8

re-up 824.5

Reuters 555.3

rev accelerate 174.10
drive 756.4

revaluation
monetization 728.23
mature thought 930.5
re-examination 937.7

revamp revise 392.12
renovate 396.17
change 851.7

reveal unclose 292.12
manifest 348.5
disclose 351.4
divulge 351.5
signify 517.17
unfold 860.7
uncover 940.4

revealed visible 31.6
open 348.10
disclosed 351.9
scriptural 683.10

revealing
noun disclosure 351.1
adj disclosive 351.10
transparent 1028.4

revel
noun treat 95.3
celebration 487.1
lark 743.6
verb go on a spree
88.28
rejoice 116.5
make merry 743.24

Revelation 683.4

revelation visibility
31.1
appearance 33.1
surprise 131.2
manifestation 348.1
disclosure 351.1
divine revelation 683.9
unfolding 860.2
intuition 933.1
discovery 940.1

revelatory manifesting
348.9
disclosive 351.10

revel in 95.12

revelling 743.3

revelry treat 95.3
conviviality 582.3
festivity 743.3

revels 743.3

revenge
noun compensation
338.1
reprisal 506.2
vengeance 507.1
verb avenge 507.4

revenue 627.1

reverb 54.6

reverberate resound
54.7
repeat 848.11
answer 938.4

reverberating resonant
54.9
reverberant 54.11

revere cherish 104.21
respect 155.4

oversweet 66.5
ornate 498.12
wealthy 618.14
precious 632.10
expensive 632.11
melodious 708.48
productive 889.9
interesting 982.19
plentiful 990.7
oily 1054.9

riches 618.1

richly intensely 247.20
expensively 632.15
plentifully 990.9

rich man 611.20

richness colourfulness
35.4
resonance 54.1
humorousness 488.1
ornateness 498.2
wealth 618.1
expensiveness 632.1
productiveness 889.1
plenty 990.2
oiliness 1054.5

rich soil 889.6

rick
noun store 386.1
storehouse 386.6
pile 769.10
verb pile 769.19

rickety unsteady 16.16
anaemic 85.60
deformed 265.12
stricken in years
303.18
loose 803.5

ricochet
noun recoil 902.2
verb recoil 902.6

rid 430.31

riddle
noun refinery 79.13
network 170.3
porousness 292.8
conundrum 522.9
arranger 807.5
unknown 929.7
bewilderment 970.3
verb perforate 292.15
strike dead 308.17
mark 517.19
be incomprehensible
522.10
segregate 772.6
classify 807.11
shoot 903.12
solve 939.2

riddled 292.19

ride
noun drive 177.7
merry-go-round
743.15
verb go on horseback
177.34
ride at anchor 182.16
weather the storm
182.40
float 182.54

kid 490.6
ridicule 508.8
rest on 900.22

ride out weather the
storm 182.40
race 757.5
be safe 1006.2

rider equestrian 178.8
postscript 254.2
hunter 311.13
judgment 598.10
bill 613.8
jockey 757.2

ridge
noun summit 198.2
head 198.6
back 217.3
ridgeline 237.5
plateau 272.4
bulge 283.3
wrinkle 291.3
verb emboss 283.12
wrinkle 291.6

ridged 291.8

ridgeway 383.2

ridicule
noun impudence 142.2
disrespect 156.1
contempt 157.1
banter 490.1
derision 508.1
deprecation 510.2
verb have the audacity
142.7
disrespect 156.4
disdain 157.3
joke 489.13
deride 508.8
deprecate 510.12

ridiculing disrespectful
156.7
derisive 508.12
condemnatory 510.22
disparaging 512.13

ridiculous humorous
488.4
absurd 922.11
unbelievable 954.10
impossible 966.7

ridiculously
humorously 488.7
foolishly 922.13

riding driving 177.6
state 231.5

riding horse 311.13

rid of 430.31

rife reported 552.15
prevalent 863.12
teeming 883.9
plentiful 990.7

riff rapids 238.10
impromptu 708.27

rifle
noun infantryman
461.9
gun 462.10
verb furrow 290.3
plunder 482.17

ransack 937.33

rifled 290.4

rifleman infantryman
461.9
shooter 903.8

rift
noun crack 224.2
valley 237.7
falling-out 456.4
break 801.4
fault 1002.2
blemish 1003.1
verb open 292.11
belch 908.28
adj cleft 224.7

rig
noun suit 5.6
equipage 179.5
lorry 179.12
rigging 180.12
equipment 385.4
caesar 575.9
verb outfit 5.40
tamper with 354.17
plot 381.9
equip 385.8
fix 964.5

rigged decked 180.17
tampered with 354.30
provided 385.13
fixed 964.8

rigging rig 180.12
cordage 271.3
intrigue 381.5
equipment 385.4
manipulation 737.20
supporter 900.2

right
noun right side 219.1
authority 417.1
rights 430.2
estate 471.4
warrant 600.6
conservative 611.13
rightfulness 637.1
due 639.2
prerogative 642.1
justice 649.1
option 737.21
accuracy 972.5
verb remedy 396.13
harmonize 787.7
arrange 807.8
adj right-hand 219.4
straight 277.6
decorous 496.10
conventional 579.5
rightful 637.3
honest 644.13
just 649.8
orthodox 687.7
apt 787.10
sane 924.4
accurate 972.16
expedient 994.5
adv directly 161.23
rightward 219.7
rightly 637.4
absolutely 793.15
exactly 972.21

excellently 998.22
phrase right! 972.24
exclam yes 332.18

right-about 163.3,
363.1

right along 846.7

right amount 990.1

right and left
extensively 158.11
all round 209.13
laterally 218.8

right and proper right
637.3
just 649.8

right angle 200.2

right-angle
perpendicular 200.12
right-angled 278.7

right away at once
829.8
promptly 844.15

right back 745.2

righteous
noun believing 692.5
adj right 637.3
honest 644.13
virtuous 653.6
godly 692.9

righteousness propriety
637.2
probity 644.1
virtue 653.1
godliness 692.2

rightful right 637.3
condign 639.8
just 649.8
legal 673.10
genuine 972.15

rightfully rightly 637.4
duly 639.11
justly 649.11

right-hand 219.4

right-handed 219.5

right-hand man
subordinate 432.5
employee 577.3

Right Honourable
648.8

rightist 611.13, 852.4

rightly rightfully 637.4
justly 649.11
accurately 972.20
expediently 994.8

right mind 924.1

right moment 842.5

rightness dextrality
219.2
decorousness 496.3
right 637.1
propriety 637.2
justice 649.1
orthodoxy 687.1
timeliness 842.1
accuracy 972.5

right now at once
829.8

now 840.16

right-of-centre right
219.4
conservative 611.25

right off at once 829.8
promptly 844.15

right-of-way
superiority 249.1
road 383.5

right on 787.13

right-on 927.15

right people society
578.6
favour 893.2

Right Reverend 648.8

rights 430.2

right side 219.1

rights issue 738.6

rights of man 642.3

right sort 659.1

right thing 653.1

right things 579.2

right to vote vote
371.6
suffrage 609.17

right wing right side
219.1
conservative 611.13

right-wing right 219.4
conservative 611.25,
852.8

right-winger right side
219.1
conservative 611.13,
852.4

right with 787.12

rigid firm 15.18, 425.7
meticulous 339.12
unyielding 361.1
stiff 580.9, 1044.11
permanent 852.7
immovable 854.15
exact 972.17

rigidity firmness 359.2,
425.2
unyieldingness 361.2
immobility 854.3
accuracy 972.5
rigidness 1044.2

rigidly unyieldingly
361.15
firmly 425.9
stiffly 580.12
permanently 852.9
exactly 972.21

rigorous acrimonious
17.14
meticulous 339.12
unyielding 361.9
firm 425.7
ascetic 667.4
violent 671.16
exact 972.17
adverse 1010.13
difficult 1012.17
cold 1022.14

rigorously meticulously
339.16
  unyieldingly 361.15
  firmly 425.9
  violently 671.25
  truly 972.18
  exactly 972.21

rigour acrimony 17.5
  meticulousness 339.3
  firmness 425.2
  asceticism 667.1
  violence 671.1
  accuracy 972.5
  adversity 1010.1
  difficulty 1012.1

rim
  noun border 211.4
  slope 237.2
  felly 280.4
  verb border 211.10

rind exterior 206.2
  shallowness 276.1
  skin 295.3
  lamina 296.2

ring
  noun ringing 54.3
  circle 280.2
  band 280.3
  bulge 283.3
  boxing 457.9, 754.1
  arena 463.1
  jewel 498.6
  clique 617.6
  insignia 647.1
  tiara 647.4
  halo 1024.14
  atomic cluster 1037.7
  verb din 53.7
  tintinnabulate 54.8
  encircle 209.7
  telephone 347.18

ringed 209.11

ringer impostor 357.6
  substitute 861.2

ring in telephone
347.18
  inaugurate 817.11
  punch the clock
831.12
  substitute 861.4

ringing
  noun tintinnabulation
54.3
  adj loud 53.11
  pealing 54.12

ringleader instigator
375.11
  leader 574.6
  boss 610.7

ring out 831.12

rings 725.7

ring the changes
  diversify 782.2
  change 851.7, 853.5

ring up 347.18

rink playground 743.11
  ice hockey 750.4

rinse

noun dye 3.16
  washing 79.5
  cleanser 79.17
  verb wash 79.19
  soak 1063.13

rinsing washing 79.5
  wetting 1063.6

riot
  noun revolt 327.4
  free-for-all 457.5
  joke 489.6
  unruliness 671.3
  commotion 809.4
  plenty 990.2
  verb vegetate 310.31
  revolt 327.7
  contend 457.13
  rage 671.11
  roister 809.10

riot in 95.12

rioting 671.3

riotous luxuriant
310.40
  rebellious 327.11
  unrestrained 430.24
  licentious 669.8
  unruly 671.19
  plentiful 990.7
  superabundant 992.19

riot police 1007.17

RIP 309.24

rip
  noun trauma 85.37
  binge 88.6
  put-down 156.3
  tide 238.13
  libertine 665.10
  break 801.4
  verb torture 96.18
  barrel 174.9
  open 292.11
  injure 393.13
  wrest 480.22

ripe mature 303.13,
407.13
  prepared 405.16
  experienced 413.28
  marriageable 563.20
  complete 793.9
  timely 842.9
  perfected 1001.9

ripen fester 12.15
  grow 14.2, 259.7
  mature 303.9, 407.8
  develop 392.10
  evolve 860.5
  perfect 1001.5

ripened mature 303.13
  experienced 413.28
  perfected 1001.9

ripeness
  noun preparedness
405.4
  marriageability 563.2
  timeliness 842.1
  adj completion 407.2

ripening
  noun maturation 303.6
  development 392.2

evolution 860.1
  adj immature 301.10

rip off 632.7

rip-off fake 354.13
  hoax 356.7
  overcharge 632.5

riposte
  noun witticism 489.7
  defence 600.2
  answer 938.1
  verb defend 600.10
  react 902.5
  answer 938.4

ripped high 87.23
  fuddled 88.33
  tortured 96.25

ripping
  noun extortion 192.6
  severance 801.2
  adj great 998.13

ripple
  noun splash 52.5
  rapids 238.10
  wave 238.14
  rough 288.2
  wrinkle 291.3
  verb babble 52.11
  wrinkle 291.6
  agitate 916.10

rippled 291.8

rippling 52.19

rise
  noun appearance 33.1
  ascent 193.1
  rising 200.5
  acclivity 204.6
  slope 237.2
  hill 237.4
  wave 238.14
  height 272.2
  improvement 392.1
  promotion 446.1
  evolution 860.1
  source 885.5
  reaction 902.1
  verb get up 23.6
  appear 33.8
  din 53.7
  move 172.5
  ascend 193.8
  arise 200.8
  incline 204.10
  billow 238.22
  grow 251.6
  tower 272.10
  levitate 298.9
  revolt 327.7
  make good 409.10
  originate 817.13

rise above accept 134.7
  loom 247.5
  defeat 411.5

rise again 306.8

rise and fall 238.22

riser 193.5

rise up ascend 193.8
  rise 200.8
  revolt 327.7

risible merry 109.15
  humorous 488.4

rising
  noun appearance 33.1
  sore 85.36
  course 172.2
  ascent 193.1
  uprising 200.5
  acclivity 204.6
  swelling 283.4
  revolt 327.4
  adj flowing 172.8
  ascending 193.14
  uphill 204.17
  increasing 251.8

rising prices 630.4

risk
  noun investment 729.3
  gamble 759.2
  unreliability 970.6
  chance 971.1
  danger 1005.1
  verb invest 729.16
  chance 759.24
  take a chance 971.12
  endanger 1005.6
  take chances 1005.7

risking 759.1

risk-taking defiance
454.1
  daring 492.5
  chance 971.1

risky risqué 666.7
  speculative 759.27
  unreliable 970.20
  chance 971.15
  hazardous 1005.10

rite celebration 487.1
  ceremony 580.4
  ritual 701.3

rite of passage 580.4

rites 504.7

Ritter 608.5

ritual
  noun custom 373.1
  formality 580.1
  ceremony 580.4
  rite 701.3
  adj ceremonious 580.8
  ritualistic 701.18

ritualistic ceremonious
580.8
  ritual 701.18

ritually 580.11

rituals 504.7

ritzy 578.13

rival
  noun competitor 452.2
  combatant 461.1
  verb contend against
451.4
  compete 457.18
  equal 789.5
  be comparable 942.7
  excel 998.11
  adj oppositional 451.8
  competitive 457.23

rivalling superior
249.12
  competitive 457.23

rivalry envy 154.1
  hostility 451.2
  competition 457.2

rive cleave 224.4
  open 292.11
  sever 801.11

riven severed 801.23
  halved 874.6

river stream 238.1
  torrent 238.5

riverside
  noun shore 234.2
  adj coastal 234.7

riveted fixed 854.14
  gripped 982.18

riveting alluring 377.8
  engrossing 982.20

riviera 234.2

RNA 560.6

roach joint 87.11
  cigarette 89.5
  remainder 256.1
  vermin 311.35

road seaway 182.10
  route 383.1
  highway 383.5
  harbour 1008.6

roadblock 1011.5

roadhouse restaurant
8.17
  inn 228.15
  entertainment 743.13

road racing 744.1

roads 1008.6

roadster 311.13

road test 941.3

road-test 941.8

roadway 383.5

roam
  noun wandering 177.3
  verb wander 177.23

roaming
  noun wandering 177.3
  adj wandering 177.37

roan
  noun appaloosa 311.11
  adj reddish-brown
40.4

roar
  noun noise 53.3
  boom 56.4
  cry 59.1
  verb be noisy 53.9
  boom 56.9
  cry 59.6, 60.2
  laugh 116.8
  sigh 318.21
  murmur 524.26
  rage 671.11
  overact 704.31

roaring thundering
56.12
  frenzied 105.25

roast
 noun dish 10.7
 meat 10.12
 celebration 487.1
 verb cook 11.4
 bad-mouth 156.6
 kid 490.6
 ridicule 508.8
 attack 510.20
 grill 937.22
 burn 1018.22
 adj cooked 11.6

roast beef 10.13

roasted 11.6

roasting
 noun cooking 11.1
 kidding 490.3
 adj hot 1018.25

rob
 noun semiliquid
  1060.5
 verb commit robbery
  482.14

robbed of 473.8

robber thief 483.1
 holdup man 483.5

robbery loss 473.1
 theft 482.3

robbing 482.3

robe
 noun garment 5.3
 blanket 295.10
 frock 702.2
 verb clothe 5.38

robed 5.44

robes clothing 5.1
 canonicals 702.1

Robin Hood
 philanthropist 143.8
 Barabbas 483.11

robot 1040.12

robotic 780.5

robust strong 15.15
 energetic 17.13
 hale 83.12

robustly 15.23

rock
 noun horse 15.8
 missile 462.18
 rock-and-roll 708.10
 Rock of Gibraltar
  854.6
 swing 915.6
 flounder 916.8
 protector 1007.5
 stone 1044.6, 1057.1
 verb impress 93.15
 agitate 105.14
 pitch 182.55
 calm 670.7
 oscillate 915.10
 flounder 916.15
 adj instrumental
  708.51
 stone 1057.10

rock-and-roll 708.10

rock bottom bottom
  199.1
 foundation 900.6

rock-bottom bottom
  199.7
 deepest 275.15
 reduced 633.9

Rockefeller 618.8

rocker refinery 79.13
 engraving tool 713.8
 oscillator 915.9

rocket
 noun lightning 174.6
 rocket plane 181.4
 skyrocket 193.7
 missile 462.18, 1072.3
 signal 517.15
 spacecraft 1073.2
 verb shoot up 193.9
 skyrocket 1072.12

rocket-propelled flying
  184.50
 jet-propelled 903.16

rock-hard unyielding
  361.9
 hard 1044.10

rocking tranquillizing
  670.15
 swinging 915.17

rocking chair 915.9

rocking horse 743.16

rock music 708.10

rock'n'roll 708.10

rocks 1005.5

rock-steady 129.2

rocky unsteady 16.16
 tired 21.7
 rugged 288.7
 unsafe 1005.11
 hard 1044.10
 stony 1057.11

rococo
 noun ornateness 498.2
 adj ornate 498.12
 freakish 869.13
 fanciful 985.20

rod shaft 273.1
 sceptre 417.9
 stick 605.2
 regalia 647.3

rodent
 noun vertebrate 311.3
 adj rodential 311.43

rodeo 769.1

rods 1037.13

roe fish 10.23
 hen 77.9
 egg 305.15
 deer 311.5

roebuck 311.5

Roger 332.19

rogue nag 311.12
 mischief-maker 322.3
 rascal 660.3
 jockey 757.2

Roland 492.8

role function 387.5,
  724.3
 part 704.10
 script 706.2
 mode 764.4

role model paragon
  659.4
 ideal 785.4

roll
 noun bun 10.30
 staccato 55.1
 boom 56.4
 gait 177.12
 barrel roll 184.14
 wave 238.14
 length 267.2
 coil 281.2
 cylinder 282.4
 record 549.1
 document 549.5
 film 714.10
 throw 759.9
 bundle 769.8
 roster 870.6
 rotation 914.1
 swing 915.6
 flounder 916.8
 verb reverberate 54.7
 drum 55.4
 boom 56.9
 warble 60.5
 progress 162.2
 travel 177.18
 stroll 177.28
 pitch 182.55
 stunt 184.40
 level 201.6
 billow 238.22
 ball 282.7
 smooth 287.5
 press 287.6
 push 903.9
 trundle 914.10
 wallow 914.13
 oscillate 915.10
 flounder 916.15
 go easily 1013.10

roll back reduce 252.7
 retrench 635.5

roll call introduction
  613.5
 roll 870.6

rolled 201.7

rolled into one 871.10

roller wave 238.14,
  915.4
 curler 281.3
 cylinder 282.4
 smoother 287.4
 rotator 914.4
 pulverizer 1049.7

roller coaster 743.15

rollicking gay 109.14
 blustering 503.4
 boisterous 671.20

roll in arrive 186.6
 indulge 669.4

rolling

role function 387.5,

noun progression
  162.1
 throwing 903.2
 rotation 914.1
 picture 1034.5
 adj resonant 54.9
 thundering 56.12
 hilly 237.8, 272.18
 wavy 281.10
 rotating 914.14
 swinging 915.17

rolling pin 282.4

rolling stock 179.14

rolling stone wanderer
  178.2
 Proteus 853.4
 rotator 914.4

roll on march on 162.3
 travel 177.18

roll out manifest 348.5
 inaugurate 817.11

roll-out 817.1

roll over 729.16

rolls 549.1

Rolls-Royce 249.4

roll up bundle 769.20
 roll 914.10

roll-up 89.5

Roman 675.29

roman type 548.6
 story 722.3

Roman Catholic
 noun Catholic 675.19
 adj Catholic 675.29

**Roman Catholic
 Church** 675.8

Roman Catholicism
  675.8

romance
 noun love affair 104.6
 fabrication 354.10
 figment of the
  imagination 985.5
 idealism 985.7
 verb narrate 722.6
 idealize 985.16

romantic
 noun visionary 985.13
 adj sentimental 93.21
 loving 104.27
 fictional 722.7
 visionary 985.24

romanticism
 sentimentality 93.8
 amorousness 104.3
 idealism 985.7

romantic love 104.3

Romany 178.4

Rome 675.8

Romeo 104.13

Romeo and Juliet
  104.18

romp
 noun amazon 76.9
 schoolgirl 302.8
 frolic 743.5

 horse race 757.3
 verb exude
  cheerfulness 109.6
 rejoice 116.5
 caper 366.6
 play 743.23

rood 170.4

roof
 noun top 198.1
 abode 228.1
 home 228.2
 house 228.5
 roofing 295.6
 verb top 295.21

roofed 295.31

roofing roof 295.6
 sticks and stones
  1052.2

rooftop top 198.1
 roof 295.6

rook 356.19

rookie recruit 461.17
 novice 572.9
 newcomer 773.4
 beginner 817.2

room
 noun latitude 158.3,
  430.4
 chamber 197.1
 interval 224.1
 quarters 228.4
 capacity 257.2
 opportunity 842.2
 verb inhabit 225.7
 house 225.10

roommate 588.3

rooms quarters 228.4
 flat 228.13

room temperature
  1018.3

room-temperature
  1018.24

roomy comfortable
  121.11
 spacious 158.10
 broad 269.6
 airy 317.11

roost
 noun quarters 228.4
 birdhouse 228.23
 verb settle 159.17
 sit 173.10

rooster cock 76.8
 poultry 311.29

root
 noun radix 310.20
 etymon 526.2
 morphology 526.3
 source 885.5
 foundation 900.6
 verb vegetate 310.31
 fix 854.9
 take root 854.10
 search 937.31

root and branch
  793.17

rooted confirmed
373.19
innate 766.8
traditional 841.12
established 854.13

root in 199.6

rootless 871.8

root out excise 255.10
search out 937.34

roots 708.11

rootstock 310.20

rope
noun cord 271.2
latitude 430.4
scaffold 605.5
verb bind 428.10,
799.9
catch 480.17

rosary 696.4

rose
noun pinkness 41.2
nozzle 239.9
insignia 647.1
heraldic device 647.2
sprinkler 1063.8
adj pink 41.8

Rosinante nag 311.12
Al Borak 311.15

roster record 549.1
roll 870.6
schedule 964.3

rostrum prow 216.3
nose 283.8
pulpit 703.13
platform 900.13

rosy pink 41.8
red-complexioned
41.9
fresh 83.13
cheerful 109.11
optimistic 124.12
thriving 1009.13

rot
noun filth 80.7
anthrax 85.40
rottenness 393.7
bullshit 520.3
blight 1000.2
verb decay 393.22

Rota 595.3

rota record 549.1
roll 870.6
schedule 964.3

rotary flowing 172.8
circuitous 913.7
rotational 914.15

rotate move 172.5
take off 184.38
invert 205.5
recur 849.5
revolve 914.9

rotating 914.14

rotation takeoff 184.8
series 811.2
sequence 814.1
round 849.3
revolution 914.1

rote 988.4

Rothschild 618.8

rotor propeller 903.6
rotator 914.4

rotten unsound 16.15
nasty 64.7
malodorous 71.5
filthy 80.23
horrid 98.19
decayed 393.40
dishonest 645.16
corrupt 654.14

rotting putrefactive
393.39
decayed 393.40

rotund corpulent
257.18
round 282.8
convex 283.13

rouge
noun redness 41.1
makeup 1015.12
verb redden 41.4

rough
noun broken ground
288.2
diagram 381.3
undevelopment 406.4
combatant 461.1
vulgarian 497.6
ruffian 593.3
golf 748.1
verb roughen 288.4
mistreat 389.5
adj acrimonious 17.14
raucous 58.15
bitter 64.6
pungent 68.6
harsh 144.24
flowing 238.24
unsmooth 288.6
coarse 294.6, 497.11
undeveloped 406.12
gruff 505.7
violent 671.16
boisterous 671.20
nonuniform 781.3
irregular 850.3
jolting 916.20
disastrous 1010.15
adv roughly 288.11

rough-and-ready
unprepared 406.8
unrefined 497.12

rough-and-tumble
noun commotion 809.4
adj boisterous 671.20

rough edges 408.1

rough-hewn 288.6

rough in 381.11

roughly harshly 144.33
approximately 223.23
rough 288.11
vulgarly 497.16
irregularly 850.4
generally 863.17

roughneck
noun vulgarian 497.6

tough 593.4
adj boorish 497.13

roughness acrimony
17.5
raucousness 58.2
pungency 68.1
harshness 144.9
airspace 184.32
unsmoothness 288.1
irregularity 294.2,
850.1
undevelopment 406.4
coarseness 497.2
gruffness 505.3
inelegance 534.1
violence 671.1

roulade
noun ornament 709.18
verb sing 708.38

roulette 759.12

round
noun drink 88.7
tedium 118.1
step 193.5
sphere 231.2
degree 245.1
circle 280.2
canon 280.9
routine 373.6
route 383.1
rondo 708.19
field 724.4
match 748.3
fight 754.3
series 811.2
turn 824.2
revolution 849.3
circuit 913.2
whirl 914.2
verb curve 279.6
circle 280.10, 913.5
round out 282.6
turn 913.6
rotate 914.9
number 1016.16
adj circular 280.11
rotund 282.8
elegant 533.6
candid 644.17
full 793.11
circuitous 913.7
adv around 209.12,
914.16

round about
adv in every direction
161.25
around 209.12
circuitously 913.9
round 914.16
prep over 159.28
through 161.27

roundabout
noun crossing 170.2
merry-go-round
743.15
detour 913.3
rotator 914.4
adj exterior 206.7
environing 209.8
convolutional 281.6

circumlocutory 538.14
complex 798.4
circuitous 913.7

round and round
windingly 281.11
alternately 849.11
changeably 853.8
round 914.16
to and fro 915.21

round-and-round
172.8

rounded circular
280.11
rotund 282.8
bulging 283.15
blunt 286.3
phonetic 524.31

rounder libertine
665.10
dissipater 669.3

roundhouse garage
197.27
repair shop 739.5

rounding bookbinding
554.14
circuitousness 913.1

roundly approximately
223.23
candidly 644.23
completely 793.14

round of applause
509.2

round off 407.6

round robin 913.2

rounds round of
pleasure 743.7
circuit 913.2

round table 423.3

round the bend 925.27

round the clock
811.10

round-the-clock 811.8

round trip journey
177.5
circuit 913.2

round up grab 472.9
assemble 769.18
drive 1068.8

roundup 769.1

rouse energize 17.10
awake 23.4
awaken 23.5
excite 105.12
elicit 192.14
arouse 375.19

roused 105.20

rousing
noun awakening 23.2
adj refreshing 9.3
energizing 17.15
terrific 247.11
provocative 375.27

rout
noun retreat 163.2
discomfiture 412.2
rabble 606.3
attendance 768.6

throng 769.4
multitude 883.3
agitation 916.1
verb overwhelm 412.8

route 383.1

routed 412.14

router 757.2

routine
noun exercise 84.2
run 373.6
manner 384.1
act 704.7
order 806.1
series 811.2
software 1041.11
adj medium 246.3
habitual 373.15
orderly 806.6
frequent 846.4
prevalent 863.12

routinely habitually
373.21
uniformly 780.7
frequently 846.6
generally 863.17

rover wanderer 178.2
pirate 483.7

roving
noun wandering 177.3
discursiveness 538.3
adj deviative 164.7
wandering 177.37
discursive 538.13
inconstant 853.7

row
noun flap 53.4
rumpus 456.6
turbulence 671.2
series 811.2
agitation 916.1
verb be noisy 53.9
navigate 182.13
paddle 182.53
scrap 456.12
push 903.9

rowdy
noun mischief-maker
322.3
combatant 461.1
vulgarian 497.6
ruffian 593.3
adj noisy 53.13
misbehaving 322.5
boorish 497.13
boisterous 671.20

rower 183.5

rowing 182.1

rowing boat 180.1

Roxburgh 554.15

royal
noun volume 554.4
potentate 575.8
adj dignified 136.12
sovereign 417.17
good 998.12

royal assent 613.4

royal blue 45.3

Royal Highness 648.2

royalist 611.13
Royal Marine 183.4
Royal Marines branch
461.20
marines 461.27
royalties 627.1
royalty sovereignty
417.8
potentate 575.8
aristocracy 608.1
nobility 608.2
dividend 624.7
rpm 174.1
rub
noun touch 73.1
contact 223.5
bone of contention
456.7
crisis 842.4
crux 1012.8
friction 1042.1
verb pain 26.7
stroke 73.8
treat 91.24
contact 223.10
polish 287.7
represent 349.8
kid 490.6
frictionize 1042.6
dry 1064.6
rubbed 287.10
rubber
noun eradicator 395.9
bridge 758.3
putty 1045.4
elastic 1046.3
verb be curious 980.3
elasticize 1046.6
adj rubbery 1046.8
rubber stamp
noun ratification 332.4
verb ratify 332.12
rubbery weak 16.12
changeable 853.6
flaccid 1045.10
rubber 1046.8
rubbing
noun touching 73.2
image 349.5
reproduction 784.2
transcript 784.4
friction 1042.1
adj in contact 223.17
frictional 1042.9
rubbish
noun remainder 256.1
derelict 370.4
rubble 391.5
nonsense 520.2
rabble 606.3
trivia 997.4
verb bad-mouth 156.6
rubble rubbish 391.5
rock 1057.1
rub in 996.14
rub off 393.20
rub shoulders with
582.17

ruby 41.6
ruck
noun wrinkle 291.3
row 456.6
rabble 606.3
game 746.3
throng 769.4
average 863.3
multitude 883.3
verb fold 291.5
wrinkle 291.6
play 746.4
rudder 573.5
ruddy red 41.6
red-complexioned
41.9
fresh 83.13
blushing 139.13
confounded 513.10
rude raucous 58.15
hale 83.12
impudent 142.10
undeveloped 406.12
coarse 497.11
discourteous 505.4
inelegant 534.2
populational 606.8
unlearned 929.14
rudely impudently
142.13
vulgarly 497.16
discourteously 505.8
rudeness raucousness
58.2
impudence 142.2
undevelopment 406.4
coarseness 497.2
discourtesy 505.1
inelegance 534.1
rudimentary basic
199.8
dwarf 258.13
undeveloped 406.12
beginning 817.15
original 885.14
rudiments elementary
education 568.5
basics 817.6
rue
noun pity 145.1
verb regret 113.6
rueful distressing 98.20
sorrowful 112.26
regretful 113.8
pitying 145.7
ruefully distressingly
98.28
sorrowfully 112.36
regretfully 113.11
pitifully 145.10
ruff
noun staccato 55.1
verb fold 291.5
ruffle
noun staccato 55.1
agitation 105.4
edging 211.7
fold 291.1
confusion 984.3

verb drum 55.4
annoy 96.13
agitate 105.14, 916.10
provoke 152.24
wrinkle 288.5
fold 291.5
beat time 708.44
disarrange 810.2
confuse 984.7
ruffled annoyed 96.21
agitated 105.23,
916.16
convolutional 281.6
rough 288.6
folded 291.7
dishevelled 809.14
confused 984.12
rug carpet 295.9
blanket 295.10
bedding 900.20
rugby 746.1
rugby football 746.1
rugby league 746.1
rugby union 746.1
rugged strong 15.15
hale 83.12
harsh 144.24
ragged 288.7
wrinkled 291.8
strict 425.6
sturdy 762.7
rugger 746.1
ruin
noun wreck 393.8
destruction 395.1
defeat 412.1
loss 473.1
verb spoil 393.10
destroy 395.10
defeat 412.6
bankrupt 625.8
seduce 665.20
rage 671.11
thwart 1011.15
ruined past hope
125.15
dilapidated 393.33
destroyed 395.28
defeated 412.14
insolvent 625.11
stale 841.14
ruining 395.26
ruinous dilapidated
393.33
destructive 395.26
ruined 395.28
disintegrative 805.5
slovenly 809.15
stale 841.14
disastrous 1010.15
ruins remainder 256.1
wreck 393.8
rule
noun mean 246.1
supremacy 249.3
straightedge 277.3
measure 300.2
norm 373.5

governance 417.5
law 419.2, 673.3,
868.4
direction 420.3
decree 420.4
government 612.1
game 745.3
model 785.1
influence 893.1
syllogism 934.6
axiom 973.2
verb command 249.11,
420.8
sway 612.14
prevail 863.10
govern 893.8
pass judgment 945.13
ruled out closed 293.9
prohibited 444.7
impossible 966.7
rule of law 612.8
rule of thumb 941.1
rule out excise 255.10
close 293.6
obliterate 395.16
make impossible 966.6
prevent 1011.14
rule over 612.14
ruler superior 249.4
straightedge 277.3
governor 575.6
potentate 575.8
rod 605.2
ruling
noun decree 420.4
law 673.3
verdict 945.5
adj powerful 18.12
chief 249.14
authoritative 417.15
governing 612.18
prevalent 863.12
well-connected 893.14
ruling class best 249.5
mastership 417.7
upper class 607.2
ruling out closure
293.1
prohibition 444.1
qualification 958.1
rum
noun spirits 88.13
adj dishonest 645.16
odd 869.11
eccentric 926.5
rumble
noun audio distortion
50.13
row 53.4
reverberation 54.2
boom 56.4
fight 457.4
report 552.6
verb reverberate 54.7
boom 56.9
murmur 524.26
see through 940.8
rumbling

noun reverberation
54.2
adj reverberating
54.11
thundering 56.12
rumbustious 671.20
rummage
noun search 937.15
verb ransack 937.33
rumour
noun report 552.6
verb publish 352.10
report 552.11
rumoured 552.15
rump buttocks 217.4
remainder 256.1
rumpled wrinkled
291.8
dishevelled 809.14
rumpus
noun row 53.4, 456.6
turbulence 671.2
commotion 809.4
verb be noisy 53.9
run
noun trauma 85.37
direction 161.1
course 172.2
sprint 174.3
migration 177.4
journey 177.5
voyage 182.6
flight 184.9
lair 228.26
stream 238.1
flow 238.4
mean 246.1
length 267.2
routine 373.6
route 383.1
path 383.2
race 457.12
engagement 704.11
impromptu 708.27
ornament 709.18
game 746.3
match 747.3
round 748.3
series 811.2
continuance 855.1
average 863.3
make 892.4
trend 895.2
verb fester 12.15
exercise 84.4
extend 158.8
move 172.5
speed 174.8
travel 177.18
migrate 177.22
navigate 182.13
pilot 182.14
float 182.54
flow 238.16
flee 368.10
nominate 371.19
hunt 382.9
injure 393.13
make haste 401.5
print 548.14

direct 573.8
guide 573.9
run for office 609.39
go into politics 610.13
smuggle 732.8
play 746.4
ski 753.4
race 757.5
elapse 820.5
endure 826.6
operate 888.5, 888.7
incur 896.4
thrust 901.12
melt 1019.21
computerize 1041.18
liquefy 1062.5
raise 1068.6

run across meet 223.11
come across 940.3

run after curry favour
138.9
fetch 176.16
pursue 382.8
cultivate 587.12

run against oppose
451.3
counteract 899.6

run at 459.18

runaway
noun fugitive 368.5
adj fugitive 368.16
escaped 369.11

run away from 368.10

run away with 368.10

run back 163.6

run before 133.14

run-down weakened
16.18
tired 21.7
unhealthy 85.53
dilapidated 393.33
worn-out 393.36

rundown airmanship
184.3
summary 557.2
iteration 848.2

run down burn out
21.5
fail 85.47
sail into 182.41
decline 393.17
arrest 429.15
capture 480.18
run over 909.7
trace 937.35
discover 940.2

rune phonogram 546.2
sorcery 690.1

runes 961.2

run for 182.35

run for it 368.10

run from 182.36

rung step 193.5
degree 245.1

run in thrust in 191.7
interpose 213.6
nick 429.16

run-in
noun row 456.6
horse racing 757.1
adj accustomed 373.16

run into meet 223.11
collide 901.13
come across 940.3

run its course come to
an end 819.6
elapse 820.5

runner speeder 174.5
sledge 179.20
gate 239.4
branch 310.18
messenger 353.1
smuggler 732.5
jockey 757.2
member 792.4

runner-up 411.2

running
noun pus 12.6
exercise 84.2
motion 172.1
direction 573.1
candidacy 609.10
operation 888.1
melting 1019.3
liquefaction 1062.1
adj flowing 172.8,
238.24
fast 174.15
written 547.22
continuous 811.8
present 837.2
prevalent 863.12
operating 888.11
adv consecutively
811.11

running away absence
222.4
flight 368.4

running mate 610.9

running out of time
821.1

running over plentiful
990.7
overfull 992.20

runny exudative 190.20
fluid 1059.4

run off print 548.14
drive out 908.14

run of the mill average
863.3
normal 868.3

run-of-the-mill 1004.8

run on march on 162.3
chatter 540.5
continue 811.4, 855.3
endure 826.6

run out
noun match 747.3
verb burn out 21.5
exit 190.12
empty 190.13
find vent 369.10
be consumed 388.4
perish 395.23
protract 538.8

play 747.4
come to an end 819.6
elapse 820.5
eject 908.13
drive out 908.14
adj not out 747.5
past 836.7
obsolete 841.15

run over overflow
238.17
iterate 848.8
overrun 909.7
think over 930.13
examine 937.24
abound 990.5
number 1016.16

run riot revolt 327.7
dissipate 669.6
run amok 671.15
riot 809.10
overspread 909.5
superabound 992.8

run smoothly 1013.10

run-through summary
557.2
production 704.13
examination 937.3

run through pervade
221.7
perforate 292.15
stab 459.25
squander 486.3

run to extend to 261.6
entreat 440.11
equal 789.5

run up improvise 365.8
go before 815.3
produce 891.8

run-up preparation
405.1
curtain raiser 815.2
forethought 960.2

run up to 405.13

runway taxiway 184.23
path 383.2

run with accomplish
407.4
hang with 582.18

rupture
noun trauma 85.37
crack 224.2
falling-out 456.4
break 801.4
verb cleave 224.4
breach 292.14
injure 393.13
break 393.23, 801.12

ruptured impaired
393.27
broken 801.24

rural rustic 233.6
natural 416.6
agricultural 1067.20

rural dean 699.2

ruse trick 356.6
stratagem 415.3

rush
noun thrill 105.2

kick 105.3
course 172.2
velocity 174.1
run 174.3
flow 238.4
jet 238.9
grass 310.5
haste 401.1
demand 421.1
attack 459.1
outburst 671.6
prematurity 844.2
trifle 997.5
verb speed 174.8
flow 238.16
hasten 401.4
make haste 401.5
charge 459.18

rushed hurried 401.11
premature 844.8

rush hour 293.3

rush in 214.5

rushing
noun furtherance
449.5
adj flowing 172.8,
238.24
fast 174.15

rush into 401.7

russet 40.4

**Russian Orthodox
Church** 675.9

rust
noun legume 310.4
decay 393.6
blight 1000.2
verb brown 40.2
redden 41.4
corrode 393.21
age 841.9
adj reddish-brown
40.4
red 41.6

rustic
noun agriculturist
1067.5
adj rural 233.6
plain-speaking 535.3

rustle
noun rustling 52.6
verb crinkle 52.12
steal 482.13

rustling
noun rustle 52.6
adj murmuring 52.18

rusty reddish-brown
40.4
red 41.6
stricken in years
303.18
unaccustomed 374.4
corroded 393.43
out of practice 414.18
stale 841.14

rut
noun sexual desire
75.5
fever of excitement
105.7

pothole 284.3
furrow 290.1
routine 373.6
path 383.2
verb lust 75.20
furrow 290.3

ruth pity 145.1
guilt 656.1

ruthless cruel 144.26
pitiless 146.3
savage 671.21

ruthlessly cruelly
144.35
pitilessly 146.4
savagely 671.27

ruthlessness cruelty
144.11
pitilessness 146.1

rutted rough 288.6
furrowed 290.4

S
adj crescent-shaped
279.11
adv south 161.16

Sabbath day of rest
20.5
magic circle 690.3
holy day 701.11

sabbatical
noun holiday 20.3
adj vacational 20.10

sable
noun blackness 38.1
heraldic device 647.2
adj black 38.8

sabotage
noun impairment
393.1
fall 395.3
verb disable 19.9
undermine 393.15
oppose 451.3
thwart 1011.15

saboteur 357.11

sabre 459.25

sabre-rattling
noun warlikeness
458.11
threat 514.1
patriotism 591.2
adj militaristic 458.22
threatening 514.3

sac 195.2

saccharine 66.5

sachet 70.6

sack
noun bag 195.2
plundering 482.6
bundle 769.8
verb load 159.15
package 212.9
catch 480.17
plunder 482.17
rage 671.11
bundle 769.20
fire 908.20

sacking plundering
482.6
unruliness 671.3

Sacrament 701.7

sacrament 701.3

sacred
noun holy 685.2
adj almighty 677.17
holy 685.7
vocal 708.50

sacrifice
noun killing 308.1
loss 473.1
relinquishment 475.1
unselfishness 652.1
oblation 696.7
verb kill 308.12
lose 473.4
relinquish 475.3
give away 478.21
not have a selfish bone
in one's body 652.3
propitiate 696.14
sell 734.8

sacrificed 475.5

sacrificial 633.9

sacrificing 652.5

sacrilege abomination
638.2
blasphemy 694.2

sacrosanct 685.7

sad soft-coloured 35.21
dark 38.9
grey 39.4
pleasureless 96.20
distressing 98.20
saddened 112.20
gloomy 112.24
disgraceful 661.11
paltry 997.21
terrible 999.9
unfortunate 1010.14

saddened 112.20

saddle
noun ridge 237.5
helm 417.10
seat 900.17
verb burden 297.13
yoke 799.10
tend 1068.7

saddled weighted
297.18
obliged 641.16

sadism perversion
75.11
cruelty 144.11

sadist sexual pervert
75.16
tormentor 96.10
beast 144.14
punisher 604.7

sadistic 144.26

sadly distressingly
98.28, 247.21
gloomily 112.31
unfortunately 1010.17

sadness darkness 38.2

wretchedness 96.6
distressfulness 98.5
sadheartedness 112.1
paltriness 997.2

safari 177.5

safari park 743.14

safe
noun treasury 729.12
adj cautious 494.8
secure 1006.4
protected 1007.21

safe and sound 1006.4

safe-conduct 443.7

safeguard
noun pass 443.7
precaution 494.3
safety 1006.1
palladium 1007.3
bodyguard 1007.14
verb defend 460.8
protect 1007.18

safeguarded 1007.21

safeguarding
noun protection
1007.1
adj protective 1007.23

safe hands 1007.2

safe haven 1008.1

safe house hiding place
346.4
retreat 1008.5

safely 1006.8

safe sex 75.7

safety match 752.3
safeness 1006.1
protection 1007.1
safeguard 1007.3

safety first 494.1

safety net support
449.3
precaution 494.3
safeguard 1007.3

safety valve outlet
190.9
precaution 494.3
safeguard 1007.3

saffron 43.4

sag
noun sinkage 194.2
hang 202.2
declining market
737.5
verb drift off course
182.29
sink 194.6
hang 202.6
decrease 252.6
curve 279.6
cheapen 633.6

saga 719.3

sage
noun master 413.13
wise man 920.1
adj wise 919.17

sagging
noun decrease 252.1
adj tired 21.7

descending 194.11
drooping 202.10

Sahara 890.2

Saharan 1064.7

sahib Mister 76.7
master 575.1
Sir 648.3

said speech 524.30
former 813.5

sail
noun sailboat 180.3
canvas 180.14
voyage 182.6
verb glide 177.35
navigate 182.13
get under way 182.19
set sail 182.20
float 182.54
fly 184.36
go easily 1013.10

sail for head for 161.9
put away for 182.35

sailing gliding 177.16
water travel 182.1
aviation 184.1

sailing boat 180.3

sailor traveller 178.1
mariner 183.1

saint
noun holy man 659.6
angel 679.1
evangelist 684.2
believer 692.4
verb glorify 662.13
sanctify 685.5
ordain 698.12

saintly blissful 97.9
virtuous 653.6
angelic 679.6
sanctified 685.8
godly 692.9

sake motive 375.1
intention 380.1

salaam
noun obeisance 155.2
crouch 912.3
verb bow 155.6, 912.9

salacious lustful 75.26
lascivious 665.29
obscene 666.9

salad salade 10.35
hotchpotch 796.6

salaried 624.22

salary
noun pay 624.4
verb pay 624.10

sale transfer 629.1
wholesale 734.1
closing-down sale
734.3

saleable 734.14

sale price 633.2

saleroom 736.5

sales 734.13

sales force 730.3

salesman 730.3

sales manager 730.3

sales pitch 734.5

salient
noun region 231.1
adj protruding 283.14
conspicuous 348.12
notable 996.19

saline 68.9

saliva digestion 2.15,
7.8
humour 2.22
spittle 13.3

salle 197.1

sallow
verb yellow 43.3
adj colourless 36.7
yellow 43.4
yellow-faced 43.6

sally
noun journey 177.5
attack 459.1
witticism 489.7
verb set out 188.8
emerge 190.11

salmon
noun marine animal
311.30
jumper 366.4
adj pink 41.8

salmon-pink 41.8

salon parlour 197.5
museum 386.9
society 578.6
social gathering
582.10
market 736.1
company 769.3

saloon bar 88.20
parlour 197.5
cabin 197.9

saloon bar 88.20

salsa 10.9

salt
noun saltiness 68.4
mariner 183.1
preservative 397.4
wit 489.1
verb flavour 63.7
tamper with 354.17
preserve 397.9
falsify accounts 628.10
adj flavoured 62.9
salty 68.9
witty 489.15

salt-and-pepper 39.4

salted 68.9

salt marsh plain 236.1
marsh 243.1

salt water ocean 240.1
water 1063.3

salty salt 68.9
crabby 110.20
nautical 182.57
witty 489.15
risqué 666.7

salubrious 81.5

salutary healthful 81.5

helpful 449.21

salute
noun obeisance 155.2
celebration 487.1
greeting 585.4
verb signal 182.52,
517.22
praise 509.12
address 524.27
greet 585.10

salvage
noun reclamation
396.2
preservation 397.1
rescue 398.1
recovery 481.3
recompense 624.3
fee 630.6
verb redeem 396.12
rescue 398.3

salvation reclamation
396.2
preservation 397.1
rescue 398.1
redemption 677.14,
685.4

salve
noun balm 86.11
moderator 670.3
ointment 1054.3
verb medicate 91.25
relieve 120.5
redeem 396.12
oil 1054.8

salvo detonation 56.3
volley 459.9
celebration 487.1
shot 903.4
qualification 958.1

Samaritan 592.1

same
noun selfsame 777.3
tie 789.3
adj identical 777.7
wall-to-wall 780.6
former 813.5

sameness triteness
117.3
tedium 118.1
identity 777.1
regularity 780.2
similarity 783.1

same way 777.9

sample
noun specimen 62.4,
785.3
part 792.1
feeler 941.4
subject 941.7
verb taste 62.7
canvass 937.29
experiment 941.8
adj typical 349.15

sampler 937.16

sampling 792.1

Samson 15.6

samurai 608.3

sanatorium 91.21

sanctimonious prudish 500.19
  zealous 692.11
  be sanctimonious 693.4

sanction
  noun ratification 332.4
  consent 441.1
  authorization 443.3
  approval 509.1
  legalization 673.2
  verb ratify 332.12
  consent 441.2
  authorize 443.11
  approve 509.9
  legalize 673.8

sanctioned authorized 443.17
  legal 673.10

sanctioning 441.4

sanctions 603.1

sanctity sanctitude 685.1
  godliness 692.2

sanctuary hiding place 346.4
  preserve 397.7
  holy of holies 703.5
  refuge 1008.1

sanctum sanctum sanctorum 197.8
  retreat 584.6, 1008.5
  sanctuary 703.5

sand
  noun minutia 258.7
  grain 1049.6
  grain of sand 1057.2
  verb grind 287.8
  buff 1042.8

sandalwood 70.4

sanding 1042.2

Sandinista 859.3

sandpaper
  noun rough 288.2
  verb grind 287.8
  buff 1042.8

sands shore 234.2
  snags 1005.5

sandstone 1057.1

sandwich
  noun sarnie 10.31
  verb interpose 213.6

sandy yellow 43.4
  granular 1049.12
  stony 1057.11
  dry 1064.7

sane intelligent 919.12
  sensible 919.18
  sane-minded 924.4
  logical 934.20
  realistic 986.6

sang-froid 854.1

sanguine
  noun introvert 92.12
  adj sanguineous 41.7
  red-complexioned 41.9

  cheerful 109.11
  hopeful 124.11
  expectant 130.11

sanitary hygienic 79.27
  healthful 81.5

sanitation 79.3, 81.2

sanity intelligence 919.1
  sensibleness 919.6
  saneness 924.1

sans absent 222.19
  without 991.17

Santa 678.13

Santa Claus giver 478.11
  cheerful giver 485.2
  Santa 678.13

sap
  noun substance 196.5
  sucker 358.2
  entrenchment 460.5
  essence 766.2
  chump 923.3
  fluid 1059.2
  verb weaken 16.10
  excavate 284.15
  undermine 393.15
  overthrow 395.20
  spiritualize 763.4

sapped 16.18

sapper excavator 284.10
  engineer 461.13

sapphire 45.3

sapping
  noun waste 473.2
  adj weakening 16.20

sarcasm wit 489.1
  irony 508.5

sarcastic caustic 144.23
  witty 489.15
  satiric 508.13

sardonic 508.13

sark 5.15

sartorial clothing 5.44
  tailored 5.47

sash waistband 5.19
  frame 266.4

sassy 142.10

Satan liar 357.9
  Satanas 680.3
  demon 680.6
  Pluto 682.5

satanic cruel 144.26
  diabolic 654.13
  execrable 999.10

Satanism diabolism 680.14
  black magic 690.2
  idolatry 697.1

sated languid 331.20
  satiated 993.6

satellite hanger-on 138.6
  follower 166.2, 616.8
  country 232.1

  escort 768.5
  moon 1070.11
  artificial satellite 1073.6

satin
  noun smooth 287.3
  smoothness 294.3
  putty 1045.4
  adj smooth 294.8

satire wit 489.1
  sarcasm 508.5
  burlesque 508.6
  lampoon 512.5

satirical witty 489.15
  satiric 508.13

satirist humourist 489.12
  lampooner 512.7
  poet 720.11

satisfaction pleasure 95.1
  contentment 107.1
  compensation 338.1
  reparation 396.6, 481.2
  observance 434.1
  duel 457.7
  payment 624.1
  recompense 624.3
  atonement 658.1
  sufficiency 990.1
  satiety 993.1

satisfactorily
  satisfyingly 107.15
  sufficiently 990.8
  tolerably 998.24

satisfactory satisfying 107.11
  convincing 952.26
  sufficient 990.6
  tolerable 998.20

satisfied pleased 95.14
  content 107.7
  belief 952.21
  satiated 993.6

satisfy feed 8.18
  gratify 95.7
  content 107.4
  indulge 427.6
  observe 434.2
  pay 624.10
  pay in full 624.13
  atone 658.4
  convince 952.18
  suffice 990.4
  satiate 993.4

satisfying pleasant 97.6
  satisfactory 107.11
  paying 624.21
  convincing 952.26
  satiating 993.7

satisfyingly pleasantly 97.12
  satisfactorily 107.15

saturated permeated 221.15
  full 793.11
  overfull 992.20
  satiated 993.6

  soaked 1063.17

saturated fat 1054.1

saturation
  colourfulness 35.4
  colour quality 35.6
  fullness 793.2
  imbuement 796.2
  overfullness 992.3
  satiety 993.1
  soaking 1063.7

Saturn 1070.9

sauce
  noun cooking 11.1
  juice 88.14
  hotchpotch 796.6
  tinge 796.7
  pulp 1061.2
  verb flavour 63.7

saucer 280.2

saucers 8.12

saucy impudent 142.10
  defiant 454.7

sauna 79.10

saunter
  noun slow motion 175.2
  walk 177.10
  gait 177.12
  verb wander 177.23
  stroll 177.28

sausage 10.20

savage
  noun barbarian 497.7, 593.5
  verb torture 96.18
  mistreat 389.5
  injure 393.13
  rage 671.11
  work evil 999.6
  adj cruel 144.26
  pitiless 146.3
  infuriated 152.32
  deadly 308.22
  warlike 458.21
  unrefined 497.12
  fierce 671.21

savaged 96.25

savagely cruelly 144.35
  pitilessly 146.4
  fiercely 671.27
  terribly 999.14

savagery cruelty 144.11
  unrefinement 497.3
  violence 671.1
  unenlightenment 929.4

save
  noun game 745.3
  verb store up 386.11
  reserve 386.12
  not use 390.5
  preserve 397.8
  rescue 398.3
  aid 449.11
  retain 474.5
  economize 635.4
  redeem 685.6

  play 745.4
  be conservative 852.6
  play safe 1006.3
  prevent 1011.14
  prep off 255.14
  excluding 772.10
  conj unless 958.16

saved
  noun believing 692.5
  adj reserved 386.15
  unused 390.12
  preserved 397.12
  angelic 679.6
  redeemed 685.9
  regenerate 692.10

save face 136.7

saver preserver 397.5
  economizer 635.3

save up store up 386.11
  reserve 386.12
  not use 390.5
  retain 474.5
  economize 635.4

saving
  noun preservation 397.1
  rescue 398.1
  economizing 635.2
  adj preservative 397.11
  benefitting 592.4
  economical 635.6
  adv, prep in deference to 155.14
  prep excluding 772.10

saving grace
  extenuation 600.5
  characteristic 864.4

savings reserve 386.3
  funds 728.14

savings account
  account 622.2
  funds 728.14

saviour preserver 397.5
  rescuer 398.2
  redeemer 592.2

savour
  noun taste 62.1
  relish 63.2
  odour 69.1
  passion 93.2
  characteristic 864.4
  verb eat 8.20
  taste 62.7
  relish 63.5
  flavour 63.7
  enjoy 95.12

savouring eating 8.1
  tasting 62.6

savoury
  noun delicacy 10.8
  appetizer 10.9
  adj edible 8.33
  flavoured 62.9
  tasty 63.8
  fragrant 70.9
  delectable 97.10

savvy

noun discrimination
943.1
verb understand 521.7

saw
noun notching 289.2
maxim 973.1
platitude 973.3
cutlery 1039.2
verb sever 801.11

sawdust remainder
256.1
powder 1049.5

sawmill 739.3

sawn-off shotgun
462.10

saxophonist 710.4

say
noun affirmation 334.1
vote 371.6
free will 430.6
remark 524.4
speech 543.2
turn 824.2
influence 893.1
verb affirm 334.5
announce 352.12
utter 524.23
state 524.24
answer 938.4
suppose 950.10
adv approximately
223.23

sayer 524.18

say goodbye to 370.5

saying affirmation
334.1
remark 524.4
maxim 973.1

say no 442.3

say nothing 51.6

say no to prohibit
444.3
disapprove 510.10

say over 848.8

say-so affirmation 334.1
command 420.1
free will 430.6

sc by interpretation
341.18
namely 864.18

scab
noun sore 85.36
crust 295.14
blackleg 727.8
blemish 1003.1
verb crust 295.27
break a strike 727.11
blemish 1003.4

scaffold block 605.5
scaffolding 900.12

scaffolding 900.12

scalded 393.27

scalding 1018.25

scale
noun range 158.2
map 159.5
ladder 193.4

step 193.5
degree 245.1
dregs 256.2
size 257.1
blanket 295.12
crust 295.14
flake 296.3
weighing 297.9
measure 300.2
gamut 709.6
break 801.4
series 811.2
verb flake 6.11
climb 193.11
layer 296.5
raid 459.20
break 801.12

scaled-down 252.10

scale down 258.9

scaling raid 459.4
disruption 801.3

scallop
noun notching 289.2
verb cook 11.4
convolve 281.4
notch 289.4

scalloped cooked 11.6
notched 289.5

scalp peel 6.8
trade 737.23

scaly flaky 296.7
powdery 1049.11

scam
noun gyp 356.9
verb gyp 356.19

scan
noun field of view 31.3
examination 937.3
verb browse 570.13
rhyme 720.14
itemize 800.7
examine 937.24
examine cursorily
937.26
receive 1035.17

scandal slander 512.3
dirt 552.8
abomination 638.2
iniquity 654.3
disgrace 661.5
immodesty 666.2

scandalous disparaging
512.13
wrong 638.3
wicked 654.16
disgraceful 661.11
immodest 666.6
terrible 999.9

scanner 1041.4

scanning
noun metrics 720.6
televising 1034.3
data transmission
1035.8
adj metric 720.16

scant
verb limit 210.5
stint 484.5

adj narrow 270.14
incomplete 794.4
sparse 884.5
meagre 991.10

scantily scarcely 248.9,
991.16
thinly 270.23
sparsely 884.8
meagrely 991.15

scantily clad 6.13

scanty narrow 270.14
incomplete 794.4
sparse 884.5
meagre 991.10
scarce 991.11

scapegoat oblation
696.7
goat 861.3
oddity 869.4

scar
noun precipice 200.3
slope 237.2
mark 517.5
blemish 1003.1
verb mark 517.19
blemish 1003.4

scarce infrequent 847.2
sparse 884.5, 991.11

scarcely to a degree
245.7
hardly 248.9
infrequently 847.4
sparsely 884.8, 991.16

scarcity infrequency
847.1
fewness 884.1
performance 891.5
scarceness 991.3

scare
noun fear 127.1
verb frighten 127.15

scarecrow frightener
127.7
figure 349.6
eyesore 1014.4

scared 127.22

scaremongering 127.7

scarf
noun joint 799.4
verb hook 799.8

scaring 127.28

scarlet red 41.6
prostitute 665.28

scarred 1003.8

scary fearful 127.23
frightening 127.28

scathing acrimonious
17.14
caustic 144.23

scathingly 144.32

scatter
noun deflection 164.2
rarity 299.1
verb deflect 164.5
radiate 171.6
interspace 224.3
rarefy 299.3

overwhelm 412.8
squander 486.3
disperse 770.4
disband 770.8
shatter 801.13
part company 801.19
loosen 803.3
disarrange 810.2

scattered deflective
164.8
interspaced 224.6
rare 299.4
defeated 412.14
dispersed 770.9
separated 801.21
confused 809.16
sparse 884.5

scattering
noun radiation 171.2
rarefaction 299.2
disruption 801.3
noncohesion 803.1
few 884.2
adj dispersive 770.11

scavenge clean 79.18
search 937.31

scavenging 937.15

scenario project 381.2
playbook 704.21
script 706.2
effect 886.1
solution 939.1

scene look 27.3
view 33.6, 712.12
outburst 152.9
setting 209.2
arena 463.1
act 704.7
scenery 704.20

scenery view 33.6
arena 463.1
decor 704.20

scenes 704.1

scenic 704.33

scent
noun odour 69.1
sense of smell 69.4
fragrance 70.1
perfumery 70.2
track 517.8
clue 517.9
hint 551.4
verb odorize 69.7
smell 69.8
perfume 70.8
catch the scent of
940.6

scented 70.9

scenting 69.3

sceptic
noun agnostic 695.12
doubter 954.4
adj agnostic 695.20

sceptical agnostic
695.20
doubting 954.9
incredulous 955.4
uncertain 970.16

scepticism agnosticism
695.6
doubt 954.2
incredulity 955.1

sceptre rod 417.9
regalia 647.3

schedule
noun plan 381.1
chronicle 831.9
list 870.1
programme 964.3
verb plan 381.8
allot 477.9
spend 626.5
list 870.8
line up 964.6

scheduled planned
381.12
preserved 397.12
listed 870.9
slated 964.9

scheduling 626.1

schema representation
349.1
plan 381.1
outline 800.4

schematic
diagrammatic 381.14
analytical 800.9

scheme
noun trick 356.6
plan 381.1
project 381.2
intrigue 381.5
stratagem 415.3
plot 722.4
outline 800.4
verb premeditate 380.7
plot 381.9
manoeuvre 415.10
come 838.6
prearrange 964.4

schemes 893.3

scheming
noun intrigue 381.5
prearrangement 964.1
adj deceitful 356.22,
645.18
calculating 381.13
cunning 415.12
cautious 494.8

scherzo 708.25

schism desertion 370.2
falling-out 456.4
sect 675.3

schizophrenia mental
disorder 92.14
dissociation 92.20
dementia praecox
925.4

schizophrenic
noun psychotic 925.17
adj psychotic 925.28

schnapps 88.13

scholar student 572.1
specialist 865.3
wise man 920.1
scientist 927.11

scholastic 928.3
scholarly scholastic
568.19
studious 570.17
learned 927.21
scientific 927.28
scholarship subsidy
478.8
studiousness 570.4
fellowship 646.7
erudition 927.5
scholastic
noun theologian 676.3
scholar 928.3
adj academic 567.13,
568.19
studious 570.17
learned 927.21
book-learned 927.22
school
noun educational
institution 567.1
teaching 568.1
sect 617.5, 675.3
style 712.8
system of belief 952.3
verb teach 568.10
adj scholastic 567.13
school age 301.1
schoolboy boy 302.5
schoolchild 572.3
schooled 927.18
schoolgirl schoolmaid
302.8
schoolchild 572.3
schooling teaching
568.1
learning 927.4
schoolmaster 571.1
school of thought
951.1
schoolroom 567.11
schoolteacher 571.1
school-work 568.1
science art 413.7
ology 927.10
science fiction 1073.1
scientific technical
927.28
exact 972.17
realistic 986.6
scientist 927.11
scintillating witty
489.15
smart 919.14
burning 1018.27
glittering 1024.35
scion sprout 302.11
branch 310.18
descendant 561.3
member 792.4
scissor 801.11
scissors 474.3
sclerosis anaemia 85.9
hardening 1044.5
scoff

noun indignity 156.2
gibe 508.2
verb gobble 8.23
ingest 187.11
jeer 508.9
gluttonize 672.4
disbelieve 695.14
scone 10.30
scoop
noun cavity 284.2
news item 552.3
piece 792.3
verb ladle 176.17
excavate 284.15
play 750.7
scoop out 284.15
scope vision 27.1
telescope 29.4
field of view 31.3
range 158.2
degree 245.1
size 257.1
latitude 430.4
meaning 518.1
legality 673.1
opportunity 842.2
scorch
noun trauma 85.37
burn 1019.6
verb brown 40.2
barrel 174.9
injure 393.13
attack 510.20
stain 1003.6
burn 1018.22,
1019.24
dry 1064.6
scorched impaired
393.27
burned 1019.30
dried 1064.9
scorching
noun burning 1019.5
adj caustic 144.23
fiery 671.22
hot 1018.25
score
noun crack 224.2
notch 289.1
furrow 290.1
representation 349.1
motive 375.1
hit 409.5
mark 517.5
line 517.6
debt 623.1
account 628.2
playbook 704.21
piece 708.5
engraving 713.2
game 745.3, 746.3,
749.2, 750.3, 750.6
round 748.3
basketball game 751.3
bridge 758.3
meat and potatoes
766.3
eleven 881.7
sum 1016.6
verb notch 289.4

furrow 290.3
score a success 409.9
acquire 472.8
mark 517.19
compose 708.46
engrave 713.9
play 745.4, 746.4,
750.7, 751.4, 752.4
play tennis 749.3
list 870.8
calculate 1016.17
scoreboard 549.10
scored notched 289.5
furrowed 290.4
scorer recorder 550.1
composer 710.20
game 750.6
scores 883.3
scoring engraving
713.2
round 748.3
scorn
noun hate 103.1
contempt 157.1
rejection 372.1
verb hate 103.5
disdain 157.3
reject 372.2
flout 454.4
be hard to please
495.8
scorned 372.3
scornful hating 103.7
contemptuous 157.8
rejective 372.4
scornfully 157.9
scorpion 311.31
scot 630.6
scotch
noun notch 289.1
mark 517.5
curb 1011.7
verb notch 289.4
mark 517.19
hinder 1011.10
thwart 1011.15
scotched 289.5
scot-free escaped
369.11
free 430.21
Scotland Yard 1007.17
Scots Guards 461.14
Scottish Highlands
231.7
scoundrel criminal
645.10
rascal 660.3
scour
noun abrasion 1042.2
verb wash 79.19
speed 174.8
traverse 177.20
polish 287.7
ransack 937.33
abrade 1042.7
scourge
noun epidemic 85.5

punishment 604.1
whip 605.1
bane 1000.1
verb whip 604.12
scouring washing 79.5
search 937.15
abrasion 1042.2
Scouse 523.7
scout
noun vanguard 216.2
secret agent 576.9
precursor 815.1
watchman 1007.10
verb look 27.13
spurn 157.4
traverse 177.20
reject 372.2
flout 454.4
scoff 508.9
reconnoitre 937.28
scouting rejection
372.1
reconnaissance 937.8
scowl
noun frown 110.9
offence 152.2
reproving look 510.8
verb look sullen
110.15
redden 152.14
scowling 110.24
scrabble
noun creeping 177.17
scribbling 547.7
verb creep 177.26
excavate 284.15
scribble 547.20
grope 937.32
scrabbled 547.23
scramble
noun creeping 177.17
mission 184.11
bustle 330.4
haste 401.1
fight 457.4
Greek 522.7
hotchpotch 796.6
jumble 809.3
commotion 809.4
verb speed 174.8
creep 177.26
hustle 330.13
make haste 401.5
contend 457.13
make unintelligible
522.12
mix 796.10
confuse 810.3
scrambled meaningless
520.6
hard to understand
522.14
mixed 796.14
scrambled eggs 10.25
scrap
noun tatter 248.3
minutia 258.7
rubbish 391.5
row 456.6

piece 792.3
verb junk 390.8
row 456.12
scrapbook notebook
549.11
compilation 554.7
scrape
noun rasp 58.3
trauma 85.37
obeisance 155.2
pickle 1012.5
abrasion 1042.2
verb grate 58.10
touch lightly 73.7
bow 155.6
contact 223.10
excavate 284.15
grind 287.8
injure 393.13
economize 635.4
engrave 713.9
abrade 1042.7
scrap heap derelict
370.4
rubbish heap 391.6
scraping
noun economizing
635.2
abrasion 1042.2
adj grating 58.16
abrasive 1042.10
scrapping discard
390.3
contention 457.1
scrappy crabby 110.20
contentious 110.26
warlike 458.21
incomplete 794.4
discontinuous 812.4
irregular 850.3
scraps remainder 256.1
refuse 391.4
scrapyard 391.6
scratch
noun feed 10.4
rasp 58.3
trauma 85.37
shallowness 276.1
furrow 290.1
bad likeness 350.2
mark 517.5
scribbling 547.7
engraving 713.2
blemish 1003.1
abrasion 1042.2
verb grate 58.10
tingle 74.5
excavate 284.15
furrow 290.3
misdraw 350.4
injure 393.13
obliterate 395.16
mark 517.19
scribble 547.20
portray 712.19
engrave 713.9
scratched furrowed
290.4
scribbled 547.23

scratching
noun audio distortion 50.13
mark 517.5
engraving 713.2
abrasion 1042.2
adj grating 58.16

scratchy irritating 26.13
grating 58.16
rugged 288.7
scribbled 547.23

scrawl
noun illegibility 522.4
scribbling 547.7
verb scribble 547.20

scrawled 547.23

scrawny lean 270.17
meagre 991.10

scream
noun screech 58.4
cry 59.1
lament 115.3
joke 489.6
verb screech 58.8
cry 59.6, 60.2
wail 115.13
sigh 318.21
murmur 524.26

screaming garish 35.19
vociferous 59.10
gaudy 501.20

scree
noun rock 1057.1
phrase deposit 176.9

screech
noun shriek 58.4
cry 59.1
verb shriek 58.8
cry 59.6, 60.2
sigh 318.21
murmur 524.26

screeching 58.14

screen
noun refinery 79.13
network 170.3
furniture 229.1
porousness 292.8
cover 295.2
veil 346.2
pretext 376.1
scenery 704.20
cinema 706.1, 706.6
arranger 807.5
safeguard 1007.3
shade 1027.1
television receiver 1034.11
verb refine 79.22
cover 295.19
conceal 346.6
defend 460.8
project 714.16
play 751.4
segregate 772.6
classify 807.11
discriminate 943.4
protect 1007.18
shade 1027.5

screened covered 295.31
protected 1007.21
shaded 1027.7

screened-in 295.31

screening
noun refinement 79.4
network 170.3
covering 295.1
concealment 346.1
basketball game 751.3
grouping 807.3
adj covering 295.35
defensive 460.11
protective 1007.23
shading 1027.6

screenplay 706.2

screen test 706.4

screenwriter 704.22

screw
noun distortion 265.1
coil 281.2
rack 605.4
match 752.3
fastening 799.3
propeller 903.6
verb distort 265.5
convolve 281.4
gyp 356.19
shaft 389.6
demand 421.5
wrest 480.22
stint 484.5
play 752.4
hook 799.8
rotate 914.9

screwdriver 1039.1

screwed 88.33

screwed up fouled up 393.29
messed up 414.22
confused 809.16

screw-top 295.5

screw up foul up 393.11
cock up 414.12
fasten 799.7
stiffen 1044.9

screw-up
noun goof 974.6
verb make a boo-boo 974.15

scribble
noun bad likeness 350.2
illegibility 522.4
scribbling 547.7
verb misdraw 350.4
scrabble 547.20

scribbled 547.23

scribbling 547.7

scribe
noun writer 547.13
author 547.15, 718.4
recorder 550.1
rabbi 699.10
verb write 547.19

script representation 349.1
writing system 546.3
handwriting 547.3
writing 547.10
type 548.6
document 549.5
playbook 704.21
screenplay 706.2

Scripture 683.2

scripture 683.1

Scriptures 683.2

scriptures 683.1

scriptwriter author 547.15, 718.4
dramatist 704.22

scrivener
noun writer 547.13
recorder 550.1
verb write 547.19

scroll
noun coil 281.2
writing 547.10
codex 547.11
record 549.1
document 549.5
rare book 554.6
roll 870.6
verb write 547.19

scrooge 484.4

scrotum 2.11

scrub
noun washing 79.5
shrubbery 310.9
woodland 310.11
brush 310.14
abrasion 1042.2
verb wash 79.19
abrade 1042.7

scrubbing washing 79.5
network 170.3
abrasion 1042.2

scruffy dirty 80.22
shabby 393.32
base 661.12
slovenly 809.15
paltry 997.21

scrum 809.4

scrum half 746.2

scrumptious 998.13

scruples compunction 113.2
conscientiousness 644.2

scrupulous demurring 325.7
meticulous 339.12
observant 434.4
fastidious 495.9
punctilious 580.10
dutiful 641.13
conscientious 644.15
doubting 954.9

scrupulously
meticulously 339.16
fastidiously 495.14

honestly 644.21

scrutiny overview 27.6
scrutiny 27.6
examination 937.3
close attention 982.4

scuba diving 367.3

scud
noun run 174.3
rainstorm 316.2
gust 318.6
foam 320.2
verb speed 174.8
float 182.54

scuffle
noun fight 457.4
struggle 725.3
verb stroll 177.28
contend 457.13
struggle 725.11

scull
noun oar 180.15
verb navigate 182.13
row 182.53

scullery 11.3

sculpted formative 262.9
sculptured 715.7

sculptor sculpture 715.1
sculptress 716.6

sculptural 715.6

sculpture
noun forming 262.5
figure 349.6
visual arts 712.1
sculpturing 715.1
glyph 715.2
verb engrave 713.9

sculptured engraved 713.11
sculpted 715.7

scum
noun slime 80.8
offal 80.9
dregs 256.2
blanket 295.12
lamina 296.2
foam 320.2
refuse 391.4
rabble 606.3
verb cover 295.19
foam 320.5

scupper
noun drain 239.5
verb disable 19.9
sink 367.8
do for 395.11

scurrilous caustic 144.23
insulting 156.8
disparaging 512.13
cursing 513.8
obscene 666.9

scurry
noun run 174.3
haste 401.1
verb speed 174.8
make haste 401.5

scurvy low 497.15
base 661.12
paltry 997.21
terrible 999.9

scuttle
noun run 174.3
gait 177.12
porch 189.6
container 195.1
haste 401.1
verb speed 174.8
stroll 177.28
capsize 182.44
sink 367.8
do for 395.11
make haste 401.5
lose one's nerve 491.8
bankrupt 625.8

scythe 279.5

sea wave 238.14
ocean 240.1, 240.3
quantity 247.3

seabed bed 199.4
ocean depths 275.4

seaboard 234.2

sea breeze 318.5

sea change revolution 851.2
conversion 857.1

seafaring
noun water travel 182.1
adj nautical 182.57

seafood 10.23

seafront
noun shore 234.2
adj coastal 234.7

sea king 483.7

seal
noun ratification 332.4
sign 517.1
print 517.7
label 517.13
signature 527.10
regalia 647.3
engraving tool 713.8
cast 784.6
mould 785.6
characteristic 864.4
verb close 293.6
ratify 332.12
resolve 359.7
sign 437.7
mark 517.19
label 517.20
adj brown 40.3

sealed close 293.12
accepted 332.14
confidential 345.14
contracted 437.11
unknown 929.17

sea level 201.3

sealing 437.3

seal of approval
ratification 332.4
approval 509.1

seal off close 293.6
quarantine 429.13

sedative hypnotic
86.12
drug 87.2
moderator 670.3
adj sleep-inducing
22.23
calmative 86.45
palliative 670.16
sedentary inert 173.14
inactive 331.17
sedge 310.5
sediment
noun dregs 256.2
verb precipitate
1043.11
phrase deposit 176.9
sedition rebelliousness
327.3
treason 645.7
seditious 327.11
seduce enamour 104.23
lure 377.5
betray 665.20
seducer beau 104.13
deceiver 357.1
tempter 377.4
philanderer 562.12
betrayer 665.12
seducing 377.8
seduction allurement
377.1
seducement 665.6
seductive desirable
100.30
alluring 377.8
seductively 377.9
see
noun diocese 698.8
verb sense 24.6
behold 27.12
attend 221.8
perceive 521.9
visit 582.19
bet 759.25
spectate 917.5
know 927.12
contemplate 930.17
detect 940.5
heed 982.6
visualize 985.15
seed
noun sperm 305.11
stone 310.29
lineage 560.4
posterity 561.1
verb plant 1067.18
seeding rainmaking
316.5
planting 1067.14
seedling sprout 302.11
plant 310.3
tree 310.10
seedy tired 21.7
shabby 393.32
slovenly 809.15
inferior 1004.9
see eye to eye concur
332.9

agree 787.6
seeing
noun vision 27.1
observation 27.2
distinctness 31.2
observatory 1070.17
adj visual 27.20
seeing that because
887.10
granting 958.13
see into perceive 521.9
investigate 937.23
see it through
prosecute to a
conclusion 360.5
go to all lengths 793.8
continue 855.3
persist 855.5
seek pursue 382.8
endeavour 403.5
solicit 440.14
hunt 937.30
be curious 980.3
seeker pursuer 382.4
petitioner 440.7
hunter 937.18
seeking
noun pursuit 382.1
questioning 937.12
adj pursuing 382.11
seek out 382.8
seek refuge 1008.7
seek to 403.8
seem 33.10
seeming
noun aspect 33.3
exteriority 206.1
sham 354.3
illusoriness 975.2
adj apparent 33.11
exterior 206.7
specious 354.27
illusory 975.9
seemingly apparently
33.12
falsely 354.35
supposedly 950.17
seem like 33.10
seem likely 967.4
seem to be 33.10
seen 31.1
see nothing 983.2
seep
noun exuding 190.6
verb exude 190.15
trickle 238.18
be damp 1063.11
seeping
noun trickle 238.7
adj soaked 1063.17
seer spectator 917.1
wise man 920.1
predictor 961.4
visionary 985.13
see that 969.11

see the difference
943.6
see the light appear
33.8
come to life 306.8
perceive 521.9
be converted 692.7
seething
noun turbulence 671.2
agitation 916.1
boiling 1019.2
soaking 1063.7
adj heated 105.22
burning 152.29
hot 1018.25
see through perceive
521.9
penetrate 940.8
see-through 1028.4
see to prepare for
405.11
operate 888.5
attend to 982.5
see to it 969.11
segment
noun straight line
277.2
portion 477.5
sect 675.3
part 792.1
section 792.2
verb analyse 800.6
apportion 801.18
segmentation analysis
800.1
separation 801.1
segregated quarantined
429.20
secluded 584.8
separated 772.8,
801.21
unrelated 775.6
segregation quarantine
429.2
seclusion 584.1
exclusiveness 772.3
differentiation 779.4
separation 801.1
distinction 943.3
discrimination 979.4
seine 356.13
seismic 671.23
seize take command
417.14
arrest 429.15
hold 474.6
understand 521.7
usurp 640.8
secure 854.8
root 854.10
stop 856.7
infest 909.6
know 927.12
seized fast 799.14
stuck 854.16
known 927.26
seize on select 371.14
think of 930.16

seize power 417.14
seizing 480.2
seizure pang 26.2
attack 85.6
anaemia 85.9
outburst 105.9
accession 417.12
arrest 429.6
hold 474.2
seizing 480.2
take 480.10
usurpation 640.3
overrunning 909.1
spasm 916.6
frenzy 925.7
seizure of power 480.2
seldom infrequently
847.4
unusually 869.17
seldom seen infrequent
847.2
sparse 884.5
select
noun best 998.8
verb make a selection
371.1
designate 517.18
appoint 615.11
specify 864.11
discriminate 943.4
adj chosen 371.26
exclusive 495.13,
772.9
best 998.16
select committee
committee 423.2
introduction 613.5
selected 371.26
selecting 371.23
selection choice 371.1
indication 517.3
excerpt 557.3
nomination 609.11
appointment 615.2
grouping 807.3
specification 864.6
selective selecting
371.23
fastidious 495.9
exclusive 495.13,
772.9
discriminating 943.7
selectively 495.14
selectivity selectiveness
371.10
fastidiousness 495.1
exclusiveness 495.5
selector 371.7
self psyche 92.28,
918.4
ego 864.5
self-absorbed unfeeling
94.9
selfish 651.5
self-absorption
unfeeling 94.1
selfishness 651.1

self-analysis 113.3
self-appointed
presumptuous 141.10
meddlesome 214.9
self-assurance
equanimity 106.3
confidence 969.5
self-assured composed
106.13
confident 969.21
self-centred unfeeling
94.9
egotistic 140.10
selfish 651.5
self-confessed accepted
332.14
disclosive 351.10
self-confidence
equanimity 106.3
pride 136.1
confidence 969.5
self-confident
composed 106.13
proud 136.8
confident 969.21
self-congratulation
140.1
self-congratulatory
vain 140.8
self-approving 502.11
self-conscious 139.12
self-consciousness
139.4
self-contained
independent 430.22
unsociable 583.5
selfish 651.5
separate 801.20
self-control
noun equanimity 106.3
patience 134.1
self-command 359.5
restraint 428.1
temperance 668.1
moderation 670.1
verb self-govern
1040.20
self-deception
deception 356.1
illusion 975.1
self-defeating 922.10
self-defence 460.1,
600.2
self-delusion 975.1
self-denial self-control
359.5
unselfishness 652.1
asceticism 667.1
temperance 668.1
moderation 670.1
self-deprecating self-
abasing 137.12
self-effacing 139.10
self-deprecation 139.2
self-destruct blow up
395.18
fall 395.22

detect 940.5

senseless unconscious 25.8
cruel 144.26
meaningless 520.6
unordered 809.12
unintelligent 921.13
foolish 922.8
unwise 922.10
insane 925.26
illogical 935.11
inanimate 1053.5

sense of humour 489.11

sense of smell 69.4

senses five senses 24.5
wits 918.2
sanity 924.1

sensibility sensibleness 24.2
feeling 93.1
sensitivity 93.4
sagacity 919.4
cognizance 927.2
discrimination 943.1
pliancy 1045.2

sensible
noun wise 920.3
adj sentient 24.11
sensitive 93.20
grateful 150.5
weighable 297.19
cheap 633.7
substantial 762.6
intelligent 919.12
reasonable 919.18
sane 924.4
knowing 927.15
logical 934.20
realistic 986.6

sensibly positively 247.19
intelligently 919.20
reasonably 934.24

sensing 933.5

sensitive sensory 24.9
responsive 24.12
sore 26.11
sensible 93.20
excitable 105.28
touchy 110.21
confidential 345.14
fastidious 495.9
discriminating 943.7
tolerant 978.11
pliant 1045.9

sensitively 143.21

sensitive to sensible 24.11
interested 982.16

sensitivity sensitiveness 24.3
sensibility 93.4
excitability 105.10
touchiness 110.5
considerateness 143.3
pity 145.1
fastidiousness 495.1
discrimination 943.1

tolerance 978.4

sensitivity to 895.1

sensory
noun brain 918.6
adj sensorial 24.9
sensual 663.5

sensual sexual 75.24
sensualist 663.5
lascivious 665.29

sensuality sexuality 75.2
sensualness 663.1
lasciviousness 665.5

sensuous sensory 24.9
delightful 97.7
sensual 663.5

sentence
noun remark 524.4
phrase 529.1
judgment 598.10
condemnation 602.1
section 792.2
verdict 945.5
maxim 973.1
verb condemn 602.3
pass judgment 945.13

sentient 24.11

sentiment feeling 93.1
sentimentality 93.8
love 104.1
idea 931.1
opinion 952.6
attitude 977.1

sentimental
sentimentalized 93.21
loving 104.27
foolish 922.8

sentimentality
sentiment 93.8
amorousness 104.3

sentinel warner 399.4
watchman 1007.10

sentry warner 399.4
watchman 1007.10

separate
verb refine 79.22
diverge 171.5
bound 211.8
partition 213.8
interspace 224.3
open 292.11
quarantine 429.13
fall out 456.10
sow dissension 456.14
divorce 566.5
disband 770.8
segregate 772.6
differentiate 779.6
apportion 792.6
analyse 800.6
divide 801.8
part company 801.19
classify 807.11
discriminate 943.4
adj secluded 584.8
different 779.7
distinct 801.20
alone 871.8

separated interspaced 224.6
distant 261.8
quarantined 429.20
widowly 566.7
secluded 584.8
alienated 589.11
segregated 772.8
unrelated 775.6
different 779.7
disjoined 801.21
alone 871.8

separately severally 801.27
particularly 864.15
singly 871.13

separateness
unrelatedness 775.1
difference 779.1
differentiation 779.4
separation 801.1
noncohesion 803.1
aloneness 871.2

separating 801.25

separation refinement 79.4
partition 213.5
distance 261.1
quarantine 429.2
falling-out 456.4
divorce 566.1
seclusion 584.1
note 709.14
disbandment 770.3
exclusiveness 772.3
differentiation 779.4
analysis 800.1
disjunction 801.1
distinction 943.3

separatism 801.1

separatist
noun dissenter 333.3
apostate 363.5
adj repudiative 363.12

sepia 40.3

sept race 559.4
lineage 560.4
community 617.2
class 808.2

septic unhealthful 82.5
diseased 85.59
putrefactive 393.39

sepulchre 309.16

sequel following 166.1
follow-up 834.2
effect 886.1

sequence following 166.1
consistency 802.2
continuity 806.2
series 811.2
logical sequence 814.1
subsequence 834.1
effect 886.1

sequential consistent 802.11
consecutive 811.9
succeeding 814.4
resultant 886.6

deducible 934.23

serenade
noun courtship 562.7
verb court 562.21
sing 708.38

serendipity discovery 940.1
chance 971.1

serene calm 106.12
pacific 464.9
equable 670.13
light 1024.31

serenely inexcitably 106.16
moderately 670.17

serenity composure 106.2
inaction 329.1
peacefulness 464.2
moderation 670.1
uniformity 780.1

Sergeant Marshal of the RAF 575.19
Field Marshal 575.20

sergeant 1007.15

serial
noun part 554.13
radiobroadcast 1033.18
television broadcast 1034.2
adj periodical 555.1
journalistic 555.5
consistent 802.11
consecutive 811.9

serial killer 308.10

series following 166.1
edition 554.5
set 769.12
kingdom 808.5
succession 811.2
sequence 814.1
round 849.3
progression 1016.8

serious zealous 101.9
sedate 106.14
solemn 111.3
great 247.6
resolute 359.11
lofty 544.14
cognitive 930.21
notable 996.19
weighty 996.20
dangerous 1005.9

seriously zealously 101.14
sedately 106.17
solemnly 111.4
positively 247.19
resolutely 359.17

serious money 618.3

seriousness zeal 101.2
sedateness 106.4
solemnity 111.1
resolution 359.1
gravity 996.3

sermon reproof 510.5
lecture 543.3

lesson 568.7

sermons 422.1

serpent snake 311.26
traitor 357.10
beast 660.7

serpentine
noun spectrum 47.6
verb convolve 281.4
adj deviative 164.7
flowing 238.24
curved 279.7
convolutional 281.6
coiled 281.7
reptile 311.46
cunning 415.12

serrated rugged 288.7
notched 289.5

serum humour 2.22
blood 2.23
antitoxin 86.27
transfusion 91.18

servant hanger-on 138.6
instrument 384.4
subordinate 432.5
subject 432.7
servitor 577.2
assistant 616.6
believer 692.4
worker 726.2

serve
noun throw 903.3
verb be inferior 250.4
act 328.4
be instrumental 384.7
avail 387.17
summon 420.11
do duty 458.18
give 478.12
work for 577.13
officiate 724.13
play tennis 749.3
shuffle 758.4
suit 787.8
tend 895.3
throw 903.10
suffice 990.4
expedite one's affair 994.3
do good 998.10

serve and volley 749.3
serve-and-volley 749.2

service
noun serving 8.10
table service 8.11
act of kindness 143.7
rigging 180.12
instrumentality 384.3
benefit 387.4
aid 449.1
military service 458.9
branch 461.20
servanthood 577.12
ceremony 580.4
divine service 696.8
rite 701.3
task 724.2
throw 903.3
verb repair 396.14

serviceable modal
384.8
useful 387.18
helpful 449.21

serviceman 396.10

services 461.19

servicing fertilization
78.3
reparation 396.6

servile slavish 138.13
inferior 250.6
subject 432.13
downtrodden 432.16
submissive 433.12
deferential 433.16
serving 577.14

serving
noun service 8.10
rigging 180.12
adj acting 328.10
helping 449.20
servitorial 577.14

servitude subjection
432.1
service 577.12

servo 1040.13

session ecclesiastical
council 423.4
conference 541.6
match 747.3
assembly 769.2
moment 823.2

Set 680.5

set
noun navigation 159.3
direction 161.1
course 172.2
flow 238.4
form 262.1
sprout 302.11
edition 554.5
clique 617.6
setting 704.19
film studio 706.3
company 769.3
suit 769.12
group 783.5
all 791.3
cohesion 802.1
class 808.2
trend 895.2
disposition 977.3
radio 1033.3
verb be pregnant
78.12
place 159.12
establish 159.16
direct 161.5
bear 161.7
sit 173.10
sink 194.6
flow 238.16
form 262.7
sharpen 285.7
heal 396.21
prime 405.9
prescribe 420.9
allot 477.9

compose 548.16,
708.46
impose 643.4
harmonize 787.7
fasten 799.7
cohere 802.6
fix 854.9
specify 864.11
tend 895.3
thicken 1043.10
solidify 1044.8
plant 1067.18
adj trite 117.9
located 159.18
circumscribed 210.6
sharp 285.8
firm 359.12
obstinate 361.8
customary 373.14
confirmed 373.19
planned 381.12
fast 799.14
cohesive 802.10
established 854.13
fixed 854.14
assured 969.20
hardened 1044.13

set about 404.3

set against
verb offset 338.5
sow dissension 456.14
antagonize 589.7
adj hostile 589.10

set an example 785.7

set a precedent 833.3

set aside
verb repeal 445.2
segregate 772.6
allow for 958.5
adj repealed 445.3

set at undertake 404.3
set to work 725.15

set back
verb daunt 127.18
slow 175.9
indent 284.14
restrain 428.7
hinder 1011.10
adj retarded 175.12

setback disappointment
132.1
regression 163.1
slowing 175.4
relapse 394.1
discomfiture 412.2
reverse 1010.3
hindrance 1011.1

set before 371.21

set down
verb abase 137.5
deposit 159.14
affirm 334.5
reprove 510.17
record 549.15
adj humbled 137.13

set fire to excite 105.12
ignite 1019.22

set foot in go to 177.25
enter 189.7

attend 221.8

set for 405.24

set forth set out 188.8
manifest 348.5
describe 349.9
make a beginning
817.8
focus on 936.3
postulate 950.12
evidence 956.8

set free rescue 398.3
liberate 431.4
acquit 601.4

set in insert 191.3
indent 284.14
blow 318.20
begin 817.7
fix 854.9

set in motion move
172.6
motivate 375.12
execute 437.9

set off set out 188.8
border 211.10
measure off 300.11
offset 338.5
kindle 375.18
allot 477.9
explode 671.14
go contrary to 778.4
differentiate 779.6
cause 885.10
discriminate 943.4
beautify 1015.15

set of three 875.1

set on
verb base on 199.6
incite 375.17
sow dissension 456.14
adj determined upon
359.16

set on fire excite
105.12
ignite 1019.22

set out set forth 188.8
plot 381.10
phrase 532.4
dispose 807.9
begin 817.7
make a beginning
817.8

set sail hoist sail
182.20
set out 188.8
begin 817.7

set the pace lead 165.2
set an example 785.7
characterize 864.10

set the record straight
420.10

set the stage 704.28

setting
noun background
209.2
nearness 223.1
arena 463.1
motif 498.7
composition 548.2

stage setting 704.19
piece 708.5
harmonization 709.2
plot 722.4
circumstances 765.2
frame 900.10
thickening 1043.4
hardening 1044.5
planting 1067.14
adj descending 194.11

setting aside repeal
445.1
allotment 477.3

setting-off 375.2

setting sun 315.2

setting-up beginning
817.1
establishment 891.4

settle settle down
159.17
dive 184.41
arrive 186.6
sink 194.6
get down 194.7
people 225.9
gravitate 297.15
waste 308.13
resolve 359.7
do for 395.11
clobber 412.9
arrange 437.8, 466.7
pacify 465.7
reconcile 465.8
compromise 468.2
attend to 604.10
pay in full 624.13
transfer 629.3
organize 807.10
fix 854.9
interchange 862.4
conform 866.3
decide 945.11
prove 956.10
make sure 969.11

settled located 159.18
inhabited 225.12
firm 359.12
confirmed 373.19
beat 412.15
contracted 437.11
paid 624.22
ended 819.8
established 854.13
fixed 854.14
proved 956.20
assured 969.20

settle down settle
159.17
land 184.43
sink 194.6
mature 303.9
be moderate 670.5

settle for be content
107.5
interchange 862.4

settle in arrive 186.6
people 225.9

settlement
establishment 159.7

peopling 225.2
country 232.1
compact 437.1
adjustment 465.4
compromise 468.1
estate 471.4
endowment 478.9
community 617.2
payment 624.1
recompense 624.3
transfer 629.1
proof 956.3

settle on light upon
194.10
come to an agreement
332.10
resolve 359.7
transfer 629.3

settler incomer 189.4
habitant 227.9
giver 478.11
newcomer 773.4
finishing stroke 819.4

settling establishment
159.7
transfer 629.1

set to undertake 404.3
quarrel 456.11
fasten 799.7

set-to row 456.6
fight 457.4
argumentation 934.4

set to work 725.15

set up refresh 9.2
provoke 152.24
establish 159.16,
891.10
erect 200.9
plan 381.8
remedy 396.13
aid 449.11
glorify 662.13
finance 729.15
order 806.4
inaugurate 817.11
cause 885.10
produce 891.8
elevate 911.5
fix 964.5

set-up 964.8

setup structure 266.1
plan 381.1
composition 795.1
order 806.1
put-up job 964.2
cinch 1013.4

set up for 354.22

seven card 758.2
heptad 881.3

seventh
noun interval 709.20
adj septimal 881.19

seventieth 881.28

Seventy 699.9

seventy 881.7

seventy-seven 881.7

sever differentiate
779.6

dissever 801.11
discriminate 943.4

several
noun plurality 882.1
number 883.2
adj proportionate
477.13
different 779.7
diversified 782.4
particular 864.12
plural 882.7
divers 883.7

several times 848.16

severance elimination
772.2
differentiation 779.4

severe acrimonious
17.14
painful 26.10
pungent 68.6
harsh 144.24
imperious 417.16
strict 425.6
inornate 499.9
gruff 505.7
plain-speaking 535.3
violent 671.16
simple 797.6
exact 972.17
difficult 1012.17
cold 1022.14

severed 801.23

severely harshly 144.33
violently 247.23,
671.25
strictly 425.8

severity acrimony 17.5
pungency 68.1
harshness 144.9
strictness 425.1
inornateness 499.4
gruffness 505.3
plain speech 535.1
violence 671.1
simplicity 797.1
accuracy 972.5
cold 1022.1

sew stitch 741.4
hook 799.8

sewage faeces 12.4
offal 80.9
refuse 391.4

sewer
noun sink 80.12
drain 239.5
cave 284.5
gutter 654.7
needleworker 741.2
sewing machine 741.3
adj cursing 513.8

sewerage faeces 12.4
offal 80.9

sewing bookbinding
554.14
needlework 741.1

sewing machine 741.3

sex
noun gender 75.1

copulation 75.7
love 104.1
verb sexualize 75.19
adj sexual 75.24

sex appeal 377.2

sex discrimination
misanthropy 590.1
discrimination 979.4

sex drive 75.2

sexed 75.24

sexiness sexuality 75.2
sex appeal 75.3
delightfulness 97.2
amorousness 104.3
attractiveness 377.2
lasciviousness 665.5

sexism sexual
preference 75.10
misanthropy 590.1
discrimination 979.4

sexist
noun misanthrope
590.2
bigot 979.5
adj misanthropic
590.3
discriminatory 979.12

sextant celestial
navigation 182.2
goniometer 278.4
semicircle 280.8

sextet cooperation
450.1
part music 708.18
measure 720.9
six 881.2

sexton 309.8

sexual sex 75.24
amorous 104.26
gametic 305.20
amatory 562.23
lascivious 665.29

sexual abuse 75.11

sexual activity 75.2

sexual assault 480.3

sexual desire desire
100.1
craving 100.6
will 323.1
ardour 1018.2

sexual fantasy
masturbation 75.8
defence mechanism
92.23

sexual freedom 75.18

sexual harassment
389.3

sexual intercourse
copulation 75.7
lovemaking 562.1

sexuality sexual nature
75.2
lasciviousness 665.5

sexual orientation
75.10

sexual pleasure 95.1

sexual power 76.2

sexual relations 75.7

sexual revolution
75.18

sexy sexual 75.24
lustful 75.26
delightful 97.7
fun 97.8
desirable 100.30
exciting 105.30
provocative 375.27
alluring 377.8
lascivious 665.29
great 998.13

shabby squalid 80.25
inadequate 250.7
worthless 391.11
shoddy 393.32
niggardly 484.8
cheap 633.7
base 661.12
slovenly 809.15
paltry 997.21
terrible 999.9
inferior 1004.9

shack 228.9

shackle
noun restraint 428.4
curb 1011.7
verb bind 428.10
confine 429.12
hamper 1011.11

shackled 428.16

shade
noun colour 35.1
degree 245.1
hint 248.4
tinge 796.7
psyche 918.4
phantom 975.4
spectre 987.1
protection 1007.1
shadow 1026.3
shader 1027.1
verb colour 35.13
blacken 38.7
cloud 319.6
conceal 346.6
portray 712.19
darken 1026.9
screen 1027.5

shaded shadowy
1026.16
screened 1027.7

shades spectacles 29.3
eyeshade 1027.2

shading
noun blackening 38.5
gradation 245.3
treatment 712.9
darkening 1026.6
televising 1034.3
picture 1034.5
adj screening 1027.6

shadow
noun omen 133.3
hanger-on 138.6
degree 245.1
hint 248.4

remainder 256.1
paper 270.7
slim 270.8
image 349.5
treatment 712.9
spirit 763.3
reflection 784.7
psyche 918.4
phantom 975.4
spectre 987.1
protection 1007.1
shade 1026.3, 1027.1
verb colour 35.13
blacken 38.7
foreshow 133.10
stay near 223.12
cloud 319.6
lurk 346.9
image 349.11
make unintelligible
522.12
trace 937.35
darken 1026.9
shade 1027.5

shadow cabinet 613.3

shadowed shadowy
1026.16
shaded 1027.7

shadowing
noun following 166.1
ambush 346.3
pursuit 382.1
surveillance 937.9
darkening 1026.6
adj shading 1027.6

shadowy inconspicuous
32.6
obscure 522.15
thin 763.6
vague 970.19
spectral 987.7
shady 1026.16
immaterial 1051.7

shady dishonest 645.16
disreputable 661.10
shadowy 1026.16
shaded 1027.7

shaft
noun quill 3.18
air passage 239.13
tower 272.6
pole 273.1
pit 275.2, 284.4
arrow 462.6
monument 549.12
base 900.8
mine 1056.6
verb screw 389.6

shag hair 3.2
head of hair 3.4
texture 294.1

shaggy hairy 3.25
rough 288.6
nappy 294.7
dishevelled 809.14

shah 575.9

shake
noun speech defect
525.1

trill 709.19
quake 916.3
flutter 916.4
wood 1052.3
verb tremble 16.8,
127.14
weaken 16.10
agitate 105.14, 916.10
thrill 105.18
frighten 127.15
daunt 127.18
unnerve 128.10
startle 131.8
face 295.23
age 303.10
speak poorly 525.7
dance 705.5
sing 708.38
thrust 901.12
oscillate 915.10
wave 915.11
pump 915.14
quake 916.11
freeze 1022.9

shake hands near
223.7
make up 465.10
greet 585.10
strike a bargain 731.18

shake hands with
587.10

shaken agitated 105.23,
916.16
unnerved 128.14
startled 131.13
confused 984.12

shaken up 916.16

shake off free oneself
from 431.8
do away with 908.21

shake out 807.13

Shaker
noun abstainer 668.4
adj abstinent 668.10

shaker 916.9

shakes jitters 128.2
DT's 925.10
chill 1022.2

shake-up rearrangement
807.7
expedient 994.2

shake up weaken 16.10
awaken 23.5
agitate 105.14, 916.10
censure 510.13
rearrange 807.13
soften 1045.6

shakily weakly 16.22
nervously 128.16
quiveringly 916.23

shaking
noun trepidation 105.5
waving 915.2
quaking 916.2
adj jittery 128.12
inarticulate 525.12
vibrating 916.17

shaky unsteady 16.16

fearful 127.23
jittery 128.12
stricken in years
303.18
unaccustomed 374.4
inarticulate 525.12
fragile 763.7
loose 803.5
shaking 916.17
unreliable 970.20
unsafe 1005.11
cold 1022.16

shallow
noun shoal 276.2
verb shoal 276.3
adj insignificant 248.6
shoal 276.5
superficial 921.20
half-learned 929.15
trivial 997.19

shallows shoal 276.2
snags 1005.5

sham
noun fakery 354.3
fake 354.13
hoax 356.7
impostor 357.6
pretext 376.1
affectation 500.1
display 501.4
verb fake 354.21
affect 500.12
adj imitation 336.8
spurious 354.26
assumed 500.16

shaman
noun shamanist 690.7
adj sorcerous 690.14

shamanic 690.14

shamanism animism
675.6
sorcery 690.1

shambles butchery
308.3
aceldama 308.11
destruction 395.1
battlefield 463.2
marketplace 736.2
jumble 809.3

shambolic 809.16

shame
noun chagrin 96.4
regret 113.1
humiliation 137.2
abomination 638.2
iniquity 654.3
disgrace 661.5
decency 664.2
verb humiliate 137.4
disgrace 661.8

shamed humiliated
137.14
in disrepute 661.13

shameful regretful
113.8
wrong 638.3
wicked 654.16
disgraceful 661.11
terrible 999.9

shamefully
disgracefully 661.16
terribly 999.14

shameless unregretful
114.4
brazen 142.11
gaudy 501.20
wrong 638.3
dishonest 645.16
hardened 654.17
immodest 666.6

shamelessly
unregretfully 114.7
brazenly 142.14
gaudily 501.27

shampoo
noun washing 79.5
cleanser 79.17
verb wash 79.19

shamrock insignia
647.1
three 875.1

shanghai coerce 424.7
seize 480.14
abduct 482.20

shank
noun member 2.7
leg 177.14, 273.6
type 548.6
verb play 748.4

shanks 177.15

shanty 228.9

shanty-town 230.6

shape
noun aspect 33.3
apparition 33.5
fitness 84.1
outline 211.2
form 262.1
figure 262.4
structure 266.1
good condition 764.3
mode 764.4
kind 808.3
characteristic 864.4
phantom 975.4
spectre 987.1
verb form 262.7,
262.8
plan 381.8
pot 742.6
compose 795.3
conform 866.3
produce 891.8
imagine 985.14

shaped formative 262.9
structural 266.6
planned 381.12
made 891.18

shapeless formless
263.4
obscure 522.15
unordered 809.12
inconstant 853.7
abnormal 869.9
vague 970.19
unshapely 1014.8

shapely well-shaped
264.5

comely 1015.18

shape up
verb form 262.8,
806.5
improve 392.7
compose 795.3
phrase don't rock the
boat 866.10

shaping
noun forming 262.5
structure 266.1
design 717.4
composition 795.1
arrangement 807.1
production 891.2
adj almighty 677.17
imaginative 985.18

shaping-up 795.1

share
noun amount 244.2
portion 477.5
lot 738.3
part 792.1
verb respond 93.11
communicate 343.7
share in 476.6
apportion 477.6
separate 792.6

shared 776.11

shareholder
participator 476.4
shareowner 737.14

share in 476.6

share issue 738.6

share out 792.6

share-out 477.1

share power 771.3

shares 738.2

share with
communicate 343.7
apportion 477.6

sharing
noun sympathy 93.5
informing 343.2
accord 455.1
participation 476.1
apportionment 477.1
association 582.6
adj participating 476.8
mutual 776.11

shark marine animal
311.30
gyp 357.4
extortionist 480.12
savage 593.5
gambler 759.21

sharp
noun cheat 357.3
note 709.14
gambler 759.21
adj acrimonious 17.14
exquisite 24.13
painful 26.10
shrill 58.14
dissonant 61.4
bitter 64.6
pungent 68.6
strong 69.10

deep-felt 93.24
distressing 98.20
penetrating 105.31
caustic 144.23
steep 204.18
angular 278.6
keen 285.8
quick 330.18
alert 339.14
deceitful 356.22
cunning 415.12
witty 489.15
gruff 505.7
violent 671.16
smart 919.14
cold 1022.14
adv suddenly 829.9
punctually 844.14

sharpen sensitize 24.7
stimulate 105.13
aggravate 119.2
intensify 251.5
edge 285.7
tool 1039.9

sharpened 285.8

sharpening 119.1

sharper cheat 357.3
gambler 759.21

sharp-eyed clear-
sighted 27.21
vigilant 339.13

sharply caustically
144.32
gruffly 505.9

sharpness acrimony
17.5
distinctness 31.2
stridency 58.1
discord 61.1
acridness 64.2
pungency 68.1
distressfulness 98.5
causticity 144.8
keenness 285.1
quickness 330.3
alertness 339.5
cunning 415.1
wittiness 489.2
gruffness 505.3
violence 671.1
smartness 919.2
cold 1022.1

shatter demolish
395.17
splinter 801.13
madden 925.24
break 1048.3
pulverize 1049.9

shattered beat 21.8
impaired 393.27
broken 801.24

shattering
noun disruption 801.3
pulverization 1049.4
adj downright 247.12

shave contact 223.10
excise 255.10
shorten 268.6
smooth 287.5

gyp 356.19
cheapen 633.6
discount 728.27

shaved 268.9

shaven 6.17

shaving hairlessness 6.4
paper 270.7
flake 296.3
piece 792.3

shavings remainder
256.1
refuse 391.4

shaw 310.12

shay 179.4

she female 77.4
self 864.5

sheaf 769.8

shear divest 6.5
excise 255.10
shorten 268.6
strip 480.24

sheath 295.17

sheathed 295.31

shed
noun hangar 184.24
hut 228.9
verb cast 6.10
waste 473.5

shedding disrobing 6.2
waste 473.2

sheen 1024.2

sheep alabaster 37.2
jumbuck 311.7
imitator 336.4
laity 700.1
conformist 866.2

sheepish penitent 113.9
blushing 139.13
ungulate 311.44

sheepishly penitently
113.12
shyly 139.15
guilty 656.5

sheepskin 549.6

sheer
noun deviation 164.1
bias 204.3
verb deviate 164.3
change course 182.30
oblique 204.9
adj perpendicular
200.12
steep 204.18
mere 248.8
thorough 793.10
unmixed 797.7
transparent 1028.4
adv perpendicularly
200.14
absolutely 793.15

sheerness verticalness
200.1
transparency 1028.1

sheet alabaster 37.2
blanket 295.10
lamina 296.2
section 792.2

hunting 382.2
gunfire 459.8
capital punishment
604.6
game 750.6
throwing 903.2
adj painful 26.10
shooting star 133.6
shoot out 283.10
shoot-out gunfire 459.8
game 750.6
shoot up grow 14.2,
259.7
spring up 193.9
protrude 283.10
vegetate 310.31
shop
noun field 724.4
market 736.1
workplace 739.1
office 739.7
verb market 733.8
shop around choose
371.13
shop 733.8
be discriminating
943.5
shop assistant 730.3
shop at 731.16
shop floor worker
726.2
workplace 739.1
shopkeeper 730.2
shoplifting 482.1
shopper 733.5
shopping 733.1
shopping around
733.1
shopping centre
metropolis 208.7
East End 230.6
marketplace 736.2
shopping mall 739.1
shopping spree 733.1
shop steward 727.4
shop-window 206.2
shore
noun border 211.4
side 218.1
coast 234.2
verb support 449.12,
900.21
adj aquatic 182.58
coastal 234.7
shoreline
noun shore 234.2
adj coastal 234.7
shore up strengthen
15.13
support 449.12,
900.21
stiffen 1044.9
shoring 900.23
shorn 252.10
shorn of 473.8
short

noun cinema 706.1
bear 737.12
verb electrify 1031.25
adj insignificant 248.6
little 258.10
brief 268.8, 827.8
low 274.7
taciturn 344.9
gruff 505.7
concise 537.6
poor 619.7
incomplete 794.4
short of 910.5
wanting 991.13
imperfect 1002.4
adv abruptly 268.13
shortage deficiency
794.2
shortcoming 910.1
want 991.4
imperfection 1002.1
short answer gibe
508.2
answer 938.1
short-circuit 1031.25
shortcoming inequality
790.1
falling short 910.1
want 991.4
imperfection 1002.1
fault 1002.2
short corner 750.3
short-cut 268.7
short distance 223.2
shorten reduce 252.7
subtract 255.9
make small 258.9
contract 260.7
abbreviate 268.6
be brief 537.5
abridge 557.5
shortened abbreviated
268.9
concise 537.6
abridged 557.6
shortening reduction
255.2
contraction 260.1
abbreviation 268.3,
537.4
shorter 252.10
shortest 250.8
shortfall deficiency
794.2
shortcoming 910.1
want 991.4
short film 706.1
shorthand
noun phonogram 546.2
stenography 547.8
adj written 547.22
stenographic 547.27
short list 870.1
short-lived 827.7
shortly briefly 268.12
gruffly 505.9
concisely 537.7

transiently 827.10
soon 844.16
shortness irascibility
110.2
littleness 258.1
briefness 268.1
lowness 274.1
taciturnity 344.2
gruffness 505.3
conciseness 537.1
brevity 827.2
short of short 910.5
wanting 991.13
short range 223.2
short-range 223.14
shorts bear 737.12
football 745.1
rugby 746.1
short shrift pitilessness
146.1
repulse 442.2
short step 223.2
short story 722.3
short supply 991.1
short-term 827.8
short time shortness
268.1
little while 827.3
short-time 827.8
short time ago 840.16
shot
noun detonation 56.3
dose 86.6, 87.19
drink 88.7
inoculation 91.16
put-down 156.3
lightning 174.6
try 403.3
ball 462.19
fee 630.6
cinematography 706.4
photograph 714.3
take 714.8
game 745.3, 749.2,
750.6
match 747.3, 752.3
round 748.3
basketball game 751.3
throw 759.9
discharge 903.4
shooter 903.8
adj variegated 47.9
unnerved 128.14
done for 395.29
belly-up 819.9
shot down 819.9
shotgun
noun gun 462.10
verb strike dead
308.17
shot in the arm 86.8
shot through variegated
47.9
permeated 221.15
apertured 292.19
should ought to 641.3
be necessary 962.10

shoulder
noun bulge 283.3
type 548.6
joint 799.4
supporter 900.2
buttress 900.4
shelf 900.14
verb support 900.21
thrust 901.12
shouldering 901.3
shoulder to shoulder
adv cooperatively
450.6
concurrently 898.5
phrase side by side
218.12
shout
noun cry 59.1
drink 88.7
cheer 116.2
laughter 116.4
verb din 53.7
cry 59.6
cheer 116.6
laugh 116.8
be manifest 348.7
proclaim 352.13
shouting 59.10
shout out 59.8
shove
noun thrust 901.2
pushing 903.1
verb set in motion
172.6
thrust 901.12
push 903.9
shovel
noun cutlery 1039.2
verb ladle 176.17
excavate 284.15
shoving
noun pushing 903.1
adj propulsive 903.14
show
noun appearance 33.2
spectacle 33.7
externalization 206.4
display 348.2, 501.4
sham 354.3
pretext 376.1
affectation 500.1
indication 517.3
stage show 704.4
theatrical performance
704.12
marketplace 736.2
illusoriness 975.2
verb show up 31.4
appear 33.8
direct to 161.6
externalize 206.5
explain 341.10
manifest 348.5
disclose 351.4
signify 517.17
teach 568.10
project 714.16
race 757.5
evidence 956.8

prove 956.10
show business show
biz 704.1
entertainment 743.13
showcase
noun display 348.2
theatrical performance
704.12
counter 736.6
transparent substance
1028.2
verb manifest 348.5
showdown poker
759.10
contrariety 778.1
shower
noun bathe 79.8
washbasin 79.12
rain 316.1
plenty 990.2
sprinkle 1063.5
sprinkler 1063.8
verb wash 79.19
rain 316.9
give 478.12
abound 990.5
shower room 79.12
showers 79.12
show how 568.10
showing
noun appearance 33.1
externalization 206.4
display 348.2
indication 517.3
adj divested 6.12
visible 31.6
manifesting 348.9
disclosive 351.10
showing-off 501.4
showing up appearance
33.1
disclosure 351.1
showman 704.23
showmanship 704.3
shown manifested
348.13
proved 956.20
shown up 957.7
show off 348.5
show-off 501.11
show of hands 371.6
showpiece 785.1
showroom display
room 197.24
saleroom 736.5
show signs of appear to
be 33.10
augur 133.12
evidence 956.8
show through show
31.4
be transparent 1028.3
show-through
noun transparency
1028.1
adj transparent 1028.4

show up show 31.4
appear 33.8
arrive 186.6
attend 221.8
overshadow 249.8
disclose 351.4
turn up 830.6, 940.9
disprove 957.4
disillusion 976.2

showy flaunting 501.19
grandiloquent 545.8

shrapnel 462.19

shred
noun scrap 248.3
piece 792.3
verb pulverize 1049.9

shredded severed
801.23
powdery 1049.11

shredder 1049.7

shredding audio
distortion 50.13
pulverization 1049.4

shrew 110.12

shrewd cunning 415.12
artful 919.15
knowing 927.15

shrewdly cunningly
415.13
intelligently 919.20

shrewdness cunning
415.1
artfulness 919.3

shriek
noun blare 53.5
screech 58.4
cry 59.1
laughter 116.4
verb blare 53.10
screech 58.8
cry 59.6
wail 115.13
laugh 116.8
sigh 318.21
murmur 524.26

shrieking garish 35.19
shrill 58.14

shrift pardon 148.2
confession 351.3

shrill
noun screech 58.4
verb screech 58.8
adj thin 58.14
dissonant 61.4

shrimp
noun runt 258.4
verb fish 382.10

shrine
noun tomb 309.16
monument 549.12
holy place 703.4
verb enclose 212.5

shrink suffer 26.8
flinch 127.13
efface oneself 139.7
recede 168.2
retract 168.3
decrease 252.6

reduce 252.7
shrivel 260.9
demur 325.4
dodge 368.8
languish 393.18
waste 473.5

shrinkage decrement
252.3
reduction 255.2
shrinking 260.3
waste 473.2

shrink from 99.5

shrinking
noun shrinkage 260.3
demur 325.2
adj fearful 127.23
reserved 139.11
receding 168.5
demurring 325.7
reticent 344.10

shrivelled dwarf
258.13
shrunk 260.13
haggard 270.20
stricken in years
303.18
wasted 393.35
dried 1064.9

shroud
noun cover 295.2
grave clothes 309.14
supporter 900.2
verb clothe 5.38
wrap 295.20
conceal 346.6
protect 1007.18

shrouded 295.31

shrub 310.9

shrubbery 310.9

shrug
noun gesture 517.14
verb accept 134.7
submit 433.6
gesture 517.21

shrug off not care
102.4
discard 390.7
submit 433.6
underestimate 949.2
dismiss 983.4

shrunk reduced 252.10
dwarf 258.13
shrunken 260.13

shrunken reduced
252.10
dwarf 258.13
shrunk 260.13
wasted 393.35
lost 473.7

shudder
noun thrill 105.2
trepidation 105.5
shake 916.3
verb be frequent 846.3
shake 916.11
freeze 1022.9

shuddering
noun hostility 99.2

constancy 846.2
shaking 916.2
adj shaking 916.17

shuffle
noun slow motion
175.2
gait 177.12
prevarication 344.4
quibble 935.4
confusion 984.3
verb stroll 177.28
dance 705.5
make up 758.4
mix 796.10
confuse 810.3
change 853.5
quibble 935.9

shuffled disorderly
809.13
confused 984.12

shuffling
noun cardplaying
758.1
disarrangement 810.1
changing 853.3
quibbling 935.5
adj slow 175.10
dilatory 845.17
inconstant 853.7
quibbling 935.14

shun avoid 157.7,
368.6
abstain 668.7

shunt
noun impact 901.3
pushing 903.1
verb avoid 164.6
remove 176.11
push 903.9

shunted 340.14

shut
verb close 293.6
turn off 856.12
adj closed 293.9

shut down close shop
293.8
go bankrupt 625.7
lay off 856.8
turn off 856.12

shutdown closure
293.1
cessation 856.1

shut in 429.12

shut-in
noun sick person 85.42
recluse 584.5
adj unhealthy 85.53
enclosed 212.10
restricted 428.15
confined 429.19

shut off
verb separate 801.8
turn off 856.12
obstruct 1011.12
adj secluded 584.8
separated 801.21

shut out
verb close 293.6
prohibit 444.3

exclude 772.4
obstruct 1011.12
adj closed 293.9
whitewashed 412.16
excluded 772.7

shutter close shop
293.8
shade 1027.5

shutter speed 714.9

shut the door 293.6

shutting 293.1

shutting down 293.1

shuttle
noun train 179.14
aircraft 181.1
air travel 184.10
loom 740.5
oscillator 915.9
spacecraft 1073.2
verb alternate 915.13

shuttle diplomacy
609.5

shut up keep one's trap
shut 51.6
close 293.6
close shop 293.8
confine 429.12
refute 957.5

shy
noun avoidance 368.1
retreat 902.3
verb start 127.12
flinch 127.13
be startled 131.5
avoid 164.6
retract 168.3
demur 325.4
hesitate 362.7
dodge 368.8
throw 903.10
quibble 935.9
adj fearful 127.23
timid 139.12
receding 168.5
demurring 325.7
wary 494.9
incomplete 794.4
alone 871.8
doubting 954.9
wanting 991.13

shy away 168.2

shy away from flinch
127.13
hesitate 362.7
avoid 368.6

shyly fearfully 127.32
timidly 139.15

shyness fearfulness
127.3
timidity 139.4
demur 325.2

siamese 239.6

sib
noun kinfolk 559.2
adj related 559.6

Siberia jumping-off
place 261.4
Hell 1022.4

Siberian 1022.14

sibling
noun kinfolk 559.2
adj related 559.6

sic 972.20

sick
noun sick person 85.42
adj ill 85.55
disconsolate 112.28
weary 118.11
insane 925.26

sick and tired of weary
118.11
satiated 993.6

sickened 96.20

sickening
noun impairment
393.1
adj nasty 64.7
offensive 98.18

sickeningly 98.26

sickle 279.5

sick leave 222.4

sickly colourless 36.7
unhealthy 85.53

sickness disease 85.1
insanity 925.1

sickness benefit
welfarism 611.8
insurance 1007.4

sick of weary 118.11
satiated 993.6

side
noun aspect 33.3
conceit 140.4
arrogance 141.1
incline 204.4
border 211.4
flank 218.1
straight line 277.2
pretensions 501.2
boasting 502.1
bluster 503.1
lineage 560.4
party 617.4
role 704.10
team 745.2, 746.2,
747.2
interest 934.14
outlook 977.2
verb remove 176.11
border 211.10
flank 218.4
adj oblique 204.13
lateral 218.6
occasional 847.3

side against refuse
442.3
oppose 451.3
go contrary to 778.4

sideboard 1052.3

sideburns 3.8

side by side
adj near 223.14
adv in parallel 203.7
aside 218.10
cooperatively 450.6

phrase cheek to cheek 218.12

sided 218.7

side door secret passage 346.5
byway 383.4

side effect adjunct 254.1
aftermath 816.3

sidekick mate 588.4
partner 616.2
escort 768.5

sideline
noun border 211.4
avocation 724.7
merchandise 735.1
tennis 749.1
hockey 750.1
basketball 751.1
verb put away 390.6

sides 704.21

sidestep avoid 164.6
go sideways 218.5
prevaricate 344.7
dodge 368.8
compromise 468.2
quibble 935.9

side street 383.4

side-to-side 218.8

sidewalk 383.2

sideways
adj flowing 172.8
side 218.6
adv laterally 218.8

side with concur 332.9
back 449.13
take sides with 450.4

siding side 218.1
sticks and stones 1052.2
wood 1052.3

Sidney 608.5

siege enclosure 212.1
besiegement 459.5

sierra 237.6

siesta 22.3

sieve
noun refinery 79.13
network 170.3
porousness 292.8
separator 801.7
arranger 807.5
verb refine 79.22
segregate 772.6
classify 807.11
discriminate 943.4

sift refine 79.22
select 371.14
discuss 541.12
segregate 772.6
classify 800.8, 807.11
investigate 937.23
discriminate 943.4

sifting refinement 79.4
classification 800.3
grouping 807.3

sigh

noun breathing 2.19
murmur 52.4
sighing 52.8
verb murmur 52.10, 524.26
moan 52.14
lament 115.10
sough 318.21

sighing 52.8

sight
noun senses 24.5
vision 27.1
look 27.3
sighthole 29.5
field of view 31.3
view 33.6
spectacle 33.7
marvel 122.2
lot 247.4
opinion 952.6
outlook 977.2
eyesore 1014.4
verb see 27.12

sighted 27.20

sightedness 27.1

sighting 940.1

sight on 161.5

sight-seeing
noun rubbernecking 917.4
adj spectating 917.7

sign
noun prognosis 91.13
omen 133.3
poster 352.7
telltale sign 517.1
signal 517.15
symbol 518.6
letter 546.1
hint 551.4
notation 709.12
substitute 861.2
miracle 869.8
evidence 956.1
number 1016.3
verb ratify 332.12
secure 438.9
gesture 517.21
signal 517.22
letter 546.6

signal
noun sign 517.1, 517.15
hint 551.4
information technology 551.7
race 756.3
radar signal 1035.11
verb make a signal 182.52
communicate 343.7
signalize 517.22
adj remarkable 247.10
communicational 347.20
notable 996.19

signalling informing 343.2
communications 347.1

signatory 332.7

signature ratification 332.4
signing 437.3
sign 517.1
identification 517.11
sign manual 527.10
makeup 554.12
bookbinding 554.14
notation 709.12
section 792.2
acknowledgment 887.2
station identification 1033.19

signed accepted 332.14
contracted 437.11
marked 517.24

signet ratification 332.4
print 517.7
label 517.13
signature 527.10
regalia 647.3

sign for 438.9

significance
ominousness 133.7
meaning 518.1
meaningfulness 518.5
distinction 662.5
importance 996.1

significant
noun sign 518.6
adj premonitory 133.16
indicative 517.23
meaningful 518.10
prominent 662.17
evidential 956.16
important 996.17

significantly ominously 133.19
meaningfully 518.13
importantly 996.25

signified 133.15

signify augur 133.12
betoken 517.17
mean 518.8
specify 864.11
evidence 956.8
matter 996.12

signifying 517.23

sign in 186.6

signing 437.3

sign language 49.3

sign off telegraph 347.19
broadcast 1033.25

sign-off 856.1

sign of the times 133.3

sign on install 191.4
telegraph 347.19
participate 476.5
be poor 619.5
broadcast 1033.25

signor 76.7

signora 77.8

signpost post 273.4

pointer 517.4

signposted 517.24

signs disease 85.1
track 517.8

sign up install 191.4
take one's turn 824.5

sign up for 615.14

silence
noun silentness 51.1
taciturnity 344.2
verb paralyse 19.10
put to silence 51.8
strike dead 308.17
extinguish 395.15
overcome 412.7
suppress 428.8
refute 957.5

silenced 412.14

silencer 51.4

silencing 395.6

silent still 51.10
taciturn 344.9
unexpressed 519.9

silently in silence 51.13
tacitly 519.13

silent majority middle class 607.5
front 609.33
party 617.4
mediocrity 1004.5

silhouette
noun outline 211.2
contour 262.2
drawing 712.13
portrait 712.15
reflection 784.7
shadow 1026.3
verb outline 211.9

silicone 1054.2

silk smooth 287.3
smoothness 294.3
putty 1045.4

silken sleek 287.10
velvety 1045.15

silks 757.1

silky threadlike 271.7
smooth 287.9, 294.8
sleek 287.10
velvety 1045.15

sill foundation 900.6
groundsel 900.9

silliness foolishness 922.1
triviality 997.3

silly
noun silly Billy 923.6
adj nonsensical 520.7
foolish 922.8
dazed 984.14
trivial 997.19

silo garner 386.7
rocket launcher 1072.10

silt
noun dregs 256.2
phrase deposit 176.9

Silver 311.15

silver
noun tableware 8.12
whiteness 37.1
alabaster 37.2
money 728.1
precious metals 728.20
verb whiten 37.5
grey 39.3
adj white 37.7
grey 39.4
eloquent 544.8
brass 1056.17

silvered white 37.7
grey 39.4

silver jubilee 849.4

silver lining 124.3

silver medal 646.2

silver screen 706.1, 706.6

silverware tableware 8.12
hard goods 735.4

silvery white 37.7
grey 39.4
melodious 708.48
brass 1056.17

similar approximate 774.8
like 783.10
comparative 942.8

similarity relation 774.1
likeness 783.1
comparability 942.3

similarly additionally 253.11
thus 765.10
correspondingly 783.18

simile similarity 783.1
comparison 942.1

simmer
noun boiling 1019.2
verb cook 11.4
burn 152.15, 1018.22
bubble 320.4
seethe 671.12
boil 1019.20

simmered 11.6

simmering
noun cooking 11.1
boiling 1019.2
adj passionate 105.29
burning 152.29
hot 1018.25

simple soft-coloured 35.21
humble 137.10
homelike 228.33
mere 248.8
artless 416.5
tasteful 496.8
plain 499.6, 797.6
clear 521.11
elegant 533.6
plain-speaking 535.3
informal 581.3

real 760.15
essential 766.9
one 871.7
mentally deficient 921.22
ignorant 929.12
gullible 953.9
genuine 972.15
easy 1013.13

simple fact 760.3

simple matter 1013.3

simple truth 972.3

simplicity prosaicness 117.2
rusticity 233.3
decrease 252.1
artlessness 416.1
restraint 496.4
plainness 499.1
clearness 521.2
elegance 533.1
plain speech 535.1
informality 581.1
purity 797.1
oneness 871.1
mental deficiency 921.9
ignorance 929.1
gullibility 953.2
facility 1013.1

simplification
explanation 341.4
streamlining 797.2
conversion 857.1
disembarrassment 1013.6

simplified reduced 252.10
streamlined 797.9

simplify reduce 252.7
explain 341.10
chasten 499.5
make clear 521.6
streamline 797.4
facilitate 1013.7

simplistic undeveloped 406.12
oversimplified 797.10
realistic 986.6

simply to a degree 248.10
artlessly 416.7
tastefully 496.11
plainly 499.10, 535.4, 797.11
intelligibly 521.13
informally 581.4
solely 871.14
easily 1013.16

simulate imitate 336.5
sham 354.21
affect 500.12
adopt 621.4
resemble 783.7

simulated spurious 354.26
assumed 500.16
similar 783.10

simulation imitation 336.1
sham 354.3
adoption 621.2
similarity 783.1

simulator 336.4

simultaneous
accompanying 768.9
instantaneous 829.4
concurrent 835.5

simultaneously
together 768.11
at that time 820.9
at once 829.8
concurrently 835.7

sin
noun iniquity 654.3
wrongdoing 655.1
misdeed 655.2
error 974.1
verb do wrong 654.8, 655.4

since
adv subsequently 834.6
ago 836.15
ever since 836.17
conj because 887.10

sincere zealous 101.9
resolute 359.11
artless 416.5
candid 644.17
genuine 972.15

sincerely zealously 101.14
resolutely 359.17
candidly 644.23

sincerity zeal 101.2
resolution 359.1
artlessness 416.1
candour 644.4
genuineness 972.7

sinewy able-bodied 15.16
vigorous 544.11
tough 1047.4

sinful wrong 638.3
wicked 654.16
wrongdoing 655.5
ungodly 695.17
bad 999.7

sing
noun musical occasion 708.32
verb warble 60.5
be pleased 95.11
exude cheerfulness 109.6
rejoice 116.5
sigh 318.21
murmur 524.26
vocalize 708.38
poetize 720.13

singalong 708.32

singed 1019.30

Singer 741.3

singer entertainer 707.1
lead 707.6

vocalist 710.13

sing-in 708.32

singing
noun vocal music 708.13
musical occasion 708.32
adj happy 95.15
vocal 708.50

single
noun celibate 565.2
match 747.3
individual 871.4
adj unmarried 565.7
simple 797.6
characteristic 864.13
one 871.7

singled-out 371.26

single-handed 871.8

single-handedly 871.13

single man 565.3

single-minded resolute 359.11
persevering 360.8
artless 416.5
engrossed 982.17

single-mindedness
resolution 359.1
perseverance 360.1
artlessness 416.1
engrossment 982.3

single out select 371.14
specify 864.11
call attention to 982.10

singles 749.1

singleton 871.4

single woman 77.5

singly simply 797.11
particularly 864.15
individually 871.13

singular
noun number 530.8
adj wonderful 122.10
particular 864.12
characteristic 864.13
odd 869.11
one 871.7
sole 871.9
eccentric 926.5

singularity particularity 864.1
characteristic 864.4
oddity 869.3
oneness 871.1
eccentricity 926.1

singularly intensely 247.20
characteristically 864.17
oddly 869.19
singly 871.13

sinister
adj ominous 133.17
oblique 204.13
left 220.4

dishonest 645.16
bad 999.7
adverse 1010.13
adv leftward 220.6

sink
noun washbasin 79.12
sump 80.12
drain 239.5
cavity 284.2
sewer 654.7
verb weaken 16.9
burn out 21.5
disappear 34.3
fail 85.47
tipple 88.24
lose heart 112.16
sadden 112.18
recede 168.2
move 172.5
capsize 182.44
go down 194.6
decrease 252.6
deepen 275.8
dish 284.12
excavate 284.15
gravitate 297.15
age 303.10
submerge 367.7
scuttle 367.8
decline 393.17
do for 395.11
founder 410.11
bankrupt 625.8
invest 729.16
play 748.4
flit 827.6
depress 912.4
come to grief 1010.10
fall on evil days 1010.11

sinker biscuit 10.29
weight 297.6

sink in impress 93.15, 930.19
mire 243.2
be remembered 988.14

sinking
noun course 172.2
deepening 275.7
submergence 367.2
depression 912.1
adj languishing 16.21
receding 168.5
flowing 172.8
descending 194.11
weighted 297.18
dying 307.33
deteriorating 393.45

sinner evildoer 593.1
wrongdoer 660.9

sinuous curved 279.7
convolutional 281.6

sinus 279.2

sip
noun drink 8.4, 88.7
sup 62.2
hint 248.4
verb drink 8.29
taste 62.7

tipple 88.24

sipping 8.3

Sir 648.3

sir 76.7

sire
noun senior 304.5
father 560.9
Sir 648.3
jockey 757.2
author 885.4
producer 891.7
verb procreate 78.8
engender 817.14
cause 885.10

Siren 377.4

siren
noun noisemaker 53.6
spirit of the sea 240.4
amphibian 311.27
tempter 377.4
warning sign 399.3
alarm 400.1
witch 593.7
water god 678.10
bewitcher 690.9
adj alluring 377.8

Sirius 1070.4

sis 559.3

sissy
noun mollycoddle 77.10
coward 491.5
adj effeminate 77.14
cowardly 491.10

Sister 648.5

sister gal 77.6
brother 559.3
member 617.11
nun 699.17
layman 700.2
likeness 783.3

sisterhood blood relationship 559.1
fellowship 587.2, 617.3
women's rights 642.4

sister-in-law 564.2

sisters 700.1

sit be pregnant 78.12
set 173.10
convene 769.17

sit around 331.12

sit back 329.2

sit down settle 159.17
sit 173.10
strike 727.10
seat oneself 912.10

sit-down conference 541.6
strike 727.5
assembly 769.2

sit down with treat with 437.6
confer 541.11

site
noun location 159.1
arena 463.1

verb locate 159.11
place 159.12
establish 159.16
sited 159.18
sit in object 333.5
participate 476.5
sit-in objection 333.2
assembly 769.2
siting 159.6
sit on participate 476.5
appropriate 480.19
try 598.19
rest on 900.22
sit out 222.7
sitter 1007.8
sit through 134.7
sitting
noun pregnancy 78.5
conference 541.6
spiritualism 689.5
assembly 769.2
adv in council 423.6
sitting position 753.3
sitting room 197.5
situated 159.18
situation location 159.1
placement 159.6
environment 209.1
position 724.5
state 764.1
outlook 977.2
predicament 1012.4
sit up rise 200.8
wait 845.12
six match 747.3
card 758.2
half a dozen 881.2
sixpence 728.7
sixteen 881.7
sixth
noun interval 709.20
quinquesection 881.14
adj senary 881.18
sixth-form college
567.4
sixth sense senses 24.5
intuition 933.1
sixtieth 881.27
sixty 881.7
sixty-four 881.7
sixty-six 881.7
sizable 247.7, 257.16
size
noun spaciousness
158.5
largeness 257.1
extent 300.3
semiliquid 1060.5
verb adjust 257.15
classify 807.11
sizeable 158.10
sizzle
noun pep 17.3
sibilation 57.1
verb sibilate 57.2

burn 152.15
barrel 174.9
sizzling
noun snap 56.2
sibilation 57.1
adj sibilant 57.3
burning 152.29
skate 177.35
skaters 750.5
skates 179.21
skating gliding 177.16
game 750.6
skeletal skeleton 2.24
lean 270.17
haggard 270.20
skeleton
noun bones 2.2
base 199.2
outline 211.2
frame 266.4, 900.10
paper 270.7
slim 270.8
corpse 307.16
diagram 381.3
wreck 393.8
abridgment 557.1
adj skeletal 2.24
sketch
noun description 349.2
diagram 381.3
treatise 556.1
abridgment 557.1
act 704.7
drawing 712.13
likeness 783.3
verb describe 349.9
plot 381.10
outline 381.11
abridge 557.5
act 704.29
portray 712.19
sketching 712.5
sketchy incomplete
794.4
imperfect 1002.4
skew
noun deviation 164.1
bias 204.3
verb squint 28.9
deflect 164.5
oblique 204.9
go sideways 218.5
unbalance 790.3
adj deflective 164.8
askew 204.14
unequal 790.4
skewed deflective 164.8
askew 204.14
unequal 790.4
skewer
noun fastening 799.3
verb perforate 292.15
stigmatize 661.9
hook 799.8
ski glide 177.35
run 753.4
skid
noun slide 194.4

verb glide 177.35
stunt 184.40
slide 194.9
go sideways 218.5
skier 753.2
skiing gliding 177.16
snow-skiing 753.1
skilful 413.22, 998.12
skilfully 413.31
skill superiority 249.1
skilfulness 413.1
art 413.7
production 891.2
memory 988.1
skilled 413.26
skilled in 413.27
skills 927.4
skim
noun gliding 177.16
verb touch lightly 73.7
speed 174.8
glide 177.35
float 182.54
slide 194.9
contact 223.10
scratch the surface
276.4
slight 340.8
browse 570.13
examine cursorily
937.26
skimpy 991.10
skin
noun skin 2.4, 295.3
exterior 206.2
shallowness 276.1
dermis 295.3
blanket 295.12
lamina 296.2
verb peel 6.8
injure 393.13
strip 480.24
overprice 632.7
abrade 1042.7
skin-deep cutaneous
2.25, 295.32
insignificant 248.6
shallow 276.5
skinner 178.9
skinny cutaneous 2.25,
295.32
lean 270.17
skins 4.2
skint 619.10
skip
noun step 177.11
leap 366.1
wastepaper basket
391.7
verb exude
cheerfulness 109.6
rejoice 116.5
stroll 177.28
beat it 188.7, 368.11
leave undone 340.7
leap 366.5
caper 366.6
dance 705.5

play 743.23
skipper 573.8
skipping
noun leaping 366.3
adj leaping 366.7
skirmish
noun fight 457.4
verb contend 457.13
skirt
noun dress 5.16
gal 77.6, 302.7
border 211.4
verb border 211.10
side 218.4
contact 223.10
evade 368.7
circle 913.5
skirted 211.12
skirting
noun edging 211.7
adj bordering 211.11
side 218.6
skirts 211.1
skis 179.21
skulking
noun shirking 368.2
adj covert 345.12
in hiding 346.14
cowering 491.13
skull cranium 198.7
Death 307.3
skunk bear 311.23
beast 660.7
sky
noun summit 198.2
height 272.2
heavens 1070.2
verb play 748.4
elevate 911.5
sky-blue 45.3
sky-high 272.15
skylight roof 295.6
shine 1024.2
skyline 201.4
skyscraper structure
266.2
tower 272.6
slab lamina 296.2
wood 1052.3
slack
noun refuse 391.4
coal dust 1020.2
verb relax 20.7, 670.9
leave undone 340.7
shirk 368.9
loosen 803.3
fight fire 1021.7
adj weak 16.12
apathetic 94.13
inert 173.14
slow 175.10
indolent 331.19
negligent 340.10
lax 426.4
wanton 665.26
loose 803.5
slovenly 809.15

dilatory 845.17
slacken relax 20.7,
670.9
relieve 120.5
slow 175.9
abate 252.8
deteriorate 393.16
moderate 670.6
loosen 803.3
lapse into disorder
809.8
delay 845.8
hinder 1011.10
slackened 175.12
slackening weakening
16.5
relief 120.1
slowing 175.4
modulation 670.2
slacker neglecter 340.5
shirker 368.3
slackness slowness
175.1
neglect 340.1
laxness 426.1
looseness 803.2
procrastination 845.5
slacks 5.18
slag dregs 256.2
refuse 391.4
strumpet 665.14
scoria 1019.16
slalom 753.3
slam
noun report 56.1
put-down 156.3
score 409.5
hit 901.4
sock 901.5
verb crack 56.6
bad-mouth 156.6
close 293.6
belt 901.15
slander
noun monstrous lie
354.12
scandal 512.3, 552.8
verb libel 512.11
slang
noun Greek 522.7
jargon 523.9
barbarism 526.6
adj jargonish 523.19
slanging 490.1
slant
noun glance 27.4
deviation 164.1
inclination 204.2
diagonal 204.7
partiality 650.3
tendency 895.1
outlook 977.2
disposition 977.3
verb incline 204.10
go sideways 218.5
pervert 265.6
misrepresent 350.3
falsify 354.16
favour 650.8

influence 893.7
adj inclining 204.15
transverse 204.19

slanted inclining
204.15
falsified 265.11
spurious 354.26
partial 650.11

slanting
noun perversion 265.2
misrepresentation
350.1
deliberate falsehood
354.9
adj inclining 204.15

slap
noun report 56.1
smack 604.3, 901.8
verb crack 56.6
clap 159.13
smack 604.11, 901.19
adv suddenly 829.9

slap in the face
provocation 152.11
snub 157.2
slap 604.3

slap on add 253.4
coat 295.24

slapping banging 56.11
whopping 257.21

slapstick
noun wit 489.1
comedy 704.6
acting 704.8
adj burlesque 508.14
comic 704.35

slash
noun trauma 85.37
diagonal 204.7
line 517.6
discount 631.1
cheapening 633.4
engraving 713.2
break 801.4
verb cut 204.11
notch 289.4
injure 393.13
attack 510.20
cheapen 633.6
sever 801.11

slashed impaired
393.27
reduced 633.9

slashing
noun engraving 713.2
severance 801.2
adj vigorous 544.11

slate
noun ballot 609.19
credit 622.1
schedule 964.3
verb face 295.23
deprecate 510.12
schedule 964.6

slated 964.9

slates 295.6

slaughter
noun killing 308.1

butchery 308.3
destruction 395.1
unruliness 671.3
verb butcher 308.16
put an end to 395.12
rage 671.11

slaughterhouse 308.11

slaughtering 308.3

slave
noun sycophant 138.3
instrument 384.4
subject 432.7
retainer 577.1
drudge 726.3
verb work hard 725.13

slave labour 726.3

slavery servility 138.1
subjection 432.1
service 577.12
work 725.4

slaving 725.17

slavish servile 138.13
downtrodden 432.16

slavishly 138.15

slay 308.12

slayer 308.10

slaying 308.1

sleaze graft 609.34
arsehole 660.6
baseness 661.3

sleazy 661.12

sled 179.20

sledge
noun sleigh 179.20
verb glide 177.35

sledgehammer
noun tool 1039.1
verb pound 901.16

sleek
verb polish 287.7
adj slick 287.10
chic 578.13
tidy 806.8
thriving 1009.13
oily 1054.9

sleep
noun rest 20.1
slumber 22.2
unconsciousness 25.2
death 307.1
verb slumber 22.13
stagnate 173.9
neglect 340.6

sleeper slumberer
22.12
band 280.3
railway 383.7

sleep in take a rest 20.8
sleep 22.13

sleeping asleep 22.22
inert 173.14
dead 307.30
latent 519.5
unalert 983.8

sleeping bag 900.20

sleeping beauty 22.12

sleeping sickness 22.6

sleepless wakeful 23.7
industrious 330.22
vigilant 339.13
alert 339.14
persevering 360.8

sleeplessness
wakefulness 23.1
alertness 339.5

sleep on 845.9

sleepwalking
noun sleep 22.2
trance 92.19
nightwalking 177.9
adj nightwalking
177.38

sleep with 75.21

sleepy drowsy 22.21
languid 331.20

sleet
noun ice 1022.5
verb hail 1022.11

sleigh
noun sledge 179.20
verb glide 177.35

sleight chicanery 356.4
trick 356.6
stratagem 415.3

sleight of hand
juggling 356.5
trick 356.6
illusoriness 975.2

slender narrow 270.14
thin 270.16
meagre 991.10
trivial 997.19
comely 1015.18

sleuth 576.10

slew
noun bias 204.3
lot 247.4
bunch 769.7
verb change course
182.30
oblique 204.9

slewed 88.33

slice
noun lamina 296.2
piece 792.3
break 801.4
verb apportion 477.6
play 748.4
separate 792.6
sever 801.11

slicing apportionment
477.1
severance 801.2

slick
noun blanket 295.12
lamina 296.2
verb polish 287.7
oil 1054.8
adj sleek 287.10
slippery 287.11
cunning 415.12
eloquent 544.8
shrewd 919.15
oily 1054.9

adv cunningly 415.13

slicker outerwear 5.13
smoother 287.4
gyp 357.4

slicks 756.1

slide
noun gliding 177.16
slip 194.4
smooth 287.3
bolt-hole 369.3
wind instrument 711.6
photograph 714.3
print 714.5
merry-go-round
743.15
verb glide 177.35
slip 194.9
decline 393.17
elapse 820.5
go easily 1013.10

sliding
noun gliding 177.16
adj deteriorating
393.45

sliding scale 624.4

slight
noun snub 157.2
nonobservance 435.1
verb ignore 157.6
turn one's back on
340.8
flout 454.4
disparage 512.8
be inattentive 983.2
dismiss 983.4
adj frail 16.14
little 258.10
thin 270.16
shallow 276.5
rare 299.4
meagre 991.10
trivial 997.19

slightest 250.8

slightly to a degree
245.7
scarcely 248.9
small 258.16
meagrely 991.15

slim
noun lanky 270.8
verb slenderize 270.13
adj thin 270.16
sparse 884.5
meagre 991.10

slime
noun filth 80.7
slop 80.8
mud 1060.8
verb dirty 80.15

slimming 270.21

slimy filthy 80.23
obsequious 138.14
flattering 511.8
viscous 1060.12
muddy 1060.14

sling
noun dressing 86.33
slingshot 462.9
throw 903.3

verb suspend 202.8
throw 903.10

slinging 903.2

slinky thin 270.16
covert 345.12
cowering 491.13

slip
noun anchor 180.16
slide 194.4
runt 258.4
paper 270.7
blanket 295.10
youngster 302.1
girl 302.6
sprout 302.11
branch 310.18
avoidance 368.1
miss 410.4
bungle 414.5
circumvention 415.5
proof 548.5
bulletin board 549.10
misdeed 655.2
clay 742.3
slipup 974.4
harbour 1008.6
mud 1060.8
verb glide 177.35
float 182.54
slide 194.9
decline 393.17
sink 410.11
miss 410.14
bungle 414.11
give 478.12
go wrong 654.9
elapse 820.5
err 974.9
fall on evil days
1010.11

slip away steal away
368.12
give one the slip 369.9

slip back regress 163.5
deteriorate 393.16
relapse 394.4
revert 858.4

slip in insert 191.3
interpose 213.6
intrude 214.5

slip off 6.6

slip out 222.8

slippage slide 194.4
deterioration 393.3

slippery slippy 287.11
deceitful 356.22
evasive 368.15
cunning 415.12
dishonest 645.16
treacherous 645.21
unreliable 970.20
precarious 1005.12
oily 1054.9

slippery slope 885.3

slipping
noun gliding 177.16
fight 754.3
adj dying 307.33
deteriorating 393.45

out of practice 414.18
slipping away 307.33
slipping back 858.1
slipstream 184.30
slip up miss 410.14
err 974.9
slit
noun crack 224.2
furrow 290.1
break 801.4
verb cleave 224.4
furrow 290.3
open 292.11
injure 393.13
sever 801.11
adj cleft 224.7
furrowed 290.4
impaired 393.27
severed 801.23
slither
noun gait 177.12
gliding 177.16
slide 194.4
verb stroll 177.28
glide 177.35
slide 194.4
slithering
noun gliding 177.16
adj reptile 311.46
sliver scrap 248.3
piece 792.3
slob bonehead 414.9
fleabag 809.7
mud 1060.8
slog
noun walk 177.10
hit 901.4
verb stroll 177.28
drudge 725.14
play 747.4
belt 901.15
slogan call to arms
458.8
catchword 526.9
motto 973.4
slogging
noun perseverance
360.1
adj persevering 360.8
labouring 725.17
slop
noun slime 80.8
offal 80.9
refuse 391.4
mud 1060.8
mud puddle 1060.9
verb overflow 238.17
moisten 1063.12
slope
noun inclination 204.2
incline 204.4
declivity 237.2
skiing 753.1
verb incline 204.10
sloped 204.15
sloping 204.15
sloppy filthy 80.23
bungling 414.20

lax 426.4
loose 803.5
slovenly 809.15
slimy 1060.14
watery 1063.16
sloshed 88.33
slot
noun crack 224.2
opening 292.1
syntax 530.2
gambling wheel
759.16
verb cleave 224.4
sloth apathy 94.4
wretchedness 96.6
unconcern 102.2
dejection 112.3
despair 125.2
slowness 175.1
inaction 329.1
indolence 331.5
languor 331.6
flock 769.5
slots 759.16
slotted 292.19
slouch
noun slow motion
175.2
gait 177.12
idler 331.8
bungler 414.8
verb stroll 177.28
sink 194.6
idle 331.12
slough
noun cast 2.5
offal 80.9
gangrene 85.39
marsh 243.1
predicament 1012.4
mud puddle 1060.9
verb shed 6.10
discard 390.7
slovenly dirty 80.22
slipshod 340.12,
809.15
ungrammatic 531.4
slow
adj dull 117.6, 921.16
leisurely 175.10, 402.6
reluctant 325.6
indolent 331.19
languid 331.20
late 845.16
dilatory 845.17
infrequent 847.2
adv slowly 175.13
late 845.19
tardily 845.20
slow down
verb relax 20.7
restrain 428.7
retrench 635.5
moderate 670.6
strike 727.10
drive 756.4
delay 845.8
stop 1011.13

phrase easy does it
175.15
slowdown slowing
175.4
decline 252.2
economizing 635.2
strike 727.5
business cycle 731.9
slowed-down retarded
175.12
restrained 428.13
slowing 175.4
slowing down slowing
175.4
restraint 428.1
slowly dully 117.10
slow 175.13
by degrees 245.6
tardily 845.20
slow-moving 175.10
slowness dullness 117.1
leisureliness 175.1,
402.2
gait 177.12
refusal 325.1
indolence 331.5
languor 331.6
delay 845.2
procrastination 845.5
infrequency 847.1
stupidity 921.3
slow to 325.6
sludge slime 80.8
refuse 391.4
ice 1022.5
mud 1060.8
slug
noun slowcoach 175.5
idler 331.8
shot 462.19
composition 548.2
space 548.7
token 728.12
sock 901.5
verb fight 754.4
belt 901.15
sluggish apathetic
94.13
unconcerned 102.7
inert 173.14
slow 175.10
flowing 238.24
languid 331.20
dilatory 845.17
dull 921.16
sluice
noun outlet 190.9
watercourse 239.2
drain 239.5
floodgate 239.11
verb wash 79.19
flood 1063.14
slum sty 80.11
hovel 228.11
slumber
noun sleep 22.2
verb sleep 22.13
stagnate 173.9

slump
noun sinkage 194.2
decline 252.2
deterioration 393.3
declining market
737.5
shortcoming 910.1
hard times 1010.6
verb sink 194.6
decline 393.17
cheapen 633.6
fall short 910.2
slumping 393.45
slums 80.11
slur
noun aspersion 512.4
stigma 661.6
execution 708.30
notation 709.12
verb slight 340.8
defame 512.9
stigmatize 661.9
examine cursorily
937.26
stain 1003.6
slurry hotchpotch
796.6
fertilizer 889.4
slush slime 80.8
talkativeness 540.1
snow 1022.8
mud 1060.8
slut hen 77.9
pig 80.13
dog 311.17
neglecter 340.5
strumpet 665.14
slob 809.7
sly covert 345.12
cunning 415.12
cautious 494.8
shrewd 919.15
slyly surreptitiously
345.18
cunningly 415.13
smack
noun report 56.1
taste 62.1
big H 87.8
hint 248.4
try 403.3
slap 604.3, 901.8
tinge 796.7
characteristic 864.4
hit 901.4
verb crack 56.6
taste 62.7
slap 604.11, 901.19
hit 901.14
adv suddenly 829.9
smacking energetic
17.13
active 330.17
smack of 63.6
small
adj humble 137.10
insignificant 248.6,
997.17
inadequate 250.7

little 258.10
thin 270.16
ungenerous 651.6
base 661.12
narrow-minded 979.10
meagre 991.10
adv little 258.16
small amount 244.2
small arms 462.1
small beer beer 88.16
trivia 997.4
small-beer 997.20
small business 731.1
small change petty
cash 728.19
trivia 997.4
smaller reduced 252.10
fewer 884.6
smallest 250.8
small fry runt 258.4
nobody 997.7
small hours foredawn
314.4
lateness 845.1
small intestine 2.16
smallish 258.10
small-minded 979.10
small number 884.2
small-scale inferior
250.6
miniature 258.12
small space limitation
210.2
short time 827.3
small talk chitchat
541.5
gossip 552.7
small-time 997.18
small town 230.1
small-town 230.11
smart
noun smarting 26.3
verb suffer 26.8
affect 93.14
resent 152.12
adj quick 330.18
alert 339.14
witty 489.15
ridiculing 508.12
fashionable 578.11
chic 578.13
tidy 806.8
brainy 919.14
computerized 1041.19
smarten 498.8
smarting
noun smart 26.3
adj sore 26.11
smartly dressily 578.18
promptly 844.15
intelligently 919.20
smash
noun debacle 395.4
hit 409.4, 901.4
collapse 410.3
defeat 412.1

verb trap 356.20
catch 480.17

snarl
noun rasp 58.3
grimace 265.4
quarrel 456.5
complex 798.2
verb jangle 58.9
growl 60.4
redden 152.14
sigh 318.21
trap 356.20
murmur 524.26
complicate 798.3
confuse 810.3
hamper 1011.11

snarled complex 798.4
dishevelled 809.14

snatch
noun seizure 480.2
blag 482.4
piece 792.3
jerk 904.3
verb jump at 101.6
seize 480.14
steal 482.13
abduct 482.20
jerk 904.5

snatching seizure 480.2
abduction 482.9

sneak
noun dastard 491.6
rascal 660.3
verb creep 177.26
lurk 346.9
cower 491.9
smuggle 732.8

sneaking
noun creeping 177.17
adj covert 345.12
in hiding 346.14
cowering 491.13

sneak preview 706.1

sneaky covert 345.12
deceitful 356.22
cunning 415.12
cowering 491.13

sneer
noun snub 157.2
verb scoff 508.9

sneer at disdain 157.3
scoff 508.9

sneering
noun ridicule 508.1
adj contemptuous
157.8
ridiculing 508.12

sneeze
noun breathing 2.19
sibilation 57.1
verb sibilate 57.2

sneezing sibilation 57.1
anaemia 85.9

snide spiteful 144.21
spurious 354.26
disparaging 512.13
hostile 589.10

sniff

noun breathing 2.19
sibilation 57.1
snub 157.2
suction 187.5
hint 551.4
verb sibilate 57.2
smell 69.8
use 87.21
draw in 187.12
scent 940.6

sniffing
noun smelling 69.3
adj sibilant 57.3

snigger
noun laughter 116.4
verb laugh 116.8

sniggering
noun ridicule 508.1
adj ridiculing 508.12

snip
noun scrap 248.3
runt 258.4
minutia 258.7
piece 792.3
verb sever 801.11

snipe
noun cigarette 89.5
verb pull the trigger
459.22
shoot 903.12

sniper infantryman
461.9
shooter 903.8

sniping 115.4

snippets 557.4

snob 141.7

snobbery snobbishness
141.6
exclusiveness 495.5

snobbish snobby
141.14
contemptuous 157.8
exclusive 495.13,
772.9

snog
noun kiss 562.4
verb neck 562.15

snooker
noun billiards 752.1
verb play 752.4

snooping 980.6

snooty 157.8

snooze
noun nap 22.3
verb get some shut-eye
22.14

snore
noun breathing 2.19
resonance 54.1
sibilation 57.1
rasp 58.3
verb sleep 22.13
resonate 54.6
sibilate 57.2
jangle 58.9

snoring
noun breathing 2.19

resonance 54.1
adj respiratory 2.30
sibilant 57.3

snorkel tube 239.6
diving bell 367.5
extinguisher 1021.3

snorkelling 367.3

snort
noun sibilation 57.1
drink 88.7
laughter 116.4
snub 157.2
verb sibilate 57.2
grunt 60.3
use 87.21
laugh 116.8
murmur 524.26

snorting
noun ridicule 508.1
adj respiratory 2.30
ridiculing 508.12

snot humour 2.22
filth 80.7

snotty contemptuous
157.8
mucous 1060.13

snout nozzle 239.9
nose 283.8

snow
noun alabaster 37.2
basuco 87.6
granular snow 1022.8
picture 1034.5
verb give 478.12
hail 1022.11

snowball
noun accumulation
769.9
snow 1022.8
verb grow 251.6
enlarge 259.5
ball 282.7

snow-covered 1022.18

snowed 87.23

snow in 1022.11

snowman figure 349.6
snow 1022.8

snowstorm storm
671.4
snow 1022.8
picture 1034.5

snow-white 37.7

snowy white 37.7
seasonal 313.9
chaste 664.4
snowlike 1022.18

snub
noun rebuff 157.2
repulse 907.2
verb rebuff 157.5
shorten 268.6
restrain 428.7
repulse 442.5, 907.3
banish 908.17
hinder 1011.10
adj shortened 268.9

snubbed 268.9

snuff
noun breathing 2.19
sibilation 57.1
rappee 89.8
suction 187.5
verb sibilate 57.2
smell 69.8
draw in 187.12
waste 308.13
fight fire 1021.7

snuffed 1021.11

snug
noun nook 197.3
adj comfortable
121.11
seaworthy 180.18
homelike 228.33
close 293.12
tidy 806.8
cosy 1006.7

snuggle nestle 121.10
cuddle 562.17

snugly 121.14

so
adj such as 783.12
adv greatly 247.15
very 247.18
how 384.9
thus 765.10
similarly 783.18
equally 789.11
accurately 972.20
conj just so 958.15
prep, conj for 380.11

so? 997.26

soak
noun drunk 88.12
rainstorm 316.2
soaking 1063.7
verb tipple 88.24
pledge 438.10
overprice 632.7
belt 901.15
overload 992.15
liquefy 1062.5
drench 1063.13

soaked fuddled 88.33
full 793.11
overfull 992.20
drenched 1063.17

soak in absorb 187.13,
570.7
filter in 189.10

soaking
noun squeezing 192.7
imbuement 796.2
liquefaction 1062.1
soakage 1063.7
adj sorbent 187.17
soaked 1063.17
wetting 1063.18

soaking-up 570.2

soak up absorb 187.13,
570.7
thirst 1064.5
dry 1064.6

so-and-so 528.2

soap

noun cleanser 79.17
verb wash 79.19

soapbox
noun platform 900.13
verb make a speech
543.9

soap opera
sentimentality 93.8
radiobroadcast
1033.18

soapy foamy 320.7
oily 1054.9

soar move 172.5
fly 184.36
take off 193.10
loom 247.5
tower 272.10

soaring
noun course 172.2
aviation 184.1
ascent 193.1
adj flowing 172.8
flying 184.50
eminent 247.9
high 272.14

so as 958.15

so as to 380.11

sob
noun lament 115.3
verb sigh 52.14,
318.21
weep 115.12
murmur 524.26
mumble 525.9

sobbing
noun sigh 52.8
weeping 115.2
adj tearful 115.21

so be it 332.20

sober
verb moderate 670.6
adj soft-coloured
35.21
dark 38.9
grey 39.4
sedate 106.14
solemn 111.3
dignified 136.12
in one's sober senses
516.3
plain-speaking 535.3
temperate 668.9
moderate 670.10
real 760.15
sensible 919.18
cognitive 930.21
weighty 996.20

sobering 996.20

soberly sedately 106.17
solemnly 111.4
dignifiedly 136.14
moderately 670.17

so big 257.24

sobriety darkness 38.2
sedateness 106.4
solemnity 111.1
proud bearing 136.2
soberness 516.1

temperance 668.1
moderation 670.1
sensibleness 919.6
sanity 924.1

so-called spurious
354.26
pretexted 376.5
nominal 527.15

soccer 745.1

sociable
noun social gathering
582.10
adj communicative
343.10
talkative 540.9
informal 581.3
social 582.22
friendly 587.15
associational 617.17

social
noun social gathering
582.10
adj public 312.16
communal 476.9
sociable 582.22
associational 617.17

social behaviour good
behaviour 321.2
behaviourism 321.3

social class class 607.1
community 617.2

social conscience
636.5

social contract 609.6

social democracy
partisanism 609.25
progressivism 611.3
central government
612.4

social democrat
progressive 611.15
socialist 611.19

social-democratic
611.31

socialism communion
476.2
partisanism 609.25
collective ownership
611.7
democratism 612.8

socialist
noun left side 220.1
collectivist 611.19
adj left 220.4
socialistic 611.31

socialite
noun person of fashion
578.7
aristocrat 607.4
adj upper-class 607.10

socialization
cultivation 392.3
communization 476.3
attachment 480.5

socialize improve 392.9
communize 476.7
attach 480.20
politicize 611.24

socializing 476.2

social life communion
476.2
social intercourse
582.4

socially 582.25

social market 611.4

social order 612.1

social psychology
312.10

social relations 582.4

social science
behaviour 321.1
science 927.10

social security welfare
143.5
subsidy 478.8
welfarism 611.8
insurance 1007.4

social service 143.5

social services 449.3

social status 607.1

social structure 607.1

social system 607.1

social welfare welfare
143.5
welfarism 611.8

social work 143.5

social worker
philanthropist 143.8
professional 726.4

societal public 312.16
communal 476.9
populational 606.8

society
noun population 227.1
humankind 312.1
culture 373.3
société 578.6
association 582.6,
617.1
people 606.1
community 617.2
fellowship 617.3
sect 675.3
laity 700.1
company 768.2
adj associational
617.17

socio-economic 731.22

sociologist 312.10

sociology 312.10

sock
noun costume 5.9
comedy 704.6
bang 901.5
punch 901.6
verb cloak 5.39
belt 901.15

socket 284.2

socks hosiery 5.28
football 745.1
rugby 746.1

Socrates 920.2

sod land 234.1
turf 310.6

arsehole 660.6

soda beverage 10.47
extinguisher 1021.3

sodden
verb soak 1063.13
adj underdone 11.8
intoxicated 88.31
soaked 1063.17

Sodom 654.7

sodomy 75.7

sofa furniture 229.1
bed 900.19

so far thus far 211.16
to a degree 248.10
until now 837.4

soft weak 16.12
impotent 19.13
soft-coloured 35.21
faint 52.16
effeminate 77.14
sensitive 93.20
sentimental 93.21
loving 104.27
comfortable 121.11
pitying 145.7
light 298.12
out of practice 414.18
unstrict 426.5
lenient 427.7
pacific 464.9
cowardly 491.10
unintoxicating 516.4
phonetic 524.31
moderate 670.10
feebleminded 921.21
gullible 953.9
easy 1013.13
nonresistive 1045.8
slimy 1060.14
pulpy 1061.6

soft drink 10.47

soften blur 32.4
muffle 51.9
feminize 77.12
affect 93.14
relieve 120.5
have pity 145.4
move 145.5
extenuate 600.12
moderate 670.6
cushion 670.8
qualify 958.3
soften up 1045.6

softened soft-coloured
35.21
muffled 52.17
penitent 113.9
restrained 670.11
qualified 958.10
soft 1045.8

softening
noun weakening 16.5
relief 120.1
extenuation 600.5
modulation 670.2
softening-up 1045.5
adj relieving 120.9
mitigating 670.14
qualifying 958.7

easing 1045.16

soft focus 32.2

soft fruit 10.36

soft furnishings 229.1

softly faintly 52.21
gently 1045.17

softness weakness 16.1
soft colour 35.3
faintness 52.1
tenderness 93.6
comfortableness 121.2
smoothness 294.3
lightness 298.1
unstrictness 426.2
cowardice 491.1
feeblemindedness
921.8
gullibility 953.2
give 1045.1
pulpiness 1061.1

soft-spoken suave
504.18
speaking 524.32

soft spot sore spot 24.4
tendency 895.1
vulnerability 1005.4

soft touch 358.2

software 1041.11

soft water 1063.3

softwood
noun wood 1052.3
adj arboreal 310.36

soggy 1063.17

soil
noun soilure 80.5
region 231.1
country 233.1
land 234.1
verb besoil 80.16
vilify 512.10
corrupt 654.10
stigmatize 661.9
seduce 665.20
stain 1003.6

soiled sullied 80.21
unchaste 665.23
stained 1003.10

soiree social gathering
582.10
assembly 769.2

so is it 332.20

so it is 332.20

sojourn
noun sojourning 225.5
verb stop 225.8

Sol 1070.14

sol 709.7

solace
noun consolation 121.4
amusement 743.1
verb comfort 121.6
amuse 743.21

solar 1070.25

solar eclipse eclipse
1026.8
sun 1070.13

solar energy energy
17.1
fuel 1020.1

solar plexus 2.12

solar system 1070.9

solar wind 1070.13

soldier
noun ant 311.32
underworld 660.11
verb shirk 368.9
serve 458.18

soldiering 368.2

soldier on keep
doggedly at 360.3
continue 855.3

sold on pleased 95.14
belief 952.21

sole
noun fish 10.23
base 199.2
foot 199.5
adj unmarried 565.7
one 871.7
unique 871.9

solely simply 797.11
exclusively 871.14

solemn sedate 106.14
dignified 111.3,
136.12
gloomy 112.24
dull 117.6
reverent 155.9
heavy 297.16
celebrative 487.3
pompous 501.22
lofty 544.14
ceremonious 580.8
pious 692.8
worshipful 696.15
weighty 996.20

solemnity sedateness
106.4
solemness 111.1
gloom 112.7
dullness 117.1
proud bearing 136.2
weight 297.1
pomp 501.6
loftiness 544.6
formality 580.1
ceremony 580.4
rite 701.3
gravity 996.3

solemnly soberly 111.4
sadly 112.31
dignifiedly 136.14
formally 580.11

solicit make advances
439.7
canvass 440.14

soliciting 665.8

solicitor petitioner
440.7
lawyer 597.1
canvasser 730.6

solicitous sensitive
24.12
anxious 126.7

considerate 143.16
careful 339.10
courteous 504.14

solid
noun solid body 1043.6
adj firm 15.18
unanimous 332.15
faithful 644.20
solvent 729.17
substantial 762.6
sturdy 762.7
crowded 769.22
complete 793.9
permanent 852.7
stable 854.12
one 871.7
reliable 969.17
valid 972.14
great 998.13
dense 1043.12
hard 1044.10

solidarity cooperation 450.1
accord 455.1
completeness 793.1
oneness 871.1

solid fuel 1072.8

solidity firmness 15.3
solvency 729.6
substantiality 762.1
completeness 793.1
stability 854.1
immobility 854.3
oneness 871.1
reliability 969.4
validity 972.6
density 1043.1
hardness 1044.1

solidly 1043.15

soliloquy 542.1

solitary
noun recluse 584.5
oddity 869.4
adj alone 584.11, 871.8
one 871.7
eccentric 926.5

solitary confinement 429.8

solitude solitariness 584.3
aloneness 871.2

solo
noun flight 184.9
soliloquy 542.1
air 708.4
aria 708.15
keyboard 711.17
verb pilot 184.37
adj alone 871.8
adv singly 871.13

soloist 710.1

Solomon Pontius Pilate 596.5
Socrates 920.2

so long as 958.15

solstice 313.7

soluble solvable 939.3
liquefiable 1062.9

solution explanation 341.4
harmonization 709.2
resolution 939.1
expedient 994.2
liquefaction 1062.1
decoction 1062.3

solve explain 341.10
resolve 939.2
liquefy 1062.5

solvency credit 622.1
soundness 729.6

solvent
noun cleanser 79.17
thinner 270.10
dissolvent 1062.4
adj unindebted 624.23
sound 729.17
disintegrative 805.5
dissolvent 1062.8

solving 939.1

soma 2.1, 1050.3

sombre
noun gloom 1026.4
verb darken 1026.9
adj soft-coloured 35.21
dark 38.9
grey 39.4
solemn 111.3
gloomy 112.24, 1026.14
ominous 133.17
lacklustre 1026.17

some
noun somewhat 244.3
plurality 882.1
adj quantitative 244.5
plural 882.7
adv approximately 244.6

somebody person 312.5
celebrity 662.9
personage 996.8

someday 838.12

somehow in some way 384.11
by chance 971.19

someone 312.5

someplace 159.26

somersault
noun overturn 205.2
verb capsize 182.44

Somerset House 549.3

something
noun some 244.3
thing 762.3
big shot 996.9
object 1050.4
prep about 223.26

something between 104.6

something else

noun different thing 779.3
dandy 998.7
adj nothing like 786.5
great 998.13

something extra extra 254.4
gratuity 478.5

something like 783.10

something of value 338.2

sometime
adj former 836.10
occasional 847.3
adv someday 838.12

sometimes 847.5

somewhat
noun some 244.3
adv to a degree 245.7, 248.10

somewhere 159.26

somewhere else
adj abstracted 984.11
adv away 222.18

son brother 559.3
descendant 561.3

son and heir 561.3

sonar 182.2

song air 708.4
vocal music 708.13
lay 708.14
poetry 720.1

song and dance
agitation 105.4
bustle 330.4
act 704.7
commotion 809.4

songbook book 554.1
score 708.28

songstress 710.13

songwriting 547.2, 718.2

sonic 50.17

son-in-law 564.2

sonny boy 302.5
descendant 561.3

sonorous sounding 50.15
loud 53.11
resonant 54.9
grandiloquent 545.8
melodious 708.48

sons 561.1

soon in the future 838.9
presently 844.16

soon enough 844.12

sooner
noun settler 227.9
adv preferably 371.28

sooner than
adv preferably 371.28
prep instead of 861.12

soon to be 839.3

soot

noun blacking 38.6
dirt 80.6
dregs 256.2
scoria 1019.16
powder 1049.5
verb blacken 38.7
dirty 80.15

soothe relieve 120.5
quiet 173.8
pacify 465.7
calm 670.7

soothing
noun palliative 86.10
relief 120.1
pacification 465.1
modulation 670.2
adj palliative 86.40
sedative 86.45
relieving 120.9
pacificatory 465.12
tranquillizing 670.15
lubricant 1054.10

soothingly 670.17

sooty dingy 38.11
dirty 80.22

sop
noun weakling 16.6
bribe 378.2
fool 923.1
verb soak 1063.13

Sophia 919.5

sophisticated
experienced 413.28
elegant 496.9
chic 578.13
ungullible 955.5
disillusioned 976.5

sophistication
experience 413.9
taste 496.1
learning 927.4
sophistry 935.1
ungullibility 955.2

soporific
noun sleep-inducer 22.10
adj sleepy 22.21
sleep-inducing 22.23
sedative 86.45
apathetic 94.13

soppy 1063.17

soprano
noun mezzo-soprano 58.6
part 708.22
voice 709.5
adj high 58.13
vocal 708.50

sorbet 10.45

sorcerer Satanist 680.15
diviner 689.16
necromancer 690.5
illusoriness 975.2

sorcery Satanism 680.14
divination 689.10, 961.2

necromancy 690.1
illusoriness 975.2

sordid squalid 80.25
greedy 100.27
niggardly 484.8
disreputable 661.10
slovenly 809.15
terrible 999.9

sore
noun soreness 26.4
anaemia 85.9
lesion 85.36
pain 96.5
adj raw 26.11
distressing 98.20
resentful 152.26
mad 152.30
hostile 589.10
disastrous 1010.15

sorely distressingly 98.28, 247.21
disastrously 1010.18

soreness sensitivity 24.3
irritation 26.4
bitterness 152.3
anger 152.5
animosity 589.4

sorghum 66.2

sorrel
noun appaloosa 311.11
adj brown 40.3

sorrow
noun affliction 96.8
sorrowing 112.10
regret 113.1
lamentation 115.1
verb distress 98.14
grieve 112.17
aggrieve 112.19
lament 115.10

sorrowful distressing 98.20
sorrowing 112.26
plaintive 115.19

sorry unhappy 112.21
regretful 113.8
low 497.15
disgraceful 661.11
paltry 997.21

sort
noun nature 766.4
kind 808.3
verb size 257.15
classify 800.8, 807.11, 808.6
discriminate 943.4

sorted arranged 807.14
classified 808.8

sortie mission 184.11
attack 459.1

sorting classification 800.3, 808.1
grouping 807.3

sorting out
classification 800.3
grouping 807.3
solution 939.1

sort of 245.7

sort out plan 381.8
  injure 393.13
  arrange 437.8, 807.8
  beat up 604.14
  disinvolve 797.5
  classify 800.8, 807.11
  think about 930.11
  solve 939.2
  discriminate 943.4
  make sure 969.11

SOS 400.1

so-so
  adj medium 246.3
  mediocre 1004.7
  adv mediocrely
    1004.11

sot 88.11

so that
  conj so 958.15
  prep, conj for 380.11

so to speak 783.19

sou 997.5

sought-after desirable
    100.30
  fashionable 578.11
  distinguished 662.16

soul passion 93.2
  heart 93.3
  substance 196.5
  interior 207.2
  life force 306.3
  person 312.5
  spirit 689.18
  something 762.3
  essence 766.2
  inner nature 766.5
  particularity 864.1
  individual 871.4
  psyche 918.4
  genius 919.8

soul-destroying 308.23

soulful 93.17

soulless unfeeling 94.9
  cruel 144.26
  animal 311.38
  inanimate 1053.5

soul mate 783.3

souls 227.1

soul-searching 113.3

sound
  noun sonance 50.1
  inlet 242.1
  feeler 941.4
  verb appear to be
    33.10
  blare 53.10
  reverberate 54.7
  ring 54.8
  take soundings 275.9
  measure 300.10
  plunge 367.6
  say 524.23
  blow a horn 708.42
  investigate 937.23
  sound out 941.9
  adj firm 15.18
  whole 83.11

orthodox 687.7
solvent 729.17
sturdy 762.7
stable 854.12
sensible 919.18
sane 924.4
logical 934.20
reliable 969.17
valid 972.14
realistic 986.6
good 998.12
intact 1001.7
unhazardous 1006.5

sounded sounding
    50.15
  speech 524.30

sound effects 1033.18

sounder telegraph
    347.2
  feeler 941.4

sounding
  noun sonation 50.4
  adj sonorous 50.15
  reverberating 54.11
  ringing 54.12

sound like appear to be
    33.10
  resemble 783.7

soundly strongly 15.23
  reasonably 934.24

soundness firmness
    15.3
  healthiness 83.2
  orthodoxy 687.1
  solvency 729.6
  substantiality 762.1
  stability 854.1
  sensibleness 919.6
  sanity 924.1
  reasonableness 934.9
  reliability 969.4
  validity 972.6
  goodness 998.1
  integrity 1001.2

sound out 941.9

soup potage 10.10
  airspace 184.32
  paper 270.7
  processing solution
    714.13
  semiliquid 1060.5

sour
  noun sourness 67.1
  vinegar 67.2
  verb acerbate 110.16
  aggravate 119.2
  adj dissonant 61.4
  flavoured 62.9
  bitter 64.6
  soured 67.5, 110.23
  pungent 68.6
  unpleasant 98.17
  discontented 108.7
  tainted 393.41

source headwaters
    238.2
  motive 375.1
  source of supply 386.4
  informant 551.5

origin 885.5

sour cream 67.2

soured sour 67.5,
    110.23
  aggravated 119.4
  disappointed 132.5
  tainted 393.41

sour grapes 512.1

sourly 110.27

souter 5.37

South 231.7

south
  noun points of the
    compass 161.3
  adj northern 161.14
  adv S 161.16
  down 194.13

South America 231.6,
    235.1

southbound 161.14

South coast 231.7

Southeast 231.7

southeast
  noun points of the
    compass 161.3
  adj northern 161.14

southerly
  adj northern 161.14
  adv south 161.16

southern 161.14

Southerner 227.11

Southern Hemisphere
    231.6

southernmost 161.14

South Pole opposites
    215.2
  jumping-off place
    261.4
  Siberia 1022.4

south pole 1031.8

South Wales 231.7

southward
  noun points of the
    compass 161.3
  adv south 161.16

southwards 161.16

Southwest 231.7

southwest
  noun points of the
    compass 161.3
  adj northern 161.14

southwestern 161.14

souvenir memory 988.1
  memento 988.7

sovereign
  noun potentate 575.8
  specie 728.4
  adj omnipotent 18.13
  chief 249.14
  regal 417.17
  independent 430.22
  governing 612.18
  almighty 677.17

sovereignty nationhood
    232.6

supremacy 249.3
governance 417.5
royalty 417.8
ownership 469.2
directorship 573.4
government 612.1

so very much 247.15

soviet council 423.1
  legislature 613.1

sow
  noun hen 77.9
  swine 311.9
  cast 1056.5
  verb disperse 770.4
  plant 1067.18

so what? who cares?
    102.11
  what does it matter?
    997.26

sowing 1067.14

spa bathing place 79.10
  fitness 84.1
  health resort 91.23
  resort 228.27

space
  noun extent 158.1
  airspace 184.32
  compartment 197.2
  interval 224.1
  region 231.1
  degree 245.1
  capacity 257.2
  distance 261.1
  opening 292.1
  latitude 430.4
  spacing 548.7
  stave 708.29
  time 820.1
  period 823.1
  opportunity 842.2
  outer space 1070.3
  verb interspace 224.3
  dispose 807.9
  adj spatial 158.9
  extraterrestrial
    1070.26

Space Age 823.6

space age 840.3

space-age 840.13

spacecraft 1073.2

spaced high 87.23
  interspaced 224.6

spaced out 224.6

spaceship rocket plane
    181.4
  spacecraft 1073.2

space shuttle aircraft
    181.1
  spacecraft 1073.2

space station 1073.5

space travel 1073.1

spacey 87.23

spacing 548.7

spacious sizeable
    158.10
  large 247.7
  voluminous 257.17

broad 269.6

spade ladle 176.17
  excavate 284.15
  cultivate 1067.17

spades 758.2

spaghetti 10.32

spall 1057.4

span
  noun rig 179.5
  short distance 223.2
  distance 261.1
  length 267.1
  breadth 269.1
  arch 279.4
  bridge 383.9
  period 823.1
  short time 827.3
  two 872.2
  verb extend 158.8
  overlie 295.30
  measure 300.10
  put together 799.5
  double 872.5

spangle
  noun glitter 1024.7
  verb variegate 47.7
  figure 498.9
  glitter 1024.24

spangled spotted 47.13
  ornamented 498.11
  illuminated 1024.39

spaniel 138.3

spanking
  noun corporal
    punishment 604.4
  adj energetic 17.13
  whopping 257.21
  active 330.17
  brand-new 840.10

spanking new 840.10

spanning 295.36

spar
  noun timber 180.13
  beam 273.3
  boxing 457.9
  lever 905.4
  verb quarrel 456.11
  contend 457.13
  fight 754.4
  argue 934.16

spare
  noun surplus 992.5
  verb have pity 145.4
  forgive 148.3
  refrain 329.3
  not use 390.5
  preserve 397.8
  exempt 430.14
  relinquish 475.3
  give away 478.21
  afford 626.7
  abstain 668.7
  adj additional 253.10
  remaining 256.7
  lean 270.17
  reserved 386.15
  unused 390.12
  leisure 402.5
  plain-speaking 535.3

economical 635.6
simple 797.6
occasional 847.3
substitute 861.8
meagre 991.10
superfluous 992.17
surplus 992.18

spare a thought for
982.5

spared forgiven 148.7
preserved 397.12
exempt 430.30

spare room 158.3

spares 861.2

spare time 402.1

sparing
noun pardon 148.2
economizing 635.2
adj forgiving 148.6
parsimonious 484.7
economical 635.6
temperate 668.9
meagre 991.10

sparingly thinly 270.23
economically 635.7
temperately 668.12
meagrely 991.15

spark
noun hint 248.4
inspiration 375.9
prompter 375.10
dandy 500.9
immediate cause 885.3
sparkle 1018.15
glitter 1024.7
verb motivate 375.12
kindle 375.18
cause 885.10
burn 1018.22
glitter 1024.24

sparking
noun inspiration 375.9
adj burning 1018.27

sparkle
noun bubbling 320.3
spirit 544.4
spark 1018.15
glitter 1024.7
verb exude
cheerfulness 109.6
bubble 320.4
joke 489.13
be brilliant 919.11
glitter 1024.24

sparkling happy 95.15
cheerful 109.11
bubbly 320.6
witty 489.15
spirited 544.12
gorgeous 1015.20
glittering 1024.35

sparkling wine 88.17

spark off kindle 375.18
cause 885.10

sparks 183.6

sparky 101.8

sparring partner 754.2

sparse dispersed 770.9

infrequent 847.2
scant 884.5
scarce 991.11

sparsely thinly 270.23
scatteringly 770.12
infrequently 847.4
sparsim 884.8
scarcely 991.16

Spartan
noun stoic 134.3
man of few words
344.5
adj patient 134.9
strict 425.6
inornate 499.9
plain-speaking 535.3
concise 537.6
abstinent 668.10
meagre 991.10

spasm pang 26.2
seizure 85.6
anaemia 85.9
pain 96.5
outburst 105.9
bustle 330.4
upheaval 671.5
revolution 859.1
convulsion 916.6
frenzy 925.7

spasmodic painful
26.10
convulsive 671.23
nonuniform 781.3
unordered 809.12
discontinuous 812.4
inconstant 853.7
jerky 916.19

spasms 916.2

spastic
noun sick person 85.42
adj convulsive 671.23
irregular 850.3
jerky 916.19
blockheaded 921.17
mentally deficient
921.22
foolish 922.8

spat
noun quarrel 456.5
young 561.2
verb quarrel 456.11

spate flow 238.4
torrent 238.5
quantity 247.3
lot 247.4
rainstorm 316.2
outburst 671.6
throng 769.4
plenty 990.2
superabundance 992.2

spatial 158.9

spattered sprinkled
770.10
spotted 1003.9

spatula palette 712.18
chisel 715.4

spawn
noun egg 305.15
young 561.2

verb lay 78.9
originate 891.12

speak sound 50.14
signal 182.52, 517.22
affirm 334.5
communicate 343.6
command 420.8
talk 523.16, 524.20
remark 524.25
address 524.27
make a speech 543.9

Speaker 610.3

speaker loudspeaker
50.8
talker 524.18, 543.4
chairman 574.5
spokesman 576.5

Speaker of the House
610.3

speak for represent
576.14
defend 600.10

speaking
noun communication
343.1
speech 524.1
utterance 524.3
public speaking 543.1
adj premonitory
133.16
talking 524.32
lifelike 783.16

speaking of 842.13

speaking out 334.2

speak of herald 133.14
signify 517.17

speak out come out
348.6
brave 492.11
speak up 524.22
be frank 644.12

speak to 524.27

speak up come out
348.6
brave 492.11
speak out 524.22

speak up for 600.10

spear
noun leaf 310.17
branch 310.18
stem 310.19
throwing spear 462.8
verb perforate 292.15
stab 459.25
catch 480.17

spearhead
noun vanguard 216.2
verb lead 165.2

special
noun train 179.14
commodity 735.2
specific 864.3
feature 865.2
adj newspaper 555.2
studentlike 572.12
detailed 765.9
other 779.8
classificational 808.7

particular 864.12
notable 996.19

Special Branch
1007.17

special case speciality
864.2
qualification 958.1

special committee
423.2

special correspondent
555.4

special edition 555.2

special effects 706.4

Special Forces 461.14

special interest
pressure group 609.31
interest 982.2

special interests 893.6

specialist
noun doctor 90.4
dentist 90.6
stockbroker 737.10
specializer 865.3
adj specialized 865.5

speciality talent 413.4
study 568.8
field 724.4
vocation 724.6
component 795.2
specialness 864.2
characteristic 864.4
specialty 865.1
science 927.10

specialization vocation
724.6
differentiation 779.4
particularization 864.7
speciality 865.1

specialize limit 210.5
differentiate 779.6
particularize 864.9
specify 864.11
feature 865.4

specialized 865.5

specialize in practice
328.8
study to be 570.15
specialize 865.4

specially 864.15

special permission
443.1

special pleading
defence 600.2
argument 934.5
sophistry 935.1

special police 1007.17

special school 567.4

special treatment
958.1

specialty field 724.4
speciality 864.2, 865.1
characteristic 864.4

species nomenclature
527.1
race 559.4
kind 808.3

kingdom 808.5
biology 1066.1

specific
noun remedy 86.1
special 864.3
adj circumscribed
210.6
detailed 765.9
classificational 808.7
particular 864.12

specifically fully
765.13
particularly 864.15

specification
circumscription 210.1
description 349.2
indication 517.3
accusation 599.1
circumstantiation
765.5
differentiation 779.4
designation 864.6
qualification 958.1
condition 958.2

specificity 765.4

specifics 760.4

specified 958.8

specify circumscribe
210.4
designate 517.18
name 527.11
itemize 765.6
differentiate 779.6
specialize 864.11
focus on 936.3
call attention to
982.10

specifying 864.6

specimen sample 62.4,
785.3
representative 349.7

specious meretricious
354.27
pretexted 376.5
sophistical 935.10
illusory 975.9

speck
noun spottiness 47.3
modicum 248.2
minutia 258.7
mark 517.5
intruder 773.2
stain 1003.3
verb variegate 47.7
mark 517.19
sprinkle 770.6
spot 1003.5

speckled spotted 47.13,
1003.9
sprinkled 770.10

specs 29.3

spectacle sight 33.7
marvel 122.2
display 501.4

spectacles 29.3

spectacular astonishing
122.12
gaudy 501.20

godly 692.9
supernatural 869.15
mental 918.7
attitudinal 977.7
spectral 987.7
immaterial 1051.7
spiritualism spiritism
689.5
immaterialism 1051.3
spiritualist
noun psychic 689.13
immaterialist 1051.4
adj idealist 1051.8
spirituality bliss 681.5
godliness 692.2
immateriality 1051.1
spiritually 977.9
spit
noun humour 2.22
saliva 13.3
sibilation 57.1
jet 238.9
point 283.9
fire iron 1019.12
verb salivate 13.6
snap 56.7
sibilate 57.2
growl 60.4
redden 152.14
jet 238.20
perforate 292.15
rain 316.9
stab 459.25
spite hate 103.1
despite 144.6
hostility 589.3
grudge 589.5
spiteful irascible
110.19
despiteful 144.21
hostile 589.10
spite of 338.9
spitfire bitch 110.12
goon 671.10
spitting 56.2
spittle 13.3
splash
noun spottiness 47.3
ripple 52.5
lap 238.8
mark 517.5
stain 1003.3
sprinkle 1063.5
verb ripple 52.11
spatter 80.18
lap 238.19
cut a dash 501.13
sprinkle 770.6
dramatize 996.16
spot 1003.5
moisten 1063.12
splashed sprinkled
770.10
spotted 1003.9
splashing
noun wetting 1063.6
adj rippling 52.19
splash out 486.3

splatter
noun rain 316.1
stain 1003.3
sprinkle 1063.5
verb drum 55.4
spatter 80.18
sprinkle 770.6
spot 1003.5
moisten 1063.12
splattered sprinkled
770.10
spotted 1003.9
splayed diverging
171.8
recumbent 201.8
spread 259.11
spleen viscera 2.14
unpleasure 96.1
ill humour 110.1
melancholy 112.5
weariness 118.3
bitterness 152.3
splendid grandiose
501.21
illustrious 662.19
good 998.12
superb 998.15
gorgeous 1015.20
bright 1024.32
splendidly intensely
247.20
grandiosely 501.28
excellently 998.22
gorgeously 1015.25
splendour grandeur
501.5
illustriousness 662.6
gorgeousness 1015.6
brightness 1024.4
spliced related 774.9
joined 799.13
spliff 87.11
splint
noun dressing 86.33
verb treat 91.24
splinter
noun scrap 248.3
paper 270.7
party 617.4
piece 792.3
break 801.4
verb shatter 801.13
splintered 801.23
splinter group 617.4
splintering 801.3
split
noun crack 224.2
opening 292.1
falling-out 456.4
shares 738.2
break 801.4
blemish 1003.1
verb laugh 116.8
beat it 188.7, 222.10,
368.11
cleave 224.4
open 292.11
break 393.23, 801.12

demolish 395.17
fall out 456.10
apportion 477.6,
801.18
sever 801.11
disintegrate 805.3
blemish 1003.4
adj cleft 224.7
impaired 393.27
severed 801.23
halved 874.6
blemished 1003.8
split off diverge 171.5
interspace 224.3
dissent 333.4
separate 801.8
split-off 224.6
split second 829.3
splitting
noun apportionment
477.1
severance 801.2
dissociation 805.2
adj violent 671.16
splitting-up 801.1
split-up disbandment
770.3
separation 801.1
split up apportion
477.6
divorce 566.5
disband 770.8
apportion 801.18
part company 801.19
spluttering staccato
55.7
fluttering 916.18
spoil
noun booty 482.11
verb mar 393.10
decay 393.22
bungle 414.11
indulge 427.6
plunder 482.17
thwart 1011.15
offend 1014.5
spoiled nasty 64.7
decayed 393.40
ruined 395.28
botched 414.21
indulged 427.9
ugly 1014.6
spoiler plunderer 483.6
motor racing 756.1
spoiling impairment
393.1
indulgence 427.3
plundering 482.6
spoils gain 472.3
booty 482.11
spoke radiation 171.2
step 193.5
curb 1011.7
spoken vernacular
523.18
speech 524.30
spoken for 421.10
spoken language 523.1

spoken word 524.3
spokes 169.1
spokesman mediator
466.3
speaker 543.4
informant 551.5
spokeswoman 576.5
spokesperson mediator
466.3
informant 551.5
spokesman 576.5
spokeswoman mediator
466.3
speaker 543.4
informant 551.5
spokesman 576.5
sponge
noun washing 79.5
bathe 79.8
dressing 86.33
drunk 88.12
parasite 138.5
sorption 187.6
porousness 292.8
air 298.2
marine animal 311.30
eradicator 395.9
pulp 1061.2
verb wash 79.19
absorb 187.13
obliterate 395.16
give 634.4
moisten 1063.12
dry 1064.6
sponging
noun washing 79.5
obsequiousness 138.2
sorption 187.6
adj obsequious 138.14
indolent 331.19
spongy sorbent 187.17
porous 292.20
pulpy 1045.11, 1061.6
sponsor
noun guarantor 438.6
supporter 616.9
financer 729.9
verb secure 438.9
patronize 449.15
finance 729.15
sponsorship
guarantorship 438.8
patronage 449.4
financing 729.2
spontaneity
voluntariness 324.2
unpremeditation 365.4
spontaneous voluntary
324.7
unpremeditated
365.11
instinctive 933.6
automated 1040.21
spontaneously
voluntarily 324.10
intuitively 933.7
spoof 356.7
spook

noun spectre 987.1
verb frighten 127.15
haunt 987.6
spooked 127.22
spooky 127.31
spoon 176.17
spoonful 248.2
spoons 8.12
sporadic contagious
85.61
dispersed 770.9
nonuniform 781.3
unordered 809.12
irregular 850.3
sporadically
scatteringly 770.12
nonuniformly 781.4
disjointedly 801.28
haphazardly 809.18
discontinuously 812.5
occasionally 847.5
irregularly 850.4
sport
noun hunting 382.2
joke 489.6
banter 490.1
fun 743.2
toy 743.16
sports 744.1
gambler 759.21
misfit 788.4
transformation 851.3
verb wear 5.43
hunt 382.9
play 743.23
gamble 759.23
sporting
noun hunting 382.2
gambling 759.1
adj fair-minded 649.9
sports 743.30
sports
noun athletics 743.8
sport 744.1
adj sporting 743.30
sportsman hunter
382.5
athlete 743.19
sportsmanship
competition 457.2
fairness 649.3
sportswear clothing 5.1
dry goods 735.3
sporty 5.46
spot
noun spottiness 47.3
soil 80.5
drink 88.7
location 159.1
modicum 248.2
mark 517.5
stigma 661.6
table 752.2
state 764.1
intruder 773.2
crisis 842.4
stain 1003.3
pickle 1012.5

signal 1035.11
verb see 27.12
variegate 47.7
soil 80.16
spatter 80.18
locate 159.11
mark 517.19
sprinkle 770.6
detect 940.5
bespot 1003.5
receive 1035.17

spotless clean 79.25
honest 644.13
chaste 653.7, 664.4
stainless 657.7
perfect 1001.6

spotlight
noun lighting 1024.19
verb manifest 348.5
emphasize 996.14
illuminate 1024.28

spot-on apt 787.10
accurate 972.16

spots 738.11

spotted dotted 47.13
soiled 80.21
located 159.18
unvirtuous 654.12
sprinkled 770.10
spotty 1003.9

spotter secret agent
576.9
tec 576.11
watchman 1007.10

spotting placement
159.6
discovery 940.1

spotty spotted 47.13,
1003.9
discontinuous 812.4
irregular 850.3
sparse 884.5

spouse 563.6

spout
noun outlet 190.9
ascent 193.1
jet 238.9
beak 239.8
rainstorm 316.2
disgorgement 908.7
verb run out 190.13
jet 238.20
declaim 543.10
erupt 671.13
overact 704.31
disgorge 908.25

sprain 393.13

sprawl
noun tumble 194.3
recumbency 201.2
oversize 257.5
verb rest 20.6
tumble 194.8
lie 201.5
spread 259.6
be long 267.5

sprawled 201.8

sprawling recumbent
201.8
spread 259.11

spray
noun perfumer 70.6
jet 238.9
branch 310.18
bouquet 310.23
foam 320.2
volley 459.9
member 792.4
shot 903.4
sprinkle 1063.5
sprinkler 1063.8
vaporizer 1065.6
verb jet 238.20
moisten 1063.12
vaporize 1065.8

sprayer 1063.8

spraying 1063.6

spread
noun meal 8.5
food 10.1
space 158.1
increase 251.1
size 257.1
expansion 259.1
breadth 269.1
blanket 295.10
publication 352.1
advertisement 352.6
option 737.21
caption 936.2
verb extend 158.8
diverge 171.5
radiate 171.6
transfer 176.10
grow 251.6
spread out 259.6
broaden 269.4
open 292.11
publish 352.10
come out 352.16
report 552.11
disperse 770.4
generalize 863.9
adj recumbent 201.8
increased 251.7
spreading 259.11
published 352.17
dispersed 770.9
phrase transference
176.1

spreading
noun expansion 259.1
publication 352.1
adj contagious 85.61
spacious 158.10
increasing 251.8
spread 259.11
dispersive 770.11
phrase transference
176.1

spread on 295.24

spread out diverge
171.5
spread 259.6
open 292.11

spread-out spread
259.11

broad 269.6

spread over cover
295.19
overspread 909.5

spreadsheet arranger
807.5
list 870.1
systems program
1041.12

spread with 295.24

spree
noun drinking bout
88.5
revel 743.6
verb go on a spree
88.28
make merry 743.24

sprig youngster 302.1
sprout 302.11
branch 310.18
member 792.4

sprightly
adj gay 109.14
active 330.17
agile 413.23
witty 489.15
adv actively 330.25

spring
noun progression
162.1
ascent 193.1
lake 241.1
springtide 313.2
leap 366.1
motive 375.1
source of supply 386.4
flock 769.6
fountainhead 885.6
recoil 902.2
elasticity 1046.1
elastic 1046.3
verb speed 174.8
distort 265.5
leap 366.5
blow up 395.18
exempt 430.14
release 431.5
recoil 902.6
give 1046.5
adj seasonal 313.9

springboard 1046.3

springbok 311.5

spring from 886.5

springing
noun leaping 366.3
release 431.2
adj ascending 193.14
leaping 366.7
recoiling 902.10

springs resort 228.27
bedding 900.20

springtime 313.2

spring up grow 14.2,
259.7
burst forth 33.9
shoot up 193.9
turn up 830.6

spring water 1063.3

springy quick 330.18
recoiling 902.10
pliant 1045.9
elastic 1046.7

sprinkle
noun rain 316.1
spray 1063.5
verb variegate 47.7
rain 316.9
baptize 701.16
besprinkle 770.6
moisten 1063.12

sprinkled spotted 47.13
spattered 770.10
sparse 884.5

sprinkler extinguisher
1021.3
sparger 1063.8

sprinkling hint 248.4
baptism 701.6
tinge 796.7
few 884.2
wetting 1063.6

sprint
noun run 174.3
verb speed 174.8

sprinter 174.5

sprite fairy 678.8
imp 680.7
spectre 987.1

sprout
noun seedling 302.11
branch 310.18
offshoot 561.4
upstart 606.7
verb grow 14.2, 259.7
vegetate 310.31

sprouting
noun growth 259.3
vegetation 310.30
adj grown 14.3,
259.12

spruce
verb clean 79.18
perfect 392.11
adj dressed up 5.45
cleaned 79.26
shapely 264.5
chic 578.13
tidy 806.8

sprung distorted 265.10
impaired 393.27
free 430.21
broken 801.24

spry active 330.17
quick 330.18
agile 413.23

spunk vim 17.2
pluck 359.3
balls 492.4
tinder 1020.6

spunky hot-tempered
110.25
ballsy 492.19

spur
noun mountain 237.6
point 283.9
projection 285.4

goad 375.8
member 792.4
verb sharpen 285.7
goad 375.15
hasten 401.4
drive 1068.8

spurious ungenuine
354.26
assumed 500.16
illegitimate 674.7

spurn
noun snub 157.2
verb scout 157.4
reject 372.2
be hard to please
495.8
have nothing to do
with 586.5
repulse 907.3
banish 908.17

spurned unloved 99.10
rejected 372.3

spur-of-the-moment
extemporaneous
365.12
hasty 401.9

spurt
noun run 174.3
ascent 193.1
jet 238.9
bustle 330.4
outburst 671.6
short time 827.3
disgorgement 908.7
verb run out 190.13
shoot up 193.9
jet 238.20
make haste 401.5
disgorge 908.25

sputnik 1073.6

spy
noun informer 551.6
secret agent 576.9
verb see 27.12
reconnoitre 937.28
detect 940.5
pry 980.4

spying observation 27.2
surveillance 937.9

spy on 27.13

squabble
noun quarrel 456.5
verb quarrel 456.11

squabbling 457.1

squad unit 461.21
team 617.7, 745.2,
746.2
ice hockey team 750.5
basketball team 751.2
company 769.3

squadron unit 461.21
navy 461.26
air force 461.28

Squadron Leader
575.19

squalid sordid 80.25
base 661.12
slovenly 809.15

stagnant inert 173.14
  passive 329.6
  languid 331.20
stagnate vegetate 173.9
  do nothing 329.2
stagnation inertness 173.4
  inaction 329.1
staid sedate 106.14
  solemn 111.3
  unimaginative 986.5
stain
  noun colour 35.8
  soil 80.5
  mark 517.5
  stigma 661.6
  taint 1003.3
  verb colour 35.13
  soil 80.16
  mark 517.19
  stigmatize 661.9
  bestain 1003.6
stained coloured 35.16
  soiled 80.21
  discoloured 1003.10
stained glass picture 712.11
  light filter 1027.4
stained glass window 712.11
staining colouring 35.11
  painting 35.12
stainless clean 79.25
  honest 644.13
  spotless 657.7
  chaste 664.4
  perfect 1001.6
stair step 193.5
  degree 245.1
staircase 193.3
stairs 193.3
stairway 193.3
stake
  noun state 231.5
  leg 273.6
  collateral 438.3
  estate 471.4
  portion 477.5
  scaffold 605.5
  bet 759.3
  burning 1019.5
  verb pledge 438.10
  bet 759.25
staked 438.12
stake out look 27.13
  circumscribe 210.4
  reconnoitre 937.28
stakes 759.5
staking 759.1
stale
  noun urine 12.5
  verb urinate 12.14
  adj insipid 65.2
  trite 117.9
  tainted 393.41
  fusty 841.14

stalemate
  noun same 789.3
  stop 856.2
  impasse 1012.6
  verb put a stop to 856.11
Stalinism communism 611.6
  absolutism 612.9
Stalinist
  noun Communist 611.18
  adj Communist 611.30
stalk
  noun journey 177.5
  gait 177.12
  shaft 273.1
  stem 310.19
  base 900.8
  search 937.15
  verb stroll 177.28
  lurk 346.9
  ambush 346.10
  hunt 382.9
  strut 501.15
  trace 937.35
stalker 382.5
stalking stealth 345.4
  pursuit 382.1
  hunting 382.2
  search 937.15
stall
  noun compartment 197.2
  hut 228.9
  barn 228.20
  pew 703.14
  booth 736.3
  procrastination 845.5
  verb lose power 184.45
  stick 410.16
  procrastinate 845.11
  stop 856.7, 1011.13
  hinder 1011.10
stallion cock 76.8
  horse 311.10
  jockey 757.2
stalls 757.1
stalwart
  noun strong man 15.6
  hero 492.8
  partisan 609.27
  supporter 616.9
  adj strong 15.15
  hale 83.12
  corpulent 257.18
  courageous 492.17
stamina strength 15.1
  pluck 359.3
  perseverance 360.1
  fortitude 492.6
  continuance 855.1
  toughness 1047.1
stammer
  noun stammering 525.3
  verb blush 139.8
  stutter 525.8

  be guilty 656.2
stammering
  noun shyness 139.4
  stuttering 525.3
  redundancy 848.3
  adj shy 139.12
  stuttering 525.13
stamp
  noun form 262.1
  ratification 332.4
  sign 517.1
  print 517.7, 548.3
  label 517.13
  type 548.6
  postage 553.5
  engraving tool 713.8
  nature 766.4
  cast 784.6
  mould 785.6
  kind 808.3
  characteristic 864.4
  stomp 901.10
  disposition 977.3
  verb impress upon 93.16
  stroll 177.28
  form 262.7
  indent 284.14
  mark 517.19
  label 517.20
  print 548.14
  fix 854.9
  stomp 901.22
stamped formative 262.9
  accepted 332.14
  engraved 713.11
stampede
  noun fear 127.1
  verb start 127.12
  put in fear 127.16
  hasten 401.4
  overwhelm 412.8
stamping bookbinding 554.14
  coining 728.24
stamp on 93.16
stamp out annihilate 761.7
  fight fire 1021.7
stance looks 33.4
  affirmation 334.1
  gesture 517.14
  round 748.3
  table 752.2
  fight 754.3
  footing 900.5
  opinion 952.6
  attitude 977.1
stand
  noun station 159.2
  standstill 173.3
  growth 310.2
  affirmation 334.1
  resistance 453.1
  engagement 704.11
  booth 736.3
  match 747.3
  stop 856.2

  footing 900.5
  base 900.8
  table 900.15
  outlook 977.2
  impasse 1012.6
  verb endure 134.5, 826.6
  settle 159.17
  be still 173.7
  stand erect 200.7
  be present 221.6
  resist 453.2
  offer resistance 453.3
  go into politics 610.13
  afford 626.7
  exist 760.8
  remain 852.5
  suffice 990.4
stand a chance 896.3
stand-alone
  independent 430.22
  separate 801.20
standard
  noun degree 245.1
  post 273.4
  measure 300.2
  rule 419.2, 868.4
  flag 647.6
  paragon 659.4
  model 785.1
  base 900.8
  test 941.2
  adj medium 246.3
  customary 373.14
  preceptive 419.4
  orthodox 687.7
  model 785.8
  interchangeable 862.5
  prevalent 863.12
  usual 868.9
  indistinguishable 944.6
  authoritative 969.18
standard-bearer leader 574.6
  boss 610.7
Standard English 523.4
standardized 807.14
standard of living 731.8
standard procedure 419.2
standards 636.1
stand back 163.6
stand behind 449.13
stand by adjoin 223.9
  stay near 223.12
  be prepared 405.14
  back 449.13
standby 616.9
stand down abandon 370.5
  resign 448.2
  make peace 465.9
  stop 856.7
  lay off 856.8

stand-down truce 465.5
  pause 856.3
stand firm 173.7
stand for endure 134.5
  sail for 182.35
  suffer 443.10
  signify 517.17
  designate 517.18
  mean 518.8
stand-in successor 816.4
  substitute 861.2
standing
  noun station 159.2
  rank 245.2
  class 607.1
  credit 622.1
  prestige 662.4
  state 764.1
  durability 826.1
  footing 900.5
  adj inert 173.14
standing against 451.1
standing committee 423.2
standing orders 373.5
standing ovation 509.2
standing room 704.15
standing to 896.6
standing up 200.11
stand in the way of 1011.15
stand off 182.36
stand on 900.22
stand out show 31.4
  loom 247.5
  protrude 283.10
  be manifest 348.7
  balk 361.7
  matter 996.12
standpoint viewpoint 27.7
  station 159.2
  outlook 977.2
stand still 173.7
standstill stand 173.3
  stop 856.2
  impasse 1012.6
stand together
  cooperate 450.3
  league 804.4
stand up not weaken 15.10
  ascend 193.8
  stand 200.7
  rise 200.8
  stay with it 360.4
  resist 453.2
  stand the test 941.10
  be true 972.8
  suffice 990.4
stand-up vertical 200.11
  ballsy 492.19

stand up and be
counted come out
348.6
vote 371.18
brave 492.11

stand up for 438.9

stand up to confront
216.8
offer resistance 453.3
meet an obligation
641.11

Stanley Cup 750.4

stanza passage 708.24
measure 720.9

staple
noun source of supply
386.4
commodity 735.2
marketplace 736.2
fastening 799.3
materials 1052.1
verb hook 799.8
adj fixed 854.14

staples 735.1

star
noun superior 249.4
winner 409.6
ace 413.14
decoration 646.5
insignia of rank 647.5
celebrity 662.9
film studio 706.3
lead 707.6
chief 996.10
first-rater 998.6
quasar 1070.8
verb rule 249.11
dramatize 704.28
act 704.29
matter 996.12
emphasize 996.14
feature 996.15
adj chief 249.14

starboard
noun right side 219.1
adj right 219.4
adv rightward 219.7

starch
noun carbohydrate 7.5
semiliquid 1060.5
verb stiffen 1044.9
adj stiff 580.9

starched stiff 580.9
rigid 1044.11

starchy stiff 580.9
rigid 1044.11
viscous 1060.12

stardom great success
409.3
distinction 662.5
notability 996.2

stare
noun gaze 27.5
verb gaze 27.15
wonder 122.5
be curious 980.3

stare at 27.15

staring distinct 31.7

conspicuous 348.12

stark
adj downright 247.12
mere 248.8
inornate 499.9
plain-speaking 535.3
simple 797.6
adv absolutely 793.15

starkly 31.8

stark-naked 6.14

starlet film studio
706.3
film actor 707.4

starlight 1024.12

star quality 377.1

starred 996.21

starry luminous
1024.30
celestial 1070.25

starry-eyed happy
95.15
visionary 985.24

stars fate 963.2
light source 1025.1
fixed stars 1070.4

Stars and Stripes
647.6

star-spangled
illuminated 1024.39
celestial 1070.25

star-studded
illuminated 1024.39
celestial 1070.25

start
noun shock 131.3
starting 188.2
point of departure
188.5
boundary 211.3
advantage 249.2
race 756.3
horse race 757.3
beginning 817.1
jerk 904.3
verb startle 127.12
be startled 131.5
set out 188.8
leap 366.5
hunt 382.9
break 393.23
propose 439.5
drive 756.4
race 757.5
come apart 801.9
begin 817.7
start off 903.13

start all over 855.6

started 182.61

starter appetizer 10.9
light source 1025.1

starters horse race
757.3
first 817.3

start going inaugurate
817.11
start 903.13

start in set to work
725.15
begin 817.7

starting 188.2

starting point 817.1

startle astonish 122.6
start 127.12
frighten 127.15
be startled 131.5
shock 131.8
alarm 400.3

startled frightened
127.25
shocked 131.13
alarmed 400.4

startling astonishing
122.12
frightening 127.28
surprising 131.11
sudden 829.5

startlingly
astonishingly 122.16
frightfully 127.34
surprisingly 131.15
suddenly 829.9

start off begin 817.7
start 903.13

start-off 188.2

start on 456.13

start out 817.7

start up burst forth
33.9
shoot up 193.9
protrude 283.10
leap 366.5
begin 817.7
make a beginning
817.8
inaugurate 817.11
start 903.13

start-up 817.1

starvation
noun violent death
307.6
fasting 515.1
want 991.4
adj meagre 991.10

starve hunger 100.19
die a natural death
307.24
kill 308.12
stint 484.5
be poor 619.5
freeze 1022.9, 1022.10

starved hungry 100.25
haggard 270.20
wasted 393.35
ill-provided 991.12

starving hungry 100.25
ill-provided 991.12

stash
noun hiding place
346.4
verb secrete 346.7
store 386.10

stat
noun print 784.5

verb copy 784.8

state
noun territory 231.5
country 232.1
grandeur 501.5
pomp 501.6
mode 764.1
verb affirm 334.5
announce 352.12
declare 524.24
phrase 532.4
specify 864.11
assert 952.12
adj public 312.16

stated circumscribed
210.6
affirmed 334.9
published 352.17
fixed 854.14
conditional 958.8
assured 969.20

statehood 232.6

stateless 160.10

stately
adj dignified 136.12
grandiose 501.21
lofty 544.14
ceremonious 580.8
adv dignifiedly 136.14

stately home 228.7

statement affirmation
334.1
account 349.3
announcement 352.2
remark 524.4
report 549.7
information 551.1
declaration 598.8
bill 628.3, 870.5
passage 708.24
premise 934.7
testimony 956.2
summation 1016.11

state of affairs 830.4

state of emergency
842.4

state of mind 977.4

state of play 764.2

state-of-the-art 840.14

state of war 458.1

state ownership 476.2

state police 1007.17

States 232.4

state school 567.4

stateside 232.4

statesman expert
413.11
stateswoman 610.2

statesmanship 609.3

static
noun audio distortion
50.13
meaninglessness 520.1
pandemonium 809.5
reception 1033.21
adj motionless 173.13
inert 173.14

passive 329.6
inactive 331.17
permanent 852.7
electric 1031.29
biostatic 1038.8

station
noun status 159.2
rank 245.2
class 607.1, 808.2
prestige 662.4
position 724.5
state 764.1
farm 1068.5
verb place 159.12

stationary motionless
173.13
passive 329.6
inactive 331.17
permanent 852.7
immovable 854.15

stationed 159.18

stationery handwriting
style 547.4
paper 1052.5

stationing 159.6

statistical probable
967.6
numerative 1016.23

statistician calculator
1016.14
mathematician
1016.15

statistics records 757.4
mathematical
probability 967.2
figures 1016.13

statuary
noun figure 349.6
sculpture 715.1
sculptor 716.6
adj sculptural 715.6

statue figure 349.6
work of art 712.10
sculpture 715.2

statuesque dignified
136.12
giant 272.16
sculptural 715.6
comely 1015.18

statuette 349.6

stature height 272.1
prestige 417.4, 662.4

status station 159.2
rank 245.2
class 607.1, 808.2
prestige 662.4
state 764.1

status-quo 852.8

statute prohibition
444.1
bill 613.8
law 673.3

statute book 673.5

statutory preceptive
419.4
legal 673.10

staunch firm 15.18, 359.12
close 293.12
devoted 587.21
faithful 644.20
strict 687.8
reliable 969.17

staunchly strongly 15.23
resolutely 359.17
faithfully 644.25

stave step 193.5
staff 273.2, 708.29
measure 720.9
supporter 900.2
wood 1052.3

stave off fend off 460.10
prevent 1011.14

stay
noun respite 20.2
sojourn 225.5
exemption 601.2
delay 845.2
stop 856.2
pause 856.3
supporter 900.2
prevention 1011.2
curb 1011.7
verb be still 173.7
slow 175.9
inhabit 225.7
sojourn 225.8
stop 293.7, 1011.13
cohere 802.6
endure 826.6
delay 845.8
postpone 845.9
wait 845.12
remain 852.5
continue 855.3
cease 856.6
put a stop to 856.11
support 900.21

stay at home keep to oneself 583.4
seclude oneself 584.7

stay-at-home
noun recluse 584.5
adj untravelled 173.15
recluse 584.10

stay awake 23.3

stay away 222.7

stayed 900.24

stayer 757.2

staying
noun habitation 225.1
prevention 1011.2
adj resident 225.13
durable 826.10
permanent 852.7
continuing 855.7

staying power
perseverance 360.1
continuance 855.1

stay of execution 845.2

stay on endure 826.6

continue 855.3

stay out of 329.4

stay put be still 173.7
cohere 802.6
stand fast 854.11

stays 5.23

STD 347.13

stead location 159.1
place 159.4

steadfast firm 359.12
persevering 360.8
devoted 587.21
faithful 644.20
uniform 780.5
durable 826.10
permanent 852.7
stable 854.12
reliable 969.17

steadfastly resolutely 359.17
faithfully 644.25
permanently 852.9

steadily inexcitably 106.16
resolutely 359.17
faithfully 644.25
moderately 670.17
regularly 780.8, 849.9
perpetually 828.10
constantly 846.7

steady
verb calm 670.7
stabilize 854.7
adj inexcitable 106.10
unnervous 129.2
firm 359.12
persevering 360.8
faithful 644.20
sturdy 762.7
uniform 780.5
orderly 806.6
continuous 811.8
perpetual 828.7
constant 846.5
stable 854.12
continuing 855.7
reliable 969.17
unhazardous 1006.5

steady stream 811.3

steak 10.17

steal creep 177.26
lurk 346.9
take 480.13
thieve 482.13
adopt 621.4
play 751.4

stealing
noun creeping 177.17
theft 482.1
adj in hiding 346.14

stealth stealthiness 345.4
cunning 415.1

stealthily 345.18

steam
noun pep 17.3
hot water 1018.10
water 1063.3

vapour 1065.1
verb cook 11.4
burn 152.15, 1018.22
piss off 152.23
navigate 182.13
let out 908.24
heat 1019.17
vaporize 1065.8

steamed cooked 11.6
mad 152.30

steamer steamboat 180.2
marine animal 311.30

steaming
noun water travel 182.1
theft 482.3
vaporization 1065.5
adj fervent 93.18
heated 105.22
burning 152.29
vaporous 1065.9

steamroller
noun pulverizer 1049.7
verb level 201.6
raze 395.19
clobber 412.9
twist one's arm 424.8
thrust 901.12

steam room 79.10

steamship 180.2

steamy lustful 75.26
fervent 93.18
heated 105.22
vaporous 1065.9

steed 311.10

steel
noun horse 15.8
sword 462.5
cutlery 1039.2
stone 1044.6
verb strengthen 15.13
callous 94.6
harden 1044.7
adj firm 425.7
brass 1056.17

steelworks 739.4

steely strong 15.15
grey 39.4
callous 94.12
pitiless 146.3
firm 359.12, 425.7
unyielding 361.9
sturdy 762.7
hard 1044.10
brass 1056.17

steep
noun precipice 200.3
slope 237.2
verb imbue 796.11
liquefy 1062.5
soak 1063.13
adj perpendicular 200.12
precipitous 204.18
unbelievable 954.10
difficult 1012.17

steeped 1063.17

steeple tower 272.6
projection 285.4

steeplechase
noun leap 366.1
leaping 366.3
verb leap 366.5

steer
noun sexlessness 75.9
cock 76.8
cattle 311.6
tip 551.3
verb direct to 161.6
bear 161.7
pilot 182.14
guide 573.9

steer clear of avoid 164.6, 368.6
keep one's distance 261.7
have nothing to do with 586.5

steering direction 161.1, 573.1
accounting 1040.7

steering committee 574.11

steering wheel 573.5

stellar chief 249.14
dramatic 704.33
celestial 1070.25

stem
noun fork 171.4
prow 216.3
tube 239.6
shaft 273.1
stalk 310.19
morphology 526.3
type 548.6
race 559.4
lineage 560.4
source 885.5
base 900.8
verb progress 162.2
fork 171.7
confront 216.8
contend against 451.4
put a stop to 856.11

stem from 886.5

stems 177.15

stench
noun odour 69.1
stink 71.1
verb stop 293.7

stencil
noun printing 548.1
picture 712.11
stencil printing 713.4
verb portray 712.19

step
noun velocity 172.4
pace 177.11
gait 177.12
stair 193.5
short distance 223.2
degree 245.1
layer 296.1
act 328.3
attempt 403.2
print 517.7

interval 709.20
process 888.2
expedient 994.2
verb barrel 174.9
walk 177.27
measure 300.10

step along 174.9

step aside avoid 164.6
dodge 368.8
separate 801.8

step by step by degrees 245.6
in order 806.10
consecutively 811.11

stepdaughter descendant 561.3
stepfather 564.3

step down 1031.25

stepfather father 560.9
stepmother 564.3

step forward 162.2

step in enter 189.7
mediate 466.6

stepmother mother 560.11
stepfather 564.3

step off 300.11

step on 909.7

step out 743.24

step over 909.8

stepped-up aggravated 119.4
increased 251.7

steppes 233.1

stepping in 466.1

stepping-stone step 193.5
bridge 383.9
opportunity 842.2

stepping-stones 193.3

stepping-up 119.1

steps stairs 193.3
precaution 494.3

stepson descendant 561.3
stepfather 564.3

step up aggravate 119.2
approach 167.3
accelerate 174.10
intensify 251.5
make good 409.10
electrify 1031.25

step-up acceleration 174.4
promotion 446.1

stereo 50.11

stereotype
noun habit 373.4
printing surface 548.8
verb autotype 548.15
make uniform 780.4
fix 854.9
generalize 863.9

stereotyped trite 117.9, 863.16
habitual 373.15

prevalent 863.12
indistinguishable
944.6

stereotyping custom
373.1
generality 863.1

sterile ineffective 19.15
sanitary 79.27
dull 117.6
fruitless 391.12
unproductive 890.4

sterility cleanness 79.1
dullness 117.1
unproductiveness
890.1

sterilization 79.3

sterilized 79.27

sterling
noun money 728.1
adj honest 644.13
monetary 728.30
genuine 972.15
superb 998.15

sterling crisis 729.7

stern
noun rear 217.1
arse 217.5
heel 217.7
adj harsh 144.24
unyielding 361.9
strict 425.6

sternly harshly 144.33
unyieldingly 361.15
strictly 425.8

steroid 7.7

stethoscope 48.8

stew
noun hotpot 10.11
drunk 88.12
vivarium 228.24
bustle 330.4
brothel 665.9
prostitute 665.16
hotchpotch 796.6
pickle 1012.5
verb cook 11.4
plaster 88.23
be impatient 135.4
redden 152.14
burn 152.15, 1018.22
seethe 671.12
boil 1019.20

steward
noun hand 183.6
crew 185.4
provider 385.6
bailiff 574.4
agent 576.3
attendant 577.5
major-domo 577.10
treasurer 729.11
jockey 757.2
guardian 1007.6
verb treat 387.12

stewardess hand 183.6
crew 185.4
attendant 577.5

stewardship vigilance
339.4
usage 387.2
directorship 573.4
protectorship 1007.2

stewed cooked 11.6
fuddled 88.33

stewing cooking 11.1
boiling 1019.2

stews dive 228.28
brothel 665.9

St George 458.8

stick
noun joint 87.11
slim 270.8
shaft 273.1
staff 273.2
rod 605.2
metronome 711.22
hockey 750.1
supporter 900.2
wood 1052.3
desert 1064.2
verb take it 134.6
place 159.12
be still 173.7
perforate 292.15
remain firm 359.9
stick to it 360.7
injure 393.13
stall 410.16
stab 459.25
hook 799.8
cohere 802.6
stabilize 854.7
root 854.10
stop 856.7
stump 970.14

stick around 845.12

stick at demur 325.4
hesitate 362.7

sticker thorn 285.5
label 517.13
adhesive 802.4

stick for 630.12

stick in insert 191.3
interpose 213.6

stickiness tenacity
802.3
sultriness 1018.6
viscosity 1060.2
humidity 1063.2

sticking
noun stabbing 459.10
fastening 799.3
cohesion 802.1
adj hesitant 362.11
cohesive 802.10
continuing 855.7

sticking point 439.3

stick it 360.7

stickler mule 361.6
perfectionist 495.6
tyrant 575.14

stick out be exposed
31.5
protrude 283.10
be manifest 348.7

stay with it 360.4

sticks gams 177.15
country 233.1
jumping-off place
261.4
game 750.3

stick to insist 421.8
hold 474.6

stick together put
together 799.5
cohere 802.6
cement 802.9

stick to it stick 360.7
persist 855.5

stick up rise 200.8
protrude 283.10
swipe 482.16
elevate 911.5

stick with 643.4

stick with it remain
firm 359.9
stick 360.7
persist 855.5

sticky sweaty 12.22
adhesive 802.12
difficult 1012.17
sultry 1018.28
viscous 1060.12
moist 1063.15

stiff
noun corpse 307.16
nag 311.12
bum 331.9
verb screw 389.6
adj fuddled 88.33
dull 117.6
seaworthy 180.18
stone-dead 307.31
unyielding 361.9
out of practice 414.18
bungling 414.20
firm 425.7
stilted 534.3, 580.9
rigid 1044.11
tough 1047.4
adv firmly 425.9

stiffen strengthen 15.13
electrify 1031.25
rigidify 1044.9
toughen 1047.3

stiffened increased
251.7
hardened 1044.13

stiffening 1044.5

stiffly unyieldingly
361.15
firmly 425.9
stiltedly 580.12

stiff neck proudling
136.3
obstinacy 361.1

stiffness dullness 117.1
unyieldingness 361.2
firmness 425.2
formality 580.1
inflexibility 1044.3
toughness 1047.1

stifle silence 51.8

suppress 106.8, 428.8
strangle 308.18
cover up 345.8
extinguish 395.15
moderate 670.6
obstruct 1011.12
burn 1018.22
fight fire 1021.7

stifled muffled 52.17
secret 345.11
suppressed 428.14
inarticulate 525.12

stifling
noun suffocation 308.6
veil of secrecy 345.3
extinction 395.6
suppression 428.2
extinguishing 1021.2
adj strong 69.10
stuffy 173.16
hindering 1011.17
sultry 1018.28

stigma sore 85.36
petal 310.26
mark 517.5
stigmatism 661.6
stain 1003.3

stile stairs 193.3
post 273.4

stiletto 459.25

still
noun silence 51.1
distillery 88.21
photograph 714.3
vaporizer 1065.6
verb silence 51.8
calm 670.7
adj silent 51.10
quiescent 173.12
motionless 173.13
dead 307.30
adv quiescently 173.18
until now 837.4
adv, conj
notwithstanding 338.8

still around 256.7

stillborn born 1.4
dead 307.30
unsuccessful 410.18

still life work of art
712.10
picture 712.11

still more 249.17

stillness 51.1

still room 386.8

stilted pompous 501.22
stiff 534.3, 580.9
grandiloquent 545.8
raised 911.9

stimulant
noun energizer 17.6
Adrenalin 86.9
drug 87.2
adj provocative 375.27

stimulate refresh 9.2
energize 17.10
sensitize 24.7
whet 105.13

elicit 192.14
motivate 375.12
interest 982.12

stimulated refreshed
9.4
excited 105.20
moved 375.30

stimulating refreshing
9.3
energizing 17.15
aphrodisiac 75.25
tonic 86.44
exciting 105.30
provocative 375.27
vehement 544.13
interesting 982.19
cool 1022.12

stimulation
refreshment 9.1
energizing 17.8
excitement 105.1
excitation 105.11
motivation 375.2
incitement 375.4
incentive 375.7
fission 1037.8

stimulus energizer 17.6
excitation 105.11
incentive 375.7
cause 885.1

sting
noun acrimony 17.5
smart 26.3
tingle 74.1
point 285.3
gyp 356.9
goad 375.8
stinger 1000.5
verb pain 26.7, 96.17
bite 68.5
tingle 74.5
affect 93.14
offend 152.21
gyp 356.19
goad 375.15

stinging
noun smart 26.3
tingle 74.1
adj acrimonious 17.14
painful 26.10
irritating 26.13
pungent 68.6
penetrating 105.31
caustic 144.23
prickly 285.10

stingy illiberal 484.9
ungenerous 651.6
sparse 884.5
meagre 991.10

stink
noun odour 69.1
stench 71.1
verb smell 69.6, 71.4

stinking nasty 64.7
odorous 69.9
malodorous 71.5
offensive 98.18
lousy 999.8

stint

noun degree 245.1
restriction 428.3
task 724.2
shift 824.3
verb limit 210.5
restrict 428.9
scrimp 484.5
stipe 310.19
stipendiary
noun beneficiary 479.4
adj endowed 478.26
stipulate stipulate for
421.7
contract 437.5
specify 864.11
suppose 950.10
make conditional
958.4
stipulated contracted
437.11
real 760.15
supposed 950.14
conditional 958.8
stipulation provision
421.2
compact 437.1
specification 864.6
condition 958.2
stir
noun agitation 105.4,
916.1
motion 172.1
activity 330.1
bustle 330.4
nick 429.9
commotion 809.4
verb awake 23.4
sensitize 24.7
affect 93.14
excite 105.12
agitate 105.14, 916.10
move 172.5
stir about 330.11
bustle 330.12
rouse 375.19
seethe 671.12, 914.12
stir-fry 11.4
stir in mix 796.10
combine 804.3
stirred 105.20
stirred up excited
105.20
agitated 916.16
stirring
noun excitation 105.11
motion 172.1
incitement 375.4
adj exciting 105.30
moving 172.7
astir 330.19
provocative 375.27
vehement 544.13
eventful 830.10
stirring up 105.11
stirring-up 375.4
stirrup ear 2.10
pommel 900.18
stir up excite 105.12

provoke 152.24
incite 375.17
rouse 375.19
mix 796.10
agitate 916.10
stitch
noun pang 26.2
scrap 248.3
piece 792.3
joint 799.4
verb sew 741.4
hook 799.8
stitching 741.1
St Leger 757.1
stock
° *noun* stem 310.19
animal life 311.1
humankind 312.1
means 384.2
store 386.1
assets 471.7
portion 477.5
laughingstock 508.7
race 559.4
lineage 560.4
show business 704.1
repertoire 704.9
merchandise 735.1
shares 738.2
source 885.5
materials 1052.1
paper 1052.5
deposit 1056.7
verb provide 385.7
adj trite 117.9
customary 373.14
usual 868.9
stockbroker broker
730.9
sharebroker 737.10
stockbroking 737.18
stock company cast
707.11
joint-stock company
737.15
insurance 1007.4
Stock Exchange 737.7
stock exchange stock
market 737.1
exchange 737.7
workplace 739.1
stocking 5.39
stockings 5.28
stock-in-trade means
384.2
equipment 385.4
store 386.1
supply 386.2
assets 471.7
merchandise 735.1
stock market 737.1,
737.7
stockpile
noun store 386.1
reserve 386.3
accumulation 769.9
verb store up 386.11
stockpiled 386.14

stockpiling 769.9
stocks shackle 428.4
pillory 605.3
stock up 386.11
stocky corpulent 257.18
stubby 268.10
stodgy dull 117.6
old-fogyish 841.17
viscous 1060.12
Stoic 668.10
stoic
noun Spartan 134.3
adj apathetic 94.13
inexcitable 106.10
patient 134.9
quiescent 173.12
stable 854.12
stoical apathetic 94.13
inexcitable 106.10
patient 134.9
quiescent 173.12
stoically inexcitably
106.16
patiently 134.11
inertly 173.20
Stoicism abstinence
668.2
Platonic philosophy
951.2
stoicism apathy 94.4
inexcitability 106.1
patience 134.1
submission 433.1
stability 854.1
stoke ignite 1019.22
fuel 1020.7
stoker railwayman
178.13
hand 183.6
stolen 482.23
stolen goods 482.11
stolid inexcitable
106.10
quiescent 173.12
stable 854.12
incurious 981.3
unimaginative 986.5
stomach
noun mouth 2.16
taste 62.1
appetite 100.7
verb take 134.8
suffer 443.10
stomp
noun stamp 901.10
verb stroll 177.28
stamp 901.22
stone
noun seed 310.29
pavement 383.6
missile 462.18
jewel 498.6
monument 549.12
plate 713.6
rock 1044.6, 1057.1
sticks and stones
1052.2

precious stone 1057.6
verb plaster 88.23
face 295.23
strike dead 308.17
pelt 459.27
execute 604.16
adj rock 1057.10
stone Age 823.5
stone-cold stone-dead
307.31
cold 1022.14
stoned high 87.23
fuddled 88.33
stone-dead 307.31
stone's throw 223.2
stone wall fence 212.4
barrier 1011.5
stonewall shut up 51.6
outwit 415.11
hinder 1011.10
stoneware 735.4
stonework 1052.2
stoning killing 308.1
lapidation 459.11
capital punishment
604.6
stony callous 94.12
rugged 288.7
hard 1044.10
rocky 1057.11
stooge
noun apple-polisher
138.4
follower 166.2, 616.8
dupe 358.1
instrument 384.4
figurehead 575.5
retainer 577.1
verb act 704.29
stool
noun defecation 12.2
faeces 12.4
toilet 12.11
verb defecate 12.13
stoop
noun descent 194.1
porch 197.21
pillar 273.5
plunge 367.1
crouch 912.3
verb condescend 137.8
fawn 138.7
give oneself airs 141.8
descend 194.5
plunge 367.6
bow down 433.10
incur disgrace 661.7
crouch 912.8
stooped 274.7
stop
noun standstill 173.3
destination 186.5
sojourn 225.5
obstruction 293.3
stopper 293.4
speech sound 524.13
punctuation 530.15
organ stop 711.19

match 747.3
delay 845.2
stoppage 856.2
prevention 1011.2
curb 1011.7
impasse 1012.6
verb muffle 51.9
daunt 127.18
quiet 173.8
sojourn 225.8
stop up 293.7
disaccustom 374.2
break the habit 374.3
cease to use 390.4
fend off 460.10
swear off 668.8
play 747.4
end 819.5
delay 845.8
cease 856.6
put a stop to 856.11
stay 1011.13
stop over 225.8
stopover 225.5
stoppage seizure 85.6
obstruction 293.3
end 819.1
delay 845.2
stop 856.2
prevention 1011.2
stopped stopped up
293.11
phonetic 524.31
late 845.16
stopper
noun stop 293.4
cover 295.5
finishing stroke 819.4
verb stop 293.7
top 295.21
stopping habitation
225.1
wadding 293.5
cessation 856.1
prevention 1011.2
stop press 552.3
stop work 20.8
storage placement
159.6
stowage 386.5
storehouse 386.6
fee 630.6
memory 1041.7
storage space 386.5
store
noun hoard 386.1
storehouse 386.6
preserve 397.7
gain 472.3
market 736.1
workplace 739.1
materials 1052.1
verb load 159.15
provide 385.7
stow 386.10
put away 390.6
stored accumulated
386.14
unused 390.12

err 974.9
muse 984.9
adj deviative 164.7
abnormal 869.9
purposeless 971.16
straying
noun deviation 164.1
wandering 177.3
adj wandering 177.37
abnormal 869.9
erroneous 974.16
streak
noun stripe 47.5
lightning 174.6
paper 270.7
furrow 290.1
line 517.6
nature 766.4
disposition 977.3
ray 1024.5
verb variegate 47.7
furrow 290.3
mark 517.19
streaked striped 47.15
netlike 170.11
streaking stripe 47.5
line 517.6
streaks 3.16
streaky 47.15
stream
noun course 172.2
wash 184.30
waterway 238.1
flow 238.4
channel 239.1
wind 318.1
class 808.2
procession 811.3
trend 895.2
plenty 990.2
ray 1024.5
verb move 172.5
travel 177.18
flow 238.16
rain 316.9
come together 769.16
classify 808.6
abound 990.5
streamed 808.8
streaming flowing
172.8, 238.24
rainy 316.10
loose 803.5
luminous 1024.30
streamline
noun straight line
277.2
verb simplify 797.4
modernize 840.6
streamlined blunt
286.3
simplified 797.9
modern 840.13
streamlining
simplification 797.2
facilitation 1013.5
stream of
consciousness
association 92.33

thoughts 930.4
Street 737.8
street 383.5
street market 736.2
street theatre 704.1
street value 630.2
streetwise 927.16
strength might 15.1
energy 17.1
power 18.1
strongness 68.3
haleness 83.3
quantity 244.1
greatness 247.1
will power 359.4
authoritativeness 417.2
vigour 544.3
substantiality 762.1
hardness 1044.1
toughness 1047.1
strengthen nourish
7.15
invigorate 15.13
intensify 251.5
grow 251.6
add to 253.5
confirm 956.11
stiffen 1044.9
toughen 1047.3
strengthened increased
251.7
hardened 1044.13
strengthening
noun invigoration 15.5
intensification 251.2
confirmation 956.4
hardening 1044.5
adj tonic 86.44
strenuous energetic
17.13
industrious 330.22
laborious 725.18
difficult 1012.17
strenuously
energetically 17.16
industriously 330.27
laboriously 725.19
with difficulty 1012.28
stress
noun psychological
stress 92.17
pain 96.5
anxiety 126.1
tension 128.3
urge 375.6
accent 524.11
metre 720.7
strain 725.2
thrust 901.2
urgency 996.4
adversity 1010.1
verb strain 725.10
thrust 901.12
emphasize 996.14
stressed neurotic 92.38
phonetic 524.31
emphatic 996.21

stressful fatiguing
21.13
adverse 1010.13
stretch
noun range 158.2
walk 177.10
distance 261.1
length 267.1
strain 725.2
exercise 725.6
period 823.1
spell 824.1
term 824.4
overextension 992.7
elasticity 1046.1
stretching 1046.2
verb exercise 84.4
extend 158.8, 1046.4
enlarge 259.4, 259.5
be long 267.5
lengthen 267.6
exaggerate 355.3
strain 725.10
suffice 990.4
overextend 992.13
adj elastic 1046.7
stretched lengthened
267.8
exaggerated 355.4
stretched-out 259.11
stretcher 900.19
stretching sleepiness
22.1
exercise 84.2
distension 259.2
lengthening 267.4
deliberate falsehood
354.9
exaggeration 355.1
overextension 992.7
extension 1046.2
stretch out reach out
261.5
be long 267.5
protract 538.8
stretch to 261.6
strewn 770.9
stricken affected 93.23
wretched 96.26
overcome 112.29
unnerved 128.14
strict meticulous
339.12
imperious 417.16
exacting 425.6
fastidious 495.9
conscientious 644.15
scripturalistic 687.8
exact 972.17
strictly meticulously
339.16
severely 425.8
truly 972.18
exactly 972.21
to be exact 972.22
strictly speaking truly
972.18
to be exact 972.22
stride

noun velocity 172.4
step 177.11
gait 177.12
distance 261.1
verb walk 177.27
stroll 177.28
rest on 900.22
strident acrimonious
17.14
stridulant 58.12
dissonant 61.4
strife quarrel 456.5
contention 457.1
strike
noun revolt 327.4
objection 333.2
attack 459.1
walkout 727.5
stop 856.2
discovery 940.1
verb impress 93.15,
930.19
delete 255.12
revolt 327.7
object 333.5
attack 459.14
launch an attack
459.17
print 548.14
slap 604.11
go on strike 727.10
play 747.4, 752.4
lay off 856.8
collide 901.13
hit 901.14
shoot 903.12
occur to 930.18
discover 940.2
strike against 901.13
strike at lash out at
459.16
hit 901.14
strike on 940.3
strike out set out 188.8
obliterate 395.16
originate 891.12
striker sitdown striker
727.6
team 745.2
strike up 708.37
striking
noun coining 728.24
adj powerful 18.12
exciting 105.30
wonderful 122.10
remarkable 247.10
conspicuous 348.12
vigorous 544.11
notable 996.19
strikingly powerfully
18.15
wonderfully 122.14
intensely 247.20
conspicuously 348.16
eloquently 544.15
string
noun step 193.5
line 267.3
cord 271.2

utterance 524.3
team 617.7
chord 711.20
company 769.3
section 792.2
series 811.2
procession 811.3
verb tune 708.36
continue 811.4
stringent acrimonious
17.14
harsh 144.24
strict 425.6
stringer 555.4
strings catch 421.3
orchestra 710.12
strings attached 421.3
stringy threadlike 271.7
tough 1047.4
viscous 1060.12
strip
noun runway 184.23
length 267.2
line 267.3, 517.6
strap 271.4
option 737.21
football 745.1
rugby 746.1
cricket 747.1
horse racing 757.1
verb divest 6.5
undress 6.7
peel 6.8
excise 255.10
simplify 797.4
dismiss 908.19
stripe
noun striping 47.5
line 267.3, 517.6
insignia of rank 647.5
nature 766.4
kind 808.3
slap 901.8
disposition 977.3
verb variegate 47.7
mark 517.19
whip 604.12
striped stripy 47.15
netlike 170.11
stripes 604.4
stripped divested 6.12
lost 473.7
indigent 619.8
stripped down 797.9
stripped of 473.8
stripper nudity 6.3
entertainer 707.1
separator 801.7
stripping unclothing
6.1
disclosure 351.1
loss 473.1
waste 473.2
simplification 797.2
disruption 801.3
disassembly 801.6
banishment 908.4
strive endeavour 403.5

contend 457.13
struggle 725.11

strive for try for 403.9
contend for 457.20

strive to 403.8

striving
noun intention 380.1
endeavour 403.1
adj contending 457.22
labouring 725.17

stroke
noun touch 73.1
seizure 85.6
paralysis 85.27
pain 96.5
act 328.3
attempt 403.2
stratagem 415.3
compliment 509.6
line 517.6
upheaval 671.5
work 725.4
match 747.3
round 748.3
game 749.2, 750.3
instant 829.3
hit 901.4
spasm 916.6
expedient 994.2
verb pet 73.8
encourage 375.21
exploit 387.16
rub 1042.6

stroke of luck 1009.3

strokes 748.3

stroking touching 73.2
massage 1042.3

stroll
noun slow motion
175.2
walk 177.10
gait 177.12
verb wander 177.23
saunter 177.28

strolling
noun walking 177.8
adj slow 175.10
travelling 177.36
wandering 177.37

strong
noun strong man 15.6
adj forceful 15.15
energetic 17.13
powerful 18.12
strong-flavoured 68.8
strong-smelling 69.10
malodorous 71.5
hale 83.12
alcoholic 88.37
great 247.6
tainted 393.41
phonetic 524.31
vigorous 544.11
sturdy 762.7
influential 893.13
tough 1047.4

strong arm power 18.1
combatant 461.1
protector 1007.5

strong-arm 424.8

strong feeling 93.2

stronghold hold 460.6
refuge 1008.1

strong in skilled in
413.27
versed in 927.19

strongly 15.23

strong man 15.6

strong-minded
strong-willed 359.15
intelligent 919.12

strong point talent
413.4
stronghold 460.6
speciality 865.1
good reasoning 934.10

strong-willed strong
15.15
strong-minded 359.15
obstinate 361.8

strontium 1037.5

stroppy crabby 110.20
insubordinate 327.9
perverse 361.11
oppositional 451.8

struck down 445.3

struck with 104.30

structural formal 266.6
semantic 518.12
linguistic 523.17
grammatical 530.17
organizational 807.15
constructional 891.15

structure
noun house 228.5
form 262.1
construction 266.1
building 266.2
texture 294.1
clearness 521.2
syntax 530.2
plot 722.4
composition 795.1
order 806.1
verb construct 266.5
compose 795.3
order 806.4

structured 266.6

structuring structure
266.1
composition 795.1
arrangement 807.1

struggle
noun endeavour 403.1
contention 457.1
fight 457.4, 725.3
verb endeavour 403.5
contend 457.13
strive 725.11
flounder 916.15
have difficulty
1012.11

struggle against 451.4

struggle for try for
403.9
contend for 457.20

struggle on 725.14

struggle with 457.17

struggling contending
457.22
labouring 725.17

strum 708.40

strummer 710.5

strung out 87.23

strut
noun gait 177.12
swagger 501.8
verb stroll 177.28
swagger 501.15

strutting
noun swagger 501.8
adj swaggering 501.23

stub cigarette 89.5
tail 217.6
label 517.13
extremity 819.2

stubbed 268.10

stubble beard 3.8
remainder 256.1
bristle 288.3
refuse 391.4

stubborn persevering
360.8
obstinate 361.8
firm 425.7
adhesive 802.12
inflexible 1044.12
tough 1047.4

stubbornly 361.14

stubbornness refusal
325.1
defiance 327.2
perseverance 360.1
obstinacy 361.1
firmness 425.2
tenacity 802.3
stiffness 1044.3
toughness 1047.1

stubby 268.10

stucco 295.25

stuck fast 799.14,
854.16
cohesive 802.10
beat 970.26
stranded 1012.27

stuck on 104.31

stuck-up conceited
140.11
contemptuous 157.8

stuck with 643.8

stud
noun sex object 75.4
guy 76.5
cock 76.8
leg 273.6
bulge 283.3
horse 311.10
print 517.7
jockey 757.2
verb variegate 47.7
roughen 288.4
sprinkle 770.6

studded spotted 47.13

knobbed 283.17
gnarled 288.8
bristly 288.9
nappy 294.7
ornamented 498.11
sprinkled 770.10
teeming 883.9
illuminated 1024.39

student pupil 572.1
scholar 928.3

student teacher 571.4

studied intentional
380.8
affected 533.9
reasoned 934.21

studio library 197.6
atelier 712.17
workplace 739.1
radio station 1033.6

studio audience 48.6

studious devoted to
studies 570.17
studentlike 572.12
learned 927.21
engrossed 982.17

studiously 927.29

study
noun diagnosis 91.12
library 197.6
intention 380.1
discussion 541.7
treatise 556.1
branch of learning
568.8
studying 570.3
work of art 712.10
drawing 712.13
office 739.7
science 927.10
consideration 930.2
thoughtfulness 930.3
examination 937.3
engrossment 982.3
abstractedness 984.2
retreat 1008.5
verb endeavour 403.5
discuss 541.12
regard studiously
570.12
consider 930.12
examine 937.24
memorize 988.17

study for 570.15

studying
noun study 570.3
adj engrossed 982.17

study to 403.8

study with 570.11

stuff
noun material 4.1
gal 77.6
substance 196.5, 762.2
equipment 385.4
essence 766.2
matter 1050.2
materials 1052.1
verb nourish 8.19
gorge 8.25
fill 196.7, 793.7

stop 293.7
gluttonize 672.4
overload 992.15
satiate 993.4

stuffed stopped 293.11
full 793.11
overfull 992.20
satiated 993.6

stuffed full 993.6

stuff in 191.7

stuffing
noun dressing 10.26
lining 196.3
extra 254.4
stopping 293.5
embalming 397.3
adj gluttonous 672.6

stuffy malodorous 71.5
dull 117.6
airless 173.16
unyielding 361.9
perverse 361.11
prudish 500.19
pompous 501.22
old-fogyish 841.17
narrow-minded 979.10
unimaginative 986.5
sultry 1018.28

stultifying restraining
428.11
neutralizing 899.9

stumble
noun tumble 194.3
collapse 410.3
bungle 414.5
flounder 916.8
slip 974.4
verb tumble 194.8
not know one's own
mind 362.6
bungle 414.11
stammer 525.8
flounder 916.15
err 974.9

stumbling 525.13

stumbling block
1011.4

stump
noun remainder 256.1
public speaking 543.1
palette 712.18
cricket 747.1
piece 792.3
extremity 819.2
platform 900.13
verb plod 175.7
stroll 177.28
make a speech 543.9
play 747.4
boggle 970.14
thwart 1011.15

stumped not out 747.5
beat 970.26

stumps 177.15

stump up 624.16

stumpy deformed
265.12
stubby 268.10

low 274.7

stun
  noun match 752.3
  verb deaden 25.4
  deafen 49.5
  din 53.7
  numb 94.8
  astonish 122.6
  terrify 127.17
  startle 131.8
  play 752.4
stung 96.23
stunned stupefied 25.7
  deaf 49.6
  terrified 127.26
stunner 1015.9
stunning deadening
  25.9
  astonishing 122.12
  frightening 127.28
  terrifying 127.29
  surprising 131.11
  great 998.13
  eye-catching 1015.21
stunningly 131.15
stunt perform aerobatics
  184.40
  shorten 268.6
stunted dwarf 258.13
  undeveloped 406.12
  incomplete 794.4
  meagre 991.10
stupendous wonderful
  122.10
  large 247.7
  huge 257.20
  extraordinary 869.14
stupid dumb 921.15
  foolish 922.8
stupidity stupidness
  921.3
  foolishness 922.1
  folly 922.4
  blunder 974.5
stupidly unintelligently
  921.25
  foolishly 922.13
stupor sopor 22.6
  unconsciousness 25.2
  trance 92.19
  apathy 94.4
  languor 331.6
sturdy strong 15.15
  firm 15.18
  hale 83.12
  stable 762.7
stutter
  noun stammering
  525.3
  verb stammer 525.8
stuttering
  noun stammering
  525.3
  constancy 846.2
  redundancy 848.3
  adj stammering 525.13
  constant 846.5

style

noun clothing 5.1
  aspect 33.3
  form 262.1
  petal 310.26
  behaviour 321.1
  preference 371.5
  manner 384.1
  skill 413.1
  motif 498.7
  name 527.3
  mode 532.2, 764.4
  fashion 578.1
  lines 712.8
  engraving tool 713.8
  race 753.3
  fight 754.3
  kind 808.3
  speciality 865.1
  verb name 527.11
  phrase 532.4
styled named 527.14
  phrased 532.5
styling naming 527.2
  design 717.4
stylish dressed up 5.45
  skilful 413.22
  modish 578.12
stylishly 578.17
stylist master of style
  532.3
  designer 716.9, 717.5
stylistic 532.5
stylized 580.7
stylus 50.11
stymied 1012.24
suave 287.9, 504.18
sub
  noun submarine 180.9
  substitute 861.2
  adj inferior 250.6
subconscious
  noun psyche 92.28
  inmost mind 918.3
  adj unconscious 92.41
subconscious mind
  918.3
subcontinent 235.1
subdivided 801.20
subdue muffle 51.9
  relieve 120.5
  conquer 412.10
  suppress 428.8
  master 432.9
  moderate 670.6
  calm 670.7
  soften 1045.6
subdued soft-coloured
  35.21
  faint 52.16
  muffled 52.17
  dejected 112.22
  reticent 344.10
  conquered 412.17
  suppressed 428.14
  quelled 432.15
  meek 433.15
  tasteful 496.8
  restrained 670.11

subject
  noun citizen 227.4
  vassal 432.7
  syntax 530.2
  study 568.8, 570.3
  passage 708.24
  plot 722.4
  topic 936.1
  examinee 937.19
  experimental subject
  941.7
  verb subjugate 432.8
  adj inferior 250.6
  dependent 432.13
subjected 432.14
subjection inferiority
  250.1
  subjugation 432.1
  submission 433.1
subjective introverted
  92.39
  partial 650.11
  intrinsic 766.7
  mental 918.7
subjectivity 766.1
subject matter 936.1
subject to
  verb impose 643.4
  adj liable to 896.6
  contingent 958.9
  conj provided 958.12
subjugation defeat
  412.1
  subjection 432.1
  appropriation 480.4
sublime
  noun style 532.2
  verb refine 79.22
  vaporize 1065.8
  adj blissful 97.9
  eminent 247.9, 662.18
  high 272.14
  lofty 544.14
  magnanimous 652.6
  raised 911.9
  gorgeous 1015.20
sublimely 1015.25
subliminal
  noun psyche 92.28
  adj subconscious
  92.41
  instinctive 933.6
submarine
  noun sub 180.9
  diving bell 367.5
  adj underwater 275.13
submerge surface
  182.47
  sink 194.6
  overflow 238.17
  submerse 367.7
  flood 1063.14
submerged invisible
  32.5
  underwater 275.13
  latent 519.5
  depressed 912.12
  soaked 1063.17

submerged in 982.17
submission resignation
  134.2
  obeisance 155.2
  submittal 433.1
  offer 439.1
  consent 441.1
submissive resigned
  134.10
  humble-hearted
  137.11
  servile 138.13
  obeisant 155.10
  obedient 326.3
  assenting 332.13
  downtrodden 432.16
  compliant 433.12
  consenting 441.4
  conformable 866.5
  pliant 1045.9
submit obey 326.2
  affirm 334.5
  nominate 371.19
  advise 422.5
  comply 433.6
  offer 439.4
  propose 439.5
  acquiesce 441.3
  yield 1045.7
submit to 433.9
subordinate
  noun inferior 250.2
  junior 432.5
  retainer 577.1
  nonessential 767.2
  verb subjugate 432.8
  classify 807.11
  adj inferior 250.6
  subject 432.13
  unessential 767.4
subordinated 432.14
subordinate to 432.17
subordination
  inferiority 250.1
  continuity 806.2
  grouping 807.3
subscribe abet 449.14
  contribute 478.14
  belong 617.15
subscriber endorser
  332.7
  giver 478.11
subscribe to assent
  332.8
  ratify 332.12
  secure 438.9
subscription ratification
  332.4
  giving 478.1
  donation 478.6
  signature 527.10
  fee 630.6
subsequent succeeding
  814.4
  after 834.4
subsequently 834.6
subservience inferiority
  250.1

affirmative 332.2
  submissiveness 433.3
subservient servile
  138.13
  inferior 250.6
  modal 384.8
  subject 432.13
  submissive 433.12
  deferential 433.16
  helping 449.20
subside move 172.5
  quiet 173.8
  sink 194.6
  decrease 252.6
  gravitate 297.15
  decline 393.17
subsidence standstill
  173.3
  sinkage 194.2
  slide 194.4
  decline 252.2
subsidiaries 792.2
subsidiarity 430.5
subsidiary
  noun nonessential
  767.2
  adj helping 449.20
  endowed 478.26
  unessential 767.4
subsiding
  noun course 172.2
  adj quiescent 173.12
  descending 194.11
  decreasing 252.11
  deteriorating 393.45
subsidize provide
  385.7
  support 449.12,
  900.21
  finance 478.19, 729.15
  treat 624.19
subsidy provision 385.1
  support 449.3, 900.1
  subvention 478.8
  treat 624.8
  financing 729.2
subsistence
  noun accommodations
  385.3
  support 449.3
  existence 760.1
  adj meagre 991.10
substance sum and
  substance 196.5
  quantity 244.1
  meaning 518.1
  summary 557.2
  warrant 600.6
  wealth 618.1
  funds 728.14
  substantiality 762.1
  stuff 762.2
  essence 766.2
  major part 791.6
  topic 936.1
  salient point 996.6
  matter 1050.2
substances 1052.1

substantial large
257.16
authoritative 417.15
meaningful 518.10
solvent 729.17
real 760.15
substantive 762.6
essential 766.9
stable 854.12
influential 893.13
reliable 969.17
valid 972.14
sufficient 990.6
important 996.17
dense 1043.12
material 1050.10

substantially
essentially 762.8,
766.11
on the whole 791.14
sufficiently 990.8

substantiate itemize
765.6
experiment 941.8
confirm 956.11
materialize 1050.9

substantiated proved
956.20
true 972.13

substantive
noun noun 530.5
adj grammatical
530.17
substantial 762.6
essential 766.9
vital 996.23

substitute
noun surrogate 92.31
deputy 576.1
successor 816.4
sub 861.2
verb exchange 861.4
adj alternate 861.8

substituted 861.9

substitute for represent
576.14
sub for 861.5

substitution defence
mechanism 92.23
compensation 338.1
exchange 861.1
substitute 861.2

subsumed 771.5

subterfuge secrecy
345.1
concealment 346.1
deception 356.1
trick 356.6
pretext 376.1
stratagem 415.3
quibbling 935.5

subterranean 275.12

subtext 519.2

subtitle
noun makeup 554.12
caption 936.2
verb focus on 936.3

subtle soft-coloured
35.21
dainty 248.7
thin 270.16, 763.6
rare 299.4
meticulous 339.12
cunning 415.12
nice 495.11
elegant 496.9
complex 798.4
shrewd 919.15
discriminating 943.7
exact 972.17

subtlety rarity 299.1
meticulousness 339.3
cunning 415.1
nicety 495.3
taste 496.1
unsubstantiality 763.1
margin 779.2
complexity 798.1
shrewdness 919.3
sophistry 935.1
discrimination 943.1
accuracy 972.5

subtly 495.14

subtract deduct 255.9
separate 801.8
calculate 1016.17

suburb 230.1

suburban environing
209.8
urban 230.11
upper-class 607.10
ordinary 1004.8

suburbia town 230.1
East End 230.6
middle class 607.5
mediocrity 1004.5

suburbs environment
209.1
East End 230.6

subversion overturn
205.2
fall 395.3
indoctrination 857.5
revolution 859.1
refutation 957.2

subversive
noun rebel 327.5
saboteur 357.11
radical 611.17
revolutionist 859.3
adj rebellious 327.11
destructive 395.26
radical 611.29
changed 851.10

subvert overturn 205.6
revolt 327.7
undermine 393.15
overthrow 395.20
change 851.7
indoctrinate 857.15
refute 957.5

subway crossing 170.2
train 179.14
cave 284.5
passageway 383.3

succeed accomplish
407.4
prevail 409.7
triumph 411.3
change hands 629.4
dramatize 704.28
follow 814.2, 816.5
substitute for 861.5
prosper 1009.7

succeed in 409.12

succeeding following
166.5
successful 409.14
successive 814.4
subsequent 834.4

success
noun superiority 249.1
successfulness 409.1
winner 409.6
victory 411.1
stage show 704.4
prosperity 1009.1
adj accomplishment
407.1

successful succeeding
409.14
victorious 411.7
prosperous 1009.12

successfully 409.15

succession accession
417.12
inheritance 479.2
lineage 560.4
posterity 561.1
devolution 629.2
series 811.2
sequence 814.1
subsequence 834.1

successive consecutive
811.9
succeeding 814.4
subsequent 834.4

successively 811.11

successor follower
166.2
survivor 256.3
heir 479.5
replacement 816.4
sequel 834.2
substitute 861.2

success story 409.3

succinct short 268.8
concise 537.6
aphoristic 973.6

succinctly shortly
268.12
concisely 537.7

succour
noun remedy 86.1
aid 449.1
verb aid 449.11
benefit 592.3

succulent
noun legume 310.4
adj edible 8.33
tasty 63.8
delectable 97.10
interesting 982.19

fluid 1059.4
pulpy 1061.6

succumb burn out 21.5
faint 25.5
die 307.19
perish 395.23
lose 412.12
submit 433.6

succumb to 433.9

such 783.3

such-and-such 528.2

such as 783.12

suchlike
noun likeness 783.3
adj such as 783.12

suck
noun drink 8.4, 88.7
suction 187.5
verb drink 8.29
draw in 187.12
draw off 192.12

sucker sprout 302.11
branch 310.18
pigeon 358.2

sucking suction 187.5
drawing 192.3

suckling 302.9

suction suck 187.5
drawing 192.3

sud 320.5

sudden
adj unexpected 131.10
impulsive 365.9
precipitate 401.10
abrupt 829.5
adv suddenly 829.9

sudden change 851.2

sudden death fatal
disease 85.2
early death 307.5

suddenly unexpectedly
131.14
short 268.13
impulsively 365.13
precipitately 401.15
sudden 829.9

suddenness
impulsiveness 365.2
hastiness 401.2
abruptness 829.2

sue petition 440.10
solicit 440.14
court 562.21
litigate 598.13

sue for 440.14

suet 10.13

suffer feel pain 26.8
ail 85.45
hurt 96.19
endure 134.5
submit 433.6
countenance 443.10
be punished 604.19
experience 830.8

sufferer sick person
85.42
victim 96.11

suffer for 604.19

suffering
noun pain 26.1, 96.5
adj pained 26.9
permissive 443.14

suffice be satisfactory
107.6
avail 387.17
do 990.4

sufficiency ability 18.2
satisfactoriness 107.3
sufficientness 990.1
tolerableness 998.3

sufficient satisfactory
107.11
valid 972.14
sufficing 990.6
tolerable 998.20

sufficiently
satisfactorily 107.15
amply 990.8

suffocate die a natural
death 307.24
strangle 308.18
extinguish 395.15
suppress 428.8
obstruct 1011.12
burn 1018.22

suffocated 428.14

suffocating
noun suppression
428.2
adj strong 69.10
stuffy 173.16
sultry 1018.28

suffocation violent
death 307.6
smothering 308.6
extinction 395.6

suffrage vote 371.6
participation 476.1
franchise 609.17

suffragette suffrage
609.17
women's rightist 642.5

suffused permeated
221.15
luminous 1024.30

Sufi 675.23

sugar
noun carbohydrate 7.5
sweetening 66.2
acid 87.9
sweetie 104.11
darling 562.6
verb sweeten 66.3

sugared 66.4

sugary 66.4

suggest promise 133.13
advise 422.5
propose 439.5
signify 517.17
mean 518.8
imply 519.4
hint 551.10
resemble 783.7
evidence 956.8
remind 988.20

adj arrogant 141.9
remarkable 247.10
greater 249.12
higher 272.19
authoritative 417.15
important 996.17
above par 998.14
superiority power 18.1
greatness 247.1
preeminence 249.1
abnormality 869.1
overrunning 909.1
importance 996.1
goodness 998.1
superlative
noun exaggeration
355.1
best 998.8
adj downright 247.12
supreme 249.13
high 272.14
exaggerated 355.4
Superman 15.6
superman 249.4
supermarket 736.1
supermodel artist's
model 785.5
beauty 1015.8
supernatural
noun supernaturalism
689.2, 869.7
adj divine 677.16
occult 689.23
supranatural 869.15
spectral 987.7
immaterial 1051.7
superpower 232.1
superseded 390.10
supersonic acoustic
50.17
transsonic 174.16
superstar
noun superior 249.4
ace 413.14
celebrity 662.9
lead 707.6
chief 996.10
first-rater 998.6
adj chief 249.14
superstition 953.3
superstitious 953.8
superstructure 266.2
supervise superintend
573.10
govern 612.12
supervising 573.13
supervision
superintendence 573.2
government 612.1
supervisor teaching
fellow 571.4
superintendent 574.2
supervisory supervising
573.13
executive 612.19
superwoman 77.5
supine apathetic 94.13

recumbent 201.8
low 274.7
languid 331.20
submissive 433.12
supper 8.6
supplant depose 447.4
substitute for 861.5
supple
verb soften 1045.6
adj timeserving 363.10
versatile 413.25
changeable 853.6
pliant 1045.9
supplement
noun adjunct 254.1
nonessential 767.2
sequel 816.1
verb add to 253.5
supplementary
additional 253.10
unessential 767.4
supplementation
addition 253.1
adjunct 254.1
suppleness
changeableness 853.1
pliancy 1045.2
supplied 385.13
supplier 385.6
supplies provisions
10.5, 385.2
store 386.1
supply
noun means 384.2
provision 385.1
fund 386.2
materials 1052.1
verb provide 385.7
furnish 478.15
supplying provision
385.1
giving 478.1
support
noun nutriment 10.3
consolation 121.4
assent 332.1
means 384.2
preservation 397.1
aid 449.1
maintenance 449.3
reinforcements 449.8
subsidy 478.8
supporter 616.9,
900.2
treat 624.8
financing 729.2
backing 900.1
confirmation 956.4
verb strengthen 15.13
comfort 121.6
give hope 124.10
endure 134.5
ratify 332.12
provide 385.7
preserve 397.8
lend support 449.12
subsidize 478.19
encourage 492.16
commend 509.11

benefit 592.3
defend 600.10
back 609.41
treat 624.19
afford 626.7
enact 704.30
finance 729.15
bear 900.21
confirm 956.11
care for 1007.19
supported approved
509.19
borne 900.24
supporter follower
166.2
suspender 202.5
attender 221.5
defender 460.7
giver 478.11
friend 588.1
upholder 616.9
financer 729.9
support 900.2
support group 449.2
supporting
adj approving 509.17
benefitting 592.4
supportive 900.23
confirming 956.18
prep behind 449.27
supporting cast 707.11
supporting role 704.10
supportive comforting
121.13
promising 124.13
supporting 900.23
confirming 956.18
support services 900.1
suppose imply 519.4
judge 945.8
assume 950.10
think 952.11
think likely 967.5
imagine 985.14
supposed implied
519.7
suppositive 950.14
supposedly 950.17
supposing
noun supposition
950.3
conj supposing that
950.19
supposing that 950.19
supposition implication
519.2
idea 931.1
prejudgment 946.1
supposal 950.3
suppress repress 106.8,
428.8
cover up 345.8
extinguish 395.15
conquer 412.10
subdue 432.9
prohibit 444.3
retain 474.5
domineer 612.16

moderate 670.6
cushion 670.8
hinder 1011.10
suppressed reticent
344.10
secret 345.11
conquered 412.17
repressed 428.14
subjugated 432.14
forgetful 989.9
suppression repression
92.24, 428.2
veil of secrecy 345.3
extinction 395.6
subdual 432.4
prohibition 444.1
retention 474.1
block 989.3
hindrance 1011.1
supra on high 272.21
before 813.6
supranational 312.16
supremacy primacy
249.3
influence 893.1
importance 996.1
superexcellence 998.2
supreme omnipotent
18.13
top 198.10
superlative 249.13
authoritative 417.15
governing 612.18
almighty 677.17
paramount 996.24
best 998.16
supremely 249.16
supremo 575.4
surcharge
noun burden 297.7
overcharge 632.5
overfullness 992.3
verb falsify accounts
628.10
overprice 632.7
overload 992.15
sure
adj expectant 130.11
secured 438.11
trustworthy 644.19
belief 952.21
evidential 956.16
inevitable 962.15
certain 969.13
reliable 969.17
confident 969.21
adv surely 969.24
exclam yeah 332.19
sure enough
adv surely 969.24
exclam yeah 332.19
sure-enough certain
969.13
true 972.13
genuine 972.15
surely
adv inevitably 962.19
certainly 969.23
sure 969.24

exclam yes 332.18
sure sign sign 517.1
proof 956.3
sure thing
noun dead certainty
969.2
good chance 971.8
adv surely 969.24
exclam yeah 332.19
surf
noun wave 238.14,
915.4
foam 320.2
verb navigate 182.13
surface
noun space 158.1
top 198.1
exterior 206.2
shallowness 276.1
texture 294.1
tennis 749.1
verb show 31.4
break water 182.47
arrive 186.6
emerge 190.11
shoot up 193.9
floor 295.22
come out 348.6
be manifest 348.7
be revealed 351.8
adj apparent 33.11
exterior 206.7
shallow 276.5
formal 580.7
insufficient 991.9
surfaced textural 294.5
covered 295.31
surfacing
noun breaking water
182.8
emergence 190.1
ground covering 199.3
adj emerging 190.18
surfeit
noun overfullness
992.3
satiety 993.1
verb fill 793.7
overload 992.15
satiate 993.4
surfing 182.11
surge
noun loudness 53.1
ascent 193.1
flow 238.4
wave 238.14, 915.4
increase 251.1
whirl 914.2
verb din 53.7
run out 190.13
ascend 193.8
flow 238.16
jet 238.20
billow 238.22
come together 769.16
whirl 914.11
surgeon 90.5
surgery operation 90.2

verb pinch 482.16
hit 901.14

swipe at lambaste
459.15
hit 901.14

swirl
noun agitation 105.4,
916.1
eddy 238.12
coil 281.2
bustle 330.4
whirl 914.2
verb eddy 238.21
convolve 281.4
whirl 914.11
agitate 916.10

swirling
noun agitation 105.4
rotation 914.1
adj rotating 914.14

swish
noun sibilation 57.1
verb ripple 52.11
rustle 52.12
sibilate 57.2
adj fashionable 578.11

switch
noun false hair 3.13
surprise 131.2
branch 310.18
rod 605.2
plot 722.4
member 792.4
change 851.1
substitution 861.1
trading 862.2
verb avoid 164.6
transfer 176.10
whip 604.12
trade 731.14
substitute 861.4
interchange 862.4

switchboard 704.16

switched 862.5

switched on high 87.23
wild about 101.11
gripped 982.18

switching corporal
punishment 604.4
televising 1034.3

switch off 856.12

swivel
noun axle 914.5
verb rotate 914.9

swivelling 914.1

swollen diseased 85.59
puffed up 136.10
increased 251.7
corpulent 257.18
distended 259.13
bulged 283.16
pompous 501.22
inflated 502.12
bombastic 545.9
full 793.11
overfull 992.20

swoon
noun stupor 22.6

unconsciousness 25.2
verb faint 25.5

swoop
noun descent 194.1
plunge 367.1
verb descend 194.5
plunge 367.6

sword
noun coercion 424.3
war 458.1
stabbing 459.10
combatant 461.1
blade 462.5
cutlery 1039.2
verb stab 459.25

sworn affirmed 334.9
promised 436.8

sworn to accepted
332.14
affirmed 334.9

swot 570.12

sycophantic obsequious
138.14
flattering 511.8

syllable
noun speech sound
524.13
word 526.1
measure 720.9
verb spell 546.7

syllabus abridgment
557.1
study 568.8

symbiosis cooperation
450.1
joining 799.1
concurrence 898.1

symbiotic cooperative
450.5
agreeing 787.9
concurrent 898.4

symbol
noun universal symbol
92.30
representation 349.1
emblem 517.2
sign 518.6
letter 546.1
insignia 647.1
notation 709.12
example 785.2
substitute 861.2
number 1016.3
verb designate 517.18

symbolic indicative
517.23
meaningful 518.10
semantic 518.12
symbolical 519.10

symbolically 536.4

symbolism symbol
92.30, 517.2
implication 519.2
occultism 689.1
ritualism 701.1

symbolize represent
349.8
designate 517.18

mean 518.8
metaphorize 536.2

symbolizing 349.13

symmetrical
symmetric 264.4
harmonious 533.8
orderly 806.6

symmetry
symmetricalness 264.1
harmony 533.2
correlation 776.1
agreement 787.1
equality 789.1
order 806.1

sympathetic sensitive
24.12, 93.20
comforting 121.13
kind 143.13
pitying 145.7
condoling 147.3
in accord 455.3
related 774.9
attracting 906.5
tolerant 978.11

sympathetically
145.10

sympathize pity 145.3
get along 455.2

sympathize with
respond 93.11
comfort 121.6
pity 145.3
condole with 147.2

sympathy sensitivity
24.3
fellow feeling 93.5
inclination 100.3
consolation 121.4
kindness 143.1
pity 145.1
condolence 147.1
patronage 449.4
accord 455.1
good terms 587.3
relation 774.1
attraction 906.1
tolerance 978.4

symphonic 708.51

symphony accord
455.1
harmony 708.3

symposium drinking
8.3
spree 88.5
forum 423.3
discussion 541.7
compilation 554.7
assembly 769.2

symptom prognosis
91.13
warning sign 399.3
sign 517.1
hint 551.4
evidence 956.1

symptomatic indicative
517.23
evidential 956.16
insufficient 991.9

symptoms 85.1

synagogue 703.2

sync
noun agreement 787.1
verb harmonize 787.7

syndicate
noun council 423.1
company 617.9
underworld 660.11
illicit business 732.1
verb combine 804.3

syndrome 85.1

synergy cooperation
450.1
concurrence 898.1

synod council 423.1
ecclesiastical council
423.4
diocese 698.8
assembly 769.2

synonym word 526.1
same 777.3

synonymous 777.8

synopsis shortening
268.3
abridgment 557.1

syntax structure 530.2
arrangement 807.1

synth 711.1

synthesis identification
777.2
composition 795.1
combination 804.1
priori reasoning 934.3

synthesized 804.5

synthetic
noun plastic 1052.6
adj imitation 336.8
spurious 354.26
similar 783.10
dialectic 934.22

syringe
noun sprinkler 1063.8
verb wash 79.19
moisten 1063.12

syrup sweetening 66.2
medicine 86.4
adhesive 802.4
semiliquid 1060.5

syrupy sweet 66.4
viscous 1060.12

system plan 381.1
manner 384.1
nature 766.4
order 806.1
orderliness 806.3
outlook 977.2
universe 1070.1

systematic uniform
780.5
orderly 806.6

systematically
regularly 780.8, 849.9
methodically 806.9

T 170.4

tab
noun bulge 283.3

insignia of rank 647.5
scenery 704.20
afterpart 816.2
verb label 517.20

table
noun meal 8.5
food 10.1
horizontal 201.3
furniture 229.1
plain 236.1
plateau 237.3, 272.4
lamina 296.2
diagram 381.3
record 549.1
notebook 549.11
pocket 752.2
outline 800.4
code 807.4
contents 870.2
board 900.15
summation 1016.11
verb put away 390.6
propose 439.5
legislate 613.9
postpone 845.9

tableau spectacle 33.7
picture 712.11

tablecloth 8.13

tables 182.2

tablespoon 8.12

tablet pill 86.7
lamina 296.2
notebook 549.11
monument 549.12

tableware dining
utensils 8.12
hard goods 735.4

tabling introduction
613.5
postponement 845.4

tabloid gaudy 501.20
newspaper 555.2

tabloid press 552.1

taboo
noun prohibition 444.1
exclusion 772.1
verb prohibit 444.3
exclude 772.4
adj prohibited 444.7
jargonish 523.19

tabs 87.9

tacit wordless 51.11
implicit 519.8

tacitly 519.13

taciturn untalkative
344.9
concise 537.6

tack
noun grub 10.2
vector 161.2
deviation 164.1
cordage 271.3
manner 384.1
harness 385.5
sewing 741.1
horse racing 757.1
fastening 799.3
inferiority 1004.3

verb deviate 164.3
change course 182.30
sew 741.4
hook 799.8
be changed 851.6

tackle
noun rigging 180.12
cordage 271.3
equipment 385.4
harness 385.5
impedimenta 471.3
game 745.3, 746.3,
750.3
purchase 905.6
lifter 911.3
verb practice 328.8
treat 387.12
take on 403.7
undertake 404.3
set to work 725.15
play 745.4, 746.4,
750.7
reel in 905.9

tackling 180.12

tacky unpleasant 98.17
shabby 393.32
adhesive 802.12
slovenly 809.15
viscous 1060.12
moist 1063.15

tact sensitivity 24.3
considerateness 143.3
skill 413.1
courtesy 504.1
intuition 933.1
discrimination 943.1

tactful sensitive 24.12
considerate 143.16
skilful 413.22
courteous 504.14
discriminating 943.7

tactfully considerately
143.21
discriminatingly
943.10

tactic stratagem 415.3
expedient 994.2

tactical planned 381.12
cunning 415.12

tactician planner 381.6
strategist 415.7

tactics behaviour 321.1
plan 381.1
machination 415.4
operation 458.5
basketball game 751.3

tactile tactual 73.10
touchable 73.11

tactless insensible 25.6
inconsiderate 144.18
careless 340.11
ill-bred 505.6
undiscriminating
944.5

tadpole fledgling
302.10
amphibian 311.27

tag

noun scrap 248.3
label 517.13
name 527.3
rabble 606.3
token 728.12
sequel 816.1
afterpart 816.2
extremity 819.2
verb add 253.4
allot 477.9
label 517.20
name 527.11

tagging 477.3

tag on 253.4

tail
noun braid 3.7
rear 217.1
arse 217.5
cauda 217.6
postscript 254.2
makeup 554.12
member 792.4
afterpart 816.2
extremity 819.2
verb trace 937.35
adj rear 217.9
caudal 217.11
final 819.11

tailed 217.11

tail end boundary
211.3
rear 217.1
piece 792.3
extremity 819.2

tail-end 819.11

tailing following 166.1
surveillance 937.9

tailor
noun tailoress 5.34
sewer 741.2
verb outfit 5.40
form 262.7
sew 741.4
harmonize 787.7

tailored custom-made
5.47
formative 262.9
apt 787.10

tailoring garment
making 5.31
sewing 741.1

tailor-made 787.10

tails formal dress 5.11
opposite side 215.3

taint
noun infection 85.4
stigma 661.6
tinge 796.7
characteristic 864.4
fault 1002.2
stain 1003.3
verb defile 80.17
infect 85.50
corrupt 393.12
stigmatize 661.9
blaspheme 694.5
work evil 999.6
stain 1003.6

tainted soiled 80.21
unhealthful 82.5
diseased 85.59
off 393.41
corrupt 654.14
unchaste 665.23
stained 1003.10

tait 248.3

take
noun explanation
341.4
catch 480.10
booty 482.11
receipts 627.1
cinematography 706.4
shot 714.8
production 892.2
verb eat 8.20
pocket 134.8
transport 176.12
interpret 341.9
submit 433.6
acquire 472.8
receive 479.6
possess 480.13
possess sexually
480.15
catch 480.17
steal 482.13
understand 521.7
adopt 621.4
entail 771.4
combine 804.3
suppose 950.10
think 952.11

take a back seat
retreat 163.6
retract 168.3
depend on 432.12

take a break take a rest
20.8
pause 856.9
interrupt 856.10

take account of take
stock 628.9
allow for 958.5
take cognizance of
982.9
calculate 1016.17

take a chance chance
759.24
risk 971.12
take chances 1005.7

take advantage of
avail oneself of 387.15
exploit 387.16
improve the occasion
842.8

take a holiday 20.9

take a long, hard look
27.14

take a look at 27.13

take an interest care
339.6
be involved 897.3

take an interest in
love 104.19
be curious 980.3
attend to 982.5

take a picture 714.14

take a stand 348.6

take a walk 177.29

take away remove
176.11
subtract 255.9

takeaway breakfast 8.6
restaurant 8.17

take away from
480.21

take back deny 335.4
recant 363.8
restore 481.4
recover 481.6
apologize 658.5

take care 494.7

take care of waste
308.13
perform 328.9
look after 339.9
bribe 378.3
accomplish 407.4
supervise 573.10
serve 577.13
attend to 604.10
operate 888.5
care for 1007.19

take chances chance
759.24
take a chance 1005.7

take charge be able
18.11
take command 417.14

take charge of 1007.19

take comfort 121.7

take down devour 8.22
abase 137.5
raze 395.19
reprove 510.17
record 549.15
fell 912.5

take effect 888.7

take for suppose
950.10
think 952.11

take for granted
expect 130.5
neglect 340.6
imply 519.4
suppose 950.10
believe 952.10

take from reduce 252.7
subtract 255.9
take away from 480.21

take heart cheer up
109.9
be comforted 121.7
be hopeful 124.8
take courage 492.14

take heed be careful
339.7
beware 494.7

take hold stir 330.11
gain influence 893.12

take home grab 472.9
receive 479.6

take in devour 8.22

see 27.12
hear 48.11
extend 158.8
receive 187.10, 585.7
enter 189.7
shorten 268.6
deceive 356.14
receive 479.6
understand 521.7
absorb 570.7
include 771.3
entail 771.4
put together 799.5
spectate 917.5

take issue 333.4

take issue with deny
335.4
oppose 451.3
dispute 457.21

take it take it on the
chin 134.6
submit 433.6
suppose 950.10
think 952.11
suffice 990.4

take it all monopolize
469.6
appropriate 480.19

take it easy
verb rest 20.6
compose oneself 106.7
take things as they
come 331.15
take one's leisure
402.4
phrase easy does it
175.15

take it on take action
328.5
endeavour 403.5

take its place 806.5

take it that 341.9

take kindly to concur
332.9
consent 441.2
approve 509.9

take legal action 673.8

take life 308.12

taken aback startled
131.13
unprepared 406.8

taken away 222.11

taken by surprise
surprised 131.12
unprepared 406.8

taken for granted to
be expected 130.14
tacit 519.8

taken ill 85.55

taken off 783.10

taken on 404.7

taken notice of 27.12

taken over 691.13

taken up 984.11

taken up with 982.17

taken with

adj pleased 95.14
fond of 104.30
prep compared to
942.11
takeoff taxiing 184.8
embarkation 188.3
point of departure
188.5
ascent 193.1
imitation 336.1
similarity 783.1
take off remove 6.6
beat it 188.7
leave the ground
193.10
kill 308.12
mimic 336.6
impersonate 349.12
improve 392.7
put an end to 395.12
gesture 517.21
discount 631.2
resemble 783.7
take on grieve 112.17
beef 115.16
practice 328.8
treat 387.12
tackle 403.7
undertake 404.3
contend against 451.4
engage 457.16
receive 479.6
employ 615.14
adopt 621.4
set to work 725.15
take out extract 192.10
excise 255.10
waste 308.13
escort 768.8
takeover appropriation
480.4
trading 737.19
combination 804.1
take over take
command 417.14
take possession 472.10
receive 479.6
appropriate 480.19
adopt 621.4
usurp 640.8
combine 804.3
succeed 814.2
takeover bid 737.19
take part 476.5
take part in 476.5
take place 830.5
take precautions
1006.3
take precedence rule
249.11
precede 813.2
take pride 136.5
taker recipient 479.3
partaker 480.11
take refuge 1008.7
take refuge in 376.4
take revenge 506.7

take risks 492.10
take root vegetate
310.31
become a habit 373.11
root 854.10
gain influence 893.12
take shape 262.8,
806.5
take sides 934.16
take stock take account
of 628.9
check 1016.20
take stock of scrutinize
27.14
examine 937.24
take the initiative
817.10
take the lead lead
165.2
take command 417.14
direct 573.8
dominate 612.15
initiate 817.10
take the place of
861.5
take the plunge be
determined 359.8
initiate 817.10
take the strain 905.9
take the trouble 324.3
take time spend time
820.6
wait 845.12
take time off 222.8
take time out 20.8
take to desire 100.14
fall in love 104.22
practice 328.8
be used to 373.12
avail oneself of 387.14
take turns 824.5
take up practice 328.8
adopt 371.15
undertake 404.3
patronize 449.15
take possession 472.10
collect 472.11
appropriate 480.19
espouse 509.13
discuss 541.12
write upon 556.5
pay in full 624.13
busy oneself with
724.11
assemble 769.18
include 771.3
enter 817.9
pick up 911.8
engross 982.13
take up arms 458.16
taking
noun receiving 479.1
possession 480.1
sexual possession
480.3
adoption 621.2
combination 804.1

overrunning 909.1
adj contagious 85.61
delightful 97.7
desirable 100.30
alluring 377.8
catching 480.25
taking away
subtraction 255.1
loss 473.1
taking 480.1
taking in reception
187.1
absorption 570.2
taking into account
945.17
taking off ascent 193.1
similarity 783.1
taking office 615.3
taking on 615.4
taking over accession
417.12
appropriation 480.4
taking place 830.9
takings 627.1
talcum 1015.12
talcum powder
1015.12
tale lie 354.11
gossip 552.7
story 719.3, 722.3
sum 1016.6
talent ability 18.2
flair 413.4
talented person 413.12
artistry 712.7
smartness 919.2
genius 919.8
talented gifted 413.29
smart 919.14
talents 413.4
talisman 691.5
talk
noun language 523.1
speech 524.1, 543.2
diction 541.3
palaver 541.3
report 552.6
gossip 552.7
lesson 568.7
verb communicate
343.6
signify 517.17
speak 523.16, 524.20
discuss 541.12
make a speech 543.9
gossip 552.12
talk about 133.14
talkative
communicative 343.10
disclosive 351.10
speaking 524.32
wordy 538.12
loquacious 540.9
talked-about reported
552.15
distinguished 662.16
well-known 927.27

talked-of distinguished
662.16
well-known 927.27
talker speaker 524.18,
543.4
conversationalist 541.8
talking
noun communication
343.1
speech 524.1
adj speaking 524.32
talking point 934.5
talk on 540.5
talk over persuade
375.23
confer 541.11
discuss 541.12
convince 952.18
talk show 1033.18
talk to 524.27
tall large 257.16
long 267.7
giant 272.16
grandiloquent 545.8
unbelievable 954.10
tally
noun label 517.13
report 549.7
account 628.2
likeness 783.3
agreement 787.1
list 870.1
sum 1016.6
verb compute 253.6
coincide 777.4
agree 787.6
list 870.8
number 1016.16
calculate 1016.17
tally of 1016.12
talons governance
417.5
clutches 474.4
control 612.2
tame
verb accustom 373.10
domesticate 432.11
moderate 670.6
tend 1068.7
adj inert 173.14
domesticated 228.34
meek 433.15
moderate 670.10
tamed domesticated
228.34
subdued 432.15
meek 433.15
tamely 433.19
tamer 1068.2
Tamil Tiger 859.3
taming habituation
373.8
subdual 432.4
tampered with 354.30
tampering 354.9
tamper with meddle
214.7

manipulate 354.17
bribe 378.3
adulterate 796.12
tampon dressing 86.33
stopping 293.5
tan
verb brown 40.2
prepare 405.6
beat up 604.14
adj brown 40.3
tandem
noun rig 179.5
adv behind 217.13
tang taste 62.1
zest 68.2
characteristic 864.4
sting 1000.5
tangent
noun convergence
169.1
neighbour 223.6
straight line 277.2
adj converging 169.3
in contact 223.17
tangential converging
169.3
in contact 223.17
tangerine 42.2
tangible
noun substance 762.2
adj touchable 73.11
manifest 348.8
substantial 762.6
tangle
noun complex 798.2
verb trap 356.20
catch 480.17
complicate 798.3
involve 897.2
hamper 1011.11
tangled 798.4
tangy 68.7
tank
noun lake 241.1
storehouse 386.6
verb package 212.9
tanker ship 180.1
tank corpsman 461.12
tanned brown 40.3
prepared 405.16
tanner 728.7
tanning embalming
397.3
larruping 604.5
Tannoy 50.11
tantalizing appetizing
63.10
delightful 97.7
desirable 100.30
exciting 105.30
disappointing 132.6
alluring 377.8
interesting 982.19
tantamount reciprocal
776.10
equivalent 789.8
Tantra 683.7

tearing
noun extortion 192.6
severance 801.2
adj circulatory 2.31

tea-room 8.17

tears 115.2

tear up 395.13

tear-up 457.4

tease
noun tormentor 96.10
disappointment 132.1
deceiver 357.1
verb annoy 96.13
disappoint 132.2
attract 377.6
importune 440.12
banter 490.5

teased 96.24

teaser tormentor 96.10
deceiver 357.1
tempter 377.4
scenery 704.20
dilemma 1012.7

teasing
noun importunity 440.3
bantering 490.2
adj annoying 98.22
disappointing 132.6
alluring 377.8
importunate 440.18
bantering 490.7
ridiculing 508.12

teaspoon 8.12

teatime 8.6

tec dick 576.11
cop 1007.16

technical skilled 413.26
occupational 724.16
specialized 865.5
scientific 927.28
insignificant 997.17

technical college 567.5

technicality technical term 526.5
complexity 798.1
speciality 865.1
insignificancy 997.6

technically truly 972.18
to be exact 972.22

technician expert 413.11
skilled worker 726.6
engineer 726.7
specialist 865.3
liveware 1041.17

Technicolor
colourfulness 35.4
cinematography 706.4

technique manner 384.1
skill 413.1
art 413.7
treatment 712.9
race 753.3

knowledge 927.1

technological 927.28

technology art 413.7
engineer 726.7
science 927.10

ted 302.4

teddy bear figure 349.6
toy 743.16

tedious dull 117.6
monotonous 118.9, 848.15
same 780.6
mediocre 1004.7

tedium unpleasure 96.1
monotony 118.1
repetitiousness 848.4

tee 748.1

teeming
noun proliferation 889.2
infestation 909.2
adj pregnant 78.18
permeated 221.15
diffuse 538.11
crowded 769.22
swarming 883.9
productive 889.9
infested 909.11
imaginative 985.18
plentiful 990.7
superabundant 992.19

teenager 302.1

teens 881.7

teetering
noun changing 853.3
alternation 915.5
adj unsteady 16.16

teeth dentition 2.8
acrimony 17.5
clutches 474.4

teetotal 668.10

tel 237.4

telecommunication
communications 343.5, 347.1
radio 1033.1

telecommunications 517.15

telegram
noun telegraph 347.14
message 552.4
verb telegraph 347.19

telegraph
noun telegraph recorder 347.2
telegram 347.14
verb telegram 347.19

telepathic
communicational 343.9
psychic 689.24

telepathy
communication 343.1
mental telepathy 689.9

telephone
noun phone 347.4
verb phone 347.18

telephone book
reference book 554.9
directory 574.10

telephone box 347.4

telephone call 347.13

telephone directory
telephone number 347.12
reference book 554.9
directory 574.10

telephone exchange
telephone office 347.7
telephone number 347.12

telephone line 347.17

telephone number 347.12

telephone numbers 618.3

Telephoto 714.3

telephoto 714.17

telescope
noun scope 29.4
observatory 1070.17
verb shorten 268.6

telescopic clear-sighted 27.21
microscopic 29.10

televised 352.17

televising 1034.3

television radio 347.3
informant 551.5
news 552.1
electronics 1032.1
TV 1034.1

television broadcast 1034.2

television channel 1034.4

televisual 1034.16

Telex 347.2

telex
noun telegram 347.14
verb telegraph 347.19

tell impress 93.15
communicate 343.7
divulge 351.5
say 524.23
inform 551.8
report 552.11
narrate 719.6, 722.6
have influence 893.10
evidence 956.8
recognize 988.12
matter 996.12
number 1016.16

tell all 351.7

tell a story 722.6

teller informant 551.5
banker 729.10

telling
noun informing 343.2
fiction 722.1
narration 722.2
numeration 1016.9
adj powerful 18.12

exciting 105.30
vigorous 544.11
influential 893.13
evidential 956.16
notable 996.19

tellingly powerfully 18.15
eloquently 544.15

telltale
noun divulgence 351.2
clue 517.9
hint 551.4
informer 551.6
newsmonger 552.9
adj tattletale 551.19

tell the truth confess 351.7
disillusion 976.2

tell the world 524.24

telly television 1034.1
television receiver 1034.11

temerity 493.1

temp worker 726.2
temperature 1018.3

temper
noun firmness 15.3
hot temper 110.4
dander 152.6
nature 766.4
disposition 977.3
mood 977.4
tempering 1044.4
verb strengthen 15.13
mature 303.9
moderate 670.6
imbue 796.11
qualify 958.3
harden 1044.7
toughen 1047.3

temperament pitch 709.4
nature 766.4
disposition 977.3

temperamental touchy 110.21
capricious 364.5
innate 766.8
attitudinal 977.7

temperamentally 977.9

temperance sedateness 106.4
sobriety 516.1
cardinal virtues 653.4
temperateness 668.1
moderation 670.1

temperate sedate 106.14
sober 516.3
moderate 668.9, 670.10
warm 1018.24
cool 1022.12

temperature 1018.3

tempered mature 303.13
restrained 670.11

qualified 958.10
case-hardened 1044.15
toughened 1047.6

tempest outburst 105.9
windstorm 318.12
storm 671.4

tempestuous turbulent 105.24, 671.18
passionate 105.29
stormy 318.23

Templar 597.1

template 785.6

temple side 218.1
fane 703.2

tempo
noun time 709.24
pulsation 915.3
adv in time 709.30

temporal
noun profane 686.2
adj unsacred 686.3
secularist 695.16
lay 700.3
chronological 820.7
transient 827.7
material 1050.10

temporarily for the moment 827.9
conditionally 958.11

temporary
noun worker 726.2
adj interim 825.4
transient 827.7
substitute 861.8
conditional 958.8
unreliable 970.20
makeshift 994.7

tempt enamour 104.23
induce 375.22
attract 377.6

temptation desire 100.11
allurement 377.1

tempted 100.21

tempting appetizing 63.10
delightful 97.7
desirable 100.30
alluring 377.8

temptress tempter 377.4
demimonde 665.15

ten card 758.2
X 881.6
doll 1015.9

tenacious resolute 359.11, 492.18
persevering 360.8
obstinate 361.8
retentive 474.8
adhesive 802.12
tough 1047.4
viscous 1060.12

tenaciously resolutely 359.17
perseveringly 360.9
obstinately 361.14
courageously 492.23

tenacity resolution
359.1
  perseverance 360.1
  obstinacy 361.1
  retention 474.1
  fortitude 492.6
  tenaciousness 802.3
  toughness 1047.1
  viscosity 1060.2

tenancy habitation
225.1
  possession 469.1

tenant
  noun inhabitant 227.2
  lodger 227.8
  occupant 470.4
  verb inhabit 225.7

Ten Commandments
636.1

tend bear 161.7
  gravitate 297.15
  look after 339.9
  serve 577.13
  have a tendency 895.3
  heed 982.6
  care for 1007.19
  groom 1068.7

tendency direction
161.1
  preference 371.5
  aptitude 413.5
  nature 766.4
  inclination 895.1
  probability 967.1
  disposition 977.3

tender
  noun attendant 577.5
  verb offer 439.4
  give 478.12
  pay 624.10
  adj sensitive 24.12,
  93.20
  sore 26.11
  soft-coloured 35.21
  loving 104.27
  kind 143.13
  pitying 145.7
  seaworthy 180.18
  light 298.12
  immature 301.10
  careful 339.10
  lenient 427.7
  unbalanced 790.5
  soft 1045.8

tender age 301.1

tender loving care
339.1

tenderly lovingly
104.32
  carefully 339.15
  softly 1045.17

tenderness sensitivity
24.3
  soreness 26.4
  sensibility 93.4
  tender feeling 93.6
  compassionateness
  145.2
  lightness 298.1

  youth 301.1
  softness 1045.1

tending to 895.5

tendon 271.2

tend to go bear 161.7
  gravitate 297.15

tenement sty 80.11
  flat 228.13
  flats 228.14

tenements 471.6

tenet rule 419.2
  belief 952.2

tenfold 881.22

ten million 881.11

tenner 728.7

tennis 749.1

tennis ball tennis
749.1
  elastic 1046.3

tennis court smooth
287.3
  playground 743.11
  tennis 749.1

tenor
  noun soprano 58.6
  direction 161.1
  meaning 518.1
  part 708.22
  voice 709.5
  mode 764.4
  nature 766.4
  transcript 784.4
  trend 895.2
  adj high 58.13
  vocal 708.50

tense
  noun present 530.12
  time 820.1
  verb strain 725.10
  stiffen 1044.9
  adj restless 105.27
  anxious 126.7
  tensed-up 128.13
  in suspense 130.12
  phonetic 524.31
  unfriendly 589.9
  rigid 1044.11

tension
  noun anxiety 126.1
  tenseness 128.3
  disaccord 456.1
  enmity 589.1
  strain 725.2
  overextension 992.7
  urgency 996.4
  voltage 1031.11
  rigidity 1044.2
  stretching 1046.2
  verb stiffen 1044.9

tent
  noun dressing 86.33
  canvas 295.8
  verb camp 225.11

tentacles 474.4

tentative
  noun attempt 403.2
  adj slow 175.10

  hesitant 362.11
  trial 403.16
  cautious 494.8
  interim 825.4
  substitute 861.8
  ignorant 929.12
  examining 937.37
  experimental 941.11
  unreliable 970.20
  makeshift 994.7

tentatively 175.13

tented 295.31

tenth
  noun quinquesection
  881.14
  adj denary 881.22

ten thousand 881.10

tenuous dainty 248.7
  infinitesimal 258.14
  thin 270.16, 763.6
  rare 299.4
  incoherent 803.4

tenure possession 469.1
  position 724.5
  term 823.3, 824.4

tepid indifferent 102.6
  warm 1018.24

term
  noun boundary 211.3
  sign 518.6
  word 526.1
  phrase 529.1
  end 819.1
  time 820.1, 823.3,
  824.4
  moment 823.2
  verb name 527.11

termed 527.14

terminal
  noun destination 186.5
  railway 383.7
  pause 524.10
  end 819.1
  stop 856.2
  output device 1041.9
  adj unhealthy 85.53
  past hope 125.15
  limital 210.10
  bordering 211.11
  dying 307.33
  deadly 308.22
  completing 407.9
  final 819.11
  disastrous 1010.15

terminate complete
407.6
  end 819.5
  cease 856.6
  result 886.4

terminated completed
407.11
  ended 819.8

terminating
  noun end 819.1
  adj ending 819.10

termination
  noun end 819.1
  cessation 856.1

  adj completion 407.2

terminology
  nomenclature 527.1
  dictionary 870.4

terminus
  noun destination 186.5
  boundary 211.3
  railway 383.7
  end 819.1
  stop 856.2
  adj completion 407.2

terms stipulation 421.2
  adjustment 465.4
  condition 958.2

terms of reference
765.2

tern 876.3

terra land 234.1
  Earth 1070.10

terrace balcony 197.22
  horizontal 201.3
  house 228.5
  platform 900.13

terraced house 228.5

terrain open space
158.4
  region 231.1
  land 234.1
  arena 463.1

terrestrial terrene
234.4
  secularist 695.16
  celestial 1070.25

terrible horrid 98.19
  terrific 127.30, 247.11
  wrong 638.3
  dreadful 999.9
  hideous 1014.11

terrible thing 638.2

terribly horridly 98.27
  frightfully 127.34
  distressingly 247.21
  dreadfully 999.14
  hideously 1014.13

terrific terrible 127.30,
247.11
  superb 998.15

terrifically frightfully
127.34
  superbly 998.23

terrified 127.26

terrify 127.17

terrifying 127.29

territorial 231.8

territorial waters
231.1

territory open space
158.4
  region 231.1
  state 231.5
  country 232.1
  land 234.1
  speciality 865.1
  sphere of influence
  893.4
  science 927.10

terror

  noun fear 127.1
  frightener 127.9
  roughneck 593.4
  goon 671.10
  adj terrifying 127.29

terrorism terrorization
127.7
  despotism 612.10
  violence 671.1
  revolutionism 859.2

terrorist alarmist 127.8
  destroyer 395.8
  revolutionist 859.3

terse taciturn 344.9
  elegant 533.6
  concise 537.6
  aphoristic 973.6

tersely 537.7

tertiary
  noun colour system
  35.7
  adj third 876.4

TESSA 622.2

test
  noun diagnosis 91.12
  shell 295.15
  measure 300.2
  examination 937.2
  trial 941.2
  verb interrogate
  937.21
  experiment 941.8
  verify 969.12
  adj experimental
  941.11

Testament 683.2

testament 478.10

test case 941.2

test drive 941.3

test-drive 941.8

tested devoted 587.21
  trustworthy 644.19
  tried 941.12
  assured 969.20

tester examiner 937.17
  experimenter 941.6

testes 2.11

testicles 2.11

testicular 2.27

testify depose 334.6
  signify 517.21
  call to witness 598.18
  attest 956.9

testify to 956.8

testimonial
  noun advertisement
  352.6
  celebration 487.1
  recommendation 509.4
  certificate 549.6
  monument 549.12
  testimony 956.2
  adj documentary
  549.18

testimony deposition
334.3
  evidence 598.9

attestation 956.2

testing
noun checkup 937.6
experiment 941.1
adj examining 937.37
experimental 941.11

testing ground 1072.7

Test Match 747.3

test out 941.9

test pilot aviator 185.1
experimenter 941.6

test tube philosopher's
stone 857.10
chemicalization 1058.6

tetanus 85.6

tetchy sensitive 24.12
touchy 110.21

tether
noun shackle 428.4
verb bind 428.10
yoke 799.10
secure 854.8

tethered bound 428.16
stuck 854.16

text rendering 341.2
representation 349.1
sign 518.6
writing 547.10
literature 547.12,
718.1
printed matter 548.10
textbook 554.10
makeup 554.12
playbook 704.21
score 708.28
section 792.2
topic 936.1
maxim 973.1

textbook book 554.1
text 554.10

textile
noun material 4.1
adj woven 740.7

textiles 735.3

textual scriptural
683.10
orthodox 687.7

textural structural
266.6
textured 294.5

texture material 4.1
network 170.3
structure 266.1
surface texture 294.1
weaving 740.1

textured rough 288.6
textural 294.5

Thais 665.15

Thalia comedy 704.6
creative thought 985.2

than
adv otherwise 779.11
prep compared to
942.11

thang 865.1

thankful 150.5

thank God 150.3

thankless unpleasant
98.17
disliked 99.9
ungrateful 151.4

thanks thanksgiving
150.2
prayer 696.4

thanksgiving thanks
150.2
prayer 696.4

thanks to by means of
384.13
because of 887.9

thank-you 150.2

that
adj this 864.14
conj lest 896.7

that applies 830.9

that be 837.2

thatch
noun head of hair 3.4
verb face 295.23

Thatcherism
programme 609.6
capitalism 611.9

Thatcherite
noun capitalist 611.20
adj capitalist 611.32

that is
adj happening 830.9
present 837.2
adv by interpretation
341.18

that is so 972.24

that is to say by
interpretation 341.18
namely 864.18

that may be 338.8

that one 864.14

that's for sure it is
certain 969.27
right on! 972.25

that's it that's the thing
787.13
right! 972.24

that's life 963.11

that's right so be it
332.20
right! 972.24

that's that
adv no ifs 959.3
phrase so be it 332.20
that's all for 819.14

that's the thing 787.13

that time 12.9

thaw
noun melting 1019.3
verb have pity 145.4
melt 1019.21
liquefy 1062.5

thawed 1062.6

thawing
noun melting 1019.3
liquefaction 1062.1
adj liquefying 1062.7

the 760.4

theatre hall 197.4
setting 209.2
enclosure 212.3
arena 463.1
battlefield 463.2
schoolroom 567.11
show business 704.1
playhouse 704.14
entertainment 743.13

theatrical
noun actor 707.2
adj emotionalistic
93.19
affected 500.15
theatric 501.24
dramatic 704.33

theatricality
emotionalism 93.9
dramatics 704.2

The City 737.1

theft taking 480.1
thievery 482.1
robbery 482.3

them authorities 575.15
self 864.5

thematic recurrent
848.13
topical 936.4

theme motif 498.7
identification 517.11
morphology 526.3
treatise 556.1
passage 708.24
plot 722.4
topic 936.1

theme park 743.14

themselves 864.5

then
adj former 836.10
adv additionally
253.11
at that time 820.9
thereat 820.11
subsequently 834.6
formerly 836.13
hence 887.7

then and there 829.8

thence hence 188.20,
887.7
in future 838.10

theologian 676.3

theological
noun theologian 676.3
adj religious 676.4

theology 675.1, 676.1

theorem premise 934.7
axiom 973.2

theoretical ideational
931.9
hypothetical 950.13

theoretically 950.16

theorist 950.7

theory harmonics 709.1
idea 931.1
theorization 950.1
explanation 950.2

opinion 952.6

theosophical 689.23

theosophy 689.1

therapeutic remedial
86.39
helpful 449.21

therapist health-care
professional 90.8
psychologist 92.10

therapy medicine 90.1
therapeutics 91.1
cure 396.7
aid 449.1

there threat 159.24
here 221.16

thereabouts 159.24

thereafter subsequently
834.6
in future 838.10

thereby 384.12

therefore accordingly
765.11
consequently 886.7
hence 887.7
all things considered
945.17

therein 207.10

there is no question
969.27

thereof 188.20

there's no way 442.7

thereupon then 820.11
subsequently 834.6

thermal
noun hot air 1018.9
adj warm 1018.24

thermometer 1018.20

thermostat 1018.20

thesaurus vocabulary
526.13
reference book 554.9
dictionary 870.4

these 864.14

these days 837.1

thesis treatise 556.1
accent 709.25
metre 720.7
round 849.3
premise 934.7
supposition 950.3

thespian
noun actor 707.2
adj dramatic 704.33

they authorities 575.15
exclusiveness 772.3
self 864.5

thick
noun middle 818.1
verb thicken 269.5,
1043.10
adj raucous 58.15
three-dimensional
269.8
luxuriant 310.40
inarticulate 525.12
teeming 883.9

stupid 921.15
dense 1043.12
viscous 1060.12
adv densely 1043.15

thicken increase 251.4
grow thick 269.5
thick 1043.10
solidify 1044.8
emulsify 1060.10

thickened 1060.12

thickening inspissation
1043.4
viscosity 1060.2

thicket thickset 310.13
bunch 769.7

thickly numerously
883.12
densely 1043.15

thickness raucousness
58.2
third dimension 269.2
layer 296.1
density 1043.1
viscosity 1060.2

thick with 883.9

thief robber 483.1
evildoer 593.1
criminal 660.10

thieving
noun theft 482.1
adj thievish 482.21

thigh member 2.7
leg 10.22, 177.14

thin
verb dilute 16.11
subtract 255.9
shrink 260.9
thin down 270.12
rarefy 299.3
dissipate 770.5
liquefy 1062.5
cultivate 1067.17
adj shrill 58.14
insipid 65.2
dainty 248.7
infinitesimal 258.14
shrunk 260.13
slender 270.16
shallow 276.5
rare 299.4
tenuous 763.6
sparse 884.5
meagre 991.10
transparent 1028.4
adv thinly 270.23

thin air 317.1
spirit 763.3

thing love affair 104.6
act 328.3
rage 578.4
something 762.3
particular 765.3
affair 830.3
mania 925.12
obsession 925.13
object 1050.4

thing for 895.1

things wardrobe 5.2

equipment 385.4
belongings 471.2
things to do 724.2
thingy 1050.5
think expect 130.5
care 339.6
intend 380.4
cogitate 930.8
suppose 950.10
opine 952.11
think about 930.11
think back 988.10
thinker wise man 920.1
intellectual 928.1
reasoner 934.11
philosopher 951.6
think hard think one's
head off 930.9
try to recall 988.21
thinking
noun thought 930.1
opinion 952.6
adj mental 918.7
cognitive 930.21
think it over 930.14
think much of respect
155.4
value 996.13
think of be considerate
143.10
bethink oneself of
930.16
judge 945.8
remember 988.10
think tank 941.5
think twice be cautious
494.5
hang in doubt 970.10
think twice about
362.7
think up originate
891.12
imagine 985.14
thinly thin 270.23
sparsely 884.8
thinned diluted 16.19
rare 299.4
dispersed 770.9
thinner colour 35.8
solvent 270.10, 1062.4
thinness insipidness
65.1
slenderness 270.4
rarity 299.1
unsubstantiality 763.1
fewness 884.1
superficiality 921.7
meagreness 991.2
transparency 1028.1
thinning
noun weakening 16.5
shrinking 260.3
rarefaction 299.2
cultivation 1067.13
adj solvent 1062.8
thin on the ground
884.5

third
noun degree 648.6
interval 709.20
tierce 877.2
irregular 1004.6
verb trisect 877.3
adj tertiary 876.4
third-class 1004.9
third force 611.2
thirdly 876.6
third part 877.2
third party arbitrator
466.4
political party 609.24
third person 530.7
third-rate 1004.9
third reading 613.5
thirds 478.9
third world 619.3
third-world country
232.1
thirst
noun craving 100.6
appetite 100.7
tendency 895.1
dryness 1064.1
verb hunger 100.19
drink up 1064.5
thirst for wish for
100.16
hunger 100.19
thirsty craving 100.24
thirsting 100.26
sorbent 187.17
dry 1064.7
thirteen 881.7
thirteenth 881.25
thirty 881.7
thirty-three 881.7
thirty-two 881.7
this 864.14
this afternoon 315.1
this big 257.24
this day
noun present 837.1
adv now 837.3
this day and age
837.1
this hour 837.1
this morning 314.1
this night 837.3
this one 864.14
this point 837.1
this single 864.14
this size 257.24
this stage 837.1
thistle thorn 285.5
insignia 647.1
this way 765.10
thong swimwear 5.29
strip 271.4
whip 605.1

Thor Jupiter Pluvius
316.6
lightning 1024.17
thoracic 283.19
thorax 283.6
thorn affliction 96.8
bramble 285.5
adhesive 802.4
bane 1000.1
thorny prickly 285.10
difficult 1012.17
thorough downright
247.12
painstaking 339.11
meticulous 339.12
confirmed 373.19
complete 407.12
cautious 494.8
thoroughgoing 793.10
thoroughbred
noun aristocrat 607.4
nobleman 608.4
jockey 757.2
adj upper-class 607.10
wellborn 608.11
thoroughly carefully
339.15
completely 793.14
perfectly 1001.10
thoroughness
painstakingness 339.2
caution 494.1
circumstantiality 765.4
completeness 793.1
those 864.14
thou 864.5
though 338.8
thought
noun expectation 130.1
considerateness 143.3
lightning 174.6
hint 248.4
advice 422.1
remark 524.4
tinge 796.7
intellect 918.1
thinking 930.1
idea 931.1
opinion 952.6
attention 982.1
adj cognitive 930.21
thoughtful solemn
111.3
considerate 143.16
careful 339.10
courteous 504.14
judicious 919.19
cognitive 930.21
thoughtfully solemnly
111.4
considerately 143.21
carefully 339.15
intelligently 919.20
contemplatively
930.23
thoughtfulness
solemnity 111.1
considerateness 143.3

thoughtless
inconsiderate 144.18
careless 340.11
unthinking 365.10
improvident 406.15
unskilful 414.15
foolish 922.8
unwise 922.10
thoughtfree 932.4
inattentive 983.6
scatterbrained 984.16
thought-out 934.21
thought-provoking
982.19
thoughts 930.4
thousand
noun M 881.10
myriad 883.4
adj numerous 883.6
thousand dollars
728.8
thousand million
881.12
thousands 618.2
thousandth 881.30
thrall subjection 432.1
subject 432.7
thrash best 249.7
clobber 412.9
whip 604.12
segregate 772.6
pound 901.16
thrashing defeat 412.1
corporal punishment
604.4
thrash out classify
800.8
argue 934.16
thread
noun kitten 16.7
filament 271.1
series 811.2
verb continue 811.4
threadbare trite 117.9
worn 393.31
threat warning 399.1
menace 514.1
danger 1005.1
threaten intimidate
127.20
forebode 133.11
warn 399.5
menace 514.2
come 838.6
be imminent 839.2
work evil 999.6
threatened augured
133.15
in danger 1005.13
threatening disease-
causing 85.52
ominous 133.17

menacing 514.3
imminent 839.3
dangerous 1005.9
threateningly 133.19
three
noun card 758.2
trio 875.1
adj triple 875.3
three-dimensional
microscopic 29.10
thick 269.8
photographic 714.17
tripartite 877.4
threefold
verb triplicate 876.2
adj triple 876.3
adv triply 876.5
three hundred 881.9
three-piece 876.3
three-pronged 877.4
three-quarter 746.2
threesome golfer 748.2
three 875.1
three times 876.5
three-year-old 757.2
threshold
noun porch 189.6
vestibule 197.19
boundary 211.3
sill 900.9
adj bordering 211.11
thrice 876.5
thrift 635.1
thrifty 635.6
thrill
noun pang 26.2
tingle 74.1
sensation 105.2
verb suffer 26.8
tingle 74.5, 105.18
delight 95.9
tickle 105.15
thrilled pleased 95.14
excited 105.20
thrilling delightful 97.7
exciting 105.30
thrillingly 105.36
thrill to 105.18
thrive grow 14.2, 259.7
have energy 17.11
flourish 1009.8
thriving grown 14.3,
259.12
productive 889.9
flourishing 1009.13
throat mouth 2.16
narrow 270.3
throaty raucous 58.15
inarticulate 525.12
throb
noun staccato 55.1
trepidation 105.5
beat 709.26
pulsation 915.3
flutter 916.4
verb suffer 26.8

resonate 54.6
drum 55.4
thrill 105.18
pulsate 915.12
flutter 916.12

throbbing
noun ache 26.5
staccato 55.1
trepidation 105.5
pulsation 915.3
adj aching 26.12
resonant 54.9
staccato 55.7
rhythmic 709.28
pulsative 915.18

throes pang 26.2
seizure 85.6
pain 96.5
compunction 113.2
spasm 916.6

thrombosis 85.6

throne
noun toilet 12.11
sovereignty 417.8
royal seat 417.11
verb install 615.12
glorify 662.13

throng
noun multitude 769.4, 883.3
verb come together 769.16

thronged 883.9

throttle paralyse 19.10
silence 51.8
strangle 308.18
suppress 428.8
seize 480.14

through
adj completed 407.11
prep over 159.28
by 161.27
by means of 384.13
during 820.14

through and through 793.17

through-and-through 793.10

throughout
adv scatteringly 770.12
all over 793.17
prep over 159.28
during 820.14

throughout the world 158.12

through the night 315.11

through thick and thin through fire and water 360.10
throughout 793.17

throw
noun blanket 295.10
match 747.3
cast 759.9
toss 903.3
verb give birth 1.3

clap 159.13
pot 742.6
play 747.4
discompose 810.4
fling 903.10
fell 912.5
fix 964.5
stump 970.14

throw at 459.28

throwaway
noun advertising matter 352.8
derelict 370.4
consumable 388.2
discard 390.3
adj unpremeditated 365.11
consumable 388.6
informal 581.3
easy 1013.13

throw away consume 388.3
discard 390.7
squander 486.3
overact 704.31
eject 908.13
do away with 908.21
attach little importance to 997.12

throwback regression 163.1
relapse 394.1
atavism 858.2

thrower 903.7

throw in insert 191.3
interpose 213.6

throw-in game 745.3
basketball game 751.3

throwing 903.2

throwing away 388.1

throwing out 908.1

thrown 970.26

thrown away 704.33

thrown over 99.10

thrown together 796.14

throw off take off 6.6
shed 6.10
dislodge 160.6
improvise 365.8
break the habit 374.3
free oneself from 431.8
say 524.23
do away with 908.21
let out 908.24

throw out discard 390.7
eject 908.13
disgorge 908.25

throw up give up 370.7
relinquish 475.3
vomit 908.26
elevate 911.5

thrum
noun staccato 55.1
verb hum 52.13

drum 55.4
strum 708.40
beat time 708.44

thrush 710.23

thrust
noun vim 17.2
manpower 18.4
acceleration 174.4
pass 459.3
major part 791.6
push 901.2
pushing 903.1
rocket propulsion 1072.8
verb clap 159.13
launch an attack 459.17
impel 901.11
push 901.12, 903.9

thrusting
noun impact 901.3
adj attacking 459.29
impelling 901.23

thrust upon urge upon 439.9
force upon 478.20

thud
noun dull thud 52.3
verb thump 52.15

thug killer 308.10
combatant 461.1
bandit 483.4
ruffian 593.3
follower 616.8
criminal 660.10

thuggery 308.2

thumb
noun finger 73.5
verb touch 73.6
fight 754.4

thumbs down refusal 442.1
veto 444.2
disapproval 510.1
ostracism 586.3
banishment 908.4

thumbs-up 332.2

thump
noun thud 52.3
hit 901.4
verb thud 52.15
drum 55.4
whip 604.12
beat time 708.44
hit 901.14
pound 901.16

thumping
noun staccato 55.1
adj staccato 55.7
terrific 247.11
whopping 257.21

thunder
noun noise 53.3
reverberation 54.2
thundering 56.5
verb din 53.7
boom 56.9
proclaim 352.13
murmur 524.26

thunderbolt surprise 131.2
lightning 174.6, 1024.17

thundering
noun reverberation 54.2
thunder 56.5
curse 513.1
adj intense 15.22
loud 53.11
reverberating 54.11
thunderous 56.12
whopping 257.21

thunderous loud 53.11
thundering 56.12

thunderstorm thunder 56.5
thundershower 316.3
storm 671.4

thundery 56.12

thus how 384.9
thusly 765.10
similarly 783.18
hence 887.7
to illustrate 956.23

thus far so far 211.16
to a degree 248.10
until now 837.4

thwart
verb disappoint 132.2
frustrate 412.11, 1011.15
neutralize 899.7
adj transverse 170.9, 204.19

thwarted 132.5

thwarting
circumvention 415.5
neutralization 899.2
frustration 1011.3

tiara jewel 498.6
regalia 647.3
triple crown 647.4

tic nervousness 128.1
shake 916.3
obsession 925.13

tick
noun thud 52.3
clicking 55.2
degree 245.1
insect 311.31
bloodsucker 311.36
mark 517.5
credit 622.1
short time 827.3
instant 829.3
verb thud 52.15
ticktock 55.5
mark 517.19
pulsate 915.12

ticked off 152.30

ticket
noun permission 443.1
label 517.13
certificate 549.6
ballot 609.19
token 728.12

verb label 517.20

ticking
noun clicking 55.2
motion 172.1
adj staccato 55.7

tickle
noun tickling 74.2
verb titillate 74.6
delight 95.9
thrill 105.15
incite 375.17
attract 377.6
fish 382.10
amuse 743.21
tap 901.18
interest 982.12

tickled pleased 95.14
amused 743.26
interested 982.16

tickling
noun tickle 74.2
adj ticklish 74.9
alluring 377.8
interesting 982.19

ticklish sensitive 24.12
tickling 74.9
touchy 110.21
unreliable 970.20
precarious 1005.12
difficult 1012.17

tidal aquatic 182.58
coastal 234.7
flowing 238.24

tidal wave wave 238.14, 915.4
returns 609.21
upheaval 671.5

tide flow 238.4
ocean 240.1
time 820.1

tidiness cleanness 79.1
orderliness 806.3

tidings 552.1

tidy
verb clean 79.18
tidy up 807.12
adj cleaned 79.26
large 257.16
trim 806.8
tolerable 998.20

tidy up 807.12

tidy-up 807.6

tie
noun intermediary 213.4
security 438.1
contest 457.3
fidelity 644.7
insignia 647.1
notation 709.12
game 745.3
relation 774.1
same 789.3
joining 799.1
dead heat 835.3
stop 856.2
verb compel 424.4
bind 428.10, 799.9

tip of the iceberg
modicum 248.2
hint 248.4
sign 517.1

tipped topped 198.12
inclining 204.15

tipping
noun bookbinding
554.14
adj inclining 204.15

tipple 8.29, 88.24

tips 3.16

tipsy intoxicated 88.31
inclining 204.15

tiptoe
noun creeping 177.17
verb creep 177.26
lurk 346.9
be cautious 494.5
adj creeping 177.39
adv on high 272.21

tip-top
noun summit 198.2
adj top 198.10
superlative 249.13
A1 998.18

tirade
noun lament 115.3
berating 510.7
wordiness 538.2
speech 543.2
verb wail 115.13

tire clothe 5.38
fatigue 21.4
burn out 21.5
oppress 98.16
be tedious 118.6

tired clothing 5.44
weary 21.7, 118.11
worn-out 393.36
aphoristic 973.6

tiredness weakness
16.1
fatigue 21.1
weariness 118.3

tired of weary 118.11
satiated 993.6

tireless industrious
330.22
persevering 360.8

tirelessly industriously
330.27
perseveringly 360.9

tiresome fatiguing
21.13
annoying 98.22
wearying 118.10
prosaic 721.5

tiring fatiguing 21.13
wearying 118.10

tissue
noun material 4.1
network 170.3
structure 266.1
organic matter 305.1
weaving 740.1
verb weave 740.6

tit 258.4

Titan strong man 15.6
Sol 1070.14

titan 257.13

titanic large 247.7
huge 257.20

tit for tat offset 338.2
measure for measure
506.3
interaction 776.3
substitution 861.1
interchange 862.1

tit-for-tat 776.10

tithe
noun donation 478.6
tax 630.9
quinquesection 881.14
verb charge 630.12
adj tenth 881.22

Titian reddish-brown
40.4
red 41.6
redheaded 41.10

titillating alluring
377.8
amusing 743.27
interesting 982.19

titillation tickle 74.2
pleasure 95.1
thrill 105.2

title
noun possession 469.1
ownership 469.2
estate 471.4
name 527.3
book 554.1
makeup 554.12
prerogative 642.1
honorific 648.1
golf 748.1
class 808.2
caption 936.2
verb name 527.11
focus on 936.3

titled named 527.14
noble 608.10

title-holder 413.15

title page label 517.13
makeup 554.12
caption 936.2

title role 704.10

tits 283.7

titter
noun ripple 52.5
laughter 116.4
verb laugh 116.8

tittle modicum 248.2
minutia 258.7
mark 517.5
punctuation 530.15

titular nominal 527.15
titulary 648.7

Tivoli 743.14

TLC 339.1

to
verb put an end to
395.12

prep at 159.27
toward 161.26
into 189.14
as far as 261.20
until 820.15
prep, conj for 380.11

to a certain extent
248.10

toad sycophant 138.3
amphibian 311.27

to a degree to some
extent 245.7
to a certain extent
248.10
relatively 774.12

to advantage usefully
387.26
helpfully 449.24
profitably 472.17
expediently 994.8

**to all intents and
purposes** equally
789.11
on the whole 791.14

to a man 332.17

to and fro reciprocally
776.12
alternately 849.11
changeably 853.8
back and forth 915.21

to-and-fro
noun alternation 915.5
verb alternate 915.13
adj alternate 915.19

to an extent 774.12

toast
noun sandwich 10.31
pledge 88.10
celebration 487.1
fine lady 500.10
verb drink 8.29
cook 11.4
drink to 88.29
burn 1018.22
adj brown 40.3

toasted 11.6

toasting
noun cooking 11.1
adj hot 1018.25

tobacco 89.1

tobacco smoke 89.1

to-be 838.8

to be desired desirable
100.30
expedient 994.5

to be exact 972.22

to be expected
adj as expected 130.14
adv imminently 839.4
normally 868.10

to be fair 649.12

to be had obtainable
472.14
accessible 965.8

to be precise 972.22

to be reckoned with
893.13

to be seen visible 31.6
manifest 348.8

to be sure
adv surely 969.24
exclam yes 332.18

to be trusted 644.19

to bits 801.29

to blame blameworthy
510.25
responsible 641.17
guilty 656.3

to boot 253.11

to come approaching
167.4
future 838.8
imminent 839.3
scheduled 964.9

to completion 407.14

tod 311.20

to date 837.4

today
noun present 837.1
adv now 837.3

toddler 302.9

to-do agitation 105.4,
916.1
bustle 330.4
commotion 809.4

toe base 199.2
foot 199.5

toed 199.9

to explain 341.18

to extremes 669.10

tofu 10.46

together
adj composed 106.13
in accord 455.3
adv unanimously
332.17
cooperatively 450.6
collectively 768.11
jointly 799.18
continuously 811.10
simultaneously 835.7
concurrently 898.5

togetherness 455.1

together on 787.12

together with with
768.12
in agreement with
787.12
among 796.17

to good effect 387.26

to good use 387.26

to guess 950.18

to hand 387.20

toil
noun work 725.4
verb work 724.12
drudge 725.14
hamper 1011.11

toilet
noun latrine 12.10
stool 12.11
bathroom 197.26

adj cursing 513.8

toiletries 735.6

toilette 5.1

toiling 725.17

to illustrate 956.23

to keep 474.10

token
noun omen 133.3
symbol 517.2
password 517.12
label 517.13
sign 518.6
record 549.1
counter 728.12
substitute 861.2
characteristic 864.4
evidence 956.1
memento 988.7
verb augur 133.12
manifest 348.5
adj cheap 633.7
substitute 861.8

to lease 615.22

tolerable bearable
107.13
goodish 998.20
mediocre 1004.7

tolerably satisfactorily
107.15
to a degree 248.10
fairly 998.24
mediocrely 1004.11

tolerance substance
abuse 87.1
patience 134.1
forgiveness 148.1
latitude 430.4
liberalism 430.10
sufferance 443.2
inaccuracy 974.2
toleration 978.4

tolerant patient 134.9
considerate 143.16
forgiving 148.6
lenient 427.7
nonrestrictive 430.25
permissive 443.14
tolerating 978.11

tolerate endure 134.5
be easy on 427.5
suffer 443.10
keep an open mind
978.7

tolerated 443.16

toleration patience
134.1
considerateness 143.3
liberalism 430.10
sufferance 443.2
tolerance 978.4

to let 615.22

toll
noun ringing 54.3
fee 630.6
tax 630.9
verb ring 54.8

tom cock 76.8
cat 311.21

shoot 903.12

torpor apathy 94.4
inertness 173.4
inaction 329.1
languor 331.6

torque band 280.3
jewel 498.6

torrent lightning 174.6
river 238.5
outburst 671.6

torrential flowing
238.24
rainy 316.10

torrid 1018.25

torso 1050.3

tortilla 10.28

tortoise slowcoach
175.5
reptile 311.25

tortuous distorted
265.10
curved 279.7
convolutional 281.6
grandiloquent 545.8

torture
noun agony 26.6
torment 96.7
harshness 98.4
penal servitude 604.2
verb pain 26.7
torment 96.18
agonize 98.12
deflect 164.5
deform 265.7
misinterpret 342.2
put to the question
604.15
work evil 999.6

tortured pained 26.9
affected 93.23
harrowed 96.25
falsified 265.11

torturing perversion
265.2
misinterpretation
342.1

Tory 611.13

Toryism partisanism
609.25
radicalism 611.5

to say nothing of
253.12

to sell 734.16

tosh 520.3

to shreds 801.29

to some degree 248.10

to some extent to a
degree 245.7
relatively 774.12

to spare remaining
256.7
unused 390.12
superfluous 992.17

toss
noun game 745.3
match 747.3
gamble 759.2

throw 903.3
flounder 916.8
even chance 971.7
verb thrill 105.18
clap 159.13
pitch 182.55
billow 238.22
gamble 759.23
throw 903.10
oscillate 915.10
flounder 916.15

tosser arsehole 660.6
thrower 903.7
chump 923.3

tossing
noun throwing 903.2
adj swinging 915.17

to such an extent
248.10

tot drink 8.4
modicum 248.2
child 302.3
dose 792.5

total
noun amount 244.2
plus sign 253.2
sum 791.2, 1016.6
verb compute 253.6
amount to 791.8
sum up 1016.18
adj great 247.6
downright 247.12
unmitigated 671.17
cumulative 769.23
comprehensive 771.7
whole 791.9
complete 793.9
thorough 793.10
universal 863.14
unqualified 959.2
sound 1001.7

total commitment
359.1

totalitarian
authoritative 417.15
governmental 612.17

totalitarianism 612.9

totality whole 791.1
wholeness 791.5
completeness 793.1
all 863.4
universe 1070.1

total lack 222.1

totalled high 87.23
disintegrative 805.5
belly-up 819.9

totalling 1016.10

total loss wreck 393.8
debacle 395.4
flop 410.2
loss 473.1

totally extremely
247.22
wholly 791.13
completely 793.14
solely 871.14
perfectly 1001.10

totally committed
671.22

total war death struggle
457.6
war 458.1

to tell the truth
truthfully 644.22
truly 972.18

totem symbol 517.2
race 559.4
familiar spirit 678.12
idol 697.3

to the amount of
adv at a price 630.17
prep to the tune of
244.7

to the bad 473.9

to the bitter end
through thick and thin
360.10
to the end 819.13

to the contrary no
335.8
by no means 335.9

to the death deathly
307.37
throughout 793.17

to the end to
completion 407.14
to the bitter end
819.13

to the eye 33.12

to the fore 216.12

to the front
adj prominent 662.17
adv before 216.12

to the full to
completion 407.14
utterly 793.16
plentifully 990.9

to the good helpfully
449.24
profitably 472.17

to the hilt completely
793.14
throughout 793.17

to the left 220.6

to the letter 972.21

to the life 783.16

to the limit to
completion 407.14
utterly 793.16

to the memory of in
honour of 487.4
in memory of 988.29

to the point
adj concise 537.6
relevant 774.11
apt 787.10
adv plainly 535.4

to the rear 217.15

to the right 219.7

to the side
adj side 218.6
adv aside 218.10

to the skies 247.15

to the tune of 244.7

to this day 837.4

to this place 159.23

tots 302.2

tottering
noun walking 177.8
changing 853.3
alternation 915.5
adj unsteady 16.16
slow 175.10
descending 194.11
stricken in years
303.18
on the wane 393.46

touch
noun senses 24.5
sense of touch 73.1
contact 223.5
hint 248.4
communication 343.1
skill 413.1
knack 413.6
motif 498.7
signal 517.15
implication 519.2
execution 708.30
tinge 796.7
tap 901.7
verb sense 24.6
feel 73.6
affect 93.14
move 145.5
contact 223.10
signal 517.22
relate to 774.5
equal 789.5
tap 901.18
be comparable 942.7

touch and go gamble
759.2, 970.8
even chance 971.7

touch-and-go uncertain
970.16
precarious 1005.12

touch down land
184.43
get down 194.7

touchdown landing
184.18
score 409.5

touched affected 93.23
penitent 113.9
insane 925.26

touching
noun feeling 73.2
contact 223.5
adj affecting 93.22
distressing 98.20
pitiful 145.8
in contact 223.17

touchingly 93.25

touchline 745.1

touch on remark
524.25
evidence 956.8
call attention to
982.10

touchstone measure
300.2
test 941.2

touchy sensitive 24.12
excitable 105.28
tetchy 110.21
partisan 456.17
precarious 1005.12

tough
noun hunk 15.7
combatant 461.1
roughneck 593.4
goon 671.10
adj firm 15.18
obdurate 361.10
strict 425.6
resolute 492.18
hard to understand
522.14
violent 671.16
laborious 725.18
sturdy 762.7
adhesive 802.12
durable 826.10
hard 1044.10
resistant 1047.4
viscous 1060.12

toughen strengthen
15.13
harden 1044.7, 1047.3
stiffen 1044.9

toughened 1044.13,
1047.6

toughening
noun strengthening
15.5
hardening 1044.5
adj hardening 1044.14

tough guy hunk 15.7
goon 671.10

tough job 1012.2

tough-minded 955.5

toughness strength
15.1
pluck 359.3
unyieldingness 361.2
strictness 425.1
fortitude 492.6
substantiality 762.1
tenacity 802.3
difficulty 1012.1
hardness 1044.1
resistance 1047.1
viscosity 1060.2

toupee 3.14

tour
noun journey 177.5
tower 272.6
route 383.1
engagement 704.11
shift 824.3
term 824.4
circuit 913.2
sight-seeing 917.4
verb journey 177.21

tour de force act 328.3
masterpiece 413.10

tourer 178.1

tour guide 574.7

touring
noun travel 177.1
adj travelling 177.36

tourism 177.1

tourist traveller 178.1
sightseer 917.3

tournament contest 457.3
tourney 743.10
football 745.1
rugby 746.1
golf 748.1
tennis 749.1
basketball 751.1

tour of duty 824.3

tour operator 177.5

tousled 809.14

tout
noun informant 551.5
touter 730.7
bookmaker 759.20
verb exaggerate 355.3

touted 355.4

touting 355.1

tow 904.4

toward at 159.27
towards 161.26
opposite to 215.7

towards 161.26

towel 1064.6

tower
noun estate 228.7
structure 266.2
turret 272.6
stronghold 460.6
marker 517.10
protector 1007.5
verb grow 14.2, 259.7
ascend 193.8
loom 247.5
soar 272.10

tower block flats 228.14
tower 272.6

towered 272.14

towering eminent 247.9
huge 257.20
high 272.14

tower of strength
strong man 15.6
stronghold 460.6
protector 1007.5

to what extent 384.9

to windward 182.68, 218.9

towing
noun pulling 904.1
adj pulling 904.6

town
noun township 230.1
state 231.5
adj urban 230.11

town centre 208.7

town hall city hall 230.5
legislature 613.1

town house house 228.5
courthouse 595.6

town planning 230.10

township town 230.1
state 231.5

townspeople 227.6

toxic
noun poison 1000.3
adj poisonous 82.7
harmful 999.12

toxicity poisonousness 82.3
harmfulness 999.5

toxicology 1000.3

toxic waste refuse 391.4
poison 1000.3

toxin evil 999.3
poison 1000.3

toy
noun dupe 358.1
caprice 364.1
instrument 384.4
trinket 498.4
laughingstock 508.7
plaything 743.16
trifle 997.5
verb make love 562.14
trifle 997.14
adj miniature 258.12

toying
noun trifling 997.8
adj fickle 364.6

trace
noun odour 69.1
hint 248.4
remainder 256.1
minutia 258.7
image 349.5
clue 517.9
record 549.1
tinge 796.7
signal 1035.11
verb represent 349.8
outline 381.11
mark 517.19
write 547.19
portray 712.19
copy 784.8
stalk 937.35
discover 940.2

trace element 1058.2

traces 517.8

tracing image 349.5
drawing 712.13
reproduction 784.2
transcript 784.4

track
noun direction 161.1
wake 182.7
routine 373.6
route 383.1
path 383.2
railway 383.7

racing 457.11
trail 517.8
hint 551.4
class 572.11
playground 743.11
cricket 747.1
athletics 755.1
motor racing 756.1
race 756.3
horse racing 757.1
aftereffect 886.3
verb traverse 177.20
hunt 382.9
trace 937.35

track and field sport 744.1
athletics 755.1

track down trace 937.35
discover 940.2

tracking pursuit 382.1
data transmission 1035.8

tracking down 382.1

track of 1016.12

track record
noun act 328.3
preparedness 405.4
statistics 757.4
adj accomplishment 407.1

tract space 158.1
housing 225.3
plot 231.4
booklet 554.11
treatise 556.1
field 1067.9

traction pulling 904.1
purchase 905.2
attraction 906.1

tractor traction engine 179.18
propeller plane 181.2

trade
noun vocation 724.6
commerce 731.1
trading 731.2, 862.2
bargain 731.5
custom 731.6
market 733.3
verb transfer 629.3
deal 731.14
speculate 737.23
change 853.5
interchange 862.4
adj commercial 731.21

trade association 617.9

trade at 731.16

trade barriers 731.1

trade centre 208.7

traded 862.5

trade deficit 731.9

trade fair 736.2

trade gap 731.9

trade in trade 731.14
deal in 731.15

trade-in 731.5

trademark patent 210.3
mannerism 500.2
label 517.13
characteristic 864.4
acknowledgment 887.2

trade off compensate 338.4
trade 731.14
interchange 862.4

trade-off offset 338.2
interaction 776.3

trade on 387.15

trader 730.2

trades 318.10

tradesmen 730.11

trades union 727.2

trade union association 617.1
trades union 727.2

trade unionism 727.1

trade unionist 727.4

trade with 731.16

trading
noun transfer 629.1
trade 731.2
stock-market trading 737.19
changing 853.3
swapping 862.2
adj commercial 731.21

tradition custom 373.1, 841.2
rule 419.2
religion 675.1
superstition 953.3

traditional customary 373.14
preceptive 419.4
conventional 579.5
orthodox 687.7
historical 719.7
mythological 841.12

traditionalism orthodoxy 687.1
conformity 866.1

traditionalist 841.8

traditionally
conventionally 579.6
conformably 866.7

traffic
noun communication 343.1
commerce 731.1
verb trade 731.14

traffic in 731.15

traffic jam obstruction 293.3
hindrance 1011.1

trafficker 730.2

trafficking 731.2

tragedy tragic drama 704.5
misfortune 1010.2

tragic horrid 98.19

heavy 704.34
disastrous 1010.15

tragically horridly 98.27
disastrously 1010.18

trail
noun odour 69.1
path 383.2
track 517.8
skiing 753.1
afterpart 816.2
aftereffect 886.3
verb follow 166.3
lag 166.4
dawdle 175.8
hang 202.6
bring up the rear 217.8
hunt 382.9
pull 904.4
trace 937.35

trailer caravan 179.19, 228.17
advertisement 352.6
afterpart 816.2

trailing
noun following 166.1
pursuit 382.1
surveillance 937.9
adj following 166.5

train
noun railway train 179.14
unit 461.21
attendance 768.6
series 811.2
procession 811.3
afterpart 816.2
verb direct 161.5
accustom 373.10
drill 568.13
be taught 570.11
play 744.2
pull 904.4
tend 1068.7

train driver 178.12

trained accustomed 373.16
skilled 413.26
informed 927.18

trainee recruit 461.17
student 572.1
beginner 817.2

trainer Link trainer 181.10
preparer 405.5
handler 571.6
boxer 754.2
jockey 757.2
stockman 1068.2

training habituation 373.8
preparation 405.1, 568.3

train of thought 930.4

trait culture 373.3
sign 517.1
characteristic 864.4

traitor rebel 327.5

verb progress 162.2
move 172.5
go 177.18
journey 177.21
phrase transportation 176.3
travelled 177.40
Traveller 311.15
traveller goer 178.1
travelling salesman 730.4
travelling
noun travel 177.1
adj moving 172.7
going 177.36
travelogue 543.3
travels 177.2
traverse
noun crosspiece 170.5
verb cross 170.6, 177.20
navigate 182.13
oppose 451.3
contradict 451.6
ski 753.4
adj transverse 170.9
travesty
noun reproduction 336.3
bad likeness 350.2
exaggeration 355.1
wit 489.1
burlesque 508.6
verb misrepresent 350.3
exaggerate 355.3
burlesque 508.11
trawl
noun snare 356.13
verb pull 904.4
trawler ship 180.1
fisher 382.6
treacherous
falsehearted 354.31
deceitful 356.22
perfidious 645.21
unreliable 970.20
unsafe 1005.11
treachery
falseheartedness 354.4
treacherousness 645.6
unreliability 970.6
treacle sweetening 66.2
adhesive 802.4
semiliquid 1060.5
tread
noun velocity 172.4
step 177.11, 193.5
gait 177.12
degree 245.1
verb walk 177.27
stamp 901.22
treading 177.8
treading water 182.11
treadmill
noun tedium 118.1
routine 373.6
pillory 605.3

work 725.4
regularity 780.2
adj tedious 118.9
treason apostasy 363.2, 857.3
petty treason 645.7
treasure
noun store 386.1
wealth 618.1
funds 728.14
collection 769.11
good thing 998.5
verb cherish 104.21
store up 386.11
hold 474.7
keep in memory 988.13
value 996.13
treasured beloved 104.24
stored 386.14
treasurer executive 574.3
payer 624.9
financial officer 729.11
treasures 561.1
treasure trove find 472.6
discovery 940.1
treasury store 386.1
storehouse 386.6
funds 728.14
cash 728.18
treasure-house 729.12
collection 769.11
treat
noun meal 8.5
delicacy 10.8
regalement 95.3
standing treat 624.8
verb remedy 86.38
practice medicine 90.14
doctor 91.24
use 321.6
handle 387.12
prepare 405.6
discuss 541.12
write upon 556.5
treat to 624.19
operate on 888.6
treatable 396.25
treated 405.16
treatise 556.1
treatment medicine 90.1
therapy 91.1
usage 387.2
preparation 405.1
discussion 541.7
treatise 556.1
script 706.2
technique 712.9
treat to 624.19
treat with negotiate 437.6
mediate 466.6
treaty 437.2

treble
noun soprano 58.6
air 708.4
part 708.22
voice 709.5
verb triplicate 876.2
adj high 58.13
vocal 708.50
triple 876.3
tree
noun timber 310.10
genealogy 560.5
scaffold 605.5
verb corner 1012.16
trek
noun migration 177.4
journey 177.5
verb journey 177.21
migrate 177.22
trekking 177.36
trellis
noun network 170.3
verb net 170.7
tremble
noun trepidation 105.5
trill 709.19
shake 916.3
verb shake 16.8, 127.14, 916.11
thrill 105.18
fidget 128.6
freeze 1022.9
trembling
noun trepidation 105.5
shaking 916.2
adj fearful 127.23
jittery 128.12
shaking 916.17
tremendous terrible 127.30
large 247.7
huge 257.20
superb 998.15
tremendously
frightfully 127.34
vastly 247.16
superbly 998.23
tremor thrill 105.2
trepidation 105.5
speech defect 525.1
trill 709.19
shake 916.3
tremulous fearful 127.23
jittery 128.12
inarticulate 525.12
shaking 916.17
trench
noun crack 224.2
channel 239.1
ocean depths 275.4
valley 284.9
trough 290.2
entrenchment 460.5
shelter 1008.3
verb intrude 214.5
cleave 224.4
channel 239.15
excavate 284.15

furrow 290.3
trenchant energetic 17.13
acrimonious 17.14
pungent 68.6
caustic 144.23
vigorous 544.11
sagacious 919.16
trend
noun direction 161.1
course 172.2
flow 238.4
fashion 578.1
drift 895.2
verb bear 161.7
deviate 164.3
flow 238.16
tend 895.3
trendy fashionable 578.11
faddish 578.15
hip 927.17
trepidation trepidity 105.5, 127.5
nervousness 128.1
agitation 916.1
trespass
noun intrusion 214.1
violation 435.2
usurpation 640.3
misdeed 655.2
lawbreaking 674.3
overstepping 909.3
verb intrude 214.5
violate 435.4
usurp 640.8
do wrong 655.4
overstep 909.9
trespassing intrusion 214.1
usurpation 640.3
lawbreaking 674.3
tresses 3.4
trestle railway 383.7
horse 900.16
Triad 660.11
triad 875.1
trial
noun annoyance 96.2
tribulation 96.9
attempt 403.2
preparation 405.1
contest 457.3
number 530.8
jury trial 598.6
experiment 941.1
test 941.2
adversity 1010.1
adj tentative 403.16
three 875.3
experimental 941.11
trial and error attempt 403.2
experiment 941.1
trial-and-error 941.11
trial by jury 598.6
trial run 941.3

trials and tribulations 96.9
triangle bell 54.4
love affair 104.6
straightedge 277.3
three 875.1
triangular trilateral 278.8
three 875.3
tripartite 877.4
triathlon sport 744.1
athletics meeting 755.2
tribal 559.7
tribalism 559.4
tribe race 559.4
company 769.3
kind 808.3
kingdom 808.5
tribunal
noun council 423.1
forum 595.1
platform 900.13
adj judicial 595.7
tribune praetor 596.2
platform 900.13
tributary
noun feeder 238.3
adj subject 432.13
tribute demand 421.1
gift 478.4
celebration 487.1
praise 509.5
fee 624.5
tax 630.9
citation 646.4
acknowledgment 887.2
trick
noun artifice 356.6
habit 373.4
pretext 376.1
intrigue 381.5
knack 413.6
stratagem 415.3
prank 489.10
mannerism 500.2
style 532.2
bridge 758.3
shift 824.3
characteristic 864.4
quirk 926.2
illusion 975.1
verb deceive 356.14
fool 356.15
live by one's wits 415.9
play a practical joke 489.14
trickery chicanery 356.4
juggling 356.5
stratagem 415.3
waggishness 489.4
finery 498.3
trickle
noun leakage 190.5
tricklet 238.7
few 884.2
verb leak 190.14

dribble 238.18

tricky deceptive 356.21
deceitful 356.22,
645.18
cunning 415.12
waggish 489.17
dishonest 645.16
treacherous 645.21
difficult 1012.17

tricolour
noun flag 647.6
adj variegated 47.9

tricycle 179.8

trident
noun fork 171.4
three 875.1
adj tripartite 877.4

tried experienced
413.28
devoted 587.21
trustworthy 644.19
well-tried 941.12
assured 969.20

trifle
noun sweets 10.38
hardly anything 248.5
thing of naught 763.2
particular 765.3
triviality 997.5
verb waste time 331.13
leave undone 340.7
make love 562.14
be foolish 922.6
dally 997.14

trifles 997.4

trifling
noun idling 331.4
dallying 997.8
adj insignificant 248.6
little 258.10
quibbling 935.14
trivial 997.19

Trigger 311.15

trigger
noun immediate cause
885.3
verb kindle 375.18
explode 671.14
cause 885.10
receive 1035.17

trigger-happy jittery
128.12
warlike 458.21

triggering 375.2

trigger off kindle
375.18
cause 885.10

trillion quadrillion
881.13
large number 1016.5

trilogy 875.1

trim
noun clothing 5.1
fitness 84.1
preparedness 405.4
ornamentation 498.1
good condition 764.3
verb trim ship 182.49

border 211.10
shorten 268.6
be a timeserver 363.9
prepare 405.6
clobber 412.9
ornament 498.8
cheapen 633.6
fasten 799.7
sever 801.11
tidy 807.12
reel in 905.9
adj in trim 180.19
shipshape 180.20
shapely 264.5
elegant 533.6
chic 578.13
tidy 806.8

trimmed rigged 180.17
bordered 211.12
shortened 268.9
ornamented 498.11

trimmer traitor 357.10
timeserver 363.4
conformist 866.2

trimming
noun edging 211.7
extra 254.4
ornamentation 498.1
bookbinding 554.14
adj timeserving 363.10

Trinity 677.9

trinity three 875.1
threeness 875.2

trio cooperation 450.1
part music 708.18
three 875.1

trip
noun journey 177.5
flight 184.9
tumble 194.3
bungle 414.5
misdeed 655.2
flock 769.5
slip 974.4
verb use 87.21
speed 174.8
stroll 177.28
tumble 194.8
trap 356.20
caper 366.6
overcome 412.7
bungle 414.11
go wrong 654.9
explode 671.14
dance 705.5
play 743.23
fell 912.5
err 974.9

tripartite 877.4

tripe kidneys 10.19
bullshit 520.3

triple
verb intensify 251.5
triplicate 876.2
adj three 875.3
triplicate 876.3

Triple Crown rugby
746.1
horse racing 757.1

triple crown tiara
647.4
three 875.1

tripod three 875.1
fire iron 1019.12

trip over tumble 194.8
come across 940.3

tripping
noun hallucination
975.7
adj high 87.23
harmonious 533.8
fluent 544.9

tripping over 940.1

trippy 87.23

triptych notebook
549.11
picture 712.11
three 875.1

trip up abase 137.5
trap 356.20
overcome 412.7
discompose 810.4
fell 912.5
make a boo-boo
974.15
distract 984.6

trite corny 117.9
habitual 373.15
commonplace 863.16
well-known 927.27
aphoristic 973.6
trivial 997.19

Triton spirit of the sea
240.4
water god 678.10

triumph
noun rejoicing 116.1
great success 409.3
victory 411.1
celebration 487.1
crowing 502.4
verb best 249.7
win through 409.13
prevail 411.3
exult 502.9

triumphal lofty 136.11
victorious 411.7

triumphalism victory
411.1
ostentation 501.1

triumphant successful
409.14
victorious 411.7
crowing 502.13

triumphantly
victoriously 411.9
exultantly 502.15

triumph over 411.5,
412.6

triumvirate
cooperation 450.1
central government
612.4
three 875.1

trivia modicum 248.2
trifles 997.4

trivial insignificant
248.6
inadequate 250.7
shallow 276.5
worthless 391.11
quibbling 935.14
trifling 997.19

trodden 201.7

troika cooperation
450.1
three 875.1

Trojan horse
subversive 357.11
language 1041.13

Trojan-horse 645.22

trolley cart 179.3
truck car 179.16

troop unit 461.21
company 769.3
flock 769.5

trooper warship 180.6
cavalryman 461.11
war-horse 461.29
policeman 1007.15

troops work force 18.9
army 461.22

trophy desire 100.11
victory 411.1
monument 549.12
laurel 646.3
tennis 749.1
memento 988.7
good thing 998.5

tropic 231.3

tropical 1018.24

tropics zone 231.3
oven 1018.11

trot
noun run 174.3
gait 177.12
child 302.3
repetitiousness 848.4
verb speed 174.8
go on horseback
177.34
beat it 188.7

trotter foot 199.5
race horse 311.14
jockey 757.2

trotters 177.15

trotting 757.1

troubadour wanderer
178.2
minstrel 710.14
poet 720.11

trouble
noun annoyance 96.2
affliction 96.8
anxiety 126.1
imposition 643.1
exertion 725.1
commotion 809.4
inconvenience 995.3
adversity 1010.1
impediment 1011.6
matter 1012.3
verb distress 96.16

vex 98.15
agitate 105.14, 916.10
concern 126.4
discompose 810.4
inconvenience 995.4
beset 1012.13

troubled annoyed
96.21
distressed 96.22
agitated 105.23,
916.16
anxious 126.7
trouble-plagued
1012.20

trouble-free perfect
1001.6
unhazardous 1006.5

troublemaker rebel
327.5
instigator 375.11
mischief-maker 593.2

troubles worry 126.2
adversity 1010.1

troubleshooter 396.10

troublesome annoying
98.22
bothersome 126.10
laborious 725.18
inconvenient 995.7
adverse 1010.13
hindering 1011.17
besetting 1012.18

troubling annoying
98.22
exciting 105.30

trough
noun airspace 184.32
wave 238.14, 915.4
channel 239.1
gutter 239.3
cavity 284.2
valley 284.9
trench 290.2
verb excavate 284.15
furrow 290.3

trounced 412.15

troupe
noun cast 707.11
company 769.3
verb act 704.29

trousered 5.44

trousers 5.18

trout 1014.4

trove find 472.6
discovery 940.1

trowel 1039.2

truancy absence 222.4
shirking 368.2

truant absentee 222.5
shirker 368.3
wretch 660.2

truce armistice 465.5
pause 856.3

truck
noun railway carriage
179.15
communication 343.1

rubbish 391.5
impedimenta 471.3
commerce 731.1
groceries 735.7
verb haul 176.13
trade 731.14
truck driver 178.10
trucker
  noun driver 178.10
  phrase carrier 176.7
truculent cruel 144.26
  warlike 458.21
  gruff 505.7
trudge
  noun slow motion
  175.2
  walk 177.10
  verb plod 175.7
  stroll 177.28
trudging
  noun walking 177.8
  adj slow 175.10
true
  noun truth 972.1
  verb harmonize 787.7
  adj straight 277.6
  firm 359.12
  observant 434.4
  devoted 587.21
  honest 644.16
  trustworthy 644.19
  faithful 644.20
  orthodox 687.7
  real 760.15
  certain 969.13
  truthful 972.13
true blue conservative
  611.13
  fidelity 644.7
true-blue devoted
  587.21
  faithful 644.20
  orthodox 687.7
  traditional 841.12
true-meaning 644.16
true to form typical
  349.15
  characteristic 864.13
truffle 10.38
truism generalization
  863.8
  axiom 973.2
truly
  adv positively 247.19
  truthfully 644.22
  really 760.16, 972.18
  certainly 969.23
  exclam yes 332.18
Trump 618.8
trump
  noun good guy 659.2
  expedient 994.2
  verb excel 249.6
trump card
  opportunity 842.2
  influence 893.1
trumpet
  noun blare 53.5

verb blare 53.10
  proclaim 352.13
  flaunt 501.17
  praise 509.12
  murmur 524.26
  blow a horn 708.42
trumpeter 710.4
truncated deformed
  265.12
  concise 537.6
  mutilated 794.5
truncheon
  noun sceptre 417.9
  verb whip 604.12
trundle push 903.9
  roll 914.10
trundling 914.1
trunk cylinder 282.4
  nose 283.8
  stem 310.19
  line 347.17
  base 900.8
  body 1050.3
trunks 5.29
truss
  noun bunch 769.7
  bundle 769.8
  supporter 900.2
  buttress 900.4
  verb bundle 769.20
  bind 799.9
trust
  noun hope 124.1
  estate 471.4
  commission 615.1
  company 617.9
  credit 622.1
  investment company
  737.16
  belief 952.1
  confidence 969.5
  verb hope 124.7
  commit 478.16
  believe 952.10
  confide in 952.17
trusted 952.23
trustee fiduciary 470.5
  recipient 479.3
  treasurer 729.11
trusteeship 615.1
trust fund 737.16
trust in believe in
  952.15
  trust 952.17
trusting artless 416.5
  trustful 952.22
  credulous 953.8
trustworthy trusty
  644.19
  believable 952.24
  reliable 969.17
  unhazardous 1006.5
trusty
  noun prisoner 429.11
  adj trustworthy 644.19
  trusting 952.22
  believable 952.24
  reliable 969.17

Truth 677.6
truth honesty 644.3
  orthodoxy 687.1
  reality 760.2
  certainty 969.1
  trueness 972.1
  self-evident truth
  972.2
  truth of the matter
  972.3
  truth 972.3
  axiom 973.2
truthful honest 644.16
  true 972.13
truthfully 644.22
truthfulness honesty
  644.3
  truth 972.1
truth of the matter
  fact 760.3
  truth 972.3
try
  noun whack 403.3
  game 746.3
  test 941.2
  verb refine 79.22
  attempt 403.6
  try hard 403.12
  try a case 598.19
  experiment 941.8
  sit in judgment 945.12
try again 403.12
try and 403.8
try for 403.9
try hard 403.12
trying
  noun experiment 941.1
  adj weakening 16.20
  fatiguing 21.13
  oppressive 98.24
  examining 937.37
  experimental 941.11
  adverse 1010.13
  troublesome 1012.18
trying for 403.17
trying-out 941.1
try on don 5.42
  experiment 941.8
try-on 941.2
try one 1010.8
try out prepare 405.6
  dramatize 704.28
  play 744.2
tryst 582.9
try to 403.8
try to find 937.30
try to reach 100.20
tsunami wave 238.14,
  915.4
  upheaval 671.5
tub
  noun bathe 79.8
  washbasin 79.12
  heavyweight 257.12
  verb wash 79.19
tubal 239.16

tubby corpulent 257.18
  stubby 268.10
tube
  noun train 179.14
  pipe 239.6
  cylinder 282.4
  wave 915.4
  electron tube 1032.10
  verb channel 176.14
tuber 310.20
tuberculosis 85.5
tubing 239.6
tubular tubate 239.16
  cylindric 282.11
tuck
  noun grub 10.2
  sweets 10.38
  fold 291.1
  verb fold 291.5
tucked 291.7
tucked-in 771.5
tucker
  noun apron 5.17
  food 10.1
  rations 10.6
  verb beat 21.6
tuck in put to bed
  22.19
  snug 121.9
  insert 191.3
tuck-in 8.8
tuff 1057.1
tuft flock 3.6
  beard 3.8
  feather 3.17
  growth 310.2
  bunch 769.7
tufted crested 3.30
  verdant 310.39
tug
  noun strain 725.2
  pull 904.2
  attraction 906.1
  verb strain 725.10
  pull 904.4
  attract 906.4
tugging
  noun pulling 904.1
  adj pulling 904.6
  attracting 906.5
tug-of-war fight 457.4
  pulling 904.1
tuition 568.1
tumble
  noun fall 194.3
  collapse 410.3
  jumble 809.3
  flounder 916.8
  verb thrill 105.18
  pitch 182.55
  fall 194.8, 395.22
  lose 412.12
  confuse 810.3
  fell 912.5
  wallow 914.13
  flounder 916.15
  confound 944.3

tumbled 809.14
tumbledown unsteady
  16.16
  descending 194.11
  dilapidated 393.33
tummy 2.17
tumour anaemia 85.9
  growth 85.38
  swelling 283.4
tumult noise 53.3
  agitation 105.4, 916.1
  bustle 330.4
  turbulence 671.2
  commotion 809.4
tumultuous noisy
  53.13
  turbulent 105.24,
  671.18
  blustering 503.4
tun 257.12
tundra plain 236.1
  Siberia 1022.4
tune
  noun melody 708.2
  harmony 708.3
  air 708.4
  pitch 709.4
  verb fit 405.8
  harmonize 708.35,
  787.7
  tune up 708.36
  organize 807.10
  rearrange 807.13
tuned 708.49
tuned in 980.5
tuneful 708.48
tune in listen in
  1033.27
  receive 1035.17
tuning revision 392.4
  fitting 405.2
  pitch 709.4
  organization 807.2
tunnel
  noun crossing 170.2
  lair 228.26
  channel 239.1
  cave 284.5
  passageway 383.3
  entrenchment 460.5
  verb deepen 275.8
  excavate 284.15
tunnelling 275.7
tunnel vision faulty
  eyesight 28.1
  narrow-mindedness
  979.1
turbine 903.6
turbulence agitation
  105.4, 916.1
  flow 184.29
  airspace 184.32
  roughness 288.1
  turmoil 671.2
  disorder 809.1
  liquidity 1059.1
turbulent noisy 53.13

tumultuous 105.24,
671.18
stormy 318.23
rebellious 327.11
bustling 330.20
disorderly 809.13
agitated 916.16

turf abode 228.1
sod 310.6
racing 457.11
arena 463.1
field 724.4
horse racing 757.1
sphere of influence
893.4

turgid distended 259.13
bulged 283.16
pompous 501.22
stiff 534.3
bombastic 545.9

turkey poultry 311.29
flop 410.2
loser 410.8

turmoil agitation 105.4,
916.1
anarchy 418.2
turbulence 671.2
jumble 809.3
commotion 809.4

turn
noun looks 33.4
inclination 100.3
start 131.3
act of kindness 143.7
deviation 164.1
journey 177.5
walk 177.10
bias 204.3
form 262.1
distortion 265.1
bend 279.3
act 328.3, 704.7
aptitude 413.5
ornament 709.18
transaction 731.4
trading 737.19
race 753.3, 756.3
bout 824.2
shift 824.3
crisis 842.4
round 849.3
change 851.1
reversion 858.1
tendency 895.1
circuitousness 913.1
circuit 913.2
whirl 914.2
disposition 977.3
verb direct 161.5
bear 161.7
deviate 164.3
change course 182.30
oblique 204.9
distort 265.5
curve 279.6
convolve 281.4
blunt 286.2
play 747.4
ski 753.4
recur 849.5

be changed 851.6
change 853.5
turn back 858.5
tend 895.3
go around 913.6
rotate 914.9

turn a blind eye take
134.8
exclude 772.4
be inattentive 983.2

turn a blind eye to
condone 148.4
neglect 340.6

turn against act the
traitor 645.15
defect 857.13

turn around 379.3

turnaround 163.3,
363.1

turn away 164.6

turn away from look
away 27.19
snub 157.5
avoid 368.6
dismiss 983.4

turn back put back
163.8
avoid 164.6
convert 857.11
change back 858.5
repulse 907.3

turn down invert 205.5
refuse 442.3

turned 393.41

turned around
adj backward 163.12
bewildered 970.24
dizzy 984.15
adv inversely 205.8

turned-off unconcerned
102.7
disapproving 510.21

turned-on wild about
101.11
excited 105.20
interested 982.16

turned-out 5.44

turned-up upturned
193.15
stubby 268.10
upcurving 279.9

turn for 413.5

turn from 379.4

turn in hit the hay
22.18
betray 645.14

turning
noun deviation 164.1
bend 279.3
convolution 281.1
circuitousness 913.1
rotation 914.1
adj deviative 164.7
convolutional 281.6
rotating 914.14

turning down 442.1

turning into 857.1

turning on 958.9

turning over 475.1

turning point crisis
842.4
crucial moment 842.5
urgency 996.4
salient point 996.6

turn into become
760.12
be changed 851.6
convert 857.11

turnip 831.6

turn left 164.3

turn of events 830.2

turn off offend 98.11
shut off 856.12
dismiss 908.19

turn-off 907.2

turn on excite 105.12
rouse 375.19
inaugurate 817.11

turn out outfit 5.40
get up 23.6
invert 205.5
equip 385.8
result 830.7, 886.4
eject 908.13
evict 908.15
dismiss 908.19
come true 972.12

turnout 179.5

turn out to be become
760.12
result 886.4

turnover pastry 10.39
overturn 205.2
sale 734.1
basketball game 751.3

turn over transfer
176.10, 629.3
capsize 182.44
overturn 205.6
deliver 478.13
sell 734.8
think over 930.13

turn right 164.3

turntable 50.11

turn to practice 328.8
avail oneself of 387.14
undertake 404.3
set to work 725.15
begin 817.7
attend to 982.5

turn up appear 33.8
be unexpected 131.6
arrive 186.6
upturn 193.13
attend 221.8
show up 830.6, 940.9
uncover 940.4
chance 971.11

turquoise 45.3

turret 272.6

turtle 311.25

Tuscan 717.2

tusk

noun teeth 2.8
verb gore 459.26

tussle
noun quarrel 456.5
fight 457.4
struggle 725.3
verb contend 457.13
struggle 725.11

tutelage patronage
449.4
teaching 568.1
instructorship 571.10
disciple 572.2
protectorship 1007.2

tutor
noun professor 571.3
tutorer 571.5
verb coach 568.11

tutorial 571.11

tutoring 568.1

tutti 708.24

tutti-frutti 10.38

tutu 5.9

tuxedo 5.11

TV television 1034.1
television receiver
1034.11

TV show 1034.2

TV station 1034.6

twaddle
noun nonsense 520.2
chatter 540.3
verb talk nonsense
520.5
chatter 540.5

twain
noun two 872.2
adj two 872.6

twang
noun rasp 58.3
accent 524.9
speech defect 525.1
verb jangle 58.9
murmur 524.26
nasalize 525.10
strum 708.40

twanging 58.3

tweak
noun pang 26.2
squeezing 260.2
jerk 904.3
verb pain 26.7
squeeze 260.8
rearrange 807.13
jerk 904.5

twee 500.18

tweedy studious 570.17
pedagogic 571.11

tweezers 192.9

twelfth 881.24

twelve 881.7

twelve o'clock 314.5

twelve-o'clock 314.7

twentieth 881.26

twentieth-century
840.13

twenty 881.7

twenty-five 881.7

twenty-five percent
880.2

twenty-four 881.7

twenty-four-hour
811.8

twenty-one 881.7

twenty-two 881.7

twice 873.5

twice as much 873.5

twice over 848.17

twig
noun sprout 302.11
branch 310.18
member 792.4
verb see 27.12
read one loud and
clear 521.8
know 927.12

twiggy
noun slim 270.8
adj lean 270.17
leafy 310.38

twilight
noun foredawn 314.4
dusk 315.3
daylight 1024.10
darkishness 1026.2
adj evening 315.8

twilight zone
ambiguity 539.1
gamble 970.8

twill fold 291.5
weave 740.6

twin
noun image 349.5
same 777.3
likeness 783.3
equal 789.4
verb assemble 769.18
coincide 777.4
double 872.5
duplicate 873.3
adj accompanying
768.9
identical 777.7
analogous 783.11
two 872.6

twine
noun cord 271.2
verb convolve 281.4
weave 740.6

twinge
noun pang 26.2
verb suffer 26.8

twinkle
noun instant 829.3
glitter 1024.7
verb glitter 1024.24

twinkling
noun instant 829.3
glitter 1024.7
adj glittering 1024.35

twinned related 774.9
two 872.6
double 873.4

twinning doubleness
872.1
duplication 873.1

twins set 783.5
pair of twins 872.4

twirl
noun eddy 238.12
coil 281.2
whirl 914.2
verb convolve 281.4
whirl 914.11

twirling 914.14

twist
noun braid 3.7
joint 87.11
chewing tobacco 89.7
surprise 131.2
deviation 164.1
bias 204.3
extra 254.4
distortion 265.1
coil 281.2
tendency 895.1
quirk 926.2
disposition 977.3
prejudice 979.3
blemish 1003.1
verb pain 26.7
stray 164.4
deflect 164.5
oblique 204.9
distort 265.5
pervert 265.6
deform 265.7
spin 271.6
convolve 281.4
misrepresent 350.3
falsify 354.16
cheat 356.18
corrupt 393.12
weave 740.6
rotate 914.9
prejudice 979.9
blemish 1003.4

twist and turn thrill
105.18
stray 164.4
convolve 281.4
live by one's wits
415.9
go roundabout 913.4
wiggle 916.14

twisted pained 26.9
distorted 265.10
falsified 265.11
spurious 354.26
complex 798.4
eccentric 926.5
discriminatory 979.12
blemished 1003.8

twisting
noun deflection 164.2
perversion 265.2
convolution 281.1
misinterpretation
342.1
misrepresentation
350.1
weaving 740.1
adj deviative 164.7

convolutional 281.6

twisty crooked 204.20
convolutional 281.6

twit
noun chump 923.3
verb warble 60.5
scoff 508.9
accuse 599.7
sing 708.38

twitch
noun pang 26.2
instant 829.3
jerk 904.3
shake 916.3
verb suffer 26.8
thrill 105.18
jerk 904.5, 916.13

twitching
noun nervousness
128.1
jerking 916.5
adj jerky 916.19

twitchy 128.12

two
noun card 758.2
twain 872.2
two 872.2
adj twain 872.6
both 872.7

two-dimensional
spatial 158.9
unimportant 997.16

two dozen 881.7

twofold 873.5

two-handed 413.25

two hundred 881.9

two-party 609.44

two-piece 873.5

twosome golfer 748.2
two 872.2

two-step 705.5

two-storey 296.6

two-time 356.14

two times again 848.17
doubly 873.5

two-way 776.11

two weeks 881.7

two-year-old 757.2

tycoon caesar 575.9
businessman 730.1
personage 996.8

tying 799.3

tying up 186.2

type
noun omen 133.3
form 262.1
measure 300.2
representative 349.7
preference 371.5
symbol 517.2
sign 518.6
print 548.6
nature 766.4
model 785.1
example 785.2
kind 808.3

speciality 865.1
oddity 869.4
disposition 977.3
verb write 547.19
classify 808.6

typescript writing
547.10
copy 548.4

typeset 548.19

typewritten 547.22

typhoon windstorm
318.12
whirlwind 318.14
storm 671.4

typical typic 349.15
indicative 517.23
model 785.8
classificational 808.7
normal 868.8

typically 868.10

typing 547.1

typist 547.18

typology 808.1

tyrannical 417.16

tyranny force 424.2
subjection 432.1
central government
612.4
absolutism 612.9
despotism 612.10

tyrant 575.14

tyre 280.4

tyres 756.1

U lordly 141.11
upper-class 607.10

ubiquitous omnipresent
221.13
almighty 677.17
thorough 793.10
recurrent 848.13

U-boat 180.9

Uffizi 386.9

ugliness raucousness
58.2
unpleasantness 98.1
crabbiness 110.3
unsightliness 1014.1

ugly unpleasant 98.17
crabby 110.20
dangerous 1005.9
unsightly 1014.6

uh-huh 332.19

UK 232.3

ulcer gastrointestinal
disease 85.29
sore 85.36

ulceration 85.36

Ulster 231.7

ulterior additional
253.10
thither 261.10
secret 345.11
extraneous 773.5

ultimate

noun acme of
perfection 1001.3
adj top 198.10
farthest 261.12
completing 407.9
mandatory 420.12
ending 819.10
final 819.11
eventual 830.11
future 838.8

ultimate aim 380.2

ultimately finally
819.12
eventually 830.12
in time 838.11

ultimatum warning
399.1
demand 421.1
condition 958.2

ultra
noun radical 611.17
adj extreme 247.13

ultramarine blue 45.3
transoceanic 261.11

ultrasonic acoustic
50.17
supersonic 174.16

ultrasound sound 50.1
X-ray 91.9

ultraviolet light
1024.1

Ulysses 178.2

umbilical 208.11

umbrella parachute
181.13
mission 184.11
safeguard 1007.3
shade 1027.1

umpire
noun arbitrator 466.4
judge 596.1, 945.6
match 747.3
game 749.2, 750.3
basketball game 751.3
verb mediate 466.6
sit in judgment 945.12

umpteenth 881.25

unabashed brazen
142.11
undaunted 492.21
immodest 666.6

unabated unweakened
15.21
undiminished 247.14
unmitigated 671.17

unable incapable 19.14
incompetent 414.19

unacceptable
inadmissible 108.10
unpraiseworthy 510.24
unwelcome 586.9

unacceptably 108.12

unaccompanied
separate 801.20
alone 871.8

unaccountable lawless
418.5

exempt 430.30
inexplicable 522.18
inconstant 853.7
fantastic 869.12
uncertain 970.16
purposeless 971.16

unaccountably
inexplicably 522.24
purposelessly 971.20

unaccounted for gone
34.5
unrevealed 346.12

unaccustomed 374.4

unaccustomed to
414.17

unacknowledged
unthanked 151.5
anonymous 528.3

unadorned mere 248.8
natural 416.6
undecorated 499.8
elegant 533.6
plain-speaking 535.3
simple 797.6

unadulterated clean
79.25
unadorned 499.8
unmixed 797.7
unqualified 959.2
genuine 972.15
perfect 1001.6

unadventurous 494.8

unaffected unmoved
94.11
unyielding 361.9
natural 416.6, 499.7
tasteful 496.8
elegant 533.6
plain-speaking 535.3
informal 581.3
undeceptive 644.18
uninfluenced 894.5
genuine 972.15

unafraid unfearing
492.20
confident 969.21

unaided
adj alone 871.8
adv singly 871.13

unaltered permanent
852.7
unchangeable 854.17
unqualified 959.2

unambiguous clear
521.11
certain 969.13

unambiguously
adj affirmative 334.8
adv positively 247.19
unanimously 332.17
intelligibly 521.13

unanimity
unanimousness 332.5
consensus 787.3

unanimous solid
332.15
agreeing 787.9

unanimously
  concurrently 332.17
  cooperatively 450.6
  in step 787.11
unannounced 131.10
unanswerable exempt
  430.30
  obvious 969.15
unanswered 956.21
unappealing 98.17
unarmed unfitted
  406.9
  unprotected 1005.14
unashamed unregretful
  114.4
  immodest 666.6
unashamedly
  unregretfully 114.7
  distressingly 247.21
unassailable 15.19
unassuming modest
  139.9
  natural 416.6, 499.7
  informal 581.3
  undeceptive 644.18
  genuine 972.15
unattached free 430.21
  separate 801.20
unattainable
  impracticable 966.8
  inaccessible 966.9
unattended separate
  801.20
  alone 871.8
  unprotected 1005.14
unattractive unpleasant
  98.17
  ugly 1014.6
unauthorized
  prohibited 444.7
  illegal 674.6
unavailable 966.9
unavoidable 962.15
unavoidably 962.19
unaware insensible
  94.10
  inexpectant 131.9
  unconscious 929.13
unaware of 929.13
unawares unexpectedly
  131.14
  innocently 657.9
  suddenly 829.9
  ignorantly 929.18
unbalanced eccentric
  160.12
  unjust 650.9
  ill-balanced 790.5
  insane 925.26
unbearable insufferable
  98.25
  downright 247.12
unbearably insufferably
  98.30
  distressingly 247.21

unbeatable
  impregnable 15.19
  peerless 249.15
unbeaten unused
  390.12
  undefeated 411.8
  new 840.7
unbecoming vulgar
  497.10
  disgraceful 661.11
  indecent 666.5
  inappropriate 788.7
unbeknown 929.17
unbelievable fantastic
  869.12
  incredible 954.10
unbelievably 954.14
unbiased impartial
  649.10
  unprejudiced 978.12
unblemished clean
  79.25
  honest 644.13
  spotless 657.7
  chaste 664.4
  perfect 1001.6
unblinking unnervous
  129.2
  alert 339.14
  undaunted 492.21
unblock unclose 292.12
  facilitate 1013.7
unborn 761.10
unbreakable firm
  15.18
  nonbreakable 1047.5
unbridled lawless
  418.5
  unrestrained 430.24
  profligate 665.25
  intemperate 669.7
  unruly 671.19
  excessive 992.16
unbroken directional
  161.12
  straight 277.6
  smooth 287.9
  unsubject 430.29
  uniform 780.5
  continuous 811.8
  constant 846.5
  undamaged 1001.8
unbuttoned
  unrestrained 430.24
  unfastened 801.22
uncannily 122.15
uncanny awesome
  122.11
  creepy 127.31
  deathly 307.29
  weird 987.9
uncaring
  noun carelessness
  340.2
  incuriosity 981.1
  adj apathetic 94.13
  unkind 144.16
  careless 340.11

unceremoniously
  581.4
uncertain
  inconspicuous 32.6
  irresolute 362.9
  ambiguous 539.4
  speculative 759.27
  relative 774.7
  irregular 850.3
  inconstant 853.7
  doubting 954.9
  unsure 970.16
  unsafe 1005.11
uncertainly irresolutely
  362.13
  irregularly 850.4
  changeably 853.8
  in an uncertain state
  970.28
uncertainty
  inconspicuousness
  32.2
  suspense 130.3
  irresolution 362.1
  ambiguity 539.1
  gamble 759.2
  relativity 774.2
  irregularity 850.1
  inconstancy 853.2
  doubt 954.2
  incertitude 970.1
  chance 971.1
  inaccuracy 974.2
  dangerousness 1005.2
unchallenged
  unanimous 332.15
  undoubted 969.16
unchanged uniform
  780.5
  permanent 852.7
  unchangeable 854.17
unchanging almighty
  677.17
  uniform 780.5
  constant 846.5
  permanent 852.7
  unchangeable 854.17
uncharted 929.17
unchecked lawless
  418.5
  unrestrained 430.24
  permitted 443.16
  candid 644.17
  permanent 852.7
  unauthoritative 970.21
uncle 559.3
unclean unwashed
  80.20
  unvirtuous 654.12
  unchaste 665.23
  obscene 666.9
  terrible 999.9
unclear inconspicuous
  32.6
  faint 52.16
  formless 263.4
  obscure 522.15
  illegible 522.19
  vague 970.19

Uncle Sam 612.3
uncluttered 797.6
uncomfortable
  distressed 96.22
  distressing 98.20
uncommitted free
  430.21
  neutral 467.7
  cautious 494.8
uncommon remarkable
  247.10
  novel 840.11
  infrequent 847.2
  unusual 869.10
  scarce 991.11
uncommonly intensely
  247.20
  infrequently 847.4
  unusually 869.17
  scarcely 991.16
uncompetitive 450.5
uncomplicated
  unadorned 499.8
  uninvolved 797.8
  easy 1013.13
uncomprehending
  undiscerning 921.14
  ignorant 929.12
uncompromising
  unyielding 361.9
  firm 425.7
uncompromisingly
  unyieldingly 361.15
  firmly 425.9
unconcerned insensible
  25.6
  apathetic 94.13
  uninterested 102.7
  nonchalant 106.15
  incurious 981.3
unconditional
  unrestricted 430.27
  thorough 793.10
  unqualified 959.2
unconditionally
  extremely 247.22
  completely 793.14
unconfirmed unproved
  957.8
  unauthoritative 970.21
unconnected
  unintelligible 522.13
  unrelated 775.6
  separate 801.20
  incoherent 803.4
  discontinuous 812.4
  illogical 935.11
unconscious
  noun psyche 92.28
  adj asleep 22.22
  senseless 25.8
  subconscious 92.41
  insensible 94.10
  unpremeditated
  365.11
  unaware 929.13
  instinctive 933.6
  involuntary 962.14

unintentional 971.17
  oblivious 983.7
  abstracted 984.11
  inanimate 1053.5
unconsciously
  innocently 657.9
  ignorantly 929.18
  involuntarily 962.18
  unintentionally 971.21
unconsciousness sleep
  22.2
  senselessness 25.2
  insensibility 94.2
  unperceptiveness
  921.2
  incognizance 929.3
  inattention 983.1
  inanimateness 1053.2
unconstitutional 674.6
uncontrollable frenzied
  105.25
  ungovernable 361.12
  rabid 925.30
  inevitable 962.15
uncontrollably
  violently 247.23
  ungovernably 361.17
  inevitably 962.19
uncontrolled lawless
  418.5
  unrestrained 430.24
  intemperate 669.7
  inconstant 853.7
uncontroversial
  969.16
unconventional
  informal 581.3
  unorthodox 867.6
  eccentric 926.5
unconvinced
  unbelieving 954.8
  uncertain 970.16
unconvincing 954.10
uncooked 406.10
uncouth countrified
  233.7
  bungling 414.20
  unrefined 497.12
  inelegant 534.2
  vulgar 666.8
uncover divest 6.5
  disinter 192.11
  unclose 292.12
  disclose 351.4
  greet 585.10
  unearth 940.4
uncovered divested
  6.12
  open 292.17
  unprotected 1005.14
uncovering unclothing
  6.1
  disinterment 192.2
  disclosure 351.1
  discovery 940.1
uncritical obedient
  326.3
  unmeticulous 340.13

uncriticizing 509.18
undiscriminating 944.5
credulous 953.8

uncritically 340.19

uncut unformed 263.5
undeveloped 406.12
undivided 791.11
complete 793.9

undamaged preserved 397.12
intact 791.10
unharmed 1001.8
safe 1006.4

undaunted persevering 360.8
undismayed 492.21

undecided irresolute 362.9
undetermined 970.18

undeclared 519.9

undefeated 411.8

undefined
inconspicuous 32.6
formless 263.4
anonymous 528.3
almighty 677.17
vague 970.19

undemanding unstrict 426.5
undiscriminating 944.5

undeniable downright 247.12
real 760.15
obvious 969.15

undeniably positively 247.19
unquestionably 969.25

under
adj lower 274.8
adv below 274.10
prep below 274.11, 432.17

under a cloud in disrepute 661.13
unreliable 954.11
doubted 954.12

under arrest 429.22

under attack
adj accused 599.15
adv under fire 459.31

underbelly mouth 2.16
bottom 199.1

undercarriage 900.6

underclass
underprivileged 606.4, 607.8
poor 619.3
unfortunate 1010.7

undercoat
noun colour 35.8
verb colour 35.13
coat 295.24

under consideration 937.39

under construction

adv in production 891.21
adj, adv in preparation 405.22

under control
adj restrained 428.13
extinguished 1021.11
adv in hand 612.20

under cover covered 295.31
concealed 346.11
in hiding 346.14
in safety 1006.6

undercover
adj covert 345.12
adv secretly 345.17

under cover of 356.23

undercurrent feeling 93.1
flow 238.4
wind 318.1
opposition 451.1
implication 519.2
counterforce 899.4
snags 1005.5

undercut sell 734.8
disprove 957.4

undercutting 750.3

underdeveloped
undeveloped 406.12
incomplete 794.4

underdevelopment 794.1

underdog 412.5

underestimate
noun underestimation 949.1
verb misestimate 949.2

underestimated 949.3

under fire
adj accused 599.15
adv under attack 459.31

underfoot
verb violate 435.4
adv below 274.10

undergo afford 626.7
experience 830.8

undergraduate
noun undergrad 572.6
adj studentlike 572.12

underground
noun train 179.14
dissent 333.1
secret passage 346.5
subversive 357.11
irregular 461.15
adj subterranean 275.12
dissenting 333.6
covert 345.12
concealed 346.11
adv beneath the sod 309.23
secretly 345.17

undergrowth 310.15

underhand

adj covert 345.12
deceitful 356.22
dishonest 645.16
adv surreptitiously 345.18

under house arrest
concealed 346.11
under arrest 429.22

under investigation 937.39

underlie base on 199.6
lie low 274.5
be latent 519.3
support 900.21

underline
noun line 517.6
verb mark 517.19
emphasize 996.14

underlined 996.21

underlining 517.6

under lock and key
jailed 429.21
in safety 1006.6

underlying basic 199.8
latent 519.5
essential 766.9

undermine weaken 16.10
sap 393.15
overthrow 395.20
refute 957.5

undermining
entrenchment 460.5
refutation 957.2

underneath
noun bottom 199.1
prep below 274.11
under 432.17

under no circumstances
adv noway 248.11
exclam by no means 335.9

underpaid 625.12

underpin 900.21

underpinning 900.6

underprivileged
noun disadvantaged 606.4
underclass 607.8
poor 619.3
adj inferior 250.6
indigent 619.8
unfortunate 1010.14

underrated 949.3

under sail 172.9

underscored 996.21

undersea 275.13

underside 199.1

under siege 459.31

understand interpret 341.9
comprehend 521.7
know 927.12
suppose 950.10

understandable
intelligible 521.10
knowable 927.25

understandably 521.13

understanding
noun unanimity 332.5
obligation 436.2
compact 437.1
accord 455.1
compromise 468.1
entente 787.2
intellect 918.1
intelligence 919.1
wise 920.3
comprehension 927.3
adj patient 134.9
pitying 145.7
in accord 455.3
intelligent 919.12
sagacious 919.16
knowing 927.15

understated 496.8

understatement
misrepresentation 350.1
restraint 496.4

understood tacit 519.8
traditional 841.12
known 927.26
supposed 950.14

understudy
noun deputy 576.1
substitute 861.2
verb represent 576.14

under surveillance 937.39

under suspicion
adj doubted 954.12
adv on trial 941.14

undertake practice 328.8
attempt 403.6
assume 404.3
commit 436.5
contract 437.5
set to work 725.15

undertaken assumed 404.7
contracted 437.11

undertaker 309.8

undertaking act 328.3
attempt 403.2
enterprise 404.1
obligation 436.2
compact 437.1
pledge 438.2
occupation 724.1

under the aegis of
adj under the protection of 1007.22
adv in the charge of 573.15

under the auspices of
adj under the protection of 1007.22
adv in the charge of 573.15

under the circumstances 765.11

under-the-counter
covert 345.12
illegal 674.6

under the hammer 734.17

under the impression 952.21

under the influence 87.22, 88.31

under the protection of 1007.22

under the stars 234.9

under the sun
adj existent 760.13
adv everywhere 158.12
on earth 234.9

under the surface
adj latent 519.5
adv internally 207.9

under the table
adj dead-drunk 88.32
adv surreptitiously 345.18

under-the-table covert 345.12
illegal 674.6

undertone murmur 52.4
milieu 209.3
meaning 518.1
implication 519.2

undertow flow 238.4
opposition 451.1
snags 1005.5

undervalued disliked 99.9
underestimated 949.3

underwater 275.13

under way
adj undertaken 404.7
happening 830.9
adv under sail 172.9
making way 182.63
adj, adv in preparation 405.22

underwear 5.22

underweight
noun weight 297.1
adj lean 270.17
lightweight 298.13

underwood 310.15

Underworld 838.2

underworld depths 275.3
gangland 660.11

under wraps secret 345.11
concealed 346.11

underwrite ratify 332.12
promise 436.4
secure 438.9
protect 1007.18

explain 341.10
manifest 348.5
disclose 351.4
amplify 538.7
unroll 860.7
result 886.4

unfolded 259.11

unfolding
noun appearance 33.1
flowering 310.24
explanation 341.4
display 348.2
disclosure 351.1
amplification 538.6
unfoldment 860.2
adj evolutionary 860.8

unforced
adj voluntary 324.7
unrestrained 430.24
adv at will 323.5

unforeseen
noun inexpectation
131.1
surprise attack 459.2
adj unexpected 131.10
sudden 829.5
chance 971.15

unforgettable never to
be forgotten 988.26
notable 996.19

unforgivable
unjustifiable 650.12
wicked 654.16

unforgiving 146.3

unfortunate
noun poor unfortunate
1010.7
adj ominous 133.17
unsuccessful 410.18
untimely 843.6
inexpedient 995.5
unlucky 1010.14

unfortunately
inauspiciously 133.20
inopportunely 843.7
inexpediently 995.8
unluckily 1010.17

unfounded false 354.25
baseless 763.8, 935.13
unproved 957.8
illusory 975.9

unfriendly unpleasant
98.17
averse 99.8
oppositional 451.8
warlike 458.21
unsociable 583.5
inhospitable 586.7
inimical 589.9

unfulfilled pleasureless
96.20
discontented 108.7
unaccomplished 408.3

unfunny 117.7

unfussy unmeticulous
340.13
inornate 499.9

ungainly bungling
414.20
ungraceful 1014.9

ungovernable 361.12

ungrateful 151.4

unguarded negligent
340.10
unthinking 365.10
artless 416.5
candid 644.17
unintentional 971.17
unalert 983.8
unprotected 1005.14

unhappily uncheerfully
112.32
regretfully 113.11
inexpediently 995.8
unfortunately 1010.17

unhappiness
unpleasure 96.1
discontent 108.1
infelicity 112.2
disapproval 510.1

unhappy pleasureless
96.20
discontented 108.7
uncheerful 112.21
disapproving 510.21
untimely 843.6
inexpedient 995.5
unfortunate 1010.14

unhappy about 113.8

unharmed undamaged
1001.8
safe 1006.4

unhealthy unhealthful
82.5
healthless 85.53
unwholesome 85.54
bad 999.7
unsafe 1005.11

unheard 929.17

unheard-of wonderful
122.10
unrenowned 661.14
novel 840.11
unusual 869.10
unknown 929.17

unheated 1022.13

unheeded 340.15

unhelpful inconsiderate
144.18
unserviceable 391.14

unhindered 430.26

unhinged dislocated
160.9
insane 925.26

unholy
noun profane 686.2
adj unsacred 686.3
ungodly 695.17
execrable 999.10

unhurried slow 175.10
leisurely 402.6

unhurt undamaged
1001.8
safe 1006.4

unicorn 647.2

unidentified
anonymous 528.3
unknown 929.17

unification affiliation
450.2
identification 777.2
joining 799.1
combination 804.1
oneness 871.1

unified unitary 871.10
indivisible 1043.13

uniform
noun livery 5.7
insignia 647.1
verb outfit 5.40
adj symmetric 264.4
smooth 287.9
equable 780.5
agreeing 787.9
simple 797.6
orderly 806.6
continuous 811.8
regular 849.6
one 871.7
indistinguishable
944.6

uniformed 5.44

uniformity symmetry
264.1
smoothness 287.1
evenness 780.1
agreement 787.1
simplicity 797.1
order 806.1
continuity 811.1
regularity 849.1
stability 854.1
conformity 866.1
oneness 871.1
indistinction 944.2

uniformly smoothly
287.12
equably 780.7
methodically 806.9
regularly 849.9

unify identify 777.5
put together 799.5
combine 804.3
reduce to unity 871.5

unifying 871.12

unilateral sided 218.7
unipartite 871.11

unimaginable
wonderful 122.10
fantastic 869.12
unbelievable 954.10
impossible 966.7

unimaginative prosaic
117.8, 721.5
plain-speaking 535.3
unfanciful 986.5

unimpeachable honest
644.13
inculpable 657.8
believable 952.24
obvious 969.15
accurate 972.16

unimpeded 430.26

unimportant humble
137.10
insignificant 248.6
of no importance
997.16

unimpressed
unaffected 94.11
unastonished 123.3

unimpressive 997.17

uninformed
inexpectant 131.9
ignorant 929.12

uninhabited 222.15

uninhibited
unrestrained 430.24
profligate 665.25
intemperate 669.7

uninitiated unskilled
414.16
ignorant 929.12

uninjured 1001.8

uninspired unaffected
94.11
unimaginative 986.5

uninspiring 117.7

unintelligible 522.13

unintended
unpremeditated
365.11
unintentional 971.17

unintentional
unpremeditated
365.11
involuntary 962.14
unintended 971.17

unintentionally on
impulse 365.14
involuntarily 962.18
without design 971.21

uninterested apathetic
94.13
unconcerned 102.7
bored 118.12
incurious 981.3

uninteresting 117.7

uninterrupted
directional 161.12
omnipresent 221.13
straight 277.6
persevering 360.8
consistent 802.11
continuous 811.8
perpetual 828.7
constant 846.5

uninvited unwanted
99.11
voluntary 324.7
unwelcome 586.9

union convergence
169.1
juxtaposition 223.3
affiliation 450.2
accord 455.1
marriage 563.1
association 617.1
relation 774.1

identification 777.2
agreement 787.1
joining 799.1
joint 799.4
combination 804.1
concurrence 898.1

unionism 727.1

unionist 727.4

Union Jack 647.6

unique
noun specific 864.3
adj wonderful 122.10
peerless 249.15
original 337.5
other 779.8
novel 840.11
infrequent 847.2
characteristic 864.13
unusual 869.10
one 871.7
sole 871.9

uniquely peerlessly
249.18
characteristically
864.17

uniqueness
nonimitation 337.1
infrequency 847.1
particularity 864.1
unusualness 869.2
oneness 871.1

unison
noun unanimity 332.5
accord 455.1
harmony 708.3
agreement 787.1
adj simultaneous
835.5

unit organization
461.21
something 762.3
one 871.3
individual 871.4

unitary combined
804.5
one 871.7
integrated 871.10

unite converge 169.2
cooperate 450.3
marry 563.14
come together 769.16
identify 777.5
put together 799.5
join 799.11
combine 804.3
unify 871.5
concur 898.2

united in accord 455.3
joined 799.13
combined 804.5
unitary 871.10
concurrent 898.4

United Kingdom
232.3

United Nations 612.7

United States 232.4

**United States of
America** 232.4

insufficient 991.9
sound 1001.7

unquestionable
downright 247.12
intrinsic 766.7
believable 952.24
obvious 969.15
true 972.13

unquestionably
positively 247.19
without question
969.25
truly 972.18

unquestioned believed
952.23
undoubted 969.16

unquestioning 959.2

unravel extract 192.10
explain 341.10
extricate 431.7
disinvolve 797.5
come apart 801.9
loosen 803.3
solve 939.2

unravelled 803.4

unravelling extrication
431.3
noncohesion 803.1
solution 939.1

unread 929.14

unreadable 522.19

unreal spurious 354.26
unrealistic 761.9
thin 763.6
illusory 975.9
imaginary 985.19

unrealistic unreal
761.9
imaginary 985.19
visionary 985.24

unreality nonexistence
761.1
illusoriness 975.2
idealism 985.7

unreason 922.2

unreasonable
capricious 364.5
overpriced 632.12
unjustifiable 650.12
unwise 922.10
fanatic 925.32
illogical 935.11
excessive 992.16

unreasonably
capriciously 364.7
exorbitantly 632.16
unjustly 650.13
foolishly 922.13
illogically 935.15
excessively 992.22

unreconstructed
impenitent 114.5
ungovernable 361.12
unsubject 430.29
conservative 611.25,
852.8

unrecorded 519.9

unrefined countrified
233.7
rough 288.6, 294.6
undeveloped 406.12
unpolished 497.12
ill-bred 505.6
inelegant 534.2
unlearned 929.14

unregulated permitted
443.16
illegal 674.6

unrelated irrelative
775.6
dissimilar 786.4

unrelenting persevering
360.8
unyielding 361.9
firm 425.7
wordy 538.12
constant 846.5

unreliability fickleness
364.3
untrustworthiness
645.4
inconstancy 853.2
unbelievability 954.3
undependability 970.6
dangerousness 1005.2

unreliable fickle 364.6
untrustworthy 645.19
inconstant 853.7
under a cloud 954.11
undependable 970.20
unsafe 1005.11

unremarkable 1004.8

unremitting
industrious 330.22
persevering 360.8
continuous 811.8
perpetual 828.7
constant 846.5
unchangeable 854.17
continuing 855.7

unrepentant 114.5

unrequited unthanked
151.5
unpaid 625.12

unreservedly agreeably
324.9
freely 430.32
candidly 644.23
completely 793.14

unresolved remaining
256.7
irresolute 362.9

unresponsive unfeeling
94.9
heartless 144.25
uninfluenceable 894.4

unrest trepidation
105.5
motion 172.1
agitation 916.1

unrestrained fervent
93.18
communicative 343.10
capricious 364.5
lawless 418.5

lax 426.4
unconstrained 430.24
candid 644.17
incontinent 665.24
intemperate 669.7
inconstant 853.7
excessive 992.16

unrestricted
undiminished 247.14
open 292.17
communicative 343.10
unconfined 430.27
thorough 793.10
unqualified 959.2

unrivalled 249.15

unromantic prosaic
721.5
genuine 972.15
realistic 986.6

unruffled unaffected
94.11
unexcited 106.11
quiescent 173.12
smooth 287.9
uniform 780.5

unruly defiant 327.10
ungovernable 361.12
anarchic 418.6
unrestrained 430.24
disorderly 671.19

unsafe 1005.11

unsaid tacit 51.11
unexpressed 519.9

unsatisfactory
dissatisfactory 108.9
disappointing 132.6
insufficient 991.9

unsatisfied lustful
75.26
pleasureless 96.20
greedy 100.27
discontented 108.7

unsavoury unpalatable
64.5
insipid 65.2
unpleasant 98.17
dishonest 645.16
disreputable 661.10

unscathed undamaged
1001.8
safe 1006.4

unscientific 935.11

unscrewed 801.22

unscrupulous
unmeticulous 340.13
dishonest 645.16

unseat dislodge 160.6
depose 447.4
disjoint 801.16

unseemly
adj vulgar 497.10
inelegant 534.2
wrong 638.3
indecent 666.5
inappropriate 788.7
inexpedient 995.5
adv vulgarly 497.16

unseen

noun invisibility 32.1
adj invisible 32.5
unheeded 340.15
unrevealed 346.12

unselfish liberal 485.4
impartial 649.10
selfless 652.5

unsentimental 986.6

unsettle agitate 105.14,
916.10
disorder 809.9
discompose 810.4
confuse 984.7

unsettled agitated
105.23, 916.16
restless 105.27
unplaced 160.10
bustling 330.20
irresolute 362.9
disorderly 809.13
irregular 850.3
inconstant 853.7
insane 925.26
unproved 957.8
undecided 970.18
confused 984.12

unsettling 105.30

unshakeable 326.3

unshaven 3.26

unsightly slovenly
809.15
ugly 1014.6

unskilled 414.16

unskilled labour 725.4

unsmiling solemn
111.3
unhappy 112.21

unsold 734.15

unsolicited voluntary
324.7
neglected 340.14

unsolved 346.12

unsophisticated artless
416.5
unadorned 499.8
unmixed 797.7
gullible 953.9

unsound infirm 16.15
unhealthy 85.53
unwholesome 85.54
unorthodox 688.9
insolvent 729.18
fragile 763.7
unwise 922.10
insane 925.26
unsubstantial 935.12
unreliable 970.20
imperfect 1002.4
unsafe 1005.11

unspeakable
noun sacred 685.2
adj horrid 98.19
indescribable 122.13
insulting 156.8
wicked 654.16
base 661.12
sacred 685.7
extraordinary 869.14

unspecified anonymous
528.3
general 863.11
vague 970.19

unspectacular 1004.8

unspoiled downright
247.12
preserved 397.12
natural 416.6
intact 791.10
unmixed 797.7
undamaged 1001.8

unspoken tacit 51.11
secret 345.11
unexpressed 519.9

unstable unsound
16.15
nonuniform 781.3
unbalanced 790.5
transient 827.7
inconstant 853.7
unreliable 970.20
unsafe 1005.11

unsteadily weakly
16.22
nonuniformly 781.4
irregularly 850.4
changeably 853.8
shakily 916.23

unsteady shaky 16.16
nonuniform 781.3
unbalanced 790.5
irregular 850.3
inconstant 853.7
fluttering 916.18
unreliable 970.20
unsafe 1005.11

unstinting 485.4

unstoppable 962.15

unstructured unformed
263.5
diffuse 538.11

unstuck 801.22

unsubstantiated 957.8

unsubtle 944.5

unsuccessful 410.18

unsuccessfully 410.19

unsuitable unacceptable
108.10
unserviceable 391.14
vulgar 497.10
wrong 638.3
inappropriate 788.7
untimely 843.6
inexpedient 995.5

unsuited unfitted 406.9
inappropriate 788.7

unsullied clean 79.25
natural 406.13
honest 644.13
spotless 657.7
chaste 664.4

unsung disliked 99.9
unexpressed 519.9
unrenowned 661.14

unsupported alone
871.8

baseless 935.13
unproved 957.8

unsure untrustworthy
645.19
ignorant 929.12
uncertain 970.16
unreliable 970.20
unconfident 970.23
unsafe 1005.11

unsurpassed peerless
249.15
best 998.16

unsuspected unknown
929.17
believed 952.23

unsuspecting
inexpectant 131.9
unaware 929.13
trusting 952.22
credulous 953.8
unprotected 1005.14

unsustainable baseless
935.13
unprovable 957.9

unsweetened 67.5

unswerving directional
161.12
straight 277.6
firm 359.12
persevering 360.8
faithful 644.20

unsympathetic
insensible 25.6
unfeeling 94.9
unkind 144.16
pitiless 146.3

untainted clean 79.25
preserved 397.12
natural 416.6
spotless 657.7
chaste 664.4
perfect 1001.6

untamed defiant
327.10
unsubject 430.29
unrefined 497.12
savage 671.21

untapped 390.12

untenable helpless
19.18
unacceptable 108.10
baseless 935.13

untested 957.8

unthinkable
unbelievable 954.10
impossible 966.7

unthinking
inconsiderate 144.18
careless 340.11
unreasoning 365.10
unintelligent 921.13
unwise 922.10
thoughtless 932.4
credulous 953.8
involuntary 962.14
unintentional 971.17

untidy dirty 80.22
slipshod 340.12

slovenly 809.15

untie loose 431.6
detach 801.10

untied adrift 182.61
unbound 430.28
liberated 431.10
unfastened 801.22

until 820.15

until now since 836.17
hitherto 837.4

untimely
adj inappropriate
788.7
unseasonable 843.6
premature 844.8
late 845.16
inexpedient 995.5
adv prematurely
844.13

unto 820.15

untold secret 345.11
unexpressed 519.9
infinite 822.3
innumerable 883.10
undecided 970.18

untouchable
noun outcast 586.4
adj unfeeling 94.9
disliked 99.9
out-of-the-way 261.9
prohibited 444.7
sacred 685.7

untouched unaffected
94.11
impenitent 114.5
unused 390.12
natural 406.13
intact 791.10
unmixed 797.7
new 840.7
unknown 929.17
undamaged 1001.8
safe 1006.4

untoward ominous
133.17
untimely 843.6
bad 999.7
adverse 1010.13

untrained
unaccustomed 374.4
unskilled 414.16

untreated 406.12

untried inexperienced
414.17
new 840.7
unproved 957.8

untroubled unexcited
106.11
unbothered 107.8
quiescent 173.12
pacific 464.9

untrue
adj false 354.25
nonobservant 435.5
unfaithful 645.20
erroneous 974.16
adv erroneously
974.20

untrustworthy
unfaithworthy 645.19
unreliable 970.20
unsafe 1005.11

unturned 277.6

untutored unskilled
414.16
unlearned 929.14

unusable 391.14

unused remaining
256.7
unaccustomed 374.4
unutilized 390.12
new 840.7
surplus 992.18

unused to
unaccustomed 374.4
inexperienced 414.17

unusual novel 840.11
infrequent 847.2
nonconforming 867.5
unordinary 869.10

unusually intensely
247.20
uncommonly 869.17

unveil divest 6.5
unclose 292.12
disclose 351.4

unveiled 6.12

unveiling display 348.2
disclosure 351.1
inauguration 817.5

unwaged 625.12

unwanted unwished
99.11
unwelcome 586.9

unwarranted
overpriced 632.12
undue 640.9
illegal 674.6
baseless 935.13
unauthoritative 970.21

unwary negligent
340.10
artless 416.5
rash 493.7
unalert 983.8

unwashed 80.20

unwavering unnervous
129.2
persevering 360.8
stable 854.12
confident 969.21

unwelcome unpleasant
98.17
unwanted 99.11,
586.9

unwell 85.55

unwieldy bulky 257.19
onerous 297.17
bungling 414.20
stiff 534.3
inconvenient 995.7
unmanageable 1012.19

unwilling disinclined
325.5
unconsenting 442.6

involuntary 962.14

unwillingly 325.8,
962.18

unwillingness 325.1,
442.1

unwind relax 20.7
compose oneself 106.7
disinvolve 797.5
unfold 860.7

unwinding idleness
331.2
unfolding 860.2

unwise unintelligent
921.13
injudicious 922.10
inexpedient 995.5

unwisely 922.13

unwitting unaware
929.13
involuntary 962.14
unintentional 971.17

unwittingly ignorantly
929.18
involuntarily 962.18
unintentionally 971.21

unworkable
unserviceable 391.14
impracticable 966.8
inexpedient 995.5

unworldly heavenly
681.12
godly 692.9
supernatural 869.15
immaterial 1051.7

unworthy
noun bad person 660.1
adj undue 640.9
wicked 654.16
worthless 997.22

unwritten unexpressed
519.9
speech 524.30
traditional 841.12

unyielding impregnable
15.19
pitiless 146.3
firm 359.12, 425.7
unbending 361.9
resistant 453.5
sturdy 762.7
immovable 854.15
uninfluenceable 894.4
inevitable 962.15
inflexible 1044.12

unzipped 801.22

up
verb ascend 193.8
increase 251.4
enlarge 259.4
elevate 911.5
adj awake 23.8
adv upward 193.16
vertically 200.13
on high 272.21
prep toward 161.26

up against
adj contrapositive
215.5

resistant 453.5
prep against 223.25

up against it in danger
1005.13
straitened 1012.26

up-and-coming 330.23

up and do 328.6

up and down
perpendicularly
200.14
alternately 849.11
to and fro 915.21

up-and-down
perpendicular 200.12
alternate 915.19

up and go 188.7

up-and-up 644.14

upbeat
noun improvement
392.1
beat 709.26
round 849.3
adj optimistic 124.12

upbringing 568.3

upcoming
noun ascent 193.1
adj approaching 167.4
ascending 193.14
imminent 839.3

update date 831.13
modernize 840.6

updating 840.3

upended 200.11

up for 405.18

up for grabs 970.18

up for sale 734.16

up front 817.18

up-front front 216.10
plain-speaking 535.3
first 817.17

upgrade
noun ascent 193.1
acclivity 204.6
improvement 392.1
verb improve 392.9
promote 446.2
adj ascending 193.14
uphill 204.17
adv slantingly 204.23

upgraded 392.13

upgrading 446.1

upheaval outburst
105.9
fall 395.3
convulsion 671.5
revolution 851.2
elevation 911.1

upheld 900.24

uphill
noun ascent 193.1
acclivity 204.6
adj ascending 193.14
upgrade 204.17
laborious 725.18
difficult 1012.17
adv up 193.16

valued at 630.14

values treatment 712.9
  target values 1040.10

value system 636.1

valuing 945.3

valve gate 239.10
  stopper 293.4
  wind instrument 711.6
  electron tube 1032.10
  cutlery 1039.2

vamp
  noun lover 104.12
  tempter 377.4
  demimonde 665.15
  overture 708.26
  impromptu 708.27
  fire fighter 1021.4
  verb enamour 104.23
  improvise 365.8
  fascinate 377.7
  perfect 392.11

vampire lover 104.12
  frightener 127.9
  tempter 377.4
  extortionist 480.12
  monster 593.6
  demimonde 665.15
  demon 680.6
  bewitcher 690.9

van leading 165.1
  wagon 179.2
  railway carriage
  179.15
  vanguard 216.2
  guard 1007.9

vandalism cruelty
  144.11
  misbehaviour 322.1
  destruction 395.1
  violence 671.1

Vanderbilt 618.8

vane 318.17

vanguard leading 165.1
  border 211.4
  van 216.2
  precursor 815.1
  novelty 840.2
  guard 1007.9

vanilla 499.8

vanish disappear 34.3
  quit 188.9
  perish 395.23
  flit 827.6

vanished absent 222.11
  no more 761.11
  past 836.7

vanishing
  noun disappearance
  34.1
  adj disappearing 34.4

vanity pride 136.1
  vainness 140.1
  futility 391.2
  boasting 502.1
  triviality 997.3

Vanity Fair 578.6

vanquished

noun loser 412.5
adj conquered 412.17

vantage viewpoint 27.7
  advantage 249.2
  sphere of influence
  893.4

vantage point 27.7

vapour
  noun fog 319.2
  spirit 763.3
  illusion 975.1
  figment of the
  imagination 985.5
  hot water 1018.10
  volatile 1065.1
  verb boast 502.6
  let out 908.24

variability relativity
  774.2
  nonuniformity 781.1
  multiformity 782.1
  irregularity 850.1
  inconstancy 853.2

variable
  noun process variable
  1040.9
  adj relative 774.7
  nonuniform 781.3
  multiform 782.3
  irregular 850.3
  changeable 853.6
  inconstant 853.7
  uncertain 970.16

variance dissent 333.1
  disagreement 456.2,
  788.1
  relativity 774.2
  difference 779.1

variant
  noun rendering 341.2
  adj different 779.7
  disagreeing 788.6

variation deviation
  164.1
  passage 708.24
  difference 779.1
  differentiation 779.4
  nonuniformity 781.1
  multiformity 782.1
  change 851.1
  inconstancy 853.2
  changing 853.3

varied different 779.7
  diversified 782.4
  mixed 796.14

variegated chromatic
  35.15
  many-coloured 47.9
  different 779.7
  nonuniform 781.3

variety sect 675.3
  show business 704.1
  miscellany 769.13
  difference 779.1
  nonuniformity 781.1
  multiformity 782.1
  kind 808.3
  kingdom 808.5
  change 851.1

inconstancy 853.2
plurality 882.1

various different 779.7
  nonuniform 781.3
  diversified 782.4
  plural 882.7
  several 883.7

variously differently
  779.10
  severally 782.5
  unequally 790.6

varnish
  noun blanket 295.12
  sham 354.3
  pretext 376.1
  extenuation 600.5
  palette 712.18
  verb colour 35.13
  pervert 265.6
  polish 287.7
  conceal 346.6
  falsify 354.16
  ornament 545.7
  extenuate 600.12

varnished 287.10

varsity
  noun team 617.7
  adj scholastic 567.13

vary deviate 164.3
  vacillate 362.8
  differ 779.5
  differentiate 779.6
  diversify 781.2, 782.2
  disguise 786.3
  disagree 788.5
  intermit 850.2
  be changed 851.6
  change 851.7, 853.5

varying different 779.7
  nonuniform 781.3

vas 2.21

vascular 2.31

vase 742.2

Vaseline 1054.2

vast spacious 158.10
  large 247.7
  huge 257.20

vastly extensively
  158.11
  immensely 247.16

vastness greatness
  247.1
  size 257.1
  hugeness 257.7

vat 386.6

Vatican papacy 698.6
  bishop's palace 703.8

Vatican Council 423.4

vaudeville 704.1

vault
  noun ascent 193.1
  compartment 197.2
  arch 279.4
  tomb 309.16
  leap 366.1
  storehouse 386.6
  treasury 729.12

heavens 1070.2
verb curve 279.6
  leap 366.5

vaulted 279.10

vaulting curvature
  279.1
  arch 279.4
  leaping 366.3

veal 10.14

vector infection 85.4
  carrier 85.43
  tack 161.2
  course 184.34
  straight line 277.2

veer
  noun deviation 164.1
  bias 204.3
  angle 278.2
  verb deviate 164.3
  change course 182.30
  oblique 204.9
  go sideways 218.5
  angle 278.5
  be changed 851.6

veering deviative 164.7
  irregular 850.3

vega plain 236.1
  grassland 310.8

vegan eater 8.16
  abstainer 668.4

vegetable
  noun plant 310.3
  adj vegetal 310.33
  passive 329.6
  languid 331.20
  permanent 852.7

vegetable oil 1054.1

vegetables 10.34

vegetarian
  noun eater 8.16
  abstainer 668.4
  adj eating 8.31
  vegetable 310.33
  abstinent 668.10

vegetarianism diet
  7.11
  eating 8.1
  abstinence 668.2

vegetation inertness
  173.4
  growth 259.3, 310.30
  plants 310.1
  inaction 329.1
  mere existence 760.6

vegetative vegetable
  310.33
  passive 329.6
  languid 331.20

vehemence acrimony
  17.5
  power 18.1
  passion 93.2, 544.5
  zeal 101.2
  rage 152.10
  industry 330.6
  violence 671.1

vehement acrimonious
  17.14

zealous 101.9
  passionate 105.29
  industrious 330.22
  emphatic 544.13
  violent 671.16

vehemently zealously
  101.14
  industriously 330.27
  eloquently 544.15
  violently 671.25

vehicle colour 35.8
  conveyance 179.1
  instrument 384.4
  stage show 704.4
  film 714.10

veil
  noun veiling 5.26
  cover 295.2
  veil of secrecy 345.3
  curtain 346.2
  pretext 376.1
  shade 1027.1
  verb cover 295.19
  keep secret 345.7
  conceal 346.6
  shade 1027.5

veiled covered 295.31
  latent 519.5
  vague 970.19
  shaded 1027.7

vein
  noun duct 2.21
  paper 270.7
  source of supply 386.4
  style 532.2
  mode 764.4
  nature 766.4
  disposition 977.3
  mood 977.4
  deposit 1056.7
  verb variegate 47.7

veined 47.15

Velcro 799.3

velocity rate 172.4
  speed 174.1
  gait 177.12

velvet comfort 121.1
  smooth 287.3
  smoothness 294.3
  putty 1045.4

velvety feathery 3.28
  smooth 287.9, 294.8
  sleek 287.10
  velvetlike 1045.15

vendee 733.5

vendetta quarrel 456.5
  revenge 507.1
  animosity 589.4

vending 734.2

vendor pedlar 730.5
  vending machine
  736.4

veneer
  noun shallowness
  276.1
  blanket 295.12
  lamina 296.2
  verb face 295.23

veneered 296.6

venerable dignified
136.12
reverend 155.12
aged 303.16
reputable 662.15
sacred 685.7
old 841.10
traditional 841.12

venerated respected
155.11
reputable 662.15

veneration respect
155.1
piety 692.1
worship 696.1

venereal sexual 75.24
aphrodisiac 75.25

vengeance revenge
507.1
deserts 639.3

vengeful 507.7

venison 10.12

venom poisonousness
82.3
rancour 144.7
animosity 589.4
violence 671.1
evil 999.3
poison 1000.3

venomous poisonous
82.7
hating 103.7
rancorous 144.22
hostile 589.10
violent 671.16
harmful 999.12

vent
noun parachute 181.13
emergence 190.1
outlet 190.9
air passage 239.13
escape 369.1
verb divulge 351.5
evacuate 908.22

ventilate deodorize
72.4
air 317.10
disclose 351.4
divulge 351.5
make public 352.11
discuss 541.12
refrigerate 1023.10

ventilation deodorizing
72.2
cross-ventilation 317.8
publication 352.1
discussion 541.7

ventilator air passage
239.13
aerator 317.9
fan 318.19
cooler 1023.3

venting emergence
190.1
evacuation 908.6

ventricular 2.29

venture

noun undertaking
404.1
investment 729.3
trading 737.19
gamble 759.2
verb attempt 403.6
dare 492.10
presume 640.6
invest 729.16
trade 737.23
chance 759.24

venture capital 386.2

ventured 404.7

venture to 403.8

venue 159.2

Venus Love 104.8
Venus de Milo
1015.10
stars 1070.4
planet 1070.9

veracity honesty 644.3
truth 972.1

veranda 197.21

verb 530.4

verbal
noun verb 530.4
adj communicational
343.9
semantic 518.12
speech 524.30
vocabular 526.18
grammatical 530.17
genuine 972.15

verbally
adj communicatively
343.12
adv orally 524.34
exactly 972.21

verbatim
adj genuine 972.15
adv exactly 972.21

verdant green 44.4
verdurous 310.39

verdict judgment
598.10
solution 939.1
decision 945.5

verge
noun border 211.4
insignia 647.1
verb bear 161.7
border 211.10
tend 895.3

verges 211.1

verification test 941.2
collation 942.2
confirmation 956.4
ensuring 969.8

verified tried 941.12
proved 956.20
true 972.13

verify experiment 941.8
collate 942.5
confirm 956.11,
969.12
check 1016.20

verily positively 247.19

truly 972.18

veritable straight
644.14
real 760.15
thorough 793.10
true 972.13

verity honesty 644.3
truth 972.1

vermilion
verb redden 41.4
adj red 41.6

vermin vertebrate
311.3
parasite 311.35
rabble 606.3
beast 660.7

vernacular
noun dead language
523.2
mother tongue 523.3
jargon 523.9
plain speech 535.1
adj local 231.9
common 497.14
colloquial 523.18
usual 868.9

veronica 691.5

versatile fickle 364.6
handy 387.20
ambidextrous 413.25
multiform 782.3

versatility
ambidexterity 413.3
nonuniformity 781.1
multiformity 782.1

verse
noun part 554.13
passage 708.24
poetry 720.1
poem 720.4
measure 720.9
section 792.2
curtain raiser 815.2
maxim 973.1
verb inform 551.8
poetize 720.13

versed 927.18

versed in skilled in
413.27
informed in 927.19

version reproduction
336.3
rendering 341.2
writing 547.10
sect 675.3
score 708.28
story 722.3

verso 220.1

versus toward 161.26
opposite to 215.7
opposed to 451.10

vert
noun heraldic device
647.2
adj green 44.4

vertical
noun upright 200.2
adj top 198.10

upright 200.11
steep 204.18
straight 277.6

vertically 200.13

vertiginous rotary
914.15
dizzy 984.15

vertigo anaemia 85.9
ear disease 85.15
dizziness 984.4

verve vim 17.2
passion 93.2
eagerness 101.1
gaiety 109.4
liveliness 330.2
spirit 544.4
lively imagination
985.4

very to a degree 245.7
exceedingly 247.18

very beginning 844.1

very best
noun best 998.8
adj best 998.16

very good 998.12

very latest 840.14

very like 783.15

very likely 967.8

very many 883.6

very much 247.15

very much alive
306.11

very same 777.3

very seldom 847.4

very thing 972.4

very top 198.2

very well
adv excellently 998.22
exclam yes 332.18

vessel duct 2.21
ship 180.1
container 195.1

vest
noun waistcoat 5.14
verb establish 159.16
endow 478.17
commission 615.10

vested clothing 5.44
established 854.13

vested interest estate
471.4
pressure group 609.31

vestibule ear 2.10
entrance 189.5
portal 197.19

vestige remainder
256.1
print 517.7
clue 517.9
record 549.1
tinge 796.7
antiquity 841.6

vestigial 256.7

vestments 702.1

vestry ecclesiastical
council 423.4
sacristy 703.9

vet
noun veterinary
surgeon 90.7
veteran 461.18
verb scrutinize 27.14
make a close study of
937.25

vetch 310.4

veteran
noun old man 304.2
campaigner 461.18
adj experienced
413.28
antiquated 841.13

veterinary 90.7

veterinary surgeon
90.7

veto
noun negative 444.2
executive veto 613.6
verb put one's veto
upon 444.5
oppose 451.3
disapprove 510.10
legislate 613.9

vetoed 444.7

vetting 27.6

vexed annoyed 96.21
worried 126.8
provoked 152.27
troubled 1012.20

vexed question 1012.7

via 161.27

viability activation 17.9
satisfactoriness 107.3
life 306.1
durability 826.1
workability 888.3
practicability 965.2

viable energizing 17.15
acceptable 107.12
living 306.11
workable 888.10
practicable 965.7
of importance 996.18

viaduct crossing 170.2
bridge 383.9

vibes 93.5

vibrant energetic 17.13
resonant 54.9

vibrate resonate 54.6
be frequent 846.3
oscillate 915.10
shake 916.11

vibrating resonant 54.9
constant 846.5
oscillating 915.15
shaking 916.17

vibration constancy
846.2
oscillation 915.1
shaking 916.2

vibrations 93.5

vibrator oscillator
915.9
  agitator 916.9
  massage 1042.3

vicar clergyman 699.2
  substitute 861.2

vicarage house 228.5
  benefice 698.9
  parsonage 703.7

vicarious 861.8

vice
  noun contractor 260.6
  misbehaviour 322.1
  deputy 576.1
  viciousness 654.1
  weakness 654.2
  wrongdoing 655.1
  substitute 861.2
  prep instead of 861.12

Vice-Admiral 575.21

vice-chairman 576.8

vice-chancellor
  principal 571.8
  executive 574.3
  vice-president 576.8

vice-president
  executive 574.3
  vice-chairman 576.8
  substitute 861.2

viceroy governor
575.13
  vice-president 576.8

vice versa inversely
205.8
  reciprocally 776.12
  contrarily 778.9

vicinity environment
209.1
  nearness 223.1
  region 231.1

vicious cruel 144.26
  vice-prone 654.11
  wicked 654.16
  savage 671.21
  bad 999.7
  harmful 999.12

vicious circle circle
280.2
  sophistry 935.1
  vicissitudes 971.5

viciously cruelly
144.35
  wickedly 654.19
  savagely 671.27
  terribly 999.14
  harmfully 999.15

vicissitudes 971.5

victim sick person
85.42
  sufferer 96.11
  dupe 358.1
  quarry 382.7
  loser 412.5
  laughingstock 508.7
  cheater 759.22
  unfortunate 1010.7

victimization
  deception 356.1

persecution 389.3

victor 409.6, 411.2

Victorian
  noun prude 500.11
  adj prudish 500.19
  antiquated 841.13

victorious 411.7

victory success 409.1
  triumph 411.1

video
  noun television 1034.1
  adj televisional
  1034.16

video camera 714.11

videotape
  noun bulletin board
  549.10
  television receiver
  1034.11
  verb record 549.15

vie compete 457.18
  be comparable 942.7
  excel 998.11

vie for 457.20

view
  noun look 27.3
  field of view 31.3
  aspect 33.3
  scene 33.6, 712.12
  intention 380.1
  estimate 945.3
  opinion 952.6
  outlook 977.2
  verb see 27.12
  look 27.13
  contemplate 930.17
  take the attitude 977.6
  heed 982.6

view as 952.11

viewer optical
  instrument 29.1
  recipient 479.3
  spectator 917.1
  televiewer 1034.12

viewfinder 29.5

viewing 27.2

viewpoint standpoint
27.7
  field of view 31.3
  aspect 33.3
  station 159.2
  outlook 977.2

vigil wakefulness 23.1
  vigilance 339.4

vigilance wariness
339.4
  curiosity 980.1
  protection 1007.1

vigilant wakeful 23.7
  wary 339.13
  prepared 405.16
  protective 1007.23

vigilantes 1007.17

vigorous strong 15.15,
544.11
  energetic 17.13
  powerful 18.12

hale 83.12
  fervent 93.18
  thriving 1009.13
  tough 1047.4

vigorously strongly
15.23
  energetically 17.16
  powerfully 18.15
  fervently 93.26
  eloquently 544.15

vigour strength 15.1
  energy 17.1
  power 18.1
  haleness 83.3
  gaiety 109.4
  force 544.3

viking mariner 183.1
  pirate 483.7

vile nasty 64.7
  malodorous 71.5
  filthy 80.23
  offensive 98.18
  low 497.15
  cursing 513.8
  knavish 645.17
  wicked 654.16
  base 661.12
  obscene 666.9
  paltry 997.21
  terrible 999.9

vilification berating
510.7
  defamation 512.2
  abuse 513.2

villa 228.7

village
  noun hamlet 230.2
  state 231.5
  adj urban 230.11

village green 310.7

villager 227.6

villain evildoer 593.1
  rascal 660.3
  role 704.10
  actor 707.2

villainous knavish
645.17
  wicked 654.16
  terrible 999.9

ville 230.1

vin 88.17

vinaigrette 70.6

vin de pays 88.17

vindicate justify 600.9
  acquit 601.4

vindication justification
600.1
  acquittal 601.1

vindictive 507.7

vine 310.4

vinegar sour 67.2
  preservative 397.4

vineyard 1067.10

vino 88.17

vintage
  noun yield 472.5

adj antiquated 841.13

vinyl 549.10

violate disobey 327.6
  misuse 389.4
  corrupt 393.12
  break 435.4
  possess sexually
  480.15
  seduce 665.20
  rage 671.11
  work evil 999.6

violation disobedience
327.1
  misuse 389.1
  mistreatment 389.2
  infraction 435.2
  sexual possession
  480.3
  wrong 638.1
  abomination 638.2
  seduction 665.6
  unruliness 671.3
  lawbreaking 674.3
  offence 674.4
  basketball game 751.3

violence acrimony 17.5
  excitability 105.10
  cruelty 144.11
  rage 152.10
  mistreatment 389.2
  coercion 424.3
  vehemence 671.1

violent acrimonious
17.14
  frenzied 105.25
  passionate 105.29
  coercive 424.12
  vehement 671.16
  rabid 925.30

violent death killing
307.6
  fatality 308.7

violently frenziedly
105.35
  furiously 247.23
  vehemently 671.25

violet
  noun purpleness 46.1
  adj purple 46.3

violinist 710.5

VIP 996.9

viper serpent 311.26
  beast 660.7

virago amazon 76.9
  bitch 110.12
  witch 593.7

virgin
  noun schoolgirl 302.8
  adj hinterland 233.9
  natural 406.13
  unmarried 565.7
  continent 664.6
  intact 791.10
  unmixed 797.7
  new 840.7
  unproductive 890.4
  unknown 929.17
  undamaged 1001.8

virginal immature
301.10
  natural 406.13
  unmarried 565.7
  continent 664.6
  new 840.7

virginity naturalness
406.3
  celibacy 565.1
  newness 840.1

virile potent 76.12
  courageous 492.17

virility power 18.1
  male sex 76.2
  maturity 303.2
  courage 492.1

virtual 519.5

virtually latently
519.11
  on the whole 791.14

virtue power 18.1
  courage 492.1
  morality 636.3
  probity 644.1
  virtuousness 653.1
  chastity 664.1
  goodness 998.1

virtues 679.3

virtuosity superiority
249.1
  skill 413.1
  musicianship 708.31

virtuoso
  noun superior 249.4
  master 413.13
  connoisseur 496.7
  musician 710.1
  first-rater 998.6
  adj skilful 413.22
  musical 708.47

virtuous honest 644.13
  good 653.6, 998.12
  chaste 664.4

virulent acrimonious
17.14
  poisonous 82.7
  rancorous 144.22
  resentful 152.26
  deadly 308.22
  hostile 589.10
  violent 671.16
  harmful 999.12

virus infection 85.4
  germ 85.41
  minutia 258.7
  organism 305.2
  poison 1000.3

visa
  noun ratification 332.4
  pass 443.7
  signature 527.10
  certificate 549.6
  verb ratify 332.12

visage looks 33.4
  face 216.4

visceral emotional
93.17
  interior 207.6

viscose 1060.12

viscount 608.4

viscountess 608.6

viscous thick 269.8
dense 1043.12
viscid 1060.12

Vishnu 677.3

visibility visibleness
31.1
airspace 184.32
manifestness 348.3

visible
noun visibility 31.1
adj visual 27.20, 31.6
apparent 33.11
manifest 348.8

visibly at sight 27.22
perceptibly 31.8
positively 247.19
to a degree 248.10
manifestly 348.14

vision
noun sight 27.1
apparition 33.5
deception 356.1
phantom 975.4
figment of the
imagination 985.5
visualization 985.6
dream 985.9
spectre 987.1
thing of beauty 1015.7
verb visualize 985.15

visionary
noun enthusiast 101.4
idealist 985.13
adj illusory 975.9
idealistic 985.24

visit
noun chat 541.4
social call 582.7
verb go to 177.25
enter 189.7
attend 221.8

visitation seizure 85.6
visit 582.7
examination 937.3
bane 1000.1

visiting 582.7

visitor traveller 178.1
incomer 189.4
attender 221.5
superintendent 574.2
guest 585.6
examiner 937.17

visit with 541.9

visor cover 356.11
eyeshade 1027.2

vista field of view 31.3
view 33.6

visual eye 2.26
ocular 27.20
visible 31.6

visual arts 712.1

visualization 985.6

visualize contemplate
930.17

vision 985.15

visually 27.22

vita 719.1

vital powerful 18.12
hale 83.12
eager 101.8
gay 109.14
organic 305.17
living 306.11
vigorous 544.11
durable 826.10
requisite 962.13
all-important 996.23

vitality strength 15.1
energy 17.1
power 18.1
haleness 83.3
eagerness 101.1
gaiety 109.4
life 306.1
vigour 544.3
toughness 1047.1

vital statistics 1016.13

vitamin 7.4

vitriol rancour 144.7
animosity 589.4

vitriolic acrimonious
17.14
pungent 68.6
rancorous 144.22
hostile 589.10

viva 937.2

vivacious energetic
17.13
eager 101.8
gay 109.14
active 330.17
spirited 544.12

vivacity animation 17.4
eagerness 101.1
gaiety 109.4
life 306.1
liveliness 330.2
spirit 544.4

vivid energetic 17.13
exquisite 24.13
colourful 35.18
eager 101.8
representational
349.13
descriptive 349.14
expressive 544.10
remembered 988.23
bright 1024.32

vividly descriptively
349.16
eloquently 544.15

vividness colourfulness
35.4
eloquence 544.1
spirit 544.4
brightness 1024.4

vivisection 801.5

vixen hen 77.9
bitch 110.12
witch 593.7

viz by interpretation
341.18

namely 864.18

vocabulary
noun jargon 523.9
lexis 526.13
reference book 554.9
dictionary 870.4
adj verbal 526.18

vocal speech 524.30
singing 708.50

vocalist 710.13

vocally 524.34

vocation motive 375.1
ministry 698.1
occupation 724.6
speciality 865.1

vocational 724.16

voce manner of
speaking 524.8
voice 709.5

vociferous noisy 53.13
vociferant 59.10

Vodafone 347.4

vogue
noun fashion 578.1
repute 662.1
adj stylish 578.12

voice
noun vote 371.6
approval 509.1
utterance 524.3
manner of speaking
524.8
speech sound 524.13
active voice 530.14
spokesman 576.5
part 708.22
voce 709.5
singer 710.13
verb publish 352.10
say 524.23
tune 708.36

voiced speech 524.30
phonetic 524.31

voices 710.16

voicing articulation
524.6
speech sound 524.13

void
noun space 158.1,
1070.3
vacuum 222.3
crack 224.2
nonexistence 761.1
verb defecate 12.13
delete 255.12
abolish 395.13
repeal 445.2
neutralize 899.7
evacuate 908.22
adj vacant 222.14
repealed 445.3
nonexistent 761.8

volatile
noun vapour 1065.1
adj light 298.10
fickle 364.6
transient 827.7
inconstant 853.7

superficial 921.20
flighty 984.17
volatilizable 1065.10

volatile oil 1054.1

volatility lightness
298.1
fickleness 364.3
superficiality 921.7
flightiness 984.5
vapourability 1065.4

volcanic fervent 93.18
excitable 105.28
passionate 105.29
hot-tempered 110.25
explosive 671.24

volcano mountain
237.6
outburst 671.6

volition will 323.1
choice 371.1

volk 559.4

volley
noun detonation 56.3
salvo 459.9
arrow 462.6
shot 903.4
verb play tennis 749.3

volleying 56.12

volt 1031.11

voltage 1031.11

volte-face
noun reverse 163.3,
363.1
conversion 857.1
verb about-face 163.10

voluble 540.9

volume loudness 53.1
space 158.1
quantity 247.3
size 257.1
capacity 257.2
book 554.1
tome 554.4
edition 554.5
part 554.13

voluminous spacious
158.10
large 247.7
capacious 257.17

voluntarily freely
324.10
intentionally 380.10

voluntary
noun overture 708.26
curtain raiser 815.2
adj volitional 323.4
volunteer 324.7
elective 371.22
intentional 380.8

volunteer
noun voluntariness
324.2
verb do voluntarily
324.4
adj voluntary 324.7

volunteering 324.2

volunteers 461.25

voluptuous sexual
75.24
delightful 97.7
sensual 663.5

vomit
noun vomiting 908.8
verb feel disgust 99.4
jet 238.20
erupt 671.13
spew 908.26

vomiting anaemia 85.9
nausea 85.30
vomition 908.8

voodoo
noun animism 675.6
sorcery 690.1
shaman 690.7
charm 691.5
bad influence 999.4
verb bewitch 691.9
adj sorcerous 690.14

voracious hungry
100.25
greedy 100.27
gluttonous 672.6

vortex agitation 105.4
wash 184.30
eddy 238.12
coil 281.2
bustle 330.4
whirl 914.2

vote
noun voting 371.6,
609.18
approval 509.1
suffrage 609.17
introduction 613.5
verb cast one's vote
371.18
participate 476.5
support 609.41

vote against 451.3

vote for 332.8

vote in 371.20

vote of no confidence
613.8

voter selector 371.7
elector 609.23

voting vote 371.6
participation 476.1
going to the polls
609.18

vouch
noun affirmation 334.1
verb depose 334.6
promise 436.4
testify 956.9

voucher
recommendation 509.4
certificate 549.6
receipt 627.2
witness 956.6

vouch for 334.6

vow
noun oath 334.4
promise 436.1
verb depose 334.6
promise 436.4

state 952.12

vowed 334.9

vowel
noun speech sound 524.13
adj phonetic 524.31

voyage
noun journey 177.5
verb traverse 177.20
journey 177.21
navigate 182.13

voyager 178.1

voyeur sexual pervert 75.16
inquisitive person 980.2

voyeurism perversion 75.11
curiosity 980.1

voyeuristic 980.5

vs 451.10

Vulcan 726.8

vulgar inferior 250.6
inelegant 497.10, 534.2
gaudy 501.20
ill-bred 505.6
vernacular 523.18
populational 606.8
base 661.12
uncouth 666.8

vulgarity inadequacy 250.3
vulgarness 497.1
discourtesy 505.1
inelegance 534.1
baseness 661.3
uncouthness 666.3

vulnerability
helplessness 19.4
unpreparedness 406.1
susceptibility 896.2
pregnability 1005.4
brittleness 1048.1

vulnerable helpless 19.18
influenceable 893.15
liable 896.5
pregnable 1005.16
brittle 1048.4

vulture 480.12

vulva 2.11

vying
noun hostility 451.2
contention 457.1
competition 457.2
adj competitive 457.23

W 161.18

wacky odd 869.11
screwy 922.9
crazy 925.27
kooky 926.6

wad
noun lot 247.4
lump 257.10
bomb 618.3
bunch 769.7

accumulation 769.9
verb fill 196.7, 793.7

wadding lining 196.3
stopping 293.5

waddle
noun slow motion 175.2
gait 177.12
verb stroll 177.28

wade 182.56

wade through study 570.12
drudge 725.14

wading 182.11

wads 618.3

wafer biscuit 10.29
paper 270.7
lamina 296.2
Eucharist 701.7

wafer-thin 270.16

waffle
noun pancake 10.43
bullshit 520.3
speech 524.1
chatter 540.3
quibbling 935.5
verb prevaricate 344.7
vacillate 362.8
talk nonsense 520.5
chatter 540.5
quibble 935.9

waft
noun puff 318.4
verb transport 176.12
buoy 298.8
blow 318.20
phrase transportation 176.3

wag
noun mischief-maker 322.3
humourist 489.12
swing 915.6
wiggle 916.7
verb oscillate 915.10
wave 915.11
wiggle 916.14

wage
noun pay 624.4
verb practice 328.8
employ 615.14

waged 624.22

wage-earners 607.7

wager
noun bet 759.3
gamble 970.8
verb chance 759.24
bet 759.25

wages 624.4

wage war contend 457.13
war 458.14

waggon 179.2

wagon waggon 179.2
police car 179.11

waif vagabond 178.3
derelict 370.4

wail
noun screech 58.4
lament 115.3
verb screech 58.8
cry 60.2
ululate 115.13
sigh 318.21
murmur 524.26

wailing
noun lamentation 115.1
adj shrill 58.14
howling 60.6
lamenting 115.18

wain 179.2

waist 818.1

waistband 5.19

waistcoat 5.14

waistline 818.1

wait
noun minstrel 710.14
delay 845.2
verb await 130.8
be patient 134.4
serve 577.13
delay 845.12

wait and see do nothing 329.2
wait 845.12

wait-and-see 134.10

waiter 577.7

wait for 130.8

waiting
noun suspense 130.3
cooling one's heels 845.3
adj expectant 130.11
serving 577.14
imminent 839.3

waiting for 130.11

waiting game patience 134.1
inaction 329.1

waiting list 870.1

waiting room 197.20

waitress 577.7

waive give up 370.7
reject 372.2
cease to use 390.4
not use 390.5
permit 443.9
repeal 445.2
relinquish 475.3
postpone 845.9
allow for 958.5

waived unused 390.12
relinquished 475.5

waiver relinquishment 370.3
discontinuance 390.2
permission 443.1
repeal 445.1
quitclaim 475.2
qualification 958.1

wake
noun wakefulness 23.1
track 182.7, 517.8

wash 184.30
last offices 309.4
social gathering 582.10
afterpart 816.2
aftereffect 886.3
verb awake 23.4
awaken 23.5
excite 105.12

wake up awake 23.4
awaken 23.5
excite 105.12
rouse 375.19
perceive 521.9
disillusion 976.2

wake up to 521.9

walk
noun slow motion 175.2
ramble 177.10
gait 177.12
sphere 231.2
route 383.1
path 383.2
race 457.12
arena 463.1
field 724.4
vocation 724.6
athletics meeting 755.2
circuit 913.2
verb disappear 34.3
exercise 84.4
ambulate 177.27
get off 369.7
be free 430.18
strike 727.10

walk away quit 188.9
abandon 370.5
dismiss 983.4

walk away from quit 188.9
discard 390.7
relinquish 475.3

walker 178.6

walk in 189.7

walking
noun exercise 84.2
ambulation 177.8
athletics meeting 755.2
adj travelling 177.36

walking stick staff 273.2
supporter 900.2

Walkman 50.11

walk-on 704.10

walk out exit 190.12
strike 727.10
lay off 856.8

walkout departure 188.1
desertion 370.2
strike 727.5
stop 856.2

walk out on 190.12

walk over win hands down 411.4

domineer 612.16

walk the streets 665.21

walk-through 704.13

walk-up 405.1

walkway 383.2

wall
noun precipice 200.3
fence 212.4
partition 213.5
slope 237.2
barrier 1011.5
verb fence 212.7
fortify 460.9

walled enclosed 212.10
partitioned 213.11
covered 295.31

wallet 729.14

wall in 212.5

walling 1052.2

wallop
noun sock 901.5
verb beat up 604.14
belt 901.15
clobber 901.17
flounder 916.15

wallow
noun marsh 243.1
flounder 916.8
verb pitch 182.55
bow 912.9
welter 914.13
flounder 916.15

wallow in enjoy 95.12
indulge 669.4

wallpaper 295.23

Wall Street finance 729.1
stock exchange 737.1, 737.7
financial district 737.8

wall-to-wall
comprehensive 771.7
same 780.6
thorough 793.10

wally 923.3

walnut 40.3

waltz
noun cinch 1013.4
verb dance 705.5

wan
verb lose colour 36.6
adj tired-looking 21.9
colourless 36.7
deathly 307.29
languid 331.20
lacklustre 1026.17

wand fitness 84.1
sceptre 417.9
insignia 647.1
wish-bringer 691.6
dowsing 961.3

wander stray 164.4, 983.3
roam 177.23
digress 538.9
misbelieve 688.8

be insane 925.20
err 974.9
muse 984.9

wanderer rover 178.2
alien 773.3
transient 827.4
planet 1070.9

wandering
noun deviation 164.1
roving 177.3
discursiveness 538.3
delirium 925.8
adj deviative 164.7
roving 177.37
discursive 538.13
unordered 809.12
irregular 850.3
inconstant 853.7
abnormal 869.9
insane 925.26
delirious 925.31
distracted 984.10

wanderings 177.2

wane
noun standstill 173.3
decline 252.2
deterioration 393.3
verb disappear 34.3
recede 168.2
move 172.5
quiet 173.8
decrease 252.6
age 303.10
decline 393.17

waning
noun standstill 173.3
decrease 252.1
adj receding 168.5
quiescent 173.12
decreasing 252.11
deteriorating 393.45

wank 75.22

wanker 923.3

wannabe 336.4

want
noun desire 100.1
absence 222.1
indigence 619.2
deficiency 794.2
requirement 962.2
lack 991.4
imperfection 1002.1
verb desire 100.14
be inferior 250.4
be poor 619.5
lack 794.3, 991.7
fall short 910.2
require 962.9
be insufficient 991.8

wantage deficiency
794.2
want 991.4

wanted desired 100.29
welcome 585.12
requisite 962.13

want for lack 794.3
fall short 910.2
be insufficient 991.8

wanting

noun desire 100.1
adj desirous 100.21
absent 222.11
bereft 473.8
nonexistent 761.8
incomplete 794.4
short of 910.5
insufficient 991.9
lacking 991.13
imperfect 1002.4

wanton
noun libertine 665.10
strumpet 665.14
verb make love 562.14
be promiscuous
665.19
dissipate 669.6
make merry 743.24
adj capricious 364.5
unrestrained 430.24
reckless 493.8
unvirtuous 654.12
wayward 665.26
inconstant 853.7

wantonly 493.11

want to 100.15

want to know inquire
937.20
be curious 980.3

war
noun contention 457.1
warfare 458.1
campaign 458.4
military science 458.6
verb contend 457.13
wage war 458.14

warble sing 60.5,
708.38
murmur 524.26

warbler bird 311.28
singer 710.13
songbird 710.23

warbling 708.13

war correspondent
555.4

ward hospital room
197.25
state 231.5
custody 429.5
dependent 432.6
defence 460.1
stronghold 460.6
constituency 609.16
protectorship 1007.2

warden principal 571.8
executive 574.3
minister 575.17
guardian 1007.6
doorkeeper 1007.12

warder guardian 1007.6
guard 1007.9

ward off dodge 368.8
fend off 460.10
repulse 907.3
prevent 1011.14

wardrobe furnishings
5.2
cupboard 197.15

ware 735.2

war effort 458.10

warehouse
noun storehouse 386.6
market 736.1
verb load 159.15
store 386.10

wares 735.1

warfare contention
457.1
war 458.1

warhead charge 462.16
rocket 1072.3

warily vigilantly 339.17
cunningly 415.13
charily 494.13

wariness vigilance
339.4
cunning 415.1
chariness 494.2
doubt 954.2
incredulity 955.1

warlike contending
457.22
militant 458.21

warlord 575.14

warm
noun guy 76.5
verb energize 17.10
redden 41.4
excite 105.12
heat 1019.17
adj chromatic 35.15
red 41.6
fervent 93.18
zealous 101.9
heated 105.22
comfortable 121.11
kind 143.13
vehement 544.13
hospitable 585.11
cordial 587.16
calid 1018.24

warmed 1019.29

warmed up 1019.29

war memorial 549.12

warmer 1019.10

warming
noun heating 1019.1
adj heating 1019.26

warming-up 817.3

warmly fervently 93.26
heatedly 105.34
kindly 143.18
eloquently 544.15
amicably 587.22

warmth animation 17.4
warmth of colour 35.2
passion 93.2
sympathy 93.5
tenderness 93.6
pleasure 95.1
zeal 101.2
kindness 143.1
vehemence 544.5
hospitality 585.1
cordiality 587.6

heat 1018.1

warm up exercise 84.4
prime 405.9
prepare oneself 405.13
make a beginning
817.8
heat 1019.17

warm-up exercise 84.2
preparation 405.1
curtain raiser 815.2

warm weather 1018.7

warn forebode 133.11
dissuade 379.3
caution 399.5
alarm 400.3
demand 421.5
admonish 422.6
threaten 514.2

warner 399.4

warning
noun forewarning
133.4
dissuasion 379.1
caution 399.1
preparation 405.1
demand 421.1
advice 422.1
threat 514.1
tip 551.3
adj premonitory
133.16
cautioning 399.7
advisory 422.8

war of words quarrel
456.5
contention 457.1
argumentation 934.4

warp
noun deviation 164.1
bias 204.3
distortion 265.1
woof 740.3
tendency 895.1
disposition 977.3
blemish 1003.1
verb deflect 164.5
lay 182.48
distort 265.5
misrepresent 350.3
falsify 354.16
corrupt 393.12
be changed 851.6
tend 895.3
prejudice 979.9
blemish 1003.4
adj supersonic 174.16

warped distorted
265.10
spurious 354.26
partial 650.11
corrupt 654.14
discriminatory 979.12
blemished 1003.8

warrant
noun ratification 332.4
oath 334.4
security 438.1
authorization 443.3
permit 443.6

certificate 549.6
summons 598.2
reason 600.6
commission 615.1
receipt 627.2
privilege 642.2
verb acknowledge
332.11
ratify 332.12
depose 334.6
promise 436.4
secure 438.9
authorize 443.11
justify 600.9
commission 615.10
state 952.12
testify 956.9
confirm 956.11

warranted accepted
332.14
affirmed 334.9
promised 436.8
secured 438.11
authorized 443.17
justified 639.9
just 649.8
assured 969.20
unhazardous 1006.5

Warrant Officer
Marshal of the RAF
575.19
Field Marshal 575.20
Admiral of the Fleet
575.21

warranty promise
436.1
security 438.1
authorization 443.3
certificate 549.6

warren sty 80.11
cave 284.5
rabbit 889.6

warring
noun war 458.1
adj clashing 61.5
contending 457.22
warlike 458.21

warship warship 180.6
war vessel 180.6

wart growth 85.38
runt 258.4
bulge 283.3
blemish 1003.1

wartime 458.1

war-torn 458.23

warts and all 972.19

wary vigilant 339.13
cunning 415.12
chary 494.9
doubting 954.9
incredulous 955.4

war zone 458.1

wash
noun colour 35.8
washing 79.5
laundering 79.6
cleanser 79.17
wake 182.7, 184.30
lap 238.8

West Midlands 231.7
westward
noun points of the
compass 161.3
adv west 161.18
westwards 161.18
wet
noun weakling 16.6
drink 88.7
left side 220.1
rain 316.1
wet weather 316.4
sucker 358.2
coward 491.5
moisture 1063.1
verb urinate 12.14
moisten 1063.12
adj frail 16.14
left 220.4
cowardly 491.10
progressive 611.27
foolish 922.8
fluid 1059.4
moist 1063.15
wetland
noun shore 234.2
marsh 243.1
adj coastal 234.7
wetlands shore 234.2
shoal 276.2
wetness liquidity
1059.1
moisture 1063.1
wetting
noun moistening
1063.6
adj dampening
1063.18
wet weather 316.4
whack
noun report 56.1
try 403.3
slap 604.3
hit 901.4
verb crack 56.6
waste 308.13
slap 604.11
hit 901.14
whacked 21.8
whacking terrific
247.11
whopping 257.21
whale
noun heavyweight
257.12
behemoth 257.14
marine animal 311.30
verb fish 382.10
whaling 257.21
wham
noun report 56.1
verb crack 56.6
belt 901.15
whammy
noun malevolence
144.4
spell 691.1
charm 691.5

verb bring bad luck
1010.12
wharf 1008.6
what 863.6
what can be done
965.1
what does it matter?
who cares? 102.11
what matter? 997.26
whatever 863.6
whatever comes 971.1
what for 887.8
what-for 604.1
what happens 830.4
what is right 649.1
what it's all about
766.3
what may be 965.1
what might be 965.1
whatnot 1050.5
what's happening
830.2
what should be 637.1
whatsit 1050.4
whatsoever 863.6
what's the difference?
who cares? 102.11
what does it matter?
997.26
what's what 972.4
what the hell 102.11
what will be will be it
is necessary 962.20
it is fated 963.11
what you will 796.6
wheat 10.4
wheel
noun cycle 179.8
circle 280.2
direction 573.1
helm 573.5
rack 605.4
potter's wheel 742.4
motor racing 756.1
roulette 759.12
round 849.3
propeller 903.6
whirl 914.2
rotator 914.4
big shot 996.9
verb recur 849.5
circle 913.5
rotate 914.9
whirl 914.11
wheelbarrow 179.3
wheelbase size 257.1
length 267.1
wheelchair-bound
85.53
wheeler 311.13
wheeling
noun circuitousness
913.1
rotation 914.1
adj rotating 914.14

wheeling and dealing
731.2
wheels member 2.7
gams 177.15
jalopy 179.10
mechanism 1039.4
wheeze
noun breathing 2.19
sibilation 57.1
stratagem 415.3
joke 489.6
prank 489.10
verb burn out 21.5
sibilate 57.2
wheezing respiratory
2.30
breathless 21.12
sibilant 57.3
when
adv at which time
820.8
adv, conj
notwithstanding 338.8
conj while 820.16
whence 188.20, 887.7
whenever when 820.8
whene'er 820.12
where 159.21
whereabouts
noun location 159.1
adv where 159.21
whereas
noun condition 958.2
conj because 887.10
conj when 820.16
whereby 384.12
where'er 159.22
wherein 207.10
whereupon when 820.8
after which 834.7
wherever 159.22
wherewithal
noun means 384.2
money 728.1
funds 728.14
adv herewith 384.12
whet
noun appetizer 10.9
incentive 375.7
verb sensitize 24.7
stimulate 105.13
intensify 251.5
sharpen 285.7
incite 375.17
whey 1059.2
whichever
noun whatever 863.6
adj every 863.15
whicker 60.2
whiff
noun odour 69.1
puff 318.4
clue 517.9
hint 551.4
tinge 796.7
verb smell 69.8
blow 318.20

while
noun time 820.1
period 823.1
meantime 825.2
verb spend 387.13
conj when 820.16
while away spend
387.13
fritter away 486.5
whilst 820.16
whim caprice 364.1
quirk 926.2
figment of the
imagination 985.5
whimper
noun lament 115.3
verb sigh 52.14
weep 115.12
whine 115.14
whimpering
noun weeping 115.2
adj plaintive 115.19
tearful 115.21
whimsical capricious
364.5
humorous 488.4
witty 489.15
inconstant 853.7
eccentric 926.5
uncertain 970.16
fanciful 985.20
whimsy caprice 364.1
capriciousness 364.2
eccentricity 926.1
figment of the
imagination 985.5
whine
noun screech 58.4
lament 115.3
verb sigh 52.14
screech 58.8
cry 60.2
whimper 115.14
murmur 524.26
nasalize 525.10
whining
noun sigh 52.8
complaint 115.4
adj shrill 58.14
howling 60.6
plaintive 115.19
whip
noun driver 178.9
goad 375.8
lash 605.1
merry-go-round
743.15
slap 901.8
verb foam 320.5
goad 375.15
hasten 401.4
clobber 412.9
pound 901.16
slap 901.19
agitate 916.10
emulsify 1060.10
drive 1068.8
whip in 191.3
whiplash goad 375.8

whip 605.1
whipped bubbly 320.6
beat 412.15
whipped cream 10.38
whipped up 105.20
whipping rigging
180.12
corporal punishment
604.4
whipping up excitation
105.11
incitement 375.4
whip up excite 105.12
improvise 365.8
incite 375.17
agitate 916.10
whirl
noun agitation 105.4
eddy 238.12
coil 281.2
bustle 330.4
round of pleasure
743.7
wheel 914.2
verb move 172.5
eddy 238.21
convolve 281.4
whirligig 914.11
whirling
noun rotation 914.1
adj rotating 914.14
whirlpool
noun eddy 238.12
whirl 914.2
verb whirl 914.11
whirlwind outburst
105.9
whirlblast 318.14
whirl 914.2
whirring
noun hum 52.7
adj humming 52.20
whisk
noun tap 901.7
agitator 916.9
verb sweep 79.23
barrel 174.9
transport 176.12
foam 320.5
tap 901.18
agitate 916.10
whisker 288.3
whiskers 3.8
whisper
noun murmur 52.4
touch 73.1
mumbling 525.4
tip 551.3
hint 551.4
report 552.6
verb murmur 52.10,
524.26
sigh 318.21
tell confidentially
345.9
publish 352.10
say 524.23
mumble 525.9

tip 551.11
adj murmuring 52.18
whispered faint 52.16
reported 552.15
whispering
noun murmur 52.4
mumbling 525.4
adj murmuring 52.18
whistle
noun blare 53.5
noisemaker 53.6
sibilation 57.1
screech 58.4
alarm 400.1
call 517.16
verb blare 53.10
sibilate 57.2
screech 58.8
warble 60.5
exude cheerfulness
109.6
rejoice 116.5
sigh 318.21
sing 708.38
blow a horn 708.42
whistler 311.12
whistles 50.13
whistle-stop 230.3
whistling
noun sibilation 57.1
adj shrill 58.14
whit 248.2
white
noun whiteness 37.1
basuco 87.6
egg 305.15
verb whiten 37.5
whitewash 37.6
adj colourless 36.7
pure white 37.7
clean 79.25
vacant 222.14
aged 303.16
spotless 657.7
chaste 664.4
Whitechapel 752.3
white-collar workers
607.5
white elephant 1011.6
white fish 10.23
white flag peace offer
465.2
signal 517.15
race 756.3
white hair 3.3
Whitehall 612.3
whitehead 1003.1
white heat 1018.5
white horse 238.14,
915.4
white-hot zealous
101.9
fiery 671.22
hot 1018.25
White House 228.5
white hunter 382.5

white-knuckle anxious
126.7
nervous 128.11
white light 1024.10
whiteness white 37.1
cleanness 79.1
innocence 657.1
chastity 664.1
glow 1018.12
white noise 57.1
white paper
announcement 352.2
state paper 549.8
information 551.1
white person 312.3
whites humour 2.22
formal dress 5.11
cricket 747.1
white supremacist
103.4
whitewash
noun appearance 33.2
whitening agent 37.4
pretext 376.1
extenuation 600.5
verb colour 35.13
whiten 37.5
white 37.6
scratch the surface
206.6
conceal 346.6
falsify 354.16
acquit 601.4
whitewashed 412.16
white water rapids
238.10
foam 320.2
white wedding 563.3
white wine 88.17
whither 159.21
whiting 37.4
whitish light 36.9
whity 37.8
whittle
noun cutlery 1039.2
verb form 262.7
sever 801.11
whittled 262.9
whiz
noun sibilation 57.1
ace 413.14
dandy 998.7
verb hum 52.13
sibilate 57.2
barrel 174.9
whizzing
noun hum 52.7
adj humming 52.20
who cares? 102.11
whoever 863.7
who knows? 929.19
whole
noun contents 196.1
quantity 244.1
inclusion 771.1
totality 791.1

all 791.3, 863.4
limit 793.5
sum 1016.6
adj sound 83.11,
1001.7
comprehensive 771.7
total 791.9
complete 793.9
one 871.7
unqualified 959.2
whole body 227.1
whole bunch 791.4
wholehearted 359.11
wholeheartedly 359.17
whole hog 791.4
whole-hog 793.10
wholeness whole 791.1
totality 791.5
completeness 793.1
particularity 864.1
oneness 871.1
goodness 998.1
soundness 1001.2
whole night 315.11
whole picture 765.2
wholesale
noun sale 734.1
verb deal in 731.15
sell 734.8
adj commercial 731.21
sales 734.13
thorough 793.10
extensive 863.13
undiscriminating
944.5
plentiful 990.7
adv cheaply 633.10
wholesaler
intermediary 213.4
merchant 730.2
whole show 791.4
wholesome healthful
81.5
sound 83.11
sane 924.4
whole story 760.4
whole truth 972.3
wholly fully 765.13
entirely 791.13
completely 793.14
solely 871.14
perfectly 1001.10
whomever 863.7
whoop
noun cry 59.1
verb cry 59.6
whoops 974.6
whoosh
noun sibilation 57.1
verb sibilate 57.2
whopping 257.21
whore
noun flirt 562.11
reprobate 660.5
strumpet 665.14
prostitute 665.16

verb be promiscuous
665.19
Who's Who 549.9
why
noun enigma 522.8
reason 885.2
adv whyever 887.8
wick 1025.7
wicked
noun bad 660.12
adj malicious 144.20
wrong 638.3
evil 654.16
wrongdoing 655.5
ungodly 695.17
bad 999.7
wickedly malevolently
144.30
evilly 654.19
wickedness malice
144.5
wrong 638.1
badness 654.4, 999.1
wrongdoing 655.1
ungodliness 695.3
wicker 170.3
wicket cricket 747.1
match 747.3
wide
noun match 747.3
adj spacious 158.10
voluminous 257.17
broad 269.6
phonetic 524.31
extensive 863.13
erroneous 974.16
broad-minded 978.8
adv far and wide
261.16
clear 261.19
wide-awake awake 23.8
alert 339.14
clear-witted 919.13
wide berth 430.4
wide-eyed 122.9
widely extensively
158.11
far and wide 261.16
widely known 927.27
widely read 927.20
widen grow 251.6
enlarge 259.4, 259.5
spread 259.6
broaden 269.4
generalize 863.9
widened increased
251.7
expanded 259.10
widening increase
251.1
expansion 259.1
wide of the mark
adj irrelevant 775.7
erroneous 974.16
adv wide 261.19
wide-open spread
259.11

open 292.17
unrestricted 430.27
wide-open spaces open
space 158.4
country 233.1
plain 236.1
wide-ranging spacious
158.10
broad 269.6
extensive 863.13
broad-minded 978.8
wide-screen 706.6
widespread spacious
158.10
spread 259.11
broad 269.6
customary 373.14
dispersed 770.9
extensive 863.13
wide world 1070.1
widow
noun survivor 256.3
widow woman 566.4
verb bereave 307.28,
566.6
widowed bereaved
307.35
widowly 566.7
widower survivor 256.3
widow 566.4
widowhood 566.3
width size 257.1
breadth 269.1
wield touch 73.6
use 387.10
wave 915.11
wife woman 77.5
married woman 563.8
wig 3.14
wiggle
noun wriggle 916.7
verb thrill 105.18
stroll 177.28
wriggle 916.14
wight 871.4
wild
noun wasteland 890.2
adj overzealous 101.12
frenzied 105.25
passionate 105.29
infuriated 152.32
hinterland 233.9
animal 311.38
defiant 327.10
ungovernable 361.12
unrestrained 430.24
reckless 493.8
foolhardy 493.9
unrefined 497.12
profligate 665.25
turbulent 671.18
unruly 671.19
boisterous 671.20
savage 671.21
absurd 922.11
rabid 925.30
distracted 984.10
fanciful 985.20

knowing 927.15
learned 927.21
ungullible 955.5
expedient 994.5
wisely 919.20
wise man intelligence
919.9
wise woman 920.1
intellectual 928.1
wise to 927.16
wish
noun desire 100.1,
100.11
will 323.1
request 440.1
verb desire 100.14
request 440.9
wishbone leg 10.22
fork 171.4
wish-bringer 691.6
wished-for desired
100.29
welcome 585.12
wish for hope for
100.16
request 440.9
wishful 100.23
wishful thinking
defence mechanism
92.23
wistfulness 100.4
deception 356.1
idealism 985.7
wishing 100.21
wish to 100.15
wishy-washy tasteless
16.17
insipid 65.2
inconstant 853.7
mediocre 1004.7
wisp
noun runt 258.4
bunch 769.7
luminescence 1024.13
verb tend 1068.7
wispy frail 16.14
thin 270.16
wistful wishful 100.23
melancholy 112.23
regretful 113.8
cognitive 930.21
wistfully desirously
100.31
melancholily 112.34
thoughtfully 930.23
wit skill 413.1
cunning 415.1
humour 489.1
humourist 489.12
intelligence 919.1
witch
noun bitch 110.12
frightener 127.9
old woman 304.3
hag 593.7
sorceress 690.8
eyesore 1014.4

verb fascinate 377.7
bewitch 691.9
adj sorcerous 690.14
witchcraft 690.1
witch doctor healer
90.9
shaman 690.7
witch-hunt persecution
389.3
investigation 937.4
with
adv, prep in spite of
338.9
prep at 159.27
plus 253.12
by means of 384.13
in cooperation with
450.8
in company with
768.12
in agreement with
787.12
among 796.17
with a difference
differently 779.10
dissimilarly 786.7
with affection 104.32
with an eye to 380.11
with authority 417.18
with a vengeance
powerfully 18.15
extremely 247.22
violently 671.25
utterly 793.16
with a view to 380.11
with both hands 485.5
with care carefully
339.15
cautiously 494.12
with caution cautiously
494.12
unbelievingly 954.13
with confidence
952.28
with difficulty
disadvantageously
995.9
difficultly 1012.28
with dignity solemnly
111.4
dignifiedly 136.14
with distinction
646.11
withdraw use 87.21
retreat 163.6
recede 168.2
retract 168.3
quit 188.9
extract 192.10
subtract 255.9
dissent 333.4
hesitate 362.7
recant 363.8
abandon 370.5
repeal 445.2
separate 801.8
stand alone 871.6

withdrawal substance
abuse 87.1
defence mechanism
92.23
unfeeling 94.1
retreat 163.2
recession 168.1
departure 188.1
extraction 192.1
dissent 333.1
recantation 363.3
abandonment 370.1
repeal 445.1
resignation 448.1
seclusion 584.1
elimination 772.2
separation 801.1
aloneness 871.2
incuriosity 981.1
withdrawal symptoms
87.1
withdraw from 448.2
withdrawing
noun recession 168.1
course 172.2
relinquishment 370.3
adj receding 168.5
withdrawn apathetic
94.13
reticent 344.10
private 345.13
aloof 583.6
secluded 584.8
alone 871.8
incurious 981.3
with ease 121.14
with enthusiasm
101.13
wither fail 85.47
decrease 252.6
shrink 260.9
age 303.10
languish 393.18
dry 1064.6
withered shrunk
260.13
haggard 270.20
stricken in years
303.18
wasted 393.35
dried 1064.9
withering
noun decrease 252.1
shrinking 260.3
waste 393.4
drying 1064.3
adj caustic 144.23
contemptuous 157.8
deteriorating 393.45
destructive 395.26
with feeling 93.25
with flying colours
successfully 409.15
ostentatiously 501.25
with great care 339.15
with gusto eagerly
101.13
gaily 109.18
actively 330.25

withheld 386.15
withhold keep secret
345.7
reserve 386.12
restrain 428.7
deny 442.4
hold back 484.6
abstain 668.7
withholding 442.1
with honour 646.11
with impunity 1006.8
within
adv in 207.10
prep in 207.13
within reach 965.8
within reason 934.24
with intent 380.10
with interest 982.21
within the law 673.10
with it
adj hip 927.17
adv in step 787.11
with love 104.32
with open arms
eagerly 101.13
willingly 324.8
hospitably 585.13
amicably 587.22
without
adv externally 206.10
prep absent 222.19
off 255.14
excluding 772.10
minus 991.17
conj unless 958.16
without a break
811.10
without being 761.8
without charge
adj gratuitous 634.5
adv gratuitously 634.6
without delay at once
829.8
promptly 844.15
without difficulty
1013.16
without doubt
positively 247.19
unquestionably 969.25
without exception
adj unqualified 959.2
adv regularly 780.8
always 828.11
universally 863.18
without fail 969.26
without foundation
763.8, 935.13
without hope 125.12
without question
willingly 324.8
unquestionably 969.25
truly 972.18
without stopping
continuously 811.10
constantly 846.7

without success
410.19
without warning
131.10
with pleasure 95.18
with precision 339.16
with pride 136.13
with relish eagerly
101.13
willingly 324.8
with respect 443.20
with safety 1006.8
with satisfaction
107.14
with skill 413.31
with speed 174.17
withstand oppose
451.3
resist 453.2
offer resistance 453.3
with the addition of
253.12
with the exception of
off 255.14
excluding 772.10
with the sun 314.8
with the wind 182.64
witless unintelligent
921.13
foolish 922.8
unwise 922.10
insane 925.26
unaware 929.13
scatterbrained 984.16
witness
noun certificate 549.6
informant 551.5
litigant 598.12
inspiration 677.15
spectator 917.1
examinee 937.19
testimony 956.2
eyewitness 956.6
verb see 27.12
attend 221.8
depose 334.6
be pious 692.6
spectate 917.5
testify 956.9
witnessing
noun observation 27.2
adj pious 692.8
witness to evidence
956.8
testify 956.9
wits 918.2
wittily 488.7, 489.18
witty humorous 488.4
amusing 489.15
wizard master 413.13
sorcerer 690.5
wizardry skill 413.1
sorcery 690.1
wizened dwarf 258.13
shrunk 260.13
haggard 270.20

whole caboodle 791.4
mechanism 1039.4
workshop 739.1
workstation workplace
739.1
output device 1041.9
work-study 568.3
work together 450.3
worktop 739.1
work up excite 105.12
provoke 152.24
incite 375.17
plan 381.8
agitate 916.10
work-up 91.12
work well succeed
409.7
go easily 1013.10
world quantity 247.3
plot 722.4
affairs 830.4
outlook 977.2
universe 1070.1
Earth 1070.10
World Bank 729.13
world champion
413.15
world-class chief
249.14
paramount 996.24
superior 998.14
World Cup trophy
646.3
rugby 746.1
worldly
noun profane 686.2
adj experienced
413.28
unsacred 686.3
secularist 695.16
realistic 986.6
material 1050.10
world of 883.3
world of difference
779.1
world over everywhere
158.12
universally 863.18
world politics politics
609.1
foreign policy 609.5
world power country
232.1
supremacy 249.3
world-record holder
413.15
worlds apart 779.7
worlds of 883.3
world view ideology
931.8
system of belief 952.3
climate 977.5
world-weary dejected
112.22
weary 118.11
languid 331.20

world-wide 863.14
WORM 1041.6
worm
noun earthworm
311.37
beast 660.7
blight 1000.2
verb creep 177.26
convolve 281.4
worming 177.17
wormwood 64.2
worn weakened 16.18
tired 21.7
tired-looking 21.9
trite 117.9
reduced 252.10
well-worn 393.31
disintegrative 805.5
stale 841.14
secondhand 841.18
worn-down tired 21.7
worn 393.31
worn-out weakened
16.18
burnt-out 21.10
used up 388.5, 393.36
disused 390.10
disintegrative 805.5
worried tormented
96.24
vexed 126.8
troubled 1012.20
worries 126.2
worry
noun annoyance 96.2
worriment 126.2
trouble 1012.3
verb annoy 96.13
distress 96.16
vex 98.15
upset 126.5
worry oneself 126.6
trouble 1012.13
worrying
noun worry 126.2
adj annoying 98.22
troublesome 126.10
worse aggravated 119.4
impaired 393.27
changed 851.10
worse and worse 119.4
worse for 393.27
worse for wear stricken
in years 303.18
worn 393.31
dilapidated 393.33
worsen irritate 96.14
aggravate 119.2
impair 393.9
deteriorate 393.16
be changed 851.6
change 851.7
worsened aggravated
119.4
impaired 393.27
worsening
noun irritation 96.3

aggravation 119.1
impairment 393.1
change 851.1
adj deteriorating
393.45
worse off aggravated
119.4
impaired 393.27
Worship 648.2
worship
noun love 104.1
respect 155.1
piety 692.1
worshipping 696.1
verb cherish 104.21
respect 155.4
adore 696.10
worshipful reverent
155.9
venerable 155.12
reputable 662.15
pious 692.8
worshipping 696.15
traditional 841.12
worshipped 155.11
worshipping
noun worship 696.1
adj reverent 155.9
worshipful 696.15
worst
noun evil 999.3
verb best 249.7
defeat 412.6
adj terrible 999.9
worst case 125.1
worst-case depressing
112.30
hopeless 125.12
wort 310.4
worth
noun benefit 387.4
assets 471.7
value 630.2
preciousness 632.2
funds 728.14
importance 996.1
goodness 998.1
adj possessing 469.9
priced 630.14
worth having 100.30
worthiness proud
bearing 136.2
eligibility 371.11
probity 644.1
worthless valueless
391.11
disadvantageous 995.6
paltry 997.21
unworthy 997.22
terrible 999.9
worthwhile valuable
387.22
gainful 472.16
expedient 994.5
worthy
noun good person
659.1
celebrity 662.9

personage 996.8
adj dignified 136.12
eligible 371.24
competent 413.24
praiseworthy 509.20
precious 632.10
warranted 639.9
honest 644.13
reputable 662.15
worthy of 639.10
would-be presumptuous
141.10
nominal 527.15
wound
noun trauma 85.37
pain 96.5
verb pain 26.7, 96.17
offend 152.21
injure 393.13
work evil 999.6
wounded 26.9, 96.23
wounding 98.17
wound up ended 819.8
past 836.7
woven webbed 170.12
loomed 740.7
wow audio distortion
50.13
smash 409.4
dandy 998.7
wracked 93.23
wrangle
noun quarrel 456.5
verb quarrel 456.11
argue 934.16
drive 1068.8
wrangler oppositionist
452.3
combatant 461.1
commoner 572.7
arguer 934.12
herder 1068.3
wrangling
noun contention 457.1
argumentation 934.4
adj partisan 456.17
wrap
noun dishabille 5.20
wrapper 295.18
cinematography 706.4
end 819.1
verb clothe 5.38
surround 209.6
enclose 212.5
package 212.9
fold 291.5
enwrap 295.20
bundle 769.20
bind 799.9
wrapped surrounded
209.10
packed 212.12
covered 295.31
wrapped in 982.17
wrapped up 769.21
wrapped up in fond of
104.30
involved in 897.5

engrossed 982.17
wrapper dishabille 5.20
wrapping 295.18
bookbinding 554.14
wrapping
noun packaging 212.2
covering 295.1
wrapper 295.18
adj environing 209.8
covering 295.35
wraps veil of secrecy
345.3
veil 346.2
wrap up shorten 268.6
wrap 295.20
abridge 557.5
bundle 769.20
bind 799.9
wrap-up 407.2
wrath anger 152.5
revenge 507.1
wreak do 328.6
inflict 643.5
wreak havoc destroy
395.10
rage 671.11
wreath circle 280.2
bouquet 310.23
trophy 646.3
heraldic device 647.2
braid 740.2
wreathed surrounded
209.10
ornamented 498.11
woven 740.7
wreck
noun nervous wreck
128.5
jalopy 179.10
ruins 393.8
destruction 395.1
debacle 395.4
misfortune 1010.2
verb disable 19.9
shipwreck 182.42
spoil 393.10
destroy 395.10
demolish 395.17
rage 671.11
wreckage 395.5
wrecked ruined 395.28
disintegrative 805.5
stranded 1012.21
wrecking 395.5
Wren 183.4
wrench
noun pang 26.2
trauma 85.37
pain 96.5
extortion 192.6
distortion 265.1
jerk 904.3
tool 1039.1
verb pain 26.7
distort 265.5
misinterpret 342.2
misrepresent 350.3
injure 393.13

vote 371.6
approval 509.1
side 934.14
verb assent 332.8
adv consentingly
441.5
exclam yea 332.18

yes indeed 332.18

yesterday
noun past 836.1
adv formerly 836.13

yesteryear 836.1

yet
adv additionally
253.11
previously 833.6
until now 837.4
adv, conj
notwithstanding 338.8

yet again 873.7

yew 115.7

yield
noun output 472.5
receipts 627.1
dividend 738.7
production 892.2
verb weaken 16.9
acknowledge 332.11
hesitate 362.7
give up 370.7
provide 385.7
cede 433.7
compromise 468.2
relinquish 475.3
give 478.12, 1045.7,
1046.5
bring in 627.4
conform 866.3
bear 891.13

yielded 475.5

yielding
noun relinquishment
370.3, 475.1
submission 433.1
compromise 468.1
bearing 891.6
adj unstrict 426.5
docile 433.13
bearing 889.10
handy 1013.15
pliant 1045.9

yield to indulge 427.6
submit to 433.9

yob 302.4

yoga asceticism 667.1
occultism 689.1
exercise 725.6

yogi ascetic 667.2
occultist 689.11
Brahman 699.12

yogurt 67.2

yoke
noun shackle 428.4
two 872.2
verb put together
799.5
hitch up 799.10
combine 804.3

league 804.4
double 872.5
tend 1068.7

yolk 305.15

Yom Kippur fast day
515.3
penance 658.3

yon
adj thither 261.10
adv yonder 261.13

yonder
adj thither 261.10
adv yon 261.13

Yorkshire 523.7

Yorkshire pudding
10.43

you 864.5

you and me 606.1

you are right 972.24

you-know-who 528.2

you name it 793.17

young
noun young people
302.2
brood 561.2
adj youngling 301.9
new 840.7

younger
noun youngster 302.1
adj junior 301.15
subsequent 834.4

younger generation
302.2

youngest 302.1

youngish 301.9

young lady 302.6

young-looking 301.9

young man 302.5

young people 302.2

young person 302.1

youngster 302.1

youngsters 561.1

you're telling me?
972.25

yourself 864.5

yourselves 864.5

yours truly 864.5

you said it 972.25

youth youthfulness
301.1
youngster 302.1
young people 302.2
boy 302.5
origin 817.4
memory 836.4

youth custody 429.5

youthful fresh 83.13
young 301.9

youth hostel 228.15

yow 311.7

yo-yo 923.3

Yukon jumping-off
place 261.4
Siberia 1022.4

yummy 97.8

yup 332.19

Z 819.1

z 929.7

zag
noun zigzag 204.8
angle 278.2
alternation 915.5
verb zigzag 204.12
angle 278.5

zany humourist 489.12
buffoon 707.10
fool 923.1

zap 308.13

zapped shot 395.29
belly-up 819.9

zeal vim 17.2
passion 93.2
ardour 101.2
anxiety 126.1
willingness 324.1
turbulence 671.2
zealousness 692.3
cause 885.9
interest 982.2

zealous fervent 93.18
ardent 101.9
anxious 126.7
willing 324.5
industrious 330.22
fiery 671.22
zealotical 692.11

zebra 47.6

Zeitgeist ethics 636.1
trend 895.2
climate 977.5

zenith summit 198.2
supremacy 249.3
height 272.2
limit 793.5

zephyr breeze 318.5
putty 1045.4

zeppelin 181.11

zero roulette 759.12
nothing 761.2
thing of naught 763.2
temperature 1018.3

zero in 797.4

zest animation 17.4
savour 63.2
zestfulness 68.2
pleasure 95.1
eagerness 101.1
gaiety 109.4

Zeus 316.6

zig
noun zigzag 204.8
angle 278.2
alternation 915.5
verb zigzag 204.12
angle 278.5

zigzag
noun deviation 164.1
zig 204.8
angle 278.2
avoidance 368.1
alternation 915.5

verb deflect 164.5
zig 204.12
angle 278.5
dodge 368.8
alternate 915.13
adj deviative 164.7
crooked 204.20
angular 278.6

zine 555.1

zing
noun pep 17.3
verb barrel 174.9

Zion 681.3

zip
noun pep 17.3
sibilation 57.1
zest 68.2
gaiety 109.4
zilch 761.3
verb sibilate 57.2
barrel 174.9

zipper
noun fastening 799.3
verb hook 799.8

zippy zestful 68.7
gay 109.14

zodiac band 280.3
orbit 1070.16
astrology 1070.20

zombie frightener
127.9
spectre 987.1

zonal 231.8

zone
noun region 231.1
band 280.3
layer 296.1
middle 818.1
orbit 1070.16
verb encircle 209.7
apportion 801.18

zoning 801.1

zoo menagerie 228.19
collection 769.11

zoological animal
311.38
biological 1066.3

zoologist 1066.2

zoology 1066.1

zoom speed 174.8
ascend 184.39
take off 193.10

zooming 193.1

Zoroastrian
noun idolater 697.4
adj Buddhist 675.32